The Top 6000 Companies in South West England

Companies with assets exceeding £3,500,000

John D Blackburn

Editor

dp

First Edition

Spring 2019

ISBN-13: 978-1-912736-23-2

ISBN-10: 1-912736-23-3

Printed in 8pt Nimbus Sans L

Designed by URW++ Design and Development GmbH

Dellam Publishing Limited

2 Heath Drive, Sutton, Surrey, SM2 5RP

Fax: 020 8770 7478 email: enquiries@dellam.com

SAN: 0177881 EAN/GLN: 5030670177882

Table of Contents

Acknowledgements

This is a long and detailed publication containing thousands of facts and figures. It is only to be expected, despite continuous and repeated editing and checking, that errors may occur. In such cases, once we are aware of any, we publish a correction on our website.

Readers are encouraged to check regularly at www.dellam.com/books for any corrections and updates.

Although we take extreme care to ensure accuracy and being up-to-date, we cannot accept responsibility for any errors or omissions.

We appreciate your interest in our publications, and your comments and suggestions are always welcome. Please contact us at enquiries@dellam.com.

Scotland
Northern Ireland
North East (England)
North West (England)
Yorkshire and The Humber
East Midlands (England)
West Midlands (England)
Wales
East of England
See London Inset
South East (England)
South West (England)

Scotland
North East (England)
North West (England)
Yorkshire and The Humber
East Midlands (England)
West Midlands (England)
Wales
East of England
London
South East (England)
South West (England)

Introduction

This study looks at all companies registered in South West England and where their total assets are more than £3,500,000.

South West England is the largest region by area (9,000 square miles) with a population of 5 million in 2016.

The region comprises the counties of Gloucestershire, Wiltshire, Somerset, Dorset, Devon and Cornwall; The largest city is Bristol; other cities are Salisbury, Bath, Wells, Gloucester, Exeter, Plymouth and Truro.

The most economically productive areas within the region are Bristol, the M4 corridor and south east Dorset, which are the areas with the best links to London. Bristol alone accounts for a quarter of the region's economy, with the surrounding areas of Gloucestershire, Somerset and Wiltshire accounting for a further quarter.

The aim of this study is to provide an overview of the key movers and shakers in South West England's corporate sector. Only key data has been isolated, particularly the company's net worth and total assets, but also its full name, date incorporated, registered office, activities, shareholders, directors (with date of birth, occupation and nationality) and number of employees.

Two indicators of size are used: net worth and total assets. These are preferable to turnover which is influenced by profit margins and whether the companies are capital or labour intensive.

A short summary of the corporate sector in South West England:

Total output (GVA), in 2016, was £127 billion (UK being £1,748 billion). Total output (GVA) per head, in 2016, was £23,091 (UK being £26,621). Economic Growth (GVA), 2010-2016, was 1.8% (UK being 1.9%).

For the labour market, May-July 2018, the employment level was 2,789,000 (UK 32,397,0000) and the employment rate was 79.2% (UK 75.5%). The unemployment level was 74,000 (UK 1,361,000) with an unemployment rate of 2.6% (UK 4%). Employment, January-March 2018, in manufacturing as percentage of total jobs was 8.4% (UK 7.7%) and in the public sector as percentage of total employment was 15.5% (UK 16.6%).

In 2018, there were 546,000 businesses (up 3%), (5,668,000 total businesses in the UK); and there were 126,000 employers (1,360,000 total employers in the UK). In 2017, there were 25,235 new businesses established (up 11%) and 30,040 businesses ceased trading (up 13%).

In 2017, there were 253,000 manufacturing jobs (9% of all jobs) and there were 12,180 manufacturing businesses. The region's largest manufacturing sectors are transport, food and drink and metals.

The number of VAT and/or PAYE based businesses in the region were in 2016: 227,000 (8.9% of UK); 2017: 234,000 (8.8%) and 2018: 232,000 (8.7%). In 2017, the region accounted for 7.2% of the UK's manufactured exports.

Standard cataloguing guidelines for company names in the profile section have been used, but there will be occurrences when the name may not be strictly alphabetical. A certain licence was adopted where it was felt that strictly alphabetical could lead to improper cataloguing. Some company names have been shortened in the league tables for aesthetic reasons.

John D Blackburn
Editor

This page is intentionally left blank

Total Assets League Table

Company	Value
St. James's Place PLC	£90,006,896,640
St. James's Place UK PLC	£59,281,297,408
Zurich Assurance Ltd	£56,042,000,384
Deutsch GB Limited	£37,340,000,256
Imperial Brands Finance PLC	£33,894,000,640
Imperial Brands PLC	£30,250,000,384
The Mortgage Works (UK) PLC	£29,825,247,232
Imperial Tobacco Limited	£29,364,000,768
EDF Energy Nuclear Generation Limited	£22,773,999,616
Colston's School	£22,319,826,944
Imperial Tobacco Holdings Limited	£19,864,000,512
Imperial Tobacco Holdings (2007) Limited	£18,849,996,800
Nationwide Covered Bonds LLP	£17,497,100,288
Imperial Tobacco Overseas Limited	£15,856,533,504
Imperial Tobacco Overseas Holdings Ltd	£14,725,650,432
Imperial Tobacco Holdings (1) Limited	£14,675,133,440
Western Power Distribution PLC	£14,014,199,808
Imperial Tobacco Overseas Holdings (2) Ltd	£13,915,634,688
Intel Corporation (UK) Limited	£13,155,995,648
Imperial Tobacco Overseas Holdings (3) Limited	£11,289,433,088
Imperial Brands Enterprise Finance Limited	£6,805,321,216
Pennon Group PLC	£6,163,800,064
Imperial Tobacco Altadis Limited	£5,900,521,984
Meggitt PLC	£4,826,500,096
WPD Distribution Network Holdings Limited	£4,563,400,192
Western Power Distribution (East Midlands) PLC	£4,174,599,936
Airbus Operations Limited	£4,032,000,000
YTL Utilities (UK) Limited	£3,994,800,128
Wessex Water Limited	£3,948,100,096
Western Power Distribution (West Midlands) PLC	£3,914,599,936
Wessex Water Services Limited	£3,788,600,064
Sensata Technologies UK Financing Co. PLC	£3,749,288,704
Curtis Banks Group PLC	£3,739,301,888
Merlin Entertainments PLC	£3,664,000,000
Innogy Renewables UK Limited	£3,566,785,024
Coates & Co. (Plymouth) Limited	£3,483,909,888
Liverpool Victoria General Insurance Group Ltd	£3,448,122,880
Agricultural Mortgage Corporation P L C (The)	£3,440,762,880
South West Water Limited	£3,376,199,936
Containers Packaging (Europe)	£3,354,524,672
Amcor Holding	£3,329,934,848
PPL UK Resources Limited	£3,296,045,312
Charcoal Newco 1 Limited	£3,222,515,968
Innogy Renewables UK Holdings Limited	£3,181,101,056
Amcor UK Finance PLC	£2,958,711,296
RWE Generation UK PLC	£2,912,000,000
Western Power Distribution (South West) PLC	£2,841,200,128
Sanlam Life & Pensions UK Limited	£2,799,240,960
Cobham PLC	£2,793,400,064
PPL WPD Limited	£2,790,500,096
Lockman Investments Limited	£2,756,776,960
RWE Generation UK Holdings Limited	£2,728,999,936
PPL WPD Investments Limited	£2,716,100,096
npower Group Limited	£2,704,000,000
Charcoal Newco 1A Limited	£2,616,719,104
npower Limited	£2,552,999,936
Liverpool Victoria Insurance Company Limited	£2,539,360,000
ST Schrader Holding Company UK Limited	£2,438,776,320
The Unite Group PLC	£2,431,600,128
Zurich Financial Services (UKISA) Limited	£2,371,699,968
PPL WEM Limited	£2,368,699,904
Viridor Limited	£2,264,699,904
Arval UK Group Limited	£2,246,295,040
Arval UK Limited	£2,239,009,024
AFP (Europe)	£2,164,116,992
LDC (Holdings) Limited	£2,160,669,952
Merlin Entertainments Group Holdings Limited	£2,147,760,128
Lockwash US Limited	£2,146,892,672
WPD Investment Holdings Limited	£2,086,499,968
U C B Home Loans Corporation Limited	£2,024,210,048
Dyson James Group Limited	£1,996,999,936
New Look Finance Limited	£1,989,880,064
Western Power Distribution (South Wales) PLC	£1,983,200,000
Meggitt International Holdings Limited	£1,912,116,992
PPL UK Investments Limited	£1,839,699,968
Allchurches Trust Limited	£1,747,378,048
ALD Automotive Limited	£1,683,751,040
WRK Merger Holding Sub Limited	£1,677,446,016
Ecclesiastical Insurance Group PLC	£1,674,995,968
Viridor Waste Limited	£1,662,620,032
Wessex Water Services Finance PLC	£1,637,037,952
Cavehurst Limited	£1,582,707,200
Aspire Defence Holdings Limited	£1,567,459,968
Aspire Defence Limited	£1,567,250,944
Meggitt Finance Limited	£1,555,165,952
Ecclesiastical Insurance Office PLC	£1,505,296,000
Aspire Defence Finance PLC	£1,495,065,984
Spirax-Sarco Engineering PLC	£1,476,499,968
GE Oil & Gas UK Limited	£1,464,344,064
Galloper Wind Farm Holding Company Limited	£1,460,001,408
Galloper Wind Farm Limited	£1,459,805,312
Pantheon International PLC	£1,440,920,064
Dyson Technology Limited	£1,344,600,064
Horizon Nuclear Power Limited	£1,333,262,976
IVC Acquisition Pikco Ltd	£1,309,311,616
IVC Acquisition Midco Ltd	£1,309,311,616
Meggitt International Limited	£1,258,050,048
Zurich Project Finance (UK) Limited	£1,230,150,016
Horizon Nuclear Power Wylfa Limited	£1,215,353,984
IVC Acquisition Ltd	£1,192,979,456
Eagle Star Holdings Limited	£1,175,712,000
WH Smith Retail Holdings Limited	£1,173,559,040
New Look Retail Group Limited	£1,153,400,064
Smiths News Holdings Limited	£1,095,200,000
British Empire Trust PLC	£1,033,065,984
Hitachi Nuclear Projects Development Europe Ltd	£1,032,843,520
Viridor Waste Management Limited	£1,029,233,024
Corialis Group Limited	£1,021,575,168
Highway Insurance Company Limited	£1,007,382,016
C & J Clark Limited	£999,000,000
McCarthy & Stone PLC	£995,200,000
Derbyshire Home Loans Limited	£987,766,016
Dyson Finance Limited	£968,896,000
Screwfix Direct Limited	£953,676,032
McCarthy & Stone Retirement Lifestyles Limited	£951,100,032
LV Capital PLC	£945,808,000
Devonport Royal Dockyard Limited	£929,006,016
National Oilwell Varco UK Limited	£906,932,992
Woodford Patient Capital Trust PLC	£905,288,000
St. James's Place Partnership Services Limited	£890,417,984
GE Infrastructure Aviation	£866,947,072
Rocma Europe	£864,371,904
Amcor European Investment Holdings Limited	£864,371,072
Dover Fluids UK Ltd	£849,145,984
Honda of The U.K. Manufacturing Limited	£841,907,968
Biopharma Credit PLC	£832,475,392
Smiths News Trading Limited	£831,900,032
GCP Student Living PLC	£825,598,016
npower Northern Limited	£825,000,000
Merlin UK Finco 1 Limited	£824,078,976
Richmond Group Limited	£822,400,000
Meggitt Properties PLC	£815,553,984
Bristol Airport (UK) No.3 Limited	£792,361,024
Dover Refrigeration & Food Equipment UK Ltd	£788,860,992
Sigma-Aldrich Company Limited	£786,110,976
Custom Sensors & Technologies Newco Ltd	£784,055,680
WH Smith Travel Holdings Limited	£760,265,024
Bristol Water PLC	£758,700,032
C. & J. Clark International Limited	£756,899,968
Merlin Attractions Operations Limited	£751,174,016
Renishaw P L C	£742,176,000
Rotork P.L.C.	£738,593,984
GE Aviation Systems Limited	£726,451,904
Vectura Group PLC	£718,499,968

Alu Holdco 2 Limited	£709,547,072
Spirax-Sarco Overseas Limited	£708,136,064
New Look Secured Issuer PLC	£699,251,968
USAF Finance II Limited	£691,670,976
Delphi Diesel Systems Limited	£685,003,008
Amigo Holdings PLC	£681,500,032
Amigo Loans Group Ltd	£680,700,032
Amigo Loans Ltd	£678,499,968
Ark Estates Holdings Limited	£673,458,496
Wincanton Holdings Limited	£672,400,000
WH Smith Travel Limited	£659,700,992
WH Smith High Street Limited	£657,331,008
Unite Integrated Solutions PLC	£653,697,024
Computershare Investments (UK) (No. 8) Ltd	£651,572,032
Synergy Health Limited	£631,299,968
Flybe Limited	£630,000,000
Alu Bidco Limited	£627,821,504
Synergy Health Holdings Limited	£624,651,008
Superdry PLC	£614,400,000
Allstar Business Solutions Limited	£613,102,016
Flybe Group PLC	£611,699,968
Wrigley Uno UK Limited	£608,644,992
Zurich Finance (UK) PLC	£601,465,984
Innogy Business Services UK Limited	£596,211,968
Innogy Gym 4 Limited	£594,499,904
PPL Island Limited	£578,700,032
Westcon Group European Operations Limited	£568,664,256
Hargreaves Lansdown Asset Management Limited	£559,984,000
Curo Group (Albion) Limited	£557,774,976
AES Overseas Holdings Limited	£554,326,336
GCP Holdco Limited	£545,132,992
Meggitt Aerospace Limited	£544,497,024
South West Airports Limited	£538,443,008
Lockman Electronic Holdings Limited	£533,881,984
Imperial Tobacco International Limited	£532,565,312
Norton Group Holdings Limited	£531,440,992
WH Smith PLC	£528,000,000
Highcliffe Holdings Limited	£518,952,992
UCLH Investors Limited	£516,920,992
Amcor Flexibles Finance Limited	£516,472,256
Tyco Electronics UK Ltd	£515,295,008
Scot Group Southern Limited	£510,403,008
Scot Group Limited	£507,384,992
JELF Insurance Brokers Limited	£507,000,000
D A S Legal Expenses Insurance Company Limited	£506,198,016
The Oasis Healthcare Group Limited	£505,504,992
MAN Truck and Bus UK Limited	£490,040,992
South West Water Finance PLC	£486,847,008
Nationwide Syndications Limited	£483,968,000
Integra Neurosciences Holdings (UK) Limited	£480,897,888
First Greater Western Limited	£479,406,016
Spembly Medical Limited	£477,470,592
Mears Group PLC	£476,006,016
DKH Retail Limited	£473,448,000
Oasis Healthcare Bidco Limited	£459,612,000
McCarthy & Stone (Developments) Limited	£457,400,000
Lombard Corporate Finance (December 3) Limited	£453,271,488
St.James's Place Management Services Limited	£449,663,008
CDS (Superstores International) Limited	£446,225,984
BNP Paribas Fleet Holdings Limited	£445,112,992
McCarthy & Stone (Extra Care Living) Limited	£432,300,000
The European Investment Trust PLC	£427,732,992
Selwood Housing Society Limited	£423,638,016
LDC (Finance) Limited	£417,388,768
Burford Beta Holdings Limited	£408,512,992
Colt Car Company Limited (The)	£407,383,008
GCP Topco Limited	£399,784,000
WH Smith Travel 2008 Limited	£399,760,000
Manlock Investments Limited	£397,488,992
KK Daytona Holding Ltd	£396,296,992
Meggitt Acquisition Limited	£393,856,000
Imerys UK Limited	£393,198,016
Integrated Accommodation Services PLC	£393,153,984
Accommodation Services (Holdings) Limited	£393,153,984
Computershare Limited	£392,791,008
WH Smith High Street Holdings Limited	£392,688,000
C-Retail Limited	£389,548,992
Rotork Overseas Limited	£387,255,008
Amcor Investments Germany	£385,739,872
Simplyhealth Group Limited	£385,600,000
Caveangle Limited	£384,883,392
Pen y Cymoedd Wind Farm Limited	£384,191,680
Catalent Pharma Solutions Limited	£376,012,992
Redde PLC	£371,996,992
Albany Molecular Research Limited	£371,956,992
Powerwave Energy Limited	£371,207,328
Kohler Holdings Ltd.	£370,097,376
Expedia Treasury Services Limited	£368,745,568
Zurich Employment Services Limited	£358,580,992
Meggitt Aerospace Holdings Limited	£357,752,000
MAT Foundry Group Limited	£357,258,368
Burford Zeta	£355,778,368
Safran Landing Systems UK Ltd	£350,319,008
Churchill Retirement PLC	£349,361,984
Dunlop Aerospace Holdings Limited	£344,784,000
Ark Estates Cody Park Limited	£337,392,544
Alliance Pharma PLC	£336,475,008
Burford Alpha Limited	£333,275,008
DMGI Land & Property Europe Ltd	£331,560,256
Imerys UK Finance Limited	£329,773,056
St. James's Place Wealth Management Group Ltd	£327,567,008
Churchill Retirement Living Limited	£322,105,984
Norbord Europe Limited	£321,731,008
Amcor Flexibles UK Holding Limited	£319,552,896
LDC (Portfolio) Limited	£316,283,520
Health Management (UCLH) Limited	£316,012,992
GLE Bidco Limited	£315,105,984
Independent Vetcare Limited	£314,777,312
Harbour Hotels Holdings Limited	£312,770,944
Octagon Healthcare Limited	£312,108,000
Perrigo UK Acquisition Limited	£311,860,000
The Wrigley Company Limited	£311,335,008
St James's Place Unit Trust Group Limited	£311,227,008
LDC (Portfolio 100) Limited	£309,812,928
Computershare Investments (UK) (No.3) Limited	£309,448,000
FB Ammonite Limited	£305,742,016
Alliance Pharmaceuticals Limited	£305,403,008
Dyson Limited	£305,300,000
Wincanton PLC	£304,800,000
Matthew Clark Bibendum Limited	£302,287,008
Amigo Loans Holdings Ltd	£302,040,992
Harbour International Limited	£298,841,984
RBSSAF (2) Limited	£297,211,008
GE Aviation UK	£295,984,320
GE Aviation Systems Group Limited	£295,213,792
Matthew Clark Bibendum (Holdings) Limited	£294,212,000
Merlin Entertainments (Asia Pacific) Limited	£292,580,000
Simplyhealth Access	£291,900,000
Amcor Holding No.1 Limited	£291,462,944
Wincanton UK Limited	£290,388,992
RNO Limited	£289,478,016
Oasis Dental Care Limited	£288,199,008
Western Bidco Limited	£287,131,008
Inspired Education (South Lanarkshire) Holdings Ltd	£285,467,008
Inspired Education (South Lanarkshire) PLC	£285,467,008
FR Aviation Group Limited	£285,001,984
Lloyds Bank General Insurance Holdings Limited	£283,356,992
Lombard Lease Finance Limited	£277,492,000
C. & J. Clark (Holdings) Limited	£275,400,000
Octagon Healthcare Group Limited	£274,484,992
FB Calluna Limited	£273,067,008
NOV Downhole Eurasia Limited	£270,615,360
Highway Insurance Group Limited	£263,574,000
Cheltenham & Gloucester PLC	£262,750,000

Company	Turnover
Assessments Topco Limited	£262,423,008
Imerys Minerals Limited	£262,400,992
Tilstone Industrial Limited	£262,218,768
Hargreaves Lansdown PLC	£261,000,000
Tilstone Holdings Limited	£260,127,888
LDC (Portfolio 20) Limited	£259,535,072
Octagon Healthcare Funding PLC	£259,472,000
Spirax-Sarco Investments Limited	£256,998,784
Road Management Services (Darrington) Limited	£256,739,008
Road Management Services (Darrington) Hldgs Ltd	£256,691,008
RWE Markinch Limited	£256,075,760
Lush Cosmetics Limited	£255,812,000
Aster Treasury PLC	£253,552,000
Western Provident Association Limited	£253,363,008
Masstock Arable (UK) Limited	£252,614,000
Kerry Ingredients (UK) Limited	£252,276,000
Ovo Group Ltd	£248,979,008
Key West (Holdings) Limited	£246,966,000
Witan Pacific Investment Trust PLC	£246,856,000
Trelleborg Holdings UK Limited	£246,784,992
Aim Altitude Limited	£246,172,000
AES Venezuela Finance	£246,105,808
Meggitt (UK) Limited	£242,303,008
Imerys Minerals Holding Limited	£241,213,472
Viridor EFW (Runcorn) Limited	£240,663,008
Triode Acquisitions UK Limited	£239,152,800
Ecotricity Group Ltd	£238,388,992
Alu Midco Limited	£234,592,368
Ocean Housing Group Limited	£232,066,000
GLE UK Topco Limited	£231,868,000
GLE Midco 2 Limited	£231,852,992
Auxillis Services Limited	£231,046,000
Bristol Airport Limited	£230,200,000
Radius Midco Limited	£230,017,760
Viridor Trident Park Limited	£229,164,000
Harbour Hotels Group Limited	£228,110,912
Rotork Controls Limited	£227,071,008
Flight Refuelling Limited	£224,836,000
Westrock Packaging Systems UK Ltd.	£224,764,992
Cooper Tyre & Rubber Company UK Limited	£224,612,432
USAF Management Limited	£223,904,464
Amcor UK Group Management Limited	£222,572,992
Synergy Health (UK) Limited	£222,024,000
Radius Holdco Limited	£220,961,776
Puma Energy (UK) Limited	£220,438,000
AgustaWestland Limited	£219,248,000
Viridor South London Limited	£219,024,992
Road Management Services (Finance) PLC	£219,012,000
MVV Environment Devonport Limited	£218,952,288
Radius Debtco Limited	£217,448,864
Helston Garages Group Limited	£215,798,000
Intrinsic Financial Services Limited	£212,014,000
St. James's Place Wealth Management PLC	£211,324,000
Princess Yachts Limited	£209,950,000
The Newcastle Estate Partnership Limited	£209,514,000
Connect Group PLC	£208,500,000
Helston Garages Limited	£208,435,008
Cambria Automobiles PLC	£208,380,000
Accord-UK Ltd	£206,463,008
Supergroup Internet Limited	£206,200,000
Charcoal CLG 1 Limited	£206,156,000
npower Direct Limited	£206,148,000
Hall & Woodhouse Limited	£206,032,992
Coastline Housing Limited	£205,478,000
Mears Limited	£205,271,008
Allied Minds PLC	£205,199,248
Optimas OE Solutions Ltd	£204,490,000
Seabank Power Limited	£203,243,008
Viridor Oxfordshire Limited	£203,128,992
Unicorn AIM VCT PLC	£201,718,000
Lombard Corporate Finance (11) Limited	£200,936,992
Dunlop Limited	£200,572,000
Ecclesiastical Planning Services Limited	£200,336,992
Babcock Marine (Devonport) Limited	£199,315,008
Radius Bidco Limited	£198,866,096
Innogy Gym 3 Limited	£198,172,960
Innogy Gym 2 Limited	£198,172,768
AES Ballylumford Holdings Limited	£198,143,824
Scottish Widows Unit Trust Managers Limited	£197,268,000
Yankee Candle Company (Europe) Limited	£196,910,000
Radius Pledgeco Limited	£196,120,448
Rocma Sterling	£195,360,992
Kohler Showers Holdings Limited	£194,523,008
The Ernest Cook Trust	£192,994,656
Nisbets PLC	£189,880,992
Xeon Smiles UK Limited	£189,474,352
Bentley Park (UK) Limited	£188,971,008
St.Austell Brewery Company Limited	£188,327,008
Colten Care Limited	£187,656,608
Sunseeker International Limited	£187,120,000
Refresco Beverages UK Limited	£185,803,008
Gooch & Housego PLC	£184,904,000
Kohler Showers Bidco Limited	£184,616,000
Lion/Jenga Bidco Limited	£180,268,000
Etex Building Performance Limited	£179,028,992
Two Rivers Housing	£178,951,008
AES Barry Operations Limited	£178,616,880
Kohler Mira Limited	£177,956,992
Future Publishing Limited	£174,655,008
Trifle Holdings Limited	£174,498,000
Dick Lovett Companies Limited	£173,172,000
Sanlam Investment Holdings UK Limited	£173,142,080
United Healthcare (Bromley) Limited	£172,479,008
Rhyl Flats Wind Farm Limited	£172,406,096
Ultimate Finance Group Limited	£171,164,992
North Devon Homes	£171,067,008
Monaghan Mushrooms Limited	£170,972,000
npower Yorkshire Limited	£170,234,000
Magners GB Limited	£169,904,000
Stannah Lifts Holdings Limited	£169,072,992
Robert Hitchins Limited	£168,838,560
Nutricia Limited	£168,623,008
Spirax-Sarco America Limited	£166,998,368
Belvedere Bidco Limited	£166,796,992
Auden McKenzie (Pharma Division) Limited	£166,636,032
GCP Bloomsbury Limited	£166,552,992
Westerleigh Group Holdings Limited	£166,490,016
Infineon Technologies Reigate Limited	£166,475,008
MGI Coutier Finance Limited	£166,159,424
Avon Rubber P.L.C.	£166,100,000
August UK Holdco Limited	£165,632,000
Constellation Software UK Holdco Ltd	£165,515,520
Amcor Packaging UK Limited	£165,104,000
Hospital Company (Swindon & Marlborough) Ltd	£163,586,000
The Hospital Company (Dartford) Limited	£162,447,008
Oxygen House Partners LLP	£162,368,000
Ochre Solutions (Holdings) Limited	£162,191,824
Ochre Solutions Limited	£162,191,824
GLE Midco Limited	£162,114,000
RWE Cogen UK Limited	£161,728,992
Hydro Holdings UK Limited	£161,635,008
Ovo Energy Ltd	£160,291,008
Dunlop Aerospace Group Limited	£160,171,008
Sunseeker International (Holdings) Limited	£159,775,008
University of Gloucestershire	£159,632,000
1pm PLC	£158,996,000
Duke Street Capital Oasis Acquisitions Limited	£157,612,992
FB Brassica Limited	£157,603,008
Low Carbon Oxygen Limited	£157,096,992
FB Brinjal Limited	£156,192,000
Openwork Limited	£155,507,008
West International Holdings Limited	£155,408,992
Amcor Flexibles UK Limited	£155,360,992
J.T.Baylis & Company Limited	£155,287,856

Company	Value
Ecotricity Wind and Sun Parks (Issuing) Limited	£153,503,552
UBB Waste (Essex) Limited	£153,354,000
Shaw Trust Limited (The)	£153,050,000
Wadworth and Company Limited	£152,864,992
Dunlop Holdings Limited	£151,507,008
Dutch Oak Tree Foundation	£150,995,184
Microsemi Semiconductor Limited	£150,416,128
GCP Topco 2 Limited	£150,071,008
Magnox Limited	£150,030,000
Belvedere Midco Limited	£149,586,000
Oasis Healthcare Midco 1 Limited	£148,962,000
Oasis Healthcare Midco 2 Limited	£148,962,000
Sanlam UK Limited	£148,436,768
Steward's Company Limited	£148,262,208
Kerry Ingredients Holdings (U.K.) Limited	£147,853,872
Sidlaw Group Limited	£146,952,000
Atlantic Inertial Systems Limited	£146,816,000
GCP Scape East Limited	£146,112,000
JISC	£145,963,008
Caledonia TLG Bidco Limited	£145,690,000
Alpha Schools (Highland) Holdings Limited	£143,529,872
Alpha Schools (Highland) Limited	£143,529,872
Compton Beauchamp Estates Limited	£143,365,056
Ecclesiastical Life Limited	£143,322,000
Openwork Holdings Limited	£141,760,000
Computershare Investor Services PLC	£141,575,008
Dunbia (UK)	£141,165,664
Teign Housing.	£141,036,992
London Bidco Limited	£140,942,000
Oasis Healthcare Limited	£140,311,008
Hobbycraft Group Limited	£140,308,992
Vectura Group Investments Limited	£140,000,000
LDC (Portfolio One) Limited	£139,830,880
Grant Almont Limited	£138,497,488
XJ4 Holding Company Limited	£137,900,992
LDC (Imperial Wharf) Limited	£137,704,560
Oasis Dental Care (Central) Limited	£137,562,000
Mulberry Company (Design) Limited	£135,358,000
Catalent CTS UK Holding Limited	£135,000,000
UBB Waste (Gloucestershire) Limited	£133,959,000
Lush Ltd.	£133,899,000
Cabot Learning Federation	£133,579,000
Spirax-Sarco Limited	£133,001,000
United Healthcare (Bromley) Group Limited	£131,774,000
London Topco Limited	£130,616,000
Patheon UK Limited	£130,475,168
John Baylis Limited.	£129,935,856
Duke Street Capital Oasis Midco Limited	£129,592,000
The White Horse Federation	£129,580,144
Merck Chemicals Ltd	£128,954,000
MTH Bidco Limited	£128,910,288
Merlin Entertainments (Sea Life) Limited	£128,717,000
Salisbury Diocesan Board of Finance (The)	£128,447,000
AES UK Holdings Ltd	£127,776,000
Alpha Schools (Highland) Project PLC	£127,670,992
Manitou Finance Limited	£127,663,000
Mole Valley Farmers Limited	£127,316,000
MTH Topco Limited	£127,278,000
Zimmer Biomet UK Limited	£127,072,000
Dentsply IH Limited	£126,242,448
Delphi Technologies Limited	£126,110,128
BWP Project Services Limited	£125,677,000
The Great Eastern Hotel Holding Company Limited	£125,604,000
Catalent U.K. Packaging Limited	£125,588,008
Smart Systems Limited	£124,464,000
MSA UK Holdings Limited	£124,140,000
Penny & Giles Controls Limited	£123,881,000
Westcountry Schools Trust	£123,808,000
Outdoor and Cycle Concepts Ltd	£123,681,000
Research Instruments Limited	£123,612,496
Unite Holdings Limited	£123,325,752
Nuon UK Ltd	£122,864,080
Stitch Bidco Limited	£122,750,000
Charles Robertson (Holdings) Limited	£122,699,552
Inspired Education (East Dunbartonshire) Limited	£122,436,000
Future PLC	£122,400,000
Good Energy Group PLC	£122,089,000
Ankers and Rawlings Developments Limited	£121,963,536
Amcor Europe Group Management	£121,473,624
Moog Wolverhampton Limited	£120,792,000
LDC (Portfolio Five) Limited	£120,304,240
Imperial Tobacco Overseas (Polska) Limited	£120,300,000
Yeo Valley Group Limited	£119,683,096
MW High Tech Projects UK Limited	£119,620,000
Zimmer U.K. Ltd.	£119,405,000
Mulberry Group PLC	£119,335,000
C & J Clark (No 1) Limited	£119,000,000
Miton UK Microcap Trust PLC	£118,839,000
Sigma - Aldrich Financial Services Limited	£118,402,248
Berkeley Leisure Group Limited (The)	£118,119,424
Baring Emerging Europe PLC	£117,991,000
Horizon Nuclear Power Oldbury Limited	£117,855,000
A-Gas International Limited	£117,706,000
LV Insurance Management Limited	£117,388,000
The Olympus Academy Trust	£117,071,952
Woodbury Limited	£116,942,192
Howard Tenens Limited	£116,751,000
Wainhomes (South West) Holdings Limited	£116,675,000
Lighthouse Schools Partnership	£116,241,816
Forelle Estates Limited	£116,187,824
Hills UK Limited	£116,141,000
Bradford and Sons Limited	£116,049,000
The Hospital Company (Dartford) Issuer PLC	£115,466,000
Help for Heroes	£115,174,000
Stitch 2 Limited	£115,008,000
Stitch 3 Limited	£114,598,000
Sterling ISA Managers Limited	£114,454,000
MSP Capital Ltd	£114,444,048
Bristol & West PLC	£114,129,000
Cooper Tire & Rubber Company Europe Limited	£113,479,000
G4S Joint Ventures Limited	£113,124,216
Bath and Wells Diocesan Board of Finance (The)	£111,976,000
USAF LP Limited	£111,950,128
Close Brewery Rentals Limited	£111,940,008
Vospers of Plymouth Limited	£111,766,088
Lombard Industrial Leasing Limited	£111,712,000
Curtiss-Wright Controls (UK) Limited	£110,833,000
Bristol Water Holdings UK Limited	£110,379,000
Ultimate Finance Limited	£109,424,000
Thrive Renewables PLC	£109,126,456
Gregory Distribution (Holdings) Limited	£109,061,000
West UC Limited	£108,755,000
G-TEKT Europe Manufacturing Limited	£108,457,000
Glide Topco Limited	£108,290,000
JB Global Limited	£108,268,648
Resource Solutions Group PLC	£107,586,000
Mulberry Company (Sales) Limited	£107,412,000
Yeo Valley Farms (Production) Limited	£107,194,480
Assessments Midco Limited	£107,128,000
Amcor Polska Holding Limited	£106,583,800
Eagle One Investment Holdings Limited	£106,350,000
Westerleigh WGH Limited	£105,283,312
Lombard Corporate Finance (December 1) Limited	£104,910,680
Cambium Networks, Ltd	£104,740,848
Landmark Information Group Limited	£104,309,632
Magellan Aerospace (UK) Limited	£104,136,000
Murray & Roberts United Kingdom Limited	£103,863,712
Westover Holdings Limited	£103,783,744
Quadrum Investments Group Limited	£103,402,000
Bristol PFI Limited	£103,384,000
Bristol PFI (Holdings) Limited	£103,384,000
The Exeter Diocesan Board of Finance Limited	£103,303,000
TRL Electronics Limited	£102,825,000
Insite Poster Midco Limited	£102,701,200

Company	Value
Cross Manufacturing Company (1938) Limited	£102,389,000
The English Heritage Trust	£102,289,000
Dunlop Aerospace Overseas Limited	£102,263,000
Porton Biopharma Limited	£102,041,000
Triventura Midco I Limited	£101,850,000
Oasis Healthcare International Limited	£101,779,000
Moog Controls Limited	£101,591,000
Forelle Estates Investments Limited	£101,550,000
Rygor Holdings Limited	£101,284,000
Corin Orthopaedics Holdings Limited	£101,035,000
International Plywood PLC	£100,867,920
Vospers Motor House Limited	£100,723,344
Unite Finance One (Holdings) Limited	£100,169,000
United Agri Products Limited	£99,827,000
Assessments Bidco Limited	£99,719,000
Rygor Group Limited	£99,084,000
Intercept Pharma Europe Ltd.	£98,879,544
Gregory Distribution Limited	£98,754,000
Vitacress Limited	£98,659,000
Crematoria Management Ltd.	£98,578,208
Investors in the Community (Leeds Schools) Holding	£98,260,400
Investors in the Community (Leeds Schools) Limited	£98,260,392
LDC (Project 110) Limited	£98,122,616
A.J. and R.G.Barber Limited	£98,000,216
Teleperformance Limited	£97,529,000
Amcor European Investments Limited	£97,343,144
LDC (MTF Portfolio) Limited	£97,299,336
Herman Miller Holdings Limited	£97,157,160
AFC Bournemouth Limited	£96,996,000
E-Mex Home Funding Limited	£96,897,000
C.G. Fry and Son Limited	£96,437,408
Oxygen House Group Limited	£96,406,064
The Bath and Wells Diocesan Academies Trust	£96,182,000
Copper Bidco Limited	£95,576,000
Infineon Technologies Newport Holding Limited	£95,515,000
The National Lighting Company Limited	£95,256,000
Truro Diocesan Board of Finance Limited (The)	£94,801,960
Stanley Security Solutions Limited	£94,554,000
Crown Pet Foods Limited	£94,547,000
Midas Group Limited	£94,294,000
Happold LLP	£94,123,000
Community 1st Cornwall Limited	£94,071,384
Advanced Insulation Holdings Limited	£94,049,472
Spitalgate Dealer Services Limited	£93,654,000
Aura Bidco Management Limited	£93,089,760
Insite Poster Investments (B) Limited	£92,453,416
R. B. Quadrangle Leasing Limited	£92,435,376
Brightside Group Limited	£92,377,000
Texas Instruments (U.K.) Limited	£92,082,160
Vision Direct Europe Ltd	£91,954,000
Herman Miller Limited	£91,829,000
Rich Products Limited	£91,686,376
Praxair Offshore Services Limited	£91,474,064
P of a Productions Limited	£91,140,000
Beckton Energy Limited	£91,139,000
Gemini Energy Limited	£91,134,000
WH Smith 1955 Limited	£91,108,000
Greenoaks Global Holdings Ltd.	£90,268,056
Alu Topco Limited	£90,087,920
Endsleigh Insurance Services Limited	£89,842,000
Nokia UK Limited	£89,805,000
Sandown Motors Limited	£89,709,000
F W S Carter & Sons Limited	£89,432,000
Triventura Bidco Limited	£89,321,000
Triventura Midco II Limited	£89,264,000
Funkypigeon.Com Limited	£89,208,784
Allan Sichel Limited	£89,157,560
Lyons Davidson Limited	£89,072,440
Ecotricity Generation Limited	£89,017,232
Westover Group Limited	£88,585,944
Endsleigh Limited	£88,560,000
Lornamead Group Limited	£88,404,000
Sensata Technologies (Europe) Limited	£88,235,400
Falmouth Exeter Plus	£88,156,000
Tabacalera de Garcia UK Limited	£88,099,704
Rygor Commercials Ltd	£87,733,000
YTL Property Holdings (UK) Limited	£87,179,000
Trago Mills Limited	£87,002,696
Eagle One Limited	£86,559,856
Nuvias Global Services Limited	£85,961,000
The Bath Priory Limited	£85,474,888
Severn Glocon Group PLC	£85,267,536
International Plywood (Importers) Limited	£84,964,792
Portman Healthcare (Holdings) Limited	£84,949,000
PFI Investments Limited	£84,332,000
Unite Accommodation Management 19 Limited	£84,228,032
HF Trust Limited	£84,115,000
Grange Motors (Brentwood) Limited	£83,744,000
New Look Senior Issuer PLC	£83,713,000
Future Holdings 2002 Limited	£83,457,000
Baglan Moor Healthcare PLC	£83,447,000
C.M. Downton (Haulage Contractors) Limited	£83,219,640
Specialist Aviation Services Group Limited	£83,136,000
Tor Currency Exchange Limited	£82,969,000
Helena Productions Limited	£82,858,000
1869 Limited	£81,651,000
Gloucester Diocesan Board of Finance	£81,511,000
Hobbycraft Trading Limited	£81,388,000
Parham Investment Limited	£81,370,448
First West of England Limited	£81,135,000
Knight Square Holdings Limited	£81,078,560
Knight Midco Limited	£81,078,560
Computershare Technology Services (UK) Limited	£80,761,000
Quantock Properties Limited	£80,617,000
King William St Limited	£80,596,160
Synergy Health Sterilisation UK Limited	£80,562,000
Amsafe Bridport Limited	£80,342,000
Tribal Education Limited	£80,133,000
Langdon Group Limited	£80,008,000
Catalent CTS (Edinburgh) Limited	£79,866,568
Aeroflex Test Solutions Limited	£79,547,000
CWC (UK Holdings) Limited	£79,349,000
Knorr-Bremse Rail Systems (UK) Limited	£79,320,000
Specialist Aviation Services Limited	£79,250,000
Triton Knoll Offshore Wind Farm Limited	£79,090,712
City West Country Limited	£79,064,000
Aura Wind (Midco) Limited	£78,908,232
ML Wind LLP	£78,818,720
Planit Software Limited	£78,791,000
Legoland US Holdings Limited	£78,511,000
Loungers Limited	£78,400,000
Computershare Voucher Services Limited	£78,372,000
Inter Rested Limited	£78,296,000
AGI UK Acquisition Limited	£78,235,000
IDEMIA UK Holding Limited	£78,048,000
Decision Insight Information Group (UK) Limited	£77,913,416
Nagel Langdons Ltd	£77,874,000
The Gurkha Welfare Trust	£77,861,000
Spandex Limited	£77,854,000
Defence Training Services Limited	£77,588,000
More Homes Bromley LLP	£77,337,464
Gamecube Amusement Limited	£77,307,424
Mercia Healthcare Limited	£77,281,000
Farrow & Ball Limited	£77,156,000
First Priorities PPP Health Services Limited	£77,119,808
The Great Eastern Hotel Company Limited	£77,076,000
Viscominvest Holding UK Limited	£76,836,000
Langham Industries Limited	£76,757,936
Wirral Schools Services Limited	£76,616,000
Churchill Retirement (Group) Limited	£76,395,000
USAF Management 10 Limited	£76,369,376
Trelleborg Offshore UK Limited	£76,286,000
Glatfelter Lydney, Ltd.	£76,239,000
npower Gas Limited	£76,190,000

Company	Value
Essex Schools (Holdings) Limited	£76,075,000
Essex Schools Limited	£76,075,000
Spandex Holding UK Ltd.	£76,069,000
Meiyume (UK) Limited	£75,902,000
Merlin Entertainments Group Limited	£75,702,000
LDC (AIB Warehouse) Limited	£75,635,024
United Bible Societies Association	£75,448,896
Excalibur Academies Trust	£75,387,872
Bristol City Holdings Limited	£75,188,080
Centaur Services Limited	£75,137,000
Millfield	£74,847,000
Education South West	£74,780,000
Smartstream Technologies Holdings Limited	£74,468,000
Centrax Holdings Limited	£73,812,576
G4S Investments Limited	£73,710,056
Tribal Group PLC	£73,642,000
Taylor Maxwell Group (2017) Limited	£73,515,168
Hopkins Estates Limited	£73,310,848
FR Aviation Limited	£73,201,000
Knight Square Limited	£73,072,136
A E Stuart Limited	£73,033,992
Burges Salmon LLP	£73,011,000
Brothers Drinks Co. Limited	£72,885,224
Lilibet Holdings Ltd	£72,847,000
The Renewable Energy Company Limited	£72,593,672
Insite Poster Investments (A) Limited	£72,462,368
MWI Supply (UK Acquisition) Limited	£72,406,152
Merlin Entertainments (Dungeons) Limited	£72,395,000
Paradigm (Sheffield BSF) Holdings Limited	£72,331,000
Paradigm (Sheffield BSF) Limited	£72,331,000
Emily Estate (UK) Limited	£72,182,080
Criterion Healthcare PLC	£72,161,000
Investment Funds Direct Limited	£71,893,000
Tay Valley Lighting (Leeds) Limited	£71,869,000
Severn Glocon Limited	£71,786,712
Westerleigh Group Limited	£71,712,384
USAF Management 6 Limited	£71,512,976
Commercial First Group Limited	£71,473,000
Halos Garden Amusement Limited	£71,441,480
Consilium Airton Limited	£71,386,000
Unite Finance One (Property) Limited	£71,368,000
Coban 2017 LLP	£71,211,000
Virtus Health Europe Limited	£71,191,824
Avon Rubber Overseas Limited	£71,149,728
Castle School Education Trust	£70,923,000
Arkell's Brewery Limited	£70,877,672
Victoria Group Holdings Limited	£70,677,000
Mears Care Limited	£70,646,000
Superior Group Limited	£70,638,920
Lilibet Finance Ltd	£70,115,000
Copper Midco 1 Limited	£70,106,000
Copper Midco 2 Limited	£70,067,000
ASM Assembly Systems Weymouth Limited	£70,066,000
Portman Healthcare Limited	£70,009,000
Libya Oil Ethiopia Limited	£69,999,696
Orbitz Worldwide (UK) Limited	£69,974,896
Sportech Holdco 2 Limited	£69,937,896
Teleperformance Holdings Limited	£69,872,000
Lifetime Training Group Limited	£69,813,320
Civitas SPV1 Limited	£69,649,712
Levitt UK Real Estate Limited	£69,594,592
Gatehouse Green Learning Trust	£69,347,672
Westerleigh Crematoria Limited	£69,266,624
Sutton Harbour Holdings PLC	£69,249,000
Andrew Brownsword Hotels Limited	£69,195,288
Earthline Exchange Limited	£69,182,688
Texas Instruments (U.K.) Holdings Limited	£69,093,568
Cartus Limited	£68,748,000
LDC (Tara House) Limited	£68,486,912
Tilstone Warehouse Holdco Limited	£68,395,800
Hochtief (UK) Construction Limited	£68,385,000
Viridor Waste Exeter Limited	£68,084,000
Thatchers (Myrtle Farm) Limited	£68,002,952
Voyager Fishing Company Limited	£67,767,088
Lush Retail Limited	£67,747,000
Ceuta Holdings Limited	£67,635,000
Texas Instruments Limited	£67,545,000
JELF Limited	£67,500,000
Fanatics UK Holdings Limited	£67,404,000
Apetito Limited	£67,337,000
Nippon Paint (Europe) Ltd.	£66,891,000
Thatchers Holdings Limited	£66,821,984
Sparex Limited	£66,808,492
Chelton Limited	£66,795,000
Customade Group Topco Limited	£66,696,000
Lornamead Acquisitions Limited	£66,672,000
Flemingo International (UK) Limited	£66,635,220
JISC Services Limited	£66,520,000
Rotolok (Holdings) Limited	£66,145,652
Customade Group Trading Limited	£66,055,000
Theobald Film Productions LLP	£66,004,000
SWK (UK) Limited	£65,711,000
Drilling Systems Group Limited	£65,630,640
Leidos Europe, Limited	£65,587,000
Signum Technology Limited	£65,568,000
Cavanna Group Limited	£65,550,968
LVTG Holdings Limited	£65,486,972
Cotswold Motor Group Limited	£65,420,232
Vantage Point Business Village Limited	£65,280,040
Jaguar Oil & Gas UK Limited	£65,244,000
Lyons Seafoods Limited	£64,945,000
Madame Tussauds Touring Exhibition Limited	£64,870,000
Care South	£64,615,000
Venturers Trust	£64,615,000
Glide Student & Residential Limited	£64,585,000
Radiodetection Limited	£64,494,000
Buro Happold Limited	£64,193,000
Amcor Mediflex Limited	£64,113,668
Somerset Care Limited	£64,092,920
1&1 UK Holdings Limited	£64,017,000
Greater Union Limited	£63,938,304
Brunelcare	£63,316,000
Tempire Investments Limited	£63,307,000
Molson Group Ltd	£63,246,000
Renaissance Miles Platting Limited	£63,190,340
Renaissance Miles Platting Holding Company Limited	£63,190,340
The Big Green Parcel Holding Company Limited	£63,096,000
Winchcombe Finance Limited	£63,088,000
Bristol Diocesan Board of Finance Limited (The)	£63,049,000
St. James's Place International Distribution Limited	£63,032,000
SPP Pumps Limited	£62,972,344
Portman Healthcare (Finance) Limited	£62,795,000
IDEMIA UK Limited	£62,759,000
Carlisle Fluid Technologies UK Limited	£62,638,308
FB Leasing Limited	£62,391,000
NOV Process & Flow Technologies UK Limited	£62,341,000
Searchflow Limited	£62,339,904
T. H. White Holdings Limited	£62,100,800
Tuffnells Parcels Express Limited	£61,923,000
Real Estate Gloucester Limited	£61,598,168
Services Support (Avon & Somerset) Limited	£61,249,000
Elemis Limited	£61,136,348
Foray Holdings Limited	£60,957,760
Wyke Farms Ltd	£60,794,000
Dartmoor Investment Trust Limited	£60,720,000
Scisys UK Holding Ltd	£60,672,000
Swallowfield PLC	£60,490,000
Clarart Ltd	£60,421,900
Atlas Elektronik UK Limited	£60,371,000
Palladian Academy Trust	£60,143,200
Urbaser Limited	£60,141,928
Combined Independents (Holdings) Limited	£60,094,856
Computershare Investments (UK) (No 7) Limited	£60,032,000
Launceston College	£59,998,848

Company	Turnover
Unite Finance Limited	£59,832,000
EW Beard (Holdings) Limited	£59,634,000
Curo Enterprise Limited	£59,200,000
Haynes Publishing Group PLC	£59,158,000
AgustaWestland Holdings Limited	£59,083,000
Cambria Automobiles (South East) Limited	£58,967,000
Stuart Partners Limited	£58,860,084
Advanced Insulation Group Limited	£58,807,056
Trelleborg Sealing Solutions UK Limited	£58,625,000
Sherborne Holdings Limited	£58,559,712
MSP Capital Two Limited	£58,506,180
The D'Oyly Carte Charitable Trust	£58,446,660
The Eden Trust	£58,411,000
John Fowler Holidays Limited	£58,404,808
Viridor Waste (Somerset) Limited	£58,277,000
Hoburne Limited	£58,185,036
Centrax Limited	£57,889,864
Ely Acquisition Limited	£57,776,000
Colten Care (1993) Limited	£57,759,868
Midas Construction Limited	£57,646,000
Wellsway Multi Academy Trust	£57,582,400
Allen & Heath Limited	£57,542,000
Dyson International Limited	£57,300,000
Troika Developments Limited	£57,226,956
USAF Holdings J Limited	£57,155,148
Padmanor Investments Limited	£56,944,256
D & R Topco Limited	£56,782,704
Wessex Garages Holdings Limited	£56,625,828
Newham Learning Partnership (Project Co) Limited	£56,619,832
Ashfield Land Limited	£56,304,600
Heritage Automotive Holdings Limited	£56,215,000
GS Yuasa Battery Sales UK Limited	£56,190,000
Dean & Reddyhoff Limited	£56,106,344
LVTG Limited	£56,032,300
Harding Brothers Retail Limited	£55,901,240
Geo Specialty Chemicals UK Limited	£55,854,648
Vero Software Limited	£55,809,000
Pittville Leasing Limited	£55,732,000
Pendennis Shipyard (Holdings) Limited	£55,715,344
Fazakerley Prison Services Limited	£55,583,512
Cambria Automobiles Property Limited	£55,536,000
SACO Group Holdings Limited	£55,488,000
USAF Management 11 Limited	£55,416,072
DS UK Midco 2 Limited	£55,328,240
Hargreaves Lansdown Fund Managers Ltd.	£55,269,000
Viridor Waste (Greater Manchester) Limited	£55,239,000
Mears Housing Management (Holdings) Limited	£55,036,352
Highship Industries Limited	£54,966,500
Heritage Automotive Limited	£54,851,000
Cornish Mutual Assurance Company,Limited	£54,734,228
Bristol Infracare Lift (3) Limited	£54,729,000
Seasons Holidays PLC	£54,522,512
Marchmont Farms Limited	£54,521,732
The Hospital Company (Dartford) Group Limited	£54,441,000
Vectura Limited	£54,300,000
Foray Motor Group Limited	£54,218,600
Remix Bidco Limited	£54,199,000
Andros UK Limited	£54,168,576
Norton Avonmouth Limited	£54,029,000
Computershare Mortgage Services Limited	£54,019,000
Parham Holdings Limited	£53,914,308
Dudley Infracare Lift (1) Limited	£53,797,000
Avantage (Cheshire) Limited	£53,761,640
Space Engineering Services Limited	£53,708,148
Goonvean Holdings Limited	£53,671,728
A.J. & R.G.Barber (Sales) Limited	£53,504,912
United Healthcare (Bromley) Holdings Limited	£53,404,000
Martin & Martin Holdings	£53,258,832
Twynham Learning	£53,253,000
Hardrock Developments Limited	£53,176,376
Ashton Gate Limited	£53,175,848
Lush Manufacturing Limited	£53,155,000
Pro - Direct Group Limited	£52,967,268
E.W. Beard Limited	£52,902,000
Avon Polymer Products Limited	£52,805,380
Cambria Automobiles Acquisitions Limited	£52,766,000
Amcor Flexibles Winterbourne Limited	£52,755,000
Thatchers Cider Company Limited	£52,640,336
South Manchester Healthcare Limited	£52,423,000
Eden Project Limited	£52,374,000
Breath Limited	£52,331,824
Toshiba Carrier UK Ltd.	£52,308,000
DAS UK Holdings Limited	£52,270,000
Wartsila Hamworthy Limited	£52,158,000
MTH Midco 1 Limited	£52,111,708
MTH Midco 2 Limited	£52,102,456
Pennyfarthing Developments Limited	£52,086,744
Appleby Westward Group Limited	£51,792,436
Sureserve Energy Services Limited	£51,748,592
A. H. Warren Trust (Holdings) Limited	£51,738,884
Glide Bidco Limited	£51,680,000
Meggitt Advanced Composites Limited	£51,612,000
Stanley Security Solutions - Europe Limited	£51,565,000
Novanta Technologies UK Limited	£51,411,000
Pearsalls Limited	£51,324,000
Fish Brothers (Holdings) Limited	£51,311,000
G4S Technology Limited	£51,248,000
Merrydown PLC	£51,247,252
Cengage Learning UK Holdings Limited	£51,173,000
E. & J. W. Glendinning (Holdings) Limited	£51,081,920
RBSSAF (6) Limited	£50,909,000
Bioreliance UK Acquisition Limited	£50,815,000
Project Darwin Bidco Limited	£50,681,000
Pro-Direct Sport Limited	£50,611,580
Stonegate Farmers Limited	£50,538,312
Corin Limited	£50,491,000
Good Energy Limited	£50,470,948
Brightside Insurance Services Limited	£50,444,000
Truro & Penwith Academy Trust	£50,399,900
Kirklees Schools Services Limited	£50,352,000
Group Silverline Limited	£50,219,000
Adey Innovation Limited	£50,185,000
Keenwork Limited	£50,167,196
Bob Martin (UK) Limited	£50,035,164
CG Hotel Holding Limited	£49,954,624
G & H US Holdings Limited	£49,952,104
St. James's Place DFM Holdings Limited	£49,902,260
Colosseum Dental UK Limited	£49,747,000
RBSSAF (8) Limited	£49,717,000
Assessments Midco 2 Limited	£49,676,000
Aspire Academy Trust	£49,631,704
Dextra Group PLC	£49,517,276
Sherborne School	£49,461,000
Royal Agricultural University	£49,351,000
TLT LLP	£49,264,000
Ecotricity Bonds PLC	£49,213,936
Mulberry Company (Europe) Limited	£49,187,000
Blue3 (London) Limited	£49,070,000
Good Energy Generation Assets No. 1 Limited	£49,050,000
WPD Property Investments Limited	£49,039,000
Sureserve Holdings Limited	£48,927,000
Gerber Emig Group Limited	£48,835,000
Aim Altitude UK Limited	£48,816,000
RMH (Guildford) LLP	£48,771,592
TRL Technology Limited	£48,694,000
Hospital Company (Swindon & Marlborough) Holdings	£48,694,000
Canford School,Limited	£48,669,292
IIC Peterborough Holding Company Limited	£48,611,112
Synergy Health Investments Limited	£48,552,000
AB Dynamics PLC	£48,528,304
Bailey Caravans Limited	£48,366,048
Pennyfarthing Homes Limited	£48,338,856
Sureserve Compliance Services Limited	£48,234,328
Butcombe Brewery Limited	£48,207,372

Company	Value
Scotsgrove Holdings Limited	£48,132,616
Angel Assistance Limited	£47,967,000
Trago Mills (South Devon) Limited	£47,949,908
University of St Mark & St John	£47,918,000
Malvern Tyres Holdings Limited	£47,773,200
Altran UK Limited	£47,669,152
Anthony Best Dynamics Limited	£47,668,184
Swegon Limited	£47,655,816
BBG Lift Accommodation Services Limited	£47,550,000
Sofa Brands International Limited	£47,549,240
IIC By Education (Peterborough Schools) Limited	£47,522,292
John Heathcoat & Company (Holdings) Limited	£47,386,000
Gainwell Limited	£47,373,820
Newland Homes Limited	£47,288,960
BHH Lift Accommodation Services Limited	£47,053,000
Bryanston School,Incorporated	£46,996,816
Rosemont Pharmaceuticals Limited	£46,942,000
DAC Beachcroft Claims Limited	£46,913,000
DS UK Topco Limited	£46,849,608
Burry and Knight Limited	£46,813,684
N. Notaro Homes Limited	£46,778,456
Richard Reeve's Foundation	£46,725,640
Alderley PLC	£46,717,000
A-Gas (UK) Limited	£46,662,000
Denplan Limited	£46,647,000
The Big Green Parcel Group Limited	£46,535,000
Haskins Holdings Limited	£46,500,000
Manitou UK Limited	£46,477,000
Aster Homes Limited	£46,471,000
Leicester BSF Company 1 Limited	£46,453,652
Eurac Limited	£46,382,000
Albion Healthcare (Oxford) Limited	£46,322,952
Haskins Garden Centres Limited	£46,242,000
Leicester BSF Company 2 Limited	£46,106,692
Flightbookers Limited	£46,053,000
Cygnet Industries Limited	£46,033,772
Insite Poster Investments (C) Limited	£46,023,872
Strongvox Limited	£45,997,916
Imerys Talc UK Holding Limited	£45,939,000
Qualasept Holdings Limited	£45,933,204
Wessex Eagle Limited	£45,913,924
Wessex Eagle Holdings Limited	£45,913,924
Star Education Investment Limited	£45,885,760
Silbury Housing Limited	£45,877,000
DS UK Midco 1 Limited	£45,871,076
Waddeton Park Limited	£45,735,360
Bradfords Building Supplies Limited	£45,587,268
Bristol, Clifton and West of England Zoological Society	£45,516,000
Knorr-Bremse Systems for Commercial Vehicles Ltd	£45,506,000
Molson Equipment Services Ltd	£45,494,000
J.Chandler & Company (Buckfast),Limited	£45,481,508
UFP Global Holdings Limited	£45,431,052
De Van Automotive Limited	£45,343,176
Grevan Cars Limited	£45,233,400
Wrafton Laboratories Limited	£45,168,000
IIC Northampton Limited	£45,075,484
IIC Northampton Holding Company Limited	£45,075,484
Spark Gas Shipping Ltd	£45,000,000
Insite Poster Properties Limited	£44,995,640
Bridgwater College Trust	£44,776,000
FJB Hotels Limited	£44,747,752
Ark Data Centres Limited	£44,666,308
BSR Group Holdings Limited	£44,645,240
Space Cooling Topco Limited	£44,577,024
Sensata Technologies Holding Company U.K.	£44,574,860
Cartus Holdings Limited	£44,552,000
Avon Group Manufacturing (Holdings) Limited	£44,452,888
Sydenhams Ltd	£44,406,808
Superior Seals Limited	£44,399,256
Little Cheyne Court Wind Farm Limited	£44,356,236
Hills Waste Solutions Limited	£44,339,000
Radius (UK) Limited	£44,335,664
Betterment Properties (Weymouth) Limited	£44,228,448
Alvis Brothers Limited	£44,160,888
Centek Holdings Limited	£43,834,500
T. H. White Limited	£43,722,356
Midsomer Norton Schools Partnership	£43,708,276
TBS Engineering Limited	£43,622,624
Birmingham Healthcare Services Limited	£43,533,000
MSP Capital Three Limited	£43,511,848
Michco 1205 Limited	£43,436,232
Michco 1204 Limited	£43,380,756
ARAG PLC	£43,260,652
BBGR Limited	£43,199,000
MWI Supply (UK Holdings) Limited	£43,181,148
Birchmere Limited	£43,157,576
Abbey Manor Group Limited	£43,132,000
The Wildfowl & Wetlands Trust	£43,123,000
Toolstream Limited	£43,113,000
JSP Limited	£43,090,000
T.D. Williamson UK International Limited	£43,004,276
Poole Lighting Limited	£42,981,936
The Priory Learning Trust	£42,929,616
Gall Thomson Environmental Limited	£42,925,000
Bristol Grammar School	£42,726,296
Openwork Services Limited	£42,450,000
Roman Group Topco Limited	£42,354,344
Torquay Boys' Grammar School	£42,291,000
Baker Estates Limited	£42,288,220
PAC Farms Limited	£42,151,860
Bathurst Estate Holdings Limited	£42,027,256
Daido Metal Europe Limited	£42,009,000
1pm (UK) Limited	£41,950,264
Volaris Group UK Holdco Ltd	£41,909,504
RW Threadneedle Street Limited	£41,761,000
Robert Braithwaite Limited	£41,591,984
Sandbanks Hotel Limited	£41,476,100
Stonegate Holdings Limited	£41,268,112
Cengage Learning (EMEA) Limited	£41,184,000
Ocean Automotive (Holdings) Limited	£41,144,008
PKL Group (UK) Limited	£41,086,000
Project Darwin Topco Limited	£41,086,000
Morrish Builders (Poole) Limited	£41,052,908
Batsford Estates (1983) Company Limited	£41,041,148
The Hospital Company (Dartford) Holdings Limited	£40,930,000
Project People Limited	£40,880,592
Children's Hospice South West	£40,879,408
Grenville Topco Limited	£40,872,036
Huachangda UK Limited	£40,842,132
Frazer-Nash Consultancy Limited	£40,840,000
The Hospital Company (Dartford) 2005 Limited	£40,777,000
United Healthcare (Bromley) Services Limited	£40,693,000
E.And J.W.Glendinning Limited	£40,682,308
Aardman Holdings Limited	£40,646,816
USAF Management 12 Limited	£40,488,288
npower Commercial Gas Limited	£40,410,000
Fiberlean Technologies Limited	£40,380,756
Sandown Dorset and Wiltshire Limited	£40,360,000
Axell Wireless Limited	£40,314,000
Roper Rhodes Limited	£40,307,844
Lancaster Leisure Limited	£40,306,864
Adey Holdings (2008) Limited	£40,300,000
Heathcoat Fabrics Limited	£40,297,000
Methodist Insurance Public Limited Company	£40,221,652
Ultrahaptics Limited	£40,218,000
Merlin Entertainments Developments Limited	£40,128,000
Turtle Bay Restaurants Limited	£40,094,312
Bristol Charities	£40,046,584
Aeronautical & GI Holdings Limited	£40,013,000
Flowbird Transport Limited	£39,974,000
Gillman Electrical Group Limited	£39,854,800
Mole Valley Feed Solutions Ltd	£39,796,000
Firstport Retirement Property Services Limited	£39,768,148
Williamson-Dickie Europe Limited	£39,725,000

Company	Amount
IIC (C & T) Limited	£39,649,104
Parragon Books Limited	£39,594,000
Bond Street Estates (Brighton) Limited	£39,573,112
Pendennis Shipyard Limited	£39,558,396
Ian Williams (Holdings) Limited	£39,502,000
Wallscourt Foundation	£39,482,000
Ambitions Academies Trust	£39,467,536
Investors in Health (C & T1) Limited	£39,452,844
Ropsley Farms Limited	£39,419,064
Phyworks Limited	£39,378,232
Renrod Holdings Limited	£39,339,352
Hayes Grange LLP	£39,297,756
Hollingsworth and Vose Company (U.K.) Limited	£39,262,000
Safran Landing Systems Services UK Ltd	£39,220,000
Blade Motor Group Limited	£39,170,140
WPD Telecoms Limited	£39,076,000
Whittington Facilities Limited	£39,021,176
Hoare Lea LLP	£38,896,000
Vygon (U.K.) Limited	£38,871,000
WH Smith Hospitals Limited	£38,831,496
The Universities and Colleges Admissions Service	£38,814,000
Stovax Heating Group Limited	£38,804,520
Charford Properties Limited	£38,778,360
Roman Bidco Limited	£38,773,176
Swindon Silicon Systems Limited	£38,756,000
By Education (Barking) Holdings Limited	£38,489,000
By Education (Barking) Limited	£38,489,000
Investment Funds Direct Group Limited	£38,405,440
PPL Midlands Limited	£38,276,000
AES K2 Limited	£38,273,000
Kawasaki Precision Machinery (UK) Limited	£38,258,240
Viridor Waste (West Sussex) Limited	£38,157,000
Hydro Building Systems UK Limited	£38,136,000
Rawle Gammon & Baker Holdings Limited	£38,095,184
The Diocese of Gloucester Academies Trust	£37,981,536
Ceres Estates Limited	£37,933,428
The Big Green Parcel Machine Limited	£37,916,000
Decision Insight Information Group (Europe) Limited	£37,852,160
Branksome Estates Ltd.	£37,782,036
North Kent Farms Limited	£37,746,080
Taunton Land Limited	£37,704,956
Kingsley Developments (S W) Limited	£37,665,416
Bland Group UK Holdings Limited	£37,622,216
Xylem Dewatering Solutions UK Ltd	£37,591,000
R. T. Keedwell Holdings Limited	£37,559,392
Hydro Components UK Ltd.	£37,498,000
The DB Food Group Limited	£37,414,076
East London Lift Accommodation Services Limited	£37,394,000
G.R. Lane Holdings Limited	£37,367,288
Praxair Surface Technologies Limited	£37,288,000
Longleat Enterprises Limited	£37,267,772
Welton Bibby and Baron Holdings Limited	£37,201,000
Welton Bibby and Baron Limited	£37,201,000
Centek Limited	£37,182,480
Watson-Marlow Limited	£37,166,968
J.C. & R.H. Palmer Limited	£37,139,700
WH Smith Promotions Limited	£37,111,552
Galpharm International Limited	£37,058,000
Dartington Hall Trust (The)	£37,026,000
RBSSAF (25) Limited	£37,024,456
Pencarrie Group Limited	£37,009,816
Doric Developments (Bath) Limited	£36,986,672
Nicolas James Holdings Limited	£36,969,836
Sustrans Limited	£36,926,000
Pencarrie Limited	£36,891,372
Brymain Investments Limited	£36,811,228
Threadneedles Hotel Limited	£36,785,604
Foot Anstey LLP	£36,780,000
Unite Accommodation Management One Hundred Ltd	£36,779,724
FIM Trustee Limited	£36,723,912
John Romans Park Homes Limited	£36,719,712
South East Cornwall Multi Academy Regional Trust	£36,541,940
First Databank UK Ltd	£36,532,924
LDC (Millennium View) Limited	£36,509,656
Newquay Education Trust	£36,502,176
Marine & Towage Services Group Limited	£36,461,876
FTI Management Limited	£36,453,096
Liverpool Schools Services Limited	£36,405,000
Sitec Engineering Limited	£36,298,000
Fish Brothers (Swindon) Limited	£36,282,000
George Banco.Com Limited	£36,269,692
Azure Sun (Holdco) Limited	£36,259,224
Peninsula Learning Trust	£36,246,816
FB Heliservices Limited	£36,221,000
New Forest PPP Health Services Limited	£36,185,192
Blue Cedar Homes Limited	£36,069,000
East London Lift Accommodation Services No2 Ltd	£36,013,000
SACO Cannon Street Limited	£35,968,000
Dover Engineered Systems UK Ltd	£35,915,000
Cheltine Limited	£35,793,928
Troy (UK) Limited	£35,772,760
Bandvulc Tyres Ltd	£35,733,764
D B Foods (Holdings) Limited	£35,648,560
Advanced Insulation Systems Limited	£35,648,136
LDC (Causewayend) Limited	£35,624,928
Onley Prison Services Limited	£35,594,560
Sanderson Recruitment PLC	£35,468,000
Batson Bidco Limited	£35,434,068
Aviation Training International Limited	£35,237,000
Elmbirch Properties P.L.C.	£35,218,180
Shiloh Limited	£35,211,816
James Hay Holdings Limited	£35,197,000
Crofty Multi Academy Trust	£35,179,688
Octagon Healthcare Holdings (Norwich) Limited	£35,179,000
Beale Limited	£35,178,000
Wessex Learning Trust	£35,168,464
Danisco (UK) Limited	£35,155,000
Power Electrics (Bristol) Limited	£35,115,620
John Gillman & Sons (Electrical) Limited	£35,071,380
The Cinnamon Trust	£35,066,008
Bistech Group PLC	£35,049,536
G.R. Lane Health Products Limited	£35,044,788
Ultimate Asset Finance Limited	£35,009,000
Glide Holdings Limited	£34,991,000
Royal Artillery Charitable Fund.	£34,985,000
Diocese of Bristol Academies Trust	£34,963,392
Qualasept Limited	£34,878,516
Bioquell PLC	£34,849,000
Salford Schools Solutions Holdco Limited	£34,837,656
Salford Schools Solutions Limited	£34,837,656
Eastman Estates Limited	£34,813,776
A-Gas Investments Limited	£34,788,000
H.P.H. Limited	£34,719,936
Cedar Care Homes Limited	£34,706,944
Gloucestershire Airport Limited	£34,626,456
Fenchurch Engineering Services Limited	£34,606,780
Southern Academy Trust	£34,605,460
Lewisia Limited	£34,569,852
Inspirational Futures Trust	£34,526,000
LDC (Skelhorne) Limited	£34,500,000
Havana West Limited	£34,432,056
Intrinsic Financial Planning Limited	£34,395,000
Victoria Wharves Limited	£34,361,000
Delphi Lockheed Automotive Limited	£34,331,788
Honda R & D Europe (U.K.) Limited	£34,327,000
Aura Wind (Holdco) Limited	£34,300,320
Wycliffe College (Incorporated)	£34,290,112
Summit Medical Limited	£34,280,104
McBraida Holdings Limited	£34,274,000
W H Bond & Sons Limited	£34,254,788
Cornwall Care Limited	£34,178,000
The British Pepper & Spice Company Limited	£34,158,128
We The Curious Limited	£34,131,000
St. James's Place Investment Administration Limited	£34,055,000

Ventrus Limited	£33,935,000	Control Techniques Dynamics Limited	£31,351,000
Horizon Nuclear Power Services Limited	£33,932,000	Partner Logistics Wisbech Limited	£31,302,264
Wyatt Homes Limited	£33,921,320	Exmouth Community College	£31,292,722
Lewis Wyatt (Construction) Limited	£33,921,224	Woolacombe Bay Holiday Village Limited	£31,284,322
MJL Cornwall Limited	£33,877,796	Latchways PLC	£31,277,000
Taylor Maxwell Timber Limited	£33,848,000	W.J.Tatem Limited	£31,217,350
Armada Investments Limited	£33,841,088	Harvey Commercial Holdings Limited	£31,190,382
Mitcham Holdings Ltd	£33,837,748	Avonbourne International Business and Enterprise	£31,048,400
Oval (1173) Limited	£33,763,000	Grenville Bidco Limited	£31,034,728
Corin Holdings Limited	£33,750,000	Clevedon Learning Trust	£30,997,492
Ceuta Healthcare Limited	£33,697,000	Plantforce Rentals Ltd	£30,968,010
Rotork UK Limited	£33,676,000	Tithegrove Holdings Limited	£30,958,760
Wessex Water Enterprises Limited	£33,658,000	Rochford Property Investments Limited	£30,910,912
Mabey Bridge Limited	£33,607,376	Dairy Partners Limited	£30,907,164
Stowell Concrete Limited	£33,541,438	Harvey Shopfitters Limited	£30,902,964
4Com PLC	£33,538,000	Humber Technology Limited	£30,890,822
Southerly Point Co-operative Multi-Academy Trust	£33,536,220	Your Energy Holdings Limited	£30,882,000
Connolly & Callaghan Limited	£33,515,824	Myoptique Group Ltd	£30,877,390
Powersystems UK Ltd	£33,470,898	Arena Business Centres Limited	£30,872,640
Hospital Company (Swindon & Marlborough) Group	£33,448,000	A D Burs Limited	£30,804,114
Genus Capital Limited	£33,441,480	Virtual Infrastructure Group Limited	£30,711,000
UK Court Services (Manchester) Limited	£33,382,840	The Dean Close Foundation	£30,709,352
Fen Farm Wind Park Limited	£33,347,496	Tribal Holdings Limited	£30,706,000
Christchurch Hotels Ltd	£33,294,980	H.Tempest Limited	£30,672,484
DTR VMS Limited	£33,294,000	Sitec Holdings Limited	£30,663,000
Dragonfly Education Trust	£33,220,776	Eagle Investments Limited	£30,660,420
Tylney Investments Limited	£33,101,516	Queensquare Farming Limited	£30,654,866
Charlton Abbotts Limited Liability Partnership	£32,992,432	Euston Trust Limited	£30,633,058
Katharine Lady Berkeley's School	£32,971,608	Dauntsey's School	£30,605,552
Howard Garages (Weston) Limited	£32,896,708	Tomy UK Co., Ltd.	£30,592,000
Ultrahaptics IP Ltd	£32,780,000	GH Clayhill Limited	£30,560,000
Southampton Harbour Hotel Ltd	£32,772,312	White Pennant Ltd	£30,531,088
Avon Automotive UK Holdings Limited	£32,729,300	St Peter's Hospice	£30,514,000
Curtiss-Wright Flow Control (UK) Limited	£32,717,000	Exeter Rugby Group PLC	£30,468,104
Taylor,Maxwell & Co.Limited	£32,698,654	Plymstock School	£30,448,756
Pro-Vets Group Limited	£32,644,906	Syreford Investments LLP	£30,432,256
Barden Corporation (U.K.) Limited (The)	£32,628,126	London & Devonshire Trust Limited	£30,357,414
Pate's Grammar School	£32,610,388	The James Tudor Foundation	£30,336,724
Waterdance Limited	£32,593,000	Quartet Community Foundation	£30,319,148
Pittards PLC.	£32,579,000	Hargreaves Lansdown Advisory Services Limited	£30,232,568
Amcor UK Group International Limited	£32,556,000	Milestones Trust	£30,178,766
B.46 Trustees Ltd.	£32,546,104	Champion Groundworks Limited	£30,174,020
Dyson Estates Limited	£32,510,000	Falmouth MAT	£30,162,048
Sitec Design Limited	£32,448,000	Pentwin Group Limited	£30,051,304
4Com Customer Services Ltd	£32,441,000	The Bath and Mendip Partnership Trust	£30,007,986
Ignition Credit PLC	£32,426,712	Vector Learning Trust	£29,976,448
SC Group-Global Limited	£32,322,148	Vitacress Salads Limited	£29,952,000
Epichem Group Limited	£32,322,000	Westcon Group Middle East Holdings Limited	£29,924,686
MG Markey Group Limited	£32,264,956	IEWC UK & Ireland Ltd	£29,885,246
Percy R Brend & Sons (Holdings) Limited	£32,238,110	Rittal-C S M Limited	£29,800,000
Willmot Pertwee Limited	£32,197,000	Viridor Waste Kent Limited	£29,742,000
Bistech PLC	£32,195,140	Stannah Lift Services Limited	£29,736,000
A. H. Warren Trust (Property) Limited	£32,070,052	The Dorset & Somerset Air Ambulance Charity	£29,666,116
John Wainwright & Co. Limited	£32,058,304	Wartsila Hamworthy International Limited	£29,652,000
Oasis Dental Care (Southern) Limited	£32,027,000	Clean Earth Energy Wind Investments Limited	£29,645,104
National Star Foundation	£32,017,252	Plymouth Cast	£29,641,712
Rock Services Limited	£31,980,000	Eldon Insurance Services Limited	£29,607,000
Bifold Group Limited	£31,960,000	Kelston Sparkes Holdings Limited	£29,567,068
Rose Bidco Limited	£31,904,000	Elbit Systems UK Limited	£29,551,728
Caterpillar Marine Power UK Limited	£31,868,000	Summerfield Developments (SW) Limited	£29,537,468
REPL International Limited	£31,806,816	Eagle One Foc Holdings Limited	£29,535,000
Hawkins Holdings Limited	£31,550,256	AGM Holdings Limited	£29,531,044
Castle Air Limited	£31,543,420	Lovehoney Limited	£29,512,000
Wellington College Academy Trust	£31,537,240	Studyhome 1992 Limited	£29,486,252
Pleroma Investments Limited	£31,494,000	Norseland Limited	£29,419,636
NOV UK Finance Limited	£31,435,028	Brunswick Limited	£29,391,830
J.Ferguson Estate,Limited	£31,430,244	Garador Limited	£29,379,902
Hospital Company (Swindon & Marlborough) 2006	£31,426,000	Garador Holdings Limited	£29,379,902
Lovehoney Group Limited	£31,419,000	Western Global Holdings Limited	£29,377,000
King Lifting Limited	£31,409,800	Pride Foods Limited	£29,362,000
Wellington School 1837	£31,407,912	Raven Mount Limited	£29,317,000
GH Gravesham Limited	£31,392,000	IESIS Limited	£29,304,612

Colten Care (2009) Limited	£29,290,244
Renishaw International Limited	£29,285,000
SHOO 788AA Limited	£29,274,732
Sherborne School for Girls	£29,240,012
London & Country Mortgages Limited	£29,239,448
Exeter School	£29,218,278
Ian Williams Limited	£29,213,000
Monkton Combe School	£29,193,324
Beylon Limited	£29,169,512
Systems Engineering & Assessment Ltd	£29,169,000
U-Drive Limited	£29,158,036
Kelston Sparkes (Group) Limited	£29,131,016
Batson Midco Limited	£29,112,000
Smith's (Gloucester) Limited	£29,105,924
Walkergate PFI Project Company Limited	£29,039,568
Sharp's Brewery Limited	£29,014,440
C. & J. Clark Overseas Limited	£29,000,000
Carnegie Investment Asset Management Limited	£28,959,774
Taunton School Educational Charity	£28,952,500
BCCB Incorporated Limited	£28,935,940
Rowe Estates Holdings Limited	£28,931,812
United Oilseeds Marketing Limited	£28,911,070
Knights Brown UK Ltd	£28,861,000
XYZ Machine Tools (Holdings) Limited	£28,845,472
Trelleborg Industrial Products UK Ltd	£28,843,000
Zogenix Europe Limited	£28,842,276
Kalel Partners	£28,817,404
Wasdell Packaging Limited	£28,707,694
Exeter and Devon Airport Limited	£28,663,000
Cavanna Homes (Devon) Limited	£28,640,672
Rowe Estates (UK) Limited	£28,621,124
TTK British Holdings Limited	£28,617,660
Western Power Distribution Investments Limited	£28,609,000
R. Tincknell & Son Limited	£28,595,040
Banner Limited	£28,588,204
St. Mary's School (Calne)	£28,575,668
Parkstone Grammar School Trust	£28,569,344
Agecroft Properties (No.2) Limited	£28,550,526
PLB Group Ltd.	£28,534,000
Corin Group Limited	£28,515,000
Danetre PFI Project Company Limited	£28,509,716
Hunt's Foodservice Ltd	£28,499,712
Bott Limited	£28,452,978
Ocean Automotive Limited	£28,404,852
Calcot Health & Leisure Company Limited	£28,389,832
Grove Village Limited	£28,381,340
Apak Group Limited	£28,324,416
Curtis Banks Limited	£28,291,000
Wartsila Water Systems Limited	£28,282,000
Rapid Racking Limited	£28,263,000
Deutsch UK	£28,236,552
Ukcloud Ltd	£28,234,000
Binx Health Limited	£28,212,368
Customade Group Midco Limited	£28,173,000
Unite Accommodation Management 6 Limited	£28,164,024
Tor Bridge Academy Trust	£28,104,928
Unite Accommodation Management Limited	£28,080,892
Knights Brown Construction Ltd	£28,070,000
Amazon Capital Ltd	£28,069,476
BA Technologies Holdings Limited	£28,061,840
Grenville Midco 1 Limited	£28,041,574
Grenville Midco 2 Limited	£28,041,574
Bay Education Trust	£28,040,000
Burts Potato Chips Limited	£28,023,802
Dyson James Limited	£28,000,000
Crediton Dairy Limited	£27,971,000
Merlin Entertainments (NBD) Limited	£27,915,000
Aspirations (Topco) Limited	£27,910,114
Earthline Limited	£27,892,744
Highbridge Caravan Centre Limited	£27,886,844
Agincare Homes Holdings Limited	£27,873,732
Grand Pier Limited	£27,858,488
Magicard Holdings Limited	£27,837,760
Advanced Insulation Limited	£27,795,880
Neal's Yard Holdings Limited	£27,741,000
Danfoss Power Solutions Limited	£27,696,000
Loungers Holdings Limited	£27,695,000
Sabre Group Limited	£27,689,720
Wasdell Holdings Limited	£27,685,870
Blackheath Farms LLP	£27,653,296
Insite Outdoor Advertising (A) Ltd	£27,645,300
Manor House Hotel (Okehampton) Limited	£27,626,784
Positive Cash Flow Finance Limited	£27,599,910
LDC (Portfolio Four) Limited	£27,577,348
Viridor Waste (Thames) Limited	£27,529,000
Seasalt Holdings Limited	£27,518,836
Livanova UK Limited	£27,514,002
West Pharmaceutical Services Cornwall Limited	£27,493,000
S Morris Limited	£27,454,680
Wherwell Farms Limited	£27,451,836
NIC Enterprises Limited	£27,438,836
Hills Quarry Products Limited	£27,423,000
Apex Dental Care Limited	£27,405,540
SGH Investments Limited	£27,386,590
C.J.L. Construction Limited	£27,306,588
Bibendum PLB Group Limited	£27,291,000
HRB Hotel Company Limited	£27,270,074
Holt Farms Limited	£27,224,996
Acraman (515) Limited	£27,162,446
Lucknam Park Hotels Limited	£27,156,884
The Castle Partnership Trust	£27,150,484
Investors in the Community (Bexley Schools) Limited	£27,065,610
Keyway Limited	£27,052,850
Twofour Group Limited	£27,024,000
LDC (Chaucer House) Limited	£27,000,000
Wimborne Academy Trust	£26,995,448
Safe House Holdings Limited	£26,987,136
Richmond Group Debt Capital Ltd	£26,966,000
Faringdon Academy of Schools	£26,958,000
Wells Cathedral School, Limited	£26,938,000
M J Church (Plant) Limited	£26,923,528
Essex Schools Holdings (Woodlands) Limited	£26,922,000
Essex Schools (Woodlands) Limited	£26,922,000
E Development (2) Limited	£26,915,000
Le Creuset U.K. Limited	£26,906,000
Academy Leasing Limited	£26,905,682
Robinson Property Company Limited	£26,870,440
Chewton Glen Hotels Limited	£26,868,612
Wind Holdings Nord Limited	£26,862,432
Learning Academies Trust	£26,861,256
Stannah Stairlifts Limited	£26,787,000
Bristol Water Holdings Limited	£26,775,000
Colten Care (2003) Limited	£26,759,364
South Dartmoor Academy	£26,741,000
Quest End Computer Services Limited	£26,718,932
Redmaids' High School	£26,592,044
Flower & Hayes Limited	£26,576,620
Marsden Estate Partnership LLP	£26,547,854
Cemetery Management Limited	£26,482,630
Amesbury Abbey Limited	£26,474,124
National Maritime Museum Cornwall Trust	£26,448,116
Bourne Group Holdings Ltd	£26,442,380
An Suidhe Wind Farm Limited	£26,436,352
API Technologies (UK) Limited	£26,362,000
Charcoal Midco 1 Limited	£26,336,000
Solsbury Inventions Limited	£26,315,796
Eurac Poole Limited	£26,308,000
F & B Profiles Limited	£26,296,284
Ashington Business Inc. Limited	£26,261,784
Nine Telecom Group Limited	£26,190,326
Cheltenham Bournside School and Sixth Form Centre	£26,148,552
County Tyre (Holdings) Limited (The)	£26,119,208
B T Q Limited	£26,105,000
Prior Park Educational Trust	£26,104,096

Company	Amount	Company	Amount
G. Crook & Sons Limited	£26,096,676	The Ted Wragg Multi Academy Trust	£24,324,076
Vanguard Healthcare Solutions Limited	£26,084,000	Aardman Animations Limited	£24,299,660
Bourne Group Ltd.	£26,061,072	SLG Allstars Limited	£24,282,406
Duffields Mills Limited	£26,048,000	Neal's Yard (Natural Remedies) Limited	£24,277,000
Dainton Group Services Limited	£25,988,524	SAFC Biosciences Limited	£24,257,000
Granary Ford LLP	£25,981,240	King's School, Bruton	£24,242,744
M.F. Freeman Holdings Limited	£25,944,796	Barnet Lighting Services Limited	£24,214,372
Still Materials Handling Limited	£25,936,000	Ken Biggs Contractors Limited	£24,213,680
Arval UK Leasing Services Limited	£25,900,000	Dick Lovett Limited	£24,204,000
F & B Profiles (Holdings) Limited	£25,885,864	Merchants' Academy Trust	£24,200,000
Atlantic Centre of Excellence Multi Academy Trust	£25,835,920	Stanborough (Developments) Limited	£24,181,312
Aspirations (Bidco) Limited	£25,833,288	Isles of Scilly Steamship Company Limited	£24,169,536
Dunkerton Properties LLP	£25,809,450	Queen Elizabeth's Hospital	£24,111,120
ASP Independent Living Limited	£25,776,000	Descartes Systems UK Limited	£24,083,372
Fairlie Holdings Limited	£25,738,728	Plus Shipping Services Limited	£24,021,000
Brunel Wind Limited	£25,728,480	The American Museum in Britain	£24,003,576
Hayesfield Girls' School	£25,522,686	White Horse Education Partnership Limited	£24,001,000
Beacon Communication Services Limited	£25,513,344	Snows Timber Limited	£23,991,670
Sloane & Pirkis LLP	£25,354,378	Mears Housing Management Limited	£23,953,000
Bracken Developments Limited	£25,311,494	Farmers First Limited	£23,940,372
Ball Aerocan UK Limited	£25,304,000	IIC Enfield Holding Company Limited	£23,939,562
Bevan Brittan LLP	£25,259,000	QE Academy Trust	£23,936,280
Reach South Academy Trust	£25,249,876	Lyell Trading Limited	£23,912,738
UK Power Solutions Limited	£25,246,000	STC (Milton Keynes) Limited	£23,910,302
Firstport Operations PD Limited	£25,222,650	Ashfords LLP	£23,909,000
Kerrier Investments Limited	£25,213,018	Sedgwick Solar Limited	£23,891,868
Peninsula Finance PLC	£25,187,324	Savencia Fromage & Dairy UK Ltd	£23,889,000
Bid PCB UK Limited	£25,178,000	Fasthosts Internet Limited	£23,873,000
Essilor Limited	£25,164,000	Solent Global Limited	£23,830,852
Vanguard Healthcare Group Limited	£25,094,000	Pleroma (UK) Limited	£23,805,000
Cathedral Schools Trust	£25,091,124	Renelec Limited	£23,802,000
Swinford Wind Farm Limited	£25,079,738	E.J. MacKelden & Sons (Bobbing) Limited	£23,770,848
Raven Mount Services Company Limited	£25,022,572	Vinci Education (Bradfield) Limited	£23,767,790
Cleveland FM Services Limited	£24,994,000	Enfield Lighting Services Limited	£23,759,416
Natatomisam Limited	£24,986,530	John Hackling (Transport) Limited	£23,748,200
Michelmores LLP	£24,974,000	Partner Logistics Gloucester Limited	£23,732,048
Wilson Tool International [Europe] Limited	£24,958,966	Cloudpay United Kingdom Limited	£23,722,000
Salcombe Harbour Hotel Limited	£24,949,928	HTP Grange Limited	£23,699,364
Southside Regeneration Limited	£24,941,968	St Christopher's C of E (Secondary) Multi Academy Trust	£23,680,018
Oxford Infracare Lift (1) Limited	£24,935,000	The Tank Museum Limited	£23,665,280
Sheldon School	£24,927,704	Hodgetts Farming Limited	£23,651,812
Seasalt Limited	£24,924,944	The Traffic Group Limited	£23,618,372
Royal Bay Care Homes Ltd	£24,907,208	Tay Valley Lighting (Newcastle and North Tyneside) Ltd	£23,597,000
Royds Withy King LLP	£24,860,522	Aspire Defence Services Limited	£23,596,000
Chatleigh Limited	£24,851,314	IoP Publishing Limited	£23,578,000
Waypoints Care Group Limited	£24,845,228	Safran UK Limited	£23,573,292
Edgeworth Investments Limited	£24,822,764	SSI Schaefer Ltd	£23,561,406
Schyde Investments Limited	£24,804,256	Cleeve School	£23,539,540
Fred Champion Groundworks Limited	£24,796,232	Newcross Healthcare Solutions Limited	£23,518,740
Orthod Group Limited	£24,762,880	Corin International Limited	£23,518,700
Robbins & Myers Holdings UK Limited	£24,759,000	Atlas Elektronik UK (Holdings) Limited	£23,500,000
Patalex III Productions Limited	£24,738,000	Ford Fuels Limited	£23,496,968
Redcliffe Homes Limited	£24,720,640	Daish's Group Limited	£23,491,366
Sharpak Bridgwater Limited	£24,717,000	Injury QED Limited	£23,490,000
XYZ Machine Tools Limited	£24,715,886	Tamura-Europe Limited	£23,449,664
Waterside Holiday Group Limited	£24,701,860	The Community Foundation for Wiltshire & Swindon	£23,436,660
Supara Limited	£24,697,156	NMS Infrastructure Limited	£23,379,162
Auxillis Limited	£24,680,000	TDK-Lambda UK Limited	£23,372,000
Exeter Finance Ltd	£24,607,380	Uphouse Farm Limited	£23,363,942
Trebartha Estates Limited	£24,601,724	SS Great Britain Trust	£23,357,742
Frizzell Financial Services Limited	£24,526,000	The Seafood Restaurant (Padstow) Limited	£23,342,000
Vision Dispensing Ltd.	£24,525,000	Hawkins Motors Limited	£23,300,538
Wolverhampton Radiology Limited	£24,508,000	King's Schools Taunton Limited	£23,281,696
Hartham Park Limited	£24,489,424	Bristol Harbour Hotel Limited	£23,254,224
E T Holdings Limited	£24,488,060	Watts of Lydney Group Limited	£23,248,000
Barnwood Group Limited	£24,469,636	DAS Services Limited	£23,224,000
Grant Engineering (UK) Limited	£24,428,624	RR Sea Hanover St. Limited	£23,171,236
Aspirations Care Limited	£24,417,152	Osprey Europe Limited	£23,170,224
Westcon Group Africa Operations Limited	£24,412,610	The Athelstan Trust	£23,154,596
IIC Barnet Holding Company Limited	£24,409,412	The Corsham School Academy Group	£23,151,972
Hydrock Group Limited	£24,373,140	Mi-Space (UK) Limited	£23,140,000
The Una Group Limited	£24,335,198	Alexandra Wharf Limited	£23,126,120

Company	Amount
Devon Air Ambulance Trust	£23,125,000
Dynamatic Limited	£23,112,000
Devonshire Homes Limited	£23,110,644
Flybe Aviation Services Limited	£23,100,000
R.J. Heathman (Contractors) Limited	£23,094,900
Bioquell UK Limited	£23,092,832
Churchdown School	£23,069,110
Tdown Hospitals (North Staffordshire Combined) Ltd	£23,065,000
Mead Realisations Limited	£23,061,220
Puma Energy Belfast Ltd	£23,035,810
Churchill Academy	£23,023,164
Fornuis UK Limited	£23,019,312
Avenue 64 Limited	£22,974,000
Red Hotels Limited	£22,957,284
The Mike Burton Group Limited	£22,946,176
ALD Automotive Group Limited	£22,945,000
Charter House Investments LLP	£22,911,906
R.T. Keedwell Limited	£22,910,808
Wild and Wolf Limited	£22,894,972
Brent Cars Limited	£22,859,718
E.I.C. Group Limited	£22,847,888
Vero UK Limited	£22,831,000
St. James's Place Acquisition Services Limited	£22,829,000
Cannon Care Homes Ltd	£22,824,840
Stovax Limited	£22,819,050
Renshaw U.K. Limited	£22,803,638
Morris & Perry (Gurney Slade Quarries) Limited	£22,787,252
Hollingsworth & Vose Company Limited	£22,786,000
Kandytoys Limited	£22,747,468
Abbey Manor Developments Ltd	£22,731,000
Stanley UK Acquisition Company Limited	£22,685,000
Cray U.K. Limited	£22,674,892
Waterfield Homes Limited	£22,668,564
Horstman Defence Systems Limited	£22,658,138
Cadeleigh Estates Limited	£22,655,774
Yelspa Limited	£22,654,498
Renelec Group Limited	£22,649,016
Plessey Group Holdings Limited	£22,635,000
Connolly & Callaghan Group Limited	£22,618,648
Integra Neurosciences Limited	£22,618,000
RP (Poundbury) LLP	£22,587,616
Freixenet Copestick Limited	£22,577,178
Bradgate Business Finance Limited	£22,569,920
Goodridge Limited	£22,569,000
Pet Food Holdings Limited	£22,513,000
Supacat Limited	£22,499,018
Theatre Royal (Plymouth) Limited	£22,427,000
Osprey Maritime Limited	£22,426,450
Uplands Retail Limited	£22,404,650
Francis Clark LLP	£22,381,000
Richmond upon Thames Schools Services Limited	£22,376,000
AUK Holding Limited	£22,364,000
The Nare Hotel Company Limited	£22,333,172
Hardware UK Limited	£22,331,000
Abercrombie & Kent Limited	£22,302,000
The Academy Trust of Melksham	£22,284,628
Next Generation Wind Holdings Limited	£22,275,700
WK Crematoria Limited	£22,253,802
Amcor Holdco 3	£22,246,996
Naim Audio Limited	£22,180,768
Nailsea School	£22,177,548
Acorn Education Trust	£22,148,080
Eurilait Limited	£22,139,296
All Saints' Academy, Cheltenham	£22,136,000
Norman Court and Sowley Farms Limited	£22,120,214
Independent Tool Consultants Limited	£22,090,612
Eagle Strategic Property Limited	£22,072,548
Larasian Limited	£22,063,290
Lower Pertwood Organic Farm Limited	£22,059,490
Newton Nottingham LLP	£22,044,322
Togs Limited	£22,032,094
Multivac U.K. Limited	£22,027,908

Company	Amount
Knorr-Bremse Investment (UK) Limited	£22,000,100
Bristol City Football Club Limited	£21,935,284
DAC Beachcroft Services Limited	£21,920,000
Allied Dunbar Assurance PLC	£21,918,000
South West Communications Group Holdings Limited	£21,904,300
Tricel Holdings (UK) Limited	£21,854,680
Haringey Schools Services Limited	£21,851,000
Summerfield Estates Ltd	£21,848,428
Hull Maternity Development Limited	£21,838,000
Magicard Ltd	£21,823,900
Arnewood Estates Limited	£21,811,796
Orthod Midco Limited	£21,808,978
Sir Thomas Rich's School	£21,796,690
Gensmile Limited	£21,776,504
WW Truck and Bus Limited	£21,763,722
Hardenhuish School Limited	£21,706,526
Invicta Motors Limited	£21,698,000
SBS International Holdings Limited	£21,690,560
1&1 Internet Limited	£21,685,000
Dick Lovett (Specialist Cars) Limited	£21,684,000
Steve Hoskin Construction Limited	£21,682,040
Universal Balancing Limited	£21,658,600
Kellaway Building Supplies Limited	£21,654,168
Integrated Care Solutions (East Kent) Limited	£21,639,000
Integrated Care Solutions (East Kent) Holdings Limited	£21,639,000
NK Facilities Limited	£21,636,000
Watts Desser Limited	£21,621,790
Shepperton Group Limited	£21,596,712
The CSIA Trust	£21,591,236
Priorgate Limited	£21,561,000
Teleperformance Contact Limited	£21,550,312
Cobalt Health	£21,539,712
Gensmile Dental Care Limited	£21,507,686
Heating Products Limited	£21,489,000
Eagle One Country Shopping Limited	£21,474,094
Buckland Care Limited	£21,471,656
West End Investments Clifton Limited	£21,446,876
Ringwood School	£21,445,478
The Royal Clarence Hotel Limited	£21,441,392
Eurogate Finance Limited	£21,428,992
Enga Limited	£21,401,108
Newent Community School and Sixth Form Centre	£21,396,848
Leaf Academy	£21,387,824
Grosvenor PPP Holdings Limited	£21,307,000
LDC (New Wakefield Street) Limited	£21,300,000
Hills Homes Developments Limited	£21,298,000
New Southgate Cemetery and Crematorium Limited	£21,292,068
Whiteoaks Investments Limited	£21,281,602
Twofour Broadcast Limited	£21,261,000
Tithegrove Limited	£21,253,848
Queen Elizabeth's School (Wimborne Minster)	£21,236,172
J E Beale Public Limited Company	£21,235,000
Abbey Manor Homes Limited	£21,174,000
Bell Contracting Limited	£21,169,748
Airsprung Furniture Limited	£21,162,000
MacTaggart & Mickel Homes England Limited	£21,157,000
St James Parade (107) Limited	£21,140,064
Framptons Limited	£21,137,248
The Crypt School	£21,133,200
GCP WL Limited	£21,116,000
Prima Dental Manufacturing Limited	£21,108,906
Rockley Manor Estate LLP	£21,107,680
Colten Care (1693) Limited	£21,075,224
Heavitree Brewery PLC (The)	£21,035,000
Patalex Productions Limited	£21,020,000
Homeloan Management Limited	£21,018,000
Adventure Learning Academy Trust	£21,016,000
Commercial Corporate Services Limited	£20,961,882
H.H.& D.E.Drew Limited	£20,959,506
Clayesmore School	£20,948,440
Wadebridge School	£20,947,204
Megahertz Limited	£20,942,912

Company	Amount
Mutual Real Estate Company Limited	£20,938,666
Good Energy Holding Company No. 1 Limited	£20,937,528
D.B. Foods Limited	£20,918,474
LDC (Radmarsh Road) Limited	£20,910,992
Creed Catering Supplies Limited	£20,905,752
Creed Foodservice Limited	£20,905,750
IBD Bikes UK Limited	£20,904,024
Actual Experience PLC	£20,882,000
Kemble Airfield Estates Limited	£20,853,460
Silicon Sensing Systems Limited	£20,840,000
Pentland Road Windfarm Limited	£20,826,146
C & C Management Services (UK) Limited	£20,820,000
Crawlands Limited	£20,811,946
Renrod Limited	£20,798,712
D & R Midco Limited	£20,793,552
D & R Cleanco Limited	£20,793,546
Whitehall Garden Centre (Holdings) Limited	£20,791,140
Eastleigh Care Group Limited	£20,784,286
Insite Outdoor Advertising Limited	£20,783,064
City West Commercials Limited	£20,768,740
First South West Limited	£20,761,000
Tamar Farms LLP	£20,757,180
Portland Port Limited	£20,748,280
3T's Leisure Ltd.	£20,719,768
MCAARP Holdings Limited	£20,689,000
Briarwood Products Limited	£20,651,624
McCarthy Investments Limited	£20,637,472
Gaiger Brothers Limited	£20,626,310
G3 Systems Limited	£20,615,844
Cavanna Homes (South West) Limited	£20,591,334
Lipson Co-operative Academy Trust	£20,552,088
The Kaleidoscope Collection Ltd	£20,544,588
Chatleigh Holdings Limited	£20,514,990
National Trust (Enterprises) Limited (The)	£20,512,000
Liverpool Victoria Life Company Limited	£20,435,000
Spectrum Medical Limited	£20,430,544
Aeronautical & General Instruments Limited	£20,429,000
IIC Redcar and Cleveland Holding Company Limited	£20,423,968
Hobbs Properties Limited	£20,421,940
Connect Academy Trust	£20,421,370
Ultimate Bridging Finance Limited	£20,409,000
Triumph International Limited	£20,384,000
SIRVA Relocation (No.1) Limited	£20,382,446
SIRVA Relocation Holdings Limited	£20,382,446
Petty, Wood & Co. Limited	£20,371,304
The First Federation Trust	£20,367,000
Jigsaw Solutions Limited	£20,360,460
Galpharm Healthcare Limited	£20,347,000
Bel Ombre Properties Limited	£20,324,320
Marine Academy Plymouth	£20,316,000
Redcar and Cleveland Lighting Services Limited	£20,307,164
Severn & Wye Smokery Limited	£20,300,836
L.B. Bentley Limited	£20,291,088
Plym Academy Trust	£20,279,692
King Edward's School, Bath	£20,252,700
PKL Topco Limited	£20,239,000
Gaming International Limited	£20,232,000
Campden BRI	£20,228,488
Cotswold Beacon Academy Trust	£20,222,326
Premier Cables Limited	£20,204,920
Novalis Trust	£20,196,264
Hoyle & Co (Bournemouth) Limited	£20,194,772
Tewkesbury School	£20,170,454
Lombard Corporate Finance (15) Limited	£20,135,000
M.A. Grigg (Agricultural) Limited	£20,123,898
Catalent CTS (Wales) Limited	£20,122,108
Dhrona Holdings Ltd	£20,100,768
Paris Presents UK Limited	£20,089,284
Pure Storage UK Limited	£20,070,044
BOFA International Ltd.	£20,065,968
Integrity Print Limited	£20,058,000
Bradbury House Properties Limited	£20,025,952
The Property Franchise Group PLC	£20,025,878
Devaron (UK) Limited	£20,000,100
Glasshouse Hotel Limited	£19,963,104
Shiner Limited	£19,954,000
Langdown Estates LLP	£19,945,812
Key Industrial Equipment Limited	£19,932,000
Seafood Trading Limited	£19,924,000
Rollalong Limited	£19,910,000
Acumed Acquisition Company Limited	£19,897,630
Organix Brands Limited	£19,884,000
Cover Construction Company Limited	£19,857,974
Cotham School	£19,851,442
P J Davidson Holdings Ltd.	£19,792,692
Lunamar (Group) Limited	£19,769,094
South Essex Insurance Brokers Limited	£19,710,412
Novia Financial PLC	£19,661,350
Mears Care (Holdings) Limited	£19,660,838
E.I.C.(Exeter) Limited	£19,616,808
Patel Brothers Limited	£19,614,156
Honda Engineering Europe Limited	£19,579,000
LDC (Project 111) Limited	£19,551,686
Rowe & Co.Cornwall (Properties) Limited	£19,539,652
Bridlington Schools Services Limited	£19,525,000
D-Tech (UK) Limited	£19,517,406
The Brandon Trust	£19,506,326
Teagle Holdings Limited	£19,496,944
WRC P.L.C.	£19,495,000
The Blue School	£19,474,308
The Cotswold School Academy Trust	£19,470,000
Blundell's School	£19,459,000
Intergraph (UK) Limited	£19,458,882
Workman Properties Limited	£19,454,496
Coastal UK Group Limited	£19,445,270
Airsprung Group PLC	£19,445,000
Ninecourt Limited	£19,435,520
Bristol Old Vic and Theatre Royal Trust Limited	£19,430,220
Cannington Enterprises Limited	£19,419,876
Peninsula Dental Social Enterprise CIC	£19,418,988
Naish Estate (Hoburne) Limited	£19,402,352
LDC (Brunel House) Limited	£19,400,000
Satnam Investments Limited	£19,395,696
St Juliens Limited	£19,383,382
Dick Lovett (Bristol) Limited	£19,375,000
Stonehaven (Healthcare) Ltd	£19,372,572
Hamworthy Combustion Engineering Limited	£19,362,000
Magna Learning Partnership	£19,338,012
Brightborough Capital Limited	£19,315,000
Lone Eagle Retail Limited	£19,288,544
Euravia Engineering & Supply Co. Limited	£19,288,274
Vitacress Herbs Limited	£19,277,000
Corfe Hills School Academy Trust	£19,271,656
New Look Limited	£19,174,000
Ultrahaptics Holdings Ltd	£19,174,000
G Plan Upholstery Limited	£19,166,664
Tapper and Son (Poole) Limited	£19,108,772
Watergate Bay Hotel Limited	£19,094,806
Opus Professional Services Group Limited	£19,045,768
Ropsley Holdings Limited	£19,020,620
Seabrook Land Developments Limited	£19,000,000
Plymouth Science Park Limited	£18,998,816
Delahunty Limited	£18,992,882
Kiwa Holdings (UK) Limited	£18,980,088
Baylis Estates Limited	£18,951,292
W.H.White Limited	£18,945,570
Deep Moor LF Limited	£18,944,824
Bambers Wind Park Limited	£18,933,472
West Pharmaceutical Services Group Limited	£18,931,000
Inspiring Schools Partnership	£18,920,988
Parragon Publishing Limited	£18,919,000
Hendra Touring Caravan & Camping Park Limited	£18,912,242
Falcon Self Drive Limited	£18,910,900
By Education (Waltham Forest) Limited	£18,860,000

Company	Amount
By Education (Waltham Forest) Holdings Limited	£18,860,000
Special Partnership Trust	£18,857,834
Parham Development Limited	£18,836,286
Eduserv	£18,810,660
The Bishop of Winchester Academy Trust	£18,795,504
Cruciform Services Limited	£18,793,000
The Commonweal School	£18,779,036
Jacksons Investments Limited	£18,778,000
Holmleigh Care Homes Limited	£18,770,116
G.E.H. Properties Limited	£18,767,880
GM Coachwork Limited	£18,757,168
Industrial Sales Limited	£18,753,284
Graphic PLC	£18,741,000
Swallowcourt Holdings Limited	£18,737,448
Metric Group Limited	£18,732,000
Gloucestershire Learning Alliance	£18,726,896
Galsworthy Wind Park Limited	£18,690,940
Chipping Campden School	£18,690,000
Masstock Group Holdings Limited	£18,678,000
St. Margaret's Somerset Hospice	£18,677,082
Eco Sustainable Solutions Limited	£18,670,000
Eco Holdings Limited	£18,670,000
Otter Nurseries Limited	£18,664,052
The Liberation Group UK Limited	£18,641,000
Styles & Brown Ltd	£18,634,048
Beechen Cliff School	£18,627,390
Bridge Multi-Academy Trust	£18,621,672
Vapormatic Company Limited (The)	£18,608,000
Hydreco Hydraulics Limited	£18,608,000
Teignmouth Learning Trust	£18,594,000
Bournemouth Transport Limited	£18,572,000
Kersfield Developments (Ensleigh South) Limited	£18,526,576
Intrinsic Mortgage Planning Limited	£18,519,000
Team Relocations Limited	£18,501,512
DJS (UK) Limited	£18,459,692
Chessington Hotel Limited	£18,446,000
Axminster Tool Centre Ltd	£18,443,076
Hydra Holdings 2015 Limited	£18,440,860
Cobell Ltd	£18,440,732
Cavendish Close Limited	£18,439,072
Milewood (Holdings) Ltd	£18,393,656
New Power Company Limited	£18,383,172
British Solar Renewables Limited	£18,365,280
Tolladine Estates Limited	£18,359,836
Gloucestershire FM Services Limited	£18,353,000
The Garland Company UK Limited	£18,351,226
Jam Bidco Limited	£18,347,494
St. Laurence School Academy Trust	£18,336,656
D.Stewart & Son, Limited	£18,333,740
Valmiera Glass UK Limited	£18,329,536
Bodmin College	£18,316,522
Green Valley Capital Limited	£18,315,476
Troika Eastleigh Properties Limited	£18,306,528
Eagle One Retail Limited	£18,293,222
Torry Harris Business Solutions (Europe) Ltd	£18,293,072
Kenton School Services Limited	£18,255,000
Firstport Property Services Limited	£18,253,764
Woodlodge Products Limited	£18,171,840
M. Baker (Property Services) Limited	£18,170,264
Sanoh UK Manufacturing Limited	£18,170,000
Haycock Holdings Limited	£18,161,562
M.B. Crocker Limited	£18,160,284
Wilton Bradley Holdings Limited	£18,150,456
Torquay Leisure Hotels Limited	£18,150,376
Gloucester Rugby Limited	£18,148,472
Breeze Motor Company Limited	£18,146,740
O'Neill and Brennan Construction Limited	£18,139,914
Creative England Limited	£18,139,646
Clarence Court Eggs Limited	£18,138,526
Datamine Corporate Limited	£18,131,546
Snapfish UK, Ltd.	£18,123,396
Bristol Community Health C.I.C.	£18,118,800
Edentree Investment Management Limited	£18,091,620
Simon Smith Retail Limited	£18,076,588
Aspect Trust	£18,044,540
W & S Waste Management Limited	£18,030,528
I Supply Energy Limited	£18,013,000
Bladeroom Holdings Limited	£18,010,000
Weardale Estates Limited	£17,998,428
D.C. Thomson Developments Limited	£17,991,504
W.L. Duffield & Sons Limited	£17,986,000
The Simian Group (Holdings) Limited	£17,976,000
David Hathaway Holdings Limited	£17,972,120
Salum Properties Limited	£17,968,806
Addison Developments Limited	£17,957,456
Shield Environmental Services Limited	£17,953,498
Troika Property Holdings Limited	£17,940,216
Veale Wasbrough Vizards LLP	£17,925,456
JELF Wellbeing Limited	£17,900,000
Smart Aluminium Extrusions Limited	£17,900,000
Bartletts Transport and Warehouses Limited	£17,898,800
Southwark Bridge Holdings Limited	£17,894,954
Firstport Limited	£17,891,656
Bank of Ireland Britain Holdings Limited	£17,881,332
Cult Clothing Cheltenham Limited	£17,847,812
Kandytoys Holdings Limited	£17,844,956
M. & P. Food Products Limited	£17,841,936
ARI Fleet UK Limited	£17,839,250
Vi - Spring Limited	£17,832,000
Bifold Fluidpower Limited	£17,826,000
Highlands Hospitality Limited	£17,825,622
Roger Young Limited	£17,808,428
Howard Tenens Distribution Limited	£17,801,196
E G Carter (Holdings) Limited	£17,799,470
E.G.Carter & Company Limited	£17,799,420
OC Sport Ltd	£17,796,284
Alessandra UK Limited	£17,768,280
Kelston Properties 2 Limited	£17,760,000
Willes Farming Limited	£17,756,324
Drilling Systems Limited	£17,738,494
WMG Property Limited	£17,700,254
Lanhydrock Estate Company (The)	£17,695,212
CRC Industries UK Limited	£17,691,564
CMOStores Group Limited	£17,684,798
Haven Investments Limited	£17,650,856
DWML Holdings Limited	£17,645,494
IXYS UK Westcode Ltd.	£17,623,000
The Gryphon Trust	£17,621,088
Deceuninck Holdings (UK) Limited	£17,619,000
Gamma Energy Limited	£17,608,826
Symonds Estates Limited	£17,608,456
LDC (Loughborough) Limited	£17,600,092
Oval (259) Limited	£17,597,724
H.B.H. Woolacotts Limited	£17,586,236
Gardiner (Holdings) Limited	£17,581,130
Rotalink Limited	£17,570,596
Wishford Schools (Group) Limited	£17,570,206
Headland Hotel Company Limited (The)	£17,558,572
Farleigh School Trust Limited	£17,552,960
Bristol Uniforms Limited	£17,537,000
Kemeneth Multi Academy Trust	£17,470,800
Uffculme Academy Trust	£17,469,882
M R Tizzard Limited	£17,462,484
Hospital Metalcraft Limited	£17,446,988
Bristol Infracare Lift (1) Limited	£17,446,000
K W Bell Group Limited	£17,400,608
Coate Water Care Company Limited	£17,398,724
SH & GS Property Group Limited	£17,398,358
Porthminster Hotel Company Limited	£17,395,096
A.E.R. Stafford Limited	£17,389,860
Chosen Hill School	£17,387,464
Robert Hitchins Investment Properties Limited	£17,381,772
Athena Racing Limited	£17,368,844
Handston Investments Limited	£17,350,550

Acumed Ltd	£17,341,860	RBS Asset Finance Europe Limited	£16,652,753
Mitutoyo (U.K.) Limited	£17,329,000	04021465 Limited	£16,639,000
ITEC Connect Ltd	£17,328,676	Wayfarer Group Limited	£16,639,000
Woodlodge Holdings Limited	£17,324,664	Taylor Maxwell Group Limited	£16,635,413
Bishop Wordsworth's Church of England Grammar	£17,319,680	Wiggin LLP	£16,627,443
Oak Tree Parks Limited	£17,233,876	Kingsbridge Risk Solutions Limited	£16,623,175
Avon Metals Limited	£17,226,724	Goodshelter Property Company Limited	£16,622,535
Harbourstar Limited	£17,225,552	Gardiner,Sons & Co.,Limited	£16,621,102
Keith Spicer Limited	£17,222,478	B.Walker & Co.(Dursley) Limited	£16,599,050
Amberon Holdings Limited	£17,209,412	Carbis Bay Hotel Limited	£16,584,720
Denmark Road High School	£17,202,878	Dream Makers Enterprises Limited	£16,576,976
LDC (Old Hospital) Limited	£17,200,000	Thurlestone Estates,Limited	£16,573,834
Europa Group Limited	£17,199,792	Garrad Hassan & Partners Limited	£16,561,736
Oldfield School	£17,186,944	Parable Trust Limited	£16,539,000
Bexley PPP Health Services Limited	£17,180,296	Shield Environmental Holdings Limited	£16,532,068
Geometry Properties Limited	£17,171,000	Soil Association Limited (The)	£16,515,526
Drilling Systems (U.K.) Limited	£17,168,952	Danesdale Land Limited	£16,500,513
Honda Logistics UK Limited	£17,167,876	Latona Leisure Limited	£16,486,379
Wessex Resolutions C.I.C.	£17,147,324	Shoals Hook Solar (UK) Limited	£16,475,081
Grist Group Limited	£17,141,994	The Hill Brush Company Ltd	£16,462,833
Fowlers of Bristol Limited	£17,140,862	McBraida PLC	£16,450,000
Haley Securities Limited	£17,122,276	The Workforce Development Trust Limited	£16,430,680
Scotts Limited	£17,115,000	Riverford Organic Farmers Limited	£16,425,112
Devonport High School for Boys Academy Trust	£17,072,000	Marden Edwards Limited	£16,406,902
Percy R.Brend & Sons (Hoteliers) Limited	£17,058,348	The Norville Group Limited	£16,401,289
Goodnews Evangelical Mission	£17,034,440	First Step Homes Limited	£16,387,058
The Amber Chemical Company Limited	£17,026,680	J+S Limited	£16,367,000
Kingham Farms Ltd	£17,023,528	Stepping Stones Resettlement Unit Limited	£16,359,750
Bart Spices Group Holdings Limited	£17,022,000	Thrings LLP	£16,353,021
Andrews Estate Agents Limited	£17,010,178	William Gilder Limited	£16,307,050
British Small Animal Veterinary Association	£17,000,650	The King's School Ottery St Mary	£16,306,503
Plymouth Marine Laboratory	£16,999,000	The Learning Academy Trust	£16,304,629
Epping PPP Maintenance (Health) Services Limited	£16,995,148	Thoranmart Limited	£16,303,000
Gwynt y Mor Offshore Wind Farm Limited	£16,992,066	Bristol Energy Limited	£16,300,078
Advance Bidco Limited	£16,991,992	Hanford School Charitable Trust Limited	£16,300,016
D & R Bidco Limited	£16,978,076	F.J. Chalke Limited	£16,291,846
Hugh Sexey's Hospital	£16,960,796	Synlatex Limited	£16,274,429
Havas EHS Discovery Limited	£16,954,000	W.D.M.Limited	£16,236,000
Pennant International Group PLC	£16,937,666	Advanced Paper Production Ltd.	£16,223,683
Conlon Limited	£16,929,776	St.James's Place International Assurance Group Ltd	£16,222,000
Horizon Organic Dairy Limited	£16,926,000	Maximum Fun Holdings Limited	£16,221,911
The John of Gaunt School	£16,921,528	Neptune (Europe) Ltd	£16,211,038
Tocris Cookson Limited	£16,915,000	Harold W Smart & Son Limited	£16,206,977
Herts & Essex PPP Health Services Limited	£16,912,396	Exeter Royal Academy for Deaf Education.	£16,197,916
Nailsworth Limited	£16,897,610	Twentieth Century Investments Limited	£16,184,873
Dorothy House Foundation Limited (The)	£16,893,984	The Buckinghamshire Group Limited	£16,182,957
The Reme Charity	£16,881,324	Via East Midlands Limited	£16,180,828
Finian Farming LLP	£16,848,108	All Saints Church of England Academy, Plymouth	£16,173,787
Credit Reporting Agency (Topco) Limited	£16,840,406	Keen Thinking Limited	£16,170,773
Parkfield Education Limited	£16,828,440	Blakell Europlacer Limited	£16,152,000
Hartridge Limited	£16,827,000	Eastern Business Park Limited	£16,150,459
Campden BRI (Chipping Campden) Limited	£16,824,616	Scisys UK Limited	£16,136,292
Toogoods Property Company Limited	£16,818,478	Andrews & Partners Limited	£16,134,347
Sidcot School	£16,814,492	Penton Securities Limited	£16,109,562
Highcliffe School	£16,809,000	Liverton Business Park 2012 Limited	£16,102,504
Cornish Farm Dairy Limited	£16,792,304	ARI Fleet, Ltd.	£16,100,000
Crane Merchandising Systems Limited	£16,789,712	DPM Estate Limited	£16,093,348
Bath Row Developments Ltd	£16,787,416	Careline UK Monitoring Limited	£16,092,703
Advance Topco Limited	£16,778,680	Woodchester Enterprises Limited	£16,070,285
Merlo UK Limited	£16,772,891	Rowan Dartington & Co. Limited	£16,058,896
Clarkson Evans Limited	£16,751,753	D. Dalton & Son Limited	£16,052,098
Opmal Limited	£16,745,798	S. Notaro Group Limited	£16,051,607
Hardware Holdings Limited	£16,728,000	Dairy Partners (Cymru Wales) Limited	£16,047,146
Stiga Ltd	£16,723,703	Genevac Limited	£16,044,858
Tarka Learning Partnership	£16,690,458	The Burgate School and Sixth Form	£16,040,391
Exe Investment Limited	£16,684,637	Gooch & Housego (UK) Limited	£16,034,000
EXE Investment Holdings Limited	£16,684,635	Postal Choices Limited	£16,005,828
Woodland Barton Renewables Limited	£16,670,861	Spire Payments Ltd	£15,980,000
Azure Sun Bidco Management Limited	£16,669,279	Horatio Investments Limited	£15,976,060
Burford Delta Limited	£16,663,000	E.J. Shanley & Son (Trowbridge) Limited	£15,969,223
Radius (Bristol) Limited	£16,660,521	The Buckinghamshire Limited	£15,964,634
AES Electric Ltd	£16,654,000	ABQ Investment UK Ltd	£15,957,481

LDC (William Morris II) Limited	£15,954,671
South Gloucestershire and Stroud Academy Trust	£15,953,000
Kingdon Holdings Limited	£15,932,550
Rowan Dartington Holdings Limited	£15,932,120
SRT Marine Systems PLC	£15,914,108
Commercial Estates Property Company Limited	£15,870,370
W.J. Watkins & Son Limited	£15,868,358
CCH Property Company Limited	£15,847,548
Gurr Johns Limited	£15,845,762
Gazco Limited	£15,844,784
Hemsley Fraser Group Limited	£15,843,216
Hinton Capital Investments Limited	£15,838,091
McCarthy & Stone (Home Equity Interests) Limited	£15,824,698
288 Group Limited	£15,820,092
Hanwey LLP	£15,817,000
Original Style Holdings Limited	£15,815,639
Canynge Bicknell Limited	£15,794,738
Dunview Limited	£15,785,040
Educate Together Academy Trust	£15,767,464
Somerset Road Education Trust	£15,759,503
West Country Motor Homes Limited	£15,754,564
Pembridge Property Development Limited	£15,753,544
Royal Wootton Bassett Academy Trust	£15,740,469
Livewell Southwest CIC	£15,733,753
Spectrum Medical Group Limited	£15,720,893
CFH Docmail Ltd	£15,669,000
Sitec Recruitment Limited	£15,660,000
Atlas Services Group Energy Ltd	£15,657,851
AIM Aviation Holdings Limited	£15,655,000
Parkham Farms Limited	£15,652,440
Farmor's School	£15,643,308
Gabriel Limited	£15,642,854
Standbetter Limited	£15,612,652
S. Notaro Limited	£15,597,073
Burrington Estates (New Homes) Limited	£15,589,759
Sharpak Yate Limited	£15,580,000
Apetito (U.K.) Holdings Limited	£15,579,000
Shelterbox Trust	£15,570,000
Albion Healthcare (Doncaster) Limited	£15,550,791
Cordash Limited	£15,542,863
Whitehall Group (Wessex) Limited	£15,531,985
Lombard Leasing Company Limited	£15,523,000
Manchester Working Limited	£15,522,000
Hannick Homes & Developments Limited	£15,519,442
QMP Group Limited	£15,510,433
Quick Move Properties Limited	£15,509,333
Maats Tech Limited	£15,488,257
GH Stone House Limited	£15,480,000
John O'Flynn Developments Limited	£15,472,338
Hodie Limited	£15,463,216
Amberon Limited	£15,441,000
Broadoak Mathematics and Computing College	£15,427,122
Intrinsic Wealth Limited	£15,425,000
Altogether Care LLP	£15,417,287
Insure & Go Insurance Services Limited	£15,400,000
LDC (Greetham Street) Limited	£15,398,947
Warren Farm Holiday Centre Limited	£15,389,974
Robinson Real Estate Limited	£15,384,383
SG Aerospace (UK) Limited	£15,380,000
Sustainable Drainage Systems Limited	£15,369,683
Vistgate Limited	£15,362,248
Rudgeway Farms Limited	£15,361,916
Tregenna Castle Hotel Limited	£15,359,892
SDS Holdings Limited	£15,353,940
Bodywise (UK) Limited	£15,353,172
Coombe Fisheries Limited	£15,352,552
Steanbow Limited	£15,330,515
Debden Schools Services Limited	£15,326,000
Plympton Academy	£15,284,163
N.H. Case Limited	£15,262,957
Wilton Bradley Limited	£15,251,798
Worldteam Limited	£15,230,361
Grasshopper 2000 Ltd.	£15,208,310
Charles Trent Limited	£15,203,830
FWSC (Ladram) Limited	£15,203,462
Eberspacher (U.K.) Limited	£15,202,317
Brightsource Limited	£15,198,893
Carco Limited	£15,192,026
Mount Road Care Home LLP	£15,190,888
B M J International Limited	£15,190,412
Badminton School Limited	£15,175,909
Lancer Scott Limited	£15,162,277
Mears Housing Portfolio (Holdings) Limited	£15,153,600
Carco Group Limited	£15,152,514
Railston Limited	£15,149,124
Capes (Hatherden) Limited	£15,143,208
Colonial Leisure Limited	£15,131,648
Catalyst Business Finance Limited	£15,117,231
Penair School	£15,108,816
W. Stevenson & Sons Limited	£15,106,957
Scarlet Hotel Limited	£15,098,242
Chulmleigh Academy Trust	£15,091,957
Merlin Entertainments Group Operations Limited	£15,078,000
Wellington Motors Limited	£15,043,739
Visage (Aberdeen) Limited	£15,039,259
Forward Developments Limited	£15,038,593
South West Communications Group Limited	£15,037,278
Tilstone Glasgow Limited	£15,035,623
Leeways Packaging Services Limited	£15,027,546
Miro Technologies Limited	£15,005,365
SPC Europe Limited	£14,988,307
CEPS PLC.	£14,978,000
Delstar International, Limited	£14,973,296
G4S IP 2 Limited	£14,951,865
Plantronics Limited	£14,944,266
Murrill Holdings Limited	£14,934,201
Integrated Care Solutions (Shropshire) Holdings Ltd	£14,932,000
Integrated Care Solutions (Shropshire) Limited	£14,932,000
Chichester Harbour Hotel Limited	£14,930,360
Thermographic Measurements Limited	£14,923,438
Westcliff Hall (Sidmouth) Limited	£14,918,348
Pritchard Patent Product Company (2001) Limited	£14,906,350
Faccombe Estates Limited	£14,895,960
Organic Milk Suppliers Co-operative Limited	£14,892,000
RW Gower Street Limited	£14,892,000
Tenens (Lakeside) Limited	£14,874,743
Finlay Plant (UK) Limited	£14,869,753
Badham Pharmacy Limited	£14,865,271
Pickwick Academy Trust	£14,859,758
Firstport Property Services No 2 Limited	£14,858,934
Barker Care Limited	£14,855,734
D. J. Commercial Limited	£14,852,716
Hackney Parish Almshouses Charity	£14,838,762
SACO The Serviced Apartment Company Limited	£14,835,715
Cobham Leasing Limited	£14,830,000
Enham Trust	£14,826,000
Critchley Group Limited	£14,824,001
Exyte Hargreaves Limited	£14,817,000
Sensitisers Group Ltd.	£14,810,518
Penlane Limited	£14,805,007
ISG Pearce Limited	£14,794,000
Yeo Valley Fruit Limited	£14,792,373
John Reid & Sons (Strucsteel) Holdings Limited	£14,781,970
Boardinghouse Windfarm Limited	£14,773,756
Zebra MTD Limited	£14,760,731
Redhorn Holdings Limited	£14,760,263
Commercial Limited	£14,756,979
Cream Care Group Limited	£14,747,459
Lucrative Investments Holdings Limited	£14,740,434
Clifford Holdco Limited	£14,724,210
Bournemouth School	£14,721,369
Newbery Metals Limited	£14,717,746
Porthia Group Limited	£14,678,049
Cheltenham Borough Homes Limited	£14,665,000

Company	Value
Roadform Civil Engineering Company Limited	£14,636,771
STVA UK Limited	£14,632,000
Duo Assets Limited	£14,628,221
Bob Pepper Holdings Limited	£14,625,472
M.F. Freeman Limited	£14,619,745
Murrill Construction Limited	£14,608,834
KCTG Japan Holdings Ltd.	£14,600,123
SAA Consultants Limited	£14,588,408
Exeter Estates Limited	£14,582,095
Abbeyfield Wessex Society Limited	£14,580,829
Alton Pancras Estate UK Ltd.	£14,560,843
Kites Enterprises Limited	£14,552,945
Eggbuckland Community College Academy Trust	£14,541,869
Darts Farm Limited	£14,540,658
Britanic Industries Limited	£14,525,320
Stroud High School	£14,512,885
Trivselhus UK Limited	£14,507,126
Ashgrove One Limited	£14,507,033
Appsbroker Limited	£14,501,297
GCL 2016 Limited	£14,500,816
Oakland Capital Developments Limited	£14,500,762
Clyst Vale Academy Trust	£14,497,180
P & S Hockin Limited	£14,491,926
L.A.L. Estates Limited	£14,487,789
The Lee Abbey Movement	£14,476,972
Swallowcourt Limited	£14,449,839
Wills Brothers Limited	£14,435,033
Malvern Tyres (Wholesale) Limited	£14,419,464
Falkirk Group Limited	£14,416,075
Bournemouth School for Girls	£14,368,545
Harrow Community Schools PFI Ltd	£14,361,496
Microsemi Storage Solutions Europe Ltd	£14,354,083
Crystalight Limited	£14,351,299
Ortho 2008 Limited	£14,347,000
Lilian Faithfull Care	£14,341,922
JGH Topco Limited	£14,330,057
Vision Direct Group Ltd	£14,327,000
JGH Group Limited	£14,325,470
Amica Care Trust	£14,317,130
Autism Wessex	£14,316,866
Gillett's (Holdings) Limited	£14,287,831
Step One Charity	£14,271,445
Powrmatic Limited	£14,261,299
Ribston Hall High School Academy Trust	£14,245,053
Lester Aldridge LLP	£14,242,265
CCR Motor Co. Ltd.	£14,240,609
Imagile Business Support Limited	£14,237,957
Kent County Crematorium Limited	£14,235,115
Eagle One Estates Limited	£14,234,004
Dart Marina Hotel Limited	£14,224,999
Cornwall Housing Limited	£14,218,000
Evans Transport Limited	£14,217,678
Towndown Limited	£14,204,805
The Bart Ingredients Co. Ltd	£14,204,000
Bristol Infracare Lift (2) Limited	£14,204,000
Horwood Homewares Limited	£14,201,342
Potensis Recruitment Limited	£14,180,332
Weldmar Hospicecare Trust	£14,178,919
Buckler's Mead School	£14,171,607
J.A. & E. Montgomery Limited	£14,170,665
Canprop I Limited	£14,167,211
Loadace Limited	£14,155,944
Legacy Properties Limited	£14,143,273
Trelleborg Retford Limited	£14,143,000
Forthglade Foods Holdings Limited	£14,130,520
West Somerset Academies Trust	£14,119,793
Parmenion Capital Partners LLP	£14,103,110
Tornagrain Gas Mill Limited	£14,097,866
Sarum Properties Limited	£14,096,172
Bath Rugby Limited	£14,084,361
Castle Hill Quarry Co.,Limited	£14,083,932
A. H. Warren Trust Limited	£14,077,828
South West Investment Group Limited	£14,077,429
Silver Arrow Investments Ltd	£14,050,061
Marleton Cross Limited	£14,012,885
Kong Company Limited	£14,011,656
Poole Grammar School	£14,001,243
AES TEP Power Investments Limited	£14,000,241
United Reformed Church (South Western Synod) Inc	£13,995,474
Maximum Fun Devon Limited	£13,991,005
Hylton Group Limited	£13,988,819
Metric Group Holdings Limited	£13,971,000
Viridor Waste (Landfill Restoration) Limited	£13,970,000
Autoparts & Diagnostics Limited	£13,962,533
Ruskin Mill Trust Limited	£13,954,748
Regulatory Finance Solutions Limited	£13,950,094
BH Live	£13,935,754
LDC (Alscot Road) Ltd	£13,929,757
Nonwovenn Ltd	£13,925,177
PSC Training & Development Group Limited	£13,921,638
Go-Pak UK Limited	£13,921,111
Honiton Community College Academy Trust	£13,910,372
Sexey's School	£13,907,795
Tintometer,Limited (The)	£13,906,210
Talbot Heath School Trust Limited	£13,905,775
MJL Plant Hire (Cornwall) Limited	£13,900,601
Go in Four Limited	£13,900,123
Langlands Farms Limited	£13,894,120
D.J.L.Securities (Barum) Limited	£13,887,341
Discovery Multi Academy Trust	£13,877,677
BWP Services (Holdings No 1) Limited	£13,858,000
A J Iles Holdings Limited	£13,830,299
Powderham Properties (Teignmouth) Limited	£13,817,295
J M Scully (Holdings) Limited	£13,811,202
The Ashley Family Foundation Limited	£13,810,470
Watchpike Limited	£13,805,332
Efret Limited	£13,798,800
Nettleton Holdings Limited	£13,789,873
E.A. Chamberlain (Holdings) Limited	£13,784,030
Golden Years Ltd	£13,783,569
Dick Lovett Sporting Limited	£13,782,000
Autograph Homes Limited	£13,771,565
Hameln Pharmaceuticals Ltd	£13,764,480
RWE Cogen UK (Hythe) Limited	£13,759,000
Maurice Lay Distributors Limited	£13,758,464
Procurri UK Limited	£13,753,000
Vistair Limited	£13,752,935
Coast Academies	£13,716,000
Maxim Integrated Products UK Limited	£13,713,274
Braddicks Leisure Limited	£13,706,349
Halsall Construction Limited	£13,689,065
Wentrow Media Limited	£13,689,039
The George Muller Charitable Trust	£13,688,276
R. Hannon Limited	£13,684,744
Merityre Specialists Limited	£13,683,872
Corinium Education Trust	£13,676,888
Red Kite Vehicle Consultants Limited	£13,675,989
Mrs D M France-Hayhurst Foundation	£13,673,486
Wessex GS Limited	£13,658,552
Devonshire Real Estate Limited	£13,651,497
Arthur David (Food with Service) Limited	£13,646,185
Stonebridge Colleges (Publishing) Limited	£13,642,611
Philip Dennis Foodservice (Holdings) Limited	£13,636,586
Bishop Fox's School	£13,636,000
Mears Housing Portfolio 2 Limited	£13,632,875
Plymouth College & St Dunstan's Abbey Schools Charity	£13,617,598
DAS Law Limited	£13,617,000
Williamsbuild Management Limited	£13,605,969
Massey Wilcox Transport Limited	£13,603,825
Mears New Homes Limited	£13,597,340
Thrive Renewables (Severn) Limited	£13,573,119
Vetswest Limited	£13,568,966
P & M Group Limited (The)	£13,557,083
Heritage Developments South West Limited	£13,538,786

Company	Amount
Devon Care Homes Holdings Limited	£13,505,354
The John Bentley School	£13,502,990
Neat Experts Holdings Limited	£13,501,278
Stage Electrics Partnership Limited	£13,499,774
The Chedington Court Estate Limited	£13,489,405
Panel Supplies Limited	£13,486,084
Teach Poole	£13,482,272
Baptist Insurance Company PLC The	£13,477,000
Severn Unival Limited	£13,474,821
Gener8 Finance Limited	£13,472,481
Vistair Group Limited	£13,471,576
Animal Friends Insurance Services Limited	£13,442,100
North Downs Farm Ltd	£13,436,000
FR Aviation Services Limited	£13,429,000
Canford Renewable Energy Limited	£13,415,170
Baglan Moor Healthcare Holdings Limited	£13,410,000
Endeavour Academy Trust	£13,402,499
The Royal Marines Charity	£13,396,808
Lombard Corporate Finance (7) Limited	£13,395,000
Principality Holdings Limited	£13,393,924
Gill Corporate Limited	£13,381,521
Civitas SPV44 Limited	£13,379,697
Bristol Fruit Sales (Bananas) Limited	£13,372,187
WW (UK) Limited	£13,366,980
Taylor Maxwell Holdings Limited	£13,356,102
Littleham 2010 Limited	£13,347,480
Pegasus Planning Group Limited	£13,345,683
Crispin School Academy Trust	£13,328,080
Combe Pafford School	£13,321,203
Hydrock Consultants Limited	£13,317,827
A.E. Rodda & Son Limited	£13,316,000
J.H.Haskins & Son Limited	£13,306,920
Gooch & Housego (Torquay) Limited	£13,289,000
MUJV Limited	£13,278,000
Kinch Fuel Oils Limited	£13,276,454
Wessex Group Limited	£13,275,912
Infoteam International Services Limited	£13,270,710
The Mead Academy Trust	£13,266,601
Pennant International Limited	£13,258,088
Montemax Limited	£13,252,340
Wiltshire Air Ambulance Charitable Trust	£13,247,727
Alliance Homes (Ventures) Ltd	£13,246,000
Urban Creation Management Limited	£13,244,141
Outsauce Financing Limited	£13,242,845
Arlington Limited	£13,236,557
Dene Magna School	£13,226,000
Bennetts Cranes Limited	£13,225,230
Overton (Gloucester) Limited	£13,209,743
Bicknell Holdings PLC	£13,205,929
Unitedhealthcare Global Medical (UK) Limited	£13,194,000
Linc Capital Limited	£13,190,354
Brighton Harbour Hotel Limited	£13,184,632
Falfish (Holdings) Limited	£13,182,682
First Resources Limited	£13,181,000
Springvale Properties Limited	£13,176,009
Matki Public Limited Company	£13,172,932
Quick Move Now Limited	£13,153,770
Veitch Family Holdings Limited	£13,152,590
RMMP Limited	£13,150,215
Areawise Limited	£13,119,208
Wilson Leisure Developments Limited	£13,115,673
West of England Developments (Taunton) No2 Limited	£13,102,617
Eagle One Holdings Limited	£13,095,000
Samatt Limited	£13,090,139
Bonhay & Eagle Property Company Limited	£13,082,851
Gillett's (Callington) Limited	£13,080,000
Eccles Special High Schools Company Limited	£13,080,000
DCM (Cornwall) Limited	£13,078,946
Huish Episcopi Academy	£13,074,442
Oxygen House Properties LLP	£13,071,199
Atlas Packaging Limited	£13,064,399
Aero Stanrew Limited	£13,060,000
Interconnect Products Limited	£13,056,976
AES TEP Power II Investments Limited	£13,056,302
Off-Piste Wines Limited	£13,053,000
Pearce Construction (Barnstaple) Limited	£13,044,554
PCBL Limited	£13,044,554
Midway Care Group Limited	£13,025,722
Gloucester Land Company Limited	£13,022,504
Severn Vale School	£13,020,965
LV Repair Services Limited	£12,991,000
Moseley Distributors Limited	£12,990,387
The Haygrove Academy Trust	£12,969,900
Philip Dennis Foodservice Limited	£12,966,706
Clyst Holdings Limited	£12,963,285
Off Site Solutions (R T) Limited	£12,958,481
Tenens Associates Limited	£12,955,563
Esteban Investments Limited	£12,930,542
LAL Language Centres Holding Ltd	£12,929,286
Vavassor Limited	£12,899,277
Jackamax Limited	£12,886,075
Coxco Holdings Limited	£12,881,495
Grange Motors (Swindon) Limited	£12,874,000
Permali Gloucester Limited	£12,866,755
Bee Green Solar Limited	£12,865,712
AGR Automation Limited	£12,863,041
Sunpower Solar Limited	£12,850,814
Forest Park Cemetery and Crematorium Limited	£12,845,374
M Baker (Retail) Limited	£12,834,470
Percy Williams & Sons,Limited	£12,828,657
Thompson Valves Limited	£12,828,000
Navisite Europe Limited	£12,825,221
Christchurch Fairmile Village LLP	£12,816,643
N P Automotive Coatings (Europe) Limited	£12,809,000
Spire Technology Limited	£12,807,144
Opus Recruitment Solutions Limited	£12,804,639
Landell Mills Limited	£12,795,417
Dribuild Limited	£12,784,946
Atkinson Equipment Limited	£12,762,745
The Hampshire Motor Investment Company Limited	£12,760,000
Cirencester Kingshill School	£12,744,945
AIM Aviation (Henshalls) Limited	£12,738,000
Brighton & Hove City Schools Services Limited	£12,735,000
Ludus Capital Limited	£12,732,000
Richard C. Bircher (Holdings) Limited	£12,730,279
WSP Textiles Limited	£12,730,000
Heltor Limited	£12,729,910
La Flor de Copan UK Limited	£12,729,625
Applied Automation (UK) Limited	£12,724,111
E.V. Naish Limited	£12,704,808
Faerch Plast Poole Ltd	£12,704,302
Mike Burton Travel Limited	£12,700,138
Kemble Farms Limited	£12,694,592
Harrier Print Ltd	£12,689,464
Butterfly Conservation	£12,676,630
OMPD Limited	£12,667,881
Falfish Limited	£12,664,380
Gooderham Farms Limited	£12,658,830
Coxley Developments Limited	£12,657,361
Vicaima Limited	£12,650,642
Quay Marinas Limited	£12,647,665
Whitsbury Farm & Stud Limited	£12,646,330
Entier Associates Limited	£12,645,678
IIC Lambeth Holding Company Limited	£12,637,827
Sartorius Stedim Lab Limited	£12,633,328
Pulsar Process Measurement Limited	£12,608,598
Howard Tenens (North West) Limited	£12,607,578
Viridor (Lancashire) Limited	£12,583,000
Sure Maintenance Limited	£12,581,860
Duke's 1823 LLP	£12,580,872
Firn Overseas Packaging Limited	£12,580,207
Plymouth City Airport Limited	£12,579,000
Plessey Semiconductors Limited	£12,579,000
The Weavers Shop Limited	£12,572,418

Company	Amount
Bristol Polytechnic Enterprises Limited	£12,561,000
Duke Street Capital Oasis Orthodontics Holdings Ltd	£12,560,000
Trust in Learning (Academies)	£12,546,927
Imagile Group Limited	£12,541,268
Redbridge PPP Health Services Limited	£12,526,138
Bloom Hearing Specialists Limited	£12,520,277
The Chester Abode Limited	£12,515,737
Cubit Group Limited	£12,503,618
Lambeth Lighting Services Limited	£12,501,229
Conway Bailey Transport Limited	£12,492,339
Country Houses Foundation	£12,483,639
Hayward Properties Limited	£12,483,067
Norseland Holdings Limited	£12,479,165
John Baylis Leisure Limited	£12,475,431
Mobile Windscreens Limited	£12,475,000
Rochling Engineering Plastics (UK) Limited	£12,474,259
EIMS Global Limited	£12,474,184
Dawson Media Direct Limited	£12,456,000
Versarien PLC	£12,454,000
WPD Smart Metering Limited	£12,441,000
Quay Marinas Group Ltd	£12,427,292
Council of Milton Abbey School Limited (The)	£12,421,954
Bristol Care Homes Development Limited	£12,418,992
Medisafe UK Limited	£12,399,256
Otter Power Limited	£12,392,271
Trapeze Group (UK) Limited	£12,387,293
Hydro International Limited	£12,384,465
Bristol Holding Limited	£12,382,257
WH Smith Hospitals Holdings Limited	£12,370,488
Churston Ferrers Grammar School	£12,363,178
Star Hydraulics Limited	£12,352,275
Chamberlayne Farms Limited	£12,345,752
NASA Umbrella Ltd	£12,338,231
Atlantis Operations (UK) Limited	£12,325,855
Allstone Sands Gravels Aggregates Trading Co. Ltd.	£12,322,013
Zurich Intermediary Group Limited	£12,320,000
Mole Avon Trading Limited	£12,305,464
Glen Mhor Limited	£12,302,121
Parker Knoll Upholstery Limited	£12,291,866
IBCOS Computers Ltd	£12,283,654
Blast Properties Limited	£12,269,739
Acrefield Investments Limited	£12,266,720
Dribuild Group Limited	£12,263,781
Lance Levy Investments Limited	£12,256,189
Securivin Limited	£12,249,468
IMC St.David's Ltd	£12,237,902
Livingstone Leisure Limited	£12,236,361
Glastonbury Festival Events Limited	£12,233,369
Wilsons Solicitors LLP	£12,230,913
A.M.B.Investments Limited	£12,230,211
BBG Lift Accommodation Services (No 2) Limited	£12,220,000
Abercrombie & Kent Europe Limited	£12,212,000
Trago Mills (Falmouth) Limited	£12,211,332
Bowmill Engineering Limited	£12,205,254
MJL Contractors Limited	£12,202,883
Openwave Systems Limited	£12,195,606
Warners Retail Group Limited	£12,194,395
Warners Retail Limited	£12,194,351
King David Tyres Limited	£12,192,158
South Western Helicopters Limited	£12,178,000
Ashley Chase Estate Limited	£12,176,474
The County Hotel Canterbury Limited	£12,175,626
Del Piero Limited	£12,173,001
Aster Property Limited	£12,167,000
Adam Bailey Limited	£12,163,598
Decision Insight Hub Limited	£12,148,110
Magellan Aerospace (Blackpool) Limited	£12,131,000
Silverleigh Limited	£12,130,946
Mitchell & Webber Limited	£12,127,728
Surgical Specialties UK Holdings Limited	£12,127,000
Daido Industrial Bearings Europe Limited	£12,117,000
Stockdale Trading Company Limited	£12,110,918

Company	Amount
Bee Green Energy Ltd.	£12,110,065
Shiptinvest Limited	£12,104,651
South Wilts Grammar School for Girls	£12,104,000
Eco-Bos Development Limited	£12,096,943
Pyman Bell (Holdings) Limited	£12,093,771
Canford Healthcare Limited	£12,089,699
Credit Reporting Agency (Holdings) Limited	£12,088,172
CAT-UK Services Limited	£12,084,000
Cohen & Griffiths Limited	£12,082,954
Blue Port Estates Limited	£12,078,435
Oxford Programs Limited	£12,058,122
Wolverhampton City and Walsall Lift Accommodation	£12,057,000
Insite Poster Investments Ltd.	£12,052,705
Alec Jarrett Limited	£12,045,957
Zuken Group Limited	£12,037,000
Cookpad Limited	£12,005,163
Sunpower Meadow LLP	£12,000,000
Woodland Barton Wind LLP	£12,000,000
Exmouth Marina Ltd	£11,998,000
Francis Bugler Limited	£11,987,163
Kernow Coatings Limited	£11,985,729
Colosseum Dental UK Partnerships Limited	£11,968,000
Succession Newco1 Limited	£11,964,000
Chief Vehicle Rentals Limited	£11,963,606
Colebrook Bosson & Saunders (Products) Limited	£11,954,506
Kaba Limited	£11,950,173
Aim Composites Limited	£11,944,000
Sunderland CLC School Services Limited	£11,937,000
Seahawk Marine Foods Limited	£11,934,845
Lemaca Limited	£11,930,929
Stonegate Group Limited	£11,913,472
Hammett Investments Limited	£11,912,749
Argyll Environmental Ltd	£11,911,261
Curzon 1234 Limited	£11,910,894
Expromet Technologies Group Limited	£11,902,748
Solar Power Generation Limited	£11,896,952
Devon Contract Waste Ltd	£11,896,505
Halewell Limited	£11,888,534
South West Investment Group (Capital) Limited	£11,888,166
Procurri Europe Limited	£11,886,000
Direct Online Services Holdings Limited	£11,885,090
Sportech Pools Limited	£11,881,000
Wildbrook Investments Limited	£11,879,457
Astra Trading Development Ltd.	£11,875,893
Alias Limited	£11,870,467
Torquay Girls' Grammar School	£11,861,683
Range Valley Extrusions Limited	£11,854,000
Galtec Holdings Limited	£11,852,774
Galtec Limited	£11,826,797
E & L Rental Properties Limited	£11,814,119
RMH (Guildford) Limited	£11,809,700
Cotteswold Dairy Limited	£11,807,811
Addpace Limited	£11,801,052
Fairlie Properties Limited	£11,799,337
Drilling Information Limited	£11,791,519
M Way Holdings Limited	£11,790,092
Wilson Leisure Limited	£11,787,524
A R & A L Keen Limited	£11,783,178
Procook Limited	£11,770,434
Tilstone Retail Limited	£11,769,810
St Austell Printing Company Limited	£11,752,066
Direct Online Services Limited	£11,747,095
NNA Limited	£11,746,527
A D Woodley Holdings Limited	£11,738,977
Greensquare Homes Limited	£11,737,951
Murray (Plymouth) Limited	£11,731,754
LDC (Constitution Street) Limited	£11,727,715
Haynes Developments Limited	£11,717,094
Asvida UK Limited	£11,717,052
LV Equity Release Limited	£11,701,000
Phoenix Learning & Care Holdings Limited	£11,688,330
C. Smart Agricultural Services Limited	£11,687,258

The Eurotech Group PLC	£11,677,000	PJFB Property Company Limited	£11,245,078
Drimbawn (UK) Limited	£11,668,000	Snapdragons Nurseries Limited	£11,234,010
South West Environmental Parks Limited	£11,663,540	Dorset Wildlife Trust	£11,233,000
G.J.Handy & Company Limited	£11,663,235	Vence LLP	£11,232,957
Sutton Harbour Services Limited	£11,653,000	Cullen Group Limited	£11,229,324
George Williamson & Co. Limited	£11,650,967	Comenius Trust	£11,228,000
Highworth Warneford School	£11,644,092	Walton Street LLP	£11,225,722
E.P.Mallory & Son,Limited	£11,636,272	Original Style Limited	£11,224,934
Bechtle Direct Limited	£11,636,244	George Bence & Sons Limited	£11,216,809
CDF Group Ltd	£11,634,000	Bashley Park Limited	£11,216,670
The Chota Estates Company Limited	£11,633,969	J C Thomas & Sons Limited	£11,209,512
ASCB Charitable Fund	£11,627,909	Spirit Packaging Limited	£11,203,883
Be Wiser Insurance Services Ltd	£11,625,000	Sheffield Parkway LLP	£11,197,490
CJ Room Ltd	£11,611,427	Plymouth Rentals Limited	£11,189,358
Sirona Care & Health C.I.C.	£11,611,000	Hardware Group Limited	£11,171,000
Wring Group Limited	£11,607,626	Prowrap Limited	£11,167,304
Master International Limited	£11,600,648	Julia's House Limited	£11,156,612
Pattersons (Holdings) Limited	£11,597,498	Stedall (Vehicle Fittings) Limited	£11,155,000
Property Consortium (Holdings) Limited	£11,584,920	Caerus Holdings Limited	£11,134,000
Tilstone Basingstoke Limited	£11,576,285	Codford Biogas Limited	£11,133,738
Monkey Island Properties Limited	£11,572,420	Inter Mediate Two Limited	£11,127,000
Bladeroom Group Limited	£11,559,000	Bridgend Custodial Services Limited	£11,124,000
Knights Brown Group Ltd	£11,543,000	Williams Southern Limited	£11,119,174
Kingsmead Academy	£11,538,811	Frazer-Nash Consultancy Group Limited	£11,115,671
Pukka Pads 2000 Limited	£11,537,558	Bluevenn Limited	£11,115,456
The Roseland Multi Academy Trust	£11,532,122	Footsure Western Limited	£11,113,770
South Devon UTC	£11,531,622	Fraser St James Investments Limited	£11,108,572
Cogent Communications UK Ltd	£11,530,934	Northern Isles Ferries Limited	£11,105,000
Burton Wold Wind Farm South Ltd	£11,521,504	Trethowans LLP	£11,096,992
Novia Financial Holdings Limited	£11,517,647	Italmatch UK Limited	£11,094,000
Porter Dodson LLP	£11,510,202	Charlcombe Limited	£11,080,837
Rothdean Limited	£11,500,483	The Sportsman Gun Centre Limited	£11,075,627
Baylis Ventures Limited	£11,500,436	Speeds Group Holdings Limited	£11,068,341
Bourne Holdings	£11,499,305	Royal Artillery Institution Limited	£11,052,180
Proper Cornish Limited	£11,491,723	Equa Multi Academy Trust	£11,048,766
Piller UK Limited	£11,490,443	M. Way & Son (Transport) Limited	£11,046,181
Lypiatt Studio Limited	£11,482,991	Harding & Sons,Limited	£11,042,513
Tileflair Limited	£11,480,708	Nu-Heat (Holdings) Limited	£11,035,923
The Ship (Derriford) Limited	£11,480,411	KPC & AT Body Properties Limited	£11,035,834
Bath and West Finance Limited	£11,477,085	Higher Kings Mill Limited	£11,031,033
Double H (Holdings) Limited	£11,465,628	Bix Developments Limited	£11,027,966
J.M.Harding & Partners Limited	£11,452,868	Outsource UK Limited	£11,019,584
Parsons Peebles Service Limited	£11,404,000	Swedish Lifestyle Homes No.1 Limited	£11,019,472
Dorset Press Limited (The)	£11,403,444	Westfield Academy Trust	£11,019,155
Senex Capital Limited	£11,397,715	Libya Oil Sudan Limited	£11,016,275
Salisbury Glass Centre Limited	£11,387,031	Euston Simmonds Limited	£11,015,052
Merlin Cinemas Limited	£11,374,349	Woods Consolidated Limited	£11,010,817
Dentalign Orthodontics LLP	£11,374,000	Preformed Line Products (Great Britain) Limited	£11,003,696
Constructor Group UK Limited	£11,373,279	GP Batteries (UK) Limited	£11,001,447
Sanderson Contract Management Limited	£11,373,000	Microensure Holdings Limited	£10,995,286
Pukka Pads UK Limited	£11,358,563	Bernard Cox Limited	£10,988,357
Satnam Limited	£11,358,004	Armstrong Bridging International Limited	£10,986,183
Spectrum Premier Homes Limited	£11,355,000	Cleancrop UK Limited	£10,970,000
Prabh Milnae Kaa Chaao Gurdwara	£11,354,980	Viper Innovations Ltd	£10,967,625
Masons Farm and Country Limited	£11,350,573	Freeways Trust	£10,966,006
James Mason Limited	£11,349,975	Town Hospitals (Southern General) Ltd	£10,965,000
Shervey Limited	£11,343,455	Omnis Investments Limited	£10,948,000
Wyse Estates Holdings Limited	£11,342,634	M.F. Freeman Group Limited	£10,943,336
KS SPV 1 Limited	£11,342,238	Lakes Bathrooms Limited	£10,938,713
Cornwall Hospice Care Limited	£11,342,047	Luxurycare (Birds Hill Nursing Home) Limited	£10,933,592
Quantum Old Manor Retirement Living LLP	£11,309,508	Cornwall Glass & Glazing Limited	£10,928,555
Wiltshire Wildlife Trust Limited	£11,309,286	Riviera Education Trust	£10,919,666
Caspian Networks Limited	£11,303,997	Desertlands Entertainment Limited	£10,918,000
TFIO Properties Limited	£11,303,345	Prolabs Holdings Limited	£10,916,200
Prolabs (UK) Limited	£11,301,848	Portland Stone Firms Limited	£10,914,293
Brean Leisure Park Ltd.	£11,291,422	FGP Systems Limited	£10,909,941
Electro Mechanical Systems Limited	£11,288,711	Mabey and Johnson Limited	£10,903,454
Bridport Limited	£11,287,000	Ellas No4 Limited	£10,901,000
The Watercress Company Limited	£11,284,768	The Heath Academy Trust	£10,900,185
F.H. Cummings	£11,272,072	China Fleet Trust	£10,893,711
The Park Academies Trust	£11,271,618	Cotswold Homes Limited	£10,889,114
Ayersmont Limited	£11,264,325	Servo Interconnect Limited	£10,879,761

Black Gold Developments (UK) Limited	£10,877,850	Sparrow Crane Hire Limited	£10,556,606
Wookey Hole Limited	£10,875,809	Grange Court (Hoburne) Limited	£10,555,164
Windmill Care Limited	£10,872,013	Pritchard Patent Product Co. Limited	£10,546,008
Westfield Medical Group Limited	£10,871,000	Bittware Limited	£10,544,325
Haseltine Lake LLP	£10,870,816	Catalent Micron Technologies Limited	£10,539,052
Walston Holdings Limited	£10,863,935	Antrak Limited	£10,536,903
SRT Marine Technology Limited	£10,856,906	Books & Stationers Limited	£10,534,982
SLX Group Limited	£10,854,183	Data Installation & Networking Services Limited	£10,532,464
Double H (Nurseries) Limited	£10,851,406	Potensis Limited	£10,524,180
Graytone Limited	£10,847,054	Westcoast (Bristol) Limited	£10,523,338
Coate Water Care Co Church View Nursing Home	£10,846,313	Barkwell Plumbing & Heating Limited	£10,522,238
KMW Properties Limited	£10,845,316	Stuarts Truck and Bus Limited	£10,509,390
Bedruthan Hotel Limited	£10,838,260	SCES Property Ltd	£10,508,968
J M Scully Limited	£10,837,784	Whitelock & Company Limited	£10,506,926
Intamarque Limited	£10,830,050	Jakemans (Confectioners) Limited	£10,503,564
Higher Drive Nursing Home (Holdings) Limited	£10,828,278	Danisco Holdings (UK) Limited	£10,503,000
The Crescent Trust Company Limited	£10,800,266	GH North Northampton Limited	£10,500,000
Knabs Ridge Wind Farm Limited	£10,799,301	Cronite Castings Limited	£10,490,101
Pinewood School Limited	£10,799,080	Nissha Medical Technologies Ltd	£10,487,000
Home Hardware Southwest Limited	£10,797,025	Balcarras School	£10,484,465
C Sparks & Sons Limited	£10,796,609	The Sheiling Special Education Trust	£10,479,119
Spinnaker International Limited	£10,792,289	Smallridge Bros Limited	£10,468,344
National Marine Aquarium Limited	£10,786,410	Cristie Software Limited	£10,464,558
Hovertravel Limited	£10,784,158	Harmer Properties Limited	£10,462,481
Spectrum Property Care Ltd	£10,784,000	Suremime Limited	£10,460,946
Cosmetic Warriors Limited	£10,777,000	Batten and Allen Limited	£10,455,140
Quality Care Group Limited	£10,772,936	Socomec U.K. Limited	£10,444,531
Torbay Schools Services Limited	£10,771,000	Weird Fish Holdings Limited	£10,444,184
Customade (UK) Limited	£10,770,000	Blanchworth Care Limited	£10,440,479
Fabrinet UK Limited	£10,758,000	Prospect Hospice Limited	£10,440,000
Saddleback Limited	£10,757,885	J.A. Darke Limited	£10,438,415
GDS INT Holdings Limited	£10,747,091	MCB Investments Limited	£10,435,870
Walker Developments (South West) Limited	£10,741,500	Quantum Swansea LLP	£10,430,771
Charles Saunders Limited	£10,735,747	Stonegate Agriculture Limited	£10,429,829
Downfield Homes Limited	£10,732,204	Jones Building Group Limited	£10,427,265
Reflex Electronics Limited	£10,726,967	Good Energy Delabole Windfarm Limited	£10,423,595
Buro Happold Consulting Engineers Limited	£10,723,000	St George's Bristol	£10,418,000
Wessex Grain Ltd.	£10,722,886	Southern England Farms Limited	£10,406,541
Verdant Community Energy C.I.C.	£10,722,364	Pipex Limited	£10,397,485
Horseworld Trust	£10,721,847	Worlds Apart Limited	£10,389,651
Crapper & Sons Landfill Limited	£10,720,309	Astrum Multi Academy Trust	£10,389,000
GEA Farm Technologies (UK) Ltd	£10,718,982	Treasure Homes Limited	£10,388,989
Bristol Port Wind Park Limited	£10,714,121	Megasteel Ltd	£10,386,990
Bowden Derra Park Limited	£10,713,248	Extreme Assets LLP	£10,384,760
Hertford PPP Health Services Limited	£10,699,192	Tay Valley Lighting (Stoke on Trent) Limited	£10,381,000
Hope and Homes for Children	£10,689,875	Millets Farm Centre Limited	£10,376,709
Barnwood Construction Limited	£10,688,758	Cabot Mews Limited	£10,370,884
Churngold Construction Holdings Limited	£10,686,000	Dick Lovett (Bath) Limited	£10,369,000
Froyle Harbour Hotel Limited	£10,685,600	Terraquest Solutions Limited	£10,367,009
Warminster School	£10,680,441	H.C. Starck Limited	£10,364,319
GTS Academy Trust	£10,657,210	Leading Edge Academies Partnership	£10,362,959
Newton Abbot Academy Trust	£10,651,712	Edge Restaurants (NW) Limited	£10,354,236
Evershot Farms Limited	£10,651,162	Birchclaim Limited	£10,353,707
Keith Pople Limited	£10,650,043	Regent's Park Healthcare Limited	£10,350,000
Turnspeed Precision Engineering Company Limited	£10,647,257	Grove Care Limited	£10,346,671
The Mare and Foal Sanctuary	£10,641,515	Christ Church C of E Primary School	£10,345,664
Shillofad Limited	£10,639,476	Canynge Bicknell (Investments) Limited	£10,345,627
CAA Property Limited	£10,635,033	Zycko Group Limited	£10,343,000
Avon Specialty Metals Limited	£10,634,772	Five Directions Limited	£10,336,485
Colyton Grammar School Academy Trust	£10,632,309	Armstrong Energy Global Limited	£10,335,397
Gapcontrol Limited	£10,629,684	The Stepping Stone Group Limited	£10,334,467
Smithcorp Limited	£10,626,013	UFT Limited	£10,331,497
Worlds Apart Holdings Limited	£10,622,899	Shearwell Data Limited	£10,327,498
Firstport Insurance Services Limited	£10,620,255	Rew Hotels Limited	£10,315,616
Limbs & Things Limited	£10,610,250	The Great British Card Company PLC	£10,315,203
Synertec Limited	£10,600,405	F.A.W. Baker's Kingston Farms Limited	£10,313,693
Junction 24 Limited	£10,594,990	Manuli Packaging (UK) Ltd.	£10,309,502
The Manchester Abode Limited	£10,588,944	Salterns Marina Limited	£10,308,996
Good Energy Hampole Windfarm Limited	£10,586,761	Alfco Investments Limited	£10,303,926
Eden Research PLC	£10,585,878	GWP Holdings Limited	£10,300,810
Quantum Salisbury Centre LLP	£10,581,663	Thrive Renewables (Caton Moor) Limited	£10,290,005
Ovo Electricity Ltd	£10,580,000	Railston Holdings Limited	£10,289,015

Company	Amount
Salisbury Plain Academies	£10,285,515
Targetgrange (Holdings) Limited	£10,285,183
M.A.C. Hotels Ltd	£10,282,649
R L Clapp and Sons (Cheesemakers) Limited	£10,271,479
Jade-Aden Services Limited	£10,269,514
Topcon Technology Limited	£10,268,470
LMR Holdings Limited	£10,267,929
Dometic UK Limited	£10,254,000
Altogether Care - Care Homes Limited	£10,249,746
Creditcall Group Limited	£10,246,317
Hitachi Information Control Systems Europe Ltd.	£10,245,204
Attivo Group Limited	£10,243,943
Clean Earth Holdings 2 Ltd	£10,243,104
TM Group (UK) Limited	£10,237,000
Trelleborg Marine Systems UK Limited	£10,222,000
Sanlam Wealth Planning Holdings UK Limited	£10,220,466
Martingate Centre Limited	£10,220,015
Newspace Containers Limited	£10,218,558
Eliquo Hydrok Limited	£10,217,374
Ramsbury Estates Limited	£10,213,695
Total Orthodontics Limited	£10,208,000
Little Venice Developments Limited	£10,206,034
Delt Shared Services Limited	£10,202,000
Zurich Advice Network Limited	£10,198,431
D.J. Contracts (Weymouth) Limited	£10,197,446
Cornish Scrumpy Holdings Limited	£10,185,911
National Milk Records PLC	£10,174,000
Five AI Limited	£10,166,011
C.P. Mikulla Limited	£10,164,068
Professional Reseller Group Limited	£10,163,716
Ashfield Land Management Limited	£10,152,973
Omega Housing Limited	£10,145,911
Beckery Properties Limited	£10,141,844
Brixham College Academy Trust	£10,141,551
Verto Homes Ltd	£10,139,048
Game and Wildlife Conservation Trust	£10,128,983
Goulds (Dorchester) Limited	£10,125,888
Lascar Electronics Limited	£10,124,324
Parkview Gloucester Ltd	£10,108,939
South Wiltshire UTC Limited	£10,099,000
Society for Endocrinology	£10,098,422
Culverdene Properties Limited	£10,097,639
Exeter Golf and Country Club,Limited (The)	£10,092,473
Signet Armorlite Europe Limited	£10,090,345
Alton Towers Resort Operations Limited	£10,090,000
Innovate Awarding Ltd	£10,080,650
Stuart Property (Holdings) Limited	£10,080,627
Barrettine Holdings Limited	£10,076,386
Frank Bruce & Company Limited	£10,074,176
Genus Capital 3 Limited	£10,055,752
Canprop Kensington Limited	£10,050,414
St. Mary's School Shaftesbury Trust	£10,048,378
Hospiscare	£10,047,938
Springfield Country Hotel (Stoborough) Limited	£10,041,288
The Dorcan Academy	£10,026,678
Plessey Lighting Limited	£10,025,000
Cornwall Air Ambulance Trust	£10,023,296
Kemble Business Park LLP	£10,023,130
WESC Foundation	£10,018,736
Earthline Holdings Limited	£10,017,626
Pool Academy	£10,015,043
Southern Healthcare (Wessex) Ltd	£10,009,847
Alvan Blanch Development Company Limited	£10,008,404
Alvan Blanch Holdings Limited	£10,008,404
Andrews Letting and Management Limited	£10,001,665
Arriva Group Limited	£10,001,622
Braunton School and Community College Academy	£9,997,987
Devonport High School for Girls	£9,996,678
Danco International PLC	£9,988,629
Orthodynamics Limited	£9,984,644
Beaudesert Park School Trust Limited	£9,971,088
Lornamead UK Limited	£9,970,000

Company	Amount
Michco 1208 Limited	£9,959,730
The Bourne Academy	£9,950,388
The Dobson Family Investment Company Limited	£9,950,020
Yate Disposables Ltd	£9,947,925
Head Ruddy Limited	£9,947,884
Quantum Group (Management) Limited	£9,946,312
D R Jones Yeovil Ltd.	£9,946,031
Magna Motor Company Limited	£9,943,413
Beaver Estates (Ashford) Investments Limited	£9,939,324
Charlcombe Homes Limited	£9,935,171
Holt JCB Holdings Limited	£9,932,000
Gardiner Bros. and Company (Leathers) Limited	£9,929,710
Nicolas James Group Limited	£9,922,439
Lovell Stone Group Holdings Limited	£9,922,428
Holt JCB Limited	£9,922,000
Midhurst Child Care Limited	£9,921,441
Braddicks Holiday Centre (Westward Ho!) Limited	£9,911,294
SMD 2013 Limited	£9,911,245
Shipton Mill Limited	£9,909,779
Preston School Academy Trust	£9,903,250
Little Bedwyn Estate Limited	£9,897,767
Proper Job Superstores Limited	£9,895,616
International Spray Solutions Limited	£9,895,036
Williamson-Dickie Europe Holdings Limited	£9,895,000
Canon Court Farm Limited	£9,890,081
Weymouth Harbour Estates Limited	£9,888,187
Vian Marketing Limited	£9,881,377
Symonds Forecourts Limited	£9,878,854
Colburn East Limited	£9,869,423
Hillside Property Company Limited	£9,869,296
LJ (Copiers) Limited	£9,868,105
Granite Associates Ltd.	£9,865,492
Steppes Travel Ltd	£9,861,713
Condition Monitoring Group Limited	£9,860,467
Cotek Papers Limited	£9,853,036
Stormfront Retail Limited	£9,852,376
Manutan Limited	£9,836,000
Excalibur Communications GB Limited	£9,835,307
I.D.S. Refrigeration Limited	£9,800,486
GDS Publishing Limited	£9,784,090
Buckclose Limited	£9,779,390
Libra Homes Limited	£9,779,352
A. L. Sayers (Holbeton) Limited	£9,778,207
I.J. McGill Transport Limited	£9,776,541
Majestic Tours Limited	£9,770,634
LTC Group87 Ltd	£9,768,864
Thames Valley Eggs (Production) Limited	£9,768,591
Solent International Limited	£9,761,316
Drew Holdings Limited	£9,758,686
Chippenham Motor Company Limited	£9,757,004
Torbay Economic Development Company Limited	£9,756,614
Pang Investments Limited	£9,753,954
H.Mustin & Son Limited	£9,751,544
Telesoft Technologies Limited	£9,749,000
CIL Management Consultants Limited	£9,735,920
Future Advanced Manufacture Ltd	£9,731,744
Cotswold Hoburne Limited	£9,723,816
Holton Homes Limited	£9,721,889
H.W.Clothier Milton-Westcombe Farms Limited	£9,717,097
Bristlewand Limited	£9,709,798
Deodara Limited	£9,699,692
Dingle Brothers Systems Limited	£9,698,567
Dudbridge Estates,Limited (The)	£9,691,693
Superior Specials Limited	£9,691,440
Shorelark Limited	£9,689,062
Stride Treglown Limited	£9,686,111
Chanctonbury Health Care Ltd	£9,681,534
H.J.Knee,Limited	£9,680,868
The Delta Education Trust	£9,661,000
Eastleigh Care Homes - Raleigh Mead Limited	£9,660,670
Plymouth Community Homes Energy Limited	£9,655,000
AFL Telecommunications Europe Ltd	£9,651,000

WTW Cinemas Limited	£9,645,008	Stanchester Community School Academy	£9,402,837
Grey Matter Limited	£9,641,000	Sportech Holdco 1 Limited	£9,401,000
Three Ways School	£9,635,480	Osprey Shipping Limited	£9,394,846
Infinergy Limited	£9,633,679	The Lodge Rest Limited	£9,391,312
New Yacht Club Limited	£9,629,375	P J Davidson Developments Ltd	£9,388,609
Compass Tractors Limited	£9,627,138	Custom Interconnect Limited	£9,377,000
Compass Agri (Holdings) Limited	£9,627,138	A & O Holdings Ltd	£9,373,245
Storm Land Securities Ltd	£9,624,300	Staysail Limited	£9,369,109
Pentewan Sands,Limited	£9,624,282	Creative Youth Network	£9,368,746
North Somerset Community Partnership CIC	£9,623,680	Waypoints Care (Upton) Limited	£9,359,081
Bristol Waste Company Limited	£9,621,916	Blackmore Vale Farm Cream Limited	£9,354,353
Futura Foods UK Limited	£9,610,670	Tyre Maintenance Limited	£9,354,051
Swindon Caravan Centre Limited	£9,599,210	Redlynch Agricultural Engineering Limited	£9,351,873
Artisan Biscuits Limited	£9,597,897	EA & JA Hiscock Limited	£9,345,521
Lovell Stone Group Limited	£9,591,321	Netcraft Ltd	£9,345,471
Perrys Holdings Limited	£9,587,939	Redvers and Denzil Rice Farms Limited	£9,344,924
GWE Business West Ltd	£9,579,594	Zuru UK Limited	£9,343,524
Wallsend Estates Limited	£9,569,466	Longhouse Ltd	£9,341,000
Walston Poultry Farm Limited	£9,567,018	Residential Trust Limited	£9,337,375
Gibbs Surfacing Limited	£9,566,819	Stroud Valleys Canal Company	£9,335,688
Structural Metal Decks Limited	£9,566,044	TM Property Searches Limited	£9,332,000
Play Sports Group Limited	£9,561,459	Nevro Medical Limited	£9,331,615
Crediton Milling Holdings Ltd	£9,556,391	Manor Renewable Energy Limited	£9,325,122
Ledex Limited	£9,554,226	The Bulldog Trust Limited	£9,324,357
Bushell & Meadows Limited	£9,554,067	Hardware Services Limited	£9,320,000
SAFC Hitech Limited	£9,549,000	Coleman UK Limited	£9,316,000
Castle Barton Limited	£9,547,859	Eelpower (Opco1) Limited	£9,312,898
Frome Solar Limited	£9,544,613	The Railway Convalescent Homes	£9,307,579
Pucklechurch Development Company Limited	£9,542,970	Tincknell Fuels Limited	£9,306,067
Carling Technologies Limited	£9,542,111	WA Consultants Limited	£9,305,933
Russell Worth Limited	£9,541,816	Metalex Products Limited	£9,300,459
Taylor-Davis Limited	£9,535,660	North Devon Hospice	£9,299,953
H R Jasper & Son (Holdings) Limited	£9,534,110	Impcross Limited	£9,296,022
Altus Holdings Limited	£9,533,815	Liskeard PPP Health Services Limited	£9,295,712
AECC University College	£9,532,000	The Redstart Learning Partnership	£9,295,474
Harris Fowler Limited	£9,526,930	Marcham Farms Limited	£9,292,502
Flash Investments LLP	£9,524,751	Tileflair Group Limited	£9,292,279
Park Home Life Limited	£9,524,606	RR Sea Strand Limited	£9,291,934
Charles Saunders Holdings Limited	£9,523,463	Unity Farm Holiday Centre Limited	£9,290,395
B.A.I. (U.K.), Limited	£9,520,492	Expolink Group Limited	£9,290,151
Port Regis School Limited	£9,516,132	P G Properties Limited	£9,287,257
A.E. Securities Limited	£9,515,386	Excalibur Communications Group Limited	£9,280,397
Jacgilden Properties Limited	£9,511,326	Lympstone Manor Ltd	£9,276,751
Catherine Harwood Bell LLP	£9,509,197	UK Shared Business Services Limited	£9,272,000
Cartus Financing Limited	£9,505,000	Barden Network Engineering Limited	£9,265,606
Emblem Holdings Limited	£9,503,912	Avon Valley Holdings Limited	£9,263,962
Five Valleys Aerospace Limited	£9,498,000	Wemyss Lodge Limited	£9,263,394
MF Bennion (Potatoes) Limited	£9,492,832	David Taylor (Garages) Limited	£9,258,494
C & O Tractors Limited	£9,491,940	JG Travel Group Limited	£9,247,006
Stride Treglown Group PLC	£9,482,861	Films at 59 Limited	£9,244,795
Endesign Limited	£9,478,542	The Simian Group Limited	£9,227,000
PADI EMEA Limited	£9,476,000	Avortex Limited	£9,220,845
R.M. Penny (Plant Hire and Demolition) Limited	£9,473,798	Corrington Estates Limited	£9,220,666
Willand Biogas LLP	£9,457,851	Acheson Construction Limited	£9,216,437
Civitas SPV2 Limited	£9,453,614	Stay Original Company Ltd	£9,215,635
Five Bees Limited	£9,453,320	Caerus Wealth Limited	£9,209,000
First Position Group Limited	£9,451,431	Smithbrewer Limited	£9,206,593
Light Group Limited	£9,444,281	Harbourside Learning Partnership	£9,205,521
Newincco 1402 Limited	£9,441,726	South West Care Homes Limited	£9,203,639
Toklon Limited	£9,438,000	Icon Two Limited	£9,203,460
Vowles Parks Limited	£9,435,101	Woodmace Limited	£9,202,693
Landscove Holidays Limited	£9,432,376	Mount International United Services Ltd	£9,185,525
Paradigm Norton Financial Planning Limited	£9,428,180	Watershed Arts Trust Limited (The)	£9,184,204
The Quality Assurance Agency for Higher Education	£9,422,507	Goldrose Management Limited	£9,183,307
Langham Farms Limited	£9,414,454	Air Bearings Limited	£9,182,187
Stephens Scown LLP	£9,414,104	Yorkshire Hydropower Limited	£9,179,482
Poeton Holdings Limited	£9,412,946	Coln Park LLP	£9,174,332
Dentalign Orthodontics Limited	£9,412,000	Locators Limited	£9,170,754
No House Limited	£9,407,975	Dextra Lighting Limited	£9,167,373
Yellow Bridge Developments LLP	£9,407,574	Abbeyfield Bristol and Keynsham Society	£9,160,838
Tout Limited	£9,407,201	Westward Building Services Limited	£9,157,471
People Source Consulting Limited	£9,406,804	David Hathaway Transport Limited	£9,154,376

Tewkesbury Park Limited £9,148,040
Stance (Europe) Limited £9,142,123
Beachdown Limited £9,141,173
AFL Services Europe Ltd £9,132,827
Deceuninck Limited £9,128,000
Clipper Contracting Group Ltd £9,127,048
The Eurostore Group Limited £9,127,000
PAL Properties South West Ltd £9,113,761
Ashfield Land (Birmingham) Limited £9,111,214
Midas Retail Limited £9,107,000
Denis May & Sons Limited £9,106,400
PK Food Concepts Ltd. £9,100,595
Westcoast Developments (2009) Limited £9,100,368
Spower Holdco 1 (UK) Ltd. £9,095,961
Bristol & Avon Transport & Recycling Ltd £9,094,276
Solent Stevedores Limited £9,089,229
Parris Tractors Limited £9,088,634
Conmed UK Ltd £9,087,784
J.H. Haynes & Co. Limited £9,084,405
Finlay Hire Limited £9,083,607
Big Van World Limited £9,079,334
Moreton C.Cullimore (Gravels) Limited £9,066,970
Gilders Transport Limited £9,065,988
Paper Converting Machine Company Limited £9,064,187
7 SFI Limited £9,064,021
Marazion Holdings Limited £9,047,347
Churngold Construction Limited £9,047,000
Dartmouth Holdings Limited £9,040,050
Somerville & Savage Solicitors £9,024,239
Steadfast Asset Management Limited £9,019,990
Northern Hydropower Limited £9,014,706
Stotts Group Limited £9,013,726
New Dawn Homes Limited £9,011,292
Horizon Motor Company Limited £9,004,396
Hautot Holdings Limited £9,000,001
Kersfield Developments (RHS) Limited £8,999,768
J F Pearce & Sons Limited £8,997,972
Strukta Group Limited £8,988,188
Freemans Event Partners (Logistics) Ltd. £8,987,732
Cofton Country Holidays Limited £8,986,900
Zycko Overseas Limited £8,975,000
The Check House Limited £8,970,912
Exeter Rugby Club Limited £8,965,851
Cheltenham Family Health Care Centre Limited £8,962,649
Big Apple Entertainments Limited £8,953,434
Iracroft Limited £8,949,465
Rowanmoor Executive Pensions Limited £8,936,000
In-Excess UK Limited £8,935,184
Dexretail Limited £8,932,118
Futuream (UK) Limited £8,932,024
West Mendip PPP Health Services Limited £8,930,736
Abbey Manor Property Holdings Limited £8,929,000
Samara Investments (2000) Limited £8,928,216
43P9 Limited £8,924,420
The Malvern Property Limited £8,912,676
Fourgate (Cheltenham) Limited £8,910,382
Burrington Estates (RS) Limited £8,901,385
Mulberry Studios Limited £8,901,371
Shirwell Limited £8,899,603
P S J Properties Ltd. £8,892,402
Electric Mobility Euro Limited £8,886,429
All Tel Communications Limited £8,884,100
Design Objectives Limited £8,881,946
Kinneir Dufort Topco Limited £8,880,250
Hazlewoods LLP £8,878,759
Gemaco Holdings Limited £8,875,148
Lloyd & Whyte Group Limited £8,872,557
Holiday Parks SW Limited £8,859,241
Avon Energy Limited £8,853,063
St. James's Place Charitable Foundation £8,852,796
Alexandra Dock Limited £8,851,181
Avonline PLC £8,839,866
Avonline Holdings Limited £8,839,866
New Earth Solutions (West) Limited £8,823,568
Parkside Holdings Limited £8,815,840
McCarthy Contracting & Development Limited £8,808,769
Brandwells Construction Company Limited £8,806,736
Ken White Holdings Limited £8,804,847
J. J. Farm Services Limited £8,796,172
Nynehead Care Limited £8,795,982
Mean Moor Community Wind Farm Limited £8,791,513
Serene LL Ltd £8,790,956
Somerdale International Limited £8,787,993
Wiltshire Heavy Building Materials (Group) Limited £8,779,430
A1 PPP Infrastructure Holdings Limited £8,777,007
Evesham Specialist Packaging Limited £8,769,060
Waycroft Multi Academy Trust £8,759,290
Robertson Developments Ltd £8,757,062
Weymouth and Portland National Sailing Academy £8,749,533
Forward Land Limited £8,748,438
Gilbert and Goode Limited £8,748,000
West Country Park Homes Limited £8,744,800
Kamm Civil Engineering Limited £8,737,705
Brightwater Estates Limited £8,737,311
Davies Holdings (Somerton) Limited £8,737,270
Powerbox International Limited £8,733,000
Stone King LLP £8,732,702
Retirement Homesearch Limited £8,732,153
Theatre Royal Bath Limited (The) £8,731,000
Parsons Construction Limited £8,730,191
Lexicon Book Company Limited £8,728,319
Xograph Healthcare Limited £8,723,884
Dick Lovett (Hungerford) Limited £8,721,000
Eastleigh Care Homes Limited £8,719,532
Moderandum Limited £8,715,365
Chevron Properties Limited £8,709,590
Wiltshire Heavy Building Materials Limited £8,707,249
J.R. Harding & Sons (Frome) Limited £8,701,460
Dart Valley Railway Ltd £8,697,152
Wave Multi Academy Trust £8,696,084
Captiva Homes Limited £8,692,279
Transmission Developments Co (GB) Limited £8,692,083
Distant Planet Productions Limited £8,680,000
Premier Developments (1995) Limited £8,678,972
Raans Estates Limited £8,676,812
Abraxas Insurance Administration Services Ltd £8,674,526
Primetower Properties Limited £8,674,135
Brighton Student Developments Ltd £8,673,213
Amulet Hotkey Ltd £8,670,531
Innsworth Technology Park Limited £8,665,450
Attwooll Holdings Limited £8,662,974
ASM Assembly Systems UK Holding Limited £8,659,000
Jackson Property Investments £8,658,496
St Gresham Limited £8,654,583
Property Consortium UK Limited £8,654,208
Exepex Estates Limited £8,649,121
James Froud and Sons Limited £8,647,994
Whole Nine Yards (UK) Limited £8,643,527
Good Energy Carloggas Solar Park (009) Limited £8,643,470
Chessington World of Adventures Operations Limited £8,640,000
Red Lion Investments Limited £8,638,244
The Huish Academy Trust £8,631,521
Snape Construction Limited £8,631,117
Appledore Shipbuilders (2004) Limited £8,625,000
Rochford Holdings Limited £8,619,873
Rochford Garden Machinery Limited £8,619,729
Pathfinder Park Homes Holdings Limited £8,617,341
Ballard School Limited £8,615,087
Dick Lovett Sports Cars Limited £8,615,000
SEAFox Dycem 1 Limited £8,597,564
SEAFox Dycem 2 Limited £8,597,375
Peninsula Care Homes Limited £8,596,073
Stannah Lifts Limited £8,589,000
Hebron & Medlock Limited £8,587,300

Ashley Grange Nursing Home Limited	£8,574,830	ESP Colour Limited	£8,263,629
Capston Limited	£8,566,705	The Calendar Club Limited	£8,251,633
Harrow House International College (Swanage) Ltd	£8,565,056	Gill Southern Limited	£8,247,756
J. V. Barrett & Co. Limited	£8,564,257	Poole Arts Trust Limited	£8,243,920
Alum Care Limited	£8,557,479	Barrett Partnership Limited	£8,243,124
Castlegate Business Park Limited	£8,556,271	Antech Limited	£8,242,622
Pacific West Foods (UK) Ltd	£8,553,860	Frame Homes (South West) Limited	£8,239,599
Buro Happold Engineers Limited	£8,548,000	Kelston Precision Gears Limited	£8,239,233
Broadway (Bristol) Engineering Co,Limited	£8,543,644	Bottlegreen Holdings Limited	£8,236,066
Specialist Journeys Limited	£8,543,356	Edmont Ltd	£8,234,053
Public Power Solutions Limited	£8,539,000	JELF Financial Planning Ltd	£8,234,000
PDQ Group Limited	£8,534,123	M.J. Baker Foodservice Limited	£8,221,283
Easton Grey Estate Limited	£8,533,091	RTB Private Equity Ltd	£8,219,446
CG Holdings Limited	£8,524,987	Shaunaks Holdings Limited	£8,218,851
Crug Mawr Solar Farm Limited	£8,522,432	Nicolas James Investments Limited	£8,218,310
Ellas No3 Limited	£8,512,000	Newincco 1401 Limited	£8,216,201
Vedbaek Limited	£8,511,267	Winton Primary School	£8,208,834
Bell Finance Limited	£8,507,126	Fluid Transfer International Limited	£8,208,000
Goadsby & Harding (Residential) Limited	£8,505,342	Corintech Limited	£8,206,066
Thorpe Park Operations Limited	£8,501,000	Sandroyd School Trust Limited	£8,194,468
Colston Property Developments LLP	£8,491,966	Torvean Limited	£8,194,355
Delphine Homecare Limited	£8,490,655	Resonance Limited	£8,191,730
Samatt (Group Services) Limited	£8,488,610	Shepperton Properties Limited	£8,190,070
Hoppings Softwood Products PLC	£8,488,000	Claverton Estates Ltd.	£8,188,546
World Snooker Limited	£8,472,727	Milord Homes Limited	£8,187,403
Diverse Abilities Plus Ltd	£8,456,319	GBE Converge Group Ltd	£8,185,861
Bristol Old Vic Theatre School Limited	£8,455,204	Heronbridge Investment Management LLP	£8,185,752
Underdown Investments Limited	£8,450,000	Discus Management Limited	£8,184,165
Buyology Ltd	£8,443,444	Bournemouth Young Men's Christian Association	£8,180,000
PP Capital 3 Limited	£8,436,394	Johnstone Safety International LLP	£8,177,000
Stanley's Biomass Limited	£8,432,459	Advanced Industrial Solutions Limited	£8,176,000
Feilden Clegg Bradley Studios LLP	£8,429,253	Eberspacher Exhaust Technology UK Limited	£8,171,783
White Rose UK Ltd	£8,425,217	Lowman Manufacturing Company Limited	£8,168,000
Tetra Pak CPS Limited	£8,418,000	St Aubyn Estates Ltd	£8,167,751
Somerset Community Foundation	£8,414,880	The Dartmouth-Kingswear Floating Bridge Co Ltd	£8,161,643
Charles Russell Transport UK Limited	£8,414,643	Crowdhill Limited	£8,158,201
Robert Welch Designs Limited	£8,409,652	Corin USA Limited	£8,152,339
Harper's Home Mix Limited	£8,396,240	Unicorn Training Group Limited	£8,149,287
Steiner Academy Frome	£8,393,711	Mildren Construction Limited	£8,148,475
Dorchester Middle School	£8,387,841	Thirsty Work Limited	£8,144,996
Caplon Limited	£8,385,426	Ridgevale Estates Limited	£8,142,708
Goadsby & Harding (Holdings) Limited	£8,384,825	Bristol and South Gloucestershire UTC	£8,142,054
Michael H Keene & Son Limited	£8,383,745	Duke Street Capital Oasis Orthodontics Limited	£8,138,000
South West Land Limited	£8,383,325	Balimark Limited	£8,136,586
Whitstone School Academy Trust	£8,378,016	Anana Limited	£8,131,263
Wessex Archaeology Limited	£8,375,275	Link Academy Trust	£8,128,982
Eastwood Park Limited	£8,373,105	Durable (UK) Limited	£8,127,359
Practical Developments (South West) Limited	£8,368,758	Yarlington Homes Limited	£8,127,000
Hestercombe Gardens Trust	£8,361,365	Withers Fruit Farm Limited	£8,124,414
DNO Consulting Limited	£8,356,549	Rowcroft House Foundation Limited	£8,119,172
Power Electrics Generators Limited	£8,349,239	BFF Nonwovens Limited	£8,116,157
W.C. Rowe (Falmouth) Limited	£8,344,331	P.O.C. Contractors Limited	£8,108,525
M.J. Abbott Limited	£8,343,333	W.G. Gould & Sons Limited	£8,108,366
Leoni Temco Limited	£8,339,000	Valeport (Holdings) Limited	£8,100,709
Horsebridge Network Systems Limited	£8,338,741	Bridge Road Limited	£8,088,658
Antonville Investments Limited	£8,338,352	Dale's Central Motors Limited	£8,085,287
Premiere Health Limited	£8,332,843	Watts Truck & Van Limited	£8,085,000
Lovewell Blake LLP	£8,332,000	Averys of Bristol Limited	£8,080,984
Ford Civil Engineering Limited	£8,330,520	West Country Park Home Estates Ltd	£8,080,901
Neptune Retail Limited	£8,327,293	C J L Rogers Properties Ltd.	£8,079,746
Stein's Trading Limited	£8,322,000	BNM Parkstone LLP	£8,075,468
PCP 2014 Limited	£8,317,974	AMCG Enterprise Limited	£8,072,126
Westcountry Garden Centres Limited	£8,314,107	Clean Earth Energy Investments Limited	£8,062,705
Manor Vets Limited	£8,306,697	GWP Group Limited	£8,054,789
St. Francis Limited	£8,305,746	Rowes Garage Limited	£8,053,875
Kimberly Audrey Limited	£8,302,887	SCA Group Limited	£8,052,173
Patalex II Productions Limited	£8,297,000	Devon Community Foundation	£8,051,837
George Estates Limited	£8,296,970	Raw Investments Limited	£8,049,217
The Plastic Surgeon Holdings Limited	£8,295,835	Sherborne Area Schools' Trust	£8,048,976
C & C Motor Caravans Ltd	£8,291,473	Gilo Industries Group Limited	£8,047,341
Ablebox Limited	£8,288,208	Yellow Bridge Investments Limited	£8,047,336
Shenton Global Limited	£8,281,563	Agincare Group Limited	£8,043,590

Crediton Milling Company Limited	£8,043,342
Feniton Park Limited	£8,039,458
C.W. Nash (Farms) Limited	£8,032,716
Westbury Care Limited	£8,029,819
P & B Weir Electrical Limited	£8,029,237
Good Energy Gas Limited	£8,025,697
RW Greenside Place Limited	£8,025,000
Edward Elgar Publishing Limited	£8,016,732
Sutton Harbour Projects Limited	£8,011,000
Bishop Fleming LLP	£8,001,925
PSW (Holdings) Ltd	£7,997,612
Persey Properties Partnership LLP	£7,995,578
Vee Bee Filtration UK Limited	£7,975,164
Mantracourt Electronics Limited	£7,961,372
Mawgan Porth Holiday Park Limited	£7,954,966
PP Capital 2 Ltd	£7,953,855
Cirrus Communication Systems Limited	£7,953,356
Specialist Journeys Midco 2 Limited	£7,952,133
D.B. Systems Holdings Limited	£7,952,121
Cotham Gardens Primary School Ltd	£7,944,998
Global Machine Tools (UK) Ltd	£7,944,084
Ultimate Trade Finance Limited	£7,939,000
Timehaste Limited	£7,936,537
The Masters Golf Company Limited	£7,936,329
Woodley Hotels Limited	£7,935,222
Hoburne Development Company Limited	£7,927,636
Romfield Holdings Limited	£7,926,266
Tyco Electronics Motors Ltd	£7,926,192
Reed Construction & Developments Limited	£7,925,169
B.J. Barkwell & Sons Limited	£7,921,203
Bank of Ireland Home Mortgages Limited	£7,915,075
Exeter Science Park Limited	£7,915,006
Second Applemead Limited	£7,911,541
Westfield Medical Limited	£7,909,000
Aceo Limited	£7,907,415
RTP-UK Ltd	£7,906,934
Castelan Limited	£7,904,818
Castelan Group Limited	£7,904,815
Barton Cold-Form (UK) Limited	£7,887,020
L. & F. Jones Holdings Limited	£7,885,261
221 Limited	£7,884,188
St Moritz (Holdings) Limited	£7,882,456
Western Forestry Company Limited	£7,882,140
Highfield Garden Centres Limited	£7,882,135
Unique Home Stays Limited	£7,881,167
Killiow Estates Limited	£7,877,629
M & G Properties (Cheltenham) Limited	£7,874,522
Prodigio Limited	£7,870,875
MAMG Infrastructure Management Limited	£7,869,401
A. Hammond & Sons Limited	£7,866,497
Somerset Bridge Ltd	£7,864,000
English Heritage Trading Limited	£7,854,000
Barmont Properties Limited	£7,851,987
Rookwood School Trust Limited	£7,845,935
Bighead Fasteners Limited	£7,842,399
Algreta Solutions Limited	£7,842,000
The Royal Air Force Charitable Trust Enterprises	£7,841,175
Latimer,Trend & Company Limited	£7,837,316
Grenadier Emperor Limited	£7,834,691
Stevens Family Property Limited	£7,833,461
Eagle One Homes Limited	£7,830,201
Bryan Brothers Holdings Limited	£7,825,842
David Foot Limited	£7,822,172
First Capital Finance Limited	£7,820,607
Hochtief PPP Solutions (UK) Limited	£7,813,000
South West Laundry Ltd	£7,811,196
Five Rivers Child Care Limited	£7,810,676
Salisbury Diocesan Board of Education (The)	£7,806,628
Taw Garages Limited	£7,804,420
Emerald Debtco Limited	£7,799,000
Whitecroft Developments Limited	£7,796,157
The Minerva Learning Trust (Dorset)	£7,794,140
Denvern Limited	£7,793,657
Wilson Investment Holdings Limited	£7,789,558
Torcare (Holdings) Limited	£7,787,163
Watts Aviation Services Limited	£7,784,723
Forest Press Hydraulics Limited	£7,779,434
Cowgrove Limited	£7,778,574
Devon Wildlife Trust	£7,772,749
Sharpness Dock Limited	£7,767,000
James Hay Administration Company Limited	£7,763,000
Georgian House (Torquay) Limited	£7,758,678
Refresh Living No. 1 Ltd	£7,758,257
Manton Riches Holdings Limited	£7,749,255
Parking Glasgow Limited	£7,749,000
Seadown Holiday Park Limited	£7,745,510
Flowbird Smart City UK Limited	£7,744,000
Jackson Developments Limited	£7,743,795
Way Group Limited	£7,736,350
London Aquarium (South Bank) Limited	£7,734,000
Montacute School	£7,733,363
Polamco Limited	£7,732,796
Civitas SPV20 Limited	£7,721,756
Neon (Holdings) Limited	£7,721,137
Shelburne Farming LLP	£7,720,653
Grist Environmental Limited	£7,717,225
Green and Fortune Holdings Limited	£7,715,889
IMI Webber Limited	£7,709,000
Senate Court (Southgate) Limited	£7,700,045
Harrow Hill Properties Limited	£7,695,213
Eagle One Village Shopping Limited	£7,689,039
Towerview West Sussex Limited	£7,684,724
Centrax Industries Limited	£7,678,511
Lily-Flame Ltd	£7,678,038
Irongate Limited	£7,677,256
Houzz UK Ltd.	£7,676,808
Powis Hotels Limited	£7,674,340
Simply Pleasure Limited	£7,669,731
Field International Holdings (Dorset) Limited	£7,667,432
Lymington Investments Limited	£7,666,361
Landmark International Holdings Limited	£7,665,930
EPTA Cold Service Ltd	£7,664,768
Darthaven Marina Limited	£7,663,854
GP & J Baker Limited	£7,659,667
Colten Developments Limited	£7,647,842
Jasun Envirocare PLC	£7,645,467
International Dance Supplies Limited	£7,644,580
Dilkes Energy Limited	£7,639,619
Endsleigh Insurances (Brokers) Limited	£7,636,171
Audience Systems Limited	£7,635,707
WHC Hire Services Ltd.	£7,634,838
Western Global Limited	£7,630,964
WJ South West Limited	£7,623,295
Thakeham Mushrooms Limited	£7,622,000
Kammbronn Homes Limited	£7,618,186
Raventree Limited	£7,614,655
Ashfield Land (Cardiff) Limited	£7,614,370
Longmayne Limited	£7,613,345
Kaikoura Investments Limited	£7,612,020
Kenneth Spencer Limited	£7,611,697
Jamie's Farm	£7,611,559
Steelinvest Limited	£7,610,154
Hometower Consultancy Limited	£7,608,218
R.J. Bateman (Engineering) Limited	£7,607,128
Pavey Group Holdings (UK) Limited	£7,605,299
Suttons Consumer Products Limited	£7,603,997
Norland College Limited	£7,602,431
Northam Farm Caravan Sales Limited	£7,597,131
Waypoints Care (Plymouth) Limited	£7,596,531
J & K Aquatics Limited	£7,592,270
Fleetwheel Limited	£7,589,965
Supergroup Concessions Limited	£7,589,000
SRT Marine System Solutions Limited	£7,582,304
Cotswold Collections Group Limited	£7,581,193

Nectar Imports Limited	£7,579,812	Connexion Technologies Limited	£7,412,000
Spire House Developments Limited	£7,576,004	Greendale Investments Ltd	£7,411,000
Lister Shearing Equipment Limited	£7,575,762	Dextra Services Limited	£7,410,768
Golden Hill Solar Limited	£7,573,840	EMS Acquisition Company Limited	£7,409,262
Executive Jet Support Limited	£7,569,254	New Docs Limited	£7,408,154
Teagle Machinery Limited	£7,563,774	Thomas Keble School	£7,408,145
B.G. Automotive Limited	£7,562,844	Gazelle Properties Limited	£7,405,999
Severn Valley Woodworks Limited	£7,562,256	Cottleston Holdings Limited	£7,397,546
Canynge Bicknell (Street) Limited	£7,560,978	Avon Wildlife Trust	£7,395,381
Empty Billy Limited	£7,558,060	Blue Port Holdings Limited	£7,394,391
PPSTS Limited	£7,553,662	Salisbury Glass Holdings Limited	£7,391,990
Techumbre Limited	£7,552,771	Bristol Polytechnic Enterprises (Developments) Limited	£7,391,000
H. Days Holdings Limited	£7,552,027	A.E.T. Transport Services Limited	£7,390,996
BDP Imports Limited	£7,542,191	Dutypoint Limited	£7,390,584
Terry Adams Residential LLP	£7,538,456	Guarantee Holdings Limited	£7,387,347
County Confectionery Limited	£7,537,566	The Old Sorting Office (Bournemouth) Limited	£7,382,827
Nicolas James Limited	£7,537,501	New Abbey Developments LLP	£7,382,342
Silverfish UK (Holdings) Limited	£7,537,500	Brickjet Limited	£7,381,916
TxtNation Holdings Limited	£7,530,723	Viridor Polymer Recycling Limited	£7,380,000
CTU General Partner Limited	£7,530,207	Watch Guru Limited	£7,378,047
Caerus Capital Group Limited	£7,528,000	ABS Wholesale Limited	£7,364,238
Coombe Castle International Limited	£7,527,533	Alder King LLP	£7,362,631
The Blue Kite Academy Trust	£7,525,641	Bell & Ross Limited	£7,356,583
Unity Tyre Company Limited	£7,525,277	RCR Flooring Products Limited	£7,352,899
Kellands (Plant Sales) Limited	£7,524,856	Prosafe Offshore Limited	£7,352,000
Devonshire Pine Limited	£7,521,873	Furlong Flooring (Wales) Ltd.	£7,350,085
Sesanti Limited	£7,519,566	Devon & Cornwall Autistic Community Trust	£7,347,498
Fernturn Holdings Limited	£7,519,000	Harmon (Form Tools) Limited	£7,346,466
Petrarch Holdings Limited	£7,515,860	M J Church Properties Limited	£7,335,589
Highdrive Property Co. Limited	£7,515,741	IIC (Leeds Schools) Fund Investment Limited	£7,329,166
Ecosurety Limited	£7,514,628	CGA Financial & Investment Services Limited	£7,319,877
Aaron Services Limited	£7,514,251	The Arthouse Glasgow Limited	£7,316,429
ACE Schools Multi Academy Trust	£7,509,972	London Eye Holdings Limited	£7,315,000
Bapton Manor Farm Limited	£7,508,354	Class 06 Limited	£7,311,075
St Stephens House Ltd	£7,503,829	Iota Properties Limited	£7,302,782
R & M Utility & Civil Engineering Services South West	£7,500,085	Cloudpay Holdings Limited	£7,296,000
Matquel Property Co. Limited	£7,498,309	LLK Property Limited	£7,294,345
Supported Independence Limited	£7,495,082	CELCSE Limited	£7,290,403
Urbina Private Equity No.3 Ltd	£7,494,346	Investors in the Community (Leeds Schools) Subdebt	£7,288,840
Tecalemit Garage Equipment Company Limited	£7,494,157	Ron Darch & Sons Co Ltd	£7,288,025
Peter Harding Practice Limited	£7,491,119	Chris Sterling Enterprises Limited	£7,279,618
F.G.Brewer & Sons (Farms) Limited	£7,488,899	Medland, Sanders and Twose Limited	£7,274,000
Leo Textiles Limited	£7,488,559	Julian & Son,Limited	£7,264,262
Ohashi Technica UK, Ltd.	£7,487,631	Complete Price Eyewear Limited	£7,258,841
County Garage (Barnstaple) Limited	£7,486,826	Swan Hotel Wells (2007) Limited	£7,256,941
Willett & Son Holdings Limited	£7,484,688	St. Luke's Hospice Plymouth	£7,250,688
Muscliff Primary School	£7,483,139	Harbour Hospitality Group Limited	£7,249,119
Den Dental Group Practice LLP	£7,482,000	Oastcrest Limited	£7,248,506
Marsh Holdings Limited	£7,481,562	Kiwa Limited	£7,247,993
Wallaby Grip Limited	£7,480,000	Winchcombe School	£7,247,000
Sideshow Ltd	£7,477,070	Walsall Lift Accommodation Services Limited	£7,245,000
Boyland and Son Limited	£7,470,753	Lightwater Valley Attractions Limited	£7,243,403
Aquamain (UK) Limited	£7,470,000	REPI Limited	£7,237,326
Loumin Estates Limited	£7,469,126	Renewable Energy Partnerships Limited	£7,235,826
St Christopher's C of E (Primary) Multi Academy Trust	£7,464,862	TJ International Limited	£7,234,084
M.E. Wynn & Co. Limited	£7,462,116	Autograph Homes (Hambrook) Limited	£7,229,776
Mi-Pac Newco Limited	£7,461,497	Ipipeline (TCP) Limited	£7,229,000
UCAS Media Limited	£7,458,000	Roco Investments Limited	£7,228,087
Hercules Site Services Limited	£7,457,529	Lansdown Properties (Cheltenham) Limited	£7,226,196
Alan Kerr Limited	£7,456,224	Langdon (Dorset) Farms	£7,223,476
Avalon Plastics Limited	£7,445,487	Verdo Renewables Ltd	£7,222,578
County of Gloucestershire Community Foundation	£7,433,425	Hale & Co. (Drybrook) Ltd	£7,220,481
International Education Systems Limited	£7,427,980	Fig Tree Court Limited	£7,219,767
Viridor Credits Environmental Company	£7,426,146	Strong Energy Solutions Limited	£7,210,598
S.J.Phillips & Sons (Kemble) Limited	£7,424,795	Paramount 21 Limited	£7,208,866
Wyvern Holdings Limited	£7,424,156	Erin Properties (Swindon) Limited	£7,201,419
Kitagawa Europe Limited	£7,422,513	Flatcable Limited	£7,199,720
Wyvern Cargo Ltd	£7,421,854	Bristol Care Homes Limited	£7,194,686
Tonic Construction Limited	£7,417,332	C F R Group Services Limited	£7,194,280
The Swanage Railway Trust	£7,416,523	Tricuro Support Ltd	£7,191,972
Arada Limited	£7,412,570	Brookside Community Primary School Academy Trust	£7,182,846
Terramond Limited	£7,412,053	Lee Abbey International Students' Club	£7,181,825

Company	Amount
Thermae Development Company Limited	£7,181,819
Warm Welcome Management Limited	£7,170,931
XJ6 Schools Holdings Limited	£7,168,010
Neptune Shipping Agency Limited	£7,165,542
Isles of Scilly Shipping Company Limited	£7,163,538
The King's School, Gloucester	£7,162,695
Amport and District Coaches Limited	£7,162,259
Hughes Hotels Limited	£7,161,794
R G Morcom Investments Limited	£7,157,848
Standard Brands (UK) Limited	£7,157,297
Phoenix Child Care Limited	£7,155,484
Garrad Hassan Group Limited	£7,154,469
Dartington Crystal (Torrington) Limited	£7,149,931
Cloverstand Limited	£7,139,730
Stonewood Properties Limited	£7,138,545
Van Courtlandt Holdings Limited	£7,138,516
European Friction Industries Limited	£7,137,328
Coln Signature Homes Limited	£7,136,777
Western Counties Roofing Limited	£7,135,879
WCR Holdings 2014 Limited	£7,135,879
Rush Group Limited	£7,134,014
Henry Ling Limited	£7,124,149
Grange Mill Investments Limited	£7,119,316
Imperial Civil Enforcement Solutions Limited	£7,119,049
Sarkis Limited	£7,115,091
R.R. Transport Limited	£7,110,555
Templegate Electrical Supplies Limited	£7,110,244
Allen Trump Holdings Limited	£7,107,906
Redwood Global Limited	£7,104,333
Simplex-Turbulo Group Limited	£7,100,537
Quay Developments (Southern) Limited	£7,092,843
Imperial Business Systems Limited	£7,085,950
Havenstone Property Limited	£7,084,137
Anglo-American Vulcanized Fibre Limited	£7,081,922
Pattersons (Bristol) Limited	£7,080,683
David Hathaway Properties Limited	£7,072,870
Sovereign Care Limited	£7,071,305
Gingerbread (Holdings) Limited	£7,069,416
Dumpton School	£7,066,961
The Pluss Organisation CIC	£7,062,000
Bath Taxis Limited	£7,061,865
Kruger Property Company Limited	£7,061,146
Alderley Systems Ltd	£7,059,602
Brean Down Caravan Park Limited	£7,058,987
Glanville Cleansing Limited	£7,057,802
AT Property Holdings Limited	£7,055,000
Ashri Limited	£7,051,478
Devon Doctors Limited	£7,045,574
Pharmaxo Pharmacy Services Limited	£7,044,014
Little Bear Solar Limited	£7,043,410
Bath Demolition Limited	£7,043,166
Synergy Health Systems Limited	£7,042,000
Westford Trade Services (UK) Ltd	£7,040,092
Avalon Sciences Limited	£7,039,238
Delphic Holdings Limited.	£7,036,562
Alchemist Ventures Limited	£7,032,887
Aish Technologies Limited	£7,032,000
Claremont Ferrand Limited	£7,031,964
Quantum Christchurch Care LLP	£7,031,882
St.James's Place (PCP) Limited	£7,023,437
Urban Creation (Charlotte Street) Ltd	£7,022,748
J Cossins & Sons Limited	£7,014,981
Monkey World Limited	£7,012,975
Oval Estates (St Peter's) Limited	£7,012,298
Huck Nets (U.K.) Limited	£7,009,775
Ashwoods Electric Motors Limited	£7,008,401
Cape Homes Limited	£7,007,866
Newquay View Resort Limited	£7,007,158
Computershare Services Limited	£7,005,000
Bowldown Farms Limited	£7,003,881
Park Garden Centre Limited	£7,001,000
Civitas SPV39 Limited	£6,999,726
Acoura Holdings Limited	£6,991,019
Henry Oliver Ltd	£6,986,526
AES Horizons Investments Limited	£6,986,000
Farley & Thompson LLP	£6,985,846
Sumac Precision Engineering Limited	£6,978,567
Hamilton Scott Estates Limited	£6,976,319
USAF Management 14 Limited	£6,967,370
Britannia Windows (UK) Limited	£6,964,144
Thrubwell Properties Limited	£6,959,070
Rockstone Surfacing Limited	£6,957,038
A.J. Brunt Limited	£6,956,778
Phoenix Learning and Care Limited	£6,955,372
Excalibur Unified Communications Limited	£6,955,241
Burrington Estates (Trispen) Limited	£6,952,709
3P Learning Limited	£6,952,639
Grensue Ltd	£6,950,378
West Town Lane Academy	£6,947,668
Bluewater Property Limited	£6,945,591
Omicways Limited	£6,943,220
Pattemore's Transport (Crewkerne) Limited	£6,942,074
S.C.C. Transport (Devizes) Limited	£6,938,352
Ansford Academy Trust	£6,937,686
Berrys Holdings Limited	£6,936,088
The Boston Tea Party Group Limited	£6,931,108
MPL Holdings (SW) Limited	£6,930,021
AES Barry Limited	£6,929,000
Redruth Facilities Limited	£6,929,000
Organic Foods, Drinks & Investments Holdings Ltd	£6,926,618
River Marketing (Holdings) Limited	£6,925,543
The Royal Institution of Cornwall	£6,924,000
Sir William Romney's School	£6,918,809
Newport Park Limited	£6,918,732
Hy. Duke & Son Limited	£6,916,900
Richpur Limited	£6,914,684
Cornwall Trust for Nature Conservation Ltd (The)	£6,914,573
MC Property Ventures Limited	£6,908,724
B4 Claims Limited	£6,905,674
Renelec Chalgrove Limited	£6,898,097
R.J. & K.D. McLean Limited	£6,896,927
Aspect Digital Media Limited	£6,895,756
Malaby Holdings Limited	£6,894,717
Westbury Park School	£6,889,889
Knights Brown Ltd	£6,888,000
West End Motors (Bodmin) Limited	£6,886,524
SAS (Dorset & Somerset) Limited	£6,881,720
St. Piran's School (GB) Limited	£6,880,148
New Earth Solutions (Kent) Limited	£6,879,931
Gloucestershire Warwickshire Steam Railway PLC	£6,876,856
Swoop Travel Limited	£6,865,315
Albert Goodman LLP	£6,863,859
Leckhampton Estates (Ullenwood) Limited	£6,863,092
Harrison Products Co Limited	£6,859,706
Burford Beta Limited	£6,859,000
Europa Equity Limited	£6,857,178
Isles of Scilly Skybus Limited	£6,857,060
Orproperty Limited	£6,856,791
Central Garages (Torbay) Limited	£6,855,736
Charminster Farm Limited	£6,855,088
Hawksworth Securities PLC	£6,844,338
H2H Pharmacy Limited	£6,842,044
Suttons Seeds Limited	£6,840,303
Arena Farnborough Limited	£6,835,886
Services Support (Avon & Somerset) Holdings Limited	£6,830,000
Royal Osteoporosis Society	£6,825,860
Wallace & Gromit's Children's Foundation	£6,825,755
F.G.Jeanes & Son Limited	£6,816,713
599 Developments Ltd	£6,813,874
Crowndell Consulting Limited	£6,810,640
Budock Vean Hotel Limited	£6,808,451
Willmott's Transport Limited	£6,807,883
Infusion GB Limited	£6,805,586
Collacombe Farm Limited	£6,804,362

Company	Value
Hydro International (Wastewater) Limited	£6,799,552
Wastenage Farms Limited	£6,799,525
Paull & Company Limited	£6,799,348
Phoenix Engineering Company Limited	£6,799,093
Weston Hospicecare Limited	£6,797,290
Premier Underwriting Limited	£6,795,548
Skyline Systems Limited	£6,795,170
EVGH Limited	£6,793,154
Stowford Mill Development Limited	£6,792,038
American Amusements Holdings Limited	£6,788,434
John Reid & Sons (Strucsteel) Limited	£6,786,778
DMT Property Services Ltd	£6,786,694
Arcade Leasing Limited	£6,782,765
South Essex PPP Health Services Limited	£6,773,428
Hinton Garage (Bath) Limited	£6,769,380
Bellwind-Edis Limited	£6,768,728
Clarity Copiers Limited	£6,765,832
Airport Business Centre Limited	£6,764,996
Barnwood Shopfitting Limited	£6,762,696
C.F. Roberts (Electrical Contractors) PLC	£6,761,839
Fish Brothers Property Investment LLP	£6,760,822
Luxurycare (Regency Manor Care Home) Limited	£6,760,324
Aqua Tamarisk LLP	£6,750,162
YPI Limited	£6,744,117
Daktronics UK Limited	£6,739,876
Richard Read Holdings Limited	£6,739,597
Swattons Limited	£6,736,723
Shepperton Builders Limited	£6,735,983
Sentry Self Storage Limited	£6,734,935
QDOS Homes Limited	£6,732,820
Weird Fish Limited	£6,730,041
Clifton High School	£6,729,000
Vysiion Limited	£6,728,382
Specialised Management Services Limited	£6,726,077
Tepe Oral Hygiene Products Limited	£6,724,063
AUL Underwriting Agency Ltd	£6,718,329
De Vere Farms Limited	£6,717,430
Dagenham Wind Park Limited	£6,713,949
The Academy for Character and Excellence	£6,706,719
Mortgage Intelligence Limited	£6,705,000
Positive Group (UK) Limited	£6,701,559
Alderley Farms Limited	£6,695,906
The Royal Bath & West of England Society	£6,695,000
Agincare UK Limited	£6,692,481
Providor Limited	£6,690,063
Merston Renewable Energy CIC	£6,689,353
Tran-AM Limited	£6,686,216
F G Pryor and Son Limited	£6,685,237
Orchardleigh Park Ltd	£6,683,008
777 Hotels Limited	£6,681,991
Pingry Solar Ltd	£6,677,521
B M Foods Limited	£6,668,833
The Ralph & Irma Sperring Charity	£6,668,578
Maximise IT Solutions Limited	£6,665,847
IESIS (Redcliff Street) Limited	£6,660,939
Thrive Renewables (Eye) Limited	£6,658,931
S. Notaro Holdings Limited	£6,658,489
Duffields (South West) Limited	£6,654,000
New Earth Solutions (Canford) Limited	£6,653,374
Jennings Industries Limited	£6,652,786
PMMR Developments Limited	£6,650,977
Torr Home	£6,649,900
Tudor Rose International Ltd	£6,649,178
Tickenham Court Farm Co.Limited	£6,647,837
The Andrew Brownsword Arts Foundation	£6,646,073
Firstport HMF Limited	£6,644,794
Cronite Castings (Distribution) Limited	£6,642,362
Lang & Potter (Holdings) Limited	£6,640,451
Sandpalm Properties Limited	£6,640,136
Higher Education Statistics Agency Limited	£6,636,780
Hatton Properties Limited	£6,636,653
F.J. Snook & Sons Limited	£6,635,359
Pastaking (UK) Limited	£6,634,283
Pennyfarthing Construction Limited	£6,633,749
Kliklok International Limited	£6,630,000
Milspeed Limited	£6,628,308
Aghoco 1256 Limited	£6,626,182
Tolchards Limited	£6,623,436
Field International Limited	£6,621,076
Air Control Industries Limited	£6,610,598
Ward Edward Limited	£6,610,201
Warners Trust PLC	£6,609,732
Devonfields Limited	£6,609,481
The Museum of East Asian Art	£6,609,164
Rowcliffe Holdings Limited	£6,607,121
M. & N. Electrical and Mechanical Services Limited	£6,605,199
D4E Mulberry Limited	£6,602,000
Call Caterlink Ltd	£6,600,534
Spenco Engineering Co. Limited	£6,598,942
The Herpetological Conservation Trust	£6,595,143
Sharpham Trust (The)	£6,594,993
Oakfield Investments Ltd	£6,589,539
Riohurst Investments Limited	£6,587,621
Scorribanda Holdings Limited	£6,586,020
Lester Brunt Wealth Management Ltd	£6,585,466
Farina Investments (UK) Limited	£6,585,385
Dexeco Limited	£6,578,201
Renelec Groundworks Limited	£6,575,797
Beat The Street (UK) Limited	£6,574,807
KS SPV 9 Limited	£6,574,209
Town Mills Craft Centre Limited	£6,569,630
Gilltown Limited	£6,566,770
IDS Transport (UK) Limited	£6,562,185
Wood Energy Limited	£6,559,130
Puckator Limited	£6,551,041
B R Hodgson Group Limited	£6,549,504
Stonebridge Associated Colleges Limited	£6,543,534
PWG Trading Limited	£6,536,894
PDQ Airspares Limited	£6,534,375
Temple Guiting Manor Limited	£6,525,554
Hautot Developments Limited	£6,524,577
Medipak Limited	£6,519,862
K & T Heating Services Limited	£6,519,147
Nylaplas Engineering Limited	£6,518,272
West Hants Lawn Tennis Company (Bournemouth) Ltd	£6,512,546
Sanlam Wealth Planning UK Limited	£6,512,490
Ultraparts Limited	£6,511,711
Calendula Assets Limited	£6,505,855
Robertson Developments Holdings Limited	£6,501,220
Giftworks Limited	£6,495,233
Harris & Harris Construction Limited	£6,494,523
Arnolfini Gallery Limited	£6,488,791
A & A Trading (U.K.) Limited	£6,488,322
Galion (Project Two) Limited	£6,488,253
Riders of Bridgwater Ltd.	£6,486,835
Plumlocations Limited	£6,484,970
Woodlands Group of Churches	£6,484,598
Torbay Cemetery and Crematorium Limited	£6,482,466
Burcombe Haulage Limited	£6,479,461
SF Ltd	£6,477,788
Appello Limited	£6,475,939
X.T.Holdings Limited	£6,475,908
MSA (Britain) Limited	£6,471,318
The White Horse Care Trust	£6,469,740
Camelot Developments Limited	£6,468,276
Nucleus Developments Limited	£6,468,026
Barton Farms Limited (The)	£6,467,231
Trelleborg Wheel Systems UK Limited	£6,467,000
SW Construction (Residential) Limited	£6,462,300
Avsan Holdings Limited	£6,457,263
R W Estates Ltd	£6,455,231
Wellesbourne Property Management Limited	£6,446,860
Pinetops Nurseries Limited	£6,442,959
MRT Castings Limited	£6,442,548

Company	Value
Wrings Transport Limited	£6,441,636
Charterbank Capital Limited	£6,440,767
The Grange (Chertsey) 2002 Ltd.	£6,434,385
Sundeala Limited	£6,432,961
Bessant Properties Limited	£6,431,456
CSE Bournemouth Limited	£6,431,000
Castle Court School Educational Trust Limited	£6,429,943
James Hay Partnership Management Limited	£6,428,000
The Linwood Fabric Company Limited	£6,425,398
Benridge Investments Limited	£6,424,362
Another Place Limited	£6,418,230
Roundhill Estate Limited	£6,418,159
West Country Business Systems (Holdings) Limited	£6,417,866
St Michael's Falmouth Limited	£6,416,730
Farmington Natural Stone Limited	£6,414,471
Hayne Securities Limited	£6,406,536
St. Moritz Developments Limited	£6,403,531
Budock Vean Holdings Limited	£6,403,279
Poeton Industries Limited	£6,398,265
East Devon Properties Limited	£6,398,234
Design Scaffolding (Bristol) Limited	£6,397,271
Devon & Exeter Spastics Society	£6,397,031
Ironburg Inventions Limited	£6,394,329
Kings Harbour Hotel Limited	£6,393,881
Paligap Limited	£6,389,840
Progressive Systems Limited	£6,387,617
Primeco Limited	£6,380,785
PMG Services (Bristol) Limited	£6,380,009
Cox & Robinson (Agricultural) Limited	£6,377,000
Beeley (Holdings) Limited	£6,376,653
Truflo Air Movement Limited	£6,376,000
Goodshelter Property (Surbiton) Limited	£6,375,866
Wildbrook Investments (Industrial) Limited	£6,372,407
Resolution Interiors Limited	£6,370,702
Newberry International Produce Ltd	£6,370,032
UK Pacific Hampton Station LLP	£6,368,693
Mark Farwell Plant Hire Limited	£6,364,596
An Daras Multi Academy Trust	£6,359,316
Stroud Metal Company Limited	£6,358,427
Pole Farming Limited	£6,358,132
Newham Transformation Partnership Limited	£6,353,977
Codestone Group Ltd.	£6,352,489
Avon Engineered Rubber Limited	£6,351,335
B.T.C. Activewear Holdings Limited	£6,346,117
Fleet Caravans Limited	£6,342,113
Mistral Holdings Limited	£6,339,096
Leafield Logistics & Technical Services Limited	£6,339,000
Llawnroc Hotel Limited	£6,336,976
Vauxhall Estates Limited	£6,325,102
Honeywell Global Tracking Limited	£6,324,465
3AB Care Limited	£6,324,070
Cameron Fuller Limited	£6,322,782
D.I.S. Limited	£6,320,973
Deeley Freed Developments Limited	£6,317,758
Foursquare Associates Limited	£6,317,447
Merriott Plastics Limited	£6,315,147
Tozers LLP	£6,310,897
Beard Group Ltd.(The)	£6,306,230
Applied Market Information Limited	£6,306,148
Inter-Line (South West) Limited.	£6,303,513
Seetru Limited	£6,303,000
Millfields Community Economic Development Trust CIC	£6,300,733
T.D. Williamson (U.K.) Limited	£6,300,173
TNT Fireworks U.K. Limited	£6,300,132
Trelleborg Rochdale Limited	£6,293,000
T.H.Brickell & Son,Limited	£6,291,928
Catering 328 Limited	£6,287,682
Ipex Capital GP LLP	£6,285,030
Meltor Developments Limited	£6,284,982
Nu-Pro Limited	£6,283,000
South West Metal Finishing Limited	£6,282,277
C R Down Farming Limited	£6,282,042

Company	Value
Chaplins Properties Limited	£6,280,572
PB Design and Developments Limited	£6,280,481
Bridge Motorcycles Limited	£6,279,382
Southtown Investment Company Limited	£6,279,382
Moor Park House Limited	£6,278,569
Tekne Holdings Limited	£6,278,470
Bridges (Electrical Engineers) Limited	£6,277,720
S'Porter International Limited	£6,276,155
Orchard Gate Ltd	£6,275,556
Devondale Electrical Distributors Limited	£6,273,861
Milewood Healthcare Ltd	£6,270,142
Crescent Motorcycle Company Limited	£6,270,015
Manual Investing Limited	£6,266,258
HSH Motor Company Limited	£6,261,351
West Cornwall Pasty Co. Limited	£6,260,000
Flowlinks Overseas Limited	£6,259,813
Greenland Stud Farm Holdings Ltd	£6,256,340
World Group Holdings Limited	£6,256,319
Austral-Asia World LLC UK Limited	£6,256,311
Cannon Care Homes 4 Limited	£6,251,770
Fairfield Farm Trust	£6,250,659
Litt Holdings Limited	£6,249,482
Blakell Europlacer (Intl) Limited	£6,249,360
Guy,Leonard & Co.Limited	£6,247,184
G. Northover & Sons Limited	£6,246,139
V12 Footwear Limited	£6,244,826
Premium Rate Numbers Ltd	£6,244,387
Henry W. Pollard & Sons Limited	£6,244,008
Waterlip Developments Limited	£6,239,397
Castle Nominees Limited	£6,236,511
Atkins Travel Limited	£6,236,457
Club Communications Ltd.	£6,234,938
Clark Projects 12 Limited	£6,232,215
Openwave II UK Limited	£6,232,113
Site Developments (Ferndown) Limited	£6,230,483
Langage Farm Limited Liability Partnership	£6,227,418
Suland Investments Limited	£6,222,252
Beauchamp House Nursing Home Limited	£6,221,000
Hayes School	£6,220,117
Kinlon Limited	£6,219,105
Utax (UK) Limited	£6,218,865
Bell Plant Limited	£6,214,846
Clifton Down Corporate Finance Limited	£6,211,385
Summerfield SD3 Limited	£6,209,780
Cher Varya Commercial Ltd	£6,208,177
Keynvor Morlift Limited	£6,207,511
Venture Multi Academy Trust	£6,203,228
St Margaret's Residences (Exeter) Limited	£6,200,648
South Manchester Healthcare (Holdings) Limited	£6,198,000
North Leaze Farm Limited	£6,197,027
MGV Engineering Limited	£6,195,503
Aster Solar Limited	£6,193,000
Preston Cherry LLP	£6,191,767
Rotable Repairs Limited	£6,187,570
Green-Line Contracts Limited	£6,184,400
Aviation & Defence Spares Limited	£6,184,321
Lanhydrock Golf Club Limited	£6,181,698
Jordans Limited	£6,177,388
Bonds Mill Estate Limited	£6,175,417
Flo Group Ltd	£6,175,179
Selwood Academy	£6,170,685
Athelney Trust PLC	£6,168,766
Oval Estates (Bath) Limited	£6,168,235
Advanced Insulation Contracting Limited	£6,167,700
Castle Motors (Trebrown) Limited	£6,162,725
Radipole Mill Investments Limited	£6,162,169
Amphastar UK Ltd	£6,161,978
T Shirt & Sons Limited	£6,161,429
Geneco Limited	£6,161,000
Secure Systems & Technologies Limited	£6,159,268
Silverfish UK Limited	£6,157,897
J.J. Saunders Limited	£6,150,557

Company	Amount
Hillcrest House Limited	£6,149,306
Sonus Networks Limited	£6,146,850
M Baker (Newquay) Limited	£6,141,287
Tauntfield Ltd	£6,140,088
Kelley Holdings Limited	£6,139,784
Old Quay House Hotel Limited	£6,137,748
Shirley-Young Limited	£6,135,752
Sheila Holdings Limited	£6,134,314
Sanderson Government and Defence Limited	£6,132,000
W B M Groundworks Limited	£6,131,939
Pathfinder Park Homes Limited	£6,129,578
Blue Scorpio Limited	£6,128,384
PSW Trading Limited	£6,123,988
Weird Fish Clothing Limited	£6,122,393
Roots Systems Limited	£6,122,305
Uni-Mill Engineering Limited	£6,122,198
Weblease Limited	£6,118,541
Henry W Pollard & Sons (Group) Limited	£6,115,067
Gordano Support Group Limited	£6,112,999
GWKS Ltd	£6,111,964
A7 Lochhead Limited	£6,111,936
Herbert Silver (Holdings) Limited	£6,110,951
Jasme Limited	£6,106,061
IP-Performance Ltd	£6,104,856
Thompson Acquisitions Limited	£6,103,689
Trelleborg Industrial Tyres UK Limited	£6,103,000
S W Group Logistics Limited	£6,101,738
Camps International Group Limited	£6,101,610
C.H.G. Holdings Limited	£6,101,304
Changvilla Investments Limited	£6,095,599
EMS Satcom UK, Ltd.	£6,095,000
Hemsley Fraser International Limited	£6,093,985
M P Filtri (UK) Limited	£6,093,900
Mylor Yacht Harbour (Holding Company) Limited	£6,091,251
Elm Developments Holdings Limited	£6,090,481
Express Contract Drying Ltd	£6,088,833
Keith Motors (Christchurch) Limited	£6,087,730
Ken Biggs Limited	£6,087,376
UDS Properties Limited	£6,087,000
Graceloft Limited	£6,075,011
Axiom Veterinary Laboratories Limited	£6,073,000
Beaulieu Property Management Limited	£6,071,406
PGI - Protection Group International Ltd.	£6,071,013
B4 Marketing Limited	£6,070,895
Wodskou Properties Limited	£6,069,767
Market Square Limited	£6,064,346
Upper Horns Farm LLP	£6,063,493
Forgeway Ltd	£6,061,899
Park Group South West Limited	£6,054,839
Bentley Slade Limited	£6,054,025
Buccaneer Holdings Limited	£6,052,766
Condor UK Holdings Limited	£6,047,903
OM Holidays Ltd	£6,047,234
Sutton Harbour Car Parks Limited	£6,039,000
Oakfield Grove Properties Limited	£6,038,770
K2 Medical Systems Limited	£6,038,289
Burrington Estates (Clyst St George) Limited	£6,038,199
Oakfield School Academy Trust	£6,035,830
Charter House Planning Limited	£6,032,040
Bruton School for Girls	£6,031,358
Ashwoods Innovations Limited	£6,029,347
NJG Contracting Limited	£6,028,922
L.E.W. Techniques Limited	£6,028,678
Chadwick Holdings Limited	£6,028,619
Black Country PPP Health Services Limited	£6,027,271
Comexposium Cereals Limited	£6,023,833
Furniture World Limited	£6,022,155
Butcombe Brewing Company Limited	£6,020,774
Waypoints Care (Verwood) Limited	£6,010,066
South Coast Building Supplies Ltd.	£6,009,651
Newcross Nursing Group Ltd	£6,008,761
Calleva Limited	£6,008,504

Company	Amount
The Parkway Hotel and Spa Limited	£6,006,972
Urban Creation (Beech House) Ltd	£6,006,355
Precast Concrete Structures Limited	£6,003,245
Bristol Water Core Holdings Limited	£6,000,000
The Thomas Freke and Lady Norton Charity	£5,999,857
Kingsleigh Primary School	£5,999,055
Regency Oldhomes Limited	£5,994,940
Vantage Point Business Park Limited	£5,993,077
Metaltech Precision Ltd	£5,991,747
Unite Accommodation Management 18 Limited	£5,979,442
The Thomas Hardye Multi Academy Trust	£5,975,000
Brickell Holdings Limited	£5,973,144
Bath Recreation Limited	£5,972,136
Longleat Bishopstrow Limited	£5,971,815
Axminster Carpets Limited	£5,970,190
Duresta Upholstery Limited	£5,969,938
Fermac Limited	£5,966,360
Whisstocks Developments Limited	£5,961,799
Lingfield Properties Limited	£5,961,504
Proco-STS Limited	£5,959,359
Regency Properties (Tadworth) Limited	£5,955,296
Harland Developments Limited	£5,953,430
Cornerstone Academy Trust	£5,953,318
Devonshire Homes (Landkey) Limited	£5,952,546
The Advantage Group UK Limited	£5,951,568
John Seymour Transport Limited	£5,946,467
Highlands House Investments Limited	£5,946,320
Hyperbiotics PLC	£5,944,005
Hindhead Investments Limited	£5,943,480
Moorlands College	£5,942,385
Alabare Christian Care Centres	£5,939,864
Tregenna Ventures Limited	£5,938,614
Zurich Community Trust (UK) Limited	£5,937,000
CDS Group Services Limited	£5,935,000
Fundamentals Limited	£5,932,842
Leweston School Trust	£5,932,230
Bill Allen's Autos Limited	£5,926,356
Scotch Corner Richmond LLP	£5,924,102
Cotswold Archaeology Limited	£5,923,945
Four Times Enterprises Limited	£5,921,454
Allum and Sidaway Limited	£5,919,197
Geotechnical Engineering Limited	£5,918,786
M Baker (Holdings) Limited	£5,916,500
Geist Europe Ltd	£5,916,007
Millstream Management Services Limited	£5,915,017
Old Mills Estates Limited	£5,914,486
W.J.Miller & Sons Limited	£5,913,980
Plymstock Properties Limited	£5,911,373
KS SPV 12 Limited	£5,910,093
Newcombe Beard Limited	£5,908,029
KTSL Limited	£5,903,790
SW Construction (No.2) Limited	£5,903,229
Ameriscot Commercial Limited	£5,903,062
Castle Motor Company Limited	£5,901,042
Olo Real Estate Limited	£5,901,021
RRH Limited	£5,900,903
NSD Ltd	£5,900,498
European Society of Endocrinology	£5,899,055
Oak Tree Mobility Limited	£5,894,782
Call To The Bar Ltd	£5,891,260
The Orchard Trust	£5,889,470
Colin Mear Limited	£5,887,864
Heritage & Wise Limited	£5,885,357
Rosemount Investments (Bristol) Limited	£5,884,206
Tetronics (International) Limited	£5,883,885
Hamblys Limited	£5,882,128
RMH (Manor House) Care LLP	£5,882,113
Somerset Wildlife Trust	£5,881,561
Bristol & London PLC	£5,880,188
Civitas SPV36 Limited	£5,880,096
Verplas Limited	£5,878,987
Lomand Homes Limited	£5,875,728

Company	Value
P & L Properties Limited	£5,874,885
Eagle One Mmiii Limited	£5,873,366
Plantlife International Wild Plant Conservation Charity	£5,871,813
Klaw Products Limited	£5,871,286
Premia Group Limited	£5,869,000
Steve Benson Farming Limited	£5,867,249
GMO Cars Limited	£5,866,741
Bituchem Holdings Limited	£5,863,159
Lee Abbey Fellowship	£5,862,314
Springwood Farms Limited	£5,859,683
Coffetek Limited	£5,854,520
Infineon Technologies UK Limited	£5,854,000
Leys Solar Energy C.I.C.	£5,853,451
Playforce Limited	£5,850,470
St Bede's Catholic College	£5,849,202
Chapple & Jenkins Ltd	£5,848,974
F & W Media International Limited	£5,846,463
P. E. Barton (Holdings) Ltd	£5,845,958
Gleneil Limited	£5,844,248
SPM Homes Ltd	£5,841,836
Wabash Technologies Limited	£5,841,482
Clean Earth Wind Turbines Ltd	£5,835,639
Forrestbrown Limited	£5,834,757
EMS Waste Services Limited	£5,832,577
Cabot Design Limited	£5,829,376
Bifold Fluidpower (Holdings) Limited	£5,828,000
Lloyd Brothers (Bristol) Limited	£5,827,426
The Crucial Sauce Company Limited	£5,825,894
JGBM Ltd	£5,822,446
HDM Leisure Limited	£5,819,194
Zynstra Limited	£5,817,710
Harlequin Homes (UK) Limited	£5,811,793
Offshore Marine Management Limited	£5,808,000
Harvey Farms (Winterbourne) Limited	£5,806,994
Stonehouse Investment Company Limited	£5,806,670
Shilston Barton Farming Limited	£5,801,610
Keelex 176 Limited	£5,800,346
R.W.Simon Limited	£5,799,482
MMT Centre Investment Limited	£5,799,000
Burrington Estates Limited	£5,798,758
G.B. Electronics Limited	£5,797,391
Midland House LLP	£5,796,658
Bayview Developments (South) Limited	£5,794,363
Way Fund Managers Limited	£5,794,142
Perseus Property Company Limited (The)	£5,792,774
Marlborough Facilities Limited	£5,792,000
CBSM 2012 Limited	£5,787,468
Natems Sugar Holdings (UK) Ltd	£5,786,252
Juniper Homes (Southville) Limited	£5,785,949
Cloverlait Limited	£5,785,344
Coldharbour Technology Limited	£5,782,647
Pulham & Sons (Coaches) Limited	£5,782,129
Bybrook Agriculture Limited	£5,781,096
John Sheppard Butchers Limited	£5,780,266
ACC Silicones Limited	£5,779,569
Tekne Shopfitting Limited	£5,773,207
Little & Cull Ltd	£5,770,682
Seiche Water Technology Group Ltd	£5,769,608
RMH (Wispers) Care LLP	£5,769,427
Lane's Storage and Removals Limited	£5,768,349
Islington Trowbridge Limited	£5,766,294
Langford Veterinary Services Limited	£5,762,021
A.J. Wooldridge Limited	£5,761,444
Glossbrook Holdings Limited	£5,759,848
Swanage Railway Company Limited	£5,759,381
People 2000 Limited	£5,754,477
Merriott Plastics Group Limited	£5,754,116
Woodcrescent Properties Limited	£5,751,541
A.C.C. Freight Management Limited	£5,750,899
Barrington Brown Estates Limited	£5,749,079
Century Casino Bath Limited	£5,744,219
Cooke Painter Limited	£5,743,004
Norco G R P Limited	£5,741,876
UK Pacific Hampton Limited	£5,741,289
Avonline Network Services Limited	£5,733,736
ME Estates Limited	£5,729,861
Flowervision (Bristol) Limited	£5,729,348
Imaging Equipment Limited	£5,722,250
Foam Techniques Limited	£5,722,015
Flollie Investments Limited	£5,717,506
Ronnies Limited	£5,711,746
Lower Easton Solar C.I.C.	£5,711,072
Creditcall Holdings Limited	£5,708,039
Hunter Stoves Limited	£5,707,865
Burkert UK Limited	£5,704,715
Vertigo Capital Limited	£5,704,030
PA Performance Limited	£5,703,873
BE Properties (Plymouth) Limited	£5,703,257
Abaco Estates Limited	£5,701,964
Hazelwood Motor Company Ltd	£5,699,636
Emotional Rescue Limited	£5,693,341
Everhot Ltd.	£5,693,231
SMV Commercials Limited	£5,689,605
Stanborough (Construction) Limited	£5,687,887
Lambtrad Ltd	£5,687,607
Wessex Products (Leasing) Limited	£5,684,751
Fairlynx Limited	£5,684,308
McGill Warmley Limited	£5,683,284
City Monument Properties Limited	£5,682,146
Cotswold Architectural Products Limited	£5,680,147
Architectural Profiles Limited	£5,677,915
Simonstone Motor Group PLC	£5,677,824
Boo Homes (Leckhampton) Limited	£5,677,605
Arrowedge Limited	£5,676,449
The Inspire Multi Academy Trust (South West)	£5,669,000
Churcham Homes Holdings Limited	£5,666,357
Ellson Homes Limited	£5,664,883
Action Accommodation Ltd	£5,663,358
UKRD Group Limited	£5,659,164
Lombard Corporate Finance (13) Limited	£5,656,000
Proper Tea LLP	£5,652,130
Knorr-Bremse SA Holding Company (UK) Ltd	£5,650,001
Cornwall Community Foundation	£5,645,651
Good Energy Rook Wood Solar Park (057) Limited	£5,644,031
William Hughes Limited	£5,638,889
David Salisbury Joinery Limited	£5,638,699
The Cornish Bakery Shops Limited	£5,637,148
Home Hardware Distribution Limited	£5,632,878
Basic Broadcasting Limited	£5,630,609
Devon Contractors Limited	£5,630,318
Walter C Parson Limited	£5,630,131
Pinder Fashions Limited	£5,627,718
Harris Construction Limited	£5,625,982
Lloyd's Property Southwest Limited	£5,620,796
The Ferne Animal Sanctuary	£5,618,548
Higher Tregarne Solar (UK) Limited	£5,618,409
Maiden Beech Academy Trust	£5,608,047
Sensata Technologies Limited	£5,605,000
Bartlett and Sons Limited	£5,603,820
TTR PT Limited	£5,602,904
Innovata Limited	£5,600,000
Holmshaw Property Holdings Limited	£5,599,574
Realhurry Limited	£5,598,671
Catalent U.K. Swindon Holding II Limited	£5,594,582
Mike Cruickshank Publishing Ltd	£5,592,468
Good Energy Woolbridge Solar Park (010) Limited	£5,592,129
Go Vocational Solutions Ltd	£5,587,786
Liverton Business Park 2011 Limited	£5,587,677
Staverton Electrical Supplies Ltd	£5,584,627
Dike & Son Limited	£5,583,100
La Hacienda Limited	£5,581,022
Davan Caravans Limited	£5,580,965
Stannah Management Services Limited	£5,576,000
B.R. Hodgson (Holdings) Limited	£5,575,506

Company	Amount
Clevedon Hall Estate Limited	£5,573,737
Evershot Construction Limited	£5,571,256
Gill Instruments Limited	£5,567,026
LV Protection Limited	£5,565,734
H.K.C. Europe Limited	£5,565,099
The Woods Group Limited	£5,563,612
M.D. Building Services Limited	£5,563,329
Bushurst Properties Limited	£5,561,916
Royal West of England Academy	£5,561,742
DFH Estates Limited	£5,559,486
Specialist Journeys Midco 1 Limited	£5,557,601
Sturts Community Trust	£5,556,076
Wheeler's (Westbury) Limited	£5,553,771
Rodgers of Plymouth Limited	£5,542,210
131 The Promenade Limited	£5,541,051
A Curious Group of Hotels LLP	£5,540,715
Inty Limited	£5,537,000
Acrefield Land Limited	£5,535,738
Carrs of Exeter Limited	£5,533,000
Silbury Housing Holdings Limited	£5,530,000
Just Go Holidays Limited	£5,526,320
Rollalong Holdings Limited	£5,526,000
Burges Salmon Company Limited	£5,526,000
Thatcher View Development Limited	£5,525,851
Worcester Properties Ltd	£5,525,149
The Animal Healthcare Company Ltd	£5,524,571
Pritchmor Holdings Limited	£5,522,869
Landmark Estates (London) Limited	£5,522,635
Nevis Marketing Limited	£5,522,317
Windward Marine Limited	£5,521,777
Truscotts (Barnstaple) Limited	£5,521,348
Alternative Money Solutions LLP	£5,520,035
Willcox Bros Limited	£5,519,477
Beacon Properties (UK) Ltd	£5,515,674
Pastaking Holdings Limited	£5,515,670
BGS 104 Sedbury Solar Park Limited	£5,508,168
Negatex Limited	£5,507,746
Roland DG (U.K.) Limited	£5,506,891
Tilstone Trade Limited	£5,505,729
KLKI Holdings Limited	£5,505,324
Canefield Ltd	£5,503,918
Flagdawn Limited	£5,501,176
Dycem Limited	£5,498,775
The Gloucestershire Association for Disability	£5,489,576
Edgehill Portfolio No.1 Limited	£5,489,217
Howard Tenens (West London) Limited	£5,481,545
Bendalls Leisure Limited	£5,480,032
Opex Logistics Limited	£5,479,946
Walton Civil Engineering and Surfacing Contractors Ltd	£5,478,320
Penny Brohn Cancer Care	£5,478,000
Three Counties Feeds Limited	£5,477,000
St Giles Farms Limited	£5,476,318
Lodge Service International Limited	£5,476,070
Community Health Facilities (Oxford) Limited	£5,472,051
Edgehill Battersea Limited	£5,469,292
RR Sea Dundee Limited	£5,467,222
Reig Jofre UK Limited	£5,463,440
St Davids Poultry Team Limited	£5,463,040
Investacast Limited	£5,460,354
Duchy Health Charity Limited	£5,457,430
AJ & Co.(Devon) Ltd	£5,451,627
Kernow Veterinary Group Limited	£5,449,800
Hampton House Properties Limited	£5,447,337
Pulse Global Holdings Limited	£5,447,101
M.H.R. Hicks Limited	£5,444,940
Reliance Scrap Metal Merchants (Parkstone) Limited	£5,442,184
Tacklestore Limited	£5,435,244
Mount Batten Sailing and Water Sports Centre	£5,431,251
Chronos Technology Limited	£5,431,242
Magdalen Victoria LLP	£5,430,187
Energy Measurement Limited	£5,428,115
Symec Technologies Limited	£5,427,721
Nanny McPhee Productions Limited	£5,426,000
G.A. Beaton Limited	£5,422,801
A & L Care Homes Holdings Limited	£5,418,745
Jensen-Faulkner Limited	£5,416,758
Portway Domestic Appliances Limited	£5,416,418
Hull Ocean Going Barges UK Ltd	£5,415,040
Rotamic Engineering Limited	£5,405,410
Pittard Garnar Services Limited	£5,400,738
Strata Service Solutions Ltd.	£5,399,868
Samara Investments Limited	£5,395,522
Elleness Limited	£5,394,754
AR Hooper and Partners Ltd	£5,393,485
Contactreal Limited	£5,392,119
MDE Consultants Ltd	£5,391,368
Beagle Technology Group Limited	£5,387,000
Whites Material Handling Limited	£5,383,356
Western Fuel Limited	£5,379,026
Stroudwater Redevelopment Partnership Limited	£5,378,287
Polymermedics Limited	£5,378,200
New Look FIN III Limited	£5,377,000
Regal Holiday Homes Limited	£5,376,116
Trade-Air Airline Support Limited	£5,375,996
ATP Holdings Limited	£5,372,845
St James Priory Project	£5,370,968
Tiger Communications (Holdings) Limited	£5,370,367
Linen Yard Investments (Crewkerne) Ltd	£5,369,287
W.R. Haines (Leasow Farms) Limited	£5,367,848
Kondor Property Company Limited	£5,364,197
Exeter Finance Group Limited	£5,361,177
Roberts Limbrick Limited	£5,359,935
Faber Brook Farm Limited	£5,356,465
EMG Limited	£5,354,388
Concrete Fabrications Limited	£5,354,035
Soar Newco Limited	£5,352,793
Stay Dry Roofing (South West) Limited	£5,352,244
CQC Limited	£5,352,113
St. Hugh's School (Carswell) Trust Limited	£5,351,992
Niall Hobhouse Limited	£5,350,801
Guy Anderson Wines Limited	£5,350,539
Civitas SPV18 Limited	£5,350,312
Marsh Court Farm Limited	£5,346,198
The Duchy Academy Trust	£5,345,775
Healthline UK Holdings Limited	£5,340,736
Brookridge Timber Limited	£5,338,963
Loran (Investments) Limited	£5,336,579
Cheshire Coppice PV Ltd	£5,336,178
Bayshill Properties Limited	£5,336,059
Get Fresh Cosmetics Ltd	£5,335,444
Brooks Hotels Limited	£5,334,488
Swettenham Estates (UK) Limited	£5,333,556
System 6 Kitchens Limited	£5,333,263
Civitas SPV3 Limited	£5,330,408
Red House Developments (Surrey) Limited	£5,329,930
Witney Holdings Limited	£5,329,286
Kingskerswell Property Management Limited	£5,329,220
Autumnus Energy Limited	£5,328,860
Motorhome Finance Limited	£5,328,701
Steve Vick International Limited	£5,325,567
Flying Visit Limited	£5,325,221
Old Mill Accountancy LLP	£5,325,035
Old Hall Investment Company Limited	£5,324,345
Bristol Music Trust	£5,323,185
Devon Air Ambulance Trading Company Limited	£5,322,711
Leehurst Swan Limited	£5,319,927
Pendine Wind Farm Limited	£5,319,362
Ashfield Land (Bridgend) Limited	£5,312,783
Majestic Limited	£5,310,681
Whiteburn Rookery Investments Limited	£5,309,104
JMC Recruitment Solutions Limited	£5,308,593
Bakers Coaches Limited	£5,298,996
Sailport PLC	£5,298,254
Talent & Enterprise Trust	£5,297,000

Company	Amount
C & P Medical Trading Limited	£5,296,407
Ladder and Fencing Industries (Newent) Limited	£5,296,300
Cadillac Plastic Limited	£5,294,890
First City Nursing Services Limited	£5,294,853
Finance Solutions Limited	£5,290,442
Caerus Wealth Solutions Limited	£5,289,000
Copano Limited	£5,288,408
Green and Fortune Limited	£5,286,796
Dartex Holdings Limited	£5,283,000
LAL Language Centres UK Ltd	£5,280,565
Dundee Merchant Wind Park Limited	£5,276,884
Orange International Investments (UK) Limited	£5,272,945
Country Care Homes Limited	£5,272,167
Wessex Building Services Limited	£5,270,484
Downland Consultants Limited	£5,270,265
T A Saunders Investments LLP	£5,269,443
Triangle Properties (Bristol) Limited	£5,265,414
Camelot Care Homes Limited	£5,265,202
North Place Developments Ltd	£5,264,305
Edgecom Estates Ltd	£5,263,334
Mobile Thinking Limited	£5,263,122
The Trade Link Company Limited	£5,263,074
Pennard Farms Limited	£5,253,824
Gwenray Capital Limited	£5,252,479
J & C Freeth Limited	£5,252,248
Flextrus Limited	£5,251,000
P B Design Holdings Limited	£5,249,479
Fonterra (Logistics) Limited	£5,248,000
Chappell Engineering Limited	£5,246,305
Solent Global Holdings Limited	£5,246,229
East Dorset Golf Club Limited	£5,246,034
Good Energy Lower End Farm Solar Park (026) Ltd	£5,245,448
Dragon Alfa Cement Limited	£5,243,830
Colin Mear Engineering Limited	£5,243,002
Magnet Sales and Service Limited	£5,242,113
Draycot Estates Limited	£5,238,240
Llexeter Limited	£5,236,864
Toyo Denso U.K. Limited	£5,234,267
Roseland Investments Ltd	£5,229,178
Quantum Homes Holdings Limited	£5,225,948
Cobham Defence Communications Limited	£5,225,000
Lyme Bay Cider Company Limited	£5,223,414
Zuken Limited	£5,221,000
Landmark Analytics Limited	£5,219,083
Universal Promotions Limited	£5,217,094
BGS 103 Hurst Solar Park Limited	£5,216,168
East Bros.(Timber) Limited	£5,214,972
MPLOY Staffing Solutions Limited	£5,214,900
Seven Fields Primary School	£5,214,655
Budweiser Budvar UK Limited	£5,214,562
R M Beckett Limited	£5,214,035
Goddard Park Community Primary School Academy	£5,210,774
St. Edward's School Cheltenham Trust	£5,210,000
GLM Trading Limited	£5,209,309
Tradestock Limited	£5,204,933
Riviera Produce Limited	£5,204,424
Avon Valley Precision Engineering Limited	£5,203,502
Sadborow Estate Limited	£5,202,979
Halix Limited	£5,202,348
The Plastic Surgeon Limited	£5,202,323
Beetles (UK) Ltd	£5,200,830
Deeley Freed Estates Limited	£5,200,606
Metropolitan Land and House Company Limited (The)	£5,200,523
Good Energy Cross Road Plantation Solar Park (028)	£5,200,441
Aegeus Properties,Limited	£5,195,513
Firstport Bespoke Property Services Limited	£5,194,626
Tecan Limited	£5,194,222
Retrac Productions Limited	£5,193,677
Philmark Estates Limited	£5,193,503
JM & CW Limited	£5,193,048
Lokaz Limited	£5,191,019
AW Frampton & Son Limited	£5,190,614
Harry J Palmer (Broadstone) Limited	£5,186,136
Wind River UK Limited	£5,177,952
Alleyford Limited	£5,176,334
Exmoor Calvert Trust	£5,175,431
Penny Lane Foods Limited	£5,175,405
Penny Lane Holdings Ltd	£5,175,005
Acerbic Ltd	£5,174,363
Warwick Fabrics (UK) Limited	£5,173,108
Marchant-Holliday School Limited	£5,172,818
Back Catalogue Distribution Ltd	£5,170,067
W.J. Meddings (Holdings) Limited	£5,169,908
J. Suttle Transport Limited	£5,169,680
Fulton Boiler Works, (Great Britain) Limited	£5,168,766
Healthcare Computing Limited	£5,167,749
Beta Marine Limited	£5,167,110
H & A Recycling Limited	£5,166,684
Cotswold Doors Ltd	£5,165,016
Pearce Seeds (Holdings) Limited	£5,164,415
SEC Properties Limited	£5,162,985
Pentrebay Properties Limited	£5,159,979
Valeport Limited	£5,156,171
Professor David Barrett Ltd	£5,152,070
Aspirations (Midlands) Limited	£5,150,836
St. Joseph's School Launceston	£5,150,315
R S T Leisure Ltd	£5,149,194
Alchemy Estates Limited	£5,144,387
Peninsula Properties (Exeter) Limited	£5,144,000
TKC Sales Newco Limited	£5,143,980
Addison Capital Limited	£5,140,105
Perivoli Investments Limited	£5,139,863
Church Farm Publow LLP	£5,139,820
Amimed Direct Limited	£5,137,588
Copperplane Limited	£5,134,937
The Levels Academy Trust	£5,133,883
SR & GM Limited	£5,123,780
Librocube Limited	£5,123,498
K.P. Europa Trading Limited	£5,122,954
Cadogan House Investment Properties Limited	£5,117,650
Growing Enterprises Ltd	£5,116,090
West Somerset Railway Public Limited Company	£5,116,000
Cannon Technologies Group Limited	£5,114,539
British Automobile Racing Club Limited	£5,114,463
Upper Belgrave Property Limited	£5,113,655
M J Stevens Ltd	£5,110,482
Enidvale Holdings Limited	£5,108,099
Quantum Teddington LLP	£5,105,978
Euro-Diesel (UK) Limited	£5,105,518
The Exeter Cash Plan	£5,105,000
Gloucestershire Wildlife Trust	£5,104,718
Foot Shop Limited	£5,104,529
BPE Solicitors LLP	£5,104,282
Hart's Haulage Limited	£5,102,729
Dart & Francis Limited	£5,101,270
Powervamp Limited	£5,099,697
Knights Green Estates Limited	£5,099,665
Countess of Brecknock Hospice Trust	£5,091,249
Blackdown Estates Limited	£5,090,000
Woodward & Co (Environmental) Limited	£5,087,912
West House Transport (S & G) Limited	£5,087,425
Bluebelt Hospitality Limited	£5,086,899
FDL Salterns Limited	£5,084,794
Centristic Limited	£5,083,631
Mayden House Limited	£5,081,062
Hampton Printing (Bristol) Limited	£5,080,421
Holmshaw Property Co Limited	£5,078,781
Taw and Torridge Coaches Limited	£5,078,433
Dorset Health Trust Limited (The)	£5,077,096
Saint Augustine's Catholic College	£5,074,942
E.Wiltshire & Son (Torquay) Limited	£5,073,146
Shooters Bottom Wind Park Ltd	£5,071,267
Literature and Latte Ltd	£5,068,017
Pokesdown Community Primary School	£5,066,360

Company	Amount
Metal Yapi (UK) Limited	£5,065,689
Riverside Aromatics Limited	£5,064,537
Roundswell Services Limited	£5,064,464
Elondale Limited	£5,064,079
Bartlett Contractors Limited	£5,064,060
Mallory Holdings Limited	£5,064,053
Kumari Care Limited	£5,063,219
Hugh Koch Associates LLP	£5,063,219
Redrock Consulting Limited	£5,062,834
Independent Agriculture Limited	£5,062,302
Industrial Common Ownership Finance Limited	£5,060,510
UK Solar Projects Limited	£5,059,083
G W Interiors Holdings Limited	£5,058,974
Malmesbury C of E Primary School	£5,056,889
GT Motorcycles (2012) Ltd	£5,055,545
Medcentres PLC	£5,054,044
Charles Russell International Limited	£5,053,089
3 Dorrits Investments Limited	£5,044,384
Coombes Forestry Limited	£5,043,164
Chafyn Grove School	£5,042,108
Mears Homecare Limited	£5,035,000
IF - Inspiring Futures Limited	£5,033,361
H & R Healthcare Limited	£5,032,315
A1 Engineering Solutions Group Ltd	£5,032,022
Britannia Parking Group Limited	£5,031,514
Octava Holdings Limited	£5,030,718
Sherborne Preparatory School	£5,030,674
Floortex Europe Limited	£5,030,441
Greenaway & Greenaway Limited	£5,029,477
Dart Abbey Enterprises Limited	£5,025,383
Obenshaw Limited	£5,023,887
Farthingford Properties Limited	£5,022,327
Shimao Limited	£5,020,431
Kingsdown Farm Ltd	£5,018,650
Computer and Design Services Limited	£5,018,061
Magna Motor Company (Wessex) Ltd	£5,015,787
Access Franchise Management Limited	£5,013,000
Muscle Foods Limited	£5,010,287
White Horse Country Club Ltd	£5,007,595
Multi Circuit Boards Limited	£5,007,317
Malaby Biogas Limited	£5,004,472
G.B Contracts Limited	£5,002,660
Porthia Limited	£5,002,476
Sol Plaatje Educational Project	£4,999,548
Gretton Solar Farm Limited	£4,994,609
Doughty Engineering Limited	£4,993,385
Paint Services Group Limited	£4,992,891
Avonline Network Services Holdings Limited	£4,992,650
The Forge Entertainment Limited	£4,990,026
Wolf Rock (Cornwall) Limited	£4,989,915
Versatile Controls Limited	£4,988,809
Union Jack Oil PLC	£4,987,523
Claybrook Limited	£4,981,391
Beyond The Bean Limited	£4,979,940
Action on Addiction	£4,979,231
Platinum One Hotels Limited	£4,977,173
Oceanview Developments Limited	£4,975,416
Wooda Farm Park Limited	£4,974,006
Bulk Hardware Limited	£4,973,491
Cannon Technologies Limited	£4,973,102
Sterling Capital Asset Finance Limited	£4,971,508
Rajani (Wholesale) Limited	£4,971,335
Brownbrink Ltd	£4,970,071
Trevose Limited	£4,969,413
Julian Barran Limited	£4,969,324
Lynton Downs Limited	£4,967,300
The Lewis-Manning Trust	£4,966,449
Pulse Printing Products Limited	£4,963,218
Wrapex Limited	£4,960,927
Bailey Holdings Limited	£4,955,442
C.T.C.H. Limited	£4,955,401
Appledore Land Limited	£4,955,308
R T Julian & Son Limited	£4,953,913
Oxford Spires Scaffolding Limited	£4,953,302
South West Peninsula Ahsn Limited	£4,952,630
Half Moon Bay Limited	£4,945,873
Centek Properties Limited	£4,945,852
Kernock Park Plants Limited	£4,945,477
H.R.Jasper & Son Limited	£4,944,988
Silversands Limited	£4,944,350
Drytac Europe Limited	£4,941,408
Happy Days South West Limited	£4,941,275
Litfield Land Limited	£4,939,913
Nu-Heat UK Limited	£4,939,497
Vendigital Limited	£4,937,399
Manawey Developments Limited	£4,937,160
Morning Star Motors Limited	£4,935,413
Fred Champion Hire Limited	£4,934,688
Chalwyn Estates Limited	£4,933,000
Jongor (Holdings) Ltd	£4,932,100
Highfield Homes of Distinction Limited	£4,931,778
Coolgate Limited	£4,931,153
Ace Welding Limited	£4,930,688
Bridgewell Holdings Limited	£4,930,373
Wyderington Limited	£4,926,820
Great American Specialty & Affinity Limited	£4,926,241
Thrive Renewables (Boardinghouse) Limited	£4,923,223
Gloucestershire Everyman Theatre Company Limited	£4,920,039
Colvase Estate Ltd	£4,918,926
Minton Investments (Industrial) Limited	£4,918,751
Javsford Investments Limited	£4,915,872
Thos.S.Penny,Limited	£4,914,754
Copyright Administration Services Limited	£4,914,294
Muc-Off Limited	£4,914,279
Accident Claims Handlers Limited	£4,911,165
West Coast Developments (Sandbanks) Limited	£4,911,049
A J Wakely & Sons Ltd.	£4,910,092
Image Factory Communications Ltd	£4,908,215
Bastins 2012 Limited	£4,906,480
Yardgate Limited	£4,906,237
Sunnybanks Homes (SW) Limited	£4,904,098
K. S. Coles Limited	£4,902,852
CHG Developments (Southampton) Limited	£4,902,852
Ophir Finance Company Limited	£4,901,585
Front Foot Investments Limited	£4,901,211
Bay Cottage Properties Limited	£4,900,467
Castlewood (Commercial) Properties Limited	£4,898,052
Puxton Limited	£4,893,062
Tamar View Nurseries Ltd	£4,892,816
BIL Group Limited	£4,892,121
Jam & Sons Limited	£4,891,082
Homeleigh Garden Centre Limited	£4,890,133
Cornelia Care Homes Limited	£4,889,658
Peter Ford Transport Limited	£4,889,452
Marlux Medical Limited	£4,888,535
Bath Quartermaster Limited	£4,887,744
Royal Arcade Limited	£4,887,681
Brotherwood Automobility Limited	£4,886,752
Pulse Roll Label Products Limited	£4,883,646
Forest Green Sun Company Limited	£4,882,828
Automotive Parts Distribution Limited	£4,882,416
Venator Capital Limited	£4,876,193
The Blue Sea Food Company Limited	£4,875,971
P.E. King (Bristol) Limited	£4,875,237
C J Cox Limited	£4,868,066
Clear-Flow Limited	£4,867,815
Chantry Court Westbury Ltd	£4,866,862
Helitune Limited	£4,866,120
The Point at Polzeath Limited	£4,862,742
Trelawny Citroen Limited	£4,861,850
Borough Green Sand Pits Limited	£4,861,527
Warrens Bakery Limited	£4,860,215
Carlos SS Properties Limited	£4,859,758
Marcatrin Limited	£4,852,469

Company	Value
Acorn Developments (SW) Limited	£4,851,365
Mallory International Limited	£4,850,964
YMCA Bath Group	£4,850,483
Kadar Developments Limited	£4,850,462
Bray and Slaughter Limited	£4,845,866
Nephos Technologies Ltd	£4,845,186
Perkins & Perry Ltd.	£4,842,980
Downs School (Charlton House) Limited (The)	£4,842,467
Rotork Midland Limited	£4,839,807
Gill Sensors & Controls Limited	£4,839,667
D C Li (Builders) Limited	£4,836,065
Devon Ceramics (Contracts) Limited	£4,833,383
Main Gate Leisure Limited	£4,832,317
Beaumonts (Leeds) Limited	£4,831,000
Woodstock Estates Limited	£4,828,765
Greiner Bio-One Limited	£4,827,444
Auma Actuators Limited	£4,826,895
P W Commercial Company Limited	£4,825,923
GRS (Holdings) Limited	£4,825,085
Turlough Limited	£4,824,269
Anstee & Ware Group Limited	£4,822,675
Alan Snow Agricultural Engineers Limited	£4,821,731
Mail Handling International Limited	£4,820,690
Seagull Developments Limited	£4,820,623
Dorset Village Bakery Limited	£4,820,517
E T M Contractors Limited	£4,818,219
Torcare Limited	£4,818,155
E.P. Keogh Contractors Ltd.	£4,816,291
Snowdrop Solutions Ltd	£4,816,232
Rosemundy Investments Limited	£4,814,673
Prenax Limited	£4,813,520
South Devon Railway Trust	£4,812,693
Blackmore Limited	£4,812,060
Overleaf Holdings Limited	£4,806,771
TKC Sales Limited	£4,805,320
British Holiday and Home Parks Association Limited	£4,804,903
Totus Engineering Limited	£4,803,964
R W Estates (Trading) Limited	£4,803,404
Sheerness Recycling Limited	£4,802,687
Fintec Group Limited	£4,801,486
S2 Residential Limited	£4,800,746
Positive Cashflow Finance (Holdings) Limited	£4,799,968
Green Gourmet Limited	£4,799,502
Jamaica Inn Bodmin Moor Holdings Limited	£4,798,750
Janspeed Technologies Limited	£4,795,763
Sidmouth Hotels Limited	£4,794,056
Dawson & King Limited	£4,793,679
The Real Live Leisure Company Limited	£4,793,577
Sparkworld Limited	£4,792,015
Stevens Homes Ltd	£4,791,832
Jongor Limited	£4,790,778
Delphine Holdings Limited	£4,789,856
Osborne Care Homes Limited	£4,788,920
Wishford P6 Limited	£4,787,377
Fylde CNC Specialists Limited	£4,787,305
Francis & Lewis International Limited	£4,786,992
Will Stone Historic Cars Ltd	£4,786,014
The Maynard School	£4,785,021
George Bence & Sons (Cheltenham) Limited	£4,784,812
Laceys Solicitors LLP	£4,783,756
Matthews Properties Limited	£4,782,171
Arno GB Limited	£4,779,533
Plymouth Age Concern	£4,779,523
Crocus Care Ltd	£4,779,111
SWM & Waste Recycling Limited	£4,778,757
IIC Northampton Funding Investment Limited	£4,777,400
Pewsey Vale School	£4,776,585
Brooke Energy (Engineering) Limited	£4,775,235
Stone Supplies (Bristol) Limited	£4,774,515
Berkeley Charterhouse Limited	£4,774,376
Qualtronyc Property Holdings Limited	£4,773,991
Mainchannel Developments Limited	£4,772,976
Torridge Transport Limited	£4,772,758
Independent Slate Supplies Limited	£4,772,666
Denhay Farms Limited	£4,772,646
AUB Enterprises Limited	£4,772,000
Medreport Services Limited	£4,771,857
Clearwater Properties Limited	£4,771,280
Serais Investments Limited	£4,771,000
Alterian Software Limited	£4,769,489
Exception Group Limited	£4,764,000
Shaunaks Limited	£4,761,875
Kings (Weymouth) Limited	£4,761,332
Orange Door Property Company Ltd	£4,758,105
Carnon Downs Garden Centre Limited	£4,756,533
Manchester and Provincial Car Parks Limited	£4,754,660
Fremington Homes Limited	£4,751,957
Penington Enterprises Limited	£4,750,177
Juniper Homes (Wilder) Limited	£4,750,068
Pennyfarthing New Homes Limited	£4,748,660
Beran Instruments Limited	£4,748,087
William Haley Engineering Limited	£4,747,655
K.D.P. Tools Limited	£4,747,160
Branksome Park Care Centre Limited	£4,745,882
Jumbocruiser Limited	£4,745,111
Malcolm Barnecutt Bakery Limited	£4,744,868
The Adelaide Lodge Care Home LLP	£4,741,876
Alan Porter Limited	£4,741,501
Susie Watson Designs Ltd	£4,740,696
Froyle Park Estates Limited	£4,740,681
Gloster Furniture Limited	£4,740,520
M.B.Wilkes Limited	£4,739,920
Gale Homes and Investments Limited	£4,736,617
West Country Vending Service Limited	£4,732,737
Dash Group (SW) Limited	£4,729,518
Pie Minister Limited	£4,729,000
BES Healthcare Ltd	£4,728,957
E W Button & Son Limited	£4,727,308
Dowdeswell Aviation LLP	£4,726,225
SDL Biomass Limited	£4,722,160
MDP (South West) Limited	£4,722,121
SCC (Holdings) Limited	£4,719,065
Test Development Company Limited (The)	£4,713,233
Snape Contracting Services Ltd	£4,712,255
M.T. Property Developments Limited	£4,710,742
Homes in Sedgemoor Limited	£4,710,000
The Three Rivers Partnership, Dorset	£4,709,615
ATEX Media Limited	£4,709,414
M H Joinery Products PLC	£4,708,097
Tricel (Gloucester) Limited	£4,704,975
Palm Equipment International Limited	£4,704,462
Greens of Cheltenham Limited	£4,703,323
Yeovil Securities Limited	£4,702,951
Sidney Pratt (Builders) Limited	£4,699,578
Holne Chase Properties Limited	£4,699,166
Hobbs Bros.Limited	£4,698,323
Coles Miller Solicitors LLP	£4,698,037
Haskins Snowhill Garden Centre Limited	£4,698,000
S G V M Holdings Limited	£4,697,535
CQC Holdings Limited	£4,696,852
Gould & Swayne Limited	£4,696,088
Vastern Timber Company Limited	£4,695,666
Equi Media Limited	£4,694,756
Bond Holdings Limited	£4,693,183
ASDAN	£4,692,535
Cornwall Development Company Ltd	£4,692,241
Simon James New Homes Limited	£4,691,624
IIC Northampton Subdebt Limited	£4,690,930
Rusty Shilling Developments Limited	£4,690,905
L. O. Clothier & Sons Limited	£4,690,065
3LINE Holdings Limited	£4,689,342
Premier Cables Holdings Limited	£4,686,635
Andrew Symons Limited	£4,682,782
Luxurycare (Aranlaw House Care Home) Ltd	£4,681,942

Company	Value
R.N. Padfield & Sons Limited	£4,680,714
Berrys Coaches (Taunton) Limited	£4,676,893
Graham and Green Limited	£4,674,218
Watermark Cotswolds Limited	£4,670,690
The Manor Collection Limited	£4,670,436
SEA (Group) Ltd.	£4,668,000
G.E. Developments Ltd	£4,665,857
Hillside Farm Investments Limited	£4,659,297
Circadian Trust	£4,657,912
Rodbourne Rail Farm Solar Park Limited	£4,657,187
The Gillingham Community and Leisure Trust Limited	£4,656,738
Harper's Holdings Limited	£4,651,836
Nuestra Familia Restaurants Ltd	£4,651,640
Horton Golf Limited	£4,648,336
Gilcrest Group Limited	£4,646,549
KWTN Solar Limited	£4,645,982
Chaffcombe Thorns Limited	£4,642,059
Exeter Canal and Quay Trust Limited (The)	£4,640,331
Eroga Die Company Limited	£4,639,911
Armoric Freight International (Holdings) Limited	£4,638,611
Kerdene Limited	£4,636,438
Thornleigh Camphill Communities Limited	£4,633,978
West Country Milk Consortium Limited	£4,633,869
Rawlings & Son (Bristol) Limited	£4,633,555
Rigibore Limited	£4,633,540
Partington Engineering Limited	£4,633,068
Alliance Leisure Services Limited	£4,632,268
River Marketing Limited	£4,632,241
Millwood Homes (Devon) Limited	£4,628,944
Securi-Flex Ltd.	£4,623,278
Quickgrind Limited	£4,619,815
2OC (Holdings) Limited	£4,619,000
K & J Logistics Limited	£4,616,110
IEP Technologies Limited	£4,615,961
Ann's Cottage (Warehouse) Limited	£4,615,897
DM Opco Limited	£4,613,249
Cab Aid Limited	£4,612,000
Pulsin Ltd	£4,611,353
Silversword Limited	£4,610,914
Sutton Chemicals & Textiles UK Limited	£4,608,616
Kiwi Holdings Limited	£4,606,872
A1 Engineering Solutions Limited	£4,606,248
Glen Foundry Limited	£4,604,299
Catalent MTI Pharma Solutions Limited	£4,602,633
Lockman Properties Limited	£4,600,000
House Property Associates Limited	£4,598,240
BASF Metals Recycling Limited	£4,596,000
BDV Atlantic Ltd	£4,595,723
Landmark Developments (Oakford House) Limited	£4,591,954
Integreon Managed Solutions Limited	£4,591,651
Albermarle Trading Limited	£4,590,530
Eko Properties Limited	£4,589,221
Perrys Recycling Limited	£4,587,751
WBW Solicitors LLP	£4,587,620
The Old Tannery (Holt) Limited	£4,587,538
Coastal Care Homes Limited	£4,587,176
Auger Torque Europe Limited	£4,587,140
Flyingfish Seafoods Company Limited	£4,586,381
West of England Investors Ltd	£4,577,471
IPS Pensions Limited	£4,576,000
Liverton 2014 Limited	£4,575,255
Trebah Garden Trust	£4,575,047
Feedco Ltd	£4,573,246
West End Precision Limited	£4,572,667
A. J. Charlton & Sons Limited	£4,571,023
Gridline Enterprises Limited	£4,569,615
Total Laminate Systems Ltd	£4,568,018
Zoeftig Group Limited	£4,566,322
D.J. Melsome Limited	£4,564,060
Skylarking UK Limited	£4,561,024
Bollingwood Limited	£4,558,469
Bowerings Animal Feeds Limited	£4,557,413

Company	Value
Crossco (284) Limited	£4,556,150
Cook and Copp Limited	£4,555,795
Acanthus Ventures Limited	£4,553,439
Birdwell School	£4,550,423
Sealock Limited	£4,547,933
Portland Harbour Authority Limited	£4,545,604
Rainbow Holdings (UK) Limited	£4,544,785
Bond Business Services Limited	£4,544,300
John Downer Productions Limited	£4,542,403
AGD Systems Limited	£4,541,866
Optimum SME Finance Limited	£4,541,400
SGW Research Limited	£4,539,842
Etavoni Limited	£4,539,473
Tempest Radford Limited	£4,539,337
Westbank Community Health and Care	£4,538,292
Keycrown Properties Limited	£4,538,127
J.Knapp & Sons Limited	£4,534,448
Atlantis 39 Limited	£4,532,023
Harkwell Labels Limited	£4,531,479
Danlers Limited	£4,530,509
Bigdug Limited	£4,529,281
Candida Investments Limited	£4,526,642
E & T Developments Limited	£4,525,261
CKF Systems Limited	£4,524,075
Altus Limited	£4,522,511
Soil Association Certification Limited	£4,521,849
C.G.Purchase and Son Limited	£4,520,858
Linton Limited	£4,520,661
Acorn Multi Academy Trust	£4,520,392
Wenand Homes Ltd	£4,518,564
Advanced Coated Products Limited	£4,518,000
Steele Davis Limited	£4,516,351
M.K. Test Systems Ltd.	£4,516,323
Minstead Investments (Boscombe) Limited	£4,514,190
Carrington Fox Developments Limited	£4,512,708
Read Construction (SW) Limited	£4,510,886
Ryan Turner Hope PLC	£4,510,783
Kranlyft UK Limited	£4,509,000
Teignbridge Propellers International Limited	£4,508,896
Gawcott Fields Community Solar Project C.I.C.	£4,508,663
DVG Limited	£4,508,536
Abbeyfield Sidmouth Society Limited (The)	£4,508,397
IIC Miles Platting Funding Investment Limited	£4,507,938
Solace Global Maritime Limited	£4,505,772
Deeley Freed (Penhalt) Limited	£4,505,762
Dartex Coatings Limited	£4,503,362
Westcountry Fruit Sales Limited	£4,503,067
Kay Transport Limited	£4,503,000
JS2 Investments Limited	£4,501,290
R. Moulding & Co. (Salisbury) Limited	£4,497,029
Troax (U.K.) Limited	£4,496,034
Eyre Holdings Limited	£4,494,698
Robotmother Limited	£4,489,815
Hewer Facilities Management Limited	£4,487,429
Plant Speed Limited	£4,486,393
Optima Defence & Security Group Limited	£4,485,349
Dart Valley Systems Limited	£4,485,084
J Gliddon & Sons Limited	£4,484,768
North Dairy Farms Limited	£4,481,802
Crediton Care & Support Homes Limited	£4,476,595
Build Supplies Limited	£4,476,066
Parkside (Barnstaple) Limited	£4,474,816
Somerset County Cars Limited	£4,473,302
Suttle Projects Limited	£4,468,916
The Greenbank Hotel (Falmouth) Limited	£4,468,024
Ladyswood Farm & Stud LLP	£4,466,300
Mycronic Ltd	£4,464,060
Banburys Limited	£4,463,039
The Mast (Bournemouth) Ltd	£4,461,656
Monmouth Facilities Limited	£4,460,000
Stuart Marsh Shoes Limited	£4,459,842
Quickmach Holdings Limited	£4,457,746

Bennah Limited	£4,456,195
Innkeeping Limited	£4,455,863
Western Commodities Ltd	£4,454,615
The George Group Limited	£4,454,187
The Property Management Group Limited	£4,453,781
Seacon (Europe) Limited	£4,452,508
Anglo-Continental Educational Group (G.B.) Limited	£4,451,000
Hewer Group Limited	£4,449,668
Totemplant Limited	£4,449,019
Creative Kernow Limited	£4,448,128
Warners of Gloucester Limited	£4,445,619
Portlemouth Estates Limited	£4,443,974
Repal Co-Gen (UK) Limited	£4,442,222
Stowell Park Estate Limited	£4,441,665
Dix Hills 516 Limited	£4,441,092
Newton Abbot Races Limited (The)	£4,439,590
Atlantis Ocean Energy PLC	£4,438,580
Rattray Milne Ltd	£4,437,873
Dart Sensors Limited	£4,437,872
EP Mallory & Son (Holdings) Limited	£4,434,234
Green Cape Limited	£4,432,203
Import Export Services Ltd	£4,429,641
Bioscientifica Limited	£4,429,193
John Cribb & Sons Ltd.	£4,427,589
Clipper Properties Limited	£4,425,442
Francis Tuthill Limited	£4,423,022
David Hunt (North Devon) Limited	£4,422,317
Up Cerne Limited	£4,421,903
Beacon Homes Limited	£4,421,154
Soldi Investments Ltd	£4,421,067
Dezac Group Holdings Limited	£4,417,457
The Dezac Group Limited	£4,417,438
The IPS Partnership PLC	£4,416,000
A.E. Maiden Limited	£4,415,752
Wallgate Limited	£4,415,428
Cultura Technologies Ltd	£4,414,662
C. Toms and Son Limited	£4,413,145
Canprop II Limited	£4,413,034
Sanctus Limited	£4,412,102
Opaltec International Limited	£4,411,897
Sarsen Stone Group Limited	£4,409,159
Sade Properties Ltd	£4,409,057
Brabon Properties Limited	£4,408,206
Trafalgar Estate Limited	£4,408,055
The Lozenge Limited	£4,406,369
Hanford Holdings Limited	£4,402,880
Senlan Securities Limited	£4,401,881
Mean Moor Wind Farm Holding Limited	£4,398,475
Procol Limited	£4,395,780
JR Cap Limited	£4,394,875
Wood Veterinary Group Limited	£4,394,246
Shiner Properties Limited	£4,393,000
Richard Read (Transport) Limited	£4,392,025
Brinkgreen Limited	£4,389,087
T.E.J. Heating (Plymouth) Limited	£4,388,567
A & B Contractors (Devon) Limited	£4,387,544
Lincolnshire Chickens Limited	£4,386,404
Crownhold PLC	£4,385,540
J.A. Cover Limited	£4,383,815
Exhibitor Limited	£4,383,753
Paragon Education & Skills Limited	£4,380,450
Shiphay Learning Academy	£4,380,242
High Tech Fabrications Limited	£4,379,636
Latimer Trend Holdings Limited	£4,376,199
Hawkins Agri Limited	£4,374,333
Fresh Homes (Bournemouth) Limited	£4,373,790
Edwin Tucker & Sons Limited	£4,372,891
Urban Creation (Shaw) Limited	£4,370,325
Cornish Potatoes Limited	£4,367,642
Avon Care Homes Limited	£4,366,714
Whitehall Garden Centres Limited	£4,366,695
Streamclare Limited	£4,366,626
Leicester BSF Holdings Company 1 Limited	£4,365,397
Lear, Browne & Dunsford Limited	£4,362,427
Clearwater Products Limited	£4,359,863
T K T Cattran Limited	£4,356,510
Dynavour Limited	£4,356,353
The Scott-Law Properties LLP	£4,356,143
T.H.Plumridge Limited	£4,353,191
Aviation Requirements Ltd	£4,351,270
Davenport & Sons Limited	£4,348,481
Arcade Rentals Limited	£4,347,314
Encore Oakdale LLP	£4,346,664
JKL Moseley Limited	£4,346,520
Bristol Properties Limited	£4,345,994
Flexiguide Limited	£4,345,132
Police Resources International Limited	£4,344,554
Cipher Corp Holding Ltd	£4,342,228
Genaray Limited	£4,340,289
IIC Miles Platting Subdebt Limited	£4,338,446
Sands Resort Hotel Limited	£4,336,162
NSEA Property Services Limited	£4,334,058
Pebley Beach Limited	£4,331,854
Tool Care Hire LLP	£4,330,538
Ted Williams Motors Limited	£4,330,326
Ignition DG Limited	£4,330,036
The Asha Foundation	£4,329,592
Vacsax Limited	£4,329,237
Buildit Gloster Limited	£4,328,003
Chibroco Limited	£4,325,589
Mendip Batch Medical Limited	£4,324,989
Durlston Court School Trust Limited	£4,324,963
PICS Telecom International Limited	£4,321,878
Winston Heights Ltd	£4,321,578
Maistro PLC	£4,320,925
Fallon Enterprises Ltd	£4,320,361
Woodward & Co (Holdings) Limited	£4,313,724
Amigo Management Services Ltd	£4,312,000
Seepex UK Limited	£4,309,582
Portway Precision Limited	£4,308,445
Blue Chip Holidays Ltd	£4,306,341
Elm Tree Estates Limited	£4,305,565
Jays Logistics (South West) Limited	£4,303,183
Pullman Premier Leisure Limited	£4,303,105
Gnome World Caravan Park Limited	£4,299,174
Elmley Foundation (The)	£4,297,688
Premier Livestock Auctions Limited	£4,297,680
April Medibroker Limited	£4,295,943
Dorset Freedom Properties Limited	£4,295,781
K.F.Bartlett Limited	£4,295,472
Spike Island Artspace Limited	£4,294,677
Ipplepen Property Limited	£4,293,564
Olympic Varnish Company Limited	£4,293,166
ETM Recycling Limited	£4,292,654
Johnan UK Limited	£4,291,538
Gompels Healthcare Limited	£4,291,203
2nd Half Limited	£4,289,138
OC Vor Ltd	£4,285,401
Apex One Limited	£4,281,672
Gantrail International Limited	£4,280,478
Sphere Property 4 Limited	£4,278,155
Heligan Gardens Limited	£4,278,127
Precision Lift Services Limited	£4,276,530
Spyscape Ltd	£4,275,446
Hennock Properties Limited	£4,272,551
Battens Solicitors Limited	£4,272,203
Stanbridge Property Developments Limited	£4,272,002
Foxmoor Limited	£4,271,889
Wood Barton Developments Limited	£4,271,659
PC Property Holdings Limited	£4,271,100
Whitehill Country Park Limited	£4,269,991
Pulse Power and Measurement Limited	£4,269,927
West Brothers (Frome) Ltd	£4,268,289
J R Bodman Limited	£4,268,042

Manor Farm (Castle Cary) Limited	£4,267,794
M. Preymesser Logistics Limited	£4,266,893
RAGM PLC	£4,265,771
NCC Operations Limited	£4,264,280
Scotty Ventures Limited	£4,262,902
WP Industrial Limited	£4,262,250
Stallcombe House	£4,262,238
S.W.T Finance Limited	£4,262,125
T2 Partnership Ltd	£4,260,108
Stanley Gibson Limited	£4,257,722
Gardner Garages Limited	£4,256,693
Western Truck Rental Limited	£4,256,620
Stilo International PLC	£4,255,000
TQ9 Partnership LLP	£4,254,113
D. H. J. Foot Limited	£4,252,624
Foxcombe Farm (Somerset) Limited	£4,251,398
Dawnhaze Limited	£4,251,112
North Harbour Properties LLP	£4,247,382
M & M Plant (Devon & Cornwall) Ltd	£4,247,345
Stochastic Holdings Ltd	£4,244,556
BBLP Holdings Limited	£4,244,117
Oliver Gillard (Southmead) Limited	£4,243,920
B. Thompson & Sons (Transport) Limited	£4,242,091
Warm Welcome Hotels (Southern) Limited	£4,241,916
SM Group (Europe) Ltd.	£4,241,137
David Greening Limited	£4,241,136
F W Rogers Garage (Saltash) Limited	£4,240,507
Chickerell Primary Academy	£4,235,298
Willow Green Developments Limited	£4,232,935
Woodfield Developments Limited	£4,232,571
Hooke Court Limited	£4,232,244
Castle Gardens Sherborne Limited	£4,228,081
Asset Services Limited	£4,225,163
Nova Group Europe Limited	£4,225,068
Automatic Industrial Machines Limited	£4,224,884
Marshalsea Hydraulics Limited	£4,223,000
United Registrar of Systems Limited	£4,222,530
Premier Double Glazed Units Limited	£4,221,045
Decision Logic Ltd	£4,218,333
The Environmental Dimension Partnership Limited	£4,217,931
Bristol Drugs Project Limited	£4,217,678
Magna Motor Company (Christchurch) Limited	£4,217,031
Shearbarn Holiday Park Limited	£4,216,931
Bluetech Systems International Ltd	£4,216,851
Tubbs (UK) Ltd	£4,216,338
McCaulay's Health & Sport Limited	£4,213,963
Central Management Catalogue Agency (UK) Limited	£4,212,720
Bibury Court Limited	£4,212,610
Koori Limited	£4,211,502
BBS Consultants & Actuaries Limited	£4,209,609
Consumer Intelligence Limited	£4,209,124
Haydn Fine Ltd	£4,208,720
Green Spinnaker Limited	£4,207,289
Helipebs (Holdings) Limited	£4,207,071
Scoliosis SOS Limited	£4,207,022
RHSG Properties Limited	£4,206,609
Beecholm Management Limited	£4,206,472
Hatchmoor Nursing Home Limited	£4,205,645
Benash Farms Limited	£4,205,302
Newport Caravans Limited	£4,204,857
Borlase Smart John Wells Trust Ltd	£4,204,737
Edenvale Turf (SW) Limited	£4,202,293
Marks Barn Farm (Crewkerne) Limited	£4,199,663
Crux Product Design Ltd	£4,199,511
Pennard Hill Farm Limited	£4,198,415
R. O'Dell (Holdings) Limited	£4,197,394
Antrak Group Limited	£4,193,269
115-116 Marine Parade Limited	£4,191,601
Drake Court Property Limited	£4,191,309
Tack Farms Limited	£4,191,204
Izit Group Limited	£4,190,079
Bamboo Technology Group Limited	£4,185,508
Manor Life Investments Limited	£4,184,271
Moreton C.Cullimore and Son,Limited	£4,181,649
White Rose School of Beauty	£4,177,959
Mar-Key Marquees Limited	£4,177,558
Brick Peers Limited	£4,175,452
Cavanna Homes (Cornwall) Limited	£4,174,841
Doveleigh Care Limited	£4,173,991
Solomon (Liskeard) Limited	£4,172,212
QIP Solutions Ltd	£4,169,215
G & R House Limited	£4,165,335
C G & D Heal Limited	£4,163,415
Peter Gabriel Limited	£4,160,751
Barnbury Enterprises Limited	£4,159,187
The Providence Projects Rehab Group Limited	£4,158,454
Blue3 (London) (Holdings) Limited	£4,157,000
Pennard Hill Farm Holdings Limited	£4,153,705
CDS Support Limited	£4,153,299
Global Furniture Alliance Limited	£4,152,328
Newlyn Art Gallery Limited	£4,152,238
Severn Glocon (Aberdeen) Ltd	£4,151,972
BP Rolls Holdings Limited	£4,151,302
Tiger Communications PLC	£4,148,382
Park Home Management Ltd	£4,148,175
Lloyd & Whyte Limited	£4,147,901
Radquill Developments Limited	£4,147,550
Longford Farms Limited	£4,145,400
Good Food and Drink Company Ltd	£4,143,002
Avondale Builders Limited	£4,141,839
New Leaf Plants Ltd	£4,141,368
J.E.Stacey & Co.Limited	£4,139,511
Cream Residential Care Limited	£4,139,048
Swannick & Kearn Properties Limited	£4,138,744
1st Machine Tool Accessories Limited	£4,137,924
Fairchild Thompson LLP	£4,136,285
Portico Business Services Limited	£4,134,397
Westbury-on-Trym Church of England Academy	£4,133,594
010 Limited	£4,131,495
McLean & Sons Ltd	£4,129,050
Alexander & Angell (Farms) Limited	£4,128,791
Latcham Direct Limited	£4,128,290
Corinthian Sports Limited	£4,127,769
Icon Scientific Limited	£4,126,336
Bristol PFI Debt Co 1 Limited	£4,126,187
Exeter Castle Management Company Limited	£4,125,764
A. & J. Woolf Properties Limited	£4,125,762
Host Properties Limited	£4,123,845
Christ Church C of E Primary School (Cheltenham)	£4,123,733
JGH Midco Limited	£4,122,087
TMB Patterns Limited	£4,121,161
Fox Elms Care Limited	£4,119,752
Carlin Boat Charter Limited	£4,119,164
Coastguard Road Limited	£4,118,887
Alchemy Promotions Limited	£4,115,570
Prideaux Developments Limited	£4,114,180
Leicester BSF Holdings Company 2 Limited	£4,113,763
Lightning Electrical Construction Limited	£4,112,716
DPRS Finance Limited	£4,109,918
Groundfix Limited	£4,109,389
J.C. Dean (Haulage) Limited	£4,109,183
Sidmouth Hotels Holdings Limited	£4,107,729
Independent Investment Analysis Limited	£4,107,099
Saab Technologies UK Limited	£4,106,611
Frontline Image Ltd	£4,106,392
Jupiter Care Ltd	£4,106,149
Two Rivers Investments Limited	£4,106,000
Symons Retail Limited	£4,105,300
C. & J. Clark (Street) Limited	£4,102,598
Orchardleigh Estates Limited	£4,102,280
Creedon Technologies Limited	£4,100,839
Clark Holdings (UK) Limited	£4,099,988
Fjords Processing Limited	£4,099,000
Ernesettle Community Solar Limited	£4,098,559

Ovan Properties Limited	£4,096,033	Cavium UK Ltd	£4,021,458
Les Smith Haulage Limited	£4,093,404	Certini Bicycle Company Limited	£4,020,746
Dawson E & E Parts (Europe) Ltd	£4,093,186	CTC (Wholesalers) Limited	£4,019,000
Ascent Publishing Limited	£4,093,000	Comax (UK) Limited	£4,018,813
Mayflower Properties (SW) Limited	£4,092,050	Paper Bag Company Holdings Limited	£4,017,771
Burnbake Campsite Limited	£4,091,749	St David's Church of England Primary Academy	£4,017,000
Haystack Dryers Limited	£4,090,243	Rockfield Farms Limited	£4,016,736
Two Eagles Investments Limited	£4,090,238	Dan-Floor U.K. Limited	£4,016,127
Cowley Bros.(Wroughton) Limited	£4,089,108	Patrico Limited	£4,016,097
Ikonic Holdings Limited	£4,089,060	Rockfish Group Limited	£4,015,763
Simonstone (Bristol) Limited	£4,088,190	Lake Consultancy and Investments Limited	£4,014,828
Ark Data Spring Park Limited	£4,088,047	E & H Drylining & Plastering Limited	£4,013,421
The Epiphany School	£4,088,003	Foscombe Properties Limited	£4,012,425
Poole Housing Partnership Limited	£4,086,641	Forgeway Holdings Ltd	£4,012,279
Guild Bristol Limited	£4,084,476	Aceaxis Limited	£4,012,145
ITP Developments Limited	£4,083,387	Raynsford Limited	£4,011,810
Langdon Transport Limited	£4,082,922	Clark Holt Limited	£4,010,171
Goonvean Aggregates Limited	£4,080,497	B.T. Jenkins Limited	£4,007,893
Elfordleigh Holdings Limited	£4,076,237	Lighthouse Property Estates Limited	£4,007,161
Asheek Living Limited	£4,075,854	Brook Food Processing Equipment Ltd	£4,006,885
Quickmach Engineering Limited	£4,075,708	Waite & Son (Jewellers) Limited	£4,005,229
Wildbrook Investments (Calne) Limited	£4,075,703	Lethbridge Primary School	£4,004,199
Invicta Motors (Maidstone) Limited	£4,075,000	WMG Group Ltd	£4,000,850
Rivermead Plastic Limited	£4,074,469	Harris Bros. and Collard Limited	£4,000,515
Thomas Ware & Sons Limited	£4,074,101	HJP Investments 2015	£3,999,982
Leighton-Boyce Properties Ltd.	£4,073,953	Abbey Business Equipment Limited	£3,999,442
PJAC (Bristol) Limited	£4,072,407	Gordon L. Poole (Southampton) Limited	£3,999,338
Longfield Hospice Care	£4,071,983	Cornbury Farm Contracting Limited	£3,999,119
Wiska UK Limited	£4,071,279	LBS (Fire Services) Limited	£3,999,000
Winners 2000 Fitness Limited	£4,070,733	Brook Enterprises Limited	£3,998,249
Pengelly Farms Limited	£4,069,214	Total Carbide Ltd	£3,995,000
Webbers Property Services Limited	£4,068,854	Autonumis Limited	£3,994,820
PJAC Developments Limited	£4,065,807	A.C. Hopkins (Taunton) Limited	£3,994,148
K W Brake and Son Limited	£4,065,772	Kat-O-Log Limited	£3,993,574
Martin and Company Limited	£4,065,243	Treveglos Farm Limited	£3,993,129
Student Rooms 4 Plymouth Ltd	£4,064,429	J.P.C.Properties (Southampton) Limited	£3,991,794
The Almanzora Group Limited	£4,063,780	Carter Projects Limited	£3,988,674
Freedom Healthnet Limited	£4,062,809	Sturtons Group Limited	£3,987,388
J Scadding & Son Property Limited	£4,062,452	AEGG Ltd	£3,986,360
Stealthlink Ltd	£4,062,436	Shaw Ridge Primary School	£3,986,349
Rochling Fibracon Limited	£4,061,349	API Holdco Limited	£3,985,312
Enoch Properties (Devon) Limited	£4,060,579	Longmeadow Properties Limited	£3,984,715
Wollen Michelmore LLP	£4,060,297	Hilcro Limited	£3,984,552
Cathedral View Limited	£4,059,953	John Ware Limited	£3,982,942
Tomy Europe (Holdings) Limited	£4,059,000	Crowdcube Limited	£3,982,327
Mecwash Systems Limited	£4,057,580	Wessex Electricals (Shaftesbury) Limited	£3,981,511
Whitehall Cricklade Ltd	£4,057,476	Cavity Trays Limited,	£3,978,978
Secure Services Limited	£4,057,430	Maxine Investments Limited	£3,978,953
Magmatic Limited	£4,056,760	Walter Maidment Limited	£3,978,565
Danbec Property Limited	£4,055,830	The Amber Foundation	£3,978,505
DDC Dolphin Limited	£4,055,780	Publica Group (Support) Limited	£3,977,312
Rendcomb College	£4,054,027	Apollo Radiators Limited	£3,977,242
The Gerrick Rose Animal Trust	£4,053,632	Shareland Investments Limited	£3,976,362
Sortimo International Limited	£4,052,218	Genie Toys PLC	£3,972,054
North Devon Tyres Ltd.	£4,051,959	The Borrowdale Gates Limited	£3,969,713
Cahill Welding Services Ltd.	£4,046,261	JFD Trawlers Limited	£3,969,617
Hoist Hire Holdings Limited	£4,046,000	Tildenet Ltd	£3,968,329
Chris Wheeler Construction Limited	£4,045,850	VES Precision Limited	£3,962,511
Pendennis Properties (Bournemouth)	£4,045,139	Juliana Group Limited	£3,960,033
Super Dooper Stores Limited	£4,043,000	Eagle One Residential Limited	£3,957,033
Bristol & Mendip Estates Limited	£4,041,691	Patalex V Productions Limited	£3,957,000
Snow Business International Ltd	£4,041,232	Click Consult Limited	£3,956,876
Old Coastguard Holiday Park Limited	£4,038,997	Western United Mines Limited	£3,956,809
E.J. Godwin (Peat Industries) Limited	£4,035,028	Avec Trade Limited	£3,956,219
Verton Limited	£4,031,464	Haskins Roundstone Garden Centre Limited	£3,956,000
Interfit Limited	£4,031,000	AEW Properties Limited	£3,947,191
Junction Road Croydon Limited	£4,030,279	Amcor UK Investments Limited	£3,946,000
The Macular Disease Society	£4,029,000	Ashfield Land (Aberdeen) Ltd	£3,944,350
Magna Manor Developments Limited	£4,027,968	Cribbs Triangle Limited	£3,943,406
Robinson Atterton Investments Limited	£4,026,112	Lantor (UK) Limited	£3,941,496
Sureway Express Transport Limited	£4,023,352	Healthcare South West Ltd	£3,941,400
Gill Akaster LLP	£4,021,988	Alertsystems Limited	£3,941,351

Company	Turnover
The Plymouth Hotel Company Limited	£3,938,136
Teachers Property Limited	£3,938,000
Agents and Properties (Taunton) Limited	£3,937,718
Brisdoc Healthcare Services Limited	£3,936,938
Dunns Motors (Holdings) Limited	£3,936,639
Cream II Limited	£3,934,767
Bowater Homes Ltd	£3,933,428
Chelverton Growth Trust PLC	£3,933,000
The Hideaway Truro Ltd	£3,932,641
Draper Ventilation Limited	£3,929,928
Alberti Limited	£3,929,549
Jenkins Marine Ltd.	£3,929,151
Bruf Contract Holdings Limited	£3,928,651
Palmer Care Ltd	£3,928,239
Kew Estates Limited	£3,926,866
Spring Mill Holdings Limited	£3,925,046
Four Quarters Polo LLP	£3,923,869
TJW Precision Engineering Limited	£3,923,749
E3 Media Limited	£3,922,938
The Renewable Design Company Limited	£3,920,678
Fulford Care Home Limited	£3,919,400
Truro Tractors Limited	£3,917,549
Amalgam Holdings Limited	£3,917,527
Tetbury Hospital Trust Limited	£3,916,335
Queen's Park Infant Academy	£3,915,238
Luke Barnett Limited	£3,914,990
A N Barr Industries Limited	£3,914,697
C.P. Button Limited	£3,912,546
Parsons Nationwide Distribution Ltd.	£3,909,133
M R Young & Sons (Rural) Limited	£3,908,953
B.R.Hodgson Facades Limited	£3,907,856
Foxmoor Business Park Limited	£3,906,575
Stephenson Property Services Limited	£3,904,193
Exeter Cash Plan Holdings Limited	£3,902,270
Troax Lee Manufacturing Limited	£3,900,986
Charlton Kings Junior School	£3,899,756
Dura Automotive Limited	£3,899,000
Private Equity Investor Limited	£3,897,000
Chrisgate Limited	£3,896,917
Alden Finance Limited	£3,896,640
Pali Text Society Limited (The)	£3,896,238
Farms for City Children Limited	£3,894,689
Compass Point Estates LLP	£3,892,975
Parsons and Joyce Contractors Limited	£3,890,872
St Margaret's Academy	£3,890,851
A.C. Crocker (Properties) Limited	£3,890,227
Civitas SPV33 Limited	£3,889,007
Tracertec Limited	£3,886,439
Krowji Limited	£3,886,066
Mmedia Group Limited	£3,884,322
Bristol Funeral Directors Limited	£3,883,766
Best Western Enterprises Limited	£3,881,953
Lightmoor Homes Limited	£3,880,420
J.T. Castle Limited	£3,879,737
Tre' Care Group Limited	£3,877,296
D. & I. Bridgman and Son Limited	£3,877,000
J. Wippell & Company Limited	£3,873,590
YYS International (UK) Limited	£3,873,173
Waters Park House Limited	£3,873,103
John Balaam Limited	£3,871,111
Chris Sedgeman Scaffolding Ltd.	£3,871,071
Peninsula Seafoods Limited	£3,869,616
S & B Property Limited	£3,869,558
P L H Property Investment Limited	£3,867,155
Armstrong Infrastructure and Property Finance Limited	£3,866,367
Ocean Learning Trust	£3,865,783
Great Western Enterprise (Holdings) Limited	£3,864,953
Certus Wholesale Ltd	£3,864,071
Square One Construction Limited	£3,858,711
A & B High Holdings Limited	£3,856,423
Shire Integrated Systems Limited	£3,855,442
April UK (Insurance Services) Ltd	£3,854,206
Cornish Concrete Products Limited	£3,852,088
PDF Erection Services Limited	£3,850,808
Mitcham Canada Holdings Limited	£3,850,001
Surereed Limited	£3,848,919
DEK-Co (UK) Ltd	£3,848,298
Ocean Village Waterside Developments Limited	£3,847,032
Frog Investments Limited	£3,842,268
Somerset Motorhome Centre Limited	£3,841,283
Eurotaxis Ltd.	£3,836,765
T.H.F. Johnson Limited	£3,836,507
Turner Property Holdings Limited	£3,835,592
Toller Beattie LLP	£3,835,495
One Holding Limited	£3,835,434
Courtwave Limited	£3,834,642
Trusart Limited	£3,831,621
Education Centre Management Limited	£3,831,000
Mikulla Leisure Limited	£3,829,674
A.J. Developments Limited	£3,829,397
Vertigo Investments Limited	£3,828,152
McCulloch Homes Limited	£3,827,823
ARFF Ltd	£3,825,938
Thorne Holdings Limited	£3,824,477
T. R. Hayes Limited	£3,820,397
Woodpecker Properties Limited	£3,819,114
Netvox Limited	£3,819,052
Liberty House (Nuneaton) Limited	£3,818,604
Triumph Engineering (UK) Co. Ltd	£3,818,404
Jamjar Print Ltd	£3,816,848
Crossman (Lansdown) Ltd	£3,814,680
Mundays Caravan Parks Limited	£3,813,597
Maxin Limited	£3,811,607
Turner UK Limited	£3,810,826
J D Wright & Son Ltd	£3,809,141
Wild Ash Limited	£3,806,384
Isedio Limited	£3,804,988
Acorn Classics House Limited	£3,804,409
M & P (Draycote) Limited	£3,804,238
Mount Vets Limited	£3,803,814
William C. Hockin (Transport) Limited	£3,801,701
Williams Ewan Limited	£3,800,933
Dopano Limited	£3,799,939
Albion Healthcare (Oxford) Holdings Limited	£3,794,469
Westward Investment Management Services (UK) Ltd	£3,794,359
Teoxane UK Limited	£3,792,919
Bilbster Wind Farm Limited	£3,792,869
Golfhill Limited	£3,791,714
A.L.Martin & Son,Limited	£3,790,979
Bristol Fluid System Technologies Limited	£3,789,969
Tewkesbury Marina Limited (The)	£3,789,121
Headlands Technologies Europe LLP	£3,786,347
Stafford Education Facilities Limited	£3,785,085
Fraser James Properties Limited	£3,784,943
Wilson & Sons (Engineering) Limited	£3,782,397
Ableway Developments Limited	£3,779,410
Salisbury Trading Limited	£3,778,698
A.K.S. (Yeovil) Limited	£3,777,460
Odstone Farms Limited	£3,776,573
Import Export Services (GRP) Limited	£3,775,793
G.A. Francis & Son Limited	£3,775,434
Findlay Publications Investments Limited	£3,771,252
TR (Fenpower) Limited	£3,766,001
Chatlease Limited	£3,765,963
Tollgate Group Limited	£3,764,703
River Reach Limited	£3,762,416
Devonshire Motors Limited	£3,762,134
Devonshire Homes (Bracken) Limited	£3,761,559
Gemma International Limited	£3,761,000
Holders of Congresbury Limited	£3,760,906
Indalo International Holdings Limited	£3,758,578
Skilled Group UK Limited	£3,758,563
Alpha Immobile Limited	£3,757,904
The Johnsons Group Limited	£3,756,393

Company	Value
Enys Estate Company Limited	£3,754,044
MR Capital Consultants Limited	£3,752,749
R.T. Property Investments Limited	£3,749,432
Datum Capital Limited	£3,745,917
Animals in Distress (Torbay and Westcountry)	£3,743,706
Dean Clarke Estate Ltd	£3,743,307
Goldmix Limited	£3,742,160
RR Sea St. Helens Limited	£3,738,382
Advanced Waste Solutions Ltd	£3,737,979
Innex Investments Ltd	£3,737,254
Hacche Retail Limited	£3,735,405
Future Publishing Holdings Limited	£3,735,000
Heber Limited	£3,732,440
Melbourne Homes Limited	£3,731,496
Aaron Heating Services Limited	£3,731,362
Peartime Limited	£3,728,925
Mzuri Limited	£3,728,355
Grounded Property Trading Limited	£3,726,434
M.R. Ratcliffe Consultants Limited	£3,726,031
Elmlea Junior School	£3,723,278
Worldwide Dive and Sail International Limited	£3,722,719
SB Holdings (Exeter) Limited	£3,722,586
Venture Engineering Group Limited	£3,721,167
R.S. Cook & Sons Limited	£3,720,926
Land & Buildings Limited	£3,720,793
Woodstock Leabank Office Furniture Limited	£3,720,367
Bristol Builders Supplies Limited	£3,720,222
Rygor Group Services Limited	£3,719,878
3MS Construction Limited	£3,719,440
Flycorp Aviation LLP	£3,716,392
Amariz Limited	£3,716,120
Otter Nurseries of Plymouth Limited	£3,715,908
Avantage (Cheshire) Holdings Limited	£3,715,446
Torchlightgroup Limited	£3,715,257
Surest Ltd	£3,713,450
Berry Head Hotel Limited	£3,709,605
Woods (Dorchester) Limited	£3,708,437
Chapters Freefolk Ltd	£3,704,730
House of Clive (Hair and Beauty) Limited	£3,704,419
Penmellyn Veterinary Group Limited	£3,702,343
Victor Properties Ltd	£3,701,961
Wahoo Learning Limited	£3,701,362
Colethrop Farm Limited	£3,701,177
The Royal Artillery Centre for Personal Development	£3,700,112
Alderbrook Road Limited	£3,699,800
Plastivan Limited	£3,699,682
Grosvenor Place Holdings Limited	£3,699,423
Sett Wind Development Limited	£3,698,707
Stag Buying Group Limited	£3,694,817
Libra Investments Limited	£3,693,723
R Tudor Holdings Limited	£3,692,297
The Bibury Club Limited	£3,691,800
Drewdeeds Limited	£3,690,805
Genus Capital 2 Limited	£3,688,658
Readam UK (Pty) Ltd	£3,687,714
Forest of Dean Stone Firms Limited	£3,686,235
Groves Park Investments Ltd	£3,686,160
Edgwicks Limited	£3,684,312
Transcribe Copier Systems Limited	£3,683,860
Quantum Teddington Development Limited	£3,683,294
Rexquote Ltd	£3,682,953
Cold Clad Ltd	£3,682,077
Warrington Homes Limited (The)	£3,681,892
Total (2014) Limited	£3,681,564
Kitto Group Public Limited Company	£3,680,423
Wool & Bovington Motors Limited	£3,679,343
Lagan Farms (Dorset) Limited	£3,679,172
Contango Investments Limited	£3,678,810
Parkhouse Hotel (Shifnal) Limited	£3,678,085
Oasis Plant Hire Limited	£3,677,783
JHAI Limited	£3,677,390
Watershore Ltd.	£3,675,842
Tamander Limited	£3,672,322
Tree Aid	£3,672,218
Acland Plant Hire Limited	£3,672,047
Oakleaze Holdings Limited	£3,671,926
The Foodservice Centre Limited	£3,671,333
Arisaig Partners (UK) Limited	£3,669,795
Oval Commercial Investments Limited	£3,669,393
Tasman House Developments Limited	£3,668,858
Camelot Care (Bridgwater) Limited	£3,668,153
BAEMS Limited	£3,665,255
BSR Connect Limited	£3,664,098
M K Property & Letting Limited	£3,663,559
Right Contract Services Limited	£3,661,444
Dunsmere Developments Limited	£3,660,848
Stoke Bishop Church of England Primary School	£3,660,525
Penrice House (St. Austell) Limited	£3,657,528
WPC Software Limited	£3,656,751
Western Mechanical Handling UK Limited	£3,654,958
Elliott Heron Limited	£3,653,412
Bellamy Wealth Management Limited	£3,652,390
Poolearth Limited	£3,651,061
Staines Trailers Ltd	£3,650,802
Teignmouth Maritime Services Limited	£3,650,670
Morrison Financial Associates Limited	£3,649,858
J.J. Acquisitions Limited	£3,649,816
The Hargrave Foundation	£3,646,183
Rollo Homes Number One Ltd	£3,644,512
Tamar Trading Co.Limited	£3,644,228
Jeremy Bishop Haulage Limited	£3,642,777
Carnegie International Asset Management Limited	£3,641,629
D.J. Contracts (Structural) Limited	£3,641,554
Pharos Care Limited	£3,641,107
City Eco Hotel Limited	£3,641,056
The Cullompton Walronds Preservation Trust	£3,640,336
Camanoe Estates Limited	£3,639,259
T. Ensor & Son Limited	£3,636,212
ARWC Consulting Ltd	£3,633,175
Reform Topco Limited	£3,630,313
DMJ Asset Management Ltd.	£3,627,633
Hoo Developments Limited	£3,626,914
JSM Property Services Limited	£3,626,127
Leckhampton Dairies Limited	£3,625,861
Bennett Gould and Partners Limited	£3,623,669
TPSFF Holdings Limited	£3,622,626
Leander Developments Limited	£3,621,884
Thornton Shipbrokers Limited	£3,621,647
MDM Developments (Southern) Limited	£3,621,513
Centaur Foods Limited	£3,620,969
HAB at Lovedon Fields Ltd	£3,620,541
Lake Inns & Leisure Limited	£3,618,389
Provenn Ltd	£3,614,245
Haine & Smith Partnership LLP	£3,611,684
Industrial Properties (Barton Hill) Limited	£3,609,695
Crown Yealm Limited	£3,606,598
Caruso Properties Limited	£3,603,496
Complete Design & Construction Limited	£3,603,299
Colburn Developments Limited	£3,602,862
Nutwell Farms Limited	£3,602,286
Route One Retail Limited	£3,601,877
B.& M. Babbage & Co. Limited	£3,601,871
Manor Lodge Developments Limited	£3,601,582
Witon Engineering Limited	£3,600,201
Race 500 Limited	£3,600,000
LCD Publishing Limited	£3,599,897
Giftstones Limited	£3,599,822
Rangemoors Limited	£3,597,401
Dunns Estates (Exeter) Limited	£3,596,851
Pine Wood Hill Limited	£3,596,523
Homer & Pardy Developments Limited	£3,595,516
Slee Blackwell Solicitors LLP	£3,594,824
Harlequinns Bowling and Leisure Limited	£3,594,732
Growth Property Limited	£3,593,236

Company	Value
Creditcall Limited	£3,592,476
RWC Construction Ltd	£3,591,940
N.A. Guppy Limited	£3,589,379
Total Plumbing Supplies Limited	£3,588,281
North Town Academy Trust	£3,587,000
Box House (Services) Ltd	£3,583,773
Perrott Hill School Trust Limited	£3,583,712
The South Bristol Church and Community Trust	£3,582,878
Minty Art Limited	£3,582,009
One Holding Investments Ltd	£3,581,971
Kinson Primary School	£3,581,160
Wildbrook Investments (Thornbury) Limited	£3,577,586
Taw Garage (Holdings) Limited	£3,576,908
Expolink Europe Limited	£3,576,154
P3 Medical Limited	£3,576,095
Chapel Barton House Co. Limited	£3,575,108
Hazel Holdings Limited	£3,575,033
JTL (Holdings) Limited	£3,572,844
Firmplot Limited	£3,572,823
Coombes Manor Farm Limited	£3,570,275
Yeo & Davey (Properties) Limited	£3,566,909
Korado Ltd	£3,565,449
Devonshire Poultry Limited	£3,564,552
Seal-Lite Windows Doors & Conservatories Limited	£3,563,400
Swan Properties Cornwall Limited	£3,560,483
Cotswold Micro Systems Limited	£3,560,450
Acorn Builders (Pewsey) Limited	£3,560,014
Mike Bayliss Holdings Limited	£3,558,923
Wagtech Projects Ltd	£3,557,919
Thurlestone Court Limited	£3,556,425
GGB Investments Ltd	£3,556,225
Freshstores Limited	£3,555,628
PSW Metals Limited	£3,555,093
Elliotts (Cheltenham) Limited	£3,553,785
Learning Academy Partnership (South West)	£3,553,000
QNH Limited	£3,551,978
Alfred Nichols (Services and Properties) Limited	£3,551,891
Chinewood Developments Limited	£3,550,992
VSGT Ltd	£3,550,733
Richards Homes Limited	£3,549,849
Sleepers Hill (Winchester) Limited	£3,549,681
Herring Shoes Limited	£3,549,109
Crystal Classics Fine Minerals Limited	£3,548,464
Mendip Forestry Limited	£3,548,035
Cotswold Seeds Limited	£3,547,532
Hatcher and Sons,Limited	£3,547,134
Aistone Properties Limited	£3,544,607
Tom Gallagher Group Limited	£3,544,601
Creanova Universal Closures Limited	£3,543,954
C3IA Solutions Limited	£3,543,671
Growth Technology Limited	£3,542,495
Abacus (Bristol) Limited	£3,540,993
ES Technology Group Limited	£3,538,613
Adtech Holdings Limited	£3,535,628
Malbury Properties Limited	£3,533,900
Premier Park Limited	£3,533,776
RRPI (UK) Ltd	£3,532,367
The Retired Nurses National Home	£3,530,635
N.V. Chichester Limited	£3,530,129
Woodmace Concrete Structures Limited	£3,527,545
De Monchy Aromatics Limited	£3,525,118
Wheeler's (Westbury) Holdings Limited	£3,525,117
Resort Estate Management Limited	£3,524,773
Altec Products Limited	£3,524,546
Axiom Process Limited	£3,524,000
APP (UK) Limited	£3,522,681
The Gilstone Partnership Limited	£3,521,978
Speed Superbikes Limited	£3,519,530
Digs Properties Limited	£3,517,275
Lester Brunt Partnership LLP	£3,517,022
Osric Finance Limited	£3,517,021
Moonraker (World) Ltd	£3,516,999
Sanctus Group Holdings Limited	£3,515,161
Hilditch Group Limited	£3,513,462
Cardiff Wind Park Limited	£3,512,855
F.N.Hues and Sons Limited	£3,512,705
Empire Homes (South West) Limited	£3,512,133
Martins of Exeter Limited	£3,511,511
Glevum Heating & Plumbing Limited	£3,508,282
Bardolf Farms Limited	£3,507,379
J & W Davis Limited	£3,506,524
Chachos Holdings Limited	£3,505,969
Hesters Way Partnership Ltd.	£3,505,054
W. Daniels Plant Hire Limited	£3,503,425
Ashbolt Limited	£3,502,620
CS LSI Solar Limited	£3,500,231

This page is intentionally left blank

Age of Companies

1800s [27]

Avon Rubber P.L.C.
George Bence & Sons Limited
Bradford and Sons Limited
British Empire Trust PLC
Clifton High School
Cobham PLC
Dunlop Holdings Limited
Ecclesiastical Insurance Office PLC
Exmouth Marina Ltd
First West of England Limited
Gardiner,Sons & Co.,Limited
Gloucester Rugby Limited
Hall & Woodhouse Limited
Hatcher and Sons,Limited
Heavitree Brewery PLC
Methodist Insurance PLC
Metropolitan Land and House Co Ltd
Porthminster Hotel Co Ltd
Raven Mount Services Co Ltd
Salisbury Diocesan Board of Finance
Steward's Co Ltd
Tintometer,Limited
Truro Diocesan Board of Finance Ltd
Edwin Tucker & Sons Limited
Wadworth and Co Ltd
Wallaby Grip Limited
Thomas Ware & Sons Limited

1900-1909 [21]

Accord-UK Ltd
Baptist Insurance Company PLC The
C. & J. Clark (Holdings) Ltd
Cornish Mutual Assurance Co Ltd
D A S Legal Expenses Insurance Co Ltd
Dart & Francis Limited
Hollingsworth & Vose Co Ltd
Imperial Tobacco Overseas Ltd
H.J.Knee,Limited
Malaby Holdings Limited
Paull & Co Ltd
Thos.S.Penny,Limited
Petty, Wood & Co. Limited
Phoenix Engineering Co Ltd
Pittards PLC.
Royal Agricultural University
Spirax-Sarco Investments Ltd
Vi - Spring Limited
John Wainwright & Co. Limited
J. Wippell & Co Ltd
Witan Pacific Investment Trust PLC

1910-1919 [23]

Abbey Manor Group Limited
Aeronautical & General Instruments
Amsafe Bridport Limited
Avon Polymer Products Limited
Bath and Wells Diocesan Board of Finance
J E Beale PLC
Bristol Diocesan Board of Finance
Cheltine Limited
C. & J. Clark International Ltd
Cooper Tire & Rubber Company Europe
Davenport & Sons Limited
G Plan Upholstery Limited
Gloucester Diocesan Board of Finance
Grand Pier Limited
Imperial Tobacco International Ltd
Martin and Co Ltd
Refresco Beverages UK Limited
J Scadding & Son Property Ltd
St.Austell Brewery Co Ltd
D.Stewart & Son, Limited
W.J.Tatem Limited
Wallgate Limited
T. H. White Holdings Limited

1920-1929 [48]

AES TEP Power II Investments Ltd
Agricultural Mortgage Corporation P L C
Andrews & Partners Limited
Apetito Limited
Arkell's Brewery Limited
Avon Rubber Overseas Limited
Banburys Limited
Bennah Limited
Bioquell PLC
Bonhay & Eagle Property Co Ltd
Bryanston School,Incorporated
Canford School,Limited
E.A. Chamberlain (Holdings) Ltd
J.Chandler & Company (Buckfast),Limited
Ecclesiastical Life Limited
Enham Trust
Exeter Diocesan Board of Finance Ltd
Exeter Golf and Country Club,Limited
Flower & Hayes Limited
Frizzell Financial Services Ltd
Harding & Sons,Limited
Helipebs (Holdings) Limited
William Hughes Limited
Invicta Motors Limited
Isles of Scilly Steamship Co Ltd
Libya Oil Ethiopia Limited
Libya Oil Sudan Limited
Henry Ling Limited
E.P.Mallory & Son,Limited
Marine & Towage Services Group Ltd
Meggitt Properties PLC
Newton Abbot Races Limited
Norland College Limited
Pride Foods Limited
Royal Artillery Charitable Fund.
Sidlaw Group Limited
Simplyhealth Access
Smiths News Trading Limited
St. Mary's School (Calne)
Stanley Security Solutions Ltd
Stedall (Vehicle Fittings) Ltd
Stroud Metal Co Ltd
Sydenhams Ltd
Trevose Limited
Watts of Lydney Group Limited
West Hants Lawn Tennis Company (Bournemouth)
Wrigley Co Ltd
Zurich Employment Services Ltd

1930-1939 [64]

Aim Composites Limited
Badminton School Limited
Bailey Caravans Limited
G.A. Beaton Limited
Bourne Holdings
Bradfords Building Supplies Ltd
Bray and Slaughter Limited
Bristol Builders Supplies Ltd
Frank Bruce & Co Ltd
Budock Vean Hotel Limited
Corrington Estates Limited
Cross Manufacturing Company (1938)
Dike & Son Limited
Dudbridge Estates,Limited
W.L. Duffield & Sons Limited
Duresta Upholstery Limited
Exyte Hargreaves Limited
Flight Refuelling Limited
Gaming International Limited
E.J. Godwin (Peat Industries) Ltd
Grasshopper 2000 Ltd.
Hobbs Bros.Limited
Hoppings Softwood Products PLC
Horwood Homewares Limited
Imerys Minerals Limited
Jakemans (Confectioners) Ltd
Kent County Crematorium Ltd
Kerry Ingredients (UK) Limited
Kohler Mira Limited
Lanhydrock Estate Company
Lexicon Book Co Ltd
Marden Edwards Limited
Marshalsea Hydraulics Limited
Martin & Martin Holdings
H.Mustin & Son Limited
Mutual Real Estate Co Ltd
NOV Process & Flow Technologies UK
New Yacht Club Limited
Nutricia Limited
Olympic Varnish Co Ltd
Pinewood School Limited
Poeton Industries Limited
Sidney Pratt (Builders) Ltd
Premier Livestock Auctions Ltd
Rawle Gammon & Baker Holdings Ltd
Rawlings & Son (Bristol) Ltd
Renshaw U.K. Limited
Rotalink Limited
Sadborow Estate Limited
Sherborne School for Girls
Shiner Limited
Simplex-Turbulo Group Limited
Society for Endocrinology
Keith Spicer Limited
Suttons Consumer Products Ltd
Thurlestone Estates,Limited
Tuffnells Parcels Express Ltd
Twentieth Century Investments Ltd
Vastern Timber Co Ltd
Waite & Son (Jewellers) Ltd
Percy Williams & Sons,Limited
Woodstock Estates Limited
Wycliffe College (Incorporated)
Xylem Dewatering Solutions UK Ltd

1940-1949 [85]

ACC Silicones Limited
AIM Aviation (Henshalls) Ltd
Aero Stanrew Limited
Amcor Packaging UK Limited
Averys of Bristol Limited
John Balaam Limited
Bapton Manor Farm Limited
Barden Corporation (U.K.) Ltd
Bourne Group Ltd.
Braddicks Holiday Centre (Westward Ho!)
T.H.Brickell & Son,Limited
Bridport Limited
Bristol Properties Limited
Broadway (Bristol) Engineering Co Ltd
Francis Bugler Limited
Capes (Hatherden) Limited
Castle Hill Quarry Co.,Limited
Charlcombe Limited
Clayesmore School

Cotteswold Dairy Limited
Moreton C.Cullimore (Gravels) Ltd
J.A. Darke Limited
E.I.C.(Exeter) Limited
East Bros.(Timber) Limited
Euston Trust Limited
Evans Transport Limited
Exepex Estates Limited
Goulds (Dorchester) Limited
Guy,Leonard & Co.Limited
Harmer Properties Limited
Haven Investments Limited
Hayward Properties Limited
Heathcoat Fabrics Limited
ISG Pearce Limited
IoP Publishing Limited
Julian & Son,Limited
Kingskerswell Property Management
J.Knapp & Sons Limited
Langdon (Dorset) Farms
Latimer,Trend & Co Ltd
Le Creuset U.K. Limited
Leoni Temco Limited
Lloyd Brothers (Bristol) Ltd
Dick Lovett Limited
MSA (Britain) Limited
Mabey and Johnson Limited
E.J. MacKelden & Sons (Bobbing) Ltd
W.J. Meddings (Holdings) Ltd
Medland, Sanders and Twose Ltd
Meggitt PLC
Merrydown PLC
E.V. Naish Limited
Paint Services Group Limited
Pearce Construction (Barnstaple) Ltd
Pendennis Properties (Bournemouth)
Pentewan Sands,Limited
Port Regis School Limited
Pritchard Patent Product Co. Ltd
Pulham & Sons (Coaches) Ltd
Salisbury Diocesan Board of Education
Seetru Limited
WH Smith Retail Holdings Ltd
Soil Association Limited
Speeds Group Holdings Limited
St Aubyn Estates Ltd
Step One Charity
Tamura-Europe Limited
Teagle Holdings Limited
H.Tempest Limited
Tickenham Court Farm Co.Limited
R. Tincknell & Son Limited
C. Toms and Son Limited
Torquay Leisure Hotels Limited
Trebartha Estates Limited
Trelleborg Sealing Solutions UK Ltd
W.D.M.Limited
WTW Cinemas Limited
Warners Trust PLC
West Brothers (Frome) Ltd
Westcliff Hall (Sidmouth) Ltd
Western Provident Association Ltd
Ian Williams (Holdings) Ltd
Ted Williams Motors Limited
Woods (Dorchester) Limited
Yeo & Davey (Properties) Ltd

1950-1959 [166]

Access Franchise Management Ltd
Aegeus Properties,Limited
AgustaWestland Limited
Bill Allen's Autos Limited
Alvis Brothers Limited
Anglo-Continental Educational Group (G.B.)
Arnewood Estates Limited
A.J. and R.G.Barber Limited
Barrett Partnership Limited
K.F.Bartlett Limited
Bashley Park Limited
J.T.Baylis & Co Ltd
Blackmore Vale Farm Cream Ltd
Alvan Blanch Development Co Ltd
Borough Green Sand Pits Ltd
Branksome Estates Ltd.
British Automobile Racing Club Ltd
Brook Enterprises Limited
Brunelcare
Burry and Knight Limited
CEPS PLC.
Campden BRI
Centrax Limited
Ceres Estates Limited
Chevron Properties Limited
L. O. Clothier & Sons Limited
H.W.Clothier Milton-Westcombe Farms
Council of Milton Abbey School Ltd
Dale's Central Motors Limited
D. Dalton & Son Limited
Davan Caravans Limited
Dawson & King Limited
Delphic Holdings Limited.
Denhay Farms Limited
Philip Dennis Foodservice Ltd
Devon Contractors Limited
H.H.& D.E.Drew Limited
Dura Automotive Limited
Eagle Investments Limited
Exeter Cash Plan
J.Ferguson Estate,Limited
Fleet Caravans Limited
Foray Motor Group Limited
James Froud and Sons Limited
Gaiger Brothers Limited
Gardiner Bros. and Company (Leathers)
E.And J.W.Glendinning Limited
J Gliddon & Sons Limited
Gooch & Housego PLC
Grange Court (Hoburne) Limited
Grange Motors (Brentwood) Ltd
H.P.H. Limited
Hammett Investments Limited
A. Hammond & Sons Limited
G.J.Handy & Co Ltd
J.H.Haskins & Son Limited
Hawkins Motors Limited
Hills UK Limited
Hills Waste Solutions Limited
Hoburne Development Co Ltd
Holders of Congresbury Limited
Holmshaw Property Co Limited
Hospital Metalcraft Limited
Hoyle & Co (Bournemouth) Ltd
F.N.Hues and Sons Limited
Industrial Properties (Barton Hill)
Infineon Technologies Reigate Ltd
J.P.C.Properties (Southampton) Ltd
Jacgilden Properties Limited
Javsford Investments Limited
Jennings Industries Limited
T.H.F. Johnson Limited
Kellands (Plant Sales) Limited
Knorr-Bremse Systems for Commercial Vehicles
Ladder and Fencing Industries (Newent)
G.R. Lane Holdings Limited
Leckhampton Dairies Limited
Liverpool Victoria Life Co Ltd
Longford Farms Limited
Lower Pertwood Organic Farm Ltd
Lynton Downs Limited
A.E. Maiden Limited
Manor Farm (Castle Cary) Ltd
Marchant-Holliday School Ltd
A.L.Martin & Son,Limited
McBraida PLC
Meggitt (UK) Limited
Meiyume (UK) Limited
Millfield
Mundays Caravan Parks Limited
Naish Estate (Hoburne) Limited
National Star Foundation
Neptune Shipping Agency Ltd
Newbery Metals Limited
Alfred Nichols (Services and Properties)
OM Holidays Ltd
Oakleaze Holdings Limited
Oasis Dental Care (Central) Ltd
Oasis Dental Care (Southern) Ltd
Oasis Dental Care Limited
Odstone Farms Limited
Ophir Finance Co Ltd
R.N. Padfield & Sons Limited
Harry J Palmer (Broadstone) Ltd
Parsons Peebles Service Ltd
Pattemore's Transport (Crewkerne)
Pennant International Limited
Perseus Property Co Ltd
Pleroma Investments Limited
T.H.Plumridge Limited
Gordon L. Poole (Southampton) Ltd
Keith Pople Limited
Preformed Line Products (Great Britain)
Principality Holdings Limited
Procurri UK Limited
C.G.Purchase and Son Limited
John Reid & Sons (Strucsteel) Ltd
Reliance Scrap Metal Merchants (Parkstone)
Rotork Controls Limited
Rotork P.L.C.
Rowe & Co.Cornwall (Properties) Ltd
Rowe Estates (UK) Limited
Rudgeway Farms Limited
S.C.C. Transport (Devizes) Ltd
Sandbanks Hotel Limited
Sandroyd School Trust Limited
Savencia Fromage & Dairy UK Ltd
Seadown Holiday Park Limited
Sensata Technologies Limited
Shepperton Builders Limited
Shiloh Limited
Allan Sichel Limited
Herbert Silver (Holdings) Ltd
R.W.Simon Limited
WH Smith 1955 Limited
F.J. Snook & Sons Limited
Solomon (Liskeard) Limited
Kenneth Spencer Limited
Spirax-Sarco Engineering PLC
Spirax-Sarco Limited
Sportech Pools Limited
Spring Mill Holdings Limited
J.E.Stacey & Co.Limited
TDK-Lambda UK Limited
Tamar Trading Co.Limited
Taylor,Maxwell & Co.Limited
Texas Instruments Limited

Thatchers Cider Co Ltd
Thornleigh Camphill Communities Ltd
Torridge Transport Limited
Trago Mills Limited
Triumph International Limited
Tyco Electronics UK Ltd
Vapormatic Co Ltd
Viridor Waste Management Ltd
Vospers Motor House Limited
Walston Holdings Limited
A. H. Warren Trust (Holdings) Ltd
Wells Cathedral School, Ltd
T. H. White Limited
Whitehall Cricklade Ltd
Wilson & Sons (Engineering) Ltd
E.Wiltshire & Son (Torquay) Ltd
Xeon Smiles UK Limited
Yeovil Securities Limited
Zurich Advice Network Limited

1960-1969 [262]

A.M.B.Investments Limited
AECC University College
ASM Assembly Systems Weymouth Ltd
Abbey Manor Homes Limited
Abbeyfield Bristol and Keynsham Society
Abbeyfield Sidmouth Society Ltd
Abbeyfield Wessex Society Ltd
Air Control Industries Limited
Allied Dunbar Assurance PLC
Amber Chemical Co Ltd
Amcor UK Group Management Ltd
Andrews Estate Agents Limited
Antonville Investments Limited
Arnolfini Gallery Limited
Automatic Industrial Machines Ltd
Avondale Builders Limited
BASF Metals Recycling Limited
F.A.W. Baker's Kingston Farms Ltd
Ballard School Limited
A.J. & R.G.Barber (Sales) Ltd
Bardolf Farms Limited
Barnwood Construction Limited
Barton Farms Limited
Beagle Technology Group Ltd
Beaudesert Park School Trust Ltd
Beaver Estates (Ashford) Investments
Berkeley Leisure Group Limited
Best Western Enterprises Ltd
Betterment Properties (Weymouth) Ltd
Ken Biggs Contractors Limited
Boyland and Son Limited
Braddicks Leisure Limited
Percy R.Brend & Sons (Hoteliers)
F.G.Brewer & Sons (Farms) Ltd
Bridge Motorcycles Limited
Bristol Old Vic and Theatre Royal Trust
Bristol Uniforms Limited
British Holiday and Home Parks Association
Bruf Contract Holdings Limited
Brymain Investments Limited
Budock Vean Holdings Limited
Burkert UK Limited
Bushell & Meadows Limited
CBSM 2012 Limited
Camanoe Estates Limited
Candida Investments Limited
Carling Technologies Limited
E.G.Carter & Co Ltd
Catalent U.K. Packaging Ltd
Caterpillar Marine Power UK Ltd
Cavity Trays Limited,
Cengage Learning (EMEA) Ltd
Centaur Services Limited
Central Garages (Torbay) Ltd
Chadwick Holdings Limited
Chaffcombe Thorns Limited
F.J. Chalke Limited
Chamberlayne Farms Limited
Changvilla Investments Limited
Chelton Limited
Chewton Glen Hotels Limited
C. & J. Clark Overseas Ltd
Combined Independents (Holdings) Ltd
Control Techniques Dynamics Ltd
Cornwall Trust for Nature Conservation
J Cossins & Sons Limited
Cotek Papers Limited
County Garage (Barnstaple) Ltd
County Tyre (Holdings) Limited
Cover Construction Co Ltd
Cowley Bros.(Wroughton) Ltd
Cox & Robinson (Agricultural) Ltd
Crediton Milling Co Ltd
Cronite Castings Limited
Moreton C.Cullimore and Son,Limited
D.J. Contracts (Structural) Ltd
D.J. Contracts (Weymouth) Ltd
D.J.L.Securities (Barum) Ltd
Dart Marina Hotel Limited
Dart Valley Railway Ltd
Devon Wildlife Trust
Dorset Wildlife Trust
Downland Consultants Limited
C.M. Downton (Haulage Contractors)
Duffields Mills Limited
Dumpton School
Easton Grey Estate Limited
Endsleigh Insurance Services Ltd
Erin Properties (Swindon) Ltd
Eroga Die Co Ltd
Essilor Limited
FR Aviation Limited
Farleigh School Trust Limited
Fernturn Holdings Limited
David Foot Limited
Forelle Estates Limited
Forward Developments Limited
John Fowler Holidays Limited
Fowlers of Bristol Limited
Framptons Limited
Fulton Boiler Works, (Great Britain)
GE Aviation Systems Limited
Gantrail International Limited
Geotechnical Engineering Ltd
Oliver Gillard (Southmead) Ltd
Gloucester Land Co Ltd
Gloucestershire Everyman Theatre Co Ltd
Gloucestershire Wildlife Trust
Greenaway & Greenaway Limited
N.A. Guppy Limited
HF Trust Limited
John Hackling (Transport) Ltd
Hale & Co. (Drybrook) Ltd
Hamworthy Combustion Engineering Ltd
Hanford Holdings Limited
J.M.Harding & Partners Ltd
Harmon (Form Tools) Limited
Harris Bros. and Collard Ltd
Harrow Hill Properties Limited
Haskins Roundstone Garden Centre Ltd
Havas EHS Discovery Limited
Haynes Developments Limited
Haynes Publishing Group PLC
Helston Garages Limited
Heltor Limited
Heritage & Wise Limited
Highdrive Property Co. Limited
Robert Hitchins Limited
Hobbs Properties Limited
Hobbycraft Trading Limited
Home Hardware Southwest Ltd
A.C. Hopkins (Taunton) Ltd
Hovertravel Limited
Iota Properties Limited
JELF Insurance Brokers Limited
JSP Limited
Alec Jarrett Limited
F.G.Jeanes & Son Limited
Jordans Limited
Kadar Developments Limited
Michael H Keene & Son Limited
Keith Motors (Christchurch) Ltd
Kerrier Investments Limited
Kliklok International Limited
Knights Brown Ltd
L.E.W. Techniques Limited
Lancaster Leisure Limited
G.R. Lane Health Products Ltd
Lane's Storage and Removals Ltd
Lee Abbey International Students' Club
Lincolnshire Chickens Limited
Lockman Investments Limited
Lodge Service International Ltd
Longleat Enterprises Limited
Malbury Properties Limited
Manawey Developments Limited
Marks Barn Farm (Crewkerne) Ltd
Matquel Property Co. Limited
Maxine Investments Limited
Merck Chemicals Ltd
Merityre Specialists Limited
Microsemi Semiconductor Ltd
W.J.Miller & Sons Limited
Mitchell & Webber Limited
Mole Valley Farmers Limited
J.A. & E. Montgomery Limited
Morning Star Motors Limited
Morris & Perry (Gurney Slade Quarries)
S Morris Limited
Moseley Distributors Limited
R. Moulding & Co. (Salisbury) Ltd
Murray & Roberts United Kingdom Ltd
National Oilwell Varco UK Ltd
Norseland Limited
S. Notaro Limited
Omicways Limited
Osric Finance Limited
Pali Text Society Limited
Paper Converting Machine Co Ltd
Park Home Life Limited
Penny & Giles Controls Limited
Perrott Hill School Trust Ltd
S.J.Phillips & Sons (Kemble) Ltd
Pittard Garnar Services Ltd
Powderham Properties (Teignmouth)
Power Electrics (Bristol) Ltd
Powrmatic Limited
Princess Yachts Limited
Pucklechurch Development Co Ltd
R W Estates Ltd
Richard Read (Transport) Ltd
Redvers and Denzil Rice Farms Ltd
Rittal-C S M Limited
Romfield Holdings Limited
Rookwood School Trust Limited

Rosemont Pharmaceuticals Ltd
Rygor Group Limited
SR & GM Limited
SSI Schaefer Ltd
Salterns Marina Limited
J.J. Saunders Limited
A. L. Sayers (Holbeton) Ltd
Scotsgrove Holdings Limited
Severn Glocon Limited
E.J. Shanley & Son (Trowbridge) Ltd
Shirley-Young Limited
Shirwell Limited
Site Developments (Ferndown) Ltd
Harold W Smart & Son Limited
Soil Association Certification Ltd
Somerset Wildlife Trust
South West Environmental Parks Ltd
Sparex Limited
St Giles Farms Limited
St James's Place Unit Trust Group
St. Hugh's School (Carswell) Trust
Stanley Security Solutions - Europe
Stannah Lifts Holdings Limited
Stonegate Farmers Limited
Streamclare Limited
Suland Investments Limited
Sunseeker International Ltd
Superior Seals Limited
Tapper and Son (Poole) Limited
Taw Garages Limited
Test Development Co Ltd
Tetronics (International) Ltd
Tewkesbury Marina Limited
Texas Instruments (U.K.) Ltd
B. Thompson & Sons (Transport) Ltd
Trago Mills (South Devon) Ltd
Universal Promotions Limited
Vitacress Herbs Limited
Vitacress Salads Limited
B.Walker & Co.(Dursley) Ltd
Wallsend Estates Limited
Walston Poultry Farm Limited
Wartsila Hamworthy Limited
Wartsila Water Systems Limited
Wasdell Packaging Limited
Watts Aviation Services Ltd
Robert Welch Designs Limited
West Country Vending Service Ltd
West End Motors (Bodmin) Ltd
West Pharmaceutical Services Cornwall
West of England Investors Ltd
Westover Holdings Limited
Westward Building Services Ltd
W.H.White Limited
M.B.Wilkes Limited
Ian Williams Limited
T.D. Williamson (U.K.) Ltd
Willmott's Transport Limited
Wiltshire Wildlife Trust Ltd
Wooda Farm Park Limited
Wool & Bovington Motors Ltd
A. & J. Woolf Properties Ltd
Wyke Farms Ltd
Xograph Healthcare Limited
Zimmer Biomet UK Limited
Zuken Group Limited
Zuken Limited

1970-1979 [361]

A & B High Holdings Limited
ALD Automotive Limited
Abbey Manor Property Holdings Ltd
Abercrombie & Kent Limited
Acorn Classics House Limited
Aim Altitude UK Limited
Airsprung Group PLC
Allchurches Trust Limited
Amcor UK Investments Limited
Ankers and Rawlings Developments Ltd
Antrak Group Limited
Apak Group Limited
Appledore Land Limited
Areawise Limited
Armada Investments Limited
Arno GB Limited
Artisan Biscuits Limited
Arval UK Leasing Services Ltd
Arval UK Limited
Atkinson Equipment Limited
Audience Systems Limited
Auma Actuators Limited
B.A.I. (U.K.), Limited
M Baker (Holdings) Limited
Bandvulc Tyres Ltd
Bank of Ireland Home Mortgages Ltd
Barker Care Limited
Barnwood Shopfitting Limited
J. V. Barrett & Co. Limited
Batten and Allen Limited
Baylis Estates Limited
Beard Group Ltd.(The)
E.W. Beard Limited
Beauchamp House Nursing Home Ltd
Bell & Ross Limited
Benash Farms Limited
Bennett Gould and Partners Ltd
L.B. Bentley Limited
Bicknell Holdings PLC
Richard C. Bircher (Holdings) Ltd
Birchmere Limited
Bix Developments Limited
Blakell Europlacer (Intl) Ltd
Blakell Europlacer Limited
Bott Limited
Bowerings Animal Feeds Limited
Bowmill Engineering Limited
Bracken Developments Limited
Brandwells Construction Co Ltd
Brean Leisure Park Ltd.
Brinkgreen Limited
Bristlewand Limited
Brotherwood Automobility Ltd
Bryan Brothers Holdings Ltd
Buckclose Limited
Bulk Hardware Limited
Bushurst Properties Limited
Cannon Technologies Limited
Carnon Downs Garden Centre Ltd
Cartus Limited
Castle Court School Educational Trust
A. J. Charlton & Sons Limited
Chrisgate Limited
Cirrus Communication Systems Ltd
R L Clapp and Sons (Cheesemakers)
Clarence Court Eggs Limited
Clarity Copiers Limited
Cloverstand Limited
Coastguard Road Limited
Cohen & Griffiths Limited
Colt Car Co Ltd
Colten Developments Limited
Computer and Design Services Ltd
R.S. Cook & Sons Limited
Corintech Limited
Cornish Concrete Products Ltd
Cotswold Architectural Products Ltd
Cotswold Hoburne Limited
Cotswold Seeds Limited
Creative Youth Network
Creed Foodservice Limited
Crescent Trust Co Ltd
Crownhold PLC
Cultura Technologies Ltd
DMGI Land & Property Europe Ltd
Danco International PLC
Dart Abbey Enterprises Limited
Darthaven Marina Limited
J.C. Dean (Haulage) Limited
Deutsch UK
Dextra Group PLC
Dorothy House Foundation Ltd
Dorset Health Trust Limited
Double H (Holdings) Limited
Double H (Nurseries) Limited
Doughty Engineering Limited
Downs School (Charlton House) Ltd
Drewdeeds Limited
Duchy Health Charity Limited
Dunlop Limited
Durlston Court School Trust Ltd
EPTA Cold Service Ltd
Eagle Star Holdings Limited
Eberspacher (U.K.) Limited
Edmont Ltd
Endsleigh Insurances (Brokers) Ltd
Enoch Properties (Devon) Ltd
European Investment Trust PLC
Evershot Farms Limited
Fabrinet UK Limited
Faccombe Estates Limited
Fairfield Farm Trust
Falfish Limited
Farms for City Children Ltd
Farrow & Ball Limited
Farthingford Properties Ltd
Firn Overseas Packaging Ltd
Fleetwheel Limited
Flowbird Transport Limited
Flybe Group PLC
Peter Ford Transport Limited
Frame Homes (South West) Ltd
Furlong Flooring (Wales) Ltd.
GEA Farm Technologies (UK) Ltd
Peter Gabriel Limited
Gemma International Limited
Gilbert and Goode Limited
Goodridge Limited
W.G. Gould & Sons Limited
Graceloft Limited
Graham and Green Limited
Graphic PLC
Gregory Distribution Limited
Gurr Johns Limited
H.B.H. Woolacotts Limited
W.R. Haines (Leasow Farms) Ltd
Hameln Pharmaceuticals Ltd
Hannick Homes & Developments Ltd
J.R. Harding & Sons (Frome) Ltd
Harrow House International College (Swanage)
David Hathaway Holdings Ltd
T. R. Hayes Limited
J.H. Haynes & Co. Limited
Headland Hotel Co Ltd
R.J. Heathman (Contractors) Ltd
Hendra Touring Caravan & Camping Park

Hinton Capital Investments Ltd
Hinton Garage (Bath) Limited
Hoburne Limited
B.R.Hodgson Facades Limited
Hopkins Estates Limited
Horizon Motor Co Ltd
House of Clive (Hair and Beauty) Ltd
Howard Garages (Weston) Ltd
Hunt's Foodservice Ltd
Hydro Building Systems UK Ltd
IBCOS Computers Ltd
IMI Webber Limited
IPS Partnership PLC
Independent Tool Consultants Ltd
Industrial Common Ownership Finance
Industrial Sales Limited
Intel Corporation (UK) Limited
Inter-Line (South West) Limited.
Intergraph (UK) Limited
Investacast Limited
Iracroft Limited
Islington Trowbridge Limited
J. J. Farm Services Limited
JGBM Ltd
H.R.Jasper & Son Limited
Jasun Envirocare PLC
B.T. Jenkins Limited
L. & F. Jones Holdings Ltd
Jongor Limited
Keenwork Limited
Kelston Precision Gears Ltd
Kelston Sparkes Holdings Ltd
Kernow Coatings Limited
Kerry Ingredients Holdings (U.K.)
Key Industrial Equipment Ltd
P.E. King (Bristol) Limited
King David Tyres Limited
Kings (Weymouth) Limited
Larasian Limited
Latchways PLC
Lear, Browne & Dunsford Ltd
Leeways Packaging Services Ltd
Linen Yard Investments (Crewkerne) Ltd
Lloyd & Whyte Group Limited
Lloyd's Property Southwest Ltd
Lombard Industrial Leasing Ltd
Lombard Leasing Co Ltd
Dick Lovett (Hungerford) Ltd
Dick Lovett Companies Limited
Lymington Investments Limited
Lypiatt Studio Limited
M. & P. Food Products Limited
Walter Maidment Limited
Manitou UK Limited
Manutan Limited
Marcatrin Limited
Market Square Limited
Marleton Cross Limited
Massey Wilcox Transport Ltd
Matki PLC
Mead Realisations Limited
D.J. Melsome Limited
Midas Construction Limited
Herman Miller Limited
Milord Homes Limited
Mitutoyo (U.K.) Limited
Mobile Windscreens Limited
Mole Avon Trading Limited
Moog Controls Limited
Mulberry Group PLC
N.V. Chichester Limited
Nagel Langdons Ltd

Naim Audio Limited
C.W. Nash (Farms) Limited
National Trust (Enterprises) Ltd
Negatex Limited
New Southgate Cemetery and Crematorium
Newlyn Art Gallery Limited
Norman Court and Sowley Farms Ltd
Norville Group Limited
Novanta Technologies UK Ltd
John O'Flynn Developments Ltd
Oak Tree Parks Limited
Obenshaw Limited
Osprey Shipping Limited
P3 Medical Limited
PAC Farms Limited
PB Design and Developments Ltd
Padmanor Investments Limited
J.C. & R.H. Palmer Limited
Parker Knoll Upholstery Ltd
Parsons and Joyce Contractors Ltd
Pattersons (Bristol) Limited
Pearce Seeds (Holdings) Ltd
Pebley Beach Limited
Penlane Limited
Pennard Hill Farm Limited
R.M. Penny (Plant Hire and Demolition)
People 2000 Limited
Perrys Recycling Limited
Piller UK Limited
Pinetops Nurseries Limited
Pipex Limited
Plymouth City Airport Limited
Henry W. Pollard & Sons Ltd
Poole Arts Trust Limited
Alan Porter Limited
Portlemouth Estates Limited
Quay Marinas Limited
Quickgrind Limited
Radiodetection Limited
Rangemoors Limited
Redcliffe Homes Limited
Renelec Limited
Renishaw International Limited
Renishaw P L C
Renrod Limited
Retrac Productions Limited
Rigibore Limited
Rochling Fibracon Limited
F W Rogers Garage (Saltash) Ltd
Rothdean Limited
Rotolok (Holdings) Limited
Rotork Overseas Limited
Rotork UK Limited
W.C. Rowe (Falmouth) Limited
S W Group Logistics Limited
SG Aerospace (UK) Limited
SM Group (Europe) Ltd.
SS Great Britain Trust
STVA UK Limited
Sailport PLC
Salisbury Glass Centre Limited
Sanlam Life & Pensions UK Ltd
Scot Group Limited
Senlan Securities Limited
Serais Investments Limited
John Seymour Transport Ltd
Shaunaks Limited
Shepperton Group Limited
Shipton Mill Limited
Smart Systems Limited
South Devon Railway Trust
South West Land Limited

Spandex Limited
C Sparks & Sons Limited
Spenco Engineering Co. Limited
Springfield Country Hotel (Stoborough)
Springvale Properties Limited
St Peter's Hospice
Stanborough (Developments) Ltd
Stannah Lift Services Limited
Stannah Lifts Limited
Stannah Stairlifts Limited
Stiga Ltd
Still Materials Handling Ltd
Stowell Concrete Limited
Surereed Limited
Swanage Railway Co Ltd
Swindon Silicon Systems Ltd
Synergy Health (UK) Limited
Taunton Land Limited
Taw and Torridge Coaches Ltd
David Taylor (Garages) Ltd
Taylor Maxwell Timber Limited
Taylor-Davis Limited
Tecalemit Garage Equipment Co Ltd
Theatre Royal Bath Limited
Thermographic Measurements Ltd
Thornton Shipbrokers Limited
Tiger Communications PLC
Tildenet Ltd
Tileflair Limited
Tincknell Fuels Limited
Torvean Limited
Totemplant Limited
Town Mills Craft Centre Ltd
Trago Mills (Falmouth) Limited
Tran-AM Limited
Trelleborg Industrial Tyres UK Ltd
Trelleborg Offshore UK Limited
Troika Developments Limited
Tyre Maintenance Limited
U C B Home Loans Corporation Ltd
Uni-Mill Engineering Limited
United Oilseeds Marketing Ltd
United Reformed Church (South Western Synod) Incorporated
Unity Tyre Co Ltd
Up Cerne Limited
Versatile Controls Limited
Viridor Waste Exeter Limited
Vospers of Plymouth Limited
Vygon (U.K.) Limited
Warners Retail Limited
Warrens Bakery Limited
Warrington Homes Limited
W.J. Watkins & Son Limited
Wessex Electricals (Shaftesbury) Ltd
West Country Motor Homes Ltd
West Country Park Home Estates Ltd
West End Precision Limited
West Somerset Railway PLC
Westcon Group Africa Operations Ltd
Westcountry Fruit Sales Ltd
Wherwell Farms Limited
Whites Material Handling Ltd
Whitsbury Farm & Stud Limited
George Williamson & Co. Ltd
Windward Marine Limited
A.J. Wooldridge Limited
M.E. Wynn & Co. Limited
X.T.Holdings Limited
Yelspa Limited
Yeo Valley Farms (Production) Ltd
Zurich Community Trust (UK) Ltd

1980-1989 [673]

288 Group Limited
A-Gas International Limited
A.E.T. Transport Services Ltd
AES Electric Ltd
ARI Fleet UK Limited
ATEX Media Limited
Aardman Animations Limited
Abacus (Bristol) Limited
Abbey Business Equipment Ltd
Abbey Manor Developments Ltd
M.J. Abbott Limited
Abercrombie & Kent Europe Ltd
Academy Leasing Limited
Acheson Construction Limited
Advanced Insulation Systems Ltd
Airsprung Furniture Limited
Alden Finance Limited
Alderley PLC
Alderley Systems Ltd
Alexander & Angell (Farms) Ltd
Alfco Investments Limited
Allstone Sands Gravels Aggregates Trading Co
Almanzora Group Limited
Altec Products Limited
Amcor Flexibles Winterbourne Ltd
Andrews Letting and Management Ltd
Appleby Westward Group Limited
Appledore Shipbuilders (2004) Ltd
Applied Market Information Ltd
Arada Limited
Architectural Profiles Limited
Arrowedge Limited
Arval UK Group Limited
Ashbolt Limited
Ashfield Land (Birmingham) Ltd
Ashley Family Foundation Ltd
Atkins Travel Limited
Atlas Packaging Limited
Autonumis Limited
Avalon Sciences Limited
Avon Wildlife Trust
Ayersmont Limited
B M J International Limited
B T Q Limited
BOFA International Ltd.
B.& M. Babbage & Co. Limited
M. Baker (Property Services) Ltd
Ball Aerocan UK Limited
Bank of Ireland Britain Holdings Ltd
Barnbury Enterprises Limited
R.J. Bateman (Engineering) Ltd
Batsford Estates (1983) Co Ltd
Beaumonts (Leeds) Limited
Beecholm Management Limited
K W Bell Group Limited
George Bence & Sons (Cheltenham)
Steve Benson Farming Limited
Bentley Slade Limited
Beran Instruments Limited
Berkeley Charterhouse Limited
Berrys Holdings Limited
Anthony Best Dynamics Limited
Beta Marine Limited
Beylon Limited
Bifold Fluidpower Limited
Ken Biggs Limited
Bistech PLC
Bituchem Holdings Limited
Bodywise (UK) Limited
Bonds Mill Estate Limited
Bournemouth Transport Limited
Box House (Services) Ltd
Brandon Trust
Bridgewell Holdings Limited
Bristol & Mendip Estates Ltd
Bristol & West PLC
Bristol Airport Limited
Bristol City Holdings Limited
Bristol Drugs Project Limited
Bristol Funeral Directors Ltd
Bristol Old Vic Theatre School Ltd
Bristol Polytechnic Enterprises (Developments)
Bristol Polytechnic Enterprises Ltd
Britanic Industries Limited
Britannia Windows (UK) Limited
Penny Brohn Cancer Care
Brookridge Timber Limited
A.J. Brunt Limited
Buccaneer Holdings Limited
Buro Happold Consulting Engineers
Buro Happold Engineers Limited
Buro Happold Limited
The Mike Burton Group Limited
Butterfly Conservation
C.P. Button Limited
Bybrook Agriculture Limited
C.J.L. Construction Limited
CAT-UK Services Limited
CFH Docmail Ltd
CKF Systems Limited
CSE Bournemouth Limited
CTC (Wholesalers) Limited
Cadillac Plastic Limited
Canynge Bicknell (Investments) Ltd
Canynge Bicknell Limited
Carco Limited
Carrs of Exeter Limited
F W S Carter & Sons Limited
N.H. Case Limited
Castle Barton Limited
Castle Gardens Sherborne Ltd
Catalent Micron Technologies Ltd
Cavendish Close Limited
Cemetery Management Limited
Cengage Learning UK Holdings Ltd
Centristic Limited
Charford Properties Limited
Chatlease Limited
Cheltenham & Gloucester PLC
Chippenham Motor Co Ltd
Chota Estates Co Ltd
Chronos Technology Limited
M J Church (Plant) Limited
Churchill Retirement (Group) Ltd
Churngold Construction Limited
Clifford Holdco Limited
Colburn Developments Limited
Colten Care Limited
Commercial Estates Property Co Ltd
Computershare Services Limited
Contactreal Limited
Coombe Castle International Ltd
Coombe Fisheries Limited
Corin Limited
Cornish Bakery Shops Limited
Cotswold Archaeology Limited
Cotswold Micro Systems Limited
County Confectionery Limited
County of Gloucestershire Community Foundation
J.A. Cover Limited
Crane Merchandising Systems Ltd
Creative Kernow Limited
Crematoria Management Ltd.
John Cribb & Sons Ltd.
Critchley Group Limited
A.C. Crocker (Properties) Ltd
M.B. Crocker Limited
G. Crook & Sons Limited
F.H. Cummings
Custom Interconnect Limited
D.I.S. Limited
Dainton Group Services Limited
Dan-Floor U.K. Limited
Danesdale Land Limited
Danfoss Power Solutions Ltd
W. Daniels Plant Hire Limited
Danisco (UK) Limited
Danisco Holdings (UK) Limited
Ron Darch & Sons Co Ltd
Dart Valley Systems Limited
Dartington Hall Trust
Datamine Corporate Limited
Arthur David (Food with Service)
Davies Holdings (Somerton) Ltd
De Monchy Aromatics Limited
Deceuninck Limited
Decision Insight Information Group (UK)
Denplan Limited
Dentsply IH Limited
Devon & Cornwall Autistic Community Trust
Devondale Electrical Distributors
Devonfields Limited
Devonport Royal Dockyard Ltd
Dezac Group Limited
Dingle Brothers Systems Ltd
Diverse Abilities Plus Ltd
Doric Developments (Bath) Ltd
Dorset Press Limited
Dover Fluids UK Ltd
John Downer Productions Ltd
Drew Holdings Limited
Drilling Systems Limited
Drytac Europe Limited
Dunsmere Developments Limited
Durable (UK) Limited
Dyson Technology Limited
E-Mex Home Funding Limited
Eagle One Estates Limited
Eagle One Homes Limited
Eagle One Limited
East Dorset Golf Club Limited
Ecclesiastical Insurance Group PLC
Electric Mobility Euro Limited
Electro Mechanical Systems Ltd
Elemis Limited
Edward Elgar Publishing Ltd
Elmley Foundation
Emotional Rescue Limited
Enga Limited
Epichem Group Limited
Etex Building Performance Ltd
Euravia Engineering & Supply Co. Ltd
Euro-Diesel (UK) Limited
European Friction Industries Ltd
Exeter Canal and Quay Trust Ltd
Exeter and Devon Airport Ltd
Eyre Holdings Limited
F & B Profiles Limited
FR Aviation Group Limited
FR Aviation Services Limited
Fermac Limited
First Databank UK Ltd

First South West Limited
Firstport Bespoke Property Services
Firstport Property Services Ltd
Firstport Property Services No 2 Ltd
Firstport Retirement Property Services
Fish Brothers (Holdings) Ltd
Flightbookers Limited
Foam Techniques Limited
Foodservice Centre Limited
D. H. J. Foot Limited
Foot Shop Limited
Footsure Western Limited
Ford Civil Engineering Limited
Ford Fuels Limited
Forest Press Hydraulics Ltd
G.A. Francis & Son Limited
M.F. Freeman Limited
C.G. Fry and Son Limited
Future Advanced Manufacture Ltd
Future Publishing Limited
G4S Technology Limited
GE Oil & Gas UK Limited
GS Yuasa Battery Sales UK Ltd
Galpharm International Limited
Galtec Holdings Limited
Galtec Limited
Gapcontrol Limited
Garador Limited
Gardiner (Holdings) Limited
Garrad Hassan & Partners Ltd
Gazco Limited
Gemaco Holdings Limited
Geometry Properties Limited
Gerber Emig Group Limited
Gilders Transport Limited
Gill Instruments Limited
Gillett's (Callington) Limited
John Gillman & Sons (Electrical)
Gloucestershire Warwickshire Steam Railway
Goadsby & Harding (Holdings) Ltd
Goadsby & Harding (Residential) Ltd
Great British Card Company PLC
Great Western Enterprise (Holdings)
Greendale Investments Ltd
David Greening Limited
Grevan Cars Limited
Grey Matter Limited
M.A. Grigg (Agricultural) Ltd
Grist Group Limited
William Haley Engineering Ltd
Halix Limited
Halsall Construction Limited
Handston Investments Limited
R. Hannon Limited
Hargreaves Lansdown Asset Management
Hargreaves Lansdown PLC
Harland Developments Limited
Harvey Shopfitters Limited
Haskins Snowhill Garden Centre Ltd
Hawksworth Securities PLC
Haycock Holdings Limited
C G & D Heal Limited
John Heathcoat & Company (Holdings)
Heber Limited
Helena Productions Limited
Highbridge Caravan Centre Ltd
Highfield Homes of Distinction Ltd
Hilcro Limited
Hillside Farm Investments Ltd
Hillside Property Co Ltd
William C. Hockin (Transport) Ltd
Hollingsworth and Vose Company (U.K.)
Holt Farms Limited
Holt JCB Limited
Holton Homes Limited
Homeloan Management Limited
Honda of The U.K. Manufacturing Ltd
Hoo Developments Limited
Horstman Defence Systems Ltd
Hospiscare
Howard Tenens Distribution Ltd
Hydro International (Wastewater) Ltd
Hydro International Limited
ITEC Connect Ltd
Imerys Talc UK Holding Limited
Imperial Business Systems Ltd
Imperial Civil Enforcement Solutions
Imperial Tobacco Holdings (1) Ltd
Imperial Tobacco Limited
Innovata Limited
Innsworth Technology Park Ltd
Integra Neurosciences Limited
Interconnect Products Limited
International Plywood (Importers)
International Plywood PLC
Investment Funds Direct Ltd
Ipipeline (TCP) Limited
Isles of Scilly Skybus Limited
J & K Aquatics Limited
Jenkins Marine Ltd.
Johnsons Group Limited
Juliana Group Limited
KLKI Holdings Limited
R. T. Keedwell Holdings Ltd
R.T. Keedwell Limited
Kellaway Building Supplies Ltd
Kelley Holdings Limited
Kinch Fuel Oils Limited
King Lifting Limited
Kitagawa Europe Limited
Kitto Group PLC
Knights Brown Construction Ltd
Knights Green Estates Limited
LAL Language Centres Holding Ltd
LAL Language Centres UK Ltd
LCD Publishing Limited
LV Equity Release Limited
LV Protection Limited
Lake Consultancy and Investments Ltd
Land & Buildings Limited
Landell Mills Limited
Langdon Group Limited
Langham Industries Limited
Lansdown Properties (Cheltenham) Ltd
Maurice Lay Distributors Ltd
Leehurst Swan Limited
Leo Textiles Limited
Leweston School Trust
D C Li (Builders) Limited
Lightning Electrical Construction
Lingfield Properties Limited
Lloyds Bank General Insurance Holdings
Loadace Limited
Locators Limited
Lockman Electronic Holdings Ltd
Lodge Rest Limited
Lombard Corporate Finance (December 1)
Lombard Corporate Finance (December 3)
Lombard Lease Finance Limited
London & Country Mortgages Ltd
London & Devonshire Trust Ltd
Longfield Hospice Care
Lornamead UK Limited
Dick Lovett (Bristol) Limited
Lowman Manufacturing Co Ltd
Lucknam Park Hotels Limited
M P Filtri (UK) Limited
MSP Capital Ltd
Macular Disease Society
Magna Motor Co Ltd
Magnox Limited
Majestic Tours Limited
Manchester and Provincial Car Parks
Manitou Finance Limited
Manor House Hotel (Okehampton) Ltd
Mantracourt Electronics Ltd
Marchmont Farms Limited
Stuart Marsh Shoes Limited
Masstock Arable (UK) Limited
Maxim Integrated Products UK Ltd
Colin Mear Engineering Ltd
Meggitt Acquisition Limited
Mendip Forestry Limited
Merlin Entertainments (Sea Life) Ltd
Mildren Construction Limited
Milestones Trust
Millwood Homes (Devon) Limited
Miro Technologies Limited
Morrish Builders (Poole) Ltd
Mortgage Works (UK) PLC
Mulberry Company (Design) Ltd
Mulberry Company (Europe) Ltd
Mulberry Company (Sales) Ltd
Multivac U.K. Limited
Murrill Construction Limited
Nare Hotel Co Ltd
Navisite Europe Limited
Neal's Yard (Natural Remedies) Ltd
Netcraft Ltd
Netvox Limited
Nevis Marketing Limited
New Look Limited
Nippon Paint (Europe) Ltd.
Nisbets PLC
North Devon Hospice
North Kent Farms Limited
G. Northover & Sons Limited
N. Notaro Homes Limited
Nylaplas Engineering Limited
O'Neill and Brennan Construction Ltd
Oasis Plant Hire Limited
Oastcrest Limited
Orchard Trust
Orthodynamics Limited
Osborne Care Homes Limited
Otter Nurseries Limited
Oval (259) Limited
P & M Group Limited
P L H Property Investment Ltd
P of a Productions Limited
PKL Group (UK) Limited
PLB Group Ltd.
PPL Midlands Limited
Palm Equipment International Ltd
Pantheon International PLC
Paramount 21 Limited
Parham Development Limited
Parham Investment Limited
Park Group South West Limited
Parkham Farms Limited
Parkway Hotel and Spa Limited
Parragon Books Limited
Walter C Parson Limited
Patalex II Productions Limited
Patalex Productions Limited
Patel Brothers Limited

Patrico Limited
Pendennis Shipyard (Holdings) Ltd
Peninsula Properties (Exeter) Ltd
Pennon Group PLC
Penny Lane Foods Limited
Pennyfarthing Construction Ltd
Penrice House (St. Austell) Ltd
Pet Food Holdings Limited
Pinder Fashions Limited
Planit Software Limited
Plantronics Limited
Plymouth Age Concern
Polamco Limited
Portway Domestic Appliances Ltd
Portway Precision Limited
Powersystems UK Ltd
Practical Developments (South West)
Praxair Surface Technologies Ltd
Prior Park Educational Trust
Progressive Systems Limited
Prospect Hospice Limited
Pullman Premier Leisure Ltd
Pyman Bell (Holdings) Limited
Quest End Computer Services Ltd
R S T Leisure Ltd
R. B. Quadrangle Leasing Ltd
Radquill Developments Limited
Railston Limited
Rajani (Wholesale) Limited
Range Valley Extrusions Ltd
Rapid Racking Limited
M.R. Ratcliffe Consultants Ltd
Raynsford Limited
Realhurry Limited
Red Kite Vehicle Consultants Ltd
Regency Oldhomes Limited
Regency Properties (Tadworth) Ltd
Resource Solutions Group PLC
Rew Hotels Limited
Rich Products Limited
Riohurst Investments Limited
River Reach Limited
Roadform Civil Engineering Co Ltd
Rochford Garden Machinery Ltd
Rochling Engineering Plastics (UK)
Rockstone Surfacing Limited
Rodgers of Plymouth Limited
C J L Rogers Properties Ltd.
Roots Systems Limited
Roper Rhodes Limited
Rowcroft House Foundation Ltd
Rowes Garage Limited
Royal Air Force Charitable Trust Enterprises
Royal Arcade Limited
Rygor Commercials Ltd
Rygor Group Services Limited
SAA Consultants Limited
SAFC Hitech Limited
SEA (Group) Ltd.
SIRVA Relocation (No.1) Ltd
SPM Homes Ltd
Saab Technologies UK Limited
Sabre Group Limited
Safran UK Limited
Samatt Limited
Sandpalm Properties Limited
Sarum Properties Limited
Satnam Investments Limited
Satnam Limited
Charles Saunders Limited
Scottish Widows Unit Trust Managers
J M Scully Limited
Seacon (Europe) Limited
Seagull Developments Limited
Seahawk Marine Foods Limited
Sealock Limited
Seasalt Limited
Secure Services Limited
Seepex UK Limited
Sentry Self Storage Limited
Severn & Wye Smokery Limited
Severn Glocon Group PLC
Severn Unival Limited
Severn Valley Woodworks Ltd
Sharpham Trust
Shaw Trust Limited
Shepperton Properties Limited
Shield Environmental Services Ltd
Sidcot School
Sigma-Aldrich Co Ltd
Signet Armorlite Europe Ltd
Silversands Limited
Skyline Systems Limited
WH Smith Promotions Limited
Snape Construction Limited
Snows Timber Limited
Socomec U.K. Limited
Sol Plaatje Educational Project
South West Communications Group Ltd
South West Investment Group (Capital)
South West Metal Finishing Ltd
South West Water Limited
South Western Helicopters Ltd
Space Engineering Services Ltd
Sparkworld Limited
Specialist Aviation Services Ltd
Spembly Medical Limited
Spirax-Sarco Overseas Limited
Spire Technology Limited
Spitalgate Dealer Services Ltd
St George's Bristol
St. Edward's School Cheltenham Trust
St. Joseph's School Launceston
St. Luke's Hospice Plymouth
St. Margaret's Somerset Hospice
St. Mary's School Shaftesbury Trust
Stallcombe House
Standbetter Limited
Star Hydraulics Limited
Chris Sterling Enterprises Ltd
Sterling ISA Managers Limited
Stevens Homes Ltd
Stovax Limited
Stowell Park Estate Limited
Stride Treglown Limited
Studyhome 1992 Limited
Supacat Limited
Superior Specials Limited
Suremime Limited
Sustrans Limited
Sutton Harbour Holdings PLC
Sutton Harbour Services Ltd
Swallowcourt Limited
Swallowfield PLC
Swegon Limited
Synergy Health Investments Ltd
Synergy Health Sterilisation UK Ltd
Synlatex Limited
System 6 Kitchens Limited
Systems Engineering & Assessment Ltd
T.E.J. Heating (Plymouth) Ltd
TBS Engineering Limited
TJW Precision Engineering Ltd
TMB Patterns Limited
TRL Technology Limited
Talbot Heath School Trust Ltd
Taylor Maxwell Holdings Ltd
Teleperformance Limited
Telesoft Technologies Limited
Temple Guiting Manor Limited
Tenens Associates Limited
Tetra Pak CPS Limited
Thames Valley Eggs (Production) Ltd
Theatre Royal (Plymouth) Ltd
Thoranmart Limited
Thorne Holdings Limited
Tithegrove Limited
Tollgate Group Limited
Tomy UK Co., Ltd.
Torcare Limited
Total Carbide Ltd
Towndown Limited
Trade-Air Airline Support Ltd
Transcribe Copier Systems Ltd
Transmission Developments Co (GB)
Treasure Homes Limited
Trelleborg Wheel Systems UK Ltd
Charles Trent Limited
Troax (U.K.) Limited
Troika Property Holdings Ltd
Trusart Limited
Turnspeed Precision Engineering Co Ltd
Twofour Broadcast Limited
Tylney Investments Limited
Ultraparts Limited
Unite Integrated Solutions PLC
United Bible Societies Association
Unitedhealthcare Global Medical (UK)
Unity Farm Holiday Centre Ltd
Utax (UK) Limited
Valeport Limited
Valmiera Glass UK Limited
Vauxhall Estates Limited
Vectura Limited
Veitch Family Holdings Limited
Verplas Limited
Vicaima Limited
Steve Vick International Ltd
Vistgate Limited
WPD Property Investments Ltd
WPD Telecoms Limited
WRC P.L.C.
Wagtech Projects Ltd
A J Wakely & Sons Ltd.
Walker Developments (South West) Ltd
John Ware Limited
Warm Welcome Hotels (Southern) Ltd
Warm Welcome Management Ltd
Warners of Gloucester Limited
Warwick Fabrics (UK) Limited
Watchpike Limited
Watercress Co Ltd
Watershed Arts Trust Limited
Waterside Holiday Group Ltd
Watts Truck & Van Limited
Weird Fish Limited
Wellesbourne Property Management Ltd
Wessex Archaeology Limited
Wessex Eagle Limited
Wessex GS Limited
Wessex Grain Ltd.
Wessex Water Enterprises Ltd
Wessex Water Limited
Wessex Water Services Limited
West Pharmaceutical Services Group
Western Counties Roofing Ltd

Western Forestry Co Ltd
Western Power Distribution (East Midlands)
Western Power Distribution (South Wales)
Western Power Distribution (South West)
Western Power Distribution Investments
Western Truck Rental Limited
Weston Hospicecare Limited
Westrock Packaging Systems UK Ltd.
Westward Investment Management Services (UK)
Chris Wheeler Construction Ltd
Wheeler's (Westbury) Limited
Whitehall Group (Wessex) Ltd
Willcox Bros Limited
Willett & Son Holdings Limited
Williams Southern Limited
Williamson-Dickie Europe Ltd
Wilson Investment Holdings Ltd
Wincanton Holdings Limited
Woodfield Developments Limited
Woodley Hotels Limited
Woodmace Limited
Woolacombe Bay Holiday Village Ltd
Worlds Apart Limited
Wyvern Cargo Ltd
XYZ Machine Tools Limited
Yate Disposables Ltd
Roger Young Limited
Zurich Financial Services (UKISA)
Zurich Intermediary Group Ltd

1990-1994 [411]

A-Gas (UK) Limited
A.K.S. (Yeovil) Limited
AES Horizons Investments Ltd
AFL Services Europe Ltd
AGD Systems Limited
ARAG PLC
Aardman Holdings Limited
Abaco Estates Limited
Ablebox Limited
Abraxas Insurance Administration Services
Acrefield Investments Limited
Air Bearings Limited
Alabare Christian Care Centres
Alberti Limited
Alias Limited
Alliance Leisure Services Ltd
Allstar Business Solutions Ltd
Amber Foundation
Amcor Flexibles UK Limited
Amcor UK Group International Ltd
American Amusements Holdings Ltd
Amulet Hotkey Ltd
Antech Limited
Applied Automation (UK) Ltd
Arlington Limited
Ascent Publishing Limited
Ashfield Land Management Ltd
Asset Services Limited
Athelney Trust PLC
Atlantis 39 Limited
Autism Wessex
Automotive Parts Distribution Ltd
Auxillis Limited
Auxillis Services Limited
Aviation & Defence Spares Ltd
Axiom Veterinary Laboratories Ltd
BIL Group Limited
Babcock Marine (Devonport) Ltd
Julian Barran Limited
Bartletts Transport and Warehouses
Bath Priory Limited
Battens Solicitors Limited
John Baylis Limited.
Beale Limited
Beaulieu Property Management Ltd
Beetles (UK) Ltd
Bell Contracting Limited
Berry Head Hotel Limited
Bibury Club Limited
Bioquell UK Limited
Birchclaim Limited
Bond Holdings Limited
Bourne Group Holdings Ltd
Bowldown Farms Limited
Briarwood Products Limited
Bridges (Electrical Engineers) Ltd
Bristol & Avon Transport & Recycling Ltd
Bristol Water Holdings Limited
Bristol Water PLC
British Small Animal Veterinary Association
Brothers Drinks Co. Limited
Mike Burton Travel Limited
Burts Potato Chips Limited
C.H.G. Holdings Limited
CCR Motor Co Ltd
CDS (Superstores International) Ltd
CGA Financial & Investment Services
Call Caterlink Ltd
Calleva Limited
Cambria Automobiles (South East) Ltd
Canford Renewable Energy Ltd
Caplon Limited
Care South
Carnegie International Asset Management
Ceuta Healthcare Limited
Chelverton Growth Trust PLC
Children's Hospice South West
C. & J. Clark (Street) Ltd
Matthew Clark Bibendum Ltd
Clipper Properties Limited
Cobham Leasing Limited
Coffetek Limited
Colebrook Bosson & Saunders (Products)
Coleman UK Limited
Colston's School
Commercial Limited
Complete Price Eyewear Limited
Computershare Mortgage Services Ltd
Corin Group Limited
Corin Holdings Limited
Corin International Limited
Corin USA Limited
Courtwave Limited
Cronite Castings (Distribution) Ltd
Crowdhill Limited
Crown Pet Foods Limited
D.B. Foods Limited
DDC Dolphin Limited
DMJ Asset Management Ltd.
DPM Estate Limited
Dairy Partners Limited
Danlers Limited
Dart Sensors Limited
Dartmoor Investment Trust Ltd
Data Installation & Networking Services
Dean & Reddyhoff Limited
Deep Moor LF Limited
Derbyshire Home Loans Limited
Descartes Systems UK Limited
Desertlands Entertainment Ltd
Devon & Exeter Spastics Society
Devonshire Homes Limited
Devonshire Motors Limited
Devonshire Pine Limited
Drilling Systems (U.K.) Ltd
Drimbawn (UK) Limited
Duffields (South West) Limited
Dyson International Limited
Dyson Limited
E T Holdings Limited
E T M Contractors Limited
EMG Limited
Earthline Limited
Eastman Estates Limited
Ecclesiastical Planning Services Ltd
Edentree Investment Management Ltd
Elmbirch Properties P.L.C.
Emerald Debtco Limited
English Heritage Trading Ltd
T. Ensor & Son Limited
Eurac Limited
Eurac Poole Limited
Eurilait Limited
Eurotaxis Ltd.
Eurotech Group PLC
Executive Jet Support Limited
Exmoor Calvert Trust
Fairlynx Limited
Falcon Self Drive Limited
Mark Farwell Plant Hire Ltd
Fazakerley Prison Services Ltd
Fenchurch Engineering Services Ltd
Films at 59 Limited
Findlay Publications Investments Ltd
Finlay Hire Limited
Firmplot Limited
Fish Brothers (Swindon) Ltd
Fjords Processing Limited
Flybe Limited
Francis & Lewis International Ltd
Frazer-Nash Consultancy Ltd
Freshstores Limited
Fundamentals Limited
Futura Foods UK Limited
G.B. Electronics Limited
GDS Publishing Limited
GP Batteries (UK) Limited
Gall Thomson Environmental Ltd
Genevac Limited
Gloster Furniture Limited
Gloucestershire Airport Ltd
Gordano Support Group Limited
Green Gourmet Limited
Greiner Bio-One Limited
Gridline Enterprises Limited
Grist Environmental Limited
Growth Technology Limited
Haley Securities Limited
Hampton House Properties Ltd
Hampton Printing (Bristol) Ltd
Hanford School Charitable Trust Ltd
Hargreaves Lansdown Fund Managers Ltd.
Harper's Home Mix Limited
Harris & Harris Construction Ltd
James Hay Holdings Limited
James Hay Partnership Management
Heligan Gardens Limited
Hemsley Fraser Group Limited
M.H.R. Hicks Limited
Higher Education Statistics Agency
Highway Insurance Group Ltd
Hochtief (UK) Construction Ltd
Honda Engineering Europe Ltd
Honda Logistics UK Limited

Honda R & D Europe (U.K.) Ltd
Howard Tenens (North West) Ltd
Hylton Group Limited
IP-Performance Ltd
IPS Pensions Limited
Impcross Limited
Independent Agriculture Ltd
Independent Slate Supplies Ltd
Innogy Renewables UK Limited
Inter Mediate Two Limited
International Education Systems Ltd
Ipplepen Property Limited
JELF Limited
JELF Wellbeing Limited
JISC Services Limited
Jackson Property Investments
Jade-Aden Services Limited
Jaguar Oil & Gas UK Limited
Jensen-Faulkner Limited
D R Jones Yeovil Ltd.
Kawasaki Precision Machinery (UK)
Kay Transport Limited
Keelex 176 Limited
Keycrown Properties Limited
L.A.L. Estates Limited
LDC (Holdings) Limited
Lakes Bathrooms Limited
Landmark Information Group Ltd
Landmark International Holdings Ltd
Landscove Holidays Limited
Latona Leisure Limited
Leander Developments Limited
Legacy Properties Limited
Limbs & Things Limited
Linwood Fabric Co Ltd
Longmayne Limited
Dick Lovett (Specialist Cars) Ltd
Dick Lovett Sporting Limited
Lush Ltd.
Lyme Bay Cider Co Ltd
Lyons Seafoods Limited
M & P (Draycote) Limited
M H Joinery Products PLC
M. & N. Electrical and Mechanical Services
M.K. Test Systems Ltd.
MAN Truck and Bus UK Limited
Magellan Aerospace (Blackpool) Ltd
Magnet Sales and Service Ltd
Mallory International Limited
Manual Investing Limited
Manuli Packaging (UK) Ltd.
Mar-Key Marquees Limited
MG Markey Group Limited
Masters Golf Co Ltd
Mawgan Porth Holiday Park Ltd
Maxin Limited
I.J. McGill Transport Limited
Mears Homecare Limited
Mears Limited
Mecwash Systems Limited
Medisafe UK Limited
Megasteel Ltd
Meggitt International Limited
Merlo UK Limited
Metalex Products Limited
Metric Group Limited
Minton Investments (Industrial) Ltd
Monkey World Limited
Museum of East Asian Art
Mycronic Ltd
Mzuri Limited
N P Automotive Coatings (Europe) Ltd
National Lighting Co Ltd
National Marine Aquarium Ltd
Nationwide Syndications Ltd
Nectar Imports Limited
Newland Homes Limited
Nokia UK Limited
Norco G R P Limited
North Dairy Farms Limited
Organix Brands Limited
Outsource UK Limited
P W Commercial Co Ltd
PADI EMEA Limited
PDQ Airspares Limited
Pang Investments Limited
Park Garden Centre Limited
Parkside (Barnstaple) Limited
Parsons Construction Limited
Pastaking (UK) Limited
Pathfinder Park Homes Limited
Pendennis Shipyard Limited
Pennyfarthing Homes Limited
Penton Securities Limited
Pittville Leasing Limited
Plantforce Rentals Ltd
Plastivan Limited
Pleroma (UK) Limited
Porthia Group Limited
Portico Business Services Ltd
Portland Harbour Authority Ltd
Portland Stone Firms Limited
Powervamp Limited
Premier Cables Limited
Primetower Properties Limited
Property Management Group Ltd
Pulse Power and Measurement Ltd
Quantock Properties Limited
R.R. Transport Limited
RCR Flooring Products Limited
REPL International Limited
RWE Cogen UK Limited
Raans Estates Limited
Residential Trust Limited
Robbins & Myers Holdings UK Ltd
Rochford Holdings Limited
Rosemundy Investments Limited
Rotork Midland Limited
Rowan Dartington & Co. Limited
Royal Bath & West of England Society
Rush Group Limited
Charles Russell International Ltd
S.W.T Finance Limited
SIRVA Relocation Holdings Ltd
Sanderson Recruitment PLC
Sandown Dorset and Wiltshire Ltd
Sanoh UK Manufacturing Limited
Sartorius Stedim Lab Limited
Scotts Limited
Seabank Power Limited
Shearwell Data Limited
John Sheppard Butchers Ltd
Shiptinvest Limited
Silverleigh Limited
Somerdale International Ltd
Somerset Care Limited
South West Investment Group Ltd
Specialist Aviation Services Group
Spectrum Premier Homes Limited
Spike Island Artspace Limited
Spinnaker International Ltd
St. Francis Limited
St. James's Place International Assurance Group
St. James's Place UK PLC
St. James's Place Wealth Management Group
St.James's Place (PCP) Limited
St.James's Place Management Services
Stag Buying Group Limited
Stannah Management Services Ltd
H.C. Starck Limited
Steele Davis Limited
Stonegate Agriculture Limited
Summerfield Developments (SW) Ltd
Summerfield Estates Ltd
J. Suttle Transport Limited
Team Relocations Limited
Tekne Shopfitting Limited
Tetbury Hospital Trust Limited
Thompson Valves Limited
Thrive Renewables (Caton Moor) Ltd
Thrive Renewables PLC
Timehaste Limited
Tocris Cookson Limited
Total Laminate Systems Ltd
Tracertec Limited
Trade Link Co Ltd
Trafalgar Estate Limited
Tre' Care Group Limited
Trebah Garden Trust
Tregenna Castle Hotel Limited
Tricel (Gloucester) Limited
Troax Lee Manufacturing Ltd
Truscotts (Barnstaple) Limited
R Tudor Holdings Limited
Turlough Limited
Ryan Turner Hope PLC
Turner Property Holdings Ltd
UCAS Media Limited
UKRD Group Limited
Unicorn Training Group Limited
United Agri Products Limited
United Registrar of Systems Ltd
Universities and Colleges Admissions Service
VES Precision Limited
Vee Bee Filtration UK Limited
Vero UK Limited
Vetswest Limited
Viridor Limited
Viridor Waste (Greater Manchester)
Viridor Waste (Somerset) Ltd
Viridor Waste (Thames) Limited
Viridor Waste Kent Limited
Viridor Waste Limited
Voyager Fishing Co Ltd
WA Consultants Limited
WW (UK) Limited
Wallscourt Foundation
Warminster School
A. H. Warren Trust Limited
Watson-Marlow Limited
M. Way & Son (Transport) Ltd
Weavers Shop Limited
Webbers Property Services Ltd
Weldmar Hospicecare Trust
Wessex Eagle Holdings Limited
Wessex Garages Holdings Ltd
Wessex Group Limited
West House Transport (S & G) Ltd
West UC Limited
Westcountry Garden Centres Ltd
Westerleigh Group Limited
Western Mechanical Handling UK Ltd
Westfield Medical Limited

Weymouth Harbour Estates Ltd
White Horse Care Trust
Wildfowl & Wetlands Trust
Wind River UK Limited
Witon Engineering Limited
Woodcrescent Properties Ltd
Woodpecker Properties Limited
Woodstock Leabank Office Furniture
Wrafton Laboratories Limited
Wrapex Limited
Lewis Wyatt (Construction) Ltd
YYS International (UK) Limited
Zurich Assurance Ltd
npower Gas Limited

1995 [104]

ABS Wholesale Limited
AES Barry Limited
AES K2 Limited
AFP (Europe)
ALD Automotive Group Limited
Aistone Properties Limited
Alchemy Estates Limited
Alertsystems Limited
Amcor Mediflex Limited
Amimed Direct Limited
Apetito (U.K.) Holdings Ltd
Avon Group Manufacturing (Holdings)
Barden Network Engineering Ltd
B.J. Barkwell & Sons Limited
Big Green Parcel Machine Ltd
Blade Motor Group Limited
Bridgend Custodial Services Ltd
D. & I. Bridgman and Son Ltd
Bristol Care Homes Limited
A D Burs Limited
Cavehurst Limited
Computershare Limited
Containers Packaging (Europe)
Cornwall Care Limited
Cotswold Motor Group Limited
Coxley Developments Limited
Culverdene Properties Limited
De Vere Farms Limited
EDF Energy Nuclear Generation Ltd
Eco Sustainable Solutions Ltd
Ecotricity Generation Limited
Eden Research PLC
Edgwicks Limited
Expolink Europe Limited
Farmington Natural Stone Ltd
Field International Limited
First Resources Limited
Foursquare Associates Limited
G.E. Developments Ltd
GLM Trading Limited
Gazelle Properties Limited
Gibbs Surfacing Limited
E. & J. W. Glendinning (Holdings)
Gloucestershire Association for Disability
Golfhill Limited
Great Eastern Hotel Co Ltd
Grosvenor Place Holdings Ltd
Half Moon Bay Limited
Hillcrest House Limited
Steve Hoskin Construction Ltd
Hydrock Consultants Limited
Imperial Tobacco Holdings Ltd
Independent Investment Analysis Ltd
JELF Financial Planning Ltd
Kamm Civil Engineering Limited
E.P. Keogh Contractors Ltd.
Keyway Limited
LDC (Portfolio One) Limited
Lewisia Limited
Litfield Land Limited
Lush Retail Limited
Manor Collection Limited
Medipak Limited
Mortgage Intelligence Limited
Mount Batten Sailing and Water Sports Centre
Newcastle Estate Partnership Ltd
Nu-Heat UK Limited
R. O'Dell (Holdings) Limited
Octagon Healthcare Limited
Original Style Limited
Osprey Maritime Limited
Oval Estates (Bath) Limited
Parham Holdings Limited
Peninsula Seafoods Limited
Premier Developments (1995) Ltd
Procol Limited
Project People Limited
Redde PLC
Renelec Chalgrove Limited
Renewable Energy Co Ltd
Richards Homes Limited
Ropsley Farms Limited
David Salisbury Joinery Ltd
Sanderson Contract Management Ltd
Screwfix Direct Limited
Seafood Trading Limited
Shareland Investments Limited
Shillofad Limited
Shire Integrated Systems Ltd
The Ralph & Irma Sperring Charity
Sumac Precision Engineering Ltd
Tolladine Estates Limited
Torbay Cemetery and Crematorium Ltd
Tribal Holdings Limited
UDS Properties Limited
Verton Limited
Victoria Wharves Limited
Wallace & Gromit's Children's Foundation
We The Curious Limited
Weardale Estates Limited
Wellington Motors Limited
West Country Park Homes Ltd
Wilson Leisure Limited
Wrings Transport Limited

1996 [136]

A & A Trading (U.K.) Limited
A.C.C. Freight Management Ltd
AES Barry Operations Limited
Aaron Services Limited
Alliance Pharmaceuticals Ltd
Altogether Care - Care Homes Ltd
April UK (Insurance Services) Ltd
Arcade Leasing Limited
Asha Foundation
Basic Broadcasting Limited
Bath Rugby Limited
Bayview Developments (South) Ltd
Bechtle Direct Limited
Bioscientifica Limited
Bittware Limited
Blackmore Limited
W H Bond & Sons Limited
Bristol City Football Club Ltd
Cannon Technologies Group Ltd
Carco Group Limited
Careline UK Monitoring Limited
Caspian Networks Limited
Castle Air Limited
Castle Motors (Trebrown) Ltd
Fred Champion Groundworks Ltd
Fred Champion Hire Limited
Coastline Housing Limited
Coates & Co. (Plymouth) Ltd
Computershare Technology Services (UK)
Cooper Tyre & Rubber Company UK Ltd
Copperplane Limited
Creditcall Limited
Crystalight Limited
Design Objectives Limited
Devon Community Foundation
Draycot Estates Limited
Dycem Limited
EMS Satcom UK, Ltd.
Eagle One Village Shopping Ltd
Eden Project Limited
Eliquo Hydrok Limited
Elondale Limited
Europa Group Limited
Exe Investment Limited
Express Contract Drying Ltd
F & B Profiles (Holdings) Ltd
Foxmoor Business Park Limited
G-TEKT Europe Manufacturing Ltd
Genie Toys PLC
Stanley Gibson Limited
Glide Student & Residential Ltd
Grant Engineering (UK) Limited
Graytone Limited
Greens of Cheltenham Limited
H.K.C. Europe Limited
Heritage Automotive Limited
Hestercombe Gardens Trust
B R Hodgson Group Limited
Hospital Company (Dartford) Group
Hospital Company (Dartford) Ltd
Huck Nets (U.K.) Limited
Hunter Stoves Limited
Imperial Brands Finance PLC
Imperial Brands PLC
KMW Properties Limited
Kaikoura Investments Limited
Kernock Park Plants Limited
Klaw Products Limited
Lagan Farms (Dorset) Limited
Lake Inns & Leisure Limited
Lanhydrock Golf Club Limited
Libra Homes Limited
Lifetime Training Group Ltd
Lightmoor Homes Limited
Liverpool Victoria Insurance Co Ltd
MRT Castings Limited
Mail Handling International Ltd
Main Gate Leisure Limited
Marazion Holdings Limited
Marcham Farms Limited
McCulloch Homes Limited
Mears Group PLC
C.P. Mikulla Limited
Monkton Combe School
Neptune (Europe) Ltd
Newberry International Produce Ltd
Newcross Healthcare Solutions Ltd
No House Limited
Oakfield Grove Properties Ltd
Oasis Healthcare Limited
Old Mills Estates Limited
Otter Nurseries of Plymouth Ltd
Pendine Wind Farm Limited

Pennant International Group PLC
Pentrebay Properties Limited
Plantlife International - The Wild Plant Conservation Charity
Plymouth Science Park Limited
Plymstock Properties Limited
Portland Port Limited
Precision Lift Services Ltd
Premier Double Glazed Units Ltd
Premiere Health Limited
Property Consortium UK Limited
C.F. Roberts (Electrical Contractors)
Rowcliffe Holdings Limited
SAFC Biosciences Limited
Samara Investments Limited
Seasons Holidays PLC
Sharpness Dock Limited
Snow Business International Ltd
Southern England Farms Limited
Sparrow Crane Hire Limited
St. James's Place PLC
Stage Electrics Partnership Ltd
Steadfast Asset Management Ltd
Stepping Stones Resettlement Unit
Stochastic Holdings Ltd
Supara Limited
Teagle Machinery Limited
Terramond Limited
Toogoods Property Co Ltd
U-Drive Limited
Unite Group PLC
Unite Holdings Limited
Vacsax Limited
Vysiion Limited
Waterdance Limited
Way Group Limited
Wessex Products (Leasing) Ltd
Westbury Care Limited
White Rose School of Beauty and Complementary Therapies
Whitelock & Co Ltd
Wildbrook Investments (Thornbury)
Wildbrook Investments Limited
Willmot Pertwee Limited
Winchcombe Finance Limited

1997 [149]

1st Machine Tool Accessories Ltd
3T's Leisure Ltd.
AES UK Holdings Ltd
ARFF Ltd
ASDAN
ASP Independent Living Limited
Ableway Developments Limited
Acumed Ltd
Addison Developments Limited
Addpace Limited
Agents and Properties (Taunton) Ltd
Airbus Operations Limited
Altran UK Limited
Amport and District Coaches Ltd
Animal Healthcare Co Ltd
Apollo Radiators Limited
Avon Valley Precision Engineering
Axminster Tool Centre Ltd
Balimark Limited
Barnwood Group Limited
John Baylis Leisure Limited
Bendalls Leisure Limited
Beyond The Bean Limited
Percy R Brend & Sons (Holdings) Ltd
Brightwater Estates Limited
C & O Tractors Limited
Centaur Foods Limited
Central Management Catalogue Agency (UK)
Cheltenham Family Health Care Centre
M J Church Properties Limited
C & J Clark (No 1) Limited
C & J Clark Limited
Club Communications Ltd.
Colethrop Farm Limited
Collacombe Farm Limited
Community Health Facilities (Oxford)
Coolgate Limited
Countess of Brecknock Hospice Trust
C J Cox Limited
Crescent Motorcycle Co Ltd
Criterion Healthcare PLC
Crossco (284) Limited
Cruciform Services Limited
Cullen Group Limited
Cullompton Walronds Preservation Trust
DAS Services Limited
DAS UK Holdings Limited
Devon Contract Waste Ltd
Dragon Alfa Cement Limited
Dunbia (UK)
E3 Media Limited
Edenvale Turf (SW) Limited
Exeter Rugby Club Limited
Exeter Rugby Group PLC
First Step Homes Limited
Firstport Insurance Services Ltd
Frontline Image Ltd
Future Publishing Holdings Ltd
Gilstone Partnership Limited
Gleneil Limited
Gooderham Farms Limited
Greater Union Limited
Greenbank Hotel (Falmouth) Ltd
Hartham Park Limited
Haskins Garden Centres Limited
Hayne Securities Limited
Hill Brush Co Ltd
Niall Hobhouse Limited
House Property Associates Ltd
Humber Technology Limited
Hydro Holdings UK Limited
I.D.S. Refrigeration Limited
IXYS UK Westcode Ltd.
Infoteam International Services Ltd
Inty Limited
Jackson Developments Limited
Julia's House Limited
K & J Logistics Limited
Kemble Farms Limited
Alan Kerr Limited
King Edward's School, Bath
King's School, Bruton
Kiwa Limited
Kumari Care Limited
LTC Group87 Ltd
Llawnroc Hotel Limited
Lush Manufacturing Limited
M & G Properties (Cheltenham) Ltd
Martins of Exeter Limited
Meggitt Aerospace Limited
Metric Group Holdings Limited
Microsemi Storage Solutions Europe Ltd
Midas Group Limited
Milspeed Limited
Moor Park House Limited
Mount International United Services Ltd
The George Muller Charitable Trust
National Maritime Museum Cornwall Trust
National Milk Records PLC
Nuon UK Ltd
Octagon Healthcare Holdings (Norwich)
Organic Milk Suppliers Co-operative
Outdoor and Cycle Concepts Ltd
Oval (1173) Limited
P & L Properties Limited
Peartime Limited
Pencarrie Limited
Petrarch Holdings Limited
Poolearth Limited
Prosafe Offshore Limited
Puckator Limited
Pulsar Process Measurement Ltd
Quality Assurance Agency for Higher Education
R.T. Property Investments Ltd
Ramsbury Estates Limited
Real Live Leisure Co Ltd
Redlynch Agricultural Engineering
Renelec Groundworks Limited
Research Instruments Limited
Riviera Produce Limited
Rockfield Farms Limited
Salum Properties Limited
Scisys UK Holding Ltd
Seal-Lite Windows Doors & Conservatories
Second Applemead Limited
Shilston Barton Farming Ltd
Stanborough (Construction) Ltd
Steppes Travel Ltd
Stride Treglown Group PLC
Surest Ltd
Swettenham Estates (UK) Ltd
Synergy Health Limited
Tasman House Developments Ltd
Thermae Development Co Ltd
Trelleborg Holdings UK Limited
Uphouse Farm Limited
Vectura Group PLC
Vero Software Limited
Viridor Waste (Landfill Restoration)
WHC Hire Services Ltd.
Walton Civil Engineering and Surfacing Contractors
Watermark Cotswolds Limited
Waters Park House Limited
Watershore Ltd.
West Country Business Systems (Holdings)
West End Investments Clifton Ltd
Wildbrook Investments (Industrial)
Woodlodge Products Limited
npower Northern Limited

1998 [146]

1pm (UK) Limited
4Com Customer Services Ltd
Aeroflex Test Solutions Ltd
Animal Friends Insurance Services
April Medibroker Limited
Arriva Group Limited
Auger Torque Europe Limited
Aviation Training International Ltd
B.G. Automotive Limited
BES Healthcare Ltd
M.J. Baker Foodservice Ltd
Bakers Coaches Limited
Bamboo Technology Group Ltd
EW Beard (Holdings) Limited
Bexley PPP Health Services Ltd
Black Country PPP Health Services

Bluevenn Limited
Bluewater Property Limited
Bristol & London PLC
British Pepper & Spice Co Ltd
C & C Motor Caravans Ltd
C & P Medical Trading Limited
Calendar Club Limited
Carnegie Investment Asset Management
Catalent CTS (Wales) Limited
Cedar Care Homes Limited
Chatleigh Limited
Cloudpay United Kingdom Ltd
Clyst Holdings Limited
Computershare Investor Services PLC
Conmed UK Ltd
Cornwall Development Co Ltd
Cornwall Glass & Glazing Ltd
Dagenham Wind Park Limited
Daido Industrial Bearings Europe Ltd
Dorset Village Bakery Limited
Dunlop Aerospace Group Limited
Dunlop Aerospace Holdings Ltd
Dunlop Aerospace Overseas Ltd
ESP Colour Limited
Eagle One Country Shopping Ltd
Eagle One Retail Limited
Ecotricity Group Ltd
Everhot Ltd.
FWSC (Ladram) Limited
Fasthosts Internet Limited
Fluid Transfer International Ltd
Cameron Fuller Limited
G.B Contracts Limited
GBE Converge Group Ltd
GM Coachwork Limited
Gainwell Limited
Get Fresh Cosmetics Ltd
Glen Mhor Limited
Grange Mill Investments Ltd
Hargreaves Lansdown Advisory Services
Hesters Way Partnership Ltd.
Hughes Hotels Limited
David Hunt (North Devon) Ltd
Imerys UK Limited
Imperial Tobacco Overseas Holdings Ltd
Infusion GB Limited
Inter Rested Limited
K.D.P. Tools Limited
Kingham Farms Ltd
Lancer Scott Limited
Lister Shearing Equipment Ltd
Little Bedwyn Estate Limited
Lloyd & Whyte Limited
Lomand Homes Limited
Longmeadow Properties Limited
M.D. Building Services Limited
Marlux Medical Limited
McCaulay's Health & Sport Ltd
Mears Care (Holdings) Limited
Mears Housing Management Ltd
Meggitt Aerospace Holdings Ltd
Merlin Cinemas Limited
Merlin Entertainments (Dungeons) Ltd
Merlin Entertainments Group Operations
Merriott Plastics Limited
Millfields Community Economic Development Trust CIC
Mylor Yacht Harbour (Holding Company)
Newcombe Beard Limited
North Devon Homes
Nu-Pro Limited
Onley Prison Services Limited
Opaltec International Limited
Openwork Services Limited
Orchardleigh Estates Limited
P G Properties Limited
PDF Erection Services Limited
PSC Training & Development Group Ltd
Paragon Education & Skills Ltd
Parragon Publishing Limited
Pen y Cymoedd Wind Farm Ltd
Pennyfarthing Developments Ltd
Permali Gloucester Limited
Phoenix Learning and Care Ltd
Police Resources International Ltd
Prodigio Limited
Providor Limited
Pukka Pads 2000 Limited
Quick Move Now Limited
Reed Construction & Developments Ltd
Renelec Group Limited
Resolution Interiors Limited
Rollalong Holdings Limited
Rollalong Limited
John Romans Park Homes Ltd
Royal West of England Academy
Safran Landing Systems Services UK Ltd
Safran Landing Systems UK Ltd
Sensitisers Group Ltd.
Sheila Holdings Limited
Sherborne Preparatory School
Sigma - Aldrich Financial Services
Silicon Sensing Systems Ltd
C. Smart Agricultural Services Ltd
Sortimo International Limited
South Bristol Church and Community Trust
South Manchester Healthcare (Holdings)
South Manchester Healthcare Ltd
Stealthlink Ltd
Stepping Stone Group Limited
W. Stevenson & Sons Limited
Stonehaven (Healthcare) Ltd
Structural Metal Decks Limited
Styles & Brown Ltd
Tamander Limited
Tauntfield Ltd
Town Hospitals (North Staffordshire Combined)
Truro Tractors Limited
United Healthcare (Bromley) Holdings
United Healthcare (Bromley) Ltd
Universal Balancing Limited
Urbaser Limited
WPC Software Limited
A. H. Warren Trust (Property) Ltd
Watch Guru Limited
Weblease Limited
Western Power Distribution (West Midlands)
Windmill Care Limited
Woods Group Limited
Yankee Candle Company (Europe) Ltd
npower Limited

1999 [171]

Accident Claims Handlers Ltd
Accommodation Services (Holdings)
Ace Welding Limited
Aceo Limited
Acorn Builders (Pewsey) Ltd
Amariz Limited
Guy Anderson Wines Limited
Arisaig Partners (UK) Limited
Ashley Chase Estate Limited
Auden McKenzie (Pharma Division) Ltd
Avon Care Homes Limited
Avonline PLC
Baglan Moor Healthcare Holdings Ltd
Baglan Moor Healthcare PLC
GP & J Baker Limited
Bambers Wind Park Limited
Bartlett Contractors Limited
Bath Demolition Limited
Blanchworth Care Limited
Bournemouth Young Men's Christian Association
Brabon Properties Limited
Brick Peers Limited
Brownbrink Ltd
The Andrew Brownsword Arts Foundation
Burcombe Haulage Limited
C.T.C.H. Limited
CQC Limited
Cadogan House Investment Properties
Campden BRI (Chipping Campden) Ltd
Cartus Holdings Limited
Catalent Pharma Solutions Ltd
Chanctonbury Health Care Ltd
Chappell Engineering Limited
Clarkson Evans Limited
Claverton Estates Ltd.
Coastal Care Homes Limited
Cobell Ltd
Compton Beauchamp Estates Ltd
Concrete Fabrications Limited
Connolly & Callaghan Limited
Crapper & Sons Landfill Ltd
Crowndell Consulting Limited
Cult Clothing Cheltenham Ltd
Deceuninck Holdings (UK) Ltd
Defence Training Services Ltd
Delphi Diesel Systems Limited
Delphi Lockheed Automotive Ltd
Delphine Homecare Limited
Devon Air Ambulance Trading Co Ltd
Devon Air Ambulance Trust
Dezac Group Holdings Limited
Dorset & Somerset Air Ambulance Charity
Hy. Duke & Son Limited
Dyson James Limited
Edgecom Estates Ltd
Eduserv
Enidvale Holdings Limited
Equi Media Limited
Euston Simmonds Limited
Evesham Specialist Packaging Ltd
Finance Solutions Limited
First City Nursing Services Ltd
Flowervision (Bristol) Limited
Flying Visit Limited
Fonterra (Logistics) Limited
Future PLC
G.E.H. Properties Limited
Garador Holdings Limited
Glen Foundry Limited
Good Energy Limited
Good Food and Drink Co Ltd
Greensquare Homes Limited
Group Silverline Limited
Gwynt y Mor Offshore Wind Farm Ltd
Hamilton Scott Estates Limited
Hatton Properties Limited
Health Management (UCLH) Ltd
Healthcare Computing Limited
Highway Insurance Co Ltd
Horizon Organic Dairy Limited
Hospital Company (Swindon & Marlborough)

Holdings
Hospital Company (Swindon & Marlborough)
IDEMIA UK Limited
Infineon Technologies UK Ltd
Integrated Accommodation Services PLC
Irongate Limited
J+S Limited
Simon James New Homes Limited
Jamjar Print Ltd
K2 Medical Systems Limited
Kaba Limited
Kemble Airfield Estates Ltd
Kenton School Services Limited
Kew Estates Limited
King's School, Gloucester
Korado Ltd
Leighton-Boyce Properties Ltd.
Lemaca Limited
Loran (Investments) Limited
Dick Lovett (Bath) Limited
Dick Lovett Sports Cars Ltd
Madame Tussauds Touring Exhibition
Magna Motor Company (Christchurch)
Marsh Court Farm Limited
Meggitt Advanced Composites Ltd
Mercia Healthcare Limited
Merlin Entertainments (Asia Pacific)
Metaltech Precision Ltd
Newcross Nursing Group Ltd
Northam Farm Caravan Sales Ltd
S. Notaro Holdings Limited
Nuvias Global Services Limited
Ohashi Technica UK, Ltd.
Openwork Holdings Limited
Orproperty Limited
Parsons Nationwide Distribution Ltd.
Patheon UK Limited
Pearsalls Limited
Plastic Surgeon Limited
Playforce Limited
Premier Underwriting Limited
Proper Cornish Limited
Pulse Printing Products Ltd
QDOS Homes Limited
R W Estates (Trading) Limited
RWE Generation UK PLC
Radius (UK) Limited
Redbridge PPP Health Services Ltd
Retirement Homesearch Limited
Riverford Organic Farmers Ltd
A.E. Rodda & Son Limited
Royal Bay Care Homes Ltd
Royal Clarence Hotel Limited
S & B Property Limited
SCA Group Limited
Sanlam Wealth Planning Holdings UK
Sanlam Wealth Planning UK Ltd
Scot Group Southern Limited
Securi-Flex Ltd.
Simian Group Limited
WH Smith Hospitals Holdings Ltd
Smithbrewer Limited
Specialised Management Services Ltd
Stilo International PLC
Stroudwater Redevelopment Partnership
Synertec Limited
TKC Sales Limited
TM Property Searches Limited
Tempest Radford Limited
Tomy Europe (Holdings) Limited
Tonic Construction Limited
Toshiba Carrier UK Ltd.
Town Hospitals (Southern General) Ltd
Tree Aid
Trelleborg Industrial Products UK Ltd
Trelleborg Marine Systems UK Ltd
Tricel Holdings (UK) Limited
Triton Knoll Offshore Wind Farm Ltd
W & S Waste Management Limited
Watergate Bay Hotel Limited
Susie Watson Designs Ltd
Wentrow Media Limited
Wessex Water Services Finance PLC
Westerleigh Crematoria Limited
Weymouth and Portland National Sailing Academy
Winners 2000 Fitness Limited
Woodchester Enterprises Ltd
Wring Group Limited
Wyatt Homes Limited
npower Commercial Gas Limited
npower Direct Limited

2000 [167]

04021465 Limited
1&1 Internet Limited
A.E. Securities Limited
AES TEP Power Investments Ltd
AES Venezuela Finance
AFL Telecommunications Europe Ltd
AGR Automation Limited
AJ & Co.(Devon) Ltd
AgustaWestland Holdings Ltd
Aish Technologies Limited
Alleyford Limited
Amica Care Trust
Angel Assistance Limited
Anglo-American Vulcanized Fibre Ltd
Ashfield Land (Cardiff) Ltd
Axell Wireless Limited
BBGR Limited
BDP Imports Limited
BNP Paribas Fleet Holdings Ltd
Bell Finance Limited
Benridge Investments Limited
Berrys Coaches (Taunton) Ltd
Blundell's School
Bowden Derra Park Limited
Breath Limited
Breeze Motor Co Ltd
Bridlington Schools Services Ltd
Brook Food Processing Equipment Ltd
Bruton School for Girls
CCH Property Co Ltd
CG Holdings Limited
Cabot Design Limited
Calcot Health & Leisure Co Ltd
Cannington Enterprises Limited
Cape Homes Limited
T K T Cattran Limited
Caveangle Limited
Cavium UK Ltd
Centrax Industries Limited
Chinewood Developments Limited
Clearwater Products Limited
Cogent Communications UK Ltd
Conlon Limited
Conway Bailey Transport Ltd
Cray U.K. Limited
Debden Schools Services Ltd
Decision Insight Hub Limited
Design Scaffolding (Bristol) Ltd
Doveleigh Care Limited
E & H Drylining & Plastering Ltd
Education Centre Management Ltd
Elm Tree Estates Limited
Eurogate Finance Limited
Eurostore Group Limited
Evershot Construction Limited
Excalibur Communications GB Ltd
F & W Media International Ltd
Farmers First Limited
First Capital Finance Limited
Flollie Investments Limited
Flybe Aviation Services Ltd
Foray Holdings Limited
Forward Land Limited
Foxmoor Limited
G4S Joint Ventures Limited
GMO Cars Limited
Gale Homes and Investments Ltd
Glanville Cleansing Limited
Good Energy Group PLC
Green-Line Contracts Limited
Haringey Schools Services Ltd
Harlequinns Bowling and Leisure Ltd
Haskins Holdings Limited
James Hay Administration Co Ltd
Haystack Dryers Limited
Helitune Limited
Helston Garages Group Limited
Herring Shoes Limited
Hitachi Information Control Systems Europe Ltd.
Hodie Limited
Holmleigh Care Homes Limited
Home Hardware Distribution Ltd
Hull Maternity Development Ltd
IMC St.David's Ltd
Innkeeping Limited
Insure & Go Insurance Services Ltd
Integra Neurosciences Holdings (UK)
JHAI Limited
Jupiter Care Ltd
KTSL Limited
Kat-O-Log Limited
Keen Thinking Limited
Kerdene Limited
Kingsbridge Risk Solutions Ltd
Kirklees Schools Services Ltd
Knorr-Bremse Investment (UK) Ltd
Knorr-Bremse Rail Systems (UK) Ltd
Kohler Holdings Ltd.
Kohler Showers Bidco Limited
Kohler Showers Holdings Ltd
LBS (Fire Services) Limited
Lightwater Valley Attractions Ltd
MAT Foundry Group Limited
Malvern Tyres (Wholesale) Ltd
Mayden House Limited
Newspace Containers Limited
Nynehead Care Limited
Ocean Automotive Limited
Openwave Systems Limited
PC Property Holdings Limited
PPL WEM Limited
Pattersons (Holdings) Limited
Perkins & Perry Ltd.
Phyworks Limited
Plessey Semiconductors Limited
Poeton Holdings Limited
Potensis Limited
Prenax Limited
Private Equity Investor Ltd
Quartet Community Foundation
RBSSAF (25) Limited

RWE Generation UK Holdings Ltd
Radius (Bristol) Limited
Red Lion Investments Limited
Riders of Bridgwater Ltd.
SBS International Holdings Ltd
SPC Europe Limited
Samara Investments (2000) Ltd
Searchflow Limited
Securivin Limited
Chris Sedgeman Scaffolding Ltd.
Sherborne School
Shooters Bottom Wind Park Ltd
Sidmouth Hotels Limited
Silverfish UK Limited
Smartstream Technologies Holdings
WH Smith Hospitals Limited
Smith's (Gloucester) Limited
Solent Stevedores Limited
Somerville & Savage Solicitors
Sonus Networks Limited
St. James's Place Wealth Management PLC
Stonebridge Associated Colleges Ltd
Sure Maintenance Limited
Swanage Railway Trust
Taunton School Educational Charity
Teleperformance Holdings Ltd
Templegate Electrical Supplies Ltd
Torbay Schools Services Ltd
Tradestock Limited
Traffic Group Limited
Triangle Properties (Bristol) Ltd
Tribal Group PLC
Tyco Electronics Motors Ltd
Vendigital Limited
Vision Dispensing Ltd.
Waterfield Homes Limited
Way Fund Managers Limited
West Country Milk Consortium Ltd
Western Commodities Ltd
White Horse Education Partnership
Williamson-Dickie Europe Holdings
Wirral Schools Services Ltd
Wiska UK Limited
A D Woodley Holdings Limited
World Snooker Limited
npower Yorkshire Limited

2001 [170]

43P9 Limited
ATP Holdings Limited
Agecroft Properties (No.2) Ltd
Albermarle Trading Limited
Albion Healthcare (Oxford) Holdings
Albion Healthcare (Oxford) Ltd
Allen & Heath Limited
Alliance Pharma PLC
Amcor Europe Group Management
Amcor Flexibles UK Holding Ltd
Amcor Holding
Amcor Holding No.1 Limited
Amcor UK Finance PLC
Anana Limited
Avon Metals Limited
Axiom Process Limited
Barmont Properties Limited
Beacon Communication Services Ltd
Bellwind-Edis Limited
MF Bennion (Potatoes) Limited
Big Van World Limited
Blue Chip Holidays Ltd
Brighton & Hove City Schools Services
Brightside Insurance Services Ltd
Brightsource Limited
Budweiser Budvar UK Limited
Carlos SS Properties Limited
Catalent U.K. Swindon Holding II Ltd
Cavanna Group Limited
Cavanna Homes (Cornwall) Ltd
Cavanna Homes (Devon) Limited
Cavanna Homes (South West) Ltd
Centek Limited
Chief Vehicle Rentals Limited
Churngold Construction Holdings Ltd
City West Country Limited
Claybrook Limited
Coate Water Care Co Ltd
Cornish Scrumpy Holdings Ltd
Cosmetic Warriors Limited
Crocus Care Ltd
Crown Yealm Limited
Cubit Group Limited
Curo Group (Albion) Limited
Curtiss-Wright Flow Control (UK) Ltd
DAC Beachcroft Claims Limited
Dartex Coatings Limited
Dartmouth-Kingswear Floating Bridge Co
Darts Farm Limited
Dawnhaze Limited
Dawson E & E Parts (Europe) Ltd
Dean Close Foundation
Delstar International, Limited
Devonshire Poultry Limited
Dometic UK Limited
E & T Developments Limited
Eagle One Foc Holdings Limited
Eagle One Holdings Limited
Eagle One Investment Holdings Ltd
Endsleigh Limited
FB Heliservices Limited
Feilden Clegg Bradley Studios LLP
Five Rivers Child Care Limited
Floortex Europe Limited
Frazer-Nash Consultancy Group Ltd
G3 Systems Limited
GH Clayhill Limited
Tom Gallagher Group Limited
Garland Company UK Limited
Giftworks Limited
Global Machine Tools (UK) Ltd
Growing Enterprises Ltd
Hardware UK Limited
Harvey Farms (Winterbourne) Ltd
Heating Products Limited
Hemsley Fraser International Ltd
Herts & Essex PPP Health Services
High Tech Fabrications Limited
Highfield Garden Centres Ltd
Hills Quarry Products Limited
Honeywell Global Tracking Ltd
Hope and Homes for Children
Horsebridge Network Systems Ltd
IDS Transport (UK) Limited
Ignition Credit PLC
Imaging Equipment Limited
Import Export Services Ltd
Interfit Limited
R T Julian & Son Limited
K.P. Europa Trading Limited
LDC (Loughborough) Limited
La Hacienda Limited
Lantor (UK) Limited
Liverpool Schools Services Ltd
Liverpool Victoria General Insurance Group
Lone Eagle Retail Limited
Lush Cosmetics Limited
M.A.C. Hotels Ltd
M.T. Property Developments Ltd
MJL Cornwall Limited
MPLOY Staffing Solutions Ltd
Mabey Bridge Limited
Majestic Limited
Mears Care Limited
Millstream Management Services Ltd
Moorlands College
Murray (Plymouth) Limited
New Power Co Ltd
Orchardleigh Park Ltd
Oxford Spires Scaffolding Ltd
Paligap Limited
Paradigm Norton Financial Planning
Perrigo UK Acquisition Limited
Plymouth Hotel Co Ltd
Plymouth Marine Laboratory
Pritchard Patent Product Company (2001)
Pritchmor Holdings Limited
Pro-Direct Sport Limited
Pulse Roll Label Products Ltd
Quickmach Engineering Limited
RAGM PLC
Redruth Facilities Limited
Richmond upon Thames Schools Services
River Marketing Limited
Roland DG (U.K.) Limited
Rotable Repairs Limited
SRT Marine Technology Limited
Selwood Housing Society Ltd
Simply Pleasure Limited
Smiths News Holdings Limited
Solent International Limited
Somerset County Cars Limited
South West Care Homes Limited
Southern Healthcare (Wessex) Ltd
St. Moritz Developments Ltd
Standard Brands (UK) Limited
Steelinvest Limited
Summit Medical Limited
Sundeala Limited
Sunderland CLC School Services Ltd
Teachers Property Limited
Thrubwell Properties Limited
Thurlestone Court Limited
Toolstream Limited
Torry Harris Business Solutions (Europe)
Total Plumbing Supplies Ltd
Trapeze Group (UK) Limited
Trelleborg Retford Limited
Tribal Education Limited
Tubbs (UK) Ltd
Two Rivers Housing
UK Court Services (Manchester) Ltd
Ultimate Asset Finance Limited
Ultimate Finance Limited
Ultimate Trade Finance Limited
Unicorn AIM VCT PLC
Unite Finance One (Holdings) Ltd
Unite Finance One (Property) Ltd
Vantage Point Business Village Ltd
Viridor Credits Environmental Company
Vowles Parks Limited
Wainhomes (South West) Holdings Ltd
Westover Group Limited
Whittington Facilities Limited
Willes Farming Limited
Wincanton PLC
Wolverhampton Radiology Ltd
Wood Energy Limited

YTL Utilities (UK) Limited
Zycko Overseas Limited

2002 [189]

A1 PPP Infrastructure Holdings Ltd
AGM Holdings Limited
Adelaide Lodge Care Home Limited Liability Partnership
Albion Healthcare (Doncaster) Ltd
Alderley Farms Limited
Amberon Limited
Amcor Investments Germany
Arena Business Centres Limited
Argyll Environmental Ltd
Ashfield Land Limited
Aspire Defence Services Ltd
B M Foods Limited
BFF Nonwovens Limited
Baring Emerging Europe PLC
Luke Barnett Limited
Barrington Brown Estates Ltd
Bifold Fluidpower (Holdings) Ltd
Birmingham Healthcare Services Ltd
Buckland Care Limited
C F R Group Services Limited
Camelot Care Homes Limited
Camps International Group Ltd
Canefield Ltd
Canon Court Farm Limited
Carlin Boat Charter Limited
Charlcombe Homes Limited
Cheltenham Borough Homes Ltd
Christchurch Hotels Ltd
Claremont Ferrand Limited
Clear-Flow Limited
Clearwater Properties Limited
Cobalt Health
Cobham Defence Communications Ltd
K. S. Coles Limited
Commercial First Group Limited
Condor UK Holdings Limited
Cotswold Homes Limited
Crediton Care & Support Homes Ltd
Curtiss-Wright Controls (UK) Ltd
D4E Mulberry Limited
Daktronics UK Limited
Delahunty Limited
Discus Management Limited
Distant Planet Productions Ltd
Dover Refrigeration & Food Equipment UK
Dundee Merchant Wind Park Ltd
Dutch Oak Tree Foundation
Dynavour Limited
Eagle One Mmiii Limited
Eastern Business Park Limited
Eastwood Park Limited
Eccles Special High Schools Co Ltd
Eden Trust
Edgehill Portfolio No.1 Ltd
Elfordleigh Holdings Limited
Endesign Limited
Exeter School
Exhibitor Limited
FB Leasing Limited
Firstport Limited
Flexiguide Limited
Forest Park Cemetery and Crematorium
Future Holdings 2002 Limited
GH North Northampton Limited
Gilcrest Group Limited
William Gilder Limited
Glastonbury Festival Events Ltd
Gompels Healthcare Limited
Gooch & Housego (Torquay) Ltd
Grange (Chertsey) 2002 Ltd.
Grange Motors (Swindon) Ltd
Grensue Ltd
HSH Motor Co Ltd
Harrow Community Schools PFI Ltd
Havana West Limited
Head Ruddy Limited
Hebron & Medlock Limited
Homeleigh Garden Centre Ltd
Hospital Company (Dartford) Holdings
ITP Developments Limited
Imperial Tobacco Overseas Holdings (2)
Infineon Technologies Newport Holding
Intrinsic Wealth Limited
Investors in the Community (Bexley Schools)
JSM Property Services Limited
Jigsaw Solutions Limited
Just Go Holidays Limited
Kranlyft UK Limited
LDC (Imperial Wharf) Limited
Lee Abbey Fellowship
Lee Abbey Movement
Liskeard PPP Health Services Ltd
Litt Holdings Limited
Lombard Corporate Finance (11) Ltd
Lombard Corporate Finance (13) Ltd
Lombard Corporate Finance (15) Ltd
Lombard Corporate Finance (7) Ltd
Loungers Limited
MDM Developments (Southern) Ltd
Magna Motor Company (Wessex) Ltd
Mallory Holdings Limited
Bob Martin (UK) Limited
Martingate Centre Limited
James Mason Limited
Merlin Entertainments Developments
Milewood Healthcare Ltd
R G Morcom Investments Ltd
Mulberry Studios Limited
NOV Downhole Eurasia Limited
NOV UK Finance Limited
Nanny McPhee Productions Ltd
Nettleton Holdings Limited
Nicolas James Limited
Ninecourt Limited
North Devon Tyres Ltd.
Oakland Capital Developments Ltd
Oceanview Developments Limited
Openwork Limited
Organic Foods, Drinks & Investments Holdings
PA Performance Limited
PDQ Group Limited
PPL UK Resources Limited
Pacific West Foods (UK) Ltd
Parking Glasgow Limited
Partington Engineering Limited
Patalex V Productions Limited
Peninsula Care Homes Limited
Peninsula Finance PLC
Penny Lane Holdings Ltd
Pennyfarthing New Homes Ltd
People Source Consulting Ltd
Plus Shipping Services Limited
Precast Concrete Structures Ltd
Proper Job Superstores Limited
RWE Cogen UK (Hythe) Limited
Renewable Energy Partnerships Ltd
Resonance Limited
Retired Nurses National Home
Road Management Services (Darrington) Holdings
Road Management Services (Darrington)
Road Management Services (Finance) PLC
Robotmother Limited
Rocma Sterling
SGW Research Limited
STC (Milton Keynes) Limited
SWM & Waste Recycling Limited
Sanderson Government and Defence Ltd
Scisys UK Limited
Scorribanda Holdings Limited
Scott-Law Properties LLP
Seasalt Holdings Limited
Secure Systems & Technologies Ltd
Shelterbox Trust
Simonstone (Bristol) Limited
Simonstone Motor Group PLC
Snapdragons Nurseries Limited
Somerset Community Foundation
Southtown Investment Co Ltd
St Gresham Limited
St Juliens Limited
St. Piran's School (GB) Ltd
Stafford Education Facilities Ltd
Supported Independence Limited
Sureway Express Transport Ltd
Sustainable Drainage Systems Ltd
TFIO Properties Limited
Tacklestore Limited
Tay Valley Lighting (Newcastle and North Tyneside)
Tay Valley Lighting (Stoke on Trent)
Teign Housing.
Teignmouth Maritime Services Ltd
J C Thomas & Sons Limited
Tout Limited
Ultimate Finance Group Limited
Unique Home Stays Limited
Unite Finance Limited
Uplands Retail Limited
Vanguard Healthcare Solutions Ltd
Vantage Point Business Park Ltd
Wayfarer Group Limited
Wemyss Lodge Limited
Wessex Building Services Ltd
Wessex Resolutions C.I.C.
Westcon Group European Operations
Western Fuel Limited
Wills Brothers Limited
Wiltshire Heavy Building Materials
Yardgate Limited
Zurich Finance (UK) PLC

2003 [190]

A & B Contractors (Devon) Ltd
APP (UK) Limited
AUB Enterprises Limited
Acorn Developments (SW) Ltd
Adey Innovation Limited
Airport Business Centre Ltd
Allum and Sidaway Limited
Alpha Immobile Limited
Amigo Loans Ltd
Ashwoods Electric Motors Ltd
Aspire Defence Holdings Ltd
Aster Property Limited
Attwooll Holdings Limited
Autoparts & Diagnostics Ltd
Avalon Plastics Limited
Aviation Requirements Ltd
Avon Energy Limited

Bart Ingredients Co. Ltd
Bartlett and Sons Limited
Bedruthan Hotel Limited
Blue Sea Food Co Ltd
Brent Cars Limited
Bristol Infracare Lift (1) Ltd
Bristol Water Core Holdings Ltd
Bristol Water Holdings UK Ltd
Andrew Brownsword Hotels Ltd
Burford Alpha Limited
Burford Beta Holdings Limited
Burford Beta Limited
Burford Delta Limited
Butcombe Brewery Limited
Butcombe Brewing Co Ltd
By Education (Barking) Holdings Ltd
By Education (Barking) Limited
CRC Industries UK Limited
Cadeleigh Estates Limited
Capston Limited
E G Carter (Holdings) Limited
J.T. Castle Limited
Cathedral View Limited
Check House Limited
Click Consult Limited
Cloudpay Holdings Limited
Coate Water Care Company (Church View Nursing Home)
Compass Tractors Limited
Computershare Investments (UK) (No.3)
Computershare Voucher Services Ltd
Constructor Group UK Limited
Consumer Intelligence Limited
Cornwall Community Foundation
Cornwall Housing Limited
Bernard Cox Limited
Crux Product Design Ltd
DMT Property Services Ltd
DNO Consulting Limited
P J Davidson Developments Ltd
J & W Davis Limited
Deeley Freed Estates Limited
Denvern Limited
E.I.C. Group Limited
Eagle Strategic Property Ltd
East London Lift Accommodation Services
Eastleigh Care Homes Limited
Ecosurety Limited
Eko Properties Limited
First Priorities PPP Health Services
Five Valleys Aerospace Limited
Flowbird Smart City UK Limited
Fornuis UK Limited
Freedom Healthnet Limited
Furniture World Limited
GH Gravesham Limited
Garrad Hassan Group Limited
Giftstones Limited
Glevum Heating & Plumbing Ltd
Go Vocational Solutions Ltd
Grove Care Limited
Grove Village Limited
H2H Pharmacy Limited
Happy Days South West Limited
Peter Harding Practice Ltd
Harkwell Labels Limited
Hart's Haulage Limited
David Hathaway Properties Ltd
David Hathaway Transport Ltd
Hawkins Agri Limited
Healthcare South West Ltd
Hertford PPP Health Services Ltd
Hospital Company (Dartford) Issuer PLC
Icon Two Limited
Imperial Brands Enterprise Finance
Imperial Tobacco Overseas (Polska)
In-Excess UK Limited
Infinergy Limited
Integrated Care Solutions (East Kent) Holdings
Integrated Care Solutions (East Kent)
JR Cap Limited
LDC (AIB Warehouse) Limited
LDC (Portfolio Four) Limited
Lang & Potter (Holdings) Ltd
Langdon Transport Limited
Langham Farms Limited
Light Group Limited
Llexeter Limited
Lovehoney Limited
Luxurycare (Aranlaw House Care Home) Ltd
Magellan Aerospace (UK) Ltd
Magmatic Limited
Marlborough Facilities Limited
Matthews Properties Limited
Maynard School
R.J. & K.D. McLean Limited
Mears Housing Management (Holdings)
Midas Retail Limited
Monaghan Mushrooms Limited
Next Generation Wind Holdings Ltd
Nicolas James Group Limited
Nucleus Developments Limited
Oakfield Investments Ltd
Ocean Housing Group Limited
Octagon Healthcare Funding PLC
Octagon Healthcare Group Ltd
Offshore Marine Management Ltd
Opex Logistics Limited
Osprey Europe Limited
P S J Properties Ltd.
PCBL Limited
PMG Services (Bristol) Limited
Palmer Care Ltd
Park Home Management Ltd
Parkside Holdings Limited
Patalex III Productions Ltd
J F Pearce & Sons Limited
Pennard Farms Limited
Pie Minister Limited
Plant Speed Limited
Platinum One Hotels Limited
Poole Lighting Limited
Prideaux Developments Limited
Priorgate Limited
Qualtronyc Property Holdings Ltd
Quay Marinas Group Ltd
RBSSAF (2) Limited
RBSSAF (6) Limited
RBSSAF (8) Limited
RRH Limited
Raven Mount Limited
Renrod Holdings Limited
Rexquote Ltd
Richpur Limited
Roundswell Services Limited
Royal Osteoporosis Society
Charles Russell Transport UK Ltd
SF Ltd
SPP Pumps Limited
SWK (UK) Limited
Sanctus Limited
Sands Resort Hotel Limited
Scarlet Hotel Limited
Sensata Technologies (Europe) Ltd
Services Support (Avon & Somerset) Holdings
Services Support (Avon & Somerset)
Sharp's Brewery Limited
South Essex PPP Health Services Ltd
St Austell Printing Co Ltd
St James Priory Project
Stay Dry Roofing (South West) Ltd
Strongvox Limited
Sureserve Holdings Limited
Swindon Caravan Centre Limited
T Shirt & Sons Limited
TNT Fireworks U.K. Limited
Tack Farms Limited
Tank Museum Limited
Terraquest Solutions Limited
Three Rivers Partnership, Dorset
Toyo Denso U.K. Limited
Underdown Investments Limited
Upper Belgrave Property Ltd
Viridor Waste (West Sussex) Ltd
Warren Farm Holiday Centre Ltd
Welton Bibby and Baron Holdings Ltd
Welton Bibby and Baron Limited
West Mendip PPP Health Services Ltd
Whitehall Garden Centres Ltd
Whitehill Country Park Limited
Wilson Leisure Developments Ltd
Wookey Hole Limited
XJ6 Schools Holdings Limited
Yarlington Homes Limited

2004 [197]

010 Limited
A Curious Group of Hotels LLP
API Holdco Limited
Albany Molecular Research Ltd
Alchemist Ventures Limited
Alder King LLP
Algreta Solutions Limited
Altogether Care LLP
Alum Care Limited
American Museum in Britain
Animals in Distress (Torbay and Westcountry)
Ann's Cottage (Warehouse) Ltd
Aquamain (UK) Limited
Ark Data Spring Park Limited
Arthouse Glasgow Limited
Aspirations (Midlands) Limited
Aspirations Care Limited
Atlas Services Group Energy Ltd
B4 Claims Limited
B4 Marketing Limited
BBG Lift Accommodation Services Ltd
BHH Lift Accommodation Services Ltd
Bath Row Developments Ltd
Beckery Properties Limited
Catherine Harwood Bell LLP
Bevan Brittan LLP
Bigdug Limited
Bloom Hearing Specialists Ltd
Bollingwood Limited
Boston Tea Party Group Limited
Brickjet Limited
Bristol Grammar School
Bristol Infracare Lift (2) Ltd
Bristol, Clifton and West of England Zoological Society
Burford Zeta
Burges Salmon LLP

CIL Management Consultants Ltd
Cab Aid Limited
Cannon Care Homes Ltd
Catalent CTS (Edinburgh) Ltd
Catering 328 Limited
Chalwyn Estates Limited
Chantry Court Westbury Ltd
Cleancrop UK Limited
Cleveland FM Services Limited
Cofton Country Holidays Ltd
Community 1st Cornwall Limited
Complete Design & Construction Ltd
Connect Group PLC
Cordash Limited
County Hotel Canterbury Ltd
Creanova Universal Closures Ltd
Creed Catering Supplies Ltd
Danetre PFI Project Co Ltd
Deeley Freed (Penhalt) Limited
Devon Doctors Limited
Downfield Homes Limited
Duo Assets Limited
Dyson Estates Limited
Earthline Holdings Limited
Edgehill Battersea Limited
Elbit Systems UK Limited
Elleness Limited
Ellson Homes Limited
Entier Associates Limited
Epping PPP Maintenance (Health) Services
Etavoni Limited
Exception Group Limited
Falmouth Exeter Plus
First Greater Western Limited
Flagdawn Limited
Flatcable Limited
Freeways Trust
Fylde CNC Specialists Limited
GE Aviation Systems Group Ltd
GH Stone House Limited
Genaray Limited
Global Furniture Alliance Ltd
Gloucestershire FM Services Ltd
Gould & Swayne Limited
Green and Fortune Limited
Gurkha Welfare Trust
Hargrave Foundation
Hartridge Limited
Heritage Developments South West Ltd
Hochtief PPP Solutions (UK) Ltd
Horton Golf Limited
IEWC UK & Ireland Ltd
IIC (C & T) Limited
Insite Poster Investments (A) Ltd
Insite Poster Properties Ltd
Investment Funds Direct Group Ltd
Investors in Health (C & T1) Ltd
Isles of Scilly Shipping Co Ltd
Johnstone Safety International LLP
Jumbocruiser Limited
K & T Heating Services Limited
King's Schools Taunton Limited
LDC (Project 110) Limited
Lambeth Lighting Services Ltd
Landmark Analytics Limited
Landmark Developments (Oakford House)
Livanova UK Limited
Lornamead Acquisitions Limited
MW High Tech Projects UK Ltd
Manlock Investments Limited
Masons Farm and Country Ltd
Maximise IT Solutions Limited
Mayflower Properties (SW) Ltd
Medreport Services Limited
Merlin Entertainments (NBD) Ltd
Merlin Entertainments Group Ltd
Mmedia Group Limited
Mole Valley Feed Solutions Ltd
Monmouth Facilities Limited
Montemax Limited
Myoptique Group Ltd
NK Facilities Limited
New Dawn Homes Limited
New Forest PPP Health Services Ltd
Newton Nottingham LLP
Norseland Holdings Limited
Northern Isles Ferries Limited
Novalis Trust
Ochre Solutions (Holdings) Ltd
Ochre Solutions Limited
Off Site Solutions (R T) Ltd
Orange International Investments (UK)
Outsauce Financing Limited
Overton (Gloucester) Limited
Oxford Infracare Lift (1) Ltd
PFI Investments Limited
PICS Telecom International Ltd
PWG Trading Limited
Pengelly Farms Limited
Philmark Estates Limited
Pluss Organisation CIC
Plymouth College and St Dunstan's Abbey
Schools Charity
Poole Housing Partnership Ltd
Porthia Limited
Postal Choices Limited
Primeco Limited
Proco-STS Limited
Queen Elizabeth's Hospital
RBS Asset Finance Europe Ltd
Redmaids' High School
Richmond Group Limited
Ridgevale Estates Limited
Rivermead Plastic Limited
Rochford Property Investments Ltd
Rotamic Engineering Limited
Route One Retail Limited
SB Holdings (Exeter) Limited
Saddleback Limited
Samatt (Group Services) Ltd
Senex Capital Limited
Servo Interconnect Limited
WH Smith PLC
Spire House Developments Ltd
Springwood Farms Limited
Stanley UK Acquisition Co Ltd
Sterling Capital Asset Finance Ltd
Sunnybanks Homes (SW) Limited
Super Dooper Stores Limited
Surgical Specialties UK Holdings Ltd
TJ International Limited
TLT LLP
TM Group (UK) Limited
TRL Electronics Limited
Tabacalera de Garcia UK Ltd
Theobald Film Productions LLP
Togs Limited
Toklon Limited
Tor Currency Exchange Limited
The James Tudor Foundation
Two Rivers Investments Limited
Una Group Limited
Unite Accommodation Management 6 Ltd
United Healthcare (Bromley) Group
United Healthcare (Bromley) Services
Vavassor Limited
Vision Direct Group Ltd
Wastenage Farms Limited
Wenand Homes Ltd
Whisstocks Developments Ltd
Wiggin LLP
Wild Ash Limited
Wildbrook Investments (Calne) Ltd
Wolverhampton City and Walsall Lift
Accommodation Services
Wood Barton Developments Ltd
Woodward & Co (Environmental) Ltd
Wyse Estates Holdings Limited
YMCA Bath Group
Yellow Bridge Investments Ltd
Yeo Valley Group Limited
Zimmer U.K. Ltd.
Zoeftig Group Limited

2005 [169]

Aceaxis Limited
Acland Plant Hire Limited
Acumed Acquisition Co Ltd
Advanced Paper Production Ltd.
Alpha Schools (Highland) Holdings
Alpha Schools (Highland) Ltd
Alpha Schools (Highland) Project PLC
Altus Limited
Amigo Management Services Ltd
An Suidhe Wind Farm Limited
Ark Data Centres Limited
Ashton Gate Limited
Aspect Digital Media Limited
Aspire Defence Limited
Atlas Elektronik UK (Holdings) Ltd
Atlas Elektronik UK Limited
Attivo Group Limited
BCCB Incorporated Limited
Barnet Lighting Services Ltd
Bath Taxis Limited
Beat The Street (UK) Limited
Big Green Parcel Group Limited
Binx Health Limited
Black Gold Developments (UK) Ltd
Blast Properties Limited
J R Bodman Limited
Bond Street Estates (Brighton) Ltd
Borlase Smart John Wells Trust Ltd
Brisdoc Healthcare Services Ltd
Bristol Airport (UK) No.3 Ltd
Bristol Charities
Bristol Port Wind Park Limited
Burnbake Campsite Limited
CDS Group Services Limited
Cahill Welding Services Ltd.
Canynge Bicknell (Street) Ltd
Captiva Homes Limited
Circadian Trust
Cloverlait Limited
Coln Park LLP
Comax (UK) Limited
Compass Point Estates LLP
Cornwall Hospice Care Limited
Cotswold Doors Ltd
Country Houses Foundation
Cream Residential Care Limited
Customade (UK) Limited
D'Oyly Carte Charitable Trust
D-Tech (UK) Limited
DAC Beachcroft Services Ltd
DAS Law Limited

Dudley Infracare Lift (1) Ltd
East London Lift Accommodation Services No2
Efret Limited
Emblem Holdings Limited
Enfield Lighting Services Ltd
European Society of Endocrinology
Fen Farm Wind Park Limited
Fox Elms Care Limited
Foxcombe Farm (Somerset) Ltd
Freixenet Copestick Limited
Fremington Homes Limited
G4S Investments Limited
GWP Group Limited
Game and Wildlife Conservation Trust
Gener8 Finance Limited
Good Energy Gas Limited
Grosvenor PPP Holdings Limited
Groundfix Limited
Hazlewoods LLP
Heronbridge Investment Management LLP
Herpetological Conservation Trust
Higher Drive Nursing Home (Holdings)
EA & JA Hiscock Limited
Homes in Sedgemoor Limited
Hospital Company (Dartford) 2005 Ltd
Hospital Company (Swindon & Marlborough) 2006
IIC (Leeds Schools) Fund Investment
IIC Barnet Holding Co Ltd
IIC By Education (Peterborough Schools)
IIC Lambeth Holding Co Ltd
IIC Northampton Limited
Inspired Education (East Dunbartonshire)
Inspired Education (South Lanarkshire) Holdings
Inspired Education (South Lanarkshire)
Integrated Care Solutions (Shropshire) Holdings
Integrated Care Solutions (Shropshire)
Integreon Managed Solutions Ltd
International Dance Supplies Ltd
Intrinsic Financial Planning Ltd
Intrinsic Financial Services Ltd
Intrinsic Mortgage Planning Ltd
Investors in the Community (Leeds Schools) Holding Co
Investors in the Community (Leeds Schools)
Investors in the Community (Leeds Schools) Subdebt
JB Global Limited
Janspeed Technologies Limited
A R & A L Keen Limited
Kelston Properties 2 Limited
King William St Limited
Knabs Ridge Wind Farm Limited
Krowji Limited
LDC (MTF Portfolio) Limited
LDC (Radmarsh Road) Limited
LV Insurance Management Ltd
La Flor de Copan UK Limited
Lascar Electronics Limited
Lily-Flame Ltd
Little Cheyne Court Wind Farm Ltd
Lokaz Limited
MDP (South West) Limited
MUJV Limited
McGill Warmley Limited
Merchants' Academy Trust
Midhurst Child Care Limited
Mikulla Leisure Limited
Muc-Off Limited
Nationwide Covered Bonds LLP
Neal's Yard Holdings Limited
Neptune Retail Limited
PSW Metals Limited
Parable Trust Limited
Pharos Care Limited
Phoenix Child Care Limited
Pole Farming Limited
Prabh Milnae Kaa Chaao Gurdwara
Proper Tea LLP
Pulsin Ltd
Puxton Limited
Qualasept Limited
Race 500 Limited
Railston Holdings Limited
Rainbow Holdings (UK) Limited
Raw Investments Limited
Redcar and Cleveland Lighting Services
Redhorn Holdings Limited
Redrock Consulting Limited
Regulatory Finance Solutions Ltd
Renaissance Miles Platting Ltd
Rhyl Flats Wind Farm Limited
Rocma Europe
Rowe Estates Holdings Limited
Royal Artillery Centre for Personal Development
SRT Marine Systems PLC
Salisbury Glass Holdings Ltd
Schyde Investments Limited
Scoliosis SOS Limited
Silversword Limited
Simplyhealth Group Limited
Sofa Brands International Ltd
Solsbury Inventions Limited
Somerset Motorhome Centre Ltd
South West Airports Limited
South West Communications Group Holdings
Stephenson Property Services Ltd
Stone King LLP
Superior Group Limited
Syreford Investments LLP
Tay Valley Lighting (Leeds) Ltd
Teoxane UK Limited
Truflo Air Movement Limited
Twofour Group Limited
Viridor Polymer Recycling Ltd
W B M Groundworks Limited
Walkergate PFI Project Co Ltd
Western Global Limited
Wild and Wolf Limited
Wiltshire Heavy Building Materials (Group)
Wincanton UK Limited

2006 [200]

1&1 UK Holdings Limited
1pm PLC
221 Limited
3P Learning Limited
A-Gas Investments Limited
A7 Lochhead Limited
AUL Underwriting Agency Ltd
Action on Addiction
Advanced Industrial Solutions Ltd
Ameriscot Commercial Limited
Anstee & Ware Group Limited
Apex Dental Care Limited
Appsbroker Limited
Armoric Freight International (Holdings)
Ashington Business Inc. Ltd
Aspire Defence Finance PLC
Avon Automotive UK Holdings Ltd
Avortex Limited
Badham Pharmacy Limited
Bailey Holdings Limited
Bayshill Properties Limited
Beachdown Limited
Big Apple Entertainments Ltd
Bilbster Wind Farm Limited
Blackdown Estates Limited
Bottlegreen Holdings Limited
Bradgate Business Finance Ltd
Brightside Group Limited
Bristol Fruit Sales (Bananas) Ltd
Bristol PFI (Holdings) Limited
Bristol PFI Debt Co 1 Limited
Bristol PFI Limited
Brunel Wind Limited
Brunswick Limited
Buyology Ltd
By Education (Waltham Forest) Holdings
By Education (Waltham Forest) Ltd
C3IA Solutions Limited
CG Hotel Holding Limited
Cambria Automobiles Acquisitions Ltd
Cambria Automobiles PLC
Cambria Automobiles Property Ltd
Camelot Developments Limited
Canford Healthcare Limited
Carrington Fox Developments Ltd
Centek Properties Limited
Centrax Holdings Limited
Certini Bicycle Co Ltd
Chessington Hotel Limited
Chester Abode Limited
City Eco Hotel Limited
Class 06 Limited
Close Brewery Rentals Limited
Coastal UK Group Limited
Coles Miller Solicitors LLP
Colosseum Dental UK Limited
Condition Monitoring Group Ltd
Cornelia Care Homes Limited
Cowgrove Limited
Cream II Limited
Creedon Technologies Limited
D. J. Commercial Limited
Daido Metal Europe Limited
Dartington Crystal (Torrington) Ltd
Dauntsey's School
Del Piero Limited
Deutsch GB Limited
Dopano Limited
Dream Makers Enterprises Ltd
Dunview Limited
Elliotts (Cheltenham) Limited
Exeter Estates Limited
Falkirk Group Limited
Farley & Thompson LLP
Flycorp Aviation LLP
Flyingfish Seafoods Co Ltd
Forest of Dean Stone Firms Ltd
Freemans Event Partners (Logistics) Ltd.
GWKS Ltd
Galpharm Healthcare Limited
Gardner Garages Limited
Glatfelter Lydney, Ltd.
Gooch & Housego (UK) Limited
Great Eastern Hotel Holding Co Ltd
H & R Healthcare Limited
Harrison Products Co Limited
Havenstone Property Limited
Hewer Facilities Management Ltd
Hilditch Group Limited

Hospital Company (Swindon & Marlborough) Group
Host Properties Limited
IIC Enfield Holding Co Ltd
IIC Miles Platting Funding Investment
IIC Miles Platting Subdebt Ltd
IIC Northampton Funding Investment
IIC Northampton Holding Co Ltd
IIC Northampton Subdebt Ltd
IIC Peterborough Holding Co Ltd
Ignition DG Limited
Imagile Business Support Ltd
Imperial Tobacco Holdings (2007) Ltd
Injury QED Limited
Intamarque Limited
J.J. Acquisitions Limited
JISC
Jays Logistics (South West) Ltd
Junction 24 Limited
Kemble Business Park LLP
Koori Limited
LDC (Project 111) Limited
LDC (William Morris II) Ltd
Lance Levy Investments Limited
Lester Aldridge LLP
Lighthouse Property Estates Ltd
Little & Cull Ltd
Lockman Properties Limited
London Eye Holdings Limited
Loumin Estates Limited
Lovehoney Group Limited
M & M Plant (Devon & Cornwall) Ltd
MJL Contractors Limited
Manchester Abode Limited
Manchester Working Limited
Masstock Group Holdings Ltd
Denis May & Sons Limited
McCarthy & Stone (Home Equity Interests)
McCarthy Investments Limited
Medcentres PLC
Melbourne Homes Limited
Minstead Investments (Boscombe) Ltd
NIC Enterprises Limited
NMS Infrastructure Limited
New Earth Solutions (Kent) Ltd
New Look Retail Group Limited
Newham Learning Partnership (Project Co)
Nicolas James Holdings Limited
Nicolas James Investments Ltd
Nissha Medical Technologies Ltd
Off-Piste Wines Limited
Old Mill Accountancy LLP
Henry Oliver Ltd
One Holding Limited
Ortho 2008 Limited
PJAC (Bristol) Limited
Parmenion Capital Partners LLP
Pastaking Holdings Limited
Perrys Holdings Limited
M. Preymesser Logistics Ltd
Professor David Barrett Ltd
RMH (Guildford) LLP
RMH (Guildford) Limited
RR Sea Strand Limited
Raventree Limited
Rendcomb College
Riverside Aromatics Limited
Robertson Developments Ltd
Rock Services Limited
Roseland Investments Ltd
Rowanmoor Executive Pensions Ltd
Rusty Shilling Developments Ltd
Salford Schools Solutions Holdco Ltd
Salford Schools Solutions Ltd
T A Saunders Investments LLP
Sensata Technologies Holding Company U.K.
Sheffield Parkway LLP
Shield Environmental Holdings Ltd
WH Smith Travel Holdings Ltd
South West Water Finance PLC
Spark Gas Shipping Ltd
Spectrum Medical Limited
St Davids Poultry Team Limited
Stormfront Retail Limited
Summerfield SD3 Limited
Sunseeker International (Holdings)
Sutton Harbour Car Parks Ltd
TQ9 Partnership LLP
TTR PT Limited
Tamar View Nurseries Ltd
Taylor Maxwell Group Limited
Tenens (Lakeside) Limited
Texas Instruments (U.K.) Holdings
Thompson Acquisitions Limited
Three Counties Feeds Limited
Tileflair Group Limited
Toller Beattie LLP
Torr Home
Triode Acquisitions UK Limited
Francis Tuthill Limited
USAF LP Limited
USAF Management Limited
University of Gloucestershire
Venator Capital Limited
Verdo Renewables Ltd
Viridor (Lancashire) Limited
Waddeton Park Limited
Ward Edward Limited
Wartsila Hamworthy International Ltd
Wasdell Holdings Limited
Wilson Tool International [Europe]
XJ4 Holding Co Ltd

2007 [183]

2OC (Holdings) Limited
Advanced Insulation Limited
Advantage Group UK Limited
Agincare Group Limited
Agincare UK Limited
Alton Towers Resort Operations Ltd
Amalgam Holdings Limited
Amcor Holdco 3
Appello Limited
Aster Homes Limited
Atlantic Inertial Systems Ltd
Avantage (Cheshire) Holdings Ltd
Avantage (Cheshire) Limited
Avon Engineered Rubber Limited
Adam Bailey Limited
Baylis Ventures Limited
Be Wiser Insurance Services Ltd
Beckton Energy Limited
Bibendum PLB Group Limited
Bibury Court Limited
Bifold Group Limited
Big Green Parcel Holding Co Ltd
Bioreliance UK Acquisition Ltd
Bland Group UK Holdings Ltd
Blue Cedar Homes Limited
Brooks Hotels Limited
Build Supplies Limited
CWC (UK Holdings) Limited
Cabot Learning Federation
Cannon Care Homes 4 Limited
Cardiff Wind Park Limited
Chafyn Grove School
Chapel Barton House Co. Ltd
Charcoal CLG 1 Limited
Charcoal Midco 1 Limited
Charcoal Newco 1 Limited
Charcoal Newco 1A Limited
Chessington World of Adventures Operations
Chibroco Limited
Churchill Retirement Living Ltd
Matthew Clark Bibendum (Holdings)
Codestone Group Ltd.
Cold Clad Ltd
Cornish Farm Dairy Limited
Country Care Homes Limited
Cristie Software Limited
Cygnet Industries Limited
Dentalign Orthodontics LLP
Dentalign Orthodontics Limited
Dexeco Limited
Dextra Lighting Limited
Dextra Services Limited
Duke Street Capital Oasis Acquisitions
Duke Street Capital Oasis Midco Ltd
Dynamatic Limited
Dyson Finance Limited
Eldon Insurance Services Ltd
Energy Measurement Limited
Williams Ewan Limited
Lilian Faithfull Care
Finlay Plant (UK) Limited
Firstport Operations PD Ltd
Flextrus Limited
Flo Group Ltd
Funkypigeon.Com Limited
Futuream (UK) Limited
G & H US Holdings Limited
G & R House Limited
G4S IP 2 Limited
GE Aviation UK
GE Infrastructure Aviation
GWE Business West Ltd
Galsworthy Wind Park Limited
Glide Holdings Limited
Green Cape Limited
Happold LLP
Harbourstar Limited
Harding Brothers Retail Ltd
Harris Construction Limited
Hatchmoor Nursing Home Limited
Hawkins Holdings Limited
Help for Heroes
Hometower Consultancy Limited
Horseworld Trust
Hydro Components UK Ltd.
I Supply Energy Limited
IIC Redcar and Cleveland Holding Co Ltd
Imperial Tobacco Overseas Holdings (3)
Innogy Business Services UK Ltd
Innogy Renewables UK Holdings Ltd
Italmatch UK Limited
JFD Trawlers Limited
Jacksons Investments Limited
Kimberly Audrey Limited
Kingsdown Farm Ltd
Kong Co Ltd
LDC (Alscot Road) Ltd
LDC (Portfolio Five) Limited
Langlands Farms Limited
Legoland US Holdings Limited
Leicester BSF Company 1 Ltd

Leicester BSF Holdings Company 1 Ltd
Lewis-Manning Trust
Liberty House (Nuneaton) Ltd
Literature and Latte Ltd
Lornamead Group Limited
MCB Investments Limited
Merlin Attractions Operations Ltd
Merlin Entertainments Group Holdings
Mi-Space (UK) Limited
Michelmores LLP
Minty Art Limited
Molson Equipment Services Ltd
Molson Group Ltd
Motorhome Finance Limited
NJG Contracting Limited
New Earth Solutions (Canford) Ltd
Oasis Healthcare International Ltd
Old Hall Investment Co Ltd
One Holding Investments Ltd
Orbitz Worldwide (UK) Limited
Oxford Programs Limited
P B Design Holdings Limited
PAL Properties South West Ltd
Panel Supplies Limited
Paradigm (Sheffield BSF) Holdings
Paradigm (Sheffield BSF) Ltd
Partner Logistics Gloucester Ltd
Partner Logistics Wisbech Ltd
Penington Enterprises Limited
Positive Cash Flow Finance Ltd
Premier Park Limited
Quantum Homes Holdings Limited
RMH (Manor House) Care LLP
RNO Limited
RR Sea Hanover St. Limited
RTP-UK Ltd
Read Construction (SW) Limited
Richard Read Holdings Limited
Real Estate Gloucester Limited
Reflex Electronics Limited
John Reid & Sons (Strucsteel) Holdings
Renaissance Miles Platting Holding Co
Resort Estate Management Ltd
Royal Artillery Institution Ltd
SEC Properties Limited
Charles Saunders Holdings Ltd
Sherborne Holdings Limited
Shervey Limited
Sitec Engineering Limited
Skilled Group UK Limited
South Essex Insurance Brokers Ltd
Stone Supplies (Bristol) Ltd
Stonehouse Investment Co Ltd
Sutton Harbour Projects Ltd
Swan Hotel Wells (2007) Ltd
Symonds Forecourts Limited
Andrew Symons Limited
Synergy Health Holdings Ltd
Synergy Health Systems Limited
Thorpe Park Operations Limited
Total Orthodontics Limited
Tozers LLP
Trelleborg Rochdale Limited
Turner UK Limited
UK Power Solutions Limited
UK Shared Business Services Ltd
USAF Management 6 Limited
Unite Accommodation Management Ltd
Upper Horns Farm LLP
Urbina Private Equity No.3 Ltd
Vence LLP
Victor Properties Ltd
Viper Innovations Ltd
Wabash Technologies Limited
Wellington College Academy Trust
West International Holdings Ltd
Westbank Community Health and Care
Westerleigh Group Holdings Ltd
Western United Mines Limited
Wilsons Solicitors LLP
Wind Holdings Nord Limited
Worldwide Dive and Sail International

2008 [157]

3AB Care Limited
4Com PLC
A & L Care Homes Holdings Ltd
A1 Engineering Solutions Ltd
AES Overseas Holdings Limited
AFC Bournemouth Limited
ARWC Consulting Ltd
ASCB Charitable Fund
AUK Holding Limited
Adey Holdings (2008) Limited
Advanced Insulation Contracting Ltd
Andros UK Limited
Arcade Rentals Limited
Ashley Grange Nursing Home Ltd
Atlantis Operations (UK) Ltd
Avon Valley Holdings Limited
BNM Parkstone LLP
Bennetts Cranes Limited
Bladeroom Group Limited
K W Brake and Son Limited
Brean Down Caravan Park Ltd
Bulldog Trust Limited
E W Button & Son Limited
C & C Management Services (UK) Ltd
Castle Nominees Limited
Cathedral Schools Trust
Chaplins Properties Limited
Chapple & Jenkins Ltd
Charter House Investments LLP
Clipper Contracting Group Ltd
Coban 2017 LLP
Colten Care (1693) Limited
Colten Care (1993) Limited
Colten Care (2003) Limited
Community Foundation for Wiltshire & Swindon
Cooke Painter Limited
Copyright Administration Services
Curtis Banks Limited
Curzon 1234 Limited
D B Foods (Holdings) Limited
DPRS Finance Limited
DTR VMS Limited
Den Dental Group Practice LLP
Direct Online Services Limited
Draper Ventilation Limited
Dribuild Limited
Drilling Information Limited
Duke Street Capital Oasis Orthodontics Holdings
Duke Street Capital Oasis Orthodontics
EMS Acquisition Co Ltd
EMS Waste Services Limited
Eco-Bos Development Limited
Exeter Royal Academy for Deaf Education.
Farina Investments (UK) Ltd
Finian Farming LLP
Fintec Group Limited
Firstport HMF Limited
AW Frampton & Son Limited
G W Interiors Holdings Limited
Golden Years Ltd
Hamblys Limited
Hercules Site Services Limited
Highship Industries Limited
Horizon Nuclear Power Limited
Howard Tenens Limited
Hydreco Hydraulics Limited
Hydrock Group Limited
IESIS Limited
Imagile Group Limited
Imperial Tobacco Altadis Ltd
Insite Poster Investments (B) Ltd
Insite Poster Investments Ltd.
Integrity Print Limited
JMC Recruitment Solutions Ltd
Jam & Sons Limited
Keynvor Morlift Limited
LJ (Copiers) Limited
Lambtrad Ltd
Latcham Direct Limited
Leafield Logistics & Technical Services
Lockwash US Limited
London Aquarium (South Bank) Ltd
MCAARP Holdings Limited
MJL Plant Hire (Cornwall) Ltd
Malvern Tyres Holdings Limited
Marsh Holdings Limited
McCarthy & Stone (Developments) Ltd
McCarthy & Stone PLC
McCarthy & Stone Retirement Lifestyles
NNA Limited
New Leaf Plants Ltd
Newham Transformation Partnership
Newport Caravans Limited
Nine Telecom Group Limited
Novia Financial Holdings Ltd
Novia Financial PLC
Old Tannery (Holt) Limited
Omnis Investments Limited
Opus Recruitment Solutions Ltd
Orthod Group Limited
Oval Commercial Investments Ltd
Oxygen House Partners LLP
Pentland Road Windfarm Limited
Portman Healthcare Limited
Positive Group (UK) Limited
Powerwave Energy Limited
Pro - Direct Group Limited
Procook Limited
Pukka Pads UK Limited
Quality Care Group Limited
RMH (Wispers) Care LLP
RWE Markinch Limited
Red Hotels Limited
Right Contract Services Ltd
Roberts Limbrick Limited
Rockfish Group Limited
Ronnies Limited
Rosemount Investments (Bristol) Ltd
Rygor Holdings Limited
SDS Holdings Limited
Salisbury Trading Limited
Sanlam UK Limited
Sheerness Recycling Limited
Sideshow Ltd
Skylarking UK Limited
Smallridge Bros Limited
WH Smith High Street Holdings Ltd
WH Smith High Street Limited
WH Smith Travel 2008 Limited
WH Smith Travel Limited

South Coast Building Supplies Ltd.
St James Parade (107) Limited
M J Stevens Ltd
Stonebridge Colleges (Publishing)
Stonegate Holdings Limited
Suttle Projects Limited
Swallowcourt Holdings Limited
TPSFF Holdings Limited
Tecan Limited
Tekne Holdings Limited
Thatchers Holdings Limited
M R Tizzard Limited
Trelawny Citroen Limited
Trethowans LLP
Tudor Rose International Ltd
USAF Management 10 Limited
Vanguard Healthcare Group Ltd
Venturers Trust
Vision Direct Europe Ltd
Vitacress Limited
Volaris Group UK Holdco Ltd
WW Truck and Bus Limited
White Rose UK Ltd
Woodlands Group of Churches
Worldteam Limited
Wrigley Uno UK Limited
Wyvern Holdings Limited

2009 [157]

A.E.R. Stafford Limited
AEGG Ltd
Actual Experience PLC
Terry Adams Residential LLP
All Saints Church of England Academy, Plymouth
All Saints' Academy, Cheltenham
Amcor European Investment Holdings
Amcor European Investments Ltd
Amcor Flexibles Finance Ltd
Amcor Polska Holding Limited
Aqua Tamarisk LLP
Ashfords LLP
Aspect Trust
Avsan Holdings Limited
BH Live
BPE Solicitors LLP
Barton Cold-Form (UK) Limited
R M Beckett Limited
Bee Green Energy Ltd.
Bessant Properties Limited
Bishop of Winchester Academy Trust
Bistech Group PLC
Brickell Holdings Limited
Brightborough Capital Limited
Bristol Infracare Lift (3) Ltd
Buildit Gloster Limited
CTU General Partner Limited
Caerus Capital Group Limited
Castle Motor Co Ltd
China Fleet Trust
Cinnamon Trust
City Monument Properties Ltd
City West Commercials Limited
Francis Clark LLP
Computershare Investments (UK) (No 7)
Coombes Forestry Limited
Cornwall Air Ambulance Trust
Crowdcube Limited
DEK-Co (UK) Ltd
DKH Retail Limited
P J Davidson Holdings Ltd.
Dawson Media Direct Limited
Delphine Holdings Limited
Devon Ceramics (Contracts) Ltd
Dyson James Group Limited
ETM Recycling Limited
Ellas No3 Limited
Ellas No4 Limited
Exeter Science Park Limited
Fish Brothers Property Investment LLP
Four Quarters Polo LLP
Geneco Limited
Gill Akaster LLP
Gillingham Community and Leisure Trust
Go-Pak UK Limited
Good Energy Delabole Windfarm Ltd
Goonvean Holdings Limited
Gregory Distribution (Holdings) Ltd
HDM Leisure Limited
Haine & Smith Partnership LLP
Hardware Services Limited
Harper's Holdings Limited
Harris Fowler Limited
Haseltine Lake LLP
Hennock Properties Limited
Horatio Investments Limited
Horizon Nuclear Power Oldbury Ltd
Horizon Nuclear Power Services Ltd
Horizon Nuclear Power Wylfa Ltd
Howard Tenens (West London) Ltd
Hugh Sexey's Hospital
IBD Bikes UK Limited
Icon Scientific Limited
Isedio Limited
Izit Group Limited
JG Travel Group Limited
Jamie's Farm
Kings Harbour Hotel Limited
Knorr-Bremse SA Holding Company (UK) Ltd
LLK Property Limited
Langage Farm Limited Liability Partnership
Langford Veterinary Services Ltd
Linton Limited
Lovell Stone Group Limited
Lozenge Limited
Magners GB Limited
Malaby Biogas Limited
McCarthy & Stone (Extra Care Living)
McLean & Sons Ltd
Midland House LLP
Moog Wolverhampton Limited
NASA Umbrella Ltd
NSEA Property Services Limited
Natatomisam Limited
New Earth Solutions (West) Ltd
North Leaze Farm Limited
Oak Tree Mobility Limited
Optima Defence & Security Group Ltd
Ovo Electricity Ltd
Ovo Energy Ltd
PK Food Concepts Ltd.
PKL Topco Limited
PPSTS Limited
PSW Trading Limited
Pharmaxo Pharmacy Services Ltd
Powerbox International Limited
Premia Group Limited
F G Pryor and Son Limited
Public Power Solutions Limited
Quadrum Investments Group Ltd
RR Sea Dundee Limited
RR Sea St. Helens Limited
RWC Construction Ltd
Railway Convalescent Homes
Regal Holiday Homes Limited
Robinson Atterton Investments Ltd
Robinson Property Co Ltd
Robinson Real Estate Limited
S'Porter International Limited
SMV Commercials Limited
SRT Marine System Solutions Ltd
Salcombe Harbour Hotel Limited
J M Scully (Holdings) Limited
Seafood Restaurant (Padstow) Ltd
Les Smith Haulage Limited
Speed Superbikes Limited
Square One Construction Ltd
Stitch Bidco Limited
Stonewood Properties Limited
Storm Land Securities Ltd
Strong Energy Solutions Ltd
Stroud Valleys Canal Company
Superdry PLC
Swinford Wind Farm Limited
Symec Technologies Limited
Taw Garage (Holdings) Limited
Teignbridge Propellers International
Thrings LLP
Thrive Renewables (Eye) Ltd
Tolchards Limited
Tool Care Hire LLP
Allen Trump Holdings Limited
UFT Limited
USAF Management 11 Limited
Vedbaek Limited
Vertigo Investments Limited
Victoria Group Holdings Ltd
Viridor EFW (Runcorn) Limited
WBW Solicitors LLP
WESC Foundation
Walsall Lift Accommodation Services
Waterlip Developments Limited
Waypoints Care (Verwood) Ltd
West Coast Developments (Sandbanks)
White Horse Country Club Ltd
Wodskou Properties Limited
J D Wright & Son Ltd

January-June 2010 [102]

2nd Half Limited
3MS Construction Limited
AES Ballylumford Holdings Ltd
Aaron Heating Services Limited
Acerbic Ltd
Agincare Homes Holdings Ltd
Albert Goodman LLP
Aspirations (Bidco) Limited
Aspirations (Topco) Limited
B.T.C. Activewear Holdings Ltd
BBS Consultants & Actuaries Ltd
BWP Project Services Limited
BWP Services (Holdings No 1) Ltd
Malcolm Barnecutt Bakery Ltd
Bart Spices Group Holdings Ltd
Bell Plant Limited
Bourne Academy
C-Retail Limited
Caerus Wealth Limited
Caerus Wealth Solutions Ltd
Chapters Freefolk Ltd
Corinthian Sports Limited
Cornbury Farm Contracting Ltd
Cornish Potatoes Limited
DVG Limited
Digs Properties Limited
Dunkerton Properties LLP

Essex Schools (Holdings) Ltd
Essex Schools Limited
Forgeway Ltd
Four Times Enterprises Limited
Geist Europe Ltd
Georgian House (Torquay) Ltd
Goodshelter Property (Surbiton) Ltd
Grant Almont Limited
Grounded Property Trading Ltd
Hackney Parish Almshouses Charity
Hanwey LLP
Hobbycraft Group Limited
Homer & Pardy Developments Ltd
Import Export Services (GRP) Ltd
Innogy Gym 2 Limited
Innogy Gym 3 Limited
Innogy Gym 4 Limited
Innovate Awarding Ltd
Invicta Motors (Maidstone) Ltd
KS SPV 1 Limited
Kiwa Holdings (UK) Limited
Knights Brown Group Ltd
Levitt UK Real Estate Limited
Littleham 2010 Limited
Lovewell Blake LLP
MWI Supply (UK Acquisition) Ltd
MWI Supply (UK Holdings) Ltd
Maats Tech Limited
Marine Academy Plymouth
Colin Mear Limited
Midway Care Group Limited
Milewood (Holdings) Ltd
Herman Miller Holdings Ltd
Nailsworth Limited
Nevro Medical Limited
New Docs Limited
North Harbour Properties LLP
Original Style Holdings Ltd
Pegasus Planning Group Limited
Plessey Group Holdings Limited
Power Electrics Generators Ltd
QNH Limited
Richard Reeve's Foundation
Royal Marines Charity
Ruskin Mill Trust Limited
S G V M Holdings Limited
Severn Glocon (Aberdeen) Ltd
Silbury Housing Holdings Ltd
Silbury Housing Limited
Smart Aluminium Extrusions Ltd
Alan Snow Agricultural Engineers
Solace Global Maritime Limited
South West Laundry Ltd
Sovereign Care Limited
Sportech Holdco 1 Limited
Sportech Holdco 2 Limited
Sportsman Gun Centre Limited
Staverton Electrical Supplies Ltd
Staysail Limited
Stitch 2 Limited
Stitch 3 Limited
Sturtons Group Limited
Supergroup Concessions Limited
Supergroup Internet Limited
Thirsty Work Limited
Treveglos Farm Limited
Turtle Bay Restaurants Limited
WPD Smart Metering Limited
Wheeler's (Westbury) Holdings Ltd
Ken White Holdings Limited
Whitecroft Developments Ltd
Whitehall Garden Centre (Holdings)
Williamsbuild Management Ltd
Yeo Valley Fruit Limited
Zogenix Europe Limited

July-December 2010 [90]

A.J. Developments Limited
ASM Assembly Systems UK Holding Ltd
Acoura Holdings Limited
Alternative Money Solutions LLP
Antrak Limited
Aspire Academy Trust
M Baker (Newquay) Limited
Banner Limited
A N Barr Industries Limited
Jeremy Bishop Haulage Limited
Bodmin College
Bristol Fluid System Technologies
British Solar Renewables Ltd
Cartus Financing Limited
Castlegate Business Park Ltd
Church Farm Publow LLP
Churchill Retirement PLC
Churston Ferrers Grammar School
Colonial Leisure Limited
Colosseum Dental UK Partnerships Ltd
Colvase Estate Ltd
Colyton Grammar School Academy Trust
Cornerstone Academy Trust
Cotswold School Academy Trust
Creative England Limited
Decision Insight Information Group (Europe)
Decision Logic Ltd
Devonshire Homes (Bracken) Ltd
EVGH Limited
Ecotricity Bonds PLC
Education South West
English Heritage Trust
Equa Multi Academy Trust
Fairlie Holdings Limited
Fairlie Properties Limited
Foot Anstey LLP
Galloper Wind Farm Limited
Goddard Park Community Primary School
Academy Trust
Goldrose Management Limited
Great American Specialty & Affinity
Hardenhuish School Limited
Higher Tregarne Solar (UK) Ltd
Huish Episcopi Academy
KS SPV 9 Limited
Kandytoys Limited
Learning Academy Trust
MVV Environment Devonport Ltd
Malvern Property Limited
Meltor Developments Limited
Midsomer Norton Schools Partnership
NCC Operations Limited
Ocean Village Waterside Developments
Omega Housing Limited
Otter Power Limited
Parkstone Grammar School Trust
Pate's Grammar School
Pennard Hill Farm Holdings Ltd
Prima Dental Manufacturing Ltd
Professional Reseller Group Ltd
RW Gower Street Limited
RW Greenside Place Limited
RW Threadneedle Street Limited
Rowan Dartington Holdings Ltd
Russell Worth Limited
Sharpak Bridgwater Limited
Sharpak Yate Limited
Sir Thomas Rich's School
South Wilts Grammar School for Girls
Spirit Packaging Limited
Stay Original Co Ltd
Stephens Scown LLP
Torquay Boys' Grammar School
Totus Engineering Limited
Troy (UK) Limited
USAF Management 12 Limited
Uffculme Academy Trust
Vector Learning Trust
Vectura Group Investments Ltd
Verto Homes Ltd
Viridor Oxfordshire Limited
WK Crematoria Limited
Waypoints Care (Plymouth) Ltd
Waypoints Care Group Limited
Wessex Learning Trust
Westcon Group Middle East Holdings
Westcountry Schools Trust
White Pennant Ltd
Workforce Development Trust Ltd
Worlds Apart Holdings Limited
Your Energy Holdings Limited

January-June 2011 [166]

599 Developments Ltd
Acorn Education Trust
Advanced Waste Solutions Ltd
Alessandra UK Limited
Alliance Homes (Ventures) Ltd
Ansford Academy Trust
Asheek Living Limited
Astra Trading Development Ltd.
Avenue 64 Limited
BBLP Holdings Limited
Balcarras School
Bath and West Finance Limited
Beechen Cliff School
Bishop Fox's School
Bishop Wordsworth's Church of England
Grammar School for Boys
Bladeroom Holdings Limited
Books & Stationers Limited
Bristol Community Health C.I.C.
Bristol Music Trust
Bristol and South Gloucestershire UTC
Brookside Community Primary School
Academy Trust
Burgate School and Sixth Form
Burges Salmon Co Ltd
CSIA Trust
Carbis Bay Hotel Limited
Carlisle Fluid Technologies UK Ltd
Castelan Limited
Castle Partnership Trust
Castlewood (Commercial) Properties
Cheltenham Bournside School and Sixth
Form Centre
Chipping Campden School
Chosen Hill School
Churchill Academy
Cirencester Kingshill School
Cleeve School
Clyst Vale Academy Trust
Coast Academies
Colten Care (2009) Limited
Commercial Corporate Services Ltd
Commonweal School
Cook and Copp Limited
Corfe Hills School Academy Trust
Corinium Education Trust

Corsham School Academy Group
Crispin School Academy Trust
Crypt School
Crystal Classics Fine Minerals Ltd
Denmark Road High School
Devonport High School for Boys Academy Trust
Devonport High School for Girls
Dexretail Limited
Dobson Family Investment Co Ltd
Elmlea Junior School
Exmouth Community College
Feniton Park Limited
Fraser St James Investments Ltd
Froyle Park Estates Limited
Geo Specialty Chemicals UK Ltd
Gryphon Trust
HTP Grange Limited
Hampshire Motor Investment Co Ltd
The Thomas Hardye Multi Academy Trust
Hayes School
Hayesfield Girls' School
Haygrove Academy Trust
Highcliffe School
Highworth Warneford School
Honiton Community College Academy Trust
Imerys Minerals Holding Ltd
Inspiring Schools Partnership
Ironburg Inventions Limited
JS2 Investments Limited
H R Jasper & Son (Holdings) Ltd
Johnan UK Limited
KS SPV 12 Limited
KWTN Solar Limited
Kemeneth Multi Academy Trust
Killiow Estates Limited
King's School Ottery St Mary
Kingsmead Academy
Latimer Trend Holdings Limited
Leading Edge Academies Partnership
Lethbridge Primary School
Lighthouse Schools Partnership
Lipson Co-operative Academy Trust
Livewell Southwest CIC
Livingstone Leisure Limited
Lyons Davidson Limited
M K Property & Letting Limited
Mare and Foal Sanctuary
Maximum Fun Devon Limited
Maximum Fun Holdings Limited
McBraida Holdings Limited
Mitcham Holdings Ltd
Mount Road Care Home LLP
North Somerset Community Partnership CIC
S. Notaro Group Limited
Oldfield School
Opmal Limited
PPL UK Investments Limited
Parkfield Education Limited
Penair School
Peninsula Learning Trust
Perivoli Investments Limited
Pewsey Vale School
Pickwick Academy Trust
Plympton Academy
Plymstock School
Polymermedics Limited
Pool Academy
Poole Grammar School
Preston School Academy Trust
Procurri Europe Limited
Property Consortium (Holdings) Ltd
Pulse Global Holdings Limited
QE Academy Trust
Quantum Group (Management) Ltd
Queensquare Farming Limited
R & M Utility & Civil Engineering Services South West
Redstart Learning Partnership
Ribston Hall High School Academy Trust
Ringwood School
Roseland Multi Academy Trust
Royal Wootton Bassett Academy Trust
Royds Withy King LLP
SACO The Serviced Apartment Co Ltd
SDL Biomass Limited
Sarsen Stone Group Limited
Shelburne Farming LLP
Sheldon School
Shiphay Learning Academy
Simian Group (Holdings) Ltd
Sirona Care & Health C.I.C.
Simon Smith Retail Limited
Snape Contracting Services Ltd
South Dartmoor Academy
South East Cornwall Multi Academy Regional Trust
Southampton Harbour Hotel Ltd
Spire Payments Ltd
St Margaret's Academy
Stance (Europe) Limited
Stanchester Community School Academy
Steanbow Limited
Stroud High School
Sunpower Meadow LLP
Swan Properties Cornwall Ltd
Symons Retail Limited
Teignmouth Learning Trust
Tor Bridge Academy Trust
Torbay Economic Development Co Ltd
Torchlightgroup Limited
Torquay Girls' Grammar School
Twynham Learning
TxtNation Holdings Limited
Ukcloud Ltd
Union Jack Oil PLC
University of St Mark & St John
Venture Multi Academy Trust
Vertigo Capital Limited
Vinci Education (Bradfield) Ltd
Waycroft Multi Academy Trust
West Somerset Academies Trust
Westbury-on-Trym Church of England Academy
Westfield Academy Trust
Winchcombe School
Wishford Schools (Group) Ltd

July-December 2011 [115]

ARI Fleet, Ltd.
Amesbury Abbey Limited
Athelstan Trust
Bath and Mendip Partnership Trust
The John Bentley School
Blue School
Boardinghouse Windfarm Limited
Bond Business Services Limited
Bournemouth School
Bournemouth School for Girls
Bridge Multi-Academy Trust
Brixham College Academy Trust
Broadoak Mathematics and Computing College
Buckler's Mead School
Burrington Estates Limited
CHG Developments (Southampton) Ltd
CQC Holdings Limited
Cabot Mews Limited
Cambium Networks, Ltd
Centek Holdings Limited
Charlton Kings Junior School
Charterbank Capital Limited
Chulmleigh Academy Trust
Churchdown School
Clean Earth Energy Investments Ltd
Clevedon Learning Trust
Computershare Investments (UK) (No. 8)
Cotham School
Cotswold Beacon Academy Trust
H. Days Holdings Limited
Dene Magna School
Dorcan Academy
Dragonfly Education Trust
E Development (2) Limited
EIMS Global Limited
FIM Trustee Limited
Falmouth MAT
Farmor's School
Field International Holdings (Dorset)
First Federation Trust
Five Bees Limited
Flash Investments LLP
GTS Academy Trust
Gloucestershire Learning Alliance
H & A Recycling Limited
Higher Kings Mill Limited
Holne Chase Properties Limited
Imerys UK Finance Limited
Independent Vetcare Limited
Kaleidoscope Collection Ltd
Katharine Lady Berkeley's School
Thomas Keble School
LVTG Holdings Limited
LVTG Limited
Learning Academy Partnership (South West)
Leicester BSF Company 2 Ltd
Leicester BSF Holdings Company 2 Ltd
Liverton Business Park 2011 Ltd
Longleat Bishopstrow Limited
Ludus Capital Limited
MMT Centre Investment Limited
Magna Learning Partnership
Maiden Beech Academy Trust
McCarthy Contracting & Development
Meggitt Finance Limited
Meggitt International Holdings Ltd
Mitcham Canada Holdings Ltd
Montacute School
Nephos Technologies Ltd
Newport Park Limited
Newton Abbot Academy Trust
Norbord Europe Limited
North Town Academy Trust
Oakfield School Academy Trust
Olympus Academy Trust
PSW (Holdings) Ltd
Park Academies Trust
Pentwin Group Limited
Plessey Lighting Limited
Henry W Pollard & Sons (Group) Ltd
Priory Learning Trust
Provenn Ltd
Charles Robertson (Holdings) Ltd
Sir William Romney's School
Saint Augustine's Catholic College
Sanlam Investment Holdings UK Ltd

Selwood Academy
Severn Vale School
Sexey's School
Shiner Properties Limited
Silverfish UK (Holdings) Ltd
Smithcorp Limited
Soldi Investments Ltd
Spandex Holding UK Ltd.
Special Partnership Trust
Spirax-Sarco America Limited
St Bede's Catholic College
St. James's Place Acquisition Services
St. James's Place Charitable Foundation
St. Laurence School Academy Trust
Staines Trailers Ltd
Tamar Farms LLP
Tarka Learning Partnership
Tepe Oral Hygiene Products Ltd
Tewkesbury School
Thakeham Mushrooms Limited
Ventrus Limited
WSP Textiles Limited
Waypoints Care (Upton) Limited
Wellsway Multi Academy Trust
West Town Lane Academy
Whitstone School Academy Trust
Wiltshire Air Ambulance Charitable Trust
Wollen Michelmore LLP
Zynstra Limited

January-March 2012 [68]

131 The Promenade Limited
777 Hotels Limited
API Technologies (UK) Limited
Ambitions Academies Trust
Assessments Bidco Limited
Assessments Midco 2 Limited
Assessments Midco Limited
Assessments Topco Limited
August UK Holdco Limited
BE Properties (Plymouth) Ltd
Braunton School and Community College Academy Trust
Clifton Down Corporate Finance Ltd
The Ernest Cook Trust
Coombes Manor Farm Limited
Copper Bidco Limited
Copper Midco 1 Limited
Copper Midco 2 Limited
Creditcall Group Limited
Creditcall Holdings Limited
Crug Mawr Solar Farm Limited
Curtis Banks Group PLC
DJS (UK) Limited
Daish's Group Limited
Dash Group (SW) Limited
Epiphany School
Essex Schools (Woodlands) Ltd
Essex Schools Holdings (Woodlands)
Faringdon Academy of Schools
Five Directions Limited
Forrestbrown Limited
Frog Investments Limited
GT Motorcycles (2012) Ltd
Gerrick Rose Animal Trust
Harrier Print Ltd
Holt JCB Holdings Limited
Jasme Limited
John of Gaunt School
Knight Midco Limited
Knight Square Holdings Limited
Knight Square Limited

LDC (Portfolio 100) Limited
LV Capital PLC
Leaf Academy
Longhouse Ltd
Loungers Holdings Limited
Lucrative Investments Holdings Ltd
Magdalen Victoria LLP
Manor Lodge Developments Ltd
Merriott Plastics Group Ltd
Multi Circuit Boards Limited
P.O.C. Contractors Limited
PGI - Protection Group International Ltd.
Bob Pepper Holdings Limited
Persey Properties Partnership LLP
Phoenix Learning & Care Holdings Ltd
Point at Polzeath Limited
Porter Dodson LLP
Premier Cables Holdings Ltd
Seven Fields Primary School
Signum Technology Limited
Stuart Partners Limited
Swoop Travel Limited
UBB Waste (Essex) Limited
Unite Accommodation Management One Hundred
Viridor Trident Park Limited
WJ South West Limited
Wadebridge School
Westcoast Developments (2009) Ltd

April-June 2012 [46]

Amazon Capital Ltd
Avec Trade Limited
Avonbourne International Business and Enterprise Academy Trust
Bastins 2012 Limited
Bridgwater College Trust
Canprop I Limited
Christ Church C of E Primary School
Clean Earth Energy Wind Investments
Crediton Milling Holdings Ltd
Mike Cruickshank Publishing Ltd
Curo Enterprise Limited
Dorchester Middle School
Foscombe Properties Limited
Froyle Harbour Hotel Limited
Gilo Industries Group Limited
Gingerbread (Holdings) Limited
Hills Homes Developments Ltd
IDEMIA UK Holding Limited
Ledex Limited
MDE Consultants Ltd
Manor Life Investments Limited
Mead Academy Trust
Megahertz Limited
Nailsea School
OC Sport Ltd
Octava Holdings Limited
Openwave II UK Limited
Palladian Academy Trust
Paris Presents UK Limited
Penmellyn Veterinary Group Ltd
Plymouth Community Homes Energy Ltd
Powis Hotels Limited
SC Group-Global Limited
SW Construction (Residential) Ltd
Sheiling Special Education Trust
Steiner Academy Frome
Student Rooms 4 Plymouth Ltd
Thrive Renewables (Severn) Ltd
Trust in Learning (Academies)
UCLH Investors Limited

Ultimate Bridging Finance Ltd
Viridor South London Limited
Virtual Infrastructure Group Ltd
WP Industrial Limited
White Horse Federation
M R Young & Sons (Rural) Ltd

July-September 2012 [51]

Academy Trust of Melksham
An Daras Multi Academy Trust
Apex One Limited
Avon Specialty Metals Limited
BSR Group Holdings Limited
M Baker (Retail) Limited
Bath and Wells Diocesan Academies Trust
Bellamy Wealth Management Ltd
Alvan Blanch Holdings Limited
Boo Homes (Leckhampton) Ltd
Britannia Parking Group Ltd
Catalyst Business Finance Ltd
Champion Groundworks Limited
Codford Biogas Limited
Connexion Technologies Limited
Corin Orthopaedics Holdings Ltd
Cotham Gardens Primary School Ltd
Diocese of Bristol Academies Trust
Diocese of Gloucester Academies Trust
Dribuild Group Limited
Excalibur Academies Trust
Excalibur Unified Communications Ltd
Gatehouse Green Learning Trust
Gillman Electrical Group Ltd
Goonvean Aggregates Limited
Hardware Group Limited
Hazelwood Motor Co Ltd
Hindhead Investments Limited
Kingsley Developments (S W) Ltd
Kinlon Limited
Launceston College
Liverton Business Park 2012 Ltd
Maistro PLC
Michco 1204 Limited
Michco 1205 Limited
Michco 1208 Limited
Newent Community School and Sixth Form Centre
OMPD Limited
Parkview Gloucester Ltd
Plymouth Rentals Limited
Prolabs (UK) Limited
Renewable Design Co Ltd
River Marketing (Holdings) Ltd
Roundhill Estate Limited
Sherborne Area Schools' Trust
St Moritz (Holdings) Limited
St. James's Place Partnership Services
T2 Partnership Ltd
Warners Retail Group Limited
Westbury Park School
World Group Holdings Limited

October-December 2012 [45]

Acrefield Land Limited
All Tel Communications Limited
Mike Bayliss Holdings Limited
Beeley (Holdings) Limited
Canprop Kensington Limited
Catalent CTS UK Holding Ltd
Catalent MTI Pharma Solutions Ltd
Chickerell Primary Academy

Christ Church C of E Primary School (Cheltenham)
De Van Automotive Limited
Dean Clarke Estate Ltd
EXE Investment Holdings Ltd
Elm Developments Holdings Ltd
Endeavour Academy Trust
Good Energy Hampole Windfarm Ltd
Goodshelter Property Co Ltd
Groves Park Investments Ltd
Growth Property Limited
Gwenray Capital Limited
HRB Hotel Co Ltd
Hitachi Nuclear Projects Development Europe
Holmshaw Property Holdings Ltd
Inspirational Futures Trust
Jackamax Limited
MGI Coutier Finance Limited
Microensure Holdings Limited
North Downs Farm Ltd
Oxygen House Group Limited
Pure Storage UK Limited
Quantum Salisbury Centre LLP
Rodbourne Rail Farm Solar Park Ltd
SLX Group Limited
Sloane & Pirkis LLP
South Devon UTC
South Wiltshire UTC Limited
St David's Church of England Primary Academy
St Stephens House Ltd
Stovax Heating Group Limited
Topcon Technology Limited
UBB Waste (Gloucestershire) Ltd
Unite Accommodation Management 18
Valeport (Holdings) Limited
Westerleigh WGH Limited
Yellow Bridge Developments LLP
npower Group Limited

January-March 2013 [59]

AB Dynamics PLC
Alchemy Promotions Limited
Asvida UK Limited
Axminster Carpets Limited
BSR Connect Limited
Bee Green Solar Limited
Birdwell School
Blue3 (London) (Holdings) Ltd
Blue3 (London) Limited
Buckinghamshire Group Limited
Buckinghamshire Limited
Castle School Education Trust
Chatleigh Holdings Limited
Combe Pafford School
Cream Care Group Limited
Delta Education Trust
East Devon Properties Limited
Exeter Castle Management Co Ltd
Front Foot Investments Limited
GCP Student Living PLC
Gemini Energy Limited
Gillett's (Holdings) Limited
Granite Associates Ltd.
Green Spinnaker Limited
Kelston Sparkes (Group) Ltd
Kites Enterprises Limited
Hugh Koch Associates LLP
Kondor Property Co Ltd
LDC (Portfolio) Limited
Laceys Solicitors LLP
Lester Brunt Partnership LLP
Libra Investments Limited
Little Venice Developments Ltd
New Look Finance Limited
Nuestra Familia Restaurants Ltd
Oasis Healthcare Bidco Limited
Oasis Healthcare Group Limited
Oasis Healthcare Midco 1 Ltd
Oasis Healthcare Midco 2 Ltd
Peninsula Dental Social Enterprise CIC
Plymouth Cast
Pokesdown Community Primary School
Positive Cashflow Finance (Holdings)
Queen's Park Infant Academy
RTB Private Equity Ltd
Royal Institution of Cornwall
SACO Group Holdings Limited
SW Construction (No.2) Limited
Shearbarn Holiday Park Limited
Sitec Holdings Limited
Solar Power Generation Limited
Stoke Bishop Church of England Primary School
Strukta Group Limited
Sturts Community Trust
TR (Fenpower) Limited
Versarien PLC
Wave Multi Academy Trust
YPI Limited
Zycko Group Limited

April-June 2013 [53]

Armstrong Energy Global Ltd
P. E. Barton (Holdings) Ltd
Bathurst Estate Holdings Ltd
Ceuta Holdings Limited
Clark Holdings (UK) Limited
Crediton Dairy Limited
Crucial Sauce Co Ltd
Dairy Partners (Cymru Wales) Ltd
Dover Engineered Systems UK Ltd
Dowdeswell Aviation LLP
Eastleigh Care Group Limited
Eastleigh Care Homes - Raleigh Mead
Emily Estate (UK) Limited
Exeter Finance Ltd
Fresh Homes (Bournemouth) Ltd
Goldmix Limited
Good Energy Carloggas Solar Park (009)
Good Energy Cross Road Plantation Solar Park (028)
Good Energy Lower End Farm Solar Park (026)
Good Energy Woolbridge Solar Park (010)
Headlands Technologies Europe LLP
P & S Hockin Limited
B.R. Hodgson (Holdings) Ltd
IEP Technologies Limited
Insite Poster Investments (C) Ltd
MGV Engineering Limited
Malmesbury C of E Primary School
Minerva Learning Trust (Dorset)
Neon (Holdings) Limited
Pencarrie Group Limited
Praxair Offshore Services Ltd
Providence Projects Rehab Group Ltd
Quantum Swansea LLP
Readam UK (Pty) Ltd
Refresh Living No. 1 Ltd
Remix Bidco Limited
Rockley Manor Estate LLP
Sarkis Limited
Scotch Corner Richmond LLP
Silver Arrow Investments Ltd
Solent Global Holdings Limited
South West Peninsula Ahsn Ltd
St Christopher's C of E (Primary) Multi Academy Trust
St Christopher's C of E (Secondary) Multi Academy Trust
Talent & Enterprise Trust
Thatchers (Myrtle Farm) Ltd
Three Ways School
Tilstone Industrial Limited
USAF Finance II Limited
Veale Wasbrough Vizards LLP
Woodland Barton Wind LLP
Workman Properties Limited
The Ted Wragg Multi Academy Trust

July-September 2013 [42]

AIM Aviation Holdings Limited
Acanthus Ventures Limited
Adventure Learning Academy Trust
Alexandra Wharf Limited
Ark Estates Cody Park Limited
Ark Estates Holdings Limited
Austral-Asia World LLC UK Ltd
Beacon Properties (UK) Ltd
Bel Ombre Properties Limited
Robert Braithwaite Limited
Bristol Care Homes Development Ltd
CAA Property Limited
Call To The Bar Ltd
Carter Projects Limited
Eggbuckland Community College Academy Trust
Fairchild Thompson LLP
Gilltown Limited
Good Energy Rook Wood Solar Park (057)
Greenoaks Global Holdings Ltd.
IESIS (Redcliff Street) Ltd
Image Factory Communications Ltd
Jones Building Group Limited
Luxurycare (Regency Manor Care Home)
Merlin Entertainments PLC
JKL Moseley Limited
New Abbey Developments LLP
Newquay View Resort Limited
OC Vor Ltd
Queen Elizabeth's School (Wimborne Minster)
Quickmach Holdings Limited
Radius Bidco Limited
Radius Holdco Limited
Radius Midco Limited
Rattray Milne Ltd
Roco Investments Limited
Sandown Motors Limited
Sesanti Limited
Southside Regeneration Limited
St Margaret's Residences (Exeter)
Sutton Chemicals & Textiles UK Ltd
Torcare (Holdings) Limited
Zebra MTD Limited

October-December 2013 [67]

Acraman (515) Limited
Aster Treasury PLC
Athena Racing Limited
Atlantic Centre of Excellence Multi Academy Trust
BA Technologies Holdings Ltd

BBG Lift Accommodation Services (No 2)
BGS 103 Hurst Solar Park Ltd
BGS 104 Sedbury Solar Park Ltd
Bluebelt Hospitality Limited
Camelot Care (Bridgwater) Ltd
Clark Holt Limited
Clark Projects 12 Limited
Colston Property Developments LLP
Crawlands Limited
DCM (Cornwall) Limited
DFH Estates Limited
Dilkes Energy Limited
Esteban Investments Limited
Extreme Assets LLP
Frome Solar Limited
GCP Scape East Limited
GDS INT Holdings Limited
Galion (Project Two) Limited
Gamma Energy Limited
George Banco.Com Limited
Gill Corporate Limited
Glide Bidco Limited
Glide Topco Limited
Gretton Solar Farm Limited
Haydn Fine Ltd
Houzz UK Ltd.
Huish Academy Trust
Insite Outdoor Advertising (A) Ltd
Ipex Capital GP LLP
Kernow Veterinary Group Ltd
LDC (Portfolio 20) Limited
Lunamar (Group) Limited
Lyell Trading Limited
ML Wind LLP
Magna Manor Developments Ltd
Manor Renewable Energy Limited
Mears New Homes Limited
Merlin UK Finco 1 Limited
Pingry Solar Ltd
Preston Cherry LLP
Property Franchise Group PLC
REPI Limited
SMD 2013 Limited
Sedgwick Solar Limited
Shaw Ridge Primary School
Snowdrop Solutions Ltd
Soar Newco Limited
Spectrum Property Care Ltd
Sphere Property 4 Limited
St. James's Place International Distribution
St. James's Place Investment Administration
Will Stone Historic Cars Ltd
Teleperformance Contact Ltd
Thrive Renewables (Boardinghouse)
Troika Eastleigh Properties Ltd
Ultrahaptics Limited
Unite Accommodation Management 19
VSGT Ltd
Western Global Holdings Ltd
Woodland Barton Renewables Ltd
Woods Consolidated Limited
Wyderington Limited

January-March 2014 [54]

Addison Capital Limited
Advanced Insulation Group Ltd
Advanced Insulation Holdings Ltd
Aeronautical & GI Holdings Ltd
Amberon Holdings Limited
BDV Atlantic Ltd
Bay Cottage Properties Limited
Bighead Fasteners Limited
Bishop Fleming LLP
Cipher Corp Holding Ltd
Coxco Holdings Limited
Deeley Freed Developments Ltd
Duchy Academy Trust
Educate Together Academy Trust
Forge Entertainment Limited
GRS (Holdings) Limited
Go in Four Limited
Golden Hill Solar Limited
Green Valley Capital Limited
Harlequin Homes (UK) Limited
IF - Inspiring Futures Limited
Insite Outdoor Advertising Ltd
JTL (Holdings) Limited
Jamaica Inn Bodmin Moor Holdings Ltd
Key West (Holdings) Limited
Kruger Property Co Ltd
LDC (Causewayend) Limited
LDC (Greetham Street) Limited
Liverton 2014 Limited
MC Property Ventures Limited
Mendip Batch Medical Limited
Mount Vets Limited
NSD Ltd
Neat Experts Holdings Limited
Newquay Education Trust
Old Sorting Office (Bournemouth) Ltd
Ovo Group Ltd
Quick Move Properties Limited
Redwood Global Limited
SGH Investments Limited
Space Cooling Topco Limited
Stowford Mill Development Ltd
A E Stuart Limited
Stuart Property (Holdings) Ltd
Stuarts Truck and Bus Limited
Sunpower Solar Limited
Targetgrange (Holdings) Ltd
Tewkesbury Park Limited
D.C. Thomson Developments Ltd
Truro & Penwith Academy Trust
Urban Creation (Shaw) Limited
WPD Distribution Network Holdings
West Cornwall Pasty Co. Ltd
Westford Trade Services (UK) Ltd

April-June 2014 [55]

3 Dorrits Investments Limited
7 SFI Limited
A1 Engineering Solutions Group Ltd
ABQ Investment UK Ltd
AMCG Enterprise Limited
Allied Minds PLC
Autumnus Energy Limited
Barrettine Holdings Limited
Belvedere Bidco Limited
Belvedere Midco Limited
Branksome Park Care Centre Ltd
Charter House Planning Limited
Cheshire Coppice PV Ltd
Colburn East Limited
Copano Limited
Delt Shared Services Limited
Deodara Limited
Dorset Freedom Properties Ltd
Duke's 1823 LLP
Dutypoint Limited
Environmental Dimension Partnership
The Thomas Freke and Lady Norton Charity
Gill Sensors & Controls Ltd
HAB at Lovedon Fields Ltd
JM & CW Limited
Landmark Estates (London) Ltd
Leckhampton Estates (Ullenwood) Ltd
MR Capital Consultants Limited
Muscle Foods Limited
Old Coastguard Holiday Park Ltd
Orchard Gate Ltd
PCP 2014 Limited
PMMR Developments Limited
Parris Tractors Limited
RHSG Properties Limited
RMMP Limited
RRPI (UK) Ltd
Radius Debtco Limited
Radius Pledgeco Limited
Regent's Park Healthcare Ltd
Repal Co-Gen (UK) Limited
Sade Properties Ltd
Shoals Hook Solar (UK) Limited
Southern Academy Trust
Stockdale Trading Co Ltd
Strata Service Solutions Ltd.
Total (2014) Limited
Virtus Health Europe Limited
WCR Holdings 2014 Limited
WMG Property Limited
T.D. Williamson UK International
Winston Heights Ltd
Wood Veterinary Group Limited
Yorkshire Hydropower Limited
Zurich Project Finance (UK) Ltd

July-September 2014 [62]

AGI UK Acquisition Limited
Aghoco 1256 Limited
Alton Pancras Estate UK Ltd.
Alu Bidco Limited
Alu Holdco 2 Limited
Alu Midco Limited
Alu Topco Limited
Arena Farnborough Limited
B.46 Trustees Ltd.
Blue Scorpio Limited
Bridge Road Limited
Brighton Harbour Hotel Limited
Bristol Energy Limited
CJ Room Ltd
Christchurch Fairmile Village LLP
Consilium Airton Limited
Constellation Software UK Holdco Ltd
Devonshire Real Estate Limited
Dhrona Holdings Ltd
C R Down Farming Limited
Earthline Exchange Limited
Elliott Heron Limited
Faber Brook Farm Limited
Flemingo International (UK) Ltd
Flowlinks Overseas Limited
J & C Freeth Limited
Good Energy Holding Company No. 1
AR Hooper and Partners Ltd
A J Iles Holdings Limited
Intercept Pharma Europe Ltd.
Jam Bidco Limited
Kersfield Developments (Ensleigh South)
LDC (Constitution Street) Ltd
LDC (Tara House) Limited
Lympstone Manor Ltd
MPL Holdings (SW) Limited
Manton Riches Holdings Limited
Mast (Bournemouth) Ltd
Millets Farm Centre Limited

Opus Professional Services Group Ltd
PPL Island Limited
PPL WPD Limited
Pembridge Property Development Ltd
Portman Healthcare (Finance) Ltd
Portman Healthcare (Holdings) Ltd
Puma Energy (UK) Limited
QIP Solutions Ltd
Quantum Christchurch Care LLP
Quantum Old Manor Retirement Living LLP
Reform Topco Limited
SACO Cannon Street Limited
ST Schrader Holding Company UK Ltd
Stein's Trading Limited
Tiger Communications (Holdings) Ltd
UK Pacific Hampton Limited
UK Pacific Hampton Station LLP
UK Solar Projects Limited
USAF Management 14 Limited
V12 Footwear Limited
West of England Developments (Taunton) No2
Western Power Distribution PLC
Woodmace Concrete Structures Ltd

October-December 2014 [47]

1869 Limited
Acorn Multi Academy Trust
Alexandra Dock Limited
BP Rolls Holdings Limited
Back Catalogue Distribution Ltd
Bay Education Trust
Cher Varya Commercial Ltd
Clean Earth Wind Turbines Ltd
Contango Investments Limited
Delphi Technologies Limited
Eberspacher Exhaust Technology UK
Ecotricity Wind and Sun Parks (Issuing)
FB Ammonite Limited
FB Brassica Limited
FB Calluna Limited
FTI Management Limited
Forest Green Sun Co Ltd
Mrs D M France-Hayhurst Foundation
Gensmile Limited
Good Energy Generation Assets No. 1
Guarantee Holdings Limited
Highlands Hospitality Limited
Hodgetts Farming Limited
Huachangda UK Limited
Juniper Homes (Southville) Ltd
LV Repair Services Limited
Leidos Europe, Limited
Liberation Group UK Limited
Mi-Pac Newco Limited
Mobile Thinking Limited
Ovan Properties Limited
Oxygen House Properties LLP
Parkhouse Hotel (Shifnal) Ltd
Porton Biopharma Limited
Potensis Recruitment Limited
Red House Developments (Surrey) Ltd
Reig Jofre UK Limited
SLG Allstars Limited
Somerset Road Education Trust
South Gloucestershire and Stroud Academy Trust
Suttons Seeds Limited
TKC Sales Newco Limited
Tempire Investments Limited
Tregenna Ventures Limited
Wellington School 1837
Whole Nine Yards (UK) Limited
Wimborne Academy Trust

January 2015 [13]

Cottleston Holdings Limited
Europa Equity Limited
FB Brinjal Limited
First Position Group Limited
Holiday Parks SW Limited
Jongor (Holdings) Ltd
Murrill Holdings Limited
Northern Hydropower Limited
Ocean Automotive (Holdings) Ltd
Premium Rate Numbers Ltd
SCC (Holdings) Limited
Safe House Holdings Limited
Woodford Patient Capital Trust PLC

February 2015 [22]

Advanced Coated Products Ltd
Blue Port Estates Limited
CS LSI Solar Limited
Charlton Abbotts Limited Liability Partnership
Dunns Motors (Holdings) Ltd
Feedco Ltd
Fraser James Properties Ltd
Gabriel Limited
Harbour Hotels Group Limited
Levels Academy Trust
Manor Vets Limited
Optimas OE Solutions Ltd
Pro-Vets Group Limited
Quantum Teddington Development Ltd
Shimao Limited
Shorelark Limited
Specialist Journeys Limited
Specialist Journeys Midco 1 Ltd
Specialist Journeys Midco 2 Ltd
Thatcher View Development Ltd
Westcoast (Bristol) Limited
Woodward & Co (Holdings) Ltd

March 2015 [28]

Aster Solar Limited
Bentley Park (UK) Limited
Bristol Holding Limited
Bristol Waste Co Ltd
Caerus Holdings Limited
Clevedon Hall Estate Limited
DS UK Midco 1 Limited
DS UK Midco 2 Limited
DS UK Topco Limited
Drilling Systems Group Limited
Green and Fortune Holdings Ltd
HJP Investments 2015
Hautot Holdings Limited
Junction Road Croydon Limited
Lovell Stone Group Holdings Ltd
Low Carbon Oxygen Limited
Miton UK Microcap Trust PLC
Moonraker (World) Ltd
Quay Developments (Southern) Ltd
RP (Poundbury) LLP
Teach Poole
Two Eagles Investments Limited
Vian Marketing Limited
Watts Desser Limited
Wilton Bradley Holdings Ltd
Wilton Bradley Limited
Withers Fruit Farm Limited
Woodbury Limited

April 2015 [21]

A & O Holdings Ltd
AEW Properties Limited
Advance Bidco Limited
Advance Topco Limited
Another Place Limited
CDF Group Ltd
Credit Reporting Agency (Holdings)
Edge Restaurants (NW) Limited
Exeter Cash Plan Holdings Ltd
George Group Limited
Hardware Holdings Limited
Hautot Developments Limited
Master International Limited
Norton Group Holdings Limited
Old Quay House Hotel Limited
Olo Real Estate Limited
Prolabs Holdings Limited
Ship (Derriford) Limited
Stonegate Group Limited
Tithegrove Holdings Limited
Tricuro Support Ltd

May 2015 [13]

3LINE Holdings Limited
Ashgrove One Limited
D & R Bidco Limited
D & R Cleanco Limited
D & R Midco Limited
D & R Topco Limited
Forelle Estates Investments Ltd
Gensmile Dental Care Limited
Mainchannel Developments Ltd
New Look Secured Issuer PLC
New Look Senior Issuer PLC
Shaunaks Holdings Limited
Snapfish UK, Ltd.

June 2015 [19]

Ashfield Land (Aberdeen) Ltd
D.B. Systems Holdings Limited
DWML Holdings Limited
Devon Care Homes Holdings Ltd
Dix Hills 516 Limited
Gawcott Fields Community Solar Project C.I.C.
Goodnews Evangelical Mission
Leys Solar Energy C.I.C.
Lower Easton Solar C.I.C.
Merston Renewable Energy CIC
Metal Yapi (UK) Limited
Ocean Learning Trust
Quantum Teddington LLP
Roman Bidco Limited
Roman Group Topco Limited
Techumbre Limited
Urban Creation (Beech House) Ltd
Venture Engineering Group Ltd
Verdant Community Energy C.I.C.

July 2015 [22]
Aura Wind (Holdco) Limited
Aura Wind (Midco) Limited
Bristol Harbour Hotel Limited
Century Casino Bath Limited
Eagle One Residential Limited
FJB Hotels Limited
Hayes Grange LLP
Highcliffe Holdings Limited
Hull Ocean Going Barges UK Ltd
Hydra Holdings 2015 Limited
LDC (Old Hospital) Limited
Morrison Financial Associates Ltd
Project Darwin Bidco Limited
Project Darwin Topco Limited
Radipole Mill Investments Ltd
Rose Bidco Limited
SHOO 788AA Limited
Serene LL Ltd
St. James's Place DFM Holdings Ltd
Westfield Medical Group Ltd
Willand Biogas LLP
YTL Property Holdings (UK) Ltd

August 2015 [15]
115-116 Marine Parade Limited
Altus Holdings Limited
Castelan Group Limited
GCP Holdco Limited
GCP Topco Limited
Hooke Court Limited
Kingdon Holdings Limited
MSA UK Holdings Limited
Mean Moor Wind Farm Holding Ltd
Monkey Island Properties Ltd
Paper Bag Company Holdings Ltd
Riviera Education Trust
Spower Holdco 1 (UK) Ltd.
Swannick & Kearn Properties Ltd
Witney Holdings Limited

September 2015 [22]
Baker Estates Limited
Blackheath Farms LLP
Chichester Harbour Hotel Ltd
Cookpad Limited
FGP Systems Limited
Faerch Plast Poole Ltd
Ferne Animal Sanctuary
Forthglade Foods Holdings Ltd
Galloper Wind Farm Holding Co Ltd
Gill Southern Limited
LDC (Brunel House) Limited
LDC (Finance) Limited
Langdown Estates LLP
North Place Developments Ltd
Prowrap Limited
Southwark Bridge Holdings Ltd
Spectrum Medical Group Limited
Stevens Family Property Ltd
Sureserve Compliance Services Ltd
Sureserve Energy Services Ltd
Urban Creation (Charlotte Street) Ltd
Worcester Properties Ltd

October 2015 [15]
Aim Altitude Limited
Certus Wholesale Ltd
Empire Homes (South West) Ltd
Gnome World Caravan Park Ltd
Granary Ford LLP
Guild Bristol Limited
Heath Academy Trust
MAMG Infrastructure Management Ltd
Moderandum Limited
PP Capital 2 Ltd
Tornagrain Gas Mill Limited
Trivselhus UK Limited
Visage (Aberdeen) Limited
Wishford P6 Limited
Wolf Rock (Cornwall) Limited

November 2015 [19]
Blue Kite Academy Trust
Bradbury House Properties Ltd
Custom Sensors & Technologies Newco Ltd
Ernesettle Community Solar Ltd
Exeter Finance Group Limited
M.F. Freeman Group Limited
Hardrock Developments Limited
Heritage Automotive Holdings Ltd
Indalo International Holdings Ltd
Kingsleigh Primary School
Kinson Primary School
LDC (Millennium View) Limited
MSP Capital Three Limited
MSP Capital Two Limited
Mistral Holdings Limited
Muscliff Primary School
Ropsley Holdings Limited
Sensata Technologies UK Financing Co.
Swedish Lifestyle Homes No.1 Ltd

December 2015 [16]
Blue Port Holdings Limited
Burton Wold Wind Farm South Ltd
Drake Court Property Limited
Harbour Hotels Holdings Ltd
Inspire Multi Academy Trust (South West)
KCTG Japan Holdings Ltd.
LDC (Chaucer House) Limited
LDC (Skelhorne) Limited
Norton Avonmouth Limited
SEAFox Dycem 1 Limited
SEAFox Dycem 2 Limited
Trifle Holdings Limited
Via East Midlands Limited
Vistair Group Limited
Vistair Limited
Winton Primary School

January 2016 [15]
Batson Bidco Limited
Batson Midco Limited
Burrington Estates (Clyst St George)
Burrington Estates (New Homes) Ltd
Philip Dennis Foodservice (Holdings)
Enys Estate Co Ltd
Fanatics UK Holdings Limited
Kammbronn Homes Limited
Knights Brown UK Ltd
Luxurycare (Birds Hill Nursing Home)
Overleaf Holdings Limited
PJAC Developments Limited
Symonds Estates Limited
Tilstone Retail Limited
Viscominvest Holding UK Ltd

February 2016 [17]
Alderbrook Road Limited
Amigo Holdings PLC
Brighton Student Developments Ltd
Caruso Properties Limited
Chachos Holdings Limited
Connolly & Callaghan Group Ltd
Fiberlean Technologies Limited
GCP WL Limited
LMR Holdings Limited
More Homes Bromley LLP
Newincco 1401 Limited
Newincco 1402 Limited
Oval Estates (St Peter's) Ltd
Slee Blackwell Solicitors LLP
Stanley's Biomass Limited
Towerview West Sussex Limited
Wahoo Learning Limited

March 2016 [31]
ACE Schools Multi Academy Trust
Calendula Assets Limited
Canprop II Limited
Comenius Trust
Danbec Property Limited
ES Technology Group Limited
Grenville Bidco Limited
Grenville Midco 1 Limited
Grenville Midco 2 Limited
Grenville Topco Limited
Hacche Retail Limited
Hazel Holdings Limited
Healthline UK Holdings Limited
Hoare Lea LLP
Ikonic Holdings Limited
KPC & AT Body Properties Ltd
Link Academy Trust
Marsden Estate Partnership LLP
Nonwovenn Ltd
Pathfinder Park Homes Holdings Ltd
Plym Academy Trust
Reme Charity
Sitec Design Limited
Sitec Recruitment Limited
TTK British Holdings Limited
Tilstone Holdings Limited
Tilstone Trade Limited
Ultrahaptics Holdings Ltd
Ultrahaptics IP Ltd
WMG Group Ltd
Woodlodge Holdings Limited

April 2016 [18]
Academy for Character and Excellence
Amphastar UK Ltd
Bid PCB UK Limited
Civitas SPV2 Limited
Civitas SPV3 Limited
Cribbs Triangle Limited
Customade Group Trading Ltd
DB Food Group Limited
DM Opco Limited
Expolink Group Limited
Magicard Ltd
Qualasept Holdings Limited
Reach South Academy Trust
Rollo Homes Number One Ltd
UFP Global Holdings Limited
Walton Street LLP
Whiteburn Rookery Investments Ltd
XYZ Machine Tools (Holdings) Ltd

May 2016 [18]

Avonline Holdings Limited
Avonline Network Services Holdings
Avonline Network Services Ltd
Brooke Energy (Engineering) Ltd
Connect Academy Trust
Dartmouth Holdings Limited
Ely Acquisition Limited
GLE Bidco Limited
Gamecube Amusement Limited
Harbourside Learning Partnership
Harvey Commercial Holdings Ltd
London Bidco Limited
London Topco Limited
Magicard Holdings Limited
Richmond Group Debt Capital Ltd
Salisbury Plain Academies
Succession Newco1 Limited
M Way Holdings Limited

June 2016 [20]

Armstrong Bridging International Ltd
Armstrong Infrastructure and Property Finance
Caledonia TLG Bidco Limited
Coln Signature Homes Limited
Customade Group Midco Limited
Customade Group Topco Limited
Dartex Holdings Limited
GLE Midco 2 Limited
GLE Midco Limited
GLE UK Topco Limited
GWP Holdings Limited
MTH Bidco Limited
MTH Midco 1 Limited
MTH Midco 2 Limited
MTH Topco Limited
Natems Sugar Holdings (UK) Ltd
Seiche Water Technology Group Ltd
Star Education Investment Ltd
Triumph Engineering (UK) Co. Ltd
USAF Holdings J Limited

July 2016 [12]

Discovery Multi Academy Trust
GCL 2016 Limited
Greenland Stud Farm Holdings Ltd
Hewer Group Limited
JGH Group Limited
JGH Midco Limited
JGH Topco Limited
Learning Academies Trust
New Look FIN III Limited
S2 Residential Limited
Spyscape Ltd
Stotts Group Limited

August 2016 [6]

Barkwell Plumbing & Heating Ltd
CELCSE Limited
Comexposium Cereals Limited
E & L Rental Properties Ltd
Kandytoys Holdings Limited
Kinneir Dufort Topco Limited

September 2016 [17]

Aura Bidco Management Limited
Burrington Estates (Trispen) Ltd
Clean Earth Holdings 2 Ltd
Crofty Multi Academy Trust
Direct Online Services Holdings Ltd
Fig Tree Court Limited
Fulford Care Home Limited
Genus Capital 2 Limited
Genus Capital Limited
Glasshouse Hotel Limited
Grenadier Emperor Limited
MacTaggart & Mickel Homes England
Orthod Midco Limited
PJFB Property Co Ltd
Pine Wood Hill Limited
SAS (Dorset & Somerset) Ltd
Zuru UK Limited

October 2016 [21]

Alterian Software Limited
Autograph Homes (Hambrook) Ltd
Autograph Homes Limited
Beacon Homes Limited
Biopharma Credit PLC
Clarart Ltd
Datum Capital Limited
FDL Salterns Limited
Five AI Limited
Genus Capital 3 Limited
Hideaway Truro Ltd
Hyperbiotics PLC
KK Daytona Holding Ltd
LDC (New Wakefield Street) Ltd
EP Mallory & Son (Holdings) Ltd
Orange Door Property Co Ltd
Puma Energy Belfast Ltd
Shenton Global Limited
Somerset Bridge Ltd
Tilstone Glasgow Limited
Tilstone Warehouse Holdco Ltd

November 2016 [19]

Action Accommodation Ltd
Bluetech Systems International Ltd
CDS Support Limited
Charminster Farm Limited
Corialis Group Limited
Devonshire Homes (Landkey) Ltd
Expromet Technologies Group Ltd
Halewell Limited
IVC Acquisition Ltd
Innex Investments Ltd
Kiwi Holdings Limited
Linc Capital Limited
Little Bear Solar Limited
ME Estates Limited
QMP Group Limited
St Michael's Falmouth Limited
Threadneedles Hotel Limited
Van Courtlandt Holdings Ltd
Western Bidco Limited

December 2016 [18]

Azure Sun (Holdco) Limited
Azure Sun Bidco Management Ltd
Bath Quartermaster Limited
Borrowdale Gates Limited
Bowater Homes Ltd
Civitas SPV1 Limited
Falfish (Holdings) Limited
IVC Acquisition Midco Ltd
IVC Acquisition Pikco Ltd
Kalel Partners
Kersfield Developments (RHS) Ltd
Lion/Jenga Bidco Limited
Nova Group Europe Limited
Optimum SME Finance Limited
P & B Weir Electrical Limited
Plumlocations Limited
Sanctus Group Holdings Limited
Tilstone Basingstoke Limited

January 2017 [16]

Ashfield Land (Bridgend) Ltd
Chedington Court Estate Ltd
Civitas SPV18 Limited
Civitas SPV20 Limited
Civitas SPV33 Limited
Civitas SPV36 Limited
Civitas SPV39 Limited
Civitas SPV44 Limited
Halos Garden Amusement Limited
International Spray Solutions Ltd
Ladyswood Farm & Stud LLP
Plastic Surgeon Holdings Ltd
Publica Group (Support) Ltd
Senate Court (Southgate) Ltd
Southerly Point Co-operative Multi-Academy Trust
WRK Merger Holding Sub Limited

February 2017 [21]

AT Property Holdings Limited
Amigo Loans Group Ltd
Amigo Loans Holdings Ltd
Ashri Limited
Ashwoods Innovations Limited
BAEMS Limited
Burrington Estates (RS) Ltd
Coldharbour Technology Limited
Dunns Estates (Exeter) Limited
Eco Holdings Limited
Fallon Enterprises Ltd
M.F. Freeman Holdings Limited
GCP Bloomsbury Limited
Robert Hitchins Investment Properties
Juniper Homes (Wilder) Limited
Play Sports Group Limited
SCES Property Ltd
SH & GS Property Group Limited
Scotty Ventures Limited
Swattons Limited
Taylor Maxwell Group (2017) Ltd

March 2017 [18]

Adtech Holdings Limited
Crossman (Lansdown) Ltd
Devaron (UK) Limited
Eelpower (Opco1) Limited
Encore Oakdale LLP
Fourgate (Cheltenham) Limited
GCP Topco 2 Limited
Nu-Heat (Holdings) Limited
Robertson Developments Holdings Ltd
Seabrook Land Developments Ltd
Sleepers Hill (Winchester) Ltd
Stanbridge Property Developments Ltd
Triventura Bidco Limited
Triventura Midco I Limited
Triventura Midco II Limited

Urban Creation Management Ltd
Weird Fish Clothing Limited
Weird Fish Holdings Limited

April 2017 [11]

Bath Recreation Limited
CMOStores Group Limited
Compass Agri (Holdings) Ltd
Cotswold Collections Group Ltd
Edgeworth Investments Limited
Harbour International Limited
Lilibet Finance Ltd
Lilibet Holdings Ltd
Pavey Group Holdings (UK) Ltd
Sidmouth Hotels Holdings Ltd
Whiteoaks Investments Limited

May 2017 [5]

Churcham Homes Holdings Ltd
Expedia Treasury Services Ltd
Mean Moor Community Wind Farm Ltd
Nutwell Farms Limited
PP Capital 3 Limited

June 2017 [7]

Astrum Multi Academy Trust
Atlantis Ocean Energy PLC
Forgeway Holdings Ltd
GGB Investments Ltd
Librocube Limited
Solent Global Limited
Willow Green Developments Ltd

July 2017

George Estates Limited

August 2017

Glossbrook Holdings Limited
Mears Housing Portfolio (Holdings)

September 2017

Harbour Hospitality Group Ltd
Lester Brunt Wealth Management Ltd
Mears Housing Portfolio 2 Ltd
Sett Wind Development Limited

October 2017 [5]

Credit Reporting Agency (Topco) Ltd
Highlands House Investments Ltd
Hoist Hire Holdings Limited
PPL WPD Investments Limited
WPD Investment Holdings Ltd

December 2017

Empty Billy Limited

February 2018

Excalibur Communications Group Ltd

March 2018

Insite Poster Midco Limited

Company Profiles

010 Limited
Incorporated: 17 February 2004
Net Worth: £2,265,565 *Total Assets:* £4,131,495
Registered Office: 37 High Street, Shepton Mallet, Somerset, BA4 5AQ
Activities: Construction of domestic buildings
Major Shareholder: Simon John Heal
Officers: Simon John Heal [1961] Director/Estate Agent

04021465 Limited
Incorporated: 26 June 2000 *Employees:* 96
Net Worth Deficit: £26,068,000 *Total Assets:* £16,639,000
Registered Office: Mallard Court, Express Park, Bridgwater, Somerset, TA6 4RN
Activities: Manufacture of soft drinks; production of mineral waters and other bottled waters
Officers: Aart Cornelis Duijzer, Secretary; Aart Cornelis Duijzer [1963] Director [Dutch]

1&1 Internet Limited
Incorporated: 22 March 2000 *Employees:* 64
Net Worth: £1,733,000 *Total Assets:* £21,685,000
Registered Office: Discovery House, 154 Southgate Street, Gloucester, GL1 2EX
Activities: Other information technology service activities
Officers: Matthias Steinberg [1975] Director [German]; Achim Weiss [1971] Director [German]; Simon Christopher Yeoman [1973] Director/General Manager

1&1 UK Holdings Limited
Incorporated: 30 March 2006
Net Worth: £63,757,000 *Total Assets:* £64,017,000
Registered Office: Discovery House, 154 Southgate Street, Gloucester, GL1 2EX
Activities: Activities of head offices
Parent: 1&1 Ionos SE
Officers: Matthias Steinberg [1975] Director [German]; Achim Weiss [1971] Director [German]; Simon Christopher Yeoman [1973] Director

115-116 Marine Parade Limited
Incorporated: 24 August 2015
Net Worth: £947,549 *Total Assets:* £4,191,601
Registered Office: Scots House, Scots Lane, Salisbury, Wilts, SP1 3TR
Activities: Buying and selling of own real estate
Parent: Uplift Property Limited
Officers: Peter Mark Cadwallader [1982] Director; Anthony Mark Leighs [1965] Director/Accountant

131 The Promenade Limited
Incorporated: 16 March 2012 *Employees:* 89
Net Worth Deficit: £469,754 *Total Assets:* £5,541,051
Registered Office: Dowdeswell Park, London Road, Charlton Kings, Cheltenham, Glos, GL52 6UT
Activities: Public houses and bars
Major Shareholder: Julian Marc Dunkerton
Officers: Wendy Elizabeth Anne Edwards [1963] Director; Gregory Clifford Francis Tufnell [1962] Director

1869 Limited
Incorporated: 22 December 2014 *Employees:* 1,074
Net Worth Deficit: £6,118,000 *Total Assets:* £81,651,000
Registered Office: 1 Hampton Park West, Melksham, Wilts, SN12 6GU
Activities: Activities of head offices
Parent: Tyrolese (789) Limited
Officers: Emma Victoria Jones, Secretary; Mark Raymond Clarke [1964] Director; Ciaran Andrew McMahon [1968] Director [Irish]; Ian Oliver [1963] Director

1pm (UK) Limited
Incorporated: 10 December 1998 *Employees:* 36
Net Worth: £6,969,078 *Total Assets:* £41,950,264
Registered Office: 2nd Floor, St James House, The Square, Lower Bristol Road, Bath, BA2 3BH
Activities: Renting and leasing of other machinery, equipment and tangible goods n.e.c.
Parent: 1pm PLC
Officers: Jennifer Bodey, Secretary; James Matthew Arthur Roberts [1977] Director; Richard Ian Smith [1961] Director

1pm PLC
Incorporated: 14 June 2006 *Employees:* 170
Net Worth: £48,075,000 *Total Assets:* £158,996,000
Registered Office: 2nd Floor, St James House, The Square, Lower Bristol Road, Bath, BA2 3BH
Activities: Security dealing on own account
Officers: Jennifer Bodey, Secretary; John Newman [1946] Director; Edward John Rimmer [1972] Director; James Matthew Arthur Roberts [1977] Director; Ronald Russell [1956] Director/Accountant; Richard Ian Smith [1961] Director; Julian Philip Telling [1960] Director

1st Machine Tool Accessories Limited
Incorporated: 27 November 1997 *Employees:* 16
Net Worth: £1,231,976 *Total Assets:* £4,137,924
Registered Office: Unit 1 The Headlands, Salisbury Road, Downton, Salisbury, Wilts, SP5 3JJ
Activities: Wholesale of machine tools
Shareholders: Stuart Wyndham Murray-Threipland; Claire Rose Murray-Threipland; Dunbeath Engineering Limited
Officers: Mark Jones, Secretary; Mark Jones [1961] Director; Stuart Wyndham Murray Threipland [1947] Director

221 Limited
Incorporated: 27 March 2006
Net Worth Deficit: £46,894 *Total Assets:* £7,884,188
Registered Office: The Old Post Office, 41-43 Market Place, Chippenham, Wilts, SN15 3HR
Activities: Other letting and operating of own or leased real estate
Parent: DLG Investments Ltd
Officers: Guy Russell Macklin, Secretary; Guy Russell Macklin [1977] Director; Lance Marcus Macklin [1974] Director; Derek Stanley Arthur Warwick [1954] Director

288 Group Limited
Incorporated: 14 March 1986 *Employees:* 203
Net Worth: £12,955,775 *Total Assets:* £15,820,092
Registered Office: Russell House, Oxford Road, Bournemouth, BH8 8EX
Activities: Retail sale via mail order houses or via Internet
Major Shareholder: Stephen Richard Allen
Officers: Peter Daniel Owen, Secretary; Stephen Richard Allen [1959] Director; Ian Glen [1973] Director/Marketing; Peter Daniel Owen [1964] Director/Company Secretary; Peter John Robinson [1969] Director

2nd Half Limited
Incorporated: 17 March 2010 *Employees:* 2
Net Worth: £1,653,998 *Total Assets:* £4,289,138
Registered Office: Lennox House, 3 Pierrepont Street, Bath, BA1 1LB
Activities: Other business support service activities n.e.c.
Shareholders: Christopher Geoffrey Lee-Barber; Evelyn Mary Lee-Barber
Officers: Christopher Geoffrey Lee-Barber [1957] Director; Evelyn Lee-Barber [1962] Director

2OC (Holdings) Limited
Incorporated: 3 July 2007
Net Worth: £4,616,000 *Total Assets:* £4,619,000
Registered Office: 2 Temple Back East, Temple Quay, Bristol, BS1 6EG
Activities: Activities of production holding companies
Parent: 2OC Ltd
Officers: Nigel Mitchell [1961] Director; Philip Reinheimer-Jones [1977] Director/Chartered Accountant

3 Dorrits Investments Limited
Incorporated: 14 April 2014 *Employees:* 2
Net Worth: £337,790 *Total Assets:* £5,044,384
Registered Office: Old Library, Chambers 21, Chipper Lane, Salisbury, Wilts, SP1 1BG
Activities: Financial intermediation not elsewhere classified
Shareholders: Patricia Ann Bridges; Paul Malcolm Bridges
Officers: Patricia Ann Bridges [1957] Director; Paul Malcolm Bridges [1958] Director

3AB Care Limited
Incorporated: 11 February 2008 *Employees:* 280
Net Worth: £819,863 *Total Assets:* £6,324,070
Registered Office: The Heathers, Quarry Road, Chipping Sodbury, Glos, BS37 6AX
Activities: Pre-primary education
Major Shareholder: Arvindhhai Ravlabhai Patel
Officers: Bipin Patel, Secretary; Arvindbhai Ravlabhai Patel [1950] Director; Hitan Arvindbhai Patel [1979] Director

3LINE Holdings Limited
Incorporated: 16 May 2015 *Employees:* 66
Net Worth: £1,055,050 *Total Assets:* £4,689,342
Registered Office: Unit 3 Wessex Trade Centre, Ringwood Road, Poole, Dorset, BH12 3PF
Activities: Activities of other holding companies n.e.c.
Major Shareholder: Keith Antony Avenell
Officers: Samantha Watts, Secretary; Keith Antony Avenell [1966] Director; Paul Dalgliesh [1971] Director/Manager; Samantha Watts [1967] Director

3MS Construction Limited
Incorporated: 5 February 2010 *Employees:* 53
Net Worth: £1,511,103 *Total Assets:* £3,719,440
Registered Office: Highgrove House, Truro Business Park, Threemilestone, Truro, Cornwall, TR4 9NH
Activities: Construction of domestic buildings
Officers: Mark Healey, Secretary; Darren Colin Healey [1962] Managing Director; Mark Paul Healey [1964] Marketing Director; Terence Raymond Kennedy [1956] Technical Director; Christopher Michael Littlejohn [1970] Financial Director; Ian McDonnell [1966] Construction Director

3P Learning Limited
Incorporated: 30 August 2006 *Employees:* 60
Net Worth: £912,177 *Total Assets:* £6,952,639
Registered Office: Bull Wharf, Redcliff Street, Bristol, BS1 6QR
Activities: Other software publishing
Parent: 3P Learning Limited
Officers: Simon Peter Yeandle, Secretary; Jayne Warburton [1957] Director/UK National Manager; Simon Peter Yeandle [1966] Director

3T's Leisure Ltd.
Incorporated: 3 February 1997 *Employees:* 79
Net Worth: £9,019,057 *Total Assets:* £20,719,768
Registered Office: South West Caravan Centre, The Airfield, Winkleigh, Devon, EX19 8DW
Activities: Agents specialised in the sale of other particular products
Shareholders: Michael John Taylor; Michael John Taylor
Officers: Adam Richard Lerwill [1977] Sales Director; Darren Brian Milsom [1977] Sales Director; Michael John Taylor [1961] Director; Sylvia Pearl Taylor [1933] Director

43P9 Limited
Incorporated: 2 March 2001
Net Worth Deficit: £1,564,416 *Total Assets:* £8,924,420
Registered Office: Lennox House, Pierrepont Street, Bath, BA1 1LB
Activities: Other service activities n.e.c.
Major Shareholder: Robert William Day
Officers: Matthew Day, Secretary; Robert William Day [1959] Director

4Com Customer Services Ltd
Incorporated: 21 July 1998 *Employees:* 78
Net Worth: £4,193,000 *Total Assets:* £32,441,000
Registered Office: One Lansdowne Plaza, 24 Christchurch Road, Bournemouth, BH1 3NE
Activities: Other telecommunications activities
Major Shareholder: Daron Hutt
Officers: Lynda Terry Cartledge, Secretary; Kevin John Beckett [1981] Director; Daron Grenville Hutt [1963] Director/Chairman & CEO; Gareth Jones [1980] Director; Gary Scutt [1976] Director/Chief Operations Officer; Andrew John Whittaker [1967] Finance Director

4Com PLC
Incorporated: 15 January 2008 *Employees:* 304
Net Worth Deficit: £5,206,000 *Total Assets:* £33,538,000
Registered Office: One Lansdowne Plaza, 24 Christchurch Road, Bournemouth, BH1 3NE
Activities: Other telecommunications activities
Major Shareholder: Daron Grenville Hutt
Officers: Andrew John Whittaker, Secretary; Dr Jamie Victoria Devereux-Hutt [1988] Director; Karen Lilian Elfallah [1959] Director; Daron Grenville Hutt [1963] Director/Chairman & CEO; Gary Scutt [1976] Director/Chief Operations Officer; Andrew John Whittaker [1967] Finance Director

599 Developments Ltd
Incorporated: 31 March 2011 *Employees:* 2
Net Worth: £2,938,623 *Total Assets:* £6,813,874
Registered Office: The New Works, Roughmoor Industrial Estate, Williton, Somerset, TA4 4RF
Activities: Buying and selling of own real estate
Shareholders: Mark Roger Grainger; Stephen Christopher Wells
Officers: Mark Dorrill, Secretary; Mark Roger Grainger [1959] Director; Stephen Christopher Wells [1967] Director

7 SFI Limited
Incorporated: 3 June 2014 *Employees:* 2
Net Worth Deficit: £743,087 *Total Assets:* £9,064,021
Registered Office: Manor Farmhouse, Tangley, Andover, Hants, SP11 0SH
Activities: Financial management
Major Shareholder: Lucinda Anabel Spurrier
Officers: Jack Marston Spurrier, Secretary; Edward John Marston Spurrier [1965] Director; Lucinda Anabel Spurrier [1966] Director

777 Hotels Limited
Incorporated: 23 February 2012 *Employees:* 63
Net Worth: £1,502,424 *Total Assets:* £6,681,991
Registered Office: Towngate House, 2-8 Parkstone Road, Poole, Dorset, BH15 2PW
Activities: Hotels and similar accommodation
Major Shareholder: Mark Andrew Bowley
Officers: Elizabeth Natasha Bowley [1992] Director; James William Bowley [1995] Director; Mark Andrew Bowley [1957] Director

A & A Trading (U.K.) Limited
Incorporated: 22 August 1996 *Employees:* 11
Net Worth: £5,194,094 *Total Assets:* £6,488,322
Registered Office: Mary Street House, Mary Street, Taunton, Somerset, TA1 3NW
Activities: Non-specialised wholesale trade
Shareholders: Dawn Fay Rosemary Pickering; Paul Edward Pickering
Officers: Dawn Fay Rosemary Pickering, Secretary; Dawn Fay Rosemary Pickering [1960] Director/Wholesale Merchant; Paul Edward Pickering [1959] Director/Wholesale Merchant

A & B Contractors (Devon) Limited
Incorporated: 26 August 2003 *Employees:* 36
Net Worth: £166,622 *Total Assets:* £4,387,544
Registered Office: Porte Farm, Kentisbury, Barnstaple, Devon, EX31 4NL
Activities: Landscape service activities
Shareholders: Richard Mark Barrow; Richard Anthony Dallyn
Officers: Catherine Jane Barrow, Secretary/Accountant; Richard Mark Barrow [1966] Director/Contractor; Richard Anthony Dallyn [1958] Director/Farmer

A & B High Holdings Limited
Incorporated: 28 March 1973
Net Worth: £3,491,693 *Total Assets:* £3,856,423
Registered Office: Marquis House, Gulworthy, Tavistock, Devon, PL19 8JE
Activities: Non-trading company
Parent: Coastpoint Limited
Officers: Adrian Arthur High, Secretary/Director; Adrian Arthur High [1950] Director; Elizabeth Anne High [1951] Director

A & L Care Homes Holdings Limited
Incorporated: 8 October 2008 *Employees:* 73
Net Worth: £1,624,824 *Total Assets:* £5,418,745
Registered Office: 7 Sandy Court, Ashleigh Way, Langage Business Park, Plymouth, PL7 5JX
Activities: Activities of head offices
Shareholder: Lisa Webb
Officers: Lisa Webb, Secretary; Lisa Webb [1966] Director

A & O Holdings Ltd
Incorporated: 23 April 2015
Net Worth: £67,063 *Total Assets:* £9,373,245
Registered Office: No 9 Portis Fields, Bristol Road, Portishead, Bristol, BS20 6PN
Activities: Other specialised construction activities n.e.c.
Shareholders: Osprey Maritime Limited; Allelys Holdings Limited
Officers: Lewis Peter Dangerfield, Secretary; David James Allely [1966] Director; Peter Charles Allely [1962] Director; Lewis Peter Dangerfield [1988] Director/Chartered Accountant; Nigel Fletcher [1966] Director

A Curious Group of Hotels LLP
Incorporated: 29 November 2004 *Employees:* 94
Net Worth: £570,000 *Total Assets:* £5,540,715
Registered Office: Cowley Manor, Cowley, Cheltenham, Glos, GL53 9NL

A-Gas (UK) Limited
Incorporated: 1 October 1992 *Employees:* 82
Net Worth: £26,886,000 *Total Assets:* £46,662,000
Registered Office: Banyard Road, Portbury, Bristol, BS20 7XH
Activities: Remediation activities and other waste management services
Parent: A-Gas International Limited
Officers: John Lawrence Ormerod [1970] Business Director; Robert Lee Parker [1973] Operations Director; Ian Victor Stewart Podmore [1973] Director; Richard Edward Marcel Stewart [1972] Finance Director

A-Gas International Limited
Incorporated: 14 November 1986
Net Worth: £90,063,000 *Total Assets:* £117,706,000
Registered Office: AGAS, Banyard Road, Portbury West, Bristol, BS20 7XH
Activities: Combined office administrative service activities
Parent: A-Gas Investments Limited
Officers: Richard Edward Marcel Stewart, Secretary; Andrew Ambrose [1962] Director [Australian]; Ian Victor Stewart Podmore [1973] Director; Richard Edward Marcel Stewart [1972] Director/Group CFO

A-Gas Investments Limited
Incorporated: 21 November 2006
Net Worth Deficit: £10,146,000 *Total Assets:* £34,788,000
Registered Office: AGAS, Banyard Road, Portbury, Bristol, BS20 7XH
Activities: Activities of head offices
Parent: A-Gas (Orb) Limited
Officers: Richard Edward Marcel Stewart, Secretary; Andrew Ambrose [1962] Managing Director [Australian]; Ian Victor Stewart Podmore [1973] Director; Richard Edward Marcel Stewart [1972] Director/Group CFO

A.C.C. Freight Management Limited
Incorporated: 5 September 1996 *Employees:* 16
Net Worth: £2,371,383 *Total Assets:* £5,750,899
Registered Office: Home Close Stables, Station Road, Iron Acton, Bristol, BS37 9TA
Activities: Freight transport by road
Parent: A.C.C. Freight Holdings Limited
Officers: Carl Jason Pickett [1973] Director/Freight-Forwarding

A.E. Securities Limited
Incorporated: 27 September 2000 *Employees:* 2
Net Worth: £5,298,870 *Total Assets:* £9,515,386
Registered Office: Mary Street House, Mary Street, Taunton, Somerset, TA1 3NW
Activities: Other letting and operating of own or leased real estate
Shareholders: Alistair Edward Charles Haimes; Eliot Brian Arthur Haimes
Officers: Eliot Brian Arthur Haimes, Secretary; Alistair Edward Charles Haimes [1975] Director; Eliot Brian Arthur Haimes [1977] Director

A.E.R. Stafford Limited
Incorporated: 27 March 2009 *Employees:* 232
Net Worth: £4,910,315 *Total Assets:* £17,389,860
Registered Office: The Avon Building, Units 137-145 South Liberty Lane, Bedminster, Bristol, BS3 2TL
Activities: Other business support service activities n.e.c.
Parent: Avon Group Manufacturing (Holdings) Limited
Officers: Ashok Ravjibhai Patel, Secretary; David John Langdell [1959] Managing Director; Ashok Ravjibhai Patel [1957] Director; Mark Andrew Rushin [1971] Director

A.E.T. Transport Services Limited
Incorporated: 1 June 1989 *Employees:* 52
Net Worth: £3,228,946 *Total Assets:* £7,390,996
Registered Office: Alan's House, 51 Holton Road, Holton Heath Trading Park, Poole, Dorset, BH16 6LT
Activities: Freight transport by road
Parent: AET Transport Group Limited
Officers: Andrew Edward Trotter, Secretary/Director; Andrew Edward Trotter [1962] Director; Sally Ann Trotter [1961] Director

A.J. Developments Limited
Incorporated: 21 December 2010 *Employees:* 14
Net Worth: £566,895 *Total Assets:* £3,829,397
Registered Office: 230 Ashley Road, Poole, Dorset, BH14 9BY
Activities: Construction of domestic buildings
Shareholders: Mark Stephen Adams; Sebastian Tony Janes
Officers: Mark Stephen Adams [1988] Director; Sebastian Tony Janes [1989] Director

A.K.S. (Yeovil) Limited
Incorporated: 30 March 1994 *Employees:* 16
Net Worth: £2,106,034 *Total Assets:* £3,777,460
Registered Office: AKS House, Addlewell Lane, Yeovil, Somerset, BA20 1RY
Activities: Sale of new cars and light motor vehicles
Major Shareholder: Anton Karl John Szulc
Officers: Darren Newbery, Secretary; Anton Karl Szulc [1963] Director/General Manager

A.M.B.Investments Limited
Incorporated: 31 March 1960 *Employees:* 2
Net Worth: £11,338,637 *Total Assets:* £12,230,211
Registered Office: 58 St Aidans Road, St George, Bristol, BS5 8RS
Activities: Other letting and operating of own or leased real estate
Shareholders: Andrew John Davison; Mark James Davison
Officers: Andrew John Davison, Secretary; Andrew John Davison [1942] Director/Chartered Accountant; Mark James Davison [1937] Director/Farmer

A1 Engineering Solutions Group Ltd
Incorporated: 24 April 2014 *Employees:* 71
Net Worth: £20,903 *Total Assets:* £5,032,022
Registered Office: Office 000, Bristol & Bath Science Park, Dirac Crescent, Emersons Green, Bristol, BS16 7FR
Activities: Other specialised construction activities n.e.c.
Shareholder: Robert Dean Frost
Officers: Michael David Atkinson [1968] Director; Dean Frost [1969] Director

A1 Engineering Solutions Limited
Incorporated: 21 February 2008 *Employees:* 71
Net Worth: £1,341,721 *Total Assets:* £4,606,248
Registered Office: Office 000, Bristol & Bath Science Park, Dirac Crescent, Emersons Green, Bristol, BS16 7FR
Activities: Manufacture of non-domestic cooling and ventilation equipment
Parent: A1 Engineering Solutions Group Ltd
Officers: Michael David Atkinson [1968] Director; Oliver Brown [1982] Director; Andrew William Dewhurst [1959] Director; Robert Dean Frost [1969] Director; Michael John Warris Hodgson [1972] Director/Chartered Accountant; Robert Pegg [1981] Director

A1 PPP Infrastructure Holdings Limited
Incorporated: 14 November 2002 *Employees:* 2
Net Worth: £5,665,274 *Total Assets:* £8,777,007
Registered Office: Third Floor, Broad Quay House, Prince Street, Bristol, BS1 4DJ
Activities: Activities of head offices
Parent: Semperian PPP Investment Partners No.2 Limited
Officers: Chris Burlton [1973] Director/Accountant; Neil Rae [1971] Director

A7 Lochhead Limited
Incorporated: 23 October 2006 *Employees:* 2
Net Worth: £853,631 *Total Assets:* £6,111,936
Registered Office: 31a The Avenue, Poole, Dorset, BH13 6LJ
Activities: Production of electricity
Shareholders: Ventus VCT PLC; Energy L Ltd
Officers: Karin Martina Hensher, Secretary; Alexander William Hensher [1977] Director; Matthew Derek George Ridley [1978] Director/Investment Manager

Aardman Animations Limited
Incorporated: 29 August 1986 *Employees:* 159
Net Worth: £19,048,808 *Total Assets:* £24,299,660
Registered Office: Gas Ferry Road, Bristol, BS1 6UN
Activities: Motion picture production activities
Parent: Aardman Holdings Limited
Officers: David Alan Sproxton, Secretary; Sean Michael Clarke [1967] Executive Director; Sarah Cox [1966] Executive Director; Kerry Anthony Lock [1969] Director/Accountant; Peter Duncan Fraser Lord [1953] Director; Paula Newport [1966] Director; Nicholas Wulstan Park [1958] Director; Carla Shelley [1964] Executive Director; David Alan Sproxton [1954] Director; Heather Anne Wright [1964] Executive Director

Aardman Holdings Limited
Incorporated: 18 December 1991 *Employees:* 280
Net Worth: £27,951,596 *Total Assets:* £40,646,816
Registered Office: Gas Ferry Road, Bristol, BS1 6UN
Activities: Activities of other holding companies n.e.c.
Parent: Aardman Employee Ownership Trustee Limited
Officers: David Alan Sproxton, Secretary; Sean Michael Clarke [1967] Executive Director; Sarah Cox [1966] Executive Director; Kerry Anthony Lock [1969] Director/Accountant; Peter Duncan Fraser Lord [1953] Director; Paula Newport [1966] Director; Nicholas Wulstan Park [1958] Director; Carla Shelley [1964] Executive Director; David Alan Sproxton [1954] Director/Animator; Heather Anne Wright [1964] Executive Director

Aaron Heating Services Limited
Incorporated: 12 April 2010
Net Worth: £3,731,362 *Total Assets:* £3,731,362
Registered Office: c/o BPE Solicitors LLP, First Floor, St James House, St James Square, Cheltenham, Glos, GL50 3PR
Activities: Plumbing, heat and air-conditioning installation
Parent: Lakehouse Compliance Services Limited
Officers: John William Charles Charlton, Secretary; John William Charles Charlton [1956] Director/Company Secretary; David Matthew Lummis [1979] Financial Director; Michael McMahon [1976] Director

Aaron Services Limited
Incorporated: 1 May 1996 *Employees:* 392
Net Worth: £2,088,829 *Total Assets:* £7,514,251
Registered Office: c/o BPE Solicitors LLP, First Floor, St James House, St James Square, Cheltenham, Glos, GL50 3PR
Activities: Plumbing, heat and air-conditioning installation
Parent: Aaron Heating Services Limited
Officers: John William Charles Charlton, Secretary; John William Charles Charlton [1956] Director/Company Secretary; David Matthew Lummis [1979] Managing Director; Michael McMahon [1976] Director; Jonathan Lee Posey [1973] Commercial Director; Rosemarie Gwen Prior [1958] Financial Director; Keith Taylor [1973] Operations Director

AB Dynamics PLC
Incorporated: 7 February 2013 *Employees:* 128
Net Worth: £38,042,728 *Total Assets:* £48,528,304
Registered Office: Middleton Drive, Bradford on Avon, Wilts, BA15 1GB
Activities: Other business support service activities n.e.c.
Officers: Robert Andrew Leonard Hart, Secretary; Anthony Best [1937] Non-Executive Director Chairman; Graham Dudley Eves [1945] Director; Robert Andrew Leonard Hart [1968] Director/Chief Financial Officer; Richard Hickinbotham [1958] Director; Matthew James Hubbard [1975] Director/Chief Operations Officer; Dr James Mathew Routh [1973] Director; Frederick Bryan Smart [1951] Director

Abaco Estates Limited
Incorporated: 8 April 1992
Net Worth Deficit: £7,448,151 *Total Assets:* £5,701,964
Registered Office: Suite 323, 89 Commercial Road, The Triangle, Bournemouth, BH2 5RR
Activities: Other letting and operating of own or leased real estate
Officers: Kathryn Joyce Keltie, Secretary; Fraser James Keltie [1958] Director/Chartered Surveyor

Abacus (Bristol) Limited
Incorporated: 13 January 1988
Net Worth: £2,480,094 *Total Assets:* £3,540,993
Registered Office: Bridge View House, Albert Road, St Philips, Bristol, BS2 0XS
Activities: Collection of non-hazardous waste
Shareholders: Linda Gweneth Beacham; Joanne Blackmore; James Henry Beacham; Simon James Beacham
Officers: Lynda Gwyneth Beacham, Secretary; James Henry Beacham [1947] Managing Director; Lynda Gwyneth Beacham [1950] Director/Secretary; Simon James Beacham [1970] Director/Administrator; Joanna Louise Blackmore [1973] Director/Secretary

Abbey Business Equipment Limited
Incorporated: 30 November 1987 *Employees:* 60
Net Worth: £1,038,764 *Total Assets:* £3,999,442
Registered Office: Units 23 & 24 Neptune Business Centre, Tewkesbury Road, Cheltenham, Glos, GL51 9FB
Activities: Wholesale of office furniture
Parent: Abbey Business Equipment Holdings Limited
Officers: David John Stevenson, Secretary/Director; David Bernard Giles [1964] Sales Director; Timothy Desmond Harris [1959] Director; Charles Richard Hastings [1959] Director; Stephen Layer [1968] Director; David John Stevenson [1960] Director; Mark Stradling [1964] Director

Abbey Manor Developments Ltd
Incorporated: 5 June 1980 *Employees:* 12
Net Worth: £14,734,000 *Total Assets:* £22,731,000
Registered Office: The Abbey, Preston Road, Yeovil, Somerset, BA20 2EN
Activities: Construction of commercial buildings
Shareholders: Nigel Richard Shaw Timmis; Anthony Richard Shaw Timmis; Susan Mary Dorron Timmis
Officers: Janine Mary King, Secretary; Emma Lucinda Shaw Galpin [1964] Director/Housewife; Judith Emma Gannon [1967] Director/Chartered Surveyor; Janine Mary King [1968] Director/Accountant; Vanessa Jayne Shaw Robertson [1963] Director/Housewife; Alastair Marcus Shaw Timmis [1990] Director/Chartered Surveyor; Anthony Richard Shaw Timmis [1936] Director; Christopher Howard Shaw Timmis [1974] Director/Management Accountant; Georgina Lucy Shaw Timmis [1987] Director/Scientist; Gillian Rose Timmis [1958] Director; Jonathan Adam Shaw Timmis [1968] Director/Chartered Surveyor; Nigel Richard Shaw Timmis [1961] Director/Structural Engineer; Susan Mary Dorron Timmis [1938] Director

Abbey Manor Group Limited
Incorporated: 1 October 1913 *Employees:* 21
Net Worth: £25,933,000 *Total Assets:* £43,132,000
Registered Office: The Abbey, Preston, Yeovil, Somerset, BA20 2EN
Activities: Construction of commercial buildings
Shareholders: Nigel Richard Shaw Timmis; Anthony Richard Shaw Timmis; Susan Mary Dorron Timmis
Officers: Janine Mary King, Secretary; Emma Lucinda Shaw Galpin [1964] Director/Housewife; Judith Emma Gannon [1967] Director/Chartered Surveyor; Janine Mary King [1968] Director/Accountant; Vanessa Jayne Shaw Robertson [1963] Director/Housewife; Anthony Richard Shaw Timmis [1936] Director; Christopher Howard Shaw Timmis [1974] Director/Management Accountant; Jonathan Adam Shaw Timmis [1968] Director/Chartered Surveyor; Nigel Richard Shaw Timmis [1961] Director/Structural Engineer; Susan Mary Dorron Timmis [1938] Director

Abbey Manor Homes Limited
Incorporated: 6 November 1968
Net Worth: £20,504,000 *Total Assets:* £21,174,000
Registered Office: The Abbey, Preston, Yeovil, Somerset, BA20 2EN
Activities: Other specialised construction activities n.e.c.
Parent: Abbey Manor Group Limited
Officers: Gillian Rose Timmis, Secretary; Emma Lucinda Shaw Galpin [1964] Director/Housewife; Vanessa Jayne Shaw Robertson [1963] Director/Housewife; Anthony Richard Shaw Timmis [1936] Director; Christopher Howard Shaw Timmis [1974] Director/Management Accountant; Jonathan Adam Shaw Timmis [1968] Director/Chartered Surveyor; Nigel Richard Shaw Timmis [1961] Director/Structural Engineer; Susan Mary Dorron Timmis [1938] Director

Abbey Manor Property Holdings Limited
Incorporated: 26 October 1973
Net Worth: £320,000 *Total Assets:* £8,929,000
Registered Office: The Abbey, Preston, Yeovil, Somerset, BA20 2EN
Activities: Other letting and operating of own or leased real estate
Parent: Abbey Manor Group Limited
Officers: Gillian Rose Timmis, Secretary; Emma Lucinda Shaw Galpin [1964] Director/Housewife; Vanessa Jayne Shaw Robertson [1963] Director/Housewife; Anthony Richard Shaw Timmis [1936] Director; Christopher Howard Shaw Timmis [1974] Director/Management Accountant; Johnathan Adam Shaw Timmis [1968] Director/Surveyor (GP); Nigel Richard Shaw Timmis [1961] Director/Structural Engineer; Susan Mary Dorron Timmis [1938] Director

Abbeyfield Bristol and Keynsham Society
Incorporated: 1 March 1966 *Employees:* 64
Net Worth: £8,778,997 *Total Assets:* £9,160,838
Registered Office: 29 Alma Vale Road, Clifton, Bristol, BS8 2HL
Activities: Residential care activities for the elderly and disabled
Officers: Fiona Baden Meaking, Secretary; Susan Hopkins [1944] Director/Retired; Michael David Innes [1950] Director/Consultant; John Harper Kane [1945] Director/Retired; Edward Langston [1953] Retired Director; Gillian Diana Margaret Oakhill [1940] Director/Retired Teacher; Sara Touzel [1971] Director/Solicitor

Abbeyfield Sidmouth Society Limited (The)
Incorporated: 27 May 1963 *Employees:* 14
Net Worth: £3,802,401 *Total Assets:* £4,508,397
Registered Office: Abbeyfield Court, Station Road, Sidmouth, Devon, EX10 8NW
Activities: Other accommodation
Officers: Robert George William Cook, Secretary; Alison Joan Cook [1938] Director/Retired; Robert George William Cook [1940] Director/Retired; Gillian Margaret Costin [1943] Director/Retired; Alan Darrant [1942] Director/Retired; Christine Edith Drew [1943] Director/Retired; Valerie Fursey [1951] Director/Retired; Michael Peter Gunn [1957] Director/Retired; Alfred David Wheaton [1951] Director/Solicitor

Abbeyfield Wessex Society Limited
Incorporated: 25 March 1963 *Employees:* 25
Net Worth: £14,217,592 *Total Assets:* £14,580,829
Registered Office: Westbourne House, 22 Poole Road, Bournemouth, BH4 9DS
Activities: Other accommodation
Officers: Keith Mitchell, Secretary; Steven Arundel [1947] Director/Retailer; Brenda Jean Biddle [1941] Director/Retired Production Manager; Katherine Jane Leishman [1946] Director/Retired; Keith Anthony Michael Millman [1942] Director/Bank Liaison Officer; Anastasia Helen Turner [1945] Director/Consultant Solicitor (Non Practising); Dr Christopher John Harold Williams [1940] Director/Retired

M.J. Abbott Limited
Incorporated: 12 July 1985 *Employees:* 122
Net Worth: £3,717,807 *Total Assets:* £8,343,333
Registered Office: Bratch Lane, Dinton, Salisbury, Wilts, SP3 5EB
Activities: Installation of industrial machinery and equipment
Shareholders: Jonathan Mark Abbott; Adrian John Abbott
Officers: Jonathan Mark Abbott, Secretary/Managing Director; Adrian John Abbott [1970] Technical Director; Jonathan Mark Abbott [1967] Managing Director; Michael John Abbott [1939] Director; Steven John Briggs [1969] Contracts Director; Andrew James Leah [1974] Finance Director; Michael John Regan [1969] Operations Director

Abercrombie & Kent Europe Limited
Incorporated: 23 May 1988 *Employees:* 68
Net Worth Deficit: £2,063,000 *Total Assets:* £12,212,000
Registered Office: St Georges House, Ambrose Street, Cheltenham, Glos, GL50 3LG
Activities: Tour operator activities
Parent: Abercrombie & Kent Group of Companies SA
Officers: Jonathan Andrew Bennett [1977] Director/General Manager; Brett Eric Fichte [1967] Director/Travel [American]; Carla Martindale [1968] Managing Director [German]; Robin Gary Perry [1975] Finance Director; Jonathan Paul White [1964] Director

Abercrombie & Kent Limited
Incorporated: 17 November 1972 *Employees:* 151
Net Worth: £1,127,000 *Total Assets:* £22,302,000
Registered Office: St Georges House, Ambrose Street, Cheltenham, Glos, GL50 3LG
Activities: Tour operator activities
Parent: Abercrombie & Kent Group of Companies SA
Officers: Brett Eric Fichte [1967] Director/Business Executive [American]; Kerry Elizabeth Golds [1967] Managing Director; Robin Gary Perry [1975] Finance Director

Ablebox Limited
Incorporated: 9 October 1990 *Employees:* 61
Net Worth: £3,495,092 *Total Assets:* £8,288,208
Registered Office: 23 Buckland Road, Pen Mill Trading Estate, Yeovil, Somerset, BA21 5HA
Activities: Manufacture of corrugated paper and paperboard, sacks and bags
Major Shareholder: Anthony Brian Lloyd
Officers: Samuel Peter Ainsworth [1975] Director; Anthony Brian Lloyd [1963] Director; Jack Anthony Cockburn Lloyd [1988] Director; Thomas Robert Cockburn Lloyd [1989] Director

Ableway Developments Limited
Incorporated: 6 February 1997 *Employees:* 6
Net Worth: £2,397,246 *Total Assets:* £3,779,410
Registered Office: Woodland Court, Truro Business Park, Truro, Cornwall, TR4 9NH
Activities: Construction of domestic buildings
Shareholders: Jon Paul Simpson; Kelly Simpson
Officers: Kelly Simpson, Secretary/Medical Receptionist; Jon Paul Simpson [1969] Director; Kelly Simpson [1971] Director/Medical Receptionist

ABQ Investment UK Ltd
Incorporated: 2 June 2014 *Employees:* 246
Net Worth: £850,933 *Total Assets:* £15,957,481
Registered Office: 27 East Overcliff Drive, Bournemouth, BH1 3AF
Activities: Hotels and similar accommodation
Major Shareholder: Shiekh Abdulla Qassim Faisal Thani Al Thani
Officers: Shiekh Abdulla Qassim Faisal Thani Al Thani [1963] Director [Qatari]

Abraxas Insurance Administration Services Ltd
Incorporated: 13 May 1994 *Employees:* 73
Net Worth: £2,172,372 *Total Assets:* £8,674,526
Registered Office: One Victoria Street, Bristol Bridge, Bristol, BS1 6AA
Activities: Other business support service activities n.e.c.
Parent: Mapfre Abraxas Software Limited
Officers: Nigel John Antony Howard-Jones [1947] Director; Jair Giovanni Marrugo Rojas [1972] Director [Colombian]; Javier Maria San Basilio [1966] Director/Reinsurance [Spanish]

ABS Wholesale Limited
Incorporated: 7 April 1995 *Employees:* 126
Net Worth: £1,667,415 *Total Assets:* £7,364,238
Registered Office: Towngate House, 2-8 Parkstone Road, Poole, Dorset, BH15 2PW
Activities: Non-trading company
Major Shareholder: Timothy Martin Hemming
Officers: Timothy Martin Hemming [1960] Director/Importer Retailer; Symon John Reeves [1974] Director

The Academy for Character and Excellence
Incorporated: 1 April 2016 *Employees:* 143
Net Worth: £4,983,640 *Total Assets:* £6,706,719
Registered Office: Shaldon Primary School, Bridge Road, Shaldon, Teignmouth, Devon, TQ14 0DD
Activities: Pre-primary education
Officers: Matthew Edward Cousins [1981] Director; Terence Anthony Falcao [1959] Director/Solicitor; Jackie Gater [1949] Director/Retired; Simon Christopher Girling [1977] Director/Recruitment; Philip Clive Mantell [1953] Director/Retired; Anneliese Helen Slader [1980] Director/Civil Servant; Roger Willoughby [1964] Director

Academy Leasing Limited
Incorporated: 19 March 1987 *Employees:* 46
Net Worth: £9,098,374 *Total Assets:* £26,905,682
Registered Office: 2nd Floor, St James House, The Square, Lower Bristol Road, Bath, BA2 3BH
Activities: Financial leasing
Parent: Speakertone Limited
Officers: Jennifer Bodey, Secretary; Edward John Rimmer [1972] Director; James Matthew Arthur Roberts [1977] Director; Richard Ian Smith [1961] Director

The Academy Trust of Melksham
Incorporated: 23 July 2012 *Employees:* 462
Previous: The Manor School
Net Worth: £19,767,788 *Total Assets:* £22,284,628
Registered Office: The WHF, Plymouth Street, Swindon, Wilts, SN1 2LB
Activities: Primary education

Acanthus Ventures Limited
Incorporated: 3 September 2013 *Employees:* 3
Net Worth: £3,998,160 *Total Assets:* £4,553,439
Registered Office: 2 Barnfield Crescent, Exeter, Devon, EX1 1QT
Activities: Other letting and operating of own or leased real estate
Shareholders: Merrill Damian Crabtree-Livesey; Neil James Crabtree-Livesey
Officers: Susan Ramsden, Secretary; Merrill Damian Crabtree-Livesey [1974] Director; Neil James Crabtree-Livesey [1971] Director

ACC Silicones Limited
Incorporated: 21 October 1948 *Employees:* 48
Net Worth: £4,617,206 *Total Assets:* £5,779,569
Registered Office: Amber House, Showground Road, Bridgwater, Somerset, TA6 6AJ
Activities: Manufacture of synthetic rubber in primary forms
Parent: Amber Chemical Company Limited
Officers: Thomas Gawlik, Secretary; Dr Ralf Bruckmann [1957] Director [German]; Levi James Cottington [1967] Director [American]; Dr Annegret Vester [1962] Director [German]; Nico Wawerek [1976] Director [German]

Access Franchise Management Limited
Incorporated: 22 November 1957
Net Worth: £4,163,000 *Total Assets:* £5,013,000
Registered Office: The Grange, Bishops Cleeve, Cheltenham, Glos, GL52 8XX
Activities: Other activities auxiliary to insurance and pension funding
Shareholders: Zurich Assurance Ltd; Zurich Assurance Ltd
Officers: Timothy James Grant [1964] Director; Shaun Tony Hicks [1968] Director; Gareth David Jenkins [1976] Director

Accident Claims Handlers Limited
Incorporated: 16 November 1999 *Employees:* 16
Net Worth: £3,808,729 *Total Assets:* £4,911,165
Registered Office: Hambrook Business Park, The Stream, Hambrook, Bristol, BS16 1RQ
Activities: Maintenance and repair of motor vehicles
Shareholders: Michael Dennis Savory; Miles Nicholas Savory
Officers: Michael Dennis Savory [1947] Director; Miles Nicholas Savory [1977] Director/Business Development

Accommodation Services (Holdings) Limited
Incorporated: 13 August 1999
Net Worth: £61,540,000 *Total Assets:* £393,153,984
Registered Office: Challenge House, International Drive, Tewkesbury Business Park, Tewkesbury, Glos, GL20 8UQ
Activities: Construction of commercial buildings
Shareholders: G4S Joint Ventures Limited; Innisfree Nominees Limited
Officers: Sandra Margaret Major, Secretary; Gaynor Birley-Smith [1966] Investment Director; Benjamin Christopher Jacob Dean [1979] Director; Christopher Elliott [1957] Director; David Robert Hardingham [1974] Director/Commercial Manager

Accord-UK Ltd
Incorporated: 30 December 1903 *Employees:* 658
Previous: Actavis UK Limited
Net Worth: £99,572,000 *Total Assets:* £206,463,008
Registered Office: Whiddon Valley, Barnstaple, Devon, EX32 8NS
Activities: Manufacture of pharmaceutical preparations
Parent: Accord Healthcare Limited
Officers: Nadine Jakes, Finance Director [German]; Dr James Burt [1974] Director/Chemical Engineer; Nadine Jakes [1975] Executive Director Finance & IT [German]; Sandra Lee [1963] Managing Director Operations; Priscilla Anne Lethbridge [1969] HR Director; Jonathan Wilson [1972] Managing Director UK

ACE Schools Multi Academy Trust
Incorporated: 2 March 2016 *Employees:* 163
Net Worth: £5,584,464 *Total Assets:* £7,509,972
Registered Office: Unit 3 Ensign House, Parkway Court, Longbridge Road, Plymouth, PL6 8LR
Activities: Primary education
Officers: Annette Tracey Benny [1966] Director/NHS Manager; Andrew Dunkley [1967] Director; Sarah Louise Gillett [1974] Director/Headteacher; Gavin Gracie [1956] Director/Management Consultant; Peter William McDonnell [1958] Director/College Principal; Edward Denis Parsons [1956] Director/HR Consultant; Dr Timothy John Searle [1968] Director/Engineer

Ace Welding Limited
Incorporated: 3 February 1999 *Employees:* 1
Net Worth: £3,681,242 *Total Assets:* £4,930,688
Registered Office: 6 Poole Road, Wimborne, Dorset, BH21 1QE
Activities: Other specialised construction activities n.e.c.
Shareholders: Steven George Norman; Katrina Fay Norman; Malcolm Paul Gray; Catherine Bernadette Gray
Officers: Katrina Fay Norman, Secretary; Malcolm Paul Gray [1957] Director/Steel Fabrication Engineer; Steven George Norman [1960] Director/Steel Fabrication Engineer

Aceaxis Limited
Incorporated: 4 October 2005 *Employees:* 31
Net Worth Deficit: £18,503,016 *Total Assets:* £4,012,145
Registered Office: 602 Delta Business Park, Welton Road, Swindon, Wilts, SN5 7XP
Activities: Wireless telecommunications activities
Officers: Nigel Hans Chapman [1963] Director/Business Development Manager; Stephen Edward Cooper [1971] Director/Chief Executive Officer; Jin Yang Kim [1976] Director/Vice President and Chief Customer Officer [South Korean]; Gwan Young Koo [1947] Director/President and Chief Executive Officer [South Korean]

Aceo Limited
Incorporated: 6 September 1999 *Employees:* 22
Net Worth: £7,297,945 *Total Assets:* £7,907,415
Registered Office: Hillside Farm, Rodley, Westbury on Severn, Glos, GL14 1QZ
Activities: Wholesale of wine, beer, spirits and other alcoholic beverages
Major Shareholder: Edward Odim
Officers: Edward Odim [1958] Director/Whisky Broker

Acerbic Ltd
Incorporated: 25 May 2010
Net Worth: £1,935,344 *Total Assets:* £5,174,363
Registered Office: 28 Clifton Wood Road, Bristol, BS8 4TW
Activities: Real estate agencies
Major Shareholder: Mark Budden Tucker
Officers: Mark Budden Tucker [1947] Director

Acheson Construction Limited
Incorporated: 5 May 1988 *Employees:* 55
Net Worth: £2,026,019 *Total Assets:* £9,216,437
Registered Office: 2A Railway Triangle Industrial Estate, Dorchester, DT1 2PJ
Activities: Construction of commercial buildings
Parent: LMR Holdings Limited
Officers: Susan Anne Murphy, Secretary; Robert Digby James Acheson [1948] Director/Building Contractor; Marcus Andre Drysdale [1971] Director/Quantity Surveyor; Colin Johnson [1952] Director/Charter Builder; Shane Mason [1961] Regional Director; Lloyd Ernest Surcouf [1945] Director/Building Contractor; Douglas Willcock [1969] Director/Quantity Surveyor

Acland Plant Hire Limited
Incorporated: 3 February 2005 *Employees:* 30
Net Worth: £2,172,931 *Total Assets:* £3,672,047
Registered Office: Sigma House, Oak View Close, Edginswell Park, Torquay, Devon, TQ2 7FF
Activities: Other specialised construction activities n.e.c.
Shareholders: Dennis John Heller; Dorothy Jane Heller
Officers: Dorothy Jane Heller, Secretary; Dennis John Heller [1950] Director; Dorothy Jane Heller [1953] Director

Acorn Builders (Pewsey) Limited
Incorporated: 15 January 1999 *Employees:* 22
Net Worth: £2,396,457 *Total Assets:* £3,560,014
Registered Office: Unit 18 Salisbury Road Business Park, Pewsey, Wilts, SN9 5PZ
Activities: Construction of domestic buildings
Major Shareholder: Mark James Baker
Officers: Mark James Baker, Secretary; Mark James Baker [1969] Director/Builder; Kevin Eric Franklin [1959] Director/Builder; Duncan Whitton [1967] Director/Building Site Manager

Acorn Classics House Limited
Incorporated: 8 March 1978 *Employees:* 2
Net Worth: £2,894,936 *Total Assets:* £3,804,409
Registered Office: 3-5 College Street, Burnham on Sea, Somerset, TA8 1AR
Activities: Activities of open-ended investment companies
Major Shareholder: John Peter Trevor Hunt
Officers: Joyce Noreen Hunt, Secretary; John Peter Trevor Hunt [1942] Director/Caravan Site Operator; Joyce Noreen Hunt [1946] Director/Secretary

Acorn Developments (SW) Limited
Incorporated: 18 August 2003
Net Worth: £57,962 *Total Assets:* £4,851,365
Registered Office: 40 Kingston House, 1 Kingston Road, Taunton, Somerset, TA2 7ED
Activities: Construction of domestic buildings
Major Shareholder: Mark Peter Thomas
Officers: Mark Peter Thomas [1978] Director/Property Developer

Acorn Education Trust
Incorporated: 1 June 2011 *Employees:* 447
Net Worth: £18,777,020 *Total Assets:* £22,148,080
Registered Office: Kingdown School, Woodcock Road, Warminster, Wilts, BA12 9DR
Activities: General secondary education
Officers: Fiona Simpson, Secretary; Andrew James Armstrong [1961] Director/Principal Safety Officer; John Cowan [1956] Director; Richard Anthony Crow [1971] Director/Charity CEO; Sara Jeane Edwards [1965] Director/Headteacher; Gillian Claire Gosling [1958] Director; Jennifer Emily Hampson [1966] Director; Richard Hendrickse [1970] Director; David George Middleton [1971] Director; Dr Kevin Robinson [1965] Director

Acorn Multi Academy Trust
Incorporated: 7 October 2014 *Employees:* 124
Net Worth: £3,273,917 *Total Assets:* £4,520,392
Registered Office: The Old Tool Office, Chard Street, Axminster, Devon, EX13 5EB
Activities: Primary education
Officers: Veronica Mary Elizabeth Dower, Secretary; Lesley Patricia Adams [1955] Director/Retired; Brian William Impey [1956] Director/Retired; Paul Middlemast [1946] Director/HR Consultant; Samantha Jane Miller [1967] Director/Accountant; Andrea Louise Rice [1965] Director/Headteacher; Clive Sedgewick [1956] Director/Minister of Religion; Mark Van de Weyer [1948] Director/Retired

Acoura Holdings Limited
Incorporated: 15 November 2010 *Employees:* 3
Net Worth Deficit: £3,381,194 *Total Assets:* £6,991,019
Registered Office: 2 Temple Back East, Temple Quay, Bristol, BS1 6EG
Activities: Other business support service activities n.e.c.
Parent: Lloyd's Register Inspection Limited
Officers: Tim George William Bailey [1973] Director; Stephen George Belton [1961] Director [New Zealander]; David Paul Butler [1979] Director; Martin James Gill [1960] Director; Stuart Kelly [1970] Director

Acraman (515) Limited
Incorporated: 20 December 2013 *Employees:* 81
Previous: Uplands Retail Holdings Limited
Net Worth: £12,551,107 *Total Assets:* £27,162,446
Registered Office: 7 Brook Office Park, Folly Brook Road, Emersons Green, Bristol, BS16 7FL
Activities: Activities of construction holding companies
Parent: Acraman (515) Limited
Officers: Michael Barker [1980] Director; Kevin Patrick Feldman [1966] Director; Alastair James Shiner [1974] Director

Acrefield Investments Limited
Incorporated: 30 November 1990
Net Worth: £5,739,934 *Total Assets:* £12,266,720
Registered Office: The Dower House, Tintinhull, Somerset, BA22 8PZ
Activities: Other letting and operating of own or leased real estate
Officers: Peter James Lockhart Smith, Secretary; Presiley FitzGenerald [1951] Director/Retired; Richard Kieran FitzGenerald [1945] Director/Barrister; Peter James Lockhart Smith [1948] Director

Acrefield Land Limited
Incorporated: 7 December 2012 *Employees:* 2
Net Worth Deficit: £154,685 *Total Assets:* £5,535,738
Registered Office: The Dower House, Farm Street, Tintinhull, Somerset, BA22 8PZ
Activities: Other letting and operating of own or leased real estate
Shareholder: Charles Fitzgerald
Officers: Richard Kieran FitzGenerald [1945] Director; Peter James Lockhart Smith [1948] Director

Action Accommodation Ltd
Incorporated: 23 November 2016
Net Worth: £2,581,849 *Total Assets:* £5,663,358
Registered Office: The Manor, Bradford Road, Bathford, Bath, BA1 8EA
Activities: Other letting and operating of own or leased real estate
Major Shareholder: Angela Mildon
Officers: Spencer Robin Mildon, Secretary; Angela Mildon [1952] Director/Property Management

Action on Addiction
Incorporated: 26 September 2006 *Employees:* 152
Net Worth: £3,114,400 *Total Assets:* £4,979,231
Registered Office: Head Office, East Knoyle, Wilts, SP3 6BE
Activities: Residential care activities for learning difficulties, mental health and substance abuse
Officers: Victoria Jane Whitworth, Secretary; Dr Henrietta Bowden-Jones [1964] Director/Psychiatrist; Hugo de Ferranti [1959] Art Dealer - Director; James Robert Drummond Smith [1960] Director; Tanya Louise Farrell [1968] Director/Lawyer; Robert Michael John Fox [1952] Director/Theatre Producer; Frances Gibb [1951] Director/Journalist; Professor Generald William Libby [1944] Director/Medical Practitioner; Edward John Lloyd [1955] Director/Chairman and CEO; Dr Angela Spatharou [1972] Director/Management Consultant [Greek]; Lisa Alexandra Villiers [1958] Director/Film Producer

Actual Experience PLC
Incorporated: 6 March 2009 *Employees:* 76
Net Worth: £20,058,000 *Total Assets:* £20,882,000
Registered Office: Quay House, The Ambury, Bath, BA1 1UA
Activities: Information technology consultancy activities
Officers: Roy Stephen Bennetts, Secretary; Roy Stephen Bennetts [1954] Director/Chief Financial Officer; Sir Bryan Victor Carsberg [1969] Non-Executive Board Director; Stephen James Davidson [1955] Director; David John Page [1967] Director; Dr Mark Alexander Reilly [1979] Commercial Director; Paul David Spence [1959] Director [American]; Robin Mark Young [1965] Director

Acumed Acquisition Company Limited
Incorporated: 5 May 2005 *Employees:* 32
Net Worth: £18,620,508 *Total Assets:* £19,897,630
Registered Office: Huebner House, The Fairground, Weyhill, Andover, Hants, SP11 0QN
Activities: Activities of head offices
Officers: Niall Alexander Hyndman [1976] Director; Nicholas Paul Ryder [1967] Director/Accountant; Nighat Tasleem Siddiqui [1966] Director/Chief Financial Officer [American]; Sharon Wolfington [1963] Director/Medical Device Executive [American]

Acumed Ltd
Incorporated: 3 November 1997 *Employees:* 32
Net Worth: £16,067,080 *Total Assets:* £17,341,860
Registered Office: Huebner House, The Fairground, Weyhill, Andover, Hants, SP11 0QN
Activities: Retail sale of medical and orthopaedic goods in specialised stores (not incl. hearing aids) n.e.c.
Officers: Niall Alexander Hyndman [1976] Managing Director; Nicholas Paul Ryder [1967] Director/Management Accountant; Nighat Tasleem Siddiqui [1966] Director/Chief Financial Officer [American]; Sharon Wolfington [1963] Director/Medical Device Executive [American]

Terry Adams Residential LLP
Incorporated: 27 July 2009
Net Worth: £7,482,260 *Total Assets:* £7,538,456
Registered Office: Greendale Court, Clyst St Mary, Exeter, Devon, EX5 1AW
Officers: Elizabeth Anne Adams [1940] Member; Terence Charles Adams [1939] Member

Addison Capital Limited
Incorporated: 10 March 2014
Net Worth: £1,145,230 *Total Assets:* £5,140,105
Registered Office: The Estate Office, Melbury Sampford, Dorchester, DT2 0LF
Activities: Activities of other holding companies n.e.c.
Major Shareholder: The Honourable Charlotte Anne Townshend
Officers: Robert Ian Sanderson [1952] Director/Chartered Accountant; The Honourable Charlotte Anne Townshend [1955] Director/Land Owner; James Reginald Townshend [1954] Director/Land Owner

Addison Developments Limited
Incorporated: 1 April 1997
Net Worth: £17,809,176 *Total Assets:* £17,957,456
Registered Office: The Estate Office, Melbury Sampford, Dorchester, DT2 0LF
Activities: Development of building projects
Shareholders: The Honourable Charlotte Anne Townshend; James Reginald Townshend; Ilchester Trustee Company Limited
Officers: Robert Ian Sanderson, Secretary; Robert Ian Sanderson [1952] Director/Accountant; The Honourable Charlotte Anne Townshend [1955] Director; James Reginald Townshend [1954] Director

Addpace Limited
Incorporated: 17 February 1997
Net Worth: £5,977,154 *Total Assets:* £11,801,052
Registered Office: Gordano Gate, Serbert Road, Portishead, Bristol, BS20 7GG
Activities: Other letting and operating of own or leased real estate
Major Shareholder: Darren Paul Evans
Officers: Paul Ashley Marks, Secretary; Darren Paul Evans [1961] Director/Golf Wholesaler

The Adelaide Lodge Care Home Limited Liability Partnership
Incorporated: 11 June 2002 *Employees:* 90
Net Worth: £3,414,439 *Total Assets:* £4,741,876
Registered Office: 31-33 Commercial Road, Poole, Dorset, BH14 0HU
Officers: Anthony Kerry FitzGenerald [1953] LLP Member; Ruth Patricia FitzGenerald [1955] LLP Member; Carolyn Adele Rosina Johnson [1959] LLP Member; Stuart Leonard Johnson [1944] LLP Member

Adey Holdings (2008) Limited
Incorporated: 31 October 2008 *Employees:* 86
Net Worth: £26,553,000 *Total Assets:* £40,300,000
Registered Office: UK Head Office, Gloucester Road, Cheltenham, Glos, GL51 8NR
Activities: Activities of head offices
Parent: London Bidco Limited
Officers: Dean Brown [1965] Finance Director; Edward Arthur Davies [1970] Director/Chief Operating Officer

Adey Innovation Limited
Incorporated: 22 December 2003 *Employees:* 17
Previous: Adey Ltd
Net Worth: £27,300,000 *Total Assets:* £50,185,000
Registered Office: UK Head Office, Gloucester Road, Cheltenham, Glos, GL51 8NR
Activities: Wholesale of hardware, plumbing and heating equipment and supplies
Parent: Adey Holdings (2008) Limited
Officers: Dean Brown [1965] Finance Director; Edward Arthur Davies [1970] Director/Chief Operating Officer

Adtech Holdings Limited
Incorporated: 2 March 2017
Net Worth: £933,427 *Total Assets:* £3,535,628
Registered Office: Unit 40 Aston Down East, Frampton Mansell, Stroud, Glos, GL6 8HX
Activities: Activities of head offices
Parent: Noar, Limited
Officers: Victoria June Conway, Secretary; Samantha Emma Deverell [1972] Director; David McKnight Hart [1952] Director; Arthur Jervoise Trafford Scott [1984] Director

Advance Bidco Limited
Incorporated: 22 April 2015 *Employees:* 3
Net Worth: £1,019,828 *Total Assets:* £16,991,992
Registered Office: Third Floor, One Brunswick Square, Bristol, BS2 8PE
Activities: Activities of head offices
Parent: Advance Topco Ltd
Officers: Graham Morrison [1981] Director/Investment Manager; Jonathan Smale Nash [1956] Director/Consultant; Andrew Paul Reynolds [1955] Director; Mark Henry Storey [1961] Director/Investment Professional; Andrew Symons [1956] Director/Business Consultant

Advance Topco Limited
Incorporated: 22 April 2015 *Employees:* 85
Net Worth Deficit: £1,802,715 *Total Assets:* £16,778,680
Registered Office: Third Floor, One Brunswick Square, Bristol, BS2 8PE
Activities: Activities of head offices
Officers: Graham Morrison [1981] Director/Investment Manager; Andrew Paul Reynolds [1955] Director; Mark Henry Storey [1961] Director/Investment Professional; Andrew Symons [1956] Director/Business Consultant

Advanced Coated Products Limited
Incorporated: 2 February 2015 *Employees:* 81
Net Worth: £431,000 *Total Assets:* £4,518,000
Registered Office: The Vineyards Industrial Estate, Gloucester Road, Cheltenham, Glos, GL51 8NH
Activities: Manufacture of other articles of paper and paperboard n.e.c.
Parent: Brightborough Capital Limited
Officers: Dr Nigel Craig Trilk [1965] Director; Martin Paul Urquhart [1968] Director

Advanced Industrial Solutions Limited
Incorporated: 30 October 2006 *Employees:* 123
Net Worth: £4,156,000 *Total Assets:* £8,176,000
Registered Office: Hurn View House, 5 Aviation Park West, Bournemouth International Airport, Christchurch, Dorset, BH23 6EW
Activities: Other building completion and finishing
Parent: Transforming Training with Technology Limited
Officers: Kevin Nigel Franklin [1962] Director; Martin Somerville [1977] Director; Paul Malcolm Stonebanks [1976] Director

Advanced Insulation Contracting Limited
Incorporated: 17 September 2008 *Employees:* 1
Net Worth: £2,763,055 *Total Assets:* £6,167,700
Registered Office: Unit E, Quedgeley West Business Park, Bristol Road, Gloucester, GL2 4PA
Activities: Other manufacturing n.e.c.
Shareholders: Growth Capital Partners GP Limited; Advanced Insulation Limited; Advanced Insulation Group Limited; Advanced Insulation Holdings Limited; Nicholas John Walter Parsons; Growth Capital Partners LLP
Officers: Andrew David Bennion [1968] Director; Andrew Mark King [1965] Director; Simon Harry Shepherd [1965] Director

Advanced Insulation Group Limited
Incorporated: 16 January 2014 *Employees:* 7
Net Worth: £28,416,956 *Total Assets:* £58,807,056
Registered Office: Unit E, Quedgeley West Business Park, Bristol Road, Gloucester, GL2 4PA
Activities: Activities of head offices
Shareholders: Growth Capital Partner GP Limited; Advanced Insulation Holdings Limited; Nicholas John Walter Parsons; Growth Capital Partners LLP
Officers: Andrew David Bennion, Secretary; Andrew David Bennion [1968] Director; Michael James Blake [1968] Investment Director; Andrew Mark King [1965] Director; Simon Harry Shepherd [1965] Director; David Arthur Williams [1946] Director

Advanced Insulation Holdings Limited
Incorporated: 16 January 2014 *Employees:* 387
Net Worth: £12,669,886 *Total Assets:* £94,049,472
Registered Office: Unit E, Quedgeley West Business Park, Bristol Road, Gloucester, GL2 4PA
Activities: Activities of head offices
Shareholders: Growth Capital Partners GP Limited; Nicholas John Walter Parsons; Growth Capital Partners LLP
Officers: Andrew David Bennion, Secretary; Andrew David Bennion [1968] Director; Michael James Blake [1968] Investment Director; Andrew Mark King [1965] Director; Simon Harry Shepherd [1965] Director; Russell Ward [1961] Director/Chairman; David Arthur Williams [1946] Director

Advanced Insulation Limited
Incorporated: 2 November 2007 *Employees:* 5
Net Worth: £1,220,528 *Total Assets:* £27,795,880
Registered Office: Unit E, Quedgeley West Business Park, Bristol Road, Gloucester, GL2 4PA
Activities: Other manufacturing n.e.c.
Shareholders: Growth Capital Partners GP Limited; Advanced Insulation Group Limited; Advanced Insulation Holdings Limited; Nicholas John Walter Parsons; Growth Capital Partners LLP
Officers: Andrew David Bennion, Secretary/Director; Andrew David Bennion [1968] Director; Andrew Mark King [1965] Director; Simon Harry Shepherd [1965] Director; David Arthur Williams [1946] Director

Advanced Insulation Systems Limited
Incorporated: 19 July 1989 *Employees:* 171
Net Worth: £11,900,078 *Total Assets:* £35,648,136
Registered Office: Unit E, Quedgeley West Business Park, Bristol Road, Gloucester, GL2 4PA
Activities: Other manufacturing n.e.c.
Shareholders: Growth Capital Partners GP Limited; Advanced Insulation Limited; Advanced Insulation Group Limited; Advanced Insulation Holdings Limited; Nicholas John Walter Parsons; Growth Capital Partners LLP
Officers: Andrew David Bennion, Secretary/Director; Andrew David Bennion [1968] Director; Andrew Mark King [1965] Director; Simon Harry Shepherd [1965] Director

Advanced Paper Production Ltd.
Incorporated: 21 September 2005 *Employees:* 6
Net Worth: £12,820,070 *Total Assets:* £16,223,683
Registered Office: 18a Littleham Road, Exmouth, Devon, EX8 2QG
Activities: Management consultancy activities other than financial management
Officers: Jennifer Catherine Rene [1954] Director/Personal Assistant

Advanced Waste Solutions Ltd
Incorporated: 24 March 2011 *Employees:* 32
Net Worth: £1,299,058 *Total Assets:* £3,737,979
Registered Office: 35 Black Moor Road, Ebblake Industrial Estate, Verwood, Dorset, BH31 6AT
Activities: Remediation activities and other waste management services
Shareholders: Bonita Louise Cahill; Michael Andrew
Officers: Michael Andrew [1947] Director; Bonita Louise Cahill [1972] Director/Company Administrator

The Advantage Group UK Limited
Incorporated: 4 June 2007 *Employees:* 10
Net Worth: £4,600,404 *Total Assets:* £5,951,568
Registered Office: One New Street, Wells, Somerset, BA5 2LA
Activities: Market research and public opinion polling
Major Shareholder: Andrew James Kemp-King
Officers: Iulia Stepan Kemp-King, Secretary; Andrew James Kemp-King [1953] Director; Iulia Stepan Kemp-King [1977] Director

Adventure Learning Academy Trust
Incorporated: 18 July 2013 *Employees:* 174
Net Worth: £18,221,000 *Total Assets:* £21,016,000
Registered Office: Fowey River Academy, Windmill, Fowey, Cornwall, PL23 1HE
Activities: Primary education
Shareholders: Paul Lloyd Jones; Lorraine Heath
Officers: Stephen Charles Baber [1953] Director/Retired; David Andrew Baker [1963] Director; Dr Alan Jonathan Edwards [1967] Director/Environmental Consultant; Adrian Wade [1971] Director; Andy Ward [1964] Director

AECC University College
Incorporated: 25 March 1960
Previous: Anglo-European College of Chiropractic
Net Worth: £5,937,000 *Total Assets:* £9,532,000
Registered Office: Parkwood Campus, Parkwood Road, Ferndown, Dorset, BH5 2DF
Activities: First-degree level higher education
Officers: Gabriele Sabine Margarete Sanger-Stevens, Secretary; Dr Martin Cecil Copp [1938] Director; Peter Charles Dingley [1956] Director/Chartered Accountant; Dr Mark Francis Gurden [1959] Director/Chiropractor; Professor Lesley Jane Haig [1969] Director/Principal; Tamara May Ramiz Hattab [1995] Director/Student; Philip Hume [1982] Director/Lecturer; Edgar Newcomb [1940] Director; Peter James Jon Roberts [1952] Director/Visiting Lecturer; Adrian Simpson [1959] Director; Dr Christopher Stephens [1956] Director; Daniel Sullivan [1996] Director/Student; Adrian Frederick Wild [1966] Director/Chartered Accountant; Judith Sonia May Worthington [1942] Director

Aegeus Properties,Limited
Incorporated: 10 July 1957
Net Worth Deficit: £71,036 *Total Assets:* £5,195,513
Registered Office: 105-107 Bath Road, Cheltenham, Glos, GL53 7LE
Activities: Buying and selling of own real estate
Parent: Ceres Estates Ltd
Officers: Sarah Louise Brewer, Secretary; Sarah Louise Brewer [1971] Director; Lisbeth Rose Parker [1955] Director

AEGG Ltd
Incorporated: 2 September 2009 *Employees:* 15
Net Worth: £469,545 *Total Assets:* £3,986,360
Registered Office: Fellows House, 46 Royce Close, West Portway Industrial Estate, Andover, Hants, SP10 3TS
Activities: Non-specialised wholesale trade
Major Shareholder: Anthony Norman Bruce Coats
Officers: Anthony Norman Bruce Coats [1952] Commercial Director

Aero Stanrew Limited
Incorporated: 22 February 1949 *Employees:* 246
Net Worth: £6,514,000 *Total Assets:* £13,060,000
Registered Office: Unit 1 Gratton Way, Roundswell Business Park, Barnstaple, Devon, EX31 3AR
Activities: Manufacture of electric motors, generators and transformers
Parent: Aero Stanrew Group Limited
Officers: Lynton David Boardman, Secretary; Lynton David Boardman [1967] Director/Solicitor; Simon Peter Carberry Evans [1974] Director; Thomas Brendan Garvey [1968] Director

Aeroflex Test Solutions Limited
Incorporated: 13 January 1998
Net Worth: £24,825,000 *Total Assets:* £79,547,000
Registered Office: c/o Cobham PLC, Brook Road, Wimborne, Dorset, BH21 2BJ
Activities: Activities of head offices
Parent: Lockman Electronic Holdings Limited
Officers: Lyn Carol Colloff, Secretary; Lyn Carol Colloff [1965] Director/Company Secretary; Kenneth John Morrison [1960] Director

Aeronautical & General Instruments Limited
Incorporated: 1 January 1915 *Employees:* 145
Net Worth: £15,598,000 *Total Assets:* £20,429,000
Registered Office: Fleets Point, Willis Way, Poole, Dorset, BH15 3SS
Activities: Manufacture of electronic measuring, testing etc. equipment, not for industrial process control
Parent: JFL Equity Investors III, L.P.
Officers: Geoffrey Barry Eeles [1949] Director

Aeronautical & GI Holdings Limited
Incorporated: 19 March 2014
Net Worth: £40,010,000 *Total Assets:* £40,013,000
Registered Office: Units A-C, Fleetspoint, Willis Way, Poole, Dorset, BH15 3SS
Activities: Activities of head offices
Parent: AGI UK Acquisition Limited
Officers: Stephen Laurence Brooks [1971] Director [American]; Geoffrey Barry Eeles [1949] Director

AES Ballylumford Holdings Limited
Incorporated: 21 May 2010
Net Worth: £109,728,592 *Total Assets:* £198,143,824
Registered Office: First Floor, 10 Temple Back, Bristol, BS1 6FL
Activities: Activities of other holding companies n.e.c.
Parent: AES UK Holdings Ltd
Officers: Paul Austin Hutchinson [1968] Director; Julie Leeburn [1983] Director/Solicitor; James Timothy McCullough [1962] Director/Complex Manager

AES Barry Limited
Incorporated: 7 December 1995
Net Worth Deficit: £67,408,000 *Total Assets:* £6,929,000
Registered Office: First Floor, 10 Temple Back, Bristol, BS1 6FL
Activities: Activities of other holding companies n.e.c.
Parent: JP Morgan Trustees and Depository Co Ltd
Officers: Paul Austin Hutchinson [1968] Director; James Timothy McCullough [1962] Director/Complex Manager

AES Barry Operations Limited
Incorporated: 10 June 1996
Net Worth: £111,560,992 *Total Assets:* £178,616,880
Registered Office: First Floor, 10 Temple Back, Bristol, BS1 6FL
Activities: Activities of other holding companies n.e.c.
Parent: AES Ballylumford Holdings Limited
Officers: Paul Austin Hutchinson [1968] Director; James Timothy McCullough [1962] Director/Complex Manager

AES Electric Ltd
Incorporated: 16 February 1988 *Employees:* 6
Net Worth Deficit: £1,259,000 *Total Assets:* £16,654,000
Registered Office: First Floor, 10 Temple Back, Bristol, BS1 6FL
Activities: Activities of other holding companies n.e.c.
Parent: AES UK Holdings Ltd
Officers: Paul John Chapman [1970] Program Director, Global Insurance-EMEA; Mark Eugene Green [1967] Director/Europe SBU President [American]; Serhiy Zuyev [1974] Director/UK & Ireland Country Manager [Ukrainian]

AES Horizons Investments Limited
Incorporated: 10 January 1992
Net Worth Deficit: £5,786,000 *Total Assets:* £6,986,000
Registered Office: First Floor, 10 Temple Back, Bristol, BS1 6FL
Activities: Activities of other holding companies n.e.c.
Parent: AES Electric Ltd
Officers: Mark Eugene Green [1967] Director/Europe SBU President [American]; Paul Austin Hutchinson [1968] Director/Market Risk Analyst; James Timothy McCullough [1962] Director/Complex Manager

AES K2 Limited
Incorporated: 7 December 1995
Net Worth: £6,178,000 *Total Assets:* £38,273,000
Registered Office: First Floor, 10 Temple Back, Bristol, BS1 6FL
Activities: Activities of other holding companies n.e.c.
Parent: AES Corp
Officers: Richard Scott Berge [1976] Commercial Director [American]; Paul Austin Hutchinson [1968] Director/Market Risk Analyst; James Timothy McCullough [1962] Director/Complex Manager, O&M

AES Overseas Holdings Limited
Incorporated: 29 January 2008
Net Worth: £552,638,400 *Total Assets:* £554,326,336
Registered Office: First Floor, 10 Temple Back, Bristol, BS1 6FL
Activities: Activities of other holding companies n.e.c.
Parent: AES Corp
Officers: Paul Austin Hutchinson [1968] Director; James Timothy McCullough [1962] Director/Complex Manager; Serhiy Zuyev [1974] Director/UK & Ireland Country Manager [Ukrainian]

AES TEP Power II Investments Limited
Incorporated: 22 March 1926
Net Worth: £12,261,676 *Total Assets:* £13,056,302
Registered Office: First Floor, 10 Temple Back, Bristol, BS1 6FL
Activities: Activities of other holding companies n.e.c.
Parent: AES TEP Power Investments Limited
Officers: Paul Austin Hutchinson [1968] Director; James Timothy McCullough [1962] Director/Complex Manager; Serhiy Zuyev [1974] Director/UK & Ireland Country Manager [Ukrainian]

AES TEP Power Investments Limited
Incorporated: 2 October 2000
Net Worth: £13,986,817 *Total Assets:* £14,000,241
Registered Office: First Floor, 10 Temple Back, Bristol, BS1 6FL
Activities: Activities of other holding companies n.e.c.
Parent: AES Corp
Officers: Paul Austin Hutchinson [1968] Director; James Timothy McCullough [1962] Director/Complex Manager; Serhiy Zuyev [1974] Director/UK & Ireland Country Manager [Ukrainian]

AES UK Holdings Ltd
Incorporated: 10 June 1997
Net Worth: £127,706,000 *Total Assets:* £127,776,000
Registered Office: First Floor, 10 Temple Back, Bristol, BS1 6FL
Activities: Activities of other holding companies n.e.c.
Parent: The AES Corporation
Officers: Paul Austin Hutchinson [1968] Director/Market Risk Analyst; James Timothy McCullough [1962] Director/Complex Manager, O&M; Sergiy Zuyev [1974] Director/UK & Ireland Country Manager [Ukrainian]

AES Venezuela Finance
Incorporated: 5 June 2000
Net Worth: £211,363,424 *Total Assets:* £246,105,808
Registered Office: First Floor, 10 Temple Back, Bristol, BS1 6FL
Activities: Activities of other holding companies n.e.c.
Parent: The AES Corporation
Officers: Paul Austin Hutchinson [1968] Director/Market Risk Analyst; James Timothy McCullough [1962] Director/Complex Manager, O&M

AEW Properties Limited
Incorporated: 2 April 2015 *Employees:* 2
Net Worth: £3,471,708 *Total Assets:* £3,947,191
Registered Office: Mary Street House, Mary Street, Taunton, Somerset, TA1 3NW
Activities: Other letting and operating of own or leased real estate
Shareholders: Albert Edward Walters; Helen Mary Walters
Officers: Stella Caroline Knight [1970] Director; Amanda Jane Tilly [1970] Director

AFC Bournemouth Limited
Incorporated: 27 June 2008 *Employees:* 575
Net Worth Deficit: £27,251,000 *Total Assets:* £96,996,000
Registered Office: Vitality Stadium, Dean Court, Kings Park, Bournemouth, BH7 7AF
Activities: Activities of sport clubs
Officers: Neill Christopher Blake [1979] Director; Jeffrey Anthony Mostyn [1945] Director/Chairman; Nicholas Rothwell [1966] Director/Wealth Management Consultant; Rico Seitz [1971] Director [Swiss]

AFL Services Europe Ltd
Incorporated: 22 April 1994 *Employees:* 75
Net Worth Deficit: £13,457,550 *Total Assets:* £9,132,827
Registered Office: Unit H, Newcombe Drive, Hawksworth Trading Estate, Swindon, Wilts, SN2 1DZ
Activities: Construction of other civil engineering projects n.e.c.
Officers: Robert Maxey Crowder, Secretary; Peter King, Secretary; Paul Bennett [1974] Director/General Manager; Joseph Edward Gallagher [1957] Director [American]

AFL Telecommunications Europe Ltd
Incorporated: 13 April 2000 *Employees:* 70
Net Worth: £2,619,000 *Total Assets:* £9,651,000
Registered Office: Unit H, Newcombe Drive, Hawksworth Trading Estate, Swindon, Wilts, SN2 1DZ
Activities: Other manufacturing n.e.c.
Parent: America Fujikura Limited
Officers: Robert Maxey Crowder, Secretary; Peter King, Secretary; Paul Bennett [1974] Director/General Manager; Kurt Dallas [1963] Managing Director [American]; Joseph Edward Gallagher [1957] Director/Businessman [American]; Akira Saita [1959] Director/Businessman [Japanese]

AFP (Europe)
Incorporated: 28 April 1995 *Employees:* 4
Net Worth: £2,063,502,336 *Total Assets:* £2,164,116,992
Registered Office: 83 Tower Road North, Warmley, Bristol, BS30 8XP
Activities: Other service activities n.e.c.
Officers: Matthew Charles Burrows [1970] Director; Christopher John Cheetham [1962] Director/Chartered Accountant; Damien Clayton [1971] Director; Richard Dixon [1963] Executive Director Tax Europe

AGD Systems Limited
Incorporated: 29 November 1991 *Employees:* 46
Net Worth: £3,321,509 *Total Assets:* £4,541,866
Registered Office: White Lion House, Gloucester Road, Staverton, Cheltenham, Glos, GL51 0TF
Activities: Manufacture of telegraph and telephone apparatus and equipment
Shareholders: AGD Group Limited; The Traffic Group Limited
Officers: Dawn Woodward, Secretary; Ian Grenville Hind [1959] Commercial Director; Peter Michael Hutchinson [1967] Managing Director; Douglas MacArthur Nelson [1959] Technical Director; Dawn Woodward [1970] Financial Director

Agecroft Properties (No.2) Limited
Incorporated: 23 February 2001 *Employees:* 2
Net Worth: £6,447,650 *Total Assets:* £28,550,526
Registered Office: Third Floor, Broad Quay House, Prince Street, Bristol, BS1 4DJ
Activities: Financial leasing
Parent: API Holdco Limited
Officers: Andrew Richard Kershaw [1965] Director/Projects Controller; Richard Little [1979] Investment Director

Agents and Properties (Taunton) Limited
Incorporated: 17 March 1997 *Employees:* 4
Net Worth: £3,549,014 *Total Assets:* £3,937,718
Registered Office: Mary Street House, Mary Street, Taunton, Somerset, TA1 3NW
Activities: Other letting and operating of own or leased real estate
Major Shareholder: Paul Edward Jacobs
Officers: Laureen Sheena Jacobs, Secretary; James Livingstone Jacobs [1975] Director; Paul Edward Jacobs [1946] Director/Management

Aghoco 1256 Limited
Incorporated: 4 September 2014
Net Worth: £847,257 *Total Assets:* £6,626,182
Registered Office: Malvern View Business Park, Stella Way, Cheltenham, Glos, GL52 7DQ
Activities: Financial intermediation not elsewhere classified
Shareholders: David John Glenn; Jeanette Glenn
Officers: David John Glenn [1955] Director; Jeanette Glenn [1955] Director

AGI UK Acquisition Limited
Incorporated: 10 July 2014
Net Worth: £16,347,000 *Total Assets:* £78,235,000
Registered Office: Fleets Point, Willis Way, Poole, Dorset, BH15 3SS
Activities: Activities of other holding companies n.e.c.
Parent: JFL Equity Investors III, LP
Officers: Stephen Laurence Brooks [1971] Director/Partner [American]; Gepffrey Barry Eeles [1949] Director; Alexander Harman [1975] Director/Investor [American]; David Leonard Rattner [1964] Director/General Counsel [American]

Agincare Group Limited
Incorporated: 26 March 2007 *Employees:* 2,081
Net Worth: £4,616,296 *Total Assets:* £8,043,590
Registered Office: Agincare House, Admiralty Buildings, Castletown, Portland, Dorset, DT5 1BB
Activities: Other business support service activities n.e.c.
Major Shareholder: Derek Edwin Luckhurst
Officers: Owen Griffiths, Secretary; Owen David Griffiths [1957] Financial Director; Mark Antony Heywood-Briggs [1979] Commercial Director; Sarah Louise Leskinen-Keel [1965] Director/Chief Operating Officer; Derek Edwin Luckhurst [1955] Director/Chairman; Raina Marina Taylor-Summerson [1970] Director

Agincare Homes Holdings Limited
Incorporated: 23 March 2010 *Employees:* 647
Net Worth: £11,774,125 *Total Assets:* £27,873,732
Registered Office: Agincare House, Admiralty Buildings, Castletown, Portland, Dorset, DT5 1BB
Activities: Other business support service activities n.e.c.
Major Shareholder: Derek Edwin Luckhurst
Officers: Owen Griffiths, Secretary; Jill Caroline Dale [1975] Operations Director; Owen David Griffiths [1957] Financial Director; Mark Antony Heywood-Briggs [1979] Commercial Director; Derek Edwin Luckhurst [1955] Director; Raina Marina Taylor-Summerson [1970] Director

Agincare UK Limited
Incorporated: 13 February 2007 *Employees:* 1,379
Net Worth: £4,420,517 *Total Assets:* £6,692,481
Registered Office: Agincare House, Admiralty Buildings, Castletown, Portland, Dorset, DT5 1BB
Activities: Other business support service activities n.e.c.
Parent: Agincare Group Ltd
Officers: Owen David Griffiths [1957] Director/Accountant; Luke Daniel Holmes [1978] Operations Director; Sarah Louise Leskinen-Keel [1965] Director; Raina Marina Taylor Summerson [1970] Director

AGM Holdings Limited
Incorporated: 19 March 2002 *Employees:* 176
Net Worth: £14,489,403 *Total Assets:* £29,531,044
Registered Office: Grand Pier, Marine Parade, Weston Super Mare, Somerset, BS23 1AL
Activities: Other business support service activities n.e.c.
Major Shareholder: Kerry Michael
Officers: Michelle Michael, Secretary; Axentis Panayiotou Demetriou [1979] Director; Kerry Michael [1959] Director; Michelle Michael [1967] Director

AGR Automation Limited
Incorporated: 16 May 2000 *Employees:* 134
Net Worth: £8,027,798 *Total Assets:* £12,863,041
Registered Office: Old Library Chambers, 21 Chipper Lane, Salisbury, Wilts, SP1 1BG
Activities: Manufacture of other special-purpose machinery n.e.c.
Shareholders: Robert Derek Samuel Gaston; Sharon Mary Gaston
Officers: Sharon Mary Gaston, Secretary; Robert Derek Samuel Gaston [1962] Director; Sharon Mary Gaston [1962] Director

Agricultural Mortgage Corporation P L C (The)
Incorporated: 12 November 1928 *Employees:* 70
Net Worth: £60,625,000 *Total Assets:* £3,440,762,880
Registered Office: Charlton Place, Charlton Road, Andover, Hants, SP10 1RE
Activities: Activities of mortgage finance companies
Parent: Lloyds Bank PLC
Officers: David Dermot Hennessey, Secretary; Paul Andrew Gordon [1967] Managing Director; Stuart Haycock [1982] Director; Alex Moore [1979] Director; Andrew John Naylor [1975] Director; Matthew Alastair Leonard Packham [1971] Director; Paul Nicholas Spencer [1963] Director

AgustaWestland Holdings Limited
Incorporated: 30 March 2000
Net Worth: £39,517,000 *Total Assets:* £59,083,000
Registered Office: Lysander Road, Yeovil, Somerset, BA20 2YB
Activities: Non-trading company
Parent: Leonardo SpA
Officers: Dr James Michael Wells, Secretary; Vittorio Lorenzo Della Bella [1961] Director [Italian]; Julian Russell [1969] Director; Dr James Wells [1972] Director and Company Secretary

AgustaWestland Limited
Incorporated: 9 May 1958
Net Worth: £170,196,000 *Total Assets:* £219,248,000
Registered Office: Lysander Road, Yeovil, Somerset, BA20 2YB
Activities: Manufacture of air and spacecraft and related machinery
Parent: Leonardo MW Ltd
Officers: Dr James Michael Wells, Secretary; Lorenzo Bertola [1967] Director [Italian]; Clive James Higgins [1977] Director

Aim Altitude Limited
Incorporated: 1 October 2015 *Employees:* 725
Net Worth: £47,075,000 *Total Assets:* £246,172,000
Registered Office: 1 Viscount Road, Aviation Business Park, Bournemouth International Airport, Hurn, Christchurch, Dorset, BH23 6BU
Activities: Activities of head offices
Parent: Avicade System Limited
Officers: Richard Mark Bower [1964] Director; Mark John Edwards [1954] Director; Jun Huang [1973] Director/Business Manager [Chinese]; Zhonghua Lyu [1968] Director/Chief Financial Officer [Chinese]; Mark Stoddart [1962] Finance Director; Tongyu Xu [1968] Director/Vice President [Chinese]

Aim Altitude UK Limited
Incorporated: 9 March 1971 *Employees:* 332
Previous: AIM Aviation (JECCO) Limited
Net Worth: £26,493,000 *Total Assets:* £48,816,000
Registered Office: 1 Viscount Road, Aviation Business Park, Bournemouth International Airport, Hurn, Christchurch, Dorset, BH23 6BU
Activities: Manufacture of air and spacecraft and related machinery
Parent: AIM Altitude Limited
Officers: Wayne Ball [1963] Operations Director; Richard Mark Bower [1964] Director; Mark Stoddart [1962] Finance Director; Colin Philip Thornton [1965] Director/Aircraft Interiors

AIM Aviation (Henshalls) Limited
Incorporated: 24 June 1940 *Employees:* 172
Net Worth: £9,068,000 *Total Assets:* £12,738,000
Registered Office: 1 Viscount Road, Aviation Business Park, Bournemouth International Airport, Hurn, Christchurch, Dorset, BH23 6BU
Activities: Manufacture of air and spacecraft and related machinery
Parent: AIM Altitude Limited
Officers: Wayne Ball [1963] Director/General Manager; Richard Mark Bower [1964] Director; Mark Stoddart [1962] Finance Director

AIM Aviation Holdings Limited
Incorporated: 27 August 2013
Net Worth Deficit: £59,137,000 *Total Assets:* £15,655,000
Registered Office: 1 Viscount Road, Aviation Business Park, Bournemouth International Airport, Hurn, Christchurch, Dorset, BH23 6BU
Activities: Activities of head offices
Parent: AIM Altitude Limited
Officers: Richard Mark Bower [1964] Commercial Director; Huang Jun [1973] Business Development Director [Chinese]; Mark Stoddart [1962] Finance Director

Aim Composites Limited
Incorporated: 28 January 1939 *Employees:* 146
Net Worth: £7,961,000 *Total Assets:* £11,944,000
Registered Office: 1 Viscount Road, Aviation Business Park, Bournemouth International Airport, Hurn, Christchurch, Dorset, BH23 6BU
Activities: Manufacture of air and spacecraft and related machinery
Parent: AIM Altitude Limited
Officers: Richard Mark Bower [1964] Director; Andrew Brown [1975] Director/Financial Controller; Mark Stoddart [1962] Finance Director

Air Bearings Limited
Incorporated: 9 February 1993 *Employees:* 67
Net Worth: £8,572,982 *Total Assets:* £9,182,187
Registered Office: Unit A, Nimrod Way, East Dorset Trade Park, Wimborne, Dorset, BH21 7HY
Activities: Machining
Parent: LVM GP Ltd
Officers: Miguel Mas Llinas [1950] Director [Spanish]; Hideaki Shimizu [1960] Representative Director [Japanese]; Nobuhiko Suzuki [1967] Director [Japanese]; Yoichi Tamamura [1963] Director [Japanese]

Air Control Industries Limited
Incorporated: 6 August 1969 *Employees:* 52
Net Worth: £5,146,534 *Total Assets:* £6,610,598
Registered Office: Air Control Industries Limited, Weycroft Avenue, Millwey Rise Industrial Estate, Axminster, Devon, EX13 5HU
Activities: Manufacture of other general-purpose machinery n.e.c.
Major Shareholder: Paul Tuffin
Officers: Kirsten Ann Da Silva, Secretary; Kirsten Ann Da Silva [1968] Finance Director; Christopher Ian Hellier [1972] Managing Director; Paul Tuffin [1963] Director/Engineer

Airbus Operations Limited
Incorporated: 20 November 1997 *Employees:* 7,956
Net Worth: £828,000,000 *Total Assets:* £4,032,000,000
Registered Office: Pegasus House, Aerospace Avenue, Filton, Bristol, BS34 7PA
Activities: Manufacture of air and spacecraft and related machinery
Parent: Airbus SE
Officers: Alison Louise Adams, Secretary; Christophe Bardin [1963] Director/Chief Accountant [French]; Katherine Susan Bennett [1967] Director/Senior Vice President, Airbus; Jean-Pierre Chassagne [1961] Director/Head of Business Transformation [French]; Mark Haisman [1964] Director/VP Procurement; John Conacher Harrison [1967] Director/Airbus General Counsel; Robert Mark Stewart [1962] HR Director

Airport Business Centre Limited
Incorporated: 15 August 2003 *Employees:* 16
Net Worth: £3,108,246 *Total Assets:* £6,764,996
Registered Office: 10 Thornbury Road, Estover, Plymouth, PL6 7PP
Activities: Other letting and operating of own or leased real estate
Parent: The Una Group Limited
Officers: Susan Young, Secretary; Derek John Brooking [1940] Director/Haulage Contractor; Ian Charles Brooking [1970] Director/Builder; Ian Graeme Dennis [1966] Director/Developer; David Anthony Pearce [1963] Finance Director; David Charles Young [1958] Director/Business Consultant

Airsprung Furniture Limited
Incorporated: 20 June 1980 *Employees:* 466
Net Worth Deficit: £145,000 *Total Assets:* £21,162,000
Registered Office: Canal Road Industrial Estate, Trowbridge, Wilts, BA14 8RL
Activities: Manufacture of mattresses
Major Shareholder: Andrew Stewart Perloff
Officers: Tean Elizabeth Dallaway, Company Secretary; Tean Elizabeth Dallaway [1967] Director; Antonio Lisanti [1957] Director; Simon Jeffrey Peters [1977] Director

Airsprung Group PLC
Incorporated: 17 September 1976 *Employees:* 478
Net Worth Deficit: £4,302,000 *Total Assets:* £19,445,000
Registered Office: Canal Road, Trowbridge, Wilts, BA14 8RQ
Activities: Activities of head offices
Major Shareholder: Andrew Stewart Perloff
Officers: Tean Elizabeth Dallaway, Secretary/Director; Tean Elizabeth Dallaway [1967] Director; Antonio Lisanti [1957] Director; Andrew Stewart Perloff [1944] Director; Simon Jeffrey Peters [1977] Director

Aish Technologies Limited
Incorporated: 14 August 2000 *Employees:* 220
Net Worth: £2,691,000 *Total Assets:* £7,032,000
Registered Office: Aish House, Broom Road, Poole, Dorset, BH12 4NL
Activities: Machining
Parent: AGI UK Acquisition Limited
Officers: Geoffrey Barry Eeles [1949] Director; Guy Brent Green [1961] Director; Suzanne Marie Tideswell [1975] Director

Aistone Properties Limited
Incorporated: 12 July 1995 *Employees:* 5
Net Worth: £3,112,550 *Total Assets:* £3,544,607
Registered Office: The Penthouse, One Fifty Victoria Road, Swindon, Wilts, SN1 3UZ
Activities: Buying and selling of own real estate
Shareholder: Judith Caroline Triggs
Officers: Peter Richard George Triggs, Secretary; Caroline Victoria Jane Rudler [1976] Director/Farm Secretary; Judith Caroline Triggs [1944] Director; Peter Richard George Triggs [1948] Director; Robert James Alexander Triggs [1973] Director/Solicitor; William Edward Charles Triggs [1979] Director/Insurance Broker

AJ & Co.(Devon) Ltd
Incorporated: 9 March 2000 *Employees:* 191
Net Worth: £2,831,965 *Total Assets:* £5,451,627
Registered Office: Ludbrook House, Ludbrook, Ivybridge, Devon, PL21 0LL
Activities: Residential nursing care facilities
Major Shareholder: David John Smallridge
Officers: David John Smallridge, Secretary; David John Smallridge [1956] Director/Farmer; Gina Marie Smallridge [1959] Director/Care Home Manager

Alabare Christian Care Centres
Incorporated: 23 April 1991 *Employees:* 238
Net Worth: £3,513,954 *Total Assets:* £5,939,864
Registered Office: Riverside House, 2 Watt Road, Salisbury, Wilts, SP2 7UD
Activities: Residential care activities for learning difficulties, mental health and substance abuse
Officers: Don Alexander [1962] Director; Malcolm Cassells [1955] Director/Accountant; Martin Clark [1961] Director; Phil Ruark Davis [1959] Director; Rev David Michael Karl Durston [1936] Director/Cathedral Canon; Richard Mark Holman [1956] Director/Retired; John Hunter [1950] Director/Retired; David Lawes [1955] Director/Project Manager; David McAuley [1961] Director/Chief Executive; Alicia Monica Proctor [1952] Director of Nursery Schools; Rev John Proctor [1953] Director/Chairman; Mark Bernard Proctor [1978] Director/Solicitor; Christine Mary Robinson [1954] Director

Albany Molecular Research Limited
Incorporated: 16 February 2004
Net Worth: £192,670,896 *Total Assets:* £371,956,992
Registered Office: First Floor, 10 Temple Back, Bristol, BS1 6FL
Activities: Manufacture of pharmaceutical preparations
Officers: Christopher Mark Davidson Froggatt [1975] Director/Chartered Accountant; Stacie Phillips [1974] Director/Attorney [American]

Albermarle Trading Limited
Incorporated: 21 February 2001
Net Worth: £4,562,076 *Total Assets:* £4,590,530
Registered Office: 22 Billet Street, Taunton, Somerset, TA1 3NG
Activities: Financial intermediation not elsewhere classified
Officers: Stephen John Dudley Hickson [1947] Director

Albert Goodman LLP
Incorporated: 29 March 2010 *Employees:* 279
Net Worth: £4,274,360 *Total Assets:* £6,863,859
Registered Office: Mary Street House, Mary Street, Taunton, Somerset, TA1 3NW
Officers: Richard Generald Bugler [1971] Member; Paul Nicholas Hake [1969] Member; Alison Jane Kerr [1966] Member; Michael James Cahill [1981] LLP Member; Joseph Nicholas Doggrell [1986] LLP Member; James Joseph Duggan [1959] LLP Member; Kevin Trevor Jutson [1977] LLP Member; Keith John Miller [1962] LLP Member; Louise Claire Osborne [1982] LLP Member; Paul Sargent [1957] LLP Member; Patrick John Tomlinson [1966] LLP Member; Christopher Walford [1977] LLP Member

Alberti Limited
Incorporated: 20 December 1993 *Employees:* 49
Net Worth: £999,557 *Total Assets:* £3,929,549
Registered Office: 3-5 College Street, Burnham on Sea, Somerset, TA8 1AR
Activities: Freight transport by road
Parent: R T Keedwell Holdings Limited
Officers: Stuart Raymond Keedwell, Secretary/Haulier; Michael Ivinson [1962] Director; Stuart Raymond Keedwell [1964] Director/Haulier

Albion Healthcare (Doncaster) Limited
Incorporated: 25 July 2002
Net Worth Deficit: £1,245,583 *Total Assets:* £15,550,791
Registered Office: Third Floor, Broad Quay House, Prince Street, Bristol, BS1 4DJ
Activities: Medical nursing home activities
Parent: Albion Healthcare (Doncaster) Holdings Limited
Officers: John Philip George [1968] Director/Solicitor; Angela Mills [1961] Director/Accountant; Neil Rae [1971] Director; Alan Campbell Ritchie [1967] Director

Albion Healthcare (Oxford) Holdings Limited
Incorporated: 16 July 2001 *Employees:* 7
Net Worth: £100 *Total Assets:* £3,794,469
Registered Office: Third Floor, Broad Quay House, Prince Street, Bristol, BS1 4DJ
Activities: Management of real estate on a fee or contract basis
Officers: Phillip Joseph Dodd [1955] Director; Philip Charles Dove [1974] Director/COO G4S FM; James Christopher Heath [1975] Director; Richard Little [1979] Investment Director; Geoffrey Alan Quaife [1955] Investment Director; Peter John Sheldrake [1959] Director; Phillip James Thorne [1961] Director

Albion Healthcare (Oxford) Limited
Incorporated: 28 August 2001 *Employees:* 7
Net Worth Deficit: £1,187,445 *Total Assets:* £46,322,952
Registered Office: Third Floor, Broad Quay House, Prince Street, Bristol, BS1 4DJ
Activities: Hospital activities
Parent: Albion Healthcare (Oxford) Holdings Limited
Officers: Phillip Joseph Dodd [1955] Director; Philip Charles Dove [1974] Director/COO G4S FM; James Christopher Heath [1975] Director; Richard Little [1979] Investment Director; Geoffrey Alan Quaife [1955] Investment Director; Peter John Sheldrake [1959] Director; Phillip James Thorne [1961] Director

Alchemist Ventures Limited
Incorporated: 22 June 2004
Net Worth: £6,965,483 *Total Assets:* £7,032,887
Registered Office: One Glass Wharf, Bristol, BS2 0ZX
Activities: Activities of extraterritorial organisations and bodies
Major Shareholder: Floris Rost Van Tonningen
Officers: Floris Rost Van Tonningen [1977] Director/Manager [Dutch]

Alchemy Estates Limited
Incorporated: 15 May 1995 *Employees:* 1
Net Worth: £2,693,971 *Total Assets:* £5,144,387
Registered Office: Stanford Park Farm, Park Lane, Stanford in the Vale, Faringdon, Oxon, SN7 8PF
Activities: Buying and selling of own real estate
Shareholders: Mark MacLachlan Russell Stoneham; Hayley Russell Stoneham
Officers: Hayley Russell Stoneham, Secretary; Hayley Russell Stoneham [1962] Director; Mark MacLachlan Russell Stoneham [1965] Director/Property Investment Consultant

Alchemy Promotions Limited
Incorporated: 28 February 2013 *Employees:* 34
Net Worth: £1,221,401 *Total Assets:* £4,115,570
Registered Office: 124 Cheltenham Road, Bristol, BS6 5RW
Activities: Other amusement and recreation activities n.e.c.
Major Shareholder: Richard Buck
Officers: Richard David Buck [1983] Director/Manager

ALD Automotive Group Limited
Incorporated: 31 October 1995
Previous: ALD Automotive Group PLC
Net Worth: £22,945,000 *Total Assets:* £22,945,000
Registered Office: Oakwood Drive, Emersons Green, Bristol, BS16 7LB
Activities: Renting and leasing of cars and light motor vehicles
Parent: Societe Generale
Officers: Anna Woodward, Secretary; Melvyn William Dawson [1959] Director; Mike Masterson [1960] Finance Director; Sadia Brigitte Ricke [1970] Director/Executive [French]; John Saffrett [1972] Director

ALD Automotive Limited
Incorporated: 20 August 1970 *Employees:* 479
Net Worth: £122,984,000 *Total Assets:* £1,683,751,040
Registered Office: Oakwood Drive, Emersons Green, Bristol, BS16 7LB
Activities: Renting and leasing of cars and light motor vehicles
Parent: ALD Automotive Group Limited
Officers: Anna Catherine Woodward, Secretary; Melvyn William Dawson [1959] Director; David Andrew Yates [1963] Sales Director

Alden Finance Limited
Incorporated: 1 July 1983 *Employees:* 2
Net Worth: £3,449,063 *Total Assets:* £3,896,640
Registered Office: 20 Newerne Street, Lydney, Glos, GL15 5RA
Activities: Financial intermediation not elsewhere classified
Shareholders: Alan Dennis Thompson; Susan Thompson
Officers: Susan Thompson, Secretary; Alan Dennis Thompson [1953] Director; Peter William Thompson [1981] Director/Car Dealer; Susan Thompson [1954] Director

Alder King LLP
Incorporated: 3 February 2004 *Employees:* 103
Net Worth: £5,712,332 *Total Assets:* £7,362,631
Registered Office: Pembroke House, 15 Pembroke Road, Clifton, Bristol, BS8 3BA
Officers: John Mark Benson [1964] Member; Christopher John Haworth [1959] Member; Andrew Burton Hughes [1966] Member; Martyn Jones [1963] Member; Simon Richard Price [1966] Member; Andrew John Ridler [1964] Member; Simon David Smith [1979] Member; Noel Peter George Stevens [1974] Member; Andrew Mark Watson [1961] Member; Peter Gordon John Barefoot [1952] LLP Member; Andrew Edmondson [1964] LLP Member; Paul Burridge Montague [1964] LLP Member; Philip John Pratt [1965] LLP Member; Adrian John Grenville Rowley [1964] LLP Member; Grant Stephen Watson [1939] LLP Member

Alderbrook Road Limited
Incorporated: 22 February 2016 *Employees:* 8
Net Worth Deficit: £26,643 *Total Assets:* £3,699,800
Registered Office: Swatton Barn, Badbury, Swindon, Wilts, SN4 0EU
Activities: Buying and selling of own real estate
Officers: Defne Kazan [1978] Director/Business Executive; Emre Kazan [1976] Director/Businessman; Adeel Ayaz Khan [1981] Director/Business Executive; Haris Ahmad Khan [1979] Director/Business Owner; Nazli Mohsin [1969] Director/Businesswoman [Canadian]; James Price [1967] Director/Business Executive; Cem Savas [1979] Director/Business Owner [Turkish]; Natalie Tomecki [1978] Director/Business Executive

Alderley Farms Limited
Incorporated: 20 August 2002 *Employees:* 3
Net Worth: £1,461,753 *Total Assets:* £6,695,906
Registered Office: Alderley House, Arnolds Field Estate, The Downs, Wickwar, Wotton under Edge, Glos, GL12 8JD
Activities: Mixed farming
Parent: Alderley PLC
Officers: Philippa Ann Slatter, Secretary; Lucinda Mary Rose [1962] Director; Nicola Jane Scott-Bowden [1963] Director/Estate Manager; Anthony James Vernon Shepherd [1931] Director/Engineer

Alderley PLC
Incorporated: 2 May 1989 *Employees:* 384
Net Worth: £29,760,000 *Total Assets:* £46,717,000
Registered Office: Alderley House, Arnolds Field Estate, The Downs, Wickwar, Wotton under Edge, Glos, GL12 8JD
Activities: Activities of head offices
Major Shareholder: Anthony James Vernon Shepherd
Officers: Philippa Ann Slatter, Secretary; Anthony Clifford Mansfield [1950] Director/Chartered Engineer; Lucinda Mary Rose [1962] Director; Anthony James Vernon Shepherd [1931] Director; Philippa Ann Slatter [1967] Director/Solicitor; Alan James Stark Wilson [1957] Director

Alderley Systems Ltd
Incorporated: 17 April 1985 *Employees:* 89
Net Worth: £1,713,689 *Total Assets:* £7,059,602
Registered Office: Alderley House, Arnolds Field Estate, The Downs, Wickwar, Wotton under Edge, Glos, GL12 8JD
Activities: Manufacture of other special-purpose machinery n.e.c.
Parent: Alderley PLC
Officers: Jeremy John Dearman [1973] Director/Accountant; Anthony James Vernon Shepherd [1931] Director; Michael Roger James Shepherd [1969] Director/Engineer; Matthew Way [1975] Director

Alertsystems Limited
Incorporated: 17 November 1995 *Employees:* 139
Net Worth: £1,604,968 *Total Assets:* £3,941,351
Registered Office: Alert House, 1 Willowside Park, Canal Road, Trowbridge, Wilts, BA14 8RH
Activities: Manufacture of electronic components
Parent: Alertsystems Group Limited
Officers: Paul James Brake [1967] Director; Mark Colin Nickels [1962] Director; Ian Colin Trayling [1959] Director

Alessandra UK Limited
Incorporated: 4 March 2011 *Employees:* 29
Net Worth: £16,309,622 *Total Assets:* £17,768,280
Registered Office: 102 Wells Road, Bath, BA2 3AL
Activities: Hotels and similar accommodation
Officers: Maurizio Iannuzzi [1958] Director [Italian]; Derek Alan Swift [1960] Director

Alexander & Angell (Farms) Limited
Incorporated: 26 April 1982 *Employees:* 23
Net Worth: £818,746 *Total Assets:* £4,128,791
Registered Office: Court Farm, Witcombe, Gloucester, GL3 4TU
Activities: Raising of swine and pigs
Parent: Alexander & Angell Limited
Officers: Jacqueline Mary Maguire, Secretary; Andrew Browning Hope [1946] Director; Caroline Mary Hope [1950] Director; Sophie Jane Hope [1985] Director/Farm Manager

Alexandra Dock Limited
Incorporated: 13 November 2014 *Employees:* 3
Net Worth: £1,107,832 *Total Assets:* £8,851,181
Registered Office: Harbour House, 60 Purewell, Christchurch, Dorset, BH23 1ES
Activities: Buying and selling of own real estate
Parent: Harbour International Limted
Officers: Stuart Andrew Bateman [1976] Director; David Francis Robbins [1967] Director/Accountant

Alexandra Wharf Limited
Incorporated: 14 August 2013
Net Worth: £89,008 *Total Assets:* £23,126,120
Registered Office: Harbour House, 60 Purewell, Christchurch, Dorset, BH23 1ES
Activities: Buying and selling of own real estate
Parent: Nicolas James Holdings Limited
Officers: Stuart Andrew Bateman [1976] Director; David Francis Robbins [1967] Finance Director

Alfco Investments Limited
Incorporated: 3 October 1983
Net Worth: £6,954,675 *Total Assets:* £10,303,926
Registered Office: c/o Shepherd Smail & Co, 21 Market Place, Cirencester, Glos, GL7 2NX
Activities: Other letting and operating of own or leased real estate
Major Shareholder: Adrian Lindsay-Fynn
Officers: Adrian Lindsay-Fynn, Secretary; Penelope Jean Lindsay Fynn [1952] Director/Housewife; Adrian Lindsay-Fynn [1948] Director/Farmer

Algreta Solutions Limited
Incorporated: 25 June 2004 *Employees:* 29
Net Worth Deficit: £1,891,000 *Total Assets:* £7,842,000
Registered Office: Aintree Avenue, White Horse Business Park, Trowbridge, Wilts, BA14 0XB
Activities: Other retail sale not in stores, stalls or markets
Parent: Lornamead Group Limited
Officers: Graham John Atherton [1961] Director; Gerard Jan Raymond [1957] Director [Australian]

Alias Limited
Incorporated: 17 December 1990 *Employees:* 21
Net Worth: £11,498,570 *Total Assets:* £11,870,467
Registered Office: D100 Delta Business Park, Great Western Way, Swindon, Wilts, SN5 7XP
Activities: Business and domestic software development
Parent: Intergraph (UK) Limited
Officers: Fleur Polly Mary Rose Eldridge, Secretary; Patrick Holcomb [1968] Director [American]; Michael Scott Moore [1969] Director [American]; David Leslie Myall [1957] Director

All Saints Church of England Academy, Plymouth
Incorporated: 30 September 2009 *Employees:* 110
Net Worth: £12,360,706 *Total Assets:* £16,173,787
Registered Office: All Saints Church of England Academy, Plymouth, Pennycross, Plymouth, PL5 3NE
Activities: General secondary education
Officers: Julie Ann Sandercock, Secretary; Clare Margaret Baker [1971] Director/Bank Official; Gareth Gwyn James Derrick [1958] Director/Councillor; Leni McCormick [1976] Director/Editor/Proof Reader [Norwegian]; Siobhan Meredith [1988] Director/Headteacher; Lee James Sargeant [1984] Director/Headteacher; Rebecca Smith [1981] Director/Communications Manager; Richard Charles Barrington Stevens [1968] Managing Director; The Reverend David John Walker Watson [1961] Director/Vicar

All Saints' Academy, Cheltenham
Incorporated: 27 February 2009 *Employees:* 138
Net Worth: £20,424,000 *Total Assets:* £22,136,000
Registered Office: All Saints Academy, Blaisdon Way, Cheltenham, Glos, GL51 0WH
Activities: General secondary education
Officers: Clover Baker, Secretary; Christopher William Chadwick [1958] Director/Actuary; Catherine Lucy Monica Etheredge [1964] Director/Mother and Housewife; Bethany Jackson [1992] Director/Teaching Assistant; John David Kyffin [1944] Director/Retired Management Accountant; Nicky Lowe [1960] Director/Businesswoman; Dermot Thomas Gerard McNiffe [1965] Director/Principal (Qualified Teacher); Susan Elizabeth Padfield [1943] Director/Retired School Teacher; Alastair Iain Palmer [1973] Director/Customer Service; James David Richardson [1978] Director/Senior Analyst; Claire Elizabeth Savory [1971] Director/Headteacher; Henry Watson [1984] Director/Consultant

All Tel Communications Limited
Incorporated: 14 December 2012 *Employees:* 154
Net Worth: £6,418,982 *Total Assets:* £8,884,100
Registered Office: Acorn Farm, Green Lane, Milbury Heath, Thornbury, Glos, GL12 8QW
Activities: Activities of other holding companies n.e.c.
Major Shareholder: Kevin John Morris
Officers: Jayne Louise Morris, Secretary; Kevin John Morris [1962] Director

Allchurches Trust Limited
Incorporated: 24 February 1972 *Employees:* 1,312
Net Worth: £582,051,008 *Total Assets:* £1,747,378,048
Registered Office: Beaufort House, Brunswick Road, Gloucester, GL1 1JZ
Activities: Other business support service activities n.e.c.
Officers: Rachael Jane Hall, Secretary; Michael Arlington [1953] Director; Caroline Janet Banszky [1953] Director; Timothy Joseph Carroll [1955] Director [Irish]; The Very Reverend Jane Barbara Hedges [1955] Director; Steven Charles Hudson [1954] Director; Karen Belinda Lund [1962] Director; Sir Laurence Henry Philip Magnus [1955] Director; Sir Philip John Courtney Mawer [1947] Director/Public Servant

Allen & Heath Limited
Incorporated: 20 February 2001 *Employees:* 113
Net Worth: £49,997,000 *Total Assets:* £57,542,000
Registered Office: Kernick Industrial Estate, Penryn, Cornwall, TR10 9LU
Activities: Manufacture of consumer electronics
Parent: Remix Bidco Limited
Officers: Stephen Jeffrey Benney [1968] Operations Director; Robin John Clark [1970] Director; Anthony Williams [1965] Director

Bill Allen's Autos Limited
Incorporated: 10 October 1953 *Employees:* 5
Net Worth: £5,696,426 *Total Assets:* £5,926,356
Registered Office: Windsor House, Bayshill Road, Cheltenham, Glos, GL50 3AT
Activities: Sale of used cars and light motor vehicles
Officers: William Sinclair Allen [1950] Director

Alleyford Limited
Incorporated: 2 October 2000
Net Worth: £3,693,051 *Total Assets:* £5,176,334
Registered Office: The Coach House, Leigh Farm, Angersleigh, Taunton, Somerset, TA3 7SY
Activities: Development of building projects
Major Shareholder: Roger Stuart Wright
Officers: Roger Stuart Wright, Secretary; Roger Stuart Wright [1959] Director/Financial Consultant Property

Alliance Homes (Ventures) Ltd
Incorporated: 12 May 2011
Net Worth: £8,287,000 *Total Assets:* £13,246,000
Registered Office: 40 Martingale Way, Portishead, Somerset, BS20 7AW
Activities: Production of electricity
Officers: Philippa Armstrong-Owen, Secretary; Katrina Michael [1966] Director/Chief Finance Officer; Louise Emma Swain [1970] Director/Chief Executive

Alliance Leisure Services Limited
Incorporated: 17 June 1992 *Employees:* 19
Net Worth: £1,558,471 *Total Assets:* £4,632,268
Registered Office: 24 Angel Crescent, Bridgwater, Somerset, TA6 3EW
Activities: Sports and recreation education
Shareholders: Alliance Finance Limited; Alliance Finance Limited; Alliance Finance Limited
Officers: Roman Mychajlo Semak, Secretary; Paul Andrew John Cluett [1964] Director; Sarah Louise Watts [1964] Director/Consultant

Alliance Pharma PLC
Incorporated: 26 June 2001 *Employees:* 182
Net Worth: £203,376,992 *Total Assets:* £336,475,008
Registered Office: Avonbridge House, Bath Road, Chippenham, Wilts, SN15 2BB
Activities: Activities of other holding companies n.e.c.
Officers: Chrysanthos Theoclis Chrysanthou, Secretary; Peter Jonathan Butterfield [1975] Director; Nigel Clifford [1959] Director; David Cook [1967] Director; John Dawson [1949] Director; Andrew Timothy Franklin [1966] Director; Richard Crispin Jones [1966] Finance Director; Joanna Le Couilliard [1963] Director

Alliance Pharmaceuticals Limited
Incorporated: 16 September 1996 *Employees:* 123
Net Worth: £43,179,000 *Total Assets:* £305,403,008
Registered Office: Avonbridge House, Bath Road, Chippenham, Wilts, SN15 2BB
Activities: Manufacture of pharmaceutical preparations
Parent: Alliance Pharma PLC
Officers: Chrysanthos Theoclis Chrysanthou, Secretary; Peter Jonathan Butterfield [1975] Director; Alexander James Hanbury Duggan [1970] Director/Chief Commercial Officer; Andrew Timothy Franklin [1966] Director; Stephen Martin Kidner [1968] Chief Scientific & Operations Director

Allied Dunbar Assurance PLC
Incorporated: 30 November 1965
Net Worth: £17,005,000 *Total Assets:* £21,918,000
Registered Office: The Grange, Bishops Cleeve, Cheltenham, Glos, GL52 8XX
Activities: Life insurance
Shareholders: Zurich Financial Services (UKISA) Limited; Zurich Financial Services (UKISA) Limited
Officers: James Richard Sykes [1961] Director; Steven Lewis Wall [1971] Director

Allied Minds PLC
Incorporated: 15 April 2014 *Employees:* 205
Net Worth: £53,734,840 *Total Assets:* £205,199,248
Registered Office: Beaufort House, 51 New North Road, Exeter, Devon, EX4 4EP
Activities: Activities of venture and development capital companies
Officers: Michael Scott Turner, Secretary; Peter Robert Dolan [1956] Director [American]; Charles Thomas Foley II [1971] Director/Academic [American]; Harry Thomas Rein [1944] Director/Private Investor [American]; Jeffery Paul Rohr [1950] Director [American]; Kevin Sharer [1948] Director [American]; Jill Smith [1958] Director [American]

Allstar Business Solutions Limited
Incorporated: 22 July 1991 *Employees:* 208
Net Worth: £402,686,016 *Total Assets:* £613,102,016
Registered Office: P O Box 1463, Windmill Hill, Whitehill Way, Swindon, Wilts, SN5 6PS
Activities: Other business support service activities n.e.c.
Parent: Fleetcor UK Acquisition Limited
Officers: Eric Richard Dey [1959] Director [American]; Alan King [1976] Director; Anita Kravos-Medimorec [1974] Director/Chief Financial Officer; Steven J Piscotta [1964] Director/Accountant [American]

Allstone Sands Gravels Aggregates Trading Co. Ltd.
Incorporated: 8 November 1983 *Employees:* 40
Net Worth: £8,410,729 *Total Assets:* £12,322,013
Registered Office: 5 Pullman Court, Great Western Road, Gloucester, GL1 3ND
Activities: Agents involved in the sale of timber and building materials
Shareholders: Richard Scott Murray Street; Simon John Ford
Officers: Lorraine Alison Ford, Secretary; Paul Thomas Ford [1960] Director; Simon John Ford [1966] Director/Builders Merchant

Allum and Sidaway Limited
Incorporated: 31 October 2003 *Employees:* 91
Net Worth: £2,999,862 *Total Assets:* £5,919,197
Registered Office: 26a High Street, Shaftesbury, Dorset, SP7 8JG
Activities: Retail sale of watches and jewellery in specialised stores
Parent: Allum and Sidaway Holdings Limited
Officers: Denise Ann Crossland, Secretary/Director; Jason Paul Allum [1970] Director; Patrick Butler [1970] Director; Denise Ann Crossland [1950] Director; Abigail Jayne Davies [1984] Director

The Almanzora Group Limited
Incorporated: 15 March 1984 *Employees:* 3
Net Worth: £3,932,410 *Total Assets:* £4,063,780
Registered Office: The Manor, Boddington, Cheltenham, Glos, GL51 0TJ
Activities: Other service activities n.e.c.
Parent: The Robert Hitchins Group Limited
Officers: Jonathan James Stewart Dunley, Secretary; Jonathan James Stewart Dunley [1970] Director; Peter John Goodhall [1958] Director; Jeremy Charles Hitchins [1954] Director; Jonathan Richard Hitchins [1950] Director; Stephen Robert Hitchins [1947] Director

Alpha Immobile Limited
Incorporated: 7 February 2003
Net Worth Deficit: £4,491,229 *Total Assets:* £3,757,904
Registered Office: 9 St Cadoc House, Temple Street, Keynsham, Bristol, BS31 1HD
Activities: Non-trading company
Shareholders: Zacharias Zachariou; Evangelia Zachariou
Officers: Georgia Spanou, Secretary; Spiridon Fylaktoglou [1973] Director/Lawyer [Greek]

Alpha Schools (Highland) Holdings Limited
Incorporated: 14 July 2005
Net Worth: £7,733,955 *Total Assets:* £143,529,872
Registered Office: First Floor, 10 Temple Back, Bristol, BS1 6FL
Activities: Development of building projects
Parent: Ash Holdco 1 Limited
Officers: Achal Prakash Bhuwania [1979] Director; Kirsty O'Brien [1982] Director

Alpha Schools (Highland) Limited
Incorporated: 15 July 2005
Net Worth: £7,683,955 *Total Assets:* £143,529,872
Registered Office: First Floor, 10 Temple Back, Bristol, BS1 6FL
Activities: Development of building projects
Parent: Alpha Schools (Highland) Holdings Limited
Officers: Achal Prakash Bhuwania [1979] Director; Kirsty O'Brien [1982] Director

Alpha Schools (Highland) Project PLC
Incorporated: 22 July 2005
Net Worth: £50,000 *Total Assets:* £127,670,992
Registered Office: First Floor, 10 Temple Back, Bristol, BS1 6FL
Activities: Development of building projects
Parent: Alpha Schools (Highland) Holdings Limited
Officers: Achal Prakash Bhuwania [1979] Director; Kirsty O'Brien [1982] Director

Altec Products Limited
Incorporated: 29 April 1987 *Employees:* 20
Net Worth: £3,417,868 *Total Assets:* £3,524,546
Registered Office: Bampfylde House, Black Torrington, Beaworthy, Devon, EX21 5PU
Activities: Manufacture of other rubber products
Major Shareholder: Graham David Honey
Officers: June Hayden, Secretary; June Alison Hayden [1965] Director; Graham David Honey [1966] Director

Alterian Software Limited
Incorporated: 19 October 2016 *Employees:* 77
Net Worth: £1,662,234 *Total Assets:* £4,769,489
Registered Office: Mapfre Building, 1 Victoria Street, Runwaye East, Bristol, BS1 6AA
Activities: Media representation services
Officers: Robert Alan Hale [1963] Director [American]

Alternative Money Solutions LLP
Incorporated: 13 December 2010
Net Worth: £5,501,060 *Total Assets:* £5,520,035
Registered Office: Hitchcocks HQ, Hitchcocks Business Park, Willand, Devon, EX15 3DA
Officers: Russell John Pawson [1960] Member; Geoffrey William Persey [1946] Member; Lucy Maria Persey [1984] Member; Maria Carina Persey [1955] Member; Richard Alan William Persey [1981] Member

Altogether Care - Care Homes Limited
Incorporated: 31 December 1996
Net Worth: £9,986,002 *Total Assets:* £10,249,746
Registered Office: 21 Glendinning Avenue, Weymouth, Dorset, DT4 7QF
Activities: Activities of head offices
Shareholders: Commander Brian Westlake; Linda Margaret Westlake
Officers: Linda Margaret Westlake, Secretary; Stephen Paul Knell [1974] Director; Brian Westlake [1944] Director; Linda Margaret Westlake [1947] Director

Altogether Care LLP
Incorporated: 28 April 2004 *Employees:* 367
Net Worth: £10,488,529 *Total Assets:* £15,417,287
Registered Office: 21 Glendinning Avenue, Weymouth, Dorset, DT4 7QF
Officers: Charlotte Lucy Crocker-Westlake [1985] Member; Steve Knell [1974] Member; Brian Westlake [1944] Member; Linda Margaret Westlake [1947] Member

Alton Pancras Estate UK Ltd.
Incorporated: 4 August 2014 *Employees:* 2
Net Worth: £11,285,280 *Total Assets:* £14,560,843
Registered Office: Estate Office, Up Cerne Manor, Up Cerne, Dorchester, DT2 7AW
Activities: Mixed farming
Officers: David Hebditch, Secretary; Dr Alexander Hartig [1954] Director [Austrian]; Hans Herzog [1945] Director [Austrian]; Severin Meister [1981] Director [Austrian]

Alton Towers Resort Operations Limited
Incorporated: 26 February 2007 *Employees:* 4
Net Worth: £9,371,000 *Total Assets:* £10,090,000
Registered Office: Link House, 25 West Street, Poole, Dorset, BH15 1LD
Activities: Activities of amusement parks and theme parks
Parent: Charcoal Midco 1 Limited
Officers: Fiona Jane Rose, Secretary; Matthew Paul Jowett [1967] Director/General Counsel and Company Secretary; Fiona Jane Rose [1964] Director/Assistant Group Company Secretary

Altran UK Limited
Incorporated: 15 January 1997 *Employees:* 390
Net Worth: £12,737,485 *Total Assets:* £47,669,152
Registered Office: 22 St Lawrence Street, Bath, BA1 1AN
Activities: Engineering related scientific and technical consulting activities
Parent: Altran UK Holding Limited
Officers: Stella Toresse, Secretary; Robert John Byrne [1964] Director; Michael John Simms [1961] Director; John Terrington [1958] Director/Manager

Altus Holdings Limited
Incorporated: 14 August 2015 *Employees:* 61
Net Worth: £6,377,387 *Total Assets:* £9,533,815
Registered Office: Royal Mead, 4-5a Railway Place, Bath, BA1 1SR
Activities: Business and domestic software development
Shareholders: David Andrew Jackson; Kevin Okell
Officers: Daniel Aidan Philip Butler, Secretary; Ben Cocks [1965] Director; David Andrew Jackson [1962] Director; Kevin Okell [1962] Director

Altus Limited
Incorporated: 8 September 2005 *Employees:* 61
Net Worth: £1,396,133 *Total Assets:* £4,522,511
Registered Office: Royal Mead, 4-5a Railway Place, Bath, BA1 1SR
Activities: Business and domestic software development
Parent: Altus Holdings Ltd
Officers: Daniel Aidan Philip Butler, Secretary; Ben Cocks [1965] Director/IT Consultant; David Andrew Jackson [1962] Director/Sales; Kevin Okell [1962] Director/Marketing

Alu Bidco Limited
Incorporated: 23 July 2014 *Employees:* 3
Net Worth: £8,346,359 *Total Assets:* £627,821,504
Registered Office: Arnolds Way, Yatton, Somerset, BS49 4QN
Activities: Activities of head offices
Parent: Alu Holdco 2 Limited
Officers: Wim John Scott Flo [1979] Director [Belgian]; Edward Anthony Robinson [1958] Director; Mark Robert West [1976] Director

Alu Holdco 2 Limited
Incorporated: 23 July 2014 *Employees:* 3
Net Worth: £113,229,128 *Total Assets:* £709,547,072
Registered Office: Arnolds Way, Yatton, Somerset, BS49 4QN
Activities: Activities of head offices
Parent: Alu Holdco 1 Limited
Officers: Wim John Scott Flo [1979] Director [Belgian]; Edward Anthony Robinson [1958] Director; Mark Robert West [1976] Director

Alu Midco Limited
Incorporated: 28 August 2014
Net Worth: £89,517,760 *Total Assets:* £234,592,368
Registered Office: Arnolds Way, Yatton, Somerset, BS49 4QN
Activities: Activities of head offices
Parent: Alu Topco Limited
Officers: Wim John Scott Flo [1979] Director [Belgian]; Edward Anthony Robinson [1958] Director; Mark Robert West [1976] Director

Alu Topco Limited
Incorporated: 28 August 2014
Net Worth: £90,087,920 *Total Assets:* £90,087,920
Registered Office: Arnolds Way, Yatton, Somerset, BS49 4QN
Activities: Activities of head offices
Parent: Corialis Group Limited
Officers: Wim John Scott Flo [1979] Director [Belgian]; Edward Anthony Robinson [1958] Director; Mark Robert West [1976] Director

Alum Care Limited
Incorporated: 23 November 2004 *Employees:* 86
Net Worth: £1,453,475 *Total Assets:* £8,557,479
Registered Office: 31-33 Commercial Road, Poole, Dorset, BH14 0HU
Activities: Other human health activities
Parent: The Buckinghamshire Group Limited
Officers: Victoria Benson, Secretary; Christopher Bialan [1957] Director/Finance Broker; David John Comyn [1954] Director [Irish]; Robert Leslie Cousins [1967] Director

Alvis Brothers Limited
Incorporated: 12 December 1951 *Employees:* 128
Net Worth: £22,422,480 *Total Assets:* £44,160,888
Registered Office: Lye Cross Farm, Redhill, Bristol, BS40 5RH
Activities: Raising of dairy cattle
Officers: Pauline Joyce Alvis, Secretary; John Alvis [1944] Director/Farmer; Michael George Alvis [1948] Director/Farmer; Peter James Alvis [1971] Director/Farmer; John Alvis Jnr [1969] Director/Farmer

Amalgam Holdings Limited
Incorporated: 13 December 2007
Previous: Amalgam Collection Ltd
Net Worth: £2,120,037 *Total Assets:* £3,917,527
Registered Office: The Power House, Romney Avenue, Lockleaze, Bristol, BS7 9ST
Activities: Activities of head offices
Parent: Danegeld Holdings Ltd
Officers: Sharon Clare Gartshore, Secretary; Leo Copeman [1973] Director; Sandy Alexander Copeman [1953] Director

Amariz Limited
Incorporated: 10 February 1999 *Employees:* 6
Net Worth: £1,644,874 *Total Assets:* £3,716,120
Registered Office: Imperial House, 1 Harley Place, Bristol, BS8 3JT
Activities: Activities of insurance agents and brokers
Major Shareholder: Amanda Jane Turner
Officers: Amanda Jane Turner, Secretary; Amanda Jane Turner [1970] Director/Office Manager

Amazon Capital Ltd
Incorporated: 20 April 2012 *Employees:* 2
Net Worth: £11,126,595 *Total Assets:* £28,069,476
Registered Office: 20 Chamberlain Street, Wells, Somerset, BA5 2PF
Activities: Security dealing on own account
Shareholders: Kane Bruce Pirie; Iwona Katarzyna Pirie
Officers: Iwona Katarzyna Pirie [1982] Director [Polish]; Kane Bruce Pirie [1970] Director

The Amber Chemical Company Limited
Incorporated: 2 December 1968
Net Worth: £17,016,300 *Total Assets:* £17,026,680
Registered Office: Amber House, Showground Road, Bridgwater, Somerset, TA6 6AJ
Activities: Activities of head offices
Officers: Thomas Gawlik, Secretary; Dr Ralf Bruckmann [1957] Director [German]; Levi James Cottington [1967] Director [American]; Dr Annegret Vester [1962] Director [German]; Nico Wawerek [1976] Director [German]

The Amber Foundation
Incorporated: 21 December 1994 *Employees:* 62
Net Worth: £3,516,517 *Total Assets:* £3,978,505
Registered Office: Ashley Court, Chawleigh, Chulmleigh, Devon, EX18 7EX
Activities: Other residential care activities n.e.c.
Officers: Paul Joseph Rosam, Secretary; Stephen Charles Lyall [1948] Director/Chartered Surveyor; Lady Penelope Mary Marland [1957] Director/Probation Officer; Lucy Henrietta Morris [1963] Director/Art Consultant; Richard John Oldfield [1955] Director/Business Executive; Bartholomew Evan Eric Smith [1955] Director/Businessman; The Honorable Arthur Nicholas Winston Soames [1948] Director/Member of Parliament

Amberon Holdings Limited
Incorporated: 9 January 2014 *Employees:* 469
Net Worth: £9,186,258 *Total Assets:* £17,209,412
Registered Office: Unit 1, 22 Aspen Way, Paignton, Devon, TQ4 7QR
Activities: Activities of other holding companies n.e.c.
Parent: Velocity Holdco Limited
Officers: Daniel James East [1979] Commercial Director; Terence David Musson [1966] Managing Director

Amberon Limited
Incorporated: 8 April 2002 *Employees:* 488
Net Worth: £6,077,000 *Total Assets:* £15,441,000
Registered Office: Unit 1, 22 Aspen Way, Paignton, Devon, TQ4 7QR
Activities: Renting and leasing of other machinery, equipment and tangible goods n.e.c.
Parent: Amberon Holdings Limited
Officers: Daniel James East [1979] Commercial Director; Terence David Musson [1966] Managing Director

Ambitions Academies Trust
Incorporated: 6 March 2012 *Employees:* 327
Net Worth: £27,625,168 *Total Assets:* £39,467,536
Registered Office: Manorside Academy, Evering Avenue, Poole, Dorset, BH12 4JG
Activities: Primary education
Officers: Sherri Lee Hawkins, Secretary; Jonathan Badger [1984] Director/House Husband; Marilyn Bramford [1954] Director/Special Needs Escort; Bernadette Mary Catling [1955] Director/Retired; Pat Marchiori-White [1942] Director; Louise Caroline Parker [1971] Director/Self Employed Bookkeeper/Part Time Mortgage Administration; Caroline Susan Sard [1958] Director/Teaching Assistant; Richard Smith [1964] Director/Civil Servant; Edward James Taylor [1937] Director/Retired

AMCG Enterprise Limited
Incorporated: 10 April 2014
Net Worth: £6,561,376 *Total Assets:* £8,072,126
Registered Office: 4 Brackley Close, Bournemouth International Airport, Christchurch, Dorset, BH23 6SE
Activities: Hotels and similar accommodation
Shareholder: Audrey Louise Wallrock
Officers: Audrey Louise Wallrock [1940] Director; Marina Louise Wallrock [1969] Director

Amcor Europe Group Management
Incorporated: 9 March 2001 *Employees:* 888
Net Worth: £88,915,712 *Total Assets:* £121,473,624
Registered Office: 83 Tower Road North, Warmley, Bristol, BS30 8XP
Activities: Activities of head offices
Officers: Matthew Charles Burrows [1970] Director; Christopher John Cheetham [1962] Director/Chartered Accountant; Damien Clayton [1971] Director; Richard Dixon [1963] Executive Director Tax Europe

Amcor European Investment Holdings Limited
Incorporated: 30 November 2009 *Employees:* 3
Net Worth: £849,227,008 *Total Assets:* £864,371,072
Registered Office: 83 Tower Road North, Warmley, Bristol, BS30 8XP
Activities: Activities of head offices
Officers: Matthew Charles Burrows [1970] Director; Christopher John Cheetham [1962] Director/Accountant; Damien Clayton [1971] Director; Richard Dixon [1963] Director/European Treasury and Tax Manager

Amcor European Investments Limited
Incorporated: 17 June 2009 *Employees:* 3
Net Worth: £94,976,104 *Total Assets:* £97,343,144
Registered Office: 83 Tower Road North, Warmley, Bristol, BS30 8XP
Activities: Activities of head offices
Officers: Matthew Charles Burrows [1970] Director; Christopher John Cheetham [1962] Director/Accountant; Damien Clayton [1971] Director; Richard Dixon [1963] Director/European Treasury and Tax Manager

Amcor Flexibles Finance Limited
Incorporated: 17 December 2009 *Employees:* 2
Net Worth: £516,472,256 *Total Assets:* £516,472,256
Registered Office: 83 Tower Road North, Warmley, Bristol, BS30 8XP
Activities: Other business support service activities n.e.c.
Officers: Matthew Charles Burrows [1970] Director; Christopher John Cheetham [1962] Director/Accountant; Damien Clayton [1971] Director; Richard Dixon [1963] Director/European Treasury and Tax Manager

Amcor Flexibles UK Holding Limited
Incorporated: 15 February 2001 *Employees:* 2
Net Worth: £125,138,792 *Total Assets:* £319,552,896
Registered Office: 83 Tower Road North, Warmley, Bristol, BS30 8XP
Activities: Activities of head offices
Officers: Matthew Charles Burrows [1970] Director; Christopher John Cheetham [1962] Director/Chartered Accountant; Damien Clayton [1971] Director; Richard Dixon [1963] Executive Director Tax Europe

Amcor Flexibles UK Limited
Incorporated: 13 April 1993 *Employees:* 510
Net Worth: £36,068,000 *Total Assets:* £155,360,992
Registered Office: 83 Tower Road North, Warmley, Bristol, BS30 8XP
Activities: Manufacture of plastic packing goods
Officers: Matthew Charles Burrows [1970] Director; Christopher John Cheetham [1962] Director/Chartered Accountant; Paul Courtney [1965] Director; Mark Suitor [1965] Director/Senior Manager Business Controlling; Debra Weetman [1964] Director/Plant General Manager

Amcor Flexibles Winterbourne Limited
Incorporated: 29 December 1989 *Employees:* 171
Net Worth: £32,156,000 *Total Assets:* £52,755,000
Registered Office: 83 Tower Road North, Warmley, Bristol, BS30 8XP
Activities: Manufacture of plastic packing goods
Officers: Matthew Charles Burrows [1970] Director; Damien Clayton [1971] Director; Stephen Morton [1968] Director/General Manager

Amcor Holdco 3
Incorporated: 1 October 2007
Net Worth: £22,246,996 *Total Assets:* £22,246,996
Registered Office: 83 Tower Road North, Warmley, Bristol, BS30 8XP
Activities: Activities of head offices
Officers: Matthew Charles Burrows [1970] Director; Damien Clayton [1971] Director; Richard Dixon [1963] Executive Director Tax Europe

Amcor Holding
Incorporated: 1 June 2001 *Employees:* 17
Net Worth: £527,753,024 *Total Assets:* £3,329,934,848
Registered Office: 83 Tower Road North, Warmley, Bristol, BS30 8XP
Activities: Activities of head offices
Officers: Matthew Charles Burrows [1970] Director; Christopher John Cheetham [1962] Director/Chartered Accountant; Damien Clayton [1971] Director; Richard Dixon [1963] Director/European Treasury and Tax Manager; Ian Gibson Wilson [1958] Director [Australian]

Amcor Holding No.1 Limited
Incorporated: 1 June 2001 *Employees:* 4
Net Worth: £229,466,320 *Total Assets:* £291,462,944
Registered Office: 83 Tower Road North, Warmley, Bristol, BS30 8XP
Activities: Activities of head offices
Officers: Matthew Charles Burrows [1970] Director; Christopher John Cheetham [1962] Director/Chartered Accountant; Damien Clayton [1971] Director; Richard Dixon [1963] Director/European Treasury and Tax Manager; Clare Smith [1958] Director/Vice President Global Pensions

Amcor Investments Germany
Incorporated: 29 May 2002
Net Worth: £59,110,216 *Total Assets:* £385,739,872
Registered Office: 83 Tower Road North, Warmley, Bristol, BS30 8XP
Activities: Activities of head offices
Officers: Olaf Seifert [1969] Plant Director [German]; Michael Stefanowski [1964] Director/Finance Officer [German]

Amcor Mediflex Limited
Incorporated: 28 April 1995 *Employees:* 3
Net Worth: £64,113,668 *Total Assets:* £64,113,668
Registered Office: 83 Tower Road North, Warmley, Bristol, BS30 8XP
Activities: Other business support service activities n.e.c.
Officers: Matthew Charles Burrows [1970] Director; Christopher John Cheetham [1962] Director/Chartered Accountant; Damien Clayton [1971] Director; Richard Dixon [1963] Director/European Treasury and Tax Manager

Amcor Packaging UK Limited
Incorporated: 29 April 1946 *Employees:* 395
Net Worth: £105,008,000 *Total Assets:* £165,104,000
Registered Office: Amcor Central Services, 83 Tower Road North, Warmley, Bristol, BS30 8XP
Activities: Manufacture of other paper and paperboard containers
Officers: Matthew Charles Burrows [1970] Director; Mariana Carter [1974] Director/Plant Manager; Mark Suitor [1965] Managing Director

Amcor Polska Holding Limited
Incorporated: 10 September 2009 *Employees:* 3
Net Worth: £106,583,800 *Total Assets:* £106,583,800
Registered Office: 83 Tower Road North, Warmley, Bristol, BS30 8XP
Activities: Activities of head offices
Officers: Matthew Charles Burrows [1970] Director; Christopher John Cheetham [1962] Director/Accountant; Richard Dixon [1963] Director/European Treasury and Tax Manager

Amcor UK Finance PLC
Incorporated: 15 February 2001 *Employees:* 4
Previous: Amcor UK Finance Limited
Net Worth: £395,960,128 *Total Assets:* £2,958,711,296
Registered Office: 83 Tower Road North, Warmley, Bristol, BS30 8XP
Activities: Other business support service activities n.e.c.
Officers: Lisa Roberts, Secretary; Matthew Charles Burrows [1970] Director; Christopher John Cheetham [1962] Director/Chartered Accountant; Damien Clayton [1971] Director; Richard Dixon [1963] Director/European Treasury and Tax Manager; Graeme Vavasseur [1972] Director/Vice President and Group Treasurer [Australian]

Amcor UK Group International Limited
Incorporated: 23 June 1993 *Employees:* 2
Net Worth: £32,556,000 *Total Assets:* £32,556,000
Registered Office: Amcor Central Services, 83 Tower Road North, Warmley, Bristol, BS30 8XP
Activities: Other business support service activities n.e.c.
Officers: Matthew Charles Burrows [1970] Director; Christopher John Cheetham [1962] Director/Chartered Accountant; Richard Dixon [1963] Executive Director Tax Europe

Amcor UK Group Management Limited
Incorporated: 26 July 1967 *Employees:* 10
Net Worth: £211,295,008 *Total Assets:* £222,572,992
Registered Office: 83 Tower Road North, Warmley, Bristol, BS30 8XP
Activities: Activities of head offices
Officers: Matthew Charles Burrows [1970] Director; Damien Clayton [1971] Director; Richard Dixon [1963] Executive Director Tax Europe; Simon Michael Swann [1957] Director

Amcor UK Investments Limited
Incorporated: 25 March 1971 *Employees:* 2
Net Worth: £484,000 *Total Assets:* £3,946,000
Registered Office: Amcor Central Services, 83 Tower Road North, Warmley, Bristol, BS30 8XP
Activities: Activities of head offices
Officers: Matthew Charles Burrows [1970] Director; Richard Dixon [1963] Executive Director Tax Europe

American Amusements Holdings Limited
Incorporated: 22 February 1993 *Employees:* 2
Net Worth: £6,464,395 *Total Assets:* £6,788,434
Registered Office: Potterne House, Potterne Way, Three Legged Cross, Wimborne, Dorset, BH21 6RS
Activities: Other amusement and recreation activities n.e.c.
Parent: Big Apple Entertainments Limited
Officers: Duncan Geoffrey Frank Moss, Secretary; Michael Richard Erle Appleton [1959] Director/Business Executive

The American Museum in Britain
Incorporated: 10 November 2004 *Employees:* 60
Net Worth: £23,875,932 *Total Assets:* £24,003,576
Registered Office: The American Museum in Britain, Claverton Manor, Bath, BA2 7BD
Activities: Museums activities
Officers: Edward William George Bayntun-Coward [1966] Director/Antiquarian Bookdealer; Richard Oliver Bernays [1943] Director/Investment Manager; Barbara T Bovender [1943] Director/Charity Volunteer [American]; O Delton Harrison Jr [1931] Director/Retired [American]; Mark E Haranzo [1959] Director/Attorney [American]; Lady Catherine Marjory Manning [1951] Director/Volunteer Activities; Virginia Rynne Richard [1943] Director/Lawyer (Retired) [American]; Stanley Deforest Scott [1933] Director/Volunteer Charities [American]; Gareth Vaughan Thomas [1957] Director; William John Tyne [1948] Director/Banker; Alfred M Vinton [1938] Director [American]; Dr Richard Harold Wendorf [1943] Museum Director [American]

Ameriscot Commercial Limited
Incorporated: 6 March 2006 *Employees:* 2
Net Worth: £5,873,010 *Total Assets:* £5,903,062
Registered Office: 31-33 Commercial Road, Poole, Dorset, BH14 0HU
Activities: Development of building projects
Major Shareholder: Robert McKay Kay
Officers: Harriet Anna Syrett, Secretary; Robert McKay Kay [1957] Director

Amesbury Abbey Limited
Incorporated: 2 September 2011 *Employees:* 4
Net Worth: £7,598,471 *Total Assets:* £26,474,124
Registered Office: Cholderton House, Cholderton, Salisbury, Wilts, SP4 0DW
Activities: Other residential care activities n.e.c.
Shareholders: Rosemary Anne Reid; Naomi Victoria Cornelius-Reid; David John Cornelius-Reid
Officers: David John Cornelius-Reid [1962] Director; Naomi Victoria Cornelius-Reid [1978] Director; Dr Rosemary Anne Reid [1959] Director/Consultant Obstetrician and Gynaecologist; Alastair Charles Watson [1969] Director

Amica Care Trust
Incorporated: 11 September 2000 *Employees:* 392
Previous: Somerset Redstone Trust
Net Worth: £13,558,519 *Total Assets:* £14,317,130
Registered Office: Gatchell House, Gatchell Oaks, Trull, Taunton, Somerset, TA3 7EG
Activities: Other human health activities
Officers: Jim Baker [1942] Director/Retired; Graham Owen Briscoe [1943] Director/Retired; Anthony Cooper [1943] Director/Retired; Vanda Crow [1955] Director/Retired; Lesley Elizabeth Darts [1950] Director/Retired; Alan Mansell Ladd [1948] Director/Retired; Adam Rawicz-Szczerbo [1956] Director/Business Executive; John David Whittaker [1951] Director/Retired

Amigo Holdings PLC
Incorporated: 24 February 2016 *Employees:* 264
Previous: Amigo Holdings Limited
Net Worth Deficit: £6,300,000 *Total Assets:* £681,500,032
Registered Office: Nova, 118-128 Commercial Road, Bournemouth, BH2 5LT
Activities: Activities of financial services holding companies
Parent: Richmond Group Limited
Officers: Nicholas Simon Beal, Secretary; Glen Paul Crawford [1968] Director/Chief Executive; Nayan Vithaldas Kisnadwala [1960] Director [American]; Roger Vincent Lovering [1959] Director; Richard Stanley Price [1961] Director; Clare Leslie Salmon [1963] Director; Stephan Wilcke [1970] Director [German]

Amigo Loans Group Ltd
Incorporated: 16 February 2017 *Employees:* 264
Net Worth: £192,400,000 *Total Assets:* £680,700,032
Registered Office: Nova Building, 118-128 Commercial Road, Bournemouth, BH2 5LT
Activities: Activities of financial services holding companies
Parent: Amigo Holdings PLC
Officers: Nicholas Simon Beal, Secretary; Nicholas Simon Beal [1971] Director; Glen Paul Crawford [1968] Director; Nayan Vithaldas Kisnadwala [1960] Director [American]

Amigo Loans Holdings Ltd
Incorporated: 16 February 2017
Net Worth: £302,040,992 *Total Assets:* £302,040,992
Registered Office: Nova Building, 118-128 Commercial Road, Bournemouth, BH2 5LT
Activities: Activities of financial services holding companies
Parent: Amigo Loans Group Ltd
Officers: Nicholas Simon Beal, Secretary; Nicholas Simon Beal [1971] Director; Glen Paul Crawford [1968] Director; Nayan Vithaldas Kisnadwala [1960] Director [American]

Amigo Loans Ltd
Incorporated: 22 July 2003
Net Worth: £190,400,000 *Total Assets:* £678,499,968
Registered Office: Nova, 118-128 Commercial Road, Bournemouth, BH2 5LT
Activities: Credit granting by non-deposit taking finance houses and other specialist consumer credit grantors
Parent: Amigo Loans Holdings Limited
Officers: Nicholas Simon Beal, Secretary; Nicholas Simon Beal [1971] Director/Laywer; Glen Paul Crawford [1968] Director; Nayan Vithaldas Kisnadwala [1960] Director [American]

Amigo Management Services Ltd
Incorporated: 14 March 2005 *Employees:* 264
Net Worth Deficit: £396,000 *Total Assets:* £4,312,000
Registered Office: Nova, 118-128 Commercial Road, Bournemouth, BH2 5LT
Activities: Financial intermediation not elsewhere classified
Parent: Amigo Loans Holdings Limited
Officers: Nicholas Simon Beal, Secretary; Nicholas Simon Beal [1971] Director/Solicitor; Glen Paul Crawford [1968] Director; Nayan Vithaldas Kisnadwala [1960] Director [American]

Amimed Direct Limited
Incorporated: 24 January 1995 *Employees:* 56
Net Worth: £591,539 *Total Assets:* £5,137,588
Registered Office: c/o Smith & Williamson LLP, Portwall Place, Portwall Lane, Bristol, BS1 6NA
Activities: Non-specialised wholesale trade
Shareholders: Juliet Elizabeth Balcombe; David Balcombe
Officers: Juliet Elizabeth Balcombe, Secretary; David Balcombe [1966] Director/Pharmaceuticals

Amphastar UK Ltd
Incorporated: 22 April 2016 *Employees:* 5
Net Worth: £2,885,593 *Total Assets:* £6,161,978
Registered Office: First Floor, 10 Temple Back, Bristol, BS1 6FL
Activities: Manufacture of basic pharmaceutical products
Officers: Jacob Liawatidewi, Secretary; Jacob Liawatidewi [1974] Director/Senior VP Corp Admin Center [American]; Mary Luo [1949] Director/Chief Operations Officer [American]; William Peters [1967] Director/Chief Financial Officer [American]; Jason Shandell [1974] Director/President [American]; Jack Zhang [1946] Director/Chief Executive Officer [Chinese]

Amport and District Coaches Limited
Incorporated: 7 February 1997 *Employees:* 14
Net Worth: £6,676,331 *Total Assets:* £7,162,259
Registered Office: Eastfield House, Amesbury Road, Thruxton, Andover, Hants, SP11 8ED
Activities: Other passenger land transport
Shareholders: Ann Marie Tedd; Philip John Tedd
Officers: Ann Marie Tedd, Secretary; Ann Marie Tedd [1940] Director/Secretary; Nigel Brian Tedd [1963] Director/Coach Operator; Philip John Tedd [1937] Director/Coach Operator

Amsafe Bridport Limited
Incorporated: 25 May 1915 *Employees:* 209
Net Worth: £48,155,000 *Total Assets:* £80,342,000
Registered Office: The Court, West Street, Bridport, Dorset, DT6 3QU
Activities: Service activities incidental to air transportation
Officers: Jason Mark Abbott [1966] Director/President; Jonathan David Crandall [1977] Director/Treasurer [American]; Lee James Stork [1979] Director/Financial Controller

Amulet Hotkey Ltd
Incorporated: 25 May 1990 *Employees:* 76
Net Worth: £4,465,587 *Total Assets:* £8,670,531
Registered Office: Unit 4 Cavalier Road, Heathfield Industrial Estate, Newton Abbot, Devon, TQ12 6TQ
Activities: Manufacture of computers and peripheral equipment
Major Shareholder: Vivien Grace Summerfield
Officers: Keith Richard Grundon [1960] Director; Antony Paul Hilliard [1972] Director; Andrew Jackson [1969] Director; Vivien Grace Summerfield [1946] Director; Mark Jonathon Tothill [1964] Finance Director

An Daras Multi Academy Trust
Incorporated: 25 July 2012 *Employees:* 106
Net Worth: £4,943,445 *Total Assets:* £6,359,316
Registered Office: Unit 4 Tamar Business Park, Pennygillam Way, Pennygillam Industrial Estate, Launceston, Cornwall, PL15 7ED
Activities: Primary education
Officers: Toni Jane Martin, Secretary; Graeme John Barriball [1967] Director; Sally Cooksey [1967] Director/Freelance Event Manager; Rebecca Couch [1981] Director/Diocesan Education Officer; Peter Damian Hague [1954] Director/Retired; William Thomas Hermon [1970] Director/Headteacher; Frederick Brian Jennings [1946] Director/Retired; Dr Nicola Murphy [1965] Director/Family Hub Co-ordinator; Claire Louise Paul [1966] Director/Child Protection Manager; Tim Woodward [1957] Director/Learning Tutor

An Suidhe Wind Farm Limited
Incorporated: 2 June 2005
Net Worth: £19,613,734 *Total Assets:* £26,436,352
Registered Office: Windmill Hill Business Park, Whitehill Way, Swindon, Wilts, SN5 6PB
Activities: Production of electricity
Parent: Innogy SE
Officers: Christopher David Barras, Secretary; Penelope Anne Sainsbury, Secretary; Kevin Dodd [1975] Director/Head of UK Asset Management and Operations; Benjamin James Freeman [1977] Director/Accountant

Anana Limited
Incorporated: 23 October 2001 *Employees:* 36
Net Worth: £3,923,277 *Total Assets:* £8,131,263
Registered Office: Anana House, Cube M4 Business Park, Bristol, BS16 1FX
Activities: Information technology consultancy activities
Shareholders: Marie Ann Woodward; Kerry Joanne Parsons; Roger Gordon Parsons; Christopher John Woodward
Officers: Marie Ann Woodward, Secretary/Business Analyst; Kerry Joanne Parsons [1970] Director/Financial Assistant; Christopher John Woodward [1970] Director/IT Consultant; Marie Ann Woodward [1963] Director

Guy Anderson Wines Limited
Incorporated: 26 October 1999 *Employees:* 14
Net Worth: £2,116,074 *Total Assets:* £5,350,539
Registered Office: Oak Apple House, North Street, Milborne Port, Sherborne, Dorset, DT9 5EW
Activities: Agents involved in the sale of food, beverages and tobacco
Shareholders: Guy Dacre Anderson; Louise Anderson
Officers: Guy Dacre Anderson, Secretary/Director; Guy Dacre Anderson [1963] Director; Louise Anderson [1963] Director

Andrews & Partners Limited
Incorporated: 3 December 1928 *Employees:* 591
Net Worth: £10,107,963 *Total Assets:* £16,134,347
Registered Office: Andrews Estate Agents, The Clockhouse, Bath Hill, Keynsham, Bristol, BS31 1HL
Activities: Real estate agencies
Parent: Andrews Charitable Trust
Officers: David Westgate, Secretary; Steven Derek Esom [1960] Director; Paul Bentley Heal [1950] Director/Chartered Accountant; David Edward Westgate [1965] Director/Chartered Surveyor

Andrews Estate Agents Limited
Incorporated: 10 August 1961 *Employees:* 347
Net Worth: £3,422,058 *Total Assets:* £17,010,178
Registered Office: The Clockhouse, Bath Hill, Keynsham, Bristol, BS31 1HL
Activities: Real estate agencies
Parent: Andrews & Partners Limited
Officers: Brett Ford, Secretary; Paul George Bumford [1956] Financial Services Director; Alison Jane Nunez [1972] Director; David Edward Westgate [1965] Director/Chartered Surveyor

Andrews Letting and Management Limited
Incorporated: 13 January 1981 *Employees:* 192
Net Worth: £5,994,865 *Total Assets:* £10,001,665
Registered Office: The Clockhouse, Bath Hill, Keynsham, Bristol, BS31 1HL
Activities: Real estate agencies
Parent: Andrews & Partners Limited
Officers: Brett Ford, Secretary; Alison Jane Nunez [1972] Managing Director; David Edward Westgate [1965] Director/Surveyor

Andros UK Limited
Incorporated: 31 July 2008 *Employees:* 206
Net Worth: £23,186,148 *Total Assets:* £54,168,576
Registered Office: Lullington Lane, Oldford, Frome, Somerset, BA11 2NQ
Activities: Liquid milk and cream production
Officers: Jean Louet [1966] Managing Director [French]; Derek George Wilson [1942] Director/President

Angel Assistance Limited
Incorporated: 5 January 2000
Previous: Helphire Legal Services Limited
Net Worth Deficit: £715,000 *Total Assets:* £47,967,000
Registered Office: Pinesgate, Lower Bristol Road, Bath, BA2 3DP
Activities: Activities of patent and copyright agents; other legal activities n.e.c.
Parent: Redde PLC
Officers: Nicholas Paul Tilley, Secretary; Mark Francis Chessman [1964] Director; Stephen Edward Oakley [1952] Director; Martin Ward [1967] Managing Director

Anglo-American Vulcanized Fibre Limited
Incorporated: 10 May 2000 *Employees:* 119
Net Worth: £5,780,624 *Total Assets:* £7,081,922
Registered Office: Delanco Works, Clovelly Road, Bideford, Devon, EX39 3EX
Activities: Other manufacturing n.e.c.
Officers: Jeremy Beer, Secretary; Robin Geoffrey Stenhouse [1959] Managing Director

Anglo-Continental Educational Group (G.B.) Limited
Incorporated: 27 March 1954 *Employees:* 77
Net Worth: £3,640,000 *Total Assets:* £4,451,000
Registered Office: 33 Wimborne Road, Bournemouth, BH2 6NA
Activities: Other education n.e.c.
Shareholders: Guido Schillig; Jane Elisabeth Schillig
Officers: Guido Schillig [1964] Director; Jane Elisabeth Schillig [1948] Director

Animal Friends Insurance Services Limited
Incorporated: 14 September 1998 *Employees:* 242
Net Worth: £5,022,698 *Total Assets:* £13,442,100
Registered Office: Animal Friends House, The Crescent, Sun Rise Way, Solstice Park, Amesbury, Wilts, SP4 7QA
Activities: Non-life insurance
Parent: Correlation One Investments Ltd
Officers: Wendy Jiang, Secretary; Johannes Jacobus Marx [1964] Director; Westley Kraig Pearson [1977] Director; Michael John Thorpe [1977] Director

The Animal Healthcare Company Ltd
Incorporated: 14 January 1997 *Employees:* 11
Net Worth: £990,866 *Total Assets:* £5,524,571
Registered Office: Hambleden House, Waterloo Court, Andover, Hants, SP10 1LQ
Activities: Other business support service activities n.e.c.
Parent: Denplan Limited
Officers: Romana Abdin [1963] Director; Deborah Jane Beaven [1963] Director/Chief Financial Officer

Animals in Distress (Torbay and Westcountry)
Incorporated: 6 July 2004 *Employees:* 67
Net Worth: £3,677,021 *Total Assets:* £3,743,706
Registered Office: Biltor Edgelands Lane, Ipplepen, Newton Abbot, Devon, TQ12 5UF
Activities: Farm animal boarding and care
Officers: Neil Leslie Thomas, Secretary; Robina Brand [1934] Director/Retired; Amy Cross-Webber [1985] Director; Generaldine Laura Dix [1949] Director/Retired; Gordon Rothwell Gooding [1940] Director/Retired; Alison Truscott [1969] Director/Business Development Professional; Patricia Tucker [1943] Director/Retired; David John Turner [1946] Director/Retired; Peter Nigel Walmsley [1951] Director/Retired

Ankers and Rawlings Developments Limited
Incorporated: 24 June 1975 *Employees:* 38
Net Worth: £83,738,608 *Total Assets:* £121,963,536
Registered Office: 22 Ringwood Road, Ferndown, Dorset, BH22 9AN
Activities: Development of building projects
Officers: Scott Lewis Rawlings, Secretary; Johnathan Ankers [1980] Director/Manager; Linda Ankers [1953] Director/Secretary; Martyn Eric Thomas Ankers [1952] Director/Builder; Timothy Ankers [1981] Director; Benjamin William Rawlings [1976] Director/Property; Sally Ann Rawlings [1954] Director/Secretary; Scott Lewis Rawlings [1975] Director/Property; Stuart Staple Rawlings [1953] Director/Builder

Ann's Cottage (Warehouse) Limited
Incorporated: 15 September 2004 *Employees:* 21
Net Worth: £1,468,546 *Total Assets:* £4,615,897
Registered Office: Unit 4 Higher Pityme Farm, Pityme Business Centre, St Minver, Wadebridge, Cornwall, PL27 6NU
Activities: Wholesale of clothing and footwear
Major Shareholder: Robert Roden Harris
Officers: Robert Roden Harris, Secretary; Rebecca Cornelius [1978] Director/Retail Chief Buyer; Emily Clare Doney [1983] Director/Accounts Assistant; Robert Roden Harris [1949] Director/Accounts Assistant Manager

Another Place Limited
Incorporated: 8 April 2015 *Employees:* 1
Net Worth Deficit: £327,812 *Total Assets:* £6,418,230
Registered Office: Watergate Bay Hotel, Watergate Bay, Newquay, Cornwall, TR8 4AA
Activities: Hotels and similar accommodation
Shareholder: Actev Limited
Officers: Henry William Howell Ashworth [1969] Director/Social Responsibility Organisation; William James McInnes Ashworth [1974] Director/Hotelier; Judith Anne Blakeburn [1959] Director/Hospitality Marketing; Joseph Davidson [1975] Finance Director; Christian John Hugo [1968] Director/Finance; Susan Jane Nye [1955] Director

Ansford Academy Trust
Incorporated: 3 June 2011 *Employees:* 83
Net Worth: £5,351,083 *Total Assets:* £6,937,686
Registered Office: Ansford Academy, Maggs Lane, Castle Cary, Somerset, BA7 7JJ
Activities: General secondary education
Officers: Susan Rebecca Graham, Secretary; Alison Jane Caroline Bennett [1955] Director/Teacher; Darrell Thomas Chainey [1971] Managing Director; Christopher Bremner Culpin [1944] Director/Writer; Stephen Mark Flanagan [1978] Director/IT Specialist [Irish]; Peter Anthony Gane [1948] Director/Retired; Terena Kirsty Harrison [1971] Director; David Healey [1967] Director; Jeremy Simon Holt [1962] Director/IT Consultant; Samara Lewis [1975] Director/Self Employed; Charles Arthur Llewellyn [1939] Director/Retired; Lee Elisabeth Mosley [1935] Director/Retired Teacher; Shonogh Ellen Pilgrim [1973] Director/Principal; David Iain Robertson [1967] Director/Geologist; Paul William Spencer [1972] Director/Customer Care Manager; Alison Candida Stephens [1970] Managing Director; Clare Mary Louise Watson [1970] Director/Solicitor

Anstee & Ware Group Limited
Incorporated: 16 November 2006
Previous: A W Property Limited
Net Worth: £4,800,000 *Total Assets:* £4,822,675
Registered Office: Anstee Coil, Bondsmill Estate, Bristol Road, Stonehouse, Glos, GL10 3RF
Activities: Development of building projects
Shareholders: William Jonathan Anstee; Michael Trigg
Officers: William Jonathan Anstee, Secretary/Director; William Jonathan Anstee [1961] Director; Michael Trigg [1944] Director

Antech Limited
Incorporated: 26 August 1994 *Employees:* 40
Net Worth: £7,420,274 *Total Assets:* £8,242,622
Registered Office: Unit 7 Newbery Commercial Centre, Exeter Airport Business Park, Exeter, Devon, EX5 2UL
Activities: Support activities for petroleum and natural gas mining
Shareholder: Antoni Krzysztof Lubicz Miszewski
Officers: Lesley Miszewska, Secretary; Michael Colin Hill [1968] Director/Investment Banker; John Richard Martin [1946] Director [American]; Antoni Krzysztof Lubicz Miszewski [1957] Director/Engineer; Janice Elizabeth Ward [1957] Director

Antonville Investments Limited
Incorporated: 10 March 1969 *Employees:* 3
Net Worth: £5,497,111 *Total Assets:* £8,338,352
Registered Office: 18 High West Street, Dorchester, DT1 1UW
Activities: Other letting and operating of own or leased real estate
Shareholder: Stephen Jeffrey Matthews
Officers: Carol Anthea Matthews, Secretary; Carol Anthea Matthews [1945] Director/Company Secretary; Derek Alan Matthews [1947] Director/Chartered Accountant; Stephen Jeffrey Matthews [1943] Director/Solicitor

Antrak Group Limited
Incorporated: 27 February 1975
Net Worth Deficit: £1,568,733 *Total Assets:* £4,193,269
Registered Office: Sudeley Lodge, Sudeley Road, Winchcombe, Cheltenham, Glos, GL54 5JB
Activities: Other business support service activities n.e.c.
Parent: Antrak Limited
Officers: Doris Sharp, Secretary; Robert Harrison Baines [1949] Director; Asoma Abu Banda [1933] Director [Ghanaian]; Kevin Alexander Douglas [1973] Director

Antrak Limited
Incorporated: 19 October 2010
Net Worth: £2,318,993 *Total Assets:* £10,536,903
Registered Office: Sudeley Lodge, Sudeley Road, Winchcombe, Cheltenham, Glos, GL54 5JB
Activities: Activities of other holding companies n.e.c.
Major Shareholder: Robert Harrison Baines
Officers: Doris Sharp, Secretary; Robert Harrison Baines [1949] Director; Asoma Abu Banda [1933] Director [Ghanaian]; Kevin Alexander Douglas [1973] Director

Apak Group Limited
Incorporated: 27 September 1979 *Employees:* 192
Net Worth: £21,657,972 *Total Assets:* £28,324,416
Registered Office: Nibley Court, 3 Turner Drive, Yate, Bristol, BS37 5YX
Activities: Other information technology service activities
Parent: Sopra Banking Software Limited
Officers: Stuart Antony Allen [1966] Director; Philippe Buisson [1961] Director [French]; Emmanuel Gillet [1970] Director [French]; Eric Pasquier [1971] Director [French]; James Matthew Powell [1971] Director

Apetito (U.K.) Holdings Limited
Incorporated: 7 November 1995
Net Worth: £15,579,000 *Total Assets:* £15,579,000
Registered Office: Canal Road, Trowbridge, Wilts, BA14 8RJ
Activities: Activities of head offices
Officers: Richard Peter Ring, Secretary/Director; Joerg Baumgart [1968] Director [German]; Paul Robert Freeston [1959] Director; Richard Peter Ring [1971] Director

Apetito Limited
Incorporated: 6 October 1928 *Employees:* 1,129
Net Worth: £47,659,000 *Total Assets:* £67,337,000
Registered Office: Canal Road, Trowbridge, Wilts, BA14 8RJ
Activities: Manufacture of prepared meals and dishes
Officers: Richard Peter Ring, Secretary/Director; Joerg Baumgart [1968] Director [German]; Wolfgang Dusterberg [1946] Director [German]; Paul Robert Freeston [1959] Director; Christian Kessy [1964] Director [German]; Richard Peter Ring [1971] Director; Ian Andrew Stone [1966] Director

Apex Dental Care Limited
Incorporated: 4 September 2006 *Employees:* 239
Net Worth: £5,762,486 *Total Assets:* £27,405,540
Registered Office: Bupa Dental Care, Vantage Office Park, Old Gloucester Road, Hambrook, Bristol, BS16 1GW
Activities: Dental practice activities
Parent: Apex Holding Ltd
Officers: Robin James Bryant [1970] Director/Dental Surgeon; Steven John Preddy [1959] Director/Dentist; Gabriela Pueyo Roberts [1974] Director/General Manager [Spanish]; Dr Ian David Wood [1956] Director/Dental Surgeon; Jake Stephen Hockley Wright [1972] Director

Apex One Limited
Incorporated: 28 September 2012
Net Worth Deficit: £882,924 *Total Assets:* £4,281,672
Registered Office: Gloucester House, 29 Brunswick Square, Gloucester, GL1 1UN
Activities: Development of building projects
Shareholders: McGurk Group Limited; Robert William Parr
Officers: Robert William Parr [1949] Director/Self Employed

API Holdco Limited
Incorporated: 13 October 2004 *Employees:* 2
Net Worth Deficit: £1,864,046 *Total Assets:* £3,985,312
Registered Office: Third Floor, Broad Quay House, Prince Street, Bristol, BS1 4DJ
Activities: Activities of head offices
Parent: Semperian PPP Investment Partners No.2 Limited
Officers: Andrew Richard Kershaw [1965] Director/Projects Controller; Richard Little [1979] Investment Director

API Technologies (UK) Limited
Incorporated: 25 January 2012 *Employees:* 276
Net Worth: £8,985,000 *Total Assets:* £26,362,000
Registered Office: SST, Brunel Court, Waterwells Business Park, Quedgeley, Gloucester, GL2 2AL
Activities: Activities of head offices
Officers: Richard John Farrington [1956] Director/Certified Chartered Accountant; Robert Edward Tavares [1961] Director [American]

Apollo Radiators Limited
Incorporated: 13 March 1997 *Employees:* 19
Net Worth: £3,256,539 *Total Assets:* £3,977,242
Registered Office: Unit 2 Madleaze Trading Estate, Bristol Road, Gloucester, GL1 5SG
Activities: Wholesale of hardware, plumbing and heating equipment and supplies
Major Shareholder: Stephen Duncan Field
Officers: Donald George Field, Secretary; Stephen Duncan Field [1960] Director

APP (UK) Limited
Incorporated: 24 January 2003 *Employees:* 3
Net Worth: £150,587 *Total Assets:* £3,522,681
Registered Office: Unit 2 Vernon Place, Meteor Business Park, Staverton, Gloucester, GL2 9QL
Activities: Agents involved in the sale of machinery, industrial equipment, ships and aircraft
Parent: Advanced Poly-Packaging Inc
Officers: Stuart Baker [1965] Director/President, Advanced Poly Packaging Inc [American]

Appello Limited
Incorporated: 26 July 2007 *Employees:* 35
Previous: Peverel Building Technologies Limited
Net Worth Deficit: £9,903,981 *Total Assets:* £6,475,939
Registered Office: Queensway House, 11 Queensway, New Milton, Hants, BH25 5NR
Activities: Activities of head offices
Parent: Knight Square Limited
Officers: Carl Burton Atkey [1964] Director/Head of Business; Tim Barclay [1964] Director/Chief Executive; Craig Barlow [1984] Finance Director

Appleby Westward Group Limited
Incorporated: 13 February 1984 *Employees:* 164
Net Worth: £17,066,660 *Total Assets:* £51,792,436
Registered Office: Moorlands Trading Estate, Saltash, Cornwall, PL12 6LX
Activities: Non-specialised wholesale of food, beverages and tobacco
Parent: Triode Acquisitions UK Limited
Officers: Jennifer Kane, Secretary; Michael Alan Boardman [1972] Director; John Clohisey [1952] Director [Irish]; Leo John Anthony Crawford [1959] Director/Chief Executive [Irish]; John Odonnell [1954] Finance Director [Irish]

Appledore Land Limited
Incorporated: 23 February 1973 *Employees:* 1
Net Worth: £4,599,274 *Total Assets:* £4,955,308
Registered Office: Binghams Melcombe, Dorchester, DT2 7PZ
Activities: Other letting and operating of own or leased real estate
Officers: Alan Douglas Deves, Secretary; Alan Douglas Deves [1962] Director/Chartered Accountant; John Christopher Langham [1951] Director/Engineer

Appledore Shipbuilders (2004) Limited
Incorporated: 5 September 1986 *Employees:* 226
Net Worth: £3,965,000 *Total Assets:* £8,625,000
Registered Office: Devonport Royal Dockyard, Devonport, Plymouth, PL1 4SG
Activities: Building of ships and floating structures
Parent: Babcock Marine Holdings (UK) Limited
Officers: Julia Mary Wood, Secretary; Derek Malcolm Jones [1971] Director; Gary Lambert [1966] Director

Applied Automation (UK) Limited
Incorporated: 17 August 1990 *Employees:* 170
Net Worth: £5,236,965 *Total Assets:* £12,724,111
Registered Office: Concept House, Eastern Wood Road, Langage Business Park, Plympton, Plymouth, PL7 5ET
Activities: Manufacture of other special-purpose machinery n.e.c.
Parent: Applied Automation (Holdings) Limited
Officers: Valerie Anne Rowe, Secretary; David Harry Rowe [1958] Director/Engineer

Applied Market Information Limited
Incorporated: 12 June 1987 *Employees:* 74
Net Worth: £2,994,759 *Total Assets:* £6,306,148
Registered Office: Third Floor, One Brunswick Square, Bristol, BS2 8PE
Activities: Publishing of directories and mailing lists
Parent: Advance Bidco Limited
Officers: John Patrick Horgan, Secretary; Andrew Beevers [1963] Director Events and Digital Publications; Darren Alan Spicer [1972] Director/Chartered Accountant; Andrew Symons [1956] Managing Director

Appsbroker Limited
Incorporated: 8 February 2006 *Employees:* 99
Previous: Appsbroker Consulting Limited
Net Worth: £2,947,839 *Total Assets:* £14,501,297
Registered Office: Appsbroker House, The Market Centre, 2 The Square, Old Town, Swindon, Wilts, SN1 3EB
Activities: Computer facilities management activities
Shareholders: Michael Tarcisius Conner; Natasha Jane Conner
Officers: Ian Harold Scott-Gall, Secretary; Michael Tarcisius Conner [1972] Director; Dr Natasha Jane Conner [1972] Director/Clinical Psychologist

April Medibroker Limited
Incorporated: 25 November 1998 *Employees:* 5
Net Worth: £3,376,759 *Total Assets:* £4,295,943
Registered Office: April House, Almondsbury Business Centre, Woodlands, Bradley Stoke, Bristol, BS32 4QH
Activities: Non-life insurance
Parent: April International SA
Officers: Beatrice Marie Gisele Ollier, Secretary; Vincent Alain Jean-Pierre de Meyer [1969] Director [French]; Isaac Lam [1978] Director/Chief Executive; M Emmanuel Jean Legras [1968] Director [French]; Beatrice Marie Gisele Ollier [1980] Director/General Secretary [French]; Peter William Taylor [1966] Director/Certified Chartered Accountant

April UK (Insurance Services) Ltd
Incorporated: 28 March 1996 *Employees:* 53
Net Worth: £1,476,399 *Total Assets:* £3,854,206
Registered Office: April House, Almondsbury Business Centre, Woodlands, Bradley Stoke, Bristol, BS32 4QH
Activities: Activities of insurance agents and brokers
Shareholders: Axeria Prevoyance Sante; April Prevoyance Sante
Officers: Peter William Taylor, Secretary; Isaac Lam [1978] Director/Chief Executive; M Emmanuel Jean Legras [1968] Director/Chairman [French]; Beatrice Marie Gisele Ollier [1980] Director/General Secretary [French]

Aqua Tamarisk LLP
Incorporated: 16 February 2009
Net Worth: £6,587,484 *Total Assets:* £6,750,162
Registered Office: 41 Commercial Road, Poole, Dorset, BH14 0HU
Officers: Fiona Mary Garvey [1967] Member; Timothy Guy Lewis [1962] Member; Susan Elizabeth Adams [1947] LLP Member; Kerry Louise Aitchison [1968] LLP Member; Rose Hazel Allchin [1945] LLP Member; Lucie Joanne Allen [1969] LLP Member; Jean Audrey Alner [1933] LLP Member; Joanne Bell [1977] LLP Member; Michael Anthony Bloxham [1935] LLP Member; Penelope Mary Bouskill [1949] LLP Member; Joan Bright [1932] LLP Member; Carole Byrne [1942] LLP Member; Annette Lynne Campbell [1952] LLP Member; Michael John Carter [1944] LLP Member; Glynis Causton [1952] LLP Member; Sandra June Cherrett [1943] LLP Member; Carolyn Philippa Clouting [1947] LLP Member; Pamela Ann Cooper [1940] LLP Member; Gareth Robert Copling [1967] LLP Member; Elsie Thersa Croft [1937] LLP Member; Karl Crompton [1972] LLP Member; Keith Crompton [1942] LLP Member; Nicole Kerstin Crompton [1977] LLP Member; Patricia Ann Crompton [1946] LLP Member; Shaun Crompton [1971] LLP Member; Helen Crowe [1975] LLP Member; Josephine Ruby Davies [1946] LLP Member; Alison Mary Dean [1966] LLP Member; Robert Adrian Dungay [1953] LLP Member; Valerie Ann Edmonds [1943] LLP Member; Janet Evans [1941] LLP Member; Robin Evans [1942] LLP Member; Antony Farrington [1989] LLP Member; Frances Mary Farrington [1945] LLP Member; Carole Ann Finch [1939] LLP Member; Mary Gertrude Finch [1949] LLP Member; Eric John Fisher [1946] LLP Member; Emma Fleur Flint [1962] LLP Member; Henry Lawrence Flint [1960] LLP Member; Judith Forster [1937] LLP Member; Beryl Marion Garvey [1940] LLP Member; Peter Garvey [1939] LLP Member; Lynda Gilbert [1953] LLP Member; Nicola Joy Godfrey [1952] LLP Member; Helen Gristwood [1965] LLP Member; Berkley George Hall [1936] LLP Member; Dianne Ruth Hall [1950] LLP Member; Maxine Thea Hall [1938] LLP Member; Patrick Geoffrey George Havill [1943] LLP Member; Alison Claire Kaye [1964] LLP Member; Andrew James Knowles [1968] LLP Member; Susan Margaret Larty [1956] LLP Member; Colin Sydney Lewis [1933] LLP Member; Mary Angela Lilley [1947] LLP Member; Robert George Maitland [1951] LLP Member; Christine Alison Marlow [1947] LLP Member; Christopher Marlow [1946] LLP Member; Hadyn Martin [1963] LLP Member; Theresa Catherine Martin [1967] LLP Member; Linda Dorothy Moore [1946] LLP Member; Sarah May Packer [1955] LLP Member; John Frederick Pollard [1943] LLP Member; Dr David Charles Pope [1944] LLP Member; Michael Prescott [1954] LLP Member; Paul Prescott [1952] LLP Member; Lynne Patricia Raymond [1949] LLP Member; Christine Sybil Reid [1934] LLP Member; Diane Jane Rockingham [1956] LLP Member; Joanna Elizabeth Roper [1971] LLP Member; Jane Alexandra Sandon Allum [1956] LLP Member; John Howard Sandon Allum [1954] LLP Member; Evelyn Snow [1964] LLP Member; Fiona Margaret Staddon [1969] LLP Member; Valerie Eve Stride [1945] LLP Member; Angela Mary Thomas [1959] LLP Member; Mary Tiller [1944] LLP Member; Michael Arthur Tombs [1937] LLP Member; Paul Malcolm Tuner [1946] LLP Member; Paul Malcolm Turner [1946] LLP Member; Sharron Wight [1958] LLP Member; Dorothy Ellen Willingham [1950] LLP Member; Peter Willingham [1950] LLP Member; Jamie Wollen [1967] LLP Member; Vivianne Francesca Wollen [1962] LLP Member; Colin Woods [1940] LLP Member; Jennifer Joan Young [1947] LLP Member

Aquamain (UK) Limited
Incorporated: 4 October 2004
Net Worth: £4,696,000 *Total Assets:* £7,470,000
Registered Office: Unit 22 Evercreech Junction, Evercreech, Shepton Mallet, Somerset, BA4 6NA
Activities: Construction of water projects
Parent: Stone Bidco Limited
Officers: Daniel O'Neill [1993] Director [Irish]; Mark Perkins [1963] Director; Jonathan Charles Richardson [1960] Director

Arada Limited
Incorporated: 8 August 1988 *Employees:* 70
Net Worth: £5,586,872 *Total Assets:* £7,412,570
Registered Office: The Fireworks, Weycroft Avenue, Millwey Rise Industrial Estate, Axminster, Devon, EX13 5HU
Activities: Other manufacturing n.e.c.
Officers: Elaine Rosemary Read, Secretary; Mark Christopher Brettell [1965] Sales & Marketing Director; Jonathon Matthew Butterworth [1972] Sales Director

ARAG PLC
Incorporated: 26 February 1991 *Employees:* 108
Net Worth: £11,171,947 *Total Assets:* £43,260,652
Registered Office: 9 Whiteladies Road, Clifton, Bristol, BS8 1NN
Activities: Non-life insurance
Major Shareholder: Paul Otto Fassbender
Officers: Robert Colin Moreton, Secretary; Anthony John Buss [1959] Managing Director; Dr. Renko Harm Dirksen [1976] Member of Board of Directors [German]; David Martin Haynes [1965] Underwriting and Marketing Director; Werner Nicoll [1954] Director [German]; Kathrin Smeja [1981] Director/Senior Head of Underwriting [German]

Arcade Leasing Limited
Incorporated: 28 June 1996
Net Worth: £5,248,806 *Total Assets:* £6,782,765
Registered Office: Syston Farm, Carsons Road, Mangotsfield, Bristol, BS16 9LL
Activities: Other letting and operating of own or leased real estate
Shareholders: Alistaire John Lawrence; James William Lawrence
Officers: John Charles Lawrence, Secretary; Karen Kathleen Caddick [1962] Director; John Charles Lawrence [1955] Director/Builder

Arcade Rentals Limited
Incorporated: 25 November 2008
Net Worth: £1,318,462 *Total Assets:* £4,347,314
Registered Office: Syston Farm, Carsons Road, Mangotsfield, Bristol, BS16 9LL
Activities: Other letting and operating of own or leased real estate
Officers: John Charles Lawrence [1955] Director

Architectural Profiles Limited
Incorporated: 3 June 1982 *Employees:* 13
Net Worth: £3,082,120 *Total Assets:* £5,677,915
Registered Office: 198 High Street, Burbage, Marlborough, Wilts, SN8 3AB
Activities: Other building completion and finishing
Major Shareholder: Andrew Peter Jerrard Dunne
Officers: Godfrey Arthur Brew, Secretary/Solicitor; Godfrey Arthur Brew [1940] Director/Solicitor; Andrew Peter Jerrard Dunne [1945] Director; David Jerrard Dunne [1982] Director/Finance

Areawise Limited
Incorporated: 29 April 1977 *Employees:* 3
Net Worth Deficit: £2,232,477 *Total Assets:* £13,119,208
Registered Office: Hitchcock House, Hilltop Park, Devizes Road, Salisbury, Wilts, SP3 4UF
Activities: Development of building projects
Major Shareholder: Lionel Maurice Froggatt
Officers: Lionel Maurice Froggatt, Secretary; Azita Froggatt [1966] Director; Lionel Maurice Froggatt [1945] Director; Pennie Michelle Rider [1969] Director/Researcher

Arena Business Centres Limited
Incorporated: 23 January 2002 *Employees:* 22
Net Worth: £12,592,040 *Total Assets:* £30,872,640
Registered Office: 118 Old Milton Road, New Milton, Hants, BH25 6EB
Activities: Other letting and operating of own or leased real estate
Shareholders: Jeffrey Marian Spolnik; Philip Scott Wilson
Officers: Jane Hamilton Wilson, Secretary/Director; Sharron Elizabeth Domanska [1964] Director; Jeffrey Marian Spolnik [1956] Director; Philip Scott Wilson [1962] Director

Arena Farnborough Limited
Incorporated: 25 September 2014
Net Worth: £32,723 *Total Assets:* £6,835,886
Registered Office: 118 Old Milton Road, New Milton, Hants, BH25 6EB
Activities: Other letting and operating of own or leased real estate
Parent: Arena Business Centres Limited
Officers: Sharron Elizabeth Domanska [1964] Director; Jeffrey Marian Spolnik [1956] Director; Philip Scott Wilson [1962] Director

ARFF Ltd
Incorporated: 4 December 1997 *Employees:* 1
Net Worth: £1,583,765 *Total Assets:* £3,825,938
Registered Office: Marsh House, Kingston St Mary, Taunton, Somerset, TA2 8HH
Activities: Other letting and operating of own or leased real estate
Major Shareholder: Andrew Robert Foster Flat
Officers: Diane Elizabeth Flatt, Secretary; Graham Glen Foster Flatt, Secretary; Andrew Robert Foster Flatt [1968] Director

Argyll Environmental Ltd
Incorporated: 28 November 2002 *Employees:* 1
Net Worth: £9,029,382 *Total Assets:* £11,911,261
Registered Office: 7 Abbey Court, Eagle Way, Sowton Industrial Estate, Exeter, Devon, EX2 7HY
Activities: Other professional, scientific and technical activities n.e.c.
Parent: DMGI Land & Property Europe Ltd
Officers: Matthew Teague, Secretary; Simon James Brown [1965] Director/Chief Executive; David William Callcott [1959] Director; Stephen John Stout [1960] Director/Chairman

ARI Fleet UK Limited
Incorporated: 29 September 1987 *Employees:* 139
Net Worth: £3,428,702 *Total Assets:* £17,839,250
Registered Office: 1 Methuen Park, Chippenham, Wilts, SN14 0GX
Activities: Maintenance and repair of motor vehicles
Shareholder: Melinda Kay Holman
Officers: James Russell Wells, Secretary; Keith Allen [1963] Managing Director; Mark Bryan [1965] Director [American]; Gernot Leinenbach [1972] Director [German]; Charles Richard Tousaw [1965] Director/Chief Commercial Officer [Canadian]; James Russell Wells [1958] Director/General Counsel [American]; Robert Lester White [1964] Director/Company President [American]

ARI Fleet, Ltd.
Incorporated: 25 November 2011
Net Worth: £3,034,330 *Total Assets:* £16,100,000
Registered Office: 1 Methuen Park, Chippenham, Wilts, SN14 0GX
Activities: Maintenance and repair of motor vehicles
Shareholder: Melinda Kay Holman
Officers: Katherine Andreola Mullin, Secretary; Keith Allen [1963] Managing Director; Brian Randall Bates [1969] Director [American]; Joseph Steward Holman [1926] Director [American]; Melinda Kay Holman [1960] Director [American]; Katherine Andreola Mullin [1954] Director [American]

Arisaig Partners (UK) Limited
Incorporated: 30 July 1999 *Employees:* 2
Net Worth: £453,212 *Total Assets:* £3,669,795
Registered Office: Rhum View, Coleford House, Coleford, Radstock, Somerset, BA3 5LU
Activities: Management consultancy activities other than financial management
Officers: John Torquil McAlpine, Secretary; James Michael Alexandroff [1958] Director/Investment Adviser; Andrew John Quenby Church [1956] Director; Thomas Julian Goddard [1958] Director

Ark Data Centres Limited
Incorporated: 16 December 2005 *Employees:* 65
Net Worth Deficit: £6,795,184 *Total Assets:* £44,666,308
Registered Office: Spring Park, Westwells Road, Hawthorn, Corsham, Wilts, SN13 9GB
Activities: Other letting and operating of own or leased real estate
Officers: Ian Stuart Perryment, Secretary; Simon Christopher Burrage [1971] Director/Solicitor; Lord Jonathan Evans [1958] Director; Brian Vincent Fitzpatrick [1962] Director; Derek McDonald [1967] Director; Huw Thomas Owen [1963] Director; Andrew John Pettit [1968] Director/Banker; Jeffrey Paul Thomas [1957] Director

Ark Data Spring Park Limited
Incorporated: 10 November 2004
Previous: Ark Spring Park Limited
Net Worth: £295,490 *Total Assets:* £4,088,047
Registered Office: Spring Park, Westwells Road, Hawthorn, Corsham, Wilts, SN13 9GB
Activities: Other letting and operating of own or leased real estate
Parent: Ark Data Centres Limited
Officers: Ian Stuart Perryment, Secretary; Simon Christopher Burrage [1971] Director/Solicitor; Derek McDonald [1967] Director; Huw Thomas Owen [1963] Director; Andrew John Pettit [1968] Director/Banker

Ark Estates Cody Park Limited
Incorporated: 30 July 2013
Net Worth: £35,661,160 *Total Assets:* £337,392,544
Registered Office: Spring Park, Westwells Road, Hawthorn, Corsham, Wilts, SN13 9GB
Activities: Other letting and operating of own or leased real estate
Parent: Ark Estates Holdings Limited
Officers: Ian Stuart Perryment, Secretary; Simon Christopher Burrage [1971] Director/Solicitor; Derek McDonald [1967] Director; Huw Thomas Owen [1963] Director; Andrew John Pettit [1968] Director

Ark Estates Holdings Limited
Incorporated: 4 September 2013 *Employees:* 4
Net Worth: £35,600,632 *Total Assets:* £673,458,496
Registered Office: Spring Park, Westwells Road, Corsham, Wilts, SN13 9GB
Activities: Other letting and operating of own or leased real estate
Officers: Ian Stuart Perryment, Secretary; Simon Christopher Burrage [1971] Director/Solicitor; William James Killick [1972] Director/Investment Advisor; Huw Thomas Owen [1963] Director; Andrew John Pettit [1968] Director

Arkell's Brewery Limited
Incorporated: 28 December 1927 *Employees:* 251
Net Worth: £44,568,540 *Total Assets:* £70,877,672
Registered Office: Kingsdown, Upper Stratton, Swindon, Wilts, SN2 7RU
Activities: Manufacture of beer
Officers: Emma Louise Defty, Secretary; Alexander Thomas Arkell [1985] Director/Head Brewer; George James Arkell [1978] Brewery Director; James Rixon Arkell [1951] Director/Chairman; Nicholas Henry Arkell [1955] Director of Brewery Co; Barry John Russell [1961] Director/Chartered Accountant

Arlington Limited
Incorporated: 14 August 1992
Net Worth: £9,431,268 *Total Assets:* £13,236,557
Registered Office: Midland House, 2 Poole Road, Bournemouth, BH2 5QY
Activities: Construction of commercial buildings
Major Shareholder: Neil Kelvin Forest
Officers: Neil Kelvin Forest [1963] Director/Chartered Surveyor; Sara Jane Forest [1963] Director

Armada Investments Limited
Incorporated: 22 October 1973 *Employees:* 21
Net Worth: £13,963,691 *Total Assets:* £33,841,088
Registered Office: Armada House, Odhams Wharf, Topsham, Exeter, Devon, EX3 0PB
Activities: Financial leasing
Major Shareholder: Kirk Martin Smith
Officers: Heather Anne Smith, Secretary; David John Drewett [1973] Director; Martin John Fishleigh [1944] Director/Chartered Accountant; Oliver Raymond Frederick Nash [1983] Director; Heather Anne Smith [1965] Director; Kirk Martin Smith [1944] Director

Armoric Freight International (Holdings) Limited
Incorporated: 6 February 2006 *Employees:* 26
Net Worth: £2,044,147 *Total Assets:* £4,638,611
Registered Office: 14 Barn Close, Langage Industrial Estate, Plymouth, PL7 5HQ
Activities: Freight transport by road
Major Shareholder: Marc Oscar Stummpenhusen Payne
Officers: Marc Oscar Stummpenhusen Payne, Secretary/Director; Marc Oscar Stummpenhusen Payne [1951] Director; Maureen Lynda Stummpenhusen Payne [1951] Director/Management Administrator

Armstrong Bridging International Limited
Incorporated: 2 June 2016
Net Worth: £225 *Total Assets:* £10,986,183
Registered Office: Delta Place, 27 Bath Road, Cheltenham, Glos, GL53 7TH
Activities: Financial intermediation not elsewhere classified
Shareholders: Andrew Jonathan Charles Newman; Robin Francis Chamberlayne; Stephen William Mahon
Officers: Robin Chamberlayne [1966] Director; Steve Mahon [1968] Director; Andrew Newman [1970] Director/Accountant

Armstrong Energy Global Limited
Incorporated: 10 May 2013
Net Worth: £7,665,879 *Total Assets:* £10,335,397
Registered Office: Delta Place, 27 Bath Road, Cheltenham, Glos, GL53 7TH
Activities: Production of electricity
Officers: Rodolfo Bigolin [1987] Director [Italian]; Robin Francis Chamberlayne [1966] Director; Dr Stephen William Mahon [1968] Director; Ramnath Nandakumar [1978] Director; Andrew Jonathan Charles Newman [1970] Director

Armstrong Infrastructure and Property Finance Limited
Incorporated: 17 June 2016
Net Worth: £364 *Total Assets:* £3,866,367
Registered Office: Delta Place, 27 Bath Road, Cheltenham, Glos, GL53 7TH
Activities: Financial intermediation not elsewhere classified
Shareholders: Andrew Jonathan Charles Newman; Robin Chamberlayne; Steve Mahon
Officers: Robin Chamberlayne [1966] Director; Stephen William Mahon [1968] Director; Andrew Jonathan Charles Newman [1970] Director

Arnewood Estates Limited
Incorporated: 18 November 1954 *Employees:* 25
Net Worth: £12,934,409 *Total Assets:* £21,811,796
Registered Office: 6th Floor, Dean Park House, 8-10 Dean Park Crescent, Bournemouth, BH1 1HP
Activities: Hotels and similar accommodation
Parent: FJB Hotels Limited
Officers: Joy Wanda Eva Barcellos, Secretary; Joy Wanda Eva Barcellos [1953] Director; John Godfrey Julius Butterworth [1946] Director; Wanda Gwendoline Helena Butterworth [1927] Director

Arno GB Limited
Incorporated: 25 August 1978 *Employees:* 55
Net Worth: £2,452,275 *Total Assets:* £4,779,533
Registered Office: Victorian House, Coronation Road, Bristol, BS3 1AA
Activities: Manufacture of office and shop furniture
Parent: Arno Holding International GmbH
Officers: Michael Derek Ernest Jones, Secretary; Mark John Aspin [1966] Sales Director; Guy Theodore Palmer [1969] Director; Steffen Bernd Rothmeier [1971] Group Development Director [German]; Prince Philipp Von Thurn Und Taxis [1975] Managing Director [German]

Arnolfini Gallery Limited
Incorporated: 28 April 1966 *Employees:* 27
Net Worth: £6,196,442 *Total Assets:* £6,488,791
Registered Office: 16 Narrow Quay, Bristol, BS1 4QA
Activities: Operation of arts facilities
Officers: Alison Hilda Comley [1962] Artistic Director; Lhosa Anne Daly [1976] Assistant Director of Operations; Michele Louise Farmer [1966] Director; Rachael Fleetwood [1972] Finance Director; Glen Maxwell Heron [1968] Director; Jane Anna Marie Roscoe [1967] Director/Executive Dean

Arriva Group Limited
Incorporated: 25 June 1998
Previous: McGurk Holdings Limited
Net Worth: £3,976,989 *Total Assets:* £10,001,622
Registered Office: Gloucester House, 29 Brunswick Square, Gloucester, GL1 1UN
Activities: Activities of construction holding companies
Parent: McGurk Group Limited
Officers: Eamonn Francis McGurk, Secretary/Director; Brian Andrew McGurk [1967] Director; Eamonn Francis McGurk [1965] Director

Arrowedge Limited
Incorporated: 6 August 1982 *Employees:* 26
Net Worth: £3,766,322 *Total Assets:* £5,676,449
Registered Office: 62 Poole Road, Westbourne, Bournemouth, BH4 9DZ
Activities: Wholesale of pharmaceutical goods
Major Shareholder: Ullas Mahendrakumar Patel
Officers: Manjula Patel, Secretary; Nainesh Mahendra Patel [1962] Director/Chemical Engineer; Ullas Mahendrakumar Patel [1956] Director; Yatin Mahendrakumar Patel [1962] Director/Businessman

The Arthouse Glasgow Limited
Incorporated: 16 June 2004 *Employees:* 42
Net Worth: £3,905,642 *Total Assets:* £7,316,429
Registered Office: 8 Gay Street, Bath, BA1 2PH
Activities: Hotels and similar accommodation
Major Shareholder: Andrew Douglas Brownsword
Officers: Peter Tyrrell, Secretary; Andrew Douglas Brownsword [1947] Director; Jeremy David Hancock [1964] Director/Tax Manager; Stephanie Hocking [1966] Director; Peter Tyrrell [1972] Director

Artisan Biscuits Limited
Incorporated: 5 October 1973 *Employees:* 141
Net Worth: £4,610,295 *Total Assets:* £9,597,897
Registered Office: 29 and 31 Walcot Street, Bath, BA1 5BN
Activities: Manufacture of rusks and biscuits; manufacture of preserved pastry goods and cakes
Officers: Paul Julian Darvill [1968] Managing Director; John Irving Siddall [1948] Director/Manager

Arval UK Group Limited
Incorporated: 12 December 1980 *Employees:* 653
Net Worth: £40,658,000 *Total Assets:* £2,246,295,040
Registered Office: Whitehill House, Windmill Hill, Swindon, Wilts, SN5 6PE
Activities: Activities of financial services holding companies
Parent: BNP Paribas Fleet Holdings Limited
Officers: Amanda Jane Parshall, Secretary; Bart Beckers [1963] Director/Chief Commercial Officer [Belgian]; Antonio Miguel Vieira Galvao Cabaca [1973] Managing Director [Portuguese]; Stephen Andrew Robert Hunt [1967] Director/Chief Executive Officer; Paul Lawrence Hyne [1979] Director/Chief Financial Officer; Thibault Marie Georges Francois Lavigne [1970] Director/Chief Finance Officer [French]; Monsieur Alain Carmelo Van Groenendael [1961] Director/Chief Executive Officer [Belgian]

Arval UK Leasing Services Limited
Incorporated: 22 May 1974
Previous: GE Commercial Finance Fleet Services Ltd.
Net Worth: £25,900,000 *Total Assets:* £25,900,000
Registered Office: Whitehill House, Windmill Hill, Swindon, Wilts, SN5 6PE
Activities: Other business support service activities n.e.c.
Parent: Arval UK Limited
Officers: Amanda Jane Parshall, Secretary; Bart Beckers [1963] Director/Chief Commercial Officer [Belgian]; Antonio Miguel Vieira Galvao Cabaca [1973] Managing Director [Portuguese]; Paul Lawrence Hyne [1979] Director/Chief Financial Officer

Arval UK Limited
Incorporated: 22 September 1972
Net Worth: £21,502,000 *Total Assets:* £2,239,009,024
Registered Office: Whitehill House, Windmill Hill, Swindon, Wilts, SN5 6PE
Activities: Financial leasing
Parent: Arval UK Group Limited
Officers: Amanda Jane Parshall, Secretary; Bart Beckers [1963] Director/Chief Commercial Officer [Belgian]; Antonio Miguel Vieira Galvao Cabaca [1973] Managing Director [Portuguese]; Paul Lawrence Hyne [1979] Director/Chief Financial Officer

ARWC Consulting Ltd
Incorporated: 25 March 2008
Net Worth: £2,674,861 *Total Assets:* £3,633,175
Registered Office: Flying Scotsman House, 70 Heathfields, Downend, Bristol, BS16 6HS
Activities: Accounting and auditing activities
Major Shareholder: Arthur Reginald Wood
Officers: Arthur Reginald Wood, Secretary; Arthur Reginald Wood [1950] Director/Accountant; Jacqueline Ann Wood [1950] Director/Property Manager

ASCB Charitable Fund
Incorporated: 17 April 2008 *Employees:* 4
Net Worth: £9,208,607 *Total Assets:* £11,627,909
Registered Office: Alexandra House, St Johns Street, Salisbury, Wilts, SP1 2SB
Activities: Other sports activities
Officers: Nigel Christopher Allison [1969] Director/Officer British Army; Suzanne Anderson [1968] Director/Army Officer; Major General Duncan Capps [1966] Director/Officer British Army; Brigadier Edward John Rafe Chamberlain [1968] Director/Government Servant; Brigadier David Clouston [1971] Director/Officer British Army; Steven Parker [1976] Director/Officer British Army; Brigadier Timothy John Seal [1965] Director/Officer British Army; Brigadier Andrew John Wingate Sturrock [1971] Director/Officer British Army; Brigadier Robert Jason Walton-Knight [1969] Director/British Army Officer

Ascent Publishing Limited
Incorporated: 22 November 1990 *Employees:* 48
Net Worth: £4,002,000 *Total Assets:* £4,093,000
Registered Office: Quay House, The Ambury, Bath, BA1 1UA
Activities: Publishing of consumer and business journals and periodicals
Parent: Future Publishing Limited
Officers: Penelope Anne Ladkin-Brand, Secretary; Zillah Ellen Byng-Thorne [1974] Director/Chief Executive; Oliver James Foster [1983] Director/Financial Controller; Penelope Anne Ladkin-Brand [1977] Director/Chief Financial Officer

ASDAN
Incorporated: 28 August 1997 *Employees:* 8
Net Worth: £4,111,496 *Total Assets:* £4,692,535
Registered Office: Wainbrook House, Hudds Vale Road, St George, Bristol, BS5 7HY
Activities: General secondary education
Officers: Sandra Dawn Slocombe, Secretary/Director of Business & Operations; David Payne Brockington [1947] Director/Education Consultant; Jennifer May Craig [1962] Director/Management Consultant; Marian Curran [1971] Director/Educational Leadership; Alison Jane Delyth [1951] Ex Director of Education; Brian Stanley Doidge [1958] Director/Chartered Manager & Chartered Marketer; Julie Ann Dyer [1956] Director/Headteacher; Stephen David Fahey [1969] Director; Naeem Iqbal [1961] Director/Healthcare NHS; Paul Jacobs [1960] Director/Education Consultant; Linda Peck [1954] Director/Education Consultant; Jack Edward Price [1985] Director/Commercial Manager; Peter Andrew Scholey [1949] Director/Education Consultant; John Francis Simpson [1951] Director; Christopher William Kerry Smith [1960] Managing Director; Jemma Patricia Stapleton [1985] Director/Head of HR Projects

The Asha Foundation
Incorporated: 6 September 1996 *Employees:* 10
Net Worth: £4,287,471 *Total Assets:* £4,329,592
Registered Office: The Asha Centre, Gunn Mill House, Lower Spout Lane, Mitcheldean, Glos, GL17 0EA
Activities: Other human health activities
Officers: Thomas Tak Leung Chan, Secretary/Management Consultant; Thomas Tak Leung Chan [1949] Director/NHS Manager; Richard David Gifford [1945] Director/Solicitor; Marie-Claire Traynor [1976] Director/Public Relations

Ashbolt Limited
Incorporated: 1 September 1982 *Employees:* 1
Net Worth: £2,626,271 *Total Assets:* £3,502,620
Registered Office: 7 & 8 Church Street, Wimborne, Dorset, BH21 1JH
Activities: Other letting and operating of own or leased real estate
Major Shareholder: Charlotte Barbara Dance
Officers: Jonathan William Dance, Secretary/Director; Charlotte Barbara Dance [1972] Director/IT Consultant

Asheek Living Limited
Incorporated: 25 February 2011 *Employees:* 2
Net Worth: £1,222,066 *Total Assets:* £4,075,854
Registered Office: Freshford House, Redcliffe Way, Bristol, BS1 6NL
Activities: Other letting and operating of own or leased real estate
Major Shareholder: Sophie Louise Ifeoma Chester-Glyn
Officers: Sophie Louise Ifeoma Chester-Glyn [1984] Director; Deian Glyn [1985] Director

Ashfield Land (Aberdeen) Ltd
Incorporated: 11 June 2015
Net Worth Deficit: £410,419 *Total Assets:* £3,944,350
Registered Office: St Catherine's Court, Berkeley Place, Clifton, Bristol, BS8 1BQ
Activities: Buying and selling of own real estate
Officers: Robin Henry Grey Faber, Secretary; Claire Louise Cope [1982] Planning Director; Robin Henry Grey Faber [1955] Director; Andrew James Fisher [1953] Director

Ashfield Land (Birmingham) Limited
Incorporated: 13 March 1989
Net Worth: £92,698 *Total Assets:* £9,111,214
Registered Office: St Catherine's Court, Berkeley Place, Clifton, Bristol, BS8 1BQ
Activities: Buying and selling of own real estate
Officers: Robin Henry Grey Faber, Secretary; Claire Louise Cope [1982] Planning Director; Robin Henry Grey Faber [1955] Director; Andrew James Fisher [1953] Director

Ashfield Land (Bridgend) Limited
Incorporated: 17 January 2017
Net Worth: £9,338 *Total Assets:* £5,312,783
Registered Office: St Catherine's Court, Berkeley Place, Clifton, Bristol, BS8 1BQ
Activities: Buying and selling of own real estate
Officers: Robin Henry Grey Faber, Secretary; Claire Louise Cope [1982] Planning Director; Robin Henry Grey Faber [1955] Director; Andrew James Fisher [1953] Director

Ashfield Land (Cardiff) Limited
Incorporated: 24 October 2000
Net Worth Deficit: £435,368 *Total Assets:* £7,614,370
Registered Office: St Catherine's Court, Berkeley Place, Clifton, Bristol, BS8 1BQ
Activities: Buying and selling of own real estate
Officers: Robin Henry Grey Faber, Secretary; Claire Louise Cope [1982] Planning Director; Robin Henry Grey Faber [1955] Director/Accountant; Andrew James Fisher [1953] Director

Ashfield Land Limited
Incorporated: 30 January 2002 *Employees:* 16
Net Worth: £20,836,326 *Total Assets:* £56,304,600
Registered Office: St Catherine's Court, Berkeley Place, Clifton, Bristol, BS8 1BQ
Activities: Buying and selling of own real estate
Officers: Robin Henry Grey Faber, Secretary/Accountant; Claire Louise Cope [1982] Planning Director; Robin Henry Grey Faber [1955] Director; Andrew James Fisher [1953] Director

Ashfield Land Management Limited
Incorporated: 1 August 1991
Net Worth Deficit: £3,476,875 *Total Assets:* £10,152,973
Registered Office: St Catherine's Court, Berkeley Place, Clifton, Bristol, BS8 1BQ
Activities: Buying and selling of own real estate
Officers: Robin Henry Grey Faber, Secretary; Claire Louise Cope [1982] Planning Director; Robin Henry Grey Faber [1955] Director/Chartered Accountant; Andrew James Fisher [1953] Director

Ashfords LLP
Incorporated: 7 January 2009 *Employees:* 461
Net Worth: £17,503,000 *Total Assets:* £23,909,000
Registered Office: Ashford House, Grenadier Road, Exeter, Devon, EX1 3LH
Officers: Michael Alistair Alden [1968] Member; Andrew Collins Betteridge [1975] Member; Timothy Ralph Heal [1968] Member; Robert Dirk Horsey [1963] Member; Mark Mallyon Lomas [1962] Member; Garry Sutherland MacKay [1970] Member; Ruth Kathryn Murray [1978] Member; Louise Jane Workman [1970] Member; Peter Lawrence Barton [1973] LLP Member; Angus James Bauer [1966] LLP Member; Alan Bennett [1972] LLP Member; Thomas James Penno Biddick [1982] LLP Member; James Darren Blackburn [1965] LLP Member; Patrick George Blake [1964] LLP Member; Victoria Bonnet [1973] LLP Member; Andy Lawrence Braithwaite [1959] LLP Member; Clare Louise Brewer [1971] LLP Member; Paul Butterworth [1963] LLP Member; Kirstin Audrey Cook [1970] LLP Member; Graham John Cridland [1968] LLP Member; James Alexander Crighton [1976] LLP Member; Paul Edward Dunbar [1964] LLP Member; Rebecca Louise Dury [1981] LLP Member; Christopher James Dyson [1980] LLP Member; David John Ellis [1963] LLP Member; Brian John Farrell [1978] LLP Member; Stuart Christopher Fleet [1960] LLP Member; Caroline Anne Frampton [1961] LLP Member; Michael Scott Gay [1972] LLP Member; Sian Louise Gibbon [1965] LLP Member; Elizabeth Gibson [1963] LLP Member; Christopher James Gregson [1957] LLP Member; Charles William Hattersley [1949] LLP Member; Giles Stanley Hawkins [1975] LLP Member; James Heath [1979] LLP Member; Brian Charles Hegarty [1961] LLP Member; James Hemsley [1973] LLP Member; Annabel Susan Charlotte Holyoak [1963] LLP Member; Stephen John Homer [1963] LLP Member; Vanessa Ruth James [1973] LLP Member; Sarah Anne Lomas [1956] LLP Member; Rory MacNiece [1968] LLP Member; Andrew Nicholas John MacMillan-Scott [1960] LLP Member; Nicola Manclark [1977] LLP Member; Mark Charles Manning [1976] LLP Member; Stuart William Mathews [1978] LLP Member; Neelash Mehta [1971] LLP Member; Mark Alexander Moore [1977] LLP Member; Stephen John Moore [1970] LLP Member; Kerry Anne Morgan-Gould [1984] LLP Member; James Barr Morris [1970] LLP Member; Robert Nicholson [1971] LLP Member; Mark Standish Doidge Northey [1969] LLP Member; Charles Benedict Pallot [1964] LLP Member; Judith Margaret Park [1958] LLP Member; Andrew Stuart Perkins [1971] LLP Member; Thomas Bernard Phipps [1961] LLP Member; Gareth David Pinwell [1963] LLP Member; David Anthony William Pomeroy [1965] LLP Member; Zoe Porter [1977] LLP Member; David Geoffrey Richardson [1980] LLP Member; Andrew Craig Rothwell [1956] LLP Member; Simon Roderick Rous [1950] LLP Member; Susan Jane Savill [1963] LLP Member; Jason Steven Squire [1970] LLP Member; Carl Bryan Steele [1971] LLP Member; Rory Suggett [1982] LLP Member; Jessica Eggay Effuah Tekyiwa Taylor [1962] LLP Member; Kate Elizabeth Topp [1976] LLP Member; John Edward Generald Anthony Toth [1961] LLP Member; Carol Jayne Turner [1966] LLP Member; Philip Daniel Turner [1971] LLP Member; Sarah Kay St.Clair Williamson [1976] LLP Member; Flora Christian Wood [1965] LLP Member; Andrew Worley [1971] LLP Member

Ashgrove One Limited
Incorporated: 7 May 2015
Net Worth: £1,343,868 *Total Assets:* £14,507,033
Registered Office: Grosvenor House, 1 New Road, Brixham, Devon, TQ5 8LZ
Activities: Activities of open-ended investment companies
Officers: Anthony James Rawson [1943] Director

Ashington Business Inc. Limited
Incorporated: 14 February 2006
Net Worth Deficit: £3,701,900 *Total Assets:* £26,261,784
Registered Office: Unit 1, 6 King Street, Frome, Somerset, BA11 1BH
Activities: Activities of head offices
Officers: Simon Barrie Hall [1971] Director

Ashley Chase Estate Limited
Incorporated: 8 October 1999 *Employees:* 129
Net Worth: £6,896,114 *Total Assets:* £12,176,474
Registered Office: Parks Farm, Litton Cheney, Dorchester, DT2 9AZ
Activities: Liquid milk and cream production
Parent: A.J. and R.G.Barber Limited
Officers: Charles Nicholas Barber [1972] Director/Farmer; Giles Kelson Barber [1968] Director/Farmer; Martin Charles Crabb [1965] Operations Director; Christopher Michael Newcombe [1965] Director/Certified Accountant; Michael John Pullin [1960] Director/Cheese Maker

The Ashley Family Foundation Limited
Incorporated: 7 October 1983
Net Worth: £13,670,974 *Total Assets:* £13,810,470
Registered Office: 6 Trull Farm Buildings, Trull, Tetbury, Glos, GL8 8SQ
Activities: Other social work activities without accommodation n.e.c.
Officers: Alex Dufort, Secretary; Laura Jane Ashley [1953] Director; Alexis Ashley-Korner [1995] Director/Teacher; Professor Oriana Baddeley [1954] Director/Academic; Anita Anne George [1959] Director/Lawyer; Martyn Christopher Gowar [1946] Director/Partner in Law Firm; Jeremy Malise McIlroy [1955] Director/Chartered Accountant; Emma Shuckburgh [1965] Director/Designer; Sue Timney [1950] Director/Designer

Ashley Grange Nursing Home Limited
Incorporated: 11 March 2008 *Employees:* 66
Net Worth: £3,049,777 *Total Assets:* £8,574,830
Registered Office: Russell House, Oxford Road, Bournemouth, BH8 8EX
Activities: Residential nursing care facilities
Shareholders: Trevor Stanley Abrahams; Mary Theresa Rita Abrahams
Officers: Trevor Stanley Abrahams, Secretary; Mary Theresa Rita Abrahams [1946] Director/Care Home Proprietor; Trevor Stanley Abrahams [1943] Director/Care Home Proprietor; Isabel Claire de La Haye [1976] Director; Paul Josue de La Haye [1965] Director

Ashri Limited
Incorporated: 6 February 2017
Net Worth Deficit: £905,656 *Total Assets:* £7,051,478
Registered Office: Delta Place, 27 Bath Road, Cheltenham, Glos, GL53 7TH
Activities: Other business support service activities n.e.c.
Shareholders: Stephen William Mahon; Robin Chamberlayne; Andrew Jonathan Charles Newman
Officers: Robin Chamberlayne [1966] Director; Stephen William Mahon [1968] Director; Andrew Jonathan Charles Newman [1970] Director

Ashton Gate Limited
Incorporated: 12 May 2005 *Employees:* 521
Net Worth Deficit: £18,299,274 *Total Assets:* £53,175,848
Registered Office: Ashton Road, Bristol, BS3 2EJ
Activities: Other business support service activities n.e.c.
Shareholders: Stephen Lansdown; Margaret Lansdown
Officers: Gavin Thomas Marshall, Secretary; Martin William Griffiths [1960] Director; Mark Robert Kelly [1979] Managing Director [Irish]; Jon Stephen Lansdown [1983] Director

Ashwoods Electric Motors Limited
Incorporated: 19 June 2003 *Employees:* 31
Previous: Ashwoods Automotive Ltd
Net Worth: £4,273,760 *Total Assets:* £7,008,401
Registered Office: Innovation Valley, Harcombe Cross, Chudleigh, Devon, TQ13 0DG
Activities: Manufacture of electrical and electronic equipment for motor vehicles and their engines
Shareholder: Oerlikon Drive Systems GmbH, Pfaffikon
Officers: Lloyd Conway Ash [1979] Director; Jeremy Simon Ellison [1961] Director; Mark David Marling Roberts [1977] Sales Director

Ashwoods Innovations Limited
Incorporated: 22 February 2017
Net Worth: £5,045,347 *Total Assets:* £6,029,347
Registered Office: Innovation Valley, Harcombe Cross, Chudleigh, Devon, TQ13 0DG
Activities: Activities of head offices
Shareholders: Oerlikon Drive Systems GmbH; Curtis Instruments Inc.
Officers: Matthes Bernd [1960] Director [Swiss]; Lloyd Conway Ash [1979] Director; Jeremy Simon Ellison [1961] Director; Robert Kress [1971] Director [American]; Nicholas Evan Marwell [1980] Director [American]; Christopher John Mourton [1949] Director; Stephen Post [1948] Vice President and Executive Director, Curtis Instruments [American]; Mark David Marling Roberts [1977] Director; Gunnar Stein [1970] Director [German]

ASM Assembly Systems UK Holding Limited
Incorporated: 3 December 2010 *Employees:* 54
Net Worth: £1,498,000 *Total Assets:* £8,659,000
Registered Office: 11 Albany Road, Granby Industrial Estate, Weymouth, Dorset, DT4 9TH
Activities: Activities of head offices
Parent: ASM Assembly Systems PTE Ltd
Officers: Christopher Shaw, Secretary; Martyn Buttle [1966] Director/Vice President R&D; Jonathan Roderick Maloney [1971] Director/Management Accountant; Mike Manfred Moehlheinrich [1965] Director/Vice President Finance [German]

ASM Assembly Systems Weymouth Limited
Incorporated: 7 November 1967 *Employees:* 446
Net Worth: £15,764,000 *Total Assets:* £70,066,000
Registered Office: 11 Albany Road, Granby Industrial Estate, Weymouth, Dorset, DT4 9TH
Activities: Manufacture of other special-purpose machinery n.e.c.
Parent: ASM Assembly Systems PTE Ltd
Officers: Christopher Shaw, Secretary; Martyn Buttle [1966] Director/Engineering Manager; Jonathan Roderick Maloney [1971] Director/Chartered Accountant; Mike Manfred Moehlheinrich [1965] Director/Chief Financial Officer [German]

ASP Independent Living Limited
Incorporated: 1 October 1997
Previous: Barchester Assisted Living Properties (Gorseway) Limited
Net Worth: £25,169,000 *Total Assets:* £25,776,000
Registered Office: Agincare House, Admiralty Buildings, Castletown, Portland, Dorset, DT5 2BB
Activities: Other human health activities
Parent: ASP Group Management Ltd
Officers: Adam John Luckhurst [1987] Director; Piers Luckhurst [1997] Director; Simon James Luckhurst [1989] Financial Director

Aspect Digital Media Limited
Incorporated: 2 September 2005
Net Worth: £10,000 *Total Assets:* £6,895,756
Registered Office: 30 Lasne Crescent, Brockworth, Gloucester, GL3 4UX
Activities: Other business support service activities n.e.c.
Parent: Aspect Investments Limited
Officers: Brian Anderson [1951] Director/Accountant; Keith Evans [1951] Director/Accountant; Paul Anthony Matthews [1957] Director/Writer/Producer; Phillip James Matthews [1958] Director/Business Consultant; Mark Alexander Rowse [1960] Director

Aspect Trust
Incorporated: 7 December 2009
Net Worth: £18,041,512 *Total Assets:* £18,044,540
Registered Office: The Wey Valley School, Dorchester Road, Weymouth, Dorset, DT3 5AN
Activities: Primary education
Officers: Robert Simon Cole, Secretary; David Bruce Douglas [1963] Director/Headteacher; Andrew Richard North [1965] Director/Regional Secretary

Aspirations (Bidco) Limited
Incorporated: 11 February 2010 *Employees:* 26
Net Worth Deficit: £38,226,388 *Total Assets:* £25,833,288
Registered Office: Aspirations, Unit 2b Cheltenham Road East, Gloucester, GL3 1JZ
Activities: Other human health activities
Parent: Aspirations (Topco) Limited
Officers: Catherine Beck [1980] Director/Partner; Christine Isabel Cameron [1972] Director

Aspirations (Midlands) Limited
Incorporated: 8 July 2004 *Employees:* 233
Net Worth: £4,344,235 *Total Assets:* £5,150,836
Registered Office: Aspirations, Unit B2 Elmbridge Court, Cheltenham Road East, Gloucester, GL3 1JZ
Activities: Other human health activities
Parent: Maymask (183) Limited
Officers: Christine Isabel Cameron [1972] Director

Aspirations (Topco) Limited
Incorporated: 11 February 2010 *Employees:* 872
Net Worth Deficit: £19,857,550 *Total Assets:* £27,910,114
Registered Office: Aspirations, Unit B2 Cheltenham Road East, Gloucester, GL3 1JZ
Activities: Other human health activities
Parent: August Equity Partners II GP Limited
Officers: Catherine Beck [1980] Director/Partner; Christine Isabel Cameron [1972] Director

Aspirations Care Limited
Incorporated: 23 April 2004 *Employees:* 614
Net Worth: £9,025,098 *Total Assets:* £24,417,152
Registered Office: Unit B2, Cheltenham Road East, Gloucester, GL3 1JZ
Activities: Other human health activities
Parent: Aspirations (Bidco) Limited
Officers: Christine Isabel Cameron [1972] Director; Dave Antony Sergeant [1963] Director

Aspire Academy Trust
Incorporated: 24 September 2010 *Employees:* 853
Net Worth: £42,048,108 *Total Assets:* £49,631,704
Registered Office: 20 St Austell Business Park, Carclaze, St Austell, Cornwall, PL25 4FD
Activities: Primary education
Officers: Victoria Edwards, Secretary; Melanie Gail Colton-Dyer [1966] Director/Company Secretary; Anna Elizabeth Harborne Corbett [1970] Director/Partner; Benjamin Couch [1978] Director/Quantity Surveyor; Andrew Robert Fielder [1957] Director/Headteacher; Michael Jorgen Larsen [1959] Director/Finance; Penelope Jane Shilston [1954] Director/Retired Headteacher; Jacqueline Frances Swain [1961] Director/Site Manager

Aspire Defence Finance PLC
Incorporated: 7 February 2006
Net Worth: £174,000 *Total Assets:* £1,495,065,984
Registered Office: Aspire Business Centre, Ordnance Road, Tidworth, Wilts, SP9 7QD
Activities: Financial intermediation not elsewhere classified
Parent: Aspire Defence Holdings Limited
Officers: Angus Robert McColl, Secretary; Andrew Jonathan Barrie [1967] Operations Director; Graham Maurice Beazley-Long [1960] Investment Management Director; David John Brooking [1967] Investment Director; Larry Jay Henry [1953] Director/Finance Manager [American]; Angus Robert McColl [1964] Director; Peter John Meffan [1964] Director/Chartered Civil Engineer; Arthur Harold Moore [1951] Director/Engineer; Chip Schneider [1963] Director/VP Finance & Treasurer [American]; Scott Springett [1968] Director/Asset Manager; Allan Thomson [1964] Director/Chief Executive; Matthew James Webber [1963] Director; Elena Giorgiana Wegener [1975] Investment Director

Aspire Defence Holdings Limited
Incorporated: 11 April 2003 *Employees:* 16
Net Worth: £10,269,000 *Total Assets:* £1,567,459,968
Registered Office: Aspire Business Centre, Ordnance Road, Tidworth, Wilts, SP9 7QD
Activities: Management of real estate on a fee or contract basis
Shareholders: KBR (U.K.) Investments Limited; Innisfree Secondary Partners 1 LLP
Officers: Angus Robert McColl, Secretary; Andrew Jonathan Barrie [1967] Operations Director; Graham Maurice Beazley-Long [1960] Investment Management Director; David John Brooking [1967] Investment Director; Larry Jay Henry [1953] Director/Finance Manager [American]; Angus Robert McColl [1964] Director/Chartered Accountant; Peter John Meffan [1964] Director/Chartered Civil Engineer; Arthur Harold Moore [1951] Director/Engineer; Chip Schneider [1963] Director/VP Finance & Treasurer [American]; Scott Springett [1968] Director/Asset Manager; Allan Thomson [1964] Director/Chief Executive; Matthew James Webber [1963] Director; Elena Giorgiana Wegener [1975] Investment Director

Aspire Defence Limited
Incorporated: 23 September 2005 *Employees:* 16
Net Worth: £10,094,000 *Total Assets:* £1,567,250,944
Registered Office: Aspire Business Centre, Ordnance Road, Tidworth, Wilts, SP9 7QD
Activities: Management of real estate on a fee or contract basis
Parent: Aspire Defence Holdings Limited
Officers: Angus Robert McColl, Secretary; Andrew Jonathan Barrie [1967] Operations Director; Graham Maurice Beazley-Long [1960] Investment Management Director; David John Brooking [1967] Investment Director; Larry Jay Henry [1953] Director/Finance Manager [American]; Angus Robert McColl [1964] Director; Peter John Meffan [1964] Director/Chartered Civil Engineer; Arthur Harold Moore [1951] Director/Engineer; Chip Schneider [1963] Director/VP Finance & Treasurer [American]; Scott Springett [1968] Director/Asset Manager; Allan Thomson [1964] Director/Chief Executive; Matthew James Webber [1963] Director; Elena Giorgiana Wegener [1975] Investment Director

Aspire Defence Services Limited
Incorporated: 8 October 2002 *Employees:* 954
Net Worth: £11,154,000 *Total Assets:* £23,596,000
Registered Office: Aspire Business Centre, Ordnance Road, Tidworth, Wilts, SP9 7QD
Activities: Management of real estate on a fee or contract basis
Parent: Kellogg Brown & Root Limited
Officers: Martin Nelhams, Secretary; James Arthur Barrett [1965] Director/Accountant; Colin Kenneth Kenton [1957] Project Director; Robert Paul Kerry [1956] Commercial Director

Assessments Bidco Limited
Incorporated: 24 February 2012
Net Worth: £18,522,000 *Total Assets:* £99,719,000
Registered Office: Merchants House North, Wapping Road, Bristol, BS1 4RW
Activities: Other publishing activities
Parent: Assessments Midco 2 Limited
Officers: Robert Dargue [1975] Director; Gregor Stanley Watson [1965] Director

Assessments Midco 2 Limited
Incorporated: 24 February 2012
Net Worth: £11,882,000 *Total Assets:* £49,676,000
Registered Office: Merchants House North, Wapping Road, Bristol, BS1 4RW
Activities: Other publishing activities
Parent: Assessments Midco Limited
Officers: Robert Dargue [1975] Director; Gregor Stanley Watson [1965] Director

Assessments Midco Limited
Incorporated: 24 February 2012
Net Worth: £50,126,000 *Total Assets:* £107,128,000
Registered Office: Merchants House North, Wapping Road, Bristol, BS1 4RW
Activities: Other publishing activities
Parent: Assessments Topco Limited
Officers: Robert Dargue [1975] Director; Gregor Stanley Watson [1965] Director

Assessments Topco Limited
Incorporated: 24 February 2012
Net Worth: £85,864,000 *Total Assets:* £262,423,008
Registered Office: Merchants House North, Wapping Road, Bristol, BS1 4RW
Activities: Activities of other holding companies n.e.c.
Parent: GLE Bidco Limited
Officers: Robert Dargue [1975] Director; Gregor Stanley Watson [1965] Director

Asset Services Limited
Incorporated: 9 February 1994 *Employees:* 58
Net Worth: £3,090,144 *Total Assets:* £4,225,163
Registered Office: 115 Victoria Road, Ferndown, Dorset, BH22 9HU
Activities: Other telecommunications activities
Major Shareholder: Alan Farthing
Officers: Alan Edward Farthing, Secretary; Suzanne Chairman [1967] Administration Director; John Evans [1973] Communications Director; Alan Edward Farthing [1961] Managing Director

Aster Homes Limited
Incorporated: 12 November 2007
Net Worth: £8,104,000 *Total Assets:* £46,471,000
Registered Office: Sarsen Court, Horton Avenue, Cannings Hill, Devizes, Wilts, SN10 2AZ
Activities: Development of building projects
Officers: David Allen Betteridge, Secretary; Dr Michael Edwin Biles [1951] Director/Retired; Bjorn Howard [1968] Director/Group Chief Executive; Andrew Philip Jackson [1951] Director; Andrew George Henry Kluth [1964] Director/Group Treasurer, UK Power Networks; Michael Barry McCullen [1962] Director; Tracey Mary Ann Peters [1969] Director/Counsellor; Michael Timothy Reece [1964] Group Operations & Assets Director; Stephen John Trusler [1961] Strategy Director; Caroline Sheila Wehrle [1972] Global Risk & Compliance Director; Amanda Susan Williams [1968] Group Development Director

Aster Property Limited
Incorporated: 3 January 2003 *Employees:* 410
Net Worth: £2,592,000 *Total Assets:* £12,167,000
Registered Office: Sarsen Court, Horton Avenue, Cannings Hill, Devizes, Wilts, SN10 2AZ
Activities: Construction of domestic buildings
Officers: David Allen Betteridge, Secretary; Dr Michael Edwin Biles [1951] Director/Retired; Bjorn Howard [1968] Director/Group Chief Executive; Andrew Philip Jackson [1951] Finance Director; Andrew George Henry Kluth [1964] Director/Group Treasurer, UK Power Networks; Michael Barry McCullen [1962] Director; Tracey Mary Ann Peters [1969] Director/Counsellor; Michael Timothy Reece [1964] Group Operations & Assets Director; Stephen John Trusler [1961] Director/Accommodation Sector LDR (Europe), Laing O'Rourke; Caroline Sheila Wehrle [1972] Global Risk & Compliance Director, Diageo PLC; Amanda Susan Williams [1968] Group Development Director

Aster Solar Limited
Incorporated: 6 March 2015
Net Worth: £6,142,000 *Total Assets:* £6,193,000
Registered Office: Sarsen Court, Horton Avenue, Canning Hill, Devizes, Wilts, SN10 2AZ
Activities: Production of electricity
Officers: David Allen Betteridge, Secretary; Timothy Charles Goulding [1978] Director/Accountant; Paul Richard Morgan [1961] Assistant Director - Treasury; Alec Charles Pegram [1962] Operations Director; Claire Seymour [1985] Director/Neighbourhood Manager

Aster Treasury PLC
Incorporated: 25 October 2013
Net Worth: £50,000 *Total Assets:* £253,552,000
Registered Office: Sarsen Court, Horton Avenue, Cannings Hill, Devizes, Wilts, SN10 2AZ
Activities: Activities of head offices
Officers: David Allen Betteridge, Secretary; Christopher Benn [1969] Finance Director; Bjorn Howard [1968] Director/Group Chief Executive; Paul Richard Morgan [1961] Director/Group Treasury Manager

Astra Trading Development Ltd.
Incorporated: 15 February 2011
Net Worth: £3,564,248 *Total Assets:* £11,875,893
Registered Office: 22 Billet Street, Taunton, Somerset, TA1 3NG
Activities: Other service activities n.e.c.
Major Shareholder: Oleksandr Tymoshenko
Officers: Stephen John Dudley Hickson [1947] Director

Astrum Multi Academy Trust
Incorporated: 14 June 2017 *Employees:* 174
Net Worth: £8,299,000 *Total Assets:* £10,389,000
Registered Office: Woodwater House, Pynes Hill, Exeter, Devon, EX2 5WR
Activities: Primary education
Officers: David James Atkins [1956] Director/School Admissions Appeals Officer; Ann Kathleen Garrard [1943] Director/PT Teacher; Alan Moray James Grant [1960] Director/Head of Schools HR; John Knight [1958] Director/Retired; Louise Beryl Parr [1961] Director/Headteacher/CEO; Premal Ghanshyam Patel [1987] Director/Accountant

Asvida UK Limited
Incorporated: 6 March 2013 *Employees:* 3
Net Worth: £11,690,066 *Total Assets:* £11,717,052
Registered Office: Bankside, 15 Love Lane, Cirencester, Glos, GL7 1TG
Activities: Activities of other holding companies n.e.c.
Officers: William Paul Frederick Bye, Secretary; Joo Kwang Choo [1972] Director [Singaporean]; Matthew George Jordan [1974] Sales Director; Thomas Sean Murphy [1966] Director [American]

AT Property Holdings Limited
Incorporated: 9 February 2017
Net Worth: £7,055,000 *Total Assets:* £7,055,000
Registered Office: Vici House, 2 Mallard Road, Sowton Industrial Estate, Exeter, Devon, EX2 7LD
Activities: Activities of other holding companies n.e.c.
Major Shareholder: Allen Trump
Officers: Allen Trump [1948] Director

ATEX Media Limited
Incorporated: 6 June 1980 *Employees:* 14
Net Worth: £267,964 *Total Assets:* £4,709,414
Registered Office: Unit A, Underwood Business Park, Wookey Hole Road, Wells, Somerset, BA5 1AF
Activities: Other information technology service activities
Parent: Constellation Software UK Holdco Ltd
Officers: John Edward Billowits [1972] Director [Canadian]; Daniel Lee [1980] Director [Canadian]

Athelney Trust PLC
Incorporated: 23 May 1994 *Employees:* 1
Net Worth: £6,145,524 *Total Assets:* £6,168,766
Registered Office: Waterside Court, Falmouth Road, Penryn, Cornwall, TR10 8AW
Activities: Activities of investment trusts
Officers: John Girdlestone, Secretary; Deborah Clare Warburton, Secretary; Norman Frank Ashton [1961] Director; David Anthony Lawman [1948] Director; Helen Elizabeth Sachdev [1965] Director

The Athelstan Trust
Incorporated: 11 July 2011 *Employees:* 411
Previous: Malmesbury School
Net Worth: £19,191,664 *Total Assets:* £23,154,596
Registered Office: Corn Gastons, Malmesbury, Wilts, SN16 0DF
Activities: General secondary education
Officers: Joanna Boyd Cummings, Secretary; Richard Boggis-Rolfe [1950] Director; Alexander Carlton Brooks [1966] Managing Director; David Glyn Collen [1970] Director/Project Manager; Kathryn Darby [1944] Director/Retired; David Charles Few [1965] Director/Chartered Civil Engineer; Karen Elizabeth Frost [1959] Director; Graeme John Martin [1962] Business Systems Director; Fiona Orwin [1977] Director/Store Manager; William Roy Webster [1969] Director/Economist

Athena Racing Limited
Incorporated: 19 December 2013 *Employees:* 82
Previous: Ben Ainslie Racing Limited
Net Worth Deficit: £44,185,856 *Total Assets:* £17,368,844
Registered Office: Towngate House, 2-8 Parkstone Road, Poole, Dorset, BH15 2PW
Activities: Other sports activities
Shareholders: Richard David Becker; Eleana Economides; George Economides
Officers: Sir Charles Benedict Ainslie [1977] Director; Christopher Andrew Cecil-Wright [1970] Managing Director; Matthew James Robinson [1979] Director/Accountant; Grant Eugene Simmer [1957] Director [Australian]

Atkins Travel Limited
Incorporated: 8 November 1988 *Employees:* 72
Net Worth: £1,801,650 *Total Assets:* £6,236,457
Registered Office: 1 Fridays Court, High Street, Ringwood, Hants, BH24 1JA
Activities: Tour operator activities
Shareholders: Thomas John Dixon; Corinthia Investments Ltd; David John Nash
Officers: Nicholas David Ashton Aubin, Secretary; Nicholas David Ashton Aubin [1964] Director/Accountant; Thomas John Dixon [1942] Managing Director; Joseph Fenech [1956] Director/Accountant [Maltese]; Joseph Pisani [1937] Director [Maltese]; David Richard Skillicorn [1959] Director

Atkinson Equipment Limited
Incorporated: 17 April 1972 *Employees:* 132
Net Worth: £8,529,793 *Total Assets:* £12,762,745
Registered Office: Moat Works, Moat Road, West Wilts Trading Estate, Westbury, Wilts, BA13 4JF
Activities: Agents specialised in the sale of other particular products
Major Shareholder: Clive Robert Atkinson
Officers: Simon Timothy Pearce, Finance Director; Clive Robert Atkinson [1955] Director; Giles Robert David Atkinson [1983] Director; Gregory Peter Atkinson [1985] Director; Janet Elizabeth Atkinson [1958] Director; Simon Timothy Pearce [1970] Finance Director

Atlantic Centre of Excellence Multi Academy Trust
Incorporated: 19 November 2013 *Employees:* 375
Net Worth: £22,128,432 *Total Assets:* £25,835,920
Registered Office: Porthbean Road, St Columb Minor, Newquay, Cornwall, TR7 3JF
Activities: Primary education
Officers: Amy Louise Sweet, Secretary; Daniella Louise Glynn [1978] Director/HR Consultant; David John Hobbs [1952] Director/Retired; Philip Lawrence Mason [1965] Director/Local Government Officer; Professor Tanya Sharron Ovenden-Hope [1968] Director/Senior Manager in Education; Antus Scott Phillips [1957] Director/Headteacher; Mark Terrance Smith [1967] Director/University Staff Member; Holly Sykes [1981] Director/Internal Audit Service Lead, Cornwall Council; Jennifer Susan Walker [1962] Director/Headteacher

Atlantic Inertial Systems Limited
Incorporated: 11 April 2007 *Employees:* 247
Net Worth: £128,771,000 *Total Assets:* £146,816,000
Registered Office: Clittaford Road, Southway, Plymouth, PL6 6DE
Activities: Manufacture of electronic measuring, testing etc. equipment, not for industrial process control
Parent: Goodrich Limited
Officers: Stuart Peter Barnes [1962] Director/Chartered Management Accountant; Justin Robert Keppy [1972] Director/President Sensors and Integrated Systems [American]; Kevin Pindard [1967] Managing Director

Atlantis 39 Limited
Incorporated: 13 March 1992 *Employees:* 3
Previous: Atlantis Energy Services Limited
Net Worth: £1,376,713 *Total Assets:* £4,532,023
Registered Office: A39 Hawksfield, Wadebridge, Cornwall, PL27 7LR
Activities: Other business support service activities n.e.c.
Officers: Vanessa Eldridge, Secretary; Benjamin David Eldridge [1980] Director; James Robert Eldridge [1974] Director/Engineer; John Sebastian Eldridge [1976] Director; Richard Anthony Eldridge [1942] Director/Engineer; Thomas Christian Eldridge [1978] Director

Atlantis Ocean Energy PLC
Incorporated: 15 June 2017
Net Worth Deficit: £192,943 *Total Assets:* £4,438,580
Registered Office: Beaufort House, 51 New North Road, Exeter, EX4 4EP
Activities: Activities of financial services holding companies
Parent: Simec Atlantis Energy Limited
Officers: Timothy James Cornelius [1976] Director [Australian]; Andrew Luke Dagley [1983] Director [Australian]

Atlantis Operations (UK) Limited
Incorporated: 25 January 2008 *Employees:* 10
Net Worth Deficit: £10,307,212 *Total Assets:* £12,325,855
Registered Office: Beaufort House, 51 New North Road, Exeter, EX4 4EP
Activities: Manufacture of engines and turbines, except aircraft, vehicle and cycle engines
Parent: Simec Atlantis Energy Limited
Officers: Timothy James Cornelius [1976] Director [Australian]; Andrew Luke Dagley [1983] Director/Chief Financial Officer [Australian]

Atlas Elektronik UK (Holdings) Limited
Incorporated: 5 October 2005
Net Worth: £23,500,000 *Total Assets:* £23,500,000
Registered Office: Dorset Innovation Park, Winfrith Newburgh, Dorchester, DT2 8ZB
Activities: Non-trading company
Parent: Thyssenkrupp AG
Officers: Nigel Charles Forbes Guild [1949] Director/Chairman of The Board

Atlas Elektronik UK Limited
Incorporated: 4 October 2005 *Employees:* 343
Net Worth: £33,655,000 *Total Assets:* £60,371,000
Registered Office: Dorset Innovation Park, Winfrith Newburgh, Dorchester, DT2 8ZB
Activities: Defence activities
Parent: Atlas Elektronik UK (Holdings) Limited
Officers: Claire Evans [1972] Director/Chief Financial Officer; Nigel Charles Forbes Guild [1949] Director/Chairman of The Board; Fred Thomas Keupp [1964] Director/Chief Sales Officer (CSO) [German]; Dr Antoni Mazur [1968] Managing Director [Canadian]; Stefan Meisel [1972] Executive Director Engineering & Group CTO [German]; John Sutcliffe [1963] Business Development Director

Atlas Packaging Limited
Incorporated: 28 July 1983 *Employees:* 137
Net Worth: £2,871,629 *Total Assets:* £13,064,399
Registered Office: Barron Way, Roundswell Business Park, Barnstaple, Devon, EX31 3TT
Activities: Manufacture of corrugated paper and paperboard, sacks and bags
Parent: West Country Packaging Ltd
Officers: Mark Christopher Reeve, Secretary; Adrian Gamble [1953] Director/Chairman; Mark Paul Leverton [1976] Director; Vincent Francis McDermott [1965] Manufacturing Director; Mark Christopher Reeve [1969] Commercial Director; Jason Gerard Sharman [1969] Managing Director; Philip Robert Sweetland [1968] Operations Director

Atlas Services Group Energy Ltd
Incorporated: 30 November 2004 *Employees:* 51
Net Worth Deficit: £358,554 *Total Assets:* £15,657,851
Registered Office: 10th Floor, Colston Tower, Colston Street, Bristol, BS1 4XE
Activities: Temporary employment agency activities
Parent: Atlas Services Group B.V.
Officers: Ronalda Verdoes, Secretary; Emma Campbell [1975] Director/Operations Manager

ATP Holdings Limited
Incorporated: 4 April 2001 *Employees:* 6
Net Worth: £1,874,716 *Total Assets:* £5,372,845
Registered Office: Vici House, 2 Mallard Road, Sowton, Exeter, Devon, EX2 7LD
Activities: Other letting and operating of own or leased real estate
Parent: Allen Trump Holdings Limited
Officers: Joanne Sarah Trump, Secretary; Allen Trump [1948] Director/Publisher

Attivo Group Limited
Incorporated: 26 August 2005 *Employees:* 78
Net Worth: £6,607,923 *Total Assets:* £10,243,943
Registered Office: Jessop House, Jessop Avenue, Cheltenham, Glos, GL50 3SH
Activities: Activities of head offices
Officers: Stephen John Bareham, Secretary; Stephen Charles Harper [1964] Managing Director

Attwooll Holdings Limited
Incorporated: 17 September 2003 *Employees:* 101
Net Worth: £7,674,428 *Total Assets:* £8,662,974
Registered Office: Whitminster Lodge, Whitminster, Glos, GL2 7LX
Activities: Other professional, scientific and technical activities n.e.c.
Officers: Heather Jane Attwooll, Secretary; Heather Jane Attwooll [1959] Director; John Anthony Attwooll [1956] Director; Nigel Philip Attwooll [1958] Director

AUB Enterprises Limited
Incorporated: 18 February 2003
Net Worth Deficit: £11,000 *Total Assets:* £4,772,000
Registered Office: Fernbarrow, Wallisdown, Poole, Dorset, BH12 5HH
Activities: Other letting and operating of own or leased real estate
Officers: Jonathan Renyard, Secretary; Professor Stuart Bartholomew [1947] Director/College Principal CEO; Michael John Webster Gibson [1954] Director/Retired; Christopher George Martin [1957] Director/Retired

Auden McKenzie (Pharma Division) Limited
Incorporated: 2 September 1999
Net Worth: £157,626,992 *Total Assets:* £166,636,032
Registered Office: Whiddon Valley, Barnstaple, Devon, EX32 8NS
Activities: Manufacture of basic pharmaceutical products
Parent: Auden McKenzie Holdings Limited
Officers: Dean Michael Cooper [1972] Director/Chartered Accountant; Kim Innes [1968] Director/General Manager

Audience Systems Limited
Incorporated: 21 February 1972 *Employees:* 115
Net Worth: £5,142,921 *Total Assets:* £7,635,707
Registered Office: 19b Washington Road, West Wilts Trading Estate, Westbury, Wilts, BA13 4JP
Activities: Manufacture of other furniture
Shareholders: Shigeyuki Fukasawa; Keiko Fukasawa; Kota Fukasawa
Officers: Steven Edgeworth, Secretary; Steven James Edgeworth [1967] Financial Director; Shigeyuki Fukasawa [1941] Director [Japanese]; Gary Pillinger [1969] Sales Director; Keith David Ritson [1961] Managing Director

Auger Torque Europe Limited
Incorporated: 31 March 1998 *Employees:* 25
Net Worth: £3,716,599 *Total Assets:* £4,587,140
Registered Office: Shipton Downs Farm, Hazleton, Cheltenham, Glos, GL54 4DX
Activities: Manufacture of earthmoving equipment
Officers: Rosemarie Margaret Payne, Secretary; Alistair Renwick Brydon [1973] Managing Director; Thomas Jurgen Friedrich [1965] Managing Director [German]; Roland Olbrich [1967] Director [German]

August UK Holdco Limited
Incorporated: 22 March 2012
Net Worth: £154,082,000 *Total Assets:* £165,632,000
Registered Office: Interface House, Interface Business Park, Bincknoll Lane, Royal Wootton Bassett, Swindon, Wilts, SN4 8SY
Activities: Activities of head offices
Parent: ST Schrader Holding Company UK Limited
Officers: Steven Beringhause [1965] Director/Chief Technology Officer [American]

AUK Holding Limited
Incorporated: 8 October 2008
Net Worth: £18,264,000 *Total Assets:* £22,364,000
Registered Office: Folly Road, Roundway, Devizes, Wilts, SN10 2HT
Activities: Non-trading company
Parent: Ball Aerocan Europe SAS
Officers: Jacob Stoehr, Secretary; Sebastien Gaspari [1977] Director/General Manager [French]; Richard John Peachey [1965] Director/Solicitor

AUL Underwriting Agency Ltd
Incorporated: 20 July 2006 *Employees:* 5
Net Worth: £4,052,873 *Total Assets:* £6,718,329
Registered Office: 37 Chamberlain Street, Wells, Somerset, BA5 2PQ
Activities: Activities of insurance agents and brokers
Shareholders: Simon David Winston Johnson; Guido Hesse
Officers: Martin James Bowe, Secretary; Johanna Harris [1967] Director; Guido Hesse [1967] Director/Insurance Broker [Swiss]; Simon David Winston Johnson [1955] Director/Underwriter; Nicholas Richard Ogilvy Romyn [1959] Director/Insurance Broker

Auma Actuators Limited
Incorporated: 1 June 1971 *Employees:* 29
Net Worth: £3,662,891 *Total Assets:* £4,826,895
Registered Office: Generation House, Yeo Bank 3, Kenn Road, Clevedon, Somerset, BS21 6TH
Activities: Agents specialised in the sale of other particular products
Officers: Matthias Paul Dinse [1954] International Sales Director [German]; Ferdinand Dirnhofer [1968] Director/Sales Manager [German]; Paul Leyshon Hopkins [1963] Director

Aura Bidco Management Limited
Incorporated: 22 September 2016
Net Worth: £15,419,252 *Total Assets:* £93,089,760
Registered Office: Windsor House, Bayshill Road, Cheltenham, Glos, GL50 3AT
Activities: Other business support service activities n.e.c.
Officers: Paula Burgess [1975] Director; Edward Arthur Wilson [1965] Investment Director

Aura Wind (Holdco) Limited
Incorporated: 8 July 2015
Previous: GSE Fit Wind Limited
Net Worth: £150,273 *Total Assets:* £34,300,320
Registered Office: Windsor House, Bayshill Road, Cheltenham, Glos, GL50 3AT
Activities: Activities of other holding companies n.e.c.
Parent: Aura Bidco Management Limited
Officers: Paula Burgess [1975] Director/Chief Operating Officer; Nicholas Tommy Cole [1978] Investment Director; Edward Arthur Wilson [1965] Director/Chief Investment Officer

Aura Wind (Midco) Limited
Incorporated: 9 July 2015
Previous: GSE Fit Wind (Midco) Limited
Net Worth Deficit: £4,615,094 *Total Assets:* £78,908,232
Registered Office: Windsor House, Bayshill Road, Cheltenham, Glos, GL50 3AT
Activities: Activities of other holding companies n.e.c.
Parent: Aura Wind (Holdco) Limited
Officers: Paula Burgess [1975] Director/Chief Operating Officer; Nicholas Tommy Cole [1978] Investment Director; Edward Arthur Wilson [1965] Director/Chief Investment Officer

Austral-Asia World LLC UK Limited
Incorporated: 23 August 2013
Net Worth: £4,532,802 *Total Assets:* £6,256,311
Registered Office: Queen Victoria House, 18 Royal Crescent, Cheltenham, Glos, GL50 3DA
Activities: Development of building projects
Parent: World Group Pacific Limited
Officers: Ian Marsh, Secretary; Anne Frances Turner [1967] Director [Australian]; Richard William Turner [1968] Director/Consultant [Australian]

Autism Wessex
Incorporated: 31 May 1990 *Employees:* 397
Net Worth: £12,190,407 *Total Assets:* £14,316,866
Registered Office: Portfield School, Parley Lane, Christchurch, Dorset, BH23 6BP
Activities: Other education n.e.c.
Officers: Jonathan Dean Beebee [1979] Director/Registered Nurse (Learning Disabilities); Gabriella Crouch [1991] Director/Head of Development and Communications; Hugh Tristram Dampney [1960] Director/Farmer; Malcolm Farrell [1949] Director/Councillor; Martin Christopher James [1948] Director/Retired; Caroline Martin [1956] Director/Freelance Writer/Proposal Writer; Harold Christopher Nash [1960] Director/Retired; Adrian John Trevett [1967] Director/Local Government Officer

Autograph Homes (Hambrook) Limited
Incorporated: 13 October 2016
Net Worth: £722,012 *Total Assets:* £7,229,776
Registered Office: The Malthouse, Durnford Street, Bristol, BS3 2AW
Activities: Development of building projects
Shareholders: Housing Growth Partnership GP LLP as a General Partner of Housing Growth Partnership LP; Housing Growth Partnership GP LLP as a General Partner of Housing Growth Partnership LP; Autograph Homes Limited
Officers: Brian John Daintith, Secretary; Paul Abson [1966] Director; Sean Anthony Cooper [1966] Director; Stephen James Devlin [1967] Director; Simon Michael Taylor [1968] Managing Director

Autograph Homes Limited
Incorporated: 11 October 2016 *Employees:* 5
Net Worth: £628,277 *Total Assets:* £13,771,565
Registered Office: The Malthouse, Durnford Street, Bristol, BS3 2AW
Activities: Development of building projects
Officers: Brian John Daintith, Secretary; Paul Abson [1966] Director; Maxine Anne Cooper [1966] Director; Sean Anthony Cooper [1966] Director; Debra Louise Devlin [1967] Director/Administrator; Stephen James Devlin [1967] Director; Simon Michael Taylor [1968] Managing Director

Automatic Industrial Machines Limited
Incorporated: 12 May 1969 *Employees:* 35
Net Worth: £3,027,165 *Total Assets:* £4,224,884
Registered Office: 6 Concorde Drive, 5c Business Centre, Clevedon, Somerset, BS21 6UH
Activities: Machining
Shareholders: Angela Louise Hemsley; Robert James Kendall
Officers: Angela Louise Hemsley, Secretary; Angela Louise Hemsley [1965] Director; Robert James Kendall [1968] Director/Engineer

Automotive Parts Distribution Limited
Incorporated: 24 May 1991 *Employees:* 95
Net Worth: £1,096,369 *Total Assets:* £4,882,416
Registered Office: 69-71 Lower Bristol Road, Bath, BA2 3BE
Activities: Wholesale trade of motor vehicle parts and accessories
Shareholder: Thomas Murray
Officers: Ewan Sinclair Daniel Murray [1974] Financial Director; Fraser Murray [1971] Director/Supply and Marketing; Thomas Murray [1943] Director

Autonumis Limited
Incorporated: 11 May 1987 *Employees:* 68
Net Worth: £3,204,625 *Total Assets:* £3,994,820
Registered Office: Aston Down Business Park, Aston Down, Minchinhampton, Stroud, Glos, GL6 8GA
Activities: Manufacture of other special-purpose machinery n.e.c.
Officers: David Robert Cole, Secretary; David Robert Cole [1948] Director; Richard John Henry Seymour [1942] Director

Autoparts & Diagnostics Limited
Incorporated: 20 March 2003 *Employees:* 140
Net Worth: £5,782,737 *Total Assets:* £13,962,533
Registered Office: 5 Shepherd Road, Gloucester, GL2 5EL
Activities: Retail trade of motor vehicle parts and accessories
Shareholders: Tristan Sean Seal; Jamie Seal
Officers: Tristan Sean Seal, Secretary; Alan Seal [1948] Director; Jamie Seal [1971] Commercial Director; Patrick Seal [1982] Director/Manager; Tristan Sean Seal [1975] Director

Autumnus Energy Limited
Incorporated: 3 June 2014
Net Worth: £4,467,881 *Total Assets:* £5,328,860
Registered Office: Unit 2a Trenant Industrial Estate, Bess Park Road, Wadebridge, Cornwall, PL27 6HB
Activities: Production of electricity
Shareholders: Clean Earth Energy Investments Ltd; Sean Jonathan Notley
Officers: Sean Jonathan Notley [1963] Director

Auxillis Limited
Incorporated: 13 July 1994
Previous: Albany Assistance Limited
Net Worth: £10,804,000 *Total Assets:* £24,680,000
Registered Office: Pinesgate, Lower Bristol Road, Bath, BA2 3DP
Activities: Financial intermediation not elsewhere classified
Parent: Redde PLC
Officers: Nicholas Paul Tilley, Secretary; Mark Francis Chessman [1964] Director; Stephen Edward Oakley [1952] Director; Martin Ward [1967] Managing Director

Auxillis Services Limited
Incorporated: 11 February 1992
Previous: Helphire Limited
Net Worth: £69,431,000 *Total Assets:* £231,046,000
Registered Office: Pinesgate, Lower Bristol Road, Bath, BA2 3DP
Activities: Renting and leasing of cars and light motor vehicles
Parent: Redde PLC
Officers: Nicholas Paul Tilley, Secretary; Mark Francis Chessman [1964] Director; Stephen Edward Oakley [1952] Director; Martin Ward [1967] Managing Director

Avalon Plastics Limited
Incorporated: 15 October 2003 *Employees:* 162
Net Worth: £3,276,309 *Total Assets:* £7,445,487
Registered Office: Unit 1 Genesis Three, Morland Road, Morlands Enterprise Park, Glastonbury, Somerset, BA6 9FZ
Activities: Manufacture of other plastic products
Parent: Beckery Properties Ltd
Officers: Helen Sarah Jones, Secretary; Keith Butler [1960] Director; Richard David Charles Winterbottom [1966] Managing Director

Avalon Sciences Limited
Incorporated: 16 July 1987 *Employees:* 57
Net Worth: £5,488,766 *Total Assets:* £7,039,238
Registered Office: Avalon House, Somerton Business Park, Somerton, Somerset, TA11 6SB
Activities: Manufacture of electronic measuring, testing etc. equipment, not for industrial process control
Officers: Sarah Tubridy, Secretary; Gary Valentine Tubridy [1958] Director/Electronic Engineer; Sarah Tubridy [1960] Director/Solicitor

Avantage (Cheshire) Holdings Limited
Incorporated: 24 April 2007
Net Worth: £999 *Total Assets:* £3,715,446
Registered Office: Third Floor, Broad Quay House, Prince Street, Bristol, BS1 4DJ
Activities: Activities of head offices
Shareholders: Your Housing Limited; DIF Infra 3 UK Limited
Officers: Louis Javier Falero [1977] Director/Fund Manager; Stephen Mark Fensom [1966] Director; Karl Hearfield [1983] Director/Accountant; Angela Louise Roshier [1975] Director/Asset Management

Avantage (Cheshire) Limited
Incorporated: 24 April 2007
Net Worth: £1,513,215 *Total Assets:* £53,761,640
Registered Office: Third Floor, Broad Quay House, Prince Street, Bristol, BS1 4DJ
Activities: Other accommodation
Parent: Avantage (Cheshire) Holdings Limited
Officers: Louis Javier Falero [1977] Director/Fund Manager; Stephen Mark Fensom [1966] Director; Karl Hearfield [1983] Director/Accountant; Angela Louise Roshier [1975] Director/Asset Management

Avec Trade Limited
Incorporated: 12 June 2012
Net Worth: £639,125 *Total Assets:* £3,956,219
Registered Office: 9 The Old Pottery, Manor Way, Verwood, Dorset, BH31 6HF
Activities: Management consultancy activities other than financial management
Officers: Rebekah Anne Beere [1975] Director/Consultant; Stefan Lanslots [1970] Director [Dutch]

Avenue 64 Limited
Incorporated: 15 June 2011 *Employees:* 2
Net Worth: £8,956,000 *Total Assets:* £22,974,000
Registered Office: c/o Cobham PLC, Brook Road, Wimborne, Dorset, BH21 2BJ
Activities: Wireless telecommunications activities
Parent: Lockman Electronic Holdings Limited
Officers: Philip Dyer, Secretary; Gavin James Baverstock [1973] Finance Director; Serge Dujardin [1959] Managing Director [Belgian]; Paul Emmanuel Kahn [1966] Director

Averys of Bristol Limited
Incorporated: 29 October 1942 *Employees:* 39
Net Worth Deficit: £3,847,433 *Total Assets:* £8,080,984
Registered Office: 9a Culver Street, Bristol, BS1 5LD
Activities: Retail sale via mail order houses or via Internet
Parent: Direct Wines Holdings Limited
Officers: David Andrew Thatcher [1962] Managing Director; James William Hartland Weir [1965] Director

Aviation & Defence Spares Limited
Incorporated: 15 February 1990 *Employees:* 17
Net Worth: £2,608,831 *Total Assets:* £6,184,321
Registered Office: Unit 3 Branksome Business Park, Bourne Valley Road, Poole, Dorset, BH12 1DW
Activities: Non-specialised wholesale trade
Shareholders: James Nicholas Molyneux Gordon; Matthew Charles Gordon; Nicholas Peter Gordon
Officers: Jennifer Ann Gordon, Secretary; James Nicholas Molyneux Gordon [1975] Sales & Marketing Director; Jennifer Ann Gordon [1941] Director; Matthew Charles Gordon [1973] Director; Nicholas Peter Gordon [1940] Director/Chairman

Aviation Requirements Ltd
Incorporated: 11 March 2003 *Employees:* 9
Net Worth: £3,209,719 *Total Assets:* £4,351,270
Registered Office: 33 Spa Road, Weymouth, Dorset, DT3 5EP
Activities: Management consultancy activities other than financial management
Shareholders: Heather Ann Gane; Stephen Edward Leggett
Officers: Heather Ann Gane, Secretary/Finance Officer; Jason Peter Becker [1971] Director/Aerospace Engineer; Daniel John Denham [1974] Director; Heather Ann Gane [1955] Director/Finance Officer; Stephen Edward Leggett [1953] Director/Engineer

Aviation Training International Limited
Incorporated: 8 January 1998 *Employees:* 78
Net Worth: £32,558,000 *Total Assets:* £35,237,000
Registered Office: Coldharbour Business Park, Sherborne, Dorset, DT9 4JW
Activities: Other professional, scientific and technical activities n.e.c.
Shareholders: The Boeing Company; AgustaWestland Limited
Officers: John Jeffrey Cooper [1967] Training and Professional Services Director [American]; David John Pitchforth [1965] Director/Engineer; Paul Michael Woodfield [1975] Finance Director

Avon Automotive UK Holdings Limited
Incorporated: 30 May 2006 *Employees:* 42
Net Worth: £23,199,044 *Total Assets:* £32,729,300
Registered Office: Unit 5 Westpoint Business Park, Bumpers Farm, Chippenham, Wilts, SN14 6RB
Activities: Manufacture of other rubber products
Parent: MGI Coutier SA
Officers: Mathieu Xavier Coutier [1975] Director/President of The Executive Board [French]; David John Ledwitch [1962] Product Line Director; Leland Jon Richards [1964] Director [American]

Avon Care Homes Limited
Incorporated: 22 April 1999 *Employees:* 66
Net Worth: £2,261,176 *Total Assets:* £4,366,714
Registered Office: Avon Care Homes Ltd, Mendip Court, Bath Road, Wells, Somerset, BA5 3DG
Activities: Other business support service activities n.e.c.
Parent: MCB Investments Limited
Officers: Maria Cristina Bila [1959] Director/Nursing Home Proprietor [Portuguese]

Avon Energy Limited
Incorporated: 9 September 2003 *Employees:* 1
Net Worth: £8,765,777 *Total Assets:* £8,853,063
Registered Office: 63 Heathfields, Downend, Bristol, BS16 6HT
Activities: Other letting and operating of own or leased real estate
Major Shareholder: Tariq Masood
Officers: Tariq Masood [1957] Director

Avon Engineered Rubber Limited
Incorporated: 22 June 2007
Net Worth: £2,357,450 *Total Assets:* £6,351,335
Registered Office: The Avon Building, Units 137-145 South Liberty Lane, Bedminster, Bristol, BS3 2TL
Activities: Manufacture of other rubber products
Parent: Avon Group Manufacturing (Holdings) Ltd
Officers: Ashok Ravjibhai Patel, Secretary; Kevin Harrop [1965] Managing Director; Ashok Ravjibhai Patel [1957] Director; Mark Andrew Rushin [1971] Director/Management

Avon Group Manufacturing (Holdings) Limited
Incorporated: 6 January 1995 *Employees:* 657
Net Worth: £16,167,043 *Total Assets:* £44,452,888
Registered Office: The Avon Building, Units 137-145 South Liberty Lane, Bedminster, Bristol, BS3 2TL
Activities: Activities of head offices
Major Shareholder: Mark Andrew Rushin
Officers: Ashok Ravjibhai Patel, Secretary; Kevin Harrop [1965] Director; Maria Lewis [1972] Director; Ahsok Ravjibhai Patel [1957] Director; Mark Andrew Rushin [1971] Director/Manager

Avon Metals Limited
Incorporated: 4 January 2001 *Employees:* 59
Net Worth: £13,309,577 *Total Assets:* £17,226,724
Registered Office: Ashville Road, Gloucester, GL2 5DA
Activities: Aluminium production
Major Shareholder: Walter Reid
Officers: Robin John Jones, Secretary; Philip John Brewer [1967] Director; Richard Lewis [1984] Commercial Director; Richard John McAlister-Martin [1967] Technical & Compliance Director; Steven Peter Munnoch [1978] Managing Director; Walter Reid [1955] Director; James William Verdon [1952] Operation Director

Avon Polymer Products Limited
Incorporated: 10 January 1918 *Employees:* 214
Net Worth: £166,895 *Total Assets:* £52,805,380
Registered Office: HQ, Hampton Park West, Semington Road, Melksham, Wilts, SN12 6NB
Activities: Manufacture of other rubber products
Parent: Avon Rubber P.L.C.
Officers: Miles Ingrey-Counter, Secretary; Miles Ingrey-Counter [1973] Director/Solicitor; Nicholas James Keveth [1969] Finance Director; Leon Klapwijk [1965] Director/Divisional Head - Protection [Dutch]; Paul Anthony McDonald [1974] Director/Divisional Head - Dairy; Craig Sage [1971] Director/Divisional Head - Dairy

Avon Rubber Overseas Limited
Incorporated: 2 October 1926
Net Worth: £54,470,196 *Total Assets:* £71,149,728
Registered Office: HQ, Hampton Park West, Semington Road, Melksham, Wilts, SN12 6NB
Activities: Activities of head offices
Parent: Avon Rubber P.L.C.
Officers: Miles Ingrey-Counter, Secretary; Miles Ingrey-Counter [1973] Director/Solicitor; Nicholas James Keveth [1969] Finance Director; Paul Anthony McDonald [1974] Director/Divisional Head - Dairy

Avon Rubber P.L.C.
Incorporated: 23 December 1890 *Employees:* 781
Net Worth: £84,800,000 *Total Assets:* £166,100,000
Registered Office: Hampton Park West, Semington Road, Melksham, Wilts, SN12 6NB
Activities: Manufacture of other rubber products
Officers: Miles Ingrey-Counter, Secretary; David Roger Evans [1946] Director/Chairman; Nicholas James Keveth [1969] Finance Director; Paul Anthony McDonald [1974] Director/Chief Executive Officer; Lady Chloe Patricia Ponsonby [1975] Director; Petrus Rudolf Maria Vervaat [1965] Director/Chief Executive [Dutch]

Avon Specialty Metals Limited
Incorporated: 2 August 2012 *Employees:* 18
Net Worth: £1,222,058 *Total Assets:* £10,634,772
Registered Office: Ashville Works, Ashville Road, Gloucester, GL2 5DA
Activities: Wholesale of metals and metal ores
Parent: Avon Metals Limited
Officers: Philip John Brewer [1967] Director; Steven David Cutler [1972] Director/MD; Richard Lewis [1984] Commercial Director; Steven Peter Munnoch [1978] Director; Walter Reid [1955] Director

Avon Valley Holdings Limited
Incorporated: 3 July 2008 *Employees:* 161
Net Worth: £4,700,537 *Total Assets:* £9,263,962
Registered Office: King Street, Wilton, Salisbury, Wilts, SP2 0AY
Activities: Activities of head offices
Shareholders: Peter Francis Lecount; Christopher Simon Brammall; David Clemo
Officers: Peter Francis Lecount, Secretary; Christopher Simon Brammall [1954] Director; David Clemo [1939] Director; Peter Francis Lecount [1956] Director

Avon Valley Precision Engineering Limited
Incorporated: 5 February 1997 *Employees:* 53
Net Worth: £1,830,529 *Total Assets:* £5,203,502
Registered Office: Unit A, 34 Bath Road, Bitton, Bristol, BS30 6HZ
Activities: Manufacture of other fabricated metal products n.e.c.
Parent: AVPE Investment Limited
Officers: Mark Edward Ashley Summers, Secretary; Clark Iles [1959] Director; Mark Edward Ashley Summers [1967] Director/Accountant

Avon Wildlife Trust
Incorporated: 2 May 1980 *Employees:* 42
Net Worth: £6,941,323 *Total Assets:* £7,395,381
Registered Office: 32 Jacobs Wells Road, Bristol, BS8 1DR
Activities: Other professional, scientific and technical activities n.e.c.
Officers: Madeleine Clara Elizabeth Bartlett [1989] Director/Programmes Officer; Emma Louise Beeston [1970] Director/Fundraising Consultant; Martin Lindsay Brasher [1953] Director/Retired Civil Servant; Christopher John Curling [1950] Director/Retired; Katharine Elizabeth Finn [1968] Director/Chartered Accountant; Michael James Harris [1981] Director/Town Planner; Professor Jane Memmott [1962] Director/University Professor; Nigel Morrison [1963] Director/Chartered Accountant; John Zac Nicholson [1974] Director/Architect; David Charles John Relph [1971] Director/Founder of Howplaceswork; Nathan Chares Rutter [1990] Director/Teacher; Malcolm Shepherd [1948] Retired Director

Avonbourne International Business and Enterprise Academy Trust
Incorporated: 23 May 2012 *Employees:* 296
Net Worth: £24,716,618 *Total Assets:* £31,048,400
Registered Office: Avonbourne International Business and Enterprise College, Harewood Avenue, Bournemouth, BH7 6NY
Activities: General secondary education
Officers: Joanne Cox, Secretary; Bernadette Bowler [1964] Director; Jonathan Robert Mills Bowser [1963] Director/Senior Building Services Manager; Deborah Teresa Godfrey-Phaure [1962] Director/Headteacher; Stephen James Ridges [1970] Director/Information Technology; Angela Mary Rook [1967] Business Services and Support Director; Councillor Lawrence Williams [1950] Director/Local Government Officer

Avondale Builders Limited
Incorporated: 15 October 1964 *Employees:* 3
Net Worth: £3,656,082 *Total Assets:* £4,141,839
Registered Office: Centenary House, Peninsula Park, Rydon Lane, Exeter, EX2 7XE
Activities: Development of building projects
Major Shareholder: Christopher John Hall
Officers: Christopher John Hall [1958] Director

Avonline Holdings Limited
Incorporated: 12 May 2016 *Employees:* 49
Net Worth: £612,705 *Total Assets:* £8,839,866
Registered Office: 42 Ashton Vale Road, Bristol, BS3 2AX
Activities: Activities of other holding companies n.e.c.
Major Shareholder: Estate of Mark David Wynn
Officers: Leila Wynn, Secretary; Helen Drew-Bradley [1963] Director; Leila Wynn [1963] Director

Avonline Network Services Holdings Limited
Incorporated: 12 May 2016 *Employees:* 61
Net Worth: £153,942 *Total Assets:* £4,992,650
Registered Office: 42 Ashton Vale Road, Bristol, BS3 2AX
Activities: Activities of other holding companies n.e.c.
Major Shareholder: Estate of Mark David Wynn
Officers: Leila Wynn, Secretary; Helen Drew-Bradley [1963] Director; Leila Wynn [1963] Director

Avonline Network Services Limited
Incorporated: 26 May 2016 *Employees:* 61
Net Worth: £895,028 *Total Assets:* £5,733,736
Registered Office: 42 Ashton Vale Road, Bristol, BS3 2AX
Activities: Wired telecommunications activities
Parent: Avonline Network Services Holdings Limited
Officers: Leila Wynn, Secretary; Helen Drew-Bradley [1963] Director; Leila Wynn [1963] Director

Avonline PLC
Incorporated: 21 April 1999 *Employees:* 49
Net Worth: £612,703 *Total Assets:* £8,839,866
Registered Office: 42-44 Ashton Vale Road, Bristol, BS3 2AX
Activities: Construction of utility projects for electricity and telecommunications
Parent: Avonline Holdings Ltd
Officers: Leila Wynn, Secretary; Helen Drew-Bradley [1963] Financial Director; Leila Wynn [1963] Director

Avortex Limited
Incorporated: 21 December 2006 *Employees:* 2
Net Worth: £21,008 *Total Assets:* £9,220,845
Registered Office: 12 Old Mills Industrial Estate, Paulton, Bristol, BS39 7SU
Activities: Agents specialised in the sale of other particular products
Shareholders: Lui Kisagun; Emir Kisagun
Officers: Lui Kisagun [1952] Director

Avsan Holdings Limited
Incorporated: 16 September 2009 *Employees:* 8
Net Worth Deficit: £4,595,834 *Total Assets:* £6,457,263
Registered Office: Bupa Dental Care, Vantage Office Park, Old Gloucester Road, Hambrook, Bristol, BS16 1GW
Activities: Activities of head offices
Parent: Xeon Smiles UK Limited
Officers: Robin James Bryant [1970] Director/Dentist; Steven John Preddy [1959] Director/Dentist; Gabriela Pueyo Roberts [1974] Director/General Manager [Spanish]; Dr Ian David Wood [1956] Director/Dentist; Jake Stephen Hockley Wright [1972] Director

Axell Wireless Limited
Incorporated: 25 July 2000 *Employees:* 139
Net Worth: £14,244,000 *Total Assets:* £40,314,000
Registered Office: c/o Cobham PLC, Brook Road, Wimborne, Dorset, BH21 2BJ
Activities: Wireless telecommunications activities
Parent: Avenue 64 Limited
Officers: Philip Dyer, Secretary; Gavin James Baverstock [1973] Finance Director; Serge Dujardin [1959] Director [Belgian]

Axiom Process Limited
Incorporated: 6 April 2001 *Employees:* 29
Net Worth: £3,524,000 *Total Assets:* £3,524,000
Registered Office: Stonedale Road, Oldends Lane Industrial Estate, Stonehouse, Glos, GL10 3RQ
Activities: Dormant company
Parent: National Oilwell Varco UK Limited
Officers: Alison May Sloan, Secretary; Robbert Oudendijk [1974] Director/Vice President Finance Europe, MENA, CIS [Dutch]; Simon Scott Reid [1982] Director/Accountant

Axiom Veterinary Laboratories Limited
Incorporated: 1 August 1990 *Employees:* 103
Net Worth: £4,110,000 *Total Assets:* £6,073,000
Registered Office: The Manor House, Brunel Road, Newton Abbot, Devon, TQ12 4PB
Activities: Veterinary activities
Parent: CVS (UK) Limited
Officers: Richard Aidan John Gilligan, Secretary; Richard Fairman [1967] Director; Simon Campbell Innes [1960] Director/Chief Executive

Axminster Carpets Limited
Incorporated: 26 March 2013 *Employees:* 141
Net Worth Deficit: £6,255,221 *Total Assets:* £5,970,190
Registered Office: Gamberlake, Woodmead Road, Axminster, Devon, EX13 5PQ
Activities: Manufacture of woven or tufted carpets and rugs
Parent: H. Dawson Sons and Company (Wool) Limited
Officers: Gary Bridge [1966] Director; Jo Harry Dawson [1972] Director; Jonathan Young [1960] Sales Director

Axminster Tool Centre Ltd
Incorporated: 4 March 1997 *Employees:* 285
Net Worth: £4,513,342 *Total Assets:* £18,443,076
Registered Office: Unit 10 Weycroft Avenue, Axminster, Devon, EX13 5PH
Activities: Wholesale of machine tools
Officers: Jane Boulton [1966] Director; Martin Joseph Brown [1961] Director; Hayley Jean Jones [1986] Director; Darran Calvin McLeod [1979] Director; Andrew John Parkhouse [1966] Director; Alan Victor Styles [1976] Director; Bernard George Styles [1949] Director; Ian Victor Styles [1957] Director; Katina Jean Styles [1958] Director; Michael Patton Trimble [1967] Director/Chartered Accountant

Ayersmont Limited
Incorporated: 21 December 1989 *Employees:* 99
Net Worth: £6,933,125 *Total Assets:* £11,264,325
Registered Office: Centenary House, Peninsula Park, Rydon Lane, Exeter, EX2 7XE
Activities: Activities of other holding companies n.e.c.
Shareholders: Leslie Martin Payton Hutchings; Patricia Ann Hardick
Officers: Leslie Martin Payton Hutchings, Secretary; Patricia Ann Hardick [1948] Director/Holiday Park Proprietor; Rory Alan Hardick [1974] Director; Leslie Martin Payton Hutchings [1947] Director/Chartered Surveyor

Azure Sun (Holdco) Limited
Incorporated: 2 December 2016
Net Worth Deficit: £265,804 *Total Assets:* £36,259,224
Registered Office: Windsor House, Bayshill Road, Cheltenham, Glos, GL50 3AT
Activities: Other business support service activities n.e.c.
Parent: Azure Sun Bidco Management Limited
Officers: Paula Burgess [1975] Director; Joseph Davis [1990] Director/Investment Manager; Edward Arthur Wilson [1965] Director

Azure Sun Bidco Management Limited
Incorporated: 2 December 2016
Net Worth Deficit: £94,747 *Total Assets:* £16,669,279
Registered Office: Windsor House, Bayshill Road, Cheltenham, Glos, GL50 3AT
Activities: Other business support service activities n.e.c.
Officers: Paula Burgess [1975] Director; Edward Arthur Wilson [1965] Director

B M Foods Limited
Incorporated: 31 December 2002 *Employees:* 218
Net Worth: £1,065,954 *Total Assets:* £6,668,833
Registered Office: c/o Bishop Fleming, 16 Queens Square, Bristol, BS1 4NT
Activities: Wholesale of meat and meat products
Parent: Indigo Food Group Limited
Officers: Mark Richard Sommers, Secretary; Peter James Hobbs [1980] Director; Mark Robert Woodington [1980] Director

B M J International Limited
Incorporated: 11 November 1987 *Employees:* 5
Net Worth: £7,709,479 *Total Assets:* £15,190,412
Registered Office: Carlson Suite, Building 7, Vantage Point Business Village, Mitcheldean, Glos, GL17 0DD
Activities: Other business support service activities n.e.c.
Officers: Brian John Bennett [1956] Director; Michael John Bennett [1949] Director

B T Q Limited
Incorporated: 27 November 1985 *Employees:* 454
Net Worth: £21,628,000 *Total Assets:* £26,105,000
Registered Office: Wathen Street, Staple Hill, Bristol, BS16 5LL
Activities: Manufacture of workwear
Shareholder: Alan David Dorrell
Officers: David Thompson, Secretary; Alan David Dorrell [1954] Director; Christine Irene Dorrell [1928] Director; Amanda Claire James [1954] Director; Ian Peter Mitchell [1966] Director

B.46 Trustees Ltd.
Incorporated: 1 September 2014 *Employees:* 193
Previous: Bourne Group Ltd
Net Worth: £15,655,843 *Total Assets:* £32,546,104
Registered Office: St Clements House, St Clements Road, Parkstone, Poole, Dorset, BH12 4GP
Activities: Activities of construction holding companies
Shareholders: Howard Davis; Stephen Philip William Govier
Officers: Howard Davis [1972] Director; Stephen Philip William Govier [1966] Director

B.A.I. (U.K.), Limited
Incorporated: 7 November 1972 *Employees:* 392
Net Worth: £4,814,483 *Total Assets:* £9,520,492
Registered Office: Millbay, Plymouth, PL1 3EW
Activities: Sea and coastal passenger water transport
Parent: BAI SA
Officers: John Joe Charles Napton, Secretary; Christophe Bernard Francois Mathieu [1968] Group Strategy & Commercial Director [French]; John Joe Charles Napton [1972] Company Secretary/Director; Jean-Marc Roue [1968] Director/Farmer & Chairman [French]; Corinne Pierrette Vintner [1962] Director/Legal and Insurance Services Manager [French]

B.G. Automotive Limited
Incorporated: 22 September 1998 *Employees:* 78
Net Worth: £5,076,398 *Total Assets:* £7,562,844
Registered Office: BGA House, Cheney Manor Industrial Estate, Swindon, Wilts, SN2 2DS
Activities: Wholesale trade of motor vehicle parts and accessories
Shareholders: British Gaskets Ltd; 4BG Group Ltd
Officers: Joanne White, Secretary; Christopher Cameron [1960] Sales Director; Matthew Greener [1979] Marketing Director; Roy David Jones [1957] Director; Yuko Jones [1962] Director [Japanese]; Andrew Thurlbourn [1961] Director

B.T.C. Activewear Holdings Limited
Incorporated: 3 February 2010
Net Worth Deficit: £152,544 *Total Assets:* £6,346,117
Registered Office: 2 Temple Back East, Temple Quay, Bristol, BS1 6EG
Activities: Activities of distribution holding companies
Parent: Falk & Ross Group (UK) Limited
Officers: Stephen Michael Pope [1960] Managing Director; Jens Wahl [1973] Director [German]

B4 Claims Limited
Incorporated: 30 September 2004 *Employees:* 3
Net Worth: £4,128,891 *Total Assets:* £6,905,674
Registered Office: 7 Farleigh Court, Old Weston Road, Flax Bourton, Bristol, BS48 1UR
Activities: Financial intermediation not elsewhere classified
Parent: B4 Group Limited
Officers: Rowena Palmer, Secretary; Anthony Richard Thomas Instrall [1968] Director; John Alexander Palmer [1961] Director

B4 Marketing Limited
Incorporated: 30 September 2004 *Employees:* 2
Net Worth Deficit: £3,941,108 *Total Assets:* £6,070,895
Registered Office: 7 Farleigh Court, Old Weston Road, Flax Bourton, Bristol, BS48 1UR
Activities: Other business support service activities n.e.c.
Parent: B4 Group Limited
Officers: Rowena Palmer, Secretary; Anthony Richard Thomas Instrall [1968] Director; John Alexander Palmer [1961] Director

BA Technologies Holdings Limited
Incorporated: 18 December 2013 *Employees:* 82
Previous: Ben Ainslie Racing (Holdings) Limited
Net Worth Deficit: £3,987,770 *Total Assets:* £28,061,840
Registered Office: Towngate House, 2-8 Parkstone Road, Poole, Dorset, BH15 2PW
Activities: Activities of other holding companies n.e.c.
Shareholder: Charles William Dunstone
Officers: Sir Charles Benedict Ainslie [1977] Director; Christopher Paul Bake [1963] Director; Sir Charles William Dunstone [1964] Director; Jon Paul Wood [1961] Director/Fund Manager

B.& M. Babbage & Co. Limited
Incorporated: 20 February 1984 *Employees:* 55
Net Worth: £2,608,521 *Total Assets:* £3,601,871
Registered Office: Deer Park, Brockhampton, Andoversford, Cheltenham, Glos, GL54 5SR
Activities: Construction of commercial buildings
Shareholders: Vance Brian Babbage; Gary Jessie Babbage
Officers: Gary Jessie Babbage, Secretary/Builder; Gary Jessie Babbage [1965] Director/Builder; Vance Brian Babbage [1960] Director/Builder

Babcock Marine (Devonport) Limited
Incorporated: 17 August 1994
Net Worth: £139,842,000 *Total Assets:* £199,315,008
Registered Office: c/o Devonport Royal Dockyard Ltd, Devonport, Plymouth, PL1 4SG
Activities: Activities of other holding companies n.e.c.
Parent: Babcock Marine & Technology Holdings Limited
Officers: Julia Mary Wood, Secretary; Gary Lambert [1966] Director; Iain Stuart Urquhart [1965] Director

Back Catalogue Distribution Ltd
Incorporated: 1 December 2014 *Employees:* 2
Net Worth: £5,076,869 *Total Assets:* £5,170,067
Registered Office: 1350-1360 Montpellier Court, Brockworth, Gloucester, GL3 4AH
Activities: Television programme production activities
Parent: Blackfinch Nominees
Officers: Terence Alan James Back [1953] Director; Richard James Cook [1978] Director

Badham Pharmacy Limited
Incorporated: 17 January 2006 *Employees:* 151
Net Worth: £4,917,455 *Total Assets:* £14,865,271
Registered Office: The Old Farmers Arms, Evesham Road, Bishops Cleeve, Cheltenham, Glos, GL52 8SA
Activities: Dispensing chemist in specialised stores
Shareholders: Peter Simon Stephen Badham; Linda Mary Badham
Officers: Peter Simon Stephen Badham, Secretary/Pharmaceutical Chemist; Charles Richard Badham [1983] Director/Pharmacist; Linda Mary Badham [1956] Director/Supervisor; Peter Simon Stephen Badham [1956] Director/Pharmaceutical Chemist; Helen Josephine Ireland [1981] Director/Pharmacist; Stephen Douglas Ireland [1980] Director/IT Consultant

Badminton School Limited
Incorporated: 10 June 1931 *Employees:* 223
Net Worth: £7,236,631 *Total Assets:* £15,175,909
Registered Office: Badminton School, Westbury Road, Westbury on Trym, Bristol, BS9 3BA
Activities: Pre-primary education
Parent: Badminton School Trust
Officers: Emma Diana Sandberg, Secretary; Dr Michael Albert John Chamberlain [1948] Director/Publisher/Company Chair; Justin Thomas Selwyn Chippendale [1966] Director/Headmaster; Andrew John Couper [1968] Director/Actuary; Professor Jennifer Daley [1965] Director/University Lecturer [American]; Helen Louise Jackson [1961] Director/Bursar; Alison Jarratt [1970] Director/Bursar; Adenrele Dlufunmilayo Joseph [1956] Director/Lawyer; Sibella Churchward Laing [1949] Director/School Governor; Justin Dominic Lewis [1959] Director/Consultancy; Sarah Jane Mumford [1957] Director/Solicitor; Dr Sophie Helen Otton [1968] Director/Doctor; Ian Edward George Ray [1954] Group Managing Director; Lynda Ann Thomas [1972] Director/Solicitor; Amy Louise Wallace [1980] Director/Deputy Head; Amanda Claire Webb [1964] Director; Heather Jane Wheelhouse [1964] Director/Accountant

BAEMS Limited
Incorporated: 21 February 2017
Net Worth: £337,807 *Total Assets:* £3,665,255
Registered Office: Grosvenor House, 1 New Road, Brixham, Devon, TQ5 8LZ
Activities: Other human health activities
Major Shareholder: Shaun David Pillinger
Officers: Shaun David Pillinger [1969] Director

Baglan Moor Healthcare Holdings Limited
Incorporated: 10 August 1999
Net Worth: £53,000 *Total Assets:* £13,410,000
Registered Office: Third Floor, Broad Quay House, Prince Street, Bristol, BS1 4DJ
Activities: Activities of head offices
Parent: Semperian PPP Investment Partners No.2 Limited
Officers: Andrew Richard Kershaw [1965] Director/Projects Controller; Richard Little [1979] Investment Director; Harvey John William Pownall [1966] Director

Baglan Moor Healthcare PLC
Incorporated: 1 March 1999
Net Worth: £4,082,000 *Total Assets:* £83,447,000
Registered Office: Third Floor, Broad Quay House, Prince Street, Bristol, BS1 4DJ
Activities: Non-trading company
Parent: Baglan Moor Healthcare Holdings Limited
Officers: Andrew Richard Kershaw [1965] Director/Projects Controller; Richard Little [1979] Investment Director; Harvey John William Pownall [1966] Director

Bailey Caravans Limited
Incorporated: 26 June 1939 *Employees:* 461
Net Worth: £7,191,399 *Total Assets:* £48,366,048
Registered Office: Bailey Caravans Ltd, South Liberty Lane, Bristol, BS3 2SS
Activities: Manufacture of caravans
Parent: Keenwork Limited
Officers: Jonathan Robert Aisbitt [1957] Director; Nicholas George Howard [1968] Technical Director; Simon Richard Howard [1966] Marketing Director; Stephen Paul Howard [1941] Director; Ian Matthew Rawlings [1979] Director; Andrew John Rowles [1963] Director; John Alexander Tanner [1960] Director; Steven Paul Trossell [1949] Director/Management Consultant

Bailey Holdings Limited
Incorporated: 27 November 2006
Net Worth: £1,976,994 *Total Assets:* £4,955,442
Registered Office: Venayr Goonearl, Scorrier, Redruth, Cornwall, TR16 5EB
Activities: Other letting and operating of own or leased real estate
Shareholder: Mark Bailey
Officers: Kathryn Mary Bailey, Secretary/Manager; Kathryn Mary Bailey [1974] Director/Manager

Adam Bailey Limited
Incorporated: 24 July 2007 *Employees:* 81
Net Worth: £2,783,661 *Total Assets:* £12,163,598
Registered Office: Chippenham Motor Company, Bumpers Way, Bumpers Farm, Chippenham, Wilts, SN14 6LF
Activities: Sale of new cars and light motor vehicles
Officers: Lauren Sophie Bailey, Secretary; Adam John Bailey [1967] Director; Jacqueline Anita Bailey [1968] Director

M Baker (Holdings) Limited
Incorporated: 27 April 1977 *Employees:* 2
Net Worth: £5,743,131 *Total Assets:* £5,916,500
Registered Office: Senate Court, Southernhay Gardens, Exeter, Devon, EX1 1NT
Activities: Activities of head offices
Shareholders: Andrew Tweedie Baker; Nicola Jane Lesser-Easby
Officers: Andrew Edward Browne [1966] Director/Accountant; Simon Hugh Gregory [1955] Director/Solicitor

M Baker (Newquay) Limited
Incorporated: 7 July 2010
Net Worth: £1,217,385 *Total Assets:* £6,141,287
Registered Office: Senate Court, Southernhay Gardens, Exeter, Devon, EX1 1NT
Activities: Other letting and operating of own or leased real estate
Parent: M Baker (Holdings) Limited
Officers: Andrew Edward Browne [1966] Director/Accountant; Simon Hugh Gregory [1955] Director/Solicitor

M. Baker (Property Services) Limited
Incorporated: 22 February 1983 *Employees:* 2
Net Worth: £5,175,774 *Total Assets:* £18,170,264
Registered Office: Senate Court, Southernhay Gardens, Exeter, Devon, EX1 1NT
Activities: Development of building projects
Shareholders: Simon Hugh Gregory; Andrew Edward Browne
Officers: Andrew Edward Browne [1966] Director/Accountant; Simon Hugh Gregory [1955] Director/Solicitor

M Baker (Retail) Limited
Incorporated: 6 September 2012
Net Worth: £1,290,846 *Total Assets:* £12,834,470
Registered Office: Senate Court, Southernhay Gardens, Southernhay, Exeter, EX1 1NT
Activities: Buying and selling of own real estate
Parent: M Baker (Holdings) Limited
Officers: Andrew Edward Browne [1966] Director/Accountant; Simon Hugh Gregory [1955] Director/Solicitor

Baker Estates Limited
Incorporated: 30 September 2015 *Employees:* 20
Net Worth: £454,939 *Total Assets:* £42,288,220
Registered Office: Green Tree House, Silverhills Road, Decoy Industrial Estate, Newton Abbot, Devon, TQ12 5LZ
Activities: Development of building projects
Shareholders: Gregory Paul Fitzgerald; John Stafford Dunningham
Officers: Ian Baker [1970] Director; John Stafford Dunningham [1936] Director; Greg Paul FitzGenerald [1964] Director

M.J. Baker Foodservice Limited
Incorporated: 18 November 1998 *Employees:* 115
Net Worth: £5,326,612 *Total Assets:* £8,221,283
Registered Office: 21 Fairfax Road, Heathfield, Newton Abbot, Devon, TQ12 6UD
Activities: Other food services
Major Shareholder: Malcolm John Baker
Officers: Elaine Grant, Secretary; Josephine Helen Baker [1969] Managing Director; Malcolm John Baker [1957] Director/Chairman; Gary Fice [1960] Buying Director; Elaine Grant [1965] Finance Director

GP & J Baker Limited
Incorporated: 28 April 1999 *Employees:* 83
Net Worth: £4,226,576 *Total Assets:* £7,659,667
Registered Office: 6 Stinsford Road, Poole, Dorset, BH17 0SW
Activities: Wholesale of wood, construction materials and sanitary equipment
Officers: Lisa Kravet, Secretary; Ellen Kravet Burke [1954] Director Fabric Manufacturer [American]; Ann Grafton [1959] Managing Director; Cary Kravet [1957] Director Fabric Manufacturer [American]; Lisa Kravet [1958] Director Fabric Manufacturer [American]

F.A.W. Baker's Kingston Farms Limited
Incorporated: 18 July 1960 *Employees:* 38
Net Worth: £3,729,169 *Total Assets:* £10,313,693
Registered Office: Leaze Farm, Haselbury Plucknett, Crewkerne, Somerset, TA18 7RJ
Activities: Raising of dairy cattle
Shareholders: Neil Christopher Baker; Christine Margaret Baker
Officers: Christine Margaret Baker, Secretary; Christine Margaret Baker [1945] Director/Farm Secretary/Farmer; Neil Christopher Baker [1972] Director/Farm Manager

Bakers Coaches Limited
Incorporated: 22 September 1998 *Employees:* 122
Net Worth: £2,254,564 *Total Assets:* £5,298,996
Registered Office: 48 Locking Road, Weston-Super-Mare, Avon, BS23 3DN
Activities: Tour operator activities
Shareholders: John Theodore Nowell Baker; Robert Herbert Reading Baker
Officers: Stephen Keith Hunt, Secretary; Kevin Fasham Abbey [1946] Director; John Theodore Nowell Baker [1944] Director; Margaret Joyce Baker [1939] Director/Travel Consultant; Robert Herbert Reading Baker [1939] Director; Amanda Jane Theresa Fletcher [1966] Director; Lionel Max Fletcher [1966] Director; Stephen Keith Hunt [1973] Financial Director; Christopher John Sims [1956] Finance Director; Andrew Granville Smith [1947] Director

John Balaam Limited
Incorporated: 10 January 1947 *Employees:* 5
Net Worth: £3,099,080 *Total Assets:* £3,871,111
Registered Office: 10 Bridge Street, Christchurch, Dorset, BH23 1EF
Activities: Other letting and operating of own or leased real estate
Shareholders: Jacqueline Anne Howells; Deborah Jayne Balaam; Linda Diane Farrow
Officers: David John Balaam [1932] Director; Deborah Jayne Balaam [1961] Business Director

Balcarras School
Incorporated: 17 January 2011 *Employees:* 189
Net Worth: £8,099,256 *Total Assets:* £10,484,465
Registered Office: Balcarras School, East End Road, Charlton Kings, Cheltenham, Glos, GL53 8QF
Activities: General secondary education
Officers: Richard Boulton [1968] Film Director; Dominic Liam Burke [1977] Director/Headteacher; Daren David Coull Hazael [1967] Director/Teacher; Clive Hodges [1950] Director/Retired; Karen Louise Holdsworth [1973] Director/Financial Controller; Sarah Jane Holtom-Fawcett [1971] Director/Social Worker; Peter Royston Horne [1966] Charity Assistant Chief Director; Pak Wai Hung [1973] Director/Restaurant Owner; Michiel Peter Huysinga [1967] Director [Dutch]; Howard Kellett [1963] Director/Clergyman; Richard John Leftley [1973] Director; Joanna Elizabeth McGuire [1966] Director/Recruitment Manager; Adrienne Joanne Niblett [1981] Director/Teacher; Bernard Stephen Roberts [1952] Director/Retired; Sarah Robertson [1964] Education Director; Rosalind May Ann Shepherd [1964] Director/Nurse; Geoffrey Peter Sparkes [1947] Director/Retired; James Philip Sweeting [1982] Director/Solicitor; Kate Lucy Wilkey [1973] Director/Administrator

Balimark Limited
Incorporated: 18 March 1997 *Employees:* 4
Net Worth: £242,237 *Total Assets:* £8,136,586
Registered Office: Ruardean Works, Varnister Road, Drybrook, Glos, GL17 9BH
Activities: Development of building projects
Parent: M F Freeman Developments Limited
Officers: Jennifer Mary Freeman, Secretary; Jennifer Mary Freeman [1947] Director/Manager; Luke Francis Freeman [1974] Director/Civil Engineer; Mervyn Francis Freeman [1945] Director; Steven King [1970] Director/Chartered Accountant; Peter Wharton [1963] Director/Chartered Accountant

Ball Aerocan UK Limited
Incorporated: 2 May 1984 *Employees:* 181
Net Worth: £19,924,000 *Total Assets:* £25,304,000
Registered Office: Folly Road, Devizes, Wilts, SN10 2HT
Activities: Manufacture of light metal packaging
Parent: AUK Holding Limited
Officers: Jacob Stoehr, Secretary; Sebastien Gaspari [1977] Director/General Manager [French]; Richard John Peachey [1965] Director/Solicitor

Ballard School Limited
Incorporated: 28 August 1962 *Employees:* 128
Net Worth: £7,310,726 *Total Assets:* £8,615,087
Registered Office: Fernhill Lane, New Milton, Hants, BH25 5SU
Activities: Pre-primary education
Officers: Rebecca Munro, Secretary; Merrielle Genevieve Billington [1952] Director/Magistrate; Peter Robert Goodfellow [1946] Director/Retired; Dr Emma Louise Halliwell [1973] Director/Consultant in Anaesthesia; Christopher Kean [1947] Director/Chartered Accountant; Fiona Elizabeth Morgan [1957] Director/Retired Solicitor; Rev Martin Robert Poole [1947] Director/Retired; Wendy Margaret Roberts [1946] Director/Retired; Susan Adrie Rogers [1960] Director/Teacher; Andrew William Stembridge [1971] Director/Hotel Manager; Jane Mary Tudor [1962] Director/Headteacher [Australian]; Anne Patricia Watson-Lee [1959] Director/Solicitor

Bambers Wind Park Limited
Incorporated: 18 October 1999
Net Worth: £16,280,143 *Total Assets:* £18,933,472
Registered Office: Lion House, Rowcroft, Stroud, Glos, GL5 3BY
Activities: Production of electricity
Parent: Ecotricity Group Limited
Officers: Thomas Cowling, Secretary; Asif Rehmanwala [1976] Director/Chief Operating Officer; Dale Vince [1961] Director/Consultant

Bamboo Technology Group Limited
Incorporated: 18 June 1998 *Employees:* 47
Previous: Total Ltd.
Net Worth: £560,844 *Total Assets:* £4,185,508
Registered Office: The Green House, 296 High Street, Cheltenham, Glos, GL50 3HQ
Activities: Other telecommunications activities
Major Shareholder: Stuart Robert Davis
Officers: Stuart Robert Davis [1971] Director; John Antony Lomer [1958] Director/Accountant; Lorrin Elizabeth White [1975] Director

Banburys Limited
Incorporated: 19 March 1925 *Employees:* 97
Net Worth: £2,961,811 *Total Assets:* £4,463,039
Registered Office: 32 High Street, Barnstaple, Devon, EX31 1BN
Activities: Other retail sale in non-specialised stores
Shareholders: David Charles Banbury; Richard John Banbury
Officers: Stuart Bennett, Secretary; David Charles Banbury [1952] Director; Peter Derren Banbury [1974] Director; Richard John Banbury [1955] Director; Robert Francis Banbury [1950] Director; Simon Elliot Banbury [1984] Director/Retailer; Stuart David Bennett [1965] Finance Director; Natasha Coddington [1973] Director/Store Manager; Andre William Potier [1931] Director/Chartered Accountant

Bandvulc Tyres Ltd
Incorporated: 30 January 1978 *Employees:* 327
Net Worth: £18,080,638 *Total Assets:* £35,733,764
Registered Office: Gillard Way, Lee Mill Industrial Estate, Ivybridge, Devon, PL21 9LN
Activities: Manufacture of rubber tyres and tubes; retreading and rebuilding of rubber tyres
Parent: Continental UK Group Holdings Limited
Officers: Mark Ingram, Secretary; Lutz Fricke [1962] Director/Business Executive [German]; Arthur Gregg [1962] Director; David Smith [1965] Director; Johannes Suttmeyer [1959] Director [German]

Bank of Ireland Britain Holdings Limited
Incorporated: 20 November 1986
Net Worth: £10,362,077 *Total Assets:* £17,881,332
Registered Office: 1 Temple Back East, Temple Quay, Bristol, BS1 6DX
Activities: Banks
Parent: Bank of Ireland UK Holdings PLC
Officers: Desmond Edward Crowley [1959] Director/Banker [Irish]; John-Anthony Greer [1977] Director/Banker; Ian Sheppard [1967] Commercial Director

Bank of Ireland Home Mortgages Limited
Incorporated: 23 August 1973
Net Worth: £3,908,748 *Total Assets:* £7,915,075
Registered Office: One Temple Quay, Temple Back East, Bristol, BS1 6DX
Activities: Non-trading company
Parent: Bank of Ireland UK Holdings PLC
Officers: John-Anthony Greer [1977] Director/Banker; Michael Patrick Joyce [1966] Director; Thomas McAreavey [1970] Director/Senior Finance Manager

Banner Limited
Incorporated: 8 December 2010 *Employees:* 110
Previous: Blue Max Banner Limited
Net Worth: £14,875,503 *Total Assets:* £28,588,204
Registered Office: Unit 5 Kennet Way, Trowbridge, Wilts, BA14 8BL
Activities: Wholesale of clothing and footwear
Parent: Blue Max Group Ltd
Officers: Bruce Royston Freeland [1967] Operations Director; Glenn Peter Leech [1975] Director/Chief Executive; Ian John Webb [1973] Director/Chief Finance Officer

Baptist Insurance Company PLC The
Incorporated: 17 February 1905
Net Worth: £6,452,000 *Total Assets:* £13,477,000
Registered Office: Beaufort House, Brunswick Road, Gloucester, GL1 1JZ
Activities: Non-life insurance
Officers: Rachael Jane Hall, Secretary; Anne Bishop [1961] Director; Malcolm Arthur Broad [1950] Director/Senior Commercial Manager; Miles Richard Buttrick [1952] Director/Retired; Malcolm Norman Hayes [1946] Director of Commercial Business; David Lane [1967] Director [Irish]; Andrew March Lawrence [1964] Director; Timothy John Rose [1959] Director; Michael Howard Tripp [1955] Director

Bapton Manor Farm Limited
Incorporated: 8 July 1946 *Employees:* 4
Net Worth: £5,518,698 *Total Assets:* £7,508,354
Registered Office: Bapton Manor, Bapton, Warminster, Wilts, BA12 0SB
Activities: Mixed farming
Shareholders: Christopher James Lyall; Christopher James Lyall (Trustee); Tracy Elizabeth Lyall (Trustee); Timothy Christian Smart (Trustee)
Officers: Christopher James Lyall, Secretary; Christopher James Lyall [1958] Director/Farmer

A.J. & R.G.Barber (Sales) Limited
Incorporated: 18 February 1963 *Employees:* 81
Net Worth: £33,893,704 *Total Assets:* £53,504,912
Registered Office: Maryland Farm, Smiths Lane, Ditcheat, Shepton Mallet, Somerset, BA4 6PR
Activities: Wholesale of dairy products, eggs and edible oils and fats
Parent: A.J. and R.G. Barber Limited
Officers: Thomas Nicholas Barber, Secretary/Farmer; Christopher Luke Barber [1966] Director/Farmer; Paul Kelson Barber [1942] Director/Farmer; Thomas Nicholas Barber [1943] Director/Farmer; Christopher Michael Newcombe [1965] Director/Certified Accountant; Michael John Pullin [1960] Director/Farmer

A.J. and R.G.Barber Limited
Incorporated: 1 July 1955 *Employees:* 369
Net Worth: £75,855,512 *Total Assets:* £98,000,216
Registered Office: Maryland Farm, Ditcheat, Shepton Mallet, Somerset, BA4 6PR
Activities: Raising of dairy cattle
Officers: Paul Kelson Barber, Secretary; Christopher Luke Barber [1966] Director/Farmer; Paul Kelson Barber [1942] Director/Farmer; Thomas Nicholas Barber [1943] Director; Christopher Michael Newcombe [1965] Director/Certified Accountant; Michael John Pullin [1960] Director/Farmer; Allan Walker [1970] Operations Director

Barden Corporation (U.K.) Limited (The)
Incorporated: 8 March 1948 *Employees:* 379
Net Worth: £26,504,696 *Total Assets:* £32,628,126
Registered Office: Plymbridge Road, Estover, Plymouth, PL6 7LH
Activities: Manufacture of bearings, gears, gearing and driving elements
Parent: Schaeffler AG
Officers: Peter Jonathan Michael Evans, Secretary; Stefan Peter Hermann Bauerreis [1972] Director/CFO Europe [German]; Jonathan Mark Everett [1966] Managing Director; Armin Necker [1976] Director [German]

Barden Network Engineering Limited
Incorporated: 29 March 1995 *Employees:* 154
Net Worth: £7,068,353 *Total Assets:* £9,265,606
Registered Office: Acorn Farm, Green Lane, Milbury Heath, Thornbury, Glos, GL12 8QW
Activities: Wired telecommunications activities
Parent: All Tel Communications Limited
Officers: Jayne Louise Morris, Secretary; Kevin John Morris [1962] Director/Operations Manager

Bardolf Farms Limited
Incorporated: 3 September 1963 *Employees:* 3
Net Worth: £2,061,085 *Total Assets:* £3,507,379
Registered Office: Burleston Farm House, Burleston, Dorchester, DT2 7EG
Activities: Mixed farming
Shareholders: Howard Jonathan Mason; Laura Elizabeth Mason
Officers: Laura Elizabeth Mason, Secretary/Housewife; Howard Jonathan Mason [1963] Director/Farmer; Laura Elizabeth Mason [1960] Director/Housewife

Baring Emerging Europe PLC
Incorporated: 11 October 2002
Net Worth: £108,333,000 *Total Assets:* £117,991,000
Registered Office: Beaufort House, 51 New North Road, Exeter, EX4 4EP
Activities: Activities of investment trusts
Officers: Frances Margaret Catherine Daley [1958] Director; Christopher Richard Granville [1963] Managing Director; Calum MacKenzie Thomson [1960] Director; Nadya Christina Wells [1970] Independent Director

Barker Care Limited
Incorporated: 29 August 1978 *Employees:* 194
Net Worth: £6,735,201 *Total Assets:* £14,855,734
Registered Office: 20 Richmond Hill, Clifton, Bristol, BS8 1BA
Activities: Medical nursing home activities
Officers: Kanoo Desai, Secretary; Ash Desai [1961] Director/Businessman; Kanoo Desai [1928] Director/Businessman; Madhu Desai [1926] Director/Businessman; Minal Desai [1966] Director

B.J. Barkwell & Sons Limited
Incorporated: 16 January 1995 *Employees:* 2
Net Worth: £2,727,641 *Total Assets:* £7,921,203
Registered Office: 31 Stallard Street, Trowbridge, Wilts, BA14 9AA
Activities: Other accommodation
Officers: Alistair Jeremy Dias [1971] Director; Jesse Herbert [1970] Director

Barkwell Plumbing & Heating Limited
Incorporated: 3 August 2016 *Employees:* 184
Net Worth: £4,378,596 *Total Assets:* £10,522,238
Registered Office: Barowe House, Beardown Road, Exeter Road Industrial Estate, Okehampton, Devon, EX20 1UA
Activities: Plumbing, heat and air-conditioning installation
Shareholders: Carol Barkwell; Robert Brian Barkwell
Officers: Carol Barkwell [1959] Director; Robert Brian Barkwell [1961] Director/Plumbing & Heating Engineer

Barmont Properties Limited
Incorporated: 17 August 2001 *Employees:* 2
Net Worth: £3,491,055 *Total Assets:* £7,851,987
Registered Office: Bath House, 6-8 Bath Street, Bristol, BS1 6HL
Activities: Renting and operating of Housing Association real estate
Shareholders: David Richard Barlow; Helen Sarah Barlow
Officers: Helen Sarah Barlow, Secretary; David Richard Barlow [1968] Managing Director

Barnbury Enterprises Limited
Incorporated: 9 January 1985 *Employees:* 28
Net Worth: £2,971,373 *Total Assets:* £4,159,187
Registered Office: 107 North Street, Martock, Somerset, TA12 6EJ
Activities: Non-specialised wholesale trade
Shareholders: Anne Pauline Frances Derrick; Brian Albert Derrick
Officers: Anne Pauline Frances Derrick, Secretary; Anne Pauline Frances Derrick [1941] Director/Secretary; Brian Albert Derrick [1936] Sales Director; Richard Byron Derrick [1967] Director/Business Development Manager; Benjamin Stanley Riley [1976] Director

Malcolm Barnecutt Bakery Limited
Incorporated: 28 May 2010 *Employees:* 206
Net Worth: £923,997 *Total Assets:* £4,744,868
Registered Office: 30 Beatrice Road, Bodmin, Cornwall, PL31 1RD
Activities: Manufacture of bread; manufacture of fresh pastry goods and cakes
Parent: Malcolm Barnecutt Bakery (Holdings) Limited
Officers: James Barnecutt, Secretary; James Barnecutt [1976] Director/Baker; Malcolm Barnecutt [1950] Director/Baker; Andrew Edmund Hallett [1969] Director

Barnet Lighting Services Limited
Incorporated: 23 November 2005
Net Worth Deficit: £2,446,416 *Total Assets:* £24,214,372
Registered Office: Third Floor, Broad Quay House, Prince Street, Bristol, BS1 4DJ
Activities: Other business support service activities n.e.c.
Parent: IIC Barnet Holding Company Limited
Officers: Paul Anthony Cartwright [1957] Director; Vikki Louise Everett [1971] Director/Project Manager; Thomas Benedict Symes [1956] Director

Luke Barnett Limited
Incorporated: 8 August 2002 *Employees:* 31
Net Worth: £2,404,672 *Total Assets:* £3,914,990
Registered Office: Bupa Dental Care, Vantage Office Park, Old Gloucester Road, Hambrook, Bristol, BS16 1GW
Activities: Dental practice activities
Parent: Xeon Smiles UK Limited
Officers: Robin James Bryant [1970] Director/Dental Surgeon; Steven John Preddy [1959] Director/Dentist; Gabriela Pueyo Roberts [1974] Director/General Manager [Spanish]; Dr Ian David Wood [1956] Director/Dental Surgeon; Jake Stephen Hockley Wright [1972] Director/Dentist

Barnwood Construction Limited
Incorporated: 24 December 1963 *Employees:* 84
Net Worth: £1,358,418 *Total Assets:* £10,688,758
Registered Office: 203 Barnwood Road, Gloucester, GL4 3HS
Activities: Construction of commercial buildings
Parent: Barnwood Group Limited
Officers: Peter Mark Evans, Secretary/Accountant; Simon William Carey [1963] Director/Chartered Surveyor; Peter Francis Evans [1958] Director/Estimator; Peter Mark Evans [1966] Director/Accountant; Stuart Michael Pearce [1962] Construction Director; David Neil Piper [1962] Director/Surveyor

Barnwood Group Limited
Incorporated: 28 April 1997 *Employees:* 237
Net Worth: £8,287,766 *Total Assets:* £24,469,636
Registered Office: 203 Barnwood Road, Gloucester, GL4 3HS
Activities: Construction of commercial buildings
Shareholder: Simon William Carey
Officers: Peter Mark Evans, Secretary/Accountant; Simon William Carey [1963] Director/Chartered Surveyor; Peter Francis Evans [1958] Director/Estimator; Peter Mark Evans [1966] Director/Accountant

Barnwood Shopfitting Limited
Incorporated: 17 November 1971 *Employees:* 102
Net Worth: £1,391,798 *Total Assets:* £6,762,696
Registered Office: 203 Barnwood Road, Gloucester, GL4 3HS
Activities: Joinery installation
Parent: Barnwood Group Limited
Officers: Peter Mark Evans, Secretary/Accountant; James William Bennett [1970] Director/Estimator; Ian Michael Brewster [1964] Director; Simon William Carey [1963] Director/Chartered Surveyor; Peter Mark Evans [1966] Director/Accountant; William John Morgan [1954] Director

A N Barr Industries Limited
Incorporated: 27 August 2010
Net Worth: £2,946,037 *Total Assets:* £3,914,697
Registered Office: Ashford House, Grenadier Road, Exeter, Devon, EX1 3LH
Activities: Management consultancy activities other than financial management
Parent: Barr Atoll Limited
Officers: Andrew Nicholson Barr [1973] Director

Julian Barran Limited
Incorporated: 18 November 1991 *Employees:* 1
Net Worth: £135,822 *Total Assets:* £4,969,324
Registered Office: Oak Apple House, North Street, Milborne Port, Sherborne, Dorset, DT9 5EW
Activities: Retail sale of antiques including antique books in stores
Major Shareholder: Julian Mark Lechmere Barran
Officers: Julian Mark Lechmere Barran [1947] Director/Fine Art Dealer

J. V. Barrett & Co. Limited
Incorporated: 5 September 1975 *Employees:* 107
Net Worth: £4,181,295 *Total Assets:* £8,564,257
Registered Office: St Ivel Way, Warmley, Bristol, BS15 5TY
Activities: Manufacture of other chemical products n.e.c.
Parent: Barrettine Holdings Ltd
Officers: Christopher Brian Randall, Secretary; Colin John Bailey [1943] Director/Company Chairman; Steven Harold Bailey [1970] Sales Director; Alan Richard Louis Greer [1959] Sales Director; Christopher Brian Randall [1968] Financial Director; David Jeffrey Spiers [1967] Production Director

Barrett Partnership Limited
Incorporated: 13 July 1951 *Employees:* 74
Previous: Hambly's (Whitstone) Limited
Net Worth: £3,730,539 *Total Assets:* £8,243,124
Registered Office: The Elms, Whitstone, Holsworthy, Devon, EX22 6TB
Activities: Other letting and operating of own or leased real estate
Shareholders: Jeanne Ann Barrett; Abel William John Barrett
Officers: Jeanne Ann Barrett, Secretary; Abel William John Barrett [1944] Director/Agricultural Engineer; Christopher Ian Barrett [1976] Director/Project Management; Jeanne Ann Barrett [1945] Director/Company Secretary; Stephen John Barrett [1972] Director/Engineer Designer

Barrettine Holdings Limited
Incorporated: 1 April 2014 *Employees:* 108
Net Worth: £6,016,737 *Total Assets:* £10,076,386
Registered Office: St Ivel Way, Warmley, Bristol, BS30 8TY
Activities: Manufacture of other chemical products n.e.c.
Shareholders: Colin John Bailey; Jeannette Bailey
Officers: Christopher Brian Randall, Secretary; Colin John Bailey [1943] Director; Steven Harold Bailey [1970] Director; Christopher Brian Randall [1968] Director; Suzanne Elizabeth Whiting [1974] Sales Director

Barrington Brown Estates Limited
Incorporated: 3 September 2002 *Employees:* 2
Net Worth: £2,171,781 *Total Assets:* £5,749,079
Registered Office: 2 Victoria Business Park, Victoria Avenue, Chard, Somerset, TA20 1HE
Activities: Development of building projects
Major Shareholder: Dominic Richard Brown
Officers: Eleanor Louise Barrington-Brown, Secretary; Dominic Richard Barrington-Brown [1979] Director

The Bart Ingredients Co. Ltd
Incorporated: 20 October 2003 *Employees:* 195
Net Worth: £8,335,000 *Total Assets:* £14,204,000
Registered Office: York Road, Bedminister, Bristol, BS3 4AD
Activities: Manufacture of sugar confectionery
Parent: Bart Spices Group Holdings Limited
Officers: David John Collard [1967] Director; James Dorman [1969] Director; Jorg Herden [1970] Director [German]

Bart Spices Group Holdings Limited
Incorporated: 16 April 2010 *Employees:* 195
Net Worth: £4,623,000 *Total Assets:* £17,022,000
Registered Office: Bart Spices Ltd, York Road, Bedminster, Bristol, BS3 4AD
Activities: Manufacture of sugar confectionery
Shareholders: Dieter Fritz Ludwig Fuchs; Josef Diekmann
Officers: David John Collard [1967] Director; Jorg Herden [1970] Director [German]

Bartlett and Sons Limited
Incorporated: 28 July 2003 *Employees:* 46
Net Worth: £5,167,576 *Total Assets:* £5,603,820
Registered Office: 5-9 Cheltenham Street, Bath, BA2 3EX
Activities: Retail sale of meat and meat products in specialised stores
Shareholders: David William Francis Bartlett; Andrew Philip Bartlett
Officers: Debora Ann Beswick, Secretary; Andrew Philip Bartlett [1963] Director/Butcher; David William Francis Bartlett [1960] Director/Butcher; Lorna Jean Bartlett [1932] Director/Butcher; William George Bartlett [1934] Director/Butcher

Bartlett Contractors Limited
Incorporated: 28 July 1999 *Employees:* 33
Net Worth: £1,692,318 *Total Assets:* £5,064,060
Registered Office: Hitchcock House, Hilltop Park, Devizes Road, Salisbury, Wilts, SP3 4UF
Activities: Construction of other civil engineering projects n.e.c.
Shareholders: Robert John Bartlett; Tina Marie Bere
Officers: Tina Marie Bere, Secretary; Robert John Bartlett [1970] Director/Contractor; Tina Marie Bere [1966] Director/Administrator

K.F.Bartlett Limited
Incorporated: 17 August 1959 *Employees:* 77
Net Worth: £2,750,016 *Total Assets:* £4,295,472
Registered Office: Marsh Green Road, Marsh Barton, Exeter, EX2 8PT
Activities: Plumbing, heat and air-conditioning installation
Shareholders: Paul Anthony Bartlett; David Bartlett
Officers: Nicola Ann Bartlett, Secretary; David Bartlett [1959] Director; Ian Scott Bartlett [1972] Director; Marie Bartlett [1934] Director/Administrator; Paul Anthony Bartlett [1961] Director; Roy William Bartlett [1943] Director; Daniel Pedrick [1973] Director; John Ponsford [1963] Director

Bartletts Transport and Warehouses Limited
Incorporated: 18 February 1993 *Employees:* 113
Net Worth: £11,518,444 *Total Assets:* £17,898,800
Registered Office: The Old Bank, The Triangle, Paulton, Bristol, BS39 7LE
Activities: Buying and selling of own real estate
Major Shareholder: Bryan Robert Bartlett
Officers: Rachael Lydia Burns, Secretary; Bryan Robert Bartlett [1939] Director; Rachael Lydia Burns [1970] Director

P. E. Barton (Holdings) Ltd
Incorporated: 22 April 2013 *Employees:* 3
Net Worth: £4,294,638 *Total Assets:* £5,845,958
Registered Office: 21 Church Road, Parkstone, Poole, Dorset, BH14 8UF
Activities: Activities of other holding companies n.e.c.
Shareholders: Ian Stuart Bailey; Jill Catherine Bailey
Officers: Ian Stuart Bailey [1965] Director; Jill Catherine Bailey [1967] Director

Barton Cold-Form (UK) Limited
Incorporated: 25 August 2009 *Employees:* 79
Net Worth Deficit: £1,130,841 *Total Assets:* £7,887,020
Registered Office: Optimas OE Solutions Ltd, Waterwells Drive, Quedgeley, Gloucester, GL2 2FR
Activities: Manufacture of fasteners and screw machine products
Parent: Optimas OE Solutions Ltd
Officers: Philip Terence Ballard [1973] Director; Rebecca Weber Goldman [1956] Director/Lawyer [American]

Barton Farms Limited (The)
Incorporated: 25 August 1966 *Employees:* 4
Net Worth: £3,761,533 *Total Assets:* £6,467,231
Registered Office: Barton House, Barton on the Heath, Moreton in Marsh, Glos, GL56 0PJ
Activities: Mixed farming
Parent: Hamish Cathie (Holdings) Limited
Officers: Gillian Aileen Bewley Cathie [1949] Director; Ian Hamish Bewley Cathie [1941] Director

BASF Metals Recycling Limited
Incorporated: 17 June 1968
Net Worth Deficit: £2,779,000 *Total Assets:* £4,596,000
Registered Office: Gate A Forest Vale Road, Forest Vale Industrial Estate, Cinderford, Glos, GL14 2PH
Activities: Precious metals production
Parent: BASF Catalysts UK Holdings Limited
Officers: Helen Victoria Koerner, Secretary; Richard John Carter [1962] Managing Director BASF UK & Ireland; Robert Smallwood [1959] Director/Site Manager

Bashley Park Limited
Incorporated: 23 June 1950 *Employees:* 87
Net Worth: £2,501,221 *Total Assets:* £11,216,670
Registered Office: 10 Hoburne Lane, Christchurch, Dorset, BH23 4HP
Activities: Holiday centres and villages
Parent: Hoburne Limited
Officers: Nicholas Stewart Putnam, Company Secretary; Rosemary Sarah Kennar [1956] Director; Timothy Richard Knight [1960] Director; Rodney Philip Tucker [1954] Director

Basic Broadcasting Limited
Incorporated: 29 March 1996 *Employees:* 1
Net Worth: £5,549,295 *Total Assets:* £5,630,609
Registered Office: 3-5 College Street, Burnham on Sea, Somerset, TA8 1AR
Activities: Sound recording and music publishing activities
Major Shareholder: Adrian Chiles
Officers: Adrian Chiles [1967] Director/Journalist

Bastins 2012 Limited
Incorporated: 17 May 2012 *Employees:* 57
Net Worth: £4,463,793 *Total Assets:* £4,906,480
Registered Office: Sigma House, Oak View Close, Edginswell Park, Torquay, Devon, TQ2 7FF
Activities: Other retail sale in non-specialised stores
Major Shareholder: Yvonne Bishop
Officers: Denise Carol Hopkins [1951] Director; Michael James Hopkins [1948] Director; Nicholas Hopkins [1981] Director

R.J. Bateman (Engineering) Limited
Incorporated: 22 May 1980 *Employees:* 66
Net Worth: £5,291,843 *Total Assets:* £7,607,128
Registered Office: 124 High Street, Midsomer Norton, Bath, BA3 2DA
Activities: Other manufacturing n.e.c.
Shareholders: Richard John Bateman; Sally Michelle Bateman
Officers: Sally Michelle Bateman, Secretary; Jason John Bateman [1969] Director/Engineer; Richard John Bateman [1941] Director/Engineer

The Bath and Mendip Partnership Trust
Incorporated: 3 August 2011 *Employees:* 604
Previous: The Partnership Trust
Net Worth: £24,641,526 *Total Assets:* £30,007,986
Registered Office: Fosse Way School, Longfellow Road, Radstock, Somerset, BA3 3AL
Activities: Other education n.e.c.
Officers: Suzy Dawn Dinning, Secretary; Richard John Denning [1949] Director/Local Government Officer; Michael James Gray [1953] Director/Construction Project Manager; Tina Hoare [1957] Director/Retired; John Nicholas Jones [1954] Director/Headmaster; Dr Hilary MacAulay [1967] Director/Executive Principal; Philip Michael Marten [1975] Director/Financial Adviser; Steven William Murphy [1955] Director; Robin Christopher Nash [1956] Director/Retired; Fiona Mary Randle [1957] Director/Local Government Officer; David Tilling [1950] Director/Executive Principal; Peter Joseph Michael Turner [1944] Director/Retired

The Bath and Wells Diocesan Academies Trust
Incorporated: 7 September 2012 *Employees:* 619
Net Worth: £77,593,000 *Total Assets:* £96,182,000
Registered Office: The Old Deanery, St Andrew's Street, Wells, Somerset, BA5 2UG
Activities: Primary education
Officers: Jason Andrew Brown, Secretary; Rosemary Lilian Bailey [1949] Director; Philip John Bowditch [1965] Director of Learning & Achievement; Oliver Cofler [1968] Logistics Director; Nigel Adrian Daniel [1954] Director/Retired Bank Manager; Roger Leslie Eggleton [1951] Director; David William Stjohn Heath [1954] Director/Board Member; Thomas John Jeffery [1958] Director/Independent Education Advisor; Duncan Charles MacRae [1971] Director/Headteacher; Donald James McGillivray [1972] Director/Architect; Gillian Patricia Minns [1956] Director/HR Consultant; Ruth Ellen Newton [1953] Director/Retired Headteacher; Dr Alexander Christie Priest [1985] Director/Chief Executive; Wendy Patricia Simmons [1940] Director/SIAMS Inspector

Bath and Wells Diocesan Board of Finance (The)
Incorporated: 6 March 1915 *Employees:* 57
Net Worth: £101,157,000 *Total Assets:* £111,976,000
Registered Office: Diocesan Office, The Old Deanery, Cathedral Green, Wells, Somerset, BA5 2UG
Activities: Activities of religious organisations
Officers: Nicholas Guy May, Secretary; Anthony Charles Blackshaw [1955] Director/Retired Headteacher; The Revd Sally Elizabeth Buddle [1961] Director/Clerk in Holy Orders; Katherine Cannell [1946] Director/Retired; John Harverd Davies [1957] Director/Dean of Wells; The Revd Canon Roger Driver [1964] Director/Clerk in Holy Orders; The Revd Bruce Steven Faulkner [1963] Director/Clerk in Holy Orders; The Venerable Anne Elizabeth Gell [1963] Director/Archdeacon of Wells; The Revd Diana Greenfield [1971] Director/Priest, Church of England; Stephen Grimshaw [1952] Director/Civil Servant; Peter Hancock [1955] Director/Bishop in The Church of England; The Revd Jane Haslam [1970] Director/Clerk in Holy Orders; The Ven Simon James Hill [1964] Director/Archdeacon; Timothy Charles Hind [1950] Director/Chartered Insurer; Christopher Richard Jenkins [1947] Director/Retired; Marilyn Lee [1950] Director/Retired; James Stephen Loring [1956] Director/Retired; Mary Elizabeth Masters [1941] Director/Retired; Harry Thomas Musselwhite [1944] Director/Retired University Manager; Robert John Norman [1953] Director Abbey House Glastonbury; Dr Axel Anthony Palmer [1952] Director/Visiting Lecturer and Examiner; The Revd Caroline Ralph [1960] Director/Clerk in Holy Orders; The Revd Andrew Nigel Thomas [1975] Director/Clerk in Holy Orders; The Right Reverend Ruth Elizabeth Worsley [1962] Director/Bishop of Taunton; Adrian Youings [1965] Director/Clerk in Holy Orders

Bath and West Finance Limited
Incorporated: 17 June 2011 *Employees:* 10
Net Worth: £503,699 *Total Assets:* £11,477,085
Registered Office: Bury Manor Offices, Woodcroft Lane, Wick, Bristol, BS30 5SH
Activities: Activities of mortgage finance companies
Major Shareholder: Martyn Scott Smith
Officers: Ian Douglas Parsons, Secretary; Matthew James Robert Anderson [1964] Director; Ian Douglas Parsons [1955] Director; Martyn Scott Smith [1961] Director

Bath Demolition Limited
Incorporated: 4 February 1999 *Employees:* 26
Net Worth: £5,346,671 *Total Assets:* £7,043,166
Registered Office: Aldermoor Way, Longwell Green, Bristol, BS30 7EU
Activities: Demolition
Officers: Donna Louise Ealey, Secretary; Paul John Ealey [1965] Director

The Bath Priory Limited
Incorporated: 6 September 1994 *Employees:* 497
Net Worth: £56,736,120 *Total Assets:* £85,474,888
Registered Office: 8 Gay Street, Bath, BA1 2PH
Activities: Hotels and similar accommodation
Major Shareholder: Andrew Douglas Brownsword
Officers: Peter Tyrrell, Secretary; Andrew Douglas Brownsword [1947] Director/Publisher; Christina June Brownsword [1951] Director/Housewife; Jeremy David Hancock [1964] Director/Tax Manager; Stephanie Hocking [1966] Director; Peter Tyrrell [1972] Director

Bath Quartermaster Limited
Incorporated: 20 December 2016
Net Worth: £4,843,339 *Total Assets:* £4,887,744
Registered Office: 84 White Horse Road, Marlborough, Wilts, SN8 2FE
Activities: Removal services
Officers: Simon Eveleigh [1946] Director/Chartered Surveyor; Christopher Chris Villiers [1976] Director

Bath Recreation Limited
Incorporated: 21 April 2017
Net Worth: £5,828,292 *Total Assets:* £5,972,136
Registered Office: Pulteney Mews, Bath, BA2 4DS
Activities: Other amusement and recreation activities n.e.c.
Officers: Stephen John Baddeley [1961] Director of Sport; Elizabeth Christine Bloor [1957] Director; Derwent William Moger Campbell [1952] Director/Solicitor; Robert Francis Carver [1959] Director/Senior Manager; David William Durdan [1946] Director/Retired; Simon George Emery [1963] Director/Builder; Geoffrey Charles Fairclough [1955] Director/Chartered Accountant; Martin John Harman [1946] Director; Michael John Laughton [1964] Director/Accountant; Angela Jane Lewis [1966] Director/Charity Worker; Keziah Evelyn Webber Moreno [1985] Director/Teacher; Christopher Dean Watt [1968] Director

Bath Row Developments Ltd
Incorporated: 24 March 2004 *Employees:* 1
Net Worth: £6,328,862 *Total Assets:* £16,787,416
Registered Office: Kelly Park, St Dominick, Saltash, Cornwall, PL12 6SQ
Activities: Other letting and operating of own or leased real estate
Major Shareholder: Alan James Fall
Officers: Graham David Wilkins, Secretary; Alan James Fall [1965] Director/Property Investment

Bath Rugby Limited
Incorporated: 12 March 1996 *Employees:* 146
Net Worth Deficit: £12,971,751 *Total Assets:* £14,084,361
Registered Office: Farleigh House, Farleigh Hungerford, Bath, BA2 7RW
Activities: Operation of sports facilities
Major Shareholder: Bruce Timothy Craig
Officers: Colin Brian Davis, Secretary; Bruce Timothy Craig [1962] Director; Lars Tarquin McDonald [1977] Managing Director

Bath Taxis Limited
Incorporated: 21 April 2005 *Employees:* 1
Previous: Simpson Raine Limited
Net Worth: £3,631,693 *Total Assets:* £7,061,865
Registered Office: 2b Paxcroft Farm Industrial Estate, Hilperton, Trowbridge, Wilts, BA14 6JB
Activities: Taxi operation
Major Shareholder: David Julian Scaramanga
Officers: Amanda Jayne Ridings [1966] Director/Manager

Bathurst Estate Holdings Limited
Incorporated: 13 June 2013
Net Worth: £28,996,154 *Total Assets:* £42,027,256
Registered Office: The Bathurst Estate Office, Cirencester Park, Cirencester, Glos, GL7 2BU
Activities: Buying and selling of own real estate
Shareholders: Keith James Bruce-Smith; Roger Hugh Knight Seelig; James Felton Somers Hervey-Bathurst; James William Jeremy Ritblat; Patrick James Russell; Michael John Chantler; Timothy Roger William Moore
Officers: Peter William James Clegg, Secretary; Keith James Bruce-Smith [1953] Director/Solicitor; James Felton Somers Hervey-Bathurst [1949] Director/Consultant; Roger Hugh Knight Seelig [1945] Director/Corporate Financier

Batsford Estates (1983) Company Limited
Incorporated: 8 March 1983 *Employees:* 10
Net Worth: £28,800,104 *Total Assets:* £41,041,148
Registered Office: The Estate Office, Batsford, Moreton in Marsh, Glos, GL56 9QF
Activities: Management of real estate on a fee or contract basis
Shareholders: Michael Dulverton; The Honourable Philip Reginald Smith; Earl of Aylesford Charles Heneage Finch-Knightley
Officers: Victoria Maryjane Jones, Secretary; The Lord Michael Dulverton [1944] Director/Landowner; Charles Heneage Finch-Knightley [1947] Director; The Honourable Philip Reginald Smith [1945] Director/Farmer; Honourable Robert Anthony Hamilton Wills [1983] Director/Land Owner

Batson Bidco Limited
Incorporated: 12 January 2016 *Employees:* 3
Net Worth Deficit: £1,658,109 *Total Assets:* £35,434,068
Registered Office: 9 Miller Court, Severn Drive, Tewkesbury Business Park, Tewkesbury, Glos, GL20 8DN
Activities: Activities of head offices
Parent: Batson Midco Limited
Officers: Andrew Guy Melville Stevens [1963] Director/Chief Finance Officer; James Douglas Robert Twining [1972] Director/Chief Executive; Steven John Wynne [1958] Director/Insurance Broker; Dorian John Zanker [1964] Director

Batson Midco Limited
Incorporated: 12 January 2016
Net Worth Deficit: £3,881,791 *Total Assets:* £29,112,000
Registered Office: 9 Miller Court, Severn Drive, Tewkesbury Business Park, Tewkesbury, Glos, GL20 8DN
Activities: Activities of head offices
Parent: Kingsbridge Group Limited
Officers: Andrew Guy Melville Stevens [1963] Director/Chief Finance Officer; James Douglas Robert Twining [1972] Director/Chief Executive; Steven John Wynne [1958] Director/Insurance Broker; Dorian John Zanker [1964] Director

Batten and Allen Limited
Incorporated: 10 October 1972 *Employees:* 114
Net Worth: £6,554,354 *Total Assets:* £10,455,140
Registered Office: Bridge End, Love Lane, Cirencester, Glos, GL7 1NQ
Activities: Manufacture of jewellery and related articles
Major Shareholder: Shawn Anthony Batten
Officers: David Stephen Legg, Secretary; Alan Thomas Batten [1938] Director/Engineer; Rosemary Hazel Batten [1936] Director/Administrator; Shawn Anthony Batten [1966] Managing Director; Tanya Jane Batten [1972] Director/Administrator; Andrew Stephen Edwards [1964] Sales Director; David Stephen Legg [1981] Director/Certified Accountant; Ian Andrew MacKinnon [1964] Managing Director; David Phillip Merchant [1982] Engineering Director

Battens Solicitors Limited
Incorporated: 13 July 1994 *Employees:* 150
Net Worth: £1,848,494 *Total Assets:* £4,272,203
Registered Office: Mansion House, Princes Street, Yeovil, Somerset, BA20 1EP
Activities: Solicitors
Officers: Stuart Roland Allen [1956] Director/Solicitor; David Henry Cary Batten [1952] Director/Solicitor; Jill Amanda Cochrane [1964] Director/Solicitor; Raymond Martin Edwards [1948] Director/Solicitor; Peter Harrison Livingstone [1964] Director/Solicitor; Robert Charles Randall [1953] Director/Lawyer; Ceri Ann Stephens [1976] Director/Solicitor; David Christopher Stephens [1952] Director/Solicitor

Bay Cottage Properties Limited
Incorporated: 7 February 2014 *Employees:* 2
Net Worth: £4,799,227 *Total Assets:* £4,900,467
Registered Office: Woodlands Grange, Woodlands Lane, Bradley Stoke, Bristol, BS32 4JY
Activities: Management of real estate on a fee or contract basis
Shareholders: Terence Brian Duke; Dorothy Eleanor Duke
Officers: Charlotte May Thomas, Secretary; Dorothy Eleanor Duke [1946] Director; Terence Brian Duke [1939] Director; Charlotte May Thomas [1977] Director

Bay Education Trust
Incorporated: 7 November 2014 *Employees:* 55
Net Worth: £20,789,000 *Total Assets:* £28,040,000
Registered Office: Paignton Community & Sports Academy, Waterleat Road, Paignton, Devon, TQ3 3WA
Activities: Primary education
Officers: Lisa Finn, Secretary; Wendy Burridge [1957] Director/Retired; Roger John Carlton [1951] Director/Reverend; Stephen Melville Criddle [1961] Director/Principal and CEO of South Devon College; Anthony William Edmond de Burgh [1973] Director/Operations Manager, Kier PLC; Jeana Johnson [1948] Director/Retired; Gavin David Jones [1977] Director/Business Consultant; Stephen Ellis Kings [1952] Director/Retired; Caroline Jeanette Knight [1963] Director/Lecturer; Andrew Stephen Medhurst [1956] Director/Retired; Kathryn Sarah Needs [1971] Director; Matthew Redwood [1958] Director/Retired; Rosalind Jane Ryman [1968] Director/General Manager

J.T.Baylis & Company Limited
Incorporated: 3 April 1957 *Employees:* 5
Net Worth: £126,108,952 *Total Assets:* £155,287,856
Registered Office: Churchfields, Westbury Hill, Bristol, BS9 3AA
Activities: Development of building projects
Parent: Baylis Trustee Company
Officers: Christopher George Walton, Secretary; John Peter David Burmester [1945] Director/Chartered Surveyor; David John Mace [1955] Director/Chartered Surveyor; Edward Whelan [1938] Director/Builder; Michael Vivian Windo [1950] Director/Project Manager

Baylis Estates Limited
Incorporated: 23 July 1976 *Employees:* 3
Net Worth: £7,845,762 *Total Assets:* £18,951,292
Registered Office: Churchfields, Westbury Hill, Bristol, BS9 3AA
Activities: Development of building projects
Parent: Baylis Trustee Company
Officers: Christopher George Walton, Secretary; John Peter David Burmester [1945] Director/Chartered Surveyor; David John Mace [1955] Director/Chartered Surveyor; James Steven Stanger [1975] Director/Chartered Surveyor; Edward Whelan [1938] Director/Builder

John Baylis Leisure Limited
Incorporated: 27 May 1997
Net Worth: £11,475,573 *Total Assets:* £12,475,431
Registered Office: Churchfields, Westbury Hill, Bristol, BS9 3AA
Activities: Other letting and operating of own or leased real estate
Parent: J T Baylis and Company Limited
Officers: Christopher George Walton, Secretary; Edward Whelan [1938] Director/Builder; Michael Vivian Windo [1950] Director

John Baylis Limited.
Incorporated: 18 November 1994 *Employees:* 3
Net Worth: £102,811,520 *Total Assets:* £129,935,856
Registered Office: Churchfields, Westbury Hill, Bristol, BS9 3AA
Activities: Other letting and operating of own or leased real estate
Shareholders: J T Baylis and Company Limited; J T Baylis and Company Limited
Officers: Christopher George Walton, Secretary; David John Mace [1955] Director/Chartered Surveyor; Edward Whelan [1938] Director/Builder; Michael Vivian Windo [1950] Director

Baylis Ventures Limited
Incorporated: 3 December 2007
Net Worth: £5,779,567 *Total Assets:* £11,500,436
Registered Office: Churchfields, Westbury Hill, Westbury on Trym, Bristol, BS9 3AA
Activities: Other letting and operating of own or leased real estate
Parent: J T Baylis and Company Limited
Officers: Christopher George Walton, Secretary; Edward Whelan [1938] Director; Michael Vivian Windo [1950] Director/Project Manager

Mike Bayliss Holdings Limited
Incorporated: 12 November 2012
Net Worth: £1,858,353 *Total Assets:* £3,558,923
Registered Office: First Floor, Unit 5, Building 6, The Mews, Brook Street, Mitcheldean, Glos, GL17 0SL
Activities: Activities of head offices
Shareholders: Michael John Bayliss; Tracy Anne Bayliss
Officers: Michael John Bayliss [1968] Managing Director; Tracy Anne Bayliss [1974] Director/Administrator

Bayshill Properties Limited
Incorporated: 9 January 2006 *Employees:* 6
Net Worth: £5,140,967 *Total Assets:* £5,336,059
Registered Office: Third Floor, 95 The Promenade, Cheltenham, Glos, GL50 1HH
Activities: Development of building projects
Officers: Andrew Charles Bays [1970] Director; John Newton Bays [1942] Director; Charles Murray Fisher [1949] Director; Mary Elizabeth Goymour [1977] Director; Nigel Ashley Walters [1953] Director

Bayview Developments (South) Limited
Incorporated: 11 March 1996 *Employees:* 4
Net Worth: £2,095,861 *Total Assets:* £5,794,363
Registered Office: The Old Exchange, 521 Wimborne Road East, Ferndown, Dorset, BH22 9NH
Activities: Development of building projects
Major Shareholder: William Lewin Buckler
Officers: William Lewin Buckler [1961] Director/Property Developer

BBG Lift Accommodation Services (No 2) Limited
Incorporated: 14 November 2013
Net Worth: £129,000 *Total Assets:* £12,220,000
Registered Office: Challenge House, International Drive, Tewkesbury Business Park, Tewkesbury, Glos, GL20 8UQ
Activities: Other letting and operating of own or leased real estate
Parent: BBG Lift Holdco (No 2) Limited
Officers: Daniel Peter Bevan, Secretary; Jamie Russell Andrews [1970] Director; Paul Simon Andrews [1970] Investment Director; Paul Edward Brand [1967] Regional Development Director; Neil Rae [1971] Director

BBG Lift Accommodation Services Limited
Incorporated: 26 March 2004
Net Worth Deficit: £5,430,000 *Total Assets:* £47,550,000
Registered Office: Challenge House, International Drive, Tewkesbury Business Park, Tewkesbury, Glos, GL20 8UQ
Activities: Other letting and operating of own or leased real estate
Parent: BHH Holdco Limited
Officers: Daniel Peter Bevan, Secretary; Jamie Russell Andrews [1970] Director; Paul Simon Andrews [1970] Investment Director; Paul Edward Brand [1967] Director; Neil Rae [1971] Director

BBGR Limited
Incorporated: 4 May 2000 *Employees:* 186
Net Worth: £13,129,000 *Total Assets:* £43,199,000
Registered Office: The Paragon, Counterslip, Bristol, BS1 6BX
Activities: Manufacture of medical and dental instruments and supplies
Parent: Essilor International
Officers: James Michael Smith [1969] Finance Director; Peter James Smith [1961] Director/Regional VP Essilor UK & Ireland

BBLP Holdings Limited
Incorporated: 26 May 2011 *Employees:* 87
Net Worth: £2,732,720 *Total Assets:* £4,244,117
Registered Office: The Tanyard, Leigh Road, Street, Somerset, BA16 0HR
Activities: Retail sale of footwear in specialised stores
Officers: Jacqueline Bemmer [1955] Finance Director; Nicholas Brine [1974] Operations Director; James William Lockyer [1967] Director; Andrew Colin Peirce [1957] Managing Director

BBS Consultants & Actuaries Limited
Incorporated: 23 February 2010 *Employees:* 85
Net Worth: £3,484,315 *Total Assets:* £4,209,609
Registered Office: Canard Court, 23-25 St Georges Road, Bristol, BS1 5UU
Activities: Other activities auxiliary to insurance and pension funding
Officers: Peter Bainbridge [1962] Director; Jude Francis Bennett [1973] Director/Consulting Actuary; Paul Bowden [1968] Director; Paul Arthur Bunzl [1962] Director; Marc Nicholas Davies [1969] Director/Administration Manager; Paul Frost [1979] Director/Administration Manager; Gavin Bryce Merchant Giles [1979] Director/Consulting Actuary; Michael Harvey [1966] Director/Consulting Actuary; James Richard Stanfield [1960] Director

BCCB Incorporated Limited
Incorporated: 8 February 2005
Net Worth: £2,341,708 *Total Assets:* £28,935,940
Registered Office: 49 High Street, Westbury on Trym, Bristol, BS9 3ED
Activities: Activities of head offices
Major Shareholder: Frederic Gaston Michel Laporte
Officers: Michael Leo Charles Goodman [1962] Director/Accountant

BDP Imports Limited
Incorporated: 12 July 2000 *Employees:* 28
Net Worth: £3,685,956 *Total Assets:* £7,542,191
Registered Office: Midway House, Herrick Way, Staverton Technology Park, Staverton, Cheltenham, Glos, GL51 6TQ
Activities: Agents involved in the sale of furniture, household goods, hardware and ironmongery
Shareholders: Martyn Simon Bell; Hugo Charles Douglas-Pennant
Officers: Hugo Charles Douglas-Pennant, Secretary/Salesman; Martyn Simon Bell [1969] Director/Salesman; Hugo Charles Douglas-Pennant [1969] Director/Salesman

BDV Atlantic Ltd
Incorporated: 20 March 2014
Net Worth Deficit: £276,497 *Total Assets:* £4,595,723
Registered Office: Apartment 1, Portland View, Dean Street, Bristol, BS2 8FE
Activities: Development of building projects
Shareholders: Nicholas Joseph Barnett; Lorna Mary Barnett
Officers: Nicholas Barnett, Secretary; Lorna Mary Barnett [1957] Director [Irish]; Nicholas Joseph Barnett [1956] Director/Property Developer [Irish]

BE Properties (Plymouth) Limited
Incorporated: 8 March 2012 *Employees:* 3
Net Worth: £2,164,376 *Total Assets:* £5,703,257
Registered Office: Unit 4 Beechwood House, Beech Avenue, Cattedown, Plymouth, PL4 0QQ
Activities: Residents property management
Parent: KPC & AT Body Properties Limited
Officers: Adele Therese Body, Secretary; Adele Therese Body [1962] Director; Kenneth Paul Cyril Body [1965] Director

Be Wiser Insurance Services Ltd
Incorporated: 12 February 2007 *Employees:* 606
Net Worth: £1,395,000 *Total Assets:* £11,625,000
Registered Office: Barrett House, Savoy Close, Andover, Hants, SP10 2HZ
Activities: Activities of insurance agents and brokers
Shareholder: Mark Andrew Bower-Dyke
Officers: Andrew John Dunkerley, Secretary; Jackie Basham [1968] Director; Vicki Beatens [1977] Director/Insurance Broker; Sharon Patricia Beckett [1961] Managing Director; James Bennett [1973] Director/Insurance Broker; Mark Andrew Bower-Dyke [1958] Director; John William Brewer [1966] Director/Insurance Broker; Mark Cliff [1961] Director; Glynn Evans [1975] Director/Insurance Broker

Beachdown Limited
Incorporated: 10 January 2006 *Employees:* 2
Net Worth: £1,893,487 *Total Assets:* £9,141,173
Registered Office: 180 Exeter Street, Plymouth, PL4 0NQ
Activities: Buying and selling of own real estate
Shareholder: George Raymond Williams
Officers: George Raymond Williams, Secretary; Matthew John Porter [1963] Director/Developer; George Raymond Williams [1961] Director/Accountant; Stefano Zucconi [1965] Director/Chartered Accountant

Beacon Communication Services Limited
Incorporated: 23 March 2001 *Employees:* 180
Net Worth: £21,758,210 *Total Assets:* £25,513,344
Registered Office: Unit E3, Pitts Cleave Industrial Estate, Tavistock, Devon, PL19 0PW
Activities: Wireless telecommunications activities
Shareholders: Mark Stephen Manton; Claire Elizabeth Manton
Officers: Claire Manton, Secretary/Accounts Manager; Mark Stephen Manton [1967] Director/Engineer

Beacon Homes Limited
Incorporated: 19 October 2016
Net Worth Deficit: £3,878 *Total Assets:* £4,421,154
Registered Office: Unit 1 Orchard Industrial Estate, Kingsbridge, Devon, TQ7 1EF
Activities: Development of building projects
Shareholder: Nicholas Brian Treseder Alford
Officers: Nicholas Brian Treseder Alford [1964] Director/Developer; Carl Ashley Woolrych Barrand [1964] Director/Chartered Surveyor; Duncan Robert Dean Harper [1967] Director/Retired Banker; Thomas Ralston Peter Raymond [1974] Director/Businessman; James Warren Harben Valentine [1964] Director/Consultant

Beacon Properties (UK) Ltd
Incorporated: 9 August 2013
Net Worth: £924,561 *Total Assets:* £5,515,674
Registered Office: Unit E3, Pitts Cleave Industrial Estate, Tavistock, Devon, PL19 0PW
Activities: Other letting and operating of own or leased real estate
Major Shareholder: Mark Stephen Manton
Officers: Claire Elizabeth Manton, Secretary; Mark Stephen Manton [1967] Director

Beagle Technology Group Limited
Incorporated: 12 December 1969 *Employees:* 83
Net Worth: £644,000 *Total Assets:* £5,387,000
Registered Office: Stony Lane, Christchurch, Dorset, BH23 1EX
Activities: Other manufacturing n.e.c.
Parent: Beagle Group Limited
Officers: John Kenneth Taylor [1964] Director-Commercial; Michael Desmond Walton [1964] Director/Business Consultant; Michael Anthony Welden [1969] Director

Beale Limited
Incorporated: 12 October 1992 *Employees:* 1,095
Previous: Beale PLC
Net Worth: £8,656,000 *Total Assets:* £35,178,000
Registered Office: 36 Old Christchurch Road, Bournemouth, BH1 1LJ
Activities: Activities of head offices
Parent: Brown Retail Holdings Limited
Officers: Tean Elizabeth Dallaway, Secretary; Anthony Richard Brown [1957] Director/Chief Executive Officer; Gellan Watt [1976] Director

J E Beale Public Limited Company
Incorporated: 1 February 1912 *Employees:* 1,095
Net Worth Deficit: £10,750,000 *Total Assets:* £21,235,000
Registered Office: 36 Old Christchurch Road, Bournemouth, BH1 1LJ
Activities: Other retail sale in non-specialised stores
Parent: Beale Limited
Officers: Tean Elizabeth Dallaway, Secretary; Anthony Richard Brown [1957] Director/Chief Executive Officer; Gellan Watt [1976] Director

EW Beard (Holdings) Limited
Incorporated: 8 December 1998 *Employees:* 309
Net Worth: £19,640,000 *Total Assets:* £59,634,000
Registered Office: Faraday Road, Swindon, Wilts, SN3 5JY
Activities: Other letting and operating of own or leased real estate
Shareholders: Mark George Beard; EA Beard Discretionary Settlement
Officers: David Brian Stockham, Secretary; Edward Alan Beard [1932] Director/Builder; Mark George Beard [1963] Director; James Chadwick Murrin [1956] Director; Neil Anthony Sherreard [1964] Director

Beard Group Ltd.(The)
Incorporated: 3 July 1975 *Employees:* 2
Net Worth: £5,998,217 *Total Assets:* £6,306,230
Registered Office: The Old Farm, Gloucester Road, Edge, Stroud, Glos, GL6 6ND
Activities: Other letting and operating of own or leased real estate
Officers: Anthony John Beard [1933] Chairman and Director; Jonathan Richard Beard [1965] Director; Jane Elizabeth Tull [1967] Director

E.W. Beard Limited
Incorporated: 2 August 1973 *Employees:* 305
Net Worth: £12,429,000 *Total Assets:* £52,902,000
Registered Office: Faraday Road, Dorcan, Swindon, Wilts, SN3 5JY
Activities: Construction of commercial buildings
Parent: EW Beard (Holdings) Limited
Officers: David Brian Stockham, Secretary; Marc Andrew Bayley [1960] Director; Edward Alan Beard [1932] Director/Builder; Mark George Beard [1963] Director/Builder; Guy Patrick Hannell [1973] Director; Andrew Mark Jenner [1969] Director/Accountant; Neil Anthony Sherreard [1964] Director

Beat The Street (UK) Limited
Incorporated: 24 November 2005 *Employees:* 146
Net Worth: £3,772,303 *Total Assets:* £6,574,807
Registered Office: Wynyard Mill, Baskerville, Malmesbury, Wilts, SN16 9BS
Activities: Other passenger land transport
Major Shareholder: Joerg Philipp
Officers: Timothy Fortnam-King, Secretary; Joerg Philipp [1968] Director/Luxury Coach Operator [Austrian]

G.A. Beaton Limited
Incorporated: 26 September 1932 *Employees:* 2
Net Worth: £4,598,253 *Total Assets:* £5,422,801
Registered Office: St Catherine's Court, Berkeley Place, Clifton, Bristol, BS8 1BQ
Activities: Other letting and operating of own or leased real estate
Shareholders: Sarah Margaret Beaton; Victoria Ann Cromwell
Officers: Sarah Margaret Beaton, Secretary; Sarah Margaret Beaton [1959] Director; Victoria Ann Cromwell [1962] Director

Beauchamp House Nursing Home Limited
Incorporated: 24 July 1973 *Employees:* 71
Net Worth: £309,000 *Total Assets:* £6,221,000
Registered Office: 39 Commercial Road, Poole, Dorset, BH14 0HU
Activities: Residential nursing care facilities
Parent: Care South
Officers: Penelope Jane Sargeant, Secretary; Lindsay Ann Ansell [1946] Director/Retired Nurse; Stephanie Claire Barnett [1973] Director; Paul Richard Causton [1947] Director/Legal Consultant; Dr Richard Day [1954] Director/Consultant Physician; Martin Richard Dyson [1946] Director/Management Consultant; Richard John Groom [1942] Director/Consultant; Charles James Holt Hunter [1946] Director; Felicity Ann Irwin [1947] Director/Public Relations Consultant; Christopher Kean [1947] Director/Consultant; Jane Stichbury [1955] Director; Hugh James Derek Webster [1946] Director/Chartered Surveyor

Beaudesert Park School Trust Limited
Incorporated: 21 August 1968 *Employees:* 152
Net Worth: £7,711,047 *Total Assets:* £9,971,088
Registered Office: Beaudesert Park School, Minchinhampton, Glos, GL6 9AF
Activities: Primary education
Officers: Claire Yvonne Kay, Secretary; Thomas Daniel Ahearne [1968] Managing Director; Carys Sian Block [1967] Director/Consultant; James Edward Bailye Cope [1966] Director/Teacher; Phillip Graham Stevens Evitt [1959] Director/Headmaster; Mark Christopher Fawcett [1967] Director; Lady Ros Ford [1957] Director/Retired; Harriet Clare I'anson [1980] Director/Lawyer; Claire Yvonne Kay [1973] Director/Housewife; Christine Lough [1955] Director/Retired; Roger Thomas Mather [1965] Finance Director; Alexandra Mary Melvin [1964] Director; Jonathan Blake Nettleton [1980] Director/Architect; Mark Christopher Spring-Rice Pyper [1947] Director/Retired Headmaster

Beaulieu Property Management Limited
Incorporated: 23 August 1990 *Employees:* 5
Net Worth: £6,054,501 *Total Assets:* £6,071,406
Registered Office: Unity Chambers, 34 High East Street, Dorchester, DT1 1HA
Activities: Buying and selling of own real estate
Major Shareholder: Jeremy Ryton Drax
Officers: Jeremy Ryton Drax, Secretary; Lisa Helen Catford [1963] Director; Peter Stephen Dove [1962] Director; Edward Quintin Drax [1971] Director/Property Investor; Jeremy Ryton Drax [1960] Director/Commercial Property Investor

Beaumonts (Leeds) Limited
Incorporated: 13 January 1983
Net Worth: £4,831,000 *Total Assets:* £4,831,000
Registered Office: Hillside Court, Bowling Hill, Chipping Sodbury, Glos, BS37 6JX
Activities: Life insurance
Parent: Beaumonts Guiseley Ltd
Officers: Caroline Wendy Godwin [1962] Director/Accountant; James Michael Pickford [1978] Director/Accountant

Beaver Estates (Ashford) Investments Limited
Incorporated: 16 August 1968 *Employees:* 3
Net Worth: £4,866,166 *Total Assets:* £9,939,324
Registered Office: West Barton, Little Silver, Cadeleigh, Tiverton, Devon, EX16 8HJ
Activities: Other letting and operating of own or leased real estate
Shareholder: Paul Edward Morris
Officers: Patrick George Williams, Secretary; Paul Edward Morris [1954] Director

Bechtle Direct Limited
Incorporated: 25 November 1996 *Employees:* 57
Net Worth: £5,723,198 *Total Assets:* £11,636,244
Registered Office: 128 High Street, Crediton, Devon, EX17 3LQ
Activities: Retail sale via mail order houses or via Internet
Officers: Ian Michael Caston, Secretary; Ian Michael Caston [1944] Director; James Richard Napp [1975] Sales Director

Beckery Properties Limited
Incorporated: 29 April 2004 *Employees:* 162
Net Worth: £4,970,953 *Total Assets:* £10,141,844
Registered Office: Unit 1 Genesis Three, Morland Road, Morlands Enterprise Park, Glastonbury, Somerset, BA6 9FZ
Activities: Other letting and operating of own or leased real estate
Shareholders: Keith Butler; John Coe
Officers: Helen Sarah Jones, Secretary/Accountant; Keith Butler [1960] Managing Director; Kyle Mark Butler [1993] Director/Auditor; John Coe [1955] Director/Property Developer

R M Beckett Limited
Incorporated: 3 November 2009 *Employees:* 46
Net Worth: £3,257,312 *Total Assets:* £5,214,035
Registered Office: Kimpton Down Stables, Kimpton Down, Andover, Hants, SP11 8PQ
Activities: Other sports activities
Shareholders: Isabelle Mary Beckett; Ralph Beckett
Officers: Isabelle Mary Beckett [1973] Director; Ralph Beckett [1971] Director

Beckton Energy Limited
Incorporated: 3 July 2007
Net Worth: £9,161,000 *Total Assets:* £91,139,000
Registered Office: One Glass Wharf, Bristol, BS2 0ZX
Activities: Other business support service activities n.e.c.
Parent: Gemini Energy Limited
Officers: Serkan Bahceci [1972] Director; Charles John Gore Hazelwood [1963] Director

Bedruthan Hotel Limited
Incorporated: 6 February 2003 *Employees:* 344
Net Worth: £9,368,174 *Total Assets:* £10,838,260
Registered Office: Bedruthan Steps Hotel, Mawgan Porth, Newquay, Cornwall, TR8 4BU
Activities: Hotels and similar accommodation
Parent: Red Hotels Limited
Officers: Emma Stratton, Secretary; Emma Stratton [1966] Director/Hotelier; Robert James Waghorn [1959] Director/Business Consultant; Rebecca Whittington [1968] Director/Hotelier

Bee Green Energy Ltd.
Incorporated: 3 June 2009 *Employees:* 3
Net Worth Deficit: £2,907,468 *Total Assets:* £12,110,065
Registered Office: The Carlson Suite, Building 7, Vantage Point Business Village, Mitcheldean, Glos, GL17 0DD
Activities: Production of electricity
Major Shareholder: Brian John Bennett
Officers: Brian John Bennett [1956] Director; Michael John Bennett [1949] Director

Bee Green Solar Limited
Incorporated: 14 January 2013
Net Worth: £483,575 *Total Assets:* £12,865,712
Registered Office: The Carlson Suite, Building 7, Vantage Point Business Village, Mitcheldean, Glos, GL17 0DD
Activities: Production of electricity
Major Shareholder: Brian John Bennett
Officers: Brian John Bennett [1956] Director

Beechen Cliff School
Incorporated: 4 March 2011 *Employees:* 204
Net Worth: £16,289,243 *Total Assets:* £18,627,390
Registered Office: Beechen Cliff School, Kipling Avenue, Bath, BA2 4RE
Activities: General secondary education
Officers: Andrew Davies [1965] Director/Headteacher; Philip Ranulph de Glanville [1968] Director/Civil Servant; Lisa Helen Doerr [1968] Managing Director; Helen Eastwood [1970] Director/Administrator; Louise Grendon [1965] Director/Lawyer; Gavin Lewis [1966] Commercial Director; Nigel Stevens [1965] Director/CEO Transdev Group; Richard Stewart [1958] Director/Teacher; Clare Louise Elisabeth Thompson [1974] Director/Head's PA/Administration Manager; Martin Rodda Williams [1966] Director/Accountant

Beecholm Management Limited
Incorporated: 9 December 1983 *Employees:* 1
Net Worth: £3,718,459 *Total Assets:* £4,206,472
Registered Office: Mole End, Shorts Green Lane, Motcombe, Shaftesbury, Dorset, SP7 9PA
Activities: Other letting and operating of own or leased real estate
Major Shareholder: Paul John Michael Zieleniewski
Officers: Jane Burton, Secretary; Paul John Michael Zieleniewski [1952] Director

Beeley (Holdings) Limited
Incorporated: 11 October 2012 *Employees:* 80
Net Worth: £2,032,012 *Total Assets:* £6,376,653
Registered Office: Mavern House, Corsham Road, Shaw, Melksham, Wilts, SN12 8EH
Activities: Activities of head offices
Shareholders: Jill James; John James Pearson
Officers: Jill James [1964] Director; John James Pearson [1966] Director

Beetles (UK) Ltd
Incorporated: 3 May 1994
Net Worth: £3,922,705 *Total Assets:* £5,200,830
Registered Office: Danbury House, Great Western Business Park, Armstrong Way, Yate, Bristol, BS37 5NG
Activities: Other letting and operating of own or leased real estate
Officers: Mark Jeremy Stevens [1954] Director/Chartered Mechanical Engineer

Bel Ombre Properties Limited
Incorporated: 5 July 2013
Net Worth: £3,027,071 *Total Assets:* £20,324,320
Registered Office: 24a High Street, Melksham, Wilts, SN12 6LA
Activities: Buying and selling of own real estate
Shareholders: Anthony Frederick James Watson; Rukshana Drupathy Watson
Officers: Anthony Frederick James Watson [1955] Director; Rukshana Drupathy Watson [1963] Director

Bell & Ross Limited
Incorporated: 5 September 1972 *Employees:* 38
Net Worth: £2,795,404 *Total Assets:* £7,356,583
Registered Office: Queensberry Hotel, Russel Street, Bath, BA1 2QF
Activities: Hotels and similar accommodation
Parent: L & H Hotels Limited
Officers: Laurence Jordan Benedict Beere, Secretary/Hotelier; Helen Louise Beere [1967] Director/Hotelier; Laurence Jordan Benedict Beere [1969] Director/Hotelier

Bell Contracting Limited
Incorporated: 8 April 1992 *Employees:* 250
Net Worth: £8,270,053 *Total Assets:* £21,169,748
Registered Office: Whimsey Industrial Estate, Steam Mills Road, Cinderford, Gloucester, GL14 3JA
Activities: Construction of domestic buildings
Shareholders: Keith William Bell; Peter Anthony Bell
Officers: Jason Bell, Secretary/Financial Director; Jason Bell [1969] Financial Director; Keith William Bell [1941] Director; Peter Anthony Bell [1961] Director; Stephen Jelf [1960] Director

Bell Finance Limited
Incorporated: 7 June 2000 *Employees:* 3
Net Worth: £1,137,857 *Total Assets:* £8,507,126
Registered Office: 2nd Floor, St James House, The Square, Lower Bristol Road, Bath, BA2 3BH
Activities: Financial intermediation not elsewhere classified
Parent: 1pm PLC
Officers: Jennifer Bodey, Secretary; John Richard Arnold [1961] Director; James Matthew Arthur Roberts [1977] Director; Richard Ian Smith [1961] Director; Ian Sullivan [1967] Director

K W Bell Group Limited
Incorporated: 20 December 1984 *Employees:* 43
Net Worth: £8,167,633 *Total Assets:* £17,400,608
Registered Office: Unit 1 Whimsey Industrial Estate, Steam Mills Road, Cinderford, Glos, GL14 3JA
Activities: Construction of domestic buildings
Shareholders: Keith William Bell; Peter Anthony Bell
Officers: Jason Bell, Secretary/Financial Director; Jason Bell [1969] Financial Director; Keith William Bell [1941] Director; Peter Anthony Bell [1961] Director; Stephen Jelf [1960] Director

Catherine Harwood Bell LLP
Incorporated: 1 April 2004 *Employees:* 90
Previous: Hall Schools of Wimbledon Limited Liability Partnership
Net Worth: £4,489,822 *Total Assets:* £9,509,197
Registered Office: Centenary House, Peninsula Park, Rydon Lane, Exeter, EX2 7XE
Officers: Timothy James Hobbs [1958] Member

Bell Plant Limited
Incorporated: 21 May 2010
Net Worth: £2,366,075 *Total Assets:* £6,214,846
Registered Office: Whimsey Industrial Estate, Steam Mills, Whimsey, Cinderford, Glos, GL14 3JA
Activities: Renting and leasing of construction and civil engineering machinery and equipment
Shareholders: Keith William Bell; Peter Anthony Bell
Officers: Keith William Bell [1941] Director; Peter Anthony Bell [1961] Director

Bellamy Wealth Management Limited
Incorporated: 19 September 2012 *Employees:* 5
Net Worth: £539,493 *Total Assets:* £3,652,390
Registered Office: Sutherlea, Purton Stoke, Swindon, Wilts, SN5 4JG
Activities: Other activities auxiliary to insurance and pension funding
Shareholders: Jon Daniel Bellamy; Karla Ann Bellamy
Officers: Jon Daniel Bellamy [1977] Director; Karla Ann Bellamy [1978] Director

Bellwind-Edis Limited
Incorporated: 29 October 2001 *Employees:* 9
Net Worth: £4,449,009 *Total Assets:* £6,768,728
Registered Office: Partnership House, 15 Crown Glass Place, Nailsea, Bristol, BS48 1RE
Activities: Other professional, scientific and technical activities n.e.c.
Major Shareholder: Kenneth John Edis
Officers: Charles Vessey Edis, Secretary; Charles Vessey Edis [1974] Director/Company Secretary; Karen Frances Edis [1957] Director/Administrator; Kenneth John Edis [1944] Director

Belvedere Bidco Limited
Incorporated: 2 May 2014
Net Worth: £8,649,000 *Total Assets:* £166,796,992
Registered Office: Brightside Park, Severn Bridge, Aust, Bristol, BS35 4BL
Activities: Activities of financial services holding companies
Parent: Belvedere Midco Ltd
Officers: Peter Bramwell Cartwright [1965] Director/Private Equity Professional; Edward John Green [1981] Director/Private Equity Investor; Robert Massey [1985] Director/Private Equity Investor; Brendan Eamon McCafferty [1967] Director; Ian Ronald Sutherland [1970] Director

Belvedere Midco Limited
Incorporated: 2 May 2014 *Employees:* 601
Net Worth Deficit: £18,898,000 *Total Assets:* £149,586,000
Registered Office: Brightside Park, Severn Bridge, Aust, Bristol, BS35 4BL
Activities: Activities of financial services holding companies
Parent: Belvedere Holdings (Guernsey) Ltd
Officers: Peter Bramwell Cartwright [1965] Director/Private Equity Professional; Edward John Green [1981] Director/Private Equity Investor; Robert Massey [1985] Director/Private Equity Investor; Brendan Eamon McCafferty [1967] Director; Ian Ronald Sutherland [1970] Director

Benash Farms Limited
Incorporated: 17 August 1978 *Employees:* 3
Net Worth: £3,416,287 *Total Assets:* £4,205,302
Registered Office: Wessex House, Challeymead Business Park, Melksham, Wilts, SN12 8BU
Activities: Other letting and operating of own or leased real estate
Shareholders: Beatrice Kate Robinson; Richard Simon William Liddiard
Officers: Beatrice Kate Robinson, Secretary; Josephine Liddiard [1933] Director; Richard Simon William Liddiard [1955] Director/Chartered Surveyor; Beatrice Kate Robinson [1962] Director

George Bence & Sons (Cheltenham) Limited
Incorporated: 29 November 1989 *Employees:* 103
Net Worth: £750,000 *Total Assets:* £4,784,812
Registered Office: 41-47 Fairview Road, Cheltenham, Glos, GL52 2EJ
Activities: Agents involved in the sale of timber and building materials
Parent: George Bence & Sons Limited
Officers: Elaine Emerton, Secretary; Christopher George Bence [1950] Director/Timber & Builders Merchant; Paul Christopher Bence [1979] Director/Builders Merchant; Carlwyn Jon Coombes [1976] Commercial Director

George Bence & Sons Limited
Incorporated: 8 June 1899 *Employees:* 103
Net Worth: £5,916,094 *Total Assets:* £11,216,809
Registered Office: 41-47 Fairview Road, Cheltenham, Glos, GL52 2EJ
Activities: Agents involved in the sale of timber and building materials
Major Shareholder: Christopher George Bence
Officers: Elaine Emerton, Secretary; Christopher George Bence [1950] Director/Builders Merchant; Matthew George Bence [1985] Director; Paul Christopher Bence [1979] Managing Director; Carlwyn Jon Coombes [1976] Commercial Director

Bendalls Leisure Limited
Incorporated: 10 April 1997 *Employees:* 80
Net Worth: £2,790,664 *Total Assets:* £5,480,032
Registered Office: Ruby Farm, Blackawton, Totnes, Devon, TQ9 7BN
Activities: Other amusement and recreation activities n.e.c.
Shareholders: Patricia Norah Bendall; Graham Wilfred Bendall
Officers: Patricia Norah Bendall, Secretary/Park Owner; Christopher Paul Bendall [1959] Director/Leisure Park Operator; Graham Wilfred Bendall [1932] Director/Chairman Leisure Park; Michael Andrew Bendall [1962] Director; Patricia Norah Bendall [1936] Director/Park Owner; Philip Graham Nicholas Bendall [1957] Director/Farmer

Bennah Limited
Incorporated: 25 May 1927 *Employees:* 1
Net Worth: £2,050,092 *Total Assets:* £4,456,195
Registered Office: Spitchwick Manor, Poundsgate, Newton Abbot, Devon, TQ13 7PB
Activities: Other letting and operating of own or leased real estate
Shareholders: Stephen Patrick William John Simpson; Steven Knight
Officers: Stephen Mark William Simpson, Secretary; Stephen Mark William Simpson [1968] Director; Stephen Patrick William John Simpson [1941] Land Agent/Director

Bennett Gould and Partners Limited
Incorporated: 16 June 1972 *Employees:* 27
Net Worth: £491,127 *Total Assets:* £3,623,669
Registered Office: 18d Ley Court, Barnett Way, Barnwood, Gloucester, GL4 3RT
Activities: Activities of insurance agents and brokers
Parent: Trans Continental Holdings (UK) Ltd
Officers: Adrian Cornelius Gyde, Secretary/Accountant; Mark Stephen Dacey [1947] Director; Adrian Cornelius Gyde [1954] Director/Accountant; Terence Leonard Martin [1951] Director [South African]; Paul Vincent [1957] Director

Bennetts Cranes Limited
Incorporated: 23 December 2008 *Employees:* 36
Net Worth: £6,749,338 *Total Assets:* £13,225,230
Registered Office: Burma Road, Sharpness, Gloucester, GL13 9UQ
Activities: Renting and leasing of other machinery, equipment and tangible goods n.e.c.
Major Shareholder: Edward Gavin Seager
Officers: Tracey Denise Pockett, Secretary; Tracey Denise Pockett [1962] Company Secretary/Director; Edward Gavin Seager [1963] Director

MF Bennion (Potatoes) Limited
Incorporated: 25 May 2001 *Employees:* 7
Net Worth: £9,189,153 *Total Assets:* £9,492,832
Registered Office: Rose Hill, Dymock, Glos, GL18 2EF
Activities: Growing of vegetables and melons, roots and tubers
Shareholders: Mark Francis Bennion; Anne Laura Bennion
Officers: Anne Bennion, Secretary; Mark Francis Bennion [1962] Director/Farmer

Benridge Investments Limited
Incorporated: 7 June 2000 *Employees:* 3
Net Worth: £5,424,211 *Total Assets:* £6,424,362
Registered Office: 10 Prince of Wales Road, Dorchester, DT1 1PW
Activities: Renting and operating of Housing Association real estate
Major Shareholder: Keith Burridge
Officers: Keith Burridge, Secretary/Property Developer; Colin Richard Burridge [1936] Director/Property Developer; Heather Jane Burridge [1962] Director; Keith Burridge [1960] Director/Property Developer

Steve Benson Farming Limited
Incorporated: 25 June 1981 *Employees:* 18
Net Worth: £2,481,581 *Total Assets:* £5,867,249
Registered Office: Unit 55 Shrivenham Hundred Business Park, Majors Road, Watchfield, Swindon, Wilts, SN6 8TY
Activities: Growing of cereals (except rice), leguminous crops and oil seeds
Major Shareholder: Stephen Francis Benson
Officers: Vicki Jane Mace, Secretary; Stephen Francis Benson [1957] Director/Agricultural Contractor

L.B. Bentley Limited
Incorporated: 28 June 1972 *Employees:* 138
Net Worth: £15,190,750 *Total Assets:* £20,291,088
Registered Office: Olympus Park, Quedgeley, Gloucester, GL2 4NF
Activities: Manufacture of other fabricated metal products n.e.c.
Major Shareholder: Maurice Mortimer Critchley
Officers: Maurice Mortimer Critchley, Secretary; Maurice Mortimer Critchley [1948] Director/Chartered Accountant; Christopher Charles Powell [1946] Director

Bentley Park (UK) Limited
Incorporated: 28 March 2015 *Employees:* 234
Net Worth Deficit: £5,803,000 *Total Assets:* £188,971,008
Registered Office: First Floor, Equinox North, Great Park Road, Bradley Stoke, Bristol, BS32 4QL
Activities: Activities of head offices
Officers: Joshua Marc Levy [1990] Director; Neil Armstrong McMyn [1969] Director/Chartered Accountant; Ronald Alexander Robson [1963] Director

The John Bentley School
Incorporated: 12 October 2011 *Employees:* 126
Net Worth: £12,877,468 *Total Assets:* £13,502,990
Registered Office: The John Bentley School, White Horse Way, Calne, Wilts, SN11 8YH
Activities: General secondary education
Officers: Lindsey Ann Wallace, Secretary; Carol Bell [1965] Director; Julie Braham [1973] Director/Senior Risk Manager; Nicola Charlotte Brennan [1972] Director/Programme Management Consultant; Dr Carolyn Cameron [1968] Director/University Lecturer; Richard Charles Carter [1980] Managing Director; Jon Lee Dodsworth [1979] Director/IT Architect; Mandy Jane Gilder [1966] Director/Housewife; Dalton Charles Godwin [1974] Director/Senior Systems Specialist; Douglas Robert Harrington [1965] Director/Civil Engineer; Suzanne Elizabeth Jacobs [1962] Director/Senior University Administrator; Hugh Pilcher-Clayton [1956] Director; Penny Shaddick [1968] Director/Head of Healthcare Partnerships; Jason Leigh David Tudor [1976] Director/Principal

Bentley Slade Limited
Incorporated: 1 November 1984 *Employees:* 1
Net Worth: £3,681,683 *Total Assets:* £6,054,025
Registered Office: 10 Bridge Street, Christchurch, Dorset, BH23 1EF
Activities: Development of building projects
Major Shareholder: David Slade
Officers: Martin George Slade, Secretary; David Slade [1955] Director

Beran Instruments Limited
Incorporated: 23 March 1984 *Employees:* 49
Net Worth: £1,551,891 *Total Assets:* £4,748,087
Registered Office: Hatchmoor Industrial Estate, Great Torrington, Devon, EX38 7HP
Activities: Manufacture of electronic measuring, testing etc. equipment, not for industrial process control
Parent: Condition Monitoring Group Limited
Officers: Rachel Jane Allen, Secretary; Rachel Jane Allen [1976] Director/Accountant; Douglas Robert Graham [1980] Director/Engineer; Gareth Maurice Lee-Richards [1945] Director; Andres Lobato [1955] Director; Freda Anne Lobato [1953] Director

Berkeley Charterhouse Limited
Incorporated: 15 April 1983 *Employees:* 1
Net Worth: £1,970,312 *Total Assets:* £4,774,376
Registered Office: 3 Temple Quay, Temple Back East, Bristol, BS1 6DZ
Activities: Other letting and operating of own or leased real estate
Major Shareholder: Christopher Charles Banks
Officers: Paul James Tarran, Secretary; Christopher Charles Banks [1949] Director

Berkeley Leisure Group Limited (The)
Incorporated: 23 December 1960 *Employees:* 214
Net Worth: £110,919,704 *Total Assets:* £118,119,424
Registered Office: West Coker House, West Coker, Yeovil, Somerset, BA22 9BW
Activities: Recreational vehicle parks, trailer parks and camping grounds
Major Shareholder: John Roland Berkley
Officers: Steve Drew, Secretary; Anne Berkley [1942] Director; John Roland Berkley [1934] Director; David Edward Curson [1961] Director; Steve Drew [1959] Director/Certified Chartered Accountant; James Stewart Leese [1955] Director; Paul Anthony Tarr [1954] Director

Berry Head Hotel Limited
Incorporated: 27 May 1994 *Employees:* 60
Net Worth: £1,747,653 *Total Assets:* £3,709,605
Registered Office: c/o Bishop Fleming, Chy Nyverow, Newham Road, Truro, Cornwall, TR1 2DP
Activities: Hotels and similar accommodation
Parent: Edward Bence Hotels Ltd
Officers: Sarah Elizabeth Bence, Secretary; Mr Edward James Bence [1986] Director/Hotel Manager; Edward John Bence [1952] Director/Hotelier and Consultant; Sarah Elizabeth Bence [1955] Director/Company Secretary; Lucinda Elizabeth Chamings [1981] Director

Berrys Coaches (Taunton) Limited
Incorporated: 21 February 2000 *Employees:* 117
Net Worth: £1,800,727 *Total Assets:* £4,676,893
Registered Office: Peter Clifford House, Great Western Way, Taunton, Somerset, TA2 6BX
Activities: Other urban, suburban or metropolitan passenger land transport (not underground, metro or similar)
Shareholders: Berrys Coaches Holdings Limited; Berrys Holdings Ltd
Officers: James Bradly Berry, Secretary; Stuart Alexander Berry [1960] Director/Coach Operator; Ian Daniells [1961] Director

Berrys Holdings Limited
Incorporated: 9 April 1985 *Employees:* 1
Net Worth: £6,386,562 *Total Assets:* £6,936,088
Registered Office: Peter Clifford House, Great Western Way, Taunton, Somerset, TA2 6BX
Activities: Other letting and operating of own or leased real estate
Parent: Berrys Property Holdings Limited
Officers: James Bradly Berry, Secretary; Stuart Alexander Berry [1960] Director/Coach Operator

BES Healthcare Ltd
Incorporated: 1 April 1998 *Employees:* 33
Previous: B.E.S. Rehab Limited
Net Worth: £1,850,513 *Total Assets:* £4,728,957
Registered Office: 131 South Liberty Lane, Ashton Vale, Bristol, BS3 2SZ
Activities: Retail sale of medical and orthopaedic goods in specialised stores (not incl. hearing aids) n.e.c.
Officers: Dr Mark Barend Ter Haar, Secretary/Marketing; Gregory Amos [1947] Director/Sales; Bornona Ashim Dasgupta [1988] Marketing Director [Indian]; Diane Elaine Hargrove [1964] Director/Sales and Marketing; Leyton Mark Stevens [1964] Director/Chief Executive Officer; Dr Mark Barend Ter Haar [1948] Director/Marketing

Bessant Properties Limited
Incorporated: 21 July 2009
Net Worth: £1,344,442 *Total Assets:* £6,431,456
Registered Office: 4 Moberly Road, Salisbury, Wilts, SP1 3BY
Activities: Other letting and operating of own or leased real estate
Shareholder: Thomas Matthew Bessant
Officers: Marie Janice Eileen Bessant [1955] Director; Thomas Matthew Bessant [1979] Director/Solicitor

Anthony Best Dynamics Limited
Incorporated: 13 August 1982 *Employees:* 128
Net Worth: £25,699,776 *Total Assets:* £47,668,184
Registered Office: Middleton Drive, Bradford on Avon, Wilts, BA15 1GB
Activities: Manufacture of other special-purpose machinery n.e.c.
Parent: AB Dynamics PLC
Officers: Robert Andrew Leonard Hart, Secretary; Anthony Best [1937] Director; Naemi Best [1935] Director; Robert Andrew Leonard Hart [1968] Director/Company Secretary; Matthew James Hubbard [1975] Director/Engineer; Dr Colin Patrick Martin [1966] Director/Engineer; Stephen John Neads [1960] Director/Engineer; Andrew James Pick [1979] Business Director - Track Testing Systems; Dr James Mathew Routh [1973] Director; Andrew Walter Rumble [1961] Director; Adrian Joby Simms [1976] Business Director - Laboratory Testing Systems

Best Western Enterprises Limited
Incorporated: 14 September 1967 *Employees:* 1
Net Worth: £3,708,473 *Total Assets:* £3,881,953
Registered Office: Rumwell Hall, Rumwell, Taunton, Somerset, TA4 1EL
Activities: Development of building projects
Shareholders: Michael John Anthony Best; Ann Best
Officers: Ann Best, Secretary; Andrew John Best [1967] Director; Ann Best [1938] Property Director; Michael John Anthony Best [1937] Property Director

Beta Marine Limited
Incorporated: 23 March 1987 *Employees:* 40
Net Worth: £3,014,816 *Total Assets:* £5,167,110
Registered Office: Davy Way, Waterwells, Quedgeley, Glos, GL2 2AD
Activities: Manufacture of engines and turbines, except aircraft, vehicle and cycle engines
Officers: John Andrew Growcoot [1953] Director; David Charles Morris [1971] Director; Sarah Louise Pugh [1972] Director and Company Secretary; Laurence Frederick Talbot [1953] Director

Betterment Properties (Weymouth) Limited
Incorporated: 10 April 1967 *Employees:* 16
Net Worth: £41,004,616 *Total Assets:* £44,228,448
Registered Office: Leanne House, 6 Avon Close, Weymouth, Dorset, DT4 9UX
Activities: Construction of domestic buildings
Major Shareholder: Mervyn Stewkesbury
Officers: Mervyn Stewkesbury, Secretary; Serena Mansfield [1971] Director; Joseph Saunders [1992] Director/Development Manager; Mervyn Stewkesbury [1933] Director/Builder

Bevan Brittan LLP
Incorporated: 9 September 2004 *Employees:* 401
Net Worth: £14,793,000 *Total Assets:* £25,259,000
Registered Office: Kings Orchard, 1 Queen Street, Bristol, BS2 0HQ
Officers: Mark Joseph Balmforth Calverley [1966] Member; Joanne Louise Easterbrook [1963] Member; Robert Mark Harrison [1966] Member; Adam James Kendall [1971] Member; Andrew Christopher Tobin [1968] Member; Jonathan Michael Turner [1973] Member; Duncan John Weir [1963] Member; Nadeem Abbas Arshad [1975] LLP Member; Judith Elizabeth Barnes [1961] LLP Member; Michael Boyd [1964] LLP Member; Alison Jane Buckingham [1967] LLP Member; Vincent Joseph Buscemi [1972] LLP Member; Lyndon Stuart Campbell [1981] LLP Member; Ian Neil Caplan [1970] LLP Member; Julie Charlton [1973] LLP Member; Virginia Liljana Cooper [1972] LLP Member; Adrian Andrew Marshall Dagnall [1963] LLP Member; Steven Eccles [1974] LLP Member; Christopher Paul Harper [1977] LLP Member; Emily Jane Heard [1971] LLP Member; David Peter Hobbs [1981] LLP Member; Timothy Miles Hodgetts [1971] LLP Member; Julian Peter Hoskins [1962] LLP Member; David Alistair Hutton [1968] LLP Member; Dr Rosemary Alison Jago [1973] LLP Member; Sarah-Jane Lamont [1967] LLP Member; Richard David Lane [1972] LLP Member; Simon Alexander Lindsay [1963] LLP Member; Joanna Clare Lloyd [1967] LLP Member; Ashley Norman [1965] LLP Member; David John Owens [1958] LLP Member; Sharon Jayne Renouf [1969] LLP Member; Louise Marie Robling [1973] LLP Member; Jodie Maree Sinclair [1970] LLP Member; Steven Mark Smith [1967] LLP Member; Hugo Offley Prideaux Stephens [1956] LLP Member; Richard Ian Stirk [1974] LLP Member; Paul Stephen Taverner [1967] LLP Member; Matthew Thomas Waters [1979] LLP Member; Wendy Mary Wilks [1967] LLP Member

Bexley PPP Health Services Limited
Incorporated: 19 May 1998 *Employees:* 3
Net Worth: £4,509,969 *Total Assets:* £17,180,296
Registered Office: Third Floor, Broad Quay House, Prince Street, Bristol, BS1 4DJ
Activities: Other specialised construction activities n.e.c.
Parent: RBIL Limited
Officers: Christopher John Blundell [1966] Regional Director; Andrew Richard Kershaw [1965] Director/Projects Controller; Richard Little [1979] Investment Director; Daniel North [1988] Investment Director

Beylon Limited
Incorporated: 14 January 1986 *Employees:* 2
Net Worth: £20,877,472 *Total Assets:* £29,169,512
Registered Office: 4th Floor, Hartwell House, 55-61 Victoria Street, Bristol, BS1 6AD
Activities: Development of building projects
Shareholders: Carla Atef Frateschi; Carlos Atef Moussa
Officers: Carla Atef Frateschi [1961] Director/Barrister; Carlos Atef Moussa [1965] Director/Property Management [French]

Beyond The Bean Limited
Incorporated: 1 April 1997
Net Worth: £3,362,590 *Total Assets:* £4,979,940
Registered Office: Unit 6 Cala Trading Estate, Ashton Vale Road, Bristol, BS3 2HA
Activities: Manufacture of other food products n.e.c.
Shareholders: Jeremy Paul Rogers; Nicola Mary Portch
Officers: Jeremy Paul Rogers, Secretary; Nicola Mary Portch [1965] Director; Jeremy Paul Rogers [1971] Director

BFF Nonwovens Limited
Incorporated: 25 October 2002 *Employees:* 68
Net Worth: £1,648,288 *Total Assets:* £8,116,157
Registered Office: BFF Business Park, Bath Road, Bridgwater, Somerset, TA6 4NZ
Activities: Manufacture of non-wovens and articles made from non-wovens, except apparel
Parent: Nonwovenn Ltd
Officers: Andrew Brownlow [1965] Managing Director; David Peter Lamb [1959] Director/Chairman

BGS 103 Hurst Solar Park Limited
Incorporated: 20 November 2013
Net Worth Deficit: £35,411 *Total Assets:* £5,216,168
Registered Office: Carlson Suite, 4th Floor, Vantage Point Business Village, Mitcheldean, Glos, GL17 0DD
Activities: Production of electricity
Officers: Brian John Bennett [1956] Director

BGS 104 Sedbury Solar Park Limited
Incorporated: 20 November 2013
Net Worth: £89,173 *Total Assets:* £5,508,168
Registered Office: Carlson Suite, 4th Floor, Vantage Point Business Village, Mitcheldean, Glos, GL17 0DD
Activities: Production of electricity
Major Shareholder: Brian John Bennett
Officers: Brian John Bennett [1956] Director

BH Live
Incorporated: 1 December 2009 *Employees:* 564
Net Worth: £3,503,948 *Total Assets:* £13,935,754
Registered Office: Bournemouth International Centre, Exeter Road, Bournemouth, BH2 5BH
Activities: Operation of arts facilities
Officers: Stephen Mark Lane, Secretary; Robert Andrew Boulton [1961] Director/Security Consultant; Robert Herbert Chapman [1942] Director; Paul Christopher Collins [1953] Director; Philip Anthony Dewhurst [1949] Director; Lyn Mary Margaret Glass [1950] Director; Philip Anthony Gowers [1968] Director/Dentist; Sandra Denise Graham [1957] Director/Solicitor; Peter Gareth Gunn [1959] Director/Chief Executive; Martin John Kimberley [1969] Director/Chief Executive; Cllr Andrew Mason Morgan [1962] Director/Local Councillor & Copywriter; Dorcas Jaqueline Williams [1962] Communications Director; Michael Raymond Wright [1949] Managing Director

BHH Lift Accommodation Services Limited
Incorporated: 19 February 2004
Net Worth Deficit: £4,649,000 *Total Assets:* £47,053,000
Registered Office: Challenge House, International Drive, Tewkesbury Business Park, Tewkesbury, Glos, GL20 8UQ
Activities: Other letting and operating of own or leased real estate
Parent: BHH Holdco Limited
Officers: Daniel Peter Bevan, Secretary; Jamie Russell Andrews [1970] Area Director; Paul Simon Andrews [1970] Investment Director; Paul Edward Brand [1967] Director; Neil Rae [1971] Director

Bibendum PLB Group Limited
Incorporated: 13 March 2007
Net Worth: £19,997,000 *Total Assets:* £27,291,000
Registered Office: Whitchurch Lane, Whitchurch, Bristol, BS14 0JZ
Activities: Wholesale of wine, beer, spirits and other alcoholic beverages
Parent: Bibendum PLB (Topco) Limited
Officers: Andrea Pozzi [1971] Director/Group Chief Operating Officer; Ewan James Robertson [1982] Finance Director; Jonathan Solesbury [1965] Director/Group Chief Financial Officer

The Bibury Club Limited
Incorporated: 3 January 1991 *Employees:* 78
Net Worth: £2,059,337 *Total Assets:* £3,691,800
Registered Office: Salisbury Racecourse, Netherhampton, Salisbury, Wilts, SP2 8PN
Activities: Activities of racehorse owners
Officers: Heather Gail Clinch [1963] Director/Public Relations; Lord William Edward Robin Hood Huntingdon [1948] Director/Thoroughbred Consultant, Farmer; Lord Alastair John Margadale of Islay [1958] Director/Landowner; Jeremy John Martin [1971] Director/Clerk of The Course/Racecourse Manager; Jeffrey Colin Smith [1945] Director; Peter William Treadgold [1963] Director/Chartered Accountant

Bibury Court Limited
Incorporated: 13 March 2007 *Employees:* 3
Net Worth: £2,995,970 *Total Assets:* £4,212,610
Registered Office: Shipton Mill, Long Newnton, Tetbury, Glos, GL8 8RP
Activities: Hotels and similar accommodation
Officers: David Roberts, Secretary; John Richard Arkwright Lister [1954] Director

Bicknell Holdings PLC
Incorporated: 14 July 1971 *Employees:* 10
Net Worth: £11,819,990 *Total Assets:* £13,205,929
Registered Office: Bicknell House, Merstham Road, Bristol, BS2 9TQ
Activities: Development of building projects
Shareholders: Brian Robert Bicknell; Stephen Barrie Bicknell
Officers: Eileen Lillian Bicknell, Secretary; Brian Robert Bicknell [1946] Director; Carl Royston Bicknell [1976] Director/Civil Engineer; Stephen Barrie Bicknell [1950] Director; John Edward Castell [1953] Director/Surveyor; Rosalind Muriel Scott [1954] Director/Group Accounts Administrator

Bid PCB UK Limited
Incorporated: 29 April 2016
Net Worth: £11,661,000 *Total Assets:* £25,178,000
Registered Office: c/o Graphic PLC, Down End, Lords Meadow Industrial Estate, Crediton, Devon, EX17 1HN
Activities: Activities of head offices
Officers: Roberto Giudici [1982] Director [Italian]; Nicola Pietralunga [1968] Director [Italian]; David John Pike [1962] Director

Bifold Fluidpower (Holdings) Limited
Incorporated: 2 December 2002
Net Worth: £1,423,000 *Total Assets:* £5,828,000
Registered Office: Rotork House, Brassmill Lane, Bath, BA1 3JQ
Activities: Activities of head offices
Parent: Bifold Group Limited
Officers: Sarah Parsons, Secretary; Jonathan Mark Davis [1966] Director/Chartered Accountant; Kevin George Hostetler [1968] Director/Chief Executive [American]

Bifold Fluidpower Limited
Incorporated: 31 January 1984 *Employees:* 171
Net Worth: £9,248,000 *Total Assets:* £17,826,000
Registered Office: Rotork House, Brassmill Lane, Bath, BA1 3JQ
Activities: Manufacture of fluid power equipment
Parent: Bifold Fluidpower (Holdings) Limited
Officers: Sarah Parsons, Secretary; Jonathan Mark Davis [1966] Director/Chartered Accountant; Kevin George Hostetler [1968] Director/Chief Executive [American]

Bifold Group Limited
Incorporated: 27 March 2007 *Employees:* 2
Net Worth Deficit: £16,452,000 *Total Assets:* £31,960,000
Registered Office: Rotork House, Brassmill Lane, Bath, BA1 3JQ
Activities: Activities of head offices
Parent: Rotork Overseas Limited
Officers: Sarah Parsons, Secretary; Jonathan Mark Davis [1966] Director/Chartered Accountant; Kevin George Hostetler [1968] Director/Chief Executive [American]

Big Apple Entertainments Limited
Incorporated: 20 June 2006 *Employees:* 158
Net Worth: £4,224,948 *Total Assets:* £8,953,434
Registered Office: Potterne House, 1 Potterne Way, Wimborne, Dorset, BH21 6RS
Activities: Other amusement and recreation activities n.e.c.
Shareholder: Michael Richard Erle Appleton
Officers: Duncan Geoffrey Frank Moss, Secretary; Michael Richard Erle Appleton [1959] Director/Leisure Operator; Duncan Geoffrey Frank Moss [1955] Director/Accountant

The Big Green Parcel Group Limited
Incorporated: 8 February 2005
Net Worth: £46,535,000 *Total Assets:* £46,535,000
Registered Office: Rowan House, Cherry Orchard North, Kembrey Park, Swindon, Wilts, SN2 8UH
Activities: Licensed carriers
Parent: The Big Green Parcel Holding Company Limited
Officers: Stuart Steven Marriner, Secretary; Peter Geoffrey Birks [1963] Director; Anthony Liam Grace [1961] Director

The Big Green Parcel Holding Company Limited
Incorporated: 21 December 2007
Net Worth: £63,096,000 *Total Assets:* £63,096,000
Registered Office: Rowan House, Cherry Orchard North, Kembrey Park, Swindon, Wilts, SN2 8UH
Activities: Freight transport by road
Parent: Smiths News Holdings Limited
Officers: Stuart Steven Marriner, Secretary; Peter Geoffrey Birks [1963] Director; Anthony Liam Grace [1961] Director

The Big Green Parcel Machine Limited
Incorporated: 13 November 1995
Net Worth: £37,916,000 *Total Assets:* £37,916,000
Registered Office: Rowan House, Cherry Orchard North, Kembrey Park, Swindon, Wilts, SN2 8UH
Activities: Unlicensed carriers
Parent: The Big Green Parcel Group Limited
Officers: Stuart Steven Marriner, Secretary; Peter Geoffrey Birks [1963] Director; Anthony Liam Grace [1961] Director

Big Van World Limited
Incorporated: 11 October 2001 *Employees:* 26
Previous: Austen Trading Limited
Net Worth: £3,644,465 *Total Assets:* £9,079,334
Registered Office: Swatton Barn, Badbury, Swindon, Wilts, SN4 0EU
Activities: Sale of used cars and light motor vehicles
Major Shareholder: Michael Stephen Austen
Officers: Evelyn Frances Austen, Secretary/Director; Michael Stephen Austen [1979] Director

Bigdug Limited
Incorporated: 19 January 2004 *Employees:* 75
Net Worth: £1,961,771 *Total Assets:* £4,529,281
Registered Office: Riga Wharf, 380 Bristol Road, Gloucester, GL2 5DH
Activities: Retail sale via mail order houses or via Internet
Parent: Newport.Takkt GmbH
Officers: Heiko Hegwein [1974] Director/Board Member [German]; Franziskus Clemens Hermann Josten [1986] Director/Board Member [German]

Ken Biggs Contractors Limited
Incorporated: 20 June 1967
Net Worth: £19,753,572 *Total Assets:* £24,213,680
Registered Office: High Street, High Littleton, Bristol, BS39 6HP
Activities: Development of building projects
Shareholders: Ann Margaret Wyatt; Nicholas John Biggs; Andrew Pitt
Officers: Ann Margaret Wyatt, Secretary; Ivy Margaret Biggs [1927] Director/Secretary; Nicholas John Biggs [1959] Director; Kathryn Elizabeth MacDuff [1979] Director/Administrator; Andrew John Wyatt [1977] Director/Procurement Manager; Ann Margaret Wyatt [1952] Director/Secretary; Paul Charles Wyatt [1951] Managing Director; Stephen Charles Wyatt [1974] Director/Contracts Manager

Ken Biggs Limited
Incorporated: 15 April 1980
Net Worth: £5,858,136 *Total Assets:* £6,087,376
Registered Office: Camerton Court, Camerton, Bath, BA2 0PU
Activities: Construction of commercial buildings
Shareholder: Nicholas John Biggs
Officers: Nicholas John Biggs, Secretary; Nicholas John Biggs [1959] Director; Paul Charles Wyatt [1951] Director

Bighead Fasteners Limited
Incorporated: 9 January 2014
Net Worth: £1,973,051 *Total Assets:* £7,842,399
Registered Office: Unit 1 Black Moor Business Park, 36a Black Moor Road, Ebblake Industrial Estate, Verwood, Dorset, BH31 6BB
Activities: Activities of other holding companies n.e.c.
Major Shareholder: Matthew Stevens
Officers: Matthew Stevens, Secretary; Martin Edward Cowell [1959] Sales Director; David Theror Dean [1959] Director/Business Executive [Swiss]; Philip Lovelace James [1962] Director; Matthew Stevens [1969] Managing Director; Stephan Zehnder [1965] Director/Certified Accountant [Swiss]

BIL Group Limited
Incorporated: 22 April 1991 *Employees:* 42
Net Worth: £3,596,507 *Total Assets:* £4,892,121
Registered Office: Porte Marsh Road, Calne, Wilts, SN11 9BW
Activities: Manufacture of other fabricated metal products n.e.c.
Shareholders: Mark Simon James Farrell; Timothy Martin Walker
Officers: Peter Robert Edmondson, Secretary; Peter Robert Edmondson [1954] Finance Director; Mark Simon James Farrell [1972] Managing Director; Timothy Martin Walker [1962] Director

Bilbster Wind Farm Limited
Incorporated: 28 April 2006
Net Worth: £2,963,852 *Total Assets:* £3,792,869
Registered Office: Windmill Hill Business Park, Whitehill Way, Swindon, Wilts, SN5 6PB
Activities: Production of electricity
Parent: Innogy Renewables UK Limited
Officers: Christopher David Barras, Secretary; Penelope Anne Sainsbury, Secretary; Kevin Dodd [1975] Director/Head of UK Asset Management and Operations; Keith Moseley [1965] Director

Binx Health Limited
Incorporated: 19 July 2005 *Employees:* 48
Previous: Atlas Genetics Limited
Net Worth Deficit: £48,528,800 *Total Assets:* £28,212,368
Registered Office: Derby Court, Epsom Square, White Horse Business Park, Trowbridge, Wilts, BA14 0XG
Activities: Research and experimental development on biotechnology
Officers: Karen Frances Yates, Secretary; John Clarkson [1957] Director; Jonathan Martin Glenn [1968] Director; Florent Gros [1968] Director [French]; Stanley Lapidus [1949] Director/Executive [American]; Jeffrey Luber [1967] Director [American]; Martin Muenchbach [1970] Director [German/Swiss]; Samar Parikh [1978] Director/Entrepreneur [American]; Pavel Rodiukov [1981] Investment Manager and Director [Russian]; Dr Joachim Rothe [1963] Director [German]; Jihua Wang [1962] Director [Chinese]; Zeev Zehavi [1953] Director/Vice President [Israeli]

Biopharma Credit PLC
Incorporated: 24 October 2016
Net Worth: £706,349,568 *Total Assets:* £832,475,392
Registered Office: 51 New North Road, Exeter, EX4 4EP
Activities: Activities of investment trusts
Officers: Colin Bond [1960] Director/Chief Financial Officer; Duncan William Allan Budge [1955] Director; Harry Abraham Hyman [1956] Director/Chartered Accountant; Stephanie Marie Leouzon [1962] Director/Advisor [American]; Jeremy William Sillem [1950] Director/Managing Partner

Bioquell PLC
Incorporated: 2 June 1925 *Employees:* 220
Net Worth: £26,760,000 *Total Assets:* £34,849,000
Registered Office: 52 Royce Close, West Portway, Andover, Hants, SP10 3TS
Activities: Activities of other holding companies n.e.c.
Officers: Georgina Nicole Pope, Secretary/Accountant; Ian Roy Johnson [1953] Director; Jay Charles Lecoque [1962] Commercial Director [American]; Michael Roy David Roller [1965] Finance Director

Bioquell UK Limited
Incorporated: 9 July 1990 *Employees:* 135
Net Worth: £10,187,962 *Total Assets:* £23,092,832
Registered Office: 52 Royce Close, West Portway, Andover, Hants, SP10 3TS
Activities: Manufacture of other special-purpose machinery n.e.c.
Parent: Bioquell PLC
Officers: Georgina Nicole Pope, Secretary; Ian Roy Johnson [1953] Director; Matthew James Parks [1978] Director/Engineer; Michael Roy David Roller [1965] Finance Director

Bioreliance UK Acquisition Limited
Incorporated: 28 February 2007
Net Worth: £50,815,000 *Total Assets:* £50,815,000
Registered Office: The Old Brickyard, New Road, Gillingham, Dorset, SP8 4XT
Activities: Other professional, scientific and technical activities n.e.c.
Parent: Merck KGaA
Officers: Peter Biro [1967] Director/US Certified Public Accountant [Dutch]; David Hannah McClelland [1972] Director/General Manager

Bioscientifica Limited
Incorporated: 25 April 1996
Net Worth: £50,009 *Total Assets:* £4,429,193
Registered Office: Starling House, 1600 Newbrick Road, Stoke Gifford, Bristol, BS34 8YU
Activities: Publishing of learned journals
Officers: David Mills, Secretary; Professor Adrian John Lavington Clark [1952] Director/Retired; Professor Eleanor Davies [1963] Director/University Professor/Scientist; David Anthony Fletcher [1978] Director; Jamie David Marwick [1977] Finance Director; Dr Barbara Maria Cristina McGowan [1966] Director/Consultant and Hon Senior Lecturer [Italian]; David Mills [1962] Finance Director; Ian Stuart Russell [1969] Director/Chief Executive; Kate Elizabeth Sargent [1982] Deputy Managing Director; Adrian Thomas Stanley [1969] Director/Vice President

Birchclaim Limited
Incorporated: 22 February 1991 *Employees:* 81
Net Worth: £3,609,298 *Total Assets:* £10,353,707
Registered Office: Sixth Floor, Dean Park House, Dean Park Crescent, Bournemouth, BH1 1HP
Activities: Development of building projects
Officers: Barbara Mary Keith [1938] Director; Jennifer Margaret Keith [1950] Director; Richard Etheridge Keith [1947] Managing Director

Richard C. Bircher (Holdings) Limited
Incorporated: 28 June 1976 *Employees:* 4
Net Worth: £7,431,356 *Total Assets:* £12,730,279
Registered Office: Ground Floor, Blackbrook Gate 1, Blackbrook Business Park, Taunton, Somerset, TA1 2PX
Activities: Raising of sheep and goats
Major Shareholder: Richard Charles Bircher
Officers: Philippa Joyce Bircher, Secretary; Philippa Joyce Bircher [1951] Director/Secretary; Richard Charles Bircher [1947] Director

Birchmere Limited
Incorporated: 4 April 1975 *Employees:* 14
Net Worth: £34,963,976 *Total Assets:* £43,157,576
Registered Office: 38 Sandbanks Road, Parkstone, Poole, Dorset, BH14 8BX
Activities: Buying and selling of own real estate
Major Shareholder: Arthur John Jeffries
Officers: Elizabeth Anne Marley, Secretary; Nicholas John Dadds [1965] Director/Property Manager; Arthur John Jeffries [1930] Director/Property Developer; Paul Antony Jeffries [1965] Director/Property Manager; Derek Harold King [1928] Director/Property Manager

Birdwell School
Incorporated: 1 March 2013 *Employees:* 52
Net Worth: £3,704,791 *Total Assets:* £4,550,423
Registered Office: Hollis Close, Long Ashton, Somerset, BS41 9AZ
Activities: Primary education
Officers: Hannah Leanne Jones, Secretary; Emma Bellis [1974] Director/Deputy Headteacher; Lucy Charlotte Durham [1986] Director/Teacher; Suzanne Easton [1970] Business Owner/Director; Robert David Goodwin [1966] Director/Senior Manager, Banking; Maxine Houghton [1973] Director; Emily Kate Jones [1974] Director/Learning Support Assistant; Catherine Emma Milne [1968] Director/Self Employed; Geoffrey Hartland Mountjoy [1959] Director/Civil Servant; Dr Tabetha Jane Newman [1975] Director/Education and Research Consultant; Louise Roberts [1984] Director/Accountant; Paul Sainsbury [1975] Director/Headmaster; Nicholas Paul Thompson [1968] Director

Birmingham Healthcare Services Limited
Incorporated: 9 August 2002 *Employees:* 2
Net Worth Deficit: £15,686,000 *Total Assets:* £43,533,000
Registered Office: Third Floor, Broad Quay House, Prince Street, Bristol, BS1 4DJ
Activities: Management of real estate on a fee or contract basis
Parent: Birmingham Healthcare Services (Holdings) Limited
Officers: David Robert Hardingham [1974] Director/Commercial Manager; Harvey John William Pownall [1966] Director

Bishop Fleming LLP
Incorporated: 18 February 2014 *Employees:* 238
Net Worth: £3,559,381 *Total Assets:* £8,001,925
Registered Office: 2nd Floor, Stratus House, Emperor Way, Exeter Business Park, Exeter, EX1 3QS
Officers: Andrew Philip Sandiford [1971] Member; Ian James Crockatt Smith [1960] Member; Allison Kaye Beer [1984] LLP Member; Richard Edward Timothy Borton [1961] LLP Member; Andrew Edward Browne [1966] LLP Member; David Michael Butler [1974] LLP Member; Philippa Mary Clarke [1972] LLP Member; Nathan Coughlin [1977] LLP Member; Charles Peter Davey [1979] LLP Member; Robert Graham Davey [1965] LLP Member; James Joseph Finnegan [1975] LLP Member; Ian John Fraser [1956] LLP Member; Timothy Michael Godfrey [1965] LLP Member; William John Hanbury [1968] LLP Member; Fleur Anne Lewis [1977] LLP Member; Paul Andrew Morris [1971] LLP Member; Simon James Morrison [1977] LLP Member; Alison Oliver [1968] LLP Member; Roger David John Pimblett [1964] LLP Member; Alexander St John Robins [1968] LLP Member; Isobel Savage [1974] LLP Member; Joseph Hargreaves Scaife [1968] LLP Member; Caroline Smale [1964] LLP Member; John Philip Talbot [1976] LLP Member; Hazel Joy Tucker [1973] LLP Member; Christine Gay Tuckerman [1960] LLP Member; Pamela Wendy Anne Tuckett [1965] LLP Member; Christopher Walklett [1971] LLP Member; Nigel Keith Warren [1960] LLP Member; Jonathan Mark Williams [1963] LLP Member; Andrew Wood [1969] LLP Member

Bishop Fox's School
Incorporated: 7 June 2011 *Employees:* 147
Net Worth: £10,992,000 *Total Assets:* £13,636,000
Registered Office: Bishop Fox's School, Bishop Fox Drive, Taunton, Somerset, TA1 3HQ
Activities: General secondary education
Officers: Karan Debra Robertson, Secretary; Anthony John Alderman [1946] Director/Police Officer; Simon Robert Baldwin [1969] Director/Programme Manager; Wendy Lee Colvin [1967] Director/Architect Senior Lecturer HE [American/British]; Anna Maria Elena Curry [1958] Director/Civil Servant; James Fletcher Browning Dryden [1975] Director/Engineering Manager; Alison Jane Jones [1969] Director/Physiotherapist; David John Joslin [1961] Director; Clare Gillian Mellor [1962] Director/HR Consultant; Aneta Maria Skut [1973] Director/Teacher [German]; David Colin Smith [1950] Director; David Ronald Stephenson [1952] Director/Retired; Kerry Tonkin [1969] Director/Headteacher; Mark Alastair Wall [1964] Director/Runs a PR and Communications Company

Jeremy Bishop Haulage Limited
Incorporated: 22 October 2010
Net Worth: £1,391,832 *Total Assets:* £3,642,777
Registered Office: The Mill, Kingsteignton Road, Newton Abbot, Devon, TQ12 2QA
Activities: Freight transport by road
Shareholders: Jane Elizabeth Bishop; Jeremy Douglas Bishop
Officers: Jane Elizabeth Bishop, Secretary; Jane Elizabeth Bishop [1964] Director/Haulier/Administrator; Jeremy Douglas Bishop [1963] Director/Haulier

The Bishop of Winchester Academy Trust
Incorporated: 29 September 2009 *Employees:* 123
Net Worth: £15,682,546 *Total Assets:* £18,795,504
Registered Office: The Bishop of Winchester Academy, Mallard Road, Bournemouth, BH8 9PW
Activities: General secondary education
Officers: Julie Margaret Tannett, Secretary; Neil Baker [1967] Director/IT Controls Manager; Elizabeth Du Lieu [1963] Director/Police Officer/Restorative Justice Officer; Janice Lesley Grey [1947] Director/Teacher; Alan Hogg [1951] Director/Retired Manager; Paul Anthony McKeown [1965] Director/Academy Principal; Simon Moore [1966] Director/GM Business Planning & Insight; Mary O'Sullivan [1962] Director of Finance & Planning [Irish]; Dr Karen Pendlebury [1960] Director/University Administrator; Elizabeth Hansford Spreadbury [1940] Director

Bishop Wordsworth's Church of England Grammar School for Boys
Incorporated: 10 February 2011 *Employees:* 79
Net Worth: £16,537,646 *Total Assets:* £17,319,680
Registered Office: 11 The Close, Salisbury, Wilts, SP1 2ED
Activities: General secondary education
Officers: David John Peerless, Secretary; Professor Andrew John Bell [1965] Executive Director; Jonathan Rupert Bowden Blake [1962] Director/Banking; Dr Graham Branagan [1968] Director/Surgeon; Kevin Gregory Martin Flynn [1958] Director/Business Coach; Dr Michael Francis-Pollin [1968] Director/Freelance Researcher of Education & Sports Coach; Dr Saboor Abdus Khan Ghauri [1964] Director/Doctor; Dr Vivian Green [1961] Director/School Teacher; Rebecca Renate Harwood Lincoln [1971] Business Development Director; Jarrod Christian Hastings [1968] Director; Monica Jill Horsburgh [1952] Director/Retired; Ben Jones [1995] Director/Teaching Assistant; James Michael Oldham [1984] Director/Teacher; The Revd Canon Edward Cleasby Probert [1958] Director/Clergyman; Jane Ranaboldo [1961] Director/Solicitor; Dr Stuart David Smallwood [1962] Director/Headmaster; Brigadier Rudi Nicholas Wertheim [1957] Director/Retired

Bistech Group PLC
Incorporated: 21 January 2009 *Employees:* 73
Net Worth: £28,645,648 *Total Assets:* £35,049,536
Registered Office: 137 Victoria Road, Ferndown, Dorset, BH22 9HX
Activities: Wired telecommunications activities
Major Shareholder: Jocelyn Emma Brown
Officers: Jonathan Kirkham, Secretary; Jocelyn Emma Brown [1969] Director; Richard Stuart Holbrook [1976] Director; Jonathan Kirkham [1978] Finance Director

Bistech PLC
Incorporated: 14 June 1988 *Employees:* 73
Net Worth: £4,431,066 *Total Assets:* £32,195,140
Registered Office: 137 Victoria Road, Ferndown, Dorset, BH22 9HX
Activities: Wired telecommunications activities
Parent: Bistech Group PLC
Officers: Jonathan Kirkham, Secretary; Jocelyn Emma Brown [1969] Director; Richard Stuart Holbrook [1976] Technical Director; Jonathan Kirkham [1978] Finance Director

Bittware Limited
Incorporated: 4 November 1996 *Employees:* 20
Previous: Nallatech Limited
Net Worth: £8,726,433 *Total Assets:* £10,544,325
Registered Office: Room 1C-114, Bristol & Bath Science Park, Dirac Crescent, Emersons Green, Bristol, BS16 7FR
Activities: Other information technology service activities
Officers: Robert John Zeitler, Secretary; Joseph W Nelligan Jr [1963] Director [American]

Bituchem Holdings Limited
Incorporated: 13 January 1989 *Employees:* 39
Net Worth: £3,745,832 *Total Assets:* £5,863,159
Registered Office: Laymore Road, Forest Vale Industrial Estate, Cinderford, Glos, GL14 2YH
Activities: Other manufacturing n.e.c.
Shareholder: Paul Paschali
Officers: Michelle Paschali, Secretary; Roger Kenneth Lord [1960] Managing Director; Yuliya Nyzhnyk Paschali [1978] Director [Cypriot]; Neofytou Panagiotis [1989] Director [Cypriot]; Michelle Paschali [1975] Director; Paul Paschali [1943] Director; Paul Paschali Jnr [1978] Director

Bix Developments Limited
Incorporated: 11 August 1970 *Employees:* 5
Net Worth: £9,306,817 *Total Assets:* £11,027,966
Registered Office: Westacott, East Buckland, Barnstaple, Devon, EX32 0TA
Activities: Other letting and operating of own or leased real estate
Shareholders: Michelle Ward; Richard Geoffrey Ward; Nicola Hockridge
Officers: Michelle Ward, Secretary; Geoffrey Herbert Ward [1929] Director; Michelle Ward [1960] Director; Rita Ward [1932] Director

Black Country PPP Health Services Limited
Incorporated: 15 September 1998
Net Worth: £929,418 *Total Assets:* £6,027,271
Registered Office: Third Floor, Broad Quay House, Prince Street, Bristol, BS1 4DJ
Activities: Other specialised construction activities n.e.c.
Parent: RBIL Limited
Officers: Andrew Richard Kershaw [1965] Director/Projects Controller; Richard Little [1979] Investment Director; Julia Sarah McCabe [1970] Regional Director

Black Gold Developments (UK) Limited
Incorporated: 21 April 2005 *Employees:* 7
Net Worth: £179,167 *Total Assets:* £10,877,850
Registered Office: Westons Point Boatyard, Turks Lane, Whitecliff, Poole, Dorset, BH14 8EW
Activities: Development of building projects
Major Shareholder: Julian Leigh Jones
Officers: Julian Leigh Jones, Secretary; Julian Leigh Jones [1961] Managing Director

Blackdown Estates Limited
Incorporated: 29 March 2006
Net Worth Deficit: £1,960,597 *Total Assets:* £5,090,000
Registered Office: Tauntfield, South Road, Taunton, Somerset, TA1 3ND
Activities: Other letting and operating of own or leased real estate
Parent: Summerfield Estates Ltd
Officers: Mark Charles Blackwell, Secretary/Director; Mark Charles Blackwell [1964] Director; James Edward Holyday [1968] Director; Richard David Ayshford Lloyd [1953] Director

Blackheath Farms LLP
Incorporated: 29 September 2015 *Employees:* 2
Net Worth: £27,341,324 *Total Assets:* £27,653,296
Registered Office: One Glass Wharf, Bristol, BS2 0ZX
Officers: Sally Ann Borrows [1957] Member; Simon Alexander Borrows [1959] Member

Blackmore Limited
Incorporated: 9 October 1996 *Employees:* 74
Net Worth: £1,065,591 *Total Assets:* £4,812,060
Registered Office: Longmead Industrial Estate, Shaftesbury, Dorset, SP7 8PX
Activities: Publishing of newspapers
Parent: T.H.Brickell & Son Limited
Officers: Stuart Ambrose Morris, Secretary/Accountant; Nigel John Hunt [1972] Production Director; Stuart Ambrose Morris [1962] Director/Accountant; Andrew John Robbins [1979] Managing Director; Peter Ronald Smith [1957] Works Director; Simon West [1971] Director/Manager

Blackmore Vale Farm Cream Limited
Incorporated: 4 November 1958 *Employees:* 123
Net Worth: £3,649,775 *Total Assets:* £9,354,353
Registered Office: Wincombe Lane, Shaftesbury, Dorset, SP7 8QD
Activities: Liquid milk and cream production
Parent: Castlewood Trust and Company Limited
Officers: Heledd Sian Highnam, Secretary; Henry Cowan [1960] Commercial Director; Jonathan Geddes [1971] Operations Director; Vaughan Heard [1971] Finance Director; James William Highnam [1965] Managing Director

Blade Motor Group Limited
Incorporated: 3 April 1995 *Employees:* 379
Net Worth: £7,227,874 *Total Assets:* £39,170,140
Registered Office: Blade House, A40 Northern Bypass, Gloucester, GL2 9BJ
Activities: Sale of new cars and light motor vehicles
Parent: Blade Motor Group Holdings Limited
Officers: Rachel Clare Flanagan, Secretary; Michael John Flanagan [1955] Managing Director; Rachel Clare Flanagan [1968] Financial Director; Jerry Martin [1957] Director

Bladeroom Group Limited
Incorporated: 21 November 2008 *Employees:* 48
Net Worth: £5,504,000 *Total Assets:* £11,559,000
Registered Office: Stella Way, Bishops Cleeve, Cheltenham, Glos, GL52 7DQ
Activities: Other information technology service activities
Parent: Bladeroom Holdings Limited
Officers: Andrew James Patrick Godden, Secretary; Michael William John Bailey [1953] Director/Chartered Accountant; Jonathan David Brindley [1984] Director; Adrian Edge [1974] Director; Andrew James Patrick Godden [1974] Director; Samuel William Hanks [1979] Director; Michael Tennent Joy [1971] Director; Peter Robin Joy [1951] Director; Martin Ian Ormerod [1976] Director; Paul Stuart Rogers [1968] Director; William Samuel Thornton [1986] Director

Bladeroom Holdings Limited
Incorporated: 12 May 2011 *Employees:* 51
Net Worth: £3,386,000 *Total Assets:* £18,010,000
Registered Office: Stella Way, Bishops Cleeve, Cheltenham, Glos, GL52 7DQ
Activities: Activities of head offices
Parent: BR Corporate Trustees Ltd for The Bladeroom Employee Ownership Trust
Officers: Andrew James Patrick Godden, Secretary; Andrew James Patrick Godden [1974] Director; Michael Tennent Joy [1971] Director/Barrister; Paul Stuart Rogers [1968] Director; Susan Caroline Rogers [1962] Director; William Samuel Thornton [1986] Director/Chief Executive

Blakell Europlacer (Intl) Limited
Incorporated: 1 June 1973 *Employees:* 3
Net Worth: £588,846 *Total Assets:* £6,249,360
Registered Office: 30 Factory Road, Upton Industrial Estate, Poole, Dorset, BH16 5SL
Activities: Installation of industrial machinery and equipment
Parent: Blakell Europlacer Limited
Officers: Tracey Jayne Shotliff, Secretary; Julian Lionel Andrew Boardman [1960] Director; Robert John Conway [1951] Director

Blakell Europlacer Limited
Incorporated: 8 July 1970 *Employees:* 156
Net Worth: £5,299,000 *Total Assets:* £16,152,000
Registered Office: 30 Factory Road, Upton Industrial Estate, Poole, Dorset, BH16 5SL
Activities: Manufacture of other special-purpose machinery n.e.c.
Parent: Parable Ruth Limited
Officers: Tracey Jayne Shotliff, Secretary; Julian Lionel Andrew Boardman [1960] Director; Robert John Conway [1951] Director/Chartered Accountant; Christopher Mark Holt [1965] Director/Electrical Engineer; Victor Eduardo Lorenzo Moreno [1962] Director [Argentinian]; Michael Dominique Scheidegger [1969] Director/Project Manager (Electronics Engineer) [Swiss]

Alvan Blanch Development Company Limited
Incorporated: 15 May 1952 *Employees:* 111
Net Worth: £3,798,912 *Total Assets:* £10,008,404
Registered Office: Chelworth Manor, Chelworth, Crudwell, Malmesbury, Wilts, SN16 9SG
Activities: Manufacture of agricultural and forestry machinery other than tractors
Major Shareholder: Andrew Alvan Blanch
Officers: Helga Blanch, Secretary; Andrew Alvan Blanch [1958] Director; James Jonathan Blanch [1946] Director/Farmer

Alvan Blanch Holdings Limited
Incorporated: 31 August 2012 *Employees:* 111
Net Worth: £3,798,912 *Total Assets:* £10,008,404
Registered Office: Chelworth Manor, Crudwell, Malmesbury, Wilts, SN16 9SG
Activities: Manufacture of agricultural and forestry machinery other than tractors
Major Shareholder: Andrew Alvan Blanch
Officers: Helga Margaretha Blanch, Secretary; Andrew Alvan Blanch [1958] Director

Blanchworth Care Limited
Incorporated: 14 December 1999 *Employees:* 199
Net Worth Deficit: £5,090,230 *Total Assets:* £10,440,479
Registered Office: The Cider Mill, Blanchworth, Stinchcombe, Dursley, Glos, GL11 6BB
Activities: Residential care activities for the elderly and disabled
Shareholders: Sally Anne Manby Roberts; Jeremy Peter Ewens Walsh
Officers: Sally Anne Manby Roberts, Secretary; Neil Tocknell, Secretary; Sally Anne Manby Roberts [1954] Director; Jeremy Peter Ewens Walsh [1950] Director

Bland Group UK Holdings Limited
Incorporated: 21 November 2007 *Employees:* 214
Net Worth: £15,056,930 *Total Assets:* £37,622,216
Registered Office: Encombe House, Estate Office, Corfe Caslte, Wareham, Dorset, BH20 5LW
Activities: Activities of head offices
Officers: Ian Mackie, Secretary; James Peter George Gaggero [1959] Director; Emily Louise Howes [1979] Director/HR; Ian Mackie [1958] Director

Blast Properties Limited
Incorporated: 5 December 2005
Net Worth Deficit: £507,294 *Total Assets:* £12,269,739
Registered Office: 69 High Street, Bideford, Devon, EX39 2AT
Activities: Development of building projects
Officers: Sheila Jane Sawyer, Secretary/Developer; Alan Charles Bristow [1959] Director/Chartered Accountant; Jamie Christian George Dellow [1971] Director/Construction; Paul John Ealey [1965] Director/Demolition; Paul William Hevingham [1958] Director/Chartered Surveyor; Phillip Anthony House [1956] Director/Property Investor; Robert Harvey Sawyer [1955] Director/Developer

Bloom Hearing Specialists Limited
Incorporated: 16 January 2004 *Employees:* 125
Net Worth: £5,743,402 *Total Assets:* £12,520,277
Registered Office: 54 Fore Street, Saltash, Cornwall, PL12 6JL
Activities: Retail sale of hearing aids
Officers: Henrik Skak Bender [1984] Director [Danish]; Jorgen Jensen [1968] Director [Danish]; Diane Newman [1965] Director/Pharmacist; Jan-Peter Rekling [1965] Director [Danish]

Blue Cedar Homes Limited
Incorporated: 4 December 2007 *Employees:* 31
Net Worth: £7,277,000 *Total Assets:* £36,069,000
Registered Office: Eagle House, 1 Babbage Way, Exeter Science Park, Exeter, Devon, EX5 2FN
Activities: Construction of domestic buildings
Major Shareholder: Mark Russell Kay
Officers: Christopher David Fayers [1962] Director/Surveyor; Paul James Goodes [1965] Director/Accountant; Nicholas Ian Hole [1961] Director/Chartered Surveyor; Jonathan Michael Symons [1970] Director; Nicholas Clive Yeo [1978] Area Director

Blue Chip Holidays Ltd
Incorporated: 13 February 2001 *Employees:* 71
Net Worth: £1,937,175 *Total Assets:* £4,306,341
Registered Office: 1 Cranmere Court, Lustleigh Close, Matford Business Park, Marsh Barton Trading Estate, Exeter, Devon, EX2 8PW
Activities: Management of real estate on a fee or contract basis
Parent: Wyndham Vacation Rentals (UK) Ltd
Officers: Garry Clark Adam [1970] Finance Director; Geoffrey John Cowley [1961] Director; Allan Thomas Lambert [1974] Managing Director

The Blue Kite Academy Trust
Incorporated: 26 November 2015 *Employees:* 157
Net Worth: £6,220,945 *Total Assets:* £7,525,641
Registered Office: Wiltshire Avenue, Swindon, Wilts, SN2 1NX
Activities: Primary education
Officers: Jane Samantha Hayward, Secretary; Hayley Brown [1976] Director/School Business Manager; Gary David Evans [1977] Director/Headteacher/CEO; Carl David Harris [1978] Executive Director; Paul Himple [1959] Director/Freelance HR Consultant; Jan Hobbs [1953] Director/Retired Deputy Headteacher; Sue Marshall [1955] Director/Retired Headteacher; Pauline Miller [1958] Director/Educational Consultant; Mark Richard Rachael [1973] Director/Accountant; Rachel Delia Soare [1975] Director/Packaging Category Manager

Blue Port Estates Limited
Incorporated: 10 February 2015 *Employees:* 2
Previous: Blue Port Estates Ltd
Net Worth: £66,390 *Total Assets:* £12,078,435
Registered Office: Unit 2 High Field Business Park, Pityme, St Minver, Wadebridge, Cornwall, PL27 6FE
Activities: Buying and selling of own real estate
Shareholders: Rupert William Hume-Kendall; Caroline Elizabeth Hume-Kendall
Officers: Caroline Elizabeth Hume-Kendall [1969] Financial Services Director; Rupert William Hume-Kendall [1962] Financial Services Director

Blue Port Holdings Limited
Incorporated: 14 December 2015
Net Worth: £2,845,454 *Total Assets:* £7,394,391
Registered Office: Unit 2 High Field Business Park, Pityme, St Minver, Wadebridge, Cornwall, PL27 6FE
Activities: Activities of head offices
Shareholders: Rupert William Hume-Kendall; Caroline Elizabeth Hume-Kendall
Officers: Caroline Elizabeth Hume-Kendall [1969] Director; Rupert William Hume-Kendall [1962] Director

The Blue School
Incorporated: 15 July 2011 *Employees:* 239
Net Worth: £13,732,067 *Total Assets:* £19,474,308
Registered Office: The Blue School, Kennion Road, Wells, Somerset, BA5 2NR
Activities: General secondary education
Officers: Robert Charles Salt, Secretary; Katrina Jane Bradley [1969] Director/Veterinary Surgeon; Rev Samuel Denyer [1974] Director/Vicar; Jane Elizabeth Gardiner [1977] Director/Teacher; David Edward Hiscox [1966] Director; Peter James Hoddinott [1968] Director; Richard Anthony Houlton [1969] Director; Allan Murray Jamieson [1971] Director/Chartered Surveyor; Keith Phimister [1967] Director/IT Manager; Elizabeth Louise Ramsay [1974] Director/Teacher; Alison Clare Richards [1954] Information Specialist/Director; Dr Elizabeth Teresa Walker [1953] Director/Professional Development Specialist (Education); Jennifer Marie Warnock [1967] Director/Housewife; Mark Robert Woodlock [1971] Director/Headteacher

Blue Scorpio Limited
Incorporated: 10 September 2014 *Employees:* 1
Net Worth: £941,894 *Total Assets:* £6,128,384
Registered Office: 33 Oldfield Road, Bath, BA2 3NE
Activities: Security dealing on own account
Major Shareholder: Steven James Medlock
Officers: Peter Phipps, Secretary; David John Medlock [1955] Director; Steven James Medlock [1991] Director

The Blue Sea Food Company Limited
Incorporated: 23 April 2003 *Employees:* 150
Net Worth: £665,186 *Total Assets:* £4,875,971
Registered Office: Wessex House, Teign Road, Newton Abbot, Devon, TQ12 4AA
Activities: Processing and preserving of fish, crustaceans and molluscs
Major Shareholder: Trevor Royston Bartlett
Officers: Trevor Royston Bartlett [1955] Director/Shell Fisherman; David William Markham [1971] Director/Food Processing; Dawn Emma Spencer [1972] Director/Food Manufacturer

Blue3 (London) (Holdings) Limited
Incorporated: 14 February 2013
Net Worth: £10,000 *Total Assets:* £4,157,000
Registered Office: Third Floor, Broad Quay House, Prince Street, Bristol, BS1 4DJ
Activities: Activities of head offices
Shareholders: Equitix Infrastructure 4 Limited; DIF Infrastructure II UK Limited
Officers: Charlotte Sophie Ellen Douglass [1978] Director/Chartered Surveyor; Erwan Benoit Fournis [1972] Director/Fund Manager [French]; Adam Charles Peel Irwin [1987] Director/ICAEW Qualified Chartered Accountant; Angela Louise Roshier [1975] Director/Finance

Blue3 (London) Limited
Incorporated: 14 February 2013
Net Worth Deficit: £77,000 *Total Assets:* £49,070,000
Registered Office: Third Floor, Broad Quay House, Prince Street, Bristol, BS1 4DJ
Activities: Construction of commercial buildings
Parent: Blue3 (London) (Holdings) Limited
Officers: Charlotte Sophie Ellen Douglass [1978] Director/Chartered Surveyor; Erwan Benoit Fournis [1972] Director/Fund Manager [French]; Adam Charles Peel Irwin [1987] Director/ICAEW Qualified Chartered Accountant; Angela Louise Roshier [1975] Director/Finance

Bluebelt Hospitality Limited
Incorporated: 15 October 2013 *Employees:* 120
Net Worth: £153,317 *Total Assets:* £5,086,899
Registered Office: Widbrook Grange, Trowbridge Road, Bradford on Avon, Wilts, BA15 1UH
Activities: Hotels and similar accommodation
Major Shareholder: Nicholas James Dent
Officers: Nicholas James Dent [1975] Telecoms Director

Bluetech Systems International Ltd
Incorporated: 4 November 2016
Net Worth: £1 *Total Assets:* £4,216,851
Registered Office: Unit D, Eagle Road, Plympton, Plymouth, PL7 5JY
Activities: Other manufacturing n.e.c.
Major Shareholder: Jeremy Bernard Lee
Officers: Dr Jeremy Bernard Lee [1957] Director; Phillip Charles Smithson [1954] Director

Bluevenn Limited
Incorporated: 8 July 1998 *Employees:* 49
Net Worth Deficit: £5,245,819 *Total Assets:* £11,115,456
Registered Office: One Redcliff Street, Bristol, BS1 6NP
Activities: Business and domestic software development
Shareholders: Neil Thomas; Steven Klin; Iain Fraser Lovatt
Officers: David Mark Jameson [1973] Director; Steven Klin [1967] Director; Iain Lovatt [1957] Director; Kevin Neil Thomas [1964] Director

Bluewater Property Limited
Incorporated: 3 February 1998 *Employees:* 4
Net Worth: £6,711,081 *Total Assets:* £6,945,591
Registered Office: Bluewater Estate, Bell Close, Plymouth, PL7 4JH
Activities: Construction of commercial buildings
Shareholder: Duncan Giles Martin
Officers: Andrew Preston, Secretary; Duncan Giles Martin [1957] Director; Andrew Preston [1965] Director

Blundell's School
Incorporated: 16 June 2000 *Employees:* 257
Net Worth: £13,812,000 *Total Assets:* £19,459,000
Registered Office: Blundells School, Blundells Road, Tiverton, Devon, EX16 4DT
Activities: Primary education
Officers: Annika Hedrich-Wiggans, Secretary; Dr. Sarah Ansell [1962] Director/Doctor; Nigel Arnold [1954] Director/Retired Police Officer; Cedric Marsden Clapp [1946] Director/Retired Chartered Accountant; Nicholas John Cryer [1967] Director/Chartered Engineer; Nigel Patrick Hall [1955] Director; Barnabas John Hurst-Bannister [1952] Director/Insurance Executive; Peter Michael Johnson [1947] Director/Retired Headmaster; Martha MacNeice [1964] Director/Barrister [Irish]; James Macpherson [1949] Director/Retired Headmaster; Jessica Mary Anne Mannix [1965] Director/Fundraiser; Revd Richard Leonard Maudsley [1955] Director; Bishop Nicholas Howard Paul McKinnel [1954] Director/Bishop; Randall Thane [1957] Director; Ian Robert George Thomas [1969] Director/Financial Planner; Dr Mark Elliott Wood [1964] Director/University Lecturer

BNM Parkstone LLP
Incorporated: 25 November 2008
Net Worth: £4,005,978 *Total Assets:* £8,075,468
Registered Office: 3 Wood Row, Throop Road, Bournemouth, BH8 0DN
Officers: Lucas Khazai [1972] Member; Mahmood Shababi [1950] Member; Sybille Bernadette Jacqueline Shababi [1963] Member; Nosratolloah Babaie Ahrestani [1946] LLP Member; Mohammad Bagher Naeimi [1951] LLP Member

BNP Paribas Fleet Holdings Limited
Incorporated: 19 May 2000
Net Worth: £445,112,992 *Total Assets:* £445,112,992
Registered Office: Whitehill House, Windmill Hill, Swindon, Wilts, SN5 6PE
Activities: Activities of financial services holding companies
Parent: Arval Service Lease SA
Officers: Amanda Jane Parshall, Secretary; Bart Beckers [1963] Director/Chief Commercial Officer [Belgian]; Antonio Miguel Vieira Galvao Cabaca [1973] Managing Director [Portuguese]; Stephen Andrew Robert Hunt [1967] Director/Chief Executive Officer; Paul Lawrence Hyne [1979] Director/Chief Financial Officer; Monsieur Alain Carmelo Van Groenendael [1961] Director/Chief Executive Officer [Belgian]

Boardinghouse Windfarm Limited
Incorporated: 21 October 2011
Net Worth: £2,097,953 *Total Assets:* £14,773,756
Registered Office: 14 High Cross, Truro, Cornwall, TR1 2AJ
Activities: Production of electricity
Parent: Thrive Renewables (Boardinghouse) Limited
Officers: Matthew Thomas Clayton [1975] Executive Director; Michael Henry Deptford [1960] Director; Timothy John Kirby [1954] Director

J R Bodman Limited
Incorporated: 26 February 2005 *Employees:* 11
Net Worth: £900,292 *Total Assets:* £4,268,042
Registered Office: Bishopbrook House, Cathedral Avenue, Wells, Somerset, BA5 1FD
Activities: Raising of swine and pigs
Major Shareholder: James Richard Bodman
Officers: Helen Louise Bodman, Secretary; Helen Louise Bodman [1966] Director/Farmer; James Richard Bodman [1963] Director/Farmer

Bodmin College
Incorporated: 3 December 2010 *Employees:* 226
Net Worth: £16,136,487 *Total Assets:* £18,316,522
Registered Office: Bodmin College, Lostwithiel Road, Bodmin, Cornwall, PL31 1DD
Activities: General secondary education
Officers: Karenza Andrews [1978] Director/Parent; Alan Edward Brown [1941] Director/Retired; Jason David Coad [1962] Director/Farmer/Accountant; Brett Elliott [1968] Director/Headmaster; Timothy Alan FitzGenerald [1973] Director; Louise Amy Irons [1972] Director/Teacher; Gareth Morris [1976] Director/Teacher; David Rushton [1961] Director/Retired Headteacher; David Trewolla [1964] Director/Environment Agency; Roy Martin Vannoey [1948] Director/Part Time Lecturer

Bodywise (UK) Limited
Incorporated: 4 May 1989 *Employees:* 17
Net Worth: £13,631,801 *Total Assets:* £15,353,172
Registered Office: 14 Lower Court Road, Almondsbury, Bristol, BS32 4DX
Activities: Manufacture of household and sanitary goods and of toilet requisites
Shareholders: Susan Penelope Hewson-Lowe; Stephen Lowe
Officers: Susan Hewson Lowe, Secretary; Susan Hewson Lowe [1952] Director/Company Secretary; Stephen Lowe [1953] Managing Director

BOFA International Ltd.
Incorporated: 13 April 1987 *Employees:* 207
Net Worth: £14,283,771 *Total Assets:* £20,065,968
Registered Office: 21-22 Balena Close, Creekmoor Industrial Estate, Poole, Dorset, BH17 7DX
Activities: Manufacture of other special-purpose machinery n.e.c.
Parent: SHOO 788AA Limited
Officers: Kevin Paul Bamford [1959] Operations Director; Haydn St John Knight [1964] Sales Director; Antony Keith Lockwood [1960] Sales & Marketing Director; James Martin Oliver [1970] Finance Director; Jeff Spethmann [1965] Director/Business Executive [American]; Matthew James Wright [1970] Supply Chain Director

Bollingwood Limited
Incorporated: 22 March 2004 *Employees:* 3
Net Worth: £2,080,363 *Total Assets:* £4,558,469
Registered Office: Towngate House, 2-8 Parkstone Road, Poole, Dorset, BH15 2PW
Activities: Other business support service activities n.e.c.
Shareholders: David Laurence John Wells; Steven John Wells; Shane Robert Wells
Officers: Steven John Wells, Secretary; David Laurence John Wells [1949] Director; Shane Robert Wells [1970] Director; Steven John Wells [1974] Director/Property Manager

W H Bond & Sons Limited
Incorporated: 20 August 1996 *Employees:* 87
Net Worth: £11,721,158 *Total Assets:* £34,254,788
Registered Office: Trerule Farm, Trerulefoot, Saltash, Cornwall, PL12 5BL
Activities: Growing of cereals (except rice), leguminous crops and oil seeds
Parent: Bond Holdings Limited
Officers: Alison Mary Bond, Secretary/Director; Alison Mary Bond [1976] Director; Christopher Ian Bond [1972] Director; Jonathan Martin Bond [1970] Director

Bond Business Services Limited
Incorporated: 11 August 2011 *Employees:* 2
Previous: Rushbury Enterprises Limited
Net Worth Deficit: £1,329,691 *Total Assets:* £4,544,300
Registered Office: Rushbury House, Winchcombe, Cheltenham, Glos, GL54 5AE
Activities: Management consultancy activities other than financial management
Shareholders: Stephen William Bond; Victoria Lee Bond
Officers: Amanda Jane Perks, Secretary; Stephen William Bond [1950] Director; Victoria Lee Bond [1964] Director

Bond Holdings Limited
Incorporated: 29 July 1994 *Employees:* 4
Net Worth: £4,594,547 *Total Assets:* £4,693,183
Registered Office: Trerule Farm, Trerulefoot, Saltash, Cornwall, PL12 5BL
Activities: Mixed farming
Shareholder: Graham Martin Bond
Officers: Alison Mary Bond, Secretary/Director; Christopher Ian Bond [1972] Director; Clare Margaret Louise Bond [1963] Director; Graham Martin Bond [1963] Director; Jonathan Martin Bond [1970] Director

Bond Street Estates (Brighton) Limited
Incorporated: 16 August 2005 *Employees:* 95
Net Worth: £5,897,788 *Total Assets:* £39,573,112
Registered Office: Harbour House, 60 Purewell, Christchurch, Dorset, BH23 1ES
Activities: Hotels and similar accommodation
Parent: Brighton Harbour Hotel Limited
Officers: Stuart Andrew Bateman [1976] Director; David Francis Robbins [1967] Finance Director; Michael Oliver Warren [1970] Director [Irish]

Bonds Mill Estate Limited
Incorporated: 18 June 1985 *Employees:* 3
Net Worth: £2,645,752 *Total Assets:* £6,175,417
Registered Office: The Manor, Boddington Lane, Boddington, Cheltenham, Glos, GL51 0TJ
Activities: Other letting and operating of own or leased real estate
Parent: The Robert Hitchins Group Limited
Officers: Jonathan James Stewart Dunley, Secretary; Jonathan James Stewart Dunley [1970] Director; Jeremy Charles Hitchins [1954] Director; Simon Jeremy Tothill [1965] Director/Chartered Surveyor

Bonhay & Eagle Property Company Limited
Incorporated: 20 March 1928
Net Worth: £6,867,016 *Total Assets:* £13,082,851
Registered Office: 2 Berkeley Cottages, Collingwood Road, Stoke, Plymouth, PL1 5QT
Activities: Buying and selling of own real estate
Officers: Richard Dudley Steer, Secretary; James Dominic Gaisford [1958] Director; Alistair Nicholas Parkin [1970] Director; Henry Robert Parkin [1970] Director

Boo Homes (Leckhampton) Limited
Incorporated: 19 July 2012 *Employees:* 4
Net Worth: £75,784 *Total Assets:* £5,677,605
Registered Office: 16 Imperial Square, Cheltenham, Glos, GL50 1QZ
Activities: Development of building projects
Shareholders: Boo Homes Limited; CAA Property Limited
Officers: Edward Arthur Davies [1970] Director; Alexander John Stuart Scott [1968] Director/Property Developer; Jillian Charlotte Scott [1968] Director/Property Developer

Books & Stationers Limited
Incorporated: 3 February 2011 *Employees:* 118
Net Worth: £8,179,630 *Total Assets:* £10,534,982
Registered Office: Greenbridge Road, Swindon, Wilts, SN3 3RX
Activities: Retail sale of newspapers and stationery in specialised stores
Parent: WH Smith High Street Holdings Limited
Officers: Ian Houghton, Secretary; Ian Houghton [1965] Director; Robert James Moorhead [1964] Director

Borlase Smart John Wells Trust Ltd
Incorporated: 21 March 2005 *Employees:* 3
Net Worth: £4,162,524 *Total Assets:* £4,204,737
Registered Office: Porthmeor Studios, Back Road West, St Ives, Cornwall, TR26 1NG
Activities: Financial intermediation not elsewhere classified
Officers: Daniel Patrick Wilson, Secretary; Eileen Boydell Amos [1978] Director/Trustee; Susan Daniel McElroy [1947] Director/Museum Curator; James Green [1967] Gallery Director; Michael Porter [1948] Director/Artist; Tamzyn Elizabeth Smith [1976] Director; Roger Towndrow [1954] Director/University Lecturer; Jane Val Baker [1947] Director; Marilyn Weston [1936] Director/Retired; Percival Ross Williams [1954] Director/Arts Manager; Daniel Patrick Wilson [1955] Director/Chartered Accountant

Borough Green Sand Pits Limited
Incorporated: 10 January 1956 *Employees:* 19
Net Worth: £2,260,488 *Total Assets:* £4,861,527
Registered Office: Swatton Barn, Badbury, Swindon, Wilts, SN4 0EU
Activities: Operation of gravel and sand pits; mining of clays and kaolin
Shareholders: Roger Keith Body; Lisa Ann Barry
Officers: Roger Keith Body, Secretary; Roger Keith Body [1951] Director; Neal Leslie Dennis [1953] Director/Chartered Accountant; Robert Henry Samuel [1943] Director/Consultant

The Borrowdale Gates Limited
Incorporated: 1 December 2016
Net Worth Deficit: £266,993 *Total Assets:* £3,969,713
Registered Office: Lowin House, Tregolls Road, Truro, Cornwall, TR1 2NA
Activities: Hotels and similar accommodation
Officers: Jan Johannes Bester [1984] Director/Fund Manager [South African]; Jacobus Adriaan Nel [1975] Director/Fund Manager [South African]

The Boston Tea Party Group Limited
Incorporated: 2 December 2004 *Employees:* 535
Net Worth: £2,720,630 *Total Assets:* £6,931,108
Registered Office: 75 Park Street, Bristol, BS1 5PF
Activities: Licenced restaurants
Shareholder: Charles Giles Clarke
Officers: Julie Lynn Centracchio [1966] Director [American]; Charles Giles Clarke [1953] Director; Thomas Rupert King [1963] Director; Sam Vernon Roberts [1974] Director

Bott Limited
Incorporated: 17 August 1977 *Employees:* 425
Net Worth: £18,652,820 *Total Assets:* £28,452,978
Registered Office: Bott Limited, Bude-Stratton Business Park, Bude, Cornwall, EX23 8LY
Activities: Manufacture of other fabricated metal products n.e.c.
Parent: Bott Internationale Holding GmbH
Officers: Simon David Fry, Secretary; Simon David Fry [1955] Financial Director; Clive Robert Woodward [1962] Director/Engineer; Kevin Adrian Woodward [1967] Director; Michael Wosnitzka [1961] Director/Engineer

Bottlegreen Holdings Limited
Incorporated: 9 August 2006
Net Worth: £1,434,486 *Total Assets:* £8,236,066
Registered Office: Manderson House, 5230 Valiant Court, Delta Way, Brockworth, Gloucester, GL3 4FE
Activities: Manufacture of soft drinks; production of mineral waters and other bottled waters
Parent: Bottle Green Drinks Company Limited
Officers: Arthur Richmond, Secretary; Elaine Birchall [1966] Director [Irish]; Arthur William Richmond [1966] Director/Accountant; Karen Salters [1970] Director

The Bourne Academy
Incorporated: 5 February 2010 *Employees:* 135
Net Worth: £6,658,018 *Total Assets:* £9,950,388
Registered Office: The Bourne Academy, Hadow Road, Bournemouth, BH10 5HS
Activities: General secondary education
Officers: Mark Avoth [1970] Director/Principal; Henry Niall Pierre Bishop [1967] Director/Teacher; Timothy Mark Brown [1977] Finance Director; Daniel Butt [1974] Director/Businessman; Pauline Calvert [1961] Director [Irish]; Susan Jane Churchill [1969] Director; Caroline Foster [1956] Director/Local Government Officer; Oliver Charles Cassels Hunter [1975] Director/Engineer; Nicola Sabina Jinks [1964] Director/Lawyer; Richard John Knott [1956] Director/Deputy Headmaster; Heidi Kate Leavesley [1973] Director/Businesswoman; Lawrence George Lewis [1969] Director/Finance; David Mastrocola [1983] Director/Teacher; David Neill [1965] Director/Teacher; Jacqueline Page [1964] Director/Vice-Principal of College; Benjamin Alastair Martin Vessey [1967] Director/Headmaster

Bourne Group Holdings Ltd
Incorporated: 10 March 1992 *Employees:* 193
Net Worth: £10,242,832 *Total Assets:* £26,442,380
Registered Office: St Clements House, St Clements Road, Parkstone, Poole, Dorset, BH12 4GP
Activities: Activities of construction holding companies
Parent: Bourne (Group) Limited
Officers: Howard Davis, Secretary; Howard Davis [1972] Director; Stephen Philip William Govier [1966] Director

Bourne Group Ltd.
Incorporated: 5 June 1946 *Employees:* 193
Previous: Bourne Construction Engineering Ltd
Net Worth: £9,898,637 *Total Assets:* £26,061,072
Registered Office: St Clements House, St Clements Road, Parkstone, Poole, Dorset, BH12 4GP
Activities: Other specialised construction activities n.e.c.
Parent: Bourne Group Holdings Limited
Officers: Howard Davis, Secretary; Karl James Butters [1970] Development Director; Howard Davis [1972] Director; Stephen Philip William Govier [1966] Director; Nicholas Michael Hatton [1966] Managing Director; Nicholas Roy Hayes [1955] Managing Director; Alan Harold Pillinger [1955] Managing Director

Bourne Holdings
Incorporated: 3 December 1936 *Employees:* 1
Net Worth: £7,112,440 *Total Assets:* £11,499,305
Registered Office: 310 Bournemouth Road, Parkstone, Poole, Dorset, BH14 9AR
Activities: Renting and operating of Housing Association real estate
Major Shareholder: John Sydenham Whitelock
Officers: Nicole Pauline Mary Whitelock, Secretary; John Sydenham Whitelock [1949] Director/Property Developer; Nicole Pauline Mary Whitelock [1956] Director/Property Developer

Bournemouth School
Incorporated: 18 August 2011 *Employees:* 97
Net Worth: £12,265,170 *Total Assets:* £14,721,369
Registered Office: Bournemouth School, East Way, Bournemouth, BH8 9PY
Activities: General secondary education
Officers: Eugene Sean Brunet [1964] Director/Educational Consultant; Sally Burrows [1957] Director/Nurse; Michele Lois Helen Gosling [1964] Director/Teacher; Michael Peter Jones [1968] Finance Director; Caroline Helen Kelleway [1963] Director; Dr Dorian Paul Lewis [1967] Director/Headmaster; Cara Frederika Lloyd-Hopkins [1972] Director/Support Staff Bournemouth School; Kate Jane Shaw [1966] Director; David John Sidwick [1961] Director; Noel Edmund Torrance Smith [1964] Director/Accountant; Simon Andrew Spendlowe [1972] Funeral Director; Alan Graham Turle [1951] Director/Solicitor; Angela Karen Turton [1963] Director/HR Consultant; Danielle Jane Watts [1973] Director; David Christopher Worden [1963] Director/Teacher

Bournemouth School for Girls
Incorporated: 13 July 2011 *Employees:* 136
Net Worth: £11,406,782 *Total Assets:* £14,368,545
Registered Office: Bournemouth School for Girls, Castle Gate Close, Castle Lane West, Bournemouth, BH8 9UJ
Activities: General secondary education
Officers: Julia Ford, Secretary; Dr Sarita Subhas Alner [1975] Director/Medical; Irene Ashton [1967] Director/Chartered Surveyor; Juliana Lisa Bowley [1957] Director/Child Care House Mother; Alistair Brien [1964] Director/Headteacher; Keith Stephen Cameron [1938] Director/Retired Army Officer; Geoffrey Darnton [1948] Director/Consultant; Robert Mark Davies [1966] Director/Network Manager; Dario Di-Felice [1965] Director/Chartered Construction Manager; Lesley Karen Fereti [1970] Director/Marketing; Paul Anthony Fitzpatrick [1963] Director/Adviser Development Consultant; Linda Jane Holman [1960] Director/Teacher; Dr John Bruce Knowles [1948] Director/Chairman; David Michael Mulliner [1961] Director/House Husband; Julian David Robbins [1968] Director; Noel David Spreadbury [1939] Director/Retired; Jane Stichbury [1955] Director/Chair Royal Bournemouth & Christchurch Hospital NHS; Dr Marliese Margaretha Symons [1967] Director/Chiropractor & Homeopath; Karen Louise Yendole [1980] Director/School Technician

Bournemouth Transport Limited
Incorporated: 27 March 1986 *Employees:* 417
Net Worth: £3,104,000 *Total Assets:* £18,572,000
Registered Office: Yeomans Way, Bournemouth, BH8 0BQ
Activities: Other urban, suburban or metropolitan passenger land transport (not underground, metro or similar)
Parent: RATP DEV UK Ltd
Officers: David Julian Squire, Secretary; Cyril Herve Carniel [1961] Director/Consultant [French]; Howard Charles Goodbourn [1961] Director/Chief Financial Officer; Philip Pannell [1962] Service Delivery Director; Ann Marie Pauline Slavin [1969] Finance Director [Irish]; David Julian Squire [1961] Managing Director

Bournemouth Young Men's Christian Association
Incorporated: 30 July 1999 *Employees:* 92
Net Worth: £3,059,000 *Total Assets:* £8,180,000
Registered Office: Delta House, 56 Westover Road, Bournemouth, BH1 2BS
Activities: Other accommodation
Officers: Jacqueline Ann Morgan, Secretary; Eamon Anthony Bundred [1961] Director/Property Developer; Richard Frank Elms [1949] Director/Retired; Colin Raymond Hartland [1949] Director/Retired; Simon Marsh [1943] Director/Retired Headteacher; Rev Ian Andrew Terry [1953] Director/Minister of Religion; David Williams [1972] Director/Judge

Bowater Homes Ltd
Incorporated: 17 December 2016 *Employees:* 4
Net Worth: £3,905,355 *Total Assets:* £3,933,428
Registered Office: Coombe, Chagford, Newton Abbot, Devon, TQ13 8DF
Activities: Other service activities n.e.c.
Shareholders: Lady Susan Mary Bowater; Euan David Vansittart Bowater
Officers: Euan David Vansittart Bowater [1935] Director; Susan Mary Bowater [1940] Director; Jackie Browne [1965] Director

Bowden Derra Park Limited
Incorporated: 20 March 2000 *Employees:* 188
Net Worth: £3,295,843 *Total Assets:* £10,713,248
Registered Office: Bowden Derra Park, Polyphant, Launceston, Cornwall, PL15 7PU
Activities: Residential care activities for learning difficulties, mental health and substance abuse
Shareholders: David Elmer Cash; Judith Cash
Officers: Judith Cash, Secretary/Residential Home; David Elmer Cash [1943] Director/Residential Home Proprietor; Judith Cash [1942] Director/Residential Home

Bowerings Animal Feeds Limited
Incorporated: 6 June 1979 *Employees:* 20
Net Worth: £3,634,979 *Total Assets:* £4,557,413
Registered Office: The Docks, Bridgwater, Somerset, TA6 3EX
Activities: Manufacture of prepared feeds for farm animals
Major Shareholder: Ben Trevelyan Bowering
Officers: Ben Trevelyan Bowering, Secretary/Director; Ben Trevelyan Bowering [1957] Director; Robert John Bowering [1959] Director/Car Salesman

Bowldown Farms Limited
Incorporated: 19 February 1992 *Employees:* 13
Net Worth: £679,479 *Total Assets:* £7,003,881
Registered Office: Estate Office, Bowldown Farm, Tetbury, Glos, GL8 8UD
Activities: Raising of sheep and goats
Shareholders: Andrew Robert Richard Vernon; Greville Edward Mervyn Vernon; Hugh Richard Mervyn Vernon; Hillhouse Estates Limited
Officers: Charles Clifford Toyn, Secretary; Andrew Robert Vernon [1979] Director; James Fitzpatrick Greville Vernon [1971] Director; Emma Mary Von Hof [1983] Director

Bowmill Engineering Limited
Incorporated: 8 June 1970 *Employees:* 180
Net Worth: £5,220,402 *Total Assets:* £12,205,254
Registered Office: 18-30 Morris Road, Nuffield, Poole, Dorset, BH17 0GG
Activities: Manufacture of other fabricated metal products n.e.c.
Major Shareholder: David Adrian Boucher
Officers: David Adrian Boucher, Secretary; David Adrian Boucher [1948] Director/Mechanical Engineer; Nicholas Epps [1960] Director/Engineer; Matthew Leyshon [1969] Director/Engineer

Box House (Services) Ltd
Incorporated: 24 May 1982 *Employees:* 1
Net Worth: £483,375 *Total Assets:* £3,583,773
Registered Office: Box House, Bath Road, Box, Corsham, Wilts, SN13 8AA
Activities: Other letting and operating of own or leased real estate
Major Shareholder: Charles Gordon Tull

Boyland and Son Limited
Incorporated: 19 April 1961 *Employees:* 3
Net Worth: £6,282,013 *Total Assets:* £7,470,753
Registered Office: Unit 14 Alder Hills Park, Alder Hills, Poole, Dorset, BH12 4AR
Activities: Activities of head offices
Major Shareholder: Peter Leonard Brent Boyland
Officers: Peter Leonard Brent Boyland, Secretary; Peter Leonard Brent Boyland [1941] Director; Charlotte Katherine Burn [1982] Director; Gail Victoria Maxted [1951] Director

BP Rolls Holdings Limited
Incorporated: 7 October 2014 *Employees:* 107
Net Worth: £445,991 *Total Assets:* £4,151,302
Registered Office: 28 Hopkinson Way, West Portway Industrial Estate, Andover, Hants, SP10 3LF
Activities: Activities of other holding companies n.e.c.
Major Shareholder: David Brian Rolls
Officers: Tariq Javaid Abul [1971] Director/Sales & Operations; David Brian Rolls [1972] Director

BPE Solicitors LLP
Incorporated: 28 September 2009 *Employees:* 11
Net Worth: £1,666,032 *Total Assets:* £5,104,282
Registered Office: St James House, St James Square, Cheltenham, Glos, GL50 3PR
Officers: Robert Kenneth Bryan [1965] Member; Lisa Claire Gettins [1971] Member; Philip James Radford [1958] Member; Anthony Alexander de Nouaille Rudge [1963] Member; Antonia Louisa Shield [1972] Member; John Kerrison Workman [1959] Member; Joanne Margaret Bewley [1970] LLP Member; Nicola Charlesworth Corner [1956] LLP Member; Iain Andrew Garfield [1975] LLP Member; Ian Glyndwr Griffiths [1968] LLP Member; Gavin Richard Hughes-Jones [1945] LLP Member; Clare Elizabeth Parkin [1974] LLP Member; Dale Mark Glyn Williams [1969] LLP Member

Brabon Properties Limited
Incorporated: 20 July 1999
Net Worth: £3,485,651 *Total Assets:* £4,408,206
Registered Office: Windsor House, Bayshill Road, Cheltenham, Glos, GL50 3AT
Activities: Development of building projects
Shareholders: Whiteshill Investments Limited; Stephen Michael Tandy
Officers: Stephen Michael Tandy, Secretary/Director; Stephen Michael Tandy [1953] Director

Bracken Developments Limited
Incorporated: 7 September 1979 *Employees:* 3
Net Worth: £18,676,764 *Total Assets:* £25,311,494
Registered Office: 483 Christchurch Road, Bournemouth, BH1 4AD
Activities: Construction of domestic buildings
Shareholder: Rodney Taylor
Officers: Dorothy Ann Taylor, Secretary; Michael Charles Marchant [1967] Director; Nadine Marie Marchant [1968] Director; Dorothy Ann Taylor [1943] Director; Gregory Taylor [1971] Director/Building Manager; Rodney Taylor [1940] Director

Bradbury House Properties Limited
Incorporated: 27 November 2015
Net Worth: £1 *Total Assets:* £20,025,952
Registered Office: First Floor, Unit 1 Bromley Yard, Bromley Road, Stanton Drew, Bristol, BS39 4DE
Activities: Activities of other holding companies n.e.c.
Parent: Bradbury House Limited
Officers: Bridie Anne Bradbury [1963] Director; Neil Bradbury [1959] Director

Braddicks Holiday Centre (Westward Ho!) Limited
Incorporated: 11 April 1947
Net Worth: £4,901,000 *Total Assets:* £9,911,294
Registered Office: 12 Chingswell Street, Bideford, Devon, EX39 2NF
Activities: Holiday centres and villages
Parent: Braddicks Leisure Ltd
Officers: Michael John Williams, Secretary; Graham John Braddick [1932] Director; Robert Leslie Hobart Braddick [1972] Director; Vikki Braddick [1972] Director; John Cooke [1976] Operations Director; Michael John Williams [1962] Finance Director

Braddicks Leisure Limited
Incorporated: 23 December 1966 *Employees:* 121
Net Worth: £7,935,504 *Total Assets:* £13,706,349
Registered Office: 12 Chingswell Street, Bideford, Devon, EX39 2NF
Activities: Licenced restaurants
Major Shareholder: Robert Leslie Hobart Braddick
Officers: Michael John Williams, Secretary; Graham John Braddick [1932] Director; Robert Leslie Hobart Braddick [1972] Director; Vikki Braddick [1972] Director; John Cooke [1976] Operations Director; Michael John Williams [1962] Finance Director

Bradford and Sons Limited
Incorporated: 9 December 1893 *Employees:* 1,280
Net Worth: £44,360,000 *Total Assets:* £116,049,000
Registered Office: 98 Hendford Hill, Yeovil, Somerset, BA20 2QR
Activities: Agents involved in the sale of timber and building materials
Officers: George Miles Bramston Adams [1956] Director/Chairman; Ian Stanton Church [1961] Managing Director, Snows Timber Ltd; Mark Andrew Eburne [1962] Director/Chief Executive Officer; Nicholas Peter Hall [1962] Director; Rachel Marie Lawrence [1979] Director/Chief Financial Officer; Alan Graham Platt [1974] Director; David Andrew Young [1974] Managing Director, Bradfords Building Supplies Ltd

Bradfords Building Supplies Limited
Incorporated: 23 August 1933 *Employees:* 687
Net Worth: £16,902,044 *Total Assets:* £45,587,268
Registered Office: 96 Hendford Hill, Yeovil, Somerset, BA20 2QT
Activities: Agents involved in the sale of timber and building materials
Parent: Bradford and Sons Limited
Officers: George Miles Bramston Adams [1956] Director/Chairman; Ian Stanton Church [1961] Director; Mark Andrew Eburne [1962] Director; Lee Brian Harwood [1975] Finance Director; Rachel Marie Lawrence [1979] Director/Chief Financial Officer; David Andrew Young [1974] Director

Bradgate Business Finance Limited
Incorporated: 1 June 2006 *Employees:* 14
Net Worth: £1,523,206 *Total Assets:* £22,569,920
Registered Office: 2nd Floor, St James House, The Square, Lower Bristol Road, Bath, BA2 3BH
Activities: Financial leasing
Parent: 1pm PLC
Officers: Jennifer Bodey, Secretary; John Richard Arnold [1961] Director; James Matthew Arthur Roberts [1977] Director; Richard Ian Smith [1961] Director; Ian Sullivan [1967] Director

Robert Braithwaite Limited
Incorporated: 2 August 2013 *Employees:* 3
Net Worth: £40,823,648 *Total Assets:* £41,591,984
Registered Office: Richmond Point, 43 Richmond Hill, Bournemouth, BH2 6LR
Activities: Activities of other holding companies n.e.c.
Major Shareholder: Robert Braithwaite
Officers: Robert Braithwaite [1943] Director; David Ward [1950] Director

K W Brake and Son Limited
Incorporated: 19 March 2008 *Employees:* 9
Net Worth: £835,007 *Total Assets:* £4,065,772
Registered Office: Wessex House, Challeymead Business Park, Melksham, Wilts, SN12 8BU
Activities: Raising of dairy cattle
Shareholders: Martyn Kenneth Brake; Kathleen Mary Brake
Officers: Kathleen Mary Brake, Secretary; Christopher Martyn Brake [1975] Director/Farmer; Jane Brake [1968] Director; Kathleen Mary Brake [1950] Director/Farmer; Martyn Kenneth Brake [1948] Director/Farmer

The Brandon Trust
Incorporated: 28 March 1989
Net Worth: £14,396,354 *Total Assets:* £19,506,326
Registered Office: Olympus House, Britannia Road, Patchway, Bristol, BS34 5TA
Activities: Residential nursing care facilities
Officers: Jeremy Colin Eastwood, Secretary; John David Adams [1951] Director/Retired; Generald Robert Howe Davies [1956] Director/Retired; Bonnie Phillips Dean [1957] Director; Merlin Jocelyn Floate [1989] Director; Christopher Peter Robert Mahood [1984] Director/Lawyer; Helen Elizabeth Marsden [1960] Director; Martin James Mohan [1959] Director; Clive Anthony Pugh [1971] Director/Partner in a Law Firm; Heather Patricia Sandilands [1963] Director/Sales Manager; Guy Roger Stenson [1973] Director - Housing Association

Brandwells Construction Company Limited
Incorporated: 24 January 1973 *Employees:* 180
Net Worth: £2,532,247 *Total Assets:* £8,806,736
Registered Office: Park House, Church Lane, St George, Bristol, BS5 7AG
Activities: Construction of roads and motorways
Major Shareholder: Andrew Dowden
Officers: Matthew Browne [1968] Director/Technical Manager; Andrew Dowden [1943] Director/Civil Engineer; Christopher Paul Dowden [1968] Director/Civil Engineer; Thomas David Hurford [1973] Director/Surveyor; Stephen Llewellyn Pugh [1965] Director; Robert Alan Schofield [1974] Director/Accountant; John Michael Stafford [1957] Director

Branksome Estates Ltd.
Incorporated: 25 March 1953 *Employees:* 2
Net Worth: £35,995,200 *Total Assets:* £37,782,036
Registered Office: 310 Bournemouth Road, Parkstone, Poole, Dorset, BH14 9AR
Activities: Development of building projects
Parent: Whitelock Investments
Officers: Nicole Pauline Mary Whitelock, Secretary; John Sydenham Whitelock [1949] Director/Builder; Josh Sydenham Kennedy Whitelock [1988] Director; Nicole Pauline Mary Whitelock [1956] Director/Company Secretary

Branksome Park Care Centre Limited
Incorporated: 30 April 2014 *Employees:* 88
Net Worth: £1,145,991 *Total Assets:* £4,745,882
Registered Office: 31-33 Commercial Road, Poole, Dorset, BH14 0HU
Activities: Other human health activities
Shareholders: Andrew Tredrea; Clare Tredrea
Officers: Andrew Tredrea [1959] Director; Clare Tredrea [1963] Director; Jack Tredrea [1992] Director/Corporate Financier

Braunton School and Community College Academy Trust
Incorporated: 14 March 2012 *Employees:* 98
Net Worth: £7,613,604 *Total Assets:* £9,997,987
Registered Office: Braunton School & Community College, Barton Lane, Braunton, Devon, EX33 2BP
Activities: General secondary education
Officers: Fay Elizabeth Johnson, Secretary; Patricia Beevers [1943] Director; Michael Cammack [1960] Director/School Principal; Andrew Clee [1970] Director/General Manager; Barrie Kim Eason [1957] Director; Tracey Justina Elliott [1974] Director; David Sidney Hartnoll [1966] Director/Self Employed Fused Glass Artist; Mark Juby [1953] Director; David Liversedge [1970] Director; Andrew Milton [1962] Director/Employee Braunton Academy; Margaret Joan Robinson [1943] Director; David Sanders [1967] Director/Physiotherapist; Pamela Elizabeth Stevens [1971] Director/Employee Devon County Council; Neil Tanton [1967] Director/IT Services Manager

Bray and Slaughter Limited
Incorporated: 5 April 1934 *Employees:* 34
Net Worth: £935,593 *Total Assets:* £4,845,866
Registered Office: Locks Mills, Parson Street, Bedminster, Bristol, BS3 5RD
Activities: Other building completion and finishing
Shareholders: Grant Martin Jefferies; Joseph Colin Payne
Officers: Matthew James Cooper [1975] Operations Director; Grant Martin Jefferies [1978] Director

Brean Down Caravan Park Limited
Incorporated: 3 September 2008 *Employees:* 8
Net Worth: £6,774,790 *Total Assets:* £7,058,987
Registered Office: 3-5 College Street, Burnham on Sea, Somerset, TA8 1AR
Activities: Recreational vehicle parks, trailer parks and camping grounds
Major Shareholder: Nicola Colls
Officers: Nicola Colls, Secretary; Nicola Colls [1972] Director/Manager; Jennifer Marilyn Davies [1947] Director

Brean Leisure Park Ltd.
Incorporated: 6 February 1970 *Employees:* 229
Net Worth: £4,152,999 *Total Assets:* £11,291,422
Registered Office: Holiday Resort Unity, Coast Road, Berrow, Burnham on Sea, Somerset, TA8 2RB
Activities: Other amusement and recreation activities n.e.c.
Shareholders: Richard John House; Bridget Denise House
Officers: Bridget Denise House, Secretary; Alan Richard House [1977] Info Technology Director; Bridget Denise House [1958] Catering Director; Richard John House [1947] Managing Director; Sarah Gayle Spottiswoode [1981] Personnel/Health & Safety Director

Breath Limited
Incorporated: 9 March 2000
Net Worth: £51,837,332 *Total Assets:* £52,331,824
Registered Office: Whiddon Valley, Barnstaple, Devon, EX32 8NS
Activities: Manufacture of pharmaceutical preparations
Parent: Arrow Group ApS
Officers: Dean Michael Cooper [1972] Director/Chartered Accountant; Kim Innes [1968] Director/General Manager

Breeze Motor Company Limited
Incorporated: 9 March 2000 *Employees:* 198
Net Worth: £2,279,256 *Total Assets:* £18,146,740
Registered Office: Mazars LLP, 5th Floor, Merck House, Seldown Lane, Poole, Dorset, BH15 1TW
Activities: Sale of new cars and light motor vehicles
Major Shareholder: John Edward Corderoy
Officers: John Edward Corderoy [1963] Director/Motor Trader

Percy R Brend & Sons (Holdings) Limited
Incorporated: 16 October 1997 *Employees:* 1,190
Net Worth: £8,888,560 *Total Assets:* £32,238,110
Registered Office: 50 The Terrace, Torquay, Devon, TQ1 1DD
Activities: Other professional, scientific and technical activities n.e.c.
Shareholders: John Edward Brend; Peter Antony Brend; Richard Percival Brend
Officers: Peter Anthony Brend, Secretary; John Edward Brend [1948] Director; Justin John Brend [1972] Director; Matthew Jonathan Brend [1993] Director; Peter Anthony Brend [1977] Director; Peter Anthony Brend [1957] Director; Richard Percival Brend [1966] Director

Percy R.Brend & Sons (Hoteliers) Limited
Incorporated: 3 June 1969 *Employees:* 1,130
Net Worth: £8,997,512 *Total Assets:* £17,058,348
Registered Office: 50 The Terrace, Torquay, Devon, TQ1 1DD
Activities: Hotels and similar accommodation
Parent: Percy R Brend & Sons (Holdings) Ltd
Officers: Peter Anthony Brend, Secretary; John Edward Brend [1948] Director; Justin John Brend [1972] Director; Matthew Jonathan Brend [1993] Director; Peter Anthony Brend [1977] Director; Peter Anthony Brend [1957] Director; Richard Percival Brend [1966] Director

Brent Cars Limited
Incorporated: 11 June 2003 *Employees:* 136
Net Worth: £3,515,059 *Total Assets:* £22,859,718
Registered Office: Carbase, Aisecome Way, Weston-Super-Mare, Avon, BS22 8NA
Activities: Sale of used cars and light motor vehicles
Major Shareholder: Steven Paul Winter
Officers: Graham Bird [1954] Director/Accountant; Kieran James Hector [1981] Finance Director; Kay Kate Twine [1962] Director/Office Manager; Steven Paul Winter [1958] Director

F.G.Brewer & Sons (Farms) Limited
Incorporated: 8 December 1960 *Employees:* 5
Net Worth: £912,877 *Total Assets:* £7,488,899
Registered Office: Ennis Barton, Fraddon, St Columb, Cornwall, TR9 6EY
Activities: Raising of dairy cattle
Shareholders: Andrew Charles Brewer; Maureen Claire Brewer
Officers: Maureen Claire Brewer, Secretary; Andrew Charles Brewer [1970] Director/Farmer; Maureen Claire Brewer [1968] Director/Housewife

Briarwood Products Limited
Incorporated: 18 February 1994 *Employees:* 23
Net Worth: £14,444,986 *Total Assets:* £20,651,624
Registered Office: Briarwood Business Park, Commerce Way, Walrow Industrial Estate, Highbridge, Somerset, TA9 4AG
Activities: Roofing activities
Major Shareholder: Alan Janes
Officers: David Bunker, Secretary; Alan Janes [1944] Director/Prefabricated Goods Supplier; Oliver Wyndham Janes [1988] Director

Brick Peers Limited
Incorporated: 5 March 1999 *Employees:* 102
Net Worth: £2,778,289 *Total Assets:* £4,175,452
Registered Office: Milton Priory House, Rowdens Road, Wells, Somerset, BA5 1UA
Activities: Construction of commercial buildings
Parent: Ambrosini Construction Group Limited
Officers: Nicola Jane Ambrosini, Secretary; Adrian Generald Ambrosini [1969] Director; Mark Raymond Ambrosini [1969] Director

T.H.Brickell & Son,Limited
Incorporated: 27 March 1941 *Employees:* 98
Net Worth: £406,618 *Total Assets:* £6,291,928
Registered Office: Longmead Industrial Estate, Shaftesbury, Dorset, SP7 8PX
Activities: Printing n.e.c.
Officers: Stuart Ambrose Morris, Secretary; Stuart Ambrose Morris [1962] Director/Accountant; Peter Ronald Smith [1957] Director

Brickell Holdings Limited
Incorporated: 17 February 2009 *Employees:* 98
Net Worth: £119,705 *Total Assets:* £5,973,144
Registered Office: Longmead Industrial Estate, Longmead, Shaftesbury, Dorset, SP7 8PX
Activities: Printing n.e.c.
Shareholder: Stuart Ambrose Morris
Officers: Christopher Norman Brickell [1946] Director; Donald Conway Davis [1932] Director/Chartered Accountant; Stuart Ambrose Morris [1962] Director/Accountant; Peter Ronald Smith [1957] Director

Brickjet Limited
Incorporated: 17 September 2004 *Employees:* 1
Net Worth Deficit: £6,016,412 *Total Assets:* £7,381,916
Registered Office: The Cider Mill, Blanchworth, Dursley, Glos, GL11 6BB
Activities: Hotels and similar accommodation
Parent: Blanchworth Care Ltd
Officers: Sally Anne Manby Roberts, Secretary; Neil Tocknell, Secretary; Sally Anne Manby Roberts [1954] Director/Chairman; Jeremy Peter Ewens Walsh [1950] Director

Bridge Motorcycles Limited
Incorporated: 28 January 1963 *Employees:* 55
Net Worth: £3,757,094 *Total Assets:* £6,279,382
Registered Office: Alphin Brook Road, Marsh Barton Trading Estate, Exeter, Devon, EX2 8RG
Activities: Sale, maintenance and repair of motorcycles and related parts and accessories
Shareholders: Stuart Anthony; Southtown Investment Company Ltd
Officers: Rebecca Elizabeth Anthony, Secretary; Daniel Francis Anthony [1977] Director/General Manager; Lee McNeil Anthony [1971] Director/General Manager; Stuart Anthony [1953] Managing Director

Bridge Multi-Academy Trust
Incorporated: 10 August 2011 *Employees:* 608
Net Worth: £14,419,576 *Total Assets:* £18,621,672
Registered Office: Higher Trebyan, Lanhydrock, Bodmin, Cornwall, PL30 5DQ
Activities: Primary education
Officers: Jeremy Alder, Secretary; Maria Jane Ashurst [1965] Director/Catering Manager; Sally Jane Crabb [1975] Director/Accountant; Rebecca Joy Evans [1983] Director/Parish Support Advisor; Judith Ann Goodchild [1941] Director/Retired; Cheryl Joy Hill [1956] Director/Retired; Adrian Lee Massey [1968] Director/Headteacher; Jane Millicent McFall [1956] Director/Consultant

Bridge Road Limited
Incorporated: 18 July 2014
Previous: Kersfield Developments (Bridge Road) Limited
Net Worth Deficit: £2,488,386 *Total Assets:* £8,088,658
Registered Office: 30 Brock Street, Bath, BA1 2LN
Activities: Development of building projects
Shareholders: David Laurence Newton; David Charles Oyler; Richard Gwynne Smith
Officers: David Laurence Newton [1966] Director; David Charles Oyler [1964] Director

Bridgend Custodial Services Limited
Incorporated: 12 April 1995
Net Worth: £2,073,000 *Total Assets:* £11,124,000
Registered Office: Challenge House, International Drive, Tewkesbury Business Park, Tewkesbury, Glos, GL20 8UQ
Activities: Private security activities
Shareholders: G4S Care and Justice Services (UK) Limited; Innisfree Nominees Limited
Officers: Daniel Peter Bevan, Secretary; Gaynor Birley Smith [1966] Investment Director; Benjamin Christopher Jacob Dean [1979] Director; Gawie Murray Nienaber [1957] Director/Lawyer; Jeremy Kenneth Petherick [1954] Director

Bridges (Electrical Engineers) Limited
Incorporated: 19 July 1993 *Employees:* 167
Net Worth: £1,283,735 *Total Assets:* £6,277,720
Registered Office: Unit 31a Second Avenue, Westfield Industrial Estate, Midsomer Norton, Radstock, Somerset, BA3 4BH
Activities: Electrical installation
Shareholder: Matthew Leslie John Bridges
Officers: John William Bridges [1950] Director/Electrical Engineer; Judith Lesley Bridges [1952] Director/Administrator; Matthew Leslie John Bridges [1978] Director/Engineer; Jason Andrew Clarke [1969] Director/Engineer; Tim Lee Cooper [1973] Director/Electrical Engineer; Darin Michael Nixon [1969] Director/Electrical Engineer; Steven William Spencer [1960] Director/General Manager

Bridgewell Holdings Limited
Incorporated: 7 March 1989 *Employees:* 5
Net Worth: £4,814,112 *Total Assets:* £4,930,373
Registered Office: 2nd Floor, 23-24 High Street, Marlborough, Wilts, SN8 1LW
Activities: Activities of head offices
Shareholder: Sonia Rosemary Carver
Officers: Sarah Jane Bohane, Secretary; Fiona Katherine Kenneth [1967] Director/Consultant; Gordon Alexander Kenneth [1941] Director/Chartered Accountant

D. & I. Bridgman and Son Limited
Incorporated: 1 May 1995 *Employees:* 54
Net Worth: £921,000 *Total Assets:* £3,877,000
Registered Office: Exmoor House, Lime Way, Pathfields Business Park, South Molton, Devon, EX36 3LH
Activities: Other retail sale not in stores, stalls or markets
Parent: Mole Valley Farmers
Officers: Bruce Korican, Secretary; Andrew Jackson [1957] Director/Chief Executive; Frederick Brian Jennings [1946] Director

Bridgwater College Trust
Incorporated: 8 June 2012 *Employees:* 54
Net Worth: £31,328,000 *Total Assets:* £44,776,000
Registered Office: Bridgwater College Academy, Parkway, Bridgwater, Somerset, TA6 4QY
Activities: General secondary education
Officers: Gregory Stephen Jones, Secretary; Andrew Alleyne Berry [1971] Director/Principal of FE College; Andrew John Lucius Burrows [1954] Director/Retired; Carole Dianne Chevalley [1946] Director/Retired; Peter Leon Elliott [1974] Director/Chief Executive; Sidney Philip Gibson [1950] Director/Retired; Jason Gunningham [1970] Director/Assistant Principal; David William Hannay [1947] Retired Director; Denys Alexander Rayner [1954] Director; Sam Reilly [1989] Director/Bridgwater College; Heather Patricia Strawbridge [1959] Director; Claire Winson [1972] Director/Section Leader - Bridgwater & Taunton College

Bridlington Schools Services Limited
Incorporated: 19 May 2000 *Employees:* 2
Net Worth Deficit: £1,644,000 *Total Assets:* £19,525,000
Registered Office: Third Floor, Broad Quay House, Prince Street, Bristol, BS1 4DJ
Activities: Management of real estate on a fee or contract basis
Parent: XJ6 Schools Holdings Limited
Officers: Julia Sarah McCabe [1970] Regional Director; Daniel North [1981] Investment Director; Alan Campbell Ritchie [1967] Director

Bridport Limited
Incorporated: 13 June 1947
Net Worth: £11,287,000 *Total Assets:* £11,287,000
Registered Office: c/o Amsafe Bridport Ltd, The Court, Bridport, Dorset, DT6 3QU
Activities: Activities of head offices
Officers: Jason Mark Abbott [1966] Director/President; Jonathan David Crandall [1977] Director/Treasurer [American]; Lee James Stork [1979] Director/Financial Controller

Brightborough Capital Limited
Incorporated: 1 December 2009 *Employees:* 191
Net Worth: £5,024,000 *Total Assets:* £19,315,000
Registered Office: The Vineyards Industrial Estate, Gloucester Road, Cheltenham, Glos, GL51 8NH
Activities: Activities of other holding companies n.e.c.
Shareholders: Nigel Craig Trilk; Martin Paul Urquhart
Officers: Dr Nigel Craig Trilk [1965] Director; Martin Paul Urquhart [1968] Director

Brighton & Hove City Schools Services Limited
Incorporated: 13 July 2001 *Employees:* 2
Net Worth: £3,175,000 *Total Assets:* £12,735,000
Registered Office: Third Floor, Broad Quay House, Prince Street, Bristol, BS1 4DJ
Activities: Management of real estate on a fee or contract basis
Parent: Brighton & Hove City Schools Services (Holdings) Limited
Officers: Christopher John Blundell [1966] Regional Director; Neil Rae [1971] Director

Brighton Harbour Hotel Limited
Incorporated: 23 July 2014
Net Worth: £5,188 *Total Assets:* £13,184,632
Registered Office: Harbour House, 60 Purewell, Christchurch, Dorset, BH23 1ES
Activities: Buying and selling of own real estate
Parent: Harbour Hotels Group Limited
Officers: Stuart Andrew Bateman [1976] Director; David Francis Robbins [1967] Finance Director; Michael Oliver Warren [1970] Director [Irish]

Brighton Student Developments Ltd
Incorporated: 10 February 2016
Net Worth: £1,655,081 *Total Assets:* £8,673,213
Registered Office: c/o North Quay House, Sutton Harbour, Plymouth, PL4 0RA
Activities: Other accommodation
Shareholders: John Michael Blackburn-Panteli; Nicola Joy Blackburn-Panteli
Officers: John Michael Blackburn-Panteli, Secretary; John Michael Blackburn-Panteli [1962] Director; Nicola Joy Blackburn-Panteli [1963] Director

Brightside Group Limited
Incorporated: 20 September 2006 *Employees:* 601
Net Worth: £52,027,000 *Total Assets:* £92,377,000
Registered Office: Brightside Park, Severn Bridge, Aust, Bristol, BS35 4BL
Activities: Activities of financial services holding companies
Parent: Belvedere Bidco Ltd
Officers: Russell James Bence [1973] Managing Director; Mark Cliff [1961] Director; Edward John Green [1981] Director/Private Equity Investor; Neil Stephen Macmillan [1962] Director; Robert Massey [1985] Director/Private Equity Investor; Brendan Eamon McCafferty [1967] Director; Ian Ronald Sutherland [1970] Director

Brightside Insurance Services Limited
Incorporated: 8 January 2001 *Employees:* 489
Net Worth: £35,601,000 *Total Assets:* £50,444,000
Registered Office: Brightside Park, Severn Bridge, Aust, Bristol, BS35 4BL
Activities: Activities of insurance agents and brokers
Parent: Brightside Group Limited
Officers: Russell James Bence [1973] Managing Director; Brendan Eamon McCafferty [1967] Director; Ian Ronald Sutherland [1970] Director

Brightsource Limited
Incorporated: 14 November 2001 *Employees:* 75
Net Worth: £189,292 *Total Assets:* £15,198,893
Registered Office: St James House, St James Square, Cheltenham, Glos, GL50 3PR
Activities: Advertising agencies
Parent: Cello Signal Group Limited
Officers: Minh Tuan Huynh, Secretary; Mark Bentley [1970] Finance Director

Brightwater Estates Limited
Incorporated: 26 September 1997
Net Worth: £2,999,466 *Total Assets:* £8,737,311
Registered Office: Shop 6 Parkland Place, 39-41 Old Milton Road, New Milton, Hants, BH25 6DJ
Activities: Other letting and operating of own or leased real estate
Officers: Karen Patrice Sinclair, Secretary/Director; Anthony John Sinclair [1948] Director; Karen Patrice Sinclair [1957] Director

Brinkgreen Limited
Incorporated: 15 May 1972 *Employees:* 3
Net Worth: £1,798,283 *Total Assets:* £4,389,087
Registered Office: Ground Floor, Southfield House, 2 Southfield Road, Westbury-on-Trym, Bristol, BS9 3BH
Activities: Buying and selling of own real estate
Shareholder: John Kenneth Lewis
Officers: Emma Katherine Muggridge, Secretary; John Kenneth Lewis [1941] Director; Emma Katherine Muggridge [1970] Director

Brisdoc Healthcare Services Limited
Incorporated: 3 August 2005 *Employees:* 298
Net Worth: £2,087,996 *Total Assets:* £3,936,938
Registered Office: c/o Bishop Fleming, 16 Queen Square, Bristol, BS1 4NT
Activities: General medical practice activities
Officers: Nigel Keith Cecil Gazzard, Secretary; Dr Katharine Alsop [1963] Director/GP; Kelvin John Blake [1971] Director; Nigel Keith Cecil Gazzard [1963] Director/Operations Manager; Margaret Hickman [1950] Director; Dr Gillian Jenkins [1958] Director/GP; Dr Ray Montague [1960] Director/General Practitioner; Dr Kathleen Ryan [1964] Medical Director; Dr Nigel William Gervase Taylor [1952] Director/Medical Practitioner

Bristlewand Limited
Incorporated: 16 July 1979 *Employees:* 127
Net Worth: £5,210,576 *Total Assets:* £9,709,798
Registered Office: Unit 3 Apple Walk, Kembrey Park, Swindon, Wilts, SN2 8BL
Activities: Construction of other civil engineering projects n.e.c.
Shareholders: Valerie Margaret Kenny; John Bernard Kenny
Officers: Claire Louise Curl, Secretary; Claire Louise Curl [1973] Director; Ian James Curtis [1961] Director; William Edward Hall [1949] Director; Alfred Nigel Douglas Hambridge [1959] Director; Richard John Hunt [1955] Managing Director

Bristol & Avon Transport & Recycling Ltd
Incorporated: 24 June 1993 *Employees:* 83
Net Worth: £4,068,232 *Total Assets:* £9,094,276
Registered Office: 432 Gloucester Road, Horfield, Bristol, BS7 8TX
Activities: Other specialised construction activities n.e.c.
Parent: Terrain Plant (Holdings) Limited
Officers: Liam Kirwan, Secretary; Kevin Patrick Berkely [1974] Director/Contractor [Irish]

Bristol & London PLC
Incorporated: 5 November 1998 *Employees:* 49
Net Worth: £1,341,211 *Total Assets:* £5,880,188
Registered Office: Harbour Place, Serbert Road, Portishead, Bristol, BS20 7GF
Activities: Renting and leasing of cars and light motor vehicles
Shareholder: Helen Sackett
Officers: Beverley Donna Jenkins, Secretary; Sandra Hart [1966] Director/Accountant; Beverley Donna Jenkins [1966] Director; Ian John Luxton [1954] Director/Accountant

Bristol & Mendip Estates Limited
Incorporated: 13 October 1981 *Employees:* 3
Net Worth Deficit: £764,845 *Total Assets:* £4,041,691
Registered Office: Old Down Farm, Emborough, Radstock, Somerset, BA3 4SA
Activities: Other letting and operating of own or leased real estate
Shareholders: Morgan John Saunders; Ian Jeffrey Saunders
Officers: Morgan John Saunders, Secretary; Ian Jeffrey Saunders [1963] Director/Farmer; Morgan John Saunders [1965] Director/Company Secretary

Bristol & West PLC
Incorporated: 21 April 1987
Net Worth: £3,441,000 *Total Assets:* £114,129,000
Registered Office: One Temple Quay, Temple Back East, Temple Quay, Bristol, BS1 6DX
Activities: Banks
Parent: Bank of Ireland UK Holdings PLC
Officers: Desmond Edward Crowley [1959] Director/Banker [Irish]; Andrew George Keating [1970] Director/Accountant [Irish]; Thomas McAreavey [1970] Director/Senior Finance Manager

Bristol Airport (UK) No.3 Limited
Incorporated: 24 March 2005 *Employees:* 285
Net Worth Deficit: £21,733,000 *Total Assets:* £792,361,024
Registered Office: Administration Building, Bristol Airport, Bristol, BS48 3DY
Activities: Activities of head offices
Officers: James Alexander Adam [1970] Director/Financier [Canadian]; David William Kerr [1963] Director/Business Executive

Bristol Airport Limited
Incorporated: 28 November 1986 *Employees:* 283
Net Worth: £173,527,008 *Total Assets:* £230,200,000
Registered Office: Bristol Airport, Bristol, BS48 3DY
Activities: Scheduled passenger air transport
Parent: South West Airports Limited
Officers: James Alexander Adam [1970] Director/Financier [Canadian]; Jason Lee Clark [1972] Director/Business Executive; Graeme Kenneth Gamble [1969] Director; David William Kerr [1963] Director/Business Executive; Janis Carol Kong [1951] Director; David Christopher Williams Lees [1967] Director/Business Executive; David Lloyd McGraw [1956] Director/Chief Financial Officer [Canadian]; Elizabeth Waddell [1963] HR Director

Bristol and South Gloucestershire UTC
Incorporated: 17 May 2011 *Employees:* 27
Net Worth: £7,120,744 *Total Assets:* £8,142,054
Registered Office: Bristol Technology & Engineering Academy, New Road, Stoke Gifford, Bristol, BS34 8SF
Activities: Technical and vocational secondary education
Officers: Sarah Joanna Curtis [1973] Director/Head of Human Resources and Communications; David Samuel Edgecumbe [1971] Director/Project Manager; Alexander Edward Henry Fitzhugh [1974] Director/Engineer; Roger John Gilbert [1961] Director/Interim Principal; Ian Latto [1965] Director/Project Manager; Kevin Massie Noakes [1971] Director/Naval Engineer; David Frederick Peck [1954] Director/Education Consultant; Julian Edward William Preston [1980] Director/Global Automation Leader; Rhian Jane Priest [1966] Director/Teacher; Andrew Read [1964] Director/Royal Navy; Antony Charles Rooke [1962] Director/Operations Manager; Jayne Marie Watkins [1969] Director/Banking

Bristol Builders Supplies Limited
Incorporated: 30 June 1933 *Employees:* 37
Net Worth: £1,941,638 *Total Assets:* £3,720,222
Registered Office: 3 Barton Hill Trading Estate, Herapath Street, Bristol, BS5 9RD
Activities: Wholesale of hardware, plumbing and heating equipment and supplies
Major Shareholder: Lee Hooper
Officers: Shelley Jayne Bunker, Secretary; Lee Hooper [1976] Logistics Director; Patrick O'Donnell [1976] Operations Director

Bristol Care Homes Development Limited
Incorporated: 12 September 2013
Net Worth: £3,649,916 *Total Assets:* £12,418,992
Registered Office: 12 Hope Square, Hotwell, Bristol, BS8 4LX
Activities: Development of building projects
Major Shareholder: Geoff Crocker
Officers: Geoffrey Alan Crocker [1952] Director/Industry Strategy Consultant; Linda Janet Warren [1964] Director/Chartered Accountant

Bristol Care Homes Limited
Incorporated: 24 March 1995 *Employees:* 277
Net Worth: £3,036,629 *Total Assets:* £7,194,686
Registered Office: 10 London Square, Portishead, Bristol, BS20 7BB
Activities: Medical nursing home activities
Major Shareholder: Geoffrey Alan Crocker
Officers: Geoffrey Alan Crocker [1952] Director/Industry Strategy Consultant; Richard John Crocker [1977] Director/Chief Executive; Linda Janet Warren [1964] Director/Chartered Accountant

Bristol Charities
Incorporated: 23 March 2005 *Employees:* 13
Net Worth: £37,707,992 *Total Assets:* £40,046,584
Registered Office: 17 St Augustines Parade, Bristol, BS1 4UL
Activities: Activities of head offices
Officers: Anne Suganthi Anketell, Secretary; Harriet Frances Bosnell [1972] Director; Richard Arthur Gore [1972] Director/Solicitor; Rachel Mary Howell [1959] Director/Retired; Dr Rosalind Penelope Kennedy [1949] Director/Retired; Andrew Guise Mennell [1955] Director/Consultant; Michelle Theresa Meredith [1953] Director/Network Co-ordinator; Jonathan Thomas O'Shea [1961] Managing Director; Olivia Lettice Spencer [1960] Director/Retired; Paul Andrew Staples [1978] Director/Senior Manager, Financial Services; Nolan Ellis Webber [1976] Investment Director

Bristol City Football Club Limited
Incorporated: 29 July 1996 *Employees:* 182
Net Worth Deficit: £60,456,432 *Total Assets:* £21,935,284
Registered Office: Ashton Gate, Bristol, BS3 2EJ
Activities: Activities of sport clubs
Shareholders: Stephen Philip Lansdown; Margaret Alison Lansdown; Bristol City Holdings Limited
Officers: Gavin Thomas Marshall, Secretary; Mark Anthony Ashton [1971] Director/Chief Executive Officer; Keith William Dawe [1950] Director/Chairman; Douglas John Harman [1948] Managing Director; Jon Stephen Lansdown [1983] Director; Gavin Thomas Marshall [1977] Director/Chief Financial Officer

Bristol City Holdings Limited
Incorporated: 13 June 1980 *Employees:* 703
Net Worth Deficit: £13,761,270 *Total Assets:* £75,188,080
Registered Office: Ashton Gate, Bristol, BS3 2EJ
Activities: Operation of sports facilities
Shareholders: Margaret Alison Lansdown; Stephen Philip Lansdown
Officers: Gavin Thomas Marshall, Secretary; Keith William Dawe [1950] Director/Chairman; Douglas John Harman [1948] Managing Director; Jon Stephen Lansdown [1983] Director

Bristol Community Health C.I.C.
Incorporated: 29 March 2011 *Employees:* 1,673
Net Worth: £3,519,560 *Total Assets:* £18,118,800
Registered Office: South Plaza, Marlborough Street, Bristol, BS1 3NX
Activities: Other human health activities
Officers: Joanna Claire Makinson, Secretary; Julia Clarke [1958] Director/Chief Executive; Georgina Louise Davin [1983] Non-Executive Director (Staff Council); Julie Dovey [1972] Director/Doctor; Aileen Paterson Fraser [1958] Director; Stephen Daniel Hughes [1955] Director/Solicitor; Rhona MacDonald [1955] Director; Joanna Claire Makinson [1983] Finance Director; Michele Jane Narey [1964] Director; Penelope Victoria Rosalie Mae Phillpotts [1980] Director; Neil Matthew Stevens [1964] Director

Bristol Diocesan Board of Finance Limited (The)
Incorporated: 20 June 1919 *Employees:* 53
Net Worth: £57,440,000 *Total Assets:* £63,049,000
Registered Office: Diocesan Office, First Floor, Hillside House, 1500 Parkway North, Newbrick Road, Stoke Gifford, Bristol, BS34 8YU
Activities: Activities of religious organisations
Officers: Oliver Charles Bouverie Home, Secretary; Raymond William Adams [1958] Director/Clerk in Holy Orders; The Ven Graham Archer [1958] Director/Archdeacon; Charles Walter Edward Ralph Buchan [1951] Director/Corporate Finance Adviser; Reverend Kathryn May Campion-Spall [1979] Director/Clerk in Holy Orders; Professor David Neville Clarke [1949] Director/Retired University Academic; Catherine Jean Davison [1950] Director/Retired; The Rt Rev Vivienne Frances Faull [1955] Director/Bishop; Bruce Anthony Finnamore [1957] Director; David Michael Hoyle [1957] Director/Dean of Bristol; The Venerable Michael Anthony Johnson [1951] Director/Archdeacon; Andrew John Shirley Lucas [1955] Executive Director; Nicholas Richard Orman [1957] Director/Chartered Civil Engineer; Lee Stephen Rayfield [1955] Director/Bishop; Rev Trudie Anne Wigley [1969] Director/Vicar

Bristol Drugs Project Limited
Incorporated: 3 April 1985 *Employees:* 136
Net Worth: £3,848,743 *Total Assets:* £4,217,678
Registered Office: 11 Brunswick Square, Bristol, BS2 8PE
Activities: Other human health activities
Officers: Rosamund Amos [1984] Director/Manager; Keith Henry Francis Aston [1938] Director/Retired; Kathleen Forgan Curling [1952] Director/Chartered Town Planner (Retired); Jonathan Mark Walker Davis [1957] Director; Dr Rosalind Penelope Kennedy [1949] Director; Michael David LEA [1962] Director/Chartered Accountant; John Ross Long [1961] Director/Police; John Michael Prior [1942] Director/Retired; Jennifer Alice Eiloart Risk [1981] Director/Customer Operations Manager; Ian Sherwood [1954] Director/Retired; Dr George Thomas Smyth [1951] Director/Medical Practitioner

Bristol Energy Limited
Incorporated: 17 July 2014 *Employees:* 161
Previous: Bristol Energy & Technology Services (Supply) Limited
Net Worth Deficit: £16,881,484 *Total Assets:* £16,300,078
Registered Office: 100 Temple Street, Bristol, BS1 6AG
Activities: Trade of electricity
Parent: Bristol Holding Limited
Officers: Merlin Michael Hyman [1969] Director/Chief Executive Officer; Marek Majewicz [1974] Finance Director; Councillor Stephen George Pearce [1956] Director/Councillor; Alexander Simon Wiseman [1957] Director

Bristol Fluid System Technologies Limited
Incorporated: 31 August 2010 *Employees:* 27
Net Worth: £2,045,017 *Total Assets:* £3,789,969
Registered Office: Unit 7 Orpen Park, Ash Ridge Road, Almondsbury, Bristol, BS32 4QD
Activities: Non-specialised wholesale trade
Major Shareholder: Simon Cooke
Officers: Simon Cooke [1970] Director

Bristol Fruit Sales (Bananas) Limited
Incorporated: 9 August 2006 *Employees:* 53
Net Worth: £6,833,305 *Total Assets:* £13,372,187
Registered Office: Unit 1 Avonside Road, Avonside Industrial Estate, Bristol, BS2 0UQ
Activities: Other processing and preserving of fruit and vegetables
Parent: Fyffes Group Limited
Officers: Brian Breathnach, Secretary; Andrew Hugh Denham Smith [1963] Director; Richard John Enright [1980] Director/Accountant [Irish]; Thomas Gerard Murphy [1960] Finance Director [Irish]; Robert Ernest Smith [1948] Managing Director

Bristol Funeral Directors Limited
Incorporated: 6 October 1988
Net Worth: £3,011,333 *Total Assets:* £3,883,766
Registered Office: Southville Lodge, Southville Road, Southville, Bristol, BS3 1DJ
Activities: Activities of other holding companies n.e.c.
Shareholders: Philip Anthony Alderwick; Austin Sheppard; Derek Gilbert Gunningham
Officers: Derek Gilbert Gunningham, Secretary/Funeral Director; Philip Anthony Alderwick [1955] Funeral Director; Derek Gilbert Gunningham [1950] Funeral Director; Austin Sheppard [1950] Funeral Director

Bristol Grammar School
Incorporated: 1 June 2004 *Employees:* 287
Net Worth: £32,371,020 *Total Assets:* £42,726,296
Registered Office: Bristol Grammar School, University Road, Bristol, BS8 1SR
Activities: Primary education
Officers: John Generald Mitchell, Secretary; Andrea Jane Arlidge [1961] Director/Headteacher; Alan Robert Barr [1958] Director/Lawyer; Cedric Nishanthan Canagarajah [1966] Director/Pro Vice Chancellor; Maria Crayton [1965] Marketing Director; Candida Jill Gil [1963] Director/Chartered Accountant; Julie Dawn Knox [1952] Director/Retired Teacher; Patrick Robert Meehan [1957] Director/Chartered Financial Planner; Dr Jane Frances O'Gallagher [1957] Director/Consultant Paediatrician; David Peter Lawton Pester [1961] Director/Lawyer; Nigel Henry Pickersgill [1955] Director/Chartered Accountant; Catherine Ghislaine Redshaw [1968] Director/Employment Lawyer; Julie Teresa Selwyn [1956] Director/University Professor; David William Shelton [1949] Director/Financial Advice Consultant; John Andrew Sisman [1969] Director/Chartered Surveyor; Doctor Dominique Joelle Thompson [1970] Director/GP; Justin Babak Vafadari [1977] Director/Headteacher; Romesh Jonathan Vaitilingam [1961] Director/Writer; Mark Robert Wilson [1961] Director/Chartered Surveyor

Bristol Harbour Hotel Limited
Incorporated: 8 July 2015 *Employees:* 79
Net Worth: £3,603,525 *Total Assets:* £23,254,224
Registered Office: Harbour House, 60 Purewell, Christchurch, Dorset, BH23 1ES
Activities: Hotels and similar accommodation
Parent: Harbour Hotels Group Limited
Officers: Stuart Andrew Bateman [1976] Director; David Francis Robbins [1967] Finance Director; Michael Oliver Warren [1970] Director [Irish]

Bristol Holding Limited
Incorporated: 12 March 2015 *Employees:* 1
Net Worth Deficit: £6,312,125 *Total Assets:* £12,382,257
Registered Office: P O Box 3176, SLT Management Suite, 9 Willway Street, Bristol, BS3 9FS
Activities: Activities of other holding companies n.e.c.
Parent: Bristol City Council
Officers: Michael John Kinski [1952] Director; David Lawrence [1953] Director/Local Government Officer

Bristol Infracare Lift (1) Limited
Incorporated: 15 September 2003
Net Worth Deficit: £3,171,000 *Total Assets:* £17,446,000
Registered Office: Challenge House, International Drive, Tewkesbury Business Park, Tewkesbury, Glos, GL20 8UQ
Activities: Other letting and operating of own or leased real estate
Parent: Bristol Infracare Lift Holdings (1) Limited
Officers: Daniel Peter Bevan, Secretary; Paul Simon Andrews [1970] Director; Sarah Ann Beaumont [1982] Director/Chartered Accountant; Richard Darch [1961] Director; Balasingham Ravi Kumar [1975] Director/Investment Manager

Bristol Infracare Lift (2) Limited
Incorporated: 29 October 2004
Net Worth Deficit: £2,109,000 *Total Assets:* £14,204,000
Registered Office: Challenge House, International Drive, Tewkesbury Business Park, Tewkesbury, Glos, GL20 8UQ
Activities: Other letting and operating of own or leased real estate
Parent: Bristol Infracare Lift Holdings (2) Limited
Officers: Daniel Peter Bevan, Secretary; Paul Simon Andrews [1970] Director/Infrastructure Developer; Sarah Ann Beaumont [1982] Director/Chartered Accountant; Richard Darch [1961] Director; Balasingham Ravi Kumar [1975] Director/Investment Manager

Bristol Infracare Lift (3) Limited
Incorporated: 23 December 2009
Net Worth Deficit: £16,324,000 *Total Assets:* £54,729,000
Registered Office: Challenge House, International Drive, Tewkesbury Business Park, Tewkesbury, Glos, GL20 8UQ
Activities: Other letting and operating of own or leased real estate
Parent: Bristol Infracare Lift Holdings (3) Limited
Officers: Daniel Peter Bevan, Secretary; Paul Simon Andrews [1970] Director/Infrastructure Developer; Sarah Ann Beaumont [1982] Director/Chartered Accountant; Richard Darch [1961] Director; Balasingham Ravi Kumar [1975] Director/Investment Manager

Bristol Music Trust
Incorporated: 16 February 2011 *Employees:* 182
Net Worth: £1,188,631 *Total Assets:* £5,323,185
Registered Office: Colston Hall, Colston Street, Bristol, BS1 5AR
Activities: Cultural education
Officers: Elizabeth Waite, Secretary; Simon Chapman [1955] Director/Retired Senior Audit Partner; Anthony John Cherry [1955] Director/Lawyer; Patricia Connor [1966] Director of BBC South West; Tanya Una Lacey [1985] Director/Artist; Sandra Eustene Meadows [1963] Director/Chief Executive Officer; Sonia Brenda Mills [1955] Director/Retired; Louise Catherine Mitchell [1956] Director/Chief Executive; Andrew Nisbet [1960] Director; Cllr Estella Jane Tincknell [1960] Director/Councillor; James Anthony Ignatius Wetz [1947] Director/Educational Researcher, Consultant, Author

Bristol Old Vic and Theatre Royal Trust Limited
Incorporated: 1 April 1963 *Employees:* 124
Net Worth: £17,327,642 *Total Assets:* £19,430,220
Registered Office: Narrow Quay House, Narrow Quay, Bristol, BS1 4QA
Activities: Artistic creation
Officers: Stephen Alan Allpress [1968] Director; Denis Andrew Southerden Burn [1953] Director; Mark Janak Dakin [1961] Technical Director; Gareth John Edwards [1971] Director/Solicitor; Dame Elizabeth Anne Lucy Forgan [1944] Director; Claire Michelle Hiscott [1969] Director/Councillor; Michael David LEA [1962] Director/Chartered Accountant; Paul Dring Morrell [1948] Director/Chartered Surveyor; Chinonyerem Odimba [1974] Writer and Director; Oliver Rawlings [1981] Communications Director; Mark Geoffrey Sullivan [1957] Commercial Director; Matthew Richard Tanner [1966] Director/Chief Executive; Cllr Estella Jane Tincknell [1960] Director/University Lecturer; Helen Mary Wilde [1951] Director

Bristol Old Vic Theatre School Limited
Incorporated: 6 October 1989 *Employees:* 32
Net Worth: £6,716,123 *Total Assets:* £8,455,204
Registered Office: 1-2 Downside Road, Clifton, Bristol, BS8 2XF
Activities: First-degree level higher education
Officers: Simon Christopher Payne, Secretary; Paul Christopher Baker [1967] Director/Chartered Surveyor; Martin John Boddy [1952] Director/University Manager; Lucy Margaret Bowden [1968] Director/Television Producer; John Sunil Das [1966] Director/Television Producer; Ruth Ann Foreman [1955] Director/Chartered Accountant; David John Halton [1949] Director/Retired; Priscilla Macquire-Samson [1948] Director/Retired; David John Marsh [1944] Director/Retired Solicitor; Morag Ann Massey [1964] Director/Producer; Vanessa Hope Wingate Stevenson [1941] Director/Retired; Guy Winearls Stobart [1955] Director/Consultant; Edwyn Jon Wilson [1965] Director/General Manager

Bristol PFI (Holdings) Limited
Incorporated: 24 March 2006
Net Worth Deficit: £22,531,000 *Total Assets:* £103,384,000
Registered Office: Third Floor, Broad Quay House, Prince Street, Bristol, BS1 4DJ
Activities: Other business support service activities n.e.c.
Parent: Bristol PFI Development Limited
Officers: Paul Alan Bannister [1959] Director; Paul Anthony Cartwright [1957] Director; Jennifer Fegan [1973] Director; Nicholas James MacKee [1976] Director/Solicitor; Jamie Pritchard [1971] Director/Accountant; Katherine Mary Rae [1980] Director/Legal Advisor; Paul Sydney Shadbolt [1957] Development Director; Thomas Benedict Symes [1956] Director

Bristol PFI Debt Co 1 Limited
Incorporated: 20 January 2006 *Employees:* 3
Net Worth: £23,177 *Total Assets:* £4,126,187
Registered Office: Third Floor, Broad Quay House, Prince Street, Bristol, BS1 4DJ
Activities: Other business support service activities n.e.c.
Parent: Skanska TAM Limited
Officers: Paul Alan Bannister [1959] Director; Jennifer Fegan [1973] Director; Katherine Mary Rae [1980] Director/Legal Advisor; Paul Sydney Shadbolt [1957] Development Director

Bristol PFI Limited
Incorporated: 24 March 2006
Net Worth Deficit: £22,531,000 *Total Assets:* £103,384,000
Registered Office: Third Floor, Broad Quay House, Prince Street, Bristol, BS1 4DJ
Activities: Other business support service activities n.e.c.
Parent: Bristol PFI (Holdings) Limited
Officers: Paul Alan Bannister [1959] Director; Paul Anthony Cartwright [1957] Director; Jennifer Fegan [1973] Director; Nicholas James MacKee [1976] Director/Solicitor; Jamie Pritchard [1971] Director/Accountant; Katherine Mary Rae [1980] Director/Legal Advisor; Paul Sydney Shadbolt [1957] Development Director; Thomas Benedict Symes [1956] Director

Bristol Polytechnic Enterprises (Developments) Limited
Incorporated: 23 May 1989
Net Worth: £891,000 *Total Assets:* £7,391,000
Registered Office: University of The West of England, Frenchay Campus, Bristol, BS16 1QY
Activities: Other letting and operating of own or leased real estate
Parent: Wallscourt Foundation
Officers: Richard Hugh Orme Boyes, Secretary; Dr Norman Michael Biddle [1940] Director/Chartered Surveyor; Christopher Arthur Booy [1952] Director/Consultant; Raymond Noel Burton [1947] Director/Consultant

Bristol Polytechnic Enterprises Limited
Incorporated: 3 March 1988
Net Worth: £12,516,000 *Total Assets:* £12,561,000
Registered Office: University of The West of England, Frenchay Capmus, Bristol, BS16 1QY
Activities: Other letting and operating of own or leased real estate
Parent: University of The West of England
Officers: Richard Hugh Orme Boyes, Secretary; William Kuh Tet Liew [1962] Director/Chartered Accountant [Malaysian]; Steven George West [1961] Director/Vice Chancellor

Bristol Port Wind Park Limited
Incorporated: 7 April 2005
Net Worth: £9,308,246 *Total Assets:* £10,714,121
Registered Office: Lion House, Rowcroft, Stroud, Glos, GL5 3BY
Activities: Production of electricity
Parent: Ecotricity Group Limited
Officers: Tom Cowling, Secretary; Asif Rehmanwala [1976] Director/Chief Operating Officer; Dale Vince [1961] Director/Consultant

Bristol Properties Limited
Incorporated: 2 October 1946
Net Worth: £1,810,564 *Total Assets:* £4,345,994
Registered Office: Cornerstone House, Midland Way, Thornbury, Bristol, BS35 2BS
Activities: Other letting and operating of own or leased real estate
Officers: Judith Ann Pearce, Secretary; David Edward Pearce [1979] Director/Chartered Surveyor; Kenneth Tim Pearce [1947] Director; Robin Charles Pearce [1973] Director/Chartered Surveyor

Bristol Uniforms Limited
Incorporated: 15 November 1961 *Employees:* 143
Net Worth: £14,296,000 *Total Assets:* £17,537,000
Registered Office: Wathen Street, Staple Hill, Bristol, BS16 5LL
Activities: Manufacture of workwear
Parent: B T Q Limited
Officers: David Thompson, Secretary; Alan David Dorrell [1954] Director; Ian Peter Mitchell [1966] Director; Edward Colston Shepherd [1974] Service Operations Director; Roger John Barlow Startin [1958] Director; David Thompson [1973] Finance Director

Bristol Waste Company Limited
Incorporated: 5 March 2015 *Employees:* 552
Net Worth: £3,775,669 *Total Assets:* £9,621,916
Registered Office: Albert Road Depot, Albert Road, Bristol, BS2 0XS
Activities: Collection of non-hazardous waste
Parent: Bristol Holding
Officers: Councillor Thomas Brook [1992] Director/Councillor; Adam Robert Henshaw [1971] Finance Director; Anthony Lawless [1958] Director; Francis Rodriguez [1964] Director; Thomas Spaul [1953] Director

Bristol Water Core Holdings Limited
Incorporated: 15 January 2003
Net Worth: £5,998,000 *Total Assets:* £6,000,000
Registered Office: Bristol Water Core Holdings Ltd, Bridgwater Road, Bristol, BS13 7AT
Activities: Activities of other holding companies n.e.c.
Parent: Bristol Water Holdings Limited
Officers: Colin Caldwell, Secretary; Indradoot Dhar [1982] Director/Investment Professional; Hajime Ichishi [1975] Director/Project Manager [Japanese]; Paul Richard Malan [1970] Director/Investment Professional

Bristol Water Holdings Limited
Incorporated: 19 July 1991
Net Worth: £26,601,000 *Total Assets:* £26,775,000
Registered Office: Bridgwater Road, Bristol, BS13 7AT
Activities: Water collection, treatment and supply
Parent: Bristol Water Holdings UK Limited
Officers: Colin Caldwell, Secretary; Indradoot Dhar [1982] Director/Investment Professional; Hajime Ichishi [1975] Director/Project Manager [Japanese]; Paul Richard Malan [1970] Director/Investment Professional

Bristol Water Holdings UK Limited
Incorporated: 5 June 2003
Net Worth: £24,494,000 *Total Assets:* £110,379,000
Registered Office: Bristol Water Holdings UK Ltd, Bridgwater Road, Bristol, BS13 7AT
Activities: Activities of head offices
Parent: CSE Water UK Limited
Officers: Colin Caldwell, Secretary; Indradoot Dhar [1982] Director/Investment Professional; Hajime Ichishi [1975] Director/Project Manager [Japanese]; Paul Richard Malan [1970] Director/Investment Professional

Bristol Water PLC
Incorporated: 12 November 1991 *Employees:* 484
Net Worth: £243,000,000 *Total Assets:* £758,700,032
Registered Office: Bristol Water PLC, Bridgwater Road, Bristol, BS13 7AT
Activities: Water collection, treatment and supply
Parent: Bristol Water Core Holdings Limited
Officers: Colin Caldwell, Secretary; Jeremy Brice Bending [1954] Director/Management Consultant; Indradoot Dhar [1982] Director/Investment Professional; Laura Ann Flowerdew [1976] Director/Chief Financial Officer; Paul Andrew Francis [1962] Director, Business Consultant; Hajime Ichishi [1975] Director/Project Manager [Japanese]; Mehran Karam [1963] Director; Keith Lawrence Ludeman [1950] Director; Paul Richard Malan [1970] Director/Investment Professional; James Edward McAuliffe [1962] Director, Accountant; Timothy Edward Tutton [1947] Director

Bristol, Clifton and West of England Zoological Society Limited
Incorporated: 15 June 2004 *Employees:* 194
Net Worth: £41,179,000 *Total Assets:* £45,516,000
Registered Office: Bristol Zoo Gardens, Guthrie Road, Bristol, BS8 3HA
Activities: Botanical and zoological gardens and nature reserves activities
Officers: Angela Mather, Secretary; Victoria Charlotte Ash [1965] Director; Christopher Arthur Booy [1952] Director/Businessman; Malcolm Arthur Broad [1950] Director/Retired; David Richard Esam [1952] Director/Solicitor; Paul Kevin Michael Kearney [1958] Director/Businessman; Claire Louise Ladkin [1962] Director/Property Developer; Charlotte Mary Ceila Moar [1967] Finance Director; Professor Steven John Neill [1956] Director/University Professor; Professor Richard David Pancost [1970] Director/Professor of Biogeochemistry [American]; Professor Joanna Susan Price [1959] Director/University Vice Chancellor

Britanic Industries Limited
Incorporated: 7 June 1985 *Employees:* 15
Net Worth: £7,419,176 *Total Assets:* £14,525,320
Registered Office: Trethella Farm, Ruan High Lanes, Truro, Cornwall, TR2 5PA
Activities: Holiday centres and villages
Shareholders: Linda Caroline Briant; Nicholas James Briant
Officers: Linda Caroline Briant, Secretary; Linda Caroline Briant [1959] Director/Office Management; Nicholas James Briant [1955] Director/Leisure Management

Britannia Parking Group Limited
Incorporated: 16 August 2012 *Employees:* 301
Net Worth: £1,007,236 *Total Assets:* £5,031,514
Registered Office: 7th Floor, County Gates House, 300 Poole Road, Poole, Dorset, BH12 1AZ
Activities: Activities of other holding companies n.e.c.
Major Shareholder: Graham Stuart
Officers: Karl Oram [1968] Director; Brian John Parker [1979] Director; Graham Stuart [1960] Director

Britannia Windows (UK) Limited
Incorporated: 8 June 1982 *Employees:* 70
Net Worth: £4,050,324 *Total Assets:* £6,964,144
Registered Office: Britannia House, Kimberley Road, Clevedon, Somerset, BS21 6QJ
Activities: Other specialised construction activities n.e.c.
Major Shareholder: Glenys Rushton
Officers: Glenys Ruston, Secretary; Hayden Rushton [1976] Director

British Automobile Racing Club Limited
Incorporated: 2 March 1953 *Employees:* 64
Net Worth: £2,311,047 *Total Assets:* £5,114,463
Registered Office: Thruxton Motor Racing Circuit, Thruxton, Andover, Hants, SP11 8PN
Activities: Operation of sports facilities
Officers: Jim Baynam [1950] Director/Consultant Engineer; Mark Philip Carter [1956] Director/Consultant Engineer; Peter Francis Chubb [1946] Director/Retired; Lionel John Felix [1942] Director/Retired; Nicholas James Frost [1956] Director; Dr Bruce Grant-Braham [1951] Director/University Lecturer; Rhodri David Jenkins [1957] Director/Management Consultant; Nicholas Hugh Pearce [1955] Director/Consultant; Anthony Scott Andrews [1946] Director/Solicitor; Jeremy Latham Smith [1962] Director/Manager; Dorothy Uwota [1967] Director/Manager; Clive Wood [1952] Director/Manager

British Empire Trust PLC
Incorporated: 6 February 1889
Previous: British Empire Securities and General Trust PLC
Net Worth: £941,680,000 *Total Assets:* £1,033,065,984
Registered Office: Beaufort House, 51 New North Road, Exeter, Devon, EX4 4EP
Activities: Activities of investment trusts
Officers: Anja Maria Balfour [1963] Director; Graham John Kitchen [1967] Director; Susan Margaret Noble [1957] Director; Nigel Mervyn Sutherland Rich [1945] Director; Calum MacKenzie Thomson [1960] Director/Chartered Accountant

British Holiday and Home Parks Association Limited
Incorporated: 22 January 1962 *Employees:* 15
Net Worth: £4,166,794 *Total Assets:* £4,804,903
Registered Office: 6 Pullman Court, Great Western Road, Gloucester, GL1 3ND
Activities: Other professional, scientific and technical activities n.e.c.
Officers: Rosalind Ann Pritchard, Secretary; Andrew David Attridge [1951] Director/Park Operator; Andrew Roger Baragwanath [1958] Director/Park Owner; Philip James Edward Brierley [1968] Director; James Anthony Burfitt [1973] Operations Director; Claire Anne-Marie Flower [1972] Director; Colin Andrew Fraser [1942] Director/Mobile Homes Proprietor; Antony Richard Harper [1966] Director; Ian Clive James [1964] Director; Sarah Elizabeth Kemp [1990] Director/Solicitor; James Kennedy [1946] Director/Accountant; Malcolm John Kent [1949] Director; Thomas Simon Marshall [1962] Director/Caravan Park Operator; Charles Huw Pendleton [1971] Director/Holiday Park Operator; Simon Generald Pollock [1956] Managing Director; Richard David Rhodes [1940] Director; Gareth John Rowland [1957] Director; Paul Richard Searle [1970] Managing Director; David Morley Thornley [1955] Director; Andrew Michael Walker [1968] Director; Henry Wild [1970] Director/Caravan Parks; Verona Woodhouse [1964] Director/Caravan Park Owner and Manager [Irish]

The British Pepper & Spice Company Limited
Incorporated: 16 February 1998 *Employees:* 247
Net Worth: £16,246,930 *Total Assets:* £34,158,128
Registered Office: Manderson House, 5230 Valiant Court, Delta Way, Gloucester Business Park, Brockworth, Gloucester, GL3 4FE
Activities: Manufacture of condiments and seasonings
Parent: BPS Holdings Ltd
Officers: Arthur Richmond, Secretary; Elaine Birchall [1966] Director [Irish]; Rachael Bouch [1968] Director; Jeremy Forskitt [1959] Operations Director; Ian Kelland [1962] Sales and Marketing Director; Arthur William Richmond [1966] Director/Financial Controller; Joseph Sloan [1946] Director; Stephen Mark Sturgess [1956] Finance Director

British Small Animal Veterinary Association
Incorporated: 20 July 1993 *Employees:* 38
Net Worth: £13,764,802 *Total Assets:* £17,000,650
Registered Office: Woodrow House, 1 Telford Way, Waterwells Business Park, Quedgeley, Gloucester, GL2 2AB
Activities: Activities of professional membership organisations
Officers: Charles Gorman, Secretary; Dr Sophie Adamantos [1976] Director/Veterinary Surgeon; Dr Krista Arnold [1963] Director/Veterinary Surgeon [Austrian/Swiss]; Dr Anneli Lisa Beese [1973] Director/Veterinary Surgeon; John Rogers Chitty [1967] Director/Veterinary Surgeon; Pascale Collins [1967] Director/Veterinary Surgeon [Belgian]; Paul Robert Cooper [1952] Director/Veterinary Surgeon; Rachel Dunlop [1969] Director/Veterinary Surgeon; Graeme Eckford [1981] Director/Veterinary Surgeon; Dr Rebecca Geddes [1982] Director/Veterinary Surgeon; David Robert Godfrey [1965] Director/Veterinary Surgeon; Charles Nicholas Gorman [1961] Director/Veterinary Surgeon; Julian Hoad [1967] Director/Veterinary Surgeon; James William Hughes [1963] Director/Veterinary Surgeon; Phillip John Lhermette [1955] Director/Veterinary Surgeon; Dr Madonna Jane Elizabeth Livingstone [1979] Director/Veterinary Surgeon; Susan Jane MacAldowie [1969] Director/Veterinary Surgeon; Dr Aisling McGrath [1987] Director/Veterinary Surgeon [Irish]; Sheldon Middleton [1980] Director/Veterinary Surgeon; Kate O'Sullivan [1964] Director/Veterinary Surgeon; Susan Paterson [1959] Director/Veterinary Surgeon; Caroline Louise Queen [1968] Director/Veterinary Surgeon; Professor Ian Ramsey [1967] Director/Veterinary Surgeon; Dr Rebecca Smith [1989] Director/Veterinary Surgeon; Dr Christopher Paul Sturgess [1961] Director/Veterinary Surgeon; Catherine Lorna Thomson [1977] Director/Veterinary Surgeon; Julia Margaret Thomson [1964] Director/Veterinary Surgeon; James Warland [1985] Director/Veterinary Surgeon; Dr Helen Watson [1968] Director/Veterinary Surgeon; Tim Williams [1983] Director/Veterinary Surgeon

British Solar Renewables Limited
Incorporated: 15 July 2010 *Employees:* 88
Net Worth: £9,367,594 *Total Assets:* £18,365,280
Registered Office: 35 and 35a The Maltings, Lower Charlton Trading Estate, Shepton Mallet, Somerset, BA4 5QE
Activities: Other specialised construction activities n.e.c.
Parent: BSR Group Holdings Limited
Officers: Charles Bondi [1972] Director/Accountant; Frances Mary Button [1971] Legal Director; Graham David Harding [1966] Director/Chief Financial Officer; David Gavin Peill [1973] Commercial Director; Kenneth Reid Ross [1968] Director

Brixham College Academy Trust
Incorporated: 14 November 2011 *Employees:* 166
Net Worth: £7,389,659 *Total Assets:* £10,141,551
Registered Office: Brixham College, Higher Ranscombe Road, Brixham, Devon, TQ5 9HF
Activities: General secondary education
Officers: Julie Ethel Chubb, Secretary; Ali Bouyamourn [1957] Director; Gareth Robert Brown [1971] Director/Teacher; Joseph Champness [1987] Director/Devon and Cornwall Police - Manager; Mark James Eager [1967] Director/Principal; Scott Fry [1986] Director/Health and Safety Manager; Doctor Emily Glover [1988] Director/Assistant Project Manager; Kathryn Miller [1969] Director; Margaret Susan Milner [1947] Director; Anthony Barrington Prowse [1945] Director; Helen Roberts [1969] Director/Absence Manager/HR Manager; Clive Mark Star [1968] Director/Technical Architect; Jean Patricia Charlotte Willder [1933] Director; Andy Wilson [1963] Director/Human Resource Manager; Sandra Eleanor Wright [1975] Director/Headteacher

Broadoak Mathematics and Computing College
Incorporated: 6 December 2011 *Employees:* 110
Net Worth: £12,646,265 *Total Assets:* £15,427,122
Registered Office: Broadoak Mathematics and Computing College, Windwhistle Road, Weston-Super-Mare, Somerset, BS23 4NP
Activities: General secondary education
Officers: Beverley Ann Lloyd-Jones, Secretary; Jacqueline Ann Ford [1960] Director of Partnership, Weston College; Rebecca Frise [1972] Director/Administrator; Hannah Hall [1986] Director/Teacher; Patrick John Horrigan [1943] Director/Management Consultant; Jason Anthony Kilduff [1977] Director/Manager in Education; Michael Thomas Gilbert Lawford [1936] Director/Business Consultant; Susan Renee Marshall [1948] Director/Retired; Kathleen McGillycuddy [1973] Director/Headteacher [Irish]; Leigh Barry Morris [1965] Director; Clare Louise Pearce [1973] Director/Schools Funding Officer; Lee Melvin Tuck [1967] Director/Applications Programmer; Clayton Geoffrey Wall [1962] Director/Local Government Officer

Broadway (Bristol) Engineering Co,Limited
Incorporated: 22 November 1945 *Employees:* 97
Net Worth: £7,402,585 *Total Assets:* £8,543,644
Registered Office: Knapps Lane, St George, Bristol, BS5 7UQ
Activities: Manufacture of air and spacecraft and related machinery
Major Shareholder: Jean Esme Brattle
Officers: Jean Esme Brattle, Secretary; Jean Esme Brattle [1923] Director; Sebastian Peter Greene [1979] Director/Engineering; Darren John Gribble [1960] Director/Technical

Penny Brohn Cancer Care
Incorporated: 17 May 1982 *Employees:* 68
Net Worth: £5,241,000 *Total Assets:* £5,478,000
Registered Office: Penny Brohn Cancer Care, Chapel Pill Lane, Pill, Bristol, BS20 0HH
Activities: Other human health activities
Officers: Jayne Dilys Mary Tucker, Secretary; Dr Victor Laurence Barley [1941] Director/Medical Practitioner; Francesca Barnes [1958] Director/Banker; Felicity Ann Biggart [1959] Director/Therapist; Rebecca Louise Granger [1971] Director; Jacqueline Tania Graves [1966] Director/Registered Nurse; Katherine Elizabeth Groombridge [1975] Director/Project Manager; Kenneth David Guy [1950] Director/Accountant; Alexander George Hamilton-Baily [1977] Director/Consultant; Stephen Jonathan Rosser [1960] Director/Solicitor; Mohammed Habedat Saddiq [1970] Director; Caroline Mary Sapsed [1938] Director/Retired; Charlotte White [1982] Director/Executive Coach and Trainer

Brook Enterprises Limited
Incorporated: 8 July 1954 *Employees:* 62
Net Worth: £3,219,434 *Total Assets:* £3,998,249
Registered Office: Mary Street House, Mary Street, Taunton, Somerset, TA1 3NW
Activities: Hotels and similar accommodation
Parent: Eyre Holdings Limited
Officers: Ilona Katherine Lamb, Secretary; Ilona Katherine Lamb [1982] Director; Ivan Alistair Strubbe [1958] Managing Director

Brook Food Processing Equipment Ltd
Incorporated: 25 July 2000 *Employees:* 44
Net Worth: £2,425,497 *Total Assets:* £4,006,885
Registered Office: The New Works, Roughmoor Industrial Estate, Williton, Somerset, TA4 4RF
Activities: Manufacture of machinery for food, beverage and tobacco processing
Parent: Brook Food Trading Ltd
Officers: Mark Dorrill, Secretary; Mark Dorrill [1967] Director/Accountant; Christopher John Lees [1965] Director; Ann Mary Wells [1986] Director; Stephen Christopher Wells [1967] Director; Kerrie-Marie Wilson [1990] Director

Brooke Energy (Engineering) Limited
Incorporated: 9 May 2016 *Employees:* 23
Net Worth: £194,819 *Total Assets:* £4,775,235
Registered Office: Jewells, Hemyock, Cullompton, Devon, EX15 3PX
Activities: Production of electricity
Officers: Timothy Kevin Ayres [1980] Director/Management; Glyn Martin Brooke [1959] Director/Operations Manager; Troy Stuart [1969] Director/Manager; Kevin Ian Thomas [1962] Director/General Manager

Brookridge Timber Limited
Incorporated: 4 March 1981 *Employees:* 70
Net Worth: £1,929,726 *Total Assets:* £5,338,963
Registered Office: Hemyock, Cullompton, Devon, EX15 3PF
Activities: Sawmilling and planing of wood
Major Shareholder: Royston David Brooke
Officers: Malcolm Chapman, Secretary; Royston David Brooke [1957] Director; Christopher Anthony Jandrell [1962] Director; Neil Lush [1965] Director

Brooks Hotels Limited
Incorporated: 28 February 2007 *Employees:* 68
Net Worth: £1,190,734 *Total Assets:* £5,334,488
Registered Office: Brooks Guesthouse, 1 Crescent Gardens, Bath, BA1 2NA
Activities: Hotels and similar accommodation
Shareholders: Andrew Dominic Brooks; Carla Maria Brooks
Officers: Andrew Dominic Brooks, Secretary; Andrew Dominic Brooks [1971] Director/Hotelier; Carla Maria Brooks [1973] Director/Hotelier [Irish]

Brookside Community Primary School Academy Trust
Incorporated: 20 May 2011 *Employees:* 120
Net Worth: £3,697,313 *Total Assets:* £7,182,846
Registered Office: Brookside Academy, Brooks Road, Street, Somerset, BA16 0PR
Activities: Primary education
Officers: Sandra Dawn Cinicola, Secretary; Dr Stuart Guy Clowes [1970] Director/IT Analyst; Kevin Cook [1977] Director/Lecturer; Craig Matthew Harris [1983] Director/Web Analytics Manager; Helen Charlotte Keast [1981] Director/Raw Material Manager; Adam Paul Kelland [1986] Director/Teacher; Jennifer Lynda Moore [1962] Director/Teacher; Julie Summerhayes [1970] Director/Head of HR & OD; Robert William Sutherland [1964] Director/School Business Manager; Brian Anthony Walton [1969] Director/Headteacher; Janet Ruth White [1954] Director/Retired

Brothers Drinks Co. Limited
Incorporated: 30 April 1992 *Employees:* 185
Net Worth: £56,965,680 *Total Assets:* £72,885,224
Registered Office: 4th Floor, St Catherines Court, Berkeley Place, Clifton, Bristol, BS8 1BQ
Activities: Distilling, rectifying and blending of spirits
Officers: Iain David Glen, Secretary; Christopher John Courage [1962] Director; Iain David Glen [1969] Director/Accountant; Jonathan Showering [1962] Director/Financial Advisor; Matthew Herbert Showering [1964] Director/Marketing Advisor

Brotherwood Automobility Limited
Incorporated: 25 January 1978 *Employees:* 59
Net Worth: £2,904,338 *Total Assets:* £4,886,752
Registered Office: Pillar Box Lane, Beer Hackett, Sherborne, Dorset, DT9 6QP
Activities: Sale of other motor vehicles
Parent: Brotherwood Holdings Limited
Officers: Rodney John Brotherwood [1945] Director/Engineer; John Paul Daniel [1971] Director; Dale Anthony Worthington [1974] Director

Brownbrink Ltd
Incorporated: 22 June 1999 *Employees:* 3
Net Worth: £1,865,625 *Total Assets:* £4,970,071
Registered Office: c/o M & M Plant (Devon & Cornwall) Limited, Trethorne Business Park, Kennards House, Launceston, Cornwall, PL15 8QE
Activities: Construction of commercial buildings
Major Shareholder: Michael Winston Davey
Officers: Barry James Northcott, Secretary; Michael Winston Davey [1968] Director/Leisure Facilities Manager

The Andrew Brownsword Arts Foundation
Incorporated: 17 March 1999
Net Worth: £6,644,903 *Total Assets:* £6,646,073
Registered Office: 4 Queen Square, Bath, BA1 2HA
Activities: Operation of arts facilities
Officers: Nicholas James Burrows, Secretary; Nicholas Bonham [1948] Director/Fine Art Auctioneer; Andrew Douglas Brownsword [1947] Director; Christina June Brownsword [1951] Director; Anthony Raymond Hepworth [1952] Director/Art Dealer

Andrew Brownsword Hotels Limited
Incorporated: 8 September 2003 *Employees:* 296
Net Worth: £64,618,228 *Total Assets:* £69,195,288
Registered Office: 8 Gay Street, Bath, BA1 2PH
Activities: Activities of head offices
Major Shareholder: Andrew Douglas Brownsword
Officers: Peter Tyrrell, Secretary; Andrew Douglas Brownsword [1947] Director/Publisher; Jeremy David Hancock [1964] Director/Tax Manager; Stephanie Hocking [1966] Director; Peter Tyrrell [1972] Director

Frank Bruce & Company Limited
Incorporated: 2 May 1936 *Employees:* 5
Net Worth: £7,272,085 *Total Assets:* £10,074,176
Registered Office: 58 St Aidans Road, St George, Bristol, BS5 8RS
Activities: Other letting and operating of own or leased real estate
Shareholder: Mark James Davison
Officers: Andrew John Davison, Secretary; Andrew John Davison [1942] Director/Chartered Accountant; Mark James Davison [1937] Director/Farmer

Bruf Contract Holdings Limited
Incorporated: 31 December 1964
Net Worth: £3,860,585 *Total Assets:* £3,928,651
Registered Office: CB Reid, Wadebridge House, Wadebridge Square, Poundbury, Dorchester, DT1 3AQ
Activities: Other letting and operating of own or leased real estate
Shareholder: Matthew Robert John Roche
Officers: Stephen Mark Goodwin, Secretary; Stephen Mark Goodwin [1963] Finance Director; Matthew Robert John Roche [1955] Director/Civil Engineer

Brunel Wind Limited
Incorporated: 5 June 2006
Net Worth Deficit: £2,661,420 *Total Assets:* £25,728,480
Registered Office: c/o Thrive Renewables PLC, Deanery Road, Bristol, BS1 5AS
Activities: Activities of production holding companies
Parent: Thrive Renewables PLC
Officers: Matthew Thomas Clayton [1975] Director; Katrina Lorraine Cross [1972] Director/Accountant; Monika Lidia Paplaczyk [1979] Director/Investment Manager [Polish]

Brunelcare
Incorporated: 31 May 1958 *Employees:* 1,200
Net Worth: £24,587,000 *Total Assets:* £63,316,000
Registered Office: Saffron Gardens, Prospect Place, Whitehall, Bristol, BS5 9FF
Activities: Other accommodation
Officers: Kevin Andrew Fairman, Secretary; Tarun Gokaldas Chotai [1963] Director/Financial Consultant [Indian]; Alison Deborah Evans [1958] Director/NHS Manager; Kevin Stuart Andrew Fairman [1961] Director/Chief Executive; Mandip Singh Hayer [1965] Director; Margaret Catherine Hehir [1957] Director/Retired [Irish]; Nicholas Stuart Hooper [1954] Director/Self-Employed Consultant; Philip Ian Hope [1955] Director/Management Consultant; Julie Steed [1962] Marketing Director; Ian Michael Turner [1962] Director/Chartered Accountant; Anthony George Wilson [1936] Director/Retired

Brunswick Limited
Incorporated: 7 June 2006 *Employees:* 2
Net Worth: £9,016,687 *Total Assets:* £29,391,830
Registered Office: c/o Francis Clark LLP, North Quay House, Sutton Harbour, Plymouth, PL4 0RA
Activities: Other letting and operating of own or leased real estate
Parent: Attlee Sinclair Limited
Officers: Russell James Hooper, Secretary/Manager; Mark Farmer [1961] Director/Venture Capitalist; Russell James Hooper [1966] Director/Manager

A.J. Brunt Limited
Incorporated: 23 March 1988 *Employees:* 13
Net Worth: £6,275,893 *Total Assets:* £6,956,778
Registered Office: Grove Lane, Marston Trading Estate, Frome, Somerset, BA11 4AT
Activities: Freight transport by road
Shareholders: Mary Amelia Brunt; Alan James Brunt
Officers: Mary Amelia Brunt, Secretary; Alan James Brunt [1950] Director/Haulier; Mary Amelia Brunt [1945] Director/Haulier

Bruton School for Girls
Incorporated: 23 October 2000 *Employees:* 76
Net Worth: £4,545,514 *Total Assets:* £6,031,358
Registered Office: Bruton School for Girls, Sunny Hill, Bruton, Somerset, BA10 0NT
Activities: Pre-primary education
Officers: Adam Hume Dunsterville Harvey Kelly, Secretary; Lisa Anne Anderson [1967] Director/Financial Adviser; Elisabeth Alison Balfour [1943] Director/Book Editor; Simon Christopher Bate [1956] Director/Chief Executive; David Henry Cary Batten [1952] Solicitor Director; Christine Anne Davidson [1942] Director/Retired; Hugh Lewelyn Davies [1941] Director/Consultant; David John Charles Hindley [1940] Director/Magistrate; Gillian Hylson-Smith [1939] Director/Retired Head; Nicholas David Jefferis [1958] Director/Management Consultant; Andrew Godfrey Lane [1945] Director; Nigel Brian Noble [1947] Director/Retired Bursar; Michael John Champion Streatfeild [1945] Director/Chartered Accountant; Elizabeth Rosemary Webbe [1963] Director/Solicitor; Diana Wood [1942] Director/Governor

Bryan Brothers Holdings Limited
Incorporated: 11 November 1975 *Employees:* 1
Net Worth: £6,703,617 *Total Assets:* £7,825,842
Registered Office: Freshford House, Redcliffe Way, Bristol, BS1 6NL
Activities: Activities of head offices
Major Shareholder: Richard Bryan
Officers: Richard James Emmett Bryan, Secretary/Director; Melissa Rose Bryan [1970] Director [American]; Richard James Emmett Bryan [1970] Director; Grant Stephen Watson [1939] Director/Chartered Surveyor

Bryanston School,Incorporated
Incorporated: 26 November 1927 *Employees:* 362
Net Worth: £35,300,960 *Total Assets:* £46,996,816
Registered Office: Bryanston House, Blandford, Dorset, DT11 0PX
Activities: General secondary education
Officers: Michael Aidan John McGovern, Secretary; Natalie Bickford [1970] Human Resources Director; Simon Foster Bowes [1951] Director/Tea Merchant; Benedict Peter Broad [1985] Director; Sebastian Orby Conran [1956] Director/Designer; Dr Katherine Maire-Anne Fleming [1978] Director of Undergraduate Admissions for English; John Andrew Francis Fortescue [1955] Director/Executive Search Recruitment; Susan Foulser [1949] Director/Consultant; Julian Rutherford Greenhill [1973] Director/Barrister; Bahman Irvani [1952] Director; Mark Aubrey Seymour Laurence [1968] Director/Consultant; Christopher George Martin [1957] Director/Retired; Victoria Mary McDonaugh [1950] Director/Teacher; Mabel Ellen McKeown [1986] Director/Charity Fundraiser; Dr Hannah Mary Pharaoh [1976] Director/Doctor; Anthony Richard Poulton [1969] Director/Solicitor; Louise Marcelle Victoria Soden [1952] Director/Education; David Mark Trick [1960] Director

Brymain Investments Limited
Incorporated: 7 April 1965 *Employees:* 5
Net Worth: £20,381,260 *Total Assets:* £36,811,228
Registered Office: 50 Clifton Down Road, Bristol, BS8 4AH
Activities: Other letting and operating of own or leased real estate
Shareholder: Michael John Romain
Officers: Margaret Rose Barrington, Secretary; David Bernard Romain [1983] Director/Solicitor; Euphemia Mary McKinnon Romain [1950] Director; Jesse Daniel Romain [1981] Director/Chartered Surveyor; Michael John Romain [1950] Director

BSR Connect Limited
Incorporated: 12 March 2013 *Employees:* 7
Previous: Renewable Energy Connections Limited
Net Worth: £1,465,528 *Total Assets:* £3,664,098
Registered Office: 35 and 35a The Maltings, Lower Charlton Trading Estate, Shepton Mallet, Somerset, BA4 5QE
Activities: Electrical installation
Parent: British Solar Renewables Limited
Officers: Frances Mary Button [1971] Director/Group Chief Legal Officer; Graham David Harding [1966] Director/Chief Financial Officer; Simon Paul Roberts [1984] Director

BSR Group Holdings Limited
Incorporated: 17 July 2012 *Employees:* 95
Previous: Sustainable Power Generation Limited
Net Worth: £9,855,437 *Total Assets:* £44,645,240
Registered Office: 35 and 35a The Maltings, Lower Charlton Trading Estate, Shepton Mallet, Somerset, BA4 5QE
Activities: Activities of head offices
Shareholders: Hemera Energy Limited; Kristian Siem
Officers: Charles Bondi [1972] Director/Accountant; Graham David Harding [1966] Director/Chief Financial Officer; Simon Paul Roberts [1984] Director; Kenneth Reid Ross [1968] Director; Jorgen Westad [1961] Director [Norwegian]

Buccaneer Holdings Limited
Incorporated: 13 September 1988 *Employees:* 263
Net Worth: £3,789,105 *Total Assets:* £6,052,766
Registered Office: 37 Rodney Road, Cheltenham, Glos, GL50 1HX
Activities: Hotels and similar accommodation
Officers: Andrew Michael Jones [1961] Operations Director; Penelope Jane Ruthven [1943] Director/Design Consultant; Timothy St Clair Ruthven [1966] Director/Public House Operator

Buckclose Limited
Incorporated: 10 April 1972 *Employees:* 11
Net Worth: £6,155,455 *Total Assets:* £9,779,390
Registered Office: 7 Sandy Court, Ashleigh Way, Langage Business Park, Plymouth, PL7 5JX
Activities: Development of building projects
Shareholder: Stuart Alan Walsh
Officers: Stuart Alan Walsh, Secretary/Director; Andrew David Walsh [1963] Director/Builder; Stuart Alan Walsh [1965] Director/Surveyor

The Buckinghamshire Group Limited
Incorporated: 15 February 2013 *Employees:* 236
Net Worth Deficit: £1,068,919 *Total Assets:* £16,182,957
Registered Office: 31-33 Commercial Road, Poole, Dorset, BH14 0HU
Activities: Other business support service activities n.e.c.
Shareholders: Christopher Bialan; Robert Leslie Cousins
Officers: Christopher Bialan [1957] Director; David John Comyn [1954] Director [Irish]; Robert Leslie Cousins [1967] Director

The Buckinghamshire Limited
Incorporated: 6 February 2013 *Employees:* 2
Net Worth: £10,634,177 *Total Assets:* £15,964,634
Registered Office: 31-33 Commercial Road, Poole, Dorset, BH14 0HU
Activities: Other residential care activities n.e.c.
Parent: The Buckinghamshire Group Limited
Officers: Christopher Bialan [1957] Director; Robert Leslie Cousins [1967] Director

Buckland Care Limited
Incorporated: 29 July 2002 *Employees:* 350
Net Worth: £5,525,724 *Total Assets:* £21,471,656
Registered Office: 13 Lagoon Road, Lilliput, Poole, Dorset, BH14 8JT
Activities: Residential nursing care facilities
Parent: Buckland Care (Holdings) Limited
Officers: Joy Elizabeth Birkett, Secretary; Joy Elizabeth Birkett [1949] Director; Roger Wilfred Birkett [1943] Director

Buckler's Mead School
Incorporated: 7 July 2011 *Employees:* 117
Net Worth: £11,268,202 *Total Assets:* £14,171,607
Registered Office: Buckler's Mead School, St John's Road, Yeovil, Somerset, BA21 4NH
Activities: General secondary education
Officers: Matthew David Wood, Secretary; Dawn Copland [1971] Director/Finance Officer; John William Crew [1950] Director/Retired; John Evans [1961] Director/Yeovil College Principal; Julia Claire Foote [1969] Director/Teacher; Denise Jacqueline Gommo [1969] Director/School Business Manager; Sara Gorrod [1963] Director/Headteacher; Malcolm Kenneth Gulliver [1954] Director/Systems Engineer; Richard Grant Hunt [1949] Director/Retired; Pauline Barbara Hutchings [1952] Director/Retired; Stephen Michael Lawes [1963] Director/Management Consultant; Suzanne Parry [1972] Director/Learning Mentor; Jane Elizabeth Purchase [1970] Director/Learning Support Assistant; Martin Leonard William Salzer [1949] Director/Engineer; Colin Kenneth Thomas [1967] Director/Teacher; Graham Underhill [1962] Director/Banker

Budock Vean Holdings Limited
Incorporated: 8 November 1965 *Employees:* 83
Net Worth: £719,840 *Total Assets:* £6,403,279
Registered Office: Budock Vean Hotel, Mawnan Smith, Falmouth, Cornwall, TR11 5LG
Activities: Activities of head offices
Shareholder: Martin Edward Barlow
Officers: Martin Edward Barlow, Secretary; Edward Haggas Barlow [1929] Director; Martin Edward Barlow [1963] Director/Accountant

Budock Vean Hotel Limited
Incorporated: 10 October 1931 *Employees:* 83
Net Worth: £1,010,218 *Total Assets:* £6,808,451
Registered Office: Budock Vean Hotel, Mawnan Smith, Falmouth, Cornwall, TR11 5LG
Activities: Hotels and similar accommodation
Parent: Budock Vean Holdings Limited
Officers: Martin Edward Barlow, Secretary; Edward Haggas Barlow [1929] Director/Hotelier; Martin Edward Barlow [1963] Director

Budweiser Budvar UK Limited
Incorporated: 24 October 2001 *Employees:* 16
Net Worth: £705,399 *Total Assets:* £5,214,562
Registered Office: 76 MacRae Road, Eden Office Park, Ham Green, Bristol, BS20 0DD
Activities: Other food services
Parent: Budweiser Budvar National Corporation
Officers: Simon Warren, Secretary; Robert Chrt [1966] Director [Czech]; Simon George [1971] Sales Director; Lubomir Lojda [1960] Director/Financial Analyst [Czech]; Renata Pankova [1972] Director/Subsidiary Manager [Czech]; Simon Peter Warren [1967] Director

Francis Bugler Limited
Incorporated: 21 September 1948 *Employees:* 44
Net Worth: £2,790,150 *Total Assets:* £11,987,163
Registered Office: Barrowfield, Broadwindsor Road, Beaminster, Dorset, DT8 3PP
Activities: Wholesale of agricultural machinery, equipment and supplies
Shareholders: Richard Gerald Bugler; John William Ralph Bugler; Pamela June Bugler
Officers: Terry Anthony Score, Secretary; John William Ralph Bugler [1958] Director/Agricultural Engineer

Build Supplies Limited
Incorporated: 17 August 2007 *Employees:* 13
Net Worth: £2,290,702 *Total Assets:* £4,476,066
Registered Office: Unit 1 South Moor, Winnards Perch, St Columb, Cornwall, TR9 6DG
Activities: Wholesale of wood, construction materials and sanitary equipment
Shareholders: Michael Tregunna; Tristan Edward Tregunna
Officers: Karen Gough, Secretary; Michael Tregunna [1981] Director; Tristan Edward Tregunna [1978] Director

Buildit Gloster Limited
Incorporated: 23 March 2009 *Employees:* 48
Net Worth: £2,814,697 *Total Assets:* £4,328,003
Registered Office: 5 Pullman Court, Great Western Road, Gloucester, GL1 3ND
Activities: Agents involved in the sale of timber and building materials
Officers: James Keyse [1975] Director; Brenda Frances Meecham [1954] Director; Derek William Meecham [1952] Director

Bulk Hardware Limited
Incorporated: 19 July 1974 *Employees:* 55
Net Worth: £3,065,380 *Total Assets:* £4,973,491
Registered Office: One New Street, Wells, Somerset, BA5 2LA
Activities: Non-specialised wholesale trade
Shareholders: Wynford Rees; Janice Elizabeth Rees
Officers: Janice Elizabeth Rees, Secretary; Gareth Rees [1969] Director; Janice Elizabeth Rees [1949] Director/Company Secretary; Wynford Rees [1948] Director

The Bulldog Trust Limited
Incorporated: 20 February 2008 *Employees:* 15
Net Worth: £9,143,089 *Total Assets:* £9,324,357
Registered Office: Alexandra House, St Johns Street, Salisbury, Wilts, SP1 2SB
Activities: Other business support service activities n.e.c.
Officers: Charles Martin Richard Hoare [1976] Director/Investment Banker; Charles Vivian Jackson [1953] Director/Retired; Robert Hamish McPherson [1976] Director/Finance; Brian Andrew Smouha [1938] Director/Retired; Alexander David Williams [1973] Director/Finance

Burcombe Haulage Limited
Incorporated: 23 September 1999 *Employees:* 54
Net Worth: £4,767,333 *Total Assets:* £6,479,461
Registered Office: Harscombe House, Darklake View, Estover, Plymouth, PL6 7TL
Activities: Freight transport by road
Shareholders: Maxine Mary Batten; Richard Thomas Batten
Officers: Maxine Mary Batten, Secretary; Roger Ackford [1968] Director; Maxine Mary Batten [1958] Director; Nicola Batten [1986] Director; Richard Thomas Batten [1957] Director/Haulier; Carina Mary Hodge [1983] Director; Stuart Gavin Wilkie [1977] Director

Burford Alpha Limited
Incorporated: 1 September 2003
Net Worth Deficit: £213,815,008 *Total Assets:* £333,275,008
Registered Office: Richmond House, Avonmouth Way, Avonmouth, Bristol, BS11 8DE
Activities: Activities of head offices
Parent: Burford Beta Holdings Limited
Officers: Julian Gleek [1958] Director

Burford Beta Holdings Limited
Incorporated: 1 September 2003
Net Worth: £325,000 *Total Assets:* £408,512,992
Registered Office: Richmond House, Avonmouth Way, Avonmouth, Bristol, BS11 8DE
Activities: Activities of head offices
Shareholders: Eldon Street (Fidenza) Limited; West Coast Capital Prestven Limited
Officers: Julian Gleek [1958] Director; Barry Porter [1962] Director/Head Real Estate Asset Management

Burford Beta Limited
Incorporated: 1 September 2003
Net Worth Deficit: £4,593,000 *Total Assets:* £6,859,000
Registered Office: Richmond House, Avonmouth Way, Avonmouth, Bristol, BS11 8DE
Activities: Buying and selling of own real estate
Parent: Burford Alpha Limited
Officers: Julian Gleek [1958] Director

Burford Delta Limited
Incorporated: 14 October 2003
Net Worth: £7,312,000 *Total Assets:* £16,663,000
Registered Office: Richmond House, Avonmouth Way, Avonmouth, Bristol, BS11 8DE
Activities: Buying and selling of own real estate
Parent: Burford Beta Limited
Officers: Julian Gleek [1958] Director

Burford Zeta
Incorporated: 26 November 2004 *Employees:* 1
Net Worth: £355,778,368 *Total Assets:* £355,778,368
Registered Office: Richmond House, Avonmouth Way, Avonmouth, Bristol, BS11 8DE
Activities: Activities of head offices
Parent: Burford Epsilon
Officers: Julian Gleek [1958] Director

The Burgate School and Sixth Form
Incorporated: 8 April 2011 *Employees:* 128
Net Worth: £14,493,128 *Total Assets:* £16,040,391
Registered Office: Salisbury Road, Fordingbridge, Hants, SP6 1EZ
Activities: General secondary education
Officers: Sarah-Jane Hewett, Secretary; Annette Elizabeth Born [1966] Finance Director; Andrew Paul Cooper [1966] Managing Director; Sally Elizabeth Firino [1977] Director/School Teacher; Wendy Sara Gregoire [1955] Director/Chartered Clinical Psychologist; Nigel John Griffiths [1951] Director/Estate Manager; Jennifer Ann Hair [1958] Director/Retired; David Jonathan Millar [1971] Director/Head of Communications; Joanna Helen Newbigging [1967] Director/Health Care Assistant; Ian Nigel Newman [1955] Funeral Director; David Michael Pover [1969] Director/Headteacher; Dr Richard Wagland [1968] Director/Lecturer

Burges Salmon Company Limited
Incorporated: 8 March 2011 *Employees:* 582
Net Worth: £248,000 *Total Assets:* £5,526,000
Registered Office: One Glass Wharf, Bristol, BS2 0ZX
Activities: Other business support service activities n.e.c.
Parent: Burges Salmon LLP
Officers: Roger Bull [1970] Director/Solicitor; Emma Victoria Dowden [1979] Director of Best Practice & Operations; James Clifford Fountaine [1971] Director/Head of Personnel; Robert Halton [1958] Director; Ann Metherall [1964] Director/Solicitor; Richard Carveth Mabyn Read [1974] Director/Solicitor; Martin Webb [1976] Director/Chief Financial Officer

Burges Salmon LLP
Incorporated: 12 March 2004 *Employees:* 582
Net Worth: £54,224,000 *Total Assets:* £73,011,000
Registered Office: One Glass Wharf, Bristol, BS2 0ZX
Officers: John Edward Barnett [1970] Member; Paul Andrew Browne [1966] Member; Roger Bull [1970] Member; Jeremy Brian Dickerson [1967] Member; Elizabeth Dunn [1966] Member; Ross Fairley [1968] Member; Christopher Michael Joseph Godfrey [1962] Member; David Russell Hall [1967] Member; Colin James Ligman [1972] Member; Ian Knut Salter [1968] Member; Christopher Shaun Tudor Seaton [1961] Member; Richard Anthony Adams [1983] LLP Member; James Austin Aveline [1972] LLP Member; Michael Ralph Barlow [1969] LLP Member; Keith Charles Beattie [1972] LLP Member; Richard John Bedford [1962] LLP Member; Philip Jonathan Beer [1974] LLP Member; Jeremy Matthew George Bell [1969] LLP Member; Julian Roderick Gerard Boswall [1965] LLP Member; Luke James Bowery [1978] LLP Member; Euan McIntosh Bremner [1975] LLP Member; Justin Haddon Clifford Briggs [1971] LLP Member; Andrew James Peter Burnette [1979] LLP Member; Ian William Carnochan [1974] LLP Member; Nicholas Stephen Churchward [1974] LLP Member; Richard James Roger Clark [1970] LLP Member; Simon Anthony Coppen [1963] LLP Member; Nathan Phillip Curtis [1980] LLP Member; Dominic James Davis [1974] LLP Member; Brioney Olivia Jean Denner [1976] LLP Member; Andrew Alexander Dunlop [1964] LLP Member; Thomas Michael Dunn [1978] LLP Member; Andrew John Eaton [1978] LLP Member; Sian Louise Edmunds [1973] LLP Member; Jonathan William Eves [1981] LLP Member; Emma Louise Folkes [1977] LLP Member; William John Metherell Gard [1963] LLP Member; Nicholas Edward Luke Graves [1969] LLP Member; Paul Simon Nicholas Haggett [1960] LLP Member; Marcus Roderick Harling [1961] LLP Member; Suzanna Claire Harvey [1979] LLP Member; Michael Patrick Hayles [1978] LLP Member; Thomas Robert Morley Hewitt [1966] LLP Member; Alice Margaret Honeywill [1981] LLP Member; Sarah Katherine Hoskinson [1977] LLP Member; John George Houlden [1974] LLP Member; Timothy Mark Illston [1958] LLP Member; Christopher Michael Jackson [1966] LLP Member; Lloyd David James [1980] LLP Member; Steven James [1970] LLP Member; Sally Jupp [1979] LLP Member; Kevin Matthew Kennedy [1972] LLP Member; Richard Edward Allen Knight [1975] LLP Member; Sarah Louise Lane [1962] LLP Member; Richard John Leeming [1967] LLP Member; Adrian James Martin [1972] LLP Member; Kari Suzanne McOrmick [1970] LLP Member; Ann Metherall [1964] LLP Member; Peter Harold Abrahall Morris [1957] LLP Member; Alastair Charles Morrison [1960] LLP Member; Simon Richard Owen [1969] LLP Member; Mark Albert Paterson [1967] LLP Member; Richard Charles Pettit [1982] LLP Member; James Edward Phillips [1978] LLP Member; Ross Edward Polkinghorne [1977] LLP Member; Nigel Francis Mark Popplewell [1957] LLP Member; Clive Anthony Pugh [1971] LLP Member; Beatrice Puoti [1967] LLP Member; Matthew John Ramus [1973] LLP Member; Richard Carveth Mabyn Read [1974] LLP Member; Patrick Cathcart Robinson [1964] LLP Member; Rachael Louise Ruane [1976] LLP Member; Helen June Scott-Lawler [1971] LLP Member; Mark Rollo Cleveland Shepherd [1973] LLP Member; Matthew Andrew Sims [1977] LLP Member; Graham Matthew Soar [1974] LLP Member; Gary Clarke Soloman [1971] LLP Member; Richard Alexander Brailsford Spink [1965] LLP Member; James Alastair Sutherland [1978] LLP Member; Simon Andrew Tilling [1981] LLP Member; Ian Ross Tucker [1976] LLP Member; Camilla Louise Usher Clark [1976] LLP Member; Michael Joseph Ward [1977] LLP Member; William Rupert Weston [1971] LLP Member; William Richard Woodall [1972] LLP Member; Christopher James Worrall [1980] LLP Member; Susannah Jane Young [1979] LLP Member

Burkert UK Limited
Incorporated: 18 December 1964 *Employees:* 31
Previous: Burkert Contromatic Limited
Net Worth: £2,780,166 *Total Assets:* £5,704,715
Registered Office: Fluid Control Centre, 1 Bridge End, Cirencester, Glos, GL7 1QY
Activities: Other business support service activities n.e.c.
Officers: Heribert Peter Hans Rohrbeck [1960] Director/Chief Executive Officer [German]; Marco Ivan Steinemann [1973] Director/General Manager [Swiss]

Burnbake Campsite Limited
Incorporated: 11 May 2005 *Employees:* 13
Net Worth Deficit: £263,653 *Total Assets:* £4,091,749
Registered Office: The Estate Office, Cow Lane, Wareham, Dorset, BH20 4RD
Activities: Recreational vehicle parks, trailer parks and camping grounds
Shareholders: Rempstone Estate Trustees Ltd; Ryder Trustees Ltd
Officers: Guy James Dudley Ryder, Secretary; Anthony William Fortescue [1962] Director/Land Agent; Douglas Ryder [1963] Director/Farmer; Guy James Dudley Ryder [1968] Director/Osteopath; Phillippa Mary Ryder [1942] Director/Housewife; Michael Lawrence Stickland [1942] Director/Planning Advisor

Buro Happold Consulting Engineers Limited
Incorporated: 2 April 1986 *Employees:* 88
Net Worth: £3,447,000 *Total Assets:* £10,723,000
Registered Office: Camden Mill, Lower Bristol Road, Bath, BA2 3DQ
Activities: Other engineering activities
Officers: Delia Conway, Secretary; Philip Stephen Dalglish [1960] Director/Consulting Engineer [New Zealander]; Alan John Harbinson [1964] Director/Consulting Engineer; Padraic Kelly [1954] Director/Consulting Engineer [Irish]; Richard Brian Marshall [1969] Director/Consulting Engineer [New Zealander]; Oliver Charles Pelham Plunkett [1972] Director/Consulting Engineer [Irish]; Christopher Jeremy Dorning Young [1954] Director/Consulting Engineer

Buro Happold Engineers Limited
Incorporated: 2 April 1986 *Employees:* 961
Net Worth: £2,778,000 *Total Assets:* £8,548,000
Registered Office: Camden Mill, Lower Bristol Road, Bath, BA2 3DQ
Activities: Other engineering activities
Officers: Delia Conway, Secretary; Neil Keith Billett [1967] Director/Consulting Engineer; James Alistair Burnley Bruce [1978] Director; Misti Louise Melville [1958] Human Resources Director [New Zealander]; Paul Rogers [1965] Director/Consulting Engineer; Neil Richard Squibbs [1961] Director/Consulting Engineer; Richard Sykes [1956] Director/Chartered Accountant

Buro Happold Limited
Incorporated: 26 August 1986
Net Worth: £23,306,000 *Total Assets:* £64,193,000
Registered Office: Camden Mill, Lower Bristol Road, Bath, BA2 3DQ
Activities: Other engineering activities
Officers: Delia Conway, Secretary; James Alistair Burnley Bruce [1978] Director; Alan John Harbinson [1964] Director/Consulting Engineer; Stephen Jolly [1966] Director/Consulting Engineer; Andrew Stuart Keelin [1966] Director/Consulting Engineer; Justin Phillips [1967] Director/Consulting Engineer; Dr Sarah Prichard [1974] Director/Consulting Engineer; Neil Richard Squibbs [1961] Director/Consulting Engineer

Burrington Estates (Clyst St George) Limited
Incorporated: 25 January 2016
Net Worth Deficit: £3,975 *Total Assets:* £6,038,199
Registered Office: Dean Clarke House, Southernhay East, Exeter, Devon, EX1 1AP
Activities: Construction of domestic buildings
Parent: Burrington Estates (Holdings) Limited
Officers: Mark David Edworthy [1969] Director; Paul Neil Scantlebury [1967] Director/Property Developer

Burrington Estates (New Homes) Limited
Incorporated: 25 January 2016 *Employees:* 24
Net Worth: £1,375,518 *Total Assets:* £15,589,759
Registered Office: Dean Clarke House, Southernhay East, Exeter, Devon, EX1 1AP
Activities: Activities of construction holding companies
Shareholders: Paul Neil Scantlebury; Mark David Edworthy
Officers: Peter Robert Andrew [1959] Non-Executive Director Chairman; Mark David Edworthy [1969] Director; Colin Stuart Palmer [1974] Director; Paul Neil Scantlebury [1967] Director/Property Developer

Burrington Estates (RS) Limited
Incorporated: 7 February 2017
Net Worth Deficit: £87,148 *Total Assets:* £8,901,385
Registered Office: Dean Clarke House, Southernhay East, Exeter, Devon, EX1 1AP
Activities: Activities of construction holding companies
Shareholders: RS Investor II, SARL; Burrington Estates (New Homes) Limited
Officers: Mark David Edworthy [1969] Director; Paul David Harrison [1976] Director; Paul Neil Scantlebury [1967] Director/Property Developer; James Ronald Whittingham [1978] Director

Burrington Estates (Trispen) Limited
Incorporated: 15 September 2016
Net Worth Deficit: £7,051 *Total Assets:* £6,952,709
Registered Office: Dean Clarke House, Southernhay East, Exeter, Devon, EX1 1AP
Activities: Construction of domestic buildings
Parent: Burrington Estates (South West) Limited
Officers: Mark David Edworthy [1969] Director; Paul Neil Scantlebury [1967] Director

Burrington Estates Limited
Incorporated: 16 September 2011 *Employees:* 6
Net Worth: £55,838 *Total Assets:* £5,798,758
Registered Office: Dean Clarke House, Southernhay East, Exeter, EX1 1AP
Activities: Management consultancy activities other than financial management
Shareholders: Paul Neil Scantlebury; Thrive Capital Investments Limited
Officers: Mark David Edworthy [1969] Director; Paul Neil Scantlebury [1967] Director/Property Developer

Burry and Knight Limited
Incorporated: 27 July 1955 *Employees:* 146
Net Worth: £41,935,400 *Total Assets:* £46,813,684
Registered Office: 10 Hoburne Lane, Christchurch, Dorset, BH23 4HP
Activities: Construction of commercial buildings
Officers: Nicholas Stewart Putnam, Company Secretary; Philippa Jane Goodwin [1970] Director; Rosemary Sarah Kennar [1956] Director; Timothy Richard Knight [1960] Director/Computer Consultant; Adrian John Osman [1943] Director; Michael Pratt [1956] Director; Mark Edward Preston [1962] Director; Marco Raffaello Simonini [1967] Director/Carpenter; Rodney Philip Tucker [1954] Director

A D Burs Limited
Incorporated: 16 May 1995 *Employees:* 226
Net Worth: £19,410,820 *Total Assets:* £30,804,114
Registered Office: Prima Dental Group, Stephenson Drive, Waterwells Business Park, Gloucester, GL2 2AG
Activities: Manufacture of medical and dental instruments and supplies
Major Shareholder: Michael Ashkin
Officers: Carl Ashkin [1963] Director/Business Executive [American]; Michael William Caputo [1947] Director [American]; Richard Oscar Muller [1956] Director

The Mike Burton Group Limited
Incorporated: 12 May 1981 *Employees:* 72
Net Worth: £5,897,308 *Total Assets:* £22,946,176
Registered Office: Carter Court, 8 Davy Way, Quedgeley, Gloucester, GL2 2DE
Activities: Other business support service activities n.e.c.
Officers: Ian Raymond Edwards, Secretary; Michael Alan Burton [1945] Chairman and Managing Director; Ian Raymond Edwards [1961] Financial Director

Mike Burton Travel Limited
Incorporated: 3 June 1991
Net Worth: £2,596,399 *Total Assets:* £12,700,138
Registered Office: Carter Court, 8 Davy Way, Quedgeley, Gloucester, GL2 2DE
Activities: Tour operator activities
Parent: The Mike Burton Group Limited
Officers: Ian Raymond Edwards, Secretary; Michael Alan Burton [1945] Director/Sports Management; Ian Raymond Edwards [1961] Director/Company Accountant

Burton Wold Wind Farm South Ltd
Incorporated: 7 December 2015 *Employees:* 4
Net Worth: £131,220 *Total Assets:* £11,521,504
Registered Office: 16 West Borough, Wimborne, Dorset, BH21 1NG
Activities: Construction of utility projects for electricity and telecommunications
Shareholders: WWS Development LLP; Infinergy Limited
Officers: Ilan Reich [1969] Director [Israeli]; Guy Lesley Rubinstein [1965] Director [Israeli]; Tjiwolt Wierda [1972] Director [Dutch]; Esbjorn Roderick Wilmar [1970] Director [Dutch]

Burts Potato Chips Limited
Incorporated: 25 November 1991 *Employees:* 209
Previous: Burts Chips Limited
Net Worth: £1,689,903 *Total Assets:* £28,023,802
Registered Office: The Klamp House, Belliver Way, Roborough, Plymouth, PL6 7BP
Activities: Manufacture of other food products n.e.c.
Parent: Andrea Holdings SA
Officers: Michael Patrick Richard Cosby, Secretary; Michael Patrick Richard Cosby [1963] Finance Director; John Leonard Joseph [1965] Operations Director; Timothy Geoffrey Kelly [1957] Director; Simon Richard Knight [1971] Sales and Marketing Director; David Alexander Nairn [1956] Director/Consultant; Jitendrakumar Maganbhai Patel [1952] Director; Yogeshchandra Maganbhai Patel [1956] Director

Bushell & Meadows Limited
Incorporated: 30 November 1962 *Employees:* 48
Net Worth: £8,164,389 *Total Assets:* £9,554,067
Registered Office: Northway Lane, Tewkesbury, Glos, GL20 8HG
Activities: Machining
Parent: Descram Limited
Officers: Clare Dovey, Secretary; Michael Attwood [1963] Director; Charles Robert Desoutter [1954] Director; George Charles Desoutter [1978] Director; William Paul Desoutter [1982] Director; Alexandra Rose Wansbrough [1977] Director

Bushurst Properties Limited
Incorporated: 25 January 1973 *Employees:* 1
Net Worth: £4,778,728 *Total Assets:* £5,561,916
Registered Office: Hawksworth, 26 Albert Road, Cheltenham, Glos, GL52 2QX
Activities: Buying and selling of own real estate
Major Shareholder: Anthony Royston Eugene Overbury
Officers: Anthony Royston Eugene Overbury, Secretary; Anthony Royston Eugene Overbury [1940] Director/Property Developer; Shirley Doreen Overbury [1945] Director

Butcombe Brewery Limited
Incorporated: 8 January 2003 *Employees:* 395
Net Worth: £5,004,378 *Total Assets:* £48,207,372
Registered Office: Cox's Green, Wrington, Bristol, BS40 5PA
Activities: Manufacture of beer
Parent: Butcombe Brewing Company Limited
Officers: Richard Stuart Grainger [1960] Director; Timothy Hubert [1962] Director; Nigel Richard Osborne [1966] Director; Jayson Peter Perfect [1979] Director

Butcombe Brewing Company Limited
Incorporated: 8 January 2003
Net Worth: £3,855,656 *Total Assets:* £6,020,774
Registered Office: Cox's Green, Wrington, Bristol, BS40 5PA
Activities: Manufacture of beer
Parent: The Liberation Group UK Limited
Officers: Richard Stuart Grainger [1960] Director; Timothy Hubert [1962] Director; Nigel Richard Osborne [1966] Director

Butterfly Conservation
Incorporated: 17 December 1987 *Employees:* 78
Net Worth: £12,304,342 *Total Assets:* £12,676,630
Registered Office: Manor Yard, East Lulworth, Wareham, Dorset, BH20 5QP
Activities: Other business support service activities n.e.c.
Officers: Julie Marie Williams, Secretary; James Asher [1950] Director/Business Manager; Fiona Barclay [1971] Managing Director; Dr Andy Barker [1959] Director/University Lecturer; Apithanny Bourne [1993] Director/Analytical Chemist; Andrew Christopher Howard Brown [1946] Director/Semi-Retired; Kathryn Dawson [1965] Director/University Administrator; Michael Dean [1947] Director/Retired; Roger Clive Dobbs [1945] Director/Retired; Dr Susan Elizabeth Foden [1953] Director/Retired; Karen Fiona Goldie-Morrison [1952] Director; Michael Frederick Johnston [1962] Director; Simon Saville [1958] Director/Retired; Nigel Symington [1948] Director/Retired; Ilija Vukomanovic [1951] Director/Retired; Chris Winnick [1953] Director/Retired

E W Button & Son Limited
Incorporated: 30 July 2008 *Employees:* 42
Net Worth: £157,824 *Total Assets:* £4,727,308
Registered Office: 12 Southgate Street, Launceston, Cornwall, PL15 9DP
Activities: Growing of vegetables and melons, roots and tubers
Shareholders: Andrew Joe Button; Andrew Tucker Button; Jean Button
Officers: Jean Button, Secretary; Andrew Tucker Button [1949] Director/Farmer; Andrew Joe Button [1974] Director/Farmer; Jean Button [1950] Director/Farmer

C.P. Button Limited
Incorporated: 22 April 1980 *Employees:* 10
Net Worth: £1,694,936 *Total Assets:* £3,912,546
Registered Office: Polshea Farm, St Tudy, Bodmin, Cornwall, PL30 3PA
Activities: Raising of dairy cattle
Shareholders: Lynn Button; Peter Mark Button
Officers: Lynn Button, Secretary; Charles Peter Button [1941] Director/Farmer; Lynn Button [1971] Director/Farmer; Peter Mark Button [1967] Director/Farmer; Wendy Maude Button [1942] Director/Farmer

Buyology Ltd
Incorporated: 26 September 2006
Net Worth: £6,871,746 *Total Assets:* £8,443,444
Registered Office: Bennetts Solicitors, Barley Wood Stables, Long Lane, Wrington, Bristol, BS40 5SA
Activities: Other retail sale in non-specialised stores
Shareholders: Robert Hoy; Sarah Jane Hoy
Officers: Isabel Hoy, Secretary; Robert Hoy [1962] Director

BWP Project Services Limited
Incorporated: 9 June 2010 *Employees:* 3
Net Worth Deficit: £29,114,000 *Total Assets:* £125,677,000
Registered Office: Third Floor, Broad Quay House, Prince Street, Bristol, BS1 4DJ
Activities: Other professional, scientific and technical activities n.e.c.
Parent: BWP Services (Holdings No. 2) Limited
Officers: Graham Baldock [1958] Executive Director Operations; Neil Rae [1971] Director; Alan Campbell Ritchie [1967] Director

BWP Services (Holdings No 1) Limited
Incorporated: 9 June 2010 *Employees:* 3
Net Worth: £50,000 *Total Assets:* £13,858,000
Registered Office: Third Floor, Broad Quay House, Prince Street, Bristol, BS1 4DJ
Activities: Other business support service activities n.e.c.
Parent: BWP Services (Holdings No 3) Limited
Officers: Graham Baldock [1958] Executive Director Operations; Neil Rae [1971] Director; Alan Campbell Ritchie [1967] Director

By Education (Barking) Holdings Limited
Incorporated: 31 October 2003
Net Worth Deficit: £979,000 *Total Assets:* £38,489,000
Registered Office: First Floor, 10 Temple Back, Bristol, BS1 6FL
Activities: Construction of commercial buildings
Parent: Infrastructure Investments (Portal) GP Limited
Officers: Angela Mills [1961] Alternate Director; John Whittington [1960] Director

By Education (Barking) Limited
Incorporated: 31 October 2003
Net Worth Deficit: £979,000 *Total Assets:* £38,489,000
Registered Office: First Floor, 10 Temple Back, Bristol, BS1 6FL
Activities: Construction of commercial buildings
Parent: By Education (Barking) Holdings Limited
Officers: Angela Mills [1961] Alternate Director; John Whittington [1960] Director

By Education (Waltham Forest) Holdings Limited
Incorporated: 24 November 2006
Net Worth Deficit: £4,624,000 *Total Assets:* £18,860,000
Registered Office: First Floor, 10 Temple Back, Bristol, BS1 6FL
Activities: Activities of head offices
Parent: Infrared Infrastructure Yield Holdings Limited
Officers: Kaushik Bhadra [1979] Director; Ross William Driver [1981] Director/Corporate Finance; Alan Paul Imber [1966] Director/Accountant; Clement David Baptiste Leverd [1986] Director [French]; Aiden Joseph McManus [1964] Director; Daniel Colin Ward [1982] Investment Director

By Education (Waltham Forest) Limited
Incorporated: 24 November 2006
Net Worth Deficit: £4,624,000 *Total Assets:* £18,860,000
Registered Office: First Floor, 10 Temple Back, Bristol, BS1 6FL
Activities: Other business support service activities n.e.c.
Parent: By Education (Waltham Forest) Holdings Limited
Officers: Kaushik Bhadra [1979] Director; Ross William Driver [1981] Director/Corporate Finance; Alan Paul Imber [1966] Director/Accountant; Clement David Baptiste Leverd [1986] Director [French]; Aiden Joseph McManus [1964] Director; Daniel Colin Ward [1982] Investment Director

Bybrook Agriculture Limited
Incorporated: 6 September 1985 *Employees:* 25
Net Worth: £4,879,904 *Total Assets:* £5,781,096
Registered Office: Bishopbrook House, Cathedral Avenue, Wells, Somerset, BA5 1FD
Activities: Raising of poultry
Major Shareholder: Charles Anthony Bloomer
Officers: James Francis Bloomer, Secretary; Charles Anthony Bloomer [1941] Director/Farmer; Charlie Bloomer [1991] Director; James Francis Bloomer [1967] Director/Farmer

C & C Management Services (UK) Limited
Incorporated: 7 November 2008 *Employees:* 17
Net Worth: £4,558,000 *Total Assets:* £20,820,000
Registered Office: Ashford House, Grenadier Road, Exeter, Devon, EX1 3LH
Activities: Management consultancy activities other than financial management
Parent: C & C Holdings (NI) Limited
Officers: Richard Alistair Evans [1974] Director/Solicitor; Stephen Glancey [1960] Director; Riona Heffernan [1980] Director/Chartered Accountant [Irish]

C & C Motor Caravans Ltd
Incorporated: 12 November 1998 *Employees:* 52
Net Worth: £1,220,308 *Total Assets:* £8,291,473
Registered Office: Chelston Business Park, Wellington, Somerset, TA21 9JE
Activities: Sale of other motor vehicles
Shareholders: Brenda Eyles; Stanley Eyles
Officers: Sandra Maria Eyles, Company Secretary; Antony David Eyles [1953] Director; Forrest Eyles [1980] Director; Rodney Eyles [1949] Director; Stanley Eyles [1925] Director; Tamsin Eyles Kavanagh [1977] Director/Publicity; Wayne Patrick Kavanagh [1976] Director

C & O Tractors Limited
Incorporated: 9 September 1997 *Employees:* 72
Net Worth: £2,591,845 *Total Assets:* £9,491,940
Registered Office: Blandford Heights, Blandford Forum, Dorset, DT11 7TF
Activities: Manufacture of agricultural tractors
Parent: C & O Holdings Limited
Officers: Lucy Rebecca Coles, Secretary; Andrew George Coles [1971] Director/Sales Representative; Samantha Jane Finlay [1968] Director; Richard Paul Spencer [1962] Group Sales Director

C & P Medical Trading Limited
Incorporated: 11 August 1998 *Employees:* 34
Net Worth: £514,168 *Total Assets:* £5,296,407
Registered Office: Unit 1 Avro Business Centre, Avro Way, Bowerhill Estate, Melksham, Wilts, SN12 6TP
Activities: Wholesale of pharmaceutical goods
Major Shareholder: Peter John Shaw
Officers: Julia Lauren Shaw, Secretary/Director; Julia Lauren Shaw [1968] Director; Peter John Shaw [1970] Managing Director

C F R Group Services Limited
Incorporated: 25 October 2002 *Employees:* 178
Net Worth: £2,776,413 *Total Assets:* £7,194,280
Registered Office: Barrington House, Kingsditch, Lane, Cheltenham, Glos, GL51 9NN
Activities: Electrical installation
Officers: Michael Barrington Roberts, Secretary/Director; Ian Robert Henderson [1958] Director; Michael Barrington Roberts [1944] Director; Paul Steven Roberts [1969] Director

C-Retail Limited
Incorporated: 28 January 2010 *Employees:* 1,412
Net Worth: £53,010,000 *Total Assets:* £389,548,992
Registered Office: Unit 60 The Runnings, Cheltenham, Glos, GL51 9NW
Activities: Retail sale of clothing in specialised stores
Parent: Superdry PLC
Officers: Edward Peter Barker [1972] Director; Simon Callander [1967] Director/Group General Counsel and Company Secretary; Euan Angus Sutherland [1969] Director

C.H.G. Holdings Limited
Incorporated: 25 April 1994
Net Worth: £4,154,360 *Total Assets:* £6,101,304
Registered Office: 37 Commercial Road, Poole, Dorset, BH14 0HU
Activities: Activities of head offices
Shareholders: Leslie Aubrey Pink; Jacqueline Pink
Officers: Jacqueline Pink, Secretary/Director; Jacqueline Pink [1953] Director; Leslie Aubrey Pink [1947] Director/Hotelier

C.J.L. Construction Limited
Incorporated: 9 December 1983 *Employees:* 255
Net Worth: £23,661,084 *Total Assets:* £27,306,588
Registered Office: Woodland Court, Sandford, Winscombe, Somerset, BS25 5QP
Activities: Construction of other civil engineering projects n.e.c.
Officers: Helen Marie Lomas, Secretary; Christopher John Lomas [1955] Managing Director; Helen Marie Lomas [1961] Director

C.T.C.H. Limited
Incorporated: 29 December 1999 *Employees:* 202
Net Worth: £4,337,054 *Total Assets:* £4,955,401
Registered Office: Cedar Lodge, Grange Road, Northway, Tewkesbury, Glos, GL20 8HZ
Activities: Residential care activities for the elderly and disabled
Major Shareholder: Antony David Cronk
Officers: Deborah Jane Smith, Secretary; Antony David Cronk [1960] Director; Daniel Antony Cronk [1986] Director

C3IA Solutions Limited
Incorporated: 17 March 2006 *Employees:* 36
Net Worth: £2,192,617 *Total Assets:* £3,543,671
Registered Office: Unit B, The Outlook, Ling Road, Poole, Dorset, BH12 4PY
Activities: Other information technology service activities
Shareholder: Matthew Howard Horan
Officers: Neville Francis Brill, Secretary; Matthew Howard Horan [1965] Director; Keith Lewis Parsons [1967] Director

CAA Property Limited
Incorporated: 25 September 2013
Net Worth: £1,474,036 *Total Assets:* £10,635,033
Registered Office: Delta Place, 27 Bath Road, Cheltenham, Glos, GL53 7TH
Activities: Buying and selling of own real estate
Shareholders: Andrea Nicola Adey; Christopher John Adey
Officers: Andrea Nicola Adey [1962] Director; Christopher John Adey [1966] Director

Cab Aid Limited
Incorporated: 13 January 2004
Net Worth: £4,264,000 *Total Assets:* £4,612,000
Registered Office: Pinesgate, Lower Bristol Road, Bath, BA2 3DP
Activities: Renting and leasing of cars and light motor vehicles
Parent: Redde PLC
Officers: Nicholas Paul Tilley, Secretary; Mark Francis Chessman [1964] Director; Stephen Edward Oakley [1952] Director; Martin Ward [1967] Managing Director

Cabot Design Limited
Incorporated: 28 February 2000 *Employees:* 19
Net Worth: £5,563,705 *Total Assets:* £5,829,376
Registered Office: 14 Long Street, Wotton under Edge, Glos, GL12 7EP
Activities: Technical testing and analysis
Shareholder: Nicholas John Kemp
Officers: Sally King, Secretary; Mervyn Davidson [1963] Director/Engineer; Nicholas John Kemp [1967] Director/Engineer

Cabot Learning Federation
Incorporated: 10 April 2007 *Employees:* 1,529
Net Worth: £108,446,000 *Total Assets:* £133,579,000
Registered Office: Federation House, King's Oak Academy, Brook Road, Bristol, BS15 4JT
Activities: General secondary education
Officers: Bryony Dale Green, Secretary; Nusrat Arshad [1972] Director; Anthony John Cherry [1955] Director/Solicitor; Adrian Coleman [1968] Director/Chartered Accountant; Susan Catherine Coombes [1971] Director/Teaching and Learning Consultant; Airlie Ann Fife [1957] Director/Service Manager; Pete Franklin [1963] Director/Local Government Officer; Jane Harrington [1966] Director/Deputy Vice Chancellor and Provost; Rhodri Iwan James [1971] Director/Senior HR Business Partner; Guy Keith-Miller [1978] Director/Higher Education; William Kuh Tet Liew [1962] Director of Finance [Malaysian]; Nicola Marilyn McAllister [1948] Director/Retired Secondary Headteacher

Cabot Mews Limited
Incorporated: 20 September 2011 *Employees:* 2
Net Worth: £3,920,455 *Total Assets:* £10,370,884
Registered Office: Springfield House, 45 Welsh Back, Bristol, BS1 4AG
Activities: Other letting and operating of own or leased real estate
Parent: CTU General Partner Limited
Officers: Scott Matthew Davidson [1963] Director; Peter Oliphant [1962] Director

Cadeleigh Estates Limited
Incorporated: 31 March 2003 *Employees:* 1
Net Worth: £11,990,496 *Total Assets:* £22,655,774
Registered Office: West Barton, Little Silver, Cadeleigh, Tiverton, Devon, EX16 8HJ
Activities: Buying and selling of own real estate
Major Shareholder: Paul Edward Morris
Officers: Patrick George Williams, Secretary; Paul Edward Morris [1954] Director

Cadillac Plastic Limited
Incorporated: 8 July 1982 *Employees:* 20
Net Worth: £4,232,814 *Total Assets:* £5,294,890
Registered Office: Rivermead Drive, Westlea, Swindon, Wilts, SN5 7YT
Activities: Agents specialised in the sale of other particular products
Officers: John Martyn Jones, Secretary; Annie Buchanan Jones [1943] Director/Business Executive; John Martyn Jones [1949] Director/Accountant; Alistair Malcolm Kennedy [1947] Director/Executive; Cecilia Joy Kennedy [1948] Director/Business Executive

Cadogan House Investment Properties Limited
Incorporated: 1 February 1999 *Employees:* 3
Net Worth: £774,239 *Total Assets:* £5,117,650
Registered Office: The Granby Building, 5 St Margarets Terrace, Weston-Super-Mare, Avon, BS23 1AH
Activities: Other letting and operating of own or leased real estate
Shareholder: Paul George Routledge
Officers: Paul George Routledge, Secretary; Paul George Routledge [1957] Director; Sharon Lesley Routledge [1960] Director

Caerus Capital Group Limited
Incorporated: 8 November 2009
Net Worth: £3,041,000 *Total Assets:* £7,528,000
Registered Office: Wiltshire Court, Farnsby Street, Swindon, Wilts, SN1 5AH
Activities: Activities of financial services holding companies
Parent: Intrinsic Financial Services Limited
Officers: David Rance [1963] Director/Accountant; Darren William John Sharkey [1970] Director/Accountant [Irish]

Caerus Holdings Limited
Incorporated: 11 March 2015 *Employees:* 13
Net Worth: £6,419,000 *Total Assets:* £11,134,000
Registered Office: Wiltshire Court, Farnsby Street, Swindon, Wilts, SN1 5AH
Activities: Activities of financial services holding companies
Parent: Caerus Capital Group Limited
Officers: David Rance [1963] Director/Accountant; Darren William John Sharkey [1970] Director/Accountant [Irish]

Caerus Wealth Limited
Incorporated: 25 June 2010
Net Worth Deficit: £1,241,000 *Total Assets:* £9,209,000
Registered Office: Wiltshire Court, Farnsby Street, Swindon, Wilts, SN1 5AH
Activities: Other business support service activities n.e.c.
Parent: Caerus Holdings Limited
Officers: David Rance [1963] Director/Accountant; Darren William John Sharkey [1970] Director/Accountant [Irish]

Caerus Wealth Solutions Limited
Incorporated: 28 June 2010
Net Worth Deficit: £1,003,000 *Total Assets:* £5,289,000
Registered Office: Wiltshire Court, Farnsby Street, Swindon, Wilts, SN1 5AH
Activities: Other business support service activities n.e.c.
Parent: Caerus Holdings Limited
Officers: David Rance [1963] Director/Accountant; Darren William John Sharkey [1970] Director/Accountant [Irish]

Cahill Welding Services Ltd.
Incorporated: 18 July 2005 *Employees:* 43
Net Worth: £1,447,223 *Total Assets:* £4,046,261
Registered Office: 5 & 6 The Saw Mills, Middlemarsh, Sherborne, Dorset, DT9 5QW
Activities: Manufacture of metal structures and parts of structures
Shareholders: Ian Anthony Cahill; David John Cahill
Officers: Cherrie Margaret Cahill, Secretary; David John Cahill [1954] Director/Steel Fabricator; Ian Anthony Cahill [1981] Director/Welder

Calcot Health & Leisure Company Limited
Incorporated: 24 November 2000 *Employees:* 440
Net Worth: £15,751,947 *Total Assets:* £28,389,832
Registered Office: Calcot Manor, Tetbury, Glos, GL8 8YJ
Activities: Hotels and similar accommodation
Major Shareholder: Michael John Christopher Stone
Officers: Richard James Ball, Secretary; Catherine Ball [1961] Director/Spa Manager; Richard James Ball [1960] Director/Hotel Manager; Nicola Jane Farquhar [1968] Director/Interior Designer; Michele Mella [1967] Director/General Manager [Italian]; Timothy St Clair Ruthven [1966] Hospitality - Director; Paul Nicholas Sadler [1963] Director/Hotel Manager; Andrew Jonathan Stone [1970] Director; Charles Robert Henry Stone [1966] Director/Businessman; Michael John Christopher Stone [1936] Director/Retired

Caledonia TLG Bidco Limited
Incorporated: 22 June 2016
Net Worth: £89,552,000 *Total Assets:* £145,690,000
Registered Office: c/o Butcombe Brewery, Havyatt Road Trading Estate, Havyatt Road, Wrington, Bristol, BS40 5PA
Activities: Dormant company
Parent: Caledonia TLG Midco Limited
Officers: Richard Stuart Grainger [1960] Director; Timothy Hubert [1962] Director; Nigel Richard Osborne [1966] Director

The Calendar Club Limited
Incorporated: 3 April 1998 *Employees:* 68
Net Worth: £2,544,656 *Total Assets:* £8,251,633
Registered Office: Exe Box, Matford Park Road, Matford, Exeter, Devon, EX2 8FD
Activities: Other retail sale in non-specialised stores
Shareholders: Marc Thomas Winkelman; Zebra MTD Ltd
Officers: Sharon Jane Colclough [1972] Director; David Philip Pike [1959] Director; Elizabeth Anne Winkelman [1985] Director/Business Owner [American]; Marc Thomas Winkelman [1957] Director [American]

Calendula Assets Limited
Incorporated: 25 March 2016 *Employees:* 2
Net Worth: £2,163,408 *Total Assets:* £6,505,855
Registered Office: 25a St Clements Road, Bournemouth, BH1 4DU
Activities: Development of building projects
Major Shareholder: Steven John Wells
Officers: David Michael Chapman [1968] Finance Director; Steven John Wells [1974] Director

Call Caterlink Ltd
Incorporated: 15 September 1993 *Employees:* 40
Net Worth: £3,085,272 *Total Assets:* £6,600,534
Registered Office: Unit 8 Bodmin Business Park, Launceston Road, Bodmin, Cornwall, PL31 2RJ
Activities: Manufacture of other food products n.e.c.
Parent: NIC Enterprises Limited
Officers: Michael Wodskou, Secretary; Patrick Aalhuizen [1965] Director [Swedish]; Thomas Ernst Bruck [1962] Director [German]; Riccardo Antonio Marcantonio [1980] Director; Nadia Millar [1968] Director; Tor Agner Osmundsen [1978] Director [Norwegian]; Bernard Bertram Pooley [1957] Finance Director; Nicholas Philip Venditti [1971] Director; Michael Wodskou [1967] Director [Danish]

Call To The Bar Ltd
Incorporated: 5 September 2013 *Employees:* 2
Net Worth: £817,481 *Total Assets:* £5,891,260
Registered Office: Kernow House, Gas Hill, Newham, Truro, Cornwall, TR1 2XP
Activities: Public houses and bars
Major Shareholder: Rolf Hugo Munding
Officers: Rolf Hugo Munding [1953] Director; Stephen John Welsh [1959] Director

Calleva Limited
Incorporated: 14 December 1993 *Employees:* 21
Net Worth: £4,621,362 *Total Assets:* £6,008,504
Registered Office: Market Way, North Petherton, Bridgwater, Somerset, TA6 6DF
Activities: Other manufacturing n.e.c.
Parent: Calleblend Limited
Officers: Wendy Shaw, Secretary; Clive Antony Griffiths [1958] Director/Food Ingredients; Edward James Ryle [1987] Director; Natasha Grace Ryle [1988] Director; Wendy Shaw [1957] Director

Camanoe Estates Limited
Incorporated: 23 May 1962 *Employees:* 40
Net Worth: £3,370,831 *Total Assets:* £3,639,259
Registered Office: Kings Buildings, Lydney, Glos, GL15 5HE
Activities: Buying and selling of own real estate
Shareholder: Simon Andrew Jonathan Porter
Officers: Simon Andrew Jonathan Porter, Secretary; Caroline Sarah Jane Constance [1969] Director; Amanda Louise Gething Lewis [1966] Director; Anne Lesley Porter [1941] Director; Dr Mark Christopher Milson Porter [1962] Director/General Practitioner (Medical); Simon Andrew Jonathan Porter [1963] Director

Cambium Networks, Ltd
Incorporated: 25 August 2011 *Employees:* 100
Net Worth: £6,142,725 *Total Assets:* £104,740,848
Registered Office: Unit B2 Linhay Business Park, Eastern Road, Ashburton, Newton Abbot, Devon, TQ13 7UP
Activities: Wireless telecommunications activities
Officers: Atul Bhatnagar [1957] Director/President and CEO of Cambium Networks [American]; Stephen Cumming [1970] Director/Chief Financial Officer; Scott Imhoff [1968] Director/Management [American]; Sally RAU [1958] Director/Lawyer [American]; Peter Strong [1960] Director/Engineer; Vibhu Vivek [1967] Director/Senior Vice President, Products [American]

Cambria Automobiles (South East) Limited
Incorporated: 29 July 1994 *Employees:* 268
Net Worth: £36,973,000 *Total Assets:* £58,967,000
Registered Office: Swindon Motor Park, Dorcan Way, Swindon, Wilts, SN3 3RA
Activities: Sale of new cars and light motor vehicles
Parent: Cambria Automobiles Acquisitions Ltd
Officers: James Anthony Mullins, Finance Director; Timothy Alex Duckers [1973] Director; Mark Jonathan James Lavery [1965] Director; James Anthony Mullins [1978] Director

Cambria Automobiles Acquisitions Limited
Incorporated: 31 March 2006
Net Worth: £6,923,000 *Total Assets:* £52,766,000
Registered Office: Swindon Motor Park, Dorcan Way, Swindon, Wilts, SN3 3RA
Activities: Financial management
Parent: Cambria Automobiles Group Ltd
Officers: James Anthony Mullins, Finance Director/Company Secretary; Mark Jonathan James Lavery [1965] Director; James Anthony Mullins [1978] Finance Director/Company Secretary

Cambria Automobiles PLC
Incorporated: 23 March 2006 *Employees:* 1,160
Net Worth: £56,627,000 *Total Assets:* £208,380,000
Registered Office: Swindon Motor Park, Dorcan Way, Swindon, Wilts, SN3 3RA
Activities: Activities of head offices
Shareholder: Nicola Lavery
Officers: James Anthony Mullins, Secretary; William Francis Charnley [1960] Director/Solicitor; Timothy Alex Duckers [1973] Director; Mark Jonathan James Lavery [1965] Director; Paul Gerard Christopher McGill [1956] Director/Accountant; James Anthony Mullins [1978] Finance Director; Philip Hilary Swatman [1949] Director

Cambria Automobiles Property Limited
Incorporated: 13 February 2006
Net Worth: £4,216,000 *Total Assets:* £55,536,000
Registered Office: Swindon Motor Park, Dorcan Way, Swindon, Wilts, SN3 3RA
Activities: Other letting and operating of own or leased real estate
Parent: Cambria Automobiles Group Ltd
Officers: James Anthony Mullins, Secretary/Director; Mark Jonathan James Lavery [1965] Director; James Anthony Mullins [1978] Director

Camelot Care (Bridgwater) Limited
Incorporated: 29 October 2013 *Employees:* 53
Net Worth: £460,032 *Total Assets:* £3,668,153
Registered Office: Harpers Cottage, Trull, Taunton, Somerset, TA3 7NZ
Activities: Residential nursing care facilities
Shareholders: Hyang Ja Teasdale; Camelot Care Limited
Officers: John Clement Teasdale, Secretary; Hyang Ja Teasdale [1954] Director

Camelot Care Homes Limited
Incorporated: 28 January 2002 *Employees:* 55
Net Worth: £1,825,118 *Total Assets:* £5,265,202
Registered Office: 1 Countess Road, Amesbury, Salisbury, Wilts, SP4 7DW
Activities: Residential nursing care facilities
Shareholders: Renuka Thillainathan; Siva Nadesan
Officers: Vasantha Nadesan [1964] Director; Renuka Thillainathan [1960] Director/Accountant

Camelot Developments Limited
Incorporated: 18 September 2006 *Employees:* 3
Net Worth: £292,342 *Total Assets:* £6,468,276
Registered Office: Winterboure Associates, 1 Frederick Place, Weymouth, Dorset, DT4 8HQ
Activities: Other building completion and finishing
Officers: David John Glover, Secretary/Builder; David John Glover [1953] Director/Builder; Richard Kingdon [1964] Director/Builder; Billy Knight [1966] Director/Builder

Campden BRI
Incorporated: 16 August 1952 *Employees:* 408
Net Worth Deficit: £888,883 *Total Assets:* £20,228,488
Registered Office: Station Road, Chipping Campden, Glos, GL55 6LD
Activities: Other research and experimental development on natural sciences and engineering
Officers: Christopher Ikpeme, Secretary; Anthony Guy Bowman [1946] Director; Robert Paul Clarke [1949] Director; Doctor Andrew Robert Davies [1958] Director/Microbiologist; Arthur Robert Heygate [1945] Director/Farmer and Flour Miller; Timothy Holmes [1966] Director/Quality Manager; Alec Louis Kyriakides [1965] Director; Philip Edward Moody [1954] Director; Alexander Paul Fraser Nelstrop [1975] Director; Professor John O'Brien [1960] Director/Scientist Nestec SA [Irish]; Helen Margaret Sisson [1965] Technical Director; Richard Julian Stride [1963] Director/Food Retail; William Brett Warburton [1955] Director; Alexander William Waugh [1958] Director/Administrator

Campden BRI (Chipping Campden) Limited
Incorporated: 7 September 1999 *Employees:* 323
Net Worth: £4,399,952 *Total Assets:* £16,824,616
Registered Office: Station Road, Chipping Campden, Glos, GL55 6LD
Activities: Other research and experimental development on natural sciences and engineering
Parent: Campden BRI
Officers: Christopher Ikpeme, Secretary; Jeremy Charles Glyn Davies [1960] Director; Martin Nigel Hall [1954] Director; Simon Christopher Huscroft [1959] Director; Christopher Ikpeme [1964] Director; Steven James Walker [1960] Director

Camps International Group Limited
Incorporated: 29 May 2002 *Employees:* 157
Previous: Camps International Limited
Net Worth: £2,578,230 *Total Assets:* £6,101,610
Registered Office: Unit 10 Kingfisher Park, Headlands Business Park, Salisbury Road, Blashford, Ringwood, Hants, BH24 3NX
Activities: Tour operator activities
Officers: Carl David Palmer, Secretary; James Michael Gallagher [1949] Director; Matthew Steven Lacey [1972] Director; Carl David Palmer [1973] Finance Director; Stuart Rees Jones [1970] Director

Candida Investments Limited
Incorporated: 14 September 1961
Net Worth: £4,124,846 *Total Assets:* £4,526,642
Registered Office: Springfield House, Chard Road, Drimpton, Beaminster, Dorset, DT8 3RF
Activities: Buying and selling of own real estate
Officers: Deborah Jean Robertson, Secretary; Elsie May Dorothy Arnold [1926] Director; Frederick Thomas Arnold [1925] Director; Jennifer Susan Healy [1949] Director; Deborah Jean Robertson [1960] Director/Company Secretary; Ann Gillian Waite [1947] Director/Retired Teacher

Canefield Ltd
Incorporated: 28 May 2002 *Employees:* 584
Net Worth: £913,933 *Total Assets:* £5,503,918
Registered Office: Aldreth, Pearcroft Road, Stonehouse, Glos, GL10 2JY
Activities: Unlicenced restaurants and cafes
Officers: Athelston Sealey [1957] Director

Canford Healthcare Limited
Incorporated: 5 December 2006 *Employees:* 1,057
Previous: Canford Healthcare PLC
Net Worth: £3,765,397 *Total Assets:* £12,089,699
Registered Office: Russell House, Oxford Road, Bournemouth, BH8 8EX
Activities: Other business support service activities n.e.c.
Shareholders: Brian Patrick Cooney; Barry Michael Lambert
Officers: Stephen Charles Bates, Secretary; Stephen Charles Bates [1965] Director; Brian Patrick Cooney [1965] Director [Irish]; Paul Kenny [1960] Director [Irish]; Barry Michael Lambert [1950] Director

Canford Renewable Energy Limited
Incorporated: 24 January 1994 *Employees:* 16
Net Worth: £5,890,511 *Total Assets:* £13,415,170
Registered Office: Energy Site Control Centre, Arena Way, Wimborne, Dorset, BH21 3BW
Activities: Raising of other animals
Major Shareholder: William Edward Riddle
Officers: Stuart Michael Hudson, Secretary; Stuart Michael Hudson [1972] Director; William Edward Riddle [1952] Director

Canford School,Limited
Incorporated: 27 June 1923 *Employees:* 429
Net Worth: £42,098,188 *Total Assets:* £48,669,292
Registered Office: The Bursary, Canford School, Wimborne, Dorset, BH21 3AD
Activities: General secondary education
Officers: Michael Beauchamp Mansel Porter, Secretary; Annette April Anthony [1963] Director/Lawyer [American]; Barry Desmond Coupe [1951] Director/Architect; Robert Walter Daubeney [1965] Director/Oil Broker; Jeremy Michael de Halpert [1947] Director/Retired; Dr Philippa Jane Dickins [1955] Director/Retired; Dr Georgina Anne Fozard [1985] Director/Doctor; Nicholas Henniker Holloway [1977] Director/Teacher; Michael Makepeace Eugene Jeffries [1944] Director; Matthew Terence Keats [1970] Director/Solicitor; Stephen Hedley Le Bas [1970] Director/Accountant; David Roger Levin [1949] Director/Headmaster; Richard Edward Thurston Nicholl [1950] Director/Retired (Headmaster); Adam Bransom Richards [1970] Director [British Virgin Islander]; Reverend John Harold Simmons [1946] Director/Chairman; James David Winn Stileman [1960] Operations Director; Annabel Laura Rose Thomas [1977] Director/Solicitor

Cannington Enterprises Limited
Incorporated: 7 April 2000 *Employees:* 40
Net Worth: £7,928,575 *Total Assets:* £19,419,876
Registered Office: Swang Farm, Cannington, Bridgwater, Somerset, TA5 2NJ
Activities: Production of electricity
Shareholders: Michael James Roe; Tim Roe
Officers: Michael James Roe, Secretary; Michael James Roe [1949] Director/Farmer; Timothy William Roe [1976] Director/Farmer

Cannon Care Homes 4 Limited
Incorporated: 3 October 2007 *Employees:* 1
Net Worth: £160,768 *Total Assets:* £6,251,770
Registered Office: 50 The Terrace, Torquay, Devon, TQ1 1DD
Activities: Activities of head offices
Parent: Cannon Care Homes Limited
Officers: Jane Canon, Secretary; Robin George Canon [1953] Director

Cannon Care Homes Ltd
Incorporated: 21 December 2004 *Employees:* 227
Net Worth: £4,879,652 *Total Assets:* £22,824,840
Registered Office: 50 The Terrace, Torquay, Devon, TQ1 1DD
Activities: Activities of head offices
Major Shareholder: Robin George Cannon
Officers: Jane Canon, Secretary; Robin George Canon [1953] Director

Cannon Technologies Group Limited
Incorporated: 26 June 1996 *Employees:* 74
Net Worth: £2,990,302 *Total Assets:* £5,114,539
Registered Office: 13 Queensway, Stem Lane Industrial Estate, New Milton, Hants, BH25 5NU
Activities: Other engineering activities
Shareholders: Edward Arnold Reddicliffe; Patricia Jennifer Reddicliffe
Officers: Edward Arnold Reddicliffe, Secretary; Matthew Goulding [1962] Director/General Manager; Edward Arnold Reddicliffe [1937] Director/Chartered Engineer

Cannon Technologies Limited
Incorporated: 22 June 1978
Net Worth: £2,867,313 *Total Assets:* £4,973,102
Registered Office: 13 Queensway, Stem Lane Industrial Estate, New Milton, Hants, BH25 5NU
Activities: Manufacture of light metal packaging
Parent: Cannon Technologies Group Limited
Officers: Edward Arnold Reddicliffe, Secretary; Matthew Goulding [1962] Director-General Manager; Edward Arnold Reddicliffe [1937] Director/Chartered Engineer

Canon Court Farm Limited
Incorporated: 24 October 2002 *Employees:* 9
Net Worth: £4,039,575 *Total Assets:* £9,890,081
Registered Office: Maltravers House, Petters Way, Yeovil, Somerset, BA20 1SH
Activities: Raising of dairy cattle
Shareholders: Alan Tizzard; Elizabeth Tizzard
Officers: Elizabeth Anne Tizzard, Secretary; Alan John Tizzard [1958] Director/Farmer; Elizabeth Anne Tizzard [1957] Director/Farmer

Canprop I Limited
Incorporated: 24 May 2012
Net Worth: £317,177 *Total Assets:* £14,167,211
Registered Office: Westbury Court, Church Road, Westbury on Trym, Bristol, BS9 3EF
Activities: Buying and selling of own real estate
Major Shareholder: Michael Robin Cannon
Officers: Christopher John Mitchell, Secretary; Michael Robin Canon [1938] Director/Retired; Christopher John Mitchell [1957] Director/Solicitor

Canprop II Limited
Incorporated: 7 March 2016
Net Worth Deficit: £23,577 *Total Assets:* £4,413,034
Registered Office: Suite 1, Westbury Court, Church Road, Westbury on Trym, Bristol, BS9 3EF
Activities: Development of building projects
Major Shareholder: Michael Robin Cannon
Officers: Marianne Sarah Mitchell, Secretary; Christopher John Mitchell [1957] Director/Solicitor

Canprop Kensington Limited
Incorporated: 10 October 2012
Net Worth: £4,222,994 *Total Assets:* £10,050,414
Registered Office: Westbury Court, Church Road, Westbury on Trym, Bristol, BS9 3EF
Activities: Buying and selling of own real estate
Major Shareholder: Michael Robin Cannon
Officers: Christopher John Mitchell [1957] Director/Solicitor

Canynge Bicknell (Investments) Limited
Incorporated: 26 August 1988
Net Worth: £5,201,929 *Total Assets:* £10,345,627
Registered Office: Bicknell House, Merstham Road, Bristol, BS2 9TQ
Activities: Other letting and operating of own or leased real estate
Parent: Canynge Bicknell Limited
Officers: Rosalind Muriel Scott, Secretary; Brian Robert Bicknell [1946] Director; John Edward Castell [1953] Director/Surveyor; Adrian Whicheloe [1953] Director

Canynge Bicknell (Street) Limited
Incorporated: 22 September 2005
Net Worth Deficit: £403,502 *Total Assets:* £7,560,978
Registered Office: Bicknell House, Merstham Road, Bristol, BS2 9TQ
Activities: Development of building projects
Shareholders: Canynge Properties Limited; Bicknell Holdings PLC; Lenfestey Estates (Holdings) Limited
Officers: Rosalind Muriel Scott, Secretary; Brian Robert Bicknell [1946] Director; John Edward Castell [1953] Director/Surveyor; Mark Lenfestey FitzGenerald [1958] Director; Adrian Whicheloe [1953] Director

Canynge Bicknell Limited
Incorporated: 12 August 1981 *Employees:* 3
Net Worth: £8,225,026 *Total Assets:* £15,794,738
Registered Office: Bicknell House, Merstham Road, Bristol, BS2 9TQ
Activities: Development of building projects
Shareholders: Bicknell Holdings PLC; Canynge Estates Limited
Officers: Rosalind Muriel Scott, Secretary; Brian Robert Bicknell [1946] Director; Mark Lenfestey FitzGenerald [1958] Director; Adrian Whicheloe [1953] Director

Cape Homes Limited
Incorporated: 18 May 2000
Net Worth: £3,394,252 *Total Assets:* £7,007,866
Registered Office: Victoria House, Churchill Road, Leckhampton, Cheltenham, Glos, GL53 7EG
Activities: Construction of other civil engineering projects n.e.c.
Major Shareholder: Mark Anthony Holland
Officers: Mark Anthony Holland, Secretary/Director; Mark Anthony Holland [1969] Director

Capes (Hatherden) Limited
Incorporated: 31 March 1948 *Employees:* 4
Net Worth: £13,716,196 *Total Assets:* £15,143,208
Registered Office: Hatherden House, Hatherden, Andover, Hants, SP11 0HX
Activities: Growing of cereals (except rice), leguminous crops and oil seeds
Major Shareholder: Jonathan James Stephen Capes
Officers: Sarah Elizabeth Blair Capes, Secretary [Australian/British]; Jonathan James Stephen Capes [1959] Director/Farmer; Matthew James Capes [1992] Director/Maths Teacher; Nina Alice Capes [1995] Director/Advertising Trainee; Sarah Elizabeth Blair Capes [1960] Director/Farming [Australian/British]

Caplon Limited
Incorporated: 6 November 1990 *Employees:* 1
Net Worth: £2,131,962 *Total Assets:* £8,385,426
Registered Office: 11 Quiet Street, Bath, BA1 2LB
Activities: Retail sale in commercial art galleries
Major Shareholder: Richard Brake
Officers: Heather Marjorie Rose Brake, Secretary; Alastair James Brake [1975] Director; Heather Marjorie Rose Brake [1937] Director/Clerical; Richard Lindsey Brake [1959] Director/Investment Banker

Capston Limited
Incorporated: 3 June 2003
Net Worth Deficit: £4,635,337 *Total Assets:* £8,566,705
Registered Office: 49 High Street, Westbury on Trym, Bristol, BS9 3ED
Activities: Activities of head offices
Shareholder: Maximino Hernandez Garcia
Officers: Andrea Gamon [1957] Director/Consultant [Austrian]; Michael Leo Charles Goodman [1962] Director/Accountant; Maximino Garcia Hernandez [1949] Director/Administrator [Spanish]

Captiva Homes Limited
Incorporated: 24 February 2005 *Employees:* 3
Net Worth: £2,293,040 *Total Assets:* £8,692,279
Registered Office: 37 Commercial Road, Poole, Dorset, BH14 0HU
Activities: Development of building projects
Shareholders: James Nicholas Pink; Justin Seth Gentleman
Officers: James Nicholas Pink, Secretary/Director; Justin Gentleman [1978] Director; James Nicholas Pink [1980] Director

Carbis Bay Hotel Limited
Incorporated: 17 February 2011 *Employees:* 2
Net Worth: £4,715,997 *Total Assets:* £16,584,720
Registered Office: Peat House, Newham Road, Truro, Cornwall, TR1 2DP
Activities: Hotels and similar accommodation
Major Shareholder: Malcolm Walter Baker
Officers: Malcolm Walter Baker [1936] Director/Hotelier; Stephen Philip Baker [1968] Director/Hotelier

Carco Group Limited
Incorporated: 10 October 1996 *Employees:* 145
Net Worth: £4,411,214 *Total Assets:* £15,152,514
Registered Office: City Motors Building, Castle Court, St Philips Causeway, Bristol, BS4 3AX
Activities: Activities of head offices
Shareholder: Robin Douglas Cook
Officers: James Maxwell Clarke [1938] Director; Richard James Cook [1963] Director; Robin Douglas Cook [1961] Director; Robert David Joce [1952] Director; James Joseph Robertson [1958] Director

Carco Limited
Incorporated: 29 December 1989 *Employees:* 145
Net Worth: £4,411,221 *Total Assets:* £15,192,026
Registered Office: City Motors Building, Castle Court, St Philips Causeway, Bristol, BS4 3AX
Activities: Sale of new cars and light motor vehicles
Parent: Carco Group Limited
Officers: James Maxwell Clarke [1938] Director; Richard James Cook [1963] Director; Robin Douglas Cook [1961] Director; Robert David Joce [1952] Director; James Joseph Robertson [1958] Director

Cardiff Wind Park Limited
Incorporated: 12 April 2007
Net Worth: £1,298,979 *Total Assets:* £3,512,855
Registered Office: Lion House, Rowcroft, Stroud, Glos, GL5 3BY
Activities: Production of electricity
Parent: Ecotricity Group Limited
Officers: Tom Cowling, Secretary; Asif Rehmanwala [1976] Director/Chief Operating Officer; Dale Vince [1961] Director/Consultant

Care South
Incorporated: 4 December 1990 *Employees:* 1,187
Net Worth: £40,186,000 *Total Assets:* £64,615,000
Registered Office: Head Office, 39 Commercial Road, Poole, Dorset, BH14 0HU
Activities: Residential care activities for the elderly and disabled
Officers: Penelope Jane Sargeant, Secretary; Lindsay Ann Ansell [1946] Director/Retired Nurse; Stephanie Claire Barnett [1973] Director; Paul Richard Causton [1947] Director/Legal Consultant; Dr Richard Day [1954] Director/Consultant Physician; Martin Richard Dyson [1946] Director/Management Consultant; Richard John Groom [1942] Director/Consultant; Charles James Holt Hunter [1946] Director; Felicity Ann Irwin [1947] Director/Public Relations Consultant; Christopher Kean [1947] Director/Consultant; Jane Stichbury [1955] Director; Hugh James Derek Webster [1946] Director/Chartered Surveyor

Careline UK Monitoring Limited
Incorporated: 26 July 1996 *Employees:* 168
Net Worth: £12,201,857 *Total Assets:* £16,092,703
Registered Office: Queensway House, 11 Queensway, New Milton, Hants, BH25 5NR
Activities: Other service activities n.e.c.
Parent: Appello Limited
Officers: Carl Burton Atkey [1964] Director/Head of Business; Tim Barclay [1964] Director/Chief Executive; Craig Barlow [1984] Finance Director

Carlin Boat Charter Limited
Incorporated: 20 November 2002 *Employees:* 2
Net Worth: £559,096 *Total Assets:* £4,119,164
Registered Office: 24 Cornwall Road, Dorchester, DT1 1RX
Activities: Sea and coastal passenger water transport
Shareholder: John Gilbert Alford
Officers: Fiona Carlin, Secretary; John Gilbert Alford [1956] Director; Patrick Paul Carlin [1957] Director

Carling Technologies Limited
Incorporated: 27 March 1969 *Employees:* 27
Net Worth: £7,341,564 *Total Assets:* £9,542,111
Registered Office: 4 Airport Business Park, Exeter Airport, Clyst, Honiton, Exeter, EX5 2UL
Activities: Manufacture of electricity distribution and control apparatus
Parent: Carling Technologies Inc
Officers: Michael Salvatore Fanzo, Secretary; Chris Sorenson [1978] Director [American]

Carlisle Fluid Technologies UK Limited
Incorporated: 2 June 2011 *Employees:* 173
Previous: Finishing Brands UK Limited
Net Worth: £52,445,136 *Total Assets:* £62,638,308
Registered Office: Ringwood Road, Bournemouth, BH11 9LH
Activities: Manufacture of other general-purpose machinery n.e.c.
Parent: Carlisle Companies Inc
Officers: Alex James Norris [1969] Director/Business Executive; Michael L Roberson [1955] Director/Solicitor [American]; Robert Michael Roche [1967] Director/Business Executive [American]; David Gavin Smith [1970] Director of Sales

Carlos SS Properties Limited
Incorporated: 28 March 2001
Net Worth: £4,313,940 *Total Assets:* £4,859,758
Registered Office: Beaufort House, 2 Cornmarket Court, Wimborne, Dorset, BH21 1JL
Activities: Buying and selling of own real estate
Major Shareholder: Carlos Brian Duncan Seton-Smith
Officers: Carlos Brian Duncan Seton-Smith, Secretary; Carlos Brian Duncan Seton Smith [1970] Director/Property Management

Carnegie International Asset Management Limited
Incorporated: 10 April 1992
Net Worth: £3,553,799 *Total Assets:* £3,641,629
Registered Office: Minerva House, Lower Bristol Road, Bath, BA2 9ER
Activities: Management consultancy activities other than financial management
Major Shareholder: Lucille Lanette de Savary
Officers: Joseph James Keefe, Secretary; Lucille Lanette de Savary [1954] Director/Consultant

Carnegie Investment Asset Management Limited
Incorporated: 13 March 1998
Net Worth: £3,928,410 *Total Assets:* £28,959,774
Registered Office: Minerva House, Lower Bristol Road, Bath, BA2 9ER
Activities: Activities of other holding companies n.e.c.
Major Shareholder: Lucille Lanette de Savary
Officers: Joseph James Keefe, Secretary; Lucille Lanette de Savary [1954] Director/Consultant

Carnon Downs Garden Centre Limited
Incorporated: 18 May 1979 *Employees:* 49
Net Worth: £4,197,385 *Total Assets:* £4,756,533
Registered Office: 8 Regent Street, Bradford on Tone, Taunton, Somerset, TA4 1HB
Activities: Other retail sale in non-specialised stores
Officers: Jacqueline Ross Kinnear Hassall, Secretary/Director; Mark Ian Hassall [1954] Director/Accountant

Carrington Fox Developments Limited
Incorporated: 27 September 2006
Net Worth Deficit: £4,043 *Total Assets:* £4,512,708
Registered Office: Scots House, 15 Scots Lane, Salisbury, Wilts, SP1 3TR
Activities: Construction of domestic buildings
Parent: Esher Homes Limited
Officers: Anthony Joseph Farrell [1948] Director [Irish]; Simon Anthony Peel [1967] Director

Carrs of Exeter Limited
Incorporated: 18 December 1989 *Employees:* 45
Net Worth: £3,606,000 *Total Assets:* £5,533,000
Registered Office: 85 Meneage Street, Helston, Cornwall, TR13 8RD
Activities: Sale of new cars and light motor vehicles
Officers: Andrew John Barrett [1963] Director; Sarah Anne Burley [1968] HR Director; Betty Vera Carr [1940] Director; David Stanley Carr [1937] Director; Jonathan Craig Glanville [1974] Director/Chartered Accountant; Thomas Moore [1980] Director/IT Manager

E.G.Carter & Company Limited
Incorporated: 5 February 1964 *Employees:* 182
Net Worth: £3,109,338 *Total Assets:* £17,799,420
Registered Office: Bybrook House, Lower Tuffley Lane, Gloucester, GL2 5EE
Activities: Construction of commercial buildings
Parent: E G Carter (Holdings) Limited
Officers: David James Carter, Secretary; Ian Christopher Brown [1967] Divisional Director; Peter Graham Burrows [1960] Divisional Director; David James Carter [1964] Director/Purchasing Manager; Michael Edward Carter [1958] Director

F W S Carter & Sons Limited
Incorporated: 3 July 1986 *Employees:* 155
Net Worth: £40,934,000 *Total Assets:* £89,432,000
Registered Office: Greendale Business Park, Woodbury Salterton, Exeter, Devon, EX5 1EW
Activities: Mixed farming
Shareholders: Rowan Charles Carter; Robin Anthony Bill Carter
Officers: Peter German, Secretary; Alec Robin Bill Carter [1974] Director; Mathew Rowan Carter [1982] Director; Robin Anthony Bill Carter [1944] Director/Farmer; Rowan Charles Carter [1953] Director/Farmer; Peter Lewin German [1953] Director

E G Carter (Holdings) Limited
Incorporated: 9 July 2003 *Employees:* 182
Net Worth: £3,109,389 *Total Assets:* £17,799,470
Registered Office: Bybrook House, Lower Tuffley Lane, Gloucester, GL2 5EE
Activities: Activities of construction holding companies
Shareholder: Michael Edward Charles Carter
Officers: David James Carter, Secretary; Ian Christopher Brown [1967] Divisional Director; Peter Graham Burrows [1960] Divisional Director; David James Carter [1964] Director/Purchasing Manager; Michael Edward Carter [1958] Director

Carter Projects Limited
Incorporated: 30 September 2013
Net Worth: £3,954,931 *Total Assets:* £3,988,674
Registered Office: Swatton Barn, Badbury, Swindon, Wilts, SN4 0EU
Activities: Other letting and operating of own or leased real estate
Shareholders: Paul Terence Carter; Sonya Carter
Officers: Paul Terence Carter [1968] Director; Sonya Carter [1975] Director/Company Secretary

Cartus Financing Limited
Incorporated: 28 July 2010 *Employees:* 4
Total Assets: £9,505,000
Registered Office: Frankland Road, Blagrove, Swindon, Wilts, SN5 8RS
Activities: Development of building projects
Parent: Cartus Limited
Officers: Richard Martin Tucker, Secretary; Robert George Abbott [1962] Director; David Andrew Pascoe [1967] Director; Ian Christopher Balfour Payne [1957] Director; Richard Martin Tucker [1957] Director

Cartus Holdings Limited
Incorporated: 11 May 1999 *Employees:* 420
Net Worth: £20,198,000 *Total Assets:* £44,552,000
Registered Office: Frankland Road, Blagrove, Swindon, Wilts, SN5 8RS
Activities: Development of building projects
Parent: Realogy Holdings Corp.
Officers: Richard Martin Tucker, Secretary; Robert George Abbott [1962] Director; David Andrew Pascoe [1967] Director; Ian Christopher Balfour Payne [1957] Director; Richard Martin Tucker [1957] Director

Cartus Limited
Incorporated: 19 June 1979
Net Worth: £12,061,000 *Total Assets:* £68,748,000
Registered Office: Frankland Road, Blagrove, Swindon, Wilts, SN5 8RS
Activities: Development of building projects
Parent: Cartus Holdings Limited
Officers: Richard Martin Tucker, Secretary; Robert George Abbott [1962] Director; David Andrew Pascoe [1967] Director; Ian Christopher Balfour Payne [1957] Director; Richard Martin Tucker [1957] Director

Caruso Properties Limited
Incorporated: 3 February 2016
Net Worth: £169,631 *Total Assets:* £3,603,496
Registered Office: Barnett & Co Accountants Ltd, 24a High Street, Melksham, Wilts, SN12 6LA
Activities: Buying and selling of own real estate
Officers: Anthony Frederick James Watson [1955] Director; Rukshana Drupathy Watson [1963] Director

N.H. Case Limited
Incorporated: 12 April 1985 *Employees:* 114
Net Worth: £10,511,890 *Total Assets:* £15,262,957
Registered Office: 21 Bennetts Field, Wincanton, Somerset, BA9 9DT
Activities: Wholesale of other food, including fish, crustaceans and molluscs
Major Shareholder: Thomas Harry Case
Officers: Thomas Harry Case, Secretary/Frozen Food Merchant; Nigel Harry Case [1943] Director/Frozen Food Merchant; Thomas Harry Case [1966] Director/Frozen Food Merchant

Caspian Networks Limited
Incorporated: 25 November 1996 *Employees:* 1,003
Net Worth: £4,924,039 *Total Assets:* £11,303,997
Registered Office: 101-105 The Horsefair, Bristol, BS1 3JR
Activities: Take-away food shops and mobile food stands
Major Shareholder: Michael Denis Guerin
Officers: Alison Wendy Guerin, Company Secretary; Alison Wendy Guerin [1960] Director; Michael Denis Guerin [1958] Director

Castelan Group Limited
Incorporated: 5 August 2015 *Employees:* 195
Net Worth: £1,118,222 *Total Assets:* £7,904,815
Registered Office: Alpha House, Sunnyside Road North, Weston Super Mare, Somerset, BS23 3QY
Activities: Activities of other holding companies n.e.c.
Shareholders: Ian Annand; Martin John Napper
Officers: Ian Annand [1964] Director; Stuart David Armstong [1978] Finance Director; Martin John Napper [1962] Director

Castelan Limited
Incorporated: 17 May 2011 *Employees:* 195
Net Worth: £1,118,222 *Total Assets:* £7,904,818
Registered Office: Alpha House, Sunnyside Road North, Weston Super Mare, Somerset, BS23 3QY
Activities: Non-life insurance
Parent: Castelan Group Limited
Officers: Ian Annand [1964] Director; Stuart David Armstong [1978] Finance Director; Martin John Napper [1962] Director

Castle Air Limited
Incorporated: 22 April 1996 *Employees:* 79
Net Worth: £6,155,700 *Total Assets:* £31,543,420
Registered Office: Head Office, Castle Air Limited, Trebrown, Liskeard, Cornwall, PL14 3PX
Activities: Non-scheduled passenger air transport
Major Shareholder: Roy Stanley Flood
Officers: Ross Kristian Bunyard [1973] Managing Director; Roy Stanley Flood [1942] Chairman of The Board and Director; Stuart John Flood [1955] Director; Robert Anthony Kneale Manning [1952] Director

Castle Barton Limited
Incorporated: 4 November 1988 *Employees:* 2
Net Worth: £3,864,061 *Total Assets:* £9,547,859
Registered Office: 165 High Street, Honiton, Devon, EX14 1LQ
Activities: Other letting and operating of own or leased real estate
Shareholders: Alison Jean Gordon; Angus Kenneth Gordon
Officers: Alison Jean Gordon, Secretary; Alison Jean Gordon [1942] Director/Administrator; Angus Kenneth Gordon [1941] Director/Chartered Surveyor

Castle Court School Educational Trust Limited
Incorporated: 18 September 1973 *Employees:* 118
Net Worth: £3,622,642 *Total Assets:* £6,429,943
Registered Office: Castle Court School, Knoll House, Knoll Lane, Corfe Mullen, Wimborne, Dorset, BH21 3RF
Activities: Pre-primary education
Officers: Nathan Philip Norris, Secretary; David William Neville Aston [1962] Director/Retired Headmaster; Danielle Grady [1979] Director/Dentist; Catherine Noelle Jack [1976] Director/Trustee; Ian Neill Johnston [1963] Director/Developer; Jonathan Morley [1957] Director/Teacher; Dr Madeline Anne Phillips [1977] Director/Doctor; Philippa Sarah Rossiter [1971] Director/Self Employed; Timothy Peter Creswell Stone [1971] Director/Solicitor

Castle Gardens Sherborne Limited
Incorporated: 18 November 1986 *Employees:* 65
Net Worth: £2,489,751 *Total Assets:* £4,228,081
Registered Office: 40 High West Street, Dorchester, DT1 1UR
Activities: Retail sale of flowers, plants, seeds, fertilizers, pet animals and pet food in specialised stores
Officers: Helen Louise Burks [1963] Director/Horticulturist; Michael David Burks [1963] Director/Horticulturist

Castle Hill Quarry Co.,Limited
Incorporated: 6 January 1941 *Employees:* 22
Net Worth: £12,986,191 *Total Assets:* £14,083,932
Registered Office: Hill Quarry, Cannington, Bridgwater, Somerset, TA5 2QF
Activities: Quarrying of ornamental and building stone, limestone, gypsum, chalk and slate
Shareholders: Philip John Butterworth; Stuart George Thorne
Officers: Susan Carolyn Compton, Secretary; Stephen Ford [1957] Director/Quarry Manager; Michael John King [1944] Director/Golf Club MD; John Eric Salmon [1948] Director/Surveyor

J.T. Castle Limited
Incorporated: 10 June 2003 *Employees:* 4
Net Worth: £1,104,207 *Total Assets:* £3,879,737
Registered Office: Hitchcock House, Hilltop Park, Devizes Road, Salisbury, Wilts, SP3 4UF
Activities: Development of building projects
Shareholders: Heather Mary Bell; Nigel Patrick Bell
Officers: Nigel Patrick Bell, Secretary/Director; Heather Mary Bell [1961] Director; Nigel Patrick Bell [1962] Director

Castle Motor Company Limited
Incorporated: 27 March 2009 *Employees:* 46
Net Worth: £4,119,388 *Total Assets:* £5,901,042
Registered Office: Castle Garage, Trebrown, Liskeard, Cornwall, PL14 3PX
Activities: Dormant company
Major Shareholder: Roy Stanley Flood
Officers: Dale Flood [1980] Director; Dean Roy Flood [1975] Director/Salesman; Roy Stanley Flood [1942] Director; Stuart John Flood [1955] Director; Robert Anthony Kneale Manning [1952] Director

Castle Motors (Trebrown) Limited
Incorporated: 22 April 1996 *Employees:* 46
Net Worth: £4,977,083 *Total Assets:* £6,162,725
Registered Office: Castle Garage, Trebrown, Liskeard, Cornwall, PL14 3PX
Activities: Sale of new cars and light motor vehicles
Parent: Castle Motor Company Ltd
Officers: Dale Flood [1980] Director; Dean Roy Flood [1975] Director/Salesman; Lee Adam Flood [1985] Director; Roy Stanley Flood [1942] Director; Stuart John Flood [1955] Director; Robert Anthony Kneale Manning [1952] Director

Castle Nominees Limited
Incorporated: 8 October 2008
Total Assets: £6,236,511
Registered Office: Springfield House, 45 Welsh Back, Bristol, BS1 4AG
Activities: Other letting and operating of own or leased real estate
Parent: Barnett Waddingham Capital Trustees Ltd
Officers: Kerry Ann Davidson [1965] Director; Scott Matthew Davidson [1963] Director

The Castle Partnership Trust
Incorporated: 3 June 2011 *Employees:* 241
Net Worth: £21,254,542 *Total Assets:* £27,150,484
Registered Office: The Castle School, Wellington Road, Taunton, Somerset, TA1 5AU
Activities: General secondary education
Shareholders: Peter Paton Haines; Karen Margaret Canham; Sheila Mary Naylor
Officers: Julie Lynn Gregory, Secretary; Christopher Atkins [1959] Director/Lecturer; Michelle Peter Fox [1968] Director/Solicitor; Carly Hatch [1975] Director/Headteacher; Marc MacCloskey [1969] Director/Hotelier [Irish]; Sheila Mary Naylor [1947] Director; Mark Richmond [1952] Director/Retired; Sarah Watson [1963] Director/Headteacher

Castle School Education Trust
Incorporated: 11 February 2013 *Employees:* 502
Net Worth: £60,689,000 *Total Assets:* £70,923,000
Registered Office: CSET, Mangotsfield School, Rodway Hill, Bristol, BS16 9LH
Activities: Primary education
Officers: Meng Kwok, Secretary; Rhona Allgood [1959] Director/Chemical Engineer; Rhiannon Wynne Clancy [1981] Director/Communications Manager; Mark Fuller [1970] Director/Training Support Officer; Paul David Harrod [1976] Director/Chief Executive Bristol Together CIC; Susannah Faith Hill [1957] Director/Retired; Andrew Levitt [1956] IT Director; Simon John MacSorley [1964] Director of Estates; Colin Ronald McDougall [1967] Director/Marketing; William George Roberts [1975] Director/Chief Executive; Penelope Susan Robinson [1948] Director/Retired; Christopher James White-Horne [1969] Director/Chartered Engineer

Castlegate Business Park Limited
Incorporated: 9 November 2010 *Employees:* 3
Net Worth: £2,739,530 *Total Assets:* £8,556,271
Registered Office: The Manor, Boddington Lane, Boddington, Cheltenham, Glos, GL51 0TJ
Activities: Other letting and operating of own or leased real estate
Parent: Robert Hitchins Limited
Officers: Jonathan James Stewart Dunley, Secretary; Jonathan James Stewart Dunley [1970] Director; Jeremy Charles Hitchins [1954] Director; Simon Jeremy Tothill [1965] Director/Chartered Surveyor

Castlewood (Commercial) Properties Limited
Incorporated: 11 April 2011 *Employees:* 2
Net Worth Deficit: £1,033,899 *Total Assets:* £4,898,052
Registered Office: 43-45 Devizes Road, Swindon, Wilts, SN1 4BG
Activities: Development of building projects
Shareholder: Arthur William Dunkley
Officers: Andrew Peter Cowley [1986] Director; Neil Cowley [1958] Director

CAT-UK Services Limited
Incorporated: 20 March 1986 *Employees:* 145
Net Worth: £834,000 *Total Assets:* £12,084,000
Registered Office: 1st Floor, St Andrews House, St Andrews Road, Avonmouth, Bristol, BS11 9DQ
Activities: Maintenance and repair of motor vehicles
Parent: CAT France SAS
Officers: Manuel Antelo [1953] Director [Italian]; Walter Alejandro Forbes [1962] Director [Argentinian]; Stuart Martin Warren [1958] Director International Development, Managing Director UK

Catalent CTS (Edinburgh) Limited
Incorporated: 4 November 2004 *Employees:* 238
Net Worth: £70,045,720 *Total Assets:* £79,866,568
Registered Office: Frankland Road, Blagrove, Swindon, Wilts, SN5 8YG
Activities: Manufacture of pharmaceutical preparations
Officers: Shaileshbhai Madhavbhai Patel, Secretary; Wetteny Joseph [1972] Director/VP Finance [American]; Shaileshbhai Madhavbhai Patel [1967] Global Director

Catalent CTS (Wales) Limited
Incorporated: 9 June 1998
Net Worth: £20,122,108 *Total Assets:* £20,122,108
Registered Office: Frankland Road, Blagrove, Swindon, Wilts, SN5 8YG
Activities: Other professional, scientific and technical activities n.e.c.
Officers: Shaileshbhai Madhavbhai Patel, Secretary; Wetteny Joseph [1972] Director/VP Finance [American]; Shaileshbhai Madhavbhai Patel [1967] Global Director

Catalent CTS UK Holding Limited
Incorporated: 20 December 2012
Net Worth Deficit: £46,426,616 *Total Assets:* £135,000,000
Registered Office: Frankland Road, Blagrove, Swindon, Wilts, SN5 8YG
Activities: Activities of production holding companies
Officers: Shaileshbhai Madhavbhai Patel, Secretary; Wetteny Joseph [1972] Director/President - Development and Clinical Services [American]; Shaileshbhai Madhavbhai Patel [1967] Global Director; Alan Robinson [1958] Director/General Manager

Catalent Micron Technologies Limited
Incorporated: 17 September 1980 *Employees:* 45
Previous: Micron Technologies Limited
Net Worth: £7,638,594 *Total Assets:* £10,539,052
Registered Office: Frankland Road, Blagrove, Swindon, Wilts, SN5 8YG
Activities: Manufacture of basic pharmaceutical products
Officers: Nyssa Forde, Secretary; Jonathan Arnold [1965] Director/President, Oral Drug Delivery; Steven Fasman [1962] Director [American]; Wetteny Joseph [1972] Director/SVP, CFO [American]

Catalent MTI Pharma Solutions Limited
Incorporated: 20 December 2012
Previous: MTI Pharma Solutions Ltd
Net Worth Deficit: £1,276,264 *Total Assets:* £4,602,633
Registered Office: Frankland Road, Blagrove, Swindon, Wilts, SN5 8YG
Activities: Manufacture of basic pharmaceutical products
Officers: Nyssa Forde, Secretary; Jonathan Arnold [1965] Director/President, Oral Drug Delivery; Steven Fasman [1962] Director [American]; Wetteny Joseph [1972] Director/SVP, CFO [American]

Catalent Pharma Solutions Limited
Incorporated: 28 April 1999 *Employees:* 17
Net Worth: £96,736,000 *Total Assets:* £376,012,992
Registered Office: Frankland Road, Blagrove, Swindon, Wilts, SN5 8YG
Activities: Activities of head offices
Officers: Alex Reed, Secretary; Kirk Walsh, Secretary; Jonathan Arnold [1965] Director/President, Oral Drug Delivery; Aristippos Gennadios [1965] Director [American]; Alessandro Maselli [1972] Director/General Manager [Italian]

Catalent U.K. Packaging Limited
Incorporated: 8 February 1962 *Employees:* 243
Net Worth: £92,892,760 *Total Assets:* £125,588,008
Registered Office: Frankland Road, Blagrove, Swindon, Wilts, SN5 8YG
Activities: Other manufacturing n.e.c.
Officers: Shaileshbhai Madhavbhai Patel, Secretary; Wetteny Joseph [1972] Director/VP Finance [American]; Shaileshbhai Madhavbhai Patel [1967] Global Director

Catalent U.K. Swindon Holding II Limited
Incorporated: 24 January 2001
Net Worth: £5,594,582 *Total Assets:* £5,594,582
Registered Office: Frankland Road, Blagrove, Swindon, Wilts, SN5 8YG
Activities: Activities of head offices
Officers: Alex Reed, Secretary; Jonathan Arnold [1965] Director/President, Oral Drug Delivery; Wetteny Joseph [1972] Director/Senior Vice President & Chief Financial Officer [American]; Alex Reed [1983] Finance Director

Catalyst Business Finance Limited
Incorporated: 26 September 2012 *Employees:* 22
Net Worth: £6,283,240 *Total Assets:* £15,117,231
Registered Office: 41 London Road, Palace Chambers, Stroud, Glos, GL5 2AJ
Activities: Factoring
Officers: Mark Batten [1957] Director; Martine Faith Catton [1970] Sales and Marketing Director; Stuart MacKay Fraser [1964] Director; Anthony Edward Kenny [1961] Director/Chartered Accountant; John Francis Soden [1952] Director

Catering 328 Limited
Incorporated: 21 April 2004 *Employees:* 90
Net Worth Deficit: £1,314,392 *Total Assets:* £6,287,682
Registered Office: Unit F, Chelworth Industrial Estate, Chelworth Road, Cricklade, Swindon, Wilts, SN6 6HE
Activities: Wholesale of fruit and vegetables
Shareholders: Sunnyfield Veg Limited; J. Pao & Co. Limited
Officers: Sue Shuk Yin Liu, Secretary; Ronny Wai Kin Liu [1960] Director; Sue Shuk Yin Liu [1961] Director; Andrew Pao [1964] Director

Caterpillar Marine Power UK Limited
Incorporated: 7 October 1968 *Employees:* 90
Net Worth: £21,900,000 *Total Assets:* £31,868,000
Registered Office: 22 Cobham Road, Ferndown Industrial Estate, Wimborne, Dorset, BH21 7PW
Activities: Manufacture of engines and turbines, except aircraft, vehicle and cycle engines
Parent: Caterpillar UK Holdings Limited
Officers: Johanna Elizabeth Deason, Secretary; Nigel John Burroughs [1964] Director/Tax Accountant; Andrew James Goldspink [1971] Director/Facility Manager; Nigel Parkinson [1967] Managing Director

Cathedral Schools Trust
Incorporated: 27 February 2008 *Employees:* 332
Previous: Bristol Cathedral Choir School
Net Worth: £20,539,948 *Total Assets:* £25,091,124
Registered Office: College Square, Bristol, BS1 5TS
Activities: General secondary education
Officers: Stephen Peter Atkinson [1953] Director/Architect; Neil Blundell [1968] Director/Principal; Nicola Boyce [1967] Director/Lawyer; Clare Alison Galliers [1965] Director/Education Consultant; David Michael Hoyle [1957] Director/Dean of Bristol Cathedral; Merlyn Pamela Ipinson-Fleming [1963] Director/Human Resources Practitioner; Michael David LEA [1962] Director/Managing Partner; Stephen Royston Parsons [1951] Director

Cathedral View Limited
Incorporated: 12 March 2003 *Employees:* 75
Net Worth: £1,961,880 *Total Assets:* £4,059,953
Registered Office: Trethowa, Probus, Truro, Cornwall, TR2 4JE
Activities: Medical nursing home activities
Parent: Cathedral View Holdings Limited
Officers: Elaine Sharp, Secretary/Care Home; Elaine Sharp [1951] Director/Care Home; Guy Sharp [1937] Director/Retired

T K T Cattran Limited
Incorporated: 22 August 2000 *Employees:* 2
Net Worth: £3,854,817 *Total Assets:* £4,356,510
Registered Office: The Sycamores, Alverton, Penzance, Cornwall, TR18 4TJ
Activities: Development of building projects
Parent: Caysha Limited
Officers: Timothy Michael Cattran, Secretary; Timothy Michael Cattran [1949] Director

Cavanna Group Limited
Incorporated: 19 April 2001 *Employees:* 108
Net Worth: £48,372,632 *Total Assets:* £65,550,968
Registered Office: Cavanna House, Riviera Park, Nicholson Road, Torquay, Devon, TQ2 7TD
Activities: Construction of domestic buildings
Officers: Brian Generald Bargent, Secretary; Brian Generald Bargent [1964] Director; Jeremy Mark Cavanna [1956] Director/House Builder; Jonathan Cavanna [1954] Director; Martin George Cavanna [1957] Director/House Builder; Keith Raymond Miller [1969] Director

Cavanna Homes (Cornwall) Limited
Incorporated: 4 June 2001
Net Worth: £1,000 *Total Assets:* £4,174,841
Registered Office: Cavanna House, Riviera Park, Nicholson Road, Torquay, Devon, TQ2 7TD
Activities: Construction of domestic buildings
Shareholder: Cavanna Group Limited
Officers: Andrew Guerin, Secretary; Brian Generald Bargent [1964] Director; Jeremy Mark Cavanna [1956] Director/House Builder; Jonathan Cavanna [1954] Director; Martin George Cavanna [1957] Director; Keith Raymond Miller [1969] Director

Cavanna Homes (Devon) Limited
Incorporated: 4 June 2001 *Employees:* 5
Net Worth: £1,000 *Total Assets:* £28,640,672
Registered Office: Cavanna House, Riviera Park, Nicholson Road, Torquay, Devon, TQ2 7TD
Activities: Construction of domestic buildings
Parent: Cavanna Group Limited
Officers: Andrew Guerin, Secretary; Brian Generald Bargent [1964] Director; Jeremy Mark Cavanna [1956] Director/House Builder; Jonathan Cavanna [1954] Director; Martin George Cavanna [1957] Director; Keith Raymond Miller [1969] Director

Cavanna Homes (South West) Limited
Incorporated: 4 June 2001 *Employees:* 5
Net Worth: £1,000 *Total Assets:* £20,591,334
Registered Office: Cavanna House, Riviera Park, Nicholson Road, Torquay, Devon, TQ2 7TD
Activities: Construction of domestic buildings
Parent: Cavanna Group Limited
Officers: Andrew Guerin, Secretary; Brian Generald Bargent [1964] Director; Jeremy Mark Cavanna [1956] Director/House Builder; Jonathan Cavanna [1954] Director; Martin George Cavanna [1957] Director; Keith Raymond Miller [1969] Director

Caveangle Limited
Incorporated: 1 March 2000
Net Worth: £379,599,200 *Total Assets:* £384,883,392
Registered Office: 2nd Floor, West Wing, Kingsgate House, Newbury Road, Andover, Hants, SP10 4DU
Activities: Activities of other holding companies n.e.c.
Parent: Integra LifeSciences Holdings Corporation
Officers: Sravan Kumar Emany [1977] Director/Senior VP, Strategy, Treasurer & Investor Relations [American]; Jeffrey Alan Mosebrook [1976] Director/VP, Corp Controller & Principle Accounting Officer [American]

Cavehurst Limited
Incorporated: 17 October 1995
Net Worth: £832,155,200 *Total Assets:* £1,582,707,200
Registered Office: Atlantic House, Aviation Park West, Bournemouth International Airport, Christchurch, Dorset, BH23 6EW
Activities: Financial intermediation not elsewhere classified
Parent: Meggitt Properties PLC
Officers: Simon Robert Grant, Secretary; Derek John O'Neill [1962] Director/Company Secretary; Marina Louise Thomas [1976] Director/Company Secretary

Cavendish Close Limited
Incorporated: 29 June 1989 *Employees:* 103
Net Worth: £12,205,654 *Total Assets:* £18,439,072
Registered Office: c/o Francis Clark LLP, North Quay House, Sutton Harbour, Plymouth, PL4 0RA
Activities: Residential nursing care facilities
Parent: Woodley Hotels Limited
Officers: Girishkumar Devchand Dhrona, Secretary/Businessman; Girishkumar Devchand Dhrona [1946] Director/Businessman; Sanjay Girishkumar Dhrona [1983] Director/Businessman; Vasantlal Devchand Jhina Dhrona [1943] Director

Cavity Trays Limited,
Incorporated: 8 July 1963
Net Worth: £1,365,479 *Total Assets:* £3,978,978
Registered Office: Greengate House, 87 Pickwick Road, Corsham, Wilts, SN13 9BY
Activities: Manufacture of other plastic products
Major Shareholder: John Louis Shillabeer
Officers: John Louis Shillabeer, Secretary; Diana Elizabeth Shillabeer [1952] Director; John Louis Shillabeer [1948] Director

Cavium UK Ltd
Incorporated: 3 April 2000 *Employees:* 12
Previous: QLogic (UK) Limited
Net Worth: £3,667,968 *Total Assets:* £4,021,458
Registered Office: 2 Temple Back East, Temple Quay, Bristol, BS1 6EG
Activities: Other information technology service activities
Parent: Cavium, Inc.
Officers: Mitchell Lee Gaynor [1959] Director/Chief Administration and Legal Officer [American]; Jean Xiaojin Hu [1963] Director/Financial Officer [American]; Marc Van Weddingen [1958] Director/Business Executive [Belgian]

CBSM 2012 Limited
Incorporated: 26 June 1961 *Employees:* 7
Net Worth: £5,540,506 *Total Assets:* £5,787,468
Registered Office: 1 Cedar House, Brook Road, Budleigh Salterton, Devon, EX9 6BB
Activities: Development of building projects
Officers: Janet Burch [1961] Director; Harry Carter [1954] Director/Architect; Ronald Nicholas Carter [1948] Director/Builder & Plant Manager; Michael Henry Gardiner [1929] Director/Accountant

CCH Property Company Limited
Incorporated: 8 December 2000
Net Worth: £4,100,867 *Total Assets:* £15,847,548
Registered Office: Centenary House, Peninsula Park, Rydon Lane, Exeter, EX2 7XE
Activities: Other letting and operating of own or leased real estate
Parent: Braundshill Holdings Limited
Officers: Graham Edward Vanstone, Secretary; David John Cobb [1961] Director/Accountant; The Hon Charles Patrick Rolle Fane Trefusis [1962] Director/Gentleman; Leigh Stuart Rix [1958] Director/Land Agent; John Christian Varley [1960] Director

CCR Motor Co. Ltd.
Incorporated: 28 June 1991 *Employees:* 77
Net Worth: £3,810,559 *Total Assets:* £14,240,609
Registered Office: 1 Vernon Court, Meteor Business Park, Cheltenham Road East, Staverton, Glos, GL2 9QG
Activities: Sale of new cars and light motor vehicles
Parent: VT Holdings Co., Ltd.
Officers: Tatsuya Suzuki, Secretary; Timothy Raymond Bagnall [1965] Managing Director; Masahide Ito [1960] Director [Japanese]; Koichi Yoshida [1971] Director [Japanese]

CDF Group Ltd
Incorporated: 23 April 2015 *Employees:* 108
Net Worth: £4,782,000 *Total Assets:* £11,634,000
Registered Office: Prigg Meadow, Ashburton, Newton Abbot, Devon, TQ13 7DF
Activities: Activities of head offices
Shareholder: Charles Frederick Cooke-Hurle
Officers: Juliet Collis [1961] Director; Charles Frederick Cooke-Hurle [1951] Director; Andrew King [1965] Director; Paul Sean Wilson [1964] Director

CDS (Superstores International) Limited
Incorporated: 20 March 1992 *Employees:* 9,030
Net Worth: £179,560,000 *Total Assets:* £446,225,984
Registered Office: Tamar House, Thornbury Road, Plymouth, PL6 7PP
Activities: Other retail sale in non-specialised stores
Major Shareholder: Sarah Jane Dawson
Officers: Christopher Frederick Dawson [1951] Director

CDS Group Services Limited
Incorporated: 20 January 2005 *Employees:* 71
Net Worth: £1,558,000 *Total Assets:* £5,935,000
Registered Office: Tamar House, Thornbury Road, Estover, Plymouth, PL6 7PT
Activities: Development of building projects
Shareholders: CDS Superstores International Limited; Sarah Jane Dawson; Christopher Frederick Dawson
Officers: Christopher Frederick Dawson [1951] Director

CDS Support Limited
Incorporated: 2 November 2016
Net Worth: £565,297 *Total Assets:* £4,153,299
Registered Office: The Bramery, Alstone Lane, Cheltenham, Glos, GL51 8HE
Activities: Other information technology service activities
Parent: Graphic Plates Ltd
Officers: Guy Adrian Van Lopik, Secretary; Fergus Robert Edward Bailie [1979] Director; Richard Henry Bradley [1969] Director; Philip Graham Walter [1958] Director

Cedar Care Homes Limited
Incorporated: 18 June 1998 *Employees:* 401
Net Worth: £14,690,307 *Total Assets:* £34,706,944
Registered Office: 20 Richmond Hill, Clifton, Bristol, BS8 2SE
Activities: Residential nursing care facilities
Shareholders: Ash Madhubhai Desai; Madhu Desai; Kanoo Desai
Officers: Ash Madhubhai Desai, Secretary; Ash Madhubhai Desai [1961] Managing Director; Kanoo Desai [1928] Director; Madhu Desai [1926] Director/Pharmacist; Minal Desai [1966] Director of Nursing

CELCSE Limited
Incorporated: 31 August 2016
Net Worth Deficit: £11,945 *Total Assets:* £7,290,403
Registered Office: Woodwater House, Pynes Hill, Exeter, EX2 5WR
Activities: Construction of utility projects for electricity and telecommunications
Shareholders: Cesar Gonzalez Otalora; Jose Manuel Zorrilla
Officers: Cesar Gonzalez Otalora [1974] Director/Chief Executive Officer [Spanish]; Jose Manuel Zorrilla [1974] Director/Chief Executive Officer [Spanish]

Cemetery Management Limited
Incorporated: 9 December 1987
Net Worth: £69,834 *Total Assets:* £26,482,630
Registered Office: Chapel View, Westerleigh Crematorium, Westerleigh Road, Westerleigh, Bristol, BS37 8QP
Activities: Dormant company
Parent: Westerleigh Crematoria Ltd
Officers: Dafydd Rhys John, Secretary; Dafydd Rhys John [1974] Director/Chartered Accountant; Ian David McArdle [1966] Director/Chartered Surveyor

Cengage Learning (EMEA) Limited
Incorporated: 13 April 1967 *Employees:* 199
Net Worth: £26,340,000 *Total Assets:* £41,184,000
Registered Office: Cheriton House, North Way, Andover, Hants, SP10 5BE
Activities: Book publishing
Parent: Cengage Learning UK Holdings Limited
Officers: Stephen Lake, Secretary; Charles Merrill Bonney II [1970] Director [American]; Hans Alexander Broich [1965] Director [German]; David Lloyd Rae [1961] Director [Australian]

Cengage Learning UK Holdings Limited
Incorporated: 10 July 1980
Net Worth: £47,417,000 *Total Assets:* £51,173,000
Registered Office: Cheriton House, North Way, Andover, Hants, SP10 5BE
Activities: Activities of head offices
Parent: Cengage Learning Holdings B.V.
Officers: Stephen Lake, Secretary; Charles Merrill Bonney II [1970] Director [American]; Hans Alexander Broich [1965] Director [German]; David Lloyd Rae [1961] Director [Australian]

Centaur Foods Limited
Incorporated: 7 February 1997 *Employees:* 23
Net Worth: £2,585,567 *Total Assets:* £3,620,969
Registered Office: Unit 2 Beaufort Trade Park, Pucklechurch Trading Estate, Pucklechurch, S Glos, BS16 9QH
Activities: Non-specialised wholesale of food, beverages and tobacco
Major Shareholder: Mark Eric Catterall
Officers: Adrian Hardy Walton, Secretary/Director/Manager; Mark Eric Catterall [1960] Director [Australian]; Adrian Hardy Walton [1967] Director/Manager

Centaur Services Limited
Incorporated: 9 January 1964 *Employees:* 262
Net Worth: £20,511,000 *Total Assets:* £75,137,000
Registered Office: Centaur House, Torbay Road, Castle Cary, Somerset, BA7 7EU
Activities: Veterinary activities
Parent: MWI Supply (UK Acquisition) Limited
Officers: Brian Topper, Secretary; John Gardner Chou [1956] Director/Business Executive [American]; James F Cleary Jr [1963] Director/CEO & President [American]; Mark Jeffrey Shaw [1962] Director/President [American]; Brian Topper [1973] Director/MD [American]

Centek Holdings Limited
Incorporated: 16 August 2011 *Employees:* 177
Net Worth: £26,993,428 *Total Assets:* £43,834,500
Registered Office: Station View, Forde Road, Newton Abbot, Devon, TQ12 4AE
Activities: Activities of other holding companies n.e.c.
Parent: Centek Technologies Limited
Officers: David Janicek [1977] Director [American]

Centek Limited
Incorporated: 15 May 2001 *Employees:* 125
Net Worth: £19,091,412 *Total Assets:* £37,182,480
Registered Office: Forde Road, Brunel Industrial Estate, Newton Abbot, Devon, TQ12 4AE
Activities: Manufacture of other fabricated metal products n.e.c.
Parent: Centek Holdings Limited
Officers: David Ball [1969] Managing Director [American]; David Coghlan [1959] Managing Director [American]; David Janicek [1977] Director [American]; Gary Watson [1963] Managing Director

Centek Properties Limited
Incorporated: 10 July 2006
Net Worth Deficit: £224,386 *Total Assets:* £4,945,852
Registered Office: Station View, Forde Road, Newton Abbot, Devon, TQ12 4AE
Activities: Other letting and operating of own or leased real estate
Parent: Centek Limited
Officers: David Janicek [1977] Director [American]

Central Garages (Torbay) Limited
Incorporated: 18 May 1961 *Employees:* 39
Net Worth: £6,381,751 *Total Assets:* £6,855,736
Registered Office: Central Garage (Brixham), Milton Street, Brixham, Devon, TQ5 0BY
Activities: Retail trade of motor vehicle parts and accessories
Shareholder: Peter Dewis Ashley
Officers: David Michael Ashley [1981] Director/Motor Engineer; Peter Dewis Ashley [1937] Director/Motor Engineer; Ross Ashley [1980] Director; Scott Michael Ashley [1975] Director/Business Manager; Simon Peter Ashley [1969] Director/Motor Engineer

Central Management Catalogue Agency (UK) Limited
Incorporated: 9 October 1997 *Employees:* 70
Net Worth: £3,440,775 *Total Assets:* £4,212,720
Registered Office: Ross House, The Square, Stow on the Wold, Glos, GL54 1AF
Activities: Agents specialised in the sale of other particular products
Major Shareholder: Robert Crawford
Officers: Robert Crawford, Secretary; Robert Crawford [1966] Director/Manager; Chris Peter Green [1966] Director/Obsolescence Management; Gary Harman [1965] Director/Codification Services; Darren Topley [1968] Managing Director

Centrax Holdings Limited
Incorporated: 4 May 2006 *Employees:* 308
Net Worth: £36,343,748 *Total Assets:* £73,812,576
Registered Office: Centrax Limited, Shaldon Road, Newton Abbot, Devon, TQ12 4SQ
Activities: Activities of head offices
Shareholder: Richard Henry Howard Barr
Officers: Ian Andrew Duffin, Secretary; Andrew Nicholson Barr [1973] Director; Charles Robert Barr [1945] Director/Joint MD and Chief Executive; Christopher Howard Barr [1978] Director; Richard Henry Howard Barr [1920] Director/Chairman; Richard Anthony Barr [1950] Director/Joint MD; Ian Andrew Duffin [1956] Director/Chartered Accountant

Centrax Industries Limited
Incorporated: 24 March 2000 *Employees:* 22
Net Worth: £3,569,661 *Total Assets:* £7,678,511
Registered Office: Centrax, Shaldon Road, Newton Abbot, Devon, TQ12 4SQ
Activities: Activities of head offices
Parent: Centrax Holdings Limited
Officers: Ian Raymond Birt, Secretary; Andrew Nicholson Barr [1973] Director; Charles Robert Barr [1945] Director; Christopher Howard Barr [1978] Director; Richard Anthony Barr [1950] Director; Richard Henry Howard Barr [1920] Director; Ian Andrew Duffin [1956] Director/Chartered Accountant

Centrax Limited
Incorporated: 29 October 1957 *Employees:* 190
Net Worth: £25,573,318 *Total Assets:* £57,889,864
Registered Office: Centrax, Shaldon Road, Newton Abbot, Devon, TQ12 4SQ
Activities: Manufacture of electric motors, generators and transformers
Officers: Ian Raymond Birt, Secretary; Andrew Nicholson Barr [1973] Director; Charles Robert Barr [1945] Director; Christopher Howard Barr [1978] Director; Richard Henry Howard Barr [1920] Director; Richard Anthony Barr [1950] Director; Ian Andrew Duffin [1956] Director/Chartered Accountant; Kevin John Steele [1958] Director

Centristic Limited
Incorporated: 9 March 1981 *Employees:* 58
Net Worth: £2,512,031 *Total Assets:* £5,083,631
Registered Office: Centristic, Cavalier Road, Heathfield Industrial Estate, Newton Abbot, Devon, TQ12 6TQ
Activities: Manufacture of metal structures and parts of structures
Major Shareholder: Alistair Roderick Grant
Officers: Alistair Roderick Grant, Secretary/Director; Alistair Roderick Grant [1952] Director; James David Hepworth [1966] Director/Construction Manager

Century Casino Bath Limited
Incorporated: 6 July 2015 *Employees:* 1
Previous: Saw Close Casino Limited
Net Worth Deficit: £164,883 *Total Assets:* £5,744,219
Registered Office: Century Casino, Saw Close, Bath, BA1 1EY
Activities: Gambling and betting activities
Parent: Century Casinos, Inc.
Officers: Nikolaus Strohriegel [1969] Director [Austrian]

CEPS PLC.
Incorporated: 30 April 1952 *Employees:* 286
Net Worth: £3,607,000 *Total Assets:* £14,978,000
Registered Office: 11 Laura Place, Bath, BA2 4BL
Activities: Activities of head offices
Shareholder: David Alistair Horner
Officers: Vivien Elizabeth Langford, Secretary; David Alistair Horner [1959] Director; Vivien Elizabeth Langford [1961] Director/Chartered Accountant; Geoffrey Charles Martin [1945] Director/Chartered Accountant; Mark David Pollard [1959] Director

Ceres Estates Limited
Incorporated: 1 May 1959 *Employees:* 6
Net Worth: £16,088,377 *Total Assets:* £37,933,428
Registered Office: 105-107 Bath Road, Cheltenham, Glos, GL53 7LE
Activities: Buying and selling of own real estate
Major Shareholder: William John Parker
Officers: Sarah Louise Brewer, Secretary; Sarah Louise Brewer [1971] Director; Lisbeth Rose Parker [1955] Director

Certini Bicycle Company Limited
Incorporated: 28 February 2006 *Employees:* 37
Net Worth: £1,179,530 *Total Assets:* £4,020,746
Registered Office: 10 Kingsmill Road, Tamar View Industrial Estate, Saltash, Cornwall, PL12 6LF
Activities: Other retail sale in non-specialised stores
Parent: Certini (Holdings) Ltd
Officers: Deborah Dare, Secretary; Robert David Carron [1962] Director; Anthony Dare [1961] Director

Certus Wholesale Ltd
Incorporated: 23 October 2015
Net Worth: £3,648,082 *Total Assets:* £3,864,071
Registered Office: 59 Regency Court, Brookbank Close, Cheltenham, Glos, GL50 3NS
Activities: Non-specialised wholesale trade
Major Shareholder: Alistair Henderson
Officers: Alistair Henderson [1981] Director

Ceuta Healthcare Limited
Incorporated: 6 October 1994 *Employees:* 168
Net Worth: £6,064,000 *Total Assets:* £33,697,000
Registered Office: Hill House, 41 Richmond Hill, Bournemouth, BH2 6HS
Activities: Other human health activities
Parent: Ceuta Holdings Limited
Officers: Edwin Charles Bessant [1953] Managing Director; Peter Andrew Burrows [1960] International Business Development Director; Christopher Charles Clarkson [1964] Sales Director; Jonathan David Connolly [1965] Marketing Director; Annette Zita D'Abreo [1962] Deputy Managing Director; Robert Edward Hester [1968] Director; Christopher James Hoole [1968] Director/Accountant; John Phillip Watmough [1959] Sales Director

Ceuta Holdings Limited
Incorporated: 14 May 2013 *Employees:* 323
Net Worth: £26,867,000 *Total Assets:* £67,635,000
Registered Office: Hill House, 41 Richmond Hill, Bournemouth, BH2 6HS
Activities: Activities of head offices
Shareholders: Edwin Charles Bessant; Juggernaut Capital Partners II LP
Officers: Robert Edward Hester, Secretary; Edwin Charles Bessant [1953] Director; Annette Zita D'Abreo [1962] Director; Robert Edward Hester [1968] Director; Craig Michael Hille [1974] Director/Investor [American]; Darrin Andrew Kleinman [1974] Director [American]; John David Shulman [1963] Director/Investor [American]

CFH Docmail Ltd
Incorporated: 21 April 1983 *Employees:* 374
Net Worth: £3,015,000 *Total Assets:* £15,669,000
Registered Office: St Peter's Park, Wells Road, Radstock, Bath, BA3 3UP
Activities: Printing n.e.c.
Parent: CFH Tradeco Limited
Officers: Simon Bunyan [1962] Director; Stephen Patrick Cray [1967] Director; Adam Michael Harwood [1963] Director; Joanne Louise Helps [1967] Director/Accountant; Bryan Joseph Knowles [1976] Director; Jonathan Lacey Marsh [1968] Director; William McFedries [1972] Director

CG Holdings Limited
Incorporated: 3 February 2000 *Employees:* 38
Net Worth: £4,674,080 *Total Assets:* £8,524,987
Registered Office: Tickenham Road, Clevedon, Somerset, BS21 6AB
Activities: Activities of other holding companies n.e.c.
Major Shareholder: Stephen Warren Day
Officers: Zoe Louise Day, Secretary; Stephen Warren Day [1962] Director; Zoe Louise Day [1964] Director/Company Secretary; Alison Jane Skedd [1963] Finance Director

CG Hotel Holding Limited
Incorporated: 21 March 2006 *Employees:* 379
Net Worth: £5,451,566 *Total Assets:* £49,954,624
Registered Office: Chewton Glen Hotel, New Milton, Hants, BH25 6QS
Activities: Other business support service activities n.e.c.
Major Shareholder: Ian Malcolm Livingstone
Officers: Richard John Livingstone [1964] Director; Leonard Kevin Sebastian [1969] Group Managing and Legal Director [Swiss]

CGA Financial & Investment Services Limited
Incorporated: 26 November 1991 *Employees:* 12
Net Worth: £1,895,468 *Total Assets:* £7,319,877
Registered Office: Chalke House, Station Road, Codford, Warminster, Wilts, BA12 0JX
Activities: Financial intermediation not elsewhere classified
Officers: William Harrison Allan [1956] Director/Financial Advisor

Chachos Holdings Limited
Incorporated: 12 February 2016 *Employees:* 2
Net Worth Deficit: £21,237 *Total Assets:* £3,505,969
Registered Office: 27 Queens Gate, Bristol, BS9 1TZ
Activities: Other letting and operating of own or leased real estate
Shareholders: Anunziata Combatti; Ian Hopkinson
Officers: Anunziata Elena Combatti [1975] Director/Housewife [Italian]; Ian Robert Hopkinson [1971] Director

Chadwick Holdings Limited
Incorporated: 4 January 1967 *Employees:* 3
Net Worth: £952,511 *Total Assets:* £6,028,619
Registered Office: Chadwick House, 6 Hallam Road, Clevedon, Somerset, BS21 7SF
Activities: Other letting and operating of own or leased real estate
Shareholder: Mervyn Willbert Douglas
Officers: Joan Marcia Douglas, Secretary; Mervyn Willbert Douglas [1943] Director; Richard James Douglas [1968] Director/Chartered Surveyor; Stuart Alexander Douglas [1965] Director/Chartered Surveyor

Chaffcombe Thorns Limited
Incorporated: 6 April 1961
Net Worth: £2,654,106 *Total Assets:* £4,642,059
Registered Office: Deer Park Farm, Buckerell, Honiton, Devon, EX14 3QD
Activities: Raising of sheep and goats
Officers: Mavis Josephine Hazel Galling, Secretary; Mavis Josephine Hazel Galling [1932] Director/Company Secretary; Ronald George Galling [1932] Director/Arbitrator

Chafyn Grove School
Incorporated: 4 June 2007 *Employees:* 105
Net Worth: £3,654,175 *Total Assets:* £5,042,108
Registered Office: Chafyn Grove School, Bourne Avenue, Salisbury, Wilts, SP1 1LR
Activities: Primary education
Officers: Michelle Louise Davies, Secretary; Katherine Lucy Brown [1968] Director/Teacher; Thomas Frederick Clay [1956] Director/Banker; Tom Yori Griffiths [1965] Director/Military Officer; Nicholas Reginald Maurice Jones [1952] Director/Communications Adviser; Helen Ruth Lello [1964] Director/Solicitor; Mark Duncan Mortimer [1967] Director/Headmaster; Michael Roy David Roller [1965] Director/Chartered Accountant; Mark Edward Curwen Wordsworth [1965] Director/Chartered Surveyor

F.J. Chalke Limited
Incorporated: 13 May 1960 *Employees:* 109
Net Worth: £6,974,213 *Total Assets:* £16,291,846
Registered Office: The Talbot Garage, Salisbury Street, Mere, Warminster, Wilts, BA12 6HE
Activities: Sale of new cars and light motor vehicles
Major Shareholder: Edward James Chalke
Officers: Richard Fox, Secretary; Edward James Chalke [1961] Managing Director; Stephen Geoffrey Fowler [1962] Director/Manager; Grahame Herbert John Fry [1952] Director/Sales Manager

Chalwyn Estates Limited
Incorporated: 11 June 2004 *Employees:* 2
Net Worth: £1,540,460 *Total Assets:* £4,933,000
Registered Office: Unit 1c Chalwyn Industrial Estate, Parkstone, Poole, Dorset, BH12 4PE
Activities: Other letting and operating of own or leased real estate
Major Shareholder: Frederick William Austin Page Roberts
Officers: Frederick William Austin Page-Roberts [1963] Director

E.A. Chamberlain (Holdings) Limited
Incorporated: 16 June 1920
Net Worth: £13,693,591 *Total Assets:* £13,784,030
Registered Office: Avening Road, Nailsworth, Stroud, Glos, GL6 0BS
Activities: Other letting and operating of own or leased real estate
Parent: Nailsworth Limited
Officers: Cecilia Diana Chamberlain, Secretary; Hector James David Chamberlain [1998] Director; James Edward Chamberlain [1958] Director/Publishing; Jasper Edward Henry Chamberlain [1992] Director

Chamberlayne Farms Limited
Incorporated: 16 January 1964
Net Worth: £4,649,747 *Total Assets:* £12,345,752
Registered Office: Maisemore Court Farm, Maisemore, Gloucester, GL2 8EY
Activities: Growing of cereals (except rice), leguminous crops and oil seeds
Officers: Humphrey John Chamberlayne, Secretary; Humphrey John Chamberlayne [1945] Director/Farmer; Jeremy Rudge Chamberlayne [1940] Director/Farmer; Luke Patrick Chamberlayne [1963] Director/Farmer; Robert Scott Chamberlayne [1972] Director/Property Developer; Robin Francis Chamberlayne [1966] Director/Financial Advisor

Champion Groundworks Limited
Incorporated: 11 September 2012 *Employees:* 261
Net Worth: £17,690,294 *Total Assets:* £30,174,020
Registered Office: Doublebois Industrial Estate, Doublebois, Liskeard, Cornwall, PL14 6LE
Activities: Other construction installation
Major Shareholder: Frederick Charles Champion
Officers: Frederick Charles Champion [1956] Director; Shaun David Champion [1981] Director; James Stephen Cleaton-Roberts [1980] Director/Quantity Surveyor

Fred Champion Groundworks Limited
Incorporated: 17 May 1996 *Employees:* 255
Net Worth: £15,725,523 *Total Assets:* £24,796,232
Registered Office: Doublebois Industrial Estate, Doublebois, Liskeard, Cornwall, PL14 6LE
Activities: Site preparation
Parent: Champion Groundworks Ltd
Officers: James Stephen Cleaton-Roberts, Secretary; Michael Vincent Caers [1960] Director/Contracts Manager; Frederick Charles Champion [1956] Director; Shaun David Champion [1981] Director; John James Cheffings [1982] Director; James Stephen Cleaton-Roberts [1980] Director/Quantity Surveyor; David Shaun Philp [1971] Director

Fred Champion Hire Limited
Incorporated: 17 May 1996 *Employees:* 6
Net Worth: £4,105,134 *Total Assets:* £4,934,688
Registered Office: Doublebois Industrial Estate, Doublebois, Liskeard, Cornwall, PL14 6LE
Activities: Renting and leasing of construction and civil engineering machinery and equipment
Parent: Champion Groundworks Ltd
Officers: James Stephen Cleaton-Roberts, Secretary; Donna Champion [1970] Director; Frederick Charles Champion [1956] Director; Shaun David Champion [1981] Director; James Stephen Cleaton-Roberts [1980] Director/Quantity Surveyor

Chanctonbury Health Care Ltd
Incorporated: 19 August 1999 *Employees:* 126
Net Worth: £1,974,003 *Total Assets:* £9,681,534
Registered Office: Windsor House, Bayshill Road, Cheltenham, Glos, GL50 3AT
Activities: Residential nursing care facilities
Shareholders: Barry Jeremy Sinclair; Barry Jeremy Sinclair
Officers: Anthony Joseph Berkovi, Secretary/Chartered Accountant; Anthony Joseph Berkovi [1947] Director/Chartered Accountant; Barry Jeremy Sinclair [1959] Director/Care Home Proprietor; Sharon Rosalind Sinclair [1963] Director/Counselling Therapist; Gregory Keith Wood [1969] Director/Management Accountant

J.Chandler & Company (Buckfast),Limited
Incorporated: 23 May 1927 *Employees:* 27
Net Worth: £38,395,232 *Total Assets:* £45,481,508
Registered Office: New Abbey House, Fyfield Road, Weyhill, Andover, Hants, SP11 8DN
Activities: Manufacture of other non-distilled fermented beverages
Officers: Jonathan William Sharp, Secretary; David Roger Charlesworth [1951] Director/Minister of Religion; Jonathan Roger Deacon [1956] Director/Chartered Accountant; Bernard Richard Joyce [1935] Director/Retired; Gary Richard Joyce [1961] Director; Jane Carol Joyce [1967] Director; Denis Morgan Moylan [1956] Director; Jonathan William Sharp [1966] Director; Father Gavin Francis Straw [1959] Director/Minister of Religion; Peter Frederick Winckley [1960] Director

Changvilla Investments Limited
Incorporated: 29 January 1960
Net Worth: £2,966,720 *Total Assets:* £6,095,599
Registered Office: Wood House, Chudleigh, Newton Abbot, Devon, TQ13 0EH
Activities: Other letting and operating of own or leased real estate
Major Shareholder: James Edward Day
Officers: Edward Reginald Day, Secretary; Coralie Anne Day [1956] Director; Edward Reginald Day [1932] Director; James Edward Day [1963] Director

Chantry Court Westbury Ltd
Incorporated: 24 September 2004 *Employees:* 1
Net Worth: £1,763,528 *Total Assets:* £4,866,862
Registered Office: 3 Bath Mews, Bath Parade, Cheltenham, Glos, GL53 7HL
Activities: Development of building projects
Parent: Mohawk Investments Ltd
Officers: David Ian Brierley [1956] Director; Noel Kelly [1954] Director [Irish]

Chapel Barton House Co. Limited
Incorporated: 14 August 2007
Net Worth: £649,539 *Total Assets:* £3,575,108
Registered Office: Chapel Barton House, High Street, Bruton, Somerset, BA10 0AE
Activities: Licenced restaurants
Shareholder: Catherine Teresa Trant
Officers: Ahmed Riza Sidki, Secretary; Ahmed Riza Sidki [1954] Director; Catherine Teresa Trant [1959] Director/Management Consultant

Chaplins Properties Limited
Incorporated: 15 July 2008 *Employees:* 84
Net Worth: £2,788,338 *Total Assets:* £6,280,572
Registered Office: Brittanic House, 51 North Hill, Plymouth, PL4 8HZ
Activities: Activities of head offices
Major Shareholder: Linda Suzanne Thompson
Officers: Michelle Mary Cummings, Secretary; Vanessa Claire Chaplin [1968] Director/Retail Manager; Linda Suzanne Thompson [1946] Director/Manager

Chappell Engineering Limited
Incorporated: 16 June 1999
Net Worth: £5,111,045 *Total Assets:* £5,246,305
Registered Office: Unit 2 Brunel Way, Stonehouse, Glos, GL10 3SX
Activities: Machining
Shareholder: James Richard Chappell
Officers: Lynn Margaret Chappell, Secretary; James Richard Chappell [1941] Director/Engineer; Lynn Margaret Chappell [1946] Director/Bookkeeper; Frank Phillips [1968] Director/Warehouse Manager; Sharon Phillips [1970] Director/General Manager

Chapple & Jenkins Ltd
Incorporated: 31 January 2008 *Employees:* 53
Net Worth: £1,850,014 *Total Assets:* £5,848,974
Registered Office: Chapple & Jenkins Warehouse, Unit 91 Station Road, Kingswood, Bristol, BS15 4NR
Activities: Non-specialised wholesale trade
Shareholder: Kevin Scott Chapple
Officers: Kevin Scott Chapple, Secretary/Director; Kevin Scott Chapple [1978] Director; Richard Chapple [1974] Director; Martin Jenkins [1978] Director; Stephen Matthew Jenkins [1980] Director

Chapters Freefolk Ltd
Incorporated: 14 January 2010
Net Worth Deficit: £14,681 *Total Assets:* £3,704,730
Registered Office: Littleworth Barn, Milton Lilbourne, Littleworth, Pewsey, Wilts, SN9 5LF
Activities: Buying and selling of own real estate
Officers: Mark Richard John Piper, Secretary; Mark Richard John Piper [1964] Director; Steven Wake [1966] Director

Charcoal CLG 1 Limited
Incorporated: 26 February 2007 *Employees:* 2
Net Worth: £206,156,000 *Total Assets:* £206,156,000
Registered Office: Link House, 25 West Street, Poole, Dorset, BH15 1LD
Activities: Activities of head offices
Officers: Fiona Jane Rose, Secretary; Matthew Paul Jowett [1967] Director/General Counsel and Company Secretary; Alistair Windybank [1972] Director

Charcoal Midco 1 Limited
Incorporated: 23 February 2007 *Employees:* 2
Net Worth: £26,336,000 *Total Assets:* £26,336,000
Registered Office: Link House, 25 West Street, Poole, Dorset, BH15 1LD
Activities: Activities of head offices
Parent: Merlin Entertainments Group Holdings Limited
Officers: Fiona Jane Rose, Secretary; Matthew Paul Jowett [1967] Director/General Counsel and Company Secretary; Fiona Jane Rose [1964] Director/Assistant Group Company Secretary

Charcoal Newco 1 Limited
Incorporated: 26 February 2007 *Employees:* 2
Net Worth: £557,920,000 *Total Assets:* £3,222,515,968
Registered Office: Link House, 25 West Street, Poole, Dorset, BH15 1LD
Activities: Activities of head offices
Shareholders: Charcoal CLG 1 Limited; Merlin Entertainments PLC
Officers: Fiona Jane Rose, Secretary; Matthew Paul Jowett [1967] Director/General Counsel and Company Secretary; Fiona Jane Rose [1964] Director/Assistant Group Company Secretary

Charcoal Newco 1A Limited
Incorporated: 27 February 2007
Net Worth: £905,875,008 *Total Assets:* £2,616,719,104
Registered Office: Link House, 25 West Street, Poole, Dorset, BH15 1LD
Activities: Activities of head offices
Parent: Charcoal Newco 1 Limited
Officers: Fiona Jane Rose, Secretary; Matthew Paul Jowett [1967] Director/General Counsel and Company Secretary; Fiona Jane Rose [1964] Director/Assistant Group Company Secretary

Charford Properties Limited
Incorporated: 6 October 1988 *Employees:* 3
Previous: Parkwater Investments Limited
Net Worth: £32,818,564 *Total Assets:* £38,778,360
Registered Office: 3 The Limes, Woodfalls Farm, Slab Lane, Salisbury, Wilts, SP5 2NE
Activities: Other letting and operating of own or leased real estate
Parent: Charford Properties Holdings Limited
Officers: Hannah Claire Grenfell Cahill [1984] Director/Business Development Manager; Nigel Kevin Grenfell Jennings [1954] Director

Charlcombe Homes Limited
Incorporated: 13 May 2002 *Employees:* 4
Net Worth: £600,100 *Total Assets:* £9,935,171
Registered Office: Ashdown, Richmond Heights, Lansdown, Bath, BA1 5QJ
Activities: Construction of domestic buildings
Officers: Alastair John Leigh Gibson, Secretary/Director; Alastair John Leigh Gibson [1963] Director; John Hartley [1957] Director

Charlcombe Limited
Incorporated: 8 September 1948 *Employees:* 5
Net Worth: £10,166,488 *Total Assets:* £11,080,837
Registered Office: Ground Floor, Southfield House, 2 Southfield Road, Westbury-on-Trym, Bristol, BS9 3BH
Activities: Other accommodation
Shareholder: Emma Katherine Muggridge
Officers: Emma Katherine Muggridge, Secretary; John Kenneth Lewis [1941] Director/Insurance Broker; Emma Katherine Muggridge [1970] Director/Surveyor

A. J. Charlton & Sons Limited
Incorporated: 15 September 1976 *Employees:* 88
Net Worth: £964,506 *Total Assets:* £4,571,023
Registered Office: The Sawmills, Buckland Down, Frome, Somerset, BA11 2RH
Activities: Sawmilling and planing of wood
Officers: Peter James Charlton, Secretary; Adrian Derek Charlton [1957] Director/Timber Merchant; Anthony James Charlton [1929] Director/Timber Merchant; David Graham Charlton [1955] Director/Timber Merchant; Peter James Charlton [1953] Director/Accountant

Charlton Abbotts Limited Liability Partnership
Incorporated: 3 February 2015 *Employees:* 4
Net Worth: £31,689,778 *Total Assets:* £32,992,432
Registered Office: Charlton Abbotts Manor, Andoversford, Glos, GL54 5TF
Officers: Edwin Maxime Bailey [1949] Member; Tristan Ward Bailey [1947] Member; Peter David Hudson [1958] Member; Louise Jane Stoten [1969] LLP Member

Charlton Kings Junior School
Incorporated: 4 July 2011 *Employees:* 37
Net Worth: £3,352,924 *Total Assets:* £3,899,756
Registered Office: East End Road, Charlton Kings, Cheltenham, Glos, GL53 8QE
Activities: Primary education
Officers: Katharine Shepherd, Secretary; Lesley Crompton [1970] Director/Teacher; Ian Davidson [1949] Director/Deputy Headteacher; Russell James Grimshaw [1969] Director/Civil Engineer; Sheena Habben [1974] Director/Human Resources Manager [British/South African]; Mark Hawkins [1978] Director/Head of Agile Delivery; Christopher Michael James Hunter [1980] Director of Financial Advice Consultancy; Nick Jukes [1986] Director/Teacher; Andrew Vincent Lackey [1974] Director/Crown Servant; Alasdair Richard Mundy [1987] Director/RAF Pilot; Lee Robert Pajak [1973] Director/Headteacher; Caroline Helen Parker [1977] Director/Teacher; Lisa Plumpton [1972] Director/Business Analyst; Susan Jane Selwood [1965] Director/Teacher; Peter Williams [1969] Director/Commercial and Project Manager

Charminster Farm Limited
Incorporated: 3 November 2016
Net Worth Deficit: £7,297 *Total Assets:* £6,855,088
Registered Office: 22 Ringwood Road, Longahm, Ferndown, Dorset, BH22 9AN
Activities: Development of building projects
Shareholders: Scott Lewis Rawlings; David Lewis Wyatt
Officers: Scott Lewis Rawlings [1975] Director; David Lewis Wyatt [1970] Director

Charter House Investments LLP
Incorporated: 20 August 2008
Net Worth: £81,917 *Total Assets:* £22,911,906
Registered Office: Minerva House, Lower Bristol Road, Bath, BA2 9ER
Officers: James Nicholas John de Savary [1982] Member; Nicholas Charles de Savary [1948] Member

Charter House Planning Limited
Incorporated: 25 June 2014 *Employees:* 12
Net Worth: £139,109 *Total Assets:* £6,032,040
Registered Office: St Mary's House, Netherhampton, Salisbury, Wilts, SP2 8PU
Activities: Other business support service activities n.e.c.
Major Shareholder: Nigel Jeremy Weir
Officers: Mr Neil Trewartha [1971] Director; Nigel Jeremy Weir [1970] Director

Charterbank Capital Limited
Incorporated: 1 July 2011 *Employees:* 3
Net Worth: £1,105,481 *Total Assets:* £6,440,767
Registered Office: 4 Southernhay West, Exeter, EX1 1JG
Activities: Activities of mortgage finance companies
Shareholders: Christopher John Eccles; Louise Sarah Eccles; Tom Neil Branson
Officers: Louise Sarah Eccles, Secretary; Thomas Neil Branson [1979] Director/Surveyor; Christopher John Eccles [1962] Director/Chartered Surveyor

Chatlease Limited
Incorporated: 25 November 1986 *Employees:* 1
Net Worth: £3,531,267 *Total Assets:* £3,765,963
Registered Office: 10 Bridge Street, Christchurch, Dorset, BH23 1EF
Activities: Development of building projects
Major Shareholder: Susan Feld
Officers: Geoffrey Donald Feld, Secretary; Susan Feld [1944] Director

Chatleigh Holdings Limited
Incorporated: 30 January 2013 *Employees:* 3
Net Worth: £14,149,220 *Total Assets:* £20,514,990
Registered Office: St George's Lodge, 33 Oldfield Road, Bath, BA2 3NE
Activities: Activities of head offices
Major Shareholder: David John Medlock
Officers: Peter Phipps, Secretary; David John Medlock [1955] Director; Peter John Medlock [1984] Director

Chatleigh Limited
Incorporated: 18 September 1998 *Employees:* 4
Net Worth: £15,862,702 *Total Assets:* £24,851,314
Registered Office: St Georges Lodge, 33 Oldfield Road, Bath, BA2 3NE
Activities: Activities of head offices
Parent: Chatleigh Holdings Limited
Officers: Peter Phipps, Secretary; David John Medlock [1955] Director; Jacqueline Mary Medlock [1958] Director; Peter John Medlock [1984] Director

The Check House Limited
Incorporated: 3 February 2003 *Employees:* 78
Net Worth: £5,983,795 *Total Assets:* £8,970,912
Registered Office: 50 The Terrace, Torquay, Devon, TQ1 1DD
Activities: Residential care activities for the elderly and disabled
Parent: Cannon Care Homes Ltd
Officers: Jane Canon, Secretary; Robin George Canon [1953] Director

The Chedington Court Estate Limited
Incorporated: 19 January 2017 *Employees:* 3
Net Worth Deficit: £534,508 *Total Assets:* £13,489,405
Registered Office: The Estate Office, Chedington Court, Chedington, Beaminster, Dorset, DT8 3HY
Activities: Activities of other holding companies n.e.c.
Shareholders: Geoffrey William Guy; Katherine Mary Guy
Officers: Russell Adrian Bowyer [1962] Director/Chartered Accountant; Dr Geoffrey William Guy [1954] Director/Doctor and PLC Chairman; Katherine Mary Guy [1959] Housewife and Director

Cheltenham & Gloucester PLC
Incorporated: 23 September 1988 *Employees:* 625
Net Worth: £174,980,992 *Total Assets:* £262,750,000
Registered Office: Barnett Way, Gloucester, GL4 3RL
Activities: Other business support service activities n.e.c.
Parent: Lloyds Bank PLC
Officers: Paul Gittins, Secretary; Robert William Fletcher [1964] Director; Christopher Gowland [1977] Director

Cheltenham Borough Homes Limited
Incorporated: 12 November 2002 *Employees:* 156
Net Worth Deficit: £3,716,000 *Total Assets:* £14,665,000
Registered Office: Cheltenham House, Clarence Street, Cheltenham, Glos, GL50 3JR
Activities: Other business support service activities n.e.c.
Parent: Cheltenham Borough Council
Officers: Helen Price, Secretary; Patricia Ann Blain [1961] Director; Shane Brimfield [1959] Director/House Husband; William Britton-Lewis [1980] Director/BP Employee; David Michael Clowes [1958] Director/Retired; Alison Christine Foster [1959] Director/Self Employed; Jason Charles Langley [1972] Director; Christopher John Mason [1960] Director/Lecturer; Una Marie Pearce-Lynch [1971] Marketing Director; Suzanne Theresa Williams [1962] Director/Councillor

Cheltenham Bournside School and Sixth Form Centre
Incorporated: 10 February 2011 *Employees:* 193
Net Worth: £22,791,620 *Total Assets:* £26,148,552
Registered Office: Warden Hill Road, Cheltenham, Glos, GL51 3EF
Activities: General secondary education
Officers: Alan Francis Hastings, Secretary; Paul Edward John Baker [1950] Finance Director; Julie Dawn Bodilly [1954] Director/Administration Manager; Gareth Burton [1979] Director/Headmaster; Nicola Jane Cox [1964] Director; Kenneth Goodwin [1957] Director/Journalist; William Scott Harvey [1949] Director; Stuart Lee Hutton [1968] Director/Chief Investment Officer; Richard Henry Knight [1955] Director/Solicitor; Antonia Carter Noble [1972] Director/Non-Practising Barrister/Cabinet Member GCC; Andrew Ponting [1952] Director/Business Development Manager; Stephen Michael Reis [1962] Director/IT Consultant; Stephen George Rudge [1952] Director; Katherine Safe [1967] Director/Teacher of Physics; Neil Walter Spurrier [1954] Director/IT Consultant; Susan Margaretta Tovell [1960] Managing Director; Samantha Candida Watson [1966] Director/Charity Fundraising Consultant; Natalie Helen Wheeler [1969] Director/Copywriter

Cheltenham Family Health Care Centre Limited
Incorporated: 6 May 1997
Net Worth: £6,585,356 *Total Assets:* £8,962,649
Registered Office: CFHCC Saint Pauls Medical Centre, 121 Swindon Road, Cheltenham, Glos, GL50 4DP
Activities: General medical practice activities
Officers: Doctor John Henry Batten [1948] Director/General Medical Practitioner; Dr Robert Chapple [1962] Director/General Practitioner; Dr Sally Louise Davies [1963] Director/Doctor; Dr Phillip Donald Fielding [1961] Director/General Practitioner; Dr Peter Thomas Smith [1974] Director/Doctor

Cheltine Limited
Incorporated: 27 July 1914 *Employees:* 9
Net Worth: £28,245,562 *Total Assets:* £35,793,928
Registered Office: 16 Suffolk Parade, Cheltenham, Glos, GL50 2AE
Activities: Other letting and operating of own or leased real estate
Officers: Rachel Isabel Ida Keighley, Secretary; Jane Mary Organ, Secretary; Richard William Holborow [1952] Director/Veterinary Surgeon; Charles Edward Keighley [1950] Director/Manager; John William Keighley [1979] Director/Management Consultant; Rachel Isabel Ida Keighley [1972] Director; Jane Mary Organ [1966] Director; James Alexander Edan Starforth Van Gils [1982] Director/Doctor; Julia Jane Van-Gils [1950] Director

Chelton Limited
Incorporated: 27 January 1967 *Employees:* 378
Net Worth: £39,284,000 *Total Assets:* £66,795,000
Registered Office: Brook Road, Wimborne, Dorset, BH21 2BJ
Activities: Manufacture of communication equipment other than telegraph, and telephone apparatus and equipment
Parent: Lockman Electronic Holdings Limited
Officers: Phillip Dyer, Secretary; Matthew Edward Bealey [1980] Director/Accountant; David Robert Bulley [1980] Director/Vice President & General Manager; Paul Emmanuel Kahn [1966] Director

Chelverton Growth Trust PLC
Incorporated: 8 November 1994
Net Worth: £3,303,000 *Total Assets:* £3,933,000
Registered Office: Suite 8, Bridge House, Courtenay Street, Newton Abbot, Devon, TQ12 2QS
Activities: Activities of investment trusts
Officers: Kevin John Allen [1955] Director/Chartered Accountant; David Alistair Horner [1959] Director/Investment Manager; Ian Paul Martin [1960] Director

Cher Varya Commercial Ltd
Incorporated: 2 December 2014
Net Worth: £314,645 *Total Assets:* £6,208,177
Registered Office: Unit 5 Riverside House, Newham, Truro, Cornwall, TR1 2XN
Activities: Other letting and operating of own or leased real estate
Parent: Cher Varya Group Ltd
Officers: Leigh Raymond Ibbotson [1961] Director; Lesley Sharon Ibbotson [1961] Director

Cheshire Coppice PV Ltd
Incorporated: 3 June 2014
Previous: Sunsave 38 (Cheshire Coppice) Limited
Net Worth Deficit: £340,299 *Total Assets:* £5,336,178
Registered Office: c/o Stephens Scown Secretarial Limited, Osprey House, Malpas Road, Truro, Cornwall, TR1 1UT
Activities: Production of electricity
Parent: BCKRS Borrower Limited
Officers: Thomas Steffen Krupke [1962] Director [German]

Chessington Hotel Limited
Incorporated: 24 January 2006 *Employees:* 204
Net Worth Deficit: £6,637,000 *Total Assets:* £18,446,000
Registered Office: Link House, 25 West Street, Poole, Dorset, BH15 1LD
Activities: Hotels and similar accommodation
Parent: Merlin Entertainments (NBD) Limited
Officers: Fiona Jane Rose, Secretary; Matthew Paul Jowett [1967] Director/General Counsel and Company Secretary; Fraser Montgomery [1970] Director/Accountant; Fiona Jane Rose [1964] Director/Assistant Group Company Secretary

Chessington World of Adventures Operations Limited
Incorporated: 26 February 2007 *Employees:* 3
Net Worth: £8,286,000 *Total Assets:* £8,640,000
Registered Office: Link House, 25 West Street, Poole, Dorset, BH15 1LD
Activities: Activities of amusement parks and theme parks
Parent: Charcoal Holdco Limited
Officers: Fiona Jane Rose, Secretary; Matthew Paul Jowett [1967] Director/General Counsel and Company Secretary; Fiona Jane Rose [1964] Director/Assistant Group Company Secretary

The Chester Abode Limited
Incorporated: 13 January 2006 *Employees:* 75
Net Worth: £12,032,290 *Total Assets:* £12,515,737
Registered Office: 8 Gay Street, Bath, BA1 2PH
Activities: Hotels and similar accommodation
Major Shareholder: Andrew Douglas Brownsword
Officers: Peter Tyrrell, Secretary; Andrew Douglas Brownsword [1947] Director; Jeremy David Hancock [1964] Director; Stephanie Hocking [1966] Director; Peter Tyrrell [1972] Director

Chevron Properties Limited
Incorporated: 22 September 1955
Net Worth: £8,704,790 *Total Assets:* £8,709,590
Registered Office: Narrow Quay House, Narrow Quay, Bristol, BS1 4QA
Activities: Activities of head offices
Major Shareholder: Michael Peter Collins
Officers: Michelle Dawn Rose [1967] Director/Lawyer

Chewton Glen Hotels Limited
Incorporated: 24 November 1965 *Employees:* 334
Net Worth: £11,450,361 *Total Assets:* £26,868,612
Registered Office: Chewton Glen Hotel, New Milton, Hants, BH25 6QS
Activities: Hotels and similar accommodation
Parent: C G Hotel Holding Limited
Officers: Ian Malcolm Livingstone [1962] Director; Andrew William Stembridge [1971] Director/Hotel Manager

CHG Developments (Southampton) Limited
Incorporated: 28 November 2011
Net Worth: £521,169 *Total Assets:* £4,902,852
Registered Office: 37 Commercial Road, Poole, Dorset, BH14 0HU
Activities: Development of building projects
Shareholders: Leslie Aubrey Pink; Jacqueline Pink
Officers: Jacqueline Pink, Secretary; Leslie Aubrey Pink [1947] Director

Chibroco Limited
Incorporated: 25 January 2007
Net Worth: £974,290 *Total Assets:* £4,325,589
Registered Office: 9 Hayward Close, Abbeymead, Gloucester, GL4 4RJ
Activities: Other letting and operating of own or leased real estate
Shareholders: Chi Kin Yip; Chi Hung Yip; Chi Shing Yip; Lai Ha Yip; Yee Fong Yip
Officers: Chi Kin Yip, Secretary/Wholesaler; Chi Hung Yip [1973] Director/Wholesaler; Chi Shing Yip [1979] Director/Wholesaler; Chi Kin Yip [1970] Director/Wholesaler; Lai Ha Yip [1971] Director/Restaurateur; Yee Fong Yip [1975] Director/Restaurateur

Chichester Harbour Hotel Limited
Incorporated: 22 September 2015 *Employees:* 51
Net Worth: £3,798,441 *Total Assets:* £14,930,360
Registered Office: Harbour House, 60 Purewell, Christchurch, Dorset, BH23 1ES
Activities: Hotels and similar accommodation
Parent: Harbour Hotels Group Limited
Officers: Stuart Andrew Bateman [1976] Director; David Francis Robbins [1967] Finance Director; Michael Oliver Warren [1970] Director [Irish]

Chickerell Primary Academy
Incorporated: 28 November 2012 *Employees:* 67
Net Worth: £3,054,326 *Total Assets:* £4,235,298
Registered Office: Chickerell Primary Academy, Rashley Road, Chickerell, Weymouth, Dorset, DT3 4AT
Activities: Primary education
Officers: Catherine Michelle Anders [1981] Director/Teacher; Elisabeth Clare Gray [1961] Director/College Lecturer; Jody Samantha Harris [1970] Director/Principal; Lorraine Mary Llewellyn [1965] Director/Vice Principal; Anne Newell [1972] Director/Firefighter; Simon Nicholas Newport [1975] Director/Transport Manager; Andrew Purnell [1970] Director/Payroll Manager; David Tattersall [1953] Director/Accountant; Stuart Arthur Charles Warren [1973] Director/Project Manager

Chief Vehicle Rentals Limited
Incorporated: 1 February 2001 *Employees:* 105
Net Worth: £1,562,741 *Total Assets:* £11,963,606
Registered Office: The Coachworks, Roundham Road, Paignton, Devon, TQ4 6DS
Activities: Renting and leasing of cars and light motor vehicles
Major Shareholder: Shaun Cunningham
Officers: Emma Louise Prudden, Secretary; Martyn Cresswell [1969] Sales Director; Shaun Cunningham [1970] Managing Director; Emma Louise Prudden [1984] Finance Director [Irish]

Children's Hospice South West
Incorporated: 17 June 1991 *Employees:* 344
Net Worth: £39,897,800 *Total Assets:* £40,879,408
Registered Office: Little Bridge House, Redlands Road, Fremington, Barnstaple, Devon, EX31 2PZ
Activities: Other human health activities
Officers: Jonathan Charles Webber, Secretary; Alan Broughton [1961] Director/Independent Investor; Stephen Lewis Hindley [1949] Director/Executive Chairman; Beverley Horler [1962] Retired Bank Director; Roger John Knight [1955] Director/Retired; Simon Christopher Langton Hewer [1962] Director/Consultant Paediatrician; Nicola Tracey Mason [1963] Director/Marketing Procurement Consultant; Patricia Morris [1952] Director/Management & Training Consultant; Elizabeth Rushton Redfern [1952] Director/Retired Nurse; Karen Elizabeth Vera Rogers [1961] Director/Headteacher; Generald Robert Sones [1955] Director/HR Consultant; David Mark Turner [1961] Director/Solicitor; Damian Nicholas Whittard [1972] Director/Economist

China Fleet Trust
Incorporated: 10 December 2009 *Employees:* 217
Net Worth: £9,236,023 *Total Assets:* £10,893,711
Registered Office: China Fleet Country Club, North Pill, Saltash, Cornwall, PL12 6LJ
Activities: Operation of sports facilities
Officers: Alexander Thomas Sharpe, Secretary; Sarah Catherine Adkins [1965] Director/Solicitor; Robert Alan Seabrook Baldry [1970] Director/Marketing Consultant; Alastair Keith Camp [1956] Director; Ian Robert Douglas [1951] Director; Christopher David Green [1961] Director/Royal Navy Warrant Officer; Gordon Charles Hannah [1973] Director/Royal Navy Warrant Officer; Laura Hodgson [1976] Director/Royal Navy Officer; Robert Edward Lowe [1969] Director/Self Employed; Trevor Mark Smith [1969] Director/Military; Richard Dennis Watts [1962] Business Director; Michael George Wood [1948] Director/Rear Admiral RN Retired, JP

Chinewood Developments Limited
Incorporated: 13 April 2000 *Employees:* 4
Net Worth: £1,425,001 *Total Assets:* £3,550,992
Registered Office: Old Library House, 4 Dean Park Crescent, Bournemouth, BH1 1LY
Activities: Other letting and operating of own or leased real estate
Officers: Clare Ellis, Secretary; Andrew Nicholas Ellis [1954] Director/Surveyor; Edward Thomas Frederick Ellis [1987] Director; James Dominic Marsden Ellis [1980] Director; Nicholas Alexander James Ellis [1982] Director

Chippenham Motor Company Limited
Incorporated: 21 November 1985 *Employees:* 79
Previous: Gemini Motor Company Limited
Net Worth: £2,103,174 *Total Assets:* £9,757,004
Registered Office: Chippenham Motor Company, Bumpers Way, Chippenham, Wilts, SN14 6LF
Activities: Sale, maintenance and repair of motorcycles and related parts and accessories
Major Shareholder: Adam John Bailey
Officers: Lauren Sophie Bailey, Secretary; Adam John Bailey [1967] Director

Chipping Campden School
Incorporated: 23 June 2011 *Employees:* 147
Net Worth: £16,692,000 *Total Assets:* £18,690,000
Registered Office: Chipping Campden School, Cider Mill Lane, Chipping Campden, Glos, GL55 6HU
Activities: General secondary education
Officers: Steven John Donnachie, Secretary; Jane Patricia Annett [1968] Director/School Teacher; David Thomas Betteley [1954] Director/Business Advisor; James William Birch [1961] Director Chartered Engineer; Alison Braithwaite [1971] Director/Marketing Consultant; Sara Jane Chandler [1955] Director/Teacher; Revd Dana Lurkse Delap [1965] Director/Vicar; Melbourne Donald Inman [1957] Director/High Court Judge; Andrew Charles Millroy Jones [1967] Director/Chartered Accountant [Australian]; John Alfred Sanderson [1966] Director; Victor John Scutt [1955] Director/Retired Headteacher; Sally Louise Steele [1972] Director; Andrew John Sunderland [1961] Director; Christopher Walker [1983] Director

Chosen Hill School
Incorporated: 3 March 2011 *Employees:* 185
Net Worth: £14,986,803 *Total Assets:* £17,387,464
Registered Office: Chosen Hill School, Brookfield Road, Churchdown, Gloucester, GL3 2PL
Activities: General secondary education
Officers: Kay Kavanagh, Secretary; Amanda Aston [1970] Director/Performance Manager; Maurice John Edgington [1956] Financial Director; Charlotte Elizabeth Fishlock [1989] Director/Teacher; Kirsten Helen Harrison [1968] Director/Headteacher; Kate Lesley Hemens [1972] Director/Office Manager; Alexander Kirby [1983] Director; Professor Nigel Francis McLoughlin [1968] Director/Higher Education Professional [Irish]; Lucy Moore [1970] Director; Naomi Jayne Murray [1976] Director/Early Years Teacher; William Ralph Parker [1982] Director/Public Sector; Susan Joan Pullen [1951] Director/Farmer's Wife

The Chota Estates Company Limited
Incorporated: 30 December 1983 *Employees:* 2
Net Worth: £10,627,488 *Total Assets:* £11,633,969
Registered Office: Westbury Court, Church Road, Westbury on Trym, Bristol, BS9 3EF
Activities: Growing of cereals (except rice), leguminous crops and oil seeds
Major Shareholder: Paul John Moore
Officers: Margaret Ann Clarke, Secretary; Paul John Moore [1947] Director

Chrisgate Limited
Incorporated: 20 December 1973 *Employees:* 1
Net Worth: £1,027,384 *Total Assets:* £3,896,917
Registered Office: 167 Victoria Road, Swindon, Wilts, SN1 3BU
Activities: Other letting and operating of own or leased real estate
Major Shareholder: Terence Percy Cain
Officers: Peter John Hulance, Secretary; Terence Percy Cain [1947] Director/Property Consultant

Christ Church C of E Primary School
Incorporated: 24 May 2012 *Employees:* 36
Net Worth: £9,715,302 *Total Assets:* £10,345,664
Registered Office: Royal Park, Clifton, Bristol, BS8 3AW
Activities: Primary education
Officers: Tamara Jordan, Secretary; Guy Adams [1966] Director/Barrister; Jessica Baum [1979] Director/Mother; Sarah Louise Blakeston [1971] Director/Pharmaceutical Consultant; Jayne Coller [1958] Director/Teacher; Anneliese Jane Crabb [1977] Director/Human Resources Consultant; Christopher Stephen Duncan [1958] Director/Design Company Owner; Elizabeth Amy Gray [1979] Director/Environmental Consultant; Georgina Jacintha Fleetwood Harford [1951] Director/Retired Teacher; Clare Jones [1970] Director/Headteacher; Victoria Richardson [1979] Director/Teacher; Amar Shah [1963] Director/Optician [Indian]; Rev Neil Edward Shepherd [1977] Director/Curate; Thomas James Skirrow [1980] Director of Operations, Tree Aid; Dr Axel Walther [1968] Director/Doctor [German]

Christ Church C of E Primary School (Cheltenham)
Incorporated: 11 October 2012 *Employees:* 26
Net Worth: £3,758,412 *Total Assets:* £4,123,733
Registered Office: Christ Church C of E Primary School, Malvern Road, Cheltenham, Glos, GL50 2NR
Activities: Primary education
Officers: Dianne Lynne Hibbert, Secretary; Duncan Cook [1976] Director/Headteacher; Matthew Charles Jenkins [1969] Director/Civil Servant; Ian Kirkwood [1946] Director/Retired; Susan Terese Lee [1946] Director/Retired; Reverend Timothy James Edward Mayfield [1960] Director/Clergy; Jennifer Ann Norman [1948] Director/Retired Teacher; Susan Elizabeth Padfield [1943] Director/Retired School Teacher; Carolyn Marianne Parikos [1972] Director/Pharmacist; Daniel Parker [1980] Director/Information Officer; Kate Elizabeth Thomson [1966] Director/Senior Lecturer; Louise Helena Osmond Treloar [1966] Director/Kitchen Assistant; Julia Elizabeth Walker [1977] Director/Teacher

Christchurch Fairmile Village LLP
Incorporated: 19 September 2014 *Employees:* 68
Net Worth: £11,640,707 *Total Assets:* £12,816,643
Registered Office: Russell House, Oxford Road, Bournemouth, BH8 8EX

Christchurch Hotels Ltd
Incorporated: 29 August 2002 *Employees:* 111
Net Worth: £3,800,537 *Total Assets:* £33,294,980
Registered Office: Harbour House, 60 Purewell, Christchurch, Dorset, BH23 1ES
Activities: Hotels and similar accommodation
Parent: Harbour Hotels Group Limited
Officers: Stuart Andrew Bateman [1976] Director; David Francis Robbins [1967] Finance Director; Michael Oliver Warren [1970] Director [Irish]

Chronos Technology Limited
Incorporated: 18 September 1986
Net Worth: £3,432,629 *Total Assets:* £5,431,242
Registered Office: Stowfield House, Upper Stowfield, Lydbrook, Glos, GL17 9PD
Activities: Other telecommunications activities
Shareholders: Charles William Townshend Curry; Angela Miriam Curry
Officers: Joanne Akers, Secretary; Angela Miriam Curry [1951] Director/Teacher; Charles William Townshend Curry [1952] Director/Chairman

Chulmleigh Academy Trust
Incorporated: 8 July 2011 *Employees:* 148
Net Worth: £12,034,009 *Total Assets:* £15,091,957
Registered Office: c/o Chulmleigh Community College, Chulmleigh, Devon, EX18 7AA
Activities: Primary education
Officers: Christina Anne Harrison, Secretary; Stephen Charles Baber [1953] Director/Retired; Keith Austin Greenwood [1963] Director/Management Retail; Michael Edward Johnson [1966] Director/Headteacher; Timothy John Coates Newman [1966] Managing Director; Paul Keith Osborne [1972] Director; Nina Nancy Philips [1973] Director; Adrian Wade [1971] Director; Dr Martin James White [1958] Director; Paul Keith Winter [1950] Director/Leadership Mentor/Development Consultant; David John Worden [1958] Director/Retired Teacher

M J Church (Plant) Limited
Incorporated: 19 October 1984 *Employees:* 327
Net Worth: £10,148,784 *Total Assets:* £26,923,528
Registered Office: Star Farm, Marshfield, Chippenham, Wilts, SN14 8LH
Activities: Remediation activities and other waste management services
Shareholders: Paula Jean Church; Michael John Church
Officers: Paula Jean Church, Secretary; Michael John Church [1952] Director/Plant Hire Contractor; Paula Jean Church [1955] Director/Housewife

Church Farm Publow LLP
Incorporated: 15 July 2010 *Employees:* 1
Net Worth: £4,985,971 *Total Assets:* £5,139,820
Registered Office: Ground Floor, 11 Manvers Street, Bath, BA1 1JQ
Officers: Joanna Patricia Dawe [1951] Member; Keith William Dawe [1950] Member

M J Church Properties Limited
Incorporated: 26 September 1997 *Employees:* 2
Net Worth: £2,156,099 *Total Assets:* £7,335,589
Registered Office: Star Farm, Marshfield, Chippenham, Wilts, SN14 8LH
Activities: Other letting and operating of own or leased real estate
Shareholders: Michael John Church; Paula Jean Church
Officers: Paula Jean Church, Secretary; Michael John Church [1952] Director; Paula Jean Church [1955] Director

Churcham Homes Holdings Limited
Incorporated: 26 May 2017 *Employees:* 4
Net Worth: £4,014,057 *Total Assets:* £5,666,357
Registered Office: Staverton Court, Staverton, Cheltenham, Glos, GL51 0UX
Activities: Activities of other holding companies n.e.c.
Shareholders: Stuart Duncan Hall; Graham James Hall
Officers: Ashley John Hall [1988] Director; Graham James Hall [1964] Director; James Stuart Hall [1987] Director; Stuart Duncan Hall [1961] Director

Churchdown School
Incorporated: 14 September 2011 *Employees:* 133
Net Worth: £19,538,062 *Total Assets:* £23,069,110
Registered Office: Winston Road, Churchdown, Gloucester, GL3 2RB
Activities: General secondary education
Officers: Shaun Anthony Lloyd, Secretary; Susan Elizabeth Belinfante [1959] Director/Teacher; Christopher John Belli [1975] Director/Headteacher; Patricia Church [1967] Director/Teacher; Simon Deane Ireland [1956] Director/Civil Servant; Matthew Peter Long [1967] Director/Plumber; Mark Perkins [1973] Director/Air Traffic Controller; Marie Walker [1957] Director/Retired; David Russell White [1966] Director/Senior Programme Manager; Christopher John Widden [1952] Director/Retired; Ian Tremayne Willoughby [1953] Director/Site Manager at Junior School; Jane Wooler [1965] Director/Senior Science Technician

Churchill Academy
Incorporated: 29 June 2011 *Employees:* 169
Net Worth: £18,915,132 *Total Assets:* £23,023,164
Registered Office: Churchill Academy & Sixth Form, Churchill Green, Churchill, Somerset, BS25 5QN
Activities: General secondary education
Officers: Christopher Rollo Hildrew, Secretary; Yolanda Valerie Chadwick [1972] Director/Teacher; Jecetinne Shen-Ju Chen-Taylor [1967] Director/Architect; Jonathan David Dewey [1966] Director/Copywriter/Communications Consultant; Christopher Stephen George [1959] Director/Retired Teacher; Ben Hardy [1978] Managing Director; Christopher Hildrew [1974] Director/Headteacher; Matthew Robert Johnson [1969] Director/Independent Financial Adviser; Jonathan Lawrence [1969] Director/IT Consultant; Louise Jocelyn Malik [1969] Director/Finance; Susan Jacqueline Marshall [1965] Director/Teacher; Margaret Baird Brown Mooney [1947] Director/Retired Headteacher; Anne Kathryn Oakley [1953] Director/Retired; Rachel Elizabeth Thompson [1964] Director/Sixth Form Manager; Andrew Terry Titerickx [1966] Director/Senior Project Manager; Sarah Marie Tucker [1987] Director/Teacher

Churchill Retirement (Group) Limited
Incorporated: 23 November 1984 *Employees:* 3
Net Worth: £76,270,000 *Total Assets:* £76,395,000
Registered Office: Churchill House, Parkside, Ringwood, Hants, BH24 3SG
Activities: Buying and selling of own real estate
Parent: Churchill Retirement PLC
Officers: Darren Mark Riley, Secretary; Dean Marlow [1971] Director/Accountant; Clinton James McCarthy [1964] Director/Builder; Spencer John McCarthy [1966] Director/Builder

Churchill Retirement Living Limited
Incorporated: 25 May 2007 *Employees:* 344
Net Worth: £105,086,000 *Total Assets:* £322,105,984
Registered Office: Churchill House, Parkside, Ringwood, Hants, BH24 3SG
Activities: Construction of domestic buildings
Parent: Churchill Retirement (Group) Limited
Officers: Darren Mark Riley, Secretary; Dean Marlow [1971] Director/Accountant; Clinton James McCarthy [1964] Director; Spencer John McCarthy [1966] Director; Martin Anthony Young [1954] Regional Managing Director

Churchill Retirement PLC
Incorporated: 3 November 2010 *Employees:* 594
Net Worth: £160,030,000 *Total Assets:* £349,361,984
Registered Office: Churchill House, Parkside, Ringwood, Hants, BH24 3SG
Activities: Buying and selling of own real estate
Shareholders: John Sidney McCarthy; Gwendoline Joan McCarthy
Officers: Darren Mark Riley, Secretary; Simon Hunter Boadle [1958] Director/Financial Adviser; Rodney Michael Harrison [1948] Director; Dean Marlow [1971] Director/Accountant; Clinton James McCarthy [1964] Director/Builder; John Sidney McCarthy [1939] Director; Spencer John McCarthy [1966] Director/Builder; William Alder Oliver [1956] Director; Martin Anthony Young [1954] Director

Churngold Construction Holdings Limited
Incorporated: 13 August 2001 *Employees:* 176
Net Worth: £2,797,000 *Total Assets:* £10,686,000
Registered Office: St Andrews House, St Andrews Road, Bristol, BS11 9DQ
Activities: Activities of head offices
Officers: James Ross Ancell [1953] Director [British/New Zealander]; Martin Glyn Best [1966] Director; Andrew Robert Brown [1964] Managing Director; Richard Kevin McCabe [1962] Director; Robert Neil Vaughan Mead [1983] Director; Timothy Stuart Ross [1948] Director

Churngold Construction Limited
Incorporated: 25 April 1985 *Employees:* 176
Net Worth: £2,461,000 *Total Assets:* £9,047,000
Registered Office: St Andrews House, St Andrews Road, Avonmouth, Bristol, BS11 9DQ
Activities: Construction of commercial buildings
Parent: Churngold Construction Holdings Limited
Officers: James Ross Ancell [1953] Director [British/New Zealander]; Martin Glyn Best [1966] Director; Andrew Robert Brown [1964] Managing Director; Richard Kevin McCabe [1962] Director; Robert Neil Vaughan Mead [1983] Director; Robert John Roughley [1981] Director

Churston Ferrers Grammar School
Incorporated: 22 November 2010 *Employees:* 93
Net Worth: £10,237,430 *Total Assets:* £12,363,178
Registered Office: Churston Ferrers Grammar School, Greenway Road, Brixham, Devon, TQ5 0LN
Activities: General secondary education
Officers: Vanessa Wolf, Secretary; Rachael Donna Brooks [1985] Director/Teacher; Steven Paul Caunter [1968] Director/Assistant Principal - Education; Matthew Cooper [1984] Director/Solicitor; Holly Jane Godsland [1991] Director/Teacher; Adrian Frances Handley [1968] Managing Director; Roni Jay [1961] Director/Writer; Elizabeth Anne Loly [1977] Director/Communications Consultant; Daniel James Mitchell [1975] Quantity Surveyor/Director; Tracey Pamela Morris [1969] Director/HR Project Manager; Robert James Owers [1964] Director/Headteacher; Robert Tyler [1970] Director

CIL Management Consultants Limited
Incorporated: 26 May 2004 *Employees:* 86
Net Worth: £5,302,951 *Total Assets:* £9,735,920
Registered Office: 12 Kingsway, Frome, Somerset, BA11 1BT
Activities: Management consultancy activities other than financial management
Parent: CIL Strategy Consultants Limited
Officers: Laura Jane Robertson, Secretary; Sebastian George Chambers [1967] Director; Thomas Fletcher [1979] Director/Management Consultant; Giles Johnson [1969] Director/Management Consultant; Alexander Marshall [1976] Director/Management Consultant; Laura Jane Robertson [1966] Director/Accountant; Jonathan Paul Whiteman [1978] Director/Consultant

The Cinnamon Trust
Incorporated: 29 August 2009 *Employees:* 79
Net Worth: £34,946,020 *Total Assets:* £35,066,008
Registered Office: 10 Market Square, Hayle, Cornwall, TR27 4HE
Activities: Social work activities without accommodation for the elderly and disabled
Officers: Dale William Band [1976] Director/Solicitor; John Richard Dale [1953] Director/Graphic Designer; Averil Regina Jarvis [1945] Director/Charity Chief Executive

Cipher Corp Holding Ltd
Incorporated: 6 February 2014 *Employees:* 1
Previous: Cipher Corp Ltd
Net Worth Deficit: £20,241 *Total Assets:* £4,342,228
Registered Office: Third Floor, 95 The Promenade, Cheltenham, Glos, GL50 1HH
Activities: Ready-made interactive leisure and entertainment software development
Major Shareholder: John Francis Weston Hunt
Officers: John Francis Weston Hunt [1963] Director/Entrepreneur [Irish]

Circadian Trust
Incorporated: 7 March 2005 *Employees:* 269
Net Worth Deficit: £1,155,242 *Total Assets:* £4,657,912
Registered Office: Bradley Stoke Leisure Centre, Bradley Stoke, Bristol, BS32 9BS
Activities: Operation of sports facilities
Officers: Juliet Kilty, Secretary; Philip David Boobier [1960] Director/Retired; Anthony William Stuart Davis [1949] Director/Councillor; Adrian Jeffrey Dawe [1956] Director/Chartered Surveyor; Benjamin James Hilton [1977] Director of Programmes; Suzanna Hinnell [1975] Director/Consultant; Neil Lorne McKen [1969] Director/Associate Lecturer; Mary Kathrine Morris [1948] Director/Councillor; Janet Eileen Raven [1957] Director/Performance Pastoral Supervisor; Derek Segger [1958] Director/Head of Plant Service Centre; Roland George Sims [1954] Director/Retired; Susan Timbrell [1964] Director/Clerical; Peter Tuodolo [1974] Director/Logistics Assistant [Nigerian]; Patrick Maico Van Beek [1974] Director/Actuary [Dutch]; Robert David Wimbush [1966] Director/Client Relationship Manager

Cirencester Kingshill School
Incorporated: 29 June 2011 *Employees:* 108
Net Worth: £11,519,236 *Total Assets:* £12,744,945
Registered Office: Cirencester Kingshill School, Kingshill Lane, Cirencester, Glos, GL7 1HS
Activities: General secondary education
Officers: Sarah Gardiner, Secretary; Rene Peter Blamey [1981] Director/Head of Operations; Claire Marie Cleaver [1973] Director/Teacher; Karen Fraser [1963] Director/Vice Principal Further Education; Penelope Rosemarie Hicks [1969] Director/Careers Coordinator; Valerie June Hindson [1964] Director/Project Manager; Andrew Robert Johnson [1946] Director/Retired Schoolteacher; Colin Stephen O'Hare [1949] Director/Examinations Officer; Christine Sophia Oates [1960] Director/Headteacher; Elizabeth Ann Owen Reed [1946] Director of Customer Services; Maureen Richards [1952] Director/Careers Adviser; Nigel Philip Robbins [1945] Director/County and District Councillor; Sebastian Gerard MacKenzie Thomas [1989] Director/Teacher; David Walklett [1952] Director/Retired

Cirrus Communication Systems Limited
Incorporated: 21 August 1979 *Employees:* 153
Net Worth: £1,062,977 *Total Assets:* £7,953,356
Registered Office: Queensway House, 11 Queensway, New Milton, Hants, BH25 5NR
Activities: Other specialised construction activities n.e.c.
Parent: Careline UK Monitoring Limited
Officers: Tim Barclay [1964] Director/Chief Executive; Craig Barlow [1984] Finance Director

City Eco Hotel Limited
Incorporated: 3 May 2006 *Employees:* 40
Net Worth: £188,630 *Total Assets:* £3,641,056
Registered Office: 4 Grove Road, Bournemouth, BH1 3AX
Activities: Hotels and similar accommodation
Shareholder: Christopher Daivd Lewis Airey
Officers: Sarah Burrows, Secretary; Christopher David Lewis Airey [1972] Managing Director; Sarah Burrows [1965] Director; Harish Gordhandas Sodha [1953] Director

City Monument Properties Limited
Incorporated: 18 September 2009 *Employees:* 1
Net Worth: £533,531 *Total Assets:* £5,682,146
Registered Office: 2 Temple Back East, Temple Quay, Bristol, BS1 6EG
Activities: Construction of commercial buildings
Parent: City & West End Properties Limited
Officers: Kay Patrick Despard [1958] Director/Chartered Surveyor

City West Commercials Limited
Incorporated: 6 February 2009 *Employees:* 144
Net Worth: £911,808 *Total Assets:* £20,768,740
Registered Office: City West Commercials Ltd, Kings Weston Lane, St Andrews Road, Avonmouth, Bristol, BS11 9BY
Activities: Sale of new cars and light motor vehicles
Shareholders: Nigel Preston Smith; Gilbran (Management) Limited
Officers: Graeson Clarke, Secretary; Graeson John Clarke [1970] Director/Dealer Principal; Jennifer Hutchings [1983] Director/Financial Controller; Paul Richmond Ridout [1977] Truck Sales Director; Nigel Preston Smith [1967] Director; Darren Richard Sweet [1971] Group Aftersales Director

City West Country Limited
Incorporated: 17 October 2001 *Employees:* 398
Net Worth: £15,851,000 *Total Assets:* £79,064,000
Registered Office: c/o Mercedes Benz of Exeter, Matford Park Road, Exeter, EX2 8FD
Activities: Sale of new cars and light motor vehicles
Officers: Michael Anthony Wickins, Secretary/Director; Gavin Robert Walker [1967] Finance Director; Anthony John Wickins [1951] Director; Michael Anthony Wickins [1970] Director

Civitas SPV1 Limited
Incorporated: 9 December 2016
Net Worth: £45,972,660 *Total Assets:* £69,649,712
Registered Office: Beaufort House, 51 New North Road, Exeter, EX4 4EP
Activities: Activities of real estate investment trusts
Parent: Civitas Social Housing PLC
Officers: Paul Ralph Bridge [1970] Director; Graham Charles Peck [1986] Director; Thomas Clifford Pridmore [1972] Director

Civitas SPV18 Limited
Incorporated: 4 January 2017
Net Worth: £3,132,734 *Total Assets:* £5,350,312
Registered Office: Beaufort House, 51 New North Road, Exeter, EX4 4EP
Activities: Buying and selling of own real estate
Parent: Civitas Social Housing PLC
Officers: Paul Ralph Bridge [1970] Director; Graham Charles Peck [1986] Director

Civitas SPV2 Limited
Incorporated: 9 April 2016
Net Worth: £6,740,220 *Total Assets:* £9,453,614
Registered Office: Beaufort House, 51 New North Road, Exeter, EX4 4EP
Activities: Buying and selling of own real estate
Officers: Paul Ralph Bridge [1970] Director; Graham Charles Peck [1986] Director; Thomas Clifford Pridmore [1972] Director

Civitas SPV20 Limited
Incorporated: 27 January 2017
Net Worth: £4,593,156 *Total Assets:* £7,721,756
Registered Office: Beaufort House, 51 New North Road, Exeter, EX4 4EP
Activities: Buying and selling of own real estate
Parent: Civitas Social Housing PLC
Officers: Paul Ralph Bridge [1970] Director; Graham Charles Peck [1986] Director

Civitas SPV3 Limited
Incorporated: 29 April 2016
Net Worth: £3,185,082 *Total Assets:* £5,330,408
Registered Office: Beaufort House, 51 New North Road, Exeter, EX4 4EP
Activities: Buying and selling of own real estate
Parent: Civitas Social Housing PLC
Officers: Paul Ralph Bridge [1970] Director; Graham Charles Peck [1986] Director; Thomas Clifford Pridmore [1972] Director

Civitas SPV33 Limited
Incorporated: 4 January 2017
Net Worth: £2,671,986 *Total Assets:* £3,889,007
Registered Office: Beaufort House, 51 New North Road, Exeter, EX4 4EP
Activities: Buying and selling of own real estate
Parent: Civitas Social Housing PLC
Officers: Paul Ralph Bridge [1970] Director; Graham Charles Peck [1986] Director

Civitas SPV36 Limited
Incorporated: 27 January 2017
Net Worth: £3,413,823 *Total Assets:* £5,880,096
Registered Office: Beaufort House, 51 New North Road, Exeter, EX4 4EP
Activities: Buying and selling of own real estate
Parent: Civitas Social Housing PLC
Officers: Paul Ralph Bridge [1970] Director; Graham Charles Peck [1986] Director

Civitas SPV39 Limited
Incorporated: 4 January 2017
Net Worth: £5,265,137 *Total Assets:* £6,999,726
Registered Office: Beaufort House, 51 New North Road, Exeter, EX4 4EP
Activities: Buying and selling of own real estate
Parent: Civitas Social Housing PLC
Officers: Paul Ralph Bridge [1970] Director; Graham Charles Peck [1986] Director

Civitas SPV44 Limited
Incorporated: 27 January 2017
Net Worth: £13,379,697 *Total Assets:* £13,379,697
Registered Office: Beaufort House, 51 New North Road, Exeter, EX4 4EP
Activities: Buying and selling of own real estate
Parent: Civitas Social Housing PLC
Officers: Paul Ralph Bridge [1970] Director; Graham Charles Peck [1986] Director

CJ Room Ltd
Incorporated: 4 August 2014 *Employees:* 442
Net Worth: £1,787,082 *Total Assets:* £11,611,427
Registered Office: McDonalds Restaurant, Great Western Way, Cockleberry Roundabout, Swindon, Wilts, SN2 1US
Activities: Unlicenced restaurants and cafes
Major Shareholder: Carl Room
Officers: Julie Ann Room, Secretary; Carl Room [1967] Director

CKF Systems Limited
Incorporated: 14 June 1988 *Employees:* 30
Net Worth: £1,522,914 *Total Assets:* £4,524,075
Registered Office: Pavilion, 1 Olympus Park, Quedgeley, Gloucester, GL2 4NF
Activities: Manufacture of lifting and handling equipment
Parent: CKF Holdings Limited
Officers: Paul Michael Swift, Secretary/Director; Paul Michael Swift [1961] Director; Bryan Stephen Wheeler [1958] Director

R L Clapp and Sons (Cheesemakers) Limited
Incorporated: 12 June 1974 *Employees:* 28
Net Worth: £4,659,624 *Total Assets:* £10,271,479
Registered Office: West Town House Farm, Baltonsborough, Glastonbury, Somerset, BA6 8RH
Activities: Liquid milk and cream production
Shareholders: Louise Frances Clapp; Simon Anthony Clapp
Officers: Louise Frances Clapp, Secretary; Jason Martin Heal, Secretary; Robert William Andrew Clapp [1975] Director/Farmer; Robert George Colston Clapp [1949] Director/Farmer; Simon Anthony Clapp [1963] Director/Farmer

Clarart Ltd
Incorporated: 19 October 2016 *Employees:* 3
Net Worth: £48,943,568 *Total Assets:* £60,421,900
Registered Office: Down Farm, Westonbirt, Tetbury, Glos, GL8 8QW
Activities: Development of building projects
Officers: Emma Claire Tomlinson [1974] Director/Veterinary Surgeon; Luke George Tomlinson [1977] Director and Professional Sport; Mark Lascelles Telford Tomlinson [1982] Director/Professional Polo Player

Claremont Ferrand Limited
Incorporated: 8 October 2002 *Employees:* 7
Previous: Claremont Homes and Property Limited
Net Worth: £1,904,621 *Total Assets:* £7,031,964
Registered Office: Springfield House, 45 Welsh Back, Bristol, BS1 4AG
Activities: Other letting and operating of own or leased real estate
Shareholders: Kerry Ann Davidson; Scott Matthew Davidson
Officers: Scott Matthew Davidson, Secretary; Kerry Ann Davidson [1965] Director; Riley Mae Davidson [1993] Director; Scott Matthew Davidson [1963] Director; Shaw Ellis Davidson [1995] Director/Illustrator; MacKenzie Florence Taylor [1990] Director

Clarence Court Eggs Limited
Incorporated: 30 July 1971 *Employees:* 4
Net Worth: £15,058,422 *Total Assets:* £18,138,526
Registered Office: Whiteoaks Farm, The Old Sidings, Corsham Road, Lacock, Chippenham, Wilts, SN15 2LZ
Activities: Raising of poultry
Parent: Stonegate Holdings Limited
Officers: James David Sheppard, Secretary; Adrian David Gott [1981] Director; James David Sheppard [1963] Director

Clarity Copiers Limited
Incorporated: 30 August 1977 *Employees:* 20
Net Worth: £4,964,115 *Total Assets:* £6,765,832
Registered Office: Clarity House, Collett Way, Newton Abbot, Devon, TQ12 4PH
Activities: Other retail sale in non-specialised stores
Parent: LJ (Copiers) Limited
Officers: Leo Thomas Whittington, Secretary; John Eldridge [1951] Director; Leo Thomas Whittington [1946] Director

C. & J. Clark (Holdings) Limited
Incorporated: 16 November 1903
Net Worth: £130,600,000 *Total Assets:* £275,400,000
Registered Office: 40 High Street, Street, Somerset, BA16 0EQ
Activities: Other business support service activities n.e.c.
Parent: C & J Clark (No 1) Limited
Officers: Elaine Ann Evans, Secretary; Stella Julie David [1962] Director; Paul Mark Kenyon [1963] Finance Director; Paul Antony Wakefield [1967] Director/Solicitor

C & J Clark (No 1) Limited
Incorporated: 1 April 1997
Net Worth: £50,300,000 *Total Assets:* £119,000,000
Registered Office: 40 High Street, Street, Somerset, BA16 0EQ
Activities: Other service activities n.e.c.
Parent: C & J Clark Limited
Officers: Elaine Ann Evans, Secretary; Paul Mark Kenyon [1963] Finance Director; Paul Antony Wakefield [1967] Director/Solicitor

C. & J. Clark (Street) Limited
Incorporated: 17 December 1992
Net Worth: £586 *Total Assets:* £4,102,598
Registered Office: 40 High Street, Street, Somerset, BA16 0EQ
Activities: Activities of head offices
Parent: C & J Clark (Holdings) Limited
Officers: Elaine Ann Evans, Secretary; Neil John Sherman [1975] Director/Accountant; Paul Antony Wakefield [1967] Director/Solicitor

Matthew Clark Bibendum (Holdings) Limited
Incorporated: 1 March 2007 *Employees:* 1,920
Previous: Matthew Clark (Holdings) Limited
Net Worth Deficit: £58,814,000 *Total Assets:* £294,212,000
Registered Office: Whitchurch Lane, Whitchurch, Bristol, BS14 0JZ
Activities: Activities of head offices
Parent: C & C Holdings (NI) Limited
Officers: Andrea Pozzi [1971] Director/Group Chief Operating Officer; Ewan Robertson [1982] Finance Director; Jonathan Solesbury [1965] Director/Group Chief Financial Officer

Matthew Clark Bibendum Limited
Incorporated: 23 October 1990 *Employees:* 1,793
Previous: Conviviality Group Limited
Net Worth Deficit: £48,134,000 *Total Assets:* £302,287,008
Registered Office: Whitchurch Lane, Bristol, BS14 0JZ
Activities: Wholesale of wine, beer, spirits and other alcoholic beverages
Parent: Matthew Clark Bibendum (Holdings) Limited
Officers: Andrea Pozzi [1971] Director/Group Chief Operating Officer; Ewan James Robertson [1982] Finance Director; Jonathan Solesbury [1965] Director/Group Chief Financial Officer

Clark Holdings (UK) Limited
Incorporated: 28 May 2013
Net Worth: £178,856 *Total Assets:* £4,099,988
Registered Office: Unit 2 Milsom Street, Cheltenham, Glos, GL50 4BA
Activities: Activities of extraterritorial organisations and bodies
Major Shareholder: Antony Barrie Clark
Officers: Antony Barrie Clark [1968] Director/Hotelier

Clark Holt Limited
Incorporated: 14 November 2013 *Employees:* 24
Net Worth: £753,447 *Total Assets:* £4,010,171
Registered Office: Hardwick House, Prospect Place, Swindon, Wilts, SN1 3LJ
Activities: Solicitors
Officers: Jonathan Mark Cape Ashbridge [1965] Director/Solicitor; Rachel Booth [1965] Director/Solicitor; Jeremy Martin Holt [1956] Director/Solicitor; Philip Mark Glyn Humphreys [1965] Director/Solicitor; Peter Robin James [1959] Director/Solicitor; Joseph Edward Gabriel Lewis [1977] Director/Solicitor; James Alexander Thorpe [1975] Director/Solicitor; Karron Whitter [1969] Director/Solicitor

C. & J. Clark International Limited
Incorporated: 17 July 1915 *Employees:* 9,553
Net Worth: £267,100,000 *Total Assets:* £756,899,968
Registered Office: 40 High Street, Street, Somerset, BA16 0EQ
Activities: Retail sale of footwear in specialised stores
Parent: C & J Clark (Holdings) Limited
Officers: Paul Antony Wakefield, Secretary; Stella Julie David [1962] Director; Paul Mark Kenyon [1963] Finance Director; Neil John Sherman [1975] Director/Accountant

C & J Clark Limited
Incorporated: 6 February 1997 *Employees:* 13,897
Net Worth: £503,900,000 *Total Assets:* £999,000,000
Registered Office: 40 High Street, Street, Somerset, BA16 0EQ
Activities: Other business support service activities n.e.c.
Officers: Paul Antony Wakefield, Secretary; Lucien Achille Alziari [1959] Director/Chief Human Resources Officer; Peter Alexander Clark [1968] Director/Executive [American]; Tanya Rose Cordrey [1966] Director/Digital Consultant; Stella Julie David [1962] Director; Paul Mark Kenyon [1963] Finance Director; Benjamin Lovell [1950] Director [American]; Thomas O'Neill [1952] Director [American]; Tobias Gunter Zimmerer [1967] Director/Shoe Technician [German]

Francis Clark LLP
Incorporated: 30 September 2009 *Employees:* 608
Net Worth: £7,716,000 *Total Assets:* £22,381,000
Registered Office: Sigma House, Oak View Close, Edginswell Park, Torquay, Devon, TQ2 7FF
Officers: Andrew Greenwood Allen [1975] Member; Michael Scott Bentley [1968] Member; Stephen John Collins [1951] Member; Nicholas Stuart Cowen [1961] Member; Nicholas Charles Farrant [1980] Member; Nicholas Henry Wyard Gooch [1966] Member; Sean Andrew Grinsted [1968] Member; Christopher Lewis Hicks [1966] Member; Andrew Henry Richards [1961] Member; James Ian Robinson [1970] Member; Martin John Aldridge [1964] LLP Member; Simon Mark Anslow [1963] LLP Member; Martin Lee Atkins [1978] LLP Member; Sharon Kathleen Austen [1971] LLP Member; Lewis John Banfield [1972] LLP Member; James Matthew Barrett [1975] LLP Member; Holly Anne Bedford [1970] LLP Member; Luke Mervyn Bennett [1963] LLP Member; Karen Ann Bowen [1966] LLP Member; Ivan Leslie Burnard [1964] LLP Member; Paul Andrew Butler [1979] LLP Member; Samuel James Chapman [1980] LLP Member; Lucinda Clare Coleman [1982] LLP Member; Paul Andrew Collings [1975] LLP Member; Paul David Crocker [1967] LLP Member; Jonathan Leonard Endacott [1967] LLP Member; Gordon Peter Fox [1963] LLP Member; Anne-Marie Gates [1964] LLP Member; Paul Christopher Giessler [1965] LLP Member; Mark Andrew Greaves [1967] LLP Member; Brian Harvey [1978] LLP Member; Stephanie Jane Henshaw [1962] LLP Member; Martin John Hobbs [1969] LLP Member; Stephen James Hobson [1958] LLP Member; Giles Duncan Hutchings [1972] LLP Member; Mark Andrew Johns [1965] LLP Member; James Andrew Hugh Killick [1965] LLP Member; Damian Edward Lannon [1968] LLP Member; Duncan Leslie [1972] LLP Member; Martin Peter Lock [1965] LLP Member; Jason Mitchell [1977] LLP Member; Glenn William Greig Nicol [1974] LLP Member; Paul Anthony O'Connell [1961] LLP Member; Susan Margaret Probyn [1960] LLP Member; Thomas William Roach [1974] LLP Member; Stuart Andrew Rogers [1977] LLP Member; John Neil Rowe [1963] LLP Member; Daniel John Sladen [1978] LLP Member; Julian Richard Smith [1960] LLP Member; Andrew Raymond Squires [1969] LLP Member; Daniel John Tout [1983] LLP Member; Julie Ann Towers [1962] LLP Member; David Keith Watton [1956] LLP Member; David Andrew Williams [1955] LLP Member; Michael Benjamin Wilson [1956] LLP Member

C. & J. Clark Overseas Limited
Incorporated: 3 January 1968
Net Worth: £27,300,000 *Total Assets:* £29,000,000
Registered Office: 40 High Street, Street, Somerset, BA16 0EQ
Activities: Manufacture of footwear
Parent: C & J Clark (Holdings) Limited
Officers: Paul Antony Wakefield, Secretary; Stella Julie David [1962] Director; Paul Mark Kenyon [1963] Finance Director

Clark Projects 12 Limited
Incorporated: 26 November 2013
Net Worth Deficit: £15,721 *Total Assets:* £6,232,215
Registered Office: Link House, 25 West Street, Poole, Dorset, BH15 1LD
Activities: Buying and selling of own real estate
Parent: Clark Estates (UK) Ltd
Officers: Stephen Geoffrey Siggs, Secretary; Marc Eric Clark [1968] Director; Stephen Geoffrey Siggs [1954] Director/Accountant

Clarkson Evans Limited
Incorporated: 17 September 1999 *Employees:* 707
Net Worth: £5,699,626 *Total Assets:* £16,751,753
Registered Office: Meteor Business Park, Cheltenham Road East, Gloucester, GL2 9QL
Activities: Electrical installation
Shareholders: Stephen Paul Evans; Sue Evans
Officers: Timothy Peter Dennis Bisp [1976] Commercial Director; Paula Kirsten Bradshaw [1968] Finance Director; Nathan Evans [1975] Business Development Director; Stephen Paul Evans [1956] Managing Director; Leigh Edwin Mason [1966] Technical Director; Lindsey Bettine Young [1978] Director/Chief Operating Officer

Class 06 Limited
Incorporated: 16 June 2006
Net Worth: £2 *Total Assets:* £7,311,075
Registered Office: Third Floor, Broad Quay House, Prince Street, Bristol, BS1 4DJ
Activities: Non-trading company
Parent: Class 98 Limited
Officers: Kenneth Andrew McLellan [1961] Regional Project Director; Alan Campbell Ritchie [1967] Director

Claverton Estates Ltd.
Incorporated: 24 March 1999 *Employees:* 3
Net Worth: £7,430,828 *Total Assets:* £8,188,546
Registered Office: 16 Whiteladies Road, Clifton, Bristol, BS8 2LG
Activities: Buying and selling of own real estate
Parent: Claverton Holdings Limited
Officers: Catherine Ann Miles Cooper, Secretary/Director; Catherine Ann Miles Cooper [1964] Director; Paul Lawrence Cooper [1964] Director/Chartered Surveyor; Daisy Offer [1933] Director

Claybrook Limited
Incorporated: 24 May 2001 *Employees:* 5
Net Worth: £2,745,427 *Total Assets:* £4,981,391
Registered Office: Strode Business Centre, Strode Road, Plympton, Plymouth, PL7 4JN
Activities: Other letting and operating of own or leased real estate
Officers: David Edwin Sykes, Secretary; Matthew Grendon Capps [1971] Director/Chartered Surveyor; David Edwin Sykes [1959] Director/Chartered Surveyor; Andrew Eric Neil Ware [1949] Director/Chartered Surveyor

Clayesmore School
Incorporated: 9 March 1940 *Employees:* 329
Net Worth: £8,311,681 *Total Assets:* £20,948,440
Registered Office: Clayesmore School, Iwerne Minster, Blandford, Dorset, DT11 8LL
Activities: Pre-primary education
Officers: Amanda Hughes, Secretary; John Ignatius Andrews [1956] Director/Solicitor; Frances Clair Deeming [1948] Director/Retired; David Charles Haywood [1945] Director/Retired; Marcia Higgs [1955] Director; Jane Elizabeth Howard [1956] Director/Retired; Timothy Charles William Ingram [1947] Director; Richard James Shaw [1954] Director; Rosemary Ann Patricia Stiven [1955] Director/School Bursar; John Douglas Stokoe [1947] Director; Michael Paul Sussman [1963] Director/Head of Innovation; Stephen Richard Symonds [1967] Director/Headmaster; Sally Wilson [1964] Director/Teacher

Clean Earth Energy Investments Limited
Incorporated: 7 July 2011
Net Worth: £7,127,163 *Total Assets:* £8,062,705
Registered Office: Unit 2a & 2b, Trenant Industrial Estate, Wadebridge, Cornwall, PL27 6HB
Activities: Production of electricity
Major Shareholder: Sean Notley
Officers: Sean Jonathan Notley [1963] Director

Clean Earth Energy Wind Investments Limited
Incorporated: 26 April 2012
Net Worth: £8,749,910 *Total Assets:* £29,645,104
Registered Office: Unit 2a & 2b, Trenant Industrial Estate, Wadebridge, Cornwall, PL27 6HB
Activities: Other business support service activities n.e.c.
Major Shareholder: Sean Jonathan Notley
Officers: Sean Jonathan Notley [1963] Director; Dean Terence Robson [1964] Director

Clean Earth Holdings 2 Ltd
Incorporated: 5 September 2016
Net Worth: £718,808 *Total Assets:* £10,243,104
Registered Office: Unit 2a & 2b Bess Park Road, Trenant Industrial Estate, Wadebridge, Cornwall, PL27 6HB
Activities: Other business support service activities n.e.c.
Parent: Clean Earth Energy Wind Investments Ltd
Officers: Sean Jonathan Notley [1963] Director; Dean Terence Robson [1964] Director

Clean Earth Wind Turbines Ltd
Incorporated: 8 October 2014
Net Worth: £376,478 *Total Assets:* £5,835,639
Registered Office: Unit 2a & 2b Bess Park Road, Trenant Industrial Estate, Wadebridge, Cornwall, PL27 6HB
Activities: Production of electricity
Parent: Clean Earth Holdings 2 Ltd
Officers: Sean Jonathan Notley [1963] Director; Dean Terence Robson [1964] Director

Cleancrop UK Limited
Incorporated: 30 November 2004
Net Worth: £10,970,000 *Total Assets:* £10,970,000
Registered Office: Station Road, Andoversford, Cheltenham, Glos, GL54 4LZ
Activities: Support activities for crop production
Parent: Agrii Holdings (UK) Limited
Officers: Peter Michael Dunne [1973] Director/Chartered Accountant [Irish]; Spencer Gareth Evans [1970] Director/Chief Financial Officer; Ronan Andrew Hughes [1968] Director [Irish]; Christopher Stephen Matthews [1957] Director; James Marshall Rennie [1957] Director

Clear-Flow Limited
Incorporated: 19 November 2002 *Employees:* 89
Net Worth: £1,967,852 *Total Assets:* £4,867,815
Registered Office: Boscawen House, St Stephen, St Austell, Cornwall, PL26 7QF
Activities: Sewerage
Parent: Goonvean Holdings Ltd
Officers: Jonathan Neil Angilley [1962] Financial Director; Honourable Evelyn Arthur Hugh Boscawen [1955] Director/Farmer; James Robert Hustler [1970] Director; Timothy Hustler [1973] Director

Clearwater Products Limited
Incorporated: 16 March 2000 *Employees:* 26
Net Worth: £1,775,607 *Total Assets:* £4,359,863
Registered Office: Shannon Place, Shannon Way, Tewkesbury, Glos, GL20 8SL
Activities: Wholesale of hardware, plumbing and heating equipment and supplies
Shareholders: James Justin Casswell; David John Stringfellow
Officers: David John Stringfellow, Secretary/Director; James Justin Casswell [1958] Director; Timothy Peter Cavanagh [1960] Director; David John Stringfellow [1955] Director

Clearwater Properties Limited
Incorporated: 10 July 2002
Net Worth: £818,044 *Total Assets:* £4,771,280
Registered Office: First Floor Offices, Wimberley Park, Knapp Lane, Brimscombe, Stroud, Glos, GL5 2TH
Activities: Other letting and operating of own or leased real estate
Major Shareholder: Alvin Mark Lindley
Officers: Susan Jayne Harper, Secretary; Alvin Mark Lindley [1956] Director

Cleeve School
Incorporated: 13 May 2011 *Employees:* 175
Net Worth: £21,246,408 *Total Assets:* £23,539,540
Registered Office: Two Hedges Road, Bishops Cleeve, Cheltenham, Glos, GL52 8AE
Activities: General secondary education
Officers: Rhian Blackman, Secretary; Alison Dawn Berry [1970] Director/Head of Stakeholder Liaison HESA; Simon Britton [1973] Director/Design Team Leader; Rachel Jane Eperjesi [1976] Director/Senior Lecturer in Primary Education; Barbara Anne Farmer [1961] Director/Teacher; Michael Paul Hartley [1978] Director/Mathematics Teacher; Emma Jane Morgan [1969] Director/Procurement and Corporate Security Specialist; Caroline Jane Pennels [1959] Director/Barrister; Tracey Pewtner [1966] Director/Marketing Project Manager; Alwyn Richards [1969] Director/Headteacher; Anthony Lee Rushton [1974] Director/IT Manager & Architect; Simon Wall [1967] Director/HR Consultant; Diane Meriel Wilson [1965] Director/Assistant Treasurer

Clevedon Hall Estate Limited
Incorporated: 20 March 2015
Net Worth Deficit: £185,039 *Total Assets:* £5,573,737
Registered Office: Clevedon Hall, Elton Road, Clevedon, Somerset, BS21 7RQ
Activities: Other letting and operating of own or leased real estate
Shareholders: Peter John McCarthy; Sally Anne Elizabeth McCarthy
Officers: John McCarthy [1982] Director; Peter John McCarthy [1948] Director

Clevedon Learning Trust
Incorporated: 6 December 2011 *Employees:* 498
Net Worth: £24,079,020 *Total Assets:* £30,997,492
Registered Office: Clevedon School, Valley Road, Clevedon, Somerset, BS21 6AH
Activities: Pre-primary education
Officers: Kaye Case [1947] Director/Headteacher Virtual School; Alister Lewis Christopher [1960] Director/Consultant; Roger Edward Grinyer [1946] Director/Retired; Paul Kieron Kennard [1971] Director; Christopher Wayne McFall [1976] Director/Sales Development Manager; Hilary Claire Neal [1952] Director/Retired; Zoe Samantha Vanstone [1971] Director; John David Wells [1962] Director/Headteacher; Clive Tredennick Wiggin [1957] Director/Sales Manager

Cleveland FM Services Limited
Incorporated: 21 December 2004
Net Worth Deficit: £4,376,000 *Total Assets:* £24,994,000
Registered Office: Third Floor, Broad Quay House, Prince Street, Bristol, BS1 4DJ
Activities: Other business support service activities n.e.c.
Parent: Cleveland FM Services (Holdings) Limited
Officers: Michael Andrew Donn [1972] Director/Investment Manager; Karen Marie Hill [1977] Director/Investment Manager; Neil Woodburn [1979] Director/Chartered Building Surveyor

Click Consult Limited
Incorporated: 13 June 2003 *Employees:* 64
Net Worth: £2,759,472 *Total Assets:* £3,956,876
Registered Office: Hill House, 41 Richmond Hill, Bournemouth, BH2 6HS
Activities: Other information technology service activities
Parent: Ceuta Holdings Limited
Officers: Matthew David Bullas [1978] Director/CEO & Founder; Peter Andrew Burrows [1960] Director; Robert Edward Hester [1968] Finance Director; Craig Michael Hille [1974] Director/Investor [American]

Clifford Holdco Limited
Incorporated: 30 April 1987 *Employees:* 202
Previous: Bathwick Tyres (Holdings) Ltd
Net Worth: £6,150,377 *Total Assets:* £14,724,210
Registered Office: Bath Road Industrial Estate, Bath Road, Chippenham, Wilts, SN14 0AB
Activities: Other letting and operating of own or leased real estate
Shareholders: Howard Morris Wayne Clifford; Sarah Anne Clifford
Officers: Sarah Anne Clifford, Secretary; Howard Morris Wayne Clifford [1953] Director; Sarah Anne Clifford [1958] Director

Clifton Down Corporate Finance Limited
Incorporated: 30 March 2012 *Employees:* 1
Net Worth: £3,271,240 *Total Assets:* £6,211,385
Registered Office: Avonbank, Clifton Down, Bristol, BS8 3HT
Activities: Financial intermediation not elsewhere classified
Major Shareholder: Anthony Edward Kenny
Officers: Anthony Edward Kenny [1961] Director; Sarah Margaret Faraday Kenny [1962] Director

Clifton High School
Incorporated: 12 September 1877 *Employees:* 128
Net Worth: £5,073,000 *Total Assets:* £6,729,000
Registered Office: College Road, Clifton, Bristol, BS8 3JD
Activities: Pre-primary education
Officers: James Caddy, Secretary; Dr Peter Charles Bodkin [1953] Director/Management Consultant; James Matthew Caddy [1965] Director; Katie Lee [1976] Director/Manager; Anthony David Marval [1943] Director/Architect; Jane Morrison [1964] Director/Head of Communications; Lise Anne Seager [1960] Director/Solicitor; Hilary Vaughan [1967] Director/Civil Engineer; Richard Whitburn [1947] Director/Educational Consultant

Clipper Contracting Group Ltd
Incorporated: 26 June 2008 *Employees:* 2,936
Net Worth: £987,200 *Total Assets:* £9,127,048
Registered Office: 1 Widcombe Street, Poundbury, Dorchester, DT1 3BS
Activities: Management consultancy activities other than financial management
Parent: Quba Investments Limited
Officers: Richard Mark King [1977] Director; Ashley Lyas [1978] Director; Roger David Lyas [1943] Director/Accountant

Clipper Properties Limited
Incorporated: 20 September 1993 *Employees:* 3
Net Worth: £2,601,290 *Total Assets:* £4,425,442
Registered Office: c/o Bishop Fleming, 16 Queen Square, Bristol, BS1 4NT
Activities: Other business support service activities n.e.c.
Shareholders: Christopher Guy Dawson; Mark Timothy Davies; Stephen Andrew Lipfriend
Officers: Christopher Guy Dawson, Secretary; Mark Timothy Davies [1962] Director/Surveyor; Christopher Guy Dawson [1956] Director/Chartered Surveyor; Stephen Andrew Lipfriend [1957] Director/Surveyor

Close Brewery Rentals Limited
Incorporated: 23 May 2006 *Employees:* 68
Net Worth: £2,398,442 *Total Assets:* £111,940,008
Registered Office: Unit 1 Kingfisher Park, Headlands Business Park, Ringwood, Hants, BH24 3NX
Activities: Other business support service activities n.e.c.
Parent: Close Brothers Limited
Officers: Luke Antony Bazzard [1965] Director/Chief Information Officer Banking Division; David Hamilton Beswick [1964] Sales Director; Theovinder Chatha [1980] Finance Director; Tim David Lupton [1978] Director/Accountant; Gary Phillips [1975] Production Director; Adrian John Sainsbury [1968] Director/Banker; David Peter Thomson [1963] Director

L. O. Clothier & Sons Limited
Incorporated: 6 April 1959 *Employees:* 6
Net Worth: £3,261,826 *Total Assets:* £4,690,065
Registered Office: Bishopbrook House, Cathedral Avenue, Wells, Somerset, BA5 1FD
Activities: Mixed farming
Major Shareholder: Lionel Osborne Clothier
Officers: Betty Eileen Clothier, Secretary; Betty Eileen Clothier [1941] Director/Farmers Wife; Lionel Osborne Clothier [1935] Director/Farmer; Nancy Clothier [1965] Director/Farmer; Stuart Lionel Clothier [1965] Director/Farmer

H.W.Clothier Milton-Westcombe Farms Limited
Incorporated: 29 December 1959 *Employees:* 18
Net Worth: £5,738,955 *Total Assets:* £9,717,097
Registered Office: Lower Farm, Westcombe, Shepton Mallet, Somerset, BA4 6ER
Activities: Raising of dairy cattle
Major Shareholder: Phyllis Mary Clothier
Officers: Christine Mary Gore, Secretary; Richard Thomas Calver [1944] Director/Farmer; Thomas Calver [1981] Director/Operations Manager; Phyllis Mary Clothier [1920] Director/Farmer; Alistair Mark Gore [1984] Director/Sales Manager; Christine Mary Gore [1953] Director

Cloudpay Holdings Limited
Incorporated: 23 September 2003 *Employees:* 280
Net Worth Deficit: £44,463,000 *Total Assets:* £7,296,000
Registered Office: Kingsgate House, Newbury Road, Andover, Hants, SP10 4DU
Activities: Activities of head offices
Parent: Cloudpay Inc.
Officers: David John Leese [1968] Director/Chief Financial Officer; Andrew Pearson [1963] Director

Cloudpay United Kingdom Limited
Incorporated: 11 June 1998 *Employees:* 78
Net Worth Deficit: £14,140,000 *Total Assets:* £23,722,000
Registered Office: Kingsgate House, Newbury Road, Andover, Hants, SP10 4DU
Activities: Data processing, hosting and related activities
Parent: Cloudpay Holdings Limited
Officers: David John Leese [1968] Director/Chief Financial Officer; Andrew Pearson [1963] Director

Cloverlait Limited
Incorporated: 8 December 2005 *Employees:* 6
Net Worth: £1,777,163 *Total Assets:* £5,785,344
Registered Office: High Point Farm, Worminster, North Wootton, Shepton Mallet, Somerset, BA4 4AJ
Activities: Raising of dairy cattle
Shareholders: Sarah Rosalie Kim King; Ben Ashley King
Officers: Sarah Rosalie Kim King, Secretary; Benjamin Ashley King [1970] Director/Farmer; Sarah Rosalie Kim King [1973] Director/Farmer

Cloverstand Limited
Incorporated: 22 March 1976 *Employees:* 4
Net Worth: £5,267,525 *Total Assets:* £7,139,730
Registered Office: Tarrant Rawston, Blandford Forum, Dorset, DT11 8SF
Activities: Mixed farming
Shareholders: Caroline Elizabeth Tory; Mark Christopher Tory
Officers: Caroline Elizabeth Tory, Secretary; Caroline Elizabeth Tory [1955] Director/Company Secretary; Paul John Tory [1980] Director/Farmer

Club Communications Ltd.
Incorporated: 24 July 1997
Net Worth: £4,002,319 *Total Assets:* £6,234,938
Registered Office: The Hub, Stonehouse Business Park, Stonehouse, Glos, GL10 3UT
Activities: Other telecommunications activities
Major Shareholder: James Edward Palmer
Officers: Mark Robert Gallie [1971] Director

Clyst Holdings Limited
Incorporated: 2 February 1998 *Employees:* 2
Net Worth: £10,793,045 *Total Assets:* £12,963,285
Registered Office: Clyst Court, Hill Barton Business Park, Clyst St Mary, Exeter, Devon, EX5 1SA
Activities: Other letting and operating of own or leased real estate
Shareholders: Ian Trevor Buckland; Peter John Hilson
Officers: Scott Paul Buckland, Secretary; Ian Trevor Buckland [1946] Director; Peter John Hilson [1948] Director

Clyst Vale Academy Trust
Incorporated: 15 March 2011 *Employees:* 130
Net Worth: £10,908,995 *Total Assets:* £14,497,180
Registered Office: Clyst Vale Community College, Station Road, Broadclyst, Exeter, Devon, EX5 3AJ
Activities: General secondary education
Officers: Racheal Ann Long, Secretary; Dr Kevin Patrick Bawn [1960] Director/Principal; Ben Brook [1966] Director/Business Manager; Paul Colin [1958] Director; Michael Adrian Davies [1976] Director/Solicitor; Ceri Elizabeth Johnson [1966] Director/Arts Council England Employee; Sophy Norris [1970] Director/Marketing Consultant; Aude Odunlade [1983] Director/Teacher [Belgian]; Melanie Prance [1962] Director/Teacher; Dorothy Elaine Ruscoe [1946] Director/Associate Professor; Simon John Sanger-Anderson [1952] Director/Solicitor; Georgina Stroud [1951] Director/Film Consultant; Laura Waycott [1983] Director/Accountant; Tina Michelle White [1972] Director/Administrator; Dr Crawford Iain Peter Winlove [1982] Director/Academic Lecturer/Researcher

CMOStores Group Limited
Incorporated: 5 April 2017 *Employees:* 45
Net Worth Deficit: £1,470,044 *Total Assets:* £17,684,798
Registered Office: Burrington Business Park, Burrington Way, Plymouth, PL5 3LX
Activities: Activities of other holding companies n.e.c.
Parent: Key Capital Partners (Nominees) Limited
Officers: Christopher Dorey [1982] Director; Andrew Albert Dunkley [1967] Director; James William Excell [1986] Director; Michael William Fell [1957] Director/Fund Manager; Robert Andrew Kavanagh [1969] Director; Dean Murray [1962] Director; Suzanne Claire Packer [1964] Director; Adrian Saunders [1977] Director; Callum Tasker [1989] Director

Coast Academies
Incorporated: 14 June 2011 *Employees:* 220
Net Worth: £10,732,000 *Total Assets:* £13,716,000
Registered Office: Eden Park Primary School, Eden Park, Brixham, Devon, TQ5 9NH
Activities: Primary education
Officers: Sarah Anne Williscroft, Secretary; Sarah Jane Bevan [1967] Director/Full Time Mother; John Harrison [1966] Director/Sales Consultant; Kenneth Kies [1960] Director/Headteacher; David Edwin Lockyer [1946] Director/Retired; Gary Nichols [1957] Business Consultant and Director; Louise Smith [1975] Director/Marketing Manager; Timothy Michael Stephens [1960] Director/Business Manager; John Douglas Taylor [1964] Human Resources Director

Coastal Care Homes Limited
Incorporated: 23 September 1999 *Employees:* 90
Net Worth: £3,767,452 *Total Assets:* £4,587,176
Registered Office: 128 High Street, Crediton, Devon, EX17 3LQ
Activities: Residential nursing care facilities
Shareholders: Guy Perring Rogers; Nicola Jayne Rogers
Officers: Nicola Jayne Rogers, Secretary/Residential Home Proprietor; Guy Perring Rogers [1963] Director/Residential Home Proprietor; Nicola Jayne Rogers [1967] Director/Residential Home Proprietor

Coastal UK Group Limited
Incorporated: 31 July 2006 *Employees:* 137
Previous: DWML Group Limited
Net Worth: £8,840,226 *Total Assets:* £19,445,270
Registered Office: 1 & 2 Mulberry Court, Lustleigh Close, Matford Business Park, Marsh Barton Trading Estate, Exeter, EX2 8PW
Activities: Recovery of sorted materials
Parent: Faco 123 Limited
Officers: Stuart Crebo [1953] Director; Emily Anne Delve [1982] Finance Director; Steven Eric Paul Hadley [1972] Director; Richard Wynford Marsh [1963] Sales and Marketing Director; Dominic Treacher [1960] Operations Director; Allan John Vodden [1949] Director/Retired

Coastguard Road Limited
Incorporated: 2 January 1974
Net Worth: £1,634,241 *Total Assets:* £4,118,887
Registered Office: Coastguard Road Limited, Devonshire Road, Heathpark, Honiton, Devon, EX14 1SD
Activities: Wholesale of clothing and footwear
Officers: Jennifer Fulls, Secretary; Gary Neal Fulls [1965] Finance Director; Henry John Fulls [1942] Director/Company Chairman; Jennifer Fulls [1940] Director/Company Secretary; Shaun Michael Fulls [1969] Marketing Director; Henry MacKenzie White Hunt [1961] Sales Director

Coastline Housing Limited
Incorporated: 27 November 1996 *Employees:* 488
Net Worth: £35,501,000 *Total Assets:* £205,478,000
Registered Office: Coastline House, 4 Barncoose Gateway Park, Pool, Redruth, Cornwall, TR15 3RQ
Activities: Renting and operating of Housing Association real estate
Officers: David Reginald Wingham, Secretary/Director; Philip Bearne [1947] Director/Self-Employed Consultant; Steven Finlay Neill Harrison [1958] Director/Retired; Derek Law Mbe [1948] Director/Retired; Fiona Joanne Perrin [1967] Director; Susan Roberts [1949] Director/Retired; Peter Stephens [1949] Director; Mervyn John Waldron [1950] Area Director of Connells Estate Agents; Allister Wilson Young [1973] Director of Finance

Coate Water Care Company (Church View Nursing Home) Limited
Incorporated: 4 November 2003 *Employees:* 250
Net Worth: £1,315,516 *Total Assets:* £10,846,313
Registered Office: 3 Lancaster Mews, South Marston Industrial Estate, Swindon, Wilts, SN3 4YF
Activities: Residential nursing care facilities
Officers: Generaldine Frances Smith, Secretary; Christopher Leonard Smith [1950] Director; Generaldine Frances Smith [1953] Director; Jamie Smith [1979] Director; Nicholas Smith [1976] Director

Coate Water Care Company Limited
Incorporated: 22 February 2001 *Employees:* 368
Net Worth: £3,162,729 *Total Assets:* £17,398,724
Registered Office: 3 Lancaster Mews, South Marston Industrial Estate, Swindon, Wilts, SN3 4YF
Activities: Other residential care activities n.e.c.
Officers: Generaldine Frances Smith, Secretary/Carer; Christopher Leonard Smith [1950] Director/Carer; Generaldine Frances Smith [1953] Director/Carer; Jamie Smith [1979] Director; Nicholas Smith [1976] Director

Coates & Co. (Plymouth) Limited
Incorporated: 8 March 1996
Previous: V & S Plymouth Limited
Net Worth: £3,483,100,928 *Total Assets:* £3,483,909,888
Registered Office: Blackfriars Distillery, 60 Southside, Plymouth, PL1 2LQ
Activities: Distilling, rectifying and blending of spirits
Parent: Chivas Atlantic Holdings Limited
Officers: Ailsa Mary Robertson Mapplebeck, Secretary; Sean Jessop Harrison [1965] Director/Distiller; MacNab Stuart [1964] Director/Chartered Accountant; Vincent Turpin [1978] Director/Chief Financial Officer [French]

Cobalt Health
Incorporated: 4 February 2002 *Employees:* 91
Previous: Cobalt Unit Appeal Fund
Net Worth: £20,957,420 *Total Assets:* £21,539,712
Registered Office: Linton House Clinic, Thirlestaine Road, Cheltenham, Glos, GL53 7AS
Activities: Specialists medical practice activities
Officers: Malcolm James MacKeith, Secretary; Professor Mark Paul Callaway [1965] Director/Doctor; Neil Robert Holbrook [1961] Director/Archeologist; Dr Susan Ruth Owen [1952] Director [American]; John Henry Parker [1949] Director; Peter Thomas Warry [1949] Director/Chairman; Professor Gordon Keith Wilcock [1945] Director/Medical Research

Coban 2017 LLP
Incorporated: 1 February 2008 *Employees:* 385
Previous: Strutt & Parker LLP
Net Worth: £69,792,000 *Total Assets:* £71,211,000
Registered Office: 15 Dyer Street, Cirencester, Glos, GL7 2PP
Officers: Patrick Alexander Beddows [1961] Member; Michael John Alexander Fiddes [1959] Member; Paul Jonathan Fosh [1959] Member; Aidan Jonathan Charles Meynell [1974] Member; Thomas Shepherd Richardson [1958] Member; Simon Peter Bland [1958] LLP Member; Richard Allan Halford Brooks [1958] LLP Member; Alastair Charles Brown [1958] LLP Member; William Edward Church [1971] LLP Member; Ralph Crathorne [1958] LLP Member; Damian Edward Cronk [1966] LLP Member; Mark James Dorman [1976] LLP Member; Kathryn Louise Eales [1976] LLP Member; Louisa Charlotte Egerton [1963] LLP Member; James Wallace Edward Fairweather [1972] LLP Member; James Ignatius Farrell [1966] LLP Member; James Angus Forbes [1974] LLP Member; James George Neil Geddes [1969] LLP Member; William Andrew Lindsay Gemmill [1965] LLP Member; Simion Paul Glenn [1969] LLP Member; Nicholas John Greene [1955] LLP Member; Andrew Drummond Hamilton [1957] LLP Member; Richard Anthony Harris [1968] LLP Member; Ian Frankland Hepburn [1952] LLP Member; Richard David Standish Herbert [1954] LLP Member; Henry Thurston Holland-Hibbert [1959] LLP Member; Andrew Hulme [1978] LLP Member; Peter Clayton Hunt [1959] LLP Member; Philip James Hutley [1951] LLP Member; Mark William Jamieson [1960] LLP Member; Simon Michael Kibblewhite [1965] LLP Member; Jonathan Mark Lambert [1967] LLP Member; Giles Lawton [1964] LLP Member; David Ronald Leppard [1954] LLP Member; Charles Ross Lochrane [1953] LLP Member; James Alexander Donald MacKenzie [1967] LLP Member; Robin Ramsay Maitland [1957] LLP Member; Andrew James Westcott Martin [1956] LLP Member; Mark James McAndrew [1964] LLP Member; Philip Joseph McKenna [1963] LLP Member; John McLarty [1975] LLP Member; Miles Ashley Meacock [1974] LLP Member; Christopher Anthony Monk [1953] LLP Member; Antony Philip Thackray Nickalls [1967] LLP Member; Timothy Ivan Page Ratcliff [1961] LLP Member; Andrew John Rettie [1958] LLP Member; Simon Christopher Roberts [1968] LLP Member; Guy Robinson [1960] LLP Member; Michael Rowlands [1969] LLP Member; Andrew Templar Scott [1960] LLP Member; Andrew Glennie Smith [1963] LLP Member; Edward Stuart Smith [1969] LLP Member; Robert Guy Orrell Spencer [1971] LLP Member; Matthew Tack [1976] LLP Member; Antony Martin Thesiger [1968] LLP Member; Rhodri Glyn Lougher Thomas [1970] LLP Member; Robin Dennis Thomas [1953] LLP Member; Simon Underhill [1959] LLP Member; Michael William Verity [1958] LLP Member; John Graham Waterton [1954] LLP Member; Nicholas David Watson [1968] LLP Member; Richard White [1971] LLP Member; Mark David Wiggin [1963] LLP Member; Rupert Michael Wiggin [1969] LLP Member; Robert Harvey Williams [1969] LLP Member; Charles Nigel Crum Willis [1969] LLP Member; Stephen Henry Wolfe [1966] LLP Member; Andrew David Yeandle [1958] LLP Member; James Alan Youatt [1972] LLP Member; Nicholas John Young [1963] LLP Member

Cobell Ltd
Incorporated: 12 November 1999 *Employees:* 54
Net Worth: £6,220,997 *Total Assets:* £18,440,732
Registered Office: The Juice House, 1 Leigham Business Units, Silverton Road, Matford Park, Exeter, Devon, EX2 8HY
Activities: Wholesale of fruit and vegetable juices, mineral water and soft drinks
Parent: Symrise Limited
Officers: Nicholas Russell [1963] Director; Heinrich Friedrich Ludwig Schaper [1956] Director/President Flavour Division [German]

Cobham Defence Communications Limited
Incorporated: 29 October 2002 *Employees:* 19
Net Worth: £874,000 *Total Assets:* £5,225,000
Registered Office: Brook Road, Wimborne, Dorset, BH21 2BJ
Activities: Manufacture of other electrical equipment
Parent: Lockman Electronic Holdings Limited
Officers: Matthew Edward Bealey, Secretary; Matthew Edward Bealey [1980] Director; Paul Emmanuel Kahn [1966] Director; Robert Anthony Pearson [1963] Director/Professional Engineer

Cobham Leasing Limited
Incorporated: 23 June 1994
Net Worth: £8,039,000 *Total Assets:* £14,830,000
Registered Office: Brook Road, Wimborne, Dorset, BH21 2BJ
Activities: Other business support service activities n.e.c.
Parent: FR Aviation Group Limited
Officers: Michael David Parry, Secretary; Paul Anthony Armstrong [1979] Director/General Manager; Michael David Parry [1975] Finance Director; Richard Duncan Stoate [1963] Director

Cobham PLC
Incorporated: 20 December 1889 *Employees:* 10,736
Net Worth: £1,027,000,000 *Total Assets:* £2,793,400,064
Registered Office: Brook Road, Wimborne, Dorset, BH21 2BJ
Activities: Activities of head offices
Officers: Lyn Carol Colloff, Secretary; Marion Clifton Blakey [1948] Director [American]; David Charles Lockwood [1962] Director/Chief Executive; John McAdam [1948] Director; Rene Medori [1957] Director [French]; David Antony Mellors [1968] Director/Chief Financial Officer; Norton Allan Schwartz [1951] Director [American]; Michael Peter Wareing [1954] Director/Accountant; Alison Jane Wood [1963] Global Director - Strategy

Codestone Group Ltd.
Incorporated: 1 October 2007 *Employees:* 100
Net Worth: £1,097,318 *Total Assets:* £6,352,489
Registered Office: 2 Nuffield Road, Nuffield Industrial Estate, Poole, Dorset, BH17 0RB
Activities: Other information technology service activities
Shareholders: Jeremy Bucknell; David Knight
Officers: Jeremy Paul Bucknell, Secretary; Jeremy Paul Bucknell [1971] Managing Director; Paul Anthony Garratt [1960] Director; Daniel Hobson [1975] Director; David Knight [1968] Director; Sean Matthews [1974] Director; Gregory John Neilson [1973] Director; Debbie Seeley [1979] Director

Codford Biogas Limited
Incorporated: 2 August 2012 *Employees:* 12
Net Worth: £7,133,638 *Total Assets:* £11,133,738
Registered Office: Upton Wold, Moreton, Moreton in Marsh, Glos, GL56 9TR
Activities: Production of electricity
Shareholders: Ian Robbin Stanley Bond; Harry Piers Shaw Bond
Officers: Harry Piers Shaw Bond [1976] Director/Chief Executive Officer; Ian Robbin Stanley Bond [1940] Director/Land Owner; Barnaby Martin Stratton [1965] Director/Farmer; Joshua Jack Stratton [1968] Director/Farmer

Coffetek Limited
Incorporated: 2 August 1993 *Employees:* 66
Net Worth: £3,703,976 *Total Assets:* £5,854,520
Registered Office: Unit 1 Portishead Business Park, Portishead, Bristol, BS20 7BX
Activities: Manufacture of machinery for food, beverage and tobacco processing
Parent: Azkoyen SA
Officers: Robert Andrew Clayton [1961] Director; Eduardo Unzu Martinez [1964] Director [Spanish]

Cofton Country Holidays Limited
Incorporated: 27 February 2004 *Employees:* 134
Net Worth: £2,881,034 *Total Assets:* £8,986,900
Registered Office: Cofton Country Holiday Park, Starcross, Dawlish, Devon, EX6 8RP
Activities: Recreational vehicle parks, trailer parks and camping grounds
Officers: Valerie Jeffery, Secretary/Holiday Camp Proprietor; Christopher William Jeffery [1981] Director/Holiday Park Proprietor; Roger George Jeffery [1968] Director/Holiday Park Proprietor; Valerie Jeffery [1944] Director/Holiday Camp Proprietor; Mellony Anne Kirby [1979] Director/Holiday Park Proprietor; Helen Christine Scott [1971] Director/Holiday Park Proprietor

Cogent Communications UK Ltd
Incorporated: 9 June 2000 *Employees:* 32
Net Worth Deficit: £183,487 *Total Assets:* £11,530,934
Registered Office: 2 Temple Back East, Temple Quay, Bristol, BS1 6EG
Activities: Other telecommunications activities
Parent: Cogent Communications Holdings, Inc.
Officers: Jana Kaidy, Secretary; Ried Zulager, Company Secretary [American]; Dave Schaeffer [1956] Director/Chairman and CEO [American]

Cohen & Griffiths Limited
Incorporated: 4 May 1971
Net Worth: £597,216 *Total Assets:* £12,082,954
Registered Office: 4 Irnham Road, Minehead, Somerset, TA24 5DG
Activities: Other business support service activities n.e.c.
Shareholders: Anthony Stradling Marsh; Nicola Frances Marsh
Officers: Nicola Frances Marsh, Secretary; Anthony Stradling Marsh [1958] Director/Marketing Executive; Nicola Frances Marsh [1961] Director

Colburn Developments Limited
Incorporated: 20 December 1984 *Employees:* 23
Net Worth: £1,192,337 *Total Assets:* £3,602,862
Registered Office: Morris Owen House, 43-45 Devizes Road, Swindon, Wilts, SN1 4BG
Activities: Development of building projects
Shareholders: Martin Orton Evans; Rosemary Evans
Officers: Martin Orton Evans, Secretary; Roger William Boor [1960] Director; Mark David Chambers [1967] Finance Director; Martin Orton Evans [1959] Director; Rosemary Evans [1959] Director

Colburn East Limited
Incorporated: 23 June 2014
Net Worth: £941,308 *Total Assets:* £9,869,423
Registered Office: 43-45 Devizes Road, Swindon, Wilts, SN1 4BG
Activities: Development of building projects
Shareholders: Martin Orton Evans; Rosemary Evans
Officers: Mark David Chambers [1967] Director; Martin Orton Evans [1959] Director; Nicholas Julian Garrett [1962] Director; Laurence David Edgar Hollingworth [1958] Director/Investment Banker

Cold Clad Ltd
Incorporated: 12 June 2007 *Employees:* 17
Net Worth: £667,425 *Total Assets:* £3,682,077
Registered Office: Sarnia House, Green Lane, Tewkesbury, Glos, GL20 8HD
Activities: Other construction installation
Major Shareholder: Jonathan Peter Pitman
Officers: Zoe Jayne Pitman, Secretary/HR Administrator; Colin James Baker [1965] Sales Director; Gareth Pitman [1984] Director/Project Manager; Jonathan Peter Pitman [1977] Director

Coldharbour Technology Limited
Incorporated: 23 February 2017
Net Worth: £5,782,647 *Total Assets:* £5,782,647
Registered Office: Midway House, Staverton Technology Park, Herrick Way, Cheltenham, Glos, GL51 6TQ
Activities: Activities of other holding companies n.e.c.
Shareholders: UIL Limited; Graham Cole; Steven David Smith
Officers: Alexander Mark Butcher [1958] Director; Graham Cole [1948] Director; Jonathan Michael Groocock [1977] Director/Fund Management; Michael John Jolliffe [1950] Director/Ship Owner; Steven David Smith [1960] Director/Accountant

Colebrook Bosson & Saunders (Products) Limited
Incorporated: 29 June 1990 *Employees:* 49
Net Worth: £6,404,675 *Total Assets:* £11,954,506
Registered Office: 1 Portal Road, Bowerhill, Melksham, Wilts, SN12 6GN
Activities: Other manufacturing n.e.c.
Parent: Herman Miller Limited
Officers: David William Audis, Secretary; David Arnold Lutz [1957] Director/Principal Corporate Development [American]; Oliver Keene Pigott [1983] Finance Director; Robert Thomas Woodbridge [1976] Director/Financial Controller

Coleman UK Limited
Incorporated: 19 October 1992 *Employees:* 10
Net Worth Deficit: £257,000 *Total Assets:* £9,316,000
Registered Office: The Courtyard, Wraxall Hill, Wraxall, Bristol, BS48 1NA
Activities: Non-specialised wholesale trade
Parent: Newell Brands Inc
Officers: Andrew Noble, Secretary; Raj Bhalchandra Dave [1974] Chief Securities Counsel (Director) [American]; Brian James Decker [1976] Director/Attorney [American]; Martin Vergien [1970] Director [German]

K. S. Coles Limited
Incorporated: 8 November 2002 *Employees:* 139
Net Worth: £3,425,647 *Total Assets:* £4,902,852
Registered Office: Chelston House Farm, Chelston, Wellington, Somerset, TA21 9HP
Activities: Growing of vegetables and melons, roots and tubers
Shareholders: Kenneth Stuart Coles; Christine Mary Coles; Paul Metford Coles
Officers: Christine Mary Coles, Secretary; Christine Mary Coles [1947] Director/Farmer; Kenneth Stuart Coles [1942] Director/Farmer; Paul Metford Coles [1968] Director/Farmer

Coles Miller Solicitors LLP
Incorporated: 28 March 2006 *Employees:* 118
Net Worth: £3,452,077 *Total Assets:* £4,698,037
Registered Office: 44-46 Parkstone Road, Poole, Dorset, BH15 2PG
Officers: Neil Anthony Robert Andrews [1969] Member; Adrian Cameron Cormack [1966] Member; Roger Mark Leedham [1960] Member; Simon Timothy Steele-Williams [1966] Member; Jason Barnett [1975] LLP Member; Lydia Barnett [1980] LLP Member; Stuart Bradford [1976] LLP Member; Ruth Helen Elkins [1973] LLP Member; Kerry Leanne Houston Kypta [1977] LLP Member; Matthew Lewis [1988] LLP Member; Richard James Perrins [1981] LLP Member; David Brian Charles Simpson [1960] LLP Member; Anthony Weber [1971] LLP Member; Christopher David Whittle [1973] LLP Member

Colethrop Farm Limited
Incorporated: 7 March 1997 *Employees:* 4
Net Worth: £2,904,814 *Total Assets:* £3,701,177
Registered Office: c/o Woodward Hale, 38 Dollar Street, Cirencester, Glos, GL7 2AN
Activities: Growing of cereals (except rice), leguminous crops and oil seeds
Major Shareholder: Marcus Beresford Heywood
Officers: Marcus Beresford Heywood, Secretary; Timothy David Hamilton [1951] Director/Chartered Surveyor; Marcus Beresford Heywood [1948] Director; Olivia Anne Heywood [1980] Director

Collacombe Farm Limited
Incorporated: 20 November 1997 *Employees:* 5
Net Worth: £6,183,398 *Total Assets:* £6,804,362
Registered Office: Collacombe Barton, Lamerton, Tavistock, Devon, PL19 8SB
Activities: Mixed farming
Shareholders: Sarah Catherine Oliver; Ian McClure Forrest
Officers: Sarah Catherine Oliver, Secretary/Director; Ian McClure Forrest [1958] Director/Chairman; Sarah Catherine Oliver [1958] Director

Coln Park LLP
Incorporated: 5 August 2005 *Employees:* 35
Net Worth: £5,456,331 *Total Assets:* £9,174,332
Registered Office: Coln Park, Claydon Pike, Lechlade, Glos, GL7 3DT

Coln Signature Homes Limited
Incorporated: 1 June 2016 *Employees:* 3
Net Worth: £478,534 *Total Assets:* £7,136,777
Registered Office: 2nd Floor, 19 Apex Court, Woodlands, Almondsbury Business Centre, Bristol, BS32 4JT
Activities: Construction of domestic buildings
Shareholders: Housing Growth Partnership GP LLP; Roger Anthony Brennan
Officers: Robert Edward Bland [1968] Director; Roger Anthony Brennan [1964] Managing Director; Kim Frances Rawsthorne [1982] Finance Director

Colonial Leisure Limited
Incorporated: 26 November 2010 *Employees:* 15
Net Worth Deficit: £880,501 *Total Assets:* £15,131,648
Registered Office: Pennsylvania Castle, Pennsylvania Road, Portland, Dorset, DT5 1HZ
Activities: Letting and operating of conference and exhibition centres
Major Shareholder: Christopher John Morris
Officers: Christopher Holleyoak [1963] Director; Christopher John Morris [1947] Director [Australian]; Joanne Eloise Peters [1982] Director

Colosseum Dental UK Limited
Incorporated: 27 September 2006 *Employees:* 555
Previous: Southern Dental Limited
Net Worth Deficit: £7,104,000 *Total Assets:* £49,747,000
Registered Office: Staverton Court, Staverton, Cheltenham, Glos, GL51 0UX
Activities: Dental practice activities
Parent: Tempire Investments Limited
Officers: Philip Buergin [1979] Director/Chief Executive Officer [Swiss]; Michael Clare [1971] Director/Chief Operating Officer; Stephen Warren Cowley [1961] Director/Dentist; Jose Fernando de Morais Lacerda Angelo [1983] Director/Dentist [Portuguese]; Daniel Fehr [1979] Director/Chief Financial Officer [Swiss]; Roderick Paul Ingham [1954] Director/Dentist; Claude Streit [1979] Director/Chief Financial Officer [Swiss]

Colosseum Dental UK Partnerships Limited
Incorporated: 25 November 2010 *Employees:* 151
Previous: Southern Dental Partnerships Limited
Net Worth: £1,548,000 *Total Assets:* £11,968,000
Registered Office: Hazelwoods, Staverton Court, Staverton, Cheltenham, Glos, GL51 0UX
Activities: Dental practice activities
Parent: Colosseum Dental UK Limited
Officers: Philip Buergin [1979] Director/Chief Executive Officer [Swiss]; Michael Clare [1971] Director/Chief Operating Officer; Daniel Fehr [1979] Director/Chief Financial Officer [Swiss]; Claude Streit [1979] Director/Chief Financial Officer [Swiss]

Colston Property Developments LLP
Incorporated: 13 November 2013
Net Worth: £2,308,594 *Total Assets:* £8,491,966
Registered Office: Q1 Quadrant Way, Hardwicke, Gloucester, GL2 2RN

Colston's School
Incorporated: 22 February 1993 *Employees:* 127
Previous: Colston's Collegiate School
Net Worth: £18,769,817,600 *Total Assets:* £22,319,826,944
Registered Office: Bell Hill, Stapleton, Bristol, BS16 1BJ
Activities: Pre-primary education
Officers: Emma Kathryn Jennings, Secretary; Sarah Bryn Allpress [1975] Director [American]; Nicholas Paul Baker [1963] Director/Company Chairman; Anne Moira Burrell [1956] Director; Gillian Cross [1957] Director/Teacher; Caroline Jane Duckworth [1961] Director/Treasurer; Martin John Hughes [1969] Director/Deputy Head; Charles James Hastings Lucas [1969] Director; Professor Joseph Peter McGeehan [1946] Director/University Professor Toshiba Research Ltd; Timothy Stuart Ross [1948] Director/Company Chairman; Dr Annela Mary Seddon [1974] Director; Jane Leslie Worthington [1951] Director; John Richard Wright [1945] Director/Accountant

Colt Car Company Limited (The)
Incorporated: 21 March 1974 *Employees:* 222
Net Worth: £17,540,000 *Total Assets:* £407,383,008
Registered Office: Watermoor, Cirencester, Glos, GL7 1LF
Activities: Sale of new cars and light motor vehicles
Parent: Mitsubishi Corporation
Officers: Carolyn Tracey Stephenson, Secretary; Hiroyuki Egami [1970] Director [Japanese]; Isao Kano [1960] Director [Japanese]; Kazuyoshi Kawakami [1969] Director [Japanese]; Keisuke Kimura [1985] Director [Japanese]; Mizuki Kuroda [1963] Finance Director [Japanese]; Robert Norris Lindley [1966] Managing Director; Hajime Machimura [1970] Director/Chairman [Japanese]; Jun Mitsuhashi [1965] Director [Japanese]

Colten Care (1693) Limited
Incorporated: 8 May 2008
Net Worth: £8,408,673 *Total Assets:* £21,075,224
Registered Office: Colten House, Forest Gate Business Park, Wellworthy Way, Ringwood, Hants, BH24 3FE
Activities: Residential care activities for the elderly and disabled
Parent: Colten Care Limited
Officers: Ian Robert Hudson, Secretary/Accountant; Mark Christopher Charles Aitchison [1968] Finance Director; George Alexander Colwell [1978] Director/Construction; Jane Colwell [1945] Director; John Colwell [1943] Director/Civil Engineer; Elaine Farrer [1964] Operations Director; Ian Robert Hudson [1948] Director/Accountant; Adrian John Otten [1940] Director/Civil Engineer; Richard Andrew Otten [1975] Director; Rosemary Otten [1946] Director

Colten Care (1993) Limited
Incorporated: 8 May 2008
Net Worth: £19,533,072 *Total Assets:* £57,759,868
Registered Office: Colten House, Forest Gate Business Park, Wellworthy Way, Ringwood, Hants, BH24 3FE
Activities: Residential care activities for the elderly and disabled
Parent: Colten Care Limited
Officers: Ian Robert Hudson, Secretary/Accountant; Mark Christopher Charles Aitchison [1968] Finance Director; George Alexander Colwell [1978] Director/Construction; Jane Colwell [1945] Director; John Colwell [1943] Director/Civil Engineer; Elaine Farrer [1964] Operations Director; Ian Robert Hudson [1948] Director/Accountant; Adrian John Otten [1940] Director/Civil Engineer; Richard Andrew Otten [1975] Director; Rosemary Otten [1946] Director

Colten Care (2003) Limited
Incorporated: 8 May 2008
Net Worth: £10,429,105 *Total Assets:* £26,759,364
Registered Office: Colten House, Forest Gate Business Park, Wellworthy Way, Ringwood, Hants, BH24 3FE
Activities: Residential care activities for the elderly and disabled
Parent: Colten Care Ltd
Officers: Ian Robert Hudson, Secretary/Accountant; Mark Christopher Charles Aitchison [1968] Finance Director; George Alexander Colwell [1978] Director/Construction; Jane Colwell [1945] Director; John Colwell [1943] Director/Civil Engineer; Elaine Farrer [1964] Operations Director; Ian Robert Hudson [1948] Director/Accountant; Adrian John Otten [1940] Director/Civil Engineer; Richard Andrew Otten [1975] Director; Rosemary Otten [1946] Director

Colten Care (2009) Limited
Incorporated: 29 June 2011
Net Worth: £4,224,211 *Total Assets:* £29,290,244
Registered Office: Colten House, Forest Gate Business Park, Wellworthy Way, Ringwood, Hants, BH24 3FE
Activities: Residential care activities for the elderly and disabled
Parent: Colten Care Limited
Officers: Ian Robert Hudson, Secretary; Mark Christopher Charles Aitchison [1968] Director/Accountant; George Alexander Colwell [1978] Director/Construction; John Colwell [1943] Director/Civil Engineer; Elaine Farrer [1964] Operations Director; Ian Robert Hudson [1948] Director/Accountant; Adrian John Otten [1940] Director/Civil Engineer; Richard Andrew Otten [1975] Director

Colten Care Limited
Incorporated: 8 February 1988 *Employees:* 1,830
Net Worth: £101,820,368 *Total Assets:* £187,656,608
Registered Office: Colten House, Forest Gate Business Park, Wellworthy Way, Ringwood, Hants, BH24 3FE
Activities: Residential care activities for the elderly and disabled
Shareholders: Adrian John Otten; John Colwell
Officers: Ian Robert Hudson, Secretary; George Alexander Colwell [1978] Director; Elaine Farrer [1964] Operations Director; Richard Andrew Otten [1975] Director

Colten Developments Limited
Incorporated: 24 August 1971 *Employees:* 18
Net Worth: £5,728,266 *Total Assets:* £7,647,842
Registered Office: Colten House, Forest Gate Business Park, Wellworthy Way, Ringwood, Hants, BH24 3FE
Activities: Construction of domestic buildings
Shareholders: Adrian John Otten; John Colwell
Officers: Ian Robert Hudson, Secretary; Mark Christopher Charles Aitchison [1968] Finance Director; George Alexander Colwell [1978] Director; Jane Colwell [1945] Director; John Colwell [1943] Director; Ian Robert Hudson [1948] Director/Chartered Accountant; Adrian John Otten [1940] Director/Civil Engineer; Richard Andrew Otten [1975] Director; Rosemary Otten [1946] Director

Colvase Estate Ltd
Incorporated: 15 December 2010 *Employees:* 4
Net Worth: £3,805,623 *Total Assets:* £4,918,926
Registered Office: Prydis Accounts Ltd, The Parade, Liskeard, Cornwall, PL14 6AF
Activities: Management of real estate on a fee or contract basis
Shareholders: Catherine Therese Angela Coles; Michael Coles
Officers: Michael Coles, Secretary; Catherine Therese Angela Coles [1963] Director; Jonathon Edward Coles [1996] Director; Michael Coles [1964] Director; Thomas Richard Coles [1993] Director/Property Management

Colyton Grammar School Academy Trust
Incorporated: 19 November 2010 *Employees:* 102
Net Worth: £8,836,527 *Total Assets:* £10,632,309
Registered Office: Whitwell Lane, Colyford, Colyton, Devon, EX24 6HN
Activities: General secondary education
Officers: Samantha Ann Smith, Secretary; Susan Burns-Price [1956] Director/School Librarian; Gordon Phillip Davis [1964] Director/Teacher; Timothy John Dyer [1958] Director/Retired; Christian John Galvin [1952] Director; Martin John Goscomb [1957] Director; Andrew Mark Gould [1965] PR Managing Director; Ian Richard Griffin [1963] Director; Kirsteen Hall [1971] Director/Civil Servant; Timothy James Harris [1969] Director/Headteacher; Isabel Ruth Knight [1967] Director/Consultant; Misty-Jane Nickells [1979] Director/Chartered Accountant; Barry John Sindall [1945] Director/Educational Consultant; Dr Jacqueline Louise Spurrier [1972] Director/Artist; Ian Victor Styles [1957] Director/Retired

Comax (UK) Limited
Incorporated: 10 January 2005
Net Worth: £1,837,937 *Total Assets:* £4,018,813
Registered Office: 2 Yeoman Road, Ringwood, Hants, BH24 3FA
Activities: Non-specialised wholesale trade
Officers: Graham Richard Moakes, Secretary; Robert John Atkins [1965] Director; Doctor James Frederick David Marsh [1945] Director/Engineer; Richard Michell [1950] Director; Graham Richard Moakes [1964] Director

Combe Pafford School
Incorporated: 1 March 2013 *Employees:* 132
Net Worth: £11,435,685 *Total Assets:* £13,321,203
Registered Office: Combe Pafford School, Steps Lane, Watcombe, Torquay, Devon, TQ2 8NL
Activities: Other education n.e.c.
Officers: Martin Avery [1979] Director/Bank Official; Mandy Biddle [1968] Director/Bank Manager; Lorna Elizabeth Cooper [1970] Director/Teacher; Elissa Bettina Emery [1984] Director/Childrens Home Manager; Jonathan Haines [1966] Director; Jane Hallwood [1952] Director/Teacher; Nicholas James [1970] Director; Michael Ernest Charles Lock [1956] Director/Headteacher; Elizabeth Moon [1951] Director/Retired; Emma Nixon [1971] Director/Learning Support Assistant; Jackie Redfern [1939] Director/Retired; John Eric Stott [1954] Director/Business Owner

Combined Independents (Holdings) Limited
Incorporated: 16 July 1963 *Employees:* 72
Net Worth: £17,930,108 *Total Assets:* £60,094,856
Registered Office: Euro House, Joule Road, West Portway, Andover, Hants, SP10 3GD
Activities: Wholesale of radio, television goods & electrical household appliances (other than records, tapes, CDs)
Officers: Marc Arnell [1968] Retail Director; James Friel [1945] Managing Director; Paul Hardy [1956] Managing Director; Simon Nicholas George Hepher [1960] Managing Director; Andrew Frederick Hill [1959] Director/Sole Trader; Philip Martyn Lord [1952] Managing Director; Fiona May Lunt [1965] Director/Sole Proprietor; Robin John Millwood [1952] Director/Electrical Retailer; Philip John Mosey [1959] Director; Timothy John Noy [1960] Director/Business Proprietor; Sarah Anne Palmer [1967] Director/Electrical Retailer; Jill Lesley Parkinson [1967] Director/Retailer; Richard James Putland [1977] Director; Steve Anthony Scogings [1972] Managing Director; Andrew Frederick Thomas [1968] Director; Graham Malcolm Todd [1946] Director/Electrical Engineer Retail Partner; Anthony Frank Tyler [1946] Director; David Brian Yelland [1962] Director

Comenius Trust
Incorporated: 8 March 2016 *Employees:* 150
Net Worth: £9,474,000 *Total Assets:* £11,228,000
Registered Office: Weston All Saints Academy, Broadmoor Lane, Weston, Bath, BA1 4JR
Activities: Primary education
Officers: Dr Anne Patricia Bull-George [1950] Director/Headteacher; Helen Clare Curran [1977] Director; Timothy Cornelius Fenton [1980] Project Director; James Richard Garforth [1947] Director/Retired; Michael James Gray [1953] Director/Senior Project Manager Construction; Philip Michael Marten [1975] Director; Thomas Stuart Peryer [1950] Director/Education Consultant; Peter Joseph Michael Turner [1944] Director/Councillor

Comexposium Cereals Limited
Incorporated: 9 August 2016 *Employees:* 9
Previous: Comexposium Haymarket Exhibitions Limited
Net Worth: £5,105,519 *Total Assets:* £6,023,833
Registered Office: 4 Colston Avenue, Bristol, BS1 4ST
Activities: Activities of exhibition and fair organisers
Shareholders: Comexposium UK Limited; Haymarket Media Group Ltd.
Officers: Martine Degremont [1959] Director [French]; Brice Delaloi [1982] Finance Director [French]; Simon Andrew Foster [1966] Director

Commercial Corporate Services Limited
Incorporated: 16 February 2011 *Employees:* 283
Net Worth: £5,586,716 *Total Assets:* £20,961,882
Registered Office: Commercial House, Old Station Drive, Leckhampton, Cheltenham, Glos, GL53 0DL
Activities: Other business support service activities n.e.c.
Shareholders: Simone Denise Hindmarch-Bye; Alastair John de Quincy Adams; Arthur Michael Stephen Hindmarch
Officers: Eileen Margaret Booth, Secretary; Alastair John Dequincy Adams [1965] Director; Arthur Michael Stephen Hindmarch [1964] Director; Simone Denise Hindmarch-Bye [1968] Director

Commercial Estates Property Company Limited
Incorporated: 2 October 1985 *Employees:* 4
Net Worth: £15,341,790 *Total Assets:* £15,870,370
Registered Office: Hawthorn House, Emperor Way, Exeter Business Park, Exeter, Devon, EX1 3QS
Activities: Other letting and operating of own or leased real estate
Shareholders: Jean Madeleine Kingdon; Karen Jean Rosser
Officers: Jean Madeleine Kingdon, Secretary; Susan Ellen Johns [1964] Director; Jean Madeleine Kingdon [1942] Director; Isabel Catherine Rosser [1990] Director/Corporate Banker; Karen Jean Rosser [1963] Director

Commercial First Group Limited
Incorporated: 14 June 2002 *Employees:* 4
Net Worth: £11,000 *Total Assets:* £71,473,000
Registered Office: Jessop House, Jessop Avenue, Cheltenham, Glos, GL50 3WG
Activities: Credit granting by non-deposit taking finance houses and other specialist consumer credit grantors
Officers: Timothy Paul Theobald, Secretary; John Fraser Stewart Barbour [1972] Operations Director; Timothy Paul Theobald [1967] Director/Chartered Accountant

Commercial Limited
Incorporated: 7 March 1991 *Employees:* 127
Net Worth: £4,320,060 *Total Assets:* £14,756,979
Registered Office: Commercial House, Old Station Drive, Leckhampton, Cheltenham, Glos, GL53 0DL
Activities: Other business support service activities n.e.c.
Parent: Commercial Corporate Services Ltd
Officers: Eileen Margaret Booth, Secretary; Alastair John de Quincy Adams [1965] Sales Director; Arthur Michael Stephen Hindmarch [1964] Managing Director; Simone Denise Hindmarch-Bye [1968] Director

The Commonweal School
Incorporated: 27 June 2011 *Employees:* 185
Net Worth: £16,336,819 *Total Assets:* £18,779,036
Registered Office: The Commonweal School, The Mall, Old Town, Swindon, Wilts, SN1 4JE
Activities: General secondary education
Officers: Joanne Sara Sear, Secretary; Dr Johanna Bakker [1952] Director/Freelance [Dutch]; Joyce Birnie [1958] Director/Senior Partnership Programmes Officer; Julian David Bourne [1967] Director/Operations Manager; Justine Karena Evans [1972] Director/Teaching Assistant; Ahmet Gurcan Fidan [1963] Director/Accountant; Erica Jane Ford [1959] Director/Speech and Language Therapist; Robert Earl St. John Linnegar [1963] Director/Headteacher; Alexandra Martin [1976] Director/Pre-School Administrator; David Miles Mason [1954] Director/Consulting Civil Engineer; Greville John Parmenter [1964] Director/Accountant; David Peter Skinner [1960] Director/Accountant; Nicholas Weaver [1962] Director/Performing Arts Technician; Lucy Whetman [1969] Director/Teacher; Genevieve Anne Williams [1955] Director/Teacher; Debra Wilson [1968] Director/Project Manager

Community 1st Cornwall Limited
Incorporated: 10 February 2004 *Employees:* 4
Net Worth: £42,646,744 *Total Assets:* £94,071,384
Registered Office: Blue Support House, 17a Moorland Road, St Austell, Cornwall, PL25 5BS
Activities: Other letting and operating of own or leased real estate
Shareholders: Equity Solutions Lift Investments Cornwall Limited; Community Health Partnerships Limited
Officers: John Connolly [1961] Director; Andrew Dwan [1965] Director; Michael Dwan [1959] Director; Balasingham Ravi Kumar [1975] Investment Director CHP South

The Community Foundation for Wiltshire & Swindon
Incorporated: 14 February 2008 *Employees:* 10
Net Worth: £22,601,064 *Total Assets:* £23,436,660
Registered Office: Sandcliff House, 21 Northgate Street, Devizes, Wilts, SN10 1JT
Activities: Other service activities n.e.c.
Officers: Rosemary Ellen MacDonald, Secretary; Denise Angela Bentley [1957] Director/Human Resources; Christpoher John Bertram Bromfield [1950] Director/Solicitor; Jason Henry Stuart Dalley [1964] Director/Investment Manager; Emma Gibbons [1968] Director/Chartered Accountant; Dame Elizabeth Louise Neville [1953] Director/Volunteer; James Paul Phipps [1979] Director; Alison Jane Radevsky [1958] Director/Consultant; Dr Andrew James Tait [1957] Director of Marketing and Communications; Steven Lewis Wall [1971] Director/Head of Business Performance Management; Susan Webber [1945] Director/Retired; William Francis Wyldbore-Smith [1948] Director

Community Health Facilities (Oxford) Limited
Incorporated: 24 July 1997 *Employees:* 3
Net Worth: £1,909,835 *Total Assets:* £5,472,051
Registered Office: Third Floor, Broad Quay House, Prince Street, Bristol, BS1 4DJ
Activities: Management of real estate on a fee or contract basis
Parent: Community Health Facilities (Holdings) Limited
Officers: Christopher John Blundell [1966] Regional Director; Andrew Richard Kershaw [1965] Director/Projects Controller; Richard Little [1979] Investment Director

Compass Agri (Holdings) Limited
Incorporated: 18 April 2017 *Employees:* 20
Net Worth: £2,904,203 *Total Assets:* £9,627,138
Registered Office: Leeward House, Fitzroy Road, Exeter Business Park, Exeter, EX1 3LJ
Activities: Activities of agricultural holding companies
Shareholders: Justin Percy William Nichols; Richard Alan John Parris
Officers: Justin Percy William Nichols [1969] Director; Richard Alan John Parris [1965] Director

Compass Point Estates LLP
Incorporated: 24 August 2005 *Employees:* 6
Net Worth: £2,604,152 *Total Assets:* £3,892,975
Registered Office: The Manager, Estates Office, Southwell Business Park, Portland, Dorset, DT5 2NA
Officers: Paul Lee [1963] Member; Gillian Paul [1965] Member

Compass Tractors Limited
Incorporated: 10 December 2003 *Employees:* 20
Net Worth: £2,904,203 *Total Assets:* £9,627,138
Registered Office: Market Way, North Petherton, Bridgwater, Somerset, TA6 6DF
Activities: Wholesale of agricultural machinery, equipment and supplies
Parent: Compass Agri (Holdings) Limited
Officers: Justin Percy William Nichols [1969] Director; Richard Alan John Parris [1965] Director/Agricultural Machinery Dealer

Complete Design & Construction Limited
Incorporated: 1 March 2004
Net Worth: £1,574,743 *Total Assets:* £3,603,299
Registered Office: 30-31 St James Place, Mangotsfield, Bristol, BS16 9JB
Activities: Development of building projects
Shareholders: Daniel William Byrne; Anton James Lavelle
Officers: Daniel William Byrne [1974] Director/Builder [Irish]; Anton James Lavelle [1977] Director/Builder [Irish]

Complete Price Eyewear Limited
Incorporated: 10 February 1993 *Employees:* 343
Net Worth: £2,203,298 *Total Assets:* £7,258,841
Registered Office: Old Town Court, 10-14 High Street, Old Town, Swindon, Wilts, SN1 3EP
Activities: Other human health activities
Major Shareholder: Damian Nicholas Kenning
Officers: Robert John Brown, Secretary; Richard Gibson [1973] Director; Damian Nicholas Kenning [1960] Director/Optician; Nicholas Paul Wingate [1971] Director/Optometrist

Compton Beauchamp Estates Limited
Incorporated: 5 October 1999
Net Worth: £114,923,280 *Total Assets:* £143,365,056
Registered Office: Upper Farm, Woolstone, Faringdon, Oxon, SN7 7QL
Activities: Growing of cereals (except rice), leguminous crops and oil seeds
Major Shareholder: Nils Wilhelm Erik Penser
Officers: Richard Kenneth Salmon, Secretary; Nils Wilhelm Erik Penser [1942] Director [Swedish]; Richard Kenneth Salmon [1952] Director; James Samuel Watson [1978] Director/Landscape Gardening Consultant

Computer and Design Services Limited
Incorporated: 26 February 1974
Net Worth: £2,076,752 *Total Assets:* £5,018,061
Registered Office: Arrowsmith Court, 10 Station Approach, Broadstone, Dorset, BH18 8AX
Activities: Business and domestic software development
Major Shareholder: Jonathan Walter Pursall Fryett
Officers: Jonathan Walter Pursall Fryett, Secretary; Ian Leslie Chambers [1960] Director/Chartered Engineer; Jonathan Walter Pursall Fryett [1950] Director/Chartered Engineer; Richard Martin Pearce [1951] Director/Software & Hardware Engineer

Computershare Investments (UK) (No 7) Limited
Incorporated: 20 October 2009 *Employees:* 3
Net Worth: £60,020,000 *Total Assets:* £60,032,000
Registered Office: The Pavilions, Bridgewater Road, Bristol, BS13 8AE
Activities: Activities of head offices
Parent: Computershare Limited
Officers: Llewellyn Kevan Botha, Secretary; Jonathan Dolbear, Secretary; Llewellyn Kevan Botha [1962] Director [South African]; James Terence Hood [1968] Director/Chartered Accountant; Nazir Sarkar [1967] Director

Computershare Investments (UK) (No. 8) Limited
Incorporated: 15 December 2011 *Employees:* 3
Net Worth: £255,427,920 *Total Assets:* £651,572,032
Registered Office: The Pavilions, Bridgwater Road, Bristol, BS13 8AE
Activities: Activities of head offices
Officers: Llewellyn Botha, Secretary; Jonathan Dolbear, Secretary; Llewellyn Kevan Botha [1962] Director/General Counsel [South African]; James Terence Hood [1968] Director/Chartered Accountant; Nazir Sarkar [1967] Director/Chartered Accountant

Computershare Investments (UK) (No.3) Limited
Incorporated: 10 September 2003 *Employees:* 4
Net Worth: £276,952,992 *Total Assets:* £309,448,000
Registered Office: The Pavilions, Bridgewater Road, Bristol, BS13 8AE
Activities: Activities of head offices
Parent: Computershare Limited
Officers: Llewellyn Kevan Botha, Secretary/Lawyer [South African]; Jonathan Dolbear, Secretary; Llewellyn Kevan Botha [1962] Director/Lawyer [South African]; James Terence Hood [1968] Director/Chartered Accountant; Nazir Sarkar [1967] Director; Ceri Ulyatt [1975] Tax Director (EMEA)

Computershare Investor Services PLC
Incorporated: 20 January 1998 *Employees:* 1,330
Net Worth: £115,073,000 *Total Assets:* £141,575,008
Registered Office: The Pavilions, Bridgewater Road, Bristol, BS13 8AE
Activities: Activities auxiliary to financial intermediation n.e.c.
Parent: Computershare Investments (UK) (No. 3) Limited
Officers: Llewellyn Kevan Botha, Secretary/Lawyer [South African]; Jonathan Dolbear, Secretary; Wai-Fong Au [1956] Director - Haralice Limited; Llewellyn Kevan Botha [1962] Director/Lawyer [South African]; Philip Charles Braithwaite [1951] Director; James Terence Hood [1968] Director/Chartered Accountant; Nazir Sarkar [1967] Director

Computershare Limited
Incorporated: 30 January 1995 *Employees:* 4
Net Worth: £284,222,016 *Total Assets:* £392,791,008
Registered Office: The Pavilions, Bridgwater Road, Bristol, BS13 8AE
Activities: Activities of head offices
Officers: Llewellyn Kevan Botha, Secretary/Lawyer [South African]; Jonathan Dolbear, Secretary; Llewellyn Kevan Botha [1962] Director/Lawyer [South African]; James Terence Hood [1968] Director/Chartered Accountant; Nazir Sarkar [1967] Director; Ceri Ulyatt [1975] Tax Director (EMEA)

Computershare Mortgage Services Limited
Incorporated: 2 February 1990
Previous: Specialist Mortgage Services Limited
Net Worth: £18,670,000 *Total Assets:* £54,019,000
Registered Office: The Pavilions, Bridgwater Road, Bristol, BS13 8AE
Activities: Financial intermediation not elsewhere classified
Parent: Computershare Investments (UK) (No. 3) Limited
Officers: Llewellyn Kevan Botha, Secretary; Jonathan Dolbear, Secretary; Peter Aeneas Ali [1974] Director of Finance; Philip Charles Braithwaite [1951] Director; Andrew Nigel Jones [1966] Director; Nicholas Stuart Robert Oldfield [1972] Director/Chartered Accountant; Jonathan Michael Pattinson [1969] Director; Garry George Stran [1965] Director

Computershare Services Limited
Incorporated: 9 October 1989 *Employees:* 1,510
Previous: Savings Management Limited
Net Worth: £1,751,000 *Total Assets:* £7,005,000
Registered Office: The Pavilions, Bridgwater Road, Bristol, BS13 8AE
Activities: Non-trading company
Parent: Computershare Investments (UK) (No. 3) Limited
Officers: Jonathan Dolbear, Secretary; Peter Aeneas Ali [1974] Finance Director; Andrew Nigel Jones [1966] Director

Computershare Technology Services (UK) Limited
Incorporated: 16 May 1996 *Employees:* 212
Net Worth: £66,213,000 *Total Assets:* £80,761,000
Registered Office: The Pavilions, Bridgwater Road, Bristol, BS13 8AE
Activities: Other information technology service activities
Parent: Computershare Limited
Officers: Llewellyn Kevan Botha, Secretary/Lawyer [South African]; Jonathan Dolbear, Secretary; Llewellyn Kevan Botha [1962] Director/Lawyer [South African]; James Terence Hood [1968] Director/Chartered Accountant; Nazir Sarkar [1967] Director

Computershare Voucher Services Limited
Incorporated: 18 November 2003 *Employees:* 24
Net Worth: £4,998,000 *Total Assets:* £78,372,000
Registered Office: The Pavilions, Bridgwater Road, Bristol, BS13 8AE
Activities: Other business support service activities n.e.c.
Parent: Computershare Investments (UK) (No. 3) Limited
Officers: Llewellyn Kevan Botha, Secretary/General Counsel [South African]; Jonathan Dolbear, Secretary; Llewellyn Kevan Botha [1962] Director/General Counsel [South African]; James Terence Hood [1968] Director/Chartered Accountant; Nazir Sarkar [1967] Director

Concrete Fabrications Limited
Incorporated: 26 January 1999 *Employees:* 107
Net Worth: £3,206,259 *Total Assets:* £5,354,035
Registered Office: 1 Cole Road, St Phillips, Bristol, BS2 0UG
Activities: Manufacture of other articles of concrete, plaster and cement
Parent: Podimore Limited
Officers: Ian Paul Elston [1975] Director; Julia Louise Russell [1978] Director; Charlotte Westlake [1964] Director/Accountant

Condition Monitoring Group Limited
Incorporated: 25 April 2006 *Employees:* 116
Net Worth: £3,930,328 *Total Assets:* £9,860,467
Registered Office: Condition Monitoring Group, Hatchmoor Industrial Estate, Torrington, Devon, EX38 7HP
Activities: Manufacture of other electrical equipment
Shareholders: Freda Anne Lobato; Gareth Maurice Lee-Richards
Officers: Rachel Jane Allen, Secretary; Rachel Jane Allen [1976] Director/Accountant; Douglas Robert Graham [1980] Director/Engineer; Gareth Maurice Lee-Richards [1945] Director/Chairman; Andres Lobato [1955] Managing Director; Freda Anne Lobato [1953] Director

Condor UK Holdings Limited
Incorporated: 22 April 2002 *Employees:* 181
Net Worth: £2,934,596 *Total Assets:* £6,047,903
Registered Office: Condor House, New Harbour Road South, Hamworthy, Poole, Dorset, BH15 4AJ
Activities: Other transportation support activities
Officers: Steven George Broomfield, Secretary; Catherine Isabelle Bates [1987] Director [Australian]; Gordon Ian Winston Parsons [1967] Director/Chairman

Conlon Limited
Incorporated: 29 November 2000 *Employees:* 191
Net Worth: £8,648,718 *Total Assets:* £16,929,776
Registered Office: Manor Farm, Calcutt, Cricklade, Swindon, Wilts, SN6 6JR
Activities: Other specialised construction activities n.e.c.
Officers: Dermot Conlon [1965] Director

Conmed UK Ltd
Incorporated: 27 March 1998 *Employees:* 62
Net Worth: £6,806,551 *Total Assets:* £9,087,784
Registered Office: 73-74 Shrivenham Hundred Business Park, Majors Road, Watchfield, Swindon, Wilts, SN6 8TY
Activities: Other business support service activities n.e.c.
Parent: Conmed Corporation
Officers: Patrick Joseph Beyer [1965] Director/President [American]; Daniel S Jonas [1964] Director/General Counsel [American]; Johonna Pelletier [1972] Director/Treasurer & Vice President, Tax [American]

Connect Academy Trust
Incorporated: 20 May 2016 *Employees:* 341
Net Worth: £15,109,440 *Total Assets:* £20,421,370
Registered Office: Leigham Primary School, Cockington Close, Leigham, Plymouth, PL6 8RF
Activities: Primary education
Officers: Louisa Jayne Tompkins, Secretary; Stuart Bellworthy [1972] Director; King Lam Kingston Ho [1968] Director/Financial Controller/Risk Manager; Christian Jenkins [1958] Director; Samuel Jones [1975] Director; Giles Francis Lawrence Freathy [1983] Director/Teacher; Lee Le Marquand [1976] Director/Business Manager; Ian Mitchell [1972] Director; Andrew Young [1967] Director/Team Lead; Dr Michael Robert Young [1947] Director

Connect Group PLC
Incorporated: 2 August 2004 *Employees:* 4,844
Net Worth Deficit: £45,900,000 *Total Assets:* £208,500,000
Registered Office: Rowan House, Cherry Orchard North, Kembrey Park, Swindon, Wilts, SN2 8UH
Activities: Activities of head offices
Officers: Stuart Steven Marriner, Secretary; Jonathan Michael Bunting [1972] Director/Chief Commercial Officer; Denise Rosemary Collis [1957] Director; Anthony Liam Grace [1961] Director; Michael John Holt [1961] Director; Paul Gareth Kennedy [1958] Director [Irish]; Jozef Opdeweegh [1966] Director/Chief Executive Officer [American/Belgian]; Mark Argent Whiteling [1963] Director

Connexion Technologies Limited
Incorporated: 27 July 2012 *Employees:* 115
Net Worth: £359,000 *Total Assets:* £7,412,000
Registered Office: CIL House, Charlton Road, Andover, Hants, SP10 3JL
Activities: Manufacture of loaded electronic boards
Major Shareholder: Craig Richard Wright
Officers: Richard Philip Eldridge, Secretary; John George Boston [1961] Director; Richard Philip Eldridge [1977] Director; Dr David Robin Stokes [1946] Director; Craig Richard Wright [1968] Director

Connolly & Callaghan Group Limited
Incorporated: 3 February 2016 *Employees:* 7
Net Worth: £19,895,856 *Total Assets:* £22,618,648
Registered Office: Hamilton House, 80 Stokes Croft, Bristol, BS1 3QY
Activities: Activities of head offices
Major Shareholder: Martin Bernard Connolly
Officers: Mary Helen Connolly [1964] Director

Connolly & Callaghan Limited
Incorporated: 17 August 1999 *Employees:* 45
Net Worth: £22,611,554 *Total Assets:* £33,515,824
Registered Office: Hamilton House, 80 Stokes Croft, Bristol, BS1 3QY
Activities: Buying and selling of own real estate
Parent: Connolly & Callaghan Group Ltd
Officers: Mary Helen Connolly [1964] Director

Consilium Airton Limited
Incorporated: 17 September 2014
Net Worth: £624,000 *Total Assets:* £71,386,000
Registered Office: Jessop House, Jessop Avenue, Cheltenham, Glos, GL50 3WG
Activities: Credit granting by non-deposit taking finance houses and other specialist consumer credit grantors
Parent: Commercial First Group Limited
Officers: Timothy Paul Theobald [1967] Director/Chartered Accountant

Constellation Software UK Holdco Ltd
Incorporated: 5 September 2014
Net Worth: £29,254,568 *Total Assets:* £165,515,520
Registered Office: Unit A1, Methuen Park, Chippenham, Wilts, SN14 0GT
Activities: Information technology consultancy activities
Officers: Darrell Peter Boxall [1970] Business Unit Manager/Director; Carrie Marks [1980] Director/Chartered Accountant; Stephen William McNally [1968] Director/Accountant; Aaron Shapiro [1987] Business Development Director [Canadian]; Paul Yancich [1985] Director/Investor [American]

Constructor Group UK Limited
Incorporated: 12 March 2003 *Employees:* 41
Net Worth: £7,324,366 *Total Assets:* £11,373,279
Registered Office: Murdock Road, Dorcan, Swindon, Wilts, SN3 5HY
Activities: Manufacture of other fabricated metal products n.e.c.
Parent: Gonvarri Material Handling AS
Officers: Andrew Stephen Leese, Secretary; Matthew Jeremy Grierson [1970] Director; Jesus Calvo Moreira [1968] Director [Spanish]; Frank Pohl [1959] Director [German]

Consumer Intelligence Limited
Incorporated: 5 November 2003 *Employees:* 74
Net Worth: £641,681 *Total Assets:* £4,209,124
Registered Office: Bath House, 6-8 Bath Street, Bristol, BS1 6HL
Activities: Other business support service activities n.e.c.
Shareholders: Ian Christopher Hughes; Maura Brigid Hughes
Officers: Ian Christopher Hughes, Secretary; Ian Christopher Hughes [1965] Director/Researcher

Contactreal Limited
Incorporated: 13 October 1988 *Employees:* 1
Net Worth: £3,783,120 *Total Assets:* £5,392,119
Registered Office: 14 Wilton Road, Salisbury, Wilts, SP2 7EE
Activities: Other letting and operating of own or leased real estate
Shareholder: Sebastian Alexander Church
Officers: Sebastian Alexander Church [1970] Director/Chartered Accountant

Containers Packaging (Europe)
Incorporated: 28 April 1995 *Employees:* 3
Net Worth: £1,161,489,152 *Total Assets:* £3,354,524,672
Registered Office: Amcor Central Services, 83 Tower Road North, Warmley, Bristol, BS30 8XP
Activities: Other service activities n.e.c.
Officers: Matthew Charles Burrows [1970] Director; Christopher John Cheetham [1962] Director/Chartered Accountant; Richard Dixon [1963] Director/European Treasury and Tax Manager

Contango Investments Limited
Incorporated: 19 November 2014
Net Worth: £425,376 *Total Assets:* £3,678,810
Registered Office: Grosvenor House, 1 New Road, Brixham, Devon, TQ5 8LZ
Activities: Activities of investment trusts
Officers: Andrew Peter Trott [1969] Director

Control Techniques Dynamics Limited
Incorporated: 19 November 1962 *Employees:* 105
Net Worth: £28,919,000 *Total Assets:* £31,351,000
Registered Office: South Way, Walworth Industrial Estate, Andover, Hants, SP10 5AB
Activities: Manufacture of electric motors, generators and transformers
Parent: Nidec Control Techniques Limited
Officers: Anthony Simmonds, Secretary; Eric Coupart [1959] Director/Engineer [French]; Guillaume de La Codre [1963] Director [French]; Keith Hedges [1951] Managing Director

Conway Bailey Transport Limited
Incorporated: 25 May 2000 *Employees:* 152
Net Worth: £5,369,575 *Total Assets:* £12,492,339
Registered Office: Venayr Goonearl, Scorrier, Redruth, Cornwall, TR16 5EB
Activities: Freight transport by road
Major Shareholder: Mark Gordon Bailey
Officers: Kathryn Mary Bailey, Secretary/Office Manager; Kathryn Mary Bailey [1974] Director/Company Secretary; Lee Daniel Wills [1985] Director

R.S. Cook & Sons Limited
Incorporated: 21 March 1972
Net Worth: £1,213,564 *Total Assets:* £3,720,926
Registered Office: Balliol House, Southernhay Gardens, Exeter, Devon, EX1 1NP
Activities: Construction of commercial buildings
Major Shareholder: Michael Reginald Cook
Officers: Cheryl Ann McNairn, Secretary; Carol Denise Cook [1959] Director; Michael Reginald Cook [1961] Director/Building Contractor; Kevin Arthur Lloyd [1981] Director

Cook and Copp Limited
Incorporated: 21 June 2011 *Employees:* 3
Net Worth: £2,432,724 *Total Assets:* £4,555,795
Registered Office: Rumwell Hall, Rumwell, Taunton, Somerset, TA4 1EL
Activities: Other letting and operating of own or leased real estate
Shareholders: Richard Franklin Mead; Patricia Mead
Officers: Sarah Mead, Secretary; Patricia Mead [1947] Director; Richard Mead [1974] Director; Sarah Mead [1977] Director

The Ernest Cook Trust
Incorporated: 12 January 2012 *Employees:* 28
Net Worth: £181,601,136 *Total Assets:* £192,994,656
Registered Office: The Estate Office, Fairford Park, Fairford, Glos, GL7 4JH
Activities: Other education n.e.c.
Officers: Dr Victoria Mary Edwards, Secretary; Andrew William Michael Christie-Miller [1950] Director/Landowner; Simon Flowerdew Eliot [1952] Director/Retired; Jenefer Dawn Greenwood [1957] Director/Chartered Surveyor; Henry Merton Henderson [1952] Director/Landowner; Mary Elizabeth Riall [1965] Director/Charity Trustee; Sir Walter Robert Alexander Ross [1950] Director/Consultant

Cooke Painter Limited
Incorporated: 13 March 2008 *Employees:* 36
Net Worth: £418,641 *Total Assets:* £5,743,004
Registered Office: 314 Wells Road, Knowle, Bristol, BS4 2QG
Activities: Solicitors
Shareholder: Andrew Michael Stone
Officers: Paul Richard Mason, Secretary; Wajid Hamid Darr [1973] Director/Solicitor; Suzanne Henderson [1978] Director/Solicitor; Andrew Michael Stone [1957] Director/Solicitor; James Robert Trescothick-Martin [1977] Director/Solicitor

Cookpad Limited
Incorporated: 28 September 2015 *Employees:* 20
Net Worth: £8,604,321 *Total Assets:* £12,005,163
Registered Office: 1-3 Broad Plain, Bristol, BS2 0JP
Activities: Other information technology service activities
Shareholder: Akimitsu Sano
Officers: Akimitsu Sano [1973] Director [Japanese]; Tomoya Yasuda [1975] Director [Japanese]

Coolgate Limited
Incorporated: 18 November 1997
Net Worth: £3,855,805 *Total Assets:* £4,931,153
Registered Office: Leeward House, Fitzroy Road, Exeter Business Park, Exeter, Devon, EX1 3LJ
Activities: Growing of cereals (except rice), leguminous crops and oil seeds
Shareholders: Charles Howard Ringrose; George David Wish; John Edward Moore; Jonathan Richard Wish; Penelope Kate Wish
Officers: Jonathan Richard Wish, Secretary; George David Wish [1932] Director/Pharmacist; Jonathan Richard Wish [1980] Director

Coombe Castle International Limited
Incorporated: 28 November 1980 *Employees:* 53
Net Worth: £3,339,812 *Total Assets:* £7,527,533
Registered Office: The Old Post Office, 41-43 Market Place, Chippenham, Wilts, SN15 3HR
Activities: Non-specialised wholesale trade
Major Shareholder: Glyn Gerald Woolley
Officers: Darren Larvin, Secretary; Darren Larvin [1971] Director; Peter Trelawney Mitchell [1960] Commercial Director; Glyn Generald Woolley [1945] Director; Susan Woolley [1946] Director

Coombe Fisheries Limited
Incorporated: 7 July 1980 *Employees:* 120
Net Worth: £6,056,363 *Total Assets:* £15,352,552
Registered Office: Riverside Road, Pottington Business Park, Barnstaple, Devon, EX31 1QN
Activities: Processing and preserving of fish, crustaceans and molluscs
Officers: Richard Alexander Charles Spear, Secretary/Director; Anthony David James Spear [1964] Director; Iain John Spear [1966] Director; Richard Alexander Charles Spear [1971] Director

Coombes Forestry Limited
Incorporated: 11 March 2009 *Employees:* 25
Net Worth: £3,304,218 *Total Assets:* £5,043,164
Registered Office: 21 Market Place, Blandford Forum, Dorset, DT11 7AF
Activities: Silviculture and other forestry activities
Major Shareholder: Jack Coombes
Officers: Jack Coombes [1981] Director/Forestry Worker; Shane Coombes [1979] Director/Forestry Worker

Coombes Manor Farm Limited
Incorporated: 24 February 2012 *Employees:* 4
Net Worth: £2,372,273 *Total Assets:* £3,570,275
Registered Office: 4 King Square, Bridgwater, Somerset, TA6 3YF
Activities: Raising of dairy cattle
Officers: Darren William Coombes [1971] Director/Farmer; Ruth Mary Coombes [1939] Director/Farmer

Cooper Tire & Rubber Company Europe Limited
Incorporated: 4 July 1918 *Employees:* 726
Net Worth: £32,786,000 *Total Assets:* £113,479,000
Registered Office: Bath Road, Melksham, Wilts, SN12 8AA
Activities: Manufacture of rubber tyres and tubes; retreading and rebuilding of rubber tyres
Parent: Cooper Tyre & Rubber Company UK Limited
Officers: Clive Weston, Secretary; Michiel Kramer [1979] Director/Business Executive; Karil Maureen Morrissey [1958] Director/Business Executive [American]; Jacobus Paulus Hendricus Van Wessum [1968] Director/Business Executive [Dutch]

Cooper Tyre & Rubber Company UK Limited
Incorporated: 25 July 1996
Net Worth: £152,115,312 *Total Assets:* £224,612,432
Registered Office: Bath Road, Melksham, Wilts, SN12 8AA
Activities: Activities of head offices
Parent: Cooper Tire & Rubber Company, Ohio
Officers: Clive Weston, Secretary; Kathleen Malloy Cindric [1981] Director/Corporate Legal Counsel [American]; Shaun Edward Graham [1970] Director/Corporate Legal Counsel [American]

Copano Limited
Incorporated: 3 April 2014 *Employees:* 1
Net Worth: £1,221,834 *Total Assets:* £5,288,408
Registered Office: Old Library Chambers, 21 Chipper Lane, Salisbury, Wilts, SP1 1BG
Activities: Other letting and operating of own or leased real estate
Shareholders: Tom Earl; Lucy Janet Earl
Officers: Tom Earl [1975] Director/Oil and Gas Trading Executive

Copper Bidco Limited
Incorporated: 12 January 2012 *Employees:* 6
Net Worth Deficit: £26,659,000 *Total Assets:* £95,576,000
Registered Office: KLAW Products, Commerce Business Centre, Commerce Close, West Wilts Trading Estate, Westbury, Wilts, BA13 4LS
Activities: Financial management
Parent: Copper Midco 2 Limited
Officers: Mike Hartman, Secretary; Mike Hartman [1965] Director/Chief Financial Officer; David Robert Hill [1966] Director; Catherine Alison Wall [1960] Director

Copper Midco 1 Limited
Incorporated: 12 January 2012
Net Worth: £293,000 *Total Assets:* £70,106,000
Registered Office: KLAW Products, Commerce Business Centre, West Wilts Trading Estate, Westbury, Wilts, BA13 4LS
Activities: Financial management
Parent: Signum Technology Limited
Officers: Mike Hartman, Secretary; Mike Hartman [1965] Director/Chief Financial Officer; David Robert Hill [1966] Director; Catherine Alison Wall [1960] Director

Copper Midco 2 Limited
Incorporated: 12 January 2012
Net Worth: £254,000 *Total Assets:* £70,067,000
Registered Office: KLAW Products, Commerce Business Centre, West Wilts Trading Estate, Westbury, Wilts, BA13 4LS
Activities: Financial management
Parent: Copper Midco 1 Limited
Officers: Mike Hartman, Secretary; Mike Hartman [1965] Director/Chief Financial Officer; David Robert Hill [1966] Director; Catherine Alison Wall [1960] Director

Copperplane Limited
Incorporated: 5 September 1996 *Employees:* 2
Net Worth: £953,416 *Total Assets:* £5,134,937
Registered Office: Leanne House, 6 Avon Close, Weymouth, Dorset, DT4 9UX
Activities: Other letting and operating of own or leased real estate
Major Shareholder: Michael William Barlow
Officers: Michael William Barlow, Secretary; Michael William Barlow [1957] Director

Copyright Administration Services Limited
Incorporated: 3 January 2008
Net Worth Deficit: £205,207 *Total Assets:* £4,914,294
Registered Office: 23 High Street, Pewsey, Wilts, SN9 5AF
Activities: Other amusement and recreation activities n.e.c.
Officers: Simon Patrick Fawcett [1962] Director; Fusun Gencsu [1957] Director [Turkish]; Tania Jayne Orchard [1964] Director

Cordash Limited
Incorporated: 4 August 2004 *Employees:* 99
Net Worth: £12,684,707 *Total Assets:* £15,542,863
Registered Office: Crosswyn House, St Ewe, St Austell, Cornwall, PL26 6EX
Activities: Non-trading company
Shareholders: Toby George Howell Ashworth; M A Ashworth Trust
Officers: Wendy Hall, Secretary; Katie Amanda Ashworth [1970] Director/Solicitor; Toby George Howell Ashworth [1967] Director; Patricia Daphne Anne Burt [1934] Director

Corfe Hills School Academy Trust
Incorporated: 21 February 2011 *Employees:* 164
Net Worth: £15,638,892 *Total Assets:* £19,271,656
Registered Office: Corfe Hills School, Higher Blandford Road, Broadstone, Dorset, BH18 9BG
Activities: General secondary education
Officers: Sheila Way, Secretary; Alison Mary Bicker [1955] Director/Teacher; Paul Bompass [1950] Director/Academy Governor; Edward David Henry Coviello [1949] Director/Chartered Accountant; Sonia Gavira [1966] Director/Executive Coach; Jennifer Susan Jefferies [1947] Director/County Councillor; Dr Sarah Louise Jordan [1958] Director/Solicitor; Jean Fiona McBain [1957] Director/Local Authority Children's Services Manager; Allan Murray [1943] Director/Teaching Assistant; Richard Mutlow [1945] Director/Retired; Dr Dirk Van Den Broek [1945] Director/Retired Business Executive [Dutch]; Paul Scott Warman [1950] Director/Retired; Patricia Zimmerman [1959] Director/Teacher

Corialis Group Limited
Incorporated: 22 November 2016
Net Worth: £318,540,608 *Total Assets:* £1,021,575,168
Registered Office: c/o Smart Systems, Arnolds Way, Yatton, Bristol, BS49 4QN
Activities: Activities of other holding companies n.e.c.
Officers: Wim Flo [1979] Director [Belgian]; Edward Anthony Robinson [1958] Director; Johan Paul Jozef Verstrepen [1961] Director/Chief Executive Officer [Belgian]; Mark Robert West [1976] Director

Corin Group Limited
Incorporated: 27 April 1994
Previous: Corin Group PLC
Net Worth: £23,968,000 *Total Assets:* £28,515,000
Registered Office: The Corinium Centre, Cirencester, Glos, GL7 1YJ
Activities: Manufacture of medical and dental instruments and supplies
Parent: Corin Orthopaedic Holdings Limited
Officers: Stefano Alfonsi [1964] Director [Italian]; Victoria Mary Silvester [1978] Director

Corin Holdings Limited
Incorporated: 13 December 1993
Net Worth: £13,074,000 *Total Assets:* £33,750,000
Registered Office: The Corinium Centre, Cirencester, Glos, GL7 1YJ
Activities: Manufacture of medical and dental instruments and supplies
Parent: Corin Group PLC
Officers: Stefano Alfonsi [1964] Director [Italian]; Victoria Mary Silvester [1978] Finance Director

Corin International Limited
Incorporated: 15 July 1992
Net Worth: £8,143,562 *Total Assets:* £23,518,700
Registered Office: The Corinium Centre, Cirencester, Glos, GL7 1YJ
Activities: Manufacture of medical and dental instruments and supplies
Parent: Corin Group PLC
Officers: Stefano Alfonsi [1964] Director [Italian]; Victoria Mary Silvester [1978] Finance Director

Corin Limited
Incorporated: 1 May 1985 *Employees:* 275
Net Worth Deficit: £11,348,000 *Total Assets:* £50,491,000
Registered Office: The Corinium Centre, Cirencester, Glos, GL7 1YJ
Activities: Manufacture of medical and dental instruments and supplies
Parent: Corin Holdings Limited
Officers: Stefano Alfonsi [1964] Director [Italian]; Russell Davies Mably [1975] Director; Victoria Mary Silvester [1978] Director/Group Financial Controller

Corin Orthopaedics Holdings Limited
Incorporated: 11 July 2012 *Employees:* 474
Net Worth: £38,128,000 *Total Assets:* £101,035,000
Registered Office: The Corinium Centre, Love Lane Industrial Estate, Cirencester, Glos, GL7 1YJ
Activities: Manufacture of medical and dental instruments and supplies
Shareholder: Marcello Comoli
Officers: Stefano Alfonsi [1964] Director [Italian]; Victoria Mary Silvester [1978] Director

Corin USA Limited
Incorporated: 14 April 1992 *Employees:* 19
Net Worth Deficit: £1,954,198 *Total Assets:* £8,152,339
Registered Office: The Corinium Centre, Love Lane Industrial Estate, Cirencester, Glos, GL7 1YJ
Activities: Manufacture of medical and dental instruments and supplies
Parent: Corin International Limited
Officers: Stefano Alfonsi [1964] Director [Italian]; Victoria Mary Silvester [1978] Finance Director

Corinium Education Trust
Incorporated: 10 February 2011 *Employees:* 126
Previous: Cirencester Deer Park School
Net Worth: £11,589,142 *Total Assets:* £13,676,888
Registered Office: Cirencester Deer Park School, Stroud Road, Cirencester, Glos, GL7 1XB
Activities: General secondary education
Officers: Martin Roger Doidge, Secretary; Susannah Gilbert [1979] Director/Economist; Chiquita Henson [1962] Director/Headteacher; Jane Lloyd [1954] Director/Retired; Claire Minett [1957] Director/Retired; Claire Amanda Mould [1969] Director; Graham Andrew Russell [1953] Director/Retired; Charles Frederick Basil Woodd [1971] Director/Actuary

Corintech Limited
Incorporated: 22 November 1977 *Employees:* 62
Net Worth: £6,183,249 *Total Assets:* £8,206,066
Registered Office: Ashford Mill, Station Road, Fordingbridge, Hants, SP6 1DZ
Activities: Manufacture of electronic components
Officers: Geoffrey Clive Andrew Allen [1954] Director/Accountant; Peter James Cross [1974] Director; Dean Charles James [1962] Marketing Director; Timothy Jordan Dench [1982] Operations Director; Julian John Navey [1961] Finance Director; Rod Stefan Piwowarski [1969] Director; Martin Skinner [1982] Sales Director; Timothy James Waterman [1962] Director

Corinthian Sports Limited
Incorporated: 12 March 2010 *Employees:* 25
Net Worth: £202,434 *Total Assets:* £4,127,769
Registered Office: Mazars LLP, 5th Floor, Merck House, Seldown Lane, Poole, Dorset, BH15 1TW
Activities: Public relations and communications activities
Parent: Corinthian (London) Holdings Limited
Officers: Mark James Hoskins [1975] Director; Gavin John O'Callaghan [1968] Director

Cornbury Farm Contracting Limited
Incorporated: 17 June 2010 *Employees:* 2
Net Worth: £1,572,125 *Total Assets:* £3,999,119
Registered Office: Cornbury Farm, West Lavington, Devizes, Wilts, SN10 4ND
Activities: Support activities for animal production (other than farm animal boarding)
Shareholders: Nicholas James Hooper; Michael Henry Hooper
Officers: Helen Marjorie Hooper, Secretary; Michael Henry Hooper [1965] Director; Nicholas James Hooper [1969] Director/Farmer

Cornelia Care Homes Limited
Incorporated: 5 April 2006
Net Worth: £7 *Total Assets:* £4,889,658
Registered Office: 1 Countess Road, Amesbury, Salisbury, Wilts, SP4 7DW
Activities: Residential nursing care facilities
Shareholders: Renuka Thillainathan; Vasantha Nadesan; Siva Nadesan
Officers: Vasantha Nadesan [1964] Director; Renuka Thillainathan [1960] Director/Accountant

Cornerstone Academy Trust
Incorporated: 9 August 2010 *Employees:* 87
Previous: Broadclyst Primary Academy Trust
Net Worth: £4,109,160 *Total Assets:* £5,953,318
Registered Office: Broadclyst Community Primary School, School Lane, Exeter, Devon, EX5 3JG
Activities: Primary education
Officers: Amy May Partridge, Secretary; Rachel Louise Billen [1976] Director/Solicitor; Jonathan Paul Bishop [1972] Director/Headteacher; Samantha Jane Chapman [1966] Director/Professional Lead, Early Years Education; Kenneth Herbert Dyson [1946] Director/Retired; Myles Gordon [1975] Director/Mortgage Protection Consultant; Will Jordan [1987] Director/Certified Chartered Accountant; Helen Litvak [1962] Marketing Director; Henry James Massey [1974] Director; Stewart David Noakes [1973] Director/Co-Founder and Board Member EMCL; Matthew James Garvey Pitts [1989] Director/Teacher; Brett Samuel Renfree [1971] Director/Retail Store Manager; Stephen John Taylor [1978] Director/IT Manager; John Tombleson Waddingham [1970] Director/Hydrologist; Paul Whitmarsh [1966] Director/Practice Manager; Bronwen Lily Williams [1992] Director/Teacher

The Cornish Bakery Shops Limited
Incorporated: 13 October 1987 *Employees:* 291
Previous: Presto Retail Limited
Net Worth: £1,148,094 *Total Assets:* £5,637,148
Registered Office: 7 Arwenack Street, Falmouth, Cornwall, TR11 3HZ
Activities: Unlicenced restaurants and cafes
Officers: Annette Claire Pellow, Secretary; Stephen John Grocutt [1963] Director; Stephen Gary Hill [1955] Director/Chartered Accountant

Cornish Concrete Products Limited
Incorporated: 23 October 1978 *Employees:* 85
Net Worth: £755,043 *Total Assets:* £3,852,088
Registered Office: Point Mills, Bissoe, Truro, Cornwall, TR4 8QZ
Activities: Other manufacturing n.e.c.
Shareholders: Estelle Moses; Hugh Harazi
Officers: Estelle Moses, Secretary; Kevin Bate [1971] Director; Hugh Harazi [1946] Director; David Jonathon Moses [1964] Director/Manager; Estelle Moses [1943] Director; Richard Edward Tatlow [1983] Director

Cornish Farm Dairy Limited
Incorporated: 13 March 2007 *Employees:* 197
Net Worth: £6,216,733 *Total Assets:* £16,792,304
Registered Office: Greymare Farm, Lostwithiel, Cornwall, PL22 0LW
Activities: Liquid milk and cream production
Shareholders: Rachel Jane Clarke; Francis William Clarke
Officers: Francis William Clarke, Secretary; Francis William Clarke [1954] Director/Farmer; George William Clarke [1988] Director; Rachel Jane Clarke [1957] Director/Farmer; Louis Jules Hydleman [1956] Director; Francis Henry Strelzyn-Clarke [1985] Director

Cornish Mutual Assurance Company,Limited
Incorporated: 10 October 1903 *Employees:* 112
Net Worth: £22,946,064 *Total Assets:* £54,734,228
Registered Office: CMA House, Newham Road, Newham, Truro, Cornwall, TR1 2SU
Activities: Non-life insurance
Officers: Margaret Patricia Schwarz, Secretary; Peter Stuart Beaumont [1967] Director/Accountant; Roger Bruce Cawse [1950] Director; Paul John Davies [1951] Chartered Director; Alan Goddard [1959] Director/Chartered Insurer; Richard Lane [1953] Director/Chartered Insurer and Chartered Manager; Paul William David Mahon [1970] Insurance Technical Director; Jeremy Paul Oatey [1967] Director/Farmer; Ian James Pawley [1947] Director/Retired Solicitor; Charles Walter Pears [1973] Director; Susannah Elizabeth Turner [1966] Director/CEO of a Community Foundation

Cornish Potatoes Limited
Incorporated: 5 March 2010
Net Worth: £4,347,404 *Total Assets:* £4,367,642
Registered Office: c/o Francis Clark LLP, North Quay House, Sutton Harbour, Plymouth, PL4 0RA
Activities: Growing of vegetables and melons, roots and tubers
Shareholders: Giles Duncan Hutchings; Louis Aidan Mathers
Officers: Edward John Rowe [1974] Director; Mark Daniel Rowe [1971] Director

Cornish Scrumpy Holdings Limited
Incorporated: 24 April 2001 *Employees:* 2
Net Worth: £8,857,481 *Total Assets:* £10,185,911
Registered Office: 7 Sandy Court, Ashleigh Way, Langage Business Park, Plymouth, PL7 5JX
Activities: Manufacture of cider and other fruit wines
Parent: Healey Holdings Limited
Officers: Kay Victoria Healey, Secretary; David John Healey [1956] Director; Jonathon Healey [1986] Director; Kay Victoria Healey [1957] Director; Sam Healey [1985] Director

Cornwall Air Ambulance Trust
Incorporated: 24 November 2009 *Employees:* 31
Net Worth: £9,470,436 *Total Assets:* £10,023,296
Registered Office: Cornwall Air Ambulance Trust Headquarters, Trevithick Downs, Newquay, Cornwall, TR8 4DY
Activities: Other business support service activities n.e.c.
Officers: Stephen James Murdoch, Secretary; Ian Brackenbury [1945] Director; Robert Richard Cowie [1953] Director/Chartered Accountant; Henry Orchard [1972] Director/Recycler; Christopher Charles Pomfret [1949] Director; Sarah Louise Pryce [1965] Director; Barbara Ann Sharples [1953] Director; Margaret Ellen Winser [1942] Director

Cornwall Care Limited
Incorporated: 13 July 1995 *Employees:* 724
Net Worth: £10,504,000 *Total Assets:* £34,178,000
Registered Office: Cornwall Care House, Truro Business Park, Threemilestone, Truro, Cornwall, TR4 9NY
Activities: Residential care activities for the elderly and disabled
Officers: Stephen James Taylor Clague, Secretary; John Keith Acornley [1953] Director; Michael John Stebbing Beadel [1959] Director/Solicitor; Dr Anthony Edward Felton [1958] Director; Generaldine Margaret Lavery [1954] Director; Colin Champion Nicholls [1946] Director/Retailer; Philip Kingdon Rees [1948] Director; Thelma Olive Sorensen [1941] Director

Cornwall Community Foundation
Incorporated: 1 July 2003 *Employees:* 6
Net Worth: £5,632,659 *Total Assets:* £5,645,651
Registered Office: Suite 1, Sheers Barton, Lawhitton, Launceston, Cornwall, PL15 9NJ
Activities: Activities of other membership organisations n.e.c.
Officers: Toby George Howell Ashworth [1967] Director; Honourable Evelyn Arthur Hugh Boscawen [1955] Director/Farmer; Kim Conchie [1956] Director/Chief Executive; Jonathan David William Cunliffe [1972] Director/Partner; John Michael Ede [1948] Director/Manager; Stamford Timothy John Galsworthy [1976] Occupation Director; Jane Margaret Hartley [1962] Director/Own Business; Deborah Mary Hinton [1944] Director/Retired; Natercia Maria Ellis Costa Dos Santos Hughes [1975] Director/Accountant [Portuguese]; Emma Mantle [1969] Director/Property Sales Consultant; Nicky Marquis [1956] Director; Daphne Janet Hildebrand Skinnard [1963] Director/Assistant Editor; Timothy John Smith [1947] Director/Chartered Accountant; Ian Taylor [1966] Director/Partner; Thomas Richard Van Oss [1957] Director/Corporate Financial Adviser; James Piran Williams [1950] Director

Cornwall Development Company Ltd
Incorporated: 17 November 1998 *Employees:* 256
Net Worth Deficit: £7,010,088 *Total Assets:* £4,692,241
Registered Office: Bickford House, Station Road, Pool, Redruth, Cornwall, TR15 3QG
Activities: Temporary employment agency activities
Parent: Corserv Ltd
Officers: Nicola Louise Pooley, Secretary/CFO; Richard Zmuda, Secretary; Dominic Jon Bostock [1976] Director; Elaine Karen Holt [1966] Director; Joseph Gerard Keohane [1967] Finance Director [Irish]; Michael Julian King [1959] Managing Director; Catherine Jane Robinson [1966] Group Managing Director

Cornwall Glass & Glazing Limited
Incorporated: 1 May 1998 *Employees:* 296
Net Worth: £1,405,997 *Total Assets:* £10,928,555
Registered Office: Old Mansion House, 9 Quay Street, Truro, Cornwall, TR1 2HE
Activities: Agents involved in the sale of timber and building materials
Shareholders: Garry David Mitchell; Mark John Mitchell; David John Mitchell
Officers: Mark John Mitchell, Secretary; Paul David Garrard [1968] Director; Angus John Herdman [1964] Sales Director; Mark James Knight [1975] Director; David John Mitchell [1945] Director/Glazier; Garry David Mitchell [1972] Director/Glazier; Mark John Mitchell [1970] Director/Glazier; Mark Norcliffe [1961] Director/Glass & Glazing; Martin Jeremy Phillips [1967] Finance Director; Martin Colin Saint [1965] Director

Cornwall Hospice Care Limited
Incorporated: 21 December 2005 *Employees:* 284
Net Worth: £10,700,784 *Total Assets:* £11,342,047
Registered Office: Mount Edgcumbe Hospice, Porthpean Road, St Austell, Cornwall, PL26 6AB
Activities: Specialists medical practice activities
Officers: Graham Ian Clarke, Secretary; Mary Allison Anson [1952] Director/Registered Care Provider/Managing Partner; Dr John Nicholas Barnes [1952] Director/Consultancy Physician; Robert Alan Brownscombe [1954] Director/Chartered Accountant; Lesley Ann Clarke [1944] Director/Retired; Dr Steve Hawkins [1954] Director/Retired G.P; Beverley MacIntyre [1957] Director/Management Consultant; Dr Colin John Philip [1955] Director/General Medical Practitioner; Graham Piercy [1960] Director; David William Renwick [1952] Director/Chief Executive; Lesley Jane Stubberfield [1950] Director/Retired; Alistair James Whyte [1959] Director/Solicitor

Cornwall Housing Limited
Incorporated: 11 February 2003 *Employees:* 385
Net Worth: £5,657,000 *Total Assets:* £14,218,000
Registered Office: Chy Trevail, Beacon Technology Park, Bodmin, Cornwall, PL31 2FR
Activities: Management of real estate on a fee or contract basis
Parent: Corserv Limited
Officers: Richard Cyril Zmuda, Secretary; Nicholas Cross [1971] Managing Director; Martin Emery [1952] Director; Jacquie Gammon [1959] Director/Councillor; John Anthony James Harris [1959] Director; Tim Andrew Jeans [1957] Director/Independent; Mary Katherine May [1949] Director/Bereavement Officer and Councillor; Mike McLening [1949] Director/Councillor; Hazel June Tearne [1947] Director/Retired; Shelley Thornton [1964] Director/Management Consultant; Dr Nigel James Williams [1946] Director/Retired

Cornwall Trust for Nature Conservation Ltd (The)
Incorporated: 15 August 1962 *Employees:* 60
Net Worth: £6,423,673 *Total Assets:* £6,914,573
Registered Office: Five Acres, Allet, Truro, Cornwall, TR4 9DJ
Activities: Other education n.e.c.
Officers: Paul Anthony Coyne [1947] Director/Retired; Stephen Harrison Crummay [1962] Director/Consultant; Frederick Anthony Currie [1947] Director/Retired; Charles Vivian David [1956] Director/Retired; Daniel Eva [1963] Director/Teacher; Dr Alan John Gowenlock [1957] Director/Retired Doctor; Russell David Horsley [1953] Director/Civil Servant; Francis MacDonald Peter Howie [1945] Director/Retired; Philip John McVey [1953] Director/Retired; Mark Nicholson [1960] Director/Copywriter; Ian Arnold Pye [1953] Director/Retired; Deirdre Ann Reeves [1953] Director/Retired PR/Marketing Consultant; Gillian Mary Saunders [1950] Director/Retired; Jean Bertha Smith [1934] Director/Retired School Teacher; David Leslie Thomas [1946] Director/Retired; Elizabeth Frances Tregenza [1945] Director/Retired; Dr Nicholas Jeremy Charles Tregenza [1945] Director; Caroline Jane Vulliamy [1948] Director/Retired Heritage at Risk Project Officer; Stephen Richard Warman [1953] Director/Retired

Corrington Estates Limited
Incorporated: 14 July 1937 *Employees:* 2
Net Worth: £8,451,810 *Total Assets:* £9,220,666
Registered Office: Beechcroft Barn, Upton Lovell, Warminster, Wilts, BA12 0JW
Activities: Other letting and operating of own or leased real estate
Shareholders: Trudy Rogers; Berkshire Trustees Limited
Officers: Jacqueline Ann Pudney, Secretary; Caroline Deborah Creagh Chapman [1960] Director; Jacqueline Ann Pudney [1963] Director and Company Secretary

The Corsham School Academy Group
Incorporated: 3 March 2011 *Employees:* 187
Net Worth: £21,491,158 *Total Assets:* £23,151,972
Registered Office: The Corsham School, The Tynings, Corsham, Wilts, SN13 9DF
Activities: General secondary education
Officers: Michelle Hocking, Secretary; Rodney Bell [1977] Director/Headteacher; Alun Davis [1971] Director/Teacher; Christopher Andrew Denton [1978] Director/Business Manager; Tom Peter Duncan Fitzpatrick [1970] Director/Solicitor; Helen Hynes [1978] Director/Health Access Team Clinical Advisor; Michael David Large [1959] Director; Professor Bernard John Morley [1959] Director/Academic; Malcolm Donald Sinclair [1961] Retired NHS Director; Gareth Spicer [1973] Director; Paul Stone [1970] Business Planning Director; Sarah Anne Truelove [1969] Director of Finance; Carole Whittingham [1961] Director/Exams and Data Manager

Cosmetic Warriors Limited
Incorporated: 22 February 2001 *Employees:* 43
Net Worth: £7,607,000 *Total Assets:* £10,777,000
Registered Office: 29 High Street, Poole, Dorset, BH15 1AB
Activities: Technical testing and analysis
Shareholder: Mark Constantine
Officers: Helen Elizabeth Ambrosen [1956] Director; Karl Joseph Bygrave [1962] Director; Margaret Joan Constantine [1953] Director/Inventor; Mark Constantine [1952] Director; Simon Constantine [1981] Director

J Cossins & Sons Limited
Incorporated: 10 March 1960 *Employees:* 14
Net Worth: £6,357,863 *Total Assets:* £7,014,981
Registered Office: Midland House, 2 Poole Road, Bournemouth, BH2 5QY
Activities: Mixed farming
Shareholders: Barbara Jean Cossins; James Richard Cossins; Alastair Richard Marcus Goodbody; John Robin Hooper
Officers: Barbara Jean Cossins, Secretary; James Richard Cossins [1957] Director/Farmer

Cotek Papers Limited
Incorporated: 5 October 1964 *Employees:* 67
Net Worth: £7,265,269 *Total Assets:* £9,853,036
Registered Office: Draycott, Moreton in Marsh, Glos, GL56 9JU
Activities: Manufacture of other articles of paper and paperboard n.e.c.
Officers: Scott Ewart Hazell, Secretary; Dr Adam Surtees Hazell [1965] Operations Director; Marian Rosalind Hazell [1929] Director; Scott Ewart Hazell [1954] Director

Cotham Gardens Primary School Ltd
Incorporated: 16 July 2012 *Employees:* 71
Previous: Colston's Primary School
Net Worth: £6,962,908 *Total Assets:* £7,944,998
Registered Office: 18 Cotham Grove, Bristol, BS6 6AL
Activities: Primary education
Officers: Adam Sheldon, Secretary; Dr Pauline Mary Allen [1953] Director/Retired Scientist; Alex Bell [1969] Director/Teacher; Catherine Olga Dunscombe [1949] Director/Semi-Retired Administrator; Emma Elizabeth Gledhill [1963] Director/Finance Manager; Iram Nazir [1972] Director/IT; Michael John Paton [1989] Director/Engineering Manager; Maxine Anorah Phillips [1963] Director/Lunchtime Assistant; Katherine Price [1971] Director/Teacher; Dr Sally Ann Reardon [1963] Director/Senior Lecturer; Dr Niklas Serning [1971] Director/Child Psychotherapist; Jamey Mynanwy Wilkinson [1977] Director/HR Advisor; Frederic Witham [1980] Director/Aerospace Engineer [British/French]; Emily Young [1984] Director/Teacher

Cotham School
Incorporated: 8 August 2011 *Employees:* 148
Net Worth: £15,794,216 *Total Assets:* £19,851,442
Registered Office: Cotham School, Cotham Lawn Road, Cotham, Bristol, BS6 6DT
Activities: General secondary education
Officers: Leanne Marie Sowersby, Secretary; Dora Lilian Alderson [1948] Director; Jack Barber [1992] Director/Teacher of Science; John Martin Bass [1964] Director/Chartered Surveyor; Massimo Bonaddio [1969] Director/Headteacher [British/Italian]; James Bowyer [1965] Director/Headteacher Education; Joanne Marguerite Butler [1968] Director/Headteacher; Edward John Carpenter [1987] Director/Network Manager; Jane Chamberlin [1970] Director/Solicitor; Jo Feather [1974] Director/Accountant; Sandra Rosa Fryer [1952] Director; Claire Louise Grocott [1965] Director; Delroy Howard Hibbert [1968] Director/Chartered Surveyor; Lucy Jane Hunt [1974] Engagement Director, Bristol Old Vic; Morag Fiona Pirie [1985] Director/HLTA; Hannah Louise Russell [1973] Director/Commissioning Manager - Bristol City Council; David Llewelyn Yorath [1945] Director/Consultant

Cotswold Archaeology Limited
Incorporated: 17 March 1989 *Employees:* 219
Net Worth: £3,235,363 *Total Assets:* £5,923,945
Registered Office: Building 11, Kemble Enterprise Park, Cirencester, Glos, GL7 6BQ
Activities: Other professional, scientific and technical activities n.e.c.
Officers: Alan Malcolm Chater [1951] Director/Chartered Accountant; Paul Peter James Cullen [1946] Director/Retired; Professor Timothy Charles Darvill [1957] Director/Professor of Archaeology; Dr Laura Helen Evis [1987] Director/Lecturer; Victoria Elizabeth Penelope Fenner [1961] Director/Development Manager; Clare Kirk [1976] Director/Marketing Consultant; Susan Barbara Parsons [1955] Director/Retired; Keith Percy Winmill [1960] Director/Company Secretary; Dr Christopher John Young [1947] Director/Retired

Cotswold Architectural Products Limited
Incorporated: 14 February 1974 *Employees:* 50
Net Worth: £3,024,233 *Total Assets:* £5,680,147
Registered Office: Manor Park Industrial Estate, Manor Road, Cheltenham, Glos, GL51 9SQ
Activities: Manufacture of locks and hinges
Officers: Ian Greaves, Secretary; Ian Greaves [1967] Director; Robert Lelio [1956] Director/Chief Financial Officer [American]; Eric William Mertz [1969] Director/Chief Executive Officer [American]; Mag Saba [1954] Director [Canadian]; Ken Stein Wilson [1971] Director

Cotswold Beacon Academy Trust
Incorporated: 4 July 2011 *Employees:* 226
Previous: Marling School
Net Worth: £18,451,964 *Total Assets:* £20,222,326
Registered Office: Cainscross Road, Stroud, Glos, GL5 4HE
Activities: Pre-primary education
Officers: Emma Louise Gray, Secretary; Graham John Ayre [1956] Director/Internal Auditor; Deborah Joan Bird [1962] Director; Helen June Cerullo [1974] Director/IT Systems Manager; Benjamin John Eagle [1980] Director/Deputy Chief Executive; John Gilbert [1952] Director/Head of Commercial Strategy; Emma Louise Gray [1967] Finance Director; Nigel Anthony Riglar [1967] Director/Local Government Officer; Stuart Lee Scott Wilson [1965] Director/Headteacher; Nathan Jon Wolstenholme [1969] Director

Cotswold Collections Group Limited
Incorporated: 19 April 2017 *Employees:* 38
Net Worth: £1,315,944 *Total Assets:* £7,581,193
Registered Office: Unit 3 Centrum Park, Tewkesbury Road, Cheltenham, Glos, GL51 9FD
Activities: Agents involved in the sale of textiles, clothing, fur, footwear and leather goods
Officers: Thomas Richard Brown, Secretary; Stuart John Binnie [1946] Director; Thomas Richard Brown [1961] Design Director; Kathryn Jane Cheesman [1959] Design Director; Mark Tristam Norwood Dugdale [1958] Director

Cotswold Doors Ltd
Incorporated: 9 June 2005 *Employees:* 33
Net Worth: £1,543,784 *Total Assets:* £5,165,016
Registered Office: Unit 1 Whelford Industrial Estate, Whelford Road, Fairford, Glos, GL7 4DT
Activities: Agents involved in the sale of timber and building materials
Major Shareholder: David Neil Campbell
Officers: Simon Campbell, Secretary/Accountant; David Neil Campbell [1951] Director; Simon Paul David Campbell [1977] Director; Nicola McDermott [1980] Director; James Alan Wilkinson [1969] Sales Director

Cotswold Hoburne Limited
Incorporated: 22 April 1971 *Employees:* 61
Net Worth: £993,921 *Total Assets:* £9,723,816
Registered Office: 10 Hoburne Lane, Christchurch, Dorset, BH23 4HP
Activities: Holiday centres and villages
Parent: Hoburne Limited
Officers: Nicholas Stewart Putnam, Company Secretary; Rosemary Sarah Kennar [1956] Director; Timothy Richard Knight [1960] Director; Rodney Philip Tucker [1954] Director

Cotswold Homes Limited
Incorporated: 19 February 2002 *Employees:* 12
Net Worth: £5,103,917 *Total Assets:* £10,889,114
Registered Office: West House, Armstrong Way, Yate, Bristol, BS37 5NG
Activities: Construction of domestic buildings
Parent: Peter Rinn Holdings Limited
Officers: Michael Glen [1964] Director/Surveyor; Liam Rinn [1984] Director/Company Secretary; Peter Charles Rinn [1950] Director [Irish]

Cotswold Micro Systems Limited
Incorporated: 29 March 1982 *Employees:* 22
Net Worth: £3,502,303 *Total Assets:* £3,560,450
Registered Office: 4 St Albans Road, Gloucester, GL2 5FW
Activities: Manufacture of loaded electronic boards
Parent: WMG Group Ltd
Officers: Emma Louise Crawford [1982] Director; Stephen John Griffin [1965] Director; Stephen Francis Whitelaw [1957] Director/Electronic Engineer

Cotswold Motor Group Limited
Incorporated: 3 March 1995 *Employees:* 353
Net Worth: £7,927,213 *Total Assets:* £65,420,232
Registered Office: Cotswold Motor Group, Corinthian Way, The Reddings, Cheltenham, Glos, GL51 6UP
Activities: Sale of new cars and light motor vehicles
Shareholders: Peter Michael Harris; Andrew Christopher Hulcoop
Officers: Mitchell Stephen James, Secretary; Peter Michael Harris [1953] Director; Andrew Christopher Hulcoop [1960] Director

The Cotswold School Academy Trust
Incorporated: 6 August 2010 *Employees:* 158
Net Worth: £17,102,000 *Total Assets:* £19,470,000
Registered Office: The Avenue, Bourton on the Water, Cheltenham, Glos, GL54 2BD
Activities: General secondary education
Officers: Kathryn Allison [1972] Director/Marketing Consultant; Lee Philip Campbell [1971] Director/Cyber Security Lecturer; Lady Mavis Dawn Dunrossil [1929] Director; Kathryn Rosemary Ellison [1964] Market Research Consultancy Director; Dr Richard John Paul Emsley [1964] Director; Robert Edward Hadley [1955] Director; William David Morgan [1975] Director/Principal; Andrew John Parker [1961] Director/Bursar; Tim Redding [1982] Director/Teacher; Cullan Riley [1970] Director/Transport and Infrastructure Planner; Catherine Roffe [1956] Director; Linda Ann Rowley [1967] Academy Improvement Director; Reverend Katrina Ruth Scott [1976] Director/Vicar; Caroline Mary Taplin [1962] H R Director; Helen Warren [1971] Director/Academia

Cotswold Seeds Limited
Incorporated: 19 March 1974 *Employees:* 17
Net Worth: £2,687,391 *Total Assets:* £3,547,532
Registered Office: Cotswold Business Village, London Road, Moreton in Marsh, Glos, GL56 0JQ
Activities: Retail sale of flowers, plants, seeds, fertilizers, pet animals and pet food in specialised stores
Major Shareholder: Ian Gerald Wilkinson
Officers: Celene Margaret Wilkinson, Secretary; Ian Generald Wilkinson [1963] Director

Cotteswold Dairy Limited
Incorporated: 1 January 1948 *Employees:* 376
Net Worth: £3,628,654 *Total Assets:* £11,807,811
Registered Office: Unit 22 Dairy Way, Northway Lane, Tewkesbury, Glos, GL20 8JE
Activities: Liquid milk and cream production
Parent: Workman Properties Limited
Officers: Louise Emma Woodward, Secretary; Wendy King [1957] Director/Accountant; Louise Emma Woodward [1969] Director and Company Secretary; George William Workman [1971] Managing Director; Gillian Marguerite Workman [1946] Director; Roger Hewins Workman [1945] Chairman/Director; Justin Michael Young [1975] Director

Cottleston Holdings Limited
Incorporated: 16 January 2015 *Employees:* 76
Net Worth: £4,913,569 *Total Assets:* £7,397,546
Registered Office: 22 Stokes Croft, Bristol, BS1 3PR
Activities: Activities of other holding companies n.e.c.
Shareholders: Lisa Michelle Gibson; Andrew William Brown
Officers: Lisa Michelle Gibson, Secretary; Andrew William Brown [1971] Director [New Zealander]; Lisa Michelle Gibson [1973] Director [New Zealander]

Council of Milton Abbey School Limited (The)
Incorporated: 26 April 1954 *Employees:* 139
Net Worth: £1,899,578 *Total Assets:* £12,421,954
Registered Office: Milton Abbey School, Milton Abbas, Blandford Forum, Dorset, DT11 0BZ
Activities: General secondary education
Officers: Neil Stephen Boulton [1950] Director/Retired; Dr Ian Geoffrey Bromilow [1956] Director/Retired; Colonel Oliver John Harben Chamberlain [1950] Director/Land Agent; Michael James Martin Dyer [1955] Director/Retired; Patrick William McGrath [1960] Director/Wine Merchant; Charles William Mitchell-Innes [1947] Director/Canon Emeritus; Matthew Damian Lloyd Noyce [1974] Director & Wealth Manager Coutts Bank; Luke James Rake [1972] Director; Jenifer Harley Simm [1948] Director/Tax Accountant and Magistrate

Countess of Brecknock Hospice Trust
Incorporated: 16 December 1997 *Employees:* 2
Net Worth: £4,907,357 *Total Assets:* £5,091,249
Registered Office: The Countess of Brecknock House, War Memorial Community Hospital, Andover, Hants, SP10 3LB
Activities: Other human health activities
Officers: Michele Gard, Secretary; Lilias Jane Benson [1940] Director; Professor Joy Carter [1955] Director/Vice-Chancellor; Dame Mary Fagan [1939] Director/Retired; Iain Robert Henderson [1948] Director/Business Consultant; Bruce Rodney Wingate Parker [1941] Director/Retired; Emma Katrina Sandy [1968] Director; Clare Mary Scheckter [1960] Director/Partner in an Organic Farm/Food Production Business; Patricia Anne West [1944] Director/County Councillor

Country Care Homes Limited
Incorporated: 12 June 2007 *Employees:* 2
Net Worth: £2 *Total Assets:* £5,272,167
Registered Office: Hill House Care Home, Little Somerford, Chippenham, Wilts, SN15 5BH
Activities: Medical nursing home activities
Shareholders: Andrew Chadwick Doveton; Norma Ann Doveton
Officers: Andrew Chadwick Doveton, Secretary; Andrew Chadwick Doveton [1949] Director/Nursing Home Proprietor; Norma Ann Doveton [1948] Director/Nursing Home Proprietor

Country Houses Foundation
Incorporated: 22 April 2005 *Employees:* 1
Net Worth: £12,407,186 *Total Assets:* £12,483,639
Registered Office: Sheephouse Farm, Uley Road, Dursley, Glos, GL11 5AD
Activities: Other business support service activities n.e.c.
Officers: David John Price, Secretary; Nicholas Charles Faithorn Barber [1940] Director; Norman William Hudson [1945] Director/Heritage Proprietor Consultant; Andrew Colin Douglas Jardine [1955] Director/Consultant; Mary Elizabeth King [1953] Director/Architect; Jeremy Gibson Dixon Musson [1965] Director/Writer & Consultant; Sir John Christopher Parsons [1946] Director/Retired; Oliver Henry James Pearcey [1951] Director/Heritage Consultant

County Confectionery Limited
Incorporated: 3 March 1988 *Employees:* 97
Net Worth: £2,957,751 *Total Assets:* £7,537,566
Registered Office: Unit 5 Penbeagle Industrial Estate, St Ives, Cornwall, TR26 2JH
Activities: Manufacture of cocoa and chocolate confectionery
Parent: NIC Enterprises Limited
Officers: David Kenneth Brian [1954] Director; Mark David Brian [1980] Commercial Director; Richard Martin Cooke [1967] Finance Director; Michael George Forrester [1956] Director; Ulrik Moes [1976] Business Development Director [Danish]; Morten Lilloen Weber [1972] Director [Danish]; Michael Wodskou [1967] Director/CEO - NIC UK [Danish]

County Garage (Barnstaple) Limited
Incorporated: 22 December 1965 *Employees:* 85
Net Worth: £3,064,497 *Total Assets:* £7,486,826
Registered Office: Coney Avenue, Hollowtree Road, Barnstaple, Devon, EX32 8QJ
Activities: Sale of new cars and light motor vehicles
Shareholder: Susan Williams
Officers: Patrick James Squire, Secretary; Wendy Elizabeth Bassom [1937] Director/Teacher/CD; Ann Veronica Lewis [1932] Director; David John Squire [1940] Director; Patrick James Squire [1945] Director; Nicholas Charles Williams [1964] Director/Chartered Accountant; Susan Williams [1939] Director; Andrew John Witherington [1962] Director

The County Hotel Canterbury Limited
Incorporated: 22 December 2004 *Employees:* 82
Net Worth: £11,682,113 *Total Assets:* £12,175,626
Registered Office: 8 Gay Street, Bath, BA1 2PH
Activities: Hotels and similar accommodation
Major Shareholder: Andrew Douglas Brownsword
Officers: Peter Tyrrell, Secretary; Andrew Douglas Brownsword [1947] Director; Jeremy David Hancock [1964] Director; Stephanie Hocking [1966] Director; Peter Tyrrell [1972] Director

County of Gloucestershire Community Foundation
Incorporated: 6 September 1989 *Employees:* 1
Net Worth: £7,363,367 *Total Assets:* £7,433,425
Registered Office: The Manor, Boddington Lane, Boddington, Cheltenham, Glos, GL51 0TJ
Activities: Other social work activities without accommodation n.e.c.
Officers: Robert Charles Berkeley [1968] Director; Tracey Clark [1980] Director; Jonathan James Stewart Dunley [1970] Director/Accountant; Christine Ellson [1945] Director/Retired; Norman Arthur Gardner [1949] Finance Director; Marcus Beresford Heywood [1948] Director/Retired; Alison Robinson [1974] Director; Richard James Stephens [1966] Director/Businessman; Martin John Surl [1957] Director/Police & Crime Commissioner; James Patrick Tabor [1950] Director/QC

County Tyre (Holdings) Limited (The)
Incorporated: 27 September 1961 *Employees:* 216
Net Worth: £5,295,448 *Total Assets:* £26,119,208
Registered Office: Malvern House, Priory Road, Gloucester, GL1 2RQ
Activities: Wholesale trade of motor vehicle parts and accessories
Parent: Malvern Tyres Holdings Limited
Officers: Christopher David Freeman [1990] Director/Office Manager; Robert Malcolm Freeman [1967] Director; Timothy James Lewis [1965] Director/Operations Manager; Alan Mark Stenning [1962] Director/Retail Manager

Courtwave Limited
Incorporated: 20 August 1993
Net Worth: £3,299,635 *Total Assets:* £3,834,642
Registered Office: Flat 8, The Grand, Elliott Street, The Hoe, Plymouth, PL1 2PE
Activities: Residents property management
Shareholders: Spear Mills Limited; Spears Mills Limited
Officers: Brian Lawrence Spear, Secretary/Director; Charles Hardwick Wahul Mills [1948] Director/Estate Agent; Brian Lawrence Spear [1947] Director

Cover Construction Company Limited
Incorporated: 17 December 1964 *Employees:* 7
Net Worth: £11,548,747 *Total Assets:* £19,857,974
Registered Office: Filkins Mill, Filkins, Lechlade, Glos, GL7 3RF
Activities: Construction of commercial buildings
Officers: Mary Jane Cover, Secretary; James Arnold Macpherson Cover [1942] Director/Builder; Mary Jane Cover [1949] Director/Housewife; Samuel James Cover [1985] Director/Graduate Rural Surveyor; Georgina Mary Goldsmith [1977] Director/Florist; Fiona Jane Tweedie [1979] Director/Speech and Language Therapist

J.A. Cover Limited
Incorporated: 14 January 1986 *Employees:* 5
Net Worth: £3,571,194 *Total Assets:* £4,383,815
Registered Office: Filkins Mill, Filkins, Lechlade, Glos, GL7 3RF
Activities: Development of building projects
Officers: Mary Jane Cover, Secretary; James Arnold Macpherson Cover [1942] Director/Builder; Mary Jane Cover [1949] Director/Housewife; Samuel James Cover [1985] Director/Graduate Rural Surveyor; Georgina Mary Goldsmith [1977] Director/Florist; Fiona Jane Tweedie [1979] Director/Speech and Language Therapist

Cowgrove Limited
Incorporated: 30 March 2006
Net Worth: £1,557,839 *Total Assets:* £7,778,574
Registered Office: 10 Bridge Street, Christchurch, Dorset, BH23 1EF
Activities: Other letting and operating of own or leased real estate
Major Shareholder: Michael Sidney Sherwood
Officers: Melanie Laura Sherwood, Secretary/Property Manager; Melanie Laura Sherwood [1965] Director/Property Manager; Michael Sidney Sherwood [1965] Director

Cowley Bros.(Wroughton) Limited
Incorporated: 24 August 1960
Net Worth: £2,094,348 *Total Assets:* £4,089,108
Registered Office: Morris Owen House, 43-45 Devizes Road, Swindon, Wilts, SN1 4BG
Activities: Construction of other civil engineering projects n.e.c.
Shareholders: Neil Cowley; Henry George Cowley
Officers: Neil Cowley, Secretary; Neil Cowley [1958] Director/Builder

Cox & Robinson (Agricultural) Limited
Incorporated: 9 March 1967 *Employees:* 31
Net Worth: £1,422,000 *Total Assets:* £6,377,000
Registered Office: Exmoor House, Lime Way, Pathfields Business Park, South Molton, Devon, EX36 3LH
Activities: Other retail sale in non-specialised stores
Parent: Mole Valley Farmers Ltd
Officers: Bruce Korican, Secretary; Graeme Maurice Cock [1965] Director; Andrew Jackson [1957] Director

C J Cox Limited
Incorporated: 19 November 1997 *Employees:* 15
Net Worth: £4,047,193 *Total Assets:* £4,868,066
Registered Office: Bagber, Sturminster Newton, Dorset, DT10 2HT
Activities: Repair of machinery
Shareholders: Christopher John Cox; Valerie Jill Cox
Officers: Valerie Jill Cox, Secretary; Christopher John Cox [1957] Director; Valerie Jill Cox [1961] Director

Bernard Cox Limited
Incorporated: 19 March 2003 *Employees:* 11
Net Worth: £6,584,112 *Total Assets:* £10,988,357
Registered Office: Hilltop Druce Farm, Puddletown, Dorchester, DT2 7SU
Activities: Growing of cereals (except rice), leguminous crops and oil seeds
Shareholders: Bernard James Cox; Elizabeth Mary May Cox
Officers: Elizabeth Mary May Cox, Secretary/Director; Bernard James Cox [1956] Director; Elizabeth Mary May Cox [1960] Director

Coxco Holdings Limited
Incorporated: 20 January 2014 *Employees:* 43
Net Worth: £11,672,637 *Total Assets:* £12,881,495
Registered Office: Burraton Road, Saltash, Cornwall, PL12 6LU
Activities: Activities of other holding companies n.e.c.
Major Shareholder: Wayne Colin Cox
Officers: Samantha Cox, Secretary; Wayne Colin Cox [1970] Managing Director

Coxley Developments Limited
Incorporated: 18 January 1995 *Employees:* 3
Net Worth: £2,437,767 *Total Assets:* £12,657,361
Registered Office: Ground Floor, Blackbrook Gate 1, Blackbrook Business Park, Taunton, Somerset, TA1 2PX
Activities: Development of building projects
Parent: SBAW Group Limited
Officers: Daniel Roy Newton, Secretary; Kevin Roy Newton [1965] Director

CQC Holdings Limited
Incorporated: 13 September 2011 *Employees:* 43
Net Worth: £3,061,348 *Total Assets:* £4,696,852
Registered Office: CQC House, 2-3 Brannam Court, Brannam Crescent, Barnstaple, Devon, EX31 3TD
Activities: Activities of production holding companies
Officers: Michael John Green, Secretary; Davina Bevan [1974] Finance Director; Christopher Jonathan Charles Chapple [1964] Director; Neil Andrew Masom [1959] Director; Simon Hobart Charles Morrish [1974] Director/Management; Ian Michael Newberry [1969] Operations Director

CQC Limited
Incorporated: 3 September 1999 *Employees:* 43
Net Worth: £3,750,439 *Total Assets:* £5,352,113
Registered Office: CQC House, 2-3 Brannam Court, Brannam Crescent, Barnstaple, Devon, EX31 3TD
Activities: Manufacture of other wearing apparel and accessories n.e.c.
Parent: CQC Holdings Limited
Officers: Michael John Green, Secretary/Management Accountant; Davina Bevan [1974] Finance Director; Christopher Jonathan Charles Chapple [1964] Director; Neil Andrew Masom [1959] Director; Simon Hobart Charles Morrish [1974] Director; Ian Michael Newberry [1969] Operations Director

Crane Merchandising Systems Limited
Incorporated: 13 March 1989 *Employees:* 109
Net Worth: £6,336,967 *Total Assets:* £16,789,712
Registered Office: Pipsmore Park, Bumpers Farm Industrial Estate, Chippenham, Wilts, SN14 6NQ
Activities: Manufacture of other special-purpose machinery n.e.c.
Parent: Crane Limited
Officers: Paul James Carver, Secretary; Paul James Carver [1968] Finance Director; Bradley Law Ellis [1968] Director/President [American]; Max Homer Mitchell [1963] Director [American]; Bradford Reams Tedder [1975] Director/President [American]; Gillian Lesley White [1961] Director/VP/GM

Crapper & Sons Landfill Limited
Incorporated: 3 February 1999 *Employees:* 38
Net Worth: £3,662,617 *Total Assets:* £10,720,309
Registered Office: Park Grounds, Brinkworth Road, Wootton Bassett, Swindon, Wilts, SN4 8DW
Activities: Other service activities n.e.c.
Officers: Roger William Crapper, Secretary/Engineer; Nicholas Francis Ash [1969] Director; Jane Marie Bowden [1968] Director; Howard Charles Crapper [1950] Director; Lawrence Crapper [1945] Director; Richard James Crapper [1971] Director; Roger William Crapper [1942] Director

Crawlands Limited
Incorporated: 15 November 2013 *Employees:* 312
Net Worth: £2,510,835 *Total Assets:* £20,811,946
Registered Office: 76 Charlton Road, Shepton Mallet, Somerset, BA4 5PD
Activities: Manufacture of other food products n.e.c.
Major Shareholder: Ian James Harvey
Officers: Ian James Harvey [1950] Director; William Robert Martin [1964] Director; Allan Warner Staples [1953] Director

Cray U.K. Limited
Incorporated: 7 March 2000 *Employees:* 63
Net Worth: £7,109,195 *Total Assets:* £22,674,892
Registered Office: Broad Quay House, Prince Street, Bristol, BS1 4DJ
Activities: Repair of computers and peripheral equipment
Parent: Cray Inc
Officers: Michael Charles Piraino, Secretary; Christopher Matthew Diddams [1981] Director/Financial Controller; Michael Charles Piraino [1967] Director/General Counsel [American]; Peter Joseph Ungaro [1968] Director/CEO Cray Inc [American]

CRC Industries UK Limited
Incorporated: 24 September 2003 *Employees:* 62
Net Worth: £15,710,454 *Total Assets:* £17,691,564
Registered Office: Ambersil House, Wylds Road, Castlefield Industrial Estate, Bridgwater, Somerset, TA6 4DD
Activities: Other manufacturing n.e.c.
Shareholders: Amy Shapiro Ufberg; Joanna Berwind Creamer; Jessica Berwind Brummett; Richard Paul Wild; Charles Graham Berwind III; James Dwight Berwind
Officers: David William Nichols, Secretary; Scott Grey [1964] Director [American]; Bruno Hereman [1958] Director [Belgian]; William James McAlister [1966] Director/Sales & Marketing

Cream Care Group Limited
Incorporated: 4 January 2013 *Employees:* 251
Net Worth: £5,248,587 *Total Assets:* £14,747,459
Registered Office: Norman's, Longrun Lane, Bishops Hull, Taunton, Somerset, TA1 5AY
Activities: Residential nursing care facilities
Shareholders: Martin Lee Reed; The Estate of Stephen John Petts
Officers: Sean Michael Davey [1967] Director/Financial Adviser; Beverley Gerontis [1962] Director; Emma Jane Mary Lewes [1970] Director; Martin Lee Reed [1962] Director

Cream II Limited
Incorporated: 2 May 2006
Net Worth: £1,408,874 *Total Assets:* £3,934,767
Registered Office: Norman's, Longrun Lane, Bishops Hull, Taunton, Somerset, TA1 5AY
Activities: Residential nursing care facilities
Parent: Cream Care Group Limited
Officers: Martin Lee Reed [1962] Director

Cream Residential Care Limited
Incorporated: 12 October 2005
Net Worth: £2,101,448 *Total Assets:* £4,139,048
Registered Office: Norman's, Longrun Lane, Bishops Hull, Taunton, Somerset, TA1 5AY
Activities: Residential nursing care facilities
Parent: Cream Care Group Limited
Officers: Martin Lee Reed [1962] Director

Creanova Universal Closures Limited
Incorporated: 1 October 2004 *Employees:* 8
Net Worth: £828,300 *Total Assets:* £3,543,954
Registered Office: 5 Shannon Point, Oakfield Close, Tewkesbury Business Park, Tewkesbury, Glos, GL20 8PF
Activities: Other manufacturing n.e.c.
Shareholder: Rodney Malcolm Druitt
Officers: Deborah Anne James, Secretary/Chartered Accountant; Robert John Druitt [1966] Director [Australian]; Rodney Malcolm Druitt [1946] Director [Australian]; Michael Furlong [1961] Director/Regional Technical Manager [Australian]; Deborah Anne James [1971] Director/Chartered Accountant; Russell Hayden Jones [1947] Director [Australian]; Harold Lienau [1957] Director [German]; George Arthur Wilson [1937] Director [Canadian]

Creative England Limited
Incorporated: 8 November 2010 *Employees:* 43
Net Worth: £801,155 *Total Assets:* £18,139,646
Registered Office: 1st Floor, College House, 32-36 College Green, Bristol, BS1 5SP
Activities: Support activities to performing arts
Officers: Karen Blackett [1971] Director; Belinda Budge [1956] Director; Matthew Coats [1965] Director/Civil Servant; Pardeep Duggal [1973] Marketing Director; Irene Rudge Graham [1967] Director/Chief Executive; Ian Livingstone [1949] Director; Daniel Kenneth Perkins [1975] Director; Neil Mahendra Rami [1967] Director/Chief Executive; Andrea Stark [1962] Director; Charles Robert Wace [1961] Director

Creative Kernow Limited
Incorporated: 31 May 1983 *Employees:* 34
Previous: Cornwall Arts Centre Trust Truro Limited
Net Worth: £708,156 *Total Assets:* £4,448,128
Registered Office: Krowji, West Park, Redruth, Cornwall, TR15 3AJ
Activities: Cultural education
Officers: Percival Ross Williams, Secretary; William Kim Conchie [1956] Director; Rosanna Jayne Elliott [1987] Theatre Director; Dinah Louise Graffy [1960] Director; Simon Paul Harvey [1974] Theatre Director; Eleanor Jubb [1982] Director/Researcher; Ross Duncan Pascoe [1960] Director/Solicitor; John Alfred Pulford [1943] Director/Management Consultant; Francis Roff Rayner [1926] Director/Retired

Creative Youth Network
Incorporated: 1 March 1973 *Employees:* 80
Net Worth: £8,789,556 *Total Assets:* £9,368,746
Registered Office: 20 Old School House, Kingswood Estate, Britannia Road, Kingswood, Bristol, BS15 8DB
Activities: Educational support services
Officers: Margaret Lily Curtis [1946] Director/Retired; William Howard Robert Durie [1941] Director/Chartered Surveyor; Lynne Elvins [1971] Director/Design Manager; Joanna Jane Grant [1964] Director; Maria Imran [2000] Director/Student; Raj Kakar-Clayton [1969] Managing Director; Michael David LEA [1962] Director/Chartered Accountant; Lucio Flavio de Souza Mesquita [1966] Director; Robert Nye [1987] Director/Wealth Management; Robyn Sandilands [1978] Director/Solicitor; Deepraj Singh [1993] Director/Professional Dance Artist; Kirsty Louise Swan [1981] Director/Solicitor

Credit Reporting Agency (Holdings) Limited
Incorporated: 9 April 2015
Net Worth: £7,911,576 *Total Assets:* £12,088,172
Registered Office: Trevithick House, Trevissome Park, Truro, Cornwall, TR4 8UN
Activities: Other information service activities n.e.c.
Parent: Credit Reporting Agency (Topco) Limited
Officers: Ian Paul Carpenter, Secretary; Ian Paul Carpenter [1979] Director; Richard David Catlin [1979] Director; Mark Alistair Champion [1973] Director/Chartered Accountant; Barry Kevin Stamp [1953] Director/Chartered Credit Manager; Christopher James Stamp [1978] Director

Credit Reporting Agency (Topco) Limited
Incorporated: 23 October 2017 *Employees:* 5
Net Worth: £10,364,250 *Total Assets:* £16,840,406
Registered Office: Trevithick House, Trevissome Park, Truro, Cornwall, TR4 8UN
Activities: Activities of credit bureaus
Officers: Ian Paul Carpenter, Secretary; Ian Paul Carpenter [1979] Director; Richard David Catlin [1979] Director; Mark Alistair Champion [1973] Director/Chartered Accountant; Barry Kevin Stamp [1953] Director; Christopher James Stamp [1978] Director

Creditcall Group Limited
Incorporated: 3 February 2012
Net Worth Deficit: £1,398,865 *Total Assets:* £10,246,317
Registered Office: Merchants House North, Wapping Road, Bristol, BS1 4RW
Activities: Business and domestic software development
Parent: Creditcall Holdings Limited
Officers: Kyle Pexton, Secretary; Justin Chen [1988] Director [American]; Kyle Pexton [1971] Director [American]; Vijay Sondhi [1964] Director [Canadian]

Creditcall Holdings Limited
Incorporated: 2 February 2012 *Employees:* 97
Net Worth Deficit: £8,051,787 *Total Assets:* £5,708,039
Registered Office: Merchants House North, Wapping Road, Bristol, BS1 4RW
Activities: Business and domestic software development
Officers: Kyle Pexton, Secretary; Justin Chen [1988] Director [American]; Kyle Pexton [1971] Director [American]; Vijay Sondhi [1964] Director [Canadian]

Creditcall Limited
Incorporated: 20 December 1996 *Employees:* 84
Net Worth Deficit: £296,371 *Total Assets:* £3,592,476
Registered Office: Merchants House North, Wapping Road, Bristol, BS1 4RW
Activities: Other telecommunications activities
Parent: Creditcall Group Limited
Officers: Kyle Pexton, Secretary; Justin Chen [1988] Director [American]; Kyle Pexton [1971] Director [American]; Vijay Sondhi [1964] Director [Canadian]

Crediton Care & Support Homes Limited
Incorporated: 26 July 2002 *Employees:* 95
Net Worth: £3,939,556 *Total Assets:* £4,476,595
Registered Office: 5 Barnfield Crescent, Exeter, Devon, EX1 1RF
Activities: Residential care activities for learning difficulties, mental health and substance abuse
Shareholders: Mary O'Sullivan; Penny O'Sullivan
Officers: Penny O'Sullivan, Secretary; Mary O'Sullivan [1930] Director; Penny O'Sullivan [1963] Director

Crediton Dairy Limited
Incorporated: 16 April 2013 *Employees:* 125
Net Worth: £18,999,000 *Total Assets:* £27,971,000
Registered Office: Head Office, Church Lane, Crediton, Devon, EX17 2AH
Activities: Liquid milk and cream production
Shareholders: Neil Angus Kennedy; Timothy Noel Smiddy
Officers: Stephen Michael Murray, Secretary; Neil Angus Kennedy [1960] Director/Businessman; Timothy Noel Smiddy [1969] Managing Director [Irish]

Crediton Milling Company Limited
Incorporated: 22 July 1964 *Employees:* 64
Net Worth: £3,090,993 *Total Assets:* £8,043,342
Registered Office: Fordton Mill, Fordton, Crediton, Devon, EX17 3DH
Activities: Manufacture of prepared feeds for farm animals
Shareholder: Mark James Gulley
Officers: Patricia Ann Gulley, Secretary; Scott John Brimilcombe [1977] Director; Russell William John Crang [1970] Director/Salesman; Mark James Gulley [1976] Director/Quality Control Manager; Patricia Ann Gulley [1949] Director/Secretary; Stephen John Gulley [1980] Director; Andrew Theo Power [1974] Director/General Manager; Michael John Vanstone [1955] Director/Sales Manager

Crediton Milling Holdings Ltd
Incorporated: 10 May 2012 *Employees:* 64
Net Worth: £5,090,831 *Total Assets:* £9,556,391
Registered Office: 128 High Street, Crediton, Devon, EX17 3LQ
Activities: Other information service activities n.e.c.
Shareholders: Stephen John Gulley; Sarah Louisa Power; Mark James Gulley
Officers: Mark James Gulley [1976] Director; Andrew Theo Power [1974] Director; Sarah Louisa Power [1974] Director

Creed Catering Supplies Limited
Incorporated: 24 March 2004 *Employees:* 344
Net Worth: £6,044,186 *Total Assets:* £20,905,752
Registered Office: Midpoint, Staverton Technology Park, Cheltenham Road, Staverton, Glos, GL51 6TQ
Activities: Non-specialised wholesale of food, beverages and tobacco
Officers: Adam Jonathan Creed [1986] Director; Barbara Creed [1942] Director; Christopher Simon Creed [1963] Managing Director; Lauren Jennifer Creed [1988] Director; Paul Martyn Creed [1962] Director; Philip George Creed [1967] Director; Steven Aneurin Creed [1967] Director; Terence Lewis Creed [1940] Director; Kirstin Nicola Hawkins [1972] Director/Certified Chartered Accountant

Creed Foodservice Limited
Incorporated: 11 August 1972 *Employees:* 344
Net Worth: £6,043,495 *Total Assets:* £20,905,750
Registered Office: Midpoint, Staverton Technology Park, Cheltenham Road, Staverton, Glos, GL51 6TQ
Activities: Non-specialised wholesale of food, beverages and tobacco
Parent: Creed Catering Supplies Limited
Officers: Christopher Simon Creed [1963] Managing Director; Paul Martyn Creed [1962] IT Director; Philip George Creed [1967] Facilities Director; Steven Aneurin Creed [1967] Director; Terence Lewis Creed [1940] Director/Chairman; Philip de Ternant [1962] Director; Karl Goodwin [1961] Director; Kirstin Nicola Hawkins [1972] Director/Certified Chartered Accountant; Martin Holmes [1965] Director; Steve Thomas Rich [1964] Operations Director; Miles Roberts [1983] Director; Philip John Vickery Mbe Dl [1976] Non Executive Director

Creedon Technologies Limited
Incorporated: 23 August 2006 *Employees:* 6
Net Worth: £1,618,521 *Total Assets:* £4,100,839
Registered Office: 17 Albert Road, Plymouth, PL2 1AB
Activities: Manufacture of consumer electronics
Parent: Creedon Technologies HK Limited
Officers: Kevin Creedon Palfreeman, Secretary; Kevin Creedon Palfreeman [1948] Director/Manager; Mark Palfreeman [1978] Director

Crematoria Management Ltd.
Incorporated: 17 July 1989 *Employees:* 120
Net Worth: £24,025,388 *Total Assets:* £98,578,208
Registered Office: Chapel View, Westerleigh Road, Westerleigh, Bristol, BS37 8QP
Activities: Funeral and related activities
Parent: Westerleigh Group Ltd
Officers: Dafydd Rhys John, Secretary; Daydd Rhys John [1974] Director/Chartered Accountant; Ian David McArdle [1966] Director/Chartered Surveyor

Crescent Motorcycle Company Limited
Incorporated: 3 December 1997 *Employees:* 46
Net Worth: £4,260,565 *Total Assets:* £6,270,015
Registered Office: 23 Black Moor Road, Ebblake Industrial Estate, Verwood, Dorset, BH31 6AX
Activities: Other sports activities
Major Shareholder: Paul Denning
Officers: John Frederick Denning, Secretary; John Frederick Denning [1940] Director/Shop Proprietor; Paul Denning [1966] Director/Manager

The Crescent Trust Company Limited
Incorporated: 7 March 1975 *Employees:* 6
Net Worth: £6,012,818 *Total Assets:* £10,800,266
Registered Office: Lee Ford, Budleigh Salterton, Devon, EX9 7AJ
Activities: Other letting and operating of own or leased real estate
Shareholder: Nigel Lindsay-Fynn
Officers: Stephen Richard Glover, Secretary; Nigel Lindsay Fynn [1942] Director/Consultant; Piers Basil Lindsay Fynn [1975] Director/Fund Manager

John Cribb & Sons Ltd.
Incorporated: 3 February 1981 *Employees:* 60
Net Worth: £1,991,804 *Total Assets:* £4,427,589
Registered Office: 117-119 Dale Valley Road, Poole, Dorset, BH15 3HZ
Activities: Wholesale of electronic and telecommunications equipment and parts
Officers: Albert John Cribb [1940] Director; David Ian Cribb [1964] Director; Rita Cribb [1943] Director; Steven John Cribb [1967] Director

Cribbs Triangle Limited
Incorporated: 28 April 2016
Net Worth Deficit: £1,017,183 *Total Assets:* £3,943,406
Registered Office: 7 Whiteladies Road, Bristol, BS8 1NN
Activities: Development of building projects
Officers: Philip Neil Briggs, Secretary; Nigel Berger [1969] Director; David Maxwell Freed [1954] Director; Andrew Dexter Maltby [1957] Director; Iain Michael Neary [1968] Director

Crispin School Academy Trust
Incorporated: 14 June 2011 *Employees:* 100
Net Worth: £9,944,468 *Total Assets:* £13,328,080
Registered Office: Crispin School, Church Road, Street, Somerset, BA16 0AD
Activities: General secondary education
Officers: Robert William Sutherland, Secretary; Walter Alexander Antonello [1954] Director/Manufacturer; Shonagh Alison Butler [1960] Director/Manager; Sandra Cinicola [1960] Director/Business Manager; Joseph Cloonan [1963] Director/Consultant [Irish]; Antony Durbacz [1960] Director; Christine Frost [1952] Director/Retired; Lesley Gaskell [1964] Director/Lawyer; Elizabeth Leyshon Leyshon [1955] Director/Retired; Alison Ruth Martin [1957] Director/Physiotherapist; Peter Christopher Bamford Millar [1960] Director; Paul Andrew Reddick [1972] Director/Teacher; Matthew Slade [1978] Director/Policeman; Simon Jeremy Williams [1978] Director/Teacher

Cristie Software Limited
Incorporated: 10 October 2007 *Employees:* 26
Net Worth: £7,915,518 *Total Assets:* £10,464,558
Registered Office: New Mill, Chestnut Lane, Stroud, Glos, GL5 3EH
Activities: Business and domestic software development
Major Shareholder: Ian Cameron
Officers: Ian Cameron, Secretary; Janet Elizabeth Blake [1951] Director; Ian Cameron [1953] Director

Critchley Group Limited
Incorporated: 30 January 1984
Net Worth: £14,824,001 *Total Assets:* £14,824,001
Registered Office: Company Secretariat, Faraday Road, Dorcan, Swindon, Wilts, SN3 5HH
Activities: Non-trading company
Parent: Tyco Electronics UK Ltd
Officers: Harold Gregory Barksdale [1964] Director/Attorney [American]; Stephen Christopher Cooper [1970] Director/Accountant; Ashley Raymond Fulford [1963] Director/Operations Manager

Criterion Healthcare PLC
Incorporated: 16 January 1997
Net Worth: £4,323,000 *Total Assets:* £72,161,000
Registered Office: Third Floor, Broad Quay House, Prince Street, Bristol, BS1 4DJ
Activities: Hospital activities
Parent: Criterion Healthcare Holdings Limited
Officers: Jonathan Peter Brown [1986] Director/Investment Manager; Rosemary Lucy Jude Deeley [1984] Director/Financial Controller; James Christopher Heath [1975] Director; Mark Geoffrey David Holden [1957] Director; Daniel Marinus Maria Vermeer [1981] Director/Senior Manager [Dutch]

A.C. Crocker (Properties) Limited
Incorporated: 21 August 1984
Net Worth: £3,513,043 *Total Assets:* £3,890,227
Registered Office: Swatton Barn, Badbury, Swindon, Wilts, SN4 0EU
Activities: Construction of commercial buildings
Shareholders: Adrian Charles Crocker; Barbara Ann Crocker
Officers: Barbara Ann Crocker, Secretary; Adrian Charles Crocker [1947] Director/Farmer

M.B. Crocker Limited
Incorporated: 16 April 1985 *Employees:* 41
Net Worth: £6,723,741 *Total Assets:* £18,160,284
Registered Office: Seniors Farm, New Street, Marnhull, Sturminster Newton, Dorset, DT10 1PZ
Activities: Raising of poultry
Major Shareholder: Mary Crocker
Officers: Paul David Crocker, Secretary; David George Hann Crocker [1933] Director/Farmer; Mary Beatrice Crocker [1934] Director/Farmer; Paul David Crocker [1962] Director/Farmer; Vivian Clive Evans [1945] Director/Certified Accountant; William John Warwick Neville [1955] Commercial Director; Graeme John Stanley [1955] Director

Crocus Care Ltd
Incorporated: 27 September 2001 *Employees:* 57
Net Worth: £727,992 *Total Assets:* £4,779,111
Registered Office: Moors Park House, Moors Park, Bishopsteignton, Teignmouth, Devon, TQ14 9RH
Activities: Residential care activities for the elderly and disabled
Major Shareholder: Paul St John Ewer
Officers: Jayne Lesley Ewer, Secretary; Paul St John Ewer [1952] Director

Crofty Multi Academy Trust
Incorporated: 1 September 2016 *Employees:* 606
Net Worth: £31,688,544 *Total Assets:* £35,179,688
Registered Office: No 2 The Seatons, Tolvaddon Energy Park, Tolvaddon, Camborne, Cornwall, TR14 0HX
Activities: Pre-primary education
Officers: Jeremy Alder, Secretary; Karen Louise Bond [1971] Director/University Administrator; Tom Arthur Hugh Briant-Evans [1978] Director/Solicitor; Michael Garfield Hosking [1949] Director/Retired; Nicholas Lake [1945] Director; Keith Charles Tipler [1949] Director/Retired; John Edward Whetter [1951] Director/Retired

Cronite Castings (Distribution) Limited
Incorporated: 13 December 1993 *Employees:* 12
Net Worth: £3,153,356 *Total Assets:* £6,642,362
Registered Office: Blacknell Lane, Crewkerne, Somerset, TA18 7YA
Activities: Wholesale of other machinery and equipment
Officers: Ann Gaynor Feetham, Secretary; Norman Lesley Manley [1954] Managing Director; Christian Marin [1966] Divisional Director [French]; Peter Roger White [1970] Sales Director; Pierre Francois Wittmann [1961] Managing Director [French]

Cronite Castings Limited
Incorporated: 14 May 1964 *Employees:* 144
Net Worth: £5,090,266 *Total Assets:* £10,490,101
Registered Office: Blacknell Lane, Crewkerne, Somerset, TA18 7YA
Activities: Casting of steel
Officers: Ann Gaynor Feetham, Secretary; Norman Lesley Manley [1954] Managing Director; Christian Marin [1966] Divisional Director [French]; Pierre Francois Wittmann [1961] Managing Director [French]

G. Crook & Sons Limited
Incorporated: 19 April 1985
Net Worth: £25,866,520 *Total Assets:* £26,096,676
Registered Office: 20 Vespasian Way, Dorchester, DT1 2RD
Activities: Other specialised construction activities n.e.c.
Major Shareholder: Barry John Crook
Officers: Barry John Crook, Secretary/Plant Operator; Barry John Crook [1958] Director/Plant Operator; Michelle Anne Handel [1964] Director/Administrator

Cross Manufacturing Company (1938) Limited
Incorporated: 23 July 1938 *Employees:* 532
Net Worth: £75,179,000 *Total Assets:* £102,389,000
Registered Office: Midford Road, Combe Down, Bath, BA2 5RR
Activities: Manufacture of other fabricated metal products n.e.c.
Shareholders: Martin John Carroll; Rodney Alan Cross; Maureen Eusebia Cross; Edward Henry Cross; Peter Grant Cross; James Robert John Cross; Richard Charles Cross; Steven St John Gordon Ross
Officers: Mark Eric Bradley, Secretary; Mark Eric Bradley [1963] Director/Chartered Accountant; Edward Henry Cross [1968] Director/Engineer; Richard Charles Cross [1967] Director/Engineer; Rodney Alan Cross [1940] Director/Chartered Engineer; Peter Francis Crudgington [1965] Director/Chartered Engineer; Martin Lovelace James [1967] Director/Engineer; Danny John Squire [1962] Director/Engineer; Paul Henry Tozer [1942] Director/Chartered Accountant

Crossco (284) Limited
Incorporated: 20 August 1997
Net Worth: £4,556,150 *Total Assets:* £4,556,150
Registered Office: East Park House, Iwerne Minster, Blandford Forum, Dorset, DT11 8LA
Activities: Non-trading company
Parent: Lewisia Limited
Officers: Erica Fiona Baker [1964] Director/Personal Assistant; Suzanne Lever [1968] Director

Crossman (Lansdown) Ltd
Incorporated: 27 March 2017
Net Worth Deficit: £2,878 *Total Assets:* £3,814,680
Registered Office: 1b Mile End, London Road, Bath, BA1 6PT
Activities: Development of building projects
Shareholders: Ellis Trading (SW) Limited; Hughes Trading Co (Bath) Limited
Officers: Simon Paul Ellis [1965] Director; Bradley Simon Hughes [1978] Director

Crowdcube Limited
Incorporated: 10 September 2009 *Employees:* 65
Net Worth: £3,104,355 *Total Assets:* £3,982,327
Registered Office: Fourth Floor, South Block, Broadwalk House, Exeter, Devon, EX1 1TS
Activities: Activities auxiliary to financial intermediation n.e.c.
Officers: William Thomas Anthony Simmons, Secretary; Timothy Brian Bunting [1963] Director/Venture Capitalist; Luke James Lang [1978] Director/Marketing Consultant; Jonathan Nicholas Hugo Sibilia [1980] Director/Venture Capitalist [French]; William Thomas Anthony Simmons [1977] Financial Director; Darren Michael Westlake [1969] Director/Product Manager; Simon James Williams [1958] Director/Chairman

Crowdhill Limited
Incorporated: 15 October 1993
Net Worth: £3,388,280 *Total Assets:* £8,158,201
Registered Office: Hitchcock House, Hilltop Park, Devizes Road, Salisbury, Wilts, SP3 4UF
Activities: Renting and operating of Housing Association real estate
Parent: Areawise Ltd
Officers: Lionel Maurice Froggatt, Secretary; Azita Froggatt [1966] Director; Lionel Maurice Froggatt [1945] Director

Crown Pet Foods Limited
Incorporated: 3 September 1992 *Employees:* 248
Net Worth: £59,337,000 *Total Assets:* £94,547,000
Registered Office: Oak Tree Meadow, Blackworthy Road, Castle Cary, Somerset, BA7 7PH
Activities: Manufacture of prepared pet foods
Parent: Pet Food Holdings Limited
Officers: Jakub Kolesa, Secretary; Jakub Kolesa [1972] Director/General Manager, Royal Canin UK & Ireland [Czech]; Michael Kunze [1966] Director/President Europe Royal Canin [German]; Loic Nicolas Serge Moutault [1971] Director [French]

Crown Yealm Limited
Incorporated: 20 September 2001 *Employees:* 4
Net Worth: £1,336,834 *Total Assets:* £3,606,598
Registered Office: Crown Yealm House, Pathfields Business Park, South Molton, Devon, EX36 3LH
Activities: Other letting and operating of own or leased real estate
Shareholders: John William Johns; Sharon Mary Johns
Officers: Sharon Mary Johns, Secretary/Director; John William Johns [1952] Director; Sharon Mary Johns [1954] Director

Crowndell Consulting Limited
Incorporated: 26 August 1999 *Employees:* 104
Net Worth: £2,449,411 *Total Assets:* £6,810,640
Registered Office: Lewinnick Lodge, Pentire, Newquay, Cornwall, TR7 1NX
Activities: Licenced restaurants
Shareholders: Jacqueline Fair; Peter Robert Fair
Officers: Peter Robert Fair, Secretary; Jacqueline Fair [1945] Director/Publican & Restaurateur; Peter Robert Fair [1956] Director/Publican & Restaurateur; Daniel Jonathan Trotter [1981] Director/Manager

Crownhold PLC
Incorporated: 16 February 1977 *Employees:* 1
Net Worth: £3,996,885 *Total Assets:* £4,385,540
Registered Office: 38-42 Newport Street, Swindon, Wilts, SN1 3DR
Activities: Development of building projects
Shareholders: Guy Peter Woodroffe Foster; Estate of Euan Woodroffe Foster (deceased)
Officers: Monica Alice Flavill, Secretary; Ann Foster [1945] Director/Opera Singer; Guy Peter Woodroffe Foster [1968] Director/Estate Agent

The Crucial Sauce Company Limited
Incorporated: 7 June 2013 *Employees:* 39
Net Worth: £2,911,944 *Total Assets:* £5,825,894
Registered Office: Manderson House, 5230 Valiant Court, Delta Way, Gloucester Business Park, Brockworth, Gloucester, GL3 4FE
Activities: Manufacture of condiments and seasonings
Parent: The British Pepper & Spice Company Ltd
Officers: Arthur William Richmond, Secretary; Elaine Birchall [1966] Director [Irish]; Rachael Bouch [1968] Director; Arthur William Richmond [1966] Director

Cruciform Services Limited
Incorporated: 23 May 1997 *Employees:* 2
Net Worth: £1,369,000 *Total Assets:* £18,793,000
Registered Office: Third Floor, Broad Quay House, Prince Street, Bristol, BS1 4DJ
Activities: Development of building projects
Parent: PFI Investments Limited
Officers: Daniel North [1981] Investment Director; Neil Rae [1971] Director

Crug Mawr Solar Farm Limited
Incorporated: 7 February 2012
Net Worth: £79,298 *Total Assets:* £8,522,432
Registered Office: The Long Barn, Manor Courtyard, Stratton on the Fosse, Radstock, Somerset, BA3 4QF
Activities: Production of electricity
Parent: CSGH Solar (1) Limited
Officers: Giuseppe La Loggia [1975] Director [Italian]; Yit Ho Tang [1974] Investment Director [Singaporean]; Christopher James Tanner [1972] Investment Director; Jonathan Simon Thompson [1963] Director

Mike Cruickshank Publishing Ltd
Incorporated: 29 May 2012 *Employees:* 2
Net Worth: £5,566,674 *Total Assets:* £5,592,468
Registered Office: c/o Businessvision, Unit 4 Sandy Court, Ashleigh Way, Plympton, Plymouth, PL7 5JX
Activities: Book publishing
Parent: Strategic Prosperity Ltd
Officers: Mike Cruickshank [1985] Director/Publisher

Crux Product Design Ltd
Incorporated: 9 September 2003 *Employees:* 27
Net Worth: £2,418,351 *Total Assets:* £4,199,511
Registered Office: Flatiron Building, 332-336 Paintworks, Bath Road, Bristol, BS4 3AR
Activities: Specialised design activities
Shareholders: James Anthony West; Mark Digby Teucher
Officers: Mark Digby Teucher, Secretary; Mark Digby Teucher [1971] Director/Design Consultant; James Anthony West [1976] Director/Engineering Consultant

The Crypt School
Incorporated: 11 January 2011 *Employees:* 129
Net Worth: £20,053,722 *Total Assets:* £21,133,200
Registered Office: Podsmead Road, Gloucester, GL2 5AE
Activities: General secondary education
Officers: Joanne Claire Hitchings, Secretary; Emma Boobyer [1974] Finance Director; Alison Margaret Borley [1969] Director/Consultant; Nicholas Charles Dyer [1969] Director/Headmaster; Dylan Brian Green [1969] Director/HR Consultant; Richard Daniel James [1950] Director; Rachael Jane Jones [1968] Director; Jason Smith [1969] Director; Glenn Webster [1963] Director; Birgit Whitman [1965] Director/Head of Research Governance [German]

Crystal Classics Fine Minerals Limited
Incorporated: 19 May 2011 *Employees:* 18
Net Worth: £1,509,555 *Total Assets:* £3,548,464
Registered Office: No 1 The Old Coach Yard, East Coker, Yeovil, Somerset, BA22 9HY
Activities: Mining of other non-ferrous metal ores
Major Shareholder: Ian Robert Bruce
Officers: Deborah Alice Boyer, Secretary; Diana Maria Bruce [1984] Director/Student [German]; Ian Robert Bruce [1969] Director/Geologist

Crystalight Limited
Incorporated: 20 November 1996
Net Worth: £1,603,343 *Total Assets:* £14,351,299
Registered Office: 6 Manor Park Business Centre, MacKenzie Way, Cheltenham, Glos, GL51 9TX
Activities: Development of building projects
Shareholders: Haleh Mirkamali; Hekmat Kaveh Baghbadrani
Officers: Haleh Mirkamali, Secretary; Hekmat Kaveh Baghbadrani [1957] Director

CS LSI Solar Limited
Incorporated: 3 February 2015
Net Worth: £3,500,231 *Total Assets:* £3,500,231
Registered Office: First Floor, 10 Temple Back, Bristol, BS1 6FL
Activities: Activities of other holding companies n.e.c.
Shareholder: London & Scottish Investments Limited
Officers: Jin Ho Park [1966] Director/Investment Manager [American]; Derek Porter [1953] Director/Chartered Accountant; Michael Jaihyun Shim [1966] Director/Attorney [American]

CSE Bournemouth Limited
Incorporated: 23 January 1980 *Employees:* 51
Net Worth: £5,321,000 *Total Assets:* £6,431,000
Registered Office: Hangar 100, Aviation Park West, Bournemouth Airport, Christchurch, Dorset, BH23 6NW
Activities: Non-scheduled passenger air transport
Parent: Oxford Aviation Holdings Limited
Officers: Shawn Christopher Fallon [1981] Director/Finance [American]; Yvette Helen Freeman [1967] Director; Andrew Leslie Preston [1965] Managing Director (Aviation Maintenance)

The CSIA Trust
Incorporated: 4 March 2011 *Employees:* 182
Previous: Camborne Science and International Academy
Net Worth: £19,280,156 *Total Assets:* £21,591,236
Registered Office: Camborne Science and International Academy, Cranberry Road, Camborne, Cornwall, TR14 7PP
Activities: General secondary education
Officers: Ian Howard Kenworthy [1954] Director/Principal; Roger James Penwarden [1948] Director/Consultant; Malcolm John Weedon [1969] Director; Dr Andrew Wetherelt [1961] Director/Lecturer

CTC (Wholesalers) Limited
Incorporated: 27 May 1983 *Employees:* 40
Net Worth: £2,586,000 *Total Assets:* £4,019,000
Registered Office: Camel House, Thorverton Road, Marsh Barton, Exeter, Devon, EX2 8FS
Activities: Non-specialised wholesale trade
Parent: CTC (Wholesalers) Holdings Limited
Officers: Stephen Geoffrey Browne [1967] Director; Nick Davey [1982] Director; John Hartshorne [1957] Director/Garage Proprietor; Ian Ralph Jacombs [1944] Director; Deborah Ann Knight [1964] Director; Angela Janet Powell [1962] Director

CTU General Partner Limited
Incorporated: 28 January 2009 *Employees:* 4
Net Worth: £580 *Total Assets:* £7,530,207
Registered Office: Springfield House, 45 Welsh Back, Bristol, BS1 4AG
Activities: Other business support service activities n.e.c.
Shareholders: Kerry Ann Davidson; Scott Matthew Davidson; Peter Oliphant; Samantha Kelly Oliphant
Officers: Kerry Ann Davidson [1965] Director; Scott Matthew Davidson [1963] Director; Peter Oliphant [1962] Director; Samantha Kelly Oliphant [1965] Director

Cubit Group Limited
Incorporated: 6 November 2001 *Employees:* 251
Net Worth: £472,003 *Total Assets:* £12,503,618
Registered Office: 4 Cedar Park, Cobham Road, Ferndown Industrial Estate, Wimborne, Dorset, BH21 7SF
Activities: Activities of head offices
Major Shareholder: Peter Gray
Officers: Peter Leigh Gray [1967] Director; Stuart Robert Lindsay [1952] Director/Chartered Accountant

Cullen Group Limited
Incorporated: 19 December 1997 *Employees:* 167
Net Worth: £5,749,237 *Total Assets:* £11,229,324
Registered Office: Freshford House, Redcliffe Way, Bristol, BS1 6NL
Activities: Other service activities n.e.c.
Major Shareholder: Stuart David Cullen
Officers: Fiona Vivienne Robson, Secretary/Office Manager; Stuart David Cullen [1960] Director; Fiona Vivienne Robson [1963] Director

Moreton C.Cullimore (Gravels) Limited
Incorporated: 16 November 1943 *Employees:* 29
Net Worth: £6,135,709 *Total Assets:* £9,066,970
Registered Office: Netherhills, Whitminster, Glos, GL2 7PD
Activities: Operation of gravel and sand pits; mining of clays and kaolin
Major Shareholder: Roger Neville Cullimore
Officers: Moreton Ferris Cullimore [1979] Director; Roger Neville Cullimore [1938] Director

Moreton C.Cullimore and Son,Limited
Incorporated: 27 January 1965 *Employees:* 48
Net Worth: £2,237,724 *Total Assets:* £4,181,649
Registered Office: Netherhills, Whitminster, Glos, GL2 7PD
Activities: Freight transport by road
Major Shareholder: Roger Neville Cullimore
Officers: Julie Angeline Cullimore [1949] Director; Moreton Ferris Cullimore [1979] Director; Roger Neville Cullimore [1938] Director

The Cullompton Walronds Preservation Trust
Incorporated: 5 March 1997
Net Worth: £3,636,508 *Total Assets:* £3,640,336
Registered Office: The Walronds, 6 Fore Street, Cullompton, Devon, EX15 1JL
Activities: Other social work activities without accommodation n.e.c.
Officers: Elizabeth Ann Sessions, Secretary; Ruth Elizabeth Lowthian Cole [1944] Director/Retired; Elizabeth Anne Labdon [1943] Director/Retired; George Robert Lloyd Maunder [1939] Director/Retired; Judith Paulette Morris [1954] Director/Cullompton Town Clerk; Elizabeth Ann Sessions [1951] Director/Retired Teacher; Diana Jane Speaight [1956] Director/Retired Teacher; Elizabeth Margaret Sutton [1950] Director/Retired; Michael John Woodcock [1936] Director/Retired

Cult Clothing Cheltenham Limited
Incorporated: 8 April 1999
Net Worth: £7,723,459 *Total Assets:* £17,847,812
Registered Office: Dowdeswell Park, London Road, Cheltenham, Glos, GL52 6UT
Activities: Development of building projects
Major Shareholder: Julian Marc Dunkerton
Officers: Julian Marc Dunkerton [1965] Director/Retailer

Cultura Technologies Ltd
Incorporated: 24 March 1976 *Employees:* 66
Net Worth: £1,951,005 *Total Assets:* £4,414,662
Registered Office: Unit A1, Methuen Park, Chippenham, Wilts, SN14 0GT
Activities: Business and domestic software development
Parent: Volaris Group UK Holdco Ltd
Officers: Robert Clay, Secretary/Director; James Arthur Baker [1960] Director/President Agri-Food [Canadian]; Robert Clay [1970] Director; Deborah Riley [1969] Finance Director

Culverdene Properties Limited
Incorporated: 26 April 1995
Net Worth: £5,246,928 *Total Assets:* £10,097,639
Registered Office: Strathaven Strathaven, 16 West Overcliff Drive, Bournemouth, BH4 8AA
Activities: Residents property management
Major Shareholder: David Keith Kelleway
Officers: Caroline Helen Kelleway, Secretary; Caroline Helen Kelleway [1963] Director/Property Manager; David Keith Kelleway [1964] Director/Estate Manager

F.H. Cummings
Incorporated: 6 May 1982 *Employees:* 13
Net Worth: £8,378,033 *Total Assets:* £11,272,072
Registered Office: Unit 19 Freeland Park, Wareham Road, Poole, Dorset, BH16 6FH
Activities: Construction of commercial buildings
Parent: F.H. Cummings (1982) Ltd
Officers: Melanie Cummings, Secretary/Director; Frederick Andrew Cummings [1972] Director; Melanie Cummings [1970] Director; Steven Cummings [1963] Director

Curo Enterprise Limited
Incorporated: 13 June 2012 *Employees:* 33
Net Worth Deficit: £16,533,000 *Total Assets:* £59,200,000
Registered Office: The Maltings, River Place, Lower Bristol Road, Bath, BA2 1EP
Activities: Development of building projects
Parent: Curo Group (Albion) Limited
Officers: Katherine Gullon, Secretary; David Ashmore [1955] Director/Group Chief Executive; Victor Manuel Silva Da Cunha [1966] Director/Group Chief Executive; Rick de Blaby [1960] Director/Chief Executive; Dr David John Haywood [1952] Director; Gerraint James Oakley [1967] Managing Director

Curo Group (Albion) Limited
Incorporated: 10 October 2001 *Employees:* 472
Net Worth: £145,380,000 *Total Assets:* £557,774,976
Registered Office: The Maltings, River Place, Lower Bristol Road, Bath, BA2 1EP
Activities: Activities of other membership organisations n.e.c.
Officers: Katherine Gullon, Secretary; David Ashmore [1955] Director; Elaine Barnes [1961] Executive Director; Victor Manuel Silva Da Cunha [1966] Director/Group Chief Executive; Rick de Blaby [1960] Director/Chief Executive; Simon David Gibbs [1958] Finance Director; Elizabeth Anne Potter [1956] Director/Self Employed; Richard Nathan Stillwell [1949] Director; Christopher John Wilson [1961] Director

Curtis Banks Group PLC
Incorporated: 2 February 2012 *Employees:* 578
Previous: Curtis Banks Group Limited
Net Worth: £44,604,000 *Total Assets:* £3,739,301,888
Registered Office: 3 Temple Quay, Temple Back East, Bristol, BS1 6DZ
Activities: Other activities auxiliary to insurance and pension funding
Shareholder: Christopher Charles Banks
Officers: Paul James Tarran, Secretary; Louis Jules Hydleman [1956] Director; Christopher Anthony James MacDonald [1961] Director; William John Rattray [1958] Director; Jane Ann Ridgley [1968] Operations Director; William Arthur Self [1982] Director; Paul James Tarran [1956] Director/Chartered Accountant

Curtis Banks Limited
Incorporated: 26 November 2008 *Employees:* 284
Net Worth: £18,096,000 *Total Assets:* £28,291,000
Registered Office: 3 Temple Quay, Temple Back East, Bristol, BS1 6DZ
Activities: Other activities auxiliary to insurance and pension funding
Parent: Curtis Banks Group PLC
Officers: Gemma Louise Millard, Secretary; Paul Alan Keepin [1978] Director; Nicola Presley [1984] Director; Jane Ann Ridgley [1968] Operations Director; Nigel Trevor Rodgers [1978] Change Director; James Robert Scott [1979] Director; William Arthur Self [1982] Director; Ian Charles Stone [1976] Director; Paul James Tarran [1956] Director/Chartered Accountant

Curtiss-Wright Controls (UK) Limited
Incorporated: 7 January 2002 *Employees:* 112
Net Worth: £59,146,000 *Total Assets:* £110,833,000
Registered Office: 15 Enterprise Way, Aviation Park West, Bournemouth International Airport, Christchurch, Dorset, BH23 6HH
Activities: Manufacture of electronic components
Officers: Paul Jude Ferdenzi, Secretary; Harry Jakubowitz, Secretary; George Patrick McDonald, Secretary; Marc Sebastian O'Casal, Secretary; Kathryn Rose Barron [1974] Director/Division Controller [Canadian]; Nigel Paul Jones [1968] Director; George Patrick McDonald [1964] Director/Associate General Counsel [American]; Kevin Michael Rayment [1969] Director/Senior Vice President; Andrew Robert Thornton [1967] Commercial Director; Glenn Edward Tynan [1958] Director/Business Executive [American]; Jason Karl Watkins [1966] Director

Curtiss-Wright Flow Control (UK) Limited
Incorporated: 27 February 2001 *Employees:* 25
Net Worth: £24,920,000 *Total Assets:* £32,717,000
Registered Office: 15 Enterprise Way, Aviation Park West, Bournemouth International Airport, Christchurch, Dorset, BH23 6HH
Activities: Manufacture of taps and valves
Officers: Paul Jude Ferdenzi, Secretary; George McDonald, Secretary; Paul Jude Ferdenzi [1967] Director/Vice President, General Counsel and Corporate Secretary [American]; Nigel Paul Jones [1968] Director; Kevin Michael Rayment [1969] Director/Senior Vice President; Andrew Robert Thornton [1967] Commercial Director; Glenn Edward Tynan [1958] Director/Accountant [American]

Curzon 1234 Limited
Incorporated: 13 November 2008 *Employees:* 177
Previous: Murray Holdings (SW) Limited
Net Worth: £1,305,217 *Total Assets:* £11,910,894
Registered Office: 44 Millbay Road, Plymouth, PL1 3FQ
Activities: Activities of head offices
Parent: Murray Holdings (SW) Limited
Officers: Kevin Alfred David Murray [1965] Director

Custom Interconnect Limited
Incorporated: 10 June 1986 *Employees:* 115
Net Worth: £4,187,000 *Total Assets:* £9,377,000
Registered Office: CIL House, Charlton Road, Andover, Hants, SP10 3JL
Activities: Manufacture of loaded electronic boards
Parent: Custom Interconnect (Holdings) Ltd
Officers: Dr Peter Barnwell, Secretary; John George Boston [1961] Managing Director; Craig Richard Wright [1968] Director/Chartered Accountant

Custom Sensors & Technologies Newco Ltd
Incorporated: 2 November 2015
Net Worth: £784,039,552 *Total Assets:* £784,055,680
Registered Office: Everdene House, Deansleigh Road, Bournemouth, BH7 7DU
Activities: Activities of other holding companies n.e.c.
Parent: Sensata Technologies UK Financing Co. PLC
Officers: Jeffrey John Cote [1966] Director [American]

Customade (UK) Limited
Incorporated: 21 December 2005 *Employees:* 201
Net Worth: £870,000 *Total Assets:* £10,770,000
Registered Office: Old End Hall, Oldends Lane, Stonehouse, Glos, GL10 3RQ
Activities: Manufacture of builders ware of plastic
Parent: Customade Group Limited
Officers: Dawn Allison Rogers, Secretary; Lance Dominic Gillett [1966] Finance Director; David Brian Leng [1962] Director/Business Executive; Neil Andrew McGill [1977] Director; John Michael Naylor-Leyland [1984] Director

Customade Group Midco Limited
Incorporated: 21 June 2016
Net Worth Deficit: £2,305,000 *Total Assets:* £28,173,000
Registered Office: Oldend Hall, Oldends Industrial Estate, Oldends Lane, Stonehouse, Glos, GL10 3RQ
Activities: Activities of production holding companies
Parent: Customade Group Topco Limited
Officers: Dawn Rogers, Secretary; Lance Dominic Gillett [1966] Finance Director; David Brian Leng [1962] Director/Business Executive; Neil Andrew McGill [1977] Director; David Alan Moore [1963] Director; John Michael Naylor-Leyland [1984] Director; Andrew David Steel [1968] Director/Partner - Private Equity

Customade Group Topco Limited
Incorporated: 20 June 2016 *Employees:* 799
Net Worth Deficit: £2,234,000 *Total Assets:* £66,696,000
Registered Office: Oldend Hall, Oldends Lane, Stonehouse, Glos, GL10 3RQ
Activities: Activities of production holding companies
Parent: Customade Group Holdco Limited
Officers: Dawn Allison Rogers, Secretary; Jonathan Edward Gatfield [1959] Director; Lance Dominic Gillett [1966] Finance Director; David Brian Leng [1962] Director/Business Executive; David Alan Moore [1963] Director; John Michael Naylor-Leyland [1984] Director; Andrew David Steel [1968] Director/Partner - Private Equity

Customade Group Trading Limited
Incorporated: 15 April 2016
Previous: Polyframe Group Limited
Net Worth Deficit: £4,862,000 *Total Assets:* £66,055,000
Registered Office: Oldend Hall, Oldends Lane, Stonehouse, Glos, GL10 3RQ
Activities: Activities of production holding companies
Parent: Customade Group Midco Ltd
Officers: Dawn Allison Rogers, Secretary; Lance Dominic Gillett [1966] Finance Director; David Brian Leng [1962] Director/Business Executive; David Alan Moore [1963] Director; John Michael Naylor-Leyland [1984] Director; Andrew David Steel [1968] Director/Partner - Private Equity

CWC (UK Holdings) Limited
Incorporated: 6 December 2007 *Employees:* 470
Net Worth: £8,273,000 *Total Assets:* £79,349,000
Registered Office: Mercedes Benz of Exeter, Matford Park Road, Exeter, Devon, EX2 8FD
Activities: Sale of new cars and light motor vehicles
Officers: Michael Anthony Wickins, Secretary/Director; Gavin Robert Walker [1967] Finance Director; Anthony John Wickins [1951] Director; Michael Anthony Wickins [1970] Director

Cygnet Industries Limited
Incorporated: 15 August 2007
Net Worth: £38,773,228 *Total Assets:* £46,033,772
Registered Office: The Estate Office, Melbury, Sampford, Dorchester, DT2 0LF
Activities: Activities of other holding companies n.e.c.
Shareholders: The Honourable Charlotte Anne Townshend; James Reginald Townshend; Ilchester Trustee Company Limited
Officers: Robert Ian Sanderson, Secretary; John Arthur Courtney Drake [1951] Director; Henry Charles Guest [1978] Director/Partner of Adelphi Capital LLP; Mark Alastair Henderson [1946] Director/Financial Adviser; The Honourable Charlotte Anne Townshend [1955] Director; James Reginald Townshend [1954] Director

D & R Bidco Limited
Incorporated: 19 May 2015
Net Worth Deficit: £3,104,104 *Total Assets:* £16,978,076
Registered Office: Portland Marina, Osprey Quay, Hamm Beach Road, Portland, Dorset, DT5 1DX
Activities: Activities of head offices
Parent: D & R Cleanco Limited
Officers: Michael Andrew Charles Prideaux [1971] Director; Richard John Reddyhoff [1952] Director

D & R Cleanco Limited
Incorporated: 19 May 2015
Net Worth: £799,970 *Total Assets:* £20,793,546
Registered Office: Portland Marina, Osprey Quay, Hamm Beach Road, Portland, Dorset, DT5 1DX
Activities: Activities of head offices
Parent: D & R Midco Limited
Officers: Michael Andrew Charles Prideaux [1971] Director; Richard John Reddyhoff [1952] Director

D & R Midco Limited
Incorporated: 19 May 2015
Net Worth: £799,922 *Total Assets:* £20,793,552
Registered Office: Portland Marina, Osprey Quay, Hamm Beach Road, Portland, Dorset, DT5 1DX
Activities: Activities of head offices
Parent: D & R Topco Limited
Officers: Michael Andrew Charles Prideaux [1971] Director; Richard John Reddyhoff [1952] Director

D & R Topco Limited
Incorporated: 18 May 2015 *Employees:* 70
Net Worth: £759,841 *Total Assets:* £56,782,704
Registered Office: Portland Marina, Osprey Quay, Hamm Beach Road, Portland, Dorset, DT5 1DX
Activities: Activities of head offices
Parent: Mansford Opportunities V LP
Officers: John Michael Dean [1939] Director; Charles Henry Knight [1966] Director/Investment Professional; Michael Andrew Charles Prideaux [1971] Director; Richard John Reddyhoff [1952] Director; David James Reynolds [1982] Director/Investment Professional

D A S Legal Expenses Insurance Company Limited
Incorporated: 28 May 1909
Net Worth: £38,541,000 *Total Assets:* £506,198,016
Registered Office: Das House, Quay Side, Temple Back, Bristol, BS1 6NH
Activities: Non-life insurance
Parent: DAS UK Holdings Limited
Officers: Catherine Jane Brown, Secretary; Brynley Case, Secretary; Andrew John Burke [1969] Director/Chief Executive Officer; Generald Cox [1954] Director; James Conroy Henderson [1975] Director [New Zealander]; Neil Stephen Macmillan [1962] Director; Karen Anne Morris [1959] Director; Gareth John Roberts [1959] Director/Solicitor; Deniss Sazonovs [1980] Director [Latvian]

D B Foods (Holdings) Limited
Incorporated: 9 September 2008 *Employees:* 277
Net Worth: £5,352,742 *Total Assets:* £35,648,560
Registered Office: Unit L, Fulcrum Business Park, Vantage Way, Poole, Dorset, BH12 4NU
Activities: Activities of head offices
Parent: The DB Food Group Limited
Officers: Ben Bayer [1970] Director; David Charles Bayer [1946] Director; Darren Carl Beale [1983] Director

The D'Oyly Carte Charitable Trust
Incorporated: 28 November 2005
Net Worth: £58,244,224 *Total Assets:* £58,446,660
Registered Office: 6 Trull Farm Buildings, Tetbury, Glos, GL8 8SQ
Activities: Other business support service activities n.e.c.
Officers: Jane Keith Thorne, Secretary; Amelia Anne Beringer [1986] Director/Solicitor; Nina Victoria Camilleri [1971] Charity Director; Henry John Freeland [1948] Director/Architect; Andrew George Wycliffe Jackson [1948] Director/Solicitor; Jeremy Leigh Pemberton [1933] Director; Dr Michael Dermod O'Brien [1938] Director/Physician; Julia Sibley [1955] Director/Chief Executive; Andrew Bowring Wimble [1957] Director/Fund Manager

D-Tech (UK) Limited
Incorporated: 5 January 2005 *Employees:* 9
Net Worth: £9,287,115 *Total Assets:* £19,517,406
Registered Office: 1325 Aztec West, Bristol, BS32 4RX
Activities: Manufacture of other special-purpose machinery n.e.c.
Parent: Schoeller-Bleckmann Oilfield Equipment AG
Officers: Manuela Brugger [1975] Director/Controller [Austrian]; Muhammad Ismail Nawaz [1960] Director/Engineer [American]; Oswald Otto [1959] Director/Controller [Austrian]

D. J. Commercial Limited
Incorporated: 3 May 2006 *Employees:* 3
Net Worth: £4,860,640 *Total Assets:* £14,852,716
Registered Office: DJ Property, Unit C, Oxford Court, Cambridge Road, Granby Industrial Estate, Weymouth, Dorset, DT4 9GH
Activities: Other letting and operating of own or leased real estate
Parent: Kathryn Jones, Michael Jones, Alan Newberry
Officers: Kathryn Jones, Secretary; Kathryn Jones [1947] Director/Secretary; Michael Jones [1973] Director/Chartered Accountant

D.B. Foods Limited
Incorporated: 12 February 1992 *Employees:* 235
Net Worth: £3,956,767 *Total Assets:* £20,918,474
Registered Office: Unit L, Fulcrum Business Park, Vantage Way, Poole, Dorset, BH12 4NU
Activities: Wholesale of meat and meat products
Parent: DB Foods (Holdings) Limited
Officers: Ben Bayer [1970] Director; David Charles Bayer [1946] Director; Patrick David Bayer [1986] Director; George Henry Charles Holliday [1976] Director; Maurice McNulty [1981] Commercial Director [Irish]; Max Henricus Maria Prudon [1976] Director [Dutch]; Stuart Nigel Robson [1966] Director/Salesman; Gary Peter Smith [1968] Finance Director

D.B. Systems Holdings Limited
Incorporated: 19 June 2015 *Employees:* 99
Net Worth Deficit: £985,307 *Total Assets:* £7,952,121
Registered Office: Spectrum 800, Ashchurch Business Park, Alexandra Way, Tewkesbury, Glos, GL20 8TD
Activities: Activities of head offices
Officers: David Charles Bulley [1968] Director; Anthony John Burgess [1963] Director; Mike Cameron-Davies [1969] Operations Director; Alastair Reece [1983] Director/Head of Content; Alexander Smart [1952] Director; James Christopher Wakefield [1966] Director

D.I.S. Limited
Incorporated: 16 August 1988 *Employees:* 60
Net Worth: £2,280,178 *Total Assets:* £6,320,973
Registered Office: Midway House, Herrick Way, Staverton Technology Park, Staverton, Cheltenham, Glos, GL51 6TQ
Activities: Plumbing, heat and air-conditioning installation
Shareholder: Darren James Bell
Officers: Raymond Bell, Secretary; Darren James Bell [1972] Director/Contract Engineer

D.J. Contracts (Structural) Limited
Incorporated: 6 June 1963 *Employees:* 2
Net Worth: £3,352,021 *Total Assets:* £3,641,554
Registered Office: DJ Property, Unit C, Oxford Court, Cambridge Road, Granby Industrial Estate, Weymouth, Dorset, DT4 9GH
Activities: Other letting and operating of own or leased real estate
Shareholders: Gregory Mudge; Alan Philip Rodgers; Kate Jones; Michael Jones
Officers: Kathryn Jones, Secretary; Kathryn Jones [1947] Director/Secretary; Michael Jones [1973] Director/Chartered Accountant

D.J. Contracts (Weymouth) Limited
Incorporated: 1 July 1969 *Employees:* 2
Net Worth: £7,060,905 *Total Assets:* £10,197,446
Registered Office: DJ Property, Unit C, Oxford Court, Cambridge Road, Granby Industrial Estate, Weymouth, Dorset, DT4 9GH
Activities: Other construction installation
Officers: Kathryn Jones, Secretary; Kathryn Jones [1947] Director/Secretary; Michael Jones [1973] Director/Chartered Accountant

D.J.L.Securities (Barum) Limited
Incorporated: 26 September 1963 *Employees:* 7
Net Worth: £6,872,750 *Total Assets:* £13,887,341
Registered Office: Loosemore House, Brannam Crescent, Roundswell Business Park, Barnstaple, Devon, EX31 3TD
Activities: Development of building projects
Shareholders: Nicholas Denis Loosemore; Mark John Loosemore; Mark John Loosemore
Officers: Karen Elizabeth LooSeniore, Secretary/Housewife; Andrew Nicholas LooSeniore [1986] Director; Karen Elizabeth LooSeniore [1957] Director/Housewife; Maria Diane LooSeniore [1964] Director/Housewife; Mark John LooSeniore [1961] Director; Nicholas Denis LooSeniore [1955] Director

D4E Mulberry Limited
Incorporated: 6 February 2002 *Employees:* 5
Net Worth Deficit: £1,751,000 *Total Assets:* £6,602,000
Registered Office: Third Floor, Broad Quay House, Prince Street, Bristol, BS1 4DJ
Activities: Management of real estate on a fee or contract basis
Parent: D4E Mulberry (Holdings) Limited
Officers: Karen Marie Hill [1977] Director; David Francis Lindesay [1960] Commercial Director; Neil Rae [1971] Director; Martin Timothy Smith [1967] Director/Banker; David Glyn Swinburn [1954] Director

DAC Beachcroft Claims Limited
Incorporated: 16 May 2001
Net Worth: £7,277,000 *Total Assets:* £46,913,000
Registered Office: Portwall Place, Portwall Lane, Bristol, BS1 9HS
Activities: Solicitors
Parent: DAC Beachcroft LLP
Officers: Anthony John Cherry [1955] Director/Solicitor; Craig Lee Dickson [1977] Director/Chief Executive Officer; Helen Louise Faulkner [1967] Director/Solicitor; James Sinclair Benedict Morris [1965] Director/Lawyer; Andrew John Cunningham Parker [1959] Director/Solicitor; Shriyesh Patel [1961] Director/Chief Financial Officer; David Egerton Pollitt [1965] Director/Solicitor; Thomas Alexander Watkinson [1975] Director/Solicitor

DAC Beachcroft Services Limited
Incorporated: 12 September 2005 *Employees:* 2,178
Net Worth: £1,918,000 *Total Assets:* £21,920,000
Registered Office: Portwall Place, Portwall Lane, Bristol, BS1 9HS
Activities: Combined office administrative service activities
Parent: DAC Beachcroft LLP
Officers: Katherine Elizabeth Farmer [1964] Director/Solicitor; David James Gillard [1962] Finance Director; Andrew Neil Keith [1965] Director/Chief Operations Officer; David Egerton Pollitt [1965] Director/Solicitor

Dagenham Wind Park Limited
Incorporated: 18 March 1998
Net Worth: £4,548,572 *Total Assets:* £6,713,949
Registered Office: Lion House, Rowcroft, Stroud, Glos, GL5 3BY
Activities: Production of electricity
Parent: Ecotricity Group Limited
Officers: Tom Cowling, Secretary; Asif Rehmanwala [1976] Director/Chief Operating Officer; Dale Vince [1961] Director/Consultant

Daido Industrial Bearings Europe Limited
Incorporated: 17 August 1998 *Employees:* 162
Net Worth Deficit: £4,576,000 *Total Assets:* £12,117,000
Registered Office: Winterhay Lane, Ilminster, Somerset, TA19 9PH
Activities: Manufacture of bearings, gears, gearing and driving elements
Parent: Daido Metal Co., Ltd
Officers: Nicola Jane Green, Secretary; Yoshitaka Emoto [1961] Director/General Manager Business Promotions [Japanese]; Nicola Jane Green [1964] Managing Director; Mark Hopkins [1967] Site Director; Naoki Kurita [1965] Director/General Manager of Finance Department [Japanese]; Kenji Shoda [1962] Director [Japanese]

Daido Metal Europe Limited
Incorporated: 10 January 2006 *Employees:* 20
Net Worth: £4,517,000 *Total Assets:* £42,009,000
Registered Office: Winterhay Lane, Ilminster, Somerset, TA19 9PH
Activities: Wholesale trade of motor vehicle parts and accessories
Parent: Daido Metal Co., Ltd
Officers: Kenji Shoda, Secretary; Kenji Shoda [1962] Managing Director DME [Japanese]; Neil Richard Medlicott Tarver [1964] Director/Business Development Manager

Dainton Group Services Limited
Incorporated: 1 October 1980 *Employees:* 43
Net Worth: £14,738,683 *Total Assets:* £25,988,524
Registered Office: Dainton Business Park, Heathfield, Newton Abbot, Devon, TQ12 6RG
Activities: Other business support service activities n.e.c.
Parent: Denvern Limited
Officers: Shaun Robert Duncan [1967] Operations Director; Paul Gregory Maddicott [1975] Director/General Manager; Andrew John Sanders [1966] Director

Dairy Partners (Cymru Wales) Limited
Incorporated: 13 May 2013 *Employees:* 78
Previous: Dansco Dairy Limited
Net Worth: £7,801,502 *Total Assets:* £16,047,146
Registered Office: Brunel Way, Stroud Water Business Park, Stonehouse, Glos, GL10 3SX
Activities: Butter and cheese production
Parent: Dairy Partners Ltd
Officers: Christina McTernan, Secretary; Clive John Bennett [1938] Director; William John Bennett [1975] Director; Robert William Peel [1966] Director

Dairy Partners Limited
Incorporated: 22 February 1994 *Employees:* 147
Net Worth: £17,464,648 *Total Assets:* £30,907,164
Registered Office: Brunel Way, Stroudwater Business Park, Oldends Lane, Stonehouse, Glos, GL10 3SX
Activities: Butter and cheese production
Shareholders: Clive John Bennett; Robert William Peel; William John Bennett
Officers: Christina McTernan, Secretary; Clive John Bennett [1938] Director; William John Bennett [1975] Director; Robert William Peel [1966] Director

Daish's Group Limited
Incorporated: 28 March 2012 *Employees:* 352
Net Worth: £5,674,290 *Total Assets:* £23,491,366
Registered Office: Devonshire Hotel, Park Hill Road, Torquay, Devon, TQ1 2DY
Activities: Activities of head offices
Major Shareholder: Jeanne Wilson
Officers: Gary Moss, Secretary; George Antony Brown [1965] Director; Paul David Harper [1981] Sales Director; Gary Moss [1952] Director/Financial Controller; Jeanne Rose Wilson [1946] Director

Daktronics UK Limited
Incorporated: 20 August 2002 *Employees:* 17
Net Worth: £2,113,361 *Total Assets:* £6,739,876
Registered Office: F16 Kestrel Court, Waterwells Drive, Quedgeley, Gloucester, GL2 2AT
Activities: Manufacture of other electrical equipment
Parent: Daktronics Inc
Officers: Martyn John Roberts, Secretary; Sheila Mae Anderson [1973] Director [American]; Patrick Alan Halliwell [1970] Managing Director; Reece Allen Kurtenbach [1964] Director [American]

Dale's Central Motors Limited
Incorporated: 14 December 1956 *Employees:* 103
Net Worth: £2,654,968 *Total Assets:* £8,085,287
Registered Office: Wheal Rose, Scorrier, Redruth, Cornwall, TR16 5BX
Activities: Sale of new cars and light motor vehicles
Officers: Margaret Dale, Secretary; Dominic Cadge [1968] Director/Company Accountant; Sara Louise Cadge [1968] Director/General Manager; Margaret Dale [1945] Director/Garage Proprietor; Tony Dale [1945] Director/Garage Proprietor; Carolyn Peters [1971] Director/General Manager; Simon Peters [1965] Director/Aftersales Manager; Jeremy Rouse [1966] Sales Director

D. Dalton & Son Limited
Incorporated: 6 April 1955 *Employees:* 15
Net Worth: £13,258,967 *Total Assets:* £16,052,098
Registered Office: Manor Farm, Bushes Road, Pimperne, Dorset, DT11 8US
Activities: Mixed farming
Officers: Timothy Michael Dalton, Secretary; Sam Sebastian Chambers [1984] Director; Douglas Peter Dalton [1982] Director; George Michael Dalton [1984] Director; Peter James Dalton [1951] Director/Farmer; Timothy Michael Dalton [1953] Director/Farmer; Lucy Caroline Lucas-Rowe [1966] Director

Dan-Floor U.K. Limited
Incorporated: 25 May 1983 *Employees:* 18
Net Worth: £3,113,538 *Total Assets:* £4,016,127
Registered Office: 106 Longmead Road, Emersons Green, Bristol, BS16 7FG
Activities: Manufacture of woven or tufted carpets and rugs
Officers: Ian Charles Dexter, Secretary/Managing Director; Nicholas David George Coburn [1959] International Sales Director; Ian Charles Dexter [1966] Managing Director; Jesper Kroejgaard Jensen [1961] Director/Financial Manager [Danish]

Danbec Property Limited
Incorporated: 9 March 2016
Net Worth: £2,415,206 *Total Assets:* £4,055,830
Registered Office: The Office, 469 Southmead Road, Westbury on Trym, Bristol, BS10 5LZ
Activities: Combined facilities support activities
Shareholder: Christopher Wyndham Wolfe
Officers: Christopher Wyndham Wolfe [1961] Director/Manager; Debra Ann Wolfe [1963] Director/Administrator

Danco International PLC
Incorporated: 5 November 1975 *Employees:* 135
Net Worth: £4,716,428 *Total Assets:* £9,988,629
Registered Office: The Pavilion Centre, Frog Lane, Coalpit Heath, Bristol, BS36 2NW
Activities: Renting and leasing of other machinery, equipment and tangible goods n.e.c.
Major Shareholder: Adrian Stephen Dann
Officers: Mary Dann, Secretary; Adrian Stephen Dann [1961] Managing Director; Mary Dann [1958] Director/Secretary; Leslie Roy Johnson [1953] Director

Danesdale Land Limited
Incorporated: 20 December 1989
Net Worth: £13,128,417 *Total Assets:* £16,500,513
Registered Office: 14 Wilton Road, Salisbury, Wilts, SP2 7EE
Activities: Management of real estate on a fee or contract basis
Officers: Tamara Jon Folkesson, Secretary; Colin Lewis Chandler [1946] Director/Management Consultant; Tamara Jon Folkesson [1967] Director

Danetre PFI Project Company Limited
Incorporated: 24 June 2004 *Employees:* 2
Net Worth Deficit: £8,107,953 *Total Assets:* £28,509,716
Registered Office: Third Floor, Broad Quay House, Prince Street, Bristol, BS1 4DJ
Activities: Other service activities n.e.c.
Parent: Danetre PFI Holding Company Limited
Officers: Richard Little [1979] Investment Director; Kenneth Andrew McLellan [1961] Regional Project Director

Danfoss Power Solutions Limited
Incorporated: 16 October 1987 *Employees:* 13
Net Worth: £24,367,000 *Total Assets:* £27,696,000
Registered Office: The Paragon, 32 Counterslip, Bristol, BS1 6BX
Activities: Other business support service activities n.e.c.
Parent: Danfoss A/S
Officers: Tom Andersen [1957] Director of Finance & Controller [Danish]; Torben Christensen [1966] Director [Danish]; Anders Stahlschmidt [1967] Director [Danish]; Nicholas Wanless [1968] Director/Accountant

W. Daniels Plant Hire Limited
Incorporated: 11 April 1983 *Employees:* 9
Net Worth: £2,990,463 *Total Assets:* £3,503,425
Registered Office: Unit L, Wallsend Industrial Estate, Cattedown, Plymouth, PL4 0RW
Activities: Other specialised construction activities n.e.c.
Major Shareholder: William Smith Daniels
Officers: Rebecca Ann Daniels [1984] Director/Company Secretary; William Matthew Daniels [1981] Director/Construction Site Manager; William Smith Daniels [1953] Director/Plant Operator

Danisco (UK) Limited
Incorporated: 27 June 1988
Net Worth: £13,886,000 *Total Assets:* £35,155,000
Registered Office: P O Box 777, High Street, Marlborough, Wilts, SN8 1XN
Activities: Manufacture of other food products n.e.c.
Parent: Danisco Holdings (UK) Limited
Officers: Adrian Paul Gough [1958] Director/Business Development Officer; Stephen Reeve [1963] Director/Accountant

Danisco Holdings (UK) Limited
Incorporated: 9 March 1984
Net Worth: £9,324,000 *Total Assets:* £10,503,000
Registered Office: 777 Market House, Ailesbury Court, High Street, Marlborough, Wilts, SN8 1AA
Activities: Activities of other holding companies n.e.c.
Parent: DowDupont Inc.
Officers: Adrian Paul Gough [1958] Director/Business Development Manager; Stephen Reeve [1963] Director/Accountant

Danlers Limited
Incorporated: 20 December 1990
Net Worth: £3,743,609 *Total Assets:* £4,530,509
Registered Office: 14a Forest Gate, Pewsham, Chippenham, Wilts, SN15 3RS
Activities: Manufacture of electric lighting equipment
Shareholder: Robert Anthony Smedley Kay
Officers: David Jonathan Smedley Kay, Secretary; David Jonathan Smedley Kay [1964] Director; Julian Joseph Kay [1967] Managing Director; Robert Anthony Smedley Kay [1935] Director/Executive Chairman; Rupert Charles Kay [1971] Director

Ron Darch & Sons Co Ltd
Incorporated: 24 February 1983 *Employees:* 51
Previous: Ron Darch & Sons Limited
Net Worth: £5,198,145 *Total Assets:* £7,288,025
Registered Office: 13a Pen Mill Trading Estate, Yeovil, Somerset, BA21 5HA
Activities: Wholesale of other fuels and related products
Officers: Simon Lee George Darch, Secretary; Andrew Tony Ronald Darch [1960] Director/Oil Distributor; Jamie Darch [1974] Director/General Manager; Jeremy Paul Darch [1962] Director/Fuel Merchant; Nigel Darch [1958] Director/Fuel Merchant; Simon Lee George Darch [1967] Director/Fuel Merchant

J.A. Darke Limited
Incorporated: 9 December 1948
Net Worth: £9,424,976 *Total Assets:* £10,438,415
Registered Office: Coleridge Farm Cottages, Chillington, Kingsbridge, Devon, TQ7 2JG
Activities: Raising of dairy cattle
Shareholders: Edward Alfred Darke; Ian Philip Darke
Officers: Brenda Marie Darke, Secretary; Edward Alfred Darke [1942] Director; Ian Philip Darke [1953] Director; Richard Charles Darke [1966] Director/Farmer

Dart & Francis Limited
Incorporated: 6 September 1905 *Employees:* 6
Net Worth: £4,871,753 *Total Assets:* £5,101,270
Registered Office: Ecclesiastical Art Works, 127a High Street, Crediton, Devon, EX17 3LQ
Activities: Other letting and operating of own or leased real estate
Shareholder: Michael Gerald Discombe
Officers: Amanda Jane Discombe [1958] Director/Secretary; Bradley Discombe [1993] Director; Hannah Fay Discombe [1984] Director; Michael Generald Discombe [1956] Director; Russell Discombe [1988] Director; Lydia Fern Richards [1986] Director

Dart Abbey Enterprises Limited
Incorporated: 5 July 1979 *Employees:* 77
Net Worth: £2,000,550 *Total Assets:* £5,025,383
Registered Office: Buckfast Abbey, Buckfast, Buckfastleigh, Devon, TQ11 0EE
Activities: Manufacture of other non-distilled fermented beverages
Parent: Buckfast Abbey Trustees Registered
Officers: Jonathan Roger Deacon, Secretary; Rev Vincent Gabriel Arnold [1931] Director/Minister of Religion; David Roger Charlesworth [1951] Director/Minister of Religion; Jonathan Roger Deacon [1956] Director/Chartered Accountant; Father Gavin Francis Straw [1959] Director/Minister of Religion

Dart Marina Hotel Limited
Incorporated: 23 May 1966 *Employees:* 85
Net Worth: £957,464 *Total Assets:* £14,224,999
Registered Office: Dart Marina Hotel, Sandquay Road, Dartmouth, Devon, TQ6 9PH
Activities: Hotels and similar accommodation
Shareholders: Richard James Wilmot Seton; William Beau Holland; Gary Noel Hitchcock
Officers: Lynda Mary Redman, Secretary; Paul Downing [1973] Managing Director; Lynda Mary Redman [1963] Finance Director; Richard James Wilmot Seton [1952] Director [New Zealander]; Anthony Philip Tucker [1950] Director

Dart Sensors Limited
Incorporated: 20 May 1994 *Employees:* 11
Net Worth: £4,229,028 *Total Assets:* £4,437,872
Registered Office: 30 Fore Street, Totnes, Devon, TQ9 5RP
Activities: Other manufacturing n.e.c.
Officers: Susan Mary King, Secretary; Edwin Ashley King [1982] Director/General Manager; John Julius King [1979] Technical Director; Susan Mary King [1950] Director/Secretary; Dr Walter John King [1944] Director/Industrial Chemist

Dart Valley Railway Ltd
Incorporated: 18 June 1965 *Employees:* 132
Previous: Dart Valley Railway PLC
Net Worth: £7,139,209 *Total Assets:* £8,697,152
Registered Office: Queens Park Station, Torbay Road, Paignton, Devon, TQ4 6AF
Activities: Passenger rail transport, interurban
Shareholder: Jeremy John Hosking
Officers: John Robert Jones, Secretary; David Ian Allan [1954] Director/Publisher; Colin Andrew Bland [1962] Director; Nicholas Geoffrey Dunn [1959] Director; John Robert Jones [1971] Director; Paul Edward Merrington [1970] Director/Shipwright/Head of Engineering

Dart Valley Systems Limited
Incorporated: 6 September 1985 *Employees:* 44
Net Worth: £3,314,526 *Total Assets:* £4,485,084
Registered Office: Kemmings Close, Long Road, Paignton, Devon, TQ4 7TW
Activities: Other specialised construction activities n.e.c.
Parent: Franke Sissons Limited
Officers: Daniel Orwin, Secretary; Roger Basler [1965] Director [Swiss]; Patrick Truttmann [1975] Director/Accountant [Swiss]

Dartex Coatings Limited
Incorporated: 27 February 2001 *Employees:* 53
Net Worth: £2,491,132 *Total Assets:* £4,503,362
Registered Office: Trelleborg International Drive, Tewkesbury Business Park, Tewkesbury, Glos, GL20 8UQ
Activities: Manufacture of other technical and industrial textiles
Parent: Dartex Holdings Limited
Officers: Vincenzo Fortunato [1960] Director Finance & Control [Italian]; Mark Anthony Jones [1962] Director/General Manager; Bengt Karl Andreas Renulf [1974] Director/Business Unit President [Swedish]

Dartex Holdings Limited
Incorporated: 3 June 2016 *Employees:* 76
Net Worth: £2,422,000 *Total Assets:* £5,283,000
Registered Office: Trelleborg International Drive, Tewkesbury Business Park, Tewkesbury, Glos, GL20 8UQ
Activities: Activities of head offices
Parent: Trelleborg Holdings UK Limited
Officers: Ingrid Charlotta Grahs [1971] Director/Lawyer [Swedish]; Niklas Anders Johansson [1973] Director/Vice President Tax [Swedish]; Lars Ivar Leijonberg [1964] Director/Vice President Internal Control [Swedish]

Darthaven Marina Limited
Incorporated: 11 September 1975 *Employees:* 44
Net Worth: £4,661,757 *Total Assets:* £7,663,854
Registered Office: Brixham Road, Kingswear, Dartmouth, Devon, TQ6 0SG
Activities: Repair and maintenance of ships and boats
Shareholders: Ann Juliet Sainthill; Kenneth John Twycross Holman
Officers: Colin Andrew Bland [1962] Director; Sophie Clare Bragg [1970] Director/Accountant; Kenneth John Twycross Holman [1956] Director/Marina Operator; Melanie Holman [1950] Director/Manager; Ann Juliet Sainthill [1950] Director/Married Woman

Dartington Crystal (Torrington) Limited
Incorporated: 28 March 2006 *Employees:* 150
Net Worth: £2,854,004 *Total Assets:* £7,149,931
Registered Office: Dartington Crystal, Town Park, School Lane, Torrington, Devon, EX38 7AN
Activities: Manufacture of hollow glass
Parent: Dartington Crystal (Holdings) Limited
Officers: Alan Ramsay, Secretary; Richard Halliday [1962] Director/Marketing and Design Manager; Neil Hughes [1968] Director; Alan Beaton Ramsay [1966] Financial Director

Dartington Hall Trust (The)
Incorporated: 14 March 1980 *Employees:* 244
Net Worth: £31,109,000 *Total Assets:* £37,026,000
Registered Office: The Elmhirst Centre, Dartington Hall, Totnes, Devon, TQ9 6EL
Activities: Post-graduate level higher education
Officers: Christopher Clive Moores, Secretary; Timothy Michael Jones [1946] Director; Dr Gregory Edward Parston [1949] Director/Executive Advisor; Sylvie Pierce [1948] Director; Robert Edward Sexton [1973] Director/Chief Executive; Sangeeta Elizabeth Singh-Watson [1969] Director/Restaurateur; Nigel Paul Topping [1965] Director/Chief Executive; Julia Unwin [1956] Non-Executive Director and Consultant; Andrew Holman Ward [1953] Director

Dartmoor Investment Trust Limited
Incorporated: 29 January 1990
Net Worth Deficit: £12,155,000 *Total Assets:* £60,720,000
Registered Office: 51 New North Road, Exeter, Devon, EX4 4EP
Activities: Financial intermediation not elsewhere classified
Major Shareholder: Nicholas Howard Lewis
Officers: Edmund Arthur Selby Lewis [1989] Director; Nicholas Howard Lewis [1954] Director/Accountant; Rosemary Jane Lewis [1987] Director; Sarah Ann Lewis [1955] Director

Dartmouth Holdings Limited
Incorporated: 3 May 2016
Net Worth: £9,040,050 *Total Assets:* £9,040,050
Registered Office: Units 1-9 Hearder Court, Beechwood Way, Langage Business Park, Plymouth, PL7 5HH
Activities: Processing and preserving of poultry meat
Shareholder: Faccenda Investments
Officers: Edward Obolensky, Secretary; Ian James Faccenda [1967] Director; Edward Obolensky [1978] Director/Chartered Accountant; Nicholas Obolensky [1977] Director

The Dartmouth-Kingswear Floating Bridge Company Limited
Incorporated: 30 July 2001 *Employees:* 15
Net Worth: £4,572,283 *Total Assets:* £8,161,643
Registered Office: Dart Marina, Sandquay Road, Dartmouth, Devon, TQ6 9PH
Activities: Inland passenger water transport
Shareholders: Richard James Wilmot Seton; William Beau Holland; Gary Noel Hitchcock
Officers: Lynda Mary Redman, Secretary; Paul Downing [1973] Managing Director; Lynda Mary Redman [1963] Finance Director; Richard James Wilmot Seton [1952] Director [New Zealander]; Anthony Philip Tucker [1950] Director

Darts Farm Limited
Incorporated: 1 October 2001 *Employees:* 137
Net Worth: £9,997,645 *Total Assets:* £14,540,658
Registered Office: Darts Farm, Topsham, Exeter, Devon, EX3 0QH
Activities: Other business support service activities n.e.c.
Shareholders: George Paul Dart; Ronald James Dart; Michael Charles Rowe Dart
Officers: Michael Charles Rowe Dart, Secretary/Retailer; George Paul Dart [1961] Director/Farmer; Michael Charles Rowe Dart [1967] Director/Retailer; Ronald James Dart [1969] Director/Retailer

DAS Law Limited
Incorporated: 7 April 2005 *Employees:* 4
Net Worth Deficit: £6,988,000 *Total Assets:* £13,617,000
Registered Office: North Quay, Temple Back, Bristol, BS1 6FL
Activities: Solicitors
Parent: DAS UK Holdings Limited
Officers: Catherine Jane Brown, Secretary; Andrew John Burke [1969] Director/Chief Executive; Brynley Richard Case [1976] Director/Solicitor; James Edward Christacos [1970] Director/Solicitor; William Ellerton [1971] Director/Solicitor

DAS Services Limited
Incorporated: 30 October 1997 *Employees:* 684
Net Worth Deficit: £8,420,000 *Total Assets:* £23,224,000
Registered Office: Das House, Quay Side, Temple Back, Bristol, BS1 6NH
Activities: Other business support service activities n.e.c.
Parent: DAS UK Holdings Limited
Officers: Catherine Jane Brown, Secretary; Kate Harriet Banks [1969] Group HR Director; Generald Cox [1954] Director; James Conroy Henderson [1975] Director [New Zealander]

DAS UK Holdings Limited
Incorporated: 29 October 1997
Net Worth: £47,156,000 *Total Assets:* £52,270,000
Registered Office: Das House, Quay Side, Temple Back, Bristol, BS1 6NH
Activities: Activities of head offices
Parent: Munchener Ruckversicherungs-Gesellschaft Aktiengesellschaft
Officers: Catherine Jane Brown, Secretary; Brynley Case, Secretary; Andrew John Burke [1969] Director/Chief Executive Officer; Generald Cox [1954] Director; James Conroy Henderson [1975] Director [New Zealander]; Neil Stephen Macmillan [1962] Director; Karen Anne Morris [1959] Director; Gareth John Roberts [1959] Director/Solicitor; Deniss Sazonovs [1980] Director [Latvian]

Dash Group (SW) Limited
Incorporated: 13 January 2012 *Employees:* 99
Net Worth: £1,323,120 *Total Assets:* £4,729,518
Registered Office: Unit 2 Barncoose Industrial Estate, Redruth, Cornwall, TR15 3RQ
Activities: Activities of head offices
Shareholders: Stephen Dash; Paul James Dash
Officers: Stephen Dash, Secretary; Pamela Dash [1946] Director; Paul Dash [1985] Director; Mr Stephen Dash [1971] Managing Director

Data Installation & Networking Services Limited
Incorporated: 22 March 1993 *Employees:* 362
Net Worth: £4,005,655 *Total Assets:* £10,532,464
Registered Office: Russell House, Oxford Road, Bournemouth, BH8 8EX
Activities: Other specialised construction activities n.e.c.
Major Shareholder: Ian Crockford
Officers: Darren Neil Bateman [1980] Finance Director; Timothy James Coppin [1970] Director; Ian Crockford [1960] Director; Nicholas Lee Crosby [1975] Sales Director; Robert Jacobs [1955] Director/Contracts; Michael Anthony Stephens [1959] Director

Datamine Corporate Limited
Incorporated: 23 March 1982 *Employees:* 2
Previous: CAE Mining Corporate Limited
Net Worth: £12,539,250 *Total Assets:* £18,131,546
Registered Office: Unit A, Underwood Business Park, Wookey Hole Road, Wells, Somerset, BA5 1AF
Activities: Other mining and quarrying n.e.c.
Officers: John Edward Billowits [1972] Director/Executive Officer [Canadian]; Damian Kevin McKay [1972] Director [Australian]

Datum Capital Limited
Incorporated: 10 October 2016 *Employees:* 32
Net Worth: £1,923,338 *Total Assets:* £3,745,917
Registered Office: Unit B, Bridge Works, Station Yard Industrial Estate, Kingsbridge, Devon, TQ7 1ES
Activities: Activities of production holding companies
Major Shareholder: Peter Benjamin Neill Scott
Officers: Peter William Anniss [1976] Director; Ian Alan John [1966] Director; Peter Benjamin Neill Scott [1972] Director/Consultant Engineer; Benjamin Widger [1975] Finance Director

Dauntsey's School
Incorporated: 11 July 2006
Net Worth: £19,867,596 *Total Assets:* £30,605,552
Registered Office: Dauntsey's School, West Lavington, Devizes, Wilts, SN10 4HE
Activities: General secondary education
Officers: Philip Mortimer Allen Nokes, Secretary; Sameera Rachel Broadhead [1973] Director/CEO; Kate Georgia Bruges [1962] Director of Learning & Development; Anthony Howard Collins [1957] Director - Semi Retired; Nicholas Blethyn Elliott [1949] Director/QC; Nicholas John Spencer Fisk [1956] Director/Chartered Accountant; David William Goodhew [1971] Director/Headmaster; Joanna Lucy Green [1966] Director/HR Assistant/Administrator; Richard Johns [1939] Director/Retired; Eleanor Anne Light [1975] Director/Business Owner; Philip James Lough [1952] Director/Retired; Charles Henry de Neufville Lucas [1948] Director/Estate Agent; Angus Stuart Macpherson [1953] Director/Accountant; Veryan Peta Nield [1962] Director/Consultant; Ian David Parker [1965] Director/Chief Executive; Dr Rachel Emma Louise Quarrell [1968] Director/Lecturer; Brigadier Peregrine Peter Rawlins [1946] Director/Retired; Frederick William Scarborough [1949] Director/Surveyor; Ian Tanter Thomas [1958] Director/Semi Retired; Lucy Fiona Walsh-Waring [1967] Director

Davan Caravans Limited
Incorporated: 13 November 1957 *Employees:* 45
Net Worth: £1,485,866 *Total Assets:* £5,580,965
Registered Office: Shepherds Way, St Georges, Weston Super Mare, Somerset, BS22 7XA
Activities: Sale of other motor vehicles
Major Shareholder: Mair Davies
Officers: Richard John Burton [1973] Director/Caravan Retailer; Glen Merrick Davies [1960] Managing Director; Mark Davies [1966] Director/Caravan Retailer; Neil Davies [1963] Director/Caravan Retailer

Davenport & Sons Limited
Incorporated: 28 December 1918 *Employees:* 4
Previous: Davenport & Son Limited
Net Worth: £2,391,577 *Total Assets:* £4,348,481
Registered Office: Woodrow House, Woodrow Farm, Stourton Caundle, Sturminster Newton, Dorset, DT10 2JJ
Activities: Other letting and operating of own or leased real estate
Shareholders: Charles Walter Fitzroy Farquhar; Patrick Henri Spencer
Officers: Elizabeth Jane Fenwick, Secretary; Elizabeth Jane Fenwick [1964] Director; Mark John Fenwick [1962] Director

Arthur David (Food with Service) Limited
Incorporated: 29 September 1986 *Employees:* 378
Previous: A David & Co Limited
Net Worth: £3,745,333 *Total Assets:* £13,646,185
Registered Office: Hillside Farm, Sutton Wick, Bishop Sutton, Bristol, BS39 5XR
Activities: Wholesale of fruit and vegetables
Major Shareholder: Arthur David
Officers: Simon Paul Cocking [1973] Director; Arthur Derrick David [1938] Director/Wholesale Fruiterer; Philip Arthur David [1962] Director; Jonathan David Evans [1967] Director/Foodservice; Daren Hill [1969] Operations Director; John Richard O'Brien [1952] Finance Director

P J Davidson Developments Ltd
Incorporated: 22 May 2003 *Employees:* 18
Previous: P J Davidson (UK) Ltd
Net Worth: £7,353,767 *Total Assets:* £9,388,609
Registered Office: 5 Millers Way, Tedburn St Mary, Exeter, Devon, EX6 6RS
Activities: Other specialised construction activities n.e.c.
Parent: P J Davidson Holdings Limited
Officers: Ronald David Isaac, Secretary; Peter James Davidson [1960] Director/Businessman

P J Davidson Holdings Ltd.
Incorporated: 21 April 2009 *Employees:* 18
Net Worth: £13,070,738 *Total Assets:* £19,792,692
Registered Office: 5 Millers Way, Tedburn St Mary, Exeter, Devon, EX6 6RS
Activities: Activities of head offices
Major Shareholder: Peter James Davidson
Officers: Ronald David Isaac, Secretary; Peter James Davidson [1960] Director/Businessman

Davies Holdings (Somerton) Limited
Incorporated: 4 October 1985 *Employees:* 4
Net Worth: £8,309,352 *Total Assets:* £8,737,270
Registered Office: Senate Court, Southernhay Gardens, Exeter, EX1 1NT
Activities: Other letting and operating of own or leased real estate
Parent: M. Baker (Property Services) Limited
Officers: Andrew Edward Browne [1966] Director; Simon Hugh Gregory [1955] Director/Solicitor

J & W Davis Limited
Incorporated: 28 February 2003 *Employees:* 12
Net Worth: £830,811 *Total Assets:* £3,506,524
Registered Office: West Bodden Farm, Doulting, Shepton Mallet, Somerset, BA4 4PU
Activities: Raising of dairy cattle
Shareholder: William Davis
Officers: Teresa Davis [1961] Director; William Davis [1949] Director/Farmer

Dawnhaze Limited
Incorporated: 29 November 2001
Net Worth: £3,372,979 *Total Assets:* £4,251,112
Registered Office: Woodlands, Staplegrove, Taunton, Somerset, TA2 6AL
Activities: Buying and selling of own real estate
Major Shareholder: Anne Underhill
Officers: Anne Underhill, Secretary/Director; Anne Underhill [1955] Director; Arthur John White [1961] Director

Dawson & King Limited
Incorporated: 10 August 1959 *Employees:* 1
Net Worth: £4,268,431 *Total Assets:* £4,793,679
Registered Office: c/o Frettens Solicitors, The Saxon Centre, 11 Bargates, Christchurch, Dorset, BH23 1PZ
Activities: Other letting and operating of own or leased real estate
Shareholder: Lucia Clair Dailey
Officers: Lucia Clair Dailey [1985] Director/Public Relations

Dawson E & E Parts (Europe) Ltd
Incorporated: 8 June 2001 *Employees:* 5
Net Worth: £2,996,770 *Total Assets:* £4,093,186
Registered Office: Unit 2 Barton Manor, Bristol, BS2 0RL
Activities: Other retail sale not in stores, stalls or markets
Parent: ESD Holdings Limited
Officers: Louisa Clare Mullin, Secretary; Martyn Lloyd Mullin [1970] Director/Engineer

Dawson Media Direct Limited
Incorporated: 20 April 2009 *Employees:* 104
Net Worth: £5,914,000 *Total Assets:* £12,456,000
Registered Office: Rowan House, Cherry Orchard North, Kembrey Park, Swindon, Wilts, SN2 8UH
Activities: Non-specialised wholesale trade
Shareholders: Smiths News Trading Limited; Dawson Book Services Limited
Officers: Stuart Steven Marriner, Secretary; Jonathan Michael Bunting [1972] Director; Anthony Liam Grace [1961] Director; Paul Lawrence Rayson [1962] Director

H. Days Holdings Limited
Incorporated: 14 December 2011 *Employees:* 398
Net Worth Deficit: £6,453,797 *Total Assets:* £7,552,027
Registered Office: Head Office, Happy Days Nurseries, Chapel Town, Summercourt, Newquay, Cornwall, TR8 5YA
Activities: Pre-primary education
Shareholders: Baronsmead Venture Trust PLC; Baronsmead Second Venture Trust PLC
Officers: Ian Mark Sanders, Secretary; Jacqueline Ann Arthur [1954] Director; Steven Cordiner [1981] Investor Director; Kim Herbert [1974] Operations Director; Kevin William Higgs [1967] Development Director; Kenneth John Lewis [1952] Director; Ian Mark Sanders [1974] Director

The DB Food Group Limited
Incorporated: 5 April 2016 *Employees:* 277
Net Worth: £7,272,740 *Total Assets:* £37,414,076
Registered Office: Unit L, Fulcrum Business Park, Vantage Way, Poole, Dorset, BH12 4NU
Activities: Activities of head offices
Shareholder: Darren Carl Beale
Officers: Ben Bayer [1970] Director; David Charles Bayer [1946] Director; Darren Carl Beale [1983] Director

DCM (Cornwall) Limited
Incorporated: 20 November 2013 *Employees:* 143
Net Worth: £3,934,157 *Total Assets:* £13,078,946
Registered Office: Wheal Rose, Scorrier, Redruth, Cornwall, TR16 5BX
Activities: Activities of other holding companies n.e.c.
Shareholder: Tony Dale
Officers: Margaret Dale, Secretary; Dominic Cadge [1968] Director/Company Accountant; Sara Cadge [1968] Director/General Manager; Margaret Dale [1945] Director/Garage Proprietor; Tony Dale [1945] Director/Garage Proprietor; Carolyn Peters [1971] Director/General Manager; Simon Peters [1965] Director/Aftersales Manager; Jeremy Rouse [1966] Sales Director

DDC Dolphin Limited
Incorporated: 4 September 1991 *Employees:* 77
Net Worth: £1,267,429 *Total Assets:* £4,055,780
Registered Office: 1st Floor, 37 Commercial Road, Poole, Dorset, BH14 0HU
Activities: Manufacture of other special-purpose machinery n.e.c.
Parent: DDC Dolphin Holdings Limited
Officers: Alan Stuart Hyde, Secretary; Brian James Calder [1956] Director; Zoe Holiday [1984] Director; Alan Stuart Hyde [1979] Director; Martin Douglas Priest [1957] Director; James Smith [1984] Director

De Monchy Aromatics Limited
Incorporated: 18 February 1982 *Employees:* 21
Net Worth: £2,240,559 *Total Assets:* £3,525,118
Registered Office: Units B & C, Holton Heath Trading Park, Blackhill Road, Poole, Dorset, BH16 6LS
Activities: Wholesale of other intermediate products
Major Shareholder: Martin Richard Gill
Officers: Susan Mary Gill, Secretary/Accountant; Henry Richard Gill [1983] Overseas Sales Director; Martin Richard Gill [1949] Director/Essential Oils Trader; Susan Mary Gill [1950] Director/Accountant; David William Graves [1940] Director/Chartered Accountant; Julie Winwood [1963] Director/Laboratory Technician

De Van Automotive Limited
Incorporated: 25 October 2012 *Employees:* 259
Net Worth: £224,127 *Total Assets:* £45,343,176
Registered Office: St Modwen House, Longbridge Road, Marsh Mills, Plymouth, PL6 8LD
Activities: Sale of new cars and light motor vehicles
Major Shareholder: Graham Paul de Val
Officers: Graham Paul de Val [1961] Director; Michael Emlyn Evans [1946] Director; Claire Jacob [1969] Director/Patent Agent; Sally Jones [1967] Director/Housewife

De Vere Farms Limited
Incorporated: 2 May 1995 *Employees:* 17
Net Worth: £3,964,604 *Total Assets:* £6,717,430
Registered Office: Beaumont, Lincombe Hill Road, Torquay, Devon, TQ1 2HN
Activities: Other letting and operating of own or leased real estate
Major Shareholder: Juan de Vere Whiteway-Wilkinson
Officers: Alexander Whiteway-Wilkinson, Secretary; Juan de Vere Whiteway-Wilkinson [1950] Director/Property Management

Dean & Reddyhoff Limited
Incorporated: 10 September 1992 *Employees:* 61
Net Worth: £15,981,751 *Total Assets:* £56,106,344
Registered Office: Portland Marina, Osprey Quay, Hamm Beach Road, Portland, Dorset, DT5 1DX
Activities: Other amusement and recreation activities n.e.c.
Parent: D & R Bidco Limited
Officers: Graham William Latham, Secretary; John Michael Dean [1939] Director; Michael Andrew Charles Prideaux [1971] Director; Richard John Reddyhoff [1952] Director/Engineer

J.C. Dean (Haulage) Limited
Incorporated: 31 January 1972 *Employees:* 27
Net Worth: £3,272,917 *Total Assets:* £4,109,183
Registered Office: Hatches Lane, Southampton Road Business Park, Salisbury, Wilts, SP1 2NZ
Activities: Freight transport by road
Major Shareholder: John Carl Dean
Officers: Trevor William Lee, Secretary; John Carl Dean [1940] Director/Haulage Contractor

Dean Clarke Estate Ltd
Incorporated: 30 November 2012
Net Worth: £1,397,538 *Total Assets:* £3,743,307
Registered Office: Dean Clarke House, Southernhay East, Exeter, Devon, EX1 1AP
Activities: Development of building projects
Parent: Burrington Estates (Commercial) Limited
Officers: Carol Edworthy, Secretary; Mark David Edworthy [1969] Director; Paul Neil Scantlebury [1967] Director/Property Developer

The Dean Close Foundation
Incorporated: 4 April 2001 *Employees:* 566
Previous: Dean Close School
Net Worth: £19,086,772 *Total Assets:* £30,709,352
Registered Office: Shelburne Road, Cheltenham, Glos, GL51 6HE
Activities: Pre-primary education
Officers: Mathew Alan Madeley, Secretary; Simon David Bullingham [1973] Director - Property Company; Kathryn Ann Carden [1958] Director; The Reverend Richard Murray Coombs [1963] Director/Clergyman; Helen Stephanie Linford Daltry [1955] Director/Sponsorship Consultant; Charles Stephen Summers Drew [1950] Director/Retired; Ian Andrew Duffin [1956] Director/Chartered Accountant; Richard Stuart Harman [1959] Director/Headmaster; Sara Louise Hirst [1953] Director/Teacher; Audrey Marsden [1955] Director/Retired; Karen Riding [1961] Director/Solicitor; Matthew Paul Smith [1959] Director; Edward Taylor [1980] Director/Adjutant 12 Regiment Royal Artillery

Debden Schools Services Limited
Incorporated: 8 February 2000 *Employees:* 2
Net Worth Deficit: £372,000 *Total Assets:* £15,326,000
Registered Office: Third Floor, Broad Quay House, Prince Street, Bristol, BS1 4DJ
Activities: Management of real estate on a fee or contract basis
Parent: XJ6 Schools Holdings Limited
Officers: Christopher John Blundell [1966] Regional Director; Neil Rae [1971] Director

Deceuninck Holdings (UK) Limited
Incorporated: 8 July 1999
Net Worth: £17,591,000 *Total Assets:* £17,619,000
Registered Office: 2 Temple Back East, Temple Quay, Bristol, BS1 6EG
Activities: Activities of head offices
Parent: Deceuninck N.V
Officers: Wim Van Acker [1973] Director/Chief Financial Officer [Belgian]; Francis Van Eeckhout [1968] Director/Chief Executive Officer [Belgian]; Bernard Vanderper [1962] Director/Sales Manager Benelux

Deceuninck Limited
Incorporated: 2 June 1981 *Employees:* 86
Net Worth: £217,000 *Total Assets:* £9,128,000
Registered Office: 2 Temple Back East, Temple Quay, Bristol, BS1 6EG
Activities: Manufacture of other plastic products
Parent: Deceuninck Holdings (UK) Limited
Officers: Wim Van Acker [1973] Director/Chief Financial Officer [Belgian]; Francis Van Eeckhout [1968] Director/Chief Executive Officer [Belgian]; Robert Lawrence McGlennon [1958] Interim Managing Director; Bernard Vanderper [1962] Director/Sales Manager Benelux

Decision Insight Hub Limited
Incorporated: 2 October 2000 *Employees:* 9
Net Worth: £3,106,042 *Total Assets:* £12,148,110
Registered Office: 5-7 Abbey Court, Eagle Way, Sowton Industrial Estate, Exeter, Devon, EX2 7HY
Activities: Data processing, hosting and related activities
Parent: Decision Insight Information Group (UK) Ltd
Officers: Matthew Teague, Secretary; Simon James Brown [1965] Director/Chief Executive; David William Callcott [1959] Director; Stephen John Stout [1960] Director/Chairman

Decision Insight Information Group (Europe) Limited
Incorporated: 4 November 2010 *Employees:* 2
Net Worth: £16,571,962 *Total Assets:* £37,852,160
Registered Office: 5-7 Abbey Court, Eagle Way, Sowton Industrial Estate, Exeter, EX2 7HY
Activities: Activities of head offices
Parent: DMGI Land & Property Europe Ltd
Officers: David William Callcott, Secretary; David William Callcott [1959] Director

Decision Insight Information Group (UK) Limited
Incorporated: 11 February 1987 *Employees:* 35
Net Worth: £26,788,772 *Total Assets:* £77,913,416
Registered Office: 5-7 Abbey Court, Eagle Way, Sowton Industrial Estate, Exeter, Devon, EX2 7HY
Activities: Data processing, hosting and related activities
Parent: DMGI Land & Property Europe Ltd
Officers: David William Callcott, Secretary; Simon James Brown [1965] Director/Chief Executive; David William Callcott [1959] Director; Stephen John Stout [1960] Director/Chairman

Decision Logic Ltd
Incorporated: 24 November 2010 *Employees:* 2
Net Worth: £2,714,536 *Total Assets:* £4,218,333
Registered Office: Unit 28 Factory Road, Upton Industrial Estate, Poole, Dorset, BH16 5SL
Activities: Manufacture of computers and peripheral equipment
Major Shareholder: Amil Gulamali
Officers: Jason Hector Blain [1970] Director/Entrepreneur; Amil Gulamali [1973] Director/IT Manager

Deeley Freed (Penhalt) Limited
Incorporated: 25 November 2004
Net Worth Deficit: £2,845,861 *Total Assets:* £4,505,762
Registered Office: 7 Whiteladies Road, Clifton, Bristol, BS8 1NN
Activities: Buying and selling of own real estate
Parent: Deeley Freed Estates Limited
Officers: Philip Neil Briggs, Secretary/Accountant; David Maxwell Freed [1954] Director; Andrew Dexter Maltby [1957] Director; Iain Michael Neary [1968] Director/Project Manager

Deeley Freed Developments Limited
Incorporated: 27 February 2014 *Employees:* 6
Net Worth: £1,453,831 *Total Assets:* £6,317,758
Registered Office: 7 Whiteladies Road, Clifton, Bristol, BS8 1NN
Activities: Buying and selling of own real estate
Shareholder: Sydney Freed (Holdings)
Officers: Philip Neil Briggs, Secretary; Philip Neil Briggs [1961] Director; David Maxwell Freed [1954] Director; Andrew Dexter Maltby [1957] Director; Iain Michael Neary [1968] Director

Deeley Freed Estates Limited
Incorporated: 8 January 2003 *Employees:* 6
Net Worth: £1,635,695 *Total Assets:* £5,200,606
Registered Office: 7 Whiteladies Road, Clifton, Bristol, BS8 1NN
Activities: Development of building projects
Parent: Deeley Freed Developments Limited
Officers: Philip Neil Briggs, Secretary/Accountant; Philip Neil Briggs [1961] Finance Director; David Maxwell Freed [1954] Director; Andrew Dexter Maltby [1957] Director; Iain Michael Neary [1968] Development Director

Deep Moor LF Limited
Incorporated: 31 October 1991
Previous: Devon Waste Management Limited
Net Worth: £12,668,638 *Total Assets:* £18,944,824
Registered Office: 1 & 2 Mulberry Court, Lustleigh Close, Matford Business Park, Marsh Barton Trading Estate, Exeter, Devon, EX2 8PW
Activities: Recovery of sorted materials
Officers: Stuart Crebo [1953] Director; Emily Anne Delve [1982] Finance Director; Steven Eric Paul Hadley [1972] Director; Richard Wynford Marsh [1963] Sales and Marketing Director; Dominic Treacher [1960] Director; Allan John Vodden [1949] Director/Retired

Defence Training Services Limited
Incorporated: 3 September 1999 *Employees:* 4
Net Worth: £8,369,000 *Total Assets:* £77,588,000
Registered Office: Third Floor, Broad Quay House, Prince Street, Bristol, BS1 4DJ
Activities: Management of real estate on a fee or contract basis
Shareholders: PFI Investments Limited; Aberdeen Infrastructure (No.3) Limited
Officers: Michael Andrew Donn [1972] Director/Investment Manager; Stephen Paul Hornby [1957] Director; Alan Campbell Ritchie [1967] Director; Martin Timothy Smith [1967] Director/Banker

DEK-Co (UK) Ltd
Incorporated: 31 March 2009
Net Worth: £430,375 *Total Assets:* £3,848,298
Registered Office: Aztec Centre, Aztec West, Almondsbury, Bristol, BS32 4TD
Activities: Financial intermediation not elsewhere classified
Major Shareholder: Anton Postolnikov
Officers: Iulian Marinescu [1969] Director/Businessman [Romanian]; Anton Postolnikov [1982] Director/Businessman [American]

Del Piero Limited
Incorporated: 14 June 2006
Net Worth Deficit: £2,648,007 *Total Assets:* £12,173,001
Registered Office: The Old School House, 75a Jacobs Wells Road, Clifton, Bristol, BS8 1DJ
Activities: Development of building projects
Shareholder: Simon Peter Arber
Officers: Simon Peter Arber [1958] Director; Michele Arcangelo Botta [1957] Director [Italian]; Nicholas Paul Bracey [1964] Director

Delahunty Limited
Incorporated: 11 December 2002 *Employees:* 4
Net Worth: £3,482,961 *Total Assets:* £18,992,882
Registered Office: 14a Forest Gate, Pewsham, Chippenham, Wilts, SN15 3RS
Activities: Retail sale of antiques including antique books in stores
Major Shareholder: Kevin Gerald Delahunty
Officers: Arabella Lilian Virginia Delahunty, Secretary; Arabella Lilian Virginia Delahunty [1950] Director; Damian John Richard Delahunty [1976] Director; Kevin Generald Delahunty [1943] Director/Antiques Dealer

Delphi Diesel Systems Limited
Incorporated: 3 November 1999 *Employees:* 2,420
Net Worth: £176,654,000 *Total Assets:* £685,003,008
Registered Office: Brunel Way, Stroudwater Business Park, Stonehouse, Glos, GL10 3SX
Activities: Manufacture of other parts and accessories for motor vehicles
Parent: Delphi Automotive Operations UK Limited
Officers: William Brenton James Allen [1986] Director/Accountant; Alan Dick [1963] Director/Vice President of Treasury; Olivier Jean Francis Lequeue [1978] Finance Director [Belgian]

Delphi Lockheed Automotive Limited
Incorporated: 25 June 1999 *Employees:* 194
Net Worth Deficit: £7,194,405 *Total Assets:* £34,331,788
Registered Office: Brunel Way, Stroudwater Business Park, Stonehouse, Glos, GL10 3SX
Activities: Wholesale trade of motor vehicle parts and accessories
Parent: Delphi Automotive Operations UK Limited
Officers: William Brenton James Allen [1986] Director/Accountant; Alan Dick [1963] Director/Vice President of Treasury; Olivier Jean Francis Lequeue [1978] Finance Director [Belgian]

Delphi Technologies Limited
Incorporated: 15 December 2014
Previous: Delphi Financial Services (UK) Limited
Net Worth: £126,110,128 *Total Assets:* £126,110,128
Registered Office: Brunel Way, Stroudwater Business Park, Stonehouse, Glos, GL10 3SX
Activities: Other professional, scientific and technical activities n.e.c.
Shareholders: Delphi Automotive Operations UK Limited; Delphi Luxembourg Limited
Officers: William Brenton James Allen [1986] Director/Accountant; Alan Dick [1963] Director/Vice President of Treasury; Olivier Jean Francis Lequeue [1978] Finance Director [Belgian]

Delphic Holdings Limited.
Incorporated: 14 November 1953
Net Worth: £6,557,533 *Total Assets:* £7,036,562
Registered Office: 7 Avon Grove, Bristol, BS9 1PJ
Activities: Other letting and operating of own or leased real estate
Shareholders: Anthony Clive Smith; Alastair John Smith
Officers: Pamela Jill Smith, Secretary; Alastair John Smith [1933] Director/Solicitor; Anthony Clive Smith [1938] Director/Chartered Accountant

Delphine Holdings Limited
Incorporated: 3 February 2009 *Employees:* 2
Net Worth: £1,680,526 *Total Assets:* £4,789,856
Registered Office: c/o Bishop Fleming, 16 Queen Square, Bristol, BS1 4NT
Activities: Dormant company
Major Shareholder: Martin and Pamela Wyatt Discretionary Settlement 2009
Officers: Dr Martin Thomas Wyatt [1949] Director/Doctor

Delphine Homecare Limited
Incorporated: 8 January 1999 *Employees:* 12
Net Worth: £3,296,393 *Total Assets:* £8,490,655
Registered Office: 1 Court Close, St Georges, Weston-Super-Mare, Avon, BS22 7AA
Activities: Other human health activities
Parent: Delphine Holdings Limited
Officers: Dr Martin Thomas Wyatt, Secretary; Dr Martin Thomas Wyatt [1959] Director

Delstar International, Limited
Incorporated: 1 October 2001 *Employees:* 62
Net Worth: £1,575,448 *Total Assets:* £14,973,296
Registered Office: c/o Bishop Fleming, 16 Queen Square, Bristol, BS1 4NT
Activities: Manufacture of non-wovens and articles made from non-wovens, except apparel
Parent: SWM Luxembourg SARL
Officers: David Timothy Cullen, Secretary; David Timothy Cullen [1966] Director/Vice President and General Manager [American]; Daniel Ray Lister [1973] Director/Executive Vice President [American]

Delt Shared Services Limited
Incorporated: 23 June 2014 *Employees:* 131
Net Worth: £3,140,000 *Total Assets:* £10,202,000
Registered Office: 2 Derriford Park, Derriford Business Park, Derriford, Plymouth, PL6 5QZ
Activities: Combined office administrative service activities
Shareholders: Plymouth City Council; NHS Northern, Eastern and Western Devon Clinical Commissioning Group (New Devon CCG)
Officers: Giles Nigel Letheren, Secretary; Lorna Margaret Collingwood-Burke [1957] Director/Chief Nursing Officer for two Devon CCGS; Nicholas Thomas Franklin [1976] Director/Network Engineer; Mark Andrew Greaves [1967] Director/Chartered Accountant; Giles Ruari Perritt [1964] Director/Local Government Officer

The Delta Education Trust
Incorporated: 30 January 2013 *Employees:* 91
Net Worth: £8,285,000 *Total Assets:* £9,661,000
Registered Office: 160 Herbert Avenue, Poole, Dorset, BH12 4HU
Activities: Other education n.e.c.
Officers: Jennifer Anne Clifford, Secretary; Andrew John Baker [1958] Director/Teacher; Mark David Bickford [1968] Director/Head of Social Investment, FSE; Laurence Keane [1961] Director/Captain, British Airways; Katie Jayne Martha Lasbury-Carter [1973] Director/Teacher; Anne Hilary Middle [1952] Director; Annice Joanne Perry [1953] Director/Headteacher; Nigel Henry Soloman [1962] Managing Director; Leanne Symonds [1973] Director/Headteacher; Sarah Margaret Watkins [1964] Director; John Matthew White [1970] Director/Chief Executive Officer; Nathan Dennis Wilkins [1974] Business Development Director, BT

Den Dental Group Practice LLP
Incorporated: 4 August 2008 *Employees:* 55
Total Assets: £7,482,000
Registered Office: Bupa Dental Care, Vantage Office Park, Old Gloucester Road, Hambrook, Bristol, BS16 1GW
Officers: Robin James Bryant [1970] Member; Steven John Preddy [1959] Member; Dr Ian David Wood [1956] Member

Dene Magna School
Incorporated: 6 July 2011 *Employees:* 90
Net Worth: £10,972,000 *Total Assets:* £13,226,000
Registered Office: Dene Magna School, Abenhall Road, Mitcheldean, Glos, GL17 0DU
Activities: General secondary education
Officers: Janet Ray, Secretary; Peter Frederick Adams [1954] Director/Exams & Community Liaison Officer; Stephen James Brady [1974] Director/Headteacher; Philip John Didcote [1967] Director/IT Consultant; Jane Foot [1967] Director/Parent; Kevin Michael Hacker [1975] Director/ICT Manager; Adam Harrington [1987] Director/Teacher; Louise Holland [1972] Director/HR; Maxine Susan Markey [1971] Director/School Governor; Michala Jane Reid [1979] Director/Teacher; Antony Alfred Rose [1960] Director/Security Officer; Dr Paul David Weiss [1970] Director/Doctor

Denhay Farms Limited
Incorporated: 7 February 1952 *Employees:* 67
Net Worth: £2,765,165 *Total Assets:* £4,772,646
Registered Office: The Paragon, Counterslip, Bristol, BS1 6BX
Activities: Raising of dairy cattle
Parent: Penntrust Limited
Officers: Duncan Knox Homan [1943] Director/Retired; Viscount Henry Lyttelton Alexander Hood [1958] Director/Solicitor; The Honourable John Samuel Hood [1959] Director/Investment Banker; James Philip Loescher [1960] Director/Accountant; Susan Elizabeth Shaw [1964] Director/Accountant; David Robert Stacey [1958] Director/Farmer; Amanda Campbell Streatfeild [1953] Director/Sales Manager; George Henry Streatfeild [1952] Director/Farmer; Simon John Streatfeild [1948] Director

Denmark Road High School
Incorporated: 22 February 2011 *Employees:* 107
Previous: High School for Girls, Gloucester
Net Worth: £15,370,854 *Total Assets:* £17,202,878
Registered Office: Denmark Road, Gloucester, GL1 3JN
Activities: General secondary education
Officers: Paramjeet Kaur Kalsi, Secretary; Barry Anthony Baxter [1951] Director/International Engineering Consultant; Jamie Douglas Colquhoun [1971] Director/Marketing Consultant; Sarah Louise Fish [1985] Director/Consultant; Claire Annette Giblin [1974] Director/Headteacher; Andrew Haigh [1964] Director/Project Manager; Laurence Desmond Lucas [1961] Director/Solicitor; Sally Jane McKinlay [1967] Tax Director; John Graham Patient [1956] Director/Data Architect; Dr Christopher John Charles Remfry [1964] Director/Doctor; Helen Victoria Spragg [1990] Director/Teacher; Katie Tucker [1985] Director/Self Employed; Dr Helen Sarah Winter [1968] Director/Medical Oncologist; Penelope Young [1971] Director/Health Visitor

Philip Dennis Foodservice (Holdings) Limited
Incorporated: 18 January 2016 *Employees:* 299
Net Worth: £4,830,170 *Total Assets:* £13,636,586
Registered Office: Mullacott Industrial Estate, Ilfracombe, Devon, EX34 8PL
Activities: Activities of distribution holding companies
Shareholders: Christopher John Dennis; Peter Joseph Dennis
Officers: Elizabeth Dennis, Secretary; Christopher John Dennis [1981] Director/Student; Elizabeth Dennis [1952] Director; John Preston Dennis [1952] Director; Peter Joseph Dennis [1986] Director/Data Analysis Consultant

Philip Dennis Foodservice Limited
Incorporated: 10 September 1956 *Employees:* 297
Net Worth: £4,600,767 *Total Assets:* £12,966,706
Registered Office: Mullacott Industrial Estate, Ilfracombe, Devon, EX34 8PL
Activities: Non-specialised wholesale of food, beverages and tobacco
Parent: Philip Dennis Foodservice (Holdings) Ltd
Officers: Stephen John Carr [1965] Managing Director; Christopher John Dennis [1981] Director/Student; Peter Joseph Dennis [1986] Director/Data Analysis Consultant

Denplan Limited
Incorporated: 22 January 1986 *Employees:* 443
Net Worth: £24,830,000 *Total Assets:* £46,647,000
Registered Office: Hambleden House, Waterloo Court, Andover, Hants, SP10 1LQ
Activities: Dental practice activities
Parent: Simplyhealth Group Limited
Officers: Romana Abdin [1963] Director; Deborah Jane Beaven [1963] Director/Chief Financial Officer

Dentalign Orthodontics Limited
Incorporated: 14 March 2007
Net Worth: £4,515,000 *Total Assets:* £9,412,000
Registered Office: Bupa Dental Care, Vantage Office Park, Old Gloucester Road, Hambrook, Bristol, BS16 1GW
Activities: Dental practice activities
Parent: Duke Street Capital Oasis Orthodontics Limited
Officers: Robin James Bryant [1970] Director/Dental Surgeon; Steven John Preddy [1959] Director/Dentist; Gabriela Pueyo Roberts [1974] Director/General Manager [Spanish]; Dr Stephen David Burleigh Taylor [1951] Director/Dentist; Dr Ian David Wood [1956] Director; Jake Stephen Hockley Wright [1972] Director

Dentalign Orthodontics LLP
Incorporated: 14 March 2007 *Employees:* 67
Total Assets: £11,374,000
Registered Office: Bupa Dental Care, Vantage Office Park, Old Gloucester Road, Hambrook, Bristol, BS16 1GW
Officers: Steven John Preddy [1959] Member; Robin James Bryant [1970] LLP Member; Adam Anthony Ryan [1960] LLP Member; Dr Stephen David Burleigh Taylor [1951] LLP Member

Dentsply IH Limited
Incorporated: 19 February 1980 *Employees:* 257
Net Worth: £33,540,852 *Total Assets:* £126,242,448
Registered Office: Dentsply IH Ltd, Brunel Way, Stonehouse, Glos, GL10 3GB
Activities: Non-specialised wholesale trade
Officers: Dr. Markus Boehringer [1964] Director/Senior Vice President [German]; Gerard Peter Campbell [1964] Director/General Manager; Robert John Winters [1960] Director/Vice President, Tax [American]

Denvern Limited
Incorporated: 4 December 2003
Net Worth: £4,063,069 *Total Assets:* £7,793,657
Registered Office: Dainton Business Park, Heathfield, Newton Abbot, Devon, TQ12 6RG
Activities: Operation of warehousing and storage facilities for land transport activities
Shareholders: Paul Gregory Maddicott; Donna Louise Maddicott
Officers: Shaun Robert Duncan [1967] Director; Donna Louise Maddicott [1973] Director; Paul Gregory Maddicott [1975] Director/General Manager

Deodara Limited
Incorporated: 8 April 2014 *Employees:* 2
Net Worth: £2,143,548 *Total Assets:* £9,699,692
Registered Office: Midland House, 2 Poole Road, Bournemouth, BH2 5QY
Activities: Security dealing on own account
Shareholders: Claire Elizabeth Bradley Locke; Glyn Anthony Stuart Locke
Officers: Claire Elizabeth Bradley Locke, Secretary; Claire Elizabeth Bradley Locke [1960] Director/Retired; Glyn Anthony Stuart Locke [1949] Director/Retired

Derbyshire Home Loans Limited
Incorporated: 10 July 1991
Net Worth: £314,595,008 *Total Assets:* £987,766,016
Registered Office: Nationwide House, Pipers Way, Swindon, Wilts, SN38 1NW
Activities: Other business support service activities n.e.c.
Parent: Nationwide Building Society
Officers: Timothy Joseph Carter [1970] Director of Product Operations; Jonathan Jasper Haydn Davy [1965] Director/Head of Collections and Recoveries; Julia Mary Roberts Dunn [1965] Director/Chief Risk Officer; Muir James Mathieson [1974] Director of Financial Controls & Information Management; Christopher Stuart Rhodes [1963] Director; Paul Wootton [1979] Director/Head of Specialist Mortgages

Descartes Systems UK Limited
Incorporated: 18 January 1990
Net Worth: £11,554,327 *Total Assets:* £24,083,372
Registered Office: 9 Avon Reach, Chippenham, Wilts, SN15 1EE
Activities: Business and domestic software development
Parent: The Descartes Systems Group Inc
Officers: Michael Roy Verhoeve, Secretary; Allan James Brett [1967] Director/Chief Financial Officer [Canadian]; John Scott Pagan [1972] Director/Lawyer [Canadian]

Desertlands Entertainment Limited
Incorporated: 26 March 1990
Net Worth: £1,196,000 *Total Assets:* £10,918,000
Registered Office: The Quadrangle, The Promenade, Cheltenham, Glos, GL50 1PX
Activities: Financial leasing
Parent: Royal Bank Leasing Limited
Officers: Stephen Paul Nixon [1970] Director/Bank Official; Keith Damian Pereira [1978] Director/Bank Official

Design Objectives Limited
Incorporated: 17 July 1996 *Employees:* 66
Net Worth: £2,500,716 *Total Assets:* £8,881,946
Registered Office: Unit 90 Woolsbridge Industrial Estate, Three Legged Cross, Wimborne, Dorset, BH21 6SP
Activities: Non-specialised wholesale trade
Officers: Owen John Bray [1982] Director; Joanna Claire Pillai [1982] Director; William George Charles Power [1982] Director

Design Scaffolding (Bristol) Limited
Incorporated: 6 March 2000 *Employees:* 46
Net Worth: £5,889,308 *Total Assets:* £6,397,271
Registered Office: Unit 3 Bakers Park, Cater Road, Bishopsworth, Bristol, BS13 7TT
Activities: Scaffold erection
Shareholders: John Patrick Boyce; Laura Jane Boyce
Officers: Hannah Louise Price, Secretary; John Patrick Boyce [1962] Director/Scaffolder

Deutsch GB Limited
Incorporated: 9 March 2006
Net Worth: £4,693,438,976 *Total Assets:* £37,340,000,256
Registered Office: Company Secretariat, Site H, Faraday Road, Swindon, Wilts, SN3 5HH
Activities: Activities of head offices
Parent: TE Connectivity Ltd
Officers: Harold Gregory Barksdale [1964] Director/Attorney [American]; Stephen Christopher Cooper [1970] Director/Accountant; Ashley Raymond Fulford [1963] Operations Director

Deutsch UK
Incorporated: 15 November 1978
Net Worth: £28,236,552 *Total Assets:* £28,236,552
Registered Office: Company Secretariat, Site H, Faraday Road, Swindon, Wilts, SN3 5HH
Activities: Non-trading company
Parent: Deutsch GB Limited
Officers: Harold Gregory Barksdale [1964] Director/Attorney [American]; Stephen Christopher Cooper [1970] Director/Accountant; Andrew Donachie [1972] Operations Director

Devaron (UK) Limited
Incorporated: 24 March 2017
Net Worth: £20,000,100 *Total Assets:* £20,000,100
Registered Office: 11th Floor, Whitefriars, Lewins Mead, Bristol, BS1 2NT
Activities: Activities of other holding companies n.e.c.
Officers: Andrew David Jessop [1978] Director/General Counsel

Devon & Cornwall Autistic Community Trust
Incorporated: 7 September 1982 *Employees:* 473
Net Worth: £4,714,002 *Total Assets:* £7,347,498
Registered Office: Lakeside Offices, The Old Cattle Market, Coronation Park, Helston, Cornwall, TR13 0SR
Activities: Other human health activities
Officers: Donald Harvey, Secretary; Trevor Charles Grose [1939] Director/Farmer; Donald Harvey [1941] Director/Quantity Surveyor; Lionel Roger James [1945] Director/Retired Headteacher; Barbara Moore [1950] Director/Clerical Officer; Julian Pykett [1943] Director of Diocesan Board of Education; Nicholas Simon Tostdevine [1960] Director/Financial Consultant

Devon & Exeter Spastics Society
Incorporated: 9 April 1991 *Employees:* 71
Net Worth: £6,348,511 *Total Assets:* £6,397,031
Registered Office: Vranch House, Pinhoe Road, Exeter, Devon, EX4 8AD
Activities: Pre-primary education
Officers: Colonel Graeme Wheeler, Secretary; Antony Jonathan Claridge Griffin [1950] Director/Retired; Penelope Anne Hale [1947] Director/Retired; Rebecca Ann Neary [1983] Director/Full Time Student; Rosemary May Pavitt [1949] Director/Retired [New Zealander]; Julia Chantal Tolman-May [1967] Director/Housewife; Dr Richard James Tomlinson [1968] Director/Paediatrician; Maureen Rosalie Charmaine Williams [1949] Director/College Lecturer; Sarah Catherine Williams [1975] Director/Full Time Carer and Mother

Devon Air Ambulance Trading Company Limited
Incorporated: 12 November 1999 *Employees:* 9
Net Worth: £189,583 *Total Assets:* £5,322,711
Registered Office: 5 Sandpiper Court, Harrington Lane, Exeter, Devon, EX4 8NS
Activities: Non-scheduled passenger air transport
Parent: Devon Air Ambulance Trust
Officers: David Robert Hawes, Secretary; Caroline Mary Creer [1967] Fundraising Director; Simon Mark Denton [1968] Director/Accountant; Helena Holt [1965] Director/Manager; Anthony John Hudson [1962] Director/Hospital Doctor; Edmund Arthur Whitmore Probert [1953] Director/Solicitor; William Anthony Richardson [1942] Director; Nicola Claire Steevenson [1980] Director/Safety Consultant; Stephen James Tyrrell [1967] Director/Sales and Business Development

Devon Air Ambulance Trust
Incorporated: 30 September 1999 *Employees:* 64
Net Worth: £21,901,000 *Total Assets:* £23,125,000
Registered Office: 5 Sandpiper Court, Harrington Lane, Exeter, EX4 8NS
Activities: Non-scheduled passenger air transport
Officers: David Robert Hawes, Secretary; Margaret Davies [1961] Director/Occupational Psychologist; Deborah Jane Fraser [1976] Regional Director; Anthony John Hudson [1962] Director/Hospital Doctor; Antony Robert Noon [1965] Director/Commercial Estate Agent; Richard David Plunkett [1970] Director/Chartered Accountant; Rachel Margaret Short [1965] Director/Lawyer; Stephen James Tyrrell [1967] Director/Management Consultant; Mark Russell Williams [1961] Director/Solicitor

Devon Care Homes Holdings Limited
Incorporated: 11 June 2015 *Employees:* 221
Net Worth: £1,183,956 *Total Assets:* £13,505,354
Registered Office: 13 Lagoon Road, Lilliput, Poole, Dorset, BH14 8JT
Activities: Activities of other holding companies n.e.c.
Shareholders: Joy Elizabeth Birkett; Roger Wilfred Birkett
Officers: Joy Elizabeth Birkett [1949] Director; Roger Wilfred Birkett [1943] Director

Devon Ceramics (Contracts) Limited
Incorporated: 6 August 2009 *Employees:* 41
Net Worth: £2,181,597 *Total Assets:* £4,833,383
Registered Office: Station Road, Totnes, Devon, TQ9 5JR
Activities: Manufacture of ceramic household and ornamental articles
Major Shareholder: Vernon John Gay
Officers: David Critchlow, Secretary; Vernon John Gay [1960] Director/Ceramics Designer

Devon Community Foundation
Incorporated: 12 August 1996 *Employees:* 11
Net Worth: £7,744,455 *Total Assets:* £8,051,837
Registered Office: Bond Pearce LLP, Ballard House, West Hoe Road, Plymouth, PL1 3AE
Activities: Other social work activities without accommodation n.e.c.
Officers: The Right Reverend Robert Ronald Atwell [1954] Director/Church of England Bishop; Edward Hugo Burnand [1969] Director; James Maxwell Griffiths Cross [1963] Director/Solicitor; Caroline Anne Harlow [1954] Director; Stephen Lewis Hindley [1949] Director/Chief Executive Officer Midas; Peter Reginald Thomas Holden [1956] Director/Financial Adviser; Sally Elizabeth Wace [1959] Director/Reporter; George James Stewart Wallis [1948] Director/Retired

Devon Contract Waste Ltd
Incorporated: 3 July 1997 *Employees:* 60
Net Worth: £5,992,736 *Total Assets:* £11,896,505
Registered Office: Enviro Hub, Marsh Barton Road, Marsh Barton Trading Estate, Exeter, Devon, EX2 8NU
Activities: Recovery of sorted materials
Major Shareholder: Simon Christopher Almond
Officers: Anne Marie Almond, Secretary; Howard Patrick Almond [1945] Director/Manager Software Development; Simon Christopher Almond [1968] Director/Businessman

Devon Contractors Limited
Incorporated: 13 May 1954 *Employees:* 38
Net Worth: £527,154 *Total Assets:* £5,630,318
Registered Office: Clyst Court, Hill Barton Business Park, Clyst St Mary, Exeter, Devon, EX5 1SA
Activities: Construction of commercial buildings
Officers: Shaun Okey Bennington, Secretary; Peter Thomas Alderson [1958] Director/Contracts Manager; Shaun Okey Bennington [1966] Director/Company Secretary; Nicholas Michael England [1969] Director/Contracts Manager; Daryn John Hunt [1964] Director/Chief Buyer

Devon Doctors Limited
Incorporated: 9 July 2004 *Employees:* 565
Net Worth: £3,295,113 *Total Assets:* £7,045,574
Registered Office: Unit 10 Manaton Court, Manaton Close, Matford Business Park, Exeter, Devon, EX2 8PF
Activities: Other human health activities
Officers: Sarah White, Secretary; Dr Trevor John Avis [1964] Director/GP; Dr Mark Eggleton [1970] Director/GP; Dr Justin Robert Geddes [1971] Director/Medical; Dr. Philippa Ann Hayes [1958] Director/GP; Ryan Hewitt [1978] Director; Dr Peter Holley [1966] Director/Doctor; Dr Bruce Davey Hughes [1970] Director/Doctor; Matthew McVicar [1984] Director; Dr Andrew Boyce Potter [1966] Director/General Practitioner; Doctor Michael Joseph William Slot [1956] Director/General Medical Practitioner

Devon Wildlife Trust
Incorporated: 23 August 1962 *Employees:* 79
Net Worth: £7,138,405 *Total Assets:* £7,772,749
Registered Office: Cricklepit Mill, Commercial Road, Exeter, Devon, EX2 4AB
Activities: Activities of other membership organisations n.e.c.
Officers: Henry James Barton, Secretary; Rebecca Anna Broad [1995] Director/Student; Andrew Paul Burns [1969] Director/Commissioned Officer, Royal Navy; Gaynor Dorothy Castle [1962] Director/Retired; Richard James Clack [1951] Director/Accountant; Francis Vernon Clarke [1963] Director/Solicitor; Andrew Charles John Cooper [1951] Director/BBC TV Series Producer/Author; Charles Edward Dixon [1954] Director/Chartered Surveyor; Suzanne Goodfellow [1951] Director/Environmental Consultant; Barry Perkins Henwood [1956] Director/Retired Doctor; Gail McKenzie [1956] Director/Communications Consultant; Dr Michael Edward Moser [1956] Director/International Environmental Consultant; Helen Nathanson [1973] Director/Housewife; Professor Victoria Denise Pope [1961] Director/Civil Servant; Nigel Wilfred Rendle [1948] Director/Retired; Trevor James Smale [1952] Director/Town Planner/Charity Manager; John Whetman [1937] Director/Horticulture

Devondale Electrical Distributors Limited
Incorporated: 30 September 1981 *Employees:* 66
Net Worth: £1,968,506 *Total Assets:* £6,273,861
Registered Office: Unit 3, 26 Marsh Green Road West, Marsh Barton Trading Estate, Exeter, Devon, EX2 8PN
Activities: Wholesale of electronic and telecommunications equipment and parts
Parent: Devondale Holdings Limited
Officers: Susan Wright, Secretary; Ian Robert Brooke [1968] Purchasing Director; David Newcombe [1950] Sales Director; Paul Melvyn Steer [1971] Director/Business Development Manager; Paul Stuart Wood [1972] Managing Director

Devonfields Limited
Incorporated: 14 January 1985 *Employees:* 7
Net Worth: £4,719,683 *Total Assets:* £6,609,481
Registered Office: Sigma House, Oak View Close, Edginswell Park, Torquay, Devon, TQ2 7FF
Activities: Development of building projects
Shareholder: The Executors of the late Mr Patrick Jeremy Kilmartin
Officers: Tim Stuart Rogers, Secretary; Annabelle Chloe Rogers [1988] Director/Clinical Psychologist; Benjamin Scott Rogers [1981] Director; Daniel Mark Rogers [1973] Director/Property Manager; Jane Elizabeth Rogers [1952] Director; Paul Oliver Rogers [1974] Director/Surveyor; Timothy Stuart Rogers [1978] Director

Devonport High School for Boys Academy Trust
Incorporated: 9 February 2011 *Employees:* 161
Net Worth: £14,108,000 *Total Assets:* £17,072,000
Registered Office: Devonport High School for Boys, Paradise Road, Plymouth, PL1 5QP
Activities: General secondary education
Officers: Geoffrey Charles Davis, Secretary; Carolyn Grace Bruce-Spencer [1964] Director/Senior Executive; Liam Bultmann [1969] Director/Barrister; Ffion Coombs [1953] Director; Diane Creber [1962] Director/Admin/Accounts; Rebecca Joanne Donnelly [1970] Director/Administrator; Rachel Grace Green [1983] Director/Teacher; Richard Paul Greenacre [1959] Director/Marine Engineer; Roger William Johnson [1941] Director/Retired; Richard George Brakespeare Killick [1963] Director; Sue Moreton [1957] Director/IAG Coordinator; Thomas Langdon Orchard [1945] Director/Accountant; Simon Pentecost [1966] Director/EHS Coordinator; Heidi Price [1966] Director/Headteacher; Daniel James John Roberts [1978] Director/Headteacher; Geoffrey John Showell [1945] Director/Retired; Maurice Arnold West [1957] Director/Chartered Surveyor

Devonport High School for Girls
Incorporated: 8 March 2011 *Employees:* 102
Net Worth: £7,987,406 *Total Assets:* £9,996,678
Registered Office: Devonport High School for Girls, Lyndhurst Road, Plymouth, PL2 3DL
Activities: General secondary education
Officers: Sarah Catherine Adkins [1965] Director/Solicitor; Jill Eileen Dolan [1944] Director/City Councillor; Robert Peter Galley [1983] Director/Teacher of Mathematics; Dr Jamie Piers Graham [1988] Director/Doctor; Maria Harrington-Seddon [1973] Director/Administration Assistant (Examinations Officer); Anita Elizabeth Hemsi [1962] Director/Teacher; Carl Hutchings [1966] Director/Resource Manager; Alison Clare Hutton [1954] Director; Ann James [1965] Director/Chief Executive; Victoria Webster [1984] Director/ICT Support Manager; Glynis Wendy Westcott [1961] Director/FE College Lecturer; Shirley Anne Williams [1955] Director/Accountant; Patricia Maria Wilton [1965] Director

Devonport Royal Dockyard Limited
Incorporated: 26 November 1986 *Employees:* 5,515
Net Worth: £503,030,016 *Total Assets:* £929,006,016
Registered Office: Devonport Royal Dockyard, Devonport, Plymouth, PL1 4SG
Activities: Building of ships and floating structures
Parent: Babcock Marine (Devonport) Limited
Officers: Julia Mary Wood, Secretary; Simon Foster [1966] Director; Stephen Amos French [1959] Director/Nuclear Engineer; Gary Lambert [1966] Director; Gavin Michael Leckie [1968] Director; Andrew David Hugh Mathews [1958] Director

Devonshire Homes (Bracken) Limited
Incorporated: 20 July 2010 *Employees:* 3
Net Worth: £3,694,803 *Total Assets:* £3,761,559
Registered Office: The Island, Lowman Green, Tiverton, Devon, EX16 4LA
Activities: Construction of domestic buildings
Parent: Devonshire Homes Limited
Officers: Owen Michael O'Callaghan, Secretary; David Philip Heathcoat Amory [1949] Director; Owen Michael O'Callaghan [1963] Director/Chartered Accountant; Daniel Francis Stephenson [1971] Director/Chartered Surveyor [Irish]

Devonshire Homes (Landkey) Limited
Incorporated: 16 November 2016
Net Worth Deficit: £2,009 *Total Assets:* £5,952,546
Registered Office: Devonshire House, Lowman Green, Tiverton, Devon, EX16 4LA
Activities: Construction of domestic buildings
Shareholders: Housing Growth Partnership GP LLP; Devonshire Homes Limited
Officers: Owen Michael O'Callaghan, Secretary; Owen Michael O'Callaghan [1963] Director; Jane Marie Pearce [1968] Sales Director; Daniel Francis Stephenson [1971] Director [Irish]

Devonshire Homes Limited
Incorporated: 1 December 1992 *Employees:* 45
Net Worth: £13,019,266 *Total Assets:* £23,110,644
Registered Office: Devonshire House, Lowman Green, Tiverton, Devon, EX16 4LA
Activities: Construction of domestic buildings
Parent: London and Devonshire Trust Limited
Officers: Owen O'Callaghan, Secretary; Charles Peter Cobb [1954] Director/Architect; David Philip Heathcoat Amory [1949] Director; Guy Charles Rawdon Langworthy [1960] Director/Building; Cristian John Neale [1972] Director/Chartered Surveyor; Owen Michael O'Callaghan [1963] Director/Chartered Accountant; Jane Marie Pearce [1968] Sales Director; Ian Smith [1956] Construction Director; Daniel Francis Stephenson [1971] Director/Chartered Surveyor [Irish]

Devonshire Motors Limited
Incorporated: 19 July 1994 *Employees:* 56
Net Worth: £851,435 *Total Assets:* £3,762,134
Registered Office: Braunton Road, Pilland Way, Barnstaple, Devon, EX31 1LQ
Activities: Sale of new cars and light motor vehicles
Shareholders: Janet Susan Jones; Nathan James Tomlinson; Graeme Stuart Dampier-Bennett
Officers: Janet Susan Jones, Secretary; Ruth Mary Cross [1936] Director; Graeme Stuart Dampier Bennett [1971] Director/Bodyshop Manager; Janet Susan Jones [1961] Director/Chartered Accountant; Leslie Martin Prater [1939] Director/Accountant; Nathan James Tomlinson [1973] Director/After Sales Manager

Devonshire Pine Limited
Incorporated: 3 April 1992 *Employees:* 139
Net Worth: £5,262,198 *Total Assets:* £7,521,873
Registered Office: Caddsdown Industrial Park, Clovelly Road, Bideford, Devon, EX39 3DX
Activities: Manufacture of other furniture
Shareholders: P & S Hockin Limited; Peter Hockin; Sharon Elaine Hockin
Officers: Mr Peter Hockin, Secretary; Peter Hockin [1961] Director; Sharon Elaine Hockin [1964] Director

Devonshire Poultry Limited
Incorporated: 4 September 2001 *Employees:* 12
Net Worth: £654,916 *Total Assets:* £3,564,552
Registered Office: Little Westcott, Drift Lane, Sheldon, Honiton, Devon, EX14 4QS
Activities: Raising of poultry
Major Shareholder: Robert John Lanning
Officers: Jacqueline Mary Lanning, Secretary; Jacqueline Mary Lanning [1970] Director/Accountant; Robert John Lanning [1971] Director/Poultry Farmer

Devonshire Real Estate Limited
Incorporated: 8 August 2014
Net Worth: £605,568 *Total Assets:* £13,651,497
Registered Office: Grosvenor House, 1 New Road, Brixham, Devon, TQ5 8LZ
Activities: Other letting and operating of own or leased real estate
Major Shareholder: Andrew Peter Trott
Officers: Andrew Peter Trott [1969] Director

Dexeco Limited
Incorporated: 2 October 2007 *Employees:* 5
Net Worth: £3,385,653 *Total Assets:* £6,578,201
Registered Office: 17 Brickfields Business Park, Gillingham, Dorset, SP8 4PX
Activities: Manufacture of electric lighting equipment
Parent: Dextra Group PLC
Officers: Rupert Henry James Martin, Secretary; Keith John Brownhill [1961] Director/Group CEO; Janie Claire Martin [1962] Director/Company Secretary; Rupert Henry James Martin [1949] Director/Group Chairman; Jonathan Ridgway [1976] Sales Director; Darren Lee Ward [1970] MD & Group Technical Director

Dexretail Limited
Incorporated: 24 January 2011 *Employees:* 9
Net Worth: £5,735,020 *Total Assets:* £8,932,118
Registered Office: 17 Brickfields Business Park, Gillingham, Dorset, SP8 4PX
Activities: Manufacture of electric lighting equipment
Parent: Dextra Group PLC
Officers: Rupert Henry James Martin, Secretary; Keith John Brownhill [1961] Director/Group CEO; James Conduit [1982] Managing Director; Janie Claire Martin [1962] Director/Company Secretary; Rupert Henry James Martin [1949] Director/Group Chairman; Duncan Paxman [1960] Sales Director; Darren Lee Ward [1970] Group Technical Director

Dextra Group PLC
Incorporated: 24 July 1978 *Employees:* 531
Net Worth: £18,961,672 *Total Assets:* £49,517,276
Registered Office: Brickfields Business Park, Gillingham, Dorset, SP8 4PX
Activities: Manufacture of electric lighting equipment
Major Shareholder: Rupert Henry James Martin
Officers: Rupert Martin, Secretary; Keith John Brownhill [1961] Director/Group CEO; Janie Claire Martin [1962] Director; Rupert Henry James Martin [1949] Director/Group Chairman; Darren Lee Ward [1970] Group Technical Director

Dextra Lighting Limited
Incorporated: 27 December 2007 *Employees:* 43
Net Worth: £4,100,744 *Total Assets:* £9,167,373
Registered Office: Brickfields Business Park, Gillingham, Dorset, SP8 4PX
Activities: Wholesale of electronic and telecommunications equipment and parts
Parent: Dextra Group PLC
Officers: Rupert Martin, Secretary; Simon Allard [1970] Managing Director; Keith John Brownhill [1961] Director/Group CEO; Steven Lewis [1964] Sales Director; Janie Claire Martin [1962] Director; Rupert Henry James Martin [1949] Director/Group Chairman; Darren Ward [1978] Group Technical Director

Dextra Services Limited
Incorporated: 27 December 2007 *Employees:* 407
Net Worth: £2,078,739 *Total Assets:* £7,410,768
Registered Office: Brickfields Business Park, Gillingham, Dorset, SP8 4PX
Activities: Manufacture of electric lighting equipment
Parent: Dextra Group PLC
Officers: Rupert Martin, Secretary; Keith John Brownhill [1961] Director/Group CEO; Shane Hansford [1970] Production Director; Janie Claire Martin [1962] Director/Company Secretary; Rupert Henry James Martin [1949] Director/Group Chairman; Nigel Penny [1966] Procurement Director; Timothy Pickford [1975] Manufacturing & Logistics Director; Darren Lee Ward [1970] Group Technical Director

Dezac Group Holdings Limited
Incorporated: 20 September 1999 *Employees:* 41
Net Worth: £2,164,637 *Total Assets:* £4,417,457
Registered Office: Dezac House, Montpellier Street, Cheltenham, Glos, GL50 1SS
Activities: Non-trading company
Shareholders: Malcolm Bradley Mills; Desmond Bryan Leon Mills
Officers: Desmond Bryan Leon Mills, Secretary; Desmond Bryan Leon Mills [1963] Managing Director; Malcolm Bradley Mills [1965] Director

The Dezac Group Limited
Incorporated: 2 November 1987 *Employees:* 41
Net Worth: £2,164,612 *Total Assets:* £4,417,438
Registered Office: Dezac House, Montpellier Street, Cheltenham, Glos, GL50 1SS
Activities: Other manufacturing n.e.c.
Shareholders: Desmond Bryan Leon Mills; Malcolm Bradley Mills
Officers: Desmond Bryan Leon Mills, Secretary; Desmond Bryan Leon Mills [1963] Managing Director; Malcolm Bradley Mills [1965] Director

DFH Estates Limited
Incorporated: 20 December 2013
Net Worth: £5,570 *Total Assets:* £5,559,486
Registered Office: Ross House, The Square, Stow on the Wold, Glos, GL54 1AF
Activities: Wholesale of flowers and plants
Shareholders: David Francis Higginson; Nicole Higginson
Officers: David Francis Higginson [1968] Director; Nicole Higginson [1968] Director

Dhrona Holdings Ltd
Incorporated: 13 August 2014 *Employees:* 103
Net Worth: £964,292 *Total Assets:* £20,100,768
Registered Office: c/o Francis Clark LLP, North Quay House, Sutton Harbour, Plymouth, PL4 0RA
Activities: Activities of head offices
Shareholders: Vasantlal Devchand Dhrona; Girishkumar Devchand Dhrona
Officers: Girishkumar Devchand Dhrona [1946] Director; Vasantlal Devchand Jhina Dhrona [1943] Director

Digs Properties Limited
Incorporated: 25 February 2010
Net Worth: £300 *Total Assets:* £3,517,275
Registered Office: 45 Oakfield Road, Clifton, Bristol, BS8 2AX
Activities: Buying and selling of own real estate
Shareholders: Kingsley Peter Webb; Edward John Ware; James Anthony Davison
Officers: James Anthony Davison [1961] Director; Edward John Ware [1960] Director; Kingsley Peter Webb [1966] Director

Dike & Son Limited
Incorporated: 28 January 1933 *Employees:* 80
Net Worth: £4,947,457 *Total Assets:* £5,583,100
Registered Office: Ring Street, Stalbridge, Dorset, DT10 2NB
Activities: Retail sale in non-specialised stores with food, beverages or tobacco predominating
Shareholder: Deirdre Kathleen Dike
Officers: Deirdre Kathleen Dike, Secretary; Andrew Thomas Dike [1975] Managing Director; Deirdre Kathleen Dike [1946] Director/Company Secretary; Adam Vincent [1981] Director/Shop Manager

Dilkes Energy Limited
Incorporated: 7 November 2013
Net Worth: £7,452,086 *Total Assets:* £7,639,619
Registered Office: Hill Farm House, Babcary, Somerton, Somerset, TA11 7EB
Activities: Production of electricity
Officers: Sarah Cruickshank, Secretary; Jennifer Wright, Secretary; Arthur Somers Llewellyn [1953] Director/Consultant; Jason Murphy [1978] Director/Accountant [Irish]

Dingle Brothers Systems Limited
Incorporated: 26 January 1988
Net Worth: £9,051,968 *Total Assets:* £9,698,567
Registered Office: Steppes, Cooksland, Bodmin, Cornwall, PL31 2AY
Activities: Other information technology service activities
Shareholders: Graham Merlin Dingle; Ronald Adrian Dingle
Officers: Graham Merlin Dingle, Secretary; Graham Merlin Dingle [1953] Director/Machinery Contractor; Morley Edwin Dingle [1950] Director/Machinery Contractor; Ronald Adrian Dingle [1946] Director/Machinery Contractor

Diocese of Bristol Academies Trust
Incorporated: 25 July 2012 *Employees:* 398
Net Worth: £29,745,184 *Total Assets:* £34,963,392
Registered Office: First Floor, Hillside House, 1500 Parkway North, Stoke Gifford, Bristol, BS34 8YU
Activities: Pre-primary education
Officers: Alistair Pickering, Secretary; Tanya Arkle [1967] Director/Education; Rachel Elizabeth Clark [1970] Director of Strategy; Iain Craig [1958] Director/Accountant (Retired); Christine Elizabeth Dursley [1953] Director/Headteacher; Lynda Eileen Fisher [1952] Director/Retired; Reverend Andrew Martin Gubbins [1965] Director/Minister of Religion; Kathleen Ann Holt [1947] Diocesan Director of Education; Rev Norma Edith McKemey [1947] Director/Associate Minister; John Douglas Morison [1954] Director/IT Consultant; Jill Yeomans [1945] Director/Retired

The Diocese of Gloucester Academies Trust
Incorporated: 19 July 2012 *Employees:* 563
Net Worth: £31,820,988 *Total Assets:* £37,981,536
Registered Office: 3 College Green, Gloucester, GL1 2LR
Activities: Educational support services
Officers: Eleanor Claire Annick Hully, Secretary; Rowen E V Scott-Berry, Secretary; The Venerable Phil John Andrew [1962] Director/Archdeacon; Timothy Rupert Brock [1967] Director/Senior Account Manager; Mervyn Charles Cowdrey [1953] Director/Retired Naval Officer; Dr Douglas Desmond Cowper [1970] Director/Chartered Engineer; Rosemary Dick [1963] Director/Chartered Accountant; Reverend Ruth Patricia Fitter [1969] Director/Vicar; Rachel Elizabeth Howie [1972] Director; Dr Kenneth David Lynch [1965] Director/Reader in Geography; Philip Eric Perks [1947] Director/Retired; Robert Westley Stokes [1973] Director/Accountant

Direct Online Services Holdings Limited
Incorporated: 23 September 2016 *Employees:* 255
Net Worth: £2,711,334 *Total Assets:* £11,885,090
Registered Office: Brearley Court, Baird Road, Waterwells Business Park, Quedgeley, Glos, GL2 2AF
Activities: Activities of other holding companies n.e.c.
Major Shareholder: William Rees
Officers: David James Cox [1960] Director; Ben Scott Crouch [1990] Director/Chief Financial Officer; Edwin D'Aubney Davies [1984] Director; Martyn Peter Rees [1961] Director; William Rees [1987] Director; Jonathan Ashley Shepherd [1974] Director

Direct Online Services Limited
Incorporated: 10 July 2008 *Employees:* 221
Net Worth: £3,023,059 *Total Assets:* £11,747,095
Registered Office: Brearley Court, Baird Road, Waterwells Business Park, Quedgeley, Gloucester, GL2 2AF
Activities: Retail sale via mail order houses or via Internet
Parent: Direct Online Sevices Holdings Limited
Officers: Sally Joanne Rees, Secretary; Philip Roger Allright [1983] Director/Transport Manager; Samantha Claire Deighton [1985] Director of Customer Relations; Stuart John Hancy [1982] Transport Director; Gregory Mark Neville [1964] Operations Director; Martyn Peter Rees [1961] Director/Commercial Manager; William Joseph Rees [1987] Director/Online Sales Manager; Marcin Piotr Samelczak [1984] Technical Director [Polish]; Daniel Robert Wilson [1980] Director/Trade Sales Manager

Discovery Multi Academy Trust
Incorporated: 6 July 2016 *Employees:* 153
Net Worth: £10,844,052 *Total Assets:* £13,877,677
Registered Office: Beechwood Primary Academy, Rockfield Avenue, Southway, Plymouth, PL6 6DX
Activities: Primary education
Officers: Sarah Alison Buckle, Secretary; Lisa Drummond [1979] Director/HR Manager; Stephen Evans [1974] Director/Area Supervisor; Julia Guy [1971] Director/Regional Manager - Banking; Darren Hart [1968] Director/Semi-Retired; Alison Wendy Nettleship [1970] Director/Headteacher; Lisa Petford [1982] Director/Finance Business Partner; Hannah Randall [1978] Director/Governor; Nina Sarlaka [1968] Director/Enterprise and Inward Investment Manager; Paul Scarsbrook [1951] Director/Head of Learning Resources; Raymond Waring [1948] Director/Retired

Discus Management Limited
Incorporated: 19 November 2002 *Employees:* 2
Net Worth: £7,882,263 *Total Assets:* £8,184,165
Registered Office: York House, Castlewood, Ashley Heath, Ringwood, Hants, BH24 2AX
Activities: Financial management
Shareholders: Douglas Grey Lingafelter; Karen Jane Lingafelter
Officers: Douglas Grey Lingafelter [1960] Director [American]; Karen Jane Lingafelter [1964] Director/Housewife

Distant Planet Productions Limited
Incorporated: 15 May 2002
Net Worth: £1,087,000 *Total Assets:* £8,680,000
Registered Office: The Quadrangle, The Promenade, Cheltenham, Glos, GL50 1PX
Activities: Financial intermediation not elsewhere classified
Parent: Royal Bank Leasing Limited
Officers: Stephen Paul Nixon [1970] Director/Bank Official; Keith Damian Pereira [1978] Director/Bank Official

Diverse Abilities Plus Ltd
Incorporated: 23 January 1981 *Employees:* 433
Net Worth: £5,906,358 *Total Assets:* £8,456,319
Registered Office: Barnabas Project Centre, 13-15 Manor Avenue, Parkstone, Poole, Dorset, BH12 4LB
Activities: Primary education
Officers: Eliezer John Kennar, Secretary; Richard Michael Peter Bavister [1978] Director/Private Banker; Martin Edward Davies [1961] Director/Solicitor; Eliezer John Kennar [1953] Director/Solicitor; Gary Leedale Knight [1964] Director/Consultant; Doctor John Beverly Peter [1943] Director/Retired; Doctor Geoffrey Lindsay Ridgway [1944] Director/Retired Clinical Microbiologist; John Allan Raymond Smith [1942] Director/Medico Legal Consultant; Nigel Trevor Still [1964] Estate Agency Director

Dix Hills 516 Limited
Incorporated: 23 June 2015 *Employees:* 5
Net Worth: £3,462,006 *Total Assets:* £4,441,092
Registered Office: Southview House, St Austell Enterprise Park, Carclaze, St Austell, Cornwall, PL25 4EJ
Activities: Activities of head offices
Officers: Timothy John McMahon [1978] Director; Simon Peter Turner [1958] Director; Ben Robert Willcocks [1978] Director; Ian Anthony Bramwell Wrigley [1955] Director; Troy Andrew Bramwell Wrigley [1978] Director

DJS (UK) Limited
Incorporated: 16 February 2012 *Employees:* 41
Net Worth: £3,562,053 *Total Assets:* £18,459,692
Registered Office: 28 Avenue Road, Parkway House, Bournemouth, BH2 5SL
Activities: Other credit granting n.e.c.
Parent: DJS Holding Limited
Officers: Steven Dixon [1965] Director; Julian John Hek [1968] Director; Daniel Joseph Ware [1984] Director; Simon James Woodhams [1971] Director

DKH Retail Limited
Incorporated: 2 November 2009 *Employees:* 178
Net Worth: £275,526,016 *Total Assets:* £473,448,000
Registered Office: Unit 60 The Runnings, Cheltenham, Glos, GL51 9NW
Activities: Wholesale of clothing and footwear
Parent: Superdry PLC
Officers: Edward Peter Barker [1972] Director; Simon Callander [1967] Director/Group General Counsel and Company Secretary; Euan Angus Sutherland [1969] Director

DM Opco Limited
Incorporated: 14 April 2016 *Employees:* 72
Net Worth Deficit: £3,566,758 *Total Assets:* £4,613,249
Registered Office: Site Control Centre, Arena Way, Wimborne, Dorset, BH21 3BW
Activities: Other service activities n.e.c.
Parent: DM Topco Limited
Officers: Brian McCabe [1972] Director [Irish]; Eamon Waters [1960] Director [Irish]

DMGI Land & Property Europe Ltd
Incorporated: 21 March 1974 *Employees:* 2
Net Worth: £196,978,736 *Total Assets:* £331,560,256
Registered Office: 5-7 Abbey Court, Eagle Way, Sowton Industrial Estate, Exeter, EX2 7HY
Activities: Activities of head offices
Parent: DMG Information Limited
Officers: David William Callcott, Secretary/Accountant; Simon James Brown [1965] Director/Chief Executive; David William Callcott [1959] Director/Accountant; Stephen John Stout [1960] Director/Chairman; Paul Adam Zwillenberg [1967] Director/CEO - Media and Publishing [British/American]

DMJ Asset Management Ltd.
Incorporated: 2 March 1990 *Employees:* 4
Previous: Hose & Hydraulics Group Limited
Net Worth: £3,239,028 *Total Assets:* £3,627,633
Registered Office: Old Drill Hall, Rocky Hill, Tavistock, Devon, PL19 0DZ
Activities: Manufacture of other rubber products
Officers: Michael Robert Yorath, Secretary; David Michael Yorath [1987] Director/Administrator; Michael Robert Yorath [1946] Director/Engineer

DMT Property Services Ltd
Incorporated: 29 July 2003 *Employees:* 2
Net Worth: £6,500,044 *Total Assets:* £6,786,694
Registered Office: Cornerstone House, Park Avenue, St Ives, Cornwall, TR26 2DN
Activities: Buying and selling of own real estate
Major Shareholder: Anne-Marie Slattery
Officers: William Joseph Barker, Secretary/Director; William Joseph Barker [1947] Director; Bernard Bertram Pooley [1957] Director/Chartered Accountant; Anne-Marie Slattery [1964] Director

DNO Consulting Limited
Incorporated: 16 October 2003 *Employees:* 25
Net Worth: £7,753,456 *Total Assets:* £8,356,549
Registered Office: 3 Sheep Street, Highworth, Wilts, SN6 7AA
Activities: Other professional, scientific and technical activities n.e.c.
Major Shareholder: Lee Joseph Mason
Officers: Lee Joseph Mason [1960] Director/Electrical Engineer

The Dobson Family Investment Company Limited
Incorporated: 17 March 2011 *Employees:* 3
Previous: Gainwell Residential Limited
Net Worth: £9,924,905 *Total Assets:* £9,950,020
Registered Office: 3 Rivergate, Temple Quay, Bristol, BS1 6GD
Activities: Fund management activities
Shareholders: Charles Edward Dobson; Julian Charles Dobson; Mary Dobson
Officers: Charles Edward Dobson [1944] Director; Julian Charles Dobson [1971] Director; Mary Dobson [1943] Director

Dometic UK Limited
Incorporated: 29 March 2001 *Employees:* 50
Net Worth: £4,900,000 *Total Assets:* £10,254,000
Registered Office: Dometic House, The Brewery, Blandford St Mary, Dorset, DT11 9LS
Activities: Wholesale of other intermediate products
Parent: Dometic Sweden AB
Officers: Amanda Joy Sutton, Secretary; Henrik Boggild [1972] Director [Danish]; Adam John Ramsden [1973] Managing Director; Juan Ramon Vargues Huerta [1959] Director/Chairman [Swedish]

Dopano Limited
Incorporated: 23 January 2006
Net Worth: £2,796,444 *Total Assets:* £3,799,939
Registered Office: Cotswold Motor Group, Corinthian Way, The Reddings, Cheltenham, Glos, GL51 6UP
Activities: Management consultancy activities other than financial management
Major Shareholder: Andrew Christopher Hulcoop
Officers: Carol Christine Hulcoop, Secretary; Andrew Christopher Hulcoop [1960] Director

The Dorcan Academy
Incorporated: 1 November 2011 *Employees:* 108
Net Worth: £8,797,017 *Total Assets:* £10,026,678
Registered Office: The Dorcan Academy, St Pauls Drive, Swindon, Wilts, SN3 5DA
Activities: General secondary education
Officers: Anne Elizabeth Cleary, Secretary; Sherryl Bareham [1967] Director/Headteacher; Joanne Brookes [1970] Director/Accountant; Peter Corkish [1986] Director/Teacher; Lisa Marie Garrett [1970] Director/Scientist; Candida Gee [1955] Director/Retired; Fiona Hardcastle [1954] Director/Learning Centre Manager; Sally-Ann Harvey [1964] Director/Customer Services Manager; Patricia Elizabeth Porter [1948] Director/Retired; Andria Ruby Thomas [1965] Director/Works in School; John James Walker [1948] Director/Retired

Dorchester Middle School
Incorporated: 4 May 2012 *Employees:* 79
Net Worth: £6,682,045 *Total Assets:* £8,387,841
Registered Office: Dorchester Middle School, Queens Avenue, Dorchester, DT1 2HS
Activities: General secondary education
Officers: John Christopher William Adams [1946] Director/Retired; Patricia Ann Bailey [1949] Director/Retired; Natasha Bousfield [1983] Director/Deputy Headteacher; Caroline Dearden [1962] Director/Executive Headteacher; Janet Margaret Dunne [1961] Director/Housewife; Jane Louise Fairless [1977] Director/Teacher; Stuart Christopher Legg [1968] Director/Fire Officer; Michael Ian Reed [1969] Director/Safety Consultant; Lisa Kerry Upchurch [1971] Director/Chartered Tax Advisor; Susan Carolyne Wood [1964] Director/Data Manager, Dorchester Middle School

Doric Developments (Bath) Limited
Incorporated: 30 May 1986 *Employees:* 99
Net Worth: £28,880,844 *Total Assets:* £36,986,672
Registered Office: Doric House, 16 Merlin Way, Bowerhill, Melksham, Wilts, SN12 6TJ
Activities: Construction of domestic buildings
Major Shareholder: Roderick Donald Timbrell-Whittle
Officers: Susan Ann Timbrell-Whittle, Secretary; Roderick Donald Timbrell-Whittle [1947] Director; Susan Ann Timbrell-Whittle [1952] Director

Dorothy House Foundation Limited (The)
Incorporated: 3 April 1978 *Employees:* 272
Net Worth: £15,855,143 *Total Assets:* £16,893,984
Registered Office: Winsley, Bradford on Avon, Wilts, BA15 2LE
Activities: Other human health activities
Officers: Anthony de Jaeger, Secretary; Dr Simon Burrell [1954] Director/Doctor; David Marcus Cavaliero [1958] Director/Solicitor; Reverend Josette Crane [1961] Director/Vicar; Christine Susan Davis [1948] Director/Social Services; James Alexander Gare [1975] Director/Chartered Accountant; Diane Patricia Hall [1957] Finance Director; Dr Mark Atkinson Hunt [1958] Director/Doctor; Ian Carlyle Lafferty [1948] Director/Retailer; Brian John Mansfield [1970] Managing Director; Charlotte Parkin [1988] Director/Senior Development Manager; Warren Francis Reid [1965] Director/Solicitor; Francesca Thompson [1958] Director; Kate Tompkins [1947] Director

The Dorset & Somerset Air Ambulance Charity
Incorporated: 13 December 1999 *Employees:* 13
Net Worth: £28,990,888 *Total Assets:* £29,666,116
Registered Office: Landacre House, Castle Road, Chelston Business Park, Wellington, Somerset, TA21 9JQ
Activities: Other professional, scientific and technical activities n.e.c.
Officers: Colin Michael Launchbury, Secretary; Dr Gillian Mary Bryce [1958] Director/Hospital Consultant; Michael John Gallagher [1955] Director; Simon Jones [1966] Director/Chief of Staff Leonardo Helicopters; Richard Ian Kennedy [1957] Director/Chartered Accountant; Michael David MacQueen Laver [1964] Director/Cabinet Maker; Hannah Mae Nobbs [1984] Director/Engineer; Anna Louise Phillips [1978] Director/Solicitor; Richard Popper [1958] Director/Fundraising & Marketing Consultant; David Charles Senior [1952] Director/Retired Aviation Manager; Glenys Taylor [1956] Director/Human Resources Consultant

Dorset Freedom Properties Limited
Incorporated: 4 June 2014 *Employees:* 3
Previous: Cotswold Commercial Properties Limited
Net Worth: £3,639,572 *Total Assets:* £4,295,781
Registered Office: Mazars LLP, 5th Floor, Merck House, Seldown Lane, Poole, Dorset, BH15 1TW
Activities: Other letting and operating of own or leased real estate
Major Shareholder: Mark Julian Griffiths
Officers: Mark Julian Griffiths [1961] Director

Dorset Health Trust Limited (The)
Incorporated: 26 August 1977
Net Worth: £5,066,713 *Total Assets:* £5,077,096
Registered Office: Unity Chambers, 34 High East Street, Dorchester, DT1 1HA
Activities: Other human health activities
Officers: Antonia Elizabeth Warren Savva, Secretary; Lavinia Frances Barbour [1949] Director; Elizabeth Brierley [1965] Director/Accountant; Dr Duncan Chambler [1982] Director/Medical Consultant; David Hugh Cove [1947] Director/Consultant Physician; Mark Declan Gibbens [1968] Director/Businessman; Sarah Heath [1973] Director/Solicitor; Patrick James Jeffery [1944] Director/Consultant Surgeon; Prof David John Leaper [1947] Director/University Professor; Caroline Joyce Nickinson [1950] Retired Charitable Trust Director; David Julian Pinder [1942] Director/Retired; Tessa Nicola Russell [1960] Director/Self Employed; Antonia Elizabeth Savva [1974] Director/Barrister; Peter John Ward [1965] Director/Medical Consultant; Doctor Simon John Winterton [1957] Director/Cardiologist; The Lady Fenella Christian Mary Wynford [1952] Director/Nurse Manager

Dorset Press Limited (The)
Incorporated: 11 October 1982 *Employees:* 109
Net Worth: £10,365,063 *Total Assets:* £11,403,444
Registered Office: 23 High East Street, Dorchester, DT1 1HD
Activities: Other service activities n.e.c.
Officers: Rita Margaret Kennett, Secretary; Anthony Victor Kennett [1938] Director; Rita Margaret Kennett [1941] Director

Dorset Village Bakery Limited
Incorporated: 21 April 1998 *Employees:* 155
Net Worth: £880,921 *Total Assets:* £4,820,517
Registered Office: Unit 2 Pinesway, Station Road, Stalbridge, Dorset, DT10 2RN
Activities: Manufacture of rusks and biscuits; manufacture of preserved pastry goods and cakes
Parent: Frontier Acquisitions Limited
Officers: Simon Leon Browne [1970] Director; Nicholas Peter Field [1978] Director; Sarah Ann Spittle [1969] Director

Dorset Wildlife Trust
Incorporated: 30 March 1961 *Employees:* 54
Previous: Dorset Trust for Nature Conservation Limited (The)
Net Worth: £10,828,000 *Total Assets:* £11,233,000
Registered Office: Brooklands Farm, Forston, Dorchester, DT2 7AA
Activities: Other education n.e.c.
Officers: Susan Elizabeth Patterson, Secretary; Henry Generald Anthony Bates [1932] Director/Material Consultant; Josephine Ruby Davies [1946] Director; Kelvyn Garth Derrick [1947] Director; John Douglas Gaye [1951] Director/Consultant; Mark George Kibblewhite [1952] Director/Soil Scientist; Giles Adrian Pugh [1966] Director/Chartered Accountant; John Roland Raymond [1946] Director/Solicitor; Alick George Simmons [1956] Director/Retired; Jeremy Ambler Thomas [1947] Director/Research Scientist; Professor Nigel Rodney Webb [1942] Director/Principal Scientific Officer/Chartered Biologist; Anne Vivienne Wheatcroft [1947] Director/Retired; James Robert White [1948] Director/Retired

Double H (Holdings) Limited
Incorporated: 11 October 1971 *Employees:* 166
Net Worth: £475,022 *Total Assets:* £11,465,628
Registered Office: 4 Cedar Park, Cobham Road, Ferndown Industrial Estate, Wimborne, Dorset, BH21 7SF
Activities: Activities of head offices
Shareholders: Neil Stevenson; David Stevenson
Officers: David Stevenson, Secretary; David Stevenson [1965] Director/Company Secretary; Neil Stevenson [1961] Director/Engineer

Double H (Nurseries) Limited
Incorporated: 17 May 1973 *Employees:* 168
Net Worth: £61,209 *Total Assets:* £10,851,406
Registered Office: 4 Cedar Park, Cobham Road, Ferndown Industrial Estate, Wimborne, Dorset, BH21 7SF
Activities: Wholesale of flowers and plants
Parent: Double H (Holdings) Limited
Officers: David Stevenson, Secretary; David Stevenson [1965] Director/Company Secretary; Neil Stevenson [1961] Director/Engineer

Doughty Engineering Limited
Incorporated: 17 February 1970 *Employees:* 62
Net Worth: £3,520,462 *Total Assets:* £4,993,385
Registered Office: Crow Arch Lane, Ringwood, Hants, BH24 1NZ
Activities: Manufacture of metal structures and parts of structures
Shareholder: Mervyn Boyd Thor Lister
Officers: Mervyn Boyd Thor Lister, Secretary; Julian Chiverton [1970] Director/Engineer; Mervyn Boyd Thor Lister [1950] Director/Engineer; Stephen Charles Wright [1976] Director/Technical Engineer

Doveleigh Care Limited
Incorporated: 28 January 2000 *Employees:* 87
Net Worth: £1,182,976 *Total Assets:* £4,173,991
Registered Office: Colcombe Wood, Colyton, Devon, EX24 6DR
Activities: Other accommodation
Shareholders: Keith Paul Mills; Elizabeth Mills
Officers: Elizabeth Mills, Secretary/Retirement Home Proprietor; Elizabeth Mills [1963] Director/Retirement Home Proprietor; Keith Paul Mills [1959] Director/Retirement Home Proprietor

Dover Engineered Systems UK Ltd
Incorporated: 15 April 2013 *Employees:* 27
Net Worth: £7,420,000 *Total Assets:* £35,915,000
Registered Office: Midland House, 2 Poole Road, Bournemouth, BH2 5QY
Activities: Other manufacturing n.e.c.
Officers: Kelly Bissett, Secretary; Kelly Simone Bissett [1972] Director; Valerie Yvonne Michelle Marie Fisson [1975] Director [Belgian]; Stefan Franken [1970] Finance Director [German]; Erling John Mitton [1971] Director

Dover Fluids UK Ltd
Incorporated: 12 October 1988 *Employees:* 5
Net Worth: £92,018,000 *Total Assets:* £849,145,984
Registered Office: Midland House, 2 Poole Road, Bournemouth, BH2 5QY
Activities: Activities of head offices
Officers: Kelly Simone Bissett, Secretary; Kelly Simone Bissett [1972] Director; Valerie Yvonne Michelle Marie Fisson [1975] Director [Belgian]; Stefan Franken [1970] Finance Director [German]; Erling John Mitton [1971] Director

Dover Refrigeration & Food Equipment UK Ltd
Incorporated: 13 March 2002
Net Worth: £717,659,008 *Total Assets:* £788,860,992
Registered Office: Midland House, 2 Poole Road, Bournemouth, BH2 5QY
Activities: Activities of head offices
Parent: Dover Fluids UK Limited
Officers: Kelly Simone Bissett, Secretary; Kelly Simone Bissett [1972] Director; Valerie Yvonne Michelle Marie Fisson [1975] Director [Belgian]; Stefan Franken [1970] Finance Director [German]; Erling John Mitton [1971] Director

Dowdeswell Aviation LLP
Incorporated: 6 June 2013
Net Worth: £4,382,475 *Total Assets:* £4,726,225
Registered Office: Dowdeswell Park, London Road, Cheltenham, Glos, GL52 6UT

C R Down Farming Limited
Incorporated: 11 August 2014 *Employees:* 13
Net Worth: £358,593 *Total Assets:* £6,282,042
Registered Office: Hayes Barton, East Budleigh, Budleigh Salterton, Exeter, Devon, EX9 7BS
Activities: Raising of swine and pigs
Shareholders: Christopher Roy Down; Katie Jane Down
Officers: Christopher Down [1970] Director/Farmer; Katie Jane Down [1972] Director/Farmer

John Downer Productions Limited
Incorporated: 5 September 1989 *Employees:* 15
Net Worth: £2,472,827 *Total Assets:* £4,542,403
Registered Office: Leighside Bridge Road, Leigh Woods, Bristol, BS8 3PB
Activities: Television programme production activities
Major Shareholder: John Leslie Keith Downer
Officers: Sara Ford, Secretary; John Leslie Keith Downer [1952] Director/Producer

Downfield Homes Limited
Incorporated: 7 January 2004 *Employees:* 2
Net Worth: £1,621,662 *Total Assets:* £10,732,204
Registered Office: Freshford House, Redcliffe Way, Bristol, BS1 6NL
Activities: Other letting and operating of own or leased real estate
Shareholders: David Peter Walker; Catherine Bronwen Walker
Officers: Catherine Bronwen Walker [1951] Director; David Peter Walker [1952] Director

Downland Consultants Limited
Incorporated: 17 October 1967 *Employees:* 2
Net Worth: £4,881,999 *Total Assets:* £5,270,265
Registered Office: Lime Court, Pathfields Business Park, South Molton, Devon, EX36 3LH
Activities: Licenced restaurants
Shareholders: Adam Lewis; Donna Eliza Bale
Officers: Stella Gertrude Lewis, Secretary; Donald Richard Lewis [1935] Director/Farmer; Stella Gertrude Lewis [1937] Director/Secretary

Downs School (Charlton House) Limited (The)
Incorporated: 15 September 1972 *Employees:* 79
Net Worth: £2,927,736 *Total Assets:* £4,842,467
Registered Office: The Downs School, Charlton House, Wraxall, Bristol, BS48 1PF
Activities: Primary education
Officers: Helen Louise Walker, Secretary; Helen Mary Archer [1959] Director/Health Visitor; Charles Rupert Guy Biggin [1973] Director/Chartered Accountant; Mark Ashley Burchfield [1970] Director; Lady Emma Jane Burgh [1967] Director/Recruitment & Property Management; Jason Mark Collard [1967] Managing Director; David Jonathan Ferris [1971] Director/Lawyer; Stephen Winfield Holliday [1962] Director/Headmaster; Nicola Anne Huggett [1969] Director/Headteacher; James Alistair George Isaacs [1969] Managing Director; Thomas Pennant Lloyd-Jones [1980] Director/Bank Official; Barnaby James Northover [1974] Director/Lawyer; Rebecca Tear [1972] Director/Headmistress; Rachel Elizabeth Thornton [1954] Director/Manager

C.M. Downton (Haulage Contractors) Limited
Incorporated: 8 May 1967 *Employees:* 1,229
Net Worth: £31,818,726 *Total Assets:* £83,219,640
Registered Office: Brook Farm, Bristol Road, Moreton Valence, Gloucester, GL2 7ND
Activities: Freight transport by road
Parent: Epiphany Operations Limited
Officers: Mark Davis, Secretary; Andrew Michael Tiffin Downton [1960] Director/Haulage Contractor; Maxwell John Downton [1964] Director/Haulage Contractor; Richard George Downton [1964] Director/Haulage Contractor; Robert Michael Emery [1969] Director/Manager; Chuang Hue Moh [1975] Director [Singaporean]; Simon Richard Pearson [1967] Director; Heath Brian Zarin [1975] Director [American]

DPM Estate Limited
Incorporated: 13 July 1992 *Employees:* 2
Net Worth: £15,645,769 *Total Assets:* £16,093,348
Registered Office: DJ Property, Unit C, Oxford Court, Cambridge Road, Granby Industrial Estate, Weymouth, Dorset, DT4 9GH
Activities: Buying and selling of own real estate
Shareholder: Kathryn Jones, Michael Jones, Alan Newberry
Officers: Kathryn Jones, Company Secretary; Kathryn Jones [1947] Director/Company Secretary; Michael Jones [1973] Director/Chartered Accountant

DPRS Finance Limited
Incorporated: 31 March 2008 *Employees:* 4
Previous: DPRS Brislington Limited
Net Worth: £684,298 *Total Assets:* £4,109,918
Registered Office: St Georges Lodge, 33 Oldfield Road, Bath, BA2 3NE
Activities: Activities of mortgage finance companies
Parent: Hebron & Medlock Limited
Officers: Peter Phipps, Secretary; David John Medlock [1955] Director; Jacqueline Mary Medlock [1958] Director; Peter John Medlock [1984] Director

Dragon Alfa Cement Limited
Incorporated: 28 November 1997 *Employees:* 11
Net Worth: £2,304,589 *Total Assets:* £5,243,830
Registered Office: The Cement Terminal, Sharpness Docks, Sharpness, Glos, GL13 9UX
Activities: Other manufacturing n.e.c.
Officers: Sandra Dawn Evans, Secretary; Maria Jose Aguado Abril [1966] Director [Spanish]; Javier Delgado Gil [1969] Director [Spanish]; Joaquin Prego Gonzalez [1972] Commercial Director [Spanish]

Dragonfly Education Trust
Incorporated: 3 August 2011 *Employees:* 283
Previous: Writhlington Academy Trust
Net Worth: £27,629,890 *Total Assets:* £33,220,776
Registered Office: Dragonfly Education Trust (Writhlington School), Knobsbury Lane, Writhlington, Radstock, Somerset, BA3 3NQ
Activities: General secondary education
Officers: Richard Anthony Chambers Akers [1971] Director/Bank Manager; Tim Lee Cooper [1973] Electrical Design Director; Linda Ruth Day [1945] Director/Retired; Mark Ivan Everett [1970] Director/Headteacher; Damian John Pascoe Knollys [1966] Director/Headteacher; Dennis John Lewis [1949] Director; Professor James Edward Smith [1964] Director/University Professor; Rachel Ann Wills [1974] Director/Chartered Accountant

Drake Court Property Limited
Incorporated: 2 December 2015 *Employees:* 2
Net Worth Deficit: £28,133 *Total Assets:* £4,191,309
Registered Office: Horizon Building, Western Wood Way, Langage Science Park, Plympton, Devon, PL7 5BG
Activities: Other letting and operating of own or leased real estate
Parent: PSC Training & Development Group Limited
Officers: Jeffery William Rowlands, Secretary; Mark John Boulting [1968] Director/Manager; Jeffery William Rowlands [1953] Director/Manager

Draper Ventilation Limited
Incorporated: 25 November 2008 *Employees:* 8
Net Worth: £898,271 *Total Assets:* £3,929,928
Registered Office: 4 King Square, Bridgwater, Somerset, TA6 3YF
Activities: Manufacture of non-domestic cooling and ventilation equipment
Major Shareholder: Paul Justin Draper
Officers: Paul Justin Draper, Secretary; Paul Justin Draper [1970] Director

Draycot Estates Limited
Incorporated: 25 April 1996
Net Worth: £4,576,806 *Total Assets:* £5,238,240
Registered Office: 4th Floor, St Catherine's Court, Berkeley Place, Clifton, Bristol, BS8 1BQ
Activities: Other letting and operating of own or leased real estate
Major Shareholder: Jeremy Edward Bent
Officers: Alison Jane Skedd, Secretary/Accountant; Jeremy Edward Bent [1951] Director; Alison Jane Skedd [1963] Finance Director

Dream Makers Enterprises Limited
Incorporated: 12 October 2006
Net Worth: £47,336 *Total Assets:* £16,576,976
Registered Office: 22 Billet Street, Taunton, Somerset, TA1 3NG
Activities: Other amusement and recreation activities n.e.c.
Officers: Stephen John Dudley Hickson [1947] Director/Accountant

Drew Holdings Limited
Incorporated: 10 September 1986 *Employees:* 81
Net Worth: £1,740,721 *Total Assets:* £9,758,686
Registered Office: Site Office, Rydon Village, Holsworthy, Devon, EX22 7HU
Activities: Activities of head offices
Officers: Josephine Lucia Maria Francis [1954] Director; Paul Ian Francis [1954] Director; David Alexander Kennedy-McGregor [1956] Director; Eugenia Rita Maria Sacchetti [1947] Director; Nicola Sacchetti [1945] Director/Restaurateur [Italian]

H.H.& D.E.Drew Limited
Incorporated: 5 April 1957 *Employees:* 121
Net Worth: £13,088,037 *Total Assets:* £20,959,506
Registered Office: Caird Avenue, New Milton, Hants, BH25 5PX
Activities: Operation of gravel and sand pits; mining of clays and kaolin
Shareholder: Hanson Quarry Product Ventures Ltd
Officers: Paul Ian Francis, Secretary; Michael Adrian Badcock [1945] Director; Robert Daniel Flower [1971] Managing Director; Paul Ian Francis [1954] Director; Kevin Adrian Harty [1955] Director [Irish]; Nicola Sacchetti [1945] Director/Restaurateur [Italian]; Charles Andrew Stubbs [1952] Director

Drewdeeds Limited
Incorporated: 14 September 1976
Net Worth: £55,421 *Total Assets:* £3,690,805
Registered Office: Gowran House, 56 Broad Street, Chipping Sodbury, Glos, BS37 6AG
Activities: Other letting and operating of own or leased real estate
Shareholders: Claire de Rosee; Maximilien Olivier Tanguy de Rosee
Officers: Claire de Rosee, Secretary; Maximilien Olivier Tanguy de Jacquier de Rosee [1975] Director; Claire de Rosee [1975] Director

Dribuild Group Limited
Incorporated: 29 August 2012 *Employees:* 61
Previous: Dribuild Holdings Limited
Net Worth: £857,200 *Total Assets:* £12,263,781
Registered Office: Freshford House, Redcliffe Way, Bristol, BS1 6NL
Activities: Activities of construction holding companies
Shareholders: Matthew Douglas Tyler; David Kipling; Michael John Holt
Officers: Michael John Holt [1965] Director; David Kipling [1966] Director; Adrian Jeremy Stuart Marshman [1974] Group Operations Director; Matthew Douglas Tyler [1970] Managing Director

Dribuild Limited
Incorporated: 1 April 2008 *Employees:* 53
Net Worth: £1,586,938 *Total Assets:* £12,784,946
Registered Office: Freshford House, Redcliffe Way, Bristol, BS1 6NL
Activities: Development of building projects
Officers: Michael John Holt [1965] Director; David Kipling [1966] Director; Adrian Jeremy Stuart Marshman [1974] Group Operations Director; Matthew Douglas Tyler [1970] Managing Director

Drilling Information Limited
Incorporated: 16 May 2008 *Employees:* 31
Net Worth: £11,637,413 *Total Assets:* £11,791,519
Registered Office: Unit 702 Sperry Way, Stonehouse Business Park, Stonehouse, Glos, GL10 3UT
Activities: Other engineering activities
Officers: Shawn Shillington [1977] Director/Lawyer [American]; Malcolm John Steel [1969] Director/Senior Vice President

Drilling Systems (U.K.) Limited
Incorporated: 6 June 1990 *Employees:* 72
Net Worth: £11,379,941 *Total Assets:* £17,168,952
Registered Office: Hurn View House, 5 Aviation Park West, Bournemouth International Airport, Hurn, Christchurch, Dorset, BH23 6EW
Activities: Manufacture of electronic measuring, testing etc. equipment, not for industrial process control
Parent: Drilling Systems Limited
Officers: Clive Jeffrey Battisby [1971] Managing Director; Kevin Nigel Franklin [1962] Director

Drilling Systems Group Limited
Incorporated: 23 March 2015 *Employees:* 4
Net Worth Deficit: £8,460,821 *Total Assets:* £65,630,640
Registered Office: Hurn View House, 5 Aviation Park West, Bournemouth International Airport, Hurn, Christchurch, Dorset, BH23 6EW
Activities: Manufacture of electronic measuring, testing etc. equipment, not for industrial process control
Parent: DS UK Midco 2 Limited
Officers: Clive Jeffrey Battisby [1971] Director; Kevin Nigel Franklin [1962] Director; Martin Somerville [1977] Director; Ihab Magdy Toma [1963] Director [Egyptian]

Drilling Systems Limited
Incorporated: 12 September 1988
Net Worth: £13,430,905 *Total Assets:* £17,738,494
Registered Office: Hurn View House, 5 Aviation Park, Bournemouth International Airport, Hurn, Christchurch, Dorset, BH23 6EW
Activities: Manufacture of electronic measuring, testing etc. equipment, not for industrial process control
Parent: Drilling Systems Group Limited
Officers: Clive Jeffrey Battisby [1971] Director; Kevin Nigel Franklin [1962] Director

Drimbawn (UK) Limited
Incorporated: 25 August 1994 *Employees:* 762
Net Worth: £4,409,000 *Total Assets:* £11,668,000
Registered Office: Stock Lane, Langford, Somerset, BS40 5ES
Activities: Growing of vegetables and melons, roots and tubers
Parent: Monaghan Mushrooms Limited
Officers: Philip Wilson, Secretary; Paul Thomas Wilson [1977] Director/Chief Operating Officer [Irish]; Philip David Wilson [1975] Divisional Director [Irish]; Ronald Christopher Wilson [1948] Director [Irish]

Drytac Europe Limited
Incorporated: 20 May 1981 *Employees:* 41
Net Worth: £1,775,365 *Total Assets:* £4,941,408
Registered Office: Drytac House, Filwood Road, Bristol, BS16 3RY
Activities: Non-specialised wholesale trade
Major Shareholder: Richard John Lisle Kelley
Officers: Angelique Kelley, Secretary; Hayden Lisle Kelley [1972] Director [Canadian]; Richard John Lisle Kelley [1944] Director [Canadian]

DS UK Midco 1 Limited
Incorporated: 24 March 2015
Net Worth Deficit: £8,868,883 *Total Assets:* £45,871,076
Registered Office: Hurn View House, 5 Aviation Park West, Bournemouth International Airport, Christchurch, Dorset, BH23 6EW
Activities: Other business support service activities n.e.c.
Parent: DS UK Topco Limited
Officers: Kevin Nigel Franklin [1962] Director; Martin Somerville [1977] Director

DS UK Midco 2 Limited
Incorporated: 24 March 2015
Net Worth: £54,919,384 *Total Assets:* £55,328,240
Registered Office: Hurn View House, 5 Aviation Park West, Bournemouth International Airport, Christchurch, Dorset, BH23 6EW
Activities: Other business support service activities n.e.c.
Parent: DS UK Midco 1 Limited
Officers: Kevin Nigel Franklin [1962] Director; Martin Somerville [1977] Director

DS UK Topco Limited
Incorporated: 24 March 2015 *Employees:* 98
Net Worth Deficit: £15,414,057 *Total Assets:* £46,849,608
Registered Office: Hurn View House, 5 Aviation Park West, Bournemouth International Airport, Christchurch, Dorset, BH23 6EW
Activities: Other business support service activities n.e.c.
Parent: Transforming Training with Technology Limited
Officers: Kevin Nigel Franklin [1962] Director; Martin Somerville [1977] Director

DTR VMS Limited
Incorporated: 22 September 2008 *Employees:* 291
Net Worth: £16,689,000 *Total Assets:* £33,294,000
Registered Office: DTR VMS Limited, Aintree Avenue, White Horse Business Park, Trowbridge, Wilts, BA14 0XB
Activities: Manufacture of other rubber products
Parent: DTR Automotive Corporation
Officers: Dongho Lee, Secretary; Bong Hwan Kim [1941] Director [South Korean]; In Hwan Kim [1963] Director [South Korean]; Sang Hun Kim [1963] Director [South Korean]

The Duchy Academy Trust
Incorporated: 13 January 2014 *Employees:* 111
Net Worth: £4,349,144 *Total Assets:* £5,345,775
Registered Office: Callington Primary School, 24 Saltash Road, Callington, Cornwall, PL17 7EF
Activities: Primary education
Officers: Julian Christopher Elliott [1971] Director/Accountant; Michael Elliott [1955] Director/Retired; Kathryn Jane Hocking [1973] Director/Acting Principal; Laetitia Mayne [1974] Director/Course Manager Lecturer; Bryan James Maywood [1966] Director/Principal; Matthew Shirley [1962] Director/Headteacher; Helen Jane Ward [1974] Director

Duchy Health Charity Limited
Incorporated: 15 July 1976
Net Worth: £5,346,563 *Total Assets:* £5,457,430
Registered Office: Peat House, Newham Road, Truro, Cornwall, TR1 2DP
Activities: Other human health activities
Officers: Mark Williams, Secretary; Dr Tamsyn Jane Anderson [1972] General Practitioner Director of Primary Care CFT; Scott Nicholas Bennett [1967] Director/Self Employed; Sally Jane Coode [1943] Director/Businesswoman; Jonathon Rawson Croggon [1965] Director/Investment Manager; Doctor John Alexander Evers [1944] Director; Timothy John Guy [1944] Director/Designer; Aldyth Hambly Staite [1950] Director/Retired Clinical Nurse Specialist; Graham Ian Murdoch [1963] Director/Solicitor; Tracie Karen North [1959] Director/University Lecturer; Carol Susan O'Brien [1943] Director/Physiotherapist; James Ivarr Robinson [1942] Director/Retired; Dr Barbara Jane Vann [1948] Director/Retired; Mary Winifred Vyvyan [1937] Director/Retired; Mark Williams [1977] Director/Chartered Accountant

Dudbridge Estates,Limited (The)
Incorporated: 13 December 1933 *Employees:* 1
Net Worth: £8,100,629 *Total Assets:* £9,691,693
Registered Office: c/o Stroud Metal Company Ltd, Dudbridge, Stroud, Glos, GL5 3EZ
Activities: Other letting and operating of own or leased real estate
Shareholders: Matthew William Large; Catherine Mary Large
Officers: Matthew William Large, Secretary; Matthew William Large [1965] Director

Dudley Infracare Lift (1) Limited
Incorporated: 12 May 2005
Net Worth Deficit: £9,710,000 *Total Assets:* £53,797,000
Registered Office: Challenge House, International Drive, Tewkesbury Business Park, Tewkesbury, Glos, GL20 8UQ
Activities: Other letting and operating of own or leased real estate
Parent: Dudley Infracare Lift Holdings (1) Limited
Officers: Daniel Peter Bevan, Secretary; Paul Simon Andrews [1970] Investment Director; Richard Darch [1961] Director; Mark William Grinonneau [1970] Director; Matthew Graham Hartland [1971] Director; Daniel Marinus Maria Vermeer [1981] Associate Director [Dutch]

W.L. Duffield & Sons Limited
Incorporated: 4 November 1936 *Employees:* 95
Net Worth: £11,396,000 *Total Assets:* £17,986,000
Registered Office: Babylon View, Pen Mill Trading Estate, Yeovil, Somerset, BA21 5HR
Activities: Manufacture of prepared feeds for farm animals
Officers: Paul Michael Chase, Secretary; Colin Stephen Beesty [1970] Director/General Manager; Paul Michael Chase [1980] Director/Certified Chartered Accountant; Alistair William Duffield [1970] Director; Martyn William Raper [1954] Director/General Manager

Duffields (South West) Limited
Incorporated: 27 February 1992 *Employees:* 48
Net Worth: £2,983,000 *Total Assets:* £6,654,000
Registered Office: Babylon View, Pen Mill Trading Estate, Yeovil, Somerset, BA21 5HR
Activities: Manufacture of prepared feeds for farm animals
Parent: Duffields Mills Limited
Officers: Paul Michael Chase, Secretary; Paul Michael Chase [1980] Director/Certified Chartered Accountant; Alistair William Duffield [1970] Director; Martyn William Raper [1954] Director/General Manager

Duffields Mills Limited
Incorporated: 20 August 1962 *Employees:* 142
Net Worth: £16,093,000 *Total Assets:* £26,048,000
Registered Office: Babylon View, Penmill Trading Estate, Yeovil, Somerset, BA21 5HR
Activities: Manufacture of prepared feeds for farm animals
Officers: Paul Michael Chase, Secretary; Robert Annable [1957] Director/Banker; Alistair William Duffield [1970] Director; Martin Edward Alan Newman [1957] Director/Engineer

Hy. Duke & Son Limited
Incorporated: 20 October 1999
Net Worth: £6,575,980 *Total Assets:* £6,916,900
Registered Office: Stafford House, 10 Prince of Wales Road, Dorchester, DT1 1PW
Activities: Retail sale in commercial art galleries
Shareholders: Garry Peter Batt; Guy John Schwinge
Officers: Garry Peter Batt, Secretary; Garry Peter Batt [1956] Director/Fine Art Auctioneer; Guy John Schwinge [1964] Director/Fine Art Auctioneer

Duke Street Capital Oasis Acquisitions Limited
Incorporated: 31 May 2007 *Employees:* 5
Net Worth Deficit: £24,394,000 *Total Assets:* £157,612,992
Registered Office: Bupa Dental Care, Vantage Office Park, Old Gloucester Road, Hambrook, Bristol, BS16 1GW
Activities: Activities of other holding companies n.e.c.
Parent: Duke Street Capital Oasis Midco Limited
Officers: Robin James Bryant [1970] Director/Dental Surgeon; Steven John Preddy [1959] Director/Dentist; Gabriela Pueyo Roberts [1974] Director/General Manager [Spanish]; Dr Ian David Wood [1956] Director; Jake Stephen Hockley Wright [1972] Director

Duke Street Capital Oasis Midco Limited
Incorporated: 31 May 2007 *Employees:* 3
Net Worth: £40,227,000 *Total Assets:* £129,592,000
Registered Office: Bupa Dental Care, Vantage Office Park, Old Gloucester Road, Hambrook, Bristol, BS16 1GW
Activities: Activities of other holding companies n.e.c.
Parent: Oasis Healthcare International Ltd
Officers: Robin James Bryant [1970] Director/Dental Surgeon; Steven John Preddy [1959] Director/Dentist; Gabriela Pueyo Roberts [1974] Director/General Manager [Spanish]; Dr Ian David Wood [1956] Director; Jake Stephen Hockley Wright [1972] Director

Duke Street Capital Oasis Orthodontics Holdings Limited
Incorporated: 10 July 2008 *Employees:* 3
Net Worth Deficit: £5,942,000 *Total Assets:* £12,560,000
Registered Office: Bupa Dental Care, Vantage Office Park, Old Gloucester Road, Hambrook, Bristol, BS16 1GW
Activities: Activities of other holding companies n.e.c.
Parent: Oasis Healthcare Limited
Officers: Steven John Preddy [1959] Director/Dentist; Gabriela Pueyo Roberts [1974] Director/General Manager [Spanish]; Jake Stephen Hockley Wright [1972] Director

Duke Street Capital Oasis Orthodontics Limited
Incorporated: 10 June 2008 *Employees:* 31
Net Worth Deficit: £10,945,000 *Total Assets:* £8,138,000
Registered Office: Bupa Dental Care, Vantage Office Park, Old Gloucester Road, Hambrook, Bristol, BS16 1GW
Activities: Activities of other holding companies n.e.c.
Parent: Duke Street Capital Oasis Orthodontics Holdings Limited
Officers: Steven John Preddy [1959] Director/Dentist; Gabriela Pueyo Roberts [1974] Director/General Manager [Spanish]; Jake Stephen Hockley Wright [1972] Director

Duke's 1823 LLP
Incorporated: 4 April 2014 *Employees:* 32
Net Worth: £12,090,339 *Total Assets:* £12,580,872
Registered Office: Duke's, Brewery Square, Dorchester, DT1 1GA
Officers: Garry Peter Batt [1956] Member; Guy John Schwinge [1964] Member

Dumpton School
Incorporated: 2 August 1968 *Employees:* 98
Net Worth: £6,519,501 *Total Assets:* £7,066,961
Registered Office: Deans Grove House, Wimborne, Dorset, BH21 7AF
Activities: Primary education
Officers: Edrys Margaret Barkham [1960] Director/Teacher; Hugh Dean Cocke [1955] Director/Retired Headmaster; Camilla Joyce Culley [1965] Director/Training Self Employed; Benjamin Davies [1970] Director; Nicholas Alexander Hopwood [1972] Marketing Director; Nicola Louise Hunter [1976] Director/Teacher; Charles John Jarrold [1965] Director/CEO British Printing Industry Federation; Dr Torlief Rene Skule [1965] Director/General Medical Practitioner [Danish]; Mark Richard Timberlake [1964] Director/Solicitor; Catherine Ann Waterman [1951] Director/Employee Relations Manager; Simon David West [1955] Director/Chartered Surveyor

Dunbia (UK)
Incorporated: 5 June 1997 *Employees:* 1,531
Previous: Dawn Meats (UK)
Net Worth: £58,145,056 *Total Assets:* £141,165,664
Registered Office: Michael House, Castle Street, Exeter, Devon, EX4 3LQ
Activities: Production of meat and poultry meat products
Parent: QDB Holdings Unlimited Compmany
Officers: Sean Breen [1958] Director [Irish]; Niall Browne [1972] Director [Irish]; James George Dobson [1953] Director; Matthew Samuel Dobson [1982] Director; Michael Queally [1963] Director [Irish]

Dundee Merchant Wind Park Limited
Incorporated: 31 January 2002
Net Worth: £4,493,434 *Total Assets:* £5,276,884
Registered Office: Lion House, Rowcroft, Stroud, Glos, GL5 3BY
Activities: Production of electricity
Parent: Ecotricty Group Limited
Officers: Tom Cowling, Secretary; Asif Rehmanwala [1976] Director/Chief Operating Officer; Dale Vince [1961] Director

Dunkerton Properties LLP
Incorporated: 28 June 2010 *Employees:* 1
Net Worth: £20,721,976 *Total Assets:* £25,809,450
Registered Office: Dowdeswell Park, London Road, Cheltenham, Glos, GL52 6UT
Officers: Julian Marc Dunkerton [1965] Member

Dunlop Aerospace Group Limited
Incorporated: 2 June 1998
Net Worth: £152,268,000 *Total Assets:* £160,171,008
Registered Office: Atlantic House, Aviation Park West, Bournemouth International Airport, Christchurch, Dorset, BH23 6EW
Activities: Non-trading company
Parent: Meggitt Acquisition Limited
Officers: Simon Robert Grant, Secretary; Ian Keith Pargeter [1965] Director/Group Financial Controller; Marina Louise Thomas [1976] Director/Company Secretary

Dunlop Aerospace Holdings Limited
Incorporated: 16 July 1998
Net Worth: £180,012,000 *Total Assets:* £344,784,000
Registered Office: Atlantic House, Aviation Park West, Bournemouth International Airport, Christchurch, Dorset, BH23 6EW
Activities: Non-trading company
Parent: Dunlop Aerospace Group Limited
Officers: Simon Robert Grant, Secretary; Ian Keith Pargeter [1965] Director/Group Financial Controller; Marina Louise Thomas [1976] Director/Company Secretary

Dunlop Aerospace Overseas Limited
Incorporated: 16 July 1998
Net Worth: £95,035,000 *Total Assets:* £102,263,000
Registered Office: Atlantic House, Aviation Park West, Bournemouth International Airport, Christchurch, Dorset, BH23 6EW
Activities: Non-trading company
Parent: Meggitt Aerospace Holdings Limited
Officers: Simon Robert Grant, Secretary; Ian Keith Pargeter [1965] Director/Group Financial Controller; Marina Louise Thomas [1976] Director/Company Secretary

Dunlop Holdings Limited
Incorporated: 12 November 1896
Net Worth: £151,450,000 *Total Assets:* £151,507,008
Registered Office: Atlantic House, Aviation Park West, Bournemouth International Airport, Christchurch, Dorset, BH23 6EW
Activities: Non-trading company
Parent: Meggitt Aerospace Holdings Limited
Officers: Simon Robert Grant, Secretary; Ian Keith Pargeter [1965] Director/Group Financial Controller; Marina Louise Thomas [1976] Director/Company Secretary

Dunlop Limited
Incorporated: 25 November 1970
Net Worth: £90,823,000 *Total Assets:* £200,572,000
Registered Office: Atlantic House, Aviation Park West, Bournemouth International Airport, Christchurch, Dorset, BH23 6EW
Activities: Non-trading company
Parent: Dunlop Holdings Limited
Officers: Simon Robert Grant, Secretary; Ian Keith Pargeter [1965] Director/Group Financial Controller; Marina Louise Thomas [1976] Director/Company Secretary

Dunns Estates (Exeter) Limited
Incorporated: 7 February 2017
Net Worth: £3,596,851 *Total Assets:* £3,596,851
Registered Office: Georges Farm, Cutsey Trull, Taunton, Somerset, TA3 7NY
Activities: Other letting and operating of own or leased real estate
Major Shareholder: Nigel Graeme Haydon Dunn
Officers: Nigel Graeme Haydon Dunn [1959] Director

Dunns Motors (Holdings) Limited
Incorporated: 12 February 2015
Net Worth: £2,378,134 *Total Assets:* £3,936,639
Registered Office: Georges Farm, Cutsey Trull, Taunton, Somerset, TA3 7NY
Activities: Other letting and operating of own or leased real estate
Shareholders: Nigel Graeme Haydon Dunn; Valerie Eileen Dunn
Officers: Nigel Graeme Haydon Dunn [1959] Director

Dunsmere Developments Limited
Incorporated: 20 November 1987 *Employees:* 5
Net Worth: £200,024 *Total Assets:* £3,660,848
Registered Office: Tangley Farmhouse, Tangley, Andover, Hants, SP11 0RZ
Activities: Construction of domestic buildings
Major Shareholder: Ala John Dale
Officers: Lesley Dale, Secretary; Alan John Dale [1949] Director/Builder

Dunview Limited
Incorporated: 30 January 2006 *Employees:* 204
Net Worth: £7,312,026 *Total Assets:* £15,785,040
Registered Office: Broadoak, Newnham on Severn, Glos, GL14 1JF
Activities: Activities of head offices
Major Shareholder: Dominic Francis Quinlan
Officers: Michelle Jane Evans, Secretary/Accountant; Michelle Jane Evans [1972] Director/Accountant; Nicola McGrail [1948] Director; Dominic Francis Quinlan [1971] Director

Duo Assets Limited
Incorporated: 30 June 2004 *Employees:* 55
Previous: Denbow Assets Limited
Net Worth: £510,762 *Total Assets:* £14,628,221
Registered Office: Silverdown House, 5 Silverdown Office Park, Fair Oak Close, Clyst, Honiton, Exeter, Devon, EX5 2UX
Activities: Other professional, scientific and technical activities n.e.c.
Shareholders: Keith Edward Darch; Patriot Fjarfesting EHF
Officers: Owen Stanley Bolt [1964] Managing Director; Keith Edward Darch [1949] Director; Patrick Doran [1959] Director; Laura Betty McAlister [1982] Director; Donna Williams [1966] Director/Accountant

Dura Automotive Limited
Incorporated: 17 December 1954
Net Worth Deficit: £15,460,000 *Total Assets:* £3,899,000
Registered Office: c/o DAC Beachcroft LLP, Portwall Place, Portwall Lane, Bristol, BS1 9HS
Activities: Manufacture of other parts and accessories for motor vehicles
Parent: Dura Holdings Limited
Officers: Pamela Lynn McIntyre [1983] Director/Corporate Controller [American]

Durable (UK) Limited
Incorporated: 21 April 1983 *Employees:* 21
Net Worth: £6,334,238 *Total Assets:* £8,127,359
Registered Office: 10 Nimrod Way, Wimborne, Dorset, BH21 7SH
Activities: Agents involved in the sale of a variety of goods
Parent: Durable Hunke und Jochheim GmbH & Co KG
Officers: Russell Shivas, Secretary; Matthias Wolfgang Gunther Laue [1965] Director [German]; Horst-Werner Maier-Hunke [1938] Director [German]; Andreas Michael Schonwalder [1963] Director/Vice President International Operations [German]; Sean David Starkey [1965] Managing Director

Duresta Upholstery Limited
Incorporated: 15 June 1938 *Employees:* 183
Net Worth: £3,068,898 *Total Assets:* £5,969,938
Registered Office: 1 Hampton Park West, Melksham, Wilts, SN12 6GU
Activities: Manufacture of other furniture
Parent: Sofa Brands International Limited
Officers: Emma Victoria Jones, Secretary/Accountant; William John Cawson [1981] Director; Clive Neville Kenyon-Brown [1960] Managing Director; Ciaran Andrew McMahon [1968] Director [Irish]; Ian Oliver [1963] Director; Philip Sharrocks [1967] Director; Colin Howard Swan [1960] Director

Durlston Court School Trust Limited
Incorporated: 23 January 1973 *Employees:* 94
Net Worth: £2,553,155 *Total Assets:* £4,324,963
Registered Office: Durlston Court School, Becton Lane, Barton on Sea, New Milton, Hants, BH25 7AQ
Activities: Primary education
Officers: Andrew Robert Thomas, Secretary; Chandra Clive Ashfield [1965] Financial Director; Angela Joan Bolam [1956] Director/Self-Employed Business Consultancy; Paul Anthony Etheridge [1957] Director/Business Owner; Peter John Hardy [1955] Director/Teacher; Dr James Russell Hickey [1971] Director/Doctor; Nicola Clare James [1968] Director/Housewife; Colin Geoffrey Lewis [1959] Director/Investment Manager; Richard Maurice Porter [1968] Managing Director; Robert Peter Wilsher [1966] Director/Retired

Dutch Oak Tree Foundation
Incorporated: 13 August 2002
Net Worth: £150,860,656 *Total Assets:* £150,995,184
Registered Office: Narrow Quay House, Narrow Quay, Bristol, BS1 4QA
Activities: Non-trading company
Officers: Pieter Willem Jacobus de Rijcke [1967] Director/CEO [Dutch]; Michael Balfour Hutchings [1948] Director/Solicitor; Pieter Van Der Meijden [1954] Director/Secretary to The Board [Dutch]

Dutypoint Limited
Incorporated: 19 May 2014 *Employees:* 64
Net Worth: £2,465,364 *Total Assets:* £7,390,584
Registered Office: Unit 11 Shepherd Road, Cole Avenue, Gloucester, GL2 5EL
Activities: Manufacture of pumps
Officers: Daniel Richard Freeman [1977] Director; Nigel Alex Freeman [1984] Director; Robert James Freeman [1972] Director; Russell Charles Freeman [1974] Director

DVG Limited
Incorporated: 8 February 2010 *Employees:* 138
Net Worth: £1,959,809 *Total Assets:* £4,508,536
Registered Office: The Chocolate Factory, Keynsham, Bristol, BS31 2AU
Activities: Veterinary activities
Officers: Amanda Jane Davis [1968] Director; David Robert Geoffrey Hillier [1962] Director

DWML Holdings Limited
Incorporated: 10 June 2015 *Employees:* 137
Previous: FACO123 Limited
Net Worth: £4,254,544 *Total Assets:* £17,645,494
Registered Office: 1 & 2 Mulberry Court, Lustleigh Close, Matford Business Park, Marsh Barton Trading Estate, Exeter, Devon, EX2 8PW
Activities: Activities of head offices
Officers: Stuart Crebo [1953] Director; Emily Anne Delve [1982] Finance Director; Steven Eric Paul Hadley [1972] Director; Richard Wynford Marsh [1963] Sales and Marketing Director; Dominic Treacher [1960] Operations Director; Allan John Vodden [1949] Director

Dycem Limited
Incorporated: 19 August 1996 *Employees:* 88
Net Worth: £2,365,418 *Total Assets:* £5,498,775
Registered Office: Unit 2-4 Ashley Trading Estate, Ashley Parade, Bristol, BS2 9BB
Activities: Manufacture of other plastic products
Parent: SEAFox Dycem 2 Limited
Officers: Michael Hugh Bell, Secretary; Iain Henry Abrahams [1959] Director/Investor; Michael Hugh Bell [1962] Director; Stewart George Cantley [1959] Director; Mark Dalziel [1959] Director; George Elliott Nicholson [1982] Director/Finance; Stanislaus Eduard Schmidt-Chiari [1984] Director/Investor [Austrian]

Dynamatic Limited
Incorporated: 10 May 2007 *Employees:* 206
Net Worth: £13,056,000 *Total Assets:* £23,112,000
Registered Office: Cheney Manor, Swindon, Wilts, SN2 2PZ
Activities: Machining
Parent: Dynamatic Technologies Limited
Officers: Geoffrey William Dore [1967] Director/Chartered Accountant; Michael John Handley [1955] Director; Steven Andrew Hayes [1972] Director/Engineer; Primila Malhoutra [1966] Director/Businesswoman; Udayant Malhoutra [1965] Director [Indian]; Arvind Mishra [1974] Managing Director [Indian]; James Tucker [1972] Director

Dynavour Limited
Incorporated: 18 January 2002 *Employees:* 42
Net Worth: £1,064,297 *Total Assets:* £4,356,353
Registered Office: Gloucester House, 29 Brunswick Square, Gloucester, GL1 1UN
Activities: Residential care activities for learning difficulties, mental health and substance abuse
Parent: McGurk Group Limited
Officers: Eamonn Francis McGurk, Secretary; Generaldine Anne Mary Ford [1970] Director; Brian Andrew McGurk [1967] Director; Eamonn Francis McGurk [1965] Director

Dyson Estates Limited
Incorporated: 1 June 2004
Net Worth: £16,710,000 *Total Assets:* £32,510,000
Registered Office: Tetbury Hill, Malmesbury, Wilts, SN16 0RP
Activities: Other business support service activities n.e.c.
Parent: Dyson James Limited
Officers: Martin William Bowen, Secretary; Martin William Bowen [1968] Director; Jorn Peter Jensen [1964] Director/Chief Financial Officer [Danish]; James Rowan [1965] Director

Dyson Finance Limited
Incorporated: 15 March 2007 *Employees:* 10
Net Worth: £27,793,000 *Total Assets:* £968,896,000
Registered Office: Dyson Limited, Tetbury Hill, Malmesbury, Wilts, SN16 0RP
Activities: Manufacture of electric domestic appliances
Parent: Dyson James Limited
Officers: Martin William Bowen, Secretary; Martin William Bowen [1968] Director; Ruth Hopkins [1966] Director of Tax & Treasury; Jorn Peter Jensen [1964] Director/Chief Financial Officer [Danish]; James Rowan [1965] Director

Dyson International Limited
Incorporated: 15 July 1991
Net Worth: £31,300,000 *Total Assets:* £57,300,000
Registered Office: Tetbury Hill, Malmesbury, Wilts, SN16 0RP
Activities: Manufacture of electric domestic appliances
Shareholders: Dyson Limited; Dyson Limited
Officers: Martin William Bowen, Secretary; Martin William Bowen [1968] Director; Jorn Peter Jensen [1964] Director/Chief Financial Officer [Danish]; James Rowan [1965] Director

Dyson James Group Limited
Incorporated: 25 November 2009 *Employees:* 9,110
Net Worth: £345,000,000 *Total Assets:* £1,996,999,936
Registered Office: Tetbury Hill, Malmesbury, Wilts, SN16 0RP
Activities: Manufacture of electric domestic appliances
Parent: Holkham Group Limited
Officers: Martin William Bowen, Secretary; Jacob Dyson [1972] Director/Design Engineer; Sir James Dyson [1947] Director/Designer; Samuel Dyson [1978] Director/Musician; David Warren Arthur East [1961] Director; Anthony Hobson [1947] Director; Jorn Peter Jensen [1964] Director/Chief Financial Officer [Danish]; Rodney O'Neal [1953] Director [American]; Ian Stuart Robertson [1958] Director; James Rowan [1965] Director

Dyson James Limited
Incorporated: 18 May 1999
Net Worth: £27,600,000 *Total Assets:* £28,000,000
Registered Office: Tetbury Hill, Malmesbury, Wilts, SN16 0RP
Activities: Manufacture of electric domestic appliances
Parent: Dyson James Group Limited
Officers: Martin William Bowen, Secretary; Martin William Bowen [1968] Director; Jorn Peter Jensen [1964] Director/Chief Financial Officer [Danish]; James Rowan [1965] Director

Dyson Limited
Incorporated: 8 July 1991 *Employees:* 873
Net Worth: £41,000,000 *Total Assets:* £305,300,000
Registered Office: Tetbury Hill, Malmesbury, Wilts, SN16 0RP
Activities: Manufacture of electric domestic appliances
Parent: Dyson James Limited
Officers: Martin William Bowen, Secretary; Martin William Bowen [1968] Director; Jorn Peter Jensen [1964] Director/Chief Financial Officer [Danish]; James Rowan [1965] Director

Dyson Technology Limited
Incorporated: 14 November 1985 *Employees:* 2,697
Net Worth: £454,200,000 *Total Assets:* £1,344,600,064
Registered Office: Tetbury Hill, Malmesbury, Wilts, SN16 0RP
Activities: Manufacture of electric domestic appliances
Parent: Dyson James Limited
Officers: Martin William Bowen, Secretary; Martin William Bowen [1968] Director; Jorn Peter Jensen [1964] Director/Chief Financial Officer [Danish]; James Rowan [1965] Director

E & H Drylining & Plastering Limited
Incorporated: 27 June 2000 *Employees:* 19
Net Worth: £2,116,002 *Total Assets:* £4,013,421
Registered Office: The Courtyard, 33 Duke Street, Trowbridge, Wilts, BA14 8EA
Activities: Plastering
Officers: Elizabeth Jane Harbour, Secretary; Richard John Dee [1969] Commercial Director; Elizabeth Jane Harbour [1953] Director/Secretary; Stephen John Harbour [1954] Managing Director

E & L Rental Properties Limited
Incorporated: 9 August 2016 *Employees:* 2
Net Worth: £5,288,256 *Total Assets:* £11,814,119
Registered Office: Abacus House, 129 North Hill, Plymouth, PL4 8JY
Activities: Other letting and operating of own or leased real estate
Shareholders: Esmail Kamaie; Linda Kamaie
Officers: Esmail Kamaie [1953] Director; Linda Kamaie [1960] Director

E & T Developments Limited
Incorporated: 20 November 2001 *Employees:* 3
Net Worth: £1,331,185 *Total Assets:* £4,525,261
Registered Office: West Park House, Milford Lane, Tamerton Foliot, Plymouth, PL5 4NG
Activities: Buying and selling of own real estate
Shareholders: Steven John Trott; Marc Edworthy
Officers: Clare Louise Trott, Secretary; Marc Edworthy [1972] Director/House Renovations; Steven John Trott [1970] Director/Electrician

E Development (2) Limited
Incorporated: 11 October 2011
Net Worth: £218,000 *Total Assets:* £26,915,000
Registered Office: 2nd Floor, Lysander House, Catbrain Lane, Cribbs Causeway, Bristol, BS10 7TQ
Activities: Activities of insurance agents and brokers
Major Shareholder: Arron Fraser Andrew Banks
Officers: Arron Fraser Andrew Banks [1966] Director/Insurance Broker; Elizabeth Bilney [1976] Director

E T Holdings Limited
Incorporated: 8 June 1994 *Employees:* 261
Net Worth: £12,644,180 *Total Assets:* £24,488,060
Registered Office: Gammaton Road, Bideford, Devon, EX39 4FG
Activities: Activities of head offices
Major Shareholder: Nigel John Evans
Officers: Susan Jayne Evans, Secretary; Alison Dunbar Evans [1941] Director; Nigel John Evans [1962] Director; Susan Jayne Evans [1968] Director; Thomas John Evans [1989] Director; Walter John Evans [1941] Director; Andrew John Taylor [1973] Finance Director

E T M Contractors Limited
Incorporated: 23 September 1994
Net Worth: £1,693,633 *Total Assets:* £4,818,219
Registered Office: 81 Hartcliffe Way, Bristol, BS3 5RN
Activities: Construction of commercial buildings
Parent: E T M Const' & Recycling Holdings Ltd
Officers: Hilary Anne McCormack, Secretary; Edward Thomas McCormack [1954] Director/Civil Engineer; Amy Louise McCormack [1985] Director; Andrew James McCormack [1982] Director

E-Mex Home Funding Limited
Incorporated: 22 April 1987
Net Worth: £15,591,000 *Total Assets:* £96,897,000
Registered Office: Nationwide House, Pipers Way, Swindon, Wilts, SN38 1NW
Activities: Financial intermediation not elsewhere classified
Parent: Nationwide Building Society
Officers: Timothy Joseph Carter [1970] Director of Product Operations; Jonathan Jasper Haydn Davy [1965] Director/Head of Collections and Recoveries; Julia Mary Roberts Dunn [1965] Director/Chief Risk Officer; Muir James Mathieson [1974] Director of Financial Controls & Information Management; Christopher Stuart Rhodes [1963] Director; Paul Wootton [1979] Director/Head of Specialist Mortgages

E.I.C. Group Limited
Incorporated: 2 April 2003 *Employees:* 163
Net Worth: £12,890,514 *Total Assets:* £22,847,888
Registered Office: Alphinbrook Road, Alphington, Exeter, Devon, EX2 8TJ
Activities: Other business support service activities n.e.c.
Shareholders: Richard James Jacobs; Clive Nicholas Jacobs
Officers: Clive Nicholas Jacobs [1949] Director; Jacqueline Louise Jacobs [1969] Director; Matthew Jacobs [1976] Director; Paul Jacobs [1974] Director; Richard James Jacobs [1944] Director

E.I.C.(Exeter) Limited
Incorporated: 1 July 1943 *Employees:* 6
Net Worth: £10,847,214 *Total Assets:* £19,616,808
Registered Office: Alphinbrook Road, Alphington, Exeter, Devon, EX2 8TJ
Activities: Other letting and operating of own or leased real estate
Parent: E.I.C. Group Limited
Officers: Jacqueline Louise Jacobs, Secretary; Clive Nicholas Jacobs [1949] Director; Jacqueline Louise Jacobs [1969] Director; Matthew Jacobs [1976] Director; Paul Jacobs [1974] Director; Richard James Jacobs [1944] Director

E3 Media Limited
Incorporated: 5 March 1997 *Employees:* 66
Net Worth: £2,806,492 *Total Assets:* £3,922,938
Registered Office: Unit 2.1-2.3 Paintworks, Bath Road, Bristol, BS4 3EH
Activities: Other information technology service activities
Parent: NGP3 Limited
Officers: Kelwyn Stuart Avery, Secretary/Director; Kelwyn Stuart Avery [1975] Director; Michael Douglas Bennett [1974] Director; Victoria Louise James [1968] Director

Eagle Investments Limited
Incorporated: 10 March 1955 *Employees:* 8
Net Worth: £26,963,144 *Total Assets:* £30,660,420
Registered Office: Eagle House, Strand, Exmouth, Devon, EX8 1AL
Activities: Construction of domestic buildings
Shareholder: Roquier Holdings Limited
Officers: Marie Evernden, Secretary; Rachael Manning, Secretary; Gary James Norton, Secretary; James Daniel Fowler [1974] Director/Fund Manager; Joanna Elizabeth Fowler [1972] Director; John Daniel Fowler [1944] Director/Property Developer; Nicholas John Fowler [1981] Director/Investment Banker; Susan Margaret Fowler [1952] Director

Eagle One Country Shopping Limited
Incorporated: 14 April 1998 *Employees:* 2
Net Worth: £8,262,431 *Total Assets:* £21,474,094
Registered Office: Eagle House, 1 Babbage Way, Exeter Science Park, Exeter, Devon, EX5 2FN
Activities: Other letting and operating of own or leased real estate
Parent: Eagle One Foc Holdings Limited
Officers: Paul James Goodes [1965] Director/Accountant; Nicholas Ian Hole [1961] Director/Chartered Surveyor; Jonathan Michael Symons [1970] Director; Paul Raymond Withers [1965] Director

Eagle One Estates Limited
Incorporated: 5 October 1983 *Employees:* 2
Net Worth: £5,918,202 *Total Assets:* £14,234,004
Registered Office: Eagle House, 1 Babbage Way, Exeter Science Park, Exeter, Devon, EX5 2FN
Activities: Other letting and operating of own or leased real estate
Parent: Eagle One Limited
Officers: Paul James Goodes [1965] Director/Accountant; Nicholas Ian Hole [1961] Director/Chartered Surveyor; Paul Raymond Withers [1965] Director

Eagle One Foc Holdings Limited
Incorporated: 9 January 2001 *Employees:* 6
Net Worth: £10,954,000 *Total Assets:* £29,535,000
Registered Office: Eagle House, 1 Babbage Way, Exeter Science Park, Exeter, Devon, EX5 2FN
Activities: Activities of other holding companies n.e.c.
Major Shareholder: Mark Russell Kay
Officers: Paul James Goodes [1965] Director/Accountant; Nicholas Ian Hole [1961] Director/Chartered Surveyor

Eagle One Holdings Limited
Incorporated: 22 February 2001 *Employees:* 7
Net Worth: £5,571,000 *Total Assets:* £13,095,000
Registered Office: Eagle House, 1 Babbage Way, Exeter Science Park, Exeter, Devon, EX5 2FN
Activities: Activities of construction holding companies
Major Shareholder: Mark Russell Kay
Officers: Paul James Goodes [1965] Director/Accountant; Nicholas Ian Hole [1961] Director/Chartered Surveyor

Eagle One Homes Limited
Incorporated: 26 November 1985 *Employees:* 7
Net Worth: £4,917,642 *Total Assets:* £7,830,201
Registered Office: Eagle House, 1 Babbage Way, Exeter Science Park, Exeter, Devon, EX5 2FN
Activities: Construction of domestic buildings
Parent: Eagle One Holdings Limited
Officers: Christopher David Fayers [1962] Director/Surveyor; Paul James Goodes [1965] Director/Accountant; Nicholas Ian Hole [1961] Director/Chartered Surveyor; Jonathan Michael Symons [1970] Director; Paul Raymond Withers [1965] Director

Eagle One Investment Holdings Limited
Incorporated: 9 January 2001 *Employees:* 40
Net Worth: £22,623,000 *Total Assets:* £106,350,000
Registered Office: Eagle House, 1 Babbage Way, Exeter Science Park, Exeter, Devon, EX5 2FN
Activities: Activities of other holding companies n.e.c.
Major Shareholder: Mark Russell Kay
Officers: Paul James Goodes [1965] Director/Accountant; Nicholas Ian Hole [1961] Director/Chartered Surveyor

Eagle One Limited
Incorporated: 24 February 1983 *Employees:* 40
Net Worth: £8,245,695 *Total Assets:* £86,559,856
Registered Office: Eagle House, 1 Babbage Way, Exeter Science Park, Exeter, Devon, EX5 2FN
Activities: Development of building projects
Parent: Eagle One Securities Limited
Officers: Christopher David Fayers [1962] Director/Surveyor; Paul James Goodes [1965] Director/Accountant; Nicholas Ian Hole [1961] Director/Chartered Surveyor; Jonathan Michael Symons [1970] Director; Paul Raymond Withers [1965] Director

Eagle One Mmiii Limited
Incorporated: 11 December 2002 *Employees:* 5
Net Worth: £1,210,249 *Total Assets:* £5,873,366
Registered Office: Eagle House, 1 Babbage Way, Exeter Science Park, Exeter, Devon, EX5 2FN
Activities: Buying and selling of own real estate
Parent: Eagle One Securities Limited
Officers: Christopher David Fayers [1962] Director/Surveyor; Paul James Goodes [1965] Director/Accountant; Nicholas Ian Hole [1961] Director/Chartered Surveyor; Paul Raymond Withers [1965] Director

Eagle One Residential Limited
Incorporated: 21 July 2015 *Employees:* 4
Net Worth: £188,675 *Total Assets:* £3,957,033
Registered Office: Eagle House, 1 Babbage Way, Exeter Science Park, Exeter, EX5 2FN
Activities: Construction of domestic buildings
Parent: Eagle One Homes Limited
Officers: Christopher David Fayers [1962] Director; Paul James Goodes [1965] Managing Director; Nicholas Ian Hole [1961] Director; Jonathan Michael Symons [1970] Director

Eagle One Retail Limited
Incorporated: 13 October 1998
Net Worth: £6,308,328 *Total Assets:* £18,293,222
Registered Office: Eagle House, 1 Babbage Way, Exeter Science Park, Exeter, Devon, EX5 2FN
Activities: Other letting and operating of own or leased real estate
Parent: Eagle One Securities Limited
Officers: Paul James Goodes [1965] Director/Accountant; Nicholas Ian Hole [1961] Director/Chartered Surveyor; Jonathan Michael Symons [1970] Director

Eagle One Village Shopping Limited
Incorporated: 12 June 1996
Net Worth: £2,691,949 *Total Assets:* £7,689,039
Registered Office: Eagle House, 1 Babbage Way, Exeter Science Park, Exeter, Devon, EX5 2FN
Activities: Other letting and operating of own or leased real estate
Parent: Eagle One Foc Holdings Limited
Officers: Paul James Goodes [1965] Director/Accountant; Nicholas Ian Hole [1961] Director/Chartered Surveyor

Eagle Star Holdings Limited
Incorporated: 22 February 1979
Net Worth: £1,175,712,000 *Total Assets:* £1,175,712,000
Registered Office: The Grange, Bishops Cleeve, Cheltenham, Glos, GL52 8XX
Activities: Activities of head offices
Shareholders: Zurich Financial Services (UKISA) Limited; Zurich Financial Services (UKISA) Limited
Officers: Helen Alison Pickford [1971] Director; James Richard Sykes [1961] Director

Eagle Strategic Property Limited
Incorporated: 15 September 2003 *Employees:* 10
Net Worth: £8,575,717 *Total Assets:* £22,072,548
Registered Office: Eagle Tower, Montpellier Drive, Cheltenham, Glos, GL50 1TA
Activities: Buying and selling of own real estate
Parent: Eagle Strategic Land Limited
Officers: Alexander James Harrington-Griffin [1984] Director; Eva Christin Harrington-Griffin [1954] Marketing Director [Swedish]; Victoria Lauren Annette Harrington-Griffin [1992] Director [Swedish]; Cherie Jane Lampitt [1978] Director

Earthline Exchange Limited
Incorporated: 16 July 2014 *Employees:* 194
Net Worth: £42,917,260 *Total Assets:* £69,182,688
Registered Office: The Upper Lime Kiln Works, Bytham Road, Ogbourne St George, Marlborough, Wilts, SN8 1TD
Activities: Activities of head offices
Shareholders: Matthew Simon Coplestone; Philip Clive Coplestone; Rodney Philip Coplestone
Officers: Matthew Simon Coplestone [1969] Director; Philip Clive Coplestone [1972] Director; Rodney Philip Coplestone [1945] Director

Earthline Holdings Limited
Incorporated: 2 March 2004 *Employees:* 3
Net Worth: £4,774,985 *Total Assets:* £10,017,626
Registered Office: The Upper Lime Kiln Works, Bytham Road, Ogbourne St George, Marlborough, Wilts, SN8 1TD
Activities: Activities of head offices
Shareholders: Philip Clive Coplestone; Matthew Simon Coplestone; Rodney Philip Coplestone
Officers: Matthew Simon Coplestone, Secretary/Director; Matthew Simon Coplestone [1969] Director; Philip Clive Coplestone [1972] Director; Rodney Philip Coplestone [1945] Director

Earthline Limited
Incorporated: 24 August 1990 *Employees:* 193
Net Worth: £3,968,705 *Total Assets:* £27,892,744
Registered Office: The Upper Lime Kiln Works, Bytham Road, Ogbourne St George, Marlborough, Wilts, SN8 1TD
Activities: Operation of gravel and sand pits; mining of clays and kaolin
Shareholders: Matthew Simon Coplestone; Rodney Philip Coplestone
Officers: Matthew Simon Coplestone, Secretary/Contractor; Matthew Simon Coplestone [1969] Director/Contractor; Philip Clive Coplestone [1972] Director/Contractor; Rodney Philip Coplestone [1945] Director/Contractor

East Bros.(Timber) Limited
Incorporated: 30 August 1945 *Employees:* 32
Net Worth: £2,582,182 *Total Assets:* £5,214,972
Registered Office: The Saw Mills, West Dean, Salisbury, Wilts, SP5 1JA
Activities: Silviculture and other forestry activities
Parent: East Brothers (Holdings) Ltd
Officers: James Andrew East, Secretary/Director; Richard John Baker [1965] Director; Andrew Charles East [1942] Director/Timber Merchant; James Andrew East [1973] Director; Roger East [1965] Director; Mark John Gilbert [1978] Director

East Devon Properties Limited
Incorporated: 21 January 2013 *Employees:* 14
Net Worth: £6,101,928 *Total Assets:* £6,398,234
Registered Office: Sigma House, Oak View Close, Edginswell Park, Torquay, Devon, TQ2 7FF
Activities: Hotels and similar accommodation
Shareholders: Nigel Robert Fowler; Adrian Charles Fowler
Officers: Adrian Charles Fowler [1966] Director; Iris Hilda Mary Fowler [1935] Director; Nigel Robert Fowler [1962] Director

East Dorset Golf Club Limited
Incorporated: 27 June 1989 *Employees:* 67
Net Worth: £2,436,654 *Total Assets:* £5,246,034
Registered Office: Stafford House, 10 Prince of Wales Road, Dorchester, DT1 1PW
Activities: Operation of sports facilities
Shareholders: Graham John Packer; Cilfa A/S
Officers: Ian Butcher, Secretary; Arthur Walter John Champion [1944] Director; Count Christian Lerche [1930] Director [Danish]

East London Lift Accommodation Services Limited
Incorporated: 7 February 2003
Net Worth Deficit: £4,502,000 *Total Assets:* £37,394,000
Registered Office: Challenge House, International Drive, Tewkesbury Business Park, Tewkesbury, Glos, GL20 8UQ
Activities: Other letting and operating of own or leased real estate
Parent: East London Lift Company Limited
Officers: Daniel Peter Bevan, Secretary; Jamie Russell Andrews [1970] Investment Director; Paul Simon Andrews [1970] Director; Henry Black [1975] Director/Chief Finance Officer; Paul Edward Brand [1967] Director; Neil Rae [1971] Director

East London Lift Accommodation Services No2 Limited
Incorporated: 3 November 2005
Net Worth Deficit: £8,552,000 *Total Assets:* £36,013,000
Registered Office: Challenge House, International Drive, Tewkesbury Business Park, Tewkesbury, Glos, GL20 8UQ
Activities: Other letting and operating of own or leased real estate
Parent: East London Lift Holdco No 2 Limited
Officers: Daniel Peter Bevan, Secretary; Jamie Russell Andrews [1970] Investment Director; Paul Simon Andrews [1970] Director; Henry Black [1975] Director/Chief Finance Officer; Paul Edward Brand [1967] Director; Neil Rae [1971] Director

Eastern Business Park Limited
Incorporated: 13 December 2002 *Employees:* 3
Net Worth: £4,409,908 *Total Assets:* £16,150,459
Registered Office: The Manor, Boddington Lane, Boddington, Cheltenham, Glos, GL51 0TJ
Activities: Other letting and operating of own or leased real estate
Parent: Robert Hitchins Limited
Officers: Jonathan James Stewart Dunley, Secretary; Jonathan James Stewart Dunley [1970] Director; Jeremy Charles Hitchins [1954] Director; Simon Jeremy Tothill [1965] Director/Chartered Surveyor

Eastleigh Care Group Limited
Incorporated: 23 April 2013 *Employees:* 320
Net Worth: £6,746,403 *Total Assets:* £20,784,286
Registered Office: 90-91 East Street, South Molton, Devon, EX36 3DF
Activities: Activities of head offices
Major Shareholder: Garry John Wilson
Officers: Garry John Wilson [1960] Director

Eastleigh Care Homes - Raleigh Mead Limited
Incorporated: 30 April 2013
Net Worth: £1,391,702 *Total Assets:* £9,660,670
Registered Office: 90-91 East Street, South Molton, Devon, EX36 3DF
Activities: Other residential care activities n.e.c.
Parent: Eastleigh Care Group Limited
Officers: Garry John Wilson [1960] Director

Eastleigh Care Homes Limited
Incorporated: 24 April 2003 *Employees:* 12
Net Worth: £5,440,963 *Total Assets:* £8,719,532
Registered Office: 90-91 East Street, South Molton, Devon, EX36 3DF
Activities: Other residential care activities n.e.c.
Parent: Eastleigh Care Group Limited
Officers: Garry John Wilson [1960] Managing Director

Eastman Estates Limited
Incorporated: 27 February 1991 *Employees:* 3
Net Worth: £16,335,168 *Total Assets:* £34,813,776
Registered Office: Bishopbrook House, Cathedral Avenue, Wells, Somerset, BA5 1FD
Activities: Other letting and operating of own or leased real estate
Parent: Eastman Holdings Limited
Officers: David Eastman, Secretary; David Eastman [1954] Director; Simon David James Eastman [1976] Director; Elizabeth Ann Evans [1980] Director

Easton Grey Estate Limited
Incorporated: 26 September 1962 *Employees:* 1
Net Worth: £7,950,749 *Total Assets:* £8,533,091
Registered Office: 7 Dollar Street, Cirencester, Glos, GL7 2AS
Activities: Buying and selling of own real estate
Officers: Richard Randolph Mullings, Secretary; John William Tremayne [1947] Director/Property & Estate Manager; Vivienne Stella Tremayne [1950] Director/Property Manager

Eastwood Park Limited
Incorporated: 2 December 2002 *Employees:* 53
Net Worth: £2,767,215 *Total Assets:* £8,373,105
Registered Office: Winchester House, Deane Gate Avenue, Taunton, Somerset, TA1 2UH
Activities: Other education n.e.c.
Shareholders: Linda Wills; John Leslie Thatcher
Officers: John Leslie Thatcher, Secretary/Director; Pauline Skane Oliver [1968] Director/Accountant; John Leslie Thatcher [1954] Director; Linda Ann Willis [1947] Director

Eberspacher (U.K.) Limited
Incorporated: 6 July 1977 *Employees:* 84
Net Worth: £11,206,066 *Total Assets:* £15,202,317
Registered Office: Climate House, Yeoman Road, Ringwood, Hants, BH24 3FA
Activities: Manufacture of electrical and electronic equipment for motor vehicles and their engines
Parent: Eberspacher (UK) Holdings Limited
Officers: Stephen George Cranfield, Secretary; Vincent Lee Lee [1958] Managing Director; Martin Heinrich Peters [1966] Director/Chief Executive Officer [German]; Dr Joerg Schernikau [1968] Managing Director [German]

Eberspacher Exhaust Technology UK Limited
Incorporated: 3 December 2014 *Employees:* 90
Net Worth Deficit: £240,171 *Total Assets:* £8,171,783
Registered Office: Climate House, Yeoman Road, Ringwood, Hants, BH24 3FA
Activities: Manufacture of other parts and accessories for motor vehicles
Parent: Eberspacher Exhaust Technology International GmbH
Officers: Neil Keith Barlow, Secretary; Heinrich Andreas Baumann [1966] Director/COO/Managing Partner [German]; Francis Maine [1972] Director/JIS Plant Manager [French]; Martin Heinrich Peters [1966] Director/CFO/Managing Partner [German]; Dr Thomas Waldhier [1962] Director [German]

Eccles Special High Schools Company Limited
Incorporated: 11 December 2002 *Employees:* 3
Net Worth: £2,520,000 *Total Assets:* £13,080,000
Registered Office: Third Floor, Broad Quay House, Prince Street, Bristol, BS1 4DJ
Activities: Management of real estate on a fee or contract basis
Parent: XJ4 Holding Company Limited
Officers: Stephen Paul Hornby [1957] Director; Richard Little [1979] Investment Director; Julia Sarah McCabe [1970] Regional Director

Ecclesiastical Insurance Group PLC
Incorporated: 26 April 1983 *Employees:* 908
Net Worth: £507,468,992 *Total Assets:* £1,674,995,968
Registered Office: Beaufort House, Brunswick Road, Gloucester, GL1 1JZ
Activities: Activities of head offices
Parent: Allchurches Trust Limited
Officers: Rachael Jane Hall, Secretary; Timothy Joseph Carroll [1955] Director [Irish]; Robert David Charles Henderson [1948] Director; Mark Christopher John Hews [1969] Director/Group Chief Executive; John Francis Hylands [1951] Director/Actuary; Andrew McIntyre [1956] Director; Mr Chris Moulder [1958] Director; Caroline Helen Taylor [1962] Director; Stephanie Jacinta Whyte [1956] Director [Irish]; Christine Louise Wilson [1958] Director/Dean

Ecclesiastical Insurance Office Public Limited Company
Incorporated: 3 August 1887 *Employees:* 1,066
Net Worth: £592,473,024 *Total Assets:* £1,505,296,000
Registered Office: Beaufort House, Brunswick Road, Gloucester, GL1 1JZ
Activities: Non-life insurance
Parent: Ecclesiastical Insurance Group PLC
Officers: Rachael Jane Hall, Secretary; Timothy Joseph Carroll [1955] Director [Irish]; Robert David Charles Henderson [1948] Director; Mark Christopher John Hews [1969] Director/Group Chief Executive; John Francis Hylands [1951] Director/Actuary; Andrew McIntyre [1956] Director; Mr Chris Moulder [1958] Director; Caroline Helen Taylor [1962] Director; Stephanie Jacinta Whyte [1956] Director [Irish]; Christine Louise Wilson [1958] Director/Dean

Ecclesiastical Life Limited
Incorporated: 19 October 1929
Net Worth: £53,250,000 *Total Assets:* £143,322,000
Registered Office: Beaufort House, Brunswick Road, Gloucester, GL1 1JZ
Activities: Life insurance
Parent: Ecclesiastical Insurance Office PLC
Officers: Rachael Jane Hall, Secretary; Mark Christopher John Hews [1969] Director/Group Chief Executive; Paul David New [1960] Director/Actuary; Paul Pickernell [1978] Director/Actuary

Ecclesiastical Planning Services Limited
Incorporated: 11 September 1991
Previous: NAFD Services Limited
Net Worth: £424,000 *Total Assets:* £200,336,992
Registered Office: Beaufort House, Brunswick Road, Gloucester, GL1 1JZ
Activities: Activities of business and employers membership organisations
Parent: Ecclesiastical Insurance Group PLC
Officers: Rachael Jane Hall, Secretary; Christopher Alan Howard Clark [1960] Director; Denise Patricia Cockrem [1962] Director/Group Chief Finance Officer; David Robert Moore [1966] Director; Paul David New [1960] Director

Eco Holdings Limited
Incorporated: 3 February 2017 *Employees:* 38
Net Worth: £7,282,000 *Total Assets:* £18,670,000
Registered Office: Richmond Point, 43 Richmond Hill, Bournemouth, BH2 6LR
Activities: Activities of head offices
Major Shareholder: Trelawney Theo Dampney
Officers: Hugh Tristram Dampney [1960] Director/Farmer; Trelawney Theo Dampney [1958] Director/Manager

Eco Sustainable Solutions Limited
Incorporated: 30 October 1995 *Employees:* 38
Net Worth: £7,282,000 *Total Assets:* £18,670,000
Registered Office: Eco, Chapel Lane, Parley, Christchurch, Dorset, BH23 6BG
Activities: Production of electricity
Parent: Eco Holdings Limited
Officers: Jonathan Mark Adams [1978] Director/Chartered Accountant; Hugh Tristram Dampney [1960] Director/Farmer; Justin Theo Dampney [1984] Director; Trelawney Theo Dampney [1958] Director/Horticulturalist; Peter Justin Hardy [1975] Director

Eco-Bos Development Limited
Incorporated: 2 September 2008 *Employees:* 1
Net Worth: £8,034,427 *Total Assets:* £12,096,943
Registered Office: Prydis Accounts Limited, The Parade, Liskeard, Cornwall, PL14 6AF
Activities: Development of building projects
Parent: Orascom Development Holding AG
Officers: Henri Simon Trahair Davies, Secretary; Khaled Galal Bichara [1971] Director/Chief Executive [Egyptian]; Pierre Louis Marie Daniellou [1958] Director/Business Executive [French]; Denis Philippe Marie Musson [1963] Director [French]; Samih Onsi Naguib Sawiris [1957] Director/Chairman [Egyptian]; Alexander Harry Yule-Smith [1965] Director

Ecosurety Limited
Incorporated: 27 March 2003 *Employees:* 33
Previous: Budget Pack Limited
Net Worth: £1,829,850 *Total Assets:* £7,514,628
Registered Office: 1190 Park Avenue, Aztec West, Almondsbury, Bristol, BS32 4FP
Activities: Remediation activities and other waste management services
Major Shareholder: Stephen Christopher Clark
Officers: Stephen Christopher Clark [1978] Director; Louise Granville-Smith [1981] Finance Director; Roderic Reginald Leefe [1961] Director/Chairman; James Michael Piper [1987] Managing Director

Ecotricity Bonds PLC
Incorporated: 8 September 2010
Net Worth: £341,390 *Total Assets:* £49,213,936
Registered Office: Lion House, Rowcroft, Stroud, Glos, GL5 3BY
Activities: Other business support service activities n.e.c.
Parent: Ecotricity Group Ltd
Officers: Tom Cowling, Secretary; Asif Rehmanwala [1976] Director/Chief Operating Officer; Dale Andrew Vince [1961] Managing Director; Kate Vince [1974] Director

Ecotricity Generation Limited
Incorporated: 23 October 1995 *Employees:* 48
Previous: Ecotricity (Next Generation) Limited
Net Worth: £66,688,312 *Total Assets:* £89,017,232
Registered Office: Lion House, Rowcroft, Stroud, Glos, GL5 3BY
Activities: Combined office administrative service activities
Parent: Ecotricity Group Limited
Officers: Tom Cowling, Secretary; Asif Rehmanwala [1976] Director/Chief Operating Officer; Dale Vince [1961] Director/Consultant

Ecotricity Group Ltd
Incorporated: 4 March 1998 *Employees:* 821
Net Worth: £59,868,000 *Total Assets:* £238,388,992
Registered Office: Lion House, Rowcroft, Stroud, Glos, GL5 3BY
Activities: Activities of head offices
Major Shareholder: Dale Andrew Vince
Officers: Thomas Cowling, Secretary; Simon John Crowfoot [1966] Director; Daniel John Goodall [1979] Director/Technology; Asif Rehmanwala [1976] Director/Chief Operating Officer; Paul Kenneth Sands [1971] Director; Emily Jane Staples [1978] Director; Dale Vince [1961] Director; Kate Vince [1974] Director

Ecotricity Wind and Sun Parks (Issuing) Limited
Incorporated: 29 October 2014
Net Worth: £6,734,189 *Total Assets:* £153,503,552
Registered Office: Lion House, Rowcroft, Stroud, Glos, GL5 3BY
Activities: Activities of other holding companies n.e.c.
Parent: Ecotricity Group Limited
Officers: Tom Cowling, Secretary; Asif Rehmanwala [1976] Director/Chief Operating Officer; Dale Andrew Vince [1961] Director

Eden Project Limited
Incorporated: 14 November 1996 *Employees:* 466
Net Worth Deficit: £31,201,000 *Total Assets:* £52,374,000
Registered Office: Bodelva, Par, Cornwall, PL24 2SG
Activities: Other education n.e.c.
Parent: The Eden Trust
Officers: Tina Dawn Bingham, Secretary; Judith Donovan [1951] Director/Business Consultant; Angela Marshall [1951] Director; Dr Michael Maunder [1963] Director; Sir Timothy Bartel Smit [1954] Director; Peter John Stewart [1958] Campaign Director; Caroline Margaret White [1953] Director; Christian Andrew Simpson Wilson [1971] Director/Solicitor; Peter John Wroe [1978] Finance Director

Eden Research PLC
Incorporated: 22 June 1995 *Employees:* 5
Net Worth: £8,513,915 *Total Assets:* £10,585,878
Registered Office: 6 Priory Court Business Park, Poulton, Cirencester, Glos, GL7 5JB
Activities: Research and experimental development on biotechnology
Officers: Alexander John Abrey, Secretary; Alexander John Abrey [1979] Director/Accountant; Robin James Scott Cridland [1967] Director/Chief Financial Officer; Sean Michael Smith [1967] Director/Chief Executive [American]; Lykele Jurrit Van Der Broek [1954] Director [Dutch]

The Eden Trust
Incorporated: 16 July 2002 *Employees:* 476
Net Worth: £14,648,000 *Total Assets:* £58,411,000
Registered Office: Bodelva, Par, Cornwall, PL24 2SG
Activities: Other education n.e.c.
Officers: Tina Dawn Bingham, Secretary; Geoffrey Neil Austin [1965] Managing Director; Dr Adam Beaumont [1972] Director; Edward Anfrid Pringle Benthall [1963] Director/Technology Investor; Jonathan Ilan Drori [1960] Director; Kevin John Havelock [1957] Director/President Refreshment Category; Dame Georgina Mary Mace [1953] Director/Professor; Lucy Blaise Parker [1953] Director/Consultant; Penny Jane Parker [1962] Director Solicitor; Richard Harry Reid [1956] Director/Advisor; Sir Ralph Ferrers Alexander Vyvyan [1960] Director

Edentree Investment Management Limited
Incorporated: 6 July 1990
Previous: Ecclesiastical Investment Management Limited
Net Worth: £9,778,442 *Total Assets:* £18,091,620
Registered Office: Beaufort House, Brunswick Road, Gloucester, GL1 1JZ
Activities: Non-trading company
Parent: Ecclesiastical Insurance Office PLC
Officers: Rachael Jane Hall, Secretary; Denise Patricia Cockrem [1962] Director/Group Chief Finance Officer; Robert David Charles Henderson [1948] Director; Robin Hepworth [1963] Director/Chief Investment Officer; Mark Christopher John Hews [1969] Director/Group Chief Executive; Richard Stormont Hughes [1957] Director; Susan Round [1958] Director of Investments

Edenvale Turf (SW) Limited
Incorporated: 20 February 1997 *Employees:* 23
Net Worth: £2,668,631 *Total Assets:* £4,202,293
Registered Office: Courtlands, Dulford, Cullompton, Devon, EX15 2EQ
Activities: Growing of other perennial crops
Shareholders: Stephen James Light; Melanie Sue Light
Officers: Melanie Sue Light, Secretary/Farmer; Generald Frederick Light [1929] Director/Retired Farmer; Melanie Sue Light [1969] Director/Company Secretary; Phyllis May Light [1931] Director/Retired Farmer; Stephen James Light [1962] Director/Landscape Contractor

EDF Energy Nuclear Generation Limited
Incorporated: 30 June 1995 *Employees:* 5,554
Net Worth: £6,134,000,128 *Total Assets:* £22,773,999,616
Registered Office: Barnett Way, Barnwood, Gloucester, GL4 3RS
Activities: Production of electricity
Parent: British Energy Generation (UK) Limited
Officers: Sarah Ellen Merritt, Secretary; Brian Cowell [1961] Director; Andrew Goddard [1975] Director; Robert Guyler [1966] Director/Accountant; Jerry Paul Haller [1963] Director; Michael James Harrison [1961] Director; John Munro [1967] Director/Engineer; David Tomblin [1976] Director/Accountant; Paul Anthony Winkle [1966] Director

Edge Restaurants (NW) Limited
Incorporated: 10 April 2015 *Employees:* 606
Net Worth: £1,753,851 *Total Assets:* £10,354,236
Registered Office: Aldreth, Pearcroft Road, Stonehouse, Glos, GL10 2JY
Activities: Unlicenced restaurants and cafes
Major Shareholder: Mark David Nuttall
Officers: Corinna Nuttall [1979] Director; Mark David Nuttall [1975] Director

Edgecom Estates Ltd
Incorporated: 11 May 1999 *Employees:* 2
Net Worth: £2,786,444 *Total Assets:* £5,263,334
Registered Office: Maltravers House, Petters Way, Yeovil, Somerset, BA20 1SH
Activities: Other letting and operating of own or leased real estate
Officers: Richard John Henry Edge, Secretary; Richard William Taylor Comstive [1966] Director/Chartered Surveyor; Richard John Henry Edge [1967] Director/Chartered Surveyor

Edgehill Battersea Limited
Incorporated: 26 August 2004
Net Worth: £1,047,841 *Total Assets:* £5,469,292
Registered Office: The Courtyard, Holt Lodge Farm, Horton, Wimborne, Dorset, BH21 7JN
Activities: Buying and selling of own real estate
Parent: Padmanor Investments Limited
Officers: Hugo Aylesford Burge, Secretary; Laura Whitford, Secretary; Oliver Aylesford Burge [1941] Director; Roger Max Davies [1942] Director; Stephen John Davies [1976] Property Director

Edgehill Portfolio No.1 Limited
Incorporated: 10 April 2002
Net Worth Deficit: £4,416,556 *Total Assets:* £5,489,217
Registered Office: The Courtyard, Holt Lodge Farm, Horton Heath, Wimborne, Dorset, BH21 7JN
Activities: Buying and selling of own real estate
Parent: Padmanor Investments Limited
Officers: Hugo Aylesford Burge [1972] Director; Oliver Aylesford Burge [1941] Director; Roger Max Davies [1942] Director; Stephen John Davies [1976] Property Director

Edgeworth Investments Limited
Incorporated: 7 April 2017
Net Worth Deficit: £42,278 *Total Assets:* £24,822,764
Registered Office: 1 Cornhill, Ilminster, Somerset, TA19 0AD
Activities: Activities of open-ended investment companies
Major Shareholder: Richard Conyngham Corfield
Officers: Timothy Ian MacLellan, Secretary; Richard Conyngham Corfield [1955] Director

Edgwicks Limited
Incorporated: 31 January 1995 *Employees:* 24
Net Worth: £3,053,882 *Total Assets:* £3,684,312
Registered Office: Northway Lane, Newtown Industrial Estate, Tewkesbury, Glos, GL20 8JG
Activities: Freight transport by road
Parent: Billot Limited
Officers: Josiane Helene Therese Milner, Secretary; Anthony Karl George Milner [1937] Director; Josiane Helene Therese Milner [1939] Director/Beautician [French]; Martyn Edgwick Milner [1969] Director/Haulier; Paul Arthur George Milner [1963] Director/Haulier

Edmont Ltd
Incorporated: 5 June 1972 *Employees:* 120
Net Worth: £2,521,038 *Total Assets:* £8,234,053
Registered Office: Edmont Ltd, Hyde Road, Upper Stratton, Swindon, Wilts, SN2 7RB
Activities: Other specialised construction activities n.e.c.
Shareholder: Arkells Brewery Ltd
Officers: Hayley Louise Paget, Secretary; Alexander Thomas Arkell [1985] Director/Head Brewer; James Rixon Arkell [1951] Director/Brewer; Emma Louise Defty [1980] Director/Financial Controller; Melanie Jane Fyans [1965] Director; Craig Royston Morton [1958] Director/Upholstery Manager; Barry John Russell [1961] Finance Director

Educate Together Academy Trust
Incorporated: 24 January 2014 *Employees:* 38
Net Worth: £15,269,046 *Total Assets:* £15,767,464
Registered Office: Avonvale Road, Redfield, Bristol, BS5 9RH
Activities: Primary education
Officers: Joanne Bradshaw, Secretary; Kathy Brown [1962] Director/University Lecturer; Dee-Anne Bruce [1983] Director/Civil Servant; Jane Lesley Dyer [1945] Director Headteacher; Rosamond Farrell [1952] Director/Headteacher; Andrew Michael Goodall [1954] Director; Jenny Grinsted [1976] Director/Author; Mandy Jane Lee [1968] Director/Head of Department - Education; Julia Ann Skinner [1952] Director/Retired; Claire Stewart-Hall [1975] Director/Educational Consultant

Education Centre Management Limited
Incorporated: 29 June 2000
Total Assets: £3,831,000
Registered Office: The Abbots House, Blackfriars, Bristol, BS1 2NZ
Activities: Other letting and operating of own or leased real estate
Parent: The Charitable Trusts for University Hospitals Bristol
Officers: Lee Aston [1970] Finance Director; Jane Elizabeth Bonnar Dean [1955] Director/Voluntary Commercial Panel Member, National Trust; Lisa Michelle Gardner [1965] Director of Finance; Paul Kevin Michael Kearney [1958] Director/Chief Executive; Peter John Scott [1947] Director/Retired

Education South West
Incorporated: 25 November 2010 *Employees:* 771
Previous: Academies South West
Net Worth: £58,222,000 *Total Assets:* £74,780,000
Registered Office: Balkwill Road, Kingsbridge, Devon, TQ7 1PL
Activities: Primary education
Officers: James Anthony Clark [1976] Director/Store Manager; Peter di Giuseppe [1945] Director/Chartered Accountant; Jeremy St John Fothergill [1953] Director/Retired; Simon Gotch [1969] Director/Company Chairman; Roger John Pope [1957] Director/Headteacher; David James Potter [1970] Director/Management Consultant; Matthew John Shanks [1971] Director/Executive Principal; Hannah Elizabeth Smith [1970] Director/Self Employed Bookkeeper; Barrie John Taylor [1963] Director/Business Development Analyst; Stephen John Tucker [1969] Director/Farmer; Lindsay John Yelland [1974] Director/Owner of Yellands Cafe Ltd

Eduserv
Incorporated: 29 April 1999 *Employees:* 119
Net Worth: £3,398,151 *Total Assets:* £18,810,660
Registered Office: 4 Portwall Lane, Bristol, BS1 6NB
Activities: Other information service activities n.e.c.
Officers: Nevil Durrant, Secretary; Nevil Durrant [1974] Finance Director

Eelpower (Opco1) Limited
Incorporated: 1 March 2017
Net Worth: £116,072 *Total Assets:* £9,312,898
Registered Office: Brook House, Anna Valley, Andover, Hants, SP11 7NG
Activities: Production of electricity
Parent: Eelpower Limited
Officers: Andrew Lubin [1966] Director/Businessman [American]; Brooks Phillip Victor Newmark [1958] Director/Businessman; Richard Stephen Partridge-Hicks [1957] Director/Businessman; Graham Frederick Peacock [1950] Director/Investor; Mark Simon [1961] Director

Efret Limited
Incorporated: 31 January 2005 *Employees:* 21
Net Worth: £2,765,193 *Total Assets:* £13,798,800
Registered Office: 118 Old Milton Road, New Milton, Hants, BH25 6EB
Activities: Freight transport by road
Shareholders: J L Duval Consulting SARL; Jean-Francois Duval
Officers: Jean-Louis Duval, Secretary/Advisor [French]; Charles Duval [1971] Director [French]; Jean-Francois Duval [1950] Director [French]; Jean-Louis Duval [1951] Director [French]; Anne Elizabeth Fournier [1949] Director; Alain Jestin [1973] Director [French]

Eggbuckland Community College Academy Trust
Incorporated: 9 July 2013 *Employees:* 214
Net Worth: £10,730,818 *Total Assets:* £14,541,869
Registered Office: Eggbuckland Community College, Westcott Close, Eggbuckland, Plymouth, PL6 5YB
Activities: General secondary education
Officers: Lorna Worthington, Secretary; Michaela Jane Bottomley [1969] Director/Civil Servant; Wendy Cavell [1953] Director/Retired; Gail Marie Clark [1955] Director; Matthew Dominic Corrigan [1965] Director/Acting Principal and CEO; Jessica Dann [1987] Director/Commercial Officer; David Fildes [1968] Director/Site Services & Process Development Manager; Debra Gilbert [1963] Director/Family Support Advisor; Rosemary Ailsa Prout [1965] Director/Graduate Training Manager; David Thomas Francis Todd [1985] Director/College Staff

EIMS Global Limited
Incorporated: 22 July 2011 *Employees:* 292
Net Worth: £3,307,560 *Total Assets:* £12,474,184
Registered Office: EIMS House, 12-14 Dean Park Crescent, Bournemouth, BH1 1HS
Activities: Market research and public opinion polling
Shareholders: Isabelle Anne Marie Edward; Jonathan Johann Edward
Officers: Jonathan Johann Edward, Secretary; Isabelle Anne Marie Edward [1968] Director [French]; Jonathan Johann Edward [1964] Director

Eko Properties Limited
Incorporated: 28 March 2003 *Employees:* 7
Net Worth: £272,435 *Total Assets:* £4,589,221
Registered Office: 14 The Paragon, Bristol, BS8 4LA
Activities: Other holiday and other collective accommodation
Major Shareholder: Keneth Aylmer
Officers: Illona Rebecca Melanie Aylmer, Secretary; Illona Rebecca Melanie Aylmer [1970] Director; Kenneth Malcolm Aylmer [1970] Director/Philanthropist

Elbit Systems UK Limited
Incorporated: 24 September 2004
Net Worth: £25,931,070 *Total Assets:* £29,551,728
Registered Office: 2 Temple Back East, Temple Quay, Bristol, BS1 6EG
Activities: Activities of head offices
Parent: Elbit Systems Ltd
Officers: David Block Temin [1955] Director/Business Executive [Israeli]; Martin Clifford St John Fausset [1957] Director; Joseph Gaspar [1948] Director [Israeli]; Ran Kril [1970] Director/Business Executive [Israeli]; Bezhalel Machlis [1963] Director/Business Executive [Israeli]; Yuval Ramon [1965] Director/Business Executive [Israeli]

Eldon Insurance Services Limited
Incorporated: 6 August 2007 *Employees:* 440
Net Worth: £3,608,000 *Total Assets:* £29,607,000
Registered Office: 2nd Floor, Lysander House, Catbrain Lane, Cribbs Causeway, Bristol, BS10 7TQ
Activities: Non-life insurance
Major Shareholder: Arron Fraser Andrew Banks
Officers: Jonathan Ian Banks [1969] Director/Lawyer; Elizabeth Bilney [1976] Director/Insurance Underwriter; Jacobus Lodewyk Coetzee [1968] Director; Robert Hayes [1977] Director/Risk Management; Alison Marshall [1978] Director and Company Secretary; Alistair Crighton Stewart [1977] Director/Solicitor

Electric Mobility Euro Limited
Incorporated: 1 September 1989 *Employees:* 32
Net Worth: £4,471,432 *Total Assets:* £8,886,429
Registered Office: Canal Way, Ilminister, Somerset, TA19 9DL
Activities: Manufacture of medical and dental instruments and supplies
Major Shareholder: Michael James Flowers
Officers: Andrew William Hearn, Secretary; Michael Flowers [1957] Director [American]; Susan Dee Flowers [1953] Director [American]; Jonathan Howard Hearth [1962] Managing Director

Electro Mechanical Systems Limited
Incorporated: 4 April 1985 *Employees:* 73
Net Worth: £8,284,235 *Total Assets:* £11,288,711
Registered Office: Units 8-12 Chalwyn Industrial Estate, St Clements Road, Parkstone, Poole, Dorset, BH12 4PE
Activities: Agents specialised in the sale of other particular products
Officers: Shaun Cole [1965] Finance Director; Michael Richard Davies [1971] Manufacturing Director; Stewart Clive Goulding [1963] Director/Sales & Marketing; John Alexander Sellings [1970] Operations Director

Elemis Limited
Incorporated: 22 July 1988 *Employees:* 505
Net Worth: £41,931,088 *Total Assets:* £61,136,348
Registered Office: Unit D, Poplar Way East, Cabot Park, Avonmouth, Bristol, BS11 0DD
Activities: Manufacture of perfumes and toilet preparations
Parent: Nemo (UK) Holdco, Ltd
Officers: Robert C Boehm, Secretary/Attorney [American]; Daniel Michael Chambers, Secretary; Michael Stephan Haringman, Secretary; Oriele Anne Dunbar [1965] Director/Chief Marketing Officer [Canadian]; Noella Gabriel [1956] Managing Director [Irish]; Michael Stephan Haringman [1944] Director/Solicitor; Marc Magliacano [1974] Director/Investor [American]; Avik Pramanik [1984] Director/Investor [American]

Elfordleigh Holdings Limited
Incorporated: 21 January 2002 *Employees:* 2
Net Worth: £2,718,053 *Total Assets:* £4,076,237
Registered Office: Elfordleigh Hotel, Colebrook, Plympton, Devon, PL7 5EB
Activities: Hotels and similar accommodation
Major Shareholder: Antal Rack
Officers: Angela Hujdurovic-Rack [1983] Director/Manager [Dutch]; Antal Rack [1946] Director [Hungarian]

Edward Elgar Publishing Limited
Incorporated: 29 July 1986 *Employees:* 66
Net Worth: £6,325,132 *Total Assets:* £8,016,732
Registered Office: Lypiatts, 15 Lansdown Road, Cheltenham, Glos, GL50 2JA
Activities: Book publishing
Shareholder: Edward James Elgar
Officers: Sandra Elgar, Secretary; Catherine Jane Elgar [1977] Director/Commissioning Editor; Edward James Elgar [1949] Director/Publisher; Emily Claire Elgar [1981] Director/Author; Laura Mary Elgar [1978] Director/Commissioning Editor; Sandra Elgar [1952] Director; Alexander James Comely Pettifer [1980] Director/Commissioning Editor; Timothy Jonathan Leslie Williams [1976] Director/Publisher

Eliquo Hydrok Limited
Incorporated: 28 August 1996 *Employees:* 23
Previous: Hydrok U.K. Ltd.
Net Worth: £2,625,476 *Total Assets:* £10,217,374
Registered Office: Unit 3 Warren Road, Indian Queens, St Columb, Cornwall, TR9 6TL
Activities: Manufacture of other fabricated metal products n.e.c.
Parent: Hydra Holdings 2015 Limited
Officers: Peter Adrian Keatley, Secretary; David Edward Armstrong [1962] Director; Lewis Jon Claud O'Brien [1982] Director/Engineer

Ellas No3 Limited
Incorporated: 28 May 2009
Net Worth: £128,000 *Total Assets:* £8,512,000
Registered Office: Challenge House, International Drive, Tewkesbury Business Park, Tewkesbury, Glos, GL20 8UQ
Activities: Other letting and operating of own or leased real estate
Parent: East London Lift Holdco No3 Limited
Officers: Daniel Peter Bevan, Secretary; Jamie Russell Andrews [1970] Investment Director; Paul Simon Andrews [1970] Commercial Director; Henry Black [1975] Director/Chief Finance Officer; Paul Edward Brand [1967] Director; Neil Rae [1971] Director

Ellas No4 Limited
Incorporated: 15 October 2009
Net Worth Deficit: £3,089,000 *Total Assets:* £10,901,000
Registered Office: Challenge House, International Drive, Tewkesbury Business Park, Tewkesbury, Glos, GL20 8UQ
Activities: Other letting and operating of own or leased real estate
Parent: East London Lift Holdco No 4 Limited
Officers: Daniel Peter Bevan, Secretary; Jamie Russell Andrews [1970] Investment Director; Paul Simon Andrews [1970] Director; Henry Black [1975] Director/Chief Finance Officer; Paul Edward Brand [1967] Director; Neil Rae [1971] Director

Elleness Limited
Incorporated: 3 June 2004
Net Worth: £5,207,728 *Total Assets:* £5,394,754
Registered Office: 496 Wallisdown Road, Bournemouth, BH11 8PT
Activities: Renting and operating of Housing Association real estate
Shareholders: Linda Witczak; Stephen Jan Witczak
Officers: Linda Witczak, Secretary; Linda Witczak [1966] Director; Stephen Jan Witczak [1965] Director

Elliott Heron Limited
Incorporated: 29 July 2014 *Employees:* 2
Net Worth: £3,312,685 *Total Assets:* £3,653,412
Registered Office: Midland House, 2 Poole Road, Bournemouth, BH2 5QY
Activities: Development of building projects
Officers: Elliott Oram [1989] Property Director

Elliotts (Cheltenham) Limited
Incorporated: 29 November 2006 *Employees:* 44
Net Worth: £1,161,232 *Total Assets:* £3,553,785
Registered Office: Pillar House, 113-115 Bath Road, Cheltenham, Glos, GL53 7LS
Activities: Other retail sale not in stores, stalls or markets
Shareholders: Nicholas Michael Elliott; Anna Christine Elliott
Officers: Anna Christine Elliott, Secretary; Anna Christine Elliott [1968] Director/Part Time Administration Assistant; Nicholas Michael Elliott [1967] Director

Ellson Homes Limited
Incorporated: 28 April 2004 *Employees:* 3
Net Worth: £231,936 *Total Assets:* £5,664,883
Registered Office: Highfield House, The Meads, Leighterton, Tetbury, Glos, GL8 8UW
Activities: Construction of domestic buildings
Shareholder: Geoffrey Alan Hanson
Officers: Emily Victoria Fromant Hanson, Secretary; Ian Anthony Gay [1967] Director/Builder; Emily Victoria Hanson [1963] Director/Developer; Geoffrey Alan Hanson [1959] Director/Property Developer

Elm Developments Holdings Limited
Incorporated: 6 November 2012 *Employees:* 2
Net Worth: £1,945,239 *Total Assets:* £6,090,481
Registered Office: Hawthorn House, Emperor Way, Exeter Business Park, Exeter, Devon, EX1 3QS
Activities: Other letting and operating of own or leased real estate
Major Shareholder: Karen Jean Rosser
Officers: Isabel Catherine Rosser [1990] Director/Corporate Banker; Karen Jean Rosser [1963] Director

Elm Tree Estates Limited
Incorporated: 23 May 2000 *Employees:* 2
Net Worth: £1,426,327 *Total Assets:* £4,305,565
Registered Office: c/o Bishop Fleming, 16 Queen Square, Bristol, BS1 4NT
Activities: Renting and operating of Housing Association real estate
Major Shareholder: Kim Elizabeth Masters
Officers: Peter Robert Masters, Secretary/Managing Director; Kim Elizabeth Masters [1954] Director/Secretary; Peter Robert Masters [1954] Managing Director

Elmbirch Properties P.L.C.
Incorporated: 13 February 1990 *Employees:* 5
Net Worth: £26,759,056 *Total Assets:* £35,218,180
Registered Office: 14 Wilton Road, Salisbury, Wilts, SP2 7EE
Activities: Management of real estate on a fee or contract basis
Officers: Tamara Jon Folkesson, Secretary; Colin Lewis Chandler [1946] Director/Management Consultant; Tamara Jon Folkesson [1967] Director

Elmlea Junior School
Incorporated: 9 May 2011 *Employees:* 35
Net Worth: £2,992,176 *Total Assets:* £3,723,278
Registered Office: The Dell, Westbury on Trym, Bristol, BS9 3UF
Activities: Primary education
Officers: Cheryl Boyle, Secretary; Gareth Beynon [1970] Director/Headteacher; Harry Burrows [1974] Director; Ian Robert Dickie [1974] Director/Environmental Consultant; Jon Robert Hollingbery [1973] Director/Accountant; Adrian Killick [1972] Director/Airline Pilot; Anna Short [1975] Director/Primary School Teacher; Ben Sillince [1980] Director/Teacher; Dr Susan Tetlow [1980] Director/Hospital Doctor; Ian Venn [1947] Director/Company Secretary; Lorraine Wright [1967] Director/Headteacher

Elmley Foundation (The)
Incorporated: 15 November 1985 *Employees:* 2
Net Worth: £3,933,990 *Total Assets:* £4,297,688
Registered Office: West Aish, Morchard Bishop, Crediton, Devon, EX17 6RX
Activities: Support activities to performing arts
Officers: Hugh Bampfield Carslake [1946] Director/Trustee; Diana Susan Johnson [1948] Director/Arts Consultant; Sally Katrina Luton [1953] Director

Elondale Limited
Incorporated: 12 July 1996 *Employees:* 45
Net Worth: £3,522,123 *Total Assets:* £5,064,079
Registered Office: Woodlands Grange, Woodlands Lane, Bradley Stoke, Bristol, BS32 4JY
Activities: Manufacture of other food products n.e.c.
Major Shareholder: Sam Jacobi
Officers: Maria Jacobi, Secretary; Sam Jacobi [1966] Director

Ely Acquisition Limited
Incorporated: 10 May 2016 *Employees:* 210
Net Worth: £6,485,000 *Total Assets:* £57,776,000
Registered Office: Shearwater House, Clevedon Hall Estate, Victoria Road, Clevedon, Somerset, BS21 7RD
Activities: Activities of head offices
Parent: Turner International Bidco Limited
Officers: Christopher Ralph Bates [1963] Director/Chief Financial Officer; Roger Peter Crook [1958] Director; Michael Gareth Brian Jennings [1969] Managing Director

Emblem Holdings Limited
Incorporated: 10 October 2005 *Employees:* 27
Net Worth: £1,688,510 *Total Assets:* £9,503,912
Registered Office: Emblem House, Pynes Hill, Exeter, Devon, EX2 5BA
Activities: Activities of head offices
Major Shareholder: David John Richardson
Officers: Nicola Jane Churchward, Secretary/Consultant; Nicola Jane Churchward [1975] Director/Consultant; David John Richardson [1971] Director; John Gerard Richardson [1940] Director

Emerald Debtco Limited
Incorporated: 13 January 1993 *Employees:* 13
Net Worth: £545,000 *Total Assets:* £7,799,000
Registered Office: One Glass Wharf, Bristol, BS2 0ZX
Activities: Activities of professional membership organisations
Officers: Timothy Derwas Dale [1975] Director; Celia Rita Jane Diepenbroek [1968] Director; Colin Nigel Dymond [1963] Director/Dairy Farmer; Arthur Richard Fearnall [1963] Producer Director; George Bright Holmes [1965] Director/Dairy Farmer; Timothy David Hosford [1957] Director/Farmer; David Hyslop [1957] Director; Angela Rosemary Rhodes [1960] Director; Hon John Hugo Trenchard Russell [1950] Director/Farmer

EMG Limited
Incorporated: 19 May 1993 *Employees:* 73
Net Worth Deficit: £267,742 *Total Assets:* £5,354,388
Registered Office: Gloucester House, 29 Brunswick Square, Gloucester, GL1 1UN
Activities: Construction of other civil engineering projects n.e.c.
Major Shareholder: Eamonn Francis McGurk
Officers: Shane Thomas Andrews [1974] Director; Jennifer Anne Jones [1961] Director; Martin James Mullaney [1988] Director

Emily Estate (UK) Limited
Incorporated: 19 April 2013 *Employees:* 20
Net Worth Deficit: £4,185,636 *Total Assets:* £72,182,080
Registered Office: Estate Office, Hadspen House, Castle Cary, Somerset, BA7 7NG
Activities: Other letting and operating of own or leased real estate
Major Shareholder: John Faulkner Seldon
Officers: Lynne Caroline Blakey [1974] Director/Accountant; Paul James Rawson [1984] Director/Architectural Consultant

Emotional Rescue Limited
Incorporated: 13 September 1985 *Employees:* 14
Net Worth: £4,402,044 *Total Assets:* £5,693,341
Registered Office: Midway House, Herrick Way, Staverton Technology Park, Staverton, Cheltenham, Glos, GL51 6TQ
Activities: Other publishing activities
Parent: ERH Limited
Officers: David Greaves [1960] Director

Empire Homes (South West) Limited
Incorporated: 23 October 2015 *Employees:* 1
Net Worth Deficit: £35,631 *Total Assets:* £3,512,133
Registered Office: The Mill, Kingsteignton Road, Newton Abbot, Devon, TQ12 2QA
Activities: Development of building projects
Major Shareholder: Ian Mitchell
Officers: Ian Robert Mitchell [1950] Director/Property Consultant

Empty Billy Limited
Incorporated: 14 December 2017
Net Worth: £314,132 *Total Assets:* £7,558,060
Registered Office: Delta Place, 27 Bath Road, Cheltenham, Glos, GL53 7TH
Activities: Fund management activities
Shareholders: David William Lloyd; Kay Frances Lloyd
Officers: David William Lloyd [1945] Director; Kay Frances Lloyd [1944] Director; Kathryn Jane Van Rooyen [1975] Director

EMS Acquisition Company Limited
Incorporated: 24 October 2008
Net Worth Deficit: £42,267,712 *Total Assets:* £7,409,262
Registered Office: Green Lane, Tewkesbury, Glos, GL20 8HD
Activities: Activities of other holding companies n.e.c.
Parent: Ademco 2 Limited
Officers: Michele Elaine Hudson [1966] Director; Allan Richards [1962] Director

EMS Satcom UK, Ltd.
Incorporated: 26 February 1996 *Employees:* 31
Net Worth: £5,872,000 *Total Assets:* £6,095,000
Registered Office: Green Lane, Ashchurch, Tewkesbury, Glos, GL20 8HD
Activities: Satellite telecommunications activities
Parent: Honeywell International Inc.
Officers: Anthony Richard Vaughan Hutchings [1956] Director

EMS Waste Services Limited
Incorporated: 21 December 2008 *Employees:* 89
Net Worth: £3,271,790 *Total Assets:* £5,832,577
Registered Office: A E Stuart & Sons, Hill Barton Business Park, Clyst St Mary, Exeter, Devon, EX5 1DR
Activities: Collection of non-hazardous waste
Parent: A E Stuart Limited
Officers: Troy Stuart, Secretary; Ross Stuart [1947] Director; Roy Anthony Raymond Stuart [1944] Director; Troy Stuart [1969] Director

Encore Oakdale LLP
Incorporated: 17 March 2017
Net Worth: £776,839 *Total Assets:* £4,346,664
Registered Office: Midland House, 2 Poole Road, Bournemouth, BH2 5QY

Endeavour Academy Trust
Incorporated: 9 October 2012 *Employees:* 140
Previous: Little Mead Academy Trust
Net Worth: £10,000,192 *Total Assets:* £13,402,499
Registered Office: Little Mead Primary Academy, Gosforth Road, Southmead, Bristol, BS10 6DS
Activities: Primary education
Officers: Maria Del Mar Trowbridge, Secretary; Barbara Mary Daykin [1959] Director/Chief Executive; Graeme Malcolm Guthrie [1950] Director/Consultant; Mehjabeen Patrick [1970] Director/Chief Financial Officer; Jane Margaret Rogers [1955] Director/Solicitor; Thomas Ward Sanday [1955] Director/Foundation Learning Course Leader; Rebecca Louise Williams [1966] Director/Project Manager

Endesign Limited
Incorporated: 14 January 2002 *Employees:* 7
Net Worth: £4,309,760 *Total Assets:* £9,478,542
Registered Office: 15 Church Street, Ilchester, Somerset, BA22 8LN
Activities: Non-specialised wholesale trade
Parent: Manton Riches Limited
Officers: Judith Elizabeth Hall, Secretary; Michael Paul Nicholas Atkins [1945] Director/Product Planner; Judith Elizabeth Hall [1958] Director/Accountant; Eef Van Leusden [1957] Director/Sales Manager [Dutch]

Endsleigh Insurance Services Limited
Incorporated: 13 August 1965 *Employees:* 770
Net Worth Deficit: £36,506,000 *Total Assets:* £89,842,000
Registered Office: Shurdington Road, Cheltenham Spa, Glos, GL51 4UE
Activities: Non-life insurance
Shareholders: Endsleigh Limited; Endsleigh Limited
Officers: Jeffery Charles Brinley [1956] Director; James Maxwell Carruthers [1954] Director; Andrew James Galbraith [1970] Director; Shakira Martin [1988] Director; Matthew Ray Neave [1982] Director/Head of Finance; Carl Anthony Shuker [1961] Director

Endsleigh Insurances (Brokers) Limited
Incorporated: 21 July 1978 *Employees:* 51
Net Worth: £3,266,476 *Total Assets:* £7,636,171
Registered Office: Shurdington Road, Cheltenham Spa, Glos, GL51 4UE
Activities: Non-life insurance
Parent: Endsleigh Insurance Services Limited
Officers: Jeffery Charles Brinley [1956] Director/Head of Finance; Andrew James Galbraith [1970] Director; Matthew Ray Neave [1982] Finance Director

Endsleigh Limited
Incorporated: 6 December 2001 *Employees:* 858
Net Worth Deficit: £50,339,000 *Total Assets:* £88,560,000
Registered Office: Shurdington Road, Cheltenham Spa, Glos, GL51 4UE
Activities: Activities of head offices
Shareholders: Trafalgar Bidco Limited; National Union of Students (UK)
Officers: Jeffery Charles Brinley [1956] Director; James Maxwell Carruthers [1954] Director; Andrew James Galbraith [1970] Director; Matthew Ray Neave [1982] Director/Head of Finance; Carl Anthony Shuker [1961] Director

Energy Measurement Limited
Incorporated: 12 June 2007
Net Worth: £4,413,200 *Total Assets:* £5,428,115
Registered Office: Stafford House, 10 Prince of Wales Road, Dorchester, DT1 1PW
Activities: Other business support service activities n.e.c.
Major Shareholder: Gary Martin Weston
Officers: Benjamin Alexander Weston, Secretary; Gary Martin Weston [1959] Director/Engineer

Enfield Lighting Services Limited
Incorporated: 22 November 2005
Net Worth Deficit: £2,647,423 *Total Assets:* £23,759,416
Registered Office: Third Floor, Broad Quay House, Prince Street, Bristol, BS1 4DJ
Activities: Other business support service activities n.e.c.
Parent: IIC Enfield Holding Company Limited
Officers: Paul Anthony Cartwright [1957] Director; Vikki Louise Everett [1971] Director/Project Manager; Thomas Benedict Symes [1956] Director

Enga Limited
Incorporated: 15 December 1989 *Employees:* 3
Net Worth: £20,140,796 *Total Assets:* £21,401,108
Registered Office: Unit 33 Clarendon Centre, Salisbury Business Park, Dairy Meadow Lane, Salisbury, Wilts, SP1 2TJ
Activities: Silviculture and other forestry activities
Officers: Donald Campbell Forsyth [1961] Director/Chartered Accountant; Digby Coulson Guy [1947] Director/Forestry Adviser; Anders Johan Magnus Koskull [1938] Director/Businessman [Swedish]; Johan Gustav Claes Koskull [1977] Director [Swedish]

English Heritage Trading Limited
Incorporated: 16 September 1994 *Employees:* 176
Net Worth: £2,028,000 *Total Assets:* £7,854,000
Registered Office: Engine House, Fire Fly Avenue, Swindon, Wilts, SN2 2EH
Activities: Other business support service activities n.e.c.
Parent: The English Heritage Trust
Officers: Victoria Barnsley [1954] Director; Charles Mark Gurassa [1956] Director; Sir Timothy James Hamilton Laurence [1955] Director/Chairman; Sir Laurence Henry Philip Magnus [1955] Director/Chairman; Katherine Lyndsay Mavor [1962] Director/CEO, Charitable Trust

The English Heritage Trust
Incorporated: 22 November 2010 *Employees:* 2,177
Net Worth: £68,113,000 *Total Assets:* £102,289,000
Registered Office: Engine House, Fire Fly Avenue, Swindon, Wilts, SN2 2EH
Activities: Operation of historical sites and buildings and similar visitor attractions
Officers: Alexander William Balfour [1971] Director/Digital Capability Specialist; Victoria Barnsley [1954] Director; Charles Mark Gurassa [1956] Director; Sukie Mary Hemming [1950] Director/Museum Official; Professor Ronald Edmund Hutton [1953] Director/Professor of History; Sir Timothy James Hamilton Laurence [1955] Director/Retired Naval Officer; Sir Laurence Henry Philip Magnus [1955] Director/Chairman; Ian McCaig [1966] Director/CEO, First Utility; Kunle Olulode [1961] Charity Director; David Adetayo Olusoga [1970] Director/TV Executive & Presenter, Author, Columnist; Sarah Elizabeth Staniforth [1953] Director; James Douglas Robert Twining [1972] Strategy Director

Enham Trust
Incorporated: 16 February 1921 *Employees:* 260
Net Worth: £5,202,000 *Total Assets:* £14,826,000
Registered Office: Enham Place, Enham Alamein, Andover, Hants, SP11 6JS
Activities: Residential care activities for the elderly and disabled
Officers: Simon Edward Guy Williams, Secretary; Professor Khalid Aziz [1953] Director; Marianne Louise Juliarne Black [1975] Director; Robert Simon Childs [1951] Director/Chief Underwriting Officer; Dawn Marie Fowler-Stevens [1972] Director; Judith Mary Gillow [1955] Director of Nursing and Organisational Development; Stuart Robert Lindsay [1952] Director/Chartered Accountant; Neil Palmer [1976] Director/Self Employed; Matthew Heath Samuel-Camps [1967] Director/Property Consultant; Clare Mary Scheckter [1960] Director/Trustee; Elizabeth Margaret Wallace [1958] Director

Enidvale Holdings Limited
Incorporated: 2 February 1999 *Employees:* 2
Net Worth: £4,676,476 *Total Assets:* £5,108,099
Registered Office: Littlecote Road, Froxfield, Marlborough, Wilts, SN8 3JY
Activities: Activities of agricultural holding companies
Major Shareholder: William Arthur Bird
Officers: Elaine Dawn Bird, Secretary; Elaine Dawn Bird [1953] Director; William Arthur Bird [1950] Director

Enoch Properties (Devon) Limited
Incorporated: 28 October 1977
Net Worth: £2,720,700 *Total Assets:* £4,060,579
Registered Office: Sigma House, Oak View Close, Edginswell Park, Torquay, Devon, TQ2 7FF
Activities: Other letting and operating of own or leased real estate
Shareholders: Richard Nicholas Enoch; Yvonne Theresa Enoch
Officers: Richard Nicholas Enoch, Secretary; Richard Nicholas Enoch [1953] Director/Helicopter Pilot; Suzanne Rachael Enoch [1979] Director/Student

T. Ensor & Son Limited
Incorporated: 4 January 1993 *Employees:* 2
Net Worth: £3,154,966 *Total Assets:* £3,636,212
Registered Office: 1 Poole Road, Wimborne, Dorset, BH21 1QA
Activities: Retail sale via stalls and markets of other goods
Major Shareholder: James Brendon George
Officers: James Brendon George, Secretary; Estelle Valerie George [1932] Director/Market Operator; James Brendon George [1964] Director/Market Operator; John James George [1935] Director/Market Operator

Entier Associates Limited
Incorporated: 24 March 2004 *Employees:* 3
Net Worth: £2,088,955 *Total Assets:* £12,645,678
Registered Office: Unit 15 Basepoint Business Centre, Oakfield Close, Tewkesbury Business Park, Tewkesbury, Glos, GL20 8SD
Activities: Other service activities n.e.c.
Shareholders: Conrad Garth Jones; Rachael Jane Jones
Officers: Rachael Jane Jones, Secretary; Conrad Garth Jones [1966] Director/Project Manager; Rachael Jane Jones [1968] Director

The Environmental Dimension Partnership Limited
Incorporated: 25 June 2014 *Employees:* 94
Net Worth: £943,170 *Total Assets:* £4,217,931
Registered Office: Tithe Barn, Barnsley Park, Barnsley, Cirencester, Glos, GL7 5EG
Activities: Environmental consulting activities
Shareholder: Benjamin James Rosedale
Officers: Tim Knowles, Secretary; Andrew Crutchley [1974] Director; Gerard Dore [1971] Director; Timothy Knowles [1976] Director; David Lewis [1974] Director; Fiona McKenzie [1973] Director; Charles Mylchreest [1979] Director; Benjamin James Rosedale [1976] Director; Tom Wigglesworth [1976] Director

Enys Estate Company Limited
Incorporated: 21 January 2016
Net Worth: £15,546 *Total Assets:* £3,754,044
Registered Office: Lea Haven, 24a North Street, Charminster, Dorchester, DT2 9QZ
Activities: Other letting and operating of own or leased real estate
Officers: Michael Byrne, Secretary; Alice Wendy Fowler [1952] Director; Professor Leonard Christopher Gordon Rogers [1954] Director

Epichem Group Limited
Incorporated: 3 January 1989
Net Worth: £32,322,000 *Total Assets:* £32,322,000
Registered Office: The Old Brickyard, New Road, Gillingham, Dorset, SP8 4XT
Activities: Activities of head offices
Parent: Sigma-Aldrich Company Limited
Officers: Peter Biro [1967] Director/US Certified Public Accountant [Dutch]; Dr Geoffrey James Irvine [1966] Director/VP Sales [New Zealander]

The Epiphany School
Incorporated: 15 March 2012 *Employees:* 56
Net Worth: £3,220,759 *Total Assets:* £4,088,003
Registered Office: The Epiphany School, Shillingstone Drive, Muscliff, Bournemouth, BH9 3PE
Activities: Primary education
Officers: Katharine Jane Fry, Secretary; Fiona Alcock [1990] Director/Teacher; David John Barter [1985] Director/Accountant; Christopher Edward Burge [1975] Director/Retail Management; Jacqueline Featherstone [1963] Director/School Business Manager; Neil William Johnson [1978] Director/Pet Shop Owner; Andy David Saunders [1962] Director/Children/Family Advisor; Helen Brida Thomas [1972] Director/Accounts Assistant; Lynne Margaret Thomas [1960] Director; Claire Elizabeth Wheeler [1978] Director/Company Secretary

Epping PPP Maintenance (Health) Services Limited
Incorporated: 6 October 2004 *Employees:* 3
Net Worth Deficit: £5,347,325 *Total Assets:* £16,995,148
Registered Office: Third Floor, Broad Quay House, Prince Street, Bristol, BS1 4DJ
Activities: Other specialised construction activities n.e.c.
Parent: RBIL Limited
Officers: Christopher John Blundell [1966] Regional Director; Andrew Richard Kershaw [1965] Director/Projects Controller; Richard Little [1979] Investment Director; Daniel North [1988] Investment Director

EPTA Cold Service Ltd
Incorporated: 5 January 1976 *Employees:* 162
Previous: Cold Service Limited
Net Worth Deficit: £2,343,238 *Total Assets:* £7,664,768
Registered Office: Avonside House, Kingfisher Park, Headlands, Ringwood, Hants, BH24 3NX
Activities: Plumbing, heat and air-conditioning installation
Parent: EPTA Service UK Limited
Officers: Massimo Andrea Albertario [1966] Director/Chief Financial Officer [Italian]; Luca Lastella [1965] Director/General Manager [Italian]; Daniele Marongiu [1959] Sales Director [Italian]; Geoffrey Charles Mills [1965] Commercial Director; Simon James Taylor [1968] Finance Director

Equa Multi Academy Trust
Incorporated: 26 November 2010 *Employees:* 104
Previous: Lavington School Limited
Net Worth: £10,583,070 *Total Assets:* £11,048,766
Registered Office: The Spring, Market Lavington, Devizes, Wilts, SN10 4EB
Activities: General secondary education
Officers: Angela Helen Marian Downing, Secretary; Mark William Bartlett [1960] Director/Teacher; Justine Bland [1969] Director/Medical Receptionist; Daniel John Davies [1963] Director/Marketing Officer; Pauline Guiney [1956] Director/Chartered Librarian; Alexander Ronald Holloway [1979] Director/IT Project Manager; Judith Holloway [1974] Director/Chief Operating Officer of Training Company; Sarah Charis Lowkis [1964] Director/Headteacher; Steven George Morse [1964] H R Director; Elanor Rachel Oddy [1970] Director/Civic Administrator; Michael William Maxwell Rees [1967] Director/Lawyer; James Christopher Rosenegk [1965] Director/Management Consultant; Philip John George Salaman [1973] Director; Lorraine Stabbins [1977] Director/Nurse (Not Currently Employed); Elliot Bruce Olav Wallace [1970] Director/Head of Strategy

Equi Media Limited
Incorporated: 10 December 1999 *Employees:* 48
Net Worth: £406,657 *Total Assets:* £4,694,756
Registered Office: Stella Building, Whitehill Way, Swindon, Wilts, SN5 6NX
Activities: Advertising agencies
Shareholders: Andrew Peter Charnock Burgess; Louise Ann Burgess
Officers: Andrew Peter Charnock Burgess [1959] Director; Louise Ann Burgess [1965] Director

Erin Properties (Swindon) Limited
Incorporated: 9 March 1966 *Employees:* 4
Net Worth: £6,651,017 *Total Assets:* £7,201,419
Registered Office: 38-42 Newport Street, Swindon, Wilts, SN1 3DR
Activities: Other letting and operating of own or leased real estate
Major Shareholder: Mary Frances Foley
Officers: Maurice Anthony Foley, Secretary/Accountant; Amanda Katherine Foley [1965] Director/Clerical Assistant; Fionuala Mary Foley [1966] Director/Estates Manager; Mary Frances Foley [1937] Director; Maurice Anthony Foley [1963] Director/Accountant

Ernesettle Community Solar Limited
Incorporated: 27 November 2015
Net Worth: £338,275 *Total Assets:* £4,098,559
Registered Office: Ballard House, West Hoe Road, Plymouth, PL1 3BJ
Activities: Production of electricity
Parent: PEC Renewables Ltd
Officers: David Charles Madge [1956] Director/Retired; Christopher John Penberthy [1964] Director/Councillor; Lee Richards [1974] Director/Programme Manager, Regen SW

Eroga Die Company Limited
Incorporated: 1 August 1967
Net Worth: £3,896,258 *Total Assets:* £4,639,911
Registered Office: Unit 6a Eastbrook Road, Eastern Avenue, Gloucester, GL4 3DB
Activities: Manufacture of tools
Shareholders: Alan Francis Townsend; Maria Dawn Peacock
Officers: Alan Francis Townsend, Secretary; Alan Francis Townsend [1972] Director/Sales and Production Manager

ES Technology Group Limited
Incorporated: 8 March 2016 *Employees:* 5
Net Worth: £597,172 *Total Assets:* £3,538,613
Registered Office: 5 Pullman Court, Great Western Road, Gloucester, GL1 3ND
Activities: Dormant company
Shareholder: Patrick Donnelly
Officers: Simon David Bent [1960] President US Operations & Director of ES Tech Group [American]; Steven Michael Bilton [1971] Director; Patrick Donnelly [1979] Director; Tracy Gill [1965] Director; Jon Samule Hood [1984] Director

ESP Colour Limited
Incorporated: 19 February 1998 *Employees:* 113
Net Worth: £1,408,709 *Total Assets:* £8,263,629
Registered Office: The Colour Hub, Milbuck Close, Elgin Drive, Swindon, Wilts, SN2 8XU
Activities: Printing n.e.c.
Major Shareholder: Paul Andrew Bradley
Officers: Paul Andrew Hudson, Secretary; Emma Jane Bradley [1973] Director; Paul Andrew Bradley [1969] Director; Nick Lee [1963] Sales Director; Simon John Smogur [1986] Finance Director

Essex Schools (Holdings) Limited
Incorporated: 16 March 2010 *Employees:* 11
Net Worth Deficit: £19,256,000 *Total Assets:* £76,075,000
Registered Office: Third Floor, Broad Quay House, Prince Street, Bristol, BS1 4DJ
Activities: Activities of head offices
Shareholders: Skanska TAM Limited; Essex LEP Limited
Officers: Paul Alan Bannister [1959] Investment Director; Emma Brown [1971] Director; Jennifer Fegan [1973] Director; Robert Alistair Martin Gillespie [1990] Director/Financial Controller; Nicholas James MacKee [1976] Director/Solicitor; John Robert Pedretti [1964] Director/General Manager [Australian]; Katherine Mary Rae [1980] Director/Legal Advisor; Paul Sydney Shadbolt [1957] Development Director; Andrew John Trow [1974] Director/Manager; Karen Williams [1973] Director; Philip Arthur Would [1971] Director/Asset Manager; Asif Yusuf [1985] Director

Essex Schools (Woodlands) Limited
Incorporated: 23 February 2012 *Employees:* 7
Net Worth Deficit: £2,155,000 *Total Assets:* £26,922,000
Registered Office: Third Floor, Broad Quay House, Prince Street, Bristol, BS1 4DJ
Activities: General secondary education
Parent: Essex Schools Holdings (Woodlands) Limited
Officers: Paul Alan Bannister [1959] Director; Jennifer Fegan [1973] Director; Nicholas James MacKee [1976] Director/Solicitor; John Robert Pedretti [1964] Director/General Manager [Australian]; Katherine Mary Rae [1980] Director/Legal Advisor; Paul Sydney Shadbolt [1957] Development Director; Andrew John Trow [1974] Director/Manager; Karen Williams [1973] Director

Essex Schools Holdings (Woodlands) Limited
Incorporated: 22 February 2012
Net Worth Deficit: £2,155,000 *Total Assets:* £26,922,000
Registered Office: Third Floor, Broad Quay House, Prince Street, Bristol, BS1 4DJ
Activities: General secondary education
Shareholders: Skanska TAM Limited; Building Schools for The Future Investments LLP; Essex LEP Limited
Officers: Paul Alan Bannister [1959] Director; Jennifer Fegan [1973] Director; Nicholas James MacKee [1976] Director/Solicitor; John Robert Pedretti [1964] Director/General Manager [Australian]; Katherine Mary Rae [1980] Director/Legal Advisor; Paul Sydney Shadbolt [1957] Development Director; Andrew John Trow [1974] Director/Manager; Karen Williams [1973] Director

Essex Schools Limited
Incorporated: 18 March 2010
Net Worth Deficit: £19,256,000 *Total Assets:* £76,075,000
Registered Office: Third Floor, Broad Quay House, Prince Street, Bristol, BS1 4DJ
Activities: General secondary education
Parent: Essex Schools (Holdings) Limited
Officers: Paul Alan Bannister [1959] Investment Director; Emma Brown [1971] Director; Jennifer Fegan [1973] Director; Robert Alistair Martin Gillespie [1990] Director/Financial Controller; Nicholas James MacKee [1976] Director/Solicitor; John Robert Pedretti [1964] Director/General Manager [Australian]; Katherine Mary Rae [1980] Director/Legal Advisor; Paul Sydney Shadbolt [1957] Development Director; Andrew John Trow [1974] Director/Manager; Karen Williams [1973] Director; Philip Arthur Would [1971] Director/Asset Manager; Asif Yusuf [1985] Director

Essilor Limited
Incorporated: 23 June 1965 *Employees:* 374
Net Worth: £6,592,000 *Total Assets:* £25,164,000
Registered Office: Cooper Road, Thornbury, Bristol, BS35 3UW
Activities: Manufacture of other plastic products
Parent: Trifle Holdings Limited
Officers: Lena Generaldine Henry [1975] Director/Executive [French]; Timothy James Precious [1972] Director; James Michael Smith [1969] Director; Peter James Smith [1961] Director/Regional VP UK & Ireland

Esteban Investments Limited
Incorporated: 7 October 2013
Net Worth: £1,910,284 *Total Assets:* £12,930,542
Registered Office: Ashton Gate Stadium, Ashton Road, Bristol, BS3 2EJ
Activities: Other letting and operating of own or leased real estate
Shareholder: Margaret Alison Lansdown
Officers: Gavin Thomas Marshall, Secretary; Martin William Griffiths [1960] Director; Jon Stephen Lansdown [1983] Director

Etavoni Limited
Incorporated: 13 September 2004 *Employees:* 29
Net Worth: £1,949,953 *Total Assets:* £4,539,473
Registered Office: Unit A, Wellsway Works, Wells Road, Radstock, Somerset, BA3 3RZ
Activities: Manufacture of other special-purpose machinery n.e.c.
Shareholder: Brian Watts
Officers: Wayne Williams, Secretary; Brian Watts [1968] Director/Engineer

Etex Building Performance Limited
Incorporated: 14 September 1987 *Employees:* 468
Previous: Siniat Limited
Net Worth: £110,608,000 *Total Assets:* £179,028,992
Registered Office: Gordano House, Marsh Lane, Easton in Gordano, Bristol, BS20 0NE
Activities: Manufacture of plaster products for construction purposes
Officers: Clive Graham Ellwood, Secretary/Accountant; Wim Schelfhout, Secretary; Neil Alexander Ash [1971] Managing Director; Jean-Louis Georges Bernard [1972] Director [French]; Clive Graham Ellwood [1958] Finance Director; Jane Elizabeth Maycock [1959] HR Director; Wim Schelfhout [1980] Finance Director [Belgian]

ETM Recycling Limited
Incorporated: 26 May 2009
Net Worth: £975,316 *Total Assets:* £4,292,654
Registered Office: 81 Hartcliffe Way, Bristol, BS3 5RN
Activities: Recovery of sorted materials
Parent: E T M Const' & Recycling Holdings Ltd
Officers: Hilary McCormack, Secretary; Amy Louise McCormack [1985] Director; Andrew McCormack [1982] Director; Edward Thomas McCormack [1954] Director

Eurac Limited
Incorporated: 13 February 1992 *Employees:* 19
Net Worth: £31,761,000 *Total Assets:* £46,382,000
Registered Office: Mannings Heath Road, Poole, Dorset, BH12 4NJ
Activities: Activities of head offices
Major Shareholder: Steve Wang
Officers: Julian Spencer William Grazebrook, Secretary; Craig Gordon [1958] Director/General Manager [American]; Julian Spencer William Grazebrook [1953] Director/Chartered Accountant; Hana Krosnar [1966] Director; Dr John George Krosnar [1943] Director; Thomas Krosnar [1971] Director; George Michael Ruhl [1955] Director/Manager [American]

Eurac Poole Limited
Incorporated: 14 February 1992 *Employees:* 205
Net Worth: £18,443,000 *Total Assets:* £26,308,000
Registered Office: Mannings Heath Road, Poole, Dorset, BH12 4NJ
Activities: Casting of iron
Officers: Julian Spencer William Grazebrook, Secretary; Hana Krosnar [1966] Managing Director; Thomas Krosnar [1971] Director

Euravia Engineering & Supply Co. Limited
Incorporated: 4 April 1988 *Employees:* 108
Net Worth: £10,765,330 *Total Assets:* £19,288,274
Registered Office: 510 Wallisdown Road, Bournemouth, BH11 8QN
Activities: Repair and maintenance of aircraft and spacecraft
Shareholder: Norman Murray Edwards
Officers: Shawn David Smith, Secretary; Jason Scott Addis [1969] Director/Vice President, European Operations; Haydn Robert Martin [1963] Corporate Director, Business Development; Elena Milantoni [1969] Director/CFO and Corporate Secretary [Canadian]; Shawn David Smith [1967] Director/Accountant; Phillip Campion Underwood [1960] Director/President

Eurilait Limited
Incorporated: 2 December 1991 *Employees:* 96
Net Worth: £1,035,280 *Total Assets:* £22,139,296
Registered Office: Leighton Lane Industrial Estate, Leighton Lane, Evercreech, Shepton Mallet, Somerset, BA4 6LQ
Activities: Wholesale of dairy products, eggs and edible oils and fats
Parent: Laita
Officers: Yvan Borgne, Secretary; Oliver Joesph Alfred Athimon [1967] Commercial Director [French]; Jean-Marie Le Bris [1974] Commercial Director [French]; James Paul Millward [1968] Managing Director

Euro-Diesel (UK) Limited
Incorporated: 7 December 1989 *Employees:* 18
Net Worth: £3,714,067 *Total Assets:* £5,105,518
Registered Office: 101-102 Cirencester Business Park, Love Lane, Cirencester, Glos, GL7 1XD
Activities: Manufacture of other general-purpose machinery n.e.c.
Officers: Giacomo Gianco Angelini, Secretary; Giacomo Gianco Angelini [1967] Finance Director [Belgian]; Jacobus Kaspers [1964] Director [Belgian]

Eurogate Finance Limited
Incorporated: 17 July 2000
Net Worth: £3,608,772 *Total Assets:* £21,428,992
Registered Office: 67 Ashley Road, Poole, Dorset, BH14 9BT
Activities: Activities of other holding companies n.e.c.
Major Shareholder: Anna Krausova
Officers: Ernest Richard Paul Donne [1962] Director/Certified Public Accountant [Irish]; Andrew Henry Irving [1965] Director

Europa Equity Limited
Incorporated: 6 January 2015 *Employees:* 291
Net Worth Deficit: £19,865,284 *Total Assets:* £6,857,178
Registered Office: Europa House, Midland Way, Thornbury, Bristol, BS35 2JX
Activities: Activities of head offices
Shareholders: Thomas John Duggan; David Maurice Saville
Officers: Ian Donald [1942] Director; Thomas John Duggan [1936] Director; David Maurice Saville [1932] Director

Europa Group Limited
Incorporated: 15 November 1996 *Employees:* 202
Net Worth: £12,159,934 *Total Assets:* £17,199,792
Registered Office: Europa House, Midland Way, Thornbury, Bristol, BS35 2JX
Activities: Activities of insurance agents and brokers
Parent: Blue Boar Holdings Limited
Officers: Mary-Anne King, Secretary; Barry Malcolm Hulbert [1938] Director/Insurance Intermediary; Mary-Anne King [1967] Finance Director; Andrew Christopher Powell [1959] Insurance Director; Scott Anthony Salter [1966] Director/Insurance

European Friction Industries Limited
Incorporated: 21 March 1986 *Employees:* 105
Net Worth: £5,902,312 *Total Assets:* £7,137,328
Registered Office: Enterprise House, 6-7 Bonville Road, Brislington, Bristol, BS4 5NZ
Activities: Manufacture of other parts and accessories for motor vehicles
Parent: EBC Holdings Limited
Officers: Tony Delwyn Prideaux [1955] Managing Director

The European Investment Trust PLC
Incorporated: 22 May 1972
Net Worth: £414,319,008 *Total Assets:* £427,732,992
Registered Office: Beaufort House, 51 New North Road, Exeter, EX4 4EP
Activities: Activities of investment trusts
Officers: Kenneth John Greig, Secretary; Susan Patricia Inglis [1964] Director; Michael William Miller Reid MacPhee [1964] Director/Investment, Self Employed; Michael Bruce Moule [1946] Director; Andrew Keith Watkins [1952] Director; Dr Michael Trevor Woodward [1957] Director

European Society of Endocrinology
Incorporated: 18 August 2005 *Employees:* 1
Net Worth: £4,336,076 *Total Assets:* £5,899,055
Registered Office: Redwood House, Brotherswood Court, Great Park Road, Almondsbury Business Park, Bradley Stoke, Bristol, BS32 4QW
Activities: Other human health activities
Officers: Professor Jerome Bertherat [1961] Director/Doctor [French]; Professor Felix Beuschlein [1969] Director/Professor Doctor [German]; Professor Andrea Giustina [1962] Director/Professor Doctor [Italian]; Professor Riccarda Granata [1966] Director/Research Scientist [Italian]; Prof Marta Juditha Korbonits [1962] Director/Doctor; Professor Beata Kos-Kudla [1963] Director/Medical Doctor [Polish]; Professor Monica Marazuela [1961] Director/Doctor Professor [Spanish]; Dr Camilla Schalin-Jantti [1964] Director/Doctor [Finnish]; Professor Aart Jan Van Der Lely [1957] Director/Doctor [Dutch]; Professor Okan Bulent Yildiz [1971] Director/Physician [Turkish]

The Eurostore Group Limited
Incorporated: 24 November 2000
Net Worth Deficit: £8,355,000 *Total Assets:* £9,127,000
Registered Office: Unit M3, Kemble Enterprise Park, Cirencester, Glos, GL7 6BQ
Activities: Activities of head offices
Parent: Manutan International SA
Officers: Monsieur Pierre-Olivier Brial, Secretary; Brigitte Auffret [1961] Director/General Manager [French]; Keith Charles Boad [1959] Managing Director; Monsieur Pierre-Olivier Brial [1973] Director/Manager [French]; Jean-Pierre Guichard [1946] Director/Chairman [French]

Eurotaxis Ltd.
Incorporated: 5 July 1991 *Employees:* 102
Net Worth: £1,171,880 *Total Assets:* £3,836,765
Registered Office: Dean Road, Yate, Bristol, BS37 5NH
Activities: Other passenger land transport
Officers: Juan Sanzo, Secretary/Taxi Hire [Spanish]; Anne Sanzo [1949] Director/Taxi Hire; Keith Alberto Sanzo [1975] Director/Transport [Spanish]; William James Sanzo [1978] Director

The Eurotech Group PLC
Incorporated: 10 May 1991 *Employees:* 154
Net Worth: £7,270,000 *Total Assets:* £11,677,000
Registered Office: Salterton Industrial Estate, Salterton Road, Exmouth, Devon, EX8 4RZ
Activities: Manufacture of electronic components
Major Shareholder: David Keith Douglas
Officers: David Keith Douglas, Finance Director; Simon Beckett [1960] Director; Anthony Derek Cornish [1952] Director; David Keith Douglas [1961] Finance Director; Keith Hole [1957] Director; Jeremy Wakeford [1963] Director

Euston Simmonds Limited
Incorporated: 22 March 1999
Net Worth: £8,555,676 *Total Assets:* £11,015,052
Registered Office: The Cedars, 35 Stoke Hill, Stoke Bishop, Bristol, BS9 1LQ
Activities: Activities of other holding companies n.e.c.
Major Shareholder: Gillian Ann Harvey
Officers: Gillian Ann Harvey, Secretary/Director; Ann Louise Blake [1982] Director; Lucie Kay Da Silva [1984] Director; Gillian Ann Harvey [1957] Director; Emma Jane King [1979] Director

Euston Trust Limited
Incorporated: 10 March 1947 *Employees:* 6
Net Worth: £26,008,744 *Total Assets:* £30,633,058
Registered Office: 35 Stoke Hill, Stoke Bishop, Bristol, BS9 1LQ
Activities: Other letting and operating of own or leased real estate
Parent: Euston Simmonds Limited
Officers: Gillian Ann Harvey, Secretary/Director; Ann Louise Blake [1982] Director; Gillian Ann Harvey [1957] Director; Lucie Kay Harvey [1984] Director; Emma Jane King [1979] Director

Evans Transport Limited
Incorporated: 27 June 1947 *Employees:* 176
Net Worth: £5,757,800 *Total Assets:* £14,217,678
Registered Office: Gammaton Road, Bideford, Devon, EX39 4FG
Activities: Freight transport by road
Parent: E T Holdings Limited
Officers: Susan Jayne Evans, Secretary; Alison Dunbar Evans [1941] Director; Nigel John Evans [1962] Director/Haulier; Susan Jayne Evans [1968] Director; Thomas John Evans [1989] Director; Walter John Evans [1941] Director/Haulier; Jonathan Raymont [1968] Director/Transport Manager; Andrew John Taylor [1973] Finance Director

Everhot Ltd.
Incorporated: 20 February 1998 *Employees:* 37
Net Worth: £3,217,667 *Total Assets:* £5,693,231
Registered Office: Coaley Mill, Coaley, Dursley, Glos, GL11 5DS
Activities: Manufacture of electric domestic appliances
Major Shareholder: Guy Richard Goring
Officers: Susan Mary Goring, Secretary; Guy Richard Goring [1969] Director/Engineer; Susan Mary Goring [1969] Sales Director

Evershot Construction Limited
Incorporated: 3 August 2000 *Employees:* 4
Net Worth: £5,456,199 *Total Assets:* £5,571,256
Registered Office: The Estate Office, Melbury Sampford, Dorchester, DT2 0LF
Activities: Development of building projects
Shareholders: The Honourable Charlotte Anne Townshend; Ilchester Trustee Company Limited; James Reginald Townshend
Officers: Robert Ian Sanderson, Secretary; Robert Ian Sanderson [1952] Director/Chartered Accountant; Marcus Kingswood Scrace [1959] Director/Chartered Surveyor; The Honourable Charlotte Anne Townshend [1955] Director; James Reginald Townshend [1954] Director

Evershot Farms Limited
Incorporated: 7 April 1971 *Employees:* 23
Net Worth: £4,438,989 *Total Assets:* £10,651,162
Registered Office: The Estate Office, Melbury Sampford, Dorchester, DT2 0LF
Activities: Mixed farming
Major Shareholder: The Honourable Charlotte Anne Townshend
Officers: Robert Ian Sanderson, Secretary; The Honourable Charlotte Anne Townshend [1955] Director; James Reginald Townshend [1954] Director

Evesham Specialist Packaging Limited
Incorporated: 21 May 1999 *Employees:* 27
Net Worth: £6,799,351 *Total Assets:* £8,769,060
Registered Office: Beaumont House, 172 Southgate Street, Gloucester, GL1 2EZ
Activities: Wholesale of other intermediate products
Shareholders: Richard Mitchell; Douglas John Wilson
Officers: Richard Mitchell, Secretary/Sales Manager; Caroline Sheila Lynch [1968] Director/Secretary; Ronan Patrick Lynch [1968] Director/Sales Manager; Duncan MacDonald [1966] Sales Director; Richard Mitchell [1966] Director/Sales Manager; Douglas John Wilson [1967] Director/Sales Manager

EVGH Limited
Incorporated: 5 October 2010 *Employees:* 69
Previous: Ecovision (Group) Limited
Net Worth Deficit: £13,801,066 *Total Assets:* £6,793,154
Registered Office: East Suite, Brimscombe Port Business Park, Brimscombe, Stroud, Glos, GL5 2QQ
Activities: Production of electricity
Officers: Stephen Pfeil, Secretary; Christopher Graham Adcock [1959] Director/Installation of Solar Panels; Neville Brauer [1953] Director; Fiona Jane Gibson [1975] Investor Director; Peter Richard Randall [1957] Director

Williams Ewan Limited
Incorporated: 4 April 2007
Net Worth Deficit: £1,808,852 *Total Assets:* £3,800,933
Registered Office: 2 Cricklade Court, Old Town, Swindon, Wilts, SN1 3EY
Activities: Buying and selling of own real estate
Shareholders: Vincent James Ewan; Robert Williams
Officers: Robert Williams, Secretary; Robert Williams [1965] Director/Property Developer

Excalibur Academies Trust
Incorporated: 17 July 2012 *Employees:* 478
Net Worth: £68,685,408 *Total Assets:* £75,387,872
Registered Office: St John's Marlborough, Granham Hill, Marlborough, Wilts, SN8 4AX
Activities: Primary education
Officers: Catherine Jane Butler [1962] Director; Emma Louise Butler [1977] Director/PR Consultant; Susan Janet Clarke [1954] Director/Company Secretary; Nicola Jane Edmondson [1968] Director; Alan Richard Buchan Gould [1968] Director/Freelance Project Management Consultant; Dr Kieran Kelly [1959] Director/University Lecturer; Lucy Clare Lee [1975] Director/Housewife; Jeanette Lynn Longhurst [1958] Director/Health & Social Care Consultant; Gillian Frances Mortimer [1962] Director/Retired; Ann Patricia Parry [1950] Director/Retired; Nicholas Simon George Swan [1954] Director/Retired; Christopher Frank William Waldon [1969] Director/Chartered Engineer; Toby Watson [1972] Director/Finance

Excalibur Communications GB Limited
Incorporated: 25 January 2000 *Employees:* 59
Net Worth: £6,074,222 *Total Assets:* £9,835,307
Registered Office: Arclite House, Century Road, Peatmoor, Swindon, Wilts, SN5 5YN
Activities: Other telecommunications activities
Parent: Excalibur Communications Limited
Officers: Peter Valentine Boucher [1971] Director/Chief Executive; Emma-Jane Jane Carter [1980] Sales & Marketing Director; Richard William Evans [1977] Finance Director; Graham Edward Charles Ford [1979] Technical Director; James Paul Phipps [1979] Director

Excalibur Communications Group Limited
Incorporated: 20 February 2018 *Employees:* 59
Net Worth: £864,589 *Total Assets:* £9,280,397
Registered Office: Arclite House, Century Road, Peatmoor, Swindon, Wilts, SN5 5YN
Activities: Activities of other holding companies n.e.c.
Shareholder: Peter Valentine Boucher
Officers: Peter Valentine Boucher [1971] Director/Chief Executive; Emma-Jane Jane Carter [1980] Sales & Marketing Director; Richard William Evans [1977] Finance Director; Graham Edward Charles Ford [1979] Technical Director; Emma Clair Phipps [1980] Director; James Paul Phipps [1979] Director

Excalibur Unified Communications Limited
Incorporated: 17 July 2012 *Employees:* 59
Net Worth: £2,710,508 *Total Assets:* £6,955,241
Registered Office: Arclite House, Century Road, Peatmoor, Swindon, Wilts, SN5 5YN
Activities: Other business support service activities n.e.c.
Parent: Excalibur Communications Group Limited
Officers: Peter Valentine Boucher [1971] Director/Chief Executive; Emma-Jane Jane Carter [1980] Sales & Marketing Director; Richard William Evans [1977] Finance Director; Graham Edward Charles Ford [1979] Technical Director; James Paul Phipps [1979] Director

Exception Group Limited
Incorporated: 30 December 2004 *Employees:* 3
Net Worth: £4,078,000 *Total Assets:* £4,764,000
Registered Office: 32 Harris Road, Port Marsh Industrial Estate, Calne, Wilts, SN11 9PT
Activities: Other business support service activities n.e.c.
Parent: Global CEM Solutions Limited
Officers: Colin Reid Campbell [1948] Director/Attorney [American]; Toh-Seng NG [1953] Director [American]

EXE Investment Holdings Limited
Incorporated: 20 November 2012
Net Worth: £16,013,543 *Total Assets:* £16,684,635
Registered Office: Unit 3c Falcon Road, Sowton Industrial Estate, Exeter, Devon, EX2 7LB
Activities: Activities of other holding companies n.e.c.
Shareholder: Guy Courtenay Bagot Brook
Officers: Guy Courtenay Bagot Brook [1960] Director; Matthew James Fripp [1977] Director; Morley Andrew Sage [1962] Director

Exe Investment Limited
Incorporated: 14 February 1996
Net Worth: £16,013,543 *Total Assets:* £16,684,637
Registered Office: Unit 3c Falcon Road, Sowton Industrial Estate, Exeter, Devon, EX2 7LB
Activities: Other letting and operating of own or leased real estate
Shareholders: EXE Investment Holdings Limited; Guy Courtenay Bagot Brook
Officers: Matthew James Fripp, Secretary; Guy Courtenay Bagot Brook [1960] Director; Matthew James Fripp [1977] Director; Morley Andrew Sage [1962] Director

Executive Jet Support Limited
Incorporated: 15 November 1994 *Employees:* 21
Net Worth: £6,077,486 *Total Assets:* £7,569,254
Registered Office: Vincients Road, Bumpers Farm Industrial Estate, Chippenham, Wilts, SN14 6NQ
Activities: Other transportation support activities
Major Shareholder: Simon Anthony Browse
Officers: Marc Richard Browse [1965] Director/Manager; Simon Anthony Browse [1969] Director

Exepex Estates Limited
Incorporated: 11 February 1947 *Employees:* 7
Net Worth: £6,572,055 *Total Assets:* £8,649,121
Registered Office: Dormy House, 43 Kingsbury Street, Marlborough, Wilts, SN8 1JE
Activities: Development of building projects
Parent: Solent Investments Limited
Officers: Anna Victoria Loader Easton, Secretary/Director; James William Alfred Loader Pittams, Secretary; Nicholas John Chase [1949] Director/Accountant; Anna Victoria Loader Easton [1964] Director/Housewife; Melanie Susan Gurney [1959] Director

Exeter and Devon Airport Limited
Incorporated: 20 July 1987 *Employees:* 303
Net Worth: £17,868,000 *Total Assets:* £28,663,000
Registered Office: Airport House, Exeter Airport, Exeter, Devon, EX5 2BD
Activities: Service activities incidental to air transportation
Parent: Regional & City Airports Holdings Limited
Officers: Katherine Georgina Cook, Secretary; Andrew Michael Bell [1979] Director/Chief Operating Officer; Clive Peter Coleman [1956] Development Director; Sir Peter Rigby [1943] Director; Matthew David Roach [1971] Director/Accountant; Stephen James Wiltshire [1974] Operations Director

Exeter Canal and Quay Trust Limited (The)
Incorporated: 17 December 1981
Net Worth: £4,275,605 *Total Assets:* £4,640,331
Registered Office: Exeter City Council Civil Offices, Paris Street, Exeter, Devon, EX1 1JN
Activities: Non-trading company
Officers: Guy Curry, Secretary; Richard Arthur Branston [1944] Director/Interviewer; Peter John Cusa [1942] Director/Architect; Peter William Edwards [1947] Director/Bus Driver; David James Harvey [1955] Director/Retired; Roger Johnson [1946] Director/Retired; Andrew Robert Leadbetter [1964] Director/Businessman; Cllr Robert Charles Newby [1954] Director/Retired; Rachel Helen Sutton [1956] Director/Councillor; Anthony John Wardle [1948] Director; Alan Williamson [1947] Director/Solicitor

The Exeter Cash Plan
Incorporated: 9 January 1953 *Employees:* 1
Previous: Engage Mutual Health
Net Worth: £2,992,000 *Total Assets:* £5,105,000
Registered Office: Lakeside House, Emperor Way, Exeter Business Park, Exeter, EX1 3FD
Activities: Non-life insurance
Parent: Exeter Cash Plan Holdings Limited
Officers: Zoe Maureen Patricia Kubiak, Secretary; Paul Austin [1965] Finance Director; David Sheldon Brand [1954] Director; Steven David Bryan [1966] Executive Director of Distribution & Marketing; Andrew Donald Sutcliffe Chapman [1958] Director/Chief Executive; Professor William Trevor Hamilton [1958] Medical Director; Helen Stodart McEwan [1964] Director/Company Executive; Stephen John Payne [1961] Director

Exeter Cash Plan Holdings Limited
Incorporated: 29 April 2015
Net Worth: £100 *Total Assets:* £3,902,270
Registered Office: Lakeside House, Emperor Way, Exeter, Devon, EX1 3FD
Activities: Other activities auxiliary to insurance and pension funding
Parent: Exeter Friendly Soceity
Officers: Zoe Maureen Patricia Kubiak, Secretary; Paul Austin [1965] Finance Director; David Sheldon Brand [1954] Director; Steven David Bryan [1966] Executive Director of Distribution & Marketing; Andrew Donald Sutcliffe Chapman [1958] Director/Chief Executive; Professor William Trevor Hamilton [1958] Medical Director; Helen Stodart McEwan [1964] Company Executive & Non-Executive Director; Stephen John Payne [1961] Director

Exeter Castle Management Company Limited
Incorporated: 5 March 2013 *Employees:* 1
Net Worth: £1,676,797 *Total Assets:* £4,125,764
Registered Office: 3 Southernhay West, Exeter, EX1 1JG
Activities: Residents property management
Major Shareholder: Derek Alan Gollop
Officers: Derek Alan Gollop [1957] Director

The Exeter Diocesan Board of Finance Limited
Incorporated: 27 November 1922 *Employees:* 62
Net Worth: £96,766,000 *Total Assets:* £103,303,000
Registered Office: The Old Deanery, The Cloisters, Exeter, Devon, EX1 1HS
Activities: Activities of religious organisations
Officers: Neil Andrew Williams, Secretary; The Right Reverend Robert Ronald Atwell [1954] Director/Clerk in Holy Orders; The Reverend David Ross Bailey [1958] Director/Clerk in Holy Orders; Mark Andrew Butchers [1959] Director/Clerk in Holy Orders; Douglas James Dettmer [1964] Director/Clerk in Holy Orders [American]; Hannah Louise Dunn [1993] Director/Self Employed; Antoinette Anne Joan Foreman [1943] Director/Retired; Giles Richard Frampton [1956] Director/Chartered Accountant; The Rev Simon George Franklin [1954] Director/Clerk in Holy Orders; The Venerable Christopher David Futcher [1958] Director/Clerk in Holy Orders; The Very Reverend Jonathan Desmond Francis Greener [1961] Director/Dean of Exeter; The Reverend Williams Peter Guy Hazlewood [1971] Director/Clerk in Holy Orders; The Reverend Edward Quincey Hobbs [1974] Director/Clerk in Holy Orders; Annie Penelope Jefferies [1949] Director/Retired Chartered Physiotherapist; Michael Stuart Jefferies [1946] Director/Retired; Stephen Anthony George Macey [1977] Director/Performance Information Analyst; Nicholas Howard Paul McKinnel [1954] Director/Clerk in Holy Orders; Robert John Mills [1949] Director/Retired; Philip Richard Mumby [1958] Director; Rev Michael John Partridge [1961] Director/Vicar; Julian Nigel Payne [1959] Director; The Right Reverend Jacqueline Ann Searle [1960] Director/Clerk in Holy Orders; Councillor Marguerite Dorothy Shapland [1948] Director; Raymond Shapland [1939] Director/Retired; The Reverend Samantha Mary Stayte [1971] Director/Clerk in Holy Orders; Michael Dermot Andrew Williams [1957] Director/Clerk in Holy Orders; Dr Michael Charles Wykes [1975] Director/Self Employed

Exeter Estates Limited
Incorporated: 18 September 2006 *Employees:* 9
Net Worth: £1,464,208 *Total Assets:* £14,582,095
Registered Office: c/o Prydis, Senate Court, Southernhay Gardens, Exeter, EX1 1NT
Activities: Retail sale of automotive fuel in specialised stores
Shareholder: Anthony George Edward Rowe
Officers: Nicholas Stephens Evans [1963] Director; Ian Charles MacLean [1957] Director; Anthony George Edward Rowe [1948] Director

Exeter Finance Group Limited
Incorporated: 10 November 2015
Net Worth Deficit: £1,033 *Total Assets:* £5,361,177
Registered Office: 3rd Floor, The Senate, Southernhay Gardens, Exeter, EX1 1UG
Activities: Other credit granting n.e.c.
Major Shareholder: Peter William Lacy Keech
Officers: Christopher John Hall [1958] Director; Peter William Lacy Keech [1954] Director

Exeter Finance Ltd
Incorporated: 20 June 2013 *Employees:* 4
Net Worth: £1,514,600 *Total Assets:* £24,607,380
Registered Office: 3rd Floor, The Senate, Southernhay Gardens, Exeter, EX1 1UG
Activities: Other credit granting n.e.c.
Parent: Exeter Finance Group Limited
Officers: Christopher John Hall [1958] Director; Peter William Lacy Keech [1954] Director

Exeter Golf and Country Club,Limited (The)
Incorporated: 13 February 1928 *Employees:* 115
Net Worth: £6,612,134 *Total Assets:* £10,092,473
Registered Office: Wear House, Countess Wear, Exeter, Devon, EX2 7AE
Activities: Activities of sport clubs
Officers: Paul Dukes [1947] Director/Hotelier; William Gannon [1951] Director; Generald Maxwell Goodison [1956] Director/Business Manager/Advisor; Peter Lacey [1944] Director/Architect; Clifford John Nightingale [1948] Director/Chartered Accountant; Deborah Ann Stevenson [1970] Director of Human Resources

Exeter Royal Academy for Deaf Education.
Incorporated: 6 May 2008 *Employees:* 193
Net Worth: £3,122,082 *Total Assets:* £16,197,916
Registered Office: 50 Topsham Road, Exeter, Devon, EX2 4NF
Activities: Other education n.e.c.
Officers: Sara Jane Papworth, Secretary; Anthony Kenneth Alexander [1948] Director/Retired; Peter Hugh Burroughs [1944] Director/Treasurer/Trustee; Rhodri Giles Davey [1974] Director/Solicitor; John Peter Alistair Dewhirst [1956] Director/Councillor; Charles Henry Hampton II [1960] Director/Partner/Lecturer [American]; Dr Janet Angela Harvey [1949] Director/Education Consultant; Stephen Ritson King [1969] Director/Insurance Broker; Jennifer Thea Sealey [1963] Director

Exeter Rugby Club Limited
Incorporated: 18 February 1997 *Employees:* 353
Net Worth: £2,050,145 *Total Assets:* £8,965,851
Registered Office: Sandy Park Stadium, Sandy Park Way, Exeter, Devon, EX2 7NN
Activities: Activities of sport clubs
Parent: Exeter Rugby Group PLC
Officers: Robert Edward John Baxter [1971] Director/Professional Rugby Union; Stephen Richard Byrne [1955] Director; Brian Lodge [1960] Director; Keiron Timothy Northcott [1960] Director/Insurance Broker; Alan Robin Quantick [1947] Director/Chartered Accountant; Anthony George Edward Rowe [1948] Director

Exeter Rugby Group PLC
Incorporated: 3 February 1997 *Employees:* 353
Net Worth: £11,099,471 *Total Assets:* £30,468,104
Registered Office: Sandy Park Stadium, Sandy Park Way, Exeter, Devon, EX2 7NN
Activities: Activities of sport clubs
Officers: Christopher John Over, Secretary; Robert Edward John Baxter [1971] Director/Professional Rugby Union; Stephen Richard Byrne [1955] Director; Mark Alistair Champion [1973] Director/Accountant; Brian Lodge [1960] Director; Keiron Timothy Northcott [1960] Director/Insurance Consultant; Christopher John Over [1952] Director/Solicitor; Alan Robin Quantick [1947] Director/Chartered Accountant; Anthony George Edward Rowe [1948] Director

Exeter School
Incorporated: 26 June 2002 *Employees:* 186
Net Worth: £23,685,276 *Total Assets:* £29,218,278
Registered Office: Victoria Park Road, Exeter, EX2 4NS
Activities: Other education n.e.c.
Officers: Miles Colin Magub Maceacharn, Secretary; Adrian Phillip Burbanks [1965] Director/Risk Management; Kevin Andrew Cheney [1950] Director/Retired Headmaster; Helen Clark [1954] Director/Home & Farm Manager; Rowan Clare Edbrooke [1961] Director/Educationalist; Paul Bernard Fisher [1954] Director/Retired; James Dominic Gaisford [1958] Director/Chartered Accountant; Dr Martin Christopher Grossel [1948] Director/University Lecturer; Brigadier Stephen Philip Hodder [1958] Director/Retired Officer; Gillian Ann Hodgetts [1968] Director/Head of Communications & Public Relations; Andrew Charles Woodley King [1949] Director/Retailer; Richard Elliott May [1964] Director/Chartered Surveyor; Alison Catherine Annetta O'Connor [1971] Director/QC; Councillor Graham John Prowse [1953] Director/Councillor; Dr Sara Catherine Smart [1956] Director/Lecturer; Ruth Marie Vigers [1963] Director/Businesswoman; Professor Anthony Francis Watkinson [1956] Director/Consultant Radiologist and Professor of Radiology

Exeter Science Park Limited
Incorporated: 24 February 2009 *Employees:* 3
Net Worth Deficit: £1,692,396 *Total Assets:* £7,915,006
Registered Office: 6 Babbage Way, Science Park, Clyst, Honiton, Exeter, EX5 2FN
Activities: Other business support service activities n.e.c.
Officers: Dr Sally Basker [1962] Director/Chief Executive Officer; Paul Clifford Chivers [1962] Director/Corporate Financier; Keri Anne Denton [1968] Director; Jane Dumeresque [1958] Director; David Ferguson [1976] Director/Head of Digital Innovation; Sean Fielding [1962] Director/University Officer; Jon-Paul Paul Hedge [1979] Director; David Geoffrey Richardson [1980] Director/Solicitor; David Norman Etheredge Rowe [1947] Director; Philip James Skinner [1960] Director/Farmer; Sir William Arnot Wakeham [1944] Director/Retired

Exhibitor Limited
Incorporated: 13 June 2002
Net Worth: £3,951,309 *Total Assets:* £4,383,753
Registered Office: 17 Black Jack Street, Cirencester, Glos, GL7 2AA
Activities: Other business support service activities n.e.c.
Officers: Kaye Bryce, Secretary/Administrator; Darren Patrick Edward Bryce [1970] Director; Kaye Bryce [1973] Director/Consultant

Exmoor Calvert Trust
Incorporated: 13 August 1991 *Employees:* 41
Net Worth: £4,695,635 *Total Assets:* £5,175,431
Registered Office: Wistlandpound, Kentisbury, Barnstaple, Devon, EX31 4SJ
Activities: Other holiday and other collective accommodation
Officers: Christopher James Gregson, Secretary; Lady Jennifer Joyce Acland [1937] Director/Lecturer; Lady Elizabeth Periam Acland Hood Gass [1940] Director/Farming; Countess Eleanor Arran [1949] Director/Farmer; Dr Thomas Leslie Bigge [1945] Director/Doctor; David Cooper [1944] Director; Michael David Patrick Ford [1956] Director; James French [1953] Director/Retired; Christopher James Gregson [1957] Director/Solicitor; Jeremy Richard Holtom [1957] Director/Chartered Surveyor; Peter John Maggs [1952] Director/Retired; Susan Joy May [1950] Director/Agriculture; Paul Bannerman Petrides [1952] Director/Retired; Philip Henry Sampson [1959] Director/Consultant; Sir David Richard Alexander Scott [1954] Director/Retired; Teresa Jane Turner [1960] Director/Accountant; William John Vandersteen [1973] Director/HR Consultant

Exmouth Community College
Incorporated: 7 March 2011 *Employees:* 328
Net Worth: £24,019,652 *Total Assets:* £31,292,722
Registered Office: Exmouth Community College, Gipsy Lane, Exmouth, Devon, EX8 3AF
Activities: General secondary education
Officers: Kim Michelle Dearsly, Secretary; Andrew John Davis [1967] Director/Principal; Raymond Davison [1945] Director/Retired University Lecturer; Jill Marion Elson [1948] Director/Retired; Dr Andrew Gelling [1965] Director/Teacher; Robert Kimbell Johnson [1949] Director/Retired; Ian Malcolm MacQueen [1947] Director; Clair Rowan McColl [1979] Director/Administration; Dr Emily Jane McGrath [1976] Director/Doctor; Lesley Miszewska [1960] Director/Company Secretary/Financial Controller; Robert Ian Mitchell [1957] Director/Chief Science Technician; Victoria Louise Raven [1967] Director/Civil Servant; Marianne Elizabeth Skinner [1960] Director/Teacher; Anna Helen Keenor Stimson [1974] Director/Researcher; Anna Sheila Streather [1961] Director/University Lecturer; Clare Tate [1979] Director/Area/Cluster Manager; Margaret Turgoose [1964] Self-Employed Director; Philip Wales [1963] Director/Academy Business Manager

Exmouth Marina Ltd
Incorporated: 26 March 1898 *Employees:* 2
Net Worth: £10,711,000 *Total Assets:* £11,998,000
Registered Office: Greendale Business Park, Woodbury Salterton, Exeter, EX5 1EW
Activities: Sea and coastal passenger water transport
Parent: FWSC (Exmouth) Ltd
Officers: Peter German, Secretary; Alec Robin Bill Carter [1974] Director; Mathew Rowan Carter [1982] Director; Robin Anthony Bill Carter [1944] Director/Farmer; Rowan Charles Carter [1953] Director/Farmer; Peter Lewin German [1953] Director

Expedia Treasury Services Limited
Incorporated: 10 May 2017
Net Worth: £30,681,576 *Total Assets:* £368,745,568
Registered Office: 2 Temple Back East, Temple Quay, Bristol, BS1 6EG
Activities: Other business support service activities n.e.c.
Parent: Expedia Group, Inc.
Officers: Robert John Dzielak [1971] Director [American]; Frances Josephine Erskine [1969] Director/Business Executive [American]; Alan Pickerill [1966] Director [American]; Lance Allen Soliday [1972] Director [American]

Expolink Europe Limited
Incorporated: 26 January 1995 *Employees:* 235
Net Worth: £389,798 *Total Assets:* £3,576,154
Registered Office: 6 Greenways Business Park, Bellinger Close, Chippenham, Wilts, SN15 1BN
Activities: Activities of call centres
Officers: Nicholas Andrew William Bacon [1961] Director; Catherine Anne Hewitt [1968] Finance Director; John Steven Wilson [1957] Director

Expolink Group Limited
Incorporated: 22 April 2016 *Employees:* 240
Net Worth: £430,496 *Total Assets:* £9,290,151
Registered Office: 6 Greenways Business Park, Bellinger Close, Chippenham, Wilts, SN15 1BN
Activities: Activities of head offices
Officers: Nicholas Andrew William Bacon [1961] Director; Catherine Anne Hewitt [1968] Finance Director; Roger Stephen Oliver [1956] Director; John Steven Wilson [1957] Director

Express Contract Drying Ltd
Incorporated: 25 June 1996
Net Worth: £4,449,451 *Total Assets:* £6,088,833
Registered Office: Flat 5.02, 2-7 Elmdale Road, Clifton, Bristol, BS8 1SZ
Activities: Manufacture of other food products n.e.c.
Major Shareholder: David Patrick McDermott
Officers: Jacqueline Spavin, Secretary; Nicholas Jonathan Ball [1973] Director/Manager; Diane May Fudge [1958] Director/Teacher; David Patrick McDermott [1949] Director; Patrick McDonagh [1972] Director/Development Manager [Irish]; Jacqueline Spavin [1957] Director/Secretary

Expromet Technologies Group Limited
Incorporated: 28 November 2016 *Employees:* 109
Net Worth: £713,160 *Total Assets:* £11,902,748
Registered Office: Mullacott Cross Trading Estate, Ilfracombe, Devon, EX34 8PL
Activities: Activities of head offices
Shareholder: Henry William Gregson
Officers: Steven Bone [1971] Director; Tony Buckland [1962] Director; Henry William Gregson [1958] Director; Alistair John Schofield [1966] Director; Christopher James Thompson [1963] Director

Extreme Assets LLP
Incorporated: 1 October 2013
Net Worth: £7,124,082 *Total Assets:* £10,384,760
Registered Office: 52 Holton Road, Holton Heath Trading Park, Poole, Dorset, BH16 6LT
Officers: Connor Jon Harrison Thorne [1995] Member; Steven Thorne [1970] Member

Exyte Hargreaves Limited
Incorporated: 7 June 1934 *Employees:* 288
Previous: MW Hargreaves Limited
Net Worth Deficit: £523,000 *Total Assets:* £14,817,000
Registered Office: Unit C1, Methuen South, Methuen Park, Bath Road, Chippenham, Wilts, SN14 0GT
Activities: Other manufacturing n.e.c.
Officers: Felicity Elaine Jackson, Secretary; Jane Fowler [1978] Finance Director; Andy Mark Sneyd [1968] Managing Director

Eyre Holdings Limited
Incorporated: 3 September 1981
Net Worth: £3,819,698 *Total Assets:* £4,494,698
Registered Office: Mary Street House, Mary Street, Taunton, Somerset, TA1 3NW
Activities: Activities of head offices
Parent: Ogier Trustee (Jersey) Limited
Officers: Ilona Katherine Lamb, Secretary; Ilona Katherine Lamb [1982] Director

F & B Profiles (Holdings) Limited
Incorporated: 23 August 1996 *Employees:* 331
Net Worth: £14,378,202 *Total Assets:* £25,885,864
Registered Office: c/o Precision Profiles, Southway Drive, Warmley, Bristol, BS30 5LW
Activities: Non-trading company
Major Shareholder: Roger Frederick Avery
Officers: Lisa Helen Sinclair, Secretary; Roger Frederick Avery [1949] Director

F & B Profiles Limited
Incorporated: 30 October 1987 *Employees:* 248
Net Worth: £13,264,822 *Total Assets:* £26,296,284
Registered Office: Southway Drive, Warmley, Bristol, BS30 5LW
Activities: Manufacture of other fabricated metal products n.e.c.
Officers: Lisa Helen Sinclair, Secretary; Roger Frederick Avery [1949] Director

F & W Media International Limited
Incorporated: 22 May 2000 *Employees:* 50
Net Worth: £681,332 *Total Assets:* £5,846,463
Registered Office: Pynes Hill Court, Pynes Hill, Rydon Lane, Exeter, EX2 5AZ
Activities: Activities of head offices
Officers: Bridget Jolliffe [1960] Director; James Anthony Charles Woollam [1977] Director

Faber Brook Farm Limited
Incorporated: 14 August 2014
Net Worth: £59,811 *Total Assets:* £5,356,465
Registered Office: Woodlands Grange, Woodlands Lane, Bradley Stoke, Bristol, BS32 4JY
Activities: Mixed farming
Shareholders: Faber Trees Limited; Jean Dyer Limited
Officers: Jean Marie Dyer [1959] Director/Farmer; Philip John Dyer [1961] Director/Farmer

Fabrinet UK Limited
Incorporated: 31 October 1977 *Employees:* 203
Previous: Exception EMS Limited
Net Worth: £4,563,000 *Total Assets:* £10,758,000
Registered Office: c/o Exception Group Limited, 32 Harris Road, Port Marsh Industrial Estate, Calne, Wilts, SN11 9PT
Activities: Manufacture of other electronic and electric wires and cables
Parent: Exception Group Limited
Officers: Simon Paul Hopcraft [1963] Director/General Manager; Toh-Seng NG [1953] Director [American]

Faccombe Estates Limited
Incorporated: 12 July 1978 *Employees:* 15
Net Worth: £13,868,302 *Total Assets:* £14,895,960
Registered Office: The Estate Office, Faccombe, Andover, Hants, SP11 0DS
Activities: Mixed farming
Parent: Etablissement Landeco Vaduz
Officers: Ian William Stark, Secretary; Alastair Brooks [1972] Director/Estate Manager; Rupert Edis [1971] Director

Faerch Plast Poole Ltd
Incorporated: 28 September 2015 *Employees:* 123
Net Worth: £3,902,923 *Total Assets:* £12,704,302
Registered Office: Faerch Plast, Fleets Lane, Poole, Dorset, BH15 3BT
Activities: Other manufacturing n.e.c.
Parent: Faerch Plast Manufacturing Limited
Officers: Tom Sand-Kristensen [1971] Director/Group CFO [Danish]

Fairchild Thompson LLP
Incorporated: 10 July 2013
Net Worth: £4,135,805 *Total Assets:* £4,136,285
Registered Office: c/o Regulatory Accounting Limited, Priam House, Fire Fly Avenue, Swindon, Wilts, SN2 2EH
Officers: Carol Jane Barber [1960] Member; Charles Barber [1998] Member; Edward Frederick Hilary Barber [1994] Member; Olivia Barber [1991] Member

Fairfield Farm Trust
Incorporated: 22 June 1977 *Employees:* 73
Previous: Fairfield Opportunity Farm (Dilton) Limited
Net Worth: £6,058,857 *Total Assets:* £6,250,659
Registered Office: 43 High Street, Dilton Marsh, Westbury, Wilts, BA13 4DL
Activities: Other education n.e.c.
Officers: Alan Best [1971] Director/Bank Official; Julie Ann Cathcart [1961] Director/Education Advisor; Martin David Cooper [1952] Director/Education Consultant; Alison Mary Irving [1943] Director; Giuseppe Antonio Melillo [1981] Director; Vicky Helen Ody [1974] Director/Accountant; Anne Marie Pelling [1965] Managing Director Butterfly Home Help

Fairlie Holdings Limited
Incorporated: 19 July 2010 *Employees:* 327
Net Worth: £9,432,162 *Total Assets:* £25,738,728
Registered Office: Minerva House, Lower Bristol Road, Bath, BA2 9ER
Activities: Activities of patent and copyright agents; other legal activities n.e.c.
Major Shareholder: John Gregory Whelan
Officers: Terry Patrick McGranaghan [1959] Finance Director; John Gregory Whelan [1946] Director/Businessman

Fairlie Properties Limited
Incorporated: 10 September 2010 *Employees:* 2
Net Worth: £1,143,625 *Total Assets:* £11,799,337
Registered Office: Minerva House, Lower Bristol Road, Bath, BA2 9ER
Activities: Other letting and operating of own or leased real estate
Parent: Fairlie Holdings Limited
Officers: Terry Patrick McGranaghan [1959] Finance Director; John Gregory Whelan [1946] Director/Businessman

Fairlynx Limited
Incorporated: 19 March 1992 *Employees:* 1
Net Worth: £4,613,706 *Total Assets:* £5,684,308
Registered Office: 7-7c Snuff Street, Devizes, Wilts, SN10 1DU
Activities: Development of building projects
Parent: Fairlynx 2010 Limited
Officers: Guy Richard Straker, Secretary; Gordon John Straker [1947] Director/Estate Agent; Guy Richard Straker [1978] Director

Lilian Faithfull Care
Incorporated: 31 December 2007 *Employees:* 317
Previous: Lilian Faithfull Homes
Net Worth: £8,677,297 *Total Assets:* £14,341,922
Registered Office: Ground Floor West, Festival House, Jessop Avenue, Cheltenham, Glos, GL50 3SH
Activities: Residential nursing care facilities
Officers: Richard Sharratt Lyons, Secretary; Janet Elizabeth Ballinger [1960] Director/Accountant; Alan John Bishop [1950] Director/Hotelier; Fiona Court [1971] Director/Consultant Oncoplastic Breast Surgeon; Eleanor Fox [1949] Director/Retired; Timothy Paul Griffin [1942] Director/Chartered Surveyor; Richard Sharratt Lyons [1944] Director/Retired Solicitor; David Nye [1939] Director/Clerk in Holy Orders; Gareth Huw Parry [1973] Director/Solicitor; Gill Pyatt [1947] Director/Headteacher; Martyn Douglas Smith [1960] Director/Chartered Accountant; Jane Gwendoline Woodley [1939] Director/Retired

Falcon Self Drive Limited
Incorporated: 24 May 1990 *Employees:* 33
Net Worth: £6,194,321 *Total Assets:* £18,910,900
Registered Office: Cornishway East, Galmington Trading Estate, Taunton, Somerset, TA1 5LZ
Activities: Renting and leasing of trucks and other heavy vehicles
Parent: Ballyvesey Holdings Limited
Officers: Harold Hugh Montgomery, Secretary; David Nigel Birkmyre [1952] Director; Harold Hugh Montgomery [1948] Director; Mark Waite [1961] Operations Director

Falfish (Holdings) Limited
Incorporated: 13 December 2016 *Employees:* 149
Net Worth: £7,251,308 *Total Assets:* £13,182,682
Registered Office: Unit 15 Cardew Industrial Estate, Redruth, Cornwall, TR15 1SS
Activities: Activities of other holding companies n.e.c.
Shareholders: William Ian Greet; Mark Ian Adrian Greet
Officers: Mark Ian Adrian Greet [1962] Managing Director; William Ian Greet [1938] Director/Retired

Falfish Limited
Incorporated: 6 July 1979 *Employees:* 144
Net Worth: £7,022,586 *Total Assets:* £12,664,380
Registered Office: 15 Cardrew Industrial Estate, Redruth, Cornwall, TR15 1SS
Activities: Wholesale of other food, including fish, crustaceans and molluscs
Parent: Falfish (Holdings) Limited
Officers: Sharon Eileen Greet, Secretary; Mark Ian Adrian Greet [1962] Managing Director; Christopher Southworth [1963] Director/General Manager

Falkirk Group Limited
Incorporated: 7 July 2006 *Employees:* 2
Net Worth: £7,105,002 *Total Assets:* £14,416,075
Registered Office: Third Floor, Broad Quay House, Prince Street, Bristol, BS1 4DJ
Activities: Other business support service activities n.e.c.
Parent: Semperian PPP Investment Partners No.2 Limited
Officers: Kenneth Andrew McLellan [1961] Regional Project Director; Alan Campbell Ritchie [1967] Director

Fallon Enterprises Ltd
Incorporated: 8 February 2017
Net Worth: £90,751 *Total Assets:* £4,320,361
Registered Office: Plym House, 3 Longbridge Road, Marsh Mills, Plymouth, PL6 8LT
Activities: Other letting and operating of own or leased real estate
Shareholders: Peter George Bennett; Josephine Marama-Eru-Tea Bennett-Ward
Officers: Peter George Bennett [1950] Director; Polly Ann Bennett [1986] Director; Sylvie Jeanne-Marie Bennett [1969] Director [French]; Josephine Marama-Eru-Tea Bennett-Ward [1982] Director

Falmouth Exeter Plus
Incorporated: 16 April 2004 *Employees:* 365
Net Worth: £26,845,000 *Total Assets:* £88,156,000
Registered Office: Falmouth Exeter Plus, Penryn Campus, Penryn, Cornwall, TR10 9FE
Activities: Educational support services
Officers: Andrew Connolly [1962] Director of Finance; Peter Mark Cox [1963] Director; Alan Gary Hill [1965] Director/Chief Information and Digital Officer; Professor David John Hosken [1965] Director/University Professor [Australian/Swiss/British]; Daniel Jones [1980] HR Director; Dr Robin Generald Kirby [1978] Director/University Strategic Advisor; Professor Alan Glen Murray [1965] Director/Deputy Vice-Chancellor; Craig Justin Nowell [1973] Director; Antony Sanders [1954] Director/Chief Executive; Michael Philip Shore-Nye [1969] Director/Chief Operating Officer

Falmouth MAT
Incorporated: 6 July 2011 *Employees:* 210
Previous: Falmouth School
Net Worth: £27,502,842 *Total Assets:* £30,162,048
Registered Office: Falmouth School, Trescobeas Road, Falmouth, Cornwall, TR11 4LH
Activities: Pre-primary education
Officers: Deborah May Pullen, Secretary; Susan Mary Godzicz [1956] Director; Michael John Ross Griffiths [1948] Director/Owns and Runs Small Property Investment Company; David Peter Nicoll [1962] Director/Community Fundraising Manager; Anthony Glyn Williams [1963] Director/Electrical Engineer; Robert Scott Wilson [1972] Director/Accountant

Fanatics UK Holdings Limited
Incorporated: 22 January 2016 *Employees:* 714
Net Worth: £24,088,000 *Total Assets:* £67,404,000
Registered Office: First Floor, 10 Temple Back, Bristol, BS1 6FL
Activities: Activities of other holding companies n.e.c.
Major Shareholder: Michael G Rubin
Officers: Lauren Levitan [1965] Director/Ecommerce Financial Management [American]; Douglas Mack [1969] Director/Business Management [American]; Caren Yeamans [1975] Director/Attorney [American]

Farina Investments (UK) Limited
Incorporated: 12 March 2008
Net Worth: £563,646 *Total Assets:* £6,585,385
Registered Office: Unit 22 Sandleheath Industrial Estate, Fordingbridge, Hants, SP6 1PA
Activities: Other business support service activities n.e.c.
Officers: Tracy Jane Davy [1963] Director/Secretary

Faringdon Academy of Schools
Incorporated: 6 March 2012 *Employees:* 432
Net Worth: £22,023,000 *Total Assets:* £26,958,000
Registered Office: Faringdon Academy of Schools, Fernham Road, Faringdon, Oxon, SN7 7LB
Activities: Primary education
Officers: Anthony James Brian Cook [1975] Director/Manager; Catherine Elizabeth Henrietta Holmes [1960] Director/Home Maker; Rachel Mary Kenyon [1968] Director/Teacher; Duncan Paul Millard [1968] Director/Chief Executive; Christine Louise Price [1960] Director/Headteacher; Paul John Turner [1954] Director/Headteacher; Jeremy John Twynam [1937] Director/Retired; Rev Paul Colin Walker [1977] Director/Reverend; Louise Warren [1967] Director/Headteacher; Cudliffe Robert Wintringham [1947] Director/Adviser/Consultant; Ian Wright [1969] Director/University Administrator

Farleigh School Trust Limited
Incorporated: 8 May 1967 *Employees:* 81
Previous: Farleigh House Trustee Limited
Net Worth: £15,384,032 *Total Assets:* £17,552,960
Registered Office: Farleigh School, Red Rice, Andover, Hants, SP11 7PW
Activities: Primary education
Officers: Paul Richard Lorimer Lane, Secretary; Keith Russell Abel [1963] Director/Business Executive; Kirsty Anderson [1970] Director/Retired Head of Pre-Prep; Charlotte Cunningham [1967] Artistic Director [Luxembourger]; Gavin John Hamilton [1956] Director/Barrister; Simon Anthony Glidden Henderson [1968] Director/Financier; Charles Ingram Evans [1975] Director/Chartered Surveyor; Oswald McBride [1966] Director/Monk; Sarah Gabrielle Raffray [1968] Director/Headmistress; Emma Elisabeth Jane Todd [1968] Director/Literary Agent; Jane Elizabeth Vyvyan [1965] Director

Farley & Thompson LLP
Incorporated: 23 November 2006 *Employees:* 11
Net Worth: £615,076 *Total Assets:* £6,985,846
Registered Office: Pine Grange, Bath Road, Bournemouth, BH1 2NU
Officers: Colin John William Chalkly Maber [1954] Member; Nicholas Paul Chetwood [1978] Member; Edward Philip Harvey [1964] Member; Caroline Gillian Mills [1963] Member; Martin John Poole [1971] Member

Farmers First Limited
Incorporated: 13 March 2000 *Employees:* 99
Net Worth: £8,793,194 *Total Assets:* £23,940,372
Registered Office: One Glass Wharf, Bristol, BS2 0ZX
Activities: Activities of agricultural holding companies
Officers: Terrence James Bayliss [1942] Director/Farmer; John Addison Geldard [1951] Director/Farmer; Michael John Gooding [1965] Director; Glyn Jones [1953] Director/Farmer; Wayne Anthony Lammas [1963] Managing Director; Stuart Thomas Morris [1955] Director/Farmer; David Trevor Owen [1948] Managing Director; Terence Ian Simpson [1962] Director/Livestock Buyer; John Henry Wescott [1969] Director

Farmington Natural Stone Limited
Incorporated: 9 November 1995
Net Worth: £3,350,744 *Total Assets:* £6,414,471
Registered Office: Farmington Quarry, Northleach, Cheltenham, Glos, GL54 3NZ
Activities: Quarrying of ornamental and building stone, limestone, gypsum, chalk and slate
Shareholder: Richard Raymond Barrow
Officers: Richard Raymond Barrow, Secretary; John James Barrow [1944] Director; Richard Raymond Barrow [1971] Director/Manager; Shane Cameron [1960] Operations Director

Farmor's School
Incorporated: 18 July 2011 *Employees:* 117
Net Worth: £14,121,977 *Total Assets:* £15,643,308
Registered Office: Farmor's School, The Park, Fairford, Glos, GL7 4JQ
Activities: General secondary education
Officers: Susan Dorey, Secretary; Samuel John Bartholomew [1979] Director/Headteacher; Stephen Alexander Conlan [1970] Director/Solicitor; Sarah Michelle Crawford [1985] Director/Teacher; Damian Michael Evans [1969] Director/Accountant; Matthew Stuart Evans [1971] Director/Headteacher; Richard Hills [1968] Executive Director [British/New Zealander]; Anthony Joseph Joslyn [1959] Director/Finance Broker; Elizabeth Knox [1947] Director/Solicitor; Claire Anne Moran [1974] Director/Consultant; Rachael Ann Mundy [1971] Director/Examinations Officer; Kay Antonia Norman [1975] Director/Curriculum Administrator; Suzanne Ruth Paton [1967] Director/Partner; Lynne Porter [1961] Director/Manager

Farms for City Children Limited
Incorporated: 12 July 1974 *Employees:* 77
Net Worth: £3,200,883 *Total Assets:* £3,894,689
Registered Office: Nethercott House, Iddesleigh, Winkleigh, Devon, EX19 8BG
Activities: Mixed farming
Officers: Clare Morpurgo, Secretary; Justin Thomas Albert [1965] Director; Richard John Ash [1959] Director/Health & Safety Manager; John Perkins Evans [1956] Director/Farmer; Simon Hugh Gregory [1955] Director/Solicitor; Frances Harris [1966] Director/University Lecturer; Charles Andrew Huntington-Whiteley [1957] Director/Chartered Surveyor; Ali Mawle [1974] Director/Head of Schools; Clare Morpurgo [1942] Director/Retired; Michael Andrew Bridge Morpurgo [1943] Director/Writer and Teacher; Peter Michael Pantlin [1950] Director/Retired

Farrow & Ball Limited
Incorporated: 18 January 1971 *Employees:* 562
Net Worth: £64,120,000 *Total Assets:* £77,156,000
Registered Office: 33 Uddens Trading Estate, Wimborne, Dorset, BH21 7NL
Activities: Manufacture of wallpaper
Parent: Farrow & Ball Holdings Limited
Officers: Richard Robert Salmond, Secretary; Martin John Ball [1960] Director of Operations; Anthony Patrick Davey [1970] Director/Chief Executive Officer; Josephine Sarah Elizabeth Rance [1970] Marketing Director; Richard Robert Salmond [1970] Finance Director

Farthingford Properties Limited
Incorporated: 4 June 1973
Net Worth: £3,630,411 *Total Assets:* £5,022,327
Registered Office: First Floor, 7 Park Street, Bristol, BS1 5NF
Activities: Other letting and operating of own or leased real estate
Parent: PJFB Property Company Limited
Officers: Joan Breach, Secretary; Joan Breach [1944] Director/Chartered Accountant; Peter John Freeman Breach [1942] Director/Chartered Accountant

Mark Farwell Plant Hire Limited
Incorporated: 20 June 1994 *Employees:* 35
Net Worth: £5,103,673 *Total Assets:* £6,364,596
Registered Office: 14a Albany Road, Weymouth, Dorset, DT4 9TH
Activities: Other specialised construction activities n.e.c.
Shareholders: Amanda Jane Farwell; Mark Henry Farwell
Officers: Amanda Jane Farwell, Company Secretary; Amanda Jane Farwell [1959] Director; Mark Henry Farwell [1962] Director

Fasthosts Internet Limited
Incorporated: 26 October 1998 *Employees:* 161
Net Worth: £5,009,000 *Total Assets:* £23,873,000
Registered Office: Discovery House, 154 Southgate Street, Gloucester, GL1 2EX
Activities: Other information technology service activities
Parent: 1&1 UK Holdings Limited
Officers: Matthias Steinberg [1975] Director [German]; Simon Christopher Yeoman [1973] Director/General Manager

Fazakerley Prison Services Limited
Incorporated: 31 October 1994
Net Worth: £13,402,309 *Total Assets:* £55,583,512
Registered Office: Third Floor, Broad Quay House, Prince Street, Bristol, BS1 4DJ
Activities: Construction of commercial buildings
Parent: G4S Joint Ventures (Fazakerley) Limited
Officers: Alan Edward Birch [1970] Director; Gawie Murray Nienaber [1957] Director/General Legal Counsel; Vaishali Jagdish Patel [1973] Director/Solicitor; Jeremy Kenneth Petherick [1954] Managing Director; Alan Campbell Ritchie [1967] Director

FB Ammonite Limited
Incorporated: 18 November 2014 *Employees:* 664
Net Worth Deficit: £72,158,000 *Total Assets:* £305,742,016
Registered Office: 33 Uddens Trading Estate, Wimborne, Dorset, BH21 7NL
Activities: Activities of head offices
Officers: Richard Robert Salmond, Secretary; Anthony Patrick Davey [1970] Director/Chief Executive Officer; Richard Robert Salmond [1970] Director/Chief Financial Officer; Joshua Schulman [1971] Director/Retail Executive [American]; Charles Richard Arklay Steel [1975] Director; Martha Shaffer Wikstrom [1956] Director [British/American]

FB Brassica Limited
Incorporated: 19 November 2014
Net Worth Deficit: £61,322,000 *Total Assets:* £157,603,008
Registered Office: 33 Uddens Trading Estate, Wimborne, Dorset, BH21 7NL
Activities: Activities of head offices
Parent: FB Ammonite Limited
Officers: Richard Robert Salmond, Secretary; Charles Richard Arklay Steel [1975] Director

FB Brinjal Limited
Incorporated: 16 January 2015
Net Worth: £8,000,000 *Total Assets:* £156,192,000
Registered Office: 33 Uddens Trading Estate, Wimborne, Dorset, BH21 7NL
Activities: Activities of head offices
Parent: FB Brassica Limited
Officers: Richard Robert Salmond, Secretary; Charles Richard Arklay Steel [1975] Director

FB Calluna Limited
Incorporated: 7 November 2014 *Employees:* 2
Net Worth: £121,031,000 *Total Assets:* £273,067,008
Registered Office: 33 Uddens Trading Estate, Wimborne, Dorset, BH21 7NL
Activities: Activities of head offices
Parent: FB Brinjal Limited
Officers: Richard Robert Salmond, Secretary; Anthony Patrick Davey [1970] Director/Chief Executive Officer; Richard Robert Salmond [1970] Director/Chief Finance Officer; Charles Richard Arklay Steel [1975] Director

FB Heliservices Limited
Incorporated: 8 January 2001 *Employees:* 619
Net Worth: £5,229,000 *Total Assets:* £36,221,000
Registered Office: Cobham PLC, Brook Road, Wimborne, Dorset, BH21 2BJ
Activities: General public administration activities
Parent: FR Aviation Group Limited
Officers: Michael David Parry, Secretary; Paul Anthony Armstrong [1979] Director/General Manager; James Albert Goodbourn [1959] Director; Michael David Parry [1975] Finance Director; Richard Duncan Stoate [1963] Director

FB Leasing Limited
Incorporated: 13 August 2002
Net Worth: £8,488,000 *Total Assets:* £62,391,000
Registered Office: Cobham PLC, Brook Road, Wimborne, Dorset, BH21 2BJ
Activities: Renting and leasing of air passenger transport equipment
Parent: FR Aviation Group Limited
Officers: Michael David Parry, Secretary; Paul Anthony Armstrong [1979] Director/General Manager; James Albert Goodbourn [1959] Director; Michael David Parry [1975] Finance Director; Richard Duncan Stoate [1963] Director

FDL Salterns Limited
Incorporated: 25 October 2016
Net Worth Deficit: £42,806 *Total Assets:* £5,084,794
Registered Office: 2 Poole Road, Bournemouth, BH2 5QY
Activities: Development of building projects
Shareholders: Housing Growth Partnership GP LLP as General Partner of Housing Growth Partnership LP; Fresh Homes (Bournemouth) Ltd
Officers: Myles Bridges [1964] Director; Richard James Edge [1981] Director; David Robert Andrew Webb [1954] Director

Feedco Ltd
Incorporated: 10 February 2015 *Employees:* 25
Net Worth: £524,042 *Total Assets:* £4,573,246
Registered Office: Postlake, Clyst St Mary, Exeter, EX5 1AP
Activities: Manufacture of prepared feeds for farm animals
Officers: Kevin John Anning [1967] Director; Jeremy William Hamilton [1980] Director; Edward James Lane [1971] Director; Martyn John Pyne [1960] Director; Kevin John Roberts [1958] Director; Wilhelmus Jacobus Maria Smit [1970] Director [Dutch]

Feilden Clegg Bradley Studios LLP
Incorporated: 17 December 2001 *Employees:* 179
Net Worth: £3,844,144 *Total Assets:* £8,429,253
Registered Office: Bath Brewery, Toll Bridge Road, Bath, BA1 7DE
Officers: Keith John Bradley [1959] Member; Peter Alexander Clegg [1950] Member; David Appel [1971] LLP Member; Simon James MacDougall Carter [1970] LLP Member; Richard Graham Collis [1970] LLP Member; Jason Jonathan Cornish [1967] LLP Member; Andrew Thomas Couling [1960] LLP Member; Simon Edward Doody [1974] LLP Member; Sara Grohmann [1971] LLP Member; Thomas Anthony Jarman [1980] LLP Member; Michael David Keys [1966] LLP Member; Hugo William Tregarthen Marrack [1970] LLP Member; Geoffrey John Rich [1969] LLP Member; Helen Elizabeth Roberts [1971] LLP Member; Rachel Elizabeth Sayers [1970] LLP Member; John Vincent Southall [1950] LLP Member; David John Stansfield [1960] LLP Member; Ian Edwards Taylor [1957] LLP Member; Andrew Michael Theobald [1964] LLP Member; Samuel Morris Tyler [1970] LLP Member; Marigold Jane Webster [1956] LLP Member; Alexander Maurice Henry Whitbread [1968] LLP Member; Amanda Whittington [1973] LLP Member

Fen Farm Wind Park Limited
Incorporated: 7 April 2005
Net Worth: £28,926,576 *Total Assets:* £33,347,496
Registered Office: Lion House, Rowcroft, Stroud, Glos, GL5 3BY
Activities: Production of electricity
Parent: Ecotricity Group Limited
Officers: Tom Cowling, Secretary; Asif Rehmanwala [1976] Director/Chief Operating Officer; Dale Vince [1961] Director/Consultant

Fenchurch Engineering Services Limited
Incorporated: 6 September 1993
Net Worth: £8,800,522 *Total Assets:* £34,606,780
Registered Office: Choweree House, 21 Boutport Street, Barnstable, Devon, EX31 1RP
Activities: Transmission of electricity
Shareholder: Edwin John Andrews
Officers: Fiona Peacey, Secretary; Edwin Andrews [1945] Director/Engineer; Fiona Peacey [1962] Director/Nurse [Australian]

Feniton Park Limited
Incorporated: 16 February 2011 *Employees:* 7
Net Worth: £200,568 *Total Assets:* £8,039,458
Registered Office: The Mews, Queen Street, Colyton, Devon, EX24 6JU
Activities: Construction of domestic buildings
Major Shareholder: David Daniel Cutler
Officers: David Daniel Cutler [1953] Director/Consultant

J.Ferguson Estate,Limited
Incorporated: 16 March 1950
Net Worth: £26,636,898 *Total Assets:* £31,430,244
Registered Office: Down Farm, Westonbirt, Tetbury, Glos, GL8 8QW
Activities: Renting and operating of Housing Association real estate
Parent: Clarart Ltd
Officers: Claire Janet Tomlinson, Secretary; Claire Janet Tomlinson [1944] Director; Emma Claire Tomlinson [1974] Director; Luke George Tomlinson [1977] Director; Mark Lascelles Telford Tomlinson [1982] Director

Fermac Limited
Incorporated: 12 April 1983 *Employees:* 62
Previous: Fermac Traffic Services Limited
Net Worth: £2,146,402 *Total Assets:* £5,966,360
Registered Office: 24a High Street, Melksham, Wilts, SN12 6LA
Activities: Freight transport by road
Parent: Rockley Holdings Limited
Officers: Stuart Morgan [1970] Director; Anthony Frederick James Watson [1955] Director; Rukshana Drupathy Watson [1963] Director

The Ferne Animal Sanctuary
Incorporated: 11 September 2015 *Employees:* 53
Net Worth: £5,518,000 *Total Assets:* £5,618,548
Registered Office: Ferne Animal Sanctuary, Wambrook, Chard, Somerset, TA20 3DH
Activities: Farm animal boarding and care
Officers: Margaret Ann Bradshaw [1947] Director; David Allan Hancock Cook [1946] Director/Retired; Graham Higgins [1987] Director; Bernadette Ann Steadman [1955] Director/Retired; Nanette Jane Wale [1947] Director/Retired

Fernturn Holdings Limited
Incorporated: 30 December 1960 *Employees:* 2
Net Worth: £7,496,000 *Total Assets:* £7,519,000
Registered Office: One Redcliff Street, Bristol, BS1 6TP
Activities: Other letting and operating of own or leased real estate
Shareholder: Sean Kingsbury
Officers: Ian John Webb, Secretary; Ruth Pryor Ovens [1974] Human Resources Director; Ian John Webb [1973] Director/Accountant

FGP Systems Limited
Incorporated: 25 September 2015 *Employees:* 127
Net Worth: £795,198 *Total Assets:* £10,909,941
Registered Office: 20-22 Cumberland Drive, Granby Industrial Estate, Weymouth, Dorset, DT4 9TB
Activities: Machining
Parent: Fundamental Engineering Ltd
Officers: Hayley Jane Bell [1982] Personal Development and HSE Director; Paul Anthony Clark [1958] Operations Director; Alexander Dunn [1953] Director; Simon Griffiths-Hughes [1970] Director of Engineering; Dan Julian Kalms [1974] Director/Chartered Accountant; Nigel John Pitman [1965] Director; David Mark Taylor [1963] Director; Sir Peter Wall [1955] Director/Chairman

Fiberlean Technologies Limited
Incorporated: 23 February 2016 *Employees:* 44
Net Worth: £24,528,568 *Total Assets:* £40,380,756
Registered Office: Par Moor Centre, Par Moor Road, Par, Cornwall, PL24 2SQ
Activities: Manufacture of other products of wood; manufacture of articles of cork, straw and plaiting materials
Shareholder: Imerys Minerals Limited
Officers: Dr Thoralf Gliese [1966] Director/Executive Vice President [German]; Olivier Hautin [1964] Director/Vice-President [Belgian]; Thierry Salmona [1954] Director/Chief Technical Officer [French]; Dr Thomas Fredrich Staehrfeldt [1966] Director/VP Research & Development Services [German]

Field International Holdings (Dorset) Limited
Incorporated: 1 September 2011 *Employees:* 125
Net Worth: £2,070,025 *Total Assets:* £7,667,432
Registered Office: 37 Commercial Road, Poole, Dorset, BH14 0HU
Activities: Activities of production holding companies
Shareholders: Marie Rose Booker; David William Booker; Mark Robert David Booker
Officers: David William Booker [1941] Director/Chairman; Marie Rose Booker [1940] Director; Mark Robert David Booker [1966] Managing Director

Field International Limited
Incorporated: 15 September 1995 *Employees:* 48
Net Worth: £926,902 *Total Assets:* £6,621,076
Registered Office: 37 Commercial Road, Poole, Dorset, BH14 0HU
Activities: Other engineering activities
Parent: Field International Holdings (Dorset) Limited
Officers: Marie Rose Booker, Secretary; Christopher Paul Allen [1956] Director; David William Booker [1941] Director/Chairman; Marie Rose Booker [1940] Director; Mark Robert David Booker [1966] Director/Chief Executive; Richard Stephen Marples [1960] Director; John William McClelland [1965] Human Resources Director [Irish]; Adam Keith Oliver [1974] Finance Director

Fig Tree Court Limited
Incorporated: 27 September 2016 *Employees:* 4
Net Worth: £6,693,515 *Total Assets:* £7,219,767
Registered Office: 54 Murhill, Limpley Stoke, Bath, BA2 7FG
Activities: Other letting and operating of own or leased real estate
Shareholders: Julian Anne Roberts; Henry Peter Mallory
Officers: Patricia Watts, Secretary; Caroline Josephine Gardner [1979] Director; Henry Peter Mallory [1971] Director; Julian Anne Roberts [1969] Director; Patricia Jane Watts [1973] Director

Films at 59 Limited
Incorporated: 1 June 1990 *Employees:* 120
Net Worth: £5,506,411 *Total Assets:* £9,244,795
Registered Office: 59 Cotham Hill, Bristol, BS6 6JR
Activities: Motion picture, video and television programme post-production activities
Shareholder: Gina Lee Fucci-Prudence
Officers: Gina Lee Fucci Prudence, Secretary [American]; Gina Lee Fucci Prudence [1966] Managing Director [American]

FIM Trustee Limited
Incorporated: 21 November 2011 *Employees:* 7
Net Worth: £31,593,164 *Total Assets:* £36,723,912
Registered Office: Alexandra House, St Johns Street, Salisbury, Wilts, SP1 2SB
Activities: Dormant company
Officers: Isobel Brown [1960] Director; Ross Stuart Campbell [1968] Director; Andrew Stuart Cowan [1962] Director/Lawyer; Neil Greenberg [1968] Director/Psychiatrist; Sir John Chalmers McColl [1952] Director; Deidre Mills [1968] Director/Chief Executive Officer; David Paul Murray [1960] Director; Hans Joseph Russell Pung [1972] Director/President of Rand Europe; Anais Stephanie Reding [1986] Director/Civil Servant; Nicholas John Roberts [1968] Director/Chief Executive Officer; Robert Neil Robson [1962] Director/Chief Executive Officer; Major General Martin John Rutledge [1954] Director/Charity Chief Executive; Andrew Christopher Ward [1967] Director/Solicitor

Finance Solutions Limited
Incorporated: 23 June 1999
Net Worth: £2,267,830 *Total Assets:* £5,290,442
Registered Office: 3 The Lynher Building, Queen Anne's Battery, Plymouth, PL4 0LP
Activities: Other credit granting n.e.c.
Shareholders: David Andrew Harrison; Robert Gateshill
Officers: David Andrew Harrison, Secretary/Director; Robert Gateshill [1944] Director; David Andrew Harrison [1953] Director

Findlay Publications Investments Limited
Incorporated: 1 December 1993
Net Worth: £3,771,252 *Total Assets:* £3,771,252
Registered Office: 9 Falcon's Gate, Dean Road Yate, Bristol, BS37 5NH
Activities: Non-trading company
Major Shareholder: Timothy Robin Rampling
Officers: Kerry Maglennon, Secretary; Timothy Robin Rampling [1957] Director

Finian Farming LLP
Incorporated: 21 February 2008 *Employees:* 27
Net Worth: £14,404,361 *Total Assets:* £16,848,108
Registered Office: McGills, Oakley House, Tetbury Road, Cirencester, Glos, GL7 1US
Officers: Anna-Maria Kennedy [1950] Member; John William Kennedy [1950] Member

Finlay Hire Limited
Incorporated: 7 January 1992
Net Worth: £2,794,332 *Total Assets:* £9,083,607
Registered Office: Unit 4 Smoke Lane Industrial Estate, Smoke Lane, Bristol, BS11 0YA
Activities: Renting and leasing of construction and civil engineering machinery and equipment
Parent: Finlay Plant (UK) Limited
Officers: Robin Nicholas Powell [1969] Director; Robert David Statham [1954] Director/Sales; Jonathan Mark Wilson [1966] Director

Finlay Plant (UK) Limited
Incorporated: 15 February 2007
Net Worth: £4,461,641 *Total Assets:* £14,869,753
Registered Office: Unit 4 Smoke Lane Industrial Estate, Smoke Lane, Bristol, BS11 0YA
Activities: Activities of head offices
Parent: Molson Group Limited
Officers: Robin Nicholas Powell [1969] Director; Robert David Statham [1954] Director; Jonathan Mark Wilson [1966] Director

Fintec Group Limited
Incorporated: 18 March 2008 *Employees:* 4
Previous: ITEC Group Limited
Net Worth: £1,015,912 *Total Assets:* £4,801,486
Registered Office: 5 Pullman Court, Great Western Road, Gloucester, GL1 3ND
Activities: Financial leasing
Major Shareholder: Jacques Duyver
Officers: Philip James Perkins [1968] Director

Firmplot Limited
Incorporated: 30 July 1992 *Employees:* 4
Net Worth: £2,844,191 *Total Assets:* £3,572,823
Registered Office: 26-28 Southernhay East, Exeter, Devon, EX1 1NS
Activities: Construction of domestic buildings
Shareholders: Edina Street; Edina Street; Graham Neil Street; Graham Neil Street
Officers: Edina Street, Secretary; Edina Street [1958] Director; Graham Neil Street [1960] Director/Builder

Firn Overseas Packaging Limited
Incorporated: 8 September 1975 *Employees:* 7
Net Worth: £3,354,685 *Total Assets:* £12,580,207
Registered Office: Northern Barn, Ashley Court, Henley, Marlborough, Wilts, SN8 3RH
Activities: Non-specialised wholesale trade
Shareholders: Nermine Elgammal; Ibrahim Elgammal; Mohammed Azzam
Officers: Paul Meechan, Secretary; Samy Azzam [1975] Director/Trader; Dr Ibrahim Elgammal [1948] Director [Canadian]; Tarek Elgammal [1983] Director [Canadian]; Paul Meechan [1966] Director/Accountant

First Capital Finance Limited
Incorporated: 18 October 2000 *Employees:* 11
Net Worth: £860,279 *Total Assets:* £7,820,607
Registered Office: Capital House, 1084-1086 Christchurch Road, Bournemouth, BH7 6DT
Activities: Financial intermediation not elsewhere classified
Officers: Sean Michael Devoy [1967] Director; Paul Gough [1972] Director [New Zealander]; David James Mogg [1970] Director/Financial Broker; Richard David Perry [1964] Director/Finance Broker; Darren Venton [1972] Director/Finance Broker

First City Nursing Services Limited
Incorporated: 6 July 1999 *Employees:* 470
Net Worth: £2,583,207 *Total Assets:* £5,294,853
Registered Office: First City House, Cheney Manor Industrial Estate, Swindon, Wilts, SN2 2QG
Activities: General medical practice activities
Shareholders: Keith Paul Trowbridge; Mary Colette Ann Trowbridge
Officers: Mary Colette Ann Trowbridge, Secretary; Keith Paul Trowbridge [1952] Director/Nurse; Mary Colette Ann Trowbridge [1956] Director/Nurse; Stephen James Trowbridge [1978] Managing Director

First Databank UK Ltd
Incorporated: 25 January 1985 *Employees:* 115
Previous: First Databank Europe Limited
Net Worth: £29,240,572 *Total Assets:* £36,532,924
Registered Office: Swallowtail House, Grenadier Road, Exeter Business Park, Exeter, Devon, EX1 3LH
Activities: Other information technology service activities
Officers: Kerri Lynn McKechnie, Secretary; Aimee Nisbet, Secretary; Gregory Hume Dorn [1968] Director [American]; Darren Joseph Nichols [1970] Managing Director; Charles Tuchinda [1975] Director/President [American]

The First Federation Trust
Incorporated: 21 October 2011 *Employees:* 361
Net Worth: £13,080,000 *Total Assets:* £20,367,000
Registered Office: Blackpool C of E Primary School, Liverton, Newton Abbot, Devon, TQ12 6JB
Activities: Primary education
Officers: Isabelle Andree Yvette Candy, Secretary; Dr Carolyn Bromfield [1948] Director/Retired University Lecturer; Ann Denner [1964] Director/Administrator; Christopher James Frankland [1980] Director/Lecturer; Andrea Elizabeth Gosling [1967] Director/General Manager; Ian James Thomas [1974] Director/Actuary; Paul Simon Walker [1977] Director/Chief Executive Officer; Alexander Peter Walmsley [1951] Director/Accountant; Rev Paul Wimsett [1958] Director/Clergyman

First Greater Western Limited
Incorporated: 27 April 2004 *Employees:* 5,863
Net Worth: £21,054,000 *Total Assets:* £479,406,016
Registered Office: Milford House, 1 Milford Street, Swindon, Wilts, SN1 1HL
Activities: Passenger rail transport, interurban
Parent: First Rail Holdings Limited
Officers: Barbara Mary Salter, Secretary; Clive Burrows [1958] Director; Dr Benjamin John Caswell [1959] Director/Accountant; Hugh Patrick Clancy [1964] Director; Kevin Gardner [1960] Director; Matthew Lawrence Golton [1967] Director; Mark Julian Hopwood [1971] Director; Stephen Montgomery [1962] Director

First Position Group Limited
Incorporated: 9 January 2015 *Employees:* 79
Previous: First Position Dance Limited
Net Worth: £2,129,271 *Total Assets:* £9,451,431
Registered Office: Harlequin House, Forde Court, Forde Road, Newton Abbot, Devon, TQ12 4BT
Activities: Wholesale of clothing and footwear
Parent: Revolution Direct Ltd
Officers: Joseph John Gelp Jr [1953] Director/Chief Executive Officer [American]; Kamlesh Raichura [1974] Director

First Priorities PPP Health Services Limited
Incorporated: 2 September 2003 *Employees:* 3
Net Worth Deficit: £12,025,627 *Total Assets:* £77,119,808
Registered Office: Third Floor, Broad Quay House, Prince Street, Bristol, BS1 4DJ
Activities: Other specialised construction activities n.e.c.
Parent: RBIL Limited
Officers: Graham John Hutt [1954] Regional Director; Andrew Richard Kershaw [1965] Director/Projects Controller; Richard Little [1979] Investment Director

First Resources Limited
Incorporated: 13 October 1995 *Employees:* 255
Net Worth Deficit: £1,861,000 *Total Assets:* £13,181,000
Registered Office: Cotswold House, 1 Crompton Road, Groundwell, Swindon, Wilts, SN25 5AW
Activities: Retail sale via mail order houses or via Internet
Shareholders: Michelle Swabey; STM Group PLC
Officers: Andrew Stuart Walsham, Secretary; Nigel Victor Swabey [1948] Director; Andrew Stuart Walsham [1964] Director/Chartered Accountant; Francesca Welbore-Ker [1957] Director/Investment Manager

First South West Limited
Incorporated: 5 October 1982 *Employees:* 695
Previous: First Devon & Cornwall Limited
Net Worth Deficit: £45,039,000 *Total Assets:* £20,761,000
Registered Office: Union Street, Camborne, Cornwall, TR14 8HF
Activities: Other urban, suburban or metropolitan passenger land transport (not underground, metro or similar)
Parent: Firstbus (South) Limited
Officers: Michael Hampson, Secretary; David Brian Alexander [1965] Regional Managing Director; Alex Paul Carter [1959] Director; Trevor Tobiasen [1952] Employee Director

First Step Homes Limited
Incorporated: 5 February 1997 *Employees:* 6
Net Worth: £7,686,886 *Total Assets:* £16,387,058
Registered Office: 30 Whiteladies Road, Clifton, Bristol, BS8 2LG
Activities: Development of building projects
Shareholders: Jane Chastney; Trevor Norman Chastney
Officers: Trevor Norman Chastney, Secretary/Surveyor; Jane Chastney [1959] Director/Part Time Teacher; Trevor Norman Chastney [1953] Director/Surveyor; Helena Maria Wysocki [1956] Director/Retired

First West of England Limited
Incorporated: 1 October 1887 *Employees:* 1,739
Previous: First Somerset & Avon Limited
Net Worth Deficit: £11,485,000 *Total Assets:* £81,135,000
Registered Office: Enterprise House, Easton Road, Bristol, BS5 0DZ
Activities: Other urban, suburban or metropolitan passenger land transport (not underground, metro or similar)
Parent: Firstbus (South) Limited
Officers: Michael Hampson, Secretary; David Brian Alexander [1965] Regional Managing Director; Ian Coyle [1967] Operations Director; James David Ferdinand Freeman [1956] Managing Director; Richard Leslie Northey [1962] Engineering Director; Rob Pymm [1971] Commercial Director; Stephen John Scott [1955] Employee Director

Firstport Bespoke Property Services Limited
Incorporated: 22 March 1982 *Employees:* 103
Previous: Pembertons Residential Limited
Net Worth: £2,116,314 *Total Assets:* £5,194,626
Registered Office: Queensway House, 11 Queensway, New Milton, Hants, BH25 5NR
Activities: Management of real estate on a fee or contract basis
Parent: Firstport Limited
Officers: Nigel Howell [1959] Director/Chief Executive Officer; Ouda Saleh [1979] Director of Finance

Firstport HMF Limited
Incorporated: 18 December 2008
Previous: Peverel HMF Limited
Net Worth: £3,051,277 *Total Assets:* £6,644,794
Registered Office: Queensway House, 11 Queensway, New Milton, Hants, BH25 5NR
Activities: Management of real estate on a fee or contract basis
Parent: Firstport Limited
Officers: Nigel Howell [1959] Director/Chief Financial Officer; Ouda Saleh [1979] Director of Finance

Firstport Insurance Services Limited
Incorporated: 11 December 1997 *Employees:* 13
Previous: Kingsborough Insurance Services Limited
Net Worth: £9,858,965 *Total Assets:* £10,620,255
Registered Office: Queensway House, 11 Queensway, New Milton, Hants, BH25 5NR
Activities: Non-life insurance
Parent: Knight Square Limited
Officers: Stuart Douglas Muncer [1977] Director/Chartered Accountant; Judith Margaret Runciman [1955] Director

Firstport Limited
Incorporated: 14 January 2002 *Employees:* 559
Previous: Peverel Property Management Limited
Net Worth Deficit: £8,900,981 *Total Assets:* £17,891,656
Registered Office: Queensway House, 11 Queensway, New Milton, Hants, BH25 5NR
Activities: Activities of head offices
Parent: Knight Square Limited
Officers: Nigel Howell [1959] Director/Chief Executive Officer; Ouda Saleh [1979] Director of Finance

Firstport Operations PD Limited
Incorporated: 13 June 2007
Previous: Peverel Operations PD Limited
Net Worth: £12,766,225 *Total Assets:* £25,222,650
Registered Office: 11 Queensway, New Milton, Hants, BH25 5NR
Activities: Management of real estate on a fee or contract basis
Shareholder: Firstport Limited
Officers: Nigel Howell [1959] Director/Chief Financial Officer; Ouda Saleh [1979] Director of Finance

Firstport Property Services Limited
Incorporated: 3 October 1986 *Employees:* 518
Previous: OM Property Management Limited
Net Worth: £12,489,718 *Total Assets:* £18,253,764
Registered Office: Queensway House, 11 Queensway, New Milton, Hants, BH25 5NR
Activities: Management of real estate on a fee or contract basis
Parent: Firstport Limited
Officers: Nigel Howell [1959] Director/Chief Executive Officer; Ouda Saleh [1979] Director of Finance

Firstport Property Services No 2 Limited
Incorporated: 16 March 1988 *Employees:* 2
Previous: OM Property Management No 2 Limited
Net Worth: £5,269,478 *Total Assets:* £14,858,934
Registered Office: Queensway House, 11 Queensway, New Milton, Hants, BH25 5NR
Activities: Management of real estate on a fee or contract basis
Parent: Firstport Limited
Officers: Nigel Howell [1959] Director/Chief Executive Officer; Ouda Saleh [1979] Director of Finance

Firstport Retirement Property Services Limited
Incorporated: 17 February 1982 *Employees:* 1,696
Previous: Peverel Management Services Limited
Net Worth: £20,212,978 *Total Assets:* £39,768,148
Registered Office: Queensway House, 11 Queensway, New Milton, Hants, BH25 5NR
Activities: Management of real estate on a fee or contract basis
Parent: Firstport Limited
Officers: Nigel Howell [1959] Director/Chief Financial Officer; Ouda Saleh [1979] Director of Finance

Fish Brothers (Holdings) Limited
Incorporated: 19 March 1982 *Employees:* 262
Net Worth: £20,407,000 *Total Assets:* £51,311,000
Registered Office: Fish Brothers, Ashworth Road, Bridgemead, Swindon, Wilts, SN5 7UZ
Activities: Sale of new cars and light motor vehicles
Shareholders: Michael Jonathan Fish; Timothy Lance Fish
Officers: Keith Eric Butler, Secretary; Antonio Antonius [1958] Director; Keith Eric Butler [1959] Finance Director; Helen Tracy Fish [1962] Director/Company Partnership; Michael Jonathan Fish [1952] Director/Garage Proprietor; Timothy Lance Fish [1955] Director/Garage Proprietor

Fish Brothers (Swindon) Limited
Incorporated: 18 February 1991 *Employees:* 260
Net Worth: £12,547,000 *Total Assets:* £36,282,000
Registered Office: Fish Brothers (Swindon), Ashworth Road, Bridgemead, Swindon, Wilts, SN5 7UZ
Activities: Sale of new cars and light motor vehicles
Parent: Fish Brothers (Holdings) Limited
Officers: Keith Eric Butler, Secretary; Keith Eric Butler [1959] Finance Director; Michael Jonathan Fish [1952] Director/Garage Proprietor; Timothy Lance Fish [1955] Director/Garage Proprietor

Fish Brothers Property Investment LLP
Incorporated: 1 May 2009
Net Worth: £3,501,487 *Total Assets:* £6,760,822
Registered Office: Ashworth Road, Bridgemead, Swindon, Wilts, SN5 7UZ
Officers: Michael Jonathan Fish [1952] Member; Timothy Lance Fish [1955] Member; Annabel Loiuse Fish [1992] LLP Member; Caroline Jane Fish [1954] LLP Member; Helen Tracy Fish [1962] LLP Member; Jonathan Charles Fish [1990] LLP Member; Julia Caroline Fish [1992] LLP Member; Lucinda Harriet Fish [1990] LLP Member; Sophie Imogen Fish [1992] LLP Member; William John Fish [1999] LLP Member

Five AI Limited
Incorporated: 12 October 2016 *Employees:* 11
Net Worth Deficit: £909,703 *Total Assets:* £10,166,011
Registered Office: Temple Studios, Temple Gate, Temple Meads, Bristol, BS1 6QA
Activities: Business and domestic software development
Parent: Five AI Inc
Officers: Stanley Boland [1960] Director/Chief Executive Officer; Laura Joanne Brown [1978] Director/Chartered Accountant; Benedict Peters [1982] Director/Business Executive; John Ewart Redford [1964] Director/Business Executive

Five Bees Limited
Incorporated: 30 August 2011
Net Worth: £1,890,047 *Total Assets:* £9,453,320
Registered Office: Stafford House, Blackbrook Park Avenue, Taunton, Somerset, TA1 2PX
Activities: Other letting and operating of own or leased real estate
Shareholders: Lisa Bromfield; David James Bromfield; Sarah Nicole Bromfield
Officers: Sharron Suzanne Best [1949] Director [Canadian]; David James Bromfield [1988] Director

Five Directions Limited
Incorporated: 21 February 2012
Net Worth: £7,678,682 *Total Assets:* £10,336,485
Registered Office: The Jetty, Sutton Wharf, Plymouth, PL4 0DW
Activities: Development of building projects
Parent: Natatomisam Limited
Officers: James Stephen Brent [1965] Director

Five Rivers Child Care Limited
Incorporated: 18 June 2001 *Employees:* 289
Net Worth: £2,068,182 *Total Assets:* £7,810,676
Registered Office: 47 Bedwin Street, Salisbury, Wilts, SP1 3UT
Activities: Other residential care activities n.e.c.
Parent: Five Rivers Ireland Limited
Officers: Jeremy Paul McConnell, Secretary; Clifford Ronald Charles Fry [1947] Director/Accountant; David Stewart Howard [1953] Director/Chairman; Pamela Jane McConnell [1955] Director

Five Valleys Aerospace Limited
Incorporated: 10 July 2003 *Employees:* 139
Net Worth: £2,680,000 *Total Assets:* £9,498,000
Registered Office: Eagle Works, London Road, Thrupp, Stroud, Gloucester, GL5 2BA
Activities: Activities of head offices
Parent: Sephton Park Fund LLP
Officers: Peter Williment, Secretary; Jason Marcus James Bailey [1964] Director; Charles Richard Foster Kemp [1957] Director/Private Equity Fund Manager; Alan Geoffrey Schroeder [1937] Director/Chairman; Peter Williment [1970] Finance Director

FJB Hotels Limited
Incorporated: 29 July 2015 *Employees:* 336
Net Worth: £33,121,306 *Total Assets:* £44,747,752
Registered Office: 6th Floor, Dean Park House, Dean Park Crescent, Bournemouth, BH1 1HP
Activities: Activities of other holding companies n.e.c.
Shareholder: Wanda Gwendoline Helena Butterworth
Officers: Joy Wanda Eva Barcellos [1953] Director; John Godfrey Julius Butterworth [1946] Director

Fjords Processing Limited
Incorporated: 10 May 1993 *Employees:* 44
Previous: Opus Maxim Limited
Net Worth: £2,437,000 *Total Assets:* £4,099,000
Registered Office: Stonedale Road, Oldends Lane, Stonehouse, Glos, GL10 3RQ
Activities: Other research and experimental development on natural sciences and engineering
Parent: National Oilwell Varco, Inc.
Officers: Alison May Sloan, Secretary; Robbert Oudendijk [1974] Director/Vice President Finance Europe, MENA, CIS [Dutch]; Simon Scott Reid [1982] Director/Accountant

Flagdawn Limited
Incorporated: 19 May 2004 *Employees:* 39
Net Worth: £2,273,274 *Total Assets:* £5,501,176
Registered Office: The Caravan Company, Dorchester Road, Wimborne, Dorset, BH21 3HA
Activities: Activities of head offices
Parent: Erusiel Limited
Officers: Paul Steven Clarke, Secretary/Director; Paul Steven Clarke [1957] Director; Andrew Michael John Scott [1956] Director

Flash Investments LLP
Incorporated: 18 October 2011
Net Worth: £9,524,751 *Total Assets:* £9,524,751
Registered Office: Unit 12 Old Mills Industrial Estate, Paulton, Bristol, BS39 7SU
Officers: Donald Peter Graber [1953] Member

Flatcable Limited
Incorporated: 19 July 2004 *Employees:* 30
Net Worth: £1,278,859 *Total Assets:* £7,199,720
Registered Office: Old Tote Buildings, Exeter Racecourse, Kennford, Exeter, Devon, EX6 7XS
Activities: Other business support service activities n.e.c.
Shareholders: David William Ough; Murray Charles Hogge
Officers: Murray Charles Hogge, Secretary/Director; Guy Edward Charles Burgoyne [1984] Director/Produce Trader; Samuel Charles Crocker [1986] Director/Trader; Murray Charles Hogge [1960] Director; Tong Theeng Lioe [1965] Director/Trader [Malaysian]; Maurice James Molloy [1963] Finance Director [Irish]; Jose Alberto Teixeira Nazare [1967] Technical Director [Portuguese]; David William Ough [1955] Director/Potato Trader

Fleet Caravans Limited
Incorporated: 7 January 1956 *Employees:* 1
Net Worth: £5,626,945 *Total Assets:* £6,342,113
Registered Office: Broadwalk House, Southernhay West, Exeter, Devon, EX1 1UA
Activities: Other business support service activities n.e.c.
Shareholders: Anthony Charles William Beard; Tozers Trust Corporation Limited
Officers: Anthony Charles William Beard, Secretary/Solicitor; Anthony Charles William Beard [1952] Director/Retired

Fleetwheel Limited
Incorporated: 8 April 1975 *Employees:* 83
Net Worth: £3,848,841 *Total Assets:* £7,589,965
Registered Office: Cotswold House, Quarry Road, Chipping Sodbury, Glos, BS37 6AX
Activities: Wholesale trade of motor vehicle parts and accessories
Parent: Picksons PLC
Officers: Colin Michael Russell, Secretary; Ian David Farbrace [1959] Director; Angela Irene Pick [1953] Director/Clerical Assistant; Colin Andrew Pick [1950] Director; Simon Andrew Pick [1981] Sales Director; Colin Michael Russell [1950] Director; Dennis Thomas [1952] Director

Flemingo International (UK) Limited
Incorporated: 17 September 2014
Net Worth Deficit: £2,230,848 *Total Assets:* £66,635,220
Registered Office: c/o Harding Retail, Avonmouth Way, Bristol, BS11 8DD
Activities: Other retail sale in non-specialised stores
Parent: Flemingo International (BVI) Limited
Officers: Carlo Bernasconi [1960] Director [Swiss]; Deepak Khetan [1973] Finance Director [Indian]

Flexiguide Limited
Incorporated: 10 July 2002 *Employees:* 43
Net Worth: £3,360,663 *Total Assets:* £4,345,132
Registered Office: Unit 9 Rodgers Industrial Estate, Yalberton Road, Paignton, Devon, TQ4 7QG
Activities: Manufacture of other fabricated metal products n.e.c.
Shareholder: Jason Benjamin Privett
Officers: Vanessa Privett, Secretary; Michael Stuart Badcott [1963] Director; Malcolm James Keat [1955] Director; Jason Benjamin Privett [1970] Director; Philip Edward Privett [1946] Director

Flextrus Limited
Incorporated: 14 September 2007 *Employees:* 29
Net Worth: £3,720,000 *Total Assets:* £5,251,000
Registered Office: No 1 Gass Close, Isleport Business Park, Highbridge, Somerset, TA9 4JT
Activities: Manufacture of plastic packing goods
Officers: David Gary Loader, Secretary; Leif Inge Asp [1962] Director/Flextrus Group CFO [Swedish]; Tomas Forsgard [1966] Managing Director [Finnish]

Flight Refuelling Limited
Incorporated: 29 October 1934 *Employees:* 485
Net Worth: £48,398,000 *Total Assets:* £224,836,000
Registered Office: Brook Road, Wimborne, Dorset, BH21 2BJ
Activities: Manufacture of plastics and rubber machinery
Parent: Cobham PLC
Officers: John Robert Gane, Secretary; James Barber [1958] Director/Sector President [American]; John Robert Gane [1971] Finance Director; Duncan Thorndike [1973] Commercial Director; Paul Watson [1964] Director/General Manager

Flightbookers Limited
Incorporated: 24 February 1982
Net Worth: £32,439,000 *Total Assets:* £46,053,000
Registered Office: 2 Temple Back East, Temple Quay, Bristol, BS1 6EG
Activities: Travel agency activities
Parent: Expedia Group, Inc.
Officers: Robert John Dzielak [1971] Director/Business Manager/Lawyer [American]; Frances Josephine Erskine [1969] Director/Business Executive [American]; Lance Allen Soliday [1972] Director/Business Manager/Accountant [American]

Flo Group Ltd
Incorporated: 29 June 2007 *Employees:* 164
Previous: Mavenwire (Europe) Ltd
Net Worth: £3,163,276 *Total Assets:* £6,175,179
Registered Office: First Floor, 10 Temple Back, Bristol, BS1 6FL
Activities: Business and domestic software development
Parent: FLO Employee Ownership Trustee Limited
Officers: Michael Jonathan Harvey [1958] Director/Logistics Consultants; Alison Frances Hatcher [1982] Director/Chief Operations Officer; Barry Thomas Hayes [1968] Director/IT Consultants; Michiel Arian Jacob Keijzer [1977] Director/Chief Executive Officer [Dutch]

Flollie Investments Limited
Incorporated: 14 December 2000 *Employees:* 93
Net Worth: £1,054,546 *Total Assets:* £5,717,506
Registered Office: 16-20 Cecil Road, Weston-Super-Mare, Somerset, BS23 2NT
Activities: Other human health activities
Shareholders: Charles Larkin; Teresa Larkin
Officers: Teresa Larkin, Secretary; Charles Larkin [1966] Director/Nursing Home Proprietor; Teresa Larkin [1969] Director/Nursing Home Proprietor

Floortex Europe Limited
Incorporated: 11 December 2001 *Employees:* 38
Net Worth: £3,479,483 *Total Assets:* £5,030,441
Registered Office: Unit 10 Miller Court, Severn Drive, Tewkesbury Business Park, Tewkesbury, Glos, GL20 8DN
Activities: Non-specialised wholesale trade
Shareholder: Steven Peter James Bull
Officers: Luisa Baravalle [1971] Operations Director [Italian]; James Steven Bull [1987] Finance Director; Steven Peter James Bull [1960] Managing Director/Chairman

Flowbird Smart City UK Limited
Incorporated: 18 August 2003 *Employees:* 89
Previous: Parkeon Limited
Net Worth: £4,121,000 *Total Assets:* £7,744,000
Registered Office: 10 Willis Way, Fleets Industrial Estate, Poole, Dorset, BH15 3SS
Activities: Other business support service activities n.e.c.
Officers: Bertrand Barthelemy [1965] Director [French]; Daniel James Hassett [1967] Director/Regional Manager

Flowbird Transport Limited
Incorporated: 5 November 1975 *Employees:* 297
Previous: Parkeon Transit Limited
Net Worth: £21,217,000 *Total Assets:* £39,974,000
Registered Office: 10 Willis Way, Fleets Industrial Estate, Poole, Dorset, BH15 3SS
Activities: Manufacture of computers and peripheral equipment
Parent: Wayfarer Group Limited
Officers: Bertrand Barthelemy [1965] Director [French]; Owen Tudor Griffith [1966] Director/Transport Systems

Flower & Hayes Limited
Incorporated: 18 May 1920 *Employees:* 16
Net Worth: £12,056,037 *Total Assets:* £26,576,620
Registered Office: Old Mills House, Old Mills, Paulton, Bristol, BS39 7SU
Activities: Construction of commercial buildings
Major Shareholder: Roderick Barry Thorner
Officers: Roderick Barry Thorner [1961] Director

Flowervision (Bristol) Limited
Incorporated: 9 June 1999 *Employees:* 42
Net Worth: £4,620,017 *Total Assets:* £5,729,348
Registered Office: Units 6 & 7 Merchants Trade Park, Tamar Road, St Phillips, Bristol, BS2 0TX
Activities: Wholesale of flowers and plants
Shareholders: Krijn van der Spijk; Andrew Haydn Jones
Officers: Sarah Louise Jones, Secretary; Andrew Haydn Jones [1969] Director/Wholesale Florist; Krijn Van Der Spijk [1967] Director/Wholesale Florist [Dutch]

Flowlinks Overseas Limited
Incorporated: 11 August 2014
Net Worth Deficit: £170,522 *Total Assets:* £6,259,813
Registered Office: First Floor, 10 Temple Back, Bristol, BS1 6FL
Activities: Non-trading company
Major Shareholder: Marcus Tullius Mussa
Officers: Marcus Tullius Mussa [1949] Director

Fluid Transfer International Limited
Incorporated: 28 October 1998 *Employees:* 50
Net Worth: £565,000 *Total Assets:* £8,208,000
Registered Office: Nailsworth Mills Estate, Avening Road, Nailsworth, Glos, GL6 0BS
Activities: Manufacture of other transport equipment n.e.c.
Parent: Flofuel Limited
Officers: Richard Sean Iles-Caine, Secretary; Steven Simon Henning [1963] Director; Richard Sean Iles-Caine [1975] Director/Accountant; George Graham Maguire [1957] Director; Daniel James Martin [1982] Sales Director; Richard Simon Mayall [1969] Director/Engineer; David Ian Peter Nairn [1965] Director/Engineer

Flybe Aviation Services Limited
Incorporated: 20 March 2000 *Employees:* 411
Net Worth: £9,500,000 *Total Assets:* £23,100,000
Registered Office: New Walker Hangar, Exeter International Airport, Clyst, Honiton, Exeter, EX5 2BA
Activities: Scheduled passenger air transport
Parent: Flybe Limited
Officers: Catherine Ledger, Secretary; Ian Richard Milne [1961] Director/Chief Financial Officer; Christine Jeanne Henriette Ourmieres-Widener [1964] Director/Chief Executive Officer [French]

Flybe Group PLC
Incorporated: 14 June 1978 *Employees:* 2,159
Net Worth: £93,100,000 *Total Assets:* £611,699,968
Registered Office: New Walker Hangar, Exeter International Airport, Clyst, Honiton, Exeter, EX5 2BA
Activities: Scheduled passenger air transport
Officers: Catherine Ledger, Secretary; Simon Timothy Laffin [1959] Director; Heather Lawrence [1969] Director; Elizabeth McMeikan [1962] Director; Ian Richard Milne [1961] Director/Chief Financial Officer; Christine Jeanne Henriette Ourmieres-Widener [1964] Director [French]

Flybe Limited
Incorporated: 1 December 1992 *Employees:* 1,748
Net Worth Deficit: £92,000,000 *Total Assets:* £630,000,000
Registered Office: New Walker Hangar, Exeter International Airport, Clyst, Honiton, Exeter, EX5 2BA
Activities: Scheduled passenger air transport
Parent: Flybe Group PLC
Officers: Catherine Ledger, Secretary; Ian Richard Milne [1961] Director/Chief Financial Officer; Christine Jeanne Henriette Ourmieres-Widener [1964] Director [French]

Flycorp Aviation LLP
Incorporated: 18 September 2006
Net Worth: £3,549,930 *Total Assets:* £3,716,392
Registered Office: Churchill House, Parkside, Ringwood, Hants, BH24 3SG
Officers: Clinton James McCarthy [1965] Member; Gwendoline Joan McCarthy [1945] Member; John Sidney McCarthy [1939] Member; Spencer John McCarthy [1966] Member

Flying Visit Limited
Incorporated: 21 October 1999 *Employees:* 39
Net Worth: £2,385,658 *Total Assets:* £5,325,221
Registered Office: Jersey Farm House, 1 Church Road, Heywood, Westbury, Wilts, BA13 4LP
Activities: Retail sale of automotive fuel in specialised stores
Major Shareholder: Steven Mark Callaway
Officers: John Richard Newman, Secretary; Mark Steven Callaway [1959] Director

Flyingfish Seafoods Company Limited
Incorporated: 19 June 2006
Net Worth: £1,990,312 *Total Assets:* £4,586,381
Registered Office: Old School Industrial Park, Moorland Road, Indian Queens, Cornwall, TR9 6JP
Activities: Wholesale of other food, including fish, crustaceans and molluscs
Shareholders: Ana-Rusila Godden; John Robert Godden
Officers: John Robert Godden [1981] Director/Manager

Foam Techniques Limited
Incorporated: 1 December 1986 *Employees:* 48
Net Worth: £4,437,220 *Total Assets:* £5,722,015
Registered Office: Units 137-145 South Liberty Lane, Bristol, BS3 2TL
Activities: Other business support service activities n.e.c.
Parent: Avon Group Manufacturing (Holdings) Limited
Officers: Ashok Ravjibhai Patel, Secretary; Ashok Ravjibhai Patel [1957] Director; Mark Andrew Rushin [1971] Group Director; Stephen Anthony Thomas [1975] Director

Fonterra (Logistics) Limited
Incorporated: 23 February 1999 *Employees:* 1
Net Worth: £4,709,000 *Total Assets:* £5,248,000
Registered Office: 100 Delta Business Park, Great Western Way, Swindon, Wilts, SN5 7XP
Activities: Service activities incidental to water transportation
Parent: Fonterra International Limited
Officers: Gulab Rai Sharma, Secretary; Mehmet Erol [1975] Director/Business Executive [Turkish]; Gulab Rai Sharma [1947] Director/Accountant

The Foodservice Centre Limited
Incorporated: 13 April 1983 *Employees:* 66
Net Worth: £582,649 *Total Assets:* £3,671,333
Registered Office: The Foodservice Centre, Cheddar Business Park, Wedmore Road, Cheddar, Somerset, BS27 3EB
Activities: Other food services
Officers: Paul Michael James, Secretary; Subir Chakravarti [1973] Sales Director; Paul Michael James [1961] Director/Accountant; Amanda Evelyn McCarthy [1965] Technical Director; Anthony Patrick Simpson [1946] Director/Food Consultant; James Patrick Simpson [1973] Director; Jeremy William Simpson [1975] Director/Commercial Manager; Peter David Wright [1950] Director

Foot Anstey LLP
Incorporated: 14 December 2010 *Employees:* 489
Net Worth: £16,547,000 *Total Assets:* £36,780,000
Registered Office: Salt Quay House, 4 North East Quay, Sutton Harbour, Plymouth, PL4 0BN
Officers: Karen Jennifer Catherine Bates [1978] Member; Simon Hugh Gregory [1955] Member; Patrick William Howarth [1970] Member; Duncan Stewart Ralph [1962] Member; John Philip Westwell [1963] Member; Christopher Stephen Worrell [1975] Member; Robert William Antrobus [1973] LLP Member; Michael Scott Squier Bird [1966] LLP Member; Deborah Anne Carrivick [1974] LLP Member; Stuart Anthony Cleak [1976] LLP Member; James Julian Collings [1980] LLP Member; Paul Andrew Cox [1974] LLP Member; Martin Cuell [1975] LLP Member; Daniel Louis Richard Cuthbert [1975] LLP Member; Lucy Jane Gill [1979] LLP Member; Marc Lee Gilston [1983] LLP Member; Andrew John Hannam [1958] LLP Member; Martin Roy Forbes Hirst [1975] LLP Member; Alan David Hughes [1972] LLP Member; Kenneth Ross Lewins [1978] LLP Member; Mark Falcon Millar [1969] LLP Member; Richard John Neary [1975] LLP Member; Jonathan Mark Oddy [1972] LLP Member; Anna Parker [1981] LLP Member; Neil Thomas Parkes [1972] LLP Member; Nathan John Peacey [1966] LLP Member; Carol Ann Phillips [1973] LLP Member; Jonathon Mark Ronald Pinder [1960] LLP Member; Jessica Pitt [1981] LLP Member; Huw William Richard Ponting [1970] LLP Member; Christopher David Pritchett [1977] LLP Member; Imam Din Qazi [1975] LLP Member; Mark Rhys-Jones [1966] LLP Member; Steven David Richards [1974] LLP Member; Joanne Sarah Rumley [1973] LLP Member; Paul Jonathan Sankey [1961] LLP Member; Emily Settle [1982] LLP Member; Peter Ian Lester Singfield [1981] LLP Member; Patrick Henry Somers [1960] LLP Member; Matthew James Stoate [1979] LLP Member; Claire Joanne Stoneman [1972] LLP Member; Ian David Stubbs [1968] LLP Member; Richard Paul Sutton [1962] LLP Member; Duncan William Sykes [1975] LLP Member; Timothy Jacob John Taylor [1969] LLP Member; Duncan Anthony Vaughan Tringham [1976] LLP Member; Richard George Walford [1973] LLP Member; Patrick Wetherall [1970] LLP Member; William David Whitt [1971] LLP Member

David Foot Limited
Incorporated: 27 April 1960 *Employees:* 34
Net Worth: £2,534,807 *Total Assets:* £7,822,172
Registered Office: Windover House, St Ann Street, Salisbury, Wilts, SP1 2DR
Activities: Growing of cereals (except rice), leguminous crops and oil seeds
Officers: Joseph Charles Foot, Secretary; Joseph Charles Foot [1980] Director/Farmer; Samuel Peter Foot [1975] Director/Farmer

D. H. J. Foot Limited
Incorporated: 10 August 1982 *Employees:* 4
Net Worth: £1,375,741 *Total Assets:* £4,252,624
Registered Office: 67b East Street, Bridport, Dorset, DT6 3LB
Activities: Other accommodation
Shareholders: Emily Foot; Tessa Foot
Officers: Joanna Fay Foot, Secretary; David Henry John Foot [1956] Director/Farmer; Joanna Fay Foot [1959] Director and Company Secretary

Foot Shop Limited
Incorporated: 10 December 1982 *Employees:* 86
Net Worth: £4,019,254 *Total Assets:* £5,104,529
Registered Office: The Tanyard, Leigh Road, Street, Somerset, BA16 0HR
Activities: Retail sale of footwear in specialised stores
Parent: BBLP Holding Limited
Officers: Jacqueline Bemmer [1955] Director; Nicholas Brine [1974] Director; James William Lockyer [1967] Director; Andrew Colin Peirce [1957] Director

Footsure Western Limited
Incorporated: 2 July 1980 *Employees:* 15
Net Worth: £4,628,721 *Total Assets:* £11,113,770
Registered Office: Units F and G Quedgeley West Business Park, Bristol Road, Hardwicke, Gloucester, GL2 4PH
Activities: Wholesale of clothing and footwear
Shareholder: Gardiner Bros and Company (Leathers) Limited
Officers: Peter Giles Gardiner, Secretary; Benjamin James Gardiner [1975] Director/Planner; James Richard Peter Gardiner [1975] Director/Accountant; Peter Giles Gardiner [1942] Director/Accountant; Richard Jolyon Gardiner [1938] Director/Accountant; Mark Douglas Holloway [1973] Operations Director; Paul Jonathan Wheeler [1969] Sales & Marketing Director

Foray Holdings Limited
Incorporated: 11 January 2000 *Employees:* 492
Net Worth: £7,887,590 *Total Assets:* £60,957,760
Registered Office: Edwards Ford, Telford Road, Salisbury, Wilts, SP2 7PF
Activities: Activities of head offices
Major Shareholder: Chris Yoxon
Officers: Helen Louise Edwards [1971] Director/Management Accountant; Simon David Moulton [1972] Director/Operations Manager; Richard Owen [1967] Director/Chairman; Christopher Yoxon [1962] Managing Director

Foray Motor Group Limited
Incorporated: 31 December 1958 *Employees:* 492
Net Worth: £5,429,205 *Total Assets:* £54,218,600
Registered Office: Telford Road, Salisbury, Wilts, SP2 7PF
Activities: Sale of new cars and light motor vehicles
Major Shareholder: Christopher Yoxon
Officers: Jason Beckley [1970] Parts Director; David Jeremy Clarke [1960] Director/Car Dealer; Helen Louise Edwards [1971] Director/Management Accountant; Simon David Moulton [1972] Operations Director; Luke William Mundy [1976] Group Service Director; Richard Owen [1967] Director/Chairman; Christopher Yoxon [1962] Director/Dealer Principal

Ford Civil Engineering Limited
Incorporated: 21 July 1982 *Employees:* 110
Net Worth: £1,958,755 *Total Assets:* £8,330,520
Registered Office: 1 Thorne Way, Woolsbridge Industrial Estate, Three Legged Cross, Wimborne, Dorset, BH21 6FB
Activities: Construction of other civil engineering projects n.e.c.
Parent: Ford Civil Engineering Holdings Limited
Officers: Linda Stella Porter, Secretary; Andy Timothy Baldwin [1963] Director; Jeremy Joseph Mark Martin [1964] Director; Linda Stella Porter [1955] Director

Ford Fuels Limited
Incorporated: 28 March 1988 *Employees:* 129
Net Worth: £7,036,790 *Total Assets:* £23,496,968
Registered Office: Farrington Fields Trading Estate, Farrington Gurney, Bristol, BS39 6UU
Activities: Wholesale of other fuels and related products
Parent: Ford Fuels (Holdings) Limited
Officers: John David Ford, Secretary; Adrian John Ford [1959] Director; John David Ford [1983] Director; Michael Ford [1959] Director; Richard Nigel Ford [1960] Director

Peter Ford Transport Limited
Incorporated: 6 January 1972 *Employees:* 2
Net Worth: £4,342,845 *Total Assets:* £4,889,452
Registered Office: 45 Park Road, Gloucester, GL1 1LP
Activities: Other letting and operating of own or leased real estate
Major Shareholder: Peter John Ford
Officers: Paul Thomas Ford, Secretary/Manager; Mark Andrew Ford [1963] Director/Manager; Paul Thomas Ford [1960] Director/Manager; Paulette Ellen Ford [1941] Director/Personal Assistant; Peter John Ford [1932] Director/Property Manager

Forelle Estates Investments Limited
Incorporated: 20 May 2015 *Employees:* 100
Net Worth: £47,020,000 *Total Assets:* £101,550,000
Registered Office: Strand House, Strand Street, Poole, Dorset, BH15 1SB
Activities: Activities of head offices
Parent: Forelle Estates Group Limited
Officers: David Robert Haikney [1959] Finance Director; Michael James Price [1967] Director

Forelle Estates Limited
Incorporated: 18 March 1963 *Employees:* 9
Net Worth: £47,808,776 *Total Assets:* £116,187,824
Registered Office: Strand House, Strand Street, Poole, Dorset, BH15 1SB
Activities: Development of building projects
Parent: Forelle Estates Holdings Ltd.
Officers: David Robert Haikney, Secretary; David Robert Haikney [1959] Finance Director; Michael James Price [1967] Director

Forest Green Sun Company Limited
Incorporated: 31 October 2014
Net Worth: £4,620,221 *Total Assets:* £4,882,828
Registered Office: Lion House, Rowcroft, Stroud, Glos, GL5 3BY
Activities: Renting and leasing of other machinery, equipment and tangible goods n.e.c.
Officers: Tom Cowling, Secretary; Asif Rehmanwala [1976] Director; Dale Andrew Vince [1961] Director

Forest of Dean Stone Firms Limited
Incorporated: 14 June 2006 *Employees:* 36
Net Worth: £2,696,165 *Total Assets:* £3,686,235
Registered Office: Staverton Court, Staverton, Cheltenham, Glos, GL51 0UX
Activities: Other business support service activities n.e.c.
Shareholders: Marcus Scott Russell; Nicholas Ian Horton; Peter Leslie Hart
Officers: Nicholas Ian Horton, Secretary; Peter Leslie Hart [1941] Director; Simon Charles Peter Hart [1978] Director; Jane Elizabeth Horton [1959] Director; Nicholas Ian Horton [1960] Director; Marcus Scott Russell [1950] Director

Forest Park Cemetery and Crematorium Limited
Incorporated: 27 November 2002 *Employees:* 13
Net Worth: £3,319,717 *Total Assets:* £12,845,374
Registered Office: Chapel View, Westerleigh Road, Westerleigh, Bristol, BS37 8QP
Activities: Funeral and related activities
Parent: Cemetery + Crematorium Services Ltd
Officers: Dafydd Rhys John, Secretary; Dafydd Rhys John [1974] Director/Chartered Accountant; Ian David McArdle [1966] Director/Chartered Surveyor

Forest Press Hydraulics Limited
Incorporated: 10 May 1984 *Employees:* 31
Net Worth: £6,950,510 *Total Assets:* £7,779,434
Registered Office: Wildin & Co, Kings Buildings, Hill Street, Lydney, Glos, GL15 5HE
Activities: Repair of machinery
Major Shareholder: Peter Francis Bullock
Officers: Peter Francis Bullock [1969] Director/Engineer

The Forge Entertainment Limited
Incorporated: 31 March 2014 *Employees:* 12
Net Worth: £230,165 *Total Assets:* £4,990,026
Registered Office: 18 Glasshouse Studios, Fryern Court Road, Fordingbridge, Hants, SP6 1QX
Activities: Television programme production activities
Major Shareholder: George Stephen John Faber
Officers: Mark William Pybus, Secretary; George Stephen John Faber [1959] Director/Television Producer; George Alasdair Ormond [1974] Director/Executive Producer; Mark William Pybus [1970] Director/Executive Producer

Forgeway Holdings Ltd
Incorporated: 11 June 2017
Net Worth: £899,392 *Total Assets:* £4,012,279
Registered Office: Forgeway, Collett Way, Newton Abbot, Devon, TQ12 4PH
Activities: Activities of other holding companies n.e.c.
Major Shareholder: Roderick Buckley
Officers: Glen Buckley [1972] Director; Laurence Edward Buckley [1946] Director; Roderick Buckley [1976] Director

Forgeway Ltd
Incorporated: 21 April 2010 *Employees:* 40
Net Worth: £3,191,029 *Total Assets:* £6,061,899
Registered Office: Forgeway, Collett Way, Newton Abbot, Devon, TQ12 4PH
Activities: Manufacture of other chemical products n.e.c.
Parent: Forgeway Holdings Ltd
Officers: Glen Buckley [1972] Director/Operations Manager; Laurence Edward Buckley [1946] Director/Lawyer; Roderick Buckley [1976] Director/Sales Manager

Fornuis UK Limited
Incorporated: 12 December 2003
Net Worth: £22,759,852 *Total Assets:* £23,019,312
Registered Office: c/o Smart Systems Limited, Arnolds Way, Yatton, Somerset, BS49 4QN
Activities: Activities of head offices
Parent: Alu Bidco Limited
Officers: Edward Anthony Robinson, Secretary/Director; Wim Flo [1979] Director [Belgian]; Edward Anthony Robinson [1958] Managing Director; Johan Paul Jozef Verstrepen [1961] Director/Chief Executive Officer [Belgian]

Forrestbrown Limited
Incorporated: 23 March 2012 *Employees:* 50
Net Worth: £3,984,764 *Total Assets:* £5,834,757
Registered Office: Grosvenor House, 149 Whiteladies Road, Clifton, Bristol, BS8 2RA
Activities: Tax consultancy
Officers: Simon Brown [1978] Director; Shane Frank [1972] Director/Chief Operating Officer [American]; Dhaval Jadav [1971] Director [American]; Michael Yirilli [1983] Director/Investor [American]

Forthglade Foods Holdings Limited
Incorporated: 9 September 2015 *Employees:* 86
Net Worth: £798,650 *Total Assets:* £14,130,520
Registered Office: Woodwater House, Pynes Hill, Exeter, Devon, EX2 5WR
Activities: Activities of head offices
Shareholder: Piper Private Equity Fund V LP
Officers: Chris David Brooking [1974] Joint Managing Director; Christopher John Max Curry [1958] Director; Generald Sean Dawson [1967] Director; Peter Christopher Edward Farquhar [1959] Director; Patrick Ashley James Horton [1967] Director; Leon Raymond Hughes [1975] Director/Associate Partner; Gerard Paul Lovell [1972] Director

Forward Developments Limited
Incorporated: 21 January 1965 *Employees:* 1
Net Worth: £13,315,391 *Total Assets:* £15,038,593
Registered Office: Woodwater Farm, Hardings Lane, Gillingham, Dorset, SP8 4HX
Activities: Growing of cereals (except rice), leguminous crops and oil seeds
Major Shareholder: Patrick Paul Sweeney
Officers: Danella Faith Sweeney, Secretary; Philippa Alice Evans-Bevan [1962] Director; Patrick Paul Sweeney [1930] Director

Forward Land Limited
Incorporated: 22 March 2000
Net Worth: £3,567,659 *Total Assets:* £8,748,438
Registered Office: 17 Imperial Square, Cheltenham, Glos, GL50 1QZ
Activities: Other letting and operating of own or leased real estate
Parent: Satnam Investments Limited
Officers: John Frederick Staite, Secretary; Satnam Singh Dhillon [1977] Director; John Frederick Staite [1948] Director/Accountant

Foscombe Properties Limited
Incorporated: 21 May 2012
Net Worth: £3,847,023 *Total Assets:* £4,012,425
Registered Office: Delta Place, 27 Bath Road, Cheltenham, Glos, GL53 7TH
Activities: Activities of other holding companies n.e.c.
Shareholders: Barbara Joan Martin; Mark Martin
Officers: Barbara Joan Martin [1955] Director; Mark Martin [1961] Director

Four Quarters Polo LLP
Incorporated: 12 October 2009 *Employees:* 19
Net Worth: £3,771,835 *Total Assets:* £3,923,869
Registered Office: 37 St Georges Road, Cheltenham, Glos, GL50 3DU
Officers: Romilla Arber [1966] Member; Simon Peter Arber [1958] Member

Four Times Enterprises Limited
Incorporated: 25 January 2010 *Employees:* 97
Net Worth: £1,753,904 *Total Assets:* £5,921,454
Registered Office: Spectrum House, Bond Street, Bristol, BS1 3LG
Activities: Activities of head offices
Shareholders: Thomas Paul Curran; Smedvig Capital AS
Officers: Thomas Paul Curran [1962] Director; John Clinton Hewett [1963] Director; Robert Peter Toms [1962] Managing Director

Fourgate (Cheltenham) Limited
Incorporated: 14 March 2017
Net Worth: £6,379,581 *Total Assets:* £8,910,382
Registered Office: Windsor House, Bayshill Road, Cheltenham, Glos, GL50 3AT
Activities: Buying and selling of own real estate
Shareholders: John Charles Gater; Julie Bridget Gater
Officers: John Charles Gater [1949] Director; Julie Bridget Gater [1949] Director

Foursquare Associates Limited
Incorporated: 20 October 1995
Net Worth: £6,314,647 *Total Assets:* £6,317,447
Registered Office: 8 Gay Street, Bath, BA1 2PH
Activities: Activities of head offices
Major Shareholder: Andrew Douglas Brownsword
Officers: Peter Tyrrell, Secretary; Andrew Douglas Brownsword [1947] Director; Peter Tyrrell [1972] Director

John Fowler Holidays Limited
Incorporated: 19 January 1965 *Employees:* 303
Net Worth: £45,226,732 *Total Assets:* £58,404,808
Registered Office: Liberty Court, Roundswell Business Park, Barnstaple, Devon, EX31 3TL
Activities: Other accommodation
Shareholders: John Fowler Holdings Limited; Susan Kathryn Steer-Fowler
Officers: Dr John Martyn William Steer-Fowler, Secretary/Managing Director; Daisy Janine Victoria Steer Fowler [1991] Director; Susan Kathryn Steer Fowler [1955] Director/Housewife; Suzy-Emma Sheila Steer Fowler [1982] Director/Managing Partner; Dr John Martyn William Steer-Fowler [1962] Managing Director

Fowlers of Bristol Limited
Incorporated: 19 December 1961 *Employees:* 166
Net Worth: £9,186,186 *Total Assets:* £17,140,862
Registered Office: 2-12 Bath Road, Pylle Hill, Bristol, BS4 3DR
Activities: Sale, maintenance and repair of motorcycles and related parts and accessories
Shareholders: Gillian Helen Johnson; Stephanie Lynn Fowler; St James Parade (107) Ltd
Officers: Neil Stanley Bennett, Secretary; Neil Stanley Bennett [1957] Finance Director; Lionel David Fowler [1946] Director; Stephanie Lyn Fowler [1947] Director; Frederick Robert Hart [1947] Director; Dr Gillian Helen Johnson [1948] Director

Fox Elms Care Limited
Incorporated: 7 February 2005 *Employees:* 90
Net Worth: £3,773,397 *Total Assets:* £4,119,752
Registered Office: 1st Floor Offices. New Wing, Agricultural House, Greville Close, Sandhurst Road, Gloucester, GL2 9RG
Activities: Other human health activities
Parent: Fox Elms Community Care Ltd
Officers: Debra Jayne Vaughan, Secretary; Christopher John Vaughan [1968] Director; Debra Jayne Vaughan [1960] Director

Foxcombe Farm (Somerset) Limited
Incorporated: 9 September 2005 *Employees:* 4
Net Worth: £649,397 *Total Assets:* £4,251,398
Registered Office: Foxcombe Farm, High Road, Galhampton, Yeovil, Somerset, BA22 7BA
Activities: Raising of dairy cattle
Major Shareholder: Jeremy Malcolm Angell
Officers: Tara Angell, Secretary; Jeremy Malcolm Angell [1971] Director/Farmer

Foxmoor Business Park Limited
Incorporated: 9 February 1996 *Employees:* 2
Previous: Foxmoor Nurseries Limited
Net Worth: £1,977,025 *Total Assets:* £3,906,575
Registered Office: The Estate Office, Foxmoor Business Park, Foxmoor Business Park Road, Wellington, Somerset, TA21 9RF
Activities: Management of real estate on a fee or contract basis
Parent: Foxmoor Limited
Officers: Gideon Robert Sumption, Secretary; Gideon Robert Sumption [1955] Director/Nurseryman; Jonathan William Honnibal Sumption [1951] Director/Nurseryman

Foxmoor Limited
Incorporated: 17 February 2000
Net Worth: £965,846 *Total Assets:* £4,271,889
Registered Office: The Estate Office, Foxmoor Business Park, Wellington, Somerset, TA21 9RF
Activities: Other letting and operating of own or leased real estate
Shareholders: Gideon Robert Sumption; Jonathan William Honnibal Sumption
Officers: Gideon Robert Sumption, Secretary/Nurseryman; Gideon Robert Sumption [1955] Director/Chartered Surveyor; Jonathan William Honnibal Sumption [1951] Director/Nurseryman

FR Aviation Group Limited
Incorporated: 8 October 1984
Net Worth: £63,225,000 *Total Assets:* £285,001,984
Registered Office: Brook Road, Wimborne, Dorset, BH21 2BJ
Activities: Other business support service activities n.e.c.
Parent: Cobham PLC
Officers: Michael David Parry, Secretary; Paul Anthony Armstrong [1979] Director/General Manager; Michael David Parry [1975] Finance Director; Richard Duncan Stoate [1963] Director

FR Aviation Limited
Incorporated: 9 April 1965 *Employees:* 298
Net Worth: £45,371,000 *Total Assets:* £73,201,000
Registered Office: Brook Road, Wimborne, Dorset, BH21 2BJ
Activities: Scheduled passenger air transport
Parent: FR Aviation Group Limited
Officers: Michael David Parry, Secretary; Paul Anthony Armstrong [1979] Director/General Manager; Michael David Parry [1975] Finance Director; Richard Duncan Stoate [1963] Director

FR Aviation Services Limited
Incorporated: 5 November 1984 *Employees:* 69
Net Worth: £10,208,000 *Total Assets:* £13,429,000
Registered Office: Brook Road, Wimborne, Dorset, BH21 2BJ
Activities: Other business support service activities n.e.c.
Parent: FR Aviation Group Limited
Officers: Michael David Parry, Secretary; Paul Anthony Armstrong [1979] Director/General Manager; Michael David Parry [1975] Finance Director; Richard Duncan Stoate [1963] Director

Frame Homes (South West) Limited
Incorporated: 15 March 1974 *Employees:* 90
Net Worth: £4,509,945 *Total Assets:* £8,239,599
Registered Office: Unit B, 483/1 Jenson House, Cardrew Industrial Estate, Redruth, Cornwall, TR15 1SS
Activities: Other construction installation
Parent: Bob Pepper Holdings Limited
Officers: Robert Andrew Pepper-Smith, Secretary; Robert David Pepper [1945] Managing Director; Michelle Pepper-Smith [1975] Director/Accounts; Robert Andrew Pepper-Smith [1971] Finance Director

AW Frampton & Son Limited
Incorporated: 14 January 2008 *Employees:* 16
Net Worth: £678,282 *Total Assets:* £5,190,614
Registered Office: 18 High West Street, Dorchester, DT1 1UW
Activities: Mixed farming
Shareholders: Alfred William Frampton; Freda Mary Margaret Frampton; Maxwell Oliver Frampton
Officers: Freda Mary Margaret Frampton, Secretary; Alfred William Frampton [1941] Director/Farmer; Amy Jane Frampton [1981] Director/Administrator; Freda Mary Margaret Frampton [1949] Director/Farmer; Maxwell Oliver Frampton [1975] Director/Farmer

Framptons Limited
Incorporated: 23 February 1968 *Employees:* 312
Net Worth: £3,252,100 *Total Assets:* £21,137,248
Registered Office: 76 Charlton Road, Shepton Mallet, Somerset, BA4 5PD
Activities: Manufacture of other food products n.e.c.
Parent: Crawlands Ltd
Officers: Ian James Harvey, Secretary; Sara Harling [1972] Sales Director; Ian James Harvey [1950] Director; Simon Hayward [1981] Managing Director; William Robert Martin [1964] Director; Allan Warner Staples [1953] Commercial Director

Mrs D M France-Hayhurst Foundation
Incorporated: 9 December 2014
Net Worth: £13,608,462 *Total Assets:* £13,673,486
Registered Office: Compass House, Lypiatt Road, Cheltenham, Glos, GL50 2QJ
Activities: Other education n.e.c.
Officers: Peter James Pierrepont Hunter [1943] Director; Phillip Robert Posnett [1974] Director; Penelope Ann Sanders [1954] Director/Solicitor; Jennifer Shearer [1949] Director/Retired; Andrew Michael Wright [1950] Director/Solicitor

Francis & Lewis International Limited
Incorporated: 8 October 1991 *Employees:* 74
Net Worth: £3,951,782 *Total Assets:* £4,786,992
Registered Office: Bellcombe Works, East Brent, Highbridge, Somerset, TA9 4DB
Activities: Manufacture of metal structures and parts of structures
Officers: Justine Rhian Garbutt [1966] Director/Civil Engineer; William John Haley [1946] Director/Engineer

G.A. Francis & Son Limited
Incorporated: 4 September 1985 *Employees:* 2
Net Worth: £3,758,444 *Total Assets:* £3,775,434
Registered Office: Sunoak, Church Lane, Winterbourne, Bristol, BS36 1SG
Activities: Construction of domestic buildings
Shareholders: Alan Don Francis; Jill Denise Francis
Officers: Alan Don Francis, Secretary/Builder; Alan Don Francis [1958] Director/Builder; Jill Denise Francis [1961] Director/Admin Officer

Fraser James Properties Limited
Incorporated: 24 February 2015 *Employees:* 2
Net Worth: £771,588 *Total Assets:* £3,784,943
Registered Office: 4 Broad Plain, Bristol, BS2 0JP
Activities: Other letting and operating of own or leased real estate
Major Shareholder: Alexander James Fraser Davies
Officers: Alexander James Fraser Davies [1975] Director/Property and Investments; Montse Riano Vilda Davies [1978] Director [Spanish]

Fraser St James Investments Limited
Incorporated: 8 June 2011 *Employees:* 5
Net Worth: £3,776,346 *Total Assets:* £11,108,572
Registered Office: 5 Uplands, Saltash, Cornwall, PL12 4NY
Activities: Development of building projects
Major Shareholder: Iain Fraser Lovett
Officers: Tracy Dunne, Secretary; Tracy Dunne [1973] Director; Iain Fraser Lovett [1968] Director

Frazer-Nash Consultancy Group Limited
Incorporated: 29 November 2001
Net Worth: £115,671 *Total Assets:* £11,115,671
Registered Office: c/o Devonport Royal Dockyard Ltd, Devonport, Plymouth, PL1 4SG
Activities: Activities of other holding companies n.e.c.
Parent: Babcock Marine Holdings (UK) Limited
Officers: Robert Ronald Burge, Secretary; Robert Ronald Burge [1966] Finance Director; Derek Malcolm Jones [1971] Director; Dr Neil Malcolm McDougall [1960] Director/Engineer; Iain Stuart Urquhart [1965] Director

Frazer-Nash Consultancy Limited
Incorporated: 27 November 1990 *Employees:* 831
Net Worth: £3,385,000 *Total Assets:* £40,840,000
Registered Office: c/o Devonport Royal Dockyard Ltd, Devonport, Plymouth, PL1 4SG
Activities: Other engineering activities
Parent: Frazer-Nash Consultancy Group Limited
Officers: Robert Ronald Burge, Secretary; Robert Ronald Burge [1966] Director/Accountant; Derek Malcolm Jones [1971] Director; Dr Neil Malcolm McDougall [1960] Director/Engineer; Iain Stuart Urquhart [1965] Director

Freedom Healthnet Limited
Incorporated: 30 June 2003
Net Worth: £1,641,910 *Total Assets:* £4,062,809
Registered Office: 4th Floor, County Gates House, 300 Poole Road, Poole, Dorset, BH12 1AZ
Activities: Activities of insurance agents and brokers
Shareholders: Nahid Salehi; Ahmed Iftekhar Saumtally; Leila Selina Saumtally; Sarah Ciranouch Saumtally
Officers: Sarah Ciranouch Saumtally, Secretary; Nahid Salehi [1952] Director/Insurance; Ahmed Iftekhar Saumtally [1952] Director; Leila Selina Saumtally [1993] Director/Sales; Sarah Ciranouch Saumtally [1982] Marketing Director

M.F. Freeman Group Limited
Incorporated: 4 November 2015 *Employees:* 4
Net Worth: £10,102,391 *Total Assets:* £10,943,336
Registered Office: Ruardean Works, Varnister Road, Drybrook, Glos, GL17 9BH
Activities: Activities of construction holding companies
Parent: M F Freeman Holdings Limited
Officers: Jennifer Mary Freeman [1947] Secretary and Director; Luke Francis Freeman [1974] Director; Mervyn Francis Freeman [1945] Director; Steven King [1970] Director/Chartered Accountant; Peter Wharton [1963] Director

M.F. Freeman Holdings Limited
Incorporated: 17 February 2017 *Employees:* 86
Net Worth: £8,152,604 *Total Assets:* £25,944,796
Registered Office: Ruardean Works, Varnister Road, Drybrook, Glos, GL17 9BH
Activities: Activities of construction holding companies
Shareholder: Luke Francis Freeman
Officers: Jennifer Mary Freeman, Secretary; Jennifer Mary Freeman [1947] Director; Luke Francis Freeman [1974] Director; Mervyn Francis Freeman [1945] Director; Steven King [1970] Director/Chartered Accountant; Peter Wharton [1963] Director

M.F. Freeman Limited
Incorporated: 19 October 1987 *Employees:* 87
Net Worth: £3,848,257 *Total Assets:* £14,619,745
Registered Office: Ruardean Works, Varnister Road, Drybrook, Glos, GL17 9BH
Activities: Construction of other civil engineering projects n.e.c.
Parent: M F Freeman Group Limited
Officers: Jennifer Mary Freeman, Secretary; Stewart Barnes [1966] Director/Management Consultant; Jennifer Mary Freeman [1945] Director/Secretary; Luke Francis Freeman [1974] Director/Construction Manager; Mervyn Francis Freeman [1945] Director/Plant Contractor; Steven King [1970] Director/Chartered Accountant; Peter Wharton [1963] Director/Chartered Accountant

Freemans Event Partners (Logistics) Ltd.
Incorporated: 14 August 2006 *Employees:* 46
Previous: SFC Event Logistics Limited
Net Worth: £5,652,994 *Total Assets:* £8,987,732
Registered Office: Unit Q2, Quadrant Distribution Centre, Quadrant Way, Hardwicke, Gloucester, GL2 2RN
Activities: Event catering activities
Parent: Freemans Event Partners Holdings Ltd
Officers: Zoe Ann Mewes, Secretary; John William Freeman [1976] Director; Stephen Thomas Freeman [1976] Director; Zoe Freeman [1984] Director

J & C Freeth Limited
Incorporated: 30 July 2014
Net Worth Deficit: £2,644 *Total Assets:* £5,252,248
Registered Office: Penhallow Farm, Ruan High Lanes, Truro, Cornwall, TR2 5LR
Activities: Mixed farming
Shareholders: James Freeth; Clare Freeth
Officers: Clare Elizabeth Freeth [1968] Director/Farmer; James Freeth [1970] Director/Farmer

Freeways Trust
Incorporated: 27 January 2004 *Employees:* 2
Net Worth: £10,901,118 *Total Assets:* £10,966,006
Registered Office: Leigh Court Day Centre, Pill Road, Abbots Leigh, Bristol, BS8 3RA
Activities: Residential care activities for learning difficulties, mental health and substance abuse
Officers: David Granville Slack, Secretary; Christopher Clement Britton [1960] Director/Building Services Consulting Engineer; Dr Leila Beatrice Cooke [1950] Director/Retired; Alison Margaret Heaton [1951] Director/Retired; Peter Laszlo [1944] Director/Retired; Franklin Selion Morton [1964] Director/Solicitor

Freixenet Copestick Limited
Incorporated: 27 May 2005 *Employees:* 29
Previous: Copestick Murray Limited
Net Worth: £2,351,225 *Total Assets:* £22,577,178
Registered Office: 8 Woodstock Court, Blenheim Road, Marlborough, Wilts, SN8 4AN
Activities: Wholesale of wine, beer, spirits and other alcoholic beverages
Parent: Henkell International GmbH
Officers: Nicholas George Bryan, Secretary; Dr Andreas Brokemper [1969] Director [German]; Damian Michael Clarke [1970] Director; Robin Peto Copestick [1963] Director; Pedro Ferrer [1958] Director [Spanish]

The Thomas Freke and Lady Norton Charity
Incorporated: 4 June 2014
Net Worth: £5,871,981 *Total Assets:* £5,999,857
Registered Office: 23 Chedworth Gate, Broome Manor, Swindon, Wilts, SN3 1NE
Activities: Other social work activities without accommodation n.e.c.
Officers: Barry Compton, Secretary; George James Arkell [1978] Director; Dr Gillian Margaret Combe [1972] Director/Doctor; Karen Margaret Mayell [1947] Director/Research Nurse; Philip John Sapwell [1950] Director/Retired; John Michael Elsworth Scott [1952] Director/Solicitor; Alison Clare Talbert [1968] Director/Accountant; Lorna Ruth Wallace [1948] Director/Retired

Fremington Homes Limited
Incorporated: 18 April 2005 *Employees:* 12
Net Worth: £2,088,633 *Total Assets:* £4,751,957
Registered Office: Lime Court, Pathfields Business Park, South Molton, Devon, EX36 3LH
Activities: Other service activities n.e.c.
Major Shareholder: Shane Amanda Stevens
Officers: Michael Stevens, Secretary; Charles Alfred Stevens [1992] Director/Operations Manager; Shane Amanda Stevens [1960] Director

Fresh Homes (Bournemouth) Limited
Incorporated: 27 June 2013
Net Worth: £2,616,537 *Total Assets:* £4,373,790
Registered Office: 2 Poole Road, Bournemouth, BH2 5QY
Activities: Development of building projects
Officers: Richard David Botterill [1948] Director; Myles Bridges [1964] Director/Surveyor; Anne Elizabeth Colwyn Foulkes [1957] Director/Retired; Jennifer Jane Bryony Hill [1955] Director/Retired; Christine Mary Webb [1958] Director/Retired; David Robert Andrew Webb [1954] Director/Consultant

Freshstores Limited
Incorporated: 3 December 1993 *Employees:* 137
Net Worth: £2,755,246 *Total Assets:* £3,555,628
Registered Office: 3rd Floor, Maltravers House, Petters Way, Yeovil, Somerset, BA20 1SQ
Activities: Retail sale of bread, cakes, flour confectionery and sugar confectionery in specialised stores
Parent: Symonds Estates Limited
Officers: John Michael Liptrot [1956] Director; Jeremy Paul Symonds [1960] Director; Julia Marie Symonds [1961] Director

Frizzell Financial Services Limited
Incorporated: 28 December 1923
Net Worth: £2,959,000 *Total Assets:* £24,526,000
Registered Office: County Gates, Bournemouth, BH1 2NF
Activities: Financial intermediation not elsewhere classified
Officers: Michael Peter Jones, Secretary; Andrew Mark Parsons [1965] Finance Director; John Trevor Perks [1970] Life Managing Director; Anthony Wayne Snow [1972] Director/Chief Risk Officer

Frog Investments Limited
Incorporated: 12 January 2012 *Employees:* 2
Net Worth: £1,599,208 *Total Assets:* £3,842,268
Registered Office: Lowin House, Tregolls Road, Truro, Cornwall, TR1 2NA
Activities: Other letting and operating of own or leased real estate
Shareholders: Annamarie Dias; James Robert Dias
Officers: Annamarie Dias [1983] Director; James Robert Dias [1978] Director/Chartered Accountant

Frome Solar Limited
Incorporated: 27 November 2013
Net Worth Deficit: £303,376 *Total Assets:* £9,544,613
Registered Office: Long Barn, Manor Courtyard, Stratton on the Fosse, Radstock, Somerset, BA3 4QF
Activities: Production of electricity
Parent: Monksham Power Limited
Officers: Yit Ho Tang [1974] Director [Singaporean]; Christopher James Tanner [1972] Director; Jonathan Simon Thompson [1963] Managing Director

Front Foot Investments Limited
Incorporated: 5 February 2013 *Employees:* 2
Net Worth: £4,732,979 *Total Assets:* £4,901,211
Registered Office: Camers, Badminton Road, Old Sodbury, Bristol, BS37 6RG
Activities: Security dealing on own account
Shareholders: Joanna Louise Denman; Michael Dennis Denman
Officers: Joanna Louise Denman [1971] Director; Michael Dennis Denman [1970] Director

Frontline Image Ltd
Incorporated: 9 April 1997 *Employees:* 100
Net Worth: £1,196,198 *Total Assets:* £4,106,392
Registered Office: Sisna Park, Estover Road, Plymouth, PL6 7FH
Activities: Finishing of textiles
Major Shareholder: David Gower
Officers: Angela Gower [1962] Director/Accountant; David Kevin Gower [1964] Director; Matthew MacKay [1983] Director; Stephen Nelson [1980] Director/Graphic Designer

James Froud and Sons Limited
Incorporated: 5 April 1950 *Employees:* 4
Net Worth: £8,137,886 *Total Assets:* £8,647,994
Registered Office: Westacott, East Buckland, Barnstaple, Devon, EX32 0TA
Activities: Other letting and operating of own or leased real estate
Major Shareholder: Geoffrey Herbert Ward
Officers: Michelle Ward, Secretary; Geoffrey Herbert Ward [1929] Director; Michelle Ward [1960] Director; Rita Ward [1932] Director

Froyle Harbour Hotel Limited
Incorporated: 20 April 2012 *Employees:* 11
Net Worth: £2,387,677 *Total Assets:* £10,685,600
Registered Office: Harbour House, 60 Purewell, Christchurch, Dorset, BH23 1ES
Activities: Hotels and similar accommodation
Parent: Harbour Hotels Group Limited
Officers: Stuart Andrew Bateman [1976] Director; David Francis Robbins [1967] Finance Director; Michael Oliver Warren [1970] Director [Irish]

Froyle Park Estates Limited
Incorporated: 28 June 2011 *Employees:* 1
Net Worth: £807,181 *Total Assets:* £4,740,681
Registered Office: Harbour House, 60 Purewell, Christchurch, Dorset, BH23 1ES
Activities: Buying and selling of own real estate
Major Shareholder: Nicolas James Roach
Officers: Stuart Andrew Bateman, Secretary; David Francis Robbins [1967] Finance Director

C.G. Fry and Son Limited
Incorporated: 28 October 1983 *Employees:* 165
Net Worth: £52,231,008 *Total Assets:* £96,437,408
Registered Office: Litton Cheney, Dorchester, DT2 9AS
Activities: Construction of domestic buildings
Shareholder: Philip George Fry
Officers: Ludovic Neil Charles Blackburn [1975] Director/Chartered Accountant; Michael Dear [1969] Director/Chartered Quantity Surveyor; Eugene Patrick Doherty [1961] Director/Architectural Technician [Irish]; Philip George Fry [1966] Director/Quantity Surveyor; Caroline June Hill [1968] Sales Director; David William Lohfink [1968] Director/Chartered Town Planner; Kevin Thomas Murch [1959] Director/Construction Manager; Michael Graham John Pinney [1969] Director

FTI Management Limited
Incorporated: 7 October 2014 *Employees:* 333
Net Worth: £8,085,041 *Total Assets:* £36,453,096
Registered Office: Gammon House, Riverside Road, Pottington Business Park, Barnstaple, Devon, EX31 1QN
Activities: Activities of head offices
Shareholders: Kevin Peter Fenlon; Paul Jay Turner
Officers: Rachel Emma Dafforn, Secretary; Bruce Peter Isaac, Secretary; Timothy Peter Isaac, Secretary; Kevin Peter Fenlon [1965] Director/Chief Executive; Robert William Isaac [1943] Director/Retired; William George Isaac [1958] Director; Paul Jay Turner [1969] Director/Accountant

Fulford Care Home Limited
Incorporated: 11 September 2016
Net Worth: £23,258 *Total Assets:* £3,919,400
Registered Office: Admiralty Buildings, Castletown, Portland, Weymouth, Dorset, DT5 1BB
Activities: Other business support service activities n.e.c.
Parent: Agincare Homes Holdings Ltd
Officers: Derek Edwin Luckhurst [1955] Director; Raina Marina Summerson [1970] Director

Cameron Fuller Limited
Incorporated: 20 February 1998 *Employees:* 21
Net Worth: £5,931,014 *Total Assets:* £6,322,782
Registered Office: Pyne Cliff, Ware Lane, Lyme Regis, Dorset, DT7 3EJ
Activities: Manufacture of other furniture
Shareholders: James Charles Cameron Fuller; Meriel Rosemary Fuller; Meriel Rosemary Fuller; James Charles Cameron Fuller
Officers: James Charles Cameron Fuller, Secretary/Director; James Charles Cameron Fuller [1967] Director; Meriel Rosemary Fuller [1967] Director

Fulton Boiler Works, (Great Britain) Limited
Incorporated: 2 August 1965 *Employees:* 58
Net Worth: £220,292 *Total Assets:* £5,168,766
Registered Office: 5 Fernhurst Road, Fishponds, Bristol, BS5 7FG
Activities: Manufacture of other special-purpose machinery n.e.c.
Shareholders: Ronald Bramley Palm (Snr); Ronald Bramley Palm (Jnr)
Officers: Melissa Obit, Secretary; Jian Chen [1962] Director/General Manager [American]; Kathy Katchmar [1959] Director/Chairman [American]; Carl Knight [1964] Managing Director; Ronald Bramley Palm Jr [1960] Director [American]; Ronald Bramley Palm Snr [1938] Director [American]

Fundamentals Limited
Incorporated: 16 June 1994 *Employees:* 64
Net Worth: £3,267,951 *Total Assets:* £5,932,842
Registered Office: Unit 2 Hillmead Enterprise Park, Marshall Road, Swindon, Wilts, SN5 5FZ
Activities: Manufacture of electricity distribution and control apparatus
Shareholders: Alison Hiscock; Jonathan Nicholas Hiscock
Officers: David Henry Bage, Secretary; David Henry Bage [1959] Director/Accountant; Martin Harris [1966] Director; Dr Jonathan Nicholas Hiscock [1973] Director; John Humble [1969] Director; Dr Vincent Paul Thornley [1971] Director/Engineer

Funkypigeon.Com Limited
Incorporated: 11 April 2007 *Employees:* 59
Previous: Spilt Ink Studio Limited
Net Worth: £4,633,878 *Total Assets:* £89,208,784
Registered Office: Greenbridge Road, Swindon, Wilts, SN3 3RX
Activities: Other retail sale not in stores, stalls or markets
Parent: WH Smith High Street Limited
Officers: Ian Houghton, Secretary; Ian Houghton [1965] Director; Robert James Moorhead [1964] Director/Accountant

Furlong Flooring (Wales) Ltd.
Incorporated: 1 March 1974 *Employees:* 54
Net Worth: £43,425 *Total Assets:* £7,350,085
Registered Office: 13 Brunel Way, Stroudwater Business Park, Stonehouse, Glos, GL10 3SX
Activities: Wholesale of furniture, carpets and lighting equipment
Parent: Furlong Holdings (UK) Ltd
Officers: Victoria Wells, Secretary; Noel Furlong [1937] Director/Chairman; Allan McDonald [1968] Sales Director; Muir O'Loghlen [1950] Director [Irish]

Furniture World Limited
Incorporated: 26 June 2003 *Employees:* 67
Net Worth: £2,077,202 *Total Assets:* £6,022,155
Registered Office: Unit 1 Cardrew Way, Cardrew Industrial Estate, Redruth, Cornwall, TR15 1SH
Activities: Retail of furniture, lighting, and similar (not musical instruments or scores) in specialised store
Parent: Neon (Holdings) Limited
Officers: Kathleen Long, Secretary; Kathleen Long [1952] Director; Marie Long [1973] Director; Roger John Long [1947] Director; Ryan Neil Long [1973] Director

Futura Foods UK Limited
Incorporated: 18 May 1993 *Employees:* 23
Net Worth: £2,093,062 *Total Assets:* £9,610,670
Registered Office: The Priory, Long Street, Dursley, Glos, GL11 4HR
Activities: Wholesale of dairy products, eggs and edible oils and fats
Parent: Nordex Holding A/S
Officers: Per Ranum Simonsen, Secretary; Martin Aagaard Pedersen [1978] Director/Commercial Development Manager [Danish]; Erik Christensen [1960] Commercial Director [Danish]; Hans Christiansen [1965] Managing Director [Danish]; Peter Mark Humphrey [1958] Director/Account Manager; Keld Hoven Pedersen [1948] Managing Director [Danish]; Per Ranum Simonsen [1962] Finance Director

Future Advanced Manufacture Ltd
Incorporated: 6 February 1981 *Employees:* 75
Net Worth: £3,895,708 *Total Assets:* £9,731,744
Registered Office: Future House, Unit F Herrick Way, Staverton Technology Park, Cheltenham, Glos, GL51 6TQ
Activities: Manufacture of air and spacecraft and related machinery
Parent: Future AM UK Ltd
Officers: Louise Claire Willis, Secretary; Arash Hatefi [1973] Quality Director; Kevin Christopher Jennings [1974] Distribution Director; Katherine Lewis [1970] Finance Director; Samuel Trevor Wesley Ogden [1974] Manufacturing Director; Craig Warrick Peterson [1975] Managing Director; Sean Nicholas Taylor [1974] Operations Director; Mark Tovey [1961] Engineering Director

Future Holdings 2002 Limited
Incorporated: 6 March 2002
Net Worth Deficit: £83,427,000 *Total Assets:* £83,457,000
Registered Office: Quay House, The Ambury, Bath, BA1 1UA
Activities: Other publishing activities
Parent: Future PLC
Officers: Penelope Ladkin-Brand, Secretary; Zillah Ellen Byng-Thorne [1974] Director; Oliver James Foster [1983] Director/Group Financial Controller; Penelope Ladkin-Brand [1977] Director

Future PLC
Incorporated: 22 April 1999 *Employees:* 582
Net Worth: £61,300,000 *Total Assets:* £122,400,000
Registered Office: Quay House, The Ambury, Bath, BA1 1UA
Activities: Other publishing activities
Officers: Penelope Ladkin-Brand, Secretary; Zillah Ellen Byng-Thorne [1974] Director; Hugo Charles Drayton [1959] Director; Rob Hattrell [1975] Director; Richard Norman Legh Huntingford [1956] Director; Penelope Ladkin-Brand [1977] Company Secretary/Director; Alan Philip Stephen Newman [1957] Director/Chairman of Audit Committee

Future Publishing Holdings Limited
Incorporated: 8 September 1997
Net Worth Deficit: £9,903,000 *Total Assets:* £3,735,000
Registered Office: Quay House, The Ambury, Bath, BA1 1UA
Activities: Other publishing activities
Parent: Future PLC
Officers: Penelope Ladkin-Brand, Secretary; Zillah Ellen Byng-Thorne [1974] Director; Oliver James Foster [1983] Director/Group Financial Controller; Penelope Ladkin-Brand [1977] Director

Future Publishing Limited
Incorporated: 10 April 1986 *Employees:* 503
Net Worth: £91,077,000 *Total Assets:* £174,655,008
Registered Office: Quay House, The Ambury, Bath, BA1 1UA
Activities: Other publishing activities
Parent: Future Holdings 2002 Limited
Officers: Penelope Ladkin-Brand, Secretary; Zillah Ellen Byng-Thorne [1974] Director; Oliver James Foster [1983] Director/Group Financial Controller; Penelope Ladkin-Brand [1977] Director

Futuream (UK) Limited
Incorporated: 6 December 2007 *Employees:* 77
Net Worth: £3,080,878 *Total Assets:* £8,932,024
Registered Office: Future House, Unit F Herrick Way, Staverton Technology Park, Cheltenham, Glos, GL51 6TQ
Activities: Other professional, scientific and technical activities n.e.c.
Major Shareholder: Craig Warrick Peterson
Officers: Louise Claire Willis, Secretary; Katherine Lewis [1970] Finance Director; Craig Warrick Peterson [1975] Managing Director; Louise Claire Willis [1979] Director

FWSC (Ladram) Limited
Incorporated: 17 September 1998 *Employees:* 126
Net Worth: £8,082,421 *Total Assets:* £15,203,462
Registered Office: Winchester House, Deane Gate Avenue, Taunton, Somerset, TA1 2UH
Activities: Recreational vehicle parks, trailer parks and camping grounds
Officers: Frances Margaret Carter, Secretary/Director; Frances Margaret Carter [1950] Director; Robin Anthony Bill Carter [1944] Director; Rowan Charles Carter [1953] Director; Zoe Anne House [1963] Director

Fylde CNC Specialists Limited
Incorporated: 8 November 2004 *Employees:* 40
Net Worth: £3,167,679 *Total Assets:* £4,787,305
Registered Office: Unit 7 Albion Close, Newtown Business Park, Poole, Dorset, BH12 3LL
Activities: Manufacture of other fabricated metal products n.e.c.
Parent: Venture Engineering Group Limited
Officers: Kate Victoria Davis [1981] Finance Director; Katie Mellor [1984] Director/Accountant; Leigh Mark Smith [1971] Director

G & H US Holdings Limited
Incorporated: 26 September 2007 *Employees:* 2
Net Worth: £37,833,092 *Total Assets:* £49,952,104
Registered Office: Dowlish Ford, Ilminster, Somerset, TA19 0PF
Activities: Activities of head offices
Parent: Gooch & Housego PLC
Officers: Gareth James Crowe, Secretary; Andrew Boteler [1966] Director/Accountant; Mark John Alexander Webster [1962] Director/Chief Executive

G & R House Limited
Incorporated: 28 February 2007 *Employees:* 4
Net Worth: £773,269 *Total Assets:* £4,165,335
Registered Office: Maltravers House, Petters Way, Yeovil, Somerset, BA20 1SH
Activities: Raising of dairy cattle
Shareholders: Graham House; Rosemary House
Officers: Rosemary House, Secretary/Farming; Graham House [1960] Director/Farming; Rosemary House [1966] Director/Farming

G Plan Upholstery Limited
Incorporated: 7 December 1917 *Employees:* 263
Net Worth: £10,020,728 *Total Assets:* £19,166,664
Registered Office: 1 Hampton Park West, Melksham, Wilts, SN12 6GU
Activities: Manufacture of other furniture
Parent: Sofa Brands International Limited
Officers: Emma Victoria Jones, Secretary/Accountant; Gareth Morgan Brown [1961] Finance Director; Stephen John Bruce [1969] Works Director; Matthew James Hudson [1968] Director; Ciaran Andrew McMahon [1968] Director [Irish]; Ian Oliver [1963] Director/Chief Executive

G W Interiors Holdings Limited
Incorporated: 27 March 2008 *Employees:* 2
Net Worth: £3,735,330 *Total Assets:* £5,058,974
Registered Office: Warren House, Blockley, Moreton in Marsh, Glos, GL56 9HL
Activities: Buying and selling of own real estate
Officers: Nigel John Stovell, Secretary; Geoffrey Peter Wall [1944] Director

G-TEKT Europe Manufacturing Limited
Incorporated: 16 September 1996 *Employees:* 808
Net Worth: £83,820,000 *Total Assets:* £108,457,000
Registered Office: Gloucester Business Park, Golf Club Lane, Brockworth, Gloucester, GL3 4AJ
Activities: Manufacture of bodies (coachwork) for motor vehicles (except caravans)
Parent: G-TEKT Corporation
Officers: Mitsuo Ishikawa [1955] Director [Japanese]; Hiroshi Seko [1961] Managing Director [Japanese]; Nicholas Jones Thomas [1972] Deputy Managing Director

G.B Contracts Limited
Incorporated: 24 December 1998 *Employees:* 2
Net Worth: £3,146,749 *Total Assets:* £5,002,660
Registered Office: GB Contracts Ltd, Chelworth Industrial Estate, Cricklade, Swindon, Wilts, SN6 6HQ
Activities: Wholesale of mining, construction and civil engineering machinery
Major Shareholder: Glenn Brooks
Officers: Glenn Brooks [1956] Director

G.B. Electronics Limited
Incorporated: 31 December 1991 *Employees:* 64
Net Worth: £1,545,708 *Total Assets:* £5,797,391
Registered Office: GBEC House, 31 Barnett Way, Gloucester, GL4 3RT
Activities: Computer facilities management activities
Parent: GBE Converge Group Limited
Officers: Sonja Joan Buttle, Secretary; Simon William Patterson, Secretary; Jason William Buttle [1971] Director/Manager; Darren Fell [1974] Director; Ian Mark Phelps [1975] Group Operations Director

G.E. Developments Ltd
Incorporated: 23 February 1995 *Employees:* 2
Net Worth: £1,506,135 *Total Assets:* £4,665,857
Registered Office: Plym House, 3 Longbridge Road, Marsh Mills, Plymouth, PL6 8LT
Activities: Construction of commercial buildings
Major Shareholder: Geoffrey Richard Easson
Officers: Brian John Hasell, Secretary; Geoffrey Richard Easson [1965] Director; Judy Easson [1970] Director

G.E.H. Properties Limited
Incorporated: 19 November 1999 *Employees:* 3
Net Worth: £2,148,554 *Total Assets:* £18,767,880
Registered Office: First Floor, 10 Temple Back, Bristol, BS1 6FL
Activities: Hotels and similar accommodation
Parent: The Great Eastern Hotel Company Limited
Officers: Robert Ryan Mangiarelli [1971] Director/Financial Executive [American]; Bradley Raymond O'Bryan [1969] Director/Financial Executive [American]; David Alan Peters [1972] Director/Attorney [American]

G3 Systems Limited
Incorporated: 26 April 2001 *Employees:* 109
Net Worth: £14,111,003 *Total Assets:* £20,615,844
Registered Office: Brunel Building, 11 Mereside, Portland, Dorset, DT5 1PY
Activities: Manufacture of other fabricated metal products n.e.c.
Parent: IAP Worldwide Services, Inc
Officers: David James Craig Jr, Secretary; Terrence Lee Derosa [1954] Director/CEO - IAP Worldwide Services Inc [American]; Iain Gordon Robertson Smith [1961] Director & General Manager

G4S Investments Limited
Incorporated: 26 September 2005
Net Worth: £44,857,876 *Total Assets:* £73,710,056
Registered Office: Third Floor, Broad Quay House, Prince Street, Bristol, BS1 4DJ
Activities: Other business support service activities n.e.c.
Parent: Semperian PPP Investment Partners No.2 Limited
Officers: Alan Edward Birch [1970] Director; Philip Charles Dove [1974] Director/COO G4S FM; Gawie Murray Nienaber [1957] Director/General Legal Counsel; Andrew Charles Mutch Rhodes [1970] Director

G4S IP 2 Limited
Incorporated: 16 October 2007 *Employees:* 2
Net Worth: £1 *Total Assets:* £14,951,865
Registered Office: Third Floor, Broad Quay House, Prince Street, Bristol, BS1 4DJ
Activities: Other business support service activities n.e.c.
Parent: Semperian PPP Investment Partners No.2 Limited
Officers: Alan Edward Birch [1970] Director; Andrew Charles Mutch Rhodes [1970] Director

G4S Joint Ventures Limited
Incorporated: 11 July 2000
Net Worth: £53,728,832 *Total Assets:* £113,124,216
Registered Office: Third Floor, Broad Quay House, Prince Street, Bristol, BS1 4DJ
Activities: Activities of head offices
Parent: G4S Investments Limited
Officers: Alan Edward Birch [1970] Director; Philip Charles Dove [1974] Director/COO G4S FM; Gawie Murray Nienaber [1957] Director/General Legal Counsel; Andrew Charles Mutch Rhodes [1970] Director

G4S Technology Limited
Incorporated: 10 May 1989 *Employees:* 158
Net Worth: £44,334,000 *Total Assets:* £51,248,000
Registered Office: Challenge House, International Drive, Tewkesbury, Glos, GL20 8UQ
Activities: Other professional, scientific and technical activities n.e.c.
Parent: G4S Regional Management (UK & I) Limited
Officers: Vaishali Jagdish Patel, Secretary; Howard Johnson [1962] Director; John Charles Kenning [1961] Director [American]

Gabriel Limited
Incorporated: 18 February 2015 *Employees:* 3
Net Worth: £15,638,694 *Total Assets:* £15,642,854
Registered Office: 2nd Floor, Stratus House, Emperor Way, Exeter Business Park, Exeter, Devon, EX1 3QS
Activities: Activities of financial services holding companies
Major Shareholder: David Francis Speakman
Officers: Richard Mark Mathias [1971] Managing Director; David Francis Speakman [1946] Director

Peter Gabriel Limited
Incorporated: 19 March 1973 *Employees:* 44
Net Worth: £1,057,216 *Total Assets:* £4,160,751
Registered Office: Mill Lane, Box, Corsham, Wilts, SN13 8PL
Activities: Sound recording and music publishing activities
Major Shareholder: Peter Brian Gabriel
Officers: David Charles Hatchman, Secretary; Peter Brian Gabriel [1950] Director/Musician; Anne Felicia Goldsworthy [1951] Director/Education Consultant; Michael David Large [1959] Managing Director

Gaiger Brothers Limited
Incorporated: 8 June 1954 *Employees:* 83
Net Worth: £13,003,175 *Total Assets:* £20,626,310
Registered Office: Kennet House, Northgate Street, Devizes, Wilts, SN10 1JT
Activities: Development of building projects
Major Shareholder: Michael Joseph Gaiger and A F Ciechan
Officers: Samuel Joseph Gaiger, Secretary/Accountant; Graham Michael Gaiger [1973] Director/Contracts Manager; James Henry Gaiger [1975] Director/Contracts Manager; Samuel Joseph Gaiger [1978] Director/Accountant

Gainwell Limited
Incorporated: 8 January 1998 *Employees:* 4
Net Worth: £46,994,576 *Total Assets:* £47,373,820
Registered Office: 3 Rivergate, Temple Quay, Bristol, BS1 6GD
Activities: Financial intermediation not elsewhere classified
Shareholder: Julian Charles Dobson
Officers: Mary Dobson, Secretary; Charles Edward Dobson [1944] Director; Julian Charles Dobson [1971] Director; Mary Dobson [1943] Director

Gale Homes and Investments Limited
Incorporated: 30 March 2000 *Employees:* 3
Net Worth: £1,367,631 *Total Assets:* £4,736,617
Registered Office: Unit C, Citrus House, 602 Wimborne Road, Bournemouth, BH9 2EN
Activities: Development of building projects
Major Shareholder: Richard John Gale
Officers: Richard John Gale, Secretary/Property Developer; Richard John Gale [1962] Director/Property Developer

Galion (Project Two) Limited
Incorporated: 31 October 2013
Net Worth: £6,297,210 *Total Assets:* £6,488,253
Registered Office: Higher Hill Farm, Butleigh Hill, Butleigh, Glastonbury, Somerset, BA6 8TW
Activities: Environmental consulting activities
Major Shareholder: Angus Crawford MacDonald
Officers: Angus Crawford MacDonald [1964] Director/Land Owner

Gall Thomson Environmental Limited
Incorporated: 13 September 1993 *Employees:* 47
Net Worth: £39,803,000 *Total Assets:* £42,925,000
Registered Office: c/o Klaw Products, Commerce Business Centre, West Wilts Trading Estate, Westbury, Wilts, BA13 4LS
Activities: Other manufacturing n.e.c.
Shareholders: Copper Bidco Limited; Copper Bidco Limited
Officers: Mike Hartman, Secretary; Mike Hartman [1965] Director/Chief Financial Officer; David Robert Hill [1966] Director; Max Philip Virgin [1979] Director; Anthony John Webber [1966] Director/General Manager

Tom Gallagher Group Limited
Incorporated: 31 August 2001 *Employees:* 36
Net Worth: £2,509,142 *Total Assets:* £3,544,601
Registered Office: M4 Service & MOT Centre, Westmead Industrial Estate, Westmead, Swindon, Wilts, SN5 7YT
Activities: Sale of other motor vehicles
Shareholders: Thomas Dennis Gallagher; Thomas Dennis Gallagher
Officers: Linda Jane Gallagher, Secretary; Martin Anthony David Gallagher [1966] Director/Sales Manager; Thomas Dennis Gallagher [1954] Director [Irish]; Charlotte Griffin [1969] Finance Director; Alan Rowland [1964] Director/After Sales Manager

Galloper Wind Farm Holding Company Limited
Incorporated: 1 September 2015
Net Worth: £118,790,296 *Total Assets:* £1,460,001,408
Registered Office: Windmill Hill Business Park, Whitehill Way, Swindon, Wilts, SN5 6PB
Activities: Activities of other holding companies n.e.c.
Shareholders: Aldeburgh Offshore Wind Investments Limited; Innogy Renewables UK Limited; Siemens AG; UK Green Investment Galloper Limited; Siemens AG; Aldeburgh Offshore Wind Investments Limited; Innogy Renewables UK Limited; UK Green Investment Galloper Limited
Officers: Christopher David Barras, Secretary; Penelope Anne Sainsbury, Secretary; Grace Arthur [1980] Director [Irish]; Paul Leslie Cowling [1960] Director; Erin Kate Eisenberg [1978] Director [American]; Matthew John Gleeson [1975] Director/Senior Vice President [Australian]; David McNamara [1962] Director/Engineer [Irish]; Christoph Friedrich Mertens [1969] Director [German]; Christian Rudiger Mockl [1973] Director [German]; Dr Karsten Moeller [1977] Director/Investment Manager [German]; Matthew Porter [1977] Associate Director; Hoffs Ruediger [1969] Director [German]; Richard Jennings Sandford [1971] Director/Head of Offshore Business Management; David Paul Tilstone [1969] Director/Investment Manager; Florian Voss [1985] Director/Investment Manager [German]

Galloper Wind Farm Limited
Incorporated: 20 July 2010
Net Worth: £118,594,176 *Total Assets:* £1,459,805,312
Registered Office: Windmill Hill Business Park, Whitehill Way, Swindon, Wilts, SN5 6PB
Activities: Construction of utility projects for electricity and telecommunications
Officers: Christopher David Barras, Secretary; Penelope Anne Sainsbury, Secretary; Grace Arthur [1980] Director [Irish]; Paul Leslie Cowling [1960] Director; Erin Kate Eisenberg [1978] Director [American]; Matthew John Gleeson [1975] Director/Senior Vice President [Australian]; David McNamara [1962] Director/Engineer [Irish]; Christoph Friedrich Mertens [1969] Director [German]; Christian Rudiger Mockl [1973] Director [German]; Dr Karsten Moeller [1977] Director/Investment Manager [German]; Matthew Porter [1977] Associate Director; Hoffs Ruediger [1969] Director [German]; Richard Jennings Sandford [1971] Director/Head of Offshore Business Management; David Paul Tilstone [1969] Director/Investment Manager; Florian Voss [1985] Director/Investment Manager [German]

Galpharm Healthcare Limited
Incorporated: 6 January 2006 *Employees:* 3
Net Worth: £18,978,000 *Total Assets:* £20,347,000
Registered Office: Wrafton, Braunton, Devon, EX33 2DL
Activities: Other business support service activities n.e.c.
Parent: Perrigo UK Acquisition Limited
Officers: Annette Corcoran, Secretary; Neil Thomas Lister [1975] Director; Dominic Rivers [1977] Director; Christopher Allan Rudd [1980] Director

Galpharm International Limited
Incorporated: 24 February 1981 *Employees:* 70
Net Worth: £18,003,000 *Total Assets:* £37,058,000
Registered Office: Wrafton, Braunton, Devon, EX33 2DL
Activities: Wholesale of pharmaceutical goods
Parent: Galpharm Healthcare Limited
Officers: Annette Corcoran, Secretary; Neil Thomas Lister [1975] Director; Dominic James Rivers [1977] Director; Christopher Allan Rudd [1980] Director

Galsworthy Wind Park Limited
Incorporated: 30 April 2007
Net Worth: £10,410,285 *Total Assets:* £18,690,940
Registered Office: Lion House, Rowcroft, Stroud, Glos, GL5 3BY
Activities: Production of electricity
Parent: Ecotricity Group Limited
Officers: Tom Cowling, Secretary; Asif Rehmanwala [1976] Director/Chief Operating Officer; Dale Vince [1961] Director/Consultant

Galtec Holdings Limited
Incorporated: 11 October 1989 *Employees:* 134
Net Worth: £6,485,626 *Total Assets:* £11,852,774
Registered Office: Carrick House, Lypiatt Road, Cheltenham, Gloucester, GL50 2QJ
Activities: Non-trading company
Officers: John Martin Handley [1962] Director/Chartered Accountant

Galtec Limited
Incorporated: 9 May 1988 *Employees:* 1
Net Worth: £5,542,305 *Total Assets:* £11,826,797
Registered Office: Carrick House, Lypiatt Road, Cheltenham, Glos, GL50 2QJ
Activities: Other specialised construction activities n.e.c.
Officers: Douglas Lee Green [1962] Director/Chief Financial Officer; John Martin Handley [1962] Director/Chartered Accountant; Peter Leggett [1967] Director/Quantity Surveyor; Thomas Lee Rayer [1986] Director/Engineer

Game and Wildlife Conservation Trust
Incorporated: 30 September 2005 *Employees:* 119
Net Worth: £9,104,067 *Total Assets:* £10,128,983
Registered Office: Burgate Manor, Fordingbridge, Hants, SP6 1EF
Activities: Other research and experimental development on natural sciences and engineering
Officers: Nicholas John Sheeran, Secretary; Richard Henry Ronald Benyon [1960] Director; Stephen John Oakley Catlin [1954] Director; Simon Chantler [1959] Director/Executive Chairman; Richard Clephane Compton [1957] Director/Landowner/Heritage Manager; Anthony Daniell [1954] Director/Company Chairman; Lord Arthur Francis Nicholas Wills Downshire [1959] Director; James Duckworth-Chad [1972] Director/Farmer; Jeremy Paul Godsmark Finnis [1956] Director/Farmer/Landowner; Edward William Fitzalan Howard [1956] Director; David James Flux [1968] Director; Dr Anthony John Hamilton [1941] Director/Company Chairman; Lara Jukes [1969] Fundraising Director; David Lionel Mayhew [1940] Director/Banker/Farmer; Stephen Peter Morant [1950] Investment Director; David Allister John Noble [1949] Director; Hugh Richard Oliver-Bellasis [1945] Farmer/Director; Sir James Edward Thornton Paice [1949] Director; Andrew Cameron Salvesen [1947] Director; John Francis Gillies Sheilds [1980] Director; Rebecca Ann Shelley [1965] Director; Emma Maude Weir [1960] Director; David Nicholas Owen Williams [1947] Director

Gamecube Amusement Limited
Incorporated: 13 May 2016
Net Worth: £76,226,992 *Total Assets:* £77,307,424
Registered Office: Gamecube, 60-66 The Horsefair, Bristol, BS1 3JQ
Activities: Activities of amusement parks and theme parks
Major Shareholder: Martin Ng
Officers: Martin NG [1989] Director; Theodora NG [1993] Marketing Director

Gaming International Limited
Incorporated: 4 March 1932 *Employees:* 79
Net Worth: £17,623,000 *Total Assets:* £20,232,000
Registered Office: Abbey Stadium, Lady Lane, Blunsdon, Swindon, Wilts, SN25 4DN
Activities: Buying and selling of own real estate
Parent: Toklon Ltd
Officers: Stephen Peter Hayward, Secretary; Phanuthep Brarypaul [1977] Director [Thai]; George Albert Edwards [1962] Director/Operations Manager; William Alexander Glass [1953] Director; Stephen Peter Hayward [1956] Director/Accountant; Clarke Anthony Osborne [1952] Director

Gamma Energy Limited
Incorporated: 5 November 2013 *Employees:* 7
Net Worth: £4,479,413 *Total Assets:* £17,608,826
Registered Office: Woodwater House, Pynes Hill, Exeter, EX2 5WR
Activities: Production of electricity
Officers: Cesar Gonzalez Otalora [1974] Director/Engineer [Spanish]; Jose Manuel Zorrilla Astudillo [1974] Director [Spanish]

Gantrail International Limited
Incorporated: 15 December 1965 *Employees:* 30
Previous: Gantry Railing International Limited
Net Worth: £1,671,103 *Total Assets:* £4,280,478
Registered Office: Sudmeadow Road, Hempsted, Gloucester, GL2 5HG
Activities: Activities of head offices
Officers: Olivier Leopold Raymond Hubert Jean Blanpain [1956] Director/Group CFO [Luxembourger]; Peter Nathan Bygrave [1978] Director; Carole Jean Cresswell [1970] Finance Director; Malcolm Paul Gray [1968] Commercial Director; Maarten Eddy Katrien Impens [1982] Director [Belgian]; Malcolm Terence Trigg [1948] Director

Gapcontrol Limited
Incorporated: 21 August 1987
Net Worth: £6,530,505 *Total Assets:* £10,629,684
Registered Office: 22 Ringwood Road, Ferndown, Dorset, BH22 9AN
Activities: Buying and selling of own real estate
Parent: Ankers and Rawlings Developments Ltd
Officers: Scott Lewis Rawlings, Secretary; Jonathan Ankers [1980] Director/Manager; Martyn Eric Thomas Ankers [1952] Director/Developer; Timothy Ankers [1981] Director; Benjamin William Rawlings [1976] Director/Property; Scott Lewis Rawlings [1975] Director/Property; Stuart Staple Rawlings [1953] Director/Builder

Garador Holdings Limited
Incorporated: 13 January 1999 *Employees:* 120
Net Worth: £26,521,192 *Total Assets:* £29,379,902
Registered Office: Bunford Lane, Yeovil, Somerset, BA20 2EJ
Activities: Manufacture of doors and windows of metal
Parent: Hormann International Beteiligungs GmbH
Officers: Alan Bacon, Secretary/Accountant; Neil Discombe [1968] Managing Director; Herr Christoph Paul Stephan Horman [1967] Director/Engineer [German]

Garador Limited
Incorporated: 1 March 1988 *Employees:* 120
Net Worth: £11,339,879 *Total Assets:* £29,379,902
Registered Office: Garador, Bunford Lane, Yeovil, Somerset, BA20 2EJ
Activities: Manufacture of doors and windows of metal
Officers: Alan Bacon, Secretary/Accountant; Neil Discombe [1968] Managing Director

Gardiner (Holdings) Limited
Incorporated: 16 October 1989 *Employees:* 120
Net Worth: £15,284,519 *Total Assets:* £17,581,130
Registered Office: 9 College Fields, Clifton, Bristol, BS8 3HP
Activities: Activities of head offices
Shareholders: Anthony George Patrick Allen; John Watson
Officers: John Watson, Secretary; Anthony George Patrick Allen [1942] Director; John Watson [1956] Director/Accountant

Gardiner Bros. and Company (Leathers) Limited
Incorporated: 23 June 1954 *Employees:* 86
Net Worth: £3,806,980 *Total Assets:* £9,929,710
Registered Office: Units F and G, Quedgeley West Business Park, Bristol Road, Hardwicke, Gloucester, GL2 4PH
Activities: Wholesale of clothing and footwear
Shareholders: Richard Jolyon Gardiner; Peter Giles Gardiner
Officers: Peter Giles Gardiner, Secretary; Benjamin James Gardiner [1975] Director/Planner; James Richard Peter Gardiner [1975] Director/Accountant; Peter Giles Gardiner [1942] Director/Accountant; Richard Jolyon Gardiner [1938] Director/Accountant; Mark Douglas Holloway [1973] Operations Director

Gardiner,Sons & Co.,Limited
Incorporated: 10 August 1893 *Employees:* 118
Net Worth: £11,537,425 *Total Assets:* £16,621,102
Registered Office: 1 Straight Street, Bristol, BS2 0FQ
Activities: Other retail sale in non-specialised stores
Officers: John Watson, Secretary; Anthony George Patrick Allen [1942] Director; Benjamin Charles Francis Allen [1970] Managing Director; Kelly Grace Bennett [1977] Director/Accountant; Shaun David Butcher [1971] Director/Retailer; John Watson [1956] Director/Accountant; Stephen David Whitcombe [1967] Director/Retailer

Gardner Garages Limited
Incorporated: 23 February 2006 *Employees:* 54
Net Worth: £959,807 *Total Assets:* £4,256,693
Registered Office: Cheltenham Service Station, Lansdown Road, Westal Green, Cheltenham, Glos, GL50 2JA
Activities: Retail sale of automotive fuel in specialised stores
Shareholders: Clive Andrew Gardner; Stella Jane Gardner
Officers: Stella Jane Gardner, Secretary; Clive Andrew Gardner [1955] Director/Chairman; Emma Jayne Gardner [1978] Managing Director; Stella Jane Gardner [1964] Director

The Garland Company UK Limited
Incorporated: 13 December 2001 *Employees:* 35
Net Worth: £1,470,666 *Total Assets:* £18,351,226
Registered Office: Second Way Centre, Second Way, Bristol, BS11 8DF
Activities: Agents involved in the sale of timber and building materials
Officers: Richard James Debacco [1941] Director/CEO [American]; David Michael Sokol [1962] Director/Vice President [American]

Garrad Hassan & Partners Limited
Incorporated: 17 January 1985 *Employees:* 192
Net Worth: £2,231,041 *Total Assets:* £16,561,736
Registered Office: One Linear Park, Avon Street, Temple Quay, Bristol, BS2 0PS
Activities: Other research and experimental development on natural sciences and engineering
Officers: Mervyn Cajetan Fernandez [1956] Director; Dr. Lars Landberg [1964] Director/Scientist [Danish]; Graeme Niall McCann [1980] Director/Engineer; Prajeev Saishankar Rasiah [1973] Director/Engineer

Garrad Hassan Group Limited
Incorporated: 17 February 2003
Net Worth: £7,143,169 *Total Assets:* £7,154,469
Registered Office: One Linear Park, Avon Street, Temple Quay, Bristol, BS2 0PS
Activities: Other research and experimental development on natural sciences and engineering
Officers: Mervyn Cajetan Fernandez [1956] Finance Director; James Lee [1972] Director/Chartered Accountant; Prajeev Saishankar Rasiah [1973] Director/Engineer

Gatehouse Green Learning Trust
Incorporated: 5 September 2012 *Employees:* 217
Previous: Redland Green School
Net Worth: £61,117,088 *Total Assets:* £69,347,672
Registered Office: Redland Green School, Redland Green, Redland Court Road, Redland, Bristol, BS6 7EH
Activities: General secondary education
Officers: Sarah Margaret Baker [1956] Director/Headteacher; Sarah Everett-Cox [1982] Director/Accountant; Lawayne Alexandria Jefferson [1954] Director/Marketing Manager [Jamaican]

Gawcott Fields Community Solar Project C.I.C.
Incorporated: 18 June 2015
Net Worth Deficit: £233,807 *Total Assets:* £4,508,663
Registered Office: Tremough Innovation Centre Communities for Renewables CIC, Tremough Innovation Centre, Penryn, Cornwall, TR10 9TA
Activities: Production of electricity
Parent: Communities for Renewables CIC
Officers: William James Burnyeat [1978] Director; Tom Cosgrove [1981] Director/Development Manager Communities; Joanna Gabbrielle Ptychandra Mallett [1966] Director Households and Communities NEF; Ian Payne [1959] Director/Chief Officer, Bucking and Winslow CAB; Anthony John Ulph [1954] Director

Gazco Limited
Incorporated: 9 March 1988 *Employees:* 165
Net Worth: £12,671,090 *Total Assets:* £15,844,784
Registered Office: Falcon Road, Sowton Industrial Estate, Exeter, Devon, EX2 7LF
Activities: Manufacture of other fabricated metal products n.e.c.
Parent: Stovax Group Limited
Officers: Andrew David Walker, Secretary; Alistair Compton [1969] Director [Zimbabwean]; Robert James Crabb [1961] Director; Edward Gerard Charles Henry [1972] Director; Ian David Kingscott [1967] Technical Director; Michael Oram [1969] Director; Andrew David Walker [1962] Director/Chartered Accountant

Gazelle Properties Limited
Incorporated: 17 August 1995 *Employees:* 1
Net Worth: £1,327,457 *Total Assets:* £7,405,999
Registered Office: 7 Regent Street, Kingswood, Bristol, BS15 8JX
Activities: Construction of commercial buildings
Shareholder: Susan Ridings
Officers: Susan Ridings [1963] Administrative Director

GBE Converge Group Ltd
Incorporated: 13 October 1998 *Employees:* 108
Previous: Simlogic Limited
Net Worth: £2,329,037 *Total Assets:* £8,185,861
Registered Office: GBEC House, 31 Barnett Way, Gloucester, GL4 3RT
Activities: Activities of other holding companies n.e.c.
Shareholders: Jason William Buttle; Sonja Joan Buttle
Officers: Sonja Joan Buttle, Secretary; Jason William Buttle [1971] Director/Manager

GCL 2016 Limited
Incorporated: 7 July 2016 *Employees:* 4
Net Worth: £816 *Total Assets:* £14,500,816
Registered Office: Moorlands Trading Estate, Saltash, Cornwall, PL12 6LX
Activities: Retail sale in non-specialised stores with food, beverages or tobacco predominating
Parent: Triode Acquisitions UK Limited
Officers: Jennifer Kane, Secretary; Michael Alan Boardman [1972] Director; John Clohisey [1952] Director [Irish]; Leo John Anthony Crawford [1959] Director [Irish]; John O'Donnell [1954] Director [Irish]

GCP Bloomsbury Limited
Incorporated: 21 February 2017
Net Worth: £70,871,000 *Total Assets:* £166,552,992
Registered Office: 51 New North Road, Exeter, EX4 4EP
Activities: Other letting and operating of own or leased real estate
Parent: GCP Holdco 2 Limited
Officers: Gillian Lyndsay Wedon Day [1964] Director/Financier; Robert Malcolm Naish [1953] Director/Chartered Surveyor; Robert Henry Haldane Peto [1950] Director/Chartered Surveyor; Marlene Wood [1962] Director/Chartered Accountant

GCP Holdco Limited
Incorporated: 27 August 2015
Net Worth: £341,820,000 *Total Assets:* £545,132,992
Registered Office: 51 New North Road, Exeter, EX4 4EP
Activities: Activities of other holding companies n.e.c.
Parent: GCP Topco Limited
Officers: Gillian Lyndsay Wedon Day [1964] Director/Financier; Robert Malcolm Naish [1953] Director/Chartered Surveyor; Robert Henry Haldane Peto [1950] Director/Chartered Surveyor; Marlene Wood [1962] Director/Chartered Accountant

GCP Scape East Limited
Incorporated: 15 November 2013
Net Worth: £102,383,000 *Total Assets:* £146,112,000
Registered Office: 51 New North Road, Exeter, EX4 4EP
Activities: Other letting and operating of own or leased real estate
Parent: GCP Holdco Limited
Officers: Gillian Lyndsay Wedon Day [1964] Director/Financier; Robert Malcolm Naish [1953] Director/Chartered Surveyor; Robert Henry Haldane Peto [1950] Director/Chartered Surveyor; Marlene Wood [1962] Director/Chartered Accountant

GCP Student Living PLC
Incorporated: 26 February 2013 *Employees:* 128
Net Worth: £574,209,984 *Total Assets:* £825,598,016
Registered Office: 51 New North Road, Exeter, EX4 4EP
Activities: Activities of real estate investment trusts
Officers: Gillian Lyndsay Wedon Day [1964] Director/Financier; Robert Malcolm Naish [1953] Director/Chartered Surveyor; Robert Henry Haldane Peto [1950] Director/Chartered Surveyor; Marlene Wood [1962] Director/Chartered Accountant

GCP Topco 2 Limited
Incorporated: 7 March 2017
Net Worth: £107,812,000 *Total Assets:* £150,071,008
Registered Office: 51 New North Road, Exeter, Devon, EX4 4EP
Activities: Activities of other holding companies n.e.c.
Parent: GCP Student Living PLC
Officers: Gillian Lyndsay Wedon Day [1964] Director/Financier; Robert Malcolm Naish [1953] Director/Chartered Surveyor; Robert Henry Haldane Peto [1950] Director/Chartered Surveyor; Marlene Wood [1962] Director/Chartered Accountant

GCP Topco Limited
Incorporated: 27 August 2015
Net Worth: £341,784,992 *Total Assets:* £399,784,000
Registered Office: 51 New North Road, Exeter, EX4 4EP
Activities: Activities of other holding companies n.e.c.
Parent: GCP Student Living PLC
Officers: Gillian Lyndsay Wedon Day [1964] Director/Financier; Robert Malcolm Naish [1953] Director/Chartered Surveyor; Robert Henry Haldane Peto [1950] Director/Chartered Surveyor; Marlene Wood [1962] Director/Chartered Accountant

GCP WL Limited
Incorporated: 3 February 2016
Net Worth: £20,547,000 *Total Assets:* £21,116,000
Registered Office: 51 New North Road, Exeter, Devon, EX4 4EP
Activities: Other letting and operating of own or leased real estate
Parent: GCP Holdco 2 Limited
Officers: Gillian Lyndsay Wedon Day [1964] Director/Financier; Robert Malcolm Naish [1953] Director/Chartered Surveyor; Robert Henry Haldane Peto [1950] Director/Chartered Surveyor; Marlene Wood [1962] Director/Chartered Accountant

GDS INT Holdings Limited
Incorporated: 13 December 2013 *Employees:* 272
Net Worth: £2,248,962 *Total Assets:* £10,747,091
Registered Office: Queen Square House, 18-21 Queen Square, Bristol, BS1 4NH
Activities: Activities of head offices
Major Shareholder: Spencer David Green
Officers: Emily Green, Secretary; Spencer David Green [1969] Director

GDS Publishing Limited
Incorporated: 3 December 1993 *Employees:* 121
Net Worth: £3,281,112 *Total Assets:* £9,784,090
Registered Office: Floor 2, Queen Square House, 18-21 Queen Square, Bristol, BS1 4NH
Activities: Activities of conference organisers
Parent: GDS INT Holdings Limited
Officers: Emily Green, Company Secretary; Spencer David Green [1969] Director/Publisher

GE Aviation Systems Group Limited
Incorporated: 26 May 2004
Net Worth: £292,793,760 *Total Assets:* £295,213,792
Registered Office: Cheltenham Road, Bishops Cleeve, Cheltenham, Glos, GL52 8SF
Activities: Activities of head offices
Parent: GE Aviation UK
Officers: Tristan Keith Chubb, Secretary; Paul Danton Laity [1959] Director/European Products & Programs Leader, Avionics; Bradley Seemayer [1981] Director; Liam Martin Slate [1980] Director/Chartered Accountant; Oliver Towers [1956] Director/VP Strategy & Customer Accounts

GE Aviation Systems Limited
Incorporated: 3 January 1963 *Employees:* 2,834
Net Worth: £342,859,552 *Total Assets:* £726,451,904
Registered Office: Cheltenham Road, Bishops Cleeve, Cheltenham, Glos, GL52 8SF
Activities: Manufacture of electronic components
Parent: GE Infrastructure Aviation
Officers: Tristan Keith Chubb, Secretary; Paul Danton Laity [1959] Director/European Products & Programs Leader, Avionics; Bradley Seemayer [1981] Director; Liam Martin Slate [1980] Director/Chartered Accountant; Oliver Towers [1956] Director/General Management

GE Aviation UK
Incorporated: 12 January 2007
Net Worth: £295,965,088 *Total Assets:* £295,984,320
Registered Office: Cheltenham Road, Bishops Cleeve, Cheltenham, Glos, GL52 8SF
Activities: Manufacture of air and spacecraft and related machinery
Parent: IGE USA Holdings
Officers: Tristan Keith Chubb [1980] Director/Solicitor; Gordon Ramsay MacGregor [1964] Director

GE Infrastructure Aviation
Incorporated: 21 September 2007
Net Worth: £866,947,072 *Total Assets:* £866,947,072
Registered Office: Cheltenham Road, Bishops Cleeve, Cheltenham, Glos, GL52 8SF
Activities: Manufacture of air and spacecraft and related machinery
Parent: GE Caledonian Limited
Officers: Tristan Keith Chubb [1980] Director/Solicitor; Gordon Ramsay MacGregor [1964] Director

GE Oil & Gas UK Limited
Incorporated: 9 October 1980 *Employees:* 2,574
Net Worth: £493,616,000 *Total Assets:* £1,464,344,064
Registered Office: 2 High Street, Nailsea, Bristol, BS48 1BS
Activities: Other business support service activities n.e.c.
Parent: Vetco International Holding 4
Officers: Lorraine Amanda Dunlop, Secretary; Dean Arnison [1964] Director; Carole Audrey Chichester [1969] Director [American]; Graham Gillies [1975] Director [Australian]; David Russell Justiss [1976] Director [American]; Benjamin Linke [1983] Director [German]; Rogerio Guimaraes Mendonca [1972] Director [Brazilian]; Carl Adam Julius Roemmele [1974] Director; Neil Saunders [1969] Director; Alasdair Murray Campbell Sloan [1967] Director; Michael Piotr Stepniak [1977] Director [American]

GEA Farm Technologies (UK) Ltd
Incorporated: 8 January 1971 *Employees:* 54
Net Worth: £3,387,555 *Total Assets:* £10,718,982
Registered Office: Wylye Works, Watery Lane, Bishopstrow, Warminster, Wilts, BA12 9HT
Activities: Manufacture of soap and detergents
Officers: Steven Murray Fifer, Secretary; Ilija Aprcovic [1966] Managing Director; Timothy John Donbavand [1967] Director; Tracey Ann O'Neill [1968] Director/Head of Human Resources UK

Geist Europe Ltd
Incorporated: 2 June 2010 *Employees:* 51
Previous: Data and Power Solutions Holdings Limited
Net Worth: £969,169 *Total Assets:* £5,916,007
Registered Office: Unit 1 The Monarch Centre, Venture Way, Priorswood Industrial Estate, Taunton, Somerset, TA2 8DE
Activities: Manufacture of electronic components
Parent: Chloride Group Limited
Officers: Eamon Rowan, Secretary; Giovanna Moschetto [1973] Director [Italian]; Eamon Rowan [1959] Director/Vice President Finance [Irish]; Theo Roger Spittel [1964] Managing Director

Gemaco Holdings Limited
Incorporated: 23 November 1988 *Employees:* 81
Net Worth: £5,429,945 *Total Assets:* £8,875,148
Registered Office: 32-40 Harwell Road, Poole, Dorset, BH17 0GE
Activities: Manufacture of other electronic and electric wires and cables
Shareholders: Paul Lodge; Allen Lodge
Officers: Allen Lodge [1967] Director/Manager; Julie Lodge [1965] Director

Gemini Energy Limited
Incorporated: 1 February 2013
Net Worth: £9,138,000 *Total Assets:* £91,134,000
Registered Office: One Glass Wharf, Bristol, BS2 0ZX
Activities: Other business support service activities n.e.c.
Parent: Water Twins Limited
Officers: Serkan Bahceci [1972] Director; Charles John Gore Hazelwood [1963] Director

Gemma International Limited
Incorporated: 2 September 1977 *Employees:* 54
Net Worth: £566,000 *Total Assets:* £3,761,000
Registered Office: Linmar House, 6 East Portway, Andover, Hants, SP10 3LU
Activities: Other publishing activities
Parent: Mr & Mrs L Rudd-Clarke 1999 Settlement
Officers: Amanda Anne Parkin [1963] Director; Christopher Pilgrim [1967] Financial Director; Timothy Lindesay Rudd Clarke [1961] Director; Declan John Salter [1959] Director/Business Consultant

Genaray Limited
Incorporated: 1 June 2004
Net Worth: £2,337,713 *Total Assets:* £4,340,289
Registered Office: One Glass Wharf, Bristol, BS2 0ZX
Activities: Other business support service activities n.e.c.
Shareholders: Raymond Spanjar; Michiel Marky Arnold Spanjar
Officers: Machiel Marky Arnold Spanjar [1946] Director [Dutch]

Geneco Limited
Incorporated: 10 March 2009 *Employees:* 7
Net Worth: £337,000 *Total Assets:* £6,161,000
Registered Office: Operations Centre, Claverton Down Road, Claverton Down, Bath, BA2 7WW
Activities: Sewerage
Parent: Wessex Water Enterprises Limited
Officers: Ruth Esme Jefferson, Secretary; Colin Frank Skellett [1945] Director; Mark Timothy Watts [1961] Director

Gener8 Finance Limited
Incorporated: 14 October 2005 *Employees:* 16
Net Worth: £3,579,039 *Total Assets:* £13,472,481
Registered Office: 2nd Floor, St James House, The Square, Lower Bristol Road, Bath, BA2 3BH
Activities: Financial intermediation not elsewhere classified
Parent: Gener8 Finance Holdings Limited
Officers: Jennifer Bodey, Secretary; Edward John Rimmer [1972] Director; James Matthew Arthur Roberts [1977] Director; Richard Ian Smith [1961] Director

Genevac Limited
Incorporated: 2 January 1990 *Employees:* 67
Net Worth: £7,504,648 *Total Assets:* £16,044,858
Registered Office: First Floor, 10 Temple Back, Bristol, BS1 6FL
Activities: Other manufacturing n.e.c.
Parent: Kimberly Audrey Limited
Officers: Michael Francis Bonner [1960] Director/Chief Financial Officer [American]; Brian Michael Larkin [1969] Director/Business Executive [American]; Michael Phillip Santoni [1969] Director/Business Executive [American]; Ian Nigel Whitehall [1970] Sales Director

Genie Toys PLC
Incorporated: 19 September 1996 *Employees:* 4
Net Worth: £3,691,119 *Total Assets:* £3,972,054
Registered Office: Genie House, St James Square, Cheltenham, Glos, GL50 3QG
Activities: Manufacture of other plastic products
Parent: Genie Toys International Limited
Officers: Alexander Jesse Norman, Secretary; Casey William Norman [1963] Director; Caspar Joe Norman [1967] Director/Writer; Sir Torquil Patrick Alexander Norman [1933] Director

Gensmile Dental Care Limited
Incorporated: 13 May 2015 *Employees:* 144
Net Worth Deficit: £1,201,469 *Total Assets:* £21,507,686
Registered Office: Easton Manor, Easton Royal, Pewsey, Wilts, SN9 5LZ
Activities: Dental practice activities
Parent: Gensmile Limited
Officers: Mark Gregory Carter, Secretary; Sarah Clare Carney-Holliday [1985] Director/Registered Dental Nurse; Andrew Kevin Fenn [1958] Director/Dentist; Simon Turton [1967] Director

Gensmile Limited
Incorporated: 31 October 2014 *Employees:* 144
Net Worth: £4,042,192 *Total Assets:* £21,776,504
Registered Office: Easton Manor, Easton Royal, Wilts, SN9 5LZ
Activities: Activities of head offices
Shareholder: Nicholas John Lowcock
Officers: Mark Gregory Carter, Secretary; Nicholas John Lowcock [1963] Director/Investor; Simon Turton [1967] Director/Investor

Genus Capital 2 Limited
Incorporated: 28 September 2016 *Employees:* 3
Net Worth Deficit: £1,100 *Total Assets:* £3,688,658
Registered Office: 2nd Floor, Stratus House, Emperor Way, Exeter Business Park, Exeter, Devon, EX1 3QS
Activities: Activities of real estate investment trusts
Parent: Genus Capital Limited
Officers: Richard Mathias [1971] Director; David Francis Speakman [1946] Director; Maureen Speakman [1951] Director

Genus Capital 3 Limited
Incorporated: 11 October 2016 *Employees:* 3
Net Worth Deficit: £1,100 *Total Assets:* £10,055,752
Registered Office: 2nd Floor, Stratus House, Emperor Way, Exeter Business Park, Exeter, Devon, EX1 3QS
Activities: Activities of real estate investment trusts
Parent: Genus Capital Limited
Officers: Richard Mathias [1971] Director; David Francis Speakman [1946] Director; Maureen Speakman [1951] Director

Genus Capital Limited
Incorporated: 20 September 2016 *Employees:* 4
Net Worth: £18,509,440 *Total Assets:* £33,441,480
Registered Office: 2nd Floor, Stratus House, Emperor Way, Exeter Business Park, Exeter, Devon, EX1 3QS
Activities: Activities of other holding companies n.e.c.
Shareholders: Anna Elizabeth Speakman Silva; Paul Speakman
Officers: Richard Mark Mathias [1971] Managing Director; David Francis Speakman [1946] Director; Maureen Speakman [1951] Director

Geo Specialty Chemicals UK Limited
Incorporated: 27 May 2011 *Employees:* 163
Net Worth: £26,352,366 *Total Assets:* £55,854,648
Registered Office: One Glass Wharf, Bristol, BS2 0ZX
Activities: Manufacture of other organic basic chemicals
Officers: Kenneth Ghazey [1956] Director/CEO of Geo Speciality Chemicals, Inc [American]; Randall Robert Lay [1954] Director [American]; Nicholas Liptrot [1960] Director

Geometry Properties Limited
Incorporated: 13 June 1986
Net Worth: £2,774,000 *Total Assets:* £17,171,000
Registered Office: New Look House, Mercery Road, Weymouth, Dorset, DT3 5HJ
Activities: Other letting and operating of own or leased real estate
Parent: New Look Limited
Officers: Laura Elizabeth Battley, Secretary; Steven Paul Challes [1959] Director; Richard John Collyer [1974] Finance Director

George Banco.Com Limited
Incorporated: 6 December 2013
Net Worth Deficit: £1,952,749 *Total Assets:* £36,269,692
Registered Office: 1st Floor, Epsom Court, Epsom Road, White Horse Business Park, Trowbridge, Wilts, BA14 0XF
Activities: Credit granting by non-deposit taking finance houses and other specialist consumer credit grantors
Parent: George Banco Limited
Officers: Reena Patel, Secretary; Miles Marius Cresswell-Turner [1962] Director; Paul Gill [1971] Director/Chief Risk Officer; Marc Richard Howells [1965] Managing Director; Peter Forbes Michael Reynolds [1966] Director; Nicholas John Teunon [1966] Director; Steven Douglas White [1968] Director

George Estates Limited
Incorporated: 5 July 2017 *Employees:* 4
Net Worth: £4,367,609 *Total Assets:* £8,296,970
Registered Office: 32 Cross Hayes, Malmesbury, Wilts, SN16 9BG
Activities: Other letting and operating of own or leased real estate
Parent: George Admas Estates LLP
Officers: George Andrew Adams [1962] Director/Property Investor

The George Group Limited
Incorporated: 22 April 2015 *Employees:* 91
Net Worth: £2,676,101 *Total Assets:* £4,454,187
Registered Office: The George Veterinary Hospital, High Street, Malmesbury, Wilts, SN16 9AU
Activities: Veterinary activities
Officers: Miles Edward Southwell Russell, Secretary; Francis John Baird [1968] Director/Veterinary Surgeon; Linda Susan Belton [1968] Director/Veterinary Surgeon; Ann Margaret Davis [1973] Director/Veterinary Surgeon; Cyril Patrick Hayes [1973] Director/Veterinary Surgeon [Irish]; Tim David Hirst [1980] Director/Veterinary Surgeon; Michael Owen Hollywood [1970] Director/Veterinary Surgeon; Thomas Alexander Oxtoby [1976] Director/Veterinary Surgeon; Richard Beresford Pearson [1960] Director/Veterinary Surgeon; Miles Edward Southwell Russell [1966] Director/Practice Manager; Laura Anne Warren Sharpe [1981] Director/Veterinary Surgeon

Georgian House (Torquay) Limited
Incorporated: 9 March 2010 *Employees:* 64
Net Worth: £2,437,730 *Total Assets:* £7,758,678
Registered Office: Georgian House, Park Hill Road, Torquay, Devon, TQ1 2DZ
Activities: Other human health activities
Shareholders: Jason Feller; Elizabeth Joan Feller
Officers: Jason Feller, Secretary; Elizabeth Joan Feller [1945] Director/Carer; Jason Feller [1971] Director/Building Developer

Geotechnical Engineering Limited
Incorporated: 14 August 1961 *Employees:* 176
Net Worth: £937,604 *Total Assets:* £5,918,786
Registered Office: Centurion House, Olympus Park, Quedgeley, Gloucester, GL2 4NF
Activities: Test drilling and boring
Major Shareholder: Andrew Brian Milne
Officers: Andrew Brian Milne, Secretary; Lyndon Allan Barton [1972] Director/Engineering Geologist; Martyn Eric Brocklesby [1969] Director/Engineering Geologist; John Christopher Wilfred Hanson [1967] Director/Chartered Geologist; Alice Lucinda Mary Milne [1960] Director/Artist; Andrew Brian Milne [1959] Managing Director; Neil Varne Parry [1965] Director/Civil Engineer

Gerber Emig Group Limited
Incorporated: 9 February 1983
Net Worth: £5,493,000 *Total Assets:* £48,835,000
Registered Office: Mallard Court, Express Park, Bridgwater, Somerset, TA6 4RN
Activities: Activities of head offices
Officers: Pieter Willem Van Meeteren, Secretary; Aart Cornelis Duijzer [1963] Managing Director [Dutch]; Johannes Henricus Wilhelmus Roelofs [1963] Managing Director [Dutch]; David John Saint [1964] Director/Executive

The Gerrick Rose Animal Trust
Incorporated: 15 February 2012
Net Worth: £3,107,455 *Total Assets:* £4,053,632
Registered Office: Unit 21 Bell Park, Bell Close, Newnham Industrial Estate, Plymouth, PL7 4FD
Activities: Other service activities n.e.c.
Officers: Anthony John Cusack, Secretary; Anthony John Cusack [1963] Director/Solicitor; Jean Clarissa Knuckey [1952] Director; Cheryl Marie Thomas [1981] Director

Get Fresh Cosmetics Ltd
Incorporated: 2 June 1998 *Employees:* 6
Net Worth: £3,687,131 *Total Assets:* £5,335,444
Registered Office: 502 Wallisdown Road, Bournemouth, BH11 8PT
Activities: Other manufacturing n.e.c.
Officers: Robert Stephen Philpott, Secretary/Managing Director; Richard Keith McAvoy [1974] Technical Director; James William Moore [1976] Operations Director; Robert Stephen Philpott [1968] Managing Director; Amir Naser Sharifi [1968] Finance Director

GGB Investments Ltd
Incorporated: 15 June 2017
Net Worth: £151,120 *Total Assets:* £3,556,225
Registered Office: Unit 8 Hornsleasow Farm, Snowshill Hill, Moreton in Marsh, Glos, GL56 9TL
Activities: Buying and selling of own real estate
Major Shareholder: George William Davies
Officers: George William Davies [1941] Director

GH Clayhill Limited
Incorporated: 20 September 2001 *Employees:* 2
Net Worth Deficit: £8,946,000 *Total Assets:* £30,560,000
Registered Office: Third Floor, Broad Quay House, Prince Street, Bristol, BS1 4DJ
Activities: Other business support service activities n.e.c.
Parent: GH Clayhill Holdings Limited
Officers: Abdul Hamid [1966] Director; Richard Little [1979] Investment Director

GH Gravesham Limited
Incorporated: 1 October 2003 *Employees:* 2
Net Worth: £4,500,000 *Total Assets:* £31,392,000
Registered Office: Third Floor, Broad Quay House, Prince Street, Bristol, BS1 4DJ
Activities: Medical nursing home activities
Parent: GH Gravesham Holdings Limited
Officers: Abdul Hamid [1966] Director; Richard Little [1979] Investment Director

GH North Northampton Limited
Incorporated: 23 July 2002 *Employees:* 2
Net Worth: £524,000 *Total Assets:* £10,500,000
Registered Office: Third Floor, Broad Quay House, Prince Street, Bristol, BS1 4DJ
Activities: Hospital activities
Parent: GH North Northampton Holdings Limited
Officers: Kenneth Andrew McLellan [1961] Regional Project Director; Neil Rae [1971] Director

GH Stone House Limited
Incorporated: 20 October 2004 *Employees:* 2
Net Worth Deficit: £725,000 *Total Assets:* £15,480,000
Registered Office: Third Floor, Broad Quay House, Prince Street, Bristol, BS1 4DJ
Activities: Medical nursing home activities
Parent: GH Stone House Holdings Limited
Officers: Abdul Hamid [1966] Director; Richard Little [1979] Investment Director

Gibbs Surfacing Limited
Incorporated: 13 April 1995 *Employees:* 75
Net Worth: £1,959,834 *Total Assets:* £9,566,819
Registered Office: 21 Turnpike Road, Blunsdon, Swindon, Wilts, SN26 7EA
Activities: Construction of roads and motorways
Officers: Vicky Ann O'Reilly, Secretary; Vincent Gibbs [1965] Director

Stanley Gibson Limited
Incorporated: 18 September 1996 *Employees:* 16
Net Worth: £1,607,891 *Total Assets:* £4,257,722
Registered Office: Fenton Court, Fenton Road, Bristol, BS7 8ND
Activities: Wholesale of meat and meat products
Major Shareholder: Robert John Bowrey
Officers: Peter Hansom, Secretary; Steven Peter Bale [1961] Technical Director; Robert John Bowrey [1965] Director/Meat Broker; Peter Benedict Hansom [1971] Director/Accountant

Giftstones Limited
Incorporated: 7 July 2003
Net Worth: £3,450,895 *Total Assets:* £3,599,822
Registered Office: c/o Lewis Ball & Co, William House, 32 Bargates, Christchurch, Dorset, BH23 1QL
Activities: Agents specialised in the sale of other particular products
Officers: Robert Alan Coram, Secretary/Gift Wholesale; John Mark Cook [1961] Director/Gift Wholesale; Robert Alan Coram [1961] Director/Gift Wholesale

Giftworks Limited
Incorporated: 1 June 2001 *Employees:* 24
Net Worth: £2,626,487 *Total Assets:* £6,495,233
Registered Office: 34 Boulevard, Weston Super Mare, Somerset, BS23 1NF
Activities: Wholesale of household goods (other than musical instruments) n.e.c
Shareholders: Giftworks (Holdings) Limited; Derrick John Grove
Officers: Lesley Binning [1965] Director/Administrator; Derrick John Grove [1962] Director/Agent

Gilbert and Goode Limited
Incorporated: 21 April 1972 *Employees:* 74
Net Worth: £5,795,000 *Total Assets:* £8,748,000
Registered Office: Stennack House, Stennack Road, St Austell, Cornwall, PL25 3SW
Activities: Development of building projects
Officers: Simon Caklais, Secretary/Construction Manager; Jonathan Peter Nathaniel Adlington [1949] Director/Retired Solicitor; Simon Caklais [1966] Managing Director; Christopher Simon Durkin [1963] Director/Semi Retired; Charles David Evans [1955] Director/Retired Accountant; Mark Gardner [1965] Director/Group Chief Executive; Simon Andrew Hembury [1961] Director/Architect; Christopher Loraine Spencer [1955] Director/Retired

Gilcrest Group Limited
Incorporated: 17 May 2002 *Employees:* 31
Net Worth: £1,525,944 *Total Assets:* £4,646,549
Registered Office: Portview Road, Avonmouth, Bristol, BS11 9LQ
Activities: Activities of head offices
Major Shareholder: Kevin Gillham
Officers: Victoria Ann Doritza Bernstein [1973] Director; Kevin Michael Mervyn Gillham [1975] Director

William Gilder Limited
Incorporated: 17 June 2002
Net Worth: £8,679,653 *Total Assets:* £16,307,050
Registered Office: Teddington Hands, Evesham Road, Tewkesbury, Glos, GL20 8NE
Activities: Wholesale of agricultural machinery, equipment and supplies
Parent: William Gilder Group Limited
Officers: Melvyn Evans [1957] Director; William Gilder [1963] Director

Gilders Transport Limited
Incorporated: 14 April 1986 *Employees:* 70
Net Worth: £3,046,129 *Total Assets:* £9,065,988
Registered Office: Marlborough Cottage, Gretton Fields, Gretton, Cheltenham, Glos, GL54 5HH
Activities: Freight transport by road
Shareholders: Grantham Gordon Gilder; Judith Elizabeth Gilder
Officers: Judith Elizabeth Gilder, Secretary; Judith Elizabeth Gilder [1946] Director/Haulage Contractor

Gill Akaster LLP
Incorporated: 6 April 2009 *Employees:* 67
Net Worth: £1,631,258 *Total Assets:* £4,021,988
Registered Office: 25 Lockyer Street, Plymouth, PL1 2QW
Officers: Jonathan James Foster Hall [1964] Member; Stephen Martyn Ramsden [1963] Member; Stephen Allen [1961] LLP Member; Anthony John Cusack [1963] LLP Member; Michelle Grove [1970] LLP Member; Matthew Keith Sheather [1975] LLP Member; David Matthew Stone [1968] LLP Member; David Wallis [1965] LLP Member; James Jonathan Walsh [1972] LLP Member

Gill Corporate Limited
Incorporated: 13 December 2013 *Employees:* 73
Net Worth: £12,596,039 *Total Assets:* £13,381,521
Registered Office: Towngate House, 2-8 Parkstone Road, Poole, Dorset, BH15 2PW
Activities: Activities of other holding companies n.e.c.
Shareholders: Lesley Henson Gill; Michael John Gill
Officers: Lesley Henson Gill [1952] Director; Michael John Gill [1947] Director

Gill Instruments Limited
Incorporated: 28 July 1988 *Employees:* 75
Net Worth: £5,084,106 *Total Assets:* £5,567,026
Registered Office: Towngate House, 2-8 Parkstone Road, Poole, Dorset, BH15 2PW
Activities: Manufacture of electronic components
Shareholders: Michael John Gill; Lesley Henson Gill; Michael John Gill
Officers: Lesley Henson Gill, Secretary; Lesley Henson Gill [1952] Director Research Administration; Michael John Gill [1947] Director Design Engineer

Gill Sensors & Controls Limited
Incorporated: 7 April 2014 *Employees:* 37
Net Worth Deficit: £1,504,827 *Total Assets:* £4,839,667
Registered Office: Towngate House, 2-8 Parkstone Road, Poole, Dorset, BH15 2PW
Activities: Manufacture of electronic components
Parent: Gill Corporate Limited
Officers: Michael John Gill [1947] Director/Design Consultant; Michael Henson Gill [1982] Director/Design Consultant; Elizabeth Deborah Phillips [1984] Director/Program Manager

Gill Southern Limited
Incorporated: 10 September 2015 *Employees:* 3
Net Worth: £860,191 *Total Assets:* £8,247,756
Registered Office: Towngate House, 2-8 Parkstone Road, Poole, Dorset, BH15 2PW
Activities: Investigation activities
Shareholders: Lesley Henson Gill; Michael John Gill; Michael John Gill
Officers: Michael Henson Gill [1982] Director; Michael John Gill [1947] Director; Elizabeth Deborah Phillips [1984] Director

Oliver Gillard (Southmead) Limited
Incorporated: 26 July 1965
Net Worth Deficit: £2,564,452 *Total Assets:* £4,243,920
Registered Office: Serridge House, Ruffer Road, Henfield, Glos, BS36 2UY
Activities: Other letting and operating of own or leased real estate
Officers: Janet Patricia Manning, Secretary; Janet Patricia Manning [1940] Director; Peter William Charles Manning [1938] Director/Service Station Operator

Gillett's (Callington) Limited
Incorporated: 15 May 1986 *Employees:* 494
Net Worth: £2,285,000 *Total Assets:* £13,080,000
Registered Office: Moorlands Trading Estate, Saltash, Cornwall, PL12 6LX
Activities: Retail sale in non-specialised stores with food, beverages or tobacco predominating
Officers: Jennifer Kane, Secretary; Michael Alan Boardman [1972] Director; John Clohisey [1952] Director [Irish]; Leo John Anthony Crawford [1959] Director [Irish]; John O'Donnell [1954] Director [Irish]

Gillett's (Holdings) Limited
Incorporated: 21 March 2013 *Employees:* 7
Net Worth: £11,301,036 *Total Assets:* £14,287,831
Registered Office: c/o Francis Clark LLP, North Quay House, Sutton Harbour, Plymouth, PL4 0RA
Activities: Retail sale in non-specialised stores with food, beverages or tobacco predominating
Major Shareholder: John Alban Gillett
Officers: Jane Alford [1967] Director/Accountant; Alan Cookson [1968] Director; Irene Gillett [1945] Director; John Alban Gillett [1941] Director

The Gillingham Community and Leisure Trust Limited
Incorporated: 3 April 2009 *Employees:* 39
Net Worth: £4,231,524 *Total Assets:* £4,656,738
Registered Office: Riversmeet, Hardings Lane, Gillingham, Dorset, SP8 4HX
Activities: Operation of sports facilities
Officers: Juliet Hillier, Secretary; Patrick Lee Andrews [1963] Director; Paul James Barber [1974] Director/Sales Manager; Sandra Kaye Barber [1975] Director/Sales Assistant; David James Hollingsworth [1972] Director/Veterinary Surgeon; Alan Michael Seldon [1968] Director/Butcher; Karen Emma Seldon [1975] Director/School Teacher; Tara Anne Whyntie [1967] Director/Administrator

John Gillman & Sons (Electrical) Limited
Incorporated: 7 October 1982 *Employees:* 172
Net Worth: £16,333,382 *Total Assets:* £35,071,380
Registered Office: Mercia Road, St Oswalds, Gloucester, GL1 2SG
Activities: Retail sale of electrical household appliances in specialised stores
Parent: Gillman Electrical Group Ltd
Officers: Annabelle Jeanette Gillman, Secretary; Adrian Gillman [1962] Director; Annabelle Jeanette Gillman [1959] Director/Company Secretary; Robert John Gillman [1955] Managing Director

Gillman Electrical Group Limited
Incorporated: 15 August 2012 *Employees:* 175
Net Worth: £20,255,764 *Total Assets:* £39,854,800
Registered Office: Mercia Road, St Oswalds Road, Gloucester, GL1 2SG
Activities: Activities of head offices
Shareholders: Robert John Gillman; Annabelle Jeanette Gillman; Adrian Gillman
Officers: Annabelle Jeanette Gillman, Secretary; Adrian Gillman [1962] Director; Annabelle Jeanette Gillman [1959] Director; Robert John Gillman [1955] Director

Gilltown Limited
Incorporated: 26 September 2013
Net Worth: £1,241,296 *Total Assets:* £6,566,770
Registered Office: 4 Cedar Park, Cobham Road, Ferndown Industrial Estate, Wimborne, Dorset, BH21 7SF
Activities: Development of building projects
Shareholders: Paul Edward Gillespie; David Anthony Townend
Officers: Paul Edward Gillespie [1947] Director; David Anthony Townend [1958] Director

Gilo Industries Group Limited
Incorporated: 19 June 2012 *Employees:* 65
Net Worth: £6,847,248 *Total Assets:* £8,047,341
Registered Office: 9 Chaldicott Barns, Tokes Lane, Semley, Shaftesbury, Dorset, SP7 9AW
Activities: Activities of other holding companies n.e.c.
Shareholder: Giles Benedict Nunez Cardozo
Officers: Murshed Al Redaini [1966] Director [Emirati]; Giles Benedict Nunez Cardozo [1979] Director/Aircraft Manufacturer; Alex Edward Head [1982] Managing Director; Robert John Martin [1969] Director; Stephan Winkler [1980] Director/Consultant [German]

The Gilstone Partnership Limited
Incorporated: 10 December 1997 *Employees:* 3
Net Worth: £666,688 *Total Assets:* £3,521,978
Registered Office: Torbay Rise, Old Mill Road, Chelston, Torquay, Devon, TQ2 6HL
Activities: Development of building projects
Shareholders: Mark Anthony David Egglestone; Timothy Peter Gilbert
Officers: Angela Dawn Egglestone, Secretary; Angela Dawn Egglestone [1957] Director/Accounts Manager; Mark Anthony David Egglestone [1960] Director; Timothy Peter Gilbert [1958] Director

Gingerbread (Holdings) Limited
Incorporated: 15 June 2012 *Employees:* 413
Net Worth: £142,395 *Total Assets:* £7,069,416
Registered Office: 1st Floor, 60-62 High Street, Hanham, Bristol, BS15 3DR
Activities: Activities of head offices
Shareholders: Anthony Werner Harry Derek Driffield; Beverley Jane Driffield
Officers: Nicola Louise Thorne, Secretary; Anthony Werner Harry Derek Driffield [1966] Director; Beverley Jane Driffield [1961] Director; Nicola Louise Thorne [1974] Company Secretary/Director

Glanville Cleansing Limited
Incorporated: 24 March 2000 *Employees:* 118
Net Worth: £2,438,922 *Total Assets:* £7,057,802
Registered Office: Unit 2 Central Court, Central Avenue, Lee Mill Industrial Estate, Ivybridge, Devon, PL21 9PE
Activities: Other specialised construction activities n.e.c.
Parent: Glanville Cleansing (Holdings) Limited
Officers: Helen Glanville, Secretary/Administration; David Alan Glanville [1962] Director/Drainage Consultant; Helen Glanville [1960] Director/Administration

Glasshouse Hotel Limited
Incorporated: 13 September 2016
Net Worth Deficit: £71,867 *Total Assets:* £19,963,104
Registered Office: Wessex Water, Operations Centre, Claverton Down Road, Claverton Down, Bath, BA2 7WW
Activities: Activities of other holding companies n.e.c.
Officers: Ruth Esme Jefferson, Secretary; Andrew Jordan [1961] Director/Executive Vice President - YTL Hotels and Properties; Pearly Poussier [1963] Finance Director [Malaysian]; Colin Frank Skellett [1945] Director

Glastonbury Festival Events Limited
Incorporated: 7 January 2002 *Employees:* 145
Previous: Glastonbury Festival 2016 Limited
Net Worth: £8,731,360 *Total Assets:* £12,233,369
Registered Office: Worthy Farm, Pilton, Shepton Mallet, Somerset, BA4 4BY
Activities: Other amusement and recreation activities n.e.c.
Major Shareholder: Michael Eavis
Officers: Elizabeth Ann Eavis, Secretary; Nicholas George Dewey [1971] Director/Manager; Emily Rose Eavis [1979] Director; Michael Eavis [1935] Director/Farmer; Paul Robert Latham [1960] Director

Glatfelter Lydney, Ltd.
Incorporated: 8 March 2006 *Employees:* 266
Net Worth: £56,559,000 *Total Assets:* £76,239,000
Registered Office: Lydney Paper Mill, Church Road, Lydney, Glos, GL15 5EJ
Activities: Manufacture of paper and paperboard
Parent: P.H. Glatfelter Company (PA)
Officers: David Carscadden [1962] Director/General Mill Manager; Dr Martin Rapp [1959] Director/Vice President & General Manager [German]; Amy Wannemacher [1966] Director of Tax [American]

GLE Bidco Limited
Incorporated: 26 May 2016
Net Worth: £132,681,000 *Total Assets:* £315,105,984
Registered Office: Merchants House North, Wapping Road, Bristol, BS1 4RW
Activities: Activities of other holding companies n.e.c.
Parent: GLE Midco 2 Limited
Officers: Robert Dargue [1975] Director; Gregor Stanley Watson [1965] Director

GLE Midco 2 Limited
Incorporated: 2 June 2016 *Employees:* 244
Net Worth: £136,006,000 *Total Assets:* £231,852,992
Registered Office: Merchants House North, Wapping Road, Bristol, BS1 4RW
Activities: Activities of other holding companies n.e.c.
Parent: GLE Midco Limited
Officers: Robert Dargue [1975] Director; Gregor Stanley Watson [1965] Director

GLE Midco Limited
Incorporated: 2 June 2016
Net Worth: £135,723,008 *Total Assets:* £162,114,000
Registered Office: Merchants House North, Wapping Road, Bristol, BS1 4RW
Activities: Activities of other holding companies n.e.c.
Parent: GLE UK Topco Limited
Officers: Robert Dargue [1975] Director; Gregor Stanley Watson [1965] Director

GLE UK Topco Limited
Incorporated: 2 June 2016 *Employees:* 244
Net Worth Deficit: £28,003,000 *Total Assets:* £231,868,000
Registered Office: Merchants House North, Wapping Road, Bristol, BS1 4RW
Activities: Activities of other holding companies n.e.c.
Shareholders: Lauren Leichtman; Arthur Edward Levine
Officers: Robert Dargue [1975] Director; Lauren Beth Leichtman [1949] Director [American]; John Martin O'Neill [1972] Director; Andrew Schwartz [1981] Director [American]; Gregor Stanley Watson [1965] Director

Glen Foundry Limited
Incorporated: 19 April 1999 *Employees:* 54
Net Worth: £2,053,898 *Total Assets:* £4,604,299
Registered Office: First Floor, 10 Temple Back, Bristol, BS1 6FL
Activities: Casting of light metals
Parent: J & L Corrigan Limited
Officers: Allan Frederick Brese, Secretary; Allan Frederick Brese [1953] Director; Graham Ross [1970] Director

Glen Mhor Limited
Incorporated: 26 March 1998 *Employees:* 50
Net Worth: £6,175,487 *Total Assets:* £12,302,121
Registered Office: First Floor, 10 Temple Back, Bristol, BS1 6FL
Activities: Hotels and similar accommodation
Shareholders: Jonathon Paul Erasmus; Victoria Clare Erasmus
Officers: Jonathon Paul Erasmus [1973] Director/Hotelier [South African]; Victoria Clare Erasmus [1977] Director/Administrator

E. & J. W. Glendinning (Holdings) Limited
Incorporated: 21 April 1995 *Employees:* 225
Net Worth: £38,822,144 *Total Assets:* £51,081,920
Registered Office: Glentor, Ashburton, Newton Abbot, Devon, TQ13 7LF
Activities: Quarrying of ornamental and building stone, limestone, gypsum, chalk and slate
Officers: Barry James Wilson, Secretary; William McLelland Beattie [1956] Director; Barry Glendinning [1963] Director/LGV Driver; Clifford John Glendinning [1959] Director/Transport Executive; Ian Forster Glendinning [1947] Director/Civil Engineer; Ann Somerscales [1942] Director/CS; Barry James Wilson [1966] Director

E.And J.W.Glendinning Limited
Incorporated: 17 November 1958 *Employees:* 225
Net Worth: £29,864,100 *Total Assets:* £40,682,308
Registered Office: Glentor, Ashburton, Newton Abbot, Devon, TQ13 7LF
Activities: Quarrying of ornamental and building stone, limestone, gypsum, chalk and slate
Parent: E and JW Glendinning (Holdings) Limited
Officers: Barry James Wilson, Secretary; Ian Neil Ashford [1948] Director; William McLelland Beattie [1956] Director/Accountant; Barry Glendinning [1963] Director/Transport Executive; Clifford John Glendinning [1959] Director/Transport Executive; Ian Forster Glendinning [1947] Director/Civil Engineer; Barry James Wilson [1966] Managing Director

Gleneil Limited
Incorporated: 4 February 1997 *Employees:* 2
Net Worth: £5,072,957 *Total Assets:* £5,844,248
Registered Office: Alford House, Alford, Castle Cary, Somerset, BA7 7PN
Activities: Buying and selling of own real estate
Shareholders: Katherine Louise Fisher Hearle; William Jeffrey Powell
Officers: William Jeffrey Powell, Secretary/Director; Katherine Louise Fisher Hearle [1959] Director & Architect; William Jeffrey Powell [1957] Director

Glevum Heating & Plumbing Limited
Incorporated: 28 April 2003 *Employees:* 62
Net Worth: £2,271,130 *Total Assets:* £3,508,282
Registered Office: Unit 6B Tuffley Park, Lower Tuffley Lane, Gloucester, GL2 5DE
Activities: Plumbing, heat and air-conditioning installation
Parent: Cornhill Investment Partners Ltd
Officers: Anish Shail Patel [1985] Director; Raj Kishore Patel [1983] Director

J Gliddon & Sons Limited
Incorporated: 21 August 1954 *Employees:* 16
Net Worth: £2,741,157 *Total Assets:* £4,484,768
Registered Office: Bank Street, Williton, Taunton, Somerset, TA4 4NG
Activities: Wholesale of agricultural machinery, equipment and supplies
Shareholder: David John Gliddon
Officers: Wendy Rachel Gliddon, Secretary; David John Gliddon [1945] Director

Glide Bidco Limited
Incorporated: 14 October 2013
Previous: Cablecom Bidco Limited
Net Worth Deficit: £27,738,000 *Total Assets:* £51,680,000
Registered Office: 1 Rivermead Court, Kenn Business Park, Windmill Road, Kenn, Clevedon, Somerset, BS21 6FT
Activities: Wired telecommunications activities
Parent: Cablecom Topco Limited
Officers: Henry Alty [1985] Director/Investor; Mark Ashley Burchfield [1970] Director; Peter Manning [1955] Director; Timothy James Pilcher [1969] Director; Catherine Allingham Richards [1973] Director/Private Equity Investor; Zoe Tindall-Doman [1972] Director

Glide Holdings Limited
Incorporated: 25 April 2007
Previous: Cablecom Networking Holdings Limited
Net Worth Deficit: £14,499,000 *Total Assets:* £34,991,000
Registered Office: 1 Rivermead Court, Kenn Business Park, Windmill Road, Kenn, Clevedon, Somerset, BS21 6FT
Activities: Wired telecommunications activities
Parent: Cablecom Bidco 2 Limited
Officers: Henry Alty [1985] Director/Investor; Mark Ashley Burchfield [1970] Director; Peter Manning [1955] Director; Timothy James Pilcher [1969] Director; Catherine Allingham Richards [1973] Director/Private Equity Investor; Zoe Tindall-Doman [1972] Director

Glide Student & Residential Limited
Incorporated: 19 April 1996 *Employees:* 122
Previous: Cablecom Networking Limited
Net Worth: £16,973,000 *Total Assets:* £64,585,000
Registered Office: 1 Rivermead Court, Kenn Business Park, Windmill Road, Kenn, Clevedon, Somerset, BS21 6FT
Activities: Wired telecommunications activities
Parent: Cablecom Networking Holdings Limited
Officers: Mark Ashley Burchfield [1970] Sales Director; Timothy James Pilcher [1969] Director; Zoe Tindall-Doman [1972] Director

Glide Topco Limited
Incorporated: 14 October 2013 *Employees:* 235
Previous: Cablecom Topco Limited
Net Worth Deficit: £38,824,000 *Total Assets:* £108,290,000
Registered Office: 1 Rivermead Court, Kenn Business Park, Windmill Road, Kenn, Clevedon, Somerset, BS21 6FT
Activities: Wired telecommunications activities
Major Shareholder: Mark Ashley Burchfield
Officers: Henry Alty [1985] Director/Investor; Mark Ashley Burchfield [1970] Director; Peter Manning [1955] Director; Timothy James Pilcher [1969] Director; Catherine Allingham Richards [1973] Director/Private Equity Investor; Zoe Tindall-Doman [1972] Director

GLM Trading Limited
Incorporated: 25 September 1995 *Employees:* 6
Net Worth: £750,674 *Total Assets:* £5,209,309
Registered Office: 11 Manvers Street, Bath, BA1 1JQ
Activities: Other service activities n.e.c.
Shareholders: Coralie Anne Joan O'Gorman; William Brendan Thomas O'Gorman
Officers: Roger Boothroyd, Secretary; Coralie Anne Joan O'Gorman [1960] Director; William Brendan Thomas O'Gorman [1957] Director/Commodity Trader

Global Furniture Alliance Limited
Incorporated: 14 April 2004 *Employees:* 25
Net Worth: £3,555,776 *Total Assets:* £4,152,328
Registered Office: 1 Long Street, Tetbury, Glos, GL8 8AA
Activities: Other business support service activities n.e.c.
Major Shareholder: James Painter
Officers: James Painter [1971] Director/Sales Manager

Global Machine Tools (UK) Ltd
Incorporated: 23 January 2001 *Employees:* 3
Net Worth: £3,944,255 *Total Assets:* £7,944,084
Registered Office: Staverton Court, Staverton, Cheltenham, Glos, GL51 0UX
Activities: Wholesale of machine tools
Parent: Global Machine Tools Holdings Limited
Officers: Graham James Hall, Secretary; Graham James Hall [1964] Director; Stuart Duncan Hall [1961] Director

Glossbrook Holdings Limited
Incorporated: 14 August 2017 *Employees:* 61
Net Worth: £62,375 *Total Assets:* £5,759,848
Registered Office: 2a Oswald Road, Bournemouth, BH9 2TQ
Activities: Activities of construction holding companies
Shareholders: Nicholas David Dunkerton; Richard Terence Fooks
Officers: Martin Allner [1963] Contracts Director; Nicholas David Dunkerton [1950] Director; Richard Terence Fooks [1968] Purchasing Director; Mark Anthony McGowan [1955] Finance Director

Gloster Furniture Limited
Incorporated: 21 January 1992 *Employees:* 8
Net Worth: £3,926,679 *Total Assets:* £4,740,520
Registered Office: Narrow Quay House, Narrow Quay, Bristol, BS1 4QA
Activities: Manufacture of other furniture
Officers: Kevin James Ryan, Secretary; Svend Loevbjerg [1970] Director [Danish]; Kevin Ryan [1961] Director/Accountant; Beat Schwendener [1969] Director [Swiss]; Angelo Corenzo Van Tol [1966] Director [Dutch]

Gloucester Diocesan Board of Finance
Incorporated: 30 December 1919 *Employees:* 164
Net Worth: £76,655,000 *Total Assets:* £81,511,000
Registered Office: Church House, College Green, Gloucester, GL1 2LY
Activities: Activities of religious organisations
Officers: Benjamin Tudur Llywelyn Preece Smith, Secretary; The Venerable Phil John Andrew [1962] Director/Clerk in Holy Orders; Reverend Stephen Craig Bishop [1968] Director/Priest; Professor Patricia Mary Broadfoot [1949] Director/Professor; Karen Czapiewski [1956] Director/Finance Lecturer; Stephen John Grindrod [1955] Director/Engineer; Christopher John Hill [1946] Director/Retired; Martin Kingston [1949] Director/Barrister; Dean Stephen David Lake [1963] Director/Dean; Richard Neale [1943] Director/Retired; Reverend Mike Parsons [1947] Director/Retired; Colin Rowland Hopwood Rank [1948] Director/Retired; Lesley Reilly [1948] Director/Retired; Helen Mary Kirkman Sammon [1957] Director/Vicar; Reverend Katrina Ruth Scott [1976] Director/Vicar; The Venerable Robert Springett [1960] Director/Clerk in Holy Orders; Michael Charles Storey [1947] Director; Bishop Rachel Treweek [1963] Director/Bishop

Gloucester Land Company Limited
Incorporated: 13 March 1961
Net Worth: £11,968,215 *Total Assets:* £13,022,504
Registered Office: The Manor, Boddington, Cheltenham, Glos, GL51 0TJ
Activities: Development of building projects
Parent: The Robert Hitchins Group Limited
Officers: Jonathan James Stewart Dunley, Secretary; Jonathan James Stewart Dunley [1970] Director; Jeremy Charles Hitchins [1954] Director; Jonathan Richard Hitchins [1950] Director; Stephen Robert Hitchins [1947] Director

Gloucester Rugby Limited
Incorporated: 12 August 1891 *Employees:* 319
Net Worth: £7,421,987 *Total Assets:* £18,148,472
Registered Office: Gloucester Rugby Club, Kingsholm, Gloucester, GL1 3AX
Activities: Activities of sport clubs
Major Shareholder: Martin George St Quinton
Officers: Mark Fairbrother, Secretary; Adam Benson [1977] Director/Chief Commercial Officer; Lance Bradley [1965] Director; Mark Fairbrother [1980] Director/Chartered Accountant; Gavin John Gleave [1966] Director; Andrew Hunt [1964] Director; Martin George St Quinton [1957] Director; Stephen Anthony Vaughan [1974] Director

Gloucestershire Airport Limited
Incorporated: 11 December 1992 *Employees:* 46
Net Worth: £24,699,078 *Total Assets:* £34,626,456
Registered Office: Terminal Building, Gloucestershire Airport, Staverton, Cheltenham, Glos, GL51 6SR
Activities: Other transportation support activities
Shareholders: Cheltenham Borough Council; Gloucester City Council
Officers: Jeremy Patrick Stephen Bennett [1965] Director/Solicitor; Elisabeth Sara Jane Carter [1958] Director/Chartered Surveyor; James Alan Head [1983] Operations Director; Peter James Hibberd [1957] Director/Retired; Dawn Patricia Melvin [1966] Director/Publisher; Michael Ian Morton [1958] Business Development Director; Mark Ryan [1969] Airport Director; Karen Elisabeth Taylor [1972] Finance Director; Adrian Gerrard Noel Tighe [1961] Director/Consultant; Roger Lee Whyborn [1952] Director/Borough Councillor (Cheltenham)

The Gloucestershire Association for Disability
Incorporated: 1 August 1995 *Employees:* 1
Net Worth: £5,266,435 *Total Assets:* £5,489,576
Registered Office: Centre for Deaf People, Colin Road, Barnwood, Gloucester, GL4 3JL
Activities: Other service activities n.e.c.
Officers: Christine Mary Ellson, Secretary; Joan Marion Davies [1953] Director/Occupational Therapist; Michael Joseph Davies [1948] Director/Retired; Christine Mary Ellson [1945] Director/Retired; Stephen John Elway [1956] Director/Retired; Maxine Yvonne Knight [1961] Director/Retired; Nora Elizabeth Lynch [1947] Director/Retired; Gail Rodway [1954] Director/Grants Manager; Terence Morris Rogers [1951] Director/Retired; Gregory Deeks Walters [1951] Director/FAB Visiting Officer - Glos County Council

Gloucestershire Everyman Theatre Company Limited
Incorporated: 22 February 1960 *Employees:* 194
Net Worth: £2,161,070 *Total Assets:* £4,920,039
Registered Office: Regent Street, Cheltenham, Glos, GL50 1HQ
Activities: Operation of arts facilities
Officers: John Kerrison Workman, Secretary; Zareen Ahmed [1955] Director/Community Animator; Jason Blackburn [1966] Director/Charity Fundraising Manager; Mark Anthony Borkowski [1958] Director; Jane Cantwell [1960] Director/Head of School of Leisure; Thornton Michael Dey [1953] Director; Mitesh Dhanak [1968] Director; Robin Hugh Herford [1946] Director; Chun Fai Kong [1963] Director/Restaurateur; Gwyneth Milner [1973] Director/Chartered Accountant; Roger James Nicholls [1942] Director/Retired; Dudley Joseph Russell [1949] Director; Clive Raymond Thomas [1962] Director/Chartered Accountant; Guy Edward Christopher Woodcock [1960] Director/Chief Executive; John Kerrison Workman [1959] Director/Solicitor

Gloucestershire FM Services Limited
Incorporated: 13 February 2004 *Employees:* 2
Net Worth Deficit: £3,812,000 *Total Assets:* £18,353,000
Registered Office: Third Floor, Broad Quay House, Prince Street, Bristol, BS1 4DJ
Activities: Other business support service activities n.e.c.
Parent: Gloucestershire FM Services (Holdings) Limited
Officers: Michael Andrew Donn [1972] Director/Investment Manager; Karen Marie Hill [1977] Director/Investment Manager

Gloucestershire Learning Alliance
Incorporated: 1 July 2011 *Employees:* 210
Net Worth: £16,163,349 *Total Assets:* £18,726,896
Registered Office: Tobyfield Road, Bishops Cleeve, Cheltenham, Glos, GL52 8NN
Activities: Primary education
Officers: Joanna Clare Duffus, Secretary; Damon James Ballinger [1972] Director/Aviation Training Manager; Louise Burridge [1969] Director/Self Employed; Christopher Thomas Cooper [1959] Director/Retired; Ian Ernest Jarvis [1967] Director/Chartered Accountant; Ruth Margaret Kessell [1964] Director/Lecturer; Ruth Elizabeth Lewis [1957] Director/Retired; Dermot Thomas Gerard McNiffe [1965] Director/Principal; Julie Elizabeth Reynolds [1964] Director/Business Consultant; Steven Ross Savory [1959] Director/Headteacher

Gloucestershire Warwickshire Steam Railway PLC
Incorporated: 28 July 1981 *Employees:* 5
Net Worth: £5,497,220 *Total Assets:* £6,876,856
Registered Office: The Railway Station, Toddington, Glos, GL54 5DT
Activities: Passenger rail transport, interurban
Officers: Richard George Johnson, Secretary; Lee Russell Alibone [1952] Director; Glyn Arthur Cornish [1949] Director; Colin James Fewell [1941] Director; Richard George Johnson [1949] Director/Solicitor; Alan George Miller [1951] Director; Ian Michael Stewart [1945] Director; Richard Charles Summers [1945] Director; Christopher John Webb [1946] Director; Richard Horton Winstanley [1951] Director

Gloucestershire Wildlife Trust
Incorporated: 21 November 1961 *Employees:* 65
Net Worth: £4,561,969 *Total Assets:* £5,104,718
Registered Office: Conservation Centre, Robinswood Hill Country Park, Reservoir Road, Gloucester, GL4 6SX
Activities: Activities of other membership organisations n.e.c.
Officers: Roger Mortlock, Secretary; Andrew James Bluett [1955] Director/Chartered Surveyor; Dr Sally Catherine Byng [1956] Director/Chief Executive; Amy Manuella Coyte [1961] Director/Consultant; Nicholas John Ford [1956] Director/Rural Property and Charity Consultant; Jane Furze [1965] Director/Business Development Consultant; Professor Anne Goodenough [1983] Director/Lecturer; Martin Charles Horwood [1962] Director/Politician; David Wyndham Jones [1964] Director/Fund Manager; Sir David Edwin Pepper [1948] Director/Retired; Anthony Edward Richardson [1954] Director/Retired; Francis Richard Seton Rundall [1951] Director/Solicitor; Mark Paul Southgate [1964] Director/Town Planner/Civil Servant

GM Coachwork Limited
Incorporated: 17 April 1998 *Employees:* 129
Net Worth: £10,620,552 *Total Assets:* £18,757,168
Registered Office: Teign Valley, Trusham, Newton Abbot, Devon, TQ13 0NX
Activities: Manufacture of other parts and accessories for motor vehicles
Officers: Linda Glynns Vooght, Secretary/Administrator; Jamie Bowden [1987] Operations Director; Nigel Collins [1955] Director; Stephen Murphy [1972] Sales Director; David Arthur William Vooght [1955] Director/Coachbuilder; Graham David Vooght [1984] Director; Linda Glynns Vooght [1959] Director/Administrator

GMO Cars Limited
Incorporated: 20 July 2000 *Employees:* 20
Net Worth: £5,410,979 *Total Assets:* £5,866,741
Registered Office: GMO Cars, Eastern Green, Penzance, Cornwall, TR18 3AS
Activities: Sale of used cars and light motor vehicles
Shareholders: Katrina Gail Orr; Gary McDonald Orr
Officers: Katrina Gail Orr, Secretary; Gary McDonald Orr [1958] Director/Motor Trader; Katrina Gail Orr [1961] Director/Secretary

Gnome World Caravan Park Limited
Incorporated: 12 October 2015 *Employees:* 12
Net Worth: £2,178,304 *Total Assets:* £4,299,174
Registered Office: Coniston House, Moorland Road, Indian Queens, Cornwall, TR9 6HN
Activities: Recreational vehicle parks, trailer parks and camping grounds
Major Shareholder: Marcus Antony Pring
Officers: Marcus Antony Pring [1969] Director

Go in Four Limited
Incorporated: 24 March 2014
Net Worth: £2,089,968 *Total Assets:* £13,900,123
Registered Office: 1 Swift Way, Bowerhill, Melksham, Wilts, SN12 6GX
Activities: Activities of head offices
Shareholders: Samuel John Gompels; Clea Gompels
Officers: Clea Gompels [1972] Director [British/Swiss]; Samuel John Gompels [1970] Director

Go Vocational Solutions Ltd
Incorporated: 17 April 2003
Net Worth: £765,585 *Total Assets:* £5,587,786
Registered Office: Clifton Heights, Triangle West, Bristol, BS8 1EJ
Activities: Business and domestic software development
Parent: LVTG Ltd
Officers: Peter James Mitchell, Secretary; Alex Phillip Khan [1977] Director; Peter James Mitchell [1971] Director

Go-Pak UK Limited
Incorporated: 8 January 2009 *Employees:* 189
Net Worth: £9,336,703 *Total Assets:* £13,921,111
Registered Office: 30-31 St James Place, Mangotsfield, Bristol, BS16 9JB
Activities: Agents involved in the sale of a variety of goods
Officers: Claire Aimee Melinda Lawley [1979] Director

Goadsby & Harding (Holdings) Limited
Incorporated: 24 November 1989 *Employees:* 30
Net Worth: £925,281 *Total Assets:* £8,384,825
Registered Office: 99 Holdenhurst Road, Bournemouth, BH8 8DY
Activities: Activities of head offices
Parent: St Gresham Limited
Officers: David Errington, Secretary; Rex David Newton Craven [1948] Director; David Errington [1955] Director; David Huck [1958] Director; Nigel Price [1959] Director

Goadsby & Harding (Residential) Limited
Incorporated: 12 December 1984 *Employees:* 209
Net Worth: £5,874,193 *Total Assets:* £8,505,342
Registered Office: 99 Holdenhurst Road, Bournemouth, BH8 8DY
Activities: Real estate agencies
Parent: Goadsby & Harding (Holdings) Limited
Officers: David Errington, Secretary; Peter Roy Atfield [1958] Director; Ian Matthew Brown [1979] Finance Director; Lynne Mary Burton [1959] Director; Rex David Newton Craven [1948] Director; Simon Gerard Cumming [1961] Director; James Dennett [1972] Director; James Richardson Doerr [1974] Director; David Errington [1955] Director; David Huck [1958] Director; Nigel Price [1959] Director; Karen Elizabeth Smith [1968] Director

Goddard Park Community Primary School Academy Trust
Incorporated: 19 August 2010 *Employees:* 155
Net Worth: £3,962,304 *Total Assets:* £5,210,774
Registered Office: Goddard Park Community Primary School, Welcombe Avenue, Swindon, Wilts, SN3 2QN
Activities: Primary education
Officers: Satnam Singh Bains [1958] Director/Health & Safety Officer; Fiona Boyd [1982] Director/Full Time Mum; Debbie Doyle [1981] Director/Receptionist; Peter Elliott [1946] Director/Retired; David Lee Godfrey [1960] Director/Administrator; Michael Harris [1966] Director/Project Manager; Simon Graham Haynes [1978] Director/IT Manager; Graham Miles [1951] Director/Retired; Eve Lorraine Pocock [1979] Director/Teaching Assistant; Reginald Charles Thoburn [1947] Director/Retired; Chris Tye [1987] Director/Teacher; Michael John Welsh [1950] Director/Headteacher

E.J. Godwin (Peat Industries) Limited
Incorporated: 17 August 1936
Net Worth: £2,793,685 *Total Assets:* £4,035,028
Registered Office: 20 Chamberlain Street, Wells, Somerset, BA5 2PF
Activities: Other manufacturing n.e.c.
Major Shareholder: Andrew Paul Rowland
Officers: Doreen Daphne Joyce Rowland, Secretary; Andrew Paul Rowland [1951] Director; Doreen Daphne Joyce Rowland [1928] Director/Company Secretary; Pamela Mary Rowland [1946] Director/Administrator

Golden Hill Solar Limited
Incorporated: 14 January 2014
Net Worth: £187,872 *Total Assets:* £7,573,840
Registered Office: The Long Barn, Manor Courtyard, Stratton on the Fosse, Radstock, Somerset, BA3 4QF
Activities: Production of electricity
Parent: Golden Hill Solar (UK) Ltd
Officers: Giuseppe La Loggia [1975] Director [Italian]; Yit Ho Tang [1974] Investment Director [Singaporean]; Christopher James Tanner [1972] Investment Director; Jonathan Simon Thompson [1963] Director

Golden Years Ltd
Incorporated: 23 June 2008 *Employees:* 81
Net Worth: £4,955,123 *Total Assets:* £13,783,569
Registered Office: 31-33 Commercial Road, Poole, Dorset, BH14 0HU
Activities: Medical nursing home activities
Officers: Dr Arujuna Sivananthan [1970] Director/Care Home Operator; Karthika Sivananthan [1973] Director/Care Operator

Goldmix Limited
Incorporated: 17 May 2013 *Employees:* 2
Net Worth: £223,722 *Total Assets:* £3,742,160
Registered Office: Wessex House, Teign Road, Newton Abbot, Devon, TQ12 4AA
Activities: Other letting and operating of own or leased real estate
Major Shareholder: Genella Barton
Officers: Genella Barton [1980] Director; Russell Anthony Toghill [1966] Director

Goldrose Management Limited
Incorporated: 8 December 2010
Net Worth: £864,765 *Total Assets:* £9,183,307
Registered Office: 11 Bredon Court, Tower Road, Newquay, Cornwall, TR7 1AW
Activities: Other letting and operating of own or leased real estate
Major Shareholder: Claire Helen Coffey
Officers: Claire Helen Coffey [1970] Director; Glen James Coffey [1969] Director

Golfhill Limited
Incorporated: 10 April 1995 *Employees:* 132
Net Worth: £1,296,637 *Total Assets:* £3,791,714
Registered Office: First Floor, CEF Building, Broomhill Way, Torquay, Devon, TQ2 7QN
Activities: Residential nursing care facilities
Parent: Shervey Limited
Officers: Tracy Anne Lowe, Secretary; David Guy Henson [1958] Director; Nicholas Shervey Meyer [1953] Director

Gompels Healthcare Limited
Incorporated: 15 April 2002
Net Worth: £2,542,886 *Total Assets:* £4,291,203
Registered Office: No 1 Swift Way, Bowerhill Industrial Estate, Melksham, Wilts, SN12 6GX
Activities: Non-specialised wholesale trade
Parent: Only Four Limited
Officers: Clea Gompels [1972] Director/Marketing [British/Swiss]; Samuel John Gompels [1970] Director/Consultant

Gooch & Housego (Torquay) Limited
Incorporated: 25 February 2002 *Employees:* 203
Net Worth: £6,994,000 *Total Assets:* £13,289,000
Registered Office: Dowlish Ford, Ilminster, Somerset, TA19 0PF
Activities: Manufacture of electronic components
Parent: Gooch & Housego PLC
Officers: Gareth James Crowe, Secretary; Andrew Boteler [1966] Director/Accountant; Mark John Alexander Webster [1962] Director/Chief Executive

Gooch & Housego (UK) Limited
Incorporated: 28 July 2006 *Employees:* 149
Net Worth: £10,932,000 *Total Assets:* £16,034,000
Registered Office: Dowlish Ford, Ilminster, Somerset, TA19 0PF
Activities: Manufacture of optical precision instruments
Parent: Gooch & Housego PLC
Officers: Gareth James Crowe, Secretary; Andrew Boteler [1966] Director/Accountant; Mark John Alexander Webster [1962] Director/Chief Executive

Gooch & Housego PLC
Incorporated: 12 December 1953 *Employees:* 866
Net Worth: £107,847,000 *Total Assets:* £184,904,000
Registered Office: Dowlish Ford, Ilminster, Somerset, TA19 0PF
Activities: Manufacture of optical precision instruments
Officers: Gareth James Crowe, Secretary; David Gregory Bauernfeind [1968] Director/Chief Financial Officer; Peter Frank Bordui [1960] Director [American]; Andrew Boteler [1966] Director/Accountant; Gary Bullard [1957] Director/Chairman; Brian Phillipson [1953] Director; Alexander Warnock [1965] Director/Chief Operating Officer; Mark John Alexander Webster [1962] Director and CEO

Good Energy Carloggas Solar Park (009) Limited
Incorporated: 15 May 2013
Net Worth Deficit: £1,138,564 *Total Assets:* £8,643,470
Registered Office: Monkton Reach, Monkton Hill, Chippenham, Wilts, SN15 1EE
Activities: Production of electricity
Parent: Good Energy Group PLC
Officers: Juliet Sarah Lovedy Davenport [1968] Director; Stephen Lloyd Rosser [1978] Director/Secretary

Good Energy Cross Road Plantation Solar Park (028) Limited
Incorporated: 6 June 2013
Net Worth Deficit: £404,998 *Total Assets:* £5,200,441
Registered Office: Monkton Reach, Monkton Hill, Chippenham, Wilts, SN15 1EE
Activities: Production of electricity
Parent: Good Energy Group PLC
Officers: Juliet Sarah Lovedy Davenport [1968] Director; Stephen Lloyd Rosser [1978] Director/Secretary

Good Energy Delabole Windfarm Limited
Incorporated: 29 May 2009
Net Worth: £2,799,705 *Total Assets:* £10,423,595
Registered Office: Monkton Reach, Monkton Hill, Chippenham, Wilts, SN15 1EE
Activities: Production of electricity
Parent: Good Energy Group PLC
Officers: Juliet Sarah Lovedy Davenport [1968] Director; Stephen Lloyd Rosser [1978] Director/Secretary

Good Energy Gas Limited
Incorporated: 6 July 2005
Net Worth: £2,858,169 *Total Assets:* £8,025,697
Registered Office: Monkton Reach, Monkton Hill, Chippenham, Wilts, SN15 1EE
Activities: Distribution of gaseous fuels through mains
Parent: Good Energy Group PLC
Officers: Stephen Lloyd Rosser, Secretary; Juliet Sarah Lovedy Davenport [1968] Chief Executive Director; Stephen Lloyd Rosser [1978] Director/Secretary

Good Energy Generation Assets No. 1 Limited
Incorporated: 17 October 2014 *Employees:* 2
Net Worth Deficit: £6,506,000 *Total Assets:* £49,050,000
Registered Office: Monkton Reach, Monkton Hill, Chippenham, Wilts, SN15 1EE
Activities: Production of electricity
Parent: Good Energy Group PLC
Officers: Juliet Sarah Lovedy Davenport [1968] Director; Stephen Lloyd Rosser [1978] Director/Secretary

Good Energy Group PLC
Incorporated: 24 May 2000 *Employees:* 331
Net Worth: £18,085,000 *Total Assets:* £122,089,000
Registered Office: Monkton Reach, Monkton Hill, Chippenham, Wilts, SN15 1EE
Activities: Production of electricity
Shareholder: Ecotricity Group Limited
Officers: Stephen Lloyd Rosser, Secretary; Juliet Sarah Lovedy Davenport [1968] Director/Executive; Timothy Jones [1971] Director/Chartered Engineer; John Neil Maltby [1962] Director; Emma Natalie Tinker [1975] Director/Investment Management; William Elliot Whitehorn [1960] Director; Nemone Louisa Wynn-Evans [1974] Director

Good Energy Hampole Windfarm Limited
Incorporated: 29 November 2012
Net Worth: £457,690 *Total Assets:* £10,586,761
Registered Office: Monkton Reach, Monkton Hill, Chippenham, Wilts, SN15 1EE
Activities: Production of electricity
Parent: Good Energy Group PLC
Officers: Juliet Sarah Lovedy Davenport [1968] Director; Stephen Lloyd Rosser [1978] Director/Secretary

Good Energy Holding Company No. 1 Limited
Incorporated: 11 September 2014 *Employees:* 2
Net Worth: £1 *Total Assets:* £20,937,528
Registered Office: Monkton Reach, Monkton Hill, Chippenham, Wilts, SN15 1EE
Activities: Production of electricity
Parent: Good Energy Group PLC
Officers: Juliet Sarah Lovedy Davenport [1968] Director; Stephen Lloyd Rosser [1978] Director/Secretary

Good Energy Limited
Incorporated: 21 December 1999 *Employees:* 331
Net Worth: £5,284,331 *Total Assets:* £50,470,948
Registered Office: Monkton Reach, Monkton Hill, Chippenham, Wilts, SN15 1EE
Activities: Trade of electricity
Parent: Good Energy Group PLC
Officers: Stephen Lloyd Rosser, Secretary; Juliet Sarah Lovedy Davenport [1968] Director/Executive; Martin John Edwards [1960] Director/Farmer; Stephen Lloyd Rosser [1978] Director/Secretary

Good Energy Lower End Farm Solar Park (026) Limited
Incorporated: 7 June 2013
Net Worth Deficit: £446,050 *Total Assets:* £5,245,448
Registered Office: Monkton Reach, Monkton Hill, Chippenham, Wilts, SN15 1EE
Activities: Production of electricity
Parent: Good Energy Group PLC
Officers: Juliet Sarah Lovedy Davenport [1968] Director; Stephen Lloyd Rosser [1978] Director/Secretary

Good Energy Rook Wood Solar Park (057) Limited
Incorporated: 4 July 2013
Net Worth Deficit: £511,789 *Total Assets:* £5,644,031
Registered Office: Monkton Reach, Monkton Hill, Chippenham, Wilts, SN15 1EE
Activities: Production of electricity
Parent: Good Energy Group PLC
Officers: Juliet Sarah Lovedy Davenport [1968] Director; Stephen Lloyd Rosser [1978] Director/Secretary

Good Energy Woolbridge Solar Park (010) Limited
Incorporated: 15 May 2013
Net Worth Deficit: £596,000 *Total Assets:* £5,592,129
Registered Office: Monkton Reach, Monkton Hill, Chippenham, Wilts, SN15 1EE
Activities: Production of electricity
Parent: Good Energy Group PLC
Officers: Juliet Sarah Lovedy Davenport [1968] Director; Stephen Lloyd Rosser [1978] Director/Secretary

Good Food and Drink Company Ltd
Incorporated: 21 April 1999 *Employees:* 94
Net Worth: £2,619,160 *Total Assets:* £4,143,002
Registered Office: The Thatched Barn Inn, Hobbs Hill, Croyde, Braunton, Devon, EX33 1LZ
Activities: Licenced restaurants
Major Shareholder: Rock Marcel Barouh
Officers: Tanya Barouh, Secretary; Rock Marcel Barouh [1961] Director/Publican; Tanya Barouh [1966] Director

Gooderham Farms Limited
Incorporated: 12 May 1997 *Employees:* 15
Net Worth: £11,597,061 *Total Assets:* £12,658,830
Registered Office: 5 Yealm View Road, Newton Ferrers, Plymouth, PL8 1AN
Activities: Support activities for crop production
Major Shareholder: Robert James Burwood Gooderham
Officers: Robert James Burwood Gooderham, Secretary/Farmer; Christine Gooderham [1959] Director; George Edward Burwood Gooderham [1990] Director/Farmer; James Robert Burwood Gooderham [1987] Director/Farmer; Pamela Mary Gooderham [1935] Director; Robert James Burwood Gooderham [1959] Director/Farmer

Goodnews Evangelical Mission
Incorporated: 22 June 2015
Net Worth: £16,737,244 *Total Assets:* £17,034,440
Registered Office: 3 The Oval Office, St Peter's Park, Cobblers Way, Radstock, Somerset, BA3 3BX
Activities: Activities of religious organisations
Officers: Hannah Griffiths, Secretary; Patricia Aisbitt [1947] Director/Accountant; Andrew Bartholomew Griffiths [1958] Charity Director; Ralph Victor Harris [1957] Director/Befriending Serviced Manager; Richard Mark Sage [1937] Director/Retired Banker

Goodridge Limited
Incorporated: 25 November 1971 *Employees:* 349
Net Worth: £15,017,000 *Total Assets:* £22,569,000
Registered Office: Dart Building, Grenadier Road, Exeter Business Park, Exeter, Devon, EX1 3QF
Activities: Manufacture of other parts and accessories for motor vehicles
Parent: RGI Star Limited
Officers: Jonathan Richardson, Secretary; Charles Robert Bolton [1964] Director/Group Chief Executive; Joseph Boucher [1983] Director/Chartered Accountant; Roger Antony Day [1960] Finance Director; Andrew Olaf Fischer [1964] Director [German]; Ian Fisher [1950] Director; Damiano Lo Giudice [1971] Director/Head of Performance and Motorsport EMEA&A [Italian]; Celso Luis Pierre [1972] Director/Chief Executive [American]; Jonathan Charles Richardson [1960] Director

Goodshelter Property (Surbiton) Limited
Incorporated: 8 June 2010 *Employees:* 2
Net Worth: £6,345,034 *Total Assets:* £6,375,866
Registered Office: Kennedy, Thurlestone, Kingsbridge, Devon, TQ7 3NP
Activities: Buying and selling of own real estate
Parent: Goodshelter Property Company Limited
Officers: Cheryll Linda Mary Beck [1961] Director; Martin Raymond Augustine Beck [1960] Director/Financial Advisor

Goodshelter Property Company Limited
Incorporated: 29 November 2012 *Employees:* 2
Net Worth: £12,862,780 *Total Assets:* £16,622,535
Registered Office: Kennedy, Thurlestone, Kingsbridge, Devon, TQ7 3NP
Activities: Buying and selling of own real estate
Shareholders: Cheryll Linda Mary Beck; Martin Raymond Augustine Beck
Officers: Cheryll Linda Mary Beck [1961] Director; Martin Raymond Augustine Beck [1960] Director/Financial Advisor

Goonvean Aggregates Limited
Incorporated: 2 August 2012 *Employees:* 30
Net Worth: £870,074 *Total Assets:* £4,080,497
Registered Office: Boscawen House, St Stephen, St Austell, Cornwall, PL26 7QF
Activities: Other mining and quarrying n.e.c.
Parent: Goonvean Holdings Ltd
Officers: Jonathan Neil Angilley [1962] Director

Goonvean Holdings Limited
Incorporated: 22 June 2009 *Employees:* 376
Net Worth: £42,828,776 *Total Assets:* £53,671,728
Registered Office: Boscawen House, St Stephen, St Austell, Cornwall, PL26 7QF
Activities: Activities of head offices
Major Shareholder: The Honourable Evelyn Arthur Hugh Boscawen
Officers: Jonathan Neil Angilley [1962] Financial Director; Honourable Evelyn Arthur Hugh Boscawen [1955] Director/Farmer

Gordano Support Group Limited
Incorporated: 15 August 1991 *Employees:* 122
Net Worth: £2,580,289 *Total Assets:* £6,112,999
Registered Office: Barns Ground, Kenn, Clevedon, Somerset, BS21 6ST
Activities: Packaging activities
Major Shareholder: Michael John Bull
Officers: Louise Susan Selwyn, Secretary; Jonathan Edward Bull [1975] Director; Michael John Bull [1934] Managing Director; Nigel John Bull [1972] Director; Anthony Frank Moore [1966] Marketing Director; Timothy James Patch [1974] Director; Peter John Roberts [1960] Director/Chartered Accountant

W.G. Gould & Sons Limited
Incorporated: 25 January 1973 *Employees:* 3
Net Worth: £4,519,020 *Total Assets:* £8,108,366
Registered Office: Foxdown, Thorne St Margaret, Wellington, Somerset, TA21 0EQ
Activities: Development of building projects
Shareholders: Wallace Geoffrey Gould Snr; Cyril Peter Gould
Officers: Cyril Peter Gould [1958] Director; Kevin William Gould [1976] Director; Wallace Geoffrey Gould [1920] Director

Gould & Swayne Limited
Incorporated: 5 March 2004 *Employees:* 27
Net Worth: £538,329 *Total Assets:* £4,696,088
Registered Office: Cranhill House, Cranhill Road, Street, Somerset, BA16 0BY
Activities: Solicitors
Parent: Culshaw Holdings Ltd
Officers: Charles Joseph Culshaw, Secretary; Charles Joseph Culshaw [1959] Director/Solicitor; Gian Carlo Floris [1983] Director/Solicitor; Jason Luke Legg [1991] Director/Solicitor; John Derek Osman [1975] Director/Solicitor

Goulds (Dorchester) Limited
Incorporated: 9 March 1946 *Employees:* 247
Net Worth: £3,900,806 *Total Assets:* £10,125,888
Registered Office: 22-23 South Street, Dorchester, DT1 1DA
Activities: Other retail sale in non-specialised stores
Officers: Brian John Tuson, Secretary; Anthony Roger Gould [1973] Director; Christopher Grant Gould [1981] Director; Roger John Gould [1948] Director; Michael Christopher Hewitson Mitchell [1949] Director; Rebecca Henrietta Murphy [1968] Director; Brian John Tuson [1961] Director

GP Batteries (UK) Limited
Incorporated: 28 April 1993 *Employees:* 9
Net Worth: £4,076,824 *Total Assets:* £11,001,447
Registered Office: Unit 17 Monument View, Chelston Business Park, Wellington, Somerset, TA21 9ND
Activities: Wholesale of electronic and telecommunications equipment and parts
Parent: GP Battery Technology (Hong Kong) Ltd
Officers: Pak Nin Ho [1953] Regional Consumer Sales Director; Gareth Neil Wheller [1968] Director; Tze Hang Wong [1963] Director/Accountant [Chinese]

Graceloft Limited
Incorporated: 3 January 1979 *Employees:* 4
Net Worth: £4,775,057 *Total Assets:* £6,075,011
Registered Office: Lakeside Offices, The Old Cattle Market, Coronation Park, Helston, Cornwall, TR13 0SR
Activities: Construction of domestic buildings
Shareholders: Susan Ann Martin; David Cyril Martin
Officers: Susan Ann Martin, Secretary; Andrea Lisa Martin [1980] Director; Claire Anne Martin [1977] Director; David Cyril Martin [1946] Director/Builder; Susan Ann Martin [1945] Director/Company Secretary

Graham and Green Limited
Incorporated: 14 June 1976 *Employees:* 90
Net Worth: £3,272,357 *Total Assets:* £4,674,218
Registered Office: 92 Walcot Street, Bath, BA1 5BG
Activities: Retail sale of hardware, paints and glass in specialised stores
Shareholders: Jamie Graham; Antonia Graham
Officers: Darren Lawrence Murphy, Secretary; Antonia Graham [1942] Director/Retailer; Jamie Campbell Graham [1973] Managing Director; Louise Graham [1981] Director of Sales and Marketing; Darren Lawrence Murphy [1968] Director/Finance and Operations

Granary Ford LLP
Incorporated: 1 October 2015
Net Worth: £25,981,240 *Total Assets:* £25,981,240
Registered Office: Centenary House, Peninsula Park, Rydon Lane, Exeter, EX2 7XE
Officers: Andrew William Michael Christie-Miller [1950] Member; Lord Gerard Nevile Mark Clinton [1934] Member; Lord Donald Thomas Younger Curry [1944] Member

Grand Pier Limited
Incorporated: 3 January 1919
Net Worth: £19,755,456 *Total Assets:* £27,858,488
Registered Office: Grand Pier, Marine Parade, Weston Super Mare, Somerset, BS23 1AL
Activities: Other service activities n.e.c.
Parent: AGM Holdings Limited
Officers: Michelle Michael, Secretary/Director; Axentis Panayiotou Demetriou [1979] Director; Kerry Michael [1959] Director; Michelle Michael [1967] Director

The Grange (Chertsey) 2002 Ltd.
Incorporated: 5 September 2002 *Employees:* 66
Net Worth: £4,109,939 *Total Assets:* £6,434,385
Registered Office: 31-33 Commercial Road, Poole, Dorset, BH14 0HU
Activities: Residential care activities for the elderly and disabled
Parent: Serene LL Ltd
Officers: Dr Arujuna Sivananthan [1970] Director/Care Home Operator; Karthika Sivananthan [1973] Director/Care Home Operator [Australian]

Grange Court (Hoburne) Limited
Incorporated: 10 December 1958 *Employees:* 79
Net Worth: £715,315 *Total Assets:* £10,555,164
Registered Office: 10 Hoburne Lane, Christchurch, Dorset, BH23 4HP
Activities: Holiday centres and villages
Parent: Hoburne Limited
Officers: Nicholas Stewart Putnam, Company Secretary; Rosemary Sarah Kennar [1956] Director; Timothy Richard Knight [1960] Director; Rodney Philip Tucker [1954] Director

Grange Mill Investments Limited
Incorporated: 22 September 1998 *Employees:* 2
Net Worth: £5,330,006 *Total Assets:* £7,119,316
Registered Office: Richmond Point, 43 Richmond Hill, Bournemouth, BH2 6LR
Activities: Construction of commercial buildings
Parent: Broadshade Group Ltd
Officers: Mandy Lorna Catto [1967] Director; Dr Stephen Kenneth Catto [1963] Director

Grange Motors (Brentwood) Limited
Incorporated: 4 December 1958 *Employees:* 348
Net Worth: £16,239,000 *Total Assets:* £83,744,000
Registered Office: Swindon Motor Park, Dorcan Way, Swindon, Wilts, SN3 3RA
Activities: Sale of new cars and light motor vehicles
Parent: Cambria Automobiles (South East) Ltd
Officers: James Anthony Mullins, Finance Director; Timothy Alex Duckers [1973] Director; Mark Jonathan James Lavery [1965] Director; James Anthony Mullins [1978] Director

Grange Motors (Swindon) Limited
Incorporated: 28 May 2002
Net Worth: £3,269,000 *Total Assets:* £12,874,000
Registered Office: Dorcan Way, Swindon, Wilts, SN3 3RA
Activities: Sale of new cars and light motor vehicles
Parent: Cambria Automobiles Acquisitions Ltd
Officers: James Anthony Mullins, Finance Director; Timothy Alex Duckers [1973] Director; Mark Jonathan James Lavery [1965] Director; James Anthony Mullins [1978] Finance Director

Granite Associates Ltd.
Incorporated: 22 February 2013 *Employees:* 4
Net Worth: £9,742,076 *Total Assets:* £9,865,492
Registered Office: Little Highlands, Blachford Road, Ivybridge, Devon, PL21 0AD
Activities: Other letting and operating of own or leased real estate
Shareholder: Patrick O'Connell
Officers: Jane Fussell [1967] Director; John O'Connell [1940] Director; Patrick O'Connell [1970] Director; Joanne Wills [1967] Director

Grant Almont Limited
Incorporated: 19 May 2010
Net Worth: £46,530 *Total Assets:* £138,497,488
Registered Office: Calcutt Court, Calcutt, Swindon, Wilts, SN6 6JR
Activities: Other specialised construction activities n.e.c.
Parent: Eastway Limited
Officers: Hayley Victoria Swain-Grainger [1970] Director

Grant Engineering (UK) Limited
Incorporated: 3 May 1996 *Employees:* 69
Net Worth: £4,958,179 *Total Assets:* £24,428,624
Registered Office: Hopton House, Hopton Industrial Estate, Devizes, Wilts, SN10 2EU
Activities: Plumbing, heat and air-conditioning installation
Shareholders: Niall John Fay; Stephen Hubert Grant
Officers: Niall John Fay, Secretary; Niall John Fay [1971] Director [Irish]; Stephen William Grant [1944] Director/Technical Manager [Irish]; Paul Wakefield [1955] Director

Graphic PLC
Incorporated: 24 December 1971 *Employees:* 176
Net Worth: £11,722,000 *Total Assets:* £18,741,000
Registered Office: Down End, Lords Meadow Industrial Estate, Crediton, Devon, EX17 1HN
Activities: Manufacture of electronic components
Parent: Bid PCB UK Ltd
Officers: Leigh Sampson, Secretary; Marco Fantoni [1971] Director [Italian]; Roberto Giudici [1982] Director [Italian]; Nicola Pietralunga [1968] Director [Italian]; David John Pike [1962] Director; Giovanni Tridenti [1968] Director [Italian]

Grasshopper 2000 Ltd.
Incorporated: 23 November 1934 *Employees:* 3
Net Worth: £15,056,084 *Total Assets:* £15,208,310
Registered Office: Bourton Far Hill Farm, Bourton on the Hill, Moreton in The Marsh, Glos, GL56 9TN
Activities: Raising of sheep and goats
Major Shareholder: Timothy David Holland-Martin
Officers: Mary Carol Luckock, Secretary; Timothy David Holland-Martin [1936] Director/Farmer

Graytone Limited
Incorporated: 6 December 1996 *Employees:* 62
Net Worth: £4,160,342 *Total Assets:* £10,847,054
Registered Office: Towngate House, 2-8 Parkstone Road, Poole, Dorset, BH15 2PW
Activities: Activities of head offices
Shareholders: Anthony Edwin Thomas Swayne; Graham Richard Yates
Officers: Nicholas Calamada Robins [1969] Finance Director; Anthony Edwin Thomas Swayne [1946] Director/Accountant; Geoffrey Colin Warde [1944] Director; Graham Richard Yates [1958] Director

Great American Specialty & Affinity Limited
Incorporated: 26 July 2010 *Employees:* 47
Net Worth: £853,813 *Total Assets:* £4,926,241
Registered Office: 32 Queen Square, Bristol, BS1 4ND
Activities: Other business support service activities n.e.c.
Parent: American Financial Group, Inc
Officers: Julian Stewart Bartlett [1967] Director; Vincent McLenaghan [1959] Director/Insurance Professional [Australian]; Jeremy Charles Webb [1959] Director/General Manager; David John Witzgall [1959] Director/Accountant [American]

The Great British Card Company PLC
Incorporated: 29 July 1980 *Employees:* 134
Net Worth: £2,976,413 *Total Assets:* £10,315,203
Registered Office: Paper House, Waterwells Drive, Gloucester, GL2 2PH
Activities: Non-specialised wholesale trade
Shareholder: Peter Allan Macbeth Reichwald
Officers: Stephen Taylor Gallagher, Secretary/Director; Nicholas Paul Adsett [1961] Director; Christopher William Richard Davies [1948] Director; Stephen Taylor Gallagher [1959] Director; Christopher Charles Powell [1946] Director; Peter Allan Macbeth Reichwald [1942] Director; Simon David Macbeth Reichwald [1968] Director; Christopher Charles Wilcox [1956] Director

The Great Eastern Hotel Company Limited
Incorporated: 7 August 1995 *Employees:* 279
Net Worth Deficit: £10,622,000 *Total Assets:* £77,076,000
Registered Office: First Floor, 10 Temple Back, Bristol, BS1 6FL
Activities: Hotels and similar accommodation
Parent: The Great Eastern Hotel Holding Company Limited
Officers: Robert Ryan Mangiarelli [1971] Director/Financial Executive [American]; Bradley Raymond O'Bryan [1969] Director/Financial Executive [American]; David Alan Peters [1972] Director/Attorney [American]

The Great Eastern Hotel Holding Company Limited
Incorporated: 6 February 2006 *Employees:* 3
Net Worth: £40,019,000 *Total Assets:* £125,604,000
Registered Office: First Floor, 10 Temple Back, Bristol, BS1 6FL
Activities: Activities of head offices
Parent: Hyatt Hotels Corporation
Officers: Robert Ryan Mangiarelli [1971] Director/Financial Executive [American]; Bradley Raymond O'Bryan [1969] Director/Financial Executive [American]; David Alan Peters [1972] Director/Attorney [American]

Great Western Enterprise (Holdings) Limited
Incorporated: 21 May 1986
Net Worth: £3,864,953 *Total Assets:* £3,864,953
Registered Office: Park House, Church Place, Swindon, Wilts, SN1 5ED
Activities: Other business support service activities n.e.c.
Officers: Tina Jane Doyle, Secretary; Nicola Alberry [1961] Director; Peter Valentine Boucher [1971] Director; Alan Fletcher [1947] Director/Bank Manager; Jack Frost [1953] Director; Michael Bernard Godfrey [1954] Director; Ian Tothill Larrard [1955] Director; James Henry Kemeys Monk [1970] Director; Andy Tait [1957] Retired Director

Greater Union Limited
Incorporated: 16 December 1997
Net Worth: £63,592,060 *Total Assets:* £63,938,304
Registered Office: First Floor, 10 Temple Back, Bristol, BS1 6FL
Activities: Non-trading company
Officers: Gregory Charles Dean [1965] Director of Finance & Accounting [Australian]; Mathew Robert Duff [1969] Director [Australian]

Green and Fortune Holdings Limited
Incorporated: 25 March 2015 *Employees:* 181
Net Worth: £492,948 *Total Assets:* £7,715,889
Registered Office: Veale Wasbrough Vizards, Narrow Quay House, Narrow Quay, Bristol, BS1 4QA
Activities: Activities of other holding companies n.e.c.
Shareholders: Peter John Millican; John Anthony Nugent
Officers: Peter John Millican [1949] Director; John Anthony Nugent [1970] Director/Chief Executive Officer

Green and Fortune Limited
Incorporated: 28 October 2004 *Employees:* 97
Net Worth: £2,493,738 *Total Assets:* £5,286,796
Registered Office: Veale Wasbrough Vizards, Narrow Quay House, Narrow Quay, Bristol, BS1 4QA
Activities: Licenced restaurants
Parent: Green and Fortune Holdings Limited
Officers: Peter John Millican [1949] Director; John Anthony Nugent [1970] Director/Chief Executive

Green Cape Limited
Incorporated: 27 April 2007
Net Worth Deficit: £302,928 *Total Assets:* £4,432,203
Registered Office: 898-902 Wimborne Road, Moordown, Bournemouth, BH9 2DW
Activities: Construction of domestic buildings
Parent: Kingsand Limited
Officers: Daniel John Colledge [1979] Director/Accountant; Ciaran Michael Lawlor [1965] Director/Chartered Accountant [Irish]; Terry Raymond Williams [1974] Director/Architect

Green Gourmet Limited
Incorporated: 2 April 1991 *Employees:* 40
Net Worth: £1,513,958 *Total Assets:* £4,799,502
Registered Office: The Moorings, Bonds Mill, Stonehouse, Glos, GL10 3RF
Activities: Manufacture of other food products n.e.c.
Shareholders: Adam James Starkey; Victoria Mary Keble-Williams
Officers: Adam James Starkey, Secretary/Managing Director; Matthew David Flynn [1979] Purchasing Director; Michael John Hanley [1978] Managing Director; Neil Humphries [1978] Director; Victoria Mary Keble-Williams [1965] Director; Adam James Starkey [1965] Director/Founder & Executive Chair

Green Spinnaker Limited
Incorporated: 4 February 2013 *Employees:* 3
Net Worth: £4,104,623 *Total Assets:* £4,207,289
Registered Office: Minerva House, Lower Bristol Road, Bath, BA2 9ER
Activities: Development of building projects
Major Shareholder: Susan Elizabeth Blatchford
Officers: David Andrew Blatchford [1966] Director; Susan Elizabeth Blatchford [1968] Director

Green Valley Capital Limited
Incorporated: 10 January 2014 *Employees:* 1
Net Worth: £3,717,288 *Total Assets:* £18,315,476
Registered Office: Portwall Place, Portwall Lane, Bristol, BS1 6NA
Activities: Activities of other holding companies n.e.c.
Major Shareholder: Thomas George Story Busher
Officers: Thomas George Story Busher [1955] Director

Green-Line Contracts Limited
Incorporated: 7 February 2000 *Employees:* 28
Net Worth: £1,977,784 *Total Assets:* £6,184,400
Registered Office: Cowfield Mill, Northway, Tewkesbury, Glos, GL20 8HG
Activities: Renting and leasing of cars and light motor vehicles
Shareholders: Nicholas Charles Green; Philip Edward Green
Officers: Nicholas Charles Green, Secretary/Director; David Duncan Green [1965] Director; Nicholas Charles Green [1960] Director; Patricia Alice Green [1939] Director; Philip Edward Green [1963] Director

Greenaway & Greenaway Limited
Incorporated: 20 June 1961
Net Worth: £1,841,327 *Total Assets:* £5,029,477
Registered Office: Transport House, Stratton, Bude, Cornwall, EX23 9NR
Activities: Other business support service activities n.e.c.
Major Shareholder: John Greenaway
Officers: John Charles Greenaway [1960] Director/Motor Engineer

The Greenbank Hotel (Falmouth) Limited
Incorporated: 15 May 1997 *Employees:* 102
Net Worth: £2,115,311 *Total Assets:* £4,468,024
Registered Office: The Greenbank Hotel, Harbourside, Falmouth, Cornwall, TR11 2SR
Activities: Support activities to performing arts
Parent: The Greenbank Hotel Ltd
Officers: Roger French, Secretary; Roger James Edward French [1945] Director; James Arthur Gatheridge [1947] Director/Leisure Complex Manager; Aaron David Pascoe [1965] Director/Hotelier; Mark Ivano Pascoe [1962] Director/Hotelier; Anthony Duncan Worden [1948] Director

Greendale Investments Ltd
Incorporated: 28 March 1988
Net Worth: £320,000 *Total Assets:* £7,411,000
Registered Office: Greendale Business Park, Woodbury Salterton, Exeter, EX5 1EW
Activities: Other letting and operating of own or leased real estate
Parent: Exmouth Marina Ltd
Officers: Peter German, Secretary; Alec Robin Bill Carter [1974] Director; Mathew Rowan Carter [1982] Director; Robin Anthony Bill Carter [1944] Director/Farmer; Rowan Charles Carter [1953] Director/Farmer; Peter Lewin German [1953] Director

David Greening Limited
Incorporated: 26 August 1987
Net Worth: £3,965,697 *Total Assets:* £4,241,136
Registered Office: Lowerfield Court, New Barn Lane, Prestbury, Cheltenham, Glos, GL52 3LB
Activities: Construction of domestic buildings
Major Shareholder: David Charles Greening
Officers: David Charles Greening [1951] Director/Builder

Greenland Stud Farm Holdings Ltd
Incorporated: 14 July 2016 *Employees:* 2
Net Worth Deficit: £1,648 *Total Assets:* £6,256,340
Registered Office: Wessex House, Challeymead Business Park, Melksham, Wilts, SN12 8BU
Activities: Other letting and operating of own or leased real estate
Major Shareholder: James Christopher Lascelles Lucas
Officers: James Christopher Lascelles Lucas [1961] Director

Greenoaks Global Holdings Ltd.
Incorporated: 18 July 2013 *Employees:* 11
Net Worth: £62,191,384 *Total Assets:* £90,268,056
Registered Office: Third Floor, 95 The Promenade, Cheltenham, Glos, GL50 1HH
Activities: Activities of other holding companies n.e.c.
Officers: Ashok Sanat Kumar Kothari [1947] Director/Executive [Indian]; Neil Mehta [1984] Managing Director [American]; Antonios Elpidoforos Papantoniou [1982] Director/Senior Executive [Greek]; Benjamin Scott Peretz [1986] Managing Director [American]

Greens of Cheltenham Limited
Incorporated: 5 January 1996
Net Worth: £4,468,497 *Total Assets:* £4,703,323
Registered Office: Stag House, The Chipping, Wotton under Edge, Glos, GL12 7AD
Activities: Other retail sale not in stores, stalls or markets
Major Shareholder: Stephen Michael Reynolds
Officers: Stephen Michael Reynolds [1959] Director/Antique Dealer

Greensquare Homes Limited
Incorporated: 19 October 1999
Net Worth: £4,525,823 *Total Assets:* £11,737,951
Registered Office: Greensquare Group, Methuen Park, Chippenham, Wilts, SN14 0GU
Activities: Development of building projects
Officers: Mandy Arnold, Secretary; Robin Thomas Bailey [1949] Director/Chairman; Barry Graham Stiles [1969] Managing Director - Construction; John Alfred Neville Tibbitts [1955] Director; Barry Wood [1956] Managing Director

Gregory Distribution (Holdings) Limited
Incorporated: 29 April 2009 *Employees:* 1,725
Net Worth: £36,334,000 *Total Assets:* £109,061,000
Registered Office: Senate Court, Southernhay Gardens, Exeter, Devon, EX1 1NT
Activities: Activities of head offices
Major Shareholder: John Kennedy Gregory
Officers: Angela Mary Butler [1967] Director; Irene Kennedy Gregory [1931] Director; John Kennedy Gregory [1958] Director; Simon Hugh Gregory [1955] Director/Solicitor; Timothy James Gregory [1963] Director/Teacher; William John Gregory [1924] Director; Paul Gerard Jefferson [1966] Director

Gregory Distribution Limited
Incorporated: 8 September 1977 *Employees:* 1,492
Net Worth: £31,210,000 *Total Assets:* £98,754,000
Registered Office: Senate Court, Southernhay Gardens, Exeter, Devon, EX1 1NT
Activities: Freight transport by road
Parent: Gregory Distribution (Holdings) Limited
Officers: Angela Mary Butler [1967] Director; John Kennedy Gregory [1958] Director/Chief Executive; Simon Hugh Gregory [1955] Director/Solicitor; Paul Gerard Jefferson [1966] Director

Greiner Bio-One Limited
Incorporated: 27 July 1992 *Employees:* 41
Net Worth: £2,690,405 *Total Assets:* £4,827,444
Registered Office: Unit 5 Stroudwater Business Park, Brunel Way, Stonehouse, Glos, GL10 3SX
Activities: Wholesale of pharmaceutical goods
Parent: Greiner Bio-One GmbH
Officers: Jonathan Frank Richard Pearson, Secretary; Noel Christopher Ennett [1958] Director/Operations Manager; Jonathan Frank Richard Pearson [1958] Director/Chartered Accountant; Thomas Milligan Woods [1958] Director/Salesman

Grenadier Emperor Limited
Incorporated: 30 September 2016
Net Worth: £594,596 *Total Assets:* £7,834,691
Registered Office: Oxygen House, Grenadier Road, Exeter Business Park, Exeter, EX1 3LH
Activities: Other letting and operating of own or leased real estate
Parent: Grenadier Estates Ltd
Officers: Eleanor Jane Adams [1972] Finance Director; George James Jennings Pawley [1986] Director/Solicitor

Grensue Ltd
Incorporated: 20 November 2002 *Employees:* 543
Net Worth: £2,700,751 *Total Assets:* £6,950,378
Registered Office: Aldreth, Pearcroft Road, Stonehouse, Glos, GL10 2JY
Activities: Take-away food shops and mobile food stands
Major Shareholder: Gregory Fox
Officers: Sue Broadbent, Secretary; Gregory Fox [1967] Director; Sue Fox [1967] Director

Grenville Bidco Limited
Incorporated: 17 March 2016 *Employees:* 7
Net Worth: £10,191,003 *Total Assets:* £31,034,728
Registered Office: Travel Chapter House, Gammaton Road, Bideford, Devon, EX39 4DF
Activities: Management consultancy activities other than financial management
Parent: Grenville Midco 2 Limited
Officers: Jayne Claire McClure [1978] Director; James Peter Morris [1978] Director

Grenville Midco 1 Limited
Incorporated: 17 March 2016
Net Worth: £13,015,000 *Total Assets:* £28,041,574
Registered Office: Travel Chapter House, Gammaton Road, Bideford, Devon, EX39 4DF
Activities: Activities of other holding companies n.e.c.
Parent: Grenville Topco Limited
Officers: Jayne Claire McClure [1978] Director; James Peter Morris [1978] Director

Grenville Midco 2 Limited
Incorporated: 17 March 2016
Net Worth: £13,015,000 *Total Assets:* £28,041,574
Registered Office: Travel Chapter House, Gammaton Road, Bideford, Devon, EX39 4DF
Activities: Activities of other holding companies n.e.c.
Parent: Grenville Midco 1 Limited
Officers: Jayne Claire McClure [1978] Director; James Peter Morris [1978] Director

Grenville Topco Limited
Incorporated: 17 March 2016 *Employees:* 189
Net Worth Deficit: £4,427,951 *Total Assets:* £40,872,036
Registered Office: Travel Chapter House, Gammaton Road, Bideford, Devon, EX39 4DF
Activities: Activities of other holding companies n.e.c.
Parent: Country Bidco Limited
Officers: Jayne Claire McClure [1978] Director; James Peter Morris [1978] Director; Sean Williams [1964] Director

Gretton Solar Farm Limited
Incorporated: 4 November 2013
Net Worth: £222,680 *Total Assets:* £4,994,609
Registered Office: Woodwater House, Pynes Hill, Exeter, Devon, EX2 5WR
Activities: Production of electricity
Officers: Sven Frauenstein [1973] Director/Chief Technology Officer [German]; Oliver Haller [1968] Director/Manager [Austrian]

Grevan Cars Limited
Incorporated: 4 October 1984 *Employees:* 259
Net Worth: £2,130,241 *Total Assets:* £45,233,400
Registered Office: St Modwen House, Longbridge Road, Marsh Mills, Plymouth, PL6 8LD
Activities: Sale of new cars and light motor vehicles
Parent: De Van Automotive Limited
Officers: Michael Emlyn Evans, Secretary/Director; Graham Paul de Val [1961] Director; Michael Emlyn Evans [1946] Director; Claire Jacob [1969] Director/Patent Agent; Sally Jones [1967] Director/Housewife

Grey Matter Limited
Incorporated: 12 October 1982 *Employees:* 107
Net Worth: £3,215,000 *Total Assets:* £9,641,000
Registered Office: 2 Prigg Meadow, Ashburton, Newton Abbot, Devon, TQ13 7DF
Activities: Wholesale of computers, computer peripheral equipment and software
Parent: CDF Group Ltd
Officers: Juliet Collis, Secretary; Juliet Collis [1961] Director/Accountant; Charles Frederick Cooke Hurle [1951] Director; Andrew King [1965] Marketing Director; Paul Sean Wilson [1964] Director/Software Consultant

Gridline Enterprises Limited
Incorporated: 28 July 1994 *Employees:* 56
Net Worth: £4,154,975 *Total Assets:* £4,569,615
Registered Office: Unit 5 Kennet Way, Canal Road Industrial Estate, Trowbridge, Wilts, BA14 8BL
Activities: Retail sale of clothing in specialised stores
Parent: F R Monkhouse Limited
Officers: Glenn Peter Leech [1975] Director; Peter John Robert Monkhouse [1970] Director; Ian John Webb [1973] Director

M.A. Grigg (Agricultural) Limited
Incorporated: 23 October 1981 *Employees:* 83
Net Worth: £17,932,572 *Total Assets:* £20,123,898
Registered Office: Pendennis, Sticker, St Austell, Cornwall, PL26 7JH
Activities: Other retail sale in non-specialised stores
Shareholders: Michael Arthur Grigg; The Estate of Ann Grigg (deceased)
Officers: Fiona Mary Kingston Grigg, Secretary; Fiona Mary Kingston Grigg [1970] Director; Michael Arthur Grigg [1942] Director/Agricultural Merchant; Sarah Ann Venning [1966] Director

Grist Environmental Limited
Incorporated: 25 October 1993 *Employees:* 160
Previous: Wiltshire Waste (Recycling) Limited
Net Worth: £2,038,794 *Total Assets:* £7,717,225
Registered Office: William Road, Devizes, Wilts, SN10 3EW
Activities: Collection of non-hazardous waste
Parent: Grist Group Limited
Officers: Adam Nigel Edgar Grist [1987] Director; James Robert Grist [1989] Director; Marcus David Grist [1991] Director; Nicole Elizabeth Grist [1995] Director; Nigel Edgar Grist [1956] Director; Paul Mortimer [1960] Director/Sales Manager

Grist Group Limited
Incorporated: 13 February 1989 *Employees:* 183
Net Worth: £7,920,878 *Total Assets:* £17,141,994
Registered Office: William Road, Devizes, Wilts, SN10 3EW
Activities: Activities of head offices
Major Shareholder: Nigel Edgar Grist
Officers: Adam Nigel Edgar Grist [1987] Director; Nigel Edgar Grist [1956] Director/Scrap Metal Dealer

Grosvenor Place Holdings Limited
Incorporated: 16 March 1995 *Employees:* 2
Net Worth: £678,804 *Total Assets:* £3,699,423
Registered Office: c/o Bishop Fleming, 16 Queen Square, Bristol, BS1 4NT
Activities: Development of building projects
Major Shareholder: Norman Brian Parfitt
Officers: Amy Georgina Parfitt, Secretary; Amy Georgina Parfitt [1976] Director; Norman Brian Parfitt [1947] Director/Farmer

Grosvenor PPP Holdings Limited
Incorporated: 29 March 2005 *Employees:* 2
Net Worth Deficit: £3,327,000 *Total Assets:* £21,307,000
Registered Office: Third Floor, Broad Quay House, Prince Street, Bristol, BS1 4DJ
Activities: Activities of head offices
Parent: Semperian (Community Health) Grosvenor Limited
Officers: Richard Little [1979] Investment Director; Neil Rae [1971] Director

Grounded Property Trading Limited
Incorporated: 23 March 2010
Net Worth: £946,523 *Total Assets:* £3,726,434
Registered Office: C V Ross & Co Limited, Unit 1, Office 1, Tower Lane Business Park, Warmley, Bristol, BS30 8XT
Activities: Buying and selling of own real estate
Officers: John Patrick Boyce [1962] Director; Laura Jane Boyce [1961] Director; Robert Hoy [1962] Director; Sarah Jane Hoy [1965] Director

Groundfix Limited
Incorporated: 11 January 2005 *Employees:* 8
Net Worth: £2,591,069 *Total Assets:* £4,109,389
Registered Office: Pilgrim House, Oxford Place, Plymouth, PL1 5AJ
Activities: Site preparation
Shareholders: Stephen Robert Hoskin; Champion Groundworks Limited
Officers: Ian John Taberner, Secretary; Frederick Charles Champion [1956] Director; Stephen Robert Hoskin [1959] Director

Group Silverline Limited
Incorporated: 29 July 1999 *Employees:* 202
Net Worth: £17,071,000 *Total Assets:* £50,219,000
Registered Office: Boundary Way, Lufton Trading Estate, Yeovil, Somerset, BA22 8HZ
Activities: Activities of other holding companies n.e.c.
Major Shareholder: James Goddard-Watts
Officers: Jon Ivan Goddard Watts [1930] Director; Darrell John Morris [1971] Director; Rory Anthony O'Donnell [1952] Director; Simon Nicholas Oakland [1969] Director/Business Executive; Nigel Francis Mark Popplewell [1957] Director/Solicitor

Grove Care Limited
Incorporated: 22 April 2003 *Employees:* 198
Net Worth: £4,240,999 *Total Assets:* £10,346,671
Registered Office: Blossom Fields, 84-86 High Street, Winterbourne, Bristol, BS36 1RB
Activities: Residential care activities for the elderly and disabled
Shareholders: Fiona Angela Jarman; Sarah McCarthy Taylor
Officers: Angela McCarthy, Secretary; Fiona Angela Jarman [1980] Director; Angela McCarthy [1943] Director [Irish]; Martin McCarthy [1950] Director [Irish]; Sarah McCarthy Taylor [1974] Director; Christopher John Taylor [1974] Director

Grove Village Limited
Incorporated: 2 January 2003
Net Worth: £9,663,204 *Total Assets:* £28,381,340
Registered Office: Third Floor, Broad Quay House, Prince Street, Bristol, BS1 4DJ
Activities: Other business support service activities n.e.c.
Parent: Grove Village Holdings Limited
Officers: Louis Javier Falero [1977] Director/Fund Manager; Michael Anthony Redford [1970] Director; Angela Louise Roshier [1975] Director/Asset Management; Paul William Warburton [1972] Director

Groves Park Investments Ltd
Incorporated: 30 November 2012
Net Worth: £818,645 *Total Assets:* £3,686,160
Registered Office: 51 Broad Street, Chipping Sodbury, Bristol, BS37 6AD
Activities: Other letting and operating of own or leased real estate
Shareholders: Christopher Brian Groves; William Stephen Park
Officers: Christopher Brian Groves [1955] Director; William Stephen Park [1960] Director

Growing Enterprises Ltd
Incorporated: 24 April 2001 *Employees:* 32
Net Worth: £3,278,131 *Total Assets:* £5,116,090
Registered Office: 3 Bath Mews, Bath Parade, Cheltenham, Glos, GL53 7HL
Activities: Retail sale of flowers, plants, seeds, fertilizers, pet animals and pet food in specialised stores
Shareholders: David Ian Brierley; Mitrecroft Limited
Officers: Louise Wendy Isaac, Secretary; David Ian Brierley [1956] Director; Noel Kelly [1954] Director/Accountant [Irish]

Growth Property Limited
Incorporated: 19 October 2012
Net Worth: £8,141 *Total Assets:* £3,593,236
Registered Office: Warren House, Blockley, Moreton in Marsh, Glos, GL56 9HL
Activities: Buying and selling of own real estate
Major Shareholder: Geoffrey Peter Wall
Officers: Geoffrey Peter Wall [1944] Director

Growth Technology Limited
Incorporated: 23 November 1992
Net Worth: £2,204,867 *Total Assets:* £3,542,495
Registered Office: Wessex House, 66 High Street, Honiton, Devon, EX14 1PD
Activities: Other service activities n.e.c.
Shareholders: Susan Grace Gunstone; Giles Wreford Gunstone
Officers: Susan Grace Gunstone, Secretary; Rachel Sarah Atkinson [1979] Director; Giles Wreford Gunstone [1949] Director; Susan Grace Gunstone [1953] Director/Administrator

GRS (Holdings) Limited
Incorporated: 13 January 2014 *Employees:* 1
Net Worth: £4,727,987 *Total Assets:* £4,825,085
Registered Office: Suffolk House, 68-70 Suffolk Road, Cheltenham, Glos, GL50 2ED
Activities: Other education n.e.c.
Major Shareholder: Cloud Bai-Yun
Officers: Dr Cloud Bai-Yun [1966] Director

The Gryphon Trust
Incorporated: 1 March 2011 *Employees:* 163
Previous: The Arnewood School
Net Worth: £15,809,848 *Total Assets:* £17,621,088
Registered Office: The Arnewood School, Gore Road, New Milton, Hants, BH25 6RS
Activities: General secondary education
Officers: Valerie Woods, Secretary; Mark Byrne [1970] Director/Head of Public Sector; Dominic Edmund Robert Coburn [1955] Director/Retired; Elizabeth Ann Cook [1938] Director; Keith Edward Craze [1952] Director/Human Resources; Alan Bryan Maugham [1943] Director/Chartered Accountant; Professor David Richards [1964] Director/University Professor/Chartered Engineer; Malcolm Edward George Walker [1955] Director; Roy George Wilkins [1951] Director/Chartered Quantity Surveyor

GS Yuasa Battery Sales UK Limited
Incorporated: 4 March 1981 *Employees:* 93
Previous: Yuasa Battery Sales (UK) Limited
Net Worth: £21,230,000 *Total Assets:* £56,190,000
Registered Office: Unit 13 Hunts Rise, South Marston Park, Swindon, Wilts, SN3 4TG
Activities: Wholesale trade of motor vehicle parts and accessories
Parent: GS Yuasa Battery Europe Ltd
Officers: John Paul McMullen, Secretary; James Noel Richard Hylton [1978] Managing Director; Pascal Marciano [1957] Director [French]; Andrew David Taylor [1965] Director; Dan Ugajin [1978] Director [Japanese]

GT Motorcycles (2012) Ltd
Incorporated: 20 February 2012 *Employees:* 41
Net Worth: £264,180 *Total Assets:* £5,055,545
Registered Office: Plym House, 3 Longbridge Road, Marsh Mills, Plymouth, PL6 8LT
Activities: Sale, maintenance and repair of motorcycles and related parts and accessories
Major Shareholder: Stephen Albert Haith
Officers: Michael William Arthur Grainger [1950] Director; Stephen Albert Haith [1963] Director

GTS Academy Trust
Incorporated: 8 July 2011 *Employees:* 87
Net Worth: £8,086,715 *Total Assets:* £10,657,210
Registered Office: Great Torrington School, Calvesford Road, Great Torrington, Devon, EX38 7DJ
Activities: General secondary education
Officers: Joanna Marie Pateman, Secretary; Sarah Jane Anstee [1968] Director/Teacher; Andrew James Bloodworth [1970] Director/Headteacher; Lucy Carmel FitzGenerald [1977] Managing Director of a HR Company; Rachel Higgs [1978] Director/Teacher; Paul David Jarrett [1970] Director/Bank Manager; Karen Lucy Meardon [1975] Director/Bookkeeper; Samantha Jayne Meeson [1966] Director/Teacher; Ian Michael Newberry [1969] Director/Head of Operations; Douglas Michael Smith [1945] Director/Sound Engineer; Peter John Villiers [1947] Director/Author; Christine Lesley Wall [1945] Director/Retired

Guarantee Holdings Limited
Incorporated: 12 December 2014 *Employees:* 116
Net Worth: £2,972,708 *Total Assets:* £7,387,347
Registered Office: 2 Pinesway, Station Road, Stalbridge, Dorset, DT10 2RN
Activities: Activities of other holding companies n.e.c.
Officers: Faith Madeline Foote [1961] Director; Lucinda Sarah Lambourne [1966] Director; Robin Michael Philpot Sheppard [1954] Director/Hotelier; Peter Norman Swan [1950] Director; Andrew John Tillard [1956] Director

Guild Bristol Limited
Incorporated: 16 October 2015
Net Worth: £772,085 *Total Assets:* £4,084,476
Registered Office: 45 Oakfield Road, Clifton, Bristol, BS8 2AX
Activities: Development of building projects
Shareholder: David William Rogers
Officers: Edward John Ware [1960] Director; Kingsley Peter Webb [1966] Director

N.A. Guppy Limited
Incorporated: 23 March 1965 *Employees:* 8
Net Worth: £1,954,472 *Total Assets:* £3,589,379
Registered Office: Croylands, Brampford Speke, Exeter, Devon, EX5 5HH
Activities: Plumbing, heat and air-conditioning installation
Major Shareholder: Norman Alfred Guppy
Officers: Ethel Elizabeth Guppy, Secretary; Ethel Elizabeth Guppy [1938] Director; Norman Charles Guppy [1957] Director; Norman Alfred Guppy [1931] Director; Stephen George Guppy [1965] Director

The Gurkha Welfare Trust
Incorporated: 8 April 2004 *Employees:* 483
Net Worth: £31,000,000 *Total Assets:* £77,861,000
Registered Office: Cross Keys House, 22 Queen Street, Salisbury, Wilts, SP1 1EY
Activities: Residential care activities for the elderly and disabled
Officers: Alexander Philip Wilder Howard, Secretary; Jeremy James Brade [1961] Director/Fund Manager; David Phillimore Clifford [1952] Director/Retired; Major General Jon Cole [1967] Director/Army Officer; Frank Seain Francis Dufficy [1953] Director/Lawyer; Major General Angus Fay [1964] Director/Government Service; Krishnabahadur Gurung [1952] Director/Retired [Nepalese]; Colonel David Gerard Hayes CBE [1953] Director/Army Officer; David James Hitchcock [1963] Director, JP Morgan; Dr John David Keeling [1958] Director/Independent Trustee; Lieutenant General Nicholas Arthur William Pope CBE [1962] Director/British Armed Forces; Colonel James Robinson [1964] Director/Army Officer; Brigadier Generald Mark Strickland [1970] Director/Army Officer; Catherine Lucy Turner [1963] Non-Executive Director and Chair; Major General Richard Wardlaw [1967] Director/British Army

Gurr Johns Limited
Incorporated: 14 November 1973 *Employees:* 22
Net Worth: £7,339,603 *Total Assets:* £15,845,762
Registered Office: 33 The Clarendon Centre, Salisbury Business Park, Dairy Meadow Lane, Salisbury, Wilts, SP1 2TJ
Activities: Other professional, scientific and technical activities n.e.c.
Major Shareholder: William Henry Smith
Officers: William Henry Smith, Secretary; Peter Richard Ensor [1948] Director/Publisher; Charles Richard Horne [1965] Managing Director [American]; Stephen John Meadowcroft [1954] Director/Valuer; William Henry Smith [1947] Director/Valuer; Simon Arthur Taylor [1957] Director/Wine Merchant

Guy,Leonard & Co.Limited
Incorporated: 3 August 1943 *Employees:* 5
Net Worth: £5,062,197 *Total Assets:* £6,247,184
Registered Office: 28 Alexandra Terrace, Exmouth, Devon, EX8 1BD
Activities: Other transportation support activities
Shareholders: David Leonardo Foa; Guido Icilio Patrick Foa
Officers: David Leonardo Foa [1973] Director/Manager; Guido Icilio Patrick Foa [1944] Director

GWE Business West Ltd
Incorporated: 15 October 2007 *Employees:* 169
Net Worth: £5,252,312 *Total Assets:* £9,579,594
Registered Office: Leigh Court Business Centre, Pill Road, Abbots Leigh, Bristol, BS8 3RA
Activities: Other business support service activities n.e.c.
Officers: Tina Jane Doyle, Secretary; Nicola Alberry [1961] Director/Company Chairman; Ian Bell [1954] Director; Richard Bonner [1969] Director; Alan Fletcher [1947] Director; Jack Frost [1953] Director; Mike Godfrey [1954] Director/Chief Engineer; Mark Edward Mason [1965] Director; Sarah Pullen [1971] Managing Director; Peter John Rilett [1950] Director/Accountant; Philip Meyrick Smith [1962] Managing Director; Iain Wolsey [1947] Director; Janine Woodcock [1968] Director

Gwenray Capital Limited
Incorporated: 29 November 2012 *Employees:* 4
Previous: Gwenray Properties Ltd
Net Worth: £176,486 *Total Assets:* £5,252,479
Registered Office: Potterne House, 1 Potterne Way, Wimborne, Dorset, BH21 6RS
Activities: Other credit granting n.e.c.
Shareholders: Raymond Higgins; Gwendoline Higgins
Officers: Raymond Higgins, Secretary; Gwendoline Higgins [1944] Director; Raymond Higgins [1941] Director

GWKS Ltd
Incorporated: 10 February 2006 *Employees:* 142
Net Worth: £1,318,022 *Total Assets:* £6,111,964
Registered Office: Goodridge Court, Goodridge Avenue, Gloucester, GL2 5EN
Activities: Site preparation
Shareholder: Eamonn Francis McGurk
Officers: Duncan Robert Hutchinson [1975] Director/Quantity Surveyor; Peter Wayne Roberts [1965] Managing Director

GWP Group Limited
Incorporated: 21 May 2005 *Employees:* 98
Net Worth: £4,803,599 *Total Assets:* £8,054,789
Registered Office: Unit 20 Chelworth Park Industrial Estate, Chelworth Road, Cricklade, Wilts, SN6 6HE
Activities: Manufacture of other paper and paperboard containers
Parent: GWP Holdings Limited
Officers: Paul Bullock, Secretary; Paul Bullock [1975] Director/Accountant; Ian Michael Cook [1959] Director; Ruth Cook [1968] Director; Andrew George James Creese [1952] Director; Ian Paul Heskins [1966] Director; David Philip Mason [1963] Director; David Bernard Pedley [1959] Managing Director

GWP Holdings Limited
Incorporated: 1 June 2016 *Employees:* 98
Net Worth: £5,956,883 *Total Assets:* £10,300,810
Registered Office: Unit 20 Chelworth Road, Cricklade, Swindon, Wilts, SN6 6HE
Activities: Manufacture of other paper and paperboard containers
Shareholders: Ruth Cook; Ian Paul Heskins
Officers: Paul Bullock, Secretary; Paul Bullock [1975] Director/Accountant; Ian Michael Cook [1959] Director; Ruth Cook [1968] Director; Ian Paul Heskins [1966] Director; David Philip Mason [1963] Director; David Bernard Pedley [1959] Director

Gwynt y Mor Offshore Wind Farm Limited
Incorporated: 18 January 1999
Net Worth Deficit: £920,333 *Total Assets:* £16,992,066
Registered Office: Windmill Hill Business Park, Whitehill Way, Swindon, Wilts, SN5 6PB
Activities: Production of electricity
Officers: Christopher David Barras, Secretary; Penelope Anne Sainsbury, Secretary; Martin Andre-Ferreira [1978] Director/FCCA Accountant; Jonathan Graham Coleridge Boles [1960] Finance Director; Andrew John Bown [1979] Investment Director; Agnieszka Cieplinska [1972] Director/Project Manager [Polish/German]; Paul Leslie Cowling [1960] Director; Christian Rudiger Mockl [1973] Director [German]; Christian Moldan [1974] Director/Project Manager [German]; Richard Jennings Sandford [1971] Director/Head of Offshore Business Management; Silke Schulte [1966] Director/Corporate Strategy and Portfolio Management [German]; Karl Ben Smith [1977] Managing Director

H & A Recycling Limited
Incorporated: 23 August 2011 *Employees:* 51
Net Worth: £654,689 *Total Assets:* £5,166,684
Registered Office: 48 Arwenack Street, Falmouth, Cornwall, TR11 3JH
Activities: Collection of non-hazardous waste
Shareholders: Geoffrey Kim Alway; Allan Martin Holmes; Allan Martin Holmes; Geoffrey Kim Alway
Officers: Geoffrey Kim Alway [1959] Director; Allan Martin Holmes [1954] Director

H & R Healthcare Limited
Incorporated: 16 May 2006
Net Worth: £2,599,806 *Total Assets:* £5,032,315
Registered Office: The Clock Tower, Farleigh Court, Old Weston Road, Flax Bourton, Bristol, BS48 1UR
Activities: Other business support service activities n.e.c.
Major Shareholder: Michael Patrick Hoskins
Officers: Anne-Marie Hoskins, Secretary; Michael Patrick Hoskins [1958] Director

H.B.H. Woolacotts Limited
Incorporated: 28 August 1973 *Employees:* 154
Net Worth: £10,824,002 *Total Assets:* £17,586,236
Registered Office: 30 Queen Street, Bude, Cornwall, EX23 8BB
Activities: Electrical installation
Major Shareholder: Martin George Hemmerle
Officers: Denise Elizabeth Blundell, Secretary; Christopher Edward Hemmerle [1986] Director/Buyer; Elizabeth Anne Hemmerle [1990] Director/Retail Manager; Helmut Karl Hemmerle [1925] Director/Chairman; Kathleen Anne Hemmerle [1960] Director; Martin George Hemmerle [1960] Director-Sales

H.K.C. Europe Limited
Incorporated: 23 December 1996 *Employees:* 60
Net Worth: £5,073,653 *Total Assets:* £5,565,099
Registered Office: Stanton House Hotel, The Avenue, Stanton Fitzwarren, Swindon, Wilts, SN6 7SD
Activities: Hotels and similar accommodation
Parent: Honda Kaihatsu Company Limited
Officers: Yasuhiro Chiyoda, Secretary; John Robert Morris, Secretary; Yasuhiro Chiyoda [1967] Director [Japanese]; Shunichi Kikuchi [1962] Director [Japanese]

H.P.H. Limited
Incorporated: 25 March 1955
Net Worth: £18,365,712 *Total Assets:* £34,719,936
Registered Office: 6 Kingsmead Square, Bath, BA1 2AB
Activities: Buying and selling of own real estate
Officers: Anne Holdoway, Secretary; Alistair Thomas John Holdoway [1959] Director/Manager; Anne Holdoway [1963] Director/Specialist Dietitian; Dr Katrine Anne Holdoway [1951] Director/Geologist; Lindsay Iain Holdoway [1961] Director/Chartered Surveyor; Lysbeth McDonald Holdoway [1953] Director/Researcher

H2H Pharmacy Limited
Incorporated: 29 December 2003 *Employees:* 19
Net Worth: £1,385,558 *Total Assets:* £6,842,044
Registered Office: 37 Great Pulteney Street, Bath, BA2 4DA
Activities: Dispensing chemist in specialised stores
Officers: Mollie Audrey Salter, Secretary; Dr Peter Huw Green [1960] Director/General Practitioner; Rosemary Christine Green [1962] Director/GP; Michael Robert Salter [1954] Director/Pharmacist; Mollie Audrey Salter [1955] Director

HAB at Lovedon Fields Ltd
Incorporated: 15 May 2014
Net Worth: £839,578 *Total Assets:* £3,620,541
Registered Office: Unit D2, Southgate Commerce Park, Frome, Somerset, BA11 2RY
Activities: Development of building projects
Shareholders: Kevin McCloud; Thomas Bernard Jarman
Officers: David Justin Irving Hamer [1970] Director/Solicitor; Jeremy William Hopwood [1959] Director/Management Consultant

Hacche Retail Limited
Incorporated: 23 March 2016 *Employees:* 50
Net Worth: £1,131,069 *Total Assets:* £3,735,405
Registered Office: Stirling House, College Road, Cheltenham, Glos, GL53 7HY
Activities: Other publishing activities
Shareholders: Leo Ian Eccles; Jean-Christophe Viollet
Officers: Ruth Ballinger [1962] Director; Leo Ian Eccles [1978] Director; Robert Paul Nock [1971] Managing Director; Nicholas James Ponting [1966] Director; Jean-Christophe Viollet [1971] Director

John Hackling (Transport) Limited
Incorporated: 10 September 1964 *Employees:* 159
Net Worth: £15,044,373 *Total Assets:* £23,748,200
Registered Office: Hackling House, Bourton Industrial Park, Bourton on the Water, Cheltenham, Glos, GL54 2EP
Activities: Freight transport by road
Parent: John Hackling (Holdings) Ltd
Officers: Diane Hackling, Secretary; Kevin John Field [1966] Director; Dale Kenneth Hackling [1978] Director; Diane Hackling [1955] Director; John Hackling [1931] Director; Kenneth John Hackling [1955] Director/Transport Contractor; Stuart Anderson Mitchell [1967] Finance Director

Hackney Parish Almshouses Charity
Incorporated: 8 June 2010
Previous: Hackney Parish Almhouses Charity
Net Worth: £13,623,335 *Total Assets:* £14,838,762
Registered Office: 6 Trull Farm Buildings, Tetbury, Glos, GL8 8SQ
Activities: Other accommodation
Officers: Joannie Ann Andrews [1943] Director/Teacher; Jacqueline Driver [1961] Director/Chartered Accountant; Reverend Alexander Strathearn Gordon [1977] Director/Minister; Councillor Margaret Gordon [1964] Director/Local Councillor; Olivia Gordon [1977] Director/Architect; David John Horder [1944] Director; Jonathan Jarrett [1990] Director/Sales Consultant; Peter James Ottino [1933] Director/Retired Solicitor; John Arthur de Clifton Parmiter [1950] Director/Chartered Surveyor; Michael George Siggs [1935] Director/Chartered Surveyor; Andrew Wilson [1969] Director/Minister; Datoru Ben Paul Workia [1951] Director/Retired

Haine & Smith Partnership LLP
Incorporated: 5 February 2009 *Employees:* 144
Net Worth: £2,813,303 *Total Assets:* £3,611,684
Registered Office: Unit 7-8 Salisbury Road Business Park, Pewsey, Wilts, SN9 5PZ
Officers: Angela Lynne Davey [1975] Member; Mark Julian Simon Saunders [1961] Member; Susan Celia Haine [1946] LLP Member; Anna Lewin [1979] LLP Member; Thomas William Pears [1983] LLP Member; Jonathan Jeremy Pillinger [1957] LLP Member; Barry Jerome Smith [1939] LLP Member; Gary Andrew Walters [1958] LLP Member

W.R. Haines (Leasow Farms) Limited
Incorporated: 20 February 1973 *Employees:* 184
Net Worth: £1,536,178 *Total Assets:* £5,367,848
Registered Office: Castle Farm, Station Road, Chipping Campden, Glos, GL55 6JD
Activities: Mixed farming
Shareholders: Martin Eric Haines; William Rimell Haines
Officers: Phoebe Mary Haines, Secretary; Martin Eric Haines [1964] Director; William Rimell Haines [1962] Director

Hale & Co. (Drybrook) Ltd
Incorporated: 29 December 1960 *Employees:* 59
Previous: Hale and Co. (Drybrook) Limited
Net Worth: £6,350,136 *Total Assets:* £7,220,481
Registered Office: The Sawmills, Nailbridge, Drybrook, Glos, GL17 9JW
Activities: Agents involved in the sale of timber and building materials
Parent: Drybrook Holdings Limited
Officers: Leslie Hale, Secretary; Jacob David Hale [1981] Director/General Manager; Jane Catherine Hale [1952] Director/Secretary; Leslie Hale [1952] Director/Chartered Accountant; Samuel Benjamin Hale [1985] Director/Building Consultant

Halewell Limited
Incorporated: 24 November 2016 *Employees:* 3
Net Worth: £9,623,323 *Total Assets:* £11,888,534
Registered Office: Old Library Chambers, 21 Chipper Lane, Salisbury, Wilts, SP1 1BG
Activities: Other business support service activities n.e.c.
Officers: Luke Callaghan [1978] Director; Mats Gunnar Heiman [1950] Director [Swedish]

William Haley Engineering Limited
Incorporated: 13 February 1986 *Employees:* 57
Net Worth: £3,611,446 *Total Assets:* £4,747,655
Registered Office: Bellcombe Works, East Brent, Highbridge, Somerset, TA9 4DB
Activities: Manufacture of metal structures and parts of structures
Officers: Will John Haley [1974] Director/General Manager; William John Haley [1946] Director/Engineer

Haley Securities Limited
Incorporated: 30 April 1990 *Employees:* 152
Net Worth: £14,531,186 *Total Assets:* £17,122,276
Registered Office: Bellcombe Works, East Brent, Highbridge, Somerset, TA9 4DB
Activities: Activities of head offices
Officers: Will John Haley [1974] Director/General Manager; William John Haley [1946] Director; Alexandra Catherine Haley Serra [1980] Director/Chartered Civil Engineer

Half Moon Bay Limited
Incorporated: 22 November 1995 *Employees:* 42
Net Worth: £3,277,692 *Total Assets:* £4,945,873
Registered Office: The Icehouse, 124 Walcot Street, Bath, BA2 5BG
Activities: Wholesale of household goods (other than musical instruments) n.e.c
Parent: The Pulteney Mews Group Limited
Officers: Sally Louise Thompson, Secretary; Peter John Thompson [1965] Director; Sally Louise Thompson [1965] Director

Halix Limited
Incorporated: 18 March 1981 *Employees:* 102
Net Worth: £1,892,960 *Total Assets:* £5,202,348
Registered Office: The Royal Exeter Hotel, Exeter Road, Bournemouth, BH2 5AG
Activities: Hotels and similar accommodation
Parent: Brewers of Nuneham Limited
Officers: Jane Susannah Brewer, Secretary; Harry Jack Brewer [1976] Director

Hall & Woodhouse Limited
Incorporated: 8 June 1898 *Employees:* 1,419
Net Worth: £118,890,000 *Total Assets:* £206,032,992
Registered Office: The Brewery, Blandford St Mary, Dorset, DT11 9LS
Activities: Manufacture of beer
Officers: Marianne Susie Jarvis, Secretary; Timothy Clarke [1957] Director; Lucinda Rachel Gray [1979] Director; David Harry Christopher Hoare [1964] Director; Mark James [1972] Director/Solicitor; Matthew Richard Kearsey [1972] Director; Dean James Livesey [1977] Director; Michael James Owen [1970] Finance Director; James Martin Scott [1959] Director; Michael Anthony Street [1947] Director; Anthony William Woodhouse [1965] Director; Mark John Michael Woodhouse [1955] Director

Halos Garden Amusement Limited
Incorporated: 23 January 2017 *Employees:* 305
Net Worth: £70,932,976 *Total Assets:* £71,441,480
Registered Office: 60-66 The Horsefair, Bristol, BS1 3DX
Activities: Gambling and betting activities
Parent: Gamecube Leisure Group Limited
Officers: Martin NG [1989] Director; Theodora NG [1993] Marketing Director

Halsall Construction Limited
Incorporated: 17 February 1989 *Employees:* 61
Net Worth: £2,619,451 *Total Assets:* £13,689,065
Registered Office: 1 Roman Way, Bath Business Park, Peasedown St John, Bath, BA2 8SG
Activities: Development of building projects
Parent: Shepperton Group Ltd
Officers: Graham Peter Braddick, Secretary; Graham Peter Braddick [1963] Finance Director; Andrew Barrie Corp [1976] Director; Gavin Kenneth Davis [1955] Director/Builder; Roy Power [1947] Director; Gary Paul Winsor [1987] Operations Director

Hamblys Limited
Incorporated: 20 November 2008 *Employees:* 65
Net Worth: £2,083,675 *Total Assets:* £5,882,128
Registered Office: Pennygillam Way, Pennygillam Industrial Estate, Launceston, Cornwall, PL15 7ED
Activities: Repair of machinery
Parent: Barrett Partnership Limited
Officers: Jeanne Ann Barrett, Secretary; Abel William John Barrett [1944] Director/Agricultural Engineer; Stephen John Barrett [1972] Director; Stephen Grenville Perryman [1959] Director/Sales Manager

Hameln Pharmaceuticals Ltd
Incorporated: 14 December 1971 *Employees:* 22
Net Worth: £9,826,141 *Total Assets:* £13,764,480
Registered Office: Nexus, Hurricane Road, Gloucester Business Park, Gloucester, GL3 4AG
Activities: Wholesale of pharmaceutical goods
Major Shareholder: Christoph Kerstein
Officers: Stephen Allen Watkin, Secretary/Managing Director; Christoph Kerstein [1961] Director/Pharmacist [German]; Stephen Allen Watkin [1967] Managing Director

Hamilton Scott Estates Limited
Incorporated: 31 August 1999 *Employees:* 2
Net Worth: £6,938,847 *Total Assets:* £6,976,319
Registered Office: 118 Old Milton Road, New Milton, Hants, BH25 6EB
Activities: Other letting and operating of own or leased real estate
Shareholders: Philip Scott Wilson; Jane Hamilton Wilson
Officers: Jane Hamilton Wilson, Secretary/Director; Jane Hamilton Wilson [1966] Director; Philip Scott Wilson [1962] Director

Hammett Investments Limited
Incorporated: 22 April 1959 *Employees:* 1
Net Worth: £10,989,147 *Total Assets:* £11,912,749
Registered Office: 6-8 Bath Street, Bristol, BS1 6HL
Activities: Other letting and operating of own or leased real estate
Major Shareholder: Margaret Patricia Hammett
Officers: Margaret Patricia Hammett, Secretary; Margaret Patricia Hammett [1952] Director/Secretary

A. Hammond & Sons Limited
Incorporated: 7 October 1959 *Employees:* 48
Net Worth: £6,047,722 *Total Assets:* £7,866,497
Registered Office: Worton House, Church Street, Sturminster Newton, Dorset, DT10 1DB
Activities: Development of building projects
Major Shareholder: Philip Lionel Hammond
Officers: Philip Lionel Hammond, Secretary; Chris Eaton [1980] Director/Quantity Surveyor; Philip Lionel Hammond [1958] Building Director; Benjamin Hobley [1968] Director; Robert John Pritchard [1958] Director/Estimating

The Hampshire Motor Investment Company Limited
Incorporated: 30 June 2011
Net Worth: £2,161,000 *Total Assets:* £12,760,000
Registered Office: Mercedes-Benz of Poole, 1 Holes Bay Road, Poole, Dorset, BH15 2BD
Activities: Other service activities n.e.c.
Parent: Sandown Motors Limited
Officers: Gareth Robert Copling, Secretary; Gareth Robert Copling [1967] Director; Gavin Alan McAllister [1981] Director

Hampton House Properties Limited
Incorporated: 23 April 1990 *Employees:* 2
Net Worth: £1,054,797 *Total Assets:* £5,447,337
Registered Office: 26-28 Southernhay East, Exeter, Devon, EX1 1NS
Activities: Other letting and operating of own or leased real estate
Major Shareholder: Rosemary Elizabeth Thomas
Officers: Rosemary Elizabeth Thomas, Secretary; Richard Brian Thomas [1953] Director/Chartered Accountant; Rosemary Elizabeth Thomas [1953] Director/Property Manager

Hampton Printing (Bristol) Limited
Incorporated: 26 June 1991 *Employees:* 59
Net Worth: £2,287,298 *Total Assets:* £5,080,421
Registered Office: Bradley Road, Royal Portbury, Bristol, BS20 7TT
Activities: Printing n.e.c.
Major Shareholder: Michael John Malpas
Officers: Michael John Malpas [1960] Director

Hamworthy Combustion Engineering Limited
Incorporated: 18 January 1962 *Employees:* 93
Net Worth: £11,346,000 *Total Assets:* £19,362,000
Registered Office: Fleets Corner, Poole, Dorset, BH17 0LA
Activities: Manufacture of ovens, furnaces and furnace burners
Parent: Koch Chemical Technology Group Limited
Officers: Paul Richard Newman, Secretary; Casey Jay Chambers [1971] Director/Business Executive [American]; Eduardo Emilio Couceiro [1968] Director/Finance Controller [Italian]; Paul Richard Newman [1966] Director/Business Executive; Anthony Saia [1959] Director

Handston Investments Limited
Incorporated: 24 October 1983 *Employees:* 1
Net Worth: £10,321,870 *Total Assets:* £17,350,550
Registered Office: Handston Court, Throop Road, Throop, Bournemouth, BH8 0DL
Activities: Other letting and operating of own or leased real estate
Major Shareholder: Graham Clifford Hands
Officers: Graham Clifford Hands [1958] Director

G.J.Handy & Company Limited
Incorporated: 8 July 1955 *Employees:* 65
Net Worth: £6,271,368 *Total Assets:* £11,663,235
Registered Office: Handy Distribution, Murdock Road, Dorcan, Swindon, Wilts, SN3 5HY
Activities: Non-specialised wholesale trade
Major Shareholder: Simon Alister Belcher
Officers: Derek Lawrence Belcher, Secretary; Stephen Bartlett [1978] Operations Director; Derek Lawrence Belcher [1947] Director/Chairman; Diane Susan Belcher [1944] Director; Simon Alister Belcher [1973] Managing Director; Mark Andrew Moseley [1969] Sales Director

Hanford Holdings Limited
Incorporated: 5 December 1962
Net Worth: £4,214,273 *Total Assets:* £4,402,880
Registered Office: Crown Chambers, Bridge Street, Salisbury, Wilts, SP1 2LZ
Activities: Other letting and operating of own or leased real estate
Parent: Pentera Trustees Limited
Officers: Audrey Catherine Spencer, Secretary; Audrey Catherine Spencer [1958] Director; Ingram Spencer [1951] Director

Hanford School Charitable Trust Limited
Incorporated: 9 January 1991 *Employees:* 62
Net Worth: £15,282,391 *Total Assets:* £16,300,016
Registered Office: Hanford School, Child Okeford, Blandford Forum, Dorset, DT11 8HN
Activities: Primary education
Officers: Felicity Speers, Secretary; Giles David Anderson [1970] Director/Publisher; Amelia Brooks [1974] Director/Headmaster's Wife; Phillip Evitt [1959] Director/Headmaster; Andrew David Hussey [1961] Director; Brigadier Alexander Thomas Lindsay Potts [1968] Director/Army Officer; Kate Mary Saker [1965] Director/Private Secretary; Michael Steinmetz [1964] Director/Sales President [American]; Christophe Nigel Paul Stourton [1965] Director/Consultant; Lucinda Jane Frances Sunnucks [1962] Director; Sarah Joan Thomas [1961] Director/Headmistress; Charlotte Watson [1960] Director/Solicitor; Catherine Cecilia White [1973] Director/Events Organiser; Clare Mary Magdalene Witheridge [1973] Marketing Director

Hannick Homes & Developments Limited
Incorporated: 5 December 1978 *Employees:* 9
Net Worth: £12,665,737 *Total Assets:* £15,519,442
Registered Office: Dammas House, Dammas Lane, Old Town, Swindon, Wilts, SN1 3EF
Activities: Development of building projects
Shareholders: Nicholas Francis Cleverley; Hannah Margaret Cleverley
Officers: Hannah Margaret Cleverley, Secretary; Hannah Margaret Cleverley [1976] Director; Nicholas Francis Cleverley [1975] Director

R. Hannon Limited
Incorporated: 14 December 1983 *Employees:* 103
Net Worth: £12,450,751 *Total Assets:* £13,684,744
Registered Office: Herridge Farm House, Collingbourne Ducis, Marlborough, Wilts, SN8 3EG
Activities: Raising of other animals
Parent: Richard Hannon Settlement
Officers: Josephine Anne Hannon, Secretary; Josephine Anne Hannon [1944] Director; Richard Hannon [1975] Director/Racehorse Trainer; Richard Michael Hannon [1945] Director/Racehorse Trainer

Hanwey LLP
Incorporated: 5 March 2010
Net Worth: £12,203,000 *Total Assets:* £15,817,000
Registered Office: 18 Whiteladies Road, Bristol, BS8 2LG
Officers: Helen Loxie Goddard-Watts [1970] Member; Mark Goddard-Watts [1961] Member; Jennifer Catherine Goddard-Watts [1938] LLP Member; Jon Ivan Goddard-Watts [1930] LLP Member

Happold LLP
Incorporated: 4 October 2007 *Employees:* 1,672
Net Worth: £34,377,000 *Total Assets:* £94,123,000
Registered Office: Camden Mill, Lower Bristol Road, Bath, BA2 3DQ
Officers: Neil Keith Billett [1967] Member; Paul Rogers [1965] Member; Neil Richard Squibbs [1961] Member; Andrew Stephen Best [1966] LLP Member; Matthew John Birchall [1971] LLP Member; Ian Booth [1972] LLP Member; Andrew Peter Comer [1955] LLP Member; Dr Michael John Cook [1955] LLP Member; Zbigniew Czajewski [1974] LLP Member; Philip Stephen Dalglish [1960] LLP Member; Michael Entwistle [2015] LLP Member; Denzil Gallagher [1970] LLP Member; Nicholas Martin Greenwood [1964] LLP Member; Alan John Harbinson [1964] LLP Member; David John Herd [1969] LLP Member; Anil Rama Hira [1955] LLP Member; Stephen Jolly [1966] LLP Member; Andrew Stuart Keelin [1966] LLP Member; Georghios Keliris [1975] LLP Member; Padraic Kelly [1954] LLP Member; Jarek Kujawa [1956] LLP Member; Davood Liaghat [1962] LLP Member; Karl Lyndon [1968] LLP Member; Ian David Maddocks [1966] LLP Member; Wolf Mangelsdorf [1967] LLP Member; Roderick Leggat Birch Manson [1965] LLP Member; Richard Brian Marshall [1969] LLP Member; Krishnendu Mukherjee [1969] LLP Member; Christian William Anderson Murdoch [1963] LLP Member; Nicholas Patrick Nelson [1959] LLP Member; Roger John Nickells [1968] LLP Member; Angus Benett Palmer [1965] LLP Member; Andrew David Parker [1963] LLP Member; Mark Phillip [1968] LLP Member; Justin Phillips [1967] LLP Member; Oliver Charles Pelham Plunkett [1972] LLP Member; Dr Sarah Prichard [1974] LLP Member; Alasdair Lawrie Robertson [1974] LLP Member; Craig Michael Schwitter [1967] LLP Member; Andrea Scotti [1978] LLP Member; Patrick John Smallbone [1958] LLP Member; Matthew Christopher Smith [1966] LLP Member; David Gavin Thompson [1965] LLP Member; Alan David Travers [1953] LLP Member; Simon Victor Wainwright [1964] LLP Member; Steven Williamson [1967] LLP Member; Christopher Jeremy Dorning Young [1954] LLP Member

Happy Days South West Limited
Incorporated: 17 June 2003 *Employees:* 193
Net Worth: £1,207,336 *Total Assets:* £4,941,275
Registered Office: Happy Days Nurseries, Chapel Town, Summercourt, Newquay, Cornwall, TR8 5YA
Activities: Pre-primary education
Parent: Happy Days Consultancy Limited
Officers: Ian Mark Sanders, Secretary; Jacqueline Ann Arthur [1954] Managing Director; Joanne Beighton [1968] Childcare & Education Director; Kim Herbert [1974] Operations Director; Kevin William Higgs [1967] Development Director; Ian Mark Sanders [1974] Finance Director

Harbour Hospitality Group Limited
Incorporated: 20 September 2017 *Employees:* 3
Net Worth Deficit: £4 *Total Assets:* £7,249,119
Registered Office: Harbour House, 60 Purewell, Christchurch, Dorset, BH23 1ES
Activities: Activities of other holding companies n.e.c.
Parent: Harbour International Limited
Officers: Stuart Andrew Bateman [1976] Director; David Francis Robbins [1967] Director/Accountant; Michael Oliver Warren [1970] Director [Irish]

Harbour Hotels Group Limited
Incorporated: 27 February 2015 *Employees:* 833
Net Worth: £40,204,040 *Total Assets:* £228,110,912
Registered Office: Harbour House, 60 Purewell, Christchurch, Dorset, BH23 1ES
Activities: Activities of head offices
Parent: Harbour Hotels Holdings Limited
Officers: Stuart Andrew Bateman [1976] Director; David Francis Robbins [1967] Finance Director; Michael Oliver Warren [1970] Director [Irish]

Harbour Hotels Holdings Limited
Incorporated: 9 December 2015 *Employees:* 854
Net Worth: £102,465,392 *Total Assets:* £312,770,944
Registered Office: Harbour House, 60 Purewell, Christchurch, Dorset, BH23 1ES
Activities: Activities of head offices
Major Shareholder: Nicolas James Roach
Officers: Stuart Andrew Bateman [1976] Director; David Francis Robbins [1967] Director

Harbour International Limited
Incorporated: 18 April 2017 *Employees:* 854
Net Worth: £48,969,440 *Total Assets:* £298,841,984
Registered Office: Harbour House, 60 Purewell, Christchurch, Dorset, BH23 1ES
Activities: Activities of other holding companies n.e.c.
Parent: Harbour Hotels Holdings Limited
Officers: Stuart Andrew Bateman [1976] Director; David Francis Robbins [1967] Director/Accountant

Harbourside Learning Partnership
Incorporated: 4 May 2016 *Employees:* 454
Net Worth: £3,611,553 *Total Assets:* £9,205,521
Registered Office: Oakdale Junior School, School Lane, Poole, Dorset, BH15 3JR
Activities: Primary education
Officers: Fiona Bannister [1971] Director/Teacher; Derek Malcolm Bayley [1972] Director/MIS Consultant; Martin James Baynham-Knight [1978] Director/Financial Strategy Manager; Rev Michael Maurice Camp [1952] Director/Parish Priest; Paul Thomas Howieson [1974] Director/Headteacher; Emma Jane Jackson [1974] Director; Brendan Gerard McCarthy [1962] Director/Retired Solicitor; Amanda Louise Procter [1971] Director/Head of Marketing; Sarah Louise Spivey [1973] Managing Director; Matthew Patrick Waterfall [1984] Director/Head of Finance

Harbourstar Limited
Incorporated: 10 September 2007 *Employees:* 43
Net Worth: £10,539,218 *Total Assets:* £17,225,552
Registered Office: Gordano Gate, Serbert Road, Portishead, Bristol, BS20 7GG
Activities: Non-specialised wholesale trade
Major Shareholder: Darren Paul Evans
Officers: Paul Ashley Marks, Secretary; Colin John Christison [1964] Director; Darren Paul Evans [1961] Director

Hardenhuish School Limited
Incorporated: 12 August 2010 *Employees:* 216
Net Worth: £20,237,698 *Total Assets:* £21,706,526
Registered Office: Hardenhuish School, Hardenhuish Lane, Chippenham, Wilts, SN14 6RJ
Activities: General secondary education
Officers: Debbie Gail Bennett [1967] Director/Teacher; Isabel Mary Blackburn [1947] Director/Retired Civil Servant; Sheila Diane Copeman [1970] Director; Sally Dellar [1976] Director/Office Manager; Trevor John Eddolls [1953] Director/Hypnotherapist; Paul Ronald Fox [1977] Director/Teacher; Robert Arthur Head [1949] Director/R & D Officer; Kirsten Mary Martin [1964] Director/Assignment Editor; Lisa Jill Percy [1971] Director/Headteacher; David Leslie Rousell [1976] Director/Proprietor Removals Company; Isabelle Lucile Michelle Semichon [1971] Director [French]; John Spencer Shaw [1969] Director/Christian Minister; Lisa Margaret Titcomb [1963] Director/Researcher; Jacqueline Rose Todd [1968] Director/Pastoral Manager; Philip Townsend [1967] Director/R&D Engineer; Vivian Arthur Vines [1947] Director/Architectural & Planning Consultant; Scott Weekes [1974] Director/Engineering Officer; Nicola Louise Wood [1963] Director

J.M.Harding & Partners Limited
Incorporated: 16 June 1960 *Employees:* 4
Net Worth: £10,281,805 *Total Assets:* £11,452,868
Registered Office: 310 Bournemouth Road, Parkstone, Poole, Dorset, BH14 9AR
Activities: Renting and operating of Housing Association real estate
Shareholder: John Sydenham Whitelock
Officers: Nicole Pauline Mary Whitelock, Secretary; Michael John Shrewsbury Harding [1948] Director/Farmer; Nicholas Anthony Harding [1954] Director; John Sydenham Whitelock [1949] Director/Building Contractor; Nicole Pauline Mary Whitelock [1956] Director

J.R. Harding & Sons (Frome) Limited
Incorporated: 25 June 1975 *Employees:* 47
Net Worth: £8,112,082 *Total Assets:* £8,701,460
Registered Office: Manor Furlong, Marston Trading Estate, Frome, Somerset, BA11 4RJ
Activities: Freight transport by road
Officers: John David Harding, Secretary; David John Harding [1964] Director; John David Harding [1945] Director; Raymond Kenneth Harding [1949] Director; Roger Keith Harding [1959] Director; Stephen Peter Harding [1955] Director

Harding & Sons,Limited
Incorporated: 23 May 1929 *Employees:* 68
Net Worth: £9,260,208 *Total Assets:* £11,042,513
Registered Office: 184 Billacombe Road, Plymstock, Plymouth, PL9 7HE
Activities: Retail sale of carpets, rugs, wall and floor coverings in specialised stores
Officers: Peter Anthony Harding, Secretary; Penelope Helen Craze [1971] Director; John Michael Harding [1947] Director; Peter Anthony Harding [1973] Director

Harding Brothers Retail Limited
Incorporated: 23 February 2007 *Employees:* 145
Net Worth: £15,566,263 *Total Assets:* £55,901,240
Registered Office: Avonmouth Way, Avonmouth, Bristol, BS11 8DD
Activities: Other retail sale in non-specialised stores
Parent: Harding Brothers Holdings Limited
Officers: Carlo Bernasconi [1960] Director [Swiss]; Mark Birnie [1969] Director; Ayyaswamy Choodamani [1958] Director/Accountant [Indian]; Neil Graham Harding [1962] Director; Deepak Khetan [1973] Finance Director [Indian]; James Keir Prescott [1968] Buying Director

Peter Harding Practice Limited
Incorporated: 16 April 2003 *Employees:* 19
Net Worth: £6,909,450 *Total Assets:* £7,491,119
Registered Office: Tucks House, Foyle Hill, Shaftesbury, Dorset, SP7 0AG
Activities: Life insurance
Major Shareholder: Peter Richard Harding
Officers: Susannah Beverley Harding, Secretary; Peter Richard Harding [1966] Director/Insurance Consultant

Hardrock Developments Limited
Incorporated: 6 November 2015
Net Worth: £2,429,904 *Total Assets:* £53,176,376
Registered Office: 45 Oakfield Road, Clifton, Bristol, BS8 2AX
Activities: Construction of domestic buildings
Officers: Christopher Mark Edwards [1970] Main Contractor Director; Francis Timothy Firmstone [1968] Director; Edward William Bernard Gunnery [1975] Director/Property Developer; Andrew Hillyer Scott [1952] Director/Investor; Archie Erskine Ward [1990] Director/Property Developer; Edward John Ware [1960] Director/Property Investor/Developer

Hardware Group Limited
Incorporated: 17 September 2012 *Employees:* 5
Net Worth: £4,083,000 *Total Assets:* £11,171,000
Registered Office: Wellington House, Kemble Enterprise Park, Kemble, Cirencester, Glos, GL7 6BQ
Activities: Wholesale of computers, computer peripheral equipment and software
Parent: Hardware Holdings Limited
Officers: David Richard Galton-Fenzi [1969] Director; Gwyn David Hicks [1971] Director/Chief Financial Officer; Stewart Holness [1966] Director; Nicholas Julian Moglia [1959] Director

Hardware Holdings Limited
Incorporated: 21 April 2015 *Employees:* 137
Net Worth: £904,000 *Total Assets:* £16,728,000
Registered Office: Wellington House, Kemble Enterprise Park, Kemble, Cirencester, Glos, GL7 6BQ
Activities: Activities of head offices
Major Shareholder: Rory James Wordsworth Sweet
Officers: David Richard Galton-Fenzi [1969] Director; Gwyn David Hicks [1971] Director/Chief Financial Officer; Stewart Holness [1966] Director; Rory James Wordsworth Sweet [1967] Director

Hardware Services Limited
Incorporated: 8 December 2009 *Employees:* 48
Net Worth Deficit: £1,361,000 *Total Assets:* £9,320,000
Registered Office: Wellington House, Kemble Enterprise Park, Kemble, Cirencester, Glos, GL7 6BQ
Activities: Other business support service activities n.e.c.
Parent: The Simian Group Limited
Officers: David Richard Galton-Fenzi [1969] Director; Gwyn David Hicks [1971] Director/Chief Financial Officer; Stewart Holness [1966] Director

Hardware UK Limited
Incorporated: 10 April 2001 *Employees:* 47
Net Worth: £7,573,000 *Total Assets:* £22,331,000
Registered Office: Wellington House, Cirencester, Glos, GL7 6BQ
Activities: Wholesale of computers, computer peripheral equipment and software
Parent: The Simian Group Limited
Officers: David Richard Galton-Fenzi [1969] Director; Gwyn David Hicks [1971] Director/Chief Financial Officer; Stewart Holness [1966] Director

The Thomas Hardye Multi Academy Trust
Incorporated: 21 June 2011 *Employees:* 294
Previous: The Thomas Hardye School
Net Worth Deficit: £203,000 *Total Assets:* £5,975,000
Registered Office: Queens Avenue, Dorchester, DT1 2ET
Activities: General secondary education
Officers: Martin Peter Baker [1956] Director; Garry Peter Batt [1956] Director/Fine Art Auctioneer; Katherine Lynne Cove [1947] Director/Retired Social Worker; Michael Foley [1961] Director/Headteacher; Matthew Charles Haines [1983] Director/Chartered Accountant; Sheila Johns [1964] Director

The Hargrave Foundation
Incorporated: 4 October 2004
Net Worth: £3,642,199 *Total Assets:* £3,646,183
Registered Office: Alexandra House, St Johns Street, Salisbury, Wilts, SP1 2SB
Activities: Other business support service activities n.e.c.
Officers: Stephen Thomas Hargrave [1955] Director; Dominic Richard Sheridan Moseley [1955] Director/Marketing Consultant; Mark Adam Parkin [1954] Director/Economist

Hargreaves Lansdown Advisory Services Limited
Incorporated: 13 February 1998 *Employees:* 145
Net Worth: £14,615,882 *Total Assets:* £30,232,568
Registered Office: 1 College Square South, Anchor Road, Bristol, BS1 5HL
Activities: Financial intermediation not elsewhere classified
Parent: Hargreaves Lansdown PLC
Officers: Alison Zobel, Secretary; Robert James Byett [1974] Compliance & Risk Director; David Dieter Davies [1977] Marketing Director; Christopher Frederick Hill [1971] Director/Chief Financial Officer; Ian James Hunter [1972] Marketing Director; Philip Michael Johnson [1971] Director/Chief Financial Officer

Hargreaves Lansdown Asset Management Limited
Incorporated: 18 March 1985
Net Worth: £114,450,000 *Total Assets:* £559,984,000
Registered Office: 1 College Square South, Anchor Road, Bristol, BS1 5HL
Activities: Activities auxiliary to financial intermediation n.e.c.
Parent: Hargreaves Lansdown PLC
Officers: Alison Zobel, Secretary; Robert James Byett [1974] Compliance & Risk Director; Heather Ruth Cooper [1963] Director/Chief People Officer; Mark William Dampier [1956] Director/Investment Manager; David Dieter Davies [1977] Director; Lee Nathan Gardhouse [1973] Director; Christopher Frederick Hill [1971] Director/Chief Financial Officer; Ian James Hunter [1972] Investment Marketing Director; Philip Michael Johnson [1971] Director/Chief Financial Officer; Christopher James Worle [1982] Digital Marketing Director

Hargreaves Lansdown Fund Managers Ltd.
Incorporated: 15 April 1992 *Employees:* 15
Net Worth: £21,906,000 *Total Assets:* £55,269,000
Registered Office: 1 College Square South, Anchor Road, Bristol, BS1 5HL
Activities: Fund management activities
Parent: Hargreaves Lansdown PLC
Officers: Alison Zobel, Secretary; Robert James Byett [1974] Compliance & Risk Director; Lee Nathan Gardhouse [1973] Director/Fund Manager; Christopher Frederick Hill [1971] Director/Chief Financial Officer; Philip Michael Johnson [1971] Director/Chief Financial Officer; Christopher James Worle [1982] Digital Marketing Director

Hargreaves Lansdown PLC
Incorporated: 10 April 1987
Net Worth: £171,800,000 *Total Assets:* £261,000,000
Registered Office: One College Square South, Anchor Road, Bristol, BS1 5HL
Activities: Activities of financial services holding companies
Officers: Alison Zobel, Secretary; Fiona Jane Clutterbuck [1958] Director; Shirley Jill Garrood [1957] Director; Christopher Frederick Hill [1971] Director/Chief Financial Officer; Philip Michael Johnson [1971] Director/Chief Financial Officer; Deanna Oppenheimer [1958] Director [American]; Roger Perkin [1948] Director; Stephen Peter Robertson [1954] Director; Jayne Elizabeth Styles [1960] Director

Haringey Schools Services Limited
Incorporated: 5 June 2000 *Employees:* 2
Net Worth: £841,000 *Total Assets:* £21,851,000
Registered Office: Third Floor, Broad Quay House, Prince Street, Bristol, BS1 4DJ
Activities: Renting and operating of Housing Association real estate
Parent: Semperian PPP Investment Partners No.2 Limited
Officers: Steven McGeown [1985] Director/Chartered Accountant

Harkwell Labels Limited
Incorporated: 14 January 2003 *Employees:* 19
Net Worth: £2,837,067 *Total Assets:* £4,531,479
Registered Office: Unit 2 Aston Way, Poole, Dorset, BH12 4FE
Activities: Other manufacturing n.e.c.
Major Shareholder: Timothy Neville Fountain
Officers: Jonathan Cooke [1970] Financial Director; Charlie Fountain [1998] Director; Harry Fountain [1998] Director; Timothy Neville Fountain [1964] Director/Printer; Ronald Barry Halliday [1955] Sales Director

Harland Developments Limited
Incorporated: 16 November 1987
Net Worth: £4,449,162 *Total Assets:* £5,953,430
Registered Office: 325 Wimborne Road West, Stapehill, Wimborne, Dorset, BH21 7NW
Activities: Other letting and operating of own or leased real estate
Parent: Harland Investments Limited
Officers: Hugh Malone, Secretary; Joseph Alexander Luxton [1989] Director/Property Developer; Rodney Alexander Luxton [1939] Director/Fleet Engineer; Derek Malone [1976] Director/Accountant; Hugh Malone [1948] Director/Chartered Accountant

Harlequin Homes (UK) Limited
Incorporated: 21 January 2014 *Employees:* 5
Net Worth: £265,084 *Total Assets:* £5,811,793
Registered Office: The Old Exchange, 521 Wimborne Road East, Ferndown, Dorset, BH22 9NH
Activities: Development of building projects
Officers: Robert John Atkins [1965] Director; Mark Andrew Wingfield [1964] Director

Harlequinns Bowling and Leisure Limited
Incorporated: 4 February 2000
Net Worth Deficit: £19,246 *Total Assets:* £3,594,732
Registered Office: Kernick Farm, Otterham, Camelford, Cornwall, PL32 9SZ
Activities: Management of real estate on a fee or contract basis
Major Shareholder: Richard Mark Quinn
Officers: Kathryn Elizabeth Quinn, Secretary; Rachael Marion Quinn [1971] Director/Manager; Richard Mark Quinn [1966] Director/Farmer

Harmer Properties Limited
Incorporated: 24 May 1940 *Employees:* 6
Net Worth: £9,186,326 *Total Assets:* £10,462,481
Registered Office: Stafford House, Blackbrook Park Avenue, Taunton, Somerset, TA1 2PX
Activities: Other letting and operating of own or leased real estate
Officers: Dr John Howard Tripp, Secretary; Gary Cox [1958] Director; Esther Anne Foster [1976] Director/Accountant; Duncan John Randell Moll [1969] Director/Business Systems Consultant; Daniel Mark Peskett [1980] Director/Marine Engineer, Royal Navy; Dr John Howard Tripp [1944] Director/Consultant Paediatrician

Harmon (Form Tools) Limited
Incorporated: 29 May 1964 *Employees:* 182
Net Worth: £2,754,551 *Total Assets:* £7,346,466
Registered Office: 3 Durrant Road, Bournemouth, BH2 6LE
Activities: Cold forming or folding
Shareholders: Robert Harmon; David Harmon; Ian Christian Harmon
Officers: Kim Lorna Harmon, Secretary; David Harmon [1958] Director; Ian Christian Harmon [1966] Director; Robert Harmon [1955] Director

Harper's Holdings Limited
Incorporated: 15 June 2009 *Employees:* 3
Net Worth: £4,318,910 *Total Assets:* £4,651,836
Registered Office: Trepolye Farm House, North Tamerton, Holsworthy, Devon, EX22 6RL
Activities: Mixed farming
Major Shareholder: William Peter Harper
Officers: Suzanne Linda Harper [1953] Director/Farmer; William Peter Harper [1955] Director/Nutritionist

Harper's Home Mix Limited
Incorporated: 4 August 1992 *Employees:* 67
Net Worth: £6,064,558 *Total Assets:* £8,396,240
Registered Office: Waldon Way, Holsworthy Industrial Estate, Holsworthy, Devon, EX22 6ER
Activities: Manufacture of prepared feeds for farm animals
Parent: Massey Bros (Feeds) Ltd
Officers: George Kynan Ardern Massey, Secretary; Andrew John Davies [1975] Operations Director; William Peter Harper [1955] Director/Animal Feed Nutritionist; Glenton Charles Johns [1971] Sales Director; George Kynan Ardern Massey [1969] Director/Animal Feed Manufacturer; Richard Thomas Massey [1944] Director/Animal Feed Manufacturer

Harrier Print Ltd
Incorporated: 29 February 2012
Net Worth: £8,990,411 *Total Assets:* £12,689,464
Registered Office: Truprint, Brunel Road, Newton Abbot, Devon, TQ12 4UH
Activities: Printing n.e.c.
Shareholder: Neil Donald Cohen
Officers: Christopher John Hughes [1966] Managing Director

Harris & Harris Construction Limited
Incorporated: 14 March 1991 *Employees:* 118
Net Worth: £2,229,387 *Total Assets:* £6,494,523
Registered Office: Unit 1e Polden Business Centre, Bristol Road, Bridgwater, Somerset, TA6 4AW
Activities: Development of building projects
Shareholders: Anthony John Harris; Jane Elizabeth Harris
Officers: Anthony John Hill, Secretary; Anthony John Harris [1962] Director/Building Developer; Gary Anthony Harris [1985] Director; Jane Elizabeth Harris [1962] Director/Secretary; John Terence Mounter [1982] Director/Quantity Surveyor

Harris Bros. and Collard Limited
Incorporated: 9 November 1961 *Employees:* 21
Net Worth: £3,354,820 *Total Assets:* £4,000,515
Registered Office: 1 East Quay Park, East Quay, Bridgwater, Somerset, TA6 4DB
Activities: Development of building projects
Major Shareholder: Stephen and Paula Travis
Officers: Paula Juliet Travis, Secretary; Stephen Mark Travis [1963] Director; Thomas Stephen Travis [1989] Director/Chartered Surveyor

Harris Construction Limited
Incorporated: 18 January 2007 *Employees:* 118
Net Worth: £1,276,837 *Total Assets:* £5,625,982
Registered Office: Unit 1e Polden Business Centre, Bristol Road, Bridgwater, Somerset, TA6 4AW
Activities: Activities of head offices
Shareholders: Anthony John Harris; Jane Elizabeth Harris
Officers: Anthony John Hill, Secretary; Anthony John Harris [1962] Director/Building Developer; Jane Elizabeth Harris [1962] Director/Secretary

Harris Fowler Limited
Incorporated: 4 August 2009 *Employees:* 92
Net Worth: £4,320,115 *Total Assets:* £9,526,930
Registered Office: 6 Hammet Street, Taunton, Somerset, TA1 1RZ
Activities: Solicitors
Shareholders: Grant Thomas Fowler; Neil Russell Williams
Officers: Grant Thomas Fowler [1966] Director/Solicitor; Andrew Christopher Holcombe [1973] Director/Senior Fee Earner; Timothy Peter Edward Jenkins [1966] Practice Director; Neil Russell Williams [1965] Director/Solicitor

Harrison Products Co Limited
Incorporated: 29 August 2006 *Employees:* 39
Net Worth: £5,273,549 *Total Assets:* £6,859,706
Registered Office: Gateway House, Draycott Business Park, Draycott, Glos, GL56 9JY
Activities: Other manufacturing n.e.c.
Shareholders: Charles Ernest Bedford; Stephanie Bedford
Officers: Stephanie Bedford, Secretary; Charles Ernest Bedford [1969] Director; Daryl Bedford [1991] Director/Sales Manager

Harrow Community Schools PFI Ltd
Incorporated: 1 February 2002
Net Worth: £630,042 *Total Assets:* £14,361,496
Registered Office: Third Floor, Broad Quay House, Prince Street, Bristol, BS1 4DJ
Activities: Other business support service activities n.e.c.
Parent: DIF Infrastructure II UK Limited
Officers: Louis Javier Falero [1977] Director/Fund Manager; Adam George Waddington [1974] Director/Asset Manager

Harrow Hill Properties Limited
Incorporated: 19 January 1962 *Employees:* 2
Net Worth: £6,366,711 *Total Assets:* £7,695,213
Registered Office: 10 Bridge Street, Christchurch, Dorset, BH23 1EF
Activities: Other letting and operating of own or leased real estate
Shareholders: Jacqueline Anne Howells; Deborah Jayne Balaam; Linda Diane Farrow
Officers: David John Balaam, Secretary; David John Balaam [1932] Director; Deborah Jayne Balaam [1961] Director/Property Management

Harrow House International College (Swanage) Ltd
Incorporated: 28 November 1974 *Employees:* 79
Net Worth: £4,422,417 *Total Assets:* £8,565,056
Registered Office: Alum House, 5 Alum Chine Road, Westbourne, Bournemouth, BH4 8DT
Activities: Other service activities n.e.c.
Major Shareholder: Robert A'barrow
Officers: Karin A'barrow, Secretary [German]; Karin A'barrow [1947] Director; Stephen Robert A'barrow [1968] Director; Robert Brian Abarrow [1935] Director; Sabine Karin Booth [1976] Director

Hart's Haulage Limited
Incorporated: 15 May 2003 *Employees:* 27
Net Worth: £4,083,214 *Total Assets:* £5,102,729
Registered Office: Highburrow Lane, Wilson Way, Redruth, Cornwall, TR15 3RN
Activities: Freight transport by road
Major Shareholder: Richard Neil Hart
Officers: Nigel Uren, Secretary; Richard Neil Hart [1969] Director/Haulier

Hartham Park Limited
Incorporated: 15 May 1997 *Employees:* 7
Previous: Hartham Park PLC
Net Worth Deficit: £2,912,669 *Total Assets:* £24,489,424
Registered Office: Hartham Park, Corsham, Wilts, SN13 0RP
Activities: Other letting and operating of own or leased real estate
Major Shareholder: Jeffrey Paul Thomas
Officers: Jeffrey Paul Thomas [1957] Director

Hartridge Limited
Incorporated: 18 February 2004 *Employees:* 52
Net Worth: £13,384,000 *Total Assets:* £16,827,000
Registered Office: Brunel Way, Stroudwater Business Park, Stonehouse, Glos, GL10 3SX
Activities: Manufacture of other special-purpose machinery n.e.c.
Parent: Delphi Automotive Operations UK Limited
Officers: William Brenton James Allen [1986] Director/Accountant; Adam Lee [1979] Business Unit Director; Olivier Jean Francis Lequeue [1978] Finance Director [Belgian]; Simon John Quantrell [1980] Director

Harvey Commercial Holdings Limited
Incorporated: 25 May 2016 *Employees:* 273
Net Worth: £12,610,272 *Total Assets:* £31,190,382
Registered Office: 19 Common Road, Hanham, Bristol, BS15 3LL
Activities: Activities of head offices
Officers: Helen Elizabeth Britton, Secretary; Andrew John Harvey [1957] Director

Harvey Farms (Winterbourne) Limited
Incorporated: 11 April 2001 *Employees:* 15
Net Worth: £3,951,842 *Total Assets:* £5,806,994
Registered Office: Manor Farm, Winterbourne Earls, Salisbury, Wilts, SP4 6HD
Activities: Mixed farming
Major Shareholder: Philip Nicholas Baker Harvey
Officers: Joseph Nicholas Harvey [1985] Director/Farmer; Philip Nicholas Baker Harvey [1957] Director/Farmer

Harvey Shopfitters Limited
Incorporated: 5 August 1981 *Employees:* 171
Net Worth: £15,706,730 *Total Assets:* £30,902,964
Registered Office: 19 Common Road, Hanham, Bristol, BS15 3LL
Activities: Other specialised construction activities n.e.c.
Officers: Helen Elizabeth Britton, Secretary; Andrew John Harvey [1957] Director/Shopfitter; Stuart Paul Jenkins [1964] Director; Steven Maurice Lodge [1963] Director; Vincent Paul Nolan [1955] Director

Haseltine Lake LLP
Incorporated: 18 March 2009 *Employees:* 151
Net Worth: £1,896,079 *Total Assets:* £10,870,816
Registered Office: Redcliff Quay, 120 Redcliff Street, Bristol, BS1 6HU
Officers: David Leslie Brown [1960] Member; Alan James Chamberlain [1980] Member; Dr Andrew John Dowling [1977] Member; Simon John Lewis Rees [1965] Member; Frances Ward Wilding [1968] Member; Patrick Michael Chapman [1985] LLP Member; Philip Davies [1972] LLP Member; Christine Lesley Fenlon [1963] LLP Member; Ashley Simon Giles [1965] LLP Member; Martin Hermann Krause [1964] LLP Member; David Nicholas Lewin [1979] LLP Member; Gwyneth Jane More O'Ferrall [1960] LLP Member; David Christopher O'Connell [1963] LLP Member; Alex Lee Rogers [1978] LLP Member; James Norman Ward [1980] LLP Member

J.H.Haskins & Son Limited
Incorporated: 14 March 1957 *Employees:* 23
Net Worth: £9,706,073 *Total Assets:* £13,306,920
Registered Office: 64 High Street, Shepton Mallet, Somerset, BA4 5AX
Activities: Sale of new cars and light motor vehicles
Officers: Rose Lilian Haskins, Secretary; Christopher George Collins [1959] Finance Director; Graham Russell Haskins [1965] Director; John Kevin Haskins [1957] Director

Haskins Garden Centres Limited
Incorporated: 9 May 1997 *Employees:* 601
Net Worth: £34,303,000 *Total Assets:* £46,242,000
Registered Office: Head Office Building, Longham, Ferndown, Dorset, BH22 9DJ
Activities: Other retail sale in non-specialised stores
Officers: John Alexander Dunlop, Secretary; John Alexander Dunlop [1959] Finance Director; Warren George Haskins [1948] Director/Chairman; Lisa Looker [1970] Director; Conna Powles [1962] Buying Director; Terrence Rodney Frederick Stockley [1944] Director; Julian Peter Winfield [1965] Director

Haskins Holdings Limited
Incorporated: 4 January 2000 *Employees:* 601
Net Worth: £34,710,000 *Total Assets:* £46,500,000
Registered Office: Haskins, Head Office Building, Longham, Ferndown, Dorset, BH22 9DJ
Activities: Non-trading company
Officers: John Alexander Dunlop, Secretary; John Alexander Dunlop [1959] Finance Director; Warren George Haskins [1948] Director; Lisa Looker [1970] Director; Conna Mary Margaret Powles [1962] Buying Director; Terrence Rodney Frederick Stockley [1944] Director; Julian Peter Winfield [1965] Director

Haskins Roundstone Garden Centre Limited
Incorporated: 13 February 1967 *Employees:* 152
Net Worth: £1,888,000 *Total Assets:* £3,956,000
Registered Office: Haskins Garden Centre, Head Office Buildings, Longham, Ferndown, Dorset, BH22 9DJ
Activities: Other retail sale in non-specialised stores
Officers: John Alexander Dunlop, Secretary; John Alexander Dunlop [1959] Finance Director; Warren George Haskins [1948] Director/Chairman; Lisa Looker [1970] Director; Conna Mary Margaret Powles [1962] Director; Julian Peter Winfield [1965] Director

Haskins Snowhill Garden Centre Limited
Incorporated: 15 September 1986 *Employees:* 98
Net Worth: £3,559,000 *Total Assets:* £4,698,000
Registered Office: Head Office Building, Longham, Ferndown, Dorset, BH22 9DJ
Activities: Other retail sale in non-specialised stores
Officers: John Alexander Dunlop, Secretary; John Alexander Dunlop [1959] Finance Director; Warren George Haskins [1948] Director; Lisa Looker [1970] Director; Conna Mary Margaret Powles [1962] Director; Julian Peter Winfield [1965] Director

Hatcher and Sons,Limited
Incorporated: 29 March 1898 *Employees:* 51
Net Worth: £2,702,411 *Total Assets:* £3,547,134
Registered Office: 11 High Street, Taunton, Somerset, TA1 3PQ
Activities: Other retail sale in non-specialised stores
Parent: Hovelands Limited
Officers: Stephen Adrian Hill, Secretary; Adrian Michael Hill [1946] Director/Retail Executive; Stephen Adrian Hill [1974] Director/Accountant; Mark Raisey [1962] Director/Retail Executive; Robert Clive Raisey [1936] Director/Accountant

Hatchmoor Nursing Home Limited
Incorporated: 23 July 2007 *Employees:* 105
Net Worth: £222,713 *Total Assets:* £4,205,645
Registered Office: 47 Boutport Street, Barnstaple, Devon, EX31 1SQ
Activities: Other human health activities
Shareholders: John Khuchmirh Singh; Solomon Satnam Singh
Officers: Solomon Satnam Singh, Secretary; John Khushmira Singh [1948] Director; Solomon Satnam Singh [1976] Director

David Hathaway Holdings Limited
Incorporated: 20 August 1976 *Employees:* 124
Net Worth: £14,605,038 *Total Assets:* £17,972,120
Registered Office: Woodward Avenue, Westerleigh Business Park, Yate, Bristol, BS37 5YS
Activities: Activities of head offices
Major Shareholder: David Roger Hathaway
Officers: Matthew David Hathaway, Secretary; Christopher Stephen Hathaway [1975] Director/Human Resources Manager; David Roger Hathaway [1943] Managing Director; James Kristian Hathaway [1972] Director/Fleet Manager; Jean Violet Hathaway [1945] Director/Secretary; Matthew David Hathaway [1970] Operations Director; Katie Jane Steeds [1981] Director/Nursery Nurse

David Hathaway Properties Limited
Incorporated: 3 January 2003
Net Worth: £4,505,313 *Total Assets:* £7,072,870
Registered Office: Woodward Avenue, Westerleigh Business Park, Yate, Bristol, BS37 5YS
Activities: Other letting and operating of own or leased real estate
Parent: David Hathaway Holdings Limited
Officers: Matthew David Hathaway, Secretary; David Roger Hathaway [1943] Managing Director; Matthew David Hathaway [1970] Operations Director

David Hathaway Transport Limited
Incorporated: 7 January 2003 *Employees:* 124
Net Worth: £6,214,329 *Total Assets:* £9,154,376
Registered Office: Woodward Avenue, Westerleigh Business Park, Yate, Bristol, BS37 5YS
Activities: Freight transport by road
Parent: David Hathaway Holdings Limited
Officers: Matthew David Hathaway, Secretary; Michelle Valerie Crocker [1966] Finance Director; Christopher Stephen Hathaway [1975] Human Resources Director; David Roger Hathaway [1943] Managing Director; James Kristian Hathaway [1972] Warehouse and Fleet Director; Matthew David Hathaway [1970] Operations Director

Hatton Properties Limited
Incorporated: 17 December 1999
Net Worth: £1,852,490 *Total Assets:* £6,636,653
Registered Office: Top Floor Office, Hatton Court Hotel, Upton Hill, Upton St Leonards, Gloucester, GL4 8DE
Activities: Activities of head offices
Parent: Hatton Logistics (Holdings) Limited
Officers: Darren Leslie Raymond Hiscox, Secretary/Director; Darren Leslie Raymond Hiscox [1966] Director; Lee Arthur Hiscox [1967] Director

Hautot Developments Limited
Incorporated: 13 April 2015 *Employees:* 1
Net Worth: £6,218,202 *Total Assets:* £6,524,577
Registered Office: Centenary House, Peninsula Park, Rydon Lane, Exeter, EX2 7XE
Activities: Development of building projects
Parent: Hautot Holdings Limited
Officers: George Norman Hautot [1942] Director/Holiday Park Owner; Joan Irene Hautot [1942] Director/Holiday Park Owner; Paul George Hautot [1976] Director/Holiday Park Manager

Hautot Holdings Limited
Incorporated: 31 March 2015
Net Worth: £8,996,425 *Total Assets:* £9,000,001
Registered Office: Centenary House, Peninsula Park, Rydon Lane, Exeter, EX2 7XE
Activities: Holiday centres and villages
Shareholders: George Norman Hautot; Joan Irene Hautot
Officers: George Norman Hautot [1942] Director/Holiday Park Owner; Joan Irene Hautot [1942] Director/Holiday Park Owner

Havana West Limited
Incorporated: 27 May 2002 *Employees:* 227
Net Worth: £6,712,614 *Total Assets:* £34,432,056
Registered Office: Minerva House, Lower Bristol Road, Bath, BA2 9ER
Activities: Hotels and similar accommodation
Major Shareholder: Lucille Lanette de Savary
Officers: Joseph James Keefe, Secretary; Lucille Lanette de Savary [1954] Director; Ian David Solkin [1966] Director/Hotelier

Havas EHS Discovery Limited
Incorporated: 19 June 1967 *Employees:* 60
Net Worth: £6,142,000 *Total Assets:* £16,954,000
Registered Office: Phoenix Way, Cirencester, Glos, GL7 1RY
Activities: Data processing, hosting and related activities
Parent: Havas UK Limited
Officers: Allan John Ross, Secretary; Alan Ralston Adamson [1966] Director/Chief Financial Officer; James George Merryweather [1981] Director/Accountant

Haven Investments Limited
Incorporated: 27 May 1946 *Employees:* 7
Net Worth: £15,893,722 *Total Assets:* £17,650,856
Registered Office: Clyst Court, Hill Barton Business Park, Clyst St Mary, Exeter, EX5 1SA
Activities: Other letting and operating of own or leased real estate
Officers: Jacqui Whitty, Secretary; Nigel Albert Cann [1945] Director; John Henry Lucas [1942] Director; Graham Douglas Murrin [1941] Director; Martin Murrin [1969] Director

Havenstone Property Limited
Incorporated: 15 August 2006
Net Worth: £3,145,499 *Total Assets:* £7,084,137
Registered Office: Lower Gawns, Blisland, Bodmin, Cornwall, PL30 4JL
Activities: Buying and selling of own real estate
Major Shareholder: John Kenneth Bowen
Officers: Robyn Susie Bowen, Secretary; John Kenneth Bowen [1950] Director/Broker

Hawkins Agri Limited
Incorporated: 10 July 2003 *Employees:* 16
Net Worth: £1,621,199 *Total Assets:* £4,374,333
Registered Office: Mary Street House, Mary Street, Taunton, Somerset, TA1 3NW
Activities: Wholesale of agricultural machinery, equipment and supplies
Major Shareholder: Jonathan Paul Hawkins
Officers: Colin Charles Hawkins, Secretary; Jonathan Paul Hawkins [1979] Director/Agricultural Engineer

Hawkins Holdings Limited
Incorporated: 16 January 2007 *Employees:* 236
Net Worth: £19,419,428 *Total Assets:* £31,550,256
Registered Office: 9 Tregarne Terrace, St Austell, Cornwall, PL25 4DD
Activities: Sale of new cars and light motor vehicles
Shareholders: Andrew James Hawkins; William Alfred John Hawkins; William John Hawkins
Officers: Andrew James Hawkins [1964] Director; Marion Wendy Hawkins [1939] Director; William Alfred John Hawkins [1936] Director; William John Hawkins [1966] Director

Hawkins Motors Limited
Incorporated: 2 July 1957 *Employees:* 236
Net Worth: £13,109,239 *Total Assets:* £23,300,538
Registered Office: 57 Gwendra Road, St Stephen, St Austell, Cornwall, PL26 7LB
Activities: Sale of new cars and light motor vehicles
Parent: Hawkins Holdings Limited
Officers: Andrew James Hawkins [1964] Director/Motor Dealership Manager; Wendy Marion Hawkins [1939] Director/Housewife; William John Hawkins [1966] Director/Sales Manager; William Alfred John Hawkins [1936] Managing Director

Hawksworth Securities PLC
Incorporated: 24 March 1988
Net Worth: £1,039,038 *Total Assets:* £6,844,338
Registered Office: 1st Floor, 7 Park Street, Bristol, BS1 5NF
Activities: Development of building projects
Parent: Hawksworth Limited
Officers: Joan Breach, Secretary; Alexander Robin Livesey Breach [1989] Director; Christopher Andrew Talbot Breach [1974] Director/Chartered Surveyor; Harry William Freeman Breach [1972] Director/Equity Research Analyst; Joan Breach [1944] Director & Secretary; Peter John Freeman Breach [1942] Director

James Hay Administration Company Limited
Incorporated: 8 September 2000 *Employees:* 535
Net Worth: £7,423,000 *Total Assets:* £7,763,000
Registered Office: Dunn's House, St Paul's Road, Salisbury, Wilts, SP2 7BF
Activities: Financial intermediation not elsewhere classified
Parent: James Hay Insurance Company Limited
Officers: Stephen John Charles Darke, Secretary; Geoffrey Stephen Clarkson [1949] Director/Solicitor; Alastair Conway [1965] Director; Keith Martin Dignam [1961] Management Consultant/Director [Irish]; Gavin Howard [1972] Director/Chief Financial Officer; Iain Beattie McCoo [1965] Director; Kathryn Elizabeth Purves [1973] Director

James Hay Holdings Limited
Incorporated: 29 May 1990
Net Worth: £22,056,000 *Total Assets:* £35,197,000
Registered Office: Dunn's House, St Pauls Road, Salisbury, Wilts, SP2 7BF
Activities: Activities of financial services holding companies
Parent: IFG UK Holdings Limited
Officers: Stephen John Charles Darke, Secretary; Alastair Conway [1965] Director; Keith Martin Dignam [1961] Management Consultant/Director [Irish]; Iain Beattie McCoo [1965] Director

James Hay Partnership Management Limited
Incorporated: 10 September 1990 *Employees:* 668
Previous: IFG Management UK Limited
Net Worth: £2,560,000 *Total Assets:* £6,428,000
Registered Office: Dunn's House, St Pauls Road, Salisbury, Wilts, SP2 7BF
Activities: Financial management
Parent: IFG UK Group Holdings Limited
Officers: Stephen John Charles Darke, Secretary; Alastair Conway [1965] Director/Chief Executive; Iain Beattie McCoo [1965] Director; Matthew James Taylor [1976] Director of Finance

Haycock Holdings Limited
Incorporated: 27 January 1988 *Employees:* 6
Net Worth: £13,393,523 *Total Assets:* £18,161,562
Registered Office: Midland House, 2 Poole Road, Bournemouth, BH2 5QY
Activities: Activities of head offices
Parent: Haycock Investments Limited
Officers: Sally Ann Meaden, Secretary; Christine Ann Haycock [1946] Director; Edward Robin Mason Haycock [1973] Director; John Christopher Haycock [1948] Director; Robin Peter Tressider Haycock [1946] Director; Rupert Bertie Haycock [1980] Director

Haydn Fine Ltd
Incorporated: 23 December 2013 *Employees:* 3
Net Worth: £2,406,540 *Total Assets:* £4,208,720
Registered Office: 2nd Floor, Stratus House, Emperor Way, Exeter, Devon, EX1 3QS
Activities: Other letting and operating of own or leased real estate
Shareholders: Kerry Ann Fine; Raymond Philip Ronald Fine
Officers: Kerry Ann Fine [1962] Director; Raymond Philip Ronald Fine [1961] Director

Hayes Grange LLP
Incorporated: 7 July 2015
Net Worth: £39,219,696 *Total Assets:* £39,297,756
Registered Office: Centenary House, Peninsula Park, Rydon Lane, Exeter, EX2 7XE
Officers: Noel George Herbert Manns [1959] Member; David James Roper Robinson [1955] Member; Edward Charles Rolle Fane Trefusis [1993] LLP Member

T. R. Hayes Limited
Incorporated: 21 March 1973 *Employees:* 46
Net Worth: £2,452,583 *Total Assets:* £3,820,397
Registered Office: 18 London Street, Walcot, Bath, BA1 5BX
Activities: Retail of furniture, lighting, and similar (not musical instruments or scores) in specialised store
Parent: Xenium Limited
Officers: Derek Richard Hayes, Secretary; Derek Richard Hayes [1937] Director/Home Furnisher; Margaret Enid Hayes [1935] Financial Director; Richard Jonathan Hayes [1972] Director

Hayes School
Incorporated: 2 March 2011 *Employees:* 67
Net Worth: £5,178,190 *Total Assets:* £6,220,117
Registered Office: Hayes School, Hayes Road, Paignton, Devon, TQ4 5PJ
Activities: Primary education
Officers: Allison Grant, Secretary; Emma Victoria Bamber [1972] Director/Deputy Headteacher; Michael Curtis [1983] Director/Head of Property Services; Sarah Giles [1976] Director/Teacher; Mark Christopher Hanbury [1974] Director/Headteacher; Marianne Harper [1976] Director/Teacher; Helen Hill [1983] Director/Isolation Officer; Alex James Howarth [1975] Director/Head of Tutorial and Leaver Progress; Helene Claire Warren [1972] Director/Teacher; Nigel Stephen Williams [1970] Director/Minister of Religion

Hayesfield Girls' School
Incorporated: 15 June 2011 *Employees:* 190
Net Worth: £22,932,030 *Total Assets:* £25,522,686
Registered Office: Hayesfield Girls' School, Upper Oldfield Park, Bath, BA2 3LA
Activities: General secondary education
Officers: Alison Norris, Secretary; Donna Baddeley [1966] Director/School Governor; Patricia Anne Bourke [1972] Director/Trustee; Roger David Chapman [1952] Director/Retired Internal Auditor; Annette Hayton [1953] Director/School Governor; Karen Jo-Anne Leigh [1972] Director/School Governor; James Matthew Robinson [1967] Director/Governor; Philip Edward Rothfield [1967] Director/School Governor; Michelle Ann Sims [1966] Director/School Governor; Dr Peter Talks [1969] Director/Governor; Mark Hamilton Whiteley [1965] Director/Governor; Roger Williams [1960] Director/School Governor; Emma Jayne Yates [1972] Director/Headteacher

The Haygrove Academy Trust
Incorporated: 10 June 2011 *Employees:* 148
Previous: Haygrove School
Net Worth: £9,686,356 *Total Assets:* £12,969,900
Registered Office: Haygrove School, Durleigh Road, Bridgwater, Somerset, TA6 7HW
Activities: General secondary education
Officers: Tracy Lee, Secretary; Lyndon Brett [1959] Director/Chartered Surveyor; Karen Margaret Canham [1960] Director/Headteacher; Mark Cooke [1963] Director of Commissioning Operations, NHS England; Ian Dyer [1959] Director/Business Owner; Trevor David Hains [1961] Director/Engineering Manager; Geoff Howe [1963] Director/Head of Radiological Protection; Tina Jane Stoel-Walker [1960] Director/Administrator; Jackie Mary Stone [1966] Director; Bozena Wierzchleyska [1964] Director/Teacher; Mark Brian Wilson [1958] Director/Accountant; Jill Witts [1957] Director/Emotional Wellbeing/Behaviour Assistant/FSW

Hayne Securities Limited
Incorporated: 11 June 1997 *Employees:* 2
Net Worth: £2,416,520 *Total Assets:* £6,406,536
Registered Office: Hayne, Corfe, Taunton, Somerset, TA3 7DB
Activities: Buying and selling of own real estate
Parent: Hayne Freeholders Limited
Officers: Christopher George, Secretary; Christopher George [1970] Operations Director; Rachel Louise George [1972] Director/Accountant

J.H. Haynes & Co. Limited
Incorporated: 20 September 1979 *Employees:* 39
Net Worth Deficit: £10,530,594 *Total Assets:* £9,084,405
Registered Office: Sparkford, Yeovil, Somerset, BA22 7JJ
Activities: Book publishing
Parent: Haynes Publishing Group P.L.C.
Officers: Richard Barker, Secretary; Richard Barker [1981] Finance Director; James Taylor Bunkum [1965] Director/Accountant; Nigel John Clements [1959] Production Director; Graham Robert Cook [1962] Director/Overseas Development; John Harold Coleman Haynes [1967] Director/Chairman; Jeremy Yates-Round [1961] Managing Director

Haynes Developments Limited
Incorporated: 29 June 1964 *Employees:* 7
Net Worth: £10,730,582 *Total Assets:* £11,717,094
Registered Office: Haynes International Motor Museum, Sparkford, Yeovil, Somerset, BA22 7LH
Activities: Development of building projects
Shareholder: Annette Constance Haynes
Officers: Annette Constance Haynes, Secretary; Annette Constance Haynes [1938] Director; Christopher Michael David Haynes [1972] Director; John Harold Coleman Haynes [1967] Director

Haynes Publishing Group Public Limited Company
Incorporated: 18 May 1960 *Employees:* 271
Net Worth: £24,987,000 *Total Assets:* £59,158,000
Registered Office: Sparkford, Yeovil, Somerset, BA22 7JJ
Activities: Activities of other holding companies n.e.c.
Officers: Richard Stephen Barker, Secretary; Richard Barker [1981] Director; Edward Bell [1949] Director; James Taylor Bunkum [1965] Director/Chief Financial Officer; Stephen David Paul Daykin [1957] Director; John Harold Coleman Haynes [1967] Managing Director; Alexander George Kwarts [1955] Managing Director [Dutch]; Peter Van Der Galien [1967] Director [Dutch]; Nina Wright [1970] Director; Jeremy Yates-Round [1961] Managing Director

Haystack Dryers Limited
Incorporated: 4 September 2000 *Employees:* 3
Net Worth: £3,776,485 *Total Assets:* £4,090,243
Registered Office: Unit 1 Pintail Business Park, 165 Christchurch Road, Ringwood, Hants, BH24 3AL
Activities: Other amusement and recreation activities n.e.c.
Officers: David John Coates, Secretary; David John Coates [1947] Director/Chartered Accountant; Paul Anthony Thomas [1971] Managing Director; Michelle Trench [1985] Director/Chartered Accountant

Hayward Properties Limited
Incorporated: 1 June 1949 *Employees:* 6
Net Worth: £9,330,665 *Total Assets:* £12,483,067
Registered Office: 59b Seamoor Road, Bournemouth, BH4 9AE
Activities: Other letting and operating of own or leased real estate
Officers: Roger Alwyn Gillett, Secretary; Gail Karen Gomez [1954] Director; Wendy Mary Griffiths [1962] Director/Conference & Events Consultant; Christopher Michael Hayward [1959] Director/Corporate Advisor; Guy Desmond Hayward [1957] Director/Construction; James Timothy Hayward [1961] Director/Business Person; Nicholas John Hayward [1957] Director

Hazel Holdings Limited
Incorporated: 11 March 2016 *Employees:* 1
Net Worth: £3,554,073 *Total Assets:* £3,575,033
Registered Office: 41 New King Street, Bath, BA1 2BN
Activities: Fund management activities
Major Shareholder: John George Rose
Officers: John George Rose [1981] Director

Hazelwood Motor Company Ltd
Incorporated: 13 September 2012 *Employees:* 3
Net Worth: £5,669,355 *Total Assets:* £5,699,636
Registered Office: c/o Mercedes Benz of Exeter, Matford Park Road, Exeter, Devon, EX2 8FD
Activities: Management consultancy activities other than financial management
Major Shareholder: Michael Anthony Wickins
Officers: Anthony John Wickins [1951] Director; Joanne Wickins [1971] Director; Michael Anthony Wickins [1970] Director

Hazlewoods LLP
Incorporated: 23 February 2005
Net Worth: £5,151,915 *Total Assets:* £8,878,759
Registered Office: Staverton Court, Staverton, Cheltenham, Glos, GL51 0UX
Officers: Rachael Anstee [1973] Member; Andrew Warner Brookes [1963] Member; Jon Maylam Cartwright [1967] Member; David Scott Clift [1967] Member; Nicholas Francis Dee [1962] Member; Ruth Dooley [1966] Member; Anthony David Flambard [1960] Member; Paul Fussell [1973] Member; Nicholas Matthew Haines [1974] Member; Mark David Harwood [1979] Member; Martin John Howard [1976] Member; Patricia Ann Kinahan [1976] Member; Scott Michael Lawrence [1972] Member; John David Lucas [1979] Member; James Raymond Morter [1974] Member; Graham Timothy Rew [1961] Member; Adam Trevor Nicholas Smail [1974] Member; Philip Arthur Swan [1960] Member; David Williams [1968] Member; Tom Woodcock [1968] Member; Richard Dade [1976] LLP Member; Peter Richard Frost [1965] LLP Member; Lucie Jessica Hammond [1968] LLP Member; Andrew Clive Harris [1974] LLP Member; Suzanne Marie Headington [1978] LLP Member; Peter Llewellyn Woodall [1967] LLP Member

HDM Leisure Limited
Incorporated: 18 June 2009
Net Worth Deficit: £74,494 *Total Assets:* £5,819,194
Registered Office: 2 Hamilton Court House, 1-3 Alum Chine Road, Bournemouth, BH4 8DT
Activities: Development of building projects
Shareholders: Graham Keith Heffer; Angeline Marie Heffer
Officers: Angeline Marie Heffer [1972] Director; Graham Keith Heffer [1967] Sales Director

Head Ruddy Limited
Incorporated: 21 November 2002 *Employees:* 4
Net Worth: £8,307,472 *Total Assets:* £9,947,884
Registered Office: Staverton Court, Staverton, Cheltenham, Glos, GL51 0UX
Activities: Other letting and operating of own or leased real estate
Shareholders: Grant Roger John Ruddy; Jasmin Head
Officers: James Maurice Ruddy, Secretary/Fish & Chip Caterer; Roger John Head [1951] Director; James Maurice Ruddy [1955] Director/Fish & Chip Caterer

Headland Hotel Company Limited (The)
Incorporated: 13 November 1973 *Employees:* 173
Net Worth: £13,136,592 *Total Assets:* £17,558,572
Registered Office: Headland Road, Newquay, Cornwall, TR7 1EW
Activities: Hotels and similar accommodation
Shareholders: John William Andrew Armstrong; Carol Jennifer Armstrong
Officers: John William Andrew Armstrong, Secretary; Carol Jennifer Armstrong [1955] Director/Hotelier; John William Andrew Armstrong [1949] Director/Hotelier; Darryl Lee Reburn [1967] Director

Headlands Technologies Europe LLP
Incorporated: 21 June 2013 *Employees:* 2
Previous: Headlands Trading (UK) LLP
Net Worth: £1,166,213 *Total Assets:* £3,786,347
Registered Office: 11th Floor, Whitefriars, Lewins Mead, Bristol, BS1 2NT

C G & D Heal Limited
Incorporated: 14 January 1988 *Employees:* 15
Net Worth: £3,719,459 *Total Assets:* £4,163,415
Registered Office: Latteridge Green Farm, Iron Acton, Bristol, BS37 9TS
Activities: Growing of cereals (except rice), leguminous crops and oil seeds
Shareholders: Christopher Gough Heal; Diane Heal
Officers: Diane Heal, Secretary; Christopher Gough Heal [1944] Director/Farmer; Diane Heal [1942] Director/Farmer; Catherine Gough Kirby [1971] Director; Annalisa Gough Wood [1968] Director

Health Management (UCLH) Limited
Incorporated: 7 May 1999
Net Worth Deficit: £63,048,000 *Total Assets:* £316,012,992
Registered Office: Third Floor, Broad Quay House, Prince Street, Bristol, BS1 4DJ
Activities: Medical nursing home activities
Parent: Health Management (UCLH) Holdings Limited
Officers: Colin John Anderson [1963] Director/Solicitor; Vikram Bhaskar [1968] Director/Portfolio Manager [Indian]; John Stephen Gordon [1962] Director; John McDonagh [1969] Director; Hannah O'Gorman [1971] Director; Ravi Parekh [1979] Director [American]; Neil Rae [1971] Director

Healthcare Computing Limited
Incorporated: 1 November 1999
Net Worth: £1,330,115 *Total Assets:* £5,167,749
Registered Office: Unit 10 Millstream Trading Estate, Christchurch Road, Ringwood, Hants, BH24 3SB
Activities: Information technology consultancy activities
Parent: Healthcare Computing Group Limited
Officers: Neil Simon Payne, Secretary; Neil Simon Payne [1978] Managing Director; Mathew Cunliffe Trudgill [1969] Director of Business Development

Healthcare South West Ltd
Incorporated: 15 April 2003 *Employees:* 10
Net Worth: £1,606,754 *Total Assets:* £3,941,400
Registered Office: 60 Staplegrove Road, Taunton, Somerset, TA1 1DJ
Activities: Other human health activities
Major Shareholder: Freda Veronica Gardner
Officers: Paul Hart, Secretary; Dr Freda Veronica Gardner [1958] Director/Clinical Psychologist

Healthline UK Holdings Limited
Incorporated: 16 March 2016
Net Worth: £3,151,047 *Total Assets:* £5,340,736
Registered Office: Carrick House, Lypiatt Road, Cheltenham, Glos, GL50 2QJ
Activities: Management consultancy activities other than financial management
Officers: Cheryl Janine Kim [1965] Director/SVP Finance [American]; David Alan Kopp [1969] Director [American]

The Heath Academy Trust
Incorporated: 5 October 2015 *Employees:* 184
Net Worth: £8,730,450 *Total Assets:* £10,900,185
Registered Office: St James CE First School, Park Lane, Alderholt, Dorset, SP6 3AJ
Activities: Primary education
Officers: Joanne Lolley, Secretary; Sharon Carter [1971] Director/Office Manager; Laura Crossley [1976] Director/Headteacher; Justine Horn [1967] Director/Headteacher & CEO for MAT; Jill Diana Christine McCall [1962] Director/School Business Management Consultant; Nicholas Delaforce Musselwhite [1970] Director/Financial Adviser; Andrew Risby [1947] Director/Retired FCCA; Jennifer Clare Taylor [1976] Director/Quality Specialist/Review Manager; Lesley Wooff [1971] Director/Personnel Manager

John Heathcoat & Company (Holdings) Limited
Incorporated: 3 July 1984 *Employees:* 480
Net Worth: £30,757,000 *Total Assets:* £47,386,000
Registered Office: Westexe, Tiverton, Devon, EX16 5LL
Activities: Activities of head offices
Officers: David Alfred Penn, Secretary; Gordon Andrew Clark [1950] Director/Management Consultant; Simon Charles Waddington [1958] Director/Chartered Accountant

Heathcoat Fabrics Limited
Incorporated: 11 March 1948 *Employees:* 479
Net Worth: £27,045,000 *Total Assets:* £40,297,000
Registered Office: Westexe, Tiverton, Devon, EX16 5LL
Activities: Weaving of textiles
Parent: John Heathcoat & Company (Holdings) Limited
Officers: David Alfred Penn, Secretary; Alan James Cockram [1955] Director/General Manager; Anna Maria Govey [1969] Director; Peter John Hill [1965] Director/General Manager; Simon James Kitchener [1962] Director/Manager; Andrew Philip MacManus [1961] Director/Engineer; John Julian Short [1959] Director/Accountant; Simon Charles Waddington [1958] Director

R.J. Heathman (Contractors) Limited
Incorporated: 16 March 1976 *Employees:* 91
Net Worth: £12,606,769 *Total Assets:* £23,094,900
Registered Office: 105-107 High Street, Worle, Weston Super Mare, Somerset, BS22 6HA
Activities: Construction of other civil engineering projects n.e.c.
Shareholders: Mark Kevin Heathman; Karen Ann Mercer
Officers: Karen Ann Mercer, Secretary; Jillian Ellen Heathman [1941] Director; Mark Kevin Heathman [1964] Director; Raymond John Heathman [1939] Director/Chairman; Kevin John Lee [1968] Director

Heating Products Limited
Incorporated: 13 June 2001 *Employees:* 85
Net Worth: £12,235,000 *Total Assets:* £21,489,000
Registered Office: Unit 7 & 8 New Fields Business Park, Stinsford Road, Poole, Dorset, BH17 0NF
Activities: Manufacture of other general-purpose machinery n.e.c.
Parent: Heating Holdings Limited
Officers: Steven Hairsine, Secretary; Shaun Barry Edwards [1968] Director/Chief Executive; Steven Hairsine [1975] Director/Chief Financial Officer; Yves Georges Radat [1968] Director/Engineer [French]; Ian Douglas Roe [1965] Director; Nicholas David Templeton Ward [1951] Director

Heavitree Brewery PLC (The)
Incorporated: 7 February 1890
Net Worth: £10,404,000 *Total Assets:* £21,035,000
Registered Office: The Heavitree Brewery PLC, Trood Lane, Matford, Exeter, EX2 8YP
Activities: Public houses and bars
Shareholder: Nicholas Henry Parnell Tucker
Officers: Nicola Jane McLean, Secretary; Graham John Crocker [1958] Director; Thomas Peter Duncan [1966] Director/Surveyor; Katherine Pease-Watkin [1965] Director/Family Mediation Project Worker; Nicholas Henry Parnell Tucker [1966] Director; William Parnell Tucker [1934] Director; Terry Wheatley [1968] Director

Heber Limited
Incorporated: 5 August 1983 *Employees:* 32
Net Worth: £3,229,004 *Total Assets:* £3,732,440
Registered Office: Belvedere Mill, Chalford, Stroud, Glos, GL6 8NT
Activities: Manufacture of loaded electronic boards
Parent: Heber Group Limited
Officers: Leslie Martin Ashton-Smith, Secretary; Leslie Martin Ashton-Smith [1960] Managing Director; Maomei Glassonbury [1975] Director; Richard John Horne [1975] Director; Graham Roderick Jackson [1957] Director; Mark Perkins [1974] Director; Ben Malcolm Thompson [1977] Director

Hebron & Medlock Limited
Incorporated: 23 July 2002 *Employees:* 5
Net Worth: £7,183,176 *Total Assets:* £8,587,300
Registered Office: St George's Lodge, 33 Oldfield Road, Bath, BA2 3NE
Activities: Other business support service activities n.e.c.
Major Shareholder: David John Medlock
Officers: Peter Phipps, Secretary; David John Medlock [1955] Director; Peter John Medlock [1984] Director; Rebecca Jane Medlock [1986] Director; Steven James Medlock [1991] Director

Helena Productions Limited
Incorporated: 11 September 1987
Net Worth Deficit: £123,000 *Total Assets:* £82,858,000
Registered Office: The Quadrangle, The Promenade, Cheltenham, Glos, GL50 1PX
Activities: Financial intermediation not elsewhere classified
Parent: Royal Bank Leasing Limited
Officers: Stephen Paul Nixon [1970] Director/Bank Official; Keith Damian Pereira [1978] Director/Bank Official

Heligan Gardens Limited
Incorporated: 12 November 1990 *Employees:* 162
Net Worth: £2,315,484 *Total Assets:* £4,278,127
Registered Office: Heligan, Pentewan, St Austell, Cornwall, PL26 6EN
Activities: Operation of historical sites and buildings and similar visitor attractions
Major Shareholder: Timothy Bartel Smit
Officers: Kathryn Elizabeth Allen, Secretary; George Elworthy [1957] Director/Manager; Dr Anthony David Kendle [1958] Director; Jeremy Alexander Bartel Smit [1980] Business Development Manager/Director; Sir Timothy Bartel Smit [1954] Director; John Richard Tremayne Willis [1962] Director/Chartered Surveyor

Helipebs (Holdings) Limited
Incorporated: 7 July 1922 *Employees:* 49
Net Worth: £3,756,054 *Total Assets:* £4,207,071
Registered Office: Premier Works, Sisson Road, Gloucester, GL2 0RE
Activities: Manufacture of fluid power equipment
Officers: John Ambler Harris, Secretary; Harry Alexander Badham [1972] Director/Manager; Ross Noden Cole [1940] Director; Geoffrey Francis Davis [1944] Director/Engineer; John Ambler Harris [1934] Director/Chartered Accountant; Eoin Joseph O'Neill [1956] Director/Management Consultant [Irish]

Helitune Limited
Incorporated: 25 April 2000 *Employees:* 35
Net Worth: £1,428,968 *Total Assets:* £4,866,120
Registered Office: Beran Instruments, Hatchmoor Industrial Estate, Torrington, Devon, EX38 7HP
Activities: Manufacture of other electrical equipment
Parent: Condition Monitoring Group Limited
Officers: Rachel Jane Allen, Secretary; Rachel Jane Allen [1976] Director/Accountant; Douglas Robert Graham [1980] Director; Gareth Maurice Lee-Richards [1945] Director/Chartered Accountant; Andres Lobato [1955] Director/Engineer; Freda Anne Lobato [1953] Director

Help for Heroes
Incorporated: 6 September 2007 *Employees:* 390
Net Worth: £107,333,000 *Total Assets:* £115,174,000
Registered Office: 14 Parkers Close, Downton Business Centre, Downton, Salisbury, Wilts, SP5 3RB
Activities: Sports and recreation education
Officers: Charles Stuart Bell [1960] Director/NHS Chief Executive; Charles Hunter Donald [1965] Director/Civil Servant; Roderick Lance Redmond Dunn [1963] Director/Consultant Surgeon; Oliver Charles Gregson [1978] Director/Banker; David Arnold Hook [1961] Director/Senior Advisor and Consultant; Professor Veronica Rosemary Hope Hailey [1956] Director/Dean of School of Management; Manroop Singh Khela [1982] Director; Charles Michael Lake [1944] Consultant and Former Director of The Royal Common; Caroline Elizabeth Armes Rylatt [1961] Director/Chief Financial Officer; Anthony Gwyn Schofield [1969] Director/Partner, Deloitte, Management Consultancy; Sir Philip Charles Cornwallis Trousdell [1948] Director/Chairman Civil Nuclear Police Authority; Robert Thomas Watsham [1952] Director/Financial Services Consultant; Thomas Geoffrey Wright [1956] Director/Investments; Philip John Yates [1960] Director/Company Consultant

Helston Garages Group Limited
Incorporated: 27 June 2000 *Employees:* 1,093
Net Worth: £92,378,000 *Total Assets:* £215,798,000
Registered Office: 85 Meneage Street, Helston, Cornwall, TR13 8RD
Activities: Activities of head offices
Shareholders: David Stanley Carr; Betty Vera Carr
Officers: Andrew John Barrett [1963] Director; Sarah Anne Burley [1968] HR Director; Betty Vera Carr [1940] Director; David Stanley Carr [1937] Director; Jonathan Craig Glanville [1974] Director/Chartered Accountant

Helston Garages Limited
Incorporated: 12 September 1961 *Employees:* 1,037
Net Worth: £79,924,000 *Total Assets:* £208,435,008
Registered Office: 85 Meneage Street, Helston, Cornwall, TR13 8RD
Activities: Sale of new cars and light motor vehicles
Officers: Andrew John Barrett [1963] Director; Sarah Anne Burley [1968] HR Director; Betty Vera Carr [1940] Director; David Stanley Carr [1937] Director; Jonathan Craig Glanville [1974] Director/Chartered Accountant

Heltor Limited
Incorporated: 14 March 1961 *Employees:* 96
Net Worth: £4,990,160 *Total Assets:* £12,729,910
Registered Office: Heathfield, Newton Abbot, Devon, TQ12 6RW
Activities: Wholesale of other fuels and related products
Parent: Heltor Holdings Limited
Officers: Nicholas Mark Gratton, Secretary; Charles Paul Kingdon [1984] Director/Chartered Surveyor; Linda Mary Kingdon [1955] Director; Paul John Kingdon [1951] Director

Hemsley Fraser Group Limited
Incorporated: 15 August 1991 *Employees:* 151
Net Worth: £4,728,400 *Total Assets:* £15,843,216
Registered Office: St James Court, 74-94 Fore Street, Saltash, Cornwall, PL12 6JW
Activities: Activities of head offices
Parent: Hemsley Fraser International Limited
Officers: Sally Hurrell, Secretary; Remi Georges Marie Blet [1978] Director/Chief Financial Officer [French]; Sir Wangping GE [1964] Director/Demos SA CEO [Chinese]; Sally Hurrell [1956] Director; Marc Richard Hutchings [1965] Director of Open and In-Company Sales; Kim SEN Liw [1950] Director/Non-Managing Executive [Singaporean]; Todd Harmon Turner [1967] Director [American]; Jean Wemaere [1946] Director [French]; Lynsey Whitmarsh [1985] Innovation Director

Hemsley Fraser International Limited
Incorporated: 12 March 2001
Net Worth: £3,020,100 *Total Assets:* £6,093,985
Registered Office: St James Court, 74-94 Fore Street, Saltash, Cornwall, PL12 6JW
Activities: Activities of head offices
Parent: Demos SA
Officers: Sally Hurrell, Secretary; Remi Georges Marie Blet [1978] Director/Chief Financial Officer [French]; Sir Wangping GE [1964] Director/Demos SA CEO [Chinese]; Sally Hurrell [1956] Director; Marc Richard Hutchings [1965] Director of Open and In-Company Sales; Kim SEN Liw [1950] Director/Non-Managing Executive [Singaporean]; Todd Harmon Turner [1967] Director; Jean Wemaere [1946] Director [French]; Lynsey Whitmarsh [1985] Innovation Director

Hendra Touring Caravan & Camping Park Limited
Incorporated: 14 April 1972 *Employees:* 114
Net Worth: £12,505,516 *Total Assets:* £18,912,242
Registered Office: Hendra Tourist Park, Hendra, Newquay, Cornwall, TR8 4NY
Activities: Holiday centres and villages
Shareholder: Robert May
Officers: Robert May, Secretary/Director; William Mark Dexter [1970] Director/Chartered Accountant; Janine Hyatt [1955] Director; Jonathan Donald Hyatt [1984] Director; Robert Kevin Hyatt [1955] Director [Canadian]; Rebecca Jane May [1967] Director; Robert May [1963] Director

Hennock Properties Limited
Incorporated: 12 February 2009
Net Worth: £3,186,233 *Total Assets:* £4,272,551
Registered Office: Alphin Brook Road, Marsh Barton, Exeter, Devon, EX2 8QF
Activities: Other letting and operating of own or leased real estate
Shareholders: Stuart Anthony; Stephen John Ody
Officers: Stuart Anthony [1953] Director; Stephen John Ody [1960] Director

Hercules Site Services Limited
Incorporated: 30 May 2008 *Employees:* 32
Net Worth: £5,029,191 *Total Assets:* £7,457,529
Registered Office: Hercules Court, Lakeside Business Park, South Cerney, Cirencester, Glos, GL7 5XL
Activities: Construction of roads and motorways
Parent: Hercules Real Estate Limited
Officers: Brusk Kivilcim Korkmaz [1979] Director/Engineer

Heritage & Wise Limited
Incorporated: 27 February 1961 *Employees:* 8
Net Worth: £5,469,947 *Total Assets:* £5,885,357
Registered Office: Westminster House, St Oswalds Road, Gloucester, GL1 2SG
Activities: Retail of furniture, lighting, and similar (not musical instruments or scores) in specialised store
Shareholders: Trustees of PD Heritage; Dunstan Heritage
Officers: Joyce Generaldine Heritage, Secretary; Michael John Davies [1944] Director/House Furnisher; Dunstan Heritage [1930] Director/House Furnisher; Joyce Generaldine Heritage [1936] Director/Secretary

Heritage Automotive Holdings Limited
Incorporated: 2 November 2015 *Employees:* 405
Net Worth: £2,423,000 *Total Assets:* £56,215,000
Registered Office: 16 Lower Road, Churchfields, Salisbury, Wilts, SP2 7QD
Activities: Management consultancy activities other than financial management
Shareholders: Richard Luis Neulaender; John Christopher Walsh
Officers: Brian Lister, Secretary; Nicholas Hinallas [1963] Director; Richard Luis Neulaender [1968] Director/Motor Dealer [German]; John Christopher Walsh [1964] Director/Motor Dealer

Heritage Automotive Limited
Incorporated: 2 January 1996 *Employees:* 402
Net Worth: £3,398,000 *Total Assets:* £54,851,000
Registered Office: 16 Lower Road, Churchfields, Salisbury, Wilts, SP2 7QD
Activities: Sale of new cars and light motor vehicles
Parent: Heritage Automotive Holdings Limited
Officers: Brian Lister, Secretary; Nicholas Hinallas [1963] Director; Richard Luis Neulaender [1968] Director/Motor Dealer [German]; John Christopher Walsh [1964] Director/Motor Dealer

Heritage Developments South West Limited
Incorporated: 14 January 2004 *Employees:* 28
Net Worth: £10,060,340 *Total Assets:* £13,538,786
Registered Office: 1a Newton Centre, Thorverton Road, Matford Business Park, Marsh Barton Trading Estate, Exeter, Devon, EX2 8GN
Activities: Construction of domestic buildings
Shareholders: David Stuart Lovell; Andrew Paul Martinovic; Stuart Anthony
Officers: David Stuart Lovell, Secretary; Stuart Anthony [1953] Director; David Stuart Lovell [1958] Director/Developer; Andrew Paul Martinovic [1966] Director

Heronbridge Investment Management LLP
Incorporated: 22 July 2005 *Employees:* 6
Net Worth: £5,754,210 *Total Assets:* £8,185,752
Registered Office: 24 Gay Street, Bath, BA1 2PD
Officers: Benoit Marie Thierry Bouchaud [1965] Member; William Bevis Comer [1965] Member; Katie Louise McMahon [1977] Member; Thomas Peter Day [1971] LLP Member

The Herpetological Conservation Trust
Incorporated: 11 March 2005
Net Worth: £6,567,123 *Total Assets:* £6,595,143
Registered Office: 655a Christchurch Road, Boscombe, Bournemouth, BH1 4AP
Activities: Non-trading company
Officers: Dr Antony Hugh Gent, Secretary; Professor Trevor John Clark Beebee [1947] Director/University Teacher; Jeremy Larick Bruce [1974] Director/Finance Executive; Janice Clemons [1952] Director/Teacher; Professor Richard Alun Griffiths [1957] Director/Professor of Biological Conservation; Howard George Inns [1955] Director/Marketing Manager; Robert Jehle [1969] Director/Senior Lecturer [Liechtensteiner]; Dr Roger Mitchell [1944] Director/Chief Scientist; Philippa Marion Perry [1937] Director/Ecological Consultant; Jonathan Webster [1952] Director/Insurance Executive

Herring Shoes Limited
Incorporated: 4 February 2000 *Employees:* 16
Net Worth: £3,255,400 *Total Assets:* £3,549,109
Registered Office: Unit 6 Station Yard Industrial Estate, Kingsbridge, Devon, TQ7 1ES
Activities: Retail sale of footwear in specialised stores
Parent: Pavers Holdings Limited
Officers: Jason Michael Paver, Secretary; Mark Andrew Granger [1961] Director; Adrian Charles Herring [1973] Director/Shoe Retailer; Jason Michael Paver [1986] Director; Stuart David Paver [1961] Director; Jason Simmonds [1970] Director

Hertford PPP Health Services Limited
Incorporated: 30 January 2003 *Employees:* 3
Net Worth Deficit: £185,294 *Total Assets:* £10,699,192
Registered Office: Third Floor, Broad Quay House, Prince Street, Bristol, BS1 4DJ
Activities: Other specialised construction activities n.e.c.
Parent: RBIL Limited
Officers: Christopher John Blundell [1966] Regional Director; Andrew Richard Kershaw [1965] Director/Projects Controller; Richard Little [1979] Investment Director

Herts & Essex PPP Health Services Limited
Incorporated: 19 January 2001 *Employees:* 3
Net Worth Deficit: £1,692,611 *Total Assets:* £16,912,396
Registered Office: Third Floor, Broad Quay House, Prince Street, Bristol, BS1 4DJ
Activities: Other specialised construction activities n.e.c.
Parent: RBIL Limited
Officers: David Robert Hardingham [1974] Director/Commercial Manager; Andrew Richard Kershaw [1965] Director/Projects Controller; Harvey John William Pownall [1966] Director

Hestercombe Gardens Trust
Incorporated: 4 December 1996 *Employees:* 57
Net Worth: £6,916,267 *Total Assets:* £8,361,365
Registered Office: Hestercombe Gardens, Cheddon Fitzpaine, Taunton, Somerset, TA2 8LQ
Activities: Operation of historical sites and buildings and similar visitor attractions
Officers: Nicholas David Francombe, Secretary; Sir Robert Andrew Burns [1943] Director/Retired Diplomat; Godfrey Pawle Davis [1949] Director; Dr Marion Harney [1951] Director/Lecturer; Marcia Jane Hill [1950] Director/Senior Recruitment Assistant; Jo Ann Matthews [1960] Director/Executive Coach; Catherine Helen O'Sullivan [1962] Director/Author; Catherine Annie Pease [1982] Director/Architect; Annie Prebensen [1958] Director/Garden Designer; Rupert Taylor [1965] Director/Management Consultant; Gemma Trudy Verdon [1968] Director/Councillor; Lady Josephine Spencer Waley-Cohen [1943] Director/Sculptor

Hesters Way Partnership Ltd.
Incorporated: 17 December 1998 *Employees:* 5
Net Worth: £3,494,562 *Total Assets:* £3,505,054
Registered Office: Hesters Way Community Resource Centre, Cassin Drive, Cheltenham, Glos, GL51 7SU
Activities: Other letting and operating of own or leased real estate
Officers: Jenny Louise Perkin, Secretary; Ryan John Barkle [1981] Director/Income Management Manager; Charlotte Jackson [1986] Director/Head of Locality at Bromford; Dr Lloyd James Peter Kilford [1978] Director/Security; Dermot Thomas Gerard McNiffe [1965] Director/School Principal; Mark Julian Saunders [1962] Director/Solicitor; Pat Marie Thornton [1936] Director/Clerical Officer

Hewer Facilities Management Limited
Incorporated: 30 May 2006 *Employees:* 133
Net Worth: £1,044,559 *Total Assets:* £4,487,429
Registered Office: Unit 3 Ambrose House, Meteor Court, Barnett Way, Barnwood, Gloucester, GL4 3GG
Activities: Electrical installation
Parent: Hewer Group Limited
Officers: Ian Wentworth Leitch, Secretary; David John Hewer [1932] Director/Contractor; Simon William Hewer [1966] Director/Contractor

Hewer Group Limited
Incorporated: 11 July 2016 *Employees:* 133
Net Worth: £1,006,798 *Total Assets:* £4,449,668
Registered Office: Unit 3 Ambrose House, Meteor Court, Barnett Way, Barnwood, Gloucester, GL4 3GG
Activities: Other letting and operating of own or leased real estate
Shareholders: Simon William Hewer; Simon William Hewer
Officers: Ian Wentworth Leitch, Secretary; Simon William Hewer [1966] Director/Contractor

HF Trust Limited
Incorporated: 10 September 1962 *Employees:* 3,447
Net Worth: £76,109,000 *Total Assets:* £84,115,000
Registered Office: 5-6 Brook Office Park, Folly Brook Road, Emersons Green, Bristol, BS16 7FL
Activities: Residential care activities for learning difficulties, mental health and substance abuse
Officers: Louisa McCann, Secretary; Amanda Jane Bunce [1957] Director/Retired Vice President - IBM; Ian Lyle Cooper [1947] Director/Retired; Professor Anthony John Holland [1948] Director/Doctor; Briony Jennifer Horvath [1979] Risk and Compliance Director; Brandon James [1978] Marketing Director; Baroness Judith Anne Jolly [1951] Director/Member of House of Lords; Simon Robert Jones [1965] Director/Chartered Accountant; Paul James Morgan [1971] Director/Fundraiser; Rajiv Patel [1971] Director, Risk and Internal Audit; Martin Laurence Taylor [1949] Director/Chartered Surveyor; Werner Andrew White [1960] Director/Self Employed

M.H.R. Hicks Limited
Incorporated: 11 October 1991 *Employees:* 2
Net Worth: £3,519,413 *Total Assets:* £5,444,940
Registered Office: Diamond Farm, Weston Road, Brean, Burnham on Sea, Somerset, TA8 2RL
Activities: Fund management activities
Shareholders: Trevor Morley Hicks; Jennifer Eileen Schofield
Officers: Carol Anne Hicks, Secretary; Joan Rosa Hicks [1922] Director/Retired; Trevor Morley Hicks [1951] Managing Director; Jennifer Eileen Schofield [1949] Director/Housewife

The Hideaway Truro Ltd
Incorporated: 4 October 2016
Net Worth Deficit: £24,904 *Total Assets:* £3,932,641
Registered Office: Riverside Studios, Newham Road, Truro, Cornwall, TR1 2SU
Activities: Other business support service activities n.e.c.
Major Shareholder: Paul John Stephens
Officers: Graham David Cuff, Secretary; Paul John Stephens [1968] Director

High Tech Fabrications Limited
Incorporated: 6 July 2001 *Employees:* 18
Net Worth: £3,699,296 *Total Assets:* £4,379,636
Registered Office: Unit 1 Crown Estate, Sudmeadow Road, Gloucester, GL2 5HG
Activities: Manufacture of other fabricated metal products n.e.c.
Shareholders: Peter John Lynch; Robert James Lynch
Officers: Robert James Lynch, Secretary; Peter John Lynch [1944] Director/Welding & Fabrication Engineer; Robert James Lynch [1972] Director/Quality & Manufacturing Manager

Highbridge Caravan Centre Limited
Incorporated: 1 November 1985 *Employees:* 160
Net Worth: £19,976,538 *Total Assets:* £27,886,844
Registered Office: 3-5 College Street, Burnham on Sea, Somerset, TA8 1AR
Activities: Sale of used cars and light motor vehicles
Parent: J & A Davies Holdings Limited
Officers: Jonathan Lee Davies [1971] Director; Lawrence Christopher Davies [1980] Director; Matthew John Davies [1972] Director; Philip Edward Davies [1978] Director

Highcliffe Holdings Limited
Incorporated: 30 July 2015 *Employees:* 1,437
Previous: Scot Group Holdings Limited
Net Worth: £96,865,000 *Total Assets:* £518,952,992
Registered Office: Scot House, Matford Park Road, Marsh Barton Trading Estate, Exeter, EX2 8AW
Activities: Activities of other holding companies n.e.c.
Major Shareholder: Nigel Clive Spokes
Officers: Nigel Clive Spokes [1960] Chairman/Director

Highcliffe School
Incorporated: 12 May 2011 *Employees:* 184
Net Worth: £13,378,000 *Total Assets:* £16,809,000
Registered Office: Highcliffe School, Parkside, Highcliffe, Christchurch, Dorset, BH23 4QD
Activities: General secondary education
Officers: Deborah Elizabeth Chaffey [1971] Director/Office Administrator; Patrick Dennis Earnshaw [1969] Director/Headteacher; Susan Elizabeth Evans [1960] Director; Nicholas Charles Geary [1941] Director/Engineer; Paul Alan Hilliard [1969] Director/Product Manager; Simon Jones [1977] Director/Teacher; John Lofts [1931] Director/Retired; Steven Midgley [1972] Director/Software Developer; Gary Dennis Moore [1963] Director/Procurement Performance Manager; Trevor Sampson [1958] Director/Builder; Matthew Sedgley [1986] Director/Teacher; Simon Joseph Welch [1970] Director/Chartered Surveyor

Highdrive Property Co. Limited
Incorporated: 1 December 1966 *Employees:* 3
Net Worth: £1,314,258 *Total Assets:* £7,515,741
Registered Office: 3 Durrant Road, Bournemouth, BH2 6NE
Activities: Construction of other civil engineering projects n.e.c.
Shareholders: Keith Peter Harrison; Nigel William Harrison
Officers: Peter Morris Harrison, Secretary; Keith Peter Harrison [1965] Director/Builder; Nigel William Harrison [1959] Director/Builder; Peter Morris Harrison [1931] Director/Property Developer

Higher Drive Nursing Home (Holdings) Limited
Incorporated: 16 May 2005 *Employees:* 2
Net Worth: £296,713 *Total Assets:* £10,828,278
Registered Office: Minerva House, Lower Bristol Road, Bath, BA2 9ER
Activities: Other business support service activities n.e.c.
Parent: Fairlie Holdings Limited
Officers: Terry Patrick McGranaghan [1959] Finance Director; John Gregory Whelan [1946] Director/Residential Nursing Home Proprietor

Higher Education Statistics Agency Limited
Incorporated: 23 November 1992 *Employees:* 129
Net Worth: £3,911,225 *Total Assets:* £6,636,780
Registered Office: 95 Promenade, Cheltenham, Glos, GL50 1HZ
Activities: Other publishing activities
Officers: Deborah Anne Lawrenson, Secretary; Paul Francis Clark [1969] Director/Chief Executive; Professor Nora Ann Colton [1962] Director/Professor; Amatey Victor Doku [1995] Director/Student Representative, Vice President; Professor Linda Sally Drew [1958] Director/Professor, Vice Chancellor; Dr Paul Michael Greatrix [1965] Director/University Registrar; David Howell [1967] Director/Chief Executive Higher Education Provider; Professor Christopher Roy Husbands [1959] Director/Vice-Chancellor; Richard Michael Jones [1990] Director/Solicitor; Professor Paul John Layzell [1957] Director/University Principal; Iain Anthony Littlejohn [1967] Director/Management Consultant; Professor Julie Elspeth Lydon [1954] Director/Vice-Chancellor, University of South Wales; Andrew McConnell [1953] Director of Finance; Tracey Slaven [1967] Director/Deputy Secretary Strategy and Planning; Professor Mark Edmund Smith [1963] Director/Vice-Chancellor

Higher Kings Mill Limited
Incorporated: 10 August 2011 *Employees:* 97
Net Worth: £8,691,891 *Total Assets:* £11,031,033
Registered Office: Higher Kings Mill Limited, Higher Kings Mill, Cullompton, Devon, EX15 1QJ
Activities: Manufacture of paper and paperboard
Shareholder: Lim Soon Huat
Officers: Mei Chin Lim, Secretary; Phaik Ngoh Goh [1968] Director [Malaysian]; Mei Chin Lim [1985] Director [Malaysian]; Soon Huat Lim [1957] Director [Malaysian]; Rodney Christopher Martin [1959] Director; Hubertus Rohe [1957] Director [German]

Higher Tregarne Solar (UK) Limited
Incorporated: 29 October 2010
Previous: AEE Renewables UK 7 Limited
Net Worth: £133,951 *Total Assets:* £5,618,409
Registered Office: The Long Barn, Manor Courtyard, Stratton on the Fosse, Radstock, Somerset, BA3 4QF
Activities: Production of electricity
Parent: CSGH Solar (1) Limited
Officers: Giuseppe La Loggia [1975] Director [Italian]; Yit Ho Tang [1974] Investment Director [Singaporean]; Christopher James Tanner [1972] Investment Director; Jonathan Simon Thompson [1963] Director

Highfield Garden Centres Limited
Incorporated: 20 March 2001 *Employees:* 131
Net Worth: £5,587,694 *Total Assets:* £7,882,135
Registered Office: Windsor House, Bayshill Road, Cheltenham, Glos, GL50 3AT
Activities: Retail sale of flowers, plants, seeds, fertilizers, pet animals and pet food in specialised stores
Parent: Western Forestry Company Limited
Officers: Timothy Robert Greenway, Secretary/Manager; Joan Elizabeth Greenway [1935] Director/Manager; Timothy Robert Greenway [1961] Director/Manager; Jonathan David Mason [1969] Director/Retail Manager

Highfield Homes of Distinction Limited
Incorporated: 27 September 1985 *Employees:* 17
Net Worth: £1,017,560 *Total Assets:* £4,931,778
Registered Office: Highfield House, Holsworthy Beacon, Holsworthy, Devon, EX22 7NF
Activities: Development of building projects
Officers: David John Watkins, Secretary; David John Watkins [1954] Managing Director

Highlands Hospitality Limited
Incorporated: 3 October 2014 *Employees:* 7
Net Worth Deficit: £2,942,345 *Total Assets:* £17,825,622
Registered Office: Stockwell House, 13 High Street, Bruton, Somerset, BA10 0AB
Activities: Hotels and similar accommodation
Shareholders: Iwan Wirth; Manuela Wirth-Hauser
Officers: Daniel Kenneth Brickell [1977] Director/Accountant; Jonathon James Cornaby [1970] Director/Accountant; Timothy Philip Jones [1954] Finance Director; Iwan Wirth [1970] Director/Art Dealer [Swiss]; Manuela Wirth-Hauser [1963] Director/Art Dealer [Swiss]; Edward John Workman [1980] Director Global Property

Highlands House Investments Limited
Incorporated: 23 October 2017 *Employees:* 2
Net Worth Deficit: £338,114 *Total Assets:* £5,946,320
Registered Office: Staverton Court, Staverton, Cheltenham, Glos, GL51 0UX
Activities: Fund management activities
Shareholders: Denise Jennifer Vincent; Raymond John Vincent
Officers: Denise Jennifer Vincent [1970] Director; Raymond John Vincent [1955] Director

Highship Industries Limited
Incorporated: 3 January 2008
Net Worth: £54,966,500 *Total Assets:* £54,966,500
Registered Office: Trym Lodge, 1 Henbury Road, Westbury on Trym, Bristol, BS9 3HQ
Activities: Manufacture of air and spacecraft and related machinery
Shareholder: Geno Invest Stiftung
Officers: Barbara Rosel Geisel [1956] Director/Sole Trader [German]

Highway Insurance Company Limited
Incorporated: 10 March 1999
Net Worth: £214,902,000 *Total Assets:* £1,007,382,016
Registered Office: Frizzell House, County Gates, Bournemouth, BH1 2NF
Activities: Non-life insurance
Parent: Highway Insurance Group Limited
Officers: Michael Peter Jones, Secretary; David Barclay Barral [1962] Director; Alan Ronald Cook [1953] Director/Chairman; Jonathan Mark Dye [1966] Director; Richard Owen Hudson [1952] Director; David Stanley Neave [1959] Director; Richard Alexander Rowney [1970] Director; Barry Duncan Smith [1954] Director; Stephen Treloar [1968] Managing Director General Insurance; Kevin Peter Wenzel [1971] Director

Highway Insurance Group Limited
Incorporated: 30 November 1994
Net Worth: £263,574,000 *Total Assets:* £263,574,000
Registered Office: County Gates, Bournemouth, BH1 2NF
Activities: Activities of head offices
Parent: Liverpool Victoria Insurance Company Limited
Officers: Michael Peter Jones, Secretary; Jonathan Mark Dye [1966] Director; Richard Alexander Rowney [1970] Director; Stephen Treloar [1968] Managing Director General Insurance

Highworth Warneford School
Incorporated: 7 June 2011 *Employees:* 161
Net Worth: £10,661,882 *Total Assets:* £11,644,092
Registered Office: Shrivenham Road, Highworth, Swindon, Wilts, SN6 7BZ
Activities: General secondary education
Officers: Phillip Henry Raymont Beaumont [1942] Director/Retired; Philip John Bole [1951] Director/Retired; Gary Robert Brown [1960] Director/Sales Agent; Suriakanthi Govender Chetty [1965] Director/Teacher [South African/British]; Louisa Jane Dibble [1963] Director/Education Officer; Clare Gevaux [1975] Director/Housewife; Lorraine Dawn Hayward [1976] Director/School Business Manager; Malcolm Stuart Holbrook [1949] Director/Business Consultant; Emma Howarth-Barnes [1974] Director/Teacher; Robin John James [1959] Director/House Husband; Gary Lewis Llewellyn [1961] Director/Chartered Town Planner; Philip Roger Mangham [1968] Director/Teacher; Mark Charles Edward Nye [1973] Director/Deputy Headteacher; Elaine Margaret Poulter [1976] Director/Housewife; Professor Andrew John Shortland [1966] Director/University Professor; Judy Caroline Smith [1962] Director/Doctor (GP); Andrew Michael Steele [1970] Director/Headteacher; Debra Lynne Tremblin [1957] Director/Library Resource Centre Manager [American]; Lynn Vardy [1945] Director/Nursery Owner; Jonathan Ellis Williams [1974] Director/Actuary

Hilcro Limited
Incorporated: 17 January 1989
Net Worth: £3,984,552 *Total Assets:* £3,984,552
Registered Office: St Matthew's House, Quays Office Park, Conference Avenue, Portishead, Bristol, BS20 7LZ
Activities: Banks
Parent: Reform Investments Ltd
Officers: Owen Tudur Cross [1943] Director; Paul Ronald Scott Lever [1940] Director

Hilditch Group Limited
Incorporated: 24 January 2006 *Employees:* 44
Net Worth: £883,386 *Total Assets:* £3,513,462
Registered Office: Hilditch, Gloucester Road Industrial Estate, Malmesbury, Wilts, SN16 9JT
Activities: Other professional, scientific and technical activities n.e.c.
Parent: Hilditch Holdings Limited
Officers: Michael Graham Hilditch, Secretary; Michael Graham Hilditch [1959] Director; Nicola Hilditch [1960] Director

The Hill Brush Company Ltd
Incorporated: 12 November 1997 *Employees:* 112
Net Worth: £13,907,323 *Total Assets:* £16,462,833
Registered Office: Norwood Park, Castle Street, Mere, Wilts, BA12 6FE
Activities: Manufacture of brooms and brushes
Shareholder: Peter Richard Coward
Officers: Andrew David Coward, Secretary; Andrew David Coward [1975] Finance/IT Director; Charles Edward Coward [1979] Director; Martin David Coward [1949] Director; Peter Richard Coward [1963] Director; Philip Wenman Coward [1951] Director

Hillcrest House Limited
Incorporated: 23 November 1995
Net Worth: £3,585,830 *Total Assets:* £6,149,306
Registered Office: Hillcrest House, Nursing Home, Barbican Road, Looe, Cornwall, PL13 1NN
Activities: Residential nursing care facilities
Shareholders: Michael James Cotton; Sharon Cotton
Officers: Michael James Cotton, Secretary/Director; Michael James Cotton [1955] Director; Sharon Cotton [1961] Director/RGN/Manager

Hills Homes Developments Limited
Incorporated: 1 May 2012 *Employees:* 22
Net Worth: £2,673,000 *Total Assets:* £21,298,000
Registered Office: Wiltshire House, County Park Business Centre, Shrivenham Road, Swindon, Wilts, SN1 2NR
Activities: Construction of domestic buildings
Parent: The Hills Group Limited
Officers: Alex Henderson, Secretary; David Ian Bevan [1965] Finance Director; Michael Patrick Hill [1968] Director; Nicholas Jonathon King [1959] Director; Alan George Pardoe [1950] Director

Hills Quarry Products Limited
Incorporated: 9 November 2001 *Employees:* 94
Net Worth: £7,103,000 *Total Assets:* £27,423,000
Registered Office: Wiltshire House, County Park Business Centre, Shrivenham Road, Swindon, Wilts, SN1 2NR
Activities: Operation of gravel and sand pits; mining of clays and kaolin
Parent: The Hills Group Limited
Officers: Alex Henderson, Secretary; Peter Frank Andrew [1962] Director; Michael Patrick Hill [1968] Director; Adrian Robert Knowles [1965] Director/Accountant; Alan George Pardoe [1950] Director

Hills UK Limited
Incorporated: 19 March 1954 *Employees:* 448
Net Worth: £67,072,000 *Total Assets:* £116,141,000
Registered Office: Wiltshire House, County Park Business Centre, Shrivenham Road, Swindon, Wilts, SN1 2NR
Activities: Development of building projects
Officers: Michael Patrick Hill, Secretary; Anthony Nelson Hill [1942] Director; Bronia Glenis Hill [1965] Director/Horse Riding Instructor; Mervyn Beverley Hill [1935] Director; Michael Patrick Hill [1968] Director; Richard Andrew Hill [1967] Director; Rosemary Margaret Hill [1940] Director; Anna Patricia Ozberk [1964] Director; Alan George Pardoe [1950] Director/Chairman

Hills Waste Solutions Limited
Incorporated: 7 September 1956 *Employees:* 250
Net Worth: £21,209,000 *Total Assets:* £44,339,000
Registered Office: Wiltshire House, County Park Business Centre, Shrivenham Road, Swindon, Wilts, SN1 2NR
Activities: Collection of non-hazardous waste
Parent: The Hills Group Limited
Officers: Alex Henderson, Secretary; Michael Patrick Hill [1968] Director; Alan George Pardoe [1950] Director/Chairman

Hillside Farm Investments Limited
Incorporated: 24 October 1986 *Employees:* 2
Net Worth: £3,889,628 *Total Assets:* £4,659,297
Registered Office: 2 Temple Street, Keynsham, Bristol, BS31 1EG
Activities: Real estate agencies
Shareholders: David Gunter; Carolyn Gunter
Officers: David John Gunter, Secretary; Carolyn Gunter [1957] Director; David Gunter [1955] Director

Hillside Property Company Limited
Incorporated: 13 May 1982 *Employees:* 5
Net Worth: £6,823,025 *Total Assets:* £9,869,296
Registered Office: Vine House, 187 Henbury Road, Henbury, Bristol, BS10 7AD
Activities: Other letting and operating of own or leased real estate
Major Shareholder: David Colin Michael Atkinson
Officers: Phillipa Atkinson, Secretary; David Colin Michael Atkinson [1960] Director; Phillipa Atkinson [1962] Director

Hindhead Investments Limited
Incorporated: 23 August 2012 *Employees:* 2
Net Worth: £5,935,884 *Total Assets:* £5,943,480
Registered Office: Pemberley Hall, Buckland Monochorum, Yelverton, Devon, PL20 7LG
Activities: Activities of other holding companies n.e.c.
Shareholders: Jeffrey Charles Deacon; Maria Bernadette Deacon
Officers: Maria Deacon, Secretary; Jeffrey Charles Deacon [1964] Director; Maria Bernadette Deacon [1966] Director

Hinton Capital Investments Limited
Incorporated: 24 September 1976 *Employees:* 2
Net Worth: £12,196,073 *Total Assets:* £15,838,091
Registered Office: Stanway House, Evesham Road, Stow on the Wold, Glos, GL54 1EJ
Activities: Development of building projects
Shareholders: Jennifer Anne Hinton; Michael John Hinton
Officers: Victoria Anne Weale, Secretary; Jennifer Anne Hinton [1943] Director; Michael John Hinton [1944] Director; William John Hinton [1971] Director; Victoria Anne Weale [1974] Director

Hinton Garage (Bath) Limited
Incorporated: 6 July 1976 *Employees:* 48
Net Worth: £6,400,632 *Total Assets:* £6,769,380
Registered Office: Western Distribution Centre, Whitchurch Lane, Whitchurch, Bristol, BS14 0BH
Activities: Maintenance and repair of motor vehicles
Shareholders: David Albert Woolcott; Janet Mary Woolcott
Officers: David Albert Woolcott, Secretary; David Albert Woolcott [1946] Director; Janet Mary Woolcott [1947] Director

EA & JA Hiscock Limited
Incorporated: 25 November 2005 *Employees:* 11
Net Worth: £2,604,192 *Total Assets:* £9,345,521
Registered Office: Bishopbrook House, Cathedral Avenue, Wells, Somerset, BA5 1FD
Activities: Raising of other animals
Shareholders: Edward Allen Hiscock; Julie Anne Hiscock
Officers: Julia Anne Hiscock, Secretary; Edward Allen Hiscock [1965] Director/Farmer; Julie Anne Hiscock [1965] Director/Farmer

Hitachi Information Control Systems Europe Ltd.
Incorporated: 2 June 2000 *Employees:* 114
Previous: The Railway Engineering Company Limited
Net Worth: £3,512,195 *Total Assets:* £10,245,204
Registered Office: Manvers House, Kingston Road, Bradford on Avon, Wilts, BA15 1AB
Activities: Other business support service activities n.e.c.
Parent: Hitachi Europe Limited
Officers: Carl William Newton, Secretary; Patrick Gerard Devlin [1972] Director/Chief Operating Officer; Satoko Fujimori [1968] Senior Director [Japanese]; Hideki Fujisawa [1968] Director/Senior Manager [Japanese]; Timothy James Gray [1965] Managing Director; Susumu Hasegawa [1967] Director/General Manager [Japanese]; Nicholas Hughes [1963] Sales Director; Nobuya Kashimura [1965] Director/Executive Chairman [Japanese]; Naotoshi Nishida [1967] Managing Director [Japanese]

Hitachi Nuclear Projects Development Europe Limited
Incorporated: 8 November 2012
Previous: Hitachi Horizon Nuclear Project Development UK Limited
Net Worth: £1,032,829,568 *Total Assets:* £1,032,843,520
Registered Office: Sunrise House, Charlton Court, Brockworth, Gloucester, GL3 4AE
Activities: Production of electricity
Parent: Hitachi, Ltd
Officers: James William Jones, Secretary; Masahide Tanigaki [1951] Director and Chairman [Japanese]

Robert Hitchins Investment Properties Limited
Incorporated: 23 February 2017
Net Worth: £2,788,300 *Total Assets:* £17,381,772
Registered Office: The Manor, Boddington Lane, Boddington, Cheltenham, Glos, GL51 0TJ
Activities: Buying and selling of own real estate
Parent: Robert Hitchins Limited
Officers: Jonathan James Stewart Dunley, Secretary; Jonathan James Stewart Dunley [1970] Director; Jeremy Charles Hitchins [1954] Director; Jonathan Richard Hitchins [1950] Director; Stephen Robert Hitchins [1947] Director; Simon Jeremy Tothill [1965] Director/Chartered Surveyor

Robert Hitchins Limited
Incorporated: 16 March 1961 *Employees:* 44
Net Worth: £99,248,192 *Total Assets:* £168,838,560
Registered Office: The Manor, Boddington, Cheltenham, Gloucester, GL51 0TJ
Activities: Development of building projects
Parent: The Robert Hitchins Group Limited
Officers: Jonathan James Stewart Dunley, Secretary; Jonathan James Stewart Dunley [1970] Director; Andrew John Hill [1958] Director; Jeremy Charles Hitchins [1954] Director; Jonathan Richard Hitchins [1950] Director; Stephen Robert Hitchins [1947] Director; Gordon Robert Jeynes [1968] Director; Simon Jeremy Tothill [1965] Director/Chartered Surveyor

HJP Investments 2015
Incorporated: 31 March 2015 *Employees:* 1
Net Worth: £3,999,982 *Total Assets:* £3,999,982
Registered Office: 1 Georges Square, Bath Street, Bristol, BS1 6BA
Activities: Activities of investment trusts
Shareholders: Hayley Joanne Parsons; Mark Douglas Loder
Officers: Hayley Joanne Parsons [1973] Director

Hoare Lea LLP
Incorporated: 14 March 2016 *Employees:* 877
Net Worth: £25,460,000 *Total Assets:* £38,896,000
Registered Office: 155 Aztec West, Almondsbury, Bristol, BS32 4UB
Officers: Ian James Durbin [1962] Member; Miles Scott Freeman [1963] Member; Gary Nicholas Tucker [1958] Member; Eduardo Luis Urinovsky [1959] Member; Mark Duncan West [1959] Member; Gary John Andrews [1968] LLP Member; David Richard Armstrong [1970] LLP Member; Simon Andrew Averill [1966] LLP Member; Jeremy David Barnes [1962] LLP Member; Ahsley Ewart Bateson [1965] LLP Member; Ian Billington [1965] LLP Member; Richard John Brown [1977] LLP Member; Stephen Buckley [1966] LLP Member; Andrew John Bullmore [1962] LLP Member; Matthew Charles Chambers [1978] LLP Member; Stephen David Clifford [1957] LLP Member; Graham Rodney Cossons [1961] LLP Member; Ian Christopher Cowley [1958] LLP Member; Nicholas Jonathan Cullen [1965] LLP Member; Steven Gary Delvin [1976] LLP Member; Colm Ceallach Dougan [1965] LLP Member; Mark Ian Doughty [1980] LLP Member; Joanne Christina Edwards [1974] LLP Member; Richard David Evans [1975] LLP Member; James Robert Ford [1980] LLP Member; Simon James French [1981] LLP Member; Karl William Friedrich [1961] LLP Member; Ian David Gow [1980] LLP Member; Russel Greenwood [1973] LLP Member; Philip James Grew [1967] LLP Member; Mark Robert Hagger [1967] LLP Member; William Miller Hannah [1969] LLP Member; Richard Wynne Harris [1964] LLP Member; Stephen John Harrison [1960] LLP Member; Matthew Edward Heaman [1966] LLP Member; Clive Joseph Higham [1964] LLP Member; Rupert Edward Horne [1966] LLP Member; Matthew Sean Jones [1969] LLP Member; Sheldon Alexander Mann [1974] LLP Member; David Matthews [1979] LLP Member; Dominic Digby Meyrick [1964] LLP Member; Richard Charles Monksmith [1977] LLP Member; Andrew Williams Morris [1964] LLP Member; Christopher Peter Myers [1966] LLP Member; Adrian James Peacock [1971] LLP Member; Andrew Neil Peggram [1977] LLP Member; Timothy James Rathbone [1963] LLP Member; Neil David Roberts [1968] LLP Member; Jonathan Craig Rush [1976] LLP Member; Simon Jonathan Russett [1968] LLP Member; Mark Anthony Ryder [1962] LLP Member; Carl John Saxon [1967] LLP Member; Justin Alexander Spencer [1970] LLP Member; David Peter Sworder [1959] LLP Member; Steven Richard Timms [1975] LLP Member; Alan Treacy [1972] LLP Member; Michael Kuen Tso [1964] LLP Member; Saul Thomas Tyler [1968] LLP Member; Matthew Michael Warner [1972] LLP Member; Andrew Thomas Warrack [1971] LLP Member; Peter James Wells [1960] LLP Member; Mark Wilson Wilkinson [1977] LLP Member; Clive Paul Williamson [1974] LLP Member; Stephen Wisby [1963] LLP Member

Hobbs Bros.Limited
Incorporated: 21 July 1932 *Employees:* 18
Net Worth: £1,054,849 *Total Assets:* £4,698,323
Registered Office: Hobbs Bros. Ltd, Spinnaker Road, Hempsted, Gloucester, GL2 5FD
Activities: Agents involved in the sale of fuels, ores, metals and industrial chemicals
Parent: Ford Fuels (Holdings) Limited
Officers: John David Ford, Secretary; Adrian John Ford [1959] Director; John David Ford [1983] Director; Michael Ford [1959] Director; Richard Nigel Ford [1960] Director

Hobbs Properties Limited
Incorporated: 8 March 1962 *Employees:* 11
Net Worth: £19,088,128 *Total Assets:* £20,421,940
Registered Office: Backwell House, Backwell, Bristol, BS48 3PL
Activities: Other letting and operating of own or leased real estate
Parent: Hobbs Holdings Limited
Officers: Sadhana Jain, Secretary; Jeremy James Hobbs [1943] Director; Julian Robert Hobbs [1951] Director; Richard John Hobbs [1965] Director/Quarrying Executive; Martin Graham Robbins [1960] Director; Judith Patricia Toogood [1938] Director

Hobbycraft Group Limited
Incorporated: 7 April 2010 *Employees:* 1,205
Net Worth Deficit: £26,951,000 *Total Assets:* £140,308,992
Registered Office: 7 Enterprise Way, Aviation Park, Bournemouth International Airport, Hurn, Christchurch, Dorset, BH23 6HG
Activities: Other retail sale of new goods in specialised stores (not commercial art galleries and opticians)
Shareholders: Bridgepoint Europe (SGP) Limited; Bridgepoint Advisers Limited
Officers: Lawrence Christensen [1943] Director; Matthew Davies [1970] Director; Dominic Martin Jordan [1966] Director; Emma Judith Sophia Watford [1977] Director; Guy Patrick Weldon [1967] Director

Hobbycraft Trading Limited
Incorporated: 22 May 1964 *Employees:* 1,201
Net Worth: £45,416,000 *Total Assets:* £81,388,000
Registered Office: 7 Enterprise Way, Aviation Park, Bournemouth International Airport, Hurn, Christchurch, Dorset, BH23 6HG
Activities: Other retail sale of new goods in specialised stores (not commercial art galleries and opticians)
Parent: Stitch Bidco Limited
Officers: Dominic Martin Jordan [1966] Operations Director; Katherine Julie Paterson [1971] Marketing Director

Niall Hobhouse Limited
Incorporated: 21 November 1997 *Employees:* 1
Net Worth: £4,058,464 *Total Assets:* £5,350,801
Registered Office: Shatwell Studios, Shatwell Lane, Yarlington, Wincanton, Somerset, BA9 8DL
Activities: Retail sale of antiques including antique books in stores
Major Shareholder: Niall Alexander Hobhouse
Officers: Niall Alexander Hobhouse [1954] Director

Hoburne Development Company Limited
Incorporated: 10 December 1958 *Employees:* 4
Net Worth: £867,528 *Total Assets:* £7,927,636
Registered Office: 10 Hoburne Lane, Christchurch, Dorset, BH23 4HP
Activities: Construction of commercial buildings
Parent: Burry and Knight Limited
Officers: Nicholas Stewart Putnam, Company Secretary; Rosemary Sarah Kennar [1956] Director; Rodney Philip Tucker [1954] Director

Hoburne Limited
Incorporated: 15 March 1973 *Employees:* 423
Net Worth: £43,850,372 *Total Assets:* £58,185,036
Registered Office: 10 Hoburne Lane, Christchurch, Dorset, BH23 4HP
Activities: Activities of head offices
Officers: Nicholas Stewart Putnam, Company Secretary; John David Butters [1981] Director; Philippa Jane Goodwin [1970] Director; Rosemary Sarah Kennar [1956] Director; Timothy Richard Knight [1960] Director/Computer Consultant; Lucy Caroline Lucas-Rowe [1966] Director; Adrian John Osman [1943] Director; Rodney Philip Tucker [1954] Director; Guy James Vigar [1957] Director/Company General Manager

Hochtief (UK) Construction Limited
Incorporated: 4 April 1990 *Employees:* 267
Net Worth: £5,848,000 *Total Assets:* £68,385,000
Registered Office: Whitehill House, Windmill Hill Business Park, Whitehill Way, Swindon, Wilts, SN5 6PE
Activities: Construction of roads and motorways
Parent: Hochtief Infrastructure GmbH
Officers: Christopher Raymond Barlow, Secretary; Lawrence Jackson [1964] Director [Irish/South African]; Jorg Laue [1972] Director [German]; Riku Tauriainen [1963] Director [Finnish]

Hochtief PPP Solutions (UK) Limited
Incorporated: 21 July 2004 *Employees:* 12
Net Worth: £4,633,000 *Total Assets:* £7,813,000
Registered Office: Whitehill House, Windmill Hill Business Park, Whitehill Way, Swindon, Wilts, SN5 6PE
Activities: Other business support service activities n.e.c.
Parent: Hochtief PPP Solutions GmbH
Officers: Jane Catherine Barber [1963] Managing Director

William C. Hockin (Transport) Limited
Incorporated: 2 April 1980 *Employees:* 23
Net Worth: £2,122,010 *Total Assets:* £3,801,701
Registered Office: Gratton Way, Roundswell Industrial Estate, Barnstaple, Devon, EX31 3NL
Activities: Freight transport by road
Shareholders: Irene Margaret Hockin; William Cyril Hockin
Officers: Irene Margaret Hockin, Secretary; Brian James Hockin [1956] Director/Accountant; Irene Margaret Hockin [1946] Director; William Cyril Hockin [1949] Director/Haulier

P & S Hockin Limited
Incorporated: 3 June 2013 *Employees:* 141
Previous: Devonshire Pine (Holdings) Limited
Net Worth: £12,173,879 *Total Assets:* £14,491,926
Registered Office: Devonshire Pine Holdings Ltd, Caddsdown Industrial Park, Bideford, Devon, EX39 3DX
Activities: Non-trading company
Shareholders: Peter Hockin; Sharon Elaine Hockin
Officers: Mr Peter Hockin, Secretary; Peter Hockin [1961] Director; Sharon Elaine Hockin [1964] Director

Hodgetts Farming Limited
Incorporated: 25 November 2014
Net Worth: £23,397,896 *Total Assets:* £23,651,812
Registered Office: 8 Gay Street, Bath, BA1 2PH
Activities: Growing of cereals (except rice), leguminous crops and oil seeds
Parent: Link Administration Holdings Limited
Officers: Nicholas James Burrows, Secretary; Nicholas James Burrows [1968] Director; Felix Edward Carter [1986] Director/Estates Manager

B.R. Hodgson (Holdings) Limited
Incorporated: 26 April 2013 *Employees:* 81
Net Worth: £2,909,874 *Total Assets:* £5,575,506
Registered Office: Naishcombe House, Golden Valley, Wick, Bristol, BS30 5TW
Activities: Activities of head offices
Officers: Alastair John Vernon Prescot, Secretary; John Andrew Dempster [1958] Director; Alastair John Vernon Prescot [1960] Director/Chartered Accountant

B.R.Hodgson Facades Limited
Incorporated: 6 December 1977 *Employees:* 66
Previous: B.R. Hodgson Limited
Net Worth: £354,362 *Total Assets:* £3,907,856
Registered Office: Naishcombe House, Golden Valley, Wick, Bristol, BS30 5TW
Activities: Construction of commercial buildings
Officers: Alastair John Vernon Prescot, Secretary; Matthew Adrian Ball [1954] Director; John Andrew Dempster [1958] Director; David Duplock [1963] Director; Jason Macer [1978] Director; Faith Parker [1959] Director; Andrew Petrie [1964] Commercial Director; Alastair John Vernon Prescot [1960] Director/Chartered Accountant

B R Hodgson Group Limited
Incorporated: 9 May 1996 *Employees:* 2
Net Worth: £4,546,010 *Total Assets:* £6,549,504
Registered Office: Naishcombe House, Golden Valley, Wick, Bristol, BS30 5TW
Activities: Buying and selling of own real estate
Major Shareholder: Geoff Valentine
Officers: Alastair John Vernon Prescot, Secretary; Geoffrey Valentine [1952] Director; Samantha Jayne Valentine [1971] Director

Hodie Limited
Incorporated: 4 January 2000 *Employees:* 3
Net Worth: £14,112,077 *Total Assets:* £15,463,216
Registered Office: Maltravers House, Petters Way, Yeovil, Somerset, BA20 1SH
Activities: Other letting and operating of own or leased real estate
Shareholders: Moderandum Limited; Trustees of Toby Bonham's 1989 Settlement
Officers: Julie Diana Elizabeth Bonham Cozens, Secretary; David Blunt [1944] Director/Barrister; Nicholas Bonham [1948] Director; Julie Diana Elizabeth Bonham Cozens [1986] Director and Company Secretary

Hoist Hire Holdings Limited
Incorporated: 12 October 2017
Net Worth: £36,000 *Total Assets:* £4,046,000
Registered Office: Mardle Way, Buckfastleigh, Devon, TQ11 0NR
Activities: Renting and leasing of construction and civil engineering machinery and equipment
Shareholders: Jeremy Paul Douce; Richard John Palk
Officers: Jeremy Paul Douce [1952] Director and Chairman; Richard John Palk [1963] Director; Katy Williamson [1985] Operations Director; Shawn Williamson [1969] Managing Director

Holders of Congresbury Limited
Incorporated: 24 April 1958 *Employees:* 21
Net Worth: £3,310,750 *Total Assets:* £3,760,906
Registered Office: The Coach House, Aust Road, Olveston, Bristol, BS35 4DE
Activities: Sale of new cars and light motor vehicles
Major Shareholder: Jacqueline Susan Baker
Officers: Phillip Neil Bryant, Secretary; Jacqueline Susan Baker [1956] Director; Phillip Neil Bryant [1957] Director/Accountant; Rex Douglas Jeffrey [1957] Director

Holiday Parks SW Limited
Incorporated: 27 January 2015 *Employees:* 41
Previous: South West Holiday Parks Limited
Net Worth Deficit: £5,120,514 *Total Assets:* £8,859,241
Registered Office: The Park, Mawgan Porth, Newquay, Cornwall, TR8 4BD
Activities: Recreational vehicle parks, trailer parks and camping grounds
Officers: Muhammad Abdul Razzak Akbar [1984] Director/Chartered Accountant; Richard Thomas Butler [1977] Director/Chartered Accountant; Demetri Dinopoulos [1979] Director/Chartered Accountant/Private Equity Professional [Greek]; Adrian Lavan Martyn [1980] Director/Accountant [Australian]

Hollingsworth & Vose Company Limited
Incorporated: 19 June 1900 *Employees:* 159
Net Worth: £9,427,000 *Total Assets:* £22,786,000
Registered Office: Postlip Mills, Winchcombe, Glos, GL54 5BB
Activities: Manufacture of other articles of paper and paperboard n.e.c.
Officers: Eileen Margaret Swain, Secretary; Jochem Hofstetter [1964] Director [German]; Joesph Kaiser [1962] Operations Director [German]; John S Madej [1965] Director/Division President -EIF [American]

Hollingsworth and Vose Company (U.K.) Limited
Incorporated: 16 September 1982 *Employees:* 211
Net Worth: £25,201,000 *Total Assets:* £39,262,000
Registered Office: Postlip Mills, Winchcombe, Cheltenham, Glos, GL54 5BB
Activities: Manufacture of other articles of paper and paperboard n.e.c.
Officers: Eileen Margaret Swain, Secretary; Jochem Hofstetter [1964] Director/Vice Principal [German]; John S Madej [1965] Director/Division President -EIF [American]

Holmleigh Care Homes Limited
Incorporated: 27 June 2000 *Employees:* 452
Net Worth: £7,671,898 *Total Assets:* £18,770,116
Registered Office: Windsor House, Bayshill Road, Cheltenham, Glos, GL50 3AT
Activities: Residential care activities for learning difficulties, mental health and substance abuse
Shareholder: Matthew Lloyd Western
Officers: Rodney Wayne Correia, Secretary/Sales Manager; Kay Diana Correia [1960] Director; Rodney Wayne Correia [1956] Director (Care Home); Matthew Lloyd Western [1973] Director

Holmshaw Property Co Limited
Incorporated: 7 May 1955
Net Worth: £4,764,979 *Total Assets:* £5,078,781
Registered Office: Staverton Court, Staverton, Cheltenham, Glos, GL51 0UX
Activities: Buying and selling of own real estate
Parent: Holmshaw Property Holdings Limited
Officers: Andrew Colin Douglas Jardine, Secretary; Andrew Colin Douglas Jardine [1955] Director/Property Consultant; Alexander James Winwood Robinson [1985] Director/Land Agent; Philip Mark St. Pier [1959] Director/Farmer

Holmshaw Property Holdings Limited
Incorporated: 3 December 2012
Net Worth: £5,598,973 *Total Assets:* £5,599,574
Registered Office: Staverton Court, Staverton, Cheltenham, Glos, GL51 0UX
Activities: Buying and selling of own real estate
Shareholders: Philip Mark St Pier; Richard St Pier; Evelyn St Pier
Officers: Andrew Colin Douglas Jardine, Secretary; Andrew Colin Douglas Jardine [1955] Director/Property Consultant; Alexander James Winwood Robinson [1985] Director/Land Agent; Philip Mark St. Pier [1959] Director/Farmer

Holne Chase Properties Limited
Incorporated: 25 November 2011 *Employees:* 2
Net Worth: £1,807,173 *Total Assets:* £4,699,166
Registered Office: Sigma House, Oak View Close, Edginswell Park, Torquay, Devon, TQ2 7FF
Activities: Other letting and operating of own or leased real estate
Shareholder: Steven Knight
Officers: Harriet Lucy Simpson [1972] Director; Richard Alexander Edward Shuldham Simpson [1969] Director

Holt Farms Limited
Incorporated: 8 September 1987 *Employees:* 50
Net Worth: £21,870,452 *Total Assets:* £27,224,996
Registered Office: Yeo Valley HQ, Rhodyate, Blagdon, Bristol, BS40 7YE
Activities: Mixed farming
Major Shareholder: Timothy William Tripp Mead
Officers: Timothy William Tripp Mead, Secretary/Farmers/Director; Adrian John Fenton [1959] Director [Irish]; Sarah Hope Mead [1964] Director/Farmer; Timothy William Tripp Mead [1963] Farmer/Director; Lesley Ann Smith [1967] Finance Director; Thomas Charles Alexanderson Wright [1983] Director

Holt JCB Holdings Limited
Incorporated: 1 March 2012 *Employees:* 113
Net Worth: £1,650,000 *Total Assets:* £9,932,000
Registered Office: Third Way, Avonmouth, Bristol, BS11 9ZG
Activities: Repair of machinery
Shareholders: Andrew John Peter Shields; Michael Andrew Winton
Officers: Michael Andrew Winton, Secretary; Andrew John Peter Shields [1979] Director; Peter Shields [1948] Director/Chairman/Director; Michael Andrew Winton [1967] Director

Holt JCB Limited
Incorporated: 26 November 1987 *Employees:* 113
Net Worth: £1,640,000 *Total Assets:* £9,922,000
Registered Office: Third Way, Avonmouth, Bristol, BS11 9ZG
Activities: Repair of machinery
Shareholders: Michael Andrew Winton; Andrew John Peter Shields
Officers: Michael Andrew Winton, Secretary/Director; Andrew John Peter Shields [1979] Director; Peter Shields [1948] Director; Michael Andrew Winton [1967] Director

Holton Homes Limited
Incorporated: 5 February 1988 *Employees:* 18
Net Worth: £2,036,771 *Total Assets:* £9,721,889
Registered Office: 2 Albany Park, Cabot Lane, Poole, Dorset, BH17 7BX
Activities: Development of building projects
Shareholders: Peter John Egerton; Clive Ashley Wingfield
Officers: Peter John Egerton, Secretary/Director; Peter John Egerton [1961] Director/Developer; Clive Ashley Wingfield [1962] Director/Developer

Home Hardware Distribution Limited
Incorporated: 4 July 2000 *Employees:* 91
Net Worth: £2,074,967 *Total Assets:* £5,632,878
Registered Office: Upcott Avenue, Pottington Business Park, Barnstaple, Devon, EX31 1NZ
Activities: Wholesale of hardware, plumbing and heating equipment and supplies
Shareholders: Home Hardware Southwest Limited; Galleon Investments (Dartford) Limited
Officers: Sean Leslie Davey, Secretary; David Copeland Adams [1949] Director/Retailer; Sean Leslie Davey [1965] Director/Chartered Accountant; Martin Brian Elliott [1961] Director

Home Hardware Southwest Limited
Incorporated: 2 March 1962 *Employees:* 163
Net Worth: £2,568,288 *Total Assets:* £10,797,025
Registered Office: Upcott Avenue, Pottington Business Park, Barnstaple, Devon, EX31 1NZ
Activities: Wholesale of china and glassware and cleaning materials
Officers: Sean Leslie Davey, Secretary; David Copeland Adams [1949] Director/Retailer; Christopher Maurice Blanchard [1952] Director/Retailer; Sean Leslie Davey [1965] Director/Chartered Accountant; Martin Brian Elliott [1961] Director; Andrew Martin Brian Lyne [1969] Director/Retailer; Jonathan Edward Mayo [1955] Director/Retailer; Nicholas Glanville Pedlar [1947] Director/Retailer; Alison Margaret Serret [1963] Director/Retailer; Robert William Watson [1954] Director/Retailer

Homeleigh Garden Centre Limited
Incorporated: 20 December 2002 *Employees:* 98
Net Worth: £2,513,580 *Total Assets:* £4,890,133
Registered Office: Homeleigh Garden Centre, Dutson, Launceston, Cornwall, PL15 9SP
Activities: Other retail sale in non-specialised stores
Shareholders: Enis Josephine Broad; Derek John Broad
Officers: Enis Josephine Broad, Secretary; Derek John Broad [1956] Director/Manager; Enis Josephine Broad [1956] Director/Manager; Robert John Broad [1985] Director/Retail Manager

Homeloan Management Limited
Incorporated: 28 January 1988 *Employees:* 948
Net Worth: £9,025,000 *Total Assets:* £21,018,000
Registered Office: The Pavilions, Bridgwater Road, Bristol, BS13 8AE
Activities: Financial intermediation not elsewhere classified
Parent: Computershare Investments (UK) (No. 3) Limited
Officers: Llewellyn Kevan Botha, Secretary; Jonathan Dolbear, Secretary; Peter Aeneas Ali [1974] Director of Finance; Philip Charles Braithwaite [1951] Director; Andrew Nigel Jones [1966] Director; Nicholas Stuart Robert Oldfield [1972] Director/Chartered Accountant; Jonathan Michael Pattinson [1969] Director; Garry George Stran [1965] Director

Homer & Pardy Developments Limited
Incorporated: 5 May 2010 *Employees:* 5
Net Worth: £365,400 *Total Assets:* £3,595,516
Registered Office: 27-29 Columbia Road, Ensbury Park, Bournemouth, BH10 4DZ
Activities: Development of building projects
Shareholders: Stewart Graham Homer; Robert James Pardy
Officers: Stewart Graham Homer [1959] Director/Mortgage Consultant; Robert James Pardy [1950] Director/Property Investor

Homes in Sedgemoor Limited
Incorporated: 18 October 2005 *Employees:* 61
Net Worth Deficit: £1,582,000 *Total Assets:* £4,710,000
Registered Office: 3rd Floor, Bridgwater House, King Square, Bridgwater, Somerset, TA6 3AR
Activities: Other accommodation
Officers: Robin Starr, Secretary; Lance John Duddridge [1967] Director/Greengrocer; David Bartholomew Ellison [1938] Director/Retired; Paul Hackett [1969] Director/Financial Consultant; Marie Hide [1978] Director/Mechanic; Janet Anita Keen [1940] Director/Councillor; David Peter Loveridge [1947] Director/Retired; Christopher Paul Moseley [1954] Director/Retired; Jane Elinor Strange [1953] Director/Management Consultant; Jenny Vernon [1959] Director

Hometower Consultancy Limited
Incorporated: 13 April 2007
Net Worth Deficit: £37,012 *Total Assets:* £7,608,218
Registered Office: 12 Old Mills Industrial Estate, Paulton, Bristol, BS39 7SU
Activities: Activities of other holding companies n.e.c.
Major Shareholder: John Joseph Bassadone
Officers: John Stewart Fuller, Secretary; Claire Louise Small [1962] Director/Administrator

Honda Engineering Europe Limited
Incorporated: 31 January 1990 *Employees:* 77
Net Worth: £4,314,000 *Total Assets:* £19,579,000
Registered Office: EGE Building, Highworth Road, South Marston, Swindon, Wilts, SN3 4TZ
Activities: Installation of industrial machinery and equipment
Parent: Honda Motor Co. Ltd
Officers: Ian Howells, Secretary/Finance Manager; Jun Nishimoto [1962] Director [Japanese]; Yoshihiko Suzuki [1961] Managing Director [Japanese]; Hiroyuki Yamamoto [1963] Director [Japanese]

Honda Logistics UK Limited
Incorporated: 24 August 1990 *Employees:* 1,219
Previous: South Marston DC Ltd
Net Worth: £11,632,741 *Total Assets:* £17,167,876
Registered Office: Unit 2 Keypoint Developement, Thornhill Road, South Marston, Swindon, Wilts, SN3 4RY
Activities: Operation of warehousing and storage facilities for land transport activities
Parent: Honda Logistics Inc
Officers: Toru Arinobu, Secretary; Isao Mizumoto [1960] Director [Japanese]; Yasumasa Shimizu [1961] Director [Japanese]; Kyuichi Yamashita [1967] Managing Director [Japanese]

Honda of The U.K. Manufacturing Limited
Incorporated: 19 February 1985 *Employees:* 3,962
Net Worth: £255,339,008 *Total Assets:* £841,907,968
Registered Office: Highworth Road, South Marston, Swindon, Wilts, SN3 4TZ
Activities: Manufacture of motor vehicles
Shareholders: Honda Motor Europe Limited; Honda Motor Co. Ltd
Officers: Ian Howells, Secretary/Finance Manager; Katsushi Inoue [1963] Managing Director [Japanese]; Jun Nishimoto [1962] Director [Japanese]

Honda R & D Europe (U.K.) Limited
Incorporated: 10 November 1992 *Employees:* 130
Net Worth: £9,157,000 *Total Assets:* £34,327,000
Registered Office: Highworth Road, South Marston, Swindon, Wilts, SN3 4TJ
Activities: Other research and experimental development on natural sciences and engineering
Parent: Honda Motor Co Ltd
Officers: Ian Howells, Secretary/Finance Manager; Hiroki Hayashi [1959] Director [Japanese]; Adrian Charles Franklin Killham [1961] Director/Chartered Engineer; Manabu Ozawa [1965] Director [Japanese]

Honeywell Global Tracking Limited
Incorporated: 6 February 2001 *Employees:* 8
Net Worth: £1,569,424 *Total Assets:* £6,324,465
Registered Office: Green Lane Business Park, Green Lane, Ashchurch, Tewkesbury, Glos, GL20 8HF
Activities: Satellite telecommunications activities
Parent: Satamatics Global Limited
Officers: Craig Denning Hodges [1978] Director/Finance Leader [American]; Thomas Park [1960] Director/Chief Commercial Officer [American]; Olivier Laille Tehio [1972] Director/Assistant General Counsel [French]

Honiton Community College Academy Trust
Incorporated: 10 June 2011 *Employees:* 116
Net Worth: £11,480,839 *Total Assets:* £13,910,372
Registered Office: Honiton Community College Academy Trust, School Lane, Honiton, Devon, EX14 1QT
Activities: General secondary education
Officers: Matthew Charles Steven Burrell, Secretary; Amy Louise Bazley [1988] Director/Teacher; Gillian Donne-Davis [1969] Director/Administrator; Margaret Ann Evans [1958] Director/Retired Accountant; Mireille Gaches-Morris [1968] Director/Office Administrator; Mark Alan Gibbs [1967] Director; Philippa Janet Gurney [1963] Director/Teacher; Siobhan Darcie Kent [1972] Director/Civil Service; Claire Louise Nuttall [1972] Director/Teaching Assistant; Lynda Kathleen Price [1951] Director/Retired; Richmal Shorter [1974] Director/Science Technician; Anthony Robert Smith [1950] Director/Retired; Glenn Norman Smith [1966] Director/Principal; Kathleen Elizabeth Smith [1949] Director/Retired Civil Servant; Sheran Patricia Taylor [1968] Director; David Vaughan Travers [1959] Director/Financial Adviser

Hoo Developments Limited
Incorporated: 29 April 1988
Net Worth: £3,008,544 *Total Assets:* £3,626,914
Registered Office: Combe, Brushford, Dulverton, Somerset, TA22 9RT
Activities: Other letting and operating of own or leased real estate
Shareholders: Julie Kelvie; Ernest John MacKelden
Officers: Julie Kelvie, Secretary; Ernest John MacKelden [1957] Director/Farmer

Hooke Court Limited
Incorporated: 28 August 2015 *Employees:* 35
Net Worth: £316,552 *Total Assets:* £4,232,244
Registered Office: Hooke Court, Hooke, Beaminster, Dorset, DT8 3NX
Activities: Educational support services
Shareholders: Mandy Cooper; Peter Cooper
Officers: Dylan Cooper [1975] Director; Christopher McConnell [1969] Director/Teacher; Sarah McConnell [1971] Director

AR Hooper and Partners Ltd
Incorporated: 1 July 2014 *Employees:* 6
Net Worth: £1,384,544 *Total Assets:* £5,393,485
Registered Office: Lower Sessland, Spreyton, Crediton, Devon, EX17 5BA
Activities: Raising of dairy cattle
Shareholders: Arthur Ronald Hooper; Marion Hooper; Rodney Arthur Hooper; Arthur Ronald Hooper; Rodney Arthur Hooper; Marion Hooper
Officers: Mrs Clara Elizabeth May Hooper, Secretary; Arthur Ronald Hooper [1937] Director/Farmer; Rodney Arthur Hooper [1966] Director/Farmer; Stuart Rodney Hooper [1986] Director/Farmer

Hope and Homes for Children
Incorporated: 3 April 2001 *Employees:* 196
Net Worth: £8,859,622 *Total Assets:* £10,689,875
Registered Office: East Clyffe Farm Barn, East Clyffe, Steeple Langford, Salisbury, Wilts, SP3 4LZ
Activities: Other social work activities without accommodation n.e.c.
Officers: Susan Elizabeth Rooke, Secretary; Matthew Graham Banks [1970] Director; Professor Andrew Bilson [1951] Director/University Professor; Victoria Jane Bruce [1970] Director/Programme Manager; Richard Cecil Greenhalgh [1944] Director; Mark William Grinonneau [1970] Director; Carol Ann Haslam [1943] Director/Television Executive; Alexander James Matheou [1970] Executive Director; Camilla Ulfsdotter Otto [1964] Director/International Civil Servant [Swedish]; Anna Julien Segall [1962] Director [Australian]; Mark Andrew Shadrack [1971] Finance Director; Malcolm John Sweeting [1957] Director/Solicitor; Dr Mike Thiedke [1973] Director/Chief Executive [German]

A.C. Hopkins (Taunton) Limited
Incorporated: 21 March 1967 *Employees:* 28
Net Worth: £3,300,950 *Total Assets:* £3,994,148
Registered Office: Ground Floor, Blackbrook Gate 1, Blackbrook Business Park, Taunton, Somerset, TA1 2PX
Activities: Wholesale of meat and meat products
Shareholders: Josephine Katherine Hopkins; Sarah Lucy Eliza Barton; Nicholas Barton; Michelmores Trust Corporation Limited
Officers: Josephine Katherine Hopkins, Secretary; Sarah Lucy Eliza Barton [1965] Director; Josephine Katherine Hopkins [1935] Director

Hopkins Estates Limited
Incorporated: 4 May 1977 *Employees:* 39
Previous: Hopkins Developments Limited
Net Worth: £42,107,812 *Total Assets:* £73,310,848
Registered Office: The Tythings Commercial Centre, Southgate Road, Wincanton, Somerset, BA9 9RZ
Activities: Mixed farming
Major Shareholder: William Ian Hopkins
Officers: William Ian Hopkins, Secretary; Nathan William Hopkins [1974] Director/Manager; William Ian Hopkins [1949] Director

Hoppings Softwood Products PLC
Incorporated: 9 May 1934 *Employees:* 64
Net Worth: £5,633,000 *Total Assets:* £8,488,000
Registered Office: 3 Southernhay West, Exeter, EX1 1JG
Activities: Support services to forestry
Shareholder: Charles Reuben Hopping
Officers: Carl Frederick Hansen, Secretary; Geoffrey Edward Alcoe [1962] Director; Andrew Court [1966] Director; Carl Frederick Hansen [1958] Director/Fellow Chartered Accountant; Charles Reuben Hopping [1953] Director; Adam Richard Pulfer [1970] Director; Joseph Charles Reevy [1955] Director/Accountant; John Michael Rhodes [1960] Director/Manager

Horatio Investments Limited
Incorporated: 19 November 2009 *Employees:* 17
Previous: Wavepower Technologies Limited
Net Worth: £5,378,443 *Total Assets:* £15,976,060
Registered Office: New Farm Offices, Hartlake, Glastonbury, Somerset, BA6 9AB
Activities: Activities of venture and development capital companies
Major Shareholder: Adam Norris
Officers: Martin Andrew Bowles [1966] Managing Director; Adam Norris [1971] Director/Investor

Horizon Motor Company Limited
Incorporated: 15 November 1971 *Employees:* 124
Net Worth: £2,948,689 *Total Assets:* £9,004,396
Registered Office: 397 Ringwood Road, Parkstone, Poole, Dorset, BH12 4LT
Activities: Sale of new cars and light motor vehicles
Major Shareholder: Colin Ross Sharpe
Officers: Simon Nicholas Rickard, Secretary; Simon Nicholas Rickard [1949] Director/Car Purchaser; Aimee Marie Sharpe [1974] Director; Christian Norman Sharpe [1979] Director; Colin Ross Sharpe [1945] Director; Margaret Ann Sharpe [1947] Director

Horizon Nuclear Power Limited
Incorporated: 30 July 2008 *Employees:* 288
Net Worth: £693,870,016 *Total Assets:* £1,333,262,976
Registered Office: Sunrise House, 1420 Charlton Court, Gloucester Business Park, Gloucester, GL3 4AE
Activities: Production of electricity
Parent: Hitachi Nuclear Projects Development Europe Limited
Officers: James William Jones, Secretary; Sir Stephen John Gomersall [1948] Director; Duncan Hawthorne [1955] Director [Canadian]; Sang Hoon David Lee [1969] Director [South Korean]; Yoshiteru Murase [1959] Director [Japanese]; Katsumi Nagasawa [1956] Director [Japanese]; Dr Timothy John Stone [1951] Director; Hidetoshi Takehara [1957] Director [Japanese]; Masahide Tanigaki [1951] Director [Japanese]

Horizon Nuclear Power Oldbury Limited
Incorporated: 6 February 2009
Net Worth: £113,520,000 *Total Assets:* £117,855,000
Registered Office: Sunrise House, 1420 Charlton Court, Gloucester Business Park, Gloucester, GL3 4AE
Activities: Production of electricity
Parent: Horizon Nuclear Power Limited
Officers: James William Jones, Secretary; Sir Stephen John Gomersall [1948] Director; Duncan Hawthorne [1955] Director [Canadian]; Sang Hoon David Lee [1969] Director [South Korean]; Katsumi Nagasawa [1956] Director [Japanese]; Dr Timothy John Stone [1951] Director; Masahide Tanigaki [1951] Director [Japanese]

Horizon Nuclear Power Services Limited
Incorporated: 6 February 2009 *Employees:* 288
Net Worth: £18,125,000 *Total Assets:* £33,932,000
Registered Office: Sunrise House, 1420 Charlton Court, Gloucester Business Park, Gloucester, GL3 4AE
Activities: Production of electricity
Parent: Horizon Nuclear Power Wylfa Limited
Officers: James William Jones, Secretary; William Alastair Stein Doig [1945] Director/Consultant; Rabih Hafez [1957] Director [Canadian]; Duncan Hawthorne [1955] Director [Canadian]; James William Jones [1964] Director/Barrister; Sang Hoon David Lee [1969] Director [South Korean]; Mark Henry Bernard Lunn [1968] Director/Engineer; Yoshiteru Murase [1959] Director/Chief Development Officer [Japanese]; Masahiko Nakane [1958] Director [Japanese]; Gwen Susan Parry-Jones [1966] Director; Dr Kenneth James Petrunik [1943] Director/Advisor/Consultant [Canadian]; Dr Timothy John Stone [1951] Director; Anthony Richard Webb [1959] Director/Nuclear Management/Assurance; Lisa Claire White [1967] HR Director

Horizon Nuclear Power Wylfa Limited
Incorporated: 6 February 2009
Net Worth: £583,147,008 *Total Assets:* £1,215,353,984
Registered Office: Sunrise House, 1420 Charlton Court, Gloucester Business Park, Gloucester, GL3 4AE
Activities: Production of electricity
Parent: Horizon Nuclear Power Wylfa Holdings Limited
Officers: James William Jones, Secretary; William Alastair Stein Doig [1945] Director/Consultant; Rabih Hafez [1957] Director [Canadian]; Duncan Hawthorne [1955] Director [Canadian]; James William Jones [1964] Director/Barrister; Sang Hoon David Lee [1969] Director [South Korean]; Mark Henry Bernard Lunn [1968] Director/Engineer; Yoshiteru Murase [1959] Director/Chief Development Officer [Japanese]; Masahiko Nakane [1958] Director [Japanese]; Gwen Susan Parry-Jones [1966] Director; Dr Kenneth James Petrunik [1943] Director/Advisor/Consultant [Canadian]; Dr Timothy John Stone [1951] Director; Anthony Richard Webb [1959] Director; Lisa Claire White [1967] HR Director

Horizon Organic Dairy Limited
Incorporated: 5 March 1999
Net Worth Deficit: £3,482,000 *Total Assets:* £16,926,000
Registered Office: Woodwater House, Pynes Hill, Exeter, Devon, EX2 5WR
Activities: Non-trading company
Officers: Paul Denayer [1969] Director/VP CFO [Belgian]; Sven Lamote [1973] Director/General Manager [Belgian]

Horsebridge Network Systems Limited
Incorporated: 23 February 2001
Net Worth Deficit: £961,820 *Total Assets:* £8,338,741
Registered Office: Unit 4 Herrick Way, Staverton Technology Park, Staverton, Cheltenham, Glos, GL51 6TQ
Activities: Information technology consultancy activities
Officers: Callum Andrew John Dick [1963] Director/Engineer; Craig Anthony Newton [1975] Director; David O'Connor [1965] Director

Horseworld Trust
Incorporated: 28 August 2007 *Employees:* 33
Net Worth: £10,661,296 *Total Assets:* £10,721,847
Registered Office: Delmar Hall, Keynes Farm, Staunton Lane, Whitchurch, Bristol, BS14 0QL
Activities: Veterinary activities
Officers: Nicola Light, Secretary/Finance Manager; Duncan John Ballard [1976] Director; Nigel Adrian Daniel [1954] Director/Retired; Leslie Barbara Dillingham [1947] Director/Retired [Canadian/British]; Andrew Dowden [1943] Managing Director; Kerry Gwyther [1959] Director/Solicitor; Ernest Richard Hemmings [1945] Director/Farmer; Michael John Neale [1954] Director/Chartered Accountant; Annette Katarina Newman [1966] Managing Director; John Lowton Newman [1945] Director/Retired; Patricia Marianne Shand [1948] Director/Livery Owner

Horstman Defence Systems Limited
Incorporated: 11 August 1980 *Employees:* 84
Net Worth: £9,430,808 *Total Assets:* £22,658,138
Registered Office: Locksbrook Road, Bath, BA1 3EX
Activities: Manufacture of other fabricated metal products n.e.c.
Shareholder: John Graham Harris
Officers: John Graham Harris [1947] Director

Horton Golf Limited
Incorporated: 26 April 2004 *Employees:* 25
Net Worth: £980,847 *Total Assets:* £4,648,336
Registered Office: Energy Site Control Centre, Arena Way, off Magna Road, Wimborne, Dorset, BH21 3BW
Activities: Other amusement and recreation activities n.e.c.
Parent: Fitzwilliam Trustees No1 and Fitzwilliam Trustees No2
Officers: Daniel Riddle, Secretary; Stuart Michael Hudson [1972] Director/General Manager; Daniel Riddle [1974] Director/Golf Manager; William Edward Riddle [1952] Director

Horwood Homewares Limited
Incorporated: 23 December 1935 *Employees:* 49
Net Worth: £12,117,675 *Total Assets:* £14,201,342
Registered Office: Avonmouth Way, Bristol, BS11 9HX
Activities: Wholesale of radio, television goods & electrical household appliances (other than records, tapes, CDs)
Parent: Horwood Homewares Holdings Limited
Officers: Nigel Stuart Hardman, Finance Director; Nigel Stuart Hardman [1951] Finance Director; Robert Joseph Jones [1976] Sales Director; Shankaran Krishnamurthy [1953] Director [Indian]; Girish Rao [1962] Director/Entrepreneur [Indian]; Neil Rosati [1964] Managing Director; Ravichandran Srinivasan [1950] Director [Indian]

Steve Hoskin Construction Limited
Incorporated: 30 August 1995 *Employees:* 286
Net Worth: £14,905,434 *Total Assets:* £21,682,040
Registered Office: Tenacres Lane, St Ive Road Industrial Estate, Pensilva, Liskeard, Cornwall, PL14 5RE
Activities: Construction of domestic buildings
Shareholder: Stephen Robert Hoskin
Officers: Charlotte Worden, Secretary; Neil Hoskin [1984] Construction Director; Stephen Robert Hoskin [1959] Director/General Construction & Civil Engineering; Charlotte Worden [1982] Company Secretary/Director

Hospiscare
Incorporated: 15 September 1987 *Employees:* 268
Net Worth: £9,378,288 *Total Assets:* £10,047,938
Registered Office: Searle House, Dryden Road, Exeter, EX2 5JJ
Activities: Other human health activities
Officers: Andrew Coleman Randall, Secretary; Matthew Bryant [1974] Director/Trustee; Geoffrey Hubert Bush [1942] Director/Retired; Dr John Alexander Coop [1955] Director/General Practitioner; Cathryn Michelle Durston [1966] Director/Trustee; Dr Sarah Jane Jackson [1975] Director/Consultant; Charlotte Leonie McGregor [1982] Director/Solicitor; Lesley Ann Murray [1950] Director/Trustee; Robert Geoffrey Pringle [1955] Director; Peter George Serjeant [1956] Director/Account; Susan Sutherland [1953] Director/Retired; Barbara Honor Sweeney [1956] Director/Clerk to Corporation, Exeter College; Ben Anthony Turner [1994] Director/Trustee; Jennifer Winslade [1968] Director/Trustee

The Hospital Company (Dartford) 2005 Limited
Incorporated: 9 May 2005 *Employees:* 3
Net Worth: £1,000 *Total Assets:* £40,777,000
Registered Office: Third Floor, Broad Quay House, Prince Street, Bristol, BS1 4DJ
Activities: Activities of head offices
Parent: The Hospital Company (Dartford) Limited
Officers: Phillip Joseph Dodd [1955] Director; David Robert Hardingham [1974] Director/Commercial Manager; Christopher James [1968] Director; Alastair James Watson [1974] Investment Director

The Hospital Company (Dartford) Group Limited
Incorporated: 29 October 1996
Net Worth: £2,007,000 *Total Assets:* £54,441,000
Registered Office: Third Floor, Broad Quay House, Prince Street, Bristol, BS1 4DJ
Activities: Construction of commercial buildings
Parent: The Hospital Company (Dartford) Holdings Limited
Officers: Phillip Joseph Dodd [1955] Director; David Robert Hardingham [1974] Director/Commercial Manager; Christopher James [1968] Director; Alastair James Watson [1974] Investment Director

The Hospital Company (Dartford) Holdings Limited
Incorporated: 6 December 2002 *Employees:* 3
Net Worth: £154,000 *Total Assets:* £40,930,000
Registered Office: Third Floor, Broad Quay House, Prince Street, Bristol, BS1 4DJ
Activities: Activities of head offices
Parent: The Hospital Company (Dartford) Holdings 2005 Limited
Officers: Phillip Joseph Dodd [1955] Director; David Robert Hardingham [1974] Director/Commercial Manager; Christopher James [1968] Director; Alastair James Watson [1974] Investment Director

The Hospital Company (Dartford) Issuer PLC
Incorporated: 21 February 2003 *Employees:* 2
Net Worth: £13,000 *Total Assets:* £115,466,000
Registered Office: Third Floor, Broad Quay House, Prince Street, Bristol, BS1 4DJ
Activities: Other business support service activities n.e.c.
Parent: The Hospital Company (Dartford) Group Limited
Officers: Phillip Joseph Dodd [1955] Director; Christopher James [1968] Director; Alastair James Watson [1974] Investment Director

The Hospital Company (Dartford) Limited
Incorporated: 29 October 1996 *Employees:* 3
Net Worth: £9,184,000 *Total Assets:* £162,447,008
Registered Office: Third Floor, Broad Quay House, Prince Street, Bristol, BS1 4DJ
Activities: Construction of commercial buildings
Parent: The Hospital Company (Dartford) Group Limited
Officers: Phillip Joseph Dodd [1955] Director; David Robert Hardingham [1974] Director/Commercial Manager; Christopher James [1968] Director; Alastair James Watson [1974] Investment Director

The Hospital Company (Swindon & Marlborough) 2006 Limited
Incorporated: 19 December 2005 *Employees:* 4
Net Worth: £180,000 *Total Assets:* £31,426,000
Registered Office: Third Floor, Broad Quay House, Prince Street, Bristol, BS1 4DJ
Activities: Medical nursing home activities
Parent: The Hospital Company (Swindon & Marlborough) Limited
Officers: Christopher John Blundell [1966] Regional Director; Richard Little [1979] Investment Director; Terence Ryan [1957] Director

The Hospital Company (Swindon & Marlborough) Group Limited
Incorporated: 14 February 2006 *Employees:* 4
Net Worth: £2,022,000 *Total Assets:* £33,448,000
Registered Office: Third Floor, Broad Quay House, Prince Street, Bristol, BS1 4DJ
Activities: Medical nursing home activities
Parent: Semperian PPP Investment Partners No.2 Limited
Officers: Christopher John Blundell [1966] Regional Director; Richard Little [1979] Investment Director; Terence Ryan [1957] Director

The Hospital Company (Swindon & Marlborough) Holdings Limited
Incorporated: 13 August 1999 *Employees:* 4
Net Worth: £10,000 *Total Assets:* £48,694,000
Registered Office: Third Floor, Broad Quay House, Prince Street, Bristol, BS1 4DJ
Activities: Medical nursing home activities
Parent: The Hospital Company (Swindon & Marlborough) Group Limited
Officers: Christopher John Blundell [1966] Regional Director; Richard Little [1979] Investment Director; Terence Ryan [1957] Director

The Hospital Company (Swindon & Marlborough) Limited
Incorporated: 12 August 1999 *Employees:* 4
Net Worth Deficit: £20,559,000 *Total Assets:* £163,586,000
Registered Office: Third Floor, Broad Quay House, Prince Street, Bristol, BS1 4DJ
Activities: Medical nursing home activities
Parent: The Hospital Company (Swindon & Marlborough) Holdings Limited
Officers: Christopher John Blundell [1966] Regional Director; Richard Little [1979] Investment Director; Terence Ryan [1957] Director

Hospital Metalcraft Limited
Incorporated: 19 October 1953 *Employees:* 162
Net Worth: £13,405,315 *Total Assets:* £17,446,988
Registered Office: Blandford Heights, Blandford Forum, Dorset, DT11 7TG
Activities: Manufacture of other fabricated metal products n.e.c.
Major Shareholder: Michael Kevin Davis
Officers: Andrew Iain Blair Smith, Secretary; Alison Yvonne Davis [1951] Director/Housewife; Michael Kevin Davis [1951] Director; Stuart Alistair Davis [1974] Director; Ian Kevin Farnfield [1972] Sales Director; Kevin Majury [1967] Operations Director; Andrew Iain Blair Smith [1957] Director/Chartered Accountant

Host Properties Limited
Incorporated: 9 January 2006
Net Worth: £13,282 *Total Assets:* £4,123,845
Registered Office: Towngate House, 2-8 Parkstone Road, Poole, Dorset, BH15 2PW
Activities: Development of building projects
Officers: Anecia Gaviana Pickup [1967] Director

House of Clive (Hair and Beauty) Limited
Incorporated: 3 August 1972 *Employees:* 218
Net Worth: £1,843,360 *Total Assets:* £3,704,419
Registered Office: Reflections House, 26 Oakfield Road, Clifton, Bristol, BS8 2AT
Activities: Hairdressing and other beauty treatment
Shareholders: Clare Cassandra Rendle; Clive Wilson Barrett
Officers: Clive Wilson Barrett [1943] Director; Clare Cassandra Rendle [1975] Director/Business Executive

House Property Associates Limited
Incorporated: 14 August 1997 *Employees:* 2
Net Worth Deficit: £543,283 *Total Assets:* £4,598,240
Registered Office: c/o Milsted Langdon LLP, Motivo House, Alvington, Yeovil, Somerset, BA20 2FG
Activities: Other business support service activities n.e.c.
Major Shareholder: Tim House
Officers: Joanne House, Secretary; Joanne House [1953] Director/Company Secretary; Timothy David House [1950] Director/Publisher

Houzz UK Ltd.
Incorporated: 13 December 2013 *Employees:* 163
Net Worth: £996,257 *Total Assets:* £7,676,808
Registered Office: 11th Floor, Whitefriars, Lewins Mead, Bristol, BS1 2NT
Activities: Management consultancy activities other than financial management
Officers: Thomas John Clayton [1976] Director/VP International Operations [American]; William Sam Veazey [1961] Director [American]

Hovertravel Limited
Incorporated: 9 December 1964 *Employees:* 85
Net Worth: £5,471,923 *Total Assets:* £10,784,158
Registered Office: Encombe House, Estate Office, Corfe Caslte, Wareham, Dorset, BH20 5LW
Activities: Sea and coastal freight water transport
Parent: Bland Group UK Holdings Limited
Officers: Ian Mackie, Secretary; Neil Chapman [1968] Director; James Peter George Gaggero [1959] Director/Company Chairman

Howard Garages (Weston) Limited
Incorporated: 17 April 1973 *Employees:* 256
Net Worth: £14,632,501 *Total Assets:* £32,896,708
Registered Office: Herluin Way, Weston Super Mare, Somerset, BS23 3YX
Activities: Sale of new cars and light motor vehicles
Parent: Howard Garages Group Limited
Officers: David Grahame Backes, Secretary; David Grahame Backes [1958] Director/Accountant; Peter Francis Coleman [1951] Director/Garage Proprietor; Peter Haynes [1966] Managing Director

Howard Tenens (North West) Limited
Incorporated: 19 August 1994 *Employees:* 5
Previous: Howard Tenens (Winsford) Limited
Net Worth: £133,121 *Total Assets:* £12,607,578
Registered Office: Tenens House, Kingfisher Business Park, London Road, Thrupp, Stroud, Glos, GL5 2BY
Activities: Operation of warehousing and storage facilities for land transport activities
Parent: Howard Tenens Limited
Officers: Simon John Emms [1975] Managing Director - Property; Benjamin John Morris [1972] Operations Director; Daniel Peter Morris [1977] Property Director; Peter Ewan Morris [1944] Managing Director; Carl David Mark Waterer [1967] Finance Director

Howard Tenens (West London) Limited
Incorporated: 24 December 2009 *Employees:* 94
Net Worth: £1,962,331 *Total Assets:* £5,481,545
Registered Office: Tenens House, Kingfisher Business Park, London Road, Thrupp, Stroud, Glos, GL5 2BY
Activities: Freight transport by road
Parent: Howard Tenens Limited
Officers: Benjamin John Morris [1972] Director; Daniel Peter Morris [1977] Director; Peter Ewan Morris [1944] Director; Carl David Mark Waterer [1967] Finance Director

Howard Tenens Distribution Limited
Incorporated: 30 November 1988
Net Worth: £7,110,758 *Total Assets:* £17,801,196
Registered Office: Tenens House, Kingfisher Business Park, London Road, Thrupp, Stroud, Glos, GL5 2BY
Activities: Buying and selling of own real estate
Officers: Julian Mark Beecham [1951] Director/Accountant; Benjamin John Morris [1972] Sales & Marketing Director; Daniel Peter Morris [1977] Group Property Director; Peter Ewan Morris [1944] Managing Director

Howard Tenens Limited
Incorporated: 5 September 2008 *Employees:* 596
Net Worth: £52,745,000 *Total Assets:* £116,751,000
Registered Office: Tenens House, Kingfisher Business Park, London Road, Thrupp, Stroud, Glos, GL5 2BY
Activities: Freight transport by road
Shareholders: Tenens PTC Limited; Peter Ewan Morris
Officers: Benjamin John Morris, Secretary; Julian Mark Beecham [1951] Director/Accountant; Jonathan Ede [1949] Director; Simon John Emms [1975] Managing Director - Property; James Hartles [1984] Director/Chief Executive Officer; Benjamin John Morris [1972] Director; Daniel Peter Morris [1977] Director; Peter Ewan Morris [1944] Managing Director; Christopher Winston Smith [1944] Director/Financial Consultant; Carl David Mark Waterer [1967] Finance Director

Hoyle & Co (Bournemouth) Limited
Incorporated: 29 March 1955 *Employees:* 2
Net Worth: £16,617,320 *Total Assets:* £20,194,772
Registered Office: 310 Bournemouth Road, Parkstone, Poole, Dorset, BH14 9AR
Activities: Renting and operating of Housing Association real estate
Shareholder: John Sydenham Whitelock
Officers: Nicole Pauline Mary Whitelock, Secretary; John Sydenham Whitelock [1949] Director/Builder; Nicole Pauline Mary Whitelock [1956] Director/Company Secretary

HRB Hotel Company Limited
Incorporated: 11 October 2012 *Employees:* 168
Net Worth: £22,867,868 *Total Assets:* £27,270,074
Registered Office: First Floor, 10 Temple Back, Bristol, BS1 6FL
Activities: Hotels and similar accommodation
Major Shareholder: His Excellency Khalaf Ahmed Khalaf Alotaiba
Officers: Khalaf Ahmed Khalaf Alotaiba [1941] Director/Group CEO [Emirati]

HSH Motor Company Limited
Incorporated: 16 September 2002 *Employees:* 110
Net Worth: £1,830,539 *Total Assets:* £6,261,351
Registered Office: One Glass Wharf, Bristol, BS2 0ZX
Activities: Sale of new cars and light motor vehicles
Shareholders: Warwick Humphries; Mrs Betty Humphries
Officers: Stephen John Bowkett [1959] Director/Accountant; Warwick Humphries [1964] Director/Dealer Principal; Paul Raymond Thomas [1963] Director/After Sales Manager

HTP Grange Limited
Incorporated: 11 January 2011
Net Worth: £7,765 *Total Assets:* £23,699,364
Registered Office: Whitehill House, Windmill Hill Business Park, Whitehill Way, Swindon, Wilts, SN5 6PE
Activities: Other business support service activities n.e.c.
Parent: HTP Grange Holdco Limited
Officers: Jane Catherine Barber, Secretary; Jane Catherine Barber [1963] Director/Chief Executive Officer; Nigel Richard Henshaw [1964] Director/Head of BSFI Asset Management; Christopher Michael Storey [1967] Project Director; Milorad Vasic [1970] Strategic Director, People

Huachangda UK Limited
Incorporated: 15 December 2014
Net Worth Deficit: £8,619 *Total Assets:* £40,842,132
Registered Office: Woodlands Grange, Woodlands Lane, Bradley Stoke, Bristol, BS32 4JY
Activities: Manufacture of other electrical equipment
Parent: Hubei Huachangda Intelligent Equipment Co., Ltd
Officers: HE Rui, Secretary; Bin Jia [1977] Director [Chinese]

Huck Nets (U.K.) Limited
Incorporated: 11 November 1996 *Employees:* 74
Net Worth: £5,638,431 *Total Assets:* £7,009,775
Registered Office: Gore Cross Business Park, Corbin Way, Bradpole, Bridport, Dorset, DT6 3UX
Activities: Manufacture of cordage, rope, twine and netting
Parent: Manfred Huck GmbH
Officers: Bernard Delbaere [1955] Director/Lawyer [Belgian]; Stefan Huck [1958] Director [German]; Jonathan Richard Legg-Bagg [1960] Director; Ian Michael Spencer [1962] Director

F.N.Hues and Sons Limited
Incorporated: 8 June 1956 *Employees:* 5
Net Worth: £3,071,421 *Total Assets:* £3,512,705
Registered Office: Cliff Farm, All Cannings, Devizes, Wilts, SN10 3NY
Activities: Mixed farming
Major Shareholder: Sally Jane Hues
Officers: James Frederick Hues, Secretary; James Frederick Hues [1977] Director/Farmer; Sally Jane Hues [1949] Director/Farmer

Hugh Sexey's Hospital
Incorporated: 15 May 2009 *Employees:* 5
Net Worth: £16,893,616 *Total Assets:* £16,960,796
Registered Office: 10 Highbury Place, Bath, BA1 6DU
Activities: Residential care activities for the elderly and disabled
Officers: Andrew Mullett, Secretary; James Anthony Fowell Buxton [1948] Director/Solicitor; Dr Susanna Davidson [1952] Director/Trustee; Julian David Cosmo de Bosdari [1951] Director/Trustee; Harriet Feilding [1959] Director; Paul Hadow [1950] Director; Sir Alexander George Hamilton Harley [1941] Director/Retired; Robin Humphry Hill [1937] Director/Trustee; Edward George Hobhouse [1960] Commercial Director; The Honourable Andrew Thomas Peter Jolliffe [1969] Director/Landowner; Ann Leslie Lee [1961] Director; Michael Mark Gusterson Stanley-Smith [1943] Director/Retired Surveyor; Lucinda Jane Frances Sunnucks [1962] Director; Elizabeth Frances Winkley [1937] Director

Hughes Hotels Limited
Incorporated: 24 July 1998 *Employees:* 66
Net Worth: £4,242,553 *Total Assets:* £7,161,794
Registered Office: 6th Floor, Dean Park House, Dean Park Crescent, Bournemouth, BH1 1HP
Activities: Hotels and similar accommodation
Shareholders: Simon John Hughes; Anthony John Hughes; June Irene Hughes
Officers: Anthony John Hughes, Secretary; Anthony John Hughes [1935] Director/Hotelier; June Irene Hughes [1941] Director; Simon John Hughes [1964] Director/Hotelier

William Hughes Limited
Incorporated: 17 October 1929 *Employees:* 103
Net Worth: £1,236,708 *Total Assets:* £5,638,889
Registered Office: Station Road, Stalbridge, Dorset, DT10 2RZ
Activities: Manufacture of wire products, chain and springs
Parent: High Tension Wires Limited
Officers: Clara Christabel Hughes, Secretary; Emma Penelope Burgon [1975] Director/Engineer; Max Ivo Arthur Hughes [1947] Director/Company Executive

The Huish Academy Trust
Incorporated: 31 October 2013 *Employees:* 78
Net Worth: £7,537,303 *Total Assets:* £8,631,521
Registered Office: Huish Primary School, Carisbrooke Gardens, Yeovil, Somerset, BA20 1AY
Activities: Primary education
Officers: Jackie Bachrach [1962] Director/Teacher; Robert James Bayley [1968] Director; Rick Peter Beaver [1956] Director/Senior Education Psychologist; Dr Brian Geary [1961] Director/Materials Engineer; Philip Lee Noone [1972] Director/Aircraft Technician Royal Navy; Pauline Price [1965] Director/Headteacher; Ceri Ann Stephens [1976] Director/Solicitor

Huish Episcopi Academy
Incorporated: 10 August 2010 *Employees:* 181
Net Worth: £9,259,276 *Total Assets:* £13,074,442
Registered Office: Huish Episcopi School, Wincanton Road, Langport, Somerset, TA10 9SS
Activities: General secondary education
Officers: Amanda Eastwood, Secretary; Christine Carol Ahmed [1979] Director/HR Consultant; Samantha Valerie Jane Baker [1968] Director/Local Government Officer; Roger Paul Clark [1965] Director/Sales & Marketing Consultant; Robert John Foster [1973] Director/Production Procurement Manager; Stephanie Julia Michell Harris [1958] Director/Journalist; Lois Amy Robson [1988] Director/Advisory Services Manager; Graham Paul Rumary [1964] Director/Technician; Anthony John Settle [1953] Director/Retired; Christopher James Wade [1971] Director/Principal; Christopher Brian Wall [1960] Director/Operations Manager

Hull Maternity Development Limited
Incorporated: 28 June 2000 *Employees:* 3
Net Worth: £1,242,000 *Total Assets:* £21,838,000
Registered Office: Third Floor, Broad Quay House, Prince Street, Bristol, BS1 4DJ
Activities: Management of real estate on a fee or contract basis
Parent: Healthcare Providers Limited
Officers: Julia Sarah McCabe [1970] Regional Director; Alan Campbell Ritchie [1967] Director

Hull Ocean Going Barges UK Ltd
Incorporated: 7 July 2015
Net Worth: £273,843 *Total Assets:* £5,415,040
Registered Office: Westerleigh Terminal, Oakleigh Green Farm Lane, Westerleigh, Bristol, BS37 8QE
Activities: Inland freight water transport
Officers: Roy Anthony Brooke [1972] Director/General Manager; Jonathan David Pegler [1965] Director/Head of Supply & Trading

Humber Technology Limited
Incorporated: 11 December 1997
Net Worth Deficit: £68,538 *Total Assets:* £30,890,822
Registered Office: 10 Saville Court, Saville Place, Clifton, Bristol, BS8 4EJ
Activities: Other business support service activities n.e.c.
Parent: J. Bollag & Cie.
Officers: Dr Josef Bollag [1942] Director/Attorney [Swiss]; Andrew Richard Lamb [1950] Director/Accountant

David Hunt (North Devon) Limited
Incorporated: 17 December 1998 *Employees:* 528
Net Worth: £73,408 *Total Assets:* £4,422,317
Registered Office: Old Station Road, Eastern Avenue, Barnstaple, Devon, EX32 8PB
Activities: Unlicenced restaurants and cafes
Major Shareholder: David Hunt
Officers: Julie Lynda Hunt, Secretary/Retailer; David Hunt [1958] Director/Franchisee

Hunt's Foodservice Ltd
Incorporated: 19 December 1974 *Employees:* 436
Net Worth: £18,087,440 *Total Assets:* £28,499,712
Registered Office: Ludbourne Road, Sherborne, Dorset, DT9 3NJ
Activities: Non-specialised wholesale of food, beverages and tobacco
Major Shareholder: Sybil Evelyn Hunt
Officers: Melvyn Dennis Norris, Secretary; Michael John Douch [1953] Director/Engineer; Richard Charles Ian Hunt [1963] Director/Farmer; Sybil Evelyn Hunt [1920] Director; Thomas Ian John Hunt [1992] Operations Director; Melvyn Dennis Norris [1961] Finance Director; Barry John Poffley [1960] Director/Chartered Accountant; Colin Froome Poffley [1934] Director/Chartered Accountant

Hunter Stoves Limited
Incorporated: 23 January 1996 *Employees:* 48
Net Worth: £2,537,932 *Total Assets:* £5,707,865
Registered Office: Trevilla Park, Slaughterbridge, Camelford, Cornwall, PL32 9TT
Activities: Manufacture of non-electric domestic appliances
Shareholders: Steven Philip Clatworthy; Paul Jeremy Grimes
Officers: Paul Jeremy Grimes, Secretary; Steven Philip Clatworthy [1957] Director/Salesman; Paul Jeremy Grimes [1953] Director/Accountant

Hydra Holdings 2015 Limited
Incorporated: 1 July 2015
Net Worth: £18,440,360 *Total Assets:* £18,440,860
Registered Office: Unit 3 Warren Road, Indian Queens, St Columb, Cornwall, TR9 6TL
Activities: Activities of production holding companies
Parent: Eliquo Water Group GmbH
Officers: David Edward Armstrong [1962] Director; Dr Dirk Brusis [1972] Director/Investment Manager [German]; Lewis Jon Claud O'Brien [1982] Director

Hydreco Hydraulics Limited
Incorporated: 19 June 2008 *Employees:* 26
Net Worth: £12,201,000 *Total Assets:* £18,608,000
Registered Office: 32 Factory Road, Poole, Dorset, BH16 5SL
Activities: Manufacture of fluid power equipment
Parent: Hydreco DBH Holdings Limited
Officers: Mark Harry Holland, Secretary; Darren Colley [1965] Director; Mark Harry Holland [1961] Director/Accountant; Katie Jane McColl [1983] Director/Chief Operating Officer

Hydro Building Systems UK Limited
Incorporated: 28 October 1971 *Employees:* 207
Previous: Sapa Building Systems Limited
Net Worth: £25,274,000 *Total Assets:* £38,136,000
Registered Office: 5300 Severn Drive, Tewkesbury Business Park, Tewkesbury, Glos, GL20 8SF
Activities: Manufacture of other fabricated metal products n.e.c.
Parent: Hydro Holdings UK Limited
Officers: Simon Nicholas Viner, Secretary; Henri Hubert Gomez [1963] Director/President [French]; Steven Mario Helsen [1978] Director [Belgian]; Mark Peter Robinson [1960] Technical Director; Nigel Keith Sissons [1957] Director; Paul Crosson Strong [1966] Sales Director; Simon Nicholas Viner [1976] Financial Director

Hydro Components UK Ltd.
Incorporated: 16 May 2007 *Employees:* 272
Previous: Sapa Components UK Limited
Net Worth: £14,670,000 *Total Assets:* £37,498,000
Registered Office: Spinnaker Park, Spinnaker Road, Gloucester, GL2 5DG
Activities: Manufacture of other fabricated metal products n.e.c.
Parent: Sapa Aluminium Holdings UK Ltd
Officers: David James Williams, Secretary; Roger Colin Ablett [1970] Director; Piotr Stanislaw Chmielewski [1974] Managing Director [Polish]; David James Williams [1978] Director/Regional Controller

Hydro Holdings UK Limited
Incorporated: 7 February 1997
Previous: Sapa Aluminium Holdings UK Limited
Net Worth: £161,522,000 *Total Assets:* £161,635,008
Registered Office: TLT LLP, One Redcliff Street, Bristol, BS1 6TP
Activities: Activities of production holding companies
Parent: Norsk Hydro ASA
Officers: Jane Sheldon, Secretary; Margit Karin Christina Steive [1964] Director/Vice President Tax [Swedish]

Hydro International (Wastewater) Limited
Incorporated: 22 May 1989 *Employees:* 31
Net Worth: £1,811,076 *Total Assets:* £6,799,552
Registered Office: Shearwater House, Clevedon Hall Estate, Victoria Road, Clevedon, Somerset, BS21 7RD
Activities: Repair of other equipment
Parent: Vexamus Limiited
Officers: Helen Rosemary Mansi, Secretary; Christopher Ralph Bates [1963] Director/Chief Financial Officer; Roger Peter Crook [1958] Commercial Director; Michael Gareth Brian Jennings [1969] Managing Director

Hydro International Limited
Incorporated: 4 January 1982 *Employees:* 42
Previous: Hydro International PLC
Net Worth: £2,648,403 *Total Assets:* £12,384,465
Registered Office: Shearwater House, Clevedon Hall Estate, Clevedon, Somerset, BS21 7RD
Activities: Agents involved in the sale of machinery, industrial equipment, ships and aircraft
Parent: Ely Acquisition Limited
Officers: Christopher Ralph Bates [1963] Director/Chief Financial Officer; Roger Peter Crook [1958] Director; Michael Gareth Brian Jennings [1969] Managing Director; James Newkirk [1964] Managing Director [American]

Hydrock Consultants Limited
Incorporated: 27 October 1995 *Employees:* 383
Net Worth: £5,822,678 *Total Assets:* £13,317,827
Registered Office: Over Court Barns, Over Lane, Almondsbury, Bristol, BS32 4DF
Activities: Other professional, scientific and technical activities n.e.c.
Parent: Hydrock Holdings Limited
Officers: Michael Yiannis Michael, Secretary; Dr Matthew Hilton [1971] Geo-Environmental Director; Dr Brian James McConnell [1964] Managing Director; Michael Yiannis Michael [1972] Finance Director

Hydrock Group Limited
Incorporated: 11 July 2008 *Employees:* 496
Net Worth: £4,142,219 *Total Assets:* £24,373,140
Registered Office: Over Court Barns, Over Lane, Almondsbury, Bristol, BS32 4DF
Activities: Other business support service activities n.e.c.
Parent: Hydrock Holdings Limited
Officers: Michael Yiannis Michael, Secretary; Michael David Casey [1950] Director; Henry David Easterbrook [1980] Director; Dr Matthew Hilton [1971] Director; Dr Brian James McConnell [1964] Director; Michael Yiannis Michael [1972] Director/Chartered Accountant

Hylton Group Limited
Incorporated: 24 December 1990 *Employees:* 102
Net Worth: £4,309,963 *Total Assets:* £13,988,819
Registered Office: Hylton, MacKenzie Way, Swindon Village, Cheltenham, Glos, GL51 9TX
Activities: Sale of new cars and light motor vehicles
Officers: Lee Andrew Koumides, Secretary; Lee Andrew Koumides [1968] Director/Accountant

Hyperbiotics PLC
Incorporated: 20 October 2016 *Employees:* 20
Net Worth: £5,409,919 *Total Assets:* £5,944,005
Registered Office: First Floor, 10 Temple Back, Bristol, BS1 6FL
Activities: Manufacture of other food products n.e.c.
Officers: Jamie Marie Amaral [1980] Director [American]; Lucas Abel Morea [1981] Director [Argentinian]; Rohit Nair [1984] Director [Indian]

I Supply Energy Limited
Incorporated: 16 January 2007 *Employees:* 167
Net Worth Deficit: £12,245,000 *Total Assets:* £18,013,000
Registered Office: 37 Commercial Road, Poole, Dorset, BH14 0HU
Activities: Trade of electricity
Parent: Vattenfall UK Sales Limited
Officers: Brendan Geoffrey Clark [1977] Finance Director; Martinus Franciscus Hagens [1971] Director [Dutch]; Erik Axel Hagland [1962] Director [Swedish]

I.D.S. Refrigeration Limited
Incorporated: 9 July 1997 *Employees:* 18
Net Worth: £3,182,662 *Total Assets:* £9,800,486
Registered Office: Green Court, Kings Weston Lane, Avonmouth, Bristol, BS11 8AZ
Activities: Non-specialised wholesale trade
Officers: Pascal Andre Dehon [1960] Director [French]; Pierre Etienne Dehon [1956] Director [French]; Pierre Donat [1958] Director/FD [French]; Allan Kristian Harper [1966] Director/Manager

IBCOS Computers Ltd
Incorporated: 21 August 1979 *Employees:* 51
Net Worth: £7,957,621 *Total Assets:* £12,283,654
Registered Office: Abacus House, Acorn Business Park, Tower Park, Poole, Dorset, BH12 4NZ
Activities: Information technology consultancy activities
Parent: IBCOS Holdings Ltd
Officers: Bonnie Jean Wilhelm, Secretary; Dexter Jonas Salna [1957] Director/Executive [Canadian]; Bonnie Jean Wilhelm [1974] Director [American]

IBD Bikes UK Limited
Incorporated: 13 August 2009 *Employees:* 62
Net Worth: £7,066,314 *Total Assets:* £20,904,024
Registered Office: Vantage Way, The Fulcrum, Poole, Dorset, BH12 4NU
Activities: Wholesale of household goods (other than musical instruments) n.e.c
Officers: Mark David Broughton, Secretary; Mark David Broughton [1979] Director/Chartered Accountant; Allison Dorothy Jenkins [1963] Director/Office Manager; Russell James Merry [1967] Director/Bike Distributor; Jeffrey Schwartz [1962] Director [Canadian]

Icon Scientific Limited
Incorporated: 20 November 2009 *Employees:* 10
Net Worth: £2,054,405 *Total Assets:* £4,126,336
Registered Office: Southview, Tarnock, Axbridge, Somerset, BS26 2SB
Activities: Other professional, scientific and technical activities n.e.c.
Parent: Sogesta Worldwide Ltd
Officers: Noel Adrian Aubrey Beauchamp [1969] Director; Kevin Fogarty [1961] Director

Icon Two Limited
Incorporated: 24 April 2003
Net Worth: £4,606,591 *Total Assets:* £9,203,460
Registered Office: Ockington, Knights Green, Dymock, Glos, GL18 2DE
Activities: Other letting and operating of own or leased real estate
Shareholders: Nicola Jane Youngs; Simon James Lewis
Officers: Penelope Ann Lewis, Secretary; John Bryan Lewis [1942] Director; Simon James Lewis [1973] Director; Nicola Jane Youngs [1975] Director

IDEMIA UK Holding Limited
Incorporated: 10 April 2012
Previous: Oberthur Technologies UK Holding Limited
Net Worth: £25,960,000 *Total Assets:* £78,048,000
Registered Office: Alexandra Way, Ashchurch Business Centre, Tewkesbury, Glos, GL20 8GA
Activities: Activities of other holding companies n.e.c.
Officers: Aaron Leslie John Davis [1973] Payment Business Director; Eric Duforest [1961] Europe Managing Director [French]; Eric Robert Quinlan [1957] Director/OT UK Country Manager

IDEMIA UK Limited
Incorporated: 8 June 1999 *Employees:* 263
Previous: Oberthur Technologies UK Limited
Net Worth: £31,030,000 *Total Assets:* £62,759,000
Registered Office: Alexandra Way, Ashchurch Business Centre, Tewkesbury, Glos, GL20 8GA
Activities: Other manufacturing n.e.c.
Parent: IDEMIA UK Holding Limited
Officers: Eric Albert Andre Duforest [1961] Managing Director [French]; Eric Robert Quinlan [1957] Director/Accountant

IDS Transport (UK) Limited
Incorporated: 19 January 2001 *Employees:* 96
Net Worth: £1,434,945 *Total Assets:* £6,562,185
Registered Office: Malvern View Business Park, Stella Way, Bishops Cleeve, Cheltenham, Glos, GL52 7DQ
Activities: Freight transport by road
Major Shareholder: Derek James Simms
Officers: Derek James Simms, Secretary/Director; Christopher Jonathon Jones [1968] Director; Derek James Simms [1963] Director

IEP Technologies Limited
Incorporated: 2 April 2013 *Employees:* 12
Net Worth: £3,385,691 *Total Assets:* £4,615,961
Registered Office: Unit 1 Neptune Business Centre, Cheltenham, Glos, GL51 9FB
Activities: Other manufacturing n.e.c.
Parent: Hoerbiger UK Limited
Officers: Randal Robert Davis [1961] Director [American]; Robert James Lade [1975] Director

IESIS (Redcliff Street) Limited
Incorporated: 6 August 2013
Net Worth: £1,984,605 *Total Assets:* £6,660,939
Registered Office: 89-95 Redcliff Street, Bristol, BS1 6LU
Activities: Other letting and operating of own or leased real estate
Parent: IESIS Limited
Officers: Robert Iestyn Lewis [1971] Director; David Franklin Steadman [1976] Director

IESIS Limited
Incorporated: 8 January 2008
Net Worth: £6,759,497 *Total Assets:* £29,304,612
Registered Office: 89-95 Redcliff Street, Bristol, BS1 6LU
Activities: Quantity surveying activities
Major Shareholder: Robert Iestyn Lewis
Officers: Matthew Melville Jones [1971] Director; Ryan John Jones [1988] Director; Robert Iestyn Lewis [1971] Director; David Franklin Steadman [1976] Director/Consultant

IEWC UK & Ireland Ltd
Incorporated: 8 December 2004 *Employees:* 107
Net Worth: £8,534,268 *Total Assets:* £29,885,246
Registered Office: 61 Gazelle Road, Weston-Super-Mare, Avon, BS24 9ES
Activities: Wholesale of electronic and telecommunications equipment and parts
Officers: John Cory McFarlane [1970] Director; Jeffrey John Siemers [1953] Director/Chief Financial Officer [American]; Michael Paul Veum [1973] Director/Chief Executive [American]

IF - Inspiring Futures Limited
Incorporated: 6 March 2014
Net Worth: £3,803,717 *Total Assets:* £5,033,361
Registered Office: Barrow House, Bishopstrow Road, Bishopstrow, Warminster, Wilts, BA12 9HU
Activities: Other education n.e.c.
Shareholders: Richard Charles Freer; Mark Richard Jeynes
Officers: Richard Charles Freer, Secretary; Caroline Anne Freer [1974] Director/Teacher; Richard Charles Henry Freer [1971] Director/Businessman; Fiona Catherine Jeynes [1965] Director/Consultant; Mark Richard Jeynes [1968] Director/Businessman

Ignition Credit PLC
Incorporated: 2 November 2001 *Employees:* 36
Net Worth: £6,032,577 *Total Assets:* £32,426,712
Registered Office: Sterling House, Green Court, Truro Business Park, Threemilestone, Truro, Cornwall, TR4 9LF
Activities: Financial leasing
Officers: Steven Charles Hunt, Secretary; Paul Caunter [1971] Sales Director; Sean Michael Devoy [1967] Director; Paul Gough [1972] Director [New Zealander]; Steven Charles Hunt [1965] Director

Ignition DG Limited
Incorporated: 14 December 2006 *Employees:* 23
Net Worth: £970,711 *Total Assets:* £4,330,036
Registered Office: Unit 1.1 Paintworks, Bath Road, Bristol, BS4 3EH
Activities: Specialised design activities
Parent: Blue Flint Group Ltd
Officers: Philip Gareth Atherton, Secretary; Philip Gareth Atherton [1974] Director/Business Improvement & Assurance; Claire Elizabeth Menzies [1959] Director/Chairman; Samantha Louise Rowe [1975] Managing Director

IIC (C & T) Limited
Incorporated: 17 May 2004
Net Worth: £841,741 *Total Assets:* £39,649,104
Registered Office: Third Floor, Broad Quay House, Prince Street, Bristol, BS1 4DJ
Activities: Other business support service activities n.e.c.
Parent: Louiseco Limited
Officers: Paul Anthony Cartwright [1957] Director; Thomas Benedict Symes [1956] Director

IIC (Leeds Schools) Fund Investment Limited
Incorporated: 17 March 2005
Net Worth: £49,871 *Total Assets:* £7,329,166
Registered Office: Third Floor, Broad Quay House, Prince Street, Bristol, BS1 4DJ
Activities: Other business support service activities n.e.c.
Parent: Louiseco Limited
Officers: Paul Anthony Cartwright [1957] Director; Richard Leonard Groome [1951] Director/Chartered Engineer; Jamie Pritchard [1971] Director/Investment Manager; Thomas Benedict Symes [1956] Director

IIC Barnet Holding Company Limited
Incorporated: 7 December 2005
Net Worth Deficit: £2,251,376 *Total Assets:* £24,409,412
Registered Office: Third Floor, Broad Quay House, Prince Street, Bristol, BS1 4DJ
Activities: Other business support service activities n.e.c.
Shareholders: Louiseco Limited; JLIF Investments Limited
Officers: Paul Anthony Cartwright [1957] Director; Vikki Louise Everett [1971] Director/Project Manager; Thomas Benedict Symes [1956] Director

IIC By Education (Peterborough Schools) Limited
Incorporated: 20 October 2005
Net Worth Deficit: £10,431,280 *Total Assets:* £47,522,292
Registered Office: Third Floor, Broad Quay House, Prince Street, Bristol, BS1 4DJ
Activities: Other business support service activities n.e.c.
Parent: IIC Peterborough Holding Company Limited
Officers: Paul Anthony Cartwright [1957] Director; Richard Leonard Groome [1951] Director/Chartered Engineer; Jamie Pritchard [1971] Director/Investment Manager; Thomas Benedict Symes [1956] Director

IIC Enfield Holding Company Limited
Incorporated: 30 January 2006
Net Worth Deficit: £2,470,748 *Total Assets:* £23,939,562
Registered Office: Third Floor, Broad Quay House, Prince Street, Bristol, BS1 4DJ
Activities: Other business support service activities n.e.c.
Shareholders: Louiseco Limited; JLIF Investments Limited
Officers: Paul Anthony Cartwright [1957] Director; Vikki Louise Everett [1971] Director/Project Manager; Thomas Benedict Symes [1956] Director

IIC Lambeth Holding Company Limited
Incorporated: 18 August 2005
Net Worth Deficit: £1,054,128 *Total Assets:* £12,637,827
Registered Office: Third Floor, Broad Quay House, Prince Street, Bristol, BS1 4DJ
Activities: Other business support service activities n.e.c.
Shareholders: Louiseco Limited; JLIF Investments Limited
Officers: Paul Anthony Cartwright [1957] Director; Vikki Louise Everett [1971] Director/Project Manager; Thomas Benedict Symes [1956] Director

IIC Miles Platting Funding Investment Limited
Incorporated: 14 September 2006
Net Worth: £400,442 *Total Assets:* £4,507,938
Registered Office: Third Floor, Broad Quay House, Prince Street, Bristol, BS1 4DJ
Activities: Other business support service activities n.e.c.
Parent: Louiseco Limited
Officers: Paul Anthony Cartwright [1957] Director; Vikki Louise Everett [1971] Director/Project Manager; Thomas Benedict Symes [1956] Director

IIC Miles Platting Subdebt Limited
Incorporated: 14 September 2006
Net Worth: £10,939 *Total Assets:* £4,338,446
Registered Office: Third Floor, Broad Quay House, Prince Street, Bristol, BS1 4DJ
Activities: Other business support service activities n.e.c.
Shareholders: IIC Miles Platting Funding Investment Limited; Louiseco Limited
Officers: Paul Anthony Cartwright [1957] Director; Vikki Louise Everett [1971] Director/Project Manager; Thomas Benedict Symes [1956] Director

IIC Northampton Funding Investment Limited
Incorporated: 13 September 2006
Net Worth: £512,419 *Total Assets:* £4,777,400
Registered Office: Third Floor, Broad Quay House, Prince Street, Bristol, BS1 4DJ
Activities: Other business support service activities n.e.c.
Parent: Louiseco Limited
Officers: Paul Anthony Cartwright [1957] Director; Vikki Louise Everett [1971] Director/Project Manager; Thomas Benedict Symes [1956] Director

IIC Northampton Holding Company Limited
Incorporated: 19 September 2006
Net Worth Deficit: £10,551,003 *Total Assets:* £45,075,484
Registered Office: Third Floor, Broad Quay House, Prince Street, Bristol, BS1 4DJ
Activities: Other business support service activities n.e.c.
Parent: Louiseco Limited
Officers: Paul Anthony Cartwright [1957] Director; Vikki Louise Everett [1971] Director/Project Manager; Thomas Benedict Symes [1956] Director

IIC Northampton Limited
Incorporated: 22 July 2005
Net Worth Deficit: £10,551,004 *Total Assets:* £45,075,484
Registered Office: Third Floor, Broad Quay House, Prince Street, Bristol, BS1 4DJ
Activities: Other business support service activities n.e.c.
Parent: IIC Northampton (Pendereds) Limited
Officers: Paul Anthony Cartwright [1957] Director; Vikki Louise Everett [1971] Director/Project Manager; Thomas Benedict Symes [1956] Director

IIC Northampton Subdebt Limited
Incorporated: 13 September 2006
Net Worth: £14,405 *Total Assets:* £4,690,930
Registered Office: Third Floor, Broad Quay House, Prince Street, Bristol, BS1 4DJ
Activities: Other business support service activities n.e.c.
Shareholders: IIC Northampton Funding Investment Limited; Louiseco Limited
Officers: Paul Anthony Cartwright [1957] Director; Vikki Louise Everett [1971] Director/Project Manager; Thomas Benedict Symes [1956] Director

IIC Peterborough Holding Company Limited
Incorporated: 8 February 2006
Net Worth Deficit: £9,342,461 *Total Assets:* £48,611,112
Registered Office: Third Floor, Broad Quay House, Prince Street, Bristol, BS1 4DJ
Activities: Other business support service activities n.e.c.
Shareholders: Louiseco Limited; JLIF Investments Limited
Officers: Paul Anthony Cartwright [1957] Director; Richard Leonard Groome [1951] Director/Chartered Engineer; Jamie Pritchard [1971] Director/Investment Manager; Thomas Benedict Symes [1956] Director

IIC Redcar and Cleveland Holding Company Limited
Incorporated: 8 May 2007
Net Worth Deficit: £3,680,615 *Total Assets:* £20,423,968
Registered Office: Third Floor, Broad Quay House, Prince Street, Bristol, BS1 4DJ
Activities: Other business support service activities n.e.c.
Shareholders: Louiseco Limited; JLIF Investments Limited
Officers: Paul Anthony Cartwright [1957] Director; Vikki Louise Everett [1971] Director/Project Manager; Thomas Benedict Symes [1956] Director

Ikonic Holdings Limited
Incorporated: 4 March 2016
Net Worth: £1,611,025 *Total Assets:* £4,089,060
Registered Office: Unit B, 6 Clifton Road, Bristol, BS8 1AG
Activities: Activities of construction holding companies
Shareholders: Peter William Hargreaves; Stephen Wayne Chant
Officers: Stephen Wayne Chant [1967] Director/Site Agent; Peter William Hargreaves [1976] Director/Site Agent

A J Iles Holdings Limited
Incorporated: 30 July 2014 *Employees:* 166
Net Worth: £9,018,543 *Total Assets:* £13,830,299
Registered Office: The Coach House, Berwick Bassett, Swindon, Wilts, SN4 9NF
Activities: Activities of construction holding companies
Shareholders: Deborah Louise Iles; Anthony James Iles
Officers: Anthony James Iles [1967] Director; Deborah Louise Iles [1970] Director

Image Factory Communications Ltd
Incorporated: 4 July 2013 *Employees:* 60
Net Worth: £1,082,911 *Total Assets:* £4,908,215
Registered Office: Image Centre, Bumpers Way, Chippenham, Wilts, SN14 6LH
Activities: Activities of other holding companies n.e.c.
Major Shareholder: Terry Robert Smith
Officers: Terry Robert Smith [1951] Director

Imagile Business Support Limited
Incorporated: 8 November 2006 *Employees:* 54
Previous: Semperian Capital Management Limited
Net Worth: £1,113,100 *Total Assets:* £14,237,957
Registered Office: Third Floor, Broad Quay House, Prince Street, Bristol, BS1 4DJ
Activities: Financial intermediation not elsewhere classified
Parent: Imagile Group Limited
Officers: Susan Taberner, Secretary; Alan Edward Birch [1970] Director; Rebecca Brunt [1972] Director; Jonathan Michael Simpson [1973] Director/Accountant

Imagile Group Limited
Incorporated: 11 November 2008 *Employees:* 3
Previous: Semperian (Holdings) Limited
Net Worth: £1,574,388 *Total Assets:* £12,541,268
Registered Office: Third Floor, Broad Quay House, Prince Street, Bristol, BS1 4DJ
Activities: Other business support service activities n.e.c.
Parent: Semperian PPP Investment Partners Group Limited
Officers: Susan Taberner, Secretary; Alan Edward Birch [1970] Director; William Robert Doughty [1968] Director/Investment Banker; Jonathan Michael Simpson [1973] Director/Accountant

Imaging Equipment Limited
Incorporated: 28 March 2001 *Employees:* 41
Net Worth Deficit: £1,114,046 *Total Assets:* £5,722,250
Registered Office: The Barn, Manor Farm, Church Lane, Chilcompton, Radstock, Somerset, BA3 4HP
Activities: Non-specialised wholesale trade
Parent: Advanced Accelerator Applications SA
Officers: Richard Samuel Cullen, Secretary; Haseeb Ahmad [1976] Director/CPO Head UK & Ireland; Oriane Fanny Lacaze [1979] Director/CCFO [French]; Barak Avraham Palatchi [1974] Director/Chief Commercial Officer [Israeli]; Prabhjeevan Singh Virk [1983] Director/Sales Manager

IMC St.David's Ltd
Incorporated: 21 February 2000 *Employees:* 4
Net Worth: £4,021,306 *Total Assets:* £12,237,902
Registered Office: Third Floor, Broad Quay House, Prince Street, Bristol, BS1 4DJ
Activities: Medical nursing home activities
Shareholders: Semperian (St.David's) Limited; Robert McAlpine Pension Scheme Capital Ventures Limited
Officers: Richard Little [1979] Investment Director; John Parnell [1972] Project Manager and Bid Director; Harvey John William Pownall [1966] Director; Robert John William Wotherspoon [1967] Director/Accountant

Imerys Minerals Holding Limited
Incorporated: 19 May 2011
Net Worth Deficit: £115,932,024 *Total Assets:* £241,213,472
Registered Office: Par Moor Centre, Par Moor Road, Par, Cornwall, PL24 2SQ
Activities: Activities of other holding companies n.e.c.
Officers: Fernando Augusto Accioly Menezes [1974] Director/VP & GM Imerys Oilfield Solutions [Brazilian/French]; Brian Robert Hanrahan [1978] Director/General Manager [American]; Edward James Quarmby [1970] Director/Tax Manager

Imerys Minerals Limited
Incorporated: 12 October 1932 *Employees:* 1,038
Net Worth: £178,079,008 *Total Assets:* £262,400,992
Registered Office: Par Moor Centre, Par Moor Road, Par, Cornwall, PL24 2SQ
Activities: Operation of gravel and sand pits; mining of clays and kaolin
Parent: Imerys UK Limited
Officers: Henri Simon Trahair-Davies, Secretary; Philippe Guy Pascal Bourg [1967] Director/Business Executive [French]; David John Clapham [1974] Director; Narender Dhayal [1981] Director/General Manager; Malcolm Francis Rogers [1958] Director/Manager; Benoit Pierre Gerard Roussel [1978] Director/Business Executive [French]; Ashley John Shopland [1966] Director

Imerys Talc UK Holding Limited
Incorporated: 20 November 1981
Net Worth: £45,890,000 *Total Assets:* £45,939,000
Registered Office: Par Moor Centre, Par Moor Road, Par, Cornwall, PL24 2SQ
Activities: Activities of other holding companies n.e.c.
Parent: Mircal SA
Officers: Henri Simon Trahair Davies, Secretary; Denis Philippe Marie Musson [1963] Director/General Counsel [French]; Laetitia Peyrat [1979] Director/In House Lawyer [French]

Imerys UK Finance Limited
Incorporated: 12 July 2011
Net Worth: £309,695,616 *Total Assets:* £329,773,056
Registered Office: Par Moor Centre, Par Moor Road, Par, Cornwall, PL24 2SQ
Activities: Activities of other holding companies n.e.c.
Parent: Imerys UK Limited
Officers: Cedric Boulier [1972] Director/Group Treasurer [French]; David John Clapham [1974] Director/Finance Manager

Imerys UK Limited
Incorporated: 26 November 1998
Net Worth: £368,736,000 *Total Assets:* £393,198,016
Registered Office: Par Moor Centre, Par Moor Road, Par, Cornwall, PL24 2SQ
Activities: Activities of head offices
Officers: Henri Simon Trahair Davies, Secretary; Denis Philippe Marie Musson [1963] Director [French]

IMI Webber Limited
Incorporated: 21 February 1979 *Employees:* 156
Net Worth: £2,198,000 *Total Assets:* £7,709,000
Registered Office: City Business Park, Easton Road, Easton, Bristol, BS5 0SP
Activities: Manufacture of taps and valves
Parent: IMI Kynoch Limited
Officers: Andrew Ball, Secretary; Peter Varwijk [1962] Managing Director [Dutch]; Paul Ward [1964] Director

Impcross Limited
Incorporated: 18 March 1994 *Employees:* 104
Net Worth: £5,478,525 *Total Assets:* £9,296,022
Registered Office: Staverton Court, Staverton, Cheltenham, Glos, GL51 0UX
Activities: Manufacture of other fabricated metal products n.e.c.
Major Shareholder: Richard Leslie Arnold
Officers: Richard Leslie Arnold, Company Secretary; Richard Leslie Arnold [1944] Director; Steven Richard Arnold [1971] Operations Director; Dale Gary Ballinger [1968] Director; John Ernest Timbrell Cook [1943] Engineering Director; Robert James Gyde [1964] Director; Terence John McGrane [1948] Director/Electrical Engineer; Andrew Ellis Weaver [1952] Director; Roger Witts [1949] Sales Director

Imperial Brands Enterprise Finance Limited
Incorporated: 5 August 2003 *Employees:* 2
Previous: Imperial Tobacco Enterprise Finance Limited
Net Worth: £5,839,497,216 *Total Assets:* £6,805,321,216
Registered Office: 121 Winterstoke Road, Bristol, BS3 2LL
Activities: Financial intermediation not elsewhere classified
Shareholders: Imperial Tobacco Limited; Imperial Tobacco Overseas Holdings (2) Limited
Officers: Gavin Paul Bonnar, Secretary; John Matthew Downing [1971] Director/Solicitor; Oliver Reginald Tant [1961] Director/Chartered Accountant; Thomas Richard William Tildesley [1973] Finance Director; Marie Ann Wall [1973] Director/Chartered Accountant; Trevor Martin Williams [1961] Director/Chartered Secretary

Imperial Brands Finance PLC
Incorporated: 14 June 1996 *Employees:* 4
Previous: Imperial Tobacco Finance PLC
Net Worth: £2,299,000,064 *Total Assets:* £33,894,000,640
Registered Office: 121 Winterstoke Road, Bristol, BS3 2LL
Activities: Financial management
Parent: Imperial Tobacco Holdings Limited
Officers: John Matthew Downing, Secretary; John Michael Jones [1971] Director/Treasurer; Oliver Reginald Tant [1961] Director/Chartered Accountant; Thomas Richard William Tildesley [1973] Finance Director; Marie Ann Wall [1973] Director/Chartered Accountant

Imperial Brands PLC
Incorporated: 6 August 1996 *Employees:* 33,300
Previous: Imperial Tobacco Group PLC
Net Worth: £5,769,999,872 *Total Assets:* £30,250,000,384
Registered Office: 121 Winterstoke Road, Bristol, BS3 2LL
Activities: Activities of head offices
Officers: John Matthew Downing, Secretary; Susan Michelle Clark [1964] Director; Alison Jane Cooper [1966] Director/Chartered Accountant; Therese Marie Esperdy [1960] Director [American]; Simon Anthony Christopher Langelier [1957] Director; Matthew Robert Phillips [1970] Director/Lawyer; Steven Paul Stanbrook [1957] Director; Oliver Reginald Tant [1961] Director/Chartered Accountant; Mark David Williamson [1957] Director/Chartered Accountant; Karen Witts [1963] Director/Accountant; Malcolm Ian Wyman [1946] Director

Imperial Business Systems Limited
Incorporated: 28 July 1988 *Employees:* 91
Net Worth: £3,824,480 *Total Assets:* £7,085,950
Registered Office: 7 Hill Street, Bristol, BS1 5PU
Activities: Non-trading company
Shareholders: Ian Iwao Yamanaka; Mehboob Neky
Officers: Ian Iwao Yamanaka, Secretary; Mehboob Neky [1951] Director/Computer Systems Consultant; Ian Iwao Yamanaka [1937] Director/Business Consultant [Canadian]

Imperial Civil Enforcement Solutions Limited
Incorporated: 28 May 1986 *Employees:* 91
Net Worth: £3,440,698 *Total Assets:* £7,119,049
Registered Office: 7 Hill Street, Bristol, BS1 5PU
Activities: Business and domestic software development
Parent: Imperial Business Systems
Officers: Jane Louise Hobbs, Secretary; Ashley Marie Bijster [1968] Director; Mehboob Neky [1951] Director/IT Consultant; Ian Iwao Yamanaka [1937] Director [Canadian]

Imperial Tobacco Altadis Limited
Incorporated: 20 August 2008
Net Worth: £5,900,521,984 *Total Assets:* £5,900,521,984
Registered Office: 121 Winterstoke Road, Bristol, BS3 2LL
Activities: Non-trading company
Parent: Imperial Tobacco Overseas Holdings (3) Limited
Officers: Gavin Paul Bonnar, Secretary; John Matthew Downing [1971] Director/Solicitor; Thomas Richard William Tildesley [1973] Finance Director; Marie Ann Wall [1973] Director/Chartered Accountant; Trevor Martin Williams [1961] Director/Chartered Secretary

Imperial Tobacco Holdings (1) Limited
Incorporated: 16 March 1989 *Employees:* 4
Net Worth: £13,742,583,808 *Total Assets:* £14,675,133,440
Registered Office: 121 Winterstoke Road, Bristol, BS3 2LL
Activities: Activities of other holding companies n.e.c.
Parent: Imperial Tobacco Limited
Officers: Gavin Paul Bonnar, Secretary; John Matthew Downing [1971] Director/Solicitor; Thomas Richard William Tildesley [1973] Finance Director; Marie Ann Wall [1973] Director/Chartered Accountant; Trevor Martin Williams [1961] Director/Chartered Secretary

Imperial Tobacco Holdings (2007) Limited
Incorporated: 3 November 2006 *Employees:* 4
Net Worth: £6,967,052,800 *Total Assets:* £18,849,996,800
Registered Office: 121 Winterstoke Road, Bristol, BS3 2LL
Activities: Activities of other holding companies n.e.c.
Parent: Imperial Brands PLC
Officers: Trevor Martin Williams, Secretary; John Matthew Downing [1971] Director/Solicitor; Oliver Reginald Tant [1961] Director/Chartered Accountant; Thomas Richard William Tildesley [1973] Finance Director; Marie Ann Wall [1973] Director/Chartered Accountant

Imperial Tobacco Holdings Limited
Incorporated: 3 August 1995
Net Worth: £8,434,999,808 *Total Assets:* £19,864,000,512
Registered Office: 121 Winterstoke Road, Bristol, BS3 2LL
Activities: Activities of other holding companies n.e.c.
Parent: Imperial Tobacco Holdings (2007) Limited
Officers: Trevor Martin Williams, Secretary; John Matthew Downing [1971] Director/Solicitor; Oliver Reginald Tant [1961] Director/Chartered Accountant; Thomas Richard William Tildesley [1973] Finance Director; Marie Ann Wall [1973] Director/Chartered Accountant

Imperial Tobacco International Limited
Incorporated: 20 July 1911 *Employees:* 90
Net Worth: £35,489,240 *Total Assets:* £532,565,312
Registered Office: 121 Winterstoke Road, Bristol, BS3 2LL
Activities: Wholesale of tobacco products
Parent: Imperial Tobacco Holdings (1) Limited
Officers: Can Gulen, Secretary; Rainer Eberlein [1960] Director [German]; Gunnar Paul Glasneck [1972] Director [German]; Can Gulen [1975] Director/Head of Finance [Turkish]; Rainer Rudolf Albrecht Hentschel [1970] Director [German]; Avelino Pinto de Oliveira [1967] Director [French]; Dr. Andreas Ripperger [1964] Director [German]

Imperial Tobacco Limited
Incorporated: 1 November 1984 *Employees:* 1,122
Net Worth: £19,793,000,448 *Total Assets:* £29,364,000,768
Registered Office: 121 Winterstoke Road, Bristol, BS3 2LL
Activities: Wholesale of tobacco products
Parent: Imperial Tobacco Holdings Limited
Officers: Trevor Martin Williams, Secretary; John Matthew Downing [1971] Director/Solicitor; Oliver Reginald Tant [1961] Director/Chartered Accountant; Thomas Richard William Tildesley [1973] Finance Director; Marie Ann Wall [1973] Director/Chartered Accountant

Imperial Tobacco Overseas (Polska) Limited
Incorporated: 7 October 2003 *Employees:* 4
Net Worth: £120,300,000 *Total Assets:* £120,300,000
Registered Office: 121 Winterstoke Road, Bristol, BS3 2LL
Activities: Activities of other holding companies n.e.c.
Parent: Imperial Tobacco Overseas Holdings (2) Limited
Officers: Gavin Paul Bonnar, Secretary; John Matthew Downing [1971] Director/Solicitor; Thomas Richard William Tildesley [1973] Finance Director; Marie Ann Wall [1973] Director/Chartered Accountant; Trevor Martin Williams [1961] Director/Chartered Secretary

Imperial Tobacco Overseas Holdings (2) Limited
Incorporated: 28 January 2002 *Employees:* 4
Net Worth: £9,252,851,712 *Total Assets:* £13,915,634,688
Registered Office: 121 Winterstoke Road, Bristol, BS3 2LL
Activities: Activities of other holding companies n.e.c.
Parent: Imperial Tobacco Overseas Holdings Limited
Officers: Gavin Paul Bonnar, Secretary; John Matthew Downing [1971] Director/Solicitor; Thomas Richard William Tildesley [1973] Finance Director; Marie Ann Wall [1973] Director/Chartered Accountant; Trevor Martin Williams [1961] Director/Chartered Secretary

Imperial Tobacco Overseas Holdings (3) Limited
Incorporated: 6 March 2007 *Employees:* 3
Net Worth: £9,399,924,736 *Total Assets:* £11,289,433,088
Registered Office: 121 Winterstoke Road, Bristol, BS3 2LL
Activities: Non-trading company
Parent: Imperial Tobacco Overseas Holdings (2) Limited
Officers: Trevor Martin Williams, Secretary; John Matthew Downing [1971] Director/Solicitor; Thomas Richard William Tildesley [1973] Finance Director; Marie Ann Wall [1973] Director/Chartered Accountant

Imperial Tobacco Overseas Holdings Ltd
Incorporated: 3 June 1998
Net Worth: £12,528,425,984 *Total Assets:* £14,725,650,432
Registered Office: 121 Winterstoke Road, Bristol, BS3 2LL
Activities: Activities of other holding companies n.e.c.
Parent: Imperial Tobacco Overseas Limited
Officers: Gavin Paul Bonnar, Secretary; John Matthew Downing [1971] Director/Solicitor; Thomas Richard William Tildesley [1973] Finance Director; Marie Ann Wall [1973] Director/Chartered Accountant; Trevor Martin Williams [1961] Director/Chartered Secretary

Imperial Tobacco Overseas Limited
Incorporated: 15 July 1903 *Employees:* 4
Net Worth: £14,667,461,632 *Total Assets:* £15,856,533,504
Registered Office: 121 Winterstoke Road, Bristol, BS3 2LL
Activities: Activities of other holding companies n.e.c.
Parent: Imperial Tobacco Holdings (1) Limited
Officers: Gavin Paul Bonnar, Secretary; John Matthew Downing [1971] Director/Solicitor; Thomas Richard William Tildesley [1973] Finance Director; Marie Ann Wall [1973] Director/Chartered Accountant; Trevor Martin Williams [1961] Director/Chartered Secretary

Import Export Services (GRP) Limited
Incorporated: 17 March 2010
Net Worth: £2,535,651 *Total Assets:* £3,775,793
Registered Office: 1 Portview Road, Avonmouth, Bristol, BS11 9LS
Activities: Installation of industrial machinery and equipment
Major Shareholder: Niels Morch Monsted
Officers: Matthew Richard Lanigan, Secretary; Niels Morch Monsted [1967] Managing Director [Danish]

Import Export Services Ltd
Incorporated: 23 May 2001 *Employees:* 54
Net Worth: £2,083,135 *Total Assets:* £4,429,641
Registered Office: 1 Portview Road, Avonmouth, Bristol, BS11 9LS
Activities: Installation of industrial machinery and equipment
Major Shareholder: Niels Morch Monsted
Officers: Matt Lanigan, Secretary; Matthew Stuart Boyd [1964] Sales Director; Niels Morch Monsted [1967] Managing Director [Danish]

In-Excess UK Limited
Incorporated: 30 May 2003 *Employees:* 123
Net Worth: £7,415,535 *Total Assets:* £8,935,184
Registered Office: Anchor House, Netherhampton Road, Harnham, Salisbury, Wilts, SP2 8RA
Activities: Other retail sale in non-specialised stores
Major Shareholder: Carl Peter Chambers
Officers: Christopher John Chambers, Secretary; Carl Peter Chambers [1960] Managing Director

Indalo International Holdings Limited
Incorporated: 18 November 2015
Net Worth: £2,621,069 *Total Assets:* £3,758,578
Registered Office: Mark Holt & Co Ltd, 7 Sandy Court, Ashleigh Way, Langage Business Park, Plympton, Plymouth, PL7 5JX
Activities: Activities of head offices
Shareholders: Julia Jennings; Jason Banks
Officers: Jason Banks [1967] Director; Julia Jennings [1971] Director

Independent Agriculture Limited
Incorporated: 8 October 1992
Net Worth Deficit: £717,666 *Total Assets:* £5,062,302
Registered Office: Andoversford, Cheltenham, Glos, GL54 4LZ
Activities: Support activities for crop production
Parent: Willmot Pertwee Limited
Officers: Spencer Gareth Evans [1970] Director/Chief Financial Officer; Ronan Andrew Hughes [1968] Director [Irish]; Christopher Stephen Matthews [1957] Director; James Marshall Rennie [1957] Director

Independent Investment Analysis Limited
Incorporated: 23 May 1995 *Employees:* 41
Net Worth: £1,666,547 *Total Assets:* £4,107,099
Registered Office: c/o Saffery Champness, St Catherine's Court, Berkeley Place, Bristol, BS8 1BQ
Activities: Activities of financial services holding companies
Shareholders: Kean Michael Seager; Janet Seager
Officers: Robert Edward James Dyte, Secretary; Robert Edward James Dyte [1971] Director/Accountant; Daniel Matthew Gregory [1972] Director/Administrator; Gavin James Haynes [1970] Director/Investment Manager; Gaynor Ann Newman [1965] Compliance Director; Kean Michael Seager [1951] Director; Simon Snook [1974] Director; Mark Robert Stone [1970] Director/Financial Advisor

Independent Slate Supplies Limited
Incorporated: 30 March 1992 *Employees:* 20
Net Worth: £2,857,456 *Total Assets:* £4,772,666
Registered Office: Whetcombe Whey, Ropers Lane, Wrington, Somerset, BS40 5NH
Activities: Agents involved in the sale of timber and building materials
Shareholders: Peter James Phipps; Victoria Mary Phipps
Officers: Marlene Puffett, Secretary; Peter James Phipps [1949] Director; Victoria Mary Phipps [1952] Director/Administrator; Anthony James Puffett [1964] Director

Independent Tool Consultants Limited
Incorporated: 4 July 1972 *Employees:* 41
Net Worth: £17,906,592 *Total Assets:* £22,090,612
Registered Office: Unit 7 Bamfurlong Industrial Park, Staverton, Cheltenham, Gloucester, GL51 6SX
Activities: Manufacture of other machine tools
Major Shareholder: Anthony James Preece
Officers: Elizabeth Helen Readstone, Secretary; Anthony James Preece [1944] Director/Engineer; Leslie James Preece [1965] Director; Wendy Ann Preece [1947] Director

Independent Vetcare Limited
Incorporated: 19 August 2011 *Employees:* 4,097
Net Worth Deficit: £47,468,988 *Total Assets:* £314,777,312
Registered Office: The Chocolate Factory, Keynsham, Bristol, BS31 2AU
Activities: Veterinary activities
Parent: IVC Acquisition Limited
Officers: Stuart Jonathan Caton [1971] Commercial Director; Paul Alexander William Cowling [1961] Director; Amanda Jane Davis [1968] Director; David Robert Geoffrey Hillier [1962] Director

Industrial Common Ownership Finance Limited
Incorporated: 17 April 1973 *Employees:* 4
Previous: Industrial Common-Ownership Finance Limited
Net Worth: £2,258,582 *Total Assets:* £5,060,510
Registered Office: Brunswick Court, Brunswick Square, Bristol, BS2 8PE
Activities: Financial intermediation not elsewhere classified
Officers: Alain Richard Demontoux, Secretary; James Alcock [1981] Director/General Manager; Andrew John Harrison [1977] Director/Management Consultant; Dan Paul Holden [1985] Co-op Director; David John Hollings [1962] Director/Business Advisor; Zena Marie King [1979] Director/Events Co-ordinator; Andrew Love [1949] Director/MP; Jon Robert Nott [1972] Director/Charity Chief Executive; Carl Pitchford [1964] Director/Consultant; Jennifer Ann Smith [1954] Director/Business Consultant; Brian James Titley [1963] Director/Co-op Development Worker; Bruce Wood [1948] Director/Development Worker

Industrial Properties (Barton Hill) Limited
Incorporated: 6 July 1959 *Employees:* 2
Net Worth: £3,416,870 *Total Assets:* £3,609,695
Registered Office: Naish Lodge, Naish Hill, Clapton in Gordano, Bristol, BS20 7RZ
Activities: Other letting and operating of own or leased real estate
Shareholder: Jonathan Philip Parker
Officers: Jayne Victoria Symons, Secretary/Food Stylist; Jason Charles Ashley Parker [1954] Director/Financial Adviser; Jonathan Philip Parker [1951] Director/Chartered Surveyor; Jayne Victoria Symons [1960] Director/Property Lettings

Industrial Sales Limited
Incorporated: 21 August 1975 *Employees:* 6
Net Worth: £14,293,724 *Total Assets:* £18,753,284
Registered Office: Daniels Industrial Estate, Bath Road, Stroud, Glos, GL5 3TJ
Activities: Other letting and operating of own or leased real estate
Shareholders: Catherine Helen Harvey; Juliet Anne Bailey
Officers: Howard Nicholas Bailey, Secretary; Howard Nicholas Bailey [1958] Director/Accountant; Juliet Anne Bailey [1955] Director; Margaret Bailey [1961] Director; Maurice Jack Bailey [1933] Director; Nancy Ruby Bailey [1932] Director; Catherine Helen Harvey [1963] Director/Property Manager

Infineon Technologies Newport Holding Limited
Incorporated: 31 January 2002
Previous: IR UK Holdings Limited
Net Worth: £30,831,000 *Total Assets:* £95,515,000
Registered Office: Infineon House, Great Western Court, Hunts Ground Road, Stoke Gifford, Glos, BS34 8HP
Activities: Activities of head offices
Officers: Alan Richard Bracher, Secretary; Lawrence Anthony Michlovich, Secretary; Andreas Brandstetter [1970] Director Affiliates & Consolidation [German]; Lawrence Anthony Michlovich [1959] Director/Lawyer [American]; Michelle Claire Thomas [1975] Finance Director

Infineon Technologies Reigate Limited
Incorporated: 10 December 1958 *Employees:* 14
Previous: International Rectifier Company (Great Britain) Limited
Net Worth: £161,119,008 *Total Assets:* £166,475,008
Registered Office: Infineon House, Great Western Court, Hunts Ground Road, Stoke Gifford, Glos, BS34 8HP
Activities: Agents specialised in the sale of other particular products
Parent: Infineon Technologies Newport Holding Limited
Officers: Alan Richard Bracher, Secretary; Lawrence Anthony Michlovich, Secretary/Lawyer [American]; Christian Uwe Apel [1963] Director/Vice President Sales & Marketing Controlling [German]; Lawrence Anthony Michlovich [1959] Director/Lawyer [American]; Michelle Claire Thomas [1975] Finance Director

Infineon Technologies UK Limited
Incorporated: 4 June 1999 *Employees:* 81
Net Worth: £1,377,000 *Total Assets:* £5,854,000
Registered Office: Infineon House, Great Western Court, Hunts Ground Road, Stoke Gifford, Bristol, BS34 8HP
Activities: Agents specialised in the sale of other particular products
Officers: Michelle Claire Thomas, Secretary; Christian Apel [1963] Director/VP Sales & Marketing Finance [German]; Ulrich Geiger [1960] Director/VP Sales Automotive Europe [German]; Paul Northey [1967] Director R&D; Austin Thomas [1966] Director/Electronics; Michelle Claire Thomas [1975] Finance Director; Jochen Vaihinger [1969] Director [German]

Infinergy Limited
Incorporated: 13 April 2003 *Employees:* 8
Net Worth: £8,254,030 *Total Assets:* £9,633,679
Registered Office: 16 West Borough, Wimborne, Dorset, BH21 1NG
Activities: Construction of utility projects for electricity and telecommunications
Parent: WW Holdco Ltd
Officers: Esbjorn Roderick Wilmar, Secretary/Director [Dutch]; Tjiwolt Wierda [1972] Director [Dutch]; Esbjorn Roderick Wilmar [1970] Director [Dutch]

Infoteam International Services Limited
Incorporated: 12 February 1997 *Employees:* 90
Net Worth: £12,327,504 *Total Assets:* £13,270,710
Registered Office: 11 Bredon Court, Tower Road, Newquay, Cornwall, TR7 1AW
Activities: Repair of electrical equipment
Major Shareholder: Glen James Coffey
Officers: Claire Helen Coffey, Secretary; Glen James Coffey [1969] Director

Infusion GB Limited
Incorporated: 23 April 1998 *Employees:* 93
Net Worth: £3,936,171 *Total Assets:* £6,805,586
Registered Office: Unit 5 The I O Centre, Hurricane Road, Gloucester Business Park, Gloucester, GL3 4AQ
Activities: Tea processing
Parent: Infusion GB Holdings Limited
Officers: Colin Bruce Philip Stevens, Secretary; Peter Barry [1967] Director/Manufacturing [Irish]; David Nicholas Brown [1964] Finance Director; Mark Andrew Minchella [1970] Director/Chartered Accountant; Colin John Smith [1961] Production Director; Peter Nigel Hastings Smith [1954] Director; Colin Bruce Philip Stevens [1966] Director/Manufacturing

Injury QED Limited
Incorporated: 11 December 2006 *Employees:* 117
Net Worth: £10,461,000 *Total Assets:* £23,490,000
Registered Office: Brightside Park, Severn Bridge, Aust, Bristol, BS35 4BL
Activities: Other business support service activities n.e.c.
Parent: Brightside Group Limited
Officers: Brendan Eamon McCafferty [1967] Director; Ian Ronald Sutherland [1970] Director

Innex Investments Ltd
Incorporated: 14 November 2016
Net Worth: £3,549,743 *Total Assets:* £3,737,254
Registered Office: Unit 66 Morelands Trading Estate, Gloucester, GL1 5RZ
Activities: Construction of commercial buildings
Major Shareholder: Parminder Bhogal
Officers: Parminder Bhogal [1972] Director

Innkeeping Limited
Incorporated: 31 March 2000 *Employees:* 2
Net Worth: £716,215 *Total Assets:* £4,455,863
Registered Office: Hailes House, Hailes, Winchcombe, Cheltenham, Glos, GL54 5PB
Activities: Other letting and operating of own or leased real estate
Shareholders: Deborah Mary Giblin; Declan Patrick Giblin
Officers: Deborah Mary Giblin, Secretary; Deborah Mary Giblin [1957] Director/Housewife [Irish]; Declan Patrick Giblin [1956] Director/Accountant [Irish]

Innogy Business Services UK Limited
Incorporated: 15 January 2007 *Employees:* 527
Previous: RWE GBS UK Limited
Net Worth Deficit: £713,000 *Total Assets:* £596,211,968
Registered Office: Windmill Hill Business Park, Whitehill Way, Swindon, Wilts, SN5 6PB
Activities: Other information technology service activities
Parent: Innogy SE
Officers: Penelope Anne Sainsbury, Secretary; Daniel Stephen Klein [1973] Director; Christopher James Pilgrim [1964] HR Director

Innogy Gym 2 Limited
Incorporated: 23 April 2010
Previous: RWE Innogy Gym 2 Limited
Net Worth Deficit: £10,917,117 *Total Assets:* £198,172,768
Registered Office: Windmill Hill Business Park, Whitehill Way, Swindon, Wilts, SN5 6PB
Activities: Activities of other holding companies n.e.c.
Parent: Innogy Renewables UK Limited
Officers: Christopher David Barras, Secretary; Paul Leslie Cowling [1960] Director; Christian Rudiger Mockl [1973] Director [German]; Richard Jennings Sandford [1971] Director/Head of Offshore Business Management

Innogy Gym 3 Limited
Incorporated: 23 April 2010
Previous: RWE Innogy Gym 3 Limited
Net Worth Deficit: £10,916,481 *Total Assets:* £198,172,960
Registered Office: Windmill Hill Business Park, Whitehill Way, Swindon, Wilts, SN5 6PB
Activities: Activities of other holding companies n.e.c.
Parent: Innogy Renewables UK Limited
Officers: Christopher David Barras, Secretary; Paul Leslie Cowling [1960] Director; Christian Rudiger Mockl [1973] Director [German]; Richard Jennings Sandford [1971] Director/Head of Offshore Business Management

Innogy Gym 4 Limited
Incorporated: 23 April 2010
Previous: RWE Innogy Gym 4 Limited
Net Worth Deficit: £32,771,252 *Total Assets:* £594,499,904
Registered Office: Windmill Hill Business Park, Whitehill Way, Swindon, Wilts, SN5 6PB
Activities: Activities of other holding companies n.e.c.
Parent: Innogy Renewables UK Limited
Officers: Christopher David Barras, Secretary; Paul Leslie Cowling [1960] Director; Christian Rudiger Mockl [1973] Director [German]; Richard Jennings Sandford [1971] Director/Head of Offshore Business Management

Innogy Renewables UK Holdings Limited
Incorporated: 12 December 2007
Previous: RWE Innogy UK Holdings Limited
Net Worth: £1,810,128,000 *Total Assets:* £3,181,101,056
Registered Office: Windmill Hill Business Park, Whitehill Way, Swindon, Wilts, SN5 6PB
Activities: Activities of other holding companies n.e.c.
Parent: Innogy SE
Officers: Christopher David Barras, Secretary; Penelope Anne Sainsbury, Secretary; Paul Leslie Cowling [1960] Director; Mary Katharine Drury [1967] Director/Chartered Mechanical Engineer; Benjamin James Freeman [1977] Director/Accountant; Michael Parker [1976] Director/Head of Onshore UK; Richard Jennings Sandford [1971] Director/Head of Offshore Business Management

Innogy Renewables UK Limited
Incorporated: 22 October 1990 *Employees:* 401
Previous: RWE Innogy UK Limited
Net Worth: £1,602,436,992 *Total Assets:* £3,566,785,024
Registered Office: Windmill Hill Business Park, Whitehill Way, Swindon, Wilts, SN5 6PB
Activities: Production of electricity
Parent: Innogy Renewables UK Holdings Limited
Officers: Christopher David Barras, Secretary; Penelope Anne Sainsbury, Secretary; Paul Leslie Cowling [1960] Director; Mary Katharine Drury [1967] Director/Chartered Mechanical Engineer; Benjamin James Freeman [1977] Director/Accountant; Cathal Hennessy [1980] Director [Irish]; Keith Moseley [1965] Director; Michael Parker [1976] Director/Head of Onshore UK; Richard Jennings Sandford [1971] Director/Head of Offshore Business Management

Innovata Limited
Incorporated: 20 July 1987
Net Worth: £2,700,000 *Total Assets:* £5,600,000
Registered Office: One Prospect West, Chippenham, Wilts, SN14 6FH
Activities: Other human health activities
Parent: Vectura Group Investments Limited
Officers: John Murphy, Secretary; John Murphy [1953] Director; James Ward-Lilley [1965] Director/Chief Executive

Innovate Awarding Ltd
Incorporated: 6 April 2010 *Employees:* 14
Previous: Lifetime Awarding Limited
Net Worth: £9,821,083 *Total Assets:* £10,080,650
Registered Office: Clifton Heights, Triangle West, Bristol, BS8 1EJ
Activities: Educational support services
Parent: Lifetime Training Group Ltd
Officers: Peter James Mitchell, Secretary; John Patrick McNamara [1953] Director [Irish]; Simon Benedict Withey [1958] Director

Innsworth Technology Park Limited
Incorporated: 15 March 1982 *Employees:* 4
Net Worth: £5,753,977 *Total Assets:* £8,665,450
Registered Office: Innsworth Lane, Gloucester, GL3 1DL
Activities: Development of building projects
Shareholder: George Edward Dowty
Officers: Jayne Thurstance, Secretary; Emma Louise Dowty [1971] Director; George Edward Dowty [1953] Director; Michael Anthony Keating [1972] Director/Accountant

Insite Outdoor Advertising (A) Ltd
Incorporated: 22 November 2013
Net Worth: £14,274,912 *Total Assets:* £27,645,300
Registered Office: Barton Hall, 29 Gloucester Street, Cirencester, Glos, GL7 2DJ
Activities: Other letting and operating of own or leased real estate
Parent: Insite Outdoor Advertising Limited
Officers: Luke Creighton [1979] Director/Chief Financial Officer; William James Killick [1972] Director/Investment Banker; Daniel Arthur John Maiden [1970] Director; Andrew John Pettit [1968] Director/Banker; Stephen John Pettit [1976] Director/Banker; Stuart Wellman [1973] Director/Property Investment

Insite Outdoor Advertising Limited
Incorporated: 29 January 2014
Net Worth: £1,141,074 *Total Assets:* £20,783,064
Registered Office: Barton Hall, 29 Gloucester Street, Cirencester, Glos, GL7 2DJ
Activities: Activities of other holding companies n.e.c.
Parent: Insite Poster Midco Limited
Officers: Luke Creighton [1979] Director/Chief Financial Officer; William James Killick [1972] Director/Investment Banker; Daniel Arthur John Maiden [1970] Director; Andrew John Pettit [1968] Director/Banker; Stephen John Pettit [1976] Director/Banker; Stuart Wellman [1973] Director/Property Investment

Insite Poster Investments (A) Limited
Incorporated: 11 October 2004
Net Worth: £44,456,652 *Total Assets:* £72,462,368
Registered Office: Barton Hall, 29 Gloucester Street, Cirencester, Glos, GL7 2DJ
Activities: Buying and selling of own real estate
Parent: Insite Poster Investments Limited
Officers: Luke Creighton [1979] Director/Chief Financial Officer; William James Killick [1972] Director/Investment Banker; Daniel Arthur John Maiden [1970] Director; Andrew John Pettit [1968] Director/Banker; Stephen John Pettit [1976] Director/Banker; Stuart Wellman [1973] Director/Property Investment

Insite Poster Investments (B) Limited
Incorporated: 13 October 2008
Net Worth: £52,549,748 *Total Assets:* £92,453,416
Registered Office: Barton Hall, 29 Gloucester Street, Cirencester, Glos, GL7 2DJ
Activities: Buying and selling of own real estate
Parent: Insite Poster Investments Limited
Officers: Luke Creighton [1979] Director/Chief Financial Officer; William James Killick [1972] Director/Investment Banker; Daniel Arthur John Maiden [1970] Director; Andrew John Petit [1968] Director/Banker; Stephen John Pettit [1976] Director/Banker; Stuart Wellman [1973] Director/Property Investment

Insite Poster Investments (C) Limited
Incorporated: 23 May 2013
Net Worth: £14,371,663 *Total Assets:* £46,023,872
Registered Office: Barton Hall, 29 Gloucester Street, Cirencester, Glos, GL7 2DJ
Activities: Buying and selling of own real estate
Parent: Insite Poster Investments Limited
Officers: Luke Creighton [1979] Director/Chief Financial Officer; William James Killick [1972] Director; Daniel Arthur John Maiden [1970] Director; Andrew John Pettit [1968] Director/Banker; Stephen John Pettit [1976] Director/Banker; Stuart Wellman [1973] Director

Insite Poster Investments Ltd.
Incorporated: 13 October 2008
Net Worth: £573,047 *Total Assets:* £12,052,705
Registered Office: Barton Hall, 29 Gloucester Street, Cirencester, Glos, GL7 2DJ
Activities: Activities of other holding companies n.e.c.
Parent: Insite Poster Midco Limited
Officers: Luke Creighton [1979] Director/Chief Financial Officer; William James Killick [1972] Director/Investment Banker; Daniel Arthur John Maiden [1970] Director; Andrew John Pettit [1968] Director/Banker; Stephen John Pettit [1976] Director/Banker; Stuart Wellman [1973] Director/Property Investment

Insite Poster Midco Limited
Incorporated: 20 March 2018
Net Worth: £102,701,200 *Total Assets:* £102,701,200
Registered Office: Barton Hall, 29 Gloucester Street, Cirencester, Glos, GL7 2DJ
Activities: Activities of other holding companies n.e.c.
Officers: Luke Creighton [1979] Director/Chief Financial Officer; William James Killick [1972] Director/Investment Banker; Daniel Arthur John Maiden [1970] Director/Chief Executive Officer; Andrew John Pettit [1968] Director/Investment Banker; Stephen John Pettit [1976] Director/Investment Banker; Stuart Wellman [1973] Director/Chief Operating Officer

Insite Poster Properties Limited
Incorporated: 26 April 2004 *Employees:* 21
Net Worth: £2,416,597 *Total Assets:* £44,995,640
Registered Office: Barton Hall, 29 Gloucester Street, Cirencester, Glos, GL7 2DJ
Activities: Buying and selling of own real estate
Parent: Insite Poster Investments Limited
Officers: Luke Creighton [1979] Director/Chief Financial Officer; William James Killick [1972] Director/Investment Banker; Daniel Arthur John Maiden [1970] Director; Andrew John Petit [1968] Director/Banker; Stephen John Pettit [1976] Director/Banker; Stuart Wellman [1973] Director/Property Investment

Inspirational Futures Trust
Incorporated: 13 December 2012 *Employees:* 198
Previous: Weston Enterprise and Entrepreneurial Learning
Net Worth: £29,676,000 *Total Assets:* £34,526,000
Registered Office: Weston College, Knightstone Campus, Knightstone Road, Weston Super Mare, Somerset, BS23 2AL
Activities: Primary education
Officers: Elspeth Freda Davis [1944] Director/Retired; Michael David Evans [1952] Director; Jacqueline Ann Ford [1960] Director; William Lowther Harding [1951] Director/Head of Human Resources

The Inspire Multi Academy Trust (South West)
Incorporated: 15 December 2015 *Employees:* 73
Net Worth: £4,638,000 *Total Assets:* £5,669,000
Registered Office: Ernesettle Community School, Biggin Hill, Plymouth, PL5 2RB
Activities: Primary education
Officers: Anita Jane Martin, Secretary; Paul William Chapman [1962] Director; Elizabeth Ann Hoodless [1963] Director; Claire Jones [1973] Director/Teacher; Gavin David Jones [1977] Director/Consultant; Aaron Robert Meredith [1979] Director; Sophia Pettit [1983] Director/Legal Executive; Carol Wood [1953] Director; Sandra-Jane Wood [1981] Director

Inspired Education (East Dunbartonshire) Limited
Incorporated: 17 February 2005
Net Worth Deficit: £27,652,000 *Total Assets:* £122,436,000
Registered Office: Third Floor, Broad Quay House, Prince Street, Bristol, BS1 4DJ
Activities: Non-trading company
Parent: Inspired Education (East Dunbartonshire) Holdings Limited
Officers: Christopher James [1968] Director; Andrew Charles Mutch Rhodes [1970] Director; Alan Campbell Ritchie [1967] Director; Richard Keith Sheehan [1975] Investment Director

Inspired Education (South Lanarkshire) Holdings Limited
Incorporated: 18 February 2005
Net Worth Deficit: £9,352,000 *Total Assets:* £285,467,008
Registered Office: Third Floor, Broad Quay House, Prince Street, Bristol, BS1 4DJ
Activities: Other business support service activities n.e.c.
Shareholder: Semperian PPP Holdings Limited
Officers: Christopher James [1968] Director; Andrew Charles Mutch Rhodes [1970] Director; Alan Campbell Ritchie [1967] Director; Richard Keith Sheehan [1975] Investment Director; Neil Woodburn [1979] Director/Chartered Building Surveyor

Inspired Education (South Lanarkshire) PLC
Incorporated: 7 July 2005
Net Worth Deficit: £9,352,000 *Total Assets:* £285,467,008
Registered Office: Third Floor, Broad Quay House, Prince Street, Bristol, BS1 4DJ
Activities: Other business support service activities n.e.c.
Parent: Inspired Education (South Lanarkshire) Holdings Limited
Officers: Christopher James [1968] Director; Andrew Charles Mutch Rhodes [1970] Director; Alan Campbell Ritchie [1967] Director; Richard Keith Sheehan [1975] Investment Director; John Edgar Allison Watt [1957] Director/Management Consultant; Neil Woodburn [1979] Director/Chartered Building Surveyor

Inspiring Schools Partnership
Incorporated: 9 March 2011 *Employees:* 353
Previous: Stoke Damerel Community College
Net Worth: £11,604,435 *Total Assets:* £18,920,988
Registered Office: Stoke Damerel Community College, Somerset Place, Plymouth, PL3 4BD
Activities: General secondary education
Officers: Anita Jane Martin, Secretary; Julia Baldie [1975] Director/HR Advisor; Richard Alan Clarke [1956] Director/Baptist Minister; Janice Cole [1962] Director/Administrator; Greg Dix [1970] Director/Chief Nurse and Operating Officer; Dr Josie Caitlin Forte [1972] Director/Optometrist; Anita Janine Frier [1969] Director/Principal; Colin Bruce Searls [1956] Director/University Lecturer; Dawn Slater [1966] Director of Clinical Practice; Wendy Tout [1970] Director/Paraprofessional FA; Mary Utton [1959] Director/Retired Headteacher

Insure & Go Insurance Services Limited
Incorporated: 21 August 2000 *Employees:* 260
Net Worth: £5,712,000 *Total Assets:* £15,400,000
Registered Office: One Victoria Street, Bristol Bridge, Bristol, BS1 6AA
Activities: Non-life insurance
Officers: Nigel John Antony Howard-Jones [1947] Director; Jair Giovanni Marrugo Rojas [1972] Director [Colombian]; Javier Maria San Basilio [1966] Director [Spanish]

Intamarque Limited
Incorporated: 10 April 2006 *Employees:* 33
Net Worth: £6,916,981 *Total Assets:* £10,830,050
Registered Office: Intamarque Distribution Centre, Alexandra Way, Ashchurch, Tewkesbury, Glos, GL20 8NB
Activities: Wholesale of household goods (other than musical instruments) n.e.c
Major Shareholder: Richard Meredith Shortt
Officers: Sophie Elizabeth Shortt, Secretary; Richard Meredith Shortt [1971] Director/Buying

Integra Neurosciences Holdings (UK) Limited
Incorporated: 9 February 2000
Net Worth: £384,152,544 *Total Assets:* £480,897,888
Registered Office: 2nd Floor, West Wing, Kingsgate House, Newbury Road, Andover, Hants, SP10 4DU
Activities: Activities of other holding companies n.e.c.
Parent: Caveangle Limited
Officers: Sravan Kumar Emany [1977] Director/Senior VP, Strategy, Treasurer & Investor Relations [American]; Jeffrey Alan Mosebrook [1976] Director/VP, Corp Controller & Principle Accounting Officer [American]

Integra Neurosciences Limited
Incorporated: 31 December 1986 *Employees:* 42
Net Worth: £11,692,000 *Total Assets:* £22,618,000
Registered Office: 2nd Floor, West Wing, Kingsgate House, Newbury Road, Andover, Hants, SP10 4DU
Activities: Manufacture of medical and dental instruments and supplies
Parent: Spembly Medical Limited
Officers: Sravan Kumar Emany [1977] Director/Senior VP, Strategy, Treasurer & Investor Relations [American]; Jeffrey Alan Mosebrook [1976] Director/VP, Corp Controller & Principle Accounting Officer [American]

Integrated Accommodation Services PLC
Incorporated: 12 August 1999
Net Worth: £61,540,000 *Total Assets:* £393,153,984
Registered Office: Challenge House, International Drive, Tewkesbury Business Park, Tewkesbury, Glos, GL20 8UQ
Activities: Construction of commercial buildings
Parent: Accommodation Services (Holdings) Limited
Officers: Sandra Margaret Major, Secretary; Gaynor Birley-Smith [1966] Investment Director; Benjamin Christopher Jacob Dean [1979] Director; Christopher Elliott [1957] Director; David Robert Hardingham [1974] Director/Commercial Manager

Integrated Care Solutions (East Kent) Holdings Limited
Incorporated: 2 September 2003
Net Worth Deficit: £5,226,000 *Total Assets:* £21,639,000
Registered Office: Third Floor, Broad Quay House, Prince Street, Bristol, BS1 4DJ
Activities: General public administration activities
Shareholders: Equitix Infrastructure 5a Limited; Kent Vanwall Limited
Officers: Benjamin David Adams [1989] Director; Fabio D'Alonzo [1976] Director [Italian]; Adam Irwin [1987] Director; Philip Arthur Would [1971] Director/Asset Manager

Integrated Care Solutions (East Kent) Limited
Incorporated: 21 February 2003
Net Worth Deficit: £5,226,000 *Total Assets:* £21,639,000
Registered Office: Third Floor, Broad Quay, Prince Street, Bristol, BS1 4DJ
Activities: Other business support service activities n.e.c.
Parent: Integrated Care Solutions (East Kent) Holdings Limited
Officers: Benjamin David Adams [1989] Director; Fabio D'Alonzo [1976] Director [Italian]; Adam Irwin [1987] Director; Philip Arthur Would [1971] Director/Asset Manager

Integrated Care Solutions (Shropshire) Holdings Limited
Incorporated: 11 March 2005
Net Worth Deficit: £2,773,000 *Total Assets:* £14,932,000
Registered Office: Third Floor, Broad Quay House, Prince Street, Bristol, BS1 4DJ
Activities: General public administration activities
Shareholders: Equitix Infrastructure 5a Limited; Equitix Healthcare Limited
Officers: Benjamin David Adams [1989] Director; Philip Arthur Would [1971] Director/Asset Manager

Integrated Care Solutions (Shropshire) Limited
Incorporated: 11 March 2005
Net Worth Deficit: £2,773,000 *Total Assets:* £14,932,000
Registered Office: Third Floor, Broad Quay, Bristol, BS1 4DJ
Activities: General public administration activities
Parent: Integrated Care Solutions (Shropshire) Holdings Limited
Officers: Benjamin David Adams [1989] Director; Philip Arthur Would [1971] Director/Asset Manager

Integreon Managed Solutions Limited
Incorporated: 15 July 2005 *Employees:* 288
Net Worth Deficit: £1,472,745 *Total Assets:* £4,591,651
Registered Office: 4th Floor, Tower Wharf, Cheese Lane, Bristol, BS2 0JJ
Activities: Other business support service activities n.e.c.
Officers: Marni Goodman Helfand, Secretary; Rishiprabh Jha, Secretary; Rishiprabh Jha, Secretary; Tushar Chandulal Gandhi [1983] Director [Indian]; Rishiprabh Jha [1972] Director/Chief Financial Officer [Indian]; Robert Dean Rowe [1960] CEO, Director and President [American]

Integrity Print Limited
Incorporated: 19 May 2008 *Employees:* 306
Net Worth: £3,000,000 *Total Assets:* £20,058,000
Registered Office: First Avenue, Westfield Trading Estate, Midsomer Norton, Bath, BA3 4BS
Activities: Other manufacturing n.e.c.
Parent: MCAARP Holdings Ltd
Officers: Arthur John Ayres, Secretary; Arthur John Ayres [1958] Finance Director; Mark Edward Cornford [1965] Managing Director

Intel Corporation (UK) Limited
Incorporated: 19 September 1973
Net Worth: £12,288,436,224 *Total Assets:* £13,155,995,648
Registered Office: Intel Corporation UK Ltd, Pipers Way, Swindon, Wilts, SN3 1RJ
Activities: Activities of head offices
Parent: Intel Overseas Funding Corporation
Officers: Tiffany Doon Silva, Secretary; Sharon Lynn Heck [1971] Tax Director [American]; Gary Kershaw [1963] Treasury Director; David John Miles [1967] Director/Head of Tax; Tiffany Doon Silva [1966] Director/Senior Counsel [American]

Inter Mediate Two Limited
Incorporated: 11 January 1990 *Employees:* 1
Previous: Enertech Group Limited
Net Worth: £11,029,000 *Total Assets:* £11,127,000
Registered Office: Sudbury House, 56 London Street, Faringdon, Oxon, SN7 7AA
Activities: Activities of head offices
Major Shareholder: Roger Frederic Hancox
Officers: Diana Hancox, Secretary; Roger Frederic Hancox [1948] Director; Daniel Rogers [1975] Director

Inter Rested Limited
Incorporated: 12 November 1998 *Employees:* 242
Net Worth: £74,203,000 *Total Assets:* £78,296,000
Registered Office: Sudbury House, 56 London Street, Faringdon, Oxon, SN7 7AA
Activities: Activities of head offices
Major Shareholder: Roger Frederic Hancox
Officers: Diana Hancox, Secretary; Roger Frederic Hancox [1948] Director

Inter-Line (South West) Limited.
Incorporated: 23 January 1976 *Employees:* 90
Net Worth: £3,778,509 *Total Assets:* £6,303,513
Registered Office: Unit 3 Woodland Close, Old Woods Trading Estate, Torquay, Devon, TQ2 7BD
Activities: Agents involved in the sale of timber and building materials
Shareholders: Beryl Elizabeth Moreing; Stanley Ralph Moreing
Officers: Beryl Elizabeth Moreing, Secretary; Deborah Ruth Bullock [1967] Director; Andrew Gene Moreing [1971] Director/Operations Manager; Beryl Elizabeth Moreing [1941] Director; Darren James Moreing [1969] Director/Logistics Manager; Stanley Ralph Moreing [1938] Director; Neil Colin Robinson [1965] Director/Finance Manager

Intercept Pharma Europe Ltd.
Incorporated: 18 September 2014 *Employees:* 47
Net Worth Deficit: £373,933,984 *Total Assets:* £98,879,544
Registered Office: One Glass Wharf, Bristol, BS2 0ZX
Activities: Wholesale of pharmaceutical goods
Parent: Intercept Pharmaceuticals, Inc.
Officers: Daniel Carey Cazel Hood, Secretary; Lisa Jane Bright [1967] Director/Business Person; Sandip Kapadia [1970] Director/Chief Financial Officer [Indian]; Dr Mark Pruzanski [1967] Director/CEO & President [Canadian]

Interconnect Products Limited
Incorporated: 27 December 1989 *Employees:* 9
Net Worth: £9,514,008 *Total Assets:* £13,056,976
Registered Office: IPL House, Templars Way, Wootton Bassett, Swindon, Wilts, SN4 7SA
Activities: Other business support service activities n.e.c.
Parent: Reflex Electronics Limited
Officers: Lin Han [1978] Director [Chinese]; David Huang [1967] Director [Chinese]

Interfit Limited
Incorporated: 14 December 2001 *Employees:* 53
Net Worth: £434,000 *Total Assets:* £4,031,000
Registered Office: Trelleborg International Drive, Tewkesbury Business Park, Tewkesbury, Glos, GL20 8UQ
Activities: Non-specialised wholesale trade
Parent: Watts Tyres Limited
Officers: Ian Elcock, Secretary; Elio Bartoli [1977] Director [Italian]; Salvatore Marino [1964] Director [Italian]; Mark Anthony Ruck [1969] Director/Accountant

Intergraph (UK) Limited
Incorporated: 30 October 1979 *Employees:* 152
Net Worth: £15,174,633 *Total Assets:* £19,458,882
Registered Office: Delta Business Park, Great Western Way, Swindon, Wilts, SN5 7XP
Activities: Information technology consultancy activities
Shareholders: Hexagon AB; Intergraph Corporation
Officers: Fleur Polly Mary Rose Eldridge, Secretary; Dean Christopher Cooke [1970] UK Director; Kevin John Holmes [1963] Director/Salesperson; Michael Scott Moore [1969] Director/Chief Financial Officer [American]; Peter Matthew Prater [1965] Sales Director

International Dance Supplies Limited
Incorporated: 13 May 2005 *Employees:* 79
Net Worth: £4,180,796 *Total Assets:* £7,644,580
Registered Office: Harlequin House, Forde Court, Forde Road, Newton Abbot, Devon, TQ12 4BT
Activities: Wholesale of clothing and footwear
Parent: First Position Group Limited
Officers: Joseph John Gelp Jr [1953] Director/Chief Executive Officer [American]; Kamlesh Raichura [1974] Managing Director

International Education Systems Limited
Incorporated: 25 October 1991 *Employees:* 98
Net Worth Deficit: £4,209,114 *Total Assets:* £7,427,980
Registered Office: Narrow Quay House, Narrow Quay, Bristol, BS1 4QA
Activities: Other education n.e.c.
Major Shareholder: Jorge Segovia Bonet
Officers: Luis Martinez, Secretary; Luis Martinez Zorzo [1959] Director/Teacher [Spanish]; Monica Segovia [1991] Marketing Director [Spanish]; Jorge Segovia Bonet [1962] Director/Businessman [Spanish]

International Plywood (Importers) Limited
Incorporated: 5 January 1981 *Employees:* 57
Net Worth: £24,720,296 *Total Assets:* £84,964,792
Registered Office: Sharvatt House, Innsworth Technology Park, Innsworth Lane, Gloucester, GL3 1DL
Activities: Non-specialised wholesale trade
Parent: International Plywood PLC
Officers: Michael Charles Walker, Secretary; David John Attwood [1948] Director; Diane Gillian Attwood [1948] Finance Director; Ian David Attwood [1973] Managing Director; Robert Charles Attwood [1977] Director; Nicholas Leslie Brinsford [1962] Sales Director; Andrew James Draper [1967] Financial Director; Scott Conrad Golding [1957] Director; Stuart Ian Watts [1970] Director/Sales Manager

International Plywood PLC
Incorporated: 17 February 1981 *Employees:* 81
Net Worth: £26,798,604 *Total Assets:* £100,867,920
Registered Office: Sharvatt House, Innsworth Technology Park, Innsworth Lane, Gloucester, GL3 1DL
Activities: Activities of distribution holding companies
Major Shareholder: David John Attwood
Officers: Michael Charles Walker, Secretary; David John Attwood [1948] Director; Diane Gillian Attwood [1948] Finance Director; Ian David Attwood [1973] Managing Director; Robert Charles Attwood [1977] Director

International Spray Solutions Limited
Incorporated: 10 January 2017 *Employees:* 3
Net Worth: £55,801 *Total Assets:* £9,895,036
Registered Office: Midway House, Staverton Technology Park, Herrick Way, Staverton, Cheltenham, Glos, GL51 6TQ
Activities: Service activities incidental to air transportation
Shareholders: Graham Nigel Cole; Steven David Smith; Steven David Smith
Officers: Graham Nigel Cole [1948] Director; Ian Downing [1969] Director; Steven David Smith [1960] Director/Accountant

Intrinsic Financial Planning Limited
Incorporated: 13 July 2005
Net Worth: £15,760,000 *Total Assets:* £34,395,000
Registered Office: Wiltshire Court, Farnsby Street, Swindon, Wilts, SN1 5AH
Activities: Activities auxiliary to financial intermediation n.e.c.
Parent: Intrinsic Financial Services Limited
Officers: Darren William John Sharkey [1970] Director/Chartered Accountant [Irish]; Andrew Bernard Thompson [1968] Director

Intrinsic Financial Services Limited
Incorporated: 22 February 2005 *Employees:* 587
Net Worth: £147,188,992 *Total Assets:* £212,014,000
Registered Office: Wiltshire Court, Farnsby Street, Swindon, Wilts, SN1 5AH
Activities: Financial intermediation not elsewhere classified
Parent: Old Mutual Wealth Holdings Limited
Officers: Keith Reginald Baldwin [1948] Director; Paul Stephen Matthews [1960] Director; Mark Oscar Satchel [1969] Director [British/South African]; Darren William John Sharkey [1970] Director/Chartered Accountant [Irish]; Gregor Ninian Stewart [1964] Director/Accountant; Andrew Bernard Thompson [1968] Managing Director - UK Distribution

Intrinsic Mortgage Planning Limited
Incorporated: 30 June 2005
Net Worth: £9,099,000 *Total Assets:* £18,519,000
Registered Office: Wiltshire Court, Farnsby Street, Swindon, Wilts, SN1 5AH
Activities: Activities auxiliary to financial intermediation n.e.c.
Parent: Intrinsic Financial Services Limited
Officers: Darren William John Sharkey [1970] Director/Chartered Accountant [Irish]; Andrew Bernard Thompson [1968] Director

Intrinsic Wealth Limited
Incorporated: 31 July 2002
Previous: Intrinsic Independent Limited
Net Worth: £3,415,000 *Total Assets:* £15,425,000
Registered Office: Wiltshire Court, Farnsby Street, Swindon, Wilts, SN1 5AH
Activities: Financial intermediation not elsewhere classified
Parent: Intrinsic Financial Services Limited
Officers: Darren William John Sharkey [1970] Director/Chartered Accountant [Irish]; Andrew Bernard Thompson [1968] Director

Inty Limited
Incorporated: 24 September 1997 *Employees:* 86
Net Worth: £2,295,000 *Total Assets:* £5,537,000
Registered Office: 170 Aztec West, Bristol, BS32 4TN
Activities: Other information technology service activities
Parent: Inty Holdings Limited
Officers: Tarek Mohamed Mohayeldin Abdelaziz Aboualam [1971] Director/Managing Partner [Egyptian]; Mohamed Aly Shawky Sobih Doukanish [1975] Director [Egyptian]; Craig Barry Marcus Joseph [1974] Director/Chief Operating Officer; Onsi Naguib Sawiris [1992] Director/Managing Partner [American]

Investacast Limited
Incorporated: 24 December 1975 *Employees:* 70
Net Worth: £3,386,933 *Total Assets:* £5,460,354
Registered Office: Investacast Ltd, Mullacott Cross Industrial Estate, Ilfracombe, Devon, EX34 8PL
Activities: Casting of steel
Parent: Investacast Ilfracombe Limited
Officers: Christopher James Thompson, Secretary/Director; Steven Bone [1971] Director; Tony Buckland [1962] Director; Henry William Gregson [1958] Director; Alistair John Schofield [1966] Director; Christopher James Thompson [1963] Director

Investment Funds Direct Group Limited
Incorporated: 6 April 2004
Net Worth: £38,338,516 *Total Assets:* £38,405,440
Registered Office: Trimbridge House, Trim Street, Bath, BA1 1HB
Activities: Activities of financial services holding companies
Shareholders: Wrap IFA Services Limited; Wrap IFA Services Limited
Officers: Tracey Graham [1965] Director; Heidi Elizabeth Johnson [1978] Director; Isobel May Langton [1963] Director; James McCourt [1967] Director; Robert Andrew Regan [1975] Director

Investment Funds Direct Limited
Incorporated: 2 February 1982 *Employees:* 398
Net Worth: £38,188,000 *Total Assets:* £71,893,000
Registered Office: Trimbridge House, Trim Street, Bath, BA1 1HB
Activities: Financial intermediation not elsewhere classified
Parent: Investment Funds Direct Group Limited
Officers: Tracey Graham [1965] Director; Heidi Elizabeth Johnson [1978] Director; Isobel May Langton [1963] Director; James McCourt [1967] Director; Robert Andrew Regan [1975] Director

Investors in Health (C & T1) Limited
Incorporated: 28 January 2004
Net Worth: £1,274,293 *Total Assets:* £39,452,844
Registered Office: Third Floor, Broad Quay House, Prince Street, Bristol, BS1 4DJ
Activities: Other business support service activities n.e.c.
Parent: Investors in Health (C & T) Holdings Limited
Officers: Paul Anthony Cartwright [1957] Director; Christopher Howlett [1967] Director; Balasingham Ravi Kumar [1975] Investment Director; Thomas Benedict Symes [1956] Director

Investors in the Community (Bexley Schools) Limited
Incorporated: 1 February 2002
Net Worth: £132,579 *Total Assets:* £27,065,610
Registered Office: Third Floor, Broad Quay House, Prince Street, Bristol, BS1 4DJ
Activities: Other business support service activities n.e.c.
Parent: Louiseco Limited
Officers: Paul Anthony Cartwright [1957] Director; Jamie Pritchard [1971] Director/Investment Manager; Thomas Benedict Symes [1956] Director

Investors in the Community (Leeds Schools) Holding Company Limited
Incorporated: 17 February 2005
Net Worth Deficit: £14,416,081 *Total Assets:* £98,260,400
Registered Office: Third Floor, Broad Quay House, Prince Street, Bristol, BS1 4DJ
Activities: Activities of head offices
Parent: Louiseco Limited
Officers: Paul Anthony Cartwright [1957] Director; Richard Leonard Groome [1951] Director/Chartered Engineer; Jamie Pritchard [1971] Director/Investment Manager; Thomas Benedict Symes [1956] Director

Investors in the Community (Leeds Schools) Limited
Incorporated: 21 January 2005
Net Worth Deficit: £14,416,090 *Total Assets:* £98,260,392
Registered Office: Third Floor, Broad Quay House, Prince Street, Bristol, BS1 4DJ
Activities: Other business support service activities n.e.c.
Parent: Investors in the Community (Leeds Schools) Holding Company Limited
Officers: Paul Anthony Cartwright [1957] Director; Richard Leonard Groome [1951] Director/Chartered Engineer; Jamie Pritchard [1971] Director/Investment Manager; Thomas Benedict Symes [1956] Director

Investors in the Community (Leeds Schools) Subdebt Limited
Incorporated: 4 March 2005
Net Worth: £6,480 *Total Assets:* £7,288,840
Registered Office: Third Floor, Broad Quay House, Prince Street, Bristol, BS1 4DJ
Activities: Other business support service activities n.e.c.
Parent: IIC (Leeds Schools) Fund Investment Limited
Officers: Paul Anthony Cartwright [1957] Director; Richard Leonard Groome [1951] Director/Chartered Engineer; Jamie Pritchard [1971] Director/Investment Manager; Thomas Benedict Symes [1956] Director

Invicta Motors (Maidstone) Limited
Incorporated: 26 January 2010 *Employees:* 55
Net Worth: £1,790,000 *Total Assets:* £4,075,000
Registered Office: Swindon Motor Park, Dorcan Way, Swindon, Wilts, SN3 3RA
Activities: Sale of new cars and light motor vehicles
Parent: Cambria Automobiles Acquisitions Ltd
Officers: James Anthony Mullins, Secretary; Timothy Alex Duckers [1973] Director; Mark Jonathan James Lavery [1965] Director; James Anthony Mullins [1978] Finance Director

Invicta Motors Limited
Incorporated: 19 December 1922 *Employees:* 148
Net Worth: £8,932,000 *Total Assets:* £21,698,000
Registered Office: Swindon Motor Park, Dorcan Way, Swindon, Wilts, SN3 3RA
Activities: Sale of new cars and light motor vehicles
Parent: Cambria Automobiles (South East) Ltd
Officers: James Anthony Mullins, Finance Director; Timothy Alex Duckers [1973] Director; Mark Jonathan James Lavery [1965] Director; James Anthony Mullins [1978] Director

IoP Publishing Limited
Incorporated: 21 April 1949 *Employees:* 346
Net Worth: £299,000 *Total Assets:* £23,578,000
Registered Office: Temple Circus, Temple Way, Bristol, BS1 6HG
Activities: Publishing of learned journals
Officers: Oliver David Callaghan [1977] Finance Director; Richard Denis Paul Charkin [1949] Director/Publisher; Kim Dovell [1965] Finance Director; Dr Olaf Ernst [1969] Commercial Director [German]; Sarah Elisabeth Flannigan [1973] Director; Professor Brian Robert Fulton [1953] Director/University Professor; Steven Richard Hall [1956] Managing Director; Professor Paul James Hardaker [1966] Director/Chief Executive; Professor Julian David Clayton Jones [1954] Director/University Professor; Rene H Olivieri [1953] Director; Bridget Pairaudeau [1968] IT Director; Antonia Karen Seymour [1971] Publishing Director

Iota Properties Limited
Incorporated: 18 August 1964
Net Worth: £7,102,782 *Total Assets:* £7,302,782
Registered Office: 5 Poole Road, Bournemouth, BH2 5QL
Activities: Other letting and operating of own or leased real estate
Officers: Jane Balmforth, Secretary; Jane Balmforth [1958] Director; Mark Julian Griffiths [1961] Director

IP-Performance Ltd
Incorporated: 5 October 1994 *Employees:* 26
Net Worth: £4,355,110 *Total Assets:* £6,104,856
Registered Office: 1-3 Merietts Court, Long Ashton Business Park, Long Ashton, Bristol, BS41 9LW
Activities: Other information technology service activities
Major Shareholder: Philip Anthony Crossley
Officers: Philip Anthony Crossley, Secretary; Philip Anthony Crossley [1957] Director; John Victor Zamick [1958] Director

Ipex Capital GP LLP
Incorporated: 14 November 2013
Net Worth: £2,630,501 *Total Assets:* £6,285,030
Registered Office: One Glass Wharf, Bristol, BS2 0ZX
Officers: Christopher John Latimer Haynes [1969] Member; Martin Gordon Robert Stapleton [1969] Member; Jonathan Patrick Moynihan [1948] LLP Member

Ipipeline (TCP) Limited
Incorporated: 30 September 1987 *Employees:* 75
Previous: The Computer Partnership Limited
Net Worth: £4,670,000 *Total Assets:* £7,229,000
Registered Office: 3rd Floor, Montpellier House, Montpellier Drive, Cheltenham, Glos, GL50 1TY
Activities: Business and domestic software development
Parent: Ipipeline Limited
Officers: Lawrence C. Berran [1971] Director/Chief Financial Officer [American]; Ashley Hale [1960] Director/Operations Manager; Ian Roger Teague [1968] Director

Ipplepen Property Limited
Incorporated: 8 January 1993 *Employees:* 2
Net Worth: £2,625,048 *Total Assets:* £4,293,564
Registered Office: Value House Stores Ltd, Clovelly Road Industrial Estate, Bideford, Devon, EX39 3HN
Activities: Other retail sale in non-specialised stores
Shareholder: Richard William, John Ford
Officers: Richard William John Ford, Secretary/Director; Michael Reginald Arthur Ford [1960] Director; Richard William John Ford [1959] Director

The IPS Partnership PLC
Incorporated: 1 November 1979 *Employees:* 45
Net Worth: £2,858,000 *Total Assets:* £4,416,000
Registered Office: Dunn's House, St Pauls Road, Salisbury, Wilts, SP2 7BF
Activities: Other professional, scientific and technical activities n.e.c.
Parent: IFG UK Holdings Limited
Officers: Stephen John Charles Darke, Secretary; Geoffrey Stephen Clarkson [1949] Director/Solicitor; Alastair Conway [1965] Director; Keith Martin Dignam [1961] Management Consultant/Director [Irish]; Gavin Howard [1972] Director/Chief Financial Officer; Iain Beattie McCoo [1965] Director; Kathryn Elizabeth Purves [1973] Director

IPS Pensions Limited
Incorporated: 16 April 1991 *Employees:* 48
Net Worth: £3,304,000 *Total Assets:* £4,576,000
Registered Office: Dunn's House, St Paul's Road, Salisbury, Wilts, SP2 7BF
Activities: Financial intermediation not elsewhere classified
Parent: IFG UK Holdings Limited
Officers: Stephen John Charles Darke, Secretary; Geoffrey Stephen Clarkson [1949] Director/Solicitor; Alastair Conway [1965] Director; Keith Martin Dignam [1961] Management Consultant/Director [Irish]; Gavin Howard [1972] Director/Chief Financial Officer; Iain Beattie McCoo [1965] Director; Kathryn Elizabeth Purves [1973] Director

Iracroft Limited
Incorporated: 22 May 1972 *Employees:* 184
Net Worth: £5,349,584 *Total Assets:* £8,949,465
Registered Office: Blandford Height Industrial Estate, Shaftesbury Lane, Blandford Forum, Dorset, DT11 7TE
Activities: Manufacture of other tanks, reservoirs and containers of metal
Shareholders: Angela Mary Simmonds; Louise Elliott
Officers: Alan Webb, Secretary; Marie-Louise Elliott [1957] Director; Wayne Kelvin Lawrence Moore [1964] Director/Chairman; Kieran Mullen [1981] Director; Nicholas David Parker [1964] Managing Director; Angela Mary Simmonds [1955] Director; Alan Webb [1960] Director/Accountant

Ironburg Inventions Limited
Incorporated: 9 May 2011 *Employees:* 3
Net Worth: £4,867,168 *Total Assets:* £6,394,329
Registered Office: 10 Market Place, Wincanton, Somerset, BA9 9LP
Activities: Other professional, scientific and technical activities n.e.c.
Officers: Duncan Ironmonger [1975] Director/Salesman; Evan Karp [1976] Director [American]; John Kim [1967] Director [American]

Irongate Limited
Incorporated: 8 October 1999 *Employees:* 7
Net Worth: £611,212 *Total Assets:* £7,677,256
Registered Office: Ashgrove Farm, Jackbarrow Road, Winstone, Cirencester, Glos, GL7 7LB
Activities: Financial intermediation not elsewhere classified
Shareholders: Edward James Scott-Hopkins; Amanda Jane Scot-Hopkins
Officers: Amanda Jane Scott Hopkins, Secretary; Amanda Jane Scott Hopkins [1965] Director/Company Secretary; Edward James Henderson Scott Hopkins [1962] Director/Financial Advisor

Isedio Limited
Incorporated: 22 September 2009
Net Worth: £1,389,410 *Total Assets:* £3,804,988
Registered Office: 339 Two Mile Hill Road, Bristol, BS15 1AN
Activities: Manufacture of metal structures and parts of structures
Major Shareholder: Shaun Anthony Spurrell
Officers: Shaun Anthony Spurrell [1967] Director

ISG Pearce Limited
Incorporated: 1 May 1946
Net Worth Deficit: £4,872,000 *Total Assets:* £14,794,000
Registered Office: Ground Floor, Unit 1200 Park House, Parkway North, Newbrick Road, Stoke Gifford, Bristol, BS34 8YU
Activities: Construction of commercial buildings
Shareholder: ISG UK Retial Limited
Officers: Nicholas James Heard, Secretary; Paul Martin Cossell [1965] Director; Robert Samuel Martin [1961] Director/General Manager; Mark Stockton [1964] Director/Accountant; Andrew Imray Taylor [1956] Director/Business Development

Isles of Scilly Shipping Company Limited
Incorporated: 12 January 2004 *Employees:* 70
Net Worth: £4,734,247 *Total Assets:* £7,163,538
Registered Office: Steamship House, Quay Street, Penzance, Cornwall, TR18 4BZ
Activities: Sea and coastal passenger water transport
Parent: Isles of Scilly Steamship Company Limited
Officers: Andrew John May [1954] Director/Flower Farmer; Stuart Kenneth Reid [1979] Director

Isles of Scilly Skybus Limited
Incorporated: 23 March 1984 *Employees:* 74
Net Worth: £1,157,759 *Total Assets:* £6,857,060
Registered Office: Top Floor, Steamship House, Quay Street, Penzance, Cornwall, TR18 4BZ
Activities: Scheduled passenger air transport
Parent: Isles of Scilly Steamship Company Limited
Officers: Andrew John May [1954] Director/Flower Farmer; Stuart Kenneth Reid [1979] Finance Director

Isles of Scilly Steamship Company Limited
Incorporated: 26 March 1920 *Employees:* 242
Net Worth: £14,721,661 *Total Assets:* £24,169,536
Registered Office: Hugh Town, St Marys, Isles of Scilly, TR21 0LJ
Activities: Sea and coastal passenger water transport
Officers: Stuart Kenneth Reid, Secretary; Peter Derek Hardaker [1943] Director/Retired; Sam Hicks [1977] Director; Stephen Martin Hicks [1954] Director/Maritime Pilot; Ian Philip Howard [1955] Director; Andrew John May [1954] Director/Flower Farmer; Gary Robert Randall [1966] Director/Chartered Accountant; Stuart Kenneth Reid [1979] Director/Chief Financial Officer; Hendrik Wiekens [1952] Joint Managing Director of Pendennis Shipyard

Islington Trowbridge Limited
Incorporated: 29 May 1979 *Employees:* 77
Net Worth: £757,477 *Total Assets:* £5,766,294
Registered Office: Trowbridge Motor Park, Canal Road, Trowbridge, Wilts, BA14 8RL
Activities: Sale of new cars and light motor vehicles
Officers: Dina Mary Christine Hatch, Secretary; Dina Mary Christine Hatch [1965] Director/Company Secretary; Nick Howe [1970] After Sales Director; Paul Colin Jones [1971] Managing Director; Roderick Donald Timbrell-Whittle [1947] Director; Susan Ann Timbrell-Whittle [1952] Director; Dylan Thomas Turner [1979] Sales Director

Italmatch UK Limited
Incorporated: 2 March 2007 *Employees:* 1
Net Worth: £8,198,000 *Total Assets:* £11,094,000
Registered Office: One Glass Wharf, Bristol, BS2 0ZX
Activities: Manufacture of other chemical products n.e.c.
Officers: Foort de Jong [1960] Director [Dutch]; Maurizio Turci [1959] Director [Italian]

ITEC Connect Ltd
Incorporated: 10 February 1988 *Employees:* 202
Net Worth: £4,620,810 *Total Assets:* £17,328,676
Registered Office: Itec House, Hawkfield Way, Whitchurch, Bristol, BS14 0BL
Activities: Other information technology service activities
Parent: Investment ITEC Connect Ltd
Officers: Susan Jennifer Bartlett, Secretary; James Arscott [1982] Director; Philip James Ford [1964] Director/Salesman; Michael David French [1952] Director/Chartered Accountant; Nicholas Luke Orme [1970] Director; Philip James Perkins [1968] Director; Ian David Stewart [1963] Director/Salesman; Benjamin Summerfield [1979] Director; Gary James Tozer [1975] Director/Sales Manager; David Charles Young [1958] Director/Business Consultant

ITP Developments Limited
Incorporated: 5 November 2002
Net Worth: £1,123,590 *Total Assets:* £4,083,387
Registered Office: The Site Office, Innsworth Technology Park, Gloucester, GL3 1DL
Activities: Development of building projects
Officers: Jayne Thurstance, Secretary; Emma Louise Dowty [1971] Director; George Edward Dowty [1953] Director/Manager; James Alexander Colin Fick [1985] Director

IVC Acquisition Ltd
Incorporated: 30 November 2016 *Employees:* 4
Net Worth: £181,552,032 *Total Assets:* £1,192,979,456
Registered Office: The Chocolate Factory, Keynsham, Bristol, BS31 2AU
Activities: Activities of other holding companies n.e.c.
Parent: IVC Acquisition Midco Ltd
Officers: Amanda Jane Davis [1968] Director; Per Gosta Franzen [1976] Director [Swedish]; David Robert Geoffrey Hillier [1962] Director; Niklas Arne Ringby [1980] Director [Swedish]

IVC Acquisition Midco Ltd
Incorporated: 5 December 2016 *Employees:* 7,418
Net Worth: £223,918,064 *Total Assets:* £1,309,311,616
Registered Office: The Chocolate Factory, Keynsham, Bristol, BS31 2AU
Activities: Activities of other holding companies n.e.c.
Parent: IVC Acquisition Pikco Ltd
Officers: Amanda Jane Davis [1968] Director; Per Gosta Franzen [1976] Director [Swedish]; David Robert Geoffrey Hillier [1962] Director; Niklas Arne Ringby [1980] Director [Swedish]

IVC Acquisition Pikco Ltd
Incorporated: 5 December 2016 *Employees:* 7,418
Net Worth: £223,793,424 *Total Assets:* £1,309,311,616
Registered Office: The Chocolate Factory, Keynsham, Bristol, BS31 2AU
Activities: Activities of other holding companies n.e.c.
Officers: Amanda Jane Davis [1968] Director; Per Gosta Franzen [1976] Director [Swedish]; David Robert Geoffrey Hillier [1962] Director; Niklas Arne Ringby [1980] Director [Swedish]

IXYS UK Westcode Ltd.
Incorporated: 28 August 1997 *Employees:* 158
Net Worth: £12,551,000 *Total Assets:* £17,623,000
Registered Office: Langley Park Way, Langley Park, Chippenham, Wilts, SN15 1GE
Activities: Manufacture of other electrical equipment
Parent: IXYS Holdings Limited
Officers: Ashley Golland, Secretary; Ashley Golland [1972] Director/Engineer; Ian Paul David Highley [1963] Director/Senior Vice President & General Manager; Marcus Gordon Waddie Ward [1969] Director/Chartered Accountant

Izit Group Limited
Incorporated: 15 May 2009 *Employees:* 1,251
Net Worth: £1,950,537 *Total Assets:* £4,190,079
Registered Office: 1 Brunswick Square, Bristol, BS2 8PE
Activities: Activities of head offices
Shareholders: Mark Thurgood; Peter Stewart Bailey; Parragon Books Ltd
Officers: Peter Stewart Bailey, Secretary; Peter Stewart Bailey [1960] Director; Malcolm Russell Hepworth [1954] Director; Jeremy Charles Marwood [1958] Director; Paul Taylor [1970] Managing Director; Mark Thurgood [1961] Director

J & K Aquatics Limited
Incorporated: 24 September 1985 *Employees:* 78
Net Worth: £2,061,958 *Total Assets:* £7,592,270
Registered Office: Market Way, North Petherton, Bridgwater, Somerset, TA6 6DF
Activities: Wholesale of other machinery and equipment
Parent: Timehaste Limited
Officers: Judith Rosina James, Secretary; Judith Rosina James [1959] Director; Paul James [1956] Director

J+S Limited
Incorporated: 16 April 1999 *Employees:* 26
Net Worth: £6,767,000 *Total Assets:* £16,367,000
Registered Office: Riverside Road, Pottington Business Park, Barnstaple, Devon, EX31 1LY
Activities: Other manufacturing n.e.c.
Parent: Systems Engineering & Assessment Ltd
Officers: Sarita Bilkhu, Secretary; Stephen Jeremy Hill [1965] Director; Andrew Stephen Thomis [1964] Director; Simon Robert Walther [1967] Director

J. J. Farm Services Limited
Incorporated: 18 December 1979
Net Worth: £2,716,311 *Total Assets:* £8,796,172
Registered Office: Far Stanley, Gretton, Winchcombe, Cheltenham, Glos, GL54 5HF
Activities: Agents involved in the sale of machinery, industrial equipment, ships and aircraft
Officers: Hannah Jenkins [1990] Director/Secretary; Martin Richard Jenkins [1967] Director/Farm Machinery Retailer

J.J. Acquisitions Limited
Incorporated: 28 September 2006 *Employees:* 4
Net Worth: £541,907 *Total Assets:* £3,649,816
Registered Office: Windover House, St Ann Street, Salisbury, Wilts, SP1 2DR
Activities: Development of building projects
Shareholders: Christian John Osorio; Ben Charles Donald Johnston
Officers: Christian Osorio, Secretary; Ben Charles Donald Johnston [1983] Director; Christian John Osorio [1982] Director

J.P.C.Properties (Southampton) Limited
Incorporated: 8 April 1957 *Employees:* 3
Net Worth: £3,795,272 *Total Assets:* £3,991,794
Registered Office: The Old Coach House, Church Street, Castle Cary, Somerset, BA7 7EJ
Activities: Development of building projects
Major Shareholder: Nicola Carol O'Dell-Shearn
Officers: Nicola Carol O'Dell-Shearn, Secretary; David Griffiths [1953] Director/Chartered Accountant; Nicola Carol O'Dell-Shearn [1982] Director/Business Executive; Rebecca O'Dell-Shearn [1976] Director/Property Manager

Jacgilden Properties Limited
Incorporated: 24 June 1959 *Employees:* 7
Net Worth: £8,647,354 *Total Assets:* £9,511,326
Registered Office: 24 Cornwall Road, Dorchester, DT1 1RX
Activities: Other letting and operating of own or leased real estate
Shareholders: Gillian Patricia Brookes; Denise Marcia Rowe
Officers: Gillian Patricia Brookes [1942] Director/Housewife; Jane McNamara [1963] Director/Physiotherapist/Pilot; Denise Marcia Rowe [1945] Director/Architect Assistant

Jackamax Limited
Incorporated: 1 November 2012 *Employees:* 1
Net Worth: £6,748,756 *Total Assets:* £12,886,075
Registered Office: c/o Francis Clark LLP, North Quay House, Sutton Harbour, Plymouth, PL4 0RA
Activities: Growing of fibre crops
Major Shareholder: Mark Daniel Rowe
Officers: Emma Rowe [1972] Director; Mark Daniel Rowe [1971] Director/Farmer

Jackson Developments Limited
Incorporated: 26 June 1997 *Employees:* 2
Net Worth: £4,786,590 *Total Assets:* £7,743,795
Registered Office: Ebenezer House, 5a Poole Road, Bournemouth, BH2 5QJ
Activities: Buying and selling of own real estate
Major Shareholder: Ann Jackson
Officers: Simon Nicholas Jackson [1966] Director

Jackson Property Investments
Incorporated: 18 March 1993
Net Worth: £1,459,921 *Total Assets:* £8,658,496
Registered Office: The Lodge, Park Road, Shepton Mallet, Somerset, BA4 5BS
Activities: Other letting and operating of own or leased real estate
Major Shareholder: Andrew Stuart Jackson
Officers: Nicola Claydon, Secretary/Accountant; Andrew Stuart Jackson [1968] Director/Accountant; Heidi Jackson [1969] Director/Housewife

Jacksons Investments Limited
Incorporated: 10 July 2007
Net Worth: £8,489,000 *Total Assets:* £18,778,000
Registered Office: Mercedes-Benz of Poole, Holes Bay Road, Poole, Dorset, BH15 2BD
Activities: Activities of head offices
Parent: Sandown Motors Limited
Officers: Gareth Robert Copling, Secretary; Gareth Robert Copling [1967] Financial Director; Gavin Alan McAllister [1981] Director

Jade-Aden Services Limited
Incorporated: 6 April 1992 *Employees:* 44
Net Worth: £4,217,525 *Total Assets:* £10,269,514
Registered Office: Tower House, Parkstone Road, Poole, Dorset, BH15 2JH
Activities: Other specialised construction activities n.e.c.
Major Shareholder: Grahame Phillip Gibson
Officers: Dawn Catherine Gibson, Secretary/Director; Dawn Catherine Gibson [1965] Director; Grahame Phillip Gibson [1962] Director

Jaguar Oil & Gas UK Limited
Incorporated: 24 April 1991
Previous: West Africa Completion Services Limited
Net Worth: £64,479,000 *Total Assets:* £65,244,000
Registered Office: 2 High Street, Nailsea, Bristol, BS48 1BS
Activities: Other business support service activities n.e.c.
Parent: Sondex Limited
Officers: Carole Audrey Chichester [1969] Director [American]; Alasdair Murray Campbell Sloan [1967] Director

Jakemans (Confectioners) Limited
Incorporated: 2 December 1938 *Employees:* 56
Net Worth: £5,203,288 *Total Assets:* £10,503,564
Registered Office: G R Lane Health Product Limited, Sisson Road, Gloucester, GL2 0GR
Activities: Manufacture of sugar confectionery
Parent: G R Lane Health Products Ltd
Officers: Paul Charles Whatley, Secretary; David Cole [1969] Director; Janet Margaret Groves [1952] Director; Jonathan Groves [1980] Commercial Director; Paul Henly [1962] Technical Director; Mark Horan [1973] Operations Director; Trevor Edward Howard [1962] Director; Aden Craig Kelly [1974] Sales Director; Hilary Lynn [1967] Marketing Director; Paul Charles Whatley [1958] Finance Director

Jam & Sons Limited
Incorporated: 29 October 2008
Net Worth: £325,334 *Total Assets:* £4,891,082
Registered Office: 10 Bridge Street, Christchurch, Dorset, BH23 1EF
Activities: Other letting and operating of own or leased real estate
Shareholders: Thomas Vyvyan Board; Benjamin Maynard Board
Officers: Jane Elizabeth Board [1947] Director; Mark Lydon Board [1945] Director

Jam Bidco Limited
Incorporated: 8 August 2014
Net Worth Deficit: £1,724,830 *Total Assets:* £18,347,494
Registered Office: ATE House, Westpark 26, Chelston, Wellington, Somerset, TA21 9AD
Activities: Manufacture of electronic measuring, testing etc. equipment, not for industrial process control
Parent: Jam Topco Limited
Officers: Alexander Charles Spencer Bowden [1974] Director; Carl John Bullock [1966] Managing Director; Jason Christopher Evans [1971] Director; Scott Andrew Fairlie [1984] Director; Michael Paul Threlfall [1964] Director

Jamaica Inn Bodmin Moor Holdings Limited
Incorporated: 15 January 2014 *Employees:* 2
Net Worth Deficit: £5,434 *Total Assets:* £4,798,750
Registered Office: Jamaica Inn, Bolventor, Launceston, Cornwall, PL15 7TS
Activities: Activities of other holding companies n.e.c.
Shareholders: Allen Richard Jackson; Elizabeth Ann Jackson
Officers: Allen Richard Jackson [1948] Director; Elizabeth Ann Jackson [1954] Director

Simon James New Homes Limited
Incorporated: 6 September 1999 *Employees:* 1
Net Worth: £966,594 *Total Assets:* £4,691,624
Registered Office: Beaufort House, 29 Oakfield Road, Clifton, Bristol, BS8 2AT
Activities: Construction of domestic buildings
Major Shareholder: Simon James Crocker
Officers: James Albert Davis, Secretary; Simon James Crocker [1971] Director

Jamie's Farm
Incorporated: 16 February 2009 *Employees:* 23
Net Worth: £5,012,754 *Total Assets:* £7,611,559
Registered Office: Hill House Farm, Ditteridge, Box, Corsham, Wilts, SN13 8QA
Activities: Mixed farming
Officers: Rebecca Ann Vian Boomer-Clark [1977] Director of Education; Peter Alexander Clegg [1950] Director/Architect; Roderick MacKinlay James [1947] Director/Architect; Sian Elisabeth Parry [1960] Director/Head of FIL Foundations; Philip Percival [1946] Director/Fund Manager; James Patrick Westhead [1966] Director/Business Executive

Jamjar Print Ltd
Incorporated: 23 July 1999 *Employees:* 34
Net Worth: £1,721,547 *Total Assets:* £3,816,848
Registered Office: Unit 1 New Queen Street, Bedminster, Bristol, BS3 4AG
Activities: Printing n.e.c.
Major Shareholder: Robert Ian Littlestone
Officers: Robert Ian Littlestone, Secretary; Edward Jenks [1985] Director; Robert Ian Littlestone [1979] Director

Janspeed Technologies Limited
Incorporated: 25 November 2005 *Employees:* 53
Net Worth: £3,258,674 *Total Assets:* £4,795,763
Registered Office: Castle Works, Castle Road, Salisbury, Wilts, SP1 3RX
Activities: Manufacture of other parts and accessories for motor vehicles
Shareholders: Mark Anthony Vaughan; Leigh Vaughan
Officers: Andrew Hillyer Scott, Secretary; Andrew Edward Cowen [1958] Director; Mark Anthony Vaughan [1962] Director

Alec Jarrett Limited
Incorporated: 10 May 1962 *Employees:* 51
Net Worth: £8,125,591 *Total Assets:* £12,045,957
Registered Office: High Street, Oldland Common, Bristol, BS30 9TN
Activities: Processing and preserving of meat
Shareholders: Robert Christopher Jarrett; Stuart Hugh Jarrett
Officers: Stuart Hugh Jarrett, Secretary; Robert Christopher Jarrett [1938] Director/Farmer and Wholesale Butcher; Stuart Hugh Jarrett [1944] Director/Farmer and Wholesale Butcher

Jasme Limited
Incorporated: 29 February 2012
Net Worth: £1,928,343 *Total Assets:* £6,106,061
Registered Office: Easterbrook Eaton Limited, Cosmopolitan House, Old Fore Street, Sidmouth, Devon, EX10 8LS
Activities: Activities of head offices
Major Shareholder: Stephen Anthony Zimmerman
Officers: Laura Jane Zimmerman [1949] Director; Stephen Anthony Zimmerman [1949] Director

H R Jasper & Son (Holdings) Limited
Incorporated: 7 March 2011 *Employees:* 103
Net Worth: £7,063,027 *Total Assets:* £9,534,110
Registered Office: Botathan Abattoir, South Petherwin, Launceston, Cornwall, PL15 7JL
Activities: Activities of head offices
Shareholder: Keith Edward Jasper
Officers: David William Jasper, Secretary; David William Jasper [1957] Director; Edward Keith Jasper [1956] Director; Graham Edward Jasper [1933] Director

H.R.Jasper & Son Limited
Incorporated: 21 April 1972 *Employees:* 99
Net Worth: £2,793,353 *Total Assets:* £4,944,988
Registered Office: Botathan, South Petherwin, Launceston, Cornwall, PL15 7JL
Activities: Processing and preserving of meat
Officers: Edward Keith Jasper, Secretary; David William Jasper [1957] Director/Farmer; Edward Keith Jasper [1956] Director/Farmer; Graham Edward Jasper [1933] Director/Farmer

Jasun Envirocare PLC
Incorporated: 25 October 1972 *Employees:* 167
Net Worth: £3,281,098 *Total Assets:* £7,645,467
Registered Office: Riverside House, Parret Way, Bridgwater, Somerset, TA6 5LB
Activities: Other manufacturing n.e.c.
Shareholders: Barbara Foot; Colin Leonard Hitch
Officers: Barbara Foot, Secretary; Graham Reginald Bentley [1966] Managing Director; Jane Penelope Bentley [1969] Director; Shaun Patrick Doran [1969] Director; Barbara Foot [1943] Director/Secretary; Colin Leonard Hitch [1966] Sales Director; Susan Anne Hitch [1967] Director

Javsford Investments Limited
Incorporated: 28 August 1959
Net Worth: £3,802,223 *Total Assets:* £4,915,872
Registered Office: Towngate House, 2-8 Parkstone Road, Poole, Dorset, BH15 2PW
Activities: Other letting and operating of own or leased real estate
Officers: John Stephen Payne, Company Secretary; Evelyn Parkhurst [1944] Director; John Stephen Payne [1965] Director

Jays Logistics (South West) Limited
Incorporated: 3 October 2006 *Employees:* 85
Net Worth: £1,560,297 *Total Assets:* £4,303,183
Registered Office: 3-5 College Street, Burnham on Sea, Somerset, TA8 1AR
Activities: Freight transport by road
Shareholders: R T Keedwell Holdings Limited; Jonathan Dennis White
Officers: Jonathan Dennis White, Secretary/Director; Stuart Raymond Keedwell [1964] Director; Paul Brian Phillips [1972] Director/Road Transport; Jonathan Dennis White [1968] Director

JB Global Limited
Incorporated: 26 September 2005 *Employees:* 1,186
Net Worth: £7,068,934 *Total Assets:* £108,268,648
Registered Office: Unit DC2 Viscount Way, South Marston Industrial Estate, Swindon, Wilts, SN3 4TN
Activities: Retail of furniture, lighting, and similar (not musical instruments or scores) in specialised store
Major Shareholder: Jason Thomas Bannister
Officers: Jason Thomas Bannister [1971] Director/Retailer; Alex Fisher [1976] Director; Julian Gillett [1969] Finance Director

F.G.Jeanes & Son Limited
Incorporated: 18 October 1960 *Employees:* 26
Net Worth: £2,343,462 *Total Assets:* £6,816,713
Registered Office: Currypool Farm, Cannington, Bridgwater, Somerset, TA5 2NH
Activities: Raising of dairy cattle
Shareholders: Francis David Jeanes; Ruth Alexandra Jeanes
Officers: Ruth Alexandra Jeanes, Secretary/Director; Francis David Jeanes [1947] Farmer/Director; Ruth Alexandra Jeanes [1953] Director

JELF Financial Planning Ltd
Incorporated: 23 June 1995
Net Worth: £4,156,000 *Total Assets:* £8,234,000
Registered Office: Hillside Court, Bowling Hill, Chipping Sodbury, Glos, BS37 6JX
Activities: Financial intermediation not elsewhere classified
Parent: Mercer Limited
Officers: Sallie Ellis, Secretary; Fiona Stewart Dunsire [1966] Director/Actuary; Grant Anthony Hughes [1973] Director/Head of Financial Planning; David Nicholas Williams [1971] Director/Accountant

JELF Insurance Brokers Limited
Incorporated: 10 February 1965
Net Worth: £470,700,000 *Total Assets:* £507,000,000
Registered Office: Hillside Court, Bowling Hill, Chipping Sodbury, Glos, BS37 6JX
Activities: Non-life insurance
Parent: Marsh Limited
Officers: Dawn Jeanette Hodges, Secretary; Jane Victoria Barker [1949] Director; Philip Andrew Barton [1962] Director; Mark Christopher Chessher [1960] Director/Accountant; John Raymond Hirst [1952] Director; Christopher John Lay [1961] Director/Insurance Broker; Jeremy Vaughan Herbert Wilson [1958] Director

JELF Limited
Incorporated: 6 October 1994 *Employees:* 1,127
Previous: JELF Public Limited Company
Net Worth: £24,900,000 *Total Assets:* £67,500,000
Registered Office: Hillside Court, Bowling Hill, Chipping Sodbury, Glos, BS37 6JX
Activities: Activities of other holding companies n.e.c.
Parent: Marsh & McLennan Companies Inc
Officers: Dawn Jeanette Hodges, Secretary; James Michael Pickford [1978] Director/Accountant

JELF Wellbeing Limited
Incorporated: 20 September 1991
Net Worth: £14,200,000 *Total Assets:* £17,900,000
Registered Office: Hillside Court, Bowling Hill, Chipping Sodbury, Glos, BS37 6JX
Activities: Non-life insurance
Parent: JELF Insurance Brokers Limited
Officers: Dawn Jeanette Hodges, Secretary; Caroline Wendy Godwin [1962] Director/Accountant; James Michael Pickford [1978] Director/Accountant

B.T. Jenkins Limited
Incorporated: 6 June 1973 *Employees:* 19
Net Worth: £2,440,948 *Total Assets:* £4,007,893
Registered Office: Woodland Court, Sandford, Winscombe, Somerset, BS25 5QP
Activities: Other specialised construction activities n.e.c.
Parent: Chasenet Limited
Officers: Christopher John Lomas [1955] Director

Jenkins Marine Ltd.
Incorporated: 11 May 1988 *Employees:* 29
Net Worth: £3,052,198 *Total Assets:* £3,929,151
Registered Office: Office Container, New Harbour Road West, Hamworthy, Poole, Dorset, BH15 4AJ
Activities: Construction of water projects
Parent: Jenkins Marine Holdings Ltd
Officers: Andrina Jenkins, Secretary; Daniel Jenkins [1978] Director/Operations Manager; Rodney Malcolm Jenkins [1945] Director/Retired

Jennings Industries Limited
Incorporated: 13 July 1959
Net Worth: £6,428,417 *Total Assets:* £6,652,786
Registered Office: Phoenix House, Combe Street, Chard, Somerset, TA20 1JE
Activities: Activities of head offices
Shareholders: Simon Charles Peter Jennings; Thomas John Jennings
Officers: Thomas John Jennings, Secretary/Director; Betty Rose Mary Jennings [1936] Director; Simon Charles Peter Jennings [1962] Director; Thomas John Jennings [1959] Director/Chartered Accountant

Jensen-Faulkner Limited
Incorporated: 24 June 1991 *Employees:* 3
Net Worth: £3,576,133 *Total Assets:* £5,416,758
Registered Office: Homefield House, Sherford, Kingsbridge, Devon, TQ7 2AT
Activities: Development of building projects
Officers: Hilary Clare Jensen, Secretary; David Andrass Jensen [1961] Director/Building Restorer; Hilary Clare Jensen [1961] Director/Secretary

JFD Trawlers Limited
Incorporated: 13 February 2007
Net Worth: £2,966,059 *Total Assets:* £3,969,617
Registered Office: Sigma House, Oak View Close, Edginswell Park, Torquay, Devon, TQ2 7FF
Activities: Marine fishing
Shareholders: John Francis Denbow; Sean Patrick Irvine
Officers: John Francis Denbow, Secretary; John Francis Denbow [1963] Director/Businessman; Sean Patrick Irvine [1959] Director/Fisherman

JG Travel Group Limited
Incorporated: 21 March 2009 *Employees:* 69
Previous: CHW Holdings Limited
Net Worth: £1,958,745 *Total Assets:* £9,247,006
Registered Office: Festival House, Jessop Avenue, Cheltenham, Glos, GL50 3SH
Activities: Other business support service activities n.e.c.
Parent: JGH Group Limited
Officers: Gary Peter Turner, Secretary; Luis Miguel Arteaga [1968] Managing Director [Spanish]; Gary Peter Turner [1969] Financial Director

JGBM Ltd
Incorporated: 18 May 1979 *Employees:* 29
Net Worth: £4,151,962 *Total Assets:* £5,822,446
Registered Office: Barn Close, Langage Business Park, Plympton, Plymouth, PL7 5HQ
Activities: Wholesale of other office machinery and equipment
Shareholders: John Peter George; Michael Andrew George
Officers: John Peter George, Secretary/Managing Director; Carol Clarke [1967] Financial Director; John Peter George [1960] General Managing Director; Michael Andrew George [1963] Marketing/IT Director

JGH Group Limited
Incorporated: 27 July 2016 *Employees:* 69
Net Worth: £676,784 *Total Assets:* £14,325,470
Registered Office: Festival House, Jessop Avenue, Cheltenham, Glos, GL50 3SH
Activities: Other business support service activities n.e.c.
Parent: JGH Midco Limited
Officers: Gary Turner, Secretary; Luis Miguel Arteaga [1968] Director [Spanish]; Gary Peter Turner [1969] Director

JGH Midco Limited
Incorporated: 27 July 2016 *Employees:* 2
Net Worth Deficit: £57,428 *Total Assets:* £4,122,087
Registered Office: Festival House, Jessop Avenue, Cheltenham, Glos, GL50 3SH
Activities: Other business support service activities n.e.c.
Parent: JGH Topco Limited
Officers: Luis Miguel Arteaga [1968] Director [Spanish]; Gary Peter Turner [1969] Director

JGH Topco Limited
Incorporated: 27 July 2016 *Employees:* 69
Net Worth: £623,231 *Total Assets:* £14,330,057
Registered Office: Festival House, Jessop Avenue, Cheltenham, Glos, GL50 3SH
Activities: Other business support service activities n.e.c.
Shareholders: Luis Miguel Arteaga; Covadonga Rodriguez; KPC II Ltd
Officers: Luis Miguel Arteaga [1968] Director [Spanish]; Hugo Edward William Robinson [1973] Director/Investment Manager

JHAI Limited
Incorporated: 26 April 2000 *Employees:* 121
Net Worth: £1,243,473 *Total Assets:* £3,677,390
Registered Office: 3 George Street, West Bay, Bridport, Dorset, DT6 4EY
Activities: Other specialised construction activities n.e.c.
Officers: Ian David Charnock [1966] Director/Building Control Inspector; Andrew Crooks [1967] Director/Building Control Inspector; Alistair Nicklin [1971] Director/Accountant FCCA; Matthew John Read [1977] Director/Chairman

Jigsaw Solutions Limited
Incorporated: 1 May 2002 *Employees:* 50
Net Worth: £6,549,029 *Total Assets:* £20,360,460
Registered Office: Bristol Road, Moreton Valence, Gloucester, GL2 7ND
Activities: Freight transport by road
Parent: Jigsaw Solutions (Holdings) Limited
Officers: Mark Davis, Secretary; Andrew Michael Tiffin Downton [1960] Director; Maxwell John Downton [1964] Director; Richard George Downton [1964] Director; Andrew John Humpherson [1965] Managing Director; Chuang Hue Moh [1975] Director [Singaporean]; Simon Richard Pearson [1967] Director; Heath Brian Zarin [1975] Director [American]

JISC
Incorporated: 17 March 2006 *Employees:* 57
Net Worth: £100,746,000 *Total Assets:* £145,963,008
Registered Office: One Castlepark, Tower Hill, Bristol, BS2 0JA
Activities: Activities of other membership organisations n.e.c.
Officers: Alice Jane Colban, Secretary; Professor Elizabeth Florence Barnes [1960] Director/Vice Chancellor; Andrew Jonathan Paul Bourne [1966] Executive Director; Susan Bowen [1974] Director/General Manager; Dr Paul Barrie Feldman [1959] Director/Chief Executive; Robin Ghurbhurun [1969] Director/Chief Executive and Principal; Professor Philip Gummett [1947] Director/Retired; Professor Paul John Layzell [1957] Director/Principal; Professor David John Maguire [1958] Director/Vice-Chancellor; Robert Gerard McWilliam [1969] Finance Director; Prof Nigel Anthony Seaton [1960] Director/University Vice-Chancellor; Jude William Thomas Sheeran [1974] Director/Manager; Professor Mark Edmund Smith [1963] Director/Vice Chancellor; Dr Robert Campbell Kennedy Thomson [1960] Director/Principal; Professor Anne Elizabeth Trefethen [1962] Director/Chief Information Officer

JISC Services Limited
Incorporated: 10 December 1993 *Employees:* 144
Previous: JISC Collections and Janet Limited
Net Worth: £6,994,000 *Total Assets:* £66,520,000
Registered Office: One Castlepark, Tower Hill, Bristol, BS2 0JA
Activities: Other telecommunications activities
Officers: Alice Jane Colban, Secretary; Alice Jane Colban [1970] Director/Chief Operating Officer and Deputy Chief Executive; Dr Paul Barrie Feldman [1959] Director/Chief Executive; Robert Roy Haymon-Collins [1959] Executive Director Customer Experience; Timothy Kidd [1962] Director/Manager; Dr Philip Richards [1968] Director/Chief Innovation Officer; Mark Anthony Wright [1958] Finance Director

JM & CW Limited
Incorporated: 23 May 2014
Net Worth: £2,208,004 *Total Assets:* £5,193,048
Registered Office: Lime Court, Pathfields Business Park, South Molton, Devon, EX36 3LH
Activities: Other letting and operating of own or leased real estate
Shareholders: Clare Winifred Clapp; Jonathan Mark Clapp
Officers: Clare Winifred Clapp [1973] Director; Jonathan Mark Clapp [1975] Director

JMC Recruitment Solutions Limited
Incorporated: 2 May 2008 *Employees:* 40
Net Worth: £443,180 *Total Assets:* £5,308,593
Registered Office: First Floor, Unit 1 Exeter International Office Park, Clyst, Honiton, Exeter, EX5 2HL
Activities: Other business support service activities n.e.c.
Parent: JMC-Group Limited
Officers: Jackie Crook, Secretary; Warren Henry Crook [1964] Director

The John of Gaunt School
Incorporated: 14 March 2012 *Employees:* 164
Net Worth: £15,942,659 *Total Assets:* £16,921,528
Registered Office: The John of Gaunt School, Wingfield Road, Trowbridge, Wilts, BA14 9EH
Activities: General secondary education
Officers: Eleanor Shergold, Secretary; Sally Anne Andrews [1967] Director/PMO Manager; Sarah Louise Bergg [1972] Director/Technical Account Manager; Tobias Samuel Corden [1985] Director/Bank Officer; Glyn Coy [1972] Director/Business Consultant; Doctor Kevin John Eames [1949] Director/Retired; Peter Howard Gear [1967] Director/Retired; Sarbjit Singh Gill [1979] Director/Teacher; Andrew Michael Hawkins [1964] Director/Site Officer; Jordan McKenzie Mockett [1992] Director/Teacher; Pamela Raymond-Heath [1976] Director/Finance Assistant; Paul James Skipp [1978] Director/Headteacher; Dr Elizabeth Jane Summerson [1950] Director/Part Time Teacher of Adults; Helen Penelope Thorne [1970] Director/Teacher; Joanna Trigg [1969] Director/Head of Customer Proposition Marketing; David Roy John Whewell [1955] Director of Education Consultancy Company; Andrew Glyn Williams [1969] Director/Engineer Surveyor; Deborah Frances Youngs [1963] Director/Parent Support Adviser

Johnan UK Limited
Incorporated: 8 February 2011 *Employees:* 9
Net Worth: £1,473,419 *Total Assets:* £4,291,538
Registered Office: Unit 3 Westerngate, Hillmead Industrial Estate, Langley Road, Swindon, Wilts, SN5 5WN
Activities: Manufacture of other parts and accessories for motor vehicles
Shareholder: Harumi Baba
Officers: Masuo Shimizu [1959] Director [Japanese]; Ken Takeuchi [1973] Director [Japanese]

T.H.F. Johnson Limited
Incorporated: 23 September 1954 *Employees:* 2
Net Worth Deficit: £51,249 *Total Assets:* £3,836,507
Registered Office: Marsh House, Coulston, Westbury, Wilts, BA13 4NZ
Activities: Growing of cereals (except rice), leguminous crops and oil seeds
Shareholders: Antony Thomas Johnson; Timothy Forbes Johnson
Officers: Antony Thomas Johnson, Secretary; Antony Thomas Johnson [1936] Director/Farmer; Molly Johnson [1940] Director; Timothy Forbes Johnson [1964] Director

The Johnsons Group Limited
Incorporated: 2 July 1986 *Employees:* 3
Net Worth: £3,317,525 *Total Assets:* £3,756,393
Registered Office: The Old Barn, Lady Farm, Chelwood, Bristol, BS39 4NN
Activities: Other letting and operating of own or leased real estate
Shareholders: James Daniel Lawrence Pearce; Claire Louise Scoble
Officers: James Daniel Lawrence Pearce [1968] Director; Claire Louise Scoble [1965] Director; Mark Thomas Shearn [1967] Director

Johnstone Safety International LLP
Incorporated: 17 December 2004 *Employees:* 31
Net Worth: £7,511,000 *Total Assets:* £8,177,000
Registered Office: Carrick House, Lypiatt Road, Cheltenham, Glos, GL50 2QJ
Officers: Sarah Helen Baker [1970] Member; Clive Johnstone [1942] Member; James Luke Johnstone [1970] Member; Joanna Mary Johnstone [1945] Member; Mark Robert Johnstone [1968] Member; Timothy William Johnstone [1975] Member; Michael John Baker [1963] LLP Member; Lisa Joy Johnstone [1971] LLP Member; Tina Johnstone [1966] LLP Member; Stephen Francis Sanders [1969] LLP Member

Jones Building Group Limited
Incorporated: 25 September 2013 *Employees:* 174
Net Worth: £4,809,890 *Total Assets:* £10,427,265
Registered Office: Willow House, Artilliary Road, Lufton Trading Estate, Yeovil, Somerset, BA22 8RP
Activities: Activities of construction holding companies
Major Shareholder: David Robert Jones
Officers: David Robert Jones [1957] Director; Mark Alexander Porter [1966] Operations Director

L. & F. Jones Holdings Limited
Incorporated: 5 November 1976 *Employees:* 264
Net Worth: £4,161,070 *Total Assets:* £7,885,261
Registered Office: Charlton Lane, Midsomer Norton, Bath, BA3 4SB
Activities: Agents involved in the sale of a variety of goods
Shareholder: Barbara Jones
Officers: Michael Anthony Byrne [1962] Finance Director; Raymond John D'Arcy [1966] Managing Director [Irish]; David Paul Jones [1968] Sales Director

D R Jones Yeovil Ltd.
Incorporated: 3 December 1993 *Employees:* 161
Net Worth: £3,721,583 *Total Assets:* £9,946,031
Registered Office: Willow House, Artillery Road, Yeovil, Somerset, BA22 8RP
Activities: Development of building projects
Parent: Jones Building Group Limited
Officers: Christopher Mark Austin [1960] Director; Craig Robert Hansell [1970] Director; David Robert Jones [1957] Director; Adrian Paul Mitchell [1948] Pre-Construction Director; Mark Alexander Porter [1966] Operations Director; Darren Leslie Robert Robins [1969] Director

Jongor (Holdings) Ltd
Incorporated: 22 January 2015 *Employees:* 1
Net Worth: £1,000,100 *Total Assets:* £4,932,100
Registered Office: Unit G, Kingsland Trading Estate, St Philips Road, Bristol, BS2 0JZ
Activities: Activities of other holding companies n.e.c.
Shareholders: Joseph Peter Nisbet; Key West (Holdings) Ltd
Officers: Joseph Nisbet [1988] Director

Jongor Limited
Incorporated: 24 August 1973 *Employees:* 85
Net Worth: £3,433,111 *Total Assets:* £4,790,778
Registered Office: Unit G, Kingsland Trading Estate, St Philips Road, Bristol, BS2 0JZ
Activities: Renting and leasing of other machinery, equipment and tangible goods n.e.c.
Parent: Jongor Trading Limited
Officers: Emma Louise Butler, Secretary; Emma Louise Butler [1982] Director/Chartered Accountant; Anthony Frederick Carter [1955] Sales Director; Stuart Paul Cole [1978] Operations Director; Joseph Nisbet [1988] Director; Jenny Anne Sharples [1975] HR Director

Jordans Limited
Incorporated: 30 November 1965 *Employees:* 74
Net Worth: £2,555,823 *Total Assets:* £6,177,388
Registered Office: First Floor, 10 Temple Back, Bristol, BS1 6FL
Activities: Data processing, hosting and related activities
Parent: Accomplish UK Holdings Limited
Officers: Jason Anthony Burgoyne [1977] Director; Paul John Cooper [1957] Director; Thomas Stephen Edwards [1965] Director; Debbie Jane Farman [1965] Director; David Rudge [1970] Director

JR Cap Limited
Incorporated: 30 May 2003
Previous: JR Farming and Estate Limited
Net Worth: £4,246,545 *Total Assets:* £4,394,875
Registered Office: 6 The Avenue, Sneyd Park, Bristol, BS9 1PA
Activities: Non-trading company
Major Shareholder: James Amschel Victor Rothschild
Officers: Jeremy Barnes [1961] Director/Chartered Accountant; James Amschel Victor Rothschild [1985] Director

JS2 Investments Limited
Incorporated: 20 May 2011
Previous: Datasharp (Holdings) Limited
Net Worth: £4,498,104 *Total Assets:* £4,501,290
Registered Office: Woodlands Court, Truro Business Park, Threemilestone, Truro, Cornwall, TR4 9NH
Activities: Activities of head offices
Shareholder: Jane Nicola Cockcroft
Officers: Jane Nicola Cockcroft [1972] Director; Dr Simon Paul McIntosh [1974] Director

JSM Property Services Limited
Incorporated: 26 November 2002 *Employees:* 2
Net Worth: £634,209 *Total Assets:* £3,626,127
Registered Office: 58 Whiteford Road, Mannamead, Plymouth, PL3 5LY
Activities: Other accommodation
Shareholders: Sandra Joy Matheson; William Grant Matheson
Officers: Sandra Joy Matheson, Secretary/Letting Agent; Sandra Joy Matheson [1965] Director/Letting Agent; William Grant Matheson [1966] Director

JSP Limited
Incorporated: 11 February 1964 *Employees:* 305
Net Worth: £29,280,000 *Total Assets:* £43,090,000
Registered Office: Carrick House, Lypiatt Road, Cheltenham, Glos, GL50 2QJ
Activities: Manufacture of other plastic products
Officers: Catharina Johanna Adriana Payne, Secretary; Sarah Helen Baker [1970] Director/PR and Advertising; Clive Johnstone [1942] Director; James Luke Johnstone [1970] Director; Joanna Mary Johnstone [1945] Director; Mark Robert Johnstone [1968] Director and Chartered Accountant; Timothy William Johnstone [1975] Director; Dr Geoffrey Thomas Knight [1943] Director/Chemist; Stephen Francis Sanders [1969] Director/Engineer

JTL (Holdings) Limited
Incorporated: 24 March 2014
Net Worth Deficit: £924,997 *Total Assets:* £3,572,844
Registered Office: Unit P, Wylds Road, Bridgwater, Somerset, TA6 4BH
Activities: Activities of head offices
Parent: Altitude (GP1) Limited
Officers: Jonathan Dibble [1960] Director; Stephen Paul Edwards [1955] Director; Philip Richard Baskeyfield Jones [1980] Director; Jonathan David Simm [1965] Director; Simon Richard White [1963] Director

Julia's House Limited
Incorporated: 14 November 1997 *Employees:* 123
Net Worth: £10,715,296 *Total Assets:* £11,156,612
Registered Office: Julia's House, Barclays House, 1 Wimborne Road, Poole, Dorset, BH15 2BB
Activities: Other human health activities
Officers: Martyn Richard Hudson, Secretary/Solicitor; Susan Anne Marie Cianchetta [1967] Director [Irish]; Brian Peter Hutchinson [1951] Director/Accountant; Elizabeth Kay Labrow [1947] Director; Warren David Munson [1973] Director/Accountant; Dr Simon Craigen Pennell [1956] Director/Medical Practitioner; Vernon Michael Phillips [1963] Director/Project Manager; Jacqueline Lesley Scrace [1974] Director; Malcolm Sevenoaks [1973] Director; Barrie Thomas [1954] Director; Christopher Robert Twaits [1976] Director/Solicitor; Peter Graham Wragg [1946] Director

R T Julian & Son Limited
Incorporated: 15 May 2001 *Employees:* 5
Net Worth Deficit: £71,475 *Total Assets:* £4,953,913
Registered Office: Treloggan Industrial Estate, Newquay, Cornwall, TR7 2SX
Activities: Other service activities n.e.c.
Parent: R T Julian & Son (Holdings) Limited
Officers: Baylor John Julian [1971] Director

Julian & Son,Limited
Incorporated: 5 March 1945 *Employees:* 42
Net Worth: £5,958,286 *Total Assets:* £7,264,262
Registered Office: 42 Station Road, St Blazey, Par, Cornwall, PL24 2LZ
Activities: Retail of furniture, lighting, and similar (not musical instruments or scores) in specialised store
Parent: Julian & Sons (Holding) Limited
Officers: Julie Wilkinson, Secretary; Annette Thomas [1962] Managing Director; Julie Wilkinson [1964] Director; Jonathan Mark Wilson [1961] Furniture Director; Robert Winch [1963] Furniture Director

Juliana Group Limited
Incorporated: 15 February 1985 *Employees:* 30
Previous: Eden-Halls Greenhouses Limited
Net Worth: £2,303,218 *Total Assets:* £3,960,033
Registered Office: The Distribution Centre, Stoke Road, Stoke Orchard, Cheltenham, Glos, GL52 7RS
Activities: Repair of machinery
Shareholders: Drivhuse AS; Juliana Drivhuse A/S
Officers: Bent Kristoffersen, Secretary; Nikolaj Staermose [1972] Managing Director [Danish]

Jumbocruiser Limited
Incorporated: 12 October 2004 *Employees:* 16
Net Worth: £3,370,657 *Total Assets:* £4,745,111
Registered Office: Sigma House, Oak View Close, Edginswell Park, Torquay, Devon, TQ2 7FF
Activities: Other passenger land transport
Shareholders: Frances Lee; Stephen Lee
Officers: Baron Stephen Alaric Lee of Coolock [1951] Director

Junction 24 Limited
Incorporated: 18 April 2006 *Employees:* 48
Net Worth: £409,553 *Total Assets:* £10,594,990
Registered Office: Puxton Park, Cowslip Lane, Hewish, Weston-Super-Mare, Somerset, BS24 6AH
Activities: Support activities for animal production (other than farm animal boarding)
Parent: Mead Realisations Limited
Officers: Katherine Patricia Hawke, Secretary/Director; Katherine Patricia Hawke [1972] Director; Alistair Daniel Derek Mead [1977] Director

Junction Road Croydon Limited
Incorporated: 27 March 2015
Net Worth Deficit: £6,282 *Total Assets:* £4,030,279
Registered Office: 3-4 Lustleigh Close, Matford Business Park, Marsh Barton Trading Estate, Exeter, EX2 8PW
Activities: Buying and selling of own real estate
Shareholder: Harry Alexander Barclay
Officers: Harry Alexander Barclay, Secretary; Simran Bhinder, Secretary; Annabel Collings, Secretary; Lorraine Percival, Secretary; Steve Percival, Secretary; Harry Alexander Barclay [1979] Director

Juniper Homes (Southville) Limited
Incorporated: 11 December 2014 *Employees:* 3
Net Worth Deficit: £993,522 *Total Assets:* £5,785,949
Registered Office: 20 Hotwell Road, Bristol, BS8 4UD
Activities: Construction of domestic buildings
Shareholders: Richard John Curtis; Jonathan Rhodri Morgan; Terry Lee Whittingham
Officers: Richard John Curtis [1969] Director/Property Developer; Jonathan Rhodri Morgan [1975] Director/Property Developer; Terry Lee Whittingham [1971] Director/Property Developer

Juniper Homes (Wilder) Limited
Incorporated: 3 February 2017
Net Worth Deficit: £248,071 *Total Assets:* £4,750,068
Registered Office: 85 Whiteladies Road, Clifton, Bristol, BS8 2NT
Activities: Development of building projects
Shareholders: Richard John Curtis; Terry Lee Whittingham; Jonathan Morgan
Officers: Richard John Curtis [1969] Director/Property Developer; Jonathan Morgan [1975] Director/Property Developer; Terry Lee Whittingham [1971] Director/Property Developer

Jupiter Care Ltd
Incorporated: 7 August 2000 *Employees:* 65
Net Worth: £1,454,782 *Total Assets:* £4,106,149
Registered Office: The Street, Kingscourt, Stroud, Glos, GL5 5DW
Activities: Residential nursing care facilities
Shareholders: Gareth Bamsey; Claire Nicola Bamsey
Officers: Claire Nicola Bamsey, Secretary; Claire Nicola Bamsey [1963] Director; Gareth Bamsey [1964] Director

Just Go Holidays Limited
Incorporated: 4 October 2002 *Employees:* 52
Net Worth: £192,091 *Total Assets:* £5,526,320
Registered Office: Festival House, Jessop Avenue, Cheltenham, Glos, GL50 3SH
Activities: Tour operator activities
Parent: JG Travel Group Limited
Officers: Gary Peter Turner, Secretary; Luis Miguel Arteaga [1968] Managing Director [Spanish]; Paul Howard Mason [1964] Operations Director; Gary Peter Turner [1969] Finance Director

K & J Logistics Limited
Incorporated: 10 April 1997 *Employees:* 2
Net Worth: £1,390,472 *Total Assets:* £4,616,110
Registered Office: 3-5 College Street, Burnham on Sea, Somerset, TA8 1AR
Activities: Freight transport by road
Parent: R T Keedwell Holdings Limited
Officers: Stuart Raymond Keedwell [1964] Director

K & T Heating Services Limited
Incorporated: 21 June 2004 *Employees:* 214
Net Worth: £1,750,415 *Total Assets:* £6,519,147
Registered Office: c/o BPE Solicitors LLP, First Floor, St James House, St James Square, Cheltenham, Glos, GL50 3PR
Activities: Plumbing, heat and air-conditioning installation
Parent: Lakehouse Compliance Services Limited
Officers: John William Charles Charlton, Secretary; John William Charles Charlton [1956] Director/Company Secretary; James William Day [1950] Director/Heating Engineer; David Greenfield [1965] Director/Heating Engineer; Michael McMahon [1976] Director

K.D.P. Tools Limited
Incorporated: 9 November 1998 *Employees:* 9
Net Worth: £4,310,803 *Total Assets:* £4,747,160
Registered Office: 4 Blackdown Park, South View Estate, Willand, Devon, EX15 2FS
Activities: Wholesale of machine tools
Shareholders: Malcolm Derek King; Stephen John King
Officers: Stephen John King, Secretary/Tool Wholesaler; Malcolm Derek King [1961] Director/Tool Wholesaler; Stephen John King [1960] Director/Tool Wholesaler

K.P. Europa Trading Limited
Incorporated: 9 January 2001 *Employees:* 5
Net Worth: £4,879,327 *Total Assets:* £5,122,954
Registered Office: Mary Street House, Mary Street, Taunton, Somerset, TA1 3NW
Activities: Sale of other motor vehicles
Officers: Dawn Fay Rosemary Pickering, Secretary; Dawn Fay Rosemary Pickering [1960] Director/Wholesale Merchant; Kevin Pickering [1964] Director/Salesman; Paul Edward Pickering [1959] Director/Wholesale Merchant; Phoebe Charmaine Pickering [1963] Director/Business Assistant

K2 Medical Systems Limited
Incorporated: 19 July 1999 *Employees:* 44
Net Worth: £3,544,045 *Total Assets:* £6,038,289
Registered Office: 26 William Prance Road, Derriford, Plymouth, PL6 5WR
Activities: Manufacture of medical and dental instruments and supplies
Parent: K2 Medical Systems Holdings Ltd
Officers: Gemma Colleen Keith, Secretary; Ian Stuart Crozier [1963] Director; Doctor Robert Duncan Falconer Keith [1963] Director/Medical Systems Engineer; James Meeson [1973] Director

Kaba Limited
Incorporated: 16 June 1999 *Employees:* 125
Net Worth: £6,479,953 *Total Assets:* £11,950,173
Registered Office: Lower Moor Way, Tiverton Business Park, Tiverton, Devon, EX16 6SS
Activities: Manufacture of locks and hinges
Officers: Shane Antony Christie, Secretary; Stephen Alfred Bewick [1966] Director; Bernhard Brinker [1965] Director/Chief Financial Officer [German]; Shane Antony Christie [1975] Finance Director; Roberto Gaspari [1959] Director/Chief Operating Officer [Italian]

Kadar Developments Limited
Incorporated: 30 April 1964 *Employees:* 4
Net Worth: £4,340,635 *Total Assets:* £4,850,462
Registered Office: 13 Harbury Road, Bristol, BS9 4PN
Activities: Other letting and operating of own or leased real estate
Parent: Plyflow Limited
Officers: David Ian Wheeler, Secretary; David Gerard Goldberg [1947] Director/Queens Counsel; Sylvia Goldberg [1920] Director; Meriel Esther Joseph [1944] Director; David Ian Wheeler [1945] Director/Chartered Surveyor

Kaikoura Investments Limited
Incorporated: 6 February 1996 *Employees:* 3
Net Worth Deficit: £905,458 *Total Assets:* £7,612,020
Registered Office: 11 Quiet Street, Bath, BA1 2LB
Activities: Buying and selling of own real estate
Shareholders: Richard Lindsey Brake; Himalia Limited
Officers: Richard Lindsey Brake, Secretary/Investment Banker; Heather Marjorie Rose Brake [1937] Director/Company Assistant; Richard Lindsey Brake [1959] Director/Investment Banker; Paul James Collis [1965] Director/Project Manager; Joanna Christine Hughes [1960] Director/Administrator

The Kaleidoscope Collection Ltd
Incorporated: 11 November 2011 *Employees:* 6
Previous: Taylor Townhouses Limited
Net Worth: £10,539,977 *Total Assets:* £20,544,588
Registered Office: 1 Lansdown Terrace, Malvern Road, Cheltenham, Glos, GL50 2JT
Activities: Hotels and similar accommodation
Shareholders: Christa Taylor; Ian John Morrison Taylor
Officers: Steven Holmes [1952] Director/Accountant; Michael Maton [1947] Director/Accountant; Christa Taylor [1959] Director/Hotelier; Ian Taylor [1960] Director/Hotelier

Kalel Partners
Incorporated: 21 December 2016
Net Worth: £1,186,478 *Total Assets:* £28,817,404
Registered Office: St Catherine's Court, Berkeley Place, Bristol, BS8 1BQ
Activities: Activities of other holding companies n.e.c.
Major Shareholder: Shuaib Arshad Chaudhary
Officers: Shuaib Arshad Chaudhary [1983] Director/Solicitor

Kamm Civil Engineering Limited
Incorporated: 20 November 1995 *Employees:* 38
Net Worth: £3,757,757 *Total Assets:* £8,737,705
Registered Office: 19 Black Moor Road, Verwood, Dorset, BH31 6AX
Activities: Construction of other civil engineering projects n.e.c.
Parent: Kamm (Holdings) Limited
Officers: Keith Reginald McWilliams, Secretary/Civil Engineering; Adam John McCormack [1969] Director/Civil Engineer; Keith Reginald McWilliams [1969] Director/Civil Engineering

Kammbronn Homes Limited
Incorporated: 19 January 2016
Net Worth: £469,442 *Total Assets:* £7,618,186
Registered Office: 12 Tresprison Business Park, Helston, Cornwall, TR13 0QD
Activities: Buying and selling of own real estate
Shareholders: MJL Cornwall Ltd; Marconi Builders and Developers Ltd
Officers: Charles Cyril Hunt [1964] Director; Nicholas Jackson [1966] Director/Architect; Matthew James Lugg [1978] Director; Neil William Perry [1958] Director

Kandytoys Holdings Limited
Incorporated: 15 August 2016 *Employees:* 60
Net Worth: £5,685,755 *Total Assets:* £17,844,956
Registered Office: Hill Barton Business Park, Sidmouth Road, Clyst St Mary, Devon, EX5 1DR
Activities: Activities of other holding companies n.e.c.
Officers: Mark Hall, Secretary; Clare Monica West, Secretary; Gary Mark Beswick [1961] Director; Mark Hall [1970] Director/Importer; Mark David Hookway [1965] Director; David Kemp Kirkby [1948] Director/Toy Importer; Frederick Martin [1982] Director

Kandytoys Limited
Incorporated: 20 September 2010 *Employees:* 60
Net Worth: £13,576,714 *Total Assets:* £22,747,468
Registered Office: Hill Barton Business Park, Sidmouth Road, Clyst St Mary, Exeter, EX5 1BR
Activities: Non-specialised wholesale trade
Officers: David Kemp Kirkby, Secretary; Clare Monica West, Secretary; Gary Mark Beswick [1961] Director; Mark Hall [1970] Director/Importer; Mark David Hookway [1965] Director; David Kemp Kirkby [1948] Director/Toy Importer; Frederick Martin [1982] Director

Kat-O-Log Limited
Incorporated: 18 October 2000 *Employees:* 3
Net Worth: £2,442,381 *Total Assets:* £3,993,574
Registered Office: Leeward House, Fitzroy Road, Exeter Business Park, Exeter, Devon, EX1 3LJ
Activities: Production of electricity
Shareholders: Diana Ruth Gamble; Adrian Gamble
Officers: Diana Ruth Gamble, Secretary/Chartered Physiotherapist; Adrian Gamble [1953] Director; Diana Ruth Gamble [1961] Director/Chartered Physiotherapist; Rev Michael Darren Gamble [1965] Director/Priest

Katharine Lady Berkeley's School
Incorporated: 7 July 2011 *Employees:* 211
Net Worth: £29,934,392 *Total Assets:* £32,971,608
Registered Office: Katharine Lady Berkeley's School, Kingswood Road, Wotton under Edge, Glos, GL12 8RB
Activities: General secondary education
Officers: Fiona Catherine Macmillan, Secretary; Peter Charles Earnsby Adams [1967] Director/Health and Safety Consultant; Joseph Christopher Blake [1988] Director/Secondary School Teacher; Margaret Clarke [1941] Director/Retired; John Edward Cordwell [1944] Director/Mayor and County Councillor; Sarah Catherine Cowan [1969] Director/Student; Andrew Phillip Harris [1955] Director/Headteacher; Sarah Catherine Haynes [1976] Director/Tax Consultant; Gillian Linda Hayward [1958] Director/Homemaker; Helen Brewster Holman [1957] Director/Retired Headteacher; Carl Peter Jenner [1964] Director/Accountant; Sarah Louise Plant [1987] Director/Senior Design Engineer; Rachel Jane Robinson [1973] Director/Charity Manager; Benjamin James Rousseau [1971] Director Healthcare Value Consultancy; Richard James Shaw [1977] Director/Secondary School Teacher

Kawasaki Precision Machinery (UK) Limited
Incorporated: 5 July 1993 *Employees:* 238
Net Worth: £15,096,494 *Total Assets:* £38,258,240
Registered Office: Ernesettle Lane, Ernesettle, Plymouth, PL5 2SA
Activities: Manufacture of fluid power equipment
Officers: Henry James Meacock, Secretary; Naoki Adachi [1958] Director/General Manager Planning Division [Japanese]; Lee Crocker [1977] General Manager - Executive Director; Shunsuke Ikuma [1968] Director [Japanese]; Yasuo Konishi [1968] Director [Japanese]; Masaki Onishi [1964] Managing Director [Japanese]

Kay Transport Limited
Incorporated: 2 July 1991 *Employees:* 140
Net Worth: £4,503,000 *Total Assets:* £4,503,000
Registered Office: Senate Court, Southernhay Gardens, Exeter, Devon, EX1 1NT
Activities: Freight transport by road
Parent: Gregory Distribution (Holdings) Limited
Officers: Angela Mary Butler [1967] Director; John Kennedy Gregory [1958] Director; Simon Hugh Gregory [1955] Director/Solicitor; Tim Prout [1964] Director/Manager

KCTG Japan Holdings Ltd.
Incorporated: 14 December 2015 *Employees:* 26
Net Worth: £8,707,321 *Total Assets:* £14,600,123
Registered Office: Fleets Corner, Poole, Dorset, BH17 0LA
Activities: Activities of other holding companies n.e.c.
Officers: Robert Joel Gibson Jr [1974] Director/General Counsel [American]; Anthony Saia [1959] Director

Thomas Keble School
Incorporated: 8 July 2011 *Employees:* 78
Net Worth: £5,955,912 *Total Assets:* £7,408,145
Registered Office: Thomas Keble School, Eastcombe, Stroud, Glos, GL6 7DY
Activities: General secondary education
Officers: Alison Louise Clarke, Secretary; Simon Bernstein [1962] Director/Charity Marketing Consultant; Mary Lorraine Beswick [1949] Director/Retired; Denise Karen Blake [1979] Director/Registered Nurse; Daniel Brunwin [1978] Director/Internal Communications Manager; Jennie Crosby [1962] Director/Teacher; Daniel Endruweit [1962] Director/Civil Servant; Jennifer Karen Evans [1962] Director/Retired; Fiona Gill [1962] Director/Children and Family Advisor; Yvonne Elizabeth Anne Hawker [1961] Director/Data Manager; Julia Sian Maunder [1969] Director/Headteacher; Nathan John Monk [1974] Director/Teacher; Jo Moran [1969] Director/Head of Division for Advice Development & Quality; Corin Alexander Hugh Norman [1973] Director/ICT Sales Manager; Ralph William Perry [1954] Director/Business Analyst; Stephen James Ponting [1957] Director/IT Manager; Karen Lesley Powell [1972] Director/School Secretary; Simon Lee Webb [1970] Director/Police Officer; James Whalley [1972] Director/Teacher

R. T. Keedwell Holdings Limited
Incorporated: 21 February 1983 *Employees:* 450
Net Worth: £16,033,904 *Total Assets:* £37,559,392
Registered Office: 3-5 College Street, Burnham on Sea, Somerset, TA8 1AR
Activities: Activities of head offices
Shareholders: Pauline Keedwell; Stuart Raymond Keedwell
Officers: Pauline Keedwell, Secretary; Pauline Keedwell [1942] Director/Secretary; Stuart Raymond Keedwell [1964] Director

R.T. Keedwell Limited
Incorporated: 12 August 1982 *Employees:* 186
Net Worth: £14,840,065 *Total Assets:* £22,910,808
Registered Office: 3-5 College Street, Burnham on Sea, Somerset, TA8 1AR
Activities: Freight transport by road
Parent: R T Keedwell Holdings Limited
Officers: Pauline Keedwell, Secretary; Andrew John Evans [1954] Director; Pauline Keedwell [1942] Director/Secretary; Stuart Raymond Keedwell [1964] Director/Haulier; Paul Brian Phillips [1972] Director/Road Transport; Jonathan Dennis White [1968] Director

Keelex 176 Limited
Incorporated: 27 July 1993 *Employees:* 97
Net Worth: £2,744,996 *Total Assets:* £5,800,346
Registered Office: Peat House, Newham Road, Truro, Cornwall, TR1 2DP
Activities: Residential care activities for learning difficulties, mental health and substance abuse
Parent: Swallowcourt Limited
Officers: Brian Robert Harris [1958] Director; Simon John Hopkins [1965] Director; Dorothy Keely [1943] Director

A R & A L Keen Limited
Incorporated: 14 March 2005 *Employees:* 13
Net Worth: £3,191,656 *Total Assets:* £11,783,178
Registered Office: 3-5 College Street, Burnham on Sea, Somerset, TA8 1AR
Activities: Sale of used cars and light motor vehicles
Major Shareholder: Amanda Louise Keen
Officers: Bianca Keen, Secretary; Amanda Louise Keen [1969] Director/Business Proprietor

Keen Thinking Limited
Incorporated: 12 June 2000 *Employees:* 52
Net Worth: £1,945,762 *Total Assets:* £16,170,773
Registered Office: The Aspen Building, Vantage Point Business Village, Mitcheldean, Glos, GL17 0DD
Activities: Other activities of employment placement agencies
Shareholders: Tom Fredrick John Atkinson; David Thornhill
Officers: Thomas Frederick John Atkinson, Secretary/Director; Thomas Frederick John Atkinson [1946] Director; David Simon Thornhill [1969] Managing Director

Michael H Keene & Son Limited
Incorporated: 9 May 1963 *Employees:* 19
Net Worth: £4,921,248 *Total Assets:* £8,383,745
Registered Office: The Moat, Anthonys Cross, Newent, Glos, GL18 1JG
Activities: Growing of cereals (except rice), leguminous crops and oil seeds
Major Shareholder: Edward Michael Keene
Officers: Megan Ann Keene, Secretary; Edward Michael Keene [1968] Director; Megan Ann Keene [1940] Director/Secretary; Michael Harold Keene [1933] Farmer/Director

Keenwork Limited
Incorporated: 27 January 1977 *Employees:* 526
Net Worth: £3,945,358 *Total Assets:* £50,167,196
Registered Office: 22-24 South Liberty Lane, Bristol, BS3 2SS
Activities: Other letting and operating of own or leased real estate
Shareholders: Simon Richard Howard; Nicholas George Howard; Robert James Howard
Officers: Stephen Paul Howard, Secretary; Nicholas George Howard [1968] Technical Director; Simon Richard Howard [1966] Director; Stephen Paul Howard [1941] Director; Valerie Margaret Howard [1942] Director

Keith Motors (Christchurch) Limited
Incorporated: 14 February 1964 *Employees:* 41
Net Worth: £919,848 *Total Assets:* £6,087,730
Registered Office: Lyndhurst Road, Christchurch, Dorset, BH23 4SB
Activities: Sale of new cars and light motor vehicles
Parent: Birchclaim Limited
Officers: Barbara Mary Keith [1938] Director/Admin Assistant; Jennifer Margaret Keith [1950] Director/Admin Assistant; Richard Etheridge Keith [1947] Sales Director

Kellands (Plant Sales) Limited
Incorporated: 23 March 1950 *Employees:* 45
Net Worth: £4,256,465 *Total Assets:* £7,524,856
Registered Office: Salmon Parade, Bridgwater, Somerset, TA6 5JY
Activities: Sale of other motor vehicles
Parent: Kellands (Holdings) Ltd
Officers: Michael Froude Hill [1934] Director; Timothy Peter Hill [1967] Joint Managing Director; Francis David Jeanes [1947] Director; Terence Leslie Edward Miller [1944] Director/Farmer; Mark Anthony Payne [1960] Joint Managing Director; Nigel John Smith [1948] Director; Paul Victor Watts [1967] Director/Chartered Accountant

Kellaway Building Supplies Limited
Incorporated: 2 April 1987 *Employees:* 215
Net Worth: £4,523,725 *Total Assets:* £21,654,168
Registered Office: Olympus House, Britannia Road, Patchway, Bristol, BS34 5TA
Activities: Agents involved in the sale of timber and building materials
Major Shareholder: Julian Ernest Milligan
Officers: Julian Ernest Milligan, Secretary/Director; Bob Denis Fleetwood [1957] Purchasing Director; Ernest Milligan [1939] Director; Julian Ernest Milligan [1968] Managing Director; Sean Morgan [1971] Branch Operations Director; Mark Nicholas Turner [1971] Finance Director

Kelley Holdings Limited
Incorporated: 18 March 1983
Net Worth: £3,733,210 *Total Assets:* £6,139,784
Registered Office: Chequers Farm, 71 Marsh Common Road, Pilning, Bristol, BS35 4JU
Activities: Buying and selling of own real estate
Major Shareholder: Robert William Kelley
Officers: Joan Kelley, Secretary; Joan Kelley [1945] Director; Robert William Kelley [1950] Director

Kelston Precision Gears Limited
Incorporated: 26 November 1973
Net Worth: £6,433,335 *Total Assets:* £8,239,233
Registered Office: Hawkfield Business Park, Hawkfield Way, Whitchurch, Bristol, BS14 0BD
Activities: Manufacture of bearings, gears, gearing and driving elements
Major Shareholder: Thomas Henry Howe
Officers: Helen Sell, Secretary; Steve Charles Heal [1967] Director/Engineer; Catherine Helena Howe [1942] Director; Thomas Henry Howe [1939] Director; Darren Sell [1968] Director; Helen Sell [1967] Director

Kelston Properties 2 Limited
Incorporated: 18 August 2005
Net Worth: £17,038,000 *Total Assets:* £17,760,000
Registered Office: Avonbank, Feeder Road, Bristol, BS2 0TB
Activities: Development of building projects
Parent: Western Power Distribution Investments Limited
Officers: Sally Ann Jones, Secretary/Accountant; Ian Robert Williams [1970] Finance Director; David Astley Withers [1958] Director/Chartered Surveyor

Kelston Sparkes (Group) Limited
Incorporated: 1 February 2013 *Employees:* 125
Net Worth: £5,590,761 *Total Assets:* £29,131,016
Registered Office: Bromley, Stanton Drew, Bristol, BS39 4DE
Activities: Renting and leasing of construction and civil engineering machinery and equipment
Parent: Kelston Sparkes Holdings Limited
Officers: Rob Stark, Secretary; Philip Graham Oddy [1957] Commercial Director; Mr Alan Kelston Sparkes [1953] Director; Robert Charles Stark [1959] Finance Director

Kelston Sparkes Holdings Limited
Incorporated: 23 October 1979 *Employees:* 147
Net Worth: £6,264,915 *Total Assets:* £29,567,068
Registered Office: Bromley, Stanton Drew, Bristol, BS39 4DE
Activities: Activities of construction holding companies
Shareholders: Robert Charles Stark; Alan Kelston Sparkes
Officers: Robert Charles Stark, Secretary; Mr Alan Kelston Sparkes [1953] Director/Construction; Robert Charles Stark [1959] Director

Kemble Airfield Estates Limited
Incorporated: 19 March 1999
Net Worth: £12,682,427 *Total Assets:* £20,853,460
Registered Office: McGills, Oakley House, Tetbury Road, Cirencester, Glos, GL7 1US
Activities: Renting and operating of Housing Association real estate
Officers: Suzannah Helen Harvey, Secretary; Christian Andrew Ackroyd [1974] Director; Suzannah Helen Harvey [1978] Director; Simon George Nuttall [1968] Director/Accountant

Kemble Business Park LLP
Incorporated: 14 December 2006
Net Worth: £2,975,438 *Total Assets:* £10,023,130
Registered Office: Manor Stables, Corsley, Warminster, Wilts, BA12 7QE
Officers: Helen Louise Aylward-Smith [1962] Member; Simon William Waterfield [1960] Member

Kemble Farms Limited
Incorporated: 7 March 1997 *Employees:* 21
Net Worth: £9,164,174 *Total Assets:* £12,694,592
Registered Office: The Bathurst Estate Office, Cirencester Park, Cirencester, Glos, GL7 2BU
Activities: Growing of cereals (except rice), leguminous crops and oil seeds
Shareholders: Roger Hugh Knight Seelig; Keith James Bruce-Smith; James William Jeremy Ritblat; James Felton Somers Hervey-Bathurst
Officers: Peter William James Clegg, Secretary; Allen Christopher Bertram Bathurst [1961] Director/Farmer and Landowner; Peter William James Clegg [1963] Director/Chief Executive; James Felton Somers Hervey-Bathurst [1949] Director/Businessman; Roger Hugh Knight Seelig [1945] Director/Corporate Financier

Kemeneth Multi Academy Trust
Incorporated: 1 June 2011 *Employees:* 165
Previous: Penryn College
Net Worth: £15,871,907 *Total Assets:* £17,470,800
Registered Office: Penryn College, Kernick Road, Penryn, Cornwall, TR10 8PZ
Activities: General secondary education
Officers: Clive Raymond Ansell [1948] Director; Adrian Christopher Bick [1965] Director/Teacher; Elizabeth Jane Brooks [1964] Director/Housewife [British/American]; Luke Everall [1968] Director/Auditor; Gillian Harries [1955] Director; Mark Steven Parsons [1959] Director/Telecom Engineer; Marian Joan Proudfoot [1935] Director; Ruth Elizabeth Rawley [1962] Director/School Administrator; Julia Roberts [1964] Director/Publishing & PR Manager; David Paul Walker [1970] Director/School Teacher

Kent County Crematorium Limited
Incorporated: 9 January 1935 *Employees:* 19
Net Worth: £5,326,313 *Total Assets:* £14,235,115
Registered Office: Chapel View, Westerleigh Crematorium, Westerleigh Road, Westerleigh, Bristol, BS37 8QP
Activities: Funeral and related activities
Parent: WK Crematoria Limited
Officers: Dafydd Rhys John, Secretary; Dafydd Rhys John [1974] Director/Chartered Accountant; Ian David McArdle [1966] Director/Chartered Surveyor

Kenton School Services Limited
Incorporated: 16 July 1999
Net Worth: £245,000 *Total Assets:* £18,255,000
Registered Office: Third Floor, Broad Quay House, Prince Street, Bristol, BS1 4DJ
Activities: Other business support service activities n.e.c.
Parent: XJ6 Schools Holdings Limited
Officers: Abdul Hamid [1966] Director; Daniel North [1981] Investment Director; Neil Rae [1971] Director

E.P. Keogh Contractors Ltd.
Incorporated: 27 September 1995
Net Worth: £2,578,856 *Total Assets:* £4,816,291
Registered Office: Bank House, 4 Wood Street, Swindon, Wilts, SN1 4AB
Activities: Development of building projects
Shareholders: Edward Paul Keogh; Ryan Lee Edward Keogh; Luke Thomas Charles Keogh
Officers: Edward Paul Leo Keogh [1960] Director/Contractor [Irish]; Luke Thomas Charles Keogh [1989] Director/Building Contractor; Ryan Lee Edward Keogh [1985] Director/Building Contractor

Kerdene Limited
Incorporated: 14 April 2000 *Employees:* 8
Net Worth: £2,381,514 *Total Assets:* £4,636,438
Registered Office: Lowin House, Tregolls Road, Truro, Cornwall, TR1 2NA
Activities: Recreational vehicle parks, trailer parks and camping grounds
Shareholders: Cher Varya Group Ltd; Tingdene Investments Limited
Officers: Christopher James Gibbard, Secretary; Christopher James Gibbard [1963] Director; Leigh Raymond Ibbotson [1961] Director

Kernock Park Plants Limited
Incorporated: 30 December 1996 *Employees:* 77
Net Worth: £4,235,659 *Total Assets:* £4,945,477
Registered Office: Kernock Park, Pillaton, Saltash, Cornwall, PL12 6RY
Activities: Plant propagation
Shareholders: Janet Patricia Harnett; Richard Frederick Harnett
Officers: Richard Frederick Harnett, Secretary; Bruce Richard Harnett [1975] Director/Horticulturist; Janet Patricia Harnett [1943] Director/Horticulturist; Richard Frederick Harnett [1939] Director/Horticulturist

Kernow Coatings Limited
Incorporated: 24 January 1973 *Employees:* 99
Net Worth: £8,249,995 *Total Assets:* £11,985,729
Registered Office: Kernow Coatings Limited, Kernick Road, Penryn, Cornwall, TR10 9DQ
Activities: Manufacture of other plastic products
Shareholders: Peter Alan Newell; Philip Mark Bartlett
Officers: Philip Mark Bartlett [1973] Technical Director; Garry Douglas Hume [1958] Operations Director; Peter Alan Newell [1960] Finance Director

Kernow Veterinary Group Limited
Incorporated: 16 October 2013 *Employees:* 5
Net Worth: £1,157,192 *Total Assets:* £5,449,800
Registered Office: Nomansland, Edgcumbe Road, Lostwithiel, Cornwall, PL22 0DZ
Activities: Veterinary activities
Officers: Andrew Cornelius [1976] Director/Veterinary Surgeon; Ronald Thomas Fraser [1958] Director/Veterinary Surgeon; Nichola Jane Paull [1956] Director/Veterinary Surgeon; Martyn Phippen [1964] Director/Veterinary Surgeon; Renay Frances Rickard [1969] Director/Practice Manager; Alistair Todd [1976] Director/Veterinary Surgeon

Alan Kerr Limited
Incorporated: 3 June 1997 *Employees:* 49
Net Worth: £821,158 *Total Assets:* £7,456,224
Registered Office: Patrick House, Blythe Way, Yalberton Industrial Estate, Paignton, Devon, TQ4 7QP
Activities: Sale of used cars and light motor vehicles
Major Shareholder: Alan Kerr
Officers: Hilary Magnani, Secretary; Alan Kerr [1939] Director/Chairman; Janice Kerr [1941] Director/Company Secretary; Stewart Kerr [1964] Director; Hilary Magnani [1959] Director; Ian Patrick Magnani [1967] Director

Kerrier Investments Limited
Incorporated: 1 February 1963 *Employees:* 3
Net Worth: £24,361,624 *Total Assets:* £25,213,018
Registered Office: c/o Francis Clark LLP, North Quay House, Sutton Harbour, Plymouth, PL4 0RA
Activities: Other letting and operating of own or leased real estate
Shareholders: Christopher Mark Simmonds; Valerie Simmonds
Officers: Valerie Simmonds, Secretary; Christine Margaret Simmonds [1967] Director; Christopher Mark Simmonds [1961] Director; Valerie Simmonds [1933] Director

Kerry Ingredients (UK) Limited
Incorporated: 12 July 1937 *Employees:* 1,699
Net Worth: £52,655,312 *Total Assets:* £252,276,000
Registered Office: Kerry, Bradley Road, Royal Portbury Dock, Bristol, BS20 7NZ
Activities: Manufacture of other food products n.e.c.
Parent: Kerry Ingredients Holdings (U.K.) Limited
Officers: Ronan Deasy, Secretary; Ronan Deasy [1964] Director/Accountant [Irish]; Trevor James Horan [1972] EMEA Country Compliance Director [Irish]; Marguerite Larkin [1971] Director/Chief Financial Officer [Irish]

Kerry Ingredients Holdings (U.K.) Limited
Incorporated: 1 December 1977
Net Worth Deficit: £31,288,402 *Total Assets:* £147,853,872
Registered Office: Kerry, Bradley Road, Royal Portbury Dock, Bristol, BS20 7NZ
Activities: Activities of other holding companies n.e.c.
Parent: Kerry Holdings (U.K.) Limited
Officers: Ronan Deasy, Secretary; Ronan Deasy [1964] Director/Accountant [Irish]; Duncan Everett [1971] Director; Cathal Henry Gunton [1977] Director/Accountant [Irish]; Trevor James Horan [1972] EMEA Country Compliance Director [Irish]; Marguerite Larkin [1971] Director/Chief Financial Officer [Irish]

Kersfield Developments (Ensleigh South) Limited
Incorporated: 21 August 2014
Net Worth Deficit: £425,674 *Total Assets:* £18,526,576
Registered Office: 30 Brock Street, Bath, BA1 2LN
Activities: Development of building projects
Shareholders: David Laurence Newton; David Charles Oyler; Richard Gwynne Smith
Officers: David Laurence Newton [1966] Director

Kersfield Developments (RHS) Limited
Incorporated: 12 December 2016 *Employees:* 2
Net Worth: £130,917 *Total Assets:* £8,999,768
Registered Office: 30 Brock Street, Bath, BA1 2LN
Activities: Development of building projects
Shareholders: David Laurence Newton; Richard Gwynne Smith; David Charles Oyler
Officers: David Laurence Newton [1966] Director

Kew Estates Limited
Incorporated: 14 June 1999 *Employees:* 2
Net Worth: £2,960,282 *Total Assets:* £3,926,866
Registered Office: Bishopbrook House, Cathedral Avenue, Wells, Somerset, BA5 1FD
Activities: Renting and operating of Housing Association real estate
Shareholders: Alasdair Bertrand Goehl; Michael James Kew
Officers: Alasdair Bertrand Goehl [1966] Director/Engineering Consultant; Michael James Kew [1972] Director/Building Contractor

Key Industrial Equipment Limited
Incorporated: 29 January 1973 *Employees:* 125
Net Worth: £13,822,000 *Total Assets:* £19,932,000
Registered Office: Blackmoor Road, Ebblake Industrial Estate, Verwood, Dorset, BH31 6AT
Activities: Non-specialised wholesale trade
Parent: Manutan Limited
Officers: Keith Charles Boad, Secretary; Keith Charles Boad [1959] Managing Director; Pierre-Oliver Brial [1973] Director/Manager [French]; Jean-Pierre Guichard [1946] Director [French]

Key West (Holdings) Limited
Incorporated: 27 March 2014 *Employees:* 1,839
Net Worth: £163,856,000 *Total Assets:* £246,966,000
Registered Office: 22 Clifton Road, Clifton, Bristol, BS8 1AQ
Activities: Activities of head offices
Major Shareholder: Andrew Nisbet
Officers: Andrew Nisbet, Secretary; Andrew Nisbet [1960] Director/Chairman; Anne Marie Nisbet [1960] Director/Business Consultant; Emily Rose Nisbet [1990] Director/Student; Joseph Peter Nisbet [1988] Director/Business Consultant

Keycrown Properties Limited
Incorporated: 30 September 1993
Net Worth: £4,457,570 *Total Assets:* £4,538,127
Registered Office: 63 Redesdale Place, Moreton in Marsh, Glos, GL56 0EF
Activities: Management consultancy activities other than financial management
Major Shareholder: Francis Terence Murphy
Officers: Susan Dawn Nursey, Secretary; Francis Terence Murphy [1949] Director

Keynvor Morlift Limited
Incorporated: 26 November 2008 *Employees:* 20
Net Worth: £2,254,091 *Total Assets:* £6,207,511
Registered Office: Iron Yard, Middle Dock, New Quay Street, Appledore, Bideford, Devon, EX39 1LU
Activities: Other business support service activities n.e.c.
Parent: Marine Asset Management Limited
Officers: Anthony Charles Glover [1976] Director; Diccon Stideford Rogers [1976] Director

Keyway Limited
Incorporated: 13 March 1995 *Employees:* 56
Previous: Keyway (Gloucester) Limited
Net Worth: £4,585,162 *Total Assets:* £27,052,850
Registered Office: Gloucester House, 29 Brunswick Square, Gloucester, GL1 1UN
Activities: Renting and leasing of construction and civil engineering machinery and equipment
Parent: Arriva Group Limited
Officers: Eamonn Francis McGurk, Secretary; Brian Andrew McGurk [1967] Operations Director; Eamonn Francis McGurk [1965] Managing Director; Patrick Joseph McGurk [1992] Director

Killiow Estates Limited
Incorporated: 25 February 2011 *Employees:* 32
Net Worth: £3,208,490 *Total Assets:* £7,877,629
Registered Office: Trevarno Farm, Prospidnick, Helston, Cornwall, TR13 0RY
Activities: Botanical and zoological gardens and nature reserves activities
Major Shareholder: Michael Roy Sagin
Officers: Michael Roy Sagin [1950] Director

Kimberly Audrey Limited
Incorporated: 23 March 2007 *Employees:* 67
Net Worth Deficit: £237,323 *Total Assets:* £8,302,887
Registered Office: First Floor, 10 Temple Back, Bristol, BS1 6FL
Activities: Activities of other holding companies n.e.c.
Officers: Michael Francis Bonner [1960] Director/Chief Financial Officer [American]; Brian Michael Larkin [1969] Director/Business Executive [American]; Michael Phillp Santoni [1969] Director/Business Executive [American]; Ian Nigel Whitehall [1970] Director/Business Executive

Kinch Fuel Oils Limited
Incorporated: 21 April 1980 *Employees:* 18
Net Worth: £11,313,664 *Total Assets:* £13,276,454
Registered Office: Redway, Hornbury Hill, Minety, Malmesbury, Wilts, SN16 9QH
Activities: Wholesale of other fuels and related products
Shareholders: Royston Charles Kinch; Pauline Margaret Kinch
Officers: Pauline Margaret Kinch, Secretary; Pauline Margaret Kinch [1954] Director/Secretary; Royston Charles Kinch [1951] Director

P.E. King (Bristol) Limited
Incorporated: 11 March 1971 *Employees:* 17
Net Worth: £2,080,643 *Total Assets:* £4,875,237
Registered Office: Two Pools Farm, Iron Acton, Bristol, BS37 9XD
Activities: Mixed farming
Shareholder: Philip King 2011 Settlement Trust
Officers: Christopher James King [1972] Director; Michael Philip King [1969] Director; Philip Edgar King [1944] Director/Farmer; Phyllis Patricia King [1945] Director

King David Tyres Limited
Incorporated: 16 July 1975 *Employees:* 119
Net Worth: £3,450,615 *Total Assets:* £12,192,158
Registered Office: Malvern House, Priory Road, Gloucester, GL1 2RQ
Activities: Maintenance and repair of motor vehicles
Parent: Malvern Tyres Holdings Limited
Officers: Christopher David Freeman [1990] Director/Office Manager; Robert Malcolm Freeman [1967] Director; Alan Mark Stenning [1962] Director/Retail Manager

King Edward's School, Bath
Incorporated: 30 June 1997 *Employees:* 275
Net Worth: £15,873,519 *Total Assets:* £20,252,700
Registered Office: North Road, Bath, BA2 6HU
Activities: Primary education
Officers: Jonathan Mark Cook Webster, Secretary; Thomas Robert John Boyce [1979] Director/Lawyer; Virginia Caroline Chalmers [1961] Director/Lawyer; Philip Gavin Cobb [1959] Director/Estate Agent; Catherine Ann Colston [1963] Director/Consultant; Simon Hugh Jackson Coombe [1962] Director/Consultant; John Isherwood [1955] Director/Barrister; Stephen Claude Lillicrap [1939] Director/Medical Physicist; David John Medlock [1955] Director; Professor Ann Brigid Millar [1965] Director/Lecturer; Daniel Garrioch Moar [1964] Director; Professor Bernard John Morley [1959] Director/Academic; Alan John Morsley [1947] Director/Retired; Paul Roper [1966] Director; Richard Paul Stevens [1949] Director/Solicitor Retired; Winifred Thomson [1942] Director/Education Adviser

King Lifting Limited
Incorporated: 15 January 1982 *Employees:* 244
Net Worth: £9,629,660 *Total Assets:* £31,409,800
Registered Office: Portwall Place, Portwall Lane, Bristol, BS1 6NA
Activities: Renting and leasing of other machinery, equipment and tangible goods n.e.c.
Major Shareholder: Robert Walter King
Officers: John Philip David McLellan, Secretary; Kieron King [1973] Director; Robert Walter King [1944] Managing Director; Sandra Jane King [1959] Director; Tristan King [1981] Director; John Philip David McLellan [1961] Director/Accountant; Andrew James Robinson [1949] Director/Management Consultant

King William St Limited
Incorporated: 30 June 2005
Net Worth: £32,333,120 *Total Assets:* £80,596,160
Registered Office: First Floor, 10 Temple Back, Bristol, BS1 6FL
Activities: Other business support service activities n.e.c.
Officers: Saad Rabea Al Khabery [1968] Director/Vice President for Finance, HR, IT [Egyptian]; Fahad Hamad M Al-Zomaia [1973] Director [Saudi Arabian]

The King's School Ottery St Mary
Incorporated: 11 March 2011 *Employees:* 128
Net Worth: £13,409,855 *Total Assets:* £16,306,503
Registered Office: The King's School, Cadhay Lane, Ottery St Mary, Devon, EX11 1RA
Activities: General secondary education
Officers: Laurence Oliver Evans, Secretary; Edward Philip Bloomfield [1943] Director/Retired; Susan Alexandra Cade [1962] Director/PR Consultant; Elizabeth Charles [1940] Director/Fitness Instructor; Stephen Ellison [1958] Director/Self-Employed Coach and Training Development Specialist; Susan Fallows [1949] Director/Retired Teacher; Dr Jason Donald Grant Fearn-Smith [1967] Director/General Practitioner; Robert Gammon [1974] Director/Headteacher; Dr Charlotte Kate Hawkins [1978] Director/Teacher; Charlotte Louise Hollingshead [1965] Director; Rebecca Seymour Jacobs [1969] Director/Teacher; Lucy Frances Kennaway [1966] Director/Owner of a Conference, Wedding and Letting Business; John Michael Lavender [1950] Director/Retired; Ruth Branwen Miles-Haynes [1972] Director/Teacher; Robin John Mitchell [1941] Director/Retired Lecturer; David Arthur Nicholson [1962] Director/Pastoral Support Worker; Alan Paterson [1963] Director/Financial Services Manager; Susan Amanda Starr [1976] Director/Barrister; Petrina Tipping [1972] Director/Educational Psychologist; Susan Caroline Wood [1966] Director/Teaching Assistant

King's School, Bruton
Incorporated: 20 January 1997 *Employees:* 306
Net Worth: £17,096,236 *Total Assets:* £24,242,744
Registered Office: King's School, Plox, Bruton, Somerset, BA10 0ED
Activities: Pre-primary education
Officers: Louis Simon Tuson, Secretary; Robin Francis Badham-Thornhill [1954] Director/Retired; Christopher Ros Stewart Birrell [1954] Director/Consultant; Richard Ian Case [1945] Director/Retired; Adam Charles Clutterbuck [1957] Director/Surveyor; Donald Mark Fisher [1960] Director/Financial Adviser; Edward George Hobhouse [1960] Director/Business Executive; Justin Broderick Hopkins [1971] Director/Solicitor; Teresa Grace Jones [1953] Director/Retired; William Alexander Jones [1949] Director/Retired; Julian David Mant [1969] Director/Lawyer; Brian Roy McConnell [1946] Director/Retired; Anthony Malcolm Douglas Palmer [1949] Director/Retired; Giles Winthrop Pretor-Pinney [1964] Finance Director; Helena Ruth Sampson [1968] Director; Jean Walker [1956] Director/Retired; Peter Wells [1957] Director/Retired

The King's School, Gloucester
Incorporated: 26 August 1999 *Employees:* 178
Net Worth: £5,174,671 *Total Assets:* £7,162,695
Registered Office: Pitt Street, Gloucester, GL1 2BG
Activities: Primary education
Officers: Jacqueline Margaret Millar, Secretary; Nicola Mary Arthy [1964] Director/Clerk in Holy Orders; Adrian Templeton Brett [1947] Director/School Bursar; Gill Brook [1958] Deputy Director of Nursing; Philip Guy Dancey [1965] Managing Director; Miles Spencer Maitland Dunkley [1967] Director; Alyson Margaret Gillespie [1952] Director/Music Teacher; Mark Hurrell [1954] Director; Robert Ingram [1948] Director/Retired; Dean Stephen David Lake [1963] Director/The Dean of Gloucester; Susan Kathleen Lewis [1955] Relationship Director; Paul Francis Markey [1960] Director; Canon Richard Mitchell [1964] Director/Precentor; Alice Elisabeth Reeve [1976] Director/Lawyer; Angela Elizabeth Sullivan [1949] Director/School Principal; Celia Stephana Margaret Thomson [1955] Director/Clerk in Holy Orders; Martin Watson [1957] Director/School Inspector; Kurt Wyman [1967] Director/Surveyor

King's Schools Taunton Limited
Incorporated: 25 March 2004 *Employees:* 284
Net Worth: £17,443,804 *Total Assets:* £23,281,696
Registered Office: 20 Holway Avenue, Taunton, Somerset, TA1 3AR
Activities: Pre-primary education
Parent: The Woodard Corporation
Officers: Simon Charles Worthy, Secretary; Dr Lynda Mary Barley [1953] Director/Social Researcher; Simon John Carder [1951] Director/Consultant; Charis Ann Cavaghan-Pack [1951] Director/Care Home Owner; Charles Francis Burnett Clark [1959] Director/Chartered Surveyor; Carolyn Ann Cooper [1968] Director/Marketing Consultant; Godfrey Pawle Davis [1949] Director; Michael David Featherstone [1951] Director/Retired; Christopher Halliwell Hirst [1947] Director/Retired Headmaster; John Edward Ransome Houghton [1948] Director/Solicitor; Dr Roger Antony Kynaston Mott [1945] Director/Retired; Linda Margaret Nash [1958] Director; Linda Clare Scott [1956] Director/Retired; Melville Fitzgibbon Trimble [1954] Director/Chartered Accountant

Kingdon Holdings Limited
Incorporated: 6 August 2015 *Employees:* 135
Net Worth: £3,632,899 *Total Assets:* £15,932,550
Registered Office: 1 Roundhead Road, Heathfield Industrial Estate, Newton Abbot, Devon, TQ12 6UE
Activities: Activities of head offices
Officers: Ian Philip Bone [1958] Director; Michael James Harris [1967] Director; Henry William Kingdon [1987] Director; Margaret Helen Kingdon [1952] Director; Nicholas Peter Kingdon [1954] Director; Victoria Clare Kingdon [1984] Director; Georgia Helen Vaines [1982] Director

Kingham Farms Ltd
Incorporated: 30 March 1998
Net Worth: £8,819,788 *Total Assets:* £17,023,528
Registered Office: Aldbourne Chase House, Stock Lane, Aldbourne, Marlborough, Wilts, SN8 2NW
Activities: Mixed farming
Major Shareholder: Brian Anthony Charles Kingham
Officers: Yvonne Goddard, Secretary; Brian Anthony Charles Kingham [1944] Director

Kings (Weymouth) Limited
Incorporated: 14 February 1979 *Employees:* 132
Net Worth: £2,607,839 *Total Assets:* £4,761,332
Registered Office: 22 New Street, Weymouth, Dorset, DT4 8DA
Activities: Hotels and similar accommodation
Shareholders: Lynne Valerie King; Fiona Jayne King
Officers: Richard George Wakely, Secretary; Fiona Jayne King [1977] Director/Hotelier; Lynne Valerie King [1952] Director/Hotelier

Kings Harbour Hotel Limited
Incorporated: 14 April 2009 *Employees:* 49
Net Worth: £1,328,154 *Total Assets:* £6,393,881
Registered Office: Harbour House, 60 Purewell, Christchurch, Dorset, BH23 1ES
Activities: Hotels and similar accommodation
Parent: Harbour Hotels Group Limimted
Officers: Stuart Andrew Bateman [1976] Director; David Francis Robbins [1967] Finance Director; Michael Oliver Warren [1970] Director [Irish]

Kingsbridge Risk Solutions Limited
Incorporated: 11 December 2000 *Employees:* 71
Net Worth: £11,818,654 *Total Assets:* £16,623,175
Registered Office: 9 Miller Court, Severn Drive, Tewkesbury Business Park, Tewkesbury, Glos, GL20 8DN
Activities: Non-life insurance
Parent: Soar Newco Limited
Officers: Marc Ratcliffe [1979] Director; Andrew Guy Melville Stevens [1963] Director/Chief Finance Officer; James Douglas Robert Twining [1972] Director/Chief Executive; Steven John Wynne [1958] Director/Insurance Broker; Thomas Wynne [1989] Director; Dorian John Zanker [1964] Director

Kingsdown Farm Ltd
Incorporated: 21 February 2007 *Employees:* 4
Net Worth: £600,974 *Total Assets:* £5,018,650
Registered Office: Bishopbrook House, Cathedral Avenue, Wells, Somerset, BA5 1FD
Activities: Growing of cereals (except rice), leguminous crops and oil seeds
Shareholders: Julian Phillips; Kate Phillips
Officers: Kate Phillips, Secretary/Farmer; Julian Phillips [1968] Director/Farmer; Kate Phillips [1969] Director/Farmer

Kingskerswell Property Management Limited
Incorporated: 9 August 1946
Net Worth: £4,152,921 *Total Assets:* £5,329,220
Registered Office: 11a Cross Street, Moretonhampstead, Newton Abbot, Devon, TQ13 8NL
Activities: Renting and operating of Housing Association real estate
Shareholders: Judith Mary Denman; Colin Newman
Officers: Judith Newman, Secretary; Colin Newman [1958] Director/Electronics Engineer; Judith Newman [1961] Director/Lawyer

Kingsleigh Primary School
Incorporated: 13 November 2015 *Employees:* 108
Net Worth: £4,241,364 *Total Assets:* £5,999,055
Registered Office: Kingsleigh Primary School, Hadow Road, Bournemouth, BH10 5HT
Activities: Primary education
Officers: Natalie Collinson [1976] Director/Company Secretary; Rachel Cornish [1976] Director/Business Administrator; Jacqueline Mary Cutler [1956] Director/School Teacher; Jacqueline Maria Edwards [1956] Director/B&B Owner; Julia Glassborow [1949] Director/Retired; Richard John Gower [1964] Director/Headteacher; Sally Jane Lissenden [1976] Director of Development; Heather Anne McKell [1952] Director/Senior Cover Supervisor; Laura Jo-Anne Ralph [1981] Director; Kevin Roberts [1966] Director/Social Worker; Natalie Saywell [1977] Director/Recruitment Consultant

Kingsley Developments (S W) Limited
Incorporated: 13 September 2012 *Employees:* 9
Net Worth: £7,506,508 *Total Assets:* £37,665,416
Registered Office: 7 Sandy Court, Ashleigh Way, Langage Business Park, Plymouth, PL7 5JX
Activities: Holiday centres and villages
Shareholder: Abraham David Kingsley Simpson
Officers: Abraham David Kingsley Simpson, Secretary; Abraham David Kingsley Simpson [1991] Managing Director; Louis William Kingsley Simpson [1985] Director

Kingsmead Academy
Incorporated: 1 March 2011 *Employees:* 118
Net Worth: £8,462,250 *Total Assets:* £11,538,811
Registered Office: Kingsmead Academy, Hartswell, Wiveliscombe, Taunton, Somerset, TA4 2NE
Activities: General secondary education
Officers: Elizabeth Caroline Pow, Secretary; Susan Harrison [1952] Director/Local Government Officer; Eva Maria Heim [1952] Director/Retired Teacher [German]; Paul Hopkins [1955] Director/IT Manager; John Hunt [1949] Director/Retired; Judith Mary Jackson [1951] Director/Solicitor; Judy Felicity Jones [1959] Director/Retired; Nicholas John Lapthorn [1973] Director/Head of Centre; Sarah Jane Lawrence [1955] Director/Self Employed; Philip Stevens [1940] Director/Furniture Maker; Daimon Paul Tilley [1967] Managing Director; David Tucker [1978] Director/Accountant; Mark Richard Williams [1979] Director/Headteacher

Kinlon Limited
Incorporated: 20 July 2012
Net Worth: £5,532,673 *Total Assets:* £6,219,105
Registered Office: Unit 16 Athelney Way, Cheltenham, Glos, GL52 6RT
Activities: Activities of other holding companies n.e.c.
Shareholders: Carl Desmond Fallon; Stephen King
Officers: Carl Desmond Fallon [1961] Director; Stephen John King [1959] Director

Kinneir Dufort Topco Limited
Incorporated: 5 August 2016 *Employees:* 79
Net Worth: £910,861 *Total Assets:* £8,880,250
Registered Office: c/o Kinneir Dufort, 5 Host Street, Bristol, BS1 5BU
Activities: Activities of other holding companies n.e.c.
Parent: Mobeus Equity Partners IV LP
Officers: Michael Norris, Secretary; Richard Anthony Babington [1974] Director; Amanda Jane Bell [1972] Commercial Director; Guy Vernon Blackburn [1979] Director; Alan Gaby [1966] Director; Merle Hall [1975] Managing Director; Craig Ian Wightman [1962] Director

Kinson Primary School
Incorporated: 16 November 2015 *Employees:* 60
Net Worth: £2,611,249 *Total Assets:* £3,581,160
Registered Office: School Lane, Kinson, Bournemouth, BH11 9DG
Activities: Primary education
Officers: Barnaby William Acworth [1952] Director/Architect; Rachael Louise Clarke [1968] Director/Company Secretary; Ann Draper [1960] Director/Workforce Development Manager; Adele Margaret Gentle [1950] Director/Retired; Melanie Jane Gillingham [1970] Director; Jonathan Lotriet [1977] Director; Miriam Damaris O'Hare [1956] Director/Scientist; Victoria Peters [1973] Director/Teacher; Rev Lee Shirvill [1968] Director/Church of England Minister; Nigel Paul Tiller [1958] Director/Civil Servant

Kirklees Schools Services Limited
Incorporated: 5 June 2000 *Employees:* 4
Net Worth: £4,826,000 *Total Assets:* £50,352,000
Registered Office: Third Floor, Broad Quay House, Prince Street, Bristol, BS1 4DJ
Activities: Renting and operating of Housing Association real estate
Parent: XJ4 Holding Company Limited
Officers: Masood Ahmed [1968] Director/Councillor; Stephen Paul Hornby [1957] Director; Richard Little [1979] Investment Director; Carole Ann Pattison [1951] Director/Councillor

Kitagawa Europe Limited
Incorporated: 6 September 1982 *Employees:* 75
Net Worth Deficit: £432,172 *Total Assets:* £7,422,513
Registered Office: Unit 1 The Headlands, Salisbury Road, Downton, Salisbury, Wilts, SP5 3JJ
Activities: Wholesale of machine tools
Shareholders: Stuart Wyndham Murray-Threipland; Kitagawa Iron Works Co Ltd
Officers: Mark Jones, Secretary; Hisashi Fujimoto [1967] Director [Japanese]; Mark Jones [1961] Director; Kazunori Kitagawa [1984] Director [Japanese]; Yuji Kitagawa [1957] Director [Japanese]; Stuart Wyndham Murray Threipland [1947] Director; Robert Wyndham Murray-Threipland [1978] Director

Kites Enterprises Limited
Incorporated: 28 March 2013 *Employees:* 3
Net Worth: £3,895,830 *Total Assets:* £14,552,945
Registered Office: Trafalgar House, The Promenade, Clifton, Bristol, BS8 3NG
Activities: Buying and selling of own real estate
Major Shareholder: Darren John Hills
Officers: Andrew Michael Fletcher [1973] Director/Chartered Accountant; Darren John Hills [1966] Director; Lynne Hills [1974] Director

Kitto Group Public Limited Company
Incorporated: 13 June 1980 *Employees:* 7
Net Worth: £3,193,949 *Total Assets:* £3,680,423
Registered Office: 174a Cheltenham Road, Bristol, BS6 5RE
Activities: Activities of construction holding companies
Major Shareholder: Beverley Graham Talbot Rowe
Officers: Cynthia Margaret Rowe, Secretary; Beverley Graham Talbot Rowe [1948] Director; Cynthia Margaret Rowe [1946] Director/Company Secretary

Kiwa Holdings (UK) Limited
Incorporated: 12 January 2010
Net Worth: £5,770,159 *Total Assets:* £18,980,088
Registered Office: Kiwa House, Malvern View Business Park, Stella Way, Bishops Cleeve, Cheltenham, Glos, GL52 7DQ
Activities: Activities of head offices
Parent: Kiwa International B.V.
Officers: Mark Stephen Horwood, Secretary; Adriaan Besemer [1961] Director [Dutch]; Linda May Campbell [1952] Director; Dr Paulus Geohardus Maria Hesselink [1959] Director [Dutch]; Luc Marie Arthur Leroy [1964] Director [Belgian]

Kiwa Limited
Incorporated: 27 November 1997 *Employees:* 144
Net Worth: £3,180,327 *Total Assets:* £7,247,993
Registered Office: Kiwa House, Malvern View Business Park, Stella Way, Bishops Cleeve, Cheltenham, Glos, GL52 7DQ
Activities: Technical testing and analysis
Parent: Kiwa Holdings (UK) Limited
Officers: Mark Stephen Horwood, Secretary; Paul Anthony Brown [1963] Director; Linda May Campbell [1952] Director; Mark Edward Crowther [1951] Director/General Manager; Mark Stephen Horwood [1964] Director; Luc Marie Arthur Leroy [1964] Director [Belgian]

Kiwi Holdings Limited
Incorporated: 25 November 2016 *Employees:* 4
Net Worth: £1,995,077 *Total Assets:* £4,606,872
Registered Office: Towngate House, 2-8 Parkstone Road, Poole, Dorset, BH15 2PW
Activities: Activities of head offices
Shareholder: Christopher John Stewart
Officers: Andrew Barnett [1968] Finance Director; Peter Burden [1974] Director; Richard James Parker [1970] Director; Christopher John Stewart [1947] Director/Chartered Accountant

KK Daytona Holding Ltd
Incorporated: 27 October 2016 *Employees:* 1,088
Net Worth: £220,896,992 *Total Assets:* £396,296,992
Registered Office: Kohler EMEA Corporate Services, Carter Court, 4 Davy Way, Quedgeley, Gloucester, GL2 2DE
Activities: Installation of industrial machinery and equipment
Officers: Karger David Kohler [1966] Director/Executive [American]; Herbert V Vollrath Kohler Jr [1939] Director/Executive [American]

Klaw Products Limited
Incorporated: 15 February 1996 *Employees:* 42
Net Worth: £765,806 *Total Assets:* £5,871,286
Registered Office: Commerce Business Centre, West Wilts Trading Estate, Westbury, Wilts, BA13 4LS
Activities: Manufacture of other fabricated metal products n.e.c.
Parent: Gall Thomson Environmental Limited
Officers: Mike Hartman, Secretary; Neil David Brisdon [1968] Director/Management Accountant; Paul Anthony Fleetwood [1969] Director; Mike Hartman [1965] Director/Chief Financial Officer; David Robert Hill [1966] Director; Anthony John Webber [1966] Director/General Manager

Kliklok International Limited
Incorporated: 21 January 1965 *Employees:* 77
Net Worth: £2,070,000 *Total Assets:* £6,630,000
Registered Office: Western Drive, Hengrove Park Estate, Bristol, BS14 0AY
Activities: Manufacture of machinery for food, beverage and tobacco processing
Parent: Bosch Packaging Technology Limited
Officers: Jonathan David Burton, Secretary; Uwe Harbauer [1964] Director/Member of The Managing Board [German]; Sebastian Kuhne [1983] Director/Engineer [German]; Bruno Oberle [1963] Director/General Manager [Swiss]

KLKI Holdings Limited
Incorporated: 11 August 1982 *Employees:* 2
Net Worth Deficit: £664,507 *Total Assets:* £5,505,324
Registered Office: Minerva House, Lower Bristol Road, Bath, BA2 9ER
Activities: Activities of other holding companies n.e.c.
Parent: Kuala Lumpur Kepong Berhad
Officers: Sue Mai Chiang, Secretary; Kay Kian Chuah [1963] Director/Accountant [Malaysian]; Hau Hian Lee [1953] Director [Malaysian]

KMW Properties Limited
Incorporated: 21 March 1996 *Employees:* 4
Net Worth: £6,237,159 *Total Assets:* £10,845,316
Registered Office: Keynsham Manor West, Manor Road, Saltford, Bristol, BS18 3AF
Activities: Buying and selling of own real estate
Officers: John Lewis Muggleton, Secretary/Building Services Engineer; Frances Katherine Anne Edwards [1954] Director/Housewife; Paul Anthony Edwards [1954] Director/Surveyor; John Lewis Muggleton [1945] Director/Building Services Engineer; Sally Muggleton [1947] Director/Housewife

Knabs Ridge Wind Farm Limited
Incorporated: 16 November 2005
Net Worth: £8,484,478 *Total Assets:* £10,799,301
Registered Office: Windmill Hill Business Park, Whitehill Way, Swindon, Wilts, SN5 6PB
Activities: Production of electricity
Parent: Innogy Renewables UK Limited
Officers: Christopher David Barras, Secretary; Penelope Anne Sainsbury, Secretary; Kevin Dodd [1975] Director/Head of UK Asset Management and Operations; Keith Moseley [1965] Director

J.Knapp & Sons Limited
Incorporated: 7 October 1948 *Employees:* 3
Net Worth: £4,183,272 *Total Assets:* £4,534,448
Registered Office: Hermes House, Fire Fly Avenue, Swindon, Wilts, SN2 2GA
Activities: Development of building projects
Parent: JKS (2015) Ltd
Officers: Caroline Dawson, Secretary/Child Minder; Caroline Dawson [1970] Director/Event Organiser; Stephen James Taylor [1968] Director/Architectural Technician

H.J.Knee,Limited
Incorporated: 2 June 1908 *Employees:* 71
Net Worth: £8,503,823 *Total Assets:* £9,680,868
Registered Office: Assento House, Goodwood Close, White Horse Business Park, Trowbridge, Wilts, BA14 0XE
Activities: Other retail sale in non-specialised stores
Shareholder: Marcus Gerald Holbrow
Officers: Andrew John Pickford, Secretary; Marcus Generald Holbrow [1954] Managing Director; Henry John Hebden Knee [1955] Director/Engineer; Richard Mark Knee [1986] Director/Engineer; Andrew John Pickford [1985] Finance Director; Ian Thomas Arthur Vidler [1972] Director

Knight Midco Limited
Incorporated: 30 January 2012 *Employees:* 3,250
Net Worth Deficit: £6,586,990 *Total Assets:* £81,078,560
Registered Office: Queensway House, 11 Queensway, New Milton, Hants, BH25 5NR
Activities: Activities of head offices
Parent: Knight Square Holdings Limited
Officers: Stuart Douglas Muncer, Secretary; Nigel Howell [1959] Director/Chief Executive Officer; Paul John Lester [1949] Director/Company Chairman

Knight Square Holdings Limited
Incorporated: 26 January 2012 *Employees:* 3,250
Net Worth Deficit: £6,544,490 *Total Assets:* £81,078,560
Registered Office: Queensway House, 11 Queensway, New Milton, Hants, BH25 5NR
Activities: Activities of head offices
Shareholders: Nigel Howell; Epiris Managers LLP; Chamonix Knight Limited
Officers: Stuart Douglas Muncer, Secretary; Simon Timothy Barclay [1964] Director; Alexander Christopher Cooper-Evans [1971] Director/Private Equity; Jane Louise Douglas Crawford [1957] Director/Partner; Alexander Jan Fortescue [1968] Director/Private Equity; Andrew John Hartley [1960] Director/Partner; Nigel Howell [1959] Director/Chief Financial Officer; Paul John Lester [1949] Director/Company Chairman; Stuart Douglas Muncer [1977] Director/Chartered Accountant; Matthew Charles Turner [1963] Director; Sam James Watkinson [1968] Director/Fund Manager

Knight Square Limited
Incorporated: 26 January 2012 *Employees:* 4
Previous: Peverel Services Limited
Net Worth Deficit: £41,543,348 *Total Assets:* £73,072,136
Registered Office: Queensway House, 11 Queensway, New Milton, Hants, BH25 5NR
Activities: Activities of head offices
Parent: Knight Midco Limited
Officers: Stuart Douglas Muncer, Secretary; Nigel Howell [1959] Director/Chief Executive Officer; Paul John Lester [1949] Director; Ouda Saleh [1979] Director of Finance

Knights Brown Construction Ltd
Incorporated: 9 December 1986 *Employees:* 226
Previous: Raymond Brown Construction Ltd
Net Worth: £8,644,000 *Total Assets:* £28,070,000
Registered Office: 160 Christchurch Road, Ringwood, Hants, BH24 3AR
Activities: Construction of other civil engineering projects n.e.c.
Parent: Knights Brown Ltd
Officers: Rupert Blake [1965] Director; Philip Crozier [1975] Director; Andrew Eilbeck [1975] Director; Guy Pitt Hardacre [1957] Director/Engineer; Mark John Isaac [1970] Plant Director; Bryan Kennedy [1966] Director; Kevin Valentine [1973] Director; Kelvin White [1960] Finance Director; Sarah Helen Whittle [1973] Director; Peter Williamson [1981] Director; Darren Thomas Wootton [1967] Director

Knights Brown Group Ltd
Incorporated: 27 January 2010 *Employees:* 6
Previous: Raymond Brown Group Limited
Net Worth: £3,644,000 *Total Assets:* £11,543,000
Registered Office: 160 Christchurch Road, Ringwood, Hants, BH24 3AR
Activities: Activities of head offices
Parent: Knights Brown Holdings Ltd
Officers: Mark John Isaac [1970] Director; Guy Pitt-Hardacre [1957] Managing Director; Kelvin White [1960] Director; Darren Thomas Wootton [1967] Commercial Director

Knights Brown Ltd
Incorporated: 5 April 1963 *Employees:* 7
Previous: Raymond Brown Ltd
Net Worth: £272,000 *Total Assets:* £6,888,000
Registered Office: 160 Christchurch Road, Ringwood, Hants, BH24 3AR
Activities: Renting and leasing of cars and light motor vehicles
Parent: Knights Brown Group Ltd
Officers: Guy Pitt Hardacre [1957] Director/Engineer; Mark John Isaac [1970] Director; Kelvin White [1960] Director; Darren Thomas Wootton [1967] Director

Knights Brown UK Ltd
Incorporated: 21 January 2016 *Employees:* 226
Previous: Knights Brown Holdings Ltd
Net Worth: £9,714,000 *Total Assets:* £28,861,000
Registered Office: 160 Christchurch Road, Ringwood, Hants, BH24 3AR
Activities: Activities of head offices
Parent: Knights Brown Holdings Ltd
Officers: Mark John Isaac [1970] Director; Guy Pitt-Hardacre [1957] Director; Kelvin White [1960] Director; Darren Thomas Wootton [1967] Director

Knights Green Estates Limited
Incorporated: 22 March 1988
Net Worth: £5,090,689 *Total Assets:* £5,099,665
Registered Office: Ockington, Knights Green, Dymock, Glos, GL18 2DE
Activities: Development of building projects
Officers: Penelope Ann Lewis, Secretary; John Bryan Lewis [1942] Director; Simon James Lewis [1973] Director; Nicola Jane Youngs [1975] Director

Knorr-Bremse Investment (UK) Limited
Incorporated: 31 March 2000
Net Worth: £100 *Total Assets:* £22,000,100
Registered Office: Knorr Bremse Rail Systems UK Ltd, Westinghouse Way, Hampton Park East, Melksham, Wilts, SN12 6TL
Activities: Activities of head offices
Parent: Knorr-Bremse Systeme fur Schienenfahrzeuge GmbH
Officers: Mark Carrol, Secretary; Paul Goodhand [1958] Managing Director; Dr Nicolas Lange [1968] Director [German]; Harald Schneider [1975] Director [German]

Knorr-Bremse Rail Systems (UK) Limited
Incorporated: 12 April 2000 *Employees:* 490
Net Worth: £21,637,000 *Total Assets:* £79,320,000
Registered Office: Westinghouse Way, Hampton Park East, Melksham, Wilts, SN12 6TL
Activities: Repair and maintenance of other transport equipment n.e.c.
Parent: Knorr-Bremse Investment (UK) Ltd
Officers: Mark Carrol, Secretary; Paul Goodhand [1958] Managing Director; Dr Nicolas Lange [1968] Director [German]

Knorr-Bremse SA Holding Company (UK) Ltd
Incorporated: 20 August 2009
Net Worth: £5,650,001 *Total Assets:* £5,650,001
Registered Office: c/o Knorr-Bremse Rail Systems (UK) Limited, Westinghouse Way, Hampton Park East, Melksham, Wilts, SN12 6TL
Activities: Activities of head offices
Parent: Knorr-Bremse Systeme fur Schienenfahrzeuge GmbH
Officers: Mark Carrol, Secretary; Paul Goodhand [1958] Managing Director

Knorr-Bremse Systems for Commercial Vehicles Limited
Incorporated: 15 February 1954 *Employees:* 50
Net Worth: £31,793,000 *Total Assets:* £45,506,000
Registered Office: Century House, Folly Brook Road, Emersons Green, Bristol, BS16 7FE
Activities: Manufacture of other parts and accessories for motor vehicles
Parent: Knorr-Bremse AG
Officers: Mark Smith, Secretary; Michael Hall [1967] Managing Director; Mark Smith [1962] Finance Director; Herr Bernd Rainer Spies [1965] Director [German]; Alexander Oliver Wagner [1978] Director/Sales & Marketing Manager [German]

Hugh Koch Associates LLP
Incorporated: 22 March 2013 *Employees:* 21
Net Worth: £1,482,962 *Total Assets:* £5,063,219
Registered Office: Carrick House, Lypiatt Road, Cheltenham, Glos, GL50 2QJ
Officers: Dr Hugh Koch [1951] Member; Margaret Susan Koch [1953] Member; Emily Jane Koch [1985] LLP Member; James William Hanns Koch [1978] LLP Member; Lyn Marie Wright [1964] LLP Member

Kohler Holdings Ltd.
Incorporated: 9 November 2000 *Employees:* 3
Net Worth: £208,164,528 *Total Assets:* £370,097,376
Registered Office: Whaddon Works, Cromwell Road, Cheltenham, Glos, GL52 5EP
Activities: Activities of head offices
Parent: Kohler Mira Limited
Officers: Thomas Gerard Adler [1960] Director/Chief Financial Officer [American]; Herbert V Kohler Junior [1939] Director/Executive [American]

Kohler Mira Limited
Incorporated: 20 November 1930 *Employees:* 772
Net Worth: £112,755,000 *Total Assets:* £177,956,992
Registered Office: Whaddon Works, Cromwell Road, Cheltenham, Glos, GL52 5EP
Activities: Manufacture of taps and valves
Parent: Kohler Showers Bidco Limited
Officers: Thomas Gerard Adler [1960] Director/Chief Financial Officer [American]; Karger David Kohler [1966] Director/Executive [American]; Herbert V Kohler Junior [1939] Director/Executive [American]

Kohler Showers Bidco Limited
Incorporated: 28 April 2000
Net Worth: £184,616,000 *Total Assets:* £184,616,000
Registered Office: Whaddon Works, Cromwell Road, Cheltenham, Glos, GL52 5EP
Activities: Manufacture of central heating radiators and boilers
Shareholders: Kohler Mira Limited; Kohler Showers Holdings Limited
Officers: Thomas Gerard Adler [1960] Director/Chief Financial Officer [American]; Herbert V Kohler Junior [1939] Director/Executive [American]

Kohler Showers Holdings Limited
Incorporated: 28 April 2000 *Employees:* 783
Net Worth: £139,416,992 *Total Assets:* £194,523,008
Registered Office: Whaddon Works, Cromwell Road, Cheltenham, Glos, GL52 5EP
Activities: Manufacture of central heating radiators and boilers
Shareholders: Kohler Mira Limited; Kohler Euro Confluence Ltd
Officers: Thomas Gerard Adler [1960] Director/Chief Financial Officer [American]; Herbert V Kohler Junior [1939] Director/Executive [American]

Kondor Property Company Limited
Incorporated: 13 March 2013
Net Worth: £1,416,328 *Total Assets:* £5,364,197
Registered Office: I-Fulflment Headquarters D2, Radar Way, Christchurch Business Park, Christchurch, Dorset, BH23 4FL
Activities: Other letting and operating of own or leased real estate
Officers: James Anthony Bartlett, Secretary; James Anthony Bartlett [1977] Managing Director I-Koncepts Ltd; Malcolm Stanley Bartlett [1945] Director/Importer; Michael Bartlett [1970] Commercial Director Kondor Ltd; Lisa Siligardi [1974] Director/Housewife [Italian]

Kong Company Limited
Incorporated: 13 August 2007 *Employees:* 32
Net Worth: £7,170,712 *Total Assets:* £14,011,656
Registered Office: Units 6-9 High Post, Salisbury, Wilts, SP4 6AT
Activities: Operation of warehousing and storage facilities for land transport activities
Parent: Kong Company LLC
Officers: Kathy Decker Frueh [1963] Director [American]; John Joseph Nelson [1946] Director [American]

Koori Limited
Incorporated: 4 September 2006 *Employees:* 2
Net Worth: £134,378 *Total Assets:* £4,211,502
Registered Office: 24 Cornwall Road, Dorchester, DT1 1RX
Activities: Development of building projects
Shareholders: Ramin Hidari; Redtale Holdings Limited
Officers: Carole Anne Hidari, Secretary; Mr Malcolm Peter Curtis [1967] Director; Ramin Hidari [1962] Director

Korado Ltd
Incorporated: 31 March 1999
Net Worth: £3,562,949 *Total Assets:* £3,565,449
Registered Office: Kernow House, Gas Hill, Newham, Truro, Cornwall, TR1 2XP
Activities: Licenced restaurants
Officers: Rolf Hugo Munding [1953] Director

KPC & AT Body Properties Limited
Incorporated: 23 March 2016 *Employees:* 4
Net Worth: £3,572,686 *Total Assets:* £11,035,834
Registered Office: Unit 4 Beechwood House, Beech Avenue, Cattedown, Plymouth, PL4 0QQ
Activities: Residents property management
Shareholders: Adele Therese Body; Kenneth Paul Cyril Body
Officers: Adele Therese Body [1962] Director; Kenneth Paul Cyril Body [1965] Director

Kranlyft UK Limited
Incorporated: 24 June 2002 *Employees:* 17
Net Worth: £3,354,000 *Total Assets:* £4,509,000
Registered Office: Unit 1 I O Centre, Cabot Park, Avonmouth, Bristol, BS11 0QL
Activities: Installation of industrial machinery and equipment
Parent: AB Kranlyft
Officers: Rune Christer Dijner [1952] Director/Businessman [Swedish]; Jurgen Vater [1967] Director/Businessman [Swedish]

Krowji Limited
Incorporated: 9 April 2005 *Employees:* 9
Net Worth Deficit: £35,768 *Total Assets:* £3,886,066
Registered Office: Krowji, West Park, Redruth, Cornwall, TR15 3AJ
Activities: Combined office administrative service activities
Parent: Creative Kernow Ltd
Officers: Percival Ross Williams, Secretary/Manager; Dinah Louise Graffy [1960] Director; Christopher James Hibbert [1950] Director/Manager; Graham Owen Frank Oldrieve [1956] Director/Chartered Surveyor

Kruger Property Company Limited
Incorporated: 26 February 2014
Net Worth: £1,610,922 *Total Assets:* £7,061,146
Registered Office: I-Fulfilment Headquarters, D2 Radar Way, Christchurch Business Park, Christchurch, Dorset, BH23 4FL
Activities: Other letting and operating of own or leased real estate
Officers: James Anthony Bartlett, Secretary; James Anthony Bartlett [1977] Director; Malcolm Stanley Bartlett [1945] Director; Michael Bartlett [1970] Director; Lisa Siligardi [1974] Director/Housewife [Italian]

KS SPV 1 Limited
Incorporated: 5 May 2010
Net Worth: £2,573,786 *Total Assets:* £11,342,238
Registered Office: c/o Francis Clark LLP, North Quay House, Sutton Harbour, Plymouth, PL4 0RA
Activities: Other business support service activities n.e.c.
Officers: Ingo Burkhardt [1973] Director [German]; Thorsten Eitle [1973] Director [German]

KS SPV 12 Limited
Incorporated: 23 February 2011 *Employees:* 2
Net Worth: £976,245 *Total Assets:* £5,910,093
Registered Office: 14 High Cross, Truro, Cornwall, TR1 2AJ
Activities: Production of electricity
Major Shareholder: Alexander Arcache
Officers: Dr Alexander Arcache [1974] Director [German]; Frank Henning Albert Bohne [1971] Director/Head of Operations [German]

KS SPV 9 Limited
Incorporated: 1 November 2010
Net Worth: £296,470 *Total Assets:* £6,574,209
Registered Office: 14 High Cross, Truro, Cornwall, TR1 2AJ
Activities: Production of electricity
Major Shareholder: Dagmar Vogt
Officers: Charles Anton Milner [1961] Director [German]; Dagmar Vogt [1964] Director [German]

KTSL Limited
Incorporated: 16 February 2000 *Employees:* 24
Net Worth: £50,725 *Total Assets:* £5,903,790
Registered Office: Unit 23 Leafield Industrial Estate, Corsham, Wilts, SN13 9RS
Activities: Information technology consultancy activities
Officers: Robert Stephen Marks [1959] Director; Timothy James McCue [1973] Director/IT Consultancy; Aaron Stuart Perrott [1976] Director/IT Consultancy; Mark Stephen Robinson [1970] Managing Director; David Round [1961] Partner & Operations Director

Kumari Care Limited
Incorporated: 21 August 1997 *Employees:* 80
Net Worth: £4,839,320 *Total Assets:* £5,063,219
Registered Office: 2 Chesterfield Buildings, Westbourne Place, Clifton, Bristol, BS8 1RU
Activities: Social work activities without accommodation for the elderly and disabled
Major Shareholder: Santosh Kumari-Chaston
Officers: Santosh Kumari-Chaston [1953] Managing Director

KWTN Solar Limited
Incorporated: 14 January 2011 *Employees:* 4
Net Worth: £1,791,283 *Total Assets:* £4,645,982
Registered Office: Coombe Farm, Roundham, Crewkerne, Somerset, TA18 8RR
Activities: Production of electricity
Shareholders: Mark Bowden Wheaton; 5T Limited
Officers: Nicholas Leslie Ronald Keeler [1962] Director; Timothy Robert Noyes [1962] Director; David Tippett [1955] Director; Mark Bowden Wheaton [1960] Director

L.A.L. Estates Limited
Incorporated: 8 November 1991
Net Worth: £9,407,040 *Total Assets:* £14,487,789
Registered Office: Down Farm, Westonbirt, Tetbury, Glos, GL8 8QW
Activities: Buying and selling of own real estate
Parent: Clarart Ltd
Officers: Claire Janet Tomlinson, Secretary/Director; Claire Janet Tomlinson [1944] Director; Emma Claire Tomlinson [1974] Director; Luke George Tomlinson [1977] Director; Mark Lascelles Telford Tomlinson [1982] Director

L.E.W. Techniques Limited
Incorporated: 20 May 1966 *Employees:* 88
Net Worth: £4,835,087 *Total Assets:* £6,028,678
Registered Office: Bindon Business Park, Cook Way, Taunton, Somerset, TA2 6BG
Activities: Manufacture of electronic components
Shareholders: Elaine Elizabeth Moll; Andrew Edward Walker
Officers: Elaine Elizabeth Moll, Secretary; Elaine Elizabeth Moll [1965] Director/Administrator; Andrew Edward Walker [1962] Director/Engineer

La Flor de Copan UK Limited
Incorporated: 25 January 2005
Net Worth: £12,729,625 *Total Assets:* £12,729,625
Registered Office: 121 Winterstoke Road, Bristol, BS3 2LL
Activities: Activities of other holding companies n.e.c.
Parent: Imperial Tobacco Overseas Holdings Limited
Officers: Gavin Paul Bonnar, Secretary; Thomas Richard William Tildesley [1973] Finance Director; Robert Dee Wilkey [1956] Director/Attorney [American]; Trevor Martin Williams [1961] Director/Chartered Secretary

La Hacienda Limited
Incorporated: 20 September 2001 *Employees:* 45
Net Worth: £3,809,793 *Total Assets:* £5,581,022
Registered Office: Hangar 27, Site C, Aston Down Airfield, Stroud, Gloucester, GL6 8HR
Activities: Wholesale of household goods (other than musical instruments) n.e.c
Parent: The Ames Companies UK Ltd.
Officers: Brian Gerard Harris [1969] Director/SVP, CFO [American]; Simon Andrew Hupfeld [1976] Director/Chief Executive Officer [Australian]; Dale Elizabeth McGrath [1961] Director/Chief Financial Operator [Australian/American]; Robert Francis Mehmel [1962] Director/Business Executive [American]

Laceys Solicitors LLP
Incorporated: 28 January 2013 *Employees:* 90
Net Worth: £2,212,814 *Total Assets:* £4,783,756
Registered Office: 5 Poole Road, Bournemouth, BH2 5QL
Officers: Philip James Day [1957] Member; Samuel Freeman [1980] Member; John Charles Munro [1974] Member; Simon Christopher Nightingale [1950] Member; Jonathan Mayson Ogden [1963] Member; Mark Robert Preece [1981] Member; Jonathan Talbot [1958] Member; Mark Richard Timberlake [1964] Member

Ladder and Fencing Industries (Newent) Limited
Incorporated: 15 August 1957 *Employees:* 41
Net Worth: £3,853,611 *Total Assets:* £5,296,300
Registered Office: Horsefair Lane, Newent, Glos, GL18 1RP
Activities: Manufacture of other products of wood; manufacture of articles of cork, straw and plaiting materials
Parent: Access Solutions Holdings Limited
Officers: Richard Jeremy Chaplin [1966] Director; David Robert Charles Neate [1973] Director; Benjamin David Richard Walker [1986] Director

Ladyswood Farm & Stud LLP
Incorporated: 12 January 2017 *Employees:* 5
Net Worth: £4,340,000 *Total Assets:* £4,466,300
Registered Office: Ladyswood Farm & Stud, Sherston, Malmesbury, Wilts, SN16 0LA
Officers: Alexander Stanley Fortescue Frost [1975] Member; Olivia Frances Frost [1978] Member

Lagan Farms (Dorset) Limited
Incorporated: 17 December 1996 *Employees:* 1
Net Worth: £3,161,518 *Total Assets:* £3,679,172
Registered Office: Park Farm, Shaftesbury Road, Gillingham, Dorset, SP8 5JG
Activities: Raising of dairy cattle
Shareholders: Clarke Trustees No. 1 Limited; Clarke Trustees No. 2 Limited
Officers: Ronald William Clarke [1952] Director/Farmer

Lake Consultancy and Investments Limited
Incorporated: 11 February 1983
Net Worth: £3,045,796 *Total Assets:* £4,014,828
Registered Office: Denzel Paddocks, Crowcombe Heathfield, Taunton, Somerset, TA4 4BS
Activities: Other information service activities n.e.c.
Shareholders: Andrew Burn; Claudia Vincent Burn
Officers: Andrew Burn, Secretary; Andrew Burn [1955] Director; Claudia Vincent Burn [1955] Director

Lake Inns & Leisure Limited
Incorporated: 28 June 1996 *Employees:* 47
Net Worth: £1,758,799 *Total Assets:* £3,618,389
Registered Office: Lowin House, Tregolls Road, Truro, Cornwall, TR1 2NA
Activities: Construction of domestic buildings
Major Shareholder: Nicholas Lake
Officers: Nicholas Lake [1945] Director/Publican

Lakes Bathrooms Limited
Incorporated: 14 August 1992 *Employees:* 136
Net Worth: £6,453,125 *Total Assets:* £10,938,713
Registered Office: Lakes Bathrooms, Alexandra Way, Ashchurch, Tewkesbury, Glos, GL20 8NB
Activities: Wholesale of household goods (other than musical instruments) n.e.c
Shareholders: Mark Stradling; Julia Katherine Martin-Jones; Bev Tamsin Brown
Officers: Alan George Craddock, Secretary; Bev Tamsin Brown [1972] Managing Director; Michael Alan Evans [1962] Operations Director; Michael John Tattam [1965] Sales & Marketing Director

LAL Language Centres Holding Ltd
Incorporated: 31 October 1980 *Employees:* 21
Net Worth: £9,045,435 *Total Assets:* £12,929,286
Registered Office: Sigma House, Oak View Close, Edginswell Park, Torquay, Devon, TQ2 7FF
Activities: Other service activities n.e.c.
Officers: Carsten Falco Becker [1974] Director [German]; Dietmar Konrad Gunz [1959] Managing Director [German]; Alexander Jocelyn Perkins [1961] Managing Director

LAL Language Centres UK Ltd
Incorporated: 23 April 1985 *Employees:* 101
Net Worth: £289,042 *Total Assets:* £5,280,565
Registered Office: Sigma House, Oak View Close, Edginswell Park, Torquay, Devon, TQ2 7FF
Activities: General secondary education
Officers: Jean Marc Bellia [1979] Director/Chief Financial Officer [Maltese]; Alexander Jocelyn Perkins [1961] Managing Director

Lambeth Lighting Services Limited
Incorporated: 16 March 2004
Net Worth Deficit: £1,190,726 *Total Assets:* £12,501,229
Registered Office: Third Floor, Broad Quay House, Prince Street, Bristol, BS1 4DJ
Activities: Other service activities n.e.c.
Parent: IIC Lambeth Holding Company Limited
Officers: Paul Anthony Cartwright [1957] Director; Vikki Louise Everett [1971] Director/Project Manager; Thomas Benedict Symes [1956] Director

Lambtrad Ltd
Incorporated: 14 April 2008 *Employees:* 577
Net Worth: £2,026,203 *Total Assets:* £5,687,607
Registered Office: Aldreth, Pearcroft Road, Stonehouse, Glos, GL10 2JY
Activities: Unlicenced restaurants and cafes
Major Shareholder: Timothy Royston Robert Lamb
Officers: Timothy Royston Robert Lamb [1967] Director

Lancaster Leisure Limited
Incorporated: 28 March 1960 *Employees:* 446
Net Worth: £24,781,868 *Total Assets:* £40,306,864
Registered Office: c/o Glover Stanbury, 30 Bear Street, Barnstaple, Devon, EX32 7DD
Activities: Activities of other holding companies n.e.c.
Shareholders: Roy Maxwell Lancaster; Rosemary Janet Lancaster
Officers: Lisa Marie Todd, Secretary; Rosemary Janet Lancaster [1934] Director/Hotelier; Roy Maxwell Lancaster [1932] Director/Hotelier; Rudi John Roy Lancaster [1964] Director/Hotelier; Sally Eileen Lancaster [1966] Director

Lance Levy Investments Limited
Incorporated: 20 February 2006
Net Worth: £8,925,555 *Total Assets:* £12,256,189
Registered Office: Calyx House, South Road, Taunton, Somerset, TA1 3DU
Activities: Other letting and operating of own or leased real estate
Parent: Lance Levy Investments 2013 Limited
Officers: Susan Jane Mitchell, Secretary; Charles Aubrey Mitchell [1953] Director

Lancer Scott Limited
Incorporated: 31 March 1998 *Employees:* 105
Net Worth: £6,970,117 *Total Assets:* £15,162,277
Registered Office: Queen Charlotte House, 53-55 Queen Charlotte Street, Bristol, BS1 4HQ
Activities: Other construction installation
Officers: Morian Cooke, Secretary; Mark Nicholas Chapman [1968] Director/Engineer; Morian Cooke [1962] Director/Building Services; Timothy Martin Dougherty [1964] Director; Robert Ivor Griffiths [1964] Director; Mark Steven Kemery [1958] Director/Building Services

Land & Buildings Limited
Incorporated: 5 September 1988 *Employees:* 3
Net Worth: £1,450,044 *Total Assets:* £3,720,793
Registered Office: 1a Trymwood Parade, Shirehampton Road, Bristol, BS9 2DP
Activities: Buying and selling of own real estate
Shareholders: Neil John Cartwright; Richard John Ernest Farrow
Officers: Neil John Cartwright, Secretary; Neil John Cartwright [1961] Director; Richard John Ernest Farrow [1958] Director/Chartered Surveyor

Landell Mills Limited
Incorporated: 16 July 1981 *Employees:* 37
Net Worth: £4,962,827 *Total Assets:* £12,795,417
Registered Office: Bryer Ash Business Park, Bradford Road, Trowbridge, Wilts, BA14 8HE
Activities: Management consultancy activities other than financial management
Parent: Landell Mills International Limited
Officers: Graham Richard Fay, Secretary; Graham Richard Fay [1955] Director/Chartered Accountant; Simon Foxwell [1975] Director; David Thomas Uglow [1971] Director

Landmark Analytics Limited
Incorporated: 17 June 2004 *Employees:* 1
Net Worth: £4,698,469 *Total Assets:* £5,219,083
Registered Office: 7 Abbey Court, Eagle Way, Sowton Industrial Estate, Exeter, EX2 7HY
Activities: Other information technology service activities
Parent: DMGI Land & Property Europe Ltd
Officers: Matthew Teague, Secretary; Simon James Brown [1965] Director/Chief Executive; David William Callcott [1959] Director; Stephen John Stout [1960] Director/Chairman

Landmark Developments (Oakford House) Limited
Incorporated: 30 September 2004
Net Worth: £587,826 *Total Assets:* £4,591,954
Registered Office: Penthouse 1, Charters, 43 Upper Oldfield Park, Bath, BA2 3LB
Activities: Development of building projects
Major Shareholder: Margaret Patricia Favager
Officers: Margaret Patricia Favager [1955] Director

Landmark Estates (London) Limited
Incorporated: 25 April 2014
Net Worth Deficit: £11,502 *Total Assets:* £5,522,635
Registered Office: Unit 9 & 10 Fridays Court, High Street, Ringwood, Hants, BH24 1AB
Activities: Development of building projects
Shareholder: James Roger Bradley
Officers: James Roger Bradley [1971] Director/Property Developer

Landmark Information Group Limited
Incorporated: 31 January 1994 *Employees:* 362
Net Worth: £81,813,384 *Total Assets:* £104,309,632
Registered Office: 7 Abbey Court, Eagle Way, Sowton Industrial Estate, Exeter, EX2 7HY
Activities: Other information technology service activities
Parent: DMGI Land & Property Europe Ltd
Officers: Matthew Teague, Secretary; Simon James Brown [1965] Director/Chief Executive; David William Callcott [1959] Director; Stephen John Stout [1960] Director/Chairman

Landmark International Holdings Limited
Incorporated: 22 September 1994 *Employees:* 1
Net Worth Deficit: £214,941 *Total Assets:* £7,665,930
Registered Office: 7 Abbey Court, Eagle Way, Sowton Industrial Estate, Exeter, EX2 7HY
Activities: Non-trading company
Parent: Landmark Information Group
Officers: David William Callcott, Finance Director; Simon James Brown [1965] Director/Chief Executive; David William Callcott [1959] Finance Director; Stephen John Stout [1960] Director/Chairman

Landscove Holidays Limited
Incorporated: 13 August 1993 *Employees:* 85
Net Worth: £5,388,291 *Total Assets:* £9,432,376
Registered Office: Centenary House, Peninsula Park, Rydon Lane, Exeter, EX2 7XE
Activities: Holiday centres and villages
Parent: Ayersmont Ltd
Officers: Rory Alan Hardick [1974] Director; Leslie Martin Payton Hutchings [1947] Director; Matilda Margot Newing [1980] Director

G.R. Lane Health Products Limited
Incorporated: 1 April 1965 *Employees:* 177
Net Worth: £8,646,956 *Total Assets:* £35,044,788
Registered Office: G R Lane Health Products Limited, Sisson Road, Gloucester, GL2 0GR
Activities: Manufacture of basic pharmaceutical products
Parent: G R Lane Holdings Ltd
Officers: Paul Charles Whatley, Secretary; David Cole [1969] Director; Janet Margaret Groves [1952] Director; Jonathan Roger Groves [1980] Commercial Director; Paul Henly [1962] Technical Director; Mark Horan [1973] Operations Director; Trevor Edward Howard [1962] Director; Aden Craig Kelly [1974] Sales Director; Hilary Lynn [1967] Marketing Director; Paul Charles Whatley [1958] Director

G.R. Lane Holdings Limited
Incorporated: 1 April 1958 *Employees:* 238
Net Worth: £15,017,777 *Total Assets:* £37,367,288
Registered Office: G R Lane Holdings Limited, Sisson Road, Gloucester, GL2 0GR
Activities: Activities of head offices
Officers: Janet Margaret Groves, Secretary; David Cole [1969] Director; Michael Edward Frost [1948] Director/Chartered Accountant; Janet Margaret Groves [1952] Director; Jonathan Roger Groves [1980] Director; Trevor Edward Howard [1962] Director; Amy Louise Power [1982] Director; Paul Simons [1938] Managing Director; Judith Helen Sissons [1954] Director; Robin James Sissons [1984] Director

Lane's Storage and Removals Limited
Incorporated: 3 May 1967 *Employees:* 85
Net Worth: £3,437,255 *Total Assets:* £5,768,349
Registered Office: Greenbottom, Chacewater, Truro, Cornwall, TR4 8QW
Activities: Removal services
Shareholders: Robert Lane; Maria Louise Russell
Officers: Maria Louise Russell, Secretary; Mark Lane [1961] Director; Michael Edward Lane [1940] Director; Robert Lane [1964] Director; Sylvia Mary Lane [1940] Director; Maria Louise Russell [1967] Director

Lang & Potter (Holdings) Limited
Incorporated: 13 January 2003 *Employees:* 256
Net Worth: £3,418,844 *Total Assets:* £6,640,451
Registered Office: Galileo Close, Newnham Industrial Estate, Plympton, Plymouth, PL7 4JW
Activities: Activities of head offices
Major Shareholder: David William Bragg Potter
Officers: Martin George Freeman [1969] Finance Director; David William Bragg Potter [1945] Director; Susan Margaret Potter [1946] Director

Langage Farm Limited Liability Partnership
Incorporated: 8 January 2009 *Employees:* 42
Net Worth: £5,452,373 *Total Assets:* £6,227,418
Registered Office: Higher Challonsleigh, Smithaleigh, Plymouth, PL7 5AY
Officers: James Robert Harvey [1964] Member; Leonard Randall Harvey [1934] Member; Wendy Elizabeth Harvey [1966] LLP Member

Langdon (Dorset) Farms
Incorporated: 10 March 1941 *Employees:* 3
Net Worth: £7,000,732 *Total Assets:* £7,223,476
Registered Office: Langdon Manor, Beaminster, Dorset, DT8 3NN
Activities: Raising of sheep and goats
Officers: Charles William White Dupont, Secretary; Angela Joy Dupont [1948] Director/Housing Association Chairman; Charles William White Dupont [1942] Director

Langdon Group Limited
Incorporated: 16 May 1988 *Employees:* 1,430
Net Worth: £45,845,000 *Total Assets:* £80,008,000
Registered Office: Showground Road, Bridgwater, Somerset, TA6 6AJ
Activities: Freight transport by road
Shareholders: Tobias Nagel; Beatrice Nagel
Officers: Renee Teresa Barrett, Secretary; Renee Teresa Barrett [1965] Financial Director; Patrick Thomas Griffiths [1969] Director; Simon Edward Holder [1952] Director/Accountant; Arran Osman [1970] Managing Director; Michael Eberhard Schymik [1959] Director [German]

Langdon Transport Limited
Incorporated: 11 February 2003
Net Worth: £1,860,095 *Total Assets:* £4,082,922
Registered Office: 38 Central Avenue, Lee Mill Industrial Estate, Ivybridge, Devon, PL21 9PE
Activities: Freight transport by road
Major Shareholder: Steve Roy Langdon
Officers: Steven Roy Langdon [1959] Director

Langdown Estates LLP
Incorporated: 10 September 2015 *Employees:* 9
Net Worth: £6,725,229 *Total Assets:* £19,945,812
Registered Office: Jolyon Suite, Lancol House, 63 Charlton Road, Andover, Hants, SP10 3JY
Officers: Maureen Valerie Langdown [1937] Member; Patrick Kelton John Langdown [1956] Member; Patrick David Langdown [1936] Member; Amanda Elizabeth Anastasia Patrice Langdown-Kirby [1964] Member

Langford Veterinary Services Limited
Incorporated: 22 January 2009 *Employees:* 152
Net Worth: £3,282,212 *Total Assets:* £5,762,021
Registered Office: Beacon House, University of Bristol, Queens Avenue, Bristol, BS8 1SE
Activities: Veterinary activities
Parent: University of Bristol
Officers: Alexis Catherine MacKay Edward, Secretary; Mick Paul Axtell [1972] Finance Director; Richard Andrew Hammond [1965] Director/Chief Executive Officer; Professor Steve Howell [1967] Director; Professor Jonathan Richard Sandy [1954] Director/Dentist; Sheena Margaret Warman [1973] Director/Veterinary Surgeon

Langham Farms Limited
Incorporated: 22 August 2003 *Employees:* 5
Net Worth: £8,690,643 *Total Assets:* £9,414,454
Registered Office: Bingham's Melcombe, Dorchester, DT2 7PZ
Activities: Mixed farming
Officers: Alan Douglas Deves, Secretary; Alan Douglas Deves [1962] Director/Chartered Accountant; Irene Elizabeth Langham [1922] Director; John Christopher Langham [1951] Director; Justin Morley Langham [1963] Director; Jill Miranda May [1961] Director

Langham Industries Limited
Incorporated: 18 April 1980 *Employees:* 286
Net Worth: £59,362,344 *Total Assets:* £76,757,936
Registered Office: Bingham's Melcombe, Dorchester, DT2 7PZ
Activities: Activities of head offices
Officers: Alan Douglas Deves, Secretary; Alan Douglas Deves [1962] Director/Chartered Accountant; Irene Elizabeth Langham [1922] Director; John Christopher Langham [1951] Director; Justin Morley Langham [1963] Director/Chartered Surveyor; Jill Miranda May [1961] Director; Sarah Rodgers [1984] Director/Accountant

Langlands Farms Limited
Incorporated: 2 March 2007
Net Worth: £4,195,908 *Total Assets:* £13,894,120
Registered Office: Hitchcocks HQ, Hitchcocks Business Park, Willand, Devon, EX15 3FA
Activities: Mixed farming
Shareholders: Richard Alan William Persey; Geoffrey William Persey; Maria Carina Persey
Officers: Richard Alan William Persey, Secretary/Farmer; Richard Alan William Persey [1981] Director/Farmer

Lanhydrock Estate Company (The)
Incorporated: 21 November 1934 *Employees:* 7
Net Worth: £8,952,441 *Total Assets:* £17,695,212
Registered Office: The Lodge,The Old Vicarage, Lanhydrock, Bodmin, Cornwall, PL30 5AD
Activities: Buying and selling of own real estate
Officers: Zara Alison Hall [1970] Director; Philip Henry Reed [1962] Director/Solicitor; Andrew Nicholas Victor Williams [1967] Director; Simon Justin Colin Williams [1972] Director

Lanhydrock Golf Club Limited
Incorporated: 18 October 1996 *Employees:* 61
Net Worth: £3,180,717 *Total Assets:* £6,181,698
Registered Office: Lanhydrock Hotel & Golf Club, Lostwithiel Road, Bodmin, Cornwall, PL30 5AQ
Activities: Hotels and similar accommodation
Shareholder: Graham Martin Bond
Officers: Clare Margaret Louise Bond, Secretary; Clare Margaret Louise Bond [1963] Director/Assistant Manager Golf Club; Graham Martin Bond [1963] Director/General Manager Golf Club

Lansdown Properties (Cheltenham) Limited
Incorporated: 4 September 1984 *Employees:* 1
Net Worth: £918,584 *Total Assets:* £7,226,196
Registered Office: Pillar House, 113-115 Bath Road, Cheltenham, Glos, GL53 7LS
Activities: Other letting and operating of own or leased real estate
Shareholders: Peter Gill; Jane Gill Maddison
Officers: Jane Gill Maddison, Secretary; Barbara Ann Gill [1938] Director; Peter Gill [1969] Director/Theatre Producer; Raymond Alan Gill [1931] Director; Jane Gill Maddison [1964] Director

Lantor (UK) Limited
Incorporated: 15 March 2001 *Employees:* 71
Net Worth: £242,559 *Total Assets:* £3,941,496
Registered Office: BFF Business Park, Bath Road, Bridgwater, Somerset, TA6 4NZ
Activities: Manufacture of non-wovens and articles made from non-wovens, except apparel
Shareholders: Nonwovens Ltd; BFF Nonwovens Limited
Officers: Andrew Michael Brownlow [1965] Director; David Peter Lamb [1959] Director/Chairman

Larasian Limited
Incorporated: 22 September 1976 *Employees:* 184
Net Worth: £17,088,964 *Total Assets:* £22,063,290
Registered Office: Module House, Whiteparish, Salisbury, Wilts, SP5 2SJ
Activities: Electrical installation
Shareholders: Brian Geoffrey Currie; Glynis Currie
Officers: Glynis Currie, Secretary; Julian John Navey, Secretary; Geoffrey Clive Andrew Allen [1954] Finance Director; Brian Geoffrey Currie [1945] Director/Engineer; Glynis Currie [1945] Director; Glynis Currie [1945] Director/Accountant; Julian John Navey [1961] Director/Chartered Accountant; Rod Stefan Piwowarski [1969] Director

Lascar Electronics Limited
Incorporated: 6 June 2005 *Employees:* 41
Net Worth: £9,149,417 *Total Assets:* £10,124,324
Registered Office: Module House, Whiteparish, Salisbury, Wilts, SP5 2SJ
Activities: Manufacture of electronic measuring, testing etc. equipment, not for industrial process control
Officers: John Burton [1970] Director; Richard James Cameron [1978] Director; Glynis Currie [1945] Director/Accountant; Alan Robert Darcy [1961] Director/Electronics Engineer; Julian John Navey [1961] Director/Chartered Accountant; Rod Stefan Piwowarski [1969] Director

Latcham Direct Limited
Incorporated: 11 September 2008
Net Worth: £1,591,353 *Total Assets:* £4,128,290
Registered Office: Unit 1 Western Drive, Hengrove, Bristol, BS14 0AZ
Activities: Printing n.e.c.
Shareholders: Michael John Hughes; Susan Jayne Hughes
Officers: Peter Charles Bachelor, Secretary; Kenneth Philip Gibbs [1960] Director; William Hornby Gore [1944] Director; Michael John Hughes [1968] Director; Susan Jayne Hughes [1963] Director/Human Resources Co-ordinator; Colin Robert Mattinson [1967] Director/Commercial Manager; Steven Christopher Morgan [1966] Production Director

Latchways PLC
Incorporated: 31 October 1974 *Employees:* 106
Net Worth: £25,820,000 *Total Assets:* £31,277,000
Registered Office: Latchways PLC, Hopton Park, Devizes, Wilts, SN10 2JP
Activities: Manufacture of other fabricated metal products n.e.c.
Parent: MSA UK Holdings Limited
Officers: Lynda Robbins, Secretary; Dr Joerdis Jens Behling [1961] Director/Vice President of Europe, MSA [German]; James M. Daugherty [1969] Director [American]; Richard William Roda [1972] Director [American]

Latimer Trend Holdings Limited
Incorporated: 6 January 2011 *Employees:* 85
Net Worth Deficit: £1,726,019 *Total Assets:* £4,376,199
Registered Office: Estover Road, Estover, Plymouth, PL6 7PY
Activities: Activities of head offices
Shareholders: Ian Campbell Crocker; Andrew Kevin Ogden; Paul Roger Opie
Officers: Ian Campbell Crocker [1960] Director/Accountant; Andrew Kevin Ogden [1960] Production Director; Paul Roger Opie [1971] Director/Customer Services Manager

Latimer,Trend & Company Limited
Incorporated: 2 May 1946 *Employees:* 85
Net Worth: £3,005,424 *Total Assets:* £7,837,316
Registered Office: Estover Road, Estover, Plymouth, PL6 7PY
Activities: Printing n.e.c.
Officers: Ian Campbell Crocker, Secretary; Ian Campbell Crocker [1960] Director/Accountant; Andrew Kevin Ogden [1960] Production Director; Paul Roger Opie [1971] Managing Director

Latona Leisure Limited
Incorporated: 6 January 1993 *Employees:* 180
Net Worth: £9,645,942 *Total Assets:* £16,486,379
Registered Office: Limpley Stoke Hotel, Woods Hill, Lower Limpley Stoke, Bath, BA2 7FZ
Activities: Hotels and similar accommodation
Shareholders: Trevor Raymond Styles; Nicholas Andre Gray
Officers: Nicholas Andre Gray, Secretary/Property Developer; Anita Rose Dodd [1959] Director/Company Secretary; Nicholas Andre Gray [1957] Director/Property Developer; Raymond John Styles [1930] Director/Builder; Trevor Raymond Styles [1957] Director/Builder

Launceston College
Incorporated: 19 July 2012 *Employees:* 416
Net Worth: £54,848,452 *Total Assets:* £59,998,848
Registered Office: Launceston College, Hurdon Road, Launceston, Cornwall, PL15 9JR
Activities: General secondary education
Officers: Tara Jade Broad, Secretary; Carla Jayne Barnard [1978] Director; Peter Crispin [1950] Director/Education Consultant; David Humphries [1953] Director/Retired Headteacher; Jack Andrew John Jackson [1964] Director/College Principal; Elaine Marshall [1962] Director; Gilly Sanders [1955] Director/Retired; Ashley John Shopland [1966] Director; Professor Fenella Theta Wojnarowska [1947] Director/Retired

Maurice Lay Distributors Limited
Incorporated: 3 November 1986 *Employees:* 84
Net Worth: £9,321,075 *Total Assets:* £13,758,464
Registered Office: Fourth Way, Avonmouth, Bristol, BS11 8DW
Activities: Wholesale of electronic and telecommunications equipment and parts
Shareholder: Maurice John Lay
Officers: Graham Terence Perry, Secretary; Daniel James Lay [1963] Sales Director; Maurice John Lay [1935] Managing Director; Graham Terence Perry [1955] Finance Director; Richard David Wood [1966] Director

LBS (Fire Services) Limited
Incorporated: 11 February 2000
Net Worth: £850,000 *Total Assets:* £3,999,000
Registered Office: Third Floor, Broad Quay House, Prince Street, Bristol, BS1 4DJ
Activities: Management of real estate on a fee or contract basis
Parent: Bandbreeze Limited
Officers: Julia Sarah McCabe [1970] Regional Director; Alan Campbell Ritchie [1967] Director

LCD Publishing Limited
Incorporated: 15 May 1984 *Employees:* 13
Net Worth: £2,758,859 *Total Assets:* £3,599,897
Registered Office: Vici House, 2 Mallard Road, Sowton, Exeter, Devon, EX2 7LD
Activities: Other service activities n.e.c.
Parent: LCD Publishing Holdings Limited
Officers: Joanne Sarah Trump, Secretary; Allen Trump [1948] Director

LDC (AIB Warehouse) Limited
Incorporated: 20 August 2003
Net Worth: £24,589,286 *Total Assets:* £75,635,024
Registered Office: South Quay, Temple Back, Bristol, BS1 6FL
Activities: Other letting and operating of own or leased real estate
Parent: LDC (Portfolio 100) Limited
Officers: Christopher Robert Szpojnarowicz, Secretary; David Faulkner [1976] Director/Deputy CFO; Joseph Julian Lister [1971] Managing Director; Richard Sauvan Smith [1974] Managing Director Operations; Christopher Robert Szpojnarowicz [1968] Director/Company Secretary/Head of Legal

LDC (Alscot Road) Ltd
Incorporated: 21 March 2007
Net Worth: £5,521,276 *Total Assets:* £13,929,757
Registered Office: South Quay, Temple Back, Bristol, BS1 6FL
Activities: Other letting and operating of own or leased real estate
Parent: LDC (Portfolio 100) Limited
Officers: Christopher Robert Szpojnarowicz, Secretary; David Faulkner [1976] Director/Deputy CFO; Joseph Julian Lister [1971] Director/Chief Financial Officer; Richard Sauvan Smith [1974] Managing Director Operations; Christopher Robert Szpojnarowicz [1968] Director/Company Secretary/Head of Legal

LDC (Brunel House) Limited
Incorporated: 3 September 2015
Net Worth: £5,167,118 *Total Assets:* £19,400,000
Registered Office: South Quay, Temple Back, Bristol, BS1 6FL
Activities: Other letting and operating of own or leased real estate
Parent: LDC (Holdings) Limited
Officers: Christopher Robert Szpojnarowicz, Secretary; David Faulkner [1976] Director/Deputy CFO; Nicholas William John Hayes [1981] Development Director; Joseph Julian Lister [1971] Director/Chief Financial Officer; Christopher Robert Szpojnarowicz [1968] Director/Head of Legal and Company Secretary

LDC (Causewayend) Limited
Incorporated: 14 February 2014
Net Worth: £5,203,797 *Total Assets:* £35,624,928
Registered Office: South Quay, Temple Back, Bristol, BS1 6FL
Activities: Other letting and operating of own or leased real estate
Parent: LDC (Finance) Limited
Officers: Christopher Robert Szpojnarowicz, Secretary; David Faulkner [1976] Director/Deputy CFO; Nicholas William John Hayes [1981] Development Director; Joseph Julian Lister [1971] Director/Chief Financial Officer; Christopher Robert Szpojnarowicz [1968] Director/Head of Legal and Company Secretary

LDC (Chaucer House) Limited
Incorporated: 2 December 2015
Net Worth: £3,958,889 *Total Assets:* £27,000,000
Registered Office: South Quay, Temple Back, Bristol, BS1 6FL
Activities: Other letting and operating of own or leased real estate
Parent: LDC (Holdings) Limited
Officers: Christopher Robert Szpojnarowicz, Secretary; David Faulkner [1976] Director/Deputy CFO; Nicholas William John Hayes [1981] Development Director; Joseph Julian Lister [1971] Director/Chief Financial Officer; Christopher Robert Szpojnarowicz [1968] Director/Head of Legal and Company Secretary

LDC (Constitution Street) Limited
Incorporated: 10 September 2014
Net Worth: £5,251,413 *Total Assets:* £11,727,715
Registered Office: South Quay, Temple Back, Bristol, BS1 6FL
Activities: Other letting and operating of own or leased real estate
Parent: LDC (Holdings) Limited
Officers: Christopher Robert Szpojnarowicz, Secretary; David Faulkner [1976] Director/Deputy CFO; Nicholas William John Hayes [1981] Development Director; Joseph Julian Lister [1971] Director/Chief Financial Officer; Christopher Robert Szpojnarowicz [1968] Director/Head of Legal and Company Secretary

LDC (Finance) Limited
Incorporated: 3 September 2015
Net Worth: £60,718,304 *Total Assets:* £417,388,768
Registered Office: South Quay, Temple Back, Bristol, BS1 6FL
Activities: Letting and operating of conference and exhibition centres
Parent: LDC (Holdings) Limited
Officers: Christopher Robert Szpojnarowicz, Secretary; David Faulkner [1976] Director/Deputy CFO; Nicholas William John Hayes [1981] Development Director; Joseph Julian Lister [1971] Director/Chief Financial Officer; Christopher Robert Szpojnarowicz [1968] Director/Head of Legal and Company Secretary

LDC (Greetham Street) Limited
Incorporated: 14 February 2014
Net Worth: £12,825,964 *Total Assets:* £15,398,947
Registered Office: South Quay, Temple Back, Bristol, BS1 6FL
Activities: Other letting and operating of own or leased real estate
Parent: LDC (Finance) Limited
Officers: Christopher Robert Szpojnarowicz, Secretary; David Faulkner [1976] Director/Deputy CFO; Nicholas William John Hayes [1981] Development Director; Joseph Julian Lister [1971] Director/Chief Financial Officer; Christopher Robert Szpojnarowicz [1968] Director/Head of Legal and Company Secretary

LDC (Holdings) Limited
Incorporated: 28 June 1991
Previous: LDC (Holdings) PLC
Net Worth: £794,384,000 *Total Assets:* £2,160,669,952
Registered Office: South Quay, Temple Back, Bristol, BS1 6FL
Activities: Other letting and operating of own or leased real estate
Parent: The Unite Group PLC
Officers: Christopher Robert Szpojnarowicz, Secretary; David Faulkner [1976] Director/Deputy CFO; Nicholas William John Hayes [1981] Development Director; Joseph Julian Lister [1971] Managing Director; Richard Sauvan Smith [1974] Managing Director; Christopher Robert Szpojnarowicz [1968] Director/Company Secretary/Head of Legal

LDC (Imperial Wharf) Limited
Incorporated: 20 September 2002
Net Worth: £77,235,240 *Total Assets:* £137,704,560
Registered Office: South Quay, Temple Back, Bristol, BS1 6FL
Activities: Other letting and operating of own or leased real estate
Parent: LDC (Holdings) Limited
Officers: Christopher Robert Szpojnarowicz, Secretary; David Faulkner [1976] Director/Deputy CFO; Joseph Julian Lister [1971] Managing Director; Christopher Robert Szpojnarowicz [1968] Director/Company Secretary/Head of Legal

LDC (Loughborough) Limited
Incorporated: 27 April 2001
Net Worth: £10,227,443 *Total Assets:* £17,600,092
Registered Office: South Quay, Temple Back, Bristol, BS1 6FL
Activities: Other letting and operating of own or leased real estate
Parent: LDC (Holdings) Limited
Officers: Christopher Robert Szpojnarowicz, Secretary; David Faulkner [1976] Director/Deputy CFO; Joseph Julian Lister [1971] Director/Chief Financial Officer; Christopher Robert Szpojnarowicz [1968] Director/Head of Legal and Company Secretary

LDC (Millennium View) Limited
Incorporated: 26 November 2015
Net Worth: £11,474,043 *Total Assets:* £36,509,656
Registered Office: South Quay, Temple Back, Bristol, BS1 6FL
Activities: Other letting and operating of own or leased real estate
Parent: LDC (Finance) Limited
Officers: Christopher Robert Szpojnarowicz, Secretary; David Faulkner [1976] Director/Deputy CFO; Nicholas William John Hayes [1981] Development Director; Joseph Julian Lister [1971] Director/Chief Financial Officer; Richard Sauvan Smith [1974] Managing Director, Operations; Christopher Robert Szpojnarowicz [1968] Director/Head of Legal and Company Secretary

LDC (MTF Portfolio) Limited
Incorporated: 8 August 2005
Net Worth: £30,452,050 *Total Assets:* £97,299,336
Registered Office: South Quay, Temple Back, Bristol, BS1 6FL
Activities: Other letting and operating of own or leased real estate
Parent: LDC (Portfolio 20) Limited
Officers: Christopher Robert Szpojnarowicz, Secretary; David Faulkner [1976] Director/Deputy CFO; Joseph Julian Lister [1971] Managing Director; Christopher Robert Szpojnarowicz [1968] Director/Company Secretary/Head of Legal

LDC (New Wakefield Street) Limited
Incorporated: 19 October 2016
Net Worth: £10,857,720 *Total Assets:* £21,300,000
Registered Office: South Quay, Temple Back, Bristol, BS1 6FL
Activities: Other letting and operating of own or leased real estate
Parent: LDC (Holdings) Limited
Officers: David Faulkner [1976] Director/Deputy CFO; Nicholas William John Hayes [1981] Development Director; Christopher Robert Szpojnarowicz [1968] Director/Head of Legal and Company Secretary

LDC (Old Hospital) Limited
Incorporated: 24 July 2015
Net Worth: £3,648,386 *Total Assets:* £17,200,000
Registered Office: South Quay, Temple Back, Bristol, BS1 6FL
Activities: Other letting and operating of own or leased real estate
Parent: LDC (Holdings) Limited
Officers: Christopher Robert Szpojnarowicz, Secretary; David Faulkner [1976] Director/Deputy CFO; Nicholas William John Hayes [1981] Development Director; Joseph Julian Lister [1971] Director/Chief Financial Officer; Christopher Robert Szpojnarowicz [1968] Director/Head of Legal and Company Secretary

LDC (Portfolio 100) Limited
Incorporated: 14 March 2012
Net Worth: £56,347,232 *Total Assets:* £309,812,928
Registered Office: South Quay, Temple Back, Bristol, BS1 6FL
Activities: Other letting and operating of own or leased real estate
Parent: LDC (Holdings) Limited
Officers: Christopher Robert Szpojnarowicz, Secretary; David Faulkner [1976] Director/Deputy CFO; Joseph Julian Lister [1971] Director/Chief Financial Officer; Richard Sauvan Smith [1974] Managing Director - Operations; Christopher Robert Szpojnarowicz [1968] Director/Company Secretary/Head of Legal

LDC (Portfolio 20) Limited
Incorporated: 5 December 2013
Net Worth: £39,686,416 *Total Assets:* £259,535,072
Registered Office: South Quay, Temple Back, Bristol, BS1 6FL
Activities: Other letting and operating of own or leased real estate
Parent: LDC (Holdings) Limited
Officers: Christopher Robert Szpojnarowicz, Secretary; David Faulkner [1976] Director/Deputy CFO; Joseph Julian Lister [1971] Director/Chief Financial Officer; Christopher Robert Szpojnarowicz [1968] Director/Head of Legal & Company Secretary

LDC (Portfolio Five) Limited
Incorporated: 2 February 2007
Net Worth: £30,946,902 *Total Assets:* £120,304,240
Registered Office: South Quay, Temple Back, Bristol, BS1 6FL
Activities: Other letting and operating of own or leased real estate
Parent: LDC (Holdings) Limited
Officers: Christopher Robert Szpojnarowicz, Secretary; David Faulkner [1976] Director/Deputy CFO; Christopher Robert Szpojnarowicz [1968] Director/Company Secretary/Head of Legal

LDC (Portfolio Four) Limited
Incorporated: 5 December 2003
Net Worth: £25,761,940 *Total Assets:* £27,577,348
Registered Office: South Quay, Temple Back, Bristol, BS1 6FL
Activities: Other letting and operating of own or leased real estate
Parent: LDC (Portfolio 100) Limited
Officers: Christopher Robert Szpojnarowicz, Secretary; David Faulkner [1976] Director/Deputy CFO; Joseph Julian Lister [1971] Managing Director; Richard Sauvan Smith [1974] Managing Director Operations; Christopher Robert Szpojnarowicz [1968] Director/Company Secretary/Head of Legal

LDC (Portfolio One) Limited
Incorporated: 3 January 1995
Net Worth: £30,794,852 *Total Assets:* £139,830,880
Registered Office: South Quay, Temple Back, Bristol, BS1 6FL
Activities: Other letting and operating of own or leased real estate
Parent: LDC (Portfolio 100) Limited
Officers: Christopher Robert Szpojnarowicz, Secretary; David Faulkner [1976] Director/Deputy CFO; Joseph Julian Lister [1971] Managing Director; Richard Sauvan Smith [1974] Managing Director Operations; Christopher Robert Szpojnarowicz [1968] Director/Company Secretary/Head of Legal

LDC (Portfolio) Limited
Incorporated: 26 February 2013
Previous: LDC (Trenchard Street) Limited
Net Worth: £65,760,372 *Total Assets:* £316,283,520
Registered Office: South Quay, Temple Back, Bristol, BS1 6FL
Activities: Other letting and operating of own or leased real estate
Parent: LDC (Finance) Limited
Officers: Christopher Robert Szpojnarowicz, Secretary; David Faulkner [1976] Director/Deputy CFO; Nicholas William John Hayes [1981] Development Director; Joseph Julian Lister [1971] Director/Chief Financial Officer; Christopher Robert Szpojnarowicz [1968] Director/Company Secretary/Head of Legal

LDC (Project 110) Limited
Incorporated: 24 March 2004
Net Worth: £26,108,968 *Total Assets:* £98,122,616
Registered Office: South Quay, Temple Back, Bristol, BS1 6FL
Activities: Other letting and operating of own or leased real estate
Parent: LDC (Portfolio 20) Limited
Officers: Christopher Robert Szpojnarowicz, Secretary; David Faulkner [1976] Director/Deputy CFO; Joseph Julian Lister [1971] Managing Director; Richard Sauvan Smith [1974] Managing Director, Operations

LDC (Project 111) Limited
Incorporated: 24 April 2006
Net Worth: £3,208,799 *Total Assets:* £19,551,686
Registered Office: South Quay, Temple Back, Bristol, BS1 6FL
Activities: Other letting and operating of own or leased real estate
Parent: LDC (Project 110) Limited
Officers: Christopher Robert Szpojnarowicz, Secretary; David Faulkner [1976] Director/Deputy CFO; Joseph Julian Lister [1971] Managing Director; Christopher Robert Szpojnarowicz [1968] Director/Head of Legal and Company Secretary

LDC (Radmarsh Road) Limited
Incorporated: 26 April 2005
Net Worth: £5,619,083 *Total Assets:* £20,910,992
Registered Office: South Quay, Temple Back, Bristol, BS1 6FL
Activities: Other letting and operating of own or leased real estate
Parent: LDC (Portfolio 100) Limited
Officers: Christopher Robert Szpojnarowicz, Secretary; David Faulkner [1976] Director/Deputy CFO; Nicholas William John Hayes [1981] Development Director; Joseph Julian Lister [1971] Director/Chief Financial Officer; Richard Sauvan Smith [1974] Managing Director Operations; Christopher Robert Szpojnarowicz [1968] Director/Company Secretary/Head of Legal

LDC (Skelhorne) Limited
Incorporated: 2 December 2015
Net Worth: £8,552,372 *Total Assets:* £34,500,000
Registered Office: South Quay, Temple Back, Bristol, BS1 6FL
Activities: Other letting and operating of own or leased real estate
Parent: LDC (Holdings) Limited
Officers: Christopher Robert Szpojnarowicz, Secretary; David Faulkner [1976] Director/Deputy CFO; Nicholas William John Hayes [1981] Development Director; Joseph Julian Lister [1971] Director/Chief Financial Officer; Christopher Robert Szpojnarowicz [1968] Director/Head of Legal and Company Secretary

LDC (Tara House) Limited
Incorporated: 11 September 2014
Net Worth: £19,921,512 *Total Assets:* £68,486,912
Registered Office: South Quay, Temple Back, Bristol, BS1 6FL
Activities: Other letting and operating of own or leased real estate
Parent: LDC (Holdings) Limited
Officers: Christopher Robert Szpojnarowicz, Secretary; David Faulkner [1976] Director/Deputy CFO; Nicholas William John Hayes [1981] Development Director; Joseph Julian Lister [1971] Director/Chief Financial Officer; Christopher Robert Szpojnarowicz [1968] Director/Head of Legal and Company Secretary

LDC (William Morris II) Limited
Incorporated: 15 November 2006
Net Worth Deficit: £910,674 *Total Assets:* £15,954,671
Registered Office: South Quay, Temple Back, Bristol, BS1 6FL
Activities: Other letting and operating of own or leased real estate
Parent: LDC (Portfolio 100) Limited
Officers: Christopher Robert Szpojnarowicz, Secretary; David Faulkner [1976] Director/Deputy CFO; Joseph Julian Lister [1971] Director/Chief Financial Officer; Richard Sauvan Smith [1974] Managing Director Operations; Christopher Robert Szpojnarowicz [1968] Director/Company Secretary/Head of Legal

Le Creuset U.K. Limited
Incorporated: 17 August 1948 *Employees:* 269
Net Worth: £18,512,000 *Total Assets:* £26,906,000
Registered Office: Le Creuset House, 83 Livingstone Road, Walworth Industrial Estate, Andover, Hants, SP10 5QZ
Activities: Wholesale of household goods (other than musical instruments) n.e.c
Officers: Mark Justin Mearns, Secretary; Nick Andrew Ryder [1961] Managing Director; Michael Frans Scheepers [1978] Commercial Director [Dutch]; Luc Torre [1956] Director [Belgian]

Leading Edge Academies Partnership
Incorporated: 3 June 2011 *Employees:* 121
Previous: Mounts Bay Academy
Net Worth: £9,048,209 *Total Assets:* £10,362,959
Registered Office: Mounts Bay Academy, Boscathnoe Lane, Penzance, Cornwall, TR18 3JT
Activities: General secondary education
Officers: Helen Rodgers, Secretary; Sarah Lesley Alexander [1979] Director/Lecturer Team Leader; Sara Jane Davey [1960] Director/Headteacher; Jackie Anne Eason [1969] Director/Governor Consultant; Jeremy Field [1953] Director/Estate Agent; Caitilin Finch [1978] Director/Self Employed; Perran Russell Gay [1959] Director/Reverend Canon; Jane Osborne [1950] Director; Philip Roe [1950] Director/Retired; David Adrian Sharp [1953] Director/Self Employed; Robin Nicholas Webb [1960] Director/Self Employed

Leaf Academy
Incorporated: 29 March 2012 *Employees:* 253
Net Worth: £15,661,541 *Total Assets:* £21,387,824
Registered Office: Leaf Academy, Duck Lane, Bournemouth, BH11 9JJ
Activities: Pre-primary education
Officers: Tanya Tracey Hall, Secretary; Beryl Baxter [1956] Director/Councillor; Brendan Oliver Booth [1980] Director; Edward George Craven [1942] Director/Retired; Samuel Robert Ellis [1979] Director/Accountant; John Godber [1951] Director/Retired; Adam Aristos Ruddle [1985] Director/Actuary; Edward James Taylor [1937] Director/Retired

Leafield Logistics & Technical Services Limited
Incorporated: 18 January 2008 *Employees:* 32
Net Worth: £4,545,000 *Total Assets:* £6,339,000
Registered Office: Lea Park, Monks Lane, Corsham, Wilts, SN13 9PH
Activities: Repair of other equipment
Officers: David Christopher Harbord [1961] Director/Chartered Accountant; Mark Edward Thistlethwayte [1964] Director; Jonathan Philip Mark Webster [1959] Managing Director

Leander Developments Limited
Incorporated: 20 March 1990 *Employees:* 7
Net Worth: £720,247 *Total Assets:* £3,621,884
Registered Office: Stratus House, Emperor Way, Exeter Business Park, Exeter, Devon, EX1 3QS
Activities: Development of building projects
Shareholders: Nicola Ann Louise Knapp; William Samuel Knapp
Officers: Jane Andrea Knapp [1946] Director; Nicola Ann Louise Knapp [1974] Director; Terence Vivian Knapp [1946] Director; William Samuel Knapp [1974] Managing Director

Lear, Browne & Dunsford Limited
Incorporated: 9 July 1973 *Employees:* 27
Net Worth: £1,794,335 *Total Assets:* £4,362,427
Registered Office: LBD House, Waterbridge Court, Matford Park Road, Exeter, EX2 8ED
Activities: Wholesale of textiles
Officers: Peter James Dunsford, Secretary; James Oliver Dunsford [1967] Director/Woollen Merchant; Mark Richard James Dunsford [1968] Director/Woollen Merchant; Peter James Dunsford [1944] Director/Woollen Merchant; Richard Dunsford [1939] Director/Woollen Merchant; Steven Paul Howard [1971] Finance Director

Learning Academies Trust
Incorporated: 19 July 2016 *Employees:* 407
Net Worth: £21,464,872 *Total Assets:* £26,861,256
Registered Office: Prince Rock Primary School, Embankment Road, Plymouth, PL4 9JF
Activities: Primary education
Officers: Kay Anita Mabin, Secretary; Carol Ann Bull [1946] Director/Retired; Jonathan Carlyle Bushby [1961] Director/Operations Manager; John James Butcher [1959] Director/Education Lecturer; Stuart Edwards [1976] Director/Solicitor; Claire Marie Fortey [1965] Director of Education; Adrian Charles King [1952] Director/Chartered Surveyor; Ciara Eve Moran [1971] Director/Headteacher; Warren O'Reilly [1975] Director/Private Hire Driver; Simon Peter Spry [1966] Director/Executive Headteacher; Ruth Woodhouse [1985] Director Plymouth Teaching School Alliance

Learning Academy Partnership (South West)
Incorporated: 21 July 2011 *Employees:* 224
Net Worth: £824,000 *Total Assets:* £3,553,000
Registered Office: Suite 4, Zealley House, Greenhill Way, Kingsteignton, Newton Abbot, Devon, TQ12 3SB
Activities: Primary education
Officers: Lynn Atkinson [1961] Director/Headteacher; Philip Kenneth Dean [1956] Finance Director; Dr Mark Graves [1969] Director/Tax Consultant; Ryan Hewitt [1978] Director/HR Consultant; Reverend Paul Ireton [1965] Director/Priest in Charge; Dr Jan Myles [1943] Director/Education Consultant; Richard Owen Vaughton [1956] Managing Director

The Learning Academy Trust
Incorporated: 1 October 2010 *Employees:* 325
Previous: Trenance Learning Academy
Net Worth: £13,302,065 *Total Assets:* £16,304,629
Registered Office: Trenance Learning Academy, Trenance Road, Newquay, Cornwall, TR7 2LU
Activities: Primary education
Officers: Clare Ridehalgh, Secretary; Gaynor Shepherd, Secretary; Michael John Andrews [1965] Director/Nursery Teacher/Owner; Robin Henry Noel Cowen [1958] Director; Kathleen Mary Crosse [1946] Director/Retired; Dr Patrick Joseph McGovern [1952] Director/Education Consultant; Susan Wendy Tym [1960] Director/Tour Operator; Paul Robert Wyatt [1946] Director/Consultant HR

Leckhampton Dairies Limited
Incorporated: 5 May 1958 *Employees:* 4
Net Worth: £3,350,312 *Total Assets:* £3,625,861
Registered Office: Church Farm, Leckhampton, Cheltenham, Glos, GL53 0QJ
Activities: Other letting and operating of own or leased real estate
Shareholder: Anne Henrietta Bernice Hicks
Officers: Jeremy William Hicks, Secretary; Anne Henrietta Bernice Hicks [1929] Director; Jeremy William Hicks [1952] Director/Solicitor; Jonathan Simon Hicks [1954] Director/Haulage Contractor; Timothy James Hicks [1955] Director/Property Developer

Leckhampton Estates (Ullenwood) Limited
Incorporated: 19 May 2014 *Employees:* 1
Previous: William Morrison (Ullenwood) Limited
Net Worth Deficit: £2,557,692 *Total Assets:* £6,863,092
Registered Office: Pillar House, 113-115 Bath Road, Cheltenham, Glos, GL53 7LS
Activities: Development of building projects
Major Shareholder: William Victor Peter Bullingham
Officers: William Victor Peter Bullingham [1943] Director

Ledex Limited
Incorporated: 4 May 2012 *Employees:* 13
Net Worth: £1,784,728 *Total Assets:* £9,554,226
Registered Office: Unit 17-20 Brickfields Business Park, Gillingham, Dorset, SP8 4PX
Activities: Manufacture of electric lighting equipment
Parent: Dextra Group PLC
Officers: Rupert Henry James Martin, Secretary; Keith John Brownhill [1961] Director/Group CEO; Janie Claire Martin [1962] Director/Group Company Secretary; Rupert Henry James Martin [1949] Director/Group Chairman; Darren Ward [1970] Group Technical Director

Lee Abbey Fellowship
Incorporated: 1 May 2002 *Employees:* 94
Net Worth: £5,441,862 *Total Assets:* £5,862,314
Registered Office: Lee Abbey, Lynton, Devon, EX35 6JJ
Activities: Activities of religious organisations
Officers: Magnus Proctor, Secretary; Mark Trevor Beedell [1956] Director/Diocesan Secretary; Graham Robert Cappleman [1956] Director/Minister; Revd Simon Charles Farrar [1956] Director/Baptist Minister; The Reverend Selina Clare Garner [1969] Director/Vicar and Youth Minister; Julia Laurel Hocking [1960] Director; Adrian Christopher Male [1959] Director; Rachel Oates [1974] Director; Magnus Proctor [1959] Director/Accountant; Revd David Charles Roland Widdows [1952] Director/Retired

Lee Abbey International Students' Club
Incorporated: 19 June 1963 *Employees:* 35
Net Worth: £4,757,073 *Total Assets:* £7,181,825
Registered Office: Lee Abbey, Lynton, Devon, EX35 6JJ
Activities: Activities of religious organisations
Officers: Magnus Proctor, Secretary; Graham Robert Cappleman [1956] Director/Minister; Emma Claire Holland [1991] Director/Producer; Revd Canon Yemi Ladipo [1937] Director/Vicar Retired [Nigerian]; Fiona Elizabeth Nouri [1962] Director/Student Support Officer; Prof Alexander Anthony Pepper [1958] Director/University Lecturer; Revd Dr Lynda Brigid Taylor [1954] Director

The Lee Abbey Movement
Incorporated: 1 May 2002 *Employees:* 121
Net Worth: £10,771,998 *Total Assets:* £14,476,972
Registered Office: Lee Abbey, Lynton, Devon, EX35 6JJ
Activities: Activities of religious organisations
Officers: Magnus Proctor, Secretary; Sister Sue Patricia Berry [1949] Director/Religious Sister and Anglican Priest; Graham Robert Cappleman [1956] Director/Minister; Revd James Keith Stuart Denniston [1949] Director/Clergyman; Susan Margaret Edmondson [1952] Director; Margaret Anne Paul [1963] Director/GP; Prof Alexander Anthony Pepper [1958] Director/University Lecturer; Reverend John Harold Simmons [1946] Director/Minister of Religion; Revd Dr Lynda Brigid Taylor [1954] Director/Retired; Stephen Adrian Weatherley [1945] Director/Consultant; Revd David Charles Roland Widdows [1952] Director/Retired

Leehurst Swan Limited
Incorporated: 19 October 1988 *Employees:* 45
Net Worth: £3,099,658 *Total Assets:* £5,319,927
Registered Office: 19 Campbell Road, Salisbury, Wilts, SP1 3BG
Activities: General secondary education
Officers: Julie Ann Bromilow, Secretary; Douglas James Gale [1959] Director/Engineer; Penny Joyce [1953] Director/Retired; Ian David McDonald [1950] Director/Retired Police Officer; Gamze Duygu Riley [1969] Director/Architectural Technician; Stephen James Spicer [1967] Director/Consultant; Richard John Thorp [1954] Director/Retired; Jonathan Paul Wansey [1953] Director/Retired; Victoria Faye Zissis [1978] Director/Airline Business

Leeways Packaging Services Limited
Incorporated: 11 November 1971 *Employees:* 82
Net Worth: £8,600,844 *Total Assets:* £15,027,546
Registered Office: Lobstock, Churcham, Gloucester, GL2 8AN
Activities: Manufacture of plastic packing goods
Parent: Leeways Holdings Limited
Officers: Lynne Walding, Secretary; Adam James Walding [1984] Director; Anthony Trevor George Walding [1956] Director; Lee Anthony Trevor Walding [1982] Director; Lynne Walding [1958] Director

Legacy Properties Limited
Incorporated: 14 June 1993 *Employees:* 6
Net Worth Deficit: £252,415 *Total Assets:* £14,143,273
Registered Office: Unit 2b Quintdown Business Park, West Road, Quintrell Downs, Cornwall, TR8 4DS
Activities: Development of building projects
Major Shareholder: Peter James Long
Officers: Samantha Anne Williams, Secretary; Linda Long [1952] Director; Nicholas Robert Long [1986] Director

Legoland US Holdings Limited
Incorporated: 7 June 2007
Net Worth: £74,617,000 *Total Assets:* £78,511,000
Registered Office: Link House, 25 West Street, Poole, Dorset, BH15 1LD
Activities: Activities of head offices
Parent: Merlin US Holdings Limited
Officers: Fiona Jane Rose, Secretary; Matthew Paul Jowett [1967] Director/General Counsel and Company Secretary; Fiona Jane Rose [1964] Director/Assistant Group Company Secretary

Leicester BSF Company 1 Limited
Incorporated: 25 May 2007 *Employees:* 4
Net Worth Deficit: £7,846,020 *Total Assets:* £46,453,652
Registered Office: Third Floor, Broad Quay House, Prince Street, Bristol, BS1 4DJ
Activities: Construction of commercial buildings
Parent: Leicester BSF Holdings Company 1 Limited
Officers: David Robert Hardingham [1974] Director/Commercial Manager; Stephen Paul Hornby [1957] Director; Colin Lemmon [1964] Operations Director; Phillip James Thorne [1961] Director

Leicester BSF Company 2 Limited
Incorporated: 21 July 2011
Net Worth: £142,059 *Total Assets:* £46,106,692
Registered Office: Third Floor, Broad Quay House, Prince Street, Bristol, BS1 4DJ
Activities: Construction of commercial buildings
Parent: Leicester BSF Holdings Company 2 Limited
Officers: David Robert Hardingham [1974] Director/Commercial Manager; Stephen Paul Hornby [1957] Director; Colin Lemmon [1964] Operations Director; Phillip James Thorne [1961] Director

Leicester BSF Holdings Company 1 Limited
Incorporated: 25 May 2007 *Employees:* 4
Net Worth: £100,000 *Total Assets:* £4,365,397
Registered Office: Third Floor, Broad Quay House, Prince Street, Bristol, BS1 4DJ
Activities: Development of building projects
Parent: Semperian Leicester PSP Limited
Officers: David Robert Hardingham [1974] Director/Commercial Manager; Stephen Paul Hornby [1957] Director; Colin Lemmon [1964] Operations Director; Phillip James Thorne [1961] Director

Leicester BSF Holdings Company 2 Limited
Incorporated: 21 July 2011 *Employees:* 4
Net Worth: £50,000 *Total Assets:* £4,113,763
Registered Office: Third Floor, Broad Quay House, Prince Street, Bristol, BS1 4DJ
Activities: Development of building projects
Parent: Semperian Leicester PSP Limited
Officers: David Robert Hardingham [1974] Director/Commercial Manager; Stephen Paul Hornby [1957] Director; Colin Lemmon [1964] Operations Director; Phillip James Thorne [1961] Director

Leidos Europe, Limited
Incorporated: 11 December 2014 *Employees:* 163
Net Worth: £10,852,000 *Total Assets:* £65,587,000
Registered Office: 8 Monarch Court, The Brooms, Emersons Green, Bristol, BS16 7FH
Activities: Other transportation support activities
Parent: Leidos Inc
Officers: Brendan Bernard Turley, Secretary; Angela Jayne Crabtree [1974] Director; Angela L Heise [1974] Director/Business Executive [American]; Graham Moore [1964] Director/Financial Executive; Matthew John Gethin Wiles [1961] Managing Director

Leighton-Boyce Properties Ltd.
Incorporated: 21 April 1999 *Employees:* 3
Net Worth: £2,824,723 *Total Assets:* £4,073,953
Registered Office: Mosaic House, 23a Northview Road, Budleigh Salteron, Devon, EX9 6DD
Activities: Other business support service activities n.e.c.
Shareholder: Oliver Stuart Leighton-Boyce
Officers: Oliver Stuart Leighton Boyce, Secretary; Oliver Stuart Leighton Boyce [1954] Director; Susan Rosemary Leighton Boyce [1956] Director

Lemaca Limited
Incorporated: 29 October 1999 *Employees:* 1,272
Net Worth: £2,004,243 *Total Assets:* £11,930,929
Registered Office: Aldreth, Pearcroft Road, Stonehouse, Glos, GL10 2JY
Activities: Take-away food shops and mobile food stands
Major Shareholder: Edward Christopher Leligdowicz
Officers: Edward Christopher Leligdowicz [1961] Director/Restaurateur

Leo Textiles Limited
Incorporated: 27 March 1981 *Employees:* 40
Net Worth: £4,975,160 *Total Assets:* £7,488,559
Registered Office: 1 Whiddon Drive, Barnstaple, Devon, EX32 8RY
Activities: Manufacture of workwear
Major Shareholder: Peter John Turner
Officers: Peter John Turner, Secretary; Linda Turner [1960] Director/Administrator [American]; Peter John Turner [1960] Managing Director

Leoni Temco Limited
Incorporated: 2 May 1947 *Employees:* 67
Net Worth: £2,988,000 *Total Assets:* £8,339,000
Registered Office: Whimsey Industrial Estate, Cinderford, Glos, GL14 3HZ
Activities: Other manufacturing n.e.c.
Parent: Leoni AG
Officers: Kerris Merab Beverley Merkitt, Secretary; Brian Paul Cutts [1971] Managing Director; Dr Alf-Joachim Harkort [1959] Senior Vice President, Managing Director [German]

Lester Aldridge LLP
Incorporated: 1 August 2006 *Employees:* 318
Net Worth: £9,030,203 *Total Assets:* £14,242,265
Registered Office: Russell House, Oxford Road, Bournemouth, BH8 8EX
Officers: Matthew Barrow [1975] Member; Susan Edwina Cowan [1959] Member; Grant Andrew Esterhuizen [1971] Member; Ann Lloyd [1976] Member; Roger Derek Woolley [1957] Member; Stephanie Louise Adams [1985] LLP Member; Thomas Charles Elliott Alder [1982] LLP Member; Paula Helen Barnes [1962] LLP Member; Kevin Barnett [1972] LLP Member; Mark Benham [1976] LLP Member; Timothy Mark Blackwell [1962] LLP Member; Laura Ann Burgess [1983] LLP Member; Joanne Elizabeth Clarke [1976] LLP Member; Martin Coward [1959] LLP Member; Claire Louise Egerton [1980] LLP Member; Christopher Paul Evans [1980] LLP Member; Richard Michael Fairbairn [1952] LLP Member; Edward Foster [1963] LLP Member; Louise Fuller [1974] LLP Member; Catharine Emma Geddes [1977] LLP Member; Peter Alan Grose [1953] LLP Member; Laura Elizabeth Guntrip [1983] LLP Member; Linda Jacques [1964] LLP Member; Victoria Jones [1973] LLP Member; Nicholas John Robert Keitley [1961] LLP Member; William George Russell Kelly [1960] LLP Member; Kurt Robert Lee [1976] LLP Member; Danielle Rebecca Montezuma [1984] LLP Member; Guy William Morgan [1968] LLP Member; Oliver Charles Phipps [1985] LLP Member; Jane Elizabeth Helen Porter [1959] LLP Member; Catherine Louise Rawles [1975] LLP Member; Suki Samra [1974] LLP Member; Rosemary Leigh Sharp [1986] LLP Member; Paula Maria Shea [1979] LLP Member; Lucy Ann Stevens [1984] LLP Member; Kate Stewart [1975] LLP Member; Simon Nicholas Stone [1948] LLP Member; Nicola Frances Sutton [1973] LLP Member; Karen Elizabeth Thompson [1959] LLP Member; Geoffrey Charles Trobridge [1955] LLP Member; Michael Richard Veal [1977] LLP Member; Lindsey Jane Watkin [1959] LLP Member; Erika Willmott [1980] LLP Member

Lester Brunt Partnership LLP
Incorporated: 19 March 2013 *Employees:* 10
Total Assets: £3,517,022
Registered Office: 7 & 8 Church Street, Wimborne, Dorset, BH21 1JH
Officers: Martin Gareth Brunt [1962] Member; Michael Stephen Lester [1953] Member

Lester Brunt Wealth Management Ltd
Incorporated: 20 September 2017 *Employees:* 13
Net Worth: £1,627 *Total Assets:* £6,585,466
Registered Office: 7 & 8 Church Street, Wimborne, Dorset, BH21 1JH
Activities: Financial management
Officers: Martin Gareth Brunt [1962] Director; Michael Stephen Lester [1953] Director

Lethbridge Primary School
Incorporated: 28 June 2011 *Employees:* 96
Net Worth: £3,520,448 *Total Assets:* £4,004,199
Registered Office: Lethbridge Primary School, Lethbridge Road, Swindon, Wilts, SN1 4BY
Activities: Primary education
Officers: Philip Roy Ashdown [1964] Director/Accountant; Terasa Joanne Beach [1971] Director; Carly Anne Chew [1989] Director/Teacher; Laura Crosby [1979] Director/IT Manager; Alexia Anne Davison [1982] Director/Teacher; Jonathan Robert Dearlove [1972] Director/Solicitor; Simone Louise Franklin [1967] Director/Training and Development Consultant; Claire Elizabeth Harmer [1967] Director/Deputy Head; Christopher Andrew Hobson [1971] Director/Electronics Engineer; Hayley Marie Jackson [1980] Director/Regional Events & Fundraising Officer; Damien John Mackman [1981] Director/Accountant; Arlene-Jane Kathy MacLaughlin [1979] Director/Corporate Banker; Lisa Joanne Mayes [1974] Director/Teacher; Nataley Maysey [1982] Director/Senior Account Manager; Doctor Kristina Mussgnug Barrett [1977] Director [German]; Annette Jane Shakespeare [1969] Director/Teacher; Caron Jayne Short [1968] Director/Teacher; Laura Anne Smith [1980] Director/Project/Change Leader; Fiona Claire Wall [1979] Director/Account Manager; Christopher Edward Webb [1987] Director/ICT Manager

The Levels Academy Trust
Incorporated: 12 February 2015 *Employees:* 103
Net Worth: £4,055,426 *Total Assets:* £5,133,883
Registered Office: Huish Episcopi Primary School, North Street, Langport, Somerset, TA10 9RW
Activities: Primary education
Officers: Heather Louise Barraclough [1973] Director/Executive Principal; Peter Henry Brandt [1965] Director/Assistant Chief Probation Officer; Martyn Canon [1973] Director/Policeman; Ros Fanshawe [1962] Director/Project Officer for Early Years; Andrew Mark Jackson [1963] Director/Teacher; Louise Ward [1978] Director/Team Leader, Social Worker

Levitt UK Real Estate Limited
Incorporated: 16 January 2010 *Employees:* 1
Net Worth: £69,111,448 *Total Assets:* £69,594,592
Registered Office: First Floor, 10 Temple Back, Bristol, BS1 6FL
Activities: Development of building projects
Major Shareholder: Jose Ramon Moras Vicente
Officers: Jason Antony Reader [1972] Director

Leweston School Trust
Incorporated: 28 July 1986 *Employees:* 131
Net Worth: £2,460,288 *Total Assets:* £5,932,230
Registered Office: Leweston School, Sherborne, Dorset, DT9 6EN
Activities: Pre-primary education
Officers: Paul Augustus Scott-Masson, Secretary; Dr Nicholas Charles George Bathurst [1954] Director/Doctor; Reverend Mark Richard Brown [1963] Director/Clergyman; Charles Lewis Comyn [1952] Director/Retired; Christopher Paul Fenton [1951] Director/Lawyer; Sarah Lucinda Gordon Wild [1959] Director/Retired Money Manager; Dermot Robert Lyndon McKechnie [1961] Director/Financial Consultant; Ian Stanton [1961] Director/Army Officer; Hugh Tatham [1974] Director/Teacher

The Lewis-Manning Trust
Incorporated: 13 June 2007 *Employees:* 85
Net Worth: £2,942,258 *Total Assets:* £4,966,449
Registered Office: 1 Crichel Mount Road, Lilliput, Poole, Dorset, BH14 8LT
Activities: Other human health activities
Officers: Timothy Lee, Secretary; Jeremy Michael Allin [1951] Director/Solicitor; Steve Harris [1978] Director/Broadcaster; Timothy Lee [1945] Retired Marketing Director (IT Sector); Elizabeth Jane Lloyd [1952] Director/Priest; Ian Marshall [1947] Director/Chartered Accountant; Anthony Charles Roberts [1934] Director/Solicitor

Lewisia Limited
Incorporated: 20 December 1995 *Employees:* 9
Net Worth: £26,925,812 *Total Assets:* £34,569,852
Registered Office: East Park House, Iwerne Minster, Blandford, Dorset, DT11 8LA
Activities: Growing of cereals (except rice), leguminous crops and oil seeds
Shareholders: Suzanne Lever; Anthony John Hunt
Officers: Erica Fiona Baker [1964] Director/Personal Assistant; Anthony John Hunt [1954] Finance Director; Suzanne Lever [1968] Director

Lexicon Book Company Limited
Incorporated: 7 July 1936
Net Worth: £6,432,974 *Total Assets:* £8,728,319
Registered Office: c/o W H Smith PLC, Greenbridge Road, Swindon, Wilts, SN3 3RX
Activities: Non-trading company
Parent: WH Smith Retail Holdings Limited
Officers: Ian Houghton, Secretary; Ian Houghton [1965] Director/Company Executive; Robert James Moorhead [1964] Director

Leys Solar Energy C.I.C.
Incorporated: 26 June 2015
Previous: Stratford Community Energy CIC
Net Worth Deficit: £357,689 *Total Assets:* £5,853,451
Registered Office: Tremough Innovation Centre, Tremough Campus, Penryn, Cornwall, TR10 9TA
Activities: Production of electricity
Parent: Heart of England Community Energy Limited
Officers: Michael Jonathan Bullock [1962] Director; Thomas John Cosgrove [1981] Director/Development Manager; Stuart Frederick Potter [1954] Director/Retired

D C Li (Builders) Limited
Incorporated: 20 August 1987 *Employees:* 20
Net Worth: £2,475,638 *Total Assets:* £4,836,065
Registered Office: Yew Tree Farm, Goodworth Clatford, Andover, Hants, SP11 7QX
Activities: Construction of domestic buildings
Shareholders: Dique Conrad Li; Helen Li
Officers: Helen Li, Secretary; Dique Conrad Li [1951] Director/Builder; Helen Li [1951] Director/Retired

The Liberation Group UK Limited
Incorporated: 7 October 2014
Net Worth Deficit: £1,775,000 *Total Assets:* £18,641,000
Registered Office: Butcombe Brewery, Havyatt Road Trading Estate, Havyatt Road, Wrington, Bristol, BS40 5PA
Activities: Activities of head offices
Officers: Richard Stuart Grainger [1960] Director; Timothy Hubert [1962] Director; Nigel Richard Osborne [1966] Director

Liberty House (Nuneaton) Limited
Incorporated: 17 December 2007 *Employees:* 3
Net Worth: £959,611 *Total Assets:* £3,818,604
Registered Office: Springfield House, 45 Welsh Back, Bristol, BS1 4AG
Activities: Other letting and operating of own or leased real estate
Shareholder: Scott Matthew Davidson
Officers: Peter Derrick Savage, Secretary/Consultant; Scott Matthew Davidson [1963] Director; Alan Roger Hampton [1947] Director; Peter Derrick Savage [1952] Director/Consultant

Libra Homes Limited
Incorporated: 22 July 1996 *Employees:* 2
Net Worth: £9,028,650 *Total Assets:* £9,779,352
Registered Office: 3 Durrant Road, Bournemouth, BH2 6NE
Activities: Other service activities n.e.c.
Major Shareholder: Andrew John Rance
Officers: Jane Sarah Rance, Secretary; Andrew John Rance [1962] Director/Civil Engineer

Libra Investments Limited
Incorporated: 28 February 2013
Net Worth: £3,434,758 *Total Assets:* £3,693,723
Registered Office: Littlewood House, Jubilee Road, Totnes, Devon, TQ9 5BP
Activities: Management consultancy activities other than financial management
Major Shareholder: Richard Charles O'Connell
Officers: Richard Charles O'Connell [1949] Director; Samantha O'Connell [1983] Director; Sheila O'Connell [1951] Director/Retired

Librocube Limited
Incorporated: 28 June 2017
Net Worth: £5,105,927 *Total Assets:* £5,123,498
Registered Office: Lowin House, Tregolls Road, Truro, Cornwall, TR1 2NA
Activities: Non-trading company
Shareholders: Keith Martin Blount; Julia Alexandra Sara Pierce
Officers: Keith Martin Blount [1973] Director; Julia Alexandra Sara Pierce [1973] Director

Libya Oil Ethiopia Limited
Incorporated: 20 November 1929
Net Worth: £8,027,242 *Total Assets:* £69,999,696
Registered Office: Narrow Quay House, Narrow Quay, Bristol, BS1 4QA
Activities: Wholesale of other fuels and related products
Parent: Libyan Investment Authority
Officers: Elmarimi Ali Ali Kashim [1953] Director/Engineer [Libyan]; Omar Elfarok Samin [1956] Director/Engineer [Libyan]

Libya Oil Sudan Limited
Incorporated: 6 December 1924
Net Worth: £4,437,735 *Total Assets:* £11,016,275
Registered Office: Narrow Quay House, Narrow Quay, Bristol, BS1 4QA
Activities: Other business support service activities n.e.c.
Parent: Libyan Investment Authority
Officers: Elmarimi Ali Kashim [1953] Director/Engineer [Libyan]; Omar Elfarok Samin [1956] Director/Engineer [Libyan]

Lifetime Training Group Limited
Incorporated: 15 October 1996 *Employees:* 884
Net Worth: £45,269,668 *Total Assets:* £69,813,320
Registered Office: Clifton Heights, Triangle West, Bristol, BS8 1EJ
Activities: Other education n.e.c.
Parent: LVTG Ltd
Officers: Peter James Mitchell, Secretary; Alex Phillip Khan [1977] Director; Peter James Mitchell [1971] Director/Chartered Accountant

Light Group Limited
Incorporated: 19 August 2003
Net Worth: £3,454,286 *Total Assets:* £9,444,281
Registered Office: The Grange, Old Gloucester Road, Cheltenham, Glos, GL51 0TF
Activities: Recreational vehicle parks, trailer parks and camping grounds
Shareholders: David Frank Light; Maria Teresa Light
Officers: Maria Teresa Light, Secretary/Caravan Park Proprietor; David Frank Light [1958] Director/Caravan Park Proprietor; Maria Teresa Light [1957] Director/Caravan Park Proprietor

Lighthouse Property Estates Limited
Incorporated: 14 July 2006 *Employees:* 7
Net Worth: £3,094,914 *Total Assets:* £4,007,161
Registered Office: The Lighthouse, Tytherington, Frome, Somerset, BA11 5BW
Activities: Hotels and similar accommodation
Officers: Jessica Williams [1997] Director/Teacher; Simon Justin Colin Williams [1972] Director/Accountant

Lighthouse Schools Partnership
Incorporated: 8 June 2011 *Employees:* 745
Previous: Gordano School
Net Worth: £95,978,704 *Total Assets:* £116,241,816
Registered Office: Gordano School, St Mary's Road, Portishead, Bristol, BS20 7QR
Activities: Pre-primary education
Officers: Clare Marie Giordmaine, Secretary; Julian William Baldwin [1957] Director/Retired Headteacher; Rachel Forbes [1973] Regional Director; Adele Jane Haysom [1969] Director/Accountant; Gary John Lewis [1969] Director/Headteacher; Mike Sewell [1967] Energy Services Director; James Robert Shepherd [1971] Area Director, Corporate; Janet Elaine Sorley [1970] Director/Chartered Engineer; David Andrew Tossell [1960] Engineering Director; Brian Wibberley [1950] Director/Retired Environment Scientist

Lightmoor Homes Limited
Incorporated: 8 August 1996
Net Worth Deficit: £698,679 *Total Assets:* £3,880,420
Registered Office: Midway House, Staverton Technology Park, Herrick Way, Staverton, Cheltenham, Glos, GL51 6TQ
Activities: Construction of domestic buildings
Major Shareholder: Keith Michael Jones
Officers: Janet Jones, Secretary; Keith Michael Jones [1955] Building Director; Stuart Michael Jones [1984] Director/Chartered Surveyor

Lightning Electrical Construction Limited
Incorporated: 9 March 1987 *Employees:* 10
Net Worth: £1,930,366 *Total Assets:* £4,112,716
Registered Office: 44 New Borough, Wimborne, Dorset, BH21 1RB
Activities: Electrical installation
Major Shareholder: Keith John Lightning
Officers: Michele Teresa Harkins, Secretary; Alison Jane Haworth, Secretary; Keith John Lightning [1947] Director

Lightwater Valley Attractions Limited
Incorporated: 12 October 2000 *Employees:* 203
Net Worth: £4,593,622 *Total Assets:* £7,243,403
Registered Office: 34 Acreman Street, Sherborne, Dorset, DT9 3NX
Activities: Activities of amusement parks and theme parks
Parent: Livingstone Leisure Limited
Officers: Ian Cunningham [1959] Director; Michael John Enright [1956] Director

Lilibet Finance Ltd
Incorporated: 12 April 2017
Net Worth: £2,940,000 *Total Assets:* £70,115,000
Registered Office: 1 Rivergate, Temple Quay, Bristol, BS1 6ED
Activities: Other retail sale not in stores, stalls or markets
Parent: Lilibet Holdings Ltd
Officers: Vincent Francis Casey [1983] Director; Stephen James Fitzpatrick [1977] Director; Adrian James Letts [1973] Director [Australian]

Lilibet Holdings Ltd
Incorporated: 12 April 2017 *Employees:* 101
Net Worth Deficit: £2,803,000 *Total Assets:* £72,847,000
Registered Office: 1 Rivergate, Temple Quay, Bristol, BS1 6ED
Activities: Other retail sale not in stores, stalls or markets
Parent: Ovo Group Ltd
Officers: Vincent Francis Casey [1983] Director; Stephen James Fitzpatrick [1977] Director; Adrian James Letts [1973] Director [Australian]

Lily-Flame Ltd
Incorporated: 4 August 2005 *Employees:* 28
Net Worth: £7,083,231 *Total Assets:* £7,678,038
Registered Office: Ground Floor, 11 Manvers Street, Bath, BA1 1JQ
Activities: Other manufacturing n.e.c.
Shareholders: Joanne Lorraine Nicholls; Lucas Miles Nicholls
Officers: Lucas Miles Nicholls, Secretary; Joanne Lorraine Nicholls [1966] Director/Manufacturer; Lucas Miles Nicholls [1968] Director/Manufacturer

Limbs & Things Limited
Incorporated: 17 August 1990 *Employees:* 146
Net Worth: £9,079,548 *Total Assets:* £10,610,250
Registered Office: Sussex Street, St Philips, Bristol, BS2 0RA
Activities: Other manufacturing n.e.c.
Officers: Anne Allin [1969] Commercial Director; Raymond Alexander Braso [1958] Director of Operations; Carolyn Margot Cooper [1943] Director/Medical Artist [Australian]; Tom Stockwell Cooper [1971] Director; Nicholas Charles Hull [1969] Managing Director; Michael John Robinson [1955] Director

Linc Capital Limited
Incorporated: 18 November 2016 *Employees:* 22
Net Worth: £8,515,964 *Total Assets:* £13,190,354
Registered Office: 15 Interface Business Park, Bincknoll Lane, Royal Wootton Bassett, Swindon, Wilts, SN4 8SY
Activities: Activities of other holding companies n.e.c.
Officers: Alun Hywel Luke [1949] Director; Christine Luke [1951] Director; Daniel Gareth Luke [1979] Managing Director; John Hywel Luke [1984] Director; Rhys David Luke [1981] Director

Lincolnshire Chickens Limited
Incorporated: 14 February 1961 *Employees:* 2
Net Worth: £3,368,039 *Total Assets:* £4,386,404
Registered Office: The Old Sidings, Corsham Road, Lacock, Wilts, SN15 2LZ
Activities: Raising of poultry
Parent: Stonegate Farmers Ltd
Officers: James David Sheppard, Secretary; Adrian David Gott [1981] Director; James David Sheppard [1963] Director

Linen Yard Investments (Crewkerne) Ltd
Incorporated: 2 June 1971 *Employees:* 5
Net Worth: £5,217,570 *Total Assets:* £5,369,287
Registered Office: 2 Linen Yard, South Street, Crewkerne, Somerset, TA18 8AB
Activities: Other letting and operating of own or leased real estate
Officers: Suzanne Marie Weekes, Secretary; Mark James Harris [1950] Director/Free Church Minister; Miriam Keen [1957] Director/Teaching Assistant; Hilary Freer Lawrence [1938] Director/Retired; Suzanne Marie Weeks [1969] Director/Secretary

Henry Ling Limited
Incorporated: 28 September 1927 *Employees:* 109
Net Worth: £6,213,745 *Total Assets:* £7,124,149
Registered Office: The Dorset Press, Dorchester, DT1 1HD
Activities: Printing n.e.c.
Officers: Rita Margaret Kennett, Secretary; Anthony Victor Kennett [1938] Director; Helen Margaret Kennett [1968] Managing Director; Mark William Kennett [1966] Financial Director; Rita Margaret Kennett [1941] Director

Lingfield Properties Limited
Incorporated: 25 January 1983
Net Worth: £2,542,317 *Total Assets:* £5,961,504
Registered Office: Bath Lodge Castle, Norton St Philip, Bath, BA2 7NH
Activities: Development of building projects
Officers: Michael Zane Hepker, Secretary/Businessman; Adrian Brian Hepker [1975] Director/Computer Consultant [South African]; Hugh Bernard Hepker [1944] Director/Businessman [South African]; Michael Zane Hepker [1945] Director/Legal Adviser

Link Academy Trust
Incorporated: 8 March 2016 *Employees:* 138
Net Worth: £6,815,151 *Total Assets:* £8,128,982
Registered Office: Landscove C of E Primary School, Landscove, Ashburton, Newton Abbot, Devon, TQ13 7LY
Activities: Primary education
Officers: Peter David Bethel [1947] Director/Retired Accountant; Isabel Jean Cherrett [1953] Director/Retired; Tracey Cleverly [1973] Director of Education; Nicola Dunford [1956] Director/C.E.O; Roy Gillard [1959] Chartered Management Accountant/Director; Jason Myles Hayward-Jones [1968] Director [British/Australian]; Cheryl Diane Mathieson [1963] Director; Simon John Niles [1969] Director/Local Government; Fiona Elisabeth Walters [1960] Farmer/Director

Linton Limited
Incorporated: 7 July 2009 *Employees:* 107
Net Worth: £1,007,586 *Total Assets:* £4,520,661
Registered Office: 1 Cole Road, St Phillips, Bristol, BS2 0UG
Activities: Non-trading company
Shareholders: Ian Paul Elston; Julia Louise Russell
Officers: Ian Paul Elston [1975] Director; Julia Louise Russell [1978] Director

The Linwood Fabric Company Limited
Incorporated: 23 March 1994 *Employees:* 46
Net Worth: £3,839,897 *Total Assets:* £6,425,398
Registered Office: 15 Headlands Business Park, Salisbury Road, Blashford, Ringwood, Hants, BH24 3PB
Activities: Wholesale of hides, skins and leather
Major Shareholder: Richard James Gloyn
Officers: Douglas John Crowther, Secretary; Diana Sonia Gloyn [1944] Director/Textile Designer; Richard James Gloyn [1943] Managing Director; Russell Barnaby Richard Gloyn [1970] Administration Director; Warrick Aaron Gloyn [1970] Sales Director

Lion/Jenga Bidco Limited
Incorporated: 13 December 2016 *Employees:* 3,002
Net Worth: £62,389,000 *Total Assets:* £180,268,000
Registered Office: 15-16 Lower Park Row, Bristol, BS1 5BN
Activities: Activities of other holding companies n.e.c.
Parent: Lion/Jenga Midco Limited
Officers: James Cocker [1982] Director/Investment Manager; Helena Duey Malchione [1990] Director/Investment Manager [American]; Matthew Wilson [1986] Director/Investment Manager

Lipson Co-operative Academy Trust
Incorporated: 11 March 2011 *Employees:* 192
Net Worth: £15,994,934 *Total Assets:* £20,552,088
Registered Office: Lipson Co-operative Academy, Bernice Terrace, Plymouth, PL4 7PG
Activities: General secondary education
Officers: Julie Bailey, Secretary; Kevin John Bishop [1965] Director/NHS Worker; Lynda Budd [1979] Director/Headteacher; James Gerard Byrne [1953] Director/Teacher [Irish]; Hugh John Galbraith Clamp [1959] Director/Education, Employability & Skills Consultant; Christopher Grant Glazier [1957] Managing Director; Adam Hodgess [1984] Director/Learning Technology Manager; Kimberly Louise Jones [1983] Director/Local Government Officer; Carrie Liann Laws [1982] Director/Chartered Legal Executive; Katherine Elizabeth Lyon [1971] Director; Debra Elaine MacLeod [1959] Director/Clerical Administration; Helen Jane Morris [1975] Director/Solicitor; Catherine Elizabeth Orchard [1971] Director; Clara Louise Southby-Tailyour [1978] Director; Lucy Hannah Taylor [1982] Director/Chartered Accountant

Liskeard PPP Health Services Limited
Incorporated: 16 January 2002
Net Worth: £696,298 *Total Assets:* £9,295,712
Registered Office: Third Floor, Broad Quay House, Prince Street, Bristol, BS1 4DJ
Activities: Other specialised construction activities n.e.c.
Parent: RBIL Limited
Officers: Graham John Hutt [1954] Regional Director; Andrew Richard Kershaw [1965] Director/Projects Controller; Andrew Charles Mutch Rhodes [1970] Director

Lister Shearing Equipment Limited
Incorporated: 21 January 1998 *Employees:* 70
Net Worth: £3,664,987 *Total Assets:* £7,575,762
Registered Office: Staverton Court, Staverton, Cheltenham, Glos, GL51 0UX
Activities: Manufacture of agricultural and forestry machinery other than tractors
Officers: Mark Stephen Grant [1975] Director; Stephen Gunson [1963] Director/Area President EMEA - Wahl GmbH

Literature and Latte Ltd
Incorporated: 8 May 2007 *Employees:* 5
Net Worth: £4,240,846 *Total Assets:* £5,068,017
Registered Office: Lowin House, Tregolls Road, Truro, Cornwall, TR1 2NA
Activities: Business and domestic software development
Parent: Librocube Limited
Officers: Julia Alexandra Sara Pierce, Secretary; Keith Martin Blount [1973] Director; David Mark Johnson [1972] Director/Sales and Marketing Commercial; Julia Alexandra Sara Pierce [1973] Director/Journalist

Litfield Land Limited
Incorporated: 31 May 1995 *Employees:* 5
Net Worth: £3,038,342 *Total Assets:* £4,939,913
Registered Office: Woodlands Grange, Woodlands Lane, Bradley Stoke, Bristol, BS32 4JY
Activities: Buying and selling of own real estate
Major Shareholder: Anna Louise Caple
Officers: Anna Louise Caple, Secretary; Simon Mark Caple [1966] Director/Land Agent

Litt Holdings Limited
Incorporated: 19 February 2002
Net Worth: £3,268,120 *Total Assets:* £6,249,482
Registered Office: Albion Dockside Building, Hanover Place, Bristol, BS1 6UT
Activities: Development of building projects
Officers: Sam Litt, Secretary/Director; Amarjit Singh Litt [1971] Director; Ranbir Singh Litt [1968] Director

Little & Cull Ltd
Incorporated: 15 March 2006 *Employees:* 106
Net Worth: £1,835,997 *Total Assets:* £5,770,682
Registered Office: Heathfield Farm, Clyst St Mary, Exeter, Devon, EX5 1AN
Activities: Event catering activities
Shareholders: Thomas Cull; Tom Roger Harb-Little
Officers: Tom Cull [1978] Joint Managing Director; Elizabeth Smith [1983] Joint Managing Director

Little Bear Solar Limited
Incorporated: 10 November 2016
Previous: Nextsolar GRHB Ltd
Net Worth Deficit: £187,914 *Total Assets:* £7,043,410
Registered Office: Tramshed, 25 Lower Park Row, Bristol, BS1 5BN
Activities: Production of electricity
Parent: New Road Solar Limited
Officers: Helen Ruth Down [1979] Director/Solicitor; Luke James Brandon Roberts [1976] Portfolio Director; Neil Anthony Wood [1980] Finance Director

Little Bedwyn Estate Limited
Incorporated: 1 June 1998
Net Worth: £5,875,687 *Total Assets:* £9,897,767
Registered Office: c/o Little Bedwyn Estate, Manor Farm, Marlborough, Wilts, SN8 3JR
Activities: Mixed farming
Parent: George Williamson & Co Limited
Officers: Philip Magor, Secretary/Director; Alexa Catherine Magor [1959] Director; Edward Charles Magor [1985] Director; Philip Magor [1956] Director/Tea Merchant

Little Cheyne Court Wind Farm Limited
Incorporated: 16 November 2005
Net Worth: £35,830,556 *Total Assets:* £44,356,236
Registered Office: Windmill Hill Business Park, Whitehill Way, Swindon, Wilts, SN5 6PB
Activities: Production of electricity
Shareholders: Greencoat UK Wind Holdco Limited; Innogy Renewables UK Limited
Officers: Christopher David Barras, Secretary; Penelope Anne Sainsbury, Secretary; Kevin Dodd [1975] Director/Head of UK Asset Management and Operations; Benjamin James Freeman [1977] Director/Accountant; Stephen Bernard Lilley [1968] Director/Investment Manager; Keith Moseley [1965] Director; Jason Paul Porter [1981] Director/Asset Manager

Little Venice Developments Limited
Incorporated: 13 February 2013 *Employees:* 1
Net Worth Deficit: £3,313,396 *Total Assets:* £10,206,034
Registered Office: Morley House, 36 Acreman Street, Sherborne, Dorset, DT9 3NX
Activities: Development of building projects
Major Shareholder: Michael Penkethman
Officers: Sarah Jane Cook, Secretary; Michael Penkethman [1964] Director

Littleham 2010 Limited
Incorporated: 23 June 2010
Net Worth Deficit: £1,018,756 *Total Assets:* £13,347,480
Registered Office: Centenary House, Peninsula Park, Rydon Lane, Exeter, EX2 7XE
Activities: Buying and selling of own real estate
Shareholders: Edward Fane Trefusis; Michael Trefusis Chamberlayne LVO
Officers: Graham Edward Vanstone, Secretary; David John Cobb [1961] Director/Accountant; Leigh Stuart Rix [1958] Director/Land Agent; John Christian Varley [1960] Director

Livanova UK Limited
Incorporated: 28 June 2004 *Employees:* 62
Previous: Sorin Group UK Limited
Net Worth: £4,077,083 *Total Assets:* £27,514,002
Registered Office: 1370 Montpellier Court, Gloucester Business Park, Gloucester, GL3 4AH
Activities: Wholesale of pharmaceutical goods
Parent: Livanova PLC
Officers: Alexander Hans-Josef Neumann [1969] Director/Vice President Corporate Legal Affairs [German]; Stefano Torelli [1961] Director [Italian]

Liverpool Schools Services Limited
Incorporated: 26 January 2001 *Employees:* 3
Net Worth: £2,589,000 *Total Assets:* £36,405,000
Registered Office: Third Floor, Broad Quay House, Prince Street, Bristol, BS1 4DJ
Activities: Management of real estate on a fee or contract basis
Parent: XJ4 Holding Company Limited
Officers: Stephen Paul Hornby [1957] Director; Richard Little [1979] Investment Director; Julia Sarah McCabe [1970] Regional Director

Liverpool Victoria General Insurance Group Limited
Incorporated: 3 December 2001
Net Worth: £768,083,968 *Total Assets:* £3,448,122,880
Registered Office: County Gates, Bournemouth, BH1 2NF
Activities: Activities of financial services holding companies
Shareholders: Allianz Holdings PLC; LV Capital PLC
Officers: Michael Peter Jones, Secretary; David Barclay Barral [1962] Director; Alan Ronald Cook [1953] Director/Chairman; Jonathan Mark Dye [1966] Director; Richard Owen Hudson [1952] Director; David Stanley Neave [1959] Director; Richard Alexander Rowney [1970] Director; Barry Duncan Smith [1954] Director; Stephen Treloar [1968] Managing Director General Insurance; Kevin Peter Wenzel [1971] Director

Liverpool Victoria Insurance Company Limited
Incorporated: 26 July 1996
Net Worth: £736,536,000 *Total Assets:* £2,539,360,000
Registered Office: County Gates, Bournemouth, BH1 2NF
Activities: Non-life insurance
Parent: Liverpool Victoria General Insurance Group Limited
Officers: Michael Peter Jones, Secretary; David Barclay Barral [1962] Director; Alan Ronald Cook [1953] Director/Chairman; Jonathan Mark Dye [1966] Director; Richard Owen Hudson [1952] Director; David Stanley Neave [1959] Director; Richard Alexander Rowney [1970] Director; Barry Duncan Smith [1954] Director; Stephen Treloar [1968] Managing Director General Insurance; Kevin Peter Wenzel [1971] Director

Liverpool Victoria Life Company Limited
Incorporated: 23 January 1958
Net Worth: £5,608,000 *Total Assets:* £20,435,000
Registered Office: County Gates, Bournemouth, BH1 2NF
Activities: Life insurance
Officers: Michael Peter Jones, Secretary; Andrew Mark Parsons [1965] Finance Director; Anthony Wayne Snow [1972] Director/Chief Risk Officer

Liverton 2014 Limited
Incorporated: 31 January 2014
Net Worth: £468,051 *Total Assets:* £4,575,255
Registered Office: Centenary House, Peninsula Park, Rydon Lane, Exeter, EX2 7XE
Activities: Production of electricity
Parent: Huntshaw Limited
Officers: Graham Edward Vanstone, Secretary; David John Cobb [1961] Director/Accountant; Leigh Stuart Rix [1958] Director/Land Agent; John Christian Varley [1960] Director; William John Wilding [1963] Director/Forestry Manager

Liverton Business Park 2011 Limited
Incorporated: 20 July 2011
Net Worth Deficit: £378,580 *Total Assets:* £5,587,677
Registered Office: Centenary House, Peninsula Park, Rydon Lane, Exeter, EX2 7XE
Activities: Other letting and operating of own or leased real estate
Major Shareholder: Edward Charles Fane Trefusis
Officers: Graham Edward Vanstone, Secretary; David John Cobb [1961] Director/Accountant; Leigh Stuart Rix [1958] Director/Land Agent; John Christian Varley [1960] Director

Liverton Business Park 2012 Limited
Incorporated: 16 July 2012
Net Worth: £9,773,894 *Total Assets:* £16,102,504
Registered Office: Centenary House, Peninsula Park, Rydon Lane, Exeter, EX2 7XE
Activities: Other letting and operating of own or leased real estate
Parent: Liverton Business Park LLP
Officers: Graham Edward Vanstone, Secretary; David John Cobb [1961] Director/Accountant; Leigh Stuart Rix [1958] Director/Land Agent; John Christian Varley [1960] Director

Livewell Southwest CIC
Incorporated: 30 March 2011 *Employees:* 2,314
Previous: Plymouth Community Healthcare CIC
Net Worth: £4,537,619 *Total Assets:* £15,733,753
Registered Office: Local Care Centre, 200 Mount Gould Road, Plymouth, PL4 7PY
Activities: Hospital activities
Shareholders: Adam Morris; Daniel O'Toole
Officers: Geoffrey Baines [1966] Director; Annette Tracey Benny [1966] Director; Dr. Michael Thomas Cooper [1964] Director/Doctor; Duncan James Steel Currall [1950] Director/Chairman; Dr. Adam Morris [1969] Director/Chief Executive; Daniel O'Toole [1971] Director of Provider Finance; David Michael Ratcliffe [1950] Director; Dawn Elizabeth Slater [1966] Director; Clare Louise Tanner [1970] Director/Management Consultant; Michelle Thomas [1966] Director of Operations; Morris Victor Watts [1958] Director

Livingstone Leisure Limited
Incorporated: 10 March 2011 *Employees:* 315
Net Worth: £3,648,974 *Total Assets:* £12,236,361
Registered Office: 34 Acreman Street, Sherborne, Dorset, DT9 3NX
Activities: Botanical and zoological gardens and nature reserves activities
Shareholders: Ian Robert Cunningham; Jennifer Anne Cunningham; Michael John Enright
Officers: Jennifer Anne Cunningham, Secretary; Ian Robert Cunningham [1959] Director; Michael John Enright [1956] Director

LJ (Copiers) Limited
Incorporated: 20 March 2008 *Employees:* 20
Net Worth: £7,937,621 *Total Assets:* £9,868,105
Registered Office: Clarity House, Collett Way, Newton Abbot, Devon, TQ12 4PH
Activities: Other information technology service activities
Shareholders: John Eldridge; Graham Alan Forward; Leo Thomas Whittington; David Turner
Officers: Leo Thomas Whittington, Secretary; John Eldridge [1951] Director; Leo Thomas Whittington [1946] Director

Llawnroc Hotel Limited
Incorporated: 17 February 1997 *Employees:* 36
Net Worth: £489,474 *Total Assets:* £6,336,976
Registered Office: 11 Bredon Court, Tower Road, Newquay, Cornwall, TR7 1AW
Activities: Hotels and similar accommodation
Officers: Claire Helen Coffey, Secretary; Glen James Coffey [1969] Director

Llexeter Limited
Incorporated: 22 October 2003 *Employees:* 34
Net Worth: £3,451,592 *Total Assets:* £5,236,864
Registered Office: Units 15-18 Greendale Business Park, Woodbury Salterton, Devon, EX5 1EW
Activities: Sale, maintenance and repair of motorcycles and related parts and accessories
Shareholders: Liangqi Xu; Bin Li
Officers: Liangqi Xu, Secretary; Bin Li [1976] Director; Liangqi Xu [1975] Director

LLK Property Limited
Incorporated: 9 December 2009
Net Worth: £620,667 *Total Assets:* £7,294,345
Registered Office: Milsted Langdon LLP, Winchester House, Deane Gate Avenue, Taunton, Somerset, TA1 2UH
Activities: Development of building projects
Shareholders: Robert Paul Heffer; Lisa Jane Heffer
Officers: Lisa Jane Heffer [1969] Director/Property Developer; Robert Paul Heffer [1969] Director

Lloyd & Whyte Group Limited
Incorporated: 6 November 1973 *Employees:* 131
Net Worth: £368,139 *Total Assets:* £8,872,557
Registered Office: Affinity House, Bindon Road, Taunton, Somerset, TA2 6AA
Activities: Other activities auxiliary to insurance and pension funding
Major Shareholder: Matthew Mervyn Pyke
Officers: Stephen Astley, Secretary/Accountant; Stephen Astley [1959] Director/Accountant; Matthew Mervyn Pyke [1970] Director/Insurance Brokers; Thomas John Williams [1955] Director

Lloyd & Whyte Limited
Incorporated: 22 December 1998 *Employees:* 50
Net Worth: £278,371 *Total Assets:* £4,147,901
Registered Office: Affinity House, Bindon Road, Taunton, Somerset, TA2 6AA
Activities: Activities of insurance agents and brokers
Parent: Lloyd & Whyte Group Ltd
Officers: Stephen Astley, Secretary/Accountant; Stephen Astley [1959] Director/Accountant; Peter Francis Lishman [1974] Director/Chartered Insurance Broker; Matthew Mervyn Pyke [1970] Director/Insurance Brokers

Lloyd Brothers (Bristol) Limited
Incorporated: 6 February 1947 *Employees:* 2
Net Worth: £4,848,778 *Total Assets:* £5,827,426
Registered Office: Stork Abbey Farm, 49 Parrys Lane, Stoke Bishop, Bristol, BS9 1AG
Activities: Other letting and operating of own or leased real estate
Officers: Martin Grahame Lloyd, Secretary; Rosalind Jane Goode [1964] Director/Chartered Surveyor

Lloyd's Property Southwest Limited
Incorporated: 2 April 1976 *Employees:* 9
Previous: Lloyds Car Sales Limited
Net Worth: £4,687,707 *Total Assets:* £5,620,796
Registered Office: Unit 4 Lodge Hill Industrial Estate, Station Road, Westbury-sub-Mendip, Wells, Somerset, BA5 1EY
Activities: Sale of used cars and light motor vehicles
Shareholder: Philip Paul Lloyd
Officers: Kenneth John Lloyd, Secretary; Henry Philip Lloyd [1987] Director/Property Developer; Hollie Elizabeth Lloyd [1988] Director/Personal Assistant; Jacob John Lloyd [1978] Director/Property Developer; Jordan Thomas Lloyd [1981] Director/Property Developer; Kenneth John Lloyd [1949] Director; Philip Paul Lloyd [1954] Director

Lloyds Bank General Insurance Holdings Limited
Incorporated: 13 April 1982
Net Worth: £283,356,000 *Total Assets:* £283,356,992
Registered Office: Charlton Place, Andover, Hants, SP10 1RE
Activities: Activities of head offices
Parent: Scottish Widows Group Limited
Officers: Joanne Margaret Jolly, Secretary; Andrea Margaret Blance [1964] Director; Kate Cheetham [1963] Director/Group General Counsel; Mark George Culmer [1962] Finance Director; Jane Elizabeth Mary Curtis [1960] Director; Michael Harris [1965] Director; John Francis Hylands [1951] Director; Antonio Lorenzo [1966] Director [Spanish]; Christopher John George Moulder [1958] Director; Sophie Jane O'Connor [1970] Director; Dr Jakob Pfaudler [1972] Community Banking Director [Austrian]; Nicholas Edward Tucker Prettejohn [1960] Director

LMR Holdings Limited
Incorporated: 16 February 2016 *Employees:* 55
Net Worth: £3,077,511 *Total Assets:* £10,267,929
Registered Office: 2A Railway Triangle Industrial Estate, Dorchester, DT1 2PJ
Activities: Activities of construction holding companies
Shareholders: Robert Digby James Acheson; Marcus Andre Drysdale; Lloyd Ernest Surcouf
Officers: Robert Digby James Acheson [1948] Director/Building Contractor; Marcus Andre Drysdale [1971] Director/Quantity Surveyor; Lloyd Ernest Surcouf [1945] Director/Building Contractor

Loadace Limited
Incorporated: 18 May 1989 *Employees:* 3
Net Worth: £8,254,054 *Total Assets:* £14,155,944
Registered Office: Woodlands, Staplegrove, Taunton, Somerset, TA2 6AL
Activities: Buying and selling of own real estate
Shareholders: Anne Underhill; Arthur John White; Sarah Jane Ling
Officers: Sarah Jane Ling, Secretary; Sarah Jane Ling [1959] Director/Secretary; Anne Underhill [1955] Director; Arthur John White [1961] Director

Locators Limited
Incorporated: 14 May 1985 *Employees:* 78
Net Worth: £2,159,559 *Total Assets:* £9,170,754
Registered Office: 36a Station Road, New Milton, Hants, BH25 6JX
Activities: Other specialised construction activities n.e.c.
Parent: Cowles Holdings Limited
Officers: Allan James Whitehead, Secretary; Brian Walter Cowles [1943] Sales Director; Nicholas Jason Hitchcock [1974] Sales Director; Anthony James Stevens [1965] Director/Accountant; Keith Anderson Stewart [1960] Director/Sales Manager

Lockman Electronic Holdings Limited
Incorporated: 18 October 1982 *Employees:* 4
Net Worth: £88,704,000 *Total Assets:* £533,881,984
Registered Office: Brook Road, Wimborne, Dorset, BH21 2BJ
Activities: Activities of head offices
Parent: Cobham PLC
Officers: Lyn Carol Colloff, Secretary; Nigel Rynd Daly [1962] Director/Business Executive; Kenneth John Morrison [1960] Director/Chartered Accountant

Lockman Investments Limited
Incorporated: 16 November 1960
Net Worth: £374,872,000 *Total Assets:* £2,756,776,960
Registered Office: Brook Road, Wimborne, Dorset, BH21 2BJ
Activities: Activities of head offices
Parent: Cobham PLC
Officers: Lyn Carol Colloff, Secretary; Nigel Rynd Daly [1962] Director/Business Executive; Kenneth John Morrison [1960] Director/Chartered Accountant

Lockman Properties Limited
Incorporated: 31 October 2006
Net Worth: £2,162,000 *Total Assets:* £4,600,000
Registered Office: Cobham PLC, Brook Road, Wimborne, Dorset, BH21 2BJ
Activities: Renting and operating of Housing Association real estate
Parent: Cobham PLC
Officers: Lyn Carol Colloff, Secretary; Nigel Rynd Daly [1962] Director/Business Executive; Michael James Kelly [1973] Director; Kenneth John Morrison [1960] Director/Accountant

Lockwash US Limited
Incorporated: 8 December 2008
Net Worth: £2,146,892,672 *Total Assets:* £2,146,892,672
Registered Office: Brook Road, Wimborne, Dorset, BH21 2BJ
Activities: Financial intermediation not elsewhere classified
Parent: Lockman Investments Limited
Officers: Lyn Carol Colloff, Secretary; Betty Jean Bible [1954] Director/Accountant [American]; Kenneth John Morrison [1960] Director/Chartered Accountant

The Lodge Rest Limited
Incorporated: 6 November 1987
Net Worth: £5,377,547 *Total Assets:* £9,391,312
Registered Office: 11-16 Philip Street, Bedminster, Bristol, BS3 4EA
Activities: Residential care activities for learning difficulties, mental health and substance abuse
Officers: Luke Hamilton Bliss [1976] Director/Chef; Matthew Thomas Bliss [1974] Director/Registered Mental Nurse; Oliver James Bliss [1981] Managing Director; Paul Edward Bliss [1986] Director/Trainee Nurse; Paul Thomas Bliss [1946] Director/Accountant

Lodge Service International Limited
Incorporated: 14 August 1961 *Employees:* 633
Net Worth: £1,102,629 *Total Assets:* £5,476,070
Registered Office: Bank House, 15 Gosditch Street, Cirencester, Glos, GL7 2AG
Activities: Activities of head offices
Major Shareholder: Stuart Roy Lodge
Officers: Stuart Roy Lodge, Secretary; John Stuart Lodge [1938] Director; Stuart Roy Lodge [1967] Director/Retail Security Consultant

Lokaz Limited
Incorporated: 11 May 2005
Net Worth: £5,111,476 *Total Assets:* £5,191,019
Registered Office: 1 Ham Close, Charlton Kings, Cheltenham, Glos, GL52 6NP
Activities: Activities of head offices
Major Shareholder: Jeffrey Lewis Arnold
Officers: Jeffrey Lewis Arnold, Secretary/Engineer; Jeffrey Lewis Arnold [1944] Director/Engineer; Lois Caroline Lythgoe [1979] Director/Treasurer; Karen Louise Smith [1983] Director/Underwriter

Lomand Homes Limited
Incorporated: 16 July 1998
Net Worth Deficit: £1,189,367 *Total Assets:* £5,875,728
Registered Office: 29 Pennsylvania Way, Portland, Dorset, DT5 1FJ
Activities: Construction of domestic buildings
Shareholder: Edward Fitzsimmons
Officers: Heather Bainbridge, Secretary; Mark Richard Coleman [1960] Director; Edward Fitzsimmons [1964] Director; John Paul Wilkins [1967] Director/Financial Services

Lombard Corporate Finance (11) Limited
Incorporated: 15 May 2002
Net Worth Deficit: £138,000 *Total Assets:* £200,936,992
Registered Office: The Quadrangle, The Promenade, Cheltenham, Glos, GL50 1PX
Activities: Financial leasing
Shareholders: The Royal Bank of Scotland PLC; Royal Bank Leasing Limited
Officers: Stephen Paul Nixon [1970] Director/Bank Official; Keith Damian Pereira [1978] Director/Bank Official

Lombard Corporate Finance (13) Limited
Incorporated: 15 May 2002
Net Worth: £973,000 *Total Assets:* £5,656,000
Registered Office: The Quadrangle, The Promenade, Cheltenham, Glos, GL50 1PX
Activities: Financial leasing
Shareholders: Royal Bank Leasing Limited; Royal Bank Leasing Limited
Officers: Stephen Paul Nixon [1970] Director/Bank Official; Keith Damian Pereira [1978] Director/Bank Official

Lombard Corporate Finance (15) Limited
Incorporated: 15 May 2002
Net Worth: £801,000 *Total Assets:* £20,135,000
Registered Office: The Quadrangle, The Promenade, Cheltenham, Glos, GL50 1PX
Activities: Financial leasing
Parent: Royal Bank Leasing Limited
Officers: Stephen Paul Nixon [1970] Director/Bank Official; Keith Damian Pereira [1978] Director/Bank Official

Lombard Corporate Finance (7) Limited
Incorporated: 16 May 2002
Net Worth: £1,190,000 *Total Assets:* £13,395,000
Registered Office: The Quadrangle, The Promenade, Cheltenham, Glos, GL50 1PX
Activities: Financial leasing
Parent: Royal Bank Leasing Limited
Officers: Stephen Paul Nixon [1970] Director/Bank Official; Keith Damian Pereira [1978] Director/Bank Official

Lombard Corporate Finance (December 1) Limited
Incorporated: 21 June 1988
Net Worth: £1,911,370 *Total Assets:* £104,910,680
Registered Office: The Quadrangle, The Promenade, Cheltenham, Glos, GL50 1PX
Activities: Financial leasing
Parent: Royal Bank Leasing Limited
Officers: Ian Andrew Ellis [1969] Director/Bank Official; David Generald Harris [1969] Director/Bank Official; Steven James Roulston [1977] Director/Bank Official

Lombard Corporate Finance (December 3) Limited
Incorporated: 8 September 1987
Net Worth: £1,420,685 *Total Assets:* £453,271,488
Registered Office: The Quadrangle, The Promenade, Cheltenham, Glos, GL50 1PX
Activities: Financial leasing
Parent: Royal Bank Leasing Limited
Officers: Ian Andrew Ellis [1969] Director/Bank Official; David Generald Harris [1969] Director/Bank Official; Steven James Roulston [1977] Director/Bank Official

Lombard Industrial Leasing Limited
Incorporated: 10 December 1973
Previous: W. & G. Industrial Leasing Limited
Net Worth: £3,647,000 *Total Assets:* £111,712,000
Registered Office: The Quadrangle, The Promenade, Cheltenham, Glos, GL50 1PX
Activities: Financial intermediation not elsewhere classified
Parent: Royal Bank Leasing Limited
Officers: Ian Andrew Ellis [1969] Director/Bank Official; David Generald Harris [1969] Director/Bank Official; Steven James Roulston [1977] Director/Bank Official

Lombard Lease Finance Limited
Incorporated: 3 July 1984
Previous: W. & G. Lease Finance Limited
Net Worth: £4,263,000 *Total Assets:* £277,492,000
Registered Office: The Quadrangle, The Promenade, Cheltenham, Glos, GL50 1PX
Activities: Financial intermediation not elsewhere classified
Parent: Royal Bank Leasing Limited
Officers: Ian Andrew Ellis [1969] Director/Bank Official; David Generald Harris [1969] Director/Bank Official; Steven James Roulston [1977] Director/Bank Official

Lombard Leasing Company Limited
Incorporated: 1 December 1971
Previous: Williams & Glyn's Leasing Company Limited
Net Worth: £2,018,000 *Total Assets:* £15,523,000
Registered Office: The Quadrangle, The Promenade, Cheltenham, Glos, GL50 1PX
Activities: Financial intermediation not elsewhere classified
Parent: Royal Bank Leasing Limited
Officers: Ian Andrew Ellis [1969] Director/Bank Official; David Generald Harris [1969] Director/Bank Official; Steven James Roulston [1977] Director/Bank Official

London & Country Mortgages Limited
Incorporated: 12 February 1986 *Employees:* 735
Net Worth: £19,173,848 *Total Assets:* £29,239,448
Registered Office: Beazer House, Lower Bristol Road, Bath, BA2 3BA
Activities: Financial intermediation not elsewhere classified
Shareholders: Experian Limited; Michael Robert Edge
Officers: Philip Ronald Cartwright [1956] Managing Director; Michael Robert Edge [1955] Director; Alexandra Brigid Kinney [1958] Director [Irish]; Clive Robert Lawson [1971] Director; David John Loftus [1961] Finance Director; Katrina Jane Machin [1966] Director

London & Devonshire Trust Limited
Incorporated: 20 January 1984 *Employees:* 74
Net Worth: £18,985,386 *Total Assets:* £30,357,414
Registered Office: The Island, Lowman Green, Tiverton, Devon, EX16 4LA
Activities: Buying and selling of own real estate
Officers: Owen O'Callaghan, Secretary; Charles Peter Cobb [1954] Director/Architect; David Philip Heathcoat Amory [1949] Director; Edward FitzGenerald Heathcoat Amory [1967] Director/Journalist; Harry James Heathcoat Amory [1977] Asset Director; Owen Michael O'Callaghan [1963] Director/Chartered Accountant; Daniel Francis Stephenson [1971] Director/Chartered Surveyor [Irish]

London Aquarium (South Bank) Limited
Incorporated: 3 April 2008
Net Worth: £7,534,000 *Total Assets:* £7,734,000
Registered Office: Link House, 25 West Street, Poole, Dorset, BH15 1LD
Activities: Other amusement and recreation activities n.e.c.
Parent: Merlin Entertainments (Sea Life) Limited
Officers: Fiona Jane Rose, Secretary; Matthew Paul Jowett [1967] Director/General Counsel and Company Secretary; Fiona Jane Rose [1964] Director/Assistant Group Company Secretary

London Bidco Limited
Incorporated: 27 May 2016 *Employees:* 8
Net Worth: £2,453,000 *Total Assets:* £140,942,000
Registered Office: UK Head Office, Gloucester Road, Cheltenham, Glos, GL51 8NR
Activities: Wholesale of hardware, plumbing and heating equipment and supplies
Parent: London Finco Limited
Officers: Dean Brown [1965] Director; Edward Arthur Davies [1970] Director

London Eye Holdings Limited
Incorporated: 24 January 2006 *Employees:* 2
Net Worth Deficit: £1,272,000 *Total Assets:* £7,315,000
Registered Office: Link House, 25 West Street, Poole, Dorset, BH15 1LD
Activities: Activities of head offices
Parent: Merlin Entertainments (NBD) Limited
Officers: Fiona Jane Rose, Secretary; Matthew Paul Jowett [1967] Director/General Counsel and Company Secretary; Fiona Jane Rose [1964] Director/Assistant Group Company Secretary

London Topco Limited
Incorporated: 26 May 2016 *Employees:* 98
Net Worth Deficit: £15,795,000 *Total Assets:* £130,616,000
Registered Office: UK Head Office, Gloucester Road, Cheltenham, Glos, GL51 8NR
Activities: Wholesale of hardware, plumbing and heating equipment and supplies
Officers: Dean Brown [1965] Director; Duncan Stanford Cooper [1961] Director; Edward Arthur Davies [1970] Director; James Richard Parkinson [1978] Director/Chief Marketing Officer; Alistair Lee Pendleton [1974] Director; Christopher John Thomas [1955] Director; John Vaughan [1966] Director; Neil Watson-Ganivet [1963] Director; Matthew Webber [1979] UK Sales Director

Lone Eagle Retail Limited
Incorporated: 13 July 2001 *Employees:* 6
Net Worth: £7,167,680 *Total Assets:* £19,288,544
Registered Office: Eagle House, 1 Babbage Way, Exeter Science Park, Exeter, Devon, EX5 2FN
Activities: Other letting and operating of own or leased real estate
Major Shareholder: Mark Russell Kay
Officers: Paul James Goodes [1965] Director/Accountant; Nicholas Ian Hole [1961] Director/Chartered Surveyor

Longfield Hospice Care
Incorporated: 25 January 1988 *Employees:* 141
Previous: Cotswold Care
Net Worth: £3,961,586 *Total Assets:* £4,071,983
Registered Office: Longfield, Burleigh Lane, Minchinhampton, Stroud, Glos, GL5 2PQ
Activities: Other human health activities
Officers: Dr Trevor Bentley [1939] Director/Retired; Neil Hampson [1962] Director/District Nurse; Bennett Harold Kushner [1952] Director/Retired; Brian Ratcliffe [1945] Director/Project Manager; Susan Reynolds [1951] Director/Retired; Dr Sarah Catherine Robinson [1948] Director/Retired; Alan Kevin Simmons [1958] Director/Wealth Management; Dr Pam Swindell [1951] Director/Retired

Longford Farms Limited
Incorporated: 14 December 1951 *Employees:* 7
Net Worth: £1,395,931 *Total Assets:* £4,145,400
Registered Office: Estate Office, Longford Castle, Salisbury, Wilts, SP5 4ED
Activities: Mixed farming
Shareholders: Helen Clark; Susan Anne Laing; The Hon Peter John Pleydell-Bouverie; William Pleydell-Bouverie (The 9th Earl of Radnor)
Officers: Karen Price, Secretary; Susan Anne Laing [1954] Director/Solicitor; The Honourable Peter John Pleydell Bouverie [1958] Director/Investment Advisor; The Hon Viscount William The 9th Earl of Radnor [1955] Director/Landowner

Longhouse Ltd
Incorporated: 2 February 2012 *Employees:* 101
Net Worth: £2,368,000 *Total Assets:* £9,341,000
Registered Office: Butland Farm House, Yealmbridge, Yealmpton, Plymouth, PL8 2EQ
Activities: Activities of head offices
Shareholders: Robert Simon Foster; Nigel John Godefroy
Officers: Robert Simon Foster [1971] Director; Nigel John Godefroy [1964] Director

Longleat Bishopstrow Limited
Incorporated: 9 September 2011 *Employees:* 76
Net Worth: £592,855 *Total Assets:* £5,971,815
Registered Office: The Longleat Estate Office, Longleat, Warminster, Wilts, BA12 7NW
Activities: Hotels and similar accommodation
Parent: Longleat Enterprises Limited
Officers: Albemarle John Cator [1953] Director/Banker; Ceawlin Henry Lazlo Thynn [1974] Director

Longleat Enterprises Limited
Incorporated: 27 January 1964 *Employees:* 709
Net Worth: £21,943,316 *Total Assets:* £37,267,772
Registered Office: The Longleat Estate Office, Longleat, Warminster, Wilts, BA12 7NW
Activities: Other amusement and recreation activities n.e.c.
Shareholders: Harry Westropp; Simon Franks; James Felton Somers Hervey-Bathurst; Albemarle John Cator
Officers: Albemarle John Cator [1953] Director; Johan Eliasch [1962] Director/Banker [Swedish]; Janie Schaffer [1961] Director; Ceawlin Henry Lazlo Thynn Lord Weymouth [1974] Director

Longmayne Limited
Incorporated: 22 October 1993 *Employees:* 7
Net Worth: £6,320,186 *Total Assets:* £7,613,345
Registered Office: Office 308, 2nd & 3rd Floors Spaces, Northgate House, Barton Court, Upper Borough Walls, Bath, BA1 1RG
Activities: Other letting and operating of own or leased real estate
Shareholders: Shelley Sadiye Duru; Spencer Tayyar Duru; Suzanne Nefica Smith
Officers: Suzanne Nefika Duru, Secretary; Spencer Tayyar Duru [1986] Director; Suzanne Nefika Duru [1980] Director

Longmeadow Properties Limited
Incorporated: 22 May 1998
Net Worth: £1,364,544 *Total Assets:* £3,984,715
Registered Office: Tregeseal, 6 Lower Port View, Saltash, Cornwall, PL12 4BY
Activities: Buying and selling of own real estate
Officers: Loraine Jean Richards, Secretary; Leslie Jean Richards [1986] Director; William John Richards [1944] Director

Loran (Investments) Limited
Incorporated: 18 August 1999
Net Worth: £4,708,213 *Total Assets:* £5,336,579
Registered Office: Marsh Court, Bridgend, Eldersfield, Gloucester, GL19 4PN
Activities: Activities of head offices
Officers: Stanley Hobson, Secretary; Andrew John Hobson [1962] Director/Chairman; Lorraine Rosemary Hobson [1959] Director/Farm Manager; Stanley Hobson [1927] Director/Accountant

Lornamead Acquisitions Limited
Incorporated: 5 November 2004
Net Worth: £66,633,000 *Total Assets:* £66,672,000
Registered Office: Aintree Avenue, White Horse Business Park, Trowbridge, Wilts, BA14 0XB
Activities: Activities of head offices
Officers: Gary David Armstrong [1965] Commercial Director; Gerard Jan Raymond [1957] Director [Australian]; Robert Adrian Sharpe [1956] Director

Lornamead Group Limited
Incorporated: 20 April 2007 *Employees:* 3
Net Worth: £48,223,000 *Total Assets:* £88,404,000
Registered Office: Aintree Avenue, White Horse Business Park, Trowbridge, Wilts, BA14 0XB
Activities: Activities of head offices
Parent: Lornamead Acquisitions Limited
Officers: Gary David Armstrong [1965] Commercial Director; Gerard Jan Raymond [1957] Director [Australian]; Robert Adrian Sharpe [1956] Director

Lornamead UK Limited
Incorporated: 1 November 1983 *Employees:* 33
Net Worth: £5,200,000 *Total Assets:* £9,970,000
Registered Office: Aintree Avenue, White Horse Business Park, Trowbridge, Wilts, BA14 0XB
Activities: Other manufacturing n.e.c.
Parent: Lornamead Group Limited
Officers: Gary David Armstrong [1965] Commercial Director; Gerard Jan Raymond [1957] Director [Australian]; Robert Adrian Sharpe [1956] Director

Loumin Estates Limited
Incorporated: 6 February 2006 *Employees:* 4
Net Worth: £1,609,122 *Total Assets:* £7,469,126
Registered Office: Third Floor, 95 The Promenade, Cheltenham, Glos, GL50 1HH
Activities: Development of building projects
Officers: John Newton Bays [1942] Director; Charles Murray Fisher [1949] Director; Mary Elizabeth Goymour [1977] Director; Nigel Ashley Walters [1953] Director

Loungers Holdings Limited
Incorporated: 7 March 2012 *Employees:* 8
Net Worth: £27,663,000 *Total Assets:* £27,695,000
Registered Office: 15-16 Lower Park Row, Bristol, BS1 5BN
Activities: Activities of other holding companies n.e.c.
Parent: Lion/Jenga Bidco Limited
Officers: Jacob Bishop [1973] Director/Restaurateur; Justin Mark Carter [1964] Director; James Cocker [1982] Director/Investment Manager; Nicholas Charles Elliot Collins [1974] Director/Restaurateur; Robert Darwent [1972] Director/Investment Manager; Gregor Grant [1966] Director/Accountant; Alexander Morton Reilley [1973] Director/Restaurateur

Loungers Limited
Incorporated: 20 November 2002 *Employees:* 3,002
Net Worth: £13,168,000 *Total Assets:* £78,400,000
Registered Office: 15-16 Lower Park Row, Bristol, BS1 5BN
Activities: Licenced restaurants
Parent: Loungers Holdings Limited
Officers: Alexander Morton Reilley, Secretary; Jacob Bishop [1973] Director/Restaurateur; Justin Mark Carter [1964] Director; James Cocker [1982] Director/Investment Manager; Nicholas Charles Elliot Collins [1974] Director/Restaurateur; Robert Darwent [1972] Director/Investment Manager; Gregor Grant [1966] Director/Accountant; Alexander Morton Reilley [1973] Director/Chairman

Lovehoney Group Limited
Incorporated: 1 December 2006 *Employees:* 265
Net Worth: £19,668,000 *Total Assets:* £31,419,000
Registered Office: 100 Locksbrook Road, Bath, BA1 3EN
Activities: Retail sale via mail order houses or via Internet
Shareholders: Honey Bidco Ltd; Neal Richard Slateford; Richard Henry Longhurst
Officers: Richard Henry Longhurst, Secretary; Richard Henry Longhurst [1969] Director; Neal Richard Slateford [1963] Director

Lovehoney Limited
Incorporated: 15 January 2003 *Employees:* 235
Net Worth: £16,387,000 *Total Assets:* £29,512,000
Registered Office: 100 Locksbrook Road, Bath, BA1 3EN
Activities: Other retail sale not in stores, stalls or markets
Parent: Lovehoney Group Ltd
Officers: Neal Richard Slateford, Secretary; Richard Henry Longhurst [1969] Managing Director; Neal Richard Slateford [1963] Director

Lovell Stone Group Holdings Limited
Incorporated: 19 March 2015 *Employees:* 63
Net Worth: £8,613,863 *Total Assets:* £9,922,428
Registered Office: Staverton Court, Staverton, Cheltenham, Glos, GL51 0UX
Activities: Activities of other holding companies n.e.c.
Major Shareholder: Peter Leslie Hart
Officers: James Peter Leslie Hart [1983] Director; Peter Leslie Hart [1941] Director; Simon Charles Peter Hart [1978] Director; Katherine Angela Robinson [1976] Director

Lovell Stone Group Limited
Incorporated: 12 May 2009 *Employees:* 49
Net Worth: £8,779,964 *Total Assets:* £9,591,321
Registered Office: Staverton Court, Staverton, Cheltenham, Glos, GL51 0UX
Activities: Other mining and quarrying n.e.c.
Parent: Lovell Stone Group Holdings Limited
Officers: Angela Ruth Hart [1948] Director; James Peter Leslie Hart [1983] Director/Sales Manager; Peter Leslie Hart [1941] Director; Simon Charles Peter Hart [1978] Director; Katherine Angela Robinson [1976] Director

Dick Lovett (Bath) Limited
Incorporated: 17 August 1999 *Employees:* 115
Previous: Wellsway Bath Limited
Net Worth: £2,627,000 *Total Assets:* £10,369,000
Registered Office: The Copse, Frankland Road, Blagrove, Swindon, Wilts, SN5 8YW
Activities: Sale of new cars and light motor vehicles
Major Shareholder: Peter Charles Lovett
Officers: Julian Winterburn, Secretary; Lynn Ross Campbell [1957] Director; Peter Charles Lovett [1950] Director; Julian Winterburn [1969] Finance Director

Dick Lovett (Bristol) Limited
Incorporated: 1 December 1982 *Employees:* 222
Net Worth: £4,431,000 *Total Assets:* £19,375,000
Registered Office: The Copse, Frankland Road, Blagrove, Swindon, Wilts, SN5 8YW
Activities: Sale of new cars and light motor vehicles
Major Shareholder: Peter Charles Lovett
Officers: Julian Winterburn, Secretary; Lynn Ross Cambell [1957] Director; Peter Charles Lovett [1950] Director; Russell John Trotman [1965] Director; Julian Winterburn [1969] Finance Director

Dick Lovett (Hungerford) Limited
Incorporated: 12 January 1972 *Employees:* 56
Net Worth: £2,409,000 *Total Assets:* £8,721,000
Registered Office: The Copse, Frankland Road, Blagrove, Swindon, Wilts, SN5 8YW
Activities: Sale of new cars and light motor vehicles
Major Shareholder: Peter Charles Lovett
Officers: Julian Winterburn, Secretary; Lynn Ross Cambell [1957] Director; Peter Charles Lovett [1950] Director; Julian Winterburn [1969] Finance Director

Dick Lovett (Specialist Cars) Limited
Incorporated: 10 December 1990 *Employees:* 206
Net Worth: £3,409,000 *Total Assets:* £21,684,000
Registered Office: The Copse, Frankland Road, Blagrove, Swindon, Wilts, SN5 8YW
Activities: Sale of new cars and light motor vehicles
Major Shareholder: Peter Charles Lovett
Officers: Julian Winterburn, Secretary; Lynn Ross Cambell [1957] Director; Peter Charles Lovett [1950] Director; Julian Winterburn [1969] Finance Director

Dick Lovett Companies Limited
Incorporated: 14 March 1973 *Employees:* 823
Net Worth: £77,089,000 *Total Assets:* £173,172,000
Registered Office: The Copse, Frankland Road, Blagrove, Swindon, Wilts, SN5 8YW
Activities: Sale of new cars and light motor vehicles
Major Shareholder: Peter Charles Lovett
Officers: Julian Winterburn, Secretary; Lynn Ross Campbell [1957] Director; Peter Charles Lovett [1950] Director; Julian Winterburn [1969] Finance Director

Dick Lovett Limited
Incorporated: 2 July 1946 *Employees:* 156
Net Worth: £10,903,000 *Total Assets:* £24,204,000
Registered Office: The Copse, Frankland Road, Blagrove, Swindon, Wilts, SN5 8YW
Activities: Sale of new cars and light motor vehicles
Major Shareholder: Peter Charles Lovett
Officers: Julian Winterburn, Secretary; Lynn Ross Cambell [1957] Director; Peter Charles Lovett [1950] Director; Julian Winterburn [1969] Finance Director

Dick Lovett Sporting Limited
Incorporated: 28 April 1993 *Employees:* 45
Net Worth: £4,977,000 *Total Assets:* £13,782,000
Registered Office: The Copse, Frankland Road, Blagrove, Swindon, Wilts, SN5 8YW
Activities: Sale of new cars and light motor vehicles
Major Shareholder: Peter Charles Lovett
Officers: Julian Winterburn, Secretary; Lynn Ross Campbell [1957] Director; Peter Charles Lovett [1950] Director; Julian Winterburn [1969] Finance Director

Dick Lovett Sports Cars Limited
Incorporated: 26 July 1999 *Employees:* 20
Net Worth: £30,000 *Total Assets:* £8,615,000
Registered Office: The Copse, Frankland Road, Blagrove, Swindon, Wilts, SN5 8YW
Activities: Sale of new cars and light motor vehicles
Major Shareholder: Peter Charles Lovett
Officers: Julian Winterburn, Secretary; Lynn Ross Cambell [1957] Director; Peter Charles Lovett [1950] Director; Julian Winterburn [1969] Finance Director

Lovewell Blake LLP
Incorporated: 14 April 2010 *Employees:* 240
Net Worth: £2,953,000 *Total Assets:* £8,332,000
Registered Office: Windsor House, Bayshill Road, Cheltenham, Glos, GL50 3AT
Officers: Philip Jeremy Bartram [1972] Member; Paul Briddon [1964] Member; Kevin Paul Bunting [1978] Member; Colin Andrew Everitt Fish [1963] Member; Neil Peter Orford [1973] Member; Steven Paul Scarlett [1970] Member; Simon Downing De-Lacy Adams [1961] LLP Member; Matthew Crawley [1981] LLP Member; Gary Andrew Flatt [1972] LLP Member; Brian James Floringer [1967] LLP Member; Rebecca Jane Gascoyne-Richards [1961] LLP Member; Mark David Haylett [1963] LLP Member; Richard Keeler [1973] LLP Member; Ryan Lincoln [1980] LLP Member; Shaun Carlton Mary [1975] LLP Member; Jamie Norton [1978] LLP Member; Mark Proctor [1977] LLP Member; Mary Elizabeth Schofield [1972] LLP Member; James Paul Shipp [1977] LLP Member; Keith Brian Shorten [1963] LLP Member; Christopher Solt [1967] LLP Member; Leigh Andrew Jon Thurston [1985] LLP Member; Andrew John Turner [1966] LLP Member; Colin Leonard Wash [1953] LLP Member; Simon Charles Watson [1971] LLP Member

Low Carbon Oxygen Limited
Incorporated: 26 March 2015
Net Worth: £44,285,224 *Total Assets:* £157,096,992
Registered Office: Oxygen House, Grenadier Road, Exeter Business Park, Exeter, EX1 3LH
Activities: Activities of other holding companies n.e.c.
Parent: Oxygen House Investments Limited
Officers: Eleanor Jane Adams [1972] Finance Director; Juan Martin Alfonso [1975] Director/Chief Financial Officer; Roy Barry Bedlow [1968] Director; Matthew Owen Gingell [1979] Director/Solicitor; Justin Michael Thesiger [1970] Operations Director; David Barclay Williamson [1965] Director/Accountant; Glenn Woodcock [1969] Director

Lower Easton Solar C.I.C.
Incorporated: 12 June 2015
Net Worth: £1,171,909 *Total Assets:* £5,711,072
Registered Office: The Long Barn, Manor Courtyard, Stratton on the Fosse, Radstock, Somerset, BA3 4QF
Activities: Production of electricity
Parent: Whitelake PV Ltd
Officers: Jonathan Simon Thompson [1963] Director

Lower Pertwood Organic Farm Limited
Incorporated: 5 May 1958 *Employees:* 8
Net Worth: £17,506,152 *Total Assets:* £22,059,490
Registered Office: Lower Pertwood Organic Farm Limited, Hindon, Salisbury, Wilts, SP3 6TA
Activities: Mixed farming
Officers: Martyn John Hurst [1947] Creative Director; Wilfred Edgar Mole [1944] Director/Farmer; Joanne Mary West [1969] Director

Lowman Manufacturing Company Limited
Incorporated: 20 January 1984 *Employees:* 3
Net Worth: £7,309,000 *Total Assets:* £8,168,000
Registered Office: The Island, Lowman Green, Tiverton, Devon, EX16 4LA
Activities: Activities of other holding companies n.e.c.
Officers: Bruce Henry Beacham, Secretary; Bruce Henry Beacham [1949] Director; David Philip Heathcoat Amory [1949] Director; Sir Ian Heathcoat Amory [1942] Director; William Francis Heathcoat Amory [1975] Director/Fund Marketing Advisor

The Lozenge Limited
Incorporated: 9 November 2009
Net Worth: £1,106,798 *Total Assets:* £4,406,369
Registered Office: Kelly Park, St Dominick, Saltash, Cornwall, PL12 6SQ
Activities: Other letting and operating of own or leased real estate
Major Shareholder: Alan James Fall
Officers: Graham Wilkins, Secretary; Alan James Fall [1965] Director

LTC Group87 Ltd
Incorporated: 12 August 1997 *Employees:* 140
Net Worth: £6,173,542 *Total Assets:* £9,768,864
Registered Office: Wixenford Depot, Colesdown Hill, Plymouth, PL9 8AA
Activities: Scaffold erection
Major Shareholder: Trevor Patrick Chinn
Officers: Gail Smith, Secretary; Michael Richard Burr [1969] Director/Surveyor; Trevor Patrick Chinn [1959] Director/Scaffolder; Robert Alexander Wills [1972] Director

Lucknam Park Hotels Limited
Incorporated: 3 February 1987 *Employees:* 141
Net Worth: £3,787,854 *Total Assets:* £27,156,884
Registered Office: Lucknam Park, Colerne, Wilts, SN14 8AZ
Activities: Hotels and similar accommodation
Officers: Sarah Jayne Reynolds, Secretary; Homayoon Amirparviz [1965] Director/Hotel General Manager; Michael Neil Farwell [1961] Director/Accountant & Business Adviser; Athanasios Laskaridis [1952] Director/Vice Chairman [Greek]; Chloe Maria Laskaridis [1982] Director/Development Manager; Grigoris Liasidis [1973] Director/Exec Assistant Manager [Cypriot]; Henry Murray [1939] Director/Hotelier

Lucrative Investments Holdings Limited
Incorporated: 1 March 2012
Net Worth: £29,721 *Total Assets:* £14,740,434
Registered Office: Wessex House, 66 High Street, Honiton, Devon, EX14 1PD
Activities: Other business support service activities n.e.c.
Officers: Dean Barrow [1970] Director

Ludus Capital Limited
Incorporated: 30 August 2011 *Employees:* 124
Net Worth: £10,023,000 *Total Assets:* £12,732,000
Registered Office: Lodgemore Mills, Stroud, Glos, GL5 3EJ
Activities: Manufacture of other textiles n.e.c.
Officers: Ewen Maitland Hamilton, Secretary; Curt Bossuyt [1959] Director [Belgian]; Ewen Maitland Hamilton [1965] Finance Director; Duncan Kettell [1965] Director; Alan Phillips [1951] Director [Belgian]; Emmanuel Schellekens [1966] Director [Belgian]; Marc Simonis [1951] Director [Belgian]; David Smith [1951] Director

Lunamar (Group) Limited
Incorporated: 21 October 2013 *Employees:* 270
Net Worth Deficit: £11,525,755 *Total Assets:* £19,769,094
Registered Office: Technology House, 18 Whiteladies Road, Bristol, BS8 2LG
Activities: Activities of other holding companies n.e.c.
Major Shareholder: Mark Goddard-Watts
Officers: Katherine Anne Gildersleeve [1976] Director/Chartered Accountant; Mark Goddard-Watts [1961] Director

Lush Cosmetics Limited
Incorporated: 16 February 2001 *Employees:* 10,976
Net Worth: £152,780,992 *Total Assets:* £255,812,000
Registered Office: 29 High Street, Poole, Dorset, BH15 1AB
Activities: Activities of head offices
Shareholder: Mark Constantine
Officers: Karl Joseph Bygrave, Secretary; Karl Joseph Bygrave [1962] Director; Margaret Joan Constantine [1953] Director/Inventor; Mark Constantine [1952] Director

Lush Ltd.
Incorporated: 17 June 1994 *Employees:* 282
Net Worth: £59,083,000 *Total Assets:* £133,899,000
Registered Office: 29 High Street, Poole, Dorset, BH15 1AB
Activities: Manufacture of perfumes and toilet preparations
Parent: Lush Cosmetics Limited
Officers: Karl Joseph Bygrave, Secretary; Rowena Jaqueline Bird [1959] Director/Retail Consultant; Karl Joseph Bygrave [1962] Director/Manager; Jack Constantine [1984] Director; Margaret Joan Constantine [1953] Director/Inventor; Mark Constantine [1952] Director; Hilary Anita Jones [1962] Director; Simon George Nicholls [1963] Director

Lush Manufacturing Limited
Incorporated: 5 March 1997 *Employees:* 1,271
Net Worth: £46,751,000 *Total Assets:* £53,155,000
Registered Office: 29 High Street, Poole, Dorset, BH15 1AB
Activities: Manufacture of perfumes and toilet preparations
Parent: Lush Limited
Officers: Karl Joseph Bygrave, Secretary; Margaret Joan Constantine [1953] Director/Inventor; David Jason Muller [1970] Director; Elizabeth Kate Smith [1976] Director/Manager

Lush Retail Limited
Incorporated: 27 July 1995 *Employees:* 3,388
Net Worth: £23,499,000 *Total Assets:* £67,747,000
Registered Office: 29 The High Street, Poole, Dorset, BH15 1AB
Activities: Retail sale of cosmetic and toilet articles in specialised stores
Parent: Lush Ltd
Officers: Karl Joseph Bygrave, Secretary; Kim Elizabeth Coles [1963] Director/Accountant; Mark Constantine [1952] Director; Paul Clifford Wheatley [1968] Property Director

Luxurycare (Aranlaw House Care Home) Ltd
Incorporated: 28 February 2003
Net Worth: £25,310 *Total Assets:* £4,681,942
Registered Office: First Floor, 5 Trinity House, 161 Old Christchurch Road, Bournemouth, BH1 1JU
Activities: Residential care activities for learning difficulties, mental health and substance abuse
Parent: Luxurycare Group Limited
Officers: Vanessa Kiran Gunputh, Secretary; Kevin Roshan Gunputh [1978] Director; Sookdeo Gunputh [1941] Director/Rest Home Partner

Luxurycare (Birds Hill Nursing Home) Limited
Incorporated: 15 January 2016
Net Worth: £13,572 *Total Assets:* £10,933,592
Registered Office: First Floor, 5 Trinity House, 161 Old Christchurch Road, Bournemouth, BH1 1JU
Activities: Residential nursing care facilities
Parent: Luxurycare Group Limited
Officers: Kevin Roshan Gunputh [1978] Director; Sookdeo Gunputh [1941] Director

Luxurycare (Regency Manor Care Home) Limited
Incorporated: 6 September 2013
Previous: Luxurycare (Regency Manor Care) Limited
Net Worth: £27,469 *Total Assets:* £6,760,324
Registered Office: First Floor, 5 Trinity House, 161 Old Christchurch Road, Bournemouth, BH1 1JU
Activities: Residential nursing care facilities
Parent: Luxurycare Group Limited
Officers: Kevin Roshan Gunputh [1978] Director; Sookdeo Gunputh [1941] Director

LV Capital PLC
Incorporated: 9 March 2012
Net Worth: £945,808,000 *Total Assets:* £945,808,000
Registered Office: County Gates, Bournemouth, BH1 2NF
Activities: Non-life insurance
Officers: Michael Peter Jones, Secretary; Andrew Mark Parsons [1965] Finance Director; Richard Alexander Rowney [1970] Director/Group Chief Executive

LV Equity Release Limited
Incorporated: 30 September 1985
Net Worth: £5,000,000 *Total Assets:* £11,701,000
Registered Office: County Gates, Bournemouth, BH1 2NF
Activities: Financial intermediation not elsewhere classified
Officers: Michael Peter Jones, Secretary; Andrew Mark Parsons [1965] Finance Director; Anthony Wayne Snow [1972] Director/Chief Risk Officer

LV Insurance Management Limited
Incorporated: 25 November 2005
Net Worth: £705,000 *Total Assets:* £117,388,000
Registered Office: County Gates, Bournemouth, BH1 2NF
Activities: Other business support service activities n.e.c.
Parent: Liverpool Victoria General Insurance Group Limited
Officers: Michael Peter Jones, Secretary; Jonathan Mark Dye [1966] Director; Richard Alexander Rowney [1970] Director/Group Chief Executive; Stephen Treloar [1968] Managing Director General Insurance

LV Protection Limited
Incorporated: 12 March 1984
Net Worth: £3,976,737 *Total Assets:* £5,565,734
Registered Office: County Gates, Bournemouth, BH1 2NF
Activities: Life insurance
Officers: Michael Peter Jones, Secretary; Andrew Mark Parsons [1965] Finance Director; Anthony Wayne Snow [1972] Director/Chief Risk Officer

LV Repair Services Limited
Incorporated: 23 December 2014
Net Worth: £10,052,000 *Total Assets:* £12,991,000
Registered Office: County Gates House, County Gates, Bournemouth, BH1 2NF
Activities: Other activities auxiliary to insurance and pension funding
Parent: Liverpool Victoria Insurance Company Limited
Officers: Michael Peter Jones, Secretary; Jonathan Mark Dye [1966] Director; Richard Alexander Rowney [1970] Director; Stephen Treloar [1968] Managing Director General Insurance

LVTG Holdings Limited
Incorporated: 8 August 2011 *Employees:* 2
Net Worth Deficit: £4,274,481 *Total Assets:* £65,486,972
Registered Office: Clifton Heights, Triangle West, Bristol, BS8 1EJ
Activities: Non-trading company
Parent: MTH Bidco Ltd
Officers: Alex Phillip Khan [1977] Director; Peter James Mitchell [1971] Director

LVTG Limited
Incorporated: 8 August 2011 *Employees:* 2
Net Worth Deficit: £2,374,366 *Total Assets:* £56,032,300
Registered Office: Clifton Heights, Triangle West, Bristol, BS8 1EJ
Activities: Non-trading company
Parent: LVTG Holdings Ltd
Officers: Alex Phillip Khan [1977] Director; Peter James Mitchell [1971] Director

Lyell Trading Limited
Incorporated: 24 October 2013
Net Worth: £22,716,444 *Total Assets:* £23,912,738
Registered Office: 1350-1360 Montpellier Court, Brockworth, Gloucester, GL3 4AH
Activities: Financial intermediation not elsewhere classified
Parent: Blackfinch Nominees Limited
Officers: Richard James Cook [1978] Director; Richard Leonard Simmonds [1979] Director/Chief Investment Officer

Lyme Bay Cider Company Limited
Incorporated: 27 August 1993
Net Worth: £2,744,107 *Total Assets:* £5,223,414
Registered Office: The Lyme Bay Winery, Shute, Seaton Junction, Axminster, Devon, EX13 7PW
Activities: Manufacture of cider and other fruit wines
Parent: Ball Capital Investment Limited
Officers: Andrew Robert Beasley, Secretary; Keith Michael Ball [1969] Director; Andrew Robert Beasley [1967] Director; James Lawrence Lambert [1981] Director

Lymington Investments Limited
Incorporated: 12 October 1978
Net Worth: £4,658,858 *Total Assets:* £7,666,361
Registered Office: 21 Churchfield Road, Poole, Dorset, BH15 2QL
Activities: Other letting and operating of own or leased real estate
Officers: David Lawrence Jenkin, Secretary; Brian Geoffrey Ford [1946] Director/Chartered Accountant; Amber Maitland Hamilton [1982] Director/Field Producer [American]; Monika Marrika Maitland [1947] Director/Housewife [German]

Lympstone Manor Ltd
Incorporated: 20 August 2014 *Employees:* 65
Net Worth: £5,029,190 *Total Assets:* £9,276,751
Registered Office: Lympstone Manor Ltd, Courtlands Lane, Exmouth, Devon, EX8 3NZ
Activities: Hotels and similar accommodation
Shareholder: Anthony George Edward Rowe
Officers: Wendy Karen Adams [1958] Director; Michael Andrew Caines [1969] Director; Michael Charles Rowe Dart [1967] Director/Retailer; Roger Paul Edwards [1965] Director; Steven George Edwards [1961] Director; David Gerrard Kirk [1966] Director; William Samuel Knapp [1974] Director; Mr Anthony George Edward Rowe [1948] Director; Rex Rozario [1935] Director

Lynton Downs Limited
Incorporated: 6 February 1958
Net Worth: £4,552,541 *Total Assets:* £4,967,300
Registered Office: Haredown Farmhouse, Great Bedwyn, Marlborough, Wilts, SN8 3ND
Activities: Raising of sheep and goats
Shareholders: Robert James Rickman; Andrew George Rickman
Officers: Robert James Rickman, Secretary/Forest Manager; Dr Andrew George Rickman [1960] Director/Engineer; Robert James Rickman [1957] Director/Forest Manager

Lyons Davidson Limited
Incorporated: 5 April 2011 *Employees:* 831
Net Worth: £19,180,220 *Total Assets:* £89,072,440
Registered Office: 43 Queen Square, Bristol, BS1 4QP
Activities: Solicitors
Parent: LD Group Holdings Limited
Officers: Gillian Angela Banbury [1966] Director/Certified Accountant; Alexandra Anne Louise Hewitt [1965] Director/Solicitor; Michelle Louise Lennaghan [1974] Director/Solicitor; Mark Savill [1967] Director/Solicitor; Richard James Squire [1955] Director/Solicitor

Lyons Seafoods Limited
Incorporated: 8 November 1994 *Employees:* 352
Net Worth: £40,598,000 *Total Assets:* £64,945,000
Registered Office: Fairfield House, Fairfield Road, Warminster, Wilts, BA12 9DA
Activities: Processing and preserving of fish, crustaceans and molluscs
Shareholder: Labeyrie Fine Foods SAS
Officers: Frederic Bouisset [1958] Director [French]; Steve Lawson [1964] Director [French]

Lypiatt Studio Limited
Incorporated: 28 February 1972 *Employees:* 7
Net Worth: £10,403,556 *Total Assets:* £11,482,991
Registered Office: Lypiatt Park, Stroud, Glos, GL6 7LL
Activities: Artistic creation
Shareholder: Eva Yvonne Chadwick
Officers: Eva Yvonne Chadwick, Secretary; Daniel Sebastian Chadwick [1965] Director/Sculptor; Eva Yvonne Chadwick [1934] Director/Administrator [French]; Simon David Chadwick [1943] Director/Sculptor; Dr Sarah Russell Marchant [1958] Director

M & G Properties (Cheltenham) Limited
Incorporated: 23 January 1997 *Employees:* 8
Net Worth: £4,514,448 *Total Assets:* £7,874,522
Registered Office: Pillar House, 113-115 Bath Road, Cheltenham, Glos, GL53 7LS
Activities: Other letting and operating of own or leased real estate
Parent: M & G Properties (Holdings) Limited
Officers: Alison Janette Edwards [1959] Director/Project Manager; Timothy Roy Edwards [1961] Director

M & M Plant (Devon & Cornwall) Ltd
Incorporated: 8 June 2006 *Employees:* 16
Net Worth: £1,532,318 *Total Assets:* £4,247,345
Registered Office: Trethorne, Kennards House, Launceston, Cornwall, PL15 8QE
Activities: Other retail sale not in stores, stalls or markets
Shareholders: Michael Winston Davey; Mark Leslie Gregory; Maria Gregory
Officers: Barry James Northcott, Secretary; Michael Winston Davey [1968] Director/Entrepreneur; Mark Leslie Gregory [1960] Director/Plant Salesman

M & P (Draycote) Limited
Incorporated: 13 February 1990 *Employees:* 43
Previous: Draycote Hotel Limited
Net Worth Deficit: £4,150,530 *Total Assets:* £3,804,238
Registered Office: Tregenna Castle Hotel, Trelyon Avenue, St Ives, Cornwall, TR26 2DE
Activities: Hotels and similar accommodation
Major Shareholder: John Howard Mason
Officers: Amanda Louise Mason, Secretary; Steven John Hewlett [1976] Director; John Howard Mason [1951] Director

M H Joinery Products PLC
Incorporated: 8 August 1994 *Employees:* 117
Net Worth: £3,052,984 *Total Assets:* £4,708,097
Registered Office: Unit 11 Parrett Way, Colley Lane Industrial Estate, Bridgwater, Somerset, TA6 5LD
Activities: Manufacture of other builders' carpentry and joinery
Shareholder: Michael John Tracey
Officers: Avril Jacqueline Saitch, Secretary; Ian Christopher Hobden [1964] Staircase Operations Director; Alan James Saitch [1957] Director/Metal Fabricators; Avril Jacqueline Saitch [1950] Director/Metal Fabricators; Michael John Tracey [1957] Director

M K Property & Letting Limited
Incorporated: 7 April 2011
Net Worth: £441,071 *Total Assets:* £3,663,559
Registered Office: 337 Holdenhurst Road, Bournemouth, BH8 8BT
Activities: Development of building projects
Major Shareholder: Michael Kaddah
Officers: Dania Kaddah [1989] Director/Promotion Model; Michael Kaddah [1948] Director/Property Developer; Sami Kaddah [1991] Director; Suzanne Kaddah [1986] Director/Estate Agent

M P Filtri (UK) Limited
Incorporated: 25 June 1987 *Employees:* 46
Net Worth: £4,381,665 *Total Assets:* £6,093,900
Registered Office: Bourton Industrial Park, Bourton on the Water, Glos, GL54 2HQ
Activities: Manufacture of other general-purpose machinery n.e.c.
Shareholders: Giovanni Pasotto; Monica Pasotto
Officers: Philip Bruce Keep, Secretary; Christopher Paul Durkin [1967] Sales Director; Sophia Elisabeth Fisher [1967] Operations Director; Philip Bruce Keep [1950] Director; Giovanni Pasotto [1962] Director/Export Department MP Filtri [Italian]; Monica Pasotto [1968] Director [Italian]

M. & N. Electrical and Mechanical Services Limited
Incorporated: 1 December 1993 *Employees:* 113
Net Worth: £3,951,815 *Total Assets:* £6,605,199
Registered Office: Unit 12 South Way, Southwell Business Park, Portland, Dorset, DT5 2NL
Activities: Other specialised construction activities n.e.c.
Major Shareholder: Gordon Matthew McFarlane
Officers: Simon James Light, Secretary; Simon James Light [1967] Director/Manager; Gordon Matthew McFarlane [1956] Managing Director

M. & P. Food Products Limited
Incorporated: 5 September 1978 *Employees:* 174
Net Worth: £9,381,893 *Total Assets:* £17,841,936
Registered Office: Tregenna Castle Hotel, Trelyon Avenue, St Ives, Cornwall, TR26 2DE
Activities: Development of building projects
Shareholder: John Howard Mason
Officers: Victoria Mason, Secretary; Steve John Hewlett [1976] Director; Amanda Louise Mason [1976] Director; John Howard Mason [1951] Director; Victoria Mason [1978] Director

M.A.C. Hotels Ltd
Incorporated: 7 February 2001 *Employees:* 98
Net Worth Deficit: £28,541,896 *Total Assets:* £10,282,649
Registered Office: Whatley Manor Hotel, Easton Grey, Malmesbury, Wilts, SN16 0RB
Activities: Hotels and similar accommodation
Parent: Ammonite Holdings Limited
Officers: Alix Landolt, Secretary; Alix Landolt [1945] Director [Swiss]; Christian Landolt [1966] Director/Hotelier [Swiss]

M.D. Building Services Limited
Incorporated: 1 May 1998 *Employees:* 241
Net Worth: £914,977 *Total Assets:* £5,563,329
Registered Office: The Malt House, Durnford Street, Ashton, Bristol, BS3 2AW
Activities: Other building completion and finishing
Parent: Radipole Mill Investments Limited
Officers: Brian John Daintith, Secretary; Sean Anthony Cooper [1966] Director; Stephen James Devlin [1967] Operations Director; Jane Nelson [1959] Director

M.K. Test Systems Ltd.
Incorporated: 14 April 1992 *Employees:* 22
Net Worth: £3,266,679 *Total Assets:* £4,516,323
Registered Office: ATE House, Westpark 26, Chelston, Wellington, Somerset, TA21 9AD
Activities: Manufacture of electronic measuring, testing etc. equipment, not for industrial process control
Parent: MK Test Group Limited
Officers: Carl John Bullock [1966] Managing Director; Jason Christopher Evans [1971] Sales Director; Michael Paul Threlfall [1964] Director/Electronics Engineer

M.T. Property Developments Limited
Incorporated: 18 January 2001
Net Worth: £430,413 *Total Assets:* £4,710,742
Registered Office: Oak Tree Cottage, Harewood Road, Calstock, Cornwall, PL18 9QN
Activities: Other letting and operating of own or leased real estate
Major Shareholder: Tracey Bernice Bennett
Officers: Tracey Bernice Bennett, Secretary; Tracey Bernice Bennett [1962] Director

Maats Tech Limited
Incorporated: 28 January 2010 *Employees:* 37
Net Worth: £11,229,550 *Total Assets:* £15,488,257
Registered Office: Office 14, Lancaster Centre, Meteor Business Park, Cheltenham Road East, Gloucester, GL2 9QL
Activities: Manufacture of lifting and handling equipment
Major Shareholder: Lisa Ann Edwards
Officers: James Edward Luxton, Secretary; Lisa Edwards [1964] Director

Mabey and Johnson Limited
Incorporated: 26 October 1943
Net Worth: £10,552,113 *Total Assets:* £10,903,454
Registered Office: Unit 9 Lydney Harbour Estate, Harbour Road, Lydney, Glos, GL15 4EJ
Activities: Manufacture of other fabricated metal products n.e.c.
Parent: Mabey Engineering (Holdings) Limited
Officers: Graeme Clive Voss, Secretary; Joanna Kate Beauchamp [1974] Director/Lawyer; Graeme Clive Voss [1970] Finance Director

Mabey Bridge Limited
Incorporated: 8 October 2001 *Employees:* 152
Net Worth: £20,780,956 *Total Assets:* £33,607,376
Registered Office: Unit 9 Lydney Harbour Estate, Harbour Road, Lydney, Glos, GL15 4EJ
Activities: Manufacture of other fabricated metal products n.e.c.
Parent: Mabey Engineering (Holdings) Limited
Officers: Shaun James Chivers [1962] Operations Director; Thomas Rasmussen [1974] Director/Civil Engineer [Irish]; Michael Treacy [1963] Director [Irish]; Graeme Clive Voss [1970] Director/Chartered Accountant

E.J. MacKelden & Sons (Bobbing) Limited
Incorporated: 5 July 1947
Net Worth: £22,501,736 *Total Assets:* £23,770,848
Registered Office: Combe, Brushford, Dulverton, Somerset, TA22 9RT
Activities: Growing of cereals (except rice), leguminous crops and oil seeds
Major Shareholder: Ernest John MacKelden
Officers: Julie Kelvie, Secretary; Ernest John MacKelden [1957] Director/Farmer

MacTaggart & Mickel Homes England Limited
Incorporated: 29 September 2016 *Employees:* 3
Net Worth Deficit: £681,000 *Total Assets:* £21,157,000
Registered Office: 4th Floor, East Cheltenham House, Clarence Street, Cheltenham, Glos, GL50 3JR
Activities: Construction of domestic buildings
Parent: MacTaggart & Mickel Group Limited
Officers: Paul John McAninch, Secretary; Joanne Matheson Casey [1958] Managing Director; Paul John McAninch [1973] Director/Certified Chartered Accountant; Andrew Alexander MacTaggart Mickel [1973] Director/Town Planner; Ross Mickel [1974] Director/General Manager; Edmund Joseph Monaghan [1964] Director/Chief Executive; David John Shaw [1961] Director

The Macular Disease Society
Incorporated: 13 October 1987 *Employees:* 49
Net Worth: £3,023,000 *Total Assets:* £4,029,000
Registered Office: Crown Chambers, South Street, Andover, Hants, SP10 2BN
Activities: Social work activities without accommodation for the elderly and disabled
Officers: Catherine Mary Yelf, Secretary; William John Best [1952] Director/Management Consultant; Cecilia Mary Bufton [1963] Director/Commercial Professional; John Herbert Dunston [1952] Director/Businessman; Toby Evans [1968] Director/Senior Manager, Audit Officer; Tim Ffytche [1936] Director/Retired; Anna Fletcher [1968] Director/Solicitor; Alison Guthrie [1955] Director/Optometrist; Alan Howell [1947] Director/Retired; Steven Alan Marris Kendall [1951] Director/Retired; Martyn Howard Long [1933] Director/Retired; Frances Luff [1965] Director/Public Affairs Consultant; Alan MacFarlane [1950] Director/Retired; Margaret Packham [1947] Director/HR Consultant; Richard Louis Piller [1961] Director/Accountant; Paul Ryb [1970] Managing Director; Stephen Robert Stacey [1955] Director/Retired

Madame Tussauds Touring Exhibition Limited
Incorporated: 15 September 1999 *Employees:* 103
Net Worth: £53,925,000 *Total Assets:* £64,870,000
Registered Office: Link House, 25 West Street, Poole, Dorset, BH15 1LD
Activities: Other amusement and recreation activities n.e.c.
Parent: Merlin Entertainments Group Holdings Limited
Officers: Fiona Jane Rose, Secretary; Matthew Paul Jowett [1967] Director/General Counsel and Company Secretary; Fiona Jane Rose [1964] Director/Assistant Group Company Secretary

Magdalen Victoria LLP
Incorporated: 13 February 2012
Net Worth: £4,613,070 *Total Assets:* £5,430,187
Registered Office: Beard Faraday Road, Dorcan, Swindon, Wilts, SN3 5JY
Officers: Mark George Beard [1963] Member; Edward Alan Beard [1932] LLP Member; James Chadwick Murrin [1956] LLP Member

Magellan Aerospace (Blackpool) Limited
Incorporated: 7 August 1990 *Employees:* 132
Net Worth: £6,957,000 *Total Assets:* £12,131,000
Registered Office: 510 Wallisdown Road, Bournemouth, BH11 8QN
Activities: Manufacture of air and spacecraft and related machinery
Shareholder: Norman Murray Edwards
Officers: Shawn David Smith, Secretary; Jason Scott Addis [1969] Director/Vice President, European Operations; Haydn Robert Martin [1963] Director; Elena Milantoni [1969] Director/CFO and Corporate Secretary [Canadian]; Shawn David Smith [1967] Director; Phillip Campion Underwood [1960] Director/President

Magellan Aerospace (UK) Limited
Incorporated: 23 September 2003 *Employees:* 892
Net Worth: £75,413,000 *Total Assets:* £104,136,000
Registered Office: 510 Wallisdown Road, Bournemouth, BH11 8QN
Activities: Other manufacturing n.e.c.
Shareholder: Norman Murray Edwards
Officers: Shawn David Smith, Secretary; Jason Scott Addis [1969] Director/Vice President, European Operations; Haydn Robert Martin [1963] Corporate Director, Business Development; Elena Milantoni [1969] Director/CFO and Corporate Secretary [Canadian]; Shawn David Smith [1967] Director/Accountant; Phillip Campion Underwood [1960] Director/President & CEO

Magicard Holdings Limited
Incorporated: 6 May 2016 *Employees:* 106
Net Worth: £322,083 *Total Assets:* £27,837,760
Registered Office: Waverley House, Hampshire Road, Granby Industrial Estate, Weymouth, Dorset, DT4 9XD
Activities: Activities of production holding companies
Officers: Ian Cliffe [1970] Director; Gordon Rodney Hague [1971] Director; Aylesh Kumar Patel [1989] Director/Investment Manager; Richard Antony Cargill Scott [1959] Director; Christopher John Thomas [1955] Non-Executive Director Chairman

Magicard Ltd
Incorporated: 14 April 2016 *Employees:* 95
Net Worth: £427,146 *Total Assets:* £21,823,900
Registered Office: Waverley House, Hampshire Road, Granby Industrial Estate, Weymouth, Dorset, DT4 9XD
Activities: Manufacture of computers and peripheral equipment
Officers: Ian Cliffe [1970] Director; Richard Antony Cargill Scott [1959] Director

Magmatic Limited
Incorporated: 18 February 2003 *Employees:* 80
Net Worth Deficit: £652,211 *Total Assets:* £4,056,760
Registered Office: Shaftesbury Chapel, Union Road, Bristol, BS2 0LP
Activities: Manufacture of other plastic products
Shareholders: Robert Law; BGF GP Limited
Officers: Trevor Bell [1957] Director/Consultant; Fiona Jane Gibson [1975] Director; Andrew Martyn Jones [1963] Director/FD; Robert Law [1977] Director; Mark Mason [1961] Commercial Director

Magna Learning Partnership
Incorporated: 30 November 2011 *Employees:* 332
Previous: St Edmund's School
Net Worth: £15,440,166 *Total Assets:* £19,338,012
Registered Office: St Edmund's School, Church Road, Laverstock, Salisbury, Wilts, SP1 1RD
Activities: General secondary education
Officers: Carina Sawyer, Secretary; Mark Allinson [1964] Director/Telecoms Manager; Mark Andrew Bower-Dyke [1958] Director/Chairman and CEO; Sarah Catherine Busby [1958] Director/Teacher; Nicola Coupe [1963] Director/School Improvement Advisor; Julia Mary Hastings [1968] Director/Management Consultant; Melissa Howarth [1975] Director/Accountant; Sharon Elizabeth McKinley [1964] Director/Business Development Manager; Neil Owen [1966] Managing Director; Kate Elizabeth Penn [1989] Director/Solicitor; Peter Radcliffe [1947] Director/Retired

Magna Manor Developments Limited
Incorporated: 19 November 2013 *Employees:* 1
Net Worth: £34,365 *Total Assets:* £4,027,968
Registered Office: Lennox House, 3 Pierrepont Street, Bath, BA1 1LB
Activities: Development of building projects
Shareholders: Michael John Watts; Jolanda Watts
Officers: Jolanda Watts, Secretary; Dr Michael John Watts [1956] Director

Magna Motor Company (Christchurch) Limited
Incorporated: 9 July 1999 *Employees:* 42
Net Worth: £1,382,322 *Total Assets:* £4,217,031
Registered Office: Horizon Motor Co Limited, 397 Ringwood Road, Poole, Dorset, BH12 4LT
Activities: Sale of new cars and light motor vehicles
Shareholders: Horizon Motor Company Limited; Magna Motor Company Limited
Officers: Aimee Marie Sharpe, Secretary; Stephen Anthony Roberts [1962] Director; Aimee Marie Sharpe [1974] Director; Christian Norman Sharpe [1979] Director; Colin Ross Sharpe [1945] Director

Magna Motor Company (Wessex) Ltd
Incorporated: 4 April 2002 *Employees:* 37
Net Worth: £1,677,213 *Total Assets:* £5,015,787
Registered Office: 397-399 Ringwood Road, Poole, Dorset, BH12 4LT
Activities: Sale of new cars and light motor vehicles
Shareholders: Stephen Anthony Roberts; Colin Ross Sharpe
Officers: Simon Nicholas Rickard, Secretary; Stephen Anthony Roberts [1962] Director; Colin Ross Sharpe [1945] Director

Magna Motor Company Limited
Incorporated: 2 December 1982 *Employees:* 74
Net Worth: £3,287,591 *Total Assets:* £9,943,413
Registered Office: 397-399 Ringwood Road, Parkstone, Poole, Dorset, BH12 4LT
Activities: Sale of new cars and light motor vehicles
Officers: Simon Nicholas Rickard, Secretary; Stephen Anthony Roberts [1962] Director/General Manager; Aimee Marie Sharpe [1974] Director; Christian Norman Sharpe [1979] Director; Colin Ross Sharpe [1945] Director

Magners GB Limited
Incorporated: 1 November 2009 *Employees:* 2
Net Worth: £37,743,000 *Total Assets:* £169,904,000
Registered Office: Ashford House, Grenadier Road, Exeter, Devon, EX1 3LH
Activities: Manufacture of cider and other fruit wines
Parent: C & C Holdings (NI) Limited
Officers: Stephen Glancey [1960] Director; Thomas Michael McCusker [1957] Managing Director; Andrea Pozzi [1971] Managing Director

Magnet Sales and Service Limited
Incorporated: 29 September 1993 *Employees:* 12
Net Worth: £4,942,269 *Total Assets:* £5,242,113
Registered Office: 31 Blackworth Industrial Estate, Highworth, Wilts, SN6 7NA
Activities: Other manufacturing n.e.c.
Major Shareholder: Ian Andrew Purvis
Officers: Ian Andrew Purvis, Secretary/Technical Sales Engineer; Andrew David Lobb [1967] Director/Manager; Ian Andrew Purvis [1959] Director/Technical Sales Engineer; Penelope Purvis [1959] Director/Teacher; Toby Alexander Purvis [1996] Director/General Manager

Magnox Limited
Incorporated: 2 June 1988 *Employees:* 2,442
Net Worth: £13,846,000 *Total Assets:* £150,030,000
Registered Office: Oldbury Technical Centre, Oldbury Naite, Thornbury, Glos, BS35 1RQ
Activities: Other service activities n.e.c.
Shareholder: Cavendish Fluor Partnership Limited
Officers: Kelly-Marie Williams, Secretary; Simon Christopher Bowen [1960] Director; Kenneth Malcolm Douglas [1970] Managing Director; Pamela Ruth Duerden [1966] Director; Paul Lloyd Edwards [1977] Director; Paul Douglas Hunt [1961] Director [American]; Susan Jee [1955] Director; John Gregory Meyer [1950] Director [American]; Anthony Moore [1956] Director; Andrew Spurr [1953] Director; Peter James Webster [1949] Director

Maiden Beech Academy Trust
Incorporated: 15 July 2011 *Employees:* 44
Net Worth: £4,017,392 *Total Assets:* £5,608,047
Registered Office: 3 Southernhay West, Exeter, Devon, EX1 1JG
Activities: Primary education
Officers: Christine Ruth Brown, Secretary; Rev Stephen Gray [1970] Director/Reverend; Kurt Hanson [1973] Director/Security Architect Consultant and Leader; Helen Hyde [1974] Director/Staff Governor; Neville Mapstone [1979] Director/Systems Manager; Florence McGhee [1983] Director/Human Resources Representative; David Moffatt [1971] Director/Parent Governor; Justine Pitman [1981] Director/Office Manager; Deborah Wakeman [1974] Director; Carl Matthew Winch [1970] Director/Headteacher

A.E. Maiden Limited
Incorporated: 11 May 1953
Net Worth: £4,237,729 *Total Assets:* £4,415,752
Registered Office: 12 St Leonards Road, Exeter, EX2 4LA
Activities: Buying and selling of own real estate
Officers: Andrew Peter Maiden, Secretary; Francesca Elizabeth Eve Dawson [1985] Director/Artist; Andrew Peter Maiden [1958] Director/Manager; Elizabeth Caroline Maiden [1958] Director/Teacher; Jed Andrew Theo Maiden [1994] Director/Architect; Zachary Andrew John Maiden [1988] Director

Walter Maidment Limited
Incorporated: 22 September 1970 *Employees:* 9
Net Worth: £2,678,307 *Total Assets:* £3,978,565
Registered Office: Manor Farm, Wilcot, Wilts, SN9 5NS
Activities: Raising of dairy cattle
Major Shareholder: Thomas Hugh Maidment
Officers: Mary Maidment, Secretary; Mary Maidment [1960] Director/Farmer [Irish]; Thomas Hugh Maidment [1956] Director/Farmer

Mail Handling International Limited
Incorporated: 23 August 1996 *Employees:* 41
Net Worth: £1,202,229 *Total Assets:* £4,820,690
Registered Office: 82 Feeder Road, Bristol, BS2 0TQ
Activities: Licensed carriers
Shareholders: Paul William Brown; Alexander Lawson
Officers: Paul William Brown, Secretary; Alexander Ritchie Lawson [1969] Director/Manager

Main Gate Leisure Limited
Incorporated: 11 July 1996 *Employees:* 102
Net Worth: £3,800,011 *Total Assets:* £4,832,317
Registered Office: Ladys Mile Farm, Exeter Road, Dawlish, Devon, EX7 0LX
Activities: Recreational vehicle parks, trailer parks and camping grounds
Parent: Ladys Mile Developments Limited
Officers: Alfred John Jeffery, Secretary; Jason Edward Jeffery [1973] Director/Camp Site Manager; Paul John Jeffery [1971] Director/Camp Site Manager

Mainchannel Developments Limited
Incorporated: 19 May 2015
Net Worth: £181,402 *Total Assets:* £4,772,976
Registered Office: 397 Christchurch Road, West Parley, Ferndown, Dorset, BH22 8SJ
Activities: Development of building projects
Major Shareholder: Paul Owen Richards
Officers: David Arthur Thomas, Secretary; Paul Owen Richards [1964] Director

Maistro PLC
Incorporated: 22 August 2012 *Employees:* 24
Previous: Blur Group PLC
Net Worth: £3,391,031 *Total Assets:* £4,320,925
Registered Office: 1a Grow On Building, 3 Babbage Way, Clyst, Honiton, Exeter, EX5 2FN
Activities: Other information technology service activities
Shareholder: Charles Street International Holdings Limited
Officers: Richard Croft, Secretary; Ian Stuart Cleverly [1969] Director/Chief Financial Officer/Accountant; Laurence Alistair John Cook [1961] Director; Richard James Croft [1963] Director/Solicitor; Preeti Mardia [1967] Director; Richard Anthony Rae [1959] Director; David Stanley Rowe [1958] Director

Majestic Limited
Incorporated: 21 November 2001 *Employees:* 3
Net Worth: £5,305,261 *Total Assets:* £5,310,681
Registered Office: 10 Somerset Place, Teignmouth, Devon, TQ14 8EN
Activities: Activities of head offices
Shareholder: Mark Wilfred Wright
Officers: Mark Wilfred Wright, Secretary/Tour Operator; James Wright [1936] Director/Tour Operator; Mark Wilfred Wright [1963] Director/Tour Operator; Rose Wright [1934] Director

Majestic Tours Limited
Incorporated: 26 October 1987 *Employees:* 37
Net Worth: £5,603,806 *Total Assets:* £9,770,634
Registered Office: 10 Somerset Place, Teignmouth, Devon, TQ14 8EN
Activities: Travel agency activities
Shareholder: Mark Wilfred Wright
Officers: Mark Wilfred Wright, Secretary; James Wright [1936] Director/Tour Operator; Mark Wilfred Wright [1963] Director/Tour Operator; Rose Wright [1934] Director

Malaby Biogas Limited
Incorporated: 3 September 2009
Net Worth: £662,216 *Total Assets:* £5,004,472
Registered Office: Bore Hill Farm, Biodigester, Deverill Road, Warminster, Wilts, BA12 8FB
Activities: Manufacture of gas
Parent: Malaby Holdings Ltd
Officers: Toby George Minter, Secretary; Thomas Frederick Minter [1965] Director; Toby George Minter [1967] Director

Malaby Holdings Limited
Incorporated: 27 September 1909
Net Worth: £6,706,665 *Total Assets:* £6,894,717
Registered Office: 3 Farleigh House, Frome Road, Bradford on Avon, Wilts, BA15 1LE
Activities: Activities of other holding companies n.e.c.
Shareholders: Thomas Frederick Minter; Toby George Minter
Officers: Toby George Minter, Secretary/Director; Nicola Gaye Minter [1967] Director/Hypnotherapist; Paula Jeanne Minter [1964] Director/Teacher [American]; Thomas Frederick Minter [1965] Director; Toby George Minter [1967] Director

Malbury Properties Limited
Incorporated: 24 July 1964 *Employees:* 2
Net Worth: £2,716,889 *Total Assets:* £3,533,900
Registered Office: 6th Floor, Dean Park House, Dean Park Crescent, Bournemouth, BH1 1HP
Activities: Development of building projects
Parent: Malbury Properties Holdings Limited
Officers: Vivien Jane Farquharson [1950] Director; Naomi Jane Farrar [1972] Director/General Manager

EP Mallory & Son (Holdings) Limited
Incorporated: 21 October 2016
Net Worth: £4,184,234 *Total Assets:* £4,434,234
Registered Office: 1-5 Bridge Street, Bath, BA2 4AP
Activities: Retail sale of watches and jewellery in specialised stores
Shareholders: Anthony Patrick Vander Woerd; Robert Henry Vander Woerd
Officers: John Vincent William Pearce, Secretary; Malcolm Leslie Bishop [1944] Director/Barrister; Anthony Patrick Van Der Woerd [1948] Director; Helen Louise Vander Woerd [1982] Director; Katie Anne Vander Woerd [1979] Director; Robert Henry Vander Woerd [1951] Director; Wendy Ann Vander Woerd [1950] Director

E.P.Mallory & Son,Limited
Incorporated: 8 November 1928 *Employees:* 41
Net Worth: £6,947,374 *Total Assets:* £11,636,272
Registered Office: 1-5 Bridge Street, Bath, BA2 4AP
Activities: Retail sale of watches and jewellery in specialised stores
Officers: John Vincent William Pearce, Secretary; Malcolm Leslie Bishop [1944] Director/Barrister; Anthony Patrick Van Der Woerd [1948] Director; Helen Louise Vander Woerd [1982] Director/Education Co-ordinator; Katie Anne Vander Woerd [1979] Director; Robert Henry Vander Woerd [1951] Director; Wendy Ann Vander Woerd [1950] Director

Mallory Holdings Limited
Incorporated: 4 January 2002 *Employees:* 32
Net Worth: £2,117,010 *Total Assets:* £5,064,053
Registered Office: Centenary House, Peninsula Park, Rydon Lane, Exeter, EX2 7XE
Activities: Other business support service activities n.e.c.
Shareholders: Ulrike Hardinge; Julian Alexander Hardinge of Penshurst
Officers: Ulrike Hardinge, Secretary/Systems Analyst [German]; Ulrike Hardinge [1957] Director/Systems Analyst [German]; Lord Julian Alexander Hardinge of Penshurst [1945] Director/Bookseller; George Alexander John Murray [1947] Director/Publisher

Mallory International Limited
Incorporated: 16 November 1994 *Employees:* 32
Net Worth: £2,058,964 *Total Assets:* £4,850,964
Registered Office: Centenary House, Peninsula Park, Rydon Lane, Exeter, EX2 7XE
Activities: Other service activities n.e.c.
Parent: Mallory International MIE Designated Activity Company
Officers: Ulrike Hardinge, Secretary/Bookseller [German]; Ulrike Hardinge [1957] Director/Bookseller [German]; Lord Julian Alexander Hardinge of Penshurst [1945] Director/Bookseller; Sophie Jane Hardinge-Walsh [1974] Director; Rachel Jimenez Dickson [1984] Director/Manager; Mathieu Julien Arnaud Peligry [1985] Director [French]; Sancha Sandling Rees [1974] Director

Malmesbury C of E Primary School
Incorporated: 11 April 2013 *Employees:* 69
Net Worth: £4,722,433 *Total Assets:* £5,056,889
Registered Office: Malmesbury C of E Primary School, Tetbury Hill, Malmesbury, Wilts, SN16 9JR
Activities: Primary education
Officers: Tina Lesley Osborne, Secretary; Judith Elizabeth Brown [1967] Director/Teaching Assistant; Julie Kay Brown [1952] Director/Nurse Manager; Charlotte Mary Cox [1971] Director/Teaching Assistant; Christopher Davies [1978] Director/Telecommunications Engineer; Deborah Michelle Hampton [1965] Director/Teacher; Melanie Jane Harris [1975] Director/Business Architect; Stephen David Heal [1968] Director/Headteacher; Brian Alexander Leitch [1976] Director/Project Manager; Daren Luscombe [1967] Director/Environmental Consultant; Dr Paula Louise Muir-McLeod [1977] Director/Teacher; Laurence Alan George Mussett [1964] Director; Christopher Simon Osborn [1979] Director/Engineer; Nigel Graham Roberts [1961] Managing Director; Rev Oliver Charles Milligan Ross [1968] Director/Vicar; Ewen Vizor [1969] Director/Teacher

The Malvern Property Limited
Incorporated: 21 December 2010 *Employees:* 135
Net Worth: £3,221,909 *Total Assets:* £8,912,676
Registered Office: Claremont House, 83 Church Road, Bishopsworth, Bristol, BS13 8JU
Activities: Buying and selling of own real estate
Shareholders: Hemsley Investment LLC; Huw Spencer Watson
Officers: Maarten Duncan Hemsley [1949] Director [American]; Helen Claire Rogers [1965] Director; Huw Spencer Watson [1958] Director

Malvern Tyres (Wholesale) Limited
Incorporated: 7 September 2000 *Employees:* 207
Net Worth: £2,048,728 *Total Assets:* £14,419,464
Registered Office: Malvern House, Priory Road, Gloucester, GL1 2RQ
Activities: Wholesale trade of motor vehicle parts and accessories
Parent: Malvern Tyres Holdings Limited
Officers: Robert Malcolm Freeman, Secretary/Operations Director; Richard Henry Knight, Secretary; Michael William Craddock [1945] Director; Christopher David Freeman [1990] Director/Office Manager; Robert Malcolm Freeman [1967] Operations Director; Alan Paul Mowbray [1956] Director/Wholesale Sales Manager; Alan Mark Stenning [1962] Director/Retail Manager

Malvern Tyres Holdings Limited
Incorporated: 14 May 2008 *Employees:* 551
Net Worth: £8,569,950 *Total Assets:* £47,773,200
Registered Office: Malvern House, Priory Road, Gloucester, GL1 2RQ
Activities: Activities of other holding companies n.e.c.
Major Shareholder: Robert Malcolm Freeman
Officers: Christopher David Freeman [1990] Director/Office Manager; Robert Malcolm Freeman [1967] Director

MAMG Infrastructure Management Limited
Incorporated: 23 October 2015
Net Worth: £175,325 *Total Assets:* £7,869,401
Registered Office: Third Floor, Broad Quay House, Prince Street, Bristol, BS1 4DJ
Activities: Other business support service activities n.e.c.
Parent: Imagile Group Limited
Officers: Susan Taberner, Secretary; Alan Edward Birch [1970] Director; Jonathan Michael Simpson [1973] Director/Accountant

MAN Truck and Bus UK Limited
Incorporated: 18 February 1992 *Employees:* 799
Net Worth: £80,792,000 *Total Assets:* £490,040,992
Registered Office: Frankland Road, Blagrove, Swindon, Wilts, SN5 8YU
Activities: Sale of other motor vehicles
Officers: Stefan Thyssen, Secretary; Johan Ulfson Bjornor [1968] Director/Head of Sales Truck [Swedish]; Patrizio Cardillo [1967] Director/Senior Vice President [German]; Thomas Hemmerich [1967] Managing Director [German]; Stefan Thyssen [1983] Finance Director [German]

Manawey Developments Limited
Incorporated: 21 October 1965
Net Worth Deficit: £932,675 *Total Assets:* £4,937,160
Registered Office: Hitchcock House, Hilltop Park, Devizes Road, Salisbury, Wilts, SP3 4UF
Activities: Development of building projects
Parent: Areawise Ltd
Officers: Azita Froggatt [1966] Director; Christopher Lionel Froggatt [1993] Director; Lionel Maurice Froggatt [1945] Director

The Manchester Abode Limited
Incorporated: 18 January 2006 *Employees:* 60
Net Worth: £9,944,748 *Total Assets:* £10,588,944
Registered Office: 8 Gay Street, Bath, BA1 2PH
Activities: Hotels and similar accommodation
Major Shareholder: Andrew Douglas Brownsword
Officers: Peter Tyrrell, Secretary; Andrew Douglas Brownsword [1947] Director; Jeremy David Hancock [1964] Director; Stephanie Hocking [1966] Director; Peter Tyrrell [1972] Director

Manchester and Provincial Car Parks Limited
Incorporated: 2 April 1987 *Employees:* 1
Net Worth: £1,983,646 *Total Assets:* £4,754,660
Registered Office: 17 Imperial Square, Cheltenham, Glos, GL50 1QZ
Activities: Other passenger land transport
Parent: Satnam Investments Ltd
Officers: John Frederick Staite, Secretary; Kuldip Singh Dhillon [1950] Director; Satnam Singh Dhillon [1977] Director/Administrator; Colin Griffiths [1963] Director/Chartered Town Planner; John Frederick Staite [1948] Director/Accountant

Manchester Working Limited
Incorporated: 23 June 2006 *Employees:* 178
Net Worth: £5,264,000 *Total Assets:* £15,522,000
Registered Office: 1390 Montpellier Court, Gloucester Business Park, Brockworth, Gloucester, GL3 4AH
Activities: Development of building projects
Parent: Morrison Facilities Services Limited
Officers: Ben Robert Westran, Secretary; Councillor Paul Gerrard Andrews [1955] Director; Carol Ann Culley [1968] Director/City Treasurer; David John Miles [1966] Director; Andrew Christopher Melville Smith [1972] Director/Chartered Accountant; Andrew Wilson [1959] Divisional Managing Director

Manitou Finance Limited
Incorporated: 24 October 1988
Net Worth: £15,888,000 *Total Assets:* £127,663,000
Registered Office: 34 Blackmoor Road, Ebblake Industrial Estate, Verwood, Dorset, BH31 6BB
Activities: Financial leasing
Shareholders: BNP Paribas SA; Manitou BF SA
Officers: Nicholas David James, Secretary; John James Patrick Bolton [1981] Director/General Manager; Jean-Michel Robert Boyer [1963] Director/CEO - Country Manager [French]; Michel Paul Denis [1965] Director/President & CEO Manitou BF [French]

Manitou UK Limited
Incorporated: 11 April 1972 *Employees:* 42
Net Worth: £9,706,000 *Total Assets:* £46,477,000
Registered Office: Ebblake Industrial Estate, Verwood, Dorset, BH31 6BB
Activities: Manufacture of lifting and handling equipment
Parent: Manitou BF
Officers: Ben Warwick, Secretary; Mark Peter Ormond [1970] Managing Director; Pierre-Francois Michel Piron [1974] Director/Sales & Marketing Controller [French]; Jean Pierre Rouault [1966] Director/Vice President Sales Northern Europe [French]

Manlock Investments Limited
Incorporated: 27 August 2004
Net Worth: £394,088,000 *Total Assets:* £397,488,992
Registered Office: Cobham PLC, Brook Road, Wimborne, Dorset, BH21 2BJ
Activities: Activities of head offices
Parent: Cobham PLC
Officers: Lyn Carol Colloff, Secretary; Nigel Rynd Daly [1962] Director/Business Executive; Kenneth John Morrison [1960] Director/Chartered Accountant

The Manor Collection Limited
Incorporated: 3 July 1995 *Employees:* 73
Net Worth: £4,344,773 *Total Assets:* £4,670,436
Registered Office: 128 High Street, Crediton, Devon, EX17 3LQ
Activities: Residential care activities for the elderly and disabled
Shareholders: Guy Perring Rogers; Nicola Jayne Rogers
Officers: Guy Perring Rogers [1963] Director/Residential Home Proprietor; Nicola Jayne Rogers [1967] Director/Residential Home Proprietor

Manor Farm (Castle Cary) Limited
Incorporated: 27 March 1954 *Employees:* 8
Net Worth: £1,893,657 *Total Assets:* £4,267,794
Registered Office: Maltravers House, Petters Way, Yeovil, Somerset, BA20 1SH
Activities: Raising of dairy cattle
Shareholders: Alistair John Churchouse; Diana Mary Churchouse
Officers: Diana Mary Churchouse, Secretary; Alistair John Churchouse [1951] Director/Farmer; Diana Mary Churchouse [1954] Director/Farmer

Manor House Hotel (Okehampton) Limited
Incorporated: 6 February 1985 *Employees:* 341
Net Worth: £18,222,200 *Total Assets:* £27,626,784
Registered Office: The Manor House Hotel, Fowley Down, Okehampton, Devon, EX20 4NA
Activities: Hotels and similar accommodation
Shareholders: Simon William James Essex; Joan Elizabeth Essex
Officers: Simon William James Essex, Secretary; Joan Elizabeth Essex [1947] Director/Hotelier; Simon William James Essex [1945] Director/Hotelier

Manor Life Investments Limited
Incorporated: 20 April 2012
Net Worth: £33,275 *Total Assets:* £4,184,271
Registered Office: Harbour House, 60 Purewell, Christchurch, Dorset, BH23 1ES
Activities: Activities of investment trusts
Parent: Nicolas James Holdings Limited
Officers: Stuart Andrew Bateman, Secretary; Stuart Andrew Bateman [1976] Director; David Francis Robbins [1967] Finance Director

Manor Lodge Developments Limited
Incorporated: 27 March 2012
Net Worth: £1,605,168 *Total Assets:* £3,601,582
Registered Office: 37 Shiphay Lane, Torquay, Devon, TQ2 7DU
Activities: Other letting and operating of own or leased real estate
Major Shareholder: David Guy Wilson
Officers: David Guy Wilson [1957] Director

Manor Renewable Energy Limited
Incorporated: 30 October 2013 *Employees:* 12
Net Worth: £4,479,012 *Total Assets:* £9,325,122
Registered Office: Unity Chambers, 34 High East Street, Dorchester, DT1 1HA
Activities: Other business support service activities n.e.c.
Shareholders: John Tye; Eric William Briar; Tobias John Mead
Officers: Eric William Briar [1966] Director/Marine Consultant; Tobias John Mead [1970] Director/Marine Consultant; John Tye [1955] Director/Marine Engineer

Manor Vets Limited
Incorporated: 17 February 2015 *Employees:* 77
Net Worth: £819,294 *Total Assets:* £8,306,697
Registered Office: The Chocolate Factory, Keynsham, Bristol, BS31 2AU
Activities: Dormant company
Parent: Pro-Vets Group Limited
Officers: Amanda Jane Davis [1968] Director; David Robert Geoffrey Hillier [1962] Director

Manton Riches Holdings Limited
Incorporated: 7 August 2014 *Employees:* 20
Net Worth: £3,057,221 *Total Assets:* £7,749,255
Registered Office: 15 Church Street, Ilchester, Somerset, BA22 8LN
Activities: Activities of head offices
Shareholders: Nicholas Atkins; Eef Van Leusden
Officers: Nicholas Atkins [1945] Director; Judith Elizabeth Hall [1958] Director/Accountant

Mantracourt Electronics Limited
Incorporated: 31 August 1983 *Employees:* 35
Net Worth: £7,311,841 *Total Assets:* £7,961,372
Registered Office: Mantracourt Electronics Ltd, The Drive, Farringdon, Exeter, EX5 2JB
Activities: Manufacture of electronic measuring, testing etc. equipment, not for industrial process control
Major Shareholder: David Richard Willmington
Officers: Hannah Rachel Brown, Secretary; Carol Joy Willmington, Secretary; Deborah Anne Willmington-Badcock, Secretary; David Richard Willmington [1952] Director/Electronics Engineer; Robert James Willmington-Badcock [1978] Director

Manual Investing Limited
Incorporated: 25 October 1993 *Employees:* 1
Net Worth: £1,848,382 *Total Assets:* £6,266,258
Registered Office: Barrow Hill House, Milborne Wick, Milborne Port, Sherborne, Dorset, DT9 4PP
Activities: Buying and selling of own real estate
Major Shareholder: Robert George Tizzard
Officers: Sarah Louise Tizzard, Secretary; Robert George Tizzard [1954] Director

Manuli Packaging (UK) Ltd.
Incorporated: 2 September 1992 *Employees:* 45
Net Worth: £3,552,767 *Total Assets:* £10,309,502
Registered Office: Unit 6 Leafield Industrial Estate, Corsham, Wilts, SN13 9SW
Activities: Manufacture of plastic packing goods
Officers: Andrew Short, Secretary; Tiziano Andreini [1972] Director [Italian]; Paul Grimes [1949] Director/Accountant; Saverio Lombardini [1967] Director [Italian]; Antonio Pecorone [1973] Director/Accountant [Italian]; Andrew Short [1945] Director

Manutan Limited
Incorporated: 4 July 1978 *Employees:* 4
Net Worth: £9,819,000 *Total Assets:* £9,836,000
Registered Office: c/o Key Industrial Equipment Ltd, Blackmoor Road, Ebblake Industrial Estate, Verwood, Dorset, BH31 6AT
Activities: Other business support service activities n.e.c.
Parent: Manutan International SA
Officers: Pierre-Olivier Brial, Secretary; Keith Charles Boad [1959] Managing Director; Pierre-Oliver Brial [1973] Director/Manager [French]; Jean-Pierre Guichard [1946] Director [French]; Xavier Emmanuel Guichard [1973] Director [French]

Mar-Key Marquees Limited
Incorporated: 30 April 1991 *Employees:* 74
Net Worth: £322,463 *Total Assets:* £4,177,558
Registered Office: Operational Centre, Throop Road, Bournemouth, BH8 0DF
Activities: Manufacture of other fabricated metal products n.e.c.
Major Shareholder: David Bryan Tabb
Officers: Linda Kathleen Williams, Secretary; Andrew James Goldie [1973] Director; Michael Richard James [1964] Director; Benjamin Scroggie [1980] Director; David Bryan Tabb [1952] Director

Marazion Holdings Limited
Incorporated: 23 December 1996 *Employees:* 244
Net Worth: £2,561,537 *Total Assets:* £9,047,347
Registered Office: Manor Office, Marazion, Cornwall, TR17 0EF
Activities: Activities of head offices
Shareholders: James Piers Southwell St Levan; Lady Mary Caroline St Levan; David Charles Hunt
Officers: Lord James Piers Southwell St Levan, Secretary; Lord James Piers Southwell St Levan [1950] Director; Lady Mary Caroline St Levan [1954] Director

Marcatrin Limited
Incorporated: 20 June 1979
Net Worth: £4,300,164 *Total Assets:* £4,852,469
Registered Office: 21a Elmlea Avenue, Stoke Bishop, Bristol, BS9 3UU
Activities: Activities of open-ended investment companies
Officers: Christopher Steven Allt [1980] Director/Property Management/Graphic Design; Janet Patricia Allt [1953] Director/Retired; John David Allt [1951] Director

Marcham Farms Limited
Incorporated: 7 August 1996 *Employees:* 10
Net Worth: £7,894,773 *Total Assets:* £9,292,502
Registered Office: Old Library Chambers, 21 Chipper Lane, Salisbury, Wilts, SP1 1BG
Activities: Growing of cereals (except rice), leguminous crops and oil seeds
Shareholders: John Lincoln Duffield; Lady Mary Jean Boyd-Carpenter
Officers: Stella Ivanova Selwood, Secretary; John Lincoln Duffield [1939] Director; Stella Ivanova Selwood [1972] Director/Secretary

Marchant-Holliday School Limited
Incorporated: 15 January 1959 *Employees:* 56
Net Worth: £5,041,765 *Total Assets:* £5,172,818
Registered Office: Marchant-Holliday School, North Cheriton, Templecombe, Somerset, BA8 0AH
Activities: Primary education
Officers: Jane Mayes, Secretary; Simon William Thorrold Sixtus Jaggard [1970] Director/Teacher; Michael Ralph Henry Liddicoat [1957] Director/Retired; Stephen Murcer [1958] Director/Banker; Lisa Jane Prior [1963] Director; Emma Louise Ramsay [1964] Director/Lawyer; Nicholas Lawrence Short [1978] Director/Civil Servant [British/Canadian]; Barbara Ann Tupper [1949] Director/Retired

Marchmont Farms Limited
Incorporated: 11 October 1983 *Employees:* 6
Net Worth: £7,338,870 *Total Assets:* £54,521,732
Registered Office: The Courtyard, Holt Lodge Farm, Horton, Wimborne, Dorset, BH21 7JN
Activities: Mixed farming
Officers: Hugo Aylesford Burge, Secretary; Laura Whitford, Secretary; Hugo Aylesford Burge [1972] Director/Company Secretary; Oliver Aylesford Burge [1941] Director

Marden Edwards Limited
Incorporated: 21 April 1931 *Employees:* 173
Net Worth: £12,036,034 *Total Assets:* £16,406,902
Registered Office: 2 Nimrod Way, East Dorset Trade Park, Wimborne, Dorset, BH21 7SH
Activities: Manufacture of other general-purpose machinery n.e.c.
Officers: Jonathan Leighton Edwards, Secretary; David Anthony Aimson [1968] Director/Accountant; Jonathan Leighton Edwards [1961] Director; Jeremy Bryan Marden [1964] Director; Wayne Kelvin Lawrence Moore [1964] Director; Michael Anthony Patey [1965] Director

The Mare and Foal Sanctuary
Incorporated: 30 March 2011 *Employees:* 105
Net Worth: £10,506,820 *Total Assets:* £10,641,515
Registered Office: Honeysuckle Farm, Haccombe-with-Combe, Newton Abbot, Devon, TQ12 4SA
Activities: Farm animal boarding and care
Officers: Nigel Julian Brown [1954] Director/Retired Banker; James Fitzpatrick [1981] Director/Communications Specialist; Elizabeth Louise Gaffer [1965] Director of Marketing; Donna Hallett [1979] Director/Deputy Manager; Robert Jonathan Lovell [1947] Director/Education Officer (Retired); Louise Harriet Sharpe [1969] Director

Marine & Towage Services Group Limited
Incorporated: 2 July 1924 *Employees:* 32
Net Worth: £9,196,027 *Total Assets:* £36,461,876
Registered Office: Kings Quay, King Street, Brixham, Devon, TQ5 9FW
Activities: Sea and coastal freight water transport
Parent: Bhagwan Marine Pty Ltd
Officers: Lauri Keven Kannikoski [1960] Director [Australian]; Jon Martin Leonard Parslow [1960] Director; Anthony Edward Wooles [1961] Director [Australian]

Marine Academy Plymouth
Incorporated: 18 March 2010 *Employees:* 215
Net Worth: £15,712,000 *Total Assets:* £20,316,000
Registered Office: c/o Universtity of Plymouth, 18 Portland Villas, Drake Circus, Plymouth, PL4 8AA
Activities: General secondary education
Officers: Anita Jane Martin, Secretary; Mark Delf [1962] Director/Head of School; Russell Geach [1979] Director/Research Manager; Adrian Hollister [1971] Director/IT Executive; Alice Mary Ludgate [1987] Director/Business Manager; Victoria Jane Matthews [1968] Director of Talent and Organisational Development; Siobhan Meredith [1988] Director/Headteacher; Justin Olosande [1965] Director; Darren Winter [1980] Director/Project Engineer; Leigh Withers [1976] Director/School Principal; Martin Wright [1977] Director/Teacher

Market Square Limited
Incorporated: 22 April 1975 *Employees:* 5
Net Worth: £4,556,839 *Total Assets:* £6,064,346
Registered Office: Ferry Cottage, Noss Mayo, Plymouth, PL8 1EU
Activities: Licenced restaurants
Officers: Angela Mary Hallett, Secretary; Angela Mary Hallett [1945] Director/Secretary; Barrie Hallett [1942] Director/Chartered Surveyor; Jonathan William Hallett [1970] Director/Designer; Simon John Hallett [1967] Director/Naval Officer; Timothy Kent Hallett [1974] Director/Chartered Surveyor

MG Markey Group Limited
Incorporated: 19 September 1991 *Employees:* 179
Net Worth: £3,966,040 *Total Assets:* £32,264,956
Registered Office: Q1 Quadrant Way, Hardwicke, Gloucester, GL2 2RN
Activities: Buying and selling of own real estate
Shareholders: Paul Francis Markey; Anthony Joseph Markey
Officers: Anthony Joseph Markey [1964] Director; Paul Francis Markey [1960] Director/Chartered Accountant

Marks Barn Farm (Crewkerne) Limited
Incorporated: 29 August 1960
Net Worth: £3,524,298 *Total Assets:* £4,199,663
Registered Office: Shutteroaks, Crewkerne, Somerset, TA18 7TR
Activities: Liquid milk and cream production
Shareholders: Hilary Freer Lawrence as Executor of The Simon Gear Lawrence Estate; Justin David Brittain Martin as Executor of The Simon Gear Lawrence Estate; Brian Mervyn Butt as Executor of The Simon Gear Lawrence Estate; Charles Francis Burnett Clarke as Trustee of The AH Warren Trust
Officers: Suzanne Weekes, Secretary; Brian Mervyn Butt [1940] Director/Chartered Accountant; Guy Coleman [1965] Director; Hilary Freer Lawrence [1938] Director/Retired; Matthew John Tufton [1979] Director/Accountant

Marlborough Facilities Limited
Incorporated: 10 July 2003 *Employees:* 3
Net Worth: £938,000 *Total Assets:* £5,792,000
Registered Office: Third Floor, Broad Quay House, Prince Street, Bristol, BS1 4DJ
Activities: Development of building projects
Parent: Chiltern Securities Limited
Officers: Graham John Hutt [1954] Regional Director; Andrew Richard Kershaw [1965] Director/Projects Controller; Richard Little [1979] Investment Director

Marleton Cross Limited
Incorporated: 11 June 1975 *Employees:* 195
Net Worth: £4,727,661 *Total Assets:* £14,012,885
Registered Office: Unit 2C, Alpha Close, Delta Drive, Tewkesbury Industrial Estate, Tewkesbury, Glos, GL20 8JF
Activities: Manufacture of household and sanitary goods and of toilet requisites
Shareholder: Bernard Leslie Robinson
Officers: Leonard John Jakeman, Secretary; Kenneth Leslie Beney [1965] Sales Director; Leonard John Jakeman [1957] Director/Chartered Accountant; Robert Edward Law [1947] Director/Accountant; Bernard Leslie Robinson [1947] Director; Lynda Robinson [1948] Director; Nicholas Paul Robinson [1970] Director

Marlux Medical Limited
Incorporated: 5 June 1998 *Employees:* 8
Net Worth: £4,597,426 *Total Assets:* £4,888,535
Registered Office: Summit Medical Limited, Industrial Park, Bourton on Water, Cheltenham, Glos, GL54 2HQ
Activities: Manufacture of medical and dental instruments and supplies
Officers: Alastair John McKay, Secretary; Daniel John Bee [1967] Director; Alec John Simpson [1969] Director

Marsden Estate Partnership LLP
Incorporated: 4 March 2016
Net Worth: £25,213,394 *Total Assets:* £26,547,854
Registered Office: Shawswell Farmhouse, Rendcombe, Glos, GL7 7HD
Officers: Caroline Patricia St Pier [1960] Member; Philip Mark St Pier [1959] Member; Evelyn Margaret Nora St Pier [1996] LLP Member; Richard Andrew Colin St Pier [1997] LLP Member

Marsh Court Farm Limited
Incorporated: 18 August 1999 *Employees:* 3
Net Worth: £3,082,944 *Total Assets:* £5,346,198
Registered Office: Marsh Court, Bridgend, Eldersfield, Gloucester, GL19 4PN
Activities: Raising of other cattle and buffaloes
Officers: Lorraine Rosemary Hobson, Secretary; Lorraine Rosemary Hobson [1959] Director/Farm Manager; Stanley Hobson [1927] Director/Accountant

Marsh Holdings Limited
Incorporated: 14 March 2008 *Employees:* 75
Net Worth: £1,171,523 *Total Assets:* £7,481,562
Registered Office: Unit 5 Merriott House, Hennock Road, Marsh Barton, Exeter, Devon, EX2 8NJ
Activities: Activities of head offices
Major Shareholder: Richard John Marsh
Officers: Michael Wall, Secretary/Director; Richard John Marsh [1965] Director; Michael Wall [1967] Director

Stuart Marsh Shoes Limited
Incorporated: 24 December 1982 *Employees:* 64
Net Worth: £3,034,857 *Total Assets:* £4,459,842
Registered Office: Hennock Court, Hennock Road East, Marsh Barton Trading Estate, Exeter, EX2 8RU
Activities: Activities of head offices
Shareholders: Stuart Marsh; Margaret Lesley Marsh
Officers: Susan Harper, Secretary; Margaret Lesley Marsh [1948] Director/Footwear Retailer; Philip Benjamin Marsh [1980] Director; Richard Peter William Marsh [1971] Director; Stuart Marsh [1946] Director/Footwear Retailer

Marshalsea Hydraulics Limited
Incorporated: 5 March 1930 *Employees:* 55
Net Worth: £3,235,000 *Total Assets:* £4,223,000
Registered Office: Rotork House, Brassmill Lane, Bath, BA1 3JQ
Activities: Manufacture of pumps
Parent: Bifold Fluidpower (Holdings) Limited
Officers: Sarah Parsons, Secretary; Jonathan Mark Davis [1966] Director/Chartered Accountant; Kevin George Hostetler [1968] Director/Chief Executive [American]

Martin & Martin Holdings
Incorporated: 14 March 1933 *Employees:* 396
Net Worth: £2,506,450 *Total Assets:* £53,258,832
Registered Office: Wemberham Lane, Yatton, Somerset, BS49 4BS
Activities: Activities of other holding companies n.e.c.
Major Shareholder: Bruce Martin
Officers: Savi Raj Madan [1965] Operations Director; Georgina Melissa Martin [1974] Director; Simon Robert Bruce Martin [1971] Director

A.L.Martin & Son,Limited
Incorporated: 1 January 1951 *Employees:* 35
Net Worth: £2,759,078 *Total Assets:* £3,790,979
Registered Office: 36 Fore Street, Okehampton, Devon, EX20 1HB
Activities: Retail sale of meat and meat products in specialised stores
Major Shareholder: Richard John Martin
Officers: Daphne Mary Martin, Secretary; Andrew John Martin [1967] Director/Butcher; Phillip Leslie Martin [1965] Director/Butcher; Richard John Martin [1941] Director/Butcher

Bob Martin (UK) Limited
Incorporated: 25 February 2002 *Employees:* 396
Net Worth: £1,128,330 *Total Assets:* £50,035,164
Registered Office: Wemberham Lane, Yatton, Bristol, BS49 4BS
Activities: Manufacture of pharmaceutical preparations
Parent: Martin & Martin Holdings
Officers: Andrew Mark Cooke [1974] Director; Andrew Michael Ford [1964] Director; Daniel Sebastian Fromm [1975] Director; Georgina Melissa Martin [1974] Director; William James Steele [1971] Director; Jeremy Paul Warne [1963] Director

Martin and Company Limited
Incorporated: 8 October 1912 *Employees:* 16
Net Worth: £2,476,930 *Total Assets:* £4,065,243
Registered Office: 19 The Promenade, Cheltenham, Glos, GL50 1LP
Activities: Retail sale of watches and jewellery in specialised stores
Major Shareholder: Ian Michael Dimmer
Officers: Pamela Helen West, Secretary; Alexandra Dimmer [1969] Director/Design & Advertising; Ian Michael Dimmer [1943] Director/Jeweller; Jonathan Dimmer [1974] Director/Jeweller; Annabel Hudson [1972] Director

Martingate Centre Limited
Incorporated: 23 January 2002 *Employees:* 2
Net Worth: £7,134,005 *Total Assets:* £10,220,015
Registered Office: 17 Market Place, Devizes, Wilts, SN10 1BA
Activities: Other letting and operating of own or leased real estate
Major Shareholder: William George Valentine Hall
Officers: John Francis Clarkson, Secretary; Andrew Edward Valentine Hall [1970] Managing Director; William George Valentine Hall [1939] Director

Martins of Exeter Limited
Incorporated: 28 January 1997 *Employees:* 17
Net Worth: £3,056,104 *Total Assets:* £3,511,511
Registered Office: Clyst Road, Sandygate, Exeter, Devon, EX2 7JL
Activities: Sale of new cars and light motor vehicles
Major Shareholder: Nicholas Robert Saunders
Officers: Nicholas Robert Saunders [1953] Director/Motor Caravan Trader

James Mason Limited
Incorporated: 17 April 2002 *Employees:* 86
Net Worth: £2,052,025 *Total Assets:* £11,349,975
Registered Office: Westcott Farm, Oakford, Tiverton, Devon, EX16 9EZ
Activities: Wholesale of agricultural machinery, equipment and supplies
Parent: Masons Farm and Country Limited
Officers: Lesley Jane Prior, Secretary/Farmer; Roger Jonathan Prior [1955] Director/Chartered Accountant

Masons Farm and Country Limited
Incorporated: 23 December 2004 *Employees:* 86
Net Worth: £2,545,576 *Total Assets:* £11,350,573
Registered Office: Westcott Farm, Oakford, Tiverton, Devon, EX16 9EZ
Activities: Wholesale of agricultural machinery, equipment and supplies
Shareholders: Roger Jonathan Prior; Lesley Jane Prior
Officers: Lesley Jane Prior, Secretary/Farmer; Roger Jonathan Prior [1955] Director/Chartered Accountant

Massey Wilcox Transport Limited
Incorporated: 20 April 1976 *Employees:* 109
Net Worth: £5,434,735 *Total Assets:* £13,603,825
Registered Office: Broadway, Chilcompton, Radstock, Somerset, BA3 4JW
Activities: Freight transport by road
Shareholder: Robert Henry Wilcox
Officers: Jill Louise Trowbridge, Secretary/Accountant; Jill Louise Trowbridge [1958] Director/Accountant; Robert Henry Wilcox [1957] Director

Masstock Arable (UK) Limited
Incorporated: 22 May 1989 *Employees:* 667
Net Worth: £22,962,000 *Total Assets:* £252,614,000
Registered Office: Andoversford, Cheltenham, Glos, GL54 4LZ
Activities: Support activities for crop production
Parent: Oval (1173) Limited
Officers: Sean Gerard Coyle [1972] Director [Irish]; Peter Michael Dunne [1973] Director/Chartered Accountant [Irish]; Spencer Gareth Evans [1970] Director/Chief Financial Officer; Ronan Andrew Hughes [1968] Director [Irish]; Thomas Joseph O'Mahony [1962] Director/Accountant [Irish]; James Marshall Rennie [1957] Director

Masstock Group Holdings Limited
Incorporated: 19 October 2006
Net Worth: £925,000 *Total Assets:* £18,678,000
Registered Office: Station Road, Andoversford, Cheltenham, Glos, GL54 4LZ
Activities: Activities of head offices
Parent: Origin Holdings (UK) Limited
Officers: Sean Gerard Coyle [1972] Director [Irish]; Peter Michael Dunne [1973] Director/Chartered Accountant [Irish]; Spencer Gareth Evans [1970] Director/Chief Financial Officer; Ronan Andrew Hughes [1968] Director [Irish]; Liam Noel Larkin [1956] Director [Irish]; Thomas Joseph O'Mahony [1962] Director/Accountant [Irish]; James Marshall Rennie [1957] Director

The Mast (Bournemouth) Ltd
Incorporated: 17 July 2014
Net Worth: £84,150 *Total Assets:* £4,461,656
Registered Office: c/o The Manchester Hotel, 56 St Michaels Road, Bournemouth, BH2 5EB
Activities: Hotels and similar accommodation
Officers: Arffan Alawa [1966] Director/Merchant [Syrian]; Khaled Alawa [1996] Director [Syrian]; Mhd Hamza Alawa [1995] Director [Syrian]; Rim Daoud Albairouti [1977] Director [Syrian]; Manal Alimam [1974] Director [Syrian]; Ammar Alkhiami [1971] Director/Investor [Syrian]; Mhd Badii Alkhimi [1998] Director [Syrian]; Omar Alkhimi [1997] Director; Alaa Alnmer [1988] Director [Syrian]; Ahmad Assi [1994] Director [Syrian]; Sara Assi [1996] Director [Syrian]; Khaled Fayoumi [1976] Director [Syrian]; Malaz Modalalh [1978] Director [Syrian]

Master International Limited
Incorporated: 22 April 2015
Net Worth: £3,421,195 *Total Assets:* £11,600,648
Registered Office: Olympus Park, Quedgeley, Gloucester, GL2 4NF
Activities: Other service activities n.e.c.
Major Shareholder: Trevor Woodgate
Officers: Trevor Woodgate [1956] Director

The Masters Golf Company Limited
Incorporated: 16 October 1990 *Employees:* 43
Net Worth: £6,346,429 *Total Assets:* £7,936,329
Registered Office: Gordano Gate, Serbert Road, Portishead, Bristol, BS20 7GG
Activities: Non-specialised wholesale trade
Major Shareholder: Darren Paul Evans
Officers: Paul Ashley Marks, Secretary; Colin John Christison [1964] Director; Darren Paul Evans [1961] Director

MAT Foundry Group Limited
Incorporated: 29 December 2000 *Employees:* 2,524
Previous: MAT Europe Holdings Limited
Net Worth: £118,117,872 *Total Assets:* £357,258,368
Registered Office: Mannings Heath Road, Poole, Dorset, BH12 4NJ
Activities: Activities of head offices
Major Shareholder: Steve Wang
Officers: Julian Spencer William Grazebrook, Secretary; Julian Spencer William Grazebrook [1953] Director/Chartered Accountant; Thomas Krosnar [1971] Director; George Michael Ruhl [1955] Director/Manager [American]; Steve Wang [1953] Director [American]

Matki Public Limited Company
Incorporated: 7 May 1971 *Employees:* 116
Net Worth: £10,556,068 *Total Assets:* £13,172,932
Registered Office: Churchward Road, Yate, Bristol, BS37 5PL
Activities: Other manufacturing n.e.c.
Shareholders: Kate Elizabeth Mossman; Kay Newsham; Per Hans Christian Mathiesen; Caroline Fiona Farrant; Caroline Terese Mathiesen; Angela Thomas
Officers: Martha Blanche Waymark Bruce, Secretary; Nicholas Francis Cunild [1982] Commercial Director; Caroline Fiona Farrant [1963] Director; Per Hans Christian Mathiesen [1931] Director [Danish]; Ross Oliver Nixon [1964] Design Director; Nicola Maria Phillips [1965] Director/Accountant

Matquel Property Co. Limited
Incorporated: 21 June 1960
Net Worth: £3,153,095 *Total Assets:* £7,498,309
Registered Office: 38 Sandbanks Road, Parkstone, Poole, Dorset, BH14 8BX
Activities: Buying and selling of own real estate
Parent: Birchmere Ltd
Officers: Elizabeth Anne Spencer, Secretary; Nicholas John Dadds [1965] Director/Property Manager; Arthur John Jeffries [1930] Director/Property Developer; Paul Antony Jeffries [1965] Director/Property Manager

Matthews Properties Limited
Incorporated: 27 January 2003 *Employees:* 2
Net Worth: £2,782,895 *Total Assets:* £4,782,171
Registered Office: Bunbury House, Stour Park, Blandford St Mary, Blandford Forum, Dorset, DT11 9LQ
Activities: Development of building projects
Shareholders: Gerrard Chatterton Matthews; Katherine Joanna Matthews
Officers: Gerrard Chatterton Matthews [1962] Director/Chartered Surveyor; Katherine Joanna Matthews [1966] Director/Secretary

Mawgan Porth Holiday Park Limited
Incorporated: 19 July 1994 *Employees:* 24
Net Worth: £6,796,942 *Total Assets:* £7,954,966
Registered Office: The Park, Mawgan Porth, Newquay, Cornwall, TR8 4BD
Activities: Recreational vehicle parks, trailer parks and camping grounds
Parent: South West Holiday Parks Limited
Officers: Muhammad Abdul Razzak Akbar [1984] Director/Chartered Accountant; Demetri Dinopoulos [1979] Director/Chartered Accountant [Greek]; Adrian Lavan Martyn [1980] Director/Accountant [Australian]

Maxim Integrated Products UK Limited
Incorporated: 21 December 1984 *Employees:* 134
Net Worth: £8,190,261 *Total Assets:* £13,713,274
Registered Office: First Floor, 10 Temple Back, Bristol, BS1 6FL
Activities: Other manufacturing n.e.c.
Officers: Mark John Casper, Secretary; Mark John Casper [1967] Director/Attorney [American]; Edwin Medlin [1957] Director/Attorney [American]

Maximise IT Solutions Limited
Incorporated: 25 August 2004 *Employees:* 25
Net Worth: £4,295,839 *Total Assets:* £6,665,847
Registered Office: Embassy House, Queens Avenue, Bristol, BS8 1SB
Activities: Business and domestic software development
Major Shareholder: Tony William David Williams
Officers: Tony William David Williams [1973] Director

Maximum Fun Devon Limited
Incorporated: 4 March 2011 *Employees:* 179
Net Worth: £2,312,689 *Total Assets:* £13,991,005
Registered Office: Crealy Great Adventure Park, Sidmouth Road, Clyst St Mary, Exeter, Devon, EX5 1DR
Activities: Activities of amusement parks and theme parks
Parent: Maximum Fun Holdings Ltd
Officers: Christopher Roy Down [1970] Director/Farmer; Katie Jane Down [1972] Director; Roy Gilbert Down [1936] Director

Maximum Fun Holdings Limited
Incorporated: 7 March 2011 *Employees:* 186
Net Worth: £7,913,818 *Total Assets:* £16,221,911
Registered Office: Crealy Great Adventure Park, Sidmouth Road, Clyst St Mary, Exeter, Devon, EX5 1DR
Activities: Other business support service activities n.e.c.
Shareholders: Christopher Roy Down; Katie Jane Down
Officers: Steven Charles Carthew [1968] Director/Certified Accountant; Christopher Roy Down [1970] Director/Farmer; Katie Jane Down [1972] Director; Roy Gilbert Down [1936] Director

Maxin Limited
Incorporated: 1 February 1993 *Employees:* 3
Net Worth: £1,695,318 *Total Assets:* £3,811,607
Registered Office: 21 Portland Square, Bristol, BS2 8SJ
Activities: Other business support service activities n.e.c.
Shareholders: Thomas Flight; Harry Stealey
Officers: Thomas Flight, Secretary; Thomas Flight [1966] Director; Harry Stealey [1960] Director

Maxine Investments Limited
Incorporated: 25 June 1962 *Employees:* 2
Net Worth: £3,769,234 *Total Assets:* £3,978,953
Registered Office: 10 Bridge Street, Christchurch, Dorset, BH23 1EF
Activities: Other letting and operating of own or leased real estate
Officers: Adrienne Rita Faiman, Secretary; Michelle Elise Abrahams [1977] Director; Adrienne Rita Faiman [1948] Director; Geoffrey Max Faiman [1948] Director; Rosalyn Eve Lesser [1974] Director

Denis May & Sons Limited
Incorporated: 16 November 2006 *Employees:* 34
Net Worth: £5,034,720 *Total Assets:* £9,106,400
Registered Office: Peat House, Newham Road, Truro, Cornwall, TR1 2DP
Activities: Manufacture of concrete products for construction purposes
Major Shareholder: Hylton John May
Officers: Edward May, Secretary; Peter John Jago [1965] Director/General Manager; Edward John May [1985] Director/Production Manager; Hylton John May [1954] Director

Mayden House Limited
Incorporated: 1 June 2000 *Employees:* 68
Net Worth: £3,035,016 *Total Assets:* £5,081,062
Registered Office: 1 Widcombe Crescent, Bath, BA2 6AH
Activities: Business and domestic software development
Shareholder: Chris May
Officers: Catherine Margaret May, Secretary; Chris David Eldridge [1975] Operations Director; Chris May [1962] Director/Software Development; Alison Sturgess-Durden [1973] Director/Business Executive

Mayflower Properties (SW) Limited
Incorporated: 29 October 2004 *Employees:* 1
Net Worth: £693,588 *Total Assets:* £4,092,050
Registered Office: 5 Chelston Business Park, Castle Road, Wellington, Somerset, TA21 9JQ
Activities: Development of building projects
Major Shareholder: James Sinclair Wood
Officers: James Sinclair Wood [1963] Director

The Maynard School
Incorporated: 4 August 2003 *Employees:* 109
Net Worth: £3,503,993 *Total Assets:* £4,785,021
Registered Office: The Maynard School, Denmark Road, Exeter, EX1 1SJ
Activities: Pre-primary education
Officers: Sandra Heather Gardner, Secretary; Lady Emma Louise Birkin [1963] Director/Venue Owner; Nicholas William Bruce-Jones [1960] Director/Armed Forces; Mark Chambers [1966] Director; Jane Elaine Chanot [1966] Director/Lawyer; James Ronald Dart [1969] Director/Self Employed; Christopher Douglas McKay Gatherer [1958] Director/Headteacher; George Alan Gibbons [1948] Director/Consultant; Henry David Luce [1963] Director; Wendy Carol Manfield [1960] Commercial Director; Caroline Ann Pascoe [1964] Director/Headmistress; Sara Madeleine Randall Johnson [1951] Director/Councillor; Lady Janet Anne Stanhope [1952] Director/Retired; Cynthia Thompson [1951] Director/Councillor; Lynn Turner [1958] Director/Veterinary Surgeon; Christina Frances Walton [1986] Director/Lecturer; Sarah Mary Witheridge [1972] Director/Solicitor

MC Property Ventures Limited
Incorporated: 17 March 2014 *Employees:* 2
Net Worth Deficit: £1,096,432 *Total Assets:* £6,908,724
Registered Office: 4 Elms Avenue, Poole, Dorset, BH14 8EF
Activities: Development of building projects
Shareholders: Carolyn Ann Butland-Beazley; Captain Michael Nicholas Butland-Beazley
Officers: Carolyn Ann Butland-Beazley, Secretary; Carolyn Ann Butland-Beazley [1959] Director/Accountant; Captain Michael Nicholas Butland-Beazley [1957] Director

MCAARP Holdings Limited
Incorporated: 19 May 2008 *Employees:* 370
Net Worth: £4,121,000 *Total Assets:* £20,689,000
Registered Office: First Avenue, Westfield Trading Estate, Midsomer Norton, Bath, BA3 4BS
Activities: Other manufacturing n.e.c.
Major Shareholder: Mark Edward Cornford
Officers: Arthur John Ayres, Secretary; Arthur John Ayres [1958] Finance Director; Mark Edward Cornford [1965] Managing Director

MCB Investments Limited
Incorporated: 19 March 2007 *Employees:* 231
Net Worth: £3,106,221 *Total Assets:* £10,435,870
Registered Office: Avon Care Homes Ltd, Mendip Court, Bath Road, Wells, Somerset, BA5 3DG
Activities: Other business support service activities n.e.c.
Major Shareholder: Maria Cristina Bila
Officers: Sandra White, Secretary; Maria Cristina Bila [1959] Director/Nursing Home Proprietor [Portuguese]

McBraida Holdings Limited
Incorporated: 21 March 2011 *Employees:* 233
Net Worth: £25,436,000 *Total Assets:* £34,274,000
Registered Office: Bridgeyate Engineeing Works, Warmley, Bristol, BS30 5JW
Activities: Activities of production holding companies
Officers: Ian Joseph McBraida [1965] Director/Engineer; Michael Peter McBraida [1938] Director/Mechanical Engineer

McBraida PLC
Incorporated: 14 May 1954 *Employees:* 180
Net Worth: £11,410,000 *Total Assets:* £16,450,000
Registered Office: Bridgeyate Engineering Works, Warmley, Bristol, BS30 5JW
Activities: Machining
Officers: Kathleen Madeline McBraida, Secretary; Ian Joseph McBraida [1965] Director/Engineer; Kathleen Madeline McBraida [1939] Director; Michael Peter McBraida [1938] Director/Mechanical Engineer

McCarthy & Stone (Developments) Limited
Incorporated: 17 June 2008 *Employees:* 128
Net Worth: £421,100,000 *Total Assets:* £457,400,000
Registered Office: Fourth Floor, 100 Holdenhurst Road, Bournemouth, BH8 8AQ
Activities: Development of building projects
Parent: McCarthy & Stone PLC
Officers: Patrick David Hole, Secretary; Rowan Clare Baker [1973] Director/Chief Financial Officer; Michael Samuel Lloyd [1978] Director - House Builder; John Michael Tonkiss [1968] Director; Nigel Alan Turner [1965] Director/Chartered Surveyor

McCarthy & Stone (Extra Care Living) Limited
Incorporated: 6 May 2009
Net Worth: £18,500,000 *Total Assets:* £432,300,000
Registered Office: Fourth Floor, 100 Holdenhurst Road, Bournemouth, BH8 8AQ
Activities: Buying and selling of own real estate
Parent: McCarthy & Stone Retirement Lifestyles Limited
Officers: Patrick David Hole, Secretary; Rowan Clare Baker [1973] Director/Chief Financial Officer; Nicholas John Dell [1960] Director/Group Property Counsel; Patrick David Hole [1966] Director/General Counsel and Company Secretary; Michael Samuel Lloyd [1978] Director - House Builder; John Michael Tonkiss [1968] Director

McCarthy & Stone (Home Equity Interests) Limited
Incorporated: 1 November 2006
Net Worth: £8,621,117 *Total Assets:* £15,824,698
Registered Office: Fourth Floor, 100 Holdenhurst Road, Bournemouth, BH8 8AQ
Activities: Buying and selling of own real estate
Parent: McCarthy & Stone Retirement Lifestyles Ltd
Officers: Patrick David Hole, Secretary; Rowan Clare Baker [1973] Director; Patrick David Hole [1966] Director/General Counsel and Company Secretary; John Michael Tonkiss [1968] Director

McCarthy & Stone PLC
Incorporated: 17 June 2008 *Employees:* 2,402
Previous: McCarthy & Stone Limited
Net Worth: £762,099,968 *Total Assets:* £995,200,000
Registered Office: Fourth Floor, 100 Holdenhurst Road, Bournemouth, BH8 8AQ
Activities: Activities of head offices
Officers: Patrick David Hole, Secretary; Rowan Clare Baker [1973] Director/Chief Financial Officer; John Peter Carter [1961] Director; Paul John Lester [1949] Director; Michael Samuel Lloyd [1978] Director - House Builder; Arun Nagwaney [1971] Director [German]; Geeta Nanda [1965] Director; Francis Eamon Nelson [1951] Director; Michael Dennis Parsons [1950] Director; John Michael Tonkiss [1968] Director; Nigel Alan Turner [1965] Director/Chartered Surveyor

McCarthy & Stone Retirement Lifestyles Limited
Incorporated: 17 June 2008 *Employees:* 981
Net Worth: £588,400,000 *Total Assets:* £951,100,032
Registered Office: Fourth Floor, 100 Holdenhurst Road, Bournemouth, BH8 8AQ
Activities: Development of building projects
Parent: McCarthy & Stone (Developments) Limited
Officers: Patrick David Hole, Secretary; Rowan Clare Baker [1973] Director/Chief Financial Officer; Gary Neil Day [1958] Director; Patrick David Hole [1966] Director/General Counsel and Company Secretary; Paula Carole Jordan [1959] Human Resources Director; Michael Samuel Lloyd [1978] Director - House Builder; John Michael Tonkiss [1968] Director; Nigel Alan Turner [1965] Director/Chartered Surveyor

McCarthy Contracting & Development Limited
Incorporated: 23 December 2011 *Employees:* 11
Net Worth: £4,437,252 *Total Assets:* £8,808,769
Registered Office: The Rockery, St James Road, Torquay, Devon, TQ1 4FT
Activities: Development of building projects
Shareholder: Sean Christopher McCarthy
Officers: Daniel McCarthy [1966] Director/Builder; Sean Christopher McCarthy [1967] Director/Surveyor

McCarthy Investments Limited
Incorporated: 6 December 2006 *Employees:* 3
Previous: McCarthy Office Investments Limited
Net Worth: £2,737,228 *Total Assets:* £20,637,472
Registered Office: Churchill House, Parkside, Ringwood, Hants, BH24 3SG
Activities: Other letting and operating of own or leased real estate
Parent: Churchill Retirement (Group) Limited
Officers: Darren Mark Riley, Secretary; Dean Marlow [1971] Director/Accountant; Clinton James McCarthy [1964] Director; Spencer John McCarthy [1966] Director

McCaulay's Health & Sport Limited
Incorporated: 20 May 1998 *Employees:* 22
Net Worth: £233,792 *Total Assets:* £4,213,963
Registered Office: Dinnaton Fitness & Golf, Ivybridge, Devon, PL21 9HU
Activities: Operation of sports facilities
Shareholders: Jamie Robert Phillips; Sarah Louise Phillips
Officers: Sarah Phillips, Secretary; James Robert Phillips [1975] Director; Sarah Louise Phillips [1976] Director

McCulloch Homes Limited
Incorporated: 6 February 1996 *Employees:* 18
Net Worth: £1,992,541 *Total Assets:* £3,827,823
Registered Office: Berkeley Coach House, Woods Hill, Limpley Stoke, Bath, BA2 7FS
Activities: Other building completion and finishing
Major Shareholder: Martin John Hill
Officers: Paul John Charles, Secretary; Martin John Hill [1953] Director/Manager; Trevor McCullough [1959] Director/Builder

I.J. McGill Transport Limited
Incorporated: 1 April 1993 *Employees:* 225
Net Worth: £2,829,105 *Total Assets:* £9,776,541
Registered Office: Broadmead Lane, Keynsham, Bristol, BS31 1ST
Activities: Freight transport by road
Shareholders: Lucy McGill; Heather Brown
Officers: Lucy McGill, Secretary; Heather Brown [1980] Director/Sales; Ian John McGill [1955] Director; Lucy McGill [1977] Director/Financial Controller; Lee Parker [1973] Director/Transport Manager; Kelly Pope [1984] Director/Administrator; Ian Stokes [1958] Director/Chartered Accountant

McGill Warmley Limited
Incorporated: 6 May 2005
Net Worth: £5,683 *Total Assets:* £5,683,284
Registered Office: Oxenleaze Farm, 88 Keevil, Trowbridge, Wilts, BA14 6NH
Activities: Other letting and operating of own or leased real estate
Shareholders: Lucy McGill; Heather Brown; Kelly Pope
Officers: Ian John McGill, Secretary/Director; Ian John McGill [1955] Director

McLean & Sons Ltd
Incorporated: 3 March 2009
Net Worth: £2,328,143 *Total Assets:* £4,129,050
Registered Office: Shunters Yard, Station Road, Semley, Shaftesbury, Dorset, SP7 9AH
Activities: Sale of new cars and light motor vehicles
Shareholder: Henry McLean
Officers: Edward McLean [1992] Director; George McLean [1987] Director/Agricultural Dealer; Henry McLean [1989] Director/Agricultural Dealer; Kim Doreen McLean [1960] Director/Agricultural Machinery Dealer; Robert John McLean [1963] Director/Agricultural Machinery Dealer; Toby McLean [1995] Director/Businessman

R.J. & K.D. McLean Limited
Incorporated: 12 March 2003 *Employees:* 8
Net Worth: £6,106,375 *Total Assets:* £6,896,927
Registered Office: Shunters Yard, Station Road, Semley, Shaftesbury, Dorset, SP7 9AH
Activities: Sale of new cars and light motor vehicles
Shareholders: Kim Doreen McLean; Robert McLean
Officers: Robert John McLean, Secretary; Kim Doreen McLean [1960] Director/Agricultural Dealers; Robert John McLean [1963] Director/Agricultural Dealers

MDE Consultants Ltd
Incorporated: 19 June 2012 *Employees:* 15
Net Worth Deficit: £369,201 *Total Assets:* £5,391,368
Registered Office: Boyces Building, 40-42 Regent Street, Clifton, Bristol, BS8 4HU
Activities: Other activities of employment placement agencies
Parent: MDE Group AS
Officers: Svein Morten Bjustveit [1977] Director [Norwegian]; Ellen Louise Nixon [1977] Director; Thomas Christopher Nixon [1978] Director

MDM Developments (Southern) Limited
Incorporated: 20 May 2002 *Employees:* 1
Net Worth: £1,127,213 *Total Assets:* £3,621,513
Registered Office: Le Beau, Arrowsmith Road, Wimborne, Dorset, BH21 3BE
Activities: Construction of domestic buildings
Officers: Mark David Matthews [1966] Director/Builder

MDP (South West) Limited
Incorporated: 28 July 2005
Net Worth: £4,096,192 *Total Assets:* £4,722,121
Registered Office: The Mill, Kingsteingnton Road, Newton Abbot, Devon, TQ12 2QA
Activities: Other specialised construction activities n.e.c.
Officers: Julie Marie Pratt, Secretary; Mark David Pratt [1970] Director/Engineer

ME Estates Limited
Incorporated: 14 November 2016 *Employees:* 1
Net Worth: £3,418,380 *Total Assets:* £5,729,861
Registered Office: Staverton Court, Staverton, Cheltenham, Glos, GL51 0UX
Activities: Buying and selling of own real estate
Major Shareholder: Mazdak Eyrumlu
Officers: Dr Mazdak Eyrumlu [1975] Director [Swedish]

The Mead Academy Trust
Incorporated: 10 April 2012 *Employees:* 190
Net Worth: £12,112,555 *Total Assets:* £13,266,601
Registered Office: The Mead Community Primary School, Hackett Place, Hilperton, Trowbridge, Wilts, BA14 7GN
Activities: Primary education
Officers: Lysbeth Rachel Bolton [1968] Director/Executive Headteacher; Jayne Louise Bullock [1973] Director/Company Co-ordinator/Company Secretary; Christian Charles Thomas Checkley [1970] Director/Management Consultant; Jonathan Peter Clark [1969] Director Property; Peter Michael Finn [1969] Director/Works for UK Space Agency; Michael Geoffrey Haines [1948] Director - Education and Training; Helen Marie Holland [1973] Director/Civil Servant; Alexandra Marie Purcell [1969] Director/Chartered Engineer; Robert Harvey Quick [1948] Director/Chartered Engineer; Tracey Louise Wright [1973] Director/Solicitor

Mead Realisations Limited
Incorporated: 19 April 1977 *Employees:* 8
Net Worth: £16,900,060 *Total Assets:* £23,061,220
Registered Office: Puxton Park, Cowslip Lane, Hewish, Weston Super Mare, Somerset, BS24 6AH
Activities: Development of building projects
Major Shareholder: Derek Richard Mead
Officers: Katherine Patricia Hawke [1972] Director; Alistair Daniel Derek Mead [1977] Director/Farmer

Mean Moor Community Wind Farm Limited
Incorporated: 30 May 2017 *Employees:* 3
Net Worth Deficit: £206,579 *Total Assets:* £8,791,513
Registered Office: c/o Thrive Renewables PLC, Deanery Road, Bristol, BS1 5AS
Activities: Activities of other holding companies n.e.c.
Parent: Energy Prospects Co-operative Limited
Officers: Matthew Thomas Clayton [1975] Director; Katrina Lorraine Cross [1972] Director/Accountant; Monika Lidia Paplaczyk [1979] Director/Investment Manager [Polish]

Mean Moor Wind Farm Holding Limited
Incorporated: 28 August 2015 *Employees:* 3
Net Worth Deficit: £9,722 *Total Assets:* £4,398,475
Registered Office: c/o Thrive Renewables PLC, Deanery Road, Bristol, BS1 5AS
Activities: Construction of utility projects for electricity and telecommunications
Parent: Mean Moor Community Wind Farm Limited
Officers: Matthew Thomas Clayton [1975] Director; Katrina Lorraine Cross [1972] Director/Accountant; Monika Lidia Paplaczyk [1979] Director/Investment Manager [Polish]

Colin Mear Engineering Limited
Incorporated: 26 August 1982 *Employees:* 88
Net Worth: £3,396,197 *Total Assets:* £5,243,002
Registered Office: Combe Wood, Combe St Nicholas, Chard, Somerset, TA20 3NL
Activities: Manufacture of machinery for food, beverage and tobacco processing
Parent: Colin Mear Limited
Officers: Paul Anthony Knight [1974] Managing Director; Juliet Maria Miller [1965] Director; Scott Drysdale Roy [1946] Director; Paul Simmons [1961] Director; David John Weatherill [1966] Sales Director

Colin Mear Limited
Incorporated: 4 February 2010 *Employees:* 88
Net Worth: £4,013,110 *Total Assets:* £5,887,864
Registered Office: CME, Combe Wood, Combe St Nicholas, Chard, Somerset, TA20 3NL
Activities: Other manufacturing n.e.c.
Shareholders: Louise Margaret Lawton; Juliet Maria Miller; Annette Lorraine Mear
Officers: Louise Margaret Lawton [1968] Director; Annette Lorraine Mear [1971] Director; Juliet Maria Miller [1965] Director

Mears Care (Holdings) Limited
Incorporated: 29 December 1998
Net Worth Deficit: £3,981,195 *Total Assets:* £19,660,838
Registered Office: 1390 Montpellier Court, Gloucester Business Park, Brockworth, Gloucester, GL3 4AH
Activities: Activities of other holding companies n.e.c.
Parent: Mears Group PLC
Officers: Ben Robert Westran [1977] Director

Mears Care Limited
Incorporated: 9 November 2001 *Employees:* 3,961
Net Worth: £3,330,000 *Total Assets:* £70,646,000
Registered Office: 1390 Montpellier Court, Gloucester Business Park, Brockworth, Gloucester, GL3 4AH
Activities: Other human health activities
Parent: Mears Care (Holdings) Limited
Officers: Andrew Christopher Melville Smith [1972] Director/Chartered Accountant; Ben Robert Westran [1977] Director

Mears Group PLC
Incorporated: 1 August 1996 *Employees:* 12,580
Net Worth: £209,494,000 *Total Assets:* £476,006,016
Registered Office: 1390 Montpellier Court, Gloucester Business Park, Brockworth, Gloucester, GL3 4AH
Activities: Activities of other holding companies n.e.c.
Officers: Ben Robert Westran, Secretary; Jason Drew Burt [1965] Director; Elizabeth Frances Corrado [1965] Director; John Geraint Davies [1954] Director; Amanda Lavinia Hillerby [1989] Director/Quality Manager; Roy Irwin [1954] Director/Housing Professional; Alan Martin Long [1962] Director; David John Miles [1966] Director; Kieran Francis Murphy [1958] Director; Andrew Christopher Melville Smith [1972] Director/Accountant; Julia Unwin [1956] Director

Mears Homecare Limited
Incorporated: 3 September 1992 *Employees:* 908
Previous: Care UK Homecare Limited
Net Worth Deficit: £4,101,000 *Total Assets:* £5,035,000
Registered Office: 1390 Montpellier Court, Gloucester Business Park, Brockworth, Gloucester, GL3 4AH
Activities: Temporary employment agency activities
Parent: Mears Care (Holdings) Limited
Officers: Ben Robert Westran, Secretary; Andrew Christopher Melville Smith [1972] Director/Accountant

Mears Housing Management (Holdings) Limited
Incorporated: 8 April 2003
Previous: Mears Housing Management Limited
Net Worth Deficit: £427,667 *Total Assets:* £55,036,352
Registered Office: 1390 Montpellier Court, Gloucester Business Park, Brockworth, Gloucester, GL3 4AH
Activities: Non-trading company
Parent: Mears Group PLC
Officers: Benjamin Robert Westran, Secretary; Andrew Christopher Melville Smith [1972] Director/Chartered Accountant; John Kenneth Taylor [1967] Managing Director; Ben Robert Westran [1977] Director/Chartered Accountant

Mears Housing Management Limited
Incorporated: 5 November 1998 *Employees:* 65
Previous: Omega Lettings Limited
Net Worth: £4,589,000 *Total Assets:* £23,953,000
Registered Office: 1390 Montpellier Court, Gloucester Business Park, Brockworth, Gloucester, GL3 4AH
Activities: Management of real estate on a fee or contract basis
Parent: Mears Housing Management Limited
Officers: Ben Robert Westran, Secretary; John Kenneth Taylor [1967] Director

Mears Housing Portfolio (Holdings) Limited
Incorporated: 10 August 2017
Net Worth: £100 *Total Assets:* £15,153,600
Registered Office: 1390 Montpellier Court, Gloucester Business Park, Brockworth, Gloucester, GL3 4AH
Activities: Other letting and operating of own or leased real estate
Parent: Mears Housing Management (Holdings) Limited
Officers: Benjamin Robert Westran, Secretary; Andrew Christopher Melville Smith [1972] Director/Chartered Accountant; John Kenneth Taylor [1967] Managing Director; Ben Robert Westran [1977] Director/Chartered Accountant

Mears Housing Portfolio 2 Limited
Incorporated: 8 September 2017
Net Worth: £100 *Total Assets:* £13,632,875
Registered Office: 1390 Montpellier Court, Gloucester Business Park, Brockworth, Gloucester, GL3 4AH
Activities: Other letting and operating of own or leased real estate
Parent: Mears Housing Portfolio (Holdings) Limited
Officers: Benjamin Robert Westran, Secretary; Andrew Christopher Melville Smith [1972] Director/Chartered Accountant; Ben Robert Westran [1977] Director/Chartered Accountant

Mears Limited
Incorporated: 6 July 1990 *Employees:* 3,307
Net Worth: £11,944,000 *Total Assets:* £205,271,008
Registered Office: 1390 Montpellier Court, Gloucester Business Park, Brockworth, Gloucester, GL3 4AH
Activities: Other building completion and finishing
Parent: Mears Group PLC
Officers: Benjamin Robert Westran, Secretary; Graham Roy Eden [1962] Director; Colin Edward Middlemass [1962] Director; David John Miles [1966] Director; Andrew Christopher Melville Smith [1972] Director/Accountant; Ben Robert Westran [1977] Director/Chartered Accountant

Mears New Homes Limited
Incorporated: 19 November 2013 *Employees:* 53
Net Worth Deficit: £1,076,729 *Total Assets:* £13,597,340
Registered Office: 1390 Montpellier Court, Gloucester Business Park, Brockworth, Gloucester, GL3 4AH
Activities: Construction of domestic buildings
Parent: Mears Limited
Officers: Timothy Michael Carpenter [1962] Managing Director; Colin Edward Middlemass [1962] Director; Ben Robert Westran [1977] Director/Chartered Accountant

Mecwash Systems Limited
Incorporated: 7 December 1993 *Employees:* 29
Net Worth: £2,549,355 *Total Assets:* £4,057,580
Registered Office: Unit A 64 Hundred, Severn Drive, Tewkesbury Business Park, Tewkesbury, Glos, GL20 8SF
Activities: Manufacture of electronic measuring, testing etc. equipment, not for industrial process control
Officers: Tom Philip Cadogan, Secretary; John Pattison [1961] Director

Medcentres PLC
Incorporated: 21 December 2006 *Employees:* 12
Net Worth: £2,214,628 *Total Assets:* £5,054,044
Registered Office: 1st Floor, Highfield House, Bartons Road, Fordingbridge, Hants, SP6 1JD
Activities: Development of building projects
Shareholders: Nicolas Jeremy Arnold; Deidre Arnold
Officers: Nicolas Jeremy Arnold, Secretary/Director; David Nicolas Arnold [1993] Director/Property Manager; Deirdre Arnold [1958] Director; James William Arnold [1990] Director/Development Manager; Michael John Arnold [1986] Director; Nicolas Jeremy Arnold [1960] Director; David Michael Chilcott [1965] Director

W.J. Meddings (Holdings) Limited
Incorporated: 20 February 1941 *Employees:* 3
Net Worth: £5,071,351 *Total Assets:* £5,169,908
Registered Office: Kingsley Close, East Way, Lee Mill Industrial Estate, Ivybridge, Devon, PL21 9LL
Activities: Activities of head offices
Shareholders: Peter McKenzie Meddings; Janice Patricia Meddings; Josephine Isabel Meddings
Officers: Janice Patricia Meddings, Secretary; Janice Patricia Meddings [1943] Director/Administration Manager; Josephine Isabel Meddings [1945] Director/Housewife; Peter McKenzie Meddings [1949] Director/Chartered Accountant

Medipak Limited
Incorporated: 28 November 1995 *Employees:* 38
Net Worth: £5,721,771 *Total Assets:* £6,519,862
Registered Office: 34 North Street, Bridgwater, Somerset, TA6 3YD
Activities: Manufacture of plastic packing goods
Officers: Denise Elizabeth Crawley, Secretary/Office Manager; Alison Jane Ball [1965] Director/Administration; Denise Elizabeth Crawley [1970] Director/Administration; Mary Culliford [1943] Director; Christopher John Powell [1986] Technical Director

Medisafe UK Limited
Incorporated: 21 August 1990 *Employees:* 73
Net Worth: £9,467,954 *Total Assets:* £12,399,256
Registered Office: Ground Floor, Stella Building, Windmill Hill Business Park, Whitehill Way, Swindon, Wilts, SN5 6NX
Activities: Manufacture of medical and dental instruments and supplies
Parent: Synergy Health Limited
Officers: Peter John Rendle [1980] Director/Chartered Accountant; Michael Tokich [1968] Director [American]; John Adam Zangerle [1966] Director and Company Secretary [American]

Medland, Sanders and Twose Limited
Incorporated: 1 January 1947 *Employees:* 89
Net Worth: £2,694,000 *Total Assets:* £7,274,000
Registered Office: c/o Medland Sanders & Twose Limited, Blundells Road, Tiverton, Devon, EX16 4DA
Activities: Sale of other motor vehicles
Shareholders: Robert Simon Foster; Nigel John Godefroy
Officers: Robert Simon Foster [1971] Director; Nigel John Godefroy [1964] Director

Medreport Services Limited
Incorporated: 1 October 2004 *Employees:* 14
Net Worth: £399,930 *Total Assets:* £4,771,857
Registered Office: The Stables, Clevedon Hall, Victoria Road, Clevedon, Somerset, BS21 7SJ
Activities: Other business support service activities n.e.c.
Officers: Eleanor Williams, Secretary; Simon Peter Munro [1978] Director/Accountant; Eleanor Williams [1978] Director and Company Secretary

Megahertz Limited
Incorporated: 17 May 2012 *Employees:* 30
Net Worth Deficit: £931,557 *Total Assets:* £20,942,912
Registered Office: Mazars LLP, 5th Floor, Merck House, Seldown Lane, Poole, Dorset, BH15 1TW
Activities: Wholesale of other machinery and equipment
Shareholder: Alexander Volov
Officers: Jonathan Ralph Flay [1971] Director

Megasteel Ltd
Incorporated: 22 November 1991 *Employees:* 5
Net Worth: £6,247,637 *Total Assets:* £10,386,990
Registered Office: Rodbourne Rail Business Centre, Grange Lane, Malmesbury, Wilts, SN16 0ES
Activities: Wholesale of metals and metal ores
Shareholders: Nigel Graham Roberts; Bella Balvinder Roberts
Officers: Nigel Graham Roberts, Secretary/Director; Bella Balvinder Roberts [1975] Director; Nigel Graham Roberts [1961] Director

Meggitt (UK) Limited
Incorporated: 8 June 1959 *Employees:* 906
Net Worth: £90,952,000 *Total Assets:* £242,303,008
Registered Office: Atlantic House, Aviation Park West, Bournemouth International Airport, Christchurch, Dorset, BH23 6EW
Activities: Manufacture of other parts and accessories for motor vehicles
Parent: Meggitt Properties PLC
Officers: Simon Robert Grant, Secretary; Louisa Sachiko Burdett [1968] Director/Chief Financial Officer; Philip Ernest Green [1956] Director/Chartered Secretary; Derek John O'Neill [1962] Director/Group Treasurer; Ian Keith Pargeter [1965] Director/Group Financial Controller; Marina Louise Thomas [1976] Director/Company Secretary; Antony Wood [1966] Director/Chief Executive

Meggitt Acquisition Limited
Incorporated: 2 April 1986
Net Worth: £32,098,000 *Total Assets:* £393,856,000
Registered Office: Atlantic House, Aviation Park West, Bournemouth International Airport, Christchurch, Dorset, BH23 6EW
Activities: Non-trading company
Parent: Meggitt International Holdings Limited
Officers: Simon Robert Grant, Secretary; Louisa Sachiko Burdett [1968] Director/Chief Financial Officer; Philip Ernest Green [1956] Director/Chartered Secretary; Marina Louise Thomas [1976] Director/Company Secretary; Antony Wood [1966] Director/Chief Executive

Meggitt Advanced Composites Limited
Incorporated: 17 November 1999
Previous: Cobham Advanced Composites Limited
Net Worth: £51,417,000 *Total Assets:* £51,612,000
Registered Office: Atlantic House, Aviation Park West, Bournemouth International Airport, Christchurch, Dorset, BH23 6EW
Activities: Dormant company
Parent: Meggitt Aerospace Limited
Officers: Simon Robert Grant, Secretary; Philip Ernest Green [1956] Director/Chartered Secretary; Ian Keith Pargeter [1965] Director/Group Financial Controller; Marina Louise Thomas [1976] Director/Company Secretary; Douglas Russell Webb [1961] Director/Chief Financial Officer

Meggitt Aerospace Holdings Limited
Incorporated: 16 July 1998
Net Worth: £357,340,992 *Total Assets:* £357,752,000
Registered Office: Atlantic House, Aviation Park West, Bournemouth International Airport, Christchurch, Dorset, BH23 6EW
Activities: Non-trading company
Parent: Dunlop Aerospace Holdings Limited
Officers: Simon Robert Grant, Secretary; Philip Ernest Green [1956] Director/Chartered Secretary; Derek John O'Neill [1962] Director/Group Treasurer; Ian Keith Pargeter [1965] Director/Group Financial Controller; Marina Louise Thomas [1976] Director/Company Secretary

Meggitt Aerospace Limited
Incorporated: 9 December 1997 *Employees:* 1,540
Net Worth: £403,585,984 *Total Assets:* £544,497,024
Registered Office: Atlantic House, Aviation Park West, Bournemouth International Airport, Christchurch, Dorset, BH23 6EW
Activities: Manufacture of other fabricated metal products n.e.c.
Parent: Dunlop Limited
Officers: Simon Robert Grant, Secretary; Louisa Sachiko Burdett [1968] Director/Chief Financial Officer; Philip Ernest Green [1956] Director/Chartered Secretary; Derek John O'Neill [1962] Director/Group Treasurer; Ian Keith Pargeter [1965] Director/Group Financial Controller; Marina Louise Thomas [1976] Director/Company Secretary; Antony Wood [1966] Director/Chief Executive

Meggitt Finance Limited
Incorporated: 19 October 2011
Net Worth: £340,843,008 *Total Assets:* £1,555,165,952
Registered Office: Atlantic House, Aviation Park West, Bournemouth International Airport, Christchurch, Dorset, BH23 6EW
Activities: Activities of head offices
Parent: Meggitt International Holdings Limited
Officers: Simon Robert Grant, Secretary; Derek John Oneill [1962] Director; Ian Keith Pargeter [1965] Director/Group Financial Controller; Marina Louise Thomas [1976] Director/Company Secretary

Meggitt International Holdings Limited
Incorporated: 19 October 2011
Net Worth: £1,902,739,968 *Total Assets:* £1,912,116,992
Registered Office: Atlantic House, Aviation Park West, Bouremouth International Airport, Christchurch, Dorset, BH23 6EW
Activities: Activities of head offices
Parent: Meggitt PLC
Officers: Simon Robert Grant, Secretary; Louisa Sachiko Burdett [1968] Director/Chief Financial Officer; Philip Ernest Green [1956] Director/Chartered Secretary; Marina Louise Thomas [1976] Director/Company Secretary; Antony Wood [1966] Director/Chief Executive

Meggitt International Limited
Incorporated: 9 November 1992
Net Worth: £389,028,000 *Total Assets:* £1,258,050,048
Registered Office: Atlantic House, Aviation Park West, Bournemouth International Airport, Christchurch, Dorset, BH23 6EW
Activities: Activities of head offices
Parent: Meggitt International Holdings Limited
Officers: Simon Robert Grant, Secretary; Louisa Sachiko Burdett [1968] Director/Chief Financial Officer; Philip Ernest Green [1956] Director/Chartered Secretary; Marina Louise Thomas [1976] Director/Company Secretary; Antony Wood [1966] Director/Chief Executive

Meggitt PLC
Incorporated: 11 April 1947 *Employees:* 11,074
Net Worth: £2,556,400,128 *Total Assets:* £4,826,500,096
Registered Office: Atlantic House, Aviation Park West, Bournemouth International Airport, Christchurch, Dorset, BH23 6EW
Activities: Activities of head offices
Officers: Marina Louise Thomas, Secretary; Guy Serge Berruyer [1951] Director [French]; Louisa Sachiko Burdett [1968] Director/Chief Financial Officer; Colin Richard Day [1955] Director; Nancy Lee Gioia [1960] Director [American]; Alison Jane Patricia Goligher [1965] Director; Philip Ernest Green [1956] Director/Chartered Secretary; Guy C Hachey [1955] Director [Canadian]; Paul Heiden [1957] Director; Sir Anthony Nigel Russell Rudd [1946] Director; Antony Wood [1966] Director/Chief Executive

Meggitt Properties PLC
Incorporated: 1 January 1929
Net Worth: £441,849,984 *Total Assets:* £815,553,984
Registered Office: Atlantic House, Aviation Park West, Bournemouth International Airport, Christchurch, Dorset, BH23 6EW
Activities: Activities of head offices
Parent: Meggitt International Holdings Limited
Officers: Simon Robert Grant, Secretary; Louisa Sachiko Burdett [1968] Director/Chief Financial Officer; Philip Ernest Green [1956] Director/Chartered Secretary; Marina Louise Thomas [1976] Director/Company Secretary; Antony Wood [1966] Director/Chief Executive

Meiyume (UK) Limited
Incorporated: 15 June 1950 *Employees:* 646
Previous: LF Beauty (UK) Limited
Net Worth: £28,370,000 *Total Assets:* £75,902,000
Registered Office: Aintree Avenue, White Horse Business Park, Trowbridge, Wilts, BA14 0XB
Activities: Manufacture of perfumes and toilet preparations
Parent: Lornamead Group Limited
Officers: Gary David Armstrong [1965] Commercial Director; Gerard Jan Raymond [1957] Director [Australian]; Robert Adrian Sharpe [1956] Director; Paul Victor Taylor [1960] Director

Melbourne Homes Limited
Incorporated: 1 June 2006
Net Worth: £1,647,829 *Total Assets:* £3,731,496
Registered Office: Pennyfarthings House, South Drive, Ossemsley, New Milton, Hants, BH25 5TL
Activities: Development of building projects
Shareholders: Mark Adams; Maria Elizabeth Adams
Officers: Mark Adams, Secretary; Maria Elizabeth Adams [1969] Director; Mark Adams [1968] Director

D.J. Melsome Limited
Incorporated: 5 May 1976 *Employees:* 1
Net Worth: £4,280,890 *Total Assets:* £4,564,060
Registered Office: Holbrook Farm, The Calfway, Bisley, Stroud, Glos, GL6 7BX
Activities: Other letting and operating of own or leased real estate
Shareholders: David John Melsome; The Executors of Mrs Rosemary Joyce Melsome
Officers: David John Melsome, Secretary; David John Melsome, Secretary; David John Melsome [1937] Director; Stephen John Melsome [1959] Director; Jacqueline Sandra Rycroft [1963] Director/Dental Assistant

Meltor Developments Limited
Incorporated: 21 October 2010
Net Worth: £5,260,794 *Total Assets:* £6,284,982
Registered Office: Winchester House, Deane Gate Avenue, Taunton, Somerset, TA1 2UH
Activities: Other letting and operating of own or leased real estate
Shareholders: Carmela de Sena; Salvatore de Sena
Officers: Salvatore de Sena [1939] Director [Italian]; Carmela Desena [1946] Director [Italian]

Mendip Batch Medical Limited
Incorporated: 28 January 2014
Net Worth: £314,063 *Total Assets:* £4,324,989
Registered Office: Pudding Pie Lane Surgery, Pudding Pie Lane, Langford, Bristol, BS40 5EL
Activities: Activities of other holding companies n.e.c.
Officers: Dr Philip Donlevy [1971] Director/General Practitioner; Dr Cordelia Feuchtwang [1961] Director/Doctor; Dr Joanna Mary King [1974] Director/General Practitioner; Dr Alan McClatchey [1956] Director/General Practitioner; Dr Samuel Partridge [1973] Director/Doctor; Shruti Devyani Patel [1968] Director/General Practitioner; Dr Richard Reed [1976] Director/Doctor; Dr Andrew Warinton [1964] Director/Doctor

Mendip Forestry Limited
Incorporated: 11 July 1984 *Employees:* 11
Net Worth: £2,816,933 *Total Assets:* £3,548,035
Registered Office: Honeybridge, Brokerswood, Westbury, Wilts, BA13 4EG
Activities: Logging
Major Shareholder: Roger John Austin
Officers: Roger John Austin, Secretary; Roger John Austin [1953] Director/Timber Buyer

Merchants' Academy Trust
Incorporated: 20 October 2005 *Employees:* 215
Previous: Merchants' Academy Withywood
Net Worth: £20,656,000 *Total Assets:* £24,200,000
Registered Office: Merchants' Academy, Gatehouse Avenue, Withywood, Bristol, BS13 9AJ
Activities: Primary education
Officers: James Ross Ancell [1953] Director [British/New Zealander]; Caroline Jane Duckworth [1961] Director/Treasurer

Mercia Healthcare Limited
Incorporated: 11 January 1999 *Employees:* 4
Net Worth: £16,780,000 *Total Assets:* £77,281,000
Registered Office: Third Floor, Broad Quay House, Prince Street, Bristol, BS1 4DJ
Activities: Other specialised construction activities n.e.c.
Parent: Mercia Healthcare (Holdings) Limited
Officers: Jonathan Nigel Edward Cowdell [1966] Director; Phillip Joseph Dodd [1955] Director; Harvey John William Pownall [1966] Director; Terence Ryan [1957] Director

Merck Chemicals Ltd
Incorporated: 25 May 1960 *Employees:* 137
Net Worth: £7,474,000 *Total Assets:* £128,954,000
Registered Office: The Old Brickyard, New Road, Gillingham, Dorset, SP8 4XT
Activities: Wholesale of chemical products
Parent: Millipore (UK) Limited
Officers: Peter Biro [1967] Director/US Certified Public Accountant [Dutch]; Victor Mark Jackson [1962] Director/Operations Manager

Merityre Specialists Limited
Incorporated: 15 May 1961 *Employees:* 247
Net Worth: £3,320,450 *Total Assets:* £13,683,872
Registered Office: Unit 33a West Way, Andover, Hants, SP10 5JG
Activities: Retail trade of motor vehicle parts and accessories
Shareholders: Noel Christopher Pope; Jolyon James Pope
Officers: Giles Derek Allen, Secretary; Dene Arnold [1964] Director; Jolyon James Pope [1952] Director; Noel Christopher Pope [1954] Director; Julian Robert Archer Spooner [1955] Director; Nicholas Harvard Taylor [1952] Director

Merlin Attractions Operations Limited
Incorporated: 7 June 2007 *Employees:* 5,906
Net Worth: £396,308,000 *Total Assets:* £751,174,016
Registered Office: Link House, 25 West Street, Poole, Dorset, BH15 1LD
Activities: Operation of historical sites and buildings and similar visitor attractions
Parent: Charcoal Midco 1 Limited
Officers: Fiona Jane Rose, Secretary; Stephanie-Jane Brooksbank [1967] Finance Director; Emma Elizabeth Catterall [1973] Director/Accountant; Fiona Eastwood [1970] Managing Director; Matthew Paul Jowett [1967] Director/General Counsel and Company Secretary; Nicholas Stephen MacKenzie [1968] Director; Fraser Montgomery [1970] Director/Accountant; Fiona Jane Rose [1964] Director/Assistant Group Company Secretary

Merlin Cinemas Limited
Incorporated: 10 November 1998 *Employees:* 333
Net Worth: £6,161,629 *Total Assets:* £11,374,349
Registered Office: Regal Theatre & Cinema, Fore Street, Redruth, Cornwall, TR15 2AZ
Activities: Support activities to performing arts
Officers: Gregory John Adams, Secretary/Office Manager; Geoffrey Greaves [1953] Director/Cinema Proprietor; Craig Thomas May [1983] Director

Merlin Entertainments (Asia Pacific) Limited
Incorporated: 10 May 1999
Net Worth: £286,049,984 *Total Assets:* £292,580,000
Registered Office: Link House, 25 West Street, Poole, Dorset, BH15 1LD
Activities: Activities of head offices
Parent: Charcoal Newco 1A Limited
Officers: Fiona Jane Rose, Secretary; Matthew Paul Jowett [1967] Director/General Counsel and Company Secretary; Fiona Jane Rose [1964] Director/Assistant Group Company Secretary

Merlin Entertainments (Dungeons) Limited
Incorporated: 20 November 1998 *Employees:* 234
Net Worth: £52,751,000 *Total Assets:* £72,395,000
Registered Office: Link House, 25 West Street, Poole, Dorset, BH15 1LD
Activities: Other amusement and recreation activities n.e.c.
Parent: Merlin Entertainments Group Operations Limited
Officers: Fiona Jane Rose, Secretary; Stephanie-Jane Brooksbank [1967] Finance Director; Matthew Paul Jowett [1967] Director/General Counsel and Company Secretary; Fraser Montgomery [1970] Director/Accountant; Fiona Jane Rose [1964] Director/Assistant Group Company Secretary

Merlin Entertainments (NBD) Limited
Incorporated: 9 January 2004 *Employees:* 2
Previous: Tussauds (NBD) Limited
Net Worth: £22,466,000 *Total Assets:* £27,915,000
Registered Office: Link House, 25 West Street, Poole, Dorset, BH15 1LD
Activities: Activities of head offices
Parent: Merlin Entertainments Group Holdings Limited
Officers: Fiona Jane Rose, Secretary; Matthew Paul Jowett [1967] Director/General Counsel and Company Secretary; Fiona Jane Rose [1964] Director/Assistant Group Company Secretary

Merlin Entertainments (Sea Life) Limited
Incorporated: 22 October 1987 *Employees:* 554
Net Worth: £91,115,000 *Total Assets:* £128,717,000
Registered Office: Link House, 25 West Street, Poole, Dorset, BH15 1LD
Activities: Other amusement and recreation activities n.e.c.
Parent: Merlin Entertainments Group Operations Limited
Officers: Fiona Jane Rose, Secretary; Stephanie-Jane Brooksbank [1967] Finance Director; Tony Grizzanti [1970] Director; Matthew Paul Jowett [1967] Director/General Counsel and Company Secretary; Fraser Montgomery [1970] Director/Accountant; Fiona Jane Rose [1964] Director/Assistant Group Company Secretary; Rene Johannes Leonardus Sleven [1980] Director/Regional General Manager, Rest of Europe [Dutch]

Merlin Entertainments Developments Limited
Incorporated: 22 November 2002 *Employees:* 261
Net Worth: £3,724,000 *Total Assets:* £40,128,000
Registered Office: Link House, 25 West Street, Poole, Dorset, BH15 1LD
Activities: Activities of head offices
Parent: Merlin Entertainments Group Operations Limited
Officers: Fiona Jane Rose, Secretary; Mark Peter Edmund Fisher [1969] Executive Director; Matthew Paul Jowett [1967] Director/General Counsel and Company Secretary; Fiona Jane Rose [1964] Director/Assistant Group Company Secretary; James Peter Williams [1983] Director

Merlin Entertainments Group Holdings Limited
Incorporated: 23 February 2007 *Employees:* 1
Net Worth: £1,190,861,056 *Total Assets:* £2,147,760,128
Registered Office: Link House, 25 West Street, Poole, Dorset, BH15 1LD
Activities: Activities of head offices
Parent: Charcoal Newco 1 Limited
Officers: Fiona Jane Rose, Secretary; Matthew Paul Jowett [1967] Director/General Counsel and Company Secretary; Fiona Jane Rose [1964] Director/Assistant Group Company Secretary

Merlin Entertainments Group Limited
Incorporated: 21 January 2004 *Employees:* 177
Net Worth: £4,442,000 *Total Assets:* £75,702,000
Registered Office: Link House, 25 West Street, Poole, Dorset, BH15 1LD
Activities: Activities of head offices
Parent: Merlin Entertainments Group Holdings Limited
Officers: Fiona Jane Rose, Secretary; Alison Chorley [1967] Director/Finance Business Partner - Digital; Matthew Paul Jowett [1967] Director/General Counsel and Company Secretary; Fiona Jane Rose [1964] Director/Assistant Group Company Secretary

Merlin Entertainments Group Operations Limited
Incorporated: 20 November 1998 *Employees:* 110
Net Worth Deficit: £6,535,000 *Total Assets:* £15,078,000
Registered Office: Link House, 25 West Street, Poole, Dorset, BH15 1LD
Activities: Other amusement and recreation activities n.e.c.
Parent: Merlin Entertainments Group Limited
Officers: Fiona Jane Rose, Secretary; Stephanie-Jane Brooksbank [1967] Finance Director; Tony Grizzanti [1970] Director; Matthew Paul Jowett [1967] Director/General Counsel and Company Secretary; Fraser Montgomery [1970] Director/Accountant; Fiona Jane Rose [1964] Director/Assistant Group Company Secretary

Merlin Entertainments PLC
Incorporated: 20 September 2013 *Employees:* 19,871
Net Worth: £1,563,000,064 *Total Assets:* £3,664,000,000
Registered Office: Link House, 25 West Street, Poole, Dorset, BH15 1LD
Activities: Activities of head offices
Officers: Matthew Jowett, Secretary; Yun Rachel Chiang [1967] Director [Chinese]; Andrew Raymond Fisher [1969] Director; Charles Mark Gurassa [1956] Director; Anne Frances Hazlitt [1963] Director; Anne-Francoise Nesmes [1971] Director/Chief Financial Officer [French]; Trudy Ann Rautio [1952] Director [American]; Soren Thorup Sorensen [1965] Director [Danish]; Sir John Michael Sunderland [1945] Director/Chairman; Nicholas John Varney [1962] Director/Chief Executive

Merlin UK Finco 1 Limited
Incorporated: 29 October 2013 *Employees:* 3
Net Worth: £374,969,984 *Total Assets:* £824,078,976
Registered Office: Link House, 25 West Street, Poole, Dorset, BH15 1LD
Activities: Non-trading company
Parent: Charcoal Newco 1 Limited
Officers: Fiona Jane Rose, Secretary; Matthew Paul Jowett [1967] Director/General Counsel and Company Secretary; Philip Pateman [1970] Director

Merlo UK Limited
Incorporated: 4 June 1993 *Employees:* 21
Net Worth: £7,292,854 *Total Assets:* £16,772,891
Registered Office: The Paddocks, Headlands Business Park, Salisbury Road, Ringwood, Hants, BH24 3PB
Activities: Agents involved in the sale of machinery, industrial equipment, ships and aircraft
Parent: Merlo S.P.A. Industria Metalmeccanica
Officers: John Leslie Iles [1937] Director; Amilcare Merlo [1934] Director [Italian]

Merriott Plastics Group Limited
Incorporated: 16 March 2012 *Employees:* 88
Net Worth: £3,639,041 *Total Assets:* £5,754,116
Registered Office: Eden Works, Blacknell Lane, Crewkerne, Somerset, TA18 7HE
Activities: Manufacture of other plastic products
Shareholder: Joy Christine Hall
Officers: Joy Christine Hall, Secretary; Ian Curtis [1961] Director; Paul Dobson [1969] Director/Accountant; Graham Patrick Goodhew [1961] Director; William Edward Hall [1949] Director; Andrew Paul Lawrence [1966] Director; Kevin Whatley [1958] Director

Merriott Plastics Limited
Incorporated: 21 January 1998 *Employees:* 42
Net Worth: £5,300,876 *Total Assets:* £6,315,147
Registered Office: Eden Works, Blacknell Lane, Crewkerne, Somerset, TA18 7HE
Activities: Manufacture of other plastic products
Parent: Merriott Plastics Group
Officers: Andrew Paul Lawrence, Secretary; Ian Curtis [1961] Director; Paul Dobson [1969] Director/Accountant; Graham Patrick Goodhew [1961] Director; William Edward Hall [1949] Director; Andrew Paul Lawrence [1966] Director/Commercial; Kevin Whatley [1958] Director

Merrydown PLC
Incorporated: 22 November 1946 *Employees:* 1
Net Worth: £26,722,968 *Total Assets:* £51,247,252
Registered Office: 5230 Valiant Court, Delta Way, Brockworth, Gloucester, GL3 4FE
Activities: Manufacture of cider and other fruit wines
Parent: SHS Group Ltd
Officers: Arthur William Richmond, Secretary; Elaine Birchall [1966] Director [Irish]; Arthur William Richmond [1966] Director/Accountant; Joseph Sloan [1946] Director/Group Chairman

Merston Renewable Energy CIC
Incorporated: 9 June 2015
Net Worth: £1,753,160 *Total Assets:* £6,689,353
Registered Office: Overmoor Farm, Neston, Corsham, Wilts, SN13 9TZ
Activities: Production of electricity
Parent: Meadow Blue Community Energy
Officers: David Cyril Barton [1956] Director; Christopher Charles Rowland [1963] Director/Community Energy and Design Consultant; Julia Chantal Waterlow [1956] Director/Retired

Metal Yapi (UK) Limited
Incorporated: 19 June 2015 *Employees:* 12
Net Worth: £738,905 *Total Assets:* £5,065,689
Registered Office: 1 Long Street, Tetbury, Glos, GL8 8AA
Activities: Manufacture of metal structures and parts of structures
Shareholders: Metal Ve Yapi Sistemleri Ticaret AS; Metal Ve Yapi Sistemleri Ticaret AS
Officers: Umut Bulbul [1976] Director [Turkish]; Peter Francis Walker [1958] Director

Metalex Products Limited
Incorporated: 14 April 1993 *Employees:* 38
Net Worth: £3,788,179 *Total Assets:* £9,300,459
Registered Office: Midland House, 2 Poole Road, Bournemouth, BH2 5QY
Activities: Other service activities n.e.c.
Shareholders: Paul Nicola; Sally Nicola
Officers: Sally Nicola, Secretary; Paul Nicola [1958] Director

Metaltech Precision Ltd
Incorporated: 13 September 1999 *Employees:* 75
Net Worth: £3,769,300 *Total Assets:* £5,991,747
Registered Office: Yonder Hill Works, Chard Junction, Chard, Somerset, TA20 4QR
Activities: Other professional, scientific and technical activities n.e.c.
Parent: MPL Holdings (SW) Limited
Officers: Jaqueline Hill, Secretary; Stephen John Hill [1968] Director/Precision Engineer; Andrew Riste [1966] Operations Director

Methodist Insurance Public Limited Company
Incorporated: 19 June 1872
Net Worth: £17,360,288 *Total Assets:* £40,221,652
Registered Office: Beaufort House, Brunswick Road, Gloucester, GL1 1JZ
Activities: Non-life insurance
Officers: Rachael Jane Hall, Secretary; Michael George Angell [1956] Church Operations Director; Rev Linda Joy Barriball [1956] Director; Colin Howard Boothman [1948] Director/Quantity Surveyor; John Coates [1952] Director; David Michael Crompton [1955] Director; Paul Harold Davis [1957] Director/Superintendent Minister; Andrew Goldsworthy Gibbs [1947] Director; John Malcolm Hamilton [1947] Director/Retired Actuary; Deborah Ann Rees [1960] Director; David Storry Walton [1956] Director

Metric Group Holdings Limited
Incorporated: 28 April 1997 *Employees:* 169
Net Worth Deficit: £3,052,000 *Total Assets:* £13,971,000
Registered Office: Metric House, Westmead Drive, Westmead Industrial Estate, Swindon, Wilts, SN5 7AD
Activities: Activities of other holding companies n.e.c.
Parent: Tri Star Security Pte. Ltd
Officers: Matthew Ridley, Secretary; Peter Austin Aylward [1962] Managing Director

Metric Group Limited
Incorporated: 21 November 1990 *Employees:* 169
Net Worth: £2,053,000 *Total Assets:* £18,732,000
Registered Office: Metric House, Westmead Drive, Westmead Industrial Estate, Swindon, Wilts, SN5 7AD
Activities: Manufacture of other electrical equipment
Parent: Metric Group Holdings Limited
Officers: Matthew Ridley, Secretary; Peter Austin Aylward [1962] Managing Director; Sandy Paul Mace [1970] R&D Director; Jessica Yi Shi [1974] Director [Chinese]

Metropolitan Land and House Company Limited (The)
Incorporated: 9 July 1878 *Employees:* 4
Net Worth: £4,616,234 *Total Assets:* £5,200,523
Registered Office: 34 High East Street, Dorchester, DT1 1HA
Activities: Development of building projects
Officers: Robin Clifford Soole, Secretary; Florent Patrice Marie Guillo-Lohan [1982] Director/Financial Controller [French]; Richard John Pickering [1960] Director; Robin Clifford Soole [1971] Director; Roger Soole [1945] Director/Accountant

MGI Coutier Finance Limited
Incorporated: 23 October 2012 *Employees:* 1
Net Worth: £30,451,604 *Total Assets:* £166,159,424
Registered Office: Unit 5 Westpoint Business Park, Bumpers Farm, Chippenham, Wilts, SN14 6RB
Activities: Manufacture of other rubber products
Officers: David John Ledwitch, Secretary; Benoit Cedric Coutier [1978] Director/Vice President Human Resources [French]; David John Ledwitch [1962] Director; Leland Jon Richards [1964] Director [American]

MGV Engineering Limited
Incorporated: 18 June 2013 *Employees:* 2
Net Worth: £511,005 *Total Assets:* £6,195,503
Registered Office: Mazars LLP, 5th Floor, Merck House, Seldown Lane, Poole, Dorset, BH15 1TW
Activities: Wholesale of other machinery and equipment
Shareholders: Andrey Mekhanik; Igor Glyanenko; Alexander Volov
Officers: Jonathan Ralph Flay [1971] Director

Mi-Pac Newco Limited
Incorporated: 10 December 2014
Net Worth: £7,461,497 *Total Assets:* £7,461,497
Registered Office: The Rear Buffer Depot, Badminton Road, Acton Turville, Badminton, Glos, GL9 1HE
Activities: Non-trading company
Major Shareholder: Richard Xavier Boissevain
Officers: Maxwell William Baines [1981] Director; Richard Xavier Boissevain [1961] Managing Director

Mi-Space (UK) Limited
Incorporated: 14 June 2007 *Employees:* 162
Net Worth: £2,321,000 *Total Assets:* £23,140,000
Registered Office: Midas House, Pynes Hill, Exeter, Devon, EX2 5WS
Activities: Construction of domestic buildings
Parent: Midas Group Limited
Officers: Duncan Fraser Rogerson, Secretary; Anthony John Eaton [1971] Divisional Director; Stephen Lewis Hindley [1949] Director/Civil Engineer; Alan Edward Hope [1965] Director; Scott George Poulter [1974] Director; Duncan Fraser Rogerson [1971] Director/Accountant

Michco 1204 Limited
Incorporated: 24 July 2012
Net Worth: £3,721,735 *Total Assets:* £43,380,756
Registered Office: 35 and 35a The Maltings, Lower Charlton Trading Estate, Shepton Mallet, Somerset, BA4 5QE
Activities: Production of electricity
Major Shareholder: Robert John Hugo Randall
Officers: Douglas Michael Friend [1980] Director; Robert John Hugo Randall [1960] Director/Financier

Michco 1205 Limited
Incorporated: 24 July 2012
Net Worth: £22,080,296 *Total Assets:* £43,436,232
Registered Office: 35 and 35a The Maltings, Lower Charlton Trading Estate, Shepton Mallet, Somerset, BA4 5QE
Activities: Production of electricity
Major Shareholder: Robert John Hugo Randall
Officers: Douglas Michael Friend [1980] Director; Robert John Hugo Randall [1960] Director/Financier

Michco 1208 Limited
Incorporated: 3 August 2012
Net Worth Deficit: £1,920 *Total Assets:* £9,959,730
Registered Office: 35 and 35a The Maltings, Lower Charlton Trading Estate, Shepton Mallet, Somerset, BA4 5QE
Activities: Activities of head offices
Shareholders: Lombard International Assurance SA; Robert John Hugo Randall
Officers: Douglas Michael Friend [1980] Director; Robert John Hugo Randall [1960] Director/Financier

Michelmores LLP
Incorporated: 22 February 2007 *Employees:* 440
Net Worth: £13,028,000 *Total Assets:* £24,974,000
Registered Office: Woodwater House, Pynes Hill, Exeter, Devon, EX2 5WR
Officers: Ian Buchanan Binnie [1962] Member; Sandra Brown [1958] Member; Richard Juxon Cobb [1969] Member; Anthony John Cockayne [1965] Member; Christopher John Hoar [1968] Member; Ian David Holyoak [1963] Member; Emma Elizabeth Honey [1970] Member; Thomas William Lawrence Hyde [1967] Member; Charles Norton Lloyd Maunder [1970] Member; Carol Ann McCormack [1961] Member; Stephen Andrew Morse [1960] Member; Andrew Richard Oldland [1965] Member; Stephen Paul Paling [1957] Member; Antony David Power [1972] Member; Timothy Charles Richards [1961] Member; Jonathan James Riley [1970] Member; Benjamin Sharples [1972] Member; Lucy Jane Smallwood [1967] Member; Simon Mark Thomas [1962] Member; Andrew Bruce Tobey [1958] Member; Vivienne Mary Williams [1976] Member; Andrew William Baines [1966] LLP Member; James Llewellyn Baker [1979] LLP Member; Simon Barnett [1958] LLP Member; Samantha Jane Billingham [1964] LLP Member; Sara Louise Chisholm-Batten [1980] LLP Member; Christopher John Close [1954] LLP Member; Joanna Mary Damerell [1962] LLP Member; Malcolm Keith Dickinson [1956] LLP Member; Richard Michael Hedger [1967] LLP Member; Ben Hogan [1978] LLP Member; Richard William Honey [1964] LLP Member; Mark Timothy Howard [1968] LLP Member; David Lainson Howe [1960] LLP Member; Melanie Hughes [1979] LLP Member; Jonathan Kitchin [1981] LLP Member; Stephen Edward McColgan [1962] LLP Member; Philip John Newhouse [1952] LLP Member; Stephen Newson [1974] LLP Member; Generald Leslie Offen [1959] LLP Member; Louise Jane Peters [1970] LLP Member; Sacha Andrew Pickering [1974] LLP Member; Jennifer Catherine Ridgway [1982] LLP Member; Philip Hunter Ryley [1960] LLP Member; Garbhan Colla Oisin Shanks [1976] LLP Member; Henry Guy Jonathan Taylor [1982] LLP Member; Thomas Michael Andrew Torkar [1978] LLP Member; James Jonathan Peter Townsend [1975] LLP Member; Alexandra Jane Olivia Watson [1979] LLP Member; Joseph Laurian Whitfield [1961] LLP Member; Peter Rhys Williams [1955] LLP Member; Philip Graeme Wolfgang [1975] LLP Member

Microensure Holdings Limited
Incorporated: 16 November 2012 *Employees:* 187
Net Worth: £9,148,063 *Total Assets:* £10,995,286
Registered Office: Parker Court, Knapp Lane, Cheltenham, Glos, GL50 3QJ
Activities: Other business support service activities n.e.c.
Shareholders: Omidyar Network Fund; Axa S.A
Officers: Arjuna Joseph Costa [1970] Director/Investor [Indian]; Robert Dommisse [1968] Executive Director M&A & Strategic Alliances [South African]; Hassan Mohamed Hassan El Shabrawishi [1980] Director [Egyptian]; Sanjeev Goel [1969] Director/Investments and Portfolio Manager [Indian]; Richard John Leftley [1973] Director; Garance Wattez-Richard [1973] Director/Head of Media Relations [French]

Microsemi Semiconductor Limited
Incorporated: 5 October 1961 *Employees:* 90
Net Worth: £30,771,396 *Total Assets:* £150,416,128
Registered Office: Portwall Place, Portwall Lane, Bristol, BS1 9HS
Activities: Manufacture of electronic components
Parent: Microsemi Corporation
Officers: James Eric Bjornholt [1970] Director/Chief Financial Officer [American]; Mohammed Nawaz Sharif [1970] Director/Vice President

Microsemi Storage Solutions Europe Ltd
Incorporated: 8 October 1997 *Employees:* 13
Previous: PMC-Sierra Europe Ltd
Net Worth: £8,811,008 *Total Assets:* £14,354,083
Registered Office: Portwall Place, Portwall Lane, Bristol, BS1 9HS
Activities: Other business support service activities n.e.c.
Parent: Microchip Technology Inc.
Officers: James Eric Bjornholt [1970] Director/Chief Financial Officer [American]; Mohammed Nawaz Sharif [1970] Director/Vice President

Midas Construction Limited
Incorporated: 14 January 1976 *Employees:* 239
Net Worth: £4,375,000 *Total Assets:* £57,646,000
Registered Office: Midas House, Pynes Hill, Exeter, Devon, EX2 5WS
Activities: Construction of commercial buildings
Parent: Midas Group Limited
Officers: Duncan Fraser Rogerson, Secretary; Stephen Lewis Hindley [1949] Director; Alan Edward Hope [1965] Director; William Andrew McAdam [1967] Director; Scott George Poulter [1974] Director; Derek Anthony Quinn [1965] Director; Duncan Fraser Rogerson [1971] Director/Accountant; Paul Stephen Strachan [1964] Director

Midas Group Limited
Incorporated: 12 September 1997 *Employees:* 482
Net Worth: £8,878,000 *Total Assets:* £94,294,000
Registered Office: Midas House, Pynes Hill, Exeter, Devon, EX2 5WS
Activities: Construction of commercial buildings
Shareholders: Michael Wesley Hocking; Stephen Lewis Hindley
Officers: Duncan Fraser Rogerson, Secretary; Stephen Lewis Hindley [1949] Director/Civil Engineer; Michael Wesley Hocking [1946] Director; Alan Edward Hope [1965] Director/Chief Executive; Scott George Poulter [1974] Commercial Director; Duncan Fraser Rogerson [1971] Director/Accountant

Midas Retail Limited
Incorporated: 19 December 2003 *Employees:* 16
Net Worth: £1,056,000 *Total Assets:* £9,107,000
Registered Office: Midas House, Pynes Hill, Exeter, Devon, EX2 5WS
Activities: Other specialised construction activities n.e.c.
Parent: Midas Group Ltd
Officers: Duncan Fraser Rogerson, Secretary; Stephen Lewis Hindley [1949] Director; Alan Edward Hope [1965] Director; Scott George Poulter [1974] Director; Duncan Fraser Rogerson [1971] Director/Accountant

Midhurst Child Care Limited
Incorporated: 19 December 2005 *Employees:* 330
Net Worth: £6,352,406 *Total Assets:* £9,921,441
Registered Office: 47 Bedwin Street, Salisbury, Wilts, SP1 3UT
Activities: Other residential care activities n.e.c.
Major Shareholder: Pamela Jane McConnell
Officers: Jeremy Paul McConnell, Secretary; Jeremy Paul McConnell [1963] Facilities Director; Pamela Jane McConnell [1955] Director

Midland House LLP
Incorporated: 30 July 2009
Net Worth: £3,340,412 *Total Assets:* £5,796,658
Registered Office: Quay House, 7 The Quay, Poole, Dorset, BH15 1HA
Officers: Karen Ruth Macey [1957] Member; Ingrid Elisabeth Juliane Walters [1950] Member; Nigel Ashley Walters [1953] Member

Midsomer Norton Schools Partnership
Incorporated: 3 September 2010 *Employees:* 583
Net Worth: £33,817,768 *Total Assets:* £43,708,276
Registered Office: Norton Hill Academy, Charlton Road, Midsomer Norton, Radstock, Somerset, BA3 4AD
Activities: General secondary education
Officers: William John Kingwell, Secretary; Robert William Arnold [1948] Director/Educational Consultant; Sarah Louise Baldwin [1972] Director/Solicitor; Dr Christian John Brace [1968] Director/Professor; Gareth Griffith [1972] Director/Headmaster; Simon Timothy Mills [1957] Director/Optician; Andrew Sinden [1954] Director/Consultant; Stuart Warrener [1951] Director/Self Employed; Alun John Williams [1974] Director/Headteacher; Sharon Ann Wiseman [1965] Director/Lecturer

Midway Care Group Limited
Incorporated: 31 March 2010 *Employees:* 380
Net Worth: £2,186,697 *Total Assets:* £13,025,722
Registered Office: Windsor House, Bayshill Road, Cheltenham, Glos, GL50 3AT
Activities: Activities of other holding companies n.e.c.
Parent: Midway Care Group Holdings Limited
Officers: Ian Geoffrey Brown [1976] Director; Matthew John Harrison [1971] Director

Mikulla Leisure Limited
Incorporated: 15 December 2005
Net Worth: £788,192 *Total Assets:* £3,829,674
Registered Office: 3-5 College Street, Burnham on Sea, Somerset, TA8 1AR
Activities: Other business support service activities n.e.c.
Parent: C.P. Mikulla Limited
Officers: Margaret Mikulla, Secretary; Christopher Paul Mikulla [1953] Director/Motor Dealer; Margaret Mikulla [1949] Director

C.P. Mikulla Limited
Incorporated: 29 January 1996 *Employees:* 13
Net Worth: £9,067,597 *Total Assets:* £10,164,068
Registered Office: 3-5 College Street, Burnham on Sea, Somerset, TA8 1AR
Activities: Sale of used cars and light motor vehicles
Shareholders: Christopher Paul Mikulla; Margaret Mikulla
Officers: Margaret Mikulla, Secretary; Christopher Paul Mikulla [1953] Director/Motor Dealer; Margaret Mikulla [1949] Company Secretary/Director

Mildren Construction Limited
Incorporated: 2 June 1987 *Employees:* 108
Net Worth: £1,876,249 *Total Assets:* £8,148,475
Registered Office: 120 Matchams Lane, Hurn, Christchurch, Dorset, BH23 6AN
Activities: Construction of commercial buildings
Major Shareholder: Christopher Stephen Wingham
Officers: Mark James Valentine, Secretary; Simon David French [1968] Managing Director; Justin Napier Galloway [1969] Pre-Construction & Business Development Director; Ashley Michael Harvey [1973] Commercial Director; Hugo Stephen Milner [1959] Design and Build Director; Mark James Valentine [1961] Financial Director; Christopher Stephen Wingham [1957] Director/Chairman

Milestones Trust
Incorporated: 16 April 1986 *Employees:* 1,081
Net Worth: £20,374,828 *Total Assets:* £30,178,766
Registered Office: Unit 10 Eclipse Office Park, High Street, Staple Hill, Bristol, BS16 5EL
Activities: Residential care activities for the elderly and disabled
Officers: Hilary Ann Pearce, Secretary; Jill Frances Hammond Broadhead [1953] Director/Solicitor; Jane Elizabeth Buswell [1957] Director/Consultant; Peter Michael Collins [1952] Director/Retired/Consultant; Verena Jayne Fuller [1966] Director; Samantha Griggs [1974] Operations Development Director; Kenneth David Guy [1950] Director/Retired; Kim Peter Heath [1956] Director/Consultant; Dr Lydia Margaret Henderson [1963] Director/Consultant; Robin Howard Nash [1937] Director/Retired; Donald Edward Nordberg [1949] Director/University Lecturer [American]; Kevin Andrew Pattison [1959] Director; Margaret Ann Shovelton [1947] Director/Retired; David Daniel Wilson [1956] Director/Consultant

Milewood (Holdings) Ltd
Incorporated: 9 June 2010 *Employees:* 304
Net Worth: £9,960,062 *Total Assets:* £18,393,656
Registered Office: 1st Floor, 1 Lakeside, Headlands Business Park, Salisbury Road, Blashford, Ringwood, Hants, BH24 3PB
Activities: Activities of other holding companies n.e.c.
Parent: Care Tree Invest Ltd
Officers: Harish Kumar Arora [1977] Director/Financial Controller; Alexandre Carpentier de Changy [1967] Director [Belgian]; Christopher Paul Hartshorne [1966] Director; Mathieu Lefebvre [1986] Director/Managing Partner [Belgian]

Milewood Healthcare Ltd
Incorporated: 7 November 2002 *Employees:* 228
Net Worth: £5,833,406 *Total Assets:* £6,270,142
Registered Office: 1st Floor, 1 Lakeside, Headlands Business Park, Salisbury Road, Blashford, Ringwood, Hants, BH24 3PB
Activities: Residential nursing care facilities
Parent: Milewood (Holdings) Ltd
Officers: Harish Kumar Arora [1977] Director/Financial Controller; Alexandre Carpentier de Changy [1967] Director [Belgian]; Christopher Paul Hartshorne [1966] Director; Mathieu Lefebvre [1986] Director/Managing Partner [Belgian]

W.J.Miller & Sons Limited
Incorporated: 19 September 1961 *Employees:* 5
Net Worth: £3,003,429 *Total Assets:* £5,913,980
Registered Office: Woodland Grange, Clanville, Andover, Hants, SP11 9JE
Activities: Mixed farming
Major Shareholder: Stephen John Douglas Miller
Officers: Stephen John Douglas Miller [1963] Director/Farmer

Herman Miller Holdings Limited
Incorporated: 23 March 2010
Net Worth: £30,851,092 *Total Assets:* £97,157,160
Registered Office: 1 Portal Road, Bowerhill, Melksham, Wilts, SN12 6GN
Activities: Manufacture of office and shop furniture
Parent: Herman Miller International Finance Luxembourg S.A.R.L
Officers: David Audis, Secretary; David Arnold Lutz [1957] Director/Principal Corporate Development [American]; Robert Thomas Woodbridge [1976] Finance Director

Herman Miller Limited
Incorporated: 22 February 1973 *Employees:* 494
Net Worth: £54,982,000 *Total Assets:* £91,829,000
Registered Office: 1 Portal Road, Bowerhill, Melksham, Wilts, SN12 6GN
Activities: Manufacture of other fabricated metal products n.e.c.
Parent: Herman Miller Holdings
Officers: David William Audis, Secretary; Jeremy Hocking [1961] Director/Business Executive; Jeffrey Stutz [1970] Director/Chief Financial Officer [American]; Joanne Margaret Williams [1965] HR Director; Robert Thomas Woodbridge [1976] Finance Director

Millets Farm Centre Limited
Incorporated: 28 August 2014 *Employees:* 107
Net Worth: £4,651,743 *Total Assets:* £10,376,709
Registered Office: 38-42 Newport Street, Swindon, Wilts, SN1 3DR
Activities: Retail sale of fruit and vegetables in specialised stores
Shareholders: Nigel John Carter; Antony David Carter
Officers: Anthony David Carter [1956] Director; Nigel John Carter [1953] Director; Sally Christina Viney [1962] Director

Millfield
Incorporated: 4 August 1953 *Employees:* 587
Net Worth: £47,680,000 *Total Assets:* £74,847,000
Registered Office: Millfield, Street, Somerset, BA16 0YD
Activities: Pre-primary education
Officers: Rachel Kay Summerhayes, Secretary; William John Bushell [1955] Director/Lloyds Broker; Ewan Alexis Cameron [1971] Director/NHS Executive; Richard James Roger Clark [1970] Director/Solicitor; Clare Cripps [1949] Director/Local Government Officer; Stephen John East [1958] Director/Chartered Accountant; Richard John Exley [1965] Director/Chartered Surveyor; Timothy Philip Griffiths [1960] Director/Chief Executive; Katherine Mary Griggs [1962] Director/Chief Executive; Christopher Halliwell Hirst [1947] Director/Retired Headteacher; Andrew Stuart Jackson [1968] Director/Accountant; John Darcy Lever [1952] Director/Retired Headmaster; Christopher Anthony James MacDonald [1961] Non-Executive Director and Corporate Adviser; John Rennie Maudslay [1953] Director/Insurance Consultant; Katharine Louise McLauchlan [1959] Director/Retired Teacher; Sara Louise Riley [1968] Director/Magistrate and Holiday Cottage Owner; Roland Dacre Rudd [1961] Director/Chairman, Finsbury; Anabel Sophia Sexton [1969] Director; Marc Alfred Liston Simon [1955] Director; Timothy Malcolm Taylor [1944] Director/Retired Headmaster and Chief Executive; Robert Patrick Thornton [1944] Director/Retired Headteacher; Richard Graham Tovey [1948] Director/Retired Headteacher; Dr Peter Marston Warner [1947] Director/Retired; David Simpson Williamson [1946] Director/Retired Bursar

Millfields Community Economic Development Trust Community Interest Company
Incorporated: 19 February 1998 *Employees:* 6
Net Worth: £470,483 *Total Assets:* £6,300,733
Registered Office: HQ, 237 Union Street, Plymouth, PL1 3HQ
Activities: Other business support service activities n.e.c.
Officers: Roger Edward Pipe, Secretary; Emma Bell [1971] Director/Teacher; Yvonne Jane Fraser [1976] Director/Self Employed Consultant; Councillor Susan Clare McDonald [1950] Director/City Councillor; Zita Anne Moyse [1944] Director/Retired; Christopher John Penberthy [1964] Director/City Councillor; Reverend Samuel Philpott [1941] Director/Parish Priest; Carole Rounsfull [1942] Director/Retired; Jean Margaret Trevaskus [1940] Director/Housewife; Janet Christine Vosper [1947] Director; Kate Watson [1979] Director/Solicitor

Millstream Management Services Limited
Incorporated: 10 September 2001 *Employees:* 198
Net Worth: £4,362,882 *Total Assets:* £5,915,017
Registered Office: Churchill House, Parkside, Ringwood, Hants, BH24 3SG
Activities: Management of real estate on a fee or contract basis
Parent: Churchill Retirement (Group) Limited
Officers: Darren Mark Riley, Secretary; Dean Marlow [1971] Director/Accountant; Clinton James McCarthy [1964] Director/Builder; Spencer John McCarthy [1966] Director/Builder

Millwood Homes (Devon) Limited
Incorporated: 14 June 1982 *Employees:* 4
Net Worth: £4,443,464 *Total Assets:* £4,628,944
Registered Office: Office 4, Dean Court Business Park, Lower Dean, Buckfastleigh, Devon, TQ11 0LT
Activities: Construction of domestic buildings
Parent: Millwood Property Investments Management Company Limited
Officers: Adrian David Hobbs, Secretary; Adrian David Hobbs [1966] Director; Alastair Bennet Fallows Salt [1948] Director; Daniel Fallows Salt [1973] Director/Civil Engineer; Pauline Margaret Salt [1947] Director

Milord Homes Limited
Incorporated: 26 July 1977
Net Worth: £5,603,947 *Total Assets:* £8,187,403
Registered Office: 14 Skylark Rise, Woolwell, Plymouth, PL6 7SN
Activities: Other letting and operating of own or leased real estate
Shareholders: Ioannis Costa Tsigarides; John Eden Tsigarides
Officers: Ioannis Costa Tsigarides, Secretary; Maureen Tsigardes [1952] Director; Filios Antony Tsigarides [1965] Director; Ioannis Costa Tsigarides [1929] Director; John Eden Tsigarides [1984] Director/Property Owner

Milspeed Limited
Incorporated: 20 January 1997 *Employees:* 29
Net Worth: £2,949,082 *Total Assets:* £6,628,308
Registered Office: Willow Court Industrial Park, Bourton on the Water, Glos, GL54 2HQ
Activities: Wholesale of textiles
Shareholders: Ian Milhench; Fiona Milhench
Officers: Ian James Milhench, Secretary; Fiona Milhench [1962] Director; Ian James Milhench [1959] Director/Marketing Agent

The Minerva Learning Trust (Dorset)
Incorporated: 7 June 2013 *Employees:* 317
Previous: The Minerva Learning Trust (Dorset) Limited
Net Worth: £4,502,048 *Total Assets:* £7,794,140
Registered Office: The Sir John Colfox Academy, Ridgeway, Bridport, Dorset, DT6 3DT
Activities: General secondary education
Officers: Clive Bath [1949] Director/Retired; Sandra Ann Brown [1939] Director/Councillor; David Hugh Jenkins [1952] Director/Public Servant; Anna Jane Ledgard [1959] Director/Producer; Alan Moss [1950] Director/Retired; Keith Vaughan Peraux [1948] Director; Julian Piper [1949] Director/Retired; Reverend Peter Jonathan Michael Stone [1971] Director/Vicar; Eric Martin Stones [1952] Managing Director; Kay Taylor [1959] Director/Headteacher; Michael John Young [1948] Retired Director of Consultancy Company

Minstead Investments (Boscombe) Limited
Incorporated: 1 March 2006
Net Worth: £2,125,055 *Total Assets:* £4,514,190
Registered Office: Ebenezer House, 5a Poole Road, Bournemouth, BH2 5QJ
Activities: Buying and selling of own real estate
Officers: John Spurling, Secretary; Stuart Alan Lees [1942] Director; John Spurling [1946] Director; Michael Brian Wilkes [1959] Director

Minton Investments (Industrial) Limited
Incorporated: 17 December 1991
Net Worth: £2,458,235 *Total Assets:* £4,918,751
Registered Office: c/o Suite 307, Eagle Tower, Montpelier Drive, Cheltenham, Glos, GL50 1TA
Activities: Other letting and operating of own or leased real estate
Shareholder: Peter Henry Simpkin
Officers: Daniel Peter Simpkin, Secretary; Adam Christopher Simpkin [1978] Director/Chartered Surveyor; Daniel Peter Simpkin [1975] Director; Peter Henry Simpkin [1945] Director

Minty Art Limited
Incorporated: 6 August 2007 *Employees:* 1
Net Worth: £3,309,105 *Total Assets:* £3,582,009
Registered Office: Portwall Place, Portwall Lane, Bristol, BS1 6NA
Activities: Other business support service activities n.e.c.
Major Shareholder: Raqib Shaw
Officers: Raqib Shaw [1974] Director/Artist

Miro Technologies Limited
Incorporated: 28 December 1983 *Employees:* 28
Net Worth Deficit: £992,852 *Total Assets:* £15,005,365
Registered Office: Building 330, The Crescent, Bristol Business Park, Bristol, BS16 1EJ
Activities: Business and domestic software development
Parent: The Boeing Company
Officers: Simon Howard Jones, Secretary; Stephen John Burnell [1963] Managing Director. UK Rotor Craft Support; Richard Stuart Mills [1963] Strategy Director, UK and Ireland; Thomas Kelley Pickett [1983] Director/Finance Manager [American]; Daniella Dina Marie Turner [1957] Director/Operations

Mistral Holdings Limited
Incorporated: 5 November 2015 *Employees:* 69
Net Worth: £3,803,230 *Total Assets:* £6,339,096
Registered Office: Eagle Tower, Montpellier Drive, Cheltenham, Glos, GL50 1TA
Activities: Non-trading company
Officers: Russell Martin Aldridge [1957] Director/Accountant; Toby Howard Barker [1977] Director/Public Relations; Michael Patrick Conway [1966] Director; Benjamin Copithorne [1974] Director; James Curtis Ford [1964] Director/Designer; Stuart Charles Fox [1964] Director; Andrew John Litchfield [1955] Director/Chairman; Josephine Lloyd [1965] Director; Jenny Miriam Marshall [1966] Director; Emma Molton [1982] Director; Timothy Read [1969] Director; Matthew Lloyd Sutton [1978] Director/Public Relations

Mitcham Canada Holdings Limited
Incorporated: 22 September 2011 *Employees:* 3
Net Worth: £3,846,565 *Total Assets:* £3,850,001
Registered Office: Unit 34 The Maltings, Charlton Estate, Shepton Mallet, Somerset, BA4 5QE
Activities: Activities of head offices
Parent: Mitcham Holdings Ltd
Officers: Robert Paul Capps [1954] Director/Chief Financial Officer [American]; Guy McKay Malden [1952] Managing Director [American]; Mark Welker [1960] Managing Director [American]

Mitcham Holdings Ltd
Incorporated: 27 May 2011
Net Worth: £27,854,680 *Total Assets:* £33,837,748
Registered Office: Unit 34 The Maltings, Charlton Estate, Shepton Mallet, Somerset, BA4 5QE
Activities: Activities of head offices
Parent: Mitcham Industries, Inc
Officers: Robert Paul Capps [1954] Director/Chief Financial Officer [American]; Guy McKay Malden [1952] Managing Director [American]; Mark Welker [1960] Managing Director [American]

Mitchell & Webber Limited
Incorporated: 22 November 1966 *Employees:* 84
Net Worth: £4,435,152 *Total Assets:* £12,127,728
Registered Office: Oil Distribution Depot, Scorrier, Redruth, Cornwall, TR16 5UT
Activities: Wholesale of petroleum and petroleum products
Officers: Roy Ernest Weedon, Secretary; Philip Ernest Mitchell [1946] Director; Frederick Eustace Webber [1936] Director/Sales Manager; Malcolm John Weedon [1969] Director/General Manager; Robert Ernest Weedon [1964] Director; Roy Ernest Weedon [1935] Director/Office Manager

Miton UK Microcap Trust PLC
Incorporated: 26 March 2015
Net Worth: £118,665,000 *Total Assets:* £118,839,000
Registered Office: Beaufort House, 51 New North Road, Exeter, EX4 4EP
Activities: Activities of investment trusts
Officers: Peter Frederick Dicks [1942] Director; Jeannette Elaine Etherden [1960] Director; Andrew David Pomfret [1960] Director; Ashe George Russell Windham [1957] Director

Mitutoyo (U.K.) Limited
Incorporated: 23 July 1979 *Employees:* 132
Net Worth: £11,798,000 *Total Assets:* £17,329,000
Registered Office: West Point Business Park, Andover, Hants, SP10 3UX
Activities: Manufacture of other special-purpose machinery n.e.c.
Officers: Jonathan Peter Brothers, Secretary; Stephen Francis Dyke [1967] Director; Raymond Penny [1965] Managing Director; Shigeyuki Sasaki [1956] Director [Japanese]; Martin Weeks [1954] Director/Manager

MJL Contractors Limited
Incorporated: 27 January 2006 *Employees:* 286
Net Worth: £4,354,456 *Total Assets:* £12,202,883
Registered Office: Unit 6 Hellys Court, Water-Ma-Trout Industrial Estate, Helston, Cornwall, TR13 0EW
Activities: Construction of other civil engineering projects n.e.c.
Parent: MJL Cornwall Limited
Officers: Jennifer Lugg, Secretary; Sylvia Margaret Jane Fisher [1960] Director/Accountant; Nicholas James Jose [1972] Director/Surveyor; Matthew James Lugg [1978] Director/Plant Hire Contractor

MJL Cornwall Limited
Incorporated: 13 February 2001 *Employees:* 288
Net Worth: £24,184,852 *Total Assets:* £33,877,796
Registered Office: Unit 6 Hellys Court, Water-Ma-Trout Industrial Estate, Helston, Cornwall, TR13 0EW
Activities: Development of building projects
Major Shareholder: Matthew James Lugg
Officers: Jennifer Lugg, Secretary; Matthew James Lugg [1978] Director/Plant Hire Contractor

MJL Plant Hire (Cornwall) Limited
Incorporated: 12 February 2008 *Employees:* 1
Net Worth: £5,710,039 *Total Assets:* £13,900,601
Registered Office: Unit 6 Hellys Court, Water-Ma-Trout Industrial Estate, Helston, Cornwall, TR13 0EW
Activities: Other specialised construction activities n.e.c.
Parent: M J L Cornwall Limited
Officers: Matthew James Lugg [1978] Director/Plant Hire Contractor

ML Wind LLP
Incorporated: 29 October 2013
Net Worth: £73,898,016 *Total Assets:* £78,818,720
Registered Office: Windmill Hill Business Park, Whitehill Way, Swindon, Wilts, SN5 6PB

Mmedia Group Limited
Incorporated: 7 December 2004 *Employees:* 43
Previous: Mobile Media Limited
Net Worth: £1,658,280 *Total Assets:* £3,884,322
Registered Office: Enterprise House, Aviation Park West, Bournemouth International Airport, Christchurch, Dorset, BH23 6NW
Activities: Advertising agencies
Parent: Mobile Media (Group) Limited
Officers: Karen Pounds, Secretary/Director; David Albert McClure Pounds [1957] Director; Karen Pounds [1965] Director

MMT Centre Investment Limited
Incorporated: 14 December 2011
Net Worth: £5,763,000 *Total Assets:* £5,799,000
Registered Office: Brightside Park, Severn Bridge, Aust, Bristol, BS35 4BL
Activities: Other letting and operating of own or leased real estate
Parent: Brightside Group Limited
Officers: Russell James Bence [1973] Managing Director; Brendan Eamon McCafferty [1967] Director; Ian Ronald Sutherland [1970] Director

Mobile Thinking Limited
Incorporated: 9 December 2014
Net Worth: £3,344,735 *Total Assets:* £5,263,122
Registered Office: 1 Market Hill, Calne, Wilts, SN11 0BT
Activities: Other telecommunications activities
Major Shareholder: James Edward Harris
Officers: James Edward Harris [1980] Director

Mobile Windscreens Limited
Incorporated: 24 May 1978 *Employees:* 421
Net Worth: £3,329,000 *Total Assets:* £12,475,000
Registered Office: St Philips Road, Bristol, BS2 0JZ
Activities: Retail trade of motor vehicle parts and accessories
Parent: Legion UK Bidco Limited
Officers: Martyn John Bennett [1959] Sales Director; Nicola Christine Coetsee [1970] Director; Martin Anthony Hubschmid [1967] Finance Director; Anders Peter Jensen [1977] Director [Swedish]; Philip Thomas Lomas [1953] Managing Director; Rizwan Joakim Rasiwala [1970] Director [Swedish]

Moderandum Limited
Incorporated: 8 October 2015 *Employees:* 6
Net Worth: £8,480,562 *Total Assets:* £8,715,365
Registered Office: The Manor Office, Cheselbourne, Dorchester, DT2 7NX
Activities: Other letting and operating of own or leased real estate
Shareholders: Eve Bonham Cozens; Michael John Bonham Cozens
Officers: Eve Bonham Cozens, Secretary; Michael Bonham Cozens, Secretary; Eve Bonham Cozens [1946] Director; Julie Diana Elizabeth Bonham Cozens [1986] Director/Teacher; Michael Jack Bonham Cozens [1988] Director; Michael Bonham Cozens [1931] Director

Mole Avon Trading Limited
Incorporated: 5 June 1973 *Employees:* 141
Net Worth: £7,481,796 *Total Assets:* £12,305,464
Registered Office: Mole Avon Centre, Joseph Locke Way, Crediton, Devon, EX17 3FD
Activities: Other retail sale in non-specialised stores
Officers: Darryl Thomas, Secretary; Alan Birmingham [1956] Director; Stuart David Crang [1955] Director/Farmer; William John Daw [1948] Director/Farmer; Michael Robert Haines [1967] Director; Leslie John Heywood [1976] Director/Farmer; John Albert Thomas Hodge [1938] Director/Farmer; Alan Paul Howland [1967] Director/Sales Manager; John Albert Thomas Lee [1959] Director/Farmer; Elizabeth Frances Priest [1970] Director/Property Management and Farmer; Margaret Janet Scarrott [1960] Director/Accountant and Farmer; Josephine Anne Holbrook Wymer [1949] Director/Consultant

Mole Valley Farmers Limited
Incorporated: 6 January 1961 *Employees:* 1,939
Net Worth: £45,096,000 *Total Assets:* £127,316,000
Registered Office: Exmoor House, Lime Way, Pathfields Business Park, South Molton, Devon, EX36 3LH
Activities: Manufacture of fertilizers and nitrogen compounds
Officers: Bruce Korican, Secretary; Stephen Colin Bone [1969] Director/Farmer; Graeme Maurice Cock [1965] Director/Farmer; Peter James Delbridge [1961] Director/Farmer; Steven Anthony Edmunds [1959] Director/Farmer; Frederick Brian Jennings [1946] Director/Farmer; Gaynor Ellen Wellwood [1968] Director/Dairy Farmer & Business Consultant; Peter George Winstone [1958] Farmer/Director

Mole Valley Feed Solutions Ltd
Incorporated: 30 September 2004 *Employees:* 319
Net Worth: £15,990,000 *Total Assets:* £39,796,000
Registered Office: Exmoor House, Lime Way, Pathfields Business Park, South Molton, Devon, EX36 3LH
Activities: Manufacture of prepared feeds for farm animals
Parent: Mole Valley Farmers Ltd
Officers: Bruce Korican, Secretary; Graeme Maurice Cock [1965] Director; Andrew Jackson [1957] Director/Chief Executive Officer

Molson Equipment Services Ltd
Incorporated: 21 September 2007 *Employees:* 89
Net Worth: £10,617,000 *Total Assets:* £45,494,000
Registered Office: Smoke Lane Industrial Estate, Avonmouth, Bristol, BS11 0YA
Activities: Wholesale of mining, construction and civil engineering machinery
Parent: Molson Group Limited
Officers: Andrew John Marsh, Secretary; Robin Nicholas Powell [1969] Director; Jonathan Mark Wilson [1966] Director

Molson Group Ltd
Incorporated: 21 September 2007 *Employees:* 141
Net Worth: £15,537,000 *Total Assets:* £63,246,000
Registered Office: Unit 4 Smoke Lane Industrial Estate, Smoke Lane, Avonmouth, Bristol, BS11 0YA
Activities: Other specialised construction activities n.e.c.
Shareholders: Robin Nicholas Powell; Jonathan Mark Wilson
Officers: Andrew John Marsh, Secretary; Robert Stephen Brown [1960] Director; William Frederick Caplan [1958] Director; Paul Leslie Oldham [1964] Director; Robin Nicholas Powell [1969] Director; Jason Lee Powles [1978] Director; Martyn John Tucker [1975] Service Director; Jonathan Mark Wilson [1966] Director

Monaghan Mushrooms Limited
Incorporated: 31 October 2003 *Employees:* 2,430
Net Worth Deficit: £1,279,000 *Total Assets:* £170,972,000
Registered Office: Stock Lane, Langford, Somerset, BS40 5ES
Activities: Other processing and preserving of fruit and vegetables
Officers: Philip Wilson, Secretary; Paul Thomas Wilson [1977] Director/Chief Operating Officer [Irish]; Philip David Wilson [1975] Divisional Director [Irish]; Ronald Christopher Wilson [1948] Director [Irish]

Monkey Island Properties Limited
Incorporated: 17 August 2015
Net Worth Deficit: £26,277 *Total Assets:* £11,572,420
Registered Office: Wessex Water, Operations Centre, Claverton Down Road, Claverton Down, Bath, BA2 7WW
Activities: Other letting and operating of own or leased real estate
Officers: Ruth Esme Jefferson, Secretary; Andrew Jordan [1961] Director/Executive Vice President - YTL Hotels and Properties; Pearly Poussier [1963] Finance Director [Malaysian]; Colin Frank Skellett [1945] Director

Monkey World Limited
Incorporated: 16 October 1990 *Employees:* 47
Net Worth: £4,169,361 *Total Assets:* £7,012,975
Registered Office: Longthorns, Wareham, Dorset, BH20 6HH
Activities: Botanical and zoological gardens and nature reserves activities
Major Shareholder: Alison Lorraine Cronin
Officers: Byron Leslie Bayford, Secretary; Dr Alison Lorraine Cronin [1966] Director [American]

Monkton Combe School
Incorporated: 23 July 1996 *Employees:* 354
Net Worth: £20,623,554 *Total Assets:* £29,193,324
Registered Office: Monkton Combe, Bath, BA2 7HG
Activities: Pre-primary education
Officers: Christopher James Bernard Alexander [1974] Director; Rev Simon Barnes [1965] Director; Rosie Coates [1957] Director; Charles Benedict Fillingham [1972] Director/Headteacher; Elizabeth Sarah Kingerley Hubbard [1970] Director/Executive Assistant; Professor Helen Eileen Langton [1959] Director; Jenny Jane Perry [1971] Director/Pharmacist; Robert Julian Pringle [1959] Director/Consultant; David John Rosser [1967] Director/Chartered Surveyor; Edward Jonathan James Shaw [1977] Director/Pastor; Mervyn Lloyd Samuel Thomas [1952] Director/Retired; Melanie Karen Townsend [1960] Director/Married Woman; Stephen Burchell Martin Burchell Martin Young [1958] Director/Chartered Accountant

Monmouth Facilities Limited
Incorporated: 23 July 2004 *Employees:* 2
Net Worth: £581,000 *Total Assets:* £4,460,000
Registered Office: Third Floor, Broad Quay House, Prince Street, Bristol, BS1 4DJ
Activities: Management of real estate on a fee or contract basis
Parent: Chiltern Securities Limited
Officers: Graham John Hutt [1954] Regional Director; Neil Rae [1971] Director

Montacute School
Incorporated: 1 August 2011 *Employees:* 98
Net Worth: £5,290,900 *Total Assets:* £7,733,363
Registered Office: Montacute School, 3 Canford Heath Road, Poole, Dorset, BH17 9NG
Activities: Other education n.e.c.
Officers: Stephen Richard Butterworth [1955] Director/Management Consultant; Wendy Byers [1960] Director/Retired; Paul Collins [1960] Director/Fire Safety Inspector; Alison Dalton [1970] Director; Janice Foster [1954] Director/Retired; Beverley Frances Gowman [1967] Director/Head of Learning; Avril Sally Jackson [1957] Director/Carer; Nicola Katherine Keynes [1959] Director/Local Government Officer; Marcia Jane Osborn [1970] Director/Teacher; Jill Owen [1959] Director/Headteacher; Jane Elizabeth Shaw [1948] Director/Retired; Tracey Jayne Smith [1965] Director/Parent Partner & Designated Safeguarding Lead; Susan Janet Watts [1957] Director/Local Government Officer

Montemax Limited
Incorporated: 3 February 2004
Net Worth: £7,091,706 *Total Assets:* £13,252,340
Registered Office: 5 Sandy Court, Ashleigh Way, Plympton, Plymouth, PL7 5JX
Activities: Buying and selling of own real estate
Officers: Mary Patricia Kathleen Abbott, Secretary; Jane Catherine Abbott [1974] Director; Mary Patricia Kathleen Abbott [1943] Director; Nicholas Robert Abbott [1971] Director; Philip Alistair John Abbott [1969] Director

J.A. & E. Montgomery Limited
Incorporated: 13 March 1968 *Employees:* 20
Net Worth: £11,443,458 *Total Assets:* £14,170,665
Registered Office: Manor Farm, North Cadbury, Yeovil, Somerset, BA22 7DW
Activities: Mixed farming
Shareholders: James Lyell Montgomery; Archibald John Montgomery
Officers: Elisabeth Jane Montgomery, Secretary; Janet Montgomery, Secretary; Archibald John Montgomery [1957] Director/Farmer; James Lyell Montgomery [1961] Director/Farmer

Moog Controls Limited
Incorporated: 29 May 1974 *Employees:* 448
Net Worth: £94,034,000 *Total Assets:* £101,591,000
Registered Office: Ashchurch, Tewkesbury, Glos, GL20 8NA
Activities: Manufacture of air and spacecraft and related machinery
Parent: Moog Inc
Officers: Peter Garrad, Secretary; Eric Burghardt [1958] Director/President [American]; Christopher John Curr [1969] Director; David Fijas [1965] Director [American]; Peter Garrad [1967] Finance Director; Mark Aidan Lawton [1968] Director; Stuart Keith McLachlan [1971] Director/Site Leader

Moog Wolverhampton Limited
Incorporated: 3 September 2009 *Employees:* 423
Net Worth: £82,115,000 *Total Assets:* £120,792,000
Registered Office: c/o Moog Controls Limited, Ashchurch, Tewkesbury, Glos, GL20 8NA
Activities: Manufacture of air and spacecraft and related machinery
Parent: Moog Inc
Officers: Peter Garrad, Secretary; Christopher Alan Head, Secretary; R Eric Burghardt [1958] Director/Accountant [American]; Stuart Keith McLachlan [1971] Director/Site Leader; David John Sharples [1960] Director

Moonraker (World) Ltd
Incorporated: 26 March 2015
Net Worth Deficit: £91,222 *Total Assets:* £3,516,999
Registered Office: Hendford Manor, Yeovil, Somerset, BA20 1UN
Activities: Other retail sale not in stores, stalls or markets
Major Shareholder: Simon John Lawrence
Officers: Simon John Lawrence [1963] Director

Moor Park House Limited
Incorporated: 2 December 1997 *Employees:* 117
Net Worth: £1,929,212 *Total Assets:* £6,278,569
Registered Office: 31-33 Commercial Road, Poole, Dorset, BH14 0HU
Activities: Other human health activities
Parent: Moor Park Home Holdings Limited
Officers: Christopher Dennis Root, Secretary/Manager; Stephen Bonnard [1976] Director/Manager; Vijayen Curthan [1975] Director/Manager; Elana Pamela Follwell [1945] Director/Manager; Christopher Dennis Root [1951] Director/Manager

Moorlands College
Incorporated: 26 June 2001
Net Worth: £5,677,178 *Total Assets:* £5,942,385
Registered Office: Moorlands College, Sopley, Christchurch, Dorset, BH23 7AT
Activities: First-degree level higher education
Officers: David Morton McLellan, Secretary; Keith Lawson Brown [1961] Director/University Lecturer; Ruth Elizabeth Flanagan [1969] Director/Teacher; Timothy Charles Goulding [1978] Director/Head of Financial Reporting; John Hurley [1948] Director/Retired; Dr Jonathan James Loose [1971] Director/Lecturer; Steven Paul May-Miller [1957] Director/Chief Executive; Donald Charles McQueen [1962] Director; Janice Marion Tuck [1957] Director/Occupational Therapist

R G Morcom Investments Limited
Incorporated: 19 April 2002
Net Worth: £4,170,272 *Total Assets:* £7,157,848
Registered Office: 23 Lockyer Street, Plymouth, PL1 2QZ
Activities: Other letting and operating of own or leased real estate
Shareholders: Rodney George Morcom; Constance June Morcom; Victoria Elizabeth Morcom
Officers: Constance June Morcom, Secretary; Rachel Morcom [1963] Director; Rodney George Morcom [1960] Director

More Homes Bromley LLP
Incorporated: 8 February 2016
Net Worth Deficit: £3,369,323 *Total Assets:* £77,337,464
Registered Office: 1390 Montpellier Court, Gloucester Business Park, Brockworth, Gloucester, GL3 4AH

Morning Star Motors Limited
Incorporated: 30 January 1962 *Employees:* 2
Net Worth: £4,902,816 *Total Assets:* £4,935,413
Registered Office: The Old Forge, Biddestone, Chippenham, Wilts, SN14 7DG
Activities: Renting and leasing of other machinery, equipment and tangible goods n.e.c.
Shareholders: Ashley Cameron Juniper; Daphne Juniper
Officers: Daphne Juniper, Secretary; Ashley Cameron Juniper [1939] Director; Daphne Juniper [1942] Director

Morris & Perry (Gurney Slade Quarries) Limited
Incorporated: 22 March 1962 *Employees:* 46
Net Worth: £19,236,760 *Total Assets:* £22,787,252
Registered Office: Tout Quarry, Charlton Adam, Somerton, Somerset, TA11 7AN
Activities: Manufacture of ready-mixed concrete
Officers: Brian Sidney Perry, Secretary; Brian Sidney Perry [1962] Managing Director; Ruth Jessica Mary Perry [1926] Director

S Morris Limited
Incorporated: 19 November 1963 *Employees:* 92
Net Worth: £21,720,188 *Total Assets:* £27,454,680
Registered Office: Tout Quarry, Charlton Adam, Somerton, Somerset, TA11 7AN
Activities: Manufacture of ready-mixed concrete
Officers: Brian Sidney Perry, Secretary; Brian Sidney Perry [1962] Managing Director; Ruth Jessica Mary Perry [1926] Director

Morrish Builders (Poole) Limited
Incorporated: 6 May 1982 *Employees:* 54
Net Worth: £24,460,198 *Total Assets:* £41,052,908
Registered Office: Unit 5a, Upton Industrial Estate, Upton, Poole, Dorset, BH16 5SL
Activities: Construction of domestic buildings
Shareholders: William Morrish; Steven Morrish; David Morrish
Officers: Steven Morrish, Secretary; David Morrish [1958] Director; Steven Morrish [1954] Director; Eugene John Charles Rapson [1963] Finance Director

Morrison Financial Associates Limited
Incorporated: 16 July 2015 *Employees:* 3
Net Worth: £1,417,551 *Total Assets:* £3,649,858
Registered Office: Ebenezer House, 5a Poole Road, Bournemouth, BH2 5QJ
Activities: Financial intermediation not elsewhere classified
Shareholders: Gary John Morrison; Pearl Mary Morrison
Officers: Gary John Morrison [1970] Director; Pearl Mary Morrison [1970] Director [Irish]

Mortgage Intelligence Limited
Incorporated: 6 February 1995 *Employees:* 53
Net Worth: £3,931,000 *Total Assets:* £6,705,000
Registered Office: Roddis House, 12 Old Christchurch Road, Bournemouth, BH1 1LG
Activities: Financial intermediation not elsewhere classified
Parent: Mortgage Intelligence Holdings Limited
Officers: Gareth Rhys Williams, Secretary; Natalie Anna Ceeney [1971] Director; Peter Curran [1966] Director; Sarah Anne Laker [1956] Director

The Mortgage Works (UK) PLC
Incorporated: 19 February 1988
Net Worth: £1,406,939,008 *Total Assets:* £29,825,247,232
Registered Office: Nationwide House, Pipers Way, Swindon, Wilts, SN38 1NW
Activities: Financial intermediation not elsewhere classified
Parent: Nationwide Building Society
Officers: Ian George Andrew [1964] Director; Timothy Joseph Carter [1970] Director of Product Operations; Jonathan Jasper Haydn Davy [1965] Director/Head of Collections and Recoveries; Julia Mary Roberts Dunn [1965] Director/Chief Risk Officer; Muir James Mathieson [1974] Director of Financial Controls & Information Management; Christopher Stuart Rhodes [1963] Director; Paul Wootton [1979] Director/Head of Specialist Mortgages

Moseley Distributors Limited
Incorporated: 10 April 1968 *Employees:* 27
Net Worth: £11,326,283 *Total Assets:* £12,990,387
Registered Office: First Floor, 10 Temple Back, Bristol, BS1 6FL
Activities: Sale of other motor vehicles
Major Shareholder: James Tweedie
Officers: James Tweedie, Secretary; James Tweedie [1953] Director

JKL Moseley Limited
Incorporated: 25 September 2013
Net Worth: £4,341,294 *Total Assets:* £4,346,520
Registered Office: 3 The Axium Centre, Dorchester Road, Lytchett Minster, Poole, Dorset, BH16 6FE
Activities: Other letting and operating of own or leased real estate
Officers: Jessica Charlotte Bryant [1990] Director/Certified Chartered Accountant; Arthur Moseley [1937] Director; Ella Mary Moseley [1936] Director; Katrina-Louise Moseley [1992] Director; Lois Maree Moseley [1998] Director

Motorhome Finance Limited
Incorporated: 19 February 2007
Net Worth: £1,475,376 *Total Assets:* £5,328,701
Registered Office: Bristol Road, Brent Knoll, Highbridge, Somerset, TA9 4HG
Activities: Other credit granting n.e.c.
Shareholders: David Ian Carp; Stephen Gary Pike
Officers: David Ian Carp, Secretary; David Ian Carp [1967] Director/Accountant; Stephen Gary Pike [1958] Director; Peter Richard Shaw [1958] Director

R. Moulding & Co. (Salisbury) Limited
Incorporated: 12 October 1964 *Employees:* 104
Net Worth: £1,947,073 *Total Assets:* £4,497,029
Registered Office: St Marys House, Netherhampton, Salisbury, Wilts, SP2 8PU
Activities: Construction of domestic buildings
Shareholders: Richard Timothy Moulding; William Alexander Moulding
Officers: William Alexander Moulding, Secretary; Robert Graham Begg [1958] Director/Building Contractors; Beverley Moulding [1966] Director/Secretary; Jane Moulding [1952] Director/Secretary; Richard Timothy Moulding [1969] Director/Builder (Building Contractor); Richard Moulding [1942] Director/Builder; William Alexander Moulding [1949] Managing Director

Mount Batten Sailing and Water Sports Centre
Incorporated: 25 August 1995
Net Worth: £2,781,455 *Total Assets:* £5,431,251
Registered Office: 70 Lawrence Road, Mount Batten, Plymstock, Plymouth, PL9 9SJ
Activities: Other business support service activities n.e.c.
Officers: Robert Zebulon Baggott [1951] Director/Consultant; Gareth Gwyn James Derrick [1958] Director/City Councillor; Timothy William Geary [1964] Director; Cllr Jeremy Goslin [1971] Director/Associate Professor; Sarah Nancy Jones [1964] Finance Director; Glenn Robert Jordan [1966] Director/Local Councillor; Adrian Douglas Kemp [1956] Director/Company Learning Manager; Cllr Michael John Edward Leaves [1948] Director; David Michael Rose [1963] Director/Head of Sport

Mount International United Services Ltd
Incorporated: 17 November 1997 *Employees:* 59
Net Worth: £4,922,518 *Total Assets:* £9,185,525
Registered Office: The Electron Building, Mount Court, Edison Close, Waterwells Business Centre, Gloucester, GL2 2FN
Activities: Repair of electronic and optical equipment
Officers: Trevor Buxton Howard, Secretary; Jeremy Alfred Gregg [1977] Director/Service Manager; Trevor Buxton Howard [1968] Director/Manager; Paul Michael Mount [1960] Director; Julie Robinson [1965] Director

Mount Road Care Home LLP
Incorporated: 27 April 2011
Net Worth: £6,007,626 *Total Assets:* £15,190,888
Registered Office: Midland House, 2 Poole Road, Bournemouth, BH2 5QY
Officers: Sarah Jane Chenevix-Trench [1959] Member; Veronica Jane Clifton Brown [1939] Member; Alistair Cecil Colvin [1936] Member; Catherine Ann Colvin [1946] Member; Charles Hubert Courage [1946] Member; James Arthur Terence Daler [1938] Member; Jonathan Richard Davie [1946] Member; Benjamin Carne Hargreaves [1946] Member; Carole Margaret Hill [1948] Member; Christopher Holdswoth Hunt [1942] Member; Andrew Charles Simon Hurst [1956] Member; Mary Katherine Lee-Steere [1943] Member; Donald Maxwell MacDonald [1938] Member; Joy Walker [1938] Member; Charles Edward Wentworth Hill [1944] Member; Ralph Wienrich [1945] Member; Richard Frederick de Leigh Wills [1935] Member

Mount Vets Limited
Incorporated: 31 March 2014
Net Worth: £878,225 *Total Assets:* £3,803,814
Registered Office: Mount Vets Limited, Taunton Road, Wellington, Somerset, TA21 9FG
Activities: Veterinary activities
Officers: James Cavanagh [1983] Director/Veterinary Surgeon; Alastair James Caygill [1970] Director/Veterinary; Eric John Chant [1967] Director/Veterinary; Charlotte Jane Freeman [1978] Director/Veterinary; Rob Mangham [1986] Director/Veterinary Surgeon; Piers Gifford Thomas Pepperell [1972] Director/Veterinary; Stuart Charles Leonard Young [1968] Director/Veterinary

MPL Holdings (SW) Limited
Incorporated: 8 August 2014 *Employees:* 105
Net Worth: £3,524,413 *Total Assets:* £6,930,021
Registered Office: Rumwell Hall, Ruwmell, Taunton, Somerset, TA4 1EL
Activities: Activities of other holding companies n.e.c.
Major Shareholder: Steve Hill
Officers: Jacqueline Ann Hill, Secretary; Jacqueline Ann Hill [1960] Director; Stephen John Hill [1968] Director

MPLOY Staffing Solutions Limited
Incorporated: 22 February 2001 *Employees:* 5,171
Net Worth: £671,793 *Total Assets:* £5,214,900
Registered Office: 4 Cedar Park, Cobham Road, Ferndown Industrial Estate, Wimborne, Dorset, BH21 7SF
Activities: Other activities of employment placement agencies
Shareholders: Matthew James Peter Swift; Mark Nash
Officers: Daniel James Keogh, Secretary; Ioana Alexandra Bandila [1990] Director [Romanian]; Anne Banks [1968] Director; Anna Milena Cebeniak [1985] Director [Polish]; Paul Dagley [1958] Director/Recruitment Consultant; Timothy Dicks [1983] Director; Beata Grudzinska [1982] Director [Polish]; Nicolette Edwina Hayton [1965] Director; Hannah Jane Howard [1988] Director; Dan Jordan [1992] Director; Leanne Marie Keeping [1976] Director; Daniel James Keogh [1966] Director/Recruitment Consultant; Karolina Kijewska [1993] Director [Polish]; Katarzyna Mieszkowska [1978] Director/Recruitment Consultant; Mark Nash [1969] Director; Ruth Patricia Ord [1953] Director/Recruitment Consultant; Jonathon Mark Raine [1979] Director; Matthew James Peter Swift [1975] Director/Recruitment Consultant; Gregory Szczepaniak [1984] Director; David Whiteman [1984] Director

MR Capital Consultants Limited
Incorporated: 23 May 2014
Net Worth: £755,427 *Total Assets:* £3,752,749
Registered Office: Easterbrook Eaton Limited, Old Fore Street, Sidmouth, Devon, EX10 8LS
Activities: Other business support service activities n.e.c.
Shareholders: Michael John Paul Marks; Rosemary Anne Marks
Officers: Michael John Paul Marks [1941] Director; Rosemary Anne Marks [1944] Director

MRT Castings Limited
Incorporated: 24 January 1996 *Employees:* 53
Net Worth: £5,130,188 *Total Assets:* £6,442,548
Registered Office: MRT Castings Ltd, South Way, Walworth Industrial Estate, Andover, Hants, SP10 5JT
Activities: Casting of light metals
Parent: Morris Rawnson & Taylor Group Ltd
Officers: Nicola Claire Rawnson, Secretary; Robert Geoffrey Baker [1958] Technical Director; Christopher Neil Rawnson [1957] Director; Kenneth John Rawnson [1945] Director; Philip James Rawnson [1975] Managing Director; Valerie Ann Rawnson [1943] Director

MSA (Britain) Limited
Incorporated: 26 June 1947 *Employees:* 18
Net Worth: £4,878,934 *Total Assets:* £6,471,318
Registered Office: Unit 2 Waller Road, Hopton Park, Devizes, Wilts, SN10 2JP
Activities: Other manufacturing n.e.c.
Parent: MSA Europe GmbH
Officers: Gail Golder, Secretary; James Michael Daugherty [1969] Tax and Treasury Director [American]; Kimberly Seaton Moore [1965] Executive HR Director [American]; Richard William Roda [1972] Director [American]

MSA UK Holdings Limited
Incorporated: 6 August 2015
Net Worth: £61,240,000 *Total Assets:* £124,140,000
Registered Office: Hopton Park, Devizes, Wilts, SN10 2JP
Activities: Activities of other holding companies n.e.c.
Parent: MSA Safety Inc
Officers: Dr Joerdis Jens Behling [1961] Director/Vice President and General Manager MSA Europe [German]; James M. Daugherty [1969] Assistant Treasurer and Director Global Tax [American]; Bob Willem Leenen [1973] Director/Vice President & President MSA International [Dutch]

MSP Capital Ltd
Incorporated: 3 February 1981 *Employees:* 14
Net Worth: £17,787,628 *Total Assets:* £114,444,048
Registered Office: Capital House, 202 Sandbanks Road, Poole, Dorset, BH14 8HA
Activities: Other credit granting n.e.c.
Shareholders: Martin Higgins; John Drinkwater
Officers: David Michael Capra [1958] Director; Martin Higgins [1969] Director; Richard James McDougall [1980] Director; Paul Graham Miracca [1975] Director/Property Developer; James Toby Page [1987] Director

MSP Capital Three Limited
Incorporated: 11 November 2015
Net Worth: £1,394,710 *Total Assets:* £43,511,848
Registered Office: Capital House, 202 Sandbanks Road, Poole, Dorset, BH14 8HA
Activities: Other credit granting n.e.c.
Major Shareholder: David Michael Capra
Officers: David Michael Capra [1958] Director; Martin Higgins [1969] Director; Richard James McDougall [1980] Director; Paul Graham Miracca [1975] Director/Property Developer; James Toby Page [1987] Director

MSP Capital Two Limited
Incorporated: 11 November 2015
Net Worth: £4,129,621 *Total Assets:* £58,506,180
Registered Office: Capital House, 202 Sandbanks Road, Poole, Dorset, BH14 8HA
Activities: Other credit granting n.e.c.
Officers: David Michael Capra [1958] Director; Martin Higgins [1969] Director; Richard James McDougall [1980] Director; Paul Graham Miracca [1975] Director/Property Developer; James Toby Page [1987] Director

MTH Bidco Limited
Incorporated: 1 June 2016 *Employees:* 5
Net Worth: £36,098,876 *Total Assets:* £128,910,288
Registered Office: Clifton Heights, Triangle West, Bristol, BS8 1EJ
Activities: Non-trading company
Parent: MTH Midco 2 Ltd
Officers: Alex Phillip Khan [1977] Director; Peter James Mitchell [1971] Director; Simon Benedict Withey [1958] Director; Adrian Michael Yurkwich [1968] Director

MTH Midco 1 Limited
Incorporated: 1 June 2016
Net Worth: £38,335,444 *Total Assets:* £52,111,708
Registered Office: Clifton Heights, Triangle West, Bristol, BS8 1EJ
Activities: Non-trading company
Parent: MTH Topco Ltd
Officers: Alex Phillip Khan [1977] Director; Peter James Mitchell [1971] Director; Simon Benedict Withey [1958] Director; Adrian Michael Yurkwich [1968] Director

MTH Midco 2 Limited
Incorporated: 1 June 2016
Net Worth: £38,395,508 *Total Assets:* £52,102,456
Registered Office: Clifton Heights, Triangle West, Bristol, BS8 1EJ
Activities: Non-trading company
Parent: MTH Midco 1 Ltd
Officers: Alex Phillip Khan [1977] Director; Peter James Mitchell [1971] Director; Simon Benedict Withey [1958] Director; Adrian Michael Yurkwich [1968] Director

MTH Topco Limited
Incorporated: 1 June 2016 *Employees:* 920
Net Worth Deficit: £9,416,000 *Total Assets:* £127,278,000
Registered Office: Clifton Heights, Triangle West, Bristol, BS8 1EJ
Activities: Non-trading company
Parent: Silverfleet Capital Partners LLP
Officers: Alex Phillip Khan [1977] Director; Peter James Mitchell [1971] Director; Simon Benedict Withey [1958] Director; Adrian Michael Yurkwich [1968] Director

Muc-Off Limited
Incorporated: 4 April 2005 *Employees:* 32
Net Worth: £1,213,521 *Total Assets:* £4,914,279
Registered Office: First Floor, Unit 1 Concept Office Park, Innovation Close, Poole, Dorset, BH12 4QT
Activities: Manufacture of other chemical products n.e.c.
Shareholders: Alexander James Trimnell; Marilyn Gratia Trimnell
Officers: Marilyn Gratia Trimnell, Secretary/Director; Alexander James Trimnell [1976] Director; Marilyn Gratia Trimnell [1949] Director

MUJV Limited
Incorporated: 27 April 2005 *Employees:* 8
Net Worth: £142,000 *Total Assets:* £13,278,000
Registered Office: Aspire Business Centre, Ordnance Road, Tidworth, Wilts, SP9 7QD
Activities: Construction of other civil engineering projects n.e.c.
Shareholders: UK Power Networks Services (Asset Management) Ltd; Veolia Water Outsourcing Limited
Officers: James Edward Towner, Secretary; John Patrick Abraham [1968] Director; Jonathan Allan [1959] Director; Xavier Aragon [1970] Director/Engineer [French]; Colin George Burke [1964] Director; Tracy Jayne Knipe [1968] Finance Director; David Paul Mitchell [1964] Director; Ian Smyth [1970] Director; James Edward Towner [1964] Director

Mulberry Company (Design) Limited
Incorporated: 5 November 1985 *Employees:* 898
Net Worth: £12,926,000 *Total Assets:* £135,358,000
Registered Office: The Rookery, Chilcompton, Bath, BA3 4EH
Activities: Manufacture of luggage, handbags and the like, saddlery and harness
Parent: Mulberry Trading Holding Company Limited
Officers: Katherine Frances Anthony Wilkinson, Secretary; Thierry Patrick Andretta [1957] Director [French]; Neil James Ritchie [1971] Director

Mulberry Company (Europe) Limited
Incorporated: 1 February 1989
Net Worth: £5,252,000 *Total Assets:* £49,187,000
Registered Office: The Rookery, Chilcompton, Bath, BA3 4EH
Activities: Activities of head offices
Parent: Mulberry Trading Holding Company Limited
Officers: Katherine Frances Anthony Wilkinson, Secretary; Thierry Patrick Andretta [1957] Director [French]; Neil James Ritchie [1971] Director

Mulberry Company (Sales) Limited
Incorporated: 17 July 1980 *Employees:* 400
Net Worth: £31,373,000 *Total Assets:* £107,412,000
Registered Office: The Rookery, Chilcompton, Bath, BA3 4EH
Activities: Retail sale of clothing in specialised stores
Parent: Mulberry Company (Europe) Limited
Officers: Katherine Frances Anthony Wilkinson, Secretary; Thierry Patrick Andretta [1957] Director [French]; Neil James Ritchie [1971] Director

Mulberry Group PLC
Incorporated: 12 August 1974 *Employees:* 1,444
Net Worth: £87,496,000 *Total Assets:* £119,335,000
Registered Office: The Rookery, Chilcompton, Bath, BA3 4EH
Activities: Activities of head offices
Shareholders: Christina Ong; Beng Seng Ong
Officers: Katherine Frances Anthony Wilkinson, Secretary; Thierry Patrick Andretta [1957] Director [French]; Christophe Oliver Cornu [1963] Director [French]; Godfrey Pawle Davis [1949] Director; Julie Lynn Gilhart [1958] Director/Fashion Consultant [American]; Steven Grapstein [1958] Director [American]; Melissa Cheng Sim Ong [1974] Director [Singaporean]; Neil James Ritchie [1971] Director; Andrew Christopher Roberts [1963] Director

Mulberry Studios Limited
Incorporated: 27 May 2002 *Employees:* 14
Net Worth: £7,372,473 *Total Assets:* £8,901,371
Registered Office: Mulberry Studios, Ide Lane, Ide, Exeter, Devon, EX2 9RY
Activities: Other publishing activities
Shareholders: Anne Michele Ablett; Paul William Ablett
Officers: Anne Michele Ablett, Secretary/Publisher; Anne Michele Ablett [1964] Director/Publisher; Paul William Ablett [1964] Director/Publisher

The George Muller Charitable Trust
Incorporated: 26 November 1997 *Employees:* 5
Net Worth: £13,534,726 *Total Assets:* £13,688,276
Registered Office: Muller House, 7 Cotham Park, Bristol, BS6 6DA
Activities: Activities of religious organisations
Officers: Anthony Clive Davies, Secretary; Anthony Clive Davies [1956] Director/Company Secretary; Quentin Timothy Starr Elston [1959] Director/Lawyer; Dr Tigist Desta Grieve [1973] Director/Research Associate, University of Bristol; Joshua Neil Kingston [1987] Director/Chartered Accountant; Edward James Marsh [1977] Director/Chartered Accountant; Stewart Douglas North [1974] Director/Church Leader; Derek James Powell [1964] Director/Church Leader; Elizabeth Flora Charlotte Small [1984] Director/Support Worker

Multi Circuit Boards Limited
Incorporated: 13 January 2012
Net Worth: £3,108,228 *Total Assets:* £5,007,317
Registered Office: 9 Pullman Way, Ringwood, Hants, BH24 1HD
Activities: Agents specialised in the sale of other particular products
Shareholders: Frank Rudiger Horstmann; Phaedra Joan Horstmann
Officers: Frank Rudiger Horstmann [1944] Director [German]; Phaedra Joan Horstmann [1945] Director [German]

Multivac U.K. Limited
Incorporated: 21 November 1984 *Employees:* 131
Net Worth: £10,445,239 *Total Assets:* £22,027,908
Registered Office: Multivac House, Rivermead Drive, Swindon, Wilts, SN5 7UY
Activities: Manufacture of other special-purpose machinery n.e.c.
Parent: Multivac Export AG
Officers: Jonathan Miners, Secretary; Hans Joachim Boeksteggers [1955] Director [German]; James Fergus Campbell [1969] Managing Director; Christian Traumann [1963] Director [German]

Mundays Caravan Parks Limited
Incorporated: 11 March 1954 *Employees:* 13
Net Worth: £3,460,707 *Total Assets:* £3,813,597
Registered Office: 3 Durrant Road, Bournemouth, BH2 6NE
Activities: Other holiday and other collective accommodation
Shareholder: Brian David William Pinson
Officers: Richard John Smedley, Secretary; Brian David William Pinson [1950] Director; John Robert Pinson [1951] Director; Lisa Jane Potts [1966] Director

Murray & Roberts United Kingdom Limited
Incorporated: 24 January 1964 *Employees:* 827
Net Worth: £74,066,472 *Total Assets:* £103,863,712
Registered Office: 6 Drakes Meadow, Penny Lane, Swindon, Wilts, SN3 3LL
Activities: Management consultancy activities other than financial management
Officers: Michael Gomes Da Costa [1964] Director/Underground Mining CEO [South African]; Trevor Naidoo [1974] Director/Underground Mining CFO [South African]

Murray (Plymouth) Limited
Incorporated: 5 March 2001 *Employees:* 157
Net Worth: £748,780 *Total Assets:* £11,731,754
Registered Office: 44 Millbay Road, Plymouth, PL1 3FQ
Activities: Sale of new cars and light motor vehicles
Parent: Murray Holdings (SW) Limited
Officers: Sharon Ann Royal, Secretary; Kevin Alfred David Murray [1965] Director/Motor Dealer

Murrill Construction Limited
Incorporated: 25 March 1985 *Employees:* 63
Net Worth: £2,390,890 *Total Assets:* £14,608,834
Registered Office: 21 Market Place, Blandford Forum, Dorset, DT11 7AF
Activities: Construction of roads and motorways
Parent: Murrill Holdings Limited
Officers: Rosemary Sargeant, Secretary; Mary Maria Mason [1963] Director; Nicholas Owen Mason [1962] Director; Anthony Ernest Sargeant [1940] Director; Rosemary Sargeant [1943] Director; Andrew John Williams [1973] Managing Director

Murrill Holdings Limited
Incorporated: 20 January 2015 *Employees:* 63
Net Worth: £2,427,239 *Total Assets:* £14,934,201
Registered Office: 21 Market Place, Blandford Forum, Dorset, DT11 7AF
Activities: Activities of other holding companies n.e.c.
Shareholders: Anthony Ernest Sargeant; Rosemary Sargeant
Officers: Mary Maria Mason [1963] Director; Nicholas Owen Mason [1962] Managing Director; Anthony Ernest Sargeant [1940] Director; Rosemary Sargeant [1943] Director

Muscle Foods Limited
Incorporated: 1 May 2014 *Employees:* 47
Net Worth: £1,135,404 *Total Assets:* £5,010,287
Registered Office: Unit L, Fulcrum Business Park, Vantage Way, Poole, Dorset, BH12 4NU
Activities: Other food services
Parent: D B Foods (Holdings) Limited
Officers: Ben Bayer [1970] Director; David Charles Bayer [1946] Director; Darren Carl Beale [1983] Director; Phil Bridgen [1978] Director; Edward Stanislaus O'Reilly [1964] Director; Nicholas Anthony Preston [1974] Director

Muscliff Primary School
Incorporated: 13 November 2015 *Employees:* 111
Net Worth: £6,012,380 *Total Assets:* £7,483,139
Registered Office: Muscliff Primary School, Broadway Lane, Throop, Bournemouth, BH8 0AB
Activities: Primary education
Officers: Lucian Andrews [1979] Director/Assistant Headteacher; David Nicholas Banks [1974] Director/Business Development Manager; Joanna Cartwright [1972] Director/Accountant; Anne Louise Crossland [1956] Director; Tracey Farwell [1971] Director/Support Services & Finance Manager; Lynette Dawn Goldborne [1955] Director/Retired; Victoria Georgina Ladbroke [1972] Director/Accountant; Caroline Lovell [1951] Director; Zoe Ann Read [1974] Director/Secondary School Teacher; Margaret Elizabeth Wyatt [1955] Director/Headteacher

The Museum of East Asian Art
Incorporated: 8 May 1990 *Employees:* 9
Net Worth: £6,570,406 *Total Assets:* £6,609,164
Registered Office: Circus Lodge, 12 Bennett Street, Bath, BA1 2QJ
Activities: Cultural education
Officers: Angelina Chee Hung Jenkins, Secretary; Stuart Duncan Balmer [1963] Director/Train Driver; Ian Frederic Hay Davison [1931] Director/Retired; Christine Mary Gore [1953] Director; Anthony Nigel Clifton Griffiths [1943] Director; Bethan Margery Jane Hutton [1968] Director; Angelina Chee Hung Jenkins [1952] Director/Retired; Brian Shane McElney [1932] Director/Retired Solicitor; Dr Stacey Pierson [1966] Director/Senior Lecturer [American]; Anne Elizabeth Shepherd [1957] Director/Retired

H.Mustin & Son Limited
Incorporated: 10 March 1939 *Employees:* 4
Net Worth: £8,166,668 *Total Assets:* £9,751,544
Registered Office: Styles Farm, Mappowder, Sturminster Newton, Dorset, DT10 2EH
Activities: Growing of cereals (except rice), leguminous crops and oil seeds
Officers: Matthew Coldicutt [1960] Director/Farm Manager; Sonia Margaret Coldicutt [1930] Director/Secretary; Rachel Margaret Munson [1961] Director/Trainee Shepherd

Mutual Real Estate Company Limited
Incorporated: 12 January 1933 *Employees:* 2
Net Worth: £18,364,056 *Total Assets:* £20,938,666
Registered Office: c/o Gervis, 4 Wick Lane, Christchurch, Dorset, BH23 1HX
Activities: Buying and selling of own real estate
Officers: Raymond John Alexander, Secretary; Andrew Philip Alexander [1972] Director/Teacher; Matthew James Alexander [1970] Managing Director; Raymond John Alexander [1938] Director/Business Consultant; Daniel John Lock [1979] Director/Student; Mary Freda Lock [1942] Director/Housewife; Sara Elizabeth Lock [1981] Director/University Student

MVV Environment Devonport Limited
Incorporated: 20 October 2010 *Employees:* 32
Net Worth: £25,949,608 *Total Assets:* £218,952,288
Registered Office: Devonport EFW CHP Facility, Creek Road, Plymouth, PL5 1FL
Activities: Treatment and disposal of non-hazardous waste
Parent: MVV Energie AG
Officers: Paul Michael Carey [1957] Director; Michael Andrew Turner [1967] Managing Director; Uwe Zickert [1969] Maintenance Director [German]

MW High Tech Projects UK Limited
Incorporated: 14 July 2004 *Employees:* 254
Net Worth Deficit: £50,749,000 *Total Assets:* £119,620,000
Registered Office: Unit C1, Methuen South Methuen Park, Bath Road, Chippenham, Wilts, SN14 0GT
Activities: Other specialised construction activities n.e.c.
Parent: M+W Germany GmbH
Officers: Felicity Elaine Jackson, Secretary; Andrew John Barrett [1965] Finance Director; Jane Fowler [1978] Finance Director

MWI Supply (UK Acquisition) Limited
Incorporated: 3 February 2010
Net Worth: £36,843,392 *Total Assets:* £72,406,152
Registered Office: Centaur House, Torbay Road, Castle Cary, Somerset, BA7 7EU
Activities: Activities of head offices
Parent: MWI Supply (UK) Ltd
Officers: Brian Topper, Secretary; John Gardner Chou [1956] Director/Business Executive [American]; James F Cleary Jr [1963] Director/CEO & President [American]; Mark Jeffrey Shaw [1962] Director/Business Executive [American]

MWI Supply (UK Holdings) Limited
Incorporated: 3 February 2010
Net Worth: £17,956,824 *Total Assets:* £43,181,148
Registered Office: Centaur House, Torbay Road, Castle Cary, Somerset, BA7 7EU
Activities: Activities of head offices
Parent: MWI Veterinary Supply Co.
Officers: Brian Topper, Secretary; John Gardner Chou [1956] Director/Business Executive [American]; James F Cleary Jr [1963] Director/CEO & President [American]; Mark Jeffrey Shaw [1962] Director/Business Executive [American]

Mycronic Ltd
Incorporated: 23 July 1990 *Employees:* 13
Net Worth: £1,714,890 *Total Assets:* £4,464,060
Registered Office: Unit 2 Concept Park, Innovation Close, Poole, Dorset, BH12 4QT
Activities: Wholesale of other intermediate products
Parent: Mycronic Technologies AB
Officers: August Torbjorn Gunnar Wingardh, Secretary; Meik Hauke [1970] Managing Director [German]; Thomas Stetter [1965] Director [German]; August Torbjorn Gunnar Wingardh [1964] Finance Director [Swedish]

Mylor Yacht Harbour (Holding Company) Limited
Incorporated: 4 December 1998 *Employees:* 9
Net Worth: £3,545,492 *Total Assets:* £6,091,251
Registered Office: Mylor Yacht Harbour, Falmouth, Cornwall, TR11 5UF
Activities: Activities of head offices
Shareholders: Dinah Louise Graffy; Roger Edmund Graffy
Officers: Roger Edmund Graffy, Secretary; Dinah Louise Graffy [1960] Director/Housewife; Roger Edmund Graffy [1957] Director; Neil Frederick Salter [1963] Director

Myoptique Group Ltd
Incorporated: 27 May 2004
Net Worth: £1,060,446 *Total Assets:* £30,877,390
Registered Office: Veale Wasbrough Vizards, Narrow Quay House, Narrow Quay, Bristol, BS1 4QA
Activities: Other retail sale not in stores, stalls or markets
Parent: Trifle Holdings Limited
Officers: Eric Pierre Antoine Martinet [1986] Director/Head of Finance, Online Division [French]; Bernhard Nuesser [1966] Director [German]; Barnaby James Streeting [1974] Director

Mzuri Limited
Incorporated: 25 September 1992 *Employees:* 22
Net Worth: £1,600,241 *Total Assets:* £3,728,355
Registered Office: Hazlewoods LLP, Windsor House, Bayshill Road, Cheltenham, Glos, GL50 3AT
Activities: Manufacture of other general-purpose machinery n.e.c.
Shareholders: Christopher Martin Lole; Samantha Kate Lole
Officers: Samantha Kate Lole, Secretary; Christopher Martin Lole [1957] Director; Samantha Kate Lole [1968] Director/Company Secretary

N P Automotive Coatings (Europe) Limited
Incorporated: 4 October 1991 *Employees:* 60
Net Worth: £8,430,000 *Total Assets:* £12,809,000
Registered Office: Britannia Trade Park, Radway Road, Swindon, Wilts, SN3 4ND
Activities: Manufacture of paints, varnishes and similar coatings, mastics and sealants
Parent: Nippon Paint (Europe) Limited
Officers: Jane Sandman, Secretary; Colin Denness [1966] Managing Director; Hiroshi Hanaoka [1966] Director [Japanese]; Minoru Iwamura [1957] Managing Director [Japanese]; Shoichi Mure [1961] Director/Vice President [Japanese]

N.V. Chichester Limited
Incorporated: 18 February 1977
Net Worth: £3,435,691 *Total Assets:* £3,530,129
Registered Office: 36a Station Road, New Milton, Hants, BH25 6JX
Activities: Other business support service activities n.e.c.
Shareholders: Nicolaas Vrijland; Rowena Mary Alexandra Vrijland
Officers: Rowena Mary Alexandra Vrijland, Secretary; Nicolaas Vrijland [1945] Director/Market Gardener [Dutch]; Rowena Mary Alexandra Vrijland [1946] Director/Market Gardener

Nagel Langdons Ltd
Incorporated: 4 October 1971 *Employees:* 1,430
Net Worth: £37,050,000 *Total Assets:* £77,874,000
Registered Office: Showground Road, Bridgwater, Somerset, TA6 6AJ
Activities: Freight transport by road
Parent: Langdon Group Ltd
Officers: Renee Teresa Barrett, Secretary; Renee Teresa Barrett [1965] Director/Chartered Accountant; Spencer Lawrence Dixon [1968] Director; Patrick Thomas Griffiths [1969] Director; Simon Edward Holder [1952] Director/Accountant; Christopher John Murt [1959] Director; Arran Osman [1970] Managing Director; Rupert Ryall [1961] Director; Michael Eberhard Schymik [1959] Director [German]

Nailsea School
Incorporated: 25 May 2012 *Employees:* 121
Net Worth: £19,975,856 *Total Assets:* £22,177,548
Registered Office: Mizzymead Road, Nailsea, Bristol, BS48 2HN
Activities: General secondary education
Officers: Melanie Argles [1978] Director/Deputy Head of Safeguarding and Quality Assurance; Claire Louise Body [1968] Director/Accountant; Debbi Buss [1970] Director/School Office Manager; Julie Catherine Cayzer [1969] Director/Veterinary Surgeon; Ewan Alistair Davidson [1969] Director/Financial Services; Dr Joanne Pamela Allen Edwards [1975] Director/Examiner; Dione Elliott [1977] Director/Headteacher; Joanna Elizabeth Hopkinson [1959] Director/Retired; Dr Neil Roy Ingram [1957] Director; Jeffrey William Morris [1957] Director/Assistant Head of House, School; Sally Claire Read [1973] Director/Civil Servant; Suzanne Marie Renny [1971] Director/Procurement Manager; Kevin Peter Royce [1962] Director/Business Development Manager; Sophie Rutty [1975] Director/Teacher; Neil John Stradling [1971] Director; Annette Christine Watts [1968] Director/Events Officer; Michael Graham West [1947] Director/Retired

Nailsworth Limited
Incorporated: 15 January 2010
Previous: Chamberlain Shareholdingco Limited
Net Worth: £247,083 *Total Assets:* £16,897,610
Registered Office: Avening Road, Nailsworth, Stroud, Glos, GL6 0BS
Activities: Non-trading company
Major Shareholder: James Edward Chamberlain
Officers: Cecilia Diana Chamberlain, Secretary; Hector James David Chamberlain [1998] Director; James Edward Chamberlain [1958] Director; Jasper Edward Henry Chamberlain [1992] Director

Naim Audio Limited
Incorporated: 4 June 1973 *Employees:* 156
Net Worth: £12,245,128 *Total Assets:* £22,180,768
Registered Office: Southampton Road, Salisbury, Wilts, SP1 2LN
Activities: Manufacture of consumer electronics
Parent: Vervent Audio Group
Officers: Roy Victor George [1953] Director/Engineer; Charles Henderson [1972] Managing Director; Jean-Louis Joseph Pettier [1961] Director/Chief Financial Officer [French]

Naish Estate (Hoburne) Limited
Incorporated: 12 October 1959 *Employees:* 97
Net Worth: £4,771,214 *Total Assets:* £19,402,352
Registered Office: 10 Hoburne Lane, Christchurch, Dorset, BH23 4HP
Activities: Holiday centres and villages
Parent: Hoburne Limited
Officers: Nicholas Stewart Putnam, Company Secretary; Rosemary Sarah Kennar [1956] Director; Timothy Richard Knight [1960] Director; Rodney Philip Tucker [1954] Director

E.V. Naish Limited
Incorporated: 19 September 1945 *Employees:* 247
Net Worth: £10,245,500 *Total Assets:* £12,704,808
Registered Office: The Felt Mills, Crow Lane, Wilton, Salisbury, Wilts, SP2 0HB
Activities: Activities of head offices
Shareholder: Geoff Naish
Officers: Geoff Naish, Secretary; Dr Pamela Jean Chamberlain [1956] Director/Analytical Chemist; Geoffrey David Naish [1959] Commercial Director

Nanny McPhee Productions Limited
Incorporated: 16 May 2002
Net Worth: £1,025,000 *Total Assets:* £5,426,000
Registered Office: The Quadrangle, The Promenade, Cheltenham, Glos, GL50 1PX
Activities: Financial leasing
Parent: Royal Bank Leasing Limited
Officers: Stephen Paul Nixon [1970] Director/Bank Official; Keith Damian Pereira [1978] Director/Bank Official

The Nare Hotel Company Limited
Incorporated: 1 December 1988 *Employees:* 99
Net Worth: £13,531,060 *Total Assets:* £22,333,172
Registered Office: Carne Beach, Veryan, Cornwall, TR2 5PF
Activities: Hotels and similar accommodation
Parent: Cordash Limited
Officers: Wendy Hall, Secretary; Katie Amanda Ashworth [1970] Director/Solicitor; Toby George Howell Ashworth [1967] Managing Director Hotelier; Patricia Daphne Anne Burt [1934] Director

NASA Umbrella Ltd
Incorporated: 4 March 2009 *Employees:* 2,049
Net Worth: £2,378,134 *Total Assets:* £12,338,231
Registered Office: Tower House, Fairfax Street, Bristol, BS1 3BN
Activities: Other business support service activities n.e.c.
Major Shareholder: David Charles Greene
Officers: Pippa Townley Elsey, Secretary; Pippa Townley Elsey [1984] Director/Secretary; David Charles Greene [1970] Director; Alex Philip Spendley [1980] Director

C.W. Nash (Farms) Limited
Incorporated: 31 August 1977 *Employees:* 6
Net Worth: £5,280,013 *Total Assets:* £8,032,716
Registered Office: Manor Farm House, Manningford Bohune, Pewsey, Wilts, SN9 6BY
Activities: Other business support service activities n.e.c.
Major Shareholder: Christopher Thomas Nash
Officers: Carol Ann Nash, Secretary; Carol Ann Nash [1967] Director/Interior Designer; Christopher Thomas Nash [1963] Director/Farmer

Natatomisam Limited
Incorporated: 13 November 2009 *Employees:* 910
Net Worth: £6,729,677 *Total Assets:* £24,986,530
Registered Office: The Jetty, Sutton Wharf, Sutton Harbour, Plymouth, PL4 0DW
Activities: Activities of open-ended investment companies
Shareholders: James Stephen Brent; Nicola Helen Brent
Officers: James Stephen Brent [1965] Director/Businessman; Nicola Helen Brent [1967] Director/Mother

Natems Sugar Holdings (UK) Ltd
Incorporated: 20 June 2016
Net Worth Deficit: £361,735 *Total Assets:* £5,786,252
Registered Office: Delta Place, 27 Bath Road, Cheltenham, Glos, GL53 7TH
Activities: Production of electricity
Officers: Robin Francis Chamberlayne [1966] Director; Stephen William Mahon [1968] Director; Andrew Jonathan Charles Newman [1970] Director; Duncan Saxon Tate [1968] Director

The National Lighting Company Limited
Incorporated: 4 November 1994 *Employees:* 545
Net Worth: £58,638,000 *Total Assets:* £95,256,000
Registered Office: 9 Cabot Lane, Creekmoor, Poole, Dorset, BH17 7BY
Activities: Activities of head offices
Shareholder: Meyer Maslo
Officers: Meyer Maslo, Secretary; Michael David Last [1968] Director/Chief Operating Officer; Elisheba Maslo [1964] Director [Swiss]; Meyer Maslo [1964] Director; Jacob Schimmel [1962] Director; Verette Schimmel-Livschitz [1964] Director/Student Midwife [Swiss]; Irwin Leo Weiler [1964] Director

National Marine Aquarium Limited
Incorporated: 31 December 1991 *Employees:* 104
Net Worth: £10,366,496 *Total Assets:* £10,786,410
Registered Office: Rope Walk, Coxside, Plymouth, PL4 0LF
Activities: Botanical and zoological gardens and nature reserves activities
Officers: Martin John Attrill [1964] Director; Ken Lewins [1978] Director/Solicitor; Mark Mallyon Lomas [1962] Director/Solicitor

National Maritime Museum Cornwall Trust
Incorporated: 8 October 1997 *Employees:* 30
Net Worth: £24,899,862 *Total Assets:* £26,448,116
Registered Office: Discovery Quay, Falmouth, Cornwall, TR11 3QY
Activities: Museums activities
Officers: Richard Mervyn Doughty, Secretary; Honourable Evelyn Arthur Hugh Boscawen [1955] Director; Jonathan David William Cunliffe [1972] Director/Estate Agent; Peter Wilton Davies [1945] Director/Retired; Robert Michael Holmes [1967] Director/Accountant; Sam Hugh D'Aquilar Hunt [1948] Director/Heritage Consultant; Tamsin Rebecca Mann [1974] Director/Solicitor; Anthony Josiah Pawlyn [1942] Director/Retired; Sara Victoria Pugh [1978] Business Director; Peter Raymond England Searle [1948] Director/Retired; Simon Patrick Sherrard [1947] Director/Company Chairman; Helen Stembridge [1969] Director/Business Coach and Project Manager; Brian Derrick Steward [1949] Director/Independent Financial Advisor; Simon Charles Tregoning [1963] Director/Holiday Cottage Agent

National Milk Records PLC
Incorporated: 6 March 1997 *Employees:* 280
Net Worth: £2,443,000 *Total Assets:* £10,174,000
Registered Office: Greenways Business Park, Fox Talbot House, Chippenham, Wilts, SN15 1BN
Activities: Support activities for animal production (other than farm animal boarding)
Officers: Mark Butcher [1958] Director; Mark Christopher Frankcom [1967] Director/Management Accountant; Mike Gallacher [1966] Director; Trevor Lloyd [1972] Director/Dairy Farmer; Andrew John Warne [1962] Managing Director

National Oilwell Varco UK Limited
Incorporated: 4 March 1966 *Employees:* 1,466
Net Worth: £776,456,000 *Total Assets:* £906,932,992
Registered Office: Stonedale Road, Oldends Lane Industrial Estate, Stonehouse, Glos, GL10 3RQ
Activities: Support activities for petroleum and natural gas mining
Parent: NOV UK Holdings Limited
Officers: Alison May Sloan, Secretary; Robbert Oudendijk [1974] Director/Vice President Finance Europe, MENA, CIS [Dutch]; Simon Scott Reid [1982] Director/Accountant

National Star Foundation
Incorporated: 20 August 1953 *Employees:* 841
Net Worth: £29,576,952 *Total Assets:* £32,017,252
Registered Office: Ullenwood Manor, Cheltenham, Glos, GL53 9QU
Activities: Post-secondary non-tertiary education
Officers: Brian Michael Chatfield [1946] Director; Timothy Cooper [1961] Director/Chief Executive; Benjamin John Higgins [1975] Director/Chief Executive; Charles Robert Victor Howes [1957] Director/Financial Consultant; Shaun David Edward Parsons [1944] Director; Barry Seamons [1937] Director/Retired; Paul Keith Styles [1950] Director; Robert Russell Thompson [1947] Director/Retired

National Trust (Enterprises) Limited (The)
Incorporated: 22 November 1972 *Employees:* 588
Net Worth: £80,000 *Total Assets:* £20,512,000
Registered Office: Heelis, Kemble Drive, Swindon, Wilts, SN2 2NA
Activities: Other retail sale in non-specialised stores
Officers: Paul Boniface, Secretary; James Hywel Bennett [1977] Director/Chartered Accountant; Timothy Roger William Moore [1946] Surveyor and Director; Orna Gabrielle Nichionna [1956] Director [Irish]; Timothy Charles Parker [1955] Director/Chairman; Sharon Pickford [1972] Director; John Russell Sell [1944] Director/Architect

Nationwide Covered Bonds LLP
Incorporated: 25 June 2005
Net Worth Deficit: £500,000 *Total Assets:* £17,497,100,288
Registered Office: Nationwide House, Pipers Way, Swindon, Wilts, SN38 1NW

Nationwide Syndications Limited
Incorporated: 7 September 1990
Net Worth: £82,856,000 *Total Assets:* £483,968,000
Registered Office: Nationwide House, Pipers Way, Swindon, Wilts, SN38 1NW
Activities: Financial intermediation not elsewhere classified
Parent: Nationwide Building Society
Officers: Anthony John Alexander [1963] Director; Heidi Billington [1971] Director; Howard Leatherland [1965] Director; Mark Martin Rennison [1960] Director

Navisite Europe Limited
Incorporated: 16 December 1988 *Employees:* 53
Net Worth: £347,879 *Total Assets:* £12,825,221
Registered Office: Business Control Ltd, Red Lion Yard, Frome Road, Bath, BA2 2PP
Activities: Data processing, hosting and related activities
Officers: Paul Andrew Lang [1966] Director/Senior Vice President Business Services [American]; Sumeet Sabharwal [1973] Director/Executive [American]

NCC Operations Limited
Incorporated: 5 July 2010 *Employees:* 260
Net Worth: £1,063,690 *Total Assets:* £4,264,280
Registered Office: National Composite Centre, Bristol & Bath Science Park, Feynman Way, Emersons Green, Bristol, BS16 7FS
Activities: Other research and experimental development on natural sciences and engineering
Parent: University of Bristol
Officers: Kenneth Mitchell, Secretary; Dr Neil Bradshaw [1961] Director; Nishan Canagarajah [1966] Director/Pro-Vice Chancellor, Bristol University; Richard Oldfield [1974] Director/Chief Executive; Jason Smerdon [1966] Director/Accountant

Neal's Yard (Natural Remedies) Limited
Incorporated: 11 November 1981 *Employees:* 523
Net Worth: £6,890,000 *Total Assets:* £24,277,000
Registered Office: Peacemarsh, Gillingham, Dorset, SP8 4EU
Activities: Manufacture of perfumes and toilet preparations
Officers: Elizabeth York, Secretary; Denise Anne Bonner [1955] Director; Anabel Kindersley [1971] Director; Barnabas Guy Kindersley [1970] Director; Peter David Kindersley [1941] Director/Publisher and Farmer; Alexander Ian Leach [1981] Sales Director; Timothy Alan Baylor Leach [1964] Director; Stephen Henry Tobitt [1965] Director/Chief Operating Officer; Susan Jane Winter [1960] Director/Product Development Manager

Neal's Yard Holdings Limited
Incorporated: 3 June 2005 *Employees:* 539
Net Worth: £7,090,000 *Total Assets:* £27,741,000
Registered Office: Peacemarsh, Gillingham, Dorset, SP8 4EU
Activities: Activities of head offices
Officers: Elizabeth York, Secretary; Barnabas Guy Kindersley [1970] Director; Juliet Elizabeth Kindersley [1940] Director; Peter David Kindersley [1941] Director/Publisher & Farmer; Harriet Rose Treuille [1967] Director

Neat Experts Holdings Limited
Incorporated: 27 March 2014 *Employees:* 58
Net Worth: £3,312,931 *Total Assets:* £13,501,278
Registered Office: Olympus House, Kingsteignton Road, Newton Abbot, Devon, TQ12 2SN
Activities: Activities of construction holding companies
Shareholder: Stephen Lloyd Willcocks Howle
Officers: Stephen Lloyd Willcocks Howle [1967] Director; Philip Richard Waggett [1966] Director

Nectar Imports Limited
Incorporated: 14 June 1990 *Employees:* 103
Net Worth: £2,574,708 *Total Assets:* £7,579,812
Registered Office: Cold Berwick Hill, Berwick St Leonard, Salisbury, Wilts, SP3 5SN
Activities: Wholesale of wine, beer, spirits and other alcoholic beverages
Parent: Fuller, Smith & Turner P.L.C.
Officers: Severine Pascale Bequin, Secretary; Simon Ray Dodd [1974] Director; Simon Emeny [1965] Director; Richard Hamilton Fleetwood Fuller [1960] Director; Jonathon David Swaine [1971] Director

Negatex Limited
Incorporated: 22 November 1976
Net Worth: £4,429,068 *Total Assets:* £5,507,746
Registered Office: Moorgate House, King Street, Newton Abbot, Devon, TQ12 2LG
Activities: Other specialised construction activities n.e.c.
Shareholders: Lloyd Vernon Howle; Brian Douglas Waggett
Officers: Lloyd Vernon Howle, Secretary; Lloyd Vernon Howle [1942] Director; Brian Douglas Waggett [1940] Director

Neon (Holdings) Limited
Incorporated: 20 June 2013 *Employees:* 67
Net Worth: £3,007,541 *Total Assets:* £7,721,137
Registered Office: c/o Francis Clark LLP, North Quay House, Sutton Harbour, Plymouth, PL4 0RA
Activities: Dormant company
Shareholders: Roger John Long; Ryan Neil Long
Officers: Ryan Neil Long [1973] Director

Nephos Technologies Ltd
Incorporated: 2 August 2011 *Employees:* 8
Net Worth: £507,189 *Total Assets:* £4,845,186
Registered Office: 312 Charminster Road, Bournemouth, BH8 9RT
Activities: Information technology consultancy activities
Shareholders: Lee Biggenden; Michael Queenan
Officers: Lee Biggenden [1980] Director/IT Sales; Michael Queenan [1981] Director/IT Sales

Neptune (Europe) Ltd
Incorporated: 24 June 1996 *Employees:* 287
Net Worth: £7,782,683 *Total Assets:* £16,211,038
Registered Office: Orion, Frankland Road, Blagrove, Swindon, Wilts, SN5 8YG
Activities: Wholesale of furniture, carpets and lighting equipment
Shareholder: Neptune Holdco Limited
Officers: John Giles Redman, Secretary; John Giles Redman [1969] Director/Technical; John Edwin Sims-Hilditch [1965] Director/Marketing & Management

Neptune Retail Limited
Incorporated: 29 March 2005 *Employees:* 78
Previous: J G E Investments Limited
Net Worth Deficit: £1,709,046 *Total Assets:* £8,327,293
Registered Office: The Neptune Building, Frankland Road, Blagrove, Swindon, Wilts, SN5 8YG
Activities: Retail of furniture, lighting, and similar (not musical instruments or scores) in specialised store
Shareholders: Hannah Jane Corinne Redman; Emma Sims-Hilditch
Officers: Giles Redman [1969] Director; Hannah Redman [1969] Director; Emma Sims-Hilditch [1966] Director; John Edwin Sims-Hilditch [1965] Director

Neptune Shipping Agency Limited
Incorporated: 17 April 1957 *Employees:* 49
Net Worth: £382,030 *Total Assets:* £7,165,542
Registered Office: Higher Sherwell, Sevenstones, Callington, Cornwall, PL17 8HU
Activities: Other transportation support activities
Shareholders: Rhonda Lynette Choroszewska; Ryszard Choroszewski
Officers: Yasmin Adams, Secretary; Rachel May, Secretary; Rhonda Lynette Choroszewska [1958] Director [Australian]; Ryszard Choroszewski [1953] Director

Netcraft Ltd
Incorporated: 4 September 1987 *Employees:* 50
Net Worth: £5,979,095 *Total Assets:* £9,345,471
Registered Office: 2 Belmont, Bath, BA1 5DZ
Activities: Other information technology service activities
Major Shareholder: Michael Hugh Prettejohn
Officers: Fiona Jane Prettejohn, Secretary; Michael Hugh Prettejohn [1962] Director/Computer Scientist

Nettleton Holdings Limited
Incorporated: 31 May 2002 *Employees:* 277
Net Worth: £3,816,786 *Total Assets:* £13,789,873
Registered Office: Lowin House, Tregolls Road, Truro, Cornwall, TR1 2NA
Activities: Activities of head offices
Shareholders: Gayle Lisa Nettleton; James Martin Nettleton
Officers: James Martin Nettleton, Secretary; Gayle Lisa Nettleton [1970] Director; James Martin Nettleton [1973] Director/Hotelier

Netvox Limited
Incorporated: 2 June 1981 *Employees:* 1
Net Worth: £3,751,945 *Total Assets:* £3,819,052
Registered Office: Deloitte & Touche LLP, 3 Rivergate, Temple Quay, Bristol, BS1 6GD
Activities: Development of building projects
Major Shareholder: Alan Vaughan Williams
Officers: Alan Vaughan Williams, Secretary; Alan Vaughan Williams [1942] Director; Huw Lewis Rhys Williams [1988] Director; Jeremy Robert Ellis Williams [1944] Director/Chartered Accountant; Margaret Elizabeth Williams [1947] Director; Rhodri David Vaughan Williams [1977] Sales and Marketing Director; Richard Owain Llewhelin Williams [1980] Director/Project Manager

Nevis Marketing Limited
Incorporated: 13 December 1988 *Employees:* 29
Net Worth: £2,485,615 *Total Assets:* £5,522,317
Registered Office: 2 Leybourne Avenue, Bournemouth, BH10 6HF
Activities: Non-specialised wholesale trade
Shareholders: Luc Marie Rigaux; Rizwan Rashid; Robert John Culverwell
Officers: Scott Thomas Empson, Secretary; Robert John Culverwell [1948] Director; Scott Thomas Empson [1971] Director; Rizwan Rashid [1961] Director [Pakistani]; Luc Rigaux [1956] Director [Belgian]

Nevro Medical Limited
Incorporated: 28 May 2010 *Employees:* 49
Net Worth: £5,858,311 *Total Assets:* £9,331,615
Registered Office: Carrick House, Lypiatt Road, Cheltenham, Glos, GL50 2QJ
Activities: Other business support service activities n.e.c.
Parent: Nevro Corp
Officers: Rami Elghandour [1978] Director/President and CEO [American]; Andrew Hugh Galligan [1956] Director [American]; Kashif Rashid [1973] Director/General Counsel [American]

New Abbey Developments LLP
Incorporated: 24 September 2013
Previous: Lewins Development LLP
Net Worth: £6,740,436 *Total Assets:* £7,382,342
Registered Office: Buckfast Abbey, Buckfast, Buckfastleigh, Devon, TQ11 0EE

New Dawn Homes Limited
Incorporated: 1 March 2004 *Employees:* 4
Net Worth: £5,201,071 *Total Assets:* £9,011,292
Registered Office: The White House, Newdawn Place, Cheltenham, Glos, GL51 0FR
Activities: Construction of domestic buildings
Major Shareholder: Angela Dawn Hughes
Officers: Liam James Hughes, Secretary; Angela Dawn Hughes [1968] Director

New Docs Limited
Incorporated: 29 June 2010 *Employees:* 1
Net Worth Deficit: £535,590 *Total Assets:* £7,408,154
Registered Office: Second Floor, The Devereux Centre, Barton Road, Tewkesbury, Glos, GL20 5GJ
Activities: Other human health activities
Officers: Dr Simon Fearn [1967] Director/Doctor; Dr Stuart Rankine Hutchison [1962] Director/Doctor; Dr Sanjay Shyamapant [1970] Director/Doctor; Dr Andrew Thomas Wales [1974] Director/Medical Practitioner

New Earth Solutions (Canford) Limited
Incorporated: 16 May 2007
Net Worth: £3,254,152 *Total Assets:* £6,653,374
Registered Office: Site Control Centre, Arena Way, Wimborne, Dorset, BH21 3BW
Activities: Other service activities n.e.c.
Parent: DM Holdco Limited
Officers: Brian McCabe [1972] Director [Irish]; Eamon Waters [1960] Director [Irish]

New Earth Solutions (Kent) Limited
Incorporated: 23 February 2006
Net Worth: £4,790,653 *Total Assets:* £6,879,931
Registered Office: Site Control Centre, Arena Way, Wimborne, Dorset, BH21 3BW
Activities: Other service activities n.e.c.
Parent: DM Holdco Limited
Officers: Brian McCabe [1972] Director [Irish]; Eamon Waters [1960] Director [Irish]

New Earth Solutions (West) Limited
Incorporated: 21 July 2009
Net Worth: £3,610,215 *Total Assets:* £8,823,568
Registered Office: Site Control Centre, Arena Way, Wimborne, Dorset, BH21 3BW
Activities: Other service activities n.e.c.
Parent: DM Holdco Limited
Officers: Brian McCabe [1972] Director [Irish]; Eamon Waters [1960] Director [Irish]

New Forest PPP Health Services Limited
Incorporated: 21 May 2004 *Employees:* 3
Net Worth Deficit: £5,736,670 *Total Assets:* £36,185,192
Registered Office: Third Floor, Broad Quay House, Prince Street, Bristol, BS1 4DJ
Activities: Other specialised construction activities n.e.c.
Parent: RBIL Limited
Officers: Graham John Hutt [1954] Regional Director; Andrew Richard Kershaw [1965] Director/Projects Controller; Richard Little [1979] Investment Director; Daniel North [1988] Investment Director

New Leaf Plants Ltd
Incorporated: 11 December 2008 *Employees:* 50
Net Worth: £3,538,921 *Total Assets:* £4,141,368
Registered Office: Ross House, The Square, Stow on the Wold, Glos, GL54 1AF
Activities: Wholesale of flowers and plants
Parent: DFH Estates Limited
Officers: David Francis Higginson, Secretary; David Francis Higginson [1968] Director

New Look FIN III Limited
Incorporated: 14 July 2016
Net Worth: £5,338,000 *Total Assets:* £5,377,000
Registered Office: New Look House, Mercery Road, Weymouth, Dorset, DT3 5HJ
Activities: Activities of head offices
Parent: New Look Finance Limited
Officers: Laura Battley, Secretary; Richard John Collyer [1974] Finance Director; Roger Brian Wightman [1964] Director/Chief Creative Officer

New Look Finance Limited
Incorporated: 26 March 2013
Net Worth: £550,220,992 *Total Assets:* £1,989,880,064
Registered Office: New Look House, Mercery Road, Weymouth, Dorset, DT3 5HJ
Activities: Activities of head offices
Parent: New Look Finance Holdings Limited
Officers: Laura Elizabeth Battley, Secretary; Richard John Collyer [1974] Finance Director; Paul John Thomas Gilbert [1962] Non-Executive Director; Alistair Kenneth McGeorge [1959] Director/Executive Chairman; Roger Brian Wightman [1964] BMD Managing Director

New Look Limited
Incorporated: 5 March 1986
Net Worth: £19,074,000 *Total Assets:* £19,174,000
Registered Office: New Look House, Mercery Road, Weymouth, Dorset, DT3 5HJ
Activities: Activities of head offices
Parent: New Look Finance Limited
Officers: Laura Elizabeth Battley, Secretary; Steven Paul Challes [1959] Director; Paul John Thomas Gilbert [1962] Non-Executive Director; Alistair Kenneth McGeorge [1959] Director/Executive Chairman; Roger Brian Wightman [1964] BMD Managing Director

New Look Retail Group Limited
Incorporated: 9 May 2006 *Employees:* 17,943
Net Worth Deficit: £560,600,000 *Total Assets:* £1,153,400,064
Registered Office: New Look House, Mercery Road, Weymouth, Dorset, DT3 5HJ
Activities: Activities of head offices
Parent: Brait SE
Officers: Laura Elizabeth Battley, Secretary; Andrew Bruce Baisley [1971] Director/Investment Professional [South African]; Richard John Collyer [1974] Director; Paul John Thomas Gilbert [1962] Director; John Andrew Gnodde [1965] Director/Investment Professional [Irish]; Alistair Kenneth McGeorge [1959] Director/Executive Chairman; Christopher Stefan Seabrooke [1953] Director [South African]; Anna Mundeep Singh [1976] Director; Tom Tar Singh [1949] Director; Roger Brian Wightman [1964] Director/Chief Creative Officer

New Look Secured Issuer PLC
Incorporated: 28 May 2015
Net Worth Deficit: £523,008,992 *Total Assets:* £699,251,968
Registered Office: New Look House, Mercery Road, Weymouth, Dorset, DT3 5HJ
Activities: Activities of head offices
Parent: New Look Finance Limited
Officers: Laura Elizabeth Battley, Secretary; Richard John Collyer [1974] Finance Director; Paul John Thomas Gilbert [1962] Director; Alistair Kenneth McGeorge [1959] Director/Executive Chairman; Roger Brian Wightman [1964] Director/Chief Creative Officer

New Look Senior Issuer PLC
Incorporated: 28 May 2015
Net Worth Deficit: £132,365,000 *Total Assets:* £83,713,000
Registered Office: New Look House, Mercery Road, Weymouth, Dorset, DT3 5HJ
Activities: Activities of head offices
Parent: New Look Finance Limited
Officers: Laura Elizabeth Battley, Secretary; Richard John Collyer [1974] Director/Group Finance Officer; Paul John Thomas Gilbert [1962] Non-Executive Director; Alistair Kenneth McGeorge [1959] Director/Executive Chairman; Roger Brian Wightman [1964] Director

New Power Company Limited
Incorporated: 4 June 2001
Net Worth: £18,381,420 *Total Assets:* £18,383,172
Registered Office: Lion House, Rowcroft, Stroud, Glos, GL5 3BY
Activities: Activities of other holding companies n.e.c.
Parent: Ecotricity Group Limited
Officers: Tom Cowling, Secretary; Asif Rehmanwala [1976] Director/Chief Operating Officer; Dale Vince [1961] Director

New Southgate Cemetery and Crematorium Limited
Incorporated: 26 September 1973 *Employees:* 16
Net Worth: £3,965,603 *Total Assets:* £21,292,068
Registered Office: Head Office, Westerleigh Crematorium, Westerleigh Road, Westerleigh, Bristol, BS37 8QP
Activities: Funeral and related activities
Parent: Cemetery + Crematorium Services Ltd
Officers: Dafydd Rhys John, Secretary; Dafydd Rhys John [1974] Director/Chartered Accountant; Ian David McArdle [1966] Director/Chartered Surveyor

New Yacht Club Limited
Incorporated: 23 January 1936 *Employees:* 29
Net Worth: £4,375,108 *Total Assets:* £9,629,375
Registered Office: Royal Motor Yacht Club, Sandbanks, Poole, Dorset, BH13 7RE
Activities: Activities of sport clubs
Officers: Sally Ann Meaden, Secretary; John Edmund Bailey [1938] Director/Design Engineer; John James Buchanan [1950] Director/Solicitor; John Graham Carr [1945] Director/Retired; Baron George Levine [1952] Director; Andrew Percy Manners [1952] Director/Sales Manager; Andrew Nigel Pearce [1952] Director/Chartered Surveyor; Jeremy Pocknell [1958] Director/Retired; James Charles Pride [1952] Director; Gill Purnell [1963] Director/Accounts Assistant; Julie Anne Reid [1959] Director/Teacher; Lewis Ridett [1993] Director/Banker; Richard Salaman [1942] Director/Retired; Martin Thomas Oliver Stanley [1957] Director/Retired; Graham Turner [1953] Director/Retired; Sally Frances Windsor [1953] Director/Public Relations Consultant; Peter WInternationale [1952] Director/Retired

Newberry International Produce Ltd
Incorporated: 11 October 1996 *Employees:* 29
Net Worth: £1,223,711 *Total Assets:* £6,370,032
Registered Office: Unit 6 & 7 Newent Business Park, Newent, Glos, GL18 1DZ
Activities: Wholesale of fruit and vegetables
Shareholders: Stuart Andrew Taylor; Gillian Louisa Pearson
Officers: Gillian Louisa Pearson [1983] Commercial Director; Leon Kristiaan Rowley [1969] Finance Director; Stuart Andrew Taylor [1984] Director

Newbery Metals Limited
Incorporated: 28 March 1956 *Employees:* 49
Previous: G.H. Newbery & Son Limited
Net Worth: £8,596,820 *Total Assets:* £14,717,746
Registered Office: Orchard Works, Ashton Road, Marsh Barton, Exeter, Devon, EX2 8LN
Activities: Wholesale of waste and scrap
Parent: Togs Limited
Officers: Mark Ashleigh Crocker, Secretary; Mark Ashleigh Crocker [1967] Director/Company Secretary; Pamela Mary Toghill [1939] Director; Russell Anthony Toghill [1966] Managing Director

The Newcastle Estate Partnership Limited
Incorporated: 10 November 1995 *Employees:* 3
Net Worth Deficit: £2,837,000 *Total Assets:* £209,514,000
Registered Office: Third Floor, Broad Quay House, Prince Street, Bristol, BS1 4DJ
Activities: Management of real estate on a fee or contract basis
Parent: Newcastle Estate Partnership Holdings Limited
Officers: Michael McGhee [1962] Director/Estate Development Manager; Kenneth Andrew McLellan [1961] Regional Project Director; Andrew Charles Mutch Rhodes [1970] Director

Newcombe Beard Limited
Incorporated: 8 December 1998 *Employees:* 1
Net Worth: £5,629,526 *Total Assets:* £5,908,029
Registered Office: 5 The Mews, Cricklade Street, Cirencester, Glos, GL7 1HY
Activities: Buying and selling of own real estate
Major Shareholder: Felicity Anne Beard
Officers: Marian Curtis, Secretary; Felicity Anne Beard [1943] Director; Jeremy Isambard Beard [1972] Director/School Teacher; Richard James Beard [1968] Director/Author; Dr Timothy Edward Beard [1965] Director/Teacher

Newcross Healthcare Solutions Limited
Incorporated: 11 April 1996 *Employees:* 2,719
Net Worth: £11,019,330 *Total Assets:* £23,518,740
Registered Office: Waterside, Berry Pomeroy, Totnes, Devon, TQ9 6LH
Activities: Temporary employment agency activities
Officers: Stephen Pattrick, Secretary; Helen Louise Chadwick [1975] Finance Director; Michelle Gorringe [1964] Director/Registered General Nurse; Tracy O'Kennedy [1969] Human Resources Director; Stephen Pattrick [1967] Company Secretary Director; Geoff Alan White [1969] Operations Director

Newcross Nursing Group Ltd
Incorporated: 24 November 1999 *Employees:* 2
Net Worth: £4,496,249 *Total Assets:* £6,008,761
Registered Office: Waterside, Berry Pomeroy, Totnes, Devon, TQ9 6LH
Activities: Temporary employment agency activities
Officers: Stephen Pattrick, Secretary; Michelle Gorringe [1964] Director; Stephen Pattrick [1967] Director

Newent Community School and Sixth Form Centre
Incorporated: 23 July 2012 *Employees:* 183
Net Worth: £19,124,134 *Total Assets:* £21,396,848
Registered Office: Newent Community School and Sixth Form Centre, Watery Lane, Newent, Glos, GL18 1QF
Activities: General secondary education
Officers: Julie Ann Price, Secretary; Guy Bodger [1956] Director; Karen Patricia Elen [1960] Director/Self Employed; Christopher Germaine [1971] Director/Teacher; Lee Michael Hampton-Whitehead [1967] Director/IT Consultant; David Ray Hogg [1961] Director/School Inspector; Alan David Johnson [1964] Director/Teacher; Helen Patricia Kelly [1969] Director/Solicitor; Jennifer Niland [1984] Director/Head of Customer Relations; David Edward Pettit [1950] Director/Retired; Graham Robert Spaull [1980] Director/Facilities and EHS Manager; Candida Spedding [1978] Director/Artist

Newham Learning Partnership (Project Co) Limited
Incorporated: 8 November 2006
Net Worth: £100,403 *Total Assets:* £56,619,832
Registered Office: Third Floor, Broad Quay House, Prince Street, Bristol, BS1 4DJ
Activities: Construction of commercial buildings
Parent: Newham Learning Partnership (Hold Co) Limited
Officers: David Ronald Baldock [1960] Director/Accountant; David Wyn Davies [1968] Director/Accountant; Hannah Holman [1980] Director; Nicholas James MacKee [1976] Director/Solicitor; Daniel Colin Ward [1982] Investment Director

Newham Transformation Partnership Limited
Incorporated: 11 December 2008
Net Worth: £224,161 *Total Assets:* £6,353,977
Registered Office: Third Floor, Broad Quay House, Prince Street, Bristol, BS1 4DJ
Activities: Construction of commercial buildings
Parent: Newham Learning Partnership (PSP) Limited
Officers: David Ronald Baldock [1960] Director/Accountant; David Wyn Davies [1968] Director/Accountant; Hannah Holman [1980] Director; Nicholas James MacKee [1976] Director/Solicitor; Daniel Colin Ward [1982] Investment Director

Newincco 1401 Limited
Incorporated: 29 February 2016 *Employees:* 5
Net Worth Deficit: £5,128,565 *Total Assets:* £8,216,201
Registered Office: c/o Dorset Village Bakery Ltd, Unit 2 Pinesway Business Park, Station Road, Stalbridge, Sturminster Newton, Dorset, DT10 2RN
Activities: Management consultancy activities other than financial management
Parent: Newincco1402
Officers: Emma Davies [1971] Director; Louise Kingston [1981] Director/Chartered Accountant; Richard Littlewood [1961] Operations Director; Simon Tovey [1966] Commercial Director

Newincco 1402 Limited
Incorporated: 26 February 2016 *Employees:* 155
Net Worth Deficit: £7,600,175 *Total Assets:* £9,441,726
Registered Office: c/o Dorset Village Bakery Ltd, Unit 2 Pinesway, Station Road Business Park, Station Road, Stalbridge, Sturminster Newton, Dorset, DT10 2RN
Activities: Management consultancy activities other than financial management
Shareholders: Livingbridge Enterprise GP LLP; Livingbridge Enterprise LLP
Officers: Emma Davies [1971] Director; Louise Kingston [1981] Director/Chartered Accountant; Richard Littlewood [1961] Operations Director; Stephen Newiss [1959] Director; Simon Tovey [1966] Commercial Director

Newland Homes Limited
Incorporated: 13 February 1991 *Employees:* 64
Net Worth: £34,275,156 *Total Assets:* £47,288,960
Registered Office: Brighouse Court, Barnett Way, Barnwood, Gloucester, GL4 3RT
Activities: Construction of domestic buildings
Shareholders: David Foreman; John Newlands McCreadie
Officers: David Foreman, Secretary; Jeremy David Drew [1964] Design Director; David Foreman [1949] Director/Residential Developer; Margaret Betty Foreman [1948] Director; John Newlands McCreadie [1957] Director/Residential Developer

Newlyn Art Gallery Limited
Incorporated: 22 April 1977 *Employees:* 23
Net Worth: £3,848,614 *Total Assets:* £4,152,238
Registered Office: The Exchange, Princes Street, Penzance, Cornwall, TR18 2NL
Activities: Operation of arts facilities
Officers: Neil Scott, Secretary; Myfanwy Barrett [1969] Managing Director, Corporate Services; Miranda Rosalind Bird [1969] Director; Bert Martin Montague Biscoe [1952] Director/Elected Member of Cornwall Council; Virginia Mary Button [1961] Director/Self Employed Writer and Curator; Andrew Paul Harper [1971] Director/Artist Lecturer; Callum Samuel Mitchell [1987] Director/Writer; Bethia Naughton-Rumbo [1987] Director/Marketing and Communications Consultant; Neil Scott [1961] Director/Retired; Liadhain Tait [1970] Director/Head of External Relations [British/American]

Newport Caravans Limited
Incorporated: 21 July 2008
Net Worth: £830,962 *Total Assets:* £4,204,857
Registered Office: 4 King Square, Bridgwater, Somerset, TA6 3YF
Activities: Other business support service activities n.e.c.
Shareholder: Robert William Lynch
Officers: Robert William Lynch, Secretary/Director; Robert William Lynch [1964] Director; Mark Kenneth Massey [1966] Director

Newport Park Limited
Incorporated: 29 November 2011
Net Worth: £61,107 *Total Assets:* £6,918,732
Registered Office: Centenary House, Peninsula Park, Rydon Lane, Exeter, EX2 7XE
Activities: Other letting and operating of own or leased real estate
Parent: Wilson Leisure Ltd
Officers: Patricia Ann Hardick [1948] Director

Newquay Education Trust
Incorporated: 26 March 2014 *Employees:* 354
Net Worth: £32,237,538 *Total Assets:* £36,502,176
Registered Office: Newquay Tretherras, Trevenson Road, Newquay, Cornwall, TR7 3BH
Activities: Primary education
Officers: Andrew Roy Keast, Secretary; Alan Geoffrey Brown [1954] Director/Cornwall Councillor; Nicholas Dixon [1969] Director/Programme Head; Sean Michael Dixon [1964] Director/Surgeon; Sarah Faith Karkeek [1951] Director; Ashley Steven Mann [1972] Director/Paramedic; Philip Lawrence Mason [1965] Director/Local Government Officer; Sebastian Parker [1954] Director; Kymberley Sarah Pinnell [1986] Director/Deputy Head

Newquay View Resort Limited
Incorporated: 25 September 2013 *Employees:* 36
Net Worth Deficit: £671,209 *Total Assets:* £7,007,158
Registered Office: Newquay View Resort, Trevelgue Road, Porth, Newquay, Cornwall, TR8 4AS
Activities: Recreational vehicle parks, trailer parks and camping grounds
Parent: Peter Bull Resorts Ltd
Officers: Barry Kenneth McGregor [1955] Managing Director; Ian Norman Smith [1964] Managing Director; Anthony Jackson Vickery [1957] Director/Chartered Accountant

Newspace Containers Limited
Incorporated: 31 October 2000 *Employees:* 122
Net Worth: £7,112,370 *Total Assets:* £10,218,558
Registered Office: Units 30-31 Lydney Harbour Estate, Harbour Road, Lydney, Glos, GL15 4EJ
Activities: Manufacture of other tanks, reservoirs and containers of metal
Parent: GCH Capital Limited
Officers: Mark Chamberlain [1957] Managing Director

Newton Abbot Academy Trust
Incorporated: 25 July 2011 *Employees:* 152
Net Worth: £7,825,869 *Total Assets:* £10,651,712
Registered Office: Newton Abbot Academy Trust, Old Exeter Road, Newton Abbot, Devon, TQ12 2NF
Activities: General secondary education
Officers: Ruth Edwina Jane Bellas, Secretary; Deborrah Back [1969] Director/Safeguarding Adults Facilitator; Claire Bird [1970] Director/Teacher; Emma Bone [1977] Director/Executive Headteacher; Linda Jane Caunter [1957] Director/Retired; Mr Paul David Cornish [1976] Director/Principal; Tamara Mary Harrison [1969] Director/Certified Chartered Accountant; Gwendoline Elizabeth Hobbs [1962] Director/Cover Supervisor; Clare Newlands [1969] Director/Housewife; Marina Joyce North [1966] Director/Administrator; Barry Christopher James Reeves [1949] Director/Retired; Charles Edward Robinson [1949] Director/Health & Safety Engineer; Dr Phil Rudling [1970] Director/Teacher; Sarah Wilkinson [1989] Director/Teacher

Newton Abbot Races Limited (The)
Incorporated: 14 February 1921 *Employees:* 179
Net Worth: £4,063,313 *Total Assets:* £4,439,590
Registered Office: Racecourse, Kingsteignton Road, Newton Abbot, Devon, TQ12 3AF
Activities: Operation of sports facilities
Officers: Patrick Gerard Masterson, Secretary/General Manager; Philip John Hobbs [1955] Director/Racehorse Trainer; Patrick Gerard Masterson [1964] Managing Director; Annette Elizabeth Merchant [1962] Director/Accountant; Richard Hugh Galabin Michelmore [1952] Director/Solicitor; George Kellock Mortimer Welch [1959] Director/Farmer

Newton Nottingham LLP
Incorporated: 5 April 2004
Net Worth: £9,448,141 *Total Assets:* £22,044,322
Registered Office: Manor Stables, Corsely, Warminster, Wilts, BA12 7QE
Officers: Ralph Congreve [1953] Member; Simon William Waterfield [1960] Member

Next Generation Wind Holdings Limited
Incorporated: 23 May 2003
Net Worth: £10,653,071 *Total Assets:* £22,275,700
Registered Office: Lion House, Rowcroft, Stroud, Glos, GL5 3BY
Activities: Activities of other holding companies n.e.c.
Parent: Ecotricity Group Limited
Officers: Tom Cowling, Secretary; Asif Rehmanwala [1976] Director/Chief Operating Officer; Dale Vince [1961] Director

NIC Enterprises Limited
Incorporated: 8 June 2006
Net Worth: £10,570,137 *Total Assets:* £27,438,836
Registered Office: Unit 8 Bodmin Business Park, Launceston Road, Bodmin, Cornwall, PL31 2RJ
Activities: Other business support service activities n.e.c.
Parent: Idun Industri AS
Officers: Michael Wodskou, Secretary; Thomas Ernst Bruck [1962] Director [German]; Riccardo Antonio Marcantonio [1980] Director; Nadia Millar [1968] Director; Tor Agner Osmundsen [1978] Director [Norwegian]; Bernard Bertram Pooley [1957] Director/Chartered Accountant; Nicholas Philip Venditti [1971] Director; Michael Wodskou [1967] Managing Director [Danish]

Alfred Nichols (Services and Properties) Limited
Incorporated: 15 April 1957
Previous: A.Nichols (Cow Mills) Limited
Net Worth: £2,735,041 *Total Assets:* £3,551,891
Registered Office: Cow Mills, Chipping Sodbury, Bristol, BS37 4AD
Activities: Manufacture of prepared feeds for farm animals
Officers: Betty Maureen Nichols, Secretary; Rev Alexander James Goodenough Cooper [1947] Director/Accountant and Priest; Susan Greenslade [1958] Director; Michael Luton [1948] Director; Ian Mackie [1959] Managing Director; Derek Nichols [1955] Director; Ivor Nichols [1928] Director/Farmer; Elizabeth Joan Woodman [1960] Director

Nicolas James Group Limited
Incorporated: 24 November 2003 *Employees:* 22
Net Worth: £931,105 *Total Assets:* £9,922,439
Registered Office: Harbour House, 60 Purewell, Christchurch, Dorset, BH23 1ES
Activities: Activities of head offices
Major Shareholder: Nicolas James Roach
Officers: Stuart Andrew Bateman, Secretary; David Francis Robbins [1967] Director/Accountant

Nicolas James Holdings Limited
Incorporated: 19 January 2006
Previous: Nicolas James Hotels Limited
Net Worth: £4,311,372 *Total Assets:* £36,969,836
Registered Office: Harbour House, 60 Purewell, Christchurch, Dorset, BH23 1ES
Activities: Activities of head offices
Parent: Nicolas James Limited
Officers: Stuart Andrew Bateman [1976] Director; David Francis Robbins [1967] Finance Director

Nicolas James Investments Limited
Incorporated: 1 December 2006 *Employees:* 1
Net Worth: £4,834,074 *Total Assets:* £8,218,310
Registered Office: Harbour House, 60 Purewell, Christchurch, Dorset, BH23 1ES
Activities: Other letting and operating of own or leased real estate
Major Shareholder: Nicolas James Roach
Officers: Stuart Andrew Bateman, Secretary; David Francis Robbins [1967] Finance Director

Nicolas James Limited
Incorporated: 4 February 2002
Net Worth: £1 *Total Assets:* £7,537,501
Registered Office: Harbour House, 60 Purewell, Christchurch, Dorset, BH23 1ES
Activities: Dormant company
Major Shareholder: Nicolas James Roach
Officers: Stuart Andrew Bateman [1976] Director; David Francis Robbins [1967] Finance Director

Nine Telecom Group Limited
Incorporated: 5 March 2008 *Employees:* 107
Net Worth Deficit: £2,933,941 *Total Assets:* £26,190,326
Registered Office: Festival House, Jessop Avenue, Cheltenham, Glos, GL50 3SP
Activities: Activities of head offices
Shareholders: James Edward Palmer; Michael Anthony Palmer
Officers: Mark Gallie [1971] Managing Director

Ninecourt Limited
Incorporated: 14 June 2002 *Employees:* 2
Net Worth: £16,371,413 *Total Assets:* £19,435,520
Registered Office: Midland House, 2 Poole Road, Bournemouth, BH2 5QY
Activities: Other letting and operating of own or leased real estate
Parent: Fiveteam Limited
Officers: David Ross Andrews [1952] Director/Accountant

Nippon Paint (Europe) Ltd.
Incorporated: 27 June 1989 *Employees:* 1
Net Worth: £65,167,000 *Total Assets:* £66,891,000
Registered Office: Britannia Trade Park, Radway Road, Swindon, Wilts, SN3 4ND
Activities: Activities of head offices
Parent: Nippon Paint Holdings Co Ltd
Officers: Seiichiro Hagihara [1969] Director/Chief Financial Officer [Japanese]; Hiroshi Hanaoka [1966] Director [Japanese]; Manabu Minami [1958] Finance Director [Japanese]; Shoichi Mure [1961] Director/Vice President [Japanese]

Nisbets PLC
Incorporated: 21 January 1983 *Employees:* 1,754
Net Worth: £114,380,000 *Total Assets:* £189,880,992
Registered Office: Nisbets PLC, Fourth Way, Bristol, BS11 8TB
Activities: Non-specialised wholesale trade
Parent: Key West (Holdings) Limited
Officers: Richard James Cromwell [1963] Marketing Director; Klaus Peter Goldenbot [1965] Director [German]; Lynn King [1973] Director; Stephen Daniel Marshall [1969] Director; Andrew Nisbet [1960] Director/Chairman; Anne Marie Nisbet [1960] Director; Deborah Jayne Preston [1972] Director; Steven Mark Robson [1960] Director; Peter Charles Sephton [1959] Director; Ian Brian Michael Sheppard [1962] Director; Robin John Anthony White [1970] Director

Nissha Medical Technologies Ltd
Incorporated: 15 November 2006
Previous: Graphic Controls Ltd
Net Worth: £2,964,000 *Total Assets:* £10,487,000
Registered Office: Torbay Business Park, Woodview Road, Paignton, Devon, TQ4 7HP
Activities: Manufacture of other articles of paper and paperboard n.e.c.
Officers: Scott Michael Bushby, Secretary; Wayne John Harper [1971] Director; Samuel Frank Heleba [1958] Director/President of Manufacturing Firm [American]; John Willis Shields [1947] Director/Marketing [Canadian]

NJG Contracting Limited
Incorporated: 14 February 2007
Net Worth: £29,580 *Total Assets:* £6,028,922
Registered Office: Harbour House, 60 Purewell, Christchurch, Dorset, BH23 1ES
Activities: Development of building projects
Major Shareholder: Nicolas James Roach
Officers: Stuart Andrew Bateman, Secretary; David Francis Robbins [1967] Finance Director

NK Facilities Limited
Incorporated: 15 January 2004 *Employees:* 3
Net Worth: £2,789,000 *Total Assets:* £21,636,000
Registered Office: Third Floor, Broad Quay House, Prince Street, Bristol, BS1 4DJ
Activities: Management of real estate on a fee or contract basis
Parent: Chiltern Securities Limited
Officers: Kathryn Louise Di-Piazza [1973] Director; Julia Sarah McCabe [1970] Regional Director; Alan Campbell Ritchie [1967] Director

NMS Infrastructure Limited
Incorporated: 22 May 2006 *Employees:* 15
Net Worth: £601,340 *Total Assets:* £23,379,162
Registered Office: Tower House, Parkstone Road, Poole, Dorset, BH15 2JH
Activities: Other business support service activities n.e.c.
Parent: NMS International Group Ltd
Officers: Adam George Roland Hatfield [1960] Director/Accountant; Frederik Louis Tsun Meng Hsu [1963] Director; Peter Jack Marks [1953] Director; Andrew Louis Oliver [1961] Director

NNA Limited
Incorporated: 21 January 2008 *Employees:* 237
Net Worth: £7,094,555 *Total Assets:* £11,746,527
Registered Office: KFC, Goodridge Avenue, Gloucester, GL2 5EA
Activities: Other business support service activities n.e.c.
Officers: Martina Elizabeth Nicholas, Secretary; Gerard Nicholas [1950] Director; Martina Elizabeth Nicholas [1960] Director; Naomi Vanessa Nicholas [1982] Director

No House Limited
Incorporated: 12 July 1996 *Employees:* 1
Net Worth: £31,118 *Total Assets:* £9,407,975
Registered Office: c/o Milsted Langdon LLP, Motivo House, Alvington, Yeovil, Somerset, BA20 2FG
Activities: Activities of other holding companies n.e.c.
Major Shareholder: Timothy David House
Officers: Joanne House, Company Secretary; Joanne House [1953] Director/Company Secretary; Timothy David House [1950] Director

Nokia UK Limited
Incorporated: 2 October 1991 *Employees:* 730
Previous: Alcatel-Lucent Telecom Limited
Net Worth Deficit: £52,781,000 *Total Assets:* £89,805,000
Registered Office: 740 Waterside Drive, Aztec West, Almondsbury, Bristol, BS32 4UF
Activities: Other telecommunications activities
Officers: Hans-Joerg Daub [1963] Director/Chief Financial Officer [German]; Ioli Tassopoulou [1984] Director/Solicitor [Greek]; Cormac Vincent Whelan [1964] Director [Irish]

Nonwovenn Ltd
Incorporated: 9 March 2016 *Employees:* 162
Net Worth: £4,326,947 *Total Assets:* £13,925,177
Registered Office: BFF Business Park, Bath Road, Bridgwater, Somerset, TA6 4NZ
Activities: Activities of head offices
Shareholders: David Peter Lamb; BGF GP Limited
Officers: Andrew Brownlow [1965] Director; NED James Dorbin [1977] Director; David Peter Lamb [1959] Director/Chairman; Mark Molyneux [1954] Non-Executive Director Chairman

Norbord Europe Limited
Incorporated: 19 December 2011 *Employees:* 754
Net Worth: £95,079,000 *Total Assets:* £321,731,008
Registered Office: Hill Village, Nadder Lane, South Molton, Devon, EX36 4HP
Activities: Manufacture of veneer sheets and wood-based panels
Parent: Norbord UK Limited
Officers: Robin Anne Lampard [1967] Director [Canadian]; Karl Morris [1961] Managing Director; Stephen John Roebuck [1956] Director

Norco G R P Limited
Incorporated: 17 December 1993 *Employees:* 106
Net Worth: £3,540,461 *Total Assets:* £5,741,876
Registered Office: 37 Commercial Road, Poole, Dorset, BH14 0HU
Activities: Other specialised construction activities n.e.c.
Parent: Norco Holdings Limited
Officers: Katie Claydon, Secretary; Mark William Northey [1973] Managing Director

Norland College Limited
Incorporated: 18 October 1923 *Employees:* 47
Previous: Norland Nursery Training College Limited
Net Worth: £6,236,636 *Total Assets:* £7,602,431
Registered Office: York Villa, York Place, London Road, Bath, BA1 6AE
Activities: Other activities of employment placement agencies
Officers: Michael Anthony Bray [1956] Finance Director; Martin Courtenay Clarke [1941] Director/Chartered Accountant; Roberta Claire Edwards [1968] Director/Copywriter Housewife; Kim Lesley England [1960] Director/HR Consultant; Julia Clare Gaskell [1964] Director/Manager of a Private Day Nursery; Rosemary Anne Heald [1961] Director/Retired Solicitor; Peter John Hymans [1955] Director/Higher Education Consultant; Christopher Edward Jenner Jerram [1953] Director/Chartered Surveyor; Christine Mary Mills [1948] Director/Management Consultant; Alastair Heyhoe Page [1962] Director/Consultant; Professor David Timms [1946] Director/Consultant; Christine Lesley Turner [1952] Director/Retired Academic

Norman Court and Sowley Farms Limited
Incorporated: 25 October 1976 *Employees:* 6
Net Worth Deficit: £921,133 *Total Assets:* £22,120,214
Registered Office: Home Farm, Norman Court, West Tytherley, Salisbury, Wilts, SP5 1NL
Activities: Mixed farming
Parent: Brickberg AB
Officers: Karl Georgeanders Bergengren, Secretary; Karl Georg Anders Bergengren [1960] Director/Farmer [Swedish]; Wilhelm Bertil Axel Bergengren [1962] Director/Portfolio Manager [Swedish]

Norseland Holdings Limited
Incorporated: 16 July 2004
Net Worth: £12,479,165 *Total Assets:* £12,479,165
Registered Office: Norseland, Somerton Road, Ilchester, Somerset, BA22 8JL
Activities: Butter and cheese production
Parent: Tine SA
Officers: James Lyndon Maffin, Secretary; Frode Djuve Fimreite [1968] Director [Norwegian]; Ketil Haddeland [1964] Director [Norwegian]; Atle Kjol Jacobsen [1971] Director [Norwegian]; Nina Kolltveit Saeter [1970] Director [Norwegian]; Espen Skarateppen [1977] Director [Norwegian]; Stuart Thomas Storey [1974] Director; John J Sullivan [1960] Director [American]

Norseland Limited
Incorporated: 8 March 1965 *Employees:* 222
Net Worth: £12,290,779 *Total Assets:* £29,419,636
Registered Office: Somerton Road, Ilchester, Yeovil, Somerset, BA22 8JL
Activities: Butter and cheese production
Parent: Tine SA
Officers: James Lyndon Maffin, Secretary; Atle Kjol Jacobsen [1971] Director [Norwegian]; James Lyndon Maffin [1970] Director/Accountant; Stuart Thomas Storey [1974] Director

North Dairy Farms Limited
Incorporated: 4 March 1991 *Employees:* 2
Net Worth: £2,992,025 *Total Assets:* £4,481,802
Registered Office: Bishopbrook House, Cathedral Avenue, Wells, Somerset, BA5 1FD
Activities: Growing of cereals (except rice), leguminous crops and oil seeds
Shareholders: Svitlana Hosie; Philip Venner; James Owen
Officers: Svitlana Hosie [1974] Director

North Devon Homes
Incorporated: 26 November 1998 *Employees:* 106
Previous: North Devon Homes Limited
Net Worth: £55,795,000 *Total Assets:* £171,067,008
Registered Office: North Devon Homes, Westacott Road, Barnstaple, Devon, EX32 8TA
Activities: Development of building projects
Officers: Philippa Jane Butler, Secretary; Dawn Evelyn Ash [1966] Director/Medically Retired; James Howard William Barrah [1971] Local Authority Director; Asad Mansur Butt [1957] Director/Social Housing Professional; Sabina Ann Goodman [1964] Finance Director; Dr Debbie Ann Hay [1962] Director/Consultant; Suzanne Carol Ingman [1957] Director/Consultant; Delyth Anne Lloyd-Evans [1959] Director/Business Executive; Scott John Murray [1971] Finance Director; Jonathan Paul Oldroyd [1961] Director; Robert William Perry Stronge [1959] Managing Director

North Devon Hospice
Incorporated: 1 February 1983 *Employees:* 195
Net Worth: £8,811,086 *Total Assets:* £9,299,953
Registered Office: North Devon Hospice, Deer Park, Newport, Barnstaple, Devon, EX32 0HU
Activities: Specialists medical practice activities
Officers: Stephen Roberts, Secretary; Sharon Bates [1969] Director/Practice Manager; Mary Elizabeth Brooks [1952] Director/Retired; David Brian Cottingham [1953] Director; Kate Jane Cox [1975] Director/Chief Executive; Alison Carol Dyer [1956] Director/Retired; Michael Reginald Arthur Ford [1960] Director; Matthew Joshua Jones [1990] Director/Publican; Peregrine John Mears [1968] Director/Chartered Architect; Thomas Parkin [1982] Director/Headmaster; Zara Jane Svensson [1966] Director/Retired; Dr Annabelle Lucy Tree [1964] Director/GP; Teresa Jane Turner [1960] Director/Accountant; Kevin Ronald Underwood [1958] Director/Commercial Property Consultant; Robert Darren Withecombe [1965] Director/Consultant

North Devon Tyres Ltd.
Incorporated: 24 January 2002 *Employees:* 64
Net Worth: £2,185,826 *Total Assets:* £4,051,959
Registered Office: 4 Ormidale Square, Tiverton Business Park, Tiverton, Devon, EX16 6TW
Activities: Maintenance and repair of motor vehicles
Major Shareholder: Trevor John Veysey
Officers: Margaret Ann Veysey, Secretary; Simon Trevor John Veysey [1980] Director; Trevor John Veysey [1956] Director

North Downs Farm Ltd
Incorporated: 13 December 2012 *Employees:* 161
Net Worth: £3,853,000 *Total Assets:* £13,436,000
Registered Office: Lower Ground Floor, 31 Lemon Street, Truro, Cornwall, TR1 2LS
Activities: Activities of head offices
Officers: Neil Angus Kennedy [1960] Director; Roger Neil Morriss [1946] Director/Creamery Manager; John William Pengelly [1943] Director/Creamery Manager; Alfred James Rodda [1943] Director/Creamery Manager; Nicholas Luke Rodda [1969] Director; Philip Ernest Rodda [1950] Director/Creamery Manager

North Harbour Properties LLP
Incorporated: 11 April 2010
Net Worth: £2,383,521 *Total Assets:* £4,247,382
Registered Office: Quay House, 7 The Quay, Poole, Dorset, BH15 1HA

North Kent Farms Limited
Incorporated: 28 October 1981 *Employees:* 4
Net Worth: £35,604,980 *Total Assets:* £37,746,080
Registered Office: Hitchcock House, Hilltop Park, Devizes Road, Salisbury, Wilts, SP3 4UF
Activities: Growing of cereals (except rice), leguminous crops and oil seeds
Shareholder: John Douglas Tremlett
Officers: Pauline Diane Tremlett, Secretary; Guy Colin Tremlett [1973] Creative Director; John Douglas Tremlett [1944] Director/Farmer; Max Lauriston Tremlett [1975] Director/Journalist; Pauline Diane Tremlett [1944] Director/Doctor

North Leaze Farm Limited
Incorporated: 20 January 2009 *Employees:* 2
Net Worth: £4,440,701 *Total Assets:* £6,197,027
Registered Office: North Leaze Farm, North Cadbury, Yeovil, Somerset, BA22 7BD
Activities: Mixed farming
Major Shareholder: Paul John Longman
Officers: Julia Anne Longman [1961] Director/Company Administration; Paul John Longman [1963] Director/Farmer

North Place Developments Ltd
Incorporated: 25 September 2015 *Employees:* 4
Net Worth: £18,528 *Total Assets:* £5,264,305
Registered Office: Ruardean Works, Varnister Road, Drybrook, Glos, GL17 9BH
Activities: Development of building projects
Parent: M F Freeman Developments Limited
Officers: Jennifer Mary Freeman [1947] Director; Luke Francis Freeman [1974] Director; Mervyn Francis Freeman [1945] Director; Steven King [1970] Director/Chartered Accountant; Peter Wharton [1963] Director/Chartered Accountant

North Somerset Community Partnership Community Interest Company
Incorporated: 18 March 2011 *Employees:* 570
Net Worth: £4,181,656 *Total Assets:* £9,623,680
Registered Office: Castlewood, Tickenham Road, Clevedon, Somerset, BS21 6FW
Activities: Medical nursing home activities
Officers: Pauline Elizabeth Gillard, Secretary; David Hamilton Baldwin [1972] Director; Judith Arden Brown [1962] Director; Nicholas John Danks [1972] Director; Sara Jane Harding [1961] Director; Lorna Harrison [1957] Director; Mary Lewis [1965] Director/Nurse; Linda Margaret Nash [1958] Director/Chairman; Philip John Saunders [1960] Director/Management Consultant; Jenny Turton [1965] Director; Hannah Margaret Young [1973] Director

North Town Academy Trust
Incorporated: 7 July 2011 *Employees:* 66
Net Worth: £2,199,000 *Total Assets:* £3,587,000
Registered Office: North Town Primary School, Staplegrove Road, Taunton, Somerset, TA1 1DF
Activities: Primary education
Officers: Emma Allaway, Secretary; Richard Martin Carpenter [1955] Director/Civil Servant; Carly Emma Catchpole [1980] Director, Training Company; Clare Greenslade [1968] Director/Accountant; Richard Hembrow [1979] Director/Defence Production Manager; Matthew Kerton [1987] Director/Teacher; Katie Knight [1987] Director/Link Worker; Heidi Treglia Kohlman [1986] Director/Teacher; Gaynor Lewis [1949] Director; Lindsey Lister [1985] Director/Teacher; Emma Charlotte Martin [1977] Director/Barrister; Amber Tansen Packer-Hughes [1976] Director/Caterer; Michael James Snowden [1965] Director/Headteacher; Adam Tidmarsh [1973] Director/Civil Servant; Katherine Marie Walters [1981] Director/Teacher; Andrea Yates [1967] Director

Northam Farm Caravan Sales Limited
Incorporated: 23 December 1999 *Employees:* 28
Net Worth: £5,041,115 *Total Assets:* £7,597,131
Registered Office: 3-5 College Street, Burnham on Sea, Somerset, TA8 1AR
Activities: Sale of used cars and light motor vehicles
Officers: David Michael Scott [1959] Director; Michael Harry Scott [1932] Director; Phillip Andrew Scott [1963] Director; Ruth Mary Scott [1933] Director

Northern Hydropower Limited
Incorporated: 20 January 2015
Net Worth: £4,625,143 *Total Assets:* £9,014,706
Registered Office: Brook House, Anna Valley, Andover, Hants, SP11 7NG
Activities: Production of electricity
Parent: Northern Hydropower Holdings Limited
Officers: John Clive Arup [1952] Director/Civil Engineer; Patrick Thomas Boyle [1974] Director; Peter Ballantyne Dixon [1950] Director; Richard Stephen Partridge-Hicks [1957] Director; Mark Simon [1961] Director; Edward Cecil Wakefield [1973] Director

Northern Isles Ferries Limited
Incorporated: 9 February 2004
Net Worth: £2,584,000 *Total Assets:* £11,105,000
Registered Office: The Quadrangle, The Promenade, Cheltenham, Glos, GL50 1PX
Activities: Financial leasing
Parent: Royal Bank Leasing Limited
Officers: Ian Andrew Ellis [1969] Director/Bank Official; David Generald Harris [1969] Director/Bank Official; Steven James Roulston [1977] Director/Bank Official

G. Northover & Sons Limited
Incorporated: 2 February 1982 *Employees:* 36
Net Worth: £2,827,079 *Total Assets:* £6,246,139
Registered Office: Northover Fuels, 22a Butts Pond Industrial Estate, Sturminster Newton, Dorset, DT10 1AZ
Activities: Agents involved in the sale of fuels, ores, metals and industrial chemicals
Shareholders: Darren Ross Northover; Neil Michael Northover
Officers: Darren Ross Northover, Secretary/Director; Darren Ross Northover [1976] Director; Neil Michael Northover [1974] Director

Norton Avonmouth Limited
Incorporated: 21 December 2015
Net Worth: £159,000 *Total Assets:* £54,029,000
Registered Office: Tamar House, Thornbury Road, Plymouth, PL6 7PP
Activities: Other letting and operating of own or leased real estate
Parent: Norton Group Holdings Limited
Officers: Christopher Frederick Dawson [1951] Director

Norton Group Holdings Limited
Incorporated: 27 April 2015 *Employees:* 9,524
Net Worth: £260,171,008 *Total Assets:* £531,440,992
Registered Office: Tamar House, Thornbury Road, Estover, Plymouth, PL6 7PP
Activities: Activities of other holding companies n.e.c.
Major Shareholder: Sarah Jane Dawson
Officers: Christopher Frederick Dawson [1951] Director

The Norville Group Limited
Incorporated: 16 May 1979 *Employees:* 226
Net Worth: £5,061,287 *Total Assets:* £16,401,289
Registered Office: Magdala Road, Gloucester, GL1 4DG
Activities: Manufacture of medical and dental instruments and supplies
Shareholder: Frank Goodwin Norville
Officers: Ian Christopher Mitchell, Secretary; Sean Micheal Donnachie [1967] Director; Robin Andrew Hughes [1958] Purchasing Director; Andrew Stuart Norville [1966] Director; Frank Goodwin Norville [1942] Director/Manufacturing Optician; Ian James Norville [1970] Director; Jennifer Margaret Norville [1942] Director/Florist

S. Notaro Group Limited
Incorporated: 26 April 2011 *Employees:* 2
Net Worth: £15,812,500 *Total Assets:* £16,051,607
Registered Office: Notaro House, Huntworth, Bridgwater, Somerset, TA7 0AJ
Activities: Development of building projects
Major Shareholder: Joseph Notaro
Officers: Antonietta Notaro [1958] Director/Secretary; Joseph Notaro [1952] Director/Builder

S. Notaro Holdings Limited
Incorporated: 25 August 1999 *Employees:* 2
Net Worth: £6,206,264 *Total Assets:* £6,658,489
Registered Office: Huntworth, Bridgwater, Somerset, TA7 0AJ
Activities: Activities of other holding companies n.e.c.
Parent: S. Notaro Group Limited
Officers: Antoinetta Notaro, Secretary; Antonietta Notaro [1958] Director/Secretary; Joseph Notaro [1952] Director/Builder

N. Notaro Homes Limited
Incorporated: 13 January 1984 *Employees:* 618
Net Worth: £19,852,308 *Total Assets:* £46,778,456
Registered Office: Queensmead Court, Bristol Road, Winscombe, Somerset, BS25 1PR
Activities: Residential nursing care facilities
Major Shareholder: Nunzio Notaro
Officers: Constance Margaret Notaro, Secretary; Constance Margaret Notaro [1956] Director/Company Secretary; Nunzio Notaro [1954] Managing Director; Sabato Dominico Notaro [1975] Finance Director

S. Notaro Limited
Incorporated: 9 April 1965 *Employees:* 9
Net Worth: £7,632,568 *Total Assets:* £15,597,073
Registered Office: Notaro House, Huntworth, Bridgwater, Somerset, TA7 0AJ
Activities: Development of building projects
Parent: S. Notaro Holdings Limited
Officers: Antoinetta Notaro, Secretary; Antonietta Notaro [1958] Director; Joseph Notaro [1952] Managing Director

NOV Downhole Eurasia Limited
Incorporated: 19 August 2002 *Employees:* 322
Net Worth: £208,846,128 *Total Assets:* £270,615,360
Registered Office: Stonedale Road, Oldends Lane, Stonehouse, Glos, GL10 3RQ
Activities: Support activities for petroleum and natural gas mining
Parent: National Oilwell Varco UK Limited
Officers: Alison May Sloan, Secretary; Robbert Oudendijk [1974] Director/Vice President Finance Europe, MENA, CIS [Dutch]; Simon Scott Reid [1982] Director/Accountant

NOV Process & Flow Technologies UK Limited
Incorporated: 13 May 1935 *Employees:* 541
Previous: Mono Pumps Limited
Net Worth: £22,789,000 *Total Assets:* £62,341,000
Registered Office: Stonedale Road, Oldends Lane Industrial Estate, Stonehouse, Glos, GL10 3RQ
Activities: Manufacture of pumps
Parent: National Oilwell Varco UK Limited
Officers: Alison May Sloan, Secretary; Robbert Oudendijk [1974] Director/Vice President Finance Europe, MENA, CIS [Dutch]; Simon Scott Reid [1982] Director/Accountant

NOV UK Finance Limited
Incorporated: 12 August 2002
Net Worth: £13,224,105 *Total Assets:* £31,435,028
Registered Office: Stonedale Road, Oldends Lane Industrial Estate, Stonehouse, Glos, GL10 3RQ
Activities: Other business support service activities n.e.c.
Parent: NOV UK Holdings Limited
Officers: Alison May Sloan, Secretary; Robbert Oudendijk [1974] Director/Vice President Finance Europe, MENA, CIS [Dutch]; Simon Scott Reid [1982] Director/Accountant

Nova Group Europe Limited
Incorporated: 6 December 2016 *Employees:* 2
Net Worth: £2,201,492 *Total Assets:* £4,225,068
Registered Office: Unit 1 Brabazon Business Park, Golf Course Lane, Filton, Bristol, BS34 7PZ
Activities: Non-trading company
Major Shareholder: Alan James Whalley
Officers: Lois Elaine Wheeler, Secretary; Gregory Beresford Hume [1961] Director/Chief Executive [Australian]; Alan James Whalley [1966] Chair/Executive Director [Australian]; Michael Douglas Whalley [1951] Director [Australian]

Novalis Trust
Incorporated: 28 April 2004 *Employees:* 208
Net Worth: £17,701,620 *Total Assets:* £20,196,264
Registered Office: Ebley House, 235 Westward Road, Ebley, Stroud, Glos, GL5 4SX
Activities: Other residential care activities n.e.c.
Officers: Paula Furley, Secretary; Matthew Alfred Bennett [1953] Director/Self Employed; Gordon William Cole [1944] Director/Consultant; Ian Michael Davies [1963] Director; Christopher Graham Lee [1948] Director/Consultant; Barbara Titmuss [1952] Director/Advanced Practitioner; Chrstine Yvonne Williams [1944] Director/Retired

Novanta Technologies UK Limited
Incorporated: 7 February 1972 *Employees:* 134
Previous: GSI Group Limited
Net Worth: £44,458,000 *Total Assets:* £51,411,000
Registered Office: 29 Holton Road, Holton Heath, Poole, Dorset, BH16 6LN
Activities: Manufacture of other machine tools
Parent: Novanta UK Investments Holding Limited
Officers: Robert Buckley [1974] Director/Financial Executive [American]; Peter Aka Lei Chang [1965] Director/Financial Controller [Chinese]; Timothy Salvatore Spinella [1966] Director/Treasurer [American]; Stephen Webb [1960] Managing Director; Brian Samuel Young [1969] Director/Professional Business Person - Executive [American]

Novia Financial Holdings Limited
Incorporated: 8 January 2008 *Employees:* 143
Net Worth: £7,942,784 *Total Assets:* £11,517,647
Registered Office: Cambridge House, Henry Street, Bath, BA1 1JS
Activities: Activities of financial services holding companies
Shareholder: David John George Royds
Officers: Julian Richard Myers, Secretary; Professor John Richard Beaumont [1957] Director; Sir Anthony Cleaver [1938] Director/Chairman; Paul Kenneth Parry [1966] Finance Director; David John George Royds [1960] Director; William George Vasilieff [1955] Director/Chief Executive Officer

Novia Financial PLC
Incorporated: 9 January 2008 *Employees:* 143
Net Worth: £15,953,892 *Total Assets:* £19,661,350
Registered Office: Cambridge House, Henry Street, Bath, BA1 1JS
Activities: Financial intermediation not elsewhere classified
Officers: Julian Richard Myers, Secretary; Professor John Richard Beaumont [1957] Director; Sir Anthony Cleaver [1938] Director/Chairman; Paul Kenneth Parry [1966] Finance Director; David John George Royds [1960] Director; William George Vasilieff [1955] Director/Chief Executive Officer

npower Commercial Gas Limited
Incorporated: 7 May 1999 *Employees:* 45
Net Worth: £6,153,000 *Total Assets:* £40,410,000
Registered Office: Windmill Hill Business Park, Whitehill Way, Swindon, Wilts, SN5 6PB
Activities: Distribution of gaseous fuels through mains
Parent: npower Limited
Officers: Glenn William Chapman, Secretary; Jason Andrew Scagell [1967] Director; Peter Russell Sharman [1967] Director

npower Direct Limited
Incorporated: 4 June 1999 *Employees:* 801
Net Worth: £52,131,000 *Total Assets:* £206,148,000
Registered Office: Windmill Hill Business Park, Whitehill Way, Swindon, Wilts, SN5 6PB
Activities: Distribution of electricity
Parent: npower Group Limited
Officers: Glenn William Chapman, Secretary; Peter Russell Sharman [1967] Director; Simon Nicholas Stacey [1965] Director/Financial Accountant

npower Gas Limited
Incorporated: 9 December 1994 *Employees:* 348
Net Worth Deficit: £193,587,008 *Total Assets:* £76,190,000
Registered Office: Windmill Hill Business Park, Whitehill Way, Swindon, Wilts, SN5 6PB
Activities: Distribution of gaseous fuels through mains
Parent: npower Limited
Officers: Glenn William Chapman, Secretary; Peter Russell Sharman [1967] Director; Simon Nicholas Stacey [1965] Director/Financial Accountant

npower Group Limited
Incorporated: 5 October 2012
Previous: npower Group PLC
Net Worth: £1,867,000,064 *Total Assets:* £2,704,000,000
Registered Office: Windmill Hill Business Park, Whitehill Way, Swindon, Wilts, SN5 6PB
Activities: Activities of other holding companies n.e.c.
Parent: Innogy SE
Officers: Glenn William Chapman, Secretary; Paul Coffey [1969] Director; Dirk Simons [1966] Director/Chief Financial Officer RWE Innogy GmbH [German]

npower Limited
Incorporated: 21 October 1998 *Employees:* 1,839
Net Worth: £246,000,000 *Total Assets:* £2,552,999,936
Registered Office: Windmill Hill Business Park, Whitehill Way, Swindon, Wilts, SN5 6PB
Activities: Distribution of electricity
Parent: npower Group Limited
Officers: Glenn William Chapman, Secretary; Christopher James Pilgrim [1964] HR Director; Jason Andrew Scagell [1967] Director; Peter Russell Sharman [1967] Director; Simon Nicholas Stacey [1965] Director/Financial Accountant; David George Titterton [1960] Director/Head of Green Deal & Obligations

npower Northern Limited
Incorporated: 10 September 1997 *Employees:* 2,986
Net Worth Deficit: £1,124,000,000 *Total Assets:* £825,000,000
Registered Office: Windmill Hill Business Park, Whitehill Way, Swindon, Wilts, SN5 6PB
Activities: Transmission of electricity
Parent: npower Group Limited
Officers: Glenn William Chapman, Secretary; Peter Russell Sharman [1967] Director; Simon Nicholas Stacey [1965] Director/Financial Accountant; David George Titterton [1960] Director/Head of Green Deal & Obligations

npower Yorkshire Limited
Incorporated: 1 March 2000 *Employees:* 274
Net Worth Deficit: £701,662,016 *Total Assets:* £170,234,000
Registered Office: Windmill Hill Business Park, Whitehill Way, Swindon, Wilts, SN5 6PB
Activities: Transmission of electricity
Parent: npower Group Limited
Officers: Glenn William Chapman, Secretary; Christopher James Pilgrim [1964] HR Director; Peter Russell Sharman [1967] Director; Simon Nicholas Stacey [1965] Director/Financial Accountant

NSD Ltd
Incorporated: 6 March 2014 *Employees:* 45
Net Worth: £1,017,404 *Total Assets:* £5,900,498
Registered Office: Orion, Frankland Road, Blagrove, Swindon, Wilts, SN5 8YG
Activities: Leasing of intellectual property and similar products, except copyright works
Parent: Neptune Holdco Limited
Officers: Giles Redman [1969] Director; John Edwin Sims-Hilditch [1965] Director

NSEA Property Services Limited
Incorporated: 17 August 2009 *Employees:* 7
Net Worth: £296,205 *Total Assets:* £4,334,058
Registered Office: The Hive, 6 Beaufighter Road, Weston Super Mare, Somerset, BS24 8EE
Activities: Other business support service activities n.e.c.
Officers: Andrew Philip Ashford [1987] Director/Technology Partner; John Nigel Brentnall [1948] Director/Solicitor; Simon Jon Gregory [1967] Director; Christopher Thomas Walford [1977] Director/Chartered Accountant; Charles Hayden Walker [1950] Director

Nu-Heat (Holdings) Limited
Incorporated: 7 March 2017 *Employees:* 107
Net Worth: £527,074 *Total Assets:* £11,035,923
Registered Office: Heathpark House, Devonshire Road, Heathpark Industrial Estate, Honiton, Devon, EX14 1SD
Activities: Activities of other holding companies n.e.c.
Parent: MNL Nominees Limited
Officers: Ole Bettum [1963] Director [Norwegian]; Ian Jeacock [1967] Director; Ashley Philip Levinson [1956] Director; Mark Andrew Millett [1975] Director; David Charles Roberts [1972] Director

Nu-Heat UK Limited
Incorporated: 29 November 1995 *Employees:* 104
Net Worth: £2,779,083 *Total Assets:* £4,939,497
Registered Office: Heathpark House, Devonshire Road, Heathpark Industrial Estate, Honiton, Devon, EX14 1SD
Activities: Other retail sale not in stores, stalls or markets
Parent: AAA Holdings
Officers: Ole Bettum [1963] Director [Norwegian]; Ian Jeacock [1967] Finance Director; Ashley Philip Levinson [1956] Director; Mark Andrew Millett [1975] Operations Director; David Charles Roberts [1972] Sales Director

Nu-Pro Limited
Incorporated: 14 April 1998 *Employees:* 103
Net Worth: £2,784,000 *Total Assets:* £6,283,000
Registered Office: Eagle Works, London Road, Thrupp, Stroud, Glos, GL5 2BA
Activities: Treatment and coating of metals
Parent: Five Valleys Aerospace Ltd
Officers: Peter Williment, Secretary; Jason Marcus James Bailey [1964] Director; Peter Williment [1970] Finance Director

Nucleus Developments Limited
Incorporated: 1 April 2003 *Employees:* 1
Net Worth: £3,224,173 *Total Assets:* £6,468,026
Registered Office: Charlcombe Grove Farm, Charlcombe, Bath, BA1 9BQ
Activities: Other letting and operating of own or leased real estate
Major Shareholder: Giles Richard Thomas
Officers: Giles Richard Thomas, Secretary; Giles Richard Thomas [1976] Director

Nuestra Familia Restaurants Ltd
Incorporated: 4 February 2013 *Employees:* 335
Net Worth: £152,170 *Total Assets:* £4,651,640
Registered Office: Aldreth, Pearcroft Road, Stonehouse, Glos, GL10 2JY
Activities: Unlicenced restaurants and cafes
Major Shareholder: Victor Antonio Arciniega
Officers: Karen Arciniega [1961] Director; Victor Antonio Arciniega [1962] Director

Nuon UK Ltd
Incorporated: 2 October 1997 *Employees:* 4
Net Worth: £122,157,680 *Total Assets:* £122,864,080
Registered Office: Abbey Warehouse, Abbey Slip, Penzance, Cornwall, TR18 4AR
Activities: Production of electricity
Shareholders: Vattenfall Wind Power Ltd; Nuon International Renewables Project B.V
Officers: Sandra Leece, Secretary; Gunnar Groebler [1972] Director [German]; Danielle Claire Lane [1975] Director; Jonas Van Mansfeld [1976] Director [Dutch]; Robert Zurawski [1976] Director [German]

Nutricia Limited
Incorporated: 3 May 1933 *Employees:* 744
Net Worth: £52,766,000 *Total Assets:* £168,623,008
Registered Office: Newmarket Avenue, Whitehorse Business Park, Trowbridge, Wilts, BA14 0XQ
Activities: Other food services
Parent: Nutricia (Cow & Gate, Milupa) Holdings Ltd
Officers: Sudip Dasgupta [1964] Finance Director [Indian]; Marc Jove Gesti [1970] Managing Director [Spanish]; Filippo Samuele Della Torre [1965] Managing Director [Italian]

Nutwell Farms Limited
Incorporated: 11 May 2017
Net Worth: £2,420,864 *Total Assets:* £3,602,286
Registered Office: 28 Alexandra Terrace, Exmouth, Devon, EX8 1BD
Activities: Other letting and operating of own or leased real estate
Major Shareholder: Nigel Patrick Lee
Officers: Nigel Patrick Lee [1966] Director/Farmer

Nuvias Global Services Limited
Incorporated: 16 November 1999 *Employees:* 94
Previous: Zycko Limited
Net Worth: £9,820,000 *Total Assets:* £85,961,000
Registered Office: Lakeview House, The Mallards, South Cerney, Cirencester, Glos, GL7 5TQ
Activities: Wholesale of computers, computer peripheral equipment and software
Parent: Zycko Overseas Limited
Officers: John Mark Havill, Secretary; David Richard Galton Fenzi [1969] Director; Julian Hodge [1970] Director; Stewart Holness [1966] Executive Director

Nylaplas Engineering Limited
Incorporated: 6 October 1982 *Employees:* 33
Net Worth: £5,835,642 *Total Assets:* £6,518,272
Registered Office: 18 Southfield Road Trading Estate, Nailsea, Bristol, BS48 1JE
Activities: Manufacture of other plastic products
Major Shareholder: Executor of The Estate of Leonora Lesley Bassett
Officers: Leonora Lesley Bassett, Secretary; Andrew Richard Bassett [1975] Technical Director; James Anthony Bassett [1974] Sales Director; Leonora Lesley Bassett [1948] Director

Nynehead Care Limited
Incorporated: 29 June 2000 *Employees:* 77
Net Worth: £3,442,775 *Total Assets:* £8,795,982
Registered Office: The Offices of Perrins Limited, The Custom House, The Strand, Barnstaple, Devon, EX31 1EU
Activities: Residential care activities for the elderly and disabled
Parent: The Stepping Stone Group Limited
Officers: John Yeates Bailey, Secretary/Director; John Yeates Bailey [1957] Director; Alyson Lynne Martin Mbe [1956] Director

R. O'Dell (Holdings) Limited
Incorporated: 6 April 1995 *Employees:* 4
Net Worth: £3,416,303 *Total Assets:* £4,197,394
Registered Office: The Old Coach House, Church Street, Castle Cary, Somerset, BA7 7EJ
Activities: Buying and selling of own real estate
Shareholders: Rebecca O'Dell-Shearn; Nicola Carol O'Dell-Shearn
Officers: Nicola Carol O'Dell-Shearn, Secretary; David Griffiths [1953] Director/Chartered Accountant; Nicola Carol O'Dell-Shearn [1982] Director/Business Executive; Rebecca O'Dell-Shearn [1976] Director/Property Manager

John O'Flynn Developments Limited
Incorporated: 8 July 1975 *Employees:* 170
Net Worth: £5,363,176 *Total Assets:* £15,472,338
Registered Office: Unit 3 Apple Walk, Kembrey Park, Swindon, Wilts, SN2 8BL
Activities: Construction of roads and motorways
Parent: Flynn Corporate Limited
Officers: Geoffrey Peter Allen [1963] Production Director; Claire Louise Curl [1973] Finance Director; Ian James Curtis [1961] Director/Chartered Accountant; William Edward Hall [1949] Director; Alfred Nigel Douglas Hambidge [1959] Managing Director

O'Neill and Brennan Construction Limited
Incorporated: 29 June 1989 *Employees:* 1,023
Net Worth: £7,103,012 *Total Assets:* £18,139,914
Registered Office: Kings Buildings, Lydney, Glos, GL15 5HE
Activities: Other construction installation
Shareholders: Patrick Gerard Brennan; Donal Gerard O'Neill
Officers: Patrick Gerard Brennan, Secretary/Manager [Irish]; David Joseph Benson [1965] Director [Irish]; Margaret Patricia Brennan [1961] Director/Teacher/Secretarial; Patrick Gerard Brennan [1959] Director [Irish]; Neil McCullough [1978] Finance Director; Eugene John Meehan [1961] Director; Ann Mary Theresa O'Neill [1956] Director/Clerical Officer; Sean Patrick O'Neill [1972] Director/Manager [Irish]; Shane Daniel O'Neill [1988] Director; Donal Gerard Oneill [1960] Director [Irish]

Oak Tree Mobility Limited
Incorporated: 25 February 2009 *Employees:* 91
Net Worth: £1,152,421 *Total Assets:* £5,894,782
Registered Office: Second Floor, St James Court, 9-12 St James Parade, Bristol, BS1 3LH
Activities: Retail sale of medical and orthopaedic goods in specialised stores (not incl. hearing aids) n.e.c.
Shareholders: Thomas James Powell; Ricky Lloyd Towler
Officers: Thomas James Powell [1983] Director; Ricky Lloyd Towler [1983] Director; Andrew David Wood [1974] Director/Chartered Accountant

Oak Tree Parks Limited
Incorporated: 21 July 1972 *Employees:* 13
Net Worth: £15,834,237 *Total Assets:* £17,233,876
Registered Office: The Office, Oaktree Park, Locking, Weston-Super-Mare, Somerset, BS24 8RG
Activities: Recreational vehicle parks, trailer parks and camping grounds
Shareholder: Noel Nation
Officers: Rachel Guilia Nation, Secretary; Catherine Rebecca Look [1966] Director; Noel Nation [1940] Director; Rachel Guilia Nation [1970] Sales Director

Oakfield Grove Properties Limited
Incorporated: 23 February 1996
Net Worth: £5,794,839 *Total Assets:* £6,038,770
Registered Office: 4th Floor, Portwall Place, Portwall Lane, Bristol, BS1 6NA
Activities: Buying and selling of own real estate
Officers: Michael Sinclair Batt [1944] Director/Chartered Accountant; Richard Francis Mannion [1947] Director/Chartered Accountant; Philip Edward Moody [1954] Director/Chartered Accountant; Michael John Neale [1954] Director/Chartered Accountant

Oakfield Investments Ltd
Incorporated: 15 January 2003
Net Worth: £6,476,095 *Total Assets:* £6,589,539
Registered Office: Units C & D, 6 The Old Coachworks, Kingsfield Lane, Longwell Green, Bristol, BS30 6DL
Activities: Other letting and operating of own or leased real estate
Major Shareholder: Nicholas Kenneth Smith
Officers: Nicholas Kenneth Smith, Secretary; Nicholas Kenneth Smith [1963] Director

Oakfield School Academy Trust
Incorporated: 5 July 2011 *Employees:* 80
Net Worth: £4,108,610 *Total Assets:* £6,035,830
Registered Office: Oakfield School, Oakfield Road, Frome, Somerset, BA11 4JF
Activities: General secondary education
Officers: Richard Timothy Glenny Cutting [1948] Director/Retired; William Joseph de Bolla [1987] Director/IT Consultant; Barry Peter Edwards [1952] Director/Semi Retired; Kate Hellard [1975] Director/Council Officer; Claire Margaret Hopkins [1970] Director/Management Consultant; Sarah Kathryn Hynds [1962] Director/Childminder; David McGrath [1983] Director; Lesley Peat [1954] Director/Teacher; Gary John Smart [1963] Director; Kate Stewart [1960] Director/Teacher; Emma Jane Wilkes [1971] Director/Headteacher

Oakland Capital Developments Limited
Incorporated: 17 December 2002 *Employees:* 47
Net Worth Deficit: £44,673 *Total Assets:* £14,500,762
Registered Office: 2nd Floor, 23-24 High Street, Marlborough, Wilts, SN8 1LW
Activities: Hotels and similar accommodation
Shareholder: Thames Valley Ventures Ltd
Officers: Sarah Jane Bohane, Secretary; Fiona Katherine Kenneth [1967] Director/Consultant; Gordon Alexander Kenneth [1941] Director/Chartered Accountant

Oakleaze Holdings Limited
Incorporated: 29 November 1955 *Employees:* 5
Net Worth: £3,381,475 *Total Assets:* £3,671,926
Registered Office: Old Crown House, 18 Market Street, Wotton under Edge, Glos, GL12 7AE
Activities: Other letting and operating of own or leased real estate
Major Shareholder: Vernon Harry Jotcham
Officers: Nicola Amanda Jotcham, Secretary/Management Accountant; Deirdre Rosamond Jotcham [1943] Director; Kerry Andrew Jotcham [1964] Director/Properties Manager; Nicola Amanda Jotcham [1966] Director/Management Accountant; Vernon Harry Jotcham [1931] Director/Building Contractor; Peter Robert Mardon [1966] Director; Katharine Anne Probert [1963] Director/Accounts Manager

Oasis Dental Care (Central) Limited
Incorporated: 21 March 1952 *Employees:* 858
Net Worth: £2,691,000 *Total Assets:* £137,562,000
Registered Office: Bupa Dental Care, Vantage Office Park, Old Gloucester Road, Hambrook, Bristol, BS16 1GW
Activities: Dental practice activities
Parent: Oasis Dental Care (Central) Holdings Limited
Officers: Robin James Bryant [1970] Director/Dental Surgeon; Ian Michael Kelly [1963] Director/Dental Surgeon; Steven John Preddy [1959] Director/Dentist; Gabriela Pueyo Roberts [1974] Director/General Manager [Spanish]; Dr Stephen David Burleigh Taylor [1951] Director/Dentist; Dr Ian David Wood [1956] Director; Jake Stephen Hockley Wright [1972] Director

Oasis Dental Care (Southern) Limited
Incorporated: 9 April 1954 *Employees:* 366
Net Worth: £14,546,000 *Total Assets:* £32,027,000
Registered Office: Bupa Dental Care, Vantage Office Park, Old Gloucester Road, Hambrook, Bristol, BS16 1GW
Activities: Dental practice activities
Parent: Oasis Dental Care (Southern) Holdings Limited
Officers: Robin James Bryant [1970] Director/Dental Surgeon; Ian Michael Kelly [1963] Director/Dental Surgeon; Steven John Preddy [1959] Director/Dentist; Gabriela Pueyo Roberts [1974] Director/General Manager [Spanish]; Dr Stephen David Burleigh Taylor [1951] Director/Dentist; Dr Ian David Wood [1956] Director; Jake Stephen Hockley Wright [1972] Director

Oasis Dental Care Limited
Incorporated: 8 February 1950 *Employees:* 888
Net Worth: £39,953,000 *Total Assets:* £288,199,008
Registered Office: Bupa Dental Care, Vantage Office Park, Old Gloucester Road, Hambrook, Bristol, BS16 1GW
Activities: Dental practice activities
Parent: Oasis Healthcare Limited
Officers: Robin James Bryant [1970] Director/Dental Surgeon; Ian Michael Kelly [1963] Director/Dental Surgeon; Steven John Preddy [1959] Director/Dentist; Gabriela Pueyo Roberts [1974] Director/General Manager [Spanish]; Dr Stephen David Burleigh Taylor [1951] Director/Dentist; Dr Ian David Wood [1956] Director; Jake Stephen Hockley Wright [1972] Director

Oasis Healthcare Bidco Limited
Incorporated: 18 February 2013 *Employees:* 3
Net Worth: £62,639,000 *Total Assets:* £459,612,000
Registered Office: Bupa Dental Care, Vantage Office Park, Old Gloucester Road, Hambrook, Bristol, BS16 1GW
Activities: Activities of other holding companies n.e.c.
Parent: Oasis Healthcare Midco 2 Ltd
Officers: Steven John Preddy [1959] Director/Dentist; Gabriela Pueyo Roberts [1974] Director/General Manager [Spanish]; Jake Stephen Hockley Wright [1972] Director

The Oasis Healthcare Group Limited
Incorporated: 15 February 2013 *Employees:* 4,691
Net Worth Deficit: £111,577,000 *Total Assets:* £505,504,992
Registered Office: Bupa Dental Care, Vantage Office Park, Old Gloucester Road, Hambrook, Bristol, BS16 1GW
Activities: Activities of other holding companies n.e.c.
Parent: Bupa Finance PLC
Officers: Steven John Preddy [1959] Director/Dentist; Gabriela Pueyo Roberts [1974] Director/General Manager [Spanish]; Charles Austen Richardson [1972] Director; Jake Stephen Hockley Wright [1972] Director

Oasis Healthcare International Limited
Incorporated: 31 May 2007 *Employees:* 5
Previous: Duke Street Capital Oasis Holdings Limited
Net Worth: £52,885,000 *Total Assets:* £101,779,000
Registered Office: Bupa Dental Care, Vantage Office Park, Old Gloucester Road, Hambrook, Bristol, BS16 1GW
Activities: Activities of other holding companies n.e.c.
Parent: Oasis Healthcare Bidco Limited
Officers: Robin James Bryant [1970] Director/Dental Surgeon; Steven John Preddy [1959] Director/Dentist; Gabriela Pueyo Roberts [1974] Director/General Manager [Spanish]; Dr Ian David Wood [1956] Director/Dental Surgeon; Jake Stephen Hockley Wright [1972] Director

Oasis Healthcare Limited
Incorporated: 1 October 1996 *Employees:* 226
Net Worth: £14,899,000 *Total Assets:* £140,311,008
Registered Office: Bupa Dental Care, Vantage Office Park, Old Gloucester Road, Hambrook, Bristol, BS16 1GW
Activities: Activities of head offices
Parent: Duke Street Capital Oasis Acquisitions Limited
Officers: Robin James Bryant [1970] Director/Dental Surgeon; Steven John Preddy [1959] Director/Dentist; Gabriela Pueyo Roberts [1974] Director/General Manager [Spanish]; Dr Stephen David Burleigh Taylor [1951] Director/Dental Surgeon; Dr Ian David Wood [1956] Director/Dental Surgeon; Jake Stephen Hockley Wright [1972] Director

Oasis Healthcare Midco 1 Limited
Incorporated: 15 February 2013 *Employees:* 2
Net Worth: £46,061,000 *Total Assets:* £148,962,000
Registered Office: Bupa Dental Care, Vantage Office Park, Old Gloucester Road, Hambrook, Bristol, BS16 1GW
Activities: Activities of other holding companies n.e.c.
Parent: The Oasis Healthcare Group Ltd
Officers: Steven John Preddy [1959] Director/Dentist; Gabriela Pueyo Roberts [1974] Director/General Manager [Spanish]; Jake Stephen Hockley Wright [1972] Director

Oasis Healthcare Midco 2 Limited
Incorporated: 15 February 2013 *Employees:* 3
Net Worth: £46,255,000 *Total Assets:* £148,962,000
Registered Office: Bupa Dental Care, Vantage Office Park, Old Gloucester Road, Hambrook, Bristol, BS16 1GW
Activities: Activities of other holding companies n.e.c.
Parent: Oasis Healthcare Midco 1 Ltd
Officers: Steven John Preddy [1959] Director/Dentist; Gabriela Pueyo Roberts [1974] Director/General Manager [Spanish]; Jake Stephen Hockley Wright [1972] Director

Oasis Plant Hire Limited
Incorporated: 31 July 1986
Net Worth: £2,959,326 *Total Assets:* £3,677,783
Registered Office: 31-33 Commercial Road, Poole, Dorset, BH14 0HU
Activities: Other letting and operating of own or leased real estate
Officers: Cherrie Evelyn Dianne Frend, Secretary; Mark Ronald Frend [1964] Director/Plant Manager; Ronald Roy Frend [1944] Director

Oastcrest Limited
Incorporated: 3 February 1984 *Employees:* 2
Net Worth: £5,872,639 *Total Assets:* £7,248,506
Registered Office: Midland House, 2 Poole Road, Bournemouth, BH2 5QY
Activities: Other letting and operating of own or leased real estate
Shareholders: Carole Virginia Allen; David Allen
Officers: Carole Virginia Allen, Secretary; Carole Virginia Allen [1939] Director; David Allen [1939] Director

Obenshaw Limited
Incorporated: 27 February 1979 *Employees:* 4
Net Worth: £4,567,241 *Total Assets:* £5,023,887
Registered Office: c/o Francis Clark LLP, North Quay House, Sutton Harbour, Plymouth, PL4 0RA
Activities: Combined office administrative service activities
Shareholders: Maria Manuela Goldsmith; David Lobb; Paul Antony Walter
Officers: David Lobb, Secretary; Maria Manuela Goldsmith [1955] Director; Matthew Hugh Goldsmith [1953] Director; David Lobb [1952] Director; Paul Antony Walter [1946] Director/Retired

OC Sport Ltd
Incorporated: 21 May 2012 *Employees:* 75
Net Worth Deficit: £1,989,274 *Total Assets:* £17,796,284
Registered Office: Mazars LLP, 5th Floor, Merck House, Seldown Lane, Poole, Dorset, BH15 1TW
Activities: Other sports activities
Officers: Mary Spradbery, Secretary; Remi Marie Ernst Duchemin [1979] Director [French]; Jean-Baptiste Marie Michel Pavin [1984] Director/CFO [French]; Roland Marie Michel Tresca [1958] Director [French]

OC Vor Ltd
Incorporated: 16 September 2013 *Employees:* 4
Net Worth Deficit: £1,226,533 *Total Assets:* £4,285,401
Registered Office: Mazars LLP, 5th Floor, Merck House, Seldown Lane, Poole, Dorset, BH15 1TW
Activities: Other sports activities
Officers: Mary Clare Spradbery, Secretary; Bruno Dubois [1959] Director [Belgian]; Herve Etienne Favre [1969] Director [Swiss]; Paul Dominic Kelly [1970] Director [Irish]

Ocean Automotive (Holdings) Limited
Incorporated: 5 January 2015 *Employees:* 267
Net Worth: £5,481,287 *Total Assets:* £41,144,008
Registered Office: 582-602 Ringwood Road, Poole, Dorset, BH12 4LY
Activities: Activities of head offices
Major Shareholder: David John Kelly
Officers: Alison Gail Ninnim, Secretary; David John Kelly [1958] Director; Alison Gail Ninnim [1970] Director; Stephen Kenneth Russell [1968] Director

Ocean Automotive Limited
Incorporated: 28 April 2000 *Employees:* 159
Net Worth: £6,154,939 *Total Assets:* £28,404,852
Registered Office: 582-602 Ringwood Road, Poole, Dorset, BH12 4LY
Activities: Sale of new cars and light motor vehicles
Parent: Ocean Automotive (Holdings) Limited
Officers: Alison Gail Ninnim, Secretary; David John Kelly [1958] Managing Director; Mark Laming [1964] Sales Director; Alison Gail Ninnim [1970] Finance Director; Stephen Kenneth Russell [1968] Director/Brand Manager

Ocean Housing Group Limited
Incorporated: 19 December 2003 *Employees:* 221
Net Worth: £28,177,000 *Total Assets:* £232,066,000
Registered Office: Stennack House, Stennack Road, Holmbush, St Austell, Cornwall, PL25 3SW
Activities: Activities of head offices
Officers: Kevin Michael Pearce, Secretary/Group Director of Resources; Jonathan Peter Nathaniel Adlington [1949] Director/Retired Solicitor; Michael Curtis Crabb [1957] Director/Retired Banker; Christopher Durkin [1963] Director/Semi Retired Consultant; Mark Gardner [1965] Director/Group Chief Executive; Kevin Michael Pearce [1965] Group Director of Resources; Andrea Julie Smith [1960] Director/Housing Consultant; Deborah Claire Wilshire [1958] Director/Consultant

Ocean Learning Trust
Incorporated: 8 June 2015 *Employees:* 241
Net Worth Deficit: £239,118 *Total Assets:* £3,865,783
Registered Office: Bethany Church of England Junior School, Knole Road, Boscombe, Bournemouth, BH1 4DJ
Activities: Primary education
Officers: Ralph Batten [1952] Director of Accountability Best Practice Network; Dominic Biles [1977] Director/Head of Human Resources; David Peter Cheeseman [1950] Director/Retired; Stuart Robert Clark [1953] Director/Retired; Simon Cox [1974] Technology Executive Director; Rev Dr Tim Matthews [1973] Director/Church Minister (C of E); Stephen Kenneth Orman [1955] Director/Executive Headteacher; Michael Jordan Thomas [1946] Director/Charity Chairman

Ocean Village Waterside Developments Limited
Incorporated: 7 December 2010
Net Worth: £646,756 *Total Assets:* £3,847,032
Registered Office: Harbour House, 60 Purewell, Christchurch, Dorset, BH23 1ES
Activities: Development of building projects
Parent: Nicolas James Holdings Limited
Officers: Stuart Andrew Bateman, Secretary; Stuart Andrew Bateman [1976] Director; David Francis Robbins [1967] Director

Oceanview Developments Limited
Incorporated: 11 July 2002 *Employees:* 5
Net Worth: £1,602,207 *Total Assets:* £4,975,416
Registered Office: 118 Old Milton Road, New Milton, Hants, BH25 6EB
Activities: Development of building projects
Shareholders: Caroline Louise Wiggins; Lee Michael Wiggins; Michael Henry Wiggins
Officers: Caroline Louise Wiggins, Secretary; Caroline Louise Wiggins [1968] Director; Lee Michael Wiggins [1964] Director; Michael Henry Wiggins [1941] Director/Retired

Ochre Solutions (Holdings) Limited
Incorporated: 25 October 2004
Net Worth Deficit: £76,186,448 *Total Assets:* £162,191,824
Registered Office: Third Floor, Broad Quay House, Prince Street, Bristol, BS1 4DJ
Activities: Medical nursing home activities
Shareholder: Infrastructure Investments (Portal) GP Limited
Officers: Colin John Anderson [1963] Director/Solicitor; Gianfranco Catrini [1972] Director/Business Executive [Italian]; Ian Richard Gethin [1971] Director/Investment Banker; David Robert Hardingham [1974] Director/Commercial Manager; Matteo Milanesi [1970] Director [Italian]; Natalia Poupard [1977] Director/Asset Manager; Geoffrey Alan Quaife [1955] Director

Ochre Solutions Limited
Incorporated: 25 October 2004
Net Worth Deficit: £76,186,448 *Total Assets:* £162,191,824
Registered Office: Third Floor, Broad Quay House, Prince Street, Bristol, BS1 4DJ
Activities: Medical nursing home activities
Parent: Ochre Solutions (Holdings) Limited
Officers: Colin John Anderson [1963] Director/Solicitor; Gianfranco Catrini [1972] Director/Business Executive [Italian]; Ian Richard Gethin [1971] Director/Investment Banker; David Robert Hardingham [1974] Director/Commercial Manager; Matteo Milanesi [1970] Director [Italian]; Natalia Poupard [1977] Director/Asset Manager; Geoffrey Alan Quaife [1955] Director

Octagon Healthcare Funding PLC
Incorporated: 18 August 2003 *Employees:* 6
Net Worth: £153,000 *Total Assets:* £259,472,000
Registered Office: Third Floor, Broad Quay House, Prince Street, Bristol, BS1 4DJ
Activities: Other business support service activities n.e.c.
Parent: Octagon Healthcare Group Limited
Officers: David John Brooking [1967] Managing Director; John Ivor Cavill [1972] Director; Sheila Jamieson Clark [1973] Director; David Francis Lindesay [1960] Commercial Director; Neil Rae [1971] Director; Peter John Sheldrake [1959] Director

Octagon Healthcare Group Limited
Incorporated: 9 July 2003
Net Worth Deficit: £56,318,000 *Total Assets:* £274,484,992
Registered Office: Third Floor, Broad Quay House, Prince Street, Bristol, BS1 4DJ
Activities: Activities of head offices
Shareholders: 3i Infrastructure Seed Assets G.P. Limited; Innisfree Nominees Limited; Semperian PPP Investment Partners No.2 Limited
Officers: David John Brooking [1967] Managing Director; John Ivor Cavill [1972] Director; Sheila Jamieson Clark [1973] Director; David Francis Lindesay [1960] Commercial Director; Neil Rae [1971] Director; Peter John Sheldrake [1959] Director

Octagon Healthcare Holdings (Norwich) Limited
Incorporated: 9 May 1997
Net Worth: £1,325,000 *Total Assets:* £35,179,000
Registered Office: Third Floor, Broad Quay House, Prince Street, Bristol, BS1 4DJ
Activities: Activities of head offices
Parent: Octagon Healthcare Group Limited
Officers: David John Brooking [1967] Managing Director; John Ivor Cavill [1972] Director; Sheila Jamieson Clark [1973] Director; David Francis Lindesay [1960] Commercial Director; Neil Rae [1971] Director; Peter John Sheldrake [1959] Director

Octagon Healthcare Limited
Incorporated: 12 October 1995
Net Worth Deficit: £18,700,000 *Total Assets:* £312,108,000
Registered Office: Third Floor, Broad Quay House, Prince Street, Bristol, BS1 4DJ
Activities: Other service activities n.e.c.
Parent: Octagon Healthcare Holdings (Norwich) Limited
Officers: David John Brooking [1967] Managing Director; John Ivor Cavill [1972] Director; Sheila Jamieson Clark [1973] Director; David Francis Lindesay [1960] Commercial Director; Neil Rae [1971] Director; Peter John Sheldrake [1959] Director

Octava Holdings Limited
Incorporated: 29 June 2012
Net Worth: £44,615 *Total Assets:* £5,030,718
Registered Office: Wessex House, 66 High Street, Honiton, Devon, EX14 1PD
Activities: Other business support service activities n.e.c.
Officers: Dean Barrow [1970] Director

Odstone Farms Limited
Incorporated: 1 January 1959 *Employees:* 2
Net Worth: £2,755,443 *Total Assets:* £3,776,573
Registered Office: Great Colleybeer, South Tawton, Okehampton, Devon, EX20 2LX
Activities: Growing of cereals (except rice), leguminous crops and oil seeds
Major Shareholder: Bob Mawle
Officers: James Robert Mawle, Secretary; Robert Ralph Mawle [1943] Director/Farmer

Off Site Solutions (R T) Limited
Incorporated: 11 June 2004 *Employees:* 190
Net Worth: £2,348,132 *Total Assets:* £12,958,481
Registered Office: Polybeam House, Hoopers Close, Isleport Business Park, Highbridge, Somerset, TA9 4JU
Activities: Other manufacturing n.e.c.
Major Shareholder: Raymond Bob Tonkinson
Officers: Lee Charles Harding, Secretary; James Antony Mark Edward Stephens [1976] Director; Richard Tonkinson [1977] Director; William Tonkinson [1979] Director

Off-Piste Wines Limited
Incorporated: 24 July 2006 *Employees:* 21
Net Worth: £4,926,000 *Total Assets:* £13,053,000
Registered Office: 8 Royal Crescent, Cheltenham, Glos, GL50 3DA
Activities: Agents involved in the sale of food, beverages and tobacco
Shareholders: Paul David James Letheren; Anthony William Vaughan Fairbank
Officers: Andrew Talbot, Secretary/Financial Controller; Anthony William Vaughan Fairbank [1963] Director; Paul David James Letheren [1967] Director; Jeremy Francis Lockspeiser [1953] Director/Chairman; Mark William Pettit [1973] Sales Director; Andrew Leslie Talbot [1979] Finance Director; Clemency Yates [1976] Sourcing and Supply Director

Offshore Marine Management Limited
Incorporated: 5 December 2003 *Employees:* 17
Net Worth: £482,000 *Total Assets:* £5,808,000
Registered Office: 55 Queen Square, Bristol, BS1 4LH
Activities: Management consultancy activities other than financial management
Officers: Robert Leo Douglas Grimmond [1969] Director [Australian]

Ohashi Technica UK, Ltd.
Incorporated: 17 December 1999 *Employees:* 30
Net Worth: £6,426,179 *Total Assets:* £7,487,631
Registered Office: Unit 6 I O Centre, Radway Road, Swindon, Wilts, SN3 4WH
Activities: Wholesale trade of motor vehicle parts and accessories
Officers: Masaya Hirose [1964] Director [Japanese]; Masato Hori [1961] Director/Executive Officer [Japanese]; Seiji Masaki [1962] Director/Executive Officer [Japanese]; Yoshiji Nakamura [1960] Director [Japanese]; Mamoru Shibasaki [1956] Director [Japanese]; Hikaru Tateiwa [1961] Managing Director [Japanese]

Old Coastguard Holiday Park Limited
Incorporated: 3 June 2014 *Employees:* 8
Net Worth: £1,115,510 *Total Assets:* £4,038,997
Registered Office: 3-5 College Street, Burnham on Sea, Somerset, TA8 1AR
Activities: Recreational vehicle parks, trailer parks and camping grounds
Officers: June Barnikel [1935] Director; Grant John Connolly [1958] Director; Kim-Marie Connolly [1965] Director; Lee Robert Connolly [1962] Director

Old Hall Investment Company Limited
Incorporated: 26 June 2007 *Employees:* 1
Net Worth: £5,318,585 *Total Assets:* £5,324,345
Registered Office: Portwall Place, Portwall Lane, Bristol, BS1 6NA
Activities: Other business support service activities n.e.c.
Officers: William Ross Warburton [1958] Director

Old Mill Accountancy LLP
Incorporated: 7 July 2006 *Employees:* 154
Net Worth: £897,830 *Total Assets:* £5,325,035
Registered Office: Maltravers House, Petters Way, Yeovil, Somerset, BA20 1SH
Officers: Michael John Butler [1967] Member; Ian James Carlson [1971] Member; Simon Mark Howard Cole [1963] Member; Jolyon Roger Geoffrey Stonehouse [1967] Member; Kevin Charles Whitmarsh [1966] Member; Julia Cary Banwell [1976] LLP Member; Lorraine Brenda Marie Bolland [1974] LLP Member; Christopher Bowles [1968] LLP Member; Amanda Jane Bradley [1967] LLP Member; Simon Peter Clark [1960] LLP Member; Stuart Alan Coombe [1982] LLP Member; Neil Cox [1977] LLP Member; James Clive Gifford [1972] LLP Member; Stuart John Grimster [1976] LLP Member; Richard Haines [1983] LLP Member; Sally Jane Harrison [1967] LLP Member; Anthony Carlo Hawes [1970] LLP Member; Rebecca Clare Hobbs [1977] LLP Member; Paula Jane Hodge [1967] LLP Member; Gavin William Jones [1973] LLP Member; Philip Stuart Kirkpatrick [1986] LLP Member; Daniel James Knight [1983] LLP Member; Timothy Lynden Lerwill [1973] LLP Member; David John Maslen [1970] LLP Member; Daniel Reece Middle [1972] LLP Member; Andrew Duncan Moore [1964] LLP Member; Adam Nicholas Morrison [1984] LLP Member; Paul Neate [1963] LLP Member; Mark John Neath [1974] LLP Member; Jonathan Andrew David Orchard [1983] LLP Member; Duncan Benedict Parkes [1973] LLP Member; David Stephen Rice [1966] LLP Member; Victoria Sian Rudham [1974] LLP Member; Mark Leonard Harold Seager [1979] LLP Member; Martin Christopher Taylor [1970] LLP Member; William Matthew Thompson [1985] LLP Member; Christopher Edward Tweedie [1964] LLP Member; Andrew Mark Vickery [1982] LLP Member; Catherine Fiona Vickery [1977] LLP Member; Andrew Wallwork [1966] LLP Member; Laura Jane Wylie [1981] LLP Member

Old Mills Estates Limited
Incorporated: 4 March 1996
Net Worth: £4,747,159 *Total Assets:* £5,914,486
Registered Office: Old Mills House, Old Mills, Paulton, Bristol, BS39 7SU
Activities: Development of building projects
Shareholder: Roderick Barry Thorner
Officers: Tracey Kim Hammond, Secretary; Lasley Jane Hall [1957] Director; Tracey Kim Hammond [1963] Director; Andrea Paget [1959] Director; Roderick Barry Thorner [1961] Director

Old Quay House Hotel Limited
Incorporated: 24 April 2015
Net Worth: £180,594 *Total Assets:* £6,137,748
Registered Office: Lowin House, Tregolls Road, Truro, Cornwall, TR1 2NA
Activities: Activities of other holding companies n.e.c.
Officers: Jan Johannes Bester [1984] Director/Fund Manager [South African]; Andre Malan [1967] Director/Fund Manager [South African]; Jacobus Adriaan Nel [1975] Director/Fund Manager [South African]

The Old Sorting Office (Bournemouth) Limited
Incorporated: 2 January 2014
Net Worth Deficit: £56,040 *Total Assets:* £7,382,827
Registered Office: 302 Charminster Road, Bournemouth, BH8 9RU
Activities: Other letting and operating of own or leased real estate
Major Shareholder: Fateh Omar Rahim
Officers: Dr Fateh Omar Rahim [1971] Director/Medical Doctor

The Old Tannery (Holt) Limited
Incorporated: 22 July 2008
Net Worth: £1,597,221 *Total Assets:* £4,587,538
Registered Office: The Courtyard, 33 Duke Street, Trowbridge, Wilts, BA14 8EA
Activities: Renting and operating of Housing Association real estate
Major Shareholder: Alix Margaret Kirkham
Officers: Alix Margaret Kirkham [1968] Director; Nicholas Robert Marshall Kirkham [1966] Director

Oldfield School
Incorporated: 17 January 2011 *Employees:* 128
Net Worth: £16,065,749 *Total Assets:* £17,186,944
Registered Office: Oldfield School, Kelston Road, Bath, BA1 9AB
Activities: General secondary education
Officers: Marya Dorothy Marriott, Secretary; Tahir Hamid Darr [1967] Director/Airline Pilot; Tom Davies [1979] Director/Bursar; Duncan Giles [1975] Director/Headmaster; Ruth Henry [1971] Director/Student Welfare Officer; Victoria Jackson [1971] Director; Verity Lewis [1980] Director/Teacher; Steven Richard MacKay [1969] Director/Headteacher; Michelle O'Doherty [1981] Director/Production Manager; Kelly Ann Ogden [1977] Director; Nicholas John Regan [1965] Director/Teacher; Joanna Symons [1973] Director/Fundraiser/Data Manager; Kevin Ward [1978] Director/Management Consultant; Stuart Paul Weatherall [1960] Director/Project Manager

Henry Oliver Ltd
Incorporated: 17 August 2006
Net Worth: £2,837,996 *Total Assets:* £6,986,526
Registered Office: 86 Shirehampton Road, Stoke Bishop, Bristol, BS9 2DR
Activities: Other letting and operating of own or leased real estate
Officers: Jonathan Henry Peevers [1951] Director

Olo Real Estate Limited
Incorporated: 24 April 2015 *Employees:* 1
Net Worth: £596,265 *Total Assets:* £5,901,021
Registered Office: c/o Bishop Fleming, Chy Nyverow, Newham Road, Truro, Cornwall, TR1 2DP
Activities: Other letting and operating of own or leased real estate
Major Shareholder: Stephen Casper
Officers: Stephen Casper, Secretary; Stephen Casper [1968] Director/Accountant

Olympic Varnish Company Limited
Incorporated: 13 August 1938
Net Worth: £3,736,345 *Total Assets:* £4,293,166
Registered Office: Val d'Or Works, Knapp Lane, Brimscombe, Stroud, Glos, GL5 2TQ
Activities: Manufacture of other paper and paperboard containers
Officers: Benjamin Paul Petyan, Secretary; Benjamin Paul Petyan [1949] Director; William Bertram Petyan [1946] Director

The Olympus Academy Trust
Incorporated: 11 November 2011 *Employees:* 765
Net Worth: £102,261,072 *Total Assets:* £117,071,952
Registered Office: Bradley Stoke Community School, Fiddlers Wood Lane, Bradley Stoke, Bristol, BS32 9BS
Activities: Primary education
Officers: Diane Ault [1971] Director/Senior Finance Manager; David Andrew Baker [1963] Director/Executive Headteacher; Paul Davies [1967] Director/Internal Auditor; Michael John Fry [1955] Director/Trustee; Isabel Prue Marsden [1965] Director/Education Consultant Teacher; Paul Richard Roberts [1972] Director/HR Manager; Kate Lindsay Sheldon [1973] Director/Homemaker; Richard William Sloan [1957] Director; Robert Charles Smyth [1955] Accountant and Director; Sarah Lois Williams [1976] Director; Timothy John Williams [1965] Director/Engineer

OM Holidays Ltd
Incorporated: 30 October 1958 *Employees:* 11
Net Worth: £3,143,754 *Total Assets:* £6,047,234
Registered Office: 10 Bridge Street, Christchurch, Dorset, BH23 1EF
Activities: Mixed farming
Parent: Weymouth Leisure Limited
Officers: Michael John Coombe [1939] Director

Omega Housing Limited
Incorporated: 19 July 2010 *Employees:* 6
Net Worth: £1,306,528 *Total Assets:* £10,145,911
Registered Office: 1390 Montpellier Court, Gloucester Business Park, Brockworth, Gloucester, GL3 4AH
Activities: Residents property management
Officers: Ben Robert Westran, Secretary; Beatrice Amia Cingtho-Taylor [1967] Director/Local Government Manager; Lucas Jordan Critchley [1982] Director; Roy Irwin [1954] Director/Housing Professional; Roger Jesse Jarman [1954] Director; Erfana Mahmood [1970] Director; Michelle Antoinette Patterson [1966] Director/Local Government Officer; Gary David Sims [1965] Director; Andrew Christopher Melville Smith [1972] Director/Chartered Accountant; Jan Taranczuk [1948] Director; John Kenneth Taylor [1967] Director

Omicways Limited
Incorporated: 31 January 1967 *Employees:* 33
Net Worth: £6,069,332 *Total Assets:* £6,943,220
Registered Office: Container Group Buying, Bude Stratton Business Park, Bude, Cornwall, EX23 8LY
Activities: Wholesale of household goods (other than musical instruments) n.e.c
Shareholders: John Alfred Varnom Marks; Patricia Josephine Marks
Officers: John Alfred Varnom Marks, Secretary; Briony Annabelle Cole [1988] Director; Damon Ballard Marks [1964] Director; Gwyneth Meirion Marks [1963] Director; John Alfred Varnom Marks [1937] Director; Niall Jack Marks [1990] Director; Patricia Josephine Marks [1938] Director; Patrick Henry Marks [1998] Director

Omnis Investments Limited
Incorporated: 1 May 2008
Net Worth: £5,891,000 *Total Assets:* £10,948,000
Registered Office: Washington House, Lydiard Fields, Swindon, Wilts, SN5 8UB
Activities: Activities auxiliary to financial intermediation n.e.c.
Parent: Openwork Holdings Limited
Officers: Kevin David Chidwick [1963] Director; Peter Davis [1960] Director; Douglas James Naismith [1959] Non-Executive Director Chairman; Dominic Paul Sheridan [1962] Director/Chief Executive Officer

OMPD Limited
Incorporated: 7 August 2012 *Employees:* 5
Net Worth: £3,017,560 *Total Assets:* £12,667,881
Registered Office: c/o Milsted Langdon LLP, Motivo House, Alvington, Yeovil, Somerset, BA20 2FG
Activities: Residents property management
Shareholders: Tim Morris Holdings Limited; James Edward Barclay Oliver
Officers: Ralph Timothy Morris [1949] Director; James Edward Barclay Oliver [1984] Director

One Holding Investments Ltd
Incorporated: 26 January 2007
Net Worth: £1,019,290 *Total Assets:* £3,581,971
Registered Office: 19 Clothier Road, Bristol, BS4 5PS
Activities: Other letting and operating of own or leased real estate
Shareholders: Munir Safdar; Jahangir Khan; KGN Sales Agency Ltd
Officers: Jahangir Khan [1975] Director; Munir Safdar [1966] Director

One Holding Limited
Incorporated: 29 March 2006 *Employees:* 48
Net Worth: £2,538,806 *Total Assets:* £3,835,434
Registered Office: 19 Clothier Road, Brislington, Bristol, BS4 5PS
Activities: Manufacture of mattresses
Shareholders: Jahanghir Khan; Munir Safdar
Officers: Munir Safdar, Secretary; Jahangir Khan [1975] Director; Munir Safdar [1966] Director

Onley Prison Services Limited
Incorporated: 14 December 1998
Net Worth: £3,912,000 *Total Assets:* £35,594,560
Registered Office: Third Floor, Broad Quay House, Prince Street, Bristol, BS1 4DJ
Activities: Public order and safety activities
Parent: G4S Joint Ventures (Onley) Limited
Officers: Alan Edward Birch [1970] Director; Gawie Murray Nienaber [1957] Director/General Legal Counsel; Vaishali Jagdish Patel [1973] Director/Solicitor; Jeremy Kenneth Petherick [1954] Managing Director; Alan Campbell Ritchie [1967] Director

Opaltec International Limited
Incorporated: 5 October 1998 *Employees:* 27
Net Worth: £1,657,622 *Total Assets:* £4,411,897
Registered Office: 118 Burcott Road, Avonmouth, Bristol, BS11 8AD
Activities: Other information technology service activities
Parent: The Hamilton Davies Group
Officers: David Whatley, Secretary; Mark Hamilton-Davies [1968] Director

Openwave II UK Limited
Incorporated: 4 May 2012 *Employees:* 69
Net Worth: £4,950,734 *Total Assets:* £6,232,113
Registered Office: 11th Floor, Whitefriars, Lewins Mead, Bristol, BS1 2NT
Activities: Other telecommunications activities
Shareholder: Pers Anders Ponuts Hermansson Lindberg
Officers: John Paul Giere [1963] Director/CEO - Openwave Mobility, Inc [American]; Anders Lidbeck [1962] Director/CFO of Enea AB Swedish Parent Company [Swedish]

Openwave Systems Limited
Incorporated: 9 October 2000 *Employees:* 69
Net Worth: £10,914,227 *Total Assets:* £12,195,606
Registered Office: 11th Floor, Whitefriars, Lewins Mead, Bristol, BS1 2NT
Activities: Activities of head offices
Shareholder: Per Anders Ponuts Hermansson Lindberg
Officers: John Paul Giere [1963] Director/CEO - Openwave Mobility, Inc [American]; Anders Lidbeck [1962] Director/CFO of Enea AB Swedish Parent Company [Swedish]

Openwork Holdings Limited
Incorporated: 24 June 1999 *Employees:* 481
Net Worth: £52,890,000 *Total Assets:* £141,760,000
Registered Office: Washington House, Lydiard Fields, Swindon, Wilts, SN5 8UB
Activities: Activities of head offices
Parent: Openwork Holdings Limited
Officers: Ian Buchanan [1964] Director; Kevin David Chidwick [1963] Director; Angela Doreen Crawford-Ingle [1952] Director; Paul Irvine Dalzell [1959] Director; Mark Duckworth [1971] Finance Director; Christopher John Rodrigues [1949] Director; Andrew John Smart [1959] Director

Openwork Limited
Incorporated: 20 March 2002
Net Worth: £88,684,000 *Total Assets:* £155,507,008
Registered Office: Washington House, Lydiard Fields, Swindon, Wilts, SN5 8UB
Activities: Financial intermediation not elsewhere classified
Parent: Openwork Holdings Limited
Officers: Kevin David Chidwick [1963] Director; Mark Duckworth [1971] Director; Ian Nicholas Lovett [1944] Director; Paul John Mitchener [1961] Governance Director; Claire Simone Oldstein [1967] Director; Andrew John Smart [1959] Director

Openwork Services Limited
Incorporated: 13 May 1998 *Employees:* 435
Net Worth: £10,909,000 *Total Assets:* £42,450,000
Registered Office: Washington House, Lydiard Fields, Swindon, Wilts, SN5 8UB
Activities: Other service activities n.e.c.
Parent: Openwork Holdings Limited
Officers: Kevin David Chidwick [1963] Director; Mark Duckworth [1971] Finance Director; Karen Juliet Morris [1970] Director

Opex Logistics Limited
Incorporated: 11 July 2003 *Employees:* 52
Previous: Isis Transport Solutions Limited
Net Worth: £2,730,720 *Total Assets:* £5,479,946
Registered Office: B2 Vantage Office Park, Old Gloucester Road, Hambrook, Bristol, BS16 1GW
Activities: Freight transport by road
Shareholders: Peter Scrivin; Geoff Pomroy
Officers: Peter Charles Scrivin, Secretary/Haulier; Geoff Pomroy [1956] Director; Peter Charles Scrivin [1981] Director

Ophir Finance Company Limited
Incorporated: 31 July 1958 *Employees:* 6
Net Worth: £2,699,265 *Total Assets:* £4,901,585
Registered Office: Towngate House, 2-8 Parkstone Road, Poole, Dorset, BH15 2PW
Activities: Development of building projects
Parent: General and Finance Facilities Limited
Officers: Stewart Jeffrey Greene, Secretary; Michael Jonathan Greene [1964] Director; Nicola Jayne Greene [1966] Director

Opmal Limited
Incorporated: 4 April 2011 *Employees:* 2
Net Worth: £915,165 *Total Assets:* £16,745,798
Registered Office: 2nd Floor, Stratus House, Emperor Way, Exeter Business Park, Exeter, EX1 3QS
Activities: Other letting and operating of own or leased real estate
Shareholders: Joseph Anton Lampo; Melanie Jane Margaret Lampo
Officers: Melanie Jane Margaret Lampo [1979] Director

Optima Defence & Security Group Limited
Incorporated: 18 February 2009 *Employees:* 39
Net Worth: £96,693 *Total Assets:* £4,485,349
Registered Office: 130 High Street, Marlborough, Wilts, SN8 1LZ
Activities: Defence activities
Shareholders: Keith Eifion Hammond; Holly Maranda Hammond
Officers: Rhys John Tudor Williams, Secretary; Stephen Richard Bishop [1964] Finance Director; Nigel Cribb [1969] Managing Director; Anthony John David Guest [1962] Director/Chief Operating Officer; Keith Eifion Hammond [1973] Director/Chief Executive; Major General Jonathan David Shaw [1957] Director/Chairman; Rhys John Tudor Williams [1965] Director/General Counsel

Optimas OE Solutions Ltd
Incorporated: 10 February 2015 *Employees:* 503
Net Worth: £75,859,000 *Total Assets:* £204,490,000
Registered Office: Optimas OE Solutions Ltd, Waterwells Drive, Quedgeley, Gloucester, GL2 2FR
Activities: Non-specialised wholesale trade
Officers: Philip Terence Ballard [1973] Director/Chartered Accountant; Rebecca Weber Goldman [1956] Director/Lawyer [American]; Michael James Tuffy [1966] Director/Executive Vice President UK

Optimum SME Finance Limited
Incorporated: 2 December 2016 *Employees:* 9
Net Worth: £103,000 *Total Assets:* £4,541,400
Registered Office: Cube M4 Business Park, Old Gloucester Road, Bristol, BS16 1FX
Activities: Factoring
Shareholders: Roger Benjamin Nagioff; Elljay Limited
Officers: Scott Lawrence Braybrook, Secretary; Scott Lawrence Braybrook [1968] Director/Chief Financial Officer; Joanna Elizabeth Nader [1970] Director; Richard John Pepler [1960] Director; Henry David Penrose Richards [1984] Director; Peter Michael Sugarman [1960] Director

Opus Professional Services Group Limited
Incorporated: 4 July 2014 *Employees:* 239
Net Worth: £2,098,222 *Total Assets:* £19,045,768
Registered Office: Portwall Place, Portwall Lane, Bristol, BS1 6NA
Activities: Other activities of employment placement agencies
Shareholders: Darren John Ryemill; Joanne Ryemill
Officers: Darren John Ryemill, Secretary; Amy Grace Golding [1985] Director; Daniel Thomas Ponting [1983] Recruitment Director; Nigel Peter Ramana [1981] Director; Darren John Ryemill [1976] Director; Ryan Speed [1983] Director

Opus Recruitment Solutions Limited
Incorporated: 11 January 2008 *Employees:* 136
Net Worth: £1,853,039 *Total Assets:* £12,804,639
Registered Office: Portwall Place, Portwall Lane, Bristol, BS1 6NA
Activities: Temporary employment agency activities
Parent: Opus Professional Services Group Limited
Officers: Darren John Ryemill, Secretary; Amy Grace Golding [1985] Director; Samuel Jenkinson [1974] Director/Recruitment; Nigel Peter Ramana [1981] Director/Recruitment Consultant; Darren John Ryemill [1976] Director; Ryan Speed [1983] Director/Recruitment

Orange Door Property Company Ltd
Incorporated: 14 October 2016
Net Worth: £9,846 *Total Assets:* £4,758,105
Registered Office: 25 Blue Water Drive, Elborough, Weston-Super-Mare, Somerset, BS24 8PF
Activities: Development of building projects
Shareholders: Catherine Jill Salmons; Paul Salmons
Officers: James Rewse Salmons [1988] Director/Nurse; Paul Salmons [1962] Director/Accountant

Orange International Investments (UK) Limited
Incorporated: 27 August 2004 *Employees:* 2
Net Worth Deficit: £952,422 *Total Assets:* £5,272,945
Registered Office: Ashford House, Grenadier Road, Exeter, Devon, EX1 3LH
Activities: Other business support service activities n.e.c.
Major Shareholder: Margeir Petursson
Officers: Mariia Brozhko [1989] Director/Business Management and Administration [Ukrainian]

Orbitz Worldwide (UK) Limited
Incorporated: 29 June 2007
Net Worth Deficit: £9,344,998 *Total Assets:* £69,974,896
Registered Office: 2 Temple Back East, Temple Quay, Bristol, BS1 6EG
Activities: Non-trading company
Parent: Expedia Group, Inc.
Officers: Robert John Dzielak [1971] Director/Business Manager/Lawyer [American]; Frances Josephine Erskine [1969] Director/Business Executive [American]; Lance Allen Soliday [1972] Director/Business Manager/Accountant [American]

Orchard Gate Ltd
Incorporated: 15 April 2014 *Employees:* 6
Net Worth: £385,129 *Total Assets:* £6,275,556
Registered Office: 10 Prince of Wales Road, Dorchester, DT1 1PW
Activities: Other letting and operating of own or leased real estate
Shareholders: Antony Peter Christie; Gail Alison Gardner
Officers: Janet Diane Christie, Secretary; Antony Peter Christie [1971] Director/Webmaster and International Marketer; Barrie Michael Christie [1943] Director/Chairman; Gail Alison Gardner [1973] Director/Chartered Marketer; Matthew Gardner [1974] Director

The Orchard Trust
Incorporated: 15 February 1989 *Employees:* 183
Net Worth: £5,673,915 *Total Assets:* £5,889,470
Registered Office: Valley Springs Lydbrook, Central Lydbrook, Lydbrook, Glos, GL17 9PP
Activities: Educational support services
Officers: Nicholas Peter Budd [1957] Director/Consultant; Rita Mary Dodsworth [1946] Director/Retired; Susan Frances Henchley [1942] Director/Retired; Elaine Hewison [1958] Director/Retired; Leon Brian Kaye [1950] Director/Retired; Robert Harry Morgan [1947] Director/Retired; Katharine Helena Morley [1964] Director/Retired; Judith Jane Morris Kaye [1948] Director/Retired; Claire Eleanor Smart [1969] Procurement Director

Orchardleigh Estates Limited
Incorporated: 7 October 1998
Net Worth: £741,388 *Total Assets:* £4,102,280
Registered Office: Orchardleigh House, Orchardleigh, Frome, Somerset, BA11 2PH
Activities: Other letting and operating of own or leased real estate
Major Shareholder: Christopher John Newby-Vincent
Officers: Christopher John Newby Vincent, Secretary; Samantha Maria Newby-Vincent [1975] Director/Assistant Horse Trainer; Christopher John Newby Vincent [1948] Director

Orchardleigh Park Ltd
Incorporated: 19 September 2001
Net Worth: £2,975,106 *Total Assets:* £6,683,008
Registered Office: Orchardleigh House, Orchardleigh, Frome, Somerset, BA11 2PH
Activities: Hotels and similar accommodation
Major Shareholder: Christopher Newby-Vincent
Officers: Christopher John Newby-Vincent, Secretary; Christopher Newby Vincent [1948] Managing Director

Organic Foods, Drinks & Investments Holdings Ltd
Incorporated: 21 June 2002
Net Worth Deficit: £5,127,014 *Total Assets:* £6,926,618
Registered Office: First Floor, 10 Temple Back, Bristol, BS1 6FL
Activities: Activities of other holding companies n.e.c.
Major Shareholder: Lynda Anne Cambouroglou
Officers: Daniella Cambouroglou [1985] Director [British/Greek]; Lynda Cambouroglou [1955] Director [British/Greek]

Organic Milk Suppliers Co-operative Limited
Incorporated: 2 June 1997 *Employees:* 20
Net Worth: £2,006,000 *Total Assets:* £14,892,000
Registered Office: 501 Parkway, Worle, Weston Super Mare, Somerset, BS22 6WA
Activities: Activities of other membership organisations n.e.c.
Officers: John Arthur Alpe [1959] Director/Farmer; Murray MacEwan Brown [1965] Director/Farmer; Bruce Warren Carlisle [1964] Director/Farmer; Timothy John Downes [1974] Director/Farmer; Lyndon Roger Charles Edwards [1963] Director/Farmer; Amanda Grist [1977] Finance Director; Richard Hampton [1972] Director; Harold Glyn Jones [1963] Farmer/Director; Neil Angus Kennedy [1960] Director; Ross Paton [1960] Director/Farmer; Sir Walter Robert Alexander Ross [1950] Director/Chartered Surveyor; Nicholas Peter George Saphir [1944] Director/Consultant; Miles Saunders [1963] Director/Farmer; George Simon Tomlinson [1944] Director/Surveyor; Graham Vallis [1960] Director/Farmer; Adam Peter Westaway [1972] Director/Farmer

Organix Brands Limited
Incorporated: 19 May 1992 *Employees:* 52
Net Worth: £13,033,000 *Total Assets:* £19,884,000
Registered Office: The Green House, 120-122 Commercial Road, Bournemouth, BH2 5LT
Activities: Non-specialised wholesale of food, beverages and tobacco
Parent: Hero Espana SA
Officers: Rachel Debra Shutler, Secretary; Markus Lenke [1969] Director [German]; Philipp Von Jagow [1978] Managing Director [German]

Original Style Holdings Limited
Incorporated: 15 January 2010 *Employees:* 250
Net Worth: £12,722,664 *Total Assets:* £15,815,639
Registered Office: Falcon Road, Sowton Industrial Estate, Exeter, Devon, EX2 7LF
Activities: Activities of head offices
Shareholder: Guy Courtenay Bagot Brook
Officers: Matthew James Fripp, Secretary; Colin Malcolm Brook [1937] Director; Guy Courtenay Bagot Brook [1960] Director; Matthew James Fripp [1977] Director; Miles Peter Jennings [1961] Director; Morley Andrew Sage [1962] Director; Christopher Alan Sowden [1964] Director

Original Style Limited
Incorporated: 3 February 1995 *Employees:* 240
Net Worth: £7,956,285 *Total Assets:* £11,224,934
Registered Office: Falcon Road, Sowton Industrial Estate, Exeter, Devon, EX2 7LF
Activities: Manufacture of ceramic tiles and flags
Shareholders: Guy Courtenay Bagot Brook; Original Style Holdings Limited
Officers: Matthew Fripp, Secretary; Guy Courtenay Bagot Brook [1960] Director; Matthew James Fripp [1977] Director/Chartered Accountant; Miles Peter Jennings [1961] Director; Christopher Alan Sowden [1964] Director

Orproperty Limited
Incorporated: 6 August 1999
Net Worth: £1,057,570 *Total Assets:* £6,856,791
Registered Office: The Forge Enterprise Centre, 3 Church Road, West Huntspill, Somerset, TA9 3RN
Activities: Development of building projects
Officers: Mark William Hamlin, Secretary/Director; Julian Philip Hamlin [1984] Director; Dr Mark William Hamlin [1954] Director; Dr Moira Anne Hamlin [1951] Director

Ortho 2008 Limited
Incorporated: 21 November 2006 *Employees:* 40
Net Worth: £12,707,000 *Total Assets:* £14,347,000
Registered Office: Bupa Dental Care, Vantage Office Park, Old Gloucester Road, Hambrook, Bristol, BS16 1GW
Activities: Dental practice activities
Parent: Duke Street Capital Oasis Orthodontics Holdings Limited
Officers: Robin James Bryant [1970] Director/Dental Surgeon; Steven John Preddy [1959] Director/Dentist; Gabriela Pueyo Roberts [1974] Director/General Manager [Spanish]; Adam Anthony Ryan [1960] Director/Dentist; Dr Ian David Wood [1956] Director/Dentist; Jake Stephen Hockley Wright [1972] Director

Orthod Group Limited
Incorporated: 14 March 2008 *Employees:* 110
Previous: Summit Medical Group Limited
Net Worth: £954,682 *Total Assets:* £24,762,880
Registered Office: c/o Summit Medical Ltd, Industrial Park, Bourton on the Water, Cheltenham, Glos, GL54 2HQ
Activities: Manufacture of medical and dental instruments and supplies
Parent: Bowmoor Bidco Limited
Officers: Alastair John McKay, Secretary; Daniel John Bee [1967] Director; Alec John Simpson [1969] Director

Orthod Midco Limited
Incorporated: 22 September 2016
Net Worth: £21,166,112 *Total Assets:* £21,808,978
Registered Office: c/o Summit Medical Ltd, Industrial Park, Bourton on the Water, Cheltenham, Glos, GL54 2HQ
Activities: Manufacture of medical and dental instruments and supplies
Officers: Alastair John McKay, Secretary; Daniel John Bee [1967] Director; Alec John Simpson [1969] Director

Orthodynamics Limited
Incorporated: 27 January 1986
Net Worth: £9,665,492 *Total Assets:* £9,984,644
Registered Office: c/o Summit Medical Ltd, Bourton on the Water Industrial Park, Bourton on The Water, Glos, GL54 2HQ
Activities: Manufacture of medical and dental instruments and supplies
Officers: Alastair John McKay, Secretary; Daniel John Bee [1967] Director; Alec John Simpson [1969] Director

Osborne Care Homes Limited
Incorporated: 18 January 1989 *Employees:* 150
Net Worth: £1,574,897 *Total Assets:* £4,788,920
Registered Office: Withey House, 26 Withey Close West, Bristol, BS9 3SX
Activities: Residential nursing care facilities
Major Shareholder: Michael Barton Slator
Officers: Joshua Alexander Slator [1980] Director/Administrator; Michael Barton Slator [1946] Director/Chartered Accountant

Osprey Europe Limited
Incorporated: 29 August 2003 *Employees:* 59
Net Worth: £18,660,602 *Total Assets:* £23,170,224
Registered Office: Talon House, Aston Way, Poole, Dorset, BH12 4FE
Activities: Non-specialised wholesale trade
Officers: Tom Robert Entwistle [1982] Sales Director; Christian Johnson [1980] Director/Partner [American]; Jonathan Wilfrid Petty [1969] Marketing Director; Scott Pfotenhauer [1954] Director/Financial Adviser [American]; Layne Rigney [1968] Director [American]; Dagne Taylor [1981] Finance Director; Robert Burns Wylie [1969] Managing Director

Osprey Maritime Limited
Incorporated: 24 July 1995 *Employees:* 26
Net Worth: £16,559,679 *Total Assets:* £22,426,450
Registered Office: No 9 Portis Fields, Bristol Road, Portishead, Bristol, BS20 6PN
Activities: Sea and coastal freight water transport
Shareholders: Nigel Fletcher; Peter Fletcher
Officers: Lewis Peter Dangerfield, Secretary; Lewis Peter Dangerfield [1988] Director/Chartered Accountant; Nigel Fletcher [1966] Director/Chartered Shipbroker; Peter Fletcher [1969] Director/Shipbroker

Osprey Shipping Limited
Incorporated: 1 August 1979 *Employees:* 26
Net Worth: £4,334,934 *Total Assets:* £9,394,846
Registered Office: No 9 Portis Fields, Bristol Road, Portishead, Bristol, BS20 6PN
Activities: Sea and coastal freight water transport
Parent: Osprey Maritime Limited
Officers: Lewis Peter Dangerfield, Secretary; Lewis Peter Dangerfield [1988] Director/Chartered Accountant; Nigel Fletcher [1966] Director/Chartered Shipbroker; Peter Fletcher [1969] Director/Shipbroker

Osric Finance Limited
Incorporated: 17 October 1962 *Employees:* 2
Net Worth: £2,836,658 *Total Assets:* £3,517,021
Registered Office: 383 Two Mile Hill Road, Kingswood, Bristol, BS15 1AD
Activities: Other letting and operating of own or leased real estate
Major Shareholder: Margaret Josephine Ledbury
Officers: Margaret Joy Eld, Secretary; Margaret Josephine Ledbury [1933] Director/School Teacher

Otter Nurseries Limited
Incorporated: 18 August 1980 *Employees:* 270
Net Worth: £14,063,231 *Total Assets:* £18,664,052
Registered Office: Gosford Road, Ottery St Mary, Devon, EX11 1LZ
Activities: Other retail sale in non-specialised stores
Shareholders: Marilyn Sylvia White; Malcolm John White
Officers: Marilyn Sylvia White, Secretary; Jacqueline Taylor [1967] Director/Buyer; Catherine White [1972] Director/IT Consultant; Malcolm John White [1941] Director/Horticulturalist; Marilyn Sylvia White [1943] Director/Horticulturalist

Otter Nurseries of Plymouth Limited
Incorporated: 26 July 1996 *Employees:* 67
Net Worth: £2,904,469 *Total Assets:* £3,715,908
Registered Office: Garden Centre, Chittleburn Hill, Brixton, Plymouth, PL8 2BL
Activities: Other retail sale in non-specialised stores
Officers: Jacqueline Taylor, Secretary; Jacqueline Taylor [1967] Director; Malcolm John White [1941] Director; Marilyn Sylvia White [1943] Director

Otter Power Limited
Incorporated: 23 September 2010
Net Worth: £5,148,431 *Total Assets:* £12,392,271
Registered Office: Rose Park Farm, Otterham Station, Camelford, Cornwall, PL32 9SW
Activities: Production of electricity
Major Shareholder: Richard Mark Quinn
Officers: Richard Mark Quinn, Secretary; Richard Mark Quinn [1966] Director and Farmer

Outdoor and Cycle Concepts Ltd
Incorporated: 6 June 1997 *Employees:* 2,024
Previous: Cotswold Outdoor Limited
Net Worth Deficit: £24,361,000 *Total Assets:* £123,681,000
Registered Office: Unit 11 Kemble Business Park, Crudwell, Malmesbury, Wilts, SN16 9SH
Activities: Retail sale of sports goods, fishing gear, camping goods, boats and bicycles
Parent: Retail Concepts N.V
Officers: Matthew Paul Smith, Secretary; Gregory Michael Nieuwenhuys [1979] Director [Dutch]; Matthew Paul Smith [1978] Finance Director

Outsauce Financing Limited
Incorporated: 3 December 2004 *Employees:* 27
Net Worth: £475,122 *Total Assets:* £13,242,845
Registered Office: St Georges House, 13-14 Ambrose Street, Cheltenham, Glos, GL50 3LG
Activities: Other business support service activities n.e.c.
Parent: Outsauce Holdings Limited
Officers: Mallory Westfield, Secretary; Richard Anthony Foster [1978] Director; Michael Henry [1963] Finance Director; Mark McAllister [1962] Director

Outsource UK Limited
Incorporated: 13 May 1991 *Employees:* 73
Net Worth: £2,519,374 *Total Assets:* £11,019,584
Registered Office: Churchward House, Fire Fly Avenue, Swindon, Wilts, SN2 2EY
Activities: Other activities of employment placement agencies
Major Shareholder: Paul Jameson
Officers: Sandra Helen Gale, Secretary; Nicholas James Dettmar [1973] Director; Sandra Helen Gale [1961] Director/Accountant; Charles Edward Hughes [1946] Director; Paul Dominic Jameson [1966] Director/Recruitment Consultant

Oval (1173) Limited
Incorporated: 18 February 1997
Net Worth: £12,182,000 *Total Assets:* £33,763,000
Registered Office: Agrii, Station Road, Andoversford, Cheltenham, Glos, GL54 4LZ
Activities: Activities of head offices
Parent: Masstock Group Holdings Limited
Officers: Peter Michael Dunne [1973] Director/Chartered Accountant [Irish]; Spencer Gareth Evans [1970] Director/Chief Financial Officer; Ronan Andrew Hughes [1968] Director [Irish]; Thomas Joseph O'Mahony [1962] Director/Accountant [Irish]; James Marshall Rennie [1957] Director

Oval (259) Limited
Incorporated: 23 July 1986 *Employees:* 61
Net Worth: £15,357,410 *Total Assets:* £17,597,724
Registered Office: Unit 4 Cropmead, Crewkerne, Somerset, TA18 7HQ
Activities: Activities of head offices
Major Shareholder: Melvyn Edward Hazell
Officers: Anita Mosley, Secretary; Melvyn Edward Hazell [1938] Director; Rose Hazell [1935] Director/Secretary

Oval Commercial Investments Limited
Incorporated: 4 March 2008
Net Worth: £630,663 *Total Assets:* £3,669,393
Registered Office: Suite 10, The Oval Office, St Peters Business Park, Cobblers Way, Radstock, Somerset, BA3 3BX
Activities: Other accommodation
Parent: Oval Estates (Bath) Limited
Officers: Alan Geoffrey Broadway, Secretary; Alan Geoffrey Broadway [1960] Director; Dean Broadway [1987] Director

Oval Estates (Bath) Limited
Incorporated: 6 October 1995 *Employees:* 2
Net Worth: £5,117,581 *Total Assets:* £6,168,235
Registered Office: Suite 10, The Oval Office, St Peters Business Park, Cobblers Way, Radstock, Somerset, BA3 3BX
Activities: Development of building projects
Major Shareholder: Alan Geoffrey Broadway
Officers: Alan Geoffrey Broadway, Secretary; Alan Geoffrey Broadway [1960] Managing Director; Dean Broadway [1987] Director

Oval Estates (St Peter's) Limited
Incorporated: 5 February 2016 *Employees:* 2
Net Worth Deficit: £113,874 *Total Assets:* £7,012,298
Registered Office: Suite 10, The Oval Office, St Peter's Business Park, Cobblers Way, Radstock, Somerset, BA3 3BX
Activities: Construction of domestic buildings
Parent: Oval Estates (Bath) Limited
Officers: Dean Broadway, Secretary; Alan Geoffrey Broadway [1960] Director

Ovan Properties Limited
Incorporated: 6 October 2014 *Employees:* 1
Net Worth: £412 *Total Assets:* £4,096,033
Registered Office: 4 Withingham Road, Poole, Dorset, BH13 6BX
Activities: Buying and selling of own real estate
Major Shareholder: Simon Ian Booth
Officers: Darren John Booth [1969] Director; Simon Ian Booth [1973] Director

Overleaf Holdings Limited
Incorporated: 26 January 2016 *Employees:* 32
Net Worth: £2,878,676 *Total Assets:* £4,806,771
Registered Office: Torchlight, Windmill Hill Business Park, Whitehill Way, Swindon, Wilts, SN5 6QR
Activities: Activities of other holding companies n.e.c.
Shareholders: Edward Charles Dickson; Sean Craig Lumley
Officers: Edward Charles Dickson [1974] Director; Sean Craig Lumley [1976] Director

Overton (Gloucester) Limited
Incorporated: 27 July 2004 *Employees:* 144
Net Worth: £7,037,794 *Total Assets:* £13,209,743
Registered Office: Overton Farm, Maisemore, Gloucester, GL2 8HR
Activities: Renting and leasing of construction and civil engineering machinery and equipment
Officers: Paul Ancell, Secretary; Steven John Chaplin [1964] Director

Ovo Electricity Ltd
Incorporated: 25 March 2009
Net Worth: £10,579,000 *Total Assets:* £10,580,000
Registered Office: 1 Rivergate, Temple Quay, Bristol, BS1 6ED
Activities: Other retail sale not in stores, stalls or markets
Parent: Ovo Energy Ltd
Officers: Vincent Casey, Secretary; Vincent Francis Casey [1983] Director; Stephen Fitzpatrick [1977] Director; Adrian James Letts [1973] Director [Australian]; Stephen Thomas Murphy [1956] Director; Niall Fraser Wass [1969] Director/Technology Executive & Advisor

Ovo Energy Ltd
Incorporated: 29 April 2009 *Employees:* 1,099
Net Worth Deficit: £78,543,000 *Total Assets:* £160,291,008
Registered Office: 1 Rivergate, Temple Quay, Bristol, BS1 6ED
Activities: Other retail sale not in stores, stalls or markets
Parent: Ovo Group Ltd
Officers: Vincent Casey, Secretary; Vincent Francis Casey [1983] Director; Stephen Fitzpatrick [1977] Director; Adrian James Letts [1973] Director [Australian]; Stephen Thomas Murphy [1956] Director; Niall Fraser Wass [1969] Director/Technology Executive & Advisor

Ovo Group Ltd
Incorporated: 27 January 2014 *Employees:* 1,263
Net Worth Deficit: £3,526,000 *Total Assets:* £248,979,008
Registered Office: 1 Rivergate, Temple Quay, Bristol, BS1 6ED
Activities: Other retail sale not in stores, stalls or markets
Parent: Imagination Industries Limited
Officers: Vincent Casey, Secretary; Vincent Francis Casey [1983] Director; Stephen James Fitzpatrick [1977] Director; Adrian James Letts [1973] Director [Australian]; Stephen Thomas Murphy [1956] Director; Daniel William Sasaki [1963] Director; Atsushi Suzuki [1972] Director [Japanese]; Niall Fraser Wass [1969] Director/Technology Executive & Advisor

Oxford Infracare Lift (1) Limited
Incorporated: 16 January 2004
Net Worth Deficit: £2,350,000 *Total Assets:* £24,935,000
Registered Office: Challenge House, International Drive, Tewkesbury Business Park, Tewkesbury, Glos, GL20 8UQ
Activities: Other letting and operating of own or leased real estate
Parent: Oxford Infracare Lift Holdings (1) Limited
Officers: Daniel Peter Bevan, Secretary; Paul Simon Andrews [1970] Investment Director; Sarah Ann Beaumont [1982] Director/Chartered Accountant; Richard Darch [1961] Director; Gareth Kenworthy [1972] Director of Finance; Balasingham Ravi Kumar [1975] Director/Investment Manager

Oxford Programs Limited
Incorporated: 8 January 2007 *Employees:* 134
Net Worth: £4,278,992 *Total Assets:* £12,058,122
Registered Office: 14 King Street, Bristol, BS1 4EF
Activities: Cultural education
Major Shareholder: William Robert Humphreys
Officers: Robert Ashton Humphreys, Secretary; George Thomas Humphreys [1983] Director; William Robert Humphreys [1981] Director/Self Employed

Oxford Spires Scaffolding Limited
Incorporated: 12 February 2001 *Employees:* 70
Net Worth: £4,199,220 *Total Assets:* £4,953,302
Registered Office: 1 Long Street, Tetbury, Glos, GL8 8AA
Activities: Scaffold erection
Major Shareholder: Karl Darren Naylon
Officers: Karl Darren Naylon [1968] Director

Oxygen House Group Limited
Incorporated: 23 November 2012
Previous: Oxygen House Investments Limited
Net Worth: £40,931,368 *Total Assets:* £96,406,064
Registered Office: Oxygen House, Grenadier Road, Exeter Business Park, Exeter, Devon, EX1 3LH
Activities: Activities of venture and development capital companies
Major Shareholder: Mark James Dixon
Officers: Roy Barry Bedlow [1968] Director; Dr Mark James Dixon [1969] Director; David Barclay Williamson [1965] Director; Glenn Woodcock [1969] Director

Oxygen House Partners LLP
Incorporated: 8 December 2008 *Employees:* 138
Previous: Andromeda Capital Partners LLP
Net Worth: £50,938,000 *Total Assets:* £162,368,000
Registered Office: Oxygen House, Grenadier Road, Exeter Business Park, Exeter, Devon, EX1 3LH
Officers: Dr Elizabeth Anne Dixon [1970] Member; Dr Mark James Dixon [1969] Member

Oxygen House Properties LLP
Incorporated: 12 December 2014
Net Worth: £12,966,614 *Total Assets:* £13,071,199
Registered Office: Oxygen House, Grenadier Road, Exeter Business Park, Exeter, Devon, EX1 3LH
Officers: David Barclay Williamson [1965] Member

P & B Weir Electrical Limited
Incorporated: 15 December 2016 *Employees:* 39
Net Worth: £64,339 *Total Assets:* £8,029,237
Registered Office: Unit 1 Leafield Trading Estate, Leafield Way, Corsham, Wilts, SN13 9SW
Activities: Manufacture of other electrical equipment
Parent: Novarc UK Limited
Officers: Michael John Credicott [1960] Business Development Director; Geraint Llewellyn-Evans [1958] Managing Director

P & L Properties Limited
Incorporated: 17 March 1997 *Employees:* 1
Net Worth: £1,619,736 *Total Assets:* £5,874,885
Registered Office: Sixth Floor, Dean Park House, 8-10 Dean Park Crescent, Bournemouth, BH1 1HP
Activities: Other letting and operating of own or leased real estate
Officers: Kate Ellen Schofield, Secretary; Peter John Schofield [1946] Director/Chartered Accountant

P & M Group Limited (The)
Incorporated: 4 November 1986 *Employees:* 123
Net Worth: £5,858,740 *Total Assets:* £13,557,083
Registered Office: Unit 3f Llanthony Business Park, Llanthony Road, Gloucester, GL2 5QT
Activities: Other manufacturing n.e.c.
Shareholders: Andrew Peter Moon; Richard Charles Moon
Officers: Andrew Peter Moon [1958] Managing Director; Gareth Edward Ross [1970] Financial Director; Adrian Roger Smith [1963] Director; Anthony Wall [1963] Director

P B Design Holdings Limited
Incorporated: 18 June 2007 *Employees:* 56
Net Worth: £3,298,687 *Total Assets:* £5,249,479
Registered Office: Units 9-10 Hithergreen Industrial Estate, Clevedon, Somerset, BS21 6XT
Activities: Activities of other holding companies n.e.c.
Parent: PB Design Employee Trustee Limited
Officers: Timothy Christopher Philip Broomfield [1954] Director/Accountant; Andrew Hooper [1955] Director/Manager

P G Properties Limited
Incorporated: 19 January 1998 *Employees:* 11
Net Worth: £847,920 *Total Assets:* £9,287,257
Registered Office: Office 1, Number One Bristol, Lewins Mead, Bristol, BS1 2NJ
Activities: Activities of other holding companies n.e.c.
Shareholders: Gregory Alexander Grant; Fiona Elizabeth Bradley
Officers: Fiona Elizabeth Bradley, Secretary; Fiona Elizabeth Bradley [1965] Finance Director; Stuart John Gaiger [1980] Director; Gregory Alexander Grant [1951] Director/Priest

P L H Property Investment Limited
Incorporated: 6 November 1987 *Employees:* 1
Net Worth: £1,903,129 *Total Assets:* £3,867,155
Registered Office: Towngate House, 2-8 Parkstone Road, Poole, Dorset, BH15 2PW
Activities: Other letting and operating of own or leased real estate
Major Shareholder: Carolyn Ann Butland-Beazley
Officers: Carolyn Ann Butland-Beazley, Secretary/Accountant; Carolyn Ann Butland-Beazley [1959] Director/Accountant

P of a Productions Limited
Incorporated: 6 June 1989
Net Worth Deficit: £276,000 *Total Assets:* £91,140,000
Registered Office: The Quadrangle, The Promenade, Cheltenham, Glos, GL50 1PX
Activities: Non-trading company
Shareholders: Lombard Corporate Finance (11) Limited; Royal Bank Leasing Limited
Officers: Stephen Paul Nixon [1970] Director/Bank Official; Keith Damian Pereira [1978] Director/Bank Official

P S J Properties Ltd.
Incorporated: 29 January 2003 *Employees:* 7
Net Worth: £7,789,453 *Total Assets:* £8,892,402
Registered Office: 107 North Street, Martock, Somerset, TA12 6EJ
Activities: Development of building projects
Major Shareholder: Philip Stanley Jessopp
Officers: Philip Stanley Jessopp, Secretary/Motorcycle Dealer; Ann Patricia Jessopp [1946] Director/Secretary; Philip Stanley Jessopp [1955] Director/Motorcycle Dealer

P W Commercial Company Limited
Incorporated: 24 November 1994 *Employees:* 62
Net Worth: £3,258,650 *Total Assets:* £4,825,923
Registered Office: Commerce House, Tewkesbury Road, Cheltenham, Glos, GL51 9AN
Activities: Wholesale of waste and scrap
Shareholders: Donald Henry Robins; Sally Ann Robins; Geoffrey Stuart Robins
Officers: Donald Henry Robins, Secretary; Donald Henry Robins [1953] Director; Geoffrey Robins [1955] Director; Sally Ann Robins [1955] Director

P.O.C. Contractors Limited
Incorporated: 17 January 2012 *Employees:* 47
Net Worth: £4,514,407 *Total Assets:* £8,108,525
Registered Office: Venture House, Calne Road, Lyneham, Chippenham, Wilts, SN15 4PP
Activities: Site preparation
Shareholders: Patrick Joseph O'Connor; Julie O'Connor; Daniel Richard O'Connor
Officers: Patrick Joseph O'Connor [1957] Director [Irish]

P3 Medical Limited
Incorporated: 21 September 1972 *Employees:* 73
Net Worth: £2,851,197 *Total Assets:* £3,576,095
Registered Office: 1 Newbridge Close, Bristol, BS4 4AX
Activities: Manufacture of medical and dental instruments and supplies
Officers: Ian McEvoy [1954] Director; Hasmukh Modi [1950] Director/Pharmacist; Simon Christopher Talbot [1963] Director

PA Performance Limited
Incorporated: 11 July 2002 *Employees:* 5
Net Worth: £5,039,405 *Total Assets:* £5,703,873
Registered Office: Freshford House, Redcliffe Way, Bristol, BS1 6NL
Activities: Non-specialised wholesale trade
Shareholders: Paula Louise Meredith; Richard Austin Meredith
Officers: Paula Louise Meredith, Secretary; Paula Louise Meredith [1966] Director; Richard Austin Meredith [1964] Sales Director

PAC Farms Limited
Incorporated: 5 August 1971
Net Worth: £40,763,524 *Total Assets:* £42,151,860
Registered Office: Coombe House, Ham Spray, Marlborough, Wilts, SN8 3QZ
Activities: Other letting and operating of own or leased real estate
Shareholders: Paul Richard Clarke; Anne Elizabeth Clarke
Officers: Anne Elizabeth Clarke, Secretary; Anne Elizabeth Clarke [1949] Director; Paul Richard Clarke [1949] Director/Bulb Grower/Farmer

Pacific West Foods (UK) Ltd
Incorporated: 29 July 2002 *Employees:* 12
Net Worth: £2,818,613 *Total Assets:* £8,553,860
Registered Office: 3 Willowside Park, Canal Road, Trowbridge, Wilts, BA14 8RH
Activities: Wholesale of other food, including fish, crustaceans and molluscs
Parent: Golden Fresh Sdn Bhd
Officers: Lisa Jayne Semple, Secretary; Geok Bee NG [1954] Director/Senior Commercial Manager [Malaysian]; Mario Eric Rose [1956] Managing Director [Australian]; Hai Earn Saw [1958] Director/Chief Executive Officer [Malaysian]; Lip Teik Saw [1962] Director [Malaysian]

R.N. Padfield & Sons Limited
Incorporated: 11 April 1958 *Employees:* 2
Net Worth: £2,494,361 *Total Assets:* £4,680,714
Registered Office: The Hawthorns, Hawthorns Lane, Corse, Gloucester, GL19 3NY
Activities: Mixed farming
Officers: Hazel Jean Padfield, Secretary/Retired Doctor; Christopher Richard Padfield [1973] Director/Farming; Hazel Jean Padfield [1948] Director/Retired Doctor; Richard William Padfield [1948] Director/Farmer

PADI EMEA Limited
Incorporated: 18 January 1991 *Employees:* 101
Net Worth: £1,331,000 *Total Assets:* £9,476,000
Registered Office: The Pavilions, Bridgwater Road, Bristol, BS13 8AE
Activities: Activities of professional membership organisations
Shareholder: Hansjoerg Wyss
Officers: Chad Michael Kuehn [1978] Director [American]; David Colin Murray [1969] Director/Chartered Accountant; Thomas A. Richardson [1955] Director/Chairman [American]; Mark Peter Spiers [1967] Director/Vice President - Sales & Marketing

Padmanor Investments Limited
Incorporated: 12 July 1978 *Employees:* 6
Net Worth: £30,302,816 *Total Assets:* £56,944,256
Registered Office: The Courtyard, Holt Lodge Farm, Horton, Wimborne, Dorset, BH21 7JN
Activities: Other letting and operating of own or leased real estate
Officers: Hugo Aylesford Burge, Secretary; Laura Whitford, Secretary; Hugo Aylesford Burge [1972] Director/Company Secretary; Oliver Aylesford Burge [1941] Director; Roger Max Davies [1942] Director; Stephen John Davies [1976] Property Director

Paint Services Group Limited
Incorporated: 23 December 1947 *Employees:* 28
Net Worth: £3,533,785 *Total Assets:* £4,992,891
Registered Office: Towngate House, 2-8 Parkstone Road, Poole, Dorset, BH15 2PW
Activities: Non-specialised wholesale trade
Parent: Graytone Limited
Officers: Nicholas Calamada Robins [1969] Finance Director; Geoffrey Colin Warde [1944] Director; Graham Richard Yates [1958] Director

PAL Properties South West Ltd
Incorporated: 24 August 2007
Net Worth: £4,891,498 *Total Assets:* £9,113,761
Registered Office: 69 High Street, Bideford, Devon, EX39 2AT
Activities: Development of building projects
Shareholders: Paul Andrew Jury; L T Tanner Developments Limited
Officers: Simon James Tanner, Secretary; Paul Andrew Jury [1961] Director; Leslie Terence Tanner [1947] Director

Pali Text Society Limited (The)
Incorporated: 7 August 1963 *Employees:* 3
Net Worth: £3,765,331 *Total Assets:* £3,896,238
Registered Office: Old Market Studios, 68 Old Market Street, Bristol, BS2 0EJ
Activities: Book publishing
Officers: Doctor Eivind George Kahrs, Secretary/University Lecturer [Norwegian]; Professor Rupert Gethin [1957] Director/University Lecturer; Doctor Eivind George Kahrs [1952] Director/University Lecturer [Norwegian]

Paligap Limited
Incorporated: 14 February 2001 *Employees:* 28
Net Worth: £797,809 *Total Assets:* £6,389,840
Registered Office: Unit 2 Danbury House, Great Western Business Park, Yate, Bristol, BS37 5NG
Activities: Non-specialised wholesale trade
Major Shareholder: Mark Brinley Aldo Edwards
Officers: Kerry Beecham, Secretary; David Christopher Lane [1969] Managing Director

Palladian Academy Trust
Incorporated: 8 May 2012 *Employees:* 422
Previous: Ralph Allen School
Net Worth: £52,699,092 *Total Assets:* £60,143,200
Registered Office: Ralph Allen School, Claverton Down Road, Combe Down, Bath, BA2 7AD
Activities: General secondary education
Officers: Johanna Mary Marsh, Secretary; Sally Jan Apps [1981] Director/Executive Headteacher; Patricia Jean Black [1950] Director/Head of Initial Teacher Training; Richard Bullard [1961] Director/Headteacher; Russell Adam Franks [1966] Software Director; Wera Benedicta Caecilie Hobhouse [1960] Director/Member of Parliament; Prof Christopher Roy James [1949] Director/University Professor; Caroline Mary Mercer [1947] Director/Retired; Margaret Ann Simmons-Bird [1957] Director of Education Transformation; Christopher James Wheeler [1977] Director/Headmaster; Roger Joseph Martin Whelan [1943] Director; Tim Withers [1962] Director/Principal; Susan Louise Wright [1961] Director/Communications Consultant

Palm Equipment International Limited
Incorporated: 14 March 1986 *Employees:* 46
Net Worth: £4,417,956 *Total Assets:* £4,704,462
Registered Office: Kenn Business Park, Kenn Road, Kenn, Clevedon, Somerset, BS21 6TH
Activities: Manufacture of other wearing apparel and accessories n.e.c.
Officers: Andrew Paul Knight, Secretary; Andrew Paul Knight [1956] Managing Director; Robert Kenneth Slee [1954] Director

Harry J Palmer (Broadstone) Limited
Incorporated: 11 February 1957 *Employees:* 7
Net Worth: £5,081,891 *Total Assets:* £5,186,136
Registered Office: 28 Old Road, Wimborne, Dorset, BH21 1EJ
Activities: Development of building projects
Parent: Harry J. Palmer Holdings Limited
Officers: Peter Harris, Secretary; Colin Palmer [1943] Director/Chairman; May Catherine Palmer [1976] Managing Director

Palmer Care Ltd
Incorporated: 24 February 2003 *Employees:* 15
Net Worth: £3,626,729 *Total Assets:* £3,928,239
Registered Office: 16 Glendinning Avenue, Weymouth, Dorset, DT4 7QF
Activities: Residential care activities for the elderly and disabled
Major Shareholder: Pamela Palmer
Officers: Steven James Palmer, Secretary/Director; Pamela Palmer [1934] Director/Care Worker

J.C. & R.H. Palmer Limited
Incorporated: 17 November 1975 *Employees:* 55
Net Worth: £34,099,496 *Total Assets:* £37,139,700
Registered Office: Old Brewery, Bridport, Dorset, DT6 4JA
Activities: Manufacture of beer
Shareholders: Anthony John Cleeves Palmer; Cleeves William Robert Palmer
Officers: Gary George Adcock, Secretary; Gary George Adcock [1963] Director/Accountant; Anthony John Cleeves Palmer [1951] Brewery Director; Cleeves William Robert Palmer [1962] Brewery Director; Emily Grace Palmer [1991] Director/Banker

Panel Supplies Limited
Incorporated: 12 June 2007 *Employees:* 34
Net Worth: £2,432,003 *Total Assets:* £13,486,084
Registered Office: Sharvatt House, Innsworth Technology Park, Innsworth Lane, Gloucester, GL3 1DL
Activities: Wholesale of wood, construction materials and sanitary equipment
Parent: International Plywood PLC
Officers: Michael Charles Walker, Secretary; Diane Gillian Attwood [1948] Director; Ian David Attwood [1973] Managing Director; Robert Charles Attwood [1977] Director; Andrew James Draper [1967] Financial Director; Scott Conrad Golding [1957] Director; Lorraine Denise O'Brien [1962] Director

Pang Investments Limited
Incorporated: 11 March 1993 *Employees:* 1
Net Worth: £4,298,497 *Total Assets:* £9,753,954
Registered Office: 4 King Square, Bridgwater, Somerset, TA6 3YF
Activities: Development of building projects
Major Shareholder: Anthony Mark Pang
Officers: Michael Anthony Pang, Secretary; Anthony Mark Pang [1962] Director/Property Developer

Pantheon International PLC
Incorporated: 16 July 1987
Previous: Pantheon International Participations PLC.
Net Worth: £1,306,764,032 *Total Assets:* £1,440,920,064
Registered Office: Beaufort House, 51 New North Road, Exeter, Devon, EX4 4EP
Activities: Activities of investment trusts
Officers: Ian Christopher Simon Barby [1945] Director; John Downing Burgess [1950] Director; Sir Laurence Henry Philip Magnus [1955] Director; David Logan Melvin [1960] Director; Susannah Elizabeth McKean Nicklin [1969] Director; John Brian Harold Christopher Anthony Singer [1951] Director; Rhoderick Martin Swire [1951] Director/Investment Manager

Paper Bag Company Holdings Limited
Incorporated: 25 August 2015
Net Worth: £1,300,885 *Total Assets:* £4,017,771
Registered Office: Unit 6 Woodlands Industrial Estate, Eden Vale Road, Westbury, Wilts, BA13 3QS
Activities: Activities of other holding companies n.e.c.
Shareholders: Judith Elizabeth Marling; Jonathan David Marling
Officers: Jonathan David Marling [1973] Director; Judith Elizabeth Marling [1972] Director

Paper Converting Machine Company Limited
Incorporated: 27 December 1962 *Employees:* 43
Net Worth: £8,021,771 *Total Assets:* £9,064,187
Registered Office: 1 Bush Park, Estover, Plymouth, PL6 7RG
Activities: Manufacture of other general-purpose machinery n.e.c.
Officers: Michael John Redwood, Secretary; Sergio Casella [1964] Managing Director [Italian]; Gregory Loran Coonrod [1956] Director/Accountant [American]; Michael John Redwood [1970] Director; Timothy Joseph Sullivan [1957] Director/Executive [American]

Parable Trust Limited
Incorporated: 26 October 2005 *Employees:* 157
Net Worth: £4,619,000 *Total Assets:* £16,539,000
Registered Office: 30 Factory Road, Upton Industrial Estate, Poole, Dorset, BH16 5SL
Activities: Activities of head offices
Officers: Tracey Jayne Shotliff, Secretary; Julian Lionel Andrew Boardman [1960] Director/Chartered Accountant; Robert John Conway [1951] Director/Chartered Accountant; Ralph Albert Hume [1947] Director/Electrical Draughtsman; Mark William Jarvis [1961] Director; Andrew David Long [1981] Director/Chartered Accountant; Rev Victor Eduardo Lorenzo Moreno [1962] Director/Minister Business Advisor [Spanish]; Tracey Jayne Shotliff [1962] Director/Finance & HR Manager

Paradigm (Sheffield BSF) Holdings Limited
Incorporated: 6 February 2007
Net Worth Deficit: £18,370,000 *Total Assets:* £72,331,000
Registered Office: Third Floor, Broad Quay House, Prince Street, Bristol, BS1 4DJ
Activities: Activities of head offices
Shareholders: Infrastructure Investments Holdings Limited; Infrared Infrastructure Yield Holdings Limited
Officers: Mark Geoffrey David Holden [1957] Director

Paradigm (Sheffield BSF) Limited
Incorporated: 6 February 2007
Net Worth Deficit: £18,370,000 *Total Assets:* £72,331,000
Registered Office: Third Floor, Broad Quay House, Prince Street, Bristol, BS1 4DJ
Activities: Other business support service activities n.e.c.
Parent: Paradigm (Sheffield BSF) Holdings Limited
Officers: Mark Geoffrey David Holden [1957] Director

Paradigm Norton Financial Planning Limited
Incorporated: 22 May 2001 *Employees:* 48
Net Worth: £4,090,282 *Total Assets:* £9,428,180
Registered Office: Paradigm House, MacRae Road, Ham Green, Bristol, BS20 0DD
Activities: Activities auxiliary to financial intermediation n.e.c.
Parent: Paradigm Norton Holdings Limited
Officers: John Peter Bigwood, Secretary; Richard John Child [1956] Director/Financial Advisor; Matthew Paul Fowler [1977] Director/Operations Manager; Kevin John Gregory [1957] Director; Barry David Horner [1960] Managing Director; William John Pratt [1972] Director

Paragon Education & Skills Limited
Incorporated: 18 March 1998 *Employees:* 219
Net Worth: £2,911,717 *Total Assets:* £4,380,450
Registered Office: Bournemouth Technology Centre, Station Approach, Ashley Road, Bournemouth, BH1 4NB
Activities: Technical and vocational secondary education
Parent: Paragon Education & Skills Group Limited
Officers: Mark David Botha [1976] Director/Chief Executive; David Hills [1970] Finance Director

Paramount 21 Limited
Incorporated: 13 September 1988 *Employees:* 118
Net Worth: £3,136,623 *Total Assets:* £7,208,866
Registered Office: Old Newton Road, Heathfield, Newton Abbot, Devon, TQ12 6RA
Activities: Manufacture of other food products n.e.c.
Shareholders: Alison Bernadette Hannaford; Paul Hannaford
Officers: Paul Hannaford, Secretary; Alison Bernadette Hannaford [1961] Director/Chairman; Jacob Devon Hannaford [1990] Director; Joshua George Hannaford [1987] Purchasing Director; Paul Hannaford [1957] Director; Stephen Lamont [1964] Production Director; Jonathan Edward Phillips [1969] Managing Director; Suzanne Thomson [1959] Sales Director; Philip James Wilkinson OBE [1953] Director

Parham Development Limited
Incorporated: 14 September 1988
Net Worth: £7,178,718 *Total Assets:* £18,836,286
Registered Office: Unity Chambers, 34 High East Street, Dorchester, DT1 1HA
Activities: Development of building projects
Parent: Parham Holdings Limited
Officers: Jeremy Ryton Drax, Secretary; Lisa Helen Catford [1963] Director; Peter Stephen Dove [1962] Director; Edward Quintin Drax [1971] Director/Property Investor; Jeremy Ryton Drax [1960] Director

Parham Holdings Limited
Incorporated: 20 September 1995 *Employees:* 6
Net Worth: £16,022,710 *Total Assets:* £53,914,308
Registered Office: Unity Chambers, 34 High East Street, Dorchester, DT1 1HA
Activities: Activities of head offices
Parent: Beaulieu Property Management Limited
Officers: Jeremy Ryton Drax, Secretary; Lisa Helen Catford [1963] Director; Peter Stephen Dove [1962] Director; Edward Quintin Drax [1971] Director/Property Investor; Jeremy Ryton Drax [1960] Director

Parham Investment Limited
Incorporated: 15 May 1989
Net Worth: £55,455,568 *Total Assets:* £81,370,448
Registered Office: Unity Chambers, 34 High East Street, Dorchester, DT1 1HA
Activities: Development of building projects
Parent: Parham Holdings Limited
Officers: Jeremy Ryton Drax, Secretary/Director; Lisa Helen Catford [1963] Director; Peter Stephen Dove [1962] Director; Edward Quintin Drax [1971] Director/Property Investor; Jeremy Ryton Drax [1960] Director

Paris Presents UK Limited
Incorporated: 3 April 2012 *Employees:* 5
Net Worth: £14,275,656 *Total Assets:* £20,089,284
Registered Office: 11th Floor, Whitefriars, Lewins Mead, Bristol, BS1 2NT
Activities: Hairdressing and other beauty treatment
Officers: William George [1961] Director/President [American]; Patrick O'Brien [1958] Director [American]; Douglas Richcreek [1966] Director/CFO and VP of Finance [American]; Robert W Wiltz [1955] Director/Chief Customer Officer [American]

The Park Academies Trust
Incorporated: 5 July 2011 *Employees:* 165
Previous: The Lydiard Park Academy
Net Worth: £10,282,998 *Total Assets:* £11,271,618
Registered Office: The Lydiard Park Academy, Grange Park Way, Grange Park, Swindon, Wilts, SN5 6HN
Activities: General secondary education
Officers: Joanne Brown, Secretary; David John Allen [1972] Director/Businessman; Louise Suzanne Bouteiller [1968] Director/Businesswoman; Frederick John Child [1949] Director/Retired; Alastair Ian Dixon-Patterson [1970] Director of Finance and Operations; Mark Anthony Edwards [1969] Director/Manager; Corinna Jayne Mazzotta [1972] Director; Scott James Robins [1992] Director/Legal Adviser; Clive Ian Zimmerman [1965] Director/Executive Principal

Park Garden Centre Limited
Incorporated: 6 April 1990 *Employees:* 92
Net Worth: £3,653,000 *Total Assets:* £7,001,000
Registered Office: Almondsbury Garden Centre, Over Lane, Almondsbury, Bristol, BS32 4BP
Activities: Retail sale of flowers, plants, seeds, fertilizers, pet animals and pet food in specialised stores
Major Shareholder: Philip John Hodges
Officers: Philip John Hodges, Secretary; Gregory Keith Cairns [1945] Director/Chartered Accountant; Alan Keith Hodges [1937] Director/Garden Centre Proprietor; Philip John Hodges [1970] Managing Director

Park Group South West Limited
Incorporated: 16 March 1989 *Employees:* 34
Net Worth: £3,338,921 *Total Assets:* £6,054,839
Registered Office: Michael House, Castle Street, Exeter, Devon, EX4 3LQ
Activities: Printing n.e.c.
Parent: PGH (South West) Limited
Officers: Elizabeth Jane Marshall, Secretary/Design Director; Edward James Marshall [1974] Sales Director; Elizabeth Jane Marshall [1972] Design Director; Kathleen Anne Marshall [1944] Director/Retail Manager

Park Home Life Limited
Incorporated: 2 April 1963 *Employees:* 14
Previous: Pine View Parks Limited
Net Worth: £5,961,807 *Total Assets:* £9,524,606
Registered Office: Park Office, Blunsdon Abbey Park, Blunsdon St Andrew, Swindon, Wilts, SN25 2DU
Activities: Other business support service activities n.e.c.
Parent: Sea Pickle Limited
Officers: Adam Joseph Griffin, Secretary; Adam Joseph Griffin [1971] Director; Kate Louise Griffin [1970] Director

Park Home Management Ltd
Incorporated: 13 January 2003 *Employees:* 1
Net Worth: £2,399,748 *Total Assets:* £4,148,175
Registered Office: Royal Mews, St Georges Place, Cheltenham, Glos, GL50 3PQ
Activities: Other letting and operating of own or leased real estate
Major Shareholder: Gary Paul Newman
Officers: Karen Newman, Secretary; Gary Paul Newman [1967] Director/Mobile Homes Manager

Parker Knoll Upholstery Limited
Incorporated: 4 July 1973 *Employees:* 259
Net Worth: £5,882,895 *Total Assets:* £12,291,866
Registered Office: 1 Hampton Park West, Melksham, Wilts, SN12 6GU
Activities: Manufacture of other furniture
Parent: Sofa Brands International Limited
Officers: Emma Victoria Jones, Secretary/Accountant; Donna Louise Bellingham [1966] Director; Gareth Morgan Brown [1961] Director; Christopher Anthony Everist [1966] Director; Ciaran Andrew McMahon [1968] Director [Irish]; Andrew Miles [1962] Director; Ian Oliver [1963] Director; Thomas White [1972] Director

Parkfield Education Limited
Incorporated: 20 May 2011 *Employees:* 55
Net Worth: £15,087,230 *Total Assets:* £16,828,440
Registered Office: Parley Lane, Hurn, Christchurch, Dorset, BH23 6DF
Activities: Primary education
Shareholder: Reverend Matthew Anthony Clayton
Officers: Maria Nikolaevna Cherskova [1977] Director/Compliance; Lynda Jean Clarke [1950] Director/Retired Education Inspector; Matthew Livingston Clarkson [1975] Director/Finance; Catherine Violet Shaw [1951] Director; Nicola Ann Shawyer [1971] Director

Parkham Farms Limited
Incorporated: 2 March 1988 *Employees:* 48
Net Worth: £10,562,414 *Total Assets:* £15,652,440
Registered Office: St John's House, Castle Street, Taunton, Somerset, TA1 4AY
Activities: Butter and cheese production
Major Shareholder: Peter Anthony Willes
Officers: Peter Anthony Willes, Secretary; Emma Louise Beer [1973] Director/Quality Assurance Officer; Sarah Jean Berry [1967] Director/Company Secretary; Peter Anthony Willes [1964] Director/Businessman

Parkhouse Hotel (Shifnal) Limited
Incorporated: 19 November 2014
Net Worth: £635,656 *Total Assets:* £3,678,085
Registered Office: Grosvenor House, 1 New Road, Brixham, Devon, TQ5 8LZ
Activities: Hotels and similar accommodation
Officers: Andrew Peter Trott [1969] Director

Parking Glasgow Limited
Incorporated: 11 September 2002
Previous: Impregilo Parking (Glasgow) Limited
Net Worth Deficit: £5,272,000 *Total Assets:* £7,749,000
Registered Office: Third Floor, Broad Quay House, Prince Street, Bristol, BS1 4DJ
Activities: Development of building projects
Parent: Semperian (Glasgow) Limited
Officers: Richard Little [1979] Investment Director; Kenneth Andrew McLellan [1961] Regional Project Director; Alan Campbell Ritchie [1967] Director

Parkside (Barnstaple) Limited
Incorporated: 30 October 1991 *Employees:* 40
Net Worth: £1,486,812 *Total Assets:* £4,474,816
Registered Office: Newport Road, Barnstaple, Devon, EX32 9BA
Activities: Sale of new cars and light motor vehicles
Shareholder: Susan Williams
Officers: Patrick James Squire, Secretary; Wendy Elizabeth Bassom [1937] Director; Ann Veronica Lewis [1932] Director; David John Squire [1940] Director; Patrick James Squire [1945] Director; Nicholas Charles Williams [1964] Director/Chartered Accountant; Susan Williams [1939] Director; Andrew John Witherington [1962] Director

Parkside Holdings Limited
Incorporated: 28 August 2003 *Employees:* 180
Net Worth: £2,094,898 *Total Assets:* £8,815,840
Registered Office: Park House, Church Lane, St George, Bristol, BS5 7AG
Activities: Activities of construction holding companies
Major Shareholder: Andrew Dowden
Officers: Matthew Browne [1968] Director/Technical Manager; Andrew Dowden [1943] Director; Christopher Paul Dowden [1968] Construction Director; Thomas David Hurford [1973] Director/Surveyor; John Michael Stafford [1957] Director

Parkstone Grammar School Trust
Incorporated: 6 December 2010 *Employees:* 202
Net Worth: £25,931,320 *Total Assets:* £28,569,344
Registered Office: Parkstone Grammar School, Sopers Lane, Poole, Dorset, BH17 7EP
Activities: General secondary education
Officers: Christine Bailey [1947] Director/Retired; Dr Suzie Jane Baverstock [1961] Director/Retired; Christopher Benn [1969] Director/Accountant; Simon John Bowden [1959] Director; Andrew David Haitly Burn [1949] Director/Arts Administrator; Kirsty Ann Cooper [1978] Director/Paraplanning; Simon Paul Dunk [1965] Director/Army Officer; David Mark Hallsworth [1966] Director/Headteacher; Matthew John Hosier [1970] Director/Clergyman; Simon James Huxter [1974] Director; Alison Nicola McMullen [1961] Director/HR Manager; Samantha Pope [1966] Director/Nurse; Ann Simmons [1941] Director/Retired Teacher; Dawn Stark [1965] Director/Insurance Administrator; John Matthew Coles Waters [1966] Director/Teacher; Michael Simon Whitaker [1956] Director/Retired; Julia Jane Wilkinson [1971] Director/Head of Careers; Trevor Howard Willis [1983] Director/Teacher; Robert Peter Wilsher [1966] Director/Accountant

Parkview Gloucester Ltd
Incorporated: 13 July 2012 *Employees:* 58
Previous: BBMAR Limited
Net Worth: £646,289 *Total Assets:* £10,108,939
Registered Office: Q1 Quadrant Way, Hardwicke, Gloucester, GL2 2RN
Activities: Residential nursing care facilities
Shareholders: Benjamin St John White; Markey Developments LLP
Officers: Ian Kimberley [1957] Director; Anthony Joseph Markey [1964] Director; Paul Francis Markey [1960] Director/Chartered Accountant; William Stuart Charles Mellstrom [1968] Director/Chartered Surveyor

The Parkway Hotel and Spa Limited
Incorporated: 20 July 1983 *Employees:* 121
Net Worth: £5,071,294 *Total Assets:* £6,006,972
Registered Office: Minerva House, Lower Bristol Road, Bath, BA2 9ER
Activities: Hotels and similar accommodation
Parent: Havana West Limited
Officers: Joseph Keefe, Secretary; Lucille Lanette de Savary [1954] Director; Ian David Solkin [1966] Director/Hotelier

Parmenion Capital Partners LLP
Incorporated: 7 September 2006 *Employees:* 90
Net Worth: £6,360,109 *Total Assets:* £14,103,110
Registered Office: 2 College Square, Anchor Road, Bristol, BS1 5UE

Parragon Books Limited
Incorporated: 9 May 1988 *Employees:* 202
Net Worth: £8,500,000 *Total Assets:* £39,594,000
Registered Office: c/o TLT LLP, One Redcliff Street, Bristol, BS1 6TP
Activities: Book publishing
Parent: Parragon Publishing Limited
Officers: Andrew Francis Thomson [1942] Director/Publisher; David Howard Eric Thomson [1973] CEO/Director

Parragon Publishing Limited
Incorporated: 12 August 1998
Net Worth: £7,658,000 *Total Assets:* £18,919,000
Registered Office: c/o TLT LLP, One Redcliff Street, Bristol, BS1 6TP
Activities: Activities of other holding companies n.e.c.
Parent: D.C. Thomson Consumer Products Limited
Officers: Andrew Francis Thomson [1942] Director; Christopher Harold William Thomson [1950] Director/Publisher; David Howard Eric Thomson [1973] Director/Chief Operating Officer

Parris Tractors Limited
Incorporated: 4 April 2014 *Employees:* 6
Net Worth: £1,590,016 *Total Assets:* £9,088,634
Registered Office: Ash House, Cook Way, Bindon Road, Taunton, Somerset, TA2 6BJ
Activities: Wholesale of agricultural machinery, equipment and supplies
Shareholders: Alan Peter Parris; Richard Alan John Parris
Officers: Alan Peter Parris [1936] Director/Farmer; Philippa Parris [1967] Director/Company Administration; Richard Alan John Parris [1965] Director/Farming; Sylvia Mary Parris [1937] Director/Farming

Walter C Parson Limited
Incorporated: 2 April 1987 *Employees:* 70
Net Worth: £3,864,908 *Total Assets:* £5,630,131
Registered Office: 51 North Hill, Plymouth, PL4 8HZ
Activities: Funeral and related activities
Shareholders: Graham Philip May; Stephen John Ware
Officers: Graham Philip May [1947] Director; David John Parslow [1958] Director; John Stephen Ware [1991] Director; Stephen John Ware [1959] Director

Parsons and Joyce Contractors Limited
Incorporated: 31 October 1978 *Employees:* 14
Net Worth: £2,185,852 *Total Assets:* £3,890,872
Registered Office: 44 Ashley Road, Poole, Dorset, BH14 9BN
Activities: Construction of domestic buildings
Major Shareholder: Mark Peter Parsons
Officers: Amanda Elizabeth Williams, Secretary; Mark Peter Parsons [1966] Director/Builder; Amanda Elizabeth Williams [1972] Director

Parsons Construction Limited
Incorporated: 30 October 1991
Net Worth: £4,832,513 *Total Assets:* £8,730,191
Registered Office: Rothman Pantall LLP, 10 St Ann Street, Salisbury, Wilts, SP1 2DN
Activities: Construction of commercial buildings
Major Shareholder: Steve Parsons
Officers: Gary Vincent, Secretary; Steven John Parsons [1962] Director/Plastering Contractor

Parsons Nationwide Distribution Ltd.
Incorporated: 7 April 1999 *Employees:* 63
Net Worth: £795,660 *Total Assets:* £3,909,133
Registered Office: Redwoods, 2 Clyst Works, Clyst Road, Topsham, Exeter, Devon, EX3 0DB
Activities: Freight transport by road
Major Shareholder: Noreen Anne Hoskin
Officers: Keith Albert Hoskin, Secretary; Noreen Anne Hoskin [1943] Director/Business Administrator

Parsons Peebles Service Limited
Incorporated: 11 January 1950 *Employees:* 196
Previous: Anstee & Ware Limited
Net Worth: £1,913,000 *Total Assets:* £11,404,000
Registered Office: St Georges Industrial Estate, St Andrews Road, Avonmouth, Bristol, BS11 9HS
Activities: Manufacture of other electrical equipment
Officers: Ashleigh Joanne Greenan [1979] Director; Gareth Lloyd Roberts [1962] Director

Partington Engineering Limited
Incorporated: 2 October 2002 *Employees:* 28
Net Worth: £3,530,952 *Total Assets:* £4,633,068
Registered Office: Holly Hill Road, Forest Vale Industrial Estate, Cinderford, Glos, GL1 2YA
Activities: Other manufacturing n.e.c.
Major Shareholder: Brian Philip Jones
Officers: James Damian Grundy [1973] Director; Brian Philip Jones [1968] Director/Manager

Partner Logistics Gloucester Limited
Incorporated: 19 July 2007 *Employees:* 28
Net Worth Deficit: £7,669,285 *Total Assets:* £23,732,048
Registered Office: Partner Logistics UK, Unilever Site, Corinium Avenue, Barnwood, Gloucester, GL4 3BW
Activities: Other business support service activities n.e.c.
Officers: Duco Robert Gijsbert Buijze [1962] Director/Netherlands [Dutch]; Jason Eugene Burnett [1976] Director [American]; Michael Joseph McClendon [1965] Director [American]; Johannes Albrecht Poelman [1973] Director [Dutch]

Partner Logistics Wisbech Limited
Incorporated: 19 July 2007 *Employees:* 38
Net Worth Deficit: £11,412,794 *Total Assets:* £31,302,264
Registered Office: Partner Logistics, Unilever Site, Corinium Avenue, Barnwood, Gloucester, GL4 3BW
Activities: Other business support service activities n.e.c.
Officers: Duco Robert Gijsbert Buijze [1962] Director [Dutch]; Jason Eugene Burnett [1976] Director [American]; Michael Joseph McClendon [1965] Director [American]; Johannes Albrecht Poelman [1973] Director [Dutch]

Pastaking (UK) Limited
Incorporated: 20 April 1994 *Employees:* 60
Net Worth: £4,580,108 *Total Assets:* £6,634,283
Registered Office: Plantation House, Milber Trading Estate, Newton Abbot, Devon, TQ12 4SG
Activities: Manufacture of other food products n.e.c.
Parent: NBGI Private Equity Fund 2 LLP
Officers: Gavin Eliot Cox [1968] Director

Pastaking Holdings Limited
Incorporated: 21 March 2006
Net Worth: £1,895,966 *Total Assets:* £5,515,670
Registered Office: Plantation House, Milber Industrial Estate, Newton Abbot, Devon, TQ12 4SG
Activities: Activities of head offices
Parent: PK Food Concepts Ltd
Officers: Gavin Eliot Cox [1968] Director

Patalex II Productions Limited
Incorporated: 6 June 1989
Net Worth: £1,003,000 *Total Assets:* £8,297,000
Registered Office: The Quadrangle, The Promenade, Cheltenham, Glos, GL50 1PX
Activities: Non-trading company
Parent: Royal Bank Leasing Limited
Officers: Stephen Paul Nixon [1970] Director/Bank Official; Keith Damian Pereira [1978] Director/Bank Official

Patalex III Productions Limited
Incorporated: 5 December 2003
Net Worth: £1,047,000 *Total Assets:* £24,738,000
Registered Office: The Quadrangle, The Promenade, Cheltenham, Glos, GL50 1PX
Activities: Financial leasing
Parent: P of a Productions Limited
Officers: Stephen Paul Nixon [1970] Director/Bank Official; Keith Damian Pereira [1978] Director/Bank Official

Patalex Productions Limited
Incorporated: 31 August 1987
Net Worth: £756,000 *Total Assets:* £21,020,000
Registered Office: The Quadrangle, The Promenade, Cheltenham, Glos, GL50 1PX
Activities: Financial leasing
Parent: Royal Bank Leasing Limited
Officers: Stephen Paul Nixon [1970] Director/Bank Official; Keith Damian Pereira [1978] Director/Bank Official

Patalex V Productions Limited
Incorporated: 15 May 2002
Net Worth: £1,015,000 *Total Assets:* £3,957,000
Registered Office: The Quadrangle, The Promenade, Cheltenham, Glos, GL50 1PX
Activities: Financial leasing
Parent: Royal Bank Leasing Limited
Officers: Stephen Paul Nixon [1970] Director/Bank Official; Keith Damian Pereira [1978] Director/Bank Official

Pate's Grammar School
Incorporated: 8 September 2010 *Employees:* 37
Net Worth: £30,614,680 *Total Assets:* £32,610,388
Registered Office: Pate's Grammar School, Princess Elizabeth Way, Cheltenham, Glos, GL51 0HG
Activities: General secondary education
Officers: Stephen Frederick Locke, Secretary; Warwick Ainsworth-Parker [1972] Managing Director (Estate Agency); Guy Bailey Bradshaw [1962] Director/Dentist; Anne Dickinson [1953] Director/Exams Officer; Jennifer Dye [1964] Director/University Academic; Russel Bryan Ellicott [1970] Director/Headteacher; Raymond Fish [1962] Director/Management Consultant; Rebecca Jayne Flaxman [1976] Director/HR Consultant; William Head [1982] Director/Teacher; Carolyn Horrocks [1969] Director; Graeme May [1969] Director/Teacher; Dr Helen Dale Moore [1970] Director/Fellow & Tutor, Associate Professor in English; Shirley Park [1963] Director/Development Manager in School

Patel Brothers Limited
Incorporated: 31 August 1987
Net Worth: £8,682,527 *Total Assets:* £19,614,156
Registered Office: The Weavers Shop, Eastern Avenue, Gloucester, GL4 3BY
Activities: Other letting and operating of own or leased real estate
Officers: Yakub Patel, Secretary; Ibrahim Patel [1954] Director/Carpet Retailer; Yakub Patel [1948] Director/Carpet Retailer; Yusuf Patel [1957] Director/Carpet Retailer

Patheon UK Limited
Incorporated: 29 April 1999 *Employees:* 312
Net Worth: £31,208,536 *Total Assets:* £130,475,168
Registered Office: Kingfisher Drive, Swindon, Wilts, SN3 5BZ
Activities: Manufacture of basic pharmaceutical products
Parent: Thermo Fisher Scientific Inc.
Officers: Nicholas Roger Clive Plummer, Secretary; Luca Andretta [1974] Director [Italian]; Nicholas Roger Clive Plummer [1970] Director and Company Secretary; Andrew Robinson [1972] Finance Director

Pathfinder Park Homes Holdings Limited
Incorporated: 4 March 2016 *Employees:* 121
Net Worth Deficit: £225,899 *Total Assets:* £8,617,341
Registered Office: Cavalier Road, Heathfield, Newton Abbot, Devon, TQ12 6FJ
Activities: Other service activities n.e.c.
Shareholders: Michael Anthony Wills; Bruce Graeme MacDonald
Officers: Mark Alistair Champion [1973] Director; Martin Frank Hember [1956] Director; John Brian Hoyle [1949] Director; Bruce Graeme MacDonald [1965] Managing Director; Michael Anthony Wills [1956] Director

Pathfinder Park Homes Limited
Incorporated: 1 March 1993 *Employees:* 121
Net Worth: £3,432,981 *Total Assets:* £6,129,578
Registered Office: Cavalier Road, Heathfield, Newton Abbot, Devon, TQ12 6FJ
Activities: Other service activities n.e.c.
Parent: Pathfinder Park Homes Holdings Limited
Officers: John Hoyle, Secretary; Mark Alistair Champion [1973] Finance Director; Martin Frank Hember [1956] Director/General Manager; John Brian Hoyle [1949] Director; Bruce Graeme MacDonald [1965] Managing Director; Michael Anthony Wills [1956] Director

Patrico Limited
Incorporated: 18 May 1983 *Employees:* 22
Net Worth: £2,161,858 *Total Assets:* £4,016,097
Registered Office: Northway Lodge, Newtown Industrial Estate, Northway Lane, Tewkesbury, Glos, GL20 8JG
Activities: Non-specialised wholesale trade
Shareholders: Valerie Ann Lanchbury; Robert John Lanchbury
Officers: Robert John Lanchbury, Secretary; John Herbert [1965] Director/General Manager; Robert John Lanchbury [1950] Director/Sales Representative

Pattemore's Transport (Crewkerne) Limited
Incorporated: 21 April 1959 *Employees:* 110
Net Worth: £2,521,249 *Total Assets:* £6,942,074
Registered Office: Mosterton Road, Misterton, Crewkerne, Somerset, TA18 8NT
Activities: Liquid milk and cream production
Shareholder: Stephen George Pattemore
Officers: Nicola Sarah Hill, Secretary; Nicola Sarah Hill [1969] Finance Director; Alex William Pattemore [1971] Transport Director; Geoffrey William Pattemore [1945] Director/Haulage Contractor; Shaun Stephen Pattemore [1974] Director; Stephen George Pattemore [1952] Director/Haulage Contractor

Pattersons (Bristol) Limited
Incorporated: 10 April 1973 *Employees:* 124
Net Worth: £2,834,786 *Total Assets:* £7,080,683
Registered Office: Pattersons, Winterstoke Road, Bristol, BS3 2NS
Activities: Wholesale of other intermediate products
Officers: Karl Blackford [1970] Group Commercial Director; Richard Briere [1973] Finance Director; Christopher John Patterson [1959] Director/Ironmonger; John Bryan Patterson [1930] Director/Ironmonger; Sheila Gail Annabel Patterson [1960] Director/Sales Executive; Mark Silcocks [1959] Director/Sales

Pattersons (Holdings) Limited
Incorporated: 1 August 2000 *Employees:* 134
Net Worth: £4,916,346 *Total Assets:* £11,597,498
Registered Office: Pattersons, Winterstoke Road, Bristol, BS3 2NS
Activities: Activities of head offices
Major Shareholder: Christopher John Patterson
Officers: Sheila Gail Annabel Patterson, Secretary; Karl Michael Blackford [1970] Group Commercial Director; Richard Briere [1973] Finance Director; Christopher John Patterson [1959] Director; John Bryan Patterson [1930] Director; Sheila Gail Annabel Patterson [1960] Director

Paull & Company Limited
Incorporated: 26 April 1906 *Employees:* 20
Net Worth: £6,336,709 *Total Assets:* £6,799,348
Registered Office: Coat Road, Martock, Somerset, TA12 6EX
Activities: Development of building projects
Shareholders: Philip Craig Paull; Fiona Mary Paull
Officers: Kate Louise Vasey, Secretary/Advertising Creative; Chloe Michelle Paull [1984] Director/Retail Assistant; Douglas Chard Paull [1980] Director/Junior Surveyor; Fiona Mary Paull [1955] Director/Retail Assistant; James Henry Paull [1987] Director/Financial Regulator; Philip Craig Paull [1952] Managing Director; Kate Louise Vasey [1980] Director/Advertising Creative

Pavey Group Holdings (UK) Limited
Incorporated: 21 April 2017
Net Worth: £6,238,610 *Total Assets:* £7,605,299
Registered Office: 50 The Terrace, Torquay, Devon, TQ1 1DD
Activities: Activities of other holding companies n.e.c.
Officers: Alistair Charles Peel, Secretary; Michael Peter Rea [1966] Director; Charles Douglas Knowles Scott [1973] Director

PB Design and Developments Limited
Incorporated: 26 June 1979 *Employees:* 56
Net Worth: £4,329,689 *Total Assets:* £6,280,481
Registered Office: Units 9-10 Hither Green Industrial Estate, Clevedon, Bristol, BS21 6XT
Activities: Manufacture of other electrical equipment
Parent: PB Design Holdings Limited
Officers: Timothy Christopher Philip Broomfield, Secretary/Accountant; Timothy Christopher Philip Broomfield [1954] Director; Mark Crocker [1966] Director/Manager; Scott Generald Edsall [1973] Sales Director [American]; Andrew Hooper [1955] Director/Manager

PC Property Holdings Limited
Incorporated: 21 March 2000
Net Worth: £2,429,426 *Total Assets:* £4,271,100
Registered Office: 23a Church Road, Poole, Dorset, BH14 8UF
Activities: Other letting and operating of own or leased real estate
Parent: PC Asset Investments Ltd
Officers: Stephen John Smith, Secretary; Donald Joseph McCarthy [1958] Director; David Daniel Morris [1969] Director

PCBL Limited
Incorporated: 28 March 2003 *Employees:* 102
Net Worth: £4,649,973 *Total Assets:* £13,044,554
Registered Office: Pearce House, Brannam Crescent, Roundswell Business Park, Barnstaple, Devon, EX31 3TD
Activities: Development of building projects
Shareholder: David Michael Parsons
Officers: Richard Andrew Bevan [1958] Director/Contracts Manager; Richard Claude Jeffs [1971] Director/Financial Controller; Paul Spencer Knox [1966] Director/Housing Manager; David Michael Parsons [1956] Director

PCP 2014 Limited
Incorporated: 24 April 2014
Net Worth Deficit: £178,085 *Total Assets:* £8,317,974
Registered Office: 3 Fry's Walk, Shepton Mallet, Somerset, BA4 5WT
Activities: Other letting and operating of own or leased real estate
Officers: Graham John Anthony Dolan, Secretary; Chung Hau [1979] Director; Deepak Jalan [1974] Director

PDF Erection Services Limited
Incorporated: 30 November 1998
Net Worth: £3,053,861 *Total Assets:* £3,850,808
Registered Office: Stafford House, 10 Prince of Wales Road, Dorchester, DT1 1PW
Activities: Construction of commercial buildings
Shareholders: Paul David Frampton; Susan Elizabeth May Frampton
Officers: Susan Elizabeth May Frampton, Secretary/Steel Erector; Paul David Frampton [1966] Director/Steel Erector; Susan Elizabeth May Frampton [1971] Director/Steel Erector

PDQ Airspares Limited
Incorporated: 1 August 1990 *Employees:* 57
Net Worth: £2,101,211 *Total Assets:* £6,534,375
Registered Office: The Office, Redbrook, Ringwood Road, Fordingbridge, Hants, SP6 2ET
Activities: Manufacture of air and spacecraft and related machinery
Parent: PDQ Group Limited
Officers: Nicholas Douglas Lewis [1969] Director; Mauricio Perini [1971] Director/Chief Financial Officer [American]; Scott Michael Tucker [1971] Director [American]

PDQ Group Limited
Incorporated: 14 June 2002 *Employees:* 63
Net Worth: £5,696,070 *Total Assets:* £8,534,123
Registered Office: The Office, Redbrook, Fordingbridge, Hants, SP6 2ET
Activities: Manufacture of air and spacecraft and related machinery
Officers: Nicholas Douglas Lewis [1969] Director; Mauricio Perini [1971] Director/Chief Financial Officer [American]; Scott Michael Tucker [1971] Director [American]

J F Pearce & Sons Limited
Incorporated: 23 March 2003 *Employees:* 93
Net Worth: £5,864,872 *Total Assets:* £8,997,972
Registered Office: Unit 1 Leighton Business Park, Wanstrow, Shepton Mallet, Somerset, BA4 4FX
Activities: Freight transport by road
Shareholders: Joseph Charles Pearce; John Robert Pearce; James Stuart Pearce
Officers: Joseph Charles Pearce, Secretary/Haulier; James Stuart Pearce [1965] Director/Haulier; John Robert Pearce [1957] Director/Haulier; Joseph Charles Pearce [1967] Director/Haulier

Pearce Construction (Barnstaple) Limited
Incorporated: 10 April 1946 *Employees:* 102
Net Worth: £4,632,388 *Total Assets:* £13,044,554
Registered Office: Pearce House, Brannam Crescent, Roundswell Business Park, Barnstaple, Devon, EX31 3TD
Activities: Development of building projects
Parent: PCBL Limited
Officers: Richard Andrew Bevan [1958] Director; Mark Robert Davis [1967] Director; Nicholas John Hopkins [1976] Director; Richard Claude Jeffs [1971] Director; Paul Spencer Knox [1966] Director; David Michael Parsons [1956] Director

Pearce Seeds (Holdings) Limited
Incorporated: 28 October 1977 *Employees:* 39
Net Worth: £951,636 *Total Assets:* £5,164,415
Registered Office: Rosedown, Sandford Orcas, Sherborne, Dorset, DT9 4SX
Activities: Agents selling agricultural raw materials, livestock, textile raw materials and semi-finished goods
Shareholders: Christine Marion Tuffin; Kenneth Leslie Tuffin
Officers: Christine Marion Tuffin, Secretary/Accounts; Timothy Arnold Henry Rutter [1965] Director; Christine Marion Tuffin [1957] Director; Kenneth Leslie Tuffin [1952] Director

Pearsalls Limited
Incorporated: 30 September 1999 *Employees:* 175
Net Worth: £41,068,000 *Total Assets:* £51,324,000
Registered Office: Tancred Street, Taunton, Somerset, TA1 1RY
Activities: Manufacture of medical and dental instruments and supplies
Parent: Surgical Specialties UK Holdings Limited
Officers: Daniel Joseph Sutherby, Secretary; Daniel Joseph Sutherby [1964] Director/Finance Officer [American]

Peartime Limited
Incorporated: 19 March 1997
Net Worth: £1,536,492 *Total Assets:* £3,728,925
Registered Office: St Ann's Manor, 6-8 St Ann Street, Salisbury, Wilts, SP1 2DN
Activities: Hotels and similar accommodation
Officers: James Thomas Whitehead, Secretary/Accountant; James Saville Palmer [1959] Director/Consultant; Rowland Andrew Palmer [1955] Director/Consultant

Pebley Beach Limited
Incorporated: 26 November 1976 *Employees:* 47
Net Worth: £1,003,070 *Total Assets:* £4,331,854
Registered Office: West Swindon Motor Park, Paddington Drive, Bridgemead, Swindon, Wilts, SN5 7SB
Activities: Sale of new cars and light motor vehicles
Parent: Pebley Beach Holdings Limited
Officers: Dominic Charles Threlfall [1970] Director

Pegasus Planning Group Limited
Incorporated: 8 June 2010 *Employees:* 232
Net Worth: £10,606,127 *Total Assets:* £13,345,683
Registered Office: Pegasus House, Querns Business Centre, Whitworth Road, Cirencester, Glos, GL7 1RT
Activities: Urban planning and landscape architectural activities
Officers: Robert Barber [1964] Director; Anthony Charles Bateman [1956] Director; Stephen Hugh Bawtree [1951] Director; Paul Burrell [1967] Director; Christopher Calvert [1978] Director; Michael Colin Carr [1969] Director; Peter Nigel Andrew Cook [1964] Director; Nicola Crouch [1971] Executive Director; David Hutchison [1976] Director; Samantha Kerby [1967] Director; Gary Lees [1967] Director; Guy Longley [1961] Director; Christopher James May [1959] Director; Jeremy Peachey [1966] Director; Paul Smith [1961] Director; James Richard Tarzey [1966] Director; Sebastian Tibenham [1979] Executive Director; Colin Paul Virtue [1975] Director; Dan Weaver [1979] Director

Pembridge Property Development Limited
Incorporated: 12 September 2014 *Employees:* 1
Net Worth Deficit: £2,051,034 *Total Assets:* £15,753,544
Registered Office: 2nd Floor, Stratus House, Emperor Way, Exeter Business Park, Exeter, Devon, EX1 3QS
Activities: Development of building projects
Officers: David Nicholas Wright [1957] Director/Entrepreneur

Pen y Cymoedd Wind Farm Limited
Incorporated: 19 January 1998 *Employees:* 3
Net Worth: £102,294,616 *Total Assets:* £384,191,680
Registered Office: Abbey Warehouse, Abbey Slip, Penzance, Cornwall, TR18 4AR
Activities: Production of electricity
Officers: Jonas Van Mansfeld, Secretary; Alper Elmas [1976] Director [Cypriot]; Jonathan David Chin O'Sullivan [1977] Director

Penair School
Incorporated: 9 March 2011 *Employees:* 120
Net Worth: £12,704,392 *Total Assets:* £15,108,816
Registered Office: Penair School, St Clement, Truro, Cornwall, TR1 1TN
Activities: General secondary education
Shareholders: David John Matthew; Nicholas Denis Vincent; Sara Louise Cadge
Officers: Elizabeth Mary Blues, Secretary; Joel Weinberg Ashton [1977] Director of Languages School; Lynne Bray [1964] Director/Lawyer; Andrew John Brigden [1955] Director/Maritime Manager; James Christian Davidson [1976] Director/Headteacher; Marie Gendall [1972] Director/HR; Henry George Arthur Lewis [1990] Director/Inclusion Manager; David John Matthew [1954] Director of Finance; Alan Derek Morgan [1952] Director/Retired; Jacqueline Parker [1962] Director/Business Manager; Antony Patrick Julyan Polglase [1962] Director/Businessman; Carolyn Mary Power [1973] Director/Deputy Headteacher; Elizabeth Mary Seale [1955] Director/Consultant

Pencarrie Group Limited
Incorporated: 22 April 2013 *Employees:* 209
Previous: Pencarrie Holdings Ltd.
Net Worth: £21,555,058 *Total Assets:* £37,009,816
Registered Office: Centenary House, Peninsula Park, Rydon Lane, Exeter, EX2 7XE
Activities: Activities of other holding companies n.e.c.
Parent: Pencarrie Holdings Limited
Officers: Nicci Claire Gratwicke [1973] Director; Sarah Louise Irving [1975] Director; Clare Victoria Persey [1975] Director

Pencarrie Limited
Incorporated: 16 May 1997 *Employees:* 207
Net Worth: £22,344,372 *Total Assets:* £36,891,372
Registered Office: Pencarrie House, South View Estate, Willand, Cullompton, Devon, EX15 2QW
Activities: Wholesale of textiles
Parent: Pencarrie Holdings Limited
Officers: Francis Leslie Bevan, Secretary; Francis Leslie Bevan [1963] Director/Chartered Accountant; Nicola Claire Gratwicke [1973] Director; Sarah Louise Irving [1975] Director; Anthony John Lock [1962] Director; Clare Victoria Persey [1975] Director

Pendennis Properties (Bournemouth)
Incorporated: 26 October 1948
Net Worth: £3,218,842 *Total Assets:* £4,045,139
Registered Office: 65c Bargates, Christchurch, Dorset, BH23 1QE
Activities: Development of building projects
Major Shareholder: Philip John Kermode
Officers: Stella Jane Unsworth, Secretary; Louise Una Kermode [1968] Director; Philip John Kermode [1965] Director/Builder; Tristan Anthony Pinckston [1966] Director/Property Developer

Pendennis Shipyard (Holdings) Limited
Incorporated: 28 July 1988 *Employees:* 402
Net Worth: £31,477,058 *Total Assets:* £55,715,344
Registered Office: The Docks, Falmouth, Cornwall, TR11 4NR
Activities: Building of pleasure and sporting boats
Officers: Ian Langley Granville, Secretary; Toby James Allies [1974] Director; Micheal John Carr [1959] Director/Naval Architect; Ian Langley Granville [1961] Director/Accountant; Anthony Arthur Hill [1942] Director/Chartered Accountant; Terence Charles Mordaunt [1947] Director; Charles Bruce Robertson [1953] Director/Retailer; Hendrik Wiekens [1952] Director

Pendennis Shipyard Limited
Incorporated: 14 November 1994 *Employees:* 394
Net Worth: £17,518,476 *Total Assets:* £39,558,396
Registered Office: The Docks, Falmouth, Cornwall, TR11 4NR
Activities: Building of pleasure and sporting boats
Parent: Pendennis Shipyard (Holdings) Limited
Officers: Ian Langley Granville, Secretary; Toby James Allies [1974] Director; Jillian Gwendoline Carr [1960] Director/Teacher; Micheal John Carr [1959] Director/Naval Architect; Ian Langley Granville [1961] Director/Accountant; Anthony Arthur Hill [1942] Director/Chartered Accountant; Stephen Frederick James Hills [1967] Director/Engineer; Charles Bruce Robertson [1953] Director/Retailer; Charles James Ross [1978] Director/Naval Architect

Pendine Wind Farm Limited
Incorporated: 16 December 1996 *Employees:* 3
Net Worth: £4,807,594 *Total Assets:* £5,319,362
Registered Office: Abbey Warehouse, Abbey Slip, Penzance, Cornwall, TR18 4AR
Activities: Production of electricity
Parent: Nuon UK Ltd
Officers: Jonas Van Mansfeld, Secretary; Alper Elmas [1976] Director [Cypriot]; Jonathan David Chin O'Sullivan [1977] Director

Pengelly Farms Limited
Incorporated: 5 July 2004 *Employees:* 12
Net Worth: £726,233 *Total Assets:* £4,069,214
Registered Office: Bishopbrook House, Cathedral Avenue, Wells, Somerset, BA5 1FD
Activities: Growing of cereals (except rice), leguminous crops and oil seeds
Shareholders: Philip Melville Rogers; Simon Rogers
Officers: Simon Rogers, Secretary/Farmer; Philip Melville Rogers [1970] Director/Farmer; Simon Rogers [1945] Director/Farmer

Penington Enterprises Limited
Incorporated: 23 April 2007 *Employees:* 1
Net Worth: £344,099 *Total Assets:* £4,750,177
Registered Office: First Floor, 10 Temple Back, Bristol, BS1 6FL
Activities: Other business support service activities n.e.c.
Officers: David William Hardacre [1945] Director/Business Consultant

Peninsula Care Homes Limited
Incorporated: 10 December 2002 *Employees:* 248
Net Worth: £3,678,123 *Total Assets:* £8,596,073
Registered Office: Parkland House Residential Home, Barley Lane, Exeter, Devon, EX4 1TA
Activities: Other service activities n.e.c.
Major Shareholder: David Charles Arnold
Officers: Caroline Jade Arnold [1982] Director/HR Manager; Isobel Arnold [1947] Director; Louise Claire Arnold [1974] Managing Director; Stephen John Arnold [1976] Director/Customer Relations

Peninsula Dental Social Enterprise CIC
Incorporated: 9 January 2013 *Employees:* 61
Net Worth: £402,644 *Total Assets:* £19,418,988
Registered Office: Finance & Sustainability, New Cooperage Building, University of Plymouth, Royal William Yard, Plymouth, PL4 8AA
Activities: Dental practice activities
Officers: Sally Crabb, Secretary; Nathan Findlay [1978] Director/Chief Operating Officer; Dr Jane Luker [1959] Director/Dental Surgeon; Alastair Sean Matthews [1962] Director/Chartered Accountant; Ewen McColl [1969] Director/Associate Professor/Consultant; Professor Christopher Jeremy Tredwin [1971] Director/Professor of Restorative Dentistry; Henry William Warren [1950] Director; Robert Vaughan Witton [1976] Director/Dental Consultant

Peninsula Finance PLC
Incorporated: 4 March 2002 *Employees:* 10
Net Worth: £4,513,792 *Total Assets:* £25,187,324
Registered Office: Studio 5-11, 5 Millbay Road, Plymouth, PL1 3LF
Activities: Activities of mortgage finance companies
Officers: Jacqueline Sandra Ashley [1950] Director; Paul Alisdair James Hussell [1962] Director; Richard Hugh Galabin Michelmore [1952] Director/Solicitor; Daniel James Rowe Palmer [1981] Director/Chief Executive

Peninsula Learning Trust
Incorporated: 15 March 2011 *Employees:* 460
Previous: Penrice Academy
Net Worth: £31,815,464 *Total Assets:* £36,246,816
Registered Office: Unit 18 St Austell Business Park, Treverbyn Road, St Austell, Cornwall, PL25 4FD
Activities: Primary education
Officers: Graham Michael Jeremy Groves, Secretary; Jeremy Keith Barnard [1964] Director/Human Resources Manager; Michael John Cooper [1949] Director/Retired; Shaun Netherton [1965] Director/Service Engineer; Kevin Michael Pearce [1965] Finance Director; John Carne Simeons [1946] Director/Retired; Gregory John Slater [1970] Director/Chartered Architect; Ramon Van de Velde [1975] Director [Dutch]

Peninsula Properties (Exeter) Limited
Incorporated: 19 October 1988
Net Worth: £5,062,000 *Total Assets:* £5,144,000
Registered Office: Peninsula House, Rydon Lane, Exeter, Devon, EX2 7HR
Activities: Development of building projects
Parent: South West Water Limited
Officers: Simon Anthony Follet Pugsley, Secretary; Karen Senior, Secretary; Susan Jane Davy [1969] Director; Louise Frances Rowe [1982] Director/Accountant

Peninsula Seafoods Limited
Incorporated: 11 May 1995 *Employees:* 5
Net Worth: £1,225,399 *Total Assets:* £3,869,616
Registered Office: Riverside Road, Pottington Business Park, Barnstaple, Devon, EX31 1QN
Activities: Wholesale of other food, including fish, crustaceans and molluscs
Shareholder: Stephen Harold Pell
Officers: Iain John Spear, Secretary/Director; Stephen Harold Pell [1965] Director; Anthony David James Spear [1964] Director; Iain John Spear [1966] Director

Penlane Limited
Incorporated: 22 November 1971 *Employees:* 3
Net Worth: £11,152,682 *Total Assets:* £14,805,007
Registered Office: St Matthew's House, Quays Office Park, Conference Avenue, Portishead, Bristol, BS20 7LZ
Activities: Other letting and operating of own or leased real estate
Shareholders: Paul Seddon; Gloria Ann Seddon
Officers: Phillippa Jane Barry, Secretary; Giles Edward Barry [1975] Director; Phillippa Jane Barry [1969] Director/Administrator; Gloria Seddon [1939] Director; Paul Seddon [1937] Director

Penmellyn Veterinary Group Limited
Incorporated: 11 May 2012 *Employees:* 6
Net Worth: £1,196,260 *Total Assets:* £3,702,343
Registered Office: The Chocolate Factory, Keynsham, Bristol, BS31 2AU
Activities: Veterinary activities
Officers: Amanda Jane Davis [1968] Director; David Robert Geoffrey Hillier [1962] Director

Pennant International Group PLC
Incorporated: 18 April 1996 *Employees:* 115
Net Worth: £13,328,127 *Total Assets:* £16,937,666
Registered Office: Pennant Court, Staverton Technology Park, Cheltenham, Glos, GL51 6TQ
Activities: Other business support service activities n.e.c.
Officers: David Clements, Secretary; Gary Robert Barnes [1966] Finance Director; David Joseph Clements [1979] Commercial Director; Simon Alick Moore [1965] Director; John Maurice Maynard Ponsonby [1955] Director; Christopher Charles Powell [1946] Director; Philip Henry Walker [1980] Director/Chartered Accountant

Pennant International Limited
Incorporated: 25 February 1958 *Employees:* 53
Previous: Pennant Training Systems Limited
Net Worth: £7,160,302 *Total Assets:* £13,258,088
Registered Office: Pennant Court, Staverton Technology Park, Gloucester Road, Cheltenham, Glos, GL51 6TL
Activities: Other manufacturing n.e.c.
Parent: Pennant International Group PLC
Officers: David Joseph Clements, Secretary; Gary Robert Barnes [1966] Finance Director; David Joseph Clements [1979] Commercial Director; Simon Alick Moore [1965] Director; John Maurice Maynard Ponsonby [1955] Director; Christopher Charles Powell [1946] Director/Chairman; Philip Henry Walker [1980] Director/Chartered Accountant

Pennard Farms Limited
Incorporated: 13 January 2003 *Employees:* 10
Net Worth: £2,440,139 *Total Assets:* £5,253,824
Registered Office: New Manor Farm, Polsham, Wells, Somerset, BA5 1RP
Activities: Raising of dairy cattle
Shareholders: Martin Herbert Hawkins; Stanley Joseph Hawkins
Officers: Martin Herbert Hawkins, Secretary; Martin Herbert Hawkins [1965] Director/Farmer; Stanley Joseph Hawkins [1967] Director/Farmer

Pennard Hill Farm Holdings Limited
Incorporated: 16 December 2010
Net Worth: £4,131,315 *Total Assets:* £4,153,705
Registered Office: 20 Chamberlain Street, Wells, Somerset, BA5 2PF
Activities: Activities of head offices
Major Shareholder: David William Chambers
Officers: Philippa Clair Chambers, Secretary; David William Chambers [1957] Director

Pennard Hill Farm Limited
Incorporated: 9 May 1975 *Employees:* 4
Net Worth: £4,113,244 *Total Assets:* £4,198,415
Registered Office: 20 Chamberlain Street, Wells, Somerset, BA5 2PF
Activities: Growing of cereals (except rice), leguminous crops and oil seeds
Parent: Pennard Hill Farm Holdings Limited
Officers: Philippa Clair Chambers, Secretary; David William Chambers [1957] Director and Farmer

Pennon Group PLC
Incorporated: 1 April 1989 *Employees:* 5,014
Net Worth: £1,340,899,968 *Total Assets:* £6,163,800,064
Registered Office: Peninsula House, Rydon Lane, Exeter, EX2 7HR
Activities: Activities of head offices
Officers: Simon Anthony Follet Pugsley, Secretary; Neil Cooper [1967] Director; Susan Jane Davy [1969] Director; Iain Richard Evans [1951] Director/Management Consultant; Christopher Loughlin [1952] Director/Chief Executive; Sir Thomas John Parker [1942] Director; Gillian Ann Rider [1954] Director

Penny & Giles Controls Limited
Incorporated: 1 April 1965 *Employees:* 521
Net Worth: £76,211,000 *Total Assets:* £123,881,000
Registered Office: 15 Enterprise Way, Aviation Park West, Bournemouth International Airport, Christchurch, Dorset, BH23 6HH
Activities: Manufacture of other electrical equipment
Parent: Curtiss-Wright Controls (UK) Limited
Officers: Paul Jude Ferdenzi, Secretary; Harry Jakubowitz, Secretary; George Patrick McDonald, Secretary; Marc Sebastian O'Casal, Secretary; Nigel Paul Jones [1968] Director; George Patrick McDonald [1964] Director/Associate General Counsel [American]; Kevin Michael Rayment [1969] Director/Senior Vice President; Andrew Robert Thornton [1967] Commercial Director; Glenn Edward Tynan [1958] Director/Vice President & CFO [American]; Jason Karl Watkins [1966] Director

R.M. Penny (Plant Hire and Demolition) Limited
Incorporated: 9 January 1975 *Employees:* 92
Net Worth: £6,644,259 *Total Assets:* £9,473,798
Registered Office: Green Street, Ston Easton, Bath, BA3 4BY
Activities: Construction of commercial buildings
Shareholders: Roger Maxwell Penny; Catherine Elizabeth Penny
Officers: Catherine Elizabeth Penny, Secretary; Thomas George Brimble [1993] Director; Catherine Elizabeth Penny [1942] Director/Plant Hire Contractor; Christopher Nigel Penny [1963] Director; Roger Maxwell Penny [1938] Director/Plant Hire Contractor; Damien James Pick [1970] Director/General Manager

Penny Lane Foods Limited
Incorporated: 15 January 1985 *Employees:* 90
Net Worth: £2,529,123 *Total Assets:* £5,175,405
Registered Office: Units 1a-1e Yeo Road, Colley Lane Industrial Estate, Bridgwater, Somerset, TA6 5NA
Activities: Production of meat and poultry meat products
Officers: Edmund James Quentin Bailhache, Secretary/Solicitor; Catherine Laura Jones, Secretary; Adrian Christopher Jones [1965] Managing Director; Catherine Laura Jones [1968] Company Secretary/Director

Penny Lane Holdings Ltd
Incorporated: 7 November 2002 *Employees:* 90
Net Worth: £2,529,123 *Total Assets:* £5,175,005
Registered Office: 1 Yeo Road, Bridgwater, Somerset, TA6 5NA
Activities: Production of meat and poultry meat products
Shareholders: Adrian Christopher Jones; Catherine Laura Jones
Officers: Edmund James Quentin Bailhache, Secretary/Solicitor; Catherine Laura Jones, Secretary; Adrian Christopher Jones [1965] Managing Director; Catherine Laura Jones [1968] Director

Thos.S.Penny,Limited
Incorporated: 25 June 1907 *Employees:* 6
Net Worth: £4,422,284 *Total Assets:* £4,914,754
Registered Office: Mary Street House, Mary Street, Taunton, Somerset, TA1 3NW
Activities: Other letting and operating of own or leased real estate
Shareholder: Stephen James Lewis Penny
Officers: Duncan Michael Bagehot Kite [1968] Director/Chartered Surveyor; Sarah Samantha Kite [1966] Director/Events Organiser; Dr Catherine Margaret Penny [1980] Director/Doctor; Elizabeth Clare Penny [1982] Director/Student; Robert Michael Lewis Penny [1985] Director/Student; Stephen James Lewis Penny [1951] Director/Chartered Surveyor

Pennyfarthing Construction Limited
Incorporated: 6 October 1989 *Employees:* 73
Net Worth: £901,603 *Total Assets:* £6,633,749
Registered Office: Pennyfarthing House, South Drive, Ossemsley, New Milton, Hants, BH25 5TL
Activities: Construction of domestic buildings
Parent: Pennyfarthing Developments Limited
Officers: Mark Adams, Secretary/Builder; Daniel Adams [1966] Director/Builder; Mark Adams [1968] Director/Builder; Trevor Ruben Adams [1942] Director/Builder; Matthew Shane Sebastian Dukes [1969] Managing Director

Pennyfarthing Developments Limited
Incorporated: 23 January 1998 *Employees:* 73
Net Worth: £19,186,468 *Total Assets:* £52,086,744
Registered Office: Pennyfarthing Farmhouse, Ossemsley, New Milton, Hants, BH25 5TL
Activities: Development of building projects
Shareholders: Mark Adams; Daniel Adams
Officers: Mark Adams, Secretary; Daniel Adams [1966] Director/Builder; Mark Adams [1968] Director/Builder; Trevor Ruben Adams [1942] Director/Builder; Matthew Shane Sebastian Dukes [1969] Managing Director

Pennyfarthing Homes Limited
Incorporated: 22 December 1994
Net Worth: £11,759,150 *Total Assets:* £48,338,856
Registered Office: Pennyfarthing House, Ossemsley, New Milton, Hants, BH25 5TL
Activities: Development of building projects
Parent: Pennyfarthing Developments Limited
Officers: Mark Adams, Secretary/Construction Company Manager; Daniel Adams [1966] Director/Builder; Mark Adams [1968] Director/Construction Company Manager; Trevor Ruben Adams [1942] Managing Director; Matthew Shane Sebastian Dukes [1969] Managing Director

Pennyfarthing New Homes Limited
Incorporated: 15 November 2002
Net Worth: £3,206,558 *Total Assets:* £4,748,660
Registered Office: Pennyfarthing House, Ossemsley, New Milton, Hants, BH25 5TL
Activities: Development of building projects
Shareholder: Pennyfarthing Developments Limited
Officers: Mark Adams, Secretary/Director; Daniel Adams [1966] Director/Builder; Mark Adams [1968] Director; Trevor Ruben Adams [1942] Director; William Stephen Cairns [1949] Director; Matthew Shane Sebastian Dukes [1969] Managing Director

Penrice House (St. Austell) Limited
Incorporated: 24 January 1980 *Employees:* 37
Net Worth: £3,603,083 *Total Assets:* £3,657,528
Registered Office: Penrice House, Porthpean, St Austell, Cornwall, PL26 6AZ
Activities: Residential care activities for the elderly and disabled
Officers: Alison Mary Phillips, Secretary; Alec Bawden [1943] Director/Retired; Margaret Katherine Bawden [1945] Director/Retired; David Stephen Boardman [1950] Director/Retired; Dr Richard Bown [1948] Director/Retired; Jennifer Burden [1981] Director/Solicitor; Doctor Paul Bentham Foster [1950] Director/Retired Medical Practitioner; Alexandra Francis [1946] Director/Retired; Dr Linda Bridget Sampson [1958] Director of Commissioning; Philip Graham Snell [1951] Director/Solicitor; Alan Percival Tregilgas [1950] Director/Accountant

Pentewan Sands,Limited
Incorporated: 5 April 1945 *Employees:* 95
Net Worth: £7,206,819 *Total Assets:* £9,624,282
Registered Office: 20 Henver Road, Newquay, Cornwall, TR7 3BJ
Activities: Holiday centres and villages
Shareholders: John Richard Tremayne Willis; Antonia Mary Damaris Willis; Peter Edward Hawley; Terence Arthur Cole; James Buller Kitson
Officers: Antonia Mary Damaris Willis, Secretary; Peter Edward Hawley [1938] Director; Antonia Mary Damaris Willis [1961] Director; John Richard Tremayne Willis [1962] Director/Surveyor; Penelope Eve Willis [1921] Director

Pentland Road Windfarm Limited
Incorporated: 1 August 2008 *Employees:* 2
Net Worth: £3,123,725 *Total Assets:* £20,826,146
Registered Office: Harpford Farm, Payton, Wellington, Somerset, TA21 0EE
Activities: Production of electricity
Shareholders: Peter John Crone; Michael David Legh Huntingford
Officers: Peter John Crone [1950] Director; Michael David Legh Huntingford [1962] Director

Penton Securities Limited
Incorporated: 19 August 1993 *Employees:* 71
Net Worth: £5,006,054 *Total Assets:* £16,109,562
Registered Office: 141 Somerford Road, Christchurch, Dorset, BH23 3PY
Activities: Sale of new cars and light motor vehicles
Major Shareholder: Robert James Wilson
Officers: Jan Dibden, Secretary; Jan Michael Dibden [1967] Finance Director; Charles William Robert Wilson [1979] Sales Director; Robert James Wilson [1946] Director; Stephen Robert Wilson [1965] Director

Pentrebay Properties Limited
Incorporated: 4 June 1996 *Employees:* 3
Net Worth: £4,884,422 *Total Assets:* £5,159,979
Registered Office: 92 Embankment Road, Cattedown, Plymouth, PL4 9HY
Activities: Buying and selling of own real estate
Officers: Carleton Mayer, Secretary; Carleton Mayer [1961] Director/Property Manager

Pentwin Group Limited
Incorporated: 16 August 2011 *Employees:* 101
Net Worth: £27,012,926 *Total Assets:* £30,051,304
Registered Office: 1 Manor Park Business Centre, MacKenzie Way, Swindon Village, Cheltenham, Glos, GL51 9TX
Activities: Activities of head offices
Major Shareholder: Anthony James Rawson
Officers: Sean Edward Rice, Secretary; Richard Cox [1934] Director; Anthony James Rawson [1943] Director

People 2000 Limited
Incorporated: 19 July 1972 *Employees:* 2
Net Worth: £5,750,140 *Total Assets:* £5,754,477
Registered Office: Atalaya, 34 Sea Road, Carlyon Bay, St Austell, Cornwall, PL25 3SF
Activities: Credit granting by non-deposit taking finance houses and other specialist consumer credit grantors
Shareholders: Peter Albert Leon Browning; Ann Victoria Browning
Officers: Ann Victoria Browning, Secretary; Alison Victoria Browning [1969] Managing Director; Ann Victoria Browning [1935] Director & Secretary; Peter Albert Leon Browning [1931] Director; Peter Frederick Woods-Browning [1972] Director/Operations Manager

People Source Consulting Limited
Incorporated: 7 March 2002 *Employees:* 40
Net Worth: £5,829,150 *Total Assets:* £9,406,804
Registered Office: 1 Georges Square, Bath Street, Bristol, BS1 6BA
Activities: Other activities of employment placement agencies
Parent: Manpower Holdings Limited
Officers: Jason Anthony Baker [1975] Director/Recruitment

Bob Pepper Holdings Limited
Incorporated: 2 February 2012 *Employees:* 128
Net Worth: £8,091,671 *Total Assets:* £14,625,472
Registered Office: Jenson House, Cardrew Industrial Estate, Redruth, Cornwall, TR15 1SS
Activities: Activities of construction holding companies
Major Shareholder: Robert David Pepper
Officers: Tracey Marie Bullen [1970] Director/Chartered Surveyor; Robert David Pepper [1945] Director/Property Developer; Michelle Pepper-Smith [1975] Director; Robert Andrew Pepper-Smith [1971] Financial Director

Perivoli Investments Limited
Incorporated: 7 February 2011 *Employees:* 2
Net Worth: £3,982,138 *Total Assets:* £5,139,863
Registered Office: Midland Bridge House, Midland Bridge Road, Bath, BA2 3FP
Activities: Other business support service activities n.e.c.
Officers: Nicholas Leycester Adams [1956] Director; Justin Neil Weir [1966] Director/Doctor

Perkins & Perry Ltd.
Incorporated: 20 March 2000 *Employees:* 42
Net Worth: £3,929,329 *Total Assets:* £4,842,980
Registered Office: The Old Carriage Works, Moresk Road, Truro, Cornwall, TR1 1DG
Activities: Roofing activities
Major Shareholder: Jacqueline Anne Perkins
Officers: Jonathan Edward Mildren, Secretary; Jonathan Edward Mildren [1968] Director/Accountant; Gillian Ann Perkins [1971] Director; Jacqueline Anne Perkins [1944] Director; Gaerth Bryan Spargo [1960] Director

Permali Gloucester Limited
Incorporated: 15 April 1998 *Employees:* 79
Net Worth: £4,637,904 *Total Assets:* £12,866,755
Registered Office: Bristol Road, Gloucester, GL1 5TT
Activities: Manufacture of plastic plates, sheets, tubes and profiles
Shareholders: Gus King; 3i Group PLC
Officers: Nicholas Baird, Secretary; Nicholas Baird [1966] Director; Paul Dennis Carter [1952] Director; Gus King [1958] Director; Michael John Bennell Smith [1964] Managing Director

Perrigo UK Acquisition Limited
Incorporated: 15 June 2001 *Employees:* 3
Net Worth: £84,227,000 *Total Assets:* £311,860,000
Registered Office: Wrafton, Braunton, Devon, EX33 2DL
Activities: Other business support service activities n.e.c.
Parent: Perrigo UK Finco Limited Partnership
Officers: James Larson, Secretary; Louis Cherico [1971] Director/Treasurer [American]; Neil Thomas Lister [1975] Director; Dominic James Rivers [1977] Director

Perrott Hill School Trust Limited
Incorporated: 23 December 1966 *Employees:* 90
Net Worth: £1,563,309 *Total Assets:* £3,583,712
Registered Office: Perrott Hill School, North Perrott, Crewkerne, Somerset, TA18 7SL
Activities: Primary education
Officers: Neil Mapletoft, Secretary; Lord John Bradbury [1940] Director/Retired; Paul Highmoor Brewster [1957] Director/Retired; Kate Phillippa Frost [1975] Director/Partner in Farming Business; Generaldine Kerton-Johnson [1944] Director/Headmistress; Richard John King [1955] Director/Solicitor; Kathryn Latham [1965] Director/Doctor; John Darcy Lever [1952] Director/Retired Headmaster; Marcus Longbottom [1969] Director/Certified Chartered Accountant; Justin Lowe [1966] Director/Chartered Surveyor; Sarah McConnell [1971] Director/Business Owner; Keith Roman Moore [1947] Marketing Director; Sarah Joan Thomas [1961] Director/Headmistress

Perrys Holdings Limited
Incorporated: 13 November 2006 *Employees:* 65
Net Worth: £7,992,672 *Total Assets:* £9,587,939
Registered Office: Recycling Limited, Rimpton Road, Marston Magna, Yeovil, Somerset, BA22 8DL
Activities: Activities of other holding companies n.e.c.
Major Shareholder: Estate of Brian Frederick Perry
Officers: Samantha Jane Perry, Secretary/Sales Manager; Ian Cook [1964] Director; Christopher James Perry [1970] Managing Director; Matthew Alexander Perry [1974] Transport Director; Samantha Jane Perry [1968] Sales Director

Perrys Recycling Limited
Incorporated: 7 January 1975 *Employees:* 64
Net Worth: £2,924,859 *Total Assets:* £4,587,751
Registered Office: Rimpton Road, Marston Magna, Yeovil, Somerset, BA22 8DL
Activities: Recovery of sorted materials
Parent: Perrys Holdings Limited
Officers: Samantha Jane Perry, Secretary/Sales Director; Christopher James Perry [1970] Managing Director; Matthew Alexander Perry [1974] Transport Director; Nicholas Shaun Perry [1959] Production Director; Samantha Jane Perry [1968] Sales Director

Perseus Property Company Limited (The)
Incorporated: 13 November 1950 *Employees:* 5
Net Worth: £2,354,055 *Total Assets:* £5,792,774
Registered Office: Pearl Assurance House, 128 Old Christchurch Road, Bournemouth, BH1 1NL
Activities: Buying and selling of own real estate
Shareholder: R E Wright Discretionary Settlement
Officers: Sarah Jane Marie Wright, Secretary; Susan Louise Rowe [1961] Director; Richard Rafael Wright [1963] Director/Deputy Secretary/Joint MD

Persey Properties Partnership LLP
Incorporated: 27 February 2012 *Employees:* 1
Net Worth: £5,120,391 *Total Assets:* £7,995,578
Registered Office: Centenary House, Peninsula Park, Rydon Lane, Exeter, EX2 7XE
Officers: Nicci Claire Gratwicke [1973] Member; Sarah Louise Irving [1975] Member; Clare Victoria Persey [1975] Member; Paul Richard Persey [1948] Member

Pet Food Holdings Limited
Incorporated: 21 September 1984
Net Worth: £22,513,000 *Total Assets:* £22,513,000
Registered Office: Oak Tree Meadow, Blackworthy Road, Castle Cary, Somerset, BA7 7PH
Activities: Activities of head offices
Parent: Mars Petcare UK Holdings Limited
Officers: Jakub Kolesa, Secretary; Jakub Kolesa [1972] Director/General Manager, Royal Canin UK & Ireland [Czech]; Michael Kunze [1966] Director/President Europe Royal Canin [German]; Loic Nicolas Serge Moutault [1971] Director [French]

Petrarch Holdings Limited
Incorporated: 3 October 1997
Net Worth Deficit: £646,024 *Total Assets:* £7,515,860
Registered Office: First Floor, 10 Temple Back, Bristol, BS1 6FL
Activities: Non-trading company
Officers: William Gwion Harries [1964] Fiduciary Management Director; Jeremy Paul Smith [1961] Client Services Director

Petty, Wood & Co. Limited
Incorporated: 28 October 1904 *Employees:* 95
Net Worth: £5,290,220 *Total Assets:* £20,371,304
Registered Office: Livingstone Road, Walworth Business Park, Andover, Hants, SP10 5NS
Activities: Non-specialised wholesale of food, beverages and tobacco
Shareholders: Sean Michael Linehan; John Potter; Giles Marc Reynolds
Officers: Sean Michael Linehan, Secretary; Sean Michael Linehan [1967] Finance Director; John Potter [1964] Director; Giles Marc Reynolds [1971] Brand Director

Pewsey Vale School
Incorporated: 8 June 2011 *Employees:* 60
Net Worth: £4,352,033 *Total Assets:* £4,776,585
Registered Office: Pewsey Vale School, Wilcot Road, Pewsey, Wilts, SN9 5EW
Activities: General secondary education
Officers: Deborah Clarke, Secretary; Mark Alsop [1956] Director/Retired Lawyer; Judith Barclay [1957] HR Director; Caroline Frances Dalrymple [1939] Director/Interior Decorator; Andrew Dang [1982] IT Director; Josephine Mary Del Mar [1969] Director; Elinor Mary Goodman [1946] Director/Journalist; Andrew Haig [1966] Director/IT Consultant; Alan John Toby MacAuslan [1953] Director/Retired; Neil Pritchard [1974] Director/Headteacher; Barbara Amy Reeder [1952] Director/Teacher; Tracy Lorraine Richards [1965] Director; Thomas Peter Robinson [1989] Director/Assistant Headteacher; David Richard Frederick Smith [1953] Director/Retired Teacher; Lynda Thomson [1965] Director/IT Consultant

PFI Investments Limited
Incorporated: 15 January 2004
Net Worth Deficit: £20,738,000 *Total Assets:* £84,332,000
Registered Office: Third Floor, Broad Quay House, Prince Street, Bristol, BS1 4DJ
Activities: Non-trading company
Parent: Semperian PPP Investment Partners Limited
Officers: Chris Burlton [1973] Director/Accountant; Jonathan Michael Simpson [1973] Director/Accountant

PGI - Protection Group International Ltd.
Incorporated: 28 February 2012 *Employees:* 95
Net Worth Deficit: £20,090,856 *Total Assets:* £6,071,013
Registered Office: Unit 13-14 Swallow Court, Sampford Peverell, Tiverton, Devon, EX16 7EJ
Activities: Private security activities
Shareholder: Mohamed Ali Mohamed Al Barwani
Officers: Dr Mohamed Ali Mohamed Al Barwani [1951] Director/Entrepreneur [Omani]; Barry Martin Roche [1973] Director; Neville Robert Storey [1962] Director

Pharmaxo Pharmacy Services Limited
Incorporated: 5 August 2009 *Employees:* 33
Net Worth: £1,964,968 *Total Assets:* £7,044,014
Registered Office: 3 Corsham Science Park, Park Lane, Corsham, Wilts, SN13 9FU
Activities: Manufacture of pharmaceutical preparations
Parent: Qualasept Pharmaxo Holdings Limited
Officers: Alison Maria Davis [1973] Director; Christopher James Fountain [1966] Director/Chartered Accountant; Christopher Dean Watt [1968] Director

Pharos Care Limited
Incorporated: 7 November 2005 *Employees:* 137
Net Worth: £380,395 *Total Assets:* £3,641,107
Registered Office: Windsor House, Bayshill Road, Cheltenham, Glos, GL50 3AT
Activities: Residential care activities for learning difficulties, mental health and substance abuse
Parent: Midway Care Group Limited
Officers: Ian Geoffrey Brown [1976] Director; Matthew John Harrison [1971] Director

S.J.Phillips & Sons (Kemble) Limited
Incorporated: 30 September 1969 *Employees:* 10
Net Worth: £5,749,039 *Total Assets:* £7,424,795
Registered Office: Kilkenny Farm, Bibury, Cirencester, Glos, GL7 5PD
Activities: Mixed farming
Shareholders: Nicholas John Phillips; Priscilla March Phillips; Anthony Oscar Colburn
Officers: Priscilla March Phillips, Secretary/Housewife; Anthony Oscar Colburn [1954] Director/Farmer; Nicholas John Phillips [1982] Director/Farmer; Priscilla March Phillips [1951] Director/Housewife

Philmark Estates Limited
Incorporated: 5 April 2004 *Employees:* 3
Net Worth: £825,407 *Total Assets:* £5,193,503
Registered Office: 37 Great Pulteney Street, Bath, BA2 4DA
Activities: Other letting and operating of own or leased real estate
Major Shareholder: Julian Mark Ottignon
Officers: Timothy Anderson, Secretary; Julian Mark Ottignon [1953] Director

Phoenix Child Care Limited
Incorporated: 12 July 2005 *Employees:* 174
Net Worth Deficit: £282,645 *Total Assets:* £7,155,484
Registered Office: First Floor, Rolle Quay House, Rolle Quay, Barnstaple, Devon, EX31 1JE
Activities: Residential care activities for learning difficulties, mental health and substance abuse
Parent: Phoenix Learning & Care Holdings Limited
Officers: Francois HR Delbaere, Secretary; Francois HR Delbaere [1981] Finance Director; Jonathan Hugh Pain [1969] Operations Director

Phoenix Engineering Company Limited
Incorporated: 22 October 1905 *Employees:* 45
Net Worth: £6,198,135 *Total Assets:* £6,799,093
Registered Office: Phoenix House, Combe Street, Chard, Somerset, TA20 1JE
Activities: Manufacture of equipment for concrete crushing and screening and roadworks
Shareholders: Simon Charles Peter Jennings; Thomas John Jennings
Officers: Thomas John Jennings, Secretary; Betty Rose Mary Jennings [1936] Director; Simon Charles Peter Jennings [1962] Director/Engineer; Thomas John Jennings [1959] Director/Chartered Accountant

Phoenix Learning & Care Holdings Limited
Incorporated: 5 January 2012 *Employees:* 319
Net Worth Deficit: £2,964,171 *Total Assets:* £11,688,330
Registered Office: First Floor, Rolle Quay, Barnstaple, Devon, EX31 1JE
Activities: Activities of head offices
Parent: Ashridge Capital (Phoenix) Limited Partnership
Officers: Francois HR Delbaere, Secretary; Michael Buckingham [1946] Director/Retired CEO; Francois HR Delbaere [1981] Finance Director; Jonathan Hugh Pain [1969] Operations Director; David Mark Sherratt [1967] Director

Phoenix Learning and Care Limited
Incorporated: 24 June 1998 *Employees:* 145
Net Worth: £5,111,769 *Total Assets:* £6,955,372
Registered Office: First Floor, Rolle Quay House, Rolle Quay, Barnstaple, Devon, EX31 1JE
Activities: Other education n.e.c.
Parent: Phoenix Child Care Limited
Officers: Francois HR Delbaere, Secretary; Francois HR Delbaere [1981] Finance Director; Jonathan Hugh Pain [1969] Operations Director

Phyworks Limited
Incorporated: 20 September 2000
Net Worth: £37,304,472 *Total Assets:* £39,378,232
Registered Office: First Floor, 10 Temple Back, Bristol, BS1 6FL
Activities: Manufacture of electronic components
Officers: Mark John Casper, Secretary; Mark John Casper [1967] Director/Assistant General Counsel [American]; Edwin Medlin [1957] Director/Attorney [American]

Pickwick Academy Trust
Incorporated: 9 March 2011 *Employees:* 276
Previous: Corsham Primary School
Net Worth: £12,981,953 *Total Assets:* £14,859,758
Registered Office: Corsham Primary School, Pound Pill, Corsham, Wilts, SN13 9YW
Activities: Primary education
Officers: Fiona Allen [1956] Director/Executive Headteacher; Gill Clark [1950] Director; Andrew Edward Valentine Hall [1970] Director/Self Employed; Rob Hayday [1967] Director/NHS Manager; David Lloyd Blake Powell [1943] Director/Town Councillor; Paul Leonard Vincent [1948] Director/Expert Care Quality Commission; Robert James Ward [1972] Director/RAF WSOp Cmn; David Willis [1948] Director/Retired

PICS Telecom International Limited
Incorporated: 4 June 2004 *Employees:* 47
Net Worth: £895,517 *Total Assets:* £4,321,878
Registered Office: Charnwood House, Marsh Road, Ashton, Bristol, BS3 2NA
Activities: Retail sale of telecommunications equipment other than mobile telephones
Parent: PICS Telecom International Corporation
Officers: Jr. Williams, Secretary; Timothy Ward Williams [1955] Director/Telecom Equipment Distributor [American]

Pie Minister Limited
Incorporated: 15 January 2003 *Employees:* 257
Net Worth: £999,000 *Total Assets:* £4,729,000
Registered Office: 24 Stokes Croft, Bristol, BS1 3PR
Activities: Manufacture of bread; manufacture of fresh pastry goods and cakes
Shareholders: Jonathan David Simon; Tristan Hogg
Officers: Gonzalo Alonso Trujillo, Secretary/Director; Tristan Richard Edward Hogg [1979] Director/Chef; Jonathan David Simon [1972] Director/Manager; Gonzalo Alonso Trujillo [1970] Director; Simon Clive Turner [1968] Director/Investment Advisor [South African/British]

Piller UK Limited
Incorporated: 19 November 1975 *Employees:* 46
Net Worth: £6,350,864 *Total Assets:* £11,490,443
Registered Office: Westgate, Phoenix Way, Cirencester, Glos, GL7 1RY
Activities: Manufacture of electric motors, generators and transformers
Parent: Langley Holdings PLC
Officers: Andrew Charles Dyke [1963] Chairman & Group Director; Mark Lee [1967] Managing Director

Pinder Fashions Limited
Incorporated: 14 February 1984 *Employees:* 25
Net Worth: £2,894,752 *Total Assets:* £5,627,718
Registered Office: Warren Trading, Beach Walk, Dawlish Warren, Dawlish, Devon, EX7 0NF
Activities: Retail sale of clothing in specialised stores
Shareholders: Garry Ninder Singh Benning; Gavin Singh Benning
Officers: Balvinder Singh Benning, Secretary; Balvinder Singh Benning [1953] Director; Bhupinder Singh Benning [1952] Director; Garry Ninder Singh Benning [1983] Director; Gavin Singh Benning [1977] Director

Pine Wood Hill Limited
Incorporated: 19 September 2016
Net Worth: £3,596,523 *Total Assets:* £3,596,523
Registered Office: Park Office, Blunsdon Abbey Park, Blunsdon St Andrew, Swindon, Wilts, SN25 2DU
Activities: Other business support service activities n.e.c.
Shareholders: Katie Sarah Marion Allen; Aaron David Griffin; Adam Joseph Griffin
Officers: Katie Sarah Marion Allen [1981] Director; Aaron David Griffin [1973] Director; Adam Joseph Griffin [1971] Director

Pinetops Nurseries Limited
Incorporated: 8 December 1976 *Employees:* 19
Net Worth: £2,905,937 *Total Assets:* £6,442,959
Registered Office: Towngate House, 2-8 Parkstone Road, Poole, Dorset, BH15 2PW
Activities: Growing of vegetables and melons, roots and tubers
Shareholders: Jean Marie Dick Paton; Jean Marie Dick Paton
Officers: Jean Marie Dick Paton [1934] Director; Rory Graham Paton [1969] Director

Pinewood School Limited
Incorporated: 19 April 1938 *Employees:* 95
Net Worth: £8,980,717 *Total Assets:* £10,799,080
Registered Office: Pinewood School, Bourton, Swindon, Wilts, SN6 8HZ
Activities: Primary education
Officers: Nicola Jane McAvoy, Secretary; Robin Francis Badham Thornhill [1954] Director/Teacher; Adrian Paul Ballard [1969] Development Director Sherborne School; Julian Charles Birch [1973] Director/Information Technology; Randal Timothy Brown [1958] Director/Retired; Peter Nigel Bryan [1960] Director of Corporate Resources & Deputy Master; James Caldwell Campbell [1950] Director/Self Employed Consultant; Nicholas Francis Cleverley [1975] Director/Surveyor; Emma Acworth Cripwell [1974] Marketing Director; Rebecca Jane Dougall [1970] Director/Headmistress; David John Fawcus [1956] Director/Chartered Accountant; Guy Peter Woodroffe Foster [1968] Director/Property Development; Catherine Ann Mary France [1969] Director/Lawyer; Nicola Anne Huggett [1969] Director/Head Independent School; Philip James Lough [1952] Director/Headmaster; Edward George Mawle [1972] Director/Financial Advisor; Richard Ian White [1955] Director/School Bursar

Pingry Solar Ltd
Incorporated: 27 November 2013
Net Worth Deficit: £674,342 *Total Assets:* £6,677,521
Registered Office: Long Barn, Manor Courtyard, Stratton on the Fosse, Radstock, Somerset, BA3 4QF
Activities: Production of electricity
Parent: Coleford Energy Limited
Officers: Jonathan Simon Thompson [1963] Managing Director

Pipex Limited
Incorporated: 12 March 1975 *Employees:* 153
Net Worth: £6,010,775 *Total Assets:* £10,397,485
Registered Office: c/o National Oilwell Varco, Stonedale Road, Oldends Lane Industrial Estate, Stonehouse, Glos, GL10 3RQ
Activities: Manufacture of other plastic products
Parent: Pipex PX Ltd
Officers: Alison May Sloan, Secretary; Robbert Oudendijk [1974] Director/Vice President Finance Europe, MENA, CIS [Dutch]; Simon Scott Reid [1982] Director/Accountant

Pittard Garnar Services Limited
Incorporated: 17 February 1964
Net Worth: £913,862 *Total Assets:* £5,400,738
Registered Office: Sherborne Road, Yeovil, Somerset, BA21 5BA
Activities: Tanning and dressing of leather; dressing and dyeing of fur
Parent: Pittards PLC
Officers: Reginald Herbert Hankey [1956] Director

Pittards PLC.
Incorporated: 5 April 1909 *Employees:* 1,647
Net Worth: £19,764,000 *Total Assets:* £32,579,000
Registered Office: Sherborne Road, Yeovil, Somerset, BA21 5BA
Activities: Tanning and dressing of leather; dressing and dyeing of fur
Officers: Reginald Herbert Hankey, Secretary; Louise Margaret Cretton [1957] Director; Godfrey Pawle Davis [1949] Director; Reginald Herbert Hankey [1956] Director; Stephen Yapp [1957] Director

Pittville Leasing Limited
Incorporated: 9 May 1994
Net Worth: £2,849,000 *Total Assets:* £55,732,000
Registered Office: The Quadrangle, The Promenade, Cheltenham, Glos, GL50 1PX
Activities: Financial intermediation not elsewhere classified
Parent: Royal Bank Leasing Limited
Officers: Ian Andrew Ellis [1969] Director/Bank Official; David Generald Harris [1969] Director/Bank Official; Steven James Roulston [1977] Director/Bank Official

PJAC (Bristol) Limited
Incorporated: 4 January 2006 *Employees:* 2
Previous: Matterhorn Capital Bristol Limited
Net Worth Deficit: £23,212 *Total Assets:* £4,072,407
Registered Office: Bath House, Bath Street, Redcliffe, Bristol, BS1 6HL
Activities: Development of building projects
Parent: PJAC Developments Limited
Officers: Julian Edward Hemmens [1980] Director; Paul Dean O'Brien [1966] Director

PJAC Developments Limited
Incorporated: 12 January 2016 *Employees:* 2
Net Worth Deficit: £8,680 *Total Assets:* £4,065,807
Registered Office: Bath House, 6-8 Bath Street, Redcliffe, Bristol, BS1 6HL
Activities: Development of building projects
Shareholders: Julian Edward Hemmens; Paul Dean O'Brien
Officers: Julian Edward Hemmens [1980] Director; Paul Dean O'Brien [1966] Director

PJFB Property Company Limited
Incorporated: 2 September 2016
Net Worth: £7,741,152 *Total Assets:* £11,245,078
Registered Office: 1st Floor, 7 Park Street, Bristol, BS1 5NF
Activities: Buying and selling of own real estate
Shareholder: Peter John Freeman Breach
Officers: Alexander Robin Livesey Breach [1989] Director; Christopher Andrew Talbot Breach [1974] Director/Chartered Surveyor; Harry William Freeman Breach [1972] Director/Equity Analyst; Joan Breach [1944] Director; Peter John Freeman Breach [1942] Director

PK Food Concepts Ltd.
Incorporated: 15 October 2009 *Employees:* 339
Net Worth Deficit: £3,493,559 *Total Assets:* £9,100,595
Registered Office: Plantation House, Milber Trading Estate, Newton Abbot, Devon, TQ12 4SG
Activities: Activities of head offices
Parent: Stage Capital Management Limited
Officers: Gavin Eliot Cox [1968] Director; James Oliver Tugwell [1993] Director/Investment Manager

PKL Group (UK) Limited
Incorporated: 25 October 1988 *Employees:* 96
Net Worth: £30,304,000 *Total Assets:* £41,086,000
Registered Office: Stella Way, Bishops Cleeve, Cheltenham, Glos, GL52 7DQ
Activities: Renting and leasing of other machinery, equipment and tangible goods n.e.c.
Parent: PKL Topco Ltd
Officers: William Edward Perry, Secretary; Christopher James Elgin Irving [1971] Director; William Edward Perry [1982] Finance Director; Christopher Charles Richards [1961] Operations Director; Peter Ferdinand Schad [1962] Director; Lee Anthony Vines [1969] Director

PKL Topco Limited
Incorporated: 22 December 2009 *Employees:* 96
Net Worth: £9,468,000 *Total Assets:* £20,239,000
Registered Office: Stella Way, Bishops Cleeve, Cheltenham, Glos, GL52 7DQ
Activities: Non-trading company
Officers: Michael William John Bailey [1953] Director; Christopher James Elgin Irving [1971] Director; Peter Robin Joy [1951] Director; Peter Ferdinand Schad [1962] Director; Lee Anthony Vines [1969] Director

Planit Software Limited
Incorporated: 26 January 1987 *Employees:* 147
Net Worth: £66,992,000 *Total Assets:* £78,791,000
Registered Office: 1370 Montpellier Court, Gloucester Business Park, Brockworth, Gloucester, GL3 4AH
Activities: Business and domestic software development
Parent: Planit Holdings Limited
Officers: Julie Randall, Secretary; Paolo Guglielmini [1977] Director/VP Business Development [Italian]; David Anthony Mills [1972] Finance Director; Julie Langhorne Randall [1961] Director

Plant Speed Limited
Incorporated: 10 March 2003 *Employees:* 20
Net Worth: £2,959,748 *Total Assets:* £4,486,393
Registered Office: River Fields Estate, Central Avenue, Hallen, Bristol, BS10 7ES
Activities: Freight transport by road
Major Shareholder: Paul Edward Lomas
Officers: Paul Edward Lomas, Secretary; David Bryans [1968] Director/Haulage Manager; Paul Edward Lomas [1966] Director/Haulage Manager

Plantforce Rentals Ltd
Incorporated: 15 January 1992 *Employees:* 99
Net Worth: £5,471,469 *Total Assets:* £30,968,010
Registered Office: Plantforce Rentals Ltd, Bristol Depot, Winterstoke Road, Weston Super Mare, Somerset, BS23 3YW
Activities: Renting and leasing of construction and civil engineering machinery and equipment
Shareholders: Robin Nicholas Powell; Jonathan Mark Powell
Officers: Christopher Bruce, Secretary/Hire Manager; William Frederick Caplan [1958] Director; Samuel Joseph Mercer [1987] Operations Director; Paul Leslie Oldham [1964] Director; Robin Nicholas Powell [1969] Director; Jason Lee Powles [1978] Director; Claire Louise Trott [1971] Managing Director; Jonathan Mark Wilson [1966] Director

Plantlife International - The Wild Plant Conservation Charity
Incorporated: 29 February 1996 *Employees:* 41
Net Worth: £5,217,645 *Total Assets:* £5,871,813
Registered Office: Brewery House, 36 Milford Street, Salisbury, Wilts, SP1 2AP
Activities: Other professional, scientific and technical activities n.e.c.
Officers: Sandra Margaret McLaren, Secretary; Simon Hugh Verdon Acland [1958] Director/Writer; Clive William Aslet [1955] Director/Writer; Richard Henry Ronald Benyon [1960] Director/Member of Parliament; Dr Katherine Drayson [1984] Director/Researcher; Professor David Arnold Hill [1958] Director/Ecologist; Philippa Mary Lyons [1953] Director/Consultant; Philip Jonathan Clifford Mould [1960] Director/Art Dealer; Robin David Payne [1961] Director/Environmental Consultant; Dr Rosetta Margaret Plummer [1955] Director/Consultant; Helen Elizabeth Priday [1957] Director; Ann Rowswell [1955] Director/Retired; Doctor Tim John Stowe [1954] Charity Director

Plantronics Limited
Incorporated: 29 November 1983 *Employees:* 87
Net Worth: £9,218,759 *Total Assets:* £14,944,266
Registered Office: Interface Business Park, Bincknall Lane, Royal Wootton Bassett, Wilts, SN4 8QQ
Activities: Other business support service activities n.e.c.
Parent: Plantronics B.V.
Officers: Paul Francis Katawicz [1967] Director/Associate General Counsel [American]; William James Pflugh [1958] Senior Director of Tax and Treasury [American]

The Plastic Surgeon Holdings Limited
Incorporated: 9 January 2017 *Employees:* 220
Net Worth: £3,174,730 *Total Assets:* £8,295,835
Registered Office: c/o TLT LLP, 1 Redcliff Street, Bristol, BS1 6TP
Activities: Non-trading company
Shareholder: Robert David Mouser
Officers: Robert Michael Henry [1954] Director; Robert David Mouser [1972] Director; Timothy Stuart Ross [1948] Director

The Plastic Surgeon Limited
Incorporated: 24 February 1999 *Employees:* 217
Net Worth: £1,047,640 *Total Assets:* £5,202,323
Registered Office: Blue Waters House, Pottery Road, Bovey Tracey, Devon, TQ13 9DS
Activities: Other building completion and finishing
Parent: The Plastic Surgeon Holdings Limited
Officers: Michael Aitken [1976] Sales Director; Gary Danson [1966] Operations Director; Ross Gardner [1978] IT Director; Robert David Mouser [1972] Director; Timothy Stuart Ross [1948] Director; Neal Whelband [1976] Finance Director

Plastivan Limited
Incorporated: 26 April 1994 *Employees:* 22
Net Worth: £1,981,740 *Total Assets:* £3,699,682
Registered Office: Unit 4 Bonville Trading Estate, Brislington, Bristol, BS4 5QU
Activities: Agents involved in the sale of timber and building materials
Officers: Stephen Louis Halford [1954] Sales Director; Bart Medard Robert Van Overschelde [1962] Director [Belgian]

Platinum One Hotels Limited
Incorporated: 28 January 2003 *Employees:* 93
Net Worth: £1,139,484 *Total Assets:* £4,977,173
Registered Office: Captains Club Hotel, Wick Ferry, Wick Lane, Christchurch, Dorset, BH23 1HU
Activities: Hotels and similar accommodation
Officers: Christopher Maurice Bradfield [1952] Director; Timothy Carl Lloyd [1963] Director/Hotelier; Rosalind Jane Morgan [1958] Director; Sarah Ross [1964] Director; Robert John Wilson [1964] Hotel Director

Play Sports Group Limited
Incorporated: 7 February 2017 *Employees:* 71
Net Worth: £6,820,490 *Total Assets:* £9,561,459
Registered Office: 30 Monmouth Street, Bath, BA1 2AP
Activities: Activities of head offices
Parent: DNI Europe Holdings Limited
Officers: Sameer Pabari [1974] Director/Business Executive; Simon Alan Wear [1971] Director; Amy Wu [1987] Director/Business Executive [American]

Playforce Limited
Incorporated: 21 June 1999 *Employees:* 38
Net Worth: £3,832,934 *Total Assets:* £5,850,470
Registered Office: 1 Pegasus Way, Bowerhill, Melksham, Wilts, SN12 6TR
Activities: Other construction installation
Parent: T.C. Landscapes Limited
Officers: Simon John Abley [1976] Director; Simon John Cashmore [1970] Director; Robert Chatwin [1984] Director; Mark Wood [1964] Director

PLB Group Ltd.
Incorporated: 2 August 1982 *Employees:* 74
Net Worth Deficit: £13,926,000 *Total Assets:* £28,534,000
Registered Office: Whitchurch Lane, Whitchurch, Bristol, BS14 0JZ
Activities: Agents involved in the sale of food, beverages and tobacco
Parent: Bibendum PLB Group Limited
Officers: Andrea Pozzi [1971] Director/Group Chief Operating Officer; Ewan James Robertson [1982] Finance Director; Jonathan Solesbury [1965] Director/Group Chief Financial Officer

Pleroma (UK) Limited
Incorporated: 15 June 1994
Net Worth: £19,563,000 *Total Assets:* £23,805,000
Registered Office: Stock Lane, Langford, Somerset, BS40 5ES
Activities: Activities of head offices
Major Shareholder: Ronald Christopher Wilson
Officers: Philip Wilson, Secretary; Philip David Wilson [1975] Director [Irish]; Ronald Christopher Wilson [1948] Director/Industrialist [Irish]

Pleroma Investments Limited
Incorporated: 2 January 1952
Net Worth: £24,373,000 *Total Assets:* £31,494,000
Registered Office: Stock Lane, Langford, Somerset, BS40 5ES
Activities: Other letting and operating of own or leased real estate
Parent: Pleroma (UK) Limited
Officers: Philip Wilson, Secretary; Philip David Wilson [1975] Director/Company Secretary [Irish]; Ronald Christopher Wilson [1948] Director/Industrialist [Irish]

Plessey Group Holdings Limited
Incorporated: 14 January 2010 *Employees:* 148
Net Worth Deficit: £26,117,000 *Total Assets:* £22,635,000
Registered Office: Tamerton Road, Roborough, Plymouth, PL6 7BQ
Activities: Activities of head offices
Shareholder: Nicolas Maurice
Officers: Gilad Engel [1978] Director/Consultant [Israeli]; Iain Charles Silvester [1961] Director/Chartered Accountant; Yaron Valler [1970] Director/Consultant [Israeli]

Plessey Lighting Limited
Incorporated: 8 December 2011
Total Assets: £10,025,000
Registered Office: Tamerton Road, Roborough, Plymouth, PL6 7BQ
Activities: Manufacture of electric lighting equipment
Parent: Plessey Semiconductors Limited
Officers: Christopher Simon Bailey [1959] Director/Accountant; Iain Charles Silvester [1961] Director/Chartered Accountant

Plessey Semiconductors Limited
Incorporated: 18 December 2000 *Employees:* 147
Net Worth: £4,370,000 *Total Assets:* £12,579,000
Registered Office: Tamerton Road, Roborough, Plymouth, PL6 7BQ
Activities: Manufacture of other electrical equipment
Parent: Plessey Group Holdings Limited
Officers: Christopher Simon Bailey [1959] Director/Finance Manager; Iain Charles Silvester [1961] Director/Chartered Accountant

Plumlocations Limited
Incorporated: 7 December 2016 *Employees:* 2
Net Worth: £2,721,592 *Total Assets:* £6,484,970
Registered Office: c/o Francis Clark LLP, North Quay House, Sutton Harbour, Plymouth, PL4 0RA
Activities: Other letting and operating of own or leased real estate
Shareholders: Stephen John Mittler; Catherine Lucy Mittler
Officers: Catherine Lucy Mittler [1964] Director; Stephen John Mittler [1959] Director

T.H.Plumridge Limited
Incorporated: 30 June 1954 *Employees:* 3
Net Worth: £4,250,755 *Total Assets:* £4,353,191
Registered Office: 52-54 Winchester Street, Salisbury, Wilts, SP1 1HG
Activities: Other letting and operating of own or leased real estate
Shareholders: Sarah Plumridge; Sarah Plumridge
Officers: Sarah Plumridge, Secretary; Robin Plumridge [1941] Director/Builder; Sarah Plumridge [1967] Director/Solicitor

Plus Shipping Services Limited
Incorporated: 9 August 2002
Net Worth: £23,829,000 *Total Assets:* £24,021,000
Registered Office: Windmill Hill Business Park, Whitehill Way, Swindon, Wilts, SN5 6PB
Activities: Distribution of gaseous fuels through mains
Parent: npower Limited
Officers: Glenn William Chapman, Secretary; Peter Russell Sharman [1967] Director; Simon Nicholas Stacey [1965] Director/Financial Accountant

The Pluss Organisation CIC
Incorporated: 6 July 2004 *Employees:* 314
Previous: The Pluss Organisation
Net Worth: £1,731,000 *Total Assets:* £7,062,000
Registered Office: Office 3, Merriott House, Hennock Road Central, Marsh Barton Trading Estate, Exeter, Devon, EX2 8NP
Activities: Manufacture of other general-purpose machinery n.e.c.
Officers: Simon Mark Charles [1967] Director/Human Resources Consultant; David Alan Evans [1977] Director/Chief Operations Officer; Steven Timothy Mark Hawkins [1963] Director/Senior Manager; Stephen Anthony Otter [1962] Director; Robert Christopher Salvoni [1964] Director; Sally Ann Elizabeth Taylor [1956] Director

Plym Academy Trust
Incorporated: 10 March 2016 *Employees:* 234
Net Worth: £16,239,962 *Total Assets:* £20,279,692
Registered Office: c/o Woodford Primary School, Litchaton Way, Plympton, Plymouth, PL7 4RR
Activities: Primary education
Officers: Lindsey Robin Johnson, Secretary; John David Agnew [1967] Director/Financial Advisor; Philip Frank Braide [1953] Director/Retired; Nicholas Brewer [1973] Director/Building Surveyor; Ian Cload [1963] Director/Headteacher; Sandra Crawford [1969] Director; Rhodri Giles Davey [1974] Director/Solicitor; Lisa Damaris Hartley [1968] Director; Deborah Louise Johns [1966] Director/Payroll Manager; Geoffrey Nelder [1955] Director/Retired; Anthony Darren Rose [1980] Director/Auditor

Plymouth Age Concern
Incorporated: 4 June 1980 *Employees:* 73
Net Worth: £4,640,773 *Total Assets:* £4,779,523
Registered Office: William & Patricia Venton Centre, Astor Drive, Mount Gould, Plymouth, PL4 9RD
Activities: Residential care activities for the elderly and disabled
Officers: Elizabeth Bombieri [1959] Director/Falls Service Lead; Elizabeth Edwards-Smith [1974] Director/Consultant; Stuart Alan Keegan [1976] Director/Army Officer; Andrea Wright [1981] Director/Certified Chartered Accountant; Benny Wright [1978] Director/Trustee

Plymouth Cast
Incorporated: 11 March 2013 *Employees:* 1,552
Net Worth: £9,664,603 *Total Assets:* £29,641,712
Registered Office: St Boniface House, Ashburton, Newton Abbot, Devon, TQ13 7JL
Activities: Primary education
Officers: Denis Alexander Anderson [1945] Director/Retired; Graham Briscoe [1943] Director/Retired; John Patrick Aubone Burnett [1945] Director/Peer/Solicitor; Maria Catherine Edwards [1961] Director/Retired; Raymond Francis Friel [1963] Director/Chief Executive; Ann Christine Harris [1945] Director/Retired Headteacher; Andrew Nicholls [1955] Director/Retired; Daniel John Rogerson [1975] Director; Laura Elaine Sprackman [1980] Director; Terrence Rodney Frederick Stockley [1944] Director/Retired; Jacqui Marie Vaughan [1969] Director/Operations Manager

Plymouth City Airport Limited
Incorporated: 21 May 1975
Net Worth: £5,416,000 *Total Assets:* £12,579,000
Registered Office: Guy's Quay, Sutton Harbour, Plymouth, PL4 0ES
Activities: Other letting and operating of own or leased real estate
Parent: Sutton Harbour Holdings PLC
Officers: Natasha Claire Gadsdon, Secretary/Chartered Accountant; Philip Howard Beinhaker [1941] Director [Canadian]; Natasha Claire Gadsdon [1970] Director/Accountant; Graham Scott Miller [1963] Director

Plymouth College and St Dunstan's Abbey Schools Charity
Incorporated: 26 July 2004 *Employees:* 222
Net Worth: £7,401,422 *Total Assets:* £13,617,598
Registered Office: Plymouth College, Ford Park, Plymouth, PL4 6RN
Activities: Pre-primary education
Officers: Sarah Jane Wills, Secretary; Penny Ann Atkinson [1972] Director/GP; Adrian Templeton Brett [1947] Director/Consultant; Kelly Marie Davis [1980] Director/Lecturer; Clare Catherine Hammond [1960] Director/Solicitor; Professor David Arthur Huntley [1945] Director/Emeritus Professor; Alison Christina Campbell Mills [1966] Director/Personal Manager; Christopher Douglas Morton [1958] Director; Samantha Charlotte Seth [1969] Director/Accountant; Dr Andrew Graham Williams [1952] Director/Retired; David Roger Woodgate [1958] Director

Plymouth Community Homes Energy Limited
Incorporated: 12 April 2012
Net Worth: £9,648,000 *Total Assets:* £9,655,000
Registered Office: Plumer House, Tailyour Road, Crownhill, Plymouth, PL6 5DH
Activities: Other construction installation
Officers: Belinda Jane Pascoe, Secretary; John Clark [1961] Director/Chief Executive; Nicholas Jackson [1966] Finance Director; Gillian Fisher Martin [1963] Director; Susan Forde Shaw [1958] Director

The Plymouth Hotel Company Limited
Incorporated: 16 July 2001 *Employees:* 81
Net Worth: £1,723,206 *Total Assets:* £3,938,136
Registered Office: The Duke of Cornwall Hotel, Millbay Road, Plymouth, PL1 3LG
Activities: Hotels and similar accommodation
Shareholders: Walter Combstock; Jonathan Morcom
Officers: Jonathan Morcom, Secretary/Hotelier; Walter Combstock [1945] Director/Hotelier; Jonathan Morcom [1971] Director/Hotelier

Plymouth Marine Laboratory
Incorporated: 13 March 2001 *Employees:* 152
Net Worth: £5,252,000 *Total Assets:* £16,999,000
Registered Office: Prospect Place, West Hoe, Plymouth, PL1 3DH
Activities: Other research and experimental development on natural sciences and engineering
Officers: Beverly Kim Tremain, Secretary/Personal Assistant; Nicholas Brian Buckland OBE [1951] Director; Sir James Michael Burnell-Nugent [1949] Director; Nigel John Godefroy [1964] Director; Timothy David Jickells [1953] Director/Professor (Science); Dr Ralph Frank Rayner [1954] Director/Marine Scientist; Simon Patrick Sherrard [1947] Director; Janice Elizabeth Timberlake [1966] HR Director; Professor Bess Berkley Ward [1954] Director/Professor of Geosciences [American]; Baroness Mary Jane Watkins [1955] Director/Emeritus Professor

Plymouth Rentals Limited
Incorporated: 23 August 2012 *Employees:* 5
Previous: Hindhead Property Management Limited
Net Worth: £1,919,777 *Total Assets:* £11,189,358
Registered Office: Pemberley Hall, Buckland Monochorum, Yelverton, Devon, PL20 7LG
Activities: Other letting and operating of own or leased real estate
Shareholders: Jeffrey Charles Deacon; Maria Bernadette Deacon
Officers: Maria Deacon, Secretary; Jeffrey Charles Deacon [1964] Director; Maria Bernadette Deacon [1966] Director

Plymouth Science Park Limited
Incorporated: 12 February 1996 *Employees:* 16
Net Worth: £11,956,201 *Total Assets:* £18,998,816
Registered Office: 1 Davy Road, Derriford, Plymouth, PL6 8BX
Activities: Other letting and operating of own or leased real estate
Officers: Ian George Pearce, Secretary; John Keith Acornley [1953] Director; David Draffan [1972] Assistant Director of Economic Development; Tudor Evans [1959] Director/Councillor; Kevin David Jones [1960] Director/University Professor; Michael Allan Legoff [1961] Director; Ian Robert Bruce McFadzen [1965] Director/Chief Executive Officer; Ian George Pearce [1959] Director; Professor Jeremy Alan Roberts [1954] Director/Deputy Vice-Chancellor Research and Enterprise; David Nicholas Thomas [1962] NHS Director

Plympton Academy
Incorporated: 11 March 2011 *Employees:* 120
Previous: Ridgeway School
Net Worth: £12,175,814 *Total Assets:* £15,284,163
Registered Office: Plympton Academy, Moorland Road, Plympton, Plymouth, PL7 2RS
Activities: General secondary education
Officers: Teresa Ann Lakeman, Secretary; Edward James Atter [1973] Director/Employment Adviser; Tina Marie Blagdon [1969] Director/Financial Adviser; Lisa Boorman [1969] Director/Principal; Susan Elizabeth Dann [1958] Director/Local Government Councillor; Martin Edmunds [1976] Director/Teacher; Margaret Elizabeth Hall [1947] Director/Retired; Paul Hutchings [1957] Director/Gas Engineer Consultant; David Parker [1975] Director/Governor; Margaret Elizabeth Turner [1958] Director/Retired; Steven Wallers [1972] Director/Governor

Plymstock Properties Limited
Incorporated: 8 February 1996 *Employees:* 3
Net Worth: £2,615,374 *Total Assets:* £5,911,373
Registered Office: Fort Stamford Country Club, Jennycliff, Plymouth, PL9 9TU
Activities: Other letting and operating of own or leased real estate
Major Shareholder: Richard John Larson
Officers: Sarah Jill Larson, Secretary; Richard John Larson [1974] Director/Electrician; Sheila Larson [1942] Director/Retired Nurse

Plymstock School
Incorporated: 9 March 2011 *Employees:* 226
Net Worth: £25,477,208 *Total Assets:* £30,448,756
Registered Office: Plymstock School, Church Road, Plymstock, Plymouth, PL9 9AZ
Activities: General secondary education
Officers: Julia Crookston, Secretary; Kevin John Bunt [1959] Director/Businessman; Robert James Diment [1978] Director/Headteacher; Andrew Donald Edwards [1957] Director/Businessman

PMG Services (Bristol) Limited
Incorporated: 23 May 2003
Net Worth: £4,637,510 *Total Assets:* £6,380,009
Registered Office: Unit 1, 38 Albert Road, St Philips, Bristol, BS2 0XA
Activities: Maintenance and repair of motor vehicles
Shareholders: Bernadette Frances McGuinness; Patrick McGuinness
Officers: Clare Evelyn McGuinness, Secretary; Bernadette Frances McGuinness [1958] Director [Irish]; Patrick McGuinness [1961] Director [Irish]

PMMR Developments Limited
Incorporated: 17 June 2014 *Employees:* 6
Net Worth: £435,352 *Total Assets:* £6,650,977
Registered Office: 37 Great Pulteney Street, Bath, BA2 4DA
Activities: Development of building projects
Parent: RMMP Limited
Officers: Mollie Audrey Salter, Secretary; Dr Peter Huw Green [1960] Director/General Practitioner; Dr Rosemary Christine Loftus [1962] Director/Doctor; Michael Robert Salter [1954] Director/Pharmacist; Mollie Audrey Salter [1955] Director

Poeton Holdings Limited
Incorporated: 19 July 2000 *Employees:* 225
Net Worth: £4,241,690 *Total Assets:* £9,412,946
Registered Office: Eastern Avenue, Gloucester, GL4 3DN
Activities: Activities of head offices
Shareholders: Anthony Russell Poeton; Rowenna Jane Poeton
Officers: Anthony Russell Poeton [1948] Director; Rowenna Poeton [1959] Director

Poeton Industries Limited
Incorporated: 26 February 1930 *Employees:* 217
Net Worth: £2,673,480 *Total Assets:* £6,398,265
Registered Office: Poeton Industries Ltd, Eastern Avenue, Gloucester, GL4 3DN
Activities: Treatment and coating of metals
Parent: Poeton Holdings Limited
Officers: Stephen Terry Elliott-Mead, Secretary; Darren John Burge [1968] Managing Director; James Russell Cooke [1981] Sales Director; Stephen Terry Elliott-Mead [1975] Director/Chartered Accountant; Alastair David McLeish [1963] Director/Consultant; Anthony Russell Poeton [1948] Director

The Point at Polzeath Limited
Incorporated: 27 January 2012 *Employees:* 35
Net Worth Deficit: £1,308,681 *Total Assets:* £4,862,742
Registered Office: 1a Eddystone Road, Wadebridge, Cornwall, PL27 7AL
Activities: Operation of sports facilities
Shareholders: Eva Eleonora Rode Davies; Jeremy Jenkin Davies
Officers: Robert David Tress Clive [1964] Director; Jeremy Jenkin Davies [1963] Director; Michael George Aidan Kershaw [1961] Director/Business Advisor; Eva Eleonora Rode Davies [1963] Director [Norwegian]

Pokesdown Community Primary School
Incorporated: 1 March 2013 *Employees:* 63
Net Worth: £3,591,275 *Total Assets:* £5,066,360
Registered Office: Pokesdown Community Primary School, Livingstone Road, Bournemouth, BH5 2AS
Activities: Primary education
Officers: Terri Louise Nelson, Secretary; Joanne Barton [1970] Director/Headteacher; Adam Leneve Biddle [1973] Director/Teacher; Kirsten Bryan-Brown [1969] Director/Full Time Mother; Mark Ian Cribb [1975] Director/Hospitality; Gemma Hill [1985] Director/Teacher; Saeed Khan Rashid [1971] Director/Lecturer; Mark Saddington [1969] Director/Head of Alumni Relations; Barras Kenneth Stone [1946] Director/Lecturer; Kevin Mark Thomas [1969] Director/Business Intelligence Analyst; Katrina May Ware [1983] Director; Dr Christopher Beaumont Wragg [1975] Director

Polamco Limited
Incorporated: 20 January 1984
Net Worth: £7,700,338 *Total Assets:* £7,732,796
Registered Office: Company Secretariat, Site H, Faraday Road, Swindon, Wilts, SN3 5HH
Activities: Non-trading company
Parent: Tyco Electronics UK Holdings Ltd
Officers: Harold Gregory Barksdale [1964] Director/VP and Corporate Secretary [American]; Richard Mark Buggy [1971] Director/Vice President Finance [American]; Stephen Christopher Cooper [1970] Finance Director

Pole Farming Limited
Incorporated: 20 October 2005 *Employees:* 18
Previous: B & J Pigs Limited
Net Worth: £1,434,430 *Total Assets:* £6,358,132
Registered Office: Bishopbrook House, Cathedral Avenue, Wells, Somerset, BA5 1FD
Activities: Raising of dairy cattle
Officers: Bernadette Pole, Secretary; Bernadette Pole [1952] Director; Graham Edward Pole [1957] Director; Judith Mary Pole [1959] Director; Ray Pole [1947] Director

Police Resources International Limited
Incorporated: 16 January 1998 *Employees:* 9
Net Worth: £3,027,914 *Total Assets:* £4,344,554
Registered Office: 1 Fair Oak Court, Clyst, Honiton, Exeter, Devon, EX5 2BB
Activities: Wholesale of clothing and footwear
Major Shareholder: Derek Alan Gollop
Officers: Alison Godwin, Secretary/Accounts Manager; Derek Alan Gollop [1957] Managing Director; Nicholas Bellamy Pitts [1938] Director/Agricultural Merchant

Henry W Pollard & Sons (Group) Limited
Incorporated: 20 September 2011 *Employees:* 52
Net Worth: £1,067,320 *Total Assets:* £6,115,067
Registered Office: 20 Monmouth Street, Bridgwater, Somerset, TA6 5EJ
Activities: Activities of other holding companies n.e.c.
Shareholders: William George Badham; Mark Richard Brown
Officers: Amanda Drewitt, Secretary; William George Badham [1953] Managing Director; Mark Richard Brown [1968] Director; Hugh Graham Dalton [1960] Business Development Director; Amanda Drewitt [1972] Financial Director

Henry W. Pollard & Sons Limited
Incorporated: 10 July 1979 *Employees:* 39
Net Worth: £1,286,169 *Total Assets:* £6,244,008
Registered Office: 20 Monmouth Street, Bridgwater, Somerset, TA6 5EJ
Activities: Development of building projects
Parent: Henry W Pollard & Sons (Group) Limited
Officers: Amanda Drewitt, Secretary; William George Badham [1953] Managing Director; Mark Richard Brown [1968] Director; Hugh Graham Dalton [1960] Business Development Director; Amanda Drewitt [1972] Financial Director; Mark Douglas Coward Smith [1956] Contract Director

Polymermedics Limited
Incorporated: 10 March 2011 *Employees:* 51
Net Worth: £1,052,045 *Total Assets:* £5,378,200
Registered Office: Plastics Plant, Bucklers Lane, St Austell, Cornwall, PL25 3FR
Activities: Manufacture of other plastic products
Major Shareholder: Mateo Klemmayer
Officers: John Reginald Colling [1975] Director; Matthias Poschmann [1955] Director [German]; Neil Gary Skyba [1976] Director

Pool Academy
Incorporated: 10 February 2011 *Employees:* 122
Net Worth: £8,267,746 *Total Assets:* £10,015,043
Registered Office: Church Road, Pool, Cornwall, TR15 3PZ
Activities: General secondary education
Officers: Philip Jones, Secretary; Mary Allison Anson [1952] Director/Care Home Operator; Frank William Baker [1954] Director/Retired; Carol Anne Bragg [1963] Director/Bank Manager; Clive John Bramley [1952] Director; Allison Ruth Burton [1963] Director/Personal Assistant; Kirsty Louisa Cotton [1978] Director/Talent Development Manager; Vicky Cox [1978] Director/Manager; Nicholas Mark Hamblin [1964] Director; Claire Louise Meakin [1982] Director/Headmistress; Sarah Jayne Newham [1964] Director/Civil Servant; Luke Samuel Roberts [1984] Director; Richard Schofield [1976] Director/Police Officer; Jennifer Elizabeth Smith [1981] Director/Teacher; Kerry Leigh Kezzibelle St Leger [1985] Director; Samantha Thompson [1974] Director

Gordon L. Poole (Southampton) Limited
Incorporated: 5 September 1956 *Employees:* 2
Net Worth: £3,711,574 *Total Assets:* £3,999,338
Registered Office: 6th Floor, Dean Park House, Dean Park Crescent, Bournemouth, BH1 1HP
Activities: Development of building projects
Shareholder: Peter John Schofield
Officers: Peter John Schofield, Secretary; Carol Margaret Ashbolt [1940] Director; Peter John Schofield [1946] Director/Chartered Accountant; Valentine Nickolette Young [1946] Director

Poole Arts Trust Limited
Incorporated: 12 May 1978 *Employees:* 207
Net Worth: £6,929,188 *Total Assets:* £8,243,920
Registered Office: Lighthouse, Kingland Road, Poole, Dorset, BH15 1UG
Activities: Operation of arts facilities
Officers: Peter John Wilson, Secretary; Spencer Clarke [1970] Director; Sally Anne Crawford [1955] Director/Retired Solicitor; Rowena Julie Gaston [1969] Development Director; Richard Hendry [1968] Director; Michael Makepeace Eugene Jeffries [1944] Director; Amanda Kampel [1963] Commercial Director; Donald Edward Nordberg [1949] Director [American]; Nicola Jane Oliver [1967] Director; Mark John Powell [1964] Director/Chief Executive; Bob Reeves [1947] Director/Retired; Amir James Sadeh [1981] Director

Poole Grammar School
Incorporated: 10 June 2011 *Employees:* 155
Net Worth: £10,950,073 *Total Assets:* £14,001,243
Registered Office: Poole Grammar School, Gravel Hill, Poole, Dorset, BH17 9JU
Activities: General secondary education
Officers: Jonathan Robert Thomas Stiby, Secretary; Andrew John Baker [1958] Director/Headteacher; Stephen Charles Bates [1965] Director/Chartered Accountant; Neil John Bichard [1962] Director/Chartered Architect; Simon John Bowden [1959] Director/Retired; Nathan Chase [1981] Director/Teacher; Adrian Clive Falck [1980] Director/Solicitor; Frances Margaret French [1962] Director; Susan Da Conceicao Fry [1969] Director/Marketing and Communications; Marika Helen Holmes-Evans [1957] Director; Stephen John Morris [1963] Social Care Director; David Mark Newell [1960] Director/University Lecturer; Joshua Phillips [1974] Director/Hospital Consultant; Dr Kenneth John Power [1956] Director/Consultant; Jayes Krasandas Rana [1971] Director/Surveyor; Dr Rhiannon Jane Smith [1968] Director/Teacher; Anita Louise Steel [1957] Financial Director; April Jayne Thomas [1965] Director/Education; Dr Emma Thompson [1986] Director/Higher Education Student Support

Poole Housing Partnership Limited
Incorporated: 26 January 2004 *Employees:* 101
Net Worth Deficit: £5,537,570 *Total Assets:* £4,086,641
Registered Office: Beech House, 28-30 Wimborne Road, Poole, Dorset, BH15 2BU
Activities: Management of real estate on a fee or contract basis
Parent: Borough of Poole
Officers: Jacqueline Barton, Secretary; Peter Frederick Adams [1938] Director/Politician; Susan Elizabeth Double [1948] Director/Retired; Robert George Dunford [1979] Director/Head of Programmes; Robert David Dustan [1964] Business Development Director; David Andrew Garner-Watts [1959] Director/Operations Manager; Joan Eveline Gordon [1950] Director/Retired; Richard Lewis Hudson [1947] Director/Retired; Sandra Elizabeth Hazel Moore [1951] Director/Councillor; Reniera Elizabeth O'Donnell [1977] Director/Local Government Officer; Elizabeth Mary Pilkington [1982] Director/Banker; Antony David Underhill [1963] Director/Engineer; Peter William Harber Woodroffe [1952] Director/Solicitor

Poole Lighting Limited
Incorporated: 22 April 2003 *Employees:* 239
Net Worth: £10,959,613 *Total Assets:* £42,981,936
Registered Office: 9 Cabot Lane, Creekmoor, Poole, Dorset, BH17 7BY
Activities: Wholesale of furniture, carpets and lighting equipment
Officers: Michael Last, Secretary; Meyer Maslo, Secretary; Michael David Last [1968] Director/Chief Operating Officer; Elisheba Maslo [1964] Director [Swiss]; Meyer Maslo [1964] Director; Jacob Schimmel [1962] Director

Poolearth Limited
Incorporated: 2 December 1997 *Employees:* 33
Net Worth: £1,314,654 *Total Assets:* £3,651,061
Registered Office: 71-73 Hyde Park Road, Mutley, Plymouth, PL3 4JN
Activities: Dispensing chemist in specialised stores
Shareholders: Raymond Blatchford; Sian Retallick
Officers: Ronald Christopher Kirk, Secretary; Raymond Blatchford [1959] Director/Plumber; Ronald Christopher Kirk [1977] Director/General Manager; Sian Retallick [1961] Director/Pharmacist

Keith Pople Limited
Incorporated: 23 November 1951 *Employees:* 6
Net Worth: £9,874,393 *Total Assets:* £10,650,043
Registered Office: Suite 302, 179 Whiteladies Road, Clifton, Bristol, BS8 2AG
Activities: Other letting and operating of own or leased real estate
Officers: Christopher John Pople [1959] Director; David Jeremy Pople [1957] Director; Nicola Pople [1965] Director; Richard Clive Pople [1955] Director/Executive Manager

Port Regis School Limited
Incorporated: 8 August 1947 *Employees:* 186
Net Worth: £7,667,358 *Total Assets:* £9,516,132
Registered Office: Motcombe House, Motcombe Park, Shaftesbury, Dorset, SP7 9QA
Activities: Primary education
Officers: Jacqueline Pugh, Secretary; Mark Jonathan Paul Aichroth [1963] Director/Chief Operating Officer; Emily Boswell [1975] Director/Teacher; Lady Cathryn Mary Cayley [1965] Director/Head of Boarding; Anthony Oswald Cumine [1955] Director/Site Agent; Stephen Edlmann [1954] Director/Lawyer; William James Rufus Gething [1959] Director/Investment Property; Jeremy John Hamer [1952] Director/Chartered Accountant; Oliver Hawkins [1976] Director/Management Consultant; Christopher John Holloway [1946] Director/Chartered Surveyor; Sarah Elizabeth James [1974] Director/Teacher; Fiona Elisabeth Stafford Loveridge [1962] Director/Principal; Dr Jamie McManus [1975] Director/Teacher; James Iain Stevenson [1962] Director/Army Brigadier; Gavin Matthew White [1968] Director/Private Investor; Judy Nicola Williamson [1954] Director/Housewife

Porter Dodson LLP
Incorporated: 14 February 2012 *Employees:* 160
Net Worth: £4,786,651 *Total Assets:* £11,510,202
Registered Office: The Close, Church Path, Yeovil, Somerset, BA20 1HH
Officers: Nicholas William Clegg [1956] Member; Robert Charles Millard Fox [1963] Member; Catherine Mary-Louise James [1974] Member; Ian Sankey [1956] Member; Evelyn Adfield [1978] LLP Member; Richard John Baker [1967] LLP Member; Scott David Bowley [1973] LLP Member; Sharon Louise Collier [1977] LLP Member; Steven Farnham [1973] LLP Member; Lesley Joan Gaskell [1954] LLP Member; Benjamin James Hingley [1982] LLP Member; Stephen St John Mahoney [1961] LLP Member; Rebecca Marshall [1968] LLP Member; Julia Helen Perrins [1960] LLP Member; Adrian Peter Richard Poole [1975] LLP Member; Beverley Jane Rockliff [1956] LLP Member; Louise Lesley Robins Sanders [1968] LLP Member; Cathryn Fiona Smith [1961] LLP Member; Victoria Walker [1971] LLP Member; Bruce Kerstin Weir [1965] LLP Member; Stephen Elis Wray [1972] LLP Member

Alan Porter Limited
Incorporated: 9 January 1973 *Employees:* 5
Net Worth: £2,768,929 *Total Assets:* £4,741,501
Registered Office: Kings Buildings, Lydney, Glos, GL15 5HE
Activities: Buying and selling of own real estate
Officers: Simon Andrew Jonathan Porter, Secretary; Caroline Sarah Jane Constance [1969] Director; Amanda Louise Gething Lewis [1966] Director; Anne Lesley Porter [1941] Director; Dr Mark Christopher Milson Porter [1962] Director; Simon Andrew Jonathan Porter [1963] Director

Porthia Group Limited
Incorporated: 5 May 1992 *Employees:* 338
Net Worth: £4,070,219 *Total Assets:* £14,678,049
Registered Office: Godrevy House, Trewidden Road, St Ives, Cornwall, TR26 2BX
Activities: Activities of other holding companies n.e.c.
Shareholders: David Brian Ellsmore; Alison Ellsmore
Officers: Ian Neville Jarvis, Secretary; Alison Ellsmore [1965] Director/Secretary; David Brian Ellsmore [1946] Director

Porthia Limited
Incorporated: 21 September 2004 *Employees:* 3
Net Worth Deficit: £793,578 *Total Assets:* £5,002,476
Registered Office: Godrevy House, Trewidden Road, St Ives, Cornwall, TR26 2BX
Activities: Development of building projects
Shareholders: David Brian Ellsmore; Alison Ellsmore
Officers: Gilly-Ann Roelofje Selzer Jarvis, Secretary; Alison Ellsmore [1965] Director/Secretary; David Brian Ellsmore [1946] Director/Developer

Porthminster Hotel Company Limited
Incorporated: 23 March 1893 *Employees:* 76
Net Worth: £4,528,754 *Total Assets:* £17,395,096
Registered Office: Harbour House, 60 Purewell, Christchurch, Dorset, BH23 1ES
Activities: Hotels and similar accommodation
Parent: Harbour Hotels Group Limited
Officers: Stuart Andrew Bateman [1976] Director; David Francis Robbins [1967] Finance Director; Michael Oliver Warren [1970] Director [Irish]

Portico Business Services Limited
Incorporated: 12 December 1990 *Employees:* 43
Net Worth: £2,035,489 *Total Assets:* £4,134,397
Registered Office: 7-9 North Parade Buildings, Bath, BA1 1NS
Activities: Non-specialised wholesale trade
Major Shareholder: Simon Richard Harrison
Officers: Barbara Jacqueline Harrison, Secretary; Andrew Clifford Harrison [1932] Director/Retailer; Simon Richard Harrison [1959] Director/Card Designer and Retailer; Carmen Sophia Long [1966] Director; Ian James McDougall [1976] Operations Director

Portland Harbour Authority Limited
Incorporated: 13 December 1994 *Employees:* 39
Net Worth: £3,380,957 *Total Assets:* £4,545,604
Registered Office: Bingham's Melcombe, Dorchester, DT2 7PZ
Activities: Sea and coastal freight water transport
Officers: Alan Douglas Deves, Secretary; Rupert Thomas Nicholas Best [1943] Director/Management Consultant; Alan Douglas Deves [1962] Director/Chartered Accountant; John Christopher Langham [1951] Director; Justin Morley Langham [1963] Director/Chartered Surveyor; William Thomas Reeves [1950] Director

Portland Port Limited
Incorporated: 13 February 1996 *Employees:* 18
Net Worth: £17,215,618 *Total Assets:* £20,748,280
Registered Office: Bingham's Melcombe, Dorchester, DT2 7PZ
Activities: Sea and coastal freight water transport
Officers: Alan Douglas Deves, Secretary; Rupert Thomas Nicholas Best [1943] Director/Management Consultant; Alan Douglas Deves [1962] Director/Chartered Accountant; John Christopher Langham [1951] Director; Justin Morley Langham [1963] Director/Chartered Surveyor; William Thomas Reeves [1950] Director

Portland Stone Firms Limited
Incorporated: 23 March 1994
Net Worth: £7,154,827 *Total Assets:* £10,914,293
Registered Office: Leanne House, 6 Avon Close, Weymouth, Dorset, DT4 9UX
Activities: Quarrying of ornamental and building stone, limestone, gypsum, chalk and slate
Officers: Emma Smith, Secretary; Mervyn Stewkesbury [1933] Director

Portlemouth Estates Limited
Incorporated: 18 November 1971 *Employees:* 4
Net Worth: £3,839,748 *Total Assets:* £4,443,974
Registered Office: 12 Southgate Street, Launceston, Cornwall, PL15 9DP
Activities: Development of building projects
Shareholder: Lady Mary Florence Jephcott
Officers: Tamsin Alice Visick, Secretary; Simon Mark Farnsworth [1967] Director/Surveyor; Lady Mary Florence Jephcott [1934] Director; Peter Graham Visick [1939] Director/Mechanical Engineer; Tamsin Alice Visick [1965] Director/Chartered Surveyor

Portman Healthcare (Finance) Limited
Incorporated: 3 July 2014
Net Worth Deficit: £3,262,000 *Total Assets:* £62,795,000
Registered Office: 6 Pittville Lawn, Cheltenham, Glos, GL52 2BD
Activities: Other human health activities
Parent: Portman Healthcare (Holdings) Ltd
Officers: Darren James Ivor Milne, Secretary; Darren James Ivor Milne [1971] Director; Sam Bernard Waley-Cohen [1982] Director/Businessman

Portman Healthcare (Holdings) Limited
Incorporated: 3 July 2014 *Employees:* 598
Net Worth Deficit: £10,375,000 *Total Assets:* £84,949,000
Registered Office: 6 Pittville Lawn, Cheltenham, Glos, GL52 2BD
Activities: Other human health activities
Shareholders: Menthe Bidco Limited; Sam Waley-Choen
Officers: Darren James Ivor Milne, Secretary; Dr Mark Howard Hamburger [1961] Director/Dentist; Darren James Ivor Milne [1971] Director; Sam Bernard Waley-Cohen [1982] Director/Businessman; Mark William Welch [1964] Director

Portman Healthcare Limited
Incorporated: 4 November 2008 *Employees:* 563
Net Worth Deficit: £5,626,000 *Total Assets:* £70,009,000
Registered Office: 6 Pittville Lawn, Cheltenham, Glos, GL52 2BD
Activities: Other human health activities
Parent: Portman Healthcare (Finance) Limited
Officers: Darren James Ivor Milne, Secretary; Dr Roy Keith Bennett [1963] Director/Dentist; Dr Gurjit Singh Bhavra [1957] Director/Dentist; Stephen James Christie [1969] Business Development Director; Terence Ian Davies [1960] Director/Orthodontist; Dr Mark Howard Hamburger [1961] Director/Dentist; Dr Stuart Harry Jacobs [1953] Director/Dental Surgeon; Christopher Mark Lucas [1962] Director/Dentist; Darren James Ivor Milne [1971] Director; Andre Philip Pettemerides [1953] Director/Dental Surgeon; Dr Rebecca Peta Sadler [1973] Director/Dentist; Christopher Ian Saunders [1985] Director/Accountant; Dr Henry Pearse Stinson [1958] Director/Dental Surgeon; Sam Bernard Waley-Cohen [1982] Director/Businessman; Mark William Welch [1964] Director/Chief Operating Officer

Porton Biopharma Limited
Incorporated: 27 November 2014 *Employees:* 313
Net Worth: £78,866,000 *Total Assets:* £102,041,000
Registered Office: Manor Farm Road, Porton, Salisbury, Wilts, SP4 0JG
Activities: Manufacture of pharmaceutical preparations
Parent: Secretary of State for Health
Officers: Nigel Richard Mowbray Mackie, Secretary; Michael Brodie [1969] Finance and Commercial Director; Nigel Stanley Brooksby [1950] Director; Barry Clare [1953] Director; Donald Richard Gleave [1963] Director/Deputy Chief Executive; Martin Hindle [1943] Director/Independent Chairman; Roger James Hinton [1958] Director/Manager

Portway Domestic Appliances Limited
Incorporated: 27 October 1989 *Employees:* 21
Net Worth: £1,403,560 *Total Assets:* £5,416,418
Registered Office: Langdowns DFK, Kingsgate House, Newbury Road, Andover, Hants, SP10 4DU
Activities: Wholesale of radio, television goods & electrical household appliances (other than records, tapes, CDs)
Major Shareholder: Kenneth White
Officers: Kenneth White, Secretary; John Bainbridge [1958] Commercial Director; Ruaraidh John Pope [1985] E Commerce Director; Jack Kenneth Victor White [1989] Sales Director; Kenneth White [1953] Director/Haulier

Portway Precision Limited
Incorporated: 24 April 1986
Net Worth: £3,991,440 *Total Assets:* £4,308,445
Registered Office: 43 Albany Road, Salisbury, Wilts, SP1 3YQ
Activities: Buying and selling of own real estate
Shareholders: John Gerard Foster; Marion Elizabeth Foster
Officers: Marion Elizabeth Foster, Secretary; John Gerard Foster [1956] Director/Chartered Accountant/Engineer; Marion Elizabeth Foster [1954] Director

Positive Cash Flow Finance Limited
Incorporated: 30 May 2007 *Employees:* 23
Net Worth: £1,964,724 *Total Assets:* £27,599,910
Registered Office: 2nd Floor, St James House, The Square, Lower Bristol Road, Bath, BA2 3BH
Activities: Factoring
Parent: Positive Cashflow Finance Holdings Ltd
Officers: Jennifer Bodey, Secretary; Philip Kevin Chesham [1966] Director; Simon Mark Cook [1960] Director; Christopher Peter Davis [1964] Director; Edward John Rimmer [1972] Director; James Matthew Arthur Roberts [1977] Director; David Richard Smith [1962] Director; Richard Ian Smith [1961] Director

Positive Cashflow Finance (Holdings) Limited
Incorporated: 8 January 2013
Net Worth: £3,449,968 *Total Assets:* £4,799,968
Registered Office: 2nd Floor, St James House, The Square, Lower Bristol Road, Bath, BA2 3BH
Activities: Activities of other holding companies n.e.c.
Parent: 1pm PLC
Officers: Jennifer Bodey, Secretary; Philip Kevin Chesham [1966] Sales Director; Simon Mark Cook [1960] Commercial Director; Christopher Peter Davis [1964] Finance Director; Edward John Rimmer [1972] Director; James Matthew Arthur Roberts [1977] Director; David Richard Smith [1962] Managing Director; Richard Ian Smith [1961] Director

Positive Group (UK) Limited
Incorporated: 5 February 2008
Net Worth: £6,700,122 *Total Assets:* £6,701,559
Registered Office: H1 The Fulcrum, Vantage Way, Poole, Dorset, BH12 4NU
Activities: Activities of head offices
Shareholders: Julie Caroline Parodi; Leslie Vincent Parodi
Officers: Leslie Vincent Parodi, Secretary; Joanna Lucie Jones [1975] Director; Calum Parodi [1986] Director/Project Manager; Leslie Vincent Parodi [1954] Managing Director

Postal Choices Limited
Incorporated: 9 June 2004 *Employees:* 112
Net Worth: £4,947,455 *Total Assets:* £16,005,828
Registered Office: 42 Martingale Way, Portishead, Bristol, BS20 7AW
Activities: Postal activities under universal service obligation
Parent: Postal Choices Holdings Limited
Officers: Suzanne Bishop, Secretary; Suzanne Bishop [1969] Director; Graham John Cooper [1951] Director; Lesley Ann Harris [1964] Sales Director; Mark Andrew Plant [1964] Commercial Director; Stephen Anthony Roberts [1962] Operations Development Director

Potensis Limited
Incorporated: 31 August 2000 *Employees:* 66
Net Worth: £8,728,680 *Total Assets:* £10,524,180
Registered Office: 2nd Floor, Whitefriars Business Centre, Whitefriars, Lewins Mead, Bristol, BS1 2NT
Activities: Other business support service activities n.e.c.
Parent: Potensis Holdings Limited
Officers: Peter Crowley [1962] Director [Irish]; Neill David Hughes [1966] Director [Irish]; Jon Ingram [1980] Director; Jared Jon Sullivan [1973] Director

Potensis Recruitment Limited
Incorporated: 4 December 2014
Net Worth: £13,972,399 *Total Assets:* £14,180,332
Registered Office: 2nd Floor, Whitefriars Business Centre, Whitefriars, Lewins Mead, Bristol, BS1 2NT
Activities: Activities of head offices
Officers: Peter Crowley [1962] Director [Irish]; Neill David Hughes [1966] Director [Irish]; Jon Ingram [1980] Director; Jared Jon Sullivan [1973] Director

Powderham Properties (Teignmouth) Limited
Incorporated: 10 July 1962 *Employees:* 4
Net Worth: £13,440,584 *Total Assets:* £13,817,295
Registered Office: 22 Union Street, Newton Abbot, Devon, TQ12 2JS
Activities: Other letting and operating of own or leased real estate
Officers: George James Burgis Hulbert [1944] Director; Richard Charles Hulbert [1951] Director

Power Electrics (Bristol) Limited
Incorporated: 9 October 1963 *Employees:* 236
Net Worth: £16,995,188 *Total Assets:* £35,115,620
Registered Office: St Ivel Way, Warmley, Bristol, BS30 8TY
Activities: Renting and leasing of other machinery, equipment and tangible goods n.e.c.
Shareholders: Andrew James Pullin; John Robert Pullin
Officers: Anthony Phillip Jenkins, Secretary; Anthony Phillip Jenkins [1965] Finance Director; Andrew James Pullin [1968] Managing Director; John Robert Pullin [1965] Managing Director

Power Electrics Generators Limited
Incorporated: 12 March 2010 *Employees:* 58
Net Worth: £3,472,840 *Total Assets:* £8,349,239
Registered Office: St Ivel Way, Warmley, Bristol, BS30 8TY
Activities: Electrical installation
Parent: Power Electrics (Bristol) Ltd
Officers: Anthony Phillip Jenkins, Secretary; Anthony Phillip Jenkins [1965] Director; Andrew James Pullin [1968] Director; John Robert Pullin [1965] Director

Powerbox International Limited
Incorporated: 6 May 2009 *Employees:* 72
Net Worth Deficit: £75,000 *Total Assets:* £8,733,000
Registered Office: Telford House, The Park, Yeovil, Somerset, BA20 1DY
Activities: Retail sale of hardware, paints and glass in specialised stores
Parent: Power Box AG
Officers: Simon Paul Bird [1971] Director/Procurement; Darrell John Morris [1971] Director; Rory Anthony O'Donnell [1952] Director/Chartered Accountant

Powersystems UK Ltd
Incorporated: 11 December 1980 *Employees:* 79
Net Worth: £24,801,528 *Total Assets:* £33,470,898
Registered Office: Powersystems UK Ltd, Badminton Road, Yate, Bristol, BS37 5GG
Activities: Electrical installation
Shareholder: Stuart John Wilsmore
Officers: Eirwyn Albert Thomas, Secretary; Rachel Clare Berry [1968] Financial Director; Derek Christopher Sinclair Earby [1949] Director; Christopher Aragorn Jenkins [1972] Director/Engineer; Eirwyn Albert Thomas [1959] Director; Stuart John Wilsmore [1963] Director

Powervamp Limited
Incorporated: 11 January 1994
Net Worth: £3,673,430 *Total Assets:* £5,099,697
Registered Office: 2 Stafford Place, Weston-Super-Mare, Somerset, BS23 2QZ
Activities: Manufacture of electric motors, generators and transformers
Shareholders: Janet Mary Roller; Richard Eyton Roller
Officers: Erwan Jalil [1977] Group OEM Service Director [French/Lebanese]; Laurent Jamet [1973] Finance Director [French]; Antoine Maguin [1961] Director/Group CEO [French]; Richard Eyton Roller [1945] Director/Consultant; Kenneth Brian Walker [1963] Commercial Director

Powerwave Energy Limited
Incorporated: 18 March 2008
Net Worth: £356,001,984 *Total Assets:* £371,207,328
Registered Office: Whaddon Works, Cromwell Road, Cheltenham, Glos, GL52 5EP
Activities: Other business support service activities n.e.c.
Parent: Kohler Holdings Limited
Officers: Thomas Gerard Adler [1960] Director/Chief Financial Officer [American]; John M Suralik [1961] Director/Executive [American]

Powis Hotels Limited
Incorporated: 19 June 2012
Net Worth: £592,606 *Total Assets:* £7,674,340
Registered Office: Lincombe Hall Hotel, Lower Woodfield Road, Torquay, Devon, TQ1 2JX
Activities: Hotels and similar accommodation
Shareholders: Brett James Powis; Joanne Powis
Officers: Brett James Powis [1967] Director/Hotelier; Joanne Powis [1968] Director/Hotelier

Powrmatic Limited
Incorporated: 27 April 1960 *Employees:* 117
Net Worth: £9,974,589 *Total Assets:* £14,261,299
Registered Office: Hort Bridge, Ilminster, Somerset, TA19 9PS
Activities: Manufacture of other fabricated metal products n.e.c.
Major Shareholder: Marilyn Skony Stamm
Officers: Marilyn Skony Stamm, Secretary; Philip Anthony Brompton [1949] Managing Director; Stuart Richard Parris [1971] Managing Director; Marilyn Skony Stamm [1951] Director [American]

PP Capital 2 Ltd
Incorporated: 3 October 2015
Net Worth Deficit: £2,232 *Total Assets:* £7,953,855
Registered Office: Bespoke Tax Accountants, Delta House, 27 Bath Road, Cheltenham, Glos, GL53 7TH
Activities: Financial intermediation not elsewhere classified
Parent: Piccadilly Pictures Services Ltd
Officers: Christopher Harold Clifford Figg [1957] Director; Robert Harley Whitehouse [1950] Director [New Zealander]

PP Capital 3 Limited
Incorporated: 2 May 2017
Net Worth Deficit: £70,481 *Total Assets:* £8,436,394
Registered Office: Bespoke Tax Accountants, Delta House, 27 Bath Road, Cheltenham, Glos, GL53 7TH
Activities: Motion picture production activities
Parent: Piccadilly Pictures (Services) Ltd
Officers: Christopher Harold Figg [1957] Director; Robert Harley Whitehouse [1950] Director [New Zealander]

PPL Island Limited
Incorporated: 13 August 2014
Net Worth: £578,700,032 *Total Assets:* £578,700,032
Registered Office: Avonbank, Feeder Road, Bristol, BS2 0TB
Activities: Other business support service activities n.e.c.
Parent: WPD Distribution Network Holdings Limited
Officers: Sally Ann Jones, Secretary; Alexander James Torok [1958] Director/Tax Vice President [American]; Ian Robert Williams [1970] Finance Director

PPL Midlands Limited
Incorporated: 1 April 1989
Net Worth: £38,009,000 *Total Assets:* £38,276,000
Registered Office: Avonbank, Feeder Road, Bristol, BS2 0TB
Activities: Activities of other holding companies n.e.c.
Parent: PPL UK Investments Limited
Officers: Sally Ann Jones, Secretary; Alexander James Torok [1958] Director/Tax Vice President [American]; Ian Robert Williams [1970] Resources and External Affairs Director

PPL UK Investments Limited
Incorporated: 25 March 2011
Net Worth: £1,227,000,064 *Total Assets:* £1,839,699,968
Registered Office: Avonbank, Feeder Road, Bristol, BS2 0TB
Activities: Other business support service activities n.e.c.
Parent: Western Power Distribution PLC
Officers: Sally Ann Jones, Secretary; Alexander James Torok [1958] Director/Tax Vice President [American]; Ian Robert Williams [1970] Resources and External Affairs Director

PPL UK Resources Limited
Incorporated: 8 August 2002
Net Worth: £1,990,426,368 *Total Assets:* £3,296,045,312
Registered Office: Avonbank, Feeder Road, Bristol, BS2 0TB
Activities: Other business support service activities n.e.c.
Parent: PPL UK Holdings, LLC
Officers: Sally Ann Jones, Secretary; Alison Jane Sleightholm [1963] Resources and External Affairs Director; Alexander James Torok [1958] Director/Tax Vice President [American]; Ian Robert Williams [1970] Resources and External Affairs Director

PPL WEM Limited
Incorporated: 6 September 2000
Net Worth: £1,979,299,968 *Total Assets:* £2,368,699,904
Registered Office: Avonbank, Feeder Road, Bristol, BS2 0TB
Activities: Activities of head offices
Parent: PPL UK Investments Limited
Officers: Sally Ann Jones, Secretary; Alexander James Torok [1958] Director/Assistant Treasurer [American]; Ian Robert Williams [1970] Resources and External Affairs Director

PPL WPD Investments Limited
Incorporated: 2 October 2017
Net Worth: £2,716,100,096 *Total Assets:* £2,716,100,096
Registered Office: Avonbank, Feeder Road, Bristol, BS2 0TB
Activities: Activities of other holding companies n.e.c.
Parent: PPL WPD Limited
Officers: Sally Ann Jones, Secretary; Alexander James Torok [1958] Director/Tax & Vice President [American]; Ian Robert Williams [1970] Finance Director

PPL WPD Limited
Incorporated: 13 August 2014
Net Worth: £2,787,300,096 *Total Assets:* £2,790,500,096
Registered Office: Avonbank, Feeder Road, Bristol, BS2 0TB
Activities: Other business support service activities n.e.c.
Parent: PPL UK Management Partners
Officers: Sally Ann Jones, Secretary; Vincent Sorgi [1971] Director/Senior Vice President and Chief Financial Officer [American]; Ian Robert Williams [1970] Finance Director

PPSTS Limited
Incorporated: 18 May 2009 *Employees:* 2
Net Worth: £5,962,330 *Total Assets:* £7,553,662
Registered Office: 9 Falcon Drive, Christchurch, Dorset, BH23 4BA
Activities: Agents involved in the sale of a variety of goods
Shareholders: Jeremy Philip Rides; Trudy Jane Rides
Officers: Jeremy Philip Rides [1965] Director; Trudy Jane Rides [1965] Director/Manager

Prabh Milnae Kaa Chaao Gurdwara
Incorporated: 7 July 2005
Net Worth: £6,686,904 *Total Assets:* £11,354,980
Registered Office: PMKC, Sikh Temple, Crampton Road, Greenbridge Estate, Greenbridge, Swindon, Wilts, SN3 3JJ
Activities: Other education n.e.c.
Officers: Savraj Singh Dhillon, Secretary; Savraj Singh Dhillon [1971] Director/Chartered Accountant; Ajit Singh Khaira [1959] Director/Quality Engineer; Kulwant Singh Sidhu [1957] Director/Maintenance Engineer; Harbhajan Singh [1943] Director/Supervisor; Simerneet Singh [1979] Director/Attorney [American]

Practical Developments (South West) Limited
Incorporated: 17 January 1986 *Employees:* 38
Net Worth: £4,080,015 *Total Assets:* £8,368,758
Registered Office: Jenson House, Cardrew Industrial Estate, Redruth, Cornwall, TR15 1SS
Activities: Other manufacturing n.e.c.
Parent: Bob Pepper Holdings Limited
Officers: Jacqueline Blanche Pepper, Secretary; Robert David Pepper [1945] Director/Property Developer; Michelle Pepper-Smith [1975] Director/Account Manager; Robert Andrew Pepper-Smith [1971] Financial Director

Sidney Pratt (Builders) Limited
Incorporated: 18 May 1937 *Employees:* 5
Net Worth: £3,455,595 *Total Assets:* £4,699,578
Registered Office: Sandy Park Farm, Old Rydon Lane, Exeter, Devon, EX2 7JW
Activities: Construction of domestic buildings
Major Shareholder: Rupert Bernard Pratt
Officers: Rupert Bernard Pratt [1966] Director/Construction Manager

Praxair Offshore Services Limited
Incorporated: 8 May 2013
Net Worth Deficit: £10,075,621 *Total Assets:* £91,474,064
Registered Office: c/o Praxair Surface Technologies Ltd, Drakes Way, Greenbridge Estate, Swindon, Wilts, SN3 3HX
Activities: Support activities for petroleum and natural gas mining
Parent: Praxair Inc.
Officers: Eduardo Figueiredo Menezes [1963] Director/Business Executive [Brazilian]; Richard Lee Steinseifer [1956] Director/Business Executive [American]

Praxair Surface Technologies Limited
Incorporated: 24 August 1989
Net Worth: £27,950,000 *Total Assets:* £37,288,000
Registered Office: Drakes Way, Swindon, Wilts, SN3 3HX
Activities: Treatment and coating of metals
Parent: Linde Public Limited Company
Officers: Richard Jeremy Ward, Secretary; Steve Cast [1971] Managing Director [British/French]; Julian Oliver [1970] Finance Director; Richard Jeremy Ward [1965] Finance Director

Precast Concrete Structures Limited
Incorporated: 23 October 2002 *Employees:* 8
Net Worth: £3,760,198 *Total Assets:* £6,003,245
Registered Office: Building 101, The Waterfront, Stonehouse Business Park, Sperry Way, Stonehouse, Glos, GL10 3UT
Activities: Other specialised construction activities n.e.c.
Major Shareholder: Graham Redvers Paddock
Officers: Susan Jean Elliott Paddock, Secretary; James Cody [1971] Director; David Joseph Howard [1956] Director; Mark James Mills [1963] Director; Graham Redvers Paddock [1962] Director/Structural Engineer

Precision Lift Services Limited
Incorporated: 18 June 1996 *Employees:* 100
Net Worth: £1,573,538 *Total Assets:* £4,276,530
Registered Office: c/o BPE Solicitors LLP, First Floor, St James House, St James Square, Cheltenham, Glos, GL50 3PR
Activities: Other specialised construction activities n.e.c.
Parent: PLS GRP Limited
Officers: John William Charles Charlton, Secretary; John William Charles Charlton [1956] Director/Company Secretary; Michael McMahon [1976] Director

Preformed Line Products (Great Britain) Limited
Incorporated: 22 February 1957 *Employees:* 77
Net Worth: £9,394,781 *Total Assets:* £11,003,696
Registered Office: East Portway, Andover, Hants, SP10 3LH
Activities: Manufacture of wire products, chain and springs
Parent: Preformed Line Products Company
Officers: Christopher Neil Bridges, Secretary; John Alexander Bentley [1972] Operations Director; Stephen William Carley [1956] Director; Dennis McKenna [1967] Director [American]; Robert Grant Ruhlman [1956] Director/President PLP [American]; Martin Jeremy Spayes [1965] Sales Director

Premia Group Limited
Incorporated: 9 June 2009
Net Worth Deficit: £581,000 *Total Assets:* £5,869,000
Registered Office: Trelleborg International Drive, Tewkesbury Business Park, Tewkesbury, Glos, GL20 8UQ
Activities: Activities of head offices
Parent: Trelleborg Holdings UK Limited
Officers: Ian Elcock, Secretary; Charlotta Ingrid Grahs [1971] Director/Senior Vice President, General Counsel & Secretary [Swedish]; Niklas Anders Johansson [1973] Director/Vice President Tax [Swedish]; Ivar Lars Leijonberg [1964] Director/VP Internal Control [Swedish]

Premier Cables Holdings Limited
Incorporated: 29 February 2012 *Employees:* 3
Net Worth: £936,726 *Total Assets:* £4,686,635
Registered Office: 61 Gazelle Road, Weston-Super-Mare, Somerset, BS24 9ES
Activities: Other business support service activities n.e.c.
Parent: IEWC UK & Ireland Ltd
Officers: Jeffrey John Siemers [1953] Director/Chief Financial Officer [American]; Michael Paul Veum [1973] Director/Chief Executive [American]; Jeffrey Weinstein [1962] Director

Premier Cables Limited
Incorporated: 20 February 1992 *Employees:* 58
Net Worth: £11,631,024 *Total Assets:* £20,204,920
Registered Office: 61 Gazelle Road, Weston-Super-Mare, Somerset, BS24 9ES
Activities: Non-specialised wholesale trade
Parent: Premier Cables Holdings Limited
Officers: Jeffrey John Siemers [1953] Director/Chief Financial Officer [American]; Michael Paul Veum [1973] Director/Chief Executive [American]; Jeffrey Weinstein [1962] Director

Premier Developments (1995) Limited
Incorporated: 18 October 1995 *Employees:* 3
Net Worth: £6,670,672 *Total Assets:* £8,678,972
Registered Office: c/o Francis Clark LLP, North Quay House, Sutton Harbour, Plymouth, PL4 0RA
Activities: Other letting and operating of own or leased real estate
Shareholders: Susan Kathryn Briscoe; Susan Margaret Briscoe; Kevin Bernard Briscoe; Robert Richard Briscoe
Officers: Kevin Bernard Briscoe, Secretary/Director; Kevin Bernard Briscoe [1961] Director; Robert Richard Briscoe [1963] Director

Premier Double Glazed Units Limited
Incorporated: 2 May 1996 *Employees:* 32
Net Worth: £2,967,250 *Total Assets:* £4,221,045
Registered Office: Moorgate House, King Street, Newton Abbot, Devon, TQ12 2LG
Activities: Manufacture of builders ware of plastic
Major Shareholder: Barry George Clarke
Officers: Jayne Camm, Secretary; Barry George Clarke [1964] Director

Premier Livestock Auctions Limited
Incorporated: 14 January 1931
Net Worth: £3,137,819 *Total Assets:* £4,297,680
Registered Office: 1 Park Gardens, Yeovil, Somerset, BA20 1DW
Activities: Support activities for animal production (other than farm animal boarding)
Major Shareholder: George Ian MacNicol
Officers: Julian Tomsett, Secretary; Adel Jean MacNicol [1949] Director; George Ian MacNicol [1983] Director/Accounts Sales Executive

Premier Park Limited
Incorporated: 22 November 2007
Net Worth: £2,929,601 *Total Assets:* £3,533,776
Registered Office: 48 Queensgate House, Queen Street, Exeter, Devon, EX4 3SR
Activities: Other service activities n.e.c.
Major Shareholder: Steven John Garratt
Officers: Steven John Garratt [1968] Director; Steven John Pettit [1986] Director

Premier Underwriting Limited
Incorporated: 28 April 1999 *Employees:* 21
Net Worth: £5,974,590 *Total Assets:* £6,795,548
Registered Office: 37 Commercial Road, Poole, Dorset, BH14 0HU
Activities: Non-life insurance
Major Shareholder: Paul Christopher Gray
Officers: Paul Christopher Gray, Secretary; Terry Patrick Cavanagh [1945] Director/Retired; Christopher Terence Cooper [1957] Development and Operations Director; Paul Christopher Gray [1960] Director/Insurance; Ian Anthony Jeffery [1961] Director/Insurance

Premiere Health Limited
Incorporated: 9 April 1996 *Employees:* 154
Net Worth: £5,251,939 *Total Assets:* £8,332,843
Registered Office: c/o Francis Clark LLP, North Quay House, Sutton Harbour, Plymouth, PL4 0RA
Activities: Other accommodation
Officers: Kevin Bernard Briscoe, Secretary/Director; Kevin Bernard Briscoe [1961] Director; Robert Richard Briscoe [1963] Director

Premium Rate Numbers Ltd
Incorporated: 8 January 2015
Net Worth: £6,176,472 *Total Assets:* £6,244,387
Registered Office: 13 Harbury Road, Bristol, BS9 4PN
Activities: Computer facilities management activities
Major Shareholder: Altaf Patel
Officers: Terence Hawthorn [1972] Finance Director; Altaf Patel [1969] Director

Prenax Limited
Incorporated: 6 April 2000 *Employees:* 28
Net Worth: £262,358 *Total Assets:* £4,813,520
Registered Office: Barrington House, Watercombe Park, Lynx Trading Estate, Yeovil, Somerset, BA20 2HL
Activities: Library activities
Officers: Jan Arie Den Hartog, Secretary; Didier Bentz [1962] Director/Chief Financial Officer [French]; Jerome Conquet [1970] Director [French]; Jan Arie Den Hartog [1981] Finance and Managing Director

Preston Cherry LLP
Incorporated: 18 November 2013
Net Worth: £6,109,268 *Total Assets:* £6,191,767
Registered Office: Manor Farm House, Horsington, Templecombe, Somerset, BA8 0EB
Officers: Brooke Cherry [1981] Member; Gareth Russell Cherry [1975] Member; Andrew Preston [1966] Member

Preston School Academy Trust
Incorporated: 3 June 2011 *Employees:* 127
Net Worth: £6,917,188 *Total Assets:* £9,903,250
Registered Office: Preston School, Monks Dale, Yeovil, Somerset, BA21 3JD
Activities: General secondary education
Officers: Daniel Stuart Edwards, Secretary; Marta Baker [1969] Director; Tania Caroline Bartlett [1974] Director/Business Development; Stephen Alan Battersby [1967] Director/Education Manager; Thomas Byrne [1969] Director/Accountant; Brian Gerwyn Chappell [1952] Director/Retired; Daniel Horsington [1981] Director/Teacher; Marc House [1973] Director/Fireman; Susan Elizabeth Johnson [1952] Director/Teaching Assistant, Preston SC; Simon Jones [1966] Director/Chief of Staff; Joanne Langley-White [1982] Director; Gregg Morrison [1980] Director/Principal; Adele Jane Sampson [1983] Director/Teacher; Robert Thomas Shire [1969] Director/Financial Adviser; Deborah Louise Sims [1970] Director/Military Leadership Trainer; Rachel Walker [1969] Director/Teacher in Charge; Leanne Marie Williams [1968] Director/Solicitor

M. Preymesser Logistics Limited
Incorporated: 16 February 2006 *Employees:* 11
Net Worth: £3,817,836 *Total Assets:* £4,266,893
Registered Office: Newcombe Drive, Hawksworth Industrial Estate, Swindon, Wilts, SN2 1DZ
Activities: Freight transport by road
Parent: M. Preymesser Beteiligungs GmbH
Officers: Michael Florian Preymesser, Secretary [German]; Michael Florian Preymesser [1971] Director [German]; Adolf Anton Winkelmeier [1961] Director/Forwarding Merchant [German]

Pride Foods Limited
Incorporated: 17 November 1925
Net Worth: £23,783,000 *Total Assets:* £29,362,000
Registered Office: Mallard Court, Express Park, Bridgwater, Somerset, TA6 4RN
Activities: Non-trading company
Officers: Pieter Willem Van Meerteren, Secretary; Aart Cornelis Duijzer [1963] Managing Director [Dutch]; Johannes Henricus Wilhelmus Roelofs [1963] Managing Director [Dutch]; David John Saint [1964] Director/Executive

Prideaux Developments Limited
Incorporated: 7 August 2003
Net Worth: £958,652 *Total Assets:* £4,114,180
Registered Office: Brynmawr Farm, Wheal Butson, St Agnes, Cornwall, TR5 0PT
Activities: Development of building projects
Major Shareholder: Louise Anne Ziar
Officers: Louise Anne Ziar, Secretary; Charles Hilary Elliott Ziar [1978] Director; Louise Anne Ziar [1976] Director

Prima Dental Manufacturing Limited
Incorporated: 27 October 2010 *Employees:* 226
Net Worth: £12,649,352 *Total Assets:* £21,108,906
Registered Office: Prima Dental Group, Waterwells Business Park, Stephenson Drive, Gloucester, GL2 2HA
Activities: Other manufacturing n.e.c.
Shareholders: A D Burs Ltd; APG Holding Company Limited
Officers: Carl Ashkin [1963] Director/Business Executive [American]; Michael William Caputo [1947] Director [American]; John Alun Jones [1957] Finance Director; Richard Oscar Muller [1956] Director

Primeco Limited
Incorporated: 16 April 2004 *Employees:* 5
Net Worth: £2,455,719 *Total Assets:* £6,380,785
Registered Office: 19 The Terrace, Torquay, Devon, TQ1 1BN
Activities: Other letting and operating of own or leased real estate
Major Shareholder: David Grant Nugent
Officers: Audrey Nugent, Secretary; David Nugent [1968] Director

Primetower Properties Limited
Incorporated: 13 June 1994
Net Worth: £4,861,388 *Total Assets:* £8,674,135
Registered Office: 1 Park Place, North Road, Poole, Dorset, BH14 0LY
Activities: Development of building projects
Shareholder: John Alec Yeoman
Officers: Michael Peter Jones, Secretary; Dr Roger James Harding [1943] Director/Private Investor; Michael Peter Jones [1968] Director/Accountant; John Alec Yeoman [1954] Director/Property Developer

Princess Yachts Limited
Incorporated: 12 August 1965 *Employees:* 2,407
Previous: Princess Yachts PLC
Net Worth: £90,360,000 *Total Assets:* £209,950,000
Registered Office: Newport Street, Stonehouse, Plymouth, PL1 3QG
Activities: Building of pleasure and sporting boats
Parent: RNO Limited
Officers: Adrian Richard Bratt, Secretary; Ian Balmforth [1964] Director; Adrian Richard Bratt [1971] Director/Solicitor; Christopher John Gates [1961] Managing Director; William Daniel Green [1976] Director; Kiran Jay Haslam [1976] Director [Australian]; Grant Andres Hooper [1965] Director; Paul George MacKenzie [1970] Director; Graham Malcolm Maxa [1969] Director; Paul Michael Turner [1975] Director; Benjamin Paul Wright [1963] Director

Principality Holdings Limited
Incorporated: 19 February 1959
Net Worth: £8,268,559 *Total Assets:* £13,393,924
Registered Office: First Floor, 7 Park Street, Bristol, BS1 5NF
Activities: Other letting and operating of own or leased real estate
Parent: Ringable Limited
Officers: Joan Breach, Secretary; Joan Breach [1944] Director; Peter John Freeman Breach [1942] Director/Chartered Accountant

Prior Park Educational Trust
Incorporated: 13 October 1980 *Employees:* 281
Net Worth: £16,298,304 *Total Assets:* £26,104,096
Registered Office: Prior Park College, Ralph Allen Drive, Bath, BA2 5AH
Activities: Primary education
Officers: Julie Kim Barr, Secretary; Anthony Christopher Martin Bury [1952] Director/Chief Executive; Dr Judith Margaret Haworth [1960] Director/Psychiatrist; Julian Ross Jarvis [1973] Director/Lawyer; Austin Michael Henry King [1949] Director/Solicitor; Peter Sean James O'Donoghue [1968] Director/Accountant; Nicola Elizabeth Levelis Pearson [1952] Director & Company Secretary; Nigel John Francis Raby [1952] Director/Professional Engineer; James Nigel Rawlinson [1956] Director/University Chaplain; Anne Elizabeth Shepherd [1957] Director/Retired Civil Servant; John Michael Shinkwin [1954] Director/Charity General Secretary; Jane Mayberry Singleton [1960] Director/University Lecturer; John Parkinson Webster [1951] Director/Architect

Priorgate Limited
Incorporated: 17 June 2003
Net Worth Deficit: £728,000 *Total Assets:* £21,561,000
Registered Office: Third Floor, Broad Quay House, Prince Street, Bristol, BS1 4DJ
Activities: Management of real estate on a fee or contract basis
Parent: Priorgate Holdings Limited
Officers: Andrew Richard Kershaw [1965] Director/Projects Controller; Richard Little [1979] Investment Director; Richard John Marshall [1970] Regional Director

The Priory Learning Trust
Incorporated: 8 July 2011 *Employees:* 603
Previous: Priory Community School
Net Worth: £32,459,752 *Total Assets:* £42,929,616
Registered Office: Priory Community School Queensway, St George's, Weston-Super-Mare, Somerset, BS22 6BP
Activities: General secondary education
Officers: Victoria Louise Butterfield [1973] Director/Barrister Currently Unregistered; Neville Coles [1966] Director/Headteacher; Ian Neil Cook [1981] Director/Chartered Accountant; Diane Patricia Davey [1958] Director; Michelle Michael [1967] Director/Solicitor; John Wilson Richardson [1944] Director/Retired; Roderick Lewis Sibley [1955] Director/Operations Manager; Hannah Woodhouse [1976] Director/Civil Servant; Dr Barry Thomas Wratten [1954] Director

Pritchard Patent Product Co. Limited
Incorporated: 18 April 1946 *Employees:* 123
Net Worth: £1,967,993 *Total Assets:* £10,546,008
Registered Office: Underleys Beer, Seaton, Devon, EX12 3NA
Activities: Non-specialised wholesale trade
Parent: Pritchard Patent Product Company (2001) Limited
Officers: Christopher Paul Noake, Secretary; Christopher Paul Noake [1969] Director/Accountant; Charles Michael Pritchard [1947] Director; Hilary Margaret Robarts-Arnold [1944] Director/Married Woman; James Henry Ben Robarts-Arnold [1977] Director/Engineer; Cherry Blanche Sargent [1957] Director/Married Woman

Pritchard Patent Product Company (2001) Limited
Incorporated: 27 April 2001 *Employees:* 176
Net Worth: £6,395,825 *Total Assets:* £14,906,350
Registered Office: Underleys Beer, Seaton, Devon, EX12 3NA
Activities: Activities of head offices
Shareholders: Charles Michael Pritchard; Hilary Margaret Robarts-Arnold; Cherry Blanche Sargent
Officers: Christopher Paul Noake, Secretary/Accountant; Christopher Paul Noake [1969] Director/Accountant; Charles Michael Pritchard [1947] Director; Hilary Margaret Robarts Arnold [1944] Director; James Henry Ben Robarts-Arnold [1977] Director/Engineer; Cherry Blanche Sargent [1957] Director

Pritchmor Holdings Limited
Incorporated: 28 March 2001 *Employees:* 64
Previous: Arcol (Holdings) Limited
Net Worth: £3,363,367 *Total Assets:* £5,522,869
Registered Office: c/o Chy Nyverow, Newham Road, Truro, Cornwall, TR1 2DP
Activities: Activities of head offices
Shareholders: Alun David Morgan; Michael Brian Pritchard
Officers: Alun David Morgan, Secretary; Alun David Morgan [1967] Technical Director; Michael Brian Pritchard [1968] Commercial Director

Private Equity Investor Limited
Incorporated: 19 January 2000
Previous: Private Equity Investor PLC
Net Worth: £3,846,000 *Total Assets:* £3,897,000
Registered Office: Suite 8, Bridge House, Courtenay Street, Newton Abbot, Devon, TQ12 2QS
Activities: Activities of venture and development capital companies
Parent: KHP 2 LP
Officers: Jared Richard Barlow [1977] Director/Finance [American]; Michael Anton Bego [1970] Director/Finance [American]

Pro - Direct Group Limited
Incorporated: 15 July 2008 *Employees:* 421
Net Worth: £29,910,144 *Total Assets:* £52,967,268
Registered Office: Torre House, Shaldon Road, Newton Abbot, Devon, TQ12 4PQ
Activities: Activities of head offices
Shareholders: Martin Wreford Lake; Adrian John Lake
Officers: Norman Wreford Lake, Secretary; Peter James Hammond [1956] Director/Accountant; Adrian John Lake [1965] Director/Sports Retailer; Martin Wreford Lake [1963] Director/Sports Retailer; Norman Wreford Lake [1936] Director/Sports Retailer

Pro-Direct Sport Limited
Incorporated: 3 July 2001 *Employees:* 402
Net Worth: £31,323,604 *Total Assets:* £50,611,580
Registered Office: Pro-Direct Sport Ltd, Shaldon Road, Newton Abbot, Devon, TQ12 4PQ
Activities: Retail sale via mail order houses or via Internet
Parent: Pro-Direct Group Limited
Officers: Norman Wreford Lake, Secretary; Peter James Hammond [1956] Director/Accountant; Adrian John Lake [1965] Director/Sports Retailer; Martin Wreford Lake [1963] Director/Sports Retailer; Norman Wreford Lake [1936] Director/Sports Retailer

Pro-Vets Group Limited
Incorporated: 16 February 2015 *Employees:* 298
Net Worth Deficit: £2,413,471 *Total Assets:* £32,644,906
Registered Office: The Chocolate Factory, Keynsham, Bristol, BS31 2AU
Activities: Dormant company
Officers: Amanda Jane Davis [1968] Director; David Robert Geoffrey Hillier [1962] Director

Proco-STS Limited
Incorporated: 24 February 2004 *Employees:* 38
Net Worth: £4,813,696 *Total Assets:* £5,959,359
Registered Office: Ground Floor, Blackbrook Gate 1, Blackbrook Business Park, Taunton, Somerset, TA1 2PX
Activities: Installation of industrial machinery and equipment
Parent: Clint Limited
Officers: Philip Andrew Hyde, Secretary; Terence Kenneth Caswell [1936] Director/Electrical Engineer; Philip Andrew Hyde [1959] Director/Engineer; Glynn Sims [1969] Director/Engineer

Procol Limited
Incorporated: 1 June 1995 *Employees:* 21
Net Worth: £3,437,276 *Total Assets:* £4,395,780
Registered Office: Kingsbury House, Kingsbury Square, Melksham, Wilts, SN12 6HL
Activities: Combined facilities support activities
Parent: Procol Holdings Limited
Officers: Darren Bew [1972] Director; Jeffrey David Moore [1971] Director

Procook Limited
Incorporated: 7 July 2008 *Employees:* 298
Net Worth: £3,229,574 *Total Assets:* £11,770,434
Registered Office: ProCook, Davy Way, Waterwells, Gloucester, GL2 2BY
Activities: Other retail sale of new goods in specialised stores (not commercial art galleries and opticians)
Shareholders: Daniel Patrick O'Neill; Sarah Jane O'Neill; Michael O'Neill
Officers: Daniel Patrick O'Neill [1965] Director; Sarah Jane O'Neill [1965] Director

Procurri Europe Limited
Incorporated: 23 May 2011
Previous: Tinglobal Holdings Limited
Net Worth: £7,781,000 *Total Assets:* £11,886,000
Registered Office: Bankside Park, 15 Love Lane, Cirencester, Glos, GL7 1YG
Activities: Other business support service activities n.e.c.
Parent: Asvida UK Limited
Officers: William Paul Frederick Bye, Secretary; Joo Kwang Choo [1972] Director/Chief Financial Officer [Singaporean]; Edward Flachbarth [1967] IT Sales Director [American]; Matthew George Jordan [1974] Director; Thomas Sean Murphy [1966] Director [American]

Procurri UK Limited
Incorporated: 18 December 1959 *Employees:* 98
Previous: Tindirect Limited
Net Worth: £7,081,000 *Total Assets:* £13,753,000
Registered Office: Bankside Park, 15 Love Lane, Cirencester, Glos, GL7 1YG
Activities: Information technology consultancy activities
Parent: Procurri Europe Limited
Officers: Matthew George Jordan [1974] Sales Director

Prodigio Limited
Incorporated: 12 November 1998 *Employees:* 2
Net Worth: £6,539,536 *Total Assets:* £7,870,875
Registered Office: 30 Gay Street, Bath, BA1 2PA
Activities: Other letting and operating of own or leased real estate
Major Shareholder: Giovanni Cicirello
Officers: Vincenzo Cannella, Secretary; Vincenzo Cannella [1966] Director/Manager; Giovanni Cicirello [1942] Director [Italian]

Professional Reseller Group Limited
Incorporated: 21 September 2010 *Employees:* 338
Net Worth: £1,188,668 *Total Assets:* £10,163,716
Registered Office: Unit 1b Newton Centre, Thorverton Road, Matford Business Park, Marsh Barton Trading Estate, Exeter, Devon, EX2 8GN
Activities: Activities of head offices
Shareholders: Michael David Fleming; Andrew Jonathan Stone
Officers: James Stuart Collard Jenkins [1972] Sales Director; Daniel Evans [1975] Finance Director; Michael David Fleming [1971] Managing Director; Nick Pattas [1968] Director; Thomas William Slack [1965] Director/Accountant; Andrew Jonathan Stone [1970] Director/Managing Partner

Professor David Barrett Ltd
Incorporated: 11 July 2006
Net Worth: £4,139,942 *Total Assets:* £5,152,070
Registered Office: Thorne House, 1a The Avenue, Tiverton, Devon, EX16 4HR
Activities: Specialists medical practice activities
Major Shareholder: Professor David Stuart Barrett
Officers: Bernice Allison, Secretary; Professor David Stuart Barrett [1958] Director/Surgeon; Mery Zanutto [1971] Director/Surgical Practitioner [Italian]

Progressive Systems Limited
Incorporated: 30 June 1986 *Employees:* 39
Net Worth: £1,000,000 *Total Assets:* £6,387,617
Registered Office: Unit 7 Cranmere Court, Lustleigh Close, Exeter, Devon, EX2 8PW
Activities: Roofing activities
Shareholder: Paul Stuart Wood
Officers: Paul Stuart Wood, Secretary; Andrew John Bassett [1968] Estimating Director; Christopher Joseph Curtis [1966] Director; Roger John Fox [1956] Director; Keith Richards [1957] Contracts Director; Paul Stuart Wood [1972] Finance Director

Project Darwin Bidco Limited
Incorporated: 21 July 2015 *Employees:* 6
Net Worth Deficit: £15,671,000 *Total Assets:* £50,681,000
Registered Office: Unit 1411 Charlton Court, Gloucester Business Park, Brockworth, Glos, GL3 4AE
Activities: Activities of head offices
Shareholders: Living Bridge EP LLP; Livingbridge GP Company Limited
Officers: Andrew James Allen [1954] Director; David John Cole [1962] Director/Chief Executive Officer; Angela Dillon [1978] Finance Director; Christa Iris Echtle [1957] Director/Chairman [German]; Steven Peak [1966] Director; Simon Peet [1990] Director; Amy Louise Yateman-Smith [1984] Director

Project Darwin Topco Limited
Incorporated: 21 July 2015 *Employees:* 67
Net Worth Deficit: £26,696,000 *Total Assets:* £41,086,000
Registered Office: Unit 1411 Charlton Court, Gloucester Business Park, Brockworth, Glos, GL3 4AE
Activities: Activities of head offices
Shareholders: Living Bridge EP LLP; Linvingbridge GP Compnay Limited
Officers: Andrew James Allen [1954] Director; David John Cole [1962] Director/Chief Executive Officer; Angela Dillon [1978] Finance Director; Christa Iris Echtle [1957] Director/Chairman [German]; Steven Peak [1966] Director; Simon Peet [1990] Director; Amy Louise Yateman-Smith [1984] Director

Project People Limited
Incorporated: 28 February 1995 *Employees:* 371
Net Worth: £6,087,040 *Total Assets:* £40,880,592
Registered Office: 1st Floor, Northgate, Whitefriars, Lewins Mead, Bristol, BS1 2NT
Activities: Other information technology service activities
Shareholders: Jayantilal Govind Koria; Savita Jayantilal Koria
Officers: Pankaj Jayantilal Koria [1965] Managing Director

Prolabs (UK) Limited
Incorporated: 30 August 2012 *Employees:* 37
Net Worth: £8,071,763 *Total Assets:* £11,301,848
Registered Office: Eagle House, Lakeside Business Park, South Cerney, Cirencester, Glos, GL7 5XL
Activities: Wholesale of computers, computer peripheral equipment and software
Parent: Prolabs Holdings Limited
Officers: Andrew Thomas Jeremiah, Secretary; Alvaro Aguirre [1966] Director [American]; Walter Scott Krzywicki [1972] Director [American]; Abhishek Majumdar [1985] Director

Prolabs Holdings Limited
Incorporated: 16 April 2015
Net Worth: £6,684,812 *Total Assets:* £10,916,200
Registered Office: Eagle House, Lakeside Business Park, South Cerney, Cirencester, Glos, GL7 5XL
Activities: Activities of other holding companies n.e.c.
Parent: Halo Technology Bidco Limited
Officers: Andrew Thomas Jeremiah, Secretary; Alvaro Aguirre [1966] Director [American]; Walter Scott Krzywicki [1972] Director [American]; Rory James Wordsworth Sweet [1967] Director

Proper Cornish Limited
Incorporated: 15 June 1999 *Employees:* 240
Net Worth: £2,114,802 *Total Assets:* £11,491,723
Registered Office: Western House, Lucknow Road, Bodmin, Cornwall, PL31 1EZ
Activities: Manufacture of bread; manufacture of fresh pastry goods and cakes
Shareholders: Philip Richard Ugalde; Christopher Ian Pauling
Officers: Yvonne Helen Hollyoak, Secretary; Generald Steven Allen [1974] Operations Director; Christopher Ian Pauling [1965] Managing Director; Paul Bowman Saunders [1966] Finance Director; Philip Richard Ugalde [1946] Director/Chairman

Proper Job Superstores Limited
Incorporated: 23 August 2002 *Employees:* 280
Net Worth: £6,347,296 *Total Assets:* £9,895,616
Registered Office: Woodlands Grange, Woodlandslane, Bradley Stoke, Bristol, BS32 4JY
Activities: Retail sale of hardware, paints and glass in specialised stores
Major Shareholder: Peter Christopher Tilley
Officers: Peter Christopher Tilley [1972] Director/Retailer

Proper Tea LLP
Incorporated: 9 June 2005
Net Worth: £1,999,599 *Total Assets:* £5,652,130
Registered Office: Real World, Mill Lane Box, Corsham, Wilts, SN13 8PL
Officers: Peter Brian Gabriel [1950] Member

Property Consortium (Holdings) Limited
Incorporated: 16 February 2011 *Employees:* 291
Net Worth: £5,836,573 *Total Assets:* £11,584,920
Registered Office: Blackdown House, Culmhead Business Centre, Culmhead, Taunton, Somerset, TA3 7DY
Activities: Activities of head offices
Major Shareholder: Jeremy Hyams
Officers: Geoff Ball [1955] Director; Matthew Joseph Brady [1976] Director; James Chatterjee [1981] Director/Chartered Accountant; Gregory Duncan Gladwell [1964] Director; Stephen Duncan Grieve [1967] Insurance Director; Jeremy Hyams [1968] Director; Alec Christopher Tarrant [1951] Director

Property Consortium UK Limited
Incorporated: 23 February 1996 *Employees:* 287
Net Worth: £3,504,608 *Total Assets:* £8,654,208
Registered Office: Blackdown House, Culmhead Business Centre, Culmhead, Taunton, Somerset, TA3 7DY
Activities: Other specialised construction activities n.e.c.
Parent: Property Consortium (Holdings) Limited
Officers: Jeremy Hyams, Secretary; Matthew Joseph Brady [1976] Managing Director; James Chatterjee [1981] Director/Chartered Accountant; Stephen Duncan Grieve [1967] Director/Chief Information Officer; Jeremy Hyams [1968] Director/Management; Alec Christopher Tarrant [1951] Director

The Property Franchise Group PLC
Incorporated: 7 October 2013 *Employees:* 48
Previous: Martinco PLC
Net Worth: £14,266,731 *Total Assets:* £20,025,878
Registered Office: 2 St Stephen's Court, St Stephen's Road, Bournemouth, BH2 6LA
Activities: Real estate agencies
Shareholder: Richard Wilson Martin
Officers: Christopher Raymond Varley, Secretary; Philip James Crooks [1959] Director/Chartered Accountant; Paul Martin James Latham [1955] Director; Richard Wilson Martin [1950] Director; David Arthur Raggett [1966] Finance Director; Ian Wilson [1962] Managing Director

The Property Management Group Limited
Incorporated: 5 April 1990 *Employees:* 9
Net Worth: £1,963,571 *Total Assets:* £4,453,781
Registered Office: 182 Gloucester Road, Bristol, BS7 8NU
Activities: Management of real estate on a fee or contract basis
Major Shareholder: Jacqueline Elizabeth Rich
Officers: Dean Jonathan Rich, Secretary; Dean Jonathan Rich [1972] Director/Accounts Manager; Jacqueline Elizabeth Rich [1972] Director/Manager

Prosafe Offshore Limited
Incorporated: 19 February 1997 *Employees:* 69
Net Worth: £6,175,000 *Total Assets:* £7,352,000
Registered Office: First Floor, 10 Temple Back, Bristol, BS1 6FL
Activities: Support activities for petroleum and natural gas mining
Parent: Prosafe (UK) Holdings Limited
Officers: Jens Berge [1977] Director/Chief Operating Officer [Norwegian]; Robin Thomas Dunlop Laird [1963] Managing Director

Prospect Hospice Limited
Incorporated: 1 May 1980 *Employees:* 207
Net Worth: £9,687,000 *Total Assets:* £10,440,000
Registered Office: Moormead Road, Wroughton, Swindon, Wilts, SN4 9BY
Activities: Hospital activities
Officers: David Barrand [1962] Director/Project Manager; Dr Fiona Baskett [1959] Director/Trustee; Clive Bassett [1966] Finance Director; Mandy Casavant [1977] Director/Trustee; Eleanor Collins [1983] Accounts Director; Angela Helen Gillibrand [1949] Director; Caroline Hallatt [1970] Director/Trustee; Douglas John Looman [1958] Director/Trustee; Dr Penny Tidbury [1956] Director/Trustee; Dr Lindsay Rosanne Whittam [1966] Director/Trustee; Timothy Graham Willis [1964] Director/Head of International Relations

Provenn Ltd
Incorporated: 21 October 2011 *Employees:* 2
Net Worth: £478,625 *Total Assets:* £3,614,245
Registered Office: Venn House, Ugborough, Ivybridge, Devon, PL21 0PE
Activities: Residents property management
Shareholders: Anchoria Ltd; Prowse Developments Ltd
Officers: Nicholas Jonathan Haigh [1956] Sales Director; Andrew John Prowse [1962] Director

The Providence Projects Rehab Group Limited
Incorporated: 29 May 2013 *Employees:* 13
Net Worth: £2,073,824 *Total Assets:* £4,158,454
Registered Office: 6 Poole Road, Wimborne, Dorset, BH21 1QE
Activities: Other human health activities
Shareholders: Paul James Spanjar; Louise Spanjar
Officers: Louise Spanjar [1977] Finance Director; Paul James Spanjar [1978] Treatment Director

Providor Limited
Incorporated: 29 April 1998 *Employees:* 301
Net Worth Deficit: £2,448,310 *Total Assets:* £6,690,063
Registered Office: c/o BPE Solicitors LLP, First Floor, St James House, St James Square, Cheltenham, Glos, GL50 3PR
Activities: Support activities for petroleum and natural gas mining
Parent: Lakehouse Energy Services Limited
Officers: John William Charles Charlton, Secretary; John William Charles Charlton [1956] Director/Company Secretary; Michael McMahon [1976] Director

Prowrap Limited
Incorporated: 10 September 2015 *Employees:* 52
Net Worth: £6,253,438 *Total Assets:* £11,167,304
Registered Office: St Catherine's Court, Berkeley Place, Clifton, Bristol, BS8 1BQ
Activities: Activities of head offices
Major Shareholder: Nick Scoon
Officers: Nicholas Jeremy Scoon [1965] Director

F G Pryor and Son Limited
Incorporated: 3 November 2009 *Employees:* 30
Net Worth: £5,396,552 *Total Assets:* £6,685,237
Registered Office: Bishopbrook House, Cathedral Avenue, Wells, Somerset, BA5 1FD
Activities: Mixed farming
Shareholders: Philip Warwick Pryor; Denise Ann Pryor
Officers: Denise Ann Pryor [1968] Director; Philip Warwick Pryor [1965] Director/Farmer

PSC Training & Development Group Limited
Incorporated: 13 February 1998 *Employees:* 130
Net Worth: £8,050,338 *Total Assets:* £13,921,638
Registered Office: Unit 4 Drakes Court, Langage Industrial Estate, Plympton, Plymouth, PL7 5JY
Activities: Activities of head offices
Major Shareholder: Anna Roseen Boulting
Officers: Jeffery William Rowlands, Secretary/Finance Director; Mark John Boulting [1968] Director/Manager; Jeffery William Rowlands [1953] Finance Director/Company Secretary

PSW (Holdings) Ltd
Incorporated: 26 October 2011 *Employees:* 101
Net Worth: £5,619,739 *Total Assets:* £7,997,612
Registered Office: c/o Francis Clark LLP, North Quay House, Sutton Harbour, Plymouth, PL4 0RA
Activities: Dormant company
Shareholders: Monique Sarah Hirshman; Andrew Armon Hirshman
Officers: Andrew Hirshman, Secretary; Andrew Armon Hirshman [1969] Director; Monique Sarah Hirshman [1966] Director

PSW Metals Limited
Incorporated: 8 March 2005 *Employees:* 8
Net Worth: £2,738,055 *Total Assets:* £3,555,093
Registered Office: The Industrial Estate, Grange Court, Westbury on Severn, Glos, GL14 1PL
Activities: Recovery of sorted materials
Parent: PSW England Limited
Officers: Julia Margaret Brooks, Secretary; Julia Margaret Brooks [1962] Director/Legal Clerk; Peter Stanley Watkins [1955] Director/Recycler

PSW Trading Limited
Incorporated: 25 June 2009 *Employees:* 101
Net Worth: £3,785,113 *Total Assets:* £6,123,988
Registered Office: c/o Francis Clark LLP, North Quay House, Sutton Harbour, Plymouth, PL4 0RA
Activities: Other business support service activities n.e.c.
Parent: PSW (Holdings) Ltd
Officers: Andrew Armon Hirshman, Secretary; Andrew Armon Hirshman [1969] Director/Jeweller; Monique Sarah Hirshman [1966] Director; Jennifer Georgina Manning [1969] Director/Area Manager

Public Power Solutions Limited
Incorporated: 22 July 2009 *Employees:* 75
Previous: Swindon Commercial Services Limited
Net Worth Deficit: £3,279,000 *Total Assets:* £8,539,000
Registered Office: Waterside Park, Darby Close, Cheney Manor Industrial Estate, Swindon, Wilts, SN2 2PN
Activities: Treatment and disposal of non-hazardous waste
Parent: Swindon Borough Council
Officers: Cheryl Louise Sloan, Secretary; Bernard Thomas Brannan [1956] Director Local Authority; Janine Gail Freeman [1971] Director/Consultant; Doctor Jeffrey James Edwin Hardy [1974] Academic, Consultant and Non-Executive Director; Dwynwen Mary Martin [1955] Director/IT Consultant; James Robert Ward [1972] Finance Director [British/Finnish]; Peter William David Watts [1941] Director/Retired

Publica Group (Support) Limited
Incorporated: 24 January 2017 *Employees:* 625
Net Worth: £13,534 *Total Assets:* £3,977,312
Registered Office: Council Offices, Trinity Road, Cirencester, Glos, GL7 1ZE
Activities: General public administration activities
Shareholders: Cotswold District Council; West Oxfordshire District Council; Cheltenham Borough Council; Forest of Dean District Council
Officers: Steve Anderson-Dixon [1958] Director; David Gary Brooks [1967] Director; Wendy Louise Flynn [1971] Director/Councillor; Dr Christine Elizabeth Gore [1961] Director/Local Government Manager; David Simon Neudegg [1960] Director/Local Government Officer; Susan Gail Pangbourne [1964] Director/Local Government Officer; Rosa-Maria Maria Stewart [1982] Director [Finnish]; James Christopher Towner [1971] Strategic Engagement Director; Frank Malcolm Wilson [1964] Director/Local Government Manager

Puckator Limited
Incorporated: 1 August 1997 *Employees:* 73
Net Worth: £2,753,006 *Total Assets:* £6,551,041
Registered Office: Lowman Works, East Taphouse, Liskeard, Cornwall, PL14 4NQ
Activities: Non-specialised wholesale trade
Parent: Puckator Holdings Limited
Officers: Caroline Ann Howard, Secretary; Nicholas Mark Howard [1956] Director/Importer; Matthew Jason Shaw [1970] Director/Sales & Marketing; Simon Jonathan Thomas [1966] Director

Pucklechurch Development Company Limited
Incorporated: 2 August 1963 *Employees:* 3
Net Worth: £5,772,656 *Total Assets:* £9,542,970
Registered Office: The Estate Office, Farleaze Farm, Farleaze, Malmesbury, Wilts, SN16 0LB
Activities: Other letting and operating of own or leased real estate
Shareholders: Jonathan Tippet Seymour-Williams; Bristol Trust Limited
Officers: Victoria Anne McGowan, Secretary; Derek Richard Febry [1938] Director; Jonathan Tippet Seymour-Williams [1954] Director

Pukka Pads 2000 Limited
Incorporated: 18 November 1998 *Employees:* 90
Net Worth: £809,090 *Total Assets:* £11,537,558
Registered Office: Towngate House, 2-8 Parkstone Road, Poole, Dorset, BH15 2PW
Activities: Manufacture of paper stationery
Parent: Pukka Pads UK Limited
Officers: Christopher Charles Stott, Secretary; Andrew James Bell [1964] Director; Michael Wayne Davis [1969] Director; Christopher Charles Stott [1967] Sales Director

Pukka Pads UK Limited
Incorporated: 17 January 2008 *Employees:* 108
Net Worth: £703,181 *Total Assets:* £11,358,563
Registered Office: Towngate House, 2-8 Parkstone Road, Poole, Dorset, BH15 2PW
Activities: Non-trading company
Major Shareholder: Christopher Charles Stott
Officers: Christopher Charles Stott, Secretary; Andrew James Bell [1964] Director; Christopher Charles Stott [1967] Sales Director

Pulham & Sons (Coaches) Limited
Incorporated: 29 March 1949 *Employees:* 72
Net Worth: £1,755,560 *Total Assets:* £5,782,129
Registered Office: Bourton Business Park, Bourton on the Water, Glos, GL54 2HQ
Activities: Other urban, suburban or metropolitan passenger land transport (not underground, metro or similar)
Major Shareholder: Andrew David Pulham
Officers: Kathryn Helen Pulham, Secretary; Andrew David Pulham [1969] Director/Coach Proprietors

Pullman Premier Leisure Limited
Incorporated: 27 September 1988
Net Worth: £2,071,520 *Total Assets:* £4,303,105
Registered Office: 97 The Esplanade, Weymouth, Dorset, DT4 7AT
Activities: Management of real estate on a fee or contract basis
Major Shareholder: Graham Donald William Roper
Officers: Graham Donald William Roper, Secretary; Stephen Charles Burden [1951] Director/Retired; Keith Jones [1936] Director/Retired Civil Servant; Graham Donald William Roper [1944] Director/Publican; Susan Jane Roper [1945] Director; Peter David Shaw [1954] Director/Publisher; Jonathan Robert Tate [1962] Director/Chartered Accountant

Pulsar Process Measurement Limited
Incorporated: 4 April 1997 *Employees:* 130
Net Worth: £10,110,412 *Total Assets:* £12,608,598
Registered Office: First Floor, 10 Temple Back, Bristol, BS1 6FL
Activities: Manufacture of electronic industrial process control equipment
Shareholders: Vavassor Ltd; Vavassor Limited
Officers: Keith Victor Beard [1953] Managing Director; Jeffery Allen Deplanty [1972] Director/Business Executive [American]; William Edgar Roller [1962] Director/Business Executive [American]; Michael Phillip Santoni [1969] Director/Business Executive [American]

Pulse Global Holdings Limited
Incorporated: 6 June 2011 *Employees:* 39
Net Worth: £599,118 *Total Assets:* £5,447,101
Registered Office: Church Road, Wick, Bristol, BS30 5PE
Activities: Manufacture of printing ink
Shareholder: Gary Paul Sheppard
Officers: Gunther Gerlach [1967] Director/Industrial Engineer [German]; David John Leigh [1956] Director; Gary Paul Sheppard [1965] Director

Pulse Power and Measurement Limited
Incorporated: 25 August 1994 *Employees:* 36
Net Worth: £2,527,274 *Total Assets:* £4,269,927
Registered Office: 65 Shrivenham Hundred Business Park, Watchfield, Swindon, Wilts, SN6 8TY
Activities: Manufacture of communication equipment other than telegraph, and telephone apparatus and equipment
Major Shareholder: Neil Edward Seager
Officers: Philippa Jane Seager, Secretary; Daniel James Bromley [1977] Technical Director; Dr Robert Ferguson Reid [1953] Director; Dr Martin Edward Ryan [1970] Managing Director; Neil Edward Seager [1961] Director/Chief Executive; Philippa Jane Seager [1962] Human Resources Director; Philip William Surman [1977] Sales Director - Power

Pulse Printing Products Limited
Incorporated: 9 November 1999 *Employees:* 38
Net Worth: £302,781 *Total Assets:* £4,963,218
Registered Office: Church Road, Wick, Bristol, BS30 5PE
Activities: Manufacture of paints, varnishes and similar coatings, mastics and sealants
Major Shareholder: Gary Paul Sheppard
Officers: Gary Paul Sheppard, Secretary/Managing Director; Gunther Gerlach [1967] Director/Industrial Engineer [German]; David John Leigh [1956] Director/Sales; Gary Paul Sheppard [1965] Managing Director

Pulse Roll Label Products Limited
Incorporated: 30 May 2001 *Employees:* 58
Net Worth: £1,716,729 *Total Assets:* £4,883,646
Registered Office: Unit U, Lawrence Drive, Yate, Bristol, BS37 5PG
Activities: Manufacture of printing ink
Shareholder: Gary Paul Sheppard
Officers: Gary Peter Seward, Secretary/Managing Director; Gary Peter Seward [1972] Managing Director; Gary Paul Sheppard [1965] Director

Pulsin Ltd
Incorporated: 28 May 2005 *Employees:* 42
Previous: Pulsin' Ltd
Net Worth: £2,573,622 *Total Assets:* £4,611,353
Registered Office: Unit 16 Brunel Court, Quedgeley, Gloucester, GL2 2AL
Activities: Manufacture of other food products n.e.c.
Shareholders: Simon James-Ashburner; Benjamin Gordon Lewis; Nicholas James Bildner
Officers: Simon Paul James-Ashburner, Secretary; Nicholas James Bildner [1978] Director/Teacher; Simon Paul James-Ashburner [1978] Director

Puma Energy (UK) Limited
Incorporated: 1 August 2014
Net Worth: £7,751,000 *Total Assets:* £220,438,000
Registered Office: Westerleigh Terminal, Oakleigh Green Farm Lane, Westerleigh, Bristol, BS37 8QE
Activities: Wholesale of petroleum and petroleum products
Officers: Roy Anthony Brooke [1972] Director/General Manager; Jonathan David Pegler [1965] Director/Head of Supply & Trading

Puma Energy Belfast Ltd
Incorporated: 7 October 2016 *Employees:* 11
Net Worth Deficit: £1,675,634 *Total Assets:* £23,035,810
Registered Office: Westerleigh Terminal, Oakleigh Green Farm Lane, Westerleigh, Bristol, BS37 8QE
Activities: Operation of warehousing and storage facilities for land transport activities
Officers: Lucy Dalrymple-Smith, Secretary; Roy Anthony Brooke [1972] Director; Colin Anthony Nicholl [1970] Director [Irish]; Gary Martin Nicholl [1968] Director [Irish]; Jonathan David Pegler [1965] Director

C.G.Purchase and Son Limited
Incorporated: 1 May 1958 *Employees:* 5
Net Worth: £4,155,913 *Total Assets:* £4,520,858
Registered Office: The Old Farm House, Lower Barnsley Farm, Wimborne, Dorset, BH21 4JA
Activities: Growing of cereals (except rice), leguminous crops and oil seeds
Major Shareholder: Simon George Purchase
Officers: Helen Margaret Purchase [1960] Director; Ian George Purchase [1956] Director/Farmer; John Richard George Purchase [1930] Director/Farmer; Simon George Purchase [1984] Director

Pure Storage UK Limited
Incorporated: 25 October 2012 *Employees:* 100
Net Worth: £14,465,344 *Total Assets:* £20,070,044
Registered Office: 11th Floor, Whitefriars, Lewins Mead, Bristol, BS1 2NT
Activities: Other information technology service activities
Officers: Mona King Yuet Chu [1972] Director, Reporting & Technical Accounting [American]; Caroline Ann Gahan [1975] Finance Director [Irish]; Alexandra Jane Gartrell [1971] Director Legal EMEA - Pure Storage, Inc

Puxton Limited
Incorporated: 2 December 2005 *Employees:* 100
Net Worth Deficit: £1,078,652 *Total Assets:* £4,893,062
Registered Office: Puxton Park, Cowslip Lane, Hewish, Weston Super Mare, Somerset, BS24 6AH
Activities: Other business support service activities n.e.c.
Parent: Mead Realisations Limited
Officers: Patricia Joan Mead, Secretary; Katherine Patricia Hawke [1972] Director; Alistair Daniel Derek Mead [1977] Director/Farmer

PWG Trading Limited
Incorporated: 12 May 2004 *Employees:* 40
Net Worth: £3,206,148 *Total Assets:* £6,536,894
Registered Office: First Floor, PWG House, 85-87 Shrivenham Hundred Business Park, Majors Road, Watchfield, Swindon, Wilts, SN6 8TY
Activities: Other retail sale not in stores, stalls or markets
Parent: Graphite Capital General Partner VII
Officers: Charles James Fox [1966] Director; Jay Pengelly [1974] Managing Director; Rajinder Thapar [1962] Director; Timothy Roy Wakeman [1946] Director

Pyman Bell (Holdings) Limited
Incorporated: 24 August 1981
Net Worth: £7,012,673 *Total Assets:* £12,093,771
Registered Office: Farm Office, Wisteria Farm, Cox Hill, North Newton, Somerset, TA7 0BT
Activities: Other letting and operating of own or leased real estate
Officers: Sir Benjamin Julian Alfred Slade [1946] Director

QDOS Homes Limited
Incorporated: 17 December 1999 *Employees:* 8
Net Worth: £2,120,309 *Total Assets:* £6,732,820
Registered Office: The Courtyard, 33 Duke Street, Trowbridge, Wilts, BA14 8EA
Activities: Construction of domestic buildings
Parent: Redhorn Holdings Ltd
Officers: Elizabeth Jane Harbour, Secretary; Elizabeth Jane Harbour [1953] Director; Stephen John Harbour [1954] Director

QE Academy Trust
Incorporated: 14 March 2011 *Employees:* 201
Net Worth: £17,883,212 *Total Assets:* £23,936,280
Registered Office: Upper School, Western Road, Crediton, Devon, EX17 3LU
Activities: General secondary education
Officers: Andrew Bennet Brook, Secretary; Keith Baker [1966] Director/Wholetime Watch Commander for Devon Somerset Fire; Stephen Michael Kentish Barnes [1951] Director/Writer; Christopher James Cooper [1969] Director/Local Government Officer; James David Gregory [1975] Director/Minister of Religion; Rosemary Elizabeth Howard [1962] Director/HR Administrator; Jacqueline Michele Laffar [1962] Director/Senior Team Leader; Rupert James Poole [1971] Director/Principal; Gemma Effie Poulton [1971] Director/Archivist; Paul Tearle [1980] Director/Teacher; Carey Jane Thorne [1958] Director/Retired Teacher; Cllr Nicholas Andrew Way [1952] Director/Councillor; Suzanne Williams [1962] Director/Chartered Accountant

QIP Solutions Ltd
Incorporated: 18 August 2014
Net Worth: £2,695,339 *Total Assets:* £4,169,215
Registered Office: 13 Queens Road, Bournemouth, BH2 6BA
Activities: Business and domestic software development
Major Shareholder: Fiona Kane
Officers: Fiona Kane [1965] Director

QMP Group Limited
Incorporated: 18 November 2016 *Employees:* 16
Previous: BCOMP 510 Limited
Net Worth: £3,922,248 *Total Assets:* £15,510,433
Registered Office: 15 Interface Business Park, Bincknoll Lane, Royal Wootton Bassett, Swindon, Wilts, SN4 8SY
Activities: Buying and selling of own real estate
Major Shareholder: Stephen George Abbley
Officers: Stephen George Abbley [1957] Director; John Gerard Michael Haugh [1966] Finance Director [Irish]

QNH Limited
Incorporated: 10 March 2010 *Employees:* 60
Net Worth: £799,442 *Total Assets:* £3,551,978
Registered Office: 5th Floor, Holland House, 20 Oxford Road, Bournemouth, BH8 8EZ
Activities: Information technology consultancy activities
Parent: ESET, Spol. S R.O.
Officers: Miroslav Mikus [1984] Sales and Marketing Director [Slovak]

Quadrum Investments Group Limited
Incorporated: 27 March 2009
Net Worth Deficit: £6,184,000 *Total Assets:* £103,402,000
Registered Office: P O Box 1463, Windmill Hill, Whitehill Way, Swindon, Wilts, SN5 6PS
Activities: Activities of head offices
Parent: Fleetcor UK Acquisition Ltd
Officers: Eric Richard Dey [1959] Director [American]; Alan King [1976] Director; Anita Kravos-Medimorec [1974] Director/Chief Financial Officer; Steven Joseph Pisciotta [1964] Director [American]

Qualasept Holdings Limited
Incorporated: 20 April 2016 *Employees:* 208
Net Worth: £13,619,092 *Total Assets:* £45,933,204
Registered Office: 3 Corsham Science Park, Park Lane, Corsham, Wilts, SN13 9FU
Activities: Manufacture of pharmaceutical preparations
Shareholders: Christopher Dean Watt; Richard John Wastnage
Officers: Richard John Wastnage [1965] Director/Pharmacist; Christopher Dean Watt [1968] Director; Maria Ann Watt [1970] Director/Pharmacist

Qualasept Limited
Incorporated: 30 August 2005 *Employees:* 169
Net Worth: £13,716,244 *Total Assets:* £34,878,516
Registered Office: 3 Corsham Science Park, Park Lane, Corsham, Wilts, SN13 9FU
Activities: Manufacture of pharmaceutical preparations
Parent: Qualasept Pharmaxo Holdings Limited
Officers: Christopher James Fountain [1966] Director/Chartered Accountant; Richard John Wastnage [1965] Director/Pharmacist; Christopher Dean Watt [1968] Director

The Quality Assurance Agency for Higher Education
Incorporated: 27 March 1997 *Employees:* 118
Net Worth: £6,056,790 *Total Assets:* £9,422,507
Registered Office: Southgate House, Southgate Street, Gloucester, GL1 1UB
Activities: First-degree level higher education
Officers: Lavinia Blackett, Secretary; Matthew Adie [1995] Director/Student; Christopher Nigel Banks [1959] Director and Independent Chair; Stephen Melville Criddle [1961] Director/Principal & CEO; Dr Vanessa Louise Davies [1959] Director General; Amatey Victor Doku [1995] Director/Vice President of The National Union of Students; Sara Kaye Drake [1955] Director/Chief Executive; Linda Margaret Duncan [1963] Director/Accountant; Professor Maria Gertrude Hinfelaar [1959] Director/Vice-Chancellor and Chief Executive [Dutch]; Oliver William Johnson [1955] Director; Professor Helen Eileen Langton [1959] Director/Vice-Chancellor; Professor Craig Austin Mahoney [1957] Director/Vice Chancellor [British/Australian]; Professor Denise Angela McAlister [1955] Director/Pro Vice Chancellor; Professor Oliver Hugh Turnbull [1964] Director/Professor of Neuropsychology; Professor Andrew Brian Wathey [1958] Director/Vice Chancellor and Chief Executive; Craig Alyn Watkins [1966] Director/Accountant; Philip Alan Stuart Wilson [1971] Director/Chief Executive, Higher Education; Professor Philip Winn [1954] Director/Head of Institute (Strathclyde University)

Quality Care Group Limited
Incorporated: 4 January 2008 *Employees:* 187
Net Worth: £4,437,522 *Total Assets:* £10,772,936
Registered Office: 31-33 Commercial Road, Poole, Dorset, BH14 0HU
Activities: Other business support service activities n.e.c.
Officers: Maria Josephine Maynard, Secretary; John Kenneth Grimes [1936] Director; Bridget Elizabeth Hardman [1951] Director; John Wilfred Hardman [1946] Director; John Anthony Raymond Harris [1941] Director; Patricia Ann Harris [1942] Director; Barry Michael Lambert [1950] Director; Barry Dwane Maynard [1944] Director; Graham Murry [1948] Director; Michelle Jane Watson [1970] Director

Qualtronyc Property Holdings Limited
Incorporated: 7 April 2003 *Employees:* 4
Net Worth: £3,387,076 *Total Assets:* £4,773,991
Registered Office: Pillar House, 113-115 Bath Road, Cheltenham, Glos, GL53 7LS
Activities: Other letting and operating of own or leased real estate
Major Shareholder: Ronald Harry Atkins
Officers: Christine Atkins, Secretary/Director; Christine Atkins [1953] Director; Deborah Elizabeth Atkins [1973] Director; Ronald Harry Atkins [1944] Director; Michael David Fereday [1962] Director

Quantock Properties Limited
Incorporated: 6 April 1993
Net Worth: £8,885,000 *Total Assets:* £80,617,000
Registered Office: Mallard Court, Express Park, Bridgwater, Somerset, TA6 4RN
Activities: Other letting and operating of own or leased real estate
Officers: Pieter Willem Van Meeteren, Secretary; Aart Cornelis Duijzer [1963] Managing Director [Dutch]; Johannes Henricus Wilhelmus Roelofs [1963] Managing Director [Dutch]; David John Saint [1964] Director/Executive

Quantum Christchurch Care LLP
Incorporated: 15 September 2014
Net Worth Deficit: £953,414 *Total Assets:* £7,031,882
Registered Office: Russell House, Oxford Road, Bournemouth, BH8 8EX

Quantum Group (Management) Limited
Incorporated: 17 January 2011 *Employees:* 1
Net Worth: £8,057,449 *Total Assets:* £9,946,312
Registered Office: 10 Bridge Street, Christchurch, Dorset, BH23 1EF
Activities: Development of building projects
Officers: Richard Oliver Bernays [1943] Director/Investment Manager; Simon Hammond [1966] Director [Irish]; David William Hines [1959] Director; Julian Mark Shaffer [1968] Director

Quantum Homes Holdings Limited
Incorporated: 9 October 2007
Net Worth: £4,484,081 *Total Assets:* £5,225,948
Registered Office: 10 Bridge Street, Christchurch, Dorset, BH23 1EF
Activities: Activities of other holding companies n.e.c.
Major Shareholder: Julian Mark Shaffer
Officers: Julian Mark Shaffer [1968] Director/Property Developer

Quantum Old Manor Retirement Living LLP
Incorporated: 13 August 2014
Net Worth: £5,845,575 *Total Assets:* £11,309,508
Registered Office: Midland House, 2 Poole Road, Bournemouth, BH2 5QY

Quantum Salisbury Centre LLP
Incorporated: 12 October 2012
Net Worth: £5,656,250 *Total Assets:* £10,581,663
Registered Office: Midland House, 2 Poole Road, Bournemouth, BH2 5QY
Officers: Richard Oliver Bernays [1943] LLP Member; Nigel Sebastian David Bulmer [1947] LLP Member; Dominic Peter Caldecott [1956] LLP Member; James Arthur Terence Daler [1938] LLP Member; Patricia Mary Daler [1943] LLP Member; Paul Greatbatch [1958] LLP Member; Michael Anthony Lambert [1929] LLP Member; Rosemary Elizabeth Skillman [1962] LLP Member; Colin Stuart Wilson [1957] LLP Member; Stephen Anthony Zimmerman [1949] LLP Member; As Trustee of Quantum Salisbury Centre Euut Gfs Trustee Limited, Corporate-LLP Member

Quantum Swansea LLP
Incorporated: 5 June 2013
Net Worth: £6,014,799 *Total Assets:* £10,430,771
Registered Office: Midland House, 2 Poole Road, Bournemouth, BH2 5QY
Officers: Michael David Brennan [1969] LLP Member; James Arthur Terence Daler [1938] LLP Member; Patricia Mary Daler [1943] LLP Member; David Lee Gilbert [1959] LLP Member; Michael Herbert Gilbert [1956] LLP Member; Paul Greatbatch [1958] LLP Member; Michael Anthony Lambert [1929] LLP Member; John Phizackerley [1962] LLP Member; Charles Rankin [1961] LLP Member; Julia Mary Royds [1959] LLP Member; Michael Robert Spalter [1969] LLP Member; Goran Trapp [1962] LLP Member

Quantum Teddington Development Limited
Incorporated: 21 February 2015
Net Worth: £3,544,238 *Total Assets:* £3,683,294
Registered Office: Midland House, 2 Poole Road, Bournemouth, BH2 5QY
Activities: Construction of commercial buildings
Officers: Julian Mark Shaffer [1968] Director

Quantum Teddington LLP
Incorporated: 9 June 2015
Net Worth: £4,925,000 *Total Assets:* £5,105,978
Registered Office: Midland House, 2 Poole Road, Bournemouth, BH2 5QY
Officers: David Sidney Bernstein [1955] LLP Member; Nigel Sebastian David Bulmer [1947] LLP Member; Mark Richard Couling [1975] LLP Member; Rupert Chandos Daniels [1945] LLP Member; Hugh Jon Foulds [1932] LLP Member; Warren George Haskins [1948] LLP Member; Alan Charles Hodson [1962] LLP Member; Robin Phillips [1958] LLP Member; Damian Thornton [1963] LLP Member

Quartet Community Foundation
Incorporated: 19 April 2000 *Employees:* 11
Net Worth: £29,907,430 *Total Assets:* £30,319,148
Registered Office: Royal Oak House, Royal Oak Avenue, Bristol, BS1 4GB
Activities: Other information service activities n.e.c.
Officers: Jonathan Mark Midelton Baker [1960] Director; Susan Elizabeth Blatchford [1968] Managing Director; Robert Henry Glanville Bourns [1956] Director/Lawyer; Merlyn Pamela Ipinson-Fleming [1963] Director/HR Specialist; Christopher Nigel Johnson [1957] Director/Banker; Annie Elizabeth Kilvington [1962] Director/Solicitor; William Edward Lee [1958] Director/Actuary - Retired; Trevor Anthony Leonard [1959] Director/Accountant; Pat Meehan [1957] Director/Chartered Financial Planner; Bina Shah [1962] Director/Marketing Consultant; Benjamin Hugh Silvey [1977] Director; Julian Philip Telling [1960] Director/Businessman; Joanna Turner [1951] Director/Retired; Helen Mary Wilde [1951] Director/Retired

Quay Developments (Southern) Limited
Incorporated: 24 March 2015 *Employees:* 1
Net Worth: £4,880,629 *Total Assets:* £7,092,843
Registered Office: Windover House, St Ann Street, Salisbury, Wilts, SP1 2DR
Activities: Activities of other holding companies n.e.c.
Officers: Alex James Hunt [1982] Director

Quay Marinas Group Ltd
Incorporated: 12 August 2003 *Employees:* 85
Previous: Quay Marinas Holdings Limited
Net Worth: £4,819,866 *Total Assets:* £12,427,292
Registered Office: A & W Building, Newfoundland Way, Portishead, Somerset, BS20 7DF
Activities: Other amusement and recreation activities n.e.c.
Shareholders: Andrew Temple Yates; Andrew Temple Yates
Officers: Paul Kerr Rye, Secretary; Simon Nicholas Haigh [1962] Director; Paul Kerr Rye [1960] Director and Company Secretary; Andrew Temple Yates [1953] Director

Quay Marinas Limited
Incorporated: 5 February 1973 *Employees:* 85
Net Worth: £6,669,351 *Total Assets:* £12,647,665
Registered Office: A & W Building, Newfoundland Way, Portishead, Somerset, BS20 7DF
Activities: Other amusement and recreation activities n.e.c.
Shareholder: Andrew Temple Yates
Officers: Paul Kerr Rye, Secretary; Simon Nicholas Haigh [1962] Managing Director; Paul Kerr Rye [1960] Director and Company Secretary; Andrew Temple Yates [1953] Director

Queen Elizabeth's Hospital
Incorporated: 28 June 2004 *Employees:* 121
Net Worth: £20,480,950 *Total Assets:* £24,111,120
Registered Office: Queen Elizabeths Hospital, Berkeley Place, Clifton, Bristol, BS8 1JX
Activities: Primary education
Officers: Rodney Nicholas Cook, Secretary; Caroline Bateson [1960] Director/Retired Headteacher; Sallie Elizabeth Blanks [1958] Director/Project Manager; John Buchanan [1959] Director/Head of Tax; Edward John Corrigan [1962] Director/Chartered Accountant; Sarah Cosgrove [1951] Director/Retired; Timothy James Davis [1964] Director/Chartered Surveyor; Richard John Hill [1960] Director/Solicitor; John Anthony Hollingdale [1950] Director/Retired; Paul Alistair Keen [1955] Director/Business Manager; Kevin Riley [1955] Director/Retired Headteacher; David Alan Smart [1961] Director/Chartered Accountant; Clive John Woodford [1960] Director/Chartered Surveyor

Queen Elizabeth's School (Wimborne Minster)
Incorporated: 18 September 2013 *Employees:* 166
Net Worth: £17,666,494 *Total Assets:* £21,236,172
Registered Office: Queen Elizabeth's School, Blandford Road, Wimborne Minster, Dorset, BH21 4DT
Activities: General secondary education
Officers: Janet Elizabeth Day, Secretary; Karen Jane Allman [1962] Human Resources Director; Rupert Andrews [1971] Director; Pola Bevan [1956] Director/Retired; Rachel Leigh Cass [1962] Director; John Connor [1962] Commercial Director; Dr Margaret Elizabeth Foster [1949] Director/Retired; Fiona Brigid Holmes [1962] Director; Emma Frances Hunt [1962] Director/Vice Chancellor; Lars William Jackson [1960] Director/Interior Designer; Stephen Nicholas Jones [1978] Director; Martin Philip McLeman [1961] Director/Headteacher; Jane Mursell [1963] Director/Teacher; Sharon Lisa Powis [1967] Director/Exams Manager; Revd Andrew John William Rowland [1960] Director/Reverend; David Sims [1968] Director/Teacher; Vikki Slade [1972] Director/Charity Worker

Queen's Park Infant Academy
Incorporated: 7 March 2013 *Employees:* 53
Net Worth: £2,732,048 *Total Assets:* £3,915,238
Registered Office: East Way, Bournemouth, BH8 9PU
Activities: Primary education
Officers: Frances Blanchard [1959] Director/Teacher; Tracey Marie Edwards [1969] Director/Headteacher; Anita Margaret Evans [1943] Director/Minister of Religion; Rafael Frias-Robles [1950] Director/Architectural Technologist [Spanish]; Valerie Margaret Green [1946] Director/Retired; Jennifer Louise Ledun [1975] Director; Michelle Ann Lucas [1971] Director/Teacher; Susan Elizabeth Varley [1969] Director/NHS Project Manager

Queensquare Farming Limited
Incorporated: 24 February 2011
Net Worth: £26,363,306 *Total Assets:* £30,654,866
Registered Office: 4 Queen Square, Bath, BA1 2HA
Activities: Growing of cereals (except rice), leguminous crops and oil seeds
Parent: Queensquare Trustee Limited
Officers: Nicholas James Burrows, Secretary; Andrew Douglas Brownsword [1947] Director; Jeremy David Hancock [1964] Director/Tax Manager

Quest End Computer Services Limited
Incorporated: 6 October 1982 *Employees:* 1
Net Worth: £16,627,966 *Total Assets:* £26,718,932
Registered Office: 7 Abbey Court, Eagle Way, Sowton Industrial Estate, Exeter, Devon, EX2 7HY
Activities: Other information technology service activities
Parent: DMGI Land & Property Europe Ltd
Officers: Matthew Teague, Secretary; Simon James Brown [1965] Director/Chief Executive; David William Callcott [1959] Finance Director; Stephen John Stout [1960] Director/Chairman

Quick Move Now Limited
Incorporated: 29 June 1998 *Employees:* 22
Previous: Quick Move Properties Limited
Net Worth: £8,167,830 *Total Assets:* £13,153,770
Registered Office: Unit 15 Interface Business Park, Binknoll Lane, Wootton Bassett, Swindon, Wilts, SN4 8SY
Activities: Buying and selling of own real estate
Parent: LINC Capital Limited
Officers: Alun Hywel Luke, Secretary; Alun Hywel Luke [1949] Director; Christine Luke [1951] Director; Daniel Gareth Luke [1979] Managing Director; John Hywel Luke [1984] Sales Director; Rhys David Luke [1981] Operations Director

Quick Move Properties Limited
Incorporated: 27 February 2014 *Employees:* 16
Net Worth: £3,923,898 *Total Assets:* £15,509,333
Registered Office: 15 Interface Business Park, Bincknoll Lane, Royal Wootton Bassett, Wilts, SN4 8SY
Activities: Buying and selling of own real estate
Parent: BCOMP 510 Limited
Officers: Stephen George Abbley [1957] Director; John Gerard Michael Haugh [1966] Finance Director [Irish]

Quickgrind Limited
Incorporated: 20 October 1975 *Employees:* 25
Net Worth: £2,342,930 *Total Assets:* £4,619,815
Registered Office: Unit 5701 Shannon Place, Shannon Way, Tewkesbury, Glos, GL20 8SL
Activities: Manufacture of tools
Shareholders: Edward James Howell; Ross Edward Howell; Patricia Anne Howell
Officers: Ross Howell, Secretary; Edward James Howell [1944] Director/Engineer; Patricia Anne Howell [1946] Director; Ross Edward Howell [1979] Director/Engineer

Quickmach Engineering Limited
Incorporated: 10 January 2001 *Employees:* 55
Net Worth: £2,062,115 *Total Assets:* £4,075,708
Registered Office: Brabazon, 1 Meteor Business Park, Cheltenham Road East, Staverton, Gloucester, GL2 9QL
Activities: Other manufacturing n.e.c.
Shareholder: Michael Quinn
Officers: Malcolm Beach [1960] Director; Peter Cornish [1975] Director; Michael Quinn [1967] Director

Quickmach Holdings Limited
Incorporated: 11 September 2013 *Employees:* 4
Net Worth: £3,444,998 *Total Assets:* £4,457,746
Registered Office: Brabazon 1, Meteor Business Park, Cheltenham Road, East Staverton, Gloucester, GL2 9QL
Activities: Activities of production holding companies
Shareholder: Michael Quinn
Officers: Kelly-Anne Cornish [1978] Director; Peter Cornish [1975] Director; Charmaine Malone [1973] Director/Finance Manager; Michael Quinn [1967] Director

R & M Utility & Civil Engineering Services South West Limited
Incorporated: 27 April 2011 *Employees:* 132
Net Worth: £2,204,380 *Total Assets:* £7,500,085
Registered Office: Unit 38d Greendale Business Park, Woodbury Salterton, Exeter, Devon, EX5 1EW
Activities: Other construction installation
Shareholders: Glynn Ford; Andrew Marshall
Officers: Glynn Ford, Secretary; Glynn Ford [1976] Director/Manager; Andrew Marshall [1976] Director/Engineer

R S T Leisure Ltd
Incorporated: 22 July 1986 *Employees:* 65
Net Worth: £85,235 *Total Assets:* £5,149,194
Registered Office: c/o Prydis, Senate Court, Southernhay Gardens, Exeter, EX1 1NT
Activities: Hotels and similar accommodation
Major Shareholder: Roger Stephen Thomas Haywood
Officers: Roger Stephen Thomas Haywood [1950] Director/Restaurateur

R W Estates (Trading) Limited
Incorporated: 12 May 1999
Net Worth: £2,179,086 *Total Assets:* £4,803,404
Registered Office: 15a Fore Street, Tiverton, Devon, EX16 6LN
Activities: Buying and selling of own real estate
Shareholder: RW Estates Ltd
Officers: Garry Jonathan Mettam, Secretary/Chartered Surveyor; Garry Jonathan Mettam [1967] Director/Chartered Surveyor; Timothy Richard Ware [1963] Director/Chartered Surveyor

R W Estates Ltd
Incorporated: 15 February 1966
Net Worth: £5,119,343 *Total Assets:* £6,455,231
Registered Office: 15a Fore Street, Tiverton, Devon, EX16 6LN
Activities: Buying and selling of own real estate
Shareholders: Garry Jonathan Mettam; David Edward Mettam
Officers: Garry Jonathan Mettam, Secretary/Chartered Surveyor; David Edward Mettam [1938] Director/Chartered Surveyor; Garry Jonathan Mettam [1967] Director/Chartered Surveyor; Laurence George David Mettam [1965] Director/Graphic Designer

R. B. Quadrangle Leasing Limited
Incorporated: 14 August 1985
Net Worth: £1,216,584 *Total Assets:* £92,435,376
Registered Office: The Quadrangle, The Promenade, Cheltenham, Glos, GL50 1PX
Activities: Financial intermediation not elsewhere classified
Parent: Royal Bank Leasing Limited
Officers: Ian Andrew Ellis [1969] Director/Bank Official; David Generald Harris [1969] Director/Bank Official; Steven James Roulston [1977] Director/Bank Official

R.R. Transport Limited
Incorporated: 20 February 1991 *Employees:* 98
Net Worth: £3,778,959 *Total Assets:* £7,110,555
Registered Office: Venayr Goonearl, Scorrier, Redruth, Cornwall, TR16 5EB
Activities: Freight transport by road
Shareholders: Mark Gordon Bailey; Kathryn Mary Bailey
Officers: Kathryn Mary Bailey, Secretary/Executive Manager; Kathryn Mary Bailey [1974] Director/Executive Manager; Lee Daniel Wills [1985] Director

R.T. Property Investments Limited
Incorporated: 16 December 1997
Net Worth: £2,571,268 *Total Assets:* £3,749,432
Registered Office: Lower Littlecott Farm, Goatacre, Calne, Wilts, SN11 9HZ
Activities: Non-specialised wholesale trade
Shareholders: Lucy Victoria Holliday; Corrie Ltd
Officers: Roderick James Hugh McLeod Corrie, Secretary/Director; Lara Rebecca Brotherton [1967] Director [American]; Roderick James Hugh McLeod Corrie [1962] Director; Lucy Victoria Holliday [1971] Director/Rentier; Thomas Brook Holliday [1962] Director/Stockbroker

Raans Estates Limited
Incorporated: 17 August 1992
Net Worth: £1,647,226 *Total Assets:* £8,676,812
Registered Office: Unit 17 Lancaster Road, Sarum Business Park, Salisbury, Wilts, SP4 6FB
Activities: Other letting and operating of own or leased real estate
Shareholders: John Richard Woodley; George Woodley; William Woodley
Officers: John Richard Woodley, Secretary/Director; George Woodley [1965] Director; John Richard Woodley [1964] Director; Joyce Lang Woodley [1926] Director; William Thomas Woodley [1967] Director

Race 500 Limited
Incorporated: 27 January 2005
Net Worth Deficit: £1,020,283 *Total Assets:* £3,600,000
Registered Office: Unit 2 Kingsland Trading Estate, St Philips Road, Bristol, BS2 0JZ
Activities: Activities of other holding companies n.e.c.
Major Shareholder: Stuart Jonathan Lacey
Officers: Benjamin James Addison, Secretary; Emma Claire Lacey [1967] Director; Stuart Jonathan Lacey [1968] Director

Radiodetection Limited
Incorporated: 18 October 1977 *Employees:* 164
Net Worth: £55,883,000 *Total Assets:* £64,494,000
Registered Office: Western Drive, Bristol, BS14 0AF
Activities: Manufacture of electronic measuring, testing etc. equipment, not for industrial process control
Parent: SPX European Holding Limited
Officers: Kevin Paul Lench [1961] Managing Director; John Nurkin [1969] Director [American]; Michael Andrew Reilly [1964] Director/Corporate Controller Chief Accountant [American]; Scott William Sproule [1969] Director/Vice President, Treasurer & CFO [American]

Radipole Mill Investments Limited
Incorporated: 29 July 2015 *Employees:* 326
Net Worth: £486,452 *Total Assets:* £6,162,169
Registered Office: Meadows Causeway, Radipole, Weymouth, Dorset, DT4 9RY
Activities: Activities of construction holding companies
Shareholders: Sean Anthony Cooper; Stephen James Devlin
Officers: Andrew Stephen Hornigold, Secretary; Maxine Anne Cooper [1966] Director; Sean Anthony Cooper [1966] Director; Stephen James Devlin [1967] Director; Andrew Stephen Hornigold [1966] Director/Solicitor

Radius (Bristol) Limited
Incorporated: 6 June 2000 *Employees:* 58
Net Worth: £3,911,052 *Total Assets:* £16,660,521
Registered Office: Whitefriars, Lewins Mead, Bristol, BS1 2NT
Activities: Other business support service activities n.e.c.
Parent: Radius (UK) Limited
Officers: Lynnet Marie Conley [1960] Director/Chief Financial Officer [American]; Alan William Mathers [1967] Director/Chief Operating Officer

Radius (UK) Limited
Incorporated: 14 April 1999
Net Worth: £21,961,112 *Total Assets:* £44,335,664
Registered Office: 11th Floor, Whitefriars, Lewins Mead, Bristol, BS1 2NT
Activities: Other business support service activities n.e.c.
Parent: Radius Debtco Limited
Officers: Lynnet Marie Conley [1960] Director/Chief Financial Officer [American]; Alan William Mathers [1967] Director/Chief Operating Officer

Radius Bidco Limited
Incorporated: 18 July 2013
Net Worth Deficit: £57,121,876 *Total Assets:* £198,866,096
Registered Office: Whitefriars, Lewins Mead, Bristol, BS1 2NT
Activities: Activities of other holding companies n.e.c.
Parent: Accomplish UK Holdings Limited
Officers: Stephen Mark Chipman [1961] Director/Chief Executive Officer [American]; Lynnet Marie Conley [1960] Director/Chief Financial Officer [American]; Alan William Mathers [1967] Director/Chief Operational Officer

Radius Debtco Limited
Incorporated: 7 April 2014
Net Worth: £162,910,992 *Total Assets:* £217,448,864
Registered Office: Whitefriars, Lewins Mead, Bristol, BS1 2NT
Activities: Other business support service activities n.e.c.
Parent: Radius Pledgeco Limited
Officers: Stephen Mark Chipman [1961] Director [American]; Lynnet Marie Conley [1960] Director/Chief Financial Officer [American]

Radius Holdco Limited
Incorporated: 18 July 2013 *Employees:* 871
Net Worth Deficit: £113,202,736 *Total Assets:* £220,961,776
Registered Office: Whitefriars, Lewins Mead, Bristol, BS1 2NT
Activities: Activities of other holding companies n.e.c.
Officers: Nicholas Charles Luckock [1972] Director/Investment Executive; Thorsten Toepfer [1978] Director/Investment Executive

Radius Midco Limited
Incorporated: 18 July 2013
Net Worth: £1,817,621 *Total Assets:* £230,017,760
Registered Office: Whitefriars, Lewins Mead, Bristol, BS1 2NT
Activities: Activities of other holding companies n.e.c.
Parent: Radius Holdco Limited
Officers: Nicholas Charles Luckock [1972] Director/Investment Executive; Thorsten Toepfer [1978] Director/Investment Executive

Radius Pledgeco Limited
Incorporated: 17 April 2014
Net Worth: £187,767,888 *Total Assets:* £196,120,448
Registered Office: Whitefriars, Lewins Mead, Bristol, BS1 2NT
Activities: Other business support service activities n.e.c.
Parent: Radius Bidco Limited
Officers: Stephen Mark Chipman [1961] Director [American]; Lynnet Marie Conley [1960] Director/Chief Financial Officer [American]

Radquill Developments Limited
Incorporated: 9 January 1980 *Employees:* 1
Net Worth: £4,040,073 *Total Assets:* £4,147,550
Registered Office: Pulham Business Park, Pulham, Dorchester, DT2 7DX
Activities: Construction of commercial buildings
Shareholders: Dawn Snashall; Michael Snashall
Officers: Dawn Margaret Rose Snashall, Secretary; Michael Snashall [1947] Director; Paul Snashall [1977] Director; Sandra Ann Snashall [1968] Director/Sales Manager

RAGM PLC
Incorporated: 11 January 2001 *Employees:* 30
Net Worth: £411,477 *Total Assets:* £4,265,771
Registered Office: Hazlewoods LLP, Windsor House, Bayshill Road, Cheltenham, Glos, GL50 3AT
Activities: Wholesale of household goods (other than musical instruments) n.e.c
Major Shareholder: Ajay Chopra
Officers: Aruna Chopra, Secretary/Director; Ajay Chopra [1964] Director/Businessman; Aruna Chopra [1964] Director

Railston Holdings Limited
Incorporated: 30 June 2005 *Employees:* 104
Net Worth: £2,543,636 *Total Assets:* £10,289,015
Registered Office: Railston Building, Whitehill Lane, Wootton Bassett, Swindon, Wilts, SN4 7DB
Activities: Non-trading company
Shareholders: Gerrard Martin O'Sullivan; Geoffrey Ivor Owen
Officers: Kathryn Jane Johnson, Secretary; Philip Richard Arnett [1984] Director; Kathryn Jane Johnson [1978] Director; Gerrard Martin O'Sullivan [1956] Director; Geoffrey Ivor Owen [1967] Financial Director; Stephen Rumsey [1953] Commercial Director

Railston Limited
Incorporated: 4 November 1983 *Employees:* 102
Net Worth: £7,406,305 *Total Assets:* £15,149,124
Registered Office: Railston House, Whitehill Lane Industrial Estate, Whitehill Lane, Wootton Bassett, Wilts, SN4 7DB
Activities: Joinery installation
Parent: Railston Holdings Limited
Officers: Kathryn Jane Johnson, Secretary; Philip Richard Arnett [1984] Director/Designer; Andrew Fox [1970] Director; Kathryn Jane Johnson [1978] Director; Gerard O'Sullivan [1956] Operations Director; Geoffrey Ivor Owen [1967] Financial Director; Stephen Rumsey [1953] Commercial Director

The Railway Convalescent Homes
Incorporated: 21 December 2009
Net Worth: £9,228,401 *Total Assets:* £9,307,579
Registered Office: Bridge House, 2 Church Street, Dawlish, Devon, EX7 9AU
Activities: Other accommodation
Officers: Brian Conyard, Secretary; Stephen James Brook [1955] Director/Electrical Engineering Consultant; John Collins [1944] Director/Accountant Retired; David Robert Crome [1964] Director/Head of On Board; Barbara Jill Davenport [1961] Director/Occupational Health Nurse; Christopher Donovan [1962] Director/Employee Relations Manager; Leonard Horwood [1948] Director/Accountant; Colin Christopher Mills [1941] Director/Retired; Peter Christopher Moakes [1943] Director/Chartered Surveyor; Philip Edward O'Hare [1969] Director/General Manager; John Franklin Land Reeves [1941] Director/Retired; Anthony David Sugden [1951] Director/Driving Instructor

Rainbow Holdings (UK) Limited
Incorporated: 11 February 2005
Net Worth: £4,542,971 *Total Assets:* £4,544,785
Registered Office: The White House, London Road, Strete Ralegh, Whimple, Exeter, Devon, EX5 2PT
Activities: Other retail sale in non-specialised stores
Major Shareholder: Ralph Jeremy White
Officers: Ralph Jeremy White, Secretary/Director; Doctor Neera White [1965] Director; Ralph Jeremy White [1956] Director

Rajani (Wholesale) Limited
Incorporated: 30 March 1982
Net Worth: £4,703,163 *Total Assets:* £4,971,335
Registered Office: Maggs Lane, Clay Hill, Bristol, BS5 7EW
Activities: Non-specialised wholesale trade
Shareholder: Rajendra Rajani
Officers: Gita Rajani, Secretary; Gita Rajani [1952] Director/Administrator; Rajendra Rajani [1951] Director/Wholesale Distributor

Ramsbury Estates Limited
Incorporated: 9 May 1997 *Employees:* 73
Net Worth: £2,703,111 *Total Assets:* £10,213,695
Registered Office: The Estate Office, Priory Farm, Axford, Marlborough, Wilts, SN8 2HA
Activities: Growing of cereals (except rice), leguminous crops and oil seeds
Major Shareholder: Carl Stefan Erling Persson
Officers: Alistair Edward Stuart Ewing, Secretary; Carl Stefan Erling Persson [1947] Director [Swedish]

Range Valley Extrusions Limited
Incorporated: 4 May 1989
Net Worth: £11,760,000 *Total Assets:* £11,854,000
Registered Office: 2 Temple Back East, Temple Quay, Bristol, BS1 6EG
Activities: Other business support service activities n.e.c.
Parent: Deceuninck Holdings (UK) Limited
Officers: Wim Van Acker [1973] Director/Chief Financial Officer [Belgian]; Francis Van Eeckhout [1968] Director/Chief Executive Officer [Belgian]; Bernard Vanderper [1962] Director/Sales Manager Benelux

Rangemoors Limited
Incorporated: 11 January 1978 *Employees:* 32
Net Worth: £2,597,073 *Total Assets:* £3,597,401
Registered Office: c/o Foot Anstey Solicitors, Senate Court, Southernhay Gardens, Exeter, Devon, EX1 1NT
Activities: Non-specialised wholesale trade
Parent: Chimney Holdings Limited
Officers: Andrew John Baker [1965] Director; Gareth Harold Down [1961] Managing Director; Robert David Pocock [1963] Director/Consultant; Allan John Vodden [1949] Director

Rapid Racking Limited
Incorporated: 21 February 1986 *Employees:* 71
Net Worth: £22,605,000 *Total Assets:* £28,263,000
Registered Office: Unit M3, Kemble Industrial Park, Kemble, Cirencester, Glos, GL7 6BQ
Activities: Retail sale via mail order houses or via Internet
Parent: Eurostore Holdings Limited
Officers: Pierre-Olivier Brial, Secretary; Brigitte Auffrett [1961] Director/General Manager [French]; Keith Charles Boad [1959] Managing Director; Monsieur Pierre-Olivier Brial [1973] Director/Manager [French]; Jean-Pierre Guichard [1946] Director/Chairman [French]

M.R. Ratcliffe Consultants Limited
Incorporated: 5 May 1987 *Employees:* 46
Net Worth: £577,866 *Total Assets:* £3,726,031
Registered Office: Wolseley House, Oriel Road, Cheltenham, Glos, GL50 1TH
Activities: Non-life insurance
Officers: Patricia Rose Ratcliffe, Secretary; Michael Richardson Ratcliffe [1945] Director; Patricia Rose Ratcliffe [1937] Director

Rattray Milne Ltd
Incorporated: 11 July 2013
Net Worth: £3,193,811 *Total Assets:* £4,437,873
Registered Office: The Old Stocks Inn, The Square, Stow on the Wold, Glos, GL54 1AF
Activities: Hotels and similar accommodation
Shareholders: Charles Buckland Cockell; Judith Anne Cockell
Officers: Charles Buckland Cockell [1950] Director; James Colvile Cockell [1977] Director; Judith Anne Cockell [1953] Director; Victoria Anne Kieldsen [1980] Director

Raven Mount Limited
Incorporated: 10 November 2003 *Employees:* 3
Net Worth: £26,917,000 *Total Assets:* £29,317,000
Registered Office: Coln Park, Claydon Pike, Lechlade, Glos, GL7 3DT
Activities: Buying and selling of own real estate
Parent: Raven Mount Group Limited
Officers: Giles Leo Rabbetts [1971] Director; Mark Sinclair [1965] Finance Director; Colin Andrew Smith [1969] Director

Raven Mount Services Company Limited
Incorporated: 7 February 1898 *Employees:* 4
Previous: Raven Property Group Limited
Net Worth: £12,342,280 *Total Assets:* £25,022,572
Registered Office: Coln Park, Claydon Pike, Lechlade, Glos, GL7 3DT
Activities: Development of building projects
Parent: Raven Mount Limited
Officers: Giles Leo Rabbetts [1971] Director; Mark Sinclair [1965] Finance Director; Colin Andrew Smith [1969] Director

Raventree Limited
Incorporated: 20 April 2006 *Employees:* 122
Net Worth: £2,223,133 *Total Assets:* £7,614,655
Registered Office: Q1 Quadrant Way, Hardwicke, Gloucester, GL2 2RN
Activities: Manufacture of kitchen furniture
Parent: MG Markey Group Limited
Officers: Anthony Joseph Markey [1964] Director; Paul Francis Markey [1960] Director/Chartered Accountant

Raw Investments Limited
Incorporated: 18 November 2005 *Employees:* 2
Net Worth: £2,834,365 *Total Assets:* £8,049,217
Registered Office: c/o Francis Clark LLP, North Quay House, Sutton Harbour, Plymouth, PL4 0RA
Activities: Development of building projects
Shareholders: Ranjit Singh Dharwar; Rajinder Kaur Singh
Officers: Dr Rajinder Kaur Dharwar, Secretary; Dr Rajinder Kaur Dharwar [1977] Director/Dentist; Dr Ranjit Singh Dharwar [1977] Director/Dentist

Rawle Gammon & Baker Holdings Limited
Incorporated: 16 December 1935 *Employees:* 333
Net Worth: £15,340,675 *Total Assets:* £38,095,184
Registered Office: Gammon House, Riverside Road, Pottington Business Park, Barnstaple, Devon, EX31 1QN
Activities: Agents involved in the sale of timber and building materials
Parent: FTI Management Limited
Officers: Rachel Emma Dafforn, Secretary; Kevin Peter Fenlon [1965] Director/Chief Executive; Andrew Gamble [1964] Operations Director; Robert William Isaac [1943] Director/Retired; Jennifer Anne Naylor [1976] Human Resources Director; Christopher Winston Smith [1944] Director/Business Consultant; Paul Jay Turner [1969] Finance Director; Colin John Worth [1946] Director/Chairman

Rawlings & Son (Bristol) Limited
Incorporated: 20 August 1937 *Employees:* 18
Net Worth: £2,411,237 *Total Assets:* £4,633,555
Registered Office: Unit 3 Crown Road, Warmley, Bristol, BS30 8JJ
Activities: Wholesale of other intermediate products
Shareholders: Jonathan Alexander George Routley; Samantha Georgina Michelle Harrisingh
Officers: Thomas David Wood, Secretary; Samantha Georgina Michelle Harrisingh [1978] Director/PR Consultant; Jonathan Alexander George Routley [1976] Director; Thomas David Wood [1976] Director

Raynsford Limited
Incorporated: 9 February 1989 *Employees:* 49
Net Worth: £1,336,801 *Total Assets:* £4,011,810
Registered Office: Raynsford, Suffolk Square, Cheltenham, Glos, GL50 2EA
Activities: Other residential care activities n.e.c.
Parent: BCOMP 469 Limited
Officers: Rachel Allan-Yorke, Secretary; Nicolas Allan-Yorke [1973] Director

RBS Asset Finance Europe Limited
Incorporated: 10 February 2004
Net Worth: £941,385 *Total Assets:* £16,652,753
Registered Office: The Quadrangle, The Promenade, Cheltenham, Glos, GL50 1PX
Activities: Financial leasing
Parent: Royal Bank Leasing Limited
Officers: Ian Andrew Ellis [1969] Director/Bank Official; David Generald Harris [1969] Director/Bank Official; Steven James Roulston [1977] Director/Bank Official

RBSSAF (2) Limited
Incorporated: 5 December 2003 *Employees:* 3
Net Worth: £2,061,000 *Total Assets:* £297,211,008
Registered Office: The Quadrangle, The Promenade, Cheltenham, Glos, GL50 1PX
Activities: Financial leasing
Parent: Royal Bank Leasing Limited
Officers: Ian Andrew Ellis [1969] Director/Bank Official; David Generald Harris [1969] Director/Bank Official; Steven James Roulston [1977] Director/Bank Official

RBSSAF (25) Limited
Incorporated: 10 May 2000
Net Worth: £921,567 *Total Assets:* £37,024,456
Registered Office: The Quadrangle, The Promenade, Cheltenham, Glos, GL50 1PX
Activities: Financial intermediation not elsewhere classified
Parent: Royal Bank Leasing Limited
Officers: Ian Andrew Ellis [1969] Director/Bank Official; David Generald Harris [1969] Director/Bank Official; Steven James Roulston [1977] Director/Bank Official

RBSSAF (6) Limited
Incorporated: 5 December 2003
Net Worth: £3,344,000 *Total Assets:* £50,909,000
Registered Office: The Quadrangle, The Promenade, Cheltenham, Glos, GL50 1PX
Activities: Financial leasing
Shareholders: Royal Bank Leasing Limited; P of a Productions Limited
Officers: Stephen Paul Nixon [1970] Director/Bank Official; Keith Damian Pereira [1978] Director/Bank Official

RBSSAF (8) Limited
Incorporated: 5 December 2003
Net Worth: £428,000 *Total Assets:* £49,717,000
Registered Office: The Quadrangle, The Promenade, Cheltenham, Glos, GL50 1PX
Activities: Financial leasing
Parent: Royal Bank Leasing Limited
Officers: Ian Andrew Ellis [1969] Director/Bank Official; David Generald Harris [1969] Director/Bank Official; Steven James Roulston [1977] Director/Bank Official

RCR Flooring Products Limited
Incorporated: 5 May 1993 *Employees:* 46
Previous: Permaban Limited
Net Worth: £4,933,181 *Total Assets:* £7,352,899
Registered Office: Mill Close, Lee Mill Industrial Estate, Ivybridge, Devon, PL21 9GL
Activities: Manufacture of other fabricated metal products n.e.c.
Parent: RCR Industrial Flooring SARL
Officers: Jennifer Stanbury, Secretary; Pietro Bortoluzzi [1964] Director [Italian]; Andrew Leonard Keen [1961] Managing Director; Jonathan Mark Tarrant [1970] Finance Director

Reach South Academy Trust
Incorporated: 27 April 2016 *Employees:* 215
Net Worth: £18,360,240 *Total Assets:* £25,249,876
Registered Office: c/o UTC Plymouth, Park Avenue, Devonport, Plymouth, PL1 4RL
Activities: Primary education
Officers: Marcus Paul Ambrose Agius [1946] Non-Executive Director Chairman of PA Consulting Group; Dean Ashton [1959] Director/Chief Executive Officer; Gurbinder Beaver [1964] Director/Chief Administrative Officer; Dr Chris Gentle [1966] Director/Business Consultant; Adrian Paul Gunn [1965] Director/Retired; Susan Clare Inglish [1953] Director/Retired; Bronwen Lynne Lacey [1955] Director/Retired; Sir Steve Lyndon Lancashire [1963] Director/Headteacher; Lady Penelope Mary Marland [1957] Director/Probation Officer; Alan Newton [1957] Director/Solicitor; Mark Harry Papworth [1965] Director; Anne Marie Stevens [1955] Director/Consultant

Richard Read (Transport) Limited
Incorporated: 21 March 1963 *Employees:* 78
Net Worth: £2,191,653 *Total Assets:* £4,392,025
Registered Office: The Transport Depot, Longhope, Glos, GL17 0QG
Activities: Wholesale trade of motor vehicle parts and accessories
Parent: Richard Read Holdings Limited
Officers: Kay Read, Secretary; Brenda Susan Herring [1949] Director; Kay Read [1962] Director; Richard Paul Read [1959] Director

Read Construction (SW) Limited
Incorporated: 1 March 2007
Net Worth: £383,879 *Total Assets:* £4,510,886
Registered Office: Site Office, Merlin Court, Cligga Head Industrial Estate, Perranporth, Cornwall, TR6 0EN
Activities: Construction of commercial buildings
Major Shareholder: Andreas Read
Officers: Andreas Read [1966] Director/Building Contractor

Richard Read Holdings Limited
Incorporated: 23 March 2007 *Employees:* 81
Net Worth: £4,398,342 *Total Assets:* £6,739,597
Registered Office: The Transport Depot, Monmouth Road, Longhope, Glos, GL17 0QG
Activities: Activities of head offices
Shareholder: Richard Paul Read
Officers: Kay Read, Secretary; Brenda Susan Herring [1949] Director; Kay Read [1962] Director; Richard Paul Read [1959] Director

Readam UK (Pty) Ltd
Incorporated: 17 June 2013
Net Worth Deficit: £621,226 *Total Assets:* £3,687,714
Registered Office: 11 Henrietta Street, Bath, BA2 6LL
Activities: Hotels and similar accommodation
Parent: Readam Holdings UK Limited
Officers: Ajay Singh Chathley [1976] Director/Property Developer [Botswanan]; Priya Chathley [1977] Director/Property Manager [Indian]

Real Estate Gloucester Limited
Incorporated: 17 October 2007
Net Worth: £24,348,512 *Total Assets:* £61,598,168
Registered Office: Partner Logistics UK, Unilever Site, Corinium Avenue, Barnwood, Gloucester, GL4 3BW
Activities: Other business support service activities n.e.c.
Officers: Duco Robert Gijsbert Buijze [1962] Director [Dutch]; Jason Eugene Burnett [1976] Director [American]; Michael Joseph McClendon [1965] Director [American]; Johannes Albrecht Poelman [1973] Director [Dutch]

The Real Live Leisure Company Limited
Incorporated: 8 October 1997 *Employees:* 46
Net Worth: £3,823,004 *Total Assets:* £4,793,577
Registered Office: Oceanarium, Pier Approach, Bournemouth, BH2 5AA
Activities: Botanical and zoological gardens and nature reserves activities
Parent: Grant Leisure Group Limited
Officers: Juan Jose Lopez Taracena, Secretary; Jesus Pablo Fernandez Moran [1966] Director/Animal Parks Division Manager [Spanish]; Juan Jose Lopez Taracena [1964] Northern Europe Division Director for Group [Spanish]

Realhurry Limited
Incorporated: 26 August 1987 *Employees:* 42
Net Worth: £1,697,885 *Total Assets:* £5,598,671
Registered Office: Dolphin House, South Way, Andover, Hants, SP10 5AG
Activities: Joinery installation
Shareholders: Clayton John Williams; Terence Patrick Foley; David Julian Penfold
Officers: David Julian Penfold, Secretary; Jason Lee May [1975] Director/Estimator/Surveyor; David Julian Penfold [1963] Director/Surveyor; Clayton John Williams [1970] Contracts Director

Red Hotels Limited
Incorporated: 27 March 2008 *Employees:* 344
Net Worth: £11,331,108 *Total Assets:* £22,957,284
Registered Office: Bedruthan House, Trenance, Mawgan Porth, Newquay, Cornwall, TR8 4BU
Activities: Combined office administrative service activities
Shareholders: Rebecca Whittington; Emma Stratton
Officers: Robert James Waghorn, Secretary; Emma Stratton [1966] Marketing Director; James Robert Waghorn [1959] Director/Business Consultant; Rebecca Whittington [1968] Director

Red House Developments (Surrey) Limited
Incorporated: 13 October 2014 *Employees:* 2
Net Worth: £456,708 *Total Assets:* £5,329,930
Registered Office: Gowran House, 56 Broad Street, Chipping Sodbury, Glos, BS37 6AG
Activities: Other professional, scientific and technical activities n.e.c.
Shareholders: Karin Maria Christina Diurlin Gow; Charles Edward Gow
Officers: Charles Edward Gow [1968] Director; Karin Maria Christina Diurlin Gow [1968] Director [Swedish]

Red Kite Vehicle Consultants Limited
Incorporated: 25 November 1982
Net Worth: £744,900 *Total Assets:* £13,675,989
Registered Office: 3 Haddons Drive, Three Legged Cross, Wimborne, Dorset, BH21 6QU
Activities: Manufacture of motor vehicles
Shareholders: David Maskell; John Reginald Edward Maskell
Officers: Sarah Chairman, Secretary; Colin Charles Frederick Maskell [1935] Director/Chairman; David Maskell [1958] Administrative Director; John Reginald Edward Maskell [1953] Managing Director

Red Lion Investments Limited
Incorporated: 5 July 2000 *Employees:* 1
Net Worth: £7,999,183 *Total Assets:* £8,638,244
Registered Office: Old Library Chambers, 21 Chipper Lane, Salisbury, Wilts, SP1 1BG
Activities: Financial intermediation not elsewhere classified
Shareholders: Frank Gage Brenan; Elizabeth Rosemary Brenan
Officers: Frank Gage Brenan [1947] Director

Redbridge PPP Health Services Limited
Incorporated: 22 March 1999 *Employees:* 3
Net Worth: £1,628,021 *Total Assets:* £12,526,138
Registered Office: Third Floor, Broad Quay House, Prince Street, Bristol, BS1 4DJ
Activities: Other specialised construction activities n.e.c.
Parent: RBIL Limited
Officers: Abdul Hamid [1966] Director; Andrew Richard Kershaw [1965] Director/Projects Controller; Daniel North [1988] Investment Director; Andrew Charles Mutch Rhodes [1970] Director

Redcar and Cleveland Lighting Services Limited
Incorporated: 20 October 2005
Net Worth Deficit: £3,797,420 *Total Assets:* £20,307,164
Registered Office: Third Floor, Broad Quay House, Prince Street, Bristol, BS1 4DJ
Activities: Other business support service activities n.e.c.
Parent: IIC Redcar and Cleveland Holding Company Limited
Officers: Paul Anthony Cartwright [1957] Director; Vikki Louise Everett [1971] Director/Project Manager; Thomas Benedict Symes [1956] Director

Redcliffe Homes Limited
Incorporated: 27 June 1979 *Employees:* 29
Net Worth: £10,389,049 *Total Assets:* £24,720,640
Registered Office: Holly House, 4 High Street, Chipping Sodbury, Glos, BS37 6AH
Activities: Construction of domestic buildings
Major Shareholder: Thomas Richard O'Connor
Officers: Jonathan Mark Evans, Secretary; Jonathan Mark Evans [1981] Finance Director; Thomas Richard O'Connor [1951] Director; Andrew George Shelbourn [1968] Construction Director

Redde PLC
Incorporated: 31 October 1995 *Employees:* 2,269
Net Worth: £160,195,008 *Total Assets:* £371,996,992
Registered Office: Pinesgate, Lower Bristol Road, Bath, BA2 3DP
Activities: Activities of head offices
Shareholder: Invesco Limited
Officers: Nicholas Paul Tilley, Secretary; Mark Francis Chessman [1964] Director; John Lewis Davies [1949] Director; Mark McCafferty [1959] Director/Chief Executive; Stephen Edward Oakley [1952] Director; Avril Palmer-Baunack [1964] Director; Martin Ward [1967] Managing Director

Redhorn Holdings Limited
Incorporated: 6 January 2005 *Employees:* 25
Net Worth: £8,333,994 *Total Assets:* £14,760,263
Registered Office: The Courtyard, 33 Duke Street, Trowbridge, Wilts, BA14 8EA
Activities: Other letting and operating of own or leased real estate
Major Shareholder: Stephen John Harbour
Officers: Elizabeth Jane Harbour, Secretary; Elizabeth Jane Harbour [1953] Director/Secretary; Stephen John Harbour [1954] Director

Redlynch Agricultural Engineering Limited
Incorporated: 11 February 1997 *Employees:* 31
Net Worth: £3,808,591 *Total Assets:* £9,351,873
Registered Office: Redlynch, Bruton, Somerset, BA10 0NH
Activities: Wholesale of agricultural machinery, equipment and supplies
Major Shareholder: Nicholas James Heal
Officers: Rebecca Flynn, Secretary; Nicholas James Heal [1960] Director; Max Morton [1953] Director; Mark Morgan Peters [1968] Sales Director

Redmaids' High School
Incorporated: 29 June 2004 *Employees:* 218
Previous: The Red Maids' School
Net Worth: £24,135,440 *Total Assets:* £26,592,044
Registered Office: Redmaids' High School, Westbury Road, Westbury on Trym, Bristol, BS9 3AW
Activities: Primary education
Officers: Mark Marshall, Secretary; Catherine Ann Atkins [1967] Director/Self Employed; Richard Francis Bacon [1964] Director/Retired; Elizabeth Spanton Clarson [1946] Director; Valerie Anne Dixon [1944] Director/Retired; Sally MacDonald Dore [1962] Director; James Robert Fox [1962] Investment Director; Elizabeth Ann Fry [1962] Director/Solicitor; Rosemary Anne Heald [1961] Director/Solicitor, Non-Practising; Michael James Henry [1949] Director/Chartered Surveyor; Andrew George Aldridge Hillman [1949] Director/Chartered Accountant; Thelma Ellen Howell [1958] Director/Health Service Manager; Christopher Sanford Martin [1938] Director/Retired; Richard John Page [1959] Director/Chartered Accountant; Timothy Coulson Phillips [1959] Director/IT Consultant; Gillian Barbara Rowcliffe [1954] Director/Retired; Anne Denise Taylor [1944] Director/Retired

Redrock Consulting Limited
Incorporated: 6 April 2005 *Employees:* 72
Net Worth: £803,973 *Total Assets:* £5,062,834
Registered Office: Pembroke House, 15 Pembroke Road, Clifton, Bristol, BS8 3BA
Activities: Information technology consultancy activities
Shareholder: Dean Harte
Officers: Dean FitzGenerald Harte, Secretary; Darren Roy Chapman [1977] Director; Benjamin Matthew Curnock [1975] Director; Gary James Drever [1962] Director; Dean FitzGenerald Harte [1970] Managing Director; Brendan James Johnston [1971] Director [Irish]; Phred Jason Steer [1970] Director

Redruth Facilities Limited
Incorporated: 29 August 2001 *Employees:* 2
Net Worth: £1,000 *Total Assets:* £6,929,000
Registered Office: Third Floor, Broad Quay House, Prince Street, Bristol, BS1 4DJ
Activities: Development of building projects
Parent: Chiltern Securities Limited
Officers: David Robert Hardingham [1974] Director/Commercial Manager; Graham John Hutt [1954] Regional Director; Daniel North [1981] Investment Director

The Redstart Learning Partnership
Incorporated: 27 May 2011 *Employees:* 140
Net Worth: £6,159,910 *Total Assets:* £9,295,474
Registered Office: The Redstart Primary School, Redstart Road, Chard, Somerset, TA20 1SD
Activities: Primary education
Officers: Elizabeth Penelope Souster, Secretary; Claire Armes [1975] Director/Police Officer; Simon John Billington [1974] Director/Senior Pastor; Martin Brook [1965] Director/Executive Principal; Joseph Nicholas Doggrell [1986] Director/Accountant; Wendy Duffield [1972] Director; Helen Elizabeth Fenn [1962] Deputy Director of Education & School Effectiveness Leader; Suzanne Wendy Flack [1967] Director/Headteacher; Theresa Gale [1966] Director of Education; Keith Andrew Hallam [1962] Director/Operations Manager; Stephen Philip Oakley John [1956] Director/Education Consultant; Catherine Jane Murton [1968] Director/Solicitor; David Patrick Scotney [1954] Director/Retired Headteacher; Eric Joseph Van Den Barselaar [1968] Director/Physiotherapist [Dutch]

Redvers and Denzil Rice Farms Limited
Incorporated: 15 March 1965 *Employees:* 120
Net Worth: £5,370,687 *Total Assets:* £9,344,924
Registered Office: Stowford Farm Meadows, East Stowford Barton, Muddiford, Barnstaple, Devon, EX31 4HW
Activities: Sale of new cars and light motor vehicles
Shareholders: Antony Denzil Rice; Deborah Jayne Noall
Officers: Evelyn Marie Rice, Secretary; Deborah Jayne Noall [1963] Director; Antony Denzil Rice [1961] Director; Evelyn Marie Rice [1938] Director; Winston Denzil Rice [1940] Director

Redwood Global Limited
Incorporated: 27 March 2014 *Employees:* 41
Net Worth: £3,892,913 *Total Assets:* £7,104,333
Registered Office: Walworth Business Park, 86 Livingstone Road, Andover, Hants, SP10 5NS
Activities: Manufacture of agricultural and forestry machinery other than tractors
Parent: Redwood Global Holdings Limited
Officers: Raymond Gardner [1977] Director/General Manager; Douglas Ghinn [1987] Director/Marketing Manager

Reed Construction & Developments Limited
Incorporated: 20 March 1998 *Employees:* 2
Net Worth: £2,146,538 *Total Assets:* £7,925,169
Registered Office: 106 High Street, Crediton, Devon, EX17 3LF
Activities: Development of building projects
Major Shareholder: Christopher Mark Reed
Officers: Hannah Diane Martin, Secretary; Christopher Mark Reed [1960] Director

Richard Reeve's Foundation
Incorporated: 17 April 2010 *Employees:* 1
Net Worth: £46,577,240 *Total Assets:* £46,725,640
Registered Office: 6 Trull Farm Buildings, Trull, Tetbury, Glos, GL8 8SQ
Activities: Other education n.e.c.
Officers: Stephen Rowland-Jones, Secretary; Michael Phillip Bennett [1950] Director/Lawyer; Cllr Vivien Tilla Cutler [1950] Director/Councillor; Jo Anne Elizabeth Emmerson [1962] Programme Director; Shannon Lucy Clare Farrington [1949] Director; Elizabeth Gallagher [1990] Director/Barrister; Michael Hudson [1947] Director/Solicitor; Reverend David Lenox Ingall [1981] Director/Clerk in Holy Orders; Mark Terence Jessett [1973] Director/Consultant; Dr Sotonye Odugbemi [1980] Director/Teacher; Generald Charles Rothwell [1963] Director/Investment Manager; Lorna Jane Russell [1989] Director/Public Affairs; Alistair Wilson [1974] Director/Investment and Finance

Reflex Electronics Limited
Incorporated: 8 October 2007 *Employees:* 9
Net Worth: £7,180,603 *Total Assets:* £10,726,967
Registered Office: Swatton Barn, Badbury, Swindon, Wilts, SN4 0EU
Activities: Activities of head offices
Officers: Lin Han [1978] Director [Chinese]; David Huang [1967] Director [Chinese]

Reform Topco Limited
Incorporated: 18 July 2014 *Employees:* 32
Net Worth Deficit: £1,736,976 *Total Assets:* £3,630,313
Registered Office: St Matthew's House, Quays Office Park, Conference Avenue, Portishead, Bristol, BS20 7LZ
Activities: Activities of other holding companies n.e.c.
Officers: John Franklyn Stratford, Secretary; Owen Tudur Cross [1943] Director; Laurence Justin Dowley [1955] Director; John Christian William Kent [1955] Director; Paul Ronald Scott Lever [1940] Director; Neil John Murphy [1963] Director; Paul Robertson Murray [1970] Director

Refresco Beverages UK Limited
Incorporated: 28 November 1919 *Employees:* 842
Previous: Refresco Gerber UK Limited
Net Worth: £29,383,000 *Total Assets:* £185,803,008
Registered Office: Mallard Court, Express Park, Bridgwater, Somerset, TA6 4RN
Activities: Manufacture of soft drinks; production of mineral waters and other bottled waters
Officers: Pieter Willem Van Meeteren, Secretary; Aart Cornelis Duijzer [1963] Managing Director [Dutch]; Johannes Henricus Wilhelmus Roelofs [1963] Managing Director [Dutch]; David John Saint [1964] Director/Executive

Refresh Living No. 1 Ltd
Incorporated: 28 June 2013
Previous: Western Gazette Building Limited
Net Worth: £51,221 *Total Assets:* £7,758,257
Registered Office: 40 Kingston House, 1 Kingston Road, Taunton, Somerset, TA2 7ED
Activities: Buying and selling of own real estate
Shareholder: Mark Peter Thomas
Officers: Mark Peter Thomas [1978] Director

Regal Holiday Homes Limited
Incorporated: 24 June 2009 *Employees:* 126
Net Worth: £537,093 *Total Assets:* £5,376,116
Registered Office: 37 Commercial Road, Poole, Dorset, BH14 0HU
Activities: Manufacture of bodies (coachwork) for motor vehicles (except caravans)
Shareholders: Nigel John Heslington; Anthony Jones
Officers: Owen Brolan [1981] Director; Michael John Clifford [1961] Director; Silvano Geranio [1969] Director [Italian]; Nigel John Heslington [1967] Director; Anthony Jones [1947] Director; Eric Jones [1952] Director; Timothy Parker [1975] Director; David Michael William Ward [1969] Director

Regency Oldhomes Limited
Incorporated: 24 March 1988 *Employees:* 102
Net Worth: £4,825,205 *Total Assets:* £5,994,940
Registered Office: 31-33 Commercial Road, Poole, Dorset, BH14 0HU
Activities: Other human health activities
Parent: Royal Bay Care Homes Ltd
Officers: Russell Leonard Wilson, Secretary/Director; Anthony Frederick Wilson [1949] Director; Russell Leonard Wilson [1947] Director

Regency Properties (Tadworth) Limited
Incorporated: 9 July 1980
Net Worth: £4,784,983 *Total Assets:* £5,955,296
Registered Office: West Barton, Little Silver, Cadeleigh, Tiverton, Devon, EX16 8HJ
Activities: Other letting and operating of own or leased real estate
Major Shareholder: Paul Edward Morris
Officers: Patrick George Williams, Secretary; Paul Edward Morris [1954] Director

Regent's Park Healthcare Limited
Incorporated: 7 April 2014
Net Worth: £1,990,100 *Total Assets:* £10,350,000
Registered Office: 28-29 Batten Road, Downton Business Centre, Salisbury, Wilts, SP5 3HU
Activities: Other service activities n.e.c.
Major Shareholder: Anil Kumar Ohri
Officers: Dr Anil Kumar Ohri [1964] Director

Regulatory Finance Solutions Limited
Incorporated: 22 June 2005 *Employees:* 63
Net Worth: £4,950,337 *Total Assets:* £13,950,094
Registered Office: Priam House, Fire Fly Avenue, Swindon, Wilts, SN2 2EH
Activities: Financial intermediation not elsewhere classified
Parent: RFS Newco 1 Limited
Officers: Charlotte Angela Forbes, Secretary; Steve Breach [1969] Director; Michael Alastair Couzens [1964] Director; Anthony Harry Howitt [1988] Director; John Turner [1965] Director

John Reid & Sons (Strucsteel) Holdings Limited
Incorporated: 19 March 2007 *Employees:* 122
Net Worth: £10,598,584 *Total Assets:* £14,781,970
Registered Office: Strucsteel House, 3 Reid Street, Christchurch, Dorset, BH23 2BT
Activities: Manufacture of metal structures and parts of structures
Major Shareholder: Michael John Reid
Officers: John Miles Sinkinson, Secretary; Simon Peter Boyd [1961] Director; Michael John Reid [1928] Director; Peter James Reid [1963] Director; Timothy John Reid [1966] Director

John Reid & Sons (Strucsteel) Limited
Incorporated: 31 December 1958 *Employees:* 122
Net Worth: £2,864,598 *Total Assets:* £6,786,778
Registered Office: 3 Reid Street, Christchurch, Dorset, BH23 2BT
Activities: Manufacture of metal structures and parts of structures
Parent: John Reid and Sons (Strucsteel) Holdings Limited
Officers: John Miles Sinkinson, Secretary; Simon Peter Boyd [1961] Managing Director; Timothy Peter Cook [1959] Commercial Director; Richard William Hanson [1969] Director; Michael John Reid [1928] Director; Peter James Reid [1963] Director/Buying Manager; Timothy John Reid [1966] Director/Drawing Office Manager

Reig Jofre UK Limited
Incorporated: 7 November 2014 *Employees:* 2
Net Worth: £5,051,563 *Total Assets:* £5,463,440
Registered Office: Unit 9A Caddsdown Business Support Centre, Caddsdown Industrial Park, Bideford, Devon, EX39 3DX
Activities: Manufacture of pharmaceutical preparations
Shareholders: Laboratorio Reig Jofre SA; Compania Espanola de Financiacion Del Desarrollo
Officers: Ignasi Biosca Reig [1968] Director [Spanish]; Gabriel Roig Zapatero [1972] Director/Chief Financial Officer [Spanish]

Reliance Scrap Metal Merchants (Parkstone) Limited
Incorporated: 6 May 1954 *Employees:* 28
Net Worth: £2,153,865 *Total Assets:* £5,442,184
Registered Office: Towngate House, 2-8 Parkstone Road, Poole, Dorset, BH15 2PW
Activities: Wholesale of waste and scrap
Shareholders: David Peter Matthews; Rosalind Matthews
Officers: Ros Matthews, Secretary; Rosalind Matthews [1952] Director

The Reme Charity
Incorporated: 2 March 2016 *Employees:* 18
Net Worth: £16,763,960 *Total Assets:* £16,881,324
Registered Office: Corp Secretariat Regimental Headquarters, REME, MOD Lyneham, Chippenham, Wilts, SN15 4XX
Activities: Defence activities
Officers: Michael James Tizard, Secretary; Major General Stephen Michael Andrews [1957] Director/Colonel Commandant REME; Michael Jeremy Ainstie Bullard [1966] Director/Army Officer; Robert Charles Fram [1965] Director/Chartered Engineer; Alastair Paul Graham [1953] Director of Corporate Affairs - Bird & Bird Asia; Paul Charles Dennis Hembery [1983] Director/Army Officer; Paul Gordon Mitchell [1962] Director/Army Officer; Colonel Clare Phillips [1970] Director/Commissioned Officer HM Forces (Army); Catherine Colleen Robinson [1951] Director/Partner, Wealth Management Firm; Colonel Daniel Gordon Scott [1969] Director/Commissioned Officer HM Forces (Army); Mark Andrew Simpson [1965] Director

Remix Bidco Limited
Incorporated: 23 May 2013
Net Worth Deficit: £4,865,000 *Total Assets:* £54,199,000
Registered Office: Kernick Industrial Estate, Penryn, Cornwall, TR10 9LU
Activities: Activities of head offices
Parent: Remix Topco Limited
Officers: Robin John Clark [1970] Director; Anthony Williams [1965] Director

Renaissance Miles Platting Holding Company Limited
Incorporated: 6 March 2007
Net Worth Deficit: £5,246,037 *Total Assets:* £63,190,340
Registered Office: Third Floor, Broad Quay House, Prince Street, Bristol, BS1 4DJ
Activities: Activities of head offices
Shareholders: IIC Miles Platting Equity Limited; Manchester Housing (MP Equity) Limited
Officers: Paul Anthony Cartwright [1957] Director; Vikki Louise Everett [1971] Director/Project Manager; Richard Martin Goulder [1971] Director/Accountant; Mark Geoffrey David Holden [1957] Director; Thomas Benedict Symes [1956] Director

Renaissance Miles Platting Limited
Incorporated: 20 October 2005
Net Worth Deficit: £5,246,037 *Total Assets:* £63,190,340
Registered Office: Third Floor, Broad Quay House, Prince Street, Bristol, BS1 4DJ
Activities: Other business support service activities n.e.c.
Parent: Renaissance Miles Platting Holding Company Limited
Officers: Paul Anthony Cartwright [1957] Director; Vikki Louise Everett [1971] Director/Project Manager; Richard Martin Goulder [1971] Director/Accountant; Mark Geoffrey David Holden [1957] Director; Thomas Benedict Symes [1956] Director

Rendcomb College
Incorporated: 31 July 2006 *Employees:* 167
Net Worth: £1,656,688 *Total Assets:* £4,054,027
Registered Office: Rendcomb College, Cirencester, Glos, GL7 7HA
Activities: Other education n.e.c.
Officers: Eleanor Louise Sharman, Secretary; Sara Elizabeth Arkle [1957] Director/Teacher; Nicholas John Ford [1956] Director/Management Consultant; Simon Hanbury [1969] Director/Self Employed; Prudence Ann Hornby [1944] Director/Retired Business Consultant; Anthony Roger Marchand [1951] Director/Retired Headmaster; Imogen Iarissa Hamilton Ormerod [1976] Director/Civil Servant; Shaun David Edward Parsons [1944] Director/Retired; Sir Francis Neville Richards [1945] Director/Retired Diplomat; Hedley Sidney Ringrose [1942] Director/Retired Arch Deacon; Henry Claude Winwood Robinson [1953] Director/Farmer; Linda Hamilton Singer [1951] Director; Major General Peter Gage Williams [1951] Director/Retired Army Officer; Richard Henry Wills [1974] Director/Farmer

Renelec Chalgrove Limited
Incorporated: 23 May 1995 *Employees:* 62
Net Worth: £1,021,788 *Total Assets:* £6,898,097
Registered Office: Brownston House, New Park Street, Devizes, Wilts, SN10 1DS
Activities: Plumbing, heat and air-conditioning installation
Officers: Robert Frederick Kennedy, Secretary; Spencer James Couse [1972] Director/Contracts Manager; Vincent Richard Couse [1946] Director; John Skeen [1960] Director

Renelec Groundworks Limited
Incorporated: 28 April 1997 *Employees:* 77
Net Worth: £809,824 *Total Assets:* £6,575,797
Registered Office: Brownston House, New Park Street, Devizes, Wilts, SN10 1DS
Activities: Site preparation
Officers: Robert Frederick Kennedy, Secretary; Scot Michael Boyd [1981] Director; Charlotte Lucia Couse [1971] Director; Lucia Theresa Couse [1975] Director; Spencer James Couse [1972] Director; Vincent Richard Couse [1946] Director; Patrick Michael O'Shea [1966] Director; John Skeen [1960] Director

Renelec Group Limited
Incorporated: 14 October 1998 *Employees:* 290
Net Worth: £3,749,047 *Total Assets:* £22,649,016
Registered Office: Brownston House, New Park Street, Devizes, Wilts, SN10 1DS
Activities: Activities of head offices
Officers: Robert Frederick Kennedy, Secretary; Spencer James Couse [1972] Director; Bernard George Crew [1947] Director; Robert Frederick Kennedy [1947] Director; John Skeen [1960] Director

Renelec Limited
Incorporated: 5 May 1972 *Employees:* 290
Net Worth: £5,174,033 *Total Assets:* £23,802,000
Registered Office: Brownston House, New Park Street, Devizes, Wilts, SN10 1DS
Activities: Other construction installation
Officers: Robert Frederick Kennedy, Secretary; Spencer James Couse [1972] Director; Vincent Richard Couse [1946] Director; Bernard George Crew [1947] Director; Andrew Keith Harper [1973] Director/Accountant; Robert Frederick Kennedy [1947] Director; John Skeen [1960] Director

The Renewable Design Company Limited
Incorporated: 24 August 2012 *Employees:* 5
Net Worth: £354,376 *Total Assets:* £3,920,678
Registered Office: 41 Rodney Road, Cheltenham, Glos, GL50 1HX
Activities: Other service activities n.e.c.
Shareholders: Julian Sowerbutts; George Hollingbery
Officers: Alastair Murray [1984] Director; Julian Neame Sowerbutts [1959] Director

The Renewable Energy Company Limited
Incorporated: 7 April 1995 *Employees:* 464
Net Worth: £22,746,508 *Total Assets:* £72,593,672
Registered Office: Lion House, Rowcroft, Stroud, Glos, GL5 3BY
Activities: Trade of electricity
Parent: Ecotricity Group Limited
Officers: Tom Cowling, Secretary; Asif Rehmanwala [1976] Director/Chief Operating Officer; Dale Vince [1961] Director/Consultant

Renewable Energy Partnerships Limited
Incorporated: 25 November 2002 *Employees:* 1
Net Worth: £7,221,019 *Total Assets:* £7,235,826
Registered Office: Stratton House, Back Lane, Stoney Stratton, Shepton Mallet, Somerset, BA4 6EA
Activities: Production of electricity
Parent: Evenevery Ltd
Officers: Richard Thomas Hadwin, Secretary; Richard Thomas Hadwin [1971] Director/Chartered Accountant

Renishaw International Limited
Incorporated: 17 May 1979
Net Worth: £26,840,000 *Total Assets:* £29,285,000
Registered Office: New Mills, Wotton under Edge, Glos, GL12 8JR
Activities: Other business support service activities n.e.c.
Parent: Renishaw PLC
Officers: Daniel John Deer [1938] Director; William Ernest Lee [1975] Director; Sir David Roberts McMurtry [1940] Director [Irish]; Allen Christopher George Roberts [1949] Director

Renishaw P L C
Incorporated: 4 April 1973 *Employees:* 4,639
Net Worth: £549,171,008 *Total Assets:* £742,176,000
Registered Office: New Mills, Wotton under Edge, Glos, GL12 8JR
Activities: Manufacture of electronic measuring, testing etc. equipment, not for industrial process control
Officers: Mark David Noble, Secretary; Ellen Carol Chesney [1962] Director/Chartered Accountant [American]; Daniel John Deer [1938] Director; Catherine Janet Glickman [1957] Director; Dr David Grant [1947] Director; David John Jeans [1950] Director; William Ernest Lee [1975] Director/Engineer; Geoffrey McFarland [1968] Director [Irish]; Sir David Roberts McMurtry [1940] Director [Irish]; Allen Christopher George Roberts [1949] Director

Renrod Holdings Limited
Incorporated: 14 November 2003 *Employees:* 239
Net Worth: £20,985,888 *Total Assets:* £39,339,352
Registered Office: 12 Meridian Motor Park, North Bradley, Trowbridge, Wilts, BA14 0BJ
Activities: Activities of head offices
Shareholders: R A Cuff Business Assets Will Trust; R A Cuff Discretionary Trust
Officers: Amanda Cuff, Secretary; Jeremy Charles Cuff [1966] Director; Richard James Cuff [1972] Director; Odette Darnell [1956] Director; Rachel Elaine McCabe [1968] Director; Martyn Read [1954] Director

Renrod Limited
Incorporated: 2 May 1975 *Employees:* 239
Net Worth: £2,306,449 *Total Assets:* £20,798,712
Registered Office: 12 Meridian Motor Park, North Bradley, Trowbridge, Wilts, BA14 0BJ
Activities: Sale of new cars and light motor vehicles
Parent: Renrod Holdings Ltd
Officers: Michael Caddick [1966] Director; Jeremy Charles Cuff [1966] Director; Richard James Cuff [1972] Director; Odette Darnell [1956] Director; Mark Gregg Greenfield [1961] Director [American]; Paul Keith Mitchell [1974] Director; Martyn Read [1954] Director

Renshaw U.K. Limited
Incorporated: 24 January 1935 *Employees:* 12
Net Worth: £18,559,576 *Total Assets:* £22,803,638
Registered Office: Renshaw Barns, Upper Woodford, Salisbury, Wilts, SP4 6FA
Activities: Other letting and operating of own or leased real estate
Officers: Shaun Barry Moore, Secretary/Chartered Surveyor; Daniel William Heward Bell [1959] Director/Stockbroker; Clare Susannah MacNamara [1964] Director; Lucinda Karen MacNamara [1968] Director; Shaun Barry Moore [1965] Director/Chartered Surveyor; Stella Kathleen Muddiman [1929] Director; Sarah Catherine Norman [1966] Director; Rose Olivia Heward Outhwaite [1956] Director

Repal Co-Gen (UK) Limited
Incorporated: 1 May 2014
Net Worth: £4,361,386 *Total Assets:* £4,442,222
Registered Office: Delta Place, 27 Bath Road, Cheltenham, Glos, GL53 7TH
Activities: Production of electricity
Officers: Tom Howe [1954] Director/Chartered Accountant; Peter Robert Hughes [1948] Director; Andrew Jonathan Charles Newman [1970] Director

REPI Limited
Incorporated: 20 December 2013 *Employees:* 1
Net Worth: £908,368 *Total Assets:* £7,237,326
Registered Office: Stratton House, Back Lane, Stoney Stratton, Shepton Mallet, Somerset, BA4 6EA
Activities: Other letting and operating of own or leased real estate
Parent: Evenevery Ltd
Officers: Richard Thomas Hadwin [1971] Director

REPL International Limited
Incorporated: 13 July 1992 *Employees:* 229
Net Worth: £10,097,266 *Total Assets:* £31,806,816
Registered Office: REPL House, Kingsdown Road, Swindon, Wilts, SN25 6PB
Activities: Manufacture of other plastic products
Officers: Amardeep Singh Dhanoa, Secretary; Graham Bernard Gardner [1948] Director/Engineer; Lyla Mehta [1977] Director/Accountant; Homi Rutton Patel [1944] Director; Rutton Homi Patel [1975] Director/Engineer/Accountant

Research Instruments Limited
Incorporated: 13 August 1997 *Employees:* 83
Net Worth: £118,992,840 *Total Assets:* £123,612,496
Registered Office: Research Instruments Ltd, Bickland Industrial Park, Falmouth, Cornwall, TR11 4TA
Activities: Manufacture of medical and dental instruments and supplies
Parent: CooperSurgical Holdings Limited
Officers: Robert Dave Auerbach [1960] Director/Executive Vice President & Chief Medical Officer [American]; Kerry Lee Blair [1957] Director/Corporate Executive [American]; David Truels Hansen [1967] President & Managing Director [Danish]; Carol Rose Kaufman [1949] Director/Legal Affairs [American]; Agostino Ricupati [1967] Director/Corporate Executive [American]; Alan Thompson Tucker [1963] Director/Chief Financial Officer [American]

Residential Trust Limited
Incorporated: 11 March 1994 *Employees:* 3
Net Worth: £6,836,586 *Total Assets:* £9,337,375
Registered Office: 4 Southernhay West, Exeter, EX1 1JG
Activities: Other letting and operating of own or leased real estate
Shareholder: Christopher John Eccles
Officers: Louise Sarah Eccles, Secretary; Christopher John Eccles [1962] Director/Chartered Surveyor; George Frederick Eccles [1989] Director/Surveyor; Louise Sarah Eccles [1961] Director/Housewife

Resolution Interiors Limited
Incorporated: 4 December 1998 *Employees:* 58
Net Worth: £744,033 *Total Assets:* £6,370,702
Registered Office: Lufton 2000 Business Park, Yeovil, Somerset, BA22 8QR
Activities: Other specialised construction activities n.e.c.
Parent: Resolution Interiors Holdings Ltd
Officers: Lucy Anne Lovell, Secretary; Paul James Bissell [1967] Operations Director; Peter James Crinks [1965] Director/Administrator; Andrew Lovell [1966] Director/Sales Marketing Executive; Lucy Anne Lovell [1967] Director/Bank Clerk; Amelia Sophie Geddes Whitcombe [1981] Commercial Director

Resonance Limited
Incorporated: 17 April 2002 *Employees:* 39
Net Worth: £442,963 *Total Assets:* £8,191,730
Registered Office: The Great Barn, 5 Scarne Court, Hurdon Road, Launceston, Cornwall, PL15 9LR
Activities: Management consultancy activities other than financial management
Shareholders: Daniel James Brewer; Nesta
Officers: Sharon Joan Gorman, Secretary; Anita Bhatia [1975] Director/Senior Analyst; Daniel James Brewer [1976] Director/Entrepreneur; Simon Leslie Chisholm [1971] Investment Director; Dr Peter John Dawe [1954] Director/Entrepreneur; Graham John Hodgkin [1966] Director/Chief Executive; Michael Leslie Perreau [1955] Director; Karen Elaine Shackleton [1962] Director/Financial Consultant

Resort Estate Management Limited
Incorporated: 8 June 2007
Net Worth: £1,704,526 *Total Assets:* £3,524,773
Registered Office: Coln Park, Claydon Pike, Lechlade, Glos, GL7 3DT
Activities: Other letting and operating of own or leased real estate
Shareholders: Raven Mount Limited; Yoo Capital Limited
Officers: Jagdish Singh Johal [1972] Finance Director; Giles Leo Rabbetts [1971] Director; Andrew Matthew Thorpe [1963] Director

Resource Solutions Group PLC
Incorporated: 1 March 1982 *Employees:* 271
Net Worth: £40,626,000 *Total Assets:* £107,586,000
Registered Office: First Floor, Clifton Down House, 54a Whiteladies Road, Clifton, Bristol, BS8 2NH
Activities: Other activities of employment placement agencies
Major Shareholder: Keith William Dawe
Officers: Anya Louise Burton, Secretary; Michael Adrian Beesley [1957] Sales Director; Joanna Patricia Dawe [1951] Director; Keith William Dawe [1950] Director; Martin William Griffiths [1960] Director/Corporate Chairman

The Retired Nurses National Home
Incorporated: 4 January 2002
Net Worth: £3,453,385 *Total Assets:* £3,530,635
Registered Office: Riverside Avenue, Bournemouth, BH7 7EE
Activities: Residential care activities for the elderly and disabled
Officers: Susan Jane Smith, Secretary; Stephen Bruce Allen [1964] Director/Chief Executive; Terence Devonport [1944] Director/Retired; Jennifer Ann Griffiths [1974] Director of Finance; Susan Jane Smith [1966] Director/Charity Secretary

Retirement Homesearch Limited
Incorporated: 20 August 1999 *Employees:* 27
Net Worth: £8,326,505 *Total Assets:* £8,732,153
Registered Office: Queensway House, 11 Queensway, New Milton, Hants, BH25 5NR
Activities: Real estate agencies
Parent: Firstport Retirement Property Services Limited
Officers: Nigel Howell [1959] Director/Chief Executive Officer; Ouda Saleh [1979] Director of Finance

Retrac Productions Limited
Incorporated: 3 November 1972 *Employees:* 57
Net Worth: £3,877,145 *Total Assets:* £5,193,677
Registered Office: Units 3-5 Techno Trading Estate, Swindon, Wilts, SN2 8HB
Activities: Machining
Shareholders: John Carter Will Trust; Irene May Carter
Officers: Irene May Carter, Secretary; Alistair James Carter [1964] Purchasing Director; Andrew John Carter [1961] Director/Engineer; Irene May Carter [1936] Bookkeeper Director; Robin Alexander Carter [1966] Director; Nicholas Edward Owen [1947] Director/Chartered Accountant

Rew Hotels Limited
Incorporated: 23 July 1986 *Employees:* 131
Net Worth: £4,981,032 *Total Assets:* £10,315,616
Registered Office: Livermead House Hotel, Sea Front, Torquay, Devon, TQ2 6QJ
Activities: Hotels and similar accommodation
Major Shareholder: Sylvia Rita Rew
Officers: Sylvia Rita Rew, Secretary; Sylvia Rita Rew [1937] Director/Hotelier; Timothy Simon James Rew [1963] Director/Hotelier

Rexquote Ltd
Incorporated: 24 October 2003 *Employees:* 27
Net Worth: £1,698,546 *Total Assets:* £3,682,953
Registered Office: Broad Gauge Business Park, Bishops Lydeard, Taunton, Somerset, TA4 3RU
Activities: Manufacture of other transport equipment n.e.c.
Shareholders: Dawn Marie Hooper; Roger John Soper
Officers: Dawn Marie Hooper, Secretary/Engineering Manufacturer; Dawn Marie Hooper [1969] Director/Engineering Manufacturer; Roger John Soper [1956] Director/Engineer

RHSG Properties Limited
Incorporated: 13 June 2014 *Employees:* 3
Net Worth: £3,701,156 *Total Assets:* £4,206,609
Registered Office: 95 West Way, Bournemouth, BH9 3DT
Activities: Other letting and operating of own or leased real estate
Major Shareholder: Jane Balmforth
Officers: Jane Balmforth [1958] Director; Marcia Sommerford [1984] Director/Administrator

Rhyl Flats Wind Farm Limited
Incorporated: 21 June 2005
Net Worth: £142,199,184 *Total Assets:* £172,406,096
Registered Office: Windmill Hill Business Park, Whitehill Way, Swindon, Wilts, SN5 6PB
Activities: Production of electricity
Shareholder: Innogy Renewables UK Limited
Officers: Christopher David Barras, Secretary; Penelope Anne Sainsbury, Secretary; Paul Leslie Cowling [1960] Director; Dr Benjamin Victor Furlong [1975] Director/Asset Manager; Stephen Bernard Lilley [1968] Director/Investment Manager; Christian Rudiger Mockl [1973] Director [German]; Jason Paul Porter [1981] Director/Asset Manager; Richard Jennings Sandford [1971] Director/Head of Offshore Business Management; Karl Ben Smith [1977] Managing Director; Alexis Eduardo Ulens [1967] Fund Director [Belgian]

Ribston Hall High School Academy Trust
Incorporated: 6 May 2011 *Employees:* 136
Net Worth: £12,598,575 *Total Assets:* £14,245,053
Registered Office: Ribston Hall High School, Stroud Road, Gloucester, GL1 5LE
Activities: General secondary education
Officers: Sandy Woodcock, Secretary; Dr Georgina Joanne Kimberely Benford [1987] Director/Lecturer; Julie Bishop [1973] Director/Science Technician - Education; Sarah Elizabeth Colombini [1980] Director/Headmistress; Nicholas Francis Davies [1966] Director/IT Consultant; Lynda Janet Frall [1974] Director; Ian Stuart Forbes Henderson [1961] Director; Doctor William Fergus O'Sullivan [1973] Director/Teacher; John Rowland Otieno [1939] Director/Barrister; Jeremy Paul Owen [1970] Director/Managing Partner; Rebecca Jane Rose [1973] Director/Teacher; Anindya SEN [1972] Director/Health & Safety Inspector; Fay White [1959] Director/Headteacher; Jane Elizabeth Windscheffel [1972] Director/System Service & Support Analyst

Rich Products Limited
Incorporated: 12 September 1984 *Employees:* 324
Net Worth: £67,224,920 *Total Assets:* £91,686,376
Registered Office: Unit 5 Pioneer Road, Andover Business Park, Andover, Hants, SP11 8EZ
Activities: Manufacture of bread; manufacture of fresh pastry goods and cakes
Major Shareholder: Bob Rich
Officers: Theresa Ann Pickard, Secretary; Richard Mario Ferranti [1960] Director [American]; William E Grieshober [1964] Director/Vice President [American]; David Edward Hunt [1968] Director/MD

Richards Homes Limited
Incorporated: 27 November 1995 *Employees:* 2
Net Worth Deficit: £506,651 *Total Assets:* £3,549,849
Registered Office: Sinair, Red Lane, Bugle, St Austell, Cornwall, PL26 8QP
Activities: Development of building projects
Shareholders: Nelson Richards; Genty Richards
Officers: Nelson Richards, Secretary/Civil Engineer; Genty Richards [1949] Director/Secretary; Nelson Richards [1950] Director/Civil Engineer

Richmond Group Debt Capital Ltd
Incorporated: 7 May 2016
Net Worth: £1,360,000 *Total Assets:* £26,966,000
Registered Office: Walton House, Richmond Hill, Bournemouth, BH2 6EX
Activities: Other credit granting n.e.c.
Parent: Richmond Group Limited
Officers: Amber Kirsty Cole, Secretary; Rachid James Benamor [1977] Director; Amber Kirsty Cole [1990] Director

Richmond Group Limited
Incorporated: 14 September 2004 *Employees:* 318
Net Worth: £352,800,000 *Total Assets:* £822,400,000
Registered Office: Walton House, 56-58 Richmond Hill, Bournemouth, BH2 6EX
Activities: Other information technology service activities
Major Shareholder: James Rachid Benamor
Officers: Amber Kirsty Cole, Secretary; James Rachid Benamor [1977] Director

Richmond upon Thames Schools Services Limited
Incorporated: 18 September 2001 *Employees:* 2
Net Worth Deficit: £1,705,000 *Total Assets:* £22,376,000
Registered Office: Third Floor, Broad Quay House, Prince Street, Bristol, BS1 4DJ
Activities: Non-trading company
Parent: Richmond upon Thames Schools Services (Holdings) Limited
Officers: Abdul Hamid [1966] Director; Neil Rae [1971] Director

Richpur Limited
Incorporated: 15 September 2003 *Employees:* 4
Net Worth: £416,708 *Total Assets:* £6,914,684
Registered Office: 6 Morston Court, Aisecome Way, Weston-Super-Mare, Avon, BS22 8NG
Activities: Other business support service activities n.e.c.
Shareholders: Joanne Purgas; Dave Sunjay Daniel Purgas; Richard Purgas; Paul Veejay Julian Purgas; Joanne Joginder Purgas; Dave Sunjay Daniel Purgas; Richard Ramroop Purgas
Officers: Joanne Joginder Purgas, Secretary/Manager; Dave Sunjay Daniel Purgas [1978] Director; Joanne Joginder Purgas [1949] Director/Manager; Paul Veejay Julian Purgas [1980] Director; Richard Ramroop Purgas [1949] Director/Manager

Riders of Bridgwater Ltd.
Incorporated: 5 December 2000 *Employees:* 77
Net Worth: £3,881,687 *Total Assets:* £6,486,835
Registered Office: 107 North Street, Martock, Somerset, TA12 6EJ
Activities: Other business support service activities n.e.c.
Major Shareholder: Philip Stanley Jessopp
Officers: Philip Stanley Jessopp, Secretary/Motorcycle Dealer; Ann Patricia Jessopp [1946] Director/Secretary; Philip Stanley Jessopp [1955] Director/Motorcycle Dealer; Susan Margaret Massey [1964] Director/Accountant

Ridgevale Estates Limited
Incorporated: 5 January 2004
Net Worth Deficit: £31,845 *Total Assets:* £8,142,708
Registered Office: Suite 1, 25-27 Wood Street, Swindon, Wilts, SN1 4AN
Activities: Development of building projects
Officers: Angela Patricia Payne, Secretary; Jaspal Gill [1953] Director

Right Contract Services Limited
Incorporated: 12 December 2008 *Employees:* 19
Net Worth: £2,713,201 *Total Assets:* £3,661,444
Registered Office: Swatton Barn, Badbury, Swindon, Wilts, SN4 0EU
Activities: Temporary employment agency activities
Shareholders: James Steel; Daryl Joseph Craft
Officers: Kelly Craft, Secretary; Daryl Joseph Craft [1979] Director; James Steel [1978] Director

Rigibore Limited
Incorporated: 7 December 1979 *Employees:* 46
Net Worth: £2,081,214 *Total Assets:* £4,633,540
Registered Office: 5 Guildford Road Industrial Estate, Hayle, Cornwall, TR27 4QZ
Activities: Manufacture of tools
Parent: Bassett Group Ltd
Officers: Anthony Bassett [1965] Director/Engineer; Roger Bassett [1941] Director/Engineer; Rosemary Bassett [1942] Director/Secretary; Richard Wintour Bennet [1966] Director/Engineer; Suzanne Bennet [1967] Director/Administrator

Ringwood School
Incorporated: 4 March 2011 *Employees:* 221
Net Worth: £19,385,196 *Total Assets:* £21,445,478
Registered Office: Ringwood School, Parsonage Barn Lane, Ringwood, Hants, BH24 1SE
Activities: General secondary education
Officers: Susan Elizabeth Bennett, Secretary; Julie Christine Breakell [1977] Director/Accountant; Huw Frank Chapman [1962] Managing Director; Margaret Copplestone [1967] Director/Further Education; Katherine Anne Freeth [1972] Director/Teacher of Education; Louisa May Hoff [1979] Director/Teacher; Annie Tess Jenkinson [1966] Director/Teacher; Vicki Molly Jane Lewis [1973] Director/Teacher; Ese Ebi Ono-Sorhue [1981] Director/Engineer; Katharine Anne Palka [1964] Director/Solicitor; Sean Gavin Palka [1966] Director/Solicitor; Clare Gillian Pittman [1972] Director/Regional Business Manager; Derek Richard Scott [1950] Director/Professional Service; David Jonathan Shering [1964] Director/Corporate Banking Manager; Leanne Symonds [1973] Director/Headteacher; Franciscus Joseph Antonius Van Hoof [1970] Managing Director; Lisa Jacqueline Welch [1969] Director/Teacher

Riohurst Investments Limited
Incorporated: 7 May 1981
Net Worth: £6,174,561 *Total Assets:* £6,587,621
Registered Office: The Courtyard, Holt Lodge Farm, Horton, Wimborne, Dorset, BH21 7JN
Activities: Other letting and operating of own or leased real estate
Parent: Padmanor Investments Limited
Officers: Hugo Aylesford Burge, Secretary; Hugo Aylesford Burge [1972] Director/Company Secretary; Oliver Aylesford Burge [1941] Director; Roger Max Davies [1942] Director; Stephen John Davies [1976] Property Director

Rittal-C S M Limited
Incorporated: 13 September 1965 *Employees:* 358
Net Worth: £12,565,000 *Total Assets:* £29,800,000
Registered Office: Broadley Industrial Park, Roborough, Plymouth, PL6 7EZ
Activities: Manufacture of other fabricated metal products n.e.c.
Parent: Rittal Holdings Ltd
Officers: Martin Glyndwr Hurst Williams, Secretary; Dr Stephen Hobbs [1956] Managing Director

River Marketing (Holdings) Limited
Incorporated: 1 August 2012 *Employees:* 101
Net Worth: £2,868,921 *Total Assets:* £6,925,543
Registered Office: Building 1, Barnwood Point Business Park, Corinium Avenue, Gloucester, GL4 3HX
Activities: Activities of head offices
Shareholder: Phillip Michael Dunk
Officers: Nicola Karen Dunk, Secretary; Nadia Lucia Diluzio [1978] Director; Philip Dunk [1969] Director; Kim Frederick Paxton [1963] Director; Claire Alison West [1978] Director

River Marketing Limited
Incorporated: 29 June 2001 *Employees:* 101
Net Worth: £1,661,604 *Total Assets:* £4,632,241
Registered Office: Building 1, Barnwood Point Business Park, Corinium Avenue, Gloucester, GL4 3HX
Activities: Other business support service activities n.e.c.
Parent: River Marketing (Holdings) Limited
Officers: Nicola Karen Dunk, Secretary; Nadia Lucia Diluzio [1978] Director; Philip Dunk [1969] Managing Director; Claire Alison West [1978] Director

River Reach Limited
Incorporated: 14 October 1987 *Employees:* 1
Net Worth Deficit: £2,753,744 *Total Assets:* £3,762,416
Registered Office: Box House, Box, Corsham, Wilts, SN13 8AA
Activities: Buying and selling of own real estate
Major Shareholder: Charles Gordon Tull

Riverford Organic Farmers Limited
Incorporated: 12 March 1999 *Employees:* 629
Previous: Riverford Organic Farms Limited
Net Worth: £9,243,008 *Total Assets:* £16,425,112
Registered Office: Wash Barn, Buckfastleigh, Devon, TQ11 0JU
Activities: Growing of vegetables and melons, roots and tubers
Shareholder: William Guy Singh-Watson
Officers: Peter Anselm Frost, Secretary; Anthony Roja Buck [1983] Director; Lee John Caddy [1970] Director; Philip Anthony Clarke [1965] Director; Robert Daniel Haward [1975] Director; Luke John King [1977] Director; William Guy Singh-Watson [1960] Director/Farmer; Mark Christian David Swanwick [1953] Director; Charlotte Louise Tickle [1980] Director; Rachel Cressida Watson [1956] Director

Rivermead Plastic Limited
Incorporated: 2 December 2004
Net Worth: £500,000 *Total Assets:* £4,074,469
Registered Office: Rivermead Drive, Westlea, Swindon, Wilts, SN5 7EX
Activities: Agents specialised in the sale of other particular products
Shareholders: Alistair Malcolm Kennedy; John Martyn Jones
Officers: John Martyn Jones, Secretary/Accountant; Annie Buchanan Jones [1943] Director/Business Executive; John Martyn Jones [1949] Director/Accountant; Alistair Malcolm Kennedy [1947] Director/Business Executive; Cecilia Joy Kennedy [1948] Director/Business Executive

Riverside Aromatics Limited
Incorporated: 26 June 2006 *Employees:* 12
Net Worth: £3,792,624 *Total Assets:* £5,064,537
Registered Office: 16-18 Slader Business Park, Witney Road, Nuffield Industrial Estate, Poole, Dorset, BH17 0GP
Activities: Wholesale of chemical products
Parent: The Riverside Group Holding Company Limited
Officers: Karen Lorraine Canon, Secretary; Karen Lorraine Canon [1962] Business Development Director; Peter Roy Canon [1961] Director

Riviera Education Trust
Incorporated: 27 August 2015 *Employees:* 194
Net Worth: £8,491,609 *Total Assets:* £10,919,666
Registered Office: c/o Oldway Primary School, Higher Polsham Road, Paignton, Devon, TQ3 2SY
Activities: Primary education
Officers: Faye Diana Steele, Secretary; Stewart John Biddles [1974] Director/Headteacher; William Charles Foulds [1980] Director/Business Executive; Paul Garside [1969] Director/Senior HR Advisor (Schools' Lead); Elaine Frances Gill [1956] Director/Headteacher; Gary Sean Hotine [1965] Director/NHS Manager; Simon Lee [1981] Director/Policeman; Josie Jennifer Medforth [1977] Director/Local Government Officer; Chris O'Connor [1976] Director/Head of School; Jamie Parffrey [1978] Director/Marquee Company; Matthew Redwood [1958] Director

Riviera Produce Limited
Incorporated: 28 October 1997 *Employees:* 2
Net Worth: £2,117,543 *Total Assets:* £5,204,424
Registered Office: Higher Trevaskis Farm, 14 Gwinear Road, Connor Downs, Hayle, Cornwall, TR27 5JQ
Activities: Wholesale of fruit and vegetables
Major Shareholder: David John Simmons
Officers: Suzanne Claire Simmons, Secretary/Farmer; David John Simmons [1960] Director/Farmer; Suzanne Claire Simmons [1960] Director/Personnel Manager

RMH (Guildford) Limited
Incorporated: 1 December 2006 *Employees:* 4
Net Worth: £1,984,115 *Total Assets:* £11,809,700
Registered Office: Harbour House, 60 Purewell, Christchurch, Dorset, BH23 1ES
Activities: Hotels and similar accommodation
Parent: Harbour Hotels Group Limited
Officers: Stuart Andrew Bateman [1976] Director; David Francis Robbins [1967] Director/Accountant; Michael Oliver Warren [1970] Director [Irish]

RMH (Guildford) LLP
Incorporated: 5 December 2006 *Employees:* 147
Net Worth: £13,887,614 *Total Assets:* £48,771,592
Registered Office: Harbour House, 60 Purewell, Christchurch, Dorset, BH23 1ES

RMH (Manor House) Care LLP
Incorporated: 22 November 2007 *Employees:* 39
Net Worth: £1,982,348 *Total Assets:* £5,882,113
Registered Office: Harbour House, 60 Purewell, Christchurch, Dorset, BH23 1ES

RMH (Wispers) Care LLP
Incorporated: 27 November 2008 *Employees:* 6
Net Worth: £2,162,260 *Total Assets:* £5,769,427
Registered Office: Harbour House, 60 Purewell, Christchurch, Dorset, BH23 1ES

RMMP Limited
Incorporated: 13 June 2014 *Employees:* 23
Net Worth: £7,533,481 *Total Assets:* £13,150,215
Registered Office: 37 Great Pulteney Street, Bath, BA2 4DA
Activities: Activities of other holding companies n.e.c.
Officers: Mollie Audrey Salter, Secretary; Dr Peter Huw Green [1960] Director/General Practitioner; Dr Rosemary Christine Loftus [1962] Director/Doctor; Michael Robert Salter [1954] Director/Pharmacist; Mollie Audrey Salter [1955] Director

RNO Limited
Incorporated: 25 October 2007 *Employees:* 2,407
Net Worth Deficit: £38,426,000 *Total Assets:* £289,478,016
Registered Office: c/o Princess Yachts Limited, Newport Street, Plymouth, PL1 3QG
Activities: Activities of extraterritorial organisations and bodies
Officers: Adrian Richard Bratt, Secretary; Adrian Richard Bratt [1971] Director/Legal Counsel; Philippe Marie Franchet [1965] Director/Partner L Capital [French]; Christopher John Gates [1961] Director; Patrick Gaston Houel [1942] Director/Administration L Capital [French]; Philippe Jean-Claude Mellier [1955] Director/Company Chairman [French]; Alfonso Pallavicini [1964] Director [Italian]; Antony Michael Sheriff [1963] Director [American]; Eduardo Salvador Velasco [1973] Investment Director L Capital [French]

Road Management Services (Darrington) Holdings Limited
Incorporated: 9 December 2002
Net Worth: £19,125,000 *Total Assets:* £256,691,008
Registered Office: Third Floor, Broad Quay House, Prince Street, Bristol, BS1 4DJ
Activities: Activities of head offices
Officers: David William Bowler [1945] Director/Lawyer; Matthew James Edwards [1985] Director/Investment Manager; Larry Jay Henry [1953] Director [American]; Richard Little [1979] Investment Director; Peter John Meffan [1964] Director; Neil Rae [1971] Director; Charles Alistair Snart [1960] Director

Road Management Services (Darrington) Limited
Incorporated: 9 December 2002
Net Worth: £19,129,000 *Total Assets:* £256,739,008
Registered Office: Third Floor, Broad Quay House, Prince Street, Bristol, BS1 4DJ
Activities: Construction of roads and motorways
Parent: Road Management Services (Darrington) Holdings Limited
Officers: David William Bowler [1945] Director/Lawyer; Matthew James Edwards [1985] Director/Investment Manager; Larry Jay Henry [1953] Director [American]; Richard Little [1979] Investment Director; Peter John Meffan [1964] Director; Neil Rae [1971] Director; Charles Alistair Snart [1960] Director

Road Management Services (Finance) PLC
Incorporated: 4 December 2002
Net Worth: £50,000 *Total Assets:* £219,012,000
Registered Office: Third Floor, Broad Quay House, Prince Street, Bristol, BS1 4DJ
Activities: Financial intermediation not elsewhere classified
Parent: Road Management Services (Darrington) Limited
Officers: David William Bowler [1945] Director/Lawyer; Matthew James Edwards [1985] Director/Investment Manager; Larry Jay Henry [1953] Director [American]; Richard Little [1979] Investment Director; Peter John Meffan [1964] Director; Neil Rae [1971] Director; Charles Alistair Snart [1960] Director

Roadform Civil Engineering Company Limited
Incorporated: 16 July 1988 *Employees:* 222
Net Worth: £9,269,728 *Total Assets:* £14,636,771
Registered Office: Roadform House, Milber Trading Estate, Newton Abbot, Devon, TQ12 4SG
Activities: Construction of commercial buildings
Shareholders: Wayne Vernon Voysey; Edgar Norman Potter
Officers: Wayne Vernon Voysey, Secretary; Edgar Norman Potter [1945] Director/Civil Engineer; Wayne Vernon Voysey [1956] Director/Civil Engineer

Robbins & Myers Holdings UK Limited
Incorporated: 20 October 1992
Net Worth: £5,480,000 *Total Assets:* £24,759,000
Registered Office: Stonedale Road, Oldends Lane Industrial Estate, Stonehouse, Glos, GL10 3RQ
Activities: Activities of head offices
Parent: NOV UK Holdings Limited
Officers: Alison May Sloan, Secretary; Robbert Oudendijk [1974] Director/Vice President Finance Europe, MENA, CIS [Dutch]; Simon Scott Reid [1982] Director/Accountant

C.F. Roberts (Electrical Contractors) PLC
Incorporated: 15 January 1996 *Employees:* 177
Net Worth: £2,602,030 *Total Assets:* £6,761,839
Registered Office: Barrington House, Kingsditch Lane, Cheltenham, Glos, GL51 9NN
Activities: Electrical installation
Officers: Matthew James Robert Thompson, Secretary; Ian Robert Henderson [1958] Managing Director; Marion Mitchell [1958] Director; Paul Steven Roberts [1969] Director; Matthew James Robert Thompson [1965] Director/Chartered Accountant; John Francis Waldron [1982] Director; Andrew David Young [1978] Director

Roberts Limbrick Limited
Incorporated: 28 July 2008 *Employees:* 94
Net Worth: £2,478,860 *Total Assets:* £5,359,935
Registered Office: The Carriage Building, Bruton Way, Gloucester, GL1 1DG
Activities: Architectural activities
Officers: Elizabeth Mary Thompson, Secretary; David Paul Billingham [1965] Director; Philip Dryden [1957] Director; Paul John Gooderson [1965] Director; Peter William Newth [1960] Director/Architect; Wayne Organ [1964] Director; Aled William Roberts [1973] Director/Architect; Joseph Luke Roberts [1975] Director; Aaron Stuart Terry [1974] Director; Elizabeth Mary Thompson [1977] Director/Accountant

Charles Robertson (Holdings) Limited
Incorporated: 14 October 2011 *Employees:* 850
Net Worth: £107,721,120 *Total Assets:* £122,699,552
Registered Office: Trago Mills, Twowatersfoot, Liskeard, Cornwall, PL14 6HY
Activities: Other retail sale in non-specialised stores
Major Shareholder: Charles Bruce Robertson
Officers: Gary Peter Lord, Secretary; Gary Peter Lord [1958] Director/Accountant; Brent Alan Pinhay [1965] Director; Charles Bruce Robertson [1953] Director; Kay Joanne Weber [1959] Director

Robertson Developments Holdings Limited
Incorporated: 17 March 2017
Net Worth: £6,501,220 *Total Assets:* £6,501,220
Registered Office: The Penthouse, Telegraph House, Calenick Street, Truro, Cornwall, TR1 2SF
Activities: Activities of construction holding companies
Shareholders: Stephenson Kenneth Dean; Robert Stephenson Dean
Officers: Robert Stephenson Dean [1964] Director; Avril Margaret Whitfield [1959] Director/Tax Professional [Australian]

Robertson Developments Ltd
Incorporated: 28 February 2006 *Employees:* 25
Net Worth: £1,353,866 *Total Assets:* £8,757,062
Registered Office: The Penthouse, Telegraph House, Calenick Street, Truro, Cornwall, TR1 2SF
Activities: Construction of commercial buildings
Major Shareholder: Robert Stephenson Dean
Officers: Robert Stephenson Dean, Secretary; Robert Stephenson Dean [1964] Director; Jason Terrence Mitchell [1972] Director; Avril Margaret Whitfield [1959] Director/Consultant [Australian]

Robinson Atterton Investments Limited
Incorporated: 21 May 2009
Net Worth: £2,725,268 *Total Assets:* £4,026,112
Registered Office: Euridge Manor Farm, Euridge, Colerne, Chippenham, Wilts, SN14 8BJ
Activities: Non-trading company
Major Shareholder: John Graham Robinson
Officers: Rhona Margaret Atterton, Secretary; Charles Spencer James Atterton [1956] Director; John Graham Robinson [1947] Director

Robinson Property Company Limited
Incorporated: 21 May 2009
Net Worth: £19,779,732 *Total Assets:* £26,870,440
Registered Office: Euridge Manor Farm, Euridge, Colerne, Chippenham, Wilts, SN14 8BJ
Activities: Other letting and operating of own or leased real estate
Major Shareholder: John Graham Robinson
Officers: Charles Spencer James Atterton [1956] Director; John Graham Robinson [1947] Director

Robinson Real Estate Limited
Incorporated: 21 May 2009 *Employees:* 1
Net Worth: £9,660,008 *Total Assets:* £15,384,383
Registered Office: Euridge Manor Farm, Euridge, Colerne, Chippenham, Wilts, SN14 8BJ
Activities: Other letting and operating of own or leased real estate
Major Shareholder: John Graham Robinson
Officers: John Graham Robinson, Secretary; Charles Spencer James Atterton [1956] Director; John Graham Robinson [1947] Director

Robotmother Limited
Incorporated: 8 February 2002 *Employees:* 6
Net Worth: £269,429 *Total Assets:* £4,489,815
Registered Office: Jubilee Wharf, Commercial Road, Penryn, Cornwall, TR10 8FG
Activities: Other letting and operating of own or leased real estate
Shareholders: Andrew John Marston; John James Shepherd Marston
Officers: Andrew John Marston, Secretary/Philosopher; Caroline Cox [1969] Director/Development Manager; Andrew John Marston [1970] Director/Philosopher

Rochford Garden Machinery Limited
Incorporated: 1 November 1988 *Employees:* 41
Net Worth: £6,017,536 *Total Assets:* £8,619,729
Registered Office: Wincanton Business Park, Wincanton, Somerset, BA9 9RS
Activities: Wholesale of agricultural machinery, equipment and supplies
Parent: Rochford Holdings Ltd
Officers: Stewart Anderson [1962] Managing Director

Rochford Holdings Limited
Incorporated: 25 March 1993 *Employees:* 41
Net Worth: £6,017,630 *Total Assets:* £8,619,873
Registered Office: Albert Goodman, Hendford Manor, Hendford, Yeovil, Somerset, BA20 1UN
Activities: Dormant company
Officers: Stewart Anderson [1962] Managing Director

Rochford Property Investments Limited
Incorporated: 6 October 2004 *Employees:* 3
Net Worth: £15,126,600 *Total Assets:* £30,910,912
Registered Office: The Office, Kings House, Little Paul Street, Kingsdown, Bristol, BS2 8FD
Activities: Renting and operating of Housing Association real estate
Shareholders: Rozalind Marie Rochford; Alastair John Rochford
Officers: Rozalind Marie Rochford, Secretary; Alastair John Rochford [1970] Director/Property Investor; Rozalind Marie Rochford [1966] Director

Rochling Engineering Plastics (UK) Limited
Incorporated: 17 September 1985 *Employees:* 76
Previous: Rochling Engineering Plastics (UK) Limited
Net Worth: £7,322,989 *Total Assets:* £12,474,259
Registered Office: Waterwells Drive, Waterwells Business Park, Quedgeley, Glos, GL2 2AA
Activities: Manufacture of other products of wood; manufacture of articles of cork, straw and plaiting materials
Officers: Elizabeth Elliott, Secretary; Dr Joachim Brunswicker [1955] Director [German]; Heinrich Josef Dirksen [1958] Director [German]; Michael Sydney Knowles [1962] Managing Director; Dietmar Telgenkamper [1966] Director [German]

Rochling Fibracon Limited
Incorporated: 7 September 1979
Previous: Fibracon Twin Limited
Net Worth: £3,188,545 *Total Assets:* £4,061,349
Registered Office: Waterwells Drive, Waterwells Business Park, Quedgeley, Gloucester, GL2 2AA
Activities: Manufacture of other plastic products
Parent: Rochling Engineering Plastics (UK) Limited
Officers: Elizabeth Elliott, Secretary; Henrich Josef Dirksen [1958] Director [German]; Mike Knowles [1962] Managing Director; Dietmar Telgenkamper [1966] Director [German]

Rock Services Limited
Incorporated: 9 October 2006 *Employees:* 30
Net Worth Deficit: £67,000 *Total Assets:* £31,980,000
Registered Office: 2nd Floor, Lysander House, Catbrain Lane, Cribbs Causeway, Bristol, BS10 7TQ
Activities: Other service activities n.e.c.
Major Shareholder: Arron Fraser Andrew Banks
Officers: Arron Fraser Andrew Banks [1966] Director/Insurance Broker; Elizabeth Bilney [1976] Director

Rockfield Farms Limited
Incorporated: 16 April 1997 *Employees:* 2
Net Worth: £3,994,556 *Total Assets:* £4,016,736
Registered Office: Wessex House, Challeymead Business Park, Melksham, Wilts, SN12 8BU
Activities: Mixed farming
Shareholders: Maurice Stuart Howes; Pauline Myfanwy Howes
Officers: Maurice Stuart Howes, Director & Secretary; Maurice Stuart Howes [1944] Director & Secretary; Pauline Myfanwy Howes [1947] Director/Farmer

Rockfish Group Limited
Incorporated: 29 October 2008 *Employees:* 203
Previous: Rockfish Grill and Seafood Market Limited
Net Worth: £82,277 *Total Assets:* £4,015,763
Registered Office: 5 South Embankment, Dartmouth, Devon, TQ6 9BH
Activities: Licenced restaurants
Shareholder: Mitchell Howard Tonks
Officers: Michael John Barnes [1949] Director; William James Julius Beckett [1977] Director; Henry Richard Melville Dimbleby [1970] Director; Stephen Paul Leadbeater [1961] Director; Mathew Prowse [1972] Director/Chef; Navneet Singh Sandhu [1980] Director; Mitchell Howard Tonks [1966] Director/Chef

Rockley Manor Estate LLP
Incorporated: 15 April 2013 *Employees:* 2
Net Worth: £18,021,024 *Total Assets:* £21,107,680
Registered Office: Rockley Manor, Rockley, Marlborough, Wilts, SN8 1RT
Officers: Dr Andrew George Rickman [1960] Member; Nichola Jane Rickman [1962] Member

Rockstone Surfacing Limited
Incorporated: 26 July 1985 *Employees:* 61
Net Worth: £4,543,838 *Total Assets:* £6,957,038
Registered Office: Central Trading Estate, Signal Way, Swindon, Wilts, SN3 1PD
Activities: Construction of roads and motorways
Shareholders: Stefan Dziubinski; Lorraine Joyce Dziubinski
Officers: Lorraine Joyce Dziubinski, Secretary; Lorraine Joyce Dziubinski [1956] Director and Secretary; Stefan Michal Dziubinski Bsc Hons [1955] Director/Civil Engineer

Rocma Europe
Incorporated: 28 July 2005 *Employees:* 3
Net Worth: £18,266,866 *Total Assets:* £864,371,904
Registered Office: Amcor Central Services, 83 Tower Road North, Warmley, Bristol, BS30 8XP
Activities: Other business support service activities n.e.c.
Officers: Matthew Charles Burrows [1970] Director; Christopher John Cheetham [1962] Director/Chartered Accountant; Richard Dixon [1963] Director/European Treasury and Tax Manager

Rocma Sterling
Incorporated: 24 April 2002 *Employees:* 3
Net Worth: £10,137,000 *Total Assets:* £195,360,992
Registered Office: 83 Tower Road North, Warmley, Bristol, BS30 8XP
Activities: Other business support service activities n.e.c.
Officers: Matthew Charles Burrows [1970] Director; Christopher John Cheetham [1962] Director/Chartered Accountant; Damien Clayton [1971] Director; Richard Dixon [1963] Director/European Treasury and Tax Manager

Roco Investments Limited
Incorporated: 11 July 2013 *Employees:* 1
Net Worth: £5,711,633 *Total Assets:* £7,228,087
Registered Office: Prideaux House, St Blazey, Par, Cornwall, PL24 2SS
Activities: Activities of mortgage finance companies
Shareholders: David John Trembath; Roger James Acock; David John Trembath
Officers: David Trembath, Secretary; Roger James Acock [1955] Director/Solicitor; David John Trembath [1948] Director/Accountant

Rodbourne Rail Farm Solar Park Limited
Incorporated: 18 October 2012
Net Worth: £523,495 *Total Assets:* £4,657,187
Registered Office: 35 and 35a The Maltings, Lower Charlton Trading Estate, Shepton Mallet, Somerset, BA4 5QE
Activities: Production of electricity
Shareholders: Robert John Hugo Randall; RRAM (Portfolio One) Limited
Officers: Douglas Michael Friend [1980] Director; Robert John Hugo Randall [1960] Director

A.E. Rodda & Son Limited
Incorporated: 31 August 1999 *Employees:* 161
Net Worth: £2,486,000 *Total Assets:* £13,316,000
Registered Office: The Creamery, Scorrier, Redruth, Cornwall, TR16 5BU
Activities: Liquid milk and cream production
Parent: North Downs Farm Ltd
Officers: Philip Ernest Rodda, Secretary/Creamery Manager; Mark Francis Duddridge [1963] Director; Peter Christopher Edward Farquhar [1959] Director; Neil Angus Kennedy [1960] Director; Roger Neil Morriss [1946] Director/Creamery Manager; John William Pengelly [1943] Director/Creamery Manager; Alfred James Rodda [1943] Director/Creamery Manager; Nicholas Luke Rodda [1969] Director; Philip Ernest Rodda [1950] Director/Creamery Manager

Rodgers of Plymouth Limited
Incorporated: 23 April 1981 *Employees:* 98
Net Worth: £1,380,234 *Total Assets:* £5,542,210
Registered Office: Brixton Road Garage, Chittleburn Hill, Brixton, Plymouth, PL8 2BL
Activities: Sale of new cars and light motor vehicles
Officers: Richard Kenneth Ackland, Secretary; Richard Kenneth Ackland [1982] Director/Motor Trade; Shane Paul Bovey [1973] Director; John Nigel Gruitt [1959] Director/Garage Manager; Adam Kingsley Hext [1991] Director; Andrew Martin Hext [1958] Director/Garage Manager; Alan Rowson Pugh [1948] Director/Garage Manager

F W Rogers Garage (Saltash) Limited
Incorporated: 11 May 1978 *Employees:* 18
Net Worth: £4,192,261 *Total Assets:* £4,240,507
Registered Office: Higher Castle Farm, Trematon, Saltash, Cornwall, PL12 4QW
Activities: Sale of new cars and light motor vehicles
Parent: Zodiac Properties (UK) Limited
Officers: Michelle Beverley Barrett, Secretary; Frederick William Rogers [1946] Director/Garage Proprietor; Sandra Mary Rogers [1946] Director

C J L Rogers Properties Ltd.
Incorporated: 10 March 1989 *Employees:* 6
Net Worth: £5,806,280 *Total Assets:* £8,079,746
Registered Office: Sigma House, Oak View Close, Torquay, Devon, TQ2 7FF
Activities: Buying and selling of own real estate
Parent: R A Piercy, M I Hasler, P O Rogers
Officers: Annabelle Chloe Pike, Secretary; Jane Elizabeth Kilmartin [1952] Director; Annabelle Chloe Pike [1988] Director/Clinical Psychologist; Benjamin Scott Rogers [1981] Director; Daniel Mark Rogers [1973] Director/Manager of Properties; Paul Oliver Rogers [1974] Director; Timothy Stuart Rogers [1978] Director

Roland DG (U.K.) Limited
Incorporated: 13 December 2001 *Employees:* 43
Net Worth: £1,146,326 *Total Assets:* £5,506,891
Registered Office: Griffin House, Windmill Road, Clevedon, Somerset, BS21 6UJ
Activities: Manufacture of computers and peripheral equipment
Parent: Roland DG Europe Holdings B.V.
Officers: Rod Mitchell, Secretary; Jeremy Paul Davies [1957] Director; Koichi Hashimoto [1961] Director [Japanese]; Elie Vic Keersmaekers [1974] Director [Belgian]; Takaaki Koshita [1967] Director [Japanese]; Naoki Nagano [1960] Director [Japanese]

Rollalong Holdings Limited
Incorporated: 19 November 1998
Net Worth: £790,000 *Total Assets:* £5,526,000
Registered Office: Woolsbridge Industrial Estate, Three Legged Cross, Wimborne, Dorset, BH21 6SF
Activities: Activities of head offices
Parent: Newship Limited
Officers: Andrew Paul Bale, Secretary; Jeremy David Clarkson [1961] Director; John Watson Newman [1945] Director

Rollalong Limited
Incorporated: 14 December 1998 *Employees:* 120
Net Worth: £7,184,000 *Total Assets:* £19,910,000
Registered Office: Woolsbridge Industrial Estate, Three Legged Cross, Wimborne, Dorset, BH21 6SF
Activities: Other specialised construction activities n.e.c.
Officers: Andrew Harrison, Secretary; Stephen Chivers [1974] Director; Jeremy David Clarkson [1961] Director; Stephen Edwin John Compson [1954] Director; Darren Edward Moore [1965] Director; John Watson Newman [1945] Director; Richard John Newman [1979] Director

Rollo Homes Number One Ltd
Incorporated: 11 April 2016
Net Worth Deficit: £1,850 *Total Assets:* £3,644,512
Registered Office: The Tramshed, 25 Lower Park Row, Bristol, BS1 5BN
Activities: Development of building projects
Officers: Paul O'Brien [1966] Director

Roman Bidco Limited
Incorporated: 26 June 2015
Net Worth: £5,367,574 *Total Assets:* £38,773,176
Registered Office: Unit 5 Kennet Way, Trowbridge, Wilts, BA14 8BL
Activities: Wholesale of textiles
Parent: Roman Group Topco Ltd
Officers: George Andrew Adams [1962] Director; Bruce Royston Freeland [1967] Director; Luke Daniel Jones [1977] Director/Financial Investments/Partner; Glenn Peter Leech [1975] Director/Chief Executive; Ian John Webb [1973] Director/Chief Finance Officer

Roman Group Topco Limited
Incorporated: 26 June 2015 *Employees:* 188
Net Worth Deficit: £808,455 *Total Assets:* £42,354,344
Registered Office: Unit 5 Kennet Way, Trowbridge, Wilts, BA14 8BL
Activities: Wholesale of clothing and footwear
Parent: MML Capital Europe VI Equity SA
Officers: George Andrew Adams [1962] Director; Roderick Hilary Brooks [1954] Director; Bruce Royston Freeland [1967] Director; Luke Daniel Jones [1977] Director/Financial Investments/Partner; Glenn Peter Leech [1975] Director/Chief Executive; Ian John Webb [1973] Director/Chief Finance Officer

John Romans Park Homes Limited
Incorporated: 4 March 1998 *Employees:* 6
Net Worth: £19,238,214 *Total Assets:* £36,719,712
Registered Office: Manchester House, High Street, Stalbridge, Sturminster Newton, Dorset, DT10 2LL
Activities: Other service activities n.e.c.
Major Shareholder: John Philip Romans
Officers: John Philip Romans [1958] Director/Park Home Owner

Romfield Holdings Limited
Incorporated: 26 September 1963 *Employees:* 2
Net Worth: £5,460,258 *Total Assets:* £7,926,266
Registered Office: Grays, West Tytherley, Salisbury, Wilts, SP5 1LD
Activities: Construction of commercial buildings
Shareholders: Lyell William Fairlie; Margaret Ann Fairlie
Officers: Margaret Ann Fairlie, Secretary; Lyell William Fairlie [1945] Director/Chartered Surveyor; Margaret Ann Fairlie [1945] Director/Solicitor

Sir William Romney's School
Incorporated: 5 July 2011 *Employees:* 97
Net Worth: £5,802,157 *Total Assets:* £6,918,809
Registered Office: Sir William Romney's School, Lowfield Road, Tetbury, Glos, GL8 8AE
Activities: General secondary education
Officers: Deborah Anderson-Dixon, Secretary; Trudi Mary Baker [1962] Director/Education Consultant; Jonathan Bell [1975] Director/Headteacher; Stephen Anthony Bishop [1968] Director/Quality Inspector; Brian Cook [1950] Director/Retired; Peter Nicholas Dillon [1991] Director/Teacher; Cllr Stephen Gartland Hirst [1944] Director/Retired; Katy Victoria Riddington [1975] Director/Head of Programmes; Jacqueline Frances Rymer [1963] Director/Teaching Assistant

Ronnies Limited
Incorporated: 4 March 2008 *Employees:* 578
Net Worth: £869,258 *Total Assets:* £5,711,746
Registered Office: Aldreth Pearcrorft Road, Stonehouse, Glos, GL10 2JY
Activities: Unlicenced restaurants and cafes
Major Shareholder: Anne Wainwright
Officers: Anne Wainwright [1961] Director

Rookwood School Trust Limited
Incorporated: 26 April 1963 *Employees:* 70
Net Worth: £3,775,464 *Total Assets:* £7,845,935
Registered Office: Rookwood School, Weyhill Road, Andover, Hants, SP10 3AL
Activities: Pre-primary education
Officers: Stephen John Bench, Secretary; Lee Ray Bedborough [1957] Director/Business Consultant; David Nicholas Alwyne Drew [1960] Director/Councillor; Carolyn Hardiman [1968] Director/Air Traffic Control Officer; Kevin John Knight [1948] Director/Retired; Michael Raymond Hamilton Lower [1954] Director/Retired; Carole Machin [1956] Director/Financial Advisor; Fiona Ann Penfold [1965] Managing Director; Victoria Jane Rutherford [1971] Director/Civil Servant (Advisor); Victoria Amanda Wickens [1965] Compliance Director

Roots Systems Limited
Incorporated: 9 November 1982 *Employees:* 61
Net Worth: £4,832,745 *Total Assets:* £6,122,305
Registered Office: 1 Millennium Place, Tiverton Business Park, Tiverton, Devon, EX16 6SB
Activities: Manufacture of other special-purpose machinery n.e.c.
Parent: Rotolok (Holdings) Ltd
Officers: Ann Joyce McCauley, Secretary; Graham Robert Hook [1951] Director/Engineer; Ann Joyce McCauley [1949] Director/Company Secretary; Daniel McCauley [1936] Director/Engineer; Sean Jonathan Swales [1968] Director/Chartered Accountant

Roper Rhodes Limited
Incorporated: 16 June 1981 *Employees:* 153
Net Worth: £32,524,820 *Total Assets:* £40,307,844
Registered Office: Brassmill Lane Trading Estate, Bath, BA1 3JF
Activities: Wholesale of household goods (other than musical instruments) n.e.c
Shareholders: Mark Roper; Paul Roper
Officers: Helen Mary Morgan, Secretary; Leigh Emery Leather [1969] Director; Mark Roper [1964] Director; Paul Roper [1966] Director; Simon Philip Taylor [1966] Director

Ropsley Farms Limited
Incorporated: 27 October 1995 *Employees:* 11
Net Worth: £25,326,436 *Total Assets:* £39,419,064
Registered Office: Crickley Barrow, Northleach, Cheltenham, Glos, GL54 3QA
Activities: Growing of cereals (except rice), leguminous crops and oil seeds
Officers: Joanne Jakeman, Secretary; Michael Murray Bertioli [1932] Director/Physicist; Patricia Mary Bertioli [1933] Director/Housewife; Anthony Oscar Colburn [1954] Director/Farmer; Andrew Herbert Lane [1957] Director/Solicitor

Ropsley Holdings Limited
Incorporated: 10 November 2015
Net Worth: £19,020,620 *Total Assets:* £19,020,620
Registered Office: Crickley Barrow, Northleach, Cheltenham, Glos, GL54 3QA
Activities: Activities of agricultural holding companies
Shareholders: Andrew Herbert Lane; Patricia Mary Bertioli; Michael Murray Bertioli
Officers: Joanne Jakeman, Secretary; Michael Murray Bertioli [1932] Director; Patricia Mary Bertioli [1933] Director/Housewife; Anthony Oscar Colburn [1954] Director/Farmer; Andrew Herbert Lane [1957] Director/Solicitor

Rose Bidco Limited
Incorporated: 31 July 2015
Total Assets: £31,904,000
Registered Office: Pinesgate, Lower Bristol Road, Bath, BA2 3DP
Activities: Activities of head offices
Parent: Redde PLC
Officers: Mark Francis Chessman [1964] Director; Stephen Edward Oakley [1952] Director; Martin Ward [1967] Managing Director

Roseland Investments Ltd
Incorporated: 6 June 2006
Net Worth: £3,141,120 *Total Assets:* £5,229,178
Registered Office: c/o Milliner Davies, Southfield House, 2 Southfield Road, Westbury on Trym, Bristol, BS9 3BH
Activities: Buying and selling of own real estate
Major Shareholder: Andrew James Robb
Officers: Andrew James Robb, Secretary; Andrew James Robb [1962] Director

The Roseland Multi Academy Trust
Incorporated: 9 March 2011 *Employees:* 105
Previous: The Roseland Community College
Net Worth: £9,942,707 *Total Assets:* £11,532,122
Registered Office: The Roseland Community School, Tregony, Truro, Cornwall, TR2 5SE
Activities: Primary education
Officers: Graham Ashton [1942] Director/Business Mentor; Christopher John Challis [1971] Director/Headmaster; Morag Leask Cunningham [1973] Director/Commercial Manager; Paul Grayston [1961] Director/Site Manager; Nigel Arthur Leslie Hyde [1962] Director/Family Support Manager; Marian Josephine Shannon [1958] Director/Retired; Kate Watson [1979] Director/Solicitor; Caroline Karenza Williams [1978] Director/Self Employed

Rosemont Pharmaceuticals Limited
Incorporated: 14 December 1967 *Employees:* 193
Net Worth: £37,358,000 *Total Assets:* £46,942,000
Registered Office: Wrafton, Braunton, Devon, EX33 2DL
Activities: Manufacture of basic pharmaceutical products
Parent: Acacia Biopharma Limited
Officers: Annette Corcoran, Secretary; Neil Thomas Lister [1975] Director; Dominic James Rivers [1977] Director; Christopher Allan Rudd [1980] Director; Howard Taylor [1966] Director

Rosemount Investments (Bristol) Limited
Incorporated: 22 April 2008 *Employees:* 2
Net Worth: £4,033,128 *Total Assets:* £5,884,206
Registered Office: Redland House, 157 Redland Road, Redland, Bristol, BS6 6YE
Activities: Other letting and operating of own or leased real estate
Shareholders: Merlynna Hawthorne; Michael James Hawthorne
Officers: Merlynna Hawthorne, Secretary; Merlynna Hawthorne [1964] Director; Michael James Hawthorne [1944] Director

Rosemundy Investments Limited
Incorporated: 30 September 1994 *Employees:* 2
Net Worth: £4,709,182 *Total Assets:* £4,814,673
Registered Office: Maningham, Illogan Churchtown, Illogan, Redruth, Cornwall, TR16 4QZ
Activities: Other letting and operating of own or leased real estate
Shareholders: Stephen Arthur Manico; Veronica Gillian Manico
Officers: Veronica Gillian Manico, Company Secretary; Stephen Arthur Manico [1947] Director; Veronica Gillian Manico [1950] Director/Company Secretary

Rotable Repairs Limited
Incorporated: 7 December 2001 *Employees:* 49
Net Worth: £2,862,553 *Total Assets:* £6,187,570
Registered Office: Mead Lane Warehouse, Mead Lane, Lydney, Glos, GL15 5EL
Activities: Manufacture of air and spacecraft and related machinery
Shareholders: Rotable Repairs Group Limited; Rotable Repairs Group Limited
Officers: Bryan Croft [1971] Director; Richard Lee Gardiner [1974] Director; Simon Christopher Hack [1970] Director; Jeffrey Johnston [1957] Director [American]; Christopher a Lawler [1967] Director [American]

Rotalink Limited
Incorporated: 6 May 1936 *Employees:* 61
Net Worth: £15,327,234 *Total Assets:* £17,570,596
Registered Office: Rotalink Limited, Unit 4 Cropmead, Crewkerne, Somerset, TA18 7HQ
Activities: Other manufacturing n.e.c.
Parent: Oval (259) Limited
Officers: Anita Mosley, Secretary; Melvyn Edward Hazell [1938] Managing Director; Oona Sarah Hazell [1969] Director; Caroline Sharon Nichol [1963] Director/Head of Operations; Matheus Vilela [1980] Director/Head of Sales [Brazilian]

Rotamic Engineering Limited
Incorporated: 12 February 2004 *Employees:* 46
Net Worth: £2,979,950 *Total Assets:* £5,405,410
Registered Office: Little Moor House, Falcon Road, Sowton Industrial Estate, Exeter, EX2 7LB
Activities: Manufacture of other fabricated metal products n.e.c.
Parent: Rotamic Holdings Limited
Officers: Mark Christopher Curtis [1956] Director/Engineer; Andrew Richard Snell [1969] Director/Works/Operation Manager; Gary Paul Squires [1979] Director/Production Manager

Rothdean Limited
Incorporated: 10 July 1972 *Employees:* 31
Net Worth: £8,642,194 *Total Assets:* £11,500,483
Registered Office: Forest Vale Road, Forest Vale Industrial Estate, Cinderford, Glos, GL14 2PH
Activities: Manufacture of trailers and semi-trailers
Shareholders: Lionel Walter George Jones; Clifford John Jones
Officers: Clifford John Jones, Secretary; Clifford John Jones [1944] Managing Director; Lionel Walter George Jones [1945] Managing Director

Rotolok (Holdings) Limited
Incorporated: 22 July 1974 *Employees:* 322
Net Worth: £41,665,352 *Total Assets:* £66,145,652
Registered Office: 1 Millennium Place, Tiverton Business Park, Tiverton, Devon, EX16 6SB
Activities: Manufacture of other special-purpose machinery n.e.c.
Officers: Ann Joyce McCauley, Secretary; Ann Joyce McCauley [1949] Director/Secretary; Daniel McCauley [1936] Director/Engineer; Sean Jonathan Swales [1968] Director/Chartered Accountant

Rotork Controls Limited
Incorporated: 21 July 1958 *Employees:* 355
Net Worth: £74,006,000 *Total Assets:* £227,071,008
Registered Office: Rotork House, Brassmill Lane, Bath, BA1 3JQ
Activities: Manufacture of bearings, gears, gearing and driving elements
Parent: Rotork PLC
Officers: Sarah Parsons, Secretary; Jonathan Mark Davis [1966] Director/Chartered Accountant; Kevin George Hostetler [1968] Director/Chief Executive [American]

Rotork Midland Limited
Incorporated: 18 May 1993 *Employees:* 72
Net Worth: £3,337,069 *Total Assets:* £4,839,807
Registered Office: Rotork House, Brassmill Lane, Bath, BA1 3JQ
Activities: Machining
Parent: Rotork Overseas Limited
Officers: Sarah Parsons, Secretary; Martin John Burton [1973] Director/General Manager; Jonathan Mark Davis [1966] Director/Chartered Accountant

Rotork Overseas Limited
Incorporated: 5 May 1971
Net Worth: £68,790,000 *Total Assets:* £387,255,008
Registered Office: Rotork House, Brassmill Lane, Bath, BA1 3JQ
Activities: Activities of head offices
Parent: Rotork PLC
Officers: Sarah Parsons, Secretary; Jonathan Mark Davis [1966] Director/Chartered Accountant; Kevin George Hostetler [1968] Director/Chief Executive [American]

Rotork P.L.C.
Incorporated: 12 February 1957 *Employees:* 3,738
Net Worth: £457,200,000 *Total Assets:* £738,593,984
Registered Office: Rotork House, Brassmill Lane, Bath, BA1 3JQ
Activities: Activities of head offices
Officers: Sarah Parsons, Secretary; Ann-Christin Gjerdseth Andersen [1966] Director/Senior Vice President [Norwegian]; Lucinda Margaret Bell [1964] Finance Director; Gary Bruce Bullard [1957] Director; Timothy Russell Cobbold [1962] Board Director; Jonathan Mark Davis [1966] Director/Chartered Accountant; Peter George Dilnot [1969] Director; Kevin George Hostetler [1968] Director/Chief Executive [American]; Sally Ann James [1949] Lawyer/Non-Executive Director; Martin James Lamb [1960] Director

Rotork UK Limited
Incorporated: 10 January 1973 *Employees:* 261
Net Worth: £24,820,000 *Total Assets:* £33,676,000
Registered Office: Rotork House, Brassmill Lane, Bath, BA1 3JQ
Activities: Machining
Parent: Rotork Controls Limited
Officers: Sarah Parsons, Secretary; Richard John Holbrook [1976] Director/Regional General Manager; David Andrew Littlejohns [1969] Director

Roundhill Estate Limited
Incorporated: 17 August 2012
Net Worth Deficit: £513,758 *Total Assets:* £6,418,159
Registered Office: Stockwell House, 13 High Street, Bruton, Somerset, BA10 0AB
Activities: Other letting and operating of own or leased real estate
Shareholders: Iwan Wirth; Manuela Wirth-Hauser
Officers: Daniel Kenneth Brickell [1977] Director/Accountant; Timothy Philip Jones [1954] Finance Director

Roundswell Services Limited
Incorporated: 19 March 2003 *Employees:* 23
Net Worth: £3,458,860 *Total Assets:* £5,064,464
Registered Office: The Offices of Perrins Limited, The Custom House, The Strand, Barnstaple, Devon, EX31 1EU
Activities: Other retail sale in non-specialised stores
Shareholders: Robert John Herbert Malek; Paul Janos Gyurgyak
Officers: Robert John Herbert Malek, Secretary; Paul Janos Gyurgyak [1962] Director; Herbert Adolph Malek [1938] Director; Patricia Malek [1933] Director; Philippa Virginia Malek [1972] Director; Robert John Herbert Malek [1962] Director

Route One Retail Limited
Incorporated: 19 March 2004 *Employees:* 84
Net Worth: £2,594,686 *Total Assets:* £3,601,877
Registered Office: The Rear Buffer Depot, Badminton Road, Acton Turville, Badminton, Glos, GL9 1HE
Activities: Retail sale of clothing in specialised stores
Major Shareholder: Richard Xavier Boissevain
Officers: Richard Xavier Boissevain [1961] Managing Director; Julia Ann Dixon [1962] Director

Rowan Dartington & Co. Limited
Incorporated: 1 October 1992 *Employees:* 198
Net Worth: £9,679,806 *Total Assets:* £16,058,896
Registered Office: St James's Place House, 1 Tetbury Road, Cirencester, Glos, GL7 1FP
Activities: Financial intermediation not elsewhere classified
Parent: Rowan Dartington Holdings Limited
Officers: John Clark Betteridge [1958] Director; Trevor Cheal [1964] Managing Director; Mr Adrian Clark [1962] Director; Glenn Cockerill [1978] Finance Director; Graham Peter Coxell [1969] Director; Nicholas James Hunt [1984] Director; Stephen Jones [1968] Distribution Director; Mark Kevin Leather [1973] Director

Rowan Dartington Holdings Limited
Incorporated: 15 December 2010
Net Worth: £15,531,438 *Total Assets:* £15,932,120
Registered Office: St James's Place House, 1 Tetbury Road, Cirencester, Glos, GL7 1FP
Activities: Activities auxiliary to financial intermediation n.e.c.
Parent: St. James's Place DFM Holdings Limited
Officers: John Clark Betteridge [1958] Director; Trevor Cheal [1964] Managing Director; Graham Peter Coxell [1969] Director

Rowanmoor Executive Pensions Limited
Incorporated: 24 April 2006 *Employees:* 160
Previous: Rowanmoor Group Limited
Net Worth: £3,337,000 *Total Assets:* £8,936,000
Registered Office: Rowanmoor House, 46-50 Castle Street, Salisbury, Wilts, SP1 3TS
Activities: Financial intermediation not elsewhere classified
Parent: Embark Group Limited
Officers: Vincent Philippe Francois Cambonie, Secretary; Vincent Philippe Francois Cambonie [1965] Director/Chief Financial Officer [French]; David Oliver Downie [1965] Director/Actuary; David John Etherington [1957] Director; David John King [1967] Managing Director; Lucy Victoria Hilaria Matthews [1963] Director/Administration Manager; Phillip Smith [1968] Director

Rowcliffe Holdings Limited
Incorporated: 5 September 1996
Net Worth: £6,057,771 *Total Assets:* £6,607,121
Registered Office: Mary Street House, Mary Street, Taunton, Somerset, TA1 3NW
Activities: Other letting and operating of own or leased real estate
Shareholder: Terence David Rowcliffe
Officers: Leah Darby [1979] Director; Nigel Anthony Hatfield [1964] Director; Naomi Charlotte Rattray [1981] Director; Nathan Tristan Rowcliffe [1974] Director; Terence David Rowcliffe [1951] Director

Rowcroft House Foundation Limited
Incorporated: 14 May 1981 *Employees:* 166
Net Worth: £7,406,445 *Total Assets:* £8,119,172
Registered Office: Rowcroft House, Avenue Road, Torquay, Devon, TQ2 5LS
Activities: Specialists medical practice activities
Officers: Sally Bryant [1957] Director/HR Consultant; Anthony Dee [1947] Director/Retired; Dr Cathryn Mary Edwards [1962] Director/Consultant Gastroenterologist; Alex Janzen [1973] Director/Chief of Staff; Philip Hugh Meek [1964] Director; Colin Michael William Pincombe [1943] Director/Retired; Dr Richard William George Ward [1951] Director/GP; John Richard Edmund Whitehead [1949] Director/Doctor

Rowe & Co.Cornwall (Properties) Limited
Incorporated: 26 May 1953
Net Worth: £10,474,623 *Total Assets:* £19,539,652
Registered Office: c/o Francis Clark LLP, North Quay House, Sutton Harbour, Plymouth, PL4 0RA
Activities: Development of building projects
Parent: Rowe Estates Holdings Ltd
Officers: Michael Greenslade [1957] Director; Christopher Roger Rowe [1972] Director; Matthew Rowe [1968] Director; Richard Jason Rowe [1966] Director; Rodney Rowe [1936] Director

W.C. Rowe (Falmouth) Limited
Incorporated: 19 December 1975 *Employees:* 331
Net Worth: £3,196,047 *Total Assets:* £8,344,331
Registered Office: Unit 1 Bickland Industrial Park, Falmouth, Cornwall, TR11 4TA
Activities: Manufacture of bread; manufacture of fresh pastry goods and cakes
Parent: Chasseron Limited
Officers: David Geoffrey Lean [1962] Finance Director; Kerry Lynch [1959] Director/Accountant; Maurice Matthews [1972] Technical Director [Irish]; Paul William Charles Pearce [1981] Marketing Director

Rowe Estates (UK) Limited
Incorporated: 26 May 1953 *Employees:* 8
Net Worth: £20,887,826 *Total Assets:* £28,621,124
Registered Office: c/o Francis Clark LLP, North Quay House, Sutton Harbour, Plymouth, PL4 0RA
Activities: Development of building projects
Parent: Rowe Estates Holdings Ltd
Officers: Michael Greenslade [1957] Director; Amanda Rowe [1964] Director; Christopher Roger Rowe [1972] Director; Matthew Rowe [1968] Director; Richard Jason Rowe [1966] Director; Rodney Rowe [1936] Director

Rowe Estates Holdings Limited
Incorporated: 17 May 2005
Net Worth: £28,929,812 *Total Assets:* £28,931,812
Registered Office: c/o Francis Clark LLP, North Quay House, Sutton Harbour, Plymouth, PL4 0RA
Activities: Activities of head offices
Officers: Christopher Roger Rowe [1972] Director; Matthew Rowe [1968] Director; Richard Jason Rowe [1966] Director; Rodney Rowe [1936] Director

Rowes Garage Limited
Incorporated: 3 May 1985 *Employees:* 119
Net Worth: £5,535,049 *Total Assets:* £8,053,875
Registered Office: 447 Wolseley Road, St Budeaux, Plymouth, PL5 1BL
Activities: Sale of new cars and light motor vehicles
Major Shareholder: Maurice Kenneth Rowe
Officers: William Donald, Secretary; Andrew James Baker [1968] Director; Shaun Darby [1962] Director; Dawn Donald [1953] Director; William Donald [1951] Director; Christine Wendy Liddicoat [1943] Director/Company Secretary; Adrian Stuart Pearce [1959] Director/Service Manager; Maurice Kenneth Rowe [1949] Director/Motor Trader; Suzanne Jayne Rowe [1955] Director

Royal Agricultural University
Incorporated: 11 August 1908 *Employees:* 210
Net Worth: £28,522,000 *Total Assets:* £49,351,000
Registered Office: Royal Agricultural University, Stroud Road, Cirencester, Glos, GL7 6JS
Activities: First-degree level higher education
Officers: Susan Maria O'Neill, Secretary; Mohamed Amersi [1960] Director/Entrepreneur [Kenyan]; Alison Helen Bernays [1950] Retired Director; Ian Stuart Cooper [1961] Director/Chartered Accountant Retired; Rt Hon Michael Jack CBE [1946] Director/Retired; Professor Jonathan Graham Kydd [1951] Director/University Professor; Alexander Lawson [1970] Director/Land Agent; Chris Musgrave [1960] Director; Colin Spencer Pett [1953] Director/Retired; Jean Roberts [1949] Director/Chartered Occupational Psychologist; James Reginald Townshend [1954] Director

The Royal Air Force Charitable Trust Enterprises
Incorporated: 10 November 1987 *Employees:* 51
Net Worth: £682,708 *Total Assets:* £7,841,175
Registered Office: Douglas Bader House, Horcott Hill, Fairford, Glos, GL7 4RB
Activities: Retail sale via mail order houses or via Internet
Officers: Christopher Andrew Murray, Secretary; Stephen Andrew Armstrong [1957] Director/Chief Executive; Colin Basnett [1961] Director/Defence and Political Adviser (Air) MBDA; Christopher Bell [1957] Director; Steven Leslie Gunyon [1955] Director of Finance; Russell Blackburn Hoyle [1949] Director; Stuart Lindsell [1973] Executive Director; Caroline Rogers [1962] Director; Alan Frank Smith [1946] Chairman and Director

Royal Arcade Limited
Incorporated: 23 June 1982 *Employees:* 13
Net Worth: £2,485,471 *Total Assets:* £4,887,681
Registered Office: 92 The Esplanade, Weymouth, Dorset, DT4 7AT
Activities: Other letting and operating of own or leased real estate
Shareholders: Kevin John Flower; Timothy Peter Flower
Officers: Margaret Ann Flower, Secretary; Dennis William Flower [1953] Director/Manager; Kevin John Flower [1973] Director/Manager; Timothy Peter Flower [1983] Director/Manager

The Royal Artillery Centre for Personal Development
Incorporated: 17 May 2005 *Employees:* 58
Net Worth: £3,516,166 *Total Assets:* £3,700,112
Registered Office: Old Fire Station, Salt Lane, Salisbury, Wilts, SP1 1DU
Activities: Technical and vocational secondary education
Officers: William James Frank Bramble [1966] Director/Army Officer; Stephen Ellison [1958] Director; Neil Alan Hopkins [1953] Director; Colonel Michael James Kelly [1965] Director/Army Officer; John Bruce Knowles [1948] Director/Retired; Colonel John Brian Musgrave [1965] Director/Army Officer; Brigadier Mark Pullan Mbe [1971] Director/Army Officer; Amanda Jane Storey [1967] Director/Solicitor

Royal Artillery Charitable Fund.
Incorporated: 23 January 1920 *Employees:* 5
Net Worth: £34,088,648 *Total Assets:* £34,985,000
Registered Office: Artillery House, Royal Artillery Barracks, Larkhill, Wilts, SP4 8QT
Activities: Other social work activities without accommodation n.e.c.
Officers: Colonel Matthew Gerard John Carter, Secretary; Colonel Hugh Scott Baker [1965] Director/HM Forces; Christopher Eldred Comport [1956] Director/Businessman; Major General David Mark Cullen [1963] Director/Businessman; Andrew John Dines [1952] Director/Management Consultant; Colonel Clive Fletcher-Wood [1946] Director/Solicitor/Advocate; Colonel Michael Kelly [1965] Director/HM Forces; James Oliver Leighton [1968] Director/Investment Manager; Colonel Giles Harry Malec [1974] Director/HM Forces; Brigadier Mark Nicholas Pountain [1957] Director; Colonel William George Prior [1954] Director/Civil Servant; Colonel Michael David Relph [1957] Director/Retired

Royal Artillery Institution Limited
Incorporated: 5 December 2007 *Employees:* 3
Net Worth: £10,894,091 *Total Assets:* £11,052,180
Registered Office: Artillery House, Royal Artillery Barracks, Larkhill, Wilts, SP4 8QT
Activities: Defence activities
Officers: Colonel Matthew Gerard John Carter, Secretary; Colonel Hugh Scott Baker [1965] Director/HM Forces; Nicholas Anthony Clissitt [1956] Director/Consultant; Major General David Mark Cullen [1963] Director/Businessman; James Ronald Murray Gower [1954] Director/Armed Forces; Simon John Rhodes Halliday [1963] Director/Businessman; Colonel Michael James Kelly [1965] Director/Officer HM Forces; Colonel Giles Harry Malec [1974] Director/HM Forces; Bryan Andrew Pugh [1980] Director/HM Forces; Mark Graham Williams [1957] Director/Businessman; Colonel Richard Anthony Winchester [1960] Director/HM Forces

The Royal Bath & West of England Society
Incorporated: 23 May 1994 *Employees:* 23
Net Worth: £6,134,000 *Total Assets:* £6,695,000
Registered Office: The Showground, Shepton Mallet, Somerset, BA4 6QN
Activities: Other social work activities without accommodation n.e.c.
Officers: Paul John Hooper, Secretary; John Alvis [1944] Director/Agriculture; Richard William John Ash [1950] Director/Manufacturer; Dr Richard Thomas Calver [1944] Director/Farmer; Robert Nicholas Foord Drewett [1959] Director/Solicitor; Michael John Felton [1955] Director/Farmer; Anthony Alan Gibson [1949] Director/Consultant; Catherine Rebecca Look [1966] Director; Lance Stuart Moir [1957] Director; Martin Thatcher [1968] Director; Rupert William Uloth [1964] Director/Journalist; Sir David James Vernon Wills [1955] Director/Farmer; Angela Betty Yeoman [1931] Director

Royal Bay Care Homes Ltd
Incorporated: 1 October 1999
Net Worth: £12,527,669 *Total Assets:* £24,907,208
Registered Office: 31-33 Commercial Road, Poole, Dorset, BH14 0HU
Activities: Development of building projects
Major Shareholder: Caroline Una Wilson
Officers: Anthony Frederick Wilson, Secretary; Jules Louise Dove [1968] Director/Group Development Manager; Anthony Frederick Wilson [1949] Director/Nursing Home Proprietor; Caroline Una Wilson [1951] Director; Jamie Russell Frederick Wilson [1984] Director/Neuro Spinal Surgeon; Russell Leonard Wilson [1947] Director/Nursing Home Proprietor; Timothy Stewart Richard Wilson [1988] Director/Media & Communications Manager

The Royal Clarence Hotel Limited
Incorporated: 21 June 1999
Net Worth: £18,107,140 *Total Assets:* £21,441,392
Registered Office: 8 Gay Street, Bath, BA1 2PH
Activities: Hotels and similar accommodation
Major Shareholder: Andrew Douglas Brownsword
Officers: Peter Tyrrell, Secretary; Andrew Douglas Brownsword [1947] Director/Publisher; Jeremy David Hancock [1964] Director/Tax Manager; Stephanie Hocking [1966] Director; Peter Tyrrell [1972] Director

The Royal Institution of Cornwall
Incorporated: 16 January 2013 *Employees:* 19
Net Worth: £6,516,000 *Total Assets:* £6,924,000
Registered Office: Royal Cornwall Museum, River Street, Truro, Cornwall, TR1 2SJ
Activities: Museums activities
Officers: Bert Martin Montague Biscoe [1952] Director; David Jonathan Bishop [1939] Director/Retired; Martin Richard Brooks [1950] Director; Mark Henwood Chanter [1957] Director; Ian Charles Doble [1947] Director; Nicholas David Johnson [1950] Director/Archaeologist; Philip John Marsden [1961] Director/Author; Melinda Jane Rickett [1960] Director; Richard John Arundell Robinson [1950] Director/Retired; Peter Charles Stethridge [1948] Director

The Royal Marines Charity
Incorporated: 1 February 2010 *Employees:* 11
Previous: Royal Marines Charitable Trust Fund
Net Worth: £13,222,720 *Total Assets:* £13,396,808
Registered Office: Building 72, Commando Training Centre, Royal Marines, Lympstone, Exmouth, Devon, EX8 5AR
Activities: Defence activities
Officers: Jonathan Ball, Secretary; Keith Breslauer [1966] Managing Director [American]; Daniel Cox [1972] Director/Banker; Brigadier Paul Richard Denning [1961] Director; Ian William Grant [1955] Director/Civil Servant; David Paul Mason [1974] Director/Royal Marine; Sara Reed [1971] Director/Communications Manager; Kim Richardson [1961] Director/Charity Worker; William John Stocks [1949] Director/Retired; Richard John Weaver [1974] Director/Accountant; Brigadier Haydn John White [1965] Director/Royal Marines Officer; James Michael Zuppinger [1963] Director/Business Executive

Royal Osteoporosis Society
Incorporated: 15 December 2003 *Employees:* 67
Previous: National Osteoporosis Society
Net Worth: £6,377,165 *Total Assets:* £6,825,860
Registered Office: Royal Osteoporosis Society, Camerton, Bath, BA2 0PJ
Activities: Other human health activities
Officers: Professor Juliet Compston [1945] Director/Clinician; Dr Anne Louise Dolan [1960] Director/Consultant; Dr Neil John Lloyd Gittoes [1966] Director/Medical Practitioner; Frances May Grigg [1958] Director/Accountant; Catherine Janet Tompkins [1947] Regional Director RCN; Caroline Trewhitt [1959] Project Director; Carole Mary Walker [1942] Director/Retired; Dr Lynne Wigens [1963] Director/Regional Chief Nurse NHS England; Tim Willett [1969] Director/Consultant

Royal West of England Academy
Incorporated: 14 May 1998 *Employees:* 24
Net Worth: £5,395,362 *Total Assets:* £5,561,742
Registered Office: Queens Road, Clifton, Bristol, BS8 1PX
Activities: Operation of arts facilities
Officers: Alison Bevan, Secretary; Yvonne Margaret Ashton [1961] Director/Chartered Accountant; Jeremy Robert Cowhig [1945] Director/Retired; Maria Crayton [1965] Director/Head of Marketing; Yvonne Crossley [1942] Gallery Director/Artist; Stewart Geddes [1961] Director/Artist; Stephen Roy Jacobson [1946] Director/Artist; Elena Marco [1974] Director/Head of Department Architecture [Spanish]; Vanessa Louise Moon [1962] Director Recruitment Consultancy; Suzanne Rolt [1967] Director; Abdulhamid Sheikh [1988] Director/Entrepreneur

Royal Wootton Bassett Academy Trust
Incorporated: 18 March 2011 *Employees:* 304
Previous: Royal Wootton Bassett Academy
Net Worth: £12,595,244 *Total Assets:* £15,740,469
Registered Office: Lime Kiln, Royal Wootton Bassett, Swindon, Wilts, SN4 7HG
Activities: General secondary education
Officers: Lindsay Allen [1973] Director; Johnathan Dudley Bourne [1961] Director/Town Clerk; David Shurland Clarke [1963] Director [Australian]; George Andrew Croxford [1961] Director/Headteacher; Tristan Michael Foot [1979] Director; Jane Helen Hext [1961] Director/Retired; Marion Sweet [1950] Director/Education Consultant

Royds Withy King LLP
Incorporated: 31 January 2011 *Employees:* 450
Previous: Withy King LLP
Net Worth: £12,972,341 *Total Assets:* £24,860,522
Registered Office: 5-6 Northumberland Buildings, Queen Square, Bath, BA1 2JE
Officers: William Simon Bassett [1971] Member; Stuart John Brazington [1966] Member; Malcolm Roger Andrew Gregory [1968] Member; Shaun O'Halloran [1968] Member; Graham Jonathan Street [1966] Member; Stewart Wilkinson [1957] Member; Richard Marcus Woodman [1957] Member; Claus Kildegaard Geel Andersen [1970] LLP Member; Andrew Nicholas Ash [1967] LLP Member; Philip Ian Banks-Welsh [1959] LLP Member; Kate Benefer [1979] LLP Member; Richard William Brooks [1969] LLP Member; Ian Richard Carrier [1971] LLP Member; Andrew Alexander Chalk [1961] LLP Member; Helen Childs [1967] LLP Member; Richard Mark Coleman [1969] LLP Member; Robert Charles Collins [1968] LLP Member; Paul Thomas Daniels [1970] LLP Member; Caroline Ann Doran [1974] LLP Member; Simon Elliman [1968] LLP Member; Richard Howard Ellis [1968] LLP Member; Peter James Foskett [1959] LLP Member; Thomas Edward Gilman [1973] LLP Member; Lauren Marie Harkin [1981] LLP Member; Louise Jane Hart [1970] LLP Member; Patrick William Hart [1963] LLP Member; David Emrys Israel [1966] LLP Member; Christopher Thomas Kane [1961] LLP Member; Kerstin Kubiak [1977] LLP Member; Jamie Lester [1976] LLP Member; Sharon Fiona MacDonald [1966] LLP Member; William Patrick Erskine MacFarlane [1980] LLP Member; James David McNeile [1964] LLP Member; James William Robert Millar Craig [1953] LLP Member; Katharine Elizabeth Mortimer [1965] LLP Member; Bharat Bhushan Nahar [1977] LLP Member; Tracy Lyn Norris-Evans [1963] LLP Member; John Darrell North [1960] LLP Member; Amanda Jane Noyce [1967] LLP Member; Gemma Elizabeth Duncombe Ospedale [1964] LLP Member; Ronald Arthur Peet [1957] LLP Member; Caroline Priest [1966] LLP Member; Becky Ricards Small [1977] LLP Member; Paul Rumley [1973] LLP Member; James Sage [1983] LLP Member; Rebecca Ann Stevens [1977] LLP Member; Edward Sefton Knut Vidnes [1978] LLP Member; Richard James White [1977] LLP Member; Angus Charles Williams [1977] LLP Member; Gareth Brook Williams [1957] LLP Member

RP (Poundbury) LLP
Incorporated: 14 March 2015 *Employees:* 2
Net Worth: £22,410,216 *Total Assets:* £22,587,616
Registered Office: C G Fry and Son Limited, Litton Cheney, Dorchester, DT2 9AW
Officers: Alastair Gilbert Martin [1960] Member

RR Sea Dundee Limited
Incorporated: 28 May 2009
Previous: Conygar Dundee Limited
Net Worth: £2,896,328 *Total Assets:* £5,467,222
Registered Office: Beaufort House, 51 New North Road, Exeter, EX4 4EP
Activities: Other letting and operating of own or leased real estate
Parent: Regional REIT Limited
Officers: Sarah Ann Campbell [1978] Director/Chartered Accountant; Derek McDonald [1967] Deputy Managing Director

RR Sea Hanover St. Limited
Incorporated: 2 November 2007
Previous: Conygar Hanover Street Limited
Net Worth: £10,036,625 *Total Assets:* £23,171,236
Registered Office: Beaufort House, 51 New North Road, Exeter, EX4 4EP
Activities: Buying and selling of own real estate
Parent: Regional REIT Limited
Officers: Sarah Ann Campbell [1978] Director/Chartered Accountant; Derek McDonald [1967] Deputy Managing Director

RR Sea St. Helens Limited
Incorporated: 28 May 2009
Previous: Conygar St Helens Limited
Net Worth: £1,811,316 *Total Assets:* £3,738,382
Registered Office: Beaufort House, 51 New North Road, Exeter, EX4 4EP
Activities: Other letting and operating of own or leased real estate
Parent: Regional REIT Limited
Officers: Sarah Ann Campbell [1978] Director/Chartered Accountant; Derek McDonald [1967] Deputy Managing Director

RR Sea Strand Limited
Incorporated: 25 August 2006
Previous: Conygar Strand Limited
Net Worth: £5,036,830 *Total Assets:* £9,291,934
Registered Office: Beaufort House, 51 New North Road, Exeter, EX4 4EP
Activities: Buying and selling of own real estate
Parent: Regional REIT Limited
Officers: Sarah Ann Campbell [1978] Director/Chartered Accountant; Derek McDonald [1967] Deputy Managing Director

RRH Limited
Incorporated: 10 February 2003 *Employees:* 45
Net Worth: £1,937,682 *Total Assets:* £5,900,903
Registered Office: The Old Brickworks, Broadway, Market Lavington, Devizes, Wilts, SN10 5RH
Activities: Renting and leasing of agricultural machinery and equipment
Parent: RRH Property Limited
Officers: Thomas Reed, Secretary; Arthur Reed [1947] Director/Management; Thomas Reed [1977] Director/Sales Manager; Sarah Young [1962] Director

RRPI (UK) Ltd
Incorporated: 9 June 2014 *Employees:* 2
Net Worth Deficit: £50,062 *Total Assets:* £3,532,367
Registered Office: 118 Old Milton Road, New Milton, Hants, BH25 6EB
Activities: Other letting and operating of own or leased real estate
Parent: P P Commercial Enterprises Limited
Officers: David Ralph, Secretary; Richard Maurice Porter [1968] Director; David Michael Ralph [1979] Director

RTB Private Equity Ltd
Incorporated: 5 February 2013 *Employees:* 2
Net Worth: £8,219,446 *Total Assets:* £8,219,446
Registered Office: The New Works, Roughmoor Industrial Estate, Williton, Somerset, TA4 4RF
Activities: Dormant company
Major Shareholder: Stephen Christopher Wells
Officers: Mark Dorrill, Secretary; Ann Mary Wells [1986] Director; Stephen Christopher Wells [1967] Director

RTP-UK Ltd
Incorporated: 27 December 2007 *Employees:* 53
Net Worth: £7,397,676 *Total Assets:* £7,906,934
Registered Office: 200 Woodlands Court, Ash Ridge Road, Bristol, S Glos, BS32 4LB
Activities: Other publishing activities
Parent: Rheinmetall AG
Officers: Robert Charles Peters [1965] Director/Merchant

Rudgeway Farms Limited
Incorporated: 17 August 1954
Net Worth: £13,780,170 *Total Assets:* £15,361,916
Registered Office: Rudgeway Farms, Tredington, Tewkesbury, Glos, GL20 7BN
Activities: Mixed farming
Shareholders: Richard Martin Harvey; Caroline Wendy Horne
Officers: Richard Martin Harvey [1965] Director/Farmer; Caroline Wendy Horne [1969] Director/Farmer

Rush Group Limited
Incorporated: 9 February 1990 *Employees:* 22
Net Worth: £1,144,190 *Total Assets:* £7,134,014
Registered Office: Old Tote Buildings, Exeter Racecourse, Kennford, Exeter, Devon, EX6 7XS
Activities: Wholesale of fruit and vegetables
Parent: Flatcable Limited
Officers: Murray Charles Hogge, Secretary; Guy Edward Charles Burgoyne [1984] Director/Produce Trader; Samuel Charles Crocker [1986] Director/Fruit Trader; Murray Charles Hogge [1960] Director/Trader; Tong Theeng Lioe [1965] Director/Commodity Trader [Malaysian]; Maurice James Molloy [1963] Finance Director [Irish]; Jose Alberto Teixeira Nazare [1967] Director/Agronomist [Portuguese]; David William Ough [1955] Director/Potato Merchant

Ruskin Mill Trust Limited
Incorporated: 13 May 2010 *Employees:* 813
Net Worth: £6,644,820 *Total Assets:* £13,954,748
Registered Office: Ruskin Mill, Mill Bottom, Old Bristol Road, Nailsworth, Glos, GL6 0LA
Activities: Other education n.e.c.
Officers: Ian Keith Clements, Secretary; Jorunn Barane [1961] Director/Lecturer [Norwegian]; Phillip Forder [1953] Director/Community Engagement Manager; Aonghus Coinn Huntly Gordon [1955] Director; Vivian Frederick Blenheim Griffiths [1948] Director/Retired; Peter Gruenewald [1959] Director/Teacher [German]; Chloe Amber Hindmarsh [1983] Director/Education Services Manager; Helen Margaret Kippax [1949] Director; Kerry Ann Shillito [1974] Director/Fundraising Executive; Nick Stuart [1958] Director/Veterinary Surgeon; Guy Vassall-Adams [1969] Director/Barrister; Victoria Wren [1972] Director/Teacher

Charles Russell International Limited
Incorporated: 17 December 1992 *Employees:* 12
Net Worth: £4,601,076 *Total Assets:* £5,053,089
Registered Office: Walton Hill Farm, Tewkesbury Road, Deerhurst, Gloucester, GL19 4BN
Activities: Freight transport by road
Shareholders: Charles Stephen Russell; Anne Elizabeth Russell
Officers: Charles Stephen Russell, Secretary; Anne Elizabeth Russell [1948] Director; Benjamin Stephen Russell [1977] Director/Manager; Charles Stephen Russell [1950] Director/Haulage Contractor; Oliver Charles Russell [1972] Director/Manager

Charles Russell Transport UK Limited
Incorporated: 8 April 2003 *Employees:* 33
Net Worth: £6,115,190 *Total Assets:* £8,414,643
Registered Office: Walton Hill Farm, Tewkesbury Road, Deerhurst, Glos, GL19 4BN
Activities: Freight transport by road
Shareholders: Anne Elizabeth Russell; Charles Stephen Russell
Officers: Anne Elizabeth Russell, Secretary; Anne Elizabeth Russell [1948] Director/Secretary; Benjamin Stephen Russell [1977] Director/Manager; Charles Stephen Russell [1950] Director/Haulage Contractor; Oliver Charles Russell [1972] Director/Manager

Russell Worth Limited
Incorporated: 2 July 2010 *Employees:* 71
Net Worth: £6,050,470 *Total Assets:* £9,541,816
Registered Office: Ashleigh Way, Langage Park Office Campus, Plympton, Plymouth, PL7 5JX
Activities: Solicitors
Shareholders: Peter John Russell; Bridgitte Elizabeth Worth
Officers: Peter John Russell [1962] Director/Solicitor

Rusty Shilling Developments Limited
Incorporated: 30 March 2006 *Employees:* 8
Net Worth Deficit: £189,877 *Total Assets:* £4,690,905
Registered Office: Q1 Quadrant Distribution Centre, Quedgeley, Gloucester, GL2 2RN
Activities: Development of building projects
Shareholder: Paul Francis Markey
Officers: Paul Francis Markey, Secretary/Chartered Accountant; Anthony Joseph Markey [1964] Director; Paul Francis Markey [1960] Director/Chartered Accountant

RW Gower Street Limited
Incorporated: 29 November 2010 *Employees:* 29
Net Worth: £6,445,000 *Total Assets:* £14,892,000
Registered Office: Wessex Water, Operations Centre, Claverton Down Road, Claverton Down, Bath, BA2 7WW
Activities: Hotels and similar accommodation
Parent: Glasshouse Hotel Limited
Officers: Ruth Esme Jefferson, Secretary; Andrew Jordan [1961] Director; Pearly Poussier [1963] Director [Malaysian]; Colin Frank Skellett [1945] Director

RW Greenside Place Limited
Incorporated: 29 November 2010 *Employees:* 64
Net Worth: £2,240,000 *Total Assets:* £8,025,000
Registered Office: Wessex Water, Operations Centre, Claverton Down Road, Claverton Down, Bath, BA2 7WW
Activities: Hotels and similar accommodation
Parent: Glasshouse Hotel Limited
Officers: Ruth Esme Jefferson, Secretary; Andrew Jordan [1961] Director; Pearly Poussier [1963] Director [Malaysian]; Colin Frank Skellett [1945] Director

RW Threadneedle Street Limited
Incorporated: 29 November 2010 *Employees:* 90
Net Worth: £11,576,000 *Total Assets:* £41,761,000
Registered Office: Wessex Water, Operations Centre, Claverton Down Road, Claverton Down, Bath, BA2 7WN
Activities: Hotels and similar accommodation
Parent: Threadneedles Hotel Limited
Officers: Ruth Esme Jefferson, Secretary; Andrew Jordan [1961] Director; Pearly Poussier [1963] Director [Malaysian]; Colin Frank Skellett [1945] Director

RWC Construction Ltd
Incorporated: 14 January 2009
Net Worth Deficit: £1,596,426 *Total Assets:* £3,591,940
Registered Office: 9 Hinton Wood Avenue, Christchurch, Dorset, BH23 5AB
Activities: Other letting and operating of own or leased real estate
Officers: Robert William Field, Secretary; Richard William Crewe [1962] Director; Sara Ann Crewe [1964] Director

RWE Cogen UK (Hythe) Limited
Incorporated: 22 May 2002 *Employees:* 4
Previous: npower Cogen (Hythe) Limited
Net Worth: £10,871,000 *Total Assets:* £13,759,000
Registered Office: Windmill Hill Business Park, Whitehill Way, Swindon, Wilts, SN5 6PB
Activities: Production of electricity
Officers: Jason Anthony Keene, Secretary; Jason Anthony Keene [1970] Director/Company Secretary; Rebecca Claire Wall [1968] Director/Financial Controller

RWE Cogen UK Limited
Incorporated: 28 June 1991 *Employees:* 14
Previous: npower Cogen Limited
Net Worth: £146,262,000 *Total Assets:* £161,728,992
Registered Office: Windmill Hill Business Park, Whitehill Way, Swindon, Wilts, SN5 6PB
Activities: Production of electricity
Parent: RWE Generation UK PLC
Officers: Jason Anthony Keene, Secretary; Jason Anthony Keene [1970] Director/Company Secretary; Rebecca Claire Wall [1968] Director/Financial Controller

RWE Generation UK Holdings Limited
Incorporated: 8 May 2000
Previous: RWE Generation UK Holdings PLC
Net Worth: £2,728,000,000 *Total Assets:* £2,728,999,936
Registered Office: Windmill Hill Business Park, Whitehill Way, Swindon, Wilts, SN5 6PB
Activities: Activities of head offices
Officers: Jason Anthony Keene, Secretary; Stephen Charles Glover [1960] Director/Manager; Mohamed Shabir Suleman [1964] Director/Head of Commercial Asset Optimisation - UK; Rebecca Claire Wall [1968] Director/Financial Controller

RWE Generation UK PLC
Incorporated: 13 December 1999 *Employees:* 1,074
Net Worth: £1,626,000,000 *Total Assets:* £2,912,000,000
Registered Office: Windmill Hill Business Park, Whitehill Way, Swindon, Wilts, SN5 6PB
Activities: Production of electricity
Parent: RWE AG
Officers: Jason Anthony Keene, Secretary; Stephen Charles Glover [1960] Director/Manager; Mohamed Shabir Suleman [1964] Director/Head of Commercial Asset Optimisation-UK; Rebecca Claire Wall [1968] Director/Financial Controller

RWE Markinch Limited
Incorporated: 23 April 2008 *Employees:* 36
Previous: RWE Innogy Markinch Limited
Net Worth: £46,767,968 *Total Assets:* £256,075,760
Registered Office: Windmill Hill Business Park, Whitehill Way, Swindon, Wilts, SN5 6PB
Activities: Production of electricity
Parent: RWE Generation UK PLC
Officers: Jason Anthony Keene, Secretary; Ian Robert Calvert [1965] Director/Chemical Engineer; Richard John Little [1968] Director/Power Station Manager; Rebecca Claire Wall [1968] Director/Financial Controller

Rygor Commercials Ltd
Incorporated: 8 February 1985 *Employees:* 615
Net Worth: £10,261,000 *Total Assets:* £87,733,000
Registered Office: The Broadway, West Wilts Trading Estate, Westbury, Wilts, BA13 4HU
Activities: Sale of other motor vehicles
Shareholders: Tim Stacey; Graham Andrew Drake; Paul Reed
Officers: Martyn Morant, Secretary; Graham Andrew Drake [1966] Director/Chartered Accountant; John Keogh [1977] Director/Sales [Irish]; Martyn Morant [1978] Director/Accountant; Paul Reed [1968] Director; Timothy Brian Stacey [1966] Director; Chris Taylor [1975] Director

Rygor Group Limited
Incorporated: 1 August 1968 *Employees:* 687
Net Worth: £10,333,000 *Total Assets:* £99,084,000
Registered Office: The Broadway, West Wilts Trading Estate, Westbury, Wilts, BA13 4JX
Activities: Other business support service activities n.e.c.
Shareholders: Tim Stacey; Graham Andrew Drake; Paul Reed
Officers: Martyn Morant, Secretary; Graham Andrew Drake [1966] Director/Chartered Accountant; Paul Reed [1968] Director; Timothy Brian Stacey [1966] Director; Bruce William Ward Whitfield [1954] Director

Rygor Group Services Limited
Incorporated: 11 February 1985 *Employees:* 38
Net Worth: £152,635 *Total Assets:* £3,719,878
Registered Office: The Broadway, West Wilts Trading Estate, Westbury, Wilts, BA13 4HU
Activities: Freight transport by road
Shareholders: Tim Stacey; Graham Andrew Drake; Paul Reed
Officers: Martyn Morant, Secretary; Graham Andrew Drake [1966] Director/Chartered Accountant; Paul Reed [1968] Director; Timothy Brian Stacey [1966] Finance Director

Rygor Holdings Limited
Incorporated: 18 February 2008 *Employees:* 687
Net Worth: £7,373,000 *Total Assets:* £101,284,000
Registered Office: The Broadway, West Wilts Trading Estate, Westbury, Wilts, BA13 4JX
Activities: Combined office administrative service activities
Shareholders: Tim Stacey; Paul Reed; Graham Andrew Drake
Officers: Martyn Morant, Secretary; Graham Andrew Drake [1966] Director/Accountant; Paul Reed [1968] Director; Timothy Brian Stacey [1966] Director/Chartered Accountant

S & B Property Limited
Incorporated: 5 January 1999 *Employees:* 63
Net Worth: £2,868,188 *Total Assets:* £3,869,558
Registered Office: Unit A, Princess Street, Bedminster, Bristol, BS3 4AG
Activities: Technical and vocational secondary education
Officers: Robin Douglas Cook [1961] Director; Stephen James Curtis [1950] Director/Self Employed; Anthony Donald Jolliffe [1942] Director/Consultant; Martyn Read [1954] Director

S G V M Holdings Limited
Incorporated: 1 June 2010
Net Worth: £3,908,381 *Total Assets:* £4,697,535
Registered Office: 61 MacRae Road, Pill, Bristol, BS20 0DD
Activities: Activities of head offices
Major Shareholder: Sidney Hodge
Officers: Elaine Evelyn Ford, Secretary; Elaine Evelyn Ford [1968] Director/School Teacher; Elinor Margaret Hodge [1970] Director/Nurse; Sidney Herbert Hodge [1940] Director

S W Group Logistics Limited
Incorporated: 25 July 1979 *Employees:* 164
Net Worth: £2,627,700 *Total Assets:* £6,101,738
Registered Office: Unit 6 Cheney Manor, Swindon, Wilts, SN2 2QJ
Activities: Freight transport by road
Major Shareholder: Pauline Knox
Officers: Pauline Knox, Secretary; Pauline Knox [1935] Director; Richard Ian Knox [1963] Director

S'Porter International Limited
Incorporated: 12 November 2009 *Employees:* 5
Net Worth: £4,463,229 *Total Assets:* £6,276,155
Registered Office: The Studios, GD International Business Village, Draycott, Moreton in Marsh, Glos, GL56 9JY
Activities: Wholesale of clothing and footwear
Officers: George William Davies [1941] Director/Retailer; Steven Harvey Goodwin [1970] Production Director; Emma Claire Trayner [1968] Director/Designer

S.C.C. Transport (Devizes) Limited
Incorporated: 19 June 1956 *Employees:* 6
Net Worth: £6,420,622 *Total Assets:* £6,938,352
Registered Office: Folly Road, Roundway, Devizes, Wilts, SN10 2HT
Activities: Other letting and operating of own or leased real estate
Officers: Mark Crook, Secretary; Mark Crook [1960] Director/Distribution Manager; Philip Howard Crook [1948] Director/Chartered Accountant

S.W.T Finance Limited
Incorporated: 22 November 1990 *Employees:* 5
Net Worth: £2,377,136 *Total Assets:* £4,262,125
Registered Office: Communications House, Moor Lane, Sowton, Exeter, Devon, EX2 7JF
Activities: Other business support service activities n.e.c.
Parent: South West Communications Group Holdings Limited
Officers: Sharon Marie Rowe, Secretary; Sarah Flowers [1965] Director; David Harry Langley [1963] Director/Administrator; Brian Lodge [1960] Director; Anthony George Edward Rowe [1948] Director; Jonathan Whiley [1968] Commercial Director

S2 Residential Limited
Incorporated: 21 July 2016
Net Worth: £340 *Total Assets:* £4,800,746
Registered Office: Unity Chambers, 34 High East Street, Dorchester, DT1 1HA
Activities: Buying and selling of own real estate
Shareholders: Simon Francis Crawley Ross Skinner; Armando Verissimo Zagalo de Lima
Officers: Armando Verissimo Zagalo de Lima [1958] Director [Portuguese]; Helena Sonia Azancot Korn [1961] Director [Portuguese]; Alexandra Sarah Henderson Ross Skinner [1963] Director; Simon Francis Crawley Ross Skinner [1963] Director

SAA Consultants Limited
Incorporated: 16 February 1988 *Employees:* 42
Net Worth: £10,926,595 *Total Assets:* £14,588,408
Registered Office: The Computer Complex, Somerset Place, Plymouth, PL3 4BB
Activities: Other software publishing
Major Shareholder: Alex Lochhead
Officers: Alex Lochhead [1951] Director/Computer Consultant

Saab Technologies UK Limited
Incorporated: 18 May 1983 *Employees:* 60
Net Worth: £3,352,423 *Total Assets:* £4,106,611
Registered Office: St Mary's House, Netherhampton, Salisbury, Wilts, SP2 8PU
Activities: Other service activities n.e.c.
Parent: Saab AB
Officers: Hans Magnus Lewis-Olsson [1964] Director/Head of Market Area EMEA for Saab [Swedish]; Maxwell Litton [1986] Director/Chief of Staff, MA Europe [Swedish/American]; Simon John Read [1976] Director of Public Safety UK; Jon Mortimer Robertson [1974] Managing Director; Andrew George Walton [1954] Director/Vice President, Head of Saab Country Unit UK; Robin Alastair Wild [1976] Director

Sabre Group Limited
Incorporated: 9 April 1986
Net Worth: £20,757,386 *Total Assets:* £27,689,720
Registered Office: 11 Witney Road, Nuffield Industrial Estate, Poole, Dorset, BH17 0GJ
Activities: Other letting and operating of own or leased real estate
Officers: Paul Anthony Freeman, Secretary; Andrew John Freeman [1964] Director; Paul Anthony Freeman [1960] Director; Thelma Dulcie Freeman [1931] Director

SACO Cannon Street Limited
Incorporated: 14 August 2014
Net Worth Deficit: £3,565,000 *Total Assets:* £35,968,000
Registered Office: 6th Floor, Embassy House, Queens Avenue, Bristol, BS8 1SB
Activities: Other letting and operating of own or leased real estate
Parent: Brookfield Asset Management Inc.
Officers: Laura Birte Brinkmann [1987] Director/Vice President [German]; Stephen McCall [1972] Director

SACO Group Holdings Limited
Incorporated: 23 January 2013 *Employees:* 294
Net Worth: £7,617,000 *Total Assets:* £55,488,000
Registered Office: 6th Floor, Embassy House, Queens Avenue, Clifton, Bristol, BS8 1SB
Activities: Activities of other holding companies n.e.c.
Parent: Brookfield Asset Management Inc.
Officers: Laura Birte Brinkmann [1987] Director/Vice President [German]; Stephen McCall [1972] Director

SACO The Serviced Apartment Company Limited
Incorporated: 18 May 2011 *Employees:* 294
Net Worth: £5,870,104 *Total Assets:* £14,835,715
Registered Office: 6th Floor, Embassy House, Queens Avenue, Clifton, Bristol, BS8 1SB
Activities: Hotels and similar accommodation
Officers: Laura Birte Brinkmann [1987] Director/Vice President [German]; Daniel Carre-Bishop [1982] Director/Accountant; James Bradley Hyler [1978] Managing Director [American]; Eric Jafari [1977] Managing Director [American]; Stephen McCall [1972] Director; Kevin O'Donnell McCrain [1979] Director/Senior Vice President [American]; Zachary Bryan Vaughan [1977] Director/Managing Partner [Canadian]

Sadborow Estate Limited
Incorporated: 5 April 1937
Net Worth: £4,055,497 *Total Assets:* £5,202,979
Registered Office: Centenary House, Peninsula Park, Rydon Lane, Exeter, EX2 7XE
Activities: Management of real estate on a fee or contract basis
Shareholders: Hamish John Bertram Eyre; Rachael Emma Young; James Alexander Walpole Eyre; Carol Ann Eyre; Charles George Samuel Eyre
Officers: Carol Ann Eyre, Secretary/Director; Carol Ann Eyre [1948] Director; Charles George Samuel Eyre [1948] Director/Chartered Surveyor

Saddleback Limited
Incorporated: 21 May 2004 *Employees:* 53
Net Worth: £5,569,697 *Total Assets:* £10,757,885
Registered Office: Unit 12 Armstrong Way, Yate, Bristol, BS37 5AH
Activities: Agents specialised in the sale of other particular products
Shareholders: Andrew James Wigmore; Sarah-Jane Wigmore
Officers: Richard Charles Mardle [1980] Director; Nicholas Mason [1979] Finance Director; Neil Michael Towns [1971] Commercial Director; Andrew Wigmore [1973] Director; Sarah Jane Wigmore [1972] Director

Sade Properties Ltd
Incorporated: 28 May 2014
Net Worth Deficit: £24,575 *Total Assets:* £4,409,057
Registered Office: 43 Horseshoe Way, Hempsted, Gloucester, GL2 5GD
Activities: Other letting and operating of own or leased real estate
Shareholders: Sativa Ltd; SHK Properties Ltd
Officers: Andrew David Bennion, Secretary; Andrew David Bennion [1968] Director; Simon Harry Shepherd [1965] Director; Edward Weeks [1946] Director; David Arthur Williams [1946] Director

SAFC Biosciences Limited
Incorporated: 1 May 1996
Net Worth: £21,250,000 *Total Assets:* £24,257,000
Registered Office: The Old Brickyard, New Road, Gillingham, Dorset, SP8 4XT
Activities: Manufacture of other chemical products n.e.c.
Parent: Sigma-Aldrich Company Limited
Officers: Peter Biro [1967] Director/US Certified Public Accountant [Dutch]; Victor Mark Jackson [1962] Director/Operations Manager

SAFC Hitech Limited
Incorporated: 7 October 1982 *Employees:* 1
Net Worth: £9,381,000 *Total Assets:* £9,549,000
Registered Office: The Old Brickyard, New Road, Gillingham, Dorset, SP8 4XT
Activities: Wholesale of chemical products
Parent: Epichem Group Limited
Officers: Peter Biro [1967] Director/US Certified Public Accountant [Dutch]; Dr Geoffrey James Irvine [1966] Director/VP Sales [New Zealander]

Safe House Holdings Limited
Incorporated: 28 January 2015 *Employees:* 376
Net Worth: £13,525,526 *Total Assets:* £26,987,136
Registered Office: 16 Queen Square, Bristol, BS1 4NT
Activities: Activities of other holding companies n.e.c.
Shareholders: Mark Robert Woodington; Peter James Hobbs
Officers: Mark Richard Sommers, Secretary; Peter James Hobbs [1980] Director; Mark Robert Woodington [1980] Director

Safran Landing Systems Services UK Ltd
Incorporated: 17 March 1998 *Employees:* 263
Previous: Messier Services Limited
Net Worth: £11,148,000 *Total Assets:* £39,220,000
Registered Office: Meteor Business Park, Cheltenham Road East, Gloucester, GL2 9QL
Activities: Repair and maintenance of aircraft and spacecraft
Officers: Andrew Glenn Devons, Secretary; Philippe Catte [1958] Customer Support Director [French]; Bruno Chiarelli [1962] Director [French]; Philippe Maurice Comminges [1959] Operations Director [French]; John Alan Doherty [1962] Sales Director; Jacques Frederic Pierre Lepont [1960] Director [French]; Sophie Lucienne Gisele Malbec [1962] Director [French]; Stephane Thomas Rollin [1976] Managing Director [French]; Christopher George Wilson [1956] Managing Director; Nigel Robert Woodford [1962] Director

Safran Landing Systems UK Ltd
Incorporated: 17 April 1998 *Employees:* 938
Previous: Messier-Dowty Limited
Net Worth: £213,371,008 *Total Assets:* £350,319,008
Registered Office: Cheltenham Road East, Gloucester, GL2 9QH
Activities: Manufacture of air and spacecraft and related machinery
Parent: Safran SA
Officers: Andrew Glenn Devons, Secretary; Olivier Blat [1968] Director/Chief Financial Officer [French]; Gilles Bouctot [1959] Director/Chief Executive Officer [French]; Darren Lee Waite [1967] Director/Vice President Customer Services; Christopher George Wilson [1956] Managing Director; Nigel Robert Woodford [1962] Director

Safran UK Limited
Incorporated: 15 October 1987 *Employees:* 53
Net Worth: £21,632,604 *Total Assets:* £23,573,292
Registered Office: Safran UK, Cheltenham Road East, Gloucester, GL2 9QH
Activities: Activities of head offices
Parent: Safran SA
Officers: Gaelle Claire Sylvie Beaud de Brive, Secretary; Adrian Paul Banks [1962] Director/Head of Shared Services; Pascal Joel Jacky Bantegnie [1968] Director/Group Treasurer [French]; Terence Patrick O'Brien [1974] Director/Chartered Accountant [Irish]

Sailport PLC
Incorporated: 22 May 1979 *Employees:* 23
Net Worth: £4,159,965 *Total Assets:* £5,298,254
Registered Office: 5th Floor, Salt Quay House, 4 North East Quay, Plymouth, PL4 0BN
Activities: Other amusement and recreation activities n.e.c.
Officers: John Shell, Secretary; Timothy James Banks [1948] Director/Retired; Charles Bush [1965] Managing Director; David Walpole Crouch [1946] Director/Retired; Robert Whitefield Shapland [1950] Director/Retired Banker; Robert Dudley Chanler West [1947] Director/Retired; Julie Ann Williams [1952] Director/Lecturer

Saint Augustine's Catholic College
Incorporated: 10 August 2011 *Employees:* 134
Net Worth: £4,455,820 *Total Assets:* £5,074,942
Registered Office: Saint Augustine's Catholic College, Wingfield Road, Trowbridge, Wilts, BA14 9EN
Activities: General secondary education
Officers: Sandra Pinner, Secretary; Simon Alford [1965] HR Director; Bernadette Mary Barrett-John [1961] Director/Retired; Joanne Angela Birkett-Wendes [1974] Director/Teacher; Jacqueline Bracey [1962] Director/Teacher; Christopher John Burton [1969] Director/Businessman; Christopher Patrick Crowther [1971] Consultant Director [Irish]; Eileen Farrell [1962] Director/Teaching Assistant; Thomas Finnegan [1965] Director/Priest [Irish]; David Forster [1969] Director/Headteacher; Cyril Norman Francis Kinsky [1954] Director/Retired Barrister; Jonathan Peter Knee [1978] Director/Manager; Richard John Laverty [1973] Director/Businessman; Sarah Louise Marshall [1969] Director/Solicitor; Jeremy McKenna [1962] Director/Retired; Katherine Anne Mines [1979] Director/Business Manager; Dr Jacqueline Patricia Papadopoulos [1961] Director/Teacher; Judith Ann Marie Starkey [1973] Director/Dentist

Salcombe Harbour Hotel Limited
Incorporated: 25 November 2009 *Employees:* 68
Net Worth: £4,134,333 *Total Assets:* £24,949,928
Registered Office: Harbour House, 60 Purewell, Christchurch, Dorset, BH23 1ES
Activities: Hotels and similar accommodation
Parent: Harbour Hotels Group Limited
Officers: Stuart Andrew Bateman [1976] Director; David Francis Robbins [1967] Finance Director; Michael Oliver Warren [1970] Director [Irish]

Salford Schools Solutions Holdco Limited
Incorporated: 15 June 2006
Net Worth Deficit: £6,063,266 *Total Assets:* £34,837,656
Registered Office: Third Floor, Broad Quay House, Prince Street, Bristol, BS1 4DJ
Activities: Activities of head offices
Shareholders: Equitix Infrastructure 5a Limited; Schools Capital Limited
Officers: Hannah Holman [1980] Director; Amit Rishi Jaysukh Thakrar [1987] Director; John Whittington [1960] Director; Philip Arthur Would [1971] Director

Salford Schools Solutions Limited
Incorporated: 15 June 2006
Net Worth Deficit: £6,063,266 *Total Assets:* £34,837,656
Registered Office: Third Floor, Broad Quay House, Prince Street, Bristol, BS1 4DJ
Activities: Activities of head offices
Parent: Salford Schools Solutions Holdco Limited
Officers: Hannah Holman [1980] Director; Amit Rishi Jaysukh Thakrar [1987] Director; John Whittington [1960] Director; Philip Arthur Would [1971] Director

Salisbury Diocesan Board of Education (The)
Incorporated: 4 February 1949 *Employees:* 23
Net Worth: £7,391,314 *Total Assets:* £7,806,628
Registered Office: The Diocesan Education Centre, The Avenue, Wilton, Wilts, SP2 0FG
Activities: Educational support services
Officers: Giles Pugh, Secretary; Michael Antram [1969] Director/Headteacher; Amanda Lisa Aze [1969] Director/Headteacher; Timothy Peter Balmforth [1954] Director/Consultant; Noel Harrison [1961] Director/Consultant; The Venerable Anthony Charles MacRow-Wood [1960] Director/Archdeacon; David Christopher Pain [1966] Director/Diocesan Secretary; Margaret Dylys Pearson [1952] Director/Management Consultant; Nigel Ieuan Rees [1956] Director/Retired; Iain McIntosh Stevenson [1954] Director/Retired; Revd Jonathan Paul Triffitt [1974] Director/Priest; Canon Joy Sheridan Tubbs [1958] Director of Education

Salisbury Diocesan Board of Finance (The)
Incorporated: 24 October 1882 *Employees:* 39
Net Worth: £123,696,000 *Total Assets:* £128,447,000
Registered Office: Church House, Crane Street, Salisbury, Wilts, SP1 2QB
Activities: Activities of religious organisations
Officers: Lucinda Jane Denise Herklots, Secretary; The Rev David Baldwin [1957] Director/Vicar; Richard Ogilvie Merlott Chitty [1962] Director/HM Forces; Gillian Clarke [1947] Director/Retired; Rosemary Karen Veronica Cook [1959] Director/Solicitor; Karen Marisa Gorham [1964] Director/Bishop; Susan Anne Groom [1963] Director/Archdeacon; The Rt Rev Nicholas Roderick Holtam [1954] Director/Bishop; Derek Parker Howshall [1948] Director/Retired; Janet Jackson [1939] Director/Chair of Governors; The Venerable Alan Jeans [1958] Director/Archdeacon of Sarum; Rev Antony Charles MacRow-Wood [1960] Director/Clerk in Holy Orders; Debrah Agnes McIsaac [1953] Director/Consultant; Margaret Morrissey [1943] Director/Retired; Elena Oderstone [1974] Director [Latvian]; Nicholas Charles Papadopulos [1966] Director/Dean; Revd Canon Andrew Nicholas Perry [1962] Director/Clerk in Holy Orders; Canon Paul Richardson [1958] Director/Canon; Nigel Peter Geoffrey Salisbury [1958] Director/Insurance Broker; Canon Thomas Mark Bews Woodhouse [1966] Director/Clerk in Holy Orders

Salisbury Glass Centre Limited
Incorporated: 4 May 1976 *Employees:* 162
Net Worth: £8,355,066 *Total Assets:* £11,387,031
Registered Office: Salisbury Glass Centre, Newton Road, Churchfields, Salisbury, Wilts, SP2 7QA
Activities: Glazing
Parent: Salisbury Glass Holdings Limited
Officers: Julie Gower, Secretary; Mark Seaward Gower [1960] Director/Glazier; Christopher Grigg [1961] Director; David William Hammond Naish [1966] Director; Ian Paton [1970] Director

Salisbury Glass Holdings Limited
Incorporated: 8 September 2005 *Employees:* 162
Net Worth: £4,359,025 *Total Assets:* £7,391,990
Registered Office: Salisbury Glass Centre, Newton Road, Churchfields, Salisbury, Wilts, SP2 7QA
Activities: Activities of head offices
Shareholders: Mark Seaward Gower; Julie Gower
Officers: Julie Gower, Secretary; Mark Seaward Gower [1960] Director; Christopher Grigg [1961] Director; David William Hammond Naish [1966] Director; Ian Paton [1970] Director

David Salisbury Joinery Limited
Incorporated: 12 April 1995 *Employees:* 130
Net Worth: £636,062 *Total Assets:* £5,638,699
Registered Office: Bennett Road, Isleport Business Park, Highbridge, Somerset, TA9 4PW
Activities: Manufacture of other builders' carpentry and joinery
Major Shareholder: David John Salisbury
Officers: Catherine Anne Salisbury, Secretary; Karen Bell Hutt [1968] Sales Director; Patrick David Clunie [1965] Finance Director; Wes James Kangurs [1976] Commercial Director; David John Salisbury [1950] Managing Director

Salisbury Plain Academies
Incorporated: 5 May 2016 *Employees:* 233
Net Worth: £7,197,804 *Total Assets:* £10,285,515
Registered Office: Avon Valley College, Durrington, Salisbury, Wilts, SP4 8HH
Activities: Pre-primary education
Officers: Rachel Diane Ure, Secretary; Nigel Charles Beckett [1966] Director/Chief Financial Officer; Amba Chawla [1964] Director/Solicitor; Jane Elizabeth MacKay [1964] Director/Student; John Lloyd Nutt [1951] Director/Chartered Engineer; David Charles Powell [1958] Director/Retired; Angela Joan Reeves [1952] Director; Clare Tunnicliffe [1963] Director/Management Consultant

Salisbury Trading Limited
Incorporated: 11 September 2008 *Employees:* 72
Net Worth: £544,257 *Total Assets:* £3,778,698
Registered Office: Finance Department, Salisbury District Hospital, Odstock Road, Salisbury, Wilts, SP2 8BJ
Activities: Other cleaning services
Parent: Salisbury NHS Foundation Trust
Officers: Ronald Stephen Burrows [1943] Non-Executive Director Chairman; Lisa Jane Hayes [1978] Director/Accountant; Kevin John Newton [1953] Managing Director [New Zealander]; David Roger Taylor [1953] Director/Accountant

Salterns Marina Limited
Incorporated: 9 July 1969 *Employees:* 81
Net Worth: £2,529,060 *Total Assets:* £10,308,996
Registered Office: Midland House, 2 Poole Road, Bournemouth, BH2 5QY
Activities: Retail sale of sports goods, fishing gear, camping goods, boats and bicycles
Shareholders: Martyn Kenneth Smith; Stuart Barry Quin; William Jackson-Moore
Officers: Mark Mandy, Secretary; Martin Richard Bizzell [1960] Director/Engineer; Jonathan Eads [1962] Director; Mark Stuart Mandy [1983] Director/Accountant; John Nicholas Jackson Smith [1954] Director/Marina Management; Nicholas John Jackson Smith [1980] Director/Manager

Salum Properties Limited
Incorporated: 27 November 1997
Net Worth: £5,151,862 *Total Assets:* £17,968,806
Registered Office: Midland House, 2 Poole Road, Bournemouth, BH2 5QY
Activities: Management of real estate on a fee or contract basis
Shareholder: Richard John Clough
Officers: Richard John Clough, Secretary; Jeremy Edward Clough [1983] Director; Margaret Roselyne Clough [1943] Director; Dr Rachel Elizabeth Clough [1980] Director/Doctor; Richard John Clough [1945] Director/Solicitor

Samara Investments (2000) Limited
Incorporated: 27 March 2000
Net Worth: £2,745,348 *Total Assets:* £8,928,216
Registered Office: Office 2, Queens Gate, Jetty Marsh Road, Newton Abbot, Devon, TQ12 2SL
Activities: Development of building projects
Major Shareholder: Ralph Brown
Officers: Ralph Brown, Secretary/Director; Ralph Brown [1964] Director; Victoria Brown [1970] Director

Samara Investments Limited
Incorporated: 17 October 1996 *Employees:* 1
Net Worth: £4,484,011 *Total Assets:* £5,395,522
Registered Office: Office 1, Queens Gate, Jetty Marsh Road, Newton Abbot, Devon, TQ12 2SL
Activities: Development of building projects
Shareholders: Ralph Brown; Sarah Antoinette Laura Wright
Officers: Ralph Brown, Secretary/Director; Marjorie Brown [1932] Director; Ralph Brown [1964] Director; Sarah Antoinette Laura Wright [1963] Director

Samatt (Group Services) Limited
Incorporated: 20 February 2004 *Employees:* 11
Net Worth: £107,829 *Total Assets:* £8,488,610
Registered Office: c/o The Devonshire Hotel Ltd, Parkhill Road, Torquay, Devon, TQ1 2DY
Activities: Activities of head offices
Major Shareholder: Jeanne Wilson
Officers: Gary Moss, Secretary; George Antony Brown [1965] Director/Finance; Gary Moss [1952] Director/Group Services; Jeanne Rose Wilson [1946] Director

Samatt Limited
Incorporated: 6 September 1983 *Employees:* 2
Net Worth: £2,027,108 *Total Assets:* £13,090,139
Registered Office: c/o The Devonshire Hotel, Park Hill Road, Torquay, Devon, TQ1 2DY
Activities: Activities of head offices
Major Shareholder: Jeanne Wilson
Officers: Jeanne Rose Wilson, Secretary; George Antony Brown [1965] Director/Finance; Jeanne Rose Wilson [1946] Director/Hotelier

Sanctus Group Holdings Limited
Incorporated: 20 December 2016 *Employees:* 10
Net Worth: £2,344,907 *Total Assets:* £3,515,161
Registered Office: Sanctus House, Sperry Way, Stonehouse, Glos, GL10 3UT
Activities: Activities of head offices
Major Shareholder: Peter Alexander Cooke
Officers: Peter Alexander Cooke [1964] Director; Shaun Edward Tolfree [1979] Director

Sanctus Limited
Incorporated: 3 September 2003 *Employees:* 31
Net Worth: £2,262,996 *Total Assets:* £4,412,102
Registered Office: Sanctus House, The Waterfront, Stonehouse Park, Stonehouse, Glos, GL10 3UT
Activities: Remediation activities and other waste management services
Parent: Sanctus Group Holding Limited
Officers: Peter Alexander Cooke, Secretary; Peter Alexander Cooke [1964] Director; Shaun Edward Tolfree [1979] Director

Sandbanks Hotel Limited
Incorporated: 3 November 1955 *Employees:* 301
Net Worth: £26,245,700 *Total Assets:* £41,476,100
Registered Office: 6th Floor, Dean Park House, 8-10 Dean Park Crescent, Bournemouth, BH1 1HP
Activities: Hotels and similar accommodation
Parent: FJB Hotels Limited
Officers: Joy Wanda Eva Barcellos, Secretary; Eva Jean Adlem [1931] Director; Joy Wanda Eva Barcellos [1953] Director; John Godfrey Julius Butterworth [1946] Director

Sanderson Contract Management Limited
Incorporated: 13 September 1995 *Employees:* 2
Net Worth: £739,000 *Total Assets:* £11,373,000
Registered Office: First Floor, Clifton Down House, 54a Whiteladies Road, Clifton, Bristol, BS8 2NH
Activities: Other activities of employment placement agencies
Shareholders: Resource Solutions Group PLC; Keith William Dawe
Officers: Anya Louise Burton, Secretary; Keith William Dawe [1950] Director; Neil Martin Edward Pollinger [1957] Director/Accountant

Sanderson Government and Defence Limited
Incorporated: 26 September 2002 *Employees:* 8
Net Worth: £3,848,000 *Total Assets:* £6,132,000
Registered Office: First Floor, Clifton Down House, 54a Whiteladies Road, Clfifton, Bristol, BS8 2NH
Activities: Other activities of employment placement agencies
Parent: Resource Solutions Group PLC
Officers: Anya Louise Burton, Secretary; Keith William Dawe [1950] Director; Martin William Griffiths [1960] Director; Nicholas Walrond [1971] Director/Account Manager

Sanderson Recruitment PLC
Incorporated: 14 April 1994 *Employees:* 66
Net Worth: £18,741,000 *Total Assets:* £35,468,000
Registered Office: First Floor, Clifton Down House, 54a, Whiteladies Road, Bristol, BS8 2NH
Activities: Other activities of employment placement agencies
Parent: Resource Solutions Group PLC
Officers: Anya Louise Burton, Secretary; Jonathan Peter Ball [1975] Director; Wiliam Thomas Boney [1978] Director/Head of Contract Delivery; Keith William Dawe [1950] Director

Sandown Dorset and Wiltshire Limited
Incorporated: 27 October 1993 *Employees:* 229
Net Worth: £9,093,000 *Total Assets:* £40,360,000
Registered Office: 1 Holes Bay Road, Poole, Dorset, BH15 2BD
Activities: Sale of new cars and light motor vehicles
Parent: Selanac Holdings Limited
Officers: Gareth Robert Copling, Secretary; Gareth Robert Copling [1967] Director/Accountant; Gavin Alan McAllister [1981] Director

Sandown Motors Limited
Incorporated: 20 August 2013 *Employees:* 430
Net Worth: £12,324,000 *Total Assets:* £89,709,000
Registered Office: Mercedes-Benz of Poole, Holes Bay Road, Poole, Dorset, BH15 2BD
Activities: Sale of new cars and light motor vehicles
Parent: Selanac Holdings Limited
Officers: Gareth Robert Copling [1967] Director/Accountant; Gavin Alan McAllister [1961] Director [South African]

Sandpalm Properties Limited
Incorporated: 24 May 1989 *Employees:* 4
Net Worth: £3,354,417 *Total Assets:* £6,640,136
Registered Office: 3 Milner Road, Westcliff, Bournemouth, BH4 8AD
Activities: Buying and selling of own real estate
Shareholders: Linda Ann Scott; Roger James Scott
Officers: Linda Ann Scott, Secretary; Linda Ann Scott [1952] Director/Company Secretary; Roger James Scott [1949] Director/Property Developer

Sandroyd School Trust Limited
Incorporated: 30 July 1955 *Employees:* 78
Net Worth: £4,007,856 *Total Assets:* £8,194,468
Registered Office: Windover House, St Ann Street, Salisbury, Wilts, SP1 2DR
Activities: Primary education
Officers: Christopher Joseph Stewart, Secretary; Simon William Theodore Barber [1970] Director/Headmaster; Jaideep Mahendrakumar Barot [1974] Director/Teacher; Hannah Bell [1971] Director/Housewife; Peter John Castleman Bourke [1967] Director/Solicitor; Elizabeth Brierley [1965] Director/Chartered Accountant; Emma Elizabeth Ann McKendrick [1963] Director/Headmistress; Charles Senff McVeigh III [1942] Director; Laura Miles [1970] Director/Housewife; Oliver Hugh Stanley [1959] Director/Executive; Rhodri Glyn Lougher Thomas [1970] Director/Chartered Surveyor; George William Whitefield [1983] Director; Felicity Anne Wilson [1971] Director/Author; Philippa Louise Zingg [1969] Marketing Director

Sands Resort Hotel Limited
Incorporated: 6 February 2003 *Employees:* 84
Net Worth: £3,720,583 *Total Assets:* £4,336,162
Registered Office: Sands Resort, Watergate Road, Porth, Cornwall, TR7 3LX
Activities: Hotels and similar accommodation
Shareholders: David Nicholas Malcolm; Susan Hodges
Officers: Matthew Dean Liddicoat, Secretary; Susan Hodges [1952] Director/Landscape Architect; Matthew Dean Liddicoat [1976] Director/Accountant; David Nicholas Malcolm [1953] Director/Hotelier; Thomas Malcolm [1984] Director/Hotel Manager; Robert James Waghorn [1959] Director/Business Consultant

Sanlam Investment Holdings UK Limited
Incorporated: 17 October 2011
Net Worth: £172,790,800 *Total Assets:* £173,142,080
Registered Office: St Bartholomew's House, Lewins Mead, Bristol, BS1 2NH
Activities: Activities of financial services holding companies
Officers: Jeremy Paul Gibson, Secretary; Jeremy Paul Gibson [1973] Finance Director; Paul Brendan Hanratty [1961] Director/Actuary [Irish]; Veronica Susan Oak [1961] Director; Ian Plenderleith [1943] Director/Banker; Jonathan Charles Polin [1959] Director; Robert Roux [1964] Director/Chief Operating Officer [South African]; James Anthony Angus Samuels [1950] Director; Thomas Fritz Van Heerden [1965] Director/Chief Operating Officer [South African]; Hugh Roderick Ward [1952] Director

Sanlam Life & Pensions UK Limited
Incorporated: 20 May 1970
Net Worth: £33,760,000 *Total Assets:* £2,799,240,960
Registered Office: St Bartholomews House, Lewins Mead, Bristol, BS1 2NH
Activities: Life insurance
Parent: Sanlam UK Limited
Officers: Juliet Mary Warren, Secretary; Jeremy Paul Gibson [1973] Director/Chartered Accountant; Paul Brendan Hanratty [1961] Director/Actuary [Irish]; Barry Stephen Laggar [1975] Director/Actuary [South African]; Nicholas Allen Parry [1962] Director/Actuary; Jonathan Charles Polin [1959] Director; James Anthony Angus Samuels [1950] Director

Sanlam UK Limited
Incorporated: 24 April 2008
Net Worth: £134,572,992 *Total Assets:* £148,436,768
Registered Office: St Bartholomews House, Lewins Mead, Bristol, BS1 2NH
Activities: Activities of head offices
Parent: Sanlam Investment Holdings UK Limited
Officers: Jeremy Paul Gibson, Secretary; Jeremy Paul Gibson [1973] Director/Chartered Accountant; Jonathan Charles Polin [1959] Director

Sanlam Wealth Planning Holdings UK Limited
Incorporated: 24 November 1999
Net Worth Deficit: £2,793,604 *Total Assets:* £10,220,466
Registered Office: St Bartholomews House, Lewins Mead, Bristol, BS1 2NH
Activities: Activities of financial services holding companies
Parent: Sanlam UK Limited
Officers: Jeremy Paul Gibson, Secretary; Jeremy Paul Gibson [1973] Finance Director; David John Mason [1971] Director; Alex James Ford Morley [1967] Director; Jonathan Charles Polin [1959] Director; John David White [1966] Director

Sanlam Wealth Planning UK Limited
Incorporated: 19 November 1999 *Employees:* 72
Net Worth: £1,664,368 *Total Assets:* £6,512,490
Registered Office: St Bartholomew's House, Lewins Mead, Bristol, BS1 2NH
Activities: Financial intermediation not elsewhere classified
Parent: Sanlam Wealth Planning Holdings UK Limited
Officers: Jeremy Paul Gibson, Secretary; Jeremy Paul Gibson [1973] Director/Chartered Accountant; David John Mason [1971] Director; Alex James Ford Morley [1967] Director; Jonathan Charles Polin [1959] Director; John David White [1966] Director

Sanoh UK Manufacturing Limited
Incorporated: 3 May 1991 *Employees:* 309
Net Worth: £12,583,000 *Total Assets:* £18,170,000
Registered Office: Grandeur Point, Fourth Way, Avonmouth, Bristol, BS11 8DL
Activities: Manufacture of other parts and accessories for motor vehicles
Officers: Russell Hill, Secretary; Paul Kenneth Davis [1964] Director; Richard Filer [1966] Operations Director; Russell Hill [1981] Director/Chartered Accountant; Masaomi Masuda [1974] Director/Certified Public Accountant [Japanese]; Kaoru Oyama [1961] Director [Japanese]; Munetoshi Sasaki [1978] Director [Japanese]

Sarkis Limited
Incorporated: 24 May 2013 *Employees:* 3
Net Worth: £6,293,106 *Total Assets:* £7,115,091
Registered Office: Chute Forest Farm House, Chute Forest, Andover, Hants, SP11 9DQ
Activities: Fund management activities
Major Shareholder: Alex Geoffrey Thistlethwayte
Officers: Neil Ashley Rothwell [1965] Director/Oil Trader; Alex Geoffrey Thistlethwayte [1967] Director/Energy Trader

Sarsen Stone Group Limited
Incorporated: 21 April 2011 *Employees:* 54
Net Worth: £1,970,326 *Total Assets:* £4,409,159
Registered Office: Stonebridge House, Nursteed Road, Devizes, Wilts, SN10 3DY
Activities: Floor and wall covering
Parent: Sarsen Group Holdings Limited
Officers: Michael John Dible [1965] Sales Director; Hamish Stuart Smith [1979] Creative & Marketing Director; Marcus Richard Smith [1975] Director

Sartorius Stedim Lab Limited
Incorporated: 17 July 1992 *Employees:* 113
Net Worth: £6,178,790 *Total Assets:* £12,633,328
Registered Office: Sperry Way, Stonehouse Park, Stonehouse, Glos, GL10 3UT
Activities: Manufacture of other plastic products
Parent: Sartorius Stedim Biotech SA
Officers: Purification Perez West, Secretary; Christopher Richard Biddell [1960] Director; Dr Joachim Kreuzburg [1965] Director [German]; Dr Ralf Lausch [1966] Director/Vice President of R&D [German]; Volker Niebel [1956] Director/Operations Manager [German]

Sarum Properties Limited
Incorporated: 16 November 1987 *Employees:* 5
Net Worth: £9,373,820 *Total Assets:* £14,096,172
Registered Office: 14 Wilton Road, Salisbury, Wilts, SP2 7EE
Activities: Management of real estate on a fee or contract basis
Parent: Elmbirch Properties PLC
Officers: Colin Lewis Chandler, Secretary; Colin Lewis Chandler [1946] Director; Tamara Jon Folkesson [1967] Director

SAS (Dorset & Somerset) Limited
Incorporated: 14 September 2016
Net Worth: £1 *Total Assets:* £6,881,720
Registered Office: Gloucestershire Airport, Staverton, Cheltenham, Glos, GL51 6SS
Activities: Service activities incidental to air transportation
Parent: Specialist Aviation Services Limited
Officers: Antonius Henricus Peter Maria Schal Schaeken [1958] Director [Dutch]; Stuart David Anthony Tozer [1981] Finance Director

Satnam Investments Limited
Incorporated: 9 October 1981 *Employees:* 13
Net Worth Deficit: £470,093 *Total Assets:* £19,395,696
Registered Office: 17 Imperial Square, Cheltenham, Glos, GL50 1QZ
Activities: Development of building projects
Officers: John Frederick Staite, Secretary; Jacqueline Dhillon [1951] Director; Kuldip Singh Dhillon [1950] Director; Satnam Singh Dhillon [1977] Director; Colin Griffiths [1963] Director/Chartered Town Planner; John Frederick Staite [1948] Director/Chartered Accountant

Satnam Limited
Incorporated: 11 December 1984
Net Worth: £8,531,949 *Total Assets:* £11,358,004
Registered Office: 17 Imperial Square, Cheltenham, Glos, GL50 1QZ
Activities: Other letting and operating of own or leased real estate
Parent: Satnam Investments Limited
Officers: John Frederick Staite, Secretary; Kuldip Singh Dhillon [1950] Director; John Frederick Staite [1948] Director/Accountant

Charles Saunders Holdings Limited
Incorporated: 22 August 2007 *Employees:* 119
Net Worth: £3,151,889 *Total Assets:* £9,523,463
Registered Office: Charles Saunders Ltd, Armstrong Way, Great Western Business Park, Yate, Glos, BS37 5NG
Activities: Activities of other holding companies n.e.c.
Major Shareholder: Darren Oliver Gaulton
Officers: Suzanne Gaulton, Secretary/Bank Worker; Darren Oliver Gaulton [1971] Director/Company Manager

T A Saunders Investments LLP
Incorporated: 12 September 2006
Net Worth: £3,654,996 *Total Assets:* £5,269,443
Registered Office: 14 Cowley Road, Nuffield Industrial Estate, Poole, Dorset, BH17 0UJ
Officers: Pamela Ann Regan [1954] Member; Jonathan James Saunders [1976] Member; Timothy Alan Saunders [1950] Member

J.J. Saunders Limited
Incorporated: 2 April 1969 *Employees:* 5
Net Worth: £3,748,870 *Total Assets:* £6,150,557
Registered Office: Old Down Farm, Emborough, Radstock, Somerset, BA3 4SA
Activities: Other letting and operating of own or leased real estate
Shareholders: Morgan John Saunders; Ian Jeffrey Saunders; James Edwin Saunders
Officers: Morgan John Saunders, Secretary; Ian Jeffrey Saunders [1963] Director/Farmer; Morgan John Saunders [1965] Director/Farmer

Charles Saunders Limited
Incorporated: 20 August 1981 *Employees:* 119
Net Worth: £4,364,172 *Total Assets:* £10,735,747
Registered Office: Charles Saunders Ltd, Armstrong Way, Great Western Business Park, Yate, Glos, BS37 5NG
Activities: Wholesale of other food, including fish, crustaceans and molluscs
Major Shareholder: Darren Oliver Gaulton
Officers: Suzanne Gaulton, Secretary/Bank Worker; Darren Oliver Gaulton [1971] Director/Company Manager

Savencia Fromage & Dairy UK Ltd
Incorporated: 6 January 1958 *Employees:* 84
Previous: ULN (UK) Limited
Net Worth: £7,560,000 *Total Assets:* £23,889,000
Registered Office: The Ham, Westbury, Wilts, BA13 4HA
Activities: Wholesale of dairy products, eggs and edible oils and fats
Parent: SFD Europarticipations B.V.
Officers: Philippe Marie, Secretary; Jerome Andre Coutant [1960] Director/Business Executive [French]; Francois Wolfovski [1958] Director [French]

A. L. Sayers (Holbeton) Limited
Incorporated: 14 April 1960
Net Worth: £4,034,033 *Total Assets:* £9,778,207
Registered Office: Carswell, Holbeton, Plymouth, PL8 1HH
Activities: Raising of dairy cattle
Major Shareholder: Geoffrey Spencer Sayers
Officers: Zoe Clare Sayers, Secretary; Geoffery Spencer Sayers [1965] Director/Farmer; Zoe Clare Sayers [1968] Director

SB Holdings (Exeter) Limited
Incorporated: 21 December 2004
Net Worth: £1,760,369 *Total Assets:* £3,722,586
Registered Office: Michael House, Castle Street, Exeter, EX4 3LQ
Activities: Other letting and operating of own or leased real estate
Shareholders: Sheila Rose Charlton; Terence Arthur Clifford Charlton
Officers: Martyn Paul Charlton, Secretary; Martyn Paul Charlton [1955] Managing Director; Nicholas Terence Charlton [1962] Director; Sheila Rose Charlton [1936] Director; Terence Arthur Clifford Charlton [1936] Director; Timothy Sean Charlton [1968] Finance Director; Katrina Jones [1958] Director

SBS International Holdings Limited
Incorporated: 31 May 2000 *Employees:* 2
Net Worth: £16,132,820 *Total Assets:* £21,690,560
Registered Office: 1690 Park Avenue, Aztec West, Almondsbury, Bristol, BS32 4RA
Activities: Activities of head offices
Parent: Smartstream Technologies Holdings Limited
Officers: Claudia Giunta, Secretary; Richard Bowler [1973] Director/Chief Financial Officer; Stephen Paul Thomas [1971] Director/Accountant

SC Group-Global Limited
Incorporated: 4 April 2012 *Employees:* 214
Previous: Supacat Group Limited
Net Worth: £16,914,964 *Total Assets:* £32,322,148
Registered Office: The Airfield, Dunkeswell Airfield, Honiton, Devon, EX14 4LF
Activities: Activities of head offices
Shareholders: Roger Simon Nicholas Ames; Nicholas Laurence Jones
Officers: Alan Shaun Mitchell, Secretary; Roger Simon Nicholas Ames [1966] Director; Elizabeth Mary Jones [1977] Director; Nicholas Laurence Jones [1942] Director/Engineer; Alan Shaun Mitchell [1966] Director; Robert Harry Talbot Rice [1963] Director

SCA Group Limited
Incorporated: 20 December 1999 *Employees:* 157
Net Worth: £1,342,768 *Total Assets:* £8,052,173
Registered Office: 7 Crane Way, Woolsbridge Industrial Park, Wimborne, Dorset, BH21 6FA
Activities: Repair and maintenance of ships and boats
Major Shareholder: Stephen Anthony King
Officers: Graham Beaton [1975] Finance Director; Lee Robin Stuart Bennett [1971] Director; Stephen Anthony King [1960] Director

J Scadding & Son Property Limited
Incorporated: 5 April 1911
Net Worth: £3,509,609 *Total Assets:* £4,062,452
Registered Office: Eugene Street, St Judes, Bristol, BS5 0TW
Activities: Other letting and operating of own or leased real estate
Officers: Bryony Elizabeth Whitlock, Secretary; Christopher John Hunt [1940] Director/Chartered Civil Structural; Mary Ann Scadding [1951] Director/Administrator; Peter Graham Scadding [1960] Director/Timber Merchant; Bryony Elizabeth Whitlock [1962] Director and Company Secretary

Scarlet Hotel Limited
Incorporated: 30 April 2003
Net Worth: £1,478,051 *Total Assets:* £15,098,242
Registered Office: Tredragon Road, Mawgan Porth, Cornwall, TR8 4DJ
Activities: Hotels and similar accommodation
Parent: Red Hotels Limited
Officers: Emma Stratton [1966] Director; Robert James Waghorn [1959] Director; Rebecca Whittington [1968] Director

SCC (Holdings) Limited
Incorporated: 27 January 2015 *Employees:* 92
Net Worth: £421,919 *Total Assets:* £4,719,065
Registered Office: Centenary House, Peninsula Park, Rydon Lane, Exeter, EX2 7XE
Activities: Activities of other holding companies n.e.c.
Major Shareholder: Nigel David Burke
Officers: Nigel David Burke [1952] Director/Dealer Principal

SCES Property Ltd
Incorporated: 17 February 2017 *Employees:* 2
Net Worth: £9,439,983 *Total Assets:* £10,508,968
Registered Office: Swampton Farm, St Mary Bourne, Andover, Hants, SP11 6EW
Activities: Other letting and operating of own or leased real estate
Shareholders: Linda MacKenzie; Lesley Carole Jeffery
Officers: Lesley Carole Jeffery [1957] Director/Farmer; Linda MacKenzie [1961] Director/Lettings Manager

Schyde Investments Limited
Incorporated: 10 January 2005 *Employees:* 11
Net Worth: £9,433,903 *Total Assets:* £24,804,256
Registered Office: Royal Mews, St Georges Place, Cheltenham, Glos, GL50 3PQ
Activities: Other letting and operating of own or leased real estate
Officers: Benjamin Lander, Secretary; Nathanael Nabil Bouris [1958] Director [Greek]; Michael Thomas Robert Edmund [1970] Director/Quantity Surveyor; Reginald Dean Hyde [1962] Director

Scisys UK Holding Ltd
Incorporated: 29 August 1997 *Employees:* 559
Previous: Scisys UK Holding PLC
Net Worth: £25,714,000 *Total Assets:* £60,672,000
Registered Office: Methuen Park, Chippenham, Wilts, SN14 0GB
Activities: Business and domestic software development
Parent: Scisys Group PLC
Officers: Natasha Louise Laird, Secretary; Stephen Brignall [1955] Director/Software Engineer; Christopher Andrew Cheetham [1959] Director/Accountant; Klaus Martin Heidrich [1960] Director [German]; David Rodney Jones [1952] Director; Dr Klaus Gunter Meng [1959] Director [German]

Scisys UK Limited
Incorporated: 14 February 2002 *Employees:* 237
Net Worth: £7,512,067 *Total Assets:* £16,136,292
Registered Office: Methuen Park, Chippenham, Wilts, SN14 0GB
Activities: Business and domestic software development
Parent: Scisys PLC
Officers: Natasha Louise Laird, Secretary; Stephen Brignall [1955] Director; Christopher Andrew Cheetham [1959] Director; David Gawthorpe [1963] Director

Scoliosis SOS Limited
Incorporated: 26 May 2005 *Employees:* 15
Net Worth: £2,264,026 *Total Assets:* £4,207,022
Registered Office: 50 The Terrace, Torquay, Devon, TQ1 1DD
Activities: Specialists medical practice activities
Shareholders: Erika Maude; Jane Maude
Officers: Jane Maude, Secretary; Erika Maude [1986] Director; Jane Maude [1946] Director

Scorribanda Holdings Limited
Incorporated: 7 May 2002
Net Worth: £1 *Total Assets:* £6,586,020
Registered Office: Ladyswood House, Sherston, Malmesbury, Wilts, SN16 0LA
Activities: Activities of head offices
Major Shareholder: Rory James Wordsworth Sweet
Officers: Serena Holdsworth, Secretary; Rory James Wordsworth Sweet [1967] Director/Chairman

Scot Group Limited
Incorporated: 5 June 1979 *Employees:* 1,437
Net Worth: £119,185,000 *Total Assets:* £507,384,992
Registered Office: Scot House, Matford Park Road, Marsh Barton Trading Estate, Exeter, EX2 8AW
Activities: Renting and leasing of cars and light motor vehicles
Parent: Scot Group Holdings Ltd
Officers: Roger Owen Hancock [1965] Sales and Operations Director; Christopher James Hume [1973] Financial Director; Nigel Clive Spokes [1960] Managing Director; Martin Wilson [1970] Managing Director

Scot Group Southern Limited
Incorporated: 18 January 1999 *Employees:* 1,437
Net Worth: £124,850,000 *Total Assets:* £510,403,008
Registered Office: Scot House, Matford Park Road, Marsh Barton Trading Estate, Exeter, EX2 8AW
Activities: Activities of head offices
Parent: Highcliffe Holdings Limited
Officers: Roger Owen Hancock [1965] Managing Director; Christopher James Hume [1973] Financial Director; Nigel Clive Spokes [1960] Director/Chairman; Martin Wilson [1970] Managing Director

Scotch Corner Richmond LLP
Incorporated: 24 April 2013
Net Worth: £83,665 *Total Assets:* £5,924,102
Registered Office: Manor Stables, Corsley, Warminster, Wilts, BA12 7QE
Officers: Peter Joseph Mullen [1955] Member; Simon William Waterfield [1960] Member

Scotsgrove Holdings Limited
Incorporated: 18 January 1967 *Employees:* 5
Net Worth: £27,153,330 *Total Assets:* £48,132,616
Registered Office: Mary Street House, Mary Street, Taunton, Somerset, TA1 3NW
Activities: Other letting and operating of own or leased real estate
Officers: Brian Edward Haimes, Secretary; Alistair Edward Charles Haimes [1975] Director; Ann Haimes [1938] Director; Brian Edward Haimes [1938] Director; Eliot Brian Arthur Haimes [1977] Director/Surveyor

The Scott-Law Properties LLP
Incorporated: 22 March 2002
Net Worth: £3,225,228 *Total Assets:* £4,356,143
Registered Office: Scott-Law House, Lynch Road Business Park, Berkeley, Glos, GL13 9TA
Officers: Christine Joan Gloria Scott [1963] Member; Timothy Nicholas Scott [1961] Member

Scottish Widows Unit Trust Managers Limited
Incorporated: 19 April 1982
Net Worth: £101,838,000 *Total Assets:* £197,268,000
Registered Office: Charlton Place, Andover, Hants, SP10 1RE
Activities: Financial intermediation not elsewhere classified
Parent: Scottish Widows Limited
Officers: Christina Ann Hankin, Secretary; Catriona Margaret Herd [1965] UK Propositions Director, Longstanding LP&I, Insurance; Sean William Lowther [1960] Director; Gavin MacNeill Stewart [1959] Director

Scotts Limited
Incorporated: 12 October 1990 *Employees:* 255
Net Worth: £4,719,000 *Total Assets:* £17,115,000
Registered Office: Cotswold House, 1 Crompton Road, Groundwell, Swindon, Wilts, SN25 5AW
Activities: Retail sale via mail order houses or via Internet
Parent: First Resources Ltd
Officers: Andrew Stuart Walsham, Secretary; Alison Jean Oldham [1966] Group Marketing Director; Nigel Victor Swabey [1948] Director; Andrew Stuart Walsham [1964] Director/Chartered Accountant

Scotty Ventures Limited
Incorporated: 23 February 2017
Net Worth Deficit: £7,721 *Total Assets:* £4,262,902
Registered Office: Scot House, Matford Park Road, Marsh Barton Trading Estate, Exeter, Devon, EX2 8AW
Activities: Other service activities n.e.c.
Shareholders: Scot Group Holdings Limited; Callum John Campbell; Warren Spokes
Officers: Callum John Campbell [1988] Corporate Director; Nigel Clive Spokes [1960] Director; Warren Spokes [1989] Corporate Director

Screwfix Direct Limited
Incorporated: 5 January 1995 *Employees:* 10,797
Net Worth: £572,606,016 *Total Assets:* £953,676,032
Registered Office: Trade House, Mead Avenue, Houndstone Business Park, Yeovil, Somerset, BA22 8RT
Activities: Agents involved in the sale of timber and building materials
Parent: Screwfix Investments Limited
Officers: Nicholas James Boyd, Secretary; Rhian Helen Bartlett [1972] Director; Elizabeth Bell [1953] HR Director; Max Nicholas Britten [1976] Director; Matthew John Compton [1972] Director; Mark Howard Lemming [1976] Director; Jonathan Mark Mewett [1968] Marketing Director; Scott Andrew Parsons [1970] Director; Steven Barry Willett [1959] Managing Director

J M Scully (Holdings) Limited
Incorporated: 1 April 2009 *Employees:* 62
Net Worth: £5,429,050 *Total Assets:* £13,811,202
Registered Office: Broad Oak Farm, Broad Oak, Sturminster Newton, Dorset, DT10 2HD
Activities: Activities of head offices
Major Shareholder: Michael Patrick Scully
Officers: Shirley Jane Scully, Secretary; John Michael Scully [1941] Director/Builder; Michael Patrick Scully [1966] Director

J M Scully Limited
Incorporated: 8 March 1983 *Employees:* 61
Net Worth: £1,972,458 *Total Assets:* £10,837,784
Registered Office: 10 Wimborne Road, Walford, Wimborne, Dorset, BH21 1NN
Activities: Other specialised construction activities n.e.c.
Officers: John Clark [1957] Contracts Director; Darren Lee Pestell [1979] Estimating Director; John Michael Scully [1941] Director/Builder; Michael Patrick Scully [1966] Managing Director; Shirley Jane Scully [1961] Director and Company Secretary; Richard Vivian [1967] Surveying Director

SDL Biomass Limited
Incorporated: 8 March 2011 *Employees:* 30
Previous: S D Launchbury Limited
Net Worth: £201,889 *Total Assets:* £4,722,160
Registered Office: Westington Quarry, Westington Hill, Chipping Campden, Glos, GL55 6EG
Activities: Logging
Major Shareholder: Samuel David Launchbury
Officers: Samuel David Launchbury [1983] Director; John Stephen Pendlebury Shelton [1959] Director

SDS Holdings Limited
Incorporated: 11 April 2008 *Employees:* 150
Net Worth: £7,640,378 *Total Assets:* £15,353,940
Registered Office: 3-5 College Street, Burnham on Sea, Somerset, TA8 1AR
Activities: Activities of construction holding companies
Major Shareholder: Patrick Gabriel Cullen
Officers: Patrick Gabriel Cullen [1967] Director [Irish]

SEA (Group) Ltd.
Incorporated: 10 October 1989
Net Worth: £1,388,000 *Total Assets:* £4,668,000
Registered Office: Beckington Castle, 17 Castle Corner, Beckington, Frome, Somerset, BA11 6TA
Activities: Activities of head offices
Parent: Cohort PLC
Officers: Sarita Bilkhu, Secretary; Stephen Jeremy Hill [1965] Managing Director; Andrew Stephen Thomis [1964] Director; Simon Robert Walther [1967] Finance Director

Seabank Power Limited
Incorporated: 13 March 1991 *Employees:* 55
Net Worth: £134,427,008 *Total Assets:* £203,243,008
Registered Office: Severn Road, Hallen, Bristol, BS10 7SP
Activities: Production of electricity
Shareholders: Electricity First Limited; SSE Seabank Investments Limited
Officers: Stuart Michael Mayer, Secretary; John Anthony Downes [1970] Director of Engineering, Generation; Alexander Hughes Honeyman [1960] Director/Business Manager; Andrew John Hunter [1958] Director; Duncan Nicholas MacRae [1970] Director; Neil Douglas McGee [1951] Director [Australian]; Iwan Rees Morgan [1961] Director of Wholesale Strategy; Wendy Tong Barnes [1960] Director/Business Executive; Chao Chung Charles Tsai [1957] Director [Canadian]

Seabrook Land Developments Limited
Incorporated: 7 March 2017
Net Worth: £95 *Total Assets:* £19,000,000
Registered Office: Darts Farm, Topsham, Exeter, Devon, EX3 0QH
Activities: Buying and selling of own real estate
Shareholders: George Paul Dart; Michael Charles Rowe Dart; Ronald James Dart
Officers: Michael Charles Rowe Dart, Secretary; George Paul Dart [1961] Director; Michael Charles Rowe Dart [1967] Director; Ronald James Dart [1969] Director

Seacon (Europe) Limited
Incorporated: 19 February 1987 *Employees:* 87
Net Worth: £3,457,709 *Total Assets:* £4,452,508
Registered Office: Company Secretariat, Site H, Faraday Road, Swindon, Wilts, SN3 5HH
Activities: Manufacture of fibre optic cables
Parent: TE Connectivity Ltd.
Officers: Harold Gregory Barksdale [1964] Director/VP Corporate and Corporate Secretary [American]; Richard Mark Buggy [1971] Director/Vice President Finance [American]; Stephen Christopher Cooper [1970] Finance Director

Seadown Holiday Park Limited
Incorporated: 14 February 1958 *Employees:* 15
Net Worth: £5,986,073 *Total Assets:* £7,745,510
Registered Office: Seadown Caravan Park, Bridge Road, Charmouth, Bridport, Dorset, DT6 6QS
Activities: Other holiday and other collective accommodation
Major Shareholder: Janet Irene Osborne
Officers: Janet Irene Osborne, Secretary; Janet Irene Osborne [1951] Company Secretary/Director

The Seafood Restaurant (Padstow) Limited
Incorporated: 27 November 2009 *Employees:* 310
Net Worth: £11,173,000 *Total Assets:* £23,342,000
Registered Office: The Seafood Restaurant, Riverside, Padstow, Cornwall, PL28 8BY
Activities: Activities of other holding companies n.e.c.
Shareholders: Christopher Richard Stein; Jill Stein
Officers: Neil John McLeod, Secretary; Neil John McLeod [1962] Finance Director; Christopher Richard Stein [1947] Director/Restaurateur; Jill Stein [1947] Director/Restaurateur

Seafood Trading Limited
Incorporated: 10 March 1995 *Employees:* 310
Net Worth: £7,849,000 *Total Assets:* £19,924,000
Registered Office: Riverside, Padstow, Cornwall, PL28 8BY
Activities: Hotels and similar accommodation
Shareholders: Christopher Richard Stein; Jill Stein
Officers: Neil John McLeod, Secretary; Neil John McLeod [1962] Director; Christopher Richard Stein [1947] Director/Restaurateur; Jill Stein [1947] Director/Restaurateur

SEAFox Dycem 1 Limited
Incorporated: 15 December 2015 *Employees:* 88
Net Worth: £621,729 *Total Assets:* £8,597,564
Registered Office: 2-4 Ashley Trading Estate, Ashley Parade, Bristol, BS2 9BB
Activities: Other manufacturing n.e.c.
Parent: SEAFox Master LLP
Officers: Michael Hugh Bell, Secretary; Iain Henry Abrahams [1959] Director/Investor; Michael Hugh Bell [1962] Director; Stewart George Cantley [1959] Director; George Elliott Nicholson [1982] Director/Finance; Stanislaus Eduard Schmidt-Chiari [1984] Director/Investor [Austrian]

SEAFox Dycem 2 Limited
Incorporated: 15 December 2015 *Employees:* 88
Net Worth Deficit: £542,894 *Total Assets:* £8,597,375
Registered Office: 2-4 Ashley Trading Estate, Ashley Parade, Bristol, BS2 9BB
Activities: Other manufacturing n.e.c.
Parent: SEAFox Dycem 1 Limited
Officers: Michael Hugh Bell, Secretary; Iain Henry Abrahams [1959] Director/Investor; Michael Hugh Bell [1962] Director; Stewart George Cantley [1959] Director; George Elliott Nicholson [1982] Director/Finance; Stanislaus Eduard Schmidt-Chiari [1984] Director/Investor [Austrian]

Seagull Developments Limited
Incorporated: 8 December 1982 *Employees:* 1
Net Worth: £4,759,003 *Total Assets:* £4,820,623
Registered Office: Eagle House, Strand, Exmouth, Devon, EX8 1AL
Activities: Construction of domestic buildings
Officers: Marie Evernden, Secretary; John Daniel Fowler, Secretary; Susan Margaret Fowler, Secretary; Rachael Manning, Secretary; Gary James Norton, Secretary; James Daniel Fowler [1974] Director; Joanna Elizabeth Fowler [1972] Director; John Daniel Fowler [1944] Director; Nicholas John Fowler [1981] Director; Susan Margaret Fowler [1952] Director/Secretary

Seahawk Marine Foods Limited
Incorporated: 22 January 1982 *Employees:* 44
Net Worth: £2,387,517 *Total Assets:* £11,934,845
Registered Office: Broadleigh House, Woodmarsh, North Bradley, Trowbridge, Wilts, BA14 0SA
Activities: Wholesale of other food, including fish, crustaceans and molluscs
Major Shareholder: Derek Michael Golding
Officers: Robin Edward Peters, Secretary; Stephen Geddes [1966] Joint Managing Director; Derek Michael Golding [1947] Chairman of The Board of Directors, Company Founder; Linda Golding [1951] Director; Keith John Maguire [1953] Joint Managing Director; Robin Edward Peters [1956] Director

Seal-Lite Windows Doors & Conservatories Limited
Incorporated: 17 October 1997 *Employees:* 52
Net Worth: £2,844,999 *Total Assets:* £3,563,400
Registered Office: 18 Rickford Road, Nailsea, Bristol, BS48 4PY
Activities: Glazing
Shareholders: Christopher John Shearn; Julian Peter Shearn
Officers: Christopher John Shearn, Secretary/Manufacturer of Doors and Windows; Christopher John Shearn [1963] Director/Manufacturer of Doors and Windows; Julian Peter Shearn [1967] Director/Maker of Doors and Windows

Sealock Limited
Incorporated: 24 May 1983 *Employees:* 25
Net Worth: £3,739,153 *Total Assets:* £4,547,933
Registered Office: Scott Close, Walworth Industrial Estate, Andover, Hants, SP10 5NU
Activities: Manufacture of other chemical products n.e.c.
Major Shareholder: Henrik Follmann
Officers: Robert Mark Ladd, Secretary; Dr Thomas Damerau [1964] Director [German]; Robert Mark Ladd [1969] Director/Accountant; Christopher Mark Young [1964] Managing Director

Searchflow Limited
Incorporated: 2 October 2000 *Employees:* 105
Net Worth: £42,214,908 *Total Assets:* £62,339,904
Registered Office: 5-7 Abbey Court, Eagle Way, Sowton Industrial Estate, Exeter, Devon, EX2 7HY
Activities: Data processing, hosting and related activities
Parent: Decision Insight Information Group (UK) Ltd
Officers: Matthew Teague, Secretary; Simon James Brown [1965] Director/Chief Executive; David William Callcott [1959] Director; Stephen John Stout [1960] Director/Chairman

Seasalt Holdings Limited
Incorporated: 15 August 2002 *Employees:* 766
Previous: Chadwick Brothers Limited
Net Worth: £10,834,087 *Total Assets:* £27,518,836
Registered Office: Unit 8 Falmouth Business Park, Bickland Water Road, Falmouth, Cornwall, TR11 4SZ
Activities: Other retail sale in non-specialised stores
Shareholder: David Alfred Chadwick
Officers: Leigh George Chadwick, Secretary/Consultant; Leigh George Chadwick [1957] Director; Neil Michael Chadwick [1966] Director/Retailer; NED James Dorbin [1977] Director; Paul Leslie Hayes [1971] Sales Director

Seasalt Limited
Incorporated: 18 May 1988 *Employees:* 766
Net Worth: £9,462,858 *Total Assets:* £24,924,944
Registered Office: Unit 8 Falmouth Business Park, Bickland Water Road, Falmouth, Cornwall, TR11 4SZ
Activities: Wholesale of clothing and footwear
Parent: Seasalt Holdings Limited
Officers: Leigh George Chadwick, Secretary/Consultant; David Alfred Chadwick [1958] Director/Retailer; Leigh George Chadwick [1957] Director/Retailer; Neil Michael Chadwick [1966] Director/Retailer; Paul Leslie Hayes [1971] Director

Seasons Holidays PLC
Incorporated: 25 November 1996 *Employees:* 385
Net Worth: £7,025,424 *Total Assets:* £54,522,512
Registered Office: Wynchgate House, Woodlands Lane, Bradley Stoke, Bristol, BS32 4JT
Activities: Holiday centres and villages
Major Shareholder: Barry Thomas Hurley
Officers: Barry Hurley, Secretary; Barry Thomas Hurley [1955] Director/Developer; Sharon Angela Jeanette Kinsella [1969] Director/Client Liaison Manager

SEC Properties Limited
Incorporated: 13 February 2007
Net Worth: £2,665,572 *Total Assets:* £5,162,985
Registered Office: 95 High Street, Street, Somerset, BA16 0EZ
Activities: Other letting and operating of own or leased real estate
Major Shareholder: Graham Leslie Phippen
Officers: Clare Elizabeth Hammond, Secretary; Graham Leslie Phippen [1947] Director

Second Applemead Limited
Incorporated: 17 February 1997 *Employees:* 2
Net Worth: £6,203,470 *Total Assets:* £7,911,541
Registered Office: Nielpahar, Hewelsfield, Glos, GL15 6UU
Activities: Other letting and operating of own or leased real estate
Shareholders: Graham John Calver; Susan Anne Calver
Officers: Susan Anne Calver, Secretary/Housewife; Graham John Calver [1942] Director/Chartered Surveyor; Guy Elliott Calver [1976] Director/Surveyor; Susan Anne Calver [1946] Director/Housewife

Secure Services Limited
Incorporated: 29 October 1984 *Employees:* 3
Net Worth: £2,973,706 *Total Assets:* £4,057,430
Registered Office: Sedgecombe House, Broad Campden, Chipping Campden, Glos, GL55 6UX
Activities: Activities of head offices
Officers: Elizabeth May Smith, Secretary; Neil Alexander Talbot Smith [1942] Director; Suzanne Carol Turner Smith [1967] Director

Secure Systems & Technologies Limited
Incorporated: 12 September 2002 *Employees:* 48
Net Worth: £4,698,935 *Total Assets:* £6,159,268
Registered Office: Brunel Court, Waterwells, Gloucester, GL2 2AL
Activities: Manufacture of computers and peripheral equipment
Parent: API Technologies (UK) Limited
Officers: Richard John Farrington [1956] Director/Certified Chartered Accountant; Robert Edward Tavares [1961] Director [American]

Securi-Flex Ltd.
Incorporated: 23 April 1999 *Employees:* 21
Net Worth: £3,271,193 *Total Assets:* £4,623,278
Registered Office: The Old School House, 3a Leckhampton Road, Cheltenham, Glos, GL53 0AX
Activities: Non-specialised wholesale trade
Major Shareholder: Stuart James Taylor
Officers: Stuart James Michael Taylor [1974] Director/Communication Cables

Securivin Limited
Incorporated: 19 September 2000
Net Worth: £1,027,991 *Total Assets:* £12,249,468
Registered Office: Hitchcock House, Hilltop Park, Devizes Road, Salisbury, Wilts, SP3 4UF
Activities: Development of building projects
Shareholders: Robin Ardern Hodges; Susan Hodges
Officers: Susan Hodges, Secretary; Robin Ardern Hodges [1950] Director; Susan Hodges [1952] Director

Chris Sedgeman Scaffolding Ltd.
Incorporated: 13 December 2000 *Employees:* 55
Net Worth: £1,798,778 *Total Assets:* £3,871,071
Registered Office: Unit 2a Long Rock Industrial Estate, Long Rock, Penzance, Cornwall, TR20 8HX
Activities: Scaffold erection
Shareholders: Linda Jane Sedgeman; Christopher John Sedgeman
Officers: Lynn Tanya Way, Secretary; Christopher John Sedgeman [1960] Managing Director; Lynn Tanya Way [1971] Finance Director

Sedgwick Solar Limited
Incorporated: 6 December 2013
Net Worth: £8,050,976 *Total Assets:* £23,891,868
Registered Office: 1350-1360 Montpellier Court, Brockworth, Gloucester, GL3 4AH
Activities: Other business support service activities n.e.c.
Parent: Sedgwick Trading Limited
Officers: Richard James Cook [1978] Director; Richard Leonard Simmonds [1979] Director/Chief Investment Officer

Seepex UK Limited
Incorporated: 9 March 1981 *Employees:* 36
Net Worth: £1,593,852 *Total Assets:* £4,309,582
Registered Office: 3 Armtech Row, Houndstone Business Park, Yeovil, Somerset, BA22 8RW
Activities: Other professional, scientific and technical activities n.e.c.
Parent: Seepex Beteilgungsgellschaft mbH
Officers: Peter Valentine McGarian, Secretary; Peter Valentine McGarian [1958] Director/Engineer; Herr Ulli Seeberger [1960] Director [German]

Seetru Limited
Incorporated: 13 October 1949 *Employees:* 127
Net Worth: £1,764,000 *Total Assets:* £6,303,000
Registered Office: Albion Dockside Works, Hanover Place, Bristol, BS1 6UT
Activities: Manufacture of taps and valves
Officers: Dr Andrew Philip Varga, Secretary; Andrew Philip Varga [1960] Director/Engineer; Dr Margaret Jai Varga [1959] Director

Seiche Water Technology Group Ltd
Incorporated: 2 June 2016 *Employees:* 80
Net Worth: £4,526,386 *Total Assets:* £5,769,608
Registered Office: The Custom House, The Strand, Barnstaple, Devon, EX31 1EU
Activities: Activities of other holding companies n.e.c.
Shareholders: Roy Wyatt; Jacqueline Kensall Wyatt
Officers: Simon Jonathan Cole [1955] Director/Accountant; Keith William Hamer [1950] Director; Jacqueline Kensall Wyatt [1958] Director; Roy Wyatt [1950] Director

Selwood Academy
Incorporated: 18 October 2011 *Employees:* 97
Net Worth: £4,236,665 *Total Assets:* £6,170,685
Registered Office: Selwood Academy, Berkley Road, Frome, Somerset, BA11 2EF
Activities: General secondary education
Officers: Helen Clare Atkins [1967] Director/Assistant Head of Care; Mandy Bailey [1958] Director/HLTA Literacy; Christopher John Bailey-Green [1947] Director/Retired; Philip Brook [1963] Director/Teacher; Clare Diana Cardnell [1953] Director/Housewife; Tabitha Marne Clayson [1970] Director; Jess Francis [1980] Director/Nurse; Jean Denise Hopegood [1960] Director/Headteacher; Kyrstie Amaryllis Kirkwood [1969] Director/Early Years Teacher; Father Neil Andrew Maxted [1958] Director/Clerk in Holy Orders; Richard John Phillips [1944] Director/Retired; Susan Jane Pothitos [1960] Director/Practice Manager; Archie Bolitho Rowe [1939] Director/Lay Pastoral & Community Worker; Susan Elizabeth Willis [1968] Director/Event Manager

Selwood Housing Society Limited
Incorporated: 26 February 2001 *Employees:* 291
Net Worth: £264,400,992 *Total Assets:* £423,638,016
Registered Office: Bryer Ash Business Park, Bradford Road, Trowbridge, Wilts, BA14 8RT
Activities: Renting and operating of Housing Association real estate
Officers: Diane Patricia Hall, Secretary; Claudia Bailey [1973] Director/Group Administration; Richard Britton [1942] Director; Chris Butters [1965] Director/Certified Chartered Accountant; Martin Large [1955] Director/Board Member; Shelia Frances Lewis [1952] Director/Board Member; Lee Stephen O'Bryan [1959] Director/Managing Partner The Camden Partnership Ltd; Martin Willard Pain [1941] Director/Retired; Bridget Anne Wayman [1956] Director/Councillor; Valerie Ann Witcomb [1948] Director/Semi Retired Accountant

Senate Court (Southgate) Limited
Incorporated: 31 January 2017 *Employees:* 7
Net Worth: £3,206,800 *Total Assets:* £7,700,045
Registered Office: c/o Prydis, Senate Court, Southernhay Gardens, Exeter, Devon, EX1 1NT
Activities: Activities of other holding companies n.e.c.
Parent: Senate Court (Holdings) Limited
Officers: Nicholas John Cross [1981] Director; Simon David Hartnell Exley [1964] Director; James Arthur Harrison Priday [1987] Director; Joseph Robert James Priday [1984] Director; Gary Robert Randall [1966] Director; Andrew Arthur Waugh [1972] Director

Senex Capital Limited
Incorporated: 19 February 2004
Net Worth: £5,553,767 *Total Assets:* £11,397,715
Registered Office: Charles Farris Ltd, Quarry Fields, Mere, Wilts, BA12 6LA
Activities: Activities of head offices
Shareholders: Richard Gordon Simpson; Joanna Alice Simpson
Officers: Susan Gale, Secretary; Susan Gale [1961] Finance Director; Joanna Alice Simpson [1959] Director

Senlan Securities Limited
Incorporated: 30 September 1971 *Employees:* 3
Net Worth: £4,252,285 *Total Assets:* £4,401,881
Registered Office: 310 Bournemouth Road, Parkstone, Poole, Dorset, BH14 9AR
Activities: Renting and operating of Housing Association real estate
Shareholder: John Sydenham Whitelock
Officers: Nicole Pauline Mary Whitelock, Secretary; Jeremy Nolan Powell [1960] Director/Surveyor; John Sydenham Whitelock [1949] Director/Builder

Sensata Technologies (Europe) Limited
Incorporated: 17 October 2003
Net Worth: £88,183,784 *Total Assets:* £88,235,400
Registered Office: Interface House, Interface Business Park, Bincknoll Lane, Royal Wootton Bassett, Swindon, Wilts, SN4 8SY
Activities: Non-trading company
Parent: Sensata Technologies Holding Company UK
Officers: Graeme Martin Thompson [1967] Managing Director

Sensata Technologies Holding Company U.K.
Incorporated: 3 November 2006
Net Worth Deficit: £86,357,072 *Total Assets:* £44,574,860
Registered Office: Interface House, Interface Business Park, Bincknoll Lane, Royal Wootton Bassett, Swindon, Wilts, SN4 8SY
Activities: Other business support service activities n.e.c.
Parent: Sensata Technologies Intermediate UK Limited
Officers: Graeme Martin Thompson [1967] Managing Director

Sensata Technologies Limited
Incorporated: 14 December 1959 *Employees:* 1
Net Worth: £5,539,000 *Total Assets:* £5,605,000
Registered Office: Interface House, Interface Business Park, Bincknoll Lane, Royal Wootton Bassett, Swindon, Wilts, SN4 8SY
Activities: Machining
Parent: Sensata Technologies Holding Company U.K.
Officers: Jeffrey John Cote [1966] Director/Chief Financial Officer [American]

Sensata Technologies UK Financing Co. PLC
Incorporated: 5 November 2015
Net Worth: £3,106,066,688 *Total Assets:* £3,749,288,704
Registered Office: Interface House, Interface Business Park, Bincknoll Lane, Royal Wootton Bassett, Swindon, Wilts, SN4 8SY
Activities: Activities of other holding companies n.e.c.
Parent: Sensata Technologies Intermediate UK Limited
Officers: Jeffrey John Cote, Secretary; Jeffrey John Cote [1966] Director/Chief Operating Officer [American]; Graeme Martin Thompson [1967] Managing Director

Sensitisers Group Ltd.
Incorporated: 19 February 1998 *Employees:* 106
Net Worth: £11,566,632 *Total Assets:* £14,810,518
Registered Office: Kernow Coatings Limited, Kernick Road, Penryn, Cornwall, TR10 9DQ
Activities: Non-trading company
Shareholders: Peter Alan Newell; Philip Mark Bartlett
Officers: Philip Mark Bartlett [1973] Technical Director; Bosiljko Colak [1963] Sales Director [American]; Peter Alan Newell [1960] Finance Director

Sentry Self Storage Limited
Incorporated: 13 June 1988 *Employees:* 10
Net Worth: £2,396,024 *Total Assets:* £6,734,935
Registered Office: 14 London Street, Andover, Hants, SP10 2PA
Activities: Operation of warehousing and storage facilities for land transport activities
Shareholders: Sidney Mark Robert Hickman; Simon Charles Robert Hickman
Officers: Simon Charles Robert Hickman, Secretary; Sidney Mark Robert Hickman [1962] Director/Storage Consultant; Simon Charles Robert Hickman [1964] Director/Storage Consultant

Serais Investments Limited
Incorporated: 23 June 1976 *Employees:* 2
Net Worth: £4,763,000 *Total Assets:* £4,771,000
Registered Office: 5th Floor, Festival House, Jessop Avenue, Cheltenham, Glos, GL50 3SH
Activities: Activities of head offices
Parent: Steinhoff UK Group Properties Limited
Officers: John Henry Robins, Secretary; Paul Stanworth [1970] Director/Accountant

Serene LL Ltd
Incorporated: 7 July 2015 *Employees:* 66
Net Worth: £371,665 *Total Assets:* £8,790,956
Registered Office: 31-33 Commercial Road, Poole, Dorset, BH14 0HU
Activities: Activities of head offices
Shareholders: Arujuna Sivananthan; Karthika Sivananthan
Officers: Dr Arujuna Sivananthan [1970] Director; Karthika Sivananthan [1973] Director

Services Support (Avon & Somerset) Holdings Limited
Incorporated: 17 April 2003
Net Worth: £50,000 *Total Assets:* £6,830,000
Registered Office: Third Floor, Broad Quay House, Prince Street, Bristol, BS1 4DJ
Activities: Activities of head offices
Shareholders: Aberdeen Infrastructure (No.3) Limited; JLIF (GP) Limited
Officers: Neeti Mukundrai Anand [1984] Director; Farid Barekati [1984] Director; David Richard Bradbury [1969] Director/Senior Investment Manager; Louis Javier Falero [1977] Director/Fund Manager; Karen Marie Hill [1977] Director/Banker; Christopher Thomas Solley [1970] Director/Investment Banker

Services Support (Avon & Somerset) Limited
Incorporated: 17 April 2003
Net Worth Deficit: £11,773,000 *Total Assets:* £61,249,000
Registered Office: Third Floor, Broad Quay House, Prince Street, Bristol, BS1 4DJ
Activities: Construction of commercial buildings
Parent: Services Support (Avon & Somerset) Holdings Limited
Officers: Neeti Mukundrai Anand [1984] Director; Farid Barekati [1984] Director; David Richard Bradbury [1969] Director/Senior Investment Manager; Louis Javier Falero [1977] Director/Fund Manager; Karen Marie Hill [1977] Director/Banker; Christopher Thomas Solley [1970] Director/Investment Banker

Servo Interconnect Limited
Incorporated: 23 September 2004
Net Worth: £10,879,761 *Total Assets:* £10,879,761
Registered Office: Company Secretariat, Site H, Faraday Road, Swindon, Wilts, SN3 5HH
Activities: Non-trading company
Parent: Deutsch UK
Officers: Harold Gregory Barksdale [1964] Director/Attorney [American]; Stephen Christopher Cooper [1970] Director/Accountant; Andrew Donachie [1972] Operations Director

Sesanti Limited
Incorporated: 28 August 2013 *Employees:* 26
Net Worth: £4,906,098 *Total Assets:* £7,519,566
Registered Office: Lambda House, Fairground Industrial Estate, Weyhill, Andover, Hants, SP11 0ST
Activities: Manufacture of optical precision instruments
Officers: Andrew James Bates [1977] Technical Director; Alison Virginia Kyle-Henney [1965] Director; Peter Timothy Kyle-Henney [1964] Director/Electronic Design Engineer; Charles Peter Stuart Mill [1979] Programmes Director; Stephen David Rood [1972] Manufacturing Director; Lee James Sturges [1968] Director/Engineer

Sett Wind Development Limited
Incorporated: 29 September 2017
Net Worth Deficit: £5,659 *Total Assets:* £3,698,707
Registered Office: 16 West Borough, Wimborne, Dorset, BH21 1NG
Activities: Activities of other holding companies n.e.c.
Shareholders: Boralex Europe SARL; Infinergy Limited
Officers: Patrick Decostre [1972] Director/Vice President and General Manager Europe [Belgian]; Sophie Annick Paule Delasnerie [1976] Directrice Juridique Europe [French]; Tjiwolt Wierda [1972] Director [Dutch]; Esbjorn Roderick Wilmar [1970] Director [Dutch]

Seven Fields Primary School
Incorporated: 6 March 2012 *Employees:* 72
Net Worth: £4,822,436 *Total Assets:* £5,214,655
Registered Office: Seven Fields Primary School, Leigh Road, Penhill, Swindon, Wilts, SN2 5DE
Activities: Other food services
Officers: Revd Alison Louise Chesworth [1968] Director/Priest; Katy Dolton [1982] Director/Team Leader - Retail; Timothy James Gilson [1967] Director/Headteacher/CEO; Andrew Kevin Hall [1964] Director/Leadership & Business Coach; Jacqueline Jane McCarthy [1965] Director/Civil Servant; Peter James McGuigan [1954] Director/Retired Soldier

Severn & Wye Smokery Limited
Incorporated: 2 May 1989 *Employees:* 138
Net Worth: £10,009,738 *Total Assets:* £20,300,836
Registered Office: Chaxhill, Westbury on Severn, Glos, GL14 1QW
Activities: Processing and preserving of fish, crustaceans and molluscs
Major Shareholder: Richard Norman Cook
Officers: Shirley Ann Cook, Secretary; Richard Norman Cook [1969] Director/Fishmonger

Severn Glocon (Aberdeen) Ltd
Incorporated: 16 March 2010 *Employees:* 35
Previous: Severn Ball Valves Ltd
Net Worth: £563,447 *Total Assets:* £4,151,972
Registered Office: Severn Glocon Ltd, Olympus Park, Quedgeley, Gloucester, GL2 4NF
Activities: Wholesale of other intermediate products
Parent: Severn Glocon Group PLC
Officers: Maurice Mortimer Critchley [1948] Director/Chartered Accountant; Colin Archibald Findlay [1957] Director; Brian Robert Wood [1955] Director/Engineer

Severn Glocon Group PLC
Incorporated: 28 May 1987 *Employees:* 855
Net Worth: £32,063,800 *Total Assets:* £85,267,536
Registered Office: c/o Severn Glocon Ltd, Olympus Park, Quedgeley, Gloucester, GL2 4NF
Activities: Manufacture of pumps
Shareholders: Maurice Mortimer Critchley; Maureen Joan Critchley
Officers: Maurice Mortimer Critchley, Secretary; Maureen Joan Critchley [1947] Director; Maurice Mortimer Critchley [1948] Director/Chartered Accountant; Peter Robert Mardon [1966] Director/Solicitor; Christopher Charles Powell [1946] Director

Severn Glocon Limited
Incorporated: 30 March 1961 *Employees:* 673
Net Worth: £21,488,584 *Total Assets:* £71,786,712
Registered Office: Olympus Park, Quedgeley, Gloucester, GL2 4NF
Activities: Manufacture of taps and valves
Parent: Severn Glocon Group PLC
Officers: Maurice Mortimer Critchley, Secretary; Maurice Mortimer Critchley [1948] Director/Accountant; Christopher Charles Powell [1946] Director

Severn Unival Limited
Incorporated: 27 May 1981 *Employees:* 117
Net Worth: £6,138,107 *Total Assets:* £13,474,821
Registered Office: c/o Severn Glocon Ltd, Olympus Park, Quedgeley, Gloucester, GL2 4NF
Activities: Manufacture of taps and valves
Parent: Severn Glocon Limited
Officers: Maurice Mortimer Critchley, Secretary; Maurice Mortimer Critchley [1948] Director/Chartered Accountant; Colin Archibald Finlay [1957] Director; Christopher Charles Powell [1946] Director

Severn Vale School
Incorporated: 14 July 2011 *Employees:* 136
Net Worth: £10,343,488 *Total Assets:* £13,020,965
Registered Office: Severn Vale School, School Lane, Quedgeley, Gloucester, GL2 4PR
Activities: General secondary education
Officers: Adrian Douglas John Ayland [1968] Director; Laura Berry [1978] Director/Local Government Officer; Amanda Louise Browne [1970] Director/Self Employed; Dr Sarah Lindsey Cockin [1971] Director/Healthcare Manager; Ahmed Ginwalla [1970] Director/Management Accountant; Susan Elizabeth Hawkins [1947] Director/Personal Assistant; Jane Beverley Ireland [1958] Director/Retired; Richard Johnson [1970] Director/Headteacher; Jane McDonnell [1964] Director/Data and Exams Officer; Ian Pogue [1965] Director; Robert Rankin [1977] Director/IT Services; Vania Jane Seymour [1977] Director/Administrator; Richard Wallace [1958] Director; Julie Williamson [1973] Director/School Teacher; Paul Wilson [1983] Director/Teacher; Stephen Richard Wilson [1971] Director/Civil Service; Professor Neil Wynn [1947] Director/Retired

Severn Valley Woodworks Limited
Incorporated: 21 May 1986 *Employees:* 70
Net Worth: £2,373,916 *Total Assets:* £7,562,256
Registered Office: Church Lane, Northwood Green, Westbury on Severn, Glos, GL14 1ND
Activities: Sawmilling and planing of wood
Shareholders: Simon John Powell Brown; Judy Brown
Officers: Terrence Charles Jenkins, Secretary; Simon John Powell Brown [1964] Director; Andrew Frederick Jenkins [1944] Director; Robin Timothy Simpson [1955] Director; Anthony James Sterry [1966] Director; David Robert Twigg [1956] Sales Director

Sexey's School
Incorporated: 8 July 2011 *Employees:* 95
Net Worth: £10,572,803 *Total Assets:* £13,907,795
Registered Office: Sexey's School, Cole Road, Bruton, Somerset, BA10 0DF
Activities: General secondary education
Officers: Reverend Justin Mark Bailey [1955] Director/Priest; Karen Elizabeth Vanessa Susan Baker [1953] Director/Town Councillor; Magnus Charles Dennis [1973] Director/Photographer; Max Charles Edgar [1973] Director/Builder; James Robert Gasson-Hargreaves [1973] Director; Anthony Law Hodges [1948] Director/Retired; Patricia Mensah [1978] Director/Manager; Emma Margaret Miller [1979] Director; Janet Lynne Wilson [1962] Director/Civil Servant (Manager)

John Seymour Transport Limited
Incorporated: 27 October 1978 *Employees:* 77
Net Worth: £1,946,605 *Total Assets:* £5,946,467
Registered Office: Gammaton Road, Bideford, Devon, EX39 4FG
Activities: Freight transport by road
Officers: Susan Jayne Evans, Secretary; Nigel John Evans [1962] Director; Susan Jayne Evans [1968] Director; Thomas John Evans [1989] Director; Andrew John Taylor [1973] Finance Director

SF Ltd
Incorporated: 13 August 2003 *Employees:* 76
Net Worth: £5,389,398 *Total Assets:* £6,477,788
Registered Office: Riverside Road, Pottington Industrial Estate, Barnstaple, Devon, EX31 1LZ
Activities: Manufacture of other fabricated metal products n.e.c.
Parent: Stamm International Corporation
Officers: Marilyn Skony Stamm, Secretary; Philip Anthony Brompton [1949] Director; Tim Alan Bedford Smith [1966] Director; Marilyn Skony Stamm [1951] Director [American]

SG Aerospace (UK) Limited
Incorporated: 26 June 1972 *Employees:* 94
Previous: Sitec Professional Services Limited
Net Worth: £3,397,000 *Total Assets:* £15,380,000
Registered Office: 33 Oldfield Road, Bath, BA2 3NE
Activities: Temporary employment agency activities
Parent: Sitec Recruitment Limited
Officers: Antony Christopher Ambridge, Secretary; James Buick [1956] Director/Engineering Manager; David John Medlock [1955] Director; Peter John Medlock [1984] Director

SGH Investments Limited
Incorporated: 7 January 2014 *Employees:* 143
Net Worth: £12,854,215 *Total Assets:* £27,386,590
Registered Office: c/o Ashfords LLP, Ashford House, Grenadier Road, Exeter, EX1 3LH
Activities: Support activities for other mining and quarrying
Major Shareholder: Donald Skene
Officers: Jill Nicola Mason [1971] Director; Alison Skene [1947] Director; Donald Skene [1945] Director; Neil Skene [1968] Director

SGW Research Limited
Incorporated: 10 July 2002
Net Worth: £555,238 *Total Assets:* £4,539,842
Registered Office: Oake House, Silver Street, West Buckland, Wellington, Somerset, TA21 9LR
Activities: Non-trading company
Major Shareholder: Sarah Lucinda Gordon-Wild
Officers: James Wild, Secretary; Sarah Lucinda Gordon Wild [1959] Director/Investment Manager; James Howard Wild [1951] Director [American]

SH & GS Property Group Limited
Incorporated: 14 February 2017 *Employees:* 2
Net Worth: £15,922,040 *Total Assets:* £17,398,358
Registered Office: The Arches, Amport, Andover, Hants, SP11 8BE
Activities: Other letting and operating of own or leased real estate
Major Shareholder: Suzanne Anita Hoare
Officers: Suzanne Anita Hoare [1958] Director/Clerical Officer; Graham Michael Swatton [1956] Director/Builder

E.J. Shanley & Son (Trowbridge) Limited
Incorporated: 8 April 1965 *Employees:* 33
Net Worth: £11,272,555 *Total Assets:* £15,969,223
Registered Office: 43 Shails Lane, Trowbridge, Wilts, BA14 8LN
Activities: Recovery of sorted materials
Shareholder: Terence Edward Shanley
Officers: Terence Edward Shanley, Secretary; Andrew James Shanley [1970] Director/Scrap Merchant; Claire Lesley Shanley [1958] Director; Paul Edward Shanley [1967] Director/Scrap Merchant; Terence Edward Shanley [1946] Director/Scrap Metal Dealer

Shareland Investments Limited
Incorporated: 20 October 1995
Net Worth: £2,743,152 *Total Assets:* £3,976,362
Registered Office: 20 East Avenue, Talbot Woods, Bournemouth, BH3 7BZ
Activities: Buying and selling of own real estate
Shareholder: Susan Denise Smith
Officers: Susan Denise Smith, Secretary; Sarah Jennifer Bevan [1984] Director; Andrew Smith [1992] Director; Helen Smith [1986] Director; Susan Denise Smith [1956] Director; Victoria Louise Smith [1981] Director/Accountant

Sharp's Brewery Limited
Incorporated: 10 April 2003 *Employees:* 114
Net Worth: £20,769,196 *Total Assets:* £29,014,440
Registered Office: Pityme Industrial Estate, Rock, Wadebridge, Cornwall, PL27 6NU
Activities: Manufacture of beer
Parent: Molson Coors Brewing Company (UK) Limited
Officers: Gemma Louise Wisniewski, Secretary; Simon Kerry [1970] Finance Director; James Christian Shearer [1980] Marketing Director; Philip Mark Whitehead [1977] Director

Sharpak Bridgwater Limited
Incorporated: 1 October 2010 *Employees:* 227
Net Worth: £8,167,000 *Total Assets:* £24,717,000
Registered Office: Colley Lane Estate, Bridgwater, Somerset, TA6 5YS
Activities: Manufacture of plastic packing goods
Officers: Francois Raymond Paul Guillin, Secretary; Bertrand Michel Marc Guillin [1972] Director [French]; Sophie Guillin-Frappier [1973] Director [French]

Sharpak Yate Limited
Incorporated: 1 October 2010 *Employees:* 173
Net Worth: £7,493,000 *Total Assets:* £15,580,000
Registered Office: Highway, Yate, Bristol, BS37 7AA
Activities: Manufacture of plastic packing goods
Officers: Francois Raymond Paul Guillin, Secretary; Bertrand Michel Marc Guillin [1972] Director [French]; Sophie Guillin-Frappier [1973] Director [French]

Sharpham Trust (The)
Incorporated: 20 August 1982 *Employees:* 16
Net Worth: £6,344,847 *Total Assets:* £6,594,993
Registered Office: Sharpham House, Ashprington, Totnes, Devon, TQ9 7UT
Activities: Other education n.e.c.
Officers: Martin Wright, Secretary; Tony Kuhl [1953] Director/Retired; William John Lana [1968] Director/Eco Entrepreneur; Charlotte Rathbone [1961] Director/Landscape Architect; Elizabeth Ann Seward [1952] Director/Charity Management Consultant; Daniel Hugh Stokes [1956] Director/Retired; Martin Clive Wright [1954] Director/Solicitor

Sharpness Dock Limited
Incorporated: 20 November 1996 *Employees:* 50
Net Worth: £6,201,000 *Total Assets:* £7,767,000
Registered Office: Victoria Group Holdings Limited, Victoria Wharf, Plymouth, PL4 0RF
Activities: Cargo handling for water transport activities
Major Shareholder: Mark Alexander Vernon Gatehouse
Officers: David Sydney Martin, Secretary; Mark Alexander Vernon Gatehouse [1949] Director; David Sydney Martin [1955] Director; Garry Martin Strickland [1962] Director

Shaunaks Holdings Limited
Incorporated: 12 May 2015 *Employees:* 119
Net Worth: £6,276,731 *Total Assets:* £8,218,851
Registered Office: Shaunak House, Netham Road, Redfield, Bristol, BS5 9PQ
Activities: Activities of other holding companies n.e.c.
Shareholders: Daljet Shaunak; Kishen Daljet Shaunak; Vishal Daljet Shaunak
Officers: Daljet Shaunak [1947] Director/Pharmacist; Kishen Daljet Shaunak [1979] Director/Chartered Accountant; Vishal Daljet Shaunak [1978] Director/Pharmacist

Shaunaks Limited
Incorporated: 24 October 1979 *Employees:* 119
Net Worth: £2,853,179 *Total Assets:* £4,761,875
Registered Office: Shaunak House, Netham Road, Redfield, Bristol, BS5 9PQ
Activities: Dispensing chemist in specialised stores
Parent: Shaunaks Holdings Ltd
Officers: Kishen Shaunak, Secretary; Daljet Shaunak [1947] Director/Pharmacist; Kishen Daljet Shaunak [1979] Director/Chartered Accountant; Vishal Daljet Shaunak [1978] Director/Pharmacist

Shaw Ridge Primary School
Incorporated: 2 October 2013 *Employees:* 63
Net Worth: £3,663,775 *Total Assets:* £3,986,349
Registered Office: Ridge Green, Shaw, Swindon, Wilts, SN5 5PU
Activities: Primary education
Officers: Jill Elizabeth Bourne [1967] Director/Children's Centre Lead; Shaun Carter [1989] Director/Teacher; Bernadette Martine Dudman [1963] Director; Julia Catherine Falaki [1962] Director; Lorraine Fleming [1976] Director/Children's Centre Worker; Philip Colin Harland [1960] Director; Julia Jane Hinns [1964] Managing Director; Neil John Linsell [1962] Director/Building Control Surveyor; Zoe Claire McCormick [1974] Director/Housewife; Andrew Christopher Morton [1978] Director/Financial Planning Consultant

Shaw Trust Limited (The)
Incorporated: 3 August 1983 *Employees:* 1,814
Net Worth: £114,535,000 *Total Assets:* £153,050,000
Registered Office: Third Floor, 10 Victoria Street, Bristol, BS1 6BN
Activities: Other activities of employment placement agencies
Officers: Nicholas Oliver Charles Carey, Secretary; Paul Michael Baldwin [1965] Director; Mike Hawker [1949] Director; Peter David Holmes [1953] Director; Paul McGee [1944] Director/Retired; Jeremy Patrick Moore [1956] Director; John Norman [1951] Director/Retired; Dr Michael Leslie Nussbaum [1946] Director; Sir Kenneth Aphunezi Olisa [1951] Director/Chairman; Christina Mary Patterson [1963] Director/Journalist; Rebecca Anne Sudworth [1967] Director

Shearbarn Holiday Park Limited
Incorporated: 14 March 2013 *Employees:* 46
Net Worth Deficit: £1,203,234 *Total Assets:* £4,216,931
Registered Office: c/o Milsted Langdon LLP, Motivo House, Alvington, Yeovil, Somerset, BA20 2FG
Activities: Recreational vehicle parks, trailer parks and camping grounds
Parent: No House Limited
Officers: Timothy David House [1950] Director

Shearwell Data Limited
Incorporated: 10 September 1992 *Employees:* 103
Net Worth: £5,616,091 *Total Assets:* £10,327,498
Registered Office: Putham Farm, Wheddon Cross, Minehead, Somerset, TA24 7AS
Activities: Other manufacturing n.e.c.
Shareholders: Webber Holdings (Exmoor) Limited; National Farmers Union Mutual Insurance Society Ltd
Officers: Carolyne Martineau Webber, Secretary/Director; Carolyne Martineau Webber [1957] Director; Richard Sydney Webber [1948] Director

Sheerness Recycling Limited
Incorporated: 9 December 2008 *Employees:* 14
Net Worth: £1,362,287 *Total Assets:* £4,802,687
Registered Office: Swatton Barn, Badbury, Swindon, Wilts, SN4 0EU
Activities: Collection of non-hazardous waste
Major Shareholder: Roger Keith Body
Officers: Robert Henry Samuel, Secretary; Roger Keith Body [1951] Director; Darren John Philpott [1966] Director

Sheffield Parkway LLP
Incorporated: 23 March 2006
Net Worth Deficit: £1,353,852 *Total Assets:* £11,197,490
Registered Office: Manor Stables, Corsley, Warminster, Wilts, BA12 7QE
Officers: Ralph Congreve [1953] Member; Simon William Waterfield [1960] Member

Sheila Holdings Limited
Incorporated: 4 March 1998 *Employees:* 2
Net Worth: £3,230,246 *Total Assets:* £6,134,314
Registered Office: 31-33 Commercial Road, Poole, Dorset, BH14 0HU
Activities: Other letting and operating of own or leased real estate
Major Shareholder: Allan Arthur Morton
Officers: Lesley Margaret Morton, Secretary; Allan Arthur Morton [1949] Director; Paul Anthony Morton [1972] Director

The Sheiling Special Education Trust
Incorporated: 22 June 2012 *Employees:* 287
Net Worth: £8,006,584 *Total Assets:* £10,479,119
Registered Office: Central Office, Horton Road, Ringwood, Hants, BH24 2EB
Activities: Other education n.e.c.
Officers: Jon Freeman [1951] Director/Author and Business Consultant; Mark Gleed [1964] Director/Compliance & Integration Manager; Jean Jevons [1985] Director/Assistant Psychologist; David Keeton [1958] Director/Deputy Headteacher; Janet Elizabeth Kenward [1956] Director/Independent Support Practitioner; Jeremy Morris [1958] Director/Business Consultancy; Julian Pyzer [1954] Director/Therapeutic Care Worker; Maggi Rigg [1951] Director/Retired

Shelburne Farming LLP
Incorporated: 7 March 2011
Net Worth: £7,581,817 *Total Assets:* £7,720,653
Registered Office: 38 Dollar Street, Cirencester, Glos, GL7 2AN
Officers: John Aidan Joseph Price [1953] Member; Victoria Juliet May Price [1994] Member

Sheldon School
Incorporated: 8 March 2011 *Employees:* 227
Net Worth: £23,503,264 *Total Assets:* £24,927,704
Registered Office: Sheldon School, Hardenhuish Lane, Chippenham, Wilts, SN14 6HJ
Activities: General secondary education
Officers: Deborah Anne Louise Andrews [1968] Director/Deputy Finance Manager; Susan Margaret Brentnall [1962] Director/Voice Teacher; Louise Carver [1963] Director/Business Consultant; Carol Ann Cradock [1954] Director/Physiotherapist; Katherine Eira Mary Hathaway [1964] Director; Caroline Jane Charlotte Hiorns [1959] Director/Author; Craig Stewart Holden [1973] Director/Police Officer; Thomas Geoffrey Jacques [1968] Director/Architect; Megan Jones [1960] Director; Elizabeth Katherine Manzi [1968] Director/Teacher; Kevin Mark Pearce [1966] Director/Governance and Controls Manager; Karen Patricia Sayers [1965] Director/Chartered Accountant; Trevor Ian Sparrow [1960] Director/Teacher; Neil Charles Bryce Spurdell [1969] Director/Headmaster; Peter Charles Thomas Story [1946] Director/Admin Officer; Judith Ann Vosper [1964] Director - Marketing and PR; Stuart David Walker [1977] Director/Account Executive; Margaret Sharon Wilson [1972] Director/Teacher

Shelterbox Trust
Incorporated: 9 December 2002 *Employees:* 104
Net Worth: £14,342,000 *Total Assets:* £15,570,000
Registered Office: Falcon House, Charles Street, Truro, Cornwall, TR1 2PH
Activities: Other human health activities
Officers: Robin Alec Bayford [1949] Director/Chartered Accountant; Richard James Christopher Bland [1972] Director/Business Strategist; William Decker [1972] Marketing Director [American]; Claire Goudsmit [1972] Director/International Humanitarian Aid Consultant; Michelle Jeuken [1970] Director/Head of Communications and Engagement [Australian]; Shekhar Mehta [1959] Director/Property Development [Indian]; Lydia Helen Poole [1979] Director/Humanitarian Consultant; James Sinclair Taylor [1948] Director/Solicitor; Greg Thacker [1945] Director/Chartered Accountant

Shenton Global Limited
Incorporated: 14 October 2016 *Employees:* 77
Net Worth: £2,267,813 *Total Assets:* £8,281,563
Registered Office: Shenton House, Walworth Road, Walworth Industrial Estate, Andover, Hants, SP10 5LH
Activities: Other engineering activities
Officers: Curtis James Meek [1992] Director; Darren Carl Meek [1979] Director; Jody Brett Meek [1984] Director

John Sheppard Butchers Limited
Incorporated: 1 July 1992 *Employees:* 138
Net Worth: £1,521,143 *Total Assets:* £5,780,266
Registered Office: Unit 6 Ashley Trading Estate, Ashley Parade, Bristol, BS2 9XS
Activities: Wholesale of meat and meat products
Parent: JSB Companies Ltd
Officers: Richard John Sheppard, Secretary; Bessie Rosina Sheppard [1923] Director; Richard John Sheppard [1952] Director/Butcher

Shepperton Builders Limited
Incorporated: 5 July 1952 *Employees:* 2
Net Worth: £5,225,535 *Total Assets:* £6,735,983
Registered Office: 11 Lansdowne Court, Bumpers Way, Bumpers Farm, Chippenham, Wilts, SN14 6RZ
Activities: Construction of domestic buildings
Parent: Shepperton Group Ltd
Officers: Graham Peter Braddick [1963] Finance Director; Gavin Kenneth Davis [1955] Managing Director

Shepperton Group Limited
Incorporated: 29 March 1977 *Employees:* 70
Net Worth: £9,407,161 *Total Assets:* £21,596,712
Registered Office: 11 Lansdowne Court, Bumpers Way, Bumpers Farm, Chippenham, Wilts, SN14 6RZ
Activities: Activities of head offices
Parent: Shepperton Ventures Ltd
Officers: Graham Peter Braddick, Secretary; Graham Peter Braddick [1963] Finance Director; Gavin Kenneth Davis [1955] Director/Builder; Roy Power [1947] Managing Director; Christopher Winston Smith [1944] Director

Shepperton Properties Limited
Incorporated: 15 April 1983
Net Worth: £4,765,695 *Total Assets:* £8,190,070
Registered Office: 11 Lansdowne Court, Bumpers Way, Bumpers Farm, Chippenham, Wilts, SN14 6RZ
Activities: Other letting and operating of own or leased real estate
Parent: Shepperton Ventures Ltd
Officers: Graham Peter Braddick [1963] Finance Director; Gavin Kenneth Davis [1955] Director/Builder; Julie Ann Davis [1960] Director; Christopher Winston Smith [1944] Director

Sherborne Area Schools' Trust
Incorporated: 4 July 2012 *Employees:* 459
Previous: The Gryphon School
Net Worth: £440,068 *Total Assets:* £8,048,976
Registered Office: The Gryphon School, Bristol Road, Sherborne, Dorset, DT9 4EQ
Activities: Primary education
Officers: Christopher Adam Vigar, Secretary; Timothy Maurice Cobden Higham Bartley [1953] Director; Antony James Cooke [1970] Director; Christopher Roy Davey [1944] Director/Retired Education Professional; Janis Margaret Maitland Hill [1949] Director/Retired Secondary School Teacher; Stephen Mark Hillier [1963] Director/Headteacher; Jill Hogben [1960] Director/Manager Dorset & Wiltshire Fire & Rescue Service; Caryl Robin Plewes [1969] Director/Governance Support Advisor; Nigel Ieuan Rees [1956] Director/Bank Manager; Peter Stuart Tait [1951] Director/Consultant [New Zealander]; Philip James Tebbatt [1968] Director/Solicitor; John Ernest Tregale [1969] Director/Vicar

Sherborne Holdings Limited
Incorporated: 10 July 2007 *Employees:* 425
Net Worth: £40,383,456 *Total Assets:* £58,559,712
Registered Office: 45-47 Ashley Road, Boscombe, Bournemouth, BH1 4LG
Activities: Activities of head offices
Shareholders: James Richard Sherborne; Charles John Sherborne
Officers: Raymond John Pride, Secretary/Director; Montague John Meyer [1944] Director; Raymond John Pride [1951] Director; Charles John Sherbone [1958] Director/Timber Merchant; James Richard Sherborne [1963] Director/Timber Merchant

Sherborne Preparatory School
Incorporated: 7 April 1998 *Employees:* 99
Net Worth: £3,600,404 *Total Assets:* £5,030,674
Registered Office: Acreman Street, Sherborne, Dorset, DT9 3NY
Activities: Primary education
Officers: Barry McMaster, Secretary; Fiona Camilla Ashley Miller [1963] Retail Director; Bernard Samuel Brown [1946] Director/Retired; Tina Cosham [1956] Director/Educational Consultant; Sarah Carolyn Edwards [1963] Director; Duncan John Fowler Watt [1963] Director/Schoolmaster; Timothy David Hague [1965] Director/Accountant; David Phillip Jones [1945] Director/Retired; Nigel Lawson Jones [1956] Director/Chartered Surveyor; Dr Dominic Luckett [1966] Director/Headmaster; John Patrick Smith [1950] Director/Retired Accountant

Sherborne School
Incorporated: 26 May 2000 *Employees:* 579
Net Worth: £37,869,000 *Total Assets:* £49,461,000
Registered Office: Sherborne School, Abbey Road, Sherborne, Dorset, DT9 3LF
Activities: General secondary education
Officers: Lucy Robins, Secretary/Bursar; Isabel Anne Cooper Burke [1956] Director/Doctor; Aubrey John Capel [1957] Director/Chartered Surveyor; Vicki Cotter [1980] Director/Lawyer; Roger Stewart Fidgen [1946] Director/Chartered Surveyor; Michael Levick French [1947] Director/Chartered Accountant; Guy Andrew Hudson [1962] Director/Self Employed; Dr Maximillian Mark Jonas [1959] Director/Medical Consultant; Angela Claire Lane [1962] Director/Accountant; Robin Anthony Langley Leach [1955] Director/Barrister; Major General Arundell David Leakey [1952] Director; Russell Lucas-Rowe [1963] Director/Farmer; George Marsh [1943] Director/Headmaster Retired; Gillian Staley [1970] Director/Health and Safety Advisor; Elaine Sarah Rivett Stallard [1956] Director/Consultant; Robert Jan Temmink [1973] Director/Barrister; Matthew James Whittell [1964] Director/Chief Financial Officer; Michael Trevenen Wilson [1960] Director/Headmaster; Eric John Woods [1951] Director/Clerk in Holy Orders

Sherborne School for Girls
Incorporated: 7 November 1935 *Employees:* 313
Net Worth: £19,249,452 *Total Assets:* £29,240,012
Registered Office: Sherborne, Dorset, DT9 3QN
Activities: General secondary education
Officers: Fiona Jane Laird Clapp, Secretary; Lady Plaxy Gillian Beatrice Arthur [1950] Director/Education; Juliet Sara Blanch [1961] Director/Lawyer; Isabel Anne Cooper Burke [1956] Director/Medical Practitioner; Dr Steven George Connors [1956] Director/Retired Headmaster; Ian Richard Davenport [1960] Director; William Jeremy Alexander Gordon [1964] Director/Solicitor; Karen Marisa Gorham [1964] Director/Bishop; Louise Drummond Hall [1966] Director/Investment Banker; Amanda Louise Harris [1982] Director/Accountant; Robin Anthony Langley Leach [1955] Director; Rupert de Gascoigne Pilkington [1946] Director/Chartered Quantity Surveyor; Robin Timothy Bezeck Price [1964] Director/Company CEO; Ann Lesley Mary Simon [1956] Director/Career Management Coach; Richard William Strang [1950] Director/Financial Consultant; Philip Charles Ward [1960] Director/Headmaster; Maria Wingfield Digby [1972] Director/Property Management; Nicholas John Stirling Wordie [1966] Director/Chartered Architect

Shervey Limited
Incorporated: 3 August 2007 *Employees:* 260
Net Worth: £1,303,088 *Total Assets:* £11,343,455
Registered Office: First Floor, CEF Building, Broomhill Way, Torquay, Devon, TQ2 7QN
Activities: Activities of other holding companies n.e.c.
Shareholders: David Guy Henson; Nicholas Shervey Meyer; Lisa Patricia Henson; Suzanne Meyer
Officers: Nicholas Shervey Meyer, Secretary; David Guy Henson [1958] Director/Head of Sales; Lisa Patricia Henson [1969] Director/Executive Assistant; Nicholas Shervey Meyer [1953] Director/Care Home Operator; Suzanne Meyer [1955] Director

Shield Environmental Holdings Limited
Incorporated: 18 September 2006 *Employees:* 362
Net Worth: £7,548,563 *Total Assets:* £16,532,068
Registered Office: Shield House, Caxton Business Park, Crown Way, Warmley, Bristol, BS30 8XJ
Activities: Remediation activities and other waste management services
Major Shareholder: Phillip Anthony House
Officers: Darren Nicholas Sheppard, Secretary; Craig Dennis [1976] Technical Director; Julian Mark House [1964] Business Development Director; Luke Phillip House [1979] Managing Director; Phillip Anthony House [1956] Director/Insulation Contractor; Robert John Miotla [1964] Operational Director

Shield Environmental Services Limited
Incorporated: 26 February 1985 *Employees:* 349
Net Worth: £12,706,861 *Total Assets:* £17,953,498
Registered Office: Shield House, Caxton Business Park, Crown Way, Warmley, Bristol, BS30 8XJ
Activities: Remediation activities and other waste management services
Major Shareholder: Phillip Anthony House
Officers: Darren Nicholas Sheppard, Secretary; Craig Dennis [1976] Technical Director; Julian Mark House [1964] Business Development Director; Luke Phillip House [1979] Managing Director; Phillip Anthony House [1956] Director; Robert John Miotla [1964] Operational Director

Shillofad Limited
Incorporated: 27 October 1995
Net Worth: £7,611,116 *Total Assets:* £10,639,476
Registered Office: The Old Smithy, Stocktons Courtyard, Overbury, Tewkesbury, Glos, GL20 7NT
Activities: Silviculture and other forestry activities
Shareholders: Timothy Mucklow; Trevor Mucklow
Officers: Heather Anne Battson, Secretary; Heather Anne Battson [1968] Director/Chartered Accountant; Duns-Scott Mucklow [1983] Director/Manager Sportswear Company [French]; Timothy Mucklow [1958] Director/Fish Farmer

Shiloh Limited
Incorporated: 2 March 1953
Net Worth: £30,198,888 *Total Assets:* £35,211,816
Registered Office: c/o Synergy Health PLC, Ground Floor, Stella Building, Windmill Hill Business Park, Swindon, Wilts, SN5 6NX
Activities: Other service activities n.e.c.
Parent: Synergy Health Holdings Limited
Officers: Tracey Anne Miles [1971] Director; Peter John Rendle [1980] Director/Chartered Accountant; Michael Joseph Tokich [1968] Director/Senior Vice President & Chief Financial Officer [American]

Shilston Barton Farming Limited
Incorporated: 30 April 1997 *Employees:* 2
Net Worth: £3,555,062 *Total Assets:* £5,801,610
Registered Office: Shilstone, Modbury, Ivybridge, Devon, PL21 0TW
Activities: Other letting and operating of own or leased real estate
Major Shareholder: Sebastian Edmund Stephen Fenwick
Officers: Rosemary Jane Mucy Fenwick, Secretary; Sebastian Edmund Stephen Fenwick [1953] Director/Property Developer

Shimao Limited
Incorporated: 5 February 2015 *Employees:* 3
Net Worth: £921,847 *Total Assets:* £5,020,431
Registered Office: St Georges Lodge, Oldfield Road, Bath, BA2 3NE
Activities: Financial intermediation not elsewhere classified
Major Shareholder: Rebecca Jane Kupa
Officers: Peter Phipps, Secretary; Rebecca Kupa [1986] Director; David John Medlock [1955] Director

Shiner Limited
Incorporated: 11 June 1936 *Employees:* 101
Net Worth: £15,672,000 *Total Assets:* £19,954,000
Registered Office: 1700 Park Avenue, Aztec West, Almondsbury, Bristol, BS32 4UA
Activities: Non-specialised wholesale trade
Shareholders: Virginia Sophie Jane Allen; Charles Nicholas Allen; Christopher John Allen
Officers: Christopher John Allen, Secretary; Charles Nicholas Allen [1973] Operations Director; Christopher John Allen [1965] Sales Director; Patricia Anne Mary Allen [1943] Director; Richard Nigel Allen [1943] Director/Retired; Virginia Sophie Jane Allen [1966] Director; Graham Scott Miller [1963] Non-Executive Director Chairman; Richard Ashley James Staite [1970] Operations Director; Victoria Sarah Nina Sutherland [1974] Marketing Director

Shiner Properties Limited
Incorporated: 2 December 2011
Net Worth: £2,466,000 *Total Assets:* £4,393,000
Registered Office: 1700 Park Avenue, Aztec West, Almondsbury, Bristol, BS32 4UA
Activities: Other letting and operating of own or leased real estate
Shareholders: Charles Nicholas Allen; Christopher John Allen; Virginia Sophie Jane Allen
Officers: Charles Nicholas Allen [1973] Director; Christopher John Allen [1965] Director; Virginia Sophie Jane Allen [1966] Director

The Ship (Derriford) Limited
Incorporated: 13 April 2015
Net Worth: £3,131,781 *Total Assets:* £11,480,411
Registered Office: Dean Clarke House, Southernhay East, Exeter, Devon, EX1 1AP
Activities: Other letting and operating of own or leased real estate
Parent: Burrington Estates (Commercial) Limited
Officers: Mark David Edworthy [1969] Director; Paul Neil Scantlebury [1967] Director

Shiphay Learning Academy
Incorporated: 16 March 2011 *Employees:* 70
Net Worth: £3,244,307 *Total Assets:* £4,380,242
Registered Office: Exe Hill, Shiphay, Torquay, Devon, TQ2 7NF
Activities: Primary education
Officers: Lawrence Shaun William May, Secretary; Clare Alison Foulds [1981] Director/HR Manager; Elaine Gill [1956] Director/Headteacher; Gary Sean Hotine [1965] IT Director; Kate Lee [1973] Director/Deputy Head; Catherine Monroe [1964] Director/Teaching Assistant; Karen Pollock [1969] Director/Deputy Head; Denise Russell [1949] Director/Consultant Teacher; Mark Andrew Tucker [1973] Director/Finance Manager NHS; Reverend Adebenga Olayinka Antony Williams [1975] Director/Minister of Religion

Shiptinvest Limited
Incorporated: 12 July 1993
Previous: Finedon Mill Limited
Net Worth: £3,356,444 *Total Assets:* £12,104,651
Registered Office: Long Newnton, Tetbury, Glos, GL8 8RP
Activities: Activities of head offices
Officers: David Roberts, Secretary; John Richard Arkwright Lister [1954] Director/Miller

Shipton Mill Limited
Incorporated: 31 October 1979 *Employees:* 57
Net Worth: £6,674,011 *Total Assets:* £9,909,779
Registered Office: Shipton Mill, Long Newnton, Tetbury, Gloucester, GL8 8RP
Activities: Grain milling
Officers: David Roberts, Secretary; John Richard Arkwright Lister [1954] Director

Shire Integrated Systems Limited
Incorporated: 8 August 1995 *Employees:* 12
Net Worth: £2,681,768 *Total Assets:* £3,855,442
Registered Office: 4-5 King Square, Bridgwater, Somerset, TA6 3YF
Activities: Plumbing, heat and air-conditioning installation
Shareholders: Marcus Lynes; Martyn Anthony Peters
Officers: Marcus Lynes, Secretary/Director; Marcus Lynes [1977] Director; Martyn Anthony Peters [1974] Director; Neil Edward Taynton [1970] Director

Shirley-Young Limited
Incorporated: 3 May 1962 *Employees:* 4
Net Worth: £4,979,788 *Total Assets:* £6,135,752
Registered Office: Whyr Farm, Winterbourne Bassett, Swindon, Wilts, SN4 9QE
Activities: Growing of cereals (except rice), leguminous crops and oil seeds
Officers: Juliet Anne Verity Handslip, Secretary; Juliet Anne Verity Handslip [1978] Director/Corporate Consultant; Deborah Anne Greene Young [1949] Director/Housewife; Peter Malcolm Gavin Young [1947] Director/Solicitor; Stefanie Claire Elizabeth Young [1980] Director/Secretary

Shirwell Limited
Incorporated: 29 September 1961 *Employees:* 6
Net Worth: £7,245,915 *Total Assets:* £8,899,603
Registered Office: Hendford Manor, Hendford, Yeovil, Somerset, BA20 1UN
Activities: Other letting and operating of own or leased real estate
Officers: Stephen William Bale, Secretary; Rory Lawrance Armitage [1992] Director/Manager; Nicholas Andrew Fereday Bale [1964] Director; Philip Lawrance Bale [1968] Director; Roger Bale [1940] Director/Company Secretary; Stephen William Bale [1971] Director/Self Employed

Shoals Hook Solar (UK) Limited
Incorporated: 30 May 2014
Net Worth: £16,935 *Total Assets:* £16,475,081
Registered Office: The Long Barn, Manor Courtyard, Stratton on the Fosse, Radstock, Somerset, BA3 4QF
Activities: Production of electricity
Parent: CSGH Solar (1) Limited
Officers: Giuseppe La Loggia [1975] Director [Italian]; Yit Ho Tang [1974] Investment Director [Singaporean]; Christopher James Tanner [1972] Investment Director; Jonathan Simon Thompson [1963] Director

SHOO 788AA Limited
Incorporated: 8 July 2015 *Employees:* 230
Net Worth: £334,286 *Total Assets:* £29,274,732
Registered Office: 21-22 Balena Close, Poole, Dorset, BH17 7DX
Activities: Manufacture of non-domestic cooling and ventilation equipment
Parent: Donaldson Company, Inc.
Officers: Antony Keith Lockwood [1960] Managing Director; James Martin Oliver [1970] Director/Chartered Accountant; Lev Schoefs [1971] Director/Business Executive [Belgian]; Todd Smith [1971] Director/Business Executive [American]; Jeff Spethmann [1965] Director/Business Executive [American]; Wim Vermeersch [1966] Director/Business Executive [Belgian]

Shooters Bottom Wind Park Ltd
Incorporated: 31 May 2000
Net Worth: £4,358,266 *Total Assets:* £5,071,267
Registered Office: Lion House, Rowcroft, Stroud, Glos, GL5 3BY
Activities: Production of electricity
Parent: Ecotricity Group Limited
Officers: Tom Cowling, Secretary; Asif Rehmanwala [1976] Director/Chief Operating Officer; Dale Vince [1961] Director/Consultant

Shorelark Limited
Incorporated: 3 February 2015 *Employees:* 73
Net Worth: £6,680,267 *Total Assets:* £9,689,062
Registered Office: Units 8-12 Chalwyn Industrial Estate, St Clements Road, Parkstone, Poole, Dorset, BH12 4PE
Activities: Activities of head offices
Major Shareholder: Stewart Clive Goulding
Officers: Shaun Cole [1965] Finance Director; Michael Richard Davies [1971] Manufacturing Director; Stewart Clive Goulding [1963] Director/Sales & Marketing; John Alexander Sellings [1970] Operations Director

Allan Sichel Limited
Incorporated: 17 March 1951 *Employees:* 150
Net Worth: £21,603,816 *Total Assets:* £89,157,560
Registered Office: The Island, Lowman Green, Tiverton, Devon, EX16 4LA
Activities: Activities of distribution holding companies
Shareholder: Peter and Diana Sichel Trust
Officers: Bruce Henry Beacham, Secretary/Director; Simon Allan Harris [1961] Director; Sir Ian Heathcoat Amory [1942] Director

Sidcot School
Incorporated: 26 January 1987 *Employees:* 253
Net Worth: £11,997,483 *Total Assets:* £16,814,492
Registered Office: Sidcot School, Oakridge Lane, Winscombe, Somerset, BS25 1PD
Activities: Pre-primary education
Officers: Steve Harris, Secretary; Timothy Norman Bond [1949] Director; Rosemary Elizabeth Carr [1964] Director/Consultant; Jonathan David Kingsley Coates [1958] Director; Andrew Flint [1958] Director/Governor; Victoria Clare Hemming [1956] Director; Christopher Hobbs [1958] Director/Consultant Solicitor; Daniel Lloyd [1973] Director; Adam John Matthews [1961] Director; Sarah Louise Prag Moore [1977] Director/Consultant; Timothy Colin Niblock [1942] Director/Professor; Nicholas Jon Pyatt [1960] Director; Andrew Thomas Ward [1958] Director/Retired Teacher; David Southall Whiting [1949] Director/Marketing Consultant

Sideshow Ltd
Incorporated: 31 July 2008 *Employees:* 22
Net Worth: £6,795,472 *Total Assets:* £7,477,070
Registered Office: Mindrum House, 25 St Clair Road, Poole, Dorset, BH13 7JP
Activities: Advertising agencies
Shareholders: Sandra Uta Fehrenbacher; Anthony Richard Hill
Officers: Sandra Uta Fehrenbacher, Secretary; Sandra Uta Fehrenbacher [1973] Director [German]; Tony Hill [1968] Director/Chairman

Sidlaw Group Limited
Incorporated: 15 October 1920
Net Worth: £140,984,992 *Total Assets:* £146,952,000
Registered Office: 83 Tower Road North, Warmley, Bristol, BS30 8XP
Activities: Activities of head offices
Officers: Matthew Charles Burrows [1970] Director; Christopher John Cheetham [1962] Director/Chartered Accountant; Damien Clayton [1971] Director; Richard Dixon [1963] Director/European Treasury and Tax Manager

Sidmouth Hotels Holdings Limited
Incorporated: 7 April 2017
Net Worth: £2 *Total Assets:* £4,107,729
Registered Office: The Esplanade, Sidmouth, Devon, EX10 8AT
Activities: Activities of other holding companies n.e.c.
Major Shareholder: Mark Seward
Officers: Mark Seward [1960] Director/Hotelier

Sidmouth Hotels Limited
Incorporated: 6 July 2000 *Employees:* 55
Net Worth: £2,076,983 *Total Assets:* £4,794,056
Registered Office: The Esplanade, Sidmouth, Devon, EX10 8AT
Activities: Hotels and similar accommodation
Parent: Sidmouth Hotels Holdings Limited
Officers: Mark Seward [1960] Director/Hotelier

Sigma - Aldrich Financial Services Limited
Incorporated: 4 December 1998 *Employees:* 1
Net Worth: £28,449,688 *Total Assets:* £118,402,248
Registered Office: The Old Brickyard, Gillingham, Dorset, SP8 4XT
Activities: Financial intermediation not elsewhere classified
Parent: Merck KGaA
Officers: Jorg Bermuller [1971] Director [German]; Linda Churchward [1970] Director/Accountant [Irish]; Barry John Deegan [1976] Director/Accountant [Irish]; James Ennis [1965] Site Director [Irish]; Carola-Catherine Knecht [1983] Director/Finance Manager [German]

Sigma-Aldrich Company Limited
Incorporated: 10 December 1987 *Employees:* 562
Net Worth: £550,531,968 *Total Assets:* £786,110,976
Registered Office: The Old Brickyard, New Road, Gillingham, Dorset, SP8 4XT
Activities: Manufacture of other chemical products n.e.c.
Parent: Merck KGaA
Officers: Peter Biro [1967] Director/US Certified Public Accountant [Dutch]; Victor Mark Jackson [1962] Director/Operations Manager

Signet Armorlite Europe Limited
Incorporated: 9 March 1987 *Employees:* 92
Net Worth: £1,091,931 *Total Assets:* £10,090,345
Registered Office: 1-7 Apollo, Olympus Park Business Centre, Quedgeley, Gloucester, GL2 4NF
Activities: Other manufacturing n.e.c.
Parent: Trifle Holdings Limited
Officers: James Michael Smith [1969] Group Financial Director; Peter James Smith [1961] Director/Regional VP Essilor UK and Ireland

Signum Technology Limited
Incorporated: 12 January 2012 *Employees:* 140
Net Worth Deficit: £36,695,000 *Total Assets:* £65,568,000
Registered Office: KLAW Products, Commerce Business Centre, Commerce Close, West Wilts Trading Estate, Westbury, Wilts, BA13 4LS
Activities: Activities of head offices
Officers: Mike Hartman, Secretary; Christopher James Braithwaite [1956] Director; Adam Robert Corbett [1981] Director/Chartered Accountant; Mike Hartman [1965] Director/Chief Financial Officer; David Robert Hill [1966] Director; Hugh Philip Lenon [1960] Director/Investment Professional; Catherine Alison Wall [1960] Director

Silbury Housing Holdings Limited
Incorporated: 4 June 2010
Total Assets: £5,530,000
Registered Office: Sarsen Court, Horton Avenue, Cannings Hill, Devizes, Wilts, SN10 2AZ
Activities: Construction of domestic buildings
Officers: David Allen Betteridge, Secretary; David Allen Betteridge [1970] Governance & Risk Director; Clare Helen Crawford [1977] Business Development Director; John Karl Pott [1964] Director/Accountant

Silbury Housing Limited
Incorporated: 7 June 2010
Net Worth Deficit: £5,255,000 *Total Assets:* £45,877,000
Registered Office: Sarsen Court, Horton Avenue, Cannings Hill, Devizes, Wilts, SN10 2AZ
Activities: Construction of domestic buildings
Parent: Silbury Housing Holdings Limited
Officers: David Allen Betteridge, Secretary; David Allen Betteridge [1970] Governance & Risk Director; Clare Helen Crawford [1977] Business Development Director; Jean Maria Dalziel [1968] Housing, Care and Support Director; Alec Charles Pegram [1962] Operations Director; John Karl Pott [1964] Director/Accountant

Silicon Sensing Systems Limited
Incorporated: 21 September 1998 *Employees:* 14
Net Worth: £17,594,000 *Total Assets:* £20,840,000
Registered Office: Clittaford Road, Southway, Plymouth, PL6 6DE
Activities: Other manufacturing n.e.c.
Officers: Norman David Cooke, Secretary; Sandra Fumei [1978] Finance Director [American]; Shogo Ishimaru [1963] Finance Director [Japanese]; Hiroaki Minami [1962] Director/Engineer [Japanese]; Geoffrey Kenneth Newman [1958] Marketing Director [American]; Kevin Pindard [1967] Managing Director; Ayumu Takahashi [1959] Director [Japanese]

Herbert Silver (Holdings) Limited
Incorporated: 15 January 1954 *Employees:* 4
Net Worth: £5,692,158 *Total Assets:* £6,110,951
Registered Office: Martin Hayes, West Hill Road, West Hill, Ottery St Mary, Devon, EX11 1TU
Activities: Other letting and operating of own or leased real estate
Shareholder: Rachel Porter
Officers: Nicholas Silver, Secretary; Caroline Dent [1978] Director/Accountant; Lorraine Last [1949] Director/Part Time Teacher; Christopher John Silver [1946] Director; Nicholas Silver [1972] Director

Silver Arrow Investments Ltd
Incorporated: 27 June 2013 *Employees:* 3
Net Worth: £2,639,238 *Total Assets:* £14,050,061
Registered Office: 11a Haven Road, Poole, Dorset, BH13 7LE
Activities: Other letting and operating of own or leased real estate
Major Shareholder: Joshua Matthew Mitchell
Officers: Joshua Matthew Mitchell [1991] Director

Silverfish UK (Holdings) Limited
Incorporated: 13 July 2011
Net Worth: £3,457,500 *Total Assets:* £7,537,500
Registered Office: Units 3b and 3c Woodacre Court, Saltash Parkway Industrial Estate, Saltash, Cornwall, PL12 6LF
Activities: Non-specialised wholesale trade
Shareholders: Sarah Jane Mabbott; Darren Mabbott
Officers: Darren Graham Mabbott [1971] Director; Sarah Jane Mabbott [1970] Director

Silverfish UK Limited
Incorporated: 20 September 2000 *Employees:* 34
Net Worth: £2,824,286 *Total Assets:* £6,157,897
Registered Office: Units 3b & 3c Woodacre Court, Saltash Parkway Industrial Estate, Burraton Road, Saltash, Cornwall, PL12 6LF
Activities: Other retail sale of new goods in specialised stores (not commercial art galleries and opticians)
Parent: Silverfish UK (Holdings) Limited
Officers: Sarah Jane Mabbott, Secretary/Administrator; Darren Graham Mabbott [1971] Director/Sales Manager; Sarah Jane Mabbott [1970] Director/Administrator

Silverleigh Limited
Incorporated: 3 August 1994 *Employees:* 110
Net Worth: £6,525,175 *Total Assets:* £12,130,946
Registered Office: 50 The Terrace, Torquay, Devon, TQ1 1DD
Activities: Residential care activities for the elderly and disabled
Parent: Cannon Care Homes 4 Limited
Officers: Jane Canon, Secretary; Robin George Canon [1953] Director

Silversands Limited
Incorporated: 19 June 1987
Net Worth: £1,556,654 *Total Assets:* £4,944,350
Registered Office: 3 Albany Park, Cabot Lane, Poole, Dorset, BH17 7BX
Activities: Information technology consultancy activities
Major Shareholder: Akif Zafer Tosunlair
Officers: Susan Jones, Secretary; Sue Jones [1965] Director; Mark Spalding [1954] Director/General Manager; Akif Zafer Tosunlar [1950] Director

Silversword Limited
Incorporated: 7 September 2005 *Employees:* 42
Net Worth Deficit: £524,054 *Total Assets:* £4,610,914
Registered Office: 31-33 Commercial Road, Poole, Dorset, BH14 0HU
Activities: Other human health activities
Shareholder: Christopher Bialan
Officers: Victoria Ann Benson, Secretary; Geoffrey Smyth, Secretary; Christopher Bialan [1957] Director; Christine Joan Smyth [1954] Director; Geoffrey Smyth [1950] Director/Retired

The Simian Group (Holdings) Limited
Incorporated: 6 April 2011
Net Worth: £5,248,000 *Total Assets:* £17,976,000
Registered Office: Wellington House, Kemble Enterprise Park, Kemble, Cirencester, Glos, GL7 6BQ
Activities: Other business support service activities n.e.c.
Parent: Hardware Group Limited
Officers: Gwyn David Hicks [1971] Director/Chief Financial Officer; Stewart Holness [1966] Director

The Simian Group Limited
Incorporated: 11 October 1999
Net Worth: £2,871,000 *Total Assets:* £9,227,000
Registered Office: Wellington House, Kemble Enterprise Park, Kemble, Cirencester, Glos, GL7 6BQ
Activities: Activities of head offices
Parent: The Simian Group (Holdings) Limited
Officers: Gwyn David Hicks [1971] Director/Chief Financial Officer; Stewart Holness [1966] Director

R.W.Simon Limited
Incorporated: 20 November 1958 *Employees:* 113
Net Worth: £3,403,056 *Total Assets:* £5,799,482
Registered Office: System Works, Hatchmoor Industrial Estate, Great Torrington, Devon, EX38 7HP
Activities: Manufacture of other plastic products
Officers: Terence Michael Hitchins, Secretary; Jonathan Gregg Simon [1949] Director/Chairman; Laila Clair Simon [1985] Director; Philip Simon [1981] Director/Banker; Robert Andrew Simon [1950] Director; Imogen Simone Woolley [1991] Director/Artist

Simonstone (Bristol) Limited
Incorporated: 8 November 2002 *Employees:* 41
Net Worth: £344,133 *Total Assets:* £4,088,190
Registered Office: 803-805 Bath Road, Brislington, Bristol, BS4 5NL
Activities: Sale of new cars and light motor vehicles
Officers: Michelle Wilson, Secretary; Michael William Hooper [1956] Director; Ian Jones [1983] Sales Director; Michelle Wilson [1966] Finance Director

Simonstone Motor Group PLC
Incorporated: 7 November 2002 *Employees:* 59
Net Worth: £643,986 *Total Assets:* £5,677,824
Registered Office: 803-805 Bath Road, Brislington, Bristol, BS4 5NL
Activities: Sale of new cars and light motor vehicles
Shareholder: Michael William Hooper
Officers: Michelle Wilson, Secretary; Michael William Hooper [1956] Director; Ian Jones [1983] Sales Director; Michelle Wilson [1966] Finance Director

Simplex-Turbulo Group Limited
Incorporated: 26 October 1935 *Employees:* 59
Net Worth: £4,778,293 *Total Assets:* £7,100,537
Registered Office: Wherwell Priory, Wherwell, Andover, Hants, SP11 7JH
Activities: Agents involved in the sale of machinery, industrial equipment, ships and aircraft
Officers: Justin Alexander Spice Brooking, Secretary; Justin Alexander Spice Brooking [1966] Finance Director; The Hon Dorothy Clare Hogg [1955] Director; The Hon James Richard Martin Hogg [1951] Director/Shipping Executive; Thomas Kaiser-Sichau [1965] Commercial Director [German]

Simply Pleasure Limited
Incorporated: 17 December 2001 *Employees:* 124
Net Worth: £2,017,157 *Total Assets:* £7,669,731
Registered Office: Towngate House, 2-8 Parkstone Road, Poole, Dorset, BH15 2PW
Activities: Other retail sale of new goods in specialised stores (not commercial art galleries and opticians)
Parent: ABS Wholesale Limited
Officers: Timothy Martin Hemming [1960] Director/Importer Retailer; Symon John Reeves [1974] Director

Simplyhealth Access
Incorporated: 11 July 1922 *Employees:* 761
Net Worth: £194,600,000 *Total Assets:* £291,900,000
Registered Office: Hambleden House, Waterloo Court, Andover, Hants, SP10 1LQ
Activities: Other human health activities
Parent: Simplyhealth Holdings Limited
Officers: Romana Abdin [1963] Director; Gil Baldwin [1960] Director; Michael Andrew Hall [1954] Director/Healthcare Insurance and Services; Richard John Harris [1952] Director; John Neil Maltby [1962] Director; Kenneth Stanton Piggott [1948] Director; Alexandra Louise Pike [1963] Director

Simplyhealth Group Limited
Incorporated: 6 May 2005 *Employees:* 1,301
Net Worth: £270,100,000 *Total Assets:* £385,600,000
Registered Office: Hambleden House, Waterloo Court, Andover, Hants, SP10 1LQ
Activities: Other human health activities
Officers: Romana Abdin [1963] Director; Gil Baldwin [1960] Director; Michael Andrew Hall [1954] Director; Richard John Harris [1952] Director; John Neil Maltby [1962] Director; Kenneth Stanton Piggott [1948] Director; Alexandra Louise Pike [1963] Director

Sir Thomas Rich's School
Incorporated: 30 July 2010 *Employees:* 154
Net Worth: £20,393,444 *Total Assets:* £21,796,690
Registered Office: Oakleaze, Longlevens, Gloucester, GL2 0LF
Activities: General secondary education
Officers: Susan Rosemary Bain, Secretary; Andrew Keith Bishop [1954] Director; Richard Thomas Goldsby [1969] Director/IT Executive; Thomas Robert Grogan [1991] Director/Solicitor; Matthew Thomas Lynch [1984] Director/Teacher; Jocelyn Major [1969] Director/Independent Financial Advisor; Dr Ian Marshall [1945] Director/Retired; Julia May [1969] Director/Solicitor; Brian McBurnie [1947] Director/Retired; Matthew Spencer Richard Morgan [1975] Director/Headmaster; Roger Anthony Ogle [1947] Business Director; Alan Sidney Pilbeam [1936] Director/Retired; Richard John Taylor Powell [1949] Director/Estate Agent; Bryan Charles Stiles [1959] Director/Semi-Retired (Banking); Janferie Jill Wilton [1944] Director; Timothy Hugh Wilton [1948] Director/Teacher

Sirona Care & Health C.I.C.
Incorporated: 30 March 2011 *Employees:* 1,192
Net Worth Deficit: £1,165,000 *Total Assets:* £11,611,000
Registered Office: 2nd Floor, Kingswood Civic Centre, High Street, Kingswood, Bristol, BS15 9TR
Activities: Other human health activities
Officers: Paul Richard Butler [1965] Director; Amanda Jane Cheesley [1958] Director; Michael Simon Knighton [1950] Director; Paul May [1946] Director; David John Purdon [1955] Director; Janet Rowse [1967] Director; Jennifer Theed [1956] Director

SIRVA Relocation (No.1) Limited
Incorporated: 14 July 1986 *Employees:* 123
Net Worth: £11,897,538 *Total Assets:* £20,382,446
Registered Office: Ground Floor, Mulberry Building, Kembrey Park, Swindon, Wilts, SN2 8UY
Activities: Other transportation support activities
Parent: SIRVA Relocation Holdings Limited
Officers: Alan Russell Cullens, Secretary; Alan Russell Cullens [1966] Director/Chartered Accountant; Steven David Marshall [1964] Director

SIRVA Relocation Holdings Limited
Incorporated: 11 December 1992 *Employees:* 122
Net Worth: £11,897,539 *Total Assets:* £20,382,446
Registered Office: Ground Floor, Mulberry Building, Kembrey Park, Swindon, Wilts, SN2 8UY
Activities: Combined office administrative service activities
Parent: SIRVA Inc
Officers: Alan Russell Cullens, Secretary; Alan Russell Cullens [1966] Director/Chartered Accountant; Steven David Marshall [1964] Director

Site Developments (Ferndown) Limited
Incorporated: 13 May 1966
Net Worth: £1,625,860 *Total Assets:* £6,230,483
Registered Office: Stafford House, 10 Prince of Wales Road, Dorchester, DT1 1PW
Activities: Development of building projects
Shareholder: Adrian Nicholas Wilkes
Officers: Michael Bruce Wilkes, Secretary; Colin Richard Burridge [1936] Director; Keith Burridge [1960] Director; Adrian Nicholas Wilkes [1947] Director; Michael Bruce Wilkes [1939] Director; Vivienne Anne Wilkes [1941] Director

Sitec Design Limited
Incorporated: 23 March 2016 *Employees:* 54
Net Worth: £26,847,000 *Total Assets:* £32,448,000
Registered Office: 33 Oldfield Road, Bath, BA2 3NE
Activities: Activities of head offices
Parent: Belcan International Limited
Officers: Antony Christopher Ambridge, Secretary; James Buick [1956] Engineering Director; Elizabeth Ferris [1966] Director/Chief Finance Officer [American]; Keith Matthews [1972] Managing Director; Neal Montour [1960] Director/President, Engineering Services [American]; Mark McKenzie Naylor [1971] Finance Director

Sitec Engineering Limited
Incorporated: 14 November 2007 *Employees:* 53
Previous: Sitec Investments Limited
Net Worth: £35,133,000 *Total Assets:* £36,298,000
Registered Office: St Georges Lodge, 33 Oldfield Road, Bath, BA2 3NE
Activities: Specialised design activities
Parent: Sitec Holdings Limited
Officers: Antony Christopher Ambridge, Secretary; James Buick [1956] Engineering Director; Elizabeth Ferris [1966] Director/Chief Finance Officer [American]; Keith Matthews [1972] Managing Director; Neal Montour [1960] Director/President, Engineering Services [American]; Mark McKenzie Naylor [1971] Finance Director

Sitec Holdings Limited
Incorporated: 8 February 2013
Net Worth: £30,154,000 *Total Assets:* £30,663,000
Registered Office: St George's Lodge, 33 Oldfield Road, Bath, BA2 3NE
Activities: Activities of head offices
Parent: Sitec Design Limited
Officers: Antony Christopher Ambridge, Secretary; Elizabeth Ferris [1966] Director/Chief Finance Officer [American]; Keith Matthews [1972] Managing Director; Neal Montour [1960] Director/President, Engineering Services [American]; Mark McKenzie Naylor [1971] Finance Director

Sitec Recruitment Limited
Incorporated: 23 March 2016 *Employees:* 92
Net Worth: £3,565,000 *Total Assets:* £15,660,000
Registered Office: 33 Oldfield Road, Bath, BA2 3NE
Activities: Activities of head offices
Parent: Belcan International Limited
Officers: Antony Christopher Ambridge, Secretary; James Buick [1956] Director; Elizabeth Ferris [1966] Director/Chief Finance Officer [American]; Keith Matthews [1972] Managing Director; Neal Montour [1960] Director/President, Engineering Services [American]; Mark McKenzie Naylor [1971] Finance Director

Skilled Group UK Limited
Incorporated: 16 October 2007
Net Worth: £3,740,077 *Total Assets:* £3,758,563
Registered Office: 10th Floor, Colston Tower, Colston Street, Bristol, BS1 4XE
Activities: Other business support service activities n.e.c.
Officers: Ronalda Verdoes, Secretary; Marcellinus Johannes Mana Burghouwt [1965] Director [Dutch]

Skylarking UK Limited
Incorporated: 21 July 2008
Previous: Skylarking Limited
Net Worth: £4,116,676 *Total Assets:* £4,561,024
Registered Office: Park House, 10 Park Street, Bristol, BS1 5HX
Activities: Performing arts
Major Shareholder: Russell Joseph Howard
Officers: David Howard, Secretary; Russell Joseph Howard [1980] Director/Comedian

Skyline Systems Limited
Incorporated: 3 August 1988 *Employees:* 3
Net Worth: £6,064,954 *Total Assets:* £6,795,170
Registered Office: Stella Way, Bishops Cleeve, Cheltenham, Glos, GL52 7DQ
Activities: Wholesale of wood, construction materials and sanitary equipment
Shareholders: Donal Ring; Diana Rawlings Co Administrator of The Estate of D Rawlings
Officers: Pauline Atkinson, Secretary; Christopher Martin [1947] Director/Manager [Irish]; Anthony Mitchell [1960] Director/Chartered Accountant

Slee Blackwell Solicitors LLP
Incorporated: 16 February 2016 *Employees:* 90
Net Worth: £2,492,708 *Total Assets:* £3,594,824
Registered Office: 10 Cross Street, Barnstaple, Devon, EX31 1BA
Officers: Nicholas John Arthur [1961] Member; Andrew John Burke [1965] Member; Lee Antony Dawkins [1960] Member; Paul Jordan [1963] Member; Louise Lydia Langabeer [1973] Member; Brett Lawrence [1974] Member; James Dominic McNally [1976] Member; Emma Louise Napper [1974] Member; Emma Jane Reed [1977] Member; Romano Sidoli [1963] Member; Naomi Grace Ireson [1988] LLP Member

Sleepers Hill (Winchester) Limited
Incorporated: 7 March 2017 *Employees:* 4
Net Worth Deficit: £4,538 *Total Assets:* £3,549,681
Registered Office: 15 Hertford Court, Hertford Road, Marlborough, Wilts, SN8 4AW
Activities: Development of building projects
Parent: Sherbourne Sleepers Hill Limited
Officers: Shaun Winston Borrett [1966] Director; Bruce James O'Grady [1967] Director/Property Developer

SLG Allstars Limited
Incorporated: 3 December 2014 *Employees:* 160
Net Worth: £19,207,944 *Total Assets:* £24,282,406
Registered Office: Liberty House, St Catherine Street, Gloucester, GL1 2BX
Activities: Activities of other holding companies n.e.c.
Shareholders: Miles Spencer Maitland Dunkley; BGF GP Limited
Officers: Lucy Jane Beresford [1980] Commercial Director; Richard Mark Buckland [1977] Director; Miles Spencer Maitland Dunkley [1967] Director; Alex Jonathan Garfitt [1982] Director/Investor; Susan Hutchings [1966] Director; Geoffrey Michael Percy [1959] Director

Sloane & Pirkis LLP
Incorporated: 29 October 2012
Net Worth: £15,668,923 *Total Assets:* £25,354,378
Registered Office: Cleave Hill Water, Manaton, Newton Abbot, Devon, TQ13 9UB
Officers: David Kevin Pirkis [1957] Member; Hugh Patrick Sloane [1955] Member

SLX Group Limited
Incorporated: 9 October 2012 *Employees:* 192
Previous: VPT1 Limited
Net Worth: £2,300,823 *Total Assets:* £10,854,183
Registered Office: Encore House, Unit 3 Britannia Road, Patchway Trading Estate, Patchway, Bristol, BS34 5TA
Activities: Activities of other holding companies n.e.c.
Shareholder: John Steven Laycock
Officers: John Steven Laycock [1948] Director; Trevor Smallwood [1947] Director; Maria Ann Townsend [1980] Director/Group CEO

SM Group (Europe) Ltd.
Incorporated: 1 April 1977 *Employees:* 31
Net Worth: £2,673,394 *Total Assets:* £4,241,137
Registered Office: Mercator House, 22 Brest Road, Derriford, Plymouth, PL6 5XP
Activities: Non-specialised wholesale trade
Major Shareholder: Christopher Paul Northmore
Officers: Raymond Arthur Badminton [1962] Director; Christopher Paul Northmore [1950] Director; Susan Monica Stubbs [1966] Director

Smallridge Bros Limited
Incorporated: 20 February 2008 *Employees:* 69
Net Worth: £3,395,370 *Total Assets:* £10,468,344
Registered Office: East Collabear, Tawstock, Barnstaple, Devon, EX31 3JZ
Activities: Sale of other motor vehicles
Shareholders: David John Smallridge; Elaine Anne Smallridge; Michael James Smallridge; Gillian Smallridge
Officers: Gillian Smallridge, Secretary; David John Shambrook [1963] Director/Agricultural Engineer; David John Smallridge [1954] Director/Agricultural Engineer; Elaine Anne Smallridge [1957] Director; Gillian Smallridge [1955] Director; Michael James Smallridge [1958] Director/Agricultural Engineer

Harold W Smart & Son Limited
Incorporated: 16 July 1964 *Employees:* 18
Net Worth: £9,305,610 *Total Assets:* £16,206,977
Registered Office: Stone End Farm, Churcham, Glos, GL2 8AA
Activities: Growing of cereals (except rice), leguminous crops and oil seeds
Shareholders: David Paul Smart; Peter Jeremy Smart
Officers: Peter Jeremy Smart, Secretary; David Paul Smart [1963] Director/Farmer; Peter Jeremy Smart [1962] Director/Farmer

C. Smart Agricultural Services Limited
Incorporated: 21 September 1998 *Employees:* 56
Net Worth: £6,453,825 *Total Assets:* £11,687,258
Registered Office: Sands House, Sands Lane, Donhead St Andrew, Shaftesbury, Dorset, SP7 9EJ
Activities: Wholesale of agricultural machinery, equipment and supplies
Shareholders: Colin Smart; Frances Patricia Smart
Officers: Christopher Payne, Secretary; Michael Mervyn Mitchell [1966] Director/Manager; Christopher Payne [1983] Financial Director; Colin Smart [1957] Sales Marketing Director; Frances Patricia Smart [1965] Director/Shepherdess; Bernard William Steele [1954] Director/Manager

Smart Aluminium Extrusions Limited
Incorporated: 15 June 2010 *Employees:* 166
Net Worth Deficit: £4,004,000 *Total Assets:* £17,900,000
Registered Office: Arnolds Way, Yatton, Somerset, BS49 4QN
Activities: Aluminium production
Parent: Fornuis UK Limited
Officers: Wim Flo [1979] Director [Belgian]; Edward Anthony Robinson [1958] Director; Johan Paul Jozef Verstrepen [1961] Director [Belgian]

Smart Systems Limited
Incorporated: 23 May 1977 *Employees:* 288
Net Worth: £106,736,000 *Total Assets:* £124,464,000
Registered Office: Arnolds Way, Yatton, Somerset, BS49 4QN
Activities: Wholesale of wood, construction materials and sanitary equipment
Parent: Fonuis UK Limited
Officers: Edward Anthony Robinson, Secretary/Director; Wim Flo [1979] Director [Belgian]; Edward Anthony Robinson [1958] Director; Johan Paul Jozef Verstrepen [1961] Director [Belgian]

Smartstream Technologies Holdings Limited
Incorporated: 28 April 2000 *Employees:* 2
Net Worth: £51,967,000 *Total Assets:* £74,468,000
Registered Office: 1690 Park Avenue, Aztec West, Almondsbury, Bristol, BS32 4RA
Activities: Activities of head offices
Parent: Smartstream Acquisitions Limited
Officers: Claudia Giunta, Secretary; Richard William Bowler [1973] Director/Chief Financial Officer; Paul Stephen Thomas [1971] Director/Accountant

SMD 2013 Limited
Incorporated: 9 December 2013 *Employees:* 109
Net Worth: £4,502,956 *Total Assets:* £9,911,245
Registered Office: The Outlook, Ling Road, Tower Park, Bournemouth, BH12 4PY
Activities: Other construction installation
Parent: Firth Steels Limited
Officers: Roger Tennant Firth [1943] Director; Benedict Pratten [1973] Director

WH Smith 1955 Limited
Incorporated: 12 May 1955
Net Worth: £86,667,000 *Total Assets:* £91,108,000
Registered Office: WH Smith PLC, Greenbridge Road, Swindon, Wilts, SN3 3RX
Activities: Activities of head offices
Parent: WH Smith Retail Holdings Limited
Officers: Ian Houghton, Secretary; Stephen Martin Clarke [1967] Director/Chief Executive; Ian Houghton [1965] Director/Company Executive; Robert James Moorhead [1964] Director/Chartered Accountant

Les Smith Haulage Limited
Incorporated: 25 July 2009 *Employees:* 43
Net Worth: £1,642,536 *Total Assets:* £4,093,404
Registered Office: Kelvin Road, Greenbridge Industrial Estate, Swindon, Wilts, SN3 3JW
Activities: Freight transport by road
Parent: Les Smith Haulage Ltd Discretionary Trust
Officers: Anthony Leslie Smith [1965] Director; Daniel Brian Smith [1966] Director; Nicholas Lee Smith [1973] Director

WH Smith High Street Holdings Limited
Incorporated: 9 April 2008
Net Worth: £106,712,000 *Total Assets:* £392,688,000
Registered Office: Greenbridge Road, Swindon, Wilts, SN3 3RX
Activities: Activities of head offices
Parent: WH Smith Retail Holdings Limited
Officers: Ian Houghton, Secretary; Stephen Martin Clarke [1967] Director/Chief Executive; Ian Houghton [1965] Director; Robert James Moorhead [1964] Director/Chartered Accountant

WH Smith High Street Limited
Incorporated: 9 April 2008 *Employees:* 8,543
Net Worth: £369,371,008 *Total Assets:* £657,331,008
Registered Office: Greenbridge Road, Swindon, Wilts, SN3 3RX
Activities: Retail sale of books in specialised stores
Parent: WH Smith High Street Holdings Limited
Officers: Ian Houghton, Secretary; Stephen Martin Clarke [1967] Director/Chief Executive; Ian Houghton [1965] Director; Robert James Moorhead [1964] Director/Chartered Accountant

WH Smith Hospitals Holdings Limited
Incorporated: 14 July 1999
Net Worth: £4,221,153 *Total Assets:* £12,370,488
Registered Office: Greenbridge Road, Swindon, Wilts, SN3 3RX
Activities: Activities of head offices
Parent: WH Smith Travel 2008 Limited
Officers: Ian Houghton, Secretary/Company Executive; Stephen Martin Clarke [1967] Director/Chief Executive; Ian Houghton [1965] Director/Company Executive; Robert James Moorhead [1964] Director/Chartered Accountant

WH Smith Hospitals Limited
Incorporated: 27 April 2000 *Employees:* 611
Net Worth: £10,254,280 *Total Assets:* £38,831,496
Registered Office: Greenbridge Road, Swindon, Wilts, SN3 3RX
Activities: Other retail sale in non-specialised stores
Parent: WH Smith Hospitals Holdings Limited
Officers: Ian Houghton, Secretary/Director; Stephen Martin Clarke [1967] Director/Chief Executive; Ian Houghton [1965] Director; Robert James Moorhead [1964] Director/Chartered Accountant

WH Smith PLC
Incorporated: 10 August 2004 *Employees:* 13,828
Net Worth: £212,000,000 *Total Assets:* £528,000,000
Registered Office: Greenbridge Road, Swindon, Wilts, SN3 3RX
Activities: Activities of head offices
Officers: Ian Houghton, Secretary; Suzanne Claire Baxter [1968] Director; Stephen Martin Clarke [1967] Director/Chief Executive; Carl David Cowling [1973] Director; Annemarie Verna Florence Durbin [1963] Director/Financial Services [British/New Zealander]; Simon Emeny [1965] Director; John William Drummond Hall [1949] Director; Robert James Moorhead [1964] Director/Chartered Accountant; Henry Eric Staunton [1948] Director; Maurice Nicholas Beech Thompson [1958] Banker and Director

WH Smith Promotions Limited
Incorporated: 26 January 1989 *Employees:* 2
Net Worth: £23,277,132 *Total Assets:* £37,111,552
Registered Office: W H Smith PLC, Greenbridge Road, Swindon, Wilts, SN3 3RX
Activities: Retail sale of newspapers and stationery in specialised stores
Parent: WH Smith Retail Holdings Limited
Officers: Ian Houghton, Secretary; Stephen Martin Clarke [1967] Marketing Director; Ian Houghton [1965] Director/Company Executive; Robert James Moorhead [1964] Director/Chartered Accountant

WH Smith Retail Holdings Limited
Incorporated: 17 August 1949 *Employees:* 12,342
Net Worth: £450,726,016 *Total Assets:* £1,173,559,040
Registered Office: Greenbridge Road, Swindon, Wilts, SN3 3RX
Activities: Activities of head offices
Parent: WH Smith PLC
Officers: Ian Houghton, Secretary; Stephen Martin Clarke [1967] Director/Chief Executive; Ian Houghton [1965] Director/Company Executive; Robert James Moorhead [1964] Director/Chartered Accountant

Simon Smith Retail Limited
Incorporated: 16 February 2011 *Employees:* 105
Net Worth: £4,361,478 *Total Assets:* £18,076,588
Registered Office: 3 Fairview Court, Fairview Road, Cheltenham, Glos, GL52 2EX
Activities: Retail sale of automotive fuel in specialised stores
Shareholders: Brian John Tew; Vicky Anne Tew
Officers: Vicky Anne Tew, Secretary; Susanna Debbie Hawkins [1976] Director; Brian John Tew [1942] Director; Julie Vanessa Anne Tew [1974] Director; Vicky Anne Tew [1948] Director

WH Smith Travel 2008 Limited
Incorporated: 9 April 2008
Net Worth: £314,760,000 *Total Assets:* £399,760,000
Registered Office: Greenbridge Road, Swindon, Wilts, SN3 3RX
Activities: Activities of head offices
Parent: WH Smith Travel Holdings Limited
Officers: Ian Houghton, Secretary; Stephen Martin Clarke [1967] Director/Chief Executive; Ian Houghton [1965] Director; Robert James Moorhead [1964] Director/Chartered Accountant

WH Smith Travel Holdings Limited
Incorporated: 20 January 2006
Net Worth: £491,304,000 *Total Assets:* £760,265,024
Registered Office: Greenbridge Road, Swindon, Wilts, SN3 3RX
Activities: Activities of head offices
Parent: WH Smith Retail Holdings Limited
Officers: Ian Houghton, Secretary; Stephen Martin Clarke [1967] Director/Chief Executive; Ian Houghton [1965] Director/Company Executive; Robert James Moorhead [1964] Director/Chartered Accountant

WH Smith Travel Limited
Incorporated: 9 April 2008 *Employees:* 3,371
Net Worth: £418,892,000 *Total Assets:* £659,700,992
Registered Office: Greenbridge Road, Swindon, Wilts, SN3 3RX
Activities: Retail sale of books in specialised stores
Parent: WH Smith Travel 2008 Limited
Officers: Ian Houghton, Secretary; Stephen Martin Clarke [1967] Director/Chief Executive; Ian Houghton [1965] Director; Robert James Moorhead [1964] Director/Chartered Accountant

Smith's (Gloucester) Limited
Incorporated: 31 May 2000 *Employees:* 476
Net Worth: £6,118,710 *Total Assets:* £29,105,924
Registered Office: Alkerton Court, Eastington, Stonehouse, Glos, GL10 3AQ
Activities: Collection of non-hazardous waste
Major Shareholder: Alan Robin Smith
Officers: Pamela Joan Broomfield, Secretary; Alan Robin Smith [1959] Director; Anne Smith [1960] Director

Smithbrewer Limited
Incorporated: 26 May 1999 *Employees:* 92
Net Worth: £5,593,343 *Total Assets:* £9,206,593
Registered Office: 22 Bolton Close, Isleport Business Park, Highbridge, Somerset, TA9 4JR
Activities: Other manufacturing n.e.c.
Shareholders: Michael John Brewer; Simon Rodney Smith
Officers: Michael John Brewer, Secretary/Director; Michael John Brewer [1959] Director; Simon Rodney Smith [1964] Director

Smithcorp Limited
Incorporated: 11 October 2011 *Employees:* 163
Net Worth: £7,343,011 *Total Assets:* £10,626,013
Registered Office: Clifton Heights, Triangle West, Bristol, BS8 1EJ
Activities: Activities of head offices
Shareholders: Daniel Nikolas Smith; Adam James Smith; Dominic Richard Smith
Officers: Andrew Mark Dodge, Secretary; James Alexander Hampton Blackiston [1976] Group IT Director; Jonathan Bolitho Edwards [1981] Director/Chief Operations Officer; James Alastair Hodkinson [1972] Director/Chief Development Officer; Adam James Smith [1969] Director; Daniel Nikolas Smith [1972] Director; Dominic Richard Smith [1975] Director/Chief Executive Officer; Samantha Emma Start [1980] Director

Smiths News Holdings Limited
Incorporated: 18 June 2001
Net Worth: £338,200,000 *Total Assets:* £1,095,200,000
Registered Office: Rowan House, Cherry Orchard North, Kembrey Park, Swindon, Wilts, SN2 8UH
Activities: Activities of head offices
Parent: Connect Group PLC
Officers: Stuart Steven Marriner, Secretary; Anthony Liam Grace [1961] Director; Jozef Opdeweegh [1966] Director/Chief Executive Officer [American/Belgian]

Smiths News Trading Limited
Incorporated: 9 March 1929 *Employees:* 1,988
Net Worth: £666,899,968 *Total Assets:* £831,900,032
Registered Office: Rowan House, Cherry Orchard North, Kembrey Park, Swindon, Wilts, SN2 8UH
Activities: Non-specialised wholesale trade
Shareholders: Smiths News Holdings Limited; Smiths News Holdings Limited
Officers: Stuart Steven Marriner, Secretary; Jonathan Michael Bunting [1972] Director; Anthony Liam Grace [1961] Director

SMV Commercials Limited
Incorporated: 17 March 2009 *Employees:* 41
Net Worth: £824,536 *Total Assets:* £5,689,605
Registered Office: 20 Brympton Way, Lynx West Trading Estate, Yeovil, Somerset, BA20 2HP
Activities: Maintenance and repair of motor vehicles
Parent: Commercial Vehicles (Yeovil) Limited
Officers: Joanna Elizabeth Fowler [1972] Director; John Daniel Fowler [1944] Director

Snapdragons Nurseries Limited
Incorporated: 20 March 2002 *Employees:* 260
Net Worth: £7,768,750 *Total Assets:* £11,234,010
Registered Office: 1 Abacus House, Newlands Road, Corsham, Wilts, SN13 0BH
Activities: Pre-primary education
Shareholders: Paul Henry Collard; Rosemary Ann Collard; Paul Henry Collard; Rosemary Ann Collard
Officers: Paul Henry Collard, Secretary/Director; Jennifer Biddel [1987] Director; James Collard [1983] Director; Paul Henry Collard [1951] Director; Rosemary Ann Collard [1954] Director

Snape Construction Limited
Incorporated: 11 December 1989 *Employees:* 39
Net Worth: £4,843,009 *Total Assets:* £8,631,117
Registered Office: Willow End, Stoke Orchard Road, Bishops Cleeve, Cheltenham, Glos, GL52 7DG
Activities: Construction of commercial buildings
Officers: Susan Mary Snape, Secretary; Andrew Bernard Snape [1969] Director/General Manager; Susan Mary Snape [1946] Director/Company Secretary

Snape Contracting Services Ltd
Incorporated: 21 March 2011 *Employees:* 27
Net Worth: £1,589,091 *Total Assets:* £4,712,255
Registered Office: Willow End, Stoke Orchard Road, Bishops Cleeve, Cheltenham, Glos, GL52 7DG
Activities: Combined facilities support activities
Officers: Darryl Peter Hawkins [1963] Contracts Director; Andrew Bernard Snape [1969] Director

Snapfish UK, Ltd.
Incorporated: 6 May 2015 *Employees:* 90
Net Worth: £3,636,897 *Total Assets:* £18,123,396
Registered Office: Dakota House, Brunel Road, Newton Abbot, Devon, TQ12 4PB
Activities: Retail sale via mail order houses or via Internet
Officers: Keith Cohen [1988] Director/Executive Vice President [American]; Chris John Hughes [1966] Managing Director; Jeffrey Sim [1968] Director/Chief Financial Officer [American]; Kurt Sturn [1958] Director [American]

F.J. Snook & Sons Limited
Incorporated: 4 May 1959 *Employees:* 6
Net Worth: £5,999,092 *Total Assets:* £6,635,359
Registered Office: Rookery Farm, Urchfont, Devizes, Wilts, SN10 4RY
Activities: Mixed farming
Shareholders: Phillip James Snook; Robert Anthony Snook
Officers: Carole Forsyth Snook, Secretary; Carole Forsyth Snook [1940] Director/Secretary; John Frederick Snook [1931] Director/Farmer

Alan Snow Agricultural Engineers Limited
Incorporated: 26 March 2010 *Employees:* 19
Net Worth: £1,592,380 *Total Assets:* £4,821,731
Registered Office: 69 High Street, Bideford, Devon, EX39 2AT
Activities: Support activities for crop production
Shareholders: Reginald Alan Snow; Diane Margaret Snow
Officers: Diane Margaret Snow [1958] Director; Reginald Alan Snow [1957] Director

Snow Business International Ltd
Incorporated: 19 April 1996 *Employees:* 34
Net Worth: £3,239,186 *Total Assets:* £4,041,232
Registered Office: The Snow Mill, Bridge Road, Ebley, Stroud, Glos, GL5 4TR
Activities: Motion picture production activities
Parent: Snow Business Holdings Ltd
Officers: Lukas Warr Buxton [1959] Commercial Director; Darcey E Crownshaw [1954] Managing Director; Symon John Doliczny [1964] Operations Director; James Christopher Partridge [1984] Director

Snowdrop Solutions Ltd
Incorporated: 5 November 2013 *Employees:* 4
Net Worth: £467,183 *Total Assets:* £4,816,232
Registered Office: 37 Great Pulteney Street, Bath, BA2 4DA
Activities: Business and domestic software development
Major Shareholder: Kenneth Hart
Officers: Kenneth Hart [1969] Director/Founder

Snows Timber Limited
Incorporated: 6 March 1981 *Employees:* 206
Net Worth: £6,530,059 *Total Assets:* £23,991,670
Registered Office: 98 Hendford Hill, Yeovil, Somerset, BA20 2QR
Activities: Sawmilling and planing of wood
Parent: Bradford and Sons Limited
Officers: George Miles Bramston Adams [1956] Director/Chairman; Ian Stanton Church [1961] Managing Director; Adam Shane Cray [1987] Finance Director; Mark Andrew Eburne [1962] Director; Rachel Marie Lawrence [1979] Director/Chief Financial Officer; Craig Campbell Willoughby [1972] Director

Soar Newco Limited
Incorporated: 1 November 2013
Net Worth: £44,222 *Total Assets:* £5,352,793
Registered Office: 9 Miller Court, Severn Drive, Tewkesbury Business Park, Tewkesbury, Glos, GL20 8DN
Activities: Activities of other holding companies n.e.c.
Parent: Batson Bidco Ltd
Officers: Andrew Guy Melville Stevens [1963] Director/Chief Finance Officer; James Douglas Robert Twining [1972] Director/Chief Executive; Steven John Wynne [1958] Director/Insurance Broker; Dorian John Zanker [1964] Director

Society for Endocrinology
Incorporated: 9 February 1939 *Employees:* 76
Net Worth: £5,467,342 *Total Assets:* £10,098,422
Registered Office: Starling House, 1600 Newbrick Road, Stoke Gifford, Bristol, BS34 8YU
Activities: Publishing of learned journals
Officers: Ian Russell, Secretary; Professor Ruth Andrew [1968] Director/University Lecturer; Professor John Howard Duncan Bassett [1965] Director/Professor of Endocrinology; Dr Kristien Boelaert [1970] Director/Reader in Endocrinology & Consultant Endocrinologist; Professor Eleanor Davies [1963] Director/University Professor/Scientist; Dr Mark Gurnell [1968] Director/Doctor of Medicine; Professor Martin Hewison [1960] Director/Research Scientist; Professor Gareth Lavery [1977] Director/Senior Research Fellow; Dr Barbara McGowan [1966] Director/Consultant Endocrinologist [Italian]; Dr Dafydd Aled Rees [1970] Director/Reader/Consultant Endocrinologist; Professor Rebecca Mary Reynolds [1967] Director/Professor of Metabolic Medicine; Prof Jeremy William Tomlinson [1970] Director/Doctor; Professor Graham Richard Williams [1960] Director/Doctor

Socomec U.K. Limited
Incorporated: 2 May 1986 *Employees:* 75
Previous: Socomec Sicon Limited
Net Worth: £1,254,728 *Total Assets:* £10,444,531
Registered Office: Unit 7-9 Lakeside Business Park, Broadway Lane, South Cerney, Cirencester, Glos, GL7 5XL
Activities: Computer facilities management activities
Parent: Socomec SAS
Officers: Colin Alan Dean [1967] Managing Director; Remy Pizzato [1959] Director [French]; Bruno Adrien Joseph Plisson [1965] Director [French]; Alan James Reed [1967] Director

Sofa Brands International Limited
Incorporated: 19 May 2005 *Employees:* 7
Net Worth: £34,497,648 *Total Assets:* £47,549,240
Registered Office: 1 Hampton Park West, Melksham, Wilts, SN12 6GU
Activities: Activities of head offices
Parent: 1869 Limited
Officers: Emma Victoria Jones, Secretary/Accountant; Mark Raymond Clarke [1964] Director/Accountant; Clive Neville Kenyon-Brown [1960] Director; Ciaran Andrew McMahon [1968] Director [Irish]; Ian Oliver [1963] Director

Soil Association Certification Limited
Incorporated: 15 June 1962 *Employees:* 115
Net Worth: £32,357 *Total Assets:* £4,521,849
Registered Office: Spear House, 51 Victoria Street, Bristol, BS1 6AD
Activities: Other business support service activities n.e.c.
Parent: Soil Association Limited
Officers: Maura Catherine Poole, Secretary; Thomas Godfrey Stafford Bourne [1979] Director; Helen Mary Browning [1961] Director/CE of Charity and Farmer; Nicholas Brian Buckland [1951] Director and Chair; David Robin Langlands [1965] Business Development Director; Brian Mahony [1956] Director; Sonny Masero [1974] Director/Entrepreneur; Craig Lynn Sams [1944] Director/Grocer; Martin Sawyer [1958] Director; Marybeth Thoren [1963] Director/Fundraising & Communications [British/American]

Soil Association Limited (The)
Incorporated: 3 May 1946 *Employees:* 253
Net Worth: £8,810,664 *Total Assets:* £16,515,526
Registered Office: Spear House, 51 Victoria Street, Bristol, BS1 6AD
Activities: Activities of other membership organisations n.e.c.
Officers: Emma Jane Hussey, Secretary; Thomas Bourne [1979] Director/Consultant; John Carson [1952] Director/Farmer; Oliver Hugh Arnold Dowding [1957] Director/Farmer; Graeme Richard Matravers [1963] Director/Farmer; Martin John Nye [1964] Director; Prof. Maria Isabel Oliver [1968] Director Field Epidemiology Service Public Health [Spanish]; Rosemary Anne Radcliffe [1944] Director/Economist; Dr Gabriel John Scally [1954] Director/Public Health Physician [Irish]

Sol Plaatje Educational Project
Incorporated: 19 January 1983
Net Worth: £4,996,728 *Total Assets:* £4,999,548
Registered Office: 130a High Street, Crediton, Devon, EX17 3LQ
Activities: Non-trading company
Officers: William Henry Frankel, Secretary; Nasima Badsha [1951] Director/Executive Manager [South African]; William Henry Frankel [1944] Director/Solicitor; Horst Gerhard Hermann Kleinschmidt [1945] Director

Solace Global Maritime Limited
Incorporated: 24 May 2010 *Employees:* 17
Net Worth: £2,882,762 *Total Assets:* £4,505,772
Registered Office: Twin Sails House, West Quay Road, Poole, Dorset, BH15 1JF
Activities: Other service activities n.e.c.
Parent: Solace Global Limited
Officers: David John Peach [1972] Director/Consultant

Solar Power Generation Limited
Incorporated: 22 February 2013
Net Worth: £8,312,809 *Total Assets:* £11,896,952
Registered Office: 35 and 35a The Maltings, Lower Charlton Trading Estate, Shepton Mallet, Somerset, BA4 5QE
Activities: Activities of head offices
Parent: BSR Group Holdings Limited
Officers: Charles Bondi [1972] Director/Accountant; Graham David Harding [1966] Director; Kenneth Reid Ross [1968] Director

Soldi Investments Ltd
Incorporated: 20 July 2011 *Employees:* 7
Net Worth: £1,748,859 *Total Assets:* £4,421,067
Registered Office: Unit 3B, St Peters Park, Cobblers Way, Radstock, Bath, BA3 3BX
Activities: Other specialised construction activities n.e.c.
Shareholders: Alexander Petheram; Katyoun Petheram
Officers: Alexander Petheram [1982] Director/Project Manager

Solent Global Holdings Limited
Incorporated: 24 May 2013 *Employees:* 3
Net Worth: £3,458,166 *Total Assets:* £5,246,229
Registered Office: 118 Old Milton Road, New Milton, Hants, BH25 6EP
Activities: Activities of other holding companies n.e.c.
Parent: Solent Global Limited
Officers: Roderick Hung [1966] Director/Businessman [Chinese]; Richard Maurice Porter [1968] Director; David Michael Ralph [1979] Finance Director

Solent Global Limited
Incorporated: 14 June 2017 *Employees:* 91
Net Worth: £9,476,458 *Total Assets:* £23,830,852
Registered Office: 118 Old Milton Road, New Milton, Hants, BH25 6EP
Activities: Activities of other holding companies n.e.c.
Shareholders: Richard Maurice Porter; Joanne Claire Porter
Officers: Richard Maurice Porter [1968] Director; David Michael Ralph [1979] Finance Director

Solent International Limited
Incorporated: 25 September 2001 *Employees:* 37
Net Worth Deficit: £206,135 *Total Assets:* £9,761,316
Registered Office: 118 Old Milton Road, New Milton, Hants, BH25 6EB
Activities: Non-specialised wholesale trade
Parent: Solent Global Holdings Limited
Officers: David Michael Ralph, Secretary; Richard Maurice Porter [1968] Director; David Michael Ralph [1979] Director

Solent Stevedores Limited
Incorporated: 23 February 2000 *Employees:* 141
Net Worth: £3,676,450 *Total Assets:* £9,089,229
Registered Office: Freshford House, Redcliffe Way, Bristol, BS1 6NL
Activities: Cargo handling for water transport activities
Parent: Cullen Group Limited
Officers: Fiona Vivienne Robson, Secretary/Office Manager; Stuart David Cullen [1960] Director/Manager; Thomas Henry Dynes [1985] Operations Director; Ian David Jacobs [1962] Operations Director; Fiona Vivienne Robson [1963] Managing Director; Jonathan Richard Williams [1984] Finance Director

Solomon (Liskeard) Limited
Incorporated: 22 April 1958
Net Worth: £3,786,513 *Total Assets:* £4,172,212
Registered Office: Trevithick House, Moorswater, Liskeard, Cornwall, PL14 4LH
Activities: Retail sale of carpets, rugs, wall and floor coverings in specialised stores
Major Shareholder: Andrew Jonathan Solomon
Officers: Pamela Jean Solomon, Secretary; Andrew Jonathan Solomon [1961] Director; Ronald Eric Solomon [1929] Director

Solsbury Inventions Limited
Incorporated: 6 September 2005
Net Worth Deficit: £10,453,414 *Total Assets:* £26,315,796
Registered Office: Unit 1, 6 King Street, Frome, Somerset, BA11 1BH
Activities: Activities of head offices
Officers: Simon Barrie Hall [1971] Director

Somerdale International Limited
Incorporated: 5 September 1990 *Employees:* 22
Net Worth: £988,258 *Total Assets:* £8,787,993
Registered Office: Unit 3H, Westpark 26, Chelston, Wellington, Somerset, TA21 9AD
Activities: Wholesale of meat and meat products
Shareholders: Stephen John Waldron; Stephen George Jones
Officers: Trevor Antony Debenham, Secretary; Trevor Debenham [1980] Director/Accountant; Frederick Nairn Glen [1948] Independent Director and Business Advisor; Alan Thomas Jenkins [1980] Director; Stephen George Jones [1951] Director; Alice Mary Rosalind Manfield [1954] Director; Jonathan Seton Sykes [1959] Director; Stephen John Waldron [1959] Director

Somerset Bridge Ltd
Incorporated: 14 October 2016
Net Worth Deficit: £95,000 *Total Assets:* £7,864,000
Registered Office: Lysander House, Catbrain Lane, Cribbs Causeway, Bristol, BS10 7TQ
Activities: Activities of insurance agents and brokers
Shareholder: Arron Fraser Andrew Banks
Officers: Elizabeth Bilney [1976] Director; Christopher John Gillighan [1978] Insurance Managing Director; Alison Marshall [1978] Finance Director

Somerset Care Limited
Incorporated: 9 October 1990 *Employees:* 3,343
Net Worth: £13,939,931 *Total Assets:* £64,092,920
Registered Office: Acacia House, Blackbrook Park Avenue, Taunton, Somerset, TA1 2PX
Activities: Other residential care activities n.e.c.
Officers: Daniel Christopher Eric Cooper, Secretary; Roger Davies [1959] Director; Angela Joy Dupont [1948] Non-Executive Director Chairman; Sarah Jane Hicks [1968] Director of Care Operations; Gary Spencer Ridewood [1966] Finance Director; Richard Peter Ring [1971] Director

Somerset Community Foundation
Incorporated: 10 September 2002 *Employees:* 7
Net Worth: £8,264,767 *Total Assets:* £8,414,880
Registered Office: Yeoman House, Bath and West Showground, Shepton Mallet, Somerset, BA4 6QN
Activities: Other service activities n.e.c.
Officers: Justin Andrew Sargent, Secretary; Jane Elizabeth Barrie [1946] Director; Christopher John Bishop [1950] Director/Chartered Public Finance Accountant; Michelle Clare Ferris [1985] Director/Accountant; Paul Nicholas Hake [1969] Director/Chartered Accountant; Martin Kitchen [1949] Director/Retired; Richard David Ayshford Lloyd [1953] Director/Chartered Surveyor; John MacDonald Lyon [1948] Director/Retired; Alastair Bruce McIntosh [1958] Director/Business Development Manager; Lucilla Mary Nelson [1955] Director/Horse Breeder; Karen Jacqueline Pearson [1953] Director; Janice Angela Ross [1951] Director/Development Worker; David Michael John Taylor [1954] Director/Retired; Sarah Anne Wakefield [1956] Director/Solicitor; Timothy John Walker [1956] Director/Lawyer

Somerset County Cars Limited
Incorporated: 28 February 2001 *Employees:* 92
Net Worth: £176,156 *Total Assets:* £4,473,302
Registered Office: Centenary House, Peninsula Park, Rydon Lane, Exeter, EX2 7XE
Activities: Sale of new cars and light motor vehicles
Parent: SCC (Holdings) Limited
Officers: Nigel David Burke [1952] Director/Dealer Principal; William Robert Campsie [1959] Director/Company Accountant; Jason Marcus Lafferty [1971] Director/Centre Principal

Somerset Motorhome Centre Limited
Incorporated: 18 January 2005 *Employees:* 20
Net Worth: £3,309,807 *Total Assets:* £3,841,283
Registered Office: Mary Street House, Mary Street, Taunton, Somerset, TA1 3NW
Activities: Sale of other motor vehicles
Shareholders: Thomas Martin Lower; Maria Doris Lower
Officers: Maria Doris Lower, Secretary; Maria Doris Lower [1966] Director; Thomas Martin Lower [1968] Director

Somerset Road Education Trust
Incorporated: 5 December 2014 *Employees:* 194
Net Worth: £14,488,102 *Total Assets:* £15,759,503
Registered Office: Exeter House, Somerset Road, Salisbury, Wilts, SP1 3BL
Activities: Primary education
Officers: Sharon Caroline Elizabeth Day, Secretary; Roy Bexon [1947] Director/Retired Civil Servant; Trevor John Philip Branch [1957] Director/IT Consultancy; Russell John Cooper [1967] Operations Director NHS; Andrew James King [1980] Director; Angus John Mayhew [1973] Healthcare Director; Robert Sean McClatchey [1965] Non-Executive Director Chairman; Michael Stafford Newton [1955] Director/Retired; Mark Thomas Podkolinski [1950] Director/Retired; Matthew Stephen Sambrook [1979] Director/Headteacher; Lynda Diane Steer [1957] Director/HR

Somerset Wildlife Trust
Incorporated: 2 September 1964 *Employees:* 55
Net Worth: £5,242,057 *Total Assets:* £5,881,561
Registered Office: 34 Wellington Road, Taunton, Somerset, TA1 5AW
Activities: Other business support service activities n.e.c.
Officers: Richard Charles Atkin [1957] Director/Retired; Matthew James Bell [1985] Director/Head of Marketing and Communications; Professor Valerie Kathleen Brown [1944] Director; Simon Hicks [1945] Director/Retired; Philip James Holms [1952] Director; Helen Lawy [1955] Director; Graeme Brown Mitchell [1960] Director; Sarah Jane Nason [1952] Director; Stephen Richard Newman [1953] Director; Melville Fitzgibbon Trimble [1954] Director

Somerville & Savage Solicitors
Incorporated: 29 February 2000 *Employees:* 12
Net Worth: £134,329 *Total Assets:* £9,024,239
Registered Office: Alderbourne, Greenway Road, St Marychurch, Torquay, Devon, TQ1 4NJ
Activities: Other business support service activities n.e.c.
Shareholders: Sarah Jane French; Michael St John French
Officers: Rosemary Lorraine Bailey, Secretary; Michael St John French [1942] Director/Solicitor; Sarah Jane French [1961] Director

Sonus Networks Limited
Incorporated: 29 March 2000 *Employees:* 41
Net Worth: £4,934,418 *Total Assets:* £6,146,850
Registered Office: Unit A, Edison House, Edison Road, Swindon, Wilts, SN3 5JX
Activities: Other telecommunications activities
Parent: Sonus Networks, Inc.
Officers: Eric Marmurek, Secretary; Daryl Edward Raiford, Secretary; Daryl Edward Raiford [1962] Director/Chief Financial Officer [American]

Sortimo International Limited
Incorporated: 23 June 1998 *Employees:* 50
Net Worth: £2,813,899 *Total Assets:* £4,052,218
Registered Office: 26-28 Southernhay East, Exeter, Devon, EX1 1NS
Activities: Wholesale trade of motor vehicle parts and accessories
Major Shareholder: Reinhold Braun
Officers: Christopher Peter Jones, Secretary; Reinhold Braun [1965] Director [German]

The South Bristol Church and Community Trust
Incorporated: 23 December 1998 *Employees:* 10
Net Worth: £3,509,023 *Total Assets:* £3,582,878
Registered Office: The Withywood Centre, Queens Road, Bristol, BS13 8QA
Activities: Other business support service activities n.e.c.
Officers: Natalie Bryce [1988] Director/Solicitor; Reverend Christopher John Dobson [1962] Director/Clerk in Holy Orders; Richard Stephen Eddy [1965] Director/Bristol City Councillor; Reverend Derek Adrian James Maddox [1964] Director/Reverend; Rev Richard Victor Sharples [1961] Director/Methodist Minister; Reverend Patrick David Stonehewer [1965] Director/Minister of Religion

South Coast Building Supplies Ltd.
Incorporated: 8 August 2008 *Employees:* 64
Net Worth: £2,083,276 *Total Assets:* £6,009,651
Registered Office: Poole Lane, Bournemouth, BH11 9DU
Activities: Wholesale of wood, construction materials and sanitary equipment
Major Shareholder: Gary David Ellis
Officers: Martine Ellis, Secretary; Gary David Ellis [1966] Director/Builder; Timothy Martin Payne [1980] Director/Accountant

South Dartmoor Academy
Incorporated: 11 March 2011 *Employees:* 372
Net Worth: £19,855,000 *Total Assets:* £26,741,000
Registered Office: South Dartmoor Community College, Balland Lane, Ashburton, Devon, TQ13 7EW
Activities: Primary education
Officers: Peter Allin Brown [1968] Director; Graeme Maurice Cock [1965] Director/Farmer; Dominic Anthony Course [1968] Director/Graphic Designer; Christopher James Elliott [1982] Director/Consultant Engineer; Andrew Donald Faulkner [1981] Director/Chartered Surveyor; Beverley Garland [1972] Director; Nigel Robert Gore [1950] Director/Retired; Sarah Khan [1979] Director; Rachel Jane Rachel Shaw [1971] Director/Headteacher

South Devon Railway Trust
Incorporated: 15 January 1974 *Employees:* 68
Net Worth: £3,264,213 *Total Assets:* £4,812,693
Registered Office: The Station, Buckfastleigh, Devon, TQ11 0DZ
Activities: Passenger rail transport, interurban
Officers: Vernon Paul Coon, Secretary; John Geoffrey Addy [1948] Director/Retired; Allan Richard Cash [1953] Director/Civil Engineer; Richard James Elliott [1946] Director/Retired; Ernest Gregory Elsworth-Wilson [1994] Director/Manager Network Rail; Edward Roy Goodridge [1956] Director/Journalist; Graham Hooper [1947] Director/Retired; John Keohane [1948] Director/Retired; Jonathan Keith Morton [1956] Director/Train Driver; Peter Charles Treglown [1954] Director/Public Relations Consultant; Denver Alfred Woodward [1944] Director/Civil Engineer

South Devon UTC
Incorporated: 14 November 2012 *Employees:* 36
Net Worth: £11,086,753 *Total Assets:* £11,531,622
Registered Office: South Devon UTC, Kingsteignton Road, Newton Abbot, Devon, TQ12 2QA
Activities: Technical and vocational secondary education
Officers: Stephen Melville Criddle [1961] Director/Principal; James Trout [1982] Director; Antony Edward Wiltshire [1956] Director

South East Cornwall Multi Academy Regional Trust
Incorporated: 24 February 2011 *Employees:* 449
Previous: Saltash Multi Academy Regional Trust
Net Worth: £30,750,634 *Total Assets:* £36,541,940
Registered Office: Saltash.Net Community School, Wearde Road, Saltash, Cornwall, PL12 4AY
Activities: Primary education
Officers: Deborah Mary Stoneman, Secretary; Dr Susan Ann Brownlow [1960] Director; Daniel Philip Buckley [1967] Director/Chief Executive Officer; Helen Casson [1979] Director/Principal; Brian Robert Cook [1948] Director/Retired; James Crisp [1969] Director/Acting Head of Duchy College Stoke Climsland; Kevin Garfield Edward George [1966] Director/Solicitor; James Buller Kitson [1952] Director/Accountant; Richard Newton Chance [1952] Director/Educational Consultant; Caleb William Mark Stevens [1997] Director/Teaching Assistant and Play Worker; Elizabeth Kate Waghorn [1961] Director/Management Consultant

South Essex Insurance Brokers Limited
Incorporated: 18 July 2007 *Employees:* 90
Net Worth: £13,550,082 *Total Assets:* £19,710,412
Registered Office: Beaufort House, Brunswick Road, Gloucester, GL1 1JZ
Activities: Non-life insurance
Parent: South Essex Insurance Holdings Ltd
Officers: Rachael Jane Hall, Secretary; Barry Fehler [1946] Director; Mark Christopher John Hews [1969] Director/Group Chief Executive; Susan Jane Middleton [1976] Commercial Director; David Robert Moore [1966] Director; Bipin Thaker [1956] Associate Director

South Essex PPP Health Services Limited
Incorporated: 24 February 2003 *Employees:* 3
Net Worth Deficit: £235,815 *Total Assets:* £6,773,428
Registered Office: Third Floor, Broad Quay House, Prince Street, Bristol, BS1 4DJ
Activities: Other specialised construction activities n.e.c.
Parent: RBIL Limited
Officers: Christopher John Blundell [1966] Regional Director; Andrew Richard Kershaw [1965] Director/Projects Controller; Andrew Charles Mutch Rhodes [1970] Director

South Gloucestershire and Stroud Academy Trust
Incorporated: 12 December 2014 *Employees:* 100
Net Worth: £14,123,000 *Total Assets:* £15,953,000
Registered Office: Stratford Road, Stroud, Glos, GL5 4AH
Activities: Primary education
Officers: Katherine Louise Lee, Secretary; Valerie Patricia Bragg [1948] Director/Education Management Consultant; Jeannie Cohen-Brand [1963] Director/Head of Enterprise and New Venture; Katharine Samantha Dawson [1963] Psychologist and Director; Philip Eames [1960] Director/Auditor; Kevin John Hamblin [1965] Director/College Principal & CEO; Nigel Ian Johnson [1954] Director/Retired; Stephen Shepherd [1975] Director/Information Technology; Stephen James Winstone [1967] Director/Principal Lecturer for Education

South Manchester Healthcare (Holdings) Limited
Incorporated: 2 February 1998 *Employees:* 4
Net Worth: £1,000 *Total Assets:* £6,198,000
Registered Office: Third Floor, Broad Quay House, Prince Street, Bristol, BS1 4DJ
Activities: Other service activities n.e.c.
Shareholder: Semperian PPP Investment Partners No.2 Limited
Officers: Gaynor Birley-Smith [1966] Investment Director; Stephen Paul Hornby [1957] Director; Richard Little [1979] Investment Director; Benjamin Michael Watson [1985] Director/Portfolio Manager

South Manchester Healthcare Limited
Incorporated: 2 February 1998 *Employees:* 4
Net Worth: £6,553,000 *Total Assets:* £52,423,000
Registered Office: Third Floor, Broad Quay House, Prince Street, Bristol, BS1 4DJ
Activities: Other service activities n.e.c.
Parent: South Manchester Healthcare (Holdings) Limited
Officers: Gaynor Birley-Smith [1966] Investment Director; Stephen Paul Hornby [1957] Director; Richard Little [1979] Investment Director; Benjamin Michael Watson [1985] Director/Portfolio Manager

South West Airports Limited
Incorporated: 24 March 2005 *Employees:* 2
Net Worth Deficit: £87,423,000 *Total Assets:* £538,443,008
Registered Office: Bristol Airport, Bristol, BS48 3DY
Activities: Activities of other holding companies n.e.c.
Parent: Bristol Airport (UK) No.3 Limited
Officers: James Alexander Adam [1970] Director/Financier [Canadian]; David William Kerr [1963] Director/Business Executive; Janis Carol Kong [1951] Director; David Lloyd McGraw [1956] Director/Chief Financial Officer [Canadian]; Elizabeth Waddell [1963] HR Director

South West Care Homes Limited
Incorporated: 7 September 2001 *Employees:* 215
Net Worth: £874,096 *Total Assets:* £9,203,639
Registered Office: Plymouth Science Park, 1 Davy Road, Derriford, Plymouth, PL6 8BX
Activities: Residential care activities for the elderly and disabled
Shareholders: Alan Anthony Beale; Sharon Elaine Beale
Officers: Sharon Elaine Beale, Secretary; Alan Anthony Beale [1957] Director/Consultant

South West Communications Group Holdings Limited
Incorporated: 29 November 2005 *Employees:* 164
Net Worth: £6,375,014 *Total Assets:* £21,904,300
Registered Office: Communications House, Moor Lane, Sowton, Exeter, Devon, EX2 7JA
Activities: Activities of head offices
Major Shareholder: Anthony George Edward Rowe
Officers: Sharon Marie Rowe, Secretary; Sarah Flowers [1965] Director; David Harry Langley [1963] Director; Brian Lodge [1960] Director; Anthony George Edward Rowe [1948] Director

South West Communications Group Limited
Incorporated: 14 November 1984 *Employees:* 142
Net Worth: £3,372,630 *Total Assets:* £15,037,278
Registered Office: Communications House, Moor Lane, Sowton, Exeter, Devon, EX2 7JF
Activities: Other telecommunications activities
Parent: South West Communications Group Holdings Limited
Officers: Sharon Marie Rowe, Secretary; Sean Michael Doyle [1974] Director of Operations; Sarah Flowers [1965] Director; John Barnaby Holdstock [1972] Director of ITC; David Harry Langley [1963] Director/Administrator; Brian Lodge [1960] Director; Anthony George Edward Rowe [1948] Director; Jonathan Whiley [1968] Commercial Director

South West Environmental Parks Limited
Incorporated: 21 February 1964 *Employees:* 266
Net Worth: £9,849,791 *Total Assets:* £11,663,540
Registered Office: Totnes Road, Paignton, Devon, TQ4 7EU
Activities: Activities of amusement parks and theme parks
Parent: Whitley Wildlife Conservation Trust
Officers: Christopher James Pyne, Secretary; Sarah Barr [1953] Director/Human Resources Professional; Dr Paul Robert Francis Chanin [1950] Director/Ecological Consultant; Andrew Charles John Cooper [1951] Director/TV Producer; Richard William John Ford [1959] Director; Sylvia Jo-An Greinig [1947] Director/Headteacher & Schools Inspector; Rachael Hill [1970] Director/Chartered Accountant; Stephen Ellis Kings [1952] Director/Retired Secondary Academy Headteacher/Principal; Beth Kathleen McLaughlin [1976] Director/Marketing Consultant; Professor Judy Patricia Ravenscroft [1965] Director/National Flood & Coastal Risk Manager; Richard Alexander Rowe [1960] Director; Mark Stephen Salmon [1975] Director; Peter Michael Collinson Stevens [1936] Director/Retired

South West Investment Group (Capital) Limited
Incorporated: 14 March 1989 *Employees:* 2
Net Worth: £8,267,497 *Total Assets:* £11,888,166
Registered Office: Lowena House, Glenthorne Court, Truro Business Park, Threemilestone, Truro, Cornwall, TR4 9NY
Activities: Other business support service activities n.e.c.
Parent: South West Investment Group Limited
Officers: Nicola Louise Pooley, Secretary/Chartered Accountant; David Ian Brown [1962] Managing Director; Richard George Coombs [1954] Director; Nicola Louise Pooley [1966] Finance Director

South West Investment Group Limited
Incorporated: 26 January 1990 *Employees:* 17
Net Worth: £10,471,785 *Total Assets:* £14,077,429
Registered Office: Lowena House, Glenthorne Court, Truro Business Park, Threemilestone, Truro, Cornwall, TR4 9NY
Activities: Financial intermediation not elsewhere classified
Officers: Nicola Louise Pooley, Secretary/Chartered Accountant; David Paul Beaumont [1964] Director/Bank Manager; Glenn Kevin Caplin [1979] Director/Local Government Officer; William Kim Conchie [1956] Director/Chief Executive Officer; Richard George Coombs [1954] Director; Elaine Lesley de Trafford [1964] Director/Bank Official; Malachy Andrew Conleth McReynolds [1949] Director/Accountant [Irish]; David John Owen [1972] Director/Chief Executive

South West Land Limited
Incorporated: 2 February 1978 *Employees:* 5
Net Worth: £6,679,616 *Total Assets:* £8,383,325
Registered Office: 23 Lockyer Street, Plymouth, PL1 2QZ
Activities: Buying and selling of own real estate
Parent: South West Land (Holdings) Limited
Officers: Primrose Anne Burnett-Hitchcock, Secretary; Janice Elizabeth Palmer, Secretary; Jacob Nicholas Burnett Hitchcock [1978] Director; Charles Denys Burnett-Hitchcock [1946] Director; Primrose Anne Burnett-Hitchcock [1939] Director; Robin Amanda Creswell [1962] Director/TV Producer; Belinda Jane Eaton [1960] Director/Artist

South West Laundry Ltd
Incorporated: 16 March 2010 *Employees:* 66
Net Worth: £4,123,876 *Total Assets:* £7,811,196
Registered Office: Units U-W, St Erth Industrial Estate, Rose-an-Grouse, Canonstown, Hayle, Cornwall, TR27 6LP
Activities: Washing and (dry-)cleaning of textile and fur products
Parent: South West Laundry Holdings Limited
Officers: Peter Egan [1972] Director [Irish]; Yvonne May Monaghan [1958] Director; Timothy James Morris [1977] Director; Wayne Retallack [1977] Director; Donald Richard Smith [1967] Director

South West Metal Finishing Limited
Incorporated: 20 April 1988 *Employees:* 145
Net Worth: £3,816,811 *Total Assets:* £6,282,277
Registered Office: Alphinbrook Road, Alphington, Exeter, Devon, EX2 8TJ
Activities: Manufacture of other fabricated metal products n.e.c.
Parent: E.I.C. (Exeter) Limited
Officers: Jacqueline Louise Jacobs, Secretary; Kevin Baker [1961] Director; Jacqueline Louise Jacobs [1969] Director; Matthew Jacobs [1976] Director; Paul Jacobs [1974] Director

South West Peninsula Ahsn Limited
Incorporated: 18 April 2013 *Employees:* 40
Net Worth: £503,632 *Total Assets:* £4,952,630
Registered Office: Vantage Point, Pynes Hill, Exeter, EX2 5FD
Activities: Other professional, scientific and technical activities n.e.c.
Officers: John Keith Acornley [1953] Director; Dr Joanna Laura Bayley [1969] Director/GP; Gavin Donald Brake [1971] Business Director; Phillip Paul Confue [1964] Director; David William Freeman [1974] Director; Dr Jonathon Gray [1964] Director; Godfrey Stuart Logan [1955] Director/Professor of Paediatric Inventory; Dr Sonja Anna Manton [1979] Director [Austrian]; Dr Stuart Monk [1979] Director; Dr Alastair James Riddell [1949] Director; Neil Matthew Stevens [1964] Director; Richard John Watson [1980] Finance Director; Louise Witts [1968] Director

South West Water Finance PLC
Incorporated: 27 February 2006
Net Worth: £12,717,000 *Total Assets:* £486,847,008
Registered Office: Peninsula House, Rydon Lane, Exeter, Devon, EX2 7HR
Activities: Financial intermediation not elsewhere classified
Parent: South West Water Limited
Officers: Scott Edward Massie, Secretary; Simon Anthony Follett Pugsley, Secretary; Karen Senior, Secretary; Paul Michael Boote [1978] Director/Accountant; Christopher Loughlin [1952] Director/Chief Executive; Simon Anthony Follet Pugsley [1968] Director/Solicitor; Louise Frances Rowe [1982] Director/Accountant

South West Water Limited
Incorporated: 1 April 1989 *Employees:* 1,433
Net Worth: £621,400,000 *Total Assets:* £3,376,199,936
Registered Office: Peninsula House, Rydon Lane, Exeter, Devon, EX2 7HR
Activities: Water collection, treatment and supply
Parent: Pennon Group PLC
Officers: Simon Anthony Follet Pugsley, Secretary; Karen Senior, Secretary; Dr Stephen Charles Bird [1958] Operations Director; Jonathan Butterworth [1962] Director; Neil Cooper [1967] Director; Iain Richard Evans [1951] Director/Management Consultant; Martin John Hagen [1951] Director; Christopher Loughlin [1952] Director/Chief Executive; Sir Thomas John Parker [1942] Director; Gillian Ann Rider [1954] Director; Louise Frances Rowe [1982] Director/Accountant; Matthew Owen John Taylor [1963] Director/Member of Parliament

South Western Helicopters Limited
Incorporated: 2 November 1989 *Employees:* 13
Net Worth: £10,351,000 *Total Assets:* £12,178,000
Registered Office: Avonbank, Feeder Road, Bristol, BS2 0TB
Activities: Other business support service activities n.e.c.
Parent: WPD Distribution Network Holdings Limited
Officers: Sally Ann Jones, Secretary; Graham Roy Halladay [1966] Operations Director; Ian Craig Smith [1971] Director/Logistics Manager; Robin Weston Tutcher [1971] Director/Chief Pilot

South Wilts Grammar School for Girls
Incorporated: 25 November 2010 *Employees:* 140
Net Worth: £10,965,000 *Total Assets:* £12,104,000
Registered Office: Stratford Road, Salisbury, Wilts, SP1 3JJ
Activities: General secondary education
Officers: Hilary Jane Angel, Secretary; Sarah Jane Byerley [1968] Director/Teacher; Michele Anne Chilcott [1968] Director/Headteacher; Christopher Child [1964] Director/Army Officer; William Rhys Davies [1975] HR Director; Neil Stuart James Goddard [1971] Director/Local Government Officer; Alma Jacqueline Goodall [1951] Director/Educational Consultant/Inspector; Sharon Louise Hackett [1972] Director/Teacher; Robert Charles Hendicott [1957] Director/Management Consultant; Julie Ann King [1964] Director/Receptionist; Nicholas Patrick Lay [1968] Director/Head of Business Development; Robert James MacDonald [1981] Director/Accountant; Elizabeth Anne Ogilvie [1960] Director/Consultant; Howard Prince [1948] Director/Chartered Engineer; Lucy Anne Rigden [1987] Director/Learning Resource Assistant; Stephen John Russell [1966] Director/House Husband; Helen Clare Stewart [1960] Director/School Bursar; Miranda Jane Thomas [1964] Director; Brigadier Gregor William Wilson [1970] Director/Army Officer

South Wiltshire UTC Limited
Incorporated: 6 November 2012 *Employees:* 33
Net Worth: £9,329,000 *Total Assets:* £10,099,000
Registered Office: South Wiltshire UTC, Wilton Road, Salisbury, Wilts, SP2 7EU
Activities: Technical and vocational secondary education
Officers: Sarah Bowler, Secretary; Nigel Ferguson [1968] Director/Royal Navy; Douglas James Gale [1959] Engineering Director; Prof Janice Griffiths [1963] Director of Enterprise; Dominique Hamilton [1968] Director/Invigilator [Belgian]; Caron Hitchen [1966] Director/Teacher; Joe Mulligan [1965] Director/Principal; Aidan Marcus Tout [1982] Director/Project Manager; Mark Leon Waddington [1970] Director/Project Engineer; Philip Whalley [1950] Director; Vivien White [1959] Director/Teacher

Southampton Harbour Hotel Ltd
Incorporated: 26 April 2011 *Employees:* 71
Net Worth: £5,939,895 *Total Assets:* £32,772,312
Registered Office: Harbour House, 60 Purewell, Christchurch, Dorset, BH23 1ES
Activities: Hotels and similar accommodation
Parent: Harbour Hospitality Group Limited
Officers: Stuart Andrew Bateman [1976] Director; David Francis Robbins [1967] Finance Director; Michael Oliver Warren [1970] Director [Irish]

Southerly Point Co-operative Multi-Academy Trust
Incorporated: 9 January 2017 *Employees:* 578
Net Worth: £28,466,076 *Total Assets:* £33,536,220
Registered Office: MAT Office, Helston Community College, Church Hill, Helston, Cornwall, TR13 8NR
Activities: Primary education
Officers: Maria Collins, Secretary; Catherine Anne Bird [1964] Director/Accountant; Donna Rosemarie Bryant [1965] Director; Sean Robin Davis [1964] Director; Alan Jeffrey Horne [1952] Director; Pamela Ann Miller [1937] Director/Retired; Kristin Lynn Prior [1976] Director [American]; Susan Ann Reynolds [1986] Director/Solicitor; Antony Sanders [1954] Managing Director; Kevin Colin Thomas [1973] Director

Southern Academy Trust
Incorporated: 14 May 2014 *Employees:* 304
Previous: Shaftesbury Academy Trust
Net Worth: £29,639,552 *Total Assets:* £34,605,460
Registered Office: Shaftesbury School, Salisbury Road, Shaftesbury, Dorset, SP7 8ER
Activities: Other education n.e.c.
Officers: Carina Louise Sawyer, Secretary; Mark Edward Blackman [1969] Director/Headteacher; Christopher Norman Brickell [1946] Director/Retired; The Revd Helen Elizabeth Dawes [1974] Director/Parish Rector; Neil Ivor John Hiscock [1972] Director/Partner; Andrew Kennard [1973] Director/Police Officer; Susan Bernadette Lacey [1966] Director/Solicitor; Margaret Dylys Pearson [1952] Director/Retired; Christopher John Wilkins [1960] Director/Town Clerk

Southern England Farms Limited
Incorporated: 1 May 1996 *Employees:* 257
Net Worth: £1,714,793 *Total Assets:* £10,406,541
Registered Office: Lambo Fraddam Road, Leedstown, Hayle, Cornwall, TR27 5PF
Activities: Growing of vegetables and melons, roots and tubers
Major Shareholder: Greville Nicholas Richards
Officers: Jane Sybilla Richards, Secretary; Greville Nicholas Richards [1972] Director/Produce Broker & Grower; Jane Sybilla Richards [1973] Director

Southern Healthcare (Wessex) Ltd
Incorporated: 5 June 2001 *Employees:* 235
Net Worth: £2,608,112 *Total Assets:* £10,009,847
Registered Office: Sefton Hall, 11 Plantation Terrace, Dawlish, Devon, EX7 9DS
Activities: Residential nursing care facilities
Shareholders: Jonathan Robert Cox; Geoffrey David Cox
Officers: David Lloyd Cox [1979] Director/IT Analyst; Geoffrey David Cox [1956] Managing Director; Jonathan Robert Cox [1950] Director/Land Manager; Tanita Cox [1992] Director

Southside Regeneration Limited
Incorporated: 24 July 2013 *Employees:* 4
Net Worth: £6,223,025 *Total Assets:* £24,941,968
Registered Office: Swatton Barn, Badbury, Swindon, Wilts, SN4 0EU
Activities: Development of building projects
Shareholder: Wolfgang Peter Egger
Officers: Robert William Middleton Brook [1966] Director/Surveyor; Dr Pamela Vera Hoerr [1973] Director [German]; Thomas Ranald Stenhouse [1978] Director

Southtown Investment Company Limited
Incorporated: 30 March 2002 *Employees:* 55
Net Worth: £4,282,332 *Total Assets:* £6,279,382
Registered Office: Bridge Motorcycles, Alphinbrook Road, Marsh Barton Trading Estate, Exeter, Devon, EX2 8RG
Activities: Activities of head offices
Major Shareholder: Stuart Anthony
Officers: Rebecca Elizabeth Anthony, Secretary; Stuart Anthony [1953] Managing Director

Southwark Bridge Holdings Limited
Incorporated: 9 September 2015 *Employees:* 105
Net Worth: £1,715,116 *Total Assets:* £17,894,954
Registered Office: Petty Wood & Co Limited, Livingstone Road, Walworth Business Park, Andover, Hants, SP10 5NS
Activities: Activities of head offices
Shareholders: Sean Michael Linehan; John Potter; Giles Marc Reynolds
Officers: Sean Michael Linehan, Secretary; Sean Michael Linehan [1967] Director/Accountant; John Potter [1964] Director; Giles Marc Reynolds [1971] Commercial Director

Sovereign Care Limited
Incorporated: 17 February 2010 *Employees:* 110
Net Worth: £1,607,282 *Total Assets:* £7,071,305
Registered Office: 31-33 Commercial Road, Poole, Dorset, BH14 0HU
Activities: Other human health activities
Shareholders: Radha Ravichandran; Thuraisamy Ravichandran
Officers: Radha Ravichandran [1965] Director; Thuraisamy Ravichandran [1958] Director

Space Cooling Topco Limited
Incorporated: 12 March 2014 *Employees:* 720
Net Worth: £1,295,129 *Total Assets:* £44,577,024
Registered Office: Causeway Central, Pioneer Park, Bristol, BS4 3QB
Activities: Activities of head offices
Shareholder: Dover Refrigeration & Food Equipment UK Ltd
Officers: John Anthony Hollingdale [1950] Director; Charles Michael Murphy [1978] Director/Accountant; Joao Eduardo Navarro de Andrade [1968] Director/Engineer [American]; Nicholas Antonio Negro [1979] Director/Chief Financial Officer, Hillphoenix Incorporated [American]; Dale Edward Nouch [1971] Director; Paul Edward Sindoni [1967] Director/President, Manufacturing Business [American]; Mark Brian Woods [1970] Director/Engineer

Space Engineering Services Limited
Incorporated: 2 November 1987 *Employees:* 716
Net Worth: £36,578,912 *Total Assets:* £53,708,148
Registered Office: Causeway Central, Pioneer Park, Bristol, BS4 3QB
Activities: Manufacture of non-domestic cooling and ventilation equipment
Parent: Space Cooling Systems Holdings Limited
Officers: Charles Michael Murphy, Secretary; John Anthony Hollingdale [1950] Director; Charles Michael Murphy [1978] Director/Accountant; Dale Edward Nouch [1971] Director/Engineer; Mark Brian Woods [1970] Director/Engineers

Spandex Holding UK Ltd.
Incorporated: 10 August 2011
Net Worth: £25,411,000 *Total Assets:* £76,069,000
Registered Office: 1600 Park Avenue, Aztec West, Almondsbury, Bristol, BS32 4UA
Activities: Non-trading company
Parent: Viscominvest Holding UK Ltd
Officers: Beverley Ann Meredith, Secretary; Robert William Jackson [1963] Director/Group Vice President; Leon Watson [1967] Director/General Manager

Spandex Limited
Incorporated: 29 June 1976 *Employees:* 155
Net Worth: £58,965,000 *Total Assets:* £77,854,000
Registered Office: 1600 Park Avenue, Aztec West, Almondsbury, Bristol, BS32 4UA
Activities: Wholesale of other intermediate products
Parent: Spandex Holding UK Ltd
Officers: Beverley Ann Meredith, Secretary; Robert William Jackson [1963] Sales Director; Leon Watson [1967] Director/General Manager

Sparex Limited
Incorporated: 19 March 1965 *Employees:* 175
Net Worth: £48,353,364 *Total Assets:* £66,808,492
Registered Office: Sparex Limited, Exeter Airport, Exeter, Devon, EX5 2LJ
Activities: Wholesale of agricultural machinery, equipment and supplies
Parent: AGCO International Limited
Officers: Mark Anthony Doggrell, Secretary; Paul William de Brissac Bernard [1963] Director/Business Development Manager; Mark Anthony Doggrell [1973] Director

Spark Gas Shipping Ltd
Incorporated: 26 June 2006
Net Worth Deficit: £73,000 *Total Assets:* £45,000,000
Registered Office: 1 Rivergate, Temple Quay, Bristol, BS1 6ED
Activities: Trade of gas through mains
Parent: Spark Energy Limited
Officers: Vincent Francis Casey [1983] Director; Stephen James Fitzpatrick [1977] Director; Chris Gauld [1978] Director; Adrian Letts [1973] Director [Australian]; Hamish Duncan Adam Osborne [1973] Director

C Sparks & Sons Limited
Incorporated: 19 July 1971 *Employees:* 146
Net Worth: £1,746,021 *Total Assets:* £10,796,609
Registered Office: Sparks Transport, Wells Road, Glastonbury, Somerset, BA6 9AG
Activities: Freight transport by road
Parent: C Sparks & Sons Holdings Limited
Officers: Adrian Cyril Sparks [1946] Director/Transport Contractor; Jonathan David Sparks [1971] Managing Director; Tristan Charles Sparks [1979] Director; Stuart Leonard Summers [1982] Director

Sparkworld Limited
Incorporated: 14 March 1985 *Employees:* 34
Net Worth: £2,364,699 *Total Assets:* £4,792,015
Registered Office: 9 Battle Road, Heathfield Industrial Estate, Newton Abbot, Devon, TQ12 6RY
Activities: Wholesale of radio, television goods & electrical household appliances (other than records, tapes, CDs)
Shareholder: Marian Yvonne Crausaz
Officers: Tristan Bernard Cook, Secretary; Tristan Bernard Cook [1977] Director/Buyer; Marian Yvonne Crausaz [1950] Director; Ian Calvin James [1947] Director

Sparrow Crane Hire Limited
Incorporated: 30 December 1996 *Employees:* 87
Net Worth: £5,324,074 *Total Assets:* £10,556,606
Registered Office: Ashmead Road, Keynsham, Bristol, BS31 1SX
Activities: Renting and leasing of other machinery, equipment and tangible goods n.e.c.
Officers: Pauline Sparrow, Secretary; Alexander George Sparrow [1986] Director; Timothy Roger Sparrow [1958] Director

SPC Europe Limited
Incorporated: 30 October 2000 *Employees:* 98
Net Worth: £6,575,732 *Total Assets:* £14,988,307
Registered Office: SPC, Cory Way, West Wilts Trading Estate, Westbury, Wilts, BA13 4QT
Activities: Manufacture of other rubber products
Parent: SPC Corporate Ltd
Officers: Marilyn Hallas, Secretary; Paul Matthew Hallas [1979] Director/Operations Manager; Stephen Hallas [1952] Director/Business Administrator

Special Partnership Trust
Incorporated: 1 August 2011 *Employees:* 324
Previous: Pencalenick
Net Worth: £14,992,885 *Total Assets:* £18,857,834
Registered Office: Pencalenick School, St Clement, Truro, Cornwall, TR1 1TE
Activities: General secondary education
Officers: Clare Kendle, Secretary; Guy John Chappell [1974] Director/Chief Executive; Stephen John Colwill [1949] Director/Senior Tribunal Chair; David Cunningham [1960] Financial Director; Hayley Maria Goleniowska [1969] Director/Author; Janet Elizabeth Hudson [1950] Director/Social Care and Chair of Governors at Doubletrees; Lisa Michelle Michell [1973] Director/Headteacher; John Rail [1946] Director/Retired; Pauline Anne Robins [1953] Director/Retired HMI/Ofsted

Specialised Management Services Limited
Incorporated: 30 April 1999 *Employees:* 92
Net Worth: £3,604,205 *Total Assets:* £6,726,077
Registered Office: Alderley House, Arnolds Field Estate, The Downs, Wickwar, Wotton under Edge, Glos, GL12 8JD
Activities: Manufacture of other special-purpose machinery n.e.c.
Parent: Alderley PLC
Officers: Richard Adrian Fox Carter [1970] Director/Accountant; David Andrew Howlett [1972] Managing Director; Gary Morrow [1985] Business Development Director

Specialist Aviation Services Group Limited
Incorporated: 12 March 1993 *Employees:* 166
Previous: Specialist Aviation Services Limited
Net Worth: £19,526,000 *Total Assets:* £83,136,000
Registered Office: Gloucestershire Airport, Staverton, Cheltenham, Glos, GL51 6SS
Activities: Non-scheduled passenger air transport
Officers: Antonius Henricus Peter Maria Schal Schaeken [1958] Director [Dutch]; Stuart David Anthony Tozer [1981] Finance Director; Kevin Robertus Van Den Nieuwenhuijzen [1984] Director [Dutch]; Jeroen Franciscus Augustinus Van Den Nieuwenhuitzen [1958] Director [Dutch]

Specialist Aviation Services Limited
Incorporated: 17 September 1984 *Employees:* 153
Previous: Police Aviation Services Limited
Net Worth: £14,795,000 *Total Assets:* £79,250,000
Registered Office: Gloucestershire Airport, Staverton, Cheltenham, Glos, GL51 6SS
Activities: Non-scheduled passenger air transport
Parent: Specialist Aviation Services Group Limited
Officers: Antonius Henricus Peter Maria Schal Schaeken [1958] Director [Dutch]; Stuart David Anthony Tozer [1981] Finance Director; Kevin Robertus Van Den Nieuwenhuijzen [1984] Director/Entrepreneur [Dutch]

Specialist Journeys Limited
Incorporated: 23 February 2015 *Employees:* 4
Net Worth Deficit: £4,045,218 *Total Assets:* £8,543,356
Registered Office: The Clock Tower, 4 Oakridge Office Park, Southampton Road, Salisbury, Wilts, SP5 3HT
Activities: Tour operator activities
Parent: Specialist Journeys Midco 2 Limited
Officers: Andrew Edward Dale [1980] Finance Director; Jackie Willis [1962] Director/Chief Executive Officer

Specialist Journeys Midco 1 Limited
Incorporated: 23 February 2015 *Employees:* 2
Net Worth Deficit: £6,700,744 *Total Assets:* £5,557,601
Registered Office: The Clock Tower, Unit 4 Oakridge Office Park, Southampton Road, Whaddon, Salisbury, Wilts, SP5 3HT
Activities: Tour operator activities
Parent: Specialist Journeys Limited
Officers: Andrew Edward Dale [1980] Finance Director; Jackie Willis [1962] Director/Chief Executive Officer

Specialist Journeys Midco 2 Limited
Incorporated: 23 February 2015 *Employees:* 2
Net Worth Deficit: £3,976,974 *Total Assets:* £7,952,133
Registered Office: The Clock Tower, 4 Oakridge Office Park, Southampton Road, Salisbury, Wilts, SP5 3HT
Activities: Tour operator activities
Parent: Specialist Journeys Midco 1 Limited
Officers: Andrew Edward Dale [1980] Finance Director; Jackie Willis [1962] Director/Chief Executive Officer

Spectrum Medical Group Limited
Incorporated: 4 September 2015 *Employees:* 96
Net Worth Deficit: £5,650,899 *Total Assets:* £15,720,893
Registered Office: Harrier 4, Meteor Business Park, Cheltenham Road East, Gloucester, GL2 9QL
Activities: Manufacture of electronic measuring, testing etc. equipment, not for industrial process control
Shareholder: Stephen Brian Turner
Officers: Mark Peter Drain [1965] Director; Jeremy Charles Hitchins [1954] Director; Stephen Brian Turner [1959] Director

Spectrum Medical Limited
Incorporated: 5 October 2006 *Employees:* 55
Net Worth: £1,901,077 *Total Assets:* £20,430,544
Registered Office: Harrier 4, Meteor Business Park, Cheltenham Road East, Gloucester, GL2 9QL
Activities: Manufacture of electronic measuring, testing etc. equipment, not for industrial process control
Parent: Spectrum Medical Group Limited
Officers: Mark Peter Drain, Secretary; Mark Peter Drain [1965] Director; Jeremy Charles Hitchins [1954] Director; Stephen Brian Turner [1959] Director

Spectrum Premier Homes Limited
Incorporated: 25 March 1994
Total Assets: £11,355,000
Registered Office: Spectrum House, Grange Road, Christchurch, Dorset, BH23 4GE
Activities: Construction of domestic buildings
Officers: Claire McKenna, Secretary; Stuart Laird [1953] Director; Barry Nethercott [1954] Director/Chief Financial Officer

Spectrum Property Care Ltd
Incorporated: 1 November 2013 *Employees:* 451
Net Worth: £4,480,000 *Total Assets:* £10,784,000
Registered Office: Spectrum House, Grange Road, Christchurch, Dorset, BH23 4GE
Activities: Combined facilities support activities
Parent: Sovereign Housing Association Limited
Officers: Claire-Marie McKenna, Secretary; Steven Michael Barford [1960] Director; Stuart Laird [1953] Director; Martin Lawton [1974] Director/M&E Manager; Simon Lindley [1961] Director/Consultant; Barry Nethercott [1954] Director/Chief Financial Officer; David Stephen Todd [1948] Director

Speed Superbikes Limited
Incorporated: 8 November 2009
Net Worth: £967,330 *Total Assets:* £3,519,530
Registered Office: 6 Trusham Road, Marsh Barton Trading Estate, Exeter, Devon, EX2 8QH
Activities: Sale, maintenance and repair of motorcycles and related parts and accessories
Major Shareholder: Graeme Stanley Burford
Officers: Graeme Stanley Burford [1963] Director/Motorcycle Dealer

Speeds Group Holdings Limited
Incorporated: 22 June 1945 *Employees:* 5
Net Worth: £10,762,175 *Total Assets:* £11,068,341
Registered Office: 53 Florence Road, Parkstone, Poole, Dorset, BH14 9JF
Activities: Other letting and operating of own or leased real estate
Shareholder: Mary Ann Brown
Officers: Lucy Jayne Filer, Secretary; Daniel Brown [1972] Director; Ian Roger Brown [1943] Director; Mary Ann Brown [1943] Director; Paul Edward Brown [1972] Director/Accounts Manager; Lucy Jayne Filer [1975] Director/Company Secretary

Spembly Medical Limited
Incorporated: 7 January 1987
Net Worth: £413,423,264 *Total Assets:* £477,470,592
Registered Office: 2nd Floor, West Wing, Kingsgate House, Newbury Road, Andover, Hants, SP10 4DU
Activities: Other human health activities
Parent: Integra Neurosciences Holdings (UK) Limited
Officers: Sravan Kumar Emany [1977] Director/Senior VP, Strategy, Treasurer & Investor Relations [American]; Jeffrey Alan Mosebrook [1976] Director/VP, Corp Controller & Principle Accounting Officer [American]

Kenneth Spencer Limited
Incorporated: 23 August 1957 *Employees:* 17
Net Worth: £5,899,875 *Total Assets:* £7,611,697
Registered Office: St Martins Farm, Zeals, Warminster, Wilts, BA12 6NZ
Activities: Mixed farming
Major Shareholder: Charles James Spencer
Officers: Charles James Spencer, Secretary; Catherine Anne Spencer [1955] Director; Charles James Spencer [1955] Director/Farmer; Flora Antonia Blades Spencer [1987] Director/Media Executive; Henry Charles Blades Spencer [1990] Director/Student; Patricia Spencer [1926] Director; Thomas Spencer [1985] Director/Mechanical Engineer

Spenco Engineering Co. Limited
Incorporated: 28 January 1976 *Employees:* 35
Net Worth: £6,250,210 *Total Assets:* £6,598,942
Registered Office: Station Road, Clyst, Honiton, Exeter, Devon, EX5 2DX
Activities: Manufacture of metal structures and parts of structures
Parent: Sparex Limited
Officers: Mark Anthony Doggrell, Secretary; Paul William de Brissac Bernard [1963] Director/Business Development Manager; Mark Anthony Doggrell [1973] Director

The Ralph & Irma Sperring Charity
Incorporated: 1 March 1995
Net Worth: £6,614,906 *Total Assets:* £6,668,578
Registered Office: Thatcher & Hallam, Island House, Midsomer Norton, Radstock, Somerset, BA3 2HJ
Activities: Other service activities n.e.c.
Officers: George Harald Hilding Persson, Secretary; Sally Blanning [1938] Director/Retired; Noreen Muriel Busby [1939] Director/Retired; Rev Christopher Generald Chiplin [1953] Director/Vicar of Midsomer Norton; Dr John Patrick Nelson Haxell [1947] Director/Retired; George Harald Hilding Persson [1977] Director/Solicitor; Lisa Joy Saunders [1979] Managing Director

Sphere Property 4 Limited
Incorporated: 30 October 2013
Net Worth: £205,681 *Total Assets:* £4,278,155
Registered Office: Towngate House, 2-8 Parkstone Road, Poole, Dorset, BH15 2PW
Activities: Buying and selling of own real estate
Major Shareholder: Alexander Barrington Collier
Officers: Alexander Barrington Collier [1978] Director/Property Development

Keith Spicer Limited
Incorporated: 18 January 1939 *Employees:* 142
Net Worth: £1,786,661 *Total Assets:* £17,222,478
Registered Office: 5 Cobham Road, Ferndown Industrial Estate, Wimborne, Dorset, BH21 7PN
Activities: Tea processing
Parent: Harris Freeman Asia Limited
Officers: Chirayu Borooah [1965] Director [American]; Maria Roberts [1962] Director [American]; Anil Shah [1955] Director/Company President [American]; Harish Shah [1952] Director [Indian]; Kishore Shah [1958] Director/Executive [American]; Peter Dylan Unsworth [1958] Director/Executive Chairman

Spike Island Artspace Limited
Incorporated: 27 June 1991 *Employees:* 22
Net Worth: £4,097,900 *Total Assets:* £4,294,677
Registered Office: 133 Cumberland Road, Bristol, BS1 6UX
Activities: Operation of arts facilities
Officers: Isabel Jane Jones, Secretary; Andy Lawrence Braithwaite [1959] Director/Solicitor; Andrew Richard Savage Cooper [1951] Director/Solicitor; Jane Therese Jackson [1955] Director/Independent Curator, Writer and Cultural Advisor; Jacqueline Mary Kingsley [1969] Director/Fundraising Specialist; Gavin Thomas Marshall [1977] Director/Chief Financial Officer; Jonathan Peter Wyndham Mosley [1967] Director/Artist; Dr Dorothy Price [1969] Director/Reader in History of Art; Alice Emily Workman [1979] Director

Spinnaker International Limited
Incorporated: 28 June 1990 *Employees:* 119
Net Worth: £7,132,319 *Total Assets:* £10,792,289
Registered Office: Spinnaker House, Saltash Parkway, Saltash, Cornwall, PL12 6LF
Activities: Manufacture of electronic components
Major Shareholder: Anthony Raymond Westington
Officers: Martin Jeremy Pascoe, Secretary/Accountant; Martin Jeremy Pascoe [1966] Director/Accountant; Anthony Raymond Westington [1968] Director General Manager; Christopher George Yandell [1981] Director; John Anthony Yandell [1948] Managing Director; Vivienne Linda Yandell [1954] Director

Spirax-Sarco America Limited
Incorporated: 1 November 2011
Net Worth: £166,957,760 *Total Assets:* £166,998,368
Registered Office: Charlton House, 15 Cirencester Road, Charlton Kings, Cheltenham, Glos, GL53 8ER
Activities: Activities of head offices
Parent: Spirax-Sarco Investments Limited
Officers: Andrew John Robson, Secretary; Kevin James Boyd [1964] Finance Director; Andrew John Robson [1963] Director/Company Secretary; John Davy Senior [1961] Director/Chartered Accountant

Spirax-Sarco Engineering PLC
Incorporated: 1 January 1958 *Employees:* 6,316
Net Worth: £608,400,000 *Total Assets:* £1,476,499,968
Registered Office: Charlton House, Cirencester Road, Charlton Kings, Cheltenham, Glos, GL53 8ER
Activities: Manufacture of pumps
Officers: Andrew John Robson, Secretary; Nicholas John Anderson [1961] Director; Kevin James Boyd [1964] Finance Director; Neil Harvey Daws [1962] Director; Peter Ian France [1968] Director; Jane Sarah May Kingston [1957] Director; James Robert Provan Pike [1955] Director; Dr Geertrui Elizabeth Schoolenberg [1958] Director [Dutch]; Clive Graeme Watson [1958] Director/FD; James Lawrence Whalen [1956] Director [American]

Spirax-Sarco Investments Limited
Incorporated: 5 January 1909
Net Worth: £48,172,180 *Total Assets:* £256,998,784
Registered Office: Charlton House, Cirencester Road, Cheltenham, Glos, GL53 8ER
Activities: Activities of head offices
Parent: Spirax-Sarco Engineering PLC
Officers: Andrew John Robson, Secretary; Kevin James Boyd [1964] Finance Director; Andrew John Robson [1963] Director/Company Secretary; John Davy Senior [1961] Director/Group Chief Accountant

Spirax-Sarco Limited
Incorporated: 19 June 1952 *Employees:* 1,119
Net Worth: £46,629,000 *Total Assets:* £133,001,000
Registered Office: Charlton House, 15 Cirencester Road, Cheltenham, Glos, GL53 8ER
Activities: Manufacture of pumps
Parent: Spirax-Sarco Engineering PLC
Officers: Andrew John Robson, Secretary; Kevin James Boyd [1964] Finance Director; Neil Harvey Daws [1962] Divisional Director; Ian Farnworth [1966] Group Supply Chain Director; Gavin Huxtable [1972] Director/Regional General Manager UK & Nordics; Paul Oakley [1966] Director; Byron Jeffery Thomas [1966] Director

Spirax-Sarco Overseas Limited
Incorporated: 10 January 1980
Net Worth: £367,257,376 *Total Assets:* £708,136,064
Registered Office: Charlton House, Cirencester Road, Cheltenham, Glos, GL53 8ER
Activities: Activities of head offices
Parent: Spirax-Sarco Engineering PLC
Officers: Andrew John Robson, Secretary; Kevin James Boyd [1964] Finance Director; Andrew John Robson [1963] Director/Company Secretary; John Davy Senior [1961] Director/Group Chief Accountant

Spire House Developments Limited
Incorporated: 2 August 2004 *Employees:* 4
Previous: Spire House Finance Limited
Net Worth: £4,233,935 *Total Assets:* £7,576,004
Registered Office: Unit 15 Interface Business Park, Binknoll Lane, Wootton Bassett, Swindon, Wilts, SN4 8SY
Activities: Buying and selling of own real estate
Parent: Spire House Holdings Limited
Officers: Stephen George Abbley [1957] Director/Manager

Spire Payments Ltd
Incorporated: 14 June 2011 *Employees:* 110
Net Worth: £6,616,000 *Total Assets:* £15,980,000
Registered Office: Units 3 & 6 Milford Trading Estate, Blakey Road, Salisbury, Wilts, SP1 2UD
Activities: Manufacture of computers and peripheral equipment
Shareholders: Greg Klein; Philippe Tartavull
Officers: Tai-Kei Cheung [1959] Director/Consultant to The Payments Industry; Alain Fernando-Santana [1962] Director [French]; Greg Klein [1966] Director [American]

Spire Technology Limited
Incorporated: 29 November 1989 *Employees:* 52
Net Worth: £4,803,311 *Total Assets:* £12,807,144
Registered Office: 5 Blackmoor Road, Ebblake Industrial Estate, Verwood, Dorset, BH31 6AX
Activities: Wholesale of computers, computer peripheral equipment and software
Major Shareholder: Victor Hugo Unt
Officers: Geoffrey Fidler, Secretary; John Appleton [1965] Director/Sales Manager; Geoffrey Fidler [1962] Director/Accountant; James Michael Philpott [1968] Director/General Manager; Paul David Turner [1976] Sales Director; Victor Hugo Unt [1955] Director

Spirit Packaging Limited
Incorporated: 29 September 2010 *Employees:* 142
Net Worth: £908,238 *Total Assets:* £11,203,883
Registered Office: Atlas Packaging Ltd, Barron Way, Roundswell Business Park, Barnstaple, Devon, EX31 3TT
Activities: Manufacture of other paper and paperboard containers
Shareholder: Adrian Gamble
Officers: Mark Reeve, Secretary; Adrian Gamble [1953] Director/Chairman; Mark Paul Leverton [1976] Director; Vincent Francis McDermott [1965] Manufacturing Director; Mark Christopher Reeve [1969] Director; Jason Gerard Sharman [1969] Director; Philip Robert Sweetland [1968] Operations Director

Spitalgate Dealer Services Limited
Incorporated: 25 June 1982 *Employees:* 16
Net Worth: £11,028,000 *Total Assets:* £93,654,000
Registered Office: Watermoor, Cirencester, Glos, GL7 1LF
Activities: Sale of new cars and light motor vehicles
Parent: Mitsubishi Corporation
Officers: Carolyn Tracey Stephenson, Secretary; Paul Andrew Brigden [1966] Managing Director; Hiroyuki Egami [1970] Director [Japanese]; Isao Kano [1960] Director [Japanese]; Kazuyoshi Kawakami [1969] Director [Japanese]; Keisuke Kimura [1985] Director [Japanese]; Mizuki Kuroda [1963] Finance Director [Japanese]; Hajime Machimura [1970] Director/Chairman [Japanese]; Jun Mitsuhashi [1965] Director [Japanese]

SPM Homes Ltd
Incorporated: 25 January 1988 *Employees:* 3
Net Worth: £2,169,538 *Total Assets:* £5,841,836
Registered Office: Brecon House, Charlton Hill, Cheltenham, Glos, GL53 9NE
Activities: Construction of domestic buildings
Major Shareholder: Huw Dewi Evans
Officers: James Walter Thomas Claughan, Secretary; Huw Dewi Evans [1949] Director

Sportech Holdco 1 Limited
Incorporated: 8 January 2010
Net Worth: £9,291,000 *Total Assets:* £9,401,000
Registered Office: Icarus House, Hawkfield Close, Hawkfield Business Park, Bristol, BS14 0BN
Activities: Activities of head offices
Parent: Sportech Group Holdings Limited
Officers: Andrew Ian Gaughan [1965] Director/Chief Executive [Canadian]; Thomas Joseph Hearne [1964] CFO and Director [Canadian]; Richard Anthony McGuire [1966] Director

Sportech Holdco 2 Limited
Incorporated: 8 January 2010
Net Worth: £69,740,856 *Total Assets:* £69,937,896
Registered Office: Icarus House, Hawkfield Close, Hawkfield Business Park, Bristol, BS14 0BN
Activities: Activities of head offices
Parent: Sportech Group Holdings Limited
Officers: Thomas Joseph Hearne [1964] CFO and Director [Canadian]; Richard Anthony McGuire [1966] Director

Sportech Pools Limited
Incorporated: 25 February 1955
Previous: The Football Pools Limited
Net Worth: £1,243,000 *Total Assets:* £11,881,000
Registered Office: Icarus House, Hawkfield Close, Hawkfield Business Park, Bristol, BS14 0BN
Activities: Other business support service activities n.e.c.
Parent: Sportech Gaming Limited
Officers: Thomas Joseph Hearne [1964] CFO and Director [Canadian]; Nicola McCabe [1980] Director/Group Financial Controller; Richard Anthony McGuire [1966] Director

The Sportsman Gun Centre Limited
Incorporated: 16 February 2010 *Employees:* 48
Net Worth: £7,407,120 *Total Assets:* £11,075,627
Registered Office: Lowin House, Tregolls Road, Truro, Cornwall, TR1 2NA
Activities: Retail sale of sports goods, fishing gear, camping goods, boats and bicycles
Major Shareholder: Gary Mark Lamburn
Officers: John Bevill Trevelyan Cattran, Secretary; John Bevill Trevelyan Cattran [1966] Director; Gary Mark Lamburn [1970] Director

Spower Holdco 1 (UK) Ltd.
Incorporated: 3 August 2015
Net Worth Deficit: £758,912 *Total Assets:* £9,095,961
Registered Office: Long Barn, Manor Courtyard, Stratton on the Fosse, Radstock, Somerset, BA3 4QF
Activities: Activities of production holding companies
Parent: CSGH Solar (1) Limited
Officers: Giuseppe La Loggia [1975] Director [Italian]; Yit Ho Tang [1974] Investment Director [Singaporean]; Christopher James Tanner [1972] Investment Director

SPP Pumps Limited
Incorporated: 21 July 2003 *Employees:* 427
Net Worth: £13,996,861 *Total Assets:* £62,972,344
Registered Office: SPP Pumps Limited, Crucible Close, Mushet Industrial Park, Coleford, Glos, GL16 8PS
Activities: Manufacture of pumps
Officers: Amit Bhalchandra Naniwadekar, Secretary; Alok Sanjay Kirloskar [1983] Managing Director; Sanjay Chandrakant Kirloskar [1957] Director [Indian]; Owen Shevlin [1952] Director; Pratap Baburao Shirke [1948] Director

Spring Mill Holdings Limited
Incorporated: 9 February 1956 *Employees:* 2
Net Worth: £3,211,868 *Total Assets:* £3,925,046
Registered Office: The Estate Office, Spring Mill, Avening Road, Nailsworth, Glos, GL6 0BS
Activities: Other letting and operating of own or leased real estate
Shareholders: Gillian Coulter; Mary Anne Purvis
Officers: Margaret Rose Davis, Secretary; Gillian Coulter [1956] Director; Margaret Rose Davis [1930] Director/Secretary; Clive Julian Sampson [1951] Director/Insurance Broker

Springfield Country Hotel (Stoborough) Limited
Incorporated: 1 April 1974 *Employees:* 38
Net Worth: £5,521,047 *Total Assets:* £10,041,288
Registered Office: 3 Durrant Road, Bournemouth, BH2 6LE
Activities: Hotels and similar accommodation
Shareholders: Josephine May Alford; Andrew Aidan Clark
Officers: John Gilbert Alford, Secretary; John Gilbert Alford [1956] Director/Hotel Manager; Josephine May Alford [1927] Director

Springvale Properties Limited
Incorporated: 22 December 1972 *Employees:* 2
Net Worth: £10,860,230 *Total Assets:* £13,176,009
Registered Office: 17 Market Place, Devizes, Wilts, SN10 1BA
Activities: Development of building projects
Major Shareholder: William George Valentine Hall
Officers: John Francis Clarkson, Secretary; Andrew Edward Valentine Hall [1970] Director; William George Valentine Hall [1939] Director

Springwood Farms Limited
Incorporated: 6 February 2004 *Employees:* 11
Net Worth: £1,488,119 *Total Assets:* £5,859,683
Registered Office: Trendles, Brockhampton Farm, Buckland Newton, Dorchester, DT2 7DJ
Activities: Raising of dairy cattle
Shareholders: John William Russell Hiscock; Caroline Anne Hiscock
Officers: Caroline Anne Hiscock, Secretary; Caroline Anne Hiscock [1963] Director/Teacher and Farmer; John William Russell Hiscock [1959] Director/Farmer; William George Allen Hiscock [1992] Director/Farmer

Spyscape Ltd
Incorporated: 26 July 2016 *Employees:* 1
Net Worth Deficit: £77,076 *Total Assets:* £4,275,446
Registered Office: 95 Promenade, Cheltenham, Glos, GL50 1HH
Activities: Ready-made interactive leisure and entertainment software development
Parent: Cipher Corp Holding Ltd
Officers: John Francis Weston Hunt [1963] Director/Entrepreneur [Irish]

Square One Construction Limited
Incorporated: 27 November 2009 *Employees:* 6
Net Worth: £599,998 *Total Assets:* £3,858,711
Registered Office: Barnsell Court, Landford, Salisbury, Wilts, SP5 2QP
Activities: Construction of commercial buildings
Shareholders: Timothy Stevens; Heather Ann Stevens
Officers: Heather Ann Stevens, Secretary; Timothy Stevens [1960] Director

SR & GM Limited
Incorporated: 3 November 1967 *Employees:* 30
Net Worth: £1,382,593 *Total Assets:* £5,123,780
Registered Office: First Floor, 10 Temple Back, Bristol, BS1 6FL
Activities: Renting and leasing of construction and civil engineering machinery and equipment
Parent: Rolling Hills Limited
Officers: Alexander Gibb Rennie, Secretary; Alexander Gibb Rennie [1943] Managing Director; Brian George Rennie [1972] Director/Manager

SRT Marine System Solutions Limited
Incorporated: 16 February 2009 *Employees:* 13
Net Worth: £3,187,420 *Total Assets:* £7,582,304
Registered Office: Wireless House, Westfield Industrial Estate, Midsomer Norton, Bath, BA3 4BS
Activities: Other professional, scientific and technical activities n.e.c.
Parent: SRT Marine Systems PLC
Officers: Richard Hurd, Secretary; Richard Hurd [1970] Director/Chartered Accountant; Neil Peniket [1973] Director; Simon Richard Tucker [1970] Director

SRT Marine Systems PLC
Incorporated: 23 May 2005 *Employees:* 56
Previous: Software Radio Technology PLC
Net Worth: £9,734,478 *Total Assets:* £15,914,108
Registered Office: Wireless House, Westfield Industrial Estate, Midsomer Norton, Bath, BA3 4BS
Activities: Activities of head offices
Officers: Richard Hurd, Secretary; Kevin Joseph Finn [1960] Director; Richard Hurd [1970] Director/Chartered Accountant; Neil Peniket [1973] Director; Simon Francis Rogers [1956] Director; Simon Richard Tucker [1970] Director

SRT Marine Technology Limited
Incorporated: 6 November 2001 *Employees:* 36
Net Worth Deficit: £3,269,583 *Total Assets:* £10,856,906
Registered Office: Wireless House, Midsomer Norton, Bath, BA3 4BS
Activities: Manufacture of other electrical equipment
Parent: SRT Marine Systems PLC
Officers: Richard Hurd, Secretary; Jonathan Michael Horne [1951] Director; Richard Hurd [1970] Director/Chartered Accountant; Neil Peniket [1973] Managing Director; Simon Francis Rogers [1956] Director; Simon Richard Tucker [1970] Commercial Director

SS Great Britain Trust
Incorporated: 27 January 1971 *Employees:* 77
Net Worth: £22,217,788 *Total Assets:* £23,357,742
Registered Office: 1 Brunel Square, Bristol, BS1 6UP
Activities: Operation of historical sites and buildings and similar visitor attractions
Officers: Angela Caroline Spreadbury, Secretary; James Whistler Berresford [1956] Director; Dr Helen Roberta Doe [1949] Director/Academic Historian; Kerry Anthony Lock [1969] Director/Accountant; James Anthony Patrick McKenna [1955] Director; Dinah Anne Moore [1950] Director/Solicitor; Samuel Patrick Mullins [1954] Director; Jan Aris Stam [1958] Director/Operations Manager [Dutch]

SSI Schaefer Ltd
Incorporated: 30 November 1960 *Employees:* 237
Net Worth: £4,616,878 *Total Assets:* £23,561,406
Registered Office: 83-84 Livingstone Road, Walworth Business Park, Andover, Hants, SP10 5QZ
Activities: Wholesale of metals and metal ores
Officers: Shailen Shah, Secretary; Udo Pfeil [1959] Director [German]; Henricus Johannes Gerardus Swinkles [1955] Managing Director [Dutch]

St Aubyn Estates Ltd
Incorporated: 4 December 1944 *Employees:* 244
Previous: Godolphin Company Limited (The)
Net Worth: £1,624,606 *Total Assets:* £8,167,751
Registered Office: Estate Office, King's Road, Marazion, Cornwall, TR17 0EL
Activities: Development of building projects
Parent: Marazion Holdings Ltd
Officers: Jonathan Ayton Haward [1959] Director; Niamh Mary Lamond [1963] Director/Chief Executive Officer [Irish]; Keith Marshall [1964] Finance Director; Felix John St Aubyn [1992] Director; Hugh James St Aubyn [1983] Director; Lord James Piers Southwell St Levan [1950] Director/Consultant; Lady Mary Caroline St Levan [1954] Director; Ramon Van de Velde [1975] Director/Chief Executive [Dutch]

St Austell Printing Company Limited
Incorporated: 20 May 2003 *Employees:* 52
Net Worth: £4,501,605 *Total Assets:* £11,752,066
Registered Office: St Austell Printing Company Limited, St Austell Business Park, St Austell, Cornwall, PL25 4FD
Activities: Printing n.e.c.
Shareholders: Peter Harold Moody; Amanda Elizabeth Moody
Officers: Beth Mayman, Secretary; Amanda Elizabeth Moody [1953] Director; Peter Harold Moody [1952] Director

St Bede's Catholic College
Incorporated: 5 October 2011 *Employees:* 134
Net Worth: £3,279,617 *Total Assets:* £5,849,202
Registered Office: St Bede's Catholic College, Long Cross, Bristol, BS11 0SU
Activities: General secondary education
Officers: Lisa Marie Barton [1981] Director/Clerical Staff; Dr Alicia Sophia Chrysostomou [1966] Director/Academic [Irish]; Teresa Gilpin [1954] Director/Retired; Maria Ann Hendricks [1967] Director; Robert James King [1982] Director/Assistant Principal; Siobhan Eileen Kinsman [1971] Director/Head of Human Resources; Kevin James Magner [1962] Director; John Garry Maher [1963] Director/Principal; Rev Colin Donald Mason [1961] Director/Priest; Jane Elizabeth Morris [1973] Director/Pharmacist; Anne Bernadette Pilkington [1952] Director; Elizabeth Mary White [1952] Director/Retired

St Christopher's C of E (Primary) Multi Academy Trust
Incorporated: 21 May 2013 *Employees:* 285
Net Worth: £1,898,313 *Total Assets:* £7,464,862
Registered Office: Unit 5 Basepoint Business Centre, Yeoford Way, Marsh Barton Trading Estate, Exeter, Devon, EX2 8LB
Activities: Primary education
Officers: Andrew Paul Bailey [1968] Director/Farmer; Julia Croughton [1967] Director of Finance and Operations; Joanne Evans [1966] Director; Paul Jones [1962] Director/Priest; Amy Laver [1978] Director/Lawyer; Nicola Prentice [1971] Director/Headteacher; Brenda Steel [1957] Director/Consultant; Dr Sean Edward Sweeney [1957] Director/Educational Consultant

St Christopher's C of E (Secondary) Multi Academy Trust
Incorporated: 12 April 2013 *Employees:* 105
Net Worth: £20,988,002 *Total Assets:* £23,680,018
Registered Office: The Ilfracombe Academy, Worth Road, Ilfracombe, Devon, EX34 9JB
Activities: General secondary education
Officers: Laura Nias, Secretary; Andrew Paul Bailey [1968] Director/Farmer; Patricia Anne Glover [1951] Director/Retired Teacher (Secondary); Alison Jane Homa [1965] Director/Hotelier; Sharon Isabel Marshall [1965] Director/Headteacher; Dr Sean Edward Sweeney [1957] Director

St David's Church of England Primary Academy
Incorporated: 7 December 2012 *Employees:* 32
Net Worth: £3,670,000 *Total Assets:* £4,017,000
Registered Office: East Street, Moreton in Marsh, Glos, GL56 0LQ
Activities: Primary education
Officers: Timothy John Brazil [1964] Director/Veterinary Surgeon; Reuben Chorley [1974] Director/Business Executive; Colin John Ellyatt [1972] Director/Headteacher; Richard Edward Harding [1973] Director; Robert Edward Jones [1972] Director/Deputy Headteacher; Victoria Jones [1975] Director/Manager; Fiona Loomes [1956] Director/Retired; Hilary Patricia Owen [1946] Director/Retired; Zoe Rodgers [1996] Director/Teacher; Neil William Sullivan [1962] Sales Director; Deborah Ann Wardlaw [1968] Director/School Business Manager; Sylvia Webster [1943] Director; Ana Whitworth [1970] Director/Teaching Assistant; Charlotte Patricia Davenport Yeates [1974] Director/Health & Safety Advisor

St Davids Poultry Team Limited
Incorporated: 10 November 2006 *Employees:* 54
Net Worth: £2,421,148 *Total Assets:* £5,463,040
Registered Office: 4 King Square, Bridgwater, Somerset, TA6 3YF
Activities: Veterinary activities
Shareholders: Alan Huw Beynon; Richard George Turner
Officers: Alan Huw Beynon, Secretary; Alan Huw Beynon [1964] Director; Richard Frederick Jackson [1987] Director [Irish]; Kerry Louise McBain [1973] Director; Kenneth Nutting [1989] Director; Richard George Turner [1957] Director

St George's Bristol
Incorporated: 9 September 1986 *Employees:* 18
Net Worth: £8,994,000 *Total Assets:* £10,418,000
Registered Office: Great George Street, Bristol, BS1 5RR
Activities: Performing arts
Officers: Lorraine Evelyn James, Secretary; Richard Bacon [1964] Director/Chartered Accountant; Sandie Teresa Foxall-Smith [1957] Director; Dr Marie-Annick Melanie Gournet-Moore [1965] Director/Academic [French]; Caroline Emma Hagen [1961] Managing Director; Ben Heald [1961] Director/Chartered Accountant; Jennifer Ann Hemming [1963] Director/Legal Consultant; Prof Nicholas Andrew John Lieven [1963] Director/Engineer; Dr John Manley [1957] Director/Scientist; Robert O'Leary [1960] Director/Architect [Irish]; Robert Boardley Suttie [1958] Director

St Giles Farms Limited
Incorporated: 28 December 1961 *Employees:* 14
Net Worth: £2,762,727 *Total Assets:* £5,476,318
Registered Office: The Estate Office, Wimborne St Giles, Wimborne, Dorset, BH21 5NA
Activities: Raising of other cattle and buffaloes
Shareholders: Brian Turnbull Julius Stevens; Charles Anthony Palmer Tompkinson; The Hon 12th Earl of Shaftesbury Nicholas Ashley Cooper
Officers: Jenna Louise Copp, Secretary; Nicholas Ashley Cooper [1979] Director/Businessman; Charles Anthony Palmer Tomkinson [1940] Director/Farmer

St Gresham Limited
Incorporated: 16 July 2002 *Employees:* 283
Net Worth: £3,082,375 *Total Assets:* £8,654,583
Registered Office: 99 Holdenhurst Road, Bournemouth, BH8 8DY
Activities: Activities of head offices
Officers: David Errington, Secretary; Rex David Newton Craven [1948] Director; David Errington [1955] Director; David Neil Huck [1958] Director/Surveyor; Nigel Price [1959] Director

St James Parade (107) Limited
Incorporated: 21 January 2008 *Employees:* 166
Net Worth: £14,289,342 *Total Assets:* £21,140,064
Registered Office: 2-12 Bath Road, Pylle Hill, Bristol, BS4 3DR
Activities: Retail trade of motor vehicle parts and accessories
Shareholders: Stephanie Lynn Fowler; Gillian Helen Johnson
Officers: Neil Stanley Bennett, Secretary; Lionel David Fowler [1946] Director; Stephanie Lyn Fowler [1947] Director; Frederick Robert Hart [1947] Director; Dr Gillian Helen Johnson [1948] Director

St James Priory Project
Incorporated: 10 April 2003 *Employees:* 14
Net Worth: £5,359,013 *Total Assets:* £5,370,968
Registered Office: St James Priory, Whitson Street, Bristol, BS1 3NZ
Activities: Residential care activities for learning difficulties, mental health and substance abuse
Officers: James Joseph Banaghan, Secretary; Michael Joseph Fitzpatrick [1943] Director/Parish Priest [Irish]; Lyn Murray [1969] Director/Chief Operating Officer; David John Shakesby [1974] Director/Solicitor; Nicole Sherwood [1941] Director/Translator; Rev Christopher Whitehead [1969] Director/Priest

St James's Place Unit Trust Group Limited
Incorporated: 10 February 1969
Net Worth: £20,225,000 *Total Assets:* £311,227,008
Registered Office: St James's Place House, 1 Tetbury Road, Cirencester, Glos, GL7 1FP
Activities: Financial intermediation not elsewhere classified
Parent: St. James's Place Wealth Management Group PLC
Officers: Andrew Martin Croft [1964] Director/Chartered Accountant; Ian Stewart Gascoigne [1956] Sales Director

St Juliens Limited
Incorporated: 6 December 2002 *Employees:* 1
Net Worth: £14,245,248 *Total Assets:* £19,383,382
Registered Office: Old Mills House, Old Mills, Paulton, Bristol, BS39 7SU
Activities: Activities of head offices
Major Shareholder: Roderick Barry Thorner
Officers: Roderick Barry Thorner [1961] Director

St Margaret's Academy
Incorporated: 16 March 2011 *Employees:* 47
Net Worth: £2,722,414 *Total Assets:* £3,890,851
Registered Office: St Margarets Academy, Barewell Road, Torquay, Devon, TQ1 4PA
Activities: Primary education
Officers: Karen Lisa Colmer, Secretary; Carole Valerie Ashworth [1991] Director/Teacher; James Michael Bennett [1981] Director/Data Analysis; James John Cree [1981] Director/Deputy Headteacher; Jonathan Whyte Dickson [1981] Director/Solicitor; Raymond Allen Hill [1949] Director/Councillor; Timothy Hughes [1970] Director/Headteacher; Myles William Key [1959] Director/Technical Support Engineer; Councillor Beryl Sylvia Louise McPhail [1931] Director/Councillor; Lisa Phillips [1970] Director/Housewife; Sara Pike [1962] Director/Deputy Headteacher; Nicole Louise Turner [1972] Director/Teacher

St Margaret's Residences (Exeter) Limited
Incorporated: 20 September 2013
Net Worth: £3,867,699 *Total Assets:* £6,200,648
Registered Office: Oxygen House, Grenadier Road, Exeter Business Park, Exeter, Devon, EX1 3LH
Activities: Other letting and operating of own or leased real estate
Parent: Grenadier Estates Ltd
Officers: Eleanor Jane Adams [1972] Finance Director; Matthew Owen Gingell [1979] Director/Solicitor; David Barclay Williamson [1965] Director/Accountant

St Michael's Falmouth Limited
Incorporated: 15 November 2016 *Employees:* 2
Net Worth Deficit: £771,054 *Total Assets:* £6,416,730
Registered Office: St Michaels Falmouth Ltd, St Michaels Hotel & Spa, Gyllygvase Beach, Falmouth, Cornwall, TR11 4NB
Activities: Hotels and similar accommodation
Shareholders: Carpenter Hotels Limited; B H Hotels Ltd
Officers: Nigel John Carpenter [1959] Director; James Simon Holte Houlston [1974] Director/Chartered Surveyor

St Moritz (Holdings) Limited
Incorporated: 23 July 2012 *Employees:* 90
Net Worth: £2,292,846 *Total Assets:* £7,882,456
Registered Office: Lowin House, Tregolls Road, Truro, Cornwall, TR1 2NA
Activities: Activities of other holding companies n.e.c.
Shareholders: Hugh Ridgway; Stephen Blakeney Ridgway
Officers: Hugh Ridgway [1954] Director; Stephen Blakeney Ridgway [1951] Director/Chief Executive

St Peter's Hospice
Incorporated: 20 November 1974 *Employees:* 432
Net Worth: £28,105,000 *Total Assets:* £30,514,000
Registered Office: St Peters Hospice, Charlton Road, Brentry, Bristol, BS10 6NL
Activities: Post-graduate level higher education
Officers: Frances McCloskey, Secretary; Claire Buchanan [1966] Director of HR; Mark Jonathan Douglas Campbell [1974] Relationship Director, Lloyds Private Clients; Doctor Shaheen Shahzadi Chaudhry [1955] Director/Freelance Trainer; Dr. James William Dodd [1978] Director/Respiratory Physician; Professor Karen Forbes [1960] Director/Doctor - Hospital Consultant; Dr Nicholas Peter Goyder [1961] Director/GP - General Medical Practitioner; Roger Anthony Stanford Isaacs [1967] Director/Chartered Accountant; Martin James Mohan [1959] Director; Paul Burridge Montague [1964] Director/Chartered Surveyor; Alison Jean Moon [1962] Director/Nurse; Darren Alan Spicer [1972] Director/Chartered Accountant; Helen Claire Staines [1958] Director/Solicitor

ST Schrader Holding Company UK Limited
Incorporated: 23 September 2014 *Employees:* 2
Net Worth: £734,002,176 *Total Assets:* £2,438,776,320
Registered Office: Interface House, Interface Business Park, Bincknoll Lane, Royal Wootton Bassett, Swindon, Wilts, SN4 8SY
Activities: Activities of other holding companies n.e.c.
Officers: Steven Beringhause [1965] Director/Chief Technology Officer [American]; Jeffrey John Cote [1966] Director [American]

St Stephens House Ltd
Incorporated: 9 November 2012
Net Worth: £2,194,311 *Total Assets:* £7,503,829
Registered Office: 45 Oakfield Road, Clifton, Bristol, BS8 2AX
Activities: Buying and selling of own real estate
Shareholder: David William Rogers
Officers: Edward John Ware [1960] Director; Kingsley Peter Webb [1966] Director

St. Edward's School Cheltenham Trust
Incorporated: 20 November 1985 *Employees:* 156
Net Worth: £4,036,000 *Total Assets:* £5,210,000
Registered Office: Cirencester Road, Charlton Kings, Cheltenham, Glos, GL53 8EY
Activities: Pre-primary education
Officers: Michael Coles, Secretary; Caroline Jane Findlay [1969] Director/Chartered Accountant; Gillian Margaret Greenwell [1956] Director/Solicitor/Regulatory Advisor; Dr Susan Honeywill [1967] Director/Teacher; Jane Barbara Jones [1953] Director/Retired; Raymond Antony McGrath [1967] Director/Management Consultant; Andrew Newland [1974] Accounts Director; Paul Anthony Potts [1959] Director/Architect

St. Francis Limited
Incorporated: 6 June 1991 *Employees:* 7
Net Worth: £3,193,804 *Total Assets:* £8,305,746
Registered Office: Centaur House, Torbay Road, Castle Cary, Somerset, BA7 7EU
Activities: Veterinary activities
Parent: MWI Supply (UK Acquisition) Limited
Officers: Brian Topper, Secretary; John Gardner Chou [1956] Director/Business Executive [American]; James F Cleary Jr [1968] Director/CEO & President [American]; Mark Jeffrey Shaw [1962] Director/Business Executive [American]

St. Hugh's School (Carswell) Trust Limited
Incorporated: 23 August 1967 *Employees:* 92
Net Worth: £3,769,428 *Total Assets:* £5,351,992
Registered Office: Carswell Manor, Faringdon, Oxon, SN7 8PT
Activities: Primary education
Officers: Alistair Stuart Hamilton, Secretary; Peter Frank Boggis [1947] Director/Farmer; Anna Coull [1960] Director/GP; Paul George Daffern [1953] Director; Christopher John Davies [1959] Director/Teacher; Judy Mary Forrest [1949] Director/Retired Headmistress; Virginia Gill [1974] Director/Teacher; James Montague Guillum Scott [1956] Director/Estate Agency; Edward Paul Lister Sandbach [1953] Director/Wine Merchant; Graham James Varney [1947] Director/Building Contractor; Alex James Wildman [1971] Director/Property Investment

St. James's Place Acquisition Services Limited
Incorporated: 5 August 2011 *Employees:* 13
Net Worth Deficit: £8,398,000 *Total Assets:* £22,829,000
Registered Office: St James's Place House, 1 Tetbury Road, Cirencester, Glos, GL7 1FP
Activities: Activities of financial services holding companies
Parent: St. James's Place Wealth Management Group PLC
Officers: Andrew Martin Croft [1964] Director; Ian Stewart Gascoigne [1956] Sales Director; Iain Rob Rayner [1972] Director

St. James's Place Charitable Foundation
Incorporated: 21 October 2011 *Employees:* 9
Previous: St. James's Place Foundation
Net Worth: £8,769,812 *Total Assets:* £8,852,796
Registered Office: St James's Place House, 1 Tetbury Road, Cirencester, Glos, GL7 1FP
Activities: Other service activities n.e.c.
Officers: David Charles Bellamy [1953] Director; Malcolm Cooper-Smith [1946] Director; Andrew Martin Croft [1964] Director; Ian Stewart Gascoigne [1956] Director; Sonia Gravestock [1957] Director; David John Lamb [1957] Director; Jonathan Neil McMahon [1975] Director/Joint Chief Operating Officer [Irish]

St. James's Place DFM Holdings Limited
Incorporated: 15 July 2015
Net Worth Deficit: £2,742,352 *Total Assets:* £49,902,260
Registered Office: St James Place House, 1 Tetbury Road, Cirencester, Glos, GL7 1FP
Activities: Activities of financial services holding companies
Parent: St James's Place PLC
Officers: Andrew Martin Croft [1964] Director/Chartered Accountant; Ian Stewart Gascoigne [1956] Sales Director; Iain Rob Rayner [1972] Director

St. James's Place International Assurance Group Limited
Incorporated: 30 June 1992
Net Worth: £15,121,000 *Total Assets:* £16,222,000
Registered Office: St James's Place House, 1 Tetbury Road, Cirencester, Glos, GL7 1FP
Activities: Activities of head offices
Parent: St. James's Place Wealth Management Group PLC
Officers: Elizabeth Janet Kelly [1965] Director/Company Secretary; Charles Frederick Basil Woodd [1971] Director/Actuary

St. James's Place International Distribution Limited
Incorporated: 2 December 2013
Net Worth Deficit: £3,811,000 *Total Assets:* £63,032,000
Registered Office: St James's Place House, 1 Tetbury Road, Cirencester, Glos, GL7 1FP
Activities: Activities of head offices
Parent: St. James's Place Wealth Management Group PLC
Officers: Andrew Martin Croft [1964] Director/Chartered Accountant; Michael Robert Gravestock [1960] Director; Ian Donald MacKenzie [1971] Director

St. James's Place Investment Administration Limited
Incorporated: 6 November 2013
Net Worth: £21,257,000 *Total Assets:* £34,055,000
Registered Office: St James's Place House, 1 Tetbury Road, Cirencester, Glos, GL7 1FP
Activities: Financial intermediation not elsewhere classified
Parent: St. James's Place Wealth Management Group PLC
Officers: Andrew Martin Croft [1964] Director/Chartered Accountant; Ian Stewart Gascoigne [1956] Sales Director; Ian Donald MacKenzie [1971] Director

St. James's Place Partnership Services Limited
Incorporated: 4 September 2012
Net Worth: £8,920,000 *Total Assets:* £890,417,984
Registered Office: St James's Place House, 1 Tetbury Road, Cirencester, Glos, GL7 1FP
Activities: Other business support service activities n.e.c.
Parent: St. James's Place Wealth Management Group PLC
Officers: Andrew Martin Croft [1964] Director; Ian Stewart Gascoigne [1956] Sales Director

St. James's Place PLC
Incorporated: 1 April 1996 *Employees:* 2,014
Net Worth: £1,059,000,000 *Total Assets:* £90,006,896,640
Registered Office: St James Place House, 1 Tetbury Road, Cirencester, Glos, GL7 1FP
Activities: Activities of head offices
Officers: Elizabeth Janet Kelly, Secretary; Iain Charles Andrew Cornish [1960] Director/Company Secretary; Andrew Martin Croft [1964] Director/Chartered Accountant; Ian Stewart Gascoigne [1956] Sales Director; Simon Jeffreys [1952] Director; Baroness Patience Jane Wheatcroft [1951] Director; Roger Philip Yates [1957] Director

St. James's Place UK PLC
Incorporated: 4 July 1991
Net Worth: £595,721,984 *Total Assets:* £59,281,297,408
Registered Office: St James's Place House, 1 Tetbury Road, Cirencester, Glos, GL7 1FP
Activities: Life insurance
Parent: St. James's Place Wealth Management Group PLC
Officers: Iain Charles Andrew Cornish [1960] Director; Andrew Martin Croft [1964] Director/Chartered Accountant; Ian Donald MacKenzie [1971] Director; Charles Frederick Basil Woodd [1971] Director/Actuary

St. James's Place Wealth Management Group Limited
Incorporated: 3 July 1991
Previous: St. James's Place Wealth Management Group PLC
Net Worth: £181,335,008 *Total Assets:* £327,567,008
Registered Office: St James's Place House, 1 Tetbury Road, Cirencester, Glos, GL7 1FP
Activities: Activities of head offices
Parent: St. James's Place PLC
Officers: Andrew Martin Croft [1964] Director/Chartered Accountant; Ian Stewart Gascoigne [1956] Sales Director

St. James's Place Wealth Management PLC
Incorporated: 24 November 2000
Net Worth: £85,684,000 *Total Assets:* £211,324,000
Registered Office: St James's Place House, 1 Tetbury Road, Cirencester, Glos, GL7 1FP
Activities: Activities auxiliary to financial intermediation n.e.c.
Parent: St. James's Place Wealth Management Group PLC
Officers: Andrew Martin Croft [1964] Director/Chartered Accountant; Ian Stewart Gascoigne [1956] Sales Director

St. Joseph's School Launceston
Incorporated: 22 December 1983 *Employees:* 65
Net Worth: £4,262,374 *Total Assets:* £5,150,315
Registered Office: St Stephens Hill, Launceston, Cornwall, PL15 8HN
Activities: Primary education
Officers: Ian Barton, Secretary; Cara Lucy Emma Amankwah [1974] Director/Parent; Paul Anthony Hicks [1957] Director/Insurance Broker; Louise Martine Holmes [1967] Director/Hotelier; David William Jasper [1957] Managing Director; Katherine Scott Flashman Kitson [1969] Director/Lawyer; Susan Lewis [1947] Director/Retired; Neil Richard Pockett [1946] Director/Education; Susan Rowe [1955] Director/ISA Employee; Jason Lee Thorns [1966] Director; Margaret Joan Warren [1953] Director/Businesswoman; Trevor Watkins [1968] Director/Manager

St. Laurence School Academy Trust
Incorporated: 8 July 2011 *Employees:* 172
Net Worth: £17,188,528 *Total Assets:* £18,336,656
Registered Office: St Laurence School, Ashley Road, Bradford on Avon, Wilts, BA15 1DZ
Activities: General secondary education
Officers: Lorna Lumb, Secretary; Revd Joanna Margaret Abecassis [1954] Director; Lauren Virginia Ash [1961] Director/Teaching Assistant; Dr Ian Stuart Blagbrough [1959] Director; Susan Jane Campbell [1959] Director/Teaching Assistant; Donal Casey [1953] Director/Valuer; Trudi Margaret Chatfield [1959] Director/Teacher; Sean Lee Cooper [1967] Director/Solicitor; Dr Michael Dooley [1961] Director/Solicitor; Lindsay Jane Driscoll [1947] Director/Solicitor; Kieran Patrick Kilgallen [1962] Director/Solicitor; Dr Peter Lambert [1965] Director/Pro-Vice-Chancellor Bath University; Mark Anthony Lee [1963] Director/Project Manager; Ingrid Louise Maher Roberts [1972] Director/HR Manager [Irish]; David William Nicholson [1951] Director/Academic Accounting; Lesley Ann Roddy [1958] Director/Bank Manager; Robert Satterthwaite [1960] Director/Retired; Fergus Colin Stewart [1962] Director/Headmaster

St. Luke's Hospice Plymouth
Incorporated: 3 July 1980 *Employees:* 273
Net Worth: £6,386,309 *Total Assets:* £7,250,688
Registered Office: St Lukes Hospice, Stamford Road, Turnchapel, Plymouth, PL9 9XA
Activities: Other human health activities
Officers: Susan Canon, Secretary; Clare Margaret Baker [1971] Director/Bank Staff; Christopher John Cavanagh [1958] Director/Chartered Civil Engineer; Fiona Patricia Field [1957] Executive Director for Transformation (Retired); Charles Oliver Maunsell Hackett [1977] Director; Julie Anne Hendry [1959] Director/Retired; Dr. Stephen Hobbs [1950] Director/Retired; Richard Mark James [1965] Director/Bank Manager; Professor Stephen Edward Newstead [1946] Director/Retired; Carol Mary Postle-Hacon [1950] Director/Retired; Christina Antoinetta Quinn [1965] Director/NHS Manager; Michael Francis Risdon [1954] Director/Retired

St. Margaret's Somerset Hospice
Incorporated: 7 January 1980 *Employees:* 265
Net Worth: £17,519,504 *Total Assets:* £18,677,082
Registered Office: Heron Drive, Bishops Hull, Taunton, Somerset, TA1 5HA
Activities: Other human health activities
Officers: Kevin Jones, Secretary; Glynis Mary Atherton [1955] Director/Retired CEO of Hospice Charity; Jennifer Sirrelle Board [1955] Director/Human Resources Consultant/Executive Coach; Patrick Joseph Colton [1966] Director/Head of Franchise UK & ROI; Dr Alison Jane Grove [1955] Director/Retired; Jonathan Charles Langdon [1956] Director/Chartered Accountant; Elizabeth Jane Moss [1959] Director/Chartered Surveyor; Thomas Graham Samuel [1969] Managing Director; Dr Deborah Jane Stalker [1960] Director/Consultant Paediatrician

St. Mary's School (Calne)
Incorporated: 13 December 1928 *Employees:* 257
Net Worth: £18,031,676 *Total Assets:* £28,575,668
Registered Office: St Mary's School, Curzon Street, Calne, Wilts, SN11 0DF
Activities: Other education n.e.c.
Officers: Daniel John Boswell, Secretary; Svante Lennart Stensson Adde [1956] Director [Swedish]; Dr Linda Maureen Ashton [1972] Technical Director; Catherine Rachel Bell [1971] Director/Charity Trustee and Parish Councillor; Professor Ann Fitz-Generald [1968] Director/University Professor [Canadian]; Martin James Seymour Harris [1965] Director/Headmaster; Christine McGregor Lough [1955] Director/Headteacher; Hedley Sidney Ringrose [1942] Director/Retired; Jonathan Stephen Smith [1966] Director/Businessman; Simon Turton [1967] Director; Victoria Jane Wilson [1950] Director/Businesswoman

St. Mary's School Shaftesbury Trust
Incorporated: 20 September 1985 *Employees:* 208
Net Worth: £4,725,082 *Total Assets:* £10,048,378
Registered Office: St Mary's School, Shaftesbury, Dorset, SP7 9LP
Activities: General secondary education
Officers: Sudipa Ghosh, Secretary; Major-General Nicholas Borton [1969] Director/Army Officer; Philip Conrath [1950] Director/Barrister; Michael Charles Farmer [1961] Director/Headmaster; Peter Tyrel Geikie-Cobb [1964] Director/Consultant; Allison Harriet Hunt [1986] Director/Teacher; Dr Kathryn Mounde [1973] Director/GP; Alexander Edward Northcott [1968] Director; Sister Marie-Christine Alice Simmonds [1956] Director; Janet Lynsey Watts [1964] Director/Teacher; Victoria Mary Younghusband [1954] Director/Lawyer

St. Moritz Developments Limited
Incorporated: 16 February 2001 *Employees:* 1
Net Worth: £264,984 *Total Assets:* £6,403,531
Registered Office: Trebetherick, Wadebridge, Cornwall, PL27 6SD
Activities: Development of building projects
Parent: St Moritz (Holdings) Limited
Officers: Hugh Ridgway, Secretary; Hugh Ridgway [1954] Director/Hotelier; Stephen Blakeney Ridgway [1951] Director/Chief Executive; William Edward Fraser Whyte [1952] Director

St. Piran's School (GB) Limited
Incorporated: 11 September 2002 *Employees:* 109
Net Worth: £458,798 *Total Assets:* £6,880,148
Registered Office: 14 Trelissick Road, Hayle, Cornwall, TR27 5HY
Activities: Post-graduate level higher education
Officers: Rajanathan Satheeskumar, Secretary; Timothy Marius Ashanta Andradi [1953] Director; Godfrey John Phillips [1950] Director

St.Austell Brewery Company Limited
Incorporated: 17 January 1910 *Employees:* 1,553
Net Worth: £100,660,000 *Total Assets:* £188,327,008
Registered Office: 63 Trevarthian Road, St Austell, Cornwall, PL25 4BY
Activities: Manufacture of beer
Officers: Colin John Stratton, Secretary; Gerard Hugh Barnes [1968] Director; Gillian Caseberry [1965] Director; Kevin Roger Georgel [1970] Director/Chief Executive; Thomas Adam Luck [1956] Director; William Franck Michelmore [1959] Director; Simon James Staughton [1959] Director; Colin John Stratton [1965] Director/Chartered Accountant; Piers Michael Thompson [1971] Director/Regional National Sales Manager; Stephen John Worrall [1969] Director

St.James's Place (PCP) Limited
Incorporated: 14 April 1992
Net Worth: £5,598,318 *Total Assets:* £7,023,437
Registered Office: St James's Place House, 1 Tetbury Road, Cirencester, Glos, GL7 1FP
Activities: Other business support service activities n.e.c.
Parent: St. James's Place Wealth Management Group PLC
Officers: Andrew Martin Croft [1964] Director/Chartered Accountant; Ian Stewart Gascoigne [1956] Sales Director

St.James's Place Management Services Limited
Incorporated: 7 November 1991 *Employees:* 1,589
Net Worth Deficit: £100,316,000 *Total Assets:* £449,663,008
Registered Office: St James's Place House, 1 Tetbury Road, Cirencester, Glos, GL7 1FP
Activities: Other business support service activities n.e.c.
Parent: St. James's Place Wealth Management Group PLC
Officers: Andrew Martin Croft [1964] Director/Chartered Accountant; Ian Stewart Gascoigne [1956] Sales Director

J.E.Stacey & Co.Limited
Incorporated: 12 May 1959 *Employees:* 43
Net Worth: £3,139,009 *Total Assets:* £4,139,511
Registered Office: Inceworth Building Works, Bodmin Street, Holsworthy, Devon, EX22 6BD
Activities: Development of building projects
Parent: J.E. Stacey & Co. (Holdings) Limited
Officers: John Addicott, Secretary; John Addicott [1955] Director/Builder/Surveyor; Lucy Jane Squire [1974] Director/Certified Chartered Accountant; Andrew Frederick Stacey [1936] Director/Builder/Surveyor; John Charles Stacey [1965] Director/Builder/Surveyor; Richard James Stacey [1963] Director/Chartered Engineer

Stafford Education Facilities Limited
Incorporated: 18 December 2002 *Employees:* 2
Net Worth: £130,854 *Total Assets:* £3,785,085
Registered Office: Third Floor, Broad Quay House, Prince Street, Bristol, BS1 4DJ
Activities: Management of real estate on a fee or contract basis
Parent: Stafford Education Facilities Holdings Limited
Officers: Richard Little [1979] Investment Director; Julia Sarah McCabe [1970] Regional Director

Stag Buying Group Limited
Incorporated: 28 January 1991 *Employees:* 13
Net Worth: £1,096,035 *Total Assets:* £3,694,817
Registered Office: The Courtyard, 221 Cheney Manor Road, Cheney Manor, Swindon, Wilts, SN2 2PE
Activities: Wholesale of clothing and footwear
Officers: David John Robshaw, Secretary; Ricky Chandler [1961] Sales Director; Sara Louise Chandler [1978] Director; Ward Robertson [1963] Director

Stage Electrics Partnership Limited
Incorporated: 7 June 1996 *Employees:* 180
Net Worth: £5,925,288 *Total Assets:* £13,499,774
Registered Office: Encore House, Unit 3 Britannia Road, Patchway Trading Estate, Patchway, Bristol, BS34 5TA
Activities: Other retail sale of new goods in specialised stores (not commercial art galleries and opticians)
Parent: SLX Group Limited
Officers: John Steven Laycock [1948] Director; Trevor Smallwood [1947] Director; Maria Ann Townsend [1980] Director/Group CEO

Staines Trailers Ltd
Incorporated: 6 July 2011 *Employees:* 38
Net Worth: £708,005 *Total Assets:* £3,650,802
Registered Office: Hunshaw Barton Farm, Huntshaw, Torrington, Devon, EX38 7HH
Activities: Manufacture of other fabricated metal products n.e.c.
Major Shareholder: Edward James Staines
Officers: Edward James Staines [1965] Director/Trailer Manufacturer

Stallcombe House
Incorporated: 27 November 1981 *Employees:* 86
Net Worth: £4,152,667 *Total Assets:* £4,262,238
Registered Office: Stallcombe House Farm, Sanctuary Lane, Woodbury Salterton, Devon, EX5 1EX
Activities: Other residential care activities n.e.c.
Officers: Elizabeth Jane Johnson [1972] Director/Lawyer; Ann Elizabeth Liverton [1946] Director/Retired; Sara Elizabeth Ann Mayhew [1970] Director/Solicitor; Dorian Osborne [1965] Director/Support Worker; Geoffrey Douglas Hall Pook [1954] Director/Civil Engineer; Christopher Mark Retallack [1947] Director of Language School; Christopher Giles Townroe [1951] Director/Retired; Eileen Elizabeth Wragg [1946] Director/Councillor

Stanborough (Construction) Limited
Incorporated: 18 November 1997 *Employees:* 6
Net Worth: £2,263,193 *Total Assets:* £5,687,887
Registered Office: 1 Longfleet Road, Poole, Dorset, BH15 2HN
Activities: Other construction installation
Major Shareholder: Justin Stuart Stanborough
Officers: Rachel Margaret Stanborough, Secretary; Justin Stuart Stanborough [1971] Director; Rachel Margaret Stanborough [1972] Director

Stanborough (Developments) Limited
Incorporated: 23 April 1971 *Employees:* 2
Net Worth: £23,877,302 *Total Assets:* £24,181,312
Registered Office: 1 Longfleet Road, Poole, Dorset, BH15 2HN
Activities: Construction of other civil engineering projects n.e.c.
Major Shareholder: John Henry Stanborough
Officers: Wendy Jane Stockley, Secretary; Beryl Eleanor Snelling [1944] Director/Housewife; John Henry Stanborough [1936] Director

Stanbridge Property Developments Limited
Incorporated: 24 March 2017 *Employees:* 3
Net Worth: £20,924 *Total Assets:* £4,272,002
Registered Office: 4 The Axium Centre, Dorchester Road, Lytchett Minster, Poole, Dorset, BH16 6FE
Activities: Buying and selling of own real estate
Shareholder: David Rodney Fairchild
Officers: Barry Collingwood Wilson Fairchild [1934] Director; David Rodney Fairchild [1959] Director; Richard Barry Fairchild [1965] Director; Russell John Fairchild [1961] Director; William James Fairchild [1968] Director

Stance (Europe) Limited
Incorporated: 19 May 2011 *Employees:* 2
Net Worth: £2,394,704 *Total Assets:* £9,142,123
Registered Office: 51 North Hill, Plymouth, PL4 8HZ
Activities: Wholesale of clothing and footwear
Officers: Jeff Kearl, Secretary; Myles Trystan Neil Hutchins [1983] Director; Jeff Kearl [1972] Director [American]; John Wilson [1968] Director/President [American]

Stanchester Community School Academy
Incorporated: 21 June 2011 *Employees:* 86
Net Worth: £7,444,695 *Total Assets:* £9,402,837
Registered Office: Stanchester Community School, East Stoke, Stoke-sub-Hamdon, Somerset, TA14 6UG
Activities: General secondary education
Officers: Rosemary Atkinson [1953] Director/Retired; Lynn Benfield [1947] Director/Retired HR Manager; Jenna Burrow [1985] Director/Teacher; Simon Darley [1961] Director/Farmer; Jane Gillespie [1955] Director; Gemma Glentworth [1985] Director/Teacher; Andy Hall [1976] Director/Royal Naval Officer; Nicola Claire Holt [1972] Director Teacher; Amy Joynes [1975] Director/Principal; Dale Newson [1966] Director; Judith Watson [1951] Director/Retired; Rachel Wellfair [1986] Director/Teacher

Standard Brands (UK) Limited
Incorporated: 15 February 2001 *Employees:* 17
Net Worth: £6,762,817 *Total Assets:* £7,157,297
Registered Office: Manderson House, 5230 Valiant Court, Delta Way, Brockworth, Gloucester, GL3 4FE
Activities: Other manufacturing n.e.c.
Parent: SHS S.B. Limited
Officers: Arthur William Richmond, Secretary; Elaine Birchall [1966] Director [Irish]; Richard Harris [1965] Sales & Marketing Director; Denis McCourt [1976] Director/Company Secretary [Irish]; Arthur William Richmond [1966] Director

Standbetter Limited
Incorporated: 3 November 1987 *Employees:* 2
Net Worth: £6,356,040 *Total Assets:* £15,612,652
Registered Office: 47 Oxford Street, Weston Super Mare, Somerset, BS23 1TN
Activities: Other letting and operating of own or leased real estate
Shareholders: Peter George Carter; Anita Carter
Officers: Peter George Carter, Secretary/Managing Director; Anita Carter [1949] Director; Nicola Carter [1980] Director; Peter George Carter [1947] Director; Richard Steven Carter [1982] Director

Stanley Security Solutions - Europe Limited
Incorporated: 30 March 1966
Net Worth: £32,269,000 *Total Assets:* £51,565,000
Registered Office: Stanley House, Bramble Road, Swindon, Wilts, SN2 8ER
Activities: Activities of head offices
Parent: SWK (UK) Limited
Officers: Steven John Costello, Secretary; Andrew Stephen Lord [1972] Director/Accountant; Matthew Giles Thomas Marriott [1971] Director/Regional General Manager; Stephanie Irene Merrifield [1978] HR Director

Stanley Security Solutions Limited
Incorporated: 6 May 1922 *Employees:* 472
Net Worth: £36,710,000 *Total Assets:* £94,554,000
Registered Office: Stanley House, Bramble Road, Swindon, Wilts, SN2 8ER
Activities: Other construction installation
Parent: Niscayah Holdings Limited
Officers: Steven John Costello, Secretary; Andrew Stephen Lord [1972] Director/Accountant; Matthew Giles Thomas Marriott [1971] Director/Regional General Manager; Stephanie Irene Merrifield [1978] HR Director

Stanley UK Acquisition Company Limited
Incorporated: 14 January 2004
Net Worth: £22,685,000 *Total Assets:* £22,685,000
Registered Office: Stanley House, Bramble Road, Swindon, Wilts, SN2 8ER
Activities: Activities of head offices
Parent: Stanley U.K. Holding Ltd.
Officers: Steven John Costello, Secretary; Steven John Costello [1980] Director/Chartered Accountant; Mark Richard Smiley [1977] Director/General Manager UK & ROI; Amit Kumar Sood [1978] Director/Accountant

Stanley's Biomass Limited
Incorporated: 9 February 2016
Net Worth Deficit: £1,558,658 *Total Assets:* £8,432,459
Registered Office: Westingon Quarry, Westington Hill, Chipping Campden, Glos, GL55 6EG
Activities: Manufacture of other products of wood; manufacture of articles of cork, straw and plaiting materials
Officers: Harry Piers Shaw Bond [1976] Director; Ian Robbin Stanley Bond [1940] Director; Samuel David Launchbury [1983] Director; John Stephen Pendlebury Shelton [1959] Director

Stannah Lift Services Limited
Incorporated: 7 November 1974 *Employees:* 828
Net Worth: £12,323,000 *Total Assets:* £29,736,000
Registered Office: Watt Close, East Portway, Andover, Hants, SP10 3SD
Activities: Manufacture of lifting and handling equipment
Parent: Stannah Lifts Holdings Limited
Officers: Deborah Lee Coveney, Secretary; Deborah Lee Coveney [1968] Director; Alan Neil Russell Stannah [1939] Director; Alastair David Stannah [1973] Director; Brian Leslie Russell Stannah [1935] Director; Jonathan Neil Stannah [1965] Director; Nicholas David Stannah [1973] Business Development Director

Stannah Lifts Holdings Limited
Incorporated: 20 March 1961 *Employees:* 2,038
Net Worth: £118,218,000 *Total Assets:* £169,072,992
Registered Office: Watt Close, East Portway, Andover, Hants, SP10 3SD
Activities: Other letting and operating of own or leased real estate
Shareholders: Alan Neil Russell Stannah; Alastair David Stannah; Helen Louise Stirrup; Jacqueline Constance Patricia Stannah; Brian Leslie Russell Stannah; Jennifer Mary Stannah; Jonathan Neil Stannah; Patrick Gordon Stannah; Nicholas David Stannah
Officers: Deborah Lee Coveney, Secretary; Alan Neil Russell Stannah [1939] Director; Alastair David Stannah [1973] Director; Brian Leslie Russell Stannah [1935] Director; Jacqueline Constance Patricia Stannah [1944] Director; Jennifer Mary Stannah [1942] Director; Jonathan Neil Stannah [1965] Director; Nicholas David Stannah [1973] Business Development Director; Helen Louise Stirrup [1976] Director

Stannah Lifts Limited
Incorporated: 7 November 1974 *Employees:* 111
Net Worth: £2,296,000 *Total Assets:* £8,589,000
Registered Office: Watt Close, East Portway, Andover, Hants, SP10 3SD
Activities: Manufacture of lifting and handling equipment
Parent: Stannah Lifts Holdings Limited
Officers: Deborah Lee Coveney, Secretary; Deborah Lee Coveney [1968] Director; Alan Neil Russell Stannah [1939] Director; Alastair David Stannah [1973] Director; Brian Leslie Russell Stannah [1935] Director; Jonathan Neil Stannah [1965] Director; Nicholas David Stannah [1973] Business Development Director

Stannah Management Services Limited
Incorporated: 21 March 1990 *Employees:* 110
Net Worth: £2,469,000 *Total Assets:* £5,576,000
Registered Office: Watt Close, East Portway, Andover, Hants, SP10 3SD
Activities: Other business support service activities n.e.c.
Parent: Stannah Lifts Holdings Limited
Officers: Deborah Lee Coveney, Secretary; Deborah Lee Coveney [1968] Director; Alan Neil Russell Stannah [1939] Director; Alastair David Stannah [1973] Director; Brian Leslie Russell Stannah [1935] Director; Jonathan Neil Stannah [1965] Director; Nicholas David Stannah [1973] Business Development Director

Stannah Stairlifts Limited
Incorporated: 23 November 1978 *Employees:* 552
Net Worth: £20,293,000 *Total Assets:* £26,787,000
Registered Office: Watt Close, East Portway, Andover, Hants, SP10 3SD
Activities: Other manufacturing n.e.c.
Parent: Stannah Lifts Holdings Limited
Officers: Deborah Lee Coveney, Secretary; Deborah Lee Coveney [1968] Director; Timothy Andrew Eagles [1969] Director/Manufacturing; Alan Neil Russell Stannah [1939] Director; Alastair David Stannah [1973] Director; Brian Leslie Russell Stannah [1935] Director; Jonathan Neil Stannah [1965] Director; Nicholas David Stannah [1973] Business Development Director

Star Education Investment Limited
Incorporated: 3 June 2016 *Employees:* 1
Net Worth Deficit: £25,509 *Total Assets:* £45,885,760
Registered Office: Fifth Floor, 100 Victoria Street, Bristol, BS1 6HZ
Activities: General secondary education
Officers: Yiding Hao [1984] Director/Chairman [Chinese]

Star Hydraulics Limited
Incorporated: 22 August 1984
Net Worth: £11,720,279 *Total Assets:* £12,352,275
Registered Office: Star Hydraulics Ltd, Severn Drive, Tewkesbury Business Park, Tewkesbury, Glos, GL20 8SF
Activities: Manufacture of fluid power equipment
Major Shareholder: Paul Shillam
Officers: Paul Shillam, Secretary; Terence Balm [1937] Director/Sales Engineer; Christian McCormick [1968] Director/Engineer; Roy Mountford [1957] Director/Engineer; Paul Shillam [1952] Director/Engineer

H.C. Starck Limited
Incorporated: 23 June 1993 *Employees:* 31
Net Worth: £6,806,347 *Total Assets:* £10,364,319
Registered Office: 1 Harris Road, Calne, Wilts, SN11 9PT
Activities: Machining
Officers: Paul Leblanc [1956] Director/Finance Executive/CFO [American]; Andreas Mader [1963] Director/Business Executive [German]; Martin Alan Smith [1971] Plant Director

Staverton Electrical Supplies Ltd
Incorporated: 19 March 2010 *Employees:* 30
Net Worth: £1,667,113 *Total Assets:* £5,584,627
Registered Office: Meteor Business Park, Cheltenham Road East, Gloucester, GL2 9QL
Activities: Wholesale of other intermediate products
Officers: Paula Kirsten Bradshaw [1968] Finance Director; Stephen Paul Evans [1956] Director/Chairman

Stay Dry Roofing (South West) Limited
Incorporated: 14 January 2003 *Employees:* 17
Net Worth: £4,359,416 *Total Assets:* £5,352,244
Registered Office: 6 Houndiscombe Road, Plymouth, PL4 6HH
Activities: Roofing activities
Major Shareholder: Clinton Pethick
Officers: Sarah Frances Gould, Secretary/Office Manager; Clinton Pethick [1973] Director

Stay Original Company Ltd
Incorporated: 29 July 2010
Previous: The Draco Pub Company Limited
Net Worth: £1,270,070 *Total Assets:* £9,215,635
Registered Office: 30 Gay Street, Bath, BA1 2PA
Activities: Hotels and similar accommodation
Major Shareholder: Robert Dudley Greacen
Officers: James Brooke-Webb [1968] Director; Patrick Gerard Gill [1958] Director/Chartered Surveyor; Robert Dudley Greacen [1964] Director

Staysail Limited
Incorporated: 30 March 2010 *Employees:* 119
Net Worth: £2,158,319 *Total Assets:* £9,369,109
Registered Office: Spinnaker House, Saltash Parkway Industrial Estate, Saltash, Cornwall, PL12 6LF
Activities: Other business support service activities n.e.c.
Shareholders: Anthony Raymond Westington; John Anthony Yandell
Officers: Anthony Raymond Westington [1968] Director; John Anthony Yandell [1948] Director

STC (Milton Keynes) Limited
Incorporated: 12 August 2002 *Employees:* 5
Net Worth: £595,500 *Total Assets:* £23,910,302
Registered Office: Third Floor, Broad Quay House, Prince Street, Bristol, BS1 4DJ
Activities: Justice and judicial activities
Parent: STC (Milton Keynes) Holdings Limited
Officers: Richard Little [1979] Investment Director; Gawie Murray Nienaber [1957] Director/General Legal Counsel; Vaishali Jagdish Patel [1973] Director/Solicitor; Jeremy Kenneth Petherick [1954] Managing Director; Alan Campbell Ritchie [1967] Director

Steadfast Asset Management Limited
Incorporated: 12 August 1996 *Employees:* 5
Net Worth: £374,865 *Total Assets:* £9,019,990
Registered Office: North Wing, Rowden House, Rowden Hill, Chippenham, Wilts, SN15 2AG
Activities: Other letting and operating of own or leased real estate
Major Shareholder: Nicholas Audley Money-Kyrle
Officers: Deborah Dunsford, Secretary; Nicholas Audley Money-Kyrle [1964] Director

Stealthlink Ltd
Incorporated: 16 February 1998 *Employees:* 11
Net Worth: £3,925,334 *Total Assets:* £4,062,436
Registered Office: Tone Motor Co, Chip Lane, Taunton, Somerset, TA1 1DU
Activities: Sale of used cars and light motor vehicles
Major Shareholder: David Jones
Officers: David Andrew Jones [1964] Director

Steanbow Limited
Incorporated: 19 April 2011 *Employees:* 27
Previous: Steanbow Contracting Limited
Net Worth: £2,429,310 *Total Assets:* £15,330,515
Registered Office: Steanbow Farm, Pilton, Shepton Mallet, Somerset, BA4 4EH
Activities: Support activities for crop production
Shareholders: Finn Christensen; Michael George Finn Christensen; Neil Stuart Christensen
Officers: Finn Christensen [1937] Director/Farmer; Michael George Finn Christensen [1965] Director/Farmer; Neil Stuart Christensen [1964] Director/Farmer

Stedall (Vehicle Fittings) Limited
Incorporated: 5 December 1924 *Employees:* 24
Net Worth: £7,132,000 *Total Assets:* £11,155,000
Registered Office: Unit 1a, Badminton Road Trading Estate, Yate, Bristol, BS37 5JS
Activities: Wholesale trade of motor vehicle parts and accessories
Major Shareholder: Fredericus Johannes Kroijmans
Officers: Darren Michael Pearce, Secretary; Branwell Rupert Horth [1961] Sales Director; Darren Michael Pearce [1972] Director

Steele Davis Limited
Incorporated: 17 June 1992 *Employees:* 81
Net Worth: £512,882 *Total Assets:* £4,516,351
Registered Office: Unit 18 Devizes Trade Centre, Hopton Industrial Estate, Devizes, Wilts, SN10 2EH
Activities: Construction of commercial buildings
Shareholders: Michael David Gingell; Alastair Lindsay Steele-Davis
Officers: Mary Beatrix Steele-Davis, Secretary; Michael David Gingell [1969] Director; Julian Mark Steele Davis [1970] Director/Building Contractor; Alastair Lindsay Steele-Davis [1945] Director/Builder

Steelinvest Limited
Incorporated: 6 July 2001 *Employees:* 15
Net Worth: £194,990 *Total Assets:* £7,610,154
Registered Office: 37 Chamberlain Street, Wells, Somerset, BA5 2PQ
Activities: Wholesale of metals and metal ores
Officers: Martin James Bowe, Secretary; David Henry Mogford [1954] Director

Stein's Trading Limited
Incorporated: 28 August 2014 *Employees:* 243
Net Worth Deficit: £498,000 *Total Assets:* £8,322,000
Registered Office: The Seafood Restaurant, Riverside, Padstow, Cornwall, PL28 8BY
Activities: Licenced restaurants
Shareholders: Christopher Richard Stein; Jill Stein
Officers: Neil John McLeod, Secretary; Neil John McLeod [1962] Finance Director; Christopher Richard Stein [1947] Director/Restaurateur; Jill Stein [1947] Director/Restaurateur

Steiner Academy Frome
Incorporated: 12 June 2012 *Employees:* 60
Net Worth: £7,725,360 *Total Assets:* £8,393,711
Registered Office: Park Road, Frome, Somerset, BA11 1EU
Activities: General secondary education
Officers: Alan Abhaya [1977] Director/Teacher; Shannon Coggins [1965] Director/Administrator; Lara Ellender [1970] Director/Speech Therapist/Project Worker in Charity Sector; Paul Anthony Georghiades [1960] Director; Clare Hein [1954] Director; Agnes Javor [1947] Director/Retired; Alexander Samuel Marson [1969] Director/Consultant; Guy Marson [1969] Director/CEO Marketing Company; Trevor Michael Mepham [1959] Director; Anna O'Kane [1975] Director; Sal Steeple [1970] Director/Social Work Manager; Martin Ivar Alexander Van Duin [1974] Director/Royal Navy Officer

Step One Charity
Incorporated: 26 February 1945 *Employees:* 126
Previous: St. Loye's Foundation
Net Worth: £11,974,193 *Total Assets:* £14,271,445
Registered Office: Beaufort House, 51 New North Road, Exeter, EX4 4EP
Activities: General secondary education
Officers: Imran Beider [1960] Director/Management Accountant; David Vaughan Hodgetts [1949] Director/Retired; Ashley Pocock [1972] Director/Certified Chartered Accountant; Edmund Arthur Whitmore Probert [1953] Director/Solicitor; Mandy Suzanne Reynolds [1970] Director of Marketing; Mark Rushbrooke Forbes Taylor [1943] Director/Retired Health Service Manager/Non-Executive Director [British/Canadian]; Robert David Williams [1962] Director of a Business Advisory and Management Consultant

Stephens Scown LLP
Incorporated: 23 July 2010 *Employees:* 312
Net Worth: £7,298,578 *Total Assets:* £9,414,104
Registered Office: Curzon House, Southernhay West, Exeter, Devon, EX1 1RS
Officers: Richard George Baker [1965] Member; Robert Michael Camp [1961] Member; James Adam Keliher [1956] Member; Michael Patrick Lowry [1957] Member; Michael John Northcott [1958] Member; Elizabeth Ann Allen [1962] LLP Member; Timothy Richard Atkins [1968] LLP Member; Richard William Bagwell [1973] LLP Member; Andrew Christopher Barton [1977] LLP Member; Michael John Stebbing Beadel [1959] LLP Member; Sonya Bedford [1973] LLP Member; Robert Nilsen Brightley [1957] LLP Member; Tobias James Claridge [1963] LLP Member; Nigel Douglas Coveney [1963] LLP Member; Brian Joseph Dolan [1967] LLP Member; Giles William Dunning [1982] LLP Member; Terence Falcao [1959] LLP Member; Simon Christopher Cox Gawler [1973] LLP Member; Phillip David Gregory [1958] LLP Member; Simon Harding [1970] LLP Member; Peter Grant Marshall [1964] LLP Member; Catherine Louise Mathews [1978] LLP Member; Scott Duncan Mitchell [1966] LLP Member; Graham Ian Murdoch [1963] LLP Member; Susanne-Maria Murray [1978] LLP Member; Hilary Ann Pitts [1963] LLP Member; Toby James Pool [1973] LLP Member; Philip Henry Reed [1962] LLP Member; Mark James Richardson [1968] LLP Member; Verity Jillian Slater [1977] LLP Member; Mark Creighton Smith [1973] LLP Member; Christopher Tofts [1977] LLP Member; Henri Simon Trahair-Davies [1971] LLP Member; Benjamin David Travers [1980] LLP Member; Helen Louise Wallwork [1979] LLP Member; William John Wilkins [1968] LLP Member; Christian Andrew Simpson Wilson [1971] LLP Member; Keith Wright [1964] LLP Member

Stephenson Property Services Limited
Incorporated: 14 November 2005 *Employees:* 1
Net Worth: £115,843 *Total Assets:* £3,904,193
Registered Office: The Penthouse, Telegraph House, Calenick Street, Truro, Cornwall, TR1 2SF
Activities: Management of real estate on a fee or contract basis
Major Shareholder: Robert Stephenson Dean
Officers: Rain Amber Brooks [1985] Director/Property Manager; Robert Stephenson Dean [1964] Director

Steppes Travel Ltd
Incorporated: 24 January 1997 *Employees:* 46
Net Worth: £1,073,745 *Total Assets:* £9,861,713
Registered Office: 51 Castle Street, Cirencester, Glos, GL7 1QD
Activities: Tour operator activities
Shareholder: Nicholas Alexander Grant Laing
Officers: Nicholas Alexander Grant Laing, Secretary/Director; Simon Charles Beeching [1958] Director; Richard Donar Dikstra [1955] Managing Director; Sir Richard Drake Kleinwort [1960] Director/Financial PR Consultant; Nicholas Alexander Grant Laing [1952] Director; Andrew John Levens [1949] Director/Accountant; Harriet Rhys Williams [1970] Director; Justin Charles Wateridge [1969] Director

The Stepping Stone Group Limited
Incorporated: 15 April 1998 *Employees:* 89
Net Worth: £2,367,819 *Total Assets:* £10,334,467
Registered Office: The Offices of Perrins Limited, The Custom House, The Strand, Barnstaple, Devon, EX31 1EU
Activities: Development of building projects
Major Shareholder: John Yeates Bailey
Officers: John Yeates Bailey, Secretary/Director; John Yeates Bailey [1957] Director; Alyson Lynne Martin Mbe [1956] Director

Stepping Stones Resettlement Unit Limited
Incorporated: 5 July 1996 *Employees:* 204
Net Worth: £14,079,259 *Total Assets:* £16,359,750
Registered Office: Broadoak, Newnham of Severn, Glos, GL14 1JF
Activities: Other human health activities
Parent: Stones Holdings Limited
Officers: Michelle Jane Evans, Secretary/Accountant; Michelle Jane Evans [1972] Director/Accountant; Nicola McGrail [1948] Director; Dominic Francis Quinlan [1971] Director

Sterling Capital Asset Finance Limited
Incorporated: 23 August 2004 *Employees:* 5
Net Worth: £2,626,357 *Total Assets:* £4,971,508
Registered Office: Hanover House, The Square, Lower Bristol Road, Bath, BA2 3BH
Activities: Credit granting by non-deposit taking finance houses and other specialist consumer credit grantors
Parent: Sterling Capital Holdings Ltd
Officers: Vida Kim Humphreys, Secretary; Fiona Anne Canon [1970] Director/General Manager; Vida Kim Humphreys [1957] Director/Accountant; Wayne Alan Humphreys [1957] Director/Financier

Chris Sterling Enterprises Limited
Incorporated: 24 April 1984 *Employees:* 5
Net Worth: £6,897,483 *Total Assets:* £7,279,618
Registered Office: 5a Hopton Road, Hopton Industrial Estate, Devizes, Wilts, SN10 2EU
Activities: Wholesale of other intermediate products
Major Shareholder: Christopher Douglas Sterling
Officers: Elizabeth Josephine Jane Smith, Secretary; Elizabeth Josephine Jane Smith [1947] Director; Christopher Douglas Sterling [1950] Director

Sterling ISA Managers Limited
Incorporated: 15 June 1989
Net Worth: £88,273,000 *Total Assets:* £114,454,000
Registered Office: The Grange, Bishops Cleeve, Cheltenham, Glos, GL52 8XX
Activities: Financial intermediation not elsewhere classified
Shareholders: Zurich Financial Services (UKISA) Limited; Zurich Financial Services (UKISA) Limited
Officers: Erica Susan Arnold [1972] Director [American]; James Thomas Gaunt Butler [1946] Director; Alasdair Christopher Gillies [1958] Director/Accountant; Helen Alison Pickford [1971] Director; James Richard Sykes [1961] Director

Stevens Family Property Limited
Incorporated: 3 September 2015 *Employees:* 4
Net Worth: £7,639,953 *Total Assets:* £7,833,461
Registered Office: Unit 1 Overton Farm, Maisemore, Gloucester, GL2 8HR
Activities: Other letting and operating of own or leased real estate
Officers: Anne Catherine Edwards [1956] Marketing Strategy Director; David Ian Stevens [1961] Director; James Robert Stevens [1962] Director/Training and Development; Robert Adrian Stevens [1961] Director

Stevens Homes Ltd
Incorporated: 14 January 1986 *Employees:* 8
Net Worth: £1,965,586 *Total Assets:* £4,791,832
Registered Office: 2 Clyst Works, Clyst Road, Topsham, Exeter, Devon, EX3 0DB
Activities: Construction of domestic buildings
Major Shareholder: Michael John Stevens
Officers: Michael John Stevens [1957] Director/Plasterer

M J Stevens Ltd
Incorporated: 25 February 2008 *Employees:* 32
Net Worth: £4,146,235 *Total Assets:* £5,110,482
Registered Office: Redwoods Chartered Certified Accountants, 2 Clyst Works, Clyst Road, Topsham, Devon, EX3 0DB
Activities: Plastering
Parent: Woodcote Holdings Limited
Officers: Louis Peter Greenaway [1991] Managing Director; Nigel Peter Greenaway [1960] Director; Alan Knowles [1967] Director

W. Stevenson & Sons Limited
Incorporated: 22 May 1998 *Employees:* 68
Net Worth: £10,826,692 *Total Assets:* £15,106,957
Registered Office: Harbour Offices, Newlyn, Penzance, Cornwall, TR18 5HB
Activities: Marine fishing
Officers: Peter Richard Frank Dobson Aylott [1965] Director/Chief Executive; Sara Cathryn Bick [1963] Director/Property Management; Marie Claire Petersen [1962] Director/Physiotherapist; Chris Rhodes [1956] Director/Chairman; Lisa Jacqueline Roberts [1964] Director/Property Management; Anthony Bryan Stevenson [1968] Director; Elizabeth Caroline Stevenson [1957] Director

Steward's Company Limited
Incorporated: 15 August 1898 *Employees:* 3
Net Worth: £148,121,984 *Total Assets:* £148,262,208
Registered Office: 124 Wells Road, Bath, BA2 3AH
Activities: Other social work activities without accommodation n.e.c.
Officers: Andrew Bartholomew Griffiths, Secretary; John Aitken [1956] Operations Director; David Crawford Bingham [1955] Director/Retired; Keith Alexander Douglas BInternationaley [1968] Director/Consultant; Dr John Henry Burness [1950] Director/Editor & Treasurer; Ian Stewart Childs [1959] Director/Retired [Irish]; Glyn John Davies [1956] Director/Chartered Accountant; Dr Joshua Michael Fitzhugh [1980] Director/Editor [American]; John Gamble [1951] Director/Retired; Andrew Bartholomew Griffiths [1958] Director/Chartered Accountant; Andrew Ian Mayo [1972] Director/Manager; Alexander Lindsay McIlhinney [1947] Director/Retired; David Norton Roberts [1955] Director/Chartered Accountant; Philip John Symons [1964] Director/Solicitor; Simon James Tomlinson [1967] Director; Paul John Young [1953] Director/Christian Worker

D.Stewart & Son, Limited
Incorporated: 2 February 1916 *Employees:* 274
Net Worth: £11,760,601 *Total Assets:* £18,333,740
Registered Office: Unit 8 Christchurch Business Park, Radar Way, Christchurch, Dorset, BH23 4FL
Activities: Retail sale of flowers, plants, seeds, fertilizers, pet animals and pet food in specialised stores
Major Shareholder: David Martin Stewart
Officers: Derek Burden, Secretary; Derek Burden [1946] Director/Accountant; Terry Michael Head [1976] Director/Retail Management; Amy Alexandra Stewart [1988] Director/Marketing & Design; David Martin Stewart [1958] Director; Sam Edward Stewart [1991] Director/Wildlife Film Maker

Stiga Ltd
Incorporated: 3 October 1972 *Employees:* 46
Previous: GGP UK Limited
Net Worth: £689,405 *Total Assets:* £16,723,703
Registered Office: Unit 8 Bluewater Estate, Bell Close, Plympton, Plymouth, PL7 4JH
Activities: Wholesale of agricultural machinery, equipment and supplies
Officers: John Francis Wisely, Secretary; Roberto Lucernoni [1955] Director [Italian]; Georg Friedrich Metz [1956] Director [German]; Gary Clifford Whitney [1962] Managing Director

Still Materials Handling Limited
Incorporated: 27 November 1979 *Employees:* 213
Net Worth Deficit: £22,122,000 *Total Assets:* £25,936,000
Registered Office: Unit 4 Jacks Way, Hill Barton Business Park, Clyst St Mary, Exeter, EX5 1FG
Activities: Agents involved in the sale of machinery, industrial equipment, ships and aircraft
Parent: Kion Group AG
Officers: Nicolas Roger Smith, Secretary/Accountant; Jean-Paul Dubois [1962] Director [Belgian]; Thomas Alfred Fischer [1959] Director/Chief Sales Officer [German]; Steven Gerrard [1965] UK Sales Director; Thorsten Hofmann [1965] Finance Director [German]; Soenke Klaus Imbeck [1974] Finance Director [German]; Gillian Angela Reed [1976] Service and Operations Director; Nicolas Roger Smith [1972] Director/Accountant

Stilo International PLC
Incorporated: 14 December 1999 *Employees:* 18
Net Worth: £3,738,000 *Total Assets:* £4,255,000
Registered Office: Regus House, Windmill Hill, Business Park, Whitehill Way, Swindon, Wilts, SN5 6QR
Activities: Activities of head offices
Officers: Liam O'Donoghue, Secretary; David William Ashman [1944] Director; Leslie Burnham [1954] Director; Liam O'Donoghue [1982] Director/Solicitor [Irish]

Stitch 2 Limited
Incorporated: 8 April 2010 *Employees:* 2
Net Worth Deficit: £21,081,000 *Total Assets:* £115,008,000
Registered Office: 7 Enterprise Way, Aviation Park, Bournemouth International Airport, Hurn, Christchurch, Dorset, BH23 6HG
Activities: Other retail sale of new goods in specialised stores (not commercial art galleries and opticians)
Parent: Hobbycraft Group Limited
Officers: Dominic Martin Jordan [1966] Operations Director; Katherine Julie Paterson [1971] Marketing Director

Stitch 3 Limited
Incorporated: 8 April 2010
Net Worth: £1,380,000 *Total Assets:* £114,598,000
Registered Office: 7 Enterprise Way, Aviation Park, Bournemouth International Airport, Hurn, Christchurch, Dorset, BH23 6HG
Activities: Other retail sale of new goods in specialised stores (not commercial art galleries and opticians)
Parent: Stitch 2 Limited
Officers: Dominic Martin Jordan [1966] Director

Stitch Bidco Limited
Incorporated: 6 November 2009 *Employees:* 2
Net Worth: £9,532,000 *Total Assets:* £122,750,000
Registered Office: 7 Enterprise Way, Aviation Park, Bournemouth International Airport, Hurn, Christchurch, Dorset, BH23 6HG
Activities: Other retail sale of new goods in specialised stores (not commercial art galleries and opticians)
Parent: Stitch 3 Limited
Officers: Dominic Martin Jordan [1966] Operations Director; Katherine Julie Paterson [1971] Marketing Director

Stochastic Holdings Ltd
Incorporated: 15 April 1996
Previous: Amphora Aromatics Limited
Net Worth: £3,705,012 *Total Assets:* £4,244,556
Registered Office: 2 Chesterfield Buildings, Westbourne Place, Clifton, Bristol, BS8 1RU
Activities: Other letting and operating of own or leased real estate
Shareholders: Peter James Carroll; Christine Anne Carroll
Officers: Peter James Carroll, Secretary/Business Executive; Christine Anne Carroll [1953] Director/Executive; Peter James Carroll [1953] Director/Business Executive

Stockdale Trading Company Limited
Incorporated: 15 May 2014 *Employees:* 2
Net Worth Deficit: £1,161,078 *Total Assets:* £12,110,918
Registered Office: Holcombe House, Painswick, Stroud, Glos, GL6 6RG
Activities: Buying and selling of own real estate
Major Shareholder: John Minshull Stockdale
Officers: John Minshull Stockdale, Secretary; John Minshull Stockdale [1967] Director; Kirsty Frances Stockdale [1973] Director

Stoke Bishop Church of England Primary School
Incorporated: 27 February 2013 *Employees:* 54
Net Worth: £2,860,033 *Total Assets:* £3,660,525
Registered Office: Stoke Bishop Church of England Primary School, Cedar Park, Stoke Bishop, Bristol, BS9 1BW
Activities: Primary education
Officers: Patricia Jean Arnold [1944] Director/Retired; Daniel Bond [1976] Director/Accountant; Kathleen Mary Conway [1968] Director/Teacher; Anna Clare Creedon [1990] Director/Ordinand; Bridget Helen Davies [1969] Director/Consultant; David Gerard Forrester [1964] Director/Headteacher; Reverend Mathew David Ineson [1969] Director/Vicar; Alexander Richard Courthope Kealy [1980] Director/Teacher; James MacKenzie Pirie [1976] Director/Business Process Outsourcing; Rachel Mary Powlesland [1970] Director/Childrens & Family Worker; Andrew William Lloyd Quinton [1978] Director/Primary School Teacher; Helena Ann Richards [1972] Director/Teacher; Beverly Margaret Richardson [1948] Director/Teacher; Helen Sian Rowe [1977] Director/Chartered Accountant; Paul William Wake [1970] Director/Regional Manager, Recycling; Heather Whittard-Jones [1979] Director/Teacher; Barbara Ann Woolwright [1954] Director/Special Needs Teaching Assistant

Will Stone Historic Cars Ltd
Incorporated: 3 December 2013 *Employees:* 2
Net Worth: £88,813 *Total Assets:* £4,786,014
Registered Office: Windsor House, The Square, Ramsbury, Marlborough, Wilts, SN8 2PE
Activities: Other service activities n.e.c.
Shareholders: William David Gilchrist Stone; Helen Kay Stone
Officers: Helen Kay Stone, Secretary; Helen Kay Stone [1976] Director; William David Gilchrist Stone [1971] Director

Stone King LLP
Incorporated: 20 September 2005 *Employees:* 208
Net Worth: £3,348,684 *Total Assets:* £8,732,702
Registered Office: 13 Queen Square, Bath, BA1 2HJ
Officers: Alison Jane Allen [1966] Member; Andrew Julian Blake [1964] Member; Jonathan Robert Burchfield [1954] Member; Graham Burns [1964] Member; Steven Richard Greenwood [1965] Member; Thomas William Morrison [1977] Member; Andrew John Mortimer [1962] Member; Hugh David Mortlock Pearce [1965] Member; Ann Nicola Phillips [1954] Member; Stephen Howard Ravenscroft [1971] Member; Timothy Rutherford [1973] Member; Nicholas Simon Joss Watson [1957] Member; Peter Mark Woodhouse [1967] Member; Andrew John Banks [1968] LLP Member; Jean Rachel Boyle [1979] LLP Member; Lee Coley [1974] LLP Member; Henrietta Tamsin Eastwood [1960] LLP Member; Hugo William Greer-Walker [1971] LLP Member; Daniel Peter Harris [1963] LLP Member; Charles Hayward [1953] LLP Member; Stephanie Margaret Howarth [1958] LLP Member; Sarah Elizabeth Lane [1973] LLP Member; Robert Grant Meakin [1963] LLP Member; Thomas Duncan Murdoch [1970] LLP Member; Miguel Angel Pereira [1974] LLP Member; Roderick Graham Smith [1971] LLP Member; Paul Sutton [1959] LLP Member; Caroline Maria Taylor [1960] LLP Member

Stone Supplies (Bristol) Limited
Incorporated: 10 April 2007 *Employees:* 15
Net Worth: £2,065,724 *Total Assets:* £4,774,515
Registered Office: Lulsgate Quarry, Felton, Bristol, BS40 9UP
Activities: Agents involved in the sale of timber and building materials
Major Shareholder: Jonathan Baskerville Clayton
Officers: Melanie Kate Clayton, Secretary; Jonathan Baskerville Clayton [1968] Director

Stonebridge Associated Colleges Limited
Incorporated: 26 January 2000
Net Worth: £1,977,338 *Total Assets:* £6,543,534
Registered Office: 42 Ocean View Road, Bude, Cornwall, EX23 8NN
Activities: Technical and vocational secondary education
Officers: Susan Mary Janse Van Rensburg, Secretary; Pienaar Jacobus Janse Van Rensburg [1957] Director/Marketing Manager; Susan Mary Janse Van Rensburg [1958] Director/College Registrar; Wayne Janse Van Rensburg [1981] Director; Kate Van Rensburg [1983] Director/Administrator

Stonebridge Colleges (Publishing) Limited
Incorporated: 23 December 2008
Net Worth: £7,427,773 *Total Assets:* £13,642,611
Registered Office: 42 Ocean View Road, Bude, Cornwall, EX23 8ST
Activities: Other publishing activities
Major Shareholder: Wayne Van Rensburg
Officers: Susan Mary Janse Van Rensburg, Secretary; Pienaar Jacobus Janse Van Rensburg [1957] Director; Susan Mary Janse Van Rensburg [1958] Director & Company Secretary; Wayne Janse Van Rensburg [1981] Director

Stonegate Agriculture Limited
Incorporated: 28 September 1992 *Employees:* 77
Previous: Thames Valley Foods Limited
Net Worth: £7,496,899 *Total Assets:* £10,429,829
Registered Office: Whiteoaks Farm, The Old Sidings, Corsham Road, Lacock, Wilts, SN15 2LZ
Activities: Manufacture of other food products n.e.c.
Parent: Stonegate Farmers Ltd
Officers: James David Sheppard, Secretary; Adrian David Gott [1981] Director; James David Sheppard [1963] Director

Stonegate Farmers Limited
Incorporated: 12 November 1962 *Employees:* 200
Net Worth: £21,522,980 *Total Assets:* £50,538,312
Registered Office: Whiteoaks Farm, The Old Sidings, Corsham Road, Lacock, Wilts, SN15 2LZ
Activities: Raising of poultry
Parent: Stonegate Holdings Limited
Officers: James David Sheppard, Secretary; Adrian David Gott [1981] Director; James David Sheppard [1963] Director

Stonegate Group Limited
Incorporated: 16 April 2015
Net Worth: £4,073,705 *Total Assets:* £11,913,472
Registered Office: Whiteoaks Farm, The Old Sidings, Corsham Road, Lacock, Chippenham, Wilts, SN15 2LZ
Activities: Raising of poultry
Parent: Gott Agri Synergy Ltd
Officers: Adrian David Gott [1981] Director; James David Sheppard [1963] Director

Stonegate Holdings Limited
Incorporated: 6 March 2008 *Employees:* 2
Net Worth: £5,085,151 *Total Assets:* £41,268,112
Registered Office: Whiteoaks Farm, The Old Sidings, Corsham Road, Lacock, Wilts, SN15 2LZ
Activities: Raising of poultry
Parent: Stonegate Group Limited
Officers: Adrian David Gott [1981] Director; James David Sheppard [1963] Director

Stonehaven (Healthcare) Ltd
Incorporated: 15 October 1998 *Employees:* 288
Net Worth: £7,810,954 *Total Assets:* £19,372,572
Registered Office: C4 Linhay Business Park, Eastern Road, Ashburton, Newton Abbot, Devon, TQ13 7UP
Activities: Residential care activities for the elderly and disabled
Shareholders: Stephen Ray Stone; Dawn Sandra Stone
Officers: Stephen Ray Stone, Secretary/Manager; Dawn Sandra Stone [1949] Director/Manager; Nathaniel Stephen Stone [1974] Director/Manager; Ralphe Hickerton George Stone [1976] Director/Manager; Stephen Ray Stone [1949] Director/Manager

Stonehouse Investment Company Limited
Incorporated: 26 June 2007 *Employees:* 1
Net Worth: £5,785,705 *Total Assets:* £5,806,670
Registered Office: Portwall Place, Portwall Lane, Bristol, BS1 6NA
Activities: Other business support service activities n.e.c.
Officers: Helen Chambers, Secretary; William Brett Warburton [1955] Director

Stonewood Properties Limited
Incorporated: 16 January 2009 *Employees:* 104
Net Worth: £2,801,694 *Total Assets:* £7,138,545
Registered Office: The Stonewood Office, West Yatton Lane, Castle Combe, Chippenham, Wilts, SN14 7EY
Activities: Buying and selling of own real estate
Shareholders: Matt Aitkenhead; Benjamin MacKay Lang
Officers: Benjamin MacKay Lang, Secretary; Matthew Aitkenhead [1967] Director; Benjamin MacKay Lang [1974] Director

Storm Land Securities Ltd
Incorporated: 17 December 2009 *Employees:* 6
Net Worth: £4,326,059 *Total Assets:* £9,624,300
Registered Office: The New Works, Roughmoor Industrial Estate, Williton, Somerset, TA4 4RF
Activities: Other letting and operating of own or leased real estate
Parent: RTB Private Equity Ltd
Officers: Mark Dorrill, Secretary; Mark Dorrill [1967] Director/Accountant; Ann Mary Wells [1986] Director; Stephen Christopher Wells [1967] Director

Stormfront Retail Limited
Incorporated: 14 September 2006 *Employees:* 316
Net Worth: £1,037,966 *Total Assets:* £9,852,376
Registered Office: Unit 1b Newton Centre, Thorverton Road, Matford Business Park, Marsh Barton Trading Estate, Exeter, Devon, EX2 8GN
Activities: Retail sale of computers, peripheral units and software in specialised stores
Parent: Professional Reseller Group
Officers: Catherine Chapman, Secretary; James Stuart Collard-Jenkins [1972] Director; Daniel Evans [1975] Finance Director; Michael David Fleming [1971] Director/IT Consultant; Thomas William Slack [1965] Director/Accountant

Stotts Group Limited
Incorporated: 13 July 2016 *Employees:* 108
Net Worth: £1,093,147 *Total Assets:* £9,013,726
Registered Office: Willmotts Business Park, Waterlip, Shepton Mallet, Somerset, BA4 4RN
Activities: Activities of other holding companies n.e.c.
Major Shareholder: Andrew Mark Stott
Officers: Maria Stott, Secretary; Andrew Mark Stott [1968] Director/Chairman

Stovax Heating Group Limited
Incorporated: 20 November 2012 *Employees:* 322
Net Worth: £33,324,618 *Total Assets:* £38,804,520
Registered Office: Falcon Road, Sowton Industrial Estate, Exeter, Devon, EX2 7LF
Activities: Activities of head offices
Parent: Nibe Industrier AB
Officers: Andrew David Walker, Secretary; Sven Henrik Otto Axelsson [1979] Director [Swedish]; Alistair Compton [1969] Director [Zimbabwean]; Robert James Crabb [1961] Director; Bengt Olof Niklas Gunnarsson [1965] Director [Swedish]; Andrew David Walker [1962] Director

Stovax Limited
Incorporated: 6 July 1981 *Employees:* 153
Net Worth: £20,586,470 *Total Assets:* £22,819,050
Registered Office: Falcon Road, Sowton Industrial Estate, Exeter, Devon, EX2 7LF
Activities: Manufacture of other fabricated metal products n.e.c.
Parent: Stovax Group Limited
Officers: Andrew David Walker, Secretary; Alistair Compton [1969] Director [Zimbabwean]; Robert James Crabb [1961] Director; Edward Gerard Charles Henry [1972] Director; Michael Oram [1969] Director; Andrew David Walker [1962] Director/Chartered Accountant

Stowell Concrete Limited
Incorporated: 27 June 1972 *Employees:* 67
Net Worth: £29,339,898 *Total Assets:* £33,541,438
Registered Office: Arnolds Way, Yatton, Somerset, BS49 4QN
Activities: Manufacture of concrete products for construction purposes
Major Shareholder: Margaret Ann Stowell
Officers: Margaret Ann Stowell, Secretary; Margaret Ann Stowell [1944] Director/Secretary; Vincent John Stowell [1965] Director/Concrete Block Manufacturer

Stowell Park Estate Limited
Incorporated: 16 January 1987 *Employees:* 24
Net Worth: £3,046,615 *Total Assets:* £4,441,665
Registered Office: The Estate Office, Yanworth, Cheltenham, Glos, GL54 3LQ
Activities: Growing of cereals (except rice), leguminous crops and oil seeds
Officers: Alexander Rowland Norton George, Secretary; Alexander Rowland Norton George [1967] Director/Resident Agent; Baroness Celia Elizabeth Vestey [1949] Director/State Registered Nurse; Lord Samuel George Armstrong Vestey [1941] Director/Merchant; The Honourable William Guy Vestey [1983] Director/Sales Representative; Rebecca Rachel Alison Williams [1972] Director/Lawyer

Stowford Mill Development Limited
Incorporated: 18 March 2014
Net Worth Deficit: £156,555 *Total Assets:* £6,792,038
Registered Office: Dean Clarke House, Southernhay East, Exeter, EX1 1AP
Activities: Construction of commercial buildings
Shareholders: Peter Ross Vans Agnew; Hamish Michael Vans Agnew
Officers: Mark David Edworthy [1969] Director; Paul Neil Scantlebury [1967] Director/Property Developer

Strata Service Solutions Ltd.
Incorporated: 15 May 2014 *Employees:* 74
Net Worth Deficit: £5,319,140 *Total Assets:* £5,399,868
Registered Office: Civic Centre, Paris Street, Exeter, Devon, EX1 1JN
Activities: Computer facilities management activities
Shareholders: Exeter City Council; East Devon District Council; Teignbridge District Council
Officers: Simon Peter Icombe Davey [1967] Director/Head of Finance, East Devon District Council; Roy David Hodgson [1971] Assistant Director Finance; Paul Nicholls [1972] Director/Local Government Officer

Streamclare Limited
Incorporated: 25 March 1963 *Employees:* 2
Previous: Streamclare PLC
Net Worth: £2,671,135 *Total Assets:* £4,366,626
Registered Office: Peat House, Newham Road, Truro, Cornwall, TR1 2DP
Activities: Buying and selling of own real estate
Officers: David Charles Hughes [1963] Director

Stride Treglown Group PLC
Incorporated: 12 November 1997 *Employees:* 319
Net Worth: £5,461,246 *Total Assets:* £9,482,861
Registered Office: Promenade House, The Promenade, Clifton Down, Bristol, BS8 3NE
Activities: Architectural activities
Officers: Darren Paul Wilkins, Secretary; Penelope Suzanne Burgess [1965] Director/Chartered Accountant; Dominic Jerome Eaton [1959] Director; David James Hunter [1963] Director; Caroline Rose May Mayes [1977] Director/Architect; Gary Victor Milliner [1963] Director; Robert James Sargent [1971] Director; David Anthony Steele [1959] Director; Graham Kennedy Stephens [1971] Director; Matthew Robert Tarling [1974] Director; Gordon Donald Arthur Tero [1967] Director; Pierre Antony Wassenaar [1969] Director/Architect; Darren Paul Wilkins [1972] Director; Alastair John Wilson [1966] Director; John Alec Wright [1966] Director

Stride Treglown Limited
Incorporated: 30 August 1983 *Employees:* 319
Net Worth: £4,600,668 *Total Assets:* £9,686,111
Registered Office: Promenade House, The Promenade, Clifton Down, Bristol, BS8 3NE
Activities: Architectural activities
Parent: Stride Treglown Group PLC
Officers: Darren Paul Wilkins, Secretary; Penelope Suzanne Burgess [1965] Director/Chartered Accountant; Dominic Jerome Eaton [1959] Director; David James Hunter [1963] Director; Caroline Rose May Mayes [1977] Director/Architect; Gary Victor Milliner [1963] Director; Robert James Sargent [1971] Director; David Anthony Steele [1959] Director; Graham Kennedy Stephens [1971] Director/Town Planner; Matthew Robert Tarling [1974] Director; Gordon Donald Arthur Tero [1967] Director; Pierre Antony Wassenaar [1969] Director/Architect; Darren Paul Wilkins [1972] Director; Alastair John Wilson [1966] Director; John Alec Wright [1966] Director

Strong Energy Solutions Limited
Incorporated: 31 October 2009 *Employees:* 4
Net Worth: £6,681,726 *Total Assets:* £7,210,598
Registered Office: Energy House, Milbury Heath Road, Buckover, Glos, GL12 8QH
Activities: Other professional, scientific and technical activities n.e.c.
Major Shareholder: Kathryn Louise Murtagh
Officers: Tim McLeman [1964] Technical Director; Fergal Murtagh [1974] Managing Director [Irish]; Jeffrey Tomlinson [1965] Director

Strongvox Limited
Incorporated: 21 July 2003 *Employees:* 55
Net Worth: £8,818,337 *Total Assets:* £45,997,916
Registered Office: York House, Blackbrook Park Avenue, Blackbrook Business Park, Taunton, Somerset, TA1 2PX
Activities: Construction of domestic buildings
Shareholders: Barry Peter Amos-Yeo; Kevin Richard Amos-Yeo
Officers: Robert Topazio, Secretary/Director; Robert Alford [1949] Director; Barry Peter Amos Yeo [1980] Director; Kevin Amos Yeo [1982] Director; Toby James Thomas Ballard [1972] Managing Director; Robert Topazio [1963] Director; Wendy Jane Trott [1966] Director

Stroud High School
Incorporated: 3 June 2011 *Employees:* 107
Net Worth: £12,961,291 *Total Assets:* £14,512,885
Registered Office: Beards Lane, Cainscross Road, Stroud, Glos, GL5 4HF
Activities: General secondary education
Officers: Pauline Marian Blacklock, Secretary; Christopher Harry Chatterton [1974] Director; Phillip Anthony John Cowley [1960] Director/Stroud High School Employee; Andrew John Cutbill [1963] Director/Banking; Dylan Harold Davies [1955] Director/Engineering Consultant; Phillip Robert Duncan [1962] Director/Surveyor; Michael Arthur Ford [1971] Director/Management Consultant; Margaret Susan Freck [1937] Director/Retired Teacher; Sally Haigh [1964] Director/Teacher; Richard Harwanko [1964] Director/Engineering Manager; Geoffrey James Marshall [1955] Director; Louise McGinty [1968] Director/Education Consultant; Mark Ian McShane [1974] Director/Stroud High School Headteacher; Jonathan Nigel Morley [1975] Director/Solicitor; Jacqueline Mary Paula Phillips [1953] Director/Homemaker; Christopher Herbert Ryland [1948] Director; Richard Wade [1964] Director/Head of Human Resources; Keith Morris Withers [1960] Director/Farmer

Stroud Metal Company Limited
Incorporated: 30 September 1926 *Employees:* 47
Net Worth: £5,208,000 *Total Assets:* £6,358,427
Registered Office: Dudbridge, Stroud, Glos, GL5 3EZ
Activities: Forging, pressing, stamping and roll-forming of metal; powder metallurgy
Parent: Dudbridge Estates Ltd
Officers: Catherine Mary Large [1969] Director; Matthew William Large [1965] Director/Accounts Executive

Stroud Valleys Canal Company
Incorporated: 26 March 2009
Net Worth: £1,608,306 *Total Assets:* £9,335,688
Registered Office: Brimscombe Mill, Brimscombe Port, Stroud, Glos, GL5 2QG
Activities: Other letting and operating of own or leased real estate
Officers: Sheila Harris, Secretary; Peter John Best [1954] Director/Retired; Kenneth Neville Burgin [1956] Director/Chief Executive of Cotswold CA; Geoffrey Frank Dyer [1948] Director/Chartered Civil Engineer; Dr David John Fletcher [1942] Director/Retired; Reginald John Gregory [1948] Director/Retired; David John Groom [1940] Director/Retired; Neville Charles Nelder [1939] Director/Retired; John Martin James Twydell [1949] Director/Retired

Stroudwater Redevelopment Partnership Limited
Incorporated: 22 February 1999
Net Worth: £2,688,157 *Total Assets:* £5,378,287
Registered Office: Royal Mews, St Georges Place, Cheltenham, Glos, GL50 3PQ
Activities: Buying and selling of own real estate
Major Shareholder: Roland John Tanner
Officers: Averil Lillian Tanner, Secretary; Roland John Tanner [1954] Director

Structural Metal Decks Limited
Incorporated: 8 May 1998 *Employees:* 107
Net Worth: £4,779,026 *Total Assets:* £9,566,044
Registered Office: The Outlook, Ling Road, Tower Park, Bournemouth, BH12 4PY
Activities: Other construction installation
Parent: SMD 2013 Limited
Officers: Benedict Pratten, Secretary; Roger Tennant Firth [1943] Director/Steel Merchant; Benedict Pratten [1973] Sales & Marketing Director; Jamie Francis Turner [1976] Technical Director; Daniel Stephen Williams [1972] Construction Director

Strukta Group Limited
Incorporated: 10 January 2013 *Employees:* 99
Net Worth: £1,950,214 *Total Assets:* £8,988,188
Registered Office: 36 Walworth Road, Andover, Hants, SP10 5LH
Activities: Wholesale of wood, construction materials and sanitary equipment
Officers: Adrian Diffey [1976] Director/Builders Merchant; Benjamin Diffey [1973] Director/Builders Merchant; Kevin Diffey [1981] Director/Builders Merchant; Mark Diffey [1971] Director/Builders Merchant; Stephen Maurice Diffey [1947] Director/Builders Merchant; David John Moggach [1949] Director/Builders Merchant; Lauren James Moggach [1984] Director/Builders Merchant; Murray Moggach [1974] Director/Builders Merchant; Myles Stuart Moggach [1986] Director/Builders Merchant; Piers Moggach [1973] Director/Builders Merchant

A E Stuart Limited
Incorporated: 3 March 2014 *Employees:* 190
Net Worth: £40,798,788 *Total Assets:* £73,033,992
Registered Office: Hill Barton Business Park, Sidmouth Road, Clyst St Mary, Exeter, Devon, EX5 1DR
Activities: Activities of agricultural holding companies
Shareholders: Troy Stuart; Ross Stuart; Roy Anthony Raymond Stuart
Officers: Ross Stuart [1947] Director; Roy Anthony Raymond Stuart [1944] Director; Troy Stuart [1969] Director

Stuart Partners Limited
Incorporated: 8 February 2012 *Employees:* 25
Net Worth: £40,230,764 *Total Assets:* £58,860,084
Registered Office: Hill Barton Business Park, Sidmouth Road, Clyst St Mary, Exeter, EX5 1DR
Activities: Mixed farming
Parent: A E Stuart Limited
Officers: Ross Stuart [1947] Director; Roy Anthony Raymond Stuart [1944] Director; Troy Stuart [1969] Director

Stuart Property (Holdings) Limited
Incorporated: 7 March 2014 *Employees:* 2
Net Worth: £3,512,589 *Total Assets:* £10,080,627
Registered Office: Hill Barton Business Park, Sidmouth Road, Clyst St Mary, Exeter, Devon, EX5 1DR
Activities: Activities of other holding companies n.e.c.
Shareholders: Ryan Stuart; Troy Stuart
Officers: Ryan Stuart [1987] Director; Troy Stuart [1969] Director

Stuarts Truck and Bus Limited
Incorporated: 4 March 2014 *Employees:* 82
Net Worth: £3,324,363 *Total Assets:* £10,509,390
Registered Office: Hill Barton Business Park, Sidmouth Road, Clyst St Mary, Exeter, Devon, EX5 1DR
Activities: Sale of other motor vehicles
Parent: A E Stuart Limited
Officers: Ross Stuart [1947] Director; Roy Anthony Raymond Stuart [1944] Director; Troy Stuart [1969] Director

Student Rooms 4 Plymouth Ltd
Incorporated: 1 May 2012
Net Worth: £1,486,987 *Total Assets:* £4,064,429
Registered Office: 104 Mannamead Road, Mannamead, Plymouth, PL3 5QH
Activities: Other letting and operating of own or leased real estate
Officers: David Edward Hendy [1964] Director/Property Developer

Studyhome 1992 Limited
Incorporated: 10 March 1989 *Employees:* 4
Net Worth: £22,163,712 *Total Assets:* £29,486,252
Registered Office: Bishopbrook House, Cathedral Avenue, Wells, Somerset, BA5 1FD
Activities: Other letting and operating of own or leased real estate
Officers: Roy Courteney William Barber [1946] Director/Chartered Surveyor; John Haydon Jackson [1943] Director/Chartered Accountant; Peter John Daughton Laws [1952] Director/Chartered Accountant

Sturtons Group Limited
Incorporated: 6 May 2010 *Employees:* 2
Net Worth: £3,918,914 *Total Assets:* £3,987,388
Registered Office: 426-436 Wimborne Road, Winton, Bournemouth, BH9 2EZ
Activities: Retail of furniture, lighting, and similar (not musical instruments or scores) in specialised store
Shareholders: David Francis Scott; Pauline Scott
Officers: David Francis Scott [1946] Director; Pauline Scott [1947] Director

Sturts Community Trust
Incorporated: 14 January 2013 *Employees:* 53
Net Worth: £4,733,764 *Total Assets:* £5,556,076
Registered Office: Sturts Farm, Three Cross Road, West Moors, Dorset, BH22 0NF
Activities: Other service activities n.e.c.
Officers: David Harvey Taylor, Secretary; Timothy David Cook [1953] Director/Chartered Surveyor; Michael Crutchley [1978] Director/Head of Healthcare; Caroline Rosemary Darby-Jenkins [1964] Director/HR Consultant; Morag Margaret Doyle [1948] Director/Retired; Gabrielle Mary Gray [1941] Director/Retired Teacher; Katherine Mary Jones [1947] Director/Retired; David Harvey Taylor [1978] Director/Company Secretary

STVA UK Limited
Incorporated: 11 December 1973 *Employees:* 30
Net Worth: £4,418,000 *Total Assets:* £14,632,000
Registered Office: St Andrews House, St Andrews Road, Avonmouth, Bristol, BS11 9DQ
Activities: Maintenance and repair of motor vehicles
Parent: STVA SA
Officers: Ian Brown, Secretary; Peter Borrmann [1965] Director [German]; Ian Brown [1954] Director; Jean-Michel Floret [1968] Director [French]; Pascal Louvigny [1962] Director [French]; Peter Giovanni Tapparo [1971] Director

Styles & Brown Ltd
Incorporated: 10 February 1998 *Employees:* 292
Net Worth: £5,113,131 *Total Assets:* £18,634,048
Registered Office: Unit 10 Weycroft Avenue, Millwey Rise Industrial Estate, Axminster, Devon, EX13 5PH
Activities: Other retail sale in non-specialised stores
Officers: Alan Victor Styles [1976] Director; Bernard George Styles [1949] Director; Ian Victor Styles [1957] Director; Katina Jean Styles [1958] Director

Succession Newco1 Limited
Incorporated: 26 May 2016
Net Worth: £11,947,000 *Total Assets:* £11,964,000
Registered Office: The Drake Building, 15 Davy Road, Plymouth Science Park, Derriford, Plymouth, PL6 8BY
Activities: Activities of financial services holding companies
Parent: Succession Finance Limited
Officers: Michael John Hill [1966] Director/Chartered Accountant; Paul Stephen Morrish [1965] Director/Management Consultant

Suland Investments Limited
Incorporated: 18 August 1964 *Employees:* 3
Net Worth: £4,298,786 *Total Assets:* £6,222,252
Registered Office: 87 Whiteladies Road, Clifton, Bristol, BS8 2NT
Activities: Other business support service activities n.e.c.
Major Shareholder: Michael Amos Gillingham
Officers: Kim Deborah Parsons, Secretary; Alan Ford Gilbertson [1946] Director/Property Management; Michael Amos Gillingham [1938] Director/Property Manager

Sumac Precision Engineering Limited
Incorporated: 18 September 1995 *Employees:* 115
Net Worth: £3,993,524 *Total Assets:* £6,978,567
Registered Office: Mary Street House, Mary Street, Taunton, Somerset, TA1 3NW
Activities: Other engineering activities
Officers: Denise Clothier, Secretary; Denise Clothier [1967] Director; John Andrew Marsh [1949] Director/Engineer; Michael Andrew Robson [1961] Director/Engineer; John Alastair Stevenson [1939] Director/Engineer

Summerfield Developments (SW) Limited
Incorporated: 17 September 1990 *Employees:* 54
Net Worth: £19,197,140 *Total Assets:* £29,537,468
Registered Office: Tauntfield South Road, Taunton, Somerset, TA1 3ND
Activities: Development of building projects
Officers: Robert Alestair Smith, Secretary; Mark Charles Blackwell [1964] Director/Accountant; James Edward Holyday [1968] Director; Richard David Ayshford Lloyd [1953] Director; Richard Mead [1974] Director; Benjamin James Trickey [1974] Director

Summerfield Estates Ltd
Incorporated: 14 December 1993
Net Worth: £9,953,082 *Total Assets:* £21,848,428
Registered Office: Tauntfield, South Road, Taunton, Somerset, TA1 3ND
Activities: Development of building projects
Parent: Tauntfield Ltd
Officers: Mark Charles Blackwell, Secretary; Mark Charles Blackwell [1964] Director/Chartered Accountant; Michael Blackwell [1937] Director; Michael James Foden [1935] Director; James Edward Holyday [1968] Director/Management Surveyor; Richard David Ayshford Lloyd [1953] Director/Chairman and Chief Executive; Dr Robert Stansell Roslin Williams [1969] Director/Conservation Biologist

Summerfield SD3 Limited
Incorporated: 11 October 2006 *Employees:* 13
Net Worth: £3,095,831 *Total Assets:* £6,209,780
Registered Office: Tauntfield, South Road, Taunton, Somerset, TA1 3ND
Activities: Development of building projects
Officers: Robert Alestair Smith, Secretary; Mark Charles Blackwell [1964] Director; James Edward Holyday [1968] Director; Phillip Andrew Lloyd [1959] Director; Richard David Ayshford Lloyd [1953] Director; Richard Mead [1974] Director

Summit Medical Limited
Incorporated: 3 April 2001 *Employees:* 98
Net Worth: £18,952,712 *Total Assets:* £34,280,104
Registered Office: Bourton on the Water Industrial Park, Bourton on The Water, Cheltenham, Glos, GL54 2HQ
Activities: Manufacture of medical and dental instruments and supplies
Officers: Alastair John McKay, Secretary; Daniel John Bee [1967] Director; Alec John Simpson [1969] Director

Sundeala Limited
Incorporated: 5 October 2001 *Employees:* 88
Net Worth: £5,026,686 *Total Assets:* £6,432,961
Registered Office: Middle Mill, Cam, Dursley, Glos, GL11 5LQ
Activities: Manufacture of paper and paperboard
Major Shareholder: Peter Charles Percival Hambro
Officers: Michael Braithwaite [1971] Supply Chain Director; Michael James Gorham [1971] Director; Leo Percival Hambro [1977] Director; Peter Charles Percival Hambro [1945] Director/Merchant Financier; Joanne Mulloy [1970] Sales Director; Wayne Price [1965] Production Director; James Wiggins [1979] Finance Director

Sunderland CLC School Services Limited
Incorporated: 5 February 2001
Net Worth: £723,000 *Total Assets:* £11,937,000
Registered Office: Third Floor, Broad Quay House, Prince Street, Bristol, BS1 4DJ
Activities: Management of real estate on a fee or contract basis
Parent: Sunderland CLC Schools Investment Company Limited
Officers: Kenneth Andrew McLellan [1961] Regional Project Director; Daniel North [1981] Investment Director; Alan Campbell Ritchie [1967] Director

Sunnybanks Homes (SW) Limited
Incorporated: 12 January 2004
Net Worth: £464,516 *Total Assets:* £4,904,098
Registered Office: 7 Sandy Court, Ashleigh Way, Langage Business Park, Plymouth, PL7 5JX
Activities: Development of building projects
Shareholders: Matthew Michael Walsh; Andrew David Walsh; Stuart Alan Walsh
Officers: Stuart Alan Walsh, Secretary/Director; Andrew David Walsh [1963] Director; Stuart Alan Walsh [1965] Director

Sunpower Meadow LLP
Incorporated: 2 June 2011
Net Worth: £12,000,000 *Total Assets:* £12,000,000
Registered Office: Hendra Holiday Park, Hendra, Newquay, Cornwall, TR8 4NY
Officers: William Mark Dexter [1970] Member; Janine Hyatt [1955] Member; Robert Kevin Hyatt [1955] Member; Rebecca Jane May [1963] Member; Robert May [1967] Member

Sunpower Solar Limited
Incorporated: 25 March 2014
Net Worth: £8,879,235 *Total Assets:* £12,850,814
Registered Office: Hendra Holiday Park, Lane, Newquay, Cornwall, TR8 4NY
Activities: Production of electricity
Parent: Helios Cornwall Limited
Officers: Robert May, Secretary; William Mark Dexter [1970] Director; Janine Hyatt [1955] Director; Jonathan Donald Hyatt [1984] Director; Robert Kevin Hyatt [1955] Director [Canadian]; Rebecca Jane May [1967] Director; Robert May [1963] Director

Sunseeker International (Holdings) Limited
Incorporated: 23 August 2006 *Employees:* 2,311
Net Worth Deficit: £73,453,000 *Total Assets:* £159,775,008
Registered Office: Sunseeker House, West Quay Road, Poole, Dorset, BH15 1JD
Activities: Activities of head offices
Major Shareholder: Wang Jianlin
Officers: Adrian James Powell, Secretary; Benxi Ding [1955] Executive Director [Chinese]; Christian Marti [1966] Director/Chief Executive Officer [German]; Dazhi Wang [1977] Director [Chinese]; Michael Wheeler [1951] Director; Lin Zhang [1972] Director [Chinese]

Sunseeker International Limited
Incorporated: 17 November 1960 *Employees:* 2,318
Net Worth Deficit: £63,466,000 *Total Assets:* £187,120,000
Registered Office: Sunseeker House, West Quay Road, Poole, Dorset, BH15 1JD
Activities: Building of ships and floating structures
Parent: Sunseeker International (Holdings) Limited
Officers: Adrian James Powell, Secretary; Benxi Ding [1955] Executive Director [Chinese]; Christian Marti [1966] Director/Chief Executive Officer [German]; Michael Hugh McMillan [1966] Director/Chief Financial Officer; Sean Robertson [1970] Sales Director; Michael Keith Straughan [1961] Director/Chief Operating Officer; Dazhi Wang [1977] Director [Chinese]; Lin Zhang [1972] Director [Chinese]

Supacat Limited
Incorporated: 26 August 1980 *Employees:* 142
Net Worth: £12,179,730 *Total Assets:* £22,499,018
Registered Office: The Airfield, Dunkeswell, Honiton, Devon, EX14 4LF
Activities: Manufacture of military fighting vehicles
Parent: SC Group-Global Limited
Officers: Alan Shaun Mitchell, Secretary; Roger Simon Nicholas Ames [1966] Director; Stephen James Austen [1971] Engineering Director; Elizabeth Mary Jones [1977] Director; Nicholas Laurence Jones [1942] Director/Engineer; Alan Shaun Mitchell [1966] Director; John Jefferys Treasure [1947] Director

Supara Limited
Incorporated: 28 May 1996
Net Worth: £18,070,446 *Total Assets:* £24,697,156
Registered Office: 17 Imperial Square, Cheltenham, Glos, GL50 1QZ
Activities: Other letting and operating of own or leased real estate
Parent: Satnam Investments Ltd
Officers: John Frederick Staite, Secretary; Kuldip Singh Dhillon [1950] Director; Satnam Singh Dhillon [1977] Director; Colin Griffiths [1963] Director/Chartered Town Planner; John Frederick Staite [1948] Director/Accountant

Super Dooper Stores Limited
Incorporated: 9 August 2004
Net Worth: £802,000 *Total Assets:* £4,043,000
Registered Office: Tamar House, Thornbury Road, Estover, Plymouth, PL6 7PT
Activities: Other retail sale in non-specialised stores
Parent: Norton Group Holdings Limited
Officers: Christopher Frederick Dawson [1951] Director

Superdry PLC
Incorporated: 2 November 2009 *Employees:* 3,266
Previous: Supergroup PLC
Net Worth: £408,500,000 *Total Assets:* £614,400,000
Registered Office: Unit 60 The Runnings, Cheltenham, Glos, GL51 9NW
Activities: Wholesale of clothing and footwear
Officers: Simon Callander, Secretary; Peter Richard Bamford [1954] Director; Edward Peter Barker [1972] Director; Penelope Lesley Hughes [1959] Director; Dennis Henry Millard [1949] Director; Timothy Martin Powell [1954] Director; John Barry Smith [1957] Director; Euan Angus Sutherland [1969] Director; Sarah Florence Wood [1973] Director

Supergroup Concessions Limited
Incorporated: 28 January 2010 *Employees:* 15
Net Worth: £6,173,000 *Total Assets:* £7,589,000
Registered Office: Unit 60 The Runnings, Cheltenham, Glos, GL51 9NW
Activities: Wholesale of clothing and footwear
Parent: Superdry PLC
Officers: Edward Peter Barker [1972] Director; Simon Callander [1967] Director/Group General Counsel and Company Secretary; Euan Angus Sutherland [1969] Director

Supergroup Internet Limited
Incorporated: 28 January 2010 *Employees:* 105
Net Worth: £18,869,000 *Total Assets:* £206,200,000
Registered Office: Unit 60 The Runnings, Cheltenham, Glos, GL51 9NW
Activities: Other retail sale not in stores, stalls or markets
Parent: Superdry PLC
Officers: Edward Peter Barker [1972] Director; Simon Callander [1967] Director/Group General Counsel and Company Secretary; Euan Angus Sutherland [1969] Director

Superior Group Limited
Incorporated: 18 April 2005 *Employees:* 202
Net Worth: £59,376,352 *Total Assets:* £70,638,920
Registered Office: Nimrod Way, Ferndown Industrial Estate, Wimborne, Dorset, BH21 7SH
Activities: Activities of other holding companies n.e.c.
Major Shareholder: Timothy John Brown
Officers: Mark Andrew Wallis, Secretary/Chartered Accountant; Timothy John Brown [1957] Director/Rubber Technologist; Mark Andrew Wallis [1960] Director/Chartered Accountant

Superior Seals Limited
Incorporated: 9 September 1966 *Employees:* 143
Net Worth: £36,206,012 *Total Assets:* £44,399,256
Registered Office: Nimrod Way, Ferndown Industrial Estate, Wimborne, Dorset, BH21 7SH
Activities: Manufacture of other rubber products
Parent: Superior Group Limited
Officers: Mark Andrew Wallis, Secretary/Chartered Accountant; David Alexander Brown [1982] Production Director; Timothy John Brown [1957] Director/Rubber Technologist; Mark Andrew Wallis [1960] Director/Chartered Accountant

Superior Specials Limited
Incorporated: 28 February 1989 *Employees:* 59
Net Worth: £7,089,689 *Total Assets:* £9,691,440
Registered Office: Nimrod Way, Ferndown Industrial Estate, Wimborne, Dorset, BH21 7SH
Activities: Manufacture of other rubber products
Parent: Superior Group Limited
Officers: Mark Andrew Wallis, Secretary/Chartered Accountant; Timothy John Brown [1957] Director/Rubber Technologist; Mark Andrew Wallis [1960] Director/Chartered Accountant

Supported Independence Limited
Incorporated: 19 February 2002 *Employees:* 93
Net Worth: £4,447,124 *Total Assets:* £7,495,082
Registered Office: 27-29 Ashley Road, Bristol, BS6 5NJ
Activities: Residential care activities for the elderly and disabled
Shareholder: Supported Independence Holdings Limited
Officers: Joseph John Kelly, Secretary; Joseph John Kelly [1964] Director/Manager; Catherine Elizabeth Twine [1972] Managing Director

Sure Maintenance Limited
Incorporated: 15 September 2000 *Employees:* 360
Net Worth: £6,838,448 *Total Assets:* £12,581,860
Registered Office: c/o BPE Solicitors LLP, First Floor, St James House, St James Square, Cheltenham, Glos, GL50 3PR
Activities: Plumbing, heat and air-conditioning installation
Parent: Speedfit Limited
Officers: John William Charles Charlton, Secretary; John William Charles Charlton [1956] Director/Company Secretary; Paul Stephen Cornes [1975] Director; Michael McMahon [1976] Director

Suremime Limited
Incorporated: 30 October 1981 *Employees:* 58
Net Worth: £5,478,498 *Total Assets:* £10,460,946
Registered Office: Home Farm Holiday Park, Burnham on Sea, Somerset, TA9 4HD
Activities: Recreational vehicle parks, trailer parks and camping grounds
Shareholders: Geoffrey Atkinson; Glenys Patricia Atkinson
Officers: Glenys Patricia Atkinson, Secretary; Geoffrey Atkinson [1955] Director; Glenys Patricia Atkinson [1954] Director/Caravan Park Operator; Steven Geoffrey Atkinson [1981] Director/Caravan Park Operator

Surereed Limited
Incorporated: 6 December 1978 *Employees:* 11
Net Worth: £2,315,715 *Total Assets:* £3,848,919
Registered Office: 10 Bridge Street, Christchurch, Dorset, BH23 1EF
Activities: Development of building projects
Major Shareholder: Peter Mons Hayward
Officers: Josephine Mary Hayward, Secretary; Peter William Hayward [1984] Director; Peter Mons Hayward [1943] Director; Stephen Mons Hayward [1986] Director

Sureserve Compliance Services Limited
Incorporated: 23 September 2015
Previous: Lakehouse Compliance Services Limited
Net Worth: £567,399 *Total Assets:* £48,234,328
Registered Office: c/o BPE Solicitors LLP, First Floor, St James House, St James Square, Cheltenham, Glos, GL50 3PR
Activities: Activities of construction holding companies
Parent: Lakehouse Holdings Limited
Officers: John William Charles Charlton, Secretary; John William Charles Charlton [1956] Director/Company Secretary; Robert Holt [1954] Director; Michael McMahon [1976] Director

Sureserve Energy Services Limited
Incorporated: 23 September 2015
Previous: Lakehouse Energy Services Limited
Net Worth: £2,122,615 *Total Assets:* £51,748,592
Registered Office: c/o BPE Solicitors LLP, First Floor, St James House, St James Square, Cheltenham, Glos, GL50 3PR
Activities: Activities of construction holding companies
Parent: Lakehouse Holdings Limited
Officers: John William Charles Charlton, Secretary; John William Charles Charlton [1956] Director/Company Secretary; Robert Holt [1954] Director; Michael McMahon [1976] Director

Sureserve Holdings Limited
Incorporated: 6 February 2003
Previous: Lakehouse Holdings Limited
Net Worth: £38,409,000 *Total Assets:* £48,927,000
Registered Office: c/o BPE Solicitors LLP, First Floor, St James House, St James Square, Cheltenham, Glos, GL50 3PR
Activities: Development of building projects
Parent: Lakehouse PLC
Officers: John William Charles Charlton, Secretary; John William Charles Charlton [1956] Director/Company Secretary; Robert Holt [1954] Director; Michael McMahon [1976] Director

Surest Ltd
Incorporated: 19 March 1997 *Employees:* 16
Net Worth: £2,051,889 *Total Assets:* £3,713,450
Registered Office: Bridge House, St Clement Street, Truro, Cornwall, TR1 1ER
Activities: Other reservation service activities n.e.c.
Shareholders: Tara Jane Physick; Mark Jordan Wilson
Officers: Tara Physick, Secretary/Director; Tara Physick [1969] Director; Mark Wilson [1965] Director

Sureway Express Transport Limited
Incorporated: 30 July 2002 *Employees:* 40
Net Worth: £1,416,288 *Total Assets:* £4,023,352
Registered Office: Unit 12 The IO Centre, Cabot Park, Moorend Farm Avenue, Avonmouth, Bristol, BS11 0QL
Activities: Freight transport by road
Shareholders: Robert John Lloyd; Julie Louise Lloyd
Officers: Caroline Jane Howell, Secretary; Julie Louise Lloyd [1967] Director; Robert John Lloyd [1964] Director

Surgical Specialties UK Holdings Limited
Incorporated: 21 October 2004
Net Worth: £12,127,000 *Total Assets:* £12,127,000
Registered Office: Tancred Street, Taunton, Somerset, TA1 1RY
Activities: Manufacture of medical and dental instruments and supplies
Parent: Surgical Specialties Corporation
Officers: Daniel Joseph Sutherby, Secretary; Victor Diaz [1961] Director/Chief Operating Officer [American]

Sustainable Drainage Systems Limited
Incorporated: 8 May 2002 *Employees:* 122
Net Worth: £8,511,084 *Total Assets:* £15,369,683
Registered Office: Clearwater House, Castlemills, Biddisham, Somerset, BS26 2RE
Activities: Manufacture of builders ware of plastic
Parent: SDS Holdings Limited
Officers: Patrick Gabriel Cullen, Secretary/Engineer [Irish]; Patrick Gabriel Cullen [1967] Director [Irish]

Sustrans Limited
Incorporated: 6 March 1984 *Employees:* 505
Net Worth: £9,875,000 *Total Assets:* £36,926,000
Registered Office: 2 Cathedral Square, College Green, Bristol, BS1 5DD
Activities: Other professional, scientific and technical activities n.e.c.
Officers: Andrew Appleby, Secretary; Claire Louise Addison [1985] Director/Communications Manager; Gwenda Lynne Berry [1953] Director/Academic; Rt Revd Dr Edward Francis Condry [1953] Director/Bishop; Mark Timothy Edgell [1961] Director/Senior Manager; Catherine Max [1966] Director/Independent Consultant; Stuart Christopher Mills [1967] Director/Chief Investment Officer; Oliver Reichardt [1976] Charity Director; Helen Elizabeth Simpson [1977] Director/Lawyer; Fiona Gillian Westwood [1971] Director/Chartered Accountant

Suttle Projects Limited
Incorporated: 28 October 2008 *Employees:* 33
Net Worth: £1,304,983 *Total Assets:* £4,468,916
Registered Office: Swanworth Quarry, Worth Matravers, Swanage, Dorset, BH19 3LE
Activities: Construction of other civil engineering projects n.e.c.
Shareholder: Joseph Martin Paine
Officers: Roger Alan Funnell [1954] Director/Merchant; Alistair Maidman [1987] Director/Civil Engineer; Joseph Martin Paine [1964] Director/Civil Engineer; Christopher John Suttle [1951] Director/Merchant Owner; Liam Wayne Tucker [1982] Director/Civil Engineering Management

J. Suttle Transport Limited
Incorporated: 26 February 1993 *Employees:* 47
Net Worth: £1,789,299 *Total Assets:* £5,169,680
Registered Office: Swanworth Quarry, Worth Matravers, Swanage, Dorset, BH19 3LE
Activities: Quarrying of ornamental and building stone, limestone, gypsum, chalk and slate
Shareholders: Roger Alan Funnell; Christopher John Suttle
Officers: Simon Clabburn [1968] Director of Quarrying; Roger Alan Funnell [1954] Director; Michael Robert James [1957] Director/Plant Manager; Sue Marshall [1980] Director/Office Manager; Joseph Martin Paine [1964] Director/Civil Engineer; Christopher John Suttle [1951] Director/Quarry Operator; John Christopher Suttle [1986] Director/Quarry & Transport Management

Sutton Chemicals & Textiles UK Limited
Incorporated: 27 September 2013
Net Worth: £149,453 *Total Assets:* £4,608,616
Registered Office: Calcutt Court, Calcutt, Swindon, Wilts, SN6 6JR
Activities: Other professional, scientific and technical activities n.e.c.
Parent: Beeston Resources Limited
Officers: Stephanie Louise Smith [1986] Director

Sutton Harbour Car Parks Limited
Incorporated: 18 December 2006
Net Worth: £5,931,000 *Total Assets:* £6,039,000
Registered Office: Guy's Quay, Sutton Harbour, Plymouth, PL4 0ES
Activities: Renting and leasing of other machinery, equipment and tangible goods n.e.c.
Officers: Natasha Claire Gadsdon, Secretary/Accountant; Philip Howard Beinhaker [1941] Director [Canadian]; Natasha Claire Gadsdon [1970] Director/Accountant; Graham Scott Miller [1963] Director

Sutton Harbour Holdings PLC
Incorporated: 21 September 1989 *Employees:* 32
Net Worth: £39,974,000 *Total Assets:* £69,249,000
Registered Office: Guy's Quay, Sutton Harbour, Plymouth, PL4 0ES
Activities: Activities of other holding companies n.e.c.
Parent: FB Investors LLP
Officers: Natasha Claire Gadsdon, Secretary/Accountant; Philip Howard Beinhaker [1941] Director [Canadian]; Natasha Claire Gadsdon [1970] Director/Accountant; Graham Scott Miller [1963] Director; Sean Jonathan Swales [1968] Director/Accountant

Sutton Harbour Projects Limited
Incorporated: 2 July 2007
Net Worth Deficit: £2,530,000 *Total Assets:* £8,011,000
Registered Office: Guy's Quay, Sutton Harbour, Plymouth, PL4 0ES
Activities: Development of building projects
Parent: Sutton Harbour Holdings PLC
Officers: Natasha Claire Gadsdon, Secretary; Philip Howard Beinhaker [1941] Director [Canadian]; Natasha Claire Gadsdon [1970] Director/Accountant; Graham Scott Miller [1963] Director; Jason William Hyde Schofield [1966] Director/Chartered Surveyor

Sutton Harbour Services Limited
Incorporated: 12 September 1989
Net Worth: £364,000 *Total Assets:* £11,653,000
Registered Office: Guy's Quay, Sutton Harbour, Plymouth, PL4 0ES
Activities: Other letting and operating of own or leased real estate
Parent: Sutton Harbour Holdings PLC
Officers: Natasha Claire Gadsdon, Secretary/Accountant; Philip Howard Beinhaker [1941] Director [Canadian]; Natasha Claire Gadsdon [1970] Director/Accountant; Graham Scott Miller [1963] Director

Suttons Consumer Products Limited
Incorporated: 7 February 1934 *Employees:* 191
Net Worth: £3,424,799 *Total Assets:* £7,603,997
Registered Office: Woodview Road, Paignton, Devon, TQ4 7NG
Activities: Wholesale of grain, unmanufactured tobacco, seeds and animal feeds
Parent: Suttons Seeds Limited
Officers: Rufus William Roberts [1971] Director; David Christopher Robinson [1956] Director

Suttons Seeds Limited
Incorporated: 10 October 2014 *Employees:* 191
Net Worth: £2,681,104 *Total Assets:* £6,840,303
Registered Office: Woodview Road, Paignton, Devon, TQ4 7NG
Activities: Other manufacturing n.e.c.
Shareholders: Rufus William Roberts; David Christopher Robinson
Officers: Rufus William Roberts [1971] Director; David Christopher Robinson [1956] Director

SW Construction (No.2) Limited
Incorporated: 14 January 2013 *Employees:* 5
Net Worth: £5,893,067 *Total Assets:* £5,903,229
Registered Office: 1350-1360 Montpellier Court, Brockworth, Gloucester, GL3 4AH
Activities: Construction of domestic buildings
Parent: Blackfinch Nominees Limited
Officers: Richard James Cook [1978] Director

SW Construction (Residential) Limited
Incorporated: 15 May 2012 *Employees:* 5
Net Worth: £6,035,465 *Total Assets:* £6,462,300
Registered Office: 1350-1360 Montpellier Court, Brockworth, Gloucester, GL3 4AH
Activities: Construction of domestic buildings
Shareholders: Blackfinch Nominees Limited; Blackfinch Investments Limited
Officers: Richard James Cook [1978] Director; Jamie Christian George Dellow [1971] Director

Swallowcourt Holdings Limited
Incorporated: 28 February 2008 *Employees:* 414
Net Worth: £8,517,377 *Total Assets:* £18,737,448
Registered Office: Peat House, Newham Road, Truro, Cornwall, TR1 2DP
Activities: Activities of head offices
Officers: Brian Robert Harris [1958] Director/Manager; Simon John Hopkins [1965] Director; Dorothy Keely [1943] Director

Swallowcourt Limited
Incorporated: 26 August 1983 *Employees:* 317
Net Worth: £6,444,681 *Total Assets:* £14,449,839
Registered Office: Peat House, Newham Road, Truro, Cornwall, TR1 2DP
Activities: Residential nursing care facilities
Shareholders: Swallowcourt Holdings Limited; Swallowcourt Holdings Limited
Officers: Brian Robert Harris [1958] Director; Simon John Hopkins [1965] Director; Dorothy Keely [1943] Director

Swallowfield PLC
Incorporated: 7 January 1986 *Employees:* 593
Net Worth: £26,943,000 *Total Assets:* £60,490,000
Registered Office: Swallowfield House, Station Road, Wellington, Somerset, TA21 8NL
Activities: Manufacture of perfumes and toilet preparations
Officers: Matthew Gazzard, Secretary; Edward John Beale [1960] Director/Chief Executive; Franklin Pinhas Berrebi [1943] Director [French]; Jane Fletcher [1967] Director/Sales & Marketing; Matthew Gazzard [1971] Group Financial Director; Brendan Hynes [1960] Director; Roger Steven McDowell [1955] Director; Timothy James Perman [1962] Director

Swan Hotel Wells (2007) Limited
Incorporated: 17 January 2007 *Employees:* 56
Net Worth: £2,201,034 *Total Assets:* £7,256,941
Registered Office: Ground Floor, Blackbrook Gate 1, Blackbrook Business Park, Taunton, Somerset, TA1 2PX
Activities: Hotels and similar accommodation
Shareholders: Danzo Development Limited; The Ashmores Childrens Settlement Trust 2004
Officers: Daniel Roy Newton, Secretary; Bruce Patrick Ashmore [1961] Director/Accountant [Irish]; Kevin Roy Newton [1965] Director

Swan Properties Cornwall Limited
Incorporated: 24 May 2011 *Employees:* 2
Net Worth: £528,003 *Total Assets:* £3,560,483
Registered Office: 48 Arwenack Street, Falmouth, Cornwall, TR11 3JH
Activities: Other letting and operating of own or leased real estate
Shareholders: David John Lord; Patience Carole Lord
Officers: David John Lord [1953] Director/Property Consultant; Patience Carole Lord [1957] Director/Property Consultant

Swanage Railway Company Limited
Incorporated: 1 February 1979 *Employees:* 39
Net Worth: £2,808,758 *Total Assets:* £5,759,381
Registered Office: The Station House, Swanage, Dorset, BH19 1HB
Activities: Other passenger land transport
Parent: Swanage Railway Trust Ltd
Officers: Peter James Milford, Secretary; Michael Arthur Gould [1949] Director/Retired; Gavin Christopher Johns [1956] Director/Retired; Andrew Leslie Moore [1950] Director; Trevor John Parsons [1943] Director/Retired; Kevin Maxwell Potts [1960] Director/Royal Navy, Pilot; Elizabeth Maureen Sellen [1954] Director/Retired; Keith Roger Usher [1954] Director/Railway Manager; Mark Robert Woolley [1965] Director/Finance Officer

The Swanage Railway Trust
Incorporated: 27 November 2000 *Employees:* 39
Net Worth: £6,972,151 *Total Assets:* £7,416,523
Registered Office: Station House, Swanage, Dorset, BH19 1HB
Activities: Operation of historical sites and buildings and similar visitor attractions
Officers: Mark Robert Woolley, Secretary; Daniel John Bennett [1985] Director/Engineer; Geoffrey William Carter [1947] Director/Retired Mechanical Engineer; Paul Trevor Clements [1942] Director/Finance Manager; Randy Coldham [1945] Director/Retired; Nicholas Stephen Coram [1969] Director/Project Manager; Beryl Rita Ezzard [1945] Director/Local Government Councillor; Jacqueline Ann Hagger [1966] Director/Part Qualified CIMA Accountant; Gavin Christopher Johns [1956] Director/Retired; Stuart Irving Magnus [1946] Director/Retired; Matthew McManus [1986] Director/Train Driver; Andrew Leslie Moore [1950] Director; Trevor John Parsons [1943] Director/Retired; Elizabeth Maureen Sellen [1954] Director/Retired; Peter Nicholas Sills [1957] Director; William Stanley Trite [1947] Director/District Councillor; Michael Alan Whitwam [1945] Director/Photographer; Mark Robert Woolley [1965] Director/IT Administrator

Swannick & Kearn Properties Limited
Incorporated: 21 August 2015
Net Worth Deficit: £62,674 *Total Assets:* £4,138,744
Registered Office: Kelsall Steele Ltd, Unit A Woodlands Court, Truro Business Park, Truro, Cornwall, TR4 9NH
Activities: Construction of domestic buildings
Officers: Valerie Iris Chenoweth, Secretary; Brian George Chenoweth [1949] Director; Shonaugh Evans [1948] Director

Swattons Limited
Incorporated: 15 February 2017 *Employees:* 3
Net Worth: £5,949,255 *Total Assets:* £6,736,723
Registered Office: 39 Central Way, Andover, Hants, SP10 5AN
Activities: Other letting and operating of own or leased real estate
Major Shareholder: Stephen Paul Swatton
Officers: Stephen Paul Swatton [1959] Director/Property Letting

Swedish Lifestyle Homes No.1 Limited
Incorporated: 18 November 2015
Previous: Swedish By Design No.1 Limited
Net Worth: £1 *Total Assets:* £11,019,472
Registered Office: Unit 18-19 Cirencester Office Park, Tetbury Road, Cirencester, Glos, GL7 6JJ
Activities: Development of building projects
Major Shareholder: Kenneth James Forster
Officers: Kenneth James Forster [1956] Director; Tore Janson [1957] Director [Swedish]

Swegon Limited
Incorporated: 25 November 1980 *Employees:* 22
Net Worth: £87,835 *Total Assets:* £47,655,816
Registered Office: Forest House, Queensway, New Milton, Hants, BH25 5NN
Activities: Plumbing, heat and air-conditioning installation
Parent: Swegon Group Aktiebolag
Officers: Andrew McKay [1962] Finance Director; Christian Olin [1968] Director/Accountant [Swedish]; Hannu Saastamoinen [1960] Director [Finnish]; Robin Vollert [1968] Managing Director [Swedish]; Beth Georgina Young [1969] Director

Swettenham Estates (UK) Limited
Incorporated: 13 March 1997
Net Worth Deficit: £252,221 *Total Assets:* £5,333,556
Registered Office: 11 Quiet Street, Bath, BA1 2LB
Activities: Buying and selling of own real estate
Major Shareholder: Campbell Bruce Horne
Officers: Joanna Christine Hughes, Secretary; Campbell Bruce Horne [1959] Director/Investment Banker

Swindon Caravan Centre Limited
Incorporated: 3 April 2003 *Employees:* 69
Net Worth: £2,417,254 *Total Assets:* £9,599,210
Registered Office: Swindon Caravan Centre, Greatfield, Wootton Bassett, Swindon, Wilts, SN4 8EQ
Activities: Other retail sale of new goods in specialised stores (not commercial art galleries and opticians)
Shareholders: Guy Richard Collister; Janet Collister
Officers: Guy Richard Collister, Secretary; Guy Richard Collister [1947] Director/Caravan Retailer; Janet Collister [1947] Director; Thomas Robert Collister [1979] Director

Swindon Silicon Systems Limited
Incorporated: 11 July 1978 *Employees:* 130
Net Worth: £26,675,000 *Total Assets:* £38,756,000
Registered Office: Interface House, Interface Business Park, Bincknoll Lane, Royal Wootton Bassett, Swindon, Wilts, SN4 8SY
Activities: Manufacture of electronic components
Parent: August UK Holdco Limited
Officers: Jeremy Edwin Loraine [1962] Managing Director

Swinford Wind Farm Limited
Incorporated: 23 June 2009 *Employees:* 3
Net Worth: £10,841,867 *Total Assets:* £25,079,738
Registered Office: Abbey Warehouse, Abbey Slip, Penzance, Cornwall, TR18 4AR
Activities: Production of electricity
Parent: Nuon UK Ltd
Officers: Jonas Van Mansfeld, Secretary; Alper Elmas [1976] Director [Cypriot]; Jonathan David Chin O'Sullivan [1977] Director

SWK (UK) Limited
Incorporated: 12 December 2003
Net Worth: £19,402,000 *Total Assets:* £65,711,000
Registered Office: Stanley House, Bramble Road, Swindon, Wilts, SN2 8ER
Activities: Activities of head offices
Parent: Stanley UK Acquisition Company Limited
Officers: Steven John Costello, Secretary; Steven John Costello [1980] Director/Chartered Accountant; Mark Richard Smiley [1977] Director/General Manager UK & ROI; Amit Kumar Sood [1978] Director/Accountant

SWM & Waste Recycling Limited
Incorporated: 1 February 2002 *Employees:* 78
Net Worth: £1,963,426 *Total Assets:* £4,778,757
Registered Office: SWM & Waste Recycling Ltd, Gratton Way, Roundswell Business Park, Barnstaple, Devon, EX31 3NL
Activities: Collection of non-hazardous waste
Officers: Shawn Richard Akers [1967] Director/Used Metal Dealer; Martin Edward Mogford [1962] Operations Director; Raymond James Penfold [1963] Director/Used Metal Dealer

Swoop Travel Limited
Incorporated: 17 February 2012 *Employees:* 20
Net Worth: £586,580 *Total Assets:* £6,865,315
Registered Office: 15 Cornwallis Crescent, Bristol, BS8 4PJ
Activities: Tour operator activities
Shareholder: Jessica Mella Hallett Errington
Officers: Luke Alexander Errington [1975] Director/Consultant

Sydenhams Ltd
Incorporated: 12 July 1920 *Employees:* 421
Net Worth: £30,626,932 *Total Assets:* £44,406,808
Registered Office: 45-47 Ashley Road, Boscombe, Bournemouth, BH1 4LG
Activities: Wholesale of wood, construction materials and sanitary equipment
Parent: Sherborne Holdings Ltd
Officers: Raymond John Pride, Secretary/Director; Ian James Brailey [1956] Director; Christopher Michael Carter [1975] Purchasing Director; Montague John Meyer [1944] Director/Timber Merchant; Raymond John Pride [1951] Director; Charles John Sherborne [1958] Director/Timber Merchant; James Richard Sherborne [1963] Director/Timber Merchant; Lee Michael Wright [1974] Operations Director

Symec Technologies Limited
Incorporated: 29 July 2009 *Employees:* 37
Net Worth: £2,005,891 *Total Assets:* £5,427,721
Registered Office: 10 Brook Office Park, Emersons Green, Bristol, BS16 7FL
Activities: Wholesale of computers, computer peripheral equipment and software
Parent: Symec Group Limited
Officers: Phillip Jonathan Bruce [1981] Director; Paul Golden [1976] Director; Adrian Lawson [1971] Director; Alex David Benjamin Whiting [1980] Director

Symonds Estates Limited
Incorporated: 29 January 2016 *Employees:* 274
Net Worth: £12,757,764 *Total Assets:* £17,608,456
Registered Office: 3rd Floor, Maltravers House, Petters Way, Yeovil, Somerset, BA20 1SP
Activities: Other letting and operating of own or leased real estate
Major Shareholder: Jeremy Paul Symonds
Officers: Jeremy Paul Symonds [1960] Director; Julia Marie Symonds [1961] Director

Symonds Forecourts Limited
Incorporated: 22 May 2007 *Employees:* 67
Net Worth: £8,606,380 *Total Assets:* £9,878,854
Registered Office: 3rd Floor, Maltravers House, Petters Way, Yeovil, Somerset, BA20 1SQ
Activities: Retail sale in non-specialised stores with food, beverages or tobacco predominating
Parent: Symonds Estates Limited
Officers: Jeremy Paul Symonds, Secretary/Director; Gary Colin Pearce [1969] Director; Jeremy Paul Symonds [1960] Director; Julia Marie Symonds [1961] Director

Andrew Symons Limited
Incorporated: 23 March 2007 *Employees:* 2
Net Worth: £1,380,847 *Total Assets:* £4,682,782
Registered Office: Michells Chartered Accountants, St John's House, Castle Street, Taunton, Somerset, TA1 4AY
Activities: Wholesale of agricultural machinery, equipment and supplies
Shareholders: Andrew Mark Symons; Lisa Francesca Symons
Officers: Lisa Francesca Symons, Secretary; Andrew Mark Symons [1962] Director/Agricultural Engineer; Lisa Francesca Symons [1967] Director/Office Administrator

Symons Retail Limited
Incorporated: 14 January 2011 *Employees:* 7
Net Worth: £2,617,857 *Total Assets:* £4,105,300
Registered Office: Red Willows, Dynas la, St Ives, Cornwall, TR26 2BU
Activities: Licenced restaurants
Major Shareholder: Timothy John Symons
Officers: Charles Henry Symons [1983] Director/Manager; Timothy John Symons [1957] Director/Manager

Synergy Health (UK) Limited
Incorporated: 15 May 1970 *Employees:* 1,046
Net Worth: £171,284,992 *Total Assets:* £222,024,000
Registered Office: Ground Floor, Stella Building, Windmill Hill Business Park, Whitehill Way, Swindon, Wilts, SN5 6NX
Activities: Other manufacturing n.e.c.
Parent: Synergy Health Holdings Limited
Officers: Dr Adrian Vincent Coward [1969] Director; Peter John Rendle [1980] Director/Chartered Accountant; Michael Joseph Tokich [1968] Director/Senior Vice President & Chief Financial Officer [American]

Synergy Health Holdings Limited
Incorporated: 10 January 2007
Net Worth: £290,548,000 *Total Assets:* £624,651,008
Registered Office: Ground Floor, Stella Building, Windmill Hill Business Park, Whitehill Way, Swindon, Wilts, SN5 6NX
Activities: Activities of other holding companies n.e.c.
Parent: Synergy Health Limited
Officers: Peter John Rendle [1980] Director/Chartered Accountant; Michael Joseph Tokich [1968] Director/Corporate Executive [American]; John Adam Zangerle [1966] Director/Secretary and General Counsel [American]

Synergy Health Investments Limited
Incorporated: 11 July 1980
Net Worth: £48,427,000 *Total Assets:* £48,552,000
Registered Office: Ground Floor, Stella Building, Windmill Hill Business Park, Whitehill Way, Swindon, Wilts, SN5 6NX
Activities: Activities of other holding companies n.e.c.
Parent: Synergy Health Sterilisation UK Limited
Officers: Peter John Rendle [1980] Director/Chartered Accountant; Michael Joseph Tokich [1968] Director/Senior Vice President & Chief Financial Officer [American]

Synergy Health Limited
Incorporated: 17 April 1997 *Employees:* 15
Previous: Synergy Health PLC
Net Worth: £317,311,008 *Total Assets:* £631,299,968
Registered Office: Ground Floor, Stella Building, Windmill Hill Business Park, Whitehill Way, Swindon, Wilts, SN5 6NX
Activities: Other human health activities
Parent: Steris PLC
Officers: Dr Adrian Vincent Coward [1969] Director; Peter John Rendle [1980] Director/Chartered Accountant; Michael Joseph Tokich [1968] Director/Senior Vice President & Chief Financial Officer [American]; John Adam Zangerle [1966] Director/Secretary and General Counsel [American]

Synergy Health Sterilisation UK Limited
Incorporated: 21 November 1983 *Employees:* 198
Net Worth: £61,296,000 *Total Assets:* £80,562,000
Registered Office: Ground Floor, Stella Building, Windmill Hill Business Park, Whitehill Way, Swindon, Wilts, SN5 6NX
Activities: Other professional, scientific and technical activities n.e.c.
Parent: Synergy Health Holdings Limited
Officers: Michael John Eaton [1973] Director; Peter John Rendle [1980] Director/Chartered Accountant; Paul Nigel Santing [1956] Director/Business Manager [Dutch]; Michael Joseph Tokich [1968] Director/Senior Vice President & Chief Financial Officer [American]

Synergy Health Systems Limited
Incorporated: 15 March 2007 *Employees:* 62
Net Worth: £5,934,000 *Total Assets:* £7,042,000
Registered Office: Ground Floor, Stella Building, Windmill Hill Business Park, Whitehill Way, Swindon, Wilts, SN5 6NX
Activities: Other information technology service activities
Parent: Synergy Health Holdings Limited
Officers: Peter John Rendle [1980] Director/Chartered Accountant; Michael Joseph Tokich [1968] Director/Senior Vice President & Chief Financial Officer [American]

Synertec Limited
Incorporated: 22 February 1999 *Employees:* 165
Net Worth: £3,853,477 *Total Assets:* £10,600,405
Registered Office: 2 Castle Road, Chelston Business Park, Wellington, Somerset, TA21 9JQ
Activities: Other information service activities n.e.c.
Officers: Mark Reuben Baldock [1961] Managing Director; Michael William Cleave [1966] Production Director; Stuart Adam Nester [1977] Development Director

Synlatex Limited
Incorporated: 7 May 1985 *Employees:* 160
Net Worth: £12,402,876 *Total Assets:* £16,274,429
Registered Office: Liberty House, St Catherine Street, Gloucester, GL1 2BX
Activities: Wholesale of perfume and cosmetics
Parent: SLG Allstars Limited
Officers: Lucy Jane Beresford [1980] Sales Director; Richard Mark Buckland [1977] Director; Timothy Cound [1963] Manufacturing Director; Miles Spencer Maitland Dunkley [1967] Managing Director; Susan Hutchings [1966] Director; Lisa Topping [1974] Manufacturing Sales Director

Syreford Investments LLP
Incorporated: 14 April 2005
Net Worth: £30,410,224 *Total Assets:* £30,432,256
Registered Office: Third Floor, 95 The Promenade, Cheltenham, Glos, GL50 1HH
Officers: Anthony Geraint Williams [1958] Member

System 6 Kitchens Limited
Incorporated: 4 April 1985 *Employees:* 68
Net Worth: £2,216,428 *Total Assets:* £5,333,263
Registered Office: 4 Christow Road, Marsh Barton, Exeter, EX2 8QP
Activities: Manufacture of kitchen furniture
Major Shareholder: Ian Foster
Officers: Mr Tom Dalton [1983] Sales Director; Ian Foster [1971] Director; Nigel Kenneth Phillip Jones [1963] Managing Director

Systems Engineering & Assessment Ltd
Incorporated: 4 October 1988 *Employees:* 307
Net Worth: £17,793,000 *Total Assets:* £29,169,000
Registered Office: Beckington Castle, 17 Castle Corner, Beckington, Frome, Somerset, BA11 6TA
Activities: Manufacture of air and spacecraft and related machinery
Parent: SEA (Group) Ltd.
Officers: Sarita Bilkhu, Secretary; Stephen Jeremy Hill [1965] Managing Director; Andrew Stephen Thomis [1964] Director; Simon Robert Walther [1967] Director

T Shirt & Sons Limited
Incorporated: 28 April 2003 *Employees:* 72
Net Worth: £1,645,062 *Total Assets:* £6,161,429
Registered Office: 11 Washington Road, West Wilts Trading Estate, Westbury, Wilts, BA13 4JP
Activities: Printing n.e.c.
Shareholders: Jonathan Guy Winstanley Lunt; Andrew Michael Winstanley Lunt
Officers: Jonathan Guy Winstanley Lunt, Secretary/T Shirt Design & Retail; Andrew Michael Winstanley Lunt [1966] Director/T Shirt Design & Retail; Jonathan Guy Winstanley Lunt [1962] Director/T Shirt Design & Retail; Darren Telfer Newman [1969] Director/Certified Chartered Accountant

T.E.J. Heating (Plymouth) Limited
Incorporated: 22 May 1989 *Employees:* 22
Net Worth: £3,173,207 *Total Assets:* £4,388,567
Registered Office: Unit 14, 63 Sisna Park Road, Estover, Plymouth, PL6 7AE
Activities: Plumbing, heat and air-conditioning installation
Major Shareholder: William Robert Jordan
Officers: David James Jordan, Secretary; David James Jordan [1961] Director; Marie Ann Jordan [1958] Director; William Robert Jordan [1959] Director/Chairman

T2 Partnership Ltd
Incorporated: 24 August 2012
Net Worth: £4,193,360 *Total Assets:* £4,260,108
Registered Office: 2 Endeavour House, Parkway Court, Longbridge Road, Plymouth, PL6 8LR
Activities: Development of building projects
Shareholders: Charles Lerschai Tharnthong; Charles Lerschai Tharnthong
Officers: Charles Lerschai Tharnthong [1954] Director/Consultant Structural Engineer; Sally Loretta Tharnthong [1954] Director/Housewife

Tabacalera de Garcia UK Limited
Incorporated: 22 December 2004 *Employees:* 3
Net Worth: £88,099,704 *Total Assets:* £88,099,704
Registered Office: 121 Winterstoke Road, Bristol, BS3 2LL
Activities: Non-trading company
Parent: Imperial Tobacco Overseas Holdings Limited
Officers: Gavin Paul Bonnar, Secretary; Thomas Richard William Tildesley [1973] Finance Director; Robert Dee Wilkey [1956] Director/Attorney [American]; Trevor Martin Williams [1961] Director/Chartered Secretary

Tack Farms Limited
Incorporated: 30 January 2003 *Employees:* 8
Net Worth: £426,292 *Total Assets:* £4,191,204
Registered Office: Staverton Court, Staverton, Cheltenham, Glos, GL51 0UX
Activities: Raising of dairy cattle
Shareholders: William Peter Lewis; William Henry Lewis
Officers: William Henry Lewis, Secretary/Farmer; Susan Marie Lewis [1965] Director/Solicitor; William Peter Lewis [1935] Director/Farmer; William Henry Lewis [1963] Director/Farmer

Tacklestore Limited
Incorporated: 19 June 2002 *Employees:* 83
Net Worth: £1,454,970 *Total Assets:* £5,435,244
Registered Office: The Old Post Office, 41-43 Market Place, Chippenham, Wilts, SN15 3HR
Activities: Other business support service activities n.e.c.
Major Shareholder: Michael Thomas Hughes
Officers: Samantha Jayne Wickens, Secretary; Michael Thomas Hughes [1960] Director/Engineer

Talbot Heath School Trust Limited
Incorporated: 9 September 1981 *Employees:* 92
Net Worth: £11,118,036 *Total Assets:* £13,905,775
Registered Office: Talbot Heath School, Rothesay Road, Bournemouth, BH4 9NJ
Activities: General secondary education
Officers: Generald William Ives, Secretary; Dr Richard Day [1954] Director/Retired; Cherry Lyn Edwards [1945] Director/Retired; Revd Rupert Anthony Higgins [1959] Director/Clergy; Diana Leadbetter [1963] Director; Dr Andrew Main [1946] Director/Associate Dean; Christine Mary Norman [1946] Director/Legal Assistant; James Robert Paget [1970] Director/Chartered Certified Accountant; Sarah Louise Richards [1962] Director/Retired; Deborah Jane Sadd [1960] Director/University Professor; Claire Saunders [1969] Director/Instructional Engineer; Rachel Susan Small [1966] Director/Solicitor; Clodie Sutcliffe [1968] Director/Police Inspector; David Anthony Townend [1958] Director

Talent & Enterprise Trust
Incorporated: 10 June 2013 *Employees:* 74
Net Worth: £3,978,000 *Total Assets:* £5,297,000
Registered Office: Marine Academy Plymouth, Trevithick Road, Plymouth, PL5 2AF
Activities: Primary education
Officers: Anita Martin, Secretary; Robert Zebulon Baggott [1951] Director/Head of Innovation Gateway; Tom Cowan [1980] Director/Lecturer; Megan Paterson Crawford [1957] Director/Professor of Education; Beth Gompertz [1959] Director/Education Executive; Maria Manning [1976] Director/Finance Executive; Gillian Fisher Martin [1963] Director/HR Executive; Simon James Payne [1963] Director/Deputy Vice Chancellor; David Hedley Jacques Sammels [1977] Director/Headteacher

Tamander Limited
Incorporated: 27 February 1998 *Employees:* 4
Net Worth: £2,471,514 *Total Assets:* £3,672,322
Registered Office: Unity Chambers, 34 High East Street, Dorchester, DT1 1HA
Activities: Motion picture production activities
Shareholders: John Mathieson; Maria Paulina Tamander
Officers: Kathleen Hobbs, Secretary; John Mathieson [1961] Director/Cameraman; Maria Paulina Tamander [1963] Director/Producer

Tamar Farms LLP
Incorporated: 28 September 2011 *Employees:* 3
Net Worth: £20,680,238 *Total Assets:* £20,757,180
Registered Office: Collacombe Barton, Lamerton, Tavistock, Devon, PL19 8SB
Officers: Ian McClure Forrest [1958] Member; Sarah Catherine Oliver [1958] Member; Jennifer Charlotte Forrest [1999] LLP Member

Tamar Trading Co.Limited
Incorporated: 8 May 1959 *Employees:* 57
Net Worth: £1,297,995 *Total Assets:* £3,644,228
Registered Office: Units 13-14 Cooksland Industrial Estate, Bodmin, Cornwall, PL31 2PZ
Activities: Agents involved in the sale of timber and building materials
Shareholders: John Addicott; Richard James Stacey; John Charles Stacey
Officers: John Addicott, Secretary; John Addicott [1955] Director/Builder/Surveyor; Lucy Jane Squire [1974] Director/Certified Chartered Accountant; Andrew Frederick Stacey [1936] Director/Builder/Surveyor; John Charles Stacey [1965] Director/Builder Surveyor; Richard James Stacey [1963] Director/Chartered Engineer

Tamar View Nurseries Ltd
Incorporated: 12 July 2006
Net Worth: £4,359,768 *Total Assets:* £4,892,816
Registered Office: Carkeel, Saltash, Cornwall, PL12 6PH
Activities: Retail sale of flowers, plants, seeds, fertilizers, pet animals and pet food in specialised stores
Shareholders: Michael Anthony Hooper; Pauline Eleanor Hooper
Officers: Pauline Eleanor Hooper, Secretary; Michael Anthony Hooper [1943] Director/Retail - Garden Centre; Pauline Eleanor Hooper [1942] Director/Retail - Garden Centre

Tamura-Europe Limited
Incorporated: 14 January 1949 *Employees:* 306
Net Worth: £2,925,741 *Total Assets:* £23,449,664
Registered Office: Tamura-Europe Limited, Clarke Avenue, Calne, Wilts, SN11 9BS
Activities: Manufacture of wiring devices
Officers: Jonathan Philip Martin, Secretary; Masahiro Asada [1959] Director [Japanese]; Norihiko Nanjo [1965] Director [Japanese]; Marco Puliti [1965] Operations Director [Italian]; Yuji Yokoyama [1964] Director/Corporate Body [Japanese]

The Tank Museum Limited
Incorporated: 13 November 2003 *Employees:* 69
Net Worth: £22,811,954 *Total Assets:* £23,665,280
Registered Office: The Tank Museum, Bovington Camp, Wareham, Dorset, BH20 6JG
Activities: Museums activities
Officers: Steven Paul Dolan, Secretary; Kathryn Adie [1945] Director/Freelance Broadcaster; William Bahlsen Bannister [1967] Director; Oliver John Louis Barnham [1944] Director; Colonel Guy Hugh John Deacon [1961] Director/Army Officer; Brigadier Ian Jonathan Gibb [1965] Director; Dr Christopher Brynley Hammond [1962] Director/Museum Manager; Jeremy James Richard Pope [1943] Director; Simon Andrew Ridgway [1950] Director; Steven Edward Rowbotham [1957] Director/Vice President GD UK; William Kenneth Suttie [1956] Director/Civil Servant; Alexander Hamilton Walters [1949] Director/Retired; David Webb [1968] Director/Chief Executive; Richard Simon Wigley [1948] Director/Retired; Anthony William Woodhouse [1965] Director

Tapper and Son (Poole) Limited
Incorporated: 7 August 1964 *Employees:* 78
Net Worth: £12,335,174 *Total Assets:* £19,108,772
Registered Office: 32-34 Parkstone Road, Poole, Dorset, BH15 2PG
Activities: Funeral and related activities
Shareholders: Steven John Tapper; Chris Tapper; Paul Christopher Tapper
Officers: Steven John Tapper, Secretary; Peter Charles Crutcher [1937] Funeral Director; Alan Rice [1957] Funeral Director; Christopher John Tapper [1942] Funeral Director; Paul Christopher Tapper [1972] Funeral Director; Steven John Tapper [1969] Funeral Director

Targetgrange (Holdings) Limited
Incorporated: 14 January 2014 *Employees:* 62
Net Worth: £5,256,538 *Total Assets:* £10,285,183
Registered Office: Redland House, 157 Redland Road, Redland, Bristol, BS6 6YE
Activities: Activities of other holding companies n.e.c.
Officers: Dilipkumar Arvindbhai Patel [1952] Director; Kaushik Arvindbhai Patel [1957] Director; Manoj Arvindbhai Patel [1962] Director; Nitinchandra Arvindbhai Patel [1958] Director

Tarka Learning Partnership
Incorporated: 11 July 2011 *Employees:* 114
Previous: Newport Community School Primary Academy
Net Worth: £12,762,976 *Total Assets:* £16,690,458
Registered Office: Newport Community School Primary Academy, Landkey Road, Newport, Barnstaple, Devon, EX32 9BW
Activities: Primary education
Officers: Maureen Cann, Secretary; Joanne Byrne [1974] Director/FE College Department Manager; Graham John Cockell [1957] Director; Andrew Roy Cotton [1965] Director/Chief Executive Officer; Neil Hookway [1967] Director/FE College Department Manager; Christopher Rice [1978] Director/Actuary; Paula Stein [1950] Director/Retired; Clare Tope [1966] Director/Lecturer

Tasman House Developments Limited
Incorporated: 9 December 1997 *Employees:* 2
Net Worth: £1,310,725 *Total Assets:* £3,668,858
Registered Office: 31 Tredenham Road, St Mawes, Truro, Cornwall, TR2 5AW
Activities: Other letting and operating of own or leased real estate
Shareholders: Michael Douglas Croft; Dina Croft
Officers: Dina Croft, Secretary/Chartered Surveyor; Dina Croft [1961] Director/Chartered Surveyor; Michael Douglas Croft [1964] Director/Property Developer

W.J.Tatem Limited
Incorporated: 14 July 1913 *Employees:* 4
Net Worth: £28,105,284 *Total Assets:* £31,217,350
Registered Office: Durnsford Mill House, Mildenhall, Marlborough, Wilts, SN8 2NG
Activities: Activities of open-ended investment companies
Officers: Linda Clare Terry Gibson, Secretary; Linda Clare Terry Gibson [1961] Director/Banker; Martin George Selwyn Gibson [1961] Director/Accountant; John George Richards Homfray [1953] Sales Director; Lancelot Peter Morrish [1956] Director/Farmer

Tauntfield Ltd
Incorporated: 14 December 1998 *Employees:* 8
Net Worth: £4,736,844 *Total Assets:* £6,140,088
Registered Office: Tauntfield, South Road, Taunton, Somerset, TA1 3ND
Activities: Development of building projects
Parent: Tauntfield Holdings Ltd
Officers: Mark Charles Blackwell, Secretary; Paul Stephen Aplin [1957] Director/Chartered Accountant; Mark Charles Blackwell [1964] Director/Accountant; James Edward Holyday [1968] Director/Management Surveyor; Richard David Ayshford Lloyd [1953] Managing Director; Julia Mary Sharp [1938] Director; Elizabeth Miriam Williams [1935] Director/Architect; Dr Robert Stansell Roslin Williams [1969] Director/Conservation Biologist

Taunton Land Limited
Incorporated: 12 October 1976 *Employees:* 7
Net Worth: £20,342,348 *Total Assets:* £37,704,956
Registered Office: Rumwell Hall, Rumwell, Taunton, Somerset, TA4 1EL
Activities: Buying and selling of own real estate
Officers: Ann Christine Jeffery, Secretary; Andrea Jane Biss [1960] Director; Caroline Ann Brain [1961] Director; Ann Christine Jeffery [1934] Director/Property Investor; Simon Frank Crispin Jeffery [1958] Director/Farmer; Elizabeth Kivell [1962] Director; Helen Sloman [1962] Director; John J Sloman [1958] Director/Security Specialist

Taunton School Educational Charity
Incorporated: 1 June 2000 *Employees:* 390
Net Worth: £16,300,800 *Total Assets:* £28,952,500
Registered Office: Taunton School, Staplegrove Road, Taunton, Somerset, TA2 6AD
Activities: Pre-primary education
Officers: Nicola Miller, Secretary; Robert Charles Aldrich [1965] Director/Consultant; Christopher Charles Butters [1965] Director/Chartered Accountant; Philip Michael Cooper [1963] Director/President Division; Mark Julian Hallas [1964] Director/Retired; Timothy George Hayden [1956] Director/Solicitor; David Hugh Hebditch [1960] Director/Chartered Surveyor; Henry Charles Vaughan Keeling [1955] Director/Retired; Dr Ian Kelham [1954] Director/Retired; Richard Ian Kennedy [1957] Director/Chartered Accountant; Reverend Nigel Carl Manges [1960] Director/Minister of Religion; Ian Moncrieff [1955] Director/Military; Keith Roman Moore [1947] Director/Retired; Hilary Quantick [1965] Director/Solicitor; Marilyn Pauline Trask [1952] Director/Retired; Elaine Mary Waymouth [1946] Director/Retired

Taw and Torridge Coaches Limited
Incorporated: 4 March 1976 *Employees:* 86
Net Worth: £1,193,123 *Total Assets:* £5,078,433
Registered Office: Grange Lane Coach Depot, Merton, Okehampton, Devon, EX20 3ED
Activities: Other passenger land transport
Shareholders: Anthony Graham Hunt; Linda Ann Hunt
Officers: Anthony Graham Hunt [1950] Director; Linda Ann Hunt [1953] Director; Mark Anthony Hunt [1978] Director; Christopher Nigel Laughton [1971] Director; Tracey Ann Laughton [1974] Director

Taw Garage (Holdings) Limited
Incorporated: 9 March 2009 *Employees:* 7
Net Worth: £364,658 *Total Assets:* £3,576,908
Registered Office: 50 The Terrace, Torquay, Devon, TQ1 1DD
Activities: Other letting and operating of own or leased real estate
Parent: Percy R Brend & Sons (Holdings) Limited
Officers: Peter Anthony Brend, Secretary; John Edward Brend [1948] Director; Justin John Brend [1972] Director; Mark Richard Brend [1993] Director; Matthew Jonathan Brend [1993] Director; Peter Anthony Brend [1957] Director; Peter Anthony Brend [1977] Director; Richard Percival Brend [1966] Director

Taw Garages Limited
Incorporated: 21 November 1967 *Employees:* 67
Net Worth: £2,945,541 *Total Assets:* £7,804,420
Registered Office: 50 The Terrace, Torquay, Devon, TQ1 1DD
Activities: Sale of new cars and light motor vehicles
Parent: Taw Garage (Holdings) Limited
Officers: Peter Anthony Brend, Secretary; John Edward Brend [1948] Director; Justin John Brend [1972] Director; Mark Richard Brend [1993] Director; Matthew Jonathan Brend [1993] Director; Peter Anthony Brend [1977] Director; Peter Anthony Brend [1957] Director; Richard Percival Brend [1966] Director

Tay Valley Lighting (Leeds) Limited
Incorporated: 2 August 2005
Net Worth Deficit: £13,988,000 *Total Assets:* £71,869,000
Registered Office: Third Floor, Broad Quay House, Princes Street, Bristol, BS1 4DJ
Activities: Other service activities n.e.c.
Parent: TVL (L) Holdings Limited
Officers: Erwan Benoit Fournis [1972] Director/Fund Manager [French]; Angela Louise Roshier [1975] Director; Adam George Waddington [1974] Director

Tay Valley Lighting (Newcastle and North Tyneside) Limited
Incorporated: 1 August 2002
Net Worth Deficit: £13,002,000 *Total Assets:* £23,597,000
Registered Office: Third Floor, Broad Quay House, Princes Street, Bristol, BS1 4DJ
Activities: Non-trading company
Parent: TVL (NNT) Holdings Limited
Officers: Erwan Benoit Fournis [1972] Director/Fund Manager [French]; Angela Louise Roshier [1975] Director; Adam George Waddington [1974] Director

Tay Valley Lighting (Stoke on Trent) Limited
Incorporated: 22 April 2002
Net Worth Deficit: £5,023,000 *Total Assets:* £10,381,000
Registered Office: Third Floor, Broad Quay House, Princes Street, Bristol, BS1 4DJ
Activities: Other service activities n.e.c.
Parent: TVL (SOT) Holdings Limited
Officers: Erwan Benoit Fournis [1972] Director/Fund Manager [French]; Angela Louise Roshier [1975] Director; Adam George Waddington [1974] Director

David Taylor (Garages) Limited
Incorporated: 27 July 1976 *Employees:* 73
Net Worth: £5,953,553 *Total Assets:* £9,258,494
Registered Office: 4 King Square, Bridgwater, Somerset, TA6 3YF
Activities: Sale of used cars and light motor vehicles
Officers: Janine Michelle Sharpless, Secretary; Janine Michelle Sharpless [1966] Director/Accounts Administrator; David Monty Taylor [1945] Director/Garage Operator; Gene Mark Taylor [1965] Director/Motor Dealer; Scott David Taylor [1970] Director/Motor Hire Salesman

Taylor Maxwell Group (2017) Limited
Incorporated: 2 February 2017 *Employees:* 180
Net Worth: £3,392,914 *Total Assets:* £73,515,168
Registered Office: Taylor Maxwell House, The Promenade, Clifton, Bristol, BS8 3NW
Activities: Activities of other holding companies n.e.c.
Officers: Mark Andrew Phillips, Secretary; Anthony John Hammond [1961] Group Director; Mark Andrew Phillips [1961] Group Financial Director; Martin Rudge [1965] Managing Director

Taylor Maxwell Group Limited
Incorporated: 1 March 2006
Net Worth: £9,690,017 *Total Assets:* £16,635,413
Registered Office: Taylor Maxwell House, The Promenade, Clifton Down, Bristol, BS8 3NW
Activities: Activities of other holding companies n.e.c.
Parent: Taylor Maxwell Group (2017) Limited
Officers: Mark Phillips, Secretary; Anthony John Hammond [1961] Director; Mark Andrew Phillips [1961] Director; Martin Alan Rudge [1965] Director

Taylor Maxwell Holdings Limited
Incorporated: 13 May 1985
Net Worth: £5,079,381 *Total Assets:* £13,356,102
Registered Office: Taylor Maxwell House, The Promenade, Clifton, Bristol, BS8 3NW
Activities: Activities of other holding companies n.e.c.
Parent: Taylor Maxwell Group Limited
Officers: Mark Phillips, Secretary; Anthony John Hammond [1961] Director; Mark Phillips [1961] Director; Martin Alan Rudge [1965] Director

Taylor Maxwell Timber Limited
Incorporated: 25 January 1977 *Employees:* 47
Net Worth: £5,153,901 *Total Assets:* £33,848,000
Registered Office: Taylor Maxwell House, The Promenade, Clifton, Bristol, BS8 3NW
Activities: Agents involved in the sale of timber and building materials
Parent: Taylor Maxwell Holdings Limited
Officers: Mark Phillips, Secretary; Neil Bowler [1974] Sales Director; Robert Guilfoyle [1976] Director; Anthony John Hammond [1961] Director; David Antony Huddlestone [1966] Director; Simon Edward Colston Janes [1978] IT Director; Kevin Duncan McKenzie [1968] Director; Alexander Moffat [1980] Sales Director; Mark Phillips [1961] Director; Martin Alan Rudge [1965] Director; Anthony Peter Shelton [1963] Director

Taylor,Maxwell & Co.Limited
Incorporated: 2 January 1950 *Employees:* 107
Net Worth: £5,498,992 *Total Assets:* £32,698,654
Registered Office: Taylor Maxwell House, The Promenade, Clifton, Bristol, BS8 3NW
Activities: Agents involved in the sale of timber and building materials
Parent: Taylor Maxwell Holdings Limited
Officers: Mark Phillips, Secretary; Adam Brian Casey [1980] Director; Deborah Margaret French [1966] National Cladding Director; Robert Guilfoyle [1976] Director; Anthony John Hammond [1961] Director; Simon Edward Colston Janes [1978] IT Director; Mark Phillips [1961] Director; Martin Rudge [1965] Director; Robin Thompson [1976] Business Development Director; Stephen Ronald Williamson [1963] National Sales Director

Taylor-Davis Limited
Incorporated: 1 May 1970 *Employees:* 85
Net Worth: £6,114,051 *Total Assets:* £9,535,660
Registered Office: Moat Works, Moat Road, West Wilts Trading Estate, Westbury, Wilts, BA13 4JF
Activities: Non-specialised wholesale trade
Parent: Atkinson Equipment Limited
Officers: Simon Timothy Pearce, Finance Director; Clive Robert Atkinson [1955] Director; Giles Robert David Atkinson [1983] Director; Gregory Peter Atkinson [1985] Director; Robert Frederick James [1957] Director; Simon Timothy Pearce [1970] Finance Director; David Rawlings [1960] Sales & Marketing Director

TBS Engineering Limited
Incorporated: 28 December 1989 *Employees:* 163
Net Worth: £29,874,036 *Total Assets:* £43,622,624
Registered Office: Tbs Engineering Ltd, Hurricane Road, Brockworth, Gloucester, GL3 4AQ
Activities: Manufacture of other special-purpose machinery n.e.c.
Parent: Mitek Holdings Inc
Officers: Vivienne Francess Empson, Secretary; Vivienne Francess Empson [1963] Financial Director; Lawrence Ernest Gardiner [1949] Director/Chairman; David John Longney [1953] Managing Director; Stephen William Minchin [1951] Production Director; Thomas Valvo [1966] Director/Chief Operating Officer [American]

TDK-Lambda UK Limited
Incorporated: 4 August 1959 *Employees:* 296
Net Worth: £17,567,000 *Total Assets:* £23,372,000
Registered Office: TDK-Lambda, Kingsley Avenue, Ilfracombe, Devon, EX34 8ES
Activities: Manufacture of electronic components
Parent: TDK-Lambda Corporation
Officers: Alan Dykes [1958] Director; Andrew John Ford [1960] Engineering Director; Adam Rawicz Szczerbo [1956] Director/Co-Executive; Philip John Scotcher [1958] Manufacturing Director; Martin Southam [1956] Director/Company Executive; Paul Swan [1971] Director/Accountant; Geoffrey William Wilby [1957] Director/General Manager; Joachim Zichlarz [1964] Director/CEO/CFO [German]

Teach Poole
Incorporated: 11 March 2015 *Employees:* 224
Net Worth: £9,400,476 *Total Assets:* £13,482,272
Registered Office: Canford Heath Infant School, Learoyd Road, Poole, Dorset, BH17 8PJ
Activities: Primary education
Officers: Kellie Groves, Secretary; Valerie Ann Arbon [1958] Director/Headteacher; Sean Frampton [1967] Director; Emma Louise Hall [1977] Director; Anne Blackwood Jolliffe [1944] Director/Centre Manager - Leisure Park; Katie Jayne Martha Lasbury-Carter [1973] Director/Executive Headteacher; Dr Christopher John McCall [1952] Director/GP; Sandra Elizabeth Hazel Moore [1951] Director/Elected Councillor; Justine Louise Riste [1971] Director; Charles Arthur Rowling [1960] Director/Manager; John Matthew White [1970] Director/Headmaster; Richard Roy Yates [1948] Director

Teachers Property Limited
Incorporated: 25 January 2001
Net Worth: £2,321,000 *Total Assets:* £3,938,000
Registered Office: County Gates, Bournemouth, BH1 2NF
Activities: Other professional, scientific and technical activities n.e.c.
Officers: Michael Peter Jones, Secretary; Andrew Mark Parsons [1965] Finance Director; John Trevor Perks [1970] Life Managing Director

Teagle Holdings Limited
Incorporated: 23 February 1943 *Employees:* 138
Net Worth: £12,068,249 *Total Assets:* £19,496,944
Registered Office: Tywarnhayle, Blackwater, Truro, Cornwall, TR4 8HQ
Activities: Manufacture of agricultural and forestry machinery other than tractors
Officers: William David Teagle, Secretary; Geoffrey Osborne [1947] Director; Fred Teagle [1940] Director; Roger Fred Teagle [1967] Director/Sales Manager; Thomas Robinson Teagle [1976] Sales Director; Thomas John Teagle [1950] Director; William David Teagle [1949] Director

Teagle Machinery Limited
Incorporated: 24 July 1996 *Employees:* 138
Net Worth: £439,062 *Total Assets:* £7,563,774
Registered Office: Tywarnhayle, Blackwater, Truro, Cornwall, TR4 8HQ
Activities: Manufacture of agricultural and forestry machinery other than tractors
Parent: Teagle Holdings Ltd
Officers: William David Teagle, Secretary; Philip Carmedy-Pye [1966] Production Director; Geoffrey Osborne [1947] Director; Glen Stephen Parry [1960] Director/Accountant; Colin John Teagle [1969] Project Director; Fred Teagle [1940] Director; Roger Fred Teagle [1967] Director/Engineer; Thomas Robinson Teagle [1976] Director/Sales Manager; Thomas John Teagle [1950] Director; William David Teagle [1949] Director; Duncan James Wilson [1967] Director/Engineer

Team Relocations Limited
Incorporated: 6 January 1992 *Employees:* 78
Net Worth: £11,842,917 *Total Assets:* £18,501,512
Registered Office: Ground Floor, Mulberry Building, Kembrey Park, Swindon, Wilts, SN2 8UY
Activities: Operation of warehousing and storage facilities for water transport activities
Parent: SIRVA Relocation Holdings Limited
Officers: Andrew Phillip Coolidge [1971] Director/Chief Operating Officer [American]; Richard Post [1970] Managing Director [Dutch]

Tecalemit Garage Equipment Company Limited
Incorporated: 1 March 1973 *Employees:* 122
Net Worth: £3,633,178 *Total Assets:* £7,494,157
Registered Office: Eagle Road, Langage Business Park, Plympton, Plymouth, PL7 5JY
Activities: Repair of other equipment
Major Shareholder: Boris Levin
Officers: James Robert Devonport, Secretary; Philip Howard Cledwyn [1956] Director/Sales Manager; James Robert Devonport [1972] Director/Accountant; Dr Boris Levin [1961] Director/Manager [German]; Enrico Zanini [1973] Director/Manager [Italian]

Tecan Limited
Incorporated: 29 October 2008 *Employees:* 101
Net Worth: £3,585,823 *Total Assets:* £5,194,222
Registered Office: Tecan Limited, Tecan Way, Granby Industrial Estate, Weymouth, Dorset, DT4 9TU
Activities: Manufacture of other fabricated metal products n.e.c.
Parent: Veco B.V.
Officers: Neil Jonathan Walker [1967] Director

Techumbre Limited
Incorporated: 12 June 2015 *Employees:* 39
Net Worth: £863,620 *Total Assets:* £7,552,771
Registered Office: Unit 7 Cranmere Court, Lustleigh Close, Exeter, Devon, EX2 8PW
Activities: Construction of commercial buildings
Shareholders: Paul Stuart Wood; Andrew John Bassett
Officers: Andrew John Bassett [1968] Director; Paul Stuart Wood [1972] Director

Teign Housing.
Incorporated: 17 December 2002 *Employees:* 83
Net Worth: £83,936,000 *Total Assets:* £141,036,992
Registered Office: Millwood House, Collett Way, Newton Abbot, Devon, TQ12 4PH
Activities: Renting and operating of Housing Association real estate
Officers: Lisa Jane Maunder, Secretary; Mary Bennell [1957] Director/Consultant; Angela Mary Edwards-Jones [1959] Director/Head of Customer Services; Andrew Jones [1958] Director/Retired; James O'Dwyer [1976] Director/Property Manager; Joanna Louise Reece [1965] Director/Acting Chief Executive; Maureen Janet Robinson [1952] Director/Older Persons Advocate; Alan John Soper [1950] Director

Teignbridge Propellers International Limited
Incorporated: 14 April 2009 *Employees:* 95
Net Worth: £179,519 *Total Assets:* £4,508,896
Registered Office: Great Western Way, Forde Road, Newton Abbot, Devon, TQ12 4AW
Activities: Manufacture of other fabricated metal products n.e.c.
Major Shareholder: David Alexander Duncan
Officers: Ian Mills, Secretary; David Alexander Duncan [1941] Director; Marlene Elsie Duncan [1941] Director; David Alan Hunt [1950] Director; Ian Mills [1957] Director/Accountant; Mark Shaun Phare [1961] Sales Director

Teignmouth Learning Trust
Incorporated: 7 February 2011 *Employees:* 181
Net Worth: £14,679,000 *Total Assets:* £18,594,000
Registered Office: Teignmouth Community School, Exeter Road, Teignmouth, Devon, TQ14 9HZ
Activities: Other education n.e.c.
Officers: Scott Robert Deeming, Secretary; Andrew Paul Flanagan [1963] Director/Chartered Accountant; Patricia Stacey Henchie [1951] Director/Retired Headteacher; Sarah Minty-Dyke [1969] Director/Parent; Mark Philip Moore [1972] Director/Policeman; James O'Connell [1973] Director/Principal; Katy Marie Quinn [1978] Director/Principal; Sarah Sabourin [1972] Director/Foster Carer; Michael John Stean [1943] Director/Retired

Teignmouth Maritime Services Limited
Incorporated: 22 November 2002 *Employees:* 45
Net Worth: £1,900,914 *Total Assets:* £3,650,670
Registered Office: TMS Ltd, Unit 20 Dawlish Business Park, Dawlish, Devon, EX7 0NH
Activities: Construction of other civil engineering projects n.e.c.
Shareholder: Peter Nigel Joseph Stenner
Officers: Giles Hamilton Squirrell [1982] Director; Peter Nigel Joseph Stenner [1962] Director

Tekne Holdings Limited
Incorporated: 13 March 2008 *Employees:* 85
Net Worth: £2,540,130 *Total Assets:* £6,278,470
Registered Office: Midland House, 2 Poole Road, Bournemouth, BH2 5QY
Activities: Activities of head offices
Major Shareholder: Edward John Sevestre
Officers: Edward John Sevestre, Secretary; Philip Mansbridge [1966] Director; Martin Noble [1948] Director/Shopfitter; Edward John Sevestre [1949] Director

Tekne Shopfitting Limited
Incorporated: 2 March 1994 *Employees:* 85
Net Worth: £2,034,867 *Total Assets:* £5,773,207
Registered Office: Midland House, 2 Poole Road, Bournemouth, BH2 5QY
Activities: Other specialised construction activities n.e.c.
Parent: Tekne Holdings Limited
Officers: Susan Emma Hall, Secretary; Marc Philip Allen [1982] Estimating Director; Philip Mansbridge [1966] Director; Peter Marsh [1955] Director/Accountant; Martin Noble [1948] Director/Shopfitter; Edward John Sevestre [1949] Director/Shopfitter; Karl John Sevestre [1984] Director

Teleperformance Contact Limited
Incorporated: 30 October 2013 *Employees:* 11
Net Worth: £3,479,701 *Total Assets:* £21,550,312
Registered Office: Spectrum House, Bond Street, Bristol, BS1 3LG
Activities: Other information service activities n.e.c.
Officers: Lucio Apollonj Ghetti [1967] Director [Italian]; Olivier Claude Jean Rigaudy [1959] Director [French]

Teleperformance Holdings Limited
Incorporated: 12 July 2000
Net Worth: £69,872,000 *Total Assets:* £69,872,000
Registered Office: Spectrum House, Bond Street, Bristol, BS1 3LG
Activities: Other telecommunications activities
Parent: Teleperformance SE
Officers: Michelle Kinsella, Secretary; Olivier Claude Jean Rigaudy [1959] Director [French]; Matthew John Sims [1973] Director; Karl Wise [1974] Director/Chief Financial Officer

Teleperformance Limited
Incorporated: 1 October 1986 *Employees:* 7,381
Net Worth: £55,545,000 *Total Assets:* £97,529,000
Registered Office: Spectrum House, Bond Street, Bristol, BS1 3LG
Activities: Other telecommunications activities
Parent: Teleperformance Holdings Limited
Officers: Michelle Kinsella, Secretary; Matthew John Sims [1973] Director; Karl Wise [1974] Director/Chief Financial Officer

Telesoft Technologies Limited
Incorporated: 8 February 1989 *Employees:* 65
Net Worth: £7,221,000 *Total Assets:* £9,749,000
Registered Office: Observatory House, Stour Park, Blandford Forum, Dorset, DT11 9LQ
Activities: Other telecommunications activities
Major Shareholder: Robert Henry Downham
Officers: Paula Jane Martin, Secretary; Mathew Downham [1981] Director; Robert Henry Downham [1950] Director/Chairman; Paula Jane Martin [1968] Finance Director; Stephen Francis Patton [1966] Sales Director; David John Price [1955] Non-Executive Director Chairman; James Martin Scott [1959] Director; Dr Alison Vincent [1964] Director

H.Tempest Limited
Incorporated: 16 June 1942 *Employees:* 788
Net Worth: £24,896,286 *Total Assets:* £30,672,484
Registered Office: The Colour Laboratory, Lelant, St Ives, Cornwall, TR26 3HU
Activities: Portrait photographic activities
Shareholders: Executors of Rose Tempest; Executors of Rose Tempest; Terence Tempest; Beric Richard John Tempest; Keith Richard Harkness
Officers: Bryan Buck, Secretary/Accountant; Matthew Charles Barton [1970] Director; Bryan Buck [1957] Director/Accountant; Barry Henry Dodge [1942] Director; Beric Richard John Tempest [1939] Director; Robert Tempest [1974] Director; Terence Tempest [1954] Director

Tempest Radford Limited
Incorporated: 20 August 1999
Net Worth: £4,418,841 *Total Assets:* £4,539,337
Registered Office: One The Centre, High Street, Gillingham, Dorset, SP8 4AB
Activities: Agents specialised in the sale of other particular products
Shareholders: Tom Tempest-Radford; Tessa Tempest-Radford
Officers: Tessa Tempest-Radford, Secretary; Celia Tempest-Radford [1996] Director; Saskia Tempest-Radford [1993] Director; Tom Tempest-Radford [1965] Director/Art Consultant

Tempire Investments Limited
Incorporated: 9 October 2014
Net Worth: £17,002,000 *Total Assets:* £63,307,000
Registered Office: c/o Hazlewoods LLP, Staverton Court, Staverton, Cheltenham, Glos, GL51 0UX
Activities: Activities of other holding companies n.e.c.
Parent: Triventura Bidco Limited
Officers: Philip Buergin [1979] Director/Chief Executive Officer [Swiss]; Michael Clare [1971] Director/Chief Operating Officer; Daniel Fehr [1979] Director/Chief Financial Officer [Swiss]; Claude Streit [1979] Director/Chief Financial Officer [Swiss]

Temple Guiting Manor Limited
Incorporated: 24 March 1988 *Employees:* 8
Net Worth Deficit: £910,511 *Total Assets:* £6,525,554
Registered Office: Temple Guiting Manor, Temple Guiting, Cheltenham, Glos, GL54 5RP
Activities: Development of building projects
Major Shareholder: Steven Ross Collins
Officers: Jane Ida Collins, Secretary; Steven Ross Collins [1952] Director

Templegate Electrical Supplies Limited
Incorporated: 13 June 2000 *Employees:* 63
Net Worth: £1,852,890 *Total Assets:* £7,110,244
Registered Office: Unit 5 Templegate Distribution Centre, Mead Street, Bristol, BS3 4RP
Activities: Wholesale of electronic and telecommunications equipment and parts
Parent: Morris McLellan Limited
Officers: Ian Ronald Dyer, Secretary; Ian Ronald Dyer [1962] Finance Director; Colin Sawyer [1964] Director

Tenens (Lakeside) Limited
Incorporated: 7 March 2006 *Employees:* 5
Net Worth: £6,664,985 *Total Assets:* £14,874,743
Registered Office: Tenens House, Kingfisher Business Park, London Road, Thrupp, Stroud, Glos, GL5 2BY
Activities: Other letting and operating of own or leased real estate
Shareholders: Tenens PTC Limited; Peter Ewan Morris
Officers: Benjamin John Morris [1972] Director; Daniel Peter Morris [1977] Director; Peter Ewan Morris [1944] Director

Tenens Associates Limited
Incorporated: 17 March 1983 *Employees:* 4
Net Worth: £12,875,606 *Total Assets:* £12,955,563
Registered Office: Tenens House, Kingfisher Business Park, London Road, Thrupp, Stroud, Glos, GL5 2BY
Activities: Buying and selling of own real estate
Parent: Ewan Associates Limited
Officers: Benjamin John Morris, Secretary; Julian Mark Beecham [1951] Director/Accountant; Benjamin John Morris [1972] Sales & Marketing Director; Daniel Peter Morris [1977] Group Property Director; Peter Ewan Morris [1944] Managing Director

Teoxane UK Limited
Incorporated: 27 October 2005 *Employees:* 19
Previous: Lifestyle Aesthetics Limited
Net Worth: £1,966,430 *Total Assets:* £3,792,919
Registered Office: 54-55 Shrivenham Hundred Business Park, Majors Road, Watchfield, Swindon, Wilts, SN6 8TY
Activities: Wholesale of perfume and cosmetics
Parent: Teoxane SA
Officers: Sandra Fishlock [1967] Director/Product Specialist

Tepe Oral Hygiene Products Limited
Incorporated: 7 July 2011 *Employees:* 19
Net Worth: £4,307,667 *Total Assets:* £6,724,063
Registered Office: Eklund House, 6 Cathedral Avenue, Wells, Somerset, BA5 1FD
Activities: Agents specialised in the sale of other particular products
Major Shareholder: Bertil Eklund
Officers: Joel Magnus Eklund [1980] Director [Swedish]; Hanna Hageberg Hammar [1977] Director/Chief Financial Officer [Swedish]; Helen Richenzhagen [1975] Director [Swedish]

Terramond Limited
Incorporated: 25 November 1996 *Employees:* 4
Net Worth: £2,209,377 *Total Assets:* £7,412,053
Registered Office: West House, Armstrong Way, Yate, Bristol, BS37 5NG
Activities: Development of building projects
Shareholders: Desmond Francis Lynch; Peter Charles Rinn
Officers: Una Marie Pearce-Lynch [1971] Director; Peter Charles Rinn [1950] Director [Irish]

Terraquest Solutions Limited
Incorporated: 31 January 2003 *Employees:* 143
Net Worth: £4,643,578 *Total Assets:* £10,367,009
Registered Office: 1390 Montpellier Court, Gloucester Business Park, Brockworth, Gloucester, GL3 4AH
Activities: Management consultancy activities other than financial management
Parent: Mears Group PLC
Officers: Geoffrey Keal [1969] Director; Andrew Christopher Melville Smith [1972] Director/Chartered Accountant; Ben Robert Westran [1977] Director

Test Development Company Limited (The)
Incorporated: 17 September 1962 *Employees:* 5
Net Worth: £3,519,332 *Total Assets:* £4,713,233
Registered Office: The Estate Office, Middleton, Longparish, Hants, SP11 6PL
Activities: Growing of cereals (except rice), leguminous crops and oil seeds
Shareholders: David William Robert Cecil; Tessa Elizabeth Wills
Officers: Seamus Peter McLaughlin, Secretary; Anna Rose Constance Wills [1990] Director/Student; Charlotte Caroline Wills [1991] Director; Edward Henry Arnold Wills [1994] Director; Gianetta Clare Clemesha Wills [1962] Director; Richard Arnold Wills [1962] Director/Farmer

Tetbury Hospital Trust Limited
Incorporated: 28 January 1992 *Employees:* 27
Net Worth: £3,546,994 *Total Assets:* £3,916,335
Registered Office: Tetbury Hospital Trust Limited, Malmesbury Road, Tetbury, Glos, GL8 8XB
Activities: Hospital activities
Officers: Anthony Walsh, Secretary; Gerard Hugh Barnes [1968] Director; Kathy Callaghan [1974] Director; Lesley Jane Kunzler [1967] Director/Charity Trustee; Jeremy Goulding Lodwick [1961] Director/Investment Manager; Anthony Henry Pooley [1945] Director/Retired; Richard William Corbet Turnor [1956] Director/Solicitor; Doctor Anthony Walsh [1946] Director/Medical Practitioner

Tetra Pak CPS Limited
Incorporated: 10 August 1981 *Employees:* 72
Net Worth: £1,109,000 *Total Assets:* £8,418,000
Registered Office: Coldharbour Business Park, Coldharbour Lane, Sherborne, Dorset, DT9 4JW
Activities: Machining
Officers: Fred Ernst Heinrich Griemsmann [1964] Director [German]; Andrew Jonathan Hyde [1958] Managing Director; Paul Mark Weller [1968] Finance Director

Tetronics (International) Limited
Incorporated: 9 July 1964 *Employees:* 50
Net Worth: £700,400 *Total Assets:* £5,883,885
Registered Office: Marston Gate, Stirling Road, South Marston Park, Swindon, Wilts, SN3 4DE
Activities: Other manufacturing n.e.c.
Shareholders: Parvis Moayedi; Tetronics Holdings Limited
Officers: Dr David Edward Deegan [1973] Technical Director; Gary John Hills [1962] Director/Accountant; Henry Lafferty [1953] Director; Paris Moayedi [1938] Director/Chairman; Graeme Stuart Rumbol [1965] Managing Director

Tewkesbury Marina Limited (The)
Incorporated: 10 October 1969 *Employees:* 11
Net Worth: £1,638,422 *Total Assets:* £3,789,121
Registered Office: The Shipyard, Bredon Road, Tewkesbury, Glos, GL20 5BY
Activities: Other service activities n.e.c.
Shareholders: Leontine Mariette Cottrell; Mark Swinfen Cottrell
Officers: Mark Swinfen Cottrell [1955] Managing Director; The Hon Mrs Fiona Caroline Mary Cottrell [1953] Director

Tewkesbury Park Limited
Incorporated: 15 January 2014 *Employees:* 91
Net Worth Deficit: £3,834,642 *Total Assets:* £9,148,040
Registered Office: Tewkesbury Park, Lincoln Green Lane, Tewkesbury, Glos, GL20 7DN
Activities: Hotels and similar accommodation
Major Shareholder: Christopher Stewart McIntosh
Officers: Christopher Stewart McIntosh [1978] Managing Director; Linda Mary McIntosh [1949] Director/Manager; Claire Frances White [1980] Director/Business Consultant

Tewkesbury School
Incorporated: 9 November 2011 *Employees:* 120
Net Worth: £17,509,580 *Total Assets:* £20,170,454
Registered Office: Tewkesbury School, Ashchurch Road, Tewkesbury, Glos, GL20 8DF
Activities: General secondary education
Officers: Julia Margaret Whybrow, Secretary; Clive Richard Ainsworth [1944] Director/Chartered Engineer; Rachel Brookes [1974] Director/Technical Policy Advisor; Nigel Peter Cottell [1954] Director; Fiona Curry [1992] Director/Marketing Manager [British/Chinese]; Pierre de Carteret [1972] Director; Edward Peter Fair [1976] Director/Teacher; Deborah Hannam [1979] Director/Mature Student; Stephen Hawkins [1952] Director/Site Manager; Dawn Healey [1964] Director/Manager; Gareth Morgan Hill [1959] Director/Retired Civil Servant; Ben Jordan [1987] Director/Manager; Richard John Machray [1977] Director/Project Manager; Susan Maizonnier [1957] Director/Underwriting Manager; Group Captain Clive Andrew Montellier OBE [1962] Director/Defence and Security; Kate Morris [1977] Director; Alison Price [1969] Director/Banking Relationship Manager; Jonathan Richard Quinn [1975] Director; Gary Mark Watson [1966] Director/Headteacher

Texas Instruments (U.K.) Holdings Limited
Incorporated: 12 April 2006
Net Worth: £69,087,152 *Total Assets:* £69,093,568
Registered Office: 1 Northumberland Buildings, Queen Square, Bath, BA1 2JB
Activities: Activities of other holding companies n.e.c.
Parent: National Semiconductor International B.V.
Officers: Peter Francis Tomlinson, Secretary/Solicitor; Dr Weisel Klaus [1965] Director/Legal Counsel [German]; Dr Gerard John McCarthy [1964] Managing Director; Adrienne Helen McGlynn [1964] Finance Director; Andreas Karl Schwaiger [1974] Director Finance & Operations [German]

Texas Instruments (U.K.) Limited
Incorporated: 9 July 1969 *Employees:* 293
Net Worth: £65,776,340 *Total Assets:* £92,082,160
Registered Office: 1 Northumberland Buildings, Queen Square, Bath, BA1 2JB
Activities: Manufacture of electronic components
Parent: Texas Instruments (U.K.) Holdings Limited
Officers: Peter Francis Tomlinson, Secretary; Dr Gerard John McCarthy [1964] Managing Director; Adrienne Helen McGlynn [1964] Finance Director; Andreas Karl Schwaiger [1974] Director Finance & Operations [German]; Dr Klaus Weisel [1965] Director/Legal Counsel [German]

Texas Instruments Limited
Incorporated: 12 November 1956 *Employees:* 39
Net Worth: £30,272,000 *Total Assets:* £67,545,000
Registered Office: 1 Northumberland Buildings, Queen Square, Bath, BA1 2JB
Activities: Manufacture of electronic components
Parent: Texas Instruments (UK) Limited
Officers: Adrienne Helen McGlynn, Secretary; Dr Gerard John McCarthy [1964] Director/Manager Greenock Wafer Fab; Andreas Karl Schwaiger [1974] Director Finance and Operations [German]; Dr Klaus Weisel [1965] EMEA Legal Director [German]

TFIO Properties Limited
Incorporated: 6 March 2002 *Employees:* 3
Net Worth: £8,819,273 *Total Assets:* £11,303,345
Registered Office: 4 King Square, Bridgwater, Somerset, TA6 3YF
Activities: Other letting and operating of own or leased real estate
Shareholder: Peter John Moore
Officers: Sarita Joan Moore, Secretary/Director; Peter John Moore [1944] Director; Sarita Joan Moore [1946] Director

Thakeham Mushrooms Limited
Incorporated: 8 July 2011 *Employees:* 253
Net Worth Deficit: £10,583,000 *Total Assets:* £7,622,000
Registered Office: Stock Lane, Langford, Bristol, BS40 5ES
Activities: Growing of vegetables and melons, roots and tubers
Parent: Monaghan Mushrooms Limited
Officers: Philip David Wilson, Secretary; Paul Thomas Wilson [1977] Director/Chief Operating Officer [Irish]; Philip David Wilson [1975] Divisional Director [Irish]; Ronald Christopher Wilson [1948] Director [Irish]

Thames Valley Eggs (Production) Limited
Incorporated: 25 February 1988 *Employees:* 2
Net Worth: £4,034,544 *Total Assets:* £9,768,591
Registered Office: Whiteoaks Farm, The Old Sidings, Corsham Road, Lacock, Wilts, SN15 2LZ
Activities: Support activities for animal production (other than farm animal boarding)
Parent: Thames Valley Foods
Officers: James David Sheppard, Secretary; Adrian David Gott [1981] Director; James David Sheppard [1963] Director

Thatcher View Development Limited
Incorporated: 4 February 2015
Net Worth Deficit: £40,285 *Total Assets:* £5,525,851
Registered Office: Harbour House, 60 Purewell, Christchurch, Dorset, BH23 1ES
Activities: Buying and selling of own real estate
Parent: Nicolas James Group Limited
Officers: Stuart Andrew Bateman, Secretary; Stuart Andrew Bateman [1976] Director; David Francis Robbins [1967] Director/Accountant

Thatchers (Myrtle Farm) Limited
Incorporated: 4 April 2013 *Employees:* 219
Net Worth: £36,439,740 *Total Assets:* £68,002,952
Registered Office: Myrtle Farm, Station Road, Sandford, Winscombe, Somerset, BS25 5RA
Activities: Activities of head offices
Shareholder: Martin Thatcher
Officers: Robert Graham Davis [1947] Director; Ann Margaret Thatcher [1944] Director; John Thatcher [1943] Director; Martin Thatcher [1968] Director

Thatchers Cider Company Limited
Incorporated: 13 June 1955 *Employees:* 166
Net Worth: £16,292,184 *Total Assets:* £52,640,336
Registered Office: Myrtle Farm, Station Road, Sandford, Winscombe, Avon, BS25 5RA
Activities: Manufacture of cider and other fruit wines
Officers: Robert Graham Davis [1947] Director; Neil Day [1973] Director/Engineer; Lord Digby Jones [1955] Director; Graham Andrew Keating [1964] Director; Christopher Milton [1963] Sales Director; Robert Charles Sandall [1968] Director; Martin Thatcher [1968] Director/Cider Manufacturer; Rupert Geoffrey Ryland Thompson [1958] Director

Thatchers Holdings Limited
Incorporated: 6 August 2008 *Employees:* 161
Net Worth: £23,626,244 *Total Assets:* £66,821,984
Registered Office: Myrtle Farm, Station Road, Sandford, Winscombe, Somerset, BS25 5RA
Activities: Activities of head offices
Shareholder: Martin Thatcher
Officers: Ann Margaret Thatcher, Secretary; Robert Graham Davis [1947] Director; Ann Margaret Thatcher [1944] Director; John Thatcher [1943] Director; Martin Thatcher [1968] Managing Director

Theatre Royal (Plymouth) Limited
Incorporated: 11 May 1981 *Employees:* 165
Net Worth: £15,984,000 *Total Assets:* £22,427,000
Registered Office: Theatre Royal, Royal Parade, Plymouth, PL1 2TR
Activities: Performing arts
Officers: Lewis Eynon, Secretary; Nicholas Brian Buckland [1951] Director/Chair, University of Plymouth; Francis Desmond Drake [1952] Director/Retired Accountant; Sarah Louise Fysh [1978] Director/Head of Content, The Met Office; Shona Elizabeth Godefroy [1970] Director/Accountant; Bronwen Lynne Lacey [1955] Director/Retired; James Thomas Pidgeon [1987] Director; Paul Lewis Woods [1949] Director/Solicitor

Theatre Royal Bath Limited (The)
Incorporated: 22 February 1979 *Employees:* 67
Net Worth: £6,093,000 *Total Assets:* £8,731,000
Registered Office: The Theatre Royal, Sawclose, Bath, BA1 1ET
Activities: Performing arts
Officers: Gabrielle Mary Akbar, Secretary; Anthony Keith Clarke [1944] Director/Registered Medical Practitioner; Dominic Jerome Eaton [1959] Director/Architect; Cosmo Joseph Fry [1957] Director; Nicholas Peter Hall [1962] Director/Chartered Accountant; Paul Bentley Heal [1950] Director/Chartered Accountant; Melanie Jean Macer [1962] Director/University Research Fellow; Victoria Ann Louise Moffatt [1973] Director; John Richard Monohan [1946] Director/Chartered Surveyor; Charlotte Lucy Walker [1972] Director/Barrister

Theobald Film Productions LLP
Incorporated: 16 June 2004
Net Worth: £63,150,000 *Total Assets:* £66,004,000
Registered Office: The Quadrangle, The Promenade, Cheltenham, Glos, GL50 1PX

Thermae Development Company Limited
Incorporated: 13 October 1997 *Employees:* 221
Net Worth: £2,467,180 *Total Assets:* £7,181,819
Registered Office: Wessex Water, Claverton Down Road, Claverton Down, Bath, BA2 7WW
Activities: Fitness facilities
Officers: Ruth Esme Jefferson, Secretary; Andrew Jordan [1961] Director/Executive Vice President - YTL Hotels and Properties; Pearly Poussier [1963] Finance Director [Malaysian]; Colin Frank Skellett [1945] Director; Seok Kah Yeoh [1965] Director/Business Person [Malaysian]

Thermographic Measurements Limited
Incorporated: 27 February 1974 *Employees:* 48
Net Worth: £11,751,570 *Total Assets:* £14,923,438
Registered Office: New Factory Unit, Reme Drive, Heathpark Industrial Estate, Honiton, Devon, EX14 1SE
Activities: Manufacture of other chemical products n.e.c.
Parent: Altonover Enterprises Limited
Officers: Russell Justin Booth, Secretary; Diana Mary Booth [1940] Director; Russell Justin Booth [1969] Director

Thirsty Work Limited
Incorporated: 14 January 2010 *Employees:* 45
Net Worth: £904,048 *Total Assets:* £8,144,996
Registered Office: c/o Francis Clark LLP, North Quay House, Sutton Harbour, Plymouth, PL4 0RA
Activities: Wholesale of fruit and vegetable juices, mineral water and soft drinks
Shareholders: William John Haviland Hiley; Andrew Brian Vickery
Officers: Matthew Stimpson [1981] Director; Andrew Brian Vickery [1964] Managing Director

J C Thomas & Sons Limited
Incorporated: 25 June 2002 *Employees:* 19
Net Worth: £9,794,561 *Total Assets:* £11,209,512
Registered Office: 16 Queen Square, Bristol, BS1 4NT
Activities: Remediation activities and other waste management services
Shareholders: Andrew Mark Thomas; Martin Peter Thomas; Joseph Charles Thomas
Officers: Martin Peter Thomas, Secretary; Andrew Mark Thomas [1986] Director/Scrap Metal Recycler; Joseph Charles Thomas [1974] Director/Scrap Metal Recycler; Martin Peter Thomas [1975] Director/Scrap Metal Recycler

B. Thompson & Sons (Transport) Limited
Incorporated: 4 April 1966 *Employees:* 65
Net Worth: £3,834,807 *Total Assets:* £4,242,091
Registered Office: Sigma House, Oak View Close, Edginswell Park, Torquay, Devon, TQ2 7FF
Activities: Freight transport by road
Major Shareholder: Alan Bernard Thompson
Officers: Alan Bernard Thompson [1945] Director/Transport Contractor; Carol Mary Thompson [1958] Director; Ian Norman Thompson [1992] Director; Ryan Benjamin Thompson [1990] Director

Thompson Acquisitions Limited
Incorporated: 18 April 2006
Net Worth: £3,262,589 *Total Assets:* £6,103,689
Registered Office: 14 Beaufort East, Bath, BA1 6QD
Activities: Retail sale of books in specialised stores
Major Shareholder: Mark Thompson
Officers: Mark Thompson [1968] Director

Thompson Valves Limited
Incorporated: 18 February 1993 *Employees:* 162
Net Worth: £6,668,000 *Total Assets:* £12,828,000
Registered Office: 17 Balena Close, Creekmoor, Poole, Dorset, BH17 7EF
Activities: Manufacture of taps and valves
Parent: Truflo International Ltd
Officers: Gino Bancalari [1962] Plant Director; Martin Geobey [1968] Managing Director - UK and Ireland Sales

D.C. Thomson Developments Limited
Incorporated: 31 March 2014
Net Worth: £9,780,008 *Total Assets:* £17,991,504
Registered Office: One Redcliff Street, Bristol, BS1 6TP
Activities: Activities of other holding companies n.e.c.
Parent: D.C. Thomson Consumer Products Limited
Officers: Gavin Stewart Jones, Secretary; Gavin Stewart Jones [1970] Financial Director; Paul Taylor [1970] Director

Thoranmart Limited
Incorporated: 6 May 1986 *Employees:* 197
Net Worth: £930,000 *Total Assets:* £16,303,000
Registered Office: Swindon Motor Park, Dorcan Way, Swindon, Wilts, SN3 3RA
Activities: Sale of new cars and light motor vehicles
Parent: Cambria Automobiles Acquisitions Ltd
Officers: James Anthony Mullins, Secretary/Director; Timothy Alex Duckers [1973] Director; Mark Jonathan James Lavery [1965] Director; James Anthony Mullins [1978] Director

Thorne Holdings Limited
Incorporated: 17 March 1987 *Employees:* 2
Net Worth: £2,860,056 *Total Assets:* £3,824,477
Registered Office: 1 Wine Street, Bristol, BS1 2BB
Activities: Activities of head offices
Shareholders: Andrew John Thorne; David Thorne; Sheila Kathleen Thorne
Officers: David Thorne, Secretary; Andrew John Thorne [1963] Director; David Thorne [1966] Director; Sheila Kathleen Thorne [1931] Director

Thornleigh Camphill Communities Limited
Incorporated: 29 June 1951 *Employees:* 186
Previous: Camphill Communities Thornbury Limited
Net Worth: £3,680,558 *Total Assets:* £4,633,978
Registered Office: Thornbury Park, Thornbury, Bristol, BS35 1HP
Activities: Other education n.e.c.
Officers: Ian Stanley Bailey [1950] Director/Social Care Practitioner; Sarah Anne Compson [1983] Director/Project Manager; Paul James Glover [1949] Director/Retired Property Consultant; Dr William Anthony Nowlan [1955] Director/Health Information Consultant; Rosemary Elizabeth Phillpot [1947] Director/Retired Camphill Co Worker Occupational; Graham Howard Snell [1957] Director/Teaching Fellow; William John Southcombe [1950] Director/Self Employed - Social Care Consultant

Thornton Shipbrokers Limited
Incorporated: 12 July 1974
Net Worth: £2,474,497 *Total Assets:* £3,621,647
Registered Office: The Old Temperance House, 34-36 Fore Street, Bovey Tracey, Devon, TQ13 9AE
Activities: Operation of warehousing and storage facilities for water transport activities
Shareholders: David Stewart Southcott; William Gordon Southcott
Officers: David Stewart Southcott, Secretary; Gordon John Southcott [1943] Director

Thorpe Park Operations Limited
Incorporated: 26 February 2007
Net Worth: £8,052,000 *Total Assets:* £8,501,000
Registered Office: Link House, 25 West Street, Poole, Dorset, BH15 1LD
Activities: Activities of amusement parks and theme parks
Parent: Charcoal Midco 1 Limited
Officers: Fiona Jane Rose, Secretary; Matthew Paul Jowett [1967] Director/General Counsel and Company Secretary; Fiona Jane Rose [1964] Director/Assistant Group Company Secretary

Threadneedles Hotel Limited
Incorporated: 28 November 2016
Net Worth Deficit: £41,496 *Total Assets:* £36,785,604
Registered Office: Wessex Water, Operations Centre, Claverton Down Road, Claverton Down, Bath, BA2 7WW
Activities: Activities of other holding companies n.e.c.
Officers: Ruth Esme Jefferson, Secretary; Andrew Jordan [1961] Director/Executive Vice President - YTL Hotels and Properties; Pearly Poussier [1963] Finance Director [Malaysian]; Colin Frank Skellett [1945] Director

Three Counties Feeds Limited
Incorporated: 11 October 2006 *Employees:* 22
Net Worth: £1,841,000 *Total Assets:* £5,477,000
Registered Office: Exmoor House, Lime Way, Pathfields Business Park, South Molton, Devon, EX36 3LH
Activities: Wholesale of agricultural machinery, equipment and supplies
Parent: Mole Valley Farmers Ltd
Officers: Bruce Korican, Secretary; Peter James Delbridge [1961] Director/Farmer; Andrew Jackson [1957] Director

The Three Rivers Partnership, Dorset
Incorporated: 17 June 2003 *Employees:* 39
Net Worth: £4,283,138 *Total Assets:* £4,709,615
Registered Office: Riversmeet, Hardings Lane, Gillingham, Dorset, SP8 4HX
Activities: Activities of other membership organisations n.e.c.
Officers: Timothy Clive Lewis Drake, Secretary; Paul James Barber [1974] Sales Director; Colonel Timothy Clive Lewis Drake [1946] Director; Hugh Mark Hebditch [1944] Director/Teacher; Robert Howard Messer [1949] Director/Retired Schoolteacher; Barry Von Clemens [1965] Director/Consultant; Philip Peter Wilson [1953] Director/Retired

Three Ways School
Incorporated: 15 April 2013 *Employees:* 189
Net Worth: £6,776,052 *Total Assets:* £9,635,480
Registered Office: Three Ways School, 180 Frome Road, Bath, BA2 5RF
Activities: Other education n.e.c.
Officers: Colin Ball [1961] Director/Senior Teaching Assistant; Graham Philip Cottle [1955] Director/Property Developer; Charles Daniel Gerrish [1950] Director/Bank Manager (Retired); Katherine Frances Hall [1966] Director/Councillor; Rodney Augustus Sidney Hodgman [1944] Director/Retired; Gillian Jordan [1964] Director/Housewife; Thomas Kavanagh [1986] Director/Teacher; Roger Donald McSweeney [1948] Director/Retired; Jenni Marcia Radford [1968] Director/Housewife; Michael Harrison Roberts [1963] Director/Business Consultant; Sarah Helen Service [1948] Director/Retired; Josephine Lois Stoaling [1977] Director/Headteacher; Debbie Lee Wells [1970] Director/Teacher [Cypriot]

Thrings LLP
Incorporated: 20 January 2009 *Employees:* 323
Net Worth: £5,090,713 *Total Assets:* £16,353,021
Registered Office: 6 Drakes Meadow, Penny Lane, Swindon, Wilts, SN3 3LL
Officers: Mark John Cullingford [1969] Member; John Hwyel Davies [1971] Member; Simon Paul Holdsworth [1968] Member; Kerrie Jane Hunt [1964] Member; Benedick Matthew Harrison Jones [1973] Member; Fiona Patricia Kellow [1968] Member; David Richard Patterson [1965] Member; Jonathan David Payne [1965] Member; Warren Francis Reid [1965] Member; Duncan Sigournay [1967] Member; Michael John Tatters [1969] Member; Neil Richard Barbour [1962] LLP Member; Rachel Denise Brooks [1969] LLP Member; Mary Louise Chant [1962] LLP Member; Richard Mark Charter [1960] LLP Member; Michael Francis Chilton [1963] LLP Member; Ramona Kate Derbyshire [1978] LLP Member; Michel William Dunmore [1971] LLP Member; Graeme Colin James Fearon [1970] LLP Member; Richard John Fidler [1958] LLP Member; Alan John Goulding [1948] LLP Member; Alastair Mark Govier [1968] LLP Member; Nicholas Aaron Jeremy Lee [1984] LLP Member; Karen Anne Lintern [1963] LLP Member; Alex Lloyd Madden [1978] LLP Member; Kevin McGuinness [1965] LLP Member; David Reginald Mears [1949] LLP Member; Jeremy Jon Nixon [1970] LLP Member; Fionnuala Mary Nolan [1966] LLP Member; Jane Oakland [1954] LLP Member; Sally Georgina Pike [1970] LLP Member; Alexander James Pyatt [1975] LLP Member; Russell Lacey Reeves [1979] LLP Member; Robert Philip Sear [1952] LLP Member; Rosalind Ann Sopel [1956] LLP Member; Michael Jonathan Tomlin [1979] LLP Member; Kate Victoria Westbrook [1978] LLP Member

Thrive Renewables (Boardinghouse) Limited
Incorporated: 20 December 2013
Previous: Triodos Renewables (Boardinghouse) Limited
Net Worth: £4,923,223 *Total Assets:* £4,923,223
Registered Office: c/o Thrive Renewables PLC, Deanery Road, Bristol, BS1 5AS
Activities: Production of electricity
Parent: Thrive Renewables PLC
Officers: Matthew Thomas Clayton [1975] Director; Katrina Lorraine Cross [1972] Director; Monika Lidia Paplaczyk [1979] Director/Investment Manager [Polish]

Thrive Renewables (Caton Moor) Limited
Incorporated: 22 May 1991
Previous: Triodos Renewables (Caton Moor) Limited
Net Worth: £1,957,941 *Total Assets:* £10,290,005
Registered Office: c/o Thrive Renewables PLC, Deanery Road, Bristol, BS1 5AS
Activities: Production of electricity
Parent: Brunel Wind Limited
Officers: Matthew Thomas Clayton [1975] Director/Investment Manager; Katrina Lorraine Cross [1972] Director/Accountant; Monika Lidia Paplaczyk [1979] Director/Investment Manager [Polish]

Thrive Renewables (Eye) Limited
Incorporated: 10 February 2009
Previous: Triodos Renewables (Eye) Limited
Net Worth: £515,004 *Total Assets:* £6,658,931
Registered Office: c/o Thrive Renewables PLC, Deanery Road, Bristol, BS1 5AS
Activities: Production of electricity
Parent: Thrive Renewables PLC
Officers: Matthew Thomas Clayton [1975] Director/Investment Manager; Katrina Lorraine Cross [1972] Director/Accountant; Monika Lidia Paplaczyk [1979] Director/Investment Manager [Polish]

Thrive Renewables (Severn) Limited
Incorporated: 25 June 2012
Previous: Triodos Renewables (Severn) Limited
Net Worth Deficit: £504,103 *Total Assets:* £13,573,119
Registered Office: c/o Thrive Renewables PLC, Deanery Road, Bristol, BS1 5AS
Activities: Production of electricity
Parent: Thrive Renewables (Bristol) Limited
Officers: Matthew Thomas Clayton [1975] Director; Katrina Lorraine Cross [1972] Director/Accountant; Monika Lidia Paplaczyk [1979] Director/Investment Manager [Polish]

Thrive Renewables PLC
Incorporated: 10 October 1994 *Employees:* 8
Previous: Triodos Renewables PLC
Net Worth: £35,168,140 *Total Assets:* £109,126,456
Registered Office: Deanery Road, Bristol, BS1 5AS
Activities: Financial intermediation not elsewhere classified
Officers: Katrina Lorraine Cross, Secretary; Matthew Thomas Clayton [1975] Director; Katrina Lorraine Cross [1972] Director/Accountant; Katie Louise Gordon [1972] Director/Analyst; Charles James Middleton [1957] Director; Colin Andrew Morgan [1965] Director/Engineer; Simon John Le Grys Roberts [1963] Director/Charity Chief Executive; Tania Louise Songini [1969] Finance Director [British/Italian]; Peter Nicholas Weston [1969] Director/Investment Manager

Thrubwell Properties Limited
Incorporated: 7 November 2001
Net Worth: £4,288,787 *Total Assets:* £6,959,070
Registered Office: Bennetts Solicitors, Barley Wood Stables, Long Lane, Wrington, Bristol, BS40 5SA
Activities: Buying and selling of own real estate
Shareholders: Robert Hoy; Sarah Jane Hoy
Officers: Sarah Jane Hoy, Secretary/Shop Sales; Robert Hoy [1962] Director; Sarah Jane Hoy [1965] Director/Shop Sales

Thurlestone Court Limited
Incorporated: 17 January 2001 *Employees:* 90
Net Worth: £2,652,582 *Total Assets:* £3,556,425
Registered Office: Head Office, Willow House, Hillside, South Brent, Devon, TQ10 9AY
Activities: Residential care activities for the elderly and disabled
Major Shareholder: Neil Simon Harvey
Officers: Brigitte Caroline Harvey, Secretary; Brigitte Caroline Harvey [1970] Director/Residential Care Homes; Neil Simon Harvey [1963] Director

Thurlestone Estates,Limited
Incorporated: 2 January 1933 *Employees:* 131
Net Worth: £11,047,198 *Total Assets:* £16,573,834
Registered Office: Thurlestone Hotel, Thurlestone, Kingsbridge, Devon, TQ7 3NN
Activities: Hotels and similar accommodation
Officers: Christian David Thomas, Secretary; Cedric Marsden Clapp [1946] Director/Consultant; David William Peter Grose [1945] Director/Hotel Proprietor; Graham Richard Ernest Grose [1951] Director/Hotel Proprietor; Matthew David Cuthbert Grose [1972] Director/Hotel Management; Simon Edward Martyn Grose [1959] Director [South African]; Lucy Caroline Sarah Harrison [1964] Director/Interior Designer; Timothy Andrew Hassell [1970] Director; Victoria Hill [1970] Director/Lawyer

Tickenham Court Farm Co.Limited
Incorporated: 8 February 1946 *Employees:* 7
Net Worth: £5,385,041 *Total Assets:* £6,647,837
Registered Office: Court Farm, Tickenham, Clevedon, Somerset, BS21 6SB
Activities: Growing of vegetables and melons, roots and tubers
Officers: Amelia Rosemary Taylor, Secretary; Florence Amelia Crispi [1977] Director/Catering; Thomas William Forrester [1975] Director/Fine Art Valuer; Lawrence Stewart Plant [1945] Director/Farmer; Zoe Erica Plant [1995] Director; Amelia Rosemary Taylor [1980] Director/Sales Person

Tiger Communications (Holdings) Limited
Incorporated: 14 July 2014 *Employees:* 41
Net Worth: £3,046,879 *Total Assets:* £5,370,367
Registered Office: 77-79 Christchurch Road, Ringwood, Hants, BH24 1DH
Activities: Other telecommunications activities
Parent: Tiger Communications Holdings No.2 Ltd
Officers: Stephen Reid McCallum, Secretary; Stephen Reid McCallum [1963] Director

Tiger Communications PLC
Incorporated: 18 May 1979 *Employees:* 39
Net Worth: £2,944,277 *Total Assets:* £4,148,382
Registered Office: Crescent House, 77-79 Christchurch Road, Ringwood, Hants, BH24 1DH
Activities: Other telecommunications activities
Shareholder: Stephen Reid McCallum
Officers: Stephen Reid McCallum, Secretary; Stephen Reid McCallum [1963] Development Director; Ben Nicklen [1980] Managing Director; John Andrew Shannon [1966] Commercial Director; Phillip Paul Smith [1968] Development Director

Tildenet Ltd
Incorporated: 1 November 1976 *Employees:* 40
Net Worth: £2,574,581 *Total Assets:* £3,968,329
Registered Office: Hartcliffe Way, Bristol, BS3 5RJ
Activities: Manufacture of cordage, rope, twine and netting
Shareholders: Andrew James Downey; Bernard Thomas Joseph Downey
Officers: Philip Eric James, Finance Director; Andrew James Downey [1971] Director; Bernard Thomas Joseph Downey [1945] Managing Director; Doctor Rebecca Juliette Brodie Gage [1968] Director/Doctor; Philip Eric James [1955] Finance Director; Paul Richard Morgan [1977] Director

Tileflair Group Limited
Incorporated: 7 December 2006 *Employees:* 86
Net Worth: £2,719,211 *Total Assets:* £9,292,279
Registered Office: Tileflair Ltd, Highwood Lane, Cribbs Causeway, Bristol, BS34 5TQ
Activities: Non-trading company
Officers: Lesley Roslyn Broadhurst, Secretary; Lesley Roslyn Broadhurst [1953] Director & Company Secretary; Peter James Broadhurst [1951] Managing Director; David Anthony Brown [1964] Director; Matthew Thomas Luckman Johnson [1963] Director

Tileflair Limited
Incorporated: 25 April 1972 *Employees:* 86
Net Worth: £7,594,964 *Total Assets:* £11,480,708
Registered Office: Highwood Lane, Cribbs Causeway, Bristol, BS34 5TQ
Activities: Non-specialised wholesale trade
Parent: Tileflair Tiles Ltd
Officers: Lesley Roslyn Broadhurst, Secretary; Lesley Roslyn Broadhurst [1953] Director & Company Secretary/Solicitor; Peter James Broadhurst [1951] Chairman & Director; David Anthony Brown [1964] Director/Sales; Matthew Thomas Luckman Johnson [1963] Managing Director

Tilstone Basingstoke Limited
Incorporated: 6 December 2016
Net Worth: £3,646,538 *Total Assets:* £11,576,285
Registered Office: Beaufort House, 51 New North Road, Exeter, EX4 4EP
Activities: Other letting and operating of own or leased real estate
Parent: Tilstone Holdings Limited
Officers: Andrew Bird [1962] Director; Neil William Kirton [1963] Director; Aimee Joan Generaldine Pitman [1966] Director/Consultant

Tilstone Glasgow Limited
Incorporated: 3 October 2016
Net Worth: £3,496,072 *Total Assets:* £15,035,623
Registered Office: Beaufort House, 51 New North Road, Exeter, EX4 4EP
Activities: Activities of real estate investment trusts
Parent: Tilstone Holdings Limited
Officers: Andrew Charles Bird [1962] Director; Neil William Kirton [1963] Director; Aimee Joan Generaldine Pitman [1966] Director/Consultant

Tilstone Holdings Limited
Incorporated: 10 March 2016
Net Worth: £16,697,184 *Total Assets:* £260,127,888
Registered Office: Beaufort House, 51 New North Road, Exeter, EX4 4EP
Activities: Other letting and operating of own or leased real estate
Parent: Warehouse REIT PLC
Officers: Andrew Charles Bird [1962] Director; Neil William Kirton [1963] Director; Aimee Joan Generaldine Pitman [1966] Director/Consultant

Tilstone Industrial Limited
Incorporated: 28 June 2013
Net Worth: £19,407,792 *Total Assets:* £262,218,768
Registered Office: Beaufort House, 51 New North Road, Exeter, EX4 4EP
Activities: Non-trading company
Parent: Tilstone Holdings Limited
Officers: Andrew Charles Bird [1962] Director; Neil William Kirton [1963] Director; Aimee Joan Generaldine Pitman [1966] Director/Consultant

Tilstone Retail Limited
Incorporated: 8 January 2016
Net Worth: £4,545,749 *Total Assets:* £11,769,810
Registered Office: Beaufort House, 51 New North Road, Exeter, EX4 4EP
Activities: Management of real estate on a fee or contract basis
Parent: Tilestone Holdings Limited
Officers: Andrew Charles Bird [1962] Director/Property; Neil William Kirton [1963] Director; Aimee Joan Generaldine Pitman [1966] Director/Consultant

Tilstone Trade Limited
Incorporated: 9 March 2016
Net Worth: £4,741,985 *Total Assets:* £5,505,729
Registered Office: Beaufort House, 51 New North Road, Exeter, EX4 4EP
Activities: Other letting and operating of own or leased real estate
Parent: Tilstone Holdings Limited
Officers: Andrew Charles Bird [1962] Director; Neil William Kirton [1963] Director; Aimee Joan Generaldine Pitman [1966] Director/Consultant

Tilstone Warehouse Holdco Limited
Incorporated: 3 October 2016 *Employees:* 4
Net Worth: £4,227,915 *Total Assets:* £68,395,800
Registered Office: Beaufort House, 51 New North Road, Exeter, EX4 4EP
Activities: Activities of real estate investment trusts
Parent: Warehouse REIT PLC
Officers: Andrew Charles Bird [1962] Director; Neil William Kirton [1963] Director; Aimee Joan Generaldine Pitman [1966] Director/Consultant

Timehaste Limited
Incorporated: 13 March 1990 *Employees:* 869
Net Worth: £5,411,193 *Total Assets:* £7,936,537
Registered Office: c/o J & K Aquatics Limited, Market Way, North Petherton, Bridgwater, Somerset, TA6 6DF
Activities: Activities of other holding companies n.e.c.
Shareholders: Judith James; Paul James
Officers: Paul James, Secretary; Judith Rosina James [1959] Director; Paul James [1956] Director

R. Tincknell & Son Limited
Incorporated: 22 April 1948 *Employees:* 41
Net Worth: £13,443,638 *Total Assets:* £28,595,040
Registered Office: Cathedral View Offices, 19 Wookey Hole Road, Wells, Somerset, BA5 2BT
Activities: Other retail sale of new goods in specialised stores (not commercial art galleries and opticians)
Shareholders: Philip Frank Tincknell; Robert James Tincknell; Diana Jane Tincknell
Officers: Philip Frank Tincknell, Secretary; Diana Jane Tincknell [1980] Director; Philip Frank Tincknell [1952] Director; Robert James Tincknell [1978] Director

Tincknell Fuels Limited
Incorporated: 15 November 1972 *Employees:* 70
Net Worth: £4,440,600 *Total Assets:* £9,306,067
Registered Office: Cathedral View Offices, 19 Wookey Hole Road, Wells, Somerset, BA5 2BT
Activities: Wholesale of other fuels and related products
Parent: Tincknell Fuels (Holdings) Limited
Officers: Philip Frank Tincknell, Secretary; Robert Frederic Ormond [1957] Managing Director; Diana Jane Tincknell [1980] Director; Jane Mary Tincknell [1955] Director; Philip Frank Tincknell [1952] Director; Robert James Tincknell [1978] Joint Managing Director

Tintometer,Limited (The)
Incorporated: 23 August 1895 *Employees:* 137
Net Worth: £6,837,223 *Total Assets:* £13,906,210
Registered Office: Lovibond House, Sun Rise Way, Amesbury, Wilts, SP4 7GR
Activities: Manufacture of other inorganic basic chemicals
Officers: Sally Page, Secretary; Paul Christopher Banning [1964] Director/Chartered Accountant; Robert Ernest Lambourne [1952] Director/Chartered Accountant; Marke Reid [1961] Director/Sales Manager; Cay Peter Voss [1942] Director [German]; Maja Carola Voss [1973] Managing Director [German]

Tithegrove Holdings Limited
Incorporated: 7 April 2015 *Employees:* 504
Net Worth: £1,440,599 *Total Assets:* £30,958,760
Registered Office: Marshgate House, Marshgate, Swindon, Wilts, SN1 2PA
Activities: Construction of domestic buildings
Shareholders: Nicholas Reilly; David Bell
Officers: David Bell [1951] Director/Chartered Accountant; Steven John Horton [1964] Director; Stephen Rodwell Rayson [1948] Director; Nicholas Reilly [1972] Director; Dino Torchia [1967] Commercial Director; Gregory Jordan Tucker [1978] Director; Christopher Raymond Waddell [1961] Construction Director; Paul Horace Walton [1947] Director

Tithegrove Limited
Incorporated: 23 March 1984 *Employees:* 495
Net Worth: £2,684,219 *Total Assets:* £21,253,848
Registered Office: Marshgate House, Marshgate, Swindon, Wilts, SN1 2PA
Activities: Construction of domestic buildings
Parent: Tithegrove Holdings Ltd
Officers: David Bell [1951] Director/Chartered Accountant; Nicholas Reilly [1972] Director; Dino Torchia [1967] Commercial Director; Gregory Jordan Tucker [1978] Director; Christopher Raymond Waddell [1961] Construction Director

M R Tizzard Limited
Incorporated: 6 May 2008 *Employees:* 8
Net Worth: £6,738,989 *Total Assets:* £17,462,484
Registered Office: North Wootton Farm, North Wootton, Sherborne, Dorset, DT9 5JW
Activities: Raising of dairy cattle
Shareholders: Michael Tizzard; Susan Tizzard
Officers: Susan Tizzard, Secretary/Farmer; Michael Tizzard [1963] Director/Farmer; Susan Tizzard [1961] Director/Farmer

TJ International Limited
Incorporated: 27 August 2004 *Employees:* 137
Net Worth: £441,244 *Total Assets:* £7,234,084
Registered Office: c/o TJ International Ltd, Trecerus Industrial Estate, Padstow, Cornwall, PL28 8RW
Activities: Printing n.e.c.
Parent: TJ International (Holdings) Limited
Officers: Andrew James Adams [1970] Finance Director; Angus Clark [1954] Director/Chief Executive; Andrew John Vosper [1959] Commercial Director; Andrew Paul Watts [1966] Director

TJW Precision Engineering Limited
Incorporated: 29 November 1983 *Employees:* 63
Net Worth: £1,443,447 *Total Assets:* £3,923,749
Registered Office: Unit A1, Draycott Business Park, Cam, Dursley, Glos, GL11 5DQ
Activities: Treatment and coating of metals
Shareholder: Helena Susan Hayes
Officers: Andrea Louise O'Cleary, Secretary; Gary Cowle [1958] Director; Shaun Cowle [1970] Director; Helena Susan Hayes [1957] Director; Robert John Hayes [1983] Director; Stephen Hedley Hayes [1955] Director

TKC Sales Limited
Incorporated: 30 September 1999 *Employees:* 28
Net Worth: £2,237,822 *Total Assets:* £4,805,320
Registered Office: The Old Spitfire Hanger, The Strand, Steeple Ashton, Trowbridge, Wilts, BA14 6EP
Activities: Non-specialised wholesale trade
Major Shareholder: Matthew Winston Thomas Woodruffe
Officers: Matthew Winston Thomas Woodruffe, Secretary/Director; Paul Wearmouth [1963] Director/Accountant; Matthew Winston Thomas Woodruffe [1965] Director

TKC Sales Newco Limited
Incorporated: 10 December 2014
Net Worth: £4,449,594 *Total Assets:* £5,143,980
Registered Office: The Old Spitfire Hanger, The Strand, Steeple Ashton, Trowbridge, Wilts, BA14 6EP
Activities: Non-trading company
Major Shareholder: Matthew Winston Thomas Woodruffe
Officers: Paul Wearmouth, Secretary; Paul Wearmouth [1963] Finance Director; Matthew Winston Thomas Woodruffe [1965] Managing Director

TLT LLP
Incorporated: 16 July 2004 *Employees:* 828
Net Worth: £23,690,000 *Total Assets:* £49,264,000
Registered Office: One Redcliff Street, Bristol, BS1 6TP
Officers: Andrew Bell [1976] Member; Sasha Elizabeth Butterworth [1960] Member; Peter Michael Carney [1969] Member; Roger David Clothier [1959] Member; Maria Louise Connolly [1975] Member; Linda Convery [1960] Member; Stephen Devlin [1957] Member; Katherine Rose Evans [1962] Member; James Alexander Forsyth [1972] Member; Andrew Derek Glynn [1961] Member; Simon Lance Kevin Goss [1967] Member; Kerry Gwyther [1959] Member; Jonathan Christopher Hoey [1968] Member; William John Hull [1971] Member; Charles Perran Jervis [1970] Member; Julia Lucas [1967] Member; Andrew David Lyon [1966] Member; Julian David Mant [1969] Member; Stuart Ashley Royden McBride [1969] Member; Thomas Peter McEntegart [1968] Member; Graeme William Ewen Orchison [1962] Member; Christopher Robert Owen [1973] Member; David Peter Pester [1961] Member; Ian David Roberts [1964] Member; Gary James Roscoe [1968] Member; Mark Andrew Routley [1968] Member; John Paul Sheridan [1975] Member; David Smithen [1967] Member; Robin Mark Staunton [1957] Member; Jonathan William Stewart [1975] Member; James George Touzel [1971] Member; Miles Adrian Trower [1972] Member; Richard George Leslie Waller [1958] Member; Graham Paul Walters [1968] Member; Ben Watson [1974] Member; Andrew Webber [1977] Member; John Bennett Wood [1972] Member; Judith Susan Clare Allen [1979] LLP Member; Brian Oetegenn Armour [1969] LLP Member; Sian Claire Ashton [1979] LLP Member; Howard Jeremy Beach [1959] LLP Member; Damien Bechelli [1978] LLP Member; James Chadwick [1978] LLP Member; Warren Leonard Clark [1984] LLP Member; Pauline Cole [1962] LLP Member; Philip Collis [1980] LLP Member; Edward James Cotton [1970] LLP Member; Pauline Cowie [1961] LLP Member; Matthew John Cox [1967] LLP Member; Christopher Alexander Crighton [1982] LLP Member; Paul Crighton [1983] LLP Member; Jason Cropper [1970] LLP Member; Elizabeth Sheila Delaney [1976] LLP Member; Piara Singh Dhooper [1973] LLP Member; Natalie Katrina Drew [1978] LLP Member; Nicholas Piers Fenner [1964] LLP Member; Edmund Peter Fiddick [1972] LLP Member; Siobhan FitzGenerald [1978] LLP Member; Matthew Christopher Forrest [1978] LLP Member; Neil Thomas Franklin [1971] LLP Member; Paul Gareth Gair [1978] LLP Member; Alice Louise Gardner [1980] LLP Member; David John Gardner [1979] LLP Member; Jon Vaughan Gill [1980] LLP Member; Neil Geoffrey Gordon [1964] LLP Member; Douglas John Gourlay [1970] LLP Member; Matthew Barry Grimwood [1984] LLP Member; Abigail Deborah Hadfield [1976] LLP Member; Jonathan Mark Hainey [1968] LLP Member; Richard Eric Hall [1973] LLP Member; Daniel Michael Halstead [1977] LLP Member; Emma Catherine Haworth [1972] LLP Member; Richard Sherwill Hayllar [1977] LLP Member; Kay Hobbs [1980] LLP Member; Susan Honeyands [1967] LLP Member; Richard Houliston [1981] LLP Member; William John Andrew Hyde [1962] LLP Member; Michael Isaacs [1969] LLP Member; David Jeremy Isaacson [1973] LLP Member; Michael Paul Issacs [1969] LLP Member; Andrew Martyn Jennings [1984] LLP Member; Jason Christian Juden [1970] LLP Member; Russell Jon Kelsall [1981] LLP Member; Katharine Anne Kimber [1979] LLP Member; Kane Kirkbride [1963] LLP Member; Daniel Rhys Lloyd [1969] LLP Member; Andrew Geoffrey Lockerbie [1977] LLP Member; Alastair Graeme Lomax [1973] LLP Member; Caroline Powlett Loudon [1977] LLP Member; Julien Luke [1973] LLP Member; Victoria June Mabbett [1974] LLP Member; Noline Matemera [1972] LLP Member; Andrew Christopher McCowan [1966] LLP Member; Stephen John McGowan [1979] LLP Member; Mark Andrew McQuillan [1971] LLP Member; Neil Roland Meakin [1959] LLP Member; Kenneth Turnbull Meldrum [1964] LLP Member; Philip Moran [1980] LLP Member; Alan Turner Munro [1975] LLP Member

TM Group (UK) Limited
Incorporated: 4 November 2004 *Employees:* 146
Net Worth: £1,287,000 *Total Assets:* £10,237,000
Registered Office: 1200 Delta Business Park, Swindon, Wilts, SN5 7XZ
Activities: Other information service activities n.e.c.
Shareholders: Balanus Limited; Connells Limited; LSL Property Services PLC
Officers: Paul Edward Albone [1968] Director; Adam Robert Castleton [1964] Director; Paul Lewis Creffield [1954] Director; David Christopher Livesey [1959] Director; Joseph David Pepper [1974] Director

TM Property Searches Limited
Incorporated: 21 May 1999 *Employees:* 146
Net Worth: £375,000 *Total Assets:* £9,332,000
Registered Office: 1200 Delta Business Park, Swindon, Wilts, SN5 7XZ
Activities: Other information service activities n.e.c.
Parent: TM Group (UK) Limited
Officers: Paul Edward Albone [1968] Director; Anthony John Bobath [1965] Director; Mark Anthony Gilbert [1972] Director; Joseph David Pepper [1974] Director

TMB Patterns Limited
Incorporated: 26 January 1984 *Employees:* 69
Net Worth: £1,946,734 *Total Assets:* £4,121,161
Registered Office: 24 Brue Avenue, Colley Lane Industrial Estate, Bridgwater, Somerset, TA6 5LT
Activities: Manufacture of tools
Major Shareholder: Martin Joseph Baker
Officers: Briony Lamorna Corbett, Secretary/Chartered Accountant; Martin Joseph Baker [1952] Chairman & Managing Director; Lee Johnathan Singleton [1966] Sales Director

TNT Fireworks U.K. Limited
Incorporated: 16 June 2003 *Employees:* 8
Net Worth: £336,040 *Total Assets:* £6,300,132
Registered Office: St Mary's House, Netherhampton, Salisbury, Wilts, SP2 8PU
Activities: Other business support service activities n.e.c.
Parent: American Promotional Events Inc
Officers: Shella Bernauer, Secretary; Terrence Carroll Anderson [1957] Director [American]; Thomas Stephen Glasgow [1958] Director/Company President

Tocris Cookson Limited
Incorporated: 5 November 1993 *Employees:* 51
Net Worth: £15,237,000 *Total Assets:* £16,915,000
Registered Office: Unit 4-6 Avonbridge Trading Estate, Atlantic Road, Bristol, BS11 9QD
Activities: Manufacture of other chemical products n.e.c.
Parent: Bio-Techne Ltd
Officers: Gina Sarah Watson, Secretary; Brenda Furlow [1958] Director/Manager [American]; Dr David Alan Peters [1969] Managing Director; Gary Stapleton [1963] Director/Vice President - Bio-Techne Europe

Togs Limited
Incorporated: 19 August 2004 *Employees:* 50
Net Worth: £18,853,336 *Total Assets:* £22,032,094
Registered Office: Orchard Works, Ashton Road, Marsh Barton, Exeter, Devon, EX2 8LN
Activities: Activities of other holding companies n.e.c.
Major Shareholder: Pamela Mary Toghill
Officers: Pamela Mary Toghill, Secretary; Pamela Mary Toghill [1939] Director; Russell Anthony Toghill [1966] Director

Toklon Limited
Incorporated: 12 February 2004 *Employees:* 160
Net Worth Deficit: £1,861,000 *Total Assets:* £9,438,000
Registered Office: Abbey Stadium, Lady Lane, Blunsdon, Swindon, Wilts, SN25 4DN
Activities: Buying and selling of own real estate
Major Shareholder: Clarke Anthony Osborne
Officers: Stephen Peter Hayward, Secretary; George Albert Edwards [1962] Director; Stephen Peter Hayward [1956] Director/Accountant; Clarke Anthony Osborne [1952] Director

Tolchards Limited
Incorporated: 23 September 2009 *Employees:* 89
Net Worth: £2,033,008 *Total Assets:* £6,623,436
Registered Office: Tolchards House, Woodland Road, Torquay, Devon, TQ2 7AX
Activities: Wholesale of wine, beer, spirits and other alcoholic beverages
Major Shareholder: James Charles Mardell
Officers: Alan Stanley Jeavons [1943] Director; James Charles Mardell [1958] Director; Karen Michelle Mardell [1971] Director; Sean Charles Mardell [1988] Commercial Director; Steven Charles Mardell [1984] Operations Director; Robert Kenneth Lewis Phillips [1952] Director

Tolladine Estates Limited
Incorporated: 26 September 1995
Net Worth: £15,137,578 *Total Assets:* £18,359,836
Registered Office: Manor Stables, Corsley, Warminster, Wilts, BA12 7QE
Activities: Buying and selling of own real estate
Major Shareholder: Simon William Waterfield
Officers: Simon William Waterfield [1960] Director/Chartered Surveyor

Toller Beattie LLP
Incorporated: 12 December 2006 *Employees:* 26
Net Worth: £764,533 *Total Assets:* £3,835,495
Registered Office: Devonshire House, Riverside Road, Pottington Business Park, Barnstaple, Devon, EX31 1QN
Officers: Deborah Baker [1961] Member; Gillian Margaret Lindquist Jones [1955] Member; Mark Simon Roome [1975] Member; Jonathan Dunkley [1971] LLP Member; David Kenneth Eastman [1981] LLP Member; Penelope Joy Glaister [1980] LLP Member; Alexandra Charlotte Jenkins [1978] LLP Member

Tollgate Group Limited
Incorporated: 26 October 1983
Net Worth: £3,751,169 *Total Assets:* £3,764,703
Registered Office: 134 High Street, Hanham, Bristol, BS15 3HF
Activities: Non-trading company
Major Shareholder: Leonard George Handy
Officers: Christopher Handy, Secretary; Christopher Handy [1968] Director/Hire Manager; Leonard George Handy [1942] Director/Property Developer

C. Toms and Son Limited
Incorporated: 6 May 1941 *Employees:* 43
Net Worth: £2,404,171 *Total Assets:* £4,413,145
Registered Office: Toms Yard, East Street, Polruan, Fowey, Cornwall, PL23 1PB
Activities: Building of ships and floating structures
Major Shareholder: John Allen Toms
Officers: Karen Toms, Secretary; John Allen Toms [1944] Director/Boat Builder; Karen Louise Toms [1970] Director/Manager; Maureen Toms [1951] Director; Paul Toms [1972] Director/Engineer

Tomy Europe (Holdings) Limited
Incorporated: 19 March 1999
Net Worth Deficit: £2,256,000 *Total Assets:* £4,059,000
Registered Office: Hembury House, Pynes Hill, Rydon Lane, Exeter, Devon, EX2 5AZ
Activities: Non-trading company
Parent: Tomy Company, Ltd
Officers: Damien Archer Weight, Secretary; Yoshikazu Abe [1971] Director/Executive Officer [Japanese]; Peter Joseph Henseler [1958] Director/President [American]; Kazuhiro Kojima [1961] Director [Japanese]; Takashi Konosu [1958] Director/Executive Managing Officer [Japanese]

Tomy UK Co., Ltd.
Incorporated: 10 May 1982 *Employees:* 78
Net Worth Deficit: £20,636,000 *Total Assets:* £30,592,000
Registered Office: Hembury House, Pynes Hill, Rydon Lane, Exeter, Devon, EX2 5AZ
Activities: Wholesale of household goods (other than musical instruments) n.e.c
Parent: Tomy Europe (Holdings) Limited
Officers: Damien Archer Weight, Secretary; Kazuhiro Kojima [1961] Representative Director, COO & CFO [Japanese]; Damien Archer Weight [1964] Finance Director

Tonic Construction Limited
Incorporated: 21 September 1999 *Employees:* 166
Net Worth: £2,610,660 *Total Assets:* £7,417,332
Registered Office: The Coach House, Berwick Bassett, Swindon, Wilts, SN4 9NF
Activities: Construction of domestic buildings
Officers: Deborah Louise Iles, Secretary/Finance Manager; Tom Hulbert [1973] Director; Anthony James Iles [1967] Managing Director; Deborah Louise Iles [1970] Director/Finance Manager; Carl Robert Jenkins [1977] Director; Ian Paul Jones [1969] Commercial Director; Emma Louise Prytherch [1975] Director

Toogoods Property Company Limited
Incorporated: 13 June 1996 *Employees:* 5
Net Worth: £7,455,534 *Total Assets:* £16,818,478
Registered Office: 33 The Clarendon Centre, Salisbury Business Park, Dairy Meadow Lane, Salisbury, Wilts, SP1 2TJ
Activities: Development of building projects
Parent: Toogoods Holdings Limited
Officers: Angela Elizabeth Toogood, Company Secretary; Angela Elizabeth Toogood [1948] Director/Company Secretary; Mark James Toogood [1974] Director; Peter John Toogood [1949] Director/Property Developer

Tool Care Hire LLP
Incorporated: 20 November 2009 *Employees:* 20
Net Worth: £2,618,789 *Total Assets:* £4,330,538
Registered Office: 9 Hennock Road Central, Marsh Barton, Exeter, Devon, EX2 8NP
Officers: Martin Bodley Phillips [1959] Member

Toolstream Limited
Incorporated: 4 September 2001 *Employees:* 198
Net Worth: £14,088,000 *Total Assets:* £43,113,000
Registered Office: Boundary Way, Lufton Trading Estate, Yeovil, Somerset, BA22 8HZ
Activities: Wholesale of other machinery and equipment
Shareholders: James Goddard-Watts; Group Silverline Limited
Officers: Benjamin Thomas Frank Bailey [1980] Director; Darrell John Morris [1971] Director; Rory Anthony O'Donnell [1952] Director/Chartered Accountant

Topcon Technology Limited
Incorporated: 29 October 2012 *Employees:* 92
Previous: Digi-Star Acquisitions UK Limited
Net Worth: £5,262,652 *Total Assets:* £10,268,470
Registered Office: Topcon Technology Ltd, Cirencester Road, Minchinhampton, Stroud, Glos, GL6 9BH
Activities: Manufacture of electronic measuring, testing etc. equipment, not for industrial process control
Parent: Topcon Americas Agriculture LLC
Officers: Neil Anthony Staite, Secretary; Ivan di Federico [1963] Director/Executive Officer [Italian]; Brian Joseph Hester [1960] Director [American]; Fabio Isala [1972] Director [Italian]; David Mudrick [1964] Director [American]; Raymond O'Connor [1962] Director [Irish]; Neil Anthony Staite [1963] Director/Accountant; Albert Zahalka [1951] Director/Executive Officer [Australian]

Tor Bridge Academy Trust
Incorporated: 30 March 2011 *Employees:* 184
Net Worth: £24,931,104 *Total Assets:* £28,104,928
Registered Office: Tor Bridge High, Miller Way, Estover, Plymouth, PL6 8UN
Activities: General secondary education
Officers: Ann Anstis, Secretary; Beryl Ann Badger [1947] Director/University Professor; Jonathan Patrick Byatt [1952] Director/Driving Instructor; Helen Michelle Cocks [1981] Director/Project Manager; Nicola Ann Dowrick [1970] Director/Health & Safety Co-ordinator; Robert Charles Alastair Hember [1971] Director/IT Network Manager; Charlie Phillip William Huitson [1950] Director; Graham Roser [1970] Director/Headteacher; James Nicholas Sambells-Perry [1987] Director/Teacher; Sarah Jane Wills [1980] Director/Accountant

Tor Currency Exchange Limited
Incorporated: 29 July 2004 *Employees:* 85
Net Worth: £17,707,000 *Total Assets:* £82,969,000
Registered Office: PZ360, St Mary's Terrace, Penzance, Cornwall, TR18 4DZ
Activities: Financial intermediation not elsewhere classified
Officers: Jonathan Matthew Beddell [1978] Director; Neil Cooper [1967] Director; Nigel John Fox [1964] Director; Keith Nigel Hatton [1958] Director; Tracy Jackson [1966] Director; Leonidas Markides [1971] Director

Torbay Cemetery and Crematorium Limited
Incorporated: 4 October 1995 *Employees:* 15
Net Worth: £1,687,197 *Total Assets:* £6,482,466
Registered Office: Chapel View, Westerleigh Crematorium, Westerleigh Road, Westerleigh, Bristol, BS37 8QP
Activities: Funeral and related activities
Parent: Crematoria Management Ltd
Officers: Dafydd Rhys John, Secretary; Dafydd Rhys John [1974] Director/Chartered Accountant; Ian David McArdle [1966] Director/Chartered Surveyor

Torbay Economic Development Company Limited
Incorporated: 14 April 2011 *Employees:* 130
Net Worth: £404,068 *Total Assets:* £9,756,614
Registered Office: Tor Hill House, Union Street, Torquay, Devon, TQ2 5QW
Activities: Other professional, scientific and technical activities n.e.c.
Parent: Council of The Borough of Torbay
Officers: Andrew Paul Sherry, Secretary; Alan Robert Archer [1948] Director; Sara Louise Bond [1971] Managing Director; Christine Carter [1955] Director/Councillor; Stephen Melville Criddle [1961] Director/College Principal and CEO; Vincent Flower [1960] Managing Director; Christopher Duncan Hart [1963] Director/Solicitor; Charles Edward Hempseed [1958] Operations Director Interframe Southwest Ltd [British/Canadian]; James Patrick Howard [1967] Director/Chartered Surveyor; Derek Alan Mills [1950] Director/Councillor; Steven Parrock [1959] Director/Chief Executive; Hazel Joy Tucker [1973] Director/Accountant; Alan John Tyerman [1948] Director/Councillor

Torbay Schools Services Limited
Incorporated: 15 February 2000 *Employees:* 3
Net Worth: £1,795,000 *Total Assets:* £10,771,000
Registered Office: Third Floor, Broad Quay House, Prince Street, Bristol, BS1 4DJ
Activities: Renting and operating of Housing Association real estate
Parent: PFI Investments Limited
Officers: Graham John Hutt [1954] Regional Director; Andrew Richard Kershaw [1965] Director/Projects Controller; Richard Little [1979] Investment Director

Torcare (Holdings) Limited
Incorporated: 22 July 2013 *Employees:* 160
Net Worth: £791,246 *Total Assets:* £7,787,163
Registered Office: c/o Francis Clark LLP, North Quay House, Sutton Harbour, Plymouth, PL4 0RA
Activities: Medical nursing home activities
Shareholders: Marie Elizabeth Fourniss; Paul Barry Fourniss
Officers: Benjamin Fourniss, Secretary; Benjamin Fourniss [1979] Director; Marie Elizabeth Fourniss [1948] Director; Paul Barry Fourniss [1946] Director; Thomas Duncan Barry Fourniss [1982] Director

Torcare Limited
Incorporated: 23 July 1986 *Employees:* 160
Net Worth: £3,123,770 *Total Assets:* £4,818,155
Registered Office: c/o Francis Clark LLP, North Quay House, Sutton Harbour, Plymouth, PL4 0RA
Activities: Residential care activities for learning difficulties, mental health and substance abuse
Parent: Torcare (Holdings) Limited
Officers: Benjamin Fourniss, Secretary; Benjamin Fourniss [1979] Director; Marie Elizabeth Fourniss [1948] Director; Paul Barry Fourniss [1946] Director; Thomas Duncan Barry Fourniss [1982] Director

Torchlightgroup Limited
Incorporated: 16 June 2011 *Employees:* 9
Net Worth: £2,743,785 *Total Assets:* £3,715,257
Registered Office: Torchlightgroup, Windmill Hill Business Park, Whitehill Way, Swindon, Wilts, SN5 6QR
Activities: Defence activities
Shareholders: Edward Charles Dickson; Sean Craig Lumley
Officers: Usman Adewale Alashe [1976] Director; Edward Charles Dickson [1974] Director; Andrew Jonathan McInerney [1968] Director; Douglas Gardner McKenna [1960] Director; Peter Lachlan Alexander Monro [1973] Director; Eugene Peter Morgan [1965] Director; Ian David Whillock [1981] Director; Janet Elizabeth Williams [1959] Director

Tornagrain Gas Mill Limited
Incorporated: 27 October 2015
Net Worth Deficit: £2,316,767 *Total Assets:* £14,097,866
Registered Office: Hill Farm House, Babcary, Somerton, Somerset, TA11 7EB
Activities: Manufacture of gas
Parent: Garston Power Limited
Officers: Sarah Cruickshank, Secretary; Jennifer Wright, Secretary; Baiju Devani [1980] Director/Senior Investment Manager; Sebastian James Speight [1967] Director

Torquay Boys' Grammar School
Incorporated: 1 October 2010 *Employees:* 239
Net Worth: £36,972,000 *Total Assets:* £42,291,000
Registered Office: Torquay Boys' Grammar School, Shiphay Manor, Shiphay, Torquay, Devon, TQ2 7EL
Activities: General secondary education
Officers: Claire Beckett, Secretary; Leonora Melina Critchlow [1950] Director/Project Officer; Vincent Flower [1960] Managing Director Shearings Hotels Ltd; Anthony Lee Hinds [1946] Director/Retired; Robert Martin Lidbetter [1946] Director/Retired; Christopher Martyn Linton [1984] Director/Solicitor; Neil Tampkins [1968] Director/Bank Officer; Christine Weston [1947] Director/Retired; Brian William Wills-Pope [1951] Director/Florist

Torquay Girls' Grammar School
Incorporated: 17 January 2011 *Employees:* 130
Net Worth: £10,235,061 *Total Assets:* £11,861,683
Registered Office: 30 Shiphay Lane, Torquay, Devon, TQ2 7DY
Activities: General secondary education
Officers: Sharon Alice Wallwork, Secretary; Beverley Ann Brown [1960] Director/Teacher; Michael Paul Cowling [1960] Director/Facilities Manager; Francisca Fung [1968] Director/Teacher; Dr Julie Ann Hutt [1964] Director/Health and Safety Consultant; Bonita Ann Matthews [1977] Director/Assistant Head of Key Stage Four; Penny Rogers [1969] Director/Solicitor; Dr Nicholas Paul Smith [1964] Director/Headteacher; Sally Ann Timmins [1967] Director/Accountant; Suzanne Julie Wright [1972] Director/Employment & Skills Officer

Torquay Leisure Hotels Limited
Incorporated: 21 February 1947 *Employees:* 413
Net Worth: £8,402,364 *Total Assets:* £18,150,376
Registered Office: Derwent Hotel, Belgrave Road, Torquay, Devon, TQ2 5HS
Activities: Hotels and similar accommodation
Parent: TLH Bidco Limited
Officers: John Finnegan [1958] Director; Jason Darrell Garside [1974] Director; Ian Piercy [1962] Director

Torr Home
Incorporated: 11 May 2006 *Employees:* 85
Net Worth: £5,801,766 *Total Assets:* £6,649,900
Registered Office: Torr Home, The Drive, Hartley, Plymouth, PL3 5SY
Activities: Residential care activities for the elderly and disabled
Officers: John Roberts, Secretary; Elizabeth Bosworth [1940] Director/Retired; Neil Geoffrey Major [1946] Director/Solicitor; John Martin Modley [1946] Director/Retired; John Roberts [1940] Director/Retired; Susan Elizabeth Stidever [1939] Director/Retired

Torridge Transport Limited
Incorporated: 3 July 1958 *Employees:* 23
Net Worth: £4,252,458 *Total Assets:* £4,772,758
Registered Office: Torridge Transport, Hill Village, South Molton, Devon, EX36 4HP
Activities: Freight transport by road
Major Shareholder: Brian James Cobbledick
Officers: Brian James Cobbledick, Secretary; Brian James Cobbledick [1948] Director; Ian Charles Cobbledick [1971] Director/Property Developer

Torry Harris Business Solutions (Europe) Ltd
Incorporated: 18 October 2001 *Employees:* 105
Net Worth: £5,046,354 *Total Assets:* £18,293,072
Registered Office: 12 The Courtyard, Woodlands, Bradley Stoke, Bristol, BS32 4NQ
Activities: Information technology consultancy activities
Parent: Torry Harris Business Solutions PVT Ltd
Officers: Gupta Sujay Boggaram Nagaraj [1976] Director/Country Manager, UK

Torvean Limited
Incorporated: 5 September 1978 *Employees:* 1
Net Worth: £4,730,969 *Total Assets:* £8,194,355
Registered Office: The Holt, Lower Aisholt, Bridgwater, Somerset, TA5 1AS
Activities: Buying and selling of own real estate
Officers: Claire Demenis, Secretary; Michael David Demenis [1985] Director/Computer Technician; Ruth Maria Demenis [1954] Director/CS

Toshiba Carrier UK Ltd.
Incorporated: 25 February 1999 *Employees:* 248
Net Worth: £23,399,000 *Total Assets:* £52,308,000
Registered Office: Porsham Close, Roborough, Plymouth, PL6 7DB
Activities: Plumbing, heat and air-conditioning installation
Parent: Foray 414 Limited
Officers: Simon Boniface, Secretary; David Ernest George Dunn [1970] Director; Jean-Francois Hendrickx [1966] Marketing Director [French]; Tony Jabbour [1977] Director [French]; Simon Ross Harden McMullen [1969] Financial Director; Shoichiro Shirakawa [1967] Director [Japanese]; Akio Tateishi [1967] Director/President (Toshiba Carrier Europe S.A.S) [Japanese]

Total (2014) Limited
Incorporated: 25 April 2014 *Employees:* 47
Net Worth: £55,826 *Total Assets:* £3,681,564
Registered Office: The Green House, 296 High Street, Cheltenham, Glos, GL50 3HQ
Activities: Other telecommunications activities
Major Shareholder: Stuart Davis
Officers: Stuart Robert Davis [1971] Director; John Antony Lomer [1958] Director/Accountant; Lorrin Elizabeth Porter [1975] Operations Director

Total Carbide Ltd
Incorporated: 29 September 1989 *Employees:* 34
Net Worth: £3,172,000 *Total Assets:* £3,995,000
Registered Office: Unit 2 Chosen View Road, Cheltenham, Glos, GL51 9LT
Activities: Other manufacturing n.e.c.
Parent: Versarien PLC
Officers: Christopher Michael Leigh, Secretary; Andreas Hohmann [1964] Director [German]; Christopher Michael Leigh [1960] Director/Chartered Accountant; Neill Gareth Ricketts [1970] Director/Chief Executive

Total Laminate Systems Ltd
Incorporated: 25 February 1993 *Employees:* 79
Net Worth: £2,584,613 *Total Assets:* £4,568,018
Registered Office: 11 Nimrod Way, East Dorset Trade Park, Wimborne, Dorset, BH21 7SH
Activities: Other manufacturing n.e.c.
Parent: Crown Laminating Limited
Officers: Jacqueline Anne Andrews, Secretary; Jacqueline Anne Andrews [1957] Director/General Manager; Kevin Anthony Lloyd [1953] Director

Total Orthodontics Limited
Incorporated: 5 March 2007 *Employees:* 77
Net Worth: £5,653,000 *Total Assets:* £10,208,000
Registered Office: Bupa Dental Care, Vantage Office Park, Old Gloucester Road, Hambrook, Bristol, BS16 1GW
Activities: Dental practice activities
Parent: Oasis Dental Care (Central) Ltd
Officers: Robin James Bryant [1970] Director/Dental Surgeon; Kenneth Rodney Ferguson [1963] Director/Orthodontist; Keith John Harvey [1966] Director/Orthodontist; Dr Richard Mark Jones [1968] Director/Orthodontist; Steven John Preddy [1959] Director/Dentist; Gabriela Pueyo Roberts [1974] Director/General Manager [Spanish]; Dr Ian David Wood [1956] Director/Dental Surgeon; Jake Stephen Hockley Wright [1972] Director

Total Plumbing Supplies Limited
Incorporated: 5 January 2001 *Employees:* 56
Net Worth: £1,901,231 *Total Assets:* £3,588,281
Registered Office: 62c Beeching Close, Furnham Road, Chard, Somerset, TA20 1BB
Activities: Wholesale of hardware, plumbing and heating equipment and supplies
Shareholder: Clive Edward Handford
Officers: Ian David Moses, Secretary; Clive Edward Handford [1957] Director; Ian David Moses [1969] Director

Totemplant Limited
Incorporated: 19 September 1972 *Employees:* 26
Net Worth: £4,352,440 *Total Assets:* £4,449,019
Registered Office: Upton Farm, Upton, Ringstead, Dorchester, DT2 8NE
Activities: Other holiday and other collective accommodation
Major Shareholder: Graham John Smith
Officers: Russell Graham Smith, Secretary; Graham John Smith [1949] Director/Contractor

Totus Engineering Limited
Incorporated: 7 October 2010 *Employees:* 67
Net Worth: £1,120,782 *Total Assets:* £4,803,964
Registered Office: Suite 5, Splatford Barton, Kennford, Exeter, Devon, EX6 7XY
Activities: Electrical installation
Parent: Totus Engineering Holdings Limited
Officers: Timothy Mark Read, Secretary; Jeremy Graham Kent [1968] Director; Antony Martin [1972] Director; Timothy Mark Read [1963] Director; Philip Dean Rock [1966] Director

Tout Limited
Incorporated: 22 July 2002 *Employees:* 144
Net Worth: £2,463,942 *Total Assets:* £9,407,201
Registered Office: Riverside Farm, Church Street, Cheddar, Somerset, BS27 3RB
Activities: Retail sale in non-specialised stores with food, beverages or tobacco predominating
Shareholders: Philip James Tout; Lesley Joy Tout
Officers: Lesley Joy Tout, Secretary; Jonathan Philip Tout [1989] Managing Director; Lesley Joy Tout [1956] Director; Philip James Tout [1956] Director

Towerview West Sussex Limited
Incorporated: 24 February 2016 *Employees:* 1
Net Worth Deficit: £47,599 *Total Assets:* £7,684,724
Registered Office: Suite A5, Arena Business Centre, 9 Nimrod Way, Ferndown Industrial Estate, Ferndown, Dorset, BH21 7UH
Activities: Construction of domestic buildings
Shareholder: Joseph Anthony Gormley
Officers: Joseph Antony Neil Gormley [1978] Director/Property Developer; Nicholas Joseph Birkett Smith [1970] Director/Construction Project Manager

Town Hospitals (North Staffordshire Combined) Limited
Incorporated: 4 December 1998 *Employees:* 3
Net Worth: £4,082,000 *Total Assets:* £23,065,000
Registered Office: Third Floor, Broad Quay House, Prince Street, Bristol, BS1 4DJ
Activities: Medical nursing home activities
Parent: Town Hospitals (North Staffordshire) Holdings Limited
Officers: Alan Edward Birch [1970] Director; David Robert Hardingham [1974] Director/Commercial Manager; Julia Sarah McCabe [1970] Regional Director

Town Hospitals (Southern General) Ltd
Incorporated: 2 June 1999 *Employees:* 3
Net Worth: £1,608,000 *Total Assets:* £10,965,000
Registered Office: Third Floor, Broad Quay House, Prince Street, Bristol, BS1 4DJ
Activities: Construction of commercial buildings
Parent: Town Hospitals (Southern General) Holdings Ltd
Officers: Alan Edward Birch [1970] Director; Kenneth Andrew McLellan [1961] Regional Project Director; Alan Campbell Ritchie [1967] Director

Town Mills Craft Centre Limited
Incorporated: 28 July 1972 *Employees:* 30
Net Worth: £3,427,008 *Total Assets:* £6,569,630
Registered Office: The Old Pottery, Pottery Road, Bovey Tracey, Devon, TQ13 9DS
Activities: Non-specialised wholesale trade
Parent: Inklefinklestein Limited
Officers: Teresa Helena Bavin, Secretary; William Russon Bavin [1950] Managing Director; Frances Dorothy Bennett [1977] Director; Sarah Campbell [1971] Sales Director [Canadian]; Phoebe Margaret Mytton [1979] Director

Towndown Limited
Incorporated: 11 April 1985 *Employees:* 2
Net Worth: £251,935 *Total Assets:* £14,204,805
Registered Office: Down Farm, Westonbirt, Tetbury, Glos, GL8 8QW
Activities: Financial intermediation not elsewhere classified
Officers: Luke George Tomlinson, Secretary; James Christopher Lascelles Lucas [1961] Director; William Arthur Henry Lascelles Lucas [1965] Director

Toyo Denso U.K. Limited
Incorporated: 10 March 2003 *Employees:* 6
Net Worth: £2,760,788 *Total Assets:* £5,234,267
Registered Office: 6 Westerngate, Langley Road, Swindon, Wilts, SN5 5WN
Activities: Manufacture of other electrical equipment
Major Shareholder: Kiyoshi Koide
Officers: Fumio Nakamura, Secretary; Kiyoshi Koide [1952] Director [Japanese]

Tozers LLP
Incorporated: 18 April 2007
Net Worth: £4,900,670 *Total Assets:* £6,310,897
Registered Office: Broadwalk House, Southernhay West, Exeter, Devon, EX1 1UA
Officers: Endurance Esaah Arthur [1967] Member; Stuart William Bramley [1961] Member; Tracey Joanna Bridgwater [1963] Member; Stephen Patrick Burtchaell [1963] Member; Francis Vernon Clarke [1963] Member; Nicholas Edward Mungo Conner [1982] Member; James Edward Evans [1972] Member; Jill Wendy Headford [1956] Member; Clair Anne Hemming [1973] Member; Stephen Charles Jennings [1977] Member; Paul Dominic Kelly [1966] Member; Tracy Gillian Lambert [1964] Member; James David Orpin [1974] Member; Simon John Sanger Anderson [1952] Member; Grainne Staunton [1981] Member; Richard Charles Thorneycroft [1955] Member; Tony Wood [1963] Member; Deborah Black [1983] LLP Member; Melanie Jane Burton [1973] LLP Member; Amy Rachel Cater [1980] LLP Member; Barry Hugh Hayes [1959] LLP Member; Julia Elizabeth Knight [1979] LLP Member; Martin James Laver [1980] LLP Member; Simon Frederick Anthony Mansfield [1984] LLP Member; Paul Llewellyn Somerled Zaleski [1977] LLP Member

TPSFF Holdings Limited
Incorporated: 20 February 2008
Previous: The Plastic Surgeon Holdings Limited
Net Worth: £1,238,620 *Total Assets:* £3,622,626
Registered Office: One Redcliff Street, Bristol, BS1 6TP
Activities: Non-trading company
Parent: The Plastic Surgeon Holdings Limited
Officers: Robert David Mouser [1972] Director; Timothy Stuart Ross [1948] Director

TQ9 Partnership LLP
Incorporated: 2 August 2006 *Employees:* 3
Net Worth: £1,574,017 *Total Assets:* £4,254,113
Registered Office: Baltic Wharf Co, St Peters Quay, Totnes, Devon, TQ9 5EW
Officers: Ian Graeme Dennis [1966] Member; Julie Dennis [1967] Member; Catherine Lucy Mittler [1964] Member; Steve Mittler [1959] Member; John Mark Yallop [1960] Member

TR (Fenpower) Limited
Incorporated: 13 February 2013
Previous: Triodos Renewables (Fenpower) Limited
Net Worth: £3,735,778 *Total Assets:* £3,766,001
Registered Office: c/o Thrive Renewables PLC, Deanery Road, Bristol, BS1 5AS
Activities: Activities of production holding companies
Shareholders: Thrive Renewables PLC; Triodos S II Luxco S.A.R.L.
Officers: Gerrit Hendrikus Engelbert Brunink [1965] Director/Senior Investment Manager [Dutch]; Matthew Thomas Clayton [1975] Director; Monika Lidia Paplaczyk [1979] Director/Investment Manager [Polish]; Vincent Ramon Van Haarlem [1972] Director/Fund Manager [Dutch]

Tracertec Limited
Incorporated: 12 May 1994 *Employees:* 34
Net Worth: £2,592,460 *Total Assets:* £3,886,439
Registered Office: Thurlestone Hotel, Thurlestone, Kingsbridge, Devon, TQ7 3NN
Activities: Hotels and similar accommodation
Parent: Thurlestone Estates Ltd
Officers: Matthew David Cuthbert Grose, Secretary; Graham Richard Ernest Grose [1951] Director/Hotel Proprietor; Matthew David Cuthbert Grose [1972] Director/Hotel Management; Timothy Andrew Hassell [1970] Director

The Trade Link Company Limited
Incorporated: 21 August 1991 *Employees:* 2
Net Worth: £5,118,168 *Total Assets:* £5,263,074
Registered Office: Mary Street House, Mary Street, Taunton, Somerset, TA1 3NW
Activities: Other business support service activities n.e.c.
Parent: Clairwood Ltd
Officers: Jane Francis Alexandra Davis [1937] Director; William Edward Davis [1938] Director

Trade-Air Airline Support Limited
Incorporated: 30 June 1980 *Employees:* 19
Net Worth: £3,799,211 *Total Assets:* £5,375,996
Registered Office: 4 Cinema Buildings, Poole Road, Bournemouth, BH4 9DW
Activities: Other retail sale not in stores, stalls or markets
Major Shareholder: Nigel Richard Webb
Officers: Kelly Marie Stratton, Secretary; Toby Russell Smith [1984] Director/Sales Executive; Kelly Marie Stratton [1982] Director/Sales Executive; Nigel Richard Webb [1948] Director/Aircraft Spares Consultant

Tradestock Limited
Incorporated: 12 June 2000 *Employees:* 41
Net Worth: £1,048,069 *Total Assets:* £5,204,933
Registered Office: Poole Works, Higher Poole, Poole, Wellington, Somerset, TA21 9HW
Activities: Other manufacturing n.e.c.
Major Shareholder: Duncan John Babington
Officers: Sevgi Babington, Secretary; Duncan John Babington [1962] Director; Keith Nye [1958] Director; David Whitney [1976] Commercial Director

Trafalgar Estate Limited
Incorporated: 13 May 1993 *Employees:* 3
Net Worth: £4,305,095 *Total Assets:* £4,408,055
Registered Office: 14 Market Place, Wells, Somerset, BA5 2RE
Activities: Growing of cereals (except rice), leguminous crops and oil seeds
Officers: Neil Michael Howlett, Secretary; Jens Kann-Rasmussen [1969] Director [Danish]; Lars Erik Kann-Rasmussen [1939] Director [Danish]; Per Skovsted [1958] Director/Businessman [Danish]

The Traffic Group Limited
Incorporated: 22 February 2000 *Employees:* 122
Previous: AGD Group Limited
Net Worth: £14,978,573 *Total Assets:* £23,618,372
Registered Office: White Lion House, Gloucester Road, Staverton, Cheltenham, Glos, GL51 0TF
Activities: Activities of head offices
Shareholder: Peter Michael Hutchinson
Officers: Dawn Woodward, Secretary; Clare Mary Coles [1963] Director; Mark Hutchinson [1949] Director; Michael Raymond Hutchinson [1941] Director; Peter Michael Hutchinson [1967] Director

Trago Mills (Falmouth) Limited
Incorporated: 26 October 1976 *Employees:* 107
Net Worth: £11,373,413 *Total Assets:* £12,211,332
Registered Office: Trago Mills, Twowatersfoot, Liskeard, Cornwall, PL14 6HY
Activities: Other retail sale in non-specialised stores
Shareholders: Charles Bruce Robertson; Kay Joanne Weber
Officers: Gary Peter Lord [1958] Director/Accountant; Brent Alan Pinhay [1965] Director; Charles Bruce Robertson [1953] Director

Trago Mills (South Devon) Limited
Incorporated: 31 March 1967 *Employees:* 454
Net Worth: £43,907,468 *Total Assets:* £47,949,908
Registered Office: Trago Mills, Twowatersfoot, Liskeard, Cornwall, PL14 6HY
Activities: Other retail sale in non-specialised stores
Parent: Charles Robertson (Holdings) Ltd
Officers: Gary Peter Lord [1958] Director/Accountant; Brent Alan Pinhay [1965] Director; Charles Bruce Robertson [1953] Director; Kay Joanne Weber [1959] Director

Trago Mills Limited
Incorporated: 4 June 1959 *Employees:* 391
Net Worth: £33,615,128 *Total Assets:* £87,002,696
Registered Office: Trago Mills, Twowatersfoot, Liskeard, Cornwall, PL14 6HY
Activities: Other retail sale in non-specialised stores
Parent: Charles Robertson (Holdings) Ltd
Officers: Gary Peter Lord [1958] Director/Accountant; Brent Alan Pinhay [1965] Director; Charles Bruce Robertson [1953] Director; Kay Joanne Weber [1959] Director

Tran-AM Limited
Incorporated: 4 June 1976
Net Worth: £3,837,494 *Total Assets:* £6,686,216
Registered Office: William House, Gore Road, New Milton, Hants, BH25 6RJ
Activities: Non-specialised wholesale trade
Officers: Ian Raymond Lloyd, Company Secretary/Director; Kay Hanmer [1964] Finance Director; Ian Raymond Lloyd [1951] Director; Peter Rowland Lloyd [1979] Marketing Director; Richard Frederick Lloyd [1947] Director; Mark David Sawyer [1962] Sales & Marketing Director

Transcribe Copier Systems Limited
Incorporated: 9 August 1983 *Employees:* 5
Net Worth Deficit: £2,477,461 *Total Assets:* £3,683,860
Registered Office: 9 Falcon's Gate, Dean Road Yate, Bristol, BS37 5NH
Activities: Wholesale of other office machinery and equipment
Officers: Kerry Maglennon, Secretary; Timothy Robin Rampling [1957] Managing Director

Transmission Developments Co (GB) Limited
Incorporated: 20 February 1985 *Employees:* 79
Net Worth: £7,237,964 *Total Assets:* £8,692,083
Registered Office: Dawkins Road, Hamworthy, Poole, Dorset, BH15 4HF
Activities: Machining
Shareholders: Ian John Osborne; Carole Anne Osborne
Officers: Carole Anne Osborne, Secretary/Director; Christopher John Cowler [1965] Director; Carole Anne Osborne [1954] Director; Ian John Osborne [1953] Director/Chairman

Trapeze Group (UK) Limited
Incorporated: 15 February 2001 *Employees:* 122
Net Worth: £4,361,907 *Total Assets:* £12,387,293
Registered Office: Unit A1, Methuen Park, Chippenham, Wilts, SN14 0GT
Activities: Business and domestic software development
Parent: Trapeze Group Europe Holding A/S
Officers: Claire Charlotte Anne Sidhu, Secretary; Dr. Charles Peter Bell [1965] Director; Carrie Marks [1980] Director/Head of Finance; Janice McPherson [1961] Director/Transport Software; Martin Timothy Porter [1954] Executive Director

Tre' Care Group Limited
Incorporated: 4 September 1991 *Employees:* 287
Net Worth: £2,129,267 *Total Assets:* £3,877,296
Registered Office: Little Trefewha Residential Home, Trefewha, Praze, Camborne, Cornwall, TR14 0JZ
Activities: Hospital activities
Shareholders: Brian David Craig; Joan Belinda Gaisford
Officers: Joan Belinda Fitzhenry, Secretary/Nurse Manager; Brian David Craig [1949] Managing Director; Donna Marie Craig [1967] Director; Joan Belinda Fitzhenry [1951] Director; Peter Francis Fitzhenry [1949] Director

Treasure Homes Limited
Incorporated: 16 September 1988 *Employees:* 172
Net Worth: £9,805,118 *Total Assets:* £10,388,989
Registered Office: Abbots Leigh Manor, Manor Road, Abbots Leigh, Bristol, BS8 3RP
Activities: Residential care activities for the elderly and disabled
Major Shareholder: David Willington Gillespie
Officers: David Willington Gillespie, Secretary; Paulina Rae Gillespie, Secretary; David Willington Gillespie [1959] Director; Paulina Rae Gillespie [1962] Director/Broadcaster

Trebah Garden Trust
Incorporated: 22 January 1990 *Employees:* 58
Net Worth: £4,323,272 *Total Assets:* £4,575,047
Registered Office: Trebah, Mawnan Smith, Cornwall, TR11 5JZ
Activities: Botanical and zoological gardens and nature reserves activities
Officers: Nigel John Burnett, Secretary; Harry Stephen Bradshaw [1955] Director; Carolyn Claire Brodie [1952] Director/Pharmacist; Robert Dudley Cooke [1943] Director/Solicitor/School Principal; Michael Douglas Harvey [1950] Director/Businessman; Tim Hubbard [1954] Director/Radio Presenter; Susan Nathan [1951] Director/Designer; Lucie Margaret Nottingham [1942] Director; Gillian Frances Pipkin [1961] Director/Secretary; Charles Robert Richardson [1953] Director; Raymond Frederick Townsend [1958] Director/Horticultural Manager; Anthony Beville Vyvyan [1935] Director/Company Secretary

Trebartha Estates Limited
Incorporated: 20 September 1940 *Employees:* 2
Net Worth: £19,619,532 *Total Assets:* £24,601,724
Registered Office: 12 Southgate Street, Launceston, Cornwall, PL15 9DP
Activities: Renting and operating of Housing Association real estate
Officers: Richard Anthony Coubrough Latham, Secretary; Jolyon Ronald Thomas Barker [1967] Director/Management Consultant; Caroline Rosemary Latham [1952] Director/Caterer; Clare Elizabeth Latham [1969] Director/Interior Designer; Patrick Brian Gaston Latham [1964] Director/Oil Trader; Robert James Latham [1953] Director/Barrister; Andrew James Robson [1963] Director/Chartered Surveyor

Tree Aid
Incorporated: 28 May 1999 *Employees:* 52
Net Worth: £1,912,716 *Total Assets:* £3,672,218
Registered Office: Brunswick Court, Brunswick Square, Bristol, BS2 8PE
Activities: Other social work activities without accommodation n.e.c.
Officers: Benedict Robert Sheahan, Secretary; Shireen Grace Chambers [1962] Director/Chief Executive Officer; Elizabeth Fiona Davis [1955] Director/Trustee; Thomas David Crispin de Pass [1974] Director/Head of Communications; Terence Jagger [1956] Director/Businessman; Nicholas Francis Pride [1960] Director; Trevor Eccles Reaney [1959] Director/Retired; Alex Simon Donald Rees [1975] Director/International Development; Philip Vallum Songhurst-Thonet [1974] Director/Business Finance; Judith Twentyman [1964] Director/Chief Operating Officer

Tregenna Castle Hotel Limited
Incorporated: 7 January 1992 *Employees:* 118
Previous: Tregenna Castle Resort Limited
Net Worth: £12,018,864 *Total Assets:* £15,359,892
Registered Office: Tregenna Castle Hotel, Trelyon Avenue, St Ives, Cornwall, TR26 2DE
Activities: Hotels and similar accommodation
Major Shareholder: John Howard Mason
Officers: Amanda Louise Mason, Secretary; Steve John Hewlett [1976] Director; John Howard Mason [1951] Director

Tregenna Ventures Limited
Incorporated: 27 November 2014
Net Worth: £196,582 *Total Assets:* £5,938,614
Registered Office: Overstream, Parsons Street, Porlock, Minehead, Somerset, TA24 8QJ
Activities: Information technology consultancy activities
Major Shareholder: Anthony John Brice
Officers: Anthony John Brice [1963] Director/Investment Management

Trelawny Citroen Limited
Incorporated: 29 February 2008 *Employees:* 30
Net Worth: £3,757,081 *Total Assets:* £4,861,850
Registered Office: Unit 5 Long Rock Industrial Estate, Long Rock, Penzance, Cornwall, TR20 8HX
Activities: Sale of new cars and light motor vehicles
Major Shareholder: Norman Martin Murrish
Officers: Norman Martin Murrish, Secretary; Nicola Murrish [1972] Director; Norman Martin Murrish [1968] Director

Trelleborg Holdings UK Limited
Incorporated: 20 January 1997 *Employees:* 3
Net Worth: £168,732,000 *Total Assets:* £246,784,992
Registered Office: Trelleborg, International Drive, Tewkesbury Business Park, Tewkesbury, Glos, GL20 8UQ
Activities: Activities of head offices
Parent: Trelleborg AB
Officers: Ian Elcock, Secretary; Charlotta Ingrid Grahs [1971] Director/Senior Vice President, General Counsel & Secretary [Swedish]; Anders Niklas Johansson [1973] Director/VP Tax [Swedish]; Lars Ivar Leijonberg [1964] Director/VP Internal Control [Swedish]

Trelleborg Industrial Products UK Ltd
Incorporated: 24 September 1999 *Employees:* 230
Net Worth: £21,510,000 *Total Assets:* £28,843,000
Registered Office: Trelleborg, International Drive, Tewkesbury Business Park, Tewkesbury, Glos, GL20 8UQ
Activities: Manufacture of other rubber products
Parent: Trelleborg Holdings UK Limited
Officers: Ian Elcock, Secretary; Maximilian Wolfgang Christian Billinger [1968] Director/Business Unit President [German]; Max Rikard Albin Persson Bokander [1973] Finance Director [Swedish]; Jean Paule Mindermann [1965] Director/President [German]

Trelleborg Industrial Tyres UK Limited
Incorporated: 4 July 1979 *Employees:* 36
Net Worth: £5,027,000 *Total Assets:* £6,103,000
Registered Office: Trelleborg International Drive, Tewkesbury Business Park, Tewkesbury, Glos, GL20 8UQ
Activities: Wholesale of other intermediate products
Parent: Watts Tyres Limited
Officers: Ian Elcock, Secretary; Elio Bartoli [1977] Director [Italian]; Salvatore Marino [1964] Finance Director [Italian]; Mark Anthony Ruck [1969] Director/Accountant

Trelleborg Marine Systems UK Limited
Incorporated: 25 January 1999 *Employees:* 47
Net Worth: £6,587,000 *Total Assets:* £10,222,000
Registered Office: Trelleborg International Drive, Tewkesbury Business Park, Tewkesbury, Glos, GL20 8UQ
Activities: Manufacture of electronic industrial process control equipment
Parent: Trelleborg Holdings UK Limited
Officers: Ian Elcock, Secretary; Richard Hepworth [1968] Managing Director; David Pendleton [1964] Managing Director

Trelleborg Offshore UK Limited
Incorporated: 17 May 1978 *Employees:* 247
Net Worth: £61,337,000 *Total Assets:* £76,286,000
Registered Office: Trelleborg, International Drive, Tewkesbury Business Park, Tewkesbury, Glos, GL20 8UQ
Activities: Manufacture of other plastic products
Shareholders: CRP Securities Limited; CRP 1998 Limited
Officers: Ian Elcock, Secretary; Merete Elisabeth Aulid [1967] Director/Controller Trelleborg Offshore [Norwegian]; John Paul Drury [1971] Managing Director; Thor Hegg Eriksen [1966] Director/President [Norwegian]

Trelleborg Retford Limited
Incorporated: 31 May 2001 *Employees:* 124
Previous: Trelleborg PPL Limited
Net Worth: £9,014,000 *Total Assets:* £14,143,000
Registered Office: International Drive, Tewkesbury Business Park, Tewkesbury, Glos, GL20 8UQ
Activities: Manufacture of other rubber products
Parent: Trelleborg Holdings UK Limited
Officers: Ian Elcock, Secretary; Alan Michael Burgess [1959] Managing Director; Terry Lee Cooper [1976] Managing Director; Thor Hegg Eriksen [1966] Director/President [Norwegian]

Trelleborg Rochdale Limited
Incorporated: 2 January 2007 *Employees:* 81
Net Worth: £1,102,000 *Total Assets:* £6,293,000
Registered Office: Trelleborg International Drive, Tewkesbury Business Park, Tewkesbury, Glos, GL20 8UQ
Activities: Manufacture of other plastic products
Parent: Trelleborg Holdings UK Limited
Officers: Ian Elcock, Secretary; Alan Michael Burgess [1959] Managing Director; Raymond Julian Cann [1971] Managing Director; Thor Hegg Eriksen [1966] Director/President [Norwegian]

Trelleborg Sealing Solutions UK Limited
Incorporated: 3 December 1947 *Employees:* 671
Net Worth: £34,296,000 *Total Assets:* £58,625,000
Registered Office: Trelleborg, International Drive, Tewkesbury Business Park, Tewkesbury, Glos, GL20 8UQ
Activities: Manufacture of other rubber products
Parent: Trelleborg Holdings UK Limited
Officers: Ian Elcock, Secretary; Kent Helmer Bergenholtz [1965] Director/BU President Global Operations Engineered Plastics [Danish]; Robert Broadley [1963] Financial Director; Kristian Brok [1965] Director/BU President [Danish]; David Brown [1959] Director/MD; Damien Roger Benoit Savary [1971] Director/Aerospace Hub Europe - General Manager [French]

Trelleborg Wheel Systems UK Limited
Incorporated: 16 July 1985 *Employees:* 13
Net Worth: £4,997,000 *Total Assets:* £6,467,000
Registered Office: Trelleborg, International Drive, Tewkesbury Business Park, Tewkesbury, Glos, GL20 8UQ
Activities: Manufacture of other rubber products
Parent: Trelleborg Holdings UK Limited
Officers: Ian Elcock, Secretary; Andrea Fabio Manenti [1969] Managing Director [Italian]; Salvatore Marino [1964] Director/Business Unit Controller [Italian]; Paolo Pompei [1971] Director/Business Unit President [Italian]

Charles Trent Limited
Incorporated: 8 April 1987 *Employees:* 162
Net Worth: £4,154,374 *Total Assets:* £15,203,830
Registered Office: Trent House, 8 St Georges Avenue, Parkstone, Poole, Dorset, BH12 4ND
Activities: Wholesale trade of motor vehicle parts and accessories
Shareholders: Marc John Trent; Jonathan Trent; Neil Trent
Officers: Marc John Trent, Secretary; Jonathan Trent [1970] Director; Marc John Trent [1966] Director; Neil Trent [1970] Director

Trethowans LLP
Incorporated: 30 December 2008 *Employees:* 182
Net Worth: £8,318,031 *Total Assets:* £11,096,992
Registered Office: London Road Office Park, London Road, Salisbury, Wilts, SP1 3HP
Officers: Mark Jason Daniels [1962] Member; Andrew James Mercer [1965] Member; Garry Paul Treagust [1967] Member; Michael William Watson [1973] Member; Christopher Louis Whiteley [1964] Member; Grainne Alen-Buckley [1960] LLP Member; Matthew James Machen Barker [1969] LLP Member; Bethany Louise Blamire [1974] LLP Member; Elizabeth Bryson [1965] LLP Member; Grant Ashley Cameron [1966] LLP Member; Karl Steven Cameron [1980] LLP Member; Andrew James Carswell [1969] LLP Member; Clare Margaret Carter [1972] LLP Member; Kathryn Casey-Evans [1979] LLP Member; Richard Cook [1958] LLP Member; Richard Mark Dollimore [1972] LLP Member; Sophie Eales [1979] LLP Member; Emma Louise Earp [1979] LLP Member; Kelvin Ian Farmaner [1974] LLP Member; Mihiri Suneeta Gajraj [1982] LLP Member; Nicholas Henry Gent [1968] LLP Member; Lucy Gleisner [1981] LLP Member; John Nicholas Hall [1965] LLP Member; James Joseph Hammersley [1983] LLP Member; Thomas Patrick Guy Hartigan [1975] LLP Member; Timothy John Higham [1972] LLP Member; Amanda Jane Inch [1963] LLP Member; James Robert Kidner [1980] LLP Member; Gavin Robert Lane [1966] LLP Member; Paul Longman [1969] LLP Member; Alexandra Mayhew [1974] LLP Member; Mark William Nixon [1982] LLP Member; Gary Martin Pick [1958] LLP Member; Caroline Mary Elsworth Probert [1960] LLP Member; Simon James Rhodes [1968] LLP Member; Kimberley Ian Singleton [1960] LLP Member; Jonathan Edward Stickland [1974] LLP Member; Marcus Somerled Thorpe [1971] LLP Member; Halina Liza Tomlinson [1977] LLP Member; Elizabeth Rosemary Webbe [1963] LLP Member; Sarah Andrea Wheadon [1970] LLP Member; Emma Wilders-Pratt [1978] LLP Member; Gareth Edward Yeoman [1961] LLP Member

Treveglos Farm Limited
Incorporated: 4 March 2010 *Employees:* 6
Net Worth: £64,183 *Total Assets:* £3,993,129
Registered Office: Lowin House, Tregolls Road, Truro, Cornwall, TR1 2NA
Activities: Raising of dairy cattle
Shareholders: Andrew David Kellow; Sally Wendy Kellow
Officers: Sally Wendy Kellow, Secretary; Andrew David Kellow [1969] Director/Farmer; Sally Wendy Kellow [1970] Director/Farmer

Trevose Limited
Incorporated: 27 June 1927 *Employees:* 76
Net Worth: £1,849,396 *Total Assets:* £4,969,413
Registered Office: Trevose Golf Clubhouse, Constantine Bay, Padstow, Cornwall, PL28 8JB
Activities: Other sports activities
Shareholders: Carolyn Elsa Gammon; William Paul Harriman
Officers: Nicholas Jonathan Gammon, Secretary/Golf; Anthony John Gammon [1965] Director/Stockbrokers Assistant; Christopher Peter Gammon [1973] Director; Nicholas Jonathan Gammon [1972] Director; William Paul Harriman [1946] Director/Solicitor; David Layton [1951] Director/Accountant

Triangle Properties (Bristol) Limited
Incorporated: 14 August 2000
Net Worth: £1,982,457 *Total Assets:* £5,265,414
Registered Office: 30 Whiteladies Road, Clifton, Bristol, BS8 2LG
Activities: Development of building projects
Officers: Trevor Norman Chastney, Secretary/Property Developer; Trevor Norman Chastney [1953] Director/Property Developer; Mark Easton [1955] Director/Property Manager; David Richard Bartlett Jones [1963] Director/Financial Advisor

Tribal Education Limited
Incorporated: 20 February 2001 *Employees:* 603
Net Worth Deficit: £28,247,000 *Total Assets:* £80,133,000
Registered Office: Kings Orchard Queen Street, St Philips, Bristol, BS2 0HQ
Activities: Educational support services
Parent: Tribal Group PLC
Officers: Richard Last [1957] Director; Mark Jeremy Pickett [1961] Finance Director

Tribal Group PLC
Incorporated: 15 December 2000 *Employees:* 925
Net Worth: £32,552,000 *Total Assets:* £73,642,000
Registered Office: Kings Orchard Queen Street, St Philips, Bristol, BS2 0HQ
Activities: Educational support services
Officers: Mark Jeremy Pickett, Secretary; Richard Last [1957] Director; Roger Steven McDowell [1955] Director; Mark Jeremy Pickett [1961] Finance Director

Tribal Holdings Limited
Incorporated: 23 March 1995
Net Worth: £11,987,000 *Total Assets:* £30,706,000
Registered Office: Kings Orchard Queen Street, St Philips, Bristol, BS2 0HQ
Activities: Activities of head offices
Parent: Tribal Group PLC
Officers: Richard Last [1957] Director; Mark Jeremy Pickett [1961] Finance Director

Tricel (Gloucester) Limited
Incorporated: 3 November 1993 *Employees:* 47
Net Worth: £1,647,018 *Total Assets:* £4,704,975
Registered Office: Fox House, Stonedale Road, Stonehouse, Glos, GL10 3SA
Activities: Manufacture of other plastic products
Parent: ACSTK Holdings Unlimited Company
Officers: Cornelius Stack, Secretary; Kevin MacKay Lawson [1958] Director; Cornelius Stack [1967] Director [Irish]; Michael Joseph Stack [1964] Director [Irish]; Richard Stuart Stack [1971] Director [Irish]; Robert Stack [1972] Director [Irish]

Tricel Holdings (UK) Limited
Incorporated: 4 November 1999
Net Worth: £2,814,380 *Total Assets:* £21,854,680
Registered Office: Foxhouse Stonedale Road, Oldends Industrial Estate, Stonehouse, Glos, GL10 3SA
Activities: Activities of head offices
Parent: ACSTK Holdings Unlimited Company
Officers: David Flahive, Secretary [Irish]; Cornelius Stack [1967] Director [Irish]; Michael Joseph Stack [1964] Director [Irish]; Richard Stuart Stack [1971] Director [Irish]; Robert Stack [1972] Director [Irish]

Tricuro Support Ltd
Incorporated: 10 April 2015 *Employees:* 1,521
Net Worth: £1,279,630 *Total Assets:* £7,191,972
Registered Office: Beech House, 28-30 Wimborne Road, Poole, Dorset, BH15 2BU
Activities: Residential care activities for learning difficulties, mental health and substance abuse
Shareholders: Dorset County Council; Bournemouth Borough Council; Borough of Poole
Officers: Philip John Rook, Secretary; Alan Bulloch [1949] Director; Colin Harold Dennis [1953] Director/Independent Chair; Susan Ladbrook [1962] HR Director; Andrea Peacock [1969] Director; Jane Elizabeth Pike [1961] Director; Philip John Rook [1973] Director/Accountant; Alison Lois Waller [1966] Managing Director

Trifle Holdings Limited
Incorporated: 3 December 2015 *Employees:* 2
Net Worth: £163,728,992 *Total Assets:* £174,498,000
Registered Office: Narrow Quay, Bristol, BS1 4QA
Activities: Non-trading company
Parent: Essilor International SAS
Officers: Thomas Simon William Burmester [1975] Director/General Manager Europe; Jonathan Richard Miles [1968] Director

Triode Acquisitions UK Limited
Incorporated: 8 August 2006
Net Worth: £81,003,728 *Total Assets:* £239,152,800
Registered Office: c/o Appleby Westward, Moorlands Trading Estate Estate, Saltash, Cornwall, PL12 6LX
Activities: Activities of head offices
Parent: The Spar Group Limited
Officers: Jennifer Kane, Secretary; John Clohisey [1952] Director [Irish]; Leo John Anthony Crawford [1959] Finance Director [Irish]; John Odonnell [1954] Director [Irish]

Triton Knoll Offshore Wind Farm Limited
Incorporated: 18 January 1999
Net Worth Deficit: £16,181,354 *Total Assets:* £79,090,712
Registered Office: Windmill Hill Business Park, Whitehill Way, Swindon, Wilts, SN5 6PB
Activities: Site preparation
Parent: Triton Knoll Holdco Limited
Officers: Christopher David Barras, Secretary; Penelope Anne Sainsbury, Secretary; Martin Andre-Ferreira [1978] Director/FCCA Accountant; Stefan Rudolf Bendig [1968] Director/Senior Financial Project Manager [German]; Paul Leslie Cowling [1960] Director; Christian Rudiger Mockl [1973] Director [German]; Richard Jennings Sandford [1971] Director/Head of Offshore Business Management; Ko Suenga [1966] Director [Japanese]; Makoto Takeuchi [1969] Director/General Manager, International Business [Japanese]; Takahiko Tanaka [1975] Director/Manager, International Business [Japanese]; Hirofumi Yuya [1970] Director [Japanese]

Triumph Engineering (UK) Co. Ltd
Incorporated: 10 June 2016
Net Worth: £21,305 *Total Assets:* £3,818,404
Registered Office: 26-28 Southernhay East, Exeter, EX1 1NS
Activities: Repair of electrical equipment
Officers: Lei Liu [1983] Director [Chinese]; Rhys Pippard [1984] Director

Triumph International Limited
Incorporated: 3 August 1954 *Employees:* 94
Net Worth: £5,977,000 *Total Assets:* £20,384,000
Registered Office: Arkwright Road, Groundwell, Swindon, Wilts, SN25 5BE
Activities: Wholesale of clothing and footwear
Parent: Triumph Universa AG
Officers: Marika Kovacs [1968] Finance Director [Dutch]

Triventura Bidco Limited
Incorporated: 27 March 2017
Total Assets: £89,321,000
Registered Office: Staverton Court, Staverton, Cheltenham, Glos, GL51 0UX
Activities: Activities of other holding companies n.e.c.
Parent: Triventura Midco II Limited
Officers: Philip Buergin [1979] Director/Chief Executive Officer [Swiss]; Daniel Fehr [1979] Director/Chief Financial Officer [Swiss]

Triventura Midco I Limited
Incorporated: 27 March 2017 *Employees:* 555
Net Worth Deficit: £7,487,000 *Total Assets:* £101,850,000
Registered Office: Staverton Court, Staverton, Cheltenham, Glos, GL51 0UX
Activities: Activities of other holding companies n.e.c.
Parent: Colosseum Dental Group AS
Officers: Philip Buergin [1979] Director/Chief Executive Officer [Swiss]; Daniel Fehr [1979] Director/Chief Financial Officer [Swiss]

Triventura Midco II Limited
Incorporated: 27 March 2017
Total Assets: £89,264,000
Registered Office: Staverton Court, Staverton, Cheltenham, Glos, GL51 0UX
Activities: Activities of other holding companies n.e.c.
Parent: Triventura Midco I Limited
Officers: Philip Buergin [1979] Director/Chief Executive Officer [Swiss]; Daniel Fehr [1979] Director/Chief Financial Officer [Swiss]

Trivselhus UK Limited
Incorporated: 16 October 2015 *Employees:* 3
Net Worth Deficit: £1,376,305 *Total Assets:* £14,507,126
Registered Office: Unit 18-19 Cirencester Office Park, Tetbury Road, Cirencester, Glos, GL7 6JJ
Activities: Other business support service activities n.e.c.
Officers: Anna Kristina Belfrage [1962] Director/Chief Financial Officer [Swedish]; Kenneth James Forster [1956] Director; Tore Janson [1957] Director [Swedish]; Viktor Pilemyr [1981] Director/Chief Financial Officer [Swedish]

TRL Electronics Limited
Incorporated: 27 April 2004
Net Worth: £102,825,000 *Total Assets:* £102,825,000
Registered Office: Sigma Close, Shannon Way, Ashchurch, Tewkesbury, Glos, GL20 8ND
Activities: Manufacture of other electrical equipment
Parent: L-3 Global Holding UK Ltd.
Officers: Peter Charles Dann, Secretary; Dan Yaakov Azmon [1963] Director/Business Executive [American]; Ronald Cook [1953] Director/Vice President; Stuart John Evans [1971] Director; Richard Alan Flitton [1963] Director; Gregory Douglas Roberts [1960] Director

TRL Technology Limited
Incorporated: 8 March 1983 *Employees:* 258
Net Worth: £28,549,000 *Total Assets:* £48,694,000
Registered Office: Sigma Close, Shannon Way, Tewkesbury, Glos, GL20 8ND
Activities: Manufacture of other electrical equipment
Parent: TRL Electronics Limited
Officers: Peter Charles Dann, Secretary; Dan Yaakov Azmon [1963] Director/Business Executive [American]; Ronald Cook [1953] Director/Vice President; Stuart John Evans [1971] Director; Richard Alan Flitton [1963] Director; Gregory Douglas Roberts [1960] Director

Troax (U.K.) Limited
Incorporated: 18 March 1983 *Employees:* 22
Net Worth: £3,128,921 *Total Assets:* £4,496,034
Registered Office: Enterprise House, Murdock Road, Dorcan, Swindon, Wilts, SN3 5HY
Activities: Manufacture of other fabricated metal products n.e.c.
Parent: Troax AB
Officers: Kevin Nicholas Cooper, Secretary; Kevin Nicholas Cooper [1963] Director/Accountant; David William Teulon [1953] Managing Director; Thomas Widstrand [1957] Director [Swedish]

Troax Lee Manufacturing Limited
Incorporated: 4 December 1990 *Employees:* 35
Net Worth: £2,922,050 *Total Assets:* £3,900,986
Registered Office: Enterprise House, Murdock Road, Swindon, Wilts, SN3 5HY
Activities: Manufacture of other fabricated metal products n.e.c.
Parent: Troax (UK) Ltd
Officers: Kevin Nicholas Cooper, Secretary; Kevin Nicholas Cooper [1963] Director/Accountant; David William Teulon [1953] Managing Director; Thomas Widstrand [1957] Director [Swedish]

Troika Developments Limited
Incorporated: 19 November 1970 *Employees:* 10
Net Worth: £31,900,912 *Total Assets:* £57,226,956
Registered Office: Midland House, 2 Poole Road, Bournemouth, BH2 5QY
Activities: Development of building projects
Major Shareholder: Nigel Ashley Walters
Officers: Ben White, Secretary; Keith Bruce McKay [1956] Director/Chartered Surveyor; Nigel Ashley Walters [1953] Director; Ben White [1985] Director/Company Secretary

Troika Eastleigh Properties Limited
Incorporated: 20 November 2013 *Employees:* 3
Net Worth: £3,653,938 *Total Assets:* £18,306,528
Registered Office: Midland House, 2 Poole Road, Bournemouth, BH2 5QY
Activities: Development of building projects
Parent: Troika Developments Limited
Officers: Ben White, Secretary; Keith Bruce McKay [1956] Director; Nigel Ashley Walters [1953] Director; Ben White [1985] Director/Company Secretary

Troika Property Holdings Limited
Incorporated: 10 April 1984 *Employees:* 3
Net Worth: £8,884,085 *Total Assets:* £17,940,216
Registered Office: Midland House, 2 Poole Road, Bournemouth, BH2 5QY
Activities: Renting and operating of Housing Association real estate
Parent: Troika Developments Limited
Officers: Ben White, Secretary; Keith Bruce McKay [1956] Director/Chartered Surveyor; Nigel Ashley Walters [1953] Director; Ben White [1985] Director/Company Secretary

Troy (UK) Limited
Incorporated: 12 July 2010 *Employees:* 61
Net Worth: £1,324,940 *Total Assets:* £35,772,760
Registered Office: Roundswell Business Park, Roundswell, Barnstaple, Devon, EX31 3TU
Activities: Non-specialised wholesale trade
Shareholders: Alexandra Jane Kilbride; Paul Philip Kilbride
Officers: Wayne David Hobbs [1958] Director; Alexandra Jane Kilbride [1969] Director; Paul Philip Kilbride [1963] Director; Richard Pymm [1959] Business Development Director; Peter David Watts [1951] Director

Truflo Air Movement Limited
Incorporated: 6 July 2005 *Employees:* 62
Net Worth: £3,533,000 *Total Assets:* £6,376,000
Registered Office: First Floor, 10 Temple Back, Bristol, BS1 6FL
Activities: Manufacture of other fabricated metal products n.e.c.
Officers: Thomas Moser [1963] Director/President [American]; Wolodymyr Pelenski [1958] Director/Accountant; Jim Sorboro [1968] Director/Chief Financial Officer [American]; Isaac Granville James Edward Wharton [1960] Managing Director

Allen Trump Holdings Limited
Incorporated: 17 March 2009
Net Worth: £7,107,906 *Total Assets:* £7,107,906
Registered Office: Vici House, 2 Mallard Road, Sowton, Exeter, Devon, EX2 7LD
Activities: Activities of other holding companies n.e.c.
Parent: AT Property Holdings Limited
Officers: Samantha Joy Cliff, Secretary; Allen Trump [1948] Director/Publisher

Truro & Penwith Academy Trust
Incorporated: 6 February 2014 *Employees:* 684
Net Worth: £43,292,240 *Total Assets:* £50,399,900
Registered Office: College Road, Truro, Cornwall, TR1 3XX
Activities: Pre-primary education
Officers: Eamonn Burns, Secretary; Dr Jennifer Blunden [1976] Director/Chief Executive; Robert Stevens Crossland [1953] Director/Retired; Susan Jane Dickinson [1962] Director/Head of Finance; Anita Lesley Firth [1969] Director/Retired; Terence Arthur Lister [1946] Director/Retired; Professor Alan George Livingston [1947] Director/Retired Ex-Principal of HE College; Andrew Stittle [1960] Director/FE Senior Manager; David Rowlands Williams [1953] Director/Retired; Margaret Ellen Winser [1942] Director/Retired; Peter John Wroe [1978] Director/Accountant

Truro Diocesan Board of Finance Limited (The)
Incorporated: 23 October 1896 *Employees:* 35
Net Worth: £92,204,880 *Total Assets:* £94,801,960
Registered Office: Church House, Woodlands Court, Truro Business Park, Threemilestone, Truro, Cornwall, TR4 9NH
Activities: Cultural education
Officers: Esther Pollard, Secretary; Revd Canon Anne Elizabeth Brown [1961] Director/Clergyperson; Dean Roger Charles Bush [1956] Director/Beneficed Clergyman; Audrey Anne Elkington [1957] Director/Minister of Religion; Christopher David Goldsmith [1954] Director; Nicolas Corin John Herian [1963] Director; Charlotte Elisabeth Irwin [1967] Director/Housewife; Andrew Keast [1963] Director/Accountant; Roger Haydyn Kirkpatrick [1965] Director/Chartered Accountant; Rev Christopher Charles McQuillen-Wright [1971] Director/Minister of Religion; The Right Reverend Philip Ian Mounstephen [1959] Director/Bishop; Lynn Parker [1954] Director/Parish Priest; Robert John Perry [1954] Director/Retired; Michael James Sturgess [1956] Director/Chartered Accountant; Dr Andrew Gibb Thompson [1951] Director/Retired; Jeremy Stephen Thorold [1959] Director/Clerk in Holy Orders; Dr Michael John Todd [1943] Director/Retired; Robin Clinton West [1950] Director/Principal Cyber Security Consultant

Truro Tractors Limited
Incorporated: 22 October 1998 *Employees:* 30
Net Worth: £960,955 *Total Assets:* £3,917,549
Registered Office: Cox Hill, Chacewater, Truro, Cornwall, TR4 8LY
Activities: Wholesale of agricultural machinery, equipment and supplies
Shareholders: Jeremy Martin Stephens; Jonathan Luther Stephens
Officers: Jeremy Martin Stephens, Secretary/Tractor Dealer; Ernestine Stephens [1942] Director/Farm Machinery Dealer; Jeremy Martin Stephens [1966] Director/Agricultural Engineer; Jonathan Luther Stephens [1968] Director/Agricultural Engineer; Martin Arnold Stephens [1943] Director/Farm Machinery Dealer

Trusart Limited
Incorporated: 9 July 1984 *Employees:* 1
Net Worth: £1,378,011 *Total Assets:* £3,831,621
Registered Office: The Holt, Lower Aisholt, Bridgwater, Somerset, TA5 1AS
Activities: Other letting and operating of own or leased real estate
Officers: Michael David Demenis, Secretary; Ruth Maria Demenis [1954] Director/Chartered Secretary

Truscotts (Barnstaple) Limited
Incorporated: 9 June 1992
Net Worth: £1,546,877 *Total Assets:* £5,521,348
Registered Office: Woodland House, Forresters Business Park, Estover Road, Plymouth, PL6 7PL
Activities: Construction of commercial buildings
Major Shareholder: Michael John Boundy
Officers: Michael John Boundy [1966] Director/Property Developer; Tamara Jane Boundy [1996] Director; Thomas Harvey Boundy [1996] Director

Trust in Learning (Academies)
Incorporated: 30 May 2012 *Employees:* 411
Net Worth: £4,205,173 *Total Assets:* £12,546,927
Registered Office: Trust House, Teyfant Road, Bristol, BS13 0RG
Activities: Pre-primary education
Officers: Clare Annette Anderson, Secretary; Andrew John Baber [1961] Director/Management Accountant; Helen Margaret Cooper [1962] Managing Director; Mark Jonathan Davies [1961] Director/Chief Executive; Louise Anne Donaghey [1977] Director/Senior Vice President - India & South Asia; Thyrone Fredrick Hodgson [1978] Director/Accountant [Australian]; Caroline Janet Jenkins [1963] Director/Family and Community Engagement Worker; Laura Kochanski [1959] Director/Retired; Nathan John Peacey [1966] Director/Solicitor; Lee Daniel Probert [1983] Director/Chief Executive; Gerard Joseph Rice [1962] Director/University Lecturer; Jacquelyne Laurinda Smith [1962] Director/Community Volunteer; Jane Walton [1965] Director/Musician

TTK British Holdings Limited
Incorporated: 24 March 2016 *Employees:* 5
Net Worth: £14,361,112 *Total Assets:* £28,617,660
Registered Office: Avonmouth Way, Bristol, BS11 9HX
Activities: Activities of other holding companies n.e.c.
Officers: Nigel Stuart Hardman, Secretary; Nigel Stuart Hardman [1951] Finance Director; Chandru Kalro [1964] Managing Director [Indian]; Shankaran Krishnamurthy [1953] Director [Indian]; Neil Rosati [1964] Purchasing Director; Jagannathan Thattai Thiruvallur [1948] Director/Chairman [Indian]

TTR PT Limited
Incorporated: 12 May 2006 *Employees:* 160
Net Worth: £723,153 *Total Assets:* £5,602,904
Registered Office: TTR Ltd, Second Floor, Waterloo House, Fleets Corner, Poole, Dorset, BH17 0HL
Activities: Technical and vocational secondary education
Parent: Route2work Limited
Officers: Andrew James Powell [1969] Director

Tubbs (UK) Ltd
Incorporated: 27 April 2001 *Employees:* 4
Net Worth: £4,203,306 *Total Assets:* £4,216,338
Registered Office: Sherston Mill, Sherston, Wilts, SN16 0NG
Activities: Development of building projects
Shareholder: Richard Mark Stafford Tubbs
Officers: Joan Eleanor Tubbs, Secretary; Christopher Stafford Tubbs [1946] Director/Chairman; Joan Eleanor Tubbs [1925] Director; Richard Mark Stafford Tubbs [1972] Managing Director

Edwin Tucker & Sons Limited
Incorporated: 1 March 1899 *Employees:* 42
Net Worth: £3,575,287 *Total Assets:* £4,372,891
Registered Office: Commercial Road, Crediton, Devon, EX17 1ER
Activities: Other manufacturing n.e.c.
Shareholder: Roy Maurice Webber
Officers: Michael Howard Churchward [1953] Director/General Manager; Jonathan Roy Maurice Webber [1958] Managing Director; Roy Maurice Browne Webber [1928] Director; Richard Parnell Wheeler [1941] Director/Chairman

The James Tudor Foundation
Incorporated: 13 July 2004 *Employees:* 2
Net Worth: £30,041,448 *Total Assets:* £30,336,724
Registered Office: Suite 8, Somerset House, 18 Canynge Road, Clifton, Bristol, BS8 3JX
Activities: Other human health activities
Officers: Sarah Jane Martha Stewart, Secretary; Robert Richard Grimes Esler [1954] Retired Director; Susan Elizabeth Evans [1958] Director/Chartered Accountant; Anne Felicity McPherson [1949] Director/Retired Solicitor; Cedric Bransden Nash [1941] Director/Retired Banker; Stephanie Katharine Wren [1957] Director/Copywriter

R Tudor Holdings Limited
Incorporated: 17 May 1991 *Employees:* 3
Previous: Advantage Chemicals Holdings Limited
Net Worth: £3,258,378 *Total Assets:* £3,692,297
Registered Office: Chapel Farm, Chapel Lane, Redmarley D'Abitot, Glos, GL19 3JF
Activities: Manufacture of other inorganic basic chemicals
Officers: Michael Joseph Bache, Secretary; Michael Joseph Bache [1953] Director/Accountant; Rachel Tudor [1971] Director/Stud Manager

Tudor Rose International Ltd
Incorporated: 4 January 2008 *Employees:* 39
Previous: Hartim Limited
Net Worth: £3,170,022 *Total Assets:* £6,649,178
Registered Office: Kingfisher Business Park, London Road, Thrupp, Stroud, Glos, GL5 2BY
Activities: Non-specialised wholesale of food, beverages and tobacco
Shareholder: Western Selection Public Limited Company
Officers: Edward John Beale [1960] Director/Chief Executive; Christopher Paul Couzins-Short [1963] Director; John Frederick Gibson [1951] Director; David Courtnall Marshall [1944] Director; John Anthony Stephenson [1965] Director

Tuffnells Parcels Express Limited
Incorporated: 26 October 1936 *Employees:* 2,857
Net Worth: £30,674,000 *Total Assets:* £61,923,000
Registered Office: Rowan House, Cherry Orchard North, Kembrey Park, Swindon, Wilts, SN2 8UH
Activities: Freight transport by road
Parent: The Big Green Parcel Machine Limited
Officers: Stuart Steven Marriner, Secretary; Peter Geoffrey Birks [1963] Director; Anthony Liam Grace [1961] Director

Turlough Limited
Incorporated: 7 December 1994 *Employees:* 3
Net Worth: £3,446,875 *Total Assets:* £4,824,269
Registered Office: 26 Berkeley Square, Bristol, BS8 1HP
Activities: Construction of domestic buildings
Officers: John Alexander Taylor, Secretary; John Alexander Taylor [1957] Director/Engineer; Audrey Ann Wilson [1957] Director/Physiotherapist [Irish]

Ryan Turner Hope PLC
Incorporated: 16 July 1992 *Employees:* 41
Net Worth: £1,288,948 *Total Assets:* £4,510,783
Registered Office: Pegasus Woodward Avenue, Westerleigh Business Park, Yate, Bristol, BS37 5YS
Activities: Other business support service activities n.e.c.
Shareholders: John Michael Ryan; John Michael Turner; John Barrie Hope
Officers: Margaret Young, Secretary; Dennis Alfred Deacon [1952] Director/Businessman; Mark Fletcher [1974] Director/Designer; John Barrie Hope [1948] Director; John Michael Ryan [1948] Director; Nicholas James Ryan [1972] Director; John Michael Turner [1947] Director

Turner Property Holdings Limited
Incorporated: 19 March 1992
Net Worth: £3,810,825 *Total Assets:* £3,835,592
Registered Office: Apartment 2, Beachside, Rock, Wadebridge, Cornwall, PL27 6FD
Activities: Other letting and operating of own or leased real estate
Parent: Turner UK Limited
Officers: Sarah May Jenks, Secretary; Dominic John Turner [1967] Sales Director

Turner UK Limited
Incorporated: 25 September 2007
Net Worth: £3,784,466 *Total Assets:* £3,810,826
Registered Office: Apartment 2, Beachside, Rock, Wadebridge, Cornwall, PL27 6FD
Activities: Other business support service activities n.e.c.
Major Shareholder: Dominic John Turner
Officers: Sarah May Jenks, Secretary; Dominic John Turner [1967] Managing Director

Turnspeed Precision Engineering Company Limited
Incorporated: 10 July 1980 *Employees:* 64
Net Worth: £5,515,133 *Total Assets:* £10,647,257
Registered Office: 3 Boundary Way, Lufton Trading Estate, Yeovil, Somerset, BA22 8HZ
Activities: Other engineering activities
Major Shareholder: Ronald James Davies
Officers: Jamie Davies, Secretary/Engineer; Jamie Davies [1974] Director; Kelly Davies [1977] Director/Payroll Administrator; Ronald James Davies [1946] Director/Precision Engineer

Turtle Bay Restaurants Limited
Incorporated: 16 January 2010 *Employees:* 1,563
Net Worth: £8,678,195 *Total Assets:* £40,094,312
Registered Office: 1340 Aztec West, Almondsbury, Bristol, BS32 4RX
Activities: Licenced restaurants
Shareholders: Ajith Jayaprakash Jayawickrema; Piper Private Equity Fund V LP
Officers: Christopher John Max Curry [1958] Director/Investment Manager; Ajith Jaya Wickrema [1962] Director; Jane Margaret O'Riordan [1964] Director; Jonathan Paul Edward Temple [1973] Finance Director; Crispin Noel Stephen Tweddell [1947] Director

Francis Tuthill Limited
Incorporated: 28 March 2006
Net Worth: £1,444,259 *Total Assets:* £4,423,022
Registered Office: 5 Pullman Court, Great Western Road, Gloucester, GL1 3ND
Activities: Maintenance and repair of motor vehicles
Officers: Richard Tuthill, Secretary; Francis Tuthill [1947] Director; Richard Francis Tuthill [1974] Director

Twentieth Century Investments Limited
Incorporated: 28 August 1935
Net Worth: £10,911,348 *Total Assets:* £16,184,873
Registered Office: Towngate House, 2-8 Parkstone Road, Poole, Dorset, BH15 2PW
Activities: Other letting and operating of own or leased real estate
Shareholders: John Stephen Payne; Evelyn Parkhurst; Christopher Michael Parkhurst
Officers: John Stephen Payne, Secretary; Evelyn Parkhurst [1944] Director; John Stephen Payne [1965] Director

Two Eagles Investments Limited
Incorporated: 23 March 2015 *Employees:* 3
Net Worth: £44,738 *Total Assets:* £4,090,238
Registered Office: 16 Queen Square, Bristol, BS1 4NT
Activities: Management of real estate on a fee or contract basis
Shareholders: Geoffrey Popper; Jonathan David Rogers; Jamie Wells
Officers: Geoffrey Paul Popper [1967] Director; Jonathan David Rogers [1969] Director; James Wells [1970] Director

Two Rivers Housing
Incorporated: 2 August 2001 *Employees:* 156
Net Worth: £41,586,000 *Total Assets:* £178,951,008
Registered Office: Rivers Meet, Cleeve Mill Lane, Newent, Glos, GL18 1DS
Activities: Renting and operating of Housing Association real estate
Officers: Garry Rupert King, Secretary/Chief Executive; John Bloxsom [1955] Director/Supported Housing Manager; Susan Elizabeth Holmes [1956] Director/Retired; Timothy Christopher Jackson [1963] Executive Director; Rita Jones [1956] Director/Shop Assistant; Yvonne Leishman [1957] Director/Retired; Jonathan Richards [1959] Director/Consultant; Neil Anthony Sutherland [1952] Director

Two Rivers Investments Limited
Incorporated: 27 May 2004 *Employees:* 146
Net Worth: £2,668,000 *Total Assets:* £4,106,000
Registered Office: 39 Commercial Road, Poole, Dorset, BH14 0HU
Activities: Residential nursing care facilities
Parent: Care South
Officers: Penelope Jane Sargeant, Secretary; Lindsay Ann Ansell [1946] Director/Retired Nurse; Stephanie Claire Barnett [1973] Director; Paul Richard Causton [1947] Director/Legal Consultant; Dr Richard Day [1954] Director/Consultant Physician; Martin Richard Dyson [1946] Director/Management Consultant; Richard John Groom [1942] Director/Consultant; Charles James Holt Hunter [1946] Director; Felicity Ann Irwin [1947] Director/Public Relations Consultant; Christopher Kean [1947] Director/Consultant; Jane Stichbury [1955] Director; Hugh James Derek Webster [1946] Director/Chartered Surveyor

Twofour Broadcast Limited
Incorporated: 23 February 1989 *Employees:* 166
Net Worth Deficit: £3,946,000 *Total Assets:* £21,261,000
Registered Office: Twofour Studios, Estover, Plymouth, PL6 7RG
Activities: Television programme production activities
Parent: Twofour Group Limited
Officers: Shireen Yvonne Abbott [1971] Director of Production; Daniel Adamson [1973] Director/TV Producer; Anthony Joseph Coe Hughes [1965] Director/Accountant; Melanie Gina Leach [1974] Director/TV Producer; Andrew MacKenzie [1970] Director/TV Producer

Twofour Group Limited
Incorporated: 28 June 2005 *Employees:* 29
Net Worth: £22,909,000 *Total Assets:* £27,024,000
Registered Office: Twofour Studios, Estover, Plymouth, PL6 7RG
Activities: Video production activities
Parent: Double Double Limited
Officers: Anthony Joseph Coe Hughes [1965] Director/Accountant; Melanie Gina Leach [1974] Director/TV Producer

Twynham Learning
Incorporated: 15 March 2011 *Employees:* 478
Previous: Twynham School
Net Worth: £44,426,000 *Total Assets:* £53,253,000
Registered Office: Twynham School, Sopers Lane, Christchurch, Dorset, BH23 1JF
Activities: Primary education
Officers: Heather Jane Watson, Secretary; Bernard Adrian Bhukal [1972] Deputy Director of Capital and Operational Estates; Gaynor Stephanie Brown [1961] Director/Administrator; Matthew James Buckey [1972] Director/Business Consultant; Lynda Jean Clarke [1950] Director/Retired; Douglas Peter Croucher [1945] Director/Retired Christian Minister; Alison Jayne Curtis [1964] Director/Assistant SENDco; Gareth Ieuan Morris [1976] Director/Education; Deborah Kay Place [1960] Director/Project Manager; Robin Peter Shonfeld [1954] Retired Director of Audit and Business Assurance; Arline Audrey Sperryn-Jones [1978] Director/Chartered Accountant; Michael Arthur Turvey [1950] Director/Retired Council Chief Executive

TxtNation Holdings Limited
Incorporated: 7 February 2011 *Employees:* 30
Net Worth: £2,719,348 *Total Assets:* £7,530,723
Registered Office: 15 Billacombe Road, Plymouth, PL9 7HX
Activities: Other telecommunications activities
Shareholders: Jonathan Gordon Rowsell; Michael Matthew Whelan
Officers: Michael Matthew Whelan [1979] Director

Tyco Electronics Motors Ltd
Incorporated: 11 February 2000
Net Worth: £7,793,477 *Total Assets:* £7,926,192
Registered Office: Company Secretariat, Faraday Road, Dorcan, Swindon, Wilts, SN3 5HH
Activities: Non-trading company
Parent: Tyco Electronics UK Holdings Ltd
Officers: Harold Gregory Barksdale [1964] Director/Attorney [American]; Stephen Christopher Cooper [1970] Director/Accountant; Ashley Raymond Fulford [1963] Director/Operations Manager

Tyco Electronics UK Ltd
Incorporated: 21 June 1955 *Employees:* 1,244
Net Worth: £429,323,008 *Total Assets:* £515,295,008
Registered Office: Company Secretariat, Faraday Road, Dorcan, Swindon, Wilts, SN3 5HH
Activities: Manufacture of electronic components
Parent: Tyco Electronics UK Holdings Ltd
Officers: Harold Gregory Barksdale [1964] Director/Attorney [American]; Stephen Christopher Cooper [1970] Director/Accountant; Andrew Donachie [1972] Operations Director; Ashley Raymond Fulford [1963] Director/Operations Manager

Tylney Investments Limited
Incorporated: 30 January 1989 *Employees:* 16
Net Worth: £28,725,280 *Total Assets:* £33,101,516
Registered Office: Elmfield House, Slab Lane, Woodfalls, Salisbury, Wilts, SP5 2ND
Activities: Other letting and operating of own or leased real estate
Shareholders: Alastair Richard Stuart Thomas; Royston Derwyn Lloyd Thomas
Officers: Alastair Richard Stuart Thomas, Secretary; Caroline Margaret Churchman [1961] Director/Accountant; Alastair Richard Stuart Thomas [1967] Director/Accountant; Royston Derwyn Lloyd Thomas [1965] Director/Estate Management

Tyre Maintenance Limited
Incorporated: 29 January 1979 *Employees:* 93
Net Worth: £1,276,409 *Total Assets:* £9,354,051
Registered Office: c/o Bandvulc Tyres Ltd, Gillard Way, Lee Mill Industrial Estate, Ivybridge, Devon, PL21 9LN
Activities: Wholesale trade of motor vehicle parts and accessories
Parent: Continental UK Group Holdings Limited
Officers: Mark Ingram, Secretary; Lutz Fricke [1962] Director/Business Executive [German]; Arthur Gregg [1962] Director; David Smith [1965] Director; Johannes Suttmeyer [1959] Director [German]

U C B Home Loans Corporation Limited
Incorporated: 31 July 1972
Net Worth: £558,336,000 *Total Assets:* £2,024,210,048
Registered Office: Nationwide House, Pipers Way, Swindon, Wilts, SN38 1NW
Activities: Financial intermediation not elsewhere classified
Parent: Nationwide Building Society
Officers: Timothy Joseph Carter [1970] Director of Product Operations; Jonathan Jasper Haydn Davy [1965] Director/Head of Collections and Recoveries; Julia Mary Roberts Dunn [1965] Director/Chief Risk Officer; Muir James Mathieson [1974] Director of Financial Controls & Information Management; Christopher Stuart Rhodes [1963] Director; Paul Wootton [1979] Director/Head of Specialist Mortgages

U-Drive Limited
Incorporated: 10 April 1996 *Employees:* 146
Net Worth: £4,993,034 *Total Assets:* £29,158,036
Registered Office: 48-56 Old Wareham Road, Parkstone, Poole, Dorset, BH12 4QR
Activities: Renting and leasing of cars and light motor vehicles
Shareholders: David Alan Hamblin; Gillian Phyllis Hamblin
Officers: Gillian Phyllis Hamblin, Secretary; David Alan Hamblin [1946] Director; Gillian Phyllis Hamblin [1948] Director/Company Secretary

UBB Waste (Essex) Limited
Incorporated: 9 March 2012
Net Worth Deficit: £28,732,000 *Total Assets:* £153,354,000
Registered Office: Ashford House, Grenadier Road, Exeter, Devon, EX1 3LH
Activities: Treatment and disposal of non-hazardous waste
Parent: UBB Waste (Essex) Holdings Limited
Officers: Christopher Stephen McCarthy [1982] Commercial Director; Javier Peiro Balaguer [1974] Managing Director Urbaser Ltd [Spanish]; Simon Rooke [1967] Director; Stephen Worthy [1976] Director

UBB Waste (Gloucestershire) Limited
Incorporated: 21 November 2012
Net Worth Deficit: £14,041,000 *Total Assets:* £133,959,000
Registered Office: Ashford House, Grenadier Road, Exeter, Devon, EX1 3LH
Activities: Treatment and disposal of non-hazardous waste
Parent: UBB Waste (Gloucestershire) Holdings Limited
Officers: Christopher Stephen McCarthy [1982] Commercial Director; Javier Peiro Balaguer [1974] Managing Director Urbaser Ltd [Spanish]; Simon Rooke [1967] Director; Stephen Worthy [1976] Director

UCAS Media Limited
Incorporated: 4 August 1992 *Employees:* 68
Net Worth: £258,000 *Total Assets:* £7,458,000
Registered Office: Rosehill, New Barn Lane, Cheltenham, Glos, GL52 3LZ
Activities: Educational support services
Parent: The Universities and Colleges Admissions Service
Officers: Danya Young, Secretary; Kevin Neil Allison [1976] Director of Finance and Corporate Services; Katie Ann Bell [1965] Director/Chief Marketing Officer; Andrew Fraser Forbes [1955] Director/Principal and Chief Executive; Sander Kristel [1970] Executive Director [Dutch]; Clare Marchant [1972] Director/Chief Executive, UCAS; Professor Karen Ann Stanton [1961] Director/Vice-Chancellor; Helena Whitehead Sturridge [1952] Director; Professor Elizabeth Tulip Treasure [1958] Director/Vice Chancellor [British/New Zealander]

UCLH Investors Limited
Incorporated: 1 June 2012 *Employees:* 5
Net Worth: £53,469,000 *Total Assets:* £516,920,992
Registered Office: Third Floor, Broad Quay House, Prince Street, Bristol, BS1 4DJ
Activities: Other business support service activities n.e.c.
Parent: UCLH Investors (Holdings) Limited
Officers: Colin John Anderson [1963] Director/Solicitor; Vikram Bhaskar [1968] Director/Portfolio Manager [Indian]; John Stephen Gordon [1962] Director; John McDonagh [1969] Director; Hannah O'Gorman [1971] Director; Ravi Parekh [1979] Director [American]; Neil Rae [1971] Director

UDS Properties Limited
Incorporated: 22 February 1995
Net Worth: £622,000 *Total Assets:* £6,087,000
Registered Office: Wincanton PLC, Methuen Park, Chippenham, Wilts, SN14 0WT
Activities: Other letting and operating of own or leased real estate
Parent: Wincanton UK Limited
Officers: Rajiv Sharma, Secretary; Adrian Maxwell Colman [1970] Director; Timothy Charles Lawlor [1970] Finance Director

Uffculme Academy Trust
Incorporated: 6 August 2010 *Employees:* 196
Net Worth: £12,949,324 *Total Assets:* £17,469,882
Registered Office: Uffculme School Chapel Hill, Uffculme, Devon, EX15 3AG
Activities: Primary education
Officers: Julia Elizabeth Adamson [1974] Director/Education Manager; Susan Jayne Brewer [1956] Director/Headteacher; Max Ainley Graesser [1957] Director/Pension Scheme Trustee; Lorraine Margaret Heath [1966] Director/Headteacher; Natalie Kaye Keeling [1981] HR Director; Jill Larcombe [1956] Director/Administration; Emma Sims-Fielding [1974] Director/Assistant Principal; Jenny Louise Sutton [1980] Director/Manager; Shaun Mark Vickery [1969] Director/Certified Chartered Accountant

UFP Global Holdings Limited
Incorporated: 19 April 2016
Net Worth: £35,961,636 *Total Assets:* £45,431,052
Registered Office: Ellenborough House, Wellington Street, Cheltenham, Glos, GL50 1YD
Activities: Activities of production holding companies
Parent: Universal Forest Products Inc
Officers: Michael Francis Mordell [1957] Director/Executive Vice President, International Operations [American]

UFT Limited
Incorporated: 4 December 2009 *Employees:* 38
Net Worth: £3,677,950 *Total Assets:* £10,331,497
Registered Office: Landell Mills, Bryer-Ash Business Park, Bradford Road, Trowbridge, Wilts, BA14 8HE
Activities: Management consultancy activities other than financial management
Shareholder: David Thomas Uglow
Officers: Graham Richard Fay, Secretary; Simon Foxwell [1975] Director; David Thomas Uglow [1971] Director

UK Court Services (Manchester) Limited
Incorporated: 20 February 2001
Net Worth: £3,832,803 *Total Assets:* £33,382,840
Registered Office: Third Floor, Broad Quay House, Prince Street, Bristol, BS1 4DJ
Activities: Construction of commercial buildings
Parent: UK Court Services (Manchester) Holdings Limited
Officers: Thomas Anthony Ashe [1955] Operations Director G4S FM [Irish]; Chris Burlton [1973] Director/Accountant; Gawie Murray Nienaber [1957] Director/General Legal Counsel; Vaishali Jagdish Patel [1973] Director/Solicitor; Alan Campbell Ritchie [1967] Director

UK Pacific Hampton Limited
Incorporated: 6 August 2014
Net Worth Deficit: £25,187 *Total Assets:* £5,741,289
Registered Office: Cats Abbey Hall, Northleach, Cheltenham, Glos, GL54 3QD
Activities: Activities of other holding companies n.e.c.
Officers: Nigel John Cadbury Wilson, Secretary; Andrew Peter Biggs [1949] Director/In House Counsel; Nigel John Cadbury Wilson [1957] Director

UK Pacific Hampton Station LLP
Incorporated: 6 August 2014
Net Worth: £5,929,945 *Total Assets:* £6,368,693
Registered Office: Cats Abbey Hall, Northleach, Cheltenham, Glos, GL54 3QD

UK Power Solutions Limited
Incorporated: 23 May 2007 *Employees:* 208
Net Worth: £2,075,000 *Total Assets:* £25,246,000
Registered Office: River View House, Bonds Mill Estate, Stonehouse, Glos, GL10 3RF
Activities: Electrical installation
Shareholder: Marshall Cooke
Officers: Andrew Wright, Secretary; Faith Patricia Wright, Secretary; Joanne Marie Wright, Secretary; Marshall Cooke [1962] Sales Director; James Ronald Trumper [1961] Director; Andrew Wright [1971] Director; Nick Wright [1974] Director

UK Shared Business Services Limited
Incorporated: 1 August 2007 *Employees:* 497
Net Worth: £3,534,000 *Total Assets:* £9,272,000
Registered Office: Polaris House, North Star Avenue, Swindon, Wilts, SN2 1FF
Activities: Research and experimental development on social sciences and humanities
Shareholders: UK Research and Innovation; Secretary of State for Business Energy and Industrial Strategy
Officers: Caroline Rachel Jenkins, Secretary; Ruth Elizabeth Elliot [1977] Finance and Commercial Director; Alice Michelle Hurrell [1975] HR Director; Timothy John Knighton [1955] Director; Graham McAlister [1955] Independent Director; Neil Thomas Phimister [1967] Finance Director; Richard James Semple [1964] Director/Chief Executive

UK Solar Projects Limited
Incorporated: 24 September 2014
Net Worth: £62,711 *Total Assets:* £5,059,083
Registered Office: Delta Place, 27 Bath Road, Cheltenham, Glos, GL53 7TH
Activities: Production of electricity
Shareholder: Lowlands Low Carbon Limited
Officers: Bernard Mark Bentley [1958] Director; John Geoffrey Bolitho [1958] Director; Robin Francis Chamberlayne [1966] Director/Chartered Financial Planner; Eileen Norah Mawle [1944] Director; Rachel Rosemary Murphy [1981] Director/Home Maker; Andrew Jonathan Charles Newman [1970] Director; Nigel John Street [1949] Director

Ukcloud Ltd
Incorporated: 3 May 2011 *Employees:* 174
Previous: Skyscape Cloud Services Ltd
Net Worth Deficit: £1,206,000 *Total Assets:* £28,234,000
Registered Office: Hartham Park, Corsham, Wilts, SN13 0RP
Activities: Other information technology service activities
Parent: Virtual Infrastructure Group Limited
Officers: Sharon Brittan [1967] Director; Dr William Thomas Ginn [1967] Director; Simon John Hansford [1965] Director; Jeremy Robin Sanders [1962] Director

UKRD Group Limited
Incorporated: 24 June 1992 *Employees:* 294
Net Worth: £939,383 *Total Assets:* £5,659,164
Registered Office: Carn Brea Studios, Barncoose Industrial Estate, Redruth, Cornwall, TR15 3RQ
Activities: Activities of head offices
Officers: Andrew Preece, Secretary; Glenn Hunter Aaronson [1957] Director [American]; Anthony David Everett [1947] Director; John Keith Hepburn [1949] Director/Banker [Canadian]; Andrew Richard Preece [1968] Director/Chartered Accountant; William James Generald Rogers [1960] Director/Chief Executive; Trevor Smallwood [1947] Director; Lord James Piers Southwell St-Levan [1950] Director

Ultimate Asset Finance Limited
Incorporated: 20 November 2001 *Employees:* 16
Net Worth: £4,032,000 *Total Assets:* £35,009,000
Registered Office: First Floor, Equinox North, Great Park Road, Bradley Stoke, Bristol, BS32 4QL
Activities: Financial leasing
Parent: Ultimate Finance Group Limited
Officers: Neil Armstrong McMyn, Secretary; Neil Armstrong McMyn [1969] Director and Company Secretary; Ronald Alexander Robson [1963] Director

Ultimate Bridging Finance Limited
Incorporated: 1 June 2012 *Employees:* 10
Previous: Ashley Business Finance Limited
Net Worth: £1,929,000 *Total Assets:* £20,409,000
Registered Office: First Floor, Equinox North, Great Park Road, Bradley Stoke, Bristol, BS32 4QL
Activities: Factoring
Parent: Ultimate Finance Group Limited
Officers: Neil Armstrong McMyn, Secretary; Neil Armstrong McMyn [1969] Director and Company Secretary; Ronald Alexander Robson [1963] Director

Ultimate Finance Group Limited
Incorporated: 10 January 2002 *Employees:* 228
Previous: Ultimate Finance Group PLC
Net Worth: £18,806,000 *Total Assets:* £171,164,992
Registered Office: First Floor, Equinox North, Great Park Road, Bradley Stoke, Bristol, BS32 4QL
Activities: Factoring
Parent: Bentley Park (UK) Limited
Officers: Neil Armstrong McMyn, Secretary; Neil Armstrong McMyn [1969] Director and Company Secretary; Ronald Alexander Robson [1963] Director

Ultimate Finance Limited
Incorporated: 20 November 2001 *Employees:* 103
Previous: Ultimate Invoice Finance Limited
Net Worth Deficit: £3,795,000 *Total Assets:* £109,424,000
Registered Office: First Floor, Equinox North, Great Park Road, Bradley Stoke, Bristol, BS32 4QL
Activities: Factoring
Parent: Ultimate Finance Group Limited
Officers: Neil Armstrong McMyn, Secretary; Neil Armstrong McMyn [1969] Director and Company Secretary; Ronald Alexander Robson [1963] Director

Ultimate Trade Finance Limited
Incorporated: 20 November 2001 *Employees:* 8
Net Worth: £446,000 *Total Assets:* £7,939,000
Registered Office: First Floor, Equinox North, Great Park Road, Bradley Stoke, Bristol, BS32 4QL
Activities: Factoring
Parent: Ultimate Finance Group Limited
Officers: Neil Armstrong McMyn, Secretary; Neil Armstrong McMyn [1969] Director and Company Secretary; Ronald Alexander Robson [1963] Director

Ultrahaptics Holdings Ltd
Incorporated: 8 March 2016 *Employees:* 70
Net Worth: £17,656,000 *Total Assets:* £19,174,000
Registered Office: The West Wing, Glass Wharf, Bristol, BS2 0EL
Activities: Activities of head offices
Shareholders: IP Venture Fund II (GP) LLP; IP2IPO Nominees Limited; IP2IPO Portfolio (GP) Limited
Officers: Dr Thomas Andrew Carter [1988] Director/Chief Technology Officer; Steven Andrew Cliffe [1963] Director; Kunal Dasgupta [1976] Director/Private Equity Investment Professional; Christopher Olds [1981] Director/Chief Financial Officer [South African]; Shiva Tiwari [1984] Alternate Director; Michael Tobin [1964] Director/Chairman; Sir Hossein Yassaie [1956] Director/Technology Entrepreneur Executive

Ultrahaptics IP Ltd
Incorporated: 8 March 2016
Net Worth Deficit: £2,834,000 *Total Assets:* £32,780,000
Registered Office: The West Wing, Glass Wharf, Bristol, BS2 0EL
Activities: Non-trading company
Parent: Ultrahaptics Holdings Limited
Officers: Dr Thomas Andrew Carter [1988] Director/Chief Technology Officer; Steven Andrew Cliffe [1963] Director

Ultrahaptics Limited
Incorporated: 19 November 2013 *Employees:* 63
Net Worth: £35,169,000 *Total Assets:* £40,218,000
Registered Office: The West Wing, Glass Wharf, Bristol, BS2 0EL
Activities: Business and domestic software development
Parent: Ultrahaptics Holdings Limited
Officers: Dr Thomas Andrew Carter [1988] Director/PhD Student; Steven Andrew Cliffe [1963] Director

Ultraparts Limited
Incorporated: 18 June 1982 *Employees:* 19
Net Worth: £6,280,015 *Total Assets:* £6,511,711
Registered Office: Braunton Road, Barnstaple, Devon, EX31 4AT
Activities: Wholesale trade of motor vehicle parts and accessories
Major Shareholder: Grahame Martin Rowley
Officers: Julie Ellen Hobbs, Secretary; Grahame Martin Rowley [1951] Director and Engineer

The Una Group Limited
Incorporated: 27 August 2004 *Employees:* 5
Net Worth: £2,735,538 *Total Assets:* £24,335,198
Registered Office: 10 Thornbury Road, Estover, Plymouth, PL6 7PW
Activities: Other letting and operating of own or leased real estate
Parent: Una Property Limited
Officers: Susan Young, Secretary; Derek John Brooking [1940] Director/Haulage Contractor; Ian Charles Brooking [1970] Director/Builder; Ian Graeme Dennis [1966] Director/Builder; David Anthony Pearce [1963] Finance Director; David Charles Young [1958] Director/Business Consultant

Underdown Investments Limited
Incorporated: 27 October 2003
Net Worth Deficit: £1,003,338 *Total Assets:* £8,450,000
Registered Office: c/o Crowe Clark Whitehill, Carrick House, Lypiatt Road, Cheltenham, Glos, GL50 2QJ
Activities: Management of real estate on a fee or contract basis
Parent: M & F Finance Ireland Ltd
Officers: Brian Francis Conroy [1949] Director/Chartered Accountant [Irish]; Albert Farrell [1945] Director/Consultant [Irish]; Jennifer McGowan [1979] Director [Irish]; Andrew Whitty [1954] Director/Chartered Accountant [Irish]

Uni-Mill Engineering Limited
Incorporated: 30 July 1979 *Employees:* 43
Net Worth: £3,154,568 *Total Assets:* £6,122,198
Registered Office: Rivermead Drive, Rivermead Industrial Estate, Westlea, Swindon, Wilts, SN5 7EX
Activities: Machining
Parent: Uni-Build (Wiltshire) Ltd
Officers: Paul Raymond Hill [1965] Production Director; Nicola Jane Ogle [1968] Director/Administration Manager; Alan David Rayner [1952] Director

Unicorn AIM VCT PLC
Incorporated: 7 August 2001
Net Worth: £201,428,000 *Total Assets:* £201,718,000
Registered Office: Suite 8, Bridge House, Courtenay Street, Newton Abbot, Devon, TQ12 2QS
Activities: Activities of venture and development capital companies
Officers: Peter Frederick Dicks [1942] Director; Maria Charlotta Ginman-Horrell [1965] Director [Finnish/British]; Jeremy John Hamer [1952] Director; Jocelin Montague St John Harris [1945] Director

Unicorn Training Group Limited
Incorporated: 18 August 1992 *Employees:* 135
Net Worth: £4,034,827 *Total Assets:* £8,149,287
Registered Office: 3rd Floor, Telephone House, 18 Christchurch Road, Bournemouth, BH1 3NE
Activities: Business and domestic software development
Shareholders: Peter Ian Phillips; Greenbrook Industries Limited
Officers: Stuart William Sawyer, Secretary; Henry Richard Green [1949] Director/Electrical Product Manufacturer; Mark Daniel Jones [1975] Sales Director; Stuart Jones [1977] IT Director; Jacqueline Kennedy [1968] Director; Neill McWilliams [1969] Director; Peter Ian Phillips [1949] Director/Training Consultant; Clive John Shelton [1955] Director; Peter Dylan Unsworth [1958] Director/Accountant; Helen Patricia Watts [1964] Director

Union Jack Oil PLC
Incorporated: 18 January 2011 *Employees:* 4
Net Worth: £4,447,526 *Total Assets:* £4,987,523
Registered Office: 6 Charlotte Street, Bath, BA1 2NE
Activities: Extraction of crude petroleum
Officers: Matthew George Small, Secretary; David Roger Bramhill [1951] Director; Graham Bull [1946] Director/Consultant Exploration Geologist; Raymond George Godson [1944] Director/Accountant; Frazer Lang [1990] Director; Joseph Bernard O'Farrell [1951] Director [Irish]

Unique Home Stays Limited
Incorporated: 2 August 2002 *Employees:* 23
Net Worth: £6,018,490 *Total Assets:* £7,881,167
Registered Office: Lantern Cottage, Trebudannon, Newquay, Cornwall, TR8 4LP
Activities: Other holiday and other collective accommodation
Major Shareholder: Sarah Ann Stanley
Officers: Sarah Ann Stanley [1963] Director

Unite Accommodation Management 18 Limited
Incorporated: 12 December 2012
Net Worth Deficit: £113 *Total Assets:* £5,979,442
Registered Office: South Quay, Temple Back, Bristol, BS1 6FL
Activities: Other letting and operating of own or leased real estate
Parent: LDC (Holdings) Limited
Officers: Christopher Robert Szpojnarowicz, Secretary; David Faulkner [1976] Director/Deputy CFO; Joseph Julian Lister [1971] Director/Chief Financial Officer; Richard Sauvan Smith [1974] Managing Director, Operations; Christopher Robert Szpojnarowicz [1968] Director/Company Secretary/Head of Legal

Unite Accommodation Management 19 Limited
Incorporated: 26 November 2013
Net Worth: £1 *Total Assets:* £84,228,032
Registered Office: South Quay, Temple Back, Bristol, BS1 6FL
Activities: Other letting and operating of own or leased real estate
Parent: LDC (Holdings) Limited
Officers: Christopher Robert Szpojnarowicz, Secretary; David Faulkner [1976] Director/Deputy CFO; Joseph Julian Lister [1971] Director/Corporate Finance Manager; Christopher Robert Szpojnarowicz [1968] Director/Head of Legal & Company Secretary

Unite Accommodation Management 6 Limited
Incorporated: 18 March 2004
Net Worth: £985 *Total Assets:* £28,164,024
Registered Office: South Quay, Temple Back, Bristol, BS1 6FL
Activities: Other letting and operating of own or leased real estate
Parent: LDC (Holdings) Limited
Officers: Christopher Robert Szpojnarowicz, Secretary; David Faulkner [1976] Director/Deputy CFO; Joseph Julian Lister [1971] Director/Corporate Finance Manager; Christopher Robert Szpojnarowicz [1968] Director/Head of Legal and Company Secretary

Unite Accommodation Management Limited
Incorporated: 29 March 2007
Previous: Unite Accommodation Management 10 Limited
Net Worth: £1 *Total Assets:* £28,080,892
Registered Office: South Quay, Temple Back, Bristol, BS1 6FL
Activities: Other letting and operating of own or leased real estate
Parent: LDC (Finance) Limited
Officers: Christopher Robert Szpojnarowicz, Secretary; David Faulkner [1976] Director/Deputy CFO; Nicholas William John Hayes [1981] Development Director; Joseph Julian Lister [1971] Finance Director; Christopher Robert Szpojnarowicz [1968] Director/Company Secretary/Head of Legal

Unite Accommodation Management One Hundred Limited
Incorporated: 13 March 2012
Net Worth: £240,492 *Total Assets:* £36,779,724
Registered Office: South Quay, Temple Back, Bristol, BS1 6FL
Activities: Other letting and operating of own or leased real estate
Parent: LDC (Portfolio 100) Limited
Officers: Christopher Robert Szpojnarowicz, Secretary; David Faulkner [1976] Director/Deputy CFO; Joseph Julian Lister [1971] Director/Chief Financial Officer; Richard Sauvan Smith [1974] Managing Director - Operations; Christopher Robert Szpojnarowicz [1968] Director/Company Secretary

Unite Finance Limited
Incorporated: 15 January 2002
Net Worth: £11,529,000 *Total Assets:* £59,832,000
Registered Office: South Quay, Temple Back, Bristol, BS1 6FL
Activities: Other letting and operating of own or leased real estate
Parent: The Unite Group PLC
Officers: Christopher Robert Szpojnarowicz, Secretary; David Faulkner [1976] Director/Deputy CFO; Joseph Julian Lister [1971] Director/Chief Financial Officer; Christopher Robert Szpojnarowicz [1968] Director/Company Secretary/Head of Legal

Unite Finance One (Holdings) Limited
Incorporated: 2 November 2001
Net Worth: £9,708,000 *Total Assets:* £100,169,000
Registered Office: South Quay, Temple Back, Bristol, BS1 6FL
Activities: Other letting and operating of own or leased real estate
Parent: Unite Finance Limited
Officers: Christopher Robert Szpojnarowicz, Secretary; David Faulkner [1976] Director/Deputy CFO; Joseph Julian Lister [1971] Director/Chief Financial Officer; Christopher Robert Szpojnarowicz [1968] Director/Company Secretary/Head of Legal

Unite Finance One (Property) Limited
Incorporated: 11 October 2001
Net Worth: £61,769,000 *Total Assets:* £71,368,000
Registered Office: South Quay, Temple Back, Bristol, BS1 6FL
Activities: Other letting and operating of own or leased real estate
Parent: Unite Finance One (Holdings) Limited
Officers: Christopher Robert Szpojnarowicz, Secretary; David Faulkner [1976] Director/Deputy CFO; Joseph Julian Lister [1971] Director/Chief Financial Officer; Richard Sauvan Smith [1974] Managing Director Operations; Christopher Robert Szpojnarowicz [1968] Director/Company Secretary/Head of Legal

The Unite Group PLC
Incorporated: 15 May 1996 *Employees:* 1,262
Net Worth: £1,728,999,936 *Total Assets:* £2,431,600,128
Registered Office: South Quay, Temple Back, Bristol, BS1 6FL
Activities: Activities of other holding companies n.e.c.
Officers: Christopher Robert Szpojnarowicz, Secretary; Richard John Akers [1961] Director; Ilaria Jane Del Beato [1966] Director; Andrew Marc Jones [1968] Director/Chief Executive Officer; Joseph Julian Lister [1971] Director/Chief Financial Officer; Elizabeth McMeikan [1962] Director; Ross John Paterson [1971] Director; Richard Sauvan Smith [1974] Managing Director, Operations; Philip Michael White [1949] Director; Sir Robert James Timothy Wilson [1949] Director/Vice Chancellor

Unite Holdings Limited
Incorporated: 19 January 1996
Previous: Unite Holdings PLC
Net Worth: £9,429,657 *Total Assets:* £123,325,752
Registered Office: South Quay, Temple Back, Bristol, BS1 6FL
Activities: Other letting and operating of own or leased real estate
Parent: The Unite Group PLC
Officers: Christopher Robert Szpojnarowicz, Secretary; David Faulkner [1976] Director/Deputy CFO; Joseph Julian Lister [1971] Director/Chief Financial Officer; Christopher Robert Szpojnarowicz [1968] Director/Company Secretary/Head of Legal

Unite Integrated Solutions PLC
Incorporated: 10 July 1989 *Employees:* 1,262
Net Worth: £13,739,000 *Total Assets:* £653,697,024
Registered Office: South Quay, Temple Back, Bristol, BS1 6FL
Activities: Other letting and operating of own or leased real estate
Parent: Unite Holdings Limited
Officers: Christopher Robert Szpojnarowicz, Secretary; David Faulkner [1976] Director/Deputy CFO; Nicholas William John Hayes [1981] Development Director; Joseph Julian Lister [1971] Director/Corporate Finance Manager; Richard Sauvan Smith [1974] Managing Director; Christopher Robert Szpojnarowicz [1968] Director/Company Secretary/Head of Legal

United Agri Products Limited
Incorporated: 10 March 1993 *Employees:* 163
Net Worth: £38,720,000 *Total Assets:* £99,827,000
Registered Office: Station Road, Andoversford, Cheltenham, Glos, GL54 4LZ
Activities: Support activities for crop production
Parent: Willmot Pertwee Limited
Officers: Peter Michael Dunne [1973] Director/Chartered Accountant [Irish]; Spencer Gareth Evans [1970] Director/Chief Financial Officer; Ronan Andrew Hughes [1968] Director [Irish]; Christopher Stephen Matthews [1957] Director; James Marshall Rennie [1957] Director

United Bible Societies Association
Incorporated: 6 June 1988 *Employees:* 95
Net Worth: £55,385,264 *Total Assets:* £75,448,896
Registered Office: United Bible Societies, Stonehill Green, Westlea, Swindon, Wilts, SN5 7PJ
Activities: Activities of religious organisations
Officers: Adrian White, Secretary; Ruben Arturo Del Re [1966] Director/General Secretary [Argentinian]; Elaine Margaret Duncan [1958] Director/Chief Executive; Efua Ghartey [1966] Director/Lawyer [Ghanaian]; Dr Jutta Henner [1968] Director/General Secretary - Austrian Bible Society [German]; Anthony Lamuel [1953] Director/General Secretary - Bible Society of Pakistan [Pakistani]; Dr Roy Lawrence Peterson [1954] Director/Administrator [American]; Dr Christoph Rosel [1964] Director/Chief Executive [German]

United Healthcare (Bromley) Group Limited
Incorporated: 22 January 2004
Net Worth Deficit: £23,555,000 *Total Assets:* £131,774,000
Registered Office: Third Floor, Broad Quay House, Prince Street, Bristol, BS1 4DJ
Activities: Medical nursing home activities
Shareholders: Semperian PPP Investment Partners No.2 Limited; Innisfree Nominees Limited
Officers: Benjamin Christopher Jacob Dean [1979] Director; Christopher James [1968] Director; David Francis Lindesay [1960] Commercial Director; Richard Little [1979] Investment Director

United Healthcare (Bromley) Holdings Limited
Incorporated: 24 March 1998
Net Worth: £621,000 *Total Assets:* £53,404,000
Registered Office: Third Floor, Broad Quay House, Prince Street, Bristol, BS1 4DJ
Activities: Activities of head offices
Parent: United Healthcare (Bromley) Group Limited
Officers: Benjamin Christopher Jacob Dean [1979] Director; Christopher James [1968] Director; David Francis Lindesay [1960] Commercial Director; Richard Little [1979] Investment Director

United Healthcare (Bromley) Limited
Incorporated: 1 July 1998
Net Worth: £16,984,000 *Total Assets:* £172,479,008
Registered Office: Third Floor, Broad Quay House, Prince Street, Bristol, BS1 4DJ
Activities: Medical nursing home activities
Parent: United Healthcare (Bromley) Holdings Limited
Officers: Benjamin Christopher Jacob Dean [1979] Director; Christopher James [1968] Director; David Francis Lindesay [1960] Commercial Director; Richard Little [1979] Investment Director

United Healthcare (Bromley) Services Limited
Incorporated: 26 February 2004
Total Assets: £40,693,000
Registered Office: Third Floor, Broad Quay House, Prince Street, Bristol, BS1 4DJ
Activities: Other business support service activities n.e.c.
Parent: United Healthcare (Bromley) Limited
Officers: Benjamin Christopher Jacob Dean [1979] Director; Christopher James [1968] Director; David Francis Lindesay [1960] Commercial Director; Richard Little [1979] Investment Director

United Oilseeds Marketing Limited
Incorporated: 14 December 1979 *Employees:* 28
Net Worth: £10,229,268 *Total Assets:* £28,911,070
Registered Office: St James House, St James Place, Gains Lane, Devizes, Wilts, SN10 1FB
Activities: Post-harvest crop activities
Parent: United Oilseed Producers Limted
Officers: Christopher John Baldwin [1958] Managing Director; Helen Casey [1969] Director/Certified Accountant; Andrew Temple Cragg [1959] Director/Farmer; Richard Anthony Hall [1964] Director/Farmer; Benjamin James Jackson [1982] Director/Farmer; Colin Sharp McGregor [1968] Director/Farmer; Troy Stuart [1969] Director/Farmer; Timothy Peter Westgarth [1973] Director/Farmer

United Reformed Church (South Western Synod) Incorporated (The)
Incorporated: 5 September 1977 *Employees:* 10
Net Worth: £13,707,062 *Total Assets:* £13,995,474
Registered Office: The Manse, Norton Fitzwarren, Taunton, Somerset, TA2 6RU
Activities: Activities of religious organisations
Officers: Dr Ian Bishop Harrison, Secretary; Raoul Nigel Vaughan Hewitt, Secretary; Rev Christopher Charles Baillie [1954] Director/Minister of Religion; Revd Richard Gillies Gray [1945] Director/Retired; Ian Bishop Harrison [1950] Director/Retired; David John Hayden [1933] Director/Retired; Gwen Margaret Jennings [1955] Director/Synod Clerk; Rev Donald MacAlister [1958] Director/Minister of Religion; Maria Mills [1957] Director/Church Worker; Rev Lythan Elisabeth Nevard [1965] Director/Minister of Religion; Margaret Jill Stidson [1939] Director/Retired; Revd Ruth Josephine Whitehead [1963] Director/Minister of Religion

United Registrar of Systems Limited
Incorporated: 25 April 1994 *Employees:* 21
Net Worth: £3,068,950 *Total Assets:* £4,222,530
Registered Office: 3-5 College Court, Burnham on Sea, Somerset, TA8 1AR
Activities: Other service activities n.e.c.
Parent: United Registrar of Systems (Holdings) Limited
Officers: Christopher Paul Lewis, Secretary; David Gurdon Riggs [1957] Managing Director

Unitedhealthcare Global Medical (UK) Limited
Incorporated: 10 February 1986 *Employees:* 79
Previous: Frontier Medex Limited
Net Worth: £8,122,000 *Total Assets:* £13,194,000
Registered Office: Beechdene House, Vantage Point Business Village, Mitcheldean, Glos, GL17 0DD
Activities: Human resources provision and management of human resources functions
Parent: UnitedHealth Group Incorporated
Officers: Brigid Spicola, Secretary; Janette Hiscock [1973] Director; John Michael Malone [1967] Director [American]

Unity Farm Holiday Centre Limited
Incorporated: 25 April 1985 *Employees:* 20
Net Worth: £5,792,988 *Total Assets:* £9,290,395
Registered Office: Holiday Resort Unity, Coast Road, Berrow, Burnham on Sea, Somerset, TA8 2RB
Activities: Recreational vehicle parks, trailer parks and camping grounds
Shareholders: Richard John House; Bridget Denise House
Officers: Bridget Denise House, Secretary; Alan Richard House [1977] Information Technical Director; Bridget Denise House [1958] Catering Director; Richard John House [1947] Managing Director; Sarah Gayle Spottiswoode [1981] Personnel/Health & Safety Director

Unity Tyre Company Limited
Incorporated: 7 January 1974 *Employees:* 27
Net Worth: £7,128,080 *Total Assets:* £7,525,277
Registered Office: 18 Bath Road, Bitton, Bristol, BS30 6HZ
Activities: Wholesale trade of motor vehicle parts and accessories
Major Shareholder: Bryan David Williams
Officers: Bryan David Williams, Secretary; Bryan David Williams [1936] Director/Chairman; David Anthony Williams [1976] Managing Director

Universal Balancing Limited
Incorporated: 17 September 1998 *Employees:* 32
Net Worth: £9,854,663 *Total Assets:* £21,658,600
Registered Office: 12 Douglas Road, Kingswood, Bristol, BS15 8PD
Activities: Manufacture of other general-purpose machinery n.e.c.
Parent: Equilibrium Industries Limited
Officers: Stephen Roy Fowler, Secretary; Stephen Roy Fowler [1970] Director/Engineer; Jon Douglas Lawrence [1970] Director [American]; David John Payne [1980] Finance Director; Julian Paul Reed [1971] Director; Ward Van de Walle [1974] Director [Belgian]; Bert Vermeersch [1967] Director [Belgian]

Universal Promotions Limited
Incorporated: 25 October 1967 *Employees:* 1
Net Worth: £1,399,591 *Total Assets:* £5,217,094
Registered Office: 1st Floor, The Syms Building, Bumpers Way, Bumpers Farm, Chippenham, Wilts, SN14 6LH
Activities: Development of building projects
Officers: John Charles Barnard, Secretary; John Charles Barnard [1957] Director/Property Developer; Patrick Temple Barnard [1935] Director/Fine Art Print Publisher; Karen Rachel Barnard Weston [1961] Director/Hotelier

The Universities and Colleges Admissions Service
Incorporated: 27 July 1993 *Employees:* 498
Net Worth: £22,846,000 *Total Assets:* £38,814,000
Registered Office: Rosehill, New Barn Lane, Cheltenham, Glos, GL52 3LZ
Activities: Educational support services
Officers: Danya Young, Secretary; Dr David John Ashton [1967] Director/Vice President and Registrar; Robert Fredrick Behrens [1952] Director/Ombudsman; Professor Joy Carter [1955] Director/Vice Chancellor University of Winchester; Thomas William Chambers [1961] Director; Andrew Fraser Forbes [1955] Director/Principal and Chief Executive; Professor Sally Louise Mapstone [1957] Director/Principal and Vice-Chancellor; Professor Edward William Peck [1959] Director/Vice-Chancellor; Gerard Patrick Pennell [1959] Director/Strategic IT Adviser; Professor Colin Bryan Riordan [1959] Director/Vice-Chancellor President; Professor Sir Steven Murray Smith [1952] Director/Vice-Chancellor and Chief Executive; Professor Karen Ann Stanton [1961] Director/University Vice Chancellor; Sian Elizabeth Thornhill [1959] Director/Executive Principal

University of Gloucestershire
Incorporated: 8 December 2006 *Employees:* 911
Net Worth: £56,811,000 *Total Assets:* £159,632,000
Registered Office: Fulwood House, University of Gloucestershire, The Park, Cheltenham, Glos, GL50 2RH
Activities: First-degree level higher education
Officers: Dr Matthew Paul Andrews, Secretary; Madiha Azizi [1997] Director/Students' Union President; Peter David Bungard [1959] Director/Chief Executive; Matthew Michael Burgess [1967] Director/Principal & CEO; Paul John Davies [1951] Director; Nicola Hermine de Iongh [1970] Director/Management Consultant; Christopher Siu Kwon Fung [1973] Director [Australian]; Maisie Louise Jerrim [1996] Director/Students' Union Education Officer; David Paul Jones [1967] Director/Lecturer; Martin Ewart Jones [1948] Director; Stephen Andrew Marston [1961] Director/Vice Chancellor; Allen Mawby [1949] Director/Business Consultancy; Stephen Generald Maycock [1952] Director; Dr Andrew John Misiura [1963] Director/University Lecturer; Karen Jane Morgan [1945] Director; Mehjabeen Patrick [1970] Director/Chief Financial Officer; Daniel Ramsay [1979] Director/Head of Academic Services; Pamela Mary Sissons [1963] Director; The Very Reverend Robert Wilfred Springett [1962] Director/Bishop; Angus Wilson Taylor [1966] Director/Chartered Surveyor

University of St Mark & St John
Incorporated: 16 May 2011 *Employees:* 269
Net Worth: £23,969,000 *Total Assets:* £47,918,000
Registered Office: University of St Mark & St John, Derriford Road, Derriford, Plymouth, PL6 8BH
Activities: First-degree level higher education
Officers: Unity Faith Stuart, Secretary; Mike Baker [1975] Director/Lecturer; Richard Dion Bayly [1951] Director/Retired; Dr Susan Ann Brownlow [1960] Director; Dr Susan Eileen Cooper [1962] Director/Senior Lecturer; Matthew William Evans [1973] Director/Chief Executive; Claire Elizabeth Gibson [1970] Managing Director; Pamela Anne Greener [1960] Director/Consultant; Alex James Hawtin [1986] Director/Finance Manager; Professor Patricia Hind [1951] Director/Professor of Management Development; Bishop Nicholas Howard Paul McKinnel [1954] Director/Bishop; Graham Evan William Thair Raikes [1957] Director of Finance; Rhys William Roberts [1994] Director/Student Union Sabbatical Officer; John Michael Searson [1963] Director of Education; Michele Indianna Shoebridge [1954] Director/Higher Education Consultant; Richard Charles Barrington Stevens [1968] Managing Director; Lynn Jean Tamsett-White [1972] Director/Professional Services Manager; Emma Louise Van Der Lugt [1970] Director/GP Practice Manager; Professor Robert Ernest Warner [1956] Director/Vice-Chancellor and Chief Executive

Up Cerne Limited
Incorporated: 18 October 1979
Net Worth: £3,679,639 *Total Assets:* £4,421,903
Registered Office: Estate Office, Up Cerne Manor, Up Cerne, Dorchester, DT2 7AW
Activities: Growing of cereals (except rice), leguminous crops and oil seeds
Officers: David Hebditch, Secretary; Michael Habsburg-Lothringen [1942] Director [Austrian]; Severin Meister [1981] Director [Austrian]; John Richard Anthony Scott-Oldfield [1933] Director/Business Consultant; Sir Richard Maurice Hilton Vickers [1928] Director/Retired

Uphouse Farm Limited
Incorporated: 18 April 1997 *Employees:* 14
Net Worth: £11,119,633 *Total Assets:* £23,363,942
Registered Office: 30 Gay Street, Bath, BA1 2PA
Activities: Raising of other animals
Shareholders: Jennifer Joice; Nigel Peter Joice
Officers: Jennifer Joice, Secretary/Retired; Jennifer Joice [1946] Director/Retired; Nigel Peter Joice [1946] Director/Farmer; Patrick Joice [1973] Director/Farmer

Uplands Retail Limited
Incorporated: 6 February 2002 *Employees:* 78
Net Worth: £10,780,521 *Total Assets:* £22,404,650
Registered Office: 7 Brook Office Park, Follybrook Road, Emersons Green, Bristol, BS16 7FL
Activities: Other construction installation
Parent: Uplands Retail Holdings Limited
Officers: Michael Barker [1980] Director; Kevin Patrick Feldman [1966] Director; Martin-James James Hall [1979] Director; Jack Rake [1989] Director; Alastair James Shiner [1974] Director

Upper Belgrave Property Limited
Incorporated: 6 October 2003 *Employees:* 2
Net Worth: £4,303,120 *Total Assets:* £5,113,655
Registered Office: 10 Upper Belgrave Road, Clifton, Bristol, BS8 2XH
Activities: Other letting and operating of own or leased real estate
Officers: Peter Godfrey Jones, Secretary/Director; Patricia Joyce Jones [1942] Director; Peter Godfrey Jones [1939] Director

Upper Horns Farm LLP
Incorporated: 25 October 2007
Net Worth: £5,961,427 *Total Assets:* £6,063,493
Registered Office: Upper Horns Farm, Vernham Dean, Andover, Hants, SP11 0LL
Officers: Denise Ann Griffiths [1961] Member; Timothy Philip Griffiths [1960] Member

Urban Creation (Beech House) Ltd
Incorporated: 25 June 2015
Net Worth: £863,604 *Total Assets:* £6,006,355
Registered Office: Woodlands Grange, Woodlands Lane, Bradley Stoke, Bristol, BS32 4JY
Activities: Other accommodation
Parent: Urban Creation Management Limited
Officers: Jonathan Brecknell [1970] Director; Sarah Jane Brecknell [1974] Director

Urban Creation (Charlotte Street) Ltd
Incorporated: 10 September 2015
Net Worth: £1,084,814 *Total Assets:* £7,022,748
Registered Office: Woodlands Grange, Woodlands Lane, Bradley Stoke, Bristol, BS32 4JY
Activities: Development of building projects
Parent: Urban Creation Management Limited
Officers: Jonathan Brecknell [1970] Director

Urban Creation (Shaw) Limited
Incorporated: 4 February 2014
Net Worth: £372,344 *Total Assets:* £4,370,325
Registered Office: Woodlands Grange, Woodlands Lane, Bradley Stoke, Bristol, BS32 4JY
Activities: Development of building projects
Parent: Urban Creation Management Limited
Officers: Jonathan Brecknell [1970] Director; Sarah Jane Brecknell [1974] Director

Urban Creation Management Limited
Incorporated: 1 March 2017
Net Worth Deficit: £878 *Total Assets:* £13,244,141
Registered Office: Woodlands Grange, Woodlands Lane, Bradley Stoke, Bristol, BS32 4JY
Activities: Financial management
Shareholders: Jonathan Brecknell; Sarah Jane Brecknell
Officers: Jonathan Brecknell [1970] Director

Urbaser Limited
Incorporated: 25 June 1998 *Employees:* 446
Net Worth: £8,215,349 *Total Assets:* £60,141,928
Registered Office: First Floor, Westmoreland House, 80-86 Bath Road, Cheltenham, Glos, GL53 7JT
Activities: Remediation activities and other waste management services
Officers: Christopher Stephen McCarthy, Secretary; Jose Daniel Fernandez [1964] Director [Spanish]; Christopher Stephen McCarthy [1982] Commercial Director; Javier Peiro Balaguer [1974] Director [Spanish]; Carlos Abilio Perez [1966] Director [Spanish]; Jose Maria Sanz [1970] Finance Director [Spanish]

Urbina Private Equity No.3 Ltd
Incorporated: 8 June 2007 *Employees:* 2
Net Worth Deficit: £1,225,196 *Total Assets:* £7,494,346
Registered Office: Freshford House, Redcliffe Way, Bristol, BS1 6NL
Activities: Buying and selling of own real estate
Officers: David Nigel Sefton Pigott, Secretary; Kenneth Nicholas King [1968] Director/Property Consultant; David Nigel Sefton Pigott [1960] Director/Property Consultant

USAF Finance II Limited
Incorporated: 13 May 2013
Net Worth: £10,000 *Total Assets:* £691,670,976
Registered Office: South Quay, Temple Back, Bristol, BS1 6FL
Activities: Other letting and operating of own or leased real estate
Parent: USAF Holdings Limited
Officers: Christopher Robert Szpojnarowicz, Secretary; David Faulkner [1976] Director/Deputy CFO; Nicholas William John Hayes [1981] Development Director; Joseph Julian Lister [1971] Director/Chief Financial Officer; Christopher Robert Szpojnarowicz [1968] Director/Company Secretary/Head of Legal

USAF Holdings J Limited
Incorporated: 6 June 2016
Net Worth: £78 *Total Assets:* £57,155,148
Registered Office: South Quay, Temple Back, Bristol, BS1 6FL
Activities: Other letting and operating of own or leased real estate
Parent: Sanne Group PLC
Officers: David Faulkner [1976] Director/Deputy CFO; Joseph Julian Lister [1971] Director/Chief Financial Officer; Christopher Robert Szpojnarowicz [1968] Director/Head of Legal and Company Secretary

USAF LP Limited
Incorporated: 28 June 2006
Net Worth: £15,573,917 *Total Assets:* £111,950,128
Registered Office: South Quay, Temple Back, Bristol, BS1 6FL
Activities: Other letting and operating of own or leased real estate
Parent: LDC (Holdings) Limited
Officers: Christopher Robert Szpojnarowicz, Secretary; David Faulkner [1976] Director/Deputy CFO; Joseph Julian Lister [1971] Director/Chief Financial Officer; Christopher Robert Szpojnarowicz [1968] Director/Company Secretary/Head of Legal

USAF Management 10 Limited
Incorporated: 3 October 2008
Net Worth: £1 *Total Assets:* £76,369,376
Registered Office: South Quay, Temple Back, Bristol, BS1 6FL
Activities: Other letting and operating of own or leased real estate
Parent: LDC (Holdings) Limited
Officers: Christopher Robert Szpojnarowicz, Secretary; David Faulkner [1976] Director/Deputy CFO; Joseph Julian Lister [1971] Director/Chief Financial Officer; Christopher Robert Szpojnarowicz [1968] Director/Company Secretary/Head of Legal

USAF Management 11 Limited
Incorporated: 20 November 2009
Net Worth: £1 *Total Assets:* £55,416,072
Registered Office: South Quay, Temple Back, Bristol, BS1 6FL
Activities: Other letting and operating of own or leased real estate
Parent: LDC (Holdings) Limited
Officers: Christopher Robert Szpojnarowicz, Secretary; David Faulkner [1976] Director/Deputy CFO; Joseph Julian Lister [1971] Director/Chief Financial Officer; Christopher Robert Szpojnarowicz [1968] Director/Company Secretary/Head of Legal

USAF Management 12 Limited
Incorporated: 3 September 2010
Net Worth Deficit: £1,843 *Total Assets:* £40,488,288
Registered Office: South Quay, Temple Back, Bristol, BS1 6FL
Activities: Other letting and operating of own or leased real estate
Parent: LDC (Holdings) Limited
Officers: Christopher Robert Szpojnarowicz, Secretary; David Faulkner [1976] Director/Deputy CFO; Joseph Julian Lister [1971] Director/Chief Financial Officer; Christopher Robert Szpojnarowicz [1968] Director/Company Secretary/Head of Legal

USAF Management 14 Limited
Incorporated: 23 September 2014
Net Worth: £1 *Total Assets:* £6,967,370
Registered Office: South Quay, Temple Back, Bristol, BS1 6FL
Activities: Other letting and operating of own or leased real estate
Parent: LDC (Holdings) Limited
Officers: Christopher Robert Szpojnarowicz, Secretary; David Faulkner [1976] Director/Deputy CFO; Joseph Julian Lister [1971] Director/Chief Financial Officer; Christopher Robert Szpojnarowicz [1968] Director/Head of Legal and Company Secretary

USAF Management 6 Limited
Incorporated: 25 April 2007
Net Worth: £1 *Total Assets:* £71,512,976
Registered Office: South Quay, Temple Back, Bristol, BS1 6FL
Activities: Other letting and operating of own or leased real estate
Parent: LDC (Holdings) Limited
Officers: David Faulkner [1976] Director/Deputy CFO; Joseph Julian Lister [1971] Managing Director; Christopher Robert Szpojnarowicz [1968] Director/Company Secretary/Head of Legal

USAF Management Limited
Incorporated: 30 June 2006
Net Worth Deficit: £99 *Total Assets:* £223,904,464
Registered Office: South Quay, Temple Back, Bristol, BS1 6FL
Activities: Other letting and operating of own or leased real estate
Parent: LDC (Holdings) Limited
Officers: Christopher Robert Szpojnarowicz, Secretary; David Faulkner [1976] Director/Deputy CFO; Joseph Julian Lister [1971] Finance Director; Christopher Robert Szpojnarowicz [1968] Director/Company Secretary/Head of Legal

Utax (UK) Limited
Incorporated: 9 May 1989 *Employees:* 49
Net Worth: £691,123 *Total Assets:* £6,218,865
Registered Office: 89 Shrivenham Hundred Business Park, Majors Road, Watchfield, Swindon, Wilts, SN6 8TY
Activities: Wholesale of other office machinery and equipment
Parent: TA Triumph-Adler GmbH
Officers: Kevin John Good, Secretary; Christopher Rheidt [1968] Managing Director [German]; Shaun Edmond Wilkinson [1967] Director

V12 Footwear Limited
Incorporated: 11 July 2014 *Employees:* 29
Net Worth: £2,371,713 *Total Assets:* £6,244,826
Registered Office: V12 Footwear Limited, Greenways Business Park, Chippenham, Wilts, SN15 1BN
Activities: Wholesale of clothing and footwear
Parent: Allington IP Limited
Officers: Andrew Turner [1967] Director; Benjamin Turner [1964] Director; Charles Kester Turner [1992] Director/Marketing Manager; George Ashton Turner [1989] Director/Operations Manager; Georgina Marie Turner [1968] Director; Mr Henry Rupert Turner [1985] Director/Sales Manager; Sarah Ann Turner [1965] Director; Mr Thomas William Turner [1987] Director/Business Development Manager

Vacsax Limited
Incorporated: 16 October 1996 *Employees:* 56
Net Worth: £3,278,523 *Total Assets:* £4,329,237
Registered Office: Western Wood Way, Langage Science Park, Plymouth, PL7 5BG
Activities: Manufacture of medical and dental instruments and supplies
Parent: Sterivac Limited
Officers: Malcolm Roger Pye, Secretary; John Peter Bennett [1955] Managing Director; Robin Richard Jones [1964] UK Sales Director; Denise Sharon Ridall [1955] Director; Diane Susan Sullivan [1962] Director

Valeport (Holdings) Limited
Incorporated: 21 November 2012 *Employees:* 85
Net Worth: £5,291,514 *Total Assets:* £8,100,709
Registered Office: Valeport Limited, St Peter's Quay, Totnes, Devon, TQ9 5EW
Activities: Activities of other holding companies n.e.c.
Major Shareholder: Charles Penruddocke Quartley
Officers: Jennifer Mary Quartley, Secretary; Phillip Anthony Harvey [1966] Finance Director; Charles Penruddocke Quartley [1948] Director/Company Chairman; Jennifer Mary Quartley [1946] Director; Matthew Quartley [1971] Managing Director

Valeport Limited
Incorporated: 26 September 1985 *Employees:* 85
Net Worth: £2,474,154 *Total Assets:* £5,156,171
Registered Office: St Peters Quay, Totnes, Devon, TQ9 5EW
Activities: Manufacture of electronic measuring, testing etc. equipment, not for industrial process control
Parent: Valeport (Holdings) Limited
Officers: Jennifer Mary Quartley, Secretary; Phillip Anthony Harvey [1966] Finance Director; Charles Penruddocke Quartley [1948] Director/Company Chairman/Engineer; Matthew Quartley [1971] Managing Director

Valmiera Glass UK Limited
Incorporated: 5 November 1987 *Employees:* 139
Net Worth: £10,014,233 *Total Assets:* £18,329,536
Registered Office: Valmiera Glass UK Limited, Westbury, Sherborne, Dorset, DT9 3RB
Activities: Weaving of textiles
Parent: AS Valmieras Stikla Skiedra
Officers: Benjamin Deubel [1987] Director [German]; Roy William Hallett Andrews [1964] Managing Director - Finance; Stefan Jugel [1971] Director/General Manager [German]; Arnis Palms [1981] Managing Director [Latvian]; Andre Heinz Schwiontek [1972] Director/Vice President [German]

Van Courtlandt Holdings Limited
Incorporated: 8 November 2016
Net Worth: £6,804,608 *Total Assets:* £7,138,516
Registered Office: Enterprise House, Holton Road, Holton Heath Trading Park, Poole, Dorset, BH16 6LT
Activities: Activities of head offices
Major Shareholder: Steven Thorne
Officers: Connor Jon Harrison Thorne [1995] Director; Steven Thorne [1970] Director

Vanguard Healthcare Group Limited
Incorporated: 3 December 2008
Net Worth Deficit: £6,235,000 *Total Assets:* £25,094,000
Registered Office: Unit 1411 Charlton Court, Gloucester Business Park, Brockworth, Glos, GL3 4AE
Activities: General medical practice activities
Parent: Livingbridge GP Company Limited
Officers: Andrew James Allen [1954] Director; David John Cole [1962] Director/Chief Executive Officer; Angela Dillon [1978] Finance Director; Steven Peak [1966] Delivery & Development Director

Vanguard Healthcare Solutions Limited
Incorporated: 27 February 2002 *Employees:* 61
Net Worth: £9,337,000 *Total Assets:* £26,084,000
Registered Office: Unit 1411 Charlton Court, Gloucester Business Park, Brockworth, Gloucester, GL3 4AE
Activities: Other human health activities
Officers: Andrew James Allen [1954] Director; David John Cole [1962] Director/Chief Executive Officer; Angela Dillon [1978] Finance Director; Christa Iris Echtle [1957] Director/Chairman [German]; Steven Peak [1966] Sales Director

Vantage Point Business Park Limited
Incorporated: 7 June 2002 *Employees:* 2
Net Worth: £2,278,787 *Total Assets:* £5,993,077
Registered Office: Floor 4, Building 7, Vantage Point Business Village, Mitcheldean, Glos, GL17 0DD
Activities: Other letting and operating of own or leased real estate
Major Shareholder: Brian John Bennett
Officers: Oliver Bennett, Secretary; Brian John Bennett [1956] Director; Michael John Bennett [1949] Director

Vantage Point Business Village Limited
Incorporated: 31 May 2001 *Employees:* 4
Net Worth: £40,387,332 *Total Assets:* £65,280,040
Registered Office: Floor 4, Building 7, Vantage Point Business Village, Mitcheldean, Glos, GL17 0DD
Activities: Other letting and operating of own or leased real estate
Major Shareholder: Brian John Bennett
Officers: Oliver Bennett, Secretary; Brian John Bennett [1956] Director; Michael John Bennett [1949] Director

Vapormatic Company Limited (The)
Incorporated: 29 September 1954 *Employees:* 99
Net Worth: £10,412,000 *Total Assets:* £18,608,000
Registered Office: Vapormatic Kestrel Way, Sowton Industrial Estate, Exeter, EX2 7LA
Activities: Wholesale of agricultural machinery, equipment and supplies
Parent: Deere & Co
Officers: Adam Ali Malik, Secretary; Zoe Ann Ashby [1979] Managing Director; Taksheung Judy Hahm [1968] Director/Financial Controller [American]

Vastern Timber Company Limited
Incorporated: 30 December 1935 *Employees:* 38
Net Worth: £2,413,455 *Total Assets:* £4,695,666
Registered Office: The Sawmills, Vastern Wharf, Royal Wootton Bassett, Wilts, SN4 7PD
Activities: Sawmilling and planing of wood
Parent: Barnes,Branch & Co.Limited
Officers: Jonathan William Barnes, Secretary; Jonathan William Barnes [1955] Director/Timber Merchant; Thomas Mayhew Barnes [1974] Director/Timber Merchants; Alan William Drewitt [1961] Director; David William Madgwick [1937] Director; Mark John Querzani [1958] Director/Sawmill Manager

Vauxhall Estates Limited
Incorporated: 3 May 1988
Net Worth: £5,150,497 *Total Assets:* £6,325,102
Registered Office: Centenary House, Peninsula Park, Rydon Lane, Exeter, EX2 7XE
Activities: Development of building projects
Major Shareholder: Christopher John Hall
Officers: Christopher John Hall [1958] Director

Vavassor Limited
Incorporated: 14 September 2004 *Employees:* 135
Net Worth: £10,738,117 *Total Assets:* £12,899,277
Registered Office: First Floor, 10 Temple Back, Bristol, BS1 6FL
Activities: Other business support service activities n.e.c.
Parent: Onicon UK Limited
Officers: Keith Victor Beard [1953] Director; Jeffery Allen Deplanty [1972] Director/Business Executive [American]; William Edgar Roller [1962] Director/Business Executive [American]; Michael Phillip Santoni [1969] Director/Business Executive [American]

Veale Wasbrough Vizards LLP
Incorporated: 5 April 2013 *Employees:* 371
Net Worth: £9,009,041 *Total Assets:* £17,925,456
Registered Office: Narrow Quay House, Narrow Quay, Bristol, BS1 4QA
Officers: Gareth John Edwards [1971] Member; Simon Richard Benedict Heald [1962] Member; Richard Andrew Philips [1963] Member; Nigel Robert Puddicombe [1954] Member; Clive St John Read [1966] Member; Yvonne Maria Spencer [1964] Member; Con Alexander [1965] LLP Member; Michelle Marie Bendall [1968] LLP Member; Simon Richard Bevan [1969] LLP Member; David John Bird [1978] LLP Member; Jeffrey Curtis Brown [1956] LLP Member; Jane Ellen Byford [1968] LLP Member; Emma Cameron [1976] LLP Member; Tabitha Christiane Cave [1970] LLP Member; Robert Matthew Peter Collier [1975] LLP Member; Allison Janine Cook [1974] LLP Member; Judith Margaret Cuxson [1958] LLP Member; John Deakin [1965] LLP Member; Jonathan Geoffrey Durham [1978] LLP Member; David Rhys Emanuel [1964] LLP Member; Paul Daniel Gershlick [1974] LLP Member; Nathan Bernard Guest [1975] LLP Member; Kathryn Ann Halliday [1965] LLP Member; Samantha Jayne Hickman [1970] LLP Member; Benjamin John Holt [1979] LLP Member; Mark Quentin Henry Hughes [1956] LLP Member; Edward John Husband [1973] LLP Member; Michael John Knowles [1965] LLP Member; Joseph Kar-Seen Kwok [1969] LLP Member; Simon John Linnitt [1971] LLP Member; Douglas Locke [1973] LLP Member; Susan Malthouse [1954] LLP Member; David Kenneth Marsden [1956] LLP Member; Mary McCrorie [1960] LLP Member; Steven James McGuigan [1977] LLP Member; Huw Charles Morgan [1963] LLP Member; Jocelyn Handley Moule [1960] LLP Member; Barnaby James Northover [1974] LLP Member; David Mark Power [1969] LLP Member; Jason Mark Prosser [1973] LLP Member; Alice Elisabeth Reeve [1976] LLP Member; Edward Jon Rimmell [1976] LLP Member; Michelle Dawn Rose [1967] LLP Member; Laura Mary Seaman [1967] LLP Member; Nicholas Smith [1959] LLP Member; Serena Anne Tierney [1957] LLP Member; Paul Voller [1955] LLP Member; Benjamin Arthur De'laval Willis [1966] LLP Member

Vector Learning Trust
Incorporated: 10 August 2010 *Employees:* 265
Previous: Holyrood Academy Trust
Net Worth: £23,776,412 *Total Assets:* £29,976,448
Registered Office: Holyrood Academy, Zembard Lane, Chard, Somerset, TA20 1JL
Activities: General secondary education
Officers: Tina Coles, Secretary; Ann Margaret Adams [1961] Director/Administrator Local Authority; Martin Brook [1965] Director/Headteacher; Ewen Cameron [1977] Managing Director; Margaret Mary Mercer [1947] Director/Retired; Michael Adrian Weston [1956] Director/Retired

Vectura Group Investments Limited
Incorporated: 13 July 2010
Net Worth: £140,000,000 *Total Assets:* £140,000,000
Registered Office: 1 Prospect West, Chippenham, Wilts, SN14 6FH
Activities: Other human health activities
Parent: Vectura Group PLC
Officers: John Murphy, Secretary; John Murphy [1953] Director; James Ward-Lilley [1965] Director/Chief Executive

Vectura Group PLC
Incorporated: 13 August 1997 *Employees:* 464
Net Worth: £578,499,968 *Total Assets:* £718,499,968
Registered Office: One Prospect West, Chippenham, Wilts, SN14 6FH
Activities: Other human health activities
Officers: John Murphy, Secretary; Dr Per-Olof Andersson [1952] Director [Swedish]; Bruno Francois Jules Angelici [1947] Director [French]; Dr Susan Elizabeth Foden [1953] Director; Paul Andrew Fry [1966] Director/Chief Financial Officer; Juliet Thompson [1966] Director; James Ward-Lilley [1965] Director/Chief Executive; Neil William Warner [1953] Director; Dr Thomas Werner [1956] Director [German]; Anne Clem Whitaker [1967] Director [American]

Vectura Limited
Incorporated: 3 February 1983 *Employees:* 221
Net Worth: £31,500,000 *Total Assets:* £54,300,000
Registered Office: One Prospect West, Chippenham, Wilts, SN14 6FH
Activities: Other human health activities
Parent: Vectura Group Investments Limited
Officers: John Murphy, Secretary; John Murphy [1953] Director; James Ward-Lilley [1965] Director/Chief Executive

Vedbaek Limited
Incorporated: 25 March 2009 *Employees:* 124
Net Worth: £2,057,140 *Total Assets:* £8,511,267
Registered Office: Pillar House, 113-115 Bath Road, Cheltenham, Glos, GL53 7LS
Activities: Information technology consultancy activities
Parent: Vedbaek Holdings Ltd
Officers: Matthew Kieron Dredge [1971] Sales Director; Ian Humphries [1963] Director; David Walker [1962] Customer Services Director

Vee Bee Filtration UK Limited
Incorporated: 11 May 1992 *Employees:* 59
Net Worth: £4,465,392 *Total Assets:* £7,975,164
Registered Office: KLAW Products, Commerce Business Centre, West Wiltshire Trading Estate, Westbury, Wilts, BA13 4LS
Activities: Manufacture of other fabricated metal products n.e.c.
Parent: Vee Bee Limited
Officers: Simon John Hale [1970] Director; Mike Hartman [1965] Director/Chief Financial Officer; David Robert Hill [1966] Director; Michael John Noakes [1965] Director; Catherine Alison Wall [1960] Director

Veitch Family Holdings Limited
Incorporated: 11 September 1984 *Employees:* 83
Net Worth: £8,328,782 *Total Assets:* £13,152,590
Registered Office: The Old Vicarage, South Stoke, Bath, BA2 7DU
Activities: Activities of head offices
Shareholders: Colin Russell Veitch; Nicholas James Veitch
Officers: Colin Russell Veitch, Secretary; Colin Russell Veitch [1958] Director; Nicholas James Veitch [1963] Director

Venator Capital Limited
Incorporated: 6 July 2006 *Employees:* 21
Previous: Venator Recruitment Limited
Net Worth: £1,955,563 *Total Assets:* £4,876,193
Registered Office: Wilson House, 2 Lorne Park Road, Bournemouth, BH1 1JN
Activities: Other activities of employment placement agencies
Major Shareholder: Alex Bonnet
Officers: Rebecca Marie Heath, Secretary; Alexander Villette Bonnet [1976] Director; Rebecca Clancy [1991] Director

Vence LLP
Incorporated: 7 December 2007
Net Worth: £11,214,063 *Total Assets:* £11,232,957
Registered Office: Ashton Gate Stadium, Ashton Road, Bristol, BS3 2EJ
Officers: Jon Stephen Lansdown [1983] Member; Stephen Philip Lansdown [1952] Member

Vendigital Limited
Incorporated: 2 October 2000 *Employees:* 48
Net Worth: £3,069,182 *Total Assets:* £4,937,399
Registered Office: Old Station House, Station Approach, Newport Street, Swindon, Wilts, SN1 3DU
Activities: Other information technology service activities
Parent: Vendigital Holdings Limited
Officers: Christopher Dennison [1953] Director; Dominic Gregory Edmund Jephcott [1969] Director; Richard Waddington [1968] Director; Alan Roy Williams [1968] Director

Ventrus Limited
Incorporated: 24 October 2011 *Employees:* 761
Previous: The Primary Academies Trust
Net Worth: £22,368,000 *Total Assets:* £33,935,000
Registered Office: Woodwater Academy, Woodwater Lane, Exeter, Devon, EX2 5AW
Activities: Primary education
Shareholder: Hugh Fraser Whittaker
Officers: Emma Jayne Emery, Secretary; Gary Clifford Chown [1969] Director/Chief Executive Officer; David Edwards [1957] Director/Retired; Nathalie Ingles [1985] Director/Senior Associate - Employment Team; Tina Louise Jafrate [1966] Transformation/Programme Director; Clare Luke [1977] Director/HR Consultant; MacDonald Tatenda Muzvimwe [1979] Director/Chartered Surveyor; Jasmin Norton [1982] Director/Banker; Caroline Sally Thomas [1979] Director/Chartered Accountant (FCA); Hugh Fraser Whittaker [1968] Director/Business Consultant

Venture Engineering Group Limited
Incorporated: 10 June 2015
Net Worth: £187,600 *Total Assets:* £3,721,167
Registered Office: Unit 7 Albion Close, Newtown Business Park, Poole, Dorset, BH12 3LL
Activities: Activities of head offices
Major Shareholder: Katie O'Neil
Officers: Kate Victoria Davis [1981] Finance Director; Katie O'Neil [1984] Director/Accountant; Leigh Mark Smith [1971] Director

Venture Multi Academy Trust
Incorporated: 18 February 2011 *Employees:* 72
Previous: Trevithick Learning Academy
Net Worth: £4,930,382 *Total Assets:* £6,203,228
Registered Office: Trevithick Learning Academy, Mount Pleasant Road, Camborne, Cornwall, TR14 7RH
Activities: Primary education
Officers: Wendy Randle, Secretary; Julia Diane Dodson [1958] Director/Retired; Harry Marcus Justin Hart [1980] Director/Fire Safety Technician; Alan Honeybone [1963] Director Optician; Sean Christopher Powers [1970] Director/Principal; Ian Raggett [1970] Director/Teacher; Philip James Robinson [1942] Director/Engineering Consultant

Venturers Trust
Incorporated: 21 February 2008 *Employees:* 581
Previous: Colston's Girls' School Trust
Net Worth: £58,466,000 *Total Assets:* £64,615,000
Registered Office: Venturers Trust, Bath Road, Arnos Vale, Bristol, BS4 3AP
Activities: Primary education
Officers: Stephen Alan Allpress [1968] Director/Engineer; James Ross Ancell [1953] Director; Alison Gail Bragg [1961] Director/Consultant; Dr Jacqueline Margery Mary Cornish [1948] Director/Doctor; Caroline Jane Duckworth [1961] Director/Treasurer; John Steven Laycock [1948] Director/Retired; Lynn Robinson [1968] Director/University Manager; Colin Frank Skellett [1945] Director/Group Chief Executive; Trevor Smallwood [1947] Director/Retired; John Watson [1956] Director

Verdant Community Energy C.I.C.
Incorporated: 24 June 2015 *Employees:* 2
Net Worth Deficit: £683,853 *Total Assets:* £10,722,364
Registered Office: c/o Communities for Renewables CIC, Tremough Innovation Centre, Penryn, Cornwall, TR10 9TA
Activities: Production of electricity
Parent: Communities for Renewables CIC
Officers: William James Burnyeat [1978] Director; Thomas John Cosgrove [1981] Director/Development Manager

Verdo Renewables Ltd
Incorporated: 5 May 2006 *Employees:* 45
Net Worth: £3,819,890 *Total Assets:* £7,222,578
Registered Office: 45 Macadam Way, West Portway Industrial Estate, Andover, Hants, SP10 3XW
Activities: Wholesale of other fuels and related products
Parent: Verdo A/S
Officers: Thomas Windfeldt Bornerup [1967] Director/Manager [Danish]; Kim Frimer [1959] Director/CEO [Danish]; Kenneth Ruby Hovgaard Jeppesen [1973] Director/CFO at Verdo Group [Danish]; Alistair David McGlynn [1969] Sales Director

Vero Software Limited
Incorporated: 5 November 1997
Net Worth: £17,150,000 *Total Assets:* £55,809,000
Registered Office: 1370 Montpellier Court, Gloucester Business Park, Brockworth, Gloucester, GL3 4AH
Activities: Business and domestic software development
Shareholders: Hexagon Manufacturing Intelligence Management Ltd; Hexagon Metrology Services Ltd
Officers: Paolo Guglielmini [1977] Director/VP Business Development [Italian]; David Anthony Mills [1972] Finance Director; Julie Langhorne Randall [1961] Finance Director

Vero UK Limited
Incorporated: 26 January 1990 *Employees:* 58
Net Worth: £16,365,000 *Total Assets:* £22,831,000
Registered Office: 1370 Montpellier Court, Gloucester Business Park, Brockworth, Gloucester, GL3 4AH
Activities: Business and domestic software development
Parent: Vero Software Ltd
Officers: Julie Langhorne Randall, Secretary/Accountant; Paolo Guglielmini [1977] Director/VP Business Development [Italian]; David Anthony Mills [1972] Finance Director; Julie Langhorne Randall [1961] Director/Accountant

Verplas Limited
Incorporated: 2 July 1986 *Employees:* 109
Net Worth: £3,414,728 *Total Assets:* £5,878,987
Registered Office: Unit 7 Verwood Industrial Estate, Blackhill, Verwood, Dorset, BH31 6HA
Activities: Other service activities n.e.c.
Parent: Indutrade UK Limited
Officers: Elton Hopkins, Secretary; Robert Charles Gamis Francis [1960] Director; Peter Ian Rowlands [1968] Managing Director

Versarien PLC
Incorporated: 25 February 2013 *Employees:* 79
Net Worth: £7,725,000 *Total Assets:* £12,454,000
Registered Office: Unit 2 Chosen View Road, Cheltenham, Glos, GL51 9LT
Activities: Other manufacturing n.e.c.
Officers: Christopher Michael Leigh, Secretary; Professor Iain Gilmour Gray [1957] Director/Engineer; Christopher Michael Leigh [1960] Director/Chartered Accountant; Neill Gareth Ricketts [1970] Director/Chief Executive

Versatile Controls Limited
Incorporated: 29 July 1977 *Employees:* 8
Net Worth: £4,445,033 *Total Assets:* £4,988,809
Registered Office: The Site Office, Innsworth Technology Park, Innsworth Lane, Gloucester, GL3 1DL
Activities: Wholesale of other machinery and equipment
Major Shareholder: Jonathan Trevor Slim
Officers: Jeremy Huw Mower [1965] Director/Mechanical Engineer; Jonathan Trevor Slim [1954] Director; William Norman Slim [1988] Director

Vertigo Capital Limited
Incorporated: 3 February 2011
Net Worth Deficit: £9,665 *Total Assets:* £5,704,030
Registered Office: 12 Old Mills Industrial Estate, Paulton, Bristol, BS39 7SU
Activities: Activities of other holding companies n.e.c.
Major Shareholder: John Arthur Bassadone
Officers: John Stewart Fuller, Secretary; Claire Louise Small [1962] Director/Administrator

Vertigo Investments Limited
Incorporated: 9 November 2009
Net Worth Deficit: £8,148 *Total Assets:* £3,828,152
Registered Office: 12 Old Mills Industrial Estate, Paulton, Bristol, BS39 7SU
Activities: Activities of other holding companies n.e.c.
Major Shareholder: John Arthur Bassadone
Officers: John Stewart Fuller, Secretary; Claire Louise Small [1962] Director/Administrator

Verto Homes Ltd
Incorporated: 30 December 2010 *Employees:* 5
Previous: Verto Group Enterprise Ltd.
Net Worth: £2,030,673 *Total Assets:* £10,139,048
Registered Office: Whyfield, Green Court, Truro Business Park, Threemilestone, Truro, Cornwall, TR4 9LF
Activities: Construction of domestic buildings
Shareholders: Thomas William David Carr; Richard James Pearce
Officers: Tom William David Carr [1984] Director; Richard James Pearce [1983] Director

Verton Limited
Incorporated: 25 September 1995 *Employees:* 37
Net Worth: £3,074,309 *Total Assets:* £4,031,464
Registered Office: Verton House, Alexandra Way, Tewkesbury, Glos, GL20 8NB
Activities: Agents specialised in the sale of other particular products
Parent: Verton Holdings Limited
Officers: Tessa Ann Cardwell Abraham [1969] Director; James Christopher Locke [1972] Director; Mark Andrew Minchella [1970] Director/Accountant

VES Precision Limited
Incorporated: 19 April 1991 *Employees:* 39
Net Worth: £2,391,806 *Total Assets:* £3,962,511
Registered Office: Unit 10 Cropmead Industrial Estate, Crewkerne, Somerset, TA18 7HQ
Activities: Machining
Major Shareholder: Rodney William Scarr
Officers: Janet Robson Scarr, Secretary; Ian William Scarr [1973] Managing Director; Rodney William Scarr [1945] Director/Chairman

Vetswest Limited
Incorporated: 19 March 1990 *Employees:* 5
Net Worth: £2,911,169 *Total Assets:* £13,568,966
Registered Office: Unit 15 Clovelly Road Industrial Estate, Bideford, Devon, EX39 3HN
Activities: Agents specialised in the sale of other particular products
Parent: MWI Supply (UK Acquisition) Ltd
Officers: Brian Topper, Secretary; John Gardner Chou [1956] Director/Business Executive [American]; James F Cleary Jr [1968] Director/CEO and President [American]; Mark Jeffrey Shaw [1962] Director/Business Executive [American]

Vi - Spring Limited
Incorporated: 24 September 1901 *Employees:* 236
Net Worth: £9,354,000 *Total Assets:* £17,832,000
Registered Office: Ernesettle Lane, Plymouth, PL5 2TT
Activities: Manufacture of mattresses
Parent: Flex Equipos de Descanso S.A.
Officers: Michael David Catovsky, Secretary; Michael David Catovsky [1976] Director; Gerardo Espana [1963] Director [Spanish]; James Anthony Gerety [1958] Director; Rafael Gonzalez Betere [1961] Managing Director Flex Group [Spanish]; Christopher Harrison [1964] Operations Director; Michael Richard Meehan [1959] Director/Chartered Accountant; Angel Moreno [1961] Finance Director [Spanish]; Alain Rauh [1963] Director [French]

Via East Midlands Limited
Incorporated: 4 December 2015 *Employees:* 578
Net Worth: £1,501,809 *Total Assets:* £16,180,828
Registered Office: Corserv Head Office, Higher Trenant Road, Wadebridge, Cornwall, PL27 6TW
Activities: Construction of roads and motorways
Shareholders: Corserv Ltd; Nottinghamshire County Council
Officers: Richard Zmuda, Secretary; Arthur Henry Hooper [1955] Director/Chairman; Joseph Gerard Keohane [1967] Finance Director [Irish]; Anthony James May [1963] Director/Local Government Chief Executive; Nigel Stevenson [1964] Director/Local Government Officer

Vian Marketing Limited
Incorporated: 26 March 2015 *Employees:* 29
Net Worth: £2,748,005 *Total Assets:* £9,881,377
Registered Office: Unit B, Halwell Business Park, Halwell, Totnes, Devon, TQ9 7LQ
Activities: Management consultancy activities other than financial management
Officers: Robert William Fairchild [1951] Director; David John Hackford [1964] Director; Robert Michael Henry [1954] Director; John Hibbard [1977] Director/Chief Executive; Helen Carlene Shears [1978] Finance Director; Roger Tushingham [1954] Director

Vicaima Limited
Incorporated: 6 September 1988 *Employees:* 97
Net Worth: £2,165,110 *Total Assets:* £12,650,642
Registered Office: 38-42 Newport Street, Swindon, Wilts, SN1 3DR
Activities: Other business support service activities n.e.c.
Officers: Frederico Miguel Tomas Da Capela, Secretary; Frederico Miguel Tomas Da Capela [1977] Commercial Director [Portuguese]; Arlindo Da Costa Leite [1961] Director [Portuguese]; Pedro Silva [1973] Director [Portuguese]

Steve Vick International Limited
Incorporated: 28 May 1981 *Employees:* 65
Net Worth: £3,055,429 *Total Assets:* £5,325,567
Registered Office: 19 Treenwood Industrial Estate, Bradford on Avon, Wilts, BA15 2AU
Activities: Manufacture of trailers and semi-trailers
Shareholders: Stephen Michael Vick; Angel Mary Domenica Vick
Officers: William Andrew White, Secretary; Anthony James Day [1950] Director/Accountant; Andrew Charles Harrison [1965] Director/Contractor; Katie Louise Higgins [1984] Sales & Marketing Director; Sean Douglas Noonan [1976] Director/Contracts Manager; Angela Mary Domenica Vick [1951] Director/Administrator; Stephen Michael Vick [1949] Managing Director; William Andrew White [1974] Director/Accountant

Victor Properties Ltd
Incorporated: 10 July 2007 *Employees:* 1
Net Worth: £1,288,933 *Total Assets:* £3,701,961
Registered Office: 49 Bristol Road, Frenchay, Bristol, BS16 1LQ
Activities: Other letting and operating of own or leased real estate
Shareholder: Tracy Anne Williams
Officers: Marlene Ann Williams, Secretary; Colin Victor Williams [1944] Director

Victoria Group Holdings Limited
Incorporated: 11 July 2009 *Employees:* 246
Net Worth: £52,978,000 *Total Assets:* £70,677,000
Registered Office: Victoria Wharf, Plymouth, PL4 0RF
Activities: Activities of head offices
Major Shareholder: Mark Alexander Vernon Gatehouse
Officers: David Sydney Martin, Secretary/Director; Christine Ann Gatehouse [1955] Director; Mark Alexander Vernon Gatehouse [1949] Managing Director; Alan Burgoyne Luscombe [1958] Director; Liam Bernard Lynch [1974] Director [Irish]; David Sydney Martin [1955] Director

Victoria Wharves Limited
Incorporated: 21 September 1995 *Employees:* 50
Net Worth: £26,290,000 *Total Assets:* £34,361,000
Registered Office: Victoria Wharf, Cattedown, Plymouth, PL4 0RF
Activities: Cargo handling for water transport activities
Major Shareholder: Mark Alexander Vernon Gatehouse
Officers: David Sydney Martin, Secretary; Mark Alexander Vernon Gatehouse [1949] Director; Liam Bernard Lynch [1974] Director [Irish]; David Sydney Martin [1955] Director; Garry Martin Strickland [1962] Director

Vinci Education (Bradfield) Limited
Incorporated: 20 January 2011
Net Worth: £104,632 *Total Assets:* £23,767,790
Registered Office: Third Floor, Broad Quay House, Prince Street, Bristol, BS1 4DJ
Activities: Other business support service activities n.e.c.
Parent: Vinci Education (Bradfield) Holdings Limited
Officers: Ian David Hudson [1964] Director; Rory John Murphy [1969] Commercial Director

Viper Innovations Ltd
Incorporated: 16 April 2007
Previous: Viper Subsea Technology Limited
Net Worth: £6,805,844 *Total Assets:* £10,967,625
Registered Office: Unit 3a Marine View Office Park, 45 Martingale Way, Portishead, Bristol, BS20 7AW
Activities: Other engineering activities
Officers: Neil Irwin Douglas [1963] Director/Manager; Stephen Michael Nodder [1962] Director/Manager

Viridor (Lancashire) Limited
Incorporated: 13 September 2006 *Employees:* 42
Net Worth: £8,364,000 *Total Assets:* £12,583,000
Registered Office: Peninsula House, Rydon Lane, Exeter, Devon, EX2 7HR
Activities: Freight transport by road
Parent: Viridor Waste Management Limited
Officers: Scott Edward Massie, Secretary; Simon Anthony Follett Pugsley, Secretary; Karen Senior, Secretary; Phillip Charles Piddington [1956] Director; Elliot Arthur James Rees [1974] Director/Accountant

Viridor Credits Environmental Company
Incorporated: 25 September 2001 *Employees:* 7
Net Worth: £2,499,109 *Total Assets:* £7,426,146
Registered Office: Aintree House, Blackbrook Park Avenue, Taunton, Somerset, TA1 2PX
Activities: Other business support service activities n.e.c.
Officers: Alison Anne Salvador, Secretary; Simon Leslie Catford [1956] Director/Retired; Daniel Alaric Peter Cooke [1967] Director/Group Head of Sustainability; Mary Prior [1942] Director/Retired; Peter Walter Renshaw [1950] Director/Retired; David Balfour Robertson [1954] Director/Retired

Viridor EFW (Runcorn) Limited
Incorporated: 31 March 2009
Net Worth Deficit: £4,929,000 *Total Assets:* £240,663,008
Registered Office: Peninsula House, Rydon Lane, Exeter, Devon, EX2 7HR
Activities: Other service activities n.e.c.
Parent: Viridor Waste Management Limited
Officers: Scott Edward Massie, Secretary; Simon Anthony Follett Pugsley, Secretary; Karen Senior, Secretary; Phillip Charles Piddington [1956] Director; Elliot Arthur James Rees [1974] Director/Accountant

Viridor Limited
Incorporated: 2 January 1990 *Employees:* 3,412
Net Worth: £716,200,000 *Total Assets:* £2,264,699,904
Registered Office: Peninsula House, Rydon Lane, Exeter, Devon, EX2 7HR
Activities: Activities of head offices
Parent: Pennon Group PLC
Officers: Scott Edward Massie, Secretary; Simon Anthony Follett Pugsley, Secretary; Karen Senior, Secretary; Phillip Charles Piddington [1956] Director; Elliot Arthur James Rees [1974] Director/Accountant; Paul Michael Ringham [1969] Director

Viridor Oxfordshire Limited
Incorporated: 12 August 2010
Net Worth: £20,290,000 *Total Assets:* £203,128,992
Registered Office: Peninsula House, Rydon Lane, Exeter, Devon, EX2 7HR
Activities: Production of electricity
Parent: Viridor Waste Management Limited
Officers: Scott Edward Massie, Secretary; Simon Anthony Follett Pugsley, Secretary; Karen Senior, Secretary; Phillip Charles Piddington [1956] Director; Elliot Arthur James Rees [1974] Director/Accountant

Viridor Polymer Recycling Limited
Incorporated: 5 July 2005 *Employees:* 39
Net Worth Deficit: £14,854,000 *Total Assets:* £7,380,000
Registered Office: Peninsula House, Rydon Lane, Exeter, Devon, EX2 7HR
Activities: Other business support service activities n.e.c.
Parent: Viridor Waste Management Limited
Officers: Scott Edward Massie, Secretary; Simon Anthony Follett Pugsley, Secretary; Karen Senior, Secretary; Phillip Charles Piddington [1956] Director; Elliot Arthur James Rees [1974] Director/Accountant

Viridor South London Limited
Incorporated: 15 June 2012
Net Worth Deficit: £3,333,000 *Total Assets:* £219,024,992
Registered Office: Peninsula House, Rydon Lane, Exeter, Devon, EX2 7HR
Activities: Production of electricity
Parent: Viridor Waste Management Limited
Officers: Scott Edward Massie, Secretary; Simon Anthony Follett Pugsley, Secretary; Karen Senior, Secretary; Phillip Charles Piddington [1956] Director; Elliot Arthur James Rees [1974] Director/Accountant

Viridor Trident Park Limited
Incorporated: 6 March 2012
Net Worth: £6,832,000 *Total Assets:* £229,164,000
Registered Office: Peninsula House, Rydon Lane, Exeter, Devon, EX2 7HR
Activities: Other service activities n.e.c.
Parent: Viridor Waste Management Limited
Officers: Scott Edward Massie, Secretary; Simon Anthony Follett Pugsley, Secretary; Karen Senior, Secretary; Phillip Charles Piddington [1956] Director; Elliot Arthur James Rees [1974] Director/Accountant

Viridor Waste (Greater Manchester) Limited
Incorporated: 8 April 1992 *Employees:* 718
Net Worth Deficit: £44,357,000 *Total Assets:* £55,239,000
Registered Office: Peninsula House, Rydon Lane, Exeter, Devon, EX2 7HR
Activities: Other service activities n.e.c.
Parent: Viridor Waste Management Limited
Officers: Scott Edward Massie, Secretary; Simon Anthony Follett Pugsley, Secretary; Karen Senior, Secretary; Phillip Charles Piddington [1956] Director; Elliot Arthur James Rees [1974] Director/Accountant; Paul Michael Ringham [1969] Director

Viridor Waste (Landfill Restoration) Limited
Incorporated: 29 July 1997
Net Worth: £145,000 *Total Assets:* £13,970,000
Registered Office: Peninsula House, Rydon Lane, Exeter, Devon, EX2 7HR
Activities: Other service activities n.e.c.
Parent: Viridor Waste Management Limited
Officers: Scott Edward Massie, Secretary; Simon Anthony Follett Pugsley, Secretary; Karen Senior, Secretary; Phillip Charles Piddington [1956] Director; Elliot Arthur James Rees [1974] Director/Accountant

Viridor Waste (Somerset) Limited
Incorporated: 23 July 1991 *Employees:* 117
Net Worth Deficit: £4,483,000 *Total Assets:* £58,277,000
Registered Office: Peninsula House, Rydon Lane, Exeter, Devon, EX2 7HR
Activities: Other business support service activities n.e.c.
Parent: Viridor Waste Management Limited
Officers: Scott Edward Massie, Secretary; Simon Anthony Follett Pugsley, Secretary; Karen Senior, Secretary; Phillip Charles Piddington [1956] Director; Elliot Arthur James Rees [1974] Director/Accountant

Viridor Waste (Thames) Limited
Incorporated: 15 November 1994 *Employees:* 108
Net Worth: £60,000 *Total Assets:* £27,529,000
Registered Office: Peninsula House, Rydon Lane, Exeter, Devon, EX2 7HR
Activities: Other service activities n.e.c.
Parent: Viridor Waste Management Limited
Officers: Scott Edward Massie, Secretary; Simon Anthony Follett Pugsley, Secretary; Karen Senior, Secretary; Phillip Charles Piddington [1956] Director; Elliot Arthur James Rees [1974] Director/Accountant

Viridor Waste (West Sussex) Limited
Incorporated: 21 October 2003
Net Worth: £6,402,000 *Total Assets:* £38,157,000
Registered Office: Peninsula House, Rydon Lane, Exeter, Devon, EX2 7HR
Activities: Collection of non-hazardous waste
Parent: Viridor Waste Limited
Officers: Scott Edward Massie, Secretary; Simon Anthony Follett Pugsley, Secretary; Karen Senior, Secretary; Phillip Charles Piddington [1956] Director; Elliot Arthur James Rees [1974] Director/Accountant

Viridor Waste Exeter Limited
Incorporated: 5 December 1978 *Employees:* 16
Net Worth Deficit: £21,161,000 *Total Assets:* £68,084,000
Registered Office: Peninsula House, Rydon Lane, Exeter, Devon, EX2 7HR
Activities: Other service activities n.e.c.
Parent: Viridor Waste Limited
Officers: Scott Edward Massie, Secretary; Simon Anthony Follett Pugsley, Secretary; Karen Senior, Secretary; Phillip Charles Piddington [1956] Director; Elliot Arthur James Rees [1974] Director/Accountant

Viridor Waste Kent Limited
Incorporated: 28 September 1992 *Employees:* 83
Net Worth Deficit: £7,923,000 *Total Assets:* £29,742,000
Registered Office: Peninsula House, Rydon Lane, Exeter, Devon, EX2 7HR
Activities: Operation of gravel and sand pits; mining of clays and kaolin
Parent: Viridor Waste Management Limited
Officers: Scott Edward Massie, Secretary; Simon Anthony Follett Pugsley, Secretary; Karen Senior, Secretary; Phillip Charles Piddington [1956] Director; Elliot Arthur James Rees [1974] Director/Accountant

Viridor Waste Limited
Incorporated: 8 November 1991
Net Worth: £344,167,008 *Total Assets:* £1,662,620,032
Registered Office: Peninsula House, Rydon Lane, Exeter, Devon, EX2 7HR
Activities: Other business support service activities n.e.c.
Parent: Viridor Limited
Officers: Scott Edward Massie, Secretary; Simon Anthony Follett Pugsley, Secretary; Karen Senior, Secretary; Phillip Charles Piddington [1956] Director; Elliot Arthur James Rees [1974] Director/Accountant

Viridor Waste Management Limited
Incorporated: 3 December 1956 *Employees:* 1,633
Net Worth: £238,356,992 *Total Assets:* £1,029,233,024
Registered Office: Peninsula House, Rydon Lane, Exeter, Devon, EX2 7HR
Activities: Other service activities n.e.c.
Parent: Viridor Waste Limited
Officers: Scott Edward Massie, Secretary; Simon Anthony Follett Pugsley, Secretary; Karen Senior, Secretary; Phillip Charles Piddington [1956] Director; Elliot Arthur James Rees [1974] Director/Accountant; Paul Michael Ringham [1969] Director

Virtual Infrastructure Group Limited
Incorporated: 11 June 2012 *Employees:* 137
Net Worth: £12,893,000 *Total Assets:* £30,711,000
Registered Office: Hartham Park, Hartham, Corsham, Wilts, SN13 0RP
Activities: Data processing, hosting and related activities
Officers: Philip Michael Dawson, Secretary; James McLelland Austin [1969] Director; Sharon Brittan [1967] Director; Dr William Thomas Ginn [1967] Director; Simon John Hansford [1965] Director; Jeremy Robin Sanders [1962] Director; Jeffrey Paul Thomas [1957] Director

Virtus Health Europe Limited
Incorporated: 14 May 2014
Net Worth: £47,248,176 *Total Assets:* £71,191,824
Registered Office: 2 Temple Back East, Temple Quay, Bristol, BS1 6EG
Activities: Activities of other holding companies n.e.c.
Officers: Conor Cuthill, Secretary; Richard Banks [1976] Director; Susan Channon [1956] Director/Chief Executive Officer [New Zealander]; Glenn Patrick Powers [1959] Director/Chief Financial Officer

Visage (Aberdeen) Limited
Incorporated: 8 October 2015 *Employees:* 3
Net Worth Deficit: £441,467 *Total Assets:* £15,039,259
Registered Office: 31-33 Commercial Road, Poole, Dorset, BH14 0HU
Activities: Buying and selling of own real estate
Parent: Visage Investments LLP
Officers: Andrew Iain Taylor [1976] Director/Property Developer

Viscominvest Holding UK Limited
Incorporated: 15 January 2016
Net Worth: £33,556,000 *Total Assets:* £76,836,000
Registered Office: 1600 Park Avenue, Aztec West, Bristol, BS32 4UA
Activities: Non-trading company
Officers: Robert William Jackson [1963] Director; Leon Watson [1967] Director

Vision Direct Europe Ltd
Incorporated: 18 March 2008 *Employees:* 3
Previous: Getlenses Ltd.
Net Worth Deficit: £18,324,000 *Total Assets:* £91,954,000
Registered Office: Narrow Quay House, Narrow Quay, Bristol, BS1 4QA
Activities: Other retail sale of new goods in specialised stores (not commercial art galleries and opticians)
Parent: Vision Direct Group Limited
Officers: Lena Generaldine Henry [1975] Director/Chief Strategy Officer [French]; Michael Benjamin Kraftman [1957] Director; Richard Alan Hayden Mark Rust [1973] Director/Accountant

Vision Direct Group Ltd
Incorporated: 10 May 2004
Previous: Getlenses Group Ltd.
Net Worth: £13,926,000 *Total Assets:* £14,327,000
Registered Office: Narrow Quay House, Narrow Quay, Bristol, BS1 4QA
Activities: Activities of head offices
Parent: Trifle Holdings Limited
Officers: Lena Generaldine Henry [1975] Director/Chief Strategy Officer [French]; Michael Benjamin Kraftman [1957] Director; Eric Pierre Antoine Martinet [1986] Director/Finance Manager [French]

Vision Dispensing Ltd.
Incorporated: 24 January 2000 *Employees:* 158
Net Worth: £21,463,000 *Total Assets:* £24,525,000
Registered Office: Narrow Quay House, Narrow Quay, Bristol, BS1 4QA
Activities: Retail sale via mail order houses or via Internet
Parent: Essilor International
Officers: Lena Generaldine Henry [1975] Director/Chief Strategy Officer [French]; Michael Benjamin Kraftman [1957] Director; Richard Alan Hayden Mark Rust [1973] Director/Accountant

Vistair Group Limited
Incorporated: 3 December 2015 *Employees:* 117
Net Worth Deficit: £8,162,152 *Total Assets:* £13,471,576
Registered Office: Springfield House, 45 Welsh Back, Bristol, BS1 4AG
Activities: Non-trading company
Parent: Synova Capital General Partner 3 Limited
Officers: Alexander Charles Spencer Bowden [1974] Director; Dominic Clarke [1971] Director/Chief Commercial Officer; Scott Andrew Fairlie [1984] Director; Dr David Clifford Rhys Hedley [1972] Director; Ian Paul George Herbert [1962] Director; Richard Alexander Houghton [1958] Director [Irish]; Robert Lloyd Morgan [1972] Director

Vistair Limited
Incorporated: 3 December 2015 *Employees:* 5
Net Worth: £4,536,757 *Total Assets:* £13,752,935
Registered Office: Springfield House, 45 Welsh Back, Bristol, BS1 4AG
Activities: Non-trading company
Parent: Vistair Group Limited
Officers: Alexander Charles Spencer Bowden [1974] Director; Dominic Clarke [1971] Director/Chief Commercial Officer; Scott Andrew Fairlie [1984] Director; Dr David Clifford Rhys Hedley [1972] Director; Ian Paul George Herbert [1962] Director; Robert Lloyd Morgan [1972] Director

Vistgate Limited
Incorporated: 8 February 1980 *Employees:* 161
Net Worth: £9,618,025 *Total Assets:* £15,362,248
Registered Office: Unit 2a/2b Victoria Business Park, Roche, St Austell, Cornwall, PL26 8LX
Activities: Marine fishing
Parent: Ocean Holdings South West Ltd
Officers: Edward James Lakeman, Secretary; Leigh Geoffrey Head Genge [1981] Director/Chartered Accountant; Edward James Lakeman [1971] Director; John Andrew Lakeman [1943] Director/Consultant

Vitacress Herbs Limited
Incorporated: 30 December 1963 *Employees:* 314
Previous: Van Heyningen Brothers Limited
Net Worth: £4,344,000 *Total Assets:* £19,277,000
Registered Office: Lower Link Farm, Lower Link, St Mary Bourne, Andover, Hants, SP11 6DB
Activities: Growing of other non-perennial crops
Parent: Vitacress Limited
Officers: Ashley Cooper, Secretary; Toby John Brinsmead [1969] Director; Simon Christopher Conway [1970] Managing Director; Ashley James Cooper [1978] Finance Director; Steven Denis Rothwell [1957] Director

Vitacress Limited
Incorporated: 26 March 2008 *Employees:* 1,425
Net Worth: £46,034,000 *Total Assets:* £98,659,000
Registered Office: Lower Link Farm, Lower Link, St Mary Bourne, Andover, Hants, SP11 6DB
Activities: Combined office administrative service activities
Major Shareholder: Joao Nuno Da Costa Oliveira Macedo Silva
Officers: Ashley Cooper, Secretary; Rui Teixeira Bastos [1946] Director [Portuguese]; Toby John Brinsmead [1969] Director; Ashley James Cooper [1978] Finance Director; Vitor Jose Moreira Dos Santos [1974] Director [Portuguese]; Steven Denis Rothwell [1957] Director

Vitacress Salads Limited
Incorporated: 17 April 1961 *Employees:* 479
Net Worth: £15,088,000 *Total Assets:* £29,952,000
Registered Office: Lower Link Farm, Lower Link, St Mary Bourne, Andover, Hants, SP11 6DB
Activities: Growing of other non-perennial crops
Officers: Ashley Cooper, Secretary; Toby John Brinsmead [1969] Director; Ashley James Cooper [1978] Finance Director; Steven Denis Rothwell [1957] Production Director; Mike Sheldon [1961] Managing Director

Volaris Group UK Holdco Ltd
Incorporated: 25 January 2008
Previous: Volaris Group UK Holdco Ltd Ltd
Net Worth: £38,019,464 *Total Assets:* £41,909,504
Registered Office: Unit A1, Methuen Park, Chippenham, Wilts, SN14 0GT
Activities: Information technology consultancy activities
Parent: Constellation Software UK Holdco Ltd
Officers: Robert Clay, Secretary/Director; James Arthur Baker [1960] Financial Director [Canadian]; Brian Beattie [1967] Director/Chief Financial Officer [Canadian]; Robert Clay [1970] Director; Mark Miller [1962] Director [Canadian]; Deborah Riley [1969] Finance Director

Vospers Motor House Limited
Incorporated: 19 June 1951 *Employees:* 645
Net Worth: £20,770,948 *Total Assets:* £100,723,344
Registered Office: Marsh Mills Retail Park, Plymouth, PL6 8AY
Activities: Sale of new cars and light motor vehicles
Parent: Vospers of Plymouth Ltd
Officers: Paul Alexander Rogers, Secretary; Benjamin Darnell [1975] Used Car Director; Mark Douglas Haslam [1969] Director; Paul Alexander Rogers [1973] Financial Director; Neil Tickner [1963] Director; Peter Jonathan Tremain [1969] Director; Nicholas Julian Dyer Vosper [1972] Director; Peter Graham Vosper [1943] Director

Vospers of Plymouth Limited
Incorporated: 29 July 1971 *Employees:* 645
Net Worth: £26,228,240 *Total Assets:* £111,766,088
Registered Office: Marsh Mills Retail Park, Plymouth, PL6 8AY
Activities: Sale of new cars and light motor vehicles
Major Shareholder: Peter Graham Vosper
Officers: Paul Alexander Rogers, Secretary; Nicholas Julian Dyer Vosper [1972] Director; Peter Graham Vosper [1943] Director

Vowles Parks Limited
Incorporated: 6 August 2001 *Employees:* 24
Net Worth: £7,604,745 *Total Assets:* £9,435,101
Registered Office: 3-5 College Street, Burnham on Sea, Somerset, TA8 1AR
Activities: Other holiday and other collective accommodation
Major Shareholder: John Adrian Vowles
Officers: Audrey Christine Vowles, Secretary/Park Manager; Audrey Christine Vowles [1944] Director/Park Manager; Jayne Elizabeth Vowles [1970] Director/Park Manager; John Adrian Vowles [1943] Director/Park Manager; Michael John Vowles [1977] Director/Park Manager

Voyager Fishing Company Limited
Incorporated: 19 July 1990 *Employees:* 4
Net Worth: £41,743,460 *Total Assets:* £67,767,088
Registered Office: First Floor, 10 Temple Back, Bristol, BS1 6FL
Activities: Marine fishing
Shareholders: Arnold John McCullough; Robert McCullough
Officers: Arnold John McCullough, Company Secretary; Arnold John McCullough [1964] Director/Share Fisherman; Iris McCullough [1940] Director; Robert Nigel McCullough [1962] Director/Share Fisherman

VSGT Ltd
Incorporated: 19 December 2013 *Employees:* 103
Net Worth: £2,069,909 *Total Assets:* £3,550,733
Registered Office: Unit 1 Polham Lane, Somerton, Somerset, TA11 6SP
Activities: Activities of head offices
Officers: Philip Richard Sinnett-Thomas, Secretary; Iain Thomas Hugh Gray [1980] Sales Director; Mark James Shobbrook [1982] IT Director; Philip Richard Sinnett-Thomas [1980] Accounts Director; Jane Vine [1977] Purchasing Director

Vygon (U.K.) Limited
Incorporated: 28 August 1973 *Employees:* 165
Net Worth: £33,537,000 *Total Assets:* £38,871,000
Registered Office: The Pierre Simonet Building, V Park, Gateway North, Latham Road, Swindon, Wilts, SN25 4DL
Activities: Wholesale of pharmaceutical goods
Parent: Vygon SA
Officers: Dale Michael Keegan, Secretary; Bertrand Cuny [1936] Director [French]; Leslie Clive Robert Davies [1972] Managing Director; Stephane Regnault [1961] Director [French]

Vysiion Limited
Incorporated: 7 June 1996 *Employees:* 90
Previous: Vysiion Public Limited Company
Net Worth: £406,496 *Total Assets:* £6,728,382
Registered Office: Connect 17, Avon Way, Langley Park, Chippenham, Wilts, SN15 1GG
Activities: Other telecommunications activities
Shareholders: Bruce Brain; Business Growth Fund PLC (A/C BGF Investments LP
Officers: Karen Yolaine Broad, Secretary; James McLelland Austin [1969] Director; Bruce Brain [1941] Director; Peter Clapton [1964] Director/Chief Executive Officer; Antonia Scarlett Jenkinson [1969] Director; Neil Scott Paton [1969] Director/Chief Operating Officer

W & S Waste Management Limited
Incorporated: 22 October 1999 *Employees:* 2
Net Worth: £14,374,768 *Total Assets:* £18,030,528
Registered Office: 14-16 Nuffield Road, Nuffield Industrial Estate, Poole, Dorset, BH17 0RB
Activities: Collection of non-hazardous waste
Shareholders: Jacqueline Rickett; Geoffrey David Thompson
Officers: Thomas Harvey, Secretary; Jacqueline Rickett [1964] Director/Secretary; Geoffrey David Thompson [1948] Director/Waste Manager

W B M Groundworks Limited
Incorporated: 20 July 2005 *Employees:* 72
Net Worth: £4,748,314 *Total Assets:* £6,131,939
Registered Office: 2 Coombe Road, Callington, Cornwall, PL17 7QG
Activities: Construction of roads and motorways
Shareholders: Martin John Nicholls; John Howard Nicholls
Officers: Meeta Jane Nicholls, Secretary/Personal Banker; Michael Follett [1974] Director/Civil Engineer; John Howard Nicholls [1948] Director/Builder; Martin John Nicholls [1972] Director

W.D.M.Limited
Incorporated: 23 January 1946 *Employees:* 149
Net Worth: £13,866,000 *Total Assets:* £16,236,000
Registered Office: North View, Soundwell Road, Staple Hill, Bristol, BS16 4NX
Activities: Manufacture of other special-purpose machinery n.e.c.
Major Shareholder: John Leslie Gardiner
Officers: Stuart Roger Thomas Smith, Secretary; Christopher John Gardiner [1963] Managing Director; John Leslie Gardiner [1945] Director/Chairman

WA Consultants Limited
Incorporated: 11 January 1994 *Employees:* 27
Net Worth: £2,886,591 *Total Assets:* £9,305,933
Registered Office: Emblem House, Pynes Hill, Exeter, Devon, EX2 5BA
Activities: Temporary employment agency activities
Major Shareholder: David John Richardson
Officers: Nicola Jane Churchward, Secretary/Consultant; Nicola Jane Churchward [1975] Director/Consultant; David John Richardson [1971] Resources Director

Wabash Technologies Limited
Incorporated: 14 August 2007
Net Worth: £1,331,079 *Total Assets:* £5,841,482
Registered Office: Interface House, Interface Business Park, Bincknoll Lane, Royal Wootton Bassett, Swindon, Wilts, SN4 8SY
Activities: Operation of warehousing and storage facilities for land transport activities
Parent: Sensata Technologies UK Financing Co PLC
Officers: Paul Chawla [1965] Director; Gerrit Hendrik Ensing [1973] Director [Dutch]

Waddeton Park Limited
Incorporated: 24 May 2006 *Employees:* 10
Net Worth: £17,996,256 *Total Assets:* £45,735,360
Registered Office: Greendale Court, Clyst St Mary, Exeter, Devon, EX5 1AW
Activities: Buying and selling of own real estate
Major Shareholder: Terence Charles Adams
Officers: Marianne Patricia Barrett Rogers, Secretary; Terence Charles Adams [1939] Director/Mining Engineer; Jonathan Mark Hoggett [1953] Director/Solicitor; Generald Walter Keay [1957] Director/Developer; Simon David Steele-Perkins [1967] Director/Developer

Wadebridge School
Incorporated: 21 March 2012 *Employees:* 159
Net Worth: £19,630,346 *Total Assets:* £20,947,204
Registered Office: Wadebridge School, Gonvena Hill, Wadebridge, Cornwall, PL27 6BU
Activities: General secondary education
Officers: Christopher John Wilson, Secretary; David Billing Barton [1959] Director/Education Consultant; Valerie Ann Crabb [1952] Director/Retired School Business Manager; Louise Jane Hanson [1969] Director/Management Accountant; Katy Holmes [1960] Director/Part Time Teacher; Carey Johanna Hume [1979] Director/HLTA; Professor Andrew David Phippen [1972] Director/Professor; Christopher Mark Sims [1972] Director/Council Officer; Ian Thurtle [1963] Director/Gardener; Sion Williams [1967] Director/Deputy Headteacher; Tina Yardley [1967] Director/Principal

Wadworth and Company Limited
Incorporated: 18 November 1889 *Employees:* 1,043
Net Worth: £83,381,000 *Total Assets:* £152,864,992
Registered Office: Northgate Brewery, Devizes, Wilts, SN10 1JW
Activities: Manufacture of beer
Officers: Alison Jane Skedd, Secretary; Nigel John Bewley Atkinson [1953] Director; Rupert Bagnall [1970] Operations Director - Managed Houses; Charles John Eric Bartholomew [1951] Managing Director/Chairman; John Edward Beard [1962] Director; Edward Scandrett Harford [1948] Director/Computer Consultant; Alison Jane Skedd [1963] Director/Accountant; Nicola Claire Stenhouse [1979] Director; Lloyd John Stephens [1957] Tenanted Trade Director; Jonathan Thomas [1964] Sales Director; Christopher Welham [1970] Director/Chief Executive Officer

Wagtech Projects Ltd
Incorporated: 14 September 1988 *Employees:* 12
Net Worth: £1,095,262 *Total Assets:* £3,557,919
Registered Office: 10 St Ann Street, Salisbury, Wilts, SP1 2DN
Activities: Manufacture of electronic measuring, testing etc. equipment, not for industrial process control
Major Shareholder: Neil Durham
Officers: Antonietta Durham [1960] Director; Neil Francis Durham [1959] Managing Director; Christopher James Stapleton [1973] Commercial Director

Wahoo Learning Limited
Incorporated: 22 February 2016
Net Worth: £2,091,290 *Total Assets:* £3,701,362
Registered Office: 13 Northern Way, Cropmead, Crewkerne, Somerset, TA18 7HJ
Activities: Activities of other holding companies n.e.c.
Major Shareholder: Lloyd Stuart Smith
Officers: Lloyd Stuart Smith [1982] Director; Patricia Joy Smith [1954] Director; Stuart Douglas Smith [1954] Director

Wainhomes (South West) Holdings Limited
Incorporated: 26 March 2001 *Employees:* 118
Net Worth: £76,176,000 *Total Assets:* £116,675,000
Registered Office: Unit 2 Exeter International Office Park, Clyst, Honiton, Exeter, EX5 2HL
Activities: Construction of domestic buildings
Parent: Wain Group Limited
Officers: Roger James Treweek, Secretary; William Francis Ainscough [1977] Director/Chartered Surveyor; William Ainscough [1948] Director; Mark Charles Harding [1964] Director; Alexander James Alan Hugo [1985] Director; Stephen Timothy Toghill [1966] Director; Roger James Treweek [1961] Finance Director; Michael John Upton [1965] Director

John Wainwright & Co. Limited
Incorporated: 19 March 1902 *Employees:* 109
Net Worth: £19,107,444 *Total Assets:* £32,058,304
Registered Office: Moons Hill Quarry, Mendip Road, Stoke St Michael, Radstock, Somerset, BA3 5JU
Activities: Quarrying of ornamental and building stone, limestone, gypsum, chalk and slate
Officers: Brian Rexworthy, Secretary; Peter Boyd Barkwill [1956] Managing Director; John Purnell Luff [1946] Director/Commercial Representative; Philip Charles Percival [1946] Director/Venture Capital Investor; Brian Rexworthy [1965] Financial Director; Christopher John Saunders [1944] Director/Partner

Waite & Son (Jewellers) Limited
Incorporated: 3 June 1935 *Employees:* 13
Net Worth: £2,099,144 *Total Assets:* £4,005,229
Registered Office: 70 The Promenade, Cheltenham, Glos, GL50 1LY
Activities: Other retail sale of new goods in specialised stores (not commercial art galleries and opticians)
Shareholders: Alexander Richard Thomas Rose; Angela Rose
Officers: Angela Rose, Secretary; Alexander Richard Thomas Rose [1984] Director; Angela Rose [1951] Director/Jeweller

A J Wakely & Sons Ltd.
Incorporated: 15 January 1986 *Employees:* 66
Net Worth: £3,743,610 *Total Assets:* £4,910,092
Registered Office: 91 East Street, Bridport, Dorset, DT6 3LB
Activities: Funeral and related activities
Shareholders: Clive James Wakely; Simon Wakely
Officers: Simon Wakely, Secretary; Clive James Wakely [1961] Funeral Director; Simon Wakely [1975] Funeral Director

B.Walker & Co.(Dursley) Limited
Incorporated: 28 November 1960 *Employees:* 13
Net Worth: £11,577,645 *Total Assets:* £16,599,050
Registered Office: 8-10 Long Street, Dursley, Glos, GL11 4HZ
Activities: Development of building projects
Shareholder: Barry Frederick Walker
Officers: Philip Barry Walker, Secretary; Barry Frederick Walker [1933] Director; Charles James Walker [1975] Director/Plumber; Philip Barry Walker [1957] Director; Susan Walker [1944] Director

Walker Developments (South West) Limited
Incorporated: 4 May 1988 *Employees:* 10
Net Worth: £3,626,278 *Total Assets:* £10,741,500
Registered Office: 6 Houndiscombe Road, Plymouth, PL4 6HH
Activities: Development of building projects
Major Shareholder: Richard Jonathan Walker
Officers: Mark Thomas, Secretary/Accountant; Damien Burley [1975] Director/Property Developer; Jonathon Pascoe [1977] Director; Richard Jonathan Walker [1959] Director

Walkergate PFI Project Company Limited
Incorporated: 4 March 2005 *Employees:* 2
Net Worth Deficit: £3,700,804 *Total Assets:* £29,039,568
Registered Office: Third Floor, Broad Quay House, Prince Street, Bristol, BS1 4DJ
Activities: Other business support service activities n.e.c.
Parent: Walkergate PFI Holding Company Limited
Officers: Kenneth Andrew McLellan [1961] Regional Project Director; Alan Campbell Ritchie [1967] Director

Wallaby Grip Limited
Incorporated: 12 December 1895
Net Worth: £1,023,000 *Total Assets:* £7,480,000
Registered Office: Atlantic House, Aviation Park West, Bournemouth International Airport, Christchurch, Dorset, BH23 6EW
Activities: Non-trading company
Parent: Meggitt Investments Limited
Officers: Simon Robert Grant, Secretary; Philip Ernest Green [1956] Director/Chartered Secretary; Marina Louise Thomas [1976] Director/Company Secretary

Wallace & Gromit's Children's Foundation
Incorporated: 11 January 1995 *Employees:* 27
Net Worth: £6,488,643 *Total Assets:* £6,825,755
Registered Office: 30-32 Upper Maudlin Street, Bristol, BS2 8DJ
Activities: Hospital activities
Officers: Nicola Kim Masters, Secretary; Simon Charles Bowden Cooper [1958] Director; Angela Susan Last [1968] Director's Assistant; Jocelyn Handley Moule [1960] Director/Solicitor; Michael Reginald Norton [1964] Director/Newspaper Editor

Wallgate Limited
Incorporated: 13 June 1919 *Employees:* 53
Net Worth: £2,879,710 *Total Assets:* £4,415,428
Registered Office: Crow Lane, Wilton, Salisbury, Wilts, SP2 0HB
Activities: Manufacture of household and sanitary goods and of toilet requisites
Parent: E V Naish Limited
Officers: Melissa Jane Poore, Secretary; Geoffrey David Naish [1959] Director; Trevor Francis Howard Powell [1955] Director

Wallscourt Foundation
Incorporated: 16 November 1994
Net Worth: £37,174,000 *Total Assets:* £39,482,000
Registered Office: University of The West of England, Frenchay Campus, Bristol, BS16 1QY
Activities: Other letting and operating of own or leased real estate
Officers: Richard Hugh Orme Boyes, Secretary; Nicholas Charles Bacon [1955] Director/Businessman; Christopher Arthur Booy [1952] Director/Consultant; Raymond Noel Burton [1947] Director/Consultant; Gillian Elizabeth Camm [1959] Director; John Steven Laycock [1948] Director/Retired; William John Marshall [1952] Director/Accountant; Simon Alick Moore [1965] Director; Karen Jane Morgan [1945] Director; Steven George West [1961] Director/Vice Chancellor

Wallsend Estates Limited
Incorporated: 29 October 1962 *Employees:* 26
Net Worth: £7,875,335 *Total Assets:* £9,569,466
Registered Office: Harscombe House, 1 Darklake View, Estover, Plymouth, PL6 7TL
Activities: Recreational vehicle parks, trailer parks and camping grounds
Shareholder: David Stewart King
Officers: Margaret Ann Langmaid, Secretary; Clare Rita King [1947] Director; David Stewart King [1942] Director; Margaret Ann Langmaid [1936] Director/Secretary; Patrick Charles Langmaid [1965] Director/Chartered Surveyor; Peter Anthony Langmaid [1935] Director

Walsall Lift Accommodation Services Limited
Incorporated: 17 April 2009
Net Worth Deficit: £2,050,000 *Total Assets:* £7,245,000
Registered Office: Challenge House, International Drive, Tewkesbury Business Park, Tewkesbury, Glos, GL20 8UQ
Activities: Other letting and operating of own or leased real estate
Parent: Walsall Holdco Limited
Officers: Daniel Peter Bevan, Secretary; Paul Simon Andrews [1970] Investment Director; Richard Darch [1961] Director; Mark William Grinonneau [1970] Director; Matthew Graham Hartland [1971] Finance Director; Neil Rae [1971] Director

Walston Holdings Limited
Incorporated: 24 December 1953 *Employees:* 71
Net Worth: £8,198,970 *Total Assets:* £10,863,935
Registered Office: East Down Packing Station, Winterborne, Whitechurch, Blandford Forum, Dorset, DT11 9AS
Activities: Mixed farming
Officers: Samantha Hebburn-Heath, Secretary; Ian Generald Friend [1964] Director/Farmer; Samantha Hebburn-Heath [1972] Director

Walston Poultry Farm Limited
Incorporated: 12 October 1961 *Employees:* 71
Net Worth: £6,775,338 *Total Assets:* £9,567,018
Registered Office: East Down Packing Station, Winterborne, Whitechurch, Blandford Forum, Dorset, DT11 9AS
Activities: Raising of poultry
Parent: Walston Holdings Limited
Officers: Samantha Hebburn-Heath, Secretary; Ian Generald Friend [1964] Director/Farmer; Samantha Hebburn-Heath [1972] Director

Walton Civil Engineering and Surfacing Contractors Limited
Incorporated: 30 October 1997 *Employees:* 82
Net Worth: £3,043,859 *Total Assets:* £5,478,320
Registered Office: Mill Brook Depot, Yellingmill Lane, Shepton Mallet, Somerset, BA4 4JT
Activities: Construction of roads and motorways
Officers: Beverly Walton, Secretary; Timothy Michael Payne [1970] Joint Managing Director; Andrew Walton [1969] Joint Managing Director

Walton Street LLP
Incorporated: 1 April 2016 *Employees:* 7
Net Worth: £11,130,000 *Total Assets:* £11,225,722
Registered Office: 4 Queen Square, Bath, BA1 2HA
Officers: Andrew Douglas Brownsword [1947] Member; Christina June Brownsword [1951] Member

Ward Edward Limited
Incorporated: 1 November 2006
Net Worth Deficit: £215,316 *Total Assets:* £6,610,201
Registered Office: 25 Sandbourne Road, Bournemouth, BH4 8JH
Activities: Other letting and operating of own or leased real estate
Shareholders: Isabelle Anne Marie Edward; Jonathan Johann Edward
Officers: Isabelle Anne Marie Edward, Secretary [French]; Isabelle Anne Marie Edward [1968] Director [French]; Jonathan Johann Edward [1964] Director

Thomas Ware & Sons Limited
Incorporated: 7 June 1890 *Employees:* 38
Net Worth: £3,357,332 *Total Assets:* £4,074,101
Registered Office: Clift House, Tannery Coronation Road, Southville, Bristol, BS3 1RN
Activities: Tanning and dressing of leather; dressing and dyeing of fur
Officers: Alistair Douglas Pierre Brearley [1977] Director/Tanner; Andrew Douglas Brearley [1944] Director; Jeremy Simon Leonard Brooks [1962] Director/Financial Planner; Jonathan Thomas Godfrey [1983] Director/Investment Manager; Peter John Setterington [1947] Director

John Ware Limited
Incorporated: 19 October 1984 *Employees:* 47
Net Worth: £1,131,117 *Total Assets:* £3,982,942
Registered Office: Head Office, 65 Alcombe Road, Alcombe, Minehead, Somerset, TA24 6BD
Activities: Specialists medical practice activities
Major Shareholder: Manraj Singh Punni
Officers: Harjinder Kaur Punni, Secretary; Manraj Singh Punni [1974] Director/Pharmacist

Warm Welcome Hotels (Southern) Limited
Incorporated: 10 February 1989 *Employees:* 106
Net Worth: £1,496,146 *Total Assets:* £4,241,916
Registered Office: 9 Lady Park Road, Livermead, Torquay, Devon, TQ2 6UA
Activities: Hotels and similar accommodation
Parent: Warm Welcome Management Limited
Officers: Peter Brian Maurice Cliff [1951] Director/Accountant; Philip Glyn Davies [1945] Director/Hotelier

Warm Welcome Management Limited
Incorporated: 13 May 1985 *Employees:* 143
Net Worth: £4,513,073 *Total Assets:* £7,170,931
Registered Office: 9 Lady Park Road, Livermead, Torquay, Devon, TQ2 6UA
Activities: Activities of head offices
Shareholder: Philip Glyn Davies
Officers: Peter Brian Maurice Cliff [1951] Director/Chartered Accountant; Philip Glyn Davies [1945] Director

Warminster School
Incorporated: 15 November 1994 *Employees:* 169
Net Worth: £6,135,335 *Total Assets:* £10,680,441
Registered Office: Warminster School, Warminster, Wilts, BA12 8PJ
Activities: Pre-primary education
Officers: Katherine Mines, Secretary; Caroline Elizabeth Drennan [1961] Director/Teacher; Charles John Barrington Goodbody [1953] Director/Solicitor; Andrew Charles Peter Kennett [1958] Director/Retired Army Officer; The Rt Hon Sir David Nicholas Ramsay Latham [1942] Director; James Ian McComas [1959] Director/Self Employed; Timothy Roger William Moore [1946] Director/Land Agent; Jeremy Edwin Montague Pakenham [1948] Director/Management Consultant; Fiona Christina Stewart [1965] Marketing Director; Richard David Stratton [1944] Director/Farmer; Tyrone Richard Urch [1965] Director/Ministry of Defence; Andrew Duncan Waters [1957] Director/Education Consultant; Duncan James Wilson [1969] Vice President & Managing Director

Warners of Gloucester Limited
Incorporated: 16 June 1986 *Employees:* 78
Net Worth: £256,956 *Total Assets:* £4,445,619
Registered Office: Eastern Avenue, Gloucester, GL4 3BS
Activities: Sale of new cars and light motor vehicles
Parent: Warners Trust PLC
Officers: Anita Helen Jenkins, Secretary; Anita Helen Jenkins [1966] Director; Mark Jones [1967] Director/Dealer Principal; David Andrew Ryland [1966] Director/Financial Controller; Christopher James Neil Smart [1965] Director/Dealer Principal; Guy David Warner [1974] Director; Michael David Warner [1947] Director

Warners Retail Group Limited
Incorporated: 20 August 2012 *Employees:* 257
Net Worth: £1,805,426 *Total Assets:* £12,194,395
Registered Office: Unit 2, 130 Bristol Road, Gloucester, GL1 5SQ
Activities: Activities of head offices
Major Shareholder: Guy David Warner
Officers: Anita Helen Jenkins, Secretary; Steven Neale [1963] Director; Guy David Warner [1974] Director; Melanie Ann Warner [1974] Director; Michael David Warner [1947] Director

Warners Retail Limited
Incorporated: 20 October 1976 *Employees:* 177
Net Worth: £369,916 *Total Assets:* £12,194,351
Registered Office: Unit 2, 130 Bristol Road, Gloucester, GL1 5SQ
Activities: Retail sale in non-specialised stores with food, beverages or tobacco predominating
Parent: Warners Retail Group
Officers: Anita Helen Jenkins, Secretary; Guy David Warner [1974] Director; Melanie Ann Warner [1974] Director; Michael David Warner [1947] Director

Warners Trust PLC
Incorporated: 26 June 1946 *Employees:* 80
Net Worth: £2,284,190 *Total Assets:* £6,609,732
Registered Office: Eastern Avenue, Gloucester, GL4 3BS
Activities: Activities of head offices
Major Shareholder: Michael David Warner
Officers: Anita Helen Jenkins, Secretary; Anita Helen Jenkins [1966] Director/Chartered Accountant; Michael David Warner [1947] Director; Rosemary Anne Warner [1950] Director

Warren Farm Holiday Centre Limited
Incorporated: 4 April 2003
Net Worth: £12,647,064 *Total Assets:* £15,389,974
Registered Office: Warren Farm Holiday Park, Brean Sands, Burnham on Sea, Somerset, TA8 2RP
Activities: Holiday centres and villages
Shareholders: Christopher John Harris; Jonathan Hugh Harris; Michael Hugh Harris
Officers: Christopher John Harris [1984] Director/Manager; Jonathan Hugh Harris [1958] Director/Holiday Park Proprietor; Michael Hugh Harris [1986] Director/Manager

A. H. Warren Trust (Holdings) Limited
Incorporated: 30 April 1954 *Employees:* 68
Net Worth: £44,714,400 *Total Assets:* £51,738,884
Registered Office: Coombe Farm, Crewkerne, Somerset, TA18 8RR
Activities: Activities of head offices
Parent: A H Warren Trust
Officers: Matthew Tufton, Secretary; John Nicholas Arnot [1942] Director/Solicitor; Guy Coleman [1965] Director; Matthew John Tufton [1979] Director/Chartered Accountant

A. H. Warren Trust (Property) Limited
Incorporated: 24 March 1998 *Employees:* 3
Net Worth: £23,254,568 *Total Assets:* £32,070,052
Registered Office: Coombe Farm, Roundham, Crewkerne, Somerset, TA18 8RR
Activities: Other letting and operating of own or leased real estate
Parent: A H Warren Trust Holdings Limited
Officers: Matthew Tufton, Secretary; John Nicholas Arnot [1942] Director; Guy Coleman [1965] Director; Matthew John Tufton [1979] Director/Chartered Accountant

A. H. Warren Trust Limited
Incorporated: 8 March 1991 *Employees:* 53
Net Worth: £1,458,858 *Total Assets:* £14,077,828
Registered Office: Coombe Farm, Crewkerne, Somerset, TA18 8RR
Activities: Raising of dairy cattle
Parent: A H Warren Trust Holdings Limited
Officers: Matthew Tufton, Secretary; John Nicholas Arnot [1942] Director; Charles Francis Burnett Clark [1959] Director/Chartered Surveyor; Guy Coleman [1965] Director; Matthew John Tufton [1979] Director/Chartered Accountant

Warrens Bakery Limited
Incorporated: 2 October 1979 *Employees:* 516
Net Worth Deficit: £25,470 *Total Assets:* £4,860,215
Registered Office: The Bakery, Boswedden Road, St Just, Penzance, Cornwall, TR19 7JP
Activities: Manufacture of bread; manufacture of fresh pastry goods and cakes
Parent: Provenance Brands Limited
Officers: Jason Jobling [1975] Director/Master Baker; Alexandra Lucy Martin [1969] Director; Nicholas Bryan Straw [1956] Director; Mark Sullivan [1960] Director; Simon David Toft [1958] Director

Warrington Homes Limited (The)
Incorporated: 14 March 1977 *Employees:* 89
Net Worth: £3,630,030 *Total Assets:* £3,681,892
Registered Office: Claremont, Gastard Road, Corsham, Wilts, SN13 9PD
Activities: Residential care activities for the elderly and disabled
Officers: Richard John Christie Mauldon, Secretary; Michael Norman Canty [1959] Director/Retired; John Malcolm Chatwin [1945] Director/Retired; Dr Nicholas John Rutherford Davis [1947] Director/Retired; Doctor Rupert Christopher Fraser Drummond [1941] Director/Retired; Kate Victoria Helen Hoffman [1964] Director/Nurse; Dina McAlpine [1967] Director; Christine Reid [1943] Director/Retired; Paul Sexton [1947] Director/Project Management; Gillian Claire Stafford [1960] Director/Manager

Wartsila Hamworthy International Limited
Incorporated: 26 June 2006
Net Worth: £12,466,000 *Total Assets:* £29,652,000
Registered Office: Fleets Corner, Poole, Dorset, BH17 0JT
Activities: Activities of head offices
Officers: Kari Hietanen [1963] Director/Group Vice President Corporate Relations and Legal [Finnish]; Timo Ensio Koponen [1969] Director/Vice President Finance & Control [Finnish]

Wartsila Hamworthy Limited
Incorporated: 18 January 1962 *Employees:* 5
Net Worth: £29,274,000 *Total Assets:* £52,158,000
Registered Office: Fleets Corner, Poole, Dorset, BH17 0JT
Activities: Activities of head offices
Officers: Kari Hietanen [1963] Director/Group Vice President; Timo Koponen [1969] Director/Vice President Finance and Control [Finnish]

Wartsila Water Systems Limited
Incorporated: 18 January 1962 *Employees:* 165
Net Worth: £400,000 *Total Assets:* £28,282,000
Registered Office: Fleets Corner, Poole, Dorset, BH17 0JT
Activities: Manufacture of fluid power equipment
Parent: Wartsila Hamworthy Limited
Officers: Timo Koponen [1969] Director/Vice President Finance & Control [Finnish]; Arto Lehtinen [1971] Director [Finnish]; Erik Rasmussen [1966] Managing Director [Danish]

Warwick Fabrics (UK) Limited
Incorporated: 6 April 1988 *Employees:* 36
Net Worth: £2,087,549 *Total Assets:* £5,173,108
Registered Office: Unit 3 Davy Way, Hardwicke, Gloucester, GL2 2BY
Activities: Finishing of textiles
Shareholders: John-Andrew Ovenstone; Cameron Thomas Warwick; Leighton Barnaby Warwick
Officers: Leighton Barnaby Warwick, Secretary; Andrew Ovenstone [1942] Director [South African]; John-Andrew Ovenstone [1968] Director [South African]; Cameron Thomas Warwick [1967] Sales and Marketing Director; Leighton Barnaby Warwick [1972] Director [Australian]

Wasdell Holdings Limited
Incorporated: 27 July 2006 *Employees:* 586
Net Worth: £16,477,415 *Total Assets:* £27,685,870
Registered Office: Units 6-8 Euro Way, Blagrove, Swindon, Wilts, SN5 8YW
Activities: Activities of head offices
Major Shareholder: Martin John Tedham
Officers: Martin John Tedham [1960] Director

Wasdell Packaging Limited
Incorporated: 25 June 1969 *Employees:* 440
Net Worth: £18,937,716 *Total Assets:* £28,707,694
Registered Office: Unit 6-8 Euro Way, Blagrove, Swindon, Wilts, SN5 8YW
Activities: Other manufacturing n.e.c.
Officers: Philip Gough [1971] Director; Martin John Tedham [1960] Director; Philip Stewart Vines [1965] Director

Wastenage Farms Limited
Incorporated: 3 December 2004 *Employees:* 10
Net Worth: £2,504,528 *Total Assets:* £6,799,525
Registered Office: Tidwell Barton, East Budleigh, Budleigh Salterton, Devon, EX9 7AG
Activities: Growing of cereals (except rice), leguminous crops and oil seeds
Major Shareholder: Diana Ruth Wastenage
Officers: Diana Ruth Wastenage, Secretary/Consultant and Farmer; Diana Ruth Wastenage [1969] Director/Consultant and Farmer; Peter Henry Wastenage [1970] Director/Farmer

Watch Guru Limited
Incorporated: 13 February 1998 *Employees:* 3
Net Worth: £6,522,290 *Total Assets:* £7,378,047
Registered Office: Windover House, St Ann Street, Salisbury, Wilts, SP1 2DR
Activities: Retail sale via mail order houses or via Internet
Major Shareholder: Tom Bolt
Officers: Fifi Bolt, Secretary; Tom Bolt [1967] Director/Retail of Watches

Watchpike Limited
Incorporated: 14 November 1988 *Employees:* 7
Net Worth: £12,073,976 *Total Assets:* £13,805,332
Registered Office: 14 Widcombe Crescent, Bath, BA2 6AH
Activities: Buying and selling of own real estate
Shareholders: Peter Keith Moore; Sarah Bridget Croft; Peter Keith Moore
Officers: Sarah Bridget Croft, Secretary; Christopher John Moore [1980] Director/Property Manager; Peter Keith Moore [1947] Director

The Watercress Company Limited
Incorporated: 10 December 1986
Net Worth: £11,194,268 *Total Assets:* £11,284,768
Registered Office: Maen, Culliford Road, Dorchester, DT1 1QQ
Activities: Wholesale of fruit and vegetables
Major Shareholder: Peter Cyril Old
Officers: Pamela May Old, Secretary; Thomas Michael Amery Matthews [1975] Technical Director; Sharon Janette Baker [1964] Finance Director; Leonard Charles Barter [1943] Director/Watercress Grower; Peter Cyril Old [1942] Director

Waterdance Limited
Incorporated: 15 October 1996 *Employees:* 12
Net Worth: £10,163,000 *Total Assets:* £32,593,000
Registered Office: Greendale Business Park, Woodbury Salterton, Exeter, EX5 1EW
Activities: Marine fishing
Parent: FWS Carter & Sons Ltd
Officers: Peter German, Secretary/Accountant; Alec Robin Bill Carter [1974] Director; Mathew Rowan Carter [1982] Director; Robin Anthony Bill Carter [1944] Director; Rowan Charles Carter [1953] Director/Farmer; Peter Lewin German [1953] Director

Waterfield Homes Limited
Incorporated: 20 July 2000 *Employees:* 15
Net Worth: £8,975,874 *Total Assets:* £22,668,564
Registered Office: 5 Sandy Court, Ashleigh Way, Plympton, Plymouth, PL7 5JX
Activities: Other letting and operating of own or leased real estate
Major Shareholder: Mathew Fairfax Conyers
Officers: Mathew Fairfax Conyers [1972] Director/Property Developer

Watergate Bay Hotel Limited
Incorporated: 5 February 1999 *Employees:* 283
Net Worth: £7,065,307 *Total Assets:* £19,094,806
Registered Office: Watergate Bay Hotel, Watergate Bay, Newquay, Cornwall, TR8 4AA
Activities: Hotels and similar accommodation
Shareholders: Mary Anne Ashworth; John Reginald Ashworth; William James McInnes Ashworth
Officers: John Reginald Howell Ashworth, Secretary; Henry William Howell Ashworth [1969] Director/Social Responsibility Organisation; John Reginald Howell Ashworth [1939] Director/Hotel Proprietor; Mary Anne Ashworth [1944] Director/Hotel Proprietor; Rosamond Elizabeth Ashworth [1976] Director/Hospitality & Sports Coach; William James McInnes Ashworth [1974] Director/Hotelier; Judith Anne Blakeburn [1959] Director/Hospitality Marketing; Benjamin Frank Harper [1979] Director; Christian John Hugo [1968] Director/Finance; Alastair Michael Stuart Young [1950] Director/Accountant

Waterlip Developments Limited
Incorporated: 4 September 2009 *Employees:* 1
Net Worth: £3,151,125 *Total Assets:* £6,239,397
Registered Office: Willmotts Business Park, Waterlip, Shepton Mallet, Somerset, BA4 4RN
Activities: Other letting and operating of own or leased real estate
Major Shareholder: Andrew Mark Stott
Officers: Andy Mark Stott [1968] Director

Watermark Cotswolds Limited
Incorporated: 12 December 1997 *Employees:* 1
Net Worth: £3,882,707 *Total Assets:* £4,670,690
Registered Office: Summer Lake, Spine Road East, South Cerney, Cirencester, Glos, GL7 5LW
Activities: Activities of head offices
Major Shareholder: Maxwell Hugh Thomas
Officers: Maxwell Hugh Thomas [1945] Director/Developer

Waters Park House Limited
Incorporated: 7 July 1997 *Employees:* 104
Net Worth: £1,876,172 *Total Assets:* £3,873,103
Registered Office: 23 Lockyer Street, Plymouth, PL1 2QZ
Activities: Other residential care activities n.e.c.
Major Shareholder: Elizabeth Anne Waters
Officers: Hayley Bowden, Secretary; Elizabeth Anne Waters [1942] Director/Nursing Home Administrator

Watershed Arts Trust Limited (The)
Incorporated: 19 January 1982 *Employees:* 91
Net Worth: £8,077,526 *Total Assets:* £9,184,204
Registered Office: Watershed Arts Trust, 1 Canons Road, Bristol, BS1 5TX
Activities: Operation of arts facilities
Officers: Lisa Michelle Gardner, Secretary; Syed Shamil Ahmed [1993] Director/Freelance Events Photographer; Paul Michael Appleby [1956] Director; Diane Elizabeth Bunyan [1951] Director/Consultant; Susan Patricia Cooper [1957] Director/Social Banker; John Durrant [1963] Creative Director; Sherrie Eugene-Hart [1964] Director/Broadcaster; Lisa Michelle Gardner [1965] Director/Accountant; Stephen John Gatfield [1958] Director/Partner; Cllr Estella Jane Tincknell [1960] Director/University Lecturer; James George Touzel [1971] Director/Solicitor; Donna Marie Whitehead [1980] Director/Pro Vice Chancellor and Dean; Stephen Michael Wilson [1961] Director/Consultant

Watershore Ltd.
Incorporated: 16 April 1997
Net Worth: £2,663,921 *Total Assets:* £3,675,842
Registered Office: Ardsley House, 18 Braidley Road, Bournemouth, BH2 6JX
Activities: Buying and selling of own real estate
Major Shareholder: Hazel Bowles
Officers: Hazel Bowles, Secretary/Valuer; Hazel Bowles [1946] Director/Valuer

Waterside Holiday Group Limited
Incorporated: 15 December 1988 *Employees:* 138
Net Worth: £19,917,992 *Total Assets:* £24,701,860
Registered Office: 10 Bridge Street, Christchurch, Dorset, BH23 1EF
Activities: Holiday centres and villages
Shareholders: Claire Vanessa Jacobs; Miranda Louise Jacobs; Olivia Jane Jacobs
Officers: Miranda Louise Jacobs, Secretary; Claire Vanessa Jacobs [1966] Director; Judith Hannah Jacobs [1943] Director; Miranda Louise Jacobs [1968] Director; Olivia Jane Jacobs [1974] Director; Gareth Vaughan Thomas [1957] Director

W.J. Watkins & Son Limited
Incorporated: 8 November 1976 *Employees:* 62
Net Worth: £5,868,113 *Total Assets:* £15,868,358
Registered Office: Highfield, The Beacon, Holsworthy, Devon, EX22 7NF
Activities: Raising of dairy cattle
Major Shareholder: David John Watkins
Officers: David John Watkins, Secretary; Hilary Christine Winifred Cobbledick [1956] Agricultural Director; David John Watkins [1954] Managing Director

Susie Watson Designs Ltd
Incorporated: 2 November 1999 *Employees:* 55
Net Worth: £1,689,338 *Total Assets:* £4,740,696
Registered Office: River House Studio, Axford, Marlborough, Wilts, SN8 2HA
Activities: Other retail sale in non-specialised stores
Shareholders: Hamish Murray Watson; Susan Diana Watson
Officers: Hamish Murray Watson, Secretary/Chartered Accountant; Hamish Murray Watson [1945] Director/Chartered Accountant; Susan Diana Watson [1949] Director/Designer & Gallery Manager

Watson-Marlow Limited
Incorporated: 14 March 1990 *Employees:* 312
Net Worth: £3,473,674 *Total Assets:* £37,166,968
Registered Office: Watson-Marlow Ltd, Bickland Water Road, Tregoniggie, Falmouth, Cornwall, TR11 4RU
Activities: Manufacture of pumps
Parent: Spirax-Sarco Engineering PLC
Officers: Mark Alan Davis, Secretary; Kevin James Boyd [1964] Finance Director; Amanda-Jane Capon [1976] Director/Human Resources Professional; Mark Alan Davis [1982] Finance Director; Darren Jason Etherington [1975] Director/Engineer; Susan Mary Godzicz [1956] Director; Andrew John Green [1955] Engineering Director; Martin James Johnston [1969] Director; Christopher Andrew Magor [1961] Director/Engineer; Simon Nicholson [1967] Director; Rachel Pallett [1969] Sales Director; Mark Andrew Rawet [1960] Director; James Lawrence Whalen [1956] Director [American]; James Henry Wright [1977] Global Supply Director

Watts Aviation Services Limited
Incorporated: 17 December 1965 *Employees:* 14
Net Worth: £5,628,295 *Total Assets:* £7,784,723
Registered Office: Mead Lane Warehouse, Mead Lane, Lydney, Glos, GL15 5EL
Activities: Non-specialised wholesale trade
Officers: Simon Christopher Hack, Secretary; Simon Christopher Hack [1970] Director/General Manager; Joseph C Heinmiller [1982] Director/Private Equity Principal [American]; Christopher a Lawler [1967] Director/Managing Principal [American]

Watts Desser Limited
Incorporated: 13 March 2015 *Employees:* 30
Net Worth: £7,754,313 *Total Assets:* £21,621,790
Registered Office: Mead Lane Warehouse, Mead Lane, Lydney, Glos, GL15 5EL
Activities: Activities of other holding companies n.e.c.
Officers: Joseph C Heinmiller [1982] Director/Principal [American]; Jeffrey Johnston [1957] Director/CEO Desser Holdings LLC [American]; Christopher a Lawler [1967] Director/Managing Principal [American]

Watts of Lydney Group Limited
Incorporated: 22 December 1920 *Employees:* 178
Net Worth: £14,208,000 *Total Assets:* £23,248,000
Registered Office: Althorpe House, High Street, Lydney, Glos, GL15 5DD
Activities: Activities of head offices
Officers: Stewart Charters [1954] Managing Director; Peter John Rilett [1950] Director/Accountant; John Campbell Thurston [1940] Director; Jonathan Piers Thurston [1973] Director/Consultant

Watts Truck & Van Limited
Incorporated: 28 July 1986 *Employees:* 102
Net Worth: £1,588,000 *Total Assets:* £8,085,000
Registered Office: Althorpe House, High Street, Lydney, Glos, GL15 5DD
Activities: Sale of other motor vehicles
Parent: WT & V Limited
Officers: Simon Jeremy Morgan Griffin [1962] Director/Dealer Principal; John Campbell Thurston [1940] Director

Wave Multi Academy Trust
Incorporated: 25 February 2013 *Employees:* 169
Previous: Acorn Academy Cornwall
Net Worth: £6,891,845 *Total Assets:* £8,696,084
Registered Office: Glynn House, Treyew Road, Truro, Cornwall, TR1 3AS
Activities: Primary education
Officers: Emma Tennant, Secretary; Julieann Carter [1964] Director/Head of Nursing; Christopher John Challis [1971] Director/Deputy Headteacher; Sandy Chapman [1953] Director/Retired; Robert John Gasson [1968] Director/Executive Headteacher; Christian Jenkins [1958] Director/Businessman; Christopher John Liles [1972] Director/Teacher; Deborah Claire Wilshire [1958] Director

M. Way & Son (Transport) Limited
Incorporated: 24 August 1994 *Employees:* 120
Net Worth: £4,370,046 *Total Assets:* £11,046,181
Registered Office: Plot 6 Pathfields Business Park, South Molton, Devon, EX36 3LH
Activities: Freight transport by road
Major Shareholder: Mervyn Frederick Way
Officers: Karen Elizabeth Smith, Secretary; Karen Elizabeth Smith [1970] Director; Kevin Smith [1965] Director; Helen Way [1951] Director; Mervyn Frederick Way [1949] Director/Haulage Contractor; Nicholas Mervyn Way [1969] Director

Way Fund Managers Limited
Incorporated: 9 June 2000
Net Worth: £1,139,208 *Total Assets:* £5,794,142
Registered Office: Cedar House, 3 Cedar Park, Cobham Road, Wimborne, Dorset, BH21 7SB
Activities: Security and commodity contracts dealing activities
Parent: Professional Partners Administration Limited
Officers: Christopher Stephen Oliver, Secretary; Vincent Neil Hoare [1959] Director/Financial Services Executive; Ian Guy Hobday [1960] Director

Way Group Limited
Incorporated: 29 February 1996 *Employees:* 6
Net Worth: £2,391,334 *Total Assets:* £7,736,350
Registered Office: Cedar House, 3 Cedar Park, Cobham Road, Wimborne, Dorset, BH21 7SB
Activities: Activities of head offices
Officers: Christopher Stephen Oliver, Secretary; Clive Nicholas Boothman [1955] Director; Richard Edwin Green [1946] Director; Ian Guy Hobday [1960] Director; Paul Wilcox [1948] Director/Senior Financial Executive

M Way Holdings Limited
Incorporated: 11 May 2016 *Employees:* 110
Net Worth: £4,985,073 *Total Assets:* £11,790,092
Registered Office: M Way & Son (Transport) Ltd, Pathfields Business Park, South Molton, Devon, EX36 3LH
Activities: Renting and leasing of other machinery, equipment and tangible goods n.e.c.
Major Shareholder: Mervyn Frederick Way
Officers: Karen Elizabeth Smith [1970] Director and Company Secretary; Mervyn Frederick Way [1949] Director/Haulier; Nicholas Mervyn Way [1969] Director/Haulage Contractor

Waycroft Multi Academy Trust
Incorporated: 27 June 2011 *Employees:* 171
Net Worth: £6,416,212 *Total Assets:* £8,759,290
Registered Office: Waycroft Academy, Selden Road, Stockwood, Bristol, BS14 8PS
Activities: Primary education
Officers: Pauline Warburton, Secretary; Cathryn Mary Atkin [1976] Director; Zena Barnes [1970] Director/OCR Partner Programme Manager; Andrew Darren Bowden [1973] Director/Training Manager; Lisa Craig [1981] Director/School Teacher; Kevin Edenborough [1972] Director/Chartered Accountant; Tracy Ann French [1967] Director/Executive Headteacher; Pamela Goold [1982] Director/Associate Financial Accountant; Gail Elizabeth Lynn [1981] Director/Senior Quality Systems Analyst; Matthew Morgan [1974] Director/Assistant Principal; Heather Morris [1976] Director/School Teacher; David Norfolk [1977] Director/IT Professional; Christopher James Osborne [1983] Director/Senior Quantity Surveyor; Iris Partridge [1971] Director/Executive Officer, Easton Community Centre [German]; Mark Andrew Rogers [1965] Director/Partner Relationship Manager; Peng Tran-Freegard [1979] Director/Bart Ingredients Co

Wayfarer Group Limited
Incorporated: 30 April 2002
Net Worth Deficit: £3,984,000 *Total Assets:* £16,639,000
Registered Office: 10 Willis Way, Fleets Industrial Estate, Poole, Dorset, BH15 3SS
Activities: Other business support service activities n.e.c.
Officers: Bertrand Barthelemy [1965] Director [French]

Waypoints Care (Plymouth) Limited
Incorporated: 25 October 2010
Net Worth: £1,644,650 *Total Assets:* £7,596,531
Registered Office: Unit 1 Pullman Business Park, Pullman Way, Ringwood, Hants, BH24 1HD
Activities: Other human health activities
Parent: Waypoints Care Group Limited
Officers: Lee Griffiths, Secretary; Andrew John Baxendine [1960] Finance Director; William Frederick Stone [1938] Director

Waypoints Care (Upton) Limited
Incorporated: 9 September 2011
Net Worth: £2,217,950 *Total Assets:* £9,359,081
Registered Office: Unit 1 Pullman Business Park, Pullman Way, Ringwood, Hants, BH24 1HD
Activities: Residential nursing care facilities
Parent: Waypoints Care Group Limited
Officers: Lee Griffiths, Secretary; Andrew John Baxendine [1960] Director; William Frederick Stone [1938] Director

Waypoints Care (Verwood) Limited
Incorporated: 17 February 2009
Net Worth: £2,122,980 *Total Assets:* £6,010,066
Registered Office: Unit 1 Pullman Business Park, Pullman Way, Ringwood, Hants, BH24 1HD
Activities: Residential nursing care facilities
Parent: Waypoints Care Group Limited
Officers: Lee Richard Griffiths, Secretary; Andrew John Baxendine [1960] Director; William Frederick Stone [1938] Director

Waypoints Care Group Limited
Incorporated: 25 August 2010 *Employees:* 265
Net Worth: £6,798,236 *Total Assets:* £24,845,228
Registered Office: Unit 1 Pullman Business Park, Pullman Way, Ringwood, Hants, BH24 1HD
Activities: Residential nursing care facilities
Shareholders: William Frederick Stone; Sally Ann Stone
Officers: Lee Griffiths, Secretary; Andrew John Baxendine [1960] Director; William Frederick Stone [1938] Director

WBW Solicitors LLP
Incorporated: 13 February 2009 *Employees:* 186
Net Worth: £2,851,623 *Total Assets:* £4,587,620
Registered Office: Church House, Queen Street, Newton Abbot, Devon, TQ12 2QP
Officers: Stephen Andrew Bulman [1966] Member; Justin Osborne [1972] Member; Tracey Jane Pearce [1962] Member; Martin White [1966] Member; Catherine Ann Causey [1970] LLP Member; Sarah Jane Couch [1968] LLP Member; Helen Davies [1964] LLP Member; Lloyd George Hale [1959] LLP Member; Michael Albert Setter [1950] LLP Member; Sarah Mary Witheridge [1972] LLP Member; Fiona Agnes Yellowlees [1965] LLP Member

WCR Holdings 2014 Limited
Incorporated: 10 April 2014 *Employees:* 41
Net Worth: £4,813,784 *Total Assets:* £7,135,879
Registered Office: Sigma House, Oak View Close, Edginswell Park, Torquay, Devon, TQ2 7FF
Activities: Activities of other holding companies n.e.c.
Shareholders: Beryl White; David Brian Charles White
Officers: Benjamin James Robinson [1984] Director; Beryl White [1934] Director/Accounts Clerk; David Brian Charles White [1965] Director/Estimator/Manager; Lesley Anne White [1959] Director/Manager

We The Curious Limited
Incorporated: 18 April 1995
Previous: At Bristol Limited
Net Worth: £32,846,000 *Total Assets:* £34,131,000
Registered Office: Anchor Road, Harbourside, Bristol, BS1 5DB
Activities: Other amusement and recreation activities n.e.c.
Officers: Simon Charles Bowden Cooper [1958] Public Affairs Director; Geoffrey Richard Gollop [1955] Director/Councillor; Nick Jones [1954] Director/Education Consultant; Dr Kathreena Kurian [1970] Director; Michael David May [1951] Director/Computer Scientist; Alan Parsons [1949] Director; Chris John Sims [1956] Director; David Alan Sproxton [1954] Director; Joanna Michelle Stringer [1977] Director; Thomas Stringer [1975] Strategy Director at Dyson; Helen Godwin Teige [1976] Director

Weardale Estates Limited
Incorporated: 18 October 1995 *Employees:* 215
Net Worth: £17,640,236 *Total Assets:* £17,998,428
Registered Office: The Estate Office, Ozleworth Park, Wotton under Edge, Glos, GL12 7QA
Activities: Hunting, trapping and related service activities
Major Shareholder: Michael John Christopher Stone
Officers: Nicola Jane Farquhar [1968] Director; Sebastian Dominic Green [1971] Director/Chartered Surveyor [Irish]; Andrew Jonathan Stone [1970] Director; Michael John Christopher Stone [1936] Director/Chairman

The Weavers Shop Limited
Incorporated: 12 November 1991 *Employees:* 16
Net Worth: £12,268,211 *Total Assets:* £12,572,418
Registered Office: The Weavers Shop, Eastern Avenue, Gloucester, GL4 3BY
Activities: Retail sale of carpets, rugs, wall and floor coverings in specialised stores
Officers: Yakub Patel, Secretary; Ibrahim Patel [1954] Director/Carpet Retailer; Yakub Patel [1948] Director/Carpet Retailer; Yusuf Patel [1957] Director/Carpet Retailer

Webbers Property Services Limited
Incorporated: 14 March 1994 *Employees:* 138
Net Worth: £2,649,061 *Total Assets:* £4,068,854
Registered Office: Bristol & West House, 39-41 Boutport Street, Barnstaple, Devon, EX31 1SA
Activities: Real estate agencies
Major Shareholder: Graham Gardner Harrison
Officers: Gary Robert Holder, Secretary/Director; Lindsay Margaret Braddick [1965] Director/Estate Agent; Graham Gardner Harrison [1948] Director/Chartered Surveyor; Gary Robert Holder [1958] Finance Director; Lee Hussell [1975] Director/Estate Agent; Peter Hugh McHugh [1953] Director/Chartered Surveyor; Malcolm Edward Prescott [1966] Director/Estate Agent; Andrew Mark Simpson [1981] Director/Estate Agent; Napoleon Chaplin Wilcox [1967] Director/Estate Agent

Weblease Limited
Incorporated: 9 March 1998
Net Worth: £3,408,089 *Total Assets:* £6,118,541
Registered Office: c/o Millener Davies, Southfield House, 2 Southfield Road, Westbury on Trym, Bristol, BS9 3BH
Activities: Other letting and operating of own or leased real estate
Major Shareholder: Andrew James Robb
Officers: Andrew James Robb, Secretary; Andrew James Robb [1962] Director

Weird Fish Clothing Limited
Incorporated: 20 March 2017 *Employees:* 3
Net Worth Deficit: £190,282 *Total Assets:* £6,122,393
Registered Office: Unit 15 Miller Court, Severn Drive, Tewkesbury Business Park, Tewkesbury, Glos, GL20 8DN
Activities: Activities of head offices
Parent: Weird Fish Holdings Limited
Officers: Dean Murray [1962] Director; Bethany Phillips [1971] Product Director; John Stockton [1960] Director

Weird Fish Holdings Limited
Incorporated: 20 March 2017 *Employees:* 151
Net Worth: £314,977 *Total Assets:* £10,444,184
Registered Office: Unit 15 Miller Court, Severn Drive, Tewkesbury Business Park, Tewkesbury, Glos, GL20 8DN
Activities: Activities of head offices
Parent: Total Capital Partners Dory Investment LP acting through its General Partner TCP General Partner Ltd
Officers: Paul Michael Brown [1979] Director; Dean Murray [1962] Director; Bethany Phillips [1971] Product Director; John Stockton [1960] Director

Weird Fish Limited
Incorporated: 4 February 1981 *Employees:* 144
Net Worth: £2,373,078 *Total Assets:* £6,730,041
Registered Office: Unit 15 Miller Court, Severn Drive, Tewkesbury Business Park, Tewkesbury, Glos, GL20 8DN
Activities: Wholesale of clothing and footwear
Parent: Total Capital Partners Dory Investment LP
Officers: Jon Goodwin, Secretary/Accountant; Dean Murray [1962] Director; Bethany Phillips [1971] Product Director; John Stockton [1960] Director

Robert Welch Designs Limited
Incorporated: 7 April 1961 *Employees:* 68
Net Worth: £4,548,756 *Total Assets:* £8,409,652
Registered Office: The Studio Shop, Lower High Street, Chipping Campden, Glos, GL55 6DY
Activities: Manufacture of cutlery
Shareholders: Alan Rupert Welch; Alice Jane Welch
Officers: Alice Jane Welch, Secretary; Alan Rupert Welch [1963] Director; Alice Jane Welch [1959] Director/Public Relations

Weldmar Hospicecare Trust
Incorporated: 10 July 1990 *Employees:* 224
Net Worth: £13,557,128 *Total Assets:* £14,178,919
Registered Office: Joseph Weld Hospice, Herringston Road, Dorchester, DT1 2SL
Activities: Residential nursing care facilities
Officers: Sheena Louise Keep, Secretary; Stephen Baynard [1950] Director/Retired; Susan Mary Davies [1943] Director/Retired Deputy Chief Constable; Viscount James Hugh Carleton Fitzharris [1970] Director/Landowner; Jayne George [1960] Fundraising & Marketing Director; Tanya Grant [1967] Director/Bursar; Susan Hawkett [1948] Director/Retired NHS Manager; Dr Clare Penelope Margaret Heath [1957] Director/Retired GP; James David Edward Joicey-Cecil [1946] Director/Chartered Accountant; Davina Lynn Smith [1947] Director/Retired; Ian Richard Stone [1945] Director/Retired

Wellesbourne Property Management Limited
Incorporated: 31 January 1989 *Employees:* 1
Net Worth: £1,244,078 *Total Assets:* £6,446,860
Registered Office: Hailstone Farm, Moreton in Marsh, Glos, GL56 9TA
Activities: Other letting and operating of own or leased real estate
Shareholders: Bryan Eccles; Ann Felicity Bowes
Officers: Ann Felicity Bowes [1944] Director; Bryan Eccles [1932] Director

Wellington College Academy Trust
Incorporated: 19 December 2007 *Employees:* 204
Net Worth: £30,046,728 *Total Assets:* £31,537,240
Registered Office: The Wellington Academy, Ludgershall Road, Tidworth, Wilts, SP11 9RR
Activities: Primary education
Officers: Sara Middleton, Secretary; John Alan Claughton [1956] Director/Development Officer; David John Cowley [1948] Director/Retired; Stephen James Crouch [1973] Finance Director; Virginia Elizabeth Rhodes [1970] Director/Headteacher; Julian Paul Thomas [1966] Director/Headmaster of Wellington College

Wellington Motors Limited
Incorporated: 14 November 1995 *Employees:* 130
Net Worth: £2,699,918 *Total Assets:* £15,043,739
Registered Office: Taunton Vale House, Summerfield Way, Chelston Business Park, Wellington, Somerset, TA21 9JE
Activities: Sale of new cars and light motor vehicles
Parent: WMG Property Limited
Officers: Michael John Finn [1960] Director/Car Sales; Matthew Holcombe [1979] Sales Director

Wellington School 1837
Incorporated: 18 November 2014 *Employees:* 104
Net Worth: £24,309,818 *Total Assets:* £31,407,912
Registered Office: Wellington School, South Street, Wellington, Somerset, TA21 8NT
Activities: General secondary education
Officers: Timothy David Williams, Secretary; Antonin James Adams [1976] Director; Anna Maria Govey [1969] Director; James William Hester [1965] Director/Banking; Linda Margaret La Velle [1949] Director/University Professor; Sarah Elizabeth Merry [1969] Director/Nurse; Sheena Page [1950] Director/Retired; Robert John Palfrey [1974] Managing Director; Vivienne Frances Stock-Williams [1945] Director/Company Secretary; Peter Stuart Tait [1951] Director/Retired [New Zealander]; John Vick [1955] Director/Retired; Samantha Juliette Vigus-Hollingsworth [1971] Director/Chartered Accountant

Wells Cathedral School, Limited
Incorporated: 18 April 1956 *Employees:* 401
Net Worth: £18,253,000 *Total Assets:* £26,938,000
Registered Office: The Bursary, Wells Cathedral School, College Road, Wells, Somerset, BA5 2SX
Activities: Pre-primary education
Officers: Peter James Knell, Secretary; Helen Mary Ball [1939] Director/Retired Headteacher Education; Barbara Christine Bates [1948] Director/Retired Teacher; David Alfred John Brown [1965] Director; Andrew Colin Campbell-Orde [1969] Director/Certified Chartered Accountant; John Harverd Davies [1957] Director/Dean; Sarah Elisabeth Flannigan [1973] Director/Chief Information Officer; Canon Nicholas Lawrence Jepson-Biddle [1971] Director/Clergyman; Timothy William Hunt Lewis [1954] Director/Retired; Robert Powell [1963] Director

Wellsway Multi Academy Trust
Incorporated: 19 August 2011 *Employees:* 559
Net Worth: £48,338,444 *Total Assets:* £57,582,400
Registered Office: Wellsway School, Chandag Road, Keynsham, Bristol, BS31 1PH
Activities: Primary education
Officers: Timothy Ian Howes, Secretary; Andrea Jane Arlidge [1961] Director/Headteacher; Malcolm Arthur Broad [1950] Director/Retired; Stephen John Glavin [1967] Director/Consultant Trainer; Marlene Morley [1950] Director; Dre Kate Jane Reynolds [1961] Director/Dean of Education; Susan Mary Robbins [1952] Director; Conor Francis Ryan [1963] Director/Writer and Consultant [Irish]; Graham Shaw [1954] Director/Retired; Dr Robert Neil Simpson [1964] Director; Timothy Barie Spratt [1958] Director/Presentation Coach; Christopher David Trout [1955] Director

Welton Bibby and Baron Holdings Limited
Incorporated: 27 January 2003 *Employees:* 312
Net Worth: £26,555,000 *Total Assets:* £37,201,000
Registered Office: 1 Quartermaster Road, West Wilts Trading Estate, Westbury, Wilts, BA13 4JT
Activities: Other business support service activities n.e.c.
Major Shareholder: Martin Michael Mettler
Officers: Michael Handke [1966] Finance Director [German]; Martin Michael Mettler [1960] Director [German]; Malcolm David Ross [1949] Director; Nicholas Richard Tomkins [1969] Director

Welton Bibby and Baron Limited
Incorporated: 28 October 2003 *Employees:* 303
Net Worth: £26,555,000 *Total Assets:* £37,201,000
Registered Office: 1 Quartermaster Road, West Wilts Trading Estate, Westbury, Wilts, BA13 4JT
Activities: Manufacture of corrugated paper and paperboard, sacks and bags
Parent: Welton Bibby and Baron Holdings Limited
Officers: Michael Handke [1966] Finance Director [German]; Martin Michael Mettler [1960] Director [German]; Malcolm David Ross [1949] Director; Nicholas Richard Tomkins [1969] Director

Wemyss Lodge Limited
Incorporated: 22 November 2002 *Employees:* 210
Net Worth: £3,773,518 *Total Assets:* £9,263,394
Registered Office: Wemyss Lodge, Ermin Street, Stratton St Margaret, Swindon, Wilts, SN3 4LH
Activities: Residential care activities for the elderly and disabled
Shareholders: Michael Freeland; Lucinda Charlotte Freeland
Officers: Lucinda Charlotte Freeland, Secretary; Lucinda Charlotte Freeland [1969] Director; Michael Freeland [1964] Director/Accountant

Wenand Homes Ltd
Incorporated: 2 April 2004
Previous: A Stephens Plumbing, Heating & Renewable Technologies Ltd
Net Worth: £4,470,010 *Total Assets:* £4,518,564
Registered Office: 117 The Ridgeway, Plympton, Plymouth, PL7 2AA
Activities: Management of real estate on a fee or contract basis
Shareholders: Andrew Stephens; Wendy Jean Stephens
Officers: Wendy Jean Stephens, Secretary; Andrew Stephens [1959] Director/Plumber; Wendy Jean Stephens [1959] Director/Bookkeeper

Wentrow Media Limited
Incorporated: 8 July 1999 *Employees:* 43
Net Worth: £7,559,920 *Total Assets:* £13,689,039
Registered Office: A'Becketts, 29 High Street, Littleton Panell, Devizes, Wilts, SN10 4EN
Activities: Publishing of consumer and business journals and periodicals
Major Shareholder: Anthony John Hill
Officers: Mandy Noden, Secretary; Anthony John Hill [1950] Director/Businessman; Benjamin Mark Hillier [1985] Director/Manager; Mandy Noden [1966] Director/Secretary

WESC Foundation
Incorporated: 18 June 2009 *Employees:* 2
Net Worth: £9,532,383 *Total Assets:* £10,018,736
Registered Office: WESC Foundation, Topsham Road, Countess Wear, Exeter, Devon, EX2 6HA
Activities: Other accommodation
Officers: Patrick Dermot MacDonald, Secretary; Derek John Fargher [1952] Director/Interim Accountant; Noel Paul Fowler [1953] Director/Retired; James Heslop [1983] Director/Sales Manager; Julie Jeffreys [1960] Director/Occupational Therapist; Christopher David Knee [1951] Director/Retired; Andrew Robert Leadbetter [1964] Director/Councillor; Tracie Linehan [1971] Director/Chief Executive; Angus Martin McNicol [1955] Director/Charity Consultant; Susanne-Maria Murray [1978] Director/Solicitor (Partner); Timothy David Williams [1961] Director/Bursar

Wessex Archaeology Limited
Incorporated: 6 April 1983 *Employees:* 297
Net Worth: £4,579,642 *Total Assets:* £8,375,275
Registered Office: Portway House, Old Sarum Park, Salisbury, Wilts, SP4 6EB
Activities: Other professional, scientific and technical activities n.e.c.
Officers: Ian Giles Phillips, Secretary; Christopher Mark Brayne [1968] Director/Chief Executive; Rosemary Karen Veronica Cook [1959] Director/Solicitor; Parvis Homayounfar Jamieson [1956] Director; Janet Nichola Johnson [1945] Director; Dr Ian Christopher Selby [1961] Director/Marine Portfolio Manager; Sarah Louise Urquhart Voaden [1966] Director; Christopher Michael Watson [1955] Property Director; Dr Rowan Pirrie Whimster [1949] Director/Consultant

Wessex Building Services Limited
Incorporated: 16 July 2002 *Employees:* 70
Net Worth: £921,794 *Total Assets:* £5,270,484
Registered Office: Wessex House, Wincombe Lane, Shaftesbury, Dorset, SP7 8PJ
Activities: Electrical installation
Parent: Wessex Group Ltd
Officers: Simon Morgan, Secretary/Director; Andrew John Benton [1961] Director; Alistair Morgan [1970] Director; Simon Morgan [1967] Director

Wessex Eagle Holdings Limited
Incorporated: 14 February 1994 *Employees:* 257
Previous: Hay Bluff Limited
Net Worth: £29,595,792 *Total Assets:* £45,913,924
Registered Office: Eagle Plant, Beeching Close, Chard, Somerset, TA20 1BB
Activities: Renting and leasing of construction and civil engineering machinery and equipment
Shareholders: Wessex Eagle Trustees Ltd; Michael John Grimoldby
Officers: Gary John Parfoot, Secretary; Nicholas Sidney Barrow [1973] Director; Nigel Peter Cox [1963] Director; Alan John Cradock [1962] Director; Michael John Grimoldby [1953] Director; Jonathan Charles Gubb [1957] Director; Gary John Parfoot [1969] Director/Accountant

Wessex Eagle Limited
Incorporated: 21 January 1981 *Employees:* 257
Net Worth: £29,537,936 *Total Assets:* £45,913,924
Registered Office: Eagle Plant, Beeching Close, Chard, Somerset, TA20 1BB
Activities: Renting and leasing of construction and civil engineering machinery and equipment
Parent: Wessex Eagle Holdings Ltd
Officers: Gary Parfoot, Secretary; Nicholas Sidney Barrow [1973] Director; Nigel Peter Cox [1963] Director/Manager; Alan John Cradock [1962] Director/Engineer; Michael John Grimoldby [1953] Director; Jonathan Charles Gubb [1957] Director; Gary John Parfoot [1969] Director/Accountant

Wessex Electricals (Shaftesbury) Limited
Incorporated: 5 May 1972 *Employees:* 160
Net Worth: £1,842,945 *Total Assets:* £3,981,511
Registered Office: Wessex House, Wincombe Lane, Shaftesbury, Dorset, SP7 8PJ
Activities: Electrical installation
Parent: Wessex Group Limited
Officers: Simon Morgan, Secretary; Stuart Keith Fisher [1960] Director; Alistair Morgan [1970] Director; Simon Morgan [1967] Director

Wessex Garages Holdings Limited
Incorporated: 21 August 1991 *Employees:* 327
Net Worth: £14,129,376 *Total Assets:* £56,625,828
Registered Office: Pennywell Road, Bristol, BS5 0TT
Activities: Sale of new cars and light motor vehicles
Parent: VT Holdings Co Ltd
Officers: Timothy Raymond Bagnall, Secretary; Timothy Raymond Bagnall [1965] Director; Keith Barry Brock [1965] Managing Director; Masahide Ito [1960] Director [Japanese]; Kazuho Takahashi [1953] Director [Japanese]

Wessex Grain Ltd.
Incorporated: 22 December 1980 *Employees:* 24
Net Worth: £1,799,425 *Total Assets:* £10,722,886
Registered Office: Henstridge Trading Estate, Templecombe, Somerset, BA8 0TN
Activities: Wholesale of grain, unmanufactured tobacco, seeds and animal feeds
Parent: BayWa AG
Officers: Graham MacDonald Sinclair, Secretary; Andrew Robert Charles MacKay [1961] Director/Agricultural Commodity Trader; Graham MacDonald Sinclair [1969] Director/Chartered Accountant

Wessex Group Limited
Incorporated: 8 January 1990 *Employees:* 376
Net Worth: £5,825,369 *Total Assets:* £13,275,912
Registered Office: Wessex House, Wincombe Lane, Shaftesbury, Dorset, SP7 8PJ
Activities: Combined facilities support activities
Shareholders: Simon Morgan; Alistair Morgan
Officers: Simon Morgan, Secretary; Robert Michael Hall [1948] Director/Retired; Donna Louise Harry [1979] Finance Director; Alistair Morgan [1970] Director; Simon Morgan [1967] Director

Wessex GS Limited
Incorporated: 17 July 1989 *Employees:* 180
Net Worth: £2,218,223 *Total Assets:* £13,658,552
Registered Office: 1 Roundhead Road, Heathfield, Newton Abbot, Devon, TQ12 6UE
Activities: Sale of other motor vehicles
Parent: Kingdon Holdings Ltd
Officers: Ian Philip Bone [1958] Director; Michael James Harris [1967] Director; Henry William Kingdon [1987] Director; Victoria Clare Kingdon [1984] Director; Georgia Helen Vaines [1982] Director

Wessex Learning Trust
Incorporated: 17 August 2010 *Employees:* 420
Previous: The Kings of Wessex Academy Trust
Net Worth: £28,948,968 *Total Assets:* £35,168,464
Registered Office: The Kings of Wessex Academy, Station Road, Cheddar, Somerset, BS27 3AQ
Activities: General secondary education
Officers: Keith William Perry, Secretary; John Edwin George Angle [1942] Director/Christian Worker; Gavin Martin Ball [1964] Director/Headteacher; James Alexander Stewart Colquhoun [1950] Director/Semi-Retired Consultant; Alan John Davies [1954] Retired Airport Director; Sheridan Tracey Flavin [1966] Director; Marie Frances May Getheridge [1950] Director/Retired Headteacher; Paul Jacobs [1960] Director/Education Consultant; Brian Kirkup [1941] Director/Retired Headteacher; Susan Ann Moreman [1968] Director/Chartered Accountant; Gareth James Smith [1966] Director/Business Consultant; Kevin John Walke [1960] Director/Composer; Gareth Dominic Woodcock [1972] Director/Chartered Building Surveyor

Wessex Products (Leasing) Limited
Incorporated: 26 July 1996 *Employees:* 25
Net Worth: £5,117,424 *Total Assets:* £5,684,751
Registered Office: Wessex House, Teign Road, Newton Abbot, Devon, TQ12 4AA
Activities: Other business support service activities n.e.c.
Parent: FW3 Limited
Officers: Bridget Jepson, Secretary/Manager; Louise Skilton [1964] Director; Nicholas Philip Skilton [1959] Director/Manager

Wessex Resolutions C.I.C.
Incorporated: 15 August 2002 *Employees:* 25
Net Worth: £461,722 *Total Assets:* £17,147,324
Registered Office: Heatherton Park Studios, Heatherton Park, Bradford on Tone, Taunton, Somerset, TA4 1EU
Activities: Other credit granting n.e.c.
Officers: Lyn Rosemary Bayley-Paxman [1968] Director; Alan David Hughes [1972] Director/Solicitor; Stephen John Keohane [1959] Director; Justin Roxburgh [1964] Director/Chief Executive; Graeme Paul Sibley [1971] Director; Andrew James Wallace [1961] Director/Company Chief Executive

Wessex Water Enterprises Limited
Incorporated: 21 July 1988 *Employees:* 36
Net Worth: £520,000 *Total Assets:* £33,658,000
Registered Office: Wessex Water, Operations Centre, Claverton Down Road, Claverton Down, Bath, BA2 7WW
Activities: Collection of non-hazardous waste
Parent: Wessex Water Limited
Officers: Ruth Esme Jefferson, Secretary; Mohammed Habedat Saddiq [1970] Director; Colin Frank Skellett [1945] Director; Mark Timothy Watts [1961] Director

Wessex Water Limited
Incorporated: 1 April 1989 *Employees:* 2,773
Net Worth: £895,900,032 *Total Assets:* £3,948,100,096
Registered Office: Wessex Water, Operations Centre, Claverton Down Road, Claverton Down, Bath, BA2 7WW
Activities: Water collection, treatment and supply
Parent: YTL Utilities (UK) Limited
Officers: Ruth Esme Jefferson, Secretary; David Martin Barclay [1954] Director; David John Elliott [1960] Director/Water Company Manager; Colin Frank Skellett [1945] Director; Mark Timothy Watts [1961] Director; Francis Sock Ping Yeoh [1954] Director/Business Person [Malaysian]; Dato Seok Hong Yeoh [1959] Director/Business Person [Malaysian]; Seok Kah Yeoh [1965] Director/Business Person [Malaysian]; Seok Kian Yeoh [1957] Director/Business Person [Malaysian]

Wessex Water Services Finance PLC
Incorporated: 28 January 1999
Net Worth: £13,000 *Total Assets:* £1,637,037,952
Registered Office: Wessex Water, Operations Centre, Claverton Down Road, Claverton Down, Bath, BA2 7WW
Activities: Banks
Parent: Wessex Water Services Limited
Officers: Ruth Esme Jefferson, Secretary; Colin Frank Skellett [1945] Director; Mark Timothy Watts [1961] Director

Wessex Water Services Limited
Incorporated: 1 April 1989 *Employees:* 2,308
Net Worth: £828,600,000 *Total Assets:* £3,788,600,064
Registered Office: Wessex Water, Operations Centre, Claverton Down Road, Claverton Down, Bath, BA2 7WW
Activities: Water collection, treatment and supply
Parent: Wessex Water Limited
Officers: Ruth Esme Jefferson, Secretary; David Martin Barclay [1954] Director; Gillian Elizabeth Camm [1959] Director; Kathleen Wai Lin Chew [1959] Director/Lawyer [Malaysian]; David Huw Davies [1956] Director; Richard John Keys [1951] Director/Accountant; Andrew Fraser Pymer [1968] Director; Fiona Clare Reynolds [1958] Director; Colin Frank Skellett [1945] Director; Mark Timothy Watts [1961] Director; Francis Sock Ping Yeoh [1954] Director/Business Person [Malaysian]; Keong Hann Yeoh [1986] Director [Malaysian]; Mark Seok Kah Yeoh [1965] Director/Business Person [Malaysian]; Dato Seok Hong Yeoh [1959] Director/Business Person [Malaysian]

West Brothers (Frome) Ltd
Incorporated: 28 January 1947
Net Worth: £3,652,679 *Total Assets:* £4,268,289
Registered Office: Hardings Ground, Lane End, Corsley, Warminster, Wilts, BA12 7PA
Activities: Other manufacturing n.e.c.
Officers: Hannah Jane Caroline West, Secretary; Joanna Mary Georgiana Pengelley [1981] Director/Housewife/Law; Michael John West [1936] Director/Chairman

West Coast Developments (Sandbanks) Limited
Incorporated: 28 October 2009
Net Worth Deficit: £337,462 *Total Assets:* £4,911,049
Registered Office: 2 Hamilton Court House, 1-3 Alum Chine Road, Bournemouth, BH4 8DT
Activities: Development of building projects
Shareholders: Angeline Marie Heffer; Graham Keith Heffer
Officers: Angeline Marie Heffer [1972] Director; Graham Keith Heffer [1967] Sales Director

West Cornwall Pasty Co. Limited
Incorporated: 6 March 2014 *Employees:* 304
Net Worth: £2,110,000 *Total Assets:* £6,260,000
Registered Office: Woodbine Farm Business Centre, Threemilestone, Truro, Cornwall, TR3 6BW
Activities: Take-away food shops and mobile food stands
Parent: Samworth Brothers Limited
Officers: Timothy James Barker, Secretary; Steven Clive Bailey [1962] Director; Barry Milton Cook [1973] Managing Director; Flor Aiden Healy [1962] Director [Irish]; Richard Alexis Robertson Marris [1968] Director; Stephen John Powell [1967] Finance Director; Mark Charles Chetwode Samworth [1970] Director

West Country Business Systems (Holdings) Limited
Incorporated: 17 June 1997 *Employees:* 78
Net Worth: £896,378 *Total Assets:* £6,417,866
Registered Office: Landmark House, Wirrall Park Road, Glastonbury, Somerset, BA6 9FR
Activities: Business and domestic software development
Parent: Westleigh Investments Holdings Ltd
Officers: William Brian James, Secretary; Charles Giles Clarke [1953] Director; Emma Louise Goodwin [1966] Director; John Nicholas Harrison [1959] Director

West Country Milk Consortium Limited
Incorporated: 13 July 2000
Net Worth: £500,344 *Total Assets:* £4,633,869
Registered Office: Rundale Barn, Rectory Lane, Cromhall, Wotton under Edge, Glos, GL12 8AN
Activities: Wholesale of dairy products, eggs and edible oils and fats
Officers: Howard Marshall, Secretary; David Crocker [1969] Director; Howard Marshall [1957] Director

West Country Motor Homes Limited
Incorporated: 18 October 1979 *Employees:* 49
Net Worth: £11,596,595 *Total Assets:* £15,754,564
Registered Office: Bristol Road, Brent Knoll, Highbridge, Somerset, TA9 4HG
Activities: Sale of other motor vehicles
Major Shareholder: Stephen Gary Pike
Officers: Stephen Gary Pike [1958] Managing Director; Peter Richard Shaw [1958] Director

West Country Park Home Estates Ltd
Incorporated: 11 June 1973 *Employees:* 4
Net Worth: £7,915,855 *Total Assets:* £8,080,901
Registered Office: Royal Mews, St Georges Place, Cheltenham, Glos, GL50 3PQ
Activities: Other accommodation
Major Shareholder: David Newman
Officers: Catherine Newman, Secretary; David Newman [1941] Director; Gary Paul Newman [1967] Managing Director

West Country Park Homes Limited
Incorporated: 14 September 1995
Net Worth: £5,176,310 *Total Assets:* £8,744,800
Registered Office: Edithmead Leisure, Highbridge, Somerset, TA9 4HE
Activities: Other amusement and recreation activities n.e.c.
Shareholders: Sally Alvy Edith Abrahams; Sarah Bareham
Officers: Sally Alvy Edith Abrahams, Secretary; Sally Alvy Edith Abrahams [1962] Director/Caravan Park Operator; Sean Abrahams [1959] Director; Sarah Bareham [1936] Director/Caravan Park Proprietor

West Country Vending Service Limited
Incorporated: 21 November 1967 *Employees:* 186
Net Worth: £2,601,541 *Total Assets:* £4,732,737
Registered Office: Bath Road, Peasedown St John, Bath, BA2 8DH
Activities: Other food services
Parent: Montagu Group Limited
Officers: Paul Martin Allen [1968] Director; Raymond Latimer Hutchinson [1949] Director; Stephen Thomas Alexander Hutchinson [1958] Director; Anne Alexandra Hutchinson-Kane [1947] Director

West End Investments Clifton Limited
Incorporated: 12 December 1997 *Employees:* 8
Net Worth: £9,661,306 *Total Assets:* £21,446,876
Registered Office: 45 Oakfield Road, Clifton, Bristol, BS8 2AX
Activities: Development of building projects
Shareholders: Edward John Ware; Kingsley Peter Webb
Officers: Kingsley Peter Webb, Secretary/Director; Edward John Ware [1960] Director; Kingsley Peter Webb [1966] Director

West End Motors (Bodmin) Limited
Incorporated: 12 July 1963 *Employees:* 62
Net Worth: £3,813,093 *Total Assets:* £6,886,524
Registered Office: Bodmin Business Park, Launceston Road, Bodmin, Cornwall, PL31 2RJ
Activities: Sale of new cars and light motor vehicles
Shareholders: Antony Brian Cook; Brian Albert Cook
Officers: Antony Brian Cook, Secretary; Antony Brian Cook [1970] Director; Brian Albert Cook [1938] Director; Anthony Patrick Martin [1953] Director/General Manager

West End Precision Limited
Incorporated: 2 November 1979 *Employees:* 57
Net Worth: £3,756,616 *Total Assets:* £4,572,667
Registered Office: Caddsdown Industrial Park, Clovelly Road, Bideford, Devon, EX39 3DX
Activities: Machining
Shareholders: Leon Paul Dziurzynski; Dawn Pauline Dziurzynski
Officers: Dawn Pauline Dziurzynski, Secretary; Dawn Pauline Dziurzynski [1957] Director/Secretary; Leon Paul Dziurzynski [1952] Director/Engineer

West Hants Lawn Tennis Company (Bournemouth) Limited (The)
Incorporated: 24 December 1925 *Employees:* 104
Net Worth: £1,638,679 *Total Assets:* £6,512,546
Registered Office: The West Hants Club, Roslin Road South, Bournemouth, BH3 7EF
Activities: Operation of sports facilities
Officers: Nicholas John Purcell Fitz-Generald, Secretary; Edwin Charles Bessant [1953] Director; Michelle Susan Bray [1969] Director/Legal Editor; Nigel Stuart Butler [1957] Director/Telecoms; Karla Frances Cooper [1975] Director/Solicitor; Mark Richard Hurd [1961] Director/Property Developer; Hayley O'Shea [1974] Director/Marketing Manager; Martin Anthony Smith [1943] Director/Accountant; Stuart Graham Smith [1946] Director/Chartered Surveyor; Simon Naunton Steele [1971] Finance Director

West House Transport (S & G) Limited
Incorporated: 27 July 1990 *Employees:* 118
Net Worth: £3,468,196 *Total Assets:* £5,087,425
Registered Office: 20 Whitehouse Street, Bedminster, Bristol, BS3 4AY
Activities: Freight transport by road
Shareholders: Raymond Michael Gallop; Ian Malcolm Duncan Dunbar
Officers: Ian Malcolm Duncan Dunbar, Secretary; Ian Malcolm Duncan Dunbar [1959] Finance Director; Raymond Michael Gallop [1949] Sales Director

West International Holdings Limited
Incorporated: 19 December 2007
Net Worth: £155,392,000 *Total Assets:* £155,408,992
Registered Office: Unit 1 & 2 Sawmills End, Barnwood, Gloucester, GL4 3DL
Activities: Other telecommunications activities
Parent: West UK Holdings Limited
Officers: Louis Brucculeri, Secretary; Louis Brucculeri [1965] Director/EVP General Counsel [American]; Nancy Jill Disman [1970] Director/Chief Administrative Officer [American]; Robert Emmet Mannix [1967] Director/EVP Chief Accounting Officer [American]; Christopher Wikoff [1974] Director/EVP Treasurer [American]

West Mendip PPP Health Services Limited
Incorporated: 30 January 2003
Net Worth Deficit: £1,720,697 *Total Assets:* £8,930,736
Registered Office: Third Floor, Broad Quay House, Prince Street, Bristol, BS1 4DJ
Activities: Other specialised construction activities n.e.c.
Parent: RBIL Limited
Officers: Graham John Hutt [1954] Regional Director; Andrew Richard Kershaw [1965] Director/Projects Controller; Daniel North [1988] Investment Director; Andrew Charles Mutch Rhodes [1970] Director

West of England Developments (Taunton) No2 Limited
Incorporated: 1 September 2014 *Employees:* 1
Net Worth: £850,617 *Total Assets:* £13,102,617
Registered Office: Kibbear House, Trull, Taunton, Somerset, TA3 7LN
Activities: Construction of domestic buildings
Major Shareholder: Andreas Lehner
Officers: Andreas Lehner [1953] Director

West of England Investors Ltd
Incorporated: 16 November 1965 *Employees:* 2
Previous: West of England Inns Limited
Net Worth: £4,365,091 *Total Assets:* £4,577,471
Registered Office: Redwoods, 2 Clyst Works, Clyst Road, Topsham, Exeter, Devon, EX3 0DB
Activities: Other service activities n.e.c.
Major Shareholder: Gerald Harrison
Officers: Jacqueline Harrison, Secretary; Generald Harrison [1938] Director; Jacqueline Harrison [1944] Director/Secretary

West Pharmaceutical Services Cornwall Limited
Incorporated: 9 April 1968 *Employees:* 159
Net Worth: £12,068,000 *Total Assets:* £27,493,000
Registered Office: Holmbush Industrial Estate, Bucklers Lane, St Austell, Cornwall, PL25 3JU
Activities: Manufacture of basic pharmaceutical products
Parent: West Pharmaceutical Services Group Ltd
Officers: Darren Pope, Secretary; Ellen Yvette Grose [1970] Operations Director; George Lloyd Miller [1955] Director/Corporate Secretary [American]; Sean Peter Parish [1974] Senior Regional Director of Finance; Dr Stephan Selke [1967] Director/Vice President - Finance [German]

West Pharmaceutical Services Group Limited
Incorporated: 24 February 1989
Net Worth: £18,931,000 *Total Assets:* £18,931,000
Registered Office: West Pharmaceutical Services Group Ltd, Bucklers Lane, St Austell, Cornwall, PL25 3JU
Activities: Activities of head offices
Parent: West Pharnmaceutical Services Inc
Officers: Darren Pope, Secretary; Ellen Yvette Grose [1970] Operations Director; George Lloyd Miller [1955] Director/Corporate Secretary [American]; Sean Peter Parish [1974] Senior Regional Director of Finance; Dr Stephan Selke [1967] Director/Vice President - Finance [German]

West Somerset Academies Trust
Incorporated: 11 May 2011 *Employees:* 241
Previous: West Somerset Academy Trust
Net Worth: £8,312,779 *Total Assets:* £14,119,793
Registered Office: Minehead Middle School, Ponsford Road, Minehead, Somerset, TA24 5RH
Activities: General secondary education
Officers: Barbara Ann O'Keefe, Secretary; Lee Baker [1968] Director/Bank Official; Jill Ewen [1962] Director/Self Employed Education Consultant; Martina Suzanne Forster [1967] Director/Housewife; Hayley Lake [1974] Director/Housewife; Geoffrey Carter Lloyd [1942] Director/Retired; Iestyn Milton-Jenkins [1970] Director/Solicitor; Nicolas Paul Mouzouri [1962] Director/Training Manager; Paul Zachary Rushforth [1963] Director/Headteacher; Deborah Shelley [1966] Director/Legal Indexer; Kathryn Louise Slader Tucker [1952] Director/Farm Business Partner; Elizabeth Jane White [1972] Director/Catering

West Somerset Railway Public Limited Company
Incorporated: 5 May 1971 *Employees:* 54
Net Worth: £3,493,000 *Total Assets:* £5,116,000
Registered Office: The Railway Station, Minehead, Somerset, TA24 5BG
Activities: Passenger rail transport, interurban
Officers: Richard Barry Auger [1946] Director/Civil Engineer; Paul William Conibeare [1963] Director/Railway Manager; Frank Moor Courtney [1945] Director; Jonathan Jones-Pratt [1983] Director; Mark Leonard Smith [1948] Director

West Town Lane Academy
Incorporated: 15 November 2011 *Employees:* 109
Net Worth: £5,679,756 *Total Assets:* £6,947,668
Registered Office: West Town Lane Academy, West Town Lane, Brislington, Bristol, BS4 5DT
Activities: Primary education
Officers: Marianne Croft [1973] Director/Housewife; Jeremy Hughes [1968] Director/Headteacher; Adrian Carl Robbins [1974] Director/Deputy Headteacher

West UC Limited
Incorporated: 4 January 1993 *Employees:* 433
Previous: Intercall Conferencing Services Limited
Net Worth: £55,127,000 *Total Assets:* £108,755,000
Registered Office: Unit 1 & 2 Sawmills End, Barnwood, Gloucester, GL4 3DL
Activities: Other telecommunications activities
Parent: West International Holdings Limited
Officers: Louis Brucculeri, Secretary; Louis Brucculeri [1965] Director/EVP General Council [American]; Nancy Jill Disman [1970] Director/Chief Administrative Officer [American]; Dale Eric Frazier [1963] Director/President of West Unified Communications Services [American]; Robert Emmet Mannix [1967] Director/EVP Chief Accounting Officer [American]; Christopher Wikoff [1974] Director/EVP Treasurer [American]

Westbank Community Health and Care
Incorporated: 10 May 2007 *Employees:* 153
Net Worth: £4,315,570 *Total Assets:* £4,538,292
Registered Office: The Healthy Living Centre, Farm House Rise, Exminster, Devon, EX6 8AT
Activities: Other service activities n.e.c.
Officers: Dr Elizabeth Sara Llewelyn Anderson [1970] Director/Accountant; James Masters [1954] Director; Keith Charles Richards [1953] Director/Retired; Brana Lynne Thorn [1955] Director/Retired; Diana Lynne White [1947] Director/Retired Health and Social Care Manager; Ian William Whyte [1955] Director

Westbury Care Limited
Incorporated: 15 April 1996 *Employees:* 152
Net Worth: £3,909,128 *Total Assets:* £8,029,819
Registered Office: The Westbury Nursing Home, Falcondale Road, Westbury on Trym, Bristol, BS9 3JH
Activities: Residential nursing care facilities
Shareholders: Gordon Norman Brooking; June Marilyn Phillips; June Marilyn Phillips
Officers: Gordon Norman Brooking, Secretary/Accountant; Gordon Norman Brooking [1944] Director/Accountant; June Marilyn Phillips [1948] Director/Nursing Home Proprietor

Westbury Park School
Incorporated: 4 July 2012 *Employees:* 61
Net Worth: £6,101,341 *Total Assets:* £6,889,889
Registered Office: 13 Bayswater Avenue, Bristol, BS6 7NU
Activities: Primary education
Officers: Richard Mark Bamber [1974] Director/Headteacher; Helen Elizabeth Clark [1968] Director/Teacher; Helen Louise Couchman [1979] Director/HR Manager; Alison Margaret Dean [1964] Director/Teaching Assistant; Tanja Engelbrecht [1972] Director/Technical Engineer/Site Manager [German]; Chris Hackett [1960] Director/Local Government Officer; Revd Emma Louise Langley [1970] Director/Parish Priest; Emma Mann [1989] Director/Teacher; Dr Virginie Mengeaud [1975] Director/Quality Assurance Consultant [French]; William James Sefton [1974] Director/Solicitor; Katherine Webb [1978] Director/Accountant; Richard Leonard Webb [1963] Director

Westbury-on-Trym Church of England Academy
Incorporated: 14 June 2011 *Employees:* 58
Net Worth: £3,071,694 *Total Assets:* £4,133,594
Registered Office: Westbury on Trym Church of England Academy, Channells Hill, Westbury on Trym, Bristol, BS9 3HZ
Activities: Primary education
Officers: Deborah Jane Baker, Secretary; Matthew Stuart Baker [1979] Director/Educational Psychologist; Francis John Edwards [1976] Director/Actuarial Consultant; Judith Mary Graham [1956] Director/Retired Primary School Teacher; Louise Elizabeth Drummond Hamer [1975] Director/Senior Teaching Assistant; Andre Hendrik Hart [1962] Director/Minister of Religion [Dutch]; Mark Anthony Hibbitt [1979] Director/Independent Financial Adviser; Alexander Baird Hirst [1974] Director/Hospitality Account Manager; Dr Anthony George Hoare [1944] Director/Partly Retired; Paul Adrian Jenkins [1960] Director/Retired; Jane Johnson [1974] Director; Joseph Patrick Littlejohn [1982] Director/Software Engineer; David Robert McGregor [1947] Director/Self Employed Education Consultant; Amanda Jayne Caroline Pritchard [1973] Director/Headteacher; Richard Simon David Sloper [1964] Director/Deputy Headteacher; Clare Warbis [1968] Director/Registered Nurse; Michael John West [1942] Director/Retired

Westcliff Hall (Sidmouth) Limited
Incorporated: 26 March 1946 *Employees:* 62
Net Worth: £3,557,744 *Total Assets:* £14,918,348
Registered Office: Harbour House, 60 Purewell, Christchurch, Dorset, BH23 1ES
Activities: Hotels and similar accommodation
Parent: Harbour Hotels Group Limited
Officers: Stuart Andrew Bateman [1976] Director; David Francis Robbins [1967] Finance Director; Michael Oliver Warren [1970] Director [Irish]

Westcoast (Bristol) Limited
Incorporated: 4 February 2015
Net Worth Deficit: £2,870,662 *Total Assets:* £10,523,338
Registered Office: Suite 2, Hamilton Court House, 1-3 Alum Chine Road, Westbourne, Bournemouth, BH4 8DT
Activities: Development of building projects
Shareholders: Graham Keith Heffer; Angeline Marie Heffer
Officers: Angeline Marie Heffer [1972] Director; Graham Keith Heffer [1967] Director

Westcoast Developments (2009) Limited
Incorporated: 1 February 2012
Net Worth: £1,122,798 *Total Assets:* £9,100,368
Registered Office: 2 Hamilton Court House, 1-3 Alum Chine Road, Bournemouth, BH4 8DT
Activities: Construction of domestic buildings
Shareholders: Graham Keith Heffer; Angeline Marie Heffer
Officers: Angeline Marie Heffer [1972] Director; Graham Keith Heffer [1967] Director

Westcon Group Africa Operations Limited
Incorporated: 23 June 1976 *Employees:* 15
Previous: Westcon Africa (UK) Limited
Net Worth Deficit: £2,779,072 *Total Assets:* £24,412,610
Registered Office: Chandlers House, Wilkinson Road, Love Lane Industrial Estate, Cirencester, Glos, GL7 1YT
Activities: Other information technology service activities
Parent: Westcon Group European Operations Limited
Officers: Daniel Owen Malcolm Jones, Secretary; David Grant [1964] Director/Chief Operating Officer; Callum Grant McGregor [1978] Director/Chartered Accountant (SA) [South African]

Westcon Group European Operations Limited
Incorporated: 8 April 2002 *Employees:* 1,079
Net Worth: £99,476,648 *Total Assets:* £568,664,256
Registered Office: Chandler's House, Wilkinson Road, Love Lane Industrial Estate, Cirencester, Glos, GL7 1YT
Activities: Other information technology service activities
Parent: Westcon International Limited
Officers: Daniel Owen Malcom Jones, Secretary; David Grant [1964] Director/Chief Operating Officer; Callum Grant McGregor [1978] Director/Chartered Accountant (SA) [South African]

Westcon Group Middle East Holdings Limited
Incorporated: 20 July 2010
Previous: Westcon Emerging Markets Limited
Net Worth: £29,924,686 *Total Assets:* £29,924,686
Registered Office: Chandlers House, Wilkinson Road, Love Lane Industrial Estate, Cirencester, Glos, GL7 1YT
Activities: Other information technology service activities
Parent: Westcon Group European Operations Limited
Officers: David Grant [1964] Commercial Director; Callum Grant McGregor [1978] Director/Chartered Accountant (SA) [South African]

Westcountry Fruit Sales Limited
Incorporated: 27 May 1970 *Employees:* 187
Net Worth: £2,781,009 *Total Assets:* £4,503,067
Registered Office: Fresh Produce Distribution Centre, Higher Argal, Budock, Falmouth, Cornwall, TR11 5PE
Activities: Wholesale of fruit and vegetables
Shareholders: Sally Elizabeth Williams; Sean Harcourt Williams
Officers: Lee Barry Andrew Bartholomew, Secretary/Financial Controller; Lee Barry Andrew Bartholomew [1968] Director/Chartered Accountant; Roger Benoni Rossignol [1974] Director/Sales and Marketing Manager; Sean Harcourt Williams [1966] Director

Westcountry Garden Centres Limited
Incorporated: 10 February 1992 *Employees:* 81
Net Worth: £7,241,507 *Total Assets:* £8,314,107
Registered Office: 8 Regent Street, Bradford on Tone, Taunton, Somerset, TA4 1HB
Activities: Other retail sale in non-specialised stores
Major Shareholder: Mark Ian Hassall
Officers: Jacqueline Ross Kinnear Hassall, Secretary; Mark Ian Hassall [1954] Director/Retail Manager

Westcountry Schools Trust
Incorporated: 6 October 2010 *Employees:* 1,349
Previous: Ivybridge Academy Trust
Net Worth: £98,320,000 *Total Assets:* £123,808,000
Registered Office: Ivybridge Community College, Harford Road, Ivybridge, Devon, PL21 0JA
Activities: Primary education
Officers: Peter Andrew Gregory, Secretary; Carl Frank Atkinson [1964] Director/Independent Financial Planner; Kevin John Bunt [1959] Director/Operations Manager; Catherine Farrin [1968] Director/Police Officer; Andrew James Flay [1974] Director/Accountant; Thomas Edward Godwin [1986] Director/Marketing Consultant; Iain Grafton [1964] Director; Sheila Margaret Jenkins [1949] Director/Retired; Anne Phyllis Newall [1954] Director/Retired; Martin Roy Pollard [1963] Strategic Director; Michael Francis Saltern [1949] Director; Simon Roland Scott [1974] Director/Retail Manager; Pamela Wendy Anne Tuckett [1965] Director/Chartered Accountant; Rebecca Louise Wood [1983] Director/Solicitor

Westerleigh Crematoria Limited
Incorporated: 1 March 1999 *Employees:* 2
Net Worth: £6,524,098 *Total Assets:* £69,266,624
Registered Office: Chapel View, Westerleigh Crematorium, Westerleigh Road, Westerleigh, Bristol, BS37 8QP
Activities: Activities of other holding companies n.e.c.
Parent: Westerleigh Group Holdings Ltd
Officers: Dafydd Rhys John, Secretary; Dafydd Rhys John [1974] Director/Chartered Accountant; Ian David McArdle [1966] Director/Chartered Surveyor

Westerleigh Group Holdings Limited
Incorporated: 10 September 2007 *Employees:* 2
Net Worth: £22,323,652 *Total Assets:* £166,490,016
Registered Office: Chapel View, Westerleigh Crematorium, Westerleigh Road, Westerleigh, Bristol, BS37 8QP
Activities: Activities of head offices
Parent: Westerleigh WGH Ltd
Officers: Dafydd Rhys John, Secretary; James Alexander Adam [1970] Director/Senior Investment Executive [Canadian]; Robert William Horsnall [1981] Director/Senior Investment Manager; Dafydd Rhys John [1974] Director/Chartered Accountant; Ian David McArdle [1966] Director/Chartered Surveyor

Westerleigh Group Limited
Incorporated: 4 September 1990 *Employees:* 23
Net Worth: £672,192 *Total Assets:* £71,712,384
Registered Office: Head Office, Westerleigh Crematorium, Westerleigh Road, Westerleigh, Bristol, BS37 8QP
Activities: Activities of head offices
Parent: Westerleigh Crematoria Ltd
Officers: Dafydd Rhys John, Secretary; Dafydd Rhys John [1974] Director/Chartered Accountant; Ian David McArdle [1966] Director/Chartered Surveyor

Westerleigh WGH Limited
Incorporated: 11 October 2012 *Employees:* 2
Previous: Antin Infrastructure WGH Limited
Net Worth: £29,755,008 *Total Assets:* £105,283,312
Registered Office: Head Office, Westerleigh Crematorium, Westerleigh Road, Westerleigh, Bristol, BS37 8QP
Activities: Other business support service activities n.e.c.
Parent: Western Bidco Limited
Officers: Dafydd Rhys John, Secretary; James Alexander Adam [1970] Director/Senior Investment Executive [Canadian]; Robert William Horsnall [1981] Director/Senior Investment Manager; Dafydd Rhys John [1974] Director/Chartered Accountant

Western Bidco Limited
Incorporated: 3 November 2016
Net Worth: £130,747,000 *Total Assets:* £287,131,008
Registered Office: Head Office, Westerleigh Crematorium, Westerleigh Road, Westerleigh, Bristol, BS37 8QP
Activities: Non-trading company
Parent: Western Topco Limited
Officers: Dafydd Rhys John, Secretary; James Alexander Adam [1970] Director/Senior Investment Executive [Canadian]; John Lewis Fyfield [1972] Director/Investment Executive; Robert William Horsnall [1981] Director/Senior Investment Manager; Dafydd Rhys John [1974] Director

Western Commodities Ltd
Incorporated: 2 November 2000 *Employees:* 43
Net Worth: £1,643,705 *Total Assets:* £4,454,615
Registered Office: Unit 13 South View Estate, Willand, Cullompton, Devon, EX15 2QW
Activities: Other processing and preserving of fruit and vegetables
Major Shareholder: Richard Alan Stoker
Officers: Peter Collier [1966] Director/Accountant; Richard Alan Stoker [1963] Director

Western Counties Roofing Limited
Incorporated: 23 March 1989 *Employees:* 41
Net Worth: £4,813,784 *Total Assets:* £7,135,879
Registered Office: Sigma House, Oak View Close, Edginswell Park, Torquay, Devon, TQ2 7FF
Activities: Roofing activities
Parent: WCR Holdings 2014 Limited
Officers: Beryl White, Secretary; Lesley Anne White, Secretary; Benjamin James Robinson [1984] Director; Beryl White [1934] Director/Accounts Clerk; David Brian Charles White [1965] Director/Surveyor; Lesley Anne White [1959] Director/Financial Administrator

Western Forestry Company Limited
Incorporated: 23 March 1987 *Employees:* 131
Net Worth: £5,794,892 *Total Assets:* £7,882,140
Registered Office: Windsor House, Bayshill Road, Cheltenham, Glos, GL50 3AT
Activities: Activities of head offices
Shareholders: Timothy Robert Greenway; Joan Elizabeth Greenway
Officers: Timothy Robert Greenway, Secretary; Joan Elizabeth Greenway [1935] Director/Sales Manageress; Timothy Robert Greenway [1961] Director/Office Manager

Western Fuel Limited
Incorporated: 20 March 2002 *Employees:* 34
Net Worth: £698,106 *Total Assets:* £5,379,026
Registered Office: Bristol Road, Bridgwater, Somerset, TA6 4BJ
Activities: Agents involved in the sale of fuels, ores, metals and industrial chemicals
Shareholder: Craig David Lamont
Officers: Angela Suzanne Lamont, Secretary; Craig David Lamont [1953] Director/Fuel Oil Distributor; Nicholas Duncan Smith [1974] Director/Manager

Western Global Holdings Limited
Incorporated: 10 December 2013 *Employees:* 127
Net Worth: £15,711,000 *Total Assets:* £29,377,000
Registered Office: Western House, Broad Lane, Yate, Bristol, BS37 7LD
Activities: Other manufacturing n.e.c.
Officers: Gregory Michael Cornell [1983] Director [Canadian]; Robert Andrew Critchley [1973] Director; Robert Scott Lennox [1984] Director [Canadian]

Western Global Limited
Incorporated: 15 April 2005 *Employees:* 43
Net Worth: £1,233,128 *Total Assets:* £7,630,964
Registered Office: Western House, Broad Lane, Yate, Bristol, BS37 7LD
Activities: Other manufacturing n.e.c.
Officers: Gregory Michael Cornell [1983] Director [Canadian]; Robert Critchley [1975] Managing Director

Western Mechanical Handling UK Limited
Incorporated: 16 December 1994 *Employees:* 39
Net Worth: £2,590,826 *Total Assets:* £3,654,958
Registered Office: Moss Side Industrial Estate, Callington, Cornwall, PL17 7SD
Activities: Manufacture of machinery for food, beverage and tobacco processing
Shareholders: Hendrika Janneke Tomlinson; John Randall Tomlinson
Officers: Hendrika Janneke Tomlinson, Secretary/Administrator [Dutch]; Hendrika Janneke Tomlinson [1950] Director/Administrator [Dutch]; John Randall Tomlinson [1951] Director/Engineer

Western Power Distribution (East Midlands) PLC
Incorporated: 1 April 1989 *Employees:* 1,888
Net Worth: £1,301,699,968 *Total Assets:* £4,174,599,936
Registered Office: Avonbank, Feeder Road, Bristol, BS2 0TB
Activities: Distribution of electricity
Parent: WPD Distribution Network Holdings Limited
Officers: Sally Ann Jones, Secretary; Anthony John Cardew [1949] Director/Company Chairman; Maurice Edwin Fletcher [1950] Director/Retired; Graham Roy Halladay [1966] Operations Director; Alison Jane Sleightholm [1963] Resources and External Affairs Director; Philip Swift [1967] Operations Director; Ian Robert Williams [1970] Resources and External Affairs Director

Western Power Distribution (South Wales) PLC
Incorporated: 1 April 1989 *Employees:* 1,039
Net Worth: £667,800,000 *Total Assets:* £1,983,200,000
Registered Office: Avonbank, Feeder Road, Bristol, BS2 0TB
Activities: Distribution of electricity
Parent: WPD Distribution Network Holdings Limited
Officers: Sally Ann Jones, Secretary; Anthony John Cardew [1949] Director/Company Chairman; Maurice Edwin Fletcher [1950] Director/Retired; Graham Roy Halladay [1966] Operations Director; Alison Jane Sleightholm [1963] Resources and External Affairs Director; Philip Swift [1967] Operations Director; Ian Robert Williams [1970] Resources and External Affairs Director

Western Power Distribution (South West) PLC
Incorporated: 1 April 1989 *Employees:* 1,544
Net Worth: £895,100,032 *Total Assets:* £2,841,200,128
Registered Office: Avonbank, Feeder Road, Bristol, BS2 0TB
Activities: Distribution of electricity
Parent: WPD Distribution Network Holdings Limited
Officers: Sally Ann Jones, Secretary; Anthony John Cardew [1949] Director/Company Chairman; Maurice Edwin Fletcher [1950] Director/Retired; Graham Roy Halladay [1966] Operations Director; Alison Jane Sleightholm [1963] Resources and External Affairs Director; Philip Swift [1967] Operations Director; Ian Robert Williams [1970] Resources and External Affairs Director

Western Power Distribution (West Midlands) PLC
Incorporated: 20 July 1998 *Employees:* 2,022
Net Worth: £1,318,800,000 *Total Assets:* £3,914,599,936
Registered Office: Avonbank, Feeder Road, Bristol, BS2 0TB
Activities: Distribution of electricity
Parent: WPD Distribution Network Holdings Limited
Officers: Sally Ann Jones, Secretary; Anthony John Cardew [1949] Director/Company Chairman; Maurice Edwin Fletcher [1950] Director/Retired; Graham Roy Halladay [1966] Operations Director; Alison Jane Sleightholm [1963] Resources and External Affairs Director; Philip Swift [1967] Operations Director; Ian Robert Williams [1970] Resources and External Director

Western Power Distribution Investments Limited
Incorporated: 4 December 1987
Net Worth: £28,293,000 *Total Assets:* £28,609,000
Registered Office: Avonbank, Feeder Road, Bristol, BS2 0TB
Activities: Activities of head offices
Parent: WPD Distribution Network Holdings Limited
Officers: Sally Ann Jones, Secretary; Ian Robert Williams [1970] Resources and External Affairs Director; David Astley Withers [1958] Director/Chartered Surveyor

Western Power Distribution PLC
Incorporated: 17 September 2014 *Employees:* 6,646
Net Worth: £4,304,200,192 *Total Assets:* £14,014,199,808
Registered Office: Avonbank, Feeder Road, Bristol, BS2 0TB
Activities: Distribution of electricity
Parent: PPL WPD Investments Limited
Officers: Sally Ann Jones, Secretary; Gregory N. Dudkin [1957] Director/President PPL Electric Utilities Co [American]; Graham Roy Halladay [1966] Operations Director; Joanne Hackett Raphael [1959] Director/Attorney [American]; Alison Jane Sleightholm [1963] Resources and External Affairs Director; Vincent Sorgi [1971] Director/Vice President & Controller [American]; Philip Swift [1967] Operations Director; Alexander James Torok [1958] Director/Assistant Treasurer [American]; Ian Robert Williams [1970] Resources and External Affairs Director

Western Provident Association Limited
Incorporated: 1 December 1949 *Employees:* 301
Net Worth: £183,303,008 *Total Assets:* £253,363,008
Registered Office: Rivergate House, Blackbrook Park, Taunton, Somerset, TA1 2PE
Activities: Non-life insurance
Officers: Nicola Anne Royle, Secretary; Rodney Adrian Bramston [1962] Director [Australian]; John Frederick Chester [1955] Director/Consultant Surgeon; Evelyn Rowland Esmond Baring Cromer [1946] Director; Jasper Anthony Gill [1973] Director/Consultant Surgeon; Andrew Nathan Haworth [1969] Director/Solicitor; Nathan Luke Irwin [1979] Director/Chartered Accountant; Henry James Kenyon [1950] Director/Chartered Accountant; Martin Cedric Kramer [1940] Director/Solicitor; Robert Edmund Lee [1957] Director/Actuary; Arthur John Pugh [1950] Director/Retired; Julian Clifford Stainton [1953] Managing Director

Western Truck Rental Limited
Incorporated: 1 April 1987
Net Worth: £1,583,650 *Total Assets:* £4,256,620
Registered Office: Roundswell Industrial Estate, Barnstaple, Devon, EX31 3NL
Activities: Renting and leasing of trucks and other heavy vehicles
Major Shareholder: Robert Dawson
Officers: Robert Dawson [1947] Director

Western United Mines Limited
Incorporated: 10 May 2007 *Employees:* 12
Net Worth: £2,236,497 *Total Assets:* £3,956,809
Registered Office: Osprey House, Malpas Road, Truro, Cornwall, TR1 1LT
Activities: Mining of iron ores
Parent: Strongbow Exploration (UK) Limited
Officers: Owen Daniel Mihalop [1973] Director/Mining Engineer; Kevin Peter Williams [1949] Director/Mine Manager; Richard David Williams [1966] Director [British/Canadian]

Westfield Academy Trust
Incorporated: 9 June 2011 *Employees:* 105
Net Worth: £7,549,617 *Total Assets:* £11,019,155
Registered Office: Westfield Academy, Stiby Road, Yeovil, Somerset, BA21 3EP
Activities: General secondary education
Officers: Lisa Jeffreys, Secretary; Simon Alan Annetts [1973] Director/Engineer; Simon Mark Bachrach [1961] Director/Chartered Accountant; Sharon Louise Brooks [1973] Director/Property Development; Michael Anthony Bunting [1969] Director/Aircraft Documentation Engineer; Simon Dallimore [1972] Director/Headteacher; Mark Edward Davidge [1969] Director/Aerospace; James Divall [1977] Director; Adam Matthew Dyer [1971] Director/Clergy; James Maxwell Hawke [1967] Director/Engineer; Laura Frances Hide [1986] Director/Education Teacher; Susan Clare Howes [1965] Director/School Teacher; Robert John Llewellyn [1983] Director/Emergency Planning Manager; Helen Jane Nourse [1965] Director/HE Student Liaison Officer; Joy Elaine Elisabeth Roberts [1970] Director; Elizabeth Waterman [1957] Director/Teacher

Westfield Medical Group Limited
Incorporated: 25 July 2015 *Employees:* 109
Net Worth: £104,000 *Total Assets:* £10,871,000
Registered Office: Second Avenue, Westfield Industrial Estate, Midsomer Norton, Radstock, Somerset, BA3 4DP
Activities: Activities of head offices
Parent: Maven Co-Invest Ropley Limited Partnership
Officers: Graham Scott Miller [1963] Director; Andrew Bryant Symmonds [1970] Director; Edward James Vero [1964] Director

Westfield Medical Limited
Incorporated: 30 November 1992 *Employees:* 109
Net Worth: £1,486,000 *Total Assets:* £7,909,000
Registered Office: Second Avenue, Westfield Industrial Estate, Midsomer Norton, Radstock, Somerset, BA3 4DP
Activities: Manufacture of other paper and paperboard containers
Parent: Westfield Medical Group Limited
Officers: James Richard Baldwin [1970] Director; Nicola Kate Browne [1973] Director; Graham Scott Miller [1963] Director; Mark Andrew Slocombe [1958] Finance Director; Edward James Vero [1964] Director; Jouni Vikman [1975] Sales Director [Finnish]

Westford Trade Services (UK) Ltd
Incorporated: 4 February 2014
Net Worth: £127,226 *Total Assets:* £7,040,092
Registered Office: 37 Chamberlain Street, Wells, Somerset, BA5 2PQ
Activities: Security and commodity contracts dealing activities
Parent: Westford Trade Services Ltd
Officers: Anthony Robert Mushens, Secretary; Hande Elmener [1975] Director [Dutch]

Weston Hospicecare Limited
Incorporated: 17 August 1989 *Employees:* 145
Net Worth: £6,366,750 *Total Assets:* £6,797,290
Registered Office: Jackson Barstow House, 28 Thornbury Road, Uphill, Weston Super Mare, Somerset, BS23 4YQ
Activities: Specialists medical practice activities
Officers: John Davey, Secretary; John Davey [1946] Director/Retired; Judi Elizabeth Driscoll [1949] Director/Retired; Hilary Jennifer Emery [1945] Director; John George Katsouris [1955] Director/Financial Adviser; Michelle Michael [1967] Director/Solicitor; Simon Richard Price [1966] Director/Chartered Surveyor; Anthony Colin Roche [1950] Director/Retired; Angela Margaret Smythe [1941] Director/Housewife; Elizabeth Turner [1961] Director/Self Employed Consultant

Westover Group Limited
Incorporated: 30 October 2001 *Employees:* 711
Net Worth: £33,776,256 *Total Assets:* £88,585,944
Registered Office: 382 Charminster Road, Bournemouth, BH8 9SA
Activities: Sale of new cars and light motor vehicles
Parent: Westover Holdings Limited
Officers: Paul Christopher Collins [1953] Director; Paul Dillon [1967] Director; Keith Joseph Martin [1943] Finance Director; Peter Charles Wood [1949] Managing Director

Westover Holdings Limited
Incorporated: 2 February 1962 *Employees:* 810
Net Worth: £44,688,436 *Total Assets:* £103,783,744
Registered Office: 382 Charminster Road, Bournemouth, BH8 9SA
Activities: Sale of new cars and light motor vehicles
Shareholder: Peter Charles Wood
Officers: Keith Joseph Martin [1943] Accountant/Director; Claire Gist Turner [1979] Director; Jennifer Caroline Wood [1951] Director/Personal Assistant; Peter Charles Wood [1949] Managing Director

Westrock Packaging Systems UK Ltd.
Incorporated: 20 May 1986 *Employees:* 99
Previous: Meadwestvaco UK Limited
Net Worth: £17,681,000 *Total Assets:* £224,764,992
Registered Office: 500 Woodward Avenue, Yate, Bristol, BS37 5YS
Activities: Manufacture of other paper and paperboard containers
Officers: Kevin Alden Maxwell, Secretary; Christina Marie Able [1973] Director/SVP Tax [American]; Kevin Alden Maxwell [1975] Director and Company Secretary [American]; Anders Olof Olsson [1967] Commercial Director

Westward Building Services Limited
Incorporated: 29 January 1964 *Employees:* 41
Net Worth: £7,210,586 *Total Assets:* £9,157,471
Registered Office: Burraton Road, Saltash, Cornwall, PL12 6LU
Activities: Agents involved in the sale of timber and building materials
Parent: Coxco Holdings Limited
Officers: Wayne Colin Cox [1970] Managing Director

Westward Investment Management Services (UK) Limited
Incorporated: 23 March 1983 *Employees:* 3
Net Worth: £3,624,388 *Total Assets:* £3,794,359
Registered Office: 19 High Street, Totnes, Devon, TQ9 5NW
Activities: Development of building projects
Major Shareholder: Carl Throgmorton
Officers: Anthony John Osborne, Secretary; Carl Throgmorton [1934] Director

Weymouth and Portland National Sailing Academy
Incorporated: 21 April 1999
Net Worth: £1,137,775 *Total Assets:* £8,749,533
Registered Office: Weymouth and Portland National Sailing Academy, Osprey Quay, Portland, Dorset, DT5 1SA
Activities: Other sports activities
Officers: Rachel Kay Sadler, Secretary; Martin John Aldridge [1965] Director/Accountant; Philippa Baily [1988] Director/Marketing Manager; David Campbell-James [1949] Director/Retired Accountant; Rodney Paul Carr [1950] Director/Chief Executive; David Wyn Griffith [1961] Director/Security Consultant; Mike Harries [1962] Local Government Director; Helen Kate Lucas [1975] Director/Professional Sailor; Ralph David Luck [1952] Director/Chartered Surveyor; Matthew Vaughan Prosser [1969] Director/Chief Executive - Local Government; Ian James Walker [1970] Director of Racing, RYA

Weymouth Harbour Estates Limited
Incorporated: 25 November 1994 *Employees:* 2
Net Worth: £8,303,699 *Total Assets:* £9,888,187
Registered Office: DJ Property, Unit C, Oxford Court, Cambridge Road, Granby Industrial Estate, Weymouth, Dorset, DT4 9GH
Activities: Other letting and operating of own or leased real estate
Shareholders: Michael Jones; Paul Jones
Officers: Kathryn Jones, Company Secretary; Kathryn Jones [1947] Director/Company Secretary; Michael Jones [1973] Director/Chartered Accountant

WHC Hire Services Ltd.
Incorporated: 21 February 1997 *Employees:* 23
Net Worth: £1,987,021 *Total Assets:* £7,634,838
Registered Office: Chargrove House, Shurdington Road, Shurdington, Cheltenham, Glos, GL51 4GA
Activities: Other specialised construction activities n.e.c.
Major Shareholder: James Hopkins Clutterbuck
Officers: Heidelinde Clutterbuck, Secretary; James Hopkins Clutterbuck [1966] Director

Chris Wheeler Construction Limited
Incorporated: 10 April 1985 *Employees:* 5
Net Worth: £3,957,986 *Total Assets:* £4,045,850
Registered Office: Church Farm, Burbage, Marlborough, Wilts, SN8 3AT
Activities: Other specialised construction activities n.e.c.
Officers: Margaret Elizabeth Wheeler, Secretary; Andrew Simon Wheeler [1977] Director; Christopher Brian Wheeler [1946] Director/Motorway Fencing Contractor; Margaret Elizabeth Wheeler [1948] Director

Wheeler's (Westbury) Holdings Limited
Incorporated: 18 March 2010 *Employees:* 3
Net Worth: £1,061,792 *Total Assets:* £3,525,117
Registered Office: 31d Link Road, West Wilts Trading Estate, Westbury, Wilts, BA13 4JB
Activities: Activities of head offices
Shareholders: Gareth Geoffrey Caldicott; Kieron Borgeat
Officers: Kieron Borgeat [1963] Managing Director; Gareth Geoffrey Caldicott [1964] Director; Darren Keith Honeywell [1973] Mechanical Director; Kevin John McNeil [1962] Director/Management Accountant; Paul Scarisbrick [1972] Purchasing and Systems Director

Wheeler's (Westbury) Limited
Incorporated: 29 November 1982 *Employees:* 94
Net Worth: £2,644,324 *Total Assets:* £5,553,771
Registered Office: 31d Link Road, West Wilts Trading Estate, Westbury, Wilts, BA13 4JB
Activities: Manufacture of other electrical equipment
Parent: Wheeler's (Westbury) Holdings Limited
Officers: Kieron Borgeat [1963] Managing Director; Gareth Geoffrey Caldicott [1964] Director/Contracts Manager; Darren Keith Honeywell [1973] Mechanical Director; Kevin John McNeil [1962] Finance Director; Paul Scarisbrick [1972] Purchasing and Systems Director

Wherwell Farms Limited
Incorporated: 17 December 1973 *Employees:* 7
Net Worth: £23,743,272 *Total Assets:* £27,451,836
Registered Office: St Catherine's Court, Berkeley Place, Clifton, Bristol, BS8 1BQ
Activities: Growing of cereals (except rice), leguminous crops and oil seeds
Parent: Keybolt (Farmers) Limited
Officers: James Earl of Brecknock, Secretary; James Earl of Brecknock [1965] Director; Florence Mary Fagan [1939] Director; Richard Wilmot Starr Jukes [1936] Director/Retired; Lady Samantha Caroline Pratt [1964] Director

Whisstocks Developments Limited
Incorporated: 11 May 2004 *Employees:* 1
Net Worth Deficit: £1,575,065 *Total Assets:* £5,961,799
Registered Office: Parklands, Lustleigh, Newton Abbot, Devon, TQ13 9SH
Activities: Buying and selling of own real estate
Major Shareholder: Stephen Vantreen
Officers: Stephen Vantreen [1949] Director/Surveyor

Ken White Holdings Limited
Incorporated: 21 May 2010 *Employees:* 87
Net Worth: £4,054,551 *Total Assets:* £8,804,847
Registered Office: Langdowns DFK, Kingsgate House, Newbury Road, Andover, Hants, SP10 4DU
Activities: Activities of head offices
Major Shareholder: Kenneth White
Officers: Jack Kenneth Victor White [1989] Director/Sales Manager; Kenneth White [1953] Director/Haulier

T. H. White Holdings Limited
Incorporated: 10 February 1914 *Employees:* 546
Net Worth: £32,229,232 *Total Assets:* £62,100,800
Registered Office: Nursteed Road, Devizes, Wilts, SN10 3EA
Activities: Activities of head offices
Officers: Peter Barker, Secretary; Richard Melbourne Dewhurst [1956] Director; Michael Ian Edwards [1964] Director/Certified Chartered Accountant; Mark Simeon Rigby [1956] Director/General Manager; Alexander David Scott [1979] Director/Chartered Engineer; David Bedingfeld Scott [1950] Director/Engineer

The White Horse Care Trust
Incorporated: 20 June 1990 *Employees:* 274
Net Worth: £3,964,981 *Total Assets:* £6,469,740
Registered Office: 603 Delta Business Park, Welton Road, Swindon, Wilts, SN5 7XF
Activities: Residential nursing care facilities
Officers: Martin Andrew Slade, Secretary; Mary Joy Gladman [1941] Director/Retired; Pamela Ann Jackson [1955] Director/Retired; Myra McConnell [1957] Director/Nurse; Malcolm Cameron Tatham Morrison [1928] Director/Consultant Orthopaedic Surgeon; Raymond Francis Nelson Norman [1951] Director/Headmaster; Jeanne Morwenna Perons [1934] Director/Solicitor; Phillip Graeme Simpson [1947] Director/Quantity Surveyor; Ian Robert McNairn Spalding [1948] Director/Retired CEO (WHCT); Peter Swinburne [1949] Director/Retired

White Horse Country Club Ltd
Incorporated: 16 June 2009 *Employees:* 9
Net Worth: £3,058,997 *Total Assets:* £5,007,595
Registered Office: The Courtyard, 33 Duke Street, Trowbridge, Wilts, BA14 8EA
Activities: Other amusement and recreation activities n.e.c.
Shareholders: Shaun Leslie Thomas May; Derek Richard Hulin
Officers: Derek Richard Hulin [1952] Director; Shaun Leslie Thomas May [1963] Director

White Horse Education Partnership Limited
Incorporated: 21 January 2000 *Employees:* 3
Net Worth: £1,317,000 *Total Assets:* £24,001,000
Registered Office: Third Floor, Broad Quay House, Prince Street, Bristol, BS1 4DJ
Activities: Other business support service activities n.e.c.
Parent: North Wiltshire Schools Limited
Officers: Graham John Hutt [1954] Regional Director; Neil Rae [1971] Director; Phillip James Thorne [1961] Director

The White Horse Federation
Incorporated: 18 May 2012 *Employees:* 1,523
Net Worth: £109,527,416 *Total Assets:* £129,580,144
Registered Office: The White Horse Federation, Plymouth Street, Swindon, Wilts, SN1 2LB
Activities: Pre-primary education
Officers: Dr. Nicholas Richard Capstick [1960] Director/Chief Executive Officer; Charlotte Eleanor Christie [1960] Director/Education Consultant; Linda Clare Terry Gibson [1961] Director/Magistrate; Charlotte Heather Hall [1970] Managing Director; Christopher John Hopton [1955] Director; Richard Douglas Marsh [1951] Director/Solicitor; Simon Nicholas McMurtrie [1966] Director/Chairman; Jillian Swinburne Norton [1964] Director/Florist; Nicholas Howard Van Zeller [1953] Director/Retired

W.H.White Limited
Incorporated: 30 June 1969 *Employees:* 7
Net Worth: £4,135,605 *Total Assets:* £18,945,570
Registered Office: Energy Site Control Centre, Arena Way, Wimborne, Dorset, BH21 3BW
Activities: Other business support service activities n.e.c.
Major Shareholder: William Edward Riddle
Officers: Stuart Michael Hudson, Secretary; Jonathan Walter Pursall Fryett [1950] Director; Stuart Michael Hudson [1972] Director; William Edward Riddle [1952] Director/Chairman

T. H. White Limited
Incorporated: 20 May 1953 *Employees:* 446
Net Worth: £15,909,260 *Total Assets:* £43,722,356
Registered Office: Nursteed Road, Devizes, Wilts, SN10 3EA
Activities: Repair and maintenance of other transport equipment n.e.c.
Parent: T H White Holdings Limited
Officers: Peter Barker, Secretary; Peter Barker [1959] Director/Company Secretary; Michael Ian Edwards [1964] Director/Chartered Accountant; Timothy James Lane [1975] Director/Business Manager; Mark Rigby [1956] Director/Sales Manager; Alexander David Scott [1979] Director/Industrial Engineer

White Pennant Ltd
Incorporated: 6 October 2010 *Employees:* 1
Previous: Iceford Trading Ltd
Net Worth: £4,477,159 *Total Assets:* £30,531,088
Registered Office: Neptune, Frankland Road, Blagrove, Swindon, Wilts, SN5 8YG
Activities: Activities of other holding companies n.e.c.
Shareholders: Bremhill Properties Limited; Lilac Dorade Ltd
Officers: John Giles Redman [1969] Director; John Edwin Sims-Hilditch [1965] Director

The White Rose School of Beauty and Complementary Therapies Limited
Incorporated: 14 March 1996 *Employees:* 119
Net Worth: £3,477,390 *Total Assets:* £4,177,959
Registered Office: 18-22 Angel Crescent, Bridgwater, Somerset, TA6 3AL
Activities: Technical and vocational secondary education
Major Shareholder: Karen Lee Cooke
Officers: Alan Keith Chambers, Secretary; Karen Lee Cooke [1963] Director/College Principal

White Rose UK Ltd
Incorporated: 9 April 2008 *Employees:* 1,104
Net Worth: £3,958,878 *Total Assets:* £8,425,217
Registered Office: McDonald's Restaurant, 13-17 New George Street, Plymouth, PL1 1QZ
Activities: Unlicenced restaurants and cafes
Major Shareholder: David Paul Wynne
Officers: Melissa Burnett, Secretary/Director; David Paul Wynne [1966] Director

Whiteburn Rookery Investments Limited
Incorporated: 29 April 2016 *Employees:* 2
Net Worth: £5,269,763 *Total Assets:* £5,309,104
Registered Office: The Rookery, Orcheston, Salisbury, Wilts, SP3 4RP
Activities: Other letting and operating of own or leased real estate
Shareholders: Simon David William Shepherd; Sarah Ruth Nutall Shepherd
Officers: Sarah Ruth Nutall Shepherd [1958] Director; Simon David William Shepherd [1958] Director/Chartered Surveyor

Whitecroft Developments Limited
Incorporated: 23 March 2010 *Employees:* 5
Net Worth Deficit: £231,128 *Total Assets:* £7,796,157
Registered Office: Hayloft, Lady Farm, Chelwood, Bristol, BS39 4NN
Activities: Development of building projects
Shareholders: Martin James David Hales; Rebecca Gabrielle Hales
Officers: Martin James David Hales [1982] Director/Property Developer; Rebecca Gabrielle Hales [1981] Director/Property Developer; Susan Margaret Hales [1956] Director/Property Developer

Whitehall Cricklade Ltd
Incorporated: 31 October 1958 *Employees:* 9
Net Worth: £2,865,924 *Total Assets:* £4,057,476
Registered Office: Chelworth Industrial Estate, Cricklade, Wilts, SN6 6HE
Activities: Operation of warehousing and storage facilities for land transport activities
Parent: Whitehall Cricklade Holdings Limited
Officers: Mark Edward Sweet, Secretary; Bruce Gould Bowie [1959] Director/Packer; Helen Margaret Bowie [1960] Director; Helen Mary Sweet [1951] Director/Housewife; Marilyn Jean Sweet [1951] Director/Housewife; Mark Edward Sweet [1953] Director; Richard Allen Sweet [1951] Director/Farm Manager

Whitehall Garden Centre (Holdings) Limited
Incorporated: 3 March 2010 *Employees:* 210
Net Worth: £13,330,320 *Total Assets:* £20,791,140
Registered Office: Corsham Road, Lacock, Chippenham, Wilts, SN15 2LZ
Activities: Activities of head offices
Major Shareholder: Peter Rowland Self
Officers: Claire Jacqueline Self [1965] Director; Peter Rowland Self [1964] Director

Whitehall Garden Centres Limited
Incorporated: 2 December 2003 *Employees:* 196
Net Worth: £542,185 *Total Assets:* £4,366,695
Registered Office: Corsham Road, Lacock, Chippenham, Wilts, SN15 2LZ
Activities: Other retail sale in non-specialised stores
Parent: Whitehall Group (Wessex) Limited
Officers: Claire Jacqueline Self [1965] Director; Peter Rowland Self [1964] Director

Whitehall Group (Wessex) Limited
Incorporated: 28 November 1986 *Employees:* 16
Net Worth: £10,430,276 *Total Assets:* £15,531,985
Registered Office: Corsham Road, Lacock, Chippenham, Wilts, SN15 2LZ
Activities: Activities of head offices
Parent: Whitehall Garden Centre (Holdings) Limited
Officers: Claire Jacqueline Self [1965] Director; Peter Rowland Self [1964] Director

Whitehill Country Park Limited
Incorporated: 4 November 2003 *Employees:* 34
Net Worth: £3,904,728 *Total Assets:* £4,269,991
Registered Office: Sigma House, Oak View Close, Edginswell Park, Torquay, Devon, TQ2 7FF
Activities: Recreational vehicle parks, trailer parks and camping grounds
Parent: Whitehill Country Holdings Limited
Officers: Faye Louise Butler [1978] Director/Teacher; Michael John Jeavons [1950] Director; Timothy John Jeavons [1982] Director/Manager

Whitelock & Company Limited
Incorporated: 2 May 1996 *Employees:* 18
Net Worth: £4,655,447 *Total Assets:* £10,506,926
Registered Office: 310 Bournemouth Road, Parkstone, Poole, Dorset, BH14 9AR
Activities: Construction of commercial buildings
Major Shareholder: John Sydenham Whitelock
Officers: Nicole Pauline Mary Whitelock, Secretary; John Sydenham Whitelock [1949] Director; Josh Sydenham Kennedy Whitelock [1988] Director; Nicole Pauline Mary Whitelock [1956] Director

Whiteoaks Investments Limited
Incorporated: 20 April 2017 *Employees:* 2
Net Worth: £21,244,906 *Total Assets:* £21,281,602
Registered Office: 40 Berkeley Square, Bristol, BS8 1HP
Activities: Financial management
Major Shareholder: Heather Frankham
Officers: Matthew Gregory Dawes [1973] Finance Director; Heather Frankham [1968] Director

Whites Material Handling Limited
Incorporated: 10 March 1976 *Employees:* 83
Net Worth: £2,847,165 *Total Assets:* £5,383,356
Registered Office: c/o Precision Profiles, Southway Drive, Warmley, Bristol, BS30 5LW
Activities: Manufacture of lifting and handling equipment
Officers: Lisa Helen Sinclair, Secretary; Roger Frederick Avery [1949] Director

Whitsbury Farm & Stud Limited
Incorporated: 14 September 1977 *Employees:* 30
Net Worth: £6,418,771 *Total Assets:* £12,646,330
Registered Office: Estate Office, Manor Farm, Whitsbury, Fordingbridge, Hants, SP6 3QP
Activities: Growing of cereals (except rice), leguminous crops and oil seeds
Shareholders: Edward John Harper; Christopher John Harper
Officers: Edward John Harper, Secretary; Christopher John Harper [1941] Director; Edward John Harper [1983] Director and Company Secretary; Nicola Wynn Harper [1949] Director

Whitstone School Academy Trust
Incorporated: 15 July 2011 *Employees:* 77
Net Worth: £6,458,064 *Total Assets:* £8,378,016
Registered Office: Whitstone School, Charlton Road, Shepton Mallet, Somerset, BA4 5PF
Activities: General secondary education
Officers: Ruth Lilian Sayer, Secretary; Stuart Andrew Byrne [1972] Director/Banker; Philip John Eavis [1938] Director; Lynne Elstob [1952] Director/Quality Reviewer; Anna Gurowich [1967] Director; Anita Susan Johnson [1966] Director; Kathleen Anne Honour Lovell [1952] Director; James Paul Millward [1968] Director; John William Parham [1956] Director/Self Employed; Zena Kay Pollard [1959] Director/Bank Official; Gillian Ann Rennard [1964] Director/Headteacher; Miranda Roberts [1965] Director/Teacher

Whittington Facilities Limited
Incorporated: 18 September 2001
Net Worth Deficit: £46,487,668 *Total Assets:* £39,021,176
Registered Office: Third Floor, Broad Quay House, Prince Street, Bristol, BS1 4DJ
Activities: Non-trading company
Parent: Uberior Investments Limited
Officers: Nigel Anthony John Brindley [1956] Director; Ian Richard Gethin [1971] Director/Investment Banker; Mark Christopher Pearce [1961] Director

Whole Nine Yards (UK) Limited
Incorporated: 10 December 2014
Net Worth Deficit: £483,617 *Total Assets:* £8,643,527
Registered Office: Saffery Champness LLP, Midland House, 2 Poole Road, Bournemouth, BH2 5QY
Activities: Buying and selling of own real estate
Major Shareholder: Khalid Abdulwahid Hassan Alrustamani
Officers: Khalid Alrustamani [1967] Director [Emirati]

Wiggin LLP
Incorporated: 28 July 2004 *Employees:* 120
Net Worth: £8,148,477 *Total Assets:* £16,627,443
Registered Office: Jessop House, Jessop Avenue, Cheltenham, Glos, GL50 3WG
Officers: John Richard Banister [1964] Member; Sean St John James [1965] Member; Adrian Mark Jones [1970] Member; Syed David Ralph Quli [1971] Member; Benjamin Miles Whitelock [1975] Member; Rachel Alexander [1975] LLP Member; Sara Louise Ashby [1968] LLP Member; Simon James Robert John Baggs [1968] LLP Member; Simon Laurence Bernholt [1975] LLP Member; Michael Hilton Charles Brader [1964] LLP Member; Michael John Browne [1984] LLP Member; Matthew James Bullock [1960] LLP Member; Anna Katharine Carboni [1963] LLP Member; Simon Richard Chalkley [1966] LLP Member; Jason Morgan Chess [1964] LLP Member; Susan Lavender Crawford [1959] LLP Member; Jason Guy Fisher [1982] LLP Member; Paul Andrew Gardner [1963] LLP Member; Neil Desmond Gillard [1971] LLP Member; Christopher Michael Hammond [1979] LLP Member; Christopher Darius Hanson [1967] LLP Member; Ciaran James Hickey [1978] LLP Member; Medwyn Jones [1955] LLP Member; Caroline Mary Kean [1960] LLP Member; Stephen John Ketteley [1973] LLP Member; Alexander Mark LEA [1978] LLP Member; Shaun Reg Lowde [1964] LLP Member; Grainne Mary Clare McKenna [1971] LLP Member; David Matthew Alexander McLeish [1977] LLP Member; Charles Henry Moore [1962] LLP Member; David Ross Naylor [1968] LLP Member; Alan Jeffrey Owens [1972] LLP Member; Gurminder Panesar [1979] LLP Member; Alexander Guy Campbell Ross [1959] LLP Member; Marcus John Rowland [1970] LLP Member; Theodore Michael Shapiro [1964] LLP Member; Ceri Ann Stoner [1977] LLP Member; Ross Alexander John Tebbs Sylvester [1982] LLP Member; Daniel Charles Whybrew [1981] LLP Member

Wild and Wolf Limited
Incorporated: 4 March 2005 *Employees:* 109
Net Worth: £3,329,279 *Total Assets:* £22,894,972
Registered Office: 20 Manvers Street, Bath, BA1 1JW
Activities: Non-specialised wholesale trade
Parent: Wild and Wolf (Holdings) Limited
Officers: Gavin Stewart Jones, Secretary; Gavin Stewart Jones [1970] Financial Director; Paul Taylor [1970] Director/Chartered Accountant

Wild Ash Limited
Incorporated: 13 October 2004
Net Worth Deficit: £3,646,306 *Total Assets:* £3,806,384
Registered Office: St Catherines Court, Berkeley Place, Clifton, Bristol, BS8 1BQ
Activities: Other letting and operating of own or leased real estate
Shareholders: The Honourable Robert Richard Guy Yerburgh; The Honourable Karen Lucinda Yerburgh
Officers: Hon Robert Richard Guy Yerburgh, Secretary; Karen Lucinda Yerbugh [1962] Director/Investment Manager; The Honourable Robert Richard Guy Yerburgh [1956] Director

Wildbrook Investments (Calne) Limited
Incorporated: 18 March 2004
Net Worth: £1,539,634 *Total Assets:* £4,075,703
Registered Office: 4 Burraton Yard, Poundbury, Dorchester, DT1 3GR
Activities: Buying and selling of own real estate
Parent: Wildbrook Investments Ltd
Officers: Tracy Ann Dabbs, Secretary; Gavin Maber [1947] Director/Surveyor

Wildbrook Investments (Industrial) Limited
Incorporated: 17 July 1997
Net Worth: £6,336,043 *Total Assets:* £6,372,407
Registered Office: 4 Burraton Yard, Poundbury, Dorchester, DT1 3GR
Activities: Buying and selling of own real estate
Parent: Wildbrook Investments Ltd
Officers: Tracy Ann Dabbs, Secretary; Gavin Maber [1947] Director/Surveyor

Wildbrook Investments (Thornbury) Limited
Incorporated: 19 November 1996
Net Worth: £2,034,816 *Total Assets:* £3,577,586
Registered Office: 4 Burraton Yard, Poundbury, Dorchester, DT1 3GR
Activities: Buying and selling of own real estate
Parent: Wildbrook Investments Ltd
Officers: Tracy Ann Dabbs, Secretary; Gavin Maber [1947] Director

Wildbrook Investments Limited
Incorporated: 9 July 1996 *Employees:* 2
Net Worth: £7,462,791 *Total Assets:* £11,879,457
Registered Office: 4 Burraton Yard, Poundbury, Dorchester, DT1 3GR
Activities: Buying and selling of own real estate
Major Shareholder: Gavin Maber
Officers: Tracy Ann Dabbs, Secretary; Gavin Maber [1947] Director/Surveyor

The Wildfowl & Wetlands Trust
Incorporated: 16 December 1993 *Employees:* 430
Net Worth: £40,795,000 *Total Assets:* £43,123,000
Registered Office: Slimbridge, Gloucester, GL2 7BT
Activities: Botanical and zoological gardens and nature reserves activities
Officers: John Leslie Rew, Secretary; Andrew David Beer [1968] Charity Director; Martin Philip Birch [1965] Director/Accountant; Barnaby Daniel Briggs [1964] Director/PR Executive; Pamela Margaret Castle [1941] Director/Solicitor; Peter Donal Day [1944] Director/Chief Executive Software Company; Professor Alastair Driver [1956] Director/Conservation Manager; Simon Henzell-Thomas [1977] Director/Head of Public Affairs; Simon Jonathan Tonge [1958] Zoo Director

M.B.Wilkes Limited
Incorporated: 10 March 1964 *Employees:* 35
Net Worth: £3,437,554 *Total Assets:* £4,739,920
Registered Office: Old Market Road, Corfe Mullen, Wimborne Minster, Dorset, BH21 3QZ
Activities: Operation of gravel and sand pits; mining of clays and kaolin
Major Shareholder: Michael Bruce Wilkes
Officers: Vivienne Anne Wilkes, Secretary/Director; David Michael Wilkes [1977] Director/Manager; Michael Bruce Wilkes [1939] Director; Paul Austin Wilkes [1967] Director; Vivienne Anne Wilkes [1941] Director

Willand Biogas LLP
Incorporated: 10 July 2015
Net Worth Deficit: £1,964,943 *Total Assets:* £9,457,851
Registered Office: Cleave Farm, Templeton, Tiverton, Devon, EX16 8BP

Willcox Bros Limited
Incorporated: 19 September 1983 *Employees:* 139
Net Worth: £3,175,734 *Total Assets:* £5,519,477
Registered Office: The Garden House, Beckspool Road, Frenchay, Bristol, BS16 1NE
Activities: Other service activities n.e.c.
Shareholders: John Cossham Willcox; Samantha Allison Hawker
Officers: Samantha Allison Hawker [1968] Director/Residential Care

Willes Farming Limited
Incorporated: 24 October 2001 *Employees:* 33
Net Worth: £14,139,763 *Total Assets:* £17,756,324
Registered Office: St Johns House, Castle Street, Taunton, Somerset, TA1 4AY
Activities: Growing of cereals (except rice), leguminous crops and oil seeds
Major Shareholder: Peter Anthony Willes
Officers: Peter Anthony Willes [1964] Director/Businessman

Willett & Son Holdings Limited
Incorporated: 4 November 1987 *Employees:* 13
Net Worth: £1,711,609 *Total Assets:* £7,484,688
Registered Office: 51 Queen Square, Bristol, BS1 4LJ
Activities: Activities of head offices
Major Shareholder: John Richard Wright
Officers: Dr Elizabeth Ann Rice, Secretary; Dr Elizabeth Ann Rice [1970] Director/Scientist; John Richard Wright [1945] Director; Jonathan Allister Wright [1972] Director/Marketing Executive

Percy Williams & Sons,Limited
Incorporated: 9 March 1938 *Employees:* 6
Net Worth: £11,199,935 *Total Assets:* £12,828,657
Registered Office: Falmouth Road, Redruth, Truro, Cornwall, TR15 2QX
Activities: Development of building projects
Officers: Alan Paul Hobson, Secretary; Arminel Heather Williams [1958] Director; Jonathan Williams [1961] Director/Solicitor; Percival Ross Williams [1954] Arts Centre Director; Sarah Williams [1967] Director; Simon Crowan Williams [1955] Director/Builder; Tamsyn Mary Williams [1958] Director

Ian Williams (Holdings) Limited
Incorporated: 27 October 1941 *Employees:* 883
Net Worth: £20,400,000 *Total Assets:* £39,502,000
Registered Office: Quarry Road, Chipping Sodbury, Glos, BS37 6JL
Activities: Activities of head offices
Major Shareholder: William John Williams
Officers: David Martin Sewell, Secretary; Andrew Havard [1966] Director; David Martin Sewell [1968] Finance Director; Richard Steven Williams [1968] Director

Ian Williams Limited
Incorporated: 17 May 1966 *Employees:* 883
Net Worth: £11,159,000 *Total Assets:* £29,213,000
Registered Office: Quarry Road, Chipping Sodbury, Glos, BS37 6JL
Activities: Painting
Major Shareholder: William John Williams
Officers: David Martin Sewell, Secretary; Andrew Havard [1966] Director; Kenneth Jones [1958] Director; David Martin Sewell [1968] Finance Director; Michael John Peter Turner [1961] Business Development Director; Richard Steven Williams [1968] Director

Ted Williams Motors Limited
Incorporated: 5 March 1946
Net Worth: £3,995,014 *Total Assets:* £4,330,326
Registered Office: 58 Hampton Road, Bristol, BS6 6JA
Activities: Sale of used cars and light motor vehicles
Major Shareholder: Edward Wallace John Williams
Officers: Edward Wallace John Williams, Secretary; Edward Wallace John Williams [1938] Director/Car Salesman; Tecla Williams [1935] Director/Secretary

Williams Southern Limited
Incorporated: 26 May 1988 *Employees:* 118
Net Worth: £3,829,623 *Total Assets:* £11,119,174
Registered Office: Southern House, Eagle Close, Langage Business Park, Plympton, Plymouth, PL7 5HZ
Activities: Construction of other civil engineering projects n.e.c.
Shareholders: Richard Rodney Williams; David Joseph Williams; John David Whittaker
Officers: Richard Rodney Williams, Secretary; John David Whittaker [1965] Director/Construction; Richard Rodney Williams [1976] Director/Construction

Williamsbuild Management Limited
Incorporated: 11 May 2010 *Employees:* 120
Net Worth: £5,407,894 *Total Assets:* £13,605,969
Registered Office: Southern House, Eagle Close, Langage Business Park, Plympton, Plymouth, PL7 5HZ
Activities: Activities of head offices
Shareholders: John David Whittaker; Richard Rodney Williams; David Joseph Williams
Officers: David Joseph Williams, Secretary; John David Whittaker [1965] Director/Construction; Richard Rodney Williams [1976] Director/Construction

George Williamson & Co. Limited
Incorporated: 7 June 1974 *Employees:* 10
Net Worth: £8,889,201 *Total Assets:* £11,650,967
Registered Office: c/o Little Bedwyn Estate, Little Bedwyn, Marlborough, Wilts, SN8 3JR
Activities: Activities of agricultural holding companies
Shareholder: Philip Magor
Officers: Philip Magor, Secretary; Alexa Catherine Magor [1959] Director; Edward Charles Magor [1985] Director/Farmer; Philip Magor [1956] Director/Farmer

T.D. Williamson (U.K.) Limited
Incorporated: 10 August 1964 *Employees:* 60
Net Worth Deficit: £11,669,721 *Total Assets:* £6,300,173
Registered Office: Faraday Road, Dorcan Way, Swindon, Wilts, SN3 5HF
Activities: Other manufacturing n.e.c.
Shareholders: Richard Brooks Williamson; Stephen Dale Williamson
Officers: Caroline Anberree [1970] Director/Vice President [French]; Johan Guillaume Solange Desaegher [1968] Director/Vice President EAM [Belgian]; Gregory Gianni Vivian Florean [1982] Finance Director [Belgian]

T.D. Williamson UK International Limited
Incorporated: 9 May 2014 *Employees:* 4
Net Worth: £8,661,796 *Total Assets:* £43,004,276
Registered Office: Faraday Road, Dorcan Way, Swindon, Wilts, SN3 5HF
Activities: Other professional, scientific and technical activities n.e.c.
Shareholders: Business Executive Richard Brooks Williamson; Stephen Dale Williamson
Officers: Tory Michael Baker [1965] Director/Vice President, Chief Financial Officer [American]; Gregory Gianni Vivian Florean [1982] Finance Director [Belgian]; Michael Rogers [1968] Director/Accountant [American]

Williamson-Dickie Europe Holdings Limited
Incorporated: 20 December 2000 *Employees:* 3
Net Worth: £3,018,000 *Total Assets:* £9,895,000
Registered Office: Second Avenue, Westfield Trading Estate, Midsomer Norton, Radstock, Somerset, BA3 4BH
Activities: Manufacture of other wearing apparel and accessories n.e.c.
Parent: VF Sagebrush Enterprises LLC
Officers: Kirk Mark Ehrlich [1963] Director/Company President; Tommaso Domenico Rossi [1983] Director; Philip Charles Williamson [1962] Director/Executive [American]

Williamson-Dickie Europe Limited
Incorporated: 30 September 1983 *Employees:* 296
Net Worth: £29,130,000 *Total Assets:* £39,725,000
Registered Office: Second Avenue, Westfield Trading Estate, Midsomer Norton, Radstock, Somerset, BA3 4BH
Activities: Manufacture of other wearing apparel and accessories n.e.c.
Parent: Williamson-Dickie Europe Holdings Limited
Officers: Sarah Cooper [1964] Merchandising Director; Kirk Mark Ehrlich [1963] Director/Company President; Tommaso Domenico Rossi [1983] Director; Philip Charles Williamson [1962] Director/Business Executive [American]

Willmot Pertwee Limited
Incorporated: 3 June 1996
Net Worth: £32,197,000 *Total Assets:* £32,197,000
Registered Office: Station Road, Andoversford, Cheltenham, Glos, GL54 4LZ
Activities: Support activities for crop production
Parent: Cleancrop UK Limited
Officers: Peter Michael Dunne [1973] Director/Chartered Accountant [Irish]; Spencer Gareth Evans [1970] Director/Chief Financial Officer; Ronan Andrew Hughes [1968] Director [Irish]; Christopher Stephen Matthews [1957] Director; James Marshall Rennie [1957] Director

Willmott's Transport Limited
Incorporated: 23 August 1961 *Employees:* 87
Net Worth: £1,287,873 *Total Assets:* £6,807,883
Registered Office: Willmotts Business Park, Waterlip, Shepton Mallet, Somerset, BA4 4RN
Activities: Operation of warehousing and storage facilities for land transport activities
Parent: ADMP Group Limited
Officers: Janice Elizabeth Buchan [1956] Finance Director; Matthew Loxton [1975] Director; Andy Mark Stott [1968] Haulage Director; Andrew Tuck [1975] Director

Willow Green Developments Limited
Incorporated: 28 June 2017 *Employees:* 2
Net Worth Deficit: £12,321 *Total Assets:* £4,232,935
Registered Office: 6 Houndiscombe Road, Plymouth, PL4 6HH
Activities: Development of building projects
Shareholders: James William Lockyer; Richard Jonathan Walker
Officers: James William Lockyer [1956] Director/Consulting Engineer; Richard Jonathan Walker [1959] Director

Wills Brothers Limited
Incorporated: 30 May 2002 *Employees:* 26
Net Worth: £1,556,210 *Total Assets:* £14,435,033
Registered Office: Trevelver Farm, St Minver, Wadebridge, Cornwall, PL27 6RJ
Activities: Raising of dairy cattle
Officers: William Anthony Richard Wills, Secretary/Farmer; James David Wills [1964] Director/Farmer; Victoria Anne Wills [1965] Director; Victoria Helen Wills [1961] Director; William Anthony Richard Wills [1958] Director/Farmer

Wilson & Sons (Engineering) Limited
Incorporated: 12 March 1957 *Employees:* 33
Net Worth: £3,327,684 *Total Assets:* £3,782,397
Registered Office: Legacy House, Tower Road North, Warmley, Bristol, BS30 8WR
Activities: Machining
Parent: Wilson Brothers (Investments) Limited
Officers: Leon Peter Wilson, Secretary; Christopher John Wilson [1966] Director/Technical Engineer; Glenn Raymond Wilson [1947] Director/Engineer

Wilson Investment Holdings Limited
Incorporated: 3 June 1988 *Employees:* 38
Net Worth: £2,886,455 *Total Assets:* £7,789,558
Registered Office: 48 Churchfields Road, Salisbury, Wilts, SP2 7NW
Activities: Sale of new cars and light motor vehicles
Shareholders: Robert James Wilson; Stephen Robert Wilson
Officers: Jan Dibden, Secretary; Charles William Robert Wilson [1979] Sales Director; Robert James Wilson [1946] Director/Motor Dealer; Stephen Robert Wilson [1965] Director/Motor Dealer

Wilson Leisure Developments Limited
Incorporated: 17 July 2003 *Employees:* 14
Net Worth: £6,049,218 *Total Assets:* £13,115,673
Registered Office: Mullacott Park, Mullacott Cross, Ilfracombe, Devon, EX34 8NB
Activities: Other holiday and other collective accommodation
Major Shareholder: William Wilson
Officers: William Wilson [1955] Director

Wilson Leisure Limited
Incorporated: 9 May 1995 *Employees:* 38
Net Worth: £8,926,245 *Total Assets:* £11,787,524
Registered Office: Centenary House, Peninsula Park, Rydon Lane, Exeter, EX2 7XE
Activities: Other accommodation
Officers: Leslie Martin Payton Hutchings, Secretary; Patricia Ann Hardick [1948] Director/Holiday Park & Residential Mobile Home Operator; Rory Alan Hardick [1974] Director/Banker; Leslie Martin Payton Hutchings [1947] Director/Chartered Surveyor; Matilda Margot Newing [1980] Director

Wilson Tool International [Europe] Limited
Incorporated: 20 July 2006 *Employees:* 181
Net Worth: £15,422,243 *Total Assets:* £24,958,966
Registered Office: Stirling Road, South Marston Industrial Estate, Swindon, Wilts, SN3 4TQ
Activities: Manufacture of other special-purpose machinery n.e.c.
Officers: Richard Renner, Secretary/Director [American]; Colin Blackwell [1952] Director; Richard Renner [1955] Director [American]; Brian Robinson [1966] Director [American]

Wilsons Solicitors LLP
Incorporated: 4 June 2007 *Employees:* 117
Net Worth: £8,807,511 *Total Assets:* £12,230,913
Registered Office: Alexandra House, St Johns Street, Salisbury, Wilts, SP1 2SB
Officers: Jane Mercedes Lonergan [1965] Member; Frances Anne Mayne [1969] Member; Michael Edward Parker [1966] Member; Benjamin Charles Thornton [1976] Member; James Anthony Aspden [1978] LLP Member; Alison Janet Bailey [1968] LLP Member; Peter John Castleman Bourke [1967] LLP Member; Fiona Campbell-White [1971] LLP Member; Timothy John Carter Clayden [1958] LLP Member; Anthony Michael Edwards [1963] LLP Member; Adam Godwin Alexander Herbert [1971] LLP Member; Peter George Jeffreys [1966] LLP Member; James Anthony Johnson [1970] LLP Member; Dominic Hugh Neville Ogden [1961] LLP Member; Stephen Craig Kenneth Oxley [1955] LLP Member; Susan Georgina Russell [1964] LLP Member; Jonathan Mark Stephens [1955] LLP Member; Belinda Susan Revell Watson [1961] LLP Member; Charlotte Watts [1980] LLP Member; Torsten St John White [1969] LLP Member; Stephen Charles Whitmore [1956] LLP Member

Wilton Bradley Holdings Limited
Incorporated: 6 March 2015 *Employees:* 236
Net Worth: £8,159,768 *Total Assets:* £18,150,456
Registered Office: 8 Wentworth Road, Heathfield Industrial Estate, Newton Abbot, Devon, TQ12 6TL
Activities: Wholesale of household goods (other than musical instruments) n.e.c
Major Shareholder: Antony William Bradley
Officers: Leigh Karen Cheetham, Secretary; Paul Kevin Arrowsmith [1967] Sales Director; Antony William Bradley [1960] Managing Director; Leigh Karen Cheetham [1959] Financial Director

Wilton Bradley Limited
Incorporated: 6 March 2015 *Employees:* 126
Net Worth: £7,211,304 *Total Assets:* £15,251,798
Registered Office: 8 Wentworth Road, Heathfield Industrial Estate, Newton Abbot, Devon, TQ12 6TL
Activities: Wholesale of clothing and footwear
Parent: Wilton Bradley Holdings Limited
Officers: Leigh Karen Cheetham, Secretary; Paul Kevin Arrowsmith [1967] Sales Director; Antony William Bradley [1960] Managing Director; Ross Bradley [1987] Director; Leigh Karen Cheetham [1959] Financial Director; Scott Anthony Eden [1975] Director; Michael Leslie Harrison [1956] Director

E.Wiltshire & Son (Torquay) Limited
Incorporated: 1 October 1958 *Employees:* 16
Net Worth: £4,345,730 *Total Assets:* £5,073,146
Registered Office: Walls Hill Quarry, Babbacombe Road, Torquay, Devon, TQ1 3TA
Activities: Manufacture of concrete products for construction purposes
Shareholders: Andrew John Wiltshire; The Estate of Amy Florence Wiltshire deceased
Officers: Janine Joan Wiltshire, Secretary; Janet Elizabeth Ploog [1954] Director; Andrew John Wiltshire [1949] Director/Quarry Manager and Concrete Merchant; Jack Wiltshire [1983] Director/Manager; Janine Joan Wiltshire [1953] Housewife/Director; Samuel Harry Wiltshire [1986] Director/Manager

Wiltshire Air Ambulance Charitable Trust
Incorporated: 11 October 2011 *Employees:* 20
Net Worth: £9,186,260 *Total Assets:* £13,247,727
Registered Office: Operations Centre, Outmarsh, Semington, Wilts, BA14 6JX
Activities: Other human health activities
Officers: Anna Karen Cole [1970] Director/Solicitor; Michael John Fellows [1961] Managing Director; Peter James Foskett [1959] Director/Solicitor; Robert MacRae Kevan [1965] Director/Operations Manager; Christopher Roy Lear [1957] Director/Retired Inventor

Wiltshire Heavy Building Materials (Group) Limited
Incorporated: 22 March 2005 *Employees:* 118
Net Worth: £1,881,502 *Total Assets:* £8,779,430
Registered Office: Hopton Park Industrial Estate, Hopton Road, Devizes, Wilts, SN10 2EY
Activities: Non-specialised wholesale trade
Shareholders: Michael Kevin McQuaid; Tracey Jane McQuaid; Philip Brown; Jeffrey David Brown
Officers: Tracey Jane McQuaid, Secretary; Jeffrey David Brown [1966] Director; Philip Brown [1967] Director; Michael Kevin McQuaid [1964] Director; Tracey Jane McQuaid [1963] Director

Wiltshire Heavy Building Materials Limited
Incorporated: 29 April 2002 *Employees:* 118
Net Worth: £1,819,201 *Total Assets:* £8,707,249
Registered Office: Hopton Park Industrial Estate, Hopton Road, Devizes, Wilts, SN10 2EY
Activities: Manufacture of ready-mixed concrete
Parent: Wiltshire Heavy Building Materials (Group) Ltd
Officers: Tracey Jane McQuaid, Secretary/Businesswomen; Jeffrey David Brown [1966] Director/Businessman; Philip Brown [1967] Director/Businessman; Michael Kevin McQuaid [1964] Director/Businessman; Tracey Jane McQuaid [1963] Director/Businesswoman

Wiltshire Wildlife Trust Limited
Incorporated: 23 July 1962 *Employees:* 82
Net Worth: £10,844,009 *Total Assets:* £11,309,286
Registered Office: Elm Tree Court, Long Street, Devizes, Wilts, SN10 1NJ
Activities: Activities of other membership organisations n.e.c.
Officers: Louise May Hale, Secretary; Richard Edward Henry Aubrey-Fletcher [1954] Director/Retired Army Officer; Maurice Frank Avent [1943] Director/Retired; Rosemary Vivien Collingborn [1950] Director/Farmer; Michael James Hodgkins [1954] Director/Retired; Matthew Jolley [1980] Director [Australian]; Denise Natalie Plummer [1950] Director/Farmer; James Benjamin Clayson Ravine [1968] Director/Conservation Consultant; Mark Charles Street [1970] Director/Chartered Surveyor

Wimborne Academy Trust
Incorporated: 19 December 2014 *Employees:* 368
Net Worth: £20,874,400 *Total Assets:* £26,995,448
Registered Office: Allenbourn Middle School, East Borough, Wimborne, Dorset, BH21 1PL
Activities: Primary education
Officers: Ross Alexander Bowell, Secretary; Dr Emma Joanne Boger [1975] Director/Public Servant - Care Quality Commission; Rev Peter Hans Breckwoldt [1957] Director/Vicar; Sarah Jane Cooper [1971] Director/Head of HR; John Park Dickson [1941] Director; Sharon Anne Eldridge [1964] Director/Health & Weight Management Consultant; Hilary Ruth Evans [1952] Director/Education Consultant; Rachel King [1977] Director/Accountant; Peter Lance Taylor [1964] Director; Elizabeth Jane West [1970] Director/Headteacher

Wincanton Holdings Limited
Incorporated: 20 August 1987
Net Worth: £121,200,000 *Total Assets:* £672,400,000
Registered Office: Wincanton PLC, Methuen Park, Chippenham, Wilts, SN14 0WT
Activities: Activities of distribution holding companies
Parent: Wincanton UK Limited
Officers: Rajiv Sharma, Secretary; Adrian Maxwell Colman [1970] Director; Christopher Paul John Fenton [1976] Director/Logistics Professionals; Timothy Charles Lawlor [1970] Finance Director

Wincanton PLC
Incorporated: 13 March 2001
Net Worth Deficit: £112,500,000 *Total Assets:* £304,800,000
Registered Office: Wincanton PLC, Methuen Park, Chippenham, Wilts, SN14 0WT
Activities: Freight transport by road
Officers: Rajiv Sharma, Secretary; Gillian Carole Barr [1958] Director; Adrian Maxwell Colman [1970] Director; Paul David Dean [1961] Director; Timothy Charles Lawlor [1970] Finance Director; Stewart Oades [1953] Director; David John Chegwidden Radcliffe [1953] Director; Dr Martin Peter AREAD CBE [1950] Director/Chairman

Wincanton UK Limited
Incorporated: 17 March 2005
Net Worth: £1,086,000 *Total Assets:* £290,388,992
Registered Office: Methuen Park, Chippenham, Wilts, SN14 0WT
Activities: Freight transport by road
Parent: Wincanton PLC
Officers: Rajiv Sharma, Secretary; Adrian Maxwell Colman [1970] Director; Timothy Charles Lawlor [1970] Finance Director

Winchcombe Finance Limited
Incorporated: 22 April 1996
Net Worth: £36,000 *Total Assets:* £63,088,000
Registered Office: The Quadrangle, The Promenade, Cheltenham, Glos, GL50 1PX
Activities: Other business support service activities n.e.c.
Parent: Royal Bank Leasing Limited
Officers: Stephen Paul Nixon [1970] Director/Bank Official; Keith Damian Pereira [1978] Director/Bank Official

Winchcombe School
Incorporated: 15 April 2011 *Employees:* 54
Net Worth: £6,073,000 *Total Assets:* £7,247,000
Registered Office: Winchcombe School, Greet Road, Winchcombe, Cheltenham, Glos, GL54 5LB
Activities: General secondary education
Officers: Lesley Joanne Lodge, Secretary; William Brooks [1956] Director/IT; Geoffrey Charles Cove [1948] Director/Retired; Neil Hall [1960] Director/School Teacher; Iain Arthur Knight [1965] Director/School Governor; Victoria Claire Leather [1974] Director/Solicitor; Amanda Jane Peck [1970] Director/Certified Accountant; Susan Janet Proctor [1953] Director/Retired; Valerie Jane Udale [1962] Director/Member of Council; Anthony Robert Wilcock [1958] Director/Civil Servant; Dr Timothy John Winder [1959] Director/Teacher

Wind Holdings Nord Limited
Incorporated: 6 July 2007
Net Worth: £2,993,421 *Total Assets:* £26,862,432
Registered Office: Lion House, Rowcroft, Stroud, Glos, GL5 3BY
Activities: Activities of head offices
Officers: Tom Cowling, Secretary; Asif Rehmanwala [1976] Director/Chief Operating Officer; Dale Vince [1961] Director/Consultant

Wind River UK Limited
Incorporated: 28 March 1991 *Employees:* 19
Net Worth Deficit: £892,479 *Total Assets:* £5,177,952
Registered Office: Pure Offices, Kembrey Park, Swindon, Wilts, SN2 2BW
Activities: Other information technology service activities
Parent: Intel Corporation
Officers: Bryan Joseph Leblanc, Secretary; James Paul Douglas [1961] Director/Business Executive [American]; Bryan Joseph Leblanc [1966] Director/Business Executive [American]

Windmill Care Limited
Incorporated: 5 November 1998 *Employees:* 146
Net Worth: £4,572,848 *Total Assets:* £10,872,013
Registered Office: Jenna House, 15 Old Sneed Park, Sneyd Park, Bristol, BS9 1RG
Activities: Residential care activities for the elderly and disabled
Shareholders: Katharine Rachel Collacott; Leonard John Collacott
Officers: Leonard John Collacott, Secretary/Care Home Operator; Katharine Rachel Collacott [1958] Director/Care Home Operator; Leonard John Collacott [1955] Director/Care Home Operator; Robert Andrew Dawes [1945] Director/Chartered Accountant

Windward Marine Limited
Incorporated: 8 June 1971 *Employees:* 111
Net Worth: £4,057,339 *Total Assets:* £5,521,777
Registered Office: The Old Rectory, Winterbourne Bassett, Swindon, Wilts, SN4 9PU
Activities: Retail sale of newspapers and stationery in specialised stores
Shareholders: Peter Robert McLuskie; Susan Elizabeth Radford
Officers: William Booth [1971] Director/Yacht Chandler; Leigh Alexander Jacobs [1969] Director/Yacht Chandler; Pip Johnstone [1978] Director/Yacht Chandler; Peter Robert McLuskie [1956] Director/Yacht Chandler; Neil David Paramor [1972] Director/Yacht Chandler; Lawrence Andrew Parr [1981] Director; Susan Elizabeth Radford [1959] Director

Winners 2000 Fitness Limited
Incorporated: 27 October 1999 *Employees:* 14
Net Worth: £2,832,794 *Total Assets:* £4,070,733
Registered Office: 168 Teignmouth Road, Torquay, Devon, TQ1 4RY
Activities: Other business support service activities n.e.c.
Major Shareholder: Benjamin Hugh Longrigg
Officers: Simon Andrew Jeffery, Secretary; Simon Andrew Jeffery [1975] Director/Fitness Club Manager; Benjamin Hugh Hemsley Longrigg [1937] Director/Trustee

Winston Heights Ltd
Incorporated: 16 May 2014
Net Worth: £3,382,987 *Total Assets:* £4,321,578
Registered Office: 21 Church Road, Parkstone, Poole, Dorset, BH14 8UF
Activities: Activities of open-ended investment companies
Major Shareholder: Edelgard Maria Harder
Officers: Victor Ian Johnston [1952] Director; John Patrick Kane [1952] Director

Winton Primary School
Incorporated: 4 December 2015 *Employees:* 110
Net Worth: £7,126,830 *Total Assets:* £8,208,834
Registered Office: Winton Primary School, Oswald Road, Bournemouth, BH9 2TG
Activities: Primary education
Officers: Jane Elizabeth Bingham [1976] Director/Business Manager; Xiola Cochrane [1993] Director/Teacher; Paul Gaston [1960] Director/Retired; Robert James Hucklesby [1950] Director; Martin Long [1973] Director/Project Manager; Richard Scott [1966] Director/Pathologist; Neil Stuart Tarchetti [1973] Director/Teacher; Robin Paul Taylor [1970] Director/Private Banker; Helen Uren [1977] Director/NHS Worker; Timothy Watts [1949] Director/Retired Headteacher; William Gerard Wherity [1953] Director/Acupuncturist

J. Wippell & Company Limited
Incorporated: 27 September 1902 *Employees:* 77
Net Worth: £3,142,301 *Total Assets:* £3,873,590
Registered Office: 88 Buller Road, St Thomas, Exeter, EX4 1DQ
Activities: Manufacture of other wearing apparel and accessories n.e.c.
Officers: Christine Ann Morrish, Secretary; Christine Ann Morrish [1952] Director; Ester Millicent Edith Randall [1946] Director/Retired; Robin Frank Harold Richardson [1954] Director

Wirral Schools Services Limited
Incorporated: 28 November 2000 *Employees:* 3
Net Worth: £11,753,000 *Total Assets:* £76,616,000
Registered Office: Third Floor, Broad Quay House, Prince Street, Bristol, BS1 4DJ
Activities: Management of real estate on a fee or contract basis
Parent: XJ4 Holding Company Limited
Officers: Stephen Paul Hornby [1957] Director; Richard Little [1979] Investment Director; Julia Sarah McCabe [1970] Regional Director

Wishford P6 Limited
Incorporated: 13 October 2015
Net Worth: £104,257 *Total Assets:* £4,787,377
Registered Office: 25-27 High Street, Corsham, Wilts, SN13 0ES
Activities: Other letting and operating of own or leased real estate
Officers: Samuel Joseph Antrobus [1978] Director

Wishford Schools (Group) Limited
Incorporated: 24 March 2011 *Employees:* 249
Previous: Wishford Schools Limited
Net Worth: £6,394,495 *Total Assets:* £17,570,206
Registered Office: 25-27 High Street, Corsham, Wilts, SN13 0ES
Activities: Primary education
Officers: Samuel Joseph Antrobus, Secretary; Samuel Joseph Antrobus [1978] Director; Benjamin Antony Patrick Hewetson [1970] Director; Gavin Michael Rowland [1953] Director

Wiska UK Limited
Incorporated: 17 January 2000 *Employees:* 33
Net Worth: £674,636 *Total Assets:* £4,071,279
Registered Office: Lowin House, Tregolls Road, Truro, Cornwall, TR1 2NA
Activities: Wholesale of electronic and telecommunications equipment and parts
Shareholders: Tanja Andrea Hoppmann; Ronald Stefan Hoppmann
Officers: William James Rich, Secretary; Ronald Stefan Hoppmann [1971] Director/Manager [German]; Tanja Andrea Hoppmann [1968] Director/Manager [German]; William James Rich [1962] Managing Director

Witan Pacific Investment Trust PLC
Incorporated: 24 January 1907
Net Worth: £244,455,008 *Total Assets:* £246,856,000
Registered Office: Beaufort House, 51 New North Road, Exeter, EX4 4EP
Activities: Activities of investment trusts
Officers: Dermot James McMeekin [1949] Director; Susan Platts-Martin [1961] Director; Christopher Mark Ralph [1962] Director/Chief Investment Officer; Andrew Stephen Robson [1958] Director; Diane Seymour-Williams [1958] Director

Withers Fruit Farm Limited
Incorporated: 13 March 2015 *Employees:* 154
Net Worth: £3,295,798 *Total Assets:* £8,124,414
Registered Office: Staverton Court, Staverton, Cheltenham, Glos, GL51 0UX
Activities: Growing of other tree and bush fruits and nuts
Shareholders: Barbara Rita Leeds; George William Leeds
Officers: Barbara Rita Leeds [1924] Director/Farmer; George William Leeds [1958] Director/Farmer; Richard George Leeds [1987] Director

Witney Holdings Limited
Incorporated: 17 August 2015
Net Worth Deficit: £11,534 *Total Assets:* £5,329,286
Registered Office: Pillar House, 113-115 Bath Road, Cheltenham, Glos, GL53 7LS
Activities: Development of building projects
Shareholder: Theophilos Karpathios
Officers: Simon David Bullingham [1973] Director; William Victor Peter Bullingham [1943] Director; Simon George Shaw Jukes [1969] Director; Gabrielle Nora Karpathios [1968] Director [British/Australian]; Theophilos Karpathios [1963] Director

Witon Engineering Limited
Incorporated: 18 March 1993 *Employees:* 42
Net Worth: £846,813 *Total Assets:* £3,600,201
Registered Office: 2nd Floor, Stratus House, Emperor Way, Exeter Business Park, Exeter, EX1 3QS
Activities: Manufacture of wire products, chain and springs
Major Shareholder: Robert Ian Sheldon
Officers: Gemma Victoria Courtney, Secretary; Robert Ian Sheldon [1945] Director/Engineer; Rosamond Sheldon [1947] Director/Secretary

WJ South West Limited
Incorporated: 1 February 2012 *Employees:* 77
Previous: WJ Roadmarkings (SW) Limited
Net Worth: £1,780,950 *Total Assets:* £7,623,295
Registered Office: Tremayne House, Westpark, Chelston, Wellington, Somerset, TA21 9AD
Activities: Other specialised construction activities n.e.c.
Parent: WJ (Group) Limited
Officers: Nigel Bayley, Secretary; Wayne Douglas Johnston [1967] Director; Terry John Trevelyan [1967] Director; Martin Webb [1967] Director

WK Crematoria Limited
Incorporated: 17 September 2010 *Employees:* 2
Net Worth: £482,501 *Total Assets:* £22,253,802
Registered Office: Chapel View, Westerleigh Road, Westerleigh, Bristol, BS37 8QP
Activities: Activities of other holding companies n.e.c.
Parent: Westerleigh Group Holdings Ltd
Officers: Dafydd Rhys John, Secretary; Dafydd Rhys John [1974] Director/Chartered Accountant; Ian David McArdle [1966] Director/Chartered Surveyor

WMG Group Ltd
Incorporated: 2 March 2016
Net Worth: £950 *Total Assets:* £4,000,850
Registered Office: 4 St Albans Road, Gloucester, GL2 5FW
Activities: Manufacture of loaded electronic boards
Officers: Donna Clare Thurlow, Secretary; Emma Louise Crawford [1982] Financial Director; Stephen John Griffin [1965] Managing Director; Manuele Mazzucato [1939] Director/Entrepreneur [Italian]; Stephen Francis Whitelaw [1957] Director

WMG Property Limited
Incorporated: 1 May 2014 *Employees:* 130
Net Worth: £4,957,767 *Total Assets:* £17,700,254
Registered Office: Taunton Vale House, Summerfield Way, Chelston Business Park, Wellington, Somerset, TA21 9JE
Activities: Other letting and operating of own or leased real estate
Major Shareholder: Michael John Finn
Officers: Michael John Finn [1960] Director; Matthew Charles Holcombe [1979] Director

Wodskou Properties Limited
Incorporated: 5 November 2009
Net Worth: £1,479,599 *Total Assets:* £6,069,767
Registered Office: Kelsall Steele Ltd, Unit A Woodlands Court, Truro Business Park, Truro, Cornwall, TR4 9NH
Activities: Other letting and operating of own or leased real estate
Major Shareholder: Michael Wodskou
Officers: Michael Wodskou [1967] Director [Danish]; Sharon Louise Wodskou [1979] Director

Wolf Rock (Cornwall) Limited
Incorporated: 26 October 2015
Net Worth Deficit: £718,231 *Total Assets:* £4,989,915
Registered Office: Old County Hall, Station Road, Truro, Cornwall, TR1 3EX
Activities: Hotels and similar accommodation
Shareholders: Andreas Read; Carl Edward Jansen
Officers: Carl Edward Jansen [1967] Director [Norwegian]; Raila Nonas Langhelle [1970] Director [Norwegian]; Andreas Read [1966] Director; Elisabeth Vardoey [1969] Director/Teacher [Norwegian]

Wollen Michelmore LLP
Incorporated: 17 November 2011 *Employees:* 135
Net Worth: £2,764,500 *Total Assets:* £4,060,297
Registered Office: Carlton House, 30 The Terrace, Torquay, Devon, TQ1 1BS
Officers: Deborah Baker [1961] Member; Maurice Clarke [1956] Member; David Kenneth Eastman [1981] Member; Christopher Duncan Hart [1963] Member; Gillian Margaret Lindqvist Jones [1955] Member; Charlotte Leonie McGregor [1982] Member; Rebecca Jane Procter [1970] Member; Mark Simon Roome [1975] Member; Shirley Joy Tull [1952] Member; Katrina Vollentine [1972] Member; Simon Alan Bean [1972] LLP Member; Amanda Bonnick [1989] LLP Member; Rachel Jane Carter [1984] LLP Member; Jonathan Dunkley [1971] LLP Member; Penelope Joy Glaister [1980] LLP Member; Marinella Hollies [1958] LLP Member; Alexandra Charlotte Jenkins [1978] LLP Member; David Kendall [1965] LLP Member; Christopher Martyn Linton [1984] LLP Member; Judith Manser [1962] LLP Member; Richard Mark Phillips [1961] LLP Member; Simon James Ross Wilson [1955] LLP Member

Wolverhampton City and Walsall Lift Accommodation Services Limited
Incorporated: 19 February 2004
Net Worth Deficit: £2,028,000 *Total Assets:* £12,057,000
Registered Office: Challenge House, International Drive, Tewkesbury Business Park, Tewkesbury, Glos, GL20 8UQ
Activities: Other letting and operating of own or leased real estate
Parent: Wolverhampton & Walsall Holdco Limited
Officers: Daniel Peter Bevan, Secretary; Paul Simon Andrews [1970] Investment Director; Richard Darch [1961] Director; Mark William Grinonneau [1970] Director; Matthew Graham Hartland [1971] Finance Director; Neil Rae [1971] Director

Wolverhampton Radiology Limited
Incorporated: 18 June 2001
Previous: Impregilo Wolverhampton Limited
Net Worth Deficit: £1,475,000 *Total Assets:* £24,508,000
Registered Office: Third Floor, Broad Quay House, Prince Street, Bristol, BS1 4DJ
Activities: Development of building projects
Shareholders: Semperian (Wolverhampton) Limited; Semperian (Wolverhampton) Ltd
Officers: Richard Little [1979] Director/Business & Financial Analyst; Alan Campbell Ritchie [1967] Director

Wood Barton Developments Limited
Incorporated: 20 July 2004 *Employees:* 2
Net Worth: £1,382,332 *Total Assets:* £4,271,659
Registered Office: 7 Shindle Park, Chillington, Kingsbridge, Devon, TQ7 2JE
Activities: Buying and selling of own real estate
Officers: Jacqueline Buckle, Secretary/Property Developer; Jacqueline Buckle [1962] Director/Property Developer; Steven Buckle [1957] Director/Property Developer; Robert Lynton Howells [1950] Director; Thelma Eileen Howells [1949] Director/Housewife

Wood Energy Limited
Incorporated: 14 August 2001
Net Worth: £514,985 *Total Assets:* £6,559,130
Registered Office: Energy House, Milbury Heath, Buckover, Wotton under Edge, Glos, GL12 8QH
Activities: Repair of other equipment
Parent: Strong Energy Solutions Ltd
Officers: Fergal Murtagh, Secretary; Tim McLeman [1964] Director; Fergal Murtagh [1974] Director [Irish]; Jeffrey Tomlinson [1965] Director

Wood Veterinary Group Limited
Incorporated: 23 May 2014 *Employees:* 4
Net Worth: £1,927,619 *Total Assets:* £4,394,246
Registered Office: 125 Bristol Road, Quedgeley, Gloucester, GL2 4ND
Activities: Veterinary activities
Officers: Jason Norbury Burgess [1968] Director/Veterinary Surgeon; Paul Cunliffe [1968] Director/Veterinary Surgeon; Graham Lethbridge Stephens [1963] Director/Veterinary Surgeon; Alastair James Sinclair Williams [1977] Director/Veterinary Surgeon

Wooda Farm Park Limited
Incorporated: 19 November 1962 *Employees:* 25
Net Worth: £4,270,645 *Total Assets:* £4,974,006
Registered Office: Wooda Farm Park, Poughill, Bude, Cornwall, EX23 9HJ
Activities: Recreational vehicle parks, trailer parks and camping grounds
Shareholders: Graeme Kenneth Colwill; Kerry Colwill
Officers: Graeme Kenneth Colwill [1962] Director; Kerry Colwill [1963] Director; Charlotte Veale [1988] Director

Woodbury Limited
Incorporated: 25 March 2015 *Employees:* 3
Net Worth: £116,919,272 *Total Assets:* £116,942,192
Registered Office: 1 Mill Steps, Winterbourne Down, Bristol, BS36 1BT
Activities: Activities of head offices
Major Shareholder: Bryan Glastonbury
Officers: Ben Glastonbury [1987] Director/IT; Bryan Glastonbury [1953] Director; James Glastonbury [1990] Director/Electrical Engineer

Woodchester Enterprises Limited
Incorporated: 4 March 1999 *Employees:* 38
Net Worth: £5,672,775 *Total Assets:* £16,070,285
Registered Office: Manderson House, 5230 Valiant Court, Delta Way, Gloucester Business Park, Brockworth, Gloucester, GL3 4FE
Activities: Manufacture of soft drinks; production of mineral waters and other bottled waters
Parent: Bottlegreen Holdings Limited
Officers: Arthur Richmond, Secretary; Elaine Birchall [1966] Director [Irish]; Arthur William Richmond [1966] Director/Accountant; Karen Salters [1970] Director

Woodcrescent Properties Limited
Incorporated: 18 March 1991
Previous: Construction & Real Estate Properties Ltd
Net Worth: £2,234,650 *Total Assets:* £5,751,541
Registered Office: C V Ross & Co Limited, Unit 1, Office 1, Tower Lane Business Park, Tower Lane, Warmley, Bristol, BS30 8XT
Activities: Buying and selling of own real estate
Shareholders: Alexander Harry Mark Horton; James Anthony Horton
Officers: Alexander Harry Mark Horton [1993] Director; James Anthony Horton [1987] Director

Woodfield Developments Limited
Incorporated: 13 November 1987 *Employees:* 3
Net Worth: £972,762 *Total Assets:* £4,232,571
Registered Office: Ruardean Works, Varnister Road, Drybrook, Glos, GL17 9BH
Activities: Other letting and operating of own or leased real estate
Parent: M F Freeman Investments Limited
Officers: Jennifer Mary Freeman [1947] Director; Luke Francis Freeman [1974] Director/Construction Manager; Mervyn Francis Freeman [1945] Director; Steven King [1970] Director/Chartered Accountant; Peter Wharton [1963] Director/Chartered Accountant

Woodford Patient Capital Trust PLC
Incorporated: 26 January 2015
Net Worth: £755,294,976 *Total Assets:* £905,288,000
Registered Office: Beaufort House, 51 New North Road, Exeter, Devon, EX4 4EP
Activities: Activities of investment trusts
Officers: Scott Selby Durrand Brown [1963] Director; Carolan Dobson [1954] Director; Steven Charles Andrew Harris [1966] Director; Alan Charles Hodson [1962] Director; Dame Pamela Louise Makin [1960] Director; Susan Jane Searle [1963] Director

Woodland Barton Renewables Limited
Incorporated: 4 November 2013
Net Worth: £11,409,406 *Total Assets:* £16,670,861
Registered Office: Hendra Holiday Park, Lane, Newquay, Cornwall, TR8 4NY
Activities: Production of electricity
Parent: Zephyrus Cornwall Ltd
Officers: Robert May, Secretary; William Mark Dexter [1970] Director/Chartered Accountant; Janine Hyatt [1955] Director; Jonathan Donald Hyatt [1984] Director; Robert Kevin Hyatt [1955] Director [Canadian]; Rebecca Jane May [1967] Director; Robert May [1963] Director

Woodland Barton Wind LLP
Incorporated: 9 May 2013
Net Worth: £12,000,000 *Total Assets:* £12,000,000
Registered Office: Hendra Holiday Park, Newquay, Cornwall, TR8 4NY
Officers: Robert Kevin Hyatt [1955] Member; Robert May [1963] Member

Woodlands Group of Churches
Incorporated: 18 April 2008 *Employees:* 40
Net Worth: £6,465,603 *Total Assets:* £6,484,598
Registered Office: Woodlands Christian Centre, Belgrave Road, Clifton, Bristol, BS8 2AA
Activities: Activities of religious organisations
Officers: Bradley Lee Askew, Secretary; Bradley Lee Askew [1977] Director; Timothy John Dobson [1962] Director/Minister; Louise Hughes [1975] Director/Doctor; Edward James Marsh [1977] Director/Accountant; David John Mitchell [1958] Director/Minister of Religion; Rev Robert Lawrence Scott-Cook [1946] Director/Minister of Religion

A D Woodley Holdings Limited
Incorporated: 28 April 2000 *Employees:* 4
Net Worth: £11,664,261 *Total Assets:* £11,738,977
Registered Office: Northfields Farm, Stretton-on-Fosse, Moreton in The Marsh, Glos, GL56 9RE
Activities: Activities of other holding companies n.e.c.
Officers: Janet Woodley, Secretary; Anne May Hodgson [1948] Director; Mary Rita Wear [1948] Director; Alan Dwight Woodley [1933] Director; John Cyril Woodley [1944] Director

Woodley Hotels Limited
Incorporated: 10 November 1982
Net Worth: £7,927,022 *Total Assets:* £7,935,222
Registered Office: c/o Francis Clark LLP, North Quay House, Sutton Harbour, Plymouth, PL4 0RA
Activities: Hotels and similar accommodation
Parent: Dhrona Holdings Limited
Officers: Girishkumar Devchand Dhrona, Secretary; Girishkumar Devchand Dhrona [1946] Director/Businessman; Vasantlal Devchand Jhina Dhrona [1943] Director/Businessman

Woodlodge Holdings Limited
Incorporated: 12 March 2016 *Employees:* 97
Net Worth: £5,946,096 *Total Assets:* £17,324,664
Registered Office: Unit 3 Babdown Airfield, Tetbury, Glos, GL8 8YL
Activities: Activities of head offices
Major Shareholder: Michael Kenneth Wooldridge
Officers: Michael Kenneth Wooldridge [1988] Director

Woodlodge Products Limited
Incorporated: 5 December 1997 *Employees:* 97
Net Worth: £10,673,202 *Total Assets:* £18,171,840
Registered Office: Unit 3 Babdown Airfield, Tetbury, Glos, GL8 8YL
Activities: Non-specialised wholesale trade
Officers: Geoffrey Paul Wooldridge, Secretary; Geoffrey Paul Wooldridge [1954] Director/Wholesaler; Michael Kenneth Wooldridge [1988] Director/Chartered Accountant

Woodmace Concrete Structures Limited
Incorporated: 18 July 2014 *Employees:* 13
Net Worth: £560,280 *Total Assets:* £3,527,545
Registered Office: 3 Durrant Road, Bournemouth, BH2 6NE
Activities: Construction of other civil engineering projects n.e.c.
Shareholders: Branksome Park Holdings Ltd; Branksome Park Holdings Limited
Officers: Tracey Catherine Fisher, Secretary; Nigel Graeme Cooper [1960] Operations Director; Russell Lewis Crate [1975] Director; John Oak [1953] Director

Woodmace Limited
Incorporated: 14 February 1986 *Employees:* 93
Net Worth: £2,790,845 *Total Assets:* £9,202,693
Registered Office: 3 Durrant Road, Bournemouth, BH2 6NE
Activities: Construction of other civil engineering projects n.e.c.
Major Shareholder: John Oak
Officers: Tracey Catherine Fisher, Secretary; Nigel Graeme Cooper [1960] Director; Russell Lewis Crate [1975] Director; Tracey Catherine Fisher [1972] Group Financial Director; John Oak [1953] Director/Civil Engineer

Woodpecker Properties Limited
Incorporated: 23 June 1993 *Employees:* 1
Net Worth: £912,951 *Total Assets:* £3,819,114
Registered Office: Leanne House, 6 Avon Close, Weymouth, Dorset, DT4 9UX
Activities: Construction of other civil engineering projects n.e.c.
Major Shareholder: Derek James Newell
Officers: Derek James Newell, Secretary/Property Developer; Derek James Newell [1944] Director/Property Developer; Judith Newell [1944] Director/Company Secretary

Woods (Dorchester) Limited
Incorporated: 21 April 1942 *Employees:* 41
Net Worth: £2,953,074 *Total Assets:* £3,708,437
Registered Office: Unity Chambers, 34 High East Street, Dorchester, DT1 1HA
Activities: Retail of furniture, lighting, and similar (not musical instruments or scores) in specialised store
Shareholder: Thomas Michael Chapman
Officers: Rupert John Aldington Edwards, Secretary; Nigel Beresford Eares Beale [1943] Director; Rupert John Aldington Edwards [1948] Director/Chartered Accountant; William Robert Aldington Edwards [1976] Director/Chartered Surveyor; Hamish Ramsay McGhee [1967] Managing Director

Woods Consolidated Limited
Incorporated: 9 December 2013 *Employees:* 263
Net Worth: £1,107,711 *Total Assets:* £11,010,817
Registered Office: Unit 2 Bumpers Way, Bumpers Farm, Chippenham, Wilts, SN14 6NG
Activities: Activities of head offices
Officers: Nicholas Paul Baker [1963] Director; Barry John Dix [1971] Director; John William Lowndes [1954] Director; Ian Paul Scarr [1966] Director

The Woods Group Limited
Incorporated: 11 November 1998 *Employees:* 108
Net Worth: £4,316,560 *Total Assets:* £5,563,612
Registered Office: Bumpers Way, Bumpers Farm Industrial Estate, Chippenham, Wilts, SN14 6NG
Activities: Other business support service activities n.e.c.
Officers: Barry John Dix, Secretary; Nicholas Paul Baker [1963] Director; Barry John Dix [1971] Financial Director; John William Lowndes [1954] Director; Ian Paul Scarr [1966] Director

Woodstock Estates Limited
Incorporated: 28 December 1931
Net Worth: £4,750,723 *Total Assets:* £4,828,765
Registered Office: Warmwell House, Warmwell, Dorchester, DT2 8HQ
Activities: Development of building projects
Shareholder: Trustees of The Ross Skinner Sambrooke Trust
Officers: Simon Francis Crawley Ross Skinner, Secretary; Paul Stuart Crawley Ross Skinner [1960] Director; Sambrooke Anthony Crawley Ross Skinner [1958] Director; Simon Francis Crawley Ross Skinner [1963] Director; Venetia Caroline Ross Skinner [1936] Director

Woodstock Leabank Office Furniture Limited
Incorporated: 12 October 1993 *Employees:* 47
Net Worth: £1,382,678 *Total Assets:* £3,720,367
Registered Office: Britannic House, 51 North Hill, Plymouth, PL4 8HZ
Activities: Wholesale of office furniture
Parent: WW (UK) Limited T/A TC Group
Officers: Christopher Facey [1973] Director; Joseph Omalley [1963] Managing Director; Daniel Anthony Wooler [1968] Director

Woodward & Co (Environmental) Limited
Incorporated: 11 May 2004 *Employees:* 21
Net Worth: £2,636,096 *Total Assets:* £5,087,912
Registered Office: Unit C1, The Courtyard, Tewkesbury Business Park, Tewkesbury, Glos, GL20 8GD
Activities: Plumbing, heat and air-conditioning installation
Parent: Woodward & Co (Holdings) Limited
Officers: Andrew James Dunning [1974] Director/Building Services Engineer; Nicholas Edward Greenland [1973] Director/Building Services Engineer; Leigh John Sampson [1972] Director/Building Services Engineer

Woodward & Co (Holdings) Limited
Incorporated: 16 February 2015 *Employees:* 3
Net Worth: £3,534,811 *Total Assets:* £4,313,724
Registered Office: Unit C1, The Courtyard, Tewkesbury Business Park, Tewkesbury, Glos, GL20 8GD
Activities: Activities of other holding companies n.e.c.
Shareholders: Andrew James Dunning; Nicholas Edward Greenland; Leigh John Sampson
Officers: Andrew James Dunning [1974] Director/Building Services Engineer; Nicholas Edward Greenland [1973] Director/Building Services Engineer; Leigh John Sampson [1972] Director/Building Services Engineer

Wookey Hole Limited
Incorporated: 9 June 2003 *Employees:* 108
Net Worth: £4,030,052 *Total Assets:* £10,875,809
Registered Office: One New Street, Wells, Somerset, BA5 2LA
Activities: Other amusement and recreation activities n.e.c.
Major Shareholder: Gerald Ward Cottle
Officers: Daniel John Medley [1973] Director

Wool & Bovington Motors Limited
Incorporated: 16 November 1960 *Employees:* 66
Net Worth: £1,755,639 *Total Assets:* £3,679,343
Registered Office: Dorchester Road, Wool, Dorset, BH20 6EH
Activities: Sale of new cars and light motor vehicles
Shareholders: Nicholas Robert Mitchell Pyne; Timothy Clive Pyne
Officers: Simon Francis Pyne [1960] Director/Manager; Timothy Clive Pyne [1956] Director/Sales Manager

Woolacombe Bay Holiday Village Limited
Incorporated: 9 October 1984 *Employees:* 160
Net Worth: £16,012,523 *Total Assets:* £31,284,322
Registered Office: c/o Glover Stanbury, 30 Bear Street, Barnstaple, Devon, EX32 7DD
Activities: Holiday centres and villages
Parent: Lancaster Leisure Limited
Officers: Lisa Marie Todd, Secretary; Rosemary Janet Lancaster [1934] Director/Hotelier; Roy Maxwell Lancaster [1932] Director/Hotelier; Rudi John Roy Lancaster [1964] Director/Hotelier; Sally Eileen Lancaster [1966] Director

A.J. Wooldridge Limited
Incorporated: 4 April 1973 *Employees:* 1
Net Worth: £4,523,059 *Total Assets:* £5,761,444
Registered Office: 22 Union Street, Newton Abbot, Devon, TQ12 2JS
Activities: Growing of cereals (except rice), leguminous crops and oil seeds
Officers: Joanne Louise Wooldridge, Secretary; Michael Richard Geoffrey Wooldridge [1968] Director/Chartered Surveyor

A. & J. Woolf Properties Limited
Incorporated: 24 November 1964 *Employees:* 1
Net Worth: £3,864,286 *Total Assets:* £4,125,762
Registered Office: 20 Newerne Street, Lydney, Glos, GL15 5RA
Activities: Development of building projects
Shareholder: Renee Cerf
Officers: Renee Cerf, Secretary/Director; Katy Bonnor [1964] Customer Service Director; Renee Cerf [1964] Director

Worcester Properties Ltd
Incorporated: 3 September 2015
Net Worth: £2,609,549 *Total Assets:* £5,525,149
Registered Office: Moorgate House, King Street, Newton Abbot, Devon, TQ12 2LG
Activities: Other letting and operating of own or leased real estate
Shareholders: Jamie Andrew Barnett; Nicola Jane Cadwallader
Officers: Jamie Andrew Barnett [1974] Director/Private Landlord; Nicola Jane Cadwallader [1969] Director/Private Landlord

The Workforce Development Trust Limited
Incorporated: 3 August 2010 *Employees:* 299
Previous: Skills for Health Limited
Net Worth: £11,007,221 *Total Assets:* £16,430,680
Registered Office: 1 Temple Way, Bristol, BS2 0BY
Activities: Other education n.e.c.
Officers: Adam James Causon, Secretary; Robert Abberley [1952] Director/Trade Union Official; Robert Calderwood [1953] Director/NHS Chief Executive; Adam James Causon [1980] Executive Director; Generald Robert Howe Davies [1956] Director/Adviser; Dr Kathleen Janet Fallon [1954] Director/Chief Executive Officer - NHS; Julian Matthew Frederick Hartley [1967] Director/Chief Executive; Rory Cassian Love [1959] Director/Freelance Development and Training Consultant; Iain Fraser MacDonald [1957] Director/Chief Executive; Jeremy Steven Newman [1959] Director/Chartered Accountant; John Rogers [1961] Director/Chief Executive; Candace Pernille West [1957] Director; Allison Jane Williams [1965] Director/NHS Chief Executive; David Leonard Wood [1956] Director

Workman Properties Limited
Incorporated: 11 June 2013 *Employees:* 378
Net Worth: £9,731,749 *Total Assets:* £19,454,496
Registered Office: Unit 22 Dairy Way, Northway Lane, Tewkesbury, Glos, GL20 8JE
Activities: Activities of head offices
Shareholders: Roger Hewins Workman; George William Workman
Officers: Louise Emma Woodward, Secretary; Wendy King [1957] Director/Accountant; Louise Emma Woodward [1969] Director and Company Secretary; George William Workman [1971] Managing Director; Gillian Marguerite Workman [1946] Director; Roger Hewins Workman [1945] Chairman/Director

World Group Holdings Limited
Incorporated: 2 August 2012
Previous: World Group LLC UK Limited
Net Worth: £3,892,247 *Total Assets:* £6,256,319
Registered Office: Queen Victoria House, 18 Royal Crescent, Cheltenham, Glos, GL50 3DA
Activities: Real estate agencies
Parent: Richard William and Anne Frances Turner
Officers: Ian Anthony Marsh, Secretary; Anne Frances Turner [1967] Director [Australian]; Richard William Turner [1968] Professional Director [Australian]

World Snooker Limited
Incorporated: 14 December 2000 *Employees:* 23
Net Worth: £4,259,949 *Total Assets:* £8,472,727
Registered Office: 75 Whiteladies Road, Clifton, Bristol, BS8 2NT
Activities: Other sports activities
Parent: World Snooker Holding Limited
Officers: Simon Paul Brownell, Secretary; Simon Paul Brownell [1985] Director/Accountant; Stephen James Dawson [1959] Director; Jason Elliott Ferguson [1969] Director; Barry Maurice William Hearn [1948] Director; Edward John Hearn [1979] Director; Nigel Terrance Oldfield [1962] Director/Self Employed; Brandon Vernon Parker [1963] Director; Miles Pearce [1970] Commercial Director [British/Canadian]

Worlds Apart Holdings Limited
Incorporated: 28 October 2010 *Employees:* 69
Net Worth: £722,826 *Total Assets:* £10,622,899
Registered Office: Unit 3 Hurling Way, St Columb Major Business Park, St Columb Major, Cornwall, TR9 6SX
Activities: Manufacture of other games and toys, n.e.c.
Parent: MTHUK Ltd
Officers: Brian Craig Lawton, Secretary; Andrew Collinson Cooper [1965] Director; Brian Craig Lawton [1978] Finance Director; Neil Trevor Shinner [1964] Director; Paul Adam Solomon [1976] Director [Australian]; Menasche Stul [1949] Director [Australian]; Jacqueline Hazel Tobias [1953] Director [Australian]

Worlds Apart Limited
Incorporated: 30 December 1981 *Employees:* 69
Net Worth: £489,578 *Total Assets:* £10,389,651
Registered Office: Unit 3 Hurling Way, St Columb Major Business Park, St Columb Major, Cornwall, TR9 6SX
Activities: Manufacture of other games and toys, n.e.c.
Parent: Worlds Apart Holdings Ltd
Officers: Brian Craig Lawton, Secretary; Andrew Collinson Cooper [1965] Director/British Marketing; Brian Craig Lawton [1978] Finance Director; Neil Trevor Shinner [1964] Director/Manufacturer; Paul Adam Solomon [1976] Director [Australian]; Menasche Stul [1949] Director [Australian]; Jacqueline Hazel Tobias [1953] Director [Australian]

Worldteam Limited
Incorporated: 7 January 2008 *Employees:* 28
Net Worth: £6,131,064 *Total Assets:* £15,230,361
Registered Office: Coast View, Torquay Road, Shaldon, Teignmouth, Devon, TQ14 0BG
Activities: Other holiday and other collective accommodation
Officers: Ben Donald [1973] Director/Teacher; Gillian Mimi Donald [1938] Director; Joshua Angus Kingsley Donald [1971] Director/Project Manager; Robert Kingsley Donald [1936] Director [Australian]

Worldwide Dive and Sail International Limited
Incorporated: 27 March 2007 *Employees:* 2
Net Worth: £118,003 *Total Assets:* £3,722,719
Registered Office: 30 Gay Street, Bath, BA1 2PA
Activities: Travel agency activities
Parent: Vision Wealth Limited
Officers: Natalie Ward, Secretary; Frank Van Der Linde [1971] Director [Dutch]; Michael Mark Shandur [1975] Director

WP Industrial Limited
Incorporated: 11 April 2012 *Employees:* 27
Net Worth: £1,590,149 *Total Assets:* £4,262,250
Registered Office: WP Industrial Ltd, Watercombe Park, Yeovil, Somerset, BA20 2HL
Activities: Wholesale of other intermediate products
Officers: Roger Barter, Secretary; Bridget Ruth Barter [1949] Director; Douglas Barter [1977] Sales Director; Kenneth Paul Barter [1941] Director; Mark Barter [1971] Director; Naomi Barter [1974] Director; Pricilla Ruth Barter [1974] Director; Roger Barter [1973] Director; Shawna Joyce Barter [1981] Director

WPC Software Limited
Incorporated: 16 February 1998 *Employees:* 30
Net Worth: £2,146,653 *Total Assets:* £3,656,751
Registered Office: Apex House, Kingsfield Lane, Longwell Green, Bristol, BS30 6DL
Activities: Other information technology service activities
Shareholders: Alan Walker; Elizabeth Jill Walker
Officers: William John Wakefield Walker, Secretary; Glenn Arthur Bewes [1982] Managing Director; Alan Stephen Plummer [1976] Technical Director; Alan Walker [1950] Director; Elizabeth Jill Walker [1951] Director

WPD Distribution Network Holdings Limited
Incorporated: 23 January 2014
Net Worth: £3,708,499,968 *Total Assets:* £4,563,400,192
Registered Office: Avonbank, Feeder Road, Bristol, BS2 0TB
Activities: Activities of head offices
Shareholders: WPD Investment Holdings Limited; PPL WEM Limited
Officers: Sally Ann Jones, Secretary; Graham Roy Halladay [1966] Operations Director; Alison Jane Sleightholm [1963] Resources and External Affairs Director; Philip Swift [1967] Operations Director; Alexander James Torok [1958] Director/Assistant Treasurer [American]; Ian Robert Williams [1970] Resources and External Affairs Director

WPD Investment Holdings Limited
Incorporated: 2 October 2017
Net Worth: £2,086,499,968 *Total Assets:* £2,086,499,968
Registered Office: Avonbank, Feeder Road, Bristol, BS2 0TB
Activities: Activities of other holding companies n.e.c.
Parent: Western Power Distribution PLC
Officers: Sally Ann Jones, Secretary; Alexander James Torok [1958] Director/Tax & Vice President [American]; Ian Robert Williams [1970] Finance Director

WPD Property Investments Limited
Incorporated: 18 April 1989 *Employees:* 4
Net Worth: £44,334,000 *Total Assets:* £49,039,000
Registered Office: Avonbank, Feeder Road, Bristol, BS2 0TB
Activities: Buying and selling of own real estate
Parent: WPD Distribution Network Holdings Limited
Officers: Sally Ann Jones, Secretary; Ian Robert Williams [1970] Finance Director; David Astley Withers [1958] Director/Chartered Surveyor

WPD Smart Metering Limited
Incorporated: 28 January 2010 *Employees:* 44
Net Worth: £9,310,000 *Total Assets:* £12,441,000
Registered Office: Avonbank, Feeder Road, Bristol, BS2 0TB
Activities: Other business support service activities n.e.c.
Parent: WPD Distribution Network Holdings Limited
Officers: Sally Ann Jones, Secretary; Graham Roy Halladay [1966] Operations Director; Ian Robert Williams [1970] Finance Director

WPD Telecoms Limited
Incorporated: 18 May 1989 *Employees:* 87
Previous: Surf Telecoms Limited
Net Worth: £30,163,000 *Total Assets:* £39,076,000
Registered Office: Avonbank, Feeder Road, Bristol, BS2 0TB
Activities: Wired telecommunications activities
Parent: WPD Distribution Network Holdings Limited
Officers: Sally Ann Jones, Secretary; Graham Roy Halladay [1966] Operations Director; Ian Robert Williams [1970] Finance Director

Wrafton Laboratories Limited
Incorporated: 16 August 1991 *Employees:* 500
Net Worth: £17,128,000 *Total Assets:* £45,168,000
Registered Office: Wrafton, Braunton, Devon, EX33 2DL
Activities: Manufacture of basic pharmaceutical products
Parent: Perrigo UK Acquisition Limited
Officers: Annette Corcoran, Secretary; Neil Thomas Lister [1975] Director; Dominic James Rivers [1977] Director; Christopher Allan Rudd [1980] Director

The Ted Wragg Multi Academy Trust
Incorporated: 28 May 2013 *Employees:* 393
Net Worth: £17,665,484 *Total Assets:* £24,324,076
Registered Office: Cranbrook Education Campus, Tillhouse Road, Cranbrook, Exeter, EX5 7EE
Activities: Pre-primary education
Officers: Alison Jean Layton-Hill, Secretary; Philip Bostock [1950] Director; Robert Bosworth [1975] Director/Education Management; Rosie Clare Denham [1987] Director/Account Manager; Linda Donnellan [1956] Director/Retired Lawyer; Professor David Hall [1960] Director/Education Researcher; Elaine Hobson [1957] Director; Richard James Jacobs [1944] Director; Moira Marder [1970] Director/Executive Headteacher; Dr. Rebecca Holly Mitchell [1981] Director/University Officer; Andrew Robert Mulcock [1963] Director/Church Leader; Sarah Louise O'Meara [1975] Director/Primary Teacher; Saxon May Spence [1929] Director/Retired; Alexander Peter Walmsley [1951] Director

Wrapex Limited
Incorporated: 20 October 1994 *Employees:* 32
Net Worth: £2,510,016 *Total Assets:* £4,960,927
Registered Office: Unit 6 Lodge Causeway Trading Estate, Lodge Causeway, Fishponds, Bristol, BS16 3JB
Activities: Manufacture of other plastic products
Parent: Prowrap Ltd
Officers: Nicholas Jeremy Scoon [1965] Director

WRC P.L.C.
Incorporated: 25 May 1988 *Employees:* 148
Net Worth Deficit: £39,815,000 *Total Assets:* £19,495,000
Registered Office: Frankland Road, Blagrove, Swindon, Wilts, SN5 8YF
Activities: Other engineering activities
Officers: Jayne Elizabeth Matwiejczyk, Secretary; Martin Frederick Bradbury [1955] Director; Ronald Eric Chapman [1958] Director; Sonia Margaret Home [1977] Director/Chief Executive; Mark William Smith [1967] Director [Irish]

J D Wright & Son Ltd
Incorporated: 9 April 2009 *Employees:* 5
Net Worth: £1,125,925 *Total Assets:* £3,809,141
Registered Office: Wessex House, Challeymead Business Park, Melksham, Wilts, SN12 8BU
Activities: Raising of dairy cattle
Shareholders: Alastair Wright; Josephine Wright
Officers: Jo Wright, Secretary; Alastair Wright [1953] Director/Farmer; James Wright [1986] Director; Jo Wright [1954] Director/Farmer

The Wrigley Company Limited
Incorporated: 21 December 1925 *Employees:* 502
Net Worth: £184,048,992 *Total Assets:* £311,335,008
Registered Office: Estover, Plymouth, PL6 7PR
Activities: Manufacture of other food products n.e.c.
Parent: Wrigley Uno UK Limited
Officers: Kevin Douglas Fox [1980] Supply Chain Director; David Arnaud Manzini [1972] Director [French]; Colin James Wright Moss [1979] Director; Johanna Maria Sprotte [1968] Director [German]; Mayela Del Rosario Stuparitz [1971] Director [American]

Wrigley Uno UK Limited
Incorporated: 31 July 2008
Net Worth: £608,644,992 *Total Assets:* £608,644,992
Registered Office: Estover, Plymouth, PL6 7PR
Activities: Manufacture of other food products n.e.c.
Officers: David Arnaud Manzini [1972] Director [French]; Colin James Wright Moss [1979] Director; Johanna Maria Sprotte [1968] Director [German]; Mayela Del Rosario Stuparitz [1971] Director [American]

Wring Group Limited
Incorporated: 21 December 1999 *Employees:* 70
Net Worth: £6,657,807 *Total Assets:* £11,607,626
Registered Office: Vale Lane, Bedminster, Bristol, BS3 5RU
Activities: Construction of other civil engineering projects n.e.c.
Parent: J E Wring Discretionary Trust
Officers: John Matthew Wring, Secretary/Director/Contractor; Dean Stuart Wring [1970] Operations Director; John Matthew Wring [1965] Director/Contractor

Wrings Transport Limited
Incorporated: 21 August 1995 *Employees:* 82
Net Worth: £2,720,859 *Total Assets:* £6,441,636
Registered Office: Freshford House, Redcliffe Way, Bristol, BS1 6NL
Activities: Freight transport by road
Major Shareholder: Stuart Brandon Wring
Officers: Royston David Wring [1943] Director; Stuart Brandon Wring [1971] Director

WRK Merger Holding Sub Limited
Incorporated: 12 January 2017
Net Worth: £736,784,640 *Total Assets:* £1,677,446,016
Registered Office: 500 Woodward Avenue, Yate, Bristol, BS37 5YS
Activities: Packaging activities
Officers: Kevin Alden Maxwell [1975] Director [American]

WSP Textiles Limited
Incorporated: 2 September 2011 *Employees:* 123
Net Worth: £9,990,000 *Total Assets:* £12,730,000
Registered Office: Lodgemore Mills, Stroud, Glos, GL5 3EJ
Activities: Manufacture of other textiles n.e.c.
Parent: Ludus Capital Limited
Officers: Ewen Maitland Hamilton, Secretary; Curt Bossuyt [1959] Director [Belgian]; Ewen Maitland Hamilton [1965] Finance Director; Duncan Kettell [1965] Director; Alan Phillips [1951] Director [Belgian]; Emmanuel Schellekens [1966] Director [Belgian]; Marc Simonis [1951] Director [Belgian]; David Smith [1951] Director

WTW Cinemas Limited
Incorporated: 29 June 1945 *Employees:* 85
Previous: Capitol (St. Austell) Limited (The)
Net Worth: £7,414,694 *Total Assets:* £9,645,008
Registered Office: Lower Treforest, 66 Westerlands Road, Wadebridge, Cornwall, PL27 7EU
Activities: Motion picture projection activities
Major Shareholder: David Ronald Williams MBE
Officers: David Ronald Williams Mbe, Secretary; Dame Lynne Janie Brindley [1950] Director/Oxford Master; Angelina Williams [1944] Director/Cinema Manager; Mark Edward Williams [1980] Director/Cinema Manager; Robert David Williams [1982] Director/Cinema Manager; David Ronald Williams Mbe [1947] Director/Cinema Manager

WW (UK) Limited
Incorporated: 12 October 1993 *Employees:* 127
Net Worth: £959,052 *Total Assets:* £13,366,980
Registered Office: Britannic House, 51 North Hill, Plymouth, PL4 8HZ
Activities: Wholesale of office furniture
Shareholders: Daniel Anthony Wooler; Georgie Suzanne Wooler; Polly Louise Webb
Officers: Christopher Facey [1973] Director; Andrew Morgan [1980] Director; Joseph O'Malley [1963] Director; Polly Louise Webb [1973] Director/Marketing Executive; Robert Anthony Webb [1939] Director; Daniel Anthony Wooler [1968] Managing Director; Georgie Suzanne Wooler [1971] Director

WW Truck and Bus Limited
Incorporated: 29 March 2008 *Employees:* 224
Net Worth: £5,410,951 *Total Assets:* £21,763,722
Registered Office: Unit 201 Burcott Road, Severnside Industrial Estate, Bristol, BS11 8AP
Activities: Sale of other motor vehicles
Major Shareholder: William Nairn
Officers: Jeffrey Robert Clarke, Secretary; Jeffrey Robert Clarke [1952] Director; Richard James Millar [1972] Director; William Nairn [1958] Director

Lewis Wyatt (Construction) Limited
Incorporated: 10 December 1990 *Employees:* 52
Net Worth: £9,097,775 *Total Assets:* £33,921,224
Registered Office: 1 Parkstone Road, Poole, Dorset, BH15 2NN
Activities: Construction of commercial buildings
Parent: Wyatt Homes Limited
Officers: James Grant, Secretary; David Lewis Wyatt [1970] Director/Builder

Wyatt Homes Limited
Incorporated: 8 April 1999 *Employees:* 52
Net Worth: £9,097,875 *Total Assets:* £33,921,320
Registered Office: 1 Parkstone Road, Poole, Dorset, BH15 2NN
Activities: Construction of commercial buildings
Major Shareholder: David Lewis Wyatt
Officers: James Grant, Secretary; David Lewis Wyatt [1970] Director/Builder

Wycliffe College (Incorporated)
Incorporated: 10 April 1931 *Employees:* 377
Net Worth: £25,288,166 *Total Assets:* £34,290,112
Registered Office: Finance Department, Wycliffe College, Regent Street, Stonehouse, Glos, GL10 2AD
Activities: Pre-primary education
Officers: Thomas Patrick Wood, Secretary; Brigadier Robin John Bacon [1956] Director/Deputy Chief Executive; Simon Kinnaird Collingridge [1968] Director/Solicitor; Caroline Jane Duckworth [1961] Director/Treasurer; Lynn Carol Duncan [1952] Director; William Robert Garrard [1970] Director; Dr Lucy Jane Hair [1970] Director/Clinical Psychologist; Susan Joy Lacey [1975] Director/Logistics and Project Management; Simon Frederick Modlin Lloyd [1957] Director/Chartered Surveyor; Graeme May [1969] Director/Deputy Head; Andrea Louise Palk [1972] Director/Adjudication Officer; James Slater [1954] Director/Surveyor

Wyderington Limited
Incorporated: 23 December 2013
Net Worth: £2,289,080 *Total Assets:* £4,926,820
Registered Office: 3 Yarrow Road, Tower Park, Poole, Dorset, BH12 4TS
Activities: Other business support service activities n.e.c.
Parent: Wyderington (Assets) Limited
Officers: Jonathan Kim Aris [1963] Director

Wyke Farms Ltd
Incorporated: 27 February 1963 *Employees:* 246
Net Worth: £18,226,000 *Total Assets:* £60,794,000
Registered Office: White House Farm, Wyke Champflower, Bruton, Somerset, BA10 0PU
Activities: Butter and cheese production
Shareholder: Richard John Clothier
Officers: Paul Edwin Hardwick, Secretary; David James Clothier [1963] Director/Farmer; Grace Louise Clothier [1929] Director; Richard William Clothier [1970] Director/Production Manager; Richard John Clothier [1943] Director/Farmer; Roger Thomas Clothier [1961] Director/Farmer; Thomas John Clothier [1965] Director/Farmer; Paul Edwin Hardwick [1956] Finance Director; Ashley William Wilson [1965] Sales Director

M.E. Wynn & Co. Limited
Incorporated: 8 January 1971 *Employees:* 5
Net Worth: £5,702,670 *Total Assets:* £7,462,116
Registered Office: Pillar House, 113-115 Bath Road, Cheltenham, Glos, GL53 7LS
Activities: Development of building projects
Major Shareholder: Sally Margaret Wynn
Officers: Sally Margaret Wynn, Secretary; Michael Edward George Wynn [1997] Director; Sally Margaret Wynn [1963] Director/Secretary; Sarah Ann Elizabeth Wynn [1999] Director

Wyse Estates Holdings Limited
Incorporated: 14 May 2004 *Employees:* 8
Net Worth: £6,691,271 *Total Assets:* £11,342,634
Registered Office: Wessex House, Teign Road, Newton Abbot, Devon, TQ12 4AA
Activities: Activities of other holding companies n.e.c.
Major Shareholder: Peter James Cousens
Officers: Elisabeth Spear, Secretary; Peter James Cousens [1965] Director/Building Developer

Wyvern Cargo Ltd
Incorporated: 12 January 1983 *Employees:* 124
Net Worth: £4,985,235 *Total Assets:* £7,421,854
Registered Office: Broom Road, Poole, Dorset, BH12 4NR
Activities: Freight transport by road
Parent: Wyvern Holdings Limited
Officers: Stephen Randolph Bennett, Secretary; Stephen Randolph Bennett [1956] Director/Accountant; John Stanley Probert [1928] Director; Evan Sparrowhawk [1961] Director

Wyvern Holdings Limited
Incorporated: 18 August 2008 *Employees:* 124
Net Worth: £5,038,031 *Total Assets:* £7,424,156
Registered Office: Broom Road, Poole, Dorset, BH12 4NR
Activities: Activities of head offices
Shareholder: Evan Sparrowhawk
Officers: Stephen Randolph Bennett, Secretary; Stephen Randolph Bennett [1956] Director/Accountant; John Stanley Probert [1928] Director; Evan Sparrowhawk [1961] Director

X.T.Holdings Limited
Incorporated: 28 July 1972
Net Worth: £6,395,319 *Total Assets:* £6,475,908
Registered Office: The Coach House, Aust Road, Olveston, Bristol, BS35 4DE
Activities: Activities of head offices
Major Shareholder: Jacqueline Susan Baker
Officers: Roger Norman Elliott Savage, Secretary; Jacqueline Susan Baker [1956] Director; Michael Frederick Baker [1953] Director

Xeon Smiles UK Limited
Incorporated: 16 March 1950 *Employees:* 727
Net Worth Deficit: £531,292 *Total Assets:* £189,474,352
Registered Office: Bupa Dental Care, Vantage Office Park, Old Gloucester Road, Hambrook, Bristol, BS16 1GW
Activities: Dental practice activities
Parent: JDH Holdings Ltd
Officers: Robin James Bryant [1970] Director/Dental Surgeon; Steven John Preddy [1959] Director/Dentist; Gabriela Pueyo Roberts [1974] Director/General Manager [Spanish]; Dr Geoffrey Clive Pullen [1955] Director/Dentist; Dr Paul Slevin [1950] Director/Dentist [Irish]; Dr Ian David Wood [1956] Director/Dental Surgeon; Jake Stephen Hockley Wright [1972] Director

XJ4 Holding Company Limited
Incorporated: 4 December 2006 *Employees:* 2
Net Worth: £2,848,000 *Total Assets:* £137,900,992
Registered Office: Third Floor, Broad Quay House, Prince Street, Bristol, BS1 4DJ
Activities: Other business support service activities n.e.c.
Parent: PFI Investments Limited
Officers: Richard Little [1979] Investment Director; Jonathan Michael Simpson [1973] Director/Accountant

XJ6 Schools Holdings Limited
Incorporated: 24 January 2003 *Employees:* 2
Net Worth: £1,329,806 *Total Assets:* £7,168,010
Registered Office: Third Floor, Broad Quay House, Prince Street, Bristol, BS1 4DJ
Activities: Activities of head offices
Parent: PFI Investments Limited
Officers: Andrew Richard Kershaw [1965] Director/Projects Controller; Alan Campbell Ritchie [1967] Director

Xograph Healthcare Limited
Incorporated: 20 October 1967 *Employees:* 59
Net Worth: £3,091,149 *Total Assets:* £8,723,884
Registered Office: Xograph House, Ebley Road, Stonehouse, Glos, GL10 2LU
Activities: Manufacture of medical and dental instruments and supplies
Parent: Xograph Group Holdings Limited
Officers: Dr Krish Soni [1974] Director

Xylem Dewatering Solutions UK Ltd
Incorporated: 16 March 1931 *Employees:* 66
Net Worth: £19,185,000 *Total Assets:* £37,591,000
Registered Office: Quenington, Fairford, Cirencester, Glos, GL7 5BX
Activities: Manufacture of pumps
Parent: Godwin Holdings
Officers: Nicola Anne Tancred, Secretary; Bruce Conrad May [1959] Director/Manufacturing Manager; Paul Andrew Morris [1978] Director/Accountant

XYZ Machine Tools (Holdings) Limited
Incorporated: 14 April 2016 *Employees:* 82
Net Worth: £6,701,033 *Total Assets:* £28,845,472
Registered Office: Centenary House, Peninsula Park, Rydon Lane, Exeter, EX2 7XE
Activities: Activities of other holding companies n.e.c.
Shareholders: Nigel Atherton; Richard Wright Leonhard
Officers: Keith Wilson, Secretary; Nigel Atherton [1961] Director/Engineer; Richard Leonhard [1944] Director/Business Owner [American]; Keith Wilson [1963] Director/Engineer

XYZ Machine Tools Limited
Incorporated: 31 October 1983 *Employees:* 82
Net Worth: £21,675,322 *Total Assets:* £24,715,886
Registered Office: Centenary House, Peninsula Park, Rydon Lane, Exeter, EX2 7XE
Activities: Manufacture of tools
Parent: XYZ Machine Tools (Holdings) Limited
Officers: Keith Wilson, Secretary/Engineer; Nigel Atherton [1961] Director/Mechanical Engineer; Richard Wright Leonhard [1944] Director/Business Owner [American]; Keith Wilson [1963] Director/Engineer

Yankee Candle Company (Europe) Limited
Incorporated: 18 March 1998 *Employees:* 552
Net Worth: £16,627,000 *Total Assets:* £196,910,000
Registered Office: Poplar Way, East Cabot Park, Avonmouth, Bristol, BS11 0YH
Activities: Wholesale of household goods (other than musical instruments) n.e.c
Parent: Newell Brands Inc
Officers: Brian James Decker [1976] Director/Attorney [American]; Ben Hartley [1976] Director/Attorney

Yardgate Limited
Incorporated: 9 April 2002 *Employees:* 4
Net Worth: £4,398,948 *Total Assets:* £4,906,237
Registered Office: 6th Floor, Dean Park House, Dean Park Crescent, Bournemouth, BH1 1HP
Activities: Activities of head offices
Shareholders: Colin Richard Toomer; Elizabeth Ann Toomer
Officers: Elizabeth Ann Toomer, Secretary; Colin Richard Toomer [1955] Director; Jack Colin Toomer [1989] Director; Richard Philip Toomer [1985] Director

Yarlington Homes Limited
Incorporated: 30 September 2003
Net Worth: £6,026,000 *Total Assets:* £8,127,000
Registered Office: Yarlington Housing Group, Lupin Way, Yeovil, Somerset, BA22 8WN
Activities: Construction of domestic buildings
Parent: Yarlington Housing Group
Officers: Gemma Burton-Connolly, Secretary; Stephen Lodge [1973] Executive Director of Growth and Development; Joanna Claire Makinson [1983] Finance Director; Caroline Louise Moore [1965] Finance Director; Lindy Morgan [1965] Director/Chairman; Wayne Morris [1953] Director/Retired; Richard Nicol [1959] Director/Retired Developer; James Daniel Overill [1993] Director/Development Officer; Michael Francis Stancombe [1953] Director/Retired Solicitor; Raymond John Thompson [1948] Director/Retired

Yate Disposables Ltd
Incorporated: 30 July 1985 *Employees:* 103
Net Worth: £1,374,282 *Total Assets:* £9,947,925
Registered Office: 26 North Road, Yate, Bristol, BS37 7PA
Activities: Wholesale of china and glassware and cleaning materials
Shareholders: Derek Thomas Aston; Catherine Diane Aston
Officers: Mary Vaughan, Secretary; Catherine Diane Aston [1951] Finance Director; Derek Thomas Aston [1951] Director; Scott James Shackleford [1978] Managing Director; Mary Vaughan [1976] Director/Chartered Accountant

Yellow Bridge Developments LLP
Incorporated: 4 December 2012 *Employees:* 17
Net Worth: £6,262,476 *Total Assets:* £9,407,574
Registered Office: 7 Farleigh Court, Old Weston Road, Flax Bourton, Bristol, BS48 1UR

Yellow Bridge Investments Limited
Incorporated: 15 June 2004 *Employees:* 2
Net Worth: £960,277 *Total Assets:* £8,047,336
Registered Office: 7 Farleigh Court, Old Weston Road, Flax Bourton, Bristol, BS48 1UR
Activities: Other letting and operating of own or leased real estate
Officers: Rowena Palmer, Secretary; Anthony Richard Thomas Instrall [1968] Director; John Alexander Palmer [1961] Director

Yelspa Limited
Incorporated: 20 December 1977 *Employees:* 20
Net Worth: £4,102,417 *Total Assets:* £22,654,498
Registered Office: Faulkners Down House, Picket Piece, Andover, Hants, SP11 6LZ
Activities: Mixed farming
Major Shareholder: Henry Godefroid Andre Marie du Val de Beaulieu
Officers: Edward Du Val de Beaulieu, Secretary; Henry Du Val de Beaulieu [1958] Director

Yeo & Davey (Properties) Limited
Incorporated: 19 May 1949 *Employees:* 4
Net Worth: £2,760,072 *Total Assets:* £3,566,909
Registered Office: School House, Upton Pyne, Exeter, Devon, EX5 5JA
Activities: Other letting and operating of own or leased real estate
Officers: Sonia Gill Clapp, Secretary; Lisa Jane Clapp [1968] Director/Businesswoman; Sonia Gill Clapp [1935] Director/Secretarial Assistant; Stewart Alexander Clapp [1954] Director/Motor Dealer; Vernon Richard Charles Clapp [1931] Director/Motor Dealer

Yeo Valley Farms (Production) Limited
Incorporated: 28 October 1976 *Employees:* 1,684
Net Worth: £40,341,280 *Total Assets:* £107,194,480
Registered Office: Yeo Valley HQ, Rhodyate, Blagdon, Somerset, BS40 7YE
Activities: Liquid milk and cream production
Parent: Yeo Valley Group Ltd
Officers: Sophie Alexandra Wells, Secretary; Adrian Jarrad Carne [1966] Director; Robert Edward Sexton [1973] Finance Director; Karl John Tucker [1968] Director

Yeo Valley Fruit Limited
Incorporated: 20 April 2010
Previous: Coombe Farm Fruits Limited
Net Worth: £4,715,161 *Total Assets:* £14,792,373
Registered Office: Yeo Valley HQ, Rhodyate, Blagdon, Bristol, BS40 7YE
Activities: Other processing and preserving of fruit and vegetables
Parent: Yeo Valley Group Ltd
Officers: Adrian Carne [1986] Director; Robert Edward Sexton [1973] Finance Director; Karl John Tucker [1968] Director

Yeo Valley Group Limited
Incorporated: 11 February 2004 *Employees:* 1,715
Net Worth: £50,188,312 *Total Assets:* £119,683,096
Registered Office: YV HQ, Rhodyate, Blagdon, Bristol, BS40 7YE
Activities: Manufacture of other milk products
Major Shareholder: Timothy William Tripp Mead
Officers: Karl John Tucker, Secretary; Adrian Jarrad Carne [1966] Director; Amanda Mary Tripp Honey [1969] Director; Timothy William Tripp Mead [1963] Director; Robert Edward Sexton [1973] Finance Director; Karl John Tucker [1968] Director; Sarah Jane Tripp Warren [1962] Director; Thomas Charles Alexanderson Wright [1983] Director

Yeovil Securities Limited
Incorporated: 12 August 1957
Net Worth: £1,415,128 *Total Assets:* £4,702,951
Registered Office: West Coker House, West Coker, Yeovil, Somerset, BA22 9BW
Activities: Financial intermediation not elsewhere classified
Officers: Steve Drew, Secretary; Anne Berkley [1942] Director; John Roland Berkley [1934] Director

YMCA Bath Group
Incorporated: 16 August 2004 *Employees:* 162
Previous: Bath Young Men's Christian Association
Net Worth: £2,873,793 *Total Assets:* £4,850,483
Registered Office: International House, Broad Street Place, Bath, BA1 5LH
Activities: Hotels and similar accommodation
Officers: Michael John Fairbeard, Company Secretary; Sarah Beresford-Smith [1968] Director/Solicitor; Richard John Caddick [1974] Director; Noreen Teresa Finnamore [1960] Managing Director; David Sidney Pendle [1943] Director/Retired; Mark Christian Pitman [1934] Director/Retired; Jonathan William Webb-Peploe [1971] Director/Self Employed

Yorkshire Hydropower Limited
Incorporated: 9 June 2014
Net Worth: £4,783,521 *Total Assets:* £9,179,482
Registered Office: Brook House, Anna Valley, Andover, Hants, SP11 7NG
Activities: Production of electricity
Parent: Yorkshire Hydropower Holdings Limited
Officers: John Clive Arup, Secretary; John Clive Arup [1952] Director/Civil Engineer; Peter Ballantyne Dixon [1950] Director; Tim John Hanford [1964] Director; Piers Malcolm Charles Millar [1971] Director; Richard Stephen Partridge-Hicks [1957] Director; Mark Simon [1961] Director

M R Young & Sons (Rural) Limited
Incorporated: 24 April 2012 *Employees:* 2
Net Worth: £3,818,812 *Total Assets:* £3,908,953
Registered Office: Whyr Farm, Winterbourne Bassett, Swindon, Wilts, SN4 9QE
Activities: Growing of cereals (except rice), leguminous crops and oil seeds
Officers: Juliet Anne Verity Handslip [1978] Director/Corporate Consultant; Deborah Anne Greene Young [1949] Director/Housewife; Peter Malcolm Gavin Young [1947] Director/Solicitor; Stefanie Claire Elizabeth Young [1980] Director/Secretary

Roger Young Limited
Incorporated: 23 December 1987 *Employees:* 119
Net Worth: £11,227,706 *Total Assets:* £17,808,428
Registered Office: Roger Young Land Rover Wood Acre, Liskeard Road, Saltash Parkway, Saltash, Cornwall, PL12 6LF
Activities: Sale of new cars and light motor vehicles
Shareholders: Roger Charles Geoffrey Young; Erica Jane Young
Officers: Erica Jane Young, Secretary; Darren Edward Hardy [1967] Director; Erica Jane Young [1962] Director/Land Rover Dealership; Matthew Young [1986] Director; Roger Charles Geoffrey Young [1957] Director/Motor Dealer; Sarah Louise Young [1987] Director

Your Energy Holdings Limited
Incorporated: 10 November 2010
Net Worth: £30,870,000 *Total Assets:* £30,882,000
Registered Office: First Floor, 10 Temple Back, Bristol, BS1 6FL
Activities: Activities of other holding companies n.e.c.
Parent: AES K2 Limited
Officers: Paul Austin Hutchinson [1968] Director; James Timothy McCullough [1962] Director/Complex Manager

YPI Limited
Incorporated: 22 January 2013 *Employees:* 49
Net Worth: £443,268 *Total Assets:* £6,744,117
Registered Office: 6th Floor, Dean Park House, Dean Park Crescent, Bournemouth, BH1 1HP
Activities: Buying and selling of own real estate
Major Shareholder: David Arthur Young
Officers: David Arthur Young [1961] Director

YTL Property Holdings (UK) Limited
Incorporated: 8 July 2015
Net Worth: £52,000 *Total Assets:* £87,179,000
Registered Office: Wessex Water, Operations Centre, Claverton Down Road, Claverton Down, Bath, BA2 7WW
Activities: Development of building projects
Parent: YTL Land and Property (UK) Ltd
Officers: Ruth Esme Jefferson, Secretary; Colin Frank Skellett [1945] Director; Mark Timothy Watts [1961] Finance Director; Mark Seok Kah Yeoh [1965] Director/Business Person [Malaysian]; Seok Hong Yeoh [1959] Director/Business Person [Malaysian]

YTL Utilities (UK) Limited
Incorporated: 18 December 2001 *Employees:* 2,817
Net Worth: £614,000,000 *Total Assets:* £3,994,800,128
Registered Office: Claverton Down Road, Claverton Down, Bath, BA2 7WW
Activities: Non-trading company
Officers: Ruth Esme Jefferson, Secretary; Colin Frank Skellett [1945] Director; Mark Timothy Watts [1961] Director; Dr Francis Sock Ping Yeoh [1954] Director/Business Person [Malaysian]; Seok Kah Yeoh [1965] Director/Business Person [Malaysian]; Seok Hong Yeoh [1959] Director/Business Person [Malaysian]; Seok Kian Yeoh [1957] Director/Business Person [Malaysian]

YYS International (UK) Limited
Incorporated: 28 October 1994 *Employees:* 20
Net Worth: £2,606,918 *Total Assets:* £3,873,173
Registered Office: Units 3-5 Tradecroft Industrial Estate, Portland, Dorset, DT5 2AF
Activities: Non-specialised wholesale trade
Shareholders: Penelope de Bear; Michael de Bear
Officers: Michael de Bear, Secretary; Rachel Elizabeth Bradwick [1967] Director/Management Accountant; Michael de Bear [1949] Director; Penelope de Bear [1945] Director/Company President

Zebra MTD Limited
Incorporated: 3 September 2013 *Employees:* 139
Net Worth: £464,003 *Total Assets:* £14,760,731
Registered Office: Exe Box, Matford Park Road, Matford Business Park, Marsh Barton Trading Estate, Exeter, EX2 8FD
Activities: Activities of head offices
Shareholders: Laurence Michael Prince; Danilo Promotions Ltd
Officers: Sharon Jane Colclough [1972] Accountant/Director; Kirsty Janet Guy [1966] Director; Anthony Richard Loveys Jervoise [1964] Director; Ashley Philip Levinson [1956] Director/Consultant; David Philip Pike [1959] Director; Seven Roy Plackett [1963] Director; Lawrence Michael Prince [1946] Director

Zimmer Biomet UK Limited
Incorporated: 13 November 1962 *Employees:* 306
Previous: Zimmer Limited
Net Worth: £74,042,000 *Total Assets:* £127,072,000
Registered Office: The Courtyard, Lancaster Place, South Marston Park, Swindon, Wilts, SN3 4FP
Activities: Wholesale of pharmaceutical goods
Parent: Zimmer UK Ltd
Officers: Bo Vendelboe, Secretary; Urs Mueller [1960] Director/Senior Legal Counsel [German]; Steven Orange [1972] Director/VP North Region; Bo Vendelboe [1969] Finance Director [Danish]

Zimmer U.K. Ltd.
Incorporated: 18 August 2004
Net Worth: £56,619,000 *Total Assets:* £119,405,000
Registered Office: The Courtyard, Lancaster Place, South Marston Park, Swindon, Wilts, SN3 4FP
Activities: Activities of other holding companies n.e.c.
Parent: Zimmer Europe Holdings B.V.
Officers: Bo Vendelboe, Secretary; Steven Orange [1972] Director/VP North Region; Jitender Singh Sahni [1965] Tax Director [German]; Bo Vendelboe [1969] Finance Director [Danish]

Zoeftig Group Limited
Incorporated: 5 April 2004 *Employees:* 1
Net Worth: £3,932,373 *Total Assets:* £4,566,322
Registered Office: Unit 11 Kings Hill Industrial Estate, Bude, Cornwall, EX23 8QN
Activities: Other business support service activities n.e.c.
Parent: Figueras Global Seating Limited
Officers: Oscar Carod Arto [1971] Director [Spanish]; Marcos Carrasquilla Dorow [1975] Director/Chief Executive Officer [Spanish]; Lluis Molins Vilata [1979] Director [Spanish]; Mandy Lorraine Williams [1966] Managing Director; Paul David Williams [1965] Director

Zogenix Europe Limited
Incorporated: 7 June 2010 *Employees:* 4
Net Worth: £4,399,528 *Total Assets:* £28,842,276
Registered Office: 11th Floor, Whitefriars, Lewins Mead, Bristol, BS1 2NT
Activities: Manufacture of basic pharmaceutical products
Parent: Zogenix Inc
Officers: Dr Stephen James Farr [1959] Director/President/COO; Michael Patrick Smith [1968] Director/EVP-CFO Zogenix Inc [American]

Zuken Group Limited
Incorporated: 3 November 1960
Net Worth: £12,036,000 *Total Assets:* £12,037,000
Registered Office: Zuken Technology Centre, 1500 Aztec West, Almondsbury, Bristol, BS32 4RF
Activities: Activities of head offices
Officers: Mark Terance Sandham, Secretary; Dr Olaf Kai-Benjamin Anatole Nixdorf [1977] Director [German]; Shinji Yukawa [1957] Director [Japanese]

Zuken Limited
Incorporated: 17 June 1969 *Employees:* 55
Net Worth Deficit: £7,223,000 *Total Assets:* £5,221,000
Registered Office: Zuken Technology Centre, 1500 Aztec West, Almondsbury, Bristol, BS32 4RF
Activities: Business and domestic software development
Officers: Mark Terance Sandham, Secretary; Kazuhiro Kariya [1960] R & D Director [Japanese]; Jinya Katsube [1942] Director [Japanese]; Shinji Yukawa [1957] Director [Japanese]

Zurich Advice Network Limited
Incorporated: 9 March 1951
Net Worth: £8,631,179 *Total Assets:* £10,198,431
Registered Office: The Grange, Bishops Cleeve, Cheltenham, Glos, GL52 8XX
Activities: Financial intermediation not elsewhere classified
Shareholders: Allied Dunbar Assurance PLC; Allied Dunbar Assurance PLC
Officers: Timothy James Grant [1964] Director; Charlotte Denise Murphy [1982] Director

Zurich Assurance Ltd
Incorporated: 2 January 1990
Net Worth: £952,000,000 *Total Assets:* £56,042,000,384
Registered Office: The Grange, Bishops Cleeve, Cheltenham, Glos, GL52 8XX
Activities: Life insurance
Shareholders: Eagle Star Holdings Limited; Eagle Star Holdings Limited
Officers: James Thomas Gaunt Butler [1946] Director; Christopher Stuart Fairclough [1950] Director; Tulsi Ratakonda Naidu [1973] Director [Indian]; Gary Paul John Shaughnessy [1966] Director; Ian Charles Robert Stuart [1948] Director [Irish]; James Richard Sykes [1961] Director

Zurich Community Trust (UK) Limited
Incorporated: 31 December 1973 *Employees:* 24
Net Worth: £5,529,000 *Total Assets:* £5,937,000
Registered Office: The Grange, Bishops Cleeve, Cheltenham, Glos, GL52 8XX
Activities: Activities of business and employers membership organisations
Shareholders: Zurich Financial Services (UKISA) Nominees Limited; Zurich Financial Services (UKISA) Limited
Officers: Timothy Paul Culling [1961] Operations Director; Andrew Michael Jepp [1963] Director; Ian Nicholas Lovett [1944] Director/Banker; Wayne Donald Myslik [1967] Director [American]; Tulsi Ratakonda Naidu [1973] Director [Indian]; Richard Peden [1973] Director; Anne Torry [1965] Director

Zurich Employment Services Limited
Incorporated: 22 November 1929 *Employees:* 1,665
Net Worth Deficit: £458,020,992 *Total Assets:* £358,580,992
Registered Office: The Grange, Bishops Cleeve, Cheltenham, Glos, GL52 8XX
Activities: Human resources provision and management of human resources functions
Parent: Zurich Financial Services (UKISA) Limited
Officers: Stephen Michael Collinson [1972] Director; John Herbert Keppel [1970] Director [New Zealander]; Helen Alison Pickford [1971] Director; James Richard Sykes [1961] Director

Zurich Finance (UK) PLC
Incorporated: 18 June 2002
Net Worth: £5,658,000 *Total Assets:* £601,465,984
Registered Office: The Grange, Bishops Cleeve, Cheltenham, Glos, GL52 8XX
Activities: Financial intermediation not elsewhere classified
Parent: Zurich Insurance Group AG
Officers: Christian Henning Peter Carl [1972] Director [French]; Aileen Mathieson [1968] Director; Helen Alison Pickford [1971] Director

Zurich Financial Services (UKISA) Limited
Incorporated: 5 November 1984
Net Worth: £1,664,600,064 *Total Assets:* £2,371,699,968
Registered Office: The Grange, Bishops Cleeve, Cheltenham, Glos, GL52 8XX
Activities: Activities of head offices
Shareholders: Allied Zurich Holdings Limited; Zurich Insurance Company Ltd
Officers: Stephen Michael Collinson [1972] Director; Tulsi Ratakonda Naidu [1973] Director [Indian]; Helen Alison Pickford [1971] Director; Johan Fredrik Solberg [1977] Director [Swedish]; Julian Temes [1972] Managing Director [Spanish]

Zurich Intermediary Group Limited
Incorporated: 29 April 1985
Net Worth: £8,260,000 *Total Assets:* £12,320,000
Registered Office: The Grange, Bishops Cleeve, Cheltenham, Glos, GL52 8XX
Activities: Financial intermediation not elsewhere classified
Shareholders: Zurich Financial Services (UKISA) Limited; Zurich Financial Services (UKISA) Limited
Officers: Christopher Horne [1977] Director; Aileen Mathieson [1968] Director; Colum O'Brien [1964] Director [Irish]; Darren West [1970] Director

Zurich Project Finance (UK) Limited
Incorporated: 11 June 2014
Net Worth: £455,000 *Total Assets:* £1,230,150,016
Registered Office: The Grange, Bishops Cleeve, Cheltenham, Glos, GL52 8XX
Activities: Activities of financial services holding companies
Shareholders: Zurich Insurance Company Ltd; Zurich Insurance Company Ltd
Officers: Christian Henning Peter Carl [1972] Director [French]; Andrew Edward Jackson [1970] Director; Helen Alison Pickford [1971] Director

Zuru UK Limited
Incorporated: 13 September 2016
Net Worth: £71,252 *Total Assets:* £9,343,524
Registered Office: First Floor, 10 Temple Back, Bristol, BS1 6FL
Activities: Non-specialised wholesale trade
Major Shareholder: Mathew Peter Mowbray
Officers: Anna Jane Mowbray [1983] Director [New Zealander]; Mathew Peter Mowbray [1980] Director [New Zealander]; Nicholas James Mowbray [1985] Director [New Zealander]

Zycko Group Limited
Incorporated: 21 January 2013
Net Worth: £6,605,000 *Total Assets:* £10,343,000
Registered Office: Lakeview House, The Mallards, South Cerney, Cirencester, Glos, GL7 5TQ
Activities: Activities of other holding companies n.e.c.
Parent: Nuvia Networks Limited
Officers: John Mark Havill, Secretary; Lee James Driscoll [1972] Director; David Richard Galton-Fenzi [1969] Director; Julian Hodge [1970] Director/Chief Financial Officer; Stewart Holness [1966] Director

Zycko Overseas Limited
Incorporated: 15 June 2001
Net Worth Deficit: £1,166,000 *Total Assets:* £8,975,000
Registered Office: Lakeview House, The Mallards, South Cerney, Cirencester, Glos, GL7 5TQ
Activities: Activities of head offices
Parent: Zycko Group Limited
Officers: John Mark Havill, Secretary; David Richard Galton-Fenzi [1969] Director; Julian Hodge [1970] Director/Chief Financial Officer

Zynstra Limited
Incorporated: 29 November 2011 *Employees:* 46
Net Worth: £5,264,781 *Total Assets:* £5,817,710
Registered Office: University of Bath Innovation Centre, Carpenter House, Broad Quay, Bath, BA1 1UD
Activities: Other software publishing
Shareholder: Octopus Titan VCT PLC
Officers: Brian Francis Buggy [1962] Director [Irish]; Andrew Michael Burton [1965] Director; Jonathan Peter Michael Craton [1965] Director; Nicholas Stuart MacKay East [1972] Director; Donald Robert Gibson [1952] Director; Jean-Frederic Lardieg [1975] Investment Director, Venture Capital [French]; Robert Willett [1946] Director

This page is intentionally left blank

Standard Industrial Classification

01110 Growing of cereals (except rice), leguminous crops and oil seeds [42]

Steve Benson Farming Limited
W H Bond & Sons Limited
Capes (Hatherden) Limited
Chamberlayne Farms Limited
Chota Estates Co Ltd
Colethrop Farm Limited
Compton Beauchamp Estates Ltd
Coolgate Limited
Bernard Cox Limited
David Foot Limited
Forward Developments Limited
C G & D Heal Limited
Hodgetts Farming Limited
T.H.F. Johnson Limited
Michael H Keene & Son Limited
Kemble Farms Limited
Kingsdown Farm Ltd
Lewisia Limited
E.J. MacKelden & Sons (Bobbing) Ltd
Marcham Farms Limited
H.Mustin & Son Limited
North Dairy Farms Limited
North Kent Farms Limited
Odstone Farms Limited
Pengelly Farms Limited
Pennard Hill Farm Limited
C.G.Purchase and Son Limited
Queensquare Farming Limited
Ramsbury Estates Limited
Ropsley Farms Limited
Shirley-Young Limited
Harold W Smart & Son Limited
Stowell Park Estate Limited
Test Development Co Ltd
Trafalgar Estate Limited
Up Cerne Limited
Wastenage Farms Limited
Wherwell Farms Limited
Whitsbury Farm & Stud Limited
Willes Farming Limited
A.J. Wooldridge Limited
M R Young & Sons (Rural) Ltd

01130 Growing of vegetables and melons, roots and tubers [13]

MF Bennion (Potatoes) Limited
E W Button & Son Limited
K. S. Coles Limited
Cornish Potatoes Limited
Drimbawn (UK) Limited
H.Mustin & Son Limited
Pengelly Farms Limited
Pinetops Nurseries Limited
Riverford Organic Farmers Ltd
Southern England Farms Limited
Thakeham Mushrooms Limited
Tickenham Court Farm Co.Limited
Wastenage Farms Limited

01160 Growing of fibre crops

Jackamax Limited

01190 Growing of other non-perennial crops

Vitacress Herbs Limited
Vitacress Salads Limited

01250 Growing of other tree and bush fruits and nuts

Michael H Keene & Son Limited
Withers Fruit Farm Limited

01290 Growing of other perennial crops

Edenvale Turf (SW) Limited

01300 Plant propagation

Kernock Park Plants Limited

01410 Raising of dairy cattle [38]

Alvis Brothers Limited
F.A.W. Baker's Kingston Farms Ltd
A.J. and R.G.Barber Limited
K W Brake and Son Limited
F.G.Brewer & Sons (Farms) Ltd
C.P. Button Limited
Canon Court Farm Limited
H.W.Clothier Milton-Westcombe Farms
Cloverlait Limited
Coombes Manor Farm Limited
J.A. Darke Limited
J & W Davis Limited
Denhay Farms Limited
David Foot Limited
Foxcombe Farm (Somerset) Ltd
G & R House Limited
AR Hooper and Partners Ltd
F.G.Jeanes & Son Limited
Kemble Farms Limited
Lagan Farms (Dorset) Limited
Walter Maidment Limited
Manor Farm (Castle Cary) Ltd
H.Mustin & Son Limited
Pennard Farms Limited
Pole Farming Limited
A. L. Sayers (Holbeton) Ltd
Springwood Farms Limited
Tack Farms Limited
M R Tizzard Limited
Trafalgar Estate Limited
Treveglos Farm Limited
A. H. Warren Trust Limited
Wastenage Farms Limited
W.J. Watkins & Son Limited
Willes Farming Limited
Wills Brothers Limited
A.J. Wooldridge Limited
J D Wright & Son Ltd

01420 Raising of other cattle and buffaloes

Marsh Court Farm Limited
St Giles Farms Limited
Whitsbury Farm & Stud Limited

01430 Raising of horses and other equines

Lagan Farms (Dorset) Limited
Whitsbury Farm & Stud Limited

01450 Raising of sheep and goats [10]

Richard C. Bircher (Holdings) Ltd
Bowldown Farms Limited
Chaffcombe Thorns Limited
Grasshopper 2000 Ltd.
Langdon (Dorset) Farms
Lynton Downs Limited
Marcham Farms Limited
Stowell Park Estate Limited
W.J. Watkins & Son Limited
Whitsbury Farm & Stud Limited

01460 Raising of swine and pigs

Alexander & Angell (Farms) Ltd
A.J. and R.G.Barber Limited
J R Bodman Limited
C R Down Farming Limited
Marcham Farms Limited
Pole Farming Limited
W.J. Watkins & Son Limited

01470 Raising of poultry [11]

Alexander & Angell (Farms) Ltd
Bybrook Agriculture Limited
Clarence Court Eggs Limited
M.B. Crocker Limited
Devonshire Poultry Limited
Lincolnshire Chickens Limited
Harold W Smart & Son Limited
Stonegate Farmers Limited
Stonegate Group Limited
Stonegate Holdings Limited
Walston Poultry Farm Limited

01490 Raising of other animals

Canford Renewable Energy Ltd
R. Hannon Limited
EA & JA Hiscock Limited
Uphouse Farm Limited

01500 Mixed farming [55]

Alderley Farms Limited
Alton Pancras Estate UK Ltd.
Alvis Brothers Limited
Bapton Manor Farm Limited
Bardolf Farms Limited
Barton Farms Limited
Bond Holdings Limited
F W S Carter & Sons Limited
L. O. Clothier & Sons Limited
Cloverstand Limited
Collacombe Farm Limited
J Cossins & Sons Limited
D. Dalton & Son Limited
Evershot Farms Limited
Faber Brook Farm Limited
Faccombe Estates Limited
Farms for City Children Ltd
AW Frampton & Son Limited
J & C Freeth Limited
W.R. Haines (Leasow Farms) Ltd
Harper's Holdings Limited
Harvey Farms (Winterbourne) Ltd
Holt Farms Limited
Hopkins Estates Limited
F.N.Hues and Sons Limited
Jackamax Limited
Jamie's Farm
F.G.Jeanes & Son Limited
T.H.F. Johnson Limited

P.E. King (Bristol) Limited
Kingham Farms Ltd
Langham Farms Limited
Langlands Farms Limited
Little Bedwyn Estate Limited
Longford Farms Limited
Lower Pertwood Organic Farm Ltd
Lynton Downs Limited
Marchmont Farms Limited
W.J.Miller & Sons Limited
J.A. & E. Montgomery Limited
Norman Court and Sowley Farms Ltd
North Leaze Farm Limited
OM Holidays Ltd
R.N. Padfield & Sons Limited
S.J.Phillips & Sons (Kemble) Ltd
F G Pryor and Son Limited
Rockfield Farms Limited
Rudgeway Farms Limited
F.J. Snook & Sons Limited
Kenneth Spencer Limited
Stuart Partners Limited
Tickenham Court Farm Co.Limited
Walston Holdings Limited
Wastenage Farms Limited
Yelspa Limited

01610 Support activities for crop production

Cleancrop UK Limited
Gooderham Farms Limited
Independent Agriculture Ltd
Masstock Arable (UK) Limited
Alan Snow Agricultural Engineers
Steanbow Limited
United Agri Products Limited
Willmot Pertwee Limited

01621 Farm animal boarding and care

Animals in Distress (Torbay and Westcountry)
Ferne Animal Sanctuary
Mare and Foal Sanctuary

01629 Support activities for animal production (other than farm animal boarding)

Cornbury Farm Contracting Ltd
Gooderham Farms Limited
Junction 24 Limited
Langdon (Dorset) Farms
National Milk Records PLC
Premier Livestock Auctions Ltd
Thames Valley Eggs (Production) Ltd

01630 Post-harvest crop activities

United Oilseeds Marketing Ltd

01700 Hunting, trapping and related service activities

Alton Pancras Estate UK Ltd.
Weardale Estates Limited

02100 Silviculture and other forestry activities

Barton Farms Limited
Coombes Forestry Limited
East Bros.(Timber) Limited
Enga Limited
Faccombe Estates Limited
Grasshopper 2000 Ltd.
Lynton Downs Limited
Shillofad Limited

02200 Logging

Mendip Forestry Limited
SDL Biomass Limited
Stowell Park Estate Limited

02400 Support services to forestry

Hoppings Softwood Products PLC
Mendip Forestry Limited

03110 Marine fishing

JFD Trawlers Limited
W. Stevenson & Sons Limited
Vistgate Limited
Voyager Fishing Co Ltd
Waterdance Limited

03120 Freshwater fishing

Grasshopper 2000 Ltd.

06100 Extraction of crude petroleum

Union Jack Oil PLC

06200 Extraction of natural gas

Union Jack Oil PLC

07100 Mining of iron ores

Western United Mines Limited

07290 Mining of other non-ferrous metal ores

Crystal Classics Fine Minerals Ltd

08110 Quarrying of ornamental and building stone, limestone, gypsum, chalk and slate

Castle Hill Quarry Co.,Limited
Farmington Natural Stone Ltd
E. & J. W. Glendinning (Holdings)
E.And J.W.Glendinning Limited
Portland Stone Firms Limited
J. Suttle Transport Limited
John Wainwright & Co. Limited

08120 Operation of gravel and sand pits; mining of clays and kaolin

Borough Green Sand Pits Ltd
Moreton C.Cullimore (Gravels) Ltd
H.H.& D.E.Drew Limited
Earthline Limited
Hills Quarry Products Limited
Imerys Minerals Limited
Viridor Waste Kent Limited
M.B.Wilkes Limited

08990 Other mining and quarrying n.e.c.

Datamine Corporate Limited
Goonvean Aggregates Limited
Lovell Stone Group Limited

09100 Support activities for petroleum and natural gas mining

Antech Limited
NOV Downhole Eurasia Limited
National Oilwell Varco UK Ltd
Praxair Offshore Services Ltd
Prosafe Offshore Limited
Providor Limited

09900 Support activities for other mining and quarrying

SGH Investments Limited

10110 Processing and preserving of meat

Denhay Farms Limited
Alec Jarrett Limited
H.R.Jasper & Son Limited

10120 Processing and preserving of poultry meat

Dartmouth Holdings Limited

10130 Production of meat and poultry meat products

Dunbia (UK)
Penny Lane Foods Limited
Penny Lane Holdings Ltd

10200 Processing and preserving of fish, crustaceans and molluscs

Blue Sea Food Co Ltd
Coombe Fisheries Limited
Lyons Seafoods Limited
Severn & Wye Smokery Limited
Vistgate Limited

10390 Other processing and preserving of fruit and vegetables

Bristol Fruit Sales (Bananas) Ltd
Monaghan Mushrooms Limited
Western Commodities Ltd
Yeo Valley Fruit Limited

10511 Liquid milk and cream production [13]

Andros UK Limited
Ashley Chase Estate Limited
F.A.W. Baker's Kingston Farms Ltd
Blackmore Vale Farm Cream Ltd
F.G.Brewer & Sons (Farms) Ltd
R L Clapp and Sons (Cheesemakers)
Cornish Farm Dairy Limited
Cotteswold Dairy Limited
Crediton Dairy Limited
Marks Barn Farm (Crewkerne) Ltd
Pattemore's Transport (Crewkerne)
A.E. Rodda & Son Limited
Yeo Valley Farms (Production) Ltd

10512 Butter and cheese production [11]

Alvis Brothers Limited
Ashley Chase Estate Limited
A.J. and R.G.Barber Limited
R L Clapp and Sons (Cheesemakers)
H.W.Clothier Milton-Westcombe Farms
Dairy Partners (Cymru Wales) Ltd
Dairy Partners Limited
Norseland Holdings Limited
Norseland Limited
Parkham Farms Limited
Wyke Farms Ltd

10519 Manufacture of other milk products

Yeo Valley Farms (Production) Ltd
Yeo Valley Group Limited

10520 Manufacture of ice cream

Yeo Valley Farms (Production) Ltd

10611 Grain milling

Shipton Mill Limited

10710 Manufacture of bread; manufacture of fresh pastry goods and cakes

Malcolm Barnecutt Bakery Ltd
Pie Minister Limited
Proper Cornish Limited
Rich Products Limited
W.C. Rowe (Falmouth) Limited
Warrens Bakery Limited

10720 Manufacture of rusks and biscuits; manufacture of preserved pastry goods and cakes

Artisan Biscuits Limited
Dorset Village Bakery Limited

10821 Manufacture of cocoa and chocolate confectionery

County Confectionery Limited

10822 Manufacture of sugar confectionery

Bart Ingredients Co. Ltd
Bart Spices Group Holdings Ltd
Jakemans (Confectioners) Ltd

10831 Tea processing

Infusion GB Limited
Keith Spicer Limited

10840 Manufacture of condiments and seasonings

Bart Ingredients Co. Ltd
Bart Spices Group Holdings Ltd
British Pepper & Spice Co Ltd
Crucial Sauce Co Ltd

10850 Manufacture of prepared meals and dishes

Apetito Limited

10890 Manufacture of other food products n.e.c. [17]

Beyond The Bean Limited
Burts Potato Chips Limited
Call Caterlink Ltd
Crawlands Limited
Danisco (UK) Limited
Elondale Limited
Express Contract Drying Ltd
Framptons Limited
Green Gourmet Limited
Hyperbiotics PLC
Kerry Ingredients (UK) Limited
Paramount 21 Limited
Pastaking (UK) Limited
Pulsin Ltd
Stonegate Agriculture Limited
Wrigley Co Ltd
Wrigley Uno UK Limited

10910 Manufacture of prepared feeds for farm animals

Bowerings Animal Feeds Limited
Crediton Milling Co Ltd
W.L. Duffield & Sons Limited
Duffields (South West) Limited
Duffields Mills Limited
Feedco Ltd
Harper's Home Mix Limited
Mole Valley Feed Solutions Ltd
Alfred Nichols (Services and Properties)

10920 Manufacture of prepared pet foods

Crown Pet Foods Limited

11010 Distilling, rectifying and blending of spirits

Brothers Drinks Co. Limited
Coates & Co. (Plymouth) Ltd

11030 Manufacture of cider and other fruit wines

Brothers Drinks Co. Limited
Cornish Scrumpy Holdings Ltd
Lyme Bay Cider Co Ltd
Magners GB Limited
Merrydown PLC
Thatchers Cider Co Ltd

11040 Manufacture of other non-distilled fermented beverages

J.Chandler & Company (Buckfast),Limited
Dart Abbey Enterprises Limited

11050 Manufacture of beer

Arkell's Brewery Limited
Butcombe Brewery Limited
Butcombe Brewing Co Ltd
Hall & Woodhouse Limited
J.C. & R.H. Palmer Limited
Sharp's Brewery Limited
St.Austell Brewery Co Ltd
Wadworth and Co Ltd

11070 Manufacture of soft drinks; production of mineral waters and other bottled waters

04021465 Limited
Bottlegreen Holdings Limited
Merrydown PLC
Refresco Beverages UK Limited
Woodchester Enterprises Ltd

13200 Weaving of textiles

Heathcoat Fabrics Limited
Valmiera Glass UK Limited

13300 Finishing of textiles

Frontline Image Ltd
Heathcoat Fabrics Limited
Valmiera Glass UK Limited
Warwick Fabrics (UK) Limited

13931 Manufacture of woven or tufted carpets and rugs

Axminster Carpets Limited
Dan-Floor U.K. Limited

13940 Manufacture of cordage, rope, twine and netting

Huck Nets (U.K.) Limited
Tildenet Ltd

13950 Manufacture of non-wovens and articles made from non-wovens, except apparel

BFF Nonwovens Limited
Delstar International, Limited
Lantor (UK) Limited

13960 Manufacture of other technical and industrial textiles

Dartex Coatings Limited
Heathcoat Fabrics Limited
Lantor (UK) Limited
Tildenet Ltd
Valmiera Glass UK Limited

13990 Manufacture of other textiles n.e.c.

Ludus Capital Limited
WSP Textiles Limited

14120 Manufacture of workwear

B T Q Limited
Bristol Uniforms Limited
Leo Textiles Limited

14190 Manufacture of other wearing apparel and accessories n.e.c.

CQC Limited
Palm Equipment International Ltd
Williamson-Dickie Europe Holdings
Williamson-Dickie Europe Ltd
J. Wippell & Co Ltd

14310 Manufacture of knitted and crocheted hosiery

Heathcoat Fabrics Limited

15110 Tanning and dressing of leather; dressing and dyeing of fur

Pittard Garnar Services Ltd
Pittards PLC.
Thomas Ware & Sons Limited

15120 Manufacture of luggage, handbags and the like, saddlery and harness

Mulberry Company (Design) Ltd
Pittards PLC.

15200 Manufacture of footwear

C. & J. Clark Overseas Ltd

16100 Sawmilling and planing of wood

W H Bond & Sons Limited
Brookridge Timber Limited
A. J. Charlton & Sons Limited
East Bros.(Timber) Limited
Severn Valley Woodworks Ltd
Snows Timber Limited
Vastern Timber Co Ltd

16210 Manufacture of veneer sheets and wood-based panels

Norbord Europe Limited

16230 Manufacture of other builders' carpentry and joinery

M H Joinery Products PLC
David Salisbury Joinery Ltd

16290 Manufacture of other products of wood; manufacture of articles of cork, straw and plaiting materials
Fiberlean Technologies Limited
Ladder and Fencing Industries (Newent)
Rochling Engineering Plastics (UK)
Stanley's Biomass Limited

17120 Manufacture of paper and paperboard
Glatfelter Lydney, Ltd.
Higher Kings Mill Limited
Sundeala Limited

17211 Manufacture of corrugated paper and paperboard, sacks and bags
Ablebox Limited
Atlas Packaging Limited
Welton Bibby and Baron Limited

17219 Manufacture of other paper and paperboard containers
Amcor Packaging UK Limited
GWP Group Limited
GWP Holdings Limited
Olympic Varnish Co Ltd
Spirit Packaging Limited
Westfield Medical Limited
Westrock Packaging Systems UK Ltd.

17220 Manufacture of household and sanitary goods and of toilet requisites
Bodywise (UK) Limited
Marleton Cross Limited
Wallgate Limited

17230 Manufacture of paper stationery
Pukka Pads 2000 Limited

17240 Manufacture of wallpaper
Farrow & Ball Limited

17290 Manufacture of other articles of paper and paperboard n.e.c.
Advanced Coated Products Ltd
Cotek Papers Limited
Hollingsworth & Vose Co Ltd
Hollingsworth and Vose Company (U.K.)
Nissha Medical Technologies Ltd

18129 Printing n.e.c. [14]
T.H.Brickell & Son,Limited
Brickell Holdings Limited
CFH Docmail Ltd
ESP Colour Limited
Hampton Printing (Bristol) Ltd
Harrier Print Ltd
Jamjar Print Ltd
Latcham Direct Limited
Latimer,Trend & Co Ltd
Henry Ling Limited
Park Group South West Limited
St Austell Printing Co Ltd
T Shirt & Sons Limited
TJ International Limited

18130 Pre-press and pre-media services
Harrier Print Ltd

18140 Binding and related services
Harrier Print Ltd
Latimer,Trend & Co Ltd

20110 Manufacture of industrial gases
Praxair Offshore Services Ltd

20130 Manufacture of other inorganic basic chemicals
Tintometer,Limited
R Tudor Holdings Limited

20140 Manufacture of other organic basic chemicals
Geo Specialty Chemicals UK Ltd

20150 Manufacture of fertilizers and nitrogen compounds
Mole Valley Farmers Limited

20170 Manufacture of synthetic rubber in primary forms
ACC Silicones Limited

20301 Manufacture of paints, varnishes and similar coatings, mastics and sealants
Farrow & Ball Limited
N P Automotive Coatings (Europe) Ltd
Pulse Printing Products Ltd

20302 Manufacture of printing ink
Pulse Global Holdings Limited
Pulse Roll Label Products Ltd

20411 Manufacture of soap and detergents
GEA Farm Technologies (UK) Ltd

20420 Manufacture of perfumes and toilet preparations
Elemis Limited
Lush Ltd.
Lush Manufacturing Limited
Meiyume (UK) Limited
Neal's Yard (Natural Remedies) Ltd
Swallowfield PLC

20590 Manufacture of other chemical products n.e.c. [10]
J. V. Barrett & Co. Limited
Barrettine Holdings Limited
Forgeway Ltd
Italmatch UK Limited
Muc-Off Limited
SAFC Biosciences Limited
Sealock Limited
Sigma-Aldrich Co Ltd
Thermographic Measurements Ltd
Tocris Cookson Limited

20600 Manufacture of man-made fibres
Fiberlean Technologies Limited

21100 Manufacture of basic pharmaceutical products [12]
Amphastar UK Ltd
Auden McKenzie (Pharma Division) Ltd
Catalent MTI Pharma Solutions Ltd
Catalent Micron Technologies Ltd
Elemis Limited
Hyperbiotics PLC
G.R. Lane Health Products Ltd
Patheon UK Limited
Rosemont Pharmaceuticals Ltd
West Pharmaceutical Services Cornwall
Wrafton Laboratories Limited
Zogenix Europe Limited

21200 Manufacture of pharmaceutical preparations [14]
Accord-UK Ltd
Albany Molecular Research Ltd
Alliance Pharmaceuticals Ltd
Breath Limited
Catalent CTS (Edinburgh) Ltd
Hyperbiotics PLC
Bob Martin (UK) Limited
Patheon UK Limited
Pharmaxo Pharmacy Services Ltd
Porton Biopharma Limited
Qualasept Holdings Limited
Qualasept Limited
Reig Jofre UK Limited
Zogenix Europe Limited

22110 Manufacture of rubber tyres and tubes; retreading and rebuilding of rubber tyres
Bandvulc Tyres Ltd
Cooper Tire & Rubber Company Europe

22190 Manufacture of other rubber products [16]
Altec Products Limited
Avon Automotive UK Holdings Ltd
Avon Engineered Rubber Limited
Avon Polymer Products Limited
Avon Rubber P.L.C.
Cooper Tire & Rubber Company Europe
DMJ Asset Management Ltd.
DTR VMS Limited
MGI Coutier Finance Limited
SPC Europe Limited
Superior Seals Limited
Superior Specials Limited
Trelleborg Industrial Products UK Ltd
Trelleborg Retford Limited
Trelleborg Sealing Solutions UK Ltd
Trelleborg Wheel Systems UK Ltd

22210 Manufacture of plastic plates, sheets, tubes and profiles
Permali Gloucester Limited

22220 Manufacture of plastic packing goods
Amcor Flexibles UK Limited
Amcor Flexibles Winterbourne Ltd
Flextrus Limited
Leeways Packaging Services Ltd
Manuli Packaging (UK) Ltd.
Medipak Limited
Sharpak Bridgwater Limited
Sharpak Yate Limited

22230 Manufacture of builders ware of plastic

Customade (UK) Limited
Premier Double Glazed Units Ltd
Sustainable Drainage Systems Ltd

22290 Manufacture of other plastic products [28]

Advanced Coated Products Ltd
Altec Products Limited
Avalon Plastics Limited
Cavity Trays Limited,
Customade (UK) Limited
Deceuninck Limited
Dycem Limited
Essilor Limited
Genie Toys PLC
JSP Limited
Kernow Coatings Limited
MGI Coutier Finance Limited
Magmatic Limited
Merriott Plastics Group Ltd
Merriott Plastics Limited
Nylaplas Engineering Limited
Palm Equipment International Ltd
Pipex Limited
Polymermedics Limited
REPL International Limited
Rochling Engineering Plastics (UK)
Rochling Fibracon Limited
Sartorius Stedim Lab Limited
R.W.Simon Limited
Trelleborg Offshore UK Limited
Trelleborg Rochdale Limited
Tricel (Gloucester) Limited
Wrapex Limited

23120 Shaping and processing of flat glass

Premier Double Glazed Units Ltd

23130 Manufacture of hollow glass

Dartington Crystal (Torrington) Ltd

23310 Manufacture of ceramic tiles and flags

Original Style Limited

23410 Manufacture of ceramic household and ornamental articles

Devon Ceramics (Contracts) Ltd

23610 Manufacture of concrete products for construction purposes

Denis May & Sons Limited
Stowell Concrete Limited
E.Wiltshire & Son (Torquay) Ltd

23620 Manufacture of plaster products for construction purposes

Etex Building Performance Ltd

23630 Manufacture of ready-mixed concrete

Hills Quarry Products Limited
Morris & Perry (Gurney Slade Quarries)
S Morris Limited
Wiltshire Heavy Building Materials

23690 Manufacture of other articles of concrete, plaster and cement

Concrete Fabrications Limited
Stowell Concrete Limited

23990 Manufacture of other non-metallic mineral products n.e.c.

Bob Martin (UK) Limited

24330 Cold forming or folding

Harmon (Form Tools) Limited

24410 Precious metals production

BASF Metals Recycling Limited
J. Wippell & Co Ltd

24420 Aluminium production

Avon Metals Limited
Smart Aluminium Extrusions Ltd

24510 Casting of iron

Eurac Poole Limited

24520 Casting of steel

Cronite Castings Limited
Investacast Limited

24530 Casting of light metals

Avon Metals Limited
Glen Foundry Limited
Investacast Limited
MRT Castings Limited

25110 Manufacture of metal structures and parts of structures [12]

Cahill Welding Services Ltd.
Centristic Limited
Doughty Engineering Limited
Francis & Lewis International Ltd
William Haley Engineering Ltd
Isedio Limited
Ladder and Fencing Industries (Newent)
Metal Yapi (UK) Limited
John Reid & Sons (Strucsteel) Holdings
John Reid & Sons (Strucsteel) Ltd
Spenco Engineering Co. Limited
Tildenet Ltd

25120 Manufacture of doors and windows of metal

Garador Holdings Limited
Garador Limited

25210 Manufacture of central heating radiators and boilers

Kohler Showers Bidco Limited
Kohler Showers Holdings Ltd

25290 Manufacture of other tanks, reservoirs and containers of metal

Iracroft Limited
Newspace Containers Limited

25500 Forging, pressing, stamping and roll-forming of metal; powder metallurgy

Stroud Metal Co Ltd

25610 Treatment and coating of metals

Nu-Pro Limited
Poeton Industries Limited
Praxair Surface Technologies Ltd
TJW Precision Engineering Ltd

25620 Machining [21]

Air Bearings Limited
Aish Technologies Limited
Automatic Industrial Machines Ltd
Bushell & Meadows Limited
Chappell Engineering Limited
Dynamatic Limited
FGP Systems Limited
McBraida PLC
Retrac Productions Limited
Rotork Midland Limited
Rotork UK Limited
Sensata Technologies Limited
Spenco Engineering Co. Limited
H.C. Starck Limited
TJW Precision Engineering Ltd
Tetra Pak CPS Limited
Transmission Developments Co (GB)
Uni-Mill Engineering Limited
VES Precision Limited
West End Precision Limited
Wilson & Sons (Engineering) Ltd

25710 Manufacture of cutlery

Robert Welch Designs Limited

25720 Manufacture of locks and hinges

Cotswold Architectural Products Ltd
Kaba Limited

25730 Manufacture of tools

Eroga Die Co Ltd
Quickgrind Limited
Rigibore Limited
TMB Patterns Limited
West End Precision Limited
XYZ Machine Tools Limited

25920 Manufacture of light metal packaging

Ball Aerocan UK Limited
Cannon Technologies Limited

25930 Manufacture of wire products, chain and springs

William Hughes Limited
Preformed Line Products (Great Britain)
Witon Engineering Limited

25940 Manufacture of fasteners and screw machine products

Barton Cold-Form (UK) Limited
Witon Engineering Limited

25990 Manufacture of other fabricated metal products n.e.c. [49]

Avon Valley Precision Engineering
BIL Group Limited
L.B. Bentley Limited
Bott Limited
Bowmill Engineering Limited
Cannon Technologies Limited
Centek Limited
Centristic Limited
Constructor Group UK Limited
Cross Manufacturing Company (1938)
Eliquo Hydrok Limited
F & B Profiles Limited
Flexiguide Limited
Fylde CNC Specialists Limited
G3 Systems Limited
Gazco Limited
High Tech Fabrications Limited
Horstman Defence Systems Ltd
Hospital Metalcraft Limited
Hydro Building Systems UK Ltd
Hydro Components UK Ltd.
Impcross Limited
Kaba Limited
Klaw Products Limited
Kohler Showers Bidco Limited
Kohler Showers Holdings Ltd
Ladder and Fencing Industries (Newent)
Latchways PLC
Mabey Bridge Limited
Mabey and Johnson Limited
Mar-Key Marquees Limited
Meggitt Aerospace Limited
Herman Miller Limited
Powrmatic Limited
RCR Flooring Products Limited
Rittal-C S M Limited
Rotamic Engineering Limited
Rotork Midland Limited
SF Ltd
South West Metal Finishing Ltd
Staines Trailers Ltd
Stovax Limited
Tecan Limited
Teignbridge Propellers International
Troax (U.K.) Limited
Troax Lee Manufacturing Ltd
Truflo Air Movement Limited
Uni-Mill Engineering Limited
Vee Bee Filtration UK Limited

26110 Manufacture of electronic components [19]

Alertsystems Limited
Corintech Limited
Curtiss-Wright Controls (UK) Ltd
Eurotech Group PLC
GE Aviation Systems Limited
Geist Europe Ltd
Gill Instruments Limited
Gill Sensors & Controls Ltd
Gooch & Housego (Torquay) Ltd
Graphic PLC
L.E.W. Techniques Limited
Microsemi Semiconductor Ltd
Phyworks Limited
Spinnaker International Ltd
Swindon Silicon Systems Ltd
TDK-Lambda UK Limited
Texas Instruments (U.K.) Ltd
Texas Instruments Limited
Tyco Electronics UK Ltd

26120 Manufacture of loaded electronic boards

Connexion Technologies Limited
Cotswold Micro Systems Limited
Custom Interconnect Limited
Heber Limited
WMG Group Ltd

26200 Manufacture of computers and peripheral equipment

Amulet Hotkey Ltd
Decision Logic Ltd
Flowbird Transport Limited
Magicard Ltd
Roland DG (U.K.) Limited
Secure Systems & Technologies Ltd
Spire Payments Ltd

26301 Manufacture of telegraph and telephone apparatus and equipment

AGD Systems Limited

26309 Manufacture of communication equipment other than telegraph, and telephone apparatus and equipment

Chelton Limited
Pulse Power and Measurement Ltd

26400 Manufacture of consumer electronics

Allen & Heath Limited
Creedon Technologies Limited
Naim Audio Limited

26511 Manufacture of electronic measuring, testing etc. equipment, not for industrial process control [20]

Aeronautical & General Instruments
Atlantic Inertial Systems Ltd
Avalon Sciences Limited
Beran Instruments Limited
Drilling Systems (U.K.) Ltd
Drilling Systems Group Limited
Drilling Systems Limited
Jam Bidco Limited
Lascar Electronics Limited
M.K. Test Systems Ltd.
Mantracourt Electronics Ltd
Mecwash Systems Limited
Radiodetection Limited
Renishaw P L C
Spectrum Medical Group Limited
Spectrum Medical Limited
Thermographic Measurements Ltd
Topcon Technology Limited
Valeport Limited
Wagtech Projects Ltd

26512 Manufacture of electronic industrial process control equipment

Lascar Electronics Limited
Meggitt Aerospace Limited
Pulsar Process Measurement Ltd
Tintometer,Limited
Trelleborg Marine Systems UK Ltd

26514 Manufacture of non-electronic industrial process control equipment

Tintometer,Limited

26701 Manufacture of optical precision instruments

Aeronautical & General Instruments
Gooch & Housego (UK) Limited
Gooch & Housego PLC
Sesanti Limited

27110 Manufacture of electric motors, generators and transformers

Aero Stanrew Limited
Centrax Limited
Control Techniques Dynamics Ltd
Piller UK Limited
Powervamp Limited

27120 Manufacture of electricity distribution and control apparatus

Carling Technologies Limited
Fundamentals Limited

27310 Manufacture of fibre optic cables

Seacon (Europe) Limited

27320 Manufacture of other electronic and electric wires and cables

Fabrinet UK Limited
Gemaco Holdings Limited
Seacon (Europe) Limited

27330 Manufacture of wiring devices

Tamura-Europe Limited

27400 Manufacture of electric lighting equipment

Danlers Limited
Dexeco Limited
Dexretail Limited
Dextra Group PLC
Dextra Services Limited
Ledex Limited
Plessey Lighting Limited

27510 Manufacture of electric domestic appliances

Dyson Finance Limited
Dyson International Limited
Dyson James Group Limited
Dyson James Limited
Dyson Limited
Dyson Technology Limited
Everhot Ltd.

27520 Manufacture of non-electric domestic appliances

Hunter Stoves Limited

27900 Manufacture of other electrical equipment [19]

Aish Technologies Limited
Cobham Defence Communications Ltd
Condition Monitoring Group Ltd
Daktronics UK Limited
Dyson James Limited
Helitune Limited
Huachangda UK Limited
IXYS UK Westcode Ltd.
Metric Group Limited
P & B Weir Electrical Limited
PB Design and Developments Ltd
Parsons Peebles Service Ltd
Penny & Giles Controls Limited
Plessey Semiconductors Limited
SRT Marine Technology Limited
TRL Electronics Limited
TRL Technology Limited
Toyo Denso U.K. Limited
Wheeler's (Westbury) Limited

28110 Manufacture of engines and turbines, except aircraft, vehicle and cycle engines

Atlantis Operations (UK) Ltd
Beta Marine Limited
Caterpillar Marine Power UK Ltd

28120 Manufacture of fluid power equipment

Bifold Fluidpower Limited
Helipebs (Holdings) Limited
Hydreco Hydraulics Limited
Kawasaki Precision Machinery (UK)
Star Hydraulics Limited
Wartsila Water Systems Limited

28131 Manufacture of pumps [10]

Dutypoint Limited
Dynamatic Limited
Marshalsea Hydraulics Limited
NOV Process & Flow Technologies UK
SPP Pumps Limited
Severn Glocon Group PLC
Spirax-Sarco Engineering PLC
Spirax-Sarco Limited
Watson-Marlow Limited
Xylem Dewatering Solutions UK Ltd

28140 Manufacture of taps and valves [11]

L.B. Bentley Limited
Bifold Fluidpower Limited
Curtiss-Wright Flow Control (UK) Ltd
IMI Webber Limited
Kohler Mira Limited
Marshalsea Hydraulics Limited
Rotork Midland Limited
Seetru Limited
Severn Glocon Limited
Severn Unival Limited
Thompson Valves Limited

28150 Manufacture of bearings, gears, gearing and driving elements

Barden Corporation (U.K.) Ltd
Daido Industrial Bearings Europe Ltd
Dynamatic Limited
Kelston Precision Gears Ltd
Rotork Controls Limited

28210 Manufacture of ovens, furnaces and furnace burners

Hamworthy Combustion Engineering Ltd

28220 Manufacture of lifting and handling equipment

CKF Systems Limited
Maats Tech Limited
Manitou UK Limited
Stannah Lift Services Limited
Stannah Lifts Limited
Whites Material Handling Ltd

28250 Manufacture of non-domestic cooling and ventilation equipment

A1 Engineering Solutions Ltd
Draper Ventilation Limited
SHOO 788AA Limited
Space Engineering Services Ltd

28290 Manufacture of other general-purpose machinery n.e.c. [10]

Air Control Industries Limited
Carlisle Fluid Technologies UK Ltd
Euro-Diesel (UK) Limited
Heating Products Limited
M P Filtri (UK) Limited
Marden Edwards Limited
Mzuri Limited
Paper Converting Machine Co Ltd
Pluss Organisation CIC
Universal Balancing Limited

28301 Manufacture of agricultural tractors

C & O Tractors Limited

28302 Manufacture of agricultural and forestry machinery other than tractors

Alvan Blanch Development Co Ltd
Alvan Blanch Holdings Limited
Lister Shearing Equipment Ltd
Redwood Global Limited
Teagle Holdings Limited
Teagle Machinery Limited

28490 Manufacture of other machine tools

Independent Tool Consultants Ltd
Novanta Technologies UK Ltd

28921 Manufacture of machinery for mining

Antech Limited

28922 Manufacture of earthmoving equipment

Auger Torque Europe Limited
Whites Material Handling Ltd

28923 Manufacture of equipment for concrete crushing and screening and roadworks

Phoenix Engineering Co Ltd

28930 Manufacture of machinery for food, beverage and tobacco processing

Brook Food Processing Equipment Ltd
Coffetek Limited
Kliklok International Limited
Colin Mear Engineering Ltd
Western Mechanical Handling UK Ltd

28960 Manufacture of plastics and rubber machinery

Flight Refuelling Limited

28990 Manufacture of other special-purpose machinery n.e.c. [25]

AGR Automation Limited
ASM Assembly Systems Weymouth Ltd
Alderley Systems Ltd
Applied Automation (UK) Ltd
Autonumis Limited
BOFA International Ltd.
Anthony Best Dynamics Limited
Bioquell UK Limited
Blakell Europlacer Limited
Crane Merchandising Systems Ltd
D-Tech (UK) Limited
DDC Dolphin Limited
Etavoni Limited
Fulton Boiler Works, (Great Britain)
Hartridge Limited
Kliklok International Limited
Marden Edwards Limited
Mitutoyo (U.K.) Limited
Multivac U.K. Limited
Roots Systems Limited
Rotolok (Holdings) Limited
Specialised Management Services Ltd
TBS Engineering Limited
W.D.M.Limited
Wilson Tool International [Europe]

29100 Manufacture of motor vehicles

Honda of The U.K. Manufacturing Ltd
Red Kite Vehicle Consultants Ltd

29201 Manufacture of bodies (coachwork) for motor vehicles (except caravans)

G-TEKT Europe Manufacturing Ltd
Regal Holiday Homes Limited

29202 Manufacture of trailers and semi-trailers

Rothdean Limited
Steve Vick International Ltd

29203 Manufacture of caravans

Bailey Caravans Limited

29310 Manufacture of electrical and electronic equipment for motor vehicles and their engines

Ashwoods Electric Motors Ltd
Eberspacher (U.K.) Limited

29320 Manufacture of other parts and accessories for motor vehicles [13]

Barden Corporation (U.K.) Ltd
Delphi Diesel Systems Limited
Dura Automotive Limited
Eberspacher Exhaust Technology UK
European Friction Industries Ltd
GM Coachwork Limited
Goodridge Limited
Iracroft Limited
Janspeed Technologies Limited
Johnan UK Limited
Knorr-Bremse Systems for Commercial Vehicles
Meggitt (UK) Limited
Sanoh UK Manufacturing Limited

30110 Building of ships and floating structures

Appledore Shipbuilders (2004) Ltd
Devonport Royal Dockyard Ltd
Sunseeker International Ltd
C. Toms and Son Limited

30120 Building of pleasure and sporting boats

Pendennis Shipyard (Holdings) Ltd
Pendennis Shipyard Limited
Princess Yachts Limited

30300 Manufacture of air and spacecraft and related machinery [21]

AIM Aviation (Henshalls) Ltd
AgustaWestland Limited
Aim Altitude UK Limited
Aim Composites Limited
Airbus Operations Limited
Broadway (Bristol) Engineering Co Ltd
Future Advanced Manufacture Ltd
GE Aviation UK
GE Infrastructure Aviation
Highship Industries Limited
Magellan Aerospace (Blackpool) Ltd
McBraida PLC
Meggitt (UK) Limited
Meggitt Aerospace Limited
Moog Controls Limited
Moog Wolverhampton Limited
PDQ Airspares Limited
PDQ Group Limited
Rotable Repairs Limited
Safran Landing Systems UK Ltd
Systems Engineering & Assessment Ltd

30400 Manufacture of military fighting vehicles

Supacat Limited

30990 Manufacture of other transport equipment n.e.c.

Aeronautical & General Instruments
Flowbird Transport Limited
Fluid Transfer International Ltd
Rexquote Ltd
Supacat Limited
Systems Engineering & Assessment Ltd

31010 Manufacture of office and shop furniture

Arno GB Limited
Herman Miller Holdings Ltd

31020 Manufacture of kitchen furniture

Raventree Limited
System 6 Kitchens Limited

31030 Manufacture of mattresses

Airsprung Furniture Limited
One Holding Limited
Vi - Spring Limited

31090 Manufacture of other furniture

Airsprung Furniture Limited
Audience Systems Limited
Devonshire Pine Limited
Duresta Upholstery Limited
Cameron Fuller Limited
G Plan Upholstery Limited
Gloster Furniture Limited
Hospital Metalcraft Limited
Parker Knoll Upholstery Ltd

32120 Manufacture of jewellery and related articles

Batten and Allen Limited

32300 Manufacture of sports goods

Tildenet Ltd

32409 Manufacture of other games and toys, n.e.c.

Magmatic Limited
Worlds Apart Holdings Limited
Worlds Apart Limited

32500 Manufacture of medical and dental instruments and supplies [24]

BBGR Limited
A D Burs Limited
Corin Group Limited
Corin Holdings Limited
Corin International Limited
Corin Limited
Corin Orthopaedics Holdings Ltd
Corin USA Limited
Electric Mobility Euro Limited
Integra Neurosciences Limited
K2 Medical Systems Limited
Marlux Medical Limited
Medisafe UK Limited
Norville Group Limited
Orthod Group Limited
Orthod Midco Limited
Orthodynamics Limited
P3 Medical Limited
Pearsalls Limited
Research Instruments Limited
Summit Medical Limited
Surgical Specialties UK Holdings Ltd
Vacsax Limited
Xograph Healthcare Limited

32910 Manufacture of brooms and brushes

Hill Brush Co Ltd

32990 Other manufacturing n.e.c. [87]

AFL Telecommunications Europe Ltd
Advanced Insulation Contracting Ltd
Advanced Insulation Limited
Advanced Insulation Systems Ltd
Anglo-American Vulcanized Fibre Ltd
Arada Limited
R.J. Bateman (Engineering) Ltd
Batten and Allen Limited
Beagle Technology Group Ltd
Bituchem Holdings Limited
Bluetech Systems International Ltd
CQC Limited
CRC Industries UK Limited
Calleva Limited
Catalent U.K. Packaging Ltd
Colebrook Bosson & Saunders (Products)
Cornish Concrete Products Ltd
Creanova Universal Closures Ltd
Dart Sensors Limited
Dezac Group Limited
Dover Engineered Systems UK Ltd
Dragon Alfa Cement Limited
H.H.& D.E.Drew Limited
European Friction Industries Ltd
Exyte Hargreaves Limited
Faerch Plast Poole Ltd
Gall Thomson Environmental Ltd
Gazco Limited
Genevac Limited
Get Fresh Cosmetics Ltd
E.J. Godwin (Peat Industries) Ltd
Harkwell Labels Limited
Harrison Products Co Limited
Huachangda UK Limited
IDEMIA UK Limited
IEP Technologies Limited
Integrity Print Limited
J+S Limited
JSP Limited
Jasun Envirocare PLC
Leoni Temco Limited
Lily-Flame Ltd
Limbs & Things Limited
Lornamead UK Limited
MCAARP Holdings Limited
MSA (Britain) Limited
Magellan Aerospace (UK) Ltd
Magnet Sales and Service Ltd
Bob Martin (UK) Limited
Matki PLC
Maxim Integrated Products UK Ltd
Colin Mear Limited
Neal's Yard (Natural Remedies) Ltd
Novanta Technologies UK Ltd
Off Site Solutions (R T) Ltd
P & M Group Limited
Partington Engineering Limited
Pennant International Limited
Practical Developments (South West)
Prima Dental Manufacturing Ltd
Quickmach Engineering Limited
Regal Holiday Homes Limited
Rotalink Limited
SEAFox Dycem 1 Limited
SEAFox Dycem 2 Limited
Shearwell Data Limited
Signet Armorlite Europe Ltd
Silicon Sensing Systems Ltd
Smithbrewer Limited
Standard Brands (UK) Limited
Stannah Stairlifts Limited

Stovax Limited
Suttons Seeds Limited
Synergy Health (UK) Limited
Tetronics (International) Ltd
Tintometer,Limited
Total Carbide Ltd
Total Laminate Systems Ltd
Tradestock Limited
Edwin Tucker & Sons Limited
Versarien PLC
Wallgate Limited
Wasdell Packaging Limited
West Brothers (Frome) Ltd
Western Global Holdings Ltd
Western Global Limited
T.D. Williamson (U.K.) Ltd

33120 Repair of machinery

Brook Food Processing Equipment Ltd
C J Cox Limited
Forest Press Hydraulics Ltd
GEA Farm Technologies (UK) Ltd
Hamblys Limited
Holt JCB Holdings Limited
Holt JCB Limited
Juliana Group Limited
Stannah Lift Services Limited

33130 Repair of electronic and optical equipment

Aeronautical & General Instruments
Mount International United Services Ltd

33140 Repair of electrical equipment

Centrax Limited
Infoteam International Services Ltd
Triumph Engineering (UK) Co. Ltd

33150 Repair and maintenance of ships and boats

Darthaven Marina Limited
SCA Group Limited
C. Toms and Son Limited

33160 Repair and maintenance of aircraft and spacecraft

AgustaWestland Limited
Euravia Engineering & Supply Co. Ltd
Safran Landing Systems Services UK Ltd

33170 Repair and maintenance of other transport equipment n.e.c.

Knorr-Bremse Rail Systems (UK) Ltd
Supacat Limited
T. H. White Limited

33190 Repair of other equipment

A1 Engineering Solutions Ltd
Hydro International (Wastewater) Ltd
Leafield Logistics & Technical Services
Space Engineering Services Ltd
Tecalemit Garage Equipment Co Ltd
Wood Energy Limited

33200 Installation of industrial machinery and equipment [13]

M.J. Abbott Limited
Blakell Europlacer (Intl) Ltd
Centrax Limited
Honda Engineering Europe Ltd
Hydro International (Wastewater) Ltd
Import Export Services (GRP) Ltd
Import Export Services Ltd
KK Daytona Holding Ltd
Kranlyft UK Limited
Proco-STS Limited
Stannah Lift Services Limited
Tecalemit Garage Equipment Co Ltd
Wood Energy Limited

35110 Production of electricity [99]

A7 Lochhead Limited
Alliance Homes (Ventures) Ltd
An Suidhe Wind Farm Limited
Armstrong Energy Global Ltd
Aster Solar Limited
Autumnus Energy Limited
BGS 103 Hurst Solar Park Ltd
BGS 104 Sedbury Solar Park Ltd
Bambers Wind Park Limited
Bee Green Energy Ltd.
Bee Green Solar Limited
Bilbster Wind Farm Limited
Boardinghouse Windfarm Limited
Bristol Port Wind Park Limited
Brooke Energy (Engineering) Ltd
Cannington Enterprises Limited
Cardiff Wind Park Limited
Cheshire Coppice PV Ltd
Clean Earth Energy Investments Ltd
Clean Earth Wind Turbines Ltd
Codford Biogas Limited
Crug Mawr Solar Farm Limited
Dagenham Wind Park Limited
Dilkes Energy Limited
Dundee Merchant Wind Park Ltd
EDF Energy Nuclear Generation Ltd
EVGH Limited
Eco Sustainable Solutions Ltd
Eelpower (Opco1) Limited
Ernesettle Community Solar Ltd
Fen Farm Wind Park Limited
Frome Solar Limited
Galsworthy Wind Park Limited
Gamma Energy Limited
Gawcott Fields Community Solar Project C.I.C.
Golden Hill Solar Limited
Good Energy Carloggas Solar Park (009)
Good Energy Cross Road Plantation Solar Park (028)
Good Energy Delabole Windfarm Ltd
Good Energy Generation Assets No. 1
Good Energy Group PLC
Good Energy Hampole Windfarm Ltd
Good Energy Holding Company No. 1
Good Energy Lower End Farm Solar Park (026)
Good Energy Rook Wood Solar Park (057)
Good Energy Woolbridge Solar Park (010)
Gretton Solar Farm Limited
Gwynt y Mor Offshore Wind Farm Ltd
Higher Tregarne Solar (UK) Ltd
Hitachi Nuclear Projects Development Europe
Horizon Nuclear Power Limited
Horizon Nuclear Power Oldbury Ltd
Horizon Nuclear Power Services Ltd
Horizon Nuclear Power Wylfa Ltd
Innogy Renewables UK Limited
KS SPV 12 Limited
KS SPV 9 Limited
KWTN Solar Limited
Kat-O-Log Limited
Knabs Ridge Wind Farm Limited
Leys Solar Energy C.I.C.
Little Bear Solar Limited
Little Cheyne Court Wind Farm Ltd
Liverton 2014 Limited
Lower Easton Solar C.I.C.
Merston Renewable Energy CIC
Michco 1204 Limited
Michco 1205 Limited
Natems Sugar Holdings (UK) Ltd
Northern Hydropower Limited
Nuon UK Ltd
Otter Power Limited
Pen y Cymoedd Wind Farm Ltd
Pendine Wind Farm Limited
Pentland Road Windfarm Limited
Pingry Solar Ltd
RWE Cogen UK (Hythe) Limited
RWE Cogen UK Limited
RWE Generation UK PLC
RWE Markinch Limited
Renewable Energy Partnerships Ltd
Repal Co-Gen (UK) Limited
Rhyl Flats Wind Farm Limited
Rodbourne Rail Farm Solar Park Ltd
Seabank Power Limited
Shoals Hook Solar (UK) Limited
Shooters Bottom Wind Park Ltd
Sunpower Solar Limited
Swinford Wind Farm Limited
Thrive Renewables (Boardinghouse)
Thrive Renewables (Caton Moor) Ltd
Thrive Renewables (Eye) Ltd
Thrive Renewables (Severn) Ltd
UK Solar Projects Limited
Verdant Community Energy C.I.C.
Viridor Oxfordshire Limited
Viridor South London Limited
Woodland Barton Renewables Ltd
Yorkshire Hydropower Limited

35120 Transmission of electricity

Fenchurch Engineering Services Ltd
Good Energy Group PLC
npower Northern Limited
npower Yorkshire Limited

35130 Distribution of electricity

Western Power Distribution (East Midlands)
Western Power Distribution (South Wales)
Western Power Distribution (South West)
Western Power Distribution (West Midlands)
Western Power Distribution PLC
npower Direct Limited
npower Limited

35140 Trade of electricity

Bristol Energy Limited
Eelpower (Opco1) Limited
Good Energy Limited
I Supply Energy Limited
Renewable Energy Co Ltd

35210 Manufacture of gas

Cannington Enterprises Limited
Eco Sustainable Solutions Ltd
Malaby Biogas Limited
Tornagrain Gas Mill Limited

35220 Distribution of gaseous fuels through mains

Good Energy Gas Limited
Plus Shipping Services Limited
npower Commercial Gas Limited
npower Direct Limited
npower Gas Limited

35230 Trade of gas through mains

Bristol Energy Limited
I Supply Energy Limited
Renewable Energy Co Ltd
Spark Gas Shipping Ltd

35300 Steam and air conditioning supply

RWE Cogen UK (Hythe) Limited

36000 Water collection, treatment and supply

Bristol Water Holdings Limited
Bristol Water PLC
Highship Industries Limited
South West Water Limited
Wessex Water Limited
Wessex Water Services Limited

37000 Sewerage

Clear-Flow Limited
Geneco Limited
South West Water Limited

38110 Collection of non-hazardous waste [13]

Abacus (Bristol) Limited
Bristol Waste Co Ltd
Cannington Enterprises Limited
EMS Waste Services Limited
Grist Environmental Limited
H & A Recycling Limited
Hills Waste Solutions Limited
SWM & Waste Recycling Limited
Sheerness Recycling Limited
Smith's (Gloucester) Limited
Viridor Waste (West Sussex) Ltd
W & S Waste Management Limited
Wessex Water Enterprises Ltd

38120 Collection of hazardous waste

Grist Environmental Limited

38210 Treatment and disposal of non-hazardous waste [12]

H.H.& D.E.Drew Limited
EMS Waste Services Limited
Grist Environmental Limited
Hills Waste Solutions Limited
MVV Environment Devonport Ltd
Public Power Solutions Limited
SWM & Waste Recycling Limited
Smith's (Gloucester) Limited
Stuart Partners Limited
UBB Waste (Essex) Limited
UBB Waste (Gloucestershire) Ltd
W & S Waste Management Limited

38220 Treatment and disposal of hazardous waste

Grist Environmental Limited
Hills Waste Solutions Limited
Public Power Solutions Limited

38320 Recovery of sorted materials [12]

Canford Renewable Energy Ltd
Coastal UK Group Limited
Deep Moor LF Limited
Devon Contract Waste Ltd
ETM Recycling Limited
Hills Waste Solutions Limited
PSW Metals Limited
Perrys Recycling Limited
SWM & Waste Recycling Limited
E.J. Shanley & Son (Trowbridge) Ltd
Viridor Oxfordshire Limited
Viridor South London Limited

39000 Remediation activities and other waste management services [10]

A-Gas (UK) Limited
Advanced Waste Solutions Ltd
M J Church (Plant) Limited
Clear-Flow Limited
Ecosurety Limited
Sanctus Limited
Shield Environmental Holdings Ltd
Shield Environmental Services Ltd
J C Thomas & Sons Limited
Urbaser Limited

41100 Development of building projects [266]

Addison Developments Limited
Alleyford Limited
Alpha Schools (Highland) Holdings
Alpha Schools (Highland) Ltd
Alpha Schools (Highland) Project PLC
Ameriscot Commercial Limited
Ankers and Rawlings Developments Ltd
Anstee & Ware Group Limited
Apex One Limited
Areawise Limited
Aster Homes Limited
Austral-Asia World LLC UK Ltd
Autograph Homes (Hambrook) Ltd
Autograph Homes Limited
Avondale Builders Limited
BDV Atlantic Ltd
M. Baker (Property Services) Ltd
Baker Estates Limited
Balimark Limited
Barrington Brown Estates Ltd
Barton Farms Limited
J.T.Baylis & Co Ltd
Baylis Estates Limited
Bayshill Properties Limited
Bayview Developments (South) Ltd
Beacon Homes Limited
Bentley Slade Limited
Best Western Enterprises Ltd
Beylon Limited
Bicknell Holdings PLC
Ken Biggs Contractors Limited
Birchclaim Limited
Black Gold Developments (UK) Ltd
Blast Properties Limited
Boo Homes (Leckhampton) Ltd
Brabon Properties Limited
Branksome Estates Ltd.
Bridge Road Limited
Bristol Care Homes Development Ltd
Buckclose Limited
CBSM 2012 Limited
CDS Group Services Limited
CHG Developments (Southampton) Ltd
Calendula Assets Limited
Canprop II Limited
Canynge Bicknell (Street) Ltd
Canynge Bicknell Limited
Captiva Homes Limited
Cartus Financing Limited
Cartus Holdings Limited
Cartus Limited
J.T. Castle Limited
Castlewood (Commercial) Properties
T K T Cattran Limited
Chantry Court Westbury Ltd
Charminster Farm Limited
Chatlease Limited
Chota Estates Co Ltd
Clarart Ltd
Colburn Developments Limited
Colburn East Limited
Complete Design & Construction Ltd
J.A. Cover Limited
Coxley Developments Limited
Cribbs Triangle Limited
Crossman (Lansdown) Ltd
Crownhold PLC
Cruciform Services Limited
Crystalight Limited
Cult Clothing Cheltenham Ltd
Curo Enterprise Limited
D.J.L.Securities (Barum) Ltd
Dean Clarke Estate Ltd
Deeley Freed Estates Limited
Del Piero Limited
Devonfields Limited
Dribuild Limited
Eagle One Limited
Eco-Bos Development Limited
Elliott Heron Limited
Empire Homes (South West) Ltd
Evershot Construction Limited
Exepex Estates Limited
FDL Salterns Limited
Fairlynx Limited
First Step Homes Limited
Five Directions Limited
Forelle Estates Limited
Forward Developments Limited
Fraser St James Investments Ltd
Fresh Homes (Bournemouth) Ltd
Gaiger Brothers Limited
Gale Homes and Investments Ltd
Gilbert and Goode Limited
Gilltown Limited
Gilstone Partnership Limited
Gloucester Land Co Ltd
W.G. Gould & Sons Limited
Green Spinnaker Limited
Greensquare Homes Limited
Grosvenor Place Holdings Ltd
Guild Bristol Limited
HAB at Lovedon Fields Ltd
HDM Leisure Limited
Halsall Construction Limited
A. Hammond & Sons Limited
Hannick Homes & Developments Ltd

Harlequin Homes (UK) Limited
Harris & Harris Construction Ltd
Harris Bros. and Collard Ltd
Hautot Developments Limited
Hawksworth Securities PLC
Haynes Developments Limited
Highfield Homes of Distinction Ltd
Hills UK Limited
Hinton Capital Investments Ltd
Robert Hitchins Limited
Holton Homes Limited
Homer & Pardy Developments Ltd
Hopkins Estates Limited
Host Properties Limited
ITP Developments Limited
Innsworth Technology Park Ltd
J.J. Acquisitions Limited
J.P.C.Properties (Southampton) Ltd
Jensen-Faulkner Limited
D R Jones Yeovil Ltd.
Juniper Homes (Wilder) Limited
Kelston Properties 2 Limited
E.P. Keogh Contractors Ltd.
Kersfield Developments (Ensleigh South)
Kersfield Developments (RHS) Ltd
J.Knapp & Sons Limited
Knights Green Estates Limited
Koori Limited
LLK Property Limited
Landmark Developments (Oakford House)
Landmark Estates (London) Ltd
Leander Developments Limited
Leckhampton Estates (Ullenwood) Ltd
Legacy Properties Limited
Leicester BSF Holdings Company 1 Ltd
Leicester BSF Holdings Company 2 Ltd
Levitt UK Real Estate Limited
Lingfield Properties Limited
Litt Holdings Limited
Little Venice Developments Ltd
Loumin Estates Limited
M K Property & Letting Limited
M. & P. Food Products Limited
MC Property Ventures Limited
MJL Cornwall Limited
Magna Manor Developments Ltd
Mainchannel Developments Ltd
Malbury Properties Limited
Manawey Developments Limited
Manchester Working Limited
Marlborough Facilities Limited
Matthews Properties Limited
Mayflower Properties (SW) Ltd
McCarthy & Stone (Developments) Ltd
McCarthy & Stone Retirement Lifestyles
McCarthy Contracting & Development
Mead Realisations Limited
Medcentres PLC
Melbourne Homes Limited
Metropolitan Land and House Co Ltd
NJG Contracting Limited
Netvox Limited
North Devon Homes
North Place Developments Ltd
S. Notaro Group Limited
S. Notaro Limited
Ocean Village Waterside Developments
Oceanview Developments Limited
Old Mills Estates Limited
Ophir Finance Co Ltd
Orange Door Property Co Ltd
Orproperty Limited
Oval Estates (Bath) Limited
P S J Properties Ltd.
PAL Properties South West Ltd
PCBL Limited
PJAC (Bristol) Limited
PJAC Developments Limited
PMMR Developments Limited
Harry J Palmer (Broadstone) Ltd
Pang Investments Limited
Parham Development Limited
Parham Investment Limited
Parking Glasgow Limited
Paull & Co Ltd
Pearce Construction (Barnstaple) Ltd
Pembridge Property Development Ltd
Pendennis Properties (Bournemouth)
Peninsula Properties (Exeter) Ltd
Pennyfarthing Developments Ltd
Pennyfarthing Homes Limited
Pennyfarthing New Homes Ltd
Henry W. Pollard & Sons Ltd
Gordon L. Poole (Southampton) Ltd
Porthia Limited
Portlemouth Estates Limited
Practical Developments (South West)
Prideaux Developments Limited
Primetower Properties Limited
Quantum Group (Management) Ltd
Raven Mount Services Co Ltd
Raw Investments Limited
Redruth Facilities Limited
Reed Construction & Developments Ltd
Richards Homes Limited
Ridgevale Estates Limited
Rollo Homes Number One Ltd
Rowe & Co.Cornwall (Properties) Ltd
Rowe Estates (UK) Limited
Royal Bay Care Homes Ltd
Rusty Shilling Developments Ltd
Samara Investments (2000) Ltd
Samara Investments Limited
Satnam Investments Limited
Securivin Limited
Site Developments (Ferndown) Ltd
Sleepers Hill (Winchester) Ltd
Southside Regeneration Limited
Springvale Properties Limited
St Aubyn Estates Ltd
St. Moritz Developments Ltd
J.E.Stacey & Co.Limited
Stepping Stone Group Limited
Summerfield Developments (SW) Ltd
Summerfield Estates Ltd
Summerfield SD3 Limited
Sunnybanks Homes (SW) Limited
Surereed Limited
Sureserve Holdings Limited
Sutton Harbour Projects Ltd
Swedish Lifestyle Homes No.1 Ltd
T2 Partnership Ltd
Tauntfield Ltd
Temple Guiting Manor Limited
Terramond Limited
Toogoods Property Co Ltd
Triangle Properties (Bristol) Ltd
Troika Developments Limited
Troika Eastleigh Properties Ltd
Tubbs (UK) Ltd
Universal Promotions Limited
Urban Creation (Charlotte Street) Ltd
Urban Creation (Shaw) Limited
Vauxhall Estates Limited
B.Walker & Co.(Dursley) Ltd
Walker Developments (South West) Ltd
West Coast Developments (Sandbanks)
West End Investments Clifton Ltd
Westcoast (Bristol) Limited
Westward Investment Management Services (UK)
Whitecroft Developments Ltd
Percy Williams & Sons,Limited
Willow Green Developments Ltd
Witney Holdings Limited
Wolverhampton Radiology Ltd
Woodstock Estates Limited
A. & J. Woolf Properties Ltd
M.E. Wynn & Co. Limited
YTL Property Holdings (UK) Ltd

41201 Construction of commercial buildings [81]

Abbey Manor Developments Ltd
Abbey Manor Group Limited
Accommodation Services (Holdings)
Acheson Construction Limited
Arlington Limited
B.& M. Babbage & Co. Limited
Barnwood Construction Limited
Barnwood Group Limited
E.W. Beard Limited
Ken Biggs Limited
Blue3 (London) Limited
Bluewater Property Limited
Brick Peers Limited
Brownbrink Ltd
Burry and Knight Limited
By Education (Barking) Holdings Ltd
By Education (Barking) Limited
E.G.Carter & Co Ltd
Churngold Construction Limited
City Monument Properties Ltd
R.S. Cook & Sons Limited
Cover Construction Co Ltd
A.C. Crocker (Properties) Ltd
F.H. Cummings
Devon Contractors Limited
Dribuild Limited
E T M Contractors Limited
Evershot Construction Limited
Fazakerley Prison Services Ltd
Flower & Hayes Limited
G.E. Developments Ltd
Gazelle Properties Limited
Gilbert and Goode Limited
Gilltown Limited
Grange Mill Investments Ltd
A. Hammond & Sons Limited
Harris & Harris Construction Ltd
Harris Bros. and Collard Ltd
Haynes Developments Limited
Robert Hitchins Limited
Hoburne Development Co Ltd
B.R.Hodgson Facades Limited
Hospital Company (Dartford) Group
Hospital Company (Dartford) Ltd
ISG Pearce Limited
Innex Investments Ltd
Integrated Accommodation Services PLC
Leicester BSF Company 1 Ltd
Leicester BSF Company 2 Ltd
Midas Construction Limited
Midas Group Limited
Mildren Construction Limited
Newham Learning Partnership (Project Co)

Newham Transformation Partnership
PDF Erection Services Limited
Parsons Construction Limited
Pearce Construction (Barnstaple) Ltd
R.M. Penny (Plant Hire and Demolition)
Quantum Teddington Development Ltd
Radquill Developments Limited
Read Construction (SW) Limited
Roadform Civil Engineering Co Ltd
Robertson Developments Ltd
Romfield Holdings Limited
Services Support (Avon & Somerset)
Snape Construction Limited
Square One Construction Ltd
J.E.Stacey & Co.Limited
Steele Davis Limited
Stowford Mill Development Ltd
Summerfield Developments (SW) Ltd
Summerfield Estates Ltd
Summerfield SD3 Limited
Techumbre Limited
Town Hospitals (Southern General) Ltd
Truscotts (Barnstaple) Limited
UK Court Services (Manchester) Ltd
Westward Investment Management Services (UK)
Whitelock & Co Ltd
Lewis Wyatt (Construction) Ltd
Wyatt Homes Limited

41202 Construction of domestic buildings [119]

010 Limited
3MS Construction Limited
A.J. Developments Limited
Ableway Developments Limited
Acheson Construction Limited
Acorn Builders (Pewsey) Ltd
Acorn Developments (SW) Ltd
Aster Property Limited
Bell Contracting Limited
K W Bell Group Limited
Betterment Properties (Weymouth) Ltd
Blue Cedar Homes Limited
Bracken Developments Limited
Brick Peers Limited
Brownbrink Ltd
Burrington Estates (Clyst St George)
Burrington Estates (Trispen) Ltd
Burry and Knight Limited
Carrington Fox Developments Ltd
E.G.Carter & Co Ltd
Cavanna Group Limited
Cavanna Homes (Cornwall) Ltd
Cavanna Homes (Devon) Limited
Cavanna Homes (South West) Ltd
Charlcombe Homes Limited
Churchill Retirement Living Ltd
Coln Signature Homes Limited
Colten Developments Limited
R.S. Cook & Sons Limited
Cotswold Homes Limited
Cover Construction Co Ltd
F.H. Cummings
Devonshire Homes (Bracken) Ltd
Devonshire Homes (Landkey) Ltd
Devonshire Homes Limited
Doric Developments (Bath) Ltd
Dribuild Limited
Dunsmere Developments Limited
Eagle Investments Limited
Eagle One Homes Limited
Eagle One Residential Limited
Ellson Homes Limited
Feniton Park Limited
Firmplot Limited
G.A. Francis & Son Limited
C.G. Fry and Son Limited
Gazelle Properties Limited
Gilbert and Goode Limited
Gilltown Limited
Graceloft Limited
Green Cape Limited
David Greening Limited
A. Hammond & Sons Limited
Hardrock Developments Limited
Harris & Harris Construction Ltd
Harris Bros. and Collard Ltd
Haynes Developments Limited
Heritage Developments South West Ltd
Highfield Homes of Distinction Ltd
Hills Homes Developments Ltd
Hoburne Development Co Ltd
B.R.Hodgson Facades Limited
Holton Homes Limited
Homer & Pardy Developments Ltd
Steve Hoskin Construction Ltd
J.J. Acquisitions Limited
Simon James New Homes Limited
Juniper Homes (Southville) Ltd
Lake Inns & Leisure Limited
D C Li (Builders) Limited
Lightmoor Homes Limited
Lomand Homes Limited
MDM Developments (Southern) Ltd
MacTaggart & Mickel Homes England
McCarthy Contracting & Development
Mears New Homes Limited
Melbourne Homes Limited
Mi-Space (UK) Limited
Millwood Homes (Devon) Limited
Morrish Builders (Poole) Ltd
R. Moulding & Co. (Salisbury) Ltd
New Dawn Homes Limited
Newland Homes Limited
Oval Estates (St Peter's) Ltd
Parsons and Joyce Contractors Ltd
Pearce Construction (Barnstaple) Ltd
Pennyfarthing Construction Ltd
Sidney Pratt (Builders) Ltd
QDOS Homes Limited
Quantum Teddington Development Ltd
Redcliffe Homes Limited
Robertson Developments Ltd
Romfield Holdings Limited
SPM Homes Ltd
SW Construction (No.2) Limited
SW Construction (Residential) Ltd
Seagull Developments Limited
Shepperton Builders Limited
Silbury Housing Holdings Ltd
Silbury Housing Limited
Spectrum Premier Homes Limited
J.E.Stacey & Co.Limited
Stevens Homes Ltd
Stowford Mill Development Ltd
Strongvox Limited
Summerfield Developments (SW) Ltd
Summerfield SD3 Limited
Swannick & Kearn Properties Ltd
Tithegrove Holdings Limited
Tithegrove Limited
Tonic Construction Limited
Towerview West Sussex Limited
Turlough Limited
Verto Homes Ltd
Wainhomes (South West) Holdings Ltd
West of England Developments (Taunton) No2
Westcoast Developments (2009) Ltd
Lewis Wyatt (Construction) Ltd
Yarlington Homes Limited

42110 Construction of roads and motorways [17]

Brandwells Construction Co Ltd
Churngold Construction Limited
Gibbs Surfacing Limited
Harris & Harris Construction Ltd
Hercules Site Services Limited
Hochtief (UK) Construction Ltd
Steve Hoskin Construction Ltd
Mildren Construction Limited
Murrill Construction Limited
John O'Flynn Developments Ltd
Road Management Services (Darrington)
Rockstone Surfacing Limited
Tithegrove Holdings Limited
Tonic Construction Limited
Via East Midlands Limited
W B M Groundworks Limited
Walton Civil Engineering and Surfacing Contractors

42130 Construction of bridges and tunnels

Hercules Site Services Limited
Hochtief (UK) Construction Ltd

42210 Construction of utility projects for fluids

Hercules Site Services Limited

42220 Construction of utility projects for electricity and telecommunications [12]

Avonline PLC
Burton Wold Wind Farm South Ltd
CELCSE Limited
Galloper Wind Farm Limited
Hitachi Nuclear Projects Development Europe
Horizon Nuclear Power Limited
Horizon Nuclear Power Oldbury Ltd
Horizon Nuclear Power Services Ltd
Horizon Nuclear Power Wylfa Ltd
Infinergy Limited
Mean Moor Wind Farm Holding Ltd
Renewable Energy Partnerships Ltd

42910 Construction of water projects

M.J. Abbott Limited
Aquamain (UK) Limited
Hercules Site Services Limited
Hydro International (Wastewater) Ltd
Jenkins Marine Ltd.

42990 Construction of other civil engineering projects n.e.c. [36]

AFL Services Europe Ltd
Ankers and Rawlings Developments Ltd
Bartlett Contractors Limited
W H Bond & Sons Limited
Brandwells Construction Co Ltd
Bristlewand Limited
C.J.L. Construction Limited
Cape Homes Limited
Churngold Construction Limited
R.S. Cook & Sons Limited
Cowley Bros.(Wroughton) Ltd
EMG Limited
Eliquo Hydrok Limited
Ford Civil Engineering Limited
M.F. Freeman Limited
R.J. Heathman (Contractors) Ltd
Highdrive Property Co. Limited
Kamm Civil Engineering Limited
Knights Brown Construction Ltd
MJL Contractors Limited
MUJV Limited
S. Notaro Limited
Parking Glasgow Limited
Radquill Developments Limited
Seagull Developments Limited
Smith's (Gloucester) Limited
Stanborough (Developments) Ltd
Suttle Projects Limited
Teignmouth Maritime Services Ltd
Tonic Construction Limited
Williams Southern Limited
Wolverhampton Radiology Ltd
Woodmace Concrete Structures Ltd
Woodmace Limited
Woodpecker Properties Limited
Wring Group Limited

43110 Demolition

Bath Demolition Limited
Wring Group Limited

43120 Site preparation

Fred Champion Groundworks Ltd
Churngold Construction Limited
GWKS Ltd
Groundfix Limited
MJL Contractors Limited
P.O.C. Contractors Limited
Renelec Groundworks Limited
Triton Knoll Offshore Wind Farm Ltd

43130 Test drilling and boring

Geotechnical Engineering Ltd

43210 Electrical installation [16]

BSR Connect Limited
Bridges (Electrical Engineers) Ltd
C F R Group Services Limited
Clarkson Evans Limited
G3 Systems Limited
H.B.H. Woolacotts Limited
Hewer Facilities Management Ltd
Larasian Limited
Lightning Electrical Construction
Power Electrics Generators Ltd
Powersystems UK Ltd
C.F. Roberts (Electrical Contractors)
Totus Engineering Limited
UK Power Solutions Limited
Wessex Building Services Ltd
Wessex Electricals (Shaftesbury) Ltd

43220 Plumbing, heat and air-conditioning installation [24]

Aaron Heating Services Limited
Aaron Services Limited
Barkwell Plumbing & Heating Ltd
K.F.Bartlett Limited
Brick Peers Limited
D.I.S. Limited
EPTA Cold Service Ltd
EVGH Limited
G3 Systems Limited
Glevum Heating & Plumbing Ltd
Grant Engineering (UK) Limited
N.A. Guppy Limited
Hewer Facilities Management Ltd
K & T Heating Services Limited
Renelec Chalgrove Limited
Shire Integrated Systems Ltd
Space Engineering Services Ltd
Sure Maintenance Limited
Swegon Limited
T.E.J. Heating (Plymouth) Ltd
Toshiba Carrier UK Ltd.
Totus Engineering Limited
Wessex Electricals (Shaftesbury) Ltd
Woodward & Co (Environmental) Ltd

43290 Other construction installation [19]

Champion Groundworks Limited
Cold Clad Ltd
D.J. Contracts (Weymouth) Ltd
Frame Homes (South West) Ltd
Gilbert and Goode Limited
Lancer Scott Limited
O'Neill and Brennan Construction Ltd
P & M Group Limited
Playforce Limited
Plymouth Community Homes Energy Ltd
R & M Utility & Civil Engineering Services South West
Renelec Limited
SMD 2013 Limited
Space Engineering Services Ltd
Stanborough (Construction) Ltd
Stanley Security Solutions Ltd
Stannah Lifts Limited
Structural Metal Decks Limited
Uplands Retail Limited

43310 Plastering

E & H Drylining & Plastering Ltd
M J Stevens Ltd

43320 Joinery installation

Barnwood Group Limited
Barnwood Shopfitting Limited
Brick Peers Limited
Larasian Limited
Railston Limited
Realhurry Limited
David Salisbury Joinery Ltd

43330 Floor and wall covering

Avonline PLC
B.R.Hodgson Facades Limited
Larasian Limited
Sarsen Stone Group Limited

43341 Painting

Ian Williams Limited

43342 Glazing

Salisbury Glass Centre Limited
Seal-Lite Windows Doors & Conservatories

43390 Other building completion and finishing [14]

Advanced Industrial Solutions Ltd
Architectural Profiles Limited
Bray and Slaughter Limited
Camelot Developments Limited
Dribuild Limited
G3 Systems Limited
Harris Bros. and Collard Ltd
M.D. Building Services Limited
McCulloch Homes Limited
Mears Limited
Plastic Surgeon Limited
Realhurry Limited
Securivin Limited
St Aubyn Estates Ltd

43910 Roofing activities

Briarwood Products Limited
Perkins & Perry Ltd.
Plymouth Community Homes Energy Ltd
Progressive Systems Limited
Stay Dry Roofing (South West) Ltd
Western Counties Roofing Ltd

43991 Scaffold erection

Design Scaffolding (Bristol) Ltd
LTC Group87 Ltd
Oxford Spires Scaffolding Ltd
SCA Group Limited
Chris Sedgeman Scaffolding Ltd.

43999 Other specialised construction activities n.e.c. [77]

A & O Holdings Ltd
A1 Engineering Solutions Group Ltd
A1 Engineering Solutions Ltd
AFL Services Europe Ltd
Abbey Manor Developments Ltd
Abbey Manor Group Limited
Abbey Manor Homes Limited
M.J. Abbott Limited
Ace Welding Limited
Acland Plant Hire Limited
Bexley PPP Health Services Ltd
Black Country PPP Health Services
Bourne Group Ltd.
Bristol & Avon Transport & Recycling Ltd
Britannia Windows (UK) Limited
British Solar Renewables Ltd
Centristic Limited
Cirrus Communication Systems Ltd
Conlon Limited
G. Crook & Sons Limited
W. Daniels Plant Hire Limited
Dart Valley Systems Limited
Data Installation & Networking Services
P J Davidson Developments Ltd
Eagle Investments Limited
Edmont Ltd
Epping PPP Maintenance (Health) Services
Mark Farwell Plant Hire Ltd
First Priorities PPP Health Services
Galtec Limited

Glanville Cleansing Limited
Grant Almont Limited
Harvey Shopfitters Limited
Hertford PPP Health Services Ltd
Herts & Essex PPP Health Services
JHAI Limited
Jade-Aden Services Limited
B.T. Jenkins Limited
Liskeard PPP Health Services Ltd
Locators Limited
M. & N. Electrical and Mechanical Services
MDP (South West) Limited
MJL Contractors Limited
MJL Cornwall Limited
MJL Plant Hire (Cornwall) Ltd
MW High Tech Projects UK Ltd
Mabey Bridge Limited
Mercia Healthcare Limited
Midas Retail Limited
Molson Group Ltd
Negatex Limited
New Forest PPP Health Services Ltd
Norco G R P Limited
R.M. Penny (Plant Hire and Demolition)
Pipex Limited
Plymouth Community Homes Energy Ltd
Precast Concrete Structures Ltd
Precision Lift Services Ltd
Property Consortium UK Limited
Redbridge PPP Health Services Ltd
Resolution Interiors Limited
Roadform Civil Engineering Co Ltd
Rollalong Limited
J M Scully Limited
Soldi Investments Ltd
South Essex PPP Health Services Ltd
Tekne Shopfitting Limited
Tithegrove Limited
Steve Vick International Ltd
WHC Hire Services Ltd.
WJ South West Limited
West Mendip PPP Health Services Ltd
Chris Wheeler Construction Ltd
Ian Williams Limited
Wood Energy Limited
Woodward & Co (Environmental) Ltd
Wring Group Limited

45111 Sale of new cars and light motor vehicles [84]

A.K.S. (Yeovil) Limited
Adam Bailey Limited
Blade Motor Group Limited
Breeze Motor Co Ltd
CCR Motor Co Ltd
CWC (UK Holdings) Limited
Cambria Automobiles (South East) Ltd
Carco Limited
Carrs of Exeter Limited
Castle Motors (Trebrown) Ltd
F.J. Chalke Limited
City West Commercials Limited
City West Country Limited
Colt Car Co Ltd
Cotswold Motor Group Limited
County Garage (Barnstaple) Ltd
Dale's Central Motors Limited
De Van Automotive Limited
Devonshire Motors Limited
Fish Brothers (Holdings) Ltd
Fish Brothers (Swindon) Ltd
Foray Motor Group Limited
GM Coachwork Limited
Grange Motors (Brentwood) Ltd
Grange Motors (Swindon) Ltd
Grevan Cars Limited
HSH Motor Co Ltd
J.H.Haskins & Son Limited
Hawkins Holdings Limited
Hawkins Motors Limited
Helston Garages Limited
Heritage Automotive Limited
Holders of Congresbury Limited
Horizon Motor Co Ltd
Howard Garages (Weston) Ltd
Hylton Group Limited
Invicta Motors (Maidstone) Ltd
Invicta Motors Limited
Islington Trowbridge Limited
Keith Motors (Christchurch) Ltd
Dick Lovett (Bath) Limited
Dick Lovett (Bristol) Limited
Dick Lovett (Hungerford) Ltd
Dick Lovett (Specialist Cars) Ltd
Dick Lovett Companies Limited
Dick Lovett Limited
Dick Lovett Sporting Limited
Dick Lovett Sports Cars Ltd
Magna Motor Company (Christchurch)
Magna Motor Company (Wessex) Ltd
Magna Motor Co Ltd
Martins of Exeter Limited
McLean & Sons Ltd
R.J. & K.D. McLean Limited
Murray (Plymouth) Limited
Ocean Automotive Limited
Parkside (Barnstaple) Limited
Pebley Beach Limited
Penton Securities Limited
Redvers and Denzil Rice Farms Ltd
Renrod Limited
Rodgers of Plymouth Limited
F W Rogers Garage (Saltash) Ltd
Rowes Garage Limited
Sandown Dorset and Wiltshire Ltd
Sandown Motors Limited
Simonstone (Bristol) Limited
Simonstone Motor Group PLC
Somerset County Cars Limited
Spitalgate Dealer Services Ltd
Taw Garages Limited
Thoranmart Limited
Trelawny Citroen Limited
Vospers Motor House Limited
Vospers of Plymouth Limited
Warners of Gloucester Limited
Wellington Motors Limited
Wessex Garages Holdings Ltd
West End Motors (Bodmin) Ltd
Westover Group Limited
Westover Holdings Limited
Wilson Investment Holdings Ltd
Wool & Bovington Motors Ltd
Roger Young Limited

45112 Sale of used cars and light motor vehicles [60]

Bill Allen's Autos Limited
Adam Bailey Limited
Big Van World Limited
Blade Motor Group Limited
Breeze Motor Co Ltd
Brent Cars Limited
CCR Motor Co Ltd
Cambria Automobiles (South East) Ltd
Carco Limited
Castle Motors (Trebrown) Ltd
Devonshire Motors Limited
Fish Brothers (Holdings) Ltd
Fish Brothers (Swindon) Ltd
GM Coachwork Limited
GMO Cars Limited
Grange Motors (Brentwood) Ltd
Grange Motors (Swindon) Ltd
Hawkins Motors Limited
Heritage Automotive Limited
Highbridge Caravan Centre Ltd
Holders of Congresbury Limited
Horizon Motor Co Ltd
Howard Garages (Weston) Ltd
Hylton Group Limited
Invicta Motors (Maidstone) Ltd
Invicta Motors Limited
Islington Trowbridge Limited
A R & A L Keen Limited
Keith Motors (Christchurch) Ltd
Alan Kerr Limited
Lloyd's Property Southwest Ltd
Dick Lovett (Bristol) Limited
Dick Lovett (Hungerford) Ltd
Dick Lovett (Specialist Cars) Ltd
Dick Lovett Companies Limited
Dick Lovett Limited
Dick Lovett Sporting Limited
Dick Lovett Sports Cars Ltd
Magna Motor Company (Christchurch)
Magna Motor Company (Wessex) Ltd
Magna Motor Co Ltd
C.P. Mikulla Limited
Murray (Plymouth) Limited
Northam Farm Caravan Sales Ltd
Ocean Automotive Limited
Parkside (Barnstaple) Limited
Pebley Beach Limited
Red Kite Vehicle Consultants Ltd
Redvers and Denzil Rice Farms Ltd
Rodgers of Plymouth Limited
Rowes Garage Limited
Simonstone (Bristol) Limited
Simonstone Motor Group PLC
Stealthlink Ltd
David Taylor (Garages) Ltd
Thoranmart Limited
Trelawny Citroen Limited
Truscotts (Barnstaple) Limited
Westover Group Limited
Ted Williams Motors Limited

45190 Sale of other motor vehicles [22]

Brotherwood Automobility Ltd
C & C Motor Caravans Ltd
City West Commercials Limited
Davan Caravans Limited
Tom Gallagher Group Limited
Hamblys Limited
K.P. Europa Trading Limited
Kellands (Plant Sales) Limited
MAN Truck and Bus UK Limited
Medland, Sanders and Twose Ltd
Moseley Distributors Limited
Redvers and Denzil Rice Farms Ltd
Rothdean Limited
Rygor Commercials Ltd
Smallridge Bros Limited
Somerset Motorhome Centre Ltd
Stuarts Truck and Bus Limited

WW Truck and Bus Limited
Watts Truck & Van Limited
Wessex GS Limited
West Country Motor Homes Ltd
T. H. White Limited

45200 Maintenance and repair of motor vehicles [65]

ARI Fleet UK Limited
ARI Fleet, Ltd.
Accident Claims Handlers Ltd
Adam Bailey Limited
Blade Motor Group Limited
Breeze Motor Co Ltd
C & C Motor Caravans Ltd
CAT-UK Services Limited
CCR Motor Co Ltd
Cambria Automobiles (South East) Ltd
Carco Limited
City West Commercials Limited
County Garage (Barnstaple) Ltd
Devonshire Motors Limited
Fish Brothers (Holdings) Ltd
Fish Brothers (Swindon) Ltd
Grange Motors (Brentwood) Ltd
Grange Motors (Swindon) Ltd
J.H.Haskins & Son Limited
Hawkins Motors Limited
Heritage Automotive Limited
Hinton Garage (Bath) Limited
Holders of Congresbury Limited
Horizon Motor Co Ltd
Howard Garages (Weston) Ltd
Hylton Group Limited
Invicta Motors (Maidstone) Ltd
Invicta Motors Limited
Islington Trowbridge Limited
Keith Motors (Christchurch) Ltd
King David Tyres Limited
Dick Lovett (Bristol) Limited
Dick Lovett (Hungerford) Ltd
Dick Lovett (Specialist Cars) Ltd
Dick Lovett Companies Limited
Dick Lovett Limited
Dick Lovett Sporting Limited
Dick Lovett Sports Cars Ltd
Magna Motor Company (Wessex) Ltd
Magna Motor Co Ltd
Murray (Plymouth) Limited
North Devon Tyres Ltd.
Ocean Automotive Limited
PMG Services (Bristol) Limited
Parkside (Barnstaple) Limited
Pattemore's Transport (Crewkerne)
Pebley Beach Limited
Rodgers of Plymouth Limited
F W Rogers Garage (Saltash) Ltd
Rowes Garage Limited
Rygor Commercials Ltd
SMV Commercials Limited
STVA UK Limited
Simonstone (Bristol) Limited
Simonstone Motor Group PLC
Stuarts Truck and Bus Limited
Thoranmart Limited
Trelawny Citroen Limited
Francis Tuthill Limited
Via East Midlands Limited
WW Truck and Bus Limited
Wellington Motors Limited
Wessex GS Limited
West Country Motor Homes Ltd
Roger Young Limited

45310 Wholesale trade of motor vehicle parts and accessories [28]

Automotive Parts Distribution Ltd
B.G. Automotive Limited
County Garage (Barnstaple) Ltd
County Tyre (Holdings) Limited
Daido Metal Europe Limited
Delphi Lockheed Automotive Ltd
Eberspacher (U.K.) Limited
Fleetwheel Limited
GS Yuasa Battery Sales UK Ltd
Johnan UK Limited
Keith Motors (Christchurch) Ltd
Knorr-Bremse Systems for Commercial Vehicles
MAN Truck and Bus UK Limited
Malvern Tyres (Wholesale) Ltd
North Devon Tyres Ltd.
Ohashi Technica UK, Ltd.
Richard Read (Transport) Ltd
Rodgers of Plymouth Limited
F W Rogers Garage (Saltash) Ltd
Sortimo International Limited
Stedall (Vehicle Fittings) Ltd
Charles Trent Limited
Tyre Maintenance Limited
Ultraparts Limited
Unity Tyre Co Ltd
WW Truck and Bus Limited
Wellington Motors Limited
Roger Young Limited

45320 Retail trade of motor vehicle parts and accessories [40]

Autoparts & Diagnostics Ltd
Adam Bailey Limited
Blade Motor Group Limited
Breeze Motor Co Ltd
C & C Motor Caravans Ltd
CCR Motor Co Ltd
Cambria Automobiles (South East) Ltd
Carco Limited
Central Garages (Torbay) Ltd
City West Commercials Limited
County Tyre (Holdings) Limited
Devonshire Motors Limited
Fish Brothers (Holdings) Ltd
Fish Brothers (Swindon) Ltd
Grange Motors (Brentwood) Ltd
Grange Motors (Swindon) Ltd
Hawkins Motors Limited
Heritage Automotive Limited
Holders of Congresbury Limited
Horizon Motor Co Ltd
Howard Garages (Weston) Ltd
Hylton Group Limited
Invicta Motors (Maidstone) Ltd
Invicta Motors Limited
Islington Trowbridge Limited
Magna Motor Company (Wessex) Ltd
Magna Motor Co Ltd
Merityre Specialists Limited
Mobile Windscreens Limited
Murray (Plymouth) Limited
Ocean Automotive Limited
Parkside (Barnstaple) Limited
Pebley Beach Limited
Simonstone (Bristol) Limited
Simonstone Motor Group PLC
St James Parade (107) Limited
Stuarts Truck and Bus Limited
Thoranmart Limited
Charles Trent Limited
Wessex GS Limited

45400 Sale, maintenance and repair of motorcycles and related parts and accessories

Bridge Motorcycles Limited
Chippenham Motor Co Ltd
Fowlers of Bristol Limited
GT Motorcycles (2012) Ltd
Llexeter Limited
Dick Lovett (Bristol) Limited
Dick Lovett Companies Limited
Speed Superbikes Limited

46110 Agents selling agricultural raw materials, livestock, textile raw materials and semi-finished goods

Pearce Seeds (Holdings) Ltd

46120 Agents involved in the sale of fuels, ores, metals and industrial chemicals

A-Gas (UK) Limited
Hobbs Bros.Limited
G. Northover & Sons Limited
Western Fuel Limited

46130 Agents involved in the sale of timber and building materials [22]

Allstone Sands Gravels Aggregates Trading Co
George Bence & Sons (Cheltenham)
George Bence & Sons Limited
Bradford and Sons Limited
Bradfords Building Supplies Ltd
Buildit Gloster Limited
Cornwall Glass & Glazing Ltd
Cotswold Doors Ltd
Garland Company UK Limited
Hale & Co. (Drybrook) Ltd
Independent Slate Supplies Ltd
Inter-Line (South West) Limited.
Kellaway Building Supplies Ltd
Paull & Co Ltd
Plastivan Limited
Rawle Gammon & Baker Holdings Ltd
Screwfix Direct Limited
Stone Supplies (Bristol) Ltd
Tamar Trading Co.Limited
Taylor Maxwell Timber Limited
Taylor,Maxwell & Co.Limited
Westward Building Services Ltd

46140 Agents involved in the sale of machinery, industrial equipment, ships and aircraft

APP (UK) Limited
Hydro International Limited
J. J. Farm Services Limited
Merlo UK Limited
Simplex-Turbulo Group Limited
Still Materials Handling Ltd

46150 Agents involved in the sale of furniture, household goods, hardware and ironmongery

BDP Imports Limited

46160 Agents involved in the sale of textiles, clothing, fur, footwear and leather goods

Cotswold Collections Group Ltd

46170 Agents involved in the sale of food, beverages and tobacco

Guy Anderson Wines Limited
Off-Piste Wines Limited
PLB Group Ltd.

46180 Agents specialised in the sale of other particular products [18]

3T's Leisure Ltd.
APP (UK) Limited
Atkinson Equipment Limited
Auma Actuators Limited
Avortex Limited
Cadillac Plastic Limited
Central Management Catalogue Agency (UK)
Electro Mechanical Systems Ltd
Giftstones Limited
Infineon Technologies Reigate Ltd
Infineon Technologies UK Ltd
Multi Circuit Boards Limited
Rivermead Plastic Limited
Saddleback Limited
Tempest Radford Limited
Tepe Oral Hygiene Products Ltd
Verton Limited
Vetswest Limited

46190 Agents involved in the sale of a variety of goods

Durable (UK) Limited
Go-Pak UK Limited
L. & F. Jones Holdings Ltd
PPSTS Limited

46210 Wholesale of grain, unmanufactured tobacco, seeds and animal feeds

Feedco Ltd
Suttons Consumer Products Ltd
Wessex Grain Ltd.

46220 Wholesale of flowers and plants

DFH Estates Limited
Double H (Nurseries) Limited
Flowervision (Bristol) Limited
New Leaf Plants Ltd

46240 Wholesale of hides, skins and leather

Linwood Fabric Co Ltd

46310 Wholesale of fruit and vegetables

Catering 328 Limited
Arthur David (Food with Service)
Newberry International Produce Ltd
Riviera Produce Limited
Rush Group Limited
Watercress Co Ltd
Westcountry Fruit Sales Ltd

46320 Wholesale of meat and meat products

B M Foods Limited
Catering 328 Limited
D.B. Foods Limited
Dunbia (UK)
Stanley Gibson Limited
A.C. Hopkins (Taunton) Ltd
John Sheppard Butchers Ltd
Somerdale International Ltd

46330 Wholesale of dairy products, eggs and edible oils and fats

A.J. & R.G.Barber (Sales) Ltd
Eurilait Limited
Futura Foods UK Limited
Savencia Fromage & Dairy UK Ltd
Somerdale International Ltd
West Country Milk Consortium Ltd

46341 Wholesale of fruit and vegetable juices, mineral water and soft drinks

Cobell Ltd
Thirsty Work Limited

46342 Wholesale of wine, beer, spirits and other alcoholic beverages [10]

Aceo Limited
Arkell's Brewery Limited
Bibendum PLB Group Limited
Matthew Clark Bibendum Ltd
Freixenet Copestick Limited
Hall & Woodhouse Limited
Nectar Imports Limited
St.Austell Brewery Co Ltd
Tolchards Limited
Wadworth and Co Ltd

46350 Wholesale of tobacco products

Imperial Tobacco International Ltd
Imperial Tobacco Limited

46370 Wholesale of coffee, tea, cocoa and spices

Beyond The Bean Limited

46380 Wholesale of other food, including fish, crustaceans and molluscs [10]

N.H. Case Limited
Catering 328 Limited
Crown Pet Foods Limited
Falfish Limited
Flyingfish Seafoods Co Ltd
Pacific West Foods (UK) Ltd
Peninsula Seafoods Limited
Charles Saunders Limited
Seahawk Marine Foods Limited
Vistgate Limited

46390 Non-specialised wholesale of food, beverages and tobacco [11]

Appleby Westward Group Limited
Arkell's Brewery Limited
Centaur Foods Limited
Creed Catering Supplies Ltd
Creed Foodservice Limited
Philip Dennis Foodservice Ltd
Hunt's Foodservice Ltd
Organix Brands Limited
Petty, Wood & Co. Limited
Stonegate Farmers Limited
Tudor Rose International Ltd

46410 Wholesale of textiles

Lear, Browne & Dunsford Ltd
Linwood Fabric Co Ltd
Milspeed Limited
Pencarrie Limited
Roman Bidco Limited
Warwick Fabrics (UK) Limited

46420 Wholesale of clothing and footwear [24]

Ann's Cottage (Warehouse) Ltd
Banner Limited
Coastguard Road Limited
Cotswold Collections Group Ltd
DKH Retail Limited
First Position Group Limited
Footsure Western Limited
Gardiner Bros. and Company (Leathers)
International Dance Supplies Ltd
Leo Textiles Limited
Mulberry Company (Design) Ltd
Police Resources International Ltd
Roman Group Topco Limited
S'Porter International Limited
Saddleback Limited
Seasalt Limited
Stag Buying Group Limited
Stance (Europe) Limited
Superdry PLC
Supergroup Concessions Limited
Triumph International Limited
V12 Footwear Limited
Weird Fish Limited
Wilton Bradley Limited

46439 Wholesale of radio, television goods & electrical household appliances (other than records, tapes, CDs)

Combined Independents (Holdings) Ltd
Horwood Homewares Limited
Portway Domestic Appliances Ltd
Sparkworld Limited

46440 Wholesale of china and glassware and cleaning materials

Home Hardware Southwest Ltd
Yate Disposables Ltd

46450 Wholesale of perfume and cosmetics

DKH Retail Limited
Lush Ltd.
Neal's Yard (Natural Remedies) Ltd
Synlatex Limited
Teoxane UK Limited

46460 Wholesale of pharmaceutical goods [10]

Arrowedge Limited
C & P Medical Trading Limited
Galpharm International Limited
Greiner Bio-One Limited
Hameln Pharmaceuticals Ltd
Intercept Pharma Europe Ltd.
Livanova UK Limited
Teoxane UK Limited
Vygon (U.K.) Limited
Zimmer Biomet UK Limited

46470 Wholesale of furniture, carpets and lighting equipment

Furlong Flooring (Wales) Ltd.
Neptune (Europe) Ltd
Poole Lighting Limited

46499 Wholesale of household goods (other than musical instruments) n.e.c [20]

Giftworks Limited
Half Moon Bay Limited
Home Hardware Southwest Ltd
Horwood Homewares Limited
IBD Bikes UK Limited
Intamarque Limited
La Hacienda Limited
Lakes Bathrooms Limited
Le Creuset U.K. Limited
Magmatic Limited
Neptune (Europe) Ltd
Omicways Limited
RAGM PLC
Roper Rhodes Limited
Stovax Limited
Tomy UK Co., Ltd.
Tradestock Limited
Wilton Bradley Holdings Ltd
Wilton Bradley Limited
Yankee Candle Company (Europe) Ltd

46510 Wholesale of computers, computer peripheral equipment and software

Grey Matter Limited
Hardware Group Limited
Hardware UK Limited
Nuvias Global Services Limited
Prolabs (UK) Limited
Spire Technology Limited
Symec Technologies Limited

46520 Wholesale of electronic and telecommunications equipment and parts [10]

John Cribb & Sons Ltd.
Devondale Electrical Distributors
Dextra Lighting Limited
GP Batteries (UK) Limited
Hardware Group Limited
IEWC UK & Ireland Ltd
Maurice Lay Distributors Ltd
Nuvias Global Services Limited
Templegate Electrical Supplies Ltd
Wiska UK Limited

46610 Wholesale of agricultural machinery, equipment and supplies [21]

Briarwood Products Limited
Francis Bugler Limited
Compass Tractors Limited
GEA Farm Technologies (UK) Ltd
William Gilder Limited
J Gliddon & Sons Limited
Hamblys Limited
Hawkins Agri Limited
James Mason Limited
Masons Farm and Country Ltd
Parris Tractors Limited
Redlynch Agricultural Engineering
Rochford Garden Machinery Ltd
Smallridge Bros Limited
C. Smart Agricultural Services Ltd
Sparex Limited
Stiga Ltd
Andrew Symons Limited
Three Counties Feeds Limited
Truro Tractors Limited
Vapormatic Co Ltd

46620 Wholesale of machine tools

1st Machine Tool Accessories Ltd
Axminster Tool Centre Ltd
Global Machine Tools (UK) Ltd
K.D.P. Tools Limited
Kitagawa Europe Limited

46630 Wholesale of mining, construction and civil engineering machinery

G.B Contracts Limited
Holt JCB Holdings Limited
Holt JCB Limited
Molson Equipment Services Ltd

46650 Wholesale of office furniture

Abbey Business Equipment Ltd
WW (UK) Limited
Woodstock Leabank Office Furniture

46660 Wholesale of other office machinery and equipment

Abbey Business Equipment Ltd
JGBM Ltd
Transcribe Copier Systems Ltd
Utax (UK) Limited

46690 Wholesale of other machinery and equipment [10]

Brook Food Processing Equipment Ltd
Cronite Castings (Distribution) Ltd
J & K Aquatics Limited
Leafield Logistics & Technical Services
MGV Engineering Limited
Megahertz Limited
Stiga Ltd
Tecalemit Garage Equipment Co Ltd
Toolstream Limited
Versatile Controls Limited

46711 Wholesale of petroleum and petroleum products

Mitchell & Webber Limited
Puma Energy (UK) Limited

46719 Wholesale of other fuels and related products

Ron Darch & Sons Co Ltd
Ford Fuels Limited
Heltor Limited
Kinch Fuel Oils Limited
Libya Oil Ethiopia Limited
Puma Energy (UK) Limited
Tincknell Fuels Limited
Verdo Renewables Ltd

46720 Wholesale of metals and metal ores

Avon Specialty Metals Limited
F & B Profiles Limited
Independent Tool Consultants Ltd
Megasteel Ltd
SSI Schaefer Ltd
Steelinvest Limited

46730 Wholesale of wood, construction materials and sanitary equipment [13]

GP & J Baker Limited
Build Supplies Limited
East Bros.(Timber) Limited
Hale & Co. (Drybrook) Ltd
Horwood Homewares Limited
Panel Supplies Limited
Skyline Systems Limited
Smart Systems Limited
South Coast Building Supplies Ltd.
Stone Supplies (Bristol) Ltd
Strukta Group Limited
Sydenhams Ltd
Wiltshire Heavy Building Materials

46740 Wholesale of hardware, plumbing and heating equipment and supplies [11]

M.J. Abbott Limited
Adey Innovation Limited
Apollo Radiators Limited
Bristol Builders Supplies Ltd
Clearwater Products Limited
Hale & Co. (Drybrook) Ltd
Home Hardware Distribution Ltd
Home Hardware Southwest Ltd
London Bidco Limited
London Topco Limited
Total Plumbing Supplies Ltd

46750 Wholesale of chemical products

Libya Oil Ethiopia Limited
Merck Chemicals Ltd
Muc-Off Limited
Riverside Aromatics Limited
SAFC Hitech Limited

46760 Wholesale of other intermediate products [16]

Avortex Limited
Beyond The Bean Limited
De Monchy Aromatics Limited
Dometic UK Limited
Evesham Specialist Packaging Ltd
Mycronic Ltd
Olympic Varnish Co Ltd
Pattersons (Bristol) Limited
Rawlings & Son (Bristol) Ltd
Severn Glocon (Aberdeen) Ltd
Spandex Limited
Staverton Electrical Supplies Ltd
Chris Sterling Enterprises Ltd
Trelleborg Industrial Tyres UK Ltd
Verton Limited
WP Industrial Limited

46770 Wholesale of waste and scrap

Eco Sustainable Solutions Ltd
Newbery Metals Limited
P W Commercial Co Ltd
Reliance Scrap Metal Merchants (Parkstone)
E.J. Shanley & Son (Trowbridge) Ltd

46900 Non-specialised wholesale trade [70]

A & A Trading (U.K.) Limited
AEGG Ltd
Amimed Direct Limited
Aviation & Defence Spares Ltd
GP & J Baker Limited
Barnbury Enterprises Limited
Bristol Fluid System Technologies
Bulk Hardware Limited
CTC (Wholesalers) Limited
Call Caterlink Ltd
Certus Wholesale Ltd
Chapple & Jenkins Ltd
Coleman UK Limited
Comax (UK) Limited
Coombe Castle International Ltd
Dawson Media Direct Limited
Dentsply IH Limited
Design Objectives Limited
Drytac Europe Limited
Endesign Limited
F & B Profiles Limited
Firn Overseas Packaging Ltd
Floortex Europe Limited
Gompels Healthcare Limited
Great British Card Company PLC
G.J.Handy & Co Ltd
Harbourstar Limited
I.D.S. Refrigeration Limited
Imaging Equipment Limited
Interfit Limited
International Plywood (Importers)
Kandytoys Limited
Key Industrial Equipment Ltd
Manuli Packaging (UK) Ltd.
Masters Golf Co Ltd
Nevis Marketing Limited
Nisbets PLC
Omicways Limited
Optimas OE Solutions Ltd
Osprey Europe Limited
PA Performance Limited
Paint Services Group Limited
Paligap Limited
Patrico Limited
Portico Business Services Ltd
Premier Cables Limited
Pritchard Patent Product Co. Ltd
Puckator Limited
R.T. Property Investments Ltd
Rajani (Wholesale) Limited
Rangemoors Limited
S'Porter International Limited
SM Group (Europe) Ltd.
Securi-Flex Ltd.
Shiner Limited
Silverfish UK (Holdings) Ltd
Smiths News Trading Limited
Solent International Limited
TKC Sales Limited
Taylor-Davis Limited
Tileflair Limited
Town Mills Craft Centre Ltd
Tran-AM Limited
Troy (UK) Limited
Watts Aviation Services Ltd
Wild and Wolf Limited
Wiltshire Heavy Building Materials (Group)
Woodlodge Products Limited
YYS International (UK) Limited
Zuru UK Limited

47110 Retail sale in non-specialised stores with food, beverages or tobacco predominating

F W S Carter & Sons Limited
Dike & Son Limited
GCL 2016 Limited
Gillett's (Callington) Limited
Gillett's (Holdings) Limited
Symonds Forecourts Limited
Tout Limited
Warners Retail Limited

47190 Other retail sale in non-specialised stores [43]

Banburys Limited
Bastins 2012 Limited
J E Beale PLC
Buyology Ltd
CDS (Superstores International) Ltd
Calendar Club Limited
Carnon Downs Garden Centre Ltd
Certini Bicycle Co Ltd
Clarity Copiers Limited
Cox & Robinson (Agricultural) Ltd
Flemingo International (UK) Ltd
Gardiner,Sons & Co.,Limited
Goulds (Dorchester) Limited
M.A. Grigg (Agricultural) Ltd
Harding Brothers Retail Ltd
Haskins Garden Centres Limited
Haskins Roundstone Garden Centre Ltd
Haskins Snowhill Garden Centre Ltd
Hatcher and Sons,Limited
Homeleigh Garden Centre Ltd
In-Excess UK Limited
Ipplepen Property Limited
H.J.Knee,Limited
Mole Avon Trading Limited
National Trust (Enterprises) Ltd
Otter Nurseries Limited
Otter Nurseries of Plymouth Ltd
Rainbow Holdings (UK) Limited
Charles Robertson (Holdings) Ltd
Roundswell Services Limited
SSI Schaefer Ltd
Seasalt Holdings Limited
Seasalt Limited
WH Smith Hospitals Limited
Styles & Brown Ltd
Super Dooper Stores Limited
Trago Mills (Falmouth) Limited
Trago Mills (South Devon) Ltd
Trago Mills Limited
Susie Watson Designs Ltd
Westcountry Garden Centres Ltd
Whitehall Garden Centres Ltd
Wilton Bradley Holdings Ltd

47210 Retail sale of fruit and vegetables in specialised stores

Millets Farm Centre Limited

47220 Retail sale of meat and meat products in specialised stores

Bartlett and Sons Limited
Dunbia (UK)
A.L.Martin & Son,Limited
Millets Farm Centre Limited

47240 Retail sale of bread, cakes, flour confectionery and sugar confectionery in specialised stores

Freshstores Limited
Millets Farm Centre Limited

47250 Retail sale of beverages in specialised stores

Millets Farm Centre Limited

47290 Other retail sale of food in specialised stores

Cotteswold Dairy Limited

47300 Retail sale of automotive fuel in specialised stores

Exeter Estates Limited
Flying Visit Limited
Gardner Garages Limited
Libya Oil Ethiopia Limited
Roundswell Services Limited
Simon Smith Retail Limited
David Taylor (Garages) Ltd
Tout Limited
Warners Retail Limited

47410 Retail sale of computers, peripheral units and software in specialised stores

Stormfront Retail Limited

47429 Retail sale of telecommunications equipment other than mobile telephones

PICS Telecom International Ltd

47510 Retail sale of textiles in specialised stores

Rajani (Wholesale) Limited
Susie Watson Designs Ltd

47520 Retail sale of hardware, paints and glass in specialised stores

Cornwall Glass & Glazing Ltd
Graham and Green Limited
G.J.Handy & Co Ltd
Powerbox International Limited
Proper Job Superstores Limited
Screwfix Direct Limited
Tamar Trading Co.Limited

47530 Retail sale of carpets, rugs, wall and floor coverings in specialised stores

Graham and Green Limited
Harding & Sons,Limited
Solomon (Liskeard) Limited
Weavers Shop Limited

47540 Retail sale of electrical household appliances in specialised stores

John Gillman & Sons (Electrical)
J Gliddon & Sons Limited
H.B.H. Woolacotts Limited
Paull & Co Ltd
Sparkworld Limited

47599 Retail of furniture, lighting, and similar (not musical instruments or scores) in specialised store [11]

Furniture World Limited
Graham and Green Limited
Harding & Sons,Limited
T. R. Hayes Limited
Heritage & Wise Limited
JB Global Limited
Julian & Son,Limited
Neptune Retail Limited
Solomon (Liskeard) Limited
Sturtons Group Limited
Woods (Dorchester) Limited

47610 Retail sale of books in specialised stores

Calendar Club Limited
Dart Abbey Enterprises Limited
WH Smith High Street Limited
WH Smith Travel Limited
Thompson Acquisitions Limited

47620 Retail sale of newspapers and stationery in specialised stores

Bastins 2012 Limited
Books & Stationers Limited
WH Smith High Street Limited
WH Smith Promotions Limited
WH Smith Travel Limited
Windward Marine Limited

47640 Retail sale of sports goods, fishing gear, camping goods, boats and bicycles

C & C Motor Caravans Ltd
Darthaven Marina Limited
Outdoor and Cycle Concepts Ltd
Salterns Marina Limited
Sportsman Gun Centre Limited

47650 Retail sale of games and toys in specialised stores

Bastins 2012 Limited
Calendar Club Limited

47710 Retail sale of clothing in specialised stores [13]

C-Retail Limited
Calendar Club Limited
J Gliddon & Sons Limited
Graham and Green Limited
Gridline Enterprises Limited
Mulberry Company (Sales) Ltd
Pinder Fashions Limited
Route One Retail Limited
Seasalt Holdings Limited
Seasalt Limited
Superdry PLC
Weird Fish Limited
Windward Marine Limited

47721 Retail sale of footwear in specialised stores [10]

BBLP Holdings Limited
C. & J. Clark International Ltd
Coastguard Road Limited
Foot Shop Limited
Herring Shoes Limited
Mulberry Company (Sales) Ltd
Route One Retail Limited
Seasalt Holdings Limited
Seasalt Limited
Superdry PLC

47722 Retail sale of leather goods in specialised stores

Mulberry Company (Sales) Ltd

47730 Dispensing chemist in specialised stores

Arrowedge Limited
Badham Pharmacy Limited
H2H Pharmacy Limited
Poolearth Limited
Shaunaks Limited

47741 Retail sale of hearing aids

Bloom Hearing Specialists Ltd

47749 Retail sale of medical and orthopaedic goods in specialised stores (not incl. hearing aids) n.e.c.

Acumed Ltd
BES Healthcare Ltd
Oak Tree Mobility Limited

47750 Retail sale of cosmetic and toilet articles in specialised stores

Lush Retail Limited
Neal's Yard (Natural Remedies) Ltd
Rajani (Wholesale) Limited

47760 Retail sale of flowers, plants, seeds, fertilizers, pet animals and pet food in specialised stores

Castle Gardens Sherborne Ltd
Cotswold Seeds Limited
Growing Enterprises Ltd
Highfield Garden Centres Ltd
Park Garden Centre Limited
D.Stewart & Son, Limited
Tamar View Nurseries Ltd
Edwin Tucker & Sons Limited

47770 Retail sale of watches and jewellery in specialised stores

Allum and Sidaway Limited
EP Mallory & Son (Holdings) Ltd
E.P.Mallory & Son,Limited
Martin and Co Ltd

47781 Retail sale in commercial art galleries

Caplon Limited
Hy. Duke & Son Limited

47789 Other retail sale of new goods in specialised stores (not commercial art galleries and opticians) [25]

Axminster Tool Centre Ltd
Dart Abbey Enterprises Limited
G.J.Handy & Co Ltd
Hobbycraft Group Limited
Hobbycraft Trading Limited
Le Creuset U.K. Limited
Martin and Co Ltd
H.Mustin & Son Limited
Paull & Co Ltd
Procook Limited
Rangemoors Limited
Silverfish UK Limited
Simply Pleasure Limited
C. Smart Agricultural Services Ltd
Stage Electrics Partnership Ltd
Stitch 2 Limited
Stitch 3 Limited
Stitch Bidco Limited
Swindon Caravan Centre Limited
Tileflair Limited
R. Tincknell & Son Limited
Vision Direct Europe Ltd
Waite & Son (Jewellers) Ltd
Windward Marine Limited
J. Wippell & Co Ltd

47791 Retail sale of antiques including antique books in stores

Julian Barran Limited
Delahunty Limited
Niall Hobhouse Limited

47799 Retail sale of other second-hand goods in stores (not incl. antiques)

Mare and Foal Sanctuary
C. Smart Agricultural Services Ltd

47890 Retail sale via stalls and markets of other goods

T. Ensor & Son Limited

47910 Retail sale via mail order houses or via Internet [25]

288 Group Limited
Averys of Bristol Limited
Bechtle Direct Limited
Bigdug Limited
Direct Online Services Limited
First Resources Limited
Herring Shoes Limited
Lovehoney Group Limited
Nisbets PLC
Pro-Direct Sport Limited
Rapid Racking Limited
Route One Retail Limited
Royal Air Force Charitable Trust Enterprises
Scotts Limited
Screwfix Direct Limited
Snapfish UK, Ltd.
Superdry PLC
Suttons Consumer Products Ltd
Thompson Acquisitions Limited
Verdo Renewables Ltd
Vision Dispensing Ltd.
Watch Guru Limited
Susie Watson Designs Ltd
Windward Marine Limited
J. Wippell & Co Ltd

47990 Other retail sale not in stores, stalls or markets [26]

Algreta Solutions Limited
D. & I. Bridgman and Son Ltd
Cox & Robinson (Agricultural) Ltd
Ron Darch & Sons Co Ltd
Dawson E & E Parts (Europe) Ltd
H.H.& D.E.Drew Limited
Elliotts (Cheltenham) Limited
Funkypigeon.Com Limited
Greens of Cheltenham Limited
Lilibet Finance Ltd
Lilibet Holdings Ltd
Lovehoney Limited
M & M Plant (Devon & Cornwall) Ltd
Moonraker (World) Ltd
Myoptique Group Ltd
Nu-Heat UK Limited
Oak Tree Mobility Limited
Ovo Electricity Ltd
Ovo Energy Ltd
Ovo Group Ltd
PWG Trading Limited
Puckator Limited
Stannah Lift Services Limited
Supergroup Internet Limited
Trade-Air Airline Support Ltd
Watch Guru Limited

49100 Passenger rail transport, interurban

Dart Valley Railway Ltd
First Greater Western Limited
Gloucestershire Warwickshire Steam Railway
South Devon Railway Trust
West Somerset Railway PLC

49200 Freight rail transport

STVA UK Limited

49319 Other urban, suburban or metropolitan passenger land transport (not underground, metro or similar)

Berrys Coaches (Taunton) Ltd
Bournemouth Transport Limited
First South West Limited
First West of England Limited
Pulham & Sons (Coaches) Ltd

49320 Taxi operation

Bath Taxis Limited

49390 Other passenger land transport

Amport and District Coaches Ltd
Beat The Street (UK) Limited
Eurotaxis Ltd.
Jumbocruiser Limited
Manchester and Provincial Car Parks
Swanage Railway Co Ltd
Taw and Torridge Coaches Ltd

49410 Freight transport by road [69]

A.C.C. Freight Management Ltd
A.E.T. Transport Services Ltd
Alberti Limited
Armoric Freight International (Holdings)
Big Green Parcel Holding Co Ltd
Jeremy Bishop Haulage Limited
A.J. Brunt Limited
Burcombe Haulage Limited
CAT-UK Services Limited
F W S Carter & Sons Limited
Conway Bailey Transport Ltd
Moreton C.Cullimore and Son,Limited
J.C. Dean (Haulage) Limited
C.M. Downton (Haulage Contractors)
Edgwicks Limited
Efret Limited
Evans Transport Limited
Fermac Limited
William Gilder Limited
Gilders Transport Limited
Gregory Distribution Limited
John Hackling (Transport) Ltd
J.R. Harding & Sons (Frome) Ltd
Hart's Haulage Limited
David Hathaway Transport Ltd
Heltor Limited
William C. Hockin (Transport) Ltd
Howard Tenens (West London) Ltd
Howard Tenens Limited
IDS Transport (UK) Limited
Jays Logistics (South West) Ltd
Jigsaw Solutions Limited
Jumbocruiser Limited
K & J Logistics Limited
Kay Transport Limited
R.T. Keedwell Limited
Langdon Group Limited
Langdon Transport Limited
Massey Wilcox Transport Ltd
I.J. McGill Transport Limited
Nagel Langdons Ltd
Opex Logistics Limited
Parsons Nationwide Distribution Ltd.
Pattemore's Transport (Crewkerne)
J F Pearce & Sons Limited
Plant Speed Limited
M. Preymesser Logistics Ltd
R.R. Transport Limited
Richard Read (Transport) Ltd
Charles Russell International Ltd
Charles Russell Transport UK Ltd
Rygor Group Services Limited
S W Group Logistics Limited
STVA UK Limited
John Seymour Transport Ltd
Les Smith Haulage Limited
C Sparks & Sons Limited
Sureway Express Transport Ltd
David Taylor (Garages) Ltd
B. Thompson & Sons (Transport) Ltd
Torridge Transport Limited
Tuffnells Parcels Express Ltd
Viridor (Lancashire) Limited
M. Way & Son (Transport) Ltd
West House Transport (S & G) Ltd
Wincanton PLC
Wincanton UK Limited
Wrings Transport Limited
Wyvern Cargo Ltd

49420 Removal services

Bath Quartermaster Limited
Lane's Storage and Removals Ltd

50100 Sea and coastal passenger water transport

B.A.I. (U.K.), Limited
Carlin Boat Charter Limited
Exmouth Marina Ltd
Isles of Scilly Shipping Co Ltd
Isles of Scilly Steamship Co Ltd

50200 Sea and coastal freight water transport [10]

B.A.I. (U.K.), Limited
Hovertravel Limited
Isles of Scilly Shipping Co Ltd
Isles of Scilly Steamship Co Ltd
Jenkins Marine Ltd.
Marine & Towage Services Group Ltd
Osprey Maritime Limited
Osprey Shipping Limited
Portland Harbour Authority Ltd
Portland Port Limited

50300 Inland passenger water transport

Dartmouth-Kingswear Floating Bridge Co
C. Toms and Son Limited

50400 Inland freight water transport

Hull Ocean Going Barges UK Ltd

51101 Scheduled passenger air transport

Bristol Airport Limited
FR Aviation Limited
Flybe Aviation Services Ltd
Flybe Group PLC
Flybe Limited
Isles of Scilly Skybus Limited
Isles of Scilly Steamship Co Ltd

51102 Non-scheduled passenger air transport

CSE Bournemouth Limited
Castle Air Limited
Devon Air Ambulance Trading Co Ltd
Devon Air Ambulance Trust
Isles of Scilly Skybus Limited
Specialist Aviation Services Group
Specialist Aviation Services Ltd

51210 Freight air transport

Isles of Scilly Skybus Limited
Isles of Scilly Steamship Co Ltd

52101 Operation of warehousing and storage facilities for water transport activities

CAT-UK Services Limited
Puma Energy (UK) Limited
Team Relocations Limited
Thornton Shipbrokers Limited
C. Toms and Son Limited

52102 Operation of warehousing and storage facilities for air transport activities

Team Relocations Limited

52103 Operation of warehousing and storage facilities for land transport activities [21]

Bath Quartermaster Limited
CAT-UK Services Limited
Denvern Limited
John Hackling (Transport) Ltd
Hinton Garage (Bath) Limited
Honda Logistics UK Limited
Howard Tenens (North West) Ltd
Howard Tenens (West London) Ltd
Howard Tenens Limited
Kong Co Ltd
Massey Wilcox Transport Ltd
Puma Energy (UK) Limited
Puma Energy Belfast Ltd
Rygor Group Services Limited
Sentry Self Storage Limited
Team Relocations Limited
Wabash Technologies Limited
Whitehall Cricklade Ltd
Willmott's Transport Limited
Wincanton PLC
Wyvern Cargo Ltd

52212 Operation of rail passenger facilities at railway stations

Swanage Railway Co Ltd

52219 Other service activities incidental to land transportation, n.e.c.

P W Commercial Co Ltd
Wincanton PLC

52220 Service activities incidental to water transportation

Fonterra (Logistics) Limited
Jenkins Marine Ltd.

52230 Service activities incidental to air transportation

Amsafe Bridport Limited
Exeter and Devon Airport Ltd
GE Infrastructure Aviation
International Spray Solutions Ltd
SAS (Dorset & Somerset) Ltd

52241 Cargo handling for water transport activities

Sharpness Dock Limited
Solent Stevedores Limited
Victoria Wharves Limited

52242 Cargo handling for air transport activities

A.C.C. Freight Management Ltd

52243 Cargo handling for land transport activities

Bath Quartermaster Limited
Wincanton PLC

52290 Other transportation support activities [10]

Condor UK Holdings Limited
Executive Jet Support Limited
Gloucestershire Airport Ltd
Guy,Leonard & Co.Limited
Hinton Garage (Bath) Limited
Import Export Services Ltd
Leidos Europe, Limited
Neptune Shipping Agency Ltd
SIRVA Relocation (No.1) Ltd
Wincanton UK Limited

53100 Postal activities under universal service obligation

Postal Choices Limited

53201 Licensed carriers

Big Green Parcel Group Limited
CFH Docmail Ltd
Mail Handling International Ltd

53202 Unlicensed carriers

Big Green Parcel Machine Ltd

55100 Hotels and similar accommodation [105]

777 Hotels Limited
ABQ Investment UK Ltd
AMCG Enterprise Limited
Alessandra UK Limited
Another Place Limited
Arnewood Estates Limited
Arthouse Glasgow Limited
Bath Priory Limited
Bedruthan Hotel Limited
Bell & Ross Limited
Berry Head Hotel Limited
Bibury Court Limited
Bluebelt Hospitality Limited
Bond Street Estates (Brighton) Ltd
Borrowdale Gates Limited
Percy R.Brend & Sons (Hoteliers)
Brickjet Limited
Bristol Harbour Hotel Limited
Brook Enterprises Limited
Brooks Hotels Limited
Buccaneer Holdings Limited
Budock Vean Hotel Limited
Calcot Health & Leisure Co Ltd
Carbis Bay Hotel Limited
Chessington Hotel Limited
Chester Abode Limited
Chewton Glen Hotels Limited
Chichester Harbour Hotel Ltd
Christchurch Hotels Ltd
City Eco Hotel Limited
County Hotel Canterbury Ltd
Dart Marina Hotel Limited
East Devon Properties Limited
Elfordleigh Holdings Limited
Froyle Harbour Hotel Limited
G.E.H. Properties Limited
Glen Mhor Limited
Great Eastern Hotel Co Ltd
Green Spinnaker Limited
H.K.C. Europe Limited
HRB Hotel Co Ltd
Halix Limited
Havana West Limited
Headland Hotel Co Ltd
Highlands Hospitality Limited
Hughes Hotels Limited
Kaleidoscope Collection Ltd
Kings (Weymouth) Limited
Kings Harbour Hotel Limited
Lanhydrock Golf Club Limited
Latona Leisure Limited
Lighthouse Property Estates Ltd
Llawnroc Hotel Limited
Longleat Bishopstrow Limited
Lucknam Park Hotels Limited
Lympstone Manor Ltd
M & P (Draycote) Limited
M.A.C. Hotels Ltd
Manchester Abode Limited
Manor House Hotel (Okehampton) Ltd
Mast (Bournemouth) Ltd
Nare Hotel Co Ltd
Oakland Capital Developments Ltd
Orchardleigh Park Ltd
Parkhouse Hotel (Shifnal) Ltd
Parkway Hotel and Spa Limited
Peartime Limited
Platinum One Hotels Limited
Plymouth Hotel Co Ltd
Porthminster Hotel Co Ltd
Powis Hotels Limited
R S T Leisure Ltd
RMH (Guildford) Limited
RW Gower Street Limited
RW Greenside Place Limited
RW Threadneedle Street Limited
Rattray Milne Ltd
Readam UK (Pty) Ltd
Rew Hotels Limited
Ridgevale Estates Limited
Royal Clarence Hotel Limited
SACO The Serviced Apartment Co Ltd
Salcombe Harbour Hotel Limited
Sandbanks Hotel Limited
Sands Resort Hotel Limited
Scarlet Hotel Limited
Seafood Trading Limited
Sidmouth Hotels Limited
Southampton Harbour Hotel Ltd
Springfield Country Hotel (Stoborough)
St Aubyn Estates Ltd
St Michael's Falmouth Limited
Stay Original Co Ltd
Swan Hotel Wells (2007) Ltd
Tewkesbury Park Limited
Thurlestone Estates,Limited
Torquay Leisure Hotels Limited
Tracertec Limited
Tregenna Castle Hotel Limited
Warm Welcome Hotels (Southern) Ltd
Watergate Bay Hotel Limited
Westcliff Hall (Sidmouth) Ltd
Wolf Rock (Cornwall) Limited
Woodley Hotels Limited
YMCA Bath Group

55201 Holiday centres and villages [16]

Bashley Park Limited
Braddicks Holiday Centre (Westward Ho!)
Britanic Industries Limited
Burry and Knight Limited
Cotswold Hoburne Limited
Grange Court (Hoburne) Limited
Hautot Holdings Limited
Hendra Touring Caravan & Camping Park

Kingsley Developments (S W) Ltd
Landscove Holidays Limited
Naish Estate (Hoburne) Limited
Pentewan Sands,Limited
Seasons Holidays PLC
Warren Farm Holiday Centre Ltd
Waterside Holiday Group Ltd
Woolacombe Bay Holiday Village Ltd

55209 Other holiday and other collective accommodation [10]

CBSM 2012 Limited
Eko Properties Limited
Exmoor Calvert Trust
Mundays Caravan Parks Limited
Seadown Holiday Park Limited
Totemplant Limited
Unique Home Stays Limited
Vowles Parks Limited
Wilson Leisure Developments Ltd
Worldteam Limited

55300 Recreational vehicle parks, trailer parks and camping grounds [24]

3T's Leisure Ltd.
Berkeley Leisure Group Limited
Brean Down Caravan Park Ltd
Burnbake Campsite Limited
Cofton Country Holidays Ltd
FWSC (Ladram) Limited
Gnome World Caravan Park Ltd
Holiday Parks SW Limited
Kerdene Limited
Light Group Limited
Main Gate Leisure Limited
Mawgan Porth Holiday Park Ltd
Newquay View Resort Limited
OM Holidays Ltd
Oak Tree Parks Limited
Old Coastguard Holiday Park Ltd
Redvers and Denzil Rice Farms Ltd
Shearbarn Holiday Park Limited
Suremime Limited
Totemplant Limited
Unity Farm Holiday Centre Ltd
Wallsend Estates Limited
Whitehill Country Park Limited
Wooda Farm Park Limited

55900 Other accommodation [24]

Abbeyfield Sidmouth Society Ltd
Abbeyfield Wessex Society Ltd
Avantage (Cheshire) Limited
B.J. Barkwell & Sons Limited
Barton Farms Limited
Bournemouth Young Men's Christian Association
Brighton Student Developments Ltd
Brunelcare
Charlcombe Limited
Doveleigh Care Limited
D. H. J. Foot Limited
John Fowler Holidays Limited
Hackney Parish Almshouses Charity
Homes in Sedgemoor Limited
JSM Property Services Limited
Oval Commercial Investments Ltd
Premiere Health Limited
Railway Convalescent Homes
Samara Investments (2000) Ltd
Samara Investments Limited
Urban Creation (Beech House) Ltd
WESC Foundation
West Country Park Home Estates Ltd
Wilson Leisure Limited

56101 Licenced restaurants [24]

Boston Tea Party Group Limited
Braddicks Holiday Centre (Westward Ho!)
Braddicks Leisure Limited
Calcot Health & Leisure Co Ltd
Chapel Barton House Co. Ltd
Chester Abode Limited
County Hotel Canterbury Ltd
Crowndell Consulting Limited
Dart Abbey Enterprises Limited
Downland Consultants Limited
Good Food and Drink Co Ltd
Green and Fortune Limited
Hall & Woodhouse Limited
Korado Ltd
Loungers Limited
Manchester Abode Limited
Market Square Limited
Rockfish Group Limited
Royal Clarence Hotel Limited
Seafood Trading Limited
Stein's Trading Limited
Swan Hotel Wells (2007) Ltd
Symons Retail Limited
Turtle Bay Restaurants Limited

56102 Unlicenced restaurants and cafes [11]

Boston Tea Party Group Limited
CJ Room Ltd
Canefield Ltd
Cornish Bakery Shops Limited
Edge Restaurants (NW) Limited
HRB Hotel Co Ltd
David Hunt (North Devon) Ltd
Lambtrad Ltd
Nuestra Familia Restaurants Ltd
Ronnies Limited
White Rose UK Ltd

56103 Take-away food shops and mobile food stands

Caspian Networks Limited
Cornish Bakery Shops Limited
Grensue Ltd
Lemaca Limited
Seafood Trading Limited
West Cornwall Pasty Co. Ltd

56210 Event catering activities

Freemans Event Partners (Logistics) Ltd.
HRB Hotel Co Ltd
Lake Inns & Leisure Limited
Little & Cull Ltd

56290 Other food services

M.J. Baker Foodservice Ltd
Budweiser Budvar UK Limited
Foodservice Centre Limited
Little & Cull Ltd
Muscle Foods Limited
Nutricia Limited
Seven Fields Primary School
West Country Vending Service Ltd

56302 Public houses and bars [17]

131 The Promenade Limited
Arkell's Brewery Limited
Bluebelt Hospitality Limited
Braddicks Holiday Centre (Westward Ho!)
Braddicks Leisure Limited
Buccaneer Holdings Limited
Butcombe Brewery Limited
Butcombe Brewing Co Ltd
Call To The Bar Ltd
Chamberlayne Farms Limited
Crowndell Consulting Limited
Hall & Woodhouse Limited
Heavitree Brewery PLC
Market Square Limited
Ramsbury Estates Limited
St.Austell Brewery Co Ltd
Wadworth and Co Ltd

58110 Book publishing

Cengage Learning (EMEA) Ltd
Mike Cruickshank Publishing Ltd
Edward Elgar Publishing Ltd
J.H. Haynes & Co. Limited
National Trust (Enterprises) Ltd
Pali Text Society Limited
Parragon Books Limited

58120 Publishing of directories and mailing lists

Applied Market Information Ltd

58130 Publishing of newspapers

Blackmore Limited

58141 Publishing of learned journals

Bioscientifica Limited
IoP Publishing Limited
Society for Endocrinology

58142 Publishing of consumer and business journals and periodicals

Ascent Publishing Limited
Blackmore Limited
Wentrow Media Limited

58190 Other publishing activities [15]

Assessments Bidco Limited
Assessments Midco 2 Limited
Assessments Midco Limited
Emotional Rescue Limited
Future Holdings 2002 Limited
Future PLC
Future Publishing Holdings Ltd
Future Publishing Limited
Gemma International Limited
Great British Card Company PLC
Hacche Retail Limited
Higher Education Statistics Agency
Mulberry Studios Limited
RTP-UK Ltd
Stonebridge Colleges (Publishing)

58290 Other software publishing

3P Learning Limited
Datamine Corporate Limited
SAA Consultants Limited
Zynstra Limited

59111 Motion picture production activities

Aardman Animations Limited
PP Capital 3 Limited
Snow Business International Ltd
Tamander Limited

59112 Video production activities

Twofour Group Limited

59113 Television programme production activities

Aardman Animations Limited
Back Catalogue Distribution Ltd
John Downer Productions Ltd
Forge Entertainment Limited
Twofour Broadcast Limited
Twofour Group Limited

59120 Motion picture, video and television programme post-production activities

Films at 59 Limited

59140 Motion picture projection activities

WTW Cinemas Limited

59200 Sound recording and music publishing activities

Basic Broadcasting Limited
Peter Gabriel Limited

61100 Wired telecommunications activities [10]

AFL Telecommunications Europe Ltd
Avonline Network Services Ltd
Barden Network Engineering Ltd
Bistech Group PLC
Bistech PLC
Glide Bidco Limited
Glide Holdings Limited
Glide Student & Residential Ltd
Glide Topco Limited
WPD Telecoms Limited

61200 Wireless telecommunications activities [13]

Aceaxis Limited
Avenue 64 Limited
Avonline Network Services Ltd
Axell Wireless Limited
Beacon Communication Services Ltd
Bistech Group PLC
Bistech PLC
Cambium Networks, Ltd
Glide Bidco Limited
Glide Holdings Limited
Glide Student & Residential Ltd
Glide Topco Limited
WPD Telecoms Limited

61300 Satellite telecommunications activities

Avonline Network Services Ltd
Avonline PLC
EMS Satcom UK, Ltd.
Honeywell Global Tracking Ltd

61900 Other telecommunications activities [30]

4Com Customer Services Ltd
4Com PLC
AFL Services Europe Ltd
Asset Services Limited
Avonline PLC
Bamboo Technology Group Ltd
Barden Network Engineering Ltd
Bistech Group PLC
Bistech PLC
Chronos Technology Limited
Club Communications Ltd.
Cogent Communications UK Ltd
Creditcall Limited
Excalibur Communications GB Ltd
JISC Services Limited
Mobile Thinking Limited
Nokia UK Limited
Openwave II UK Limited
Sonus Networks Limited
South West Communications Group Ltd
Teleperformance Holdings Ltd
Teleperformance Limited
Telesoft Technologies Limited
Tiger Communications (Holdings) Ltd
Tiger Communications PLC
Total (2014) Limited
TxtNation Holdings Limited
Vysiion Limited
West International Holdings Ltd
West UC Limited

62011 Ready-made interactive leisure and entertainment software development

Aardman Animations Limited
Cipher Corp Holding Ltd
Spyscape Ltd

62012 Business and domestic software development [35]

Alias Limited
Altus Holdings Limited
Altus Limited
Bluevenn Limited
CFH Docmail Ltd
Computer and Design Services Ltd
Creditcall Group Limited
Creditcall Holdings Limited
Cristie Software Limited
Cultura Technologies Ltd
Descartes Systems UK Limited
Five AI Limited
Flo Group Ltd
Go Vocational Solutions Ltd
Imperial Civil Enforcement Solutions
Ipipeline (TCP) Limited
Literature and Latte Ltd
Maximise IT Solutions Limited
Mayden House Limited
Miro Technologies Limited
Planit Software Limited
QIP Solutions Ltd
SAA Consultants Limited
Scisys UK Holding Ltd
Scisys UK Limited
Snowdrop Solutions Ltd
Trapeze Group (UK) Limited
Ultrahaptics Limited
Unicorn Training Group Limited
Vero Software Limited
Vero UK Limited
Verto Homes Ltd
West Country Business Systems (Holdings)
Zuken Limited
Zynstra Limited

62020 Information technology consultancy activities [26]

Actual Experience PLC
Anana Limited
Constellation Software UK Holdco Ltd
Creditcall Limited
Datamine Corporate Limited
Grey Matter Limited
Healthcare Computing Limited
Horsebridge Network Systems Ltd
IBCOS Computers Ltd
Imperial Civil Enforcement Solutions
Intergraph (UK) Limited
KTSL Limited
Maximise IT Solutions Limited
Nephos Technologies Ltd
Procurri UK Limited
QNH Limited
Redrock Consulting Limited
SAA Consultants Limited
Scisys UK Holding Ltd
Scisys UK Limited
Silversands Limited
Torry Harris Business Solutions (Europe)
Tregenna Ventures Limited
Ultrahaptics Limited
Vedbaek Limited
Volaris Group UK Holdco Ltd

62030 Computer facilities management activities

Appsbroker Limited
Creditcall Group Limited
Creditcall Holdings Limited
G.B. Electronics Limited
Premium Rate Numbers Ltd
Scisys UK Limited
Socomec U.K. Limited
Strata Service Solutions Ltd.

62090 Other information technology service activities [56]

1&1 Internet Limited
ATEX Media Limited
Apak Group Limited
Bittware Limited
Bladeroom Group Limited
C3IA Solutions Limited
CDS Support Limited
Cavium UK Ltd
Click Consult Limited
Codestone Group Ltd.
Cogent Communications UK Ltd
Computershare Technology Services (UK)
Cookpad Limited
Creditcall Group Limited
Creditcall Holdings Limited
Data Installation & Networking Services
Dingle Brothers Systems Ltd
Drilling Systems (U.K.) Ltd
Drilling Systems Group Limited
Drilling Systems Limited
E3 Media Limited
Fasthosts Internet Limited
First Databank UK Ltd

G.B. Electronics Limited
Grey Matter Limited
Healthcare Computing Limited
IP-Performance Ltd
ITEC Connect Ltd
Innogy Business Services UK Ltd
Inty Limited
LJ (Copiers) Limited
Landmark Analytics Limited
Landmark Information Group Ltd
Maistro PLC
Mayden House Limited
Netcraft Ltd
Opaltec International Limited
Project People Limited
Pure Storage UK Limited
Quest End Computer Services Ltd
Richmond Group Limited
SAA Consultants Limited
Scisys UK Holding Ltd
Scisys UK Limited
Snowdrop Solutions Ltd
Symec Technologies Limited
Synergy Health Systems Limited
Torry Harris Business Solutions (Europe)
Ukcloud Ltd
Ultrahaptics Limited
Vendigital Limited
WPC Software Limited
Westcon Group Africa Operations Ltd
Westcon Group European Operations
Westcon Group Middle East Holdings
Wind River UK Limited

63110 Data processing, hosting and related activities [17]

Bistech PLC
CFH Docmail Ltd
Cloudpay United Kingdom Ltd
Computershare Technology Services (UK)
Decision Insight Hub Limited
Decision Insight Information Group (UK)
Havas EHS Discovery Limited
Higher Education Statistics Agency
Jordans Limited
Latcham Direct Limited
Mayden House Limited
National Milk Records PLC
Navisite Europe Limited
Searchflow Limited
Teleperformance Limited
Virtual Infrastructure Group Ltd
Zynstra Limited

63120 Web portals

Glide Bidco Limited
Glide Holdings Limited
Glide Student & Residential Ltd
Glide Topco Limited
Mayden House Limited

63990 Other information service activities n.e.c. [12]

Credit Reporting Agency (Holdings)
Creditcall Group Limited
Creditcall Holdings Limited
Crediton Milling Holdings Ltd
Eduserv
Higher Education Statistics Agency
Lake Consultancy and Investments Ltd
Quartet Community Foundation
Synertec Limited
TM Group (UK) Limited
TM Property Searches Limited
Teleperformance Contact Ltd

64191 Banks

Bank of Ireland Britain Holdings Ltd
Bristol & West PLC
Hilcro Limited
Wessex Water Services Finance PLC

64201 Activities of agricultural holding companies

Compass Agri (Holdings) Ltd
Enidvale Holdings Limited
Farmers First Limited
Ropsley Holdings Limited
A E Stuart Limited
George Williamson & Co. Ltd

64202 Activities of production holding companies [17]

2OC (Holdings) Limited
Brunel Wind Limited
CQC Holdings Limited
Catalent CTS UK Holding Ltd
Customade Group Midco Limited
Customade Group Topco Limited
Customade Group Trading Ltd
Datum Capital Limited
Field International Holdings (Dorset)
Hydra Holdings 2015 Limited
Hydro Holdings UK Limited
Magicard Holdings Limited
McBraida Holdings Limited
Quickmach Holdings Limited
Spower Holdco 1 (UK) Ltd.
TR (Fenpower) Limited
UFP Global Holdings Limited

64203 Activities of construction holding companies [27]

Acraman (515) Limited
Arriva Group Limited
B.46 Trustees Ltd.
Bourne Group Holdings Ltd
Burrington Estates (New Homes) Ltd
Burrington Estates (RS) Ltd
E G Carter (Holdings) Limited
Dribuild Group Limited
Eagle One Holdings Limited
M.F. Freeman Group Limited
M.F. Freeman Holdings Limited
Glossbrook Holdings Limited
Ikonic Holdings Limited
A J Iles Holdings Limited
Jones Building Group Limited
Kelston Sparkes Holdings Ltd
Kitto Group PLC
LMR Holdings Limited
Neat Experts Holdings Limited
Parkside Holdings Limited
Bob Pepper Holdings Limited
Radipole Mill Investments Ltd
Robertson Developments Holdings Ltd
SDS Holdings Limited
Sureserve Compliance Services Ltd
Sureserve Energy Services Ltd
Tauntfield Ltd

64204 Activities of distribution holding companies

B.T.C. Activewear Holdings Ltd
Philip Dennis Foodservice (Holdings)
International Plywood PLC
Allan Sichel Limited
Wincanton Holdings Limited

64205 Activities of financial services holding companies [25]

Amigo Holdings PLC
Amigo Loans Group Ltd
Amigo Loans Holdings Ltd
Arval UK Group Limited
Atlantis Ocean Energy PLC
BNP Paribas Fleet Holdings Ltd
Belvedere Bidco Limited
Belvedere Midco Limited
Brightside Group Limited
Caerus Capital Group Limited
Caerus Holdings Limited
Gabriel Limited
Hargreaves Lansdown PLC
James Hay Holdings Limited
Independent Investment Analysis Ltd
Investment Funds Direct Group Ltd
Liverpool Victoria General Insurance Group
Novia Financial Holdings Ltd
Richmond Group Limited
Sanlam Investment Holdings UK Ltd
Sanlam Wealth Planning Holdings UK
St. James's Place Acquisition Services
St. James's Place DFM Holdings Ltd
Succession Newco1 Limited
Zurich Project Finance (UK) Ltd

64209 Activities of other holding companies n.e.c. [266]

3LINE Holdings Limited
AES Ballylumford Holdings Ltd
AES Barry Limited
AES Barry Operations Limited
AES Electric Ltd
AES Horizons Investments Ltd
AES K2 Limited
AES Overseas Holdings Limited
AES TEP Power II Investments Ltd
AES TEP Power Investments Ltd
AES UK Holdings Ltd
AES Venezuela Finance
AGI UK Acquisition Limited
AT Property Holdings Limited
Aardman Holdings Limited
Addison Capital Limited
All Tel Communications Limited
Alliance Pharma PLC
Amberon Holdings Limited
Antrak Limited
Assessments Topco Limited
Asvida UK Limited
Aura Wind (Holdco) Limited
Aura Wind (Midco) Limited
Avonline Holdings Limited
Avonline Network Services Holdings
Ayersmont Limited
BA Technologies Holdings Ltd
BP Rolls Holdings Limited
Babcock Marine (Devonport) Ltd
P. E. Barton (Holdings) Ltd
Bighead Fasteners Limited
Bioquell PLC

Bistech Group PLC
Bradbury House Properties Ltd
Robert Braithwaite Limited
Brightborough Capital Limited
Bristol Funeral Directors Ltd
Bristol Holding Limited
Bristol Water Core Holdings Ltd
Britannia Parking Group Ltd
CG Holdings Limited
CMOStores Group Limited
CS LSI Solar Limited
Carnegie Investment Asset Management
Castelan Group Limited
Caveangle Limited
Centek Holdings Limited
Chedington Court Estate Ltd
Churcham Homes Holdings Ltd
Coldharbour Technology Limited
Corialis Group Limited
Cottleston Holdings Limited
Coxco Holdings Limited
Custom Sensors & Technologies Newco Ltd
Cygnet Industries Limited
DCM (Cornwall) Limited
Danisco Holdings (UK) Limited
Devaron (UK) Limited
Devon Care Homes Holdings Ltd
Direct Online Services Holdings Ltd
Duke Street Capital Oasis Acquisitions
Duke Street Capital Oasis Midco Ltd
Duke Street Capital Oasis Orthodontics Holdings
Duke Street Capital Oasis Orthodontics
EMS Acquisition Co Ltd
EXE Investment Holdings Ltd
Eagle One Foc Holdings Limited
Eagle One Investment Holdings Ltd
Ecotricity Wind and Sun Parks (Issuing)
Eurogate Finance Limited
Euston Simmonds Limited
Excalibur Communications Group Ltd
FJB Hotels Limited
Falfish (Holdings) Limited
Fanatics UK Holdings Limited
Forgeway Holdings Ltd
Foscombe Properties Limited
Frazer-Nash Consultancy Group Ltd
GBE Converge Group Ltd
GCP Holdco Limited
GCP Topco 2 Limited
GCP Topco Limited
GLE Bidco Limited
GLE Midco 2 Limited
GLE Midco Limited
GLE UK Topco Limited
Galloper Wind Farm Holding Co Ltd
Genus Capital Limited
Gill Corporate Limited
Gilo Industries Group Limited
Glasshouse Hotel Limited
Glide Bidco Limited
Glide Holdings Limited
Glide Topco Limited
Green Valley Capital Limited
Green and Fortune Holdings Ltd
Greenoaks Global Holdings Ltd.
Grenville Midco 1 Limited
Grenville Midco 2 Limited
Grenville Topco Limited
Group Silverline Limited
Guarantee Holdings Limited
Harbour Hospitality Group Ltd
Harbour International Limited
Haynes Publishing Group PLC
Highcliffe Holdings Limited
Hilcro Limited
Hindhead Investments Limited
Hometower Consultancy Limited
IDEMIA UK Holding Limited
IVC Acquisition Ltd
IVC Acquisition Midco Ltd
IVC Acquisition Pikco Ltd
Image Factory Communications Ltd
Imerys Minerals Holding Ltd
Imerys Talc UK Holding Limited
Imerys UK Finance Limited
Imperial Tobacco Holdings (1) Ltd
Imperial Tobacco Holdings (2007) Ltd
Imperial Tobacco Holdings Ltd
Imperial Tobacco Limited
Imperial Tobacco Overseas (Polska)
Imperial Tobacco Overseas Holdings (2)
Imperial Tobacco Overseas Holdings Ltd
Imperial Tobacco Overseas Ltd
Innogy Gym 2 Limited
Innogy Gym 3 Limited
Innogy Gym 4 Limited
Innogy Renewables UK Holdings Ltd
Insite Outdoor Advertising Ltd
Insite Poster Investments Ltd.
Insite Poster Midco Limited
Integra Neurosciences Holdings (UK)
JELF Limited
Jamaica Inn Bodmin Moor Holdings Ltd
Jongor (Holdings) Ltd
KCTG Japan Holdings Ltd.
KLKI Holdings Limited
Kalel Partners
Kandytoys Holdings Limited
Kerry Ingredients Holdings (U.K.)
Kimberly Audrey Limited
Kinlon Limited
Kinneir Dufort Topco Limited
La Flor de Copan UK Limited
Lancaster Leisure Limited
Linc Capital Limited
Lion/Jenga Bidco Limited
Loungers Holdings Limited
Lovell Stone Group Holdings Ltd
Low Carbon Oxygen Limited
Lowman Manufacturing Co Ltd
Lunamar (Group) Limited
MPL Holdings (SW) Limited
MSA UK Holdings Limited
Malaby Holdings Limited
Malvern Tyres Holdings Limited
Martin & Martin Holdings
Mean Moor Community Wind Farm Ltd
Mears Care (Holdings) Limited
Mears Group PLC
Mendip Batch Medical Limited
Metric Group Holdings Limited
Midway Care Group Limited
Milewood (Holdings) Ltd
Murrill Holdings Limited
New Power Co Ltd
Next Generation Wind Holdings Ltd
No House Limited
Norton Group Holdings Limited
S. Notaro Holdings Limited
Nu-Heat (Holdings) Limited
Oasis Healthcare Bidco Limited
Oasis Healthcare Group Limited
Oasis Healthcare International Ltd
Oasis Healthcare Midco 1 Ltd
Oasis Healthcare Midco 2 Ltd
Old Quay House Hotel Limited
Organic Foods, Drinks & Investments Holdings
Overleaf Holdings Limited
P B Design Holdings Limited
P G Properties Limited
PPL Midlands Limited
PPL WPD Investments Limited
Paper Bag Company Holdings Ltd
Parragon Publishing Limited
Pavey Group Holdings (UK) Ltd
Pencarrie Group Limited
Perrys Holdings Limited
Henry W Pollard & Sons (Group) Ltd
Porthia Group Limited
Positive Cashflow Finance (Holdings)
Prolabs Holdings Limited
Quantum Homes Holdings Limited
Quay Developments (Southern) Ltd
RMMP Limited
Race 500 Limited
Radius Bidco Limited
Radius Holdco Limited
Radius Midco Limited
Reform Topco Limited
Richmond Group Limited
SACO Group Holdings Limited
SCC (Holdings) Limited
SLG Allstars Limited
SLX Group Limited
ST Schrader Holding Company UK Ltd
Safe House Holdings Limited
Charles Saunders Holdings Ltd
Seafood Restaurant (Padstow) Ltd
Seiche Water Technology Group Ltd
Senate Court (Southgate) Ltd
Sensata Technologies UK Financing Co.
Sett Wind Development Limited
Shaunaks Holdings Limited
Shervey Limited
Sidmouth Hotels Holdings Ltd
Soar Newco Limited
Solent Global Holdings Limited
Solent Global Limited
South West Airports Limited
St Moritz (Holdings) Limited
Stotts Group Limited
Stuart Property (Holdings) Ltd
Superior Group Limited
Sutton Harbour Holdings PLC
Synergy Health Holdings Ltd
Synergy Health Investments Ltd
TTK British Holdings Limited
Targetgrange (Holdings) Ltd
Taylor Maxwell Group (2017) Ltd
Taylor Maxwell Group Limited
Taylor Maxwell Holdings Ltd
Tempire Investments Limited
Texas Instruments (U.K.) Holdings
D.C. Thomson Developments Ltd
Threadneedles Hotel Limited
Timehaste Limited
R. Tincknell & Son Limited
Togs Limited
Triventura Bidco Limited
Triventura Midco I Limited
Triventura Midco II Limited
Allen Trump Holdings Limited
UK Pacific Hampton Limited
Unite Group PLC

Valeport (Holdings) Limited
Vertigo Capital Limited
Vertigo Investments Limited
Virtus Health Europe Limited
WCR Holdings 2014 Limited
WK Crematoria Limited
WPD Investment Holdings Ltd
Wahoo Learning Limited
Watts Desser Limited
Westerleigh Crematoria Limited
White Pennant Ltd
A D Woodley Holdings Limited
Woodward & Co (Holdings) Ltd
Wyse Estates Holdings Limited
XYZ Machine Tools (Holdings) Ltd
Your Energy Holdings Limited
Zimmer U.K. Ltd.
Zycko Group Limited
npower Group Limited

64301 Activities of investment trusts [13]

Athelney Trust PLC
Baring Emerging Europe PLC
Biopharma Credit PLC
British Empire Trust PLC
Chelverton Growth Trust PLC
Contango Investments Limited
European Investment Trust PLC
HJP Investments 2015
Manor Life Investments Limited
Miton UK Microcap Trust PLC
Pantheon International PLC
Witan Pacific Investment Trust PLC
Woodford Patient Capital Trust PLC

64303 Activities of venture and development capital companies

Allied Minds PLC
Brightborough Capital Limited
Horatio Investments Limited
Oxygen House Group Limited
Private Equity Investor Ltd
Unicorn AIM VCT PLC

64304 Activities of open-ended investment companies

Acorn Classics House Limited
Ashgrove One Limited
Edgeworth Investments Limited
Marcatrin Limited
Natatomisam Limited
W.J.Tatem Limited
Winston Heights Ltd

64306 Activities of real estate investment trusts

Civitas SPV1 Limited
GCP Student Living PLC
Genus Capital 2 Limited
Genus Capital 3 Limited
Tilstone Glasgow Limited
Tilstone Warehouse Holdco Ltd

64910 Financial leasing [26]

Academy Leasing Limited
Agecroft Properties (No.2) Ltd
Armada Investments Limited
Arval UK Limited
Richard C. Bircher (Holdings) Ltd
Bradgate Business Finance Ltd
Desertlands Entertainment Ltd
Fintec Group Limited
Ignition Credit PLC
Lombard Corporate Finance (11) Ltd
Lombard Corporate Finance (13) Ltd
Lombard Corporate Finance (15) Ltd
Lombard Corporate Finance (7) Ltd
Lombard Corporate Finance (December 1)
Lombard Corporate Finance (December 3)
Manitou Finance Limited
Nanny McPhee Productions Ltd
Northern Isles Ferries Limited
Patalex III Productions Ltd
Patalex Productions Limited
Patalex V Productions Limited
RBS Asset Finance Europe Ltd
RBSSAF (2) Limited
RBSSAF (6) Limited
RBSSAF (8) Limited
Ultimate Asset Finance Limited

64921 Credit granting by non-deposit taking finance houses and other specialist consumer credit grantors

Amigo Loans Ltd
Commercial First Group Limited
Consilium Airton Limited
George Banco.Com Limited
Kingsley Developments (S W) Ltd
People 2000 Limited
Sterling Capital Asset Finance Ltd

64922 Activities of mortgage finance companies

Agricultural Mortgage Corporation P L C
Bath and West Finance Limited
Charterbank Capital Limited
DPRS Finance Limited
Peninsula Finance PLC
Roco Investments Limited

64929 Other credit granting n.e.c. [13]

Academy Leasing Limited
DJS (UK) Limited
Exeter Finance Group Limited
Exeter Finance Ltd
Finance Solutions Limited
Gwenray Capital Limited
MSP Capital Ltd
MSP Capital Three Limited
MSP Capital Two Limited
Motorhome Finance Limited
Richmond Group Debt Capital Ltd
Richmond Group Limited
Wessex Resolutions C.I.C.

64991 Security dealing on own account

1pm PLC
Amazon Capital Ltd
Blue Scorpio Limited
Deodara Limited
Front Foot Investments Limited

64992 Factoring

Catalyst Business Finance Ltd
Optimum SME Finance Limited
Positive Cash Flow Finance Ltd
Ultimate Bridging Finance Ltd
Ultimate Finance Group Limited
Ultimate Finance Limited
Ultimate Trade Finance Limited

64999 Financial intermediation not elsewhere classified [82]

3 Dorrits Investments Limited
Academy Leasing Limited
Aghoco 1256 Limited
Albermarle Trading Limited
Alden Finance Limited
Amigo Management Services Ltd
Armstrong Bridging International Ltd
Armstrong Infrastructure and Property Finance
Aspire Defence Finance PLC
Auxillis Limited
B4 Claims Limited
Bank of Ireland Britain Holdings Ltd
Bell Finance Limited
Berkeley Leisure Group Limited
Borlase Smart John Wells Trust Ltd
CGA Financial & Investment Services
Catalyst Business Finance Ltd
Cavehurst Limited
Clifton Down Corporate Finance Ltd
Computershare Mortgage Services Ltd
DEK-Co (UK) Ltd
Dartmoor Investment Trust Ltd
Distant Planet Productions Ltd
E-Mex Home Funding Limited
First Capital Finance Limited
Frizzell Financial Services Ltd
Gainwell Limited
Gener8 Finance Limited
Hargreaves Lansdown Advisory Services
James Hay Administration Co Ltd
Helena Productions Limited
Homeloan Management Limited
IPS Pensions Limited
Imagile Business Support Ltd
Imperial Brands Enterprise Finance
Industrial Common Ownership Finance
Intrinsic Financial Services Ltd
Intrinsic Wealth Limited
Investment Funds Direct Ltd
Irongate Limited
JELF Financial Planning Ltd
LV Equity Release Limited
Lockwash US Limited
Lombard Industrial Leasing Ltd
Lombard Lease Finance Limited
Lombard Leasing Co Ltd
London & Country Mortgages Ltd
Lyell Trading Limited
Morrison Financial Associates Ltd
Mortgage Intelligence Limited
Mortgage Works (UK) PLC
Nationwide Syndications Ltd
Novia Financial PLC
Openwork Limited
PP Capital 2 Ltd
PP Capital 3 Limited
Pittville Leasing Limited
R. B. Quadrangle Leasing Ltd
RBSSAF (25) Limited

Red Lion Investments Limited
Regulatory Finance Solutions Ltd
Road Management Services (Finance) PLC
Rowan Dartington & Co. Limited
Rowanmoor Executive Pensions Ltd
Sanlam Wealth Planning UK Ltd
Scottish Widows Unit Trust Managers
Shimao Limited
Sigma - Aldrich Financial Services
South West Investment Group Ltd
South West Water Finance PLC
St James's Place Unit Trust Group
St. James's Place Investment Administration
Sterling ISA Managers Limited
Thrive Renewables PLC
Tor Currency Exchange Limited
Towndown Limited
U C B Home Loans Corporation Ltd
Wessex Water Services Finance PLC
Yeovil Securities Limited
Zurich Advice Network Limited
Zurich Finance (UK) PLC
Zurich Intermediary Group Ltd

65110 Life insurance

Allied Dunbar Assurance PLC
Beaumonts (Leeds) Limited
Ecclesiastical Life Limited
Peter Harding Practice Ltd
LV Protection Limited
Liverpool Victoria Life Co Ltd
Sanlam Life & Pensions UK Ltd
St. James's Place UK PLC
Zurich Assurance Ltd

65120 Non-life insurance [29]

ARAG PLC
Accident Claims Handlers Ltd
Animal Friends Insurance Services
April Medibroker Limited
Baptist Insurance Company PLC The
Beaumonts (Leeds) Limited
Castelan Limited
Cornish Mutual Assurance Co Ltd
D A S Legal Expenses Insurance Co Ltd
Ecclesiastical Insurance Office PLC
Eldon Insurance Services Ltd
Endsleigh Insurance Services Ltd
Endsleigh Insurances (Brokers) Ltd
Exeter Cash Plan
Firstport Insurance Services Ltd
Highway Insurance Co Ltd
Insure & Go Insurance Services Ltd
JELF Insurance Brokers Limited
JELF Wellbeing Limited
Kingsbridge Risk Solutions Ltd
LV Capital PLC
LV Protection Limited
Liverpool Victoria Insurance Co Ltd
Methodist Insurance PLC
Mortgage Intelligence Limited
Premier Underwriting Limited
M.R. Ratcliffe Consultants Ltd
South Essex Insurance Brokers Ltd
Western Provident Association Ltd

65202 Non-life reinsurance

Animal Friends Insurance Services
JELF Insurance Brokers Limited
JELF Wellbeing Limited

65300 Pension funding

Beaumonts (Leeds) Limited
Ecclesiastical Life Limited
Sanlam Life & Pensions UK Ltd

66120 Security and commodity contracts dealing activities

Way Fund Managers Limited
Westford Trade Services (UK) Ltd

66190 Activities auxiliary to financial intermediation n.e.c. [11]

Computershare Investor Services PLC
Crowdcube Limited
Hargreaves Lansdown Asset Management
Intrinsic Financial Planning Ltd
Intrinsic Mortgage Planning Ltd
London & Country Mortgages Ltd
Omnis Investments Limited
Paradigm Norton Financial Planning
Rowan Dartington Holdings Ltd
Sanlam Wealth Planning UK Ltd
St. James's Place Wealth Management PLC

66220 Activities of insurance agents and brokers [13]

ARAG PLC
AUL Underwriting Agency Ltd
Amariz Limited
April UK (Insurance Services) Ltd
Be Wiser Insurance Services Ltd
Bennett Gould and Partners Ltd
Brightside Insurance Services Ltd
E Development (2) Limited
Europa Group Limited
Freedom Healthnet Limited
Lloyd & Whyte Limited
London & Country Mortgages Ltd
Somerset Bridge Ltd

66290 Other activities auxiliary to insurance and pension funding

Access Franchise Management Ltd
BBS Consultants & Actuaries Ltd
Bellamy Wealth Management Ltd
Curtis Banks Group PLC
Curtis Banks Limited
Exeter Cash Plan Holdings Ltd
LV Repair Services Limited
Lloyd & Whyte Group Limited
Property Consortium UK Limited

66300 Fund management activities

Dobson Family Investment Co Ltd
Empty Billy Limited
Hargreaves Lansdown Fund Managers Ltd.
Hazel Holdings Limited
M.H.R. Hicks Limited
Highlands House Investments Ltd
Kingsley Developments (S W) Ltd
Sarkis Limited

68100 Buying and selling of own real estate [212]

115-116 Marine Parade Limited
599 Developments Ltd
Abbey Manor Developments Ltd
Abbey Manor Group Limited
Aegeus Properties,Limited
Aistone Properties Limited
Alchemy Estates Limited
Alderbrook Road Limited
Alexandra Dock Limited
Alexandra Wharf Limited
Ashfield Land (Aberdeen) Ltd
Ashfield Land (Birmingham) Ltd
Ashfield Land (Bridgend) Ltd
Ashfield Land (Cardiff) Ltd
Ashfield Land Limited
Ashfield Land Management Ltd
M Baker (Retail) Limited
Bartletts Transport and Warehouses
Bathurst Estate Holdings Ltd
Baylis Estates Limited
Beachdown Limited
Beaulieu Property Management Ltd
Bel Ombre Properties Limited
Bentley Slade Limited
Birchmere Limited
Blue Port Estates Limited
Bonhay & Eagle Property Co Ltd
Brighton Harbour Hotel Limited
Brinkgreen Limited
Burford Beta Limited
Burford Delta Limited
Bushurst Properties Limited
CAA Property Limited
CBSM 2012 Limited
Cadeleigh Estates Limited
Camanoe Estates Limited
Candida Investments Limited
Canprop I Limited
Canprop Kensington Limited
Carlos SS Properties Limited
Caruso Properties Limited
T K T Cattran Limited
Ceres Estates Limited
Chantry Court Westbury Ltd
Chapters Freefolk Ltd
Chatlease Limited
Churchill Retirement (Group) Ltd
Churchill Retirement Living Ltd
Churchill Retirement PLC
Civitas SPV18 Limited
Civitas SPV2 Limited
Civitas SPV20 Limited
Civitas SPV3 Limited
Civitas SPV33 Limited
Civitas SPV36 Limited
Civitas SPV39 Limited
Civitas SPV44 Limited
Clark Projects 12 Limited
Claverton Estates Ltd.
Connolly & Callaghan Limited
Cover Construction Co Ltd
Coxley Developments Limited
Crystalight Limited
DMT Property Services Ltd
DPM Estate Limited
Dawnhaze Limited
Deeley Freed (Penhalt) Limited
Deeley Freed Developments Ltd
Digs Properties Limited
E & T Developments Limited

Eagle Investments Limited
Eagle One Mmiii Limited
Eagle Strategic Property Ltd
Easton Grey Estate Limited
Edgehill Battersea Limited
Edgehill Portfolio No.1 Ltd
Williams Ewan Limited
First Step Homes Limited
Fourgate (Cheltenham) Limited
Froyle Park Estates Limited
G W Interiors Holdings Limited
G.E. Developments Ltd
GGB Investments Ltd
Gaming International Limited
Gapcontrol Limited
Gleneil Limited
Goodshelter Property (Surbiton) Ltd
Goodshelter Property Co Ltd
Greensquare Homes Limited
Grounded Property Trading Ltd
Growth Property Limited
Gwenray Capital Limited
H.P.H. Limited
Havenstone Property Limited
Hayne Securities Limited
Robert Hitchins Investment Properties
B R Hodgson Group Limited
Holmshaw Property Co Limited
Holmshaw Property Holdings Ltd
Holton Homes Limited
Howard Tenens Distribution Ltd
Insite Poster Investments (A) Ltd
Insite Poster Investments (B) Ltd
Insite Poster Investments (C) Ltd
Insite Poster Properties Ltd
J.P.C.Properties (Southampton) Ltd
Jackson Developments Limited
Junction Road Croydon Limited
KMW Properties Limited
Kaikoura Investments Limited
Kammbronn Homes Limited
Kelley Holdings Limited
Kingsley Developments (S W) Ltd
Kites Enterprises Limited
L.A.L. Estates Limited
Land & Buildings Limited
Lanhydrock Estate Company
Leander Developments Limited
Legacy Properties Limited
Levitt UK Real Estate Limited
Litfield Land Limited
Littleham 2010 Limited
Loadace Limited
London & Devonshire Trust Ltd
Longmeadow Properties Limited
MC Property Ventures Limited
ME Estates Limited
A.E. Maiden Limited
Malvern Property Limited
Manual Investing Limited
Market Square Limited
MG Markey Group Limited
Matquel Property Co. Limited
McCarthy & Stone (Extra Care Living)
McCarthy & Stone (Home Equity Interests)
McCarthy & Stone Retirement Lifestyles
Medcentres PLC
Minstead Investments (Boscombe) Ltd
Montemax Limited
Mutual Real Estate Co Ltd
Newcombe Beard Limited
R. O'Dell (Holdings) Limited
Oakfield Grove Properties Ltd
Oceanview Developments Limited
Ovan Properties Limited
P G Properties Limited
PJFB Property Co Ltd
Pentrebay Properties Limited
Perseus Property Co Ltd
Alan Porter Limited
Porthia Limited
Portway Precision Limited
QMP Group Limited
Quick Move Now Limited
Quick Move Properties Limited
R W Estates (Trading) Limited
R W Estates Ltd
RR Sea Hanover St. Limited
RR Sea Strand Limited
Raven Mount Limited
Raw Investments Limited
Refresh Living No. 1 Ltd
River Reach Limited
C J L Rogers Properties Ltd.
Romfield Holdings Limited
Roseland Investments Ltd
S2 Residential Limited
Samara Investments (2000) Ltd
Samara Investments Limited
Sandpalm Properties Limited
Seabrook Land Developments Ltd
Seagull Developments Limited
Shareland Investments Limited
Shirley-Young Limited
South West Land Limited
Sphere Property 4 Limited
Spire House Developments Ltd
St Stephens House Ltd
Stanbridge Property Developments Ltd
Stockdale Trading Co Ltd
Stonewood Properties Limited
Streamclare Limited
Stroudwater Redevelopment Partnership
Summerfield Developments (SW) Ltd
Summerfield Estates Ltd
Summerfield SD3 Limited
Swettenham Estates (UK) Ltd
Tauntfield Ltd
Taunton Land Limited
Tenens Associates Limited
Thatcher View Development Ltd
Thrubwell Properties Limited
Toklon Limited
Tolladine Estates Limited
Torvean Limited
Troika Developments Limited
Tubbs (UK) Ltd
Urbina Private Equity No.3 Ltd
Visage (Aberdeen) Limited
WPD Property Investments Ltd
Waddeton Park Limited
Watchpike Limited
Watershore Ltd.
Whisstocks Developments Ltd
Whole Nine Yards (UK) Limited
Wildbrook Investments (Calne) Ltd
Wildbrook Investments (Industrial)
Wildbrook Investments (Thornbury)
Wildbrook Investments Limited
Wood Barton Developments Ltd
Woodcrescent Properties Ltd
YPI Limited

68201 Renting and operating of Housing Association real estate [34]

Barmont Properties Limited
Benridge Investments Limited
Bourne Holdings
Buckclose Limited
Coastline Housing Limited
Connolly & Callaghan Limited
Crowdhill Limited
E & T Developments Limited
Elleness Limited
Elm Tree Estates Limited
J.Ferguson Estate,Limited
Grosvenor Place Holdings Ltd
J.M.Harding & Partners Ltd
Haringey Schools Services Ltd
Hoyle & Co (Bournemouth) Ltd
Kemble Airfield Estates Ltd
Kew Estates Limited
Kingskerswell Property Management
Kirklees Schools Services Ltd
Lockman Properties Limited
Longmeadow Properties Limited
North Devon Homes
Oakfield Grove Properties Ltd
Old Tannery (Holt) Limited
Raw Investments Limited
Rochford Property Investments Ltd
Selwood Housing Society Ltd
Senlan Securities Limited
Teign Housing.
Torbay Schools Services Ltd
Trebartha Estates Limited
Troika Developments Limited
Troika Property Holdings Ltd
Two Rivers Housing

68202 Letting and operating of conference and exhibition centres

Colonial Leisure Limited
LDC (Finance) Limited

68209 Other letting and operating of own or leased real estate [557]

221 Limited
599 Developments Ltd
A.E. Securities Limited
A.M.B.Investments Limited
AEW Properties Limited
ARFF Ltd
ATP Holdings Limited
AUB Enterprises Limited
Abaco Estates Limited
Abbey Manor Property Holdings Ltd
Acanthus Ventures Limited
Acrefield Investments Limited
Acrefield Land Limited
Action Accommodation Ltd
Addpace Limited
Agents and Properties (Taunton) Ltd
Airport Business Centre Ltd
Aistone Properties Limited
Alfco Investments Limited
Bill Allen's Autos Limited
Altec Products Limited
Alton Pancras Estate UK Ltd.
Ankers and Rawlings Developments Ltd
Anstee & Ware Group Limited
Antonville Investments Limited
Appledore Land Limited
Arcade Leasing Limited

Arcade Rentals Limited
Arena Business Centres Limited
Arena Farnborough Limited
Ark Data Centres Limited
Ark Data Spring Park Limited
Ark Estates Cody Park Limited
Ark Estates Holdings Limited
Arriva Group Limited
Ashbolt Limited
Asheek Living Limited
Avon Energy Limited
BBG Lift Accommodation Services (No 2)
BBG Lift Accommodation Services Ltd
BHH Lift Accommodation Services Ltd
Bailey Holdings Limited
M Baker (Newquay) Limited
John Balaam Limited
Barrett Partnership Limited
Barrington Brown Estates Ltd
Bath Row Developments Ltd
Baylis Estates Limited
John Baylis Leisure Limited
John Baylis Limited.
Baylis Ventures Limited
Beacon Properties (UK) Ltd
EW Beard (Holdings) Limited
Beard Group Ltd.(The)
G.A. Beaton Limited
Beaver Estates (Ashford) Investments
Beckery Properties Limited
Beecholm Management Limited
Beetles (UK) Ltd
Bel Ombre Properties Limited
Benash Farms Limited
Bennah Limited
Berkeley Charterhouse Limited
Berrys Holdings Limited
Bessant Properties Limited
Bicknell Holdings PLC
Ken Biggs Limited
Birchclaim Limited
Birchmere Limited
Bix Developments Limited
Blackdown Estates Limited
Bluewater Property Limited
Bonds Mill Estate Limited
Bonhay & Eagle Property Co Ltd
Box House (Services) Ltd
Braddicks Holiday Centre (Westward Ho!)
Braddicks Leisure Limited
Brightwater Estates Limited
Brinkgreen Limited
Bristol & Mendip Estates Ltd
Bristol Infracare Lift (1) Ltd
Bristol Infracare Lift (2) Ltd
Bristol Infracare Lift (3) Ltd
Bristol Polytechnic Enterprises (Developments)
Bristol Polytechnic Enterprises Ltd
Bristol Properties Limited
Frank Bruce & Co Ltd
Bruf Contract Holdings Limited
Brunswick Limited
Brymain Investments Limited
Burford Delta Limited
CCH Property Co Ltd
CG Holdings Limited
Cabot Mews Limited
Cadogan House Investment Properties
Cambria Automobiles Property Ltd
Canynge Bicknell (Investments) Ltd
Carter Projects Limited
Caruso Properties Limited
Castle Barton Limited
Castle Nominees Limited
Castlegate Business Park Ltd
T K T Cattran Limited
Centek Properties Limited
Chachos Holdings Limited
Chadwick Holdings Limited
Chaffcombe Thorns Limited
Chalwyn Estates Limited
E.A. Chamberlain (Holdings) Ltd
Chamberlayne Farms Limited
Changvilla Investments Limited
Charford Properties Limited
Charlcombe Limited
Chatlease Limited
Cheltine Limited
Cher Varya Commercial Ltd
Chibroco Limited
Chinewood Developments Limited
Chrisgate Limited
M J Church Properties Limited
Claremont Ferrand Limited
Claybrook Limited
Clearwater Properties Limited
Clevedon Hall Estate Limited
Clifford Holdco Limited
Clyst Holdings Limited
Commercial Estates Property Co Ltd
Community 1st Cornwall Limited
Connolly & Callaghan Limited
Contactreal Limited
Cook and Copp Limited
Copano Limited
Copperplane Limited
Corrington Estates Limited
Cover Construction Co Ltd
J.A. Cover Limited
Cowgrove Limited
Coxley Developments Limited
Crescent Trust Co Ltd
Crown Yealm Limited
Crystalight Limited
Cult Clothing Cheltenham Ltd
D. J. Commercial Limited
D.J. Contracts (Structural) Ltd
D.J. Contracts (Weymouth) Ltd
D.J.L.Securities (Barum) Ltd
DMT Property Services Ltd
Dart & Francis Limited
Davenport & Sons Limited
Davies Holdings (Somerton) Ltd
Dawnhaze Limited
Dawson & King Limited
De Vere Farms Limited
Delphic Holdings Limited.
Devonshire Real Estate Limited
Dorset Freedom Properties Ltd
Downfield Homes Limited
Drake Court Property Limited
Draycot Estates Limited
Drewdeeds Limited
Dudbridge Estates,Limited
Dudley Infracare Lift (1) Ltd
Dunns Estates (Exeter) Limited
Dunns Motors (Holdings) Ltd
E & L Rental Properties Ltd
E.I.C.(Exeter) Limited
Eagle One Country Shopping Ltd
Eagle One Estates Limited
Eagle One Retail Limited
Eagle One Village Shopping Ltd
Eagle Strategic Property Ltd
East London Lift Accommodation Services
East London Lift Accommodation Services No2
Eastern Business Park Limited
Eastman Estates Limited
Edgecom Estates Ltd
Education Centre Management Ltd
Ellas No3 Limited
Ellas No4 Limited
Elm Developments Holdings Ltd
Emily Estate (UK) Limited
Enoch Properties (Devon) Ltd
Enys Estate Co Ltd
Erin Properties (Swindon) Ltd
Esteban Investments Limited
Euston Trust Limited
Williams Ewan Limited
Exe Investment Limited
Exeter Estates Limited
Fairlie Properties Limited
Fallon Enterprises Ltd
Farthingford Properties Ltd
Feniton Park Limited
Fernturn Holdings Limited
Fig Tree Court Limited
First Step Homes Limited
Five Bees Limited
Peter Ford Transport Limited
Forelle Estates Limited
Forward Developments Limited
Forward Land Limited
Foxmoor Limited
Fraser James Properties Ltd
Frog Investments Limited
James Froud and Sons Limited
G.B Contracts Limited
G.E. Developments Ltd
GCP Bloomsbury Limited
GCP Scape East Limited
GCP WL Limited
Gale Homes and Investments Ltd
Gapcontrol Limited
Gazelle Properties Limited
Geometry Properties Limited
George Estates Limited
Oliver Gillard (Southmead) Ltd
Gleneil Limited
Goldmix Limited
Goldrose Management Limited
Granite Associates Ltd.
Greendale Investments Ltd
Greenland Stud Farm Holdings Ltd
Greensquare Homes Limited
Grenadier Emperor Limited
Groves Park Investments Ltd
Guild Bristol Limited
H.P.H. Limited
Hamilton Scott Estates Limited
Hammett Investments Limited
Hampton House Properties Ltd
Handston Investments Limited
Hanford Holdings Limited
Harland Developments Limited
Harmer Properties Limited
Harrow Hill Properties Limited
Hartham Park Limited
J.H.Haskins & Son Limited
David Hathaway Properties Ltd
Haven Investments Limited
Havenstone Property Limited
Haydn Fine Ltd

Haynes Developments Limited
Hayward Properties Limited
Head Ruddy Limited
Hennock Properties Limited
Hesters Way Partnership Ltd.
Hewer Group Limited
Highlands Hospitality Limited
Hillside Property Co Ltd
Hobbs Properties Limited
Hodie Limited
Holne Chase Properties Limited
Hoo Developments Limited
Hopkins Estates Limited
IESIS (Redcliff Street) Ltd
Icon Two Limited
Ikonic Holdings Limited
Industrial Properties (Barton Hill)
Industrial Sales Limited
Innkeeping Limited
Insite Outdoor Advertising (A) Ltd
Insite Poster Investments (A) Ltd
Insite Poster Investments (B) Ltd
Insite Poster Investments (C) Ltd
Insite Poster Properties Ltd
Iota Properties Limited
J.P.C.Properties (Southampton) Ltd
JM & CW Limited
Jacgilden Properties Limited
Jackson Property Investments
Jam & Sons Limited
Javsford Investments Limited
Johnsons Group Limited
KMW Properties Limited
Kadar Developments Limited
Kat-O-Log Limited
Keenwork Limited
Kelley Holdings Limited
Kerrier Investments Limited
J.Knapp & Sons Limited
Kondor Property Co Ltd
Kruger Property Co Ltd
LDC (AIB Warehouse) Limited
LDC (Alscot Road) Ltd
LDC (Brunel House) Limited
LDC (Causewayend) Limited
LDC (Chaucer House) Limited
LDC (Constitution Street) Ltd
LDC (Greetham Street) Limited
LDC (Holdings) Limited
LDC (Imperial Wharf) Limited
LDC (Loughborough) Limited
LDC (MTF Portfolio) Limited
LDC (Millennium View) Limited
LDC (New Wakefield Street) Ltd
LDC (Old Hospital) Limited
LDC (Portfolio 100) Limited
LDC (Portfolio 20) Limited
LDC (Portfolio Five) Limited
LDC (Portfolio Four) Limited
LDC (Portfolio One) Limited
LDC (Portfolio) Limited
LDC (Project 110) Limited
LDC (Project 111) Limited
LDC (Radmarsh Road) Limited
LDC (Skelhorne) Limited
LDC (Tara House) Limited
LDC (William Morris II) Ltd
Lake Consultancy and Investments Ltd
Lance Levy Investments Limited
Langdon (Dorset) Farms
Langlands Farms Limited
Lanhydrock Estate Company
Lansdown Properties (Cheltenham) Ltd
Leckhampton Dairies Limited
Legacy Properties Limited
Levitt UK Real Estate Limited
Lewisia Limited
Liberty House (Nuneaton) Ltd
Lighthouse Property Estates Ltd
Linen Yard Investments (Crewkerne) Ltd
Liverton Business Park 2011 Ltd
Liverton Business Park 2012 Ltd
Lloyd Brothers (Bristol) Ltd
Lloyd's Property Southwest Ltd
Lone Eagle Retail Limited
Longmayne Limited
Lozenge Limited
Lymington Investments Limited
M & G Properties (Cheltenham) Ltd
M.T. Property Developments Ltd
MMT Centre Investment Limited
E.J. MacKelden & Sons (Bobbing) Ltd
Manchester and Provincial Car Parks
Manor Lodge Developments Ltd
Market Square Limited
Marks Barn Farm (Crewkerne) Ltd
Martingate Centre Limited
Matquel Property Co. Limited
Maxine Investments Limited
McCarthy Investments Limited
McGill Warmley Limited
Mears Housing Portfolio (Holdings)
Mears Housing Portfolio 2 Ltd
D.J. Melsome Limited
Meltor Developments Limited
Milord Homes Limited
Minton Investments (Industrial) Ltd
Moderandum Limited
Monkey Island Properties Ltd
R G Morcom Investments Ltd
JKL Moseley Limited
Mutual Real Estate Co Ltd
Netvox Limited
Newcombe Beard Limited
Newport Park Limited
Nicolas James Investments Ltd
Ninecourt Limited
Norton Avonmouth Limited
Nucleus Developments Limited
Nutwell Farms Limited
R. O'Dell (Holdings) Limited
Oakfield Investments Ltd
Oakleaze Holdings Limited
Oasis Plant Hire Limited
Oastcrest Limited
Old Sorting Office (Bournemouth) Ltd
Henry Oliver Ltd
Olo Real Estate Limited
One Holding Investments Ltd
Ophir Finance Co Ltd
Opmal Limited
Orchard Gate Ltd
Orchardleigh Estates Limited
Osric Finance Limited
Oxford Infracare Lift (1) Ltd
P & L Properties Limited
P G Properties Limited
P L H Property Investment Ltd
PAC Farms Limited
PC Property Holdings Limited
PCP 2014 Limited
Padmanor Investments Limited
Park Home Management Ltd
Patel Brothers Limited
Penlane Limited
Thos.S.Penny,Limited
Philmark Estates Limited
Pleroma Investments Limited
Plumlocations Limited
T.H.Plumridge Limited
Plymouth City Airport Limited
Plymouth Rentals Limited
Plymouth Science Park Limited
Plymstock Properties Limited
Keith Pople Limited
Porthia Group Limited
Powderham Properties (Teignmouth)
Premier Developments (1995) Ltd
Premier Livestock Auctions Ltd
Primeco Limited
Principality Holdings Limited
Prodigio Limited
Pucklechurch Development Co Ltd
Pyman Bell (Holdings) Limited
Qualtronyc Property Holdings Ltd
Quantock Properties Limited
R.T. Property Investments Ltd
REPI Limited
RHSG Properties Limited
RR Sea Dundee Limited
RR Sea Hanover St. Limited
RR Sea St. Helens Limited
RRPI (UK) Ltd
RWC Construction Ltd
Raans Estates Limited
Readam UK (Pty) Ltd
Redhorn Holdings Limited
Refresh Living No. 1 Ltd
Regency Properties (Tadworth) Ltd
Renshaw U.K. Limited
Residential Trust Limited
Resort Estate Management Ltd
Riohurst Investments Limited
Robinson Property Co Ltd
Robinson Real Estate Limited
Robotmother Limited
Romfield Holdings Limited
Rosemount Investments (Bristol) Ltd
Rosemundy Investments Limited
Roundhill Estate Limited
Rowcliffe Holdings Limited
Rowe & Co.Cornwall (Properties) Ltd
Rowe Estates (UK) Limited
Royal Arcade Limited
S.C.C. Transport (Devizes) Ltd
SACO Cannon Street Limited
SB Holdings (Exeter) Limited
SCES Property Ltd
SEC Properties Limited
SH & GS Property Group Limited
Sabre Group Limited
Sade Properties Ltd
Samara Investments (2000) Ltd
Samara Investments Limited
Satnam Limited
J.J. Saunders Limited
J Scadding & Son Property Ltd
Schyde Investments Limited
Scotsgrove Holdings Limited
Second Applemead Limited
Sheila Holdings Limited
Shepperton Properties Limited
Shilston Barton Farming Ltd
Shiner Properties Limited
Ship (Derriford) Limited
Shirley-Young Limited

Shirwell Limited
Herbert Silver (Holdings) Ltd
Silver Arrow Investments Ltd
Speeds Group Holdings Limited
Spring Mill Holdings Limited
St Margaret's Residences (Exeter)
St Stephens House Ltd
Standbetter Limited
Stannah Lifts Holdings Limited
Steadfast Asset Management Ltd
Stevens Family Property Ltd
Stochastic Holdings Ltd
Storm Land Securities Ltd
Stowell Park Estate Limited
Stroud Valleys Canal Company
Student Rooms 4 Plymouth Ltd
Studyhome 1992 Limited
Summerfield Estates Ltd
Supara Limited
Super Dooper Stores Limited
Surereed Limited
Sutton Harbour Services Ltd
Swan Properties Cornwall Ltd
Swattons Limited
Symonds Estates Limited
TFIO Properties Limited
Tasman House Developments Ltd
Tauntfield Ltd
Taw Garage (Holdings) Limited
Tenens (Lakeside) Limited
Tickenham Court Farm Co.Limited
Tilstone Basingstoke Limited
Tilstone Holdings Limited
Tilstone Trade Limited
R. Tincknell & Son Limited
Triangle Properties (Bristol) Ltd
Trusart Limited
Truscotts (Barnstaple) Limited
Tubbs (UK) Ltd
Turner Property Holdings Ltd
Twentieth Century Investments Ltd
Tylney Investments Limited
UDS Properties Limited
USAF Finance II Limited
USAF Holdings J Limited
USAF LP Limited
USAF Management 10 Limited
USAF Management 11 Limited
USAF Management 12 Limited
USAF Management 14 Limited
USAF Management 6 Limited
USAF Management Limited
Una Group Limited
Unite Accommodation Management 18
Unite Accommodation Management 19
Unite Accommodation Management 6 Ltd
Unite Accommodation Management Ltd
Unite Accommodation Management One Hundred
Unite Finance Limited
Unite Finance One (Holdings) Ltd
Unite Finance One (Property) Ltd
Unite Holdings Limited
Unite Integrated Solutions PLC
Upper Belgrave Property Ltd
Urbina Private Equity No.3 Ltd
Vantage Point Business Park Ltd
Vantage Point Business Village Ltd
Victor Properties Ltd
WMG Property Limited
WPD Property Investments Ltd
B.Walker & Co.(Dursley) Ltd
Wallscourt Foundation
Walsall Lift Accommodation Services
Ward Edward Limited
A. H. Warren Trust (Property) Ltd
Watchpike Limited
Waterfield Homes Limited
Waterlip Developments Limited
Weblease Limited
Wellesbourne Property Management Ltd
West End Investments Clifton Ltd
Weymouth Harbour Estates Ltd
Whisstocks Developments Ltd
Whiteburn Rookery Investments Ltd
Wild Ash Limited
Wildbrook Investments (Calne) Ltd
Wildbrook Investments (Industrial)
Wildbrook Investments (Thornbury)
Wildbrook Investments Limited
Percy Williams & Sons,Limited
Wishford P6 Limited
Wodskou Properties Limited
Wolverhampton City and Walsall Lift Accommodation Services
Woodfield Developments Limited
A.J. Wooldridge Limited
Worcester Properties Ltd
M.E. Wynn & Co. Limited
Yarlington Homes Limited
Yellow Bridge Investments Ltd
Yeo & Davey (Properties) Ltd

68310 Real estate agencies [11]

Acerbic Ltd
Andrews & Partners Limited
Andrews Estate Agents Limited
Andrews Letting and Management Ltd
Goadsby & Harding (Residential) Ltd
Hillside Farm Investments Ltd
Property Franchise Group PLC
Retirement Homesearch Limited
Verto Homes Ltd
Webbers Property Services Ltd
World Group Holdings Limited

68320 Management of real estate on a fee or contract basis [78]

Albion Healthcare (Oxford) Holdings
Altec Products Limited
Aspire Defence Holdings Ltd
Aspire Defence Limited
Aspire Defence Services Ltd
Aster Property Limited
Batsford Estates (1983) Co Ltd
Bay Cottage Properties Limited
Bexley PPP Health Services Ltd
Birmingham Healthcare Services Ltd
Black Country PPP Health Services
Blue Chip Holidays Ltd
Bridlington Schools Services Ltd
Brighton & Hove City Schools Services
CBSM 2012 Limited
T K T Cattran Limited
Colvase Estate Ltd
Community Health Facilities (Oxford)
Contactreal Limited
Cornwall Housing Limited
D4E Mulberry Limited
Danesdale Land Limited
Debden Schools Services Ltd
Defence Training Services Ltd
Eccles Special High Schools Co Ltd
Elmbirch Properties P.L.C.
Epping PPP Maintenance (Health) Services
Williams Ewan Limited
Firstport Bespoke Property Services
Firstport HMF Limited
Firstport Operations PD Ltd
Firstport Property Services Ltd
Firstport Property Services No 2 Ltd
Firstport Retirement Property Services
Foxmoor Business Park Limited
Goadsby & Harding (Residential) Ltd
Haringey Schools Services Ltd
Harlequinns Bowling and Leisure Ltd
Herts & Essex PPP Health Services
Hull Maternity Development Ltd
ITP Developments Limited
Insite Outdoor Advertising Ltd
Insite Poster Properties Ltd
Kirklees Schools Services Ltd
LBS (Fire Services) Limited
Liskeard PPP Health Services Ltd
Liverpool Schools Services Ltd
Marlborough Facilities Limited
Mears Housing Management Ltd
Millstream Management Services Ltd
Monmouth Facilities Limited
NK Facilities Limited
Newcastle Estate Partnership Ltd
P G Properties Limited
Poole Housing Partnership Ltd
Premium Rate Numbers Ltd
Priorgate Limited
Property Management Group Ltd
Pullman Premier Leisure Ltd
Redbridge PPP Health Services Ltd
Redruth Facilities Limited
Sadborow Estate Limited
Salum Properties Limited
Sarum Properties Limited
St Aubyn Estates Ltd
Stafford Education Facilities Ltd
Stephenson Property Services Ltd
Sunderland CLC School Services Ltd
Tilstone Retail Limited
Torbay Schools Services Ltd
Two Eagles Investments Limited
Underdown Investments Limited
Webbers Property Services Ltd
Wellesbourne Property Management Ltd
Wenand Homes Ltd
Wildbrook Investments (Calne) Ltd
Wildbrook Investments (Thornbury)
Wirral Schools Services Ltd

69102 Solicitors

Battens Solicitors Limited
Clark Holt Limited
Cooke Painter Limited
DAC Beachcroft Claims Limited
DAS Law Limited
Gould & Swayne Limited
Harris Fowler Limited
Lyons Davidson Limited
Russell Worth Limited

69109 Activities of patent and copyright agents; other legal activities n.e.c.

Angel Assistance Limited
Fairlie Holdings Limited
TM Group (UK) Limited
TM Property Searches Limited

69201 Accounting and auditing activities
ARWC Consulting Ltd
Jordans Limited

69203 Tax consultancy
Forrestbrown Limited

70100 Activities of head offices [525]
1&1 UK Holdings Limited
1869 Limited
A & L Care Homes Holdings Ltd
A-Gas Investments Limited
A1 PPP Infrastructure Holdings Ltd
AIM Aviation Holdings Limited
API Holdco Limited
API Technologies (UK) Limited
ASM Assembly Systems UK Holding Ltd
Abbey Manor Group Limited
Acumed Acquisition Co Ltd
Adey Holdings (2008) Limited
Adtech Holdings Limited
Advance Bidco Limited
Advance Topco Limited
Advanced Insulation Group Ltd
Advanced Insulation Holdings Ltd
Aeroflex Test Solutions Ltd
Aeronautical & GI Holdings Ltd
Aim Altitude Limited
Airsprung Group PLC
Alderley PLC
Altogether Care - Care Homes Ltd
Alu Bidco Limited
Alu Holdco 2 Limited
Alu Midco Limited
Alu Topco Limited
Amalgam Holdings Limited
Amber Chemical Co Ltd
Amcor Europe Group Management
Amcor European Investment Holdings
Amcor European Investments Ltd
Amcor Flexibles UK Holding Ltd
Amcor Holdco 3
Amcor Holding
Amcor Holding No.1 Limited
Amcor Investments Germany
Amcor Packaging UK Limited
Amcor Polska Holding Limited
Amcor UK Group Management Ltd
Amcor UK Investments Limited
Apetito (U.K.) Holdings Ltd
Appello Limited
Arval UK Group Limited
Ashington Business Inc. Ltd
Ashwoods Innovations Limited
Aster Treasury PLC
Attivo Group Limited
August UK Holdco Limited
Avantage (Cheshire) Holdings Ltd
Avon Group Manufacturing (Holdings)
Avon Rubber Overseas Limited
Avon Valley Holdings Limited
Avsan Holdings Limited
BCCB Incorporated Limited
BNP Paribas Fleet Holdings Ltd
BSR Group Holdings Limited
Baglan Moor Healthcare Holdings Ltd
M Baker (Holdings) Limited
Batson Bidco Limited
Batson Midco Limited
J.T.Baylis & Co Ltd
Mike Bayliss Holdings Limited
Beale Limited
EW Beard (Holdings) Limited
Beeley (Holdings) Limited
Bentley Park (UK) Limited
Bicknell Holdings PLC
Bid PCB UK Limited
Bifold Fluidpower (Holdings) Ltd
Bifold Group Limited
Bladeroom Holdings Limited
Bland Group UK Holdings Ltd
Blue Port Holdings Limited
Blue3 (London) (Holdings) Ltd
Bond Holdings Limited
Boyland and Son Limited
Bridgewell Holdings Limited
Bridport Limited
Brightside Group Limited
Bristol Airport (UK) No.3 Ltd
Bristol Charities
Bristol Water Holdings UK Ltd
Andrew Brownsword Hotels Ltd
Bruf Contract Holdings Limited
Bryan Brothers Holdings Ltd
Budock Vean Holdings Limited
Burford Alpha Limited
Burford Beta Holdings Limited
Burford Zeta
By Education (Waltham Forest) Holdings
C.H.G. Holdings Limited
CDF Group Ltd
CEPS PLC.
Cambria Automobiles PLC
Cannon Care Homes 4 Limited
Cannon Care Homes Ltd
Capston Limited
Carco Group Limited
F W S Carter & Sons Limited
Catalent Pharma Solutions Ltd
Catalent U.K. Swindon Holding II Ltd
Cengage Learning UK Holdings Ltd
Centrax Holdings Limited
Centrax Industries Limited
Ceuta Holdings Limited
Chaplins Properties Limited
Charcoal CLG 1 Limited
Charcoal Midco 1 Limited
Charcoal Newco 1 Limited
Charcoal Newco 1A Limited
Chatleigh Holdings Limited
Chatleigh Limited
Chevron Properties Limited
Churngold Construction Holdings Ltd
C. & J. Clark (Street) Ltd
Matthew Clark Bibendum (Holdings)
Cloudpay Holdings Limited
Coastguard Road Limited
Cobham PLC
Commercial First Group Limited
Computershare Investments (UK) (No 7)
Computershare Investments (UK) (No. 8)
Computershare Investments (UK) (No.3)
Computershare Limited
Connect Group PLC
Connolly & Callaghan Group Ltd
Cooper Tyre & Rubber Company UK Ltd
Creanova Universal Closures Ltd
Cronite Castings (Distribution) Ltd
Cubit Group Limited
Curzon 1234 Limited
D & R Bidco Limited
D & R Cleanco Limited
D & R Midco Limited
D & R Topco Limited
D B Foods (Holdings) Limited
D.B. Systems Holdings Limited
DAS UK Holdings Limited
DB Food Group Limited
DMGI Land & Property Europe Ltd
DWML Holdings Limited
Daish's Group Limited
Dartex Holdings Limited
Dash Group (SW) Limited
P J Davidson Holdings Ltd.
Deceuninck Holdings (UK) Ltd
Decision Insight Information Group (Europe)
Deutsch GB Limited
Dhrona Holdings Ltd
Dix Hills 516 Limited
Double H (Holdings) Limited
Dover Fluids UK Ltd
Dover Refrigeration & Food Equipment UK
Drew Holdings Limited
Dunview Limited
Dyson International Limited
Dyson James Group Limited
E T Holdings Limited
Eagle Star Holdings Limited
Earthline Exchange Limited
Earthline Holdings Limited
Eastleigh Care Group Limited
Ecclesiastical Insurance Group PLC
Eco Holdings Limited
Ecotricity Group Ltd
Elbit Systems UK Limited
Ely Acquisition Limited
Emblem Holdings Limited
Endsleigh Limited
Epichem Group Limited
Essex Schools (Holdings) Ltd
Eurac Limited
Europa Equity Limited
Eurostore Group Limited
Expolink Group Limited
Expromet Technologies Group Ltd
Eyre Holdings Limited
F & W Media International Ltd
FB Ammonite Limited
FB Brassica Limited
FB Brinjal Limited
FB Calluna Limited
FTI Management Limited
Finlay Plant (UK) Limited
Firstport Limited
Five Valleys Aerospace Limited
Flagdawn Limited
Foray Holdings Limited
Forelle Estates Investments Ltd
Fornuis UK Limited
Forthglade Foods Holdings Ltd
Four Times Enterprises Limited
Foursquare Associates Limited
G & H US Holdings Limited
G4S Joint Ventures Limited
GDS INT Holdings Limited
GE Aviation Systems Group Ltd
Gaming International Limited
Gantrail International Limited
Gardiner (Holdings) Limited
Gensmile Limited
Gerber Emig Group Limited
Gilcrest Group Limited
Gillman Electrical Group Ltd
Gingerbread (Holdings) Limited
Go in Four Limited

Goadsby & Harding (Holdings) Ltd
Goonvean Holdings Limited
Graytone Limited
Great Eastern Hotel Holding Co Ltd
Gregory Distribution (Holdings) Ltd
Grist Group Limited
Grosvenor PPP Holdings Limited
Grosvenor Place Holdings Ltd
Haley Securities Limited
Harbour Hotels Group Limited
Harbour Hotels Holdings Ltd
Hardware Holdings Limited
Harris Construction Limited
Harvey Commercial Holdings Ltd
David Hathaway Holdings Ltd
Hatton Properties Limited
Haycock Holdings Limited
Haynes Publishing Group PLC
John Heathcoat & Company (Holdings)
Helston Garages Group Limited
Hemsley Fraser Group Limited
Hemsley Fraser International Ltd
Highway Insurance Group Ltd
Hills UK Limited
Hoburne Limited
B.R. Hodgson (Holdings) Ltd
B R Hodgson Group Limited
Hospital Company (Dartford) 2005 Ltd
Hospital Company (Dartford) Holdings
Hydro International Limited
Imerys UK Limited
Imperial Brands PLC
Indalo International Holdings Ltd
Infineon Technologies Newport Holding
Intel Corporation (UK) Limited
Inter Mediate Two Limited
Inter Rested Limited
International Plywood PLC
Investors in the Community (Leeds Schools) Holding Co
Izit Group Limited
JS2 Investments Limited
JTL (Holdings) Limited
Jacksons Investments Limited
Jasme Limited
H R Jasper & Son (Holdings) Ltd
Jennings Industries Limited
R. T. Keedwell Holdings Ltd
Keenwork Limited
Key West (Holdings) Limited
Kingdon Holdings Limited
Kitto Group PLC
Kiwa Holdings (UK) Limited
Kiwi Holdings Limited
Knight Midco Limited
Knight Square Holdings Limited
Knight Square Limited
Knights Brown Group Ltd
Knights Brown UK Ltd
Knorr-Bremse Investment (UK) Ltd
Knorr-Bremse SA Holding Company (UK) Ltd
Kohler Holdings Ltd.
LV Capital PLC
G.R. Lane Holdings Limited
Lang & Potter (Holdings) Ltd
Langham Industries Limited
Larasian Limited
Latimer Trend Holdings Limited
Legoland US Holdings Limited
Liberation Group UK Limited
Lloyds Bank General Insurance Holdings
Lockman Electronic Holdings Ltd
Lockman Investments Limited
Lodge Service International Ltd
Lokaz Limited
London Eye Holdings Limited
Longhouse Ltd
Loran (Investments) Limited
Lornamead Acquisitions Limited
Lornamead Group Limited
Lush Cosmetics Limited
MAT Foundry Group Limited
MWI Supply (UK Acquisition) Ltd
MWI Supply (UK Holdings) Ltd
Majestic Limited
Manlock Investments Limited
Manton Riches Holdings Limited
Marazion Holdings Limited
Marsh Holdings Limited
Stuart Marsh Shoes Limited
Masstock Group Holdings Ltd
McCarthy & Stone PLC
Medcentres PLC
W.J. Meddings (Holdings) Ltd
Meggitt Finance Limited
Meggitt International Holdings Ltd
Meggitt International Limited
Meggitt PLC
Meggitt Properties PLC
Merlin Entertainments (Asia Pacific)
Merlin Entertainments (NBD) Ltd
Merlin Entertainments Developments
Merlin Entertainments Group Holdings
Merlin Entertainments Group Ltd
Merlin Entertainments PLC
Michco 1208 Limited
Mitcham Canada Holdings Ltd
Mitcham Holdings Ltd
Mulberry Company (Europe) Ltd
Mulberry Group PLC
Mylor Yacht Harbour (Holding Company)
E.V. Naish Limited
National Lighting Co Ltd
Neal's Yard Holdings Limited
Nettleton Holdings Limited
New Look FIN III Limited
New Look Finance Limited
New Look Limited
New Look Retail Group Limited
New Look Secured Issuer PLC
New Look Senior Issuer PLC
New Power Co Ltd
Nicolas James Group Limited
Nicolas James Holdings Limited
Nine Telecom Group Limited
Nippon Paint (Europe) Ltd.
Nonwovenn Ltd
North Downs Farm Ltd
Oasis Healthcare Limited
Ocean Automotive (Holdings) Ltd
Ocean Housing Group Limited
Octagon Healthcare Group Ltd
Octagon Healthcare Holdings (Norwich)
Openwave Systems Limited
Openwork Holdings Limited
Organic Foods, Drinks & Investments Holdings
Original Style Holdings Ltd
Oval (1173) Limited
Oval (259) Limited
PAC Farms Limited
PK Food Concepts Ltd.
PPL WEM Limited
PSC Training & Development Group Ltd
Parable Trust Limited
Paradigm (Sheffield BSF) Holdings
Parham Holdings Limited
Pastaking Holdings Limited
Pattersons (Holdings) Limited
Pennard Hill Farm Holdings Ltd
Pennon Group PLC
Pentwin Group Limited
Pet Food Holdings Limited
Phoenix Learning & Care Holdings Ltd
Play Sports Group Limited
Pleroma (UK) Limited
Plessey Group Holdings Limited
Poeton Holdings Limited
Porthia Group Limited
Positive Group (UK) Limited
Potensis Recruitment Limited
Premia Group Limited
Principality Holdings Limited
Pritchard Patent Product Company (2001)
Pritchmor Holdings Limited
Pro - Direct Group Limited
Professional Reseller Group Ltd
Project Darwin Bidco Limited
Project Darwin Topco Limited
Property Consortium (Holdings) Ltd
Prowrap Limited
Quadrum Investments Group Ltd
RWE Generation UK Holdings Ltd
Richard Read Holdings Limited
Redde PLC
Redhorn Holdings Limited
Reflex Electronics Limited
Remix Bidco Limited
Renaissance Miles Platting Holding Co
Renelec Group Limited
Renrod Holdings Limited
River Marketing (Holdings) Ltd
Road Management Services (Darrington) Holdings
Robbins & Myers Holdings UK Ltd
Rollalong Holdings Limited
Rose Bidco Limited
Rotork Overseas Limited
Rotork P.L.C.
Rowe Estates Holdings Limited
S G V M Holdings Limited
SBS International Holdings Ltd
SC Group-Global Limited
SEA (Group) Ltd.
SRT Marine Systems PLC
SWK (UK) Limited
Safran UK Limited
Salford Schools Solutions Holdco Ltd
Salford Schools Solutions Ltd
Salisbury Glass Holdings Ltd
Samatt (Group Services) Ltd
Samatt Limited
Sanctus Group Holdings Limited
Sanlam UK Limited
Satnam Investments Limited
Scorribanda Holdings Limited
Scot Group Southern Limited
J M Scully (Holdings) Limited
Secure Services Limited
Senex Capital Limited
Serais Investments Limited
Serene LL Ltd
Services Support (Avon & Somerset) Holdings
Shepperton Group Limited
Sherborne Holdings Limited

Shiptinvest Limited
Shorelark Limited
Sidlaw Group Limited
Signum Technology Limited
Simian Group Limited
Sitec Design Limited
Sitec Holdings Limited
Sitec Recruitment Limited
Smartstream Technologies Holdings
WH Smith 1955 Limited
WH Smith High Street Holdings Ltd
WH Smith Hospitals Holdings Ltd
WH Smith PLC
WH Smith Retail Holdings Ltd
WH Smith Travel 2008 Limited
WH Smith Travel Holdings Ltd
Smithcorp Limited
Smiths News Holdings Limited
Sofa Brands International Ltd
Solar Power Generation Limited
Solsbury Inventions Limited
South West Communications Group Holdings
Southtown Investment Co Ltd
Southwark Bridge Holdings Ltd
Space Cooling Topco Limited
Spirax-Sarco America Limited
Spirax-Sarco Investments Ltd
Spirax-Sarco Overseas Limited
Sportech Holdco 1 Limited
Sportech Holdco 2 Limited
St Gresham Limited
St Juliens Limited
St. James's Place International Assurance Group
St. James's Place International Distribution
St. James's Place PLC
St. James's Place Wealth Management Group
Stanley Security Solutions - Europe
Stanley UK Acquisition Co Ltd
Stannah Lifts Holdings Limited
Stepping Stone Group Limited
Stilo International PLC
Stovax Heating Group Limited
Sunseeker International (Holdings)
Swallowcourt Holdings Limited
Tekne Holdings Limited
Teleperformance Holdings Ltd
Thatchers (Myrtle Farm) Ltd
Thatchers Holdings Limited
D.C. Thomson Developments Ltd
Thorne Holdings Limited
Traffic Group Limited
Trelleborg Holdings UK Limited
Tribal Holdings Limited
Tricel Holdings (UK) Limited
Triode Acquisitions UK Limited
Troika Developments Limited
UKRD Group Limited
Ultrahaptics Holdings Ltd
United Healthcare (Bromley) Holdings
VSGT Ltd
Van Courtlandt Holdings Ltd
Veitch Family Holdings Limited
Venture Engineering Group Ltd
Victoria Group Holdings Ltd
Viridor Limited
Vision Direct Group Ltd
WPD Distribution Network Holdings
Warm Welcome Management Ltd
Warners Retail Group Limited
Warners Trust PLC
A. H. Warren Trust (Holdings) Ltd
Wartsila Hamworthy International Ltd
Wartsila Hamworthy Limited
Wasdell Holdings Limited
Watermark Cotswolds Limited
Watts of Lydney Group Limited
Way Group Limited
Weird Fish Clothing Limited
Weird Fish Holdings Limited
West Pharmaceutical Services Group
Westerleigh Group Holdings Ltd
Westerleigh Group Limited
Western Forestry Co Ltd
Western Power Distribution Investments
Westfield Medical Group Ltd
Wheeler's (Westbury) Holdings Ltd
Ken White Holdings Limited
T. H. White Holdings Limited
Whitehall Garden Centre (Holdings)
Whitehall Group (Wessex) Ltd
Willett & Son Holdings Limited
Ian Williams (Holdings) Ltd
Williamsbuild Management Ltd
Wind Holdings Nord Limited
Woodbury Limited
Woodlodge Holdings Limited
Woods Consolidated Limited
Workman Properties Limited
Wyvern Holdings Limited
X.T.Holdings Limited
XJ6 Schools Holdings Limited
Yardgate Limited
Zebra MTD Limited
Zuken Group Limited
Zurich Financial Services (UKISA)
Zycko Overseas Limited

70210 Public relations and communications activities

Corinthian Sports Limited

70221 Financial management [15]

7 SFI Limited
Bridgewell Holdings Limited
Cambria Automobiles Acquisitions Ltd
Copper Bidco Limited
Copper Midco 1 Limited
Copper Midco 2 Limited
Discus Management Limited
James Hay Partnership Management
B.R. Hodgson (Holdings) Ltd
Imperial Brands Finance PLC
Lester Brunt Wealth Management Ltd
REPI Limited
Signum Technology Limited
Urban Creation Management Ltd
Whiteoaks Investments Limited

70229 Management consultancy activities other than financial management [46]

Advanced Paper Production Ltd.
Altus Limited
Applied Market Information Ltd
Arisaig Partners (UK) Limited
Avec Trade Limited
Aviation Requirements Ltd
A N Barr Industries Limited
Barrett Partnership Limited
Berkeley Charterhouse Limited
Beylon Limited
Bond Business Services Limited
Burrington Estates Limited
C & C Management Services (UK) Ltd
CIL Management Consultants Ltd
Carnegie International Asset Management
Catalent Pharma Solutions Ltd
Clipper Contracting Group Ltd
Copper Bidco Limited
Dopano Limited
FB Calluna Limited
Flo Group Ltd
Freixenet Copestick Limited
Grenville Bidco Limited
Hazelwood Motor Co Ltd
Healthline UK Holdings Limited
Hemsley Fraser International Ltd
Heritage Automotive Holdings Ltd
Houzz UK Ltd.
Jordans Limited
Keycrown Properties Limited
Kites Enterprises Limited
Landell Mills Limited
Libra Investments Limited
Medcentres PLC
Murray & Roberts United Kingdom Ltd
Newincco 1401 Limited
Newincco 1402 Limited
Offshore Marine Management Ltd
Premium Rate Numbers Ltd
RTP-UK Ltd
Renewable Energy Partnerships Ltd
Resonance Limited
Royal Air Force Charitable Trust Enterprises
Terraquest Solutions Limited
UFT Limited
Vian Marketing Limited

71111 Architectural activities

Lake Consultancy and Investments Ltd
Roberts Limbrick Limited
Stride Treglown Group PLC
Stride Treglown Limited

71112 Urban planning and landscape architectural activities

Pegasus Planning Group Limited

71121 Engineering design activities for industrial process and production

Adey Innovation Limited
AgustaWestland Limited
Bluetech Systems International Ltd
Honda Engineering Europe Ltd
Versarien PLC

71122 Engineering related scientific and technical consulting activities

Altran UK Limited
Antech Limited
Aviation Requirements Ltd
Fiberlean Technologies Limited
Maats Tech Limited

71129 Other engineering activities [17]

Buro Happold Consulting Engineers
Buro Happold Engineers Limited
Buro Happold Limited
Cannon Technologies Group Ltd
Drilling Information Limited
Field International Limited
Forest Press Hydraulics Ltd
Frazer-Nash Consultancy Ltd
Import Export Services (GRP) Ltd
Parsons Peebles Service Ltd
RTP-UK Ltd
Shenton Global Limited
Sumac Precision Engineering Ltd
Supacat Limited
Turnspeed Precision Engineering Co Ltd
Viper Innovations Ltd
WRC P.L.C.

71200 Technical testing and analysis

Adey Innovation Limited
Anthony Best Dynamics Limited
Cabot Design Limited
Cosmetic Warriors Limited
Import Export Services (GRP) Ltd
Kiwa Limited
Patheon UK Limited

72110 Research and experimental development on biotechnology

Allied Minds PLC
Binx Health Limited
Eden Research PLC

72190 Other research and experimental development on natural sciences and engineering [22]

Adey Innovation Limited
Allied Minds PLC
Campden BRI
Campden BRI (Chipping Campden) Ltd
Catalent MTI Pharma Solutions Ltd
Creanova Universal Closures Ltd
Dart Sensors Limited
Dyson James Limited
Dyson Technology Limited
Fiberlean Technologies Limited
Fjords Processing Limited
Frazer-Nash Consultancy Ltd
Game and Wildlife Conservation Trust
Garrad Hassan & Partners Ltd
Garrad Hassan Group Limited
Honda R & D Europe (U.K.) Ltd
Infineon Technologies Reigate Ltd
Infineon Technologies UK Ltd
NCC Operations Limited
Plymouth Marine Laboratory
Spinnaker International Ltd
WRC P.L.C.

72200 Research and experimental development on social sciences and humanities

UK Shared Business Services Ltd

73110 Advertising agencies

Brightsource Limited
Equi Media Limited
Havas EHS Discovery Limited
Mmedia Group Limited
Sideshow Ltd

73120 Media representation services

Alterian Software Limited

73200 Market research and public opinion polling

Advantage Group UK Limited
Applied Market Information Ltd
EIMS Global Limited

74100 Specialised design activities

Arno GB Limited
Crux Product Design Ltd
GEA Farm Technologies (UK) Ltd
Hemsley Fraser Group Limited
Ignition DG Limited
Maats Tech Limited
Sitec Engineering Limited
Stanley Security Solutions Ltd
Robert Welch Designs Limited

74201 Portrait photographic activities

H.Tempest Limited

74901 Environmental consulting activities

Environmental Dimension Partnership
Galion (Project Two) Limited
Kiwa Limited
Public Power Solutions Limited
SDL Biomass Limited
Verto Homes Ltd

74902 Quantity surveying activities

IESIS Limited

74909 Other professional, scientific and technical activities n.e.c. [47]

Argyll Environmental Ltd
Attwooll Holdings Limited
Auden McKenzie (Pharma Division) Ltd
Aviation Training International Ltd
Avon Wildlife Trust
BWP Project Services Limited
Bellwind-Edis Limited
Bioreliance UK Acquisition Ltd
Bluetech Systems International Ltd
Percy R Brend & Sons (Holdings) Ltd
British Holiday and Home Parks Association
Campden BRI
Campden BRI (Chipping Campden) Ltd
Catalent CTS (Wales) Limited
Chaffcombe Thorns Limited
Cotswold Archaeology Limited
DNO Consulting Limited
Delphi Technologies Limited
Dorset & Somerset Air Ambulance Charity
Duo Assets Limited
Futuream (UK) Limited
G4S Technology Limited
Gurr Johns Limited
Hilditch Group Limited
Hydrock Consultants Limited
IESIS Limited
IPS Partnership PLC
Icon Scientific Limited
Import Export Services (GRP) Ltd
Import Export Services Ltd
Ironburg Inventions Limited
Kiwa Limited
Metaltech Precision Ltd
Plantlife International - The Wild Plant Conservation Charity
Red House Developments (Surrey) Ltd
SRT Marine System Solutions Ltd
Seepex UK Limited
South West Peninsula Ahsn Ltd
Strong Energy Solutions Ltd
Sustrans Limited
Sutton Chemicals & Textiles UK Ltd
Synergy Health Sterilisation UK Ltd
Teachers Property Limited
Torbay Economic Development Co Ltd
Wessex Archaeology Limited
T.D. Williamson (U.K.) Ltd
T.D. Williamson UK International

74990 Non-trading company [98]

A & B High Holdings Limited
ABS Wholesale Limited
AUK Holding Limited
AgustaWestland Holdings Ltd
Alpha Immobile Limited
Atlas Elektronik UK (Holdings) Ltd
Avon Wildlife Trust
Baglan Moor Healthcare PLC
Bank of Ireland Home Mortgages Ltd
Class 06 Limited
Computershare Services Limited
Cordash Limited
Critchley Group Limited
Crossco (284) Limited
Deutsch UK
Dezac Group Holdings Limited
Dunlop Aerospace Group Limited
Dunlop Aerospace Holdings Ltd
Dunlop Aerospace Overseas Ltd
Dunlop Holdings Limited
Dunlop Limited
Dutch Oak Tree Foundation
Edentree Investment Management Ltd
Exeter Canal and Quay Trust Ltd
F & B Profiles (Holdings) Ltd
Findlay Publications Investments Ltd
Flowlinks Overseas Limited
GBE Converge Group Ltd
Galtec Holdings Limited
Greater Union Limited
Haskins Holdings Limited
Herpetological Conservation Trust
P & S Hockin Limited
Horizon Organic Dairy Limited
Imperial Business Systems Ltd
Imperial Tobacco Altadis Ltd
Imperial Tobacco Overseas Holdings (3)
Inspired Education (East Dunbartonshire)
JR Cap Limited
LVTG Holdings Limited
LVTG Limited
Landmark International Holdings Ltd
Lexicon Book Co Ltd
Librocube Limited
Linton Limited
MTH Bidco Limited
MTH Midco 1 Limited
MTH Midco 2 Limited
MTH Topco Limited
Mears Housing Management (Holdings)
Meggitt Acquisition Limited
Meggitt Aerospace Holdings Ltd
Merlin UK Finco 1 Limited
Mi-Pac Newco Limited
Mistral Holdings Limited

Mulberry Company (Europe) Ltd
Nailsworth Limited
Nova Group Europe Limited
Orbitz Worldwide (UK) Limited
P of a Productions Limited
PFI Investments Limited
PKL Topco Limited
Patalex II Productions Limited
Petrarch Holdings Limited
Plastic Surgeon Holdings Ltd
Polamco Limited
Pride Foods Limited
Pukka Pads UK Limited
Railston Holdings Limited
Richmond upon Thames Schools Services
Robinson Atterton Investments Ltd
SGW Research Limited
Scorribanda Holdings Limited
Sensata Technologies (Europe) Ltd
Sensitisers Group Ltd.
Servo Interconnect Limited
Sol Plaatje Educational Project
Spandex Holding UK Ltd.
TKC Sales Newco Limited
TPSFF Holdings Limited
Tabacalera de Garcia UK Ltd
Tay Valley Lighting (Newcastle and North Tyneside)
Tileflair Group Limited
Tilstone Industrial Limited
Tollgate Group Limited
Tomy Europe (Holdings) Limited
Trifle Holdings Limited
Tyco Electronics Motors Ltd
Ultrahaptics IP Ltd
Viscominvest Holding UK Ltd
Vistair Group Limited
Vistair Limited
Wallaby Grip Limited
Westerleigh Crematoria Limited
Western Bidco Limited
Whittington Facilities Limited
XJ6 Schools Holdings Limited
YTL Utilities (UK) Limited

75000 Veterinary activities [13]

Axiom Veterinary Laboratories Ltd
Centaur Services Limited
DVG Limited
George Group Limited
Horseworld Trust
Independent Vetcare Limited
Kernow Veterinary Group Ltd
Langford Veterinary Services Ltd
Mount Vets Limited
Penmellyn Veterinary Group Ltd
St Davids Poultry Team Limited
St. Francis Limited
Wood Veterinary Group Limited

77110 Renting and leasing of cars and light motor vehicles [13]

ALD Automotive Group Limited
ALD Automotive Limited
Accident Claims Handlers Ltd
Arval UK Limited
Auxillis Services Limited
Bristol & London PLC
Cab Aid Limited
Chief Vehicle Rentals Limited
Green-Line Contracts Limited
Knights Brown Ltd
F W Rogers Garage (Saltash) Ltd
Scot Group Limited
U-Drive Limited

77120 Renting and leasing of trucks and other heavy vehicles

Auxillis Services Limited
Bailey Holdings Limited
Falcon Self Drive Limited
Green-Line Contracts Limited
Western Truck Rental Limited

77291 Renting and leasing of media entertainment equipment

H.B.H. Woolacotts Limited

77310 Renting and leasing of agricultural machinery and equipment

RRH Limited

77320 Renting and leasing of construction and civil engineering machinery and equipment [14]

Bell Plant Limited
W H Bond & Sons Limited
Fred Champion Hire Limited
M J Church (Plant) Limited
Finlay Hire Limited
Hale & Co. (Drybrook) Ltd
Hoist Hire Holdings Limited
Kelston Sparkes (Group) Ltd
Keyway Limited
Overton (Gloucester) Limited
Plantforce Rentals Ltd
SR & GM Limited
Wessex Eagle Holdings Limited
Wessex Eagle Limited

77342 Renting and leasing of freight water transport equipment

Jenkins Marine Ltd.

77351 Renting and leasing of air passenger transport equipment

FB Leasing Limited

77390 Renting and leasing of other machinery, equipment and tangible goods n.e.c. [18]

1pm (UK) Limited
Amberon Limited
Bennetts Cranes Limited
Danco International PLC
Forest Green Sun Co Ltd
Gazelle Properties Limited
Jongor Limited
Kat-O-Log Limited
King Lifting Limited
MJL Plant Hire (Cornwall) Ltd
Morning Star Motors Limited
PKL Group (UK) Limited
Power Electrics (Bristol) Ltd
Sadborow Estate Limited
Sparrow Crane Hire Limited
Stanley Security Solutions Ltd
Sutton Harbour Car Parks Ltd
M Way Holdings Limited

77400 Leasing of intellectual property and similar products, except copyright works

NSD Ltd
National Trust (Enterprises) Ltd

78109 Other activities of employment placement agencies [13]

Keen Thinking Limited
MDE Consultants Ltd
MPLOY Staffing Solutions Ltd
Norland College Limited
Opus Professional Services Group Ltd
Outsource UK Limited
People Source Consulting Ltd
Resource Solutions Group PLC
Sanderson Contract Management Ltd
Sanderson Government and Defence Ltd
Sanderson Recruitment PLC
Shaw Trust Limited
Venator Capital Limited

78200 Temporary employment agency activities [12]

Atlas Services Group Energy Ltd
Cornwall Development Co Ltd
Mears Homecare Limited
Newcross Healthcare Solutions Ltd
Newcross Nursing Group Ltd
Opus Recruitment Solutions Ltd
Outsource UK Limited
Project People Limited
Right Contract Services Ltd
SG Aerospace (UK) Limited
Sanderson Government and Defence Ltd
WA Consultants Limited

78300 Human resources provision and management of human resources functions

Atlas Services Group Energy Ltd
Clipper Contracting Group Ltd
Unitedhealthcare Global Medical (UK)
Zurich Employment Services Ltd

79110 Travel agency activities

Flightbookers Limited
Majestic Tours Limited
Worldwide Dive and Sail International

79120 Tour operator activities [12]

Abercrombie & Kent Europe Ltd
Abercrombie & Kent Limited
Atkins Travel Limited
Bakers Coaches Limited
Mike Burton Travel Limited
Camps International Group Ltd
Just Go Holidays Limited
Specialist Journeys Limited
Specialist Journeys Midco 1 Ltd
Specialist Journeys Midco 2 Ltd
Steppes Travel Ltd
Swoop Travel Limited

79901 Activities of tourist guides

Abercrombie & Kent Europe Ltd

79909 Other reservation service activities n.e.c.

Scarlet Hotel Limited
Surest Ltd
Swoop Travel Limited
Unitedhealthcare Global Medical (UK)

80100 Private security activities

Bridgend Custodial Services Ltd
PGI - Protection Group International Ltd.

80200 Security systems service activities

G.B. Electronics Limited
Stanley Security Solutions Ltd

80300 Investigation activities

Gill Southern Limited

81100 Combined facilities support activities

Danbec Property Limited
Procol Limited
Snape Contracting Services Ltd
Spectrum Property Care Ltd
Wessex Group Limited
Ian Williams Limited

81299 Other cleaning services

Clear-Flow Limited
PMG Services (Bristol) Limited
Salisbury Trading Limited

81300 Landscape service activities

A & B Contractors (Devon) Ltd

82110 Combined office administrative service activities [11]

A-Gas International Limited
DAC Beachcroft Services Ltd
Delt Shared Services Limited
Ecotricity Generation Limited
Krowji Limited
Obenshaw Limited
Red Hotels Limited
Rygor Holdings Limited
SIRVA Relocation Holdings Ltd
Toklon Limited
Vitacress Limited

82190 Photocopying, document preparation and other specialised office support activities

ITEC Connect Ltd

82200 Activities of call centres

EIMS Global Limited
Expolink Europe Limited

82301 Activities of exhibition and fair organisers

Comexposium Cereals Limited

82302 Activities of conference organisers

Applied Market Information Ltd
GDS Publishing Limited

82912 Activities of credit bureaus

Credit Reporting Agency (Topco) Ltd

82920 Packaging activities

Gordano Support Group Limited
WRK Merger Holding Sub Limited

82990 Other business support service activities n.e.c. [323]

2nd Half Limited
A.E.R. Stafford Limited
AB Dynamics PLC
AGM Holdings Limited
Abraxas Insurance Administration Services
Academy Leasing Limited
Accident Claims Handlers Ltd
Acoura Holdings Limited
Agincare Group Limited
Agincare Homes Holdings Ltd
Agincare UK Limited
Allchurches Trust Limited
Allstar Business Solutions Ltd
Allstone Sands Gravels Aggregates Trading Co
Amcor Flexibles Finance Ltd
Amcor Mediflex Limited
Amcor UK Finance PLC
Amcor UK Group International Ltd
Animal Healthcare Co Ltd
Antrak Group Limited
Arval UK Group Limited
Arval UK Leasing Services Ltd
Ashri Limited
Ashton Gate Limited
Aspect Digital Media Limited
Atlantis 39 Limited
Aura Bidco Management Limited
Avon Care Homes Limited
Azure Sun (Holdco) Limited
Azure Sun Bidco Management Ltd
B M J International Limited
B4 Marketing Limited
BWP Services (Holdings No 1) Ltd
Barnet Lighting Services Ltd
Julian Barran Limited
Beckton Energy Limited
Bollingwood Limited
Brighton & Hove City Schools Services
Bristol PFI (Holdings) Limited
Bristol PFI Debt Co 1 Limited
Bristol PFI Limited
Buckinghamshire Group Limited
Bulldog Trust Limited
Burges Salmon Co Ltd
Burkert UK Limited
The Mike Burton Group Limited
Butterfly Conservation
By Education (Waltham Forest) Ltd
CG Hotel Holding Limited
CTU General Partner Limited
Caerus Wealth Limited
Caerus Wealth Solutions Ltd
Call Caterlink Ltd
Canford Healthcare Limited
Cartus Financing Limited
Cartus Limited
Charter House Planning Limited
Cheltenham & Gloucester PLC
Cheltenham Borough Homes Ltd
C. & J. Clark (Holdings) Ltd
C & J Clark Limited
Clean Earth Energy Wind Investments
Clean Earth Holdings 2 Ltd
Cleveland FM Services Limited
Clipper Properties Limited
Close Brewery Rentals Limited
Cobham Leasing Limited
Cohen & Griffiths Limited
Commercial Corporate Services Ltd
Commercial Limited
Computershare Voucher Services Ltd
Conmed UK Ltd
Consumer Intelligence Limited
Cornwall Air Ambulance Trust
Cornwall Glass & Glazing Ltd
Country Houses Foundation
Coxley Developments Limited
Creditcall Limited
D'Oyly Carte Charitable Trust
DAS Services Limited
DS UK Midco 1 Limited
DS UK Midco 2 Limited
DS UK Topco Limited
Dainton Group Services Limited
Danfoss Power Solutions Ltd
Darts Farm Limited
Derbyshire Home Loans Limited
Digs Properties Limited
Dyson Estates Limited
E.I.C. Group Limited
EIMS Global Limited
Ecotricity Bonds PLC
Energy Measurement Limited
Enfield Lighting Services Ltd
English Heritage Trading Ltd
Equi Media Limited
Williams Ewan Limited
Excalibur Unified Communications Ltd
Exception Group Limited
Exeter Science Park Limited
Exhibitor Limited
Expedia Treasury Services Ltd
FB Leasing Limited
FR Aviation Group Limited
FR Aviation Services Limited
Falkirk Group Limited
Farina Investments (UK) Ltd
Flatcable Limited
Fleet Caravans Limited
Flowbird Smart City UK Limited
Foam Techniques Limited
Forest of Dean Stone Firms Ltd
Fulford Care Home Limited
G4S IP 2 Limited
G4S Investments Limited
GE Oil & Gas UK Limited
GH Clayhill Limited
GWE Business West Ltd
Galpharm Healthcare Limited
Gemini Energy Limited
Genaray Limited
J Gliddon & Sons Limited
Global Furniture Alliance Ltd
Gloucestershire FM Services Ltd
Good Energy Group PLC
W.G. Gould & Sons Limited
Great American Specialty & Affinity
Great Western Enterprise (Holdings)
Greenaway & Greenaway Limited
Grove Village Limited
H & R Healthcare Limited
HTP Grange Limited
Halewell Limited
Hardware Services Limited
Hargrave Foundation
Harrow Community Schools PFI Ltd
Hebron & Medlock Limited
Hideaway Truro Ltd
Higher Drive Nursing Home (Holdings)
Hitachi Information Control Systems Europe Ltd.

Hochtief PPP Solutions (UK) Ltd
Hospital Company (Dartford) Issuer PLC
House Property Associates Ltd
Humber Technology Limited
Hydrock Group Limited
IIC (C & T) Limited
IIC (Leeds Schools) Fund Investment
IIC Barnet Holding Co Ltd
IIC By Education (Peterborough Schools)
IIC Enfield Holding Co Ltd
IIC Lambeth Holding Co Ltd
IIC Miles Platting Funding Investment
IIC Miles Platting Subdebt Ltd
IIC Northampton Funding Investment
IIC Northampton Holding Co Ltd
IIC Northampton Limited
IIC Northampton Subdebt Ltd
IIC Peterborough Holding Co Ltd
IIC Redcar and Cleveland Holding Co Ltd
ITEC Connect Ltd
Imagile Group Limited
Injury QED Limited
Inspired Education (South Lanarkshire) Holdings
Inspired Education (South Lanarkshire)
Integrated Care Solutions (East Kent)
Integreon Managed Solutions Ltd
Interconnect Products Limited
Investors in Health (C & T1) Ltd
Investors in the Community (Bexley Schools)
Investors in the Community (Leeds Schools)
Investors in the Community (Leeds Schools) Subdebt
JELF Limited
JG Travel Group Limited
JGH Group Limited
JGH Midco Limited
JGH Topco Limited
JMC Recruitment Solutions Ltd
Jaguar Oil & Gas UK Limited
KS SPV 1 Limited
Kenton School Services Limited
Keynvor Morlift Limited
King William St Limited
LV Insurance Management Ltd
Leighton-Boyce Properties Ltd.
Libya Oil Sudan Limited
Lucrative Investments Holdings Ltd
MAMG Infrastructure Management Ltd
MCB Investments Limited
MR Capital Consultants Limited
Mallory Holdings Limited
Manor Renewable Energy Limited
Manutan Limited
Maximum Fun Holdings Limited
Maxin Limited
Medreport Services Limited
Microensure Holdings Limited
Microsemi Storage Solutions Europe Ltd
Mikulla Leisure Limited
Millfields Community Economic Development Trust CIC
Minty Art Limited
Mount Batten Sailing and Water Sports Centre
N.V. Chichester Limited
NASA Umbrella Ltd
NIC Enterprises Limited
NMS Infrastructure Limited
NNA Limited
NOV UK Finance Limited
NSEA Property Services Limited
C.W. Nash (Farms) Limited
Nevro Medical Limited
Newport Caravans Limited
Newspace Containers Limited
Ocean Housing Group Limited
Octagon Healthcare Funding PLC
Octava Holdings Limited
Old Hall Investment Co Ltd
Orange International Investments (UK)
Outsauce Financing Limited
PPL Island Limited
PPL UK Investments Limited
PPL UK Resources Limited
PPL WPD Limited
PSW Trading Limited
Paradigm (Sheffield BSF) Ltd
Parham Development Limited
Park Home Life Limited
Partner Logistics Gloucester Ltd
Partner Logistics Wisbech Ltd
Patheon UK Limited
Penington Enterprises Limited
Pennant International Group PLC
People 2000 Limited
Perivoli Investments Limited
Perrigo UK Acquisition Limited
Pine Wood Hill Limited
Plantronics Limited
Plymouth Science Park Limited
Potensis Limited
Powerwave Energy Limited
Premier Cables Holdings Ltd
Procurri Europe Limited
Project People Limited
Puxton Limited
Quality Care Group Limited
Quantum Group (Management) Ltd
Radius (Bristol) Limited
Radius (UK) Limited
Radius Debtco Limited
Radius Pledgeco Limited
Range Valley Extrusions Ltd
Real Estate Gloucester Limited
Redcar and Cleveland Lighting Services
Renaissance Miles Platting Ltd
Renishaw International Limited
Richpur Limited
Riders of Bridgwater Ltd.
River Marketing Limited
Rocma Europe
Rocma Sterling
Rygor Group Limited
S.C.C. Transport (Devizes) Ltd
S.W.T Finance Limited
Sanlam Investment Holdings UK Ltd
Sedgwick Solar Limited
Sensata Technologies Holding Company U.K.
Shearwell Data Limited
Simian Group (Holdings) Ltd
Skilled Group UK Limited
Soil Association Certification Ltd
Somerset Wildlife Trust
Somerville & Savage Solicitors
South Bristol Church and Community Trust
South West Investment Group (Capital)
South Western Helicopters Ltd
Sportech Pools Limited
St. James's Place Partnership Services
St.James's Place (PCP) Limited
St.James's Place Management Services
Stannah Management Services Ltd
Staysail Limited
Stiga Ltd
Stonehouse Investment Co Ltd
Suland Investments Limited
Sure Maintenance Limited
TNT Fireworks U.K. Limited
Tacklestore Limited
Tamander Limited
Team Relocations Limited
Trade Link Co Ltd
Transcribe Copier Systems Ltd
Trivselhus UK Limited
Ryan Turner Hope PLC
Turner UK Limited
UCLH Investors Limited
Underdown Investments Limited
United Healthcare (Bromley) Services
Vavassor Limited
Vicaima Limited
Vinci Education (Bradfield) Ltd
Viridor Credits Environmental Company
Viridor Polymer Recycling Ltd
Viridor Waste (Somerset) Ltd
Viridor Waste Limited
WPD Smart Metering Limited
WRC P.L.C.
Wagtech Projects Ltd
Walkergate PFI Project Co Ltd
Wayfarer Group Limited
Welton Bibby and Baron Holdings Ltd
Wessex Products (Leasing) Ltd
West Country Milk Consortium Ltd
Westerleigh WGH Limited
White Horse Education Partnership
W.H.White Limited
Winchcombe Finance Limited
Winners 2000 Fitness Limited
Woods Group Limited
A. & J. Woolf Properties Ltd
Wyderington Limited
XJ4 Holding Co Ltd
Zoeftig Group Limited
Zurich Employment Services Ltd
Zurich Financial Services (UKISA)

84110 General public administration activities

Cornwall Development Co Ltd
FB Heliservices Limited
GE Aviation Systems Limited
Integrated Care Solutions (East Kent) Holdings
Integrated Care Solutions (Shropshire) Holdings
Integrated Care Solutions (Shropshire)
Publica Group (Support) Ltd

84220 Defence activities

Atlas Elektronik UK Limited
Aviation Requirements Ltd
GE Aviation Systems Limited
Optima Defence & Security Group Ltd
Reme Charity
Royal Artillery Institution Ltd
Royal Marines Charity
Systems Engineering & Assessment Ltd
Torchlightgroup Limited

84230 Justice and judicial activities

STC (Milton Keynes) Limited

84240 Public order and safety activities

Fazakerley Prison Services Ltd
Onley Prison Services Limited
UK Court Services (Manchester) Ltd

85100 Pre-primary education [42]

3AB Care Limited
Academy for Character and Excellence
Badminton School Limited
Ballard School Limited
Bruton School for Girls
Castle Court School Educational Trust
Clayesmore School
Clevedon Learning Trust
Clifton High School
Colston's School
Cotswold Beacon Academy Trust
Crofty Multi Academy Trust
H. Days Holdings Limited
Dean Close Foundation
Devon & Exeter Spastics Society
Diocese of Bristol Academies Trust
Falmouth MAT
Happy Days South West Limited
King's School, Bruton
King's Schools Taunton Limited
Leaf Academy
Leweston School Trust
Lighthouse Schools Partnership
Maynard School
Millfield
Monkton Combe School
Plymouth College and St Dunstan's Abbey Schools Charity
Rookwood School Trust Limited
Salisbury Plain Academies
Seven Fields Primary School
Sidcot School
Snapdragons Nurseries Limited
St. Edward's School Cheltenham Trust
Taunton School Educational Charity
Truro & Penwith Academy Trust
Trust in Learning (Academies)
Warminster School
Wells Cathedral School, Ltd
White Horse Federation
The Ted Wragg Multi Academy Trust
Wycliffe College (Incorporated)
YMCA Bath Group

85200 Primary education [165]

ACE Schools Multi Academy Trust
Academy Trust of Melksham
Academy for Character and Excellence
Acorn Multi Academy Trust
Adventure Learning Academy Trust
Ambitions Academies Trust
An Daras Multi Academy Trust
Aspect Trust
Aspire Academy Trust
Astrum Multi Academy Trust
Atlantic Centre of Excellence Multi Academy Trust
Badminton School Limited
Ballard School Limited
Bath and Wells Diocesan Academies Trust
Bay Education Trust
Beaudesert Park School Trust Ltd
Birdwell School
Blue Kite Academy Trust
Blundell's School
Bridge Multi-Academy Trust
Bristol Grammar School
Brookside Community Primary School Academy Trust
Bruton School for Girls
Castle Court School Educational Trust
Castle School Education Trust
Chafyn Grove School
Charlton Kings Junior School
Chickerell Primary Academy
Christ Church C of E Primary School
Christ Church C of E Primary School (Cheltenham)
Chulmleigh Academy Trust
Clayesmore School
Clevedon Learning Trust
Clifton High School
Coast Academies
Colston's School
Comenius Trust
Connect Academy Trust
Cornerstone Academy Trust
Cotham Gardens Primary School Ltd
Cotswold Beacon Academy Trust
Crofty Multi Academy Trust
Dean Close Foundation
Devon & Exeter Spastics Society
Diocese of Bristol Academies Trust
Discovery Multi Academy Trust
Diverse Abilities Plus Ltd
Downs School (Charlton House) Ltd
Duchy Academy Trust
Dumpton School
Durlston Court School Trust Ltd
Educate Together Academy Trust
Education South West
Elmlea Junior School
Endeavour Academy Trust
Epiphany School
Excalibur Academies Trust
Falmouth MAT
Faringdon Academy of Schools
Farleigh School Trust Limited
Farms for City Children Ltd
First Federation Trust
Gloucestershire Learning Alliance
Goddard Park Community Primary School Academy Trust
Hanford School Charitable Trust Ltd
Harbourside Learning Partnership
Hayes School
Heath Academy Trust
Huish Academy Trust
Inspirational Futures Trust
Inspire Multi Academy Trust (South West)
King Edward's School, Bath
King's School, Bruton
King's School, Gloucester
King's Schools Taunton Limited
Kingsleigh Primary School
Kinson Primary School
Leaf Academy
Learning Academies Trust
Learning Academy Partnership (South West)
Learning Academy Trust
Lethbridge Primary School
Levels Academy Trust
Leweston School Trust
Lighthouse Schools Partnership
Link Academy Trust
Maiden Beech Academy Trust
Malmesbury C of E Primary School
Marchant-Holliday School Ltd
Maynard School
Mead Academy Trust
Merchants' Academy Trust
Millfield
Monkton Combe School
Muscliff Primary School
Newquay Education Trust
North Town Academy Trust
Ocean Learning Trust
Olympus Academy Trust
Parkfield Education Limited
Peninsula Learning Trust
Perrott Hill School Trust Ltd
Pickwick Academy Trust
Pinewood School Limited
Plym Academy Trust
Plymouth Cast
Plymouth College and St Dunstan's Abbey Schools Charity
Pokesdown Community Primary School
Port Regis School Limited
Prior Park Educational Trust
Queen Elizabeth's Hospital
Queen's Park Infant Academy
Reach South Academy Trust
Redmaids' High School
Redstart Learning Partnership
Riviera Education Trust
Rookwood School Trust Limited
Roseland Multi Academy Trust
Salisbury Plain Academies
Sandroyd School Trust Limited
Seven Fields Primary School
Shaw Ridge Primary School
Sherborne Area Schools' Trust
Sherborne Preparatory School
Shiphay Learning Academy
Sidcot School
Somerset Road Education Trust
South Dartmoor Academy
South East Cornwall Multi Academy Regional Trust
South Gloucestershire and Stroud Academy Trust
Southerly Point Co-operative Multi-Academy Trust
St Christopher's C of E (Primary) Multi Academy Trust
St David's Church of England Primary Academy
St Margaret's Academy
St. Edward's School Cheltenham Trust
St. Hugh's School (Carswell) Trust
St. Joseph's School Launceston
Stoke Bishop Church of England Primary School
Talent & Enterprise Trust
Tarka Learning Partnership
Taunton School Educational Charity
Teach Poole
Truro & Penwith Academy Trust
Trust in Learning (Academies)
Twynham Learning
Uffculme Academy Trust
Ventrus Limited
Venture Multi Academy Trust
Venturers Trust
Warminster School
Wave Multi Academy Trust
Waycroft Multi Academy Trust
Wellington College Academy Trust

Wells Cathedral School, Ltd
Wellsway Multi Academy Trust
West Town Lane Academy
Westbury Park School
Westbury-on-Trym Church of England Academy
Westcountry Schools Trust
White Horse Federation
Wimborne Academy Trust
Winton Primary School
Wishford Schools (Group) Ltd
The Ted Wragg Multi Academy Trust
Wycliffe College (Incorporated)

85310 General secondary education [223]

ACE Schools Multi Academy Trust
ASDAN
Academy Trust of Melksham
Acorn Education Trust
Adventure Learning Academy Trust
All Saints Church of England Academy, Plymouth
All Saints' Academy, Cheltenham
Ambitions Academies Trust
Ansford Academy Trust
Aspect Trust
Astrum Multi Academy Trust
Athelstan Trust
Avonbourne International Business and Enterprise Academy Trust
Badminton School Limited
Balcarras School
Ballard School Limited
Bay Education Trust
Beechen Cliff School
The John Bentley School
Bishop Fox's School
Bishop Wordsworth's Church of England Grammar School for Boys
Bishop of Winchester Academy Trust
Blue School
Blundell's School
Bodmin College
Bourne Academy
Bournemouth School
Bournemouth School for Girls
Braunton School and Community College Academy Trust
Bridgwater College Trust
Bristol Grammar School
Brixham College Academy Trust
Broadoak Mathematics and Computing College
Bruton School for Girls
Bryanston School,Incorporated
Buckler's Mead School
Burgate School and Sixth Form
CSIA Trust
Cabot Learning Federation
Canford School,Limited
Castle Court School Educational Trust
Castle Partnership Trust
Castle School Education Trust
Cathedral Schools Trust
Cheltenham Bournside School and Sixth Form Centre
Chipping Campden School
Chosen Hill School
Chulmleigh Academy Trust
Churchdown School
Churchill Academy
Churston Ferrers Grammar School
Cirencester Kingshill School
Clayesmore School
Cleeve School
Clevedon Learning Trust
Clifton High School
Clyst Vale Academy Trust
Colston's School
Colyton Grammar School Academy Trust
Commonweal School
Corfe Hills School Academy Trust
Corinium Education Trust
Corsham School Academy Group
Cotham School
Cotswold Beacon Academy Trust
Cotswold School Academy Trust
Council of Milton Abbey School Ltd
Crispin School Academy Trust
Crypt School
Dauntsey's School
Dean Close Foundation
Dene Magna School
Denmark Road High School
Devon & Exeter Spastics Society
Devonport High School for Boys Academy Trust
Devonport High School for Girls
Diocese of Bristol Academies Trust
Diverse Abilities Plus Ltd
Dorcan Academy
Dorchester Middle School
Dragonfly Education Trust
Education South West
Eggbuckland Community College Academy Trust
Equa Multi Academy Trust
Essex Schools (Woodlands) Ltd
Essex Schools Holdings (Woodlands)
Essex Schools Limited
Excalibur Academies Trust
Exmouth Community College
Falmouth MAT
Faringdon Academy of Schools
Farmor's School
GTS Academy Trust
Gatehouse Green Learning Trust
Gryphon Trust
Hanford School Charitable Trust Ltd
Hardenhuish School Limited
The Thomas Hardye Multi Academy Trust
Hayesfield Girls' School
Haygrove Academy Trust
Highcliffe School
Highworth Warneford School
Honiton Community College Academy Trust
Huish Episcopi Academy
Inspirational Futures Trust
Inspiring Schools Partnership
John of Gaunt School
Katharine Lady Berkeley's School
Thomas Keble School
Kemeneth Multi Academy Trust
King Edward's School, Bath
King's School Ottery St Mary
King's School, Bruton
King's School, Gloucester
King's Schools Taunton Limited
Kingsmead Academy
LAL Language Centres UK Ltd
Launceston College
Leading Edge Academies Partnership
Leaf Academy
Leehurst Swan Limited
Leweston School Trust
Lighthouse Schools Partnership
Lipson Co-operative Academy Trust
Magna Learning Partnership
Marine Academy Plymouth
Maynard School
Merchants' Academy Trust
Midsomer Norton Schools Partnership
Millfield
Minerva Learning Trust (Dorset)
Monkton Combe School
Nailsea School
Newent Community School and Sixth Form Centre
Newton Abbot Academy Trust
Oakfield School Academy Trust
Oldfield School
Olympus Academy Trust
Palladian Academy Trust
Park Academies Trust
Parkfield Education Limited
Parkstone Grammar School Trust
Pate's Grammar School
Penair School
Peninsula Learning Trust
Pewsey Vale School
Pinewood School Limited
Plymouth Cast
Plymouth College and St Dunstan's Abbey Schools Charity
Plympton Academy
Plymstock School
Pool Academy
Poole Grammar School
Preston School Academy Trust
Prior Park Educational Trust
Priory Learning Trust
QE Academy Trust
Queen Elizabeth's Hospital
Queen Elizabeth's School (Wimborne Minster)
Redmaids' High School
Ribston Hall High School Academy Trust
Ringwood School
Sir William Romney's School
Rookwood School Trust Limited
Roseland Multi Academy Trust
Royal Wootton Bassett Academy Trust
Saint Augustine's Catholic College
Salisbury Plain Academies
Selwood Academy
Severn Vale School
Sexey's School
Sheldon School
Sherborne Area Schools' Trust
Sherborne School
Sherborne School for Girls
Sidcot School
Sir Thomas Rich's School
South Dartmoor Academy
South East Cornwall Multi Academy Regional Trust
South Gloucestershire and Stroud Academy Trust
South Wilts Grammar School for Girls
Southerly Point Co-operative Multi-Academy Trust
Special Partnership Trust
St Bede's Catholic College
St Christopher's C of E (Secondary) Multi Academy Trust
St. Edward's School Cheltenham Trust

St. Joseph's School Launceston
St. Laurence School Academy Trust
St. Mary's School Shaftesbury Trust
Stanchester Community School Academy
Star Education Investment Ltd
Steiner Academy Frome
Step One Charity
Stroud High School
Talbot Heath School Trust Ltd
Taunton School Educational Charity
Tewkesbury School
Tor Bridge Academy Trust
Torquay Boys' Grammar School
Torquay Girls' Grammar School
Truro & Penwith Academy Trust
Trust in Learning (Academies)
Twynham Learning
Uffculme Academy Trust
Vector Learning Trust
Ventrus Limited
Venturers Trust
Wadebridge School
Warminster School
Wave Multi Academy Trust
Wellington College Academy Trust
Wellington School 1837
Wells Cathedral School, Ltd
Wellsway Multi Academy Trust
Wessex Learning Trust
West Somerset Academies Trust
Westcountry Schools Trust
Westfield Academy Trust
White Horse Federation
Whitstone School Academy Trust
Winchcombe School
The Ted Wragg Multi Academy Trust
Wycliffe College (Incorporated)

85320 Technical and vocational secondary education [15]

ASDAN
Bristol and South Gloucestershire UTC
Inspirational Futures Trust
Leaf Academy
Paragon Education & Skills Ltd
Preston School Academy Trust
Royal Artillery Centre for Personal Development
S & B Property Limited
South Devon UTC
South Gloucestershire and Stroud Academy Trust
South Wiltshire UTC Limited
Step One Charity
Stonebridge Associated Colleges Ltd
TTR PT Limited
White Rose School of Beauty and Complementary Therapies

85410 Post-secondary non-tertiary education

The Thomas Hardye Multi Academy Trust
National Star Foundation

85421 First-degree level higher education [10]

AECC University College
Bristol Old Vic Theatre School Ltd
Moorlands College
Norland College Limited
Quality Assurance Agency for Higher Education
Royal Agricultural University
Step One Charity
University of Gloucestershire
University of St Mark & St John
Westcountry Schools Trust

85422 Post-graduate level higher education [10]

AECC University College
Bristol Old Vic Theatre School Ltd
Dartington Hall Trust
Quality Assurance Agency for Higher Education
Royal Agricultural University
St Peter's Hospice
St. Piran's School (GB) Ltd
University of Gloucestershire
University of St Mark & St John
Westcountry Schools Trust

85510 Sports and recreation education

Alliance Leisure Services Ltd
Exmoor Calvert Trust
Help for Heroes

85520 Cultural education

Bristol Music Trust
Creative Kernow Limited
Museum of East Asian Art
Oxford Programs Limited
Truro Diocesan Board of Finance Ltd
Wells Cathedral School, Ltd

85590 Other education n.e.c. [50]

ACE Schools Multi Academy Trust
Anglo-Continental Educational Group (G.B.)
Autism Wessex
Bath and Mendip Partnership Trust
Bioscientifica Limited
Combe Pafford School
The Ernest Cook Trust
Cornwall Trust for Nature Conservation
Dartington Hall Trust
Delta Education Trust
Dorset Wildlife Trust
Eastwood Park Limited
Eden Project Limited
Eden Trust
Excalibur Academies Trust
Exeter Royal Academy for Deaf Education.
Exeter School
Fairfield Farm Trust
Mrs D M France-Hayhurst Foundation
GRS (Holdings) Limited
Game and Wildlife Conservation Trust
Hemsley Fraser Group Limited
IF - Inspiring Futures Limited
International Education Systems Ltd
Jamie's Farm
Lifetime Training Group Ltd
Montacute School
National Star Foundation
Norland College Limited
Phoenix Learning and Care Ltd
Prabh Milnae Kaa Chaao Gurdwara
Quality Assurance Agency for Higher Education
Richard Reeve's Foundation
Rendcomb College
Ruskin Mill Trust Limited
Seven Fields Primary School
Sharpham Trust
Sheiling Special Education Trust
Society for Endocrinology
Somerset Road Education Trust
Southern Academy Trust
St Peter's Hospice
St. Mary's School (Calne)
Teignmouth Learning Trust
Thornleigh Camphill Communities Ltd
Three Ways School
Unicorn Training Group Limited
WESC Foundation
Wallscourt Foundation
Workforce Development Trust Ltd

85600 Educational support services [20]

ACE Schools Multi Academy Trust
Academy for Character and Excellence
Astrum Multi Academy Trust
Creative Youth Network
Diocese of Bristol Academies Trust
Diocese of Gloucester Academies Trust
Falmouth Exeter Plus
Higher Education Statistics Agency
Hooke Court Limited
Horseworld Trust
Innovate Awarding Ltd
Orchard Trust
Quality Assurance Agency for Higher Education
Salisbury Diocesan Board of Education
South Gloucestershire and Stroud Academy Trust
Tribal Education Limited
Tribal Group PLC
UCAS Media Limited
Universities and Colleges Admissions Service
Wallscourt Foundation

86101 Hospital activities

Albion Healthcare (Oxford) Ltd
Criterion Healthcare PLC
GH North Northampton Limited
Livewell Southwest CIC
Prospect Hospice Limited
Tetbury Hospital Trust Limited
Tre' Care Group Limited
Wallace & Gromit's Children's Foundation

86102 Medical nursing home activities [25]

3AB Care Limited
Albion Healthcare (Doncaster) Ltd
Barker Care Limited
Bristol Care Homes Limited
Cathedral View Limited
Country Care Homes Limited
GH Gravesham Limited
GH Stone House Limited
Golden Years Ltd
Health Management (UCLH) Ltd
Hospital Company (Dartford) Group
Hospital Company (Dartford) Ltd
Hospital Company (Swindon & Marlborough) 2006
Hospital Company (Swindon & Marlborough) Group

Hospital Company (Swindon & Marlborough) Holdings
Hospital Company (Swindon & Marlborough)
IMC St.David's Ltd
North Somerset Community Partnership CIC
Ochre Solutions (Holdings) Ltd
Ochre Solutions Limited
Torcare (Holdings) Limited
Town Hospitals (North Staffordshire Combined)
Town Hospitals (Southern General) Ltd
United Healthcare (Bromley) Group
United Healthcare (Bromley) Ltd

86210 General medical practice activities

Brisdoc Healthcare Services Ltd
Cheltenham Family Health Care Centre
First City Nursing Services Ltd
Vanguard Healthcare Group Ltd

86220 Specialists medical practice activities [10]

Cobalt Health
Cornwall Hospice Care Limited
North Devon Hospice
North Somerset Community Partnership CIC
Professor David Barrett Ltd
Rowcroft House Foundation Ltd
Scoliosis SOS Limited
St Peter's Hospice
John Ware Limited
Weston Hospicecare Limited

86230 Dental practice activities [15]

Apex Dental Care Limited
Luke Barnett Limited
Colosseum Dental UK Limited
Colosseum Dental UK Partnerships Ltd
Denplan Limited
Dentalign Orthodontics Limited
Gensmile Dental Care Limited
Oasis Dental Care (Central) Ltd
Oasis Dental Care (Southern) Ltd
Oasis Dental Care Limited
Oasis Healthcare Limited
Ortho 2008 Limited
Peninsula Dental Social Enterprise CIC
Total Orthodontics Limited
Xeon Smiles UK Limited

86900 Other human health activities [74]

ASP Independent Living Limited
Alum Care Limited
Amica Care Trust
Asha Foundation
Aspirations (Bidco) Limited
Aspirations (Midlands) Limited
Aspirations (Topco) Limited
Aspirations Care Limited
BAEMS Limited
Bioscientifica Limited
Branksome Park Care Centre Ltd
Bristol Community Health C.I.C.
Bristol Drugs Project Limited
Penny Brohn Cancer Care
Ceuta Healthcare Limited
Children's Hospice South West
Cobalt Health
Complete Price Eyewear Limited
Conmed UK Ltd
Cornwall Hospice Care Limited
Countess of Brecknock Hospice Trust
Delphine Homecare Limited
Devon & Cornwall Autistic Community Trust
Devon & Exeter Spastics Society
Devon Doctors Limited
Dorothy House Foundation Ltd
Dorset Health Trust Limited
Duchy Health Charity Limited
European Society of Endocrinology
Exmoor Calvert Trust
Flollie Investments Limited
Fox Elms Care Limited
Georgian House (Torquay) Ltd
Hatchmoor Nursing Home Limited
Healthcare South West Ltd
Hospiscare
Hyperbiotics PLC
Innovata Limited
Julia's House Limited
Lewis-Manning Trust
Longfield Hospice Care
Mears Care Limited
Mears Homecare Limited
Moor Park House Limited
New Docs Limited
North Somerset Community Partnership CIC
Portman Healthcare (Finance) Ltd
Portman Healthcare (Holdings) Ltd
Portman Healthcare Limited
Prospect Hospice Limited
Providence Projects Rehab Group Ltd
Regency Oldhomes Limited
Royal Osteoporosis Society
Shelterbox Trust
Silversword Limited
Simplyhealth Access
Simplyhealth Group Limited
Sirona Care & Health C.I.C.
Society for Endocrinology
Sovereign Care Limited
Spembly Medical Limited
St. Luke's Hospice Plymouth
St. Margaret's Somerset Hospice
Stepping Stones Resettlement Unit
Synergy Health Limited
The James Tudor Foundation
Unitedhealthcare Global Medical (UK)
Vanguard Healthcare Solutions Ltd
Vectura Group Investments Ltd
Vectura Group PLC
Vectura Limited
WESC Foundation
Waypoints Care (Plymouth) Ltd
Wiltshire Air Ambulance Charitable Trust

87100 Residential nursing care facilities [37]

AJ & Co.(Devon) Ltd
Ashley Grange Nursing Home Ltd
Beauchamp House Nursing Home Ltd
Brandon Trust
Buckland Care Limited
Camelot Care (Bridgwater) Ltd
Camelot Care Homes Limited
Cavendish Close Limited
Cedar Care Homes Limited
Chanctonbury Health Care Ltd
Coastal Care Homes Limited
Coate Water Care Company (Church View Nursing Home)
Cornelia Care Homes Limited
Cream Care Group Limited
Cream II Limited
Cream Residential Care Limited
Lilian Faithfull Care
Golfhill Limited
Hillcrest House Limited
Jupiter Care Ltd
Luxurycare (Birds Hill Nursing Home)
Luxurycare (Regency Manor Care Home)
Milewood Healthcare Ltd
N. Notaro Homes Limited
Osborne Care Homes Limited
Parkview Gloucester Ltd
Southern Healthcare (Wessex) Ltd
Swallowcourt Limited
Tre' Care Group Limited
Two Rivers Investments Limited
Waypoints Care (Plymouth) Ltd
Waypoints Care (Upton) Limited
Waypoints Care (Verwood) Ltd
Waypoints Care Group Limited
Weldmar Hospicecare Trust
Westbury Care Limited
White Horse Care Trust

87200 Residential care activities for learning difficulties, mental health and substance abuse [21]

Action on Addiction
Alabare Christian Care Centres
Bowden Derra Park Limited
Brandon Trust
Crediton Care & Support Homes Ltd
Devon & Cornwall Autistic Community Trust
Dynavour Limited
Freeways Trust
HF Trust Limited
Holmleigh Care Homes Limited
Keelex 176 Limited
Lodge Rest Limited
Luxurycare (Aranlaw House Care Home) Ltd
Milewood Healthcare Ltd
Orchard Trust
Pharos Care Limited
Phoenix Child Care Limited
St James Priory Project
Torcare Limited
Tricuro Support Ltd
White Horse Care Trust

87300 Residential care activities for the elderly and disabled [46]

Abbeyfield Bristol and Keynsham Society
Abbeyfield Wessex Society Ltd
Blanchworth Care Limited
Brunelcare
C.T.C.H. Limited
Care South
Check House Limited
Colten Care (1693) Limited
Colten Care (1993) Limited
Colten Care (2003) Limited
Colten Care (2009) Limited
Colten Care Limited
Cornwall Care Limited
Crocus Care Ltd
Doveleigh Care Limited
Enham Trust
Lilian Faithfull Care
Grange (Chertsey) 2002 Ltd.
Grove Care Limited

Gurkha Welfare Trust
Hugh Sexey's Hospital
Jupiter Care Ltd
Manor Collection Limited
Milestones Trust
Milewood Healthcare Ltd
Nynehead Care Limited
Osborne Care Homes Limited
Palmer Care Ltd
Penrice House (St. Austell) Ltd
Plymouth Age Concern
Retired Nurses National Home
Silverleigh Limited
Sirona Care & Health C.I.C.
South West Care Homes Limited
Stonehaven (Healthcare) Ltd
Supported Independence Limited
Swallowcourt Limited
Thurlestone Court Limited
Torcare (Holdings) Limited
Torr Home
Tre' Care Group Limited
Treasure Homes Limited
Tricuro Support Ltd
Warrington Homes Limited
Wemyss Lodge Limited
Windmill Care Limited

87900 Other residential care activities n.e.c. [18]

Amber Foundation
Amesbury Abbey Limited
Autism Wessex
Buckinghamshire Limited
Coate Water Care Co Ltd
Diverse Abilities Plus Ltd
Eastleigh Care Homes - Raleigh Mead
Eastleigh Care Homes Limited
Five Rivers Child Care Limited
Help for Heroes
Midhurst Child Care Limited
National Star Foundation
Novalis Trust
Raynsford Limited
Somerset Care Limited
Stallcombe House
WESC Foundation
Waters Park House Limited

88100 Social work activities without accommodation for the elderly and disabled [12]

Bristol Charities
Brunelcare
Cinnamon Trust
Crocus Care Ltd
Enham Trust
First City Nursing Services Ltd
Gurkha Welfare Trust
Kumari Care Limited
Macular Disease Society
Plymouth Age Concern
Tricuro Support Ltd
Weldmar Hospicecare Trust

88910 Child day-care activities

Brandon Trust

88990 Other social work activities without accommodation n.e.c. [25]

Ashley Family Foundation Ltd
Autism Wessex
Brandon Trust
Bristol Drugs Project Limited
Cornwall Housing Limited
County of Gloucestershire Community Foundation
Cullompton Walronds Preservation Trust
Devon Community Foundation
Diverse Abilities Plus Ltd
Duchy Health Charity Limited
Five Rivers Child Care Limited
The Thomas Freke and Lady Norton Charity
HF Trust Limited
Hope and Homes for Children
Milewood Healthcare Ltd
Royal Artillery Charitable Fund.
Royal Bath & West of England Society
Royal Marines Charity
Shaw Trust Limited
Sirona Care & Health C.I.C.
Stepping Stones Resettlement Unit
Steward's Co Ltd
Tree Aid
Tricuro Support Ltd
Wessex Resolutions C.I.C.

90010 Performing arts

Skylarking UK Limited
St George's Bristol
Theatre Royal (Plymouth) Ltd
Theatre Royal Bath Limited

90020 Support activities to performing arts

Creative England Limited
Creative Kernow Limited
Elmley Foundation
Greenbank Hotel (Falmouth) Ltd
Krowji Limited
Merlin Cinemas Limited

90030 Artistic creation

Aardman Animations Limited
Bristol Old Vic Theatre School Ltd
Bristol Old Vic and Theatre Royal Trust
Lypiatt Studio Limited
Magmatic Limited
St George's Bristol

90040 Operation of arts facilities [16]

Arnolfini Gallery Limited
BH Live
Bristol Music Trust
The Andrew Brownsword Arts Foundation
Creative Kernow Limited
Dartington Hall Trust
Eden Trust
Gloucestershire Everyman Theatre Co Ltd
Krowji Limited
Newlyn Art Gallery Limited
Poole Arts Trust Limited
Royal West of England Academy
Spike Island Artspace Limited
St George's Bristol
Theatre Royal Bath Limited
Watershed Arts Trust Limited

91011 Library activities

Cornwall Trust for Nature Conservation
Prenax Limited

91020 Museums activities

American Museum in Britain
Museum of East Asian Art
National Maritime Museum Cornwall Trust
Royal Institution of Cornwall
Tank Museum Limited

91030 Operation of historical sites and buildings and similar visitor attractions

Dartington Hall Trust
English Heritage Trust
Heligan Gardens Limited
Hestercombe Gardens Trust
Merlin Attractions Operations Ltd
SS Great Britain Trust
Swanage Railway Trust

91040 Botanical and zoological gardens and nature reserves activities [14]

Bristol, Clifton and West of England Zoological Society
Cornwall Trust for Nature Conservation
Dorset Wildlife Trust
Eden Project Limited
Eden Trust
Heligan Gardens Limited
Killiow Estates Limited
Livingstone Leisure Limited
Monkey World Limited
National Marine Aquarium Ltd
Real Live Leisure Co Ltd
Somerset Wildlife Trust
Trebah Garden Trust
Wildfowl & Wetlands Trust

92000 Gambling and betting activities

Braddicks Leisure Limited
Century Casino Bath Limited
Halos Garden Amusement Limited
National Trust (Enterprises) Ltd

93110 Operation of sports facilities [19]

BH Live
Bath Rugby Limited
Bristol City Holdings Limited
British Automobile Racing Club Ltd
Brownbrink Ltd
Burry and Knight Limited
China Fleet Trust
Circadian Trust
East Dorset Golf Club Limited
Gaming International Limited
Gillingham Community and Leisure Trust
Killiow Estates Limited
McCaulay's Health & Sport Ltd
Newton Abbot Races Limited
Point at Polzeath Limited
Tewkesbury Park Limited
Tickenham Court Farm Co.Limited
Tylney Investments Limited
West Hants Lawn Tennis Company (Bournemouth)

93120 Activities of sport clubs [11]

AFC Bournemouth Limited
Bath Rugby Limited
Bristol City Football Club Ltd
Calcot Health & Leisure Co Ltd
Exeter Golf and Country Club,Limited
Exeter Rugby Club Limited
Exeter Rugby Group PLC
Gloucester Rugby Limited
Lanhydrock Golf Club Limited
New Yacht Club Limited
West Hants Lawn Tennis Company (Bournemouth)

93130 Fitness facilities

Circadian Trust
Tewkesbury Park Limited
Thermae Development Co Ltd
YMCA Bath Group

93191 Activities of racehorse owners

Bibury Club Limited

93199 Other sports activities [10]

ASCB Charitable Fund
Athena Racing Limited
R M Beckett Limited
Crescent Motorcycle Co Ltd
R. Hannon Limited
OC Sport Ltd
OC Vor Ltd
Trevose Limited
Weymouth and Portland National Sailing Academy
World Snooker Limited

93210 Activities of amusement parks and theme parks

Alton Towers Resort Operations Ltd
Chessington World of Adventures Operations
Gamecube Amusement Limited
Halos Garden Amusement Limited
Lightwater Valley Attractions Ltd
Maximum Fun Devon Limited
Merlin Attractions Operations Ltd
South West Environmental Parks Ltd
Thorpe Park Operations Limited

93290 Other amusement and recreation activities n.e.c. [36]

Alchemy Promotions Limited
American Amusements Holdings Ltd
Bath Recreation Limited
Bendalls Leisure Limited
Big Apple Entertainments Ltd
Brean Leisure Park Ltd.
Copyright Administration Services
Dean & Reddyhoff Limited
Dream Makers Enterprises Ltd
Eden Trust
Exeter Golf and Country Club,Limited
Five Directions Limited
Gamecube Amusement Limited
Glastonbury Festival Events Ltd
Greenbank Hotel (Falmouth) Ltd
Halos Garden Amusement Limited
Haystack Dryers Limited
Horton Golf Limited
Lanhydrock Estate Company
London Aquarium (South Bank) Ltd
Longleat Enterprises Limited
Madame Tussauds Touring Exhibition
Merlin Attractions Operations Ltd
Merlin Entertainments (Dungeons) Ltd
Merlin Entertainments (Sea Life) Ltd
Merlin Entertainments Group Operations
Puxton Limited
Quay Marinas Group Ltd
Quay Marinas Limited
Royal Air Force Charitable Trust Enterprises
Royal Arcade Limited
Sailport PLC
We The Curious Limited
West Country Park Homes Ltd
White Horse Country Club Ltd
Wookey Hole Limited

94110 Activities of business and employers membership organisations

Campden BRI
Ecclesiastical Planning Services Ltd
Home Hardware Southwest Ltd
Zurich Community Trust (UK) Ltd

94120 Activities of professional membership organisations

British Small Animal Veterinary Association
Emerald Debtco Limited
PADI EMEA Limited

94910 Activities of religious organisations [14]

Bath and Wells Diocesan Board of Finance
Bristol Diocesan Board of Finance
Exeter Diocesan Board of Finance Ltd
Gloucester Diocesan Board of Finance
Goodnews Evangelical Mission
Lee Abbey Fellowship
Lee Abbey International Students' Club
Lee Abbey Movement
Moorlands College
The George Muller Charitable Trust
Salisbury Diocesan Board of Finance
United Bible Societies Association
United Reformed Church (South Western Synod) Incorporated
Woodlands Group of Churches

94990 Activities of other membership organisations n.e.c. [15]

Bioscientifica Limited
Cornwall Community Foundation
Cornwall Trust for Nature Conservation
Curo Group (Albion) Limited
Devon Wildlife Trust
Ecosurety Limited
Gloucestershire Wildlife Trust
Horseworld Trust
JISC
Organic Milk Suppliers Co-operative
Society for Endocrinology
Soil Association Limited
Swanage Railway Trust
Three Rivers Partnership, Dorset
Wiltshire Wildlife Trust Ltd

95110 Repair of computers and peripheral equipment

Cray U.K. Limited
Healthcare Computing Limited

95220 Repair of household appliances and home and garden equipment

H.B.H. Woolacotts Limited

95250 Repair of watches, clocks and jewellery

Allum and Sidaway Limited

96010 Washing and (dry-)cleaning of textile and fur products

South West Laundry Ltd

96020 Hairdressing and other beauty treatment

House of Clive (Hair and Beauty) Ltd
Paris Presents UK Limited

96030 Funeral and related activities [13]

Crematoria Management Ltd.
Forest Park Cemetery and Crematorium
Kent County Crematorium Ltd
New Southgate Cemetery and Crematorium
Walter C Parson Limited
Tapper and Son (Poole) Limited
Torbay Cemetery and Crematorium Ltd
WK Crematoria Limited
A J Wakely & Sons Ltd.
Westerleigh Crematoria Limited
Westerleigh Group Holdings Ltd
Westerleigh Group Limited
Woods (Dorchester) Limited

96040 Physical well-being activities

Help for Heroes

96090 Other service activities n.e.c. [85]

43P9 Limited
AFP (Europe)
Almanzora Group Limited
Astra Trading Development Ltd.
Bowater Homes Ltd
By Education (Barking) Holdings Ltd
By Education (Barking) Limited
Careline UK Monitoring Limited
C & J Clark (No 1) Limited
Community Foundation for Wiltshire & Swindon
Containers Packaging (Europe)
Crapper & Sons Landfill Ltd
Cullen Group Limited
DM Opco Limited
Danetre PFI Project Co Ltd
Dorset Press Limited
Entier Associates Limited
Fremington Homes Limited
GE Aviation Systems Limited
GE Infrastructure Aviation
GLM Trading Limited
Gerrick Rose Animal Trust
Gloucestershire Association for Disability
Grand Pier Limited
Greensquare Homes Limited
Growth Technology Limited
Hampshire Motor Investment Co Ltd
Harrow House International College (Swanage)
Help for Heroes
R T Julian & Son Limited
LAL Language Centres Holding Ltd
LCD Publishing Limited
Lambeth Lighting Services Ltd

Libra Homes Limited
Magnox Limited
Mallory International Limited
Master International Limited
Metalex Products Limited
New Earth Solutions (Canford) Ltd
New Earth Solutions (Kent) Ltd
New Earth Solutions (West) Ltd
Octagon Healthcare Limited
Openwork Services Limited
Pathfinder Park Homes Holdings Ltd
Pathfinder Park Homes Limited
Peninsula Care Homes Limited
Pluss Organisation CIC
Premier Park Limited
Regent's Park Healthcare Ltd
Renewable Design Co Ltd
Rock Services Limited
John Romans Park Homes Ltd
Royal Air Force Charitable Trust Enterprises
Saab Technologies UK Limited
Scotty Ventures Limited
Shiloh Limited
Solace Global Maritime Limited
Somerset Community Foundation
South Manchester Healthcare (Holdings)
South Manchester Healthcare Ltd
The Ralph & Irma Sperring Charity
St. James's Place Charitable Foundation
Will Stone Historic Cars Ltd
Sturts Community Trust
Tay Valley Lighting (Leeds) Ltd
Tay Valley Lighting (Stoke on Trent)
Tewkesbury Marina Limited
Thirsty Work Limited
Tree Aid
United Registrar of Systems Ltd
Unitedhealthcare Global Medical (UK)
Verplas Limited
Viridor EFW (Runcorn) Limited
Viridor Trident Park Limited
Viridor Waste (Greater Manchester)
Viridor Waste (Landfill Restoration)
Viridor Waste (Somerset) Ltd
Viridor Waste (Thames) Limited
Viridor Waste Exeter Limited
Viridor Waste Management Ltd
West of England Investors Ltd
Westbank Community Health and Care
Willcox Bros Limited
Wiltshire Air Ambulance Charitable Trust
Roger Young Limited

98000 Residents property management [10]

BE Properties (Plymouth) Ltd
Cornish Potatoes Limited
Courtwave Limited
Culverdene Properties Limited
Exeter Castle Management Co Ltd
KPC & AT Body Properties Ltd
OMPD Limited
Omega Housing Limited
Provenn Ltd
QMP Group Limited

99000 Activities of extraterritorial organisations and bodies

Alchemist Ventures Limited
Clark Holdings (UK) Limited
RNO Limited

99999 Dormant company [17]

Axiom Process Limited
Caledonia TLG Bidco Limited
Castle Motor Co Ltd
Cemetery Management Limited
Crossco (284) Limited
Delphine Holdings Limited
ES Technology Group Limited
FIM Trustee Limited
Manor Vets Limited
Meggitt Advanced Composites Ltd
Neon (Holdings) Limited
Nicolas James Limited
PSW (Holdings) Ltd
Pro-Vets Group Limited
RTB Private Equity Ltd
Rochford Holdings Limited
Wyvern Holdings Limited

Printed in 8pt Nimbus Sans L

Designed by URW++ Design and Development GmbH

Dellam Publishing Limited

2 Heath Drive, Sutton, Surrey, SM2 5RP

Fax: 020 8770 7478 email: enquiries@dellam.com

SAN: 0177881 EAN/GLN: 5030670177882

www.ingramcontent.com/pod-product-compliance
Lightning Source LLC
LaVergne TN
LVHW082004200926
848481LV00010B/2804
9781912736232